Chambers Pocket Dictionary

Chambers Pocket Dictionary

Dictionaries Manager

Catherine Schwarz

Managing Editor

George Davidson

Editors

Elaine Higgleton, Howard Sargeant
Anne Seaton

Chambers

CHAMBERS
An imprint of Larousse plc
43–45 Annandale Street
Edinburgh EH7 4AZ

First published by W & R Chambers Ltd 1992
Reprinted 1994

We have made every effort to mark as such all words which we believe to be trademarks. We should also like to make it clear that the presence of a word in the book, whether marked or unmarked, in no way affects its legal status as a trademark.

A CIP catalogue record for this book is available from the British Library

ISBN 0-550-10583-2

Computing services by University of St. Andrews
Typeset in England by Butler & Tanner Ltd
Printed in England by Clays Ltd, St Ives, plc

Contents

Preface

In creating the *Chambers Pocket Dictionary,* the editors have attached particular importance to ensuring that the dictionary is easy to use. Great attention has been paid to the fullness and helpfulness of the definitions, which are written in clear, modern, non-technical language. Wherever possible all the information required for complete understanding of the defined word has been included in the definition itself; there is no need for the user to jump from place to place in the dictionary in search of a full explanation.

As a medium-sized dictionary, with 60 000 references and 80 000 definitions, the *Pocket* has concentrated on the main core of English vocabulary, with good coverage of the English spoken in the United Kingdom but not ignoring the English of other parts of the world. The *Pocket* is completely up to date in its coverage of the language of the modern world, especially the terminology of science and the computer industry. And although a dictionary such as the *Pocket* must inevitably omit many of the less common words of English, room has still been found for words that are no longer current but which the reader may well come across in literature. The dictionary is particularly strong in its coverage of idiomatic phrases.

Careful page design and clear modern typefaces, together with the absence of the unfamiliar symbols used in many dictionaries to indicate pronunciation, have resulted in an uncluttered, easy-to-use book.

The *Pocket Dictionary* has been created from a brand-new dictionary database developed by Chambers, drawing on the accumulated expertise of a century and a half of dictionary publishing and using to the full the editorial resources underlying *Chambers English Dictionary.*

With wide coverage of colloquial and formal language, old words and new, everyday vocabulary and the specialist terminology of science and technology, in a book that is both easy to handle and easy to read, the *Pocket Dictionary* is unrivalled in its clarity, its comprehensiveness and its authority by any dictionary of a comparable size.

Using the dictionary

1. The basic structure of an entry

The first word of an entry, printed in **bold type,** is the word to be defined. It is known as the 'headword'. If two or more headwords have the same spelling, they are distinguished by superscript numbers, e.g. **cape**[1] (= an item of clothing), **cape**[2] (= a section of coastline).

The next element of an entry after the headword is generally a grammatical label, indicating whether the word is a noun, verb, adjective, etc. This is printed in *italic* type. The grammatical labels used in this dictionary are listed among the abbreviations on pages xii and xiii. Explanations of the grammatical terms used can be found in the dictionary. The following points should also be noted:

> when a verb is both transitive and intransitive, the order of the labels indicates the relative frequency of the two uses, i.e. '*v* (*tr* & *intr*)' means that the verb is more frequently used transitively than intransitively;
>
> '*n* (*pl*)' means that the headword is plural; '*n* (in *pl*)' means that the headword is singular, but with a particular meaning is used only in the plural; '*n* (*sing*)' marks a word (e.g. **physics**) that by its form appears to be plural but which is in fact used as a singular noun.

The definition (in type like this), gives the meaning of the word. Parentheses '()' are used to mark off optional parts of definitions, such as objects of transitive verbs.

The word origin or 'etymology', enclosed in square brackets '[]', indicates the origin of the word, generally by giving in *italic* the 'source-word' from which the English word is derived. The language labels used in the etymologies can be found in the list of abbreviations on pages xii and xiii. They are for the most part self-explanatory, but the following points should be noted:

> 'Gr' refers to the language of ancient Greece, modern Greek being labelled 'ModGr';
>
> 'Norse' means Old Norse (see **Norse** in the dictionary);
>
> in foreign languages other than Greek, the language label on its own refers to the modern language, older stages of the language being labelled with 'O', e.g. ODut (= Old Dutch);

in the case of English, three stages of the language are recognised — 'Old English' (labelled 'OE') up to about 1150, Middle English (labelled 'MidE') between 1150 and 1500, and Modern English (unlabelled) from 1500 to the present day.

2. Words that belong to more than one part of speech

A change of part of speech is indicated by a dash followed by a grammatical label; a word belonging to more than one part of speech is, however, sometimes treated thus:

moo *v* (*intr*) & *n* (to make) the long low sound of a cow.

3. Words that have more than one meaning

Many words require more than one definition. In this dictionary, the most common meanings are generally given first, with rarer, older, etc. meanings coming after. Each definition is separately numbered; closely related meanings are treated together under one number, separated by semi-colons.

4. Words that have more than one form

If a word may be spelt in more than one way, both (or all) forms are shown in the dictionary, linked by 'or':

absinthe or **absinth** *n* a strong green alcoholic drink ....

The commoner spelling is entered first.

5. Other bold items in headword entries

Immediately after the definitions of the headword there may be other words in bold type, as in the entry for **jest**:

jest *n* a joke or prank. — *adv* **jestingly**. — **in jest** as a joke; not seriously.

Such bold items will be either 'derivatives' or 'phrases'.

Derivatives are formed by the addition of a suffix (or word-ending) such as *-ly* or *-ness* to the headword. Such words require no definition as their meaning is easily deducible from the meanings of the headword and the suffix.

Phrases containing the headword follow the derivative. Among the phrases, only phrasal verbs (i.e. phrases consisting of a verb plus one or two adverbs or prepositions, e.g. **put up with, come down, see off**) have grammatical labels.

6. Classification labels

Labels that indicate some restriction in the use of a word, or a certain meaning of a word, such as *slang* or *comput,* are printed in *italics* in parentheses after the part of speech label. If a label applies to more than one part of speech, it stands before the first part of speech. The meanings of the abbreviated labels are explained on pages xii and xiii.

7. Help with word formation and spelling difficulties

Irregular plurals of nouns and tenses and participles of verbs, and noun and verb forms which often cause spelling problems, are printed in a ***sloped bold*** type immediately following the part of speech label:

for nouns, all irregular plurals are given (e.g. **alumnus**, ***alumni***), and regular ones (such as **activity**, ***activities***; **radio**, ***radios***; **valley**, ***valleys***) about which there is sometimes uncertainty.

for verbs, irregular past tenses and past participles are listed (with only one form being given where the past tense and past participle are identical, e.g. **abide**, ***abode***, two forms being given where they are not identical, e.g. **write**, ***wrote***, ***written***), and also all regular formations (such as **accompany**, ***accompanies***, ***accompanied***; **abhor**, ***abhorring***, ***abhorred***; **offer**, ***offering***, ***offered***) that sometimes cause difficulty.

for adjectives, changes similar to those listed above (e.g. **big**, ***bigger***, ***biggest*** and **silly**, ***sillier***, ***silliest***) are indicated.

Most of these changes are shown in a shortened but clear and straightforward form: for example, the change from **alumnus** to ***alumni*** is shown by ***-ni***; the doubling of the final **r** of ***abhor*** in ***abhorring*** and ***abhorred*** is indicated by ***-rr-*** and the non-doubling of the final **r** of **offer** is shown by ***-r-***; and the change of **y** to **i** in ***sillier*** and ***silliest*** is shown by ***-ier*** and ***-iest***.

8. Other bold words

Below the entry for the headword, there may be entries for one or more related words:

accomplish *v* (*tr*) **1** to manage to do. **2** to complete.
— *adj* **accomplishable.** [OFr *acomplir*]
accomplished *adj* **1** clever or skilled. **2** ....
accomplishment *n* **1** a skill, esp. a social one ....

Such words (in this case **accomplished** and **accomplishment**) are called 'subheads'; each new subhead begins on a new line. Unlike the derivatives that are part of the headword entry, subheads are always defined. The entries for subheads have the same structure as those of headwords.

9. Abbreviations and symbols

Abbreviations are included in the headwords in the text, as are symbols such as **¢** and **®**. Other symbols such as **%** and **√** are to be found in the appendix of symbols on page 1065.

10. Other information

A label *cap* at a definition means that although the word is generally spelt with an initial small letter, it is spelt with a capital letter when used in the sense indicated by that particular definition.

A label 'with **the**' at a definition means that the word is always preceded by 'the' when used in the sense indicated by that definition.

The *Pocket Dictionary* provides information on the correct prepositions to use after verbs, adjectives and nouns; these are printed in **bold** type in parentheses. For example, the first definition of **look** reads '(*intr*; **at**) to turn the eyes in a certain direction so as to see'. Here, the **at** in parentheses indicates that when used in this sense, **look** may be followed by **at**. The seventh definition of **look** reads '(*intr* with **into**) to investigate', which means that in this sense, **look** must be followed by **into** and cannot be used alone. This same rule applies to adverbs such as **away**, **in**, **off** or **up** that are commonly used with many verbs and which may appear in parentheses in verb entries: if the adverb is preceded by 'with', it must follow the verb when the verb is used in that particular sense, whereas if the adverb is not preceded by 'with', its presence is optional.

If the hyphen of a bold hyphenated word appears at the end of a line, it is replaced by an = sign to show that it is a full part of the word and not simply a hyphen that has been inserted because the word has been split across two lines.

Abbreviations used in the dictionary

abbrev. or *abbrev*	abbreviation
AD	*anno domini* (see dictionary)
adj	adjective
adv	adverb
anat	anatomy
antiq	antiquities
archaeol	archaeology
archit	architecture
arith	arithmetic
astrol	astrology
astron	astronomy
Austr	Australia(n)
aux	auxiliary
b.	born
BC	before Christ
biochem	biochemistry
biol	biology
bot	botany
Br	British
c.	*circa* (Latin), about
cap, caps	capital(s)
cent.	century
chem	chemistry
Chin	Chinese
cm	centimetre
C of E	Church of England
coll	colloquial
comb fm	combining form
compar. or *compar*	comparative
cmpds	compounds
comput	computing
conj	conjunction
Czech	Czechoslovakian
d.	died
Dan	Danish
derog	derogatorily
dimin.	diminutive
Dut	Dutch
E	east; English
econ	economics
e.g.	*exempli gratia* (Latin), for example
esp.	especially
etc.	*et cetera* (Latin), and so on
ety.	etymology
electr	electricity; electrical
Eng	English
engin	engineering
euph	euphemistic
facet	facetious
fem.	feminine
fig	figurative
Finn	Finnish
fort	fortification
Fr	French
geog	geography
geol	geology
geom	geometry
Ger	German
Gr	Greek
gram	grammar
Hebr	Hebrew
hist	history
Hung	Hungarian
i.e.	*id est* (Latin), that is
imit.	imitative
interj	interjection
intr	intransitive
Ital	Italian
Jap	Japanese
kg	kilogram
km	kilometre
Lat	Latin
lb	pound
lit.	literally
math	mathematics
mech	mechanics
med	medicine
metall	metallurgy
meteorol	meteorology
Mid	Middle
mil	military
Mod	Modern
mus	music
mythol	mythology
N	north
n	noun
NAm	North American (= of both the USA and Canada)
naut	nautical
neg	negative
Norw	Norwegian
nuc	nuclear
NZ	New Zealand
O	Old
orig.	originally
pathol	pathology

Pers	Persian	sfx. or *sfx*	suffix
pfx. or *pfx*	prefix	*sing*	singular
philos	philosophy	*sociol*	sociology
phon	phonetics	Span	Spanish
physiol	physiology	superl. or *superl*	superlative
pl	plural	*surg*	surgery
Pol	Polish	Swed	Swedish
Port	Portuguese	*tech*	technology
prep	preposition	*telecomm*	telecommunications
prob.	probably	*tr*	transitive
pron	pronoun	Turk	Turkish
psychol	psychology	*TV*	television
RC	Roman Catholic	*US*	United States
relig	religion	usu.	usually
Rom	Roman	*v*	verb
Russ	Russian	*vulg*	vulgar
S	south	W	west
SAfr	South Africa(n)	*zool*	zoology
Scot	Scottish		

A

A[1] or **a** *n* ***As*** or ***A's, a's*** **1** the first letter of the English alphabet. **2** (usu. **A**) (a mark indicating) the highest grade or quality. **3** (only **A**; *mus*) the sixth note in the scale of C major. **4** (only **A**) a musical key with the note A as its base. — **from A to B** from one place to another. — **from A to Z** from the beginning to the end; completely.
A1 or **A-1** *adj* (*coll*) of the highest quality; first-class.
A-road *n* in the UK, a main road.
A-side *n* the main song or piece of music on a small record or single. ◇ See also **B-side**.
A[2] *abbrev* **1** ampere. **2** atomic: *A-bomb.* **3** alto. **4** answer. **5** advanced. **6** America. **7** Australia. **8** Associate (of a society, etc.).
A level or **Advanced level** *n* **1** an examination in a single subject in England, Wales and Northern Ireland for which school and college students study until about the age of 18. **2** a pass in such an examination.
Å *abbrev* angstrom.
a[1] and **an** — **a** is used before words beginning with a consonant or consonant sound (e.g. *one*, *unit*) and **an** before words beginning with a vowel or vowel sound (e.g. *heir*, *honour* or *hour*) — *indefinite article* **1** one. **2** used before a word describing quantity: *a dozen eggs*; *a lot of books.* **3** any; every: *A fire is hot.* **4** each or every; per: *once a day*; *60p a pound.* **5** one of a stated type: *He thinks he's a real Romeo.* [OE *an*, one]
a[2] *abbrev* **1** *ante*, (Lat) before. **2** acre.
a[3] *prep*, now usu. as *pfx* **1** to or towards: *ashore.* **2** in the process or state of: *abuzz.* **3** on: *afire.* **4** in: *nowadays.* [OE *an*, on]
a-[1] *pfx* (**an-** before a vowel) not; without; opposite to: *amoral*; *asymmetrical*; *agnostic.* [Gr]
a-[2] *pfx* of: *akin*; *afresh.* [OE *of*]
AA *abbrev* **1** Automobile Association, a British organisation which helps drivers with breakdowns or technical problems, gives travel information, etc. ◇ See also **RAC**. **2** Alcoholics Anonymous, an association for alcoholics who are trying to give up alcohol completely.
AAA *abbrev* **1** (*Br*) Amateur Athletic Association. **2** (*US*) American Automobile Association. ◇ See also **AA**.
aardvark *n* an African mammal with a long snout, that feeds on ants. [Dut *aarde*, earth + *vark*, pig]
AB *abbrev* **1** (*Br*) able seaman. **2** (*US*) *artium baccalaureus* (Lat), Bachelor of Arts.
aback : **taken aback** surprised or shocked, esp. by something unpleasant or unexpected. [OE *on bæc*, on back]
abacus *n* **1** a frame holding a number of wires along which small balls can be moved, used for counting. **2** (*archit*) the flat upper part of a column or capital. [Lat, from Gr *abax*, drawing-board]
abaft *adv* in or towards the stern of a ship. — *prep* behind. [**a**[3] + OE *bæftan*, after]
abalone *n* a kind of edible shellfish with a shell lined with mother-of-pearl. [Span *abulón*]
abandon *v* **-n-** (*tr*) **1** to give up completely: *abandon hope.* **2** to leave (a person, post of responsibility, etc.) usually intending not to return. **3** to leave (a place of danger or difficulty, etc.) intending either not to return at all or not until the danger or difficulty is past. **4** to give up to another person's control. **5** (**to**) to let (oneself) be overcome by strong emotion, passion, etc. — *n* uncontrolled, uninhibited, reckless feelings. — *n* **abandonment**. — **abandon ship** to leave a ship because of danger. [OFr *abandoner*, to put under someone's control]
abandoned *adj* **1** having been abandoned. **2** having, or behaving as if one has, no sense of shame or morality.
abase *v* (*tr*) to humiliate or degrade (a person or oneself). — *n* **abasement.** [OFr *abaissier*, from Lat *bassus*, low]
abashed *adj* embarrassed and ashamed, esp. because of shyness. [OFr *esbahir*, to astound]
abate *v* (*intr* & *tr*) to become or make less strong or severe. — *n* **abatement**. [OFr *abatre*, to bring down]
abattoir *n* a slaughterhouse. [OFr *abatre*, to bring down]
abbacy *n* **-ies** the office or authority of an abbot or abbess. [Lat *abbatia*, abbey]
abbess *n* a woman in charge of a group of nuns living in an abbey. [OFr *abbesse*]
abbey *n* **-eys** **1** a group of nuns or monks living as a community under an abbot or abbess. **2** the buildings occupied by such a community. **3** a church associated with such a community. [OFr *abeie*]
abbot *n* the man in charge of a group of monks living in an abbey. [Lat *abbas*, from Aramaic *abba*, father]
abbr. or **abbrev.** *abbrev* **1** abbreviation. **2** abbreviated.
abbreviate *v* (*tr*) to shorten, esp. to represent (a long word) by a shortened form. — *n* **abbreviation**. [Lat *abbreviare*, to shorten]
ABC[1] *n* ***ABCs*** or ***ABC's*** **1** the alphabet. **2** the basic facts about a subject, esp. when arranged alphabetically in a book. **3** an alphabetical guide.
ABC[2] *abbrev* **1** American Broadcasting Company. **2** Australian Broadcasting Corporation.

abdicate *v* **1** (*intr* & *tr*) to give up one's right to (the throne). **2** (*tr*) to refuse or fail to carry out (one's responsibilities). — *n* **abdication**. [Lat *ab-*, away, from + *dicare*, to proclaim]

abdomen *n* **1** the front part of the body containing the stomach, bowels and other organs used in digesting food. **2** the rear part of the body of insects, spiders, crabs, etc. — *adj* **abdominal**. [Lat]

abduct *v* (*tr*) to take (someone) away illegally by force or deception. — *n* **abduction**. — *n* **abductor**. [Lat *abducere*, to lead away]

abeam *adv* in a line at right angles to the length of a ship or aircraft. [**a**[3] + **beam**]

Aberdeen Angus *n* a Scottish breed of cattle with a black coat and no horns. [*Aberdeen* and *Angus*, in Scotland]

aberrant *adj* changing or departing from what is normal or accepted as standard. — *n* **aberrance** and **aberrancy**, ***-ies***. [Lat *aberrare*, to wander away]

aberration *n* a temporary, usu. brief and often surprising change from what is normal or accepted as standard. **2** a usu. temporary, brief and sudden drop in standards of behaviour, thought, etc.

abet *v* ***-tt-*** (*tr*; esp. *legal*; **in**) to help or encourage (someone) to do something wrong. — *n* **abetter** or (esp. *legal*) **abettor**. [OFr *abeter*, to entice]

abeyance *n* **1** (of laws, customs, etc.) the condition, usu. temporary, of not being used or followed: *fall into abeyance*. **2** (of a position e.g. a peerage) the state, usu. temporary, of not being filled or occupied. [OFr *abeance*, from *a*, to + *baer*, to gape]

abhor *v* ***-rr-*** (*tr*) to hate or dislike very much (usu. something one considers morally wrong). — *n* **abhorrence**. [Lat *ab-* from, away + *horrere*, to shudder]

abhorrent *adj* (**to**) hated or disliked. — *adv* **abhorrently**.

abide *v* ***abode*** or ***abided*** **1** (*tr*; used with **can** or **could**) to put up with or tolerate. **2** (*intr* with **by**) to follow, stay faithful to or obey (a decision, rule, etc.). **3** (*intr*; *old*) to live. [OE *abidan*]

abiding *adj* permanent, lasting or continuing for a long time.

ability *n* ***-ies*** **1** the power, skill or knowledge to do something. **2** great skill or intelligence. [OFr *ablete*, from Lat *habilitas*, suitability]

-ability. See **-able**.

abject *adj* **1** (of conditions, etc.) extremely sad, miserable or poor; wretched. **2** (used of people) showing lack of courage or pride, etc.; shameful. — *n* **abjection**. — *adv* **abjectly**. — *n* **abjectness**. [Lat *abjicere*, to throw away]

abjure *v* (*tr*) to promise solemnly, esp. under oath, to stop believing, doing, etc. (something). — *n* **abjuration**. [Lat *ab*, away, from + *jurare*, to swear]

ablative *n* (*gram*) the case which, esp. in Latin, expresses the place, means, manner or instrument of an action. — *adj* of or in the ablative case. [Lat *ablativus*, from *ablatus*, carried off, removed]

ablaze *adj* **1** burning, esp. strongly. **2** brightly lit. **3** (**with**) feeling extremely strong emotion. [**a**[3] + **blaze**]

able *adj* **1** having the necessary knowledge, power, time, opportunity, etc. to do something. **2** clever, skilful. — *adv* **ably**. [Lat *habilis*, handy]

able-bodied *adj* fit and healthy. — *n* (*pl*) fit and healthy people.

able seaman *n* (also **able-bodied seaman**) a sailor able to perform all duties, with more training and a higher rating than an ordinary seaman.

-able *sfx* forming adjectives meaning **1** that may or must be: *eatable*; *payable*. **2** that may be the subject of: *objectionable*. **3** that is suitable for: *seasonable*; *fashionable*. — *n sfx* **-ability**. — *adv sfx* **-ably**. ◇ See also **-ible**. [Lat *-abilis*]

ablution *n* (usu. in *pl*) **1** the washing of parts of the body as part of a religious ceremony. **2** (*coll*) the ordinary washing of oneself. **3** a place for washing oneself in a camp, on board ship, etc. [Lat *abluere*, to wash away]

ably. See **able**.

ABM *abbrev* anti-ballistic missile, a type of rocket which can destroy an enemy's ballistic missile in the air.

abnegation *n* **1** the act of giving up something one has or would like to have. **2** the act of renouncing a doctrine, etc. [Lat *abnegare*, to deny]

abnormal *adj* not normal; different from what is expected or usual. — *n* **abnormality**, ***-ies***. — *adv* **abnormally**. [Fr *anormal*, from Gr *anomalos*; influenced in form by Lat *abnormis*, unconventional]

Abo or **abo** *n* ***-os*** (*offensive slang*) an Australian aborigine. — *adj* aboriginal. [Short for **aborigine**]

aboard *adv* & *prep* **1** on, on to, in or into (a ship, train, aircraft, etc.) **2** (*naut*) alongside. [MidE *aborde*]

abode[1] *n* (*formal*) the house or place where someone lives. — **of no fixed abode** (esp. *Br legal*) having no regular home or address. [**abide**]

abode[2]. See **abide**.

abolish *v* (*tr*) to stop or put an end to (customs, laws, etc.). [Fr *abolir*]

abolition *n* **1** the act of abolishing something; the state of being abolished. **2** (*hist*) the abolishing of slavery.

abolitionist *n* a person who tries to abolish a custom or practice, esp. capital punishment or (*hist*) slavery.

A-bomb. See **atom bomb**.

abominable *adj* **1** greatly disliked, usu. because morally bad. **2** (*coll*) very bad. — *adv* **abominably**. [Lat *abominari*, to hate]

abominable snowman *n* ***-men*** a yeti. [Tibetan *metohkangmi*, snowfield man-bear]

abominate *v* (*tr*) to dislike or hate greatly. [Lat *abominari*]

abomination *n* **1** anything one hates or dislikes greatly. **2** great dislike or hatred.

aborigine *n* **1** (usu. **Aborigine**) a member of the race of people forming the original inhabitants of Australia. (The noun **Aboriginal** is now the preferred form when speaking about the original inhabitants of Australia; **Aborigine** may be considered offensive by people living in Australia.) **2** a member of any race of people who were the first people to live in a country or region, esp. as compared to later arrivals. — *n* & *adj* **aboriginal** or **Aboriginal**. [Lat *aborigines*, a race of pre-Roman inhabitants of Italy, from *ab origine*, from the beginning]

abort *v* **1** (*intr*) to lose a baby because it is born before it has developed enough to survive outside the womb; to miscarry. **2** (*intr*) (of a baby) to be lost in this way. **3** (*tr*) to remove (a baby) from the womb of (a woman) before it has developed enough to be able to survive on its own. **4** (*tr* & *intr*) to stop (a plan, space flight, etc.), or to be stopped, earlier than expected and before reaching a successful conclusion, usu. because of technical problems or danger. [Lat *abortus*, miscarried]

abortion *n* **1** an operation to abort a baby. **2** the natural failure of a pregnancy, usu. because there is something wrong with the baby; a miscarriage. **3** the failure of a plan, project, etc. **4** anything which has failed to grow properly or enough. — *n* **abortionist**.

abortive *adj* unsuccessful. — *adv* **abortively**.

abound *v* (*intr*) **1** to exist in large numbers. **2** (**in, with**) to be rich in or filled with. — *adj* **abounding**. [Lat *abundare*, to overflow]

about *prep* **1** concerning; relating to; on the subject of. **2** near to. **3** around; centring on. **4** here and there in; at points throughout. **5** all around; surrounding. **6** occupied or busy with: *What are you about?* **7** on the person of. — *adv* **1** nearly or just over; approximately. **2** nearby; close: *Is there anyone about?* **3** scattered here and there. **4** all around; in all directions. **5** in or to the opposite direction: *turn about*. **6** on the move; in action: *be up and about again after an illness*. — **about to** on the point of. — **not about to** determined not to. — **that's about it** or **all** almost everything that needs to be said or done has been. [OE *onbutan*]

about turn or **face** *n* **1** a turn made so that one is facing in the opposite direction. **2** a complete change of direction. — *v* **about-turn** or **about-face** (*intr*) to turn round so as to be facing in the opposite direction.

above *prep* **1** higher than; over. **2** more or greater than in quantity or degree. **3** higher or superior to in rank, importance, ability, etc. **4** too good or great for: *above petty quarrels*. **5** too good, respected, etc. to be affected by or subject to. **6** too difficult to be understood by; beyond the abilities of. — *adv* **1** at, in or to a higher position, place, rank, etc. **2** in addition: *over and above*. **3** in an earlier passage of written or printed text. **4** (*literary*) in heaven. — *adj* appearing or mentioned in an earlier or preceding passage of written or printed text. — *n* something already mentioned. — **above all** most of all; more than anything else. — **above and beyond** more than is required by. — **above oneself** thinking that one is more important than one is; conceited, arrogant. [OE *abufan*]

above-board *adj* honest; open; not secret.

abracadabra *interj* a word which supposedly has magic power, often used by people when doing magic tricks.

abrade *v* (*tr*) to scrape or wear away, esp. by rubbing. [Lat *abradere*, to scrape away]

abrasion *n* **1** a damaged area of skin, rock, etc., which has been worn away by scraping or rubbing. **2** the act of scraping or rubbing away. [Lat *abradere*, to scrape away]

abrasive *adj* **1** able to damage skin, rock, etc. by rubbing and scraping. **2** able to polish or make smooth by rubbing. **3** (of people or their actions) likely to annoy others by being harsh and rude. — *n* an abrasive substance. — *adv* **abrasively**. — *n* **abrasiveness**. [Lat *abradere*, to scrape away]

abreast *adv* side by side and facing in the same direction. — *adj* (**of**) up to date (with); with the most recent information: *keep abreast of events*. [**a**[3] + **breast**]

abridge *v* (*tr*) to make (a book, etc.) shorter. — *adj* **abridged**. — *n* **abridgement** or **abridgment**. [OFr *abregier*, from Lat *abbreviare*, to abbreviate]

abroad *adv* **1** in or to a foreign country or countries. **2** in circulation; at large. **3** over a wide area; in different directions. **4** (*old*) out of or away from one's home. [MidE *abrod*]

abrogate *v* (*tr*) to cancel (a law, agreement, etc.) formally or officially. — *n* **abrogation**. [Lat *abrogare*]

abrupt *adj* **1** sudden and unexpected; very quick. **2** (esp. of speech, etc.) rather sharp and rude. **3** steep. — *adv* **abruptly**. — *n* **abruptness**. [Lat *abrumpere*, to break off]

abscess *n* a painful and inflammed swelling in a part of the body, containing pus. [Lat. *abscessus*, going away]

abscissa *n* **-as** or **-ae** (*math*) a co-ordinate which gives the position of a point measured along the horizontal line of a graph. ◇ See also **ordinate**. [Lat *abscissus*, cut off]

abscond *v* (*intr*) to depart or leave quickly and usu. secretly, esp. because one has done something wrong and wants to avoid punishment or arrest. — *n* **absconder**. [Lat *abscondere*, to hide]

abseil *v* (*intr*) to go down the side of a mountain, etc. using a double rope wound round the body and fixed to a point higher up. — *n* an act of abseiling. — *n* **abseiling**. [Ger *abseilen*, from *ab*, down + *Seil*, rope]

absence *n* **1** the state of being away from work, etc. **2** the time when a person is away from work, etc. **3** the state of not existing or being lacking. — **absence of mind** a lack of attention or concentration. [Lat *absentia*, from *abesse*, to be away]

absent *adj* **1** not in its or one's expected place; not present. **2** not existing, esp. where normally to be expected. **3** showing that one is not paying attention or concentrating. — *v* (*tr*; **from**) to keep (oneself) away.

absently *adv* in a way which shows one is not paying attention or concentrating.

absent-minded *adj* not noticing what one is doing or what is going on around one, esp. because one is thinking about something else; preoccupied. — *adv* **absent-mindedly**. — *n* **absent-mindedness**.

absentee *n* a person who is not present where he or she ought to be. [**absent**]

absenteeism *n* frequent and continued absence from work, school, etc.

absentee landlord *n* a landlord who does not live in the property he lets out.

absentia. See **in absentia**.

absinthe or **absinth** *n* a strong, green alcoholic drink flavoured with substances from certain plants, such as aniseed and wormwood. [Fr *absinthe*, from Lat *absinthium*, wormwood]

absolute *adj* **1** complete; total; perfect. **2** without limits; not controlled by anything or anyone else. **3** certain; undoubted. **4** not measured in comparison with other things; not relative: *an absolute standard*. **5** pure; not mixed with anything else. **6** (*gram*) (of a part of a sentence, etc.) not dependent on the rest of the sentence, but able to stand alone. ◇ See also **relative** (sense **6**) — *n* **1** a rule, standard, etc. which is thought to be true or right in all situations. **2** (usu. *cap* with **the**; *philos*) that which can exist without being related to anything else. — *n* **absoluteness**.

absolutely *adv* **1** completely. **2** independently of anything else. **3** (*coll*) in actual fact; really; very much. **4** (usu. with **no**, **none**, etc.) at all. **5** yes; certainly.

absolute majority *n* a number of votes for a candidate in an election which is greater than the number of votes received by all the other candidates put together.

absolute pitch see under **pitch**[1].

absolute zero *n* the lowest temperature theoretically possible, 0 K (−273·15°C, or −459·67°F).

absolutism *n* the theory or practice of government by a person who has total power. — *n* & *adj* **absolutist**.

absolution *n* the formal forgiving of a person's sins, esp. by a priest. [Lat *absolutio*, acquittal]

absolve *v* (*tr*) **1** (**from**, **of**) to release or pronounce free from a promise, duty, blame, etc.. **2** (of a priest) to forgive (someone) formally for the sins he or she has committed. [Lat *absolvere*, to loosen]

absorb *v* (*tr*) **1** to take in, suck up (heat, liquid, knowledge, etc.). **2** to receive or take in as part of oneself or itself. **3** to have all of the attention or interest of. **4** to reduce or lessen (the shock, force, impact, etc. of something). — *adj* **absorbed**. — *adv* **absorbedly**. — *adj* **absorbing**. [Lat *ab*, away, from + *sorbere*, to suck in]

absorbency *n* **-ies** **1** the ability to absorb liquids, etc. **2** the degree to which something is able to absorb liquids, etc. — *n* & *adj* **absorbent**.

absorption *n* **1** the act of taking in, sucking up or absorbing, or the process of being taken in, absorbed, etc. **2** the state of having all one's interest or attention occupied by something. — *adj* **absorptive**. [Lat *absorptio*]

abstain *v* (*intr*; **from**) **1** to choose not to (start to) do, take, etc. (something). **2** to choose not to vote in an election. — *n* **abstainer**. ◇ See also **abstention** and **abstinence**. [Lat *ab*, away, from + *tenere*, to hold]

abstemious *adj* (of people, habits, etc.) taking food, alcohol, etc. in very limited amounts; moderate or restrained in what one eats or drinks. — *adv* **abstemiously**. — *n* **abstemiousness**. [Lat *abstemius*, from *abs*, away, from + *temetum*, strong drink]

abstention *n* **1** the act of choosing not to do something, esp. not to take food or alcohol. **2** a refusal to vote; a person who has abstained from voting. [Lat *abstinere*, to abstain]

abstinence *n* the practice or state of choosing not to do or take something, esp. alcohol. — *adj* **abstinent**. [Lat *abstinere*, to abstain]

abstract *adj* **1** referring to something which exists only as an idea or quality. **2** concerned with ideas and theory rather than with things which really exist or could exist. **3** (of art forms, esp. painting) representing the subject by shapes and patterns, etc. rather than in the shape or form it actually has. — *n* **1** a brief statement of the main points (of a book, speech, etc.). **2** an abstract idea, theory, etc. **3** an example of abstract painting, etc. — *v* (*tr*) **1** to take out or remove. **2** to summarise (a book, speech, etc.). — *n* **abstractness**. — **in the abstract** in theory rather than in reality. [Lat *abs*, away, from + *trahere*, to draw]

abstracted *adj* thinking about something so much that one does not notice what is happening around one. — *adv* **abstractedly**.

abstraction *n* **1** the act, or an example of, abstracting. **2** something which exists as a general idea rather than as an actual example. **3** the state of thinking about something so much that one does not notice what is happening around one.

abstruse *adj* hard to understand. — *adv* **abstrusely**. — *n* **abstruseness**. [Lat *abstrusus*, pushed away]

absurd *adj* not at all suitable; ridiculous. — *n* **absurdity**, **-*ies***. — *adv* **absurdly**. — *n* **absurdness**. [Lat *absurdus*, out of tune]

ABTA *abbrev* Association of British Travel Agents.

abundance *n* **1** a large amount, sometimes more than is needed. **2** wealth. [OFr *abundance*, from Lat *abundare*, to overflow]

abundant *adj* **1** existing in large amounts. **2** (**in**) having or providing an abundance of something.

abundantly *adv* **1** very; completely. **2** in large amounts.

abuse *v* (*tr*) **1** to use (one's position, power, etc.) wrongly. **2** to treat (someone or something) cruelly or wrongly. **3** to speak rudely or insultingly to or about (someone). — *n* **1** wrong use of one's position, power, etc. **2** bad or cruel treatment of someone or something. **3** rude or insulting words said to or about someone. [Lat *abusus*, using up, wasting]

abusive *adj* insulting or rude; using insulting or rude language. — *adv* **abusively**. — *n* **abusiveness**.

abut *v* **-*tt*- 1** (*intr*; **against**, **on**) (of countries, areas of land, buildings, etc.) to join, touch or lean (against another). **2** (*tr*) to lean on or touch (something): *a wall abutting the house*. [OFr *abouter*, to touch with an end]

abutment *n* the support at the end of an arch, e.g. in a bridge or similar structure.

abuzz *adj* in a state of noisy activity or excitement. [**a**^{3} + **buzz**]

abysmal *adj* **1** (*coll*) extremely bad. **2** very deep; very great: *abysmal ignorance*. — *adv* **abysmally**. [OFr *abisme*, abyss]

abyss *n* **1** a very large and deep hole. **2** hell. [Lat *abyssus*, from Gr *abyssos*, bottomless]

AC *abbrev* alternating current.

Ac *symbol* (*chem*) actinium.

a/c *abbrev* account.

acacia *n* a shrub or small tree with small yellow or white flowers. [Gr *akakia*]

academy *n* **-*ies* 1** a school or college giving training in a particular subject or skill. **2** a society which encourages the study of science, literature, art or music. **3** in Scotland, a school for children between the ages of 11 and 18. [Gr *Akademeia*, the garden outside Athens where the philosopher Plato taught]

academic *adj* **1** to do with learning, study, education or teaching. **2** to do with a university, college or academy. **3** theoretical rather than practical. **4** of no practical importance, e.g. because impossible or unreal: *What we would do with a car is quite academic, since we can't afford a car*. **5** intelligent, and happy when studying or learning. — *n* a member of the teaching or research staff at a university or college. — *adv* **academically**.

academician *n* a member of an academy (sense **2**), esp. the Royal Academy of Arts, the Académie Française, or the USSR Academy of Sciences.

Academy Award or **Oscar** *n* any of the various prizes given each year by the American Academy of Motion Picture Arts and Sciences to the best film, actor, actress, etc.

acanthus *n* **1** a plant or shrub with prickly leaves. **2** (*archit*) a stone carving of an acanthus leaf used for decorations on columns. [Gr *akanthos*]

ACAS *abbrev* Advisory, Conciliation and Arbitration Service, an organisation which helps settle disagreements between employers and workers.

acc. *abbrev* **1** (also **acct.**) account. **2** accusative.

accede *v* (*intr*; **to**) **1** to take office, esp. to become king or queen. **2** to agree: *accede to the proposal*. **3** to join with others in a formal agreement. [Lat *accedere*, to go near]

accelerate *v* **1** (*intr* & *tr*) to (cause to) increase speed. **2** (*intr*) to be completed more quickly. **3** (*tr*) to make (something) happen sooner. [Lat *accelare*]

acceleration *n* **1** an increasing of speed; the rate of increase of speed. **2** the power of a vehicle to increase speed quickly.

accelerator *n* **1** the pedal or lever that is pressed to make a vehicle move faster by increasing the speed of its engine. **2** any of various substances or devices which make something work, happen, move, etc. faster.

accent *n* **1** the particular way words are pronounced by people who live in a particular place, belong to a particular social group, etc. **2** emphasis or stress put on a particular syllable in speaking. **3** a mark put over or under a letter or syllable to show how it is pronounced. **4** a feature, mark or characteristic which makes something distinct or special. **5** emphasis or stress placed on certain notes or chords in a piece of music. — *v* (*tr*) **1** to pronounce with an accent. **2** to write accents on. **3** to emphasise or stress. [Lat *accentus*]

accentuate *v* (*tr*) to emphasise or make more evident or prominent. — *n* **accentuation**. [Lat *accentuare*]

accept *v* **1** (*tr*) to agree to take or receive (something offered). **2** (*tr* & *intr*) to agree to (a suggestion, proposal, etc.). **3** (*tr*) to agree to do (a job, etc.) or take on (a responsibility, etc.). **4** (*tr*) to believe to be true or correct. **5** (*tr*) to be willing to listen to and follow (advice, etc.). **6** (*tr*) to be willing to suffer or take (blame, etc.). **7** (*tr*) to take as suitable or appropriate: *won't accept cheques*. **8** (*tr*) to allow into a group, treat as a colleague, etc. **9** (*tr*) to tolerate calmly. [Lat *acceptare*, to receive]

acceptable *adj* **1** worth accepting. **2** welcome or pleasing; suitable. **3** good enough, but usu. only just; tolerable. — *n* **acceptability**. — *adv* **acceptably**.

acceptance *n* **1** the act or state of accepting something. **2** favourable or positive reception of something.

access *n* **1** a means of approaching or entering a place. **2** the right, opportunity or ability to use, approach, meet with or enter. **3** a sudden and usually brief period of strong emotion. — *v* (*tr*) to get and be able to use (information, files, etc.) on a computer. [Lat *accessus*, from *ad*, to + *cedere*, to go]

accessible *adj* **1** able to be reached easily. **2** willing to talk to or have friendly discussions with other people. **3** easy to understand and enjoy or get some benefit from. — *n* **accessibility**. — *adv* **accessibly**.

access road *n* a minor road built specially to give access to a house, etc.

access time *n* the length of time it takes to get information out of the computer it is stored in.

accessary. See **accessory**.

accessible. See **access**.

accession *n* **1** the act or process of taking up a new office or responsibility, or becoming a king or queen. **2** a person or thing added, e.g. a new book to a library. **3** the formal act of agreeing to, and coming under the rules of, an international agreement or treaty. [Lat *accedere*, to accede]

accessory *n* **-ies 1** something additional to, but less important than, something else. **2** an item of dress, such as a bag, hat, etc., which goes with a dress, coat, etc. **3** (also **accessary**; *legal*) a person who helps a criminal do something wrong. — *adj* adding to something but only in a minor way. — **accessory before** or **after the fact** (*legal*) a person who helps a criminal before or after the crime. [Lat *accessorius*]

accident *n* **1** an unexpected event which causes damage or harm. **2** something which happens without planning or intention; chance: *managed it by accident*. [Lat *accidere*, to happen]

accidental *adj* happening or done by accident; not planned. — *n* **1** a sign, such as a sharp or flat, put in front of a note in written music to show that it is to be played higher or lower. **2** something which is not a necessary feature of something. — *adv* **accidentally**.

accident-prone *adj* (of a person) frequently causing or involved in accidents, usually minor ones.

acclaim *v* (*tr*) **1** to declare (someone) to be (something) with noisy enthusiasm. **2** to receive or welcome with noisy enthusiasm. — *n* a shout of applause or welcome. [Lat *acclamare*]

acclamation *n* a loud showing of approval, agreement, applause, etc.

acclimatise or **-ize** *v* (*tr* & *intr*) to make or become accustomed to a new place, situation, climate, etc. — *n* **acclimatisation** or **-z-**. [Fr *acclimater*, from *climat*, climate]

acclivity *n* **-ies** (*formal*) an upward slope. ◇ See also **declivity**. [Lat *acclivitas*]

accolade *n* **1** a sign or expression of great praise or approval. **2** a touch on the shoulder with a sword when giving a person a knighthood. [OFr *accoler*, to embrace]

accommodate *v* (*tr*) **1** to provide (someone) with a place in which to stay. **2** to be large enough for; to be able to hold. **3** to do what (someone) wants; to do (someone) a favour. **4** (**to**) to change (e.g. one's habits or plans) in order to be more like, more acceptable to, or more helpful to (someone or something): *accommodate oneself to one's surroundings*. [Lat *accommodare*, to adapt]

accommodating *adj* helpful; willing to do what another person wants. — *adv* **accommodatingly**.

accommodation *n* **1** (in *pl* in *US*) a room or rooms in a house or hotel in which to live. **2** willingness to accept other people's wishes, etc. **3** (in *pl*; *US*) a reserved place on a bus, train, ship or aircraft.

accommodation address *n* an address used on letters to a person who cannot give, or does not want to give, his or her permanent address.

accommodation ladder *n* a small ladder on the side of a large ship by means of which one can get to or from a smaller boat.

accompaniment *n* **1** something that happens or exists at the same time as something else, or which comes with something else. **2** music played to support a singer or other musical instrument. [**accompany**]

accompanist *n* a person who plays a musical instrument to support another player or a singer. [**accompany**]

accompany *v* **-ies**, **-ied** (*tr*) **1** to come or go with. **2** to be done or found with. **3** to play a musical instrument to support (someone who is playing another instrument or singing). [OFr *accompagnier*, from *a*, to + *compaignon*, companion]

accomplice *n* a person who helps another commit a crime. [MidE *complice*, from Lat *complex*, joined]

accomplish *v* (*tr*) **1** to manage to do. **2** to complete. — *adj* **accomplishable**. [OFr *acomplir*]

accomplished *adj* **1** clever or skilled. **2** completed or finished.

accomplishment *n* **1** a skill, esp. a social one, which one has developed through practice. **2** something special or remarkable which has been done; an achievement. **3** the finishing or completing of something.

accord *v* **1** (*intr*; **with**) to agree or be in harmony. **2** (*tr*) to give (a welcome, etc.) or grant (permission, a request, etc.). — *n* agreement or consent; harmony. — **of**

one's own accord willingly; without being told to or forced to. — **with one accord** with everyone in agreement and acting at the same time. [OFr *acorder*, from Lat *ad*, to + *cor*, heart]

accordance *n* agreement or harmony: *in accordance with the law*.

according *adv* **1** (with **to**) as said or told by: *according to my doctor*. **2** (with **to**) in agreement with: *live according to one's principles*. **3** (with **as**; *formal*) in proportion as; depending on whether: *contribute money according as one is able*.

accordingly *adv* **1** in an appropriate way: *act accordingly*. **2** therefore; for that reason.

accordion *n* a musical instrument consisting of two box-like parts joined by a folding middle section, played by pushing the box-like parts together and pulling them apart again to create a sound which is changed into different notes by pressing a series of buttons and piano-like keys with the fingers. — *n* **accordionist**. [Ger *Akkordion*, from Fr *accorder* or Ital *accordare*, to harmonise]

accost *v* (*tr*) **1** to approach and speak to (someone), esp. boldly or in a threatening way. **2** (of a prostitute) to offer to have sexual intercourse with (a person) in return for money. [Lat *accostare*]

account *n* **1** a description or report. **2** an explanation, esp. of one's behaviour. **3** an arrangement by which a bank or building society allows a person to have banking or credit facilities; a deposit of money in a bank or building society. **4** a statement of the money owed to someone for goods or services. **5** (usu. in *pl*) a record of money received and spent. **6** an arrangement by which a shop allows a person to buy goods on credit and pay for them later. **7** importance or value. **8** behalf or sake. — *v* (*tr*; *formal*) to consider (someone or something) to be (something). — *v* **account for** (*tr*) **1** to give a reason or explanation for. **2** to make or give a reckoning of (money spent, etc.). **3** to destroy or kill. — **bring to account** to punish for something wrong that has been done. — **by all accounts** according to general opinion. — **call to account** to demand an explanation from, esp. for something bad or foolish that has been done. — **give a good** or **poor account of oneself** to give a good or bad performance; to make a good or bad impression. — **hold to account** to consider responsible. — **leave out of account** not to consider (a problem, factor, etc.) when making a decision, calculation, etc. — **on account 1** to be paid for at a later date. **2** as partial payment. — **on account of** because of. — **on no account** not for any reason. — **on one's own account 1** on one's own responsibility. **2** for one's own benefit. — **put to good account** to use (a situation, ability, etc.) to one's advantage. — **take into account** or **take account of** to consider (a problem, opinion, etc.) when making a decision, etc. — **turn to good account** to use to one's advantage. [OFr *aconter*]

accountable *adj* **1** responsible; having to explain or defend one's actions or conduct. **2** explicable. — *n* **accountability**.

accountancy *n* the profession of preparing and keeping the financial records of a business company, etc. — *n* **accountant**.

accounting *n* the skill or practice of preparing or keeping the financial records of a company, etc.

accoutrements *n* (*pl*) **1** equipment. **2** a soldier's equipment apart from his or her clothes and weapons. [OFr *acoustrer*, to equip]

accredit *v* **-t-** (*tr*) **1** (**to, with**) to attribute (a saying, action, etc.) to (a person): *accredit the saying to him*; *accredit her with inventing the word*. **2** (**to, at**) to send (a diplomat, etc.) to a foreign country with official authority. **3** to state officially that (something) is of a satisfactory standard. — *n* **accreditation**. [OFr *acrediter*]

accredited *adj* **1** officially recognised. **2** (of a belief, etc.) generally accepted.

accretion *n* **1** an extra layer of material which has formed on something else. **2** the process of separate things growing into one. **3** continued growth by the forming of new layers, as e.g. in trees. [Lat *accretio*, growing together]

accrue *v* **1** (*intr*; **to, from**) to come in addition, as a product, result or development. **2** (*intr*) to fall to naturally. **3** (*tr*) to collect: *accrue a collection of antique vases*. — *n* **accrual**. [OFr *acrue*, from Lat *accrescere*, to grow together]

acct. See **acc**.

acculturation *n* the process of one group of people becoming more like another group of people in behaviour, customs, etc., usu. because of living near them for a long time. [Lat *ad*, to + **culture**]

accumulate *v* **1** (*tr*) to collect or gather (something) in an increasing quantity. **2** (*intr*) to grow greater in number or quantity. — *n* **accumulation**. [Lat *accumulare*, from *cumulus*, heap]

accumulative *adj* **1** becoming greater over a period of time. **2** tending to gather, buy, etc. many things. — *adv* **accumulatively**.

accumulator *n* **1** a type of electric battery which can be recharged. **2** (*Br*; also **accumulator bet**) a bet on four or more races, where the original money bet and any money won are bet on the next race, so that the better either wins a lot of money or loses it all. **3** a part of a computer which holds the results of operations performed.

accuracy *n* exactness; the state of being absolutely correct and making no mistakes, esp. through careful effort. [**accurate**]

accurate *adj* **1** exact; absolutely correct; making no mistakes. **2** agreeing exactly with the truth or a standard. — *adv* **accurately**. [Lat *accuratus*, performed with care]

accursed *adj* **1** (*coll*) disliked or hated. **2** having been cursed. — *adv* **accursedly**. [OE *acursod*]

accusation. See **accuse**.

accusative (*gram*) *n* in certain languages, e.g. Latin, Greek and German, the grammatical case of a noun, etc. when it is the object of an action or the point towards which something is moving. — *adj* of or in the accusative. [Lat *accusativus*]

accuse *v* (*tr*; **of**) to charge (a person) with having done something wrong. — *n* **accuser**. — *adj* **accusing**. — *adv* **accusingly**. — **the accused** the person or people accused of disobeying or breaking the law. — **stand accused** (*legal*) to be the person in a court case who is accused of having broken or disobeyed the law. [Lat *accusare*]

accusation *n* **1** the act of accusing someone of having done something wrong. **2** (*legal*) a statement charging a person with having committed a crime.

accustom *v* **-m-** (*tr*; **to**) to make (oneself, someone) used to. [OFr *acostumer*]

accustomed *adj* **1** (with **to**) used to; familiar with; experienced in. **2** usual; customary.

AC/DC or **ac/dc** *abbrev* alternating current/direct current. — *adj* (*slang*) sexually attracted to both men and women.

ace *n* **1** (*cards*) the card in each of the four suits with a single symbol on it, having either the highest value or the value one. **2** a person who is extremely good at something. **3** a fighter pilot who has shot down a lot of enemy aircraft. **4** (*tennis*, etc.) a serve that is so fast and cleverly placed that the opposing player cannot hit the ball back. — *adj* (*coll*) excellent. — **an ace up one's sleeve** a hidden or secret advantage, argument, etc. that will help one to beat an opponent. — **hold all the aces** to be in a powerful or winning position. — **play one's ace** to put into action a plan for the final defeat of one's opponent. — **within an ace of** very close to. [OFr *as*, from Lat *as*, unit]

acerbic *adj* **1** bitter and sour in taste. **2** bitter and harsh in manner, speech, etc. — *n* **acerbity**. [Lat *acerbus*, sour]

acetate *n* **1** a salt of acetic acid. **2** a smooth, shiny, man-made material. **[acetic]**

acetic *adj* of or like vinegar. [Lat *acetum*, vinegar]

acetic acid *n* the clear, liquid acid that gives vinegar its sour taste.

acetone *n* (*chem*) a strong-smelling, colourless liquid used as a solvent. **[acetic]**

acetylene *n* (*chem*) a colourless gas which burns with a bright flame, used for lighting and in welding. **[acetic]**

ache *v* (*intr*) **1** to feel or be the source of a dull, continuous pain. **2** (with **for**) to want (something) very much. — *n* a dull, continuous pain. — *adj* **achy**, ***-ier***, ***-iest***. [OE *acan*, to ache; *æce*, an ache]

achieve *v* **1** (*tr*) to reach, realise or attain (a goal, ambition, etc.), esp. through hard work. **2** (*tr*) to earn or gain (a reputation, etc.). **3** (*intr*) to be successful. — *adj* **achievable**. — *n* **achiever**. [OFr *achever*]

achievement *n* **1** the gaining of something, usually after working hard for it. **2** something that has been done or gained by effort.

Achilles' heel *n* a person's weak or vulnerable point. [From *Achilles*, a hero in the *Iliad*, who was invulnerable to weapons except in his heel]

Achilles' tendon *n* the tendon that connects the muscles in the calf of the leg to the heel.

achromatic *adj* **1** having no colour. **2** transmitting light without separating it into the colours which go to form it. — *adj* **achromatically**. [Gr *a*, without + *khroma*, colour]

achy. See **ache**.

acid *n* **1** any of a group of substances, usu. in the form of liquids, that contain hydrogen, are usu. sour, and are able to dissolve metals and form salts. **2** any sour substance. **3** (*slang*) LSD. — *adj* **1** containing acid; sour to taste. **2** (of remarks, etc.) expressing bitterness or anger. — *n* **acidity**, ***-ies***. — *adv* **acidly**. [Lat *acidus*, sour]

acidic *adj* like, or containing, acid.

acidify *v* ***-ies***, ***-ied*** (*tr* & *intr*) to make or become acid. — *n* **acidification**.

Acid House *n* (also no *caps*) a type of electronically produced disco music with a repetitive, hypnotic beat, often associated with the use of certain drugs, and usu. played at very large parties.

acid rain *n* rain that contains harmful acids formed from waste gases released into the atmosphere from factories, etc.

acid test *n* a test that will show whether something is as good, strong, valuable, etc. as it is claimed to be.

ack-ack *adj* (*old coll*) anti-aircraft. [Formerly, British signaller's code for the letters *AA*, standing for *anti-aircraft*]

acknowledge *v* (*tr*) **1** to admit or accept the truth of (a fact or situation). **2** to accept as valid or legal; to recognise. **3** to report that one has received (what has been sent). **4** to express thanks for. **5** to show that one has noticed or recognised (someone), by greeting them, nodding one's head, etc. **6** to accept someone (as something); to accept a person's claim to be (something). [Old verb *acknow*, to acknowledge]

acknowledgement or **acknowledgment** *n* **1** the act of acknowledging someone or something. **2** something done, given or said to acknowledge something.

acme *n* the highest point of achievement, success, excellence, etc. [Gr]
acne *n* an unhealthy condition of skin, esp. greasy skin, in which many red spots form on the face, shoulders or back. [Lat]
acolyte *n* **1** a person who assists a priest in certain religious ceremonies. **2** an assistant or attendant. [Lat *acolytus*, from Gr *akolouthos*, follower]
aconite *n* **1** (also **monkshood** and **wolfsbane**) a poisonous wild plant with hood-like blue or yellow flowers. **2** a drug obtained from the roots of this plant. [Lat *aconitum*]
acorn *n* the nut-like fruit of the oak tree, which has a cup-shaped outer case. [OE *æcern*]
acoustic *adj* **1** of sound, the sense of hearing, or acoustics. **2** (of a musical instrument) not using electricity. **3** (of building materials, etc.) absorbing sound. — *adv* **acoustically**. [Gr *akoustikos*, from *akouein*, to hear]
acoustic coupler *n* an instrument that makes it possible for computers to pass information by means of an ordinary telephone.
acoustics *n* **1** (*pl*) the qualities of a room, hall, theatre, etc. that make it a good or bad place in which to listen to music or other sounds. **2** (*sing*) the science of sound.
acquaint *v* (*tr*; **with**) to make (a person) aware of or familiar with something. [OFr *acointer*]
acquaintance *n* **1** slight knowledge of something or someone. **2** someone whom one knows slightly. — *n* **acquaintanceship**. — **make the acquaintance of** to get to know.
acquainted *adj* **1** (**with**) knowing someone personally but not very well. **2** (with **with**) familiar with: *acquainted with her books.*
acquiesce *v* (*intr*; **in, to**) to accept (something) without objection. — *n* **acquiescence**. — *adj* **acquiescent**. — *adv* **acquiescently**. [Lat *acquiescere*]
acquire *v* (*tr*) **1** to get, gain or develop, esp. through skill or effort. **2** to achieve or reach (a reputation). [Lat *acquirere*]
acquired immune deficiency syndrome see **AIDS**.
acquired taste *n* **1** a liking for something that develops as one has more experience of it. **2** the thing liked.
acquirement *n* something learned or developed through hard work and not a natural gift.
acquisition *n* **1** a thing obtained or acquired, esp. through hard work or effort. **2** the act of obtaining, developing or acquiring a skill, etc. [Lat *acquisitio*]
acquisitive *adj* very eager to obtain and possess things. — *n* **acquisitiveness**. [Lat *acquisitivus*]
acquit *v* **-tt-** (*tr*) **1** (**of**) to declare (an accused person) to be innocent (of the crime, etc. he or she has been accused of). **2** to conduct (oneself) or behave or perform in a particular way. [OFr *aquiter*]
acquittal *n* **1** a declaration in a court of law that someone is not guilty of the crime, etc. of which he or she has been accused. **2** performance of a duty.
acre *n* **1** a unit of measurement for land, equal to 4840 square yards or 4047 square metres. **2** (in *pl*) a large area of land. [OE *æcer*, field]
acreage *n* the number of acres in a piece of land.
acrid *adj* **1** having a very strong, bitter taste or smell. **2** (of speech, manner, etc.) sharp or bitter. — *n* **acridity**. — *adv* **acridly**. [Lat *acer*, sharp, keen]
acrimony *n* bitterness in feeling, temper or speech. — *adj* **acrimonious**. — *adv* **acrimoniously**. [Lat *acrimonia*]
acrobat *n* an entertainer, e.g. in a circus, who performs skilful balancing acts and other athletic tricks. — *adj* **acrobatic**. — *adv* **acrobatically**. [Fr *acrobate*, from Gr *akrobatos*, walking on tiptoe]
acrobatics *n* **1** (*sing*) the art or skill of an acrobat. **2** (in *pl*) acrobatic movements.
acronym *n* a word made from the first letters or syllables of other words, e.g. *NATO* is an acronym of *N*orth *A*tlantic *T*reaty *O*rganisation. [Gr *akron*, point, end + *onyma*, name]
acrophobia *n* fear of heights. [Gr *akron*, point, summit + *phobos*, fear]
acropolis *n* the upper fortified part or citadel of an ancient Greek city, esp. Athens. [Gr *akron*, point, summit + *polis*, city]
across *prep* **1** to, at or on the other side of. **2** from one side of to the other. **3** so as to cross: *arms folded across the chest.* — *adv* **1** to, at or on the other side. **2** from one side to the other. — **across the board** general; applying in all cases. [**a**[3] + **cross**]
acrostic *n* a poem in which the first letters in each line form a word or proverb. [Gr *akron*, end + *stichos*, line]
acrylic *n* **1** a man-made material made from acrylic acid. **2** same as **acrylic resin**. — *adj* of the material acrylic. [Lat *acer*, sharp + *olere*, to smell]
acrylic acid *n* a type of naturally occurring acid used in the manufacture of paints, resins, materials, etc.
acrylic resin *n* a type of resin made from acrylic acid, used as a rubber, and in making paints and plastics.
act *n* **1** a thing done; a deed. **2** the process of doing something: *caught in the act.* **3** behaviour that is intended to make an impression on people and is not a sincere expression of feeling. **4** a short piece of entertainment, usu. one of a series in a show; the person or people performing this. **5** a major division of a play, opera, etc. ◇See also **scene**. **6** a formal decision reached or a law passed by a law-making body. — *v* **1** (*intr*) to behave. **2** (*intr*) to do something: *need to act fast.* **3** (*intr*; **as, for**)

to perform the actions or functions (of). **4** (*intr*) to perform in a play or film. **5** (*tr*) to perform (a part) in a play or film; to perform (a play). **6** (*tr*) to show (feelings one does not really have). **7** (*intr*; **on**, **upon**) to have an effect or influence on. — **act of God** an event beyond human control, esp. a natural disaster such as an earthquake. — *v* **act on** or **upon** (*tr*) to follow (advice, etc.); to obey (instructions, etc.). — *v* **act out** (*tr*) to express (one's feelings, fears, etc.) in one's behaviour, usu. unconsciously. — *v* **act up** (*intr*; *coll*) **1** (of a machine, etc.) not to work properly. **2** to behave badly. — **get in on the act** (*coll*) to start taking part in some profitable activity, plan, etc. in order to share in the benefits. — **get one's act together** (*coll*) to organise oneself and one's work efficiently. ◇ See also **actor** and **actress**. [Lat *actum*, thing done]

acting *n* the profession or art of performing in a play or film. — *adj* temporarily doing someone else's job or duties.

actinium *n* a radioactive metallic element (symbol **Ac**) found in pitchblende. [Gr *aktis*, ray (from its being radioactive)]

action *n* **1** the process of doing something: *put ideas into action.* **2** something done. **3** activity, force or energy: *a woman of action.* **4** a movement or gesture. **5** the working part of a machine, instrument, etc.; a mechanism. **6** a battle; fighting. **7** (with **the**) the events of a play, film, etc. **8** (*coll*) exciting activity or events going on around one: *get a piece of the action.* **9** a legal case. — **out of action** not working. [Lat *actio*, from *agere*, to do, drive]

actionable *adj* giving reasonable cause for legal action.

action-packed *adj* (*coll*) filled with exciting activity.

action replay *n* the repeating, often in slow-motion, of a piece of film on television, esp. of some important act such as scoring a goal.

action stations *n* (*pl*) positions taken by soldiers who are ready for battle, etc.

activate *v* (*tr*) **1** to make (something) start working or go into operation. **2** to make (something) radioactive. **3** to make (a chemical reaction) happen faster. — *n* **activation**. **[active]**

active *adj* **1** moving, working and doing things; full of energy. **2** operating; working. **3** having an effect: *the active ingredients.* **4** radioactive. **5** (of verbs) in the form that is used when the subject of the sentence performs the action of the verb. ◇ See also **passive**. — *n* **1** (also **active voice**) the form a verb takes when its subject performs its action. **2** a verb in the active. — *adv* **actively**. [Lat *activus*]

activist *n* a person who is very active, esp. as a member of a political group.

activity *n* **-ies 1** the state of being active or busy. **2** (often in *pl*) something that people do, esp. for pleasure, interest, exercise, etc. [Lat *activitas*]

actor *n* a man or woman whose job is performing in plays or films. [Lat *actor*, doer]

actress *n* a woman whose job is performing in plays or films.

actual *adj* existing as fact; real; not imagined, estimated or guessed. [Lat *actualis*]

actuality *n* **-ies 1** fact; reality. **2** (in *pl*) an existing condition.

actually *adv* **1** really; in fact. **2** (used esp. when surprised) as a matter of fact.

actuary *n* **-ies** a person whose job is to calculate what the risks of insurance are, and give advice to insurance companies, etc. on what price to charge. — *adj* **actuarial**. [Lat *actuarius*, clerk]

actuate *v* (*tr*) **1** to cause (a mechanism, etc.) to go into action. **2** to cause (someone) to act the way he or she does. — *n* **actuation**. [Lat *actuare*, from *actus*, act]

acuity *n* sharpness or acuteness, e.g. of the mind or senses. [Lat *acuitas*, from *acus*, needle]

acumen *n* the ability to judge quickly and well; keen insight. [Lat *acumen*, point, from *acus*, needle]

acupuncture *n* an orig. Chinese method of treating illness and pain by sticking needles into the patient's skin at certain points. — *n* **acupuncturist**. [Lat *acus*, needle + **puncture**]

acute *adj* **1** extremely severe; very bad. **2** (of the senses) keen, good or sharp; penetrating. **3** (of mental powers, etc.) quick and very good. **4** (of an illness) quickly becoming severe. ◇ See also **chronic**. **5** (of a sound) high, sharp and shrill. **6** (of an angle) less than 90°. — *n* an acute accent. — *adv* **acutely**. — *n* **acuteness**. [Lat *acuere*, to sharpen]

acute accent *n* a mark (´) over a vowel in some languages, showing pronunciation.

-acy *sfx* forming nouns meaning **1** quality: *accuracy*. **2** state, condition, office, etc.: *supremacy*; *piracy*. [Lat *-acia*]

AD or **A.D.** *abbrev* **Anno Domini**. ◇ See also **BC**.

ad *n coll* short form of **advertisement**.

adman *n* (*coll*) a man whose job is to produce or write advertisements for commercial organisations, etc.

adage *n* a proverb or maxim. [Fr, from Lat *adagium*]

adagio (*mus*) *adv* slowly. — *n* **-os** a slow movement or piece of music. [Ital]

Adam *n* the first man, according to the Bible. — **not know someone from Adam** not to know someone well enough to be able to recognise him or her. [Hebr *adam*, man]

adam's apple *n* the slight lump, part of the thyroid gland, that projects from the front of a man's neck.

adamant *adj* (**about**) completely determined; not likely to change one's mind or opinion. — *adv* **adamantly**. [OFr *adamaunt*, from Lat *adamas*, hard steel]

adapt *v* **1** (*tr* & *intr*; **to**) to change (something, oneself, etc.) so as to fit new circumstances, etc.; to make suitable for a new purpose. **2** (*tr*) to alter or modify. [Lat *ad*, to + *aptare*, to fit]

adaptable *adj* **1** (of a person) good at fitting into new circumstances, situations, etc. **2** that can be adapted. — *n* **adaptability**.

adaptation *n* **1** a thing which is adapted. **2** the process of adapting.

adaptor *n* **1** a type of electrical plug used for connecting a plug of one type to a socket of another type, or for connecting several plugs to the same socket. **2** (also **adapter**) a person who adapts.

ADC *abbrev* **aide-de-camp**.

add *v* (*tr*) **1** (**to, together**) to put together or combine (two or more things) or put (something) together with something else. **2** to put (two or more numbers) together to get their total. **3** to say or write (something) further. — *adj* **added**. — *v* **add in** (*tr*) to include, esp. as an extra. — *v* **add on** (*tr*; **to**) to attach (something) to something else. ◇ See also **add-on** below. — *v* **add up 1** (*tr*) to find the total of. **2** (*intr*; with **to**) to be or amount to. **3** (*intr*; *coll*) to make sense. [Lat *addere*, from *ad*, to + *dare*, to put]

add-on *n* **1** anything added to supplement something else. **2** a piece of computer equipment, or an extra computer program, which can be added to a computer to increase its functions. **3** an extra charge added to the basic charge of something.

addendum *n* **-da 1** an addition. **2** (usu. in *pl*) something missed out from a book, etc., added to the end. [Lat *addere*, to add]

adder *n* the common viper, a poisonous snake with a black zig-zag pattern on its back, found in northern parts of Europe and Asia. [OE *nædre*; in MidE *a nadder* became understood to be *an adder*]

addict *n* **1** a person who has a harmful habit, esp. drug-taking, and is unable to stop it. **2** (*coll*) a person who is extremely fond of a hobby, etc.: *a chess addict*. — *adj* **addicted (to)**. — *n* **addiction**. [Lat *addicere*, to surrender]

addictive *adj* causing users, etc. to become addicts: *addictive drugs*.

addition *n* **1** the act, or operation, of adding. **2** a person or thing that is added. — **in addition to** as well as; besides. [Lat *additio*, from *addere*, to add]

additional *adj* extra; more than usual. — *adv* **additionally**.

additive *n* a substance that is added, e.g. one added to food to keep it fresh longer or improve its taste or colour, etc. [Lat *additivus*]

addle *v* **1** (*tr*) to confuse or muddle. **2** (*intr*) (of an egg) to go bad. — *adj* **addled**. [OE *adela*, mud]

addle-brained *adj* confused; crazy.

address *n* **1** the number or name of the house or building, and the name of the street and town, where a person lives or works. **2** a speech or lecture. **3** a number giving the place in a computer memory where a particular piece of information is stored. — *v* (*tr*) **1** to put the name and address on (an envelope, etc.). **2** to make a speech, give a lecture, etc. to. **3** to speak to. **4** to give one's attention to (a problem, etc.). — **address oneself to 1** to speak or write to. **2** to deal with (a problem, matter, etc.). [OFr *adresser*]

addressee *n* the person to whom a letter, etc. is addressed.

form of address *n* the word or words used as a title before a person's name; the form of words used in speaking to someone on a formal or ceremonial occasion.

adduce *v* (*tr*) to mention (a fact) as a supporting reason, piece of evidence, etc. — *adj* **adducible**. [Lat *ad*, to + *ducere*, to lead]

adenoids *n* (*pl*) a mass of soft flesh projecting from the back of the throat, behind the nose, which can become swollen and require removal by surgery. [Gr *adenoiedes*, from *aden*, gland]

adenoidal *adj* **1** relating to the adenoids. **2** having the sound made by someone with swollen adenoids.

adept *adj* (**at**) skilful at doing something; proficient. — *n* an expert at something. — *adv* **adeptly**. [Lat *adeptus*, having attained an art]

adequate *adj* **1** (**for**) enough; sufficient. **2** (**to**) able to do (a particular job, task, etc.). **3** only just satisfactory. — *n* **adequacy**. — *adv* **adequately**. [Lat *ad*, to + *aequus*, equal]

adhere *v* (*intr*) **1** (**to**) to stick. **2** (**to**) to remain loyal (to a religion, etc.). **3** (with **to**) to follow (a plan, rule, etc.) exactly. [Lat *ad*, to + *haerere*, to stick]

adherent *n* a follower; a supporter. — *adj* sticking or adhering to. — *n* **adherence**.

adhesion *n* **1** the process of sticking or adhering. **2** the ability to stick or join surfaces together. **3** (*med*; often in *pl*) a condition that develops esp. after surgery, with thin layers of material forming between organs inside the body and sticking them together, so that further surgery is needed to separate them. [Lat *adhaesio*]

adhesive *adj* sticky; able to make things stick together. — *n* any substance used to stick things together. [Fr *adhésif*, from Lat *adhaerere*, to adhere]

ad hoc *adj* & *adv* for one particular purpose, situation, etc. only. [Lat, to this]

adieu *n* ***adieus*** or ***adieux*** a goodbye. — *interj* goodbye. [Fr, from *à*, to + *dieu*, God]

ad infinitum *adv* for ever; without limit. [Lat]

adipose *adj* containing, or consisting of, fat; fatty. — *n* **adiposity**. [Lat *adiposus*, from *adeps*, soft fat]

adj *abbrev* **adjective**.

adjacent *adj* (**to**) lying beside or next to: *adjacent houses*. [Lat *adjacere*, to lie by the side of]

adjective *n* a word that describes a noun or pronoun, as *dark* describes *hair* in *She has dark hair*, and *sad* describes *her* in *The book made her sad*. — *adj* **adjectival**. — *adv* **adjectivally**. [Lat *adjicere*, to throw to, apply]

adjoin *v* (*tr*) to be next to and joined to (something). — *adj* **adjoining**. [OFr *ajoindre*, from Lat *ad*, to + *jungere*, to join]

adjourn *v* **1** (*tr*) to put off (a meeting, etc.) to another time. **2** (*tr*) to finish (a meeting, etc.), intending to continue it at another time or place. **3** (*intr*; **to**) to move to another place, usu. for refreshment or rest. **4** (*intr*) to finish a meeting and separate. — *n* **adjournment**. [OFr *ajorner*]

adjudge *v* (*tr*) to declare or judge officially. — *n* **ajudgement** or **ajudgment**. [OFr *ajuger*, from Lat *adjudicare*, to adjudicate]

adjudicate *v* **1** (*intr*) to act as judge in a court, competition, etc. **2** (*tr*) to give a decision on (a disagreement between two parties, etc.). — *n* **adjudication**. — *n* **adjudicator**. [Lat *adjudicare*, from *judex*, judge]

adjunct *n* **1** something attached or added to something else but not an essential part of it. **2** a person who is below someone else in rank. **3** (*gram*) a word or clause that adds information about the subject, etc. of a sentence. [Lat *adjungere*, to join to]

adjure *v* (*tr*; *formal*) to request, beg or command solemnly. — *n* **adjuration**. [Lat *adjurare*, to swear to]

adjust *v* **1** (*tr*) to change slightly so as to be more suitable for a situation, etc. **2** (*tr*) to change or alter, esp. only slightly, to make more correct or accurate. **3** (*tr*) to calculate or assess (the amount of money payable in an insurance claim, etc.) **4** (*intr*; **to**) to change so that one fits in or becomes suited. — *adj* **adjustable**. — *n* **adjustment**. [OFr *ajuster*, to make conform to]

adjutant *n* an army officer who does administrative work. [Lat *adjutare*, to assist]

ad-lib *v* **-bb-** (*intr* & *tr*) to say (something) without preparation, esp. when one has forgotten one's lines or to fill up time; to improvise (music, etc.). — *adv* (**ad lib**) **1** without preparation. **2** (*coll*) without limit; freely. — *adj* (**ad-lib**) (of speeches, etc.) made up as the speaker speaks; improvised. [Short for Lat *ad libitum*, at pleasure]

Adm. *abbrev* Admiral.

adman. See **ad**.

admin *n* (*coll*) short form of **administration**.

administer *v* **1** (*tr*) to manage, govern or direct (one's affairs, an organisation, etc.). **2** (*tr*) to give out formally: *administer justice*. **3** (*tr*) to supervise a person taking (an oath). **4** (*tr*) to apply or provide (medicine). **5** (*tr*) to give: *administer a rebuke*. **6** (*intr*) to act as an administrator. [Lat *administrare*]

administrate *v* **1** (*tr*) to administer (a company, organisation, etc.). **2** (*intr*) to act as an administrator.

administration *n* **1** the directing, managing or governing of a company's affairs, etc. **2** a period of government by a particular party, etc. **3** (*US*) a period of government by a particular president. **4** the group of people who manage a company's affairs or run the business of government.

administrative *adj* of or concerned with administration. — *adv* **administratively**.

administrator *n* a person who manages, governs, directs, etc. the affairs of an organisation, estate, etc.

admirable. See **admire**.

admiral *n* **1** a high-ranking naval officer commanding a fleet of ships. **2** a name applied to several species of butterfly. [OFr *amiral*, from Arabic *amir-al-bahr*, lord of the sea]

admiral of the fleet *n* the highest-ranking admiral in the Royal Navy.

Admiralty *n* (with **the**; *Br hist*) the government department that managed the Royal Navy until this task was taken over by the Ministry of Defence in 1964.

admire *v* (*tr*) to regard with respect or approval. — *n* **admiration**. — *adj* **admiring**. — *adv* **admiringly**. [Lat *admirari*]

admirable *adj* **1** worthy of being admired. **2** very good; excellent. — *adv* **admirably**.

admirer *n* **1** someone who admires a particular person or thing. **2** a man who is attracted to a particular woman.

admissible *adj* that can be allowed or accepted, esp. as proof in a court of law. — *n* **admissibility**. [Lat *admissibilis*, from *admittere*, to admit]

admission *n* **1** the act of allowing in or being allowed in. **2** the cost of entry. **3** an act of admitting the truth of something. [Lat *admissio*]

admit *v* **-tt- 1** (*tr* & *intr*) to agree to the truth of (something), esp. unwillingly. **2** (*tr* & *intr*; **to**) to agree that one has done (something bad, wrong, etc.) or is guilty of (a crime, etc.). **3** (*tr*) to allow to enter. **4** (*tr*) to allow to take part in; to accept as a member or patient. **5** (*tr*; *formal*) to have room for: *a room admitting forty people*. — *v* **admit of** (*tr*) to allow as possible. [Lat *admittere*]

admittance *n* **1** the right to enter; permission to enter. **2** the act of entering; entry.

admittedly *adv* as is known to be true; as one must admit.

admixture *n* **1** a thing added to the main ingredient of something. **2** the mixing in of something extra. [Lat *ad*, to + *miscere*, to mix]

admonish *v* (*tr*) **1** to warn. **2** to scold or tell off firmly but mildly. **3** to advise or urge. — *adv* **admonishingly**. [OFr *amonester*]

admonition *n* a scolding or warning. [Lat *admonitio*, from *admonere*, to admonish]

admonitory *adj* containing a scolding or warning.

ad nauseam *adv* to the point of producing disgust; excessively. [Lat, to sickness]

ado *n* ***ados*** difficulty or trouble; fuss or bustle. — **without more** or **further ado** without any more delay; immediately. [MidE *at do*, to do]

adobe *n* **1** a kind of building material made of clay and straw, which is dried in the sun. **2** a sun-dried brick made from such material. **3** a building made from such bricks. [Span, from Arabic *at tub*, the brick]

adolescent *adj* **1** (of young people) at the stage of development between child and adult, usu. between the ages of 13 and 16. **2** (*coll*) (of behaviour) silly; immature. — *n* a young person between childhood and adulthood. — *n* **adolescence**. [Lat *adolescere*, to grow up]

Adonis *n* a handsome young man. [In Greek mythology, the name of a young man loved by the goddess Aphrodite]

adopt *v* **1** (*tr* & *intr*) to take (a child of other parents) into one's own family, becoming its legal parent. **2** (*tr*) to take up (a habit, position, policy, etc.). **3** (*tr*) to take (an idea, etc.) over from someone else. **4** (*tr*) to choose formally (esp. a candidate in an election). — *adj* **adopted**. — *n* **adoption**. [OFr *adopter*, from Lat *ad*, to + *optare*, to choose]

adoptive *adj* that adopts or is adopted.

adore *v* (*tr*) **1** to love deeply. **2** (*coll*) to like very much. **3** to worship (a god). — *n* **adoration**. — *n* **adorer**. — *adj* **adoring**. — *adv* **adoringly**.

adorable *adj* **1** worthy of being adored. **2** (*coll*) very charming and attractive. — *adv* **adorably**. [Lat *adorare*, from *ad*, to + *orare*, to pray]

adorn *v* (*tr*) **1** to decorate. **2** to add beauty to. — *n* **adornment**. [Lat *adornare*]

ADP *abbrev* automatic data processing, the processing of large quantities of data by computer as part of a company's daily routine, to provide the information the company needs every day.

adrenal *adj* **1** on or near the kidneys. **2** of the adrenal glands. [Lat *ad*, to + **renal**]

adrenal gland *n* either of the two glands which produce adrenalin, situated above the kidneys.

adrenalin or **adrenaline** *n* **1** a hormone produced by the adrenal glands when one is angry, excited or frightened, which causes the heart to beat faster so that more energy is available in case one needs to act suddenly. **2** this hormone taken from animals or (*cap*; ®) made from chemicals, used as a drug.

adrift *adj* & *adv* **1** (of a boat) not tied up; floating about without being steered. **2** without help or guidance. **3** (*coll*) off course. [**a**[3] + **drift**]

adroit *adj* quick and clever in action or thought. — *adj* **adroitly**. — *n* **adroitness**. [Fr *à droit*, according to the right, rightly]

adsorb *v* (*tr*) (of a solid) to hold (a thin layer of gas, liquid, etc.) on its surface causing a thin film to form. — *adj* **adsorbent**. — *n* **adsorption**. [Lat *ad*, to + *sorbere*, to suck in]

adulate *v* (*tr*) to praise or flatter far too much. — *n* **adulation**. — *adj* **adulatory**. [Lat *adulari*, to fawn upon]

adult *adj* **1** fully grown; mature. **2** typical of, or suitable for, a fully grown person. **3** (esp. of films) concerned with sex, and therefore not suitable for children. — *n* a fully grown person, animal, bird or plant. — *n* **adulthood**. [Lat *adultus*, grown-up]

adulterate *v* (*tr*) to add a substance to (something) so that it is no longer pure. — *n* **adulteration**. [Lat *adulterare*]

adultery *n* ***-ies*** sexual relations between a married person and a person who is not his or her spouse. — *n* **adulterer**. — *n* **adulteress**. — *adj* **adulterous**. — *adv* **adulterously**. [Lat *adulterare*, to defile]

adumbrate *v* (*tr*) **1** to indicate or describe in a general way. **2** to suggest or indicate (something likely to happen in the future); to foreshadow. **3** to throw a shadow over. — *n* **adumbration**. [Lat *adumbrare*, to shade in, sketch]

adv *abbrev* adverb.

advance *v* **1** (*tr* & *intr*) to put, move or go forward, sometimes in a threatening way. **2** (*intr*) to make progress. **3** (*tr*) to help the progress of; to improve or promote. **4** (*tr*) to propose or suggest (an idea, etc.). **5** (*tr*) to put at an earlier time or date than that previously planned. **6** (*tr*) to pay (money) to (someone) before payment is due; to lend (a sum of money) to (someone). **7** (*tr* & *intr*) to increase (a price) or be increased. — *n* **1** progress; a move forward. **2** a payment made before it is due. **3** money lent to someone. **4** an increase, esp. in price. **5** (in *pl*) friendly or sexual approaches to a person. — *adj* done, made or given beforehand. — **in advance** ahead in time, place or development. [OFr *avancer*, from Lat *abante*, in front]

advanced *adj* **1** having progressed or developed well or far. **2** modern; new; revolutionary.

Advanced level see **A level** at **A**[2].

advancement *n* **1** progress and development. **2** promotion in rank or improvement in status. **3** payment in advance.

advantage *n* **1** a favourable circumstance; benefit or usefulness. **2** a circumstance that may help one to succeed, win, etc. **3** superiority over another. **4** (*tennis*) the point scored after deuce. — **have the advantage of** to know something that is not known to (another person); to be in a better position than (someone else). — **take advantage of 1** to make use of (a situation, a person's good nature, etc.) in such a way as to benefit oneself. **2** (*old*) to seduce. — **to advantage** in such a way as to emphasise the good qualities. — **to one's advantage** of benefit or importance to one. — **turn to advantage** to use (a circumstance, a situation, etc.) in such a way as to get some benefit from it. [OFr *avantage*, from *avant*, before; see also ety. for **advance**]

advantaged *adj* having a good social or financial situation.

advantageous *adj* giving help or benefit in some way. — *adv* **advantageously**. — *n* **advantageousness**.

advent *n* **1** coming or arrival; first appearance. **2** (*cap*) the period including the four Sundays before Christmas. **3** (*cap*) the first or second coming of Christ. [Lat *adventus*, arrival]

Adventist *n* a member of a Christian group which believes the second coming of Christ will happen very soon.

adventitious *adj* happening by chance; accidental. — *adv* **adventitiously**. [Lat *adventicius*, coming from the outside]

adventure *n* **1** an exciting and often dangerous experience, such as a journey. **2** the excitement of risk or danger: *a sense of adventure*. [Lat *adventurus*, about to happen]

adventure playground *n* a playground with things for children to climb on and equipment for them to build with.

adventurer and **adventuress** *n* **1** a man, or a woman, who is willing to use any means, dishonest, immoral or dangerous, to make money, obtain power, etc. **2** a man, or a woman, who is eager for adventure.

adventurous *adj* **1** ready to act boldly and take risks; enjoying adventure; daring. **2** full of excitement, danger, daring activities, etc. — *adv* **adventurously**.

adverb *n* a word or group of words which describes or adds to the meaning of a verb, adjective or another adverb, such as *very* and *quietly* in *They were talking very quietly*. — *adj* **adverbial**. — *adv* **adverbially**. [Lat *adverbium*, a word added after]

adversary *n* **-ies 1** an opponent in a competition, etc. **2** an enemy. [Lat *adversarius*]

adversarial *adj* **1** involving opposition. **2** hostile.

adverse *adj* **1** unfavourable to one's interests. **2** disapproving. **3** hurtful. **4** (of winds) coming from in front of one and not from behind. — *adv* **adversely**. [Lat *adversus*, hostile]

adversity *n* **-ies 1** circumstances that cause trouble or sorrow. **2** an event or circumstance that causes trouble or sorrow; a misfortune.

advert[1] *n* (*coll*) short form of **advertisement**.

advert[2] *v* (*intr*; *formal*; **to**) to refer to or mention in speaking or writing. [OFr *avertir*, from Lat *advertere*, to direct one's attention to]

advertise *v* **1** (*tr*) to draw attention to or describe (goods for sale, services offered, etc.) in newspapers, on the television, etc., to encourage people to buy or use them. **2** (*tr*) to make known publically or generally. **3** (*intr*; usu. with **for**) to ask for or seek (something or someone) by putting a notice in a newspaper, shop window, etc. — *n* **advertiser**. [OFr *avertir*, from Lat *advertere*, to direct one's attention to]

advertisement *n* a public notice, announcement, picture, etc. in a newspaper, on a wall in the street, etc., which advertises something; a short television film advertising something.

advertising *n* the business of producing advertisements for goods.

advice *n* **1** suggestions or opinions given to someone about what he or she should do in a particular situation. **2** in business, etc., an official note about a transaction, etc. — **take advice 1** to ask someone for his or her opinion about what one should do. **2** to act on advice given. [OFr *avis*]

advise *v* **1** (*tr*) to give advice to. **2** (*tr*) to recommend. **3** (*tr*; **of**) to inform. **4** (*tr* & *intr*; **on**) to act as an adviser to someone. — *n* **adviser** or **advisor**. [OFr *aviser*]

advisable *adj* **1** (of action to be taken, etc.) to be recommended; wise. **2** sensible. — *n* **advisability**.

advised *adj* (esp. *in cmpds*) considered; judged: *well-advised*; *ill-advised*.

advisedly *adv* after careful thought; on purpose.

advisory *adj* giving advice.

advocaat *n* a liqueur made from raw eggs, sugar and brandy. [Dut *advocaatenborrel*, a lawyer's drink, orig. to clear the throat]

advocacy *n* **1** recommendation or active support of an idea, etc. **2** the function or job of an advocate, e.g. in a particular trial. [Lat *advocatia*, from *advocatus*, legal counsellor]

advocate *n* **1** esp. in Scotland, a lawyer who speaks for the defence or prosecution in a trial. ◇ See also **barrister**, **solicitor**. **2** a person who supports or recommends an idea, proposal, etc. — *v* (*tr*) to recommend or support (an idea, proposal, etc.), esp. in public. [OFr *avocat*, from Lat *advocatus*, legal adviser]

adze *n* a heavy tool with a blade at right angles to its handle, used for cutting and shaping wood. [OE *adesa*]

aegis: **under the aegis of** under the supervision and with the support of (an official organisation, etc.). [Gr *aigis*, the shield belonging to Zeus in Greek mythology]

aeolian harp *n* a box-like musical instrument which has strings stretched across a hole, and which makes musical sounds when the wind passes through it. [Lat *Aeolus*, god of the winds]

aeon or **eon** *n* **1** a very long period of time. **2** (*geol*) the longest stage in the formation of the earth, comprising two or more eras. [Lat, from Gr *aion*, an age]

aerate *v* (*tr*) **1** to force gas, esp. carbon dioxide, into (a liquid), e.g. when making fizzy drinks. **2** to put oxygen into (the blood) by breathing. **3** to expose to the air, esp. in order to introduce oxygen. — *n* **aeration**. [Lat *aer*, air]

aerial *n* a wire or rod on a radio or television set, able to send or receive signals. — *adj* **1** in or belonging to the air. **2** like air; ethereal. **3** in or from aircraft. — *adv* **aerially**. [Lat *aerius*, from *aer*, air]

aerie *n*. Same as **eyrie**.

aero- *comb fm* **1** of air: *aerodynamics*. **2** of aircraft: *aerodrome*. [Gr *aer*, air]

aerobatics *n* **1** (*pl*) dangerous and difficult movements of an aeroplane, such as flying upside down, etc. **2** (*sing*) the art of making an aeroplane perform such movements. — *adj* **aerobatic**. [**aero-** + **acrobatics**]

aerobic *adj* **1** (of living organisms or technical processes, etc.) dependent on a supply of oxygen. **2** relating to aerobics. **3** (of exercises) serving to increase the amount of oxygen in the blood. [**aero-** + Gr *bios*, life]

aerobics *n* **1** (*sing*) a system of physical exercise consisting of rapidly repeated, energetic movements, which increases the supply of oxygen in the blood and strengthens the heart and lungs. **2** (*pl*) energetic exercises.

aerodrome *n* (esp. *Br*) an airfield for private or military aircraft. [**aero-** + Gr *dromos*, course]

aerodynamics *n* **1** (*sing*) the scientific study of forces acting on objects as they move through the air. **2** (*pl*) the qualities required for fast and efficient movement through the air. [**aero-** + **dynamics**]

aerodynamic *adj* **1** relating to aerodynamics. **2** making effective use of aerodynamics so as to move fast through the air. — *adv* **aerodynamically**.

aerofoil *n* a structure, e.g. a wing, tail plane, etc. with a curved surface, designed to give lift when flying. [**aero-** + **foil**[2]]

aerogramme or **aerogram** *n* a thin piece of paper on which to write letters for sending by air, designed so that it can be folded and sealed without being put into an envelope. [**aero-** + **-gram**]

aeronautics *n* (*sing*) the science, art or practice of movement or travel through the air. — *adj* **aeronautic** or **aeronautical**. [**aero-** + **nautical**]

aeroplane *n* a vehicle with wings and one or more engines, designed for flying through the air. [**aero-** + **plane**[2]]

aerosol *n* **1** a mixture of liquid or solid particles and gas, packed under pressure, which is released from a container in the form of a fine spray. **2** a container holding such a mixture. [**aero-** + **sol**[2]]

aerospace *n* **1** the earth's atmosphere and outer space beyond it. **2** the branch of technology or of industry concerned with the flight of aircraft and space vehicles. [**aero-** + **space**]

aesthete *n* a person who has or claims to have a special appreciation of art and beauty. [Gr *aisthetes*, one who perceives]

aesthetic *adj* **1** able to appreciate beauty. **2** artistic; tasteful. — *adv* **aesthetically**. [Gr *aisthetikos*, from *aisthanesthai*, to perceive]

aesthetics *n* (*sing*) **1** the branch of philosophy concerned with the study of the principles of beauty, esp. in art. **2** the principles of good taste and the appreciation of beauty.

aether. Same as **ether** (senses **2** and **3**).

aetiology *n* **1** the science or philosophy of causes. **2** the study of the origins or causes of disease. — *adj* **aetiological**. — *adv* **aetiologically**. [Lat *aetiologia*, from Gr *aitia*, cause + *logos*, discourse]

AF *abbrev* audio frequency.

afar *adv* at a distance; far away. — **from afar** from a great distance. [**a**[3] + **far**]

affable *adj* pleasant and friendly in manner; easy to talk to. — *n* **affability**. — *adv* **affably**. [Lat *affabilis*, from *affari*, to speak to]

affair *n* **1** a concern, matter, or thing to be done. **2** an event or connected series of events. **3** a sexual relationship between people at least one of whom is married to someone else. **4** (in *pl*) matters of importance and public interest: *current affairs*. **5** (in *pl*) private or public business matters. [OFr *afaire*, from *a*, to + *faire*, to do]

affect[1] *v* (*tr*) **1** to have an effect on. **2** to cause (someone) to feel strong emotions, esp. sadness or pity. **3** (of diseases) to attack or infect. [Lat *afficere*]

affecting *adj* causing people to feel strong emotion, esp. sadness, pity, sympathy, joy, etc.

affect[2] *v* (*tr*) **1** to pretend to feel or have. **2** to use, wear, etc. (something) in a way that is intended to attract attention. **3** to have an obvious liking for: *affect fast cars*. [OFr *affecter*, from Lat *afficere*, to affect[1]]

affectation *n* **1** unnatural behaviour or pretence which is intended to impress people. **2** the act of pretending.

affected *adj* **1** not genuine; false; pretended. **2** (of a manner of speaking or behaving) put on to impress people. — *adv* **affectedly**.

affection *n* **1** (**for**) love or strong liking. **2** (in *pl*) feelings: *play on his affections*. **3** a disease. [Lat *affectio*, from *afficere*, to affect[1]]

affectionate *adj* (with **towards**) showing love. — *adv* **affectionately**.

afferent *adj* (*med*) (of a nerve) carrying impulses to the brain. ◇ See also **efferent**. [Lat *afferre*, from *ad*, to + *ferre*, to carry]

affianced *adj* (*old*) engaged to be married. [OFr *afiancer*, to pledge in marriage]

affidavit *n* a written statement, sworn to be true by the person who makes it, for use as evidence in a court of law. [Lat *affidavit*, he or she swears on oath]

affiliate *v* (*tr* & *intr*; **with, to**) to join (a person or a smaller organisation) to a group or another, larger, organisation as its associate or branch. — *n* a person or an organisation, etc. having an association with a group or larger body. — *n* **affiliation**. [Lat *affiliatus*, adopted]

affiliation order *n* (*legal*) a court order instructing a man to pay money towards the support of his illegitimate child.

affinity *n* **-ies 1 (for, to, between)** a strong natural liking for or feeling of attraction or closeness towards someone or something. **2 (with)** relationship, esp. by marriage. **3 (with, between)** similarity in appearance, structure, etc., esp. one suggesting relatedness. **4 (for)** chemical attraction between substances; readiness to combine chemically with another substance and remain in combination. [Lat *affinitas*, from *affinis*, neighbouring]

affirm *v* **1** (*tr*) to state positively and firmly; to state as a fact. **2** (*tr*) to uphold or confirm (an idea, belief, etc.). **3** (*intr*) in a court of law, to promise solemnly to tell the truth, without swearing a religious oath. — *n* **affirmation**. [OFr *afermer*, from Lat *ad*, to + *firmare*, to make firm]

affirmative *adj* expressing agreement; giving the answer 'yes'. — *n* an affirmative word or phrase. — *adv* **affirmatively**.

affix *v* (*tr*; **to**) to attach or fasten. — *n* a word or syllable added to the beginning or end of a word to form another, related, word, e.g. *un-* to *happy* to make *unhappy*, and *-ness* to *sad* to make *sadness*; a prefix or suffix. [Lat *affixus*, fastened to]

afflict *v* (*tr*) to cause (someone) physical or mental suffering. [Lat *affligere*, to cast down]

affliction *n* (something which causes) distress or suffering.

affluent *adj* having more than enough money; rich. — *n* **affluence**. [Lat *affluere*, to flow freely]

afford *v* (*tr*) **1** (used with **can, could, be able**) to have enough money, time, etc. to spend on (something). **2** (used with **can, could, be able**) to be able (to do something), or allow (something) to happen, without risk: *I can't afford to lose my job.* **3** to give; to provide: *a room affording a view of the sea.* — *adj* **affordable**. [OE *geforthian*, to further, promote]

afforest *v* (*tr*) to plant trees on. — *n* **afforestation**. [Lat *afforestare*]

affray *n* a fight in a public place; a breach of the peace by fighting. [OFr *esfrei*]

affront *n* an insult, esp. one delivered in public. — *v* (*tr*) **1** to insult, esp. in public. **2** to offend the pride of; to embarrass. [OFr *afronter*, to slap in the face]

Afghan *adj* belonging to Afghanistan or its inhabitants. — *n* **1** (also **Afghani**) a citizen of, or person born in, Afghanistan. **2** the official language of Afghanistan. **3** (also **Afghan hound**) a type of tall, thin dog with long silky hair, orig. used for hunting. [Persian]

aficionado *n* **-os** a person who takes an enthusiastic interest in a particular sport or pastime. [Span]

afield *adv* to or at a distance; away from home: *far afield.* [OE; **a**[3] + **field**]

afire *adj* & *adv* on fire; burning. [**a**[3] + **fire**]

aflame *adj* **1** in flames; burning. **2** very excited. [**a**[3] + **flame**]

afloat *adj* & *adv* **1** floating. **2** at sea; aboard ship. **3** out of debt; financially secure. [OE; **a**[3] + **float**]

afoot *adj* & *adv* being prepared or already in progress. [**a**[3] + **foot**]

afore *adv* & *prep* (*old* or *dialect*) before. [OE *onforan*]

afore- *comb fm* before; previously. [**afore**]

aforementioned *adj* already mentioned. — *n* (*sing* or *pl*) a person or group of people already mentioned.

aforesaid *adj* said or mentioned already.

aforethought: **with malice aforethought** (*legal*) (of a criminal act) done deliberately; planned beforehand.

a fortiori *adv* & *adj* for a stronger reason. [Lat]

afraid *adj* **1 (of)** feeling fear; frightened. **2** worried about the result of doing something and therefore avoiding it. **3** politely sorry: *I'm afraid we're going to be late.* [Past tense of the old verb *affray*, to disturb or frighten]

afresh *adv* again, esp. from the beginning; with a fresh start. [**a-**[2] + **fresh**]

African *adj* belonging to the continent of Africa, its inhabitants or languages. — *n* **1** a person born or living in Africa. **2** a person who does not live in Africa but whose ancestors came from Africa. [Lat *Africanus*]

African violet *n* a tropical plant from E Africa, with purple, white or pink flowers and hairy leaves, usu. grown indoors in Britain.

Afrikaans *n* one of the official languages of South Africa, developed from Dutch. [Dut *Afrikaans*, African]

Afrikaner *n* a white inhabitant of S Africa whose native language is Afrikaans and who is usu. of Dutch descent. [Dut *Afrikaans*, African]

Afro *n* **-os** (also without *cap*) a hairstyle consisting of thick, bushy curls standing out from the head. [**Afro-**]

Afro- *comb fm* African. [Lat *Afer*, African]

Afro-American *n* an American whose ancestors came from Africa. — *adj* of Afro-Americans, their music, culture, etc.

Afro-Caribbean *n* a person living in the Caribbean whose ancestors came orig. from Africa. — *adj* of Afro-Caribbeans, their music, culture, etc.

aft *adv* & *adj* at or towards the stern, rear or tail. [OE *æftan*, behind]

after *prep* **1** coming later in time than. **2** following in position; behind. **3** next to and following in importance, order, arrangement, etc. **4** because of; considering: *You can't expect to be promoted after that mistake.* **5** in spite of: *He's still no better after all that medicine.* **6** about: *ask after her.* **7** in pursuit of: *run after him.* **8** (of a painting or other work of art) in the style or manner of (someone else). **9** given the same name as; in imitation of: *called her Mary after her aunt.* **10** (*US*) past (an hour): *It's twenty after six.* — *adv* later in time. **2** behind in place. — *conj* after the time when. — *adj* **1** later; following: *in after years.* **2** further towards the stern of a ship: *after cabins.* ◇ See also **aft.** — **after all 1** in spite of all that has happened or been said. **2** in spite of what is or was expected. — **after one's own heart** of exactly the kind one likes. — **after you** please go before me. — **be after** to be pursuing or chasing (a person or animal). [OE *æfter*]

afterbirth *n* the blood, placenta, etc. which comes out of the womb after the birth of a baby.

aftercare *n* care and support given to someone after a period of treatment, a surgical operation, a prison sentence, etc.

after-effect *n* a circumstance or event, usu. an unpleasant one, that follows as the result of something.

afterglow *n* **1** a glow remaining in the sky after the sun has set. **2** an impression or feeling, usu. a pleasant one, that remains when the experience, etc. that caused it is over.

afterlife *n* the continued existence of one's spirit or soul after one's death.

aftermath *n* circumstances that follow and are a result of something, esp. a great and terrible event. [OE *mæth*, mowing]

afternoon see separate entry.

afters *n* (*pl*; *Br coll*) dessert; pudding.

aftershave *n* a scented lotion for putting on the face after shaving.

aftertaste *n* the taste that remains in the mouth after one has eaten or drunk something.

afterthought *n* an idea thought of after the main plan, etc. has been formed.

afterwards or **afterward** *adv* later; following (an earlier event of time).

afternoon *n* the period of the day between noon and the evening. [MidE; **after** + **noon**]

Ag *symbol* (*chem*) silver. [Lat *argentum*, silver]

again *adv* **1** once more; another time. **2** back to a previous condition, situation, etc.: *get well again.* **3** in addition: *twice as much again.* **4** however; on the other hand: *He might come, but then again he might not.* **5** further; besides. — **again and again, time and time again** or **over and over again** very often; repeatedly. [OE *ongean*]

against *prep* **1** close to or leaning on; in contact with. **2** into collision with. **3** in opposition to: *against the law.* **4** in contrast to: *against a dark background.* **5** with a bad or unfavourable effect on: *His youth is against him.* **6** as a protection from; in anticipation of or preparation for. **7** in return for: *exchange rate against the franc.* — **as against** in comparison with. — **have something against (someone** or **something)** to have a reason for disliking or disapproving of (someone or something). [MidE *ageynes*]

agape[1] *adj* **1** (of the mouth) open wide. **2** (of a person) very surprised. [**a**[3] + **gape**]

agape[2] *n* Christian brotherly love, as opposed to erotic love. [Gr *agape*, love]

agar *n* a type of jelly obtained from seaweed, used esp. in medicine and cookery. [Malay]

agaric *n* any fungus with a cap and stalk, such as the edible mushroom. [Lat *agaricum*]

agate *n* a type of semi-precious stone with layers of different colours. [OFr *agathes*]

agave *n* an American plant with thorny leaves from which fibres such as sisal are produced. [Lat]

age *n* **1** the length of time a person or thing has existed. **2** a particular stage in life. **3** the fact of being old. **4** a period in the geological development or history of the world marked by some particular feature. **5** (usu. in *pl*; *coll*) a very long time. — *v* ***ageing*** or ***aging*** **1** (*intr*) to show signs of growing old. **2** (*intr*) to grow old. **3** (*intr*) to mature. **4** (*tr*) to cause to seem older or look old. — *n* & *adj* **ageing** or **aging**. — **act** or **be one's age** to behave sensibly. — **come of age** to become legally old enough to have an adult's rights and duties. — **of an age** of the same, or a similar, age. — **over age** too old. — **under age** too young to be legally allowed to do something, e.g. buy alcohol. [OFr *aage*, from Lat *aetas*]

aged *adj* **1** having a particular age. **2** very old. — *n* old people as a group.

age group or **bracket** *n* the people between two particular ages, considered as a group.

ageism or **agism** *n* the practice of treating people differently, usu. unfairly, on the grounds of age only, esp. because they are too old. — *n* & *adj* **ageist** or **agist**.

ageless *adj* never growing old or fading; never looking older. — *n* **agelessness**.

age limit *n* the age under or over which one may not do something.

age of consent *n* the age at which one may marry or have a sexual relationship without breaking the law.

age-old *adj* done, known, etc. for a very long time.

-age *sfx* meaning **1** a collection or set: *baggage.* **2** an action: *breakage.* **3** the result of an action or event: *wreckage*. **4** a condition: *bondage*. **5** home, house or place of: *orphanage*; *anchorage*. **6** cost: *postage*. [OFr]

agency *n* **-ies 1** an office or business providing a particular service. **2** an active part played by someone in bringing something about. **3** (*US*) a government department providing a particular service. **4** the business of an agent. [Lat *agere*, to do]

agenda *n* a list of things to be done or discussed; a written list of subjects to be dealt with at a meeting, etc. [Lat, things to be done]

agent *n* **1** a person who represents an organisation and acts on its behalf; a person who deals with someone else's business matters, etc. **2** (also **secret agent**) a spy. **3** a substance that is used for producing a particular result. **4** a person who is the cause of something. [Lat *agens*, from *agere*, to do]

agent provocateur *n* ***agents provocateurs*** a person employed to lead others in illegal acts for which they will be punished. [Fr]

agglomerate *v* (*tr* & *intr*) to make into or become an untidy mass. — *n* **1** an untidy mass or collection of things. **2** a type of stone formed from small pieces of volcanic rock melted into a mass. — *adj* formed into a mass. — *n* **agglomeration**. [Lat *agglomerare*, to wind on to a ball]

agglutinate *v* **1** (*tr*) to stick or glue together. **2** (*tr* & *intr*; *gram*) (of a language) to create (words) by joining together (simpler words or word elements, each of which corresponds to a particular element of meaning). — *n* **agglutination**. — *adj* **agglutinative**. [Lat *agglutinare*, to glue together]

aggrandise or **-ize** *v* (*tr*) **1** to increase the power, wealth, etc. of (a person, country, etc.). **2** to make (someone or something) seem greater than he, she or it really is. — *n* **aggrandisement** or **-z-**. [OFr *aggrandir*]

aggravate *v* (*tr*) **1** to make (a bad situation, an illness, etc.) worse. **2** to make (someone) angry; to annoy. — *adj* **aggravating**. — *adv* **aggravatingly**. — *n* **aggravation**. [Lat *aggravare*, to make heavier or worse]

aggregate *n* **1** a collection of separate units brought together; a total. **2** the sand and broken stone that are mixed with water and cement to make concrete. **3** rock, e.g. granite, formed from a mixture of different minerals. — *adj* (of separate units) combined together. — *v* **1** (*tr* & *intr*) to combine or be combined into a single unit or whole. **2** (*tr*; *coll*) to amount to. **3** (*tr*; *formal*) to add as a member to a society, group, etc. — *n* **aggregation**. — **in the aggregate** taken all together. — **on aggregate** in total. [Lat *aggregare*, to herd or bring together]

aggression *n* **1** the act of attacking another person or country without being provoked; an instance of hostile behaviour towards someone. **2** the tendency to make unprovoked attacks. **3** hostile feelings or behaviour. [Lat *aggredi*, to attack]

aggressive *adj* **1** (of a person) always ready to attack; hostile. **2** (of a person) strong and determined; self-assertive. **3** (of an action) hostile. — *adv* **aggressively**. — *n* **aggressiveness**.

aggressor *n* in a fight, war, etc., the person, group or country that attacks first, esp. if the attack is unprovoked.

aggrieved *adj* **1** angry, hurt or upset because one feels that one has been badly or unfairly treated. **2** (*legal*) having suffered because of someone else's illegal behaviour. [OFr *agrever*, to press heavily upon]

aggro *n* (*Br slang*) **1** fighting; violent or threatening behaviour. **2** problems or difficulties. [Abbrev. of **aggression** in sense **1** and of **aggravation** in sense **2**]

aghast *adj* filled with fear or horror. [OE *gæstan*, to frighten]

agile *adj* able to move, change direction, etc. quickly and easily; nimble; active. — *adv* **agilely**. — *n* **agility**. [Lat *agilis*, from *agere*, to do]

agin *prep* (*Scot* or *coll*) against. [OE *ongean*, opposite to]

agitate *v* **1** (*tr*) to excite or trouble (a person, his or her feelings, nerves, etc.) **2** (*intr*; **for**, **against**) to try to stir up public opinion for or against, or concern for, something. **3** (*tr*) to shake or stir (a liquid). — *adj* **agitated**. — *adv* **agitatedly**. [Lat *agitare*]

agitation *n* **1** public discussion for or against something. **2** a disturbed or nervous state of mind; anxiety.

agitator *n* **1** a person who tries continually to stir up public feeling, esp. over serious political or social issues. **2** a tool or machine for stirring or shaking a liquid.

agitprop *n* the spreading of political propaganda, esp. by communists. [Russ *agitatsiya*, agitation + *propaganda*, propaganda]

aglow *adj* & *adv* shining with colour or warmth; glowing. [**a**[3] + **glow**]

AGM *abbrev* annual general meeting, a meeting of a society, public company, etc. held once a year, for discussing the past year's work or progress and choosing a new committee, board of directors, etc.

agnostic *n* a person who believes that one can know only about material things and so believes that nothing can be known about the existence of God. — *adj* of or relating to this view. — *n* **agnosticism**. [Gr *agnostos*, not known]

ago *adv* in the past; earlier. [OE *agan*, to pass by]

agog *adj* very interested and excited; eager to know more. — *adv* eagerly; expectantly. [OFr *en gogues*, in fun]

agonise or **-ize** *v* **1** (*intr*; **about**, **over**) to worry intensely or suffer great anxiety about. **2** (*tr*) to cause great anxiety or worry to. [Gr *agonizesthai*, to struggle]

agonised or **-z-** *adj* suffering or showing great anxiety, worry or agony.

agonising or **-z-** *adj* causing great bodily or mental suffering. — *adv* **agonisingly** or **-z-**.

agony *n* **-*ies*** severe bodily or mental pain. [Lat *agonia*, from Gr *agon*, struggle]

agony aunt *n* (*coll*) a person who answers letters sent in to an agony column.

agony column *n* part of a newspaper or magazine where advice is offered to readers who write in with their problems.

agoraphobia *n* an illogical fear of open and public places. — *n* & *adj* **agoraphobic**. [Gr *agora*, market-place + *phobos*, fear]

AGR *abbrev* advance gas-cooled (nuclear) reactor.

agrarian *adj* of or concerning land and its uses, esp. farming. [Lat *agrarius*, from *ager*, field]

agree *v* **1** (*intr*; **with**, **about**, **on**, **over**) to be of the same opinion as someone else about something. **2** (*intr*; **to**) to say yes to a suggestion, request or instruction. **3** (*intr*; **on**, **upon**) to reach a joint decision about something after discussion. **4** (*tr*) to reach agreement about (something). **5** (*intr* with **with**) to be suitable or good for: *Milk doesn't agree with me*. **6** (*intr*; **with**) to be consistent. **7** (*intr*; *gram*; **with**) to have the same number, person, gender or case.— **agree to differ** (of two or more people) to agree to accept each other's different opinions and still remain friends. — **be agreed** to have reached the same conclusion. [OFr *agreer*]

agreeable *adj* **1** (of things) pleasant. **2** (of people) friendly. **3** (**to**) (of people) willing to accept a suggestion, etc. — *adv* **agreeably**.

agreement *n* **1** a contract or promise. **2** a joint decision made after discussion. **3** the state of holding the same opinion. **4** (*gram*) the state of having the same number, person, gender or case.

agriculture *n* the science of cultivating the land, esp. for growing crops or rearing animals. — *adj* **agricultural**. [Lat *ager*, field + *cultura*, cultivation]

agriculturalist or **agriculturist** *n* an expert on agriculture.

agro- *comb fm* agricultural: *agrochemical*. [Lat *ager*, field]

aground *adj* & *adv* (of ships) stuck on the bottom of the sea or rocks, usu. in shallow water. [MidE; **a**³ + **ground**]

ague *n* **1** (*old*) malaria. **2** a fit of shivering. [OFr *fievre ague*, acute fever]

AH *abbrev* for *anno Hegirae*, (Lat) in the year of the Hegira.

ah *interj* used to express surprise, sympathy, admiration, pleasure, etc., according to the intonation of the speaker's voice.

aha *interj* used to express pleasure, satisfaction, triumph or surprise, according to the intonation of the speaker's voice.

ahead *adv* **1** at or in the front; forwards. **2** earlier in time; before. **3** in the lead; further advanced: *ahead on points*. — **ahead of** in advance of. — **get ahead** to make progress, esp. socially. [**a**³ + **head**]

ahem *interj* a sound made in the back of the throat, used to gain people's attention or express doubt or disapproval.

-aholic or **-oholic** *comb fm* (*coll*) addicted to: *chocoholic* (addicted to chocolate); *workaholic*. [**alcoholic**]

ahoy *interj* (*naut*) a shout to greet or attract the attention of another ship. [**ah** + **hoy**]

AI *abbrev* **1** artificial intelligence. **2** artificial insemination.

AID *abbrev* artificial insemination by donor.

aid *n* **1** help. **2** help or support in the form of money, supplies or services given to people who need it. **3** a person or thing that helps do something: *a hearing-aid*. — *v* (*tr*) **1** to help or support (someone). **2** to help (something) happen; to promote. — **aid and abet** (*legal*) to help and encourage (someone) to do something wrong, esp. disobey the law. — **in aid of** for the purpose of; in support of. — **what's this in aid of?** (*coll*) what is the reason for, or purpose of, this? [OFr *aidier*]

aide *n* an assistant or adviser, esp. to the head of a government. [Fr]

aide-de-camp *n* ***aides-de-camp*** an officer in the armed forces who acts as assistant to a senior officer.

aide-mémoire *n* ***aides-mémoire*** something that helps one to remember something, esp. a note listing the main points mentioned in a paper, speech, etc. [Fr]

AIDS or **Aids** *abbrev* acquired immune deficiency syndrome, a condition transmitted by a virus which attacks the body's system of defence against disease, leaving the sufferer extremely vulnerable to disease and likely to die eventually from any one that he or she catches.

aikido *n* a Japanese form of self-defence, based on a system of locks and holds and the movements of the attacker or opponent. [Jap *ai*, to harmonise + *ki*, breath + *do*, way]

ail *v* **1** (*intr*) to be ill and weak. **2** (*tr*; *old*) to cause pain or trouble to. — *adj* **ailing**. [OE *eglan*, to trouble]

ailment *n* an illness, esp. a minor one.

aileron *n* a flap on the back of an aircraft wing which helps it balance. [Fr, dimin. of *aile*, wing]

aim *v* **1** (*tr* & *intr*; **at**, **for**) to point or direct (a weapon, attack, remark, etc.) at (someone or something). **2** (*intr*) to plan, intend or try. — *n* **1** what a person, etc. intends to do; the achievement aimed at. **2** the ability to hit what is aimed at: *good aim*. — **take aim** to point a weapon (at someone or something) so that if the

weapon is used it will hit its target. [OFr *esmer*, from Lat *aestimare*, to estimate]
aimless *adj* without any purpose. — *adv* **aimlessly**. — *n* **aimlessness**.

ain't (*coll*) short for **1** am not; is not; are not. **2** has not; have not.

air *n* **1** the mixture of gases, consisting mainly of oxygen, nitrogen and carbon dioxide, which people and animals breathe and which forms the earth's atmosphere. **2** the space above and around the earth, where birds and aircraft fly. **3** an appearance, look or manner. **4** (in *pl*) behaviour put on to impress others, to show off, etc.: *put on airs*; *airs and graces*. **5** a tune. **6** a breeze. **7** the space above the ground thought of as the medium through which radio and television signals are sent. ◇ See also **on** or **off the air** below. — *v* **1** (*tr* & *intr*) to hang (laundry) in a warm, dry place to make it completely dry or to remove unpleasant smells; (of laundry) to be hung in a warm, dry place for this purpose. **2** (*tr* & *intr*) to let fresh air into (a room, etc.); (of a room, etc.) to become cooler or fresher in this way. **3** (*tr*) to make warm (the sheets and blankets of a bed, esp. one that has not been used recently). **4** (*tr*) to make (one's thoughts, opinions, etc.) known publicly. **5** (*tr*; *old*) to make a show of or parade. **6** (*tr* & *intr*; *US*) to broadcast or be broadcast on radio or television. — **by air** in an aircraft. — **a change of air** a beneficial change from one's usual routine. — **clear the air** to remove or reduce misunderstanding or disagreement by speaking openly and honestly. — **in the air 1** (of projects, etc.) uncertain or undecided. **2** (of opinions, news, etc.) being generally considered, thought or talked about. — **into thin air** mysteriously and leaving no trace. — **on** or **off the air** broadcasting or not broadcasting on radio or television. — **take the air** (*old*) to go for a walk. — **take to the air** to start to fly. — **walk on air** to be very happy. [OFr]

air base *n* a centre from which military aircraft operate.

air bed *n* an inflated mattress.

airborne *adj* **1** (of aircraft) flying in the air, having just taken off. **2** transported by air.

air brake *n* a brake on large vehicles operated by compressed air.

air brick *n* a brick with small holes, put into the side of a building to allow ventilation.

airbrush *n* an instrument for painting which uses compressed air to form a spray. — *v* (*tr*) to paint using an air brush.

Airbus® *n* an aircraft which can carry a large number of passengers, esp. on short flights.

air chief marshal *n* (*Br*) an air force officer equal in rank to a general or admiral.

air commodore *n* (*Br*) a senior officer in the air force.

air-conditioning *n* **1** the apparatus used to control the temperature, dryness or dampness, and sometimes the cleanness, of the air in a building, room, etc. **2** the controlling of room temperature, etc. using such apparatus. — *adj* **air-conditioned**. — *n* **air-conditioner**.

air cover *n* the use of aircraft to protect against enemy attack.

aircraft *n* ***aircraft*** any of various types of machine which can fly in the air.

aircraft carrier *n* a large naval warship with a flat deck which aircraft can take off from and land on.

aircraftman and **aircraftwoman** *n* (*Br*) a man or woman of the lowest rank in the air force.

aircrew *n* the people in an aircraft who are responsible for flying it and looking after the passengers.

air cushion *n* **1** a cushion that can be filled with air. **2** a pocket of air used for supporting a hovercraft, etc.

air-drop *n* a delivery of military equipment, troops, supplies, etc. by air. — *v* (*tr*) to deliver by aircraft.

airfield *n* a small airport, usu. with very few buildings, where small private or military aircraft are kept, and where they may take off and land.

air force *n* that part of a country's defence forces which uses aircraft for fighting.

airgun *n* a gun that uses air under pressure to fire small pellets.

air hostess *n* (*Br*) a woman member of an airliner's crew, responsible for the comfort of passengers.

airing *n* **1** the act of airing (laundry, a room, the sheets, etc. on a bed, etc.) or fact of being aired. **2** the stating and discussing of opinions, etc. publicly. **3** a short walk, etc. taken in order to get some fresh air.

airing-cupboard *n* a heated cupboard in which laundry is put to become completely dry and warm.

air lane *n* a route through the air regularly used by aircraft.

airless *adj* **1** (of the weather) unpleasantly warm, with no wind. **2** (of a room) lacking cool, fresh air; stuffy.

air letter same as **aerogramme**.

airlift *n* the transporting of large numbers of people or large amounts of goods in aircraft when other routes are blocked. — *v* (*tr*) to transport in this way.

airline *n* a company or organisation which provides a regular transport service for passengers or cargo by aircraft.

airliner *n* a large passenger aeroplane.

airlock *n* **1** a bubble of air in a pipe which prevents liquid from flowing along the pipe. **2** a small room with controllable air pressure and two entrances, which allows a person to pass between places with different air pressures (e.g. between outer space and a spaceship) without air escaping, or between air and water (e.g. between

the sea and a submarine) without water getting in.
airmail *n* **1** the system of carrying mail by air. **2** mail carried by air.
airman or **airwoman** *n* a pilot or member of the crew of an aeroplane, esp. in an air force.
air miss *n* a situation in which two aircraft on different routes come dangerously close together.
airplane *n* (*NAm*) an aeroplane.
air pocket *n* an area of reduced pressure in the air or a downward current which can cause an aircraft to suddenly lose height.
airport *n* a place where civil aircraft arrive and depart, with facilities for passengers and cargo, etc.
air raid *n* an attack by aircraft.
air-rifle *n* a rifle that is fired by air under pressure.
air-sea rescue *n* the use of both aircraft and boats to rescue people from the sea.
airship *n* a type of aircraft that consists of a long gas-filled balloon-like structure with an engine to make it move and a room-like structure under it for passengers or cargo.
airsick *adj* sick due to the motion of an aircraft. — *n* **airsickness**.
airspace *n* the part of the sky directly above a country, considered as part of the country.
airstrip *n* a strip of ground where aircraft can land and take off but which has no facilities.
air terminal *n* an office or other place in a town from where passengers are taken, usu. by bus, to an airport nearby.
airtight *adj* **1** (of a container, etc.) which air cannot get into, out of, or through. **2** (of an opinion, argument, etc.) having no weak points.
airtime *n* the length of time given to a particular item or programme on television or radio.
air-to-air *adj* (of a weapon) from one aircraft to another in flight.
air-traffic control *n* the organisation which manages the safe passage of aircraft through the sky by sending the aircraft radio messages.
air vice-marshal *n* a senior rank in the air force.
airwaves *n* (*pl*) the radio waves used by radio and television stations for their broadcasts.
airway *n* **1** a route regularly followed by aircraft. **2** (usu. in *pl*) an airline.
airwoman see **airman**.
airworthy *adj* (of aircraft) in a condition to fly safely. — *n* **airworthiness**.
airy *adj* **-ier**, **-iest** **1** with plenty of fresh, cool air. **2** not thinking about or dealing with something as seriously as one should; flippant. **3** lively; light-hearted. — *adv* **airily**. — *n* **airiness**.
airy-fairy *adj* (*coll*) showing or suggesting a lack of sense or good planning; not based on facts or on awareness of real situations.
aisle *n* **1** a passage between rows of seats, e.g. in a church or theatre. **2** the side part of the inside of a church. [Lat *ala*, wing; spelling influenced by **isle**]
aitch *n* the letter H or h. — **drop one's aitches** to fail to pronounce the sound of the letter *h* when it comes at the beginning of words. [OFr *ache*]
aitchbone *n* **1** the rump bone in cattle. **2** a cut of beef from this. [OFr *nache*, from Lat *natis*, buttocks]
ajar *adj* & *adv* partly open. [OE *on*, on + *cierr*, turn]
AK *abbrev* Alaska.
AKA or **aka** *abbrev* also known as.
akimbo *adj* & *adv* with hand on hip and elbow bent outward. [MidE *in kenebowe*, in a sharp bend]
akin *adj* **1** (with **to**) similar to. **2** related by blood. [**a-**[2] + **kin**]
AL *abbrev* Alabama.
Al *symbol* (*chem*) aluminium.
-al *sfx* **1** forming adjectives meaning 'related to': *parental*. **2** forming nouns meaning 'the action of': *arrival*.
Ala. *abbrev* Alabama.
alabaster *n* a type of white stone used for ornaments, etc. — *adj* of or like alabaster. [OFr *alabastre*]
à la carte *adv* & *adj* (of a meal in a restaurant) with each dish priced and ordered separately. [Fr]
alacrity *n* quick and cheerful enthusiasm. [Lat *alacritas*]
à la mode *adj* & *adv* in fashion; according to current fashion. [Fr]
alarm *n* **1** sudden fear produced by becoming aware of danger. **2** a noise warning of danger. **3** a bell, etc. which sounds to warn of danger or, e.g. on a clock, to waken a person from sleep. **4** an alarm clock. — *v* (*tr*) **1** to frighten. **2** to warn of danger. **3** to fit an alarm on (a house, car, etc.). — **give, raise** or **sound the alarm** to give warning of danger by shouting, ringing a bell, etc. [OFr *alarme*, from Ital *all'arme*, to arms]
alarm clock *n* a clock that can be set to make a noise at a particular time to wake someone up.
alarming *adj* disturbing or frightening. — *adv* **alarmingly**.
alarmist *n* a person who feels or spreads unnecessary alarm. — *adj* causing unnecessary alarm. — *n* **alarmism**.
Alas. *abbrev* Alaska.
alas *interj* (*old* or *lit*) used to express grief or misfortune. [OFr]
alb *n* a long white garment reaching to the feet, worn by some Christian priests. [Lat *albus*, white]
albatross *n* a large, long-winged gull-like sea bird of the southern oceans. [Port *alcatraz*, pelican]
albeit *conj* even if; although. [MidE *al be it*, although it be]
albino *n* **-os** a person or animal with no natural colour in their skin and hair (which

are white) or eyes (which are pink). — *n* **albinism**. [Port, from Lat *albus*, white]

album *n* **1** a book with blank pages for holding photographs, stamps, etc. **2** a long-playing record. [Lat, blank tablet, from *albus*, white]

albumen *n* the white part of an egg. [Lat, white of egg, from *albus*, white]

albumin *n* a protein found in egg white and blood. [See ety. for **albumen**]

alchemy *n* medieval chemistry, one of whose aims was to discover how to make gold from other metals. — *n* **alchemist**. [Lat *alchymia*, from Arabic *al*, the + *kimiya*, from Gr *kemeia*, transmutation]

alcohol *n* **1** a colourless, flammable liquid made by the fermentation or distillation of sugar, used in making drinks, solvents, etc. **2** any drink containing this liquid, such as wine or beer. **3** (*chem*) any of a number of compounds of similar structure to that of the alcohol found in beer, etc. [Arabic *al*, the + *kohl*, kohl]

alcohol abuse *n* drinking alcohol (sense **2**) to the point where it becomes harmful.

alcoholic *adj* of, containing or caused by alcohol. — *n* a person who is addicted to alcohol (sense **1** or **2**). — *adv* **alcoholically**.

alcoholism *n* the disease of being addicted to alcohol (sense **1 or 2**) and drinking so much that it is harmful.

alcove *n* a recess in the wall of a room or garden. [Span *alcoba*, from Arabic *al*, the + *qubbah*, vault]

aldehyde *n* a liquid with a suffocating smell, formed by combining alcohol with oxygen. [Abbrev. of Lat *alcohol dehydrogenatum*, alcohol derived from hydrogen]

al dente *adj* (of pasta) cooked so as to remain firm when bitten. [Ital, to the tooth]

alder *n* a tree with catkins and toothed leaves, which grows in damp areas. [OE *alor*]

alderman *n* **1** (in England and Wales until 1974) a member of a town, county or borough council elected by fellow councillors, below the rank of mayor. **2** (in the US and Canada) a member of the governing body of a city. [OE *ealdormann*, nobleman of the highest rank]

ale *n* **1** a strong beer which is fermented in the cask. **2** beer. [OE *ealu*]

alehouse *n* (*old*) an inn or public house.

aleatory *adj* depending on chance. [Lat *aleator*, dice-player]

alert *adj* **1** thinking and acting quickly. **2** (**to**) watchful and aware. — *n* **1** a warning of danger. **2** the period of time covered by such a warning. — *v* (*tr*; **to**) to warn (someone) of danger; to make (someone) aware of a fact, etc. — *adv* **alertly**. — *n* **alertness**. — **on the alert** watchful. [Fr *alerte*, from Ital *all'erta*, to the watch-tower]

Aleut *n* ***Aleut*** or ***Aleuts*** **1** a member of a people, related to the Inuit, inhabiting the Aleutian Islands and part of Alaska. **2** the language of this people. — *adj* **Aleut** and **Aleutian**. [Russ]

alexandrine *n* a verse of six iambic feet (in English) or twelve syllables (in French). — *adj* (of verse) written in alexandrines. [Fr *Alexandre*, Alexander the Great, the subject of an Old French romance written in this metre]

alfalfa *n* **1** a type of plant grown for food, esp. for animals. **2** the young edible shoots of this plant, often eaten in salads, etc. [Span, from Arabic *al-fasfasah*]

alfresco *adj* & *adv* in the open air. [Ital]

alga *n* ***algae*** (usu. in *pl*) a plant which grows in water or on moist ground, with no stem, leaves or flowers, e.g. seaweed. [Lat, seaweed]

algebra *n* a branch of mathematics that uses letters and other symbols to represent numbers in calculations and equations. — *adj* **algebraic**. — *adv* **algebraically**. [Ital and Span, from Arabic *al-jebr*, from *al*, the + *jebr*, reunion of broken parts]

-algia *comb fm* pain in the part of the body stated: *neuralgia*. [Gr *algos*, pain]

ALGOL *n* a computer programming language. [**algorithmic language**]

algorithm *n* a process or set of rules used for solving problems, calculations, etc., esp. by computer. — *adj* **algorithmic**. [Lat *algorismus*, from *Al-Khwarizmi*, 9th-century Arab mathematician]

alias *n* a false or assumed name. — *adv* also known as. [Lat, at another time, otherwise]

alibi *n* **1** a plea of being somewhere else when a crime was committed. **2** (*coll*) an excuse. [Lat, elsewhere]

alien *n* **1** a foreign-born resident of a country who has not adopted that country's nationality. **2** an inhabitant of another planet, esp. in science fiction stories. **3** a plant introduced to an area by people rather than by nature. — *adj* **1** foreign. **2** (with **to**) not in keeping with; unfamiliar to. [Lat *alienus*, foreign]

alienable *adj* (*legal*) (of property) able to be transferred to another owner.

alienate *v* (*tr*) **1** to make (someone) feel unfriendly or strange. **2** to make (someone) feel unwelcome or isolated. **3** (*legal*) to transfer ownership of (property) to another person. — *n* **alienation**.

alight[1] *adj* **1** on fire. **2** (**with**) lighted up. [MidE; **a**[3] + **light**[1]]

alight[2] *v* (*intr*) **1** (*old*; **from**) to get down from or out of (a vehicle). **2** (with **on**) to settle or land on. [OE *alihtan*]

align *v* **1** (*tr*) to put in a straight line or bring into line. **2** (*tr* & *intr*; **with**) to bring (oneself, someone, a country) into agreement with others, a political belief, cause, etc. — *n* **alignment**. [Fr *à ligne*, into line]

alike *adj* like one another; similar. — *adv* in a similar manner. [OE *gelic*]

alimentary *adj* of or relating to food and nutrition. [Lat *alimentarius*, from *alere*, to nourish]

alimentary canal *n* the passage along which food passes as it is digested, from the mouth to the anus.

alimony *n* (*legal*) money for support paid by a man to his wife or by a woman to her husband, when they are legally separated or divorced. ◇ See also **maintenance**. [Lat *alimonia*, nourishment]

aliphatic *adj* (*chem*) (of organic compounds) with carbon atoms in chains rather than rings. ◇ See also **aromatic**. [Gr *aleiphar*, oil]

aliquot *adj* (*math*) (of numbers) able to be divided into another number without any remainder: *3 is an aliquot part of 9*. [Lat, some, several]

alive *adj* **1** living; having life; in existence. **2** lively; active. **3** (with **to**) aware of; sensitive to. **4** (**with**) full of. — **alive and kicking** living and active. [OE *on life*, in life]

alkali *n* a substance which reacts with an acid to form a salt. [Arabic *al-qaly*, calcinated ashes]

alkaline *adj* containing an alkali; acting like an alkali. — *n* **alkalinity**.

alkaloid *n* any of several organic compounds containing nitrogen, found in plants, e.g. morphine and quinine.

all *adj* **1** the whole amount, number or extent of; every. **2** the greatest possible: *run with all speed*. **3** any whatever: *beyond all doubt*. — *n* **1** every one of the people or things concerned; the whole of (something). **2** one's whole strength, resources, etc.: *give one's all*. **3** (in scores in games) each. — *adv* **1** entirely, quite. **2** (*coll*) very: *go all shy*. — **after all** in spite of what has been said, been done or happened. — **all along** the whole time. — **all and sundry** everyone. — **all but** very nearly: *He all but drowned*. — **all in 1** (*coll*) exhausted. **2** with all expenses included. — **all in all** considering everything. — **all over 1** finished. **2** everywhere in or on: *all over the world*. **3** (*coll*) exactly what one would expect from someone: *That's her all over*. — **all right 1** unhurt; safe. **2** adequate; satisfactory; satisfactorily; properly. **3** used to express agreement or approval. — **all there** (*coll*) completely sane; mentally alert. — **all told** including everyone or everything. — **be all for** be very much in favour of. — **for all that** in spite of. — **in all** all together. [OE *eall*]

all-American *adj* typically American in quality, appearance, etc.

all clear *n* a signal or statement that the threat of danger is over.

all-in wrestling *n* a style of wrestling with few rules or restrictions.

all-out *adj* using all one's strength, powers, etc.

all-purpose *adj* useful for many different purposes.

all-round *adj* **1** having many different skills. **2** including everyone or everything: *an all-round education*.

all-rounder *n* a person with a lot of different skills.

allspice see separate entry.

all-time *adj* (*coll*) **1** (of e.g. a sporting record) best to date; unsurpassed. **2** of great and permanent importance: *one of the all-time greats of jazz*.

alla breve *adj* & *adv* (*mus*) played quickly with two beats to the bar instead of four. [Ital, at the breve, there orig. being one breve to the bar]

allay *v* (*tr*) to make (pain, fear, suspicion, etc.) less intense. [OE *alecgan*]

allegation *n* an unproved claim, statement or assertion. [Lat *allegatio*, from *allegare*, to allege]

allege *v* (*tr*) to claim or declare to be the case, usu. without proof. — *adj* **alleged**. — *adv* **allegedly**. [OFr *aleguer*, from Lat *allegare*, to allege, mixed with OFr *alegier*, from Lat *alleviare*, to justify, lighten]

allegiance *n* duty to support, obey and be loyal to one's government, sovereign, etc. [MidE *aliegiaunce*, from OFr *liege*, liege]

allegory *n* **-*ies*** a story, play, poem, picture, etc. in which the characters represent moral or spiritual ideas or messages. — *adj* **allegorical**. — *adv* **allegorically**. [OFr *allegorie*, from Gr *allos*, other + *agoreuein*, to speak]

allegorise or **-ize** *v* (*tr*) to put in the form of an allegory.

allegro (*mus*) *adj* & *adv* in a quick, lively manner. — *n* **-*os*** a piece of music to be played like this. [Ital]

alleluia or **hallelujah** *interj* praise the Lord. [Gr *allelouia*, from Hebr *halleluyah*, praise Jehovah]

allergen *n* a substance that causes an allergy, e.g. pollen. [**allergy**]

allergy *n* **-*ies*** **1** sensitivity of the body to some substance (e.g. dust, pollen, a food) which causes an adverse reaction (such as a rash or sneezing) in a person with this sensitivity when he or she comes into contact with that substance. **2** (*coll*) a dislike. [Gr *allos*, other + *ergia*, activity]

allergic *adj* (**to**) having an allergy: *allergic to shellfish*.

alleviate *v* (*tr*) to make (pain, a problem, suffering, etc.) less severe. — *n* **alleviation**. [Lat *alleviare*, to lighten]

alley *n* **-*eys*** **1** (also **alleyway**) a narrow passage behind or between buildings. **2** a long narrow channel used for bowling or skittles. **3** a path through a garden or park. [OFr *alee*, passage, from *aler*, to go]

alliance. See **ally**.

alligator *n* a kind of large reptile closely related to the crocodile but with a broader and shorter head, found in America and China. [Span *el lagarto*, the lizard]

alliteration *n* the repetition of the same sound at the beginning of each word or each stressed word in a phrase, as in *sing a song of sixpence*. — *adj* **alliterative**. — *adv* **alliteratively**. [Lat *alliteratio*, from *ad*, to + *littera*, letter]

alliterate *v* (*intr*) to use or show alliteration.

allocate *v* (*tr*) to give, set apart or assign (something) to someone or for some particular purpose. — *n* **allocation**. [Lat *ad*, to + *locus*, place]

allot *v* **-tt-** (*tr*) to give to (each of a group) a share of or place in (something). [OFr *aloter*]

allotment *n* **1** a small part of a larger piece of public ground rented to a person to grow vegetables, etc. **2** the act of allotting.

allotropy *n* the existence of an element in two or more different physical forms, e.g. oxygen (O_2 in the atmosphere) and ozone (O_3). — *adj* **allotropic**. [Gr *allos*, other + *tropos*, manner]

allow *v* **1** (*tr*) to permit (someone to do something, something to happen, etc.). **2** (*intr* with **for**) to take into consideration when judging or deciding. **3** (*tr*) to give or provide: *allow £10 for food.* **4** (*tr*) to admit or agree to (a point, claim, etc.). **5** (*tr*) to permit (oneself to do something). [OFr *aloer*]

allowable *adj* able to be admitted or accepted. — *adv* **allowably**.

allowance *n* **1** a fixed sum of money, amount of something, etc. given regularly. **2** something allowed. — **make allowances for 1** to take into consideration in one's plans. **2** to judge (a person) less severely, or expect less of (a person), because of special problems or difficulties he or she has.

allowedly *adv* as is generally admitted or believed.

alloy *n* a mixture of two or more metals. — *v* (*tr*) to mix (metals) together. [OFr *alei*, from Lat *alligare*, to bind]

allspice *n* the berry of the pimento, used as a spice.

allude *v* (*intr* with **to**) to speak of indirectly or mention in passing. [Lat *alludere*]

allure *n* attractiveness, appeal or charm. — *v* (*tr*) to attract, charm or fascinate. — *n* **allurement**. — *adj* **alluring**. — *adv* **alluringly**. [OFr *alurer*, from *a*, to + *lurer*, to lure]

allusion *n* an indirect reference. [Lat *allusio*, from *alure*, to allure]

allusive *adj* referring indirectly. — *adv* **allusively**.

alluvium *n* **-ia** fertile soil and sand, etc. deposited by rivers or floods, esp. in river valleys. — *adj* **alluvial**. [Lat *alluvius*, washed up]

ally *n* **-ies** a country or person, etc. that has formally agreed to help and support another. — *v* (*tr*; **with, to**) to join (oneself, one's country, etc.) to another by political agreement, marriage, friendship, etc. [OFr *aleier*, from Lat *alligare*, to bind]

alliance *n* **1** the state of being allied. **2** an agreement or treaty by which people, countries, etc. ally themselves with one another.

allied *adj* **1** joined by political agreement or treaty. **2** (*cap*) of Britain and her allies in the First and Second World Wars. **3** similar; related.

alma mater *n* the school, college or university that one attended, and from which one graduated. [Lat, bountiful mother]

almanac *n* a book, published yearly, with a calendar, information about the moon and stars, religious festivals, public holidays, etc. [Lat *almanach*, from Arabic *al*, the + *manakh*, calendar]

almighty *adj* **1** having complete power. **2** (*coll*) very great. — *adv* (*coll*) extremely. [OE *ælmihtig*]

the Almighty *n* God.

almond *n* **1** a kind of small tree related to the peach. **2** the nut-like seed from the fruit of this tree. [OFr *almende*]

almond-eyed *adj* with long, almond-shaped eyes.

almoner *n* (*old*) a medical social worker. [OFr *aumonier*]

almost *adv* nearly but not quite. [OE *ælmæst*]

alms *n* (*pl*; *hist*) donations of money, food, etc. to the poor. [OE *ælmesse*, from Gr *eleemosyne*]

alms-house *n* (*hist*) a house for the poor, paid for by charity.

aloe *n* **1** a type of plant or tree with fleshy leaves. **2** (usu. in *pl*) a bitter drug made from aloe leaves. [OE *alewe*]

aloe vera *n* a type of aloe, of which the juice from the leaves is supposed to have healing powers and is used in cosmetics.

aloft *adv* **1** in the air; overhead. **2** (*naut*) in a ship's rigging. [Norse *a lopti*, in the sky]

alone *adj* & *adv* without anyone else; by oneself; apart from other people. — **go it alone** (*coll*) to act on one's own and without help. — **leave (someone** or **something) alone** to stop bothering (someone) or interfering with (something). [MidE *al one*, all one]

along *adv* **1** in some direction: *saw him walking along*. **2** in company with others: *go along for the ride.* **3** into a more advanced state: *coming along nicely.* — *prep* beside or over all or part of the length of. — **along with** in addition to; as well as. [OE *andlang*]

alongside *prep* close to the side of. — *adv* to or at the side.

aloof *adj* unfriendly and distant. — *adv* (**from**) away; apart; distant: *stand aloof from the group.* — *adv* **aloofly**. — *n* **aloofness**. [a[3] + *loof*, luff]

aloud *adv* **1** loud enough to be able to be heard; not silently. **2** loudly. [**a**[3] + **loud**]

alp *n* **1** a high mountain. **2** in Switzerland, pasture land on a mountainside. [Lat *Alpes*, the Alps, a mountain range running through Switzerland, France and Italy]

alpine *adj* **1** of alps or high mountains. **2** (*cap*) of the Alps. — *n* a plant growing in high mountain areas.

alpaca *n* **1** a S American animal, related to the llama, with long silky hair. **2** the wool or cloth made from this animal's hair. [Span, from Aymara (a S American Indian language) *allpaqa*]

alpha *n* **1** the first letter of the Greek alphabet (A, α). **2** (a mark indicating) the best or top grade. — **alpha and omega 1** the beginning and the end. **2** the most important part. [Gr]

alpha particle *n* a helium nucleus given off by radioactive substances.

alpha ray *n* a stream of alpha particles.

alphabet *n* the set of letters, usu. in a fixed order, used in writing. [Gr *alphabetos*, from *alpha* + *beta*, the first two letters of the Greek alphabet]

alphabetical or **alphabetic** *adj* in the form of an alphabet; in the order of the letters of an alphabet. — *adv* **alphabetically**.

alphabetise or **-ize** *v* (*tr*) to arrange or list alphabetically.

alphanumeric or **alphanumerical** *adj* **1** containing both letters and numbers. **2** (of a machine) using instructions which consist of letters and numbers; able to display information in the form of letters and numbers. — *adv* **alphanumerically**. [**alphabet** + **numerical**]

alpine. See **alp**.

already *adv* **1** before the present time or the time in question. **2** so soon or so early: *already showing musical talent as a young child.* [MidE *al redy*, completely ready]

alright *adj*, *interj* & *adv* (*coll*) a less acceptable spelling of **all right**.

Alsatian *n* **1** a large, wolf-like dog, often used as a guard dog or by the police. **2** a person living in, or from, Alsace, a region in N E France. [Lat *Alsatia*, Alsace]

also *adv* in addition; too; besides. [OE *ealswa*, all so, wholly]

also-ran *n* **1** a horse, dog, person, etc. not finishing in one of the top three places in a race. **2** an unimportant, undistinguished person.

altar *n* **1** a special table at the front of a Christian church, near which the priest stands. **2** a table on which sacrifices are made to a god. — **lead to the altar** to marry (a woman). [OE *alter*, from Lat *altaria*]

altar boy *n* a young man or boy who assists a priest during a service.

altarpiece *n* a religious picture or carving above and behind an altar.

high altar *n* the main altar in a large church which has more than one altar.

alter *v* **-r-** (*tr* & *intr*) to make or become different. — *adj* **alterable**. — *n* **alteration**. [OFr *alterer*, from Lat *alter*, other]

altercation *n* a heated argument. [Lat *altercari*, to quarrel]

alter ego *n* **-os 1** a person's second or alternative character. **2** a very close and trusted friend. [Lat, other self]

alternate *adj* **1** arranged or coming one after the other by turns: *alternate periods of misery and joy*. **2** (with *pl* nouns) every other; one out of two: *alternate Mondays.* **3** alternative. — *v* **1** (*intr* & *tr*; **with**) to (cause to) succeed or follow each other by turns. **2** (*intr* with **between**) to change from one thing to another by turns. — *adv* **alternately**. — *n* **alternation**. [Lat *alternare*, to do things by turns]

alternate angles *n* (*pl*) two equal angles which lie at opposite ends and on opposite sides of a line which intersects two parallel lines.

alternating current *n* an electric current that reverses its direction at regular periods. ◇ See also **direct current**.

alternator *n* a machine which produces an alternating current.

alternative *adj* **1** available as a choice between two or more possibilities. **2** (of a lifestyle, culture, etc.) different from what is usually done, esp. in being less conventional or materialistic, and more natural. — *n* **1** the possibility of choice between two or more things. **2** any one of two or more choices or possibilities. [Lat *alternare*, to do things by turns]

alternatively *adv* as an alternative.

alternator. See **alternate**.

although *conj* in spite of the fact that; apart from the fact that; though. [MidE *al thogh*, all though]

altimeter *n* an instrument for measuring height above sea or ground level. [Lat *altus*, high + **-meter**]

altitude *n* height, esp. above sea level, or of a star above the horizon. [Lat *altitudo*, from *altus*, high]

alto *n* **-os 1** the lowest female singing voice. **2** the highest adult male singing voice. **3** a singer with an alto voice. **4** a part or piece of music written for a voice or instrument at this pitch. — *adj* (of a musical instrument, etc.) with this pitch. [Ital, from Lat *altus*, high]

altogether *adv* **1** completely. **2** on the whole. **3** taking everything into consideration. — **in the altogether** (*coll*) naked. [MidE *altogeder*, all together]

altruism *n* an unselfish concern for the welfare of other people. — *n* **altruist**. — *adj* **altruistic**. — *adv* **altruistically**. [Fr *altruisme*, from Ital *altrui*, someone else]

alum *n* a mineral salt, a compound of aluminium and potassium, used in dyeing, tanning, etc. [Lat *alumen*]

aluminium *n* a light, silvery metallic element (symbol **Al**) which is not corroded by the air. [**alum**]

alumnus *n* **-ni** a former pupil or student of a school, college or university. [Lat, pupil]

alveolar *adj* (of a sound) produced by putting the tip of the tongue against the ridge behind the upper front teeth, e.g. *t* and *n*. [Lat *alveolus*, small cavity]

always *adv* **1** at all times. **2** continually. **3** in any case; if necessary: *You could always help her if she can't manage alone.* [MidE *alwayes*]

alyssum *n* a garden plant with clusters of white, yellow or mauve flowers. [Gr *alysson*]

Alzheimer's Disease *n* a disease affecting the brain which attacks mainly middle-aged and elderly people, making them become muddled and forgetful. [Alois *Alzheimer* (1864–1915), German neurologist]

AM *abbrev* amplitude modulation.

Am *symbol* (*chem*) americium.

am. See **be**.

a.m. *abbrev* for *ante meridiem*, (Lat) before midday; in the morning. ◇ See also **p.m.**

amalgam *n* **1** a mixture or blend. **2** a mixture of mercury with any other metal. [Lat *amalgama*]

amalgamate *v* **1** (*tr* & *intr*) to join together or unite to form a single unit, organisation, etc. **2** (*intr*) (of metals) to form an alloy with mercury. — *n* **amalgamation**. **[amalgam]**

amanuensis *n* **-enses** a literary assistant or secretary, esp. one who writes from dictation or copies from manuscripts. [Lat, from *a*, from + *manus*, hand]

amaranth *n* **1** a plant with small green, red or purple flowers. **2** (*poetic*) an imaginary flower that never fades. [Gr *amarantos*, everlasting]

amaryllis *n* a lily-like plant native to S Africa, with large, trumpet-like white, pink or red flowers. [Gr and Lat, the name of a shepherdess in Virgil's *Eclogues*]

amass *v* (*tr*) to gather or collect (money, possessions, knowledge, etc.) in great quantity. [Fr *amasser*]

amateur *n* **1** a person who takes part in a sport, pastime, etc. as a hobby and without being paid for it. **2** a person who is not very skilled in an activity, etc. — *adj* of amateurs; not professional. — *n* **amateurism**. [Fr, from Lat *amator*, lover]

amateurish *adj* not very skilful; inexperienced. — *adv* **amateurishly**. — *n* **amateurishness**.

amatory *adj* of or showing sexual love. [Lat *amatorius*, loving]

amaze *v* (*tr*) to surprise greatly; to astonish. — *adj* **amazed**. — *adv* **amazedly**. — *n* **amazement**. — *adj* **amazing**. — *adv* **amazingly**. [OE *amasian*]

Amazon *n* **1** (*Gr mythol*) a member of a nation of women warriors from Scythia. **2** a very strong woman, usu. one who is good at sport. — *adj* **Amazonian** . [Gr]

ambassador *n* **1** a diplomat of the highest rank appointed by his or her government to act for or represent their country abroad. **2** a representative, messenger, or agent of. — *adj* **ambassadorial**. — *n* **ambassadorship**. [OFr *ambassateur*, from Lat *ambactus*, servant]

ambassadress *n* **1** a woman ambassador. **2** the wife of an ambassador.

amber *n* a hard, clear, yellow or brownish fossil resin used in jewellery. — *adj* made of, or coloured like, amber. [OFr *ambre*, from Arabic *anbar*, ambergris]

ambergris *n* a strong-smelling, grey, wax-like substance found in the intestines of the sperm whale, used in some perfumes. [OFr *ambre gris*, grey amber]

ambidextrous *adj* able to use both hands equally well. — *adv* **ambidextrously**. [Lat *ambi-*, both + *dexter*, right]

ambience or **ambiance** *n* the surroundings or atmosphere of a place. [Lat, from *ambi-*, about + *ire*, to go]

ambient *adj* (of air, temperature, etc.) surrounding.

ambiguous *adj* having more than one possible meaning; not clear. — *adv* **ambiguously**. — *n* **ambiguousness**. [Lat *ambiguus*, from *ambi-*, both ways + *agere*, to drive]

ambiguity *n* **-ies** **1** uncertainty of meaning. **2** an ambiguous word or statement.

ambit *n* range, extent or bounds. [Lat *ambitus*, from *ambi-*, about + *ire*, to go]

ambition *n* **1** a strong desire for success, fame or power. **2** a thing one desires to do or achieve. [Lat *ambitio*, going round, canvassing, from *ambi-*, about + *ire*, to go]

ambitious *adj* **1** having a strong desire for success, etc. **2** requiring hard work and skill. — *adv* **ambitiously**. — *n* **ambitiousness**.

ambivalence *n* the state of holding two opposite views about a person or subject at the same time. — *adj* **ambivalent**. — *adv* **ambivalently**. [Lat *ambi-*, both + *valere*, to be worth]

amble *v* (*intr*) to walk without hurrying; to stroll. — *n* a leisurely walk. [OFr *ambler*, from Lat *ambulare*, to walk about]

ambrosia *n* **1** (*Gr mythol*) the food of the gods, which gave them eternal youth and beauty. **2** something with a delicious taste or smell. [Gr, from *ambrotos*, immortal]

ambulance *n* a specially equipped vehicle for carrying sick or injured people to hospital. [Lat *ambulare*, to walk about]

ambush *n* **1** the act of lying in wait to attack someone by surprise. **2** an attack made in this way. **3** the person or people making such an attack. **4** the place of concealment from which the attack is made. — *v* (*tr*) to lie in wait for or attack (someone) in this way. [OFr *embuschier*, to place men in the woods]

ameliorate *v* (*tr* & *intr*) to make or become better. — *n* **amelioration**. [OFr *ameillorer*, from Lat *melior*, better]

amen *interj* (usu. said at the end of a prayer) so be it. [Hebr, certainly]

amenable *adj* **1** ready to accept advice or guidance. **2** legally responsible. [OFr *amener*, to lead to]

amend *v* (*tr*) to correct, improve or make minor changes to (a book, document, etc.). — *n* **amendment**. — **make amends for** to make up for or compensate for some injury, insult, etc. ◇ See also **emend**. [OFr *amender*, from Lat *emendare*]

amenity *n* **-ies 1** anything that makes life more comfortable and pleasant. **2** pleasantness of situation. **3** a public facility. [Lat *amoenus*, pleasant]

American *adj* of the United States of America or the American continent, the people who live or were born there, and the languages they speak. — *n* a person born or living in the United States of America, or the American continent. [*America*, from *Amerigo* Vespucci (1454–1512), Italian navigator]

American football *n* a game like Rugby, played by two teams of eleven players wearing heavily padded and protective clothing, with an oval ball.

American Indian *n* a member of any of the original peoples of N America.

Americanism *n* a word, phrase, custom, etc. that is characteristic of Americans.

americium *n* a radioactive white metallic element (symbol **Am**) produced artificially from plutonium and uranium. [*America*, where it was first produced]

amethyst *n* a type of purple or violet quartz used as a gemstone. — *adj* purple or violet in colour. [Gr *amethystos*, not drunken; the stone was supposed to prevent drunkenness.]

Amharic *n* the official language of Ethiopia, related to Hebrew and Arabic. — *adj* of or in this language. [*Amhara*, region in Ethiopia]

amiable *adj* likeable; friendly, pleasant and good-tempered. — *n* **amiability**. — *adv* **amiably**. [Lat *amicabilis*, amicable, confused with OFr *amable*, lovable]

amicable *adj* friendly. — *n* **amicability**. — *adv* **amicably**. [Lat *amicabilis*, from *amicus*, friend]

amid or **amidst** *prep* in the middle of; among. [OE *onmiddan*, in the centre]

amide *n* a compound formed from ammonia, in which an acid or metal radical takes the place of one or more of the hydrogen atoms. **[ammonia]**

amidships *adv* (also **midships**) in, into or near the middle of a ship. **[amid + ship]**

amine *n* a compound formed from ammonia, in which one or more hydrocarbon radicals take the place of one or more of the hydrogen atoms. **[ammonia]**

amino acid *n* an organic compound occurring naturally in plant and animal tissues, one of the basic ingredients of protein. **[amine + acid]**

amir. Same as **emir**.

amiss *adj* wrong; out of order. — *adv* wrongly. — **take (something) amiss** to be upset or offended by (something). [MidE]

amity *n* (*formal*) friendship. [OFr *amitie*, from Lat *amicus*, friend]

ammeter *n* an instrument used to measure an electric current, usu. in amperes. **[ampere + -meter]**

ammo *n* (*coll*) short form of **ammunition**.

ammonia *n* a strong-smelling gas used in making fertilisers, glue, etc. [Lat *sal ammoniacus*, salt of Ammon, ammonia in salt form first found near a temple to the god Ammon in Libya]

ammonite *n* a coil-shaped fossilised shell. [Lat *ammonites*, horn of Ammon]

ammunition *n* **1** bullets, shells, bombs, etc. made to be fired from a weapon. **2** facts, etc. which can be used against someone in an argument. [Fr *amunitions*, military supplies]

amnesia *n* loss of memory. — *n* **amnesiac**. — *adj* **amnesic**. [Gr, forgetfulness]

amnesty *n* **-ies 1** a general pardon, esp. for people guilty of political crimes. **2** a period of time during which criminals may admit to crimes, hand in weapons, etc., without being punished. [Gr *amnestia*, oblivion]

amniocentesis *n* **-eses** a test, done on a sample of the amniotic fluid taken from a pregnant woman, to find out whether the child she is carrying is healthy. [*amnion*, the membrane enclosing the foetus + *centesis*, puncture]

amniotic fluid *n* the fluid surrounding the foetus in the womb. [*amnion*, the membrane enclosing the foetus]

amoeba *n* **-ae** or **-as** a microscopic, single-celled organism which can change shape, and which usu. lives in water. — *adj* **amoebic**. [Gr *amoibe*, change]

amok or **amuck**: **run amok** or **amuck** to rush about madly, attacking everybody and everything. [Malay *amoq*, frenzied]

among or **amongst** *prep* (used of more than two things, people, etc.) **1** in the middle of: *among friends*. **2** between: *divide it among them*. **3** in the group or number of: *among his best plays*. **4** with one another: *decide among yourselves*. [OE *ongemang*]

amoral *adj* having no moral standards or principles. — *n* **amorality**. **[a-[1] + moral]**

amorous *adj* showing, feeling, or relating to love, esp. sexual love. — *adv* **amorously**. — *n* **amorousness**. [Lat *amorosus*, from *amor*, love]

amorphous *adj* with no definite shape or structure. [Gr *amorphos*, shapeless]

amortise or **-ize** *v* (*tr*) to gradually pay off (a debt) by regular payments of money. — *n* **amortisation** or **-z-**. [OFr *amortir*, to kill]

amount *n* a quantity; a total or extent: *a large amount of money*. — *v* (*intr* with **to**) to be equal or add up to in size, number, etc. [OFr *amonter*, to climb up]

amour *n* (*old*) a love affair, esp. one that is kept secret. [Fr, love]

amour-propre *n* self-esteem. [Fr]

amp *n* **1** an ampere. **2** (*coll*) an amplifier. [Abbrev.]

ampere *n* the unit by which an electric current is measured. [A M *Ampère* (1775–1836), French physicist]

amperage *n* the strength of an electrical current, measured in amperes.

ampersand *n* the sign **&**, meaning 'and'. [Short form of *and per se and*, 'and' by itself means 'and']

amphetamine *n* a drug, often taken illegally, which makes a depressed person feel happier and more energetic. [*A*lpha *m*ethyl *phe*nethyl + **amine**]

amphibian *n* **1** a creature, such as a frog or toad, that spends part of its life on land and part in water. **2** a vehicle able to operate both on land and in water. [Gr *amphi*, both + *bios*, life]

amphibious *adj* **1** living or operating both on land and in water. **2** (of a military attack, etc.) using troops landed from the sea.

amphitheatre *n* (*hist*) a round building without a roof, with tiers of seats round a central open area, used as a theatre. [Gr *amphi*, around + *theatron*, theatre]

amphora *n* ***-ras*** or ***-rae*** (*hist*) a Greek or Roman narrow-necked jar with a handle on each side and a pointed bottom, used to hold wine. [Lat, from Gr *amphi*, on both sides + *phoreus*, bearer]

ample *adj* **1** more than enough; plenty. **2** extensive, abundant. **3** (esp. of people) very large. [Lat *amplus*]

amply *adv* well; more than is necessary.

amplify *v* ***-ies***, ***-ied*** **1** (*tr*) to make (a sound or electrical signal) stronger. **2** (*tr* & *intr*; **on, upon**) to add detail to (a story, etc.). — *n* **amplification**. [Lat *amplificare*, from *amplus*, ample]

amplifier *n* a machine for increasing the strength of electrical signals, esp. so as to increase sound.

amplitude *n* **1** spaciousness, wide range or extent. **2** (*physics*) the maximum distance between the middle and either the top or bottom of a wave. [Lat *amplitudo*, from *amplus*, ample]

ampoule *n* a small, sealed container, usu. of glass, for holding a drug to be injected. [Fr]

ampulla *n* ***-ae*** **1** (*hist*) a small round glass bottle with two handles, used by ancient Romans for holding oil, perfume or wine. **2** a container for oil, water or wine used in religious ceremonies. [Lat]

amputate *v* (*tr*) to cut off (part or all of a limb). — *n* **amputation**. [Lat *amputare*, to cut off]

amputee *n* someone who has had a limb amputated.

amt. *abbrev* amount.

amuck. See **amok**.

amulet *n* a small object or jewel worn to protect the wearer from evil or disease. [Lat *amuletum*]

amuse *v* (*tr*) **1** to make (someone) laugh. **2** to keep (someone) entertained and interested. — *adj* **amused**. — *adv* **amusedly**. — *adj* **amusing**. — *adv* **amusingly**. [OFr *amuser*, to cause to muse]

amusement *n* **1** the state of being amused. **2** something that amuses. **3** a machine for riding on or playing games of chance.

amusement arcade *n* a public building with machines for gambling, video games, etc.

amusement park *n* (*NAm*) a funfair.

an. See **a**[1].

an-. See **a-**[1].

anabaptist *n* (also *cap*; *hist*) a member of a Protestant sect which believes in adult baptism. [Gr *ana*, again + *baptizein*, to dip]

anabolic steroid *n* an artificial hormone which can be used as a drug to increase muscle strength and size. [**anabolism**]

anabolism *n* chemical reactions in plants and animals by which complex substances are built up from simpler ones. [Gr *ana*, up + *bole*, throw]

anachronism *n* **1** the attribution of something to a historical period in which it did not exist. **2** a person, thing or attitude that is out of date and old-fashioned. — *adj* **anachronistic**. — *adv* **anachronistically**. [Gr *ana*, backwards + *chronos*, time]

anaconda *n* a very large S American snake. [Sinhalese *henakandaya*, the name of a Sri Lankan snake]

anaemia *n* a condition in which there are not enough red cells in the blood, causing tiredness and paleness. [Gr *an*, without + *haima*, blood]

anaemic *adj* **1** suffering from anaemia. **2** pale or weak; lacking in energy. — *adv* **anaemically**.

anaesthesia *n* loss of consciousness (**general anaesthesia**) or of feeling in a part of the body (**local anaesthesia**), caused esp. by gas or drugs given before an operation. [Gr *an*, without + *aisthesis*, feeling]

anaesthetic *n* a drug or gas that causes either total unconsciousness (**general anaesthetic**) or lack of feeling in part of the body (**local anaesthetic**), so that surgery may be performed without pain.

anaesthetise or **-ize** *v* (*tr*) to give an anaesthetic to (someone).

anaesthetist *n* a doctor who gives anaesthetics to patients.

anaglypta *n* plain white wallpaper with a raised pattern on it, usu. for painting over. [Gr *anaglyptos*, in low relief]

anagram *n* a word, phrase or sentence formed from the letters of another. [Gr *ana*, back + *gramma*, letter]

anal. See **anus**.

analgesia *n* the state of not being able to feel pain even though one is awake. [Gr *an*, not + *algeein*, to feel pain]

analgesic *n* a drug which is used to reduce or relieve pain. — *adj* pain-relieving.

analogous *adj* similar or alike in some ways. — *adv* **analogously**. [Gr *analogos*, proportionate]

analogue *n* **1** anything that is like something else. **2** a physical quantity which varies according to variations in some other physical quantity and which is used to measure or record them, as the movement of the hands on a traditional **analogue watch** measure the passage of time. ◇ See also **digital**. [*Gr analogos*, analogous]

analogue computer *n* a computer that uses variations in voltage to represent numbers in calculations.

analogy *n* **-ies 1** a likeness or similarity in some ways. **2** a way of reasoning which makes it possible to explain one thing or event by comparing it with something else. — *adj* **analogical**. — *adv* **analogically**. [Gr *analogia*, from *analogos*, analogous]

analyse *v* (*tr*) **1** to examine the structure or content of (something) in detail. **2** to work out the ingredients or component parts of (esp. a chemical compound). **3** to psychoanalyse (someone). — *adj* **analysable**. [Gr *analyein*, to undo, set free]

analysis *n* **-yses 1** a detailed examination of the structure and content of something. **2** a statement of the results of such an examination. **3** (esp. *NAm*) psychoanalysis. — **in the final analysis** after everything has been considered.

analyst *n* **1** someone who is skilled in analysis, esp. chemical, political or economic. **2** (esp. *NAm*) a psychoanalyst.

analytic or **analytical** *adj* **1** concerning or involving analysis. **2** examining or able to examine things in detail to learn or make judgements about them. — *adv* **analytically**.

anapaest *n* (*poetry*) a foot consisting of two short or unstressed beats followed by one long or stressed beat. — *adj* **anapaestic**. [Gr *anapaistos*, reversed, because it is the reverse of a **dactyl**]

anarchy *n* **1** confusion and lack of order, esp. political; the failure of law and government. **2** the absence of law and government. — *adj* **anarchic**. — *adv* **anarchically**. [Gr *an*, without + *arche*, government]

anarchism *n* a political belief that governments and laws are unnecessary and should be abolished.

anarchist *n* **1** a person who believes in anarchism. **2** a person who tries to overthrow the government by violence. **3** a person who tries to cause disorder of any kind.— *adj* **anarchistic**. — *adv* **anarchistically**.

anathema *n* **1** a person or thing one detests. **2** (in the Christian church) a person or doctrine that has been cursed or denounced. [Gr, thing devoted to evil]

anathematise or **-ize** *v* (*tr* & *intr*) to curse or denounce.

anatomy *n* **-ies 1** the science of the structure of the human or animal body, or plants, esp. studied through dissection. **2** the structure of an animal or plant. **3** (*coll*) a person's body. — *adj* **anatomical**. — *adv* **anatomically**. [Gr *anatome*, dissection]

anatomist *n* a person skilled in anatomy.

ANC *abbrev* African National Congress.

-ance *sfx* forming nouns indicating a state, quality or action: *abundance*; *performance*. [Fr, from Lat *-antia*]

ancestor *n* **1** a person who was a member of one's family a long time ago, and from whom one is descended. **2** a forerunner. [Lat *antecessor*, from *ante*, before + *cedere*, to go]

ancestral *adj* of or inherited from one's ancestors.

ancestry *n* **-ies** one's family descent.

anchor *n* **1** a heavy piece of metal with hooks which dig into the seabed, attached by a cable to a ship and used to restrict its movement. **2** a weight used to hold a balloon to the ground. **3** anything that gives security or stability. ◇ See also under **anchorman**. — *v* **1** (*tr*) to fasten (a ship or balloon) using an anchor. **2** (*tr*) to fasten securely. **3** (*intr*) to drop an anchor and become moored by it; to be moored by an anchor. [OE *ancor*]

anchorage *n* **1** a place where a ship may anchor. **2** a safe place in which to rest. **3** the act of anchoring.

anchorman or (esp. sense **1**) **anchorwoman** *n* **1** a man or woman who presents a television programme and is responsible for keeping the discussion running smoothly, linking up with reporters outside, etc. **2** (also **anchor**) a man or woman running last in a relay team.

anchorite *n* a man or woman who, for religious reasons, lives alone and separate from other people. [Gr *anachoretes*, from *ana*, apart + *choreein*, to withdraw]

anchovy *n* **-ies** a small fish of the herring family, with a strong, salty taste, usu. preserved in oil. [Span and Port *anchova*]

ancient *adj* **1** dating from very long ago. **2** very old. **3** dating from before the end of the Roman Empire in AD 476. — *n* (usu. in *pl*) people who lived in the ancient world, esp. Greeks and Romans. [OFr *ancien*, from Lat *antianus*, former, old]

ancient history *n* **1** the history of the countries surrounding the Mediterranean, esp. Greece, Italy and Egypt, before the end of the Roman Empire in AD 476. **2** (*coll*) information, news, etc. one has known for a long time.

ancillary *adj* **1** helping or giving support to e.g. medical services. **2** being used as an extra. [Lat *ancillaris*, from *ancilla*, maidservant]

-ancy *sfx* forming nouns indicating (something which shows) a state or quality: *expectancy*. [Lat *-antia*]

and *conj* (used to join two or more statements, words or clauses) **1** used to show addition: *two and two*. **2** used to show a result or reason: *fall and bang one's head*. **3** used to show repetition or duration: *It rained and rained*. **4** used to show progression: *bigger and bigger*. **5** used to show variety or contrast: *There are good cars and bad cars*. **6** (*coll*) used instead of *to* after some verbs: *come and try*. — **and/or** either or both (of two possibilities stated): *cakes and/or biscuits*. [OE]

andante *adj* & *adv* (*mus*) played rather slowly. — *n* a piece of music to be played like this. [Ital, from *andare*, to go]

andiron *n* an iron bar, usu. one of a pair, supporting logs and coal in a fireplace. [OFr *andier*]

androgynous *adj* (of a person, animal or plant) with both male and female characteristics. [Gr *androgynos*, from *aner*, man + *gyne*, woman]

android *n* a robot that looks, moves and behaves like a human. [Gr *aner*, man]

anecdote *n* a short, interesting and usu. amusing account of an incident. — *adj* **anecdotal**. [Gr *anekdota*, unpublished things, from *an*, not + *ekdotos*, published]

anemia (*US*). Same as **anaemia**.

anemometer *n* an instrument for measuring the speed and strength of the wind. [Gr *anemos*, wind + **-meter**]

anemone *n* a plant related to the buttercup, with red, purple, blue or white flowers. [Gr, windflower]

aneroid barometer or **aneroid** *n* a barometer consisting of a container with some of the air removed from inside it, which detects changes in air pressure and indicates them by a pointer on the barometer's lid. [Gr *a*, without + *neros*, water]

anesthesia and **anesthetic** (*US*). Same as **anaesthesia** and **anaesthetic**.

aneurysm or **aneurism** *n* a condition in which an artery becomes unnaturally swollen and large. [Gr *aneurysma*, from *ana*, up + *eurys*, wide]

anew *adv* **1** again. **2** in a different way. [MidE; **of** + **new**]

angel *n* **1** a messenger or attendant of God. **2** a representation of this in human form, with a halo and wings. **3** (*coll*) a very good, helpful, pure or beautiful person. **4** (*coll*) a person who puts money into an enterprise, esp. in the theatre. — **angels on horseback** oysters wrapped in slices of bacon, grilled until crisp. [Gr *angelos*, messenger]

angel cake *n* a light sponge cake.

angelfish *n* a small tropical fish with very large fins.

angelic *adj* of or like an angel, esp. in being pure, innocent and very good. — *adv* **angelically**.

angelica *n* **1** a pleasant-smelling plant, used in medicine and cooking. **2** the stalks of this plant, coated in sugar and used as a decoration for food. [Lat *herba angelica*, angelic herb]

angelus *n* **1** a Roman Catholic prayer said in the morning, at noon and at sunset, in honour of the Incarnation. **2** a bell rung to announce these prayers. [Lat *Angelus domini*, the angel of the Lord, the opening words of the prayer]

anger *n* a feeling of great or violent displeasure. — *v* **-r-** (*tr*) to make angry; to displease. [Norse *angr*, grief]

angry *adj* **-ier**, **-iest 1** feeling or showing anger. **2** (of a wound) red and sore-looking. **3** dark and stormy: *an angry sky*. — *adv* **angrily**.

angina or **angina pectoris** *n* a disease of the heart in which periods of sudden poor blood supply to the heart cause sharp pain in the chest and left arm. [Lat *angina*, a throat disease + *pectus*, breast]

Angle *n* (usu. in *pl*) a member of a N German tribe who settled in N and E England and southern Scotland in the 5th century. [OE *Angel*]

angle[1] *n* **1** the space between two straight lines or surfaces that meet. **2** the amount by which one line slopes away from another. **3** a corner. **4** a point of view; an aspect; a way of considering or being involved in something. — *v* **1** (*tr* & *intr*) to move in or place at an angle. **2** (*tr*) to present (a news story, information, etc.) from a particular point of view. [Lat *angulus*]

angle[2] *v* (*intr*) **1** to use a rod and line to try to catch fish. **2** (with **for**) to try to get in an indirect way: *angle for compliments*. — *n* **angler**. — *n* **angling**. [OE *angul*, hook]

Anglican *adj* of or relating to the Church of England and any other church in communion with it. — *n* a member of an Anglican Church. — *n* **Anglicanism**. [Lat *Anglicanus*, from *Anglus*, Angle]

anglicise or **-ize** *v* (*tr*) to make English in form or character. — *n* **anglicisation** or **-z-**. [Lat *Anglus*, Angle + **-ise**]

anglicism *n* a word or custom that is peculiar to the English.

Anglo- *comb fm* English; British; of English or British origin: *an Anglo-American*. [Lat *Anglus*, English]

Anglo-Catholic *n* a member of an Anglican Church which emphasises the church's Roman Catholic traditions. — *adj* of Anglo-Catholics. — *n* **Anglo-Catholicism**.

Anglo-Indian *n* **1** a person of British descent who has lived in India for a long time. **2** a person of mixed English and Indian descent. — *adj* of Anglo-Indians.

Anglo-Norman *n* **1** the Old French dialect introduced into England by the Norman invaders in 1066, and spoken in England by the aristocracy for about two hundred years. **2** a Norman inhabitant of England after 1066. — *adj* of the Anglo-Norman language or people.

anglophile *n* a person who admires England and the English. [**Anglo-** + Gr *philos*, friend]
anglophobe *n* a person who hates or fears England and the English. [**Anglo-** + Gr *phobos*, fear]
anglophone *n* an English-speaking person, esp. in states where other languages are also spoken. [**Anglo-** + Gr *phone*, voice]
Anglo-Saxon *n* **1** a member of any of the Germanic tribes which settled in England and parts of Scotland in the 5th century. **2** Old English, the English language before about 1150. — *adj* of the Anglo-Saxons or the Old English language.
angora *n* **1** a kind of goat, cat or rabbit with long silky hair. **2** the wool or cloth made from the hair of an angora rabbit or goat. — *adj* made from such wool or cloth. [*Angora*, old name for Ankara, capital of Turkey]
angostura *n* the bitter bark of a tree, used orig. to reduce fever, and now used to flavour drinks. [*Angostura*, now called Ciudad Bolívar, a town in Venezuela]
Angostura bitters® *n* a bitter liquid for flavouring drinks, made from angostura bark.
angry. See **anger**.
angst *n* a feeling of anxiety caused by the uncertainties of human existence. [Ger]
angstrom *n* a unit used to measure light wavelengths, X-rays, etc. [Anders J *Ångström* (1814–74), Swedish physicist]
anguish *n* great pain or suffering, esp. of the mind. [Lat *angustia*, tightness]
anguished *adj* feeling, showing or suggesting great pain.
angular *adj* **1** (of a person, etc.) thin and bony; sharp or awkward in manner. **2** having an angle or angles. **3** measured by an angle: *angular distance*. — *n* **angularity**. [Lat *angularis*, from *angulus*, angle]
anhydrous *adj* (of a chemical compound) containing no water. [Gr *an*, without + *hydor*, water]
aniline *n* a poisonous, oily liquid obtained from coal tar, and used for making dyes, drugs, plastics and explosives. [Arabic *an-nil*, indigo, from which it was first obtained]
animadversion *n* criticism or censure. [Lat *animus*, mind + *ad*, to + *vertere*, to turn]
animal *n* **1** a living being which can feel things and move when it wants. **2** any living being other than man, esp. one with four legs. **3** a person who behaves in a rough, uncivilised way. **4** (*coll*) a person or thing. — *adj* **1** of, from or like an animal. **2** of the physical desires of animals; brutal; sensual. [Lat *animalis*, having breath]
animalise or **-ize** *v* (*tr*) to make (a person) brutal or sensual.
animalism *n* **1** the state of having the physical desires of an animal. **2** the belief that man is no better than other animals.
animality *n* **1** animal nature or behaviour. **2** the state of being an animal, esp. a lower animal.
animalcule *n* a microscopic animal. [Lat *animalculum*]
animate *v* (*tr*) **1** to give life to. **2** to make lively. **3** to record (still drawings telling a story) on film in such a way as to make the images seem to move: *animated cartoon*. — *adj* alive. — *adj* **animated**. — *adv* **animatedly**. [Lat *animare*, from *anima*, breath, life or soul]
animation *n* **1** liveliness, vivacity. **2** the techniques used to record still drawings on film in such a way as to make the images seem to move.
animator *n* a person who does the drawings to be made into animated films and cartoons.
animatronics *n* the art of animating the lifelike figure of a person, animal, etc. by electronic means. [**animate** + **electronics**]
animism *n* the belief that plants and natural phenomena (e.g. rivers, mountains, etc.) have souls. — *n* **animist**. — *adj* **animistic**. [Lat *anima*, soul]
animosity *n* **-ies** a strong dislike or hatred. [Lat *animositas*]
animus *n* a feeling of strong dislike or hatred. [Lat, spirit, soul]
anion *n* (*electr*) a negatively charged ion. ◇ See also **cation**. [Gr *ana*, up + *ienai*, to go]
anise *n* a Mediterranean plant with liquorice-flavoured seeds. [Gr *anison*]
aniseed *n* the liquorice-flavoured seeds from this plant, used in making sweets, drinks and some medicines.
ankle *n* **1** the joint connecting the leg and the foot. **2** the part of the leg just above the foot. [OE *ancleow*]
anklet *n* a chain or ring worn around the ankle.
ankylosis *n* an abnormal stiffening of a joint, caused by bone disease, injury or surgery. [Gr]
annals *n* (*pl*) **1** a yearly historical record of events. **2** regular reports of an organisation's work. — *n* **annalist**. [Lat *annales* (*libri*), yearly (books)]
anneal *v* (*tr*) to heat (metal, glass, etc.) then let it cool slowly, esp. to toughen it. — *n* **annealing**. [OE *onælan*, to burn]
annelid *n* a worm with a long body made up of rings or segments. [Lat *annellus*, little ring]
annex *v* (*tr*) **1** to take possession of (land, territory), esp. by conquest or occupation. **2** to add or attach (something) to something larger. **3** (*coll*) to take without permission.— *n* **annexation**. [Lat *annectere*, to tie to]
annexe or **annex** *n* a building added on to, or used as an addition to, another.
annihilate *v* (*tr*) **1** to destroy completely. **2** to defeat or crush, esp. in an argument. —

n **annihilation**. [Lat *annihilare*, from *ad*, to + *nihil*, nothing]

anniversary *n* **-*ies*** **1** the date on which some event took place in a previous year. **2** the celebration of this event on the same date each year. [Lat *anniversarius*, from *annus*, year + *vertere*, to turn]

Anno Domini *n* **1** Latin for 'in the year of our Lord', used in giving dates since the birth of Christ. **2** (*coll*) old age.

annotate *v* (*tr*) to add notes and explanations to (a book, etc.). — *n* **annotation**. — *n* **annotator**. [Lat *annotare*]

announce *v* (*tr*) **1** to make known publicly. **2** to make known (someone's) arrival. **3** to be a sign of: *dark clouds announcing a storm*. — *n* **announcement**. [Lat *annuntiare*]

announcer *n* a person who introduces programmes on radio or television.

annoy *v* (*tr*) **1** to anger or distress. **2** to harass or pester, esp. sexually. — *n* **annoyance**. — *adj* **annoyed**. — *adj* **annoying**. — *adv* **annoyingly**. [Lat *inodiare*, to cause aversion]

annual *adj* **1** happening every year. **2** lasting for a year. — *n* **1** a plant that lives for only one year. **2** a book published every year, esp. an illustrated gift-book for children. — *adv* **annually**. [Lat *annualis*, from *annus*, year]

annual general meeting see **AGM**.

annualise or **-ize** *v* (*tr*) to calculate (rates of interest, inflation, etc.) for a year based on the figures for only part of it.

annuity *n* **-*ies*** **1** a yearly grant or allowance. **2** money invested providing a fixed amount of interest every year. [Lat *annuitas*, from *annus*, year]

annul *v* **-*ll*-** (*tr*) to declare publicly that (a marriage, legal contract, etc.) is no longer valid. — *n* **annulment**. [Lat *annullare*, from *ad*, to + *nullus*, none]

annular *adj* ring-shaped. [Lat *annularis*, from *anulus*, ring]

annular eclipse *n* an eclipse of the sun during which a ring of light can be seen around the moon's shadow.

annulate *adj* formed from or marked with rings. [Lat *annulatus*, from *anulus*, ring]

Annunciation *n* **1** (with **the**) the announcement by the angel Gabriel to Mary that she would conceive Christ. **2** the festival celebrating this, on 25 March; Lady Day. [Lat *annuntiare*]

anode *n* **1** the positive electrode in an electrolytic cell, which attracts electrons. **2** a negative terminal in a dry cell battery. ◇ See also **cathode**. [Gr *anodos*, way up, from *ana*, up + *hodos*, way]

anodise or **-ize** *v* (*tr*) to coat (a metal) with a protective oxide covering by electrolysis. [**anode**]

anodyne *n* & *adj* **1** (anything which is) able to relieve physical pain or mental distress. **2** (anything which is) able to prevent argument or criticism. [Gr *an*, without + *odyne*, pain]

anoint *v* (*tr*) to put oil or ointment on (esp. a person's head) as part of a religious ceremony, e.g. baptism. — *n* **anointment**. [Lat *inungere*, from *in*, on + *ungere*, to smear with oil]

anomaly *n* **-*ies*** something which is unusual or different from what is normal. [Gr *an*, without + *homalos*, even]

anomalous *adj* different from the usual; irregular. — *adv* **anomalously**.

anomie or **anomy** *n* a lack of moral standards in a person or social group. [Gr *an*, without + *nomos*, law]

anon *adv* (*old*) soon. [OE *on an*, into one]

anon. *abbrev* anonymous.

anonymous *adj* **1** having no name. **2** (of an act, piece of writing, etc.) by a person whose name is not known or not given. **3** without character. — *n* **anonymity**. — *adv* **anonymously**. [Gr *an*, without + *onoma*, name]

anorak *n* a hooded waterproof jacket. [Inuit]

anorexia or **anorexia nervosa** *n* an illness in which the sufferer (usu. a young girl) refuses to eat, and loses so much weight that his or her life is in danger — often caused by an obsession about weight or by emotional problems. — *n* & *adj* **anorexic**. [Gr *an*, without + *orexis*, longing]

another *adj* & *pron* **1** one more. **2** one more of the same kind: *another Thatcher*. **3** one of a different kind: *another country*. [MidE; **an other**]

anserine *adj* of or like a goose. [Lat *anser*, goose]

answer *n* **1** something said or done in reply or response to a question, request, letter, etc. **2** the solution to a mathematical problem. — *v* **-*r*-** **1** (*tr* & *intr*; **to**) to make a reply or answer. **2** (*tr*) to react or respond to (a doorbell, the telephone, etc.). **3** (*intr* with **for** or **to**) to be responsible (to someone for something). **4** (*tr* & *intr*) to be suitable (for something). **5** (*tr*) to match or be the same ás, esp. a description. **6** (*intr* with **for**) to be punished for (something). — **answer back** to reply rudely. [OE *andswaru*]

answerable *adj* (**to**, **for**) responsible for; accountable. — *n* **answerability**. — *adv* **answerably**.

answering machine *n* a machine which records telephone messages when one is absent.

answering service *n* a company which takes messages and answers telephone calls for its customers.

ant *n* a small, often wingless insect, which lives in organised colonies and is usu. thought of as very hard-working. [OE *æmette*]

anteater *n* a S African animal with a long snout, which mainly eats termites.

ant hill *n* a heap of earth built by ants over their nest.

-ant *sfx* (a person, thing, etc.) which has a quality or function or performs an action: *assistant*; *pleasant*. [Lat]

antacid *adj* (of medicines, etc.) able to lessen acidity, esp. in the stomach. — *n* an antacid medicine. [**anti-** (sense **1**) + **acid**]

antagonist *n* an opponent, enemy or adversary. — *adj* **antagonistic**. — *adv* **antagonistically**. [Gr *anti*, against + *agon*, contest]

antagonise or **-ize** *v* (*tr*) to make (someone) feel anger or hostility.

antagonism *n* openly expressed dislike or opposition.

Antarctic *n* (with **the**) the area round the South Pole. — *adj* of the area round the South Pole. [Gr *anti*, against + *arktikos*, the Arctic]

Antarctic Circle *n* an imaginary line drawn round the Earth at a latitude of 66° 32′ S, marking the limits of the Antarctic.

ante *n* **1** a stake put up by a player in poker before receiving any cards. **2** an advance payment. — *v* (*tr*; **up**) **1** to put up as a stake. **2** to pay. [Lat, before]

ante- *comb fm* before in place or time: *anteroom*; *antenatal*. [Lat *ante*, before]

antecedent *n* **1** an event or circumstance which precedes another. **2** (*gram*) a word or phrase to which another word, esp. a relative pronoun, refers. **3** (usu. in *pl*) a person's past history. — *adj* going before in time. — *n* **antecedence**. [Lat *ante*, before + *cedere*, to go]

antechamber *n* an anteroom. [**ante-** + **chamber**]

antedate *v* (*tr*) **1** to belong to an earlier period than. **2** to put a date (on a document, letter, etc.) that is earlier than the actual date. [**ante-** + **date**]

antediluvian *adj* **1** belonging to the time before the Flood. **2** (*facet*) very old or old-fashioned. [**ante-** + Lat *dilivium*, flood]

antelope *n* **-lope** or **-lopes** any of several types of graceful, deer-like animal with horns, related to the goat. [Gr *antholops*]

ante meridiem. See **a.m.**

antenatal *adj* before birth; during pregnancy. [**ante-** + Lat *natalis*, of one's birth]

antenna *n* **1** **-ae** one of a pair of feelers on the head of some insects, crabs, etc. used for touching. **2** **-nas** an aerial. [Lat, yard of a mast]

antepenultimate *n* & *adj* (anything or anyone that is) third from last. [**ante-** + **penultimate**]

anterior *adj* **1** earlier in time. **2** at or nearer the front. [Lat, from *ante*, before]

anteroom *n* a small room which opens into another, more important, room. [**ante-** + **room**]

anthem *n* **1** a usu. complicated piece of music sung by a church choir, usu. with words from the Bible. **2** a song of praise or celebration, esp. of a nation: *national anthem*. [OE *antefn*, from Lat *antiphona*, antiphon]

anther *n* that part of a flower's stamen containing the pollen. [Gr *anthos*, flower]

anthology *n* **-ies** a collection of pieces of poetry or other writing. — *n* **anthologist**. [Gr *anthos*, flower + *logia*, gathering]

anthracite *n* very hard coal that burns almost without any smoke or flames. [Gr *anthrax*, coal]

anthrax *n* a dangerous disease of sheep and cattle that may be given to human beings. [Gr, coal, carbuncle]

anthropo- *comb fm* of or like human beings. [Gr *anthropos*, man]

anthropocentric *adj* believing that mankind is the most important thing in existence. — *adv* **anthropocentrically**. [**anthropo-** + **-centric**]

anthropoid *adj* like a human being in form. — *n* an ape that is like a human being in form, e.g. the gorilla. — *adv* **anthropoidal**. [Gr *anthropoeides*, man-like]

anthropology *n* the study of human beings, esp. their society, customs and beliefs. — *adj* **anthropological** . — *adv* **anthropologically**. — *n* **anthropologist**. [**anthropo-** + **-logy**]

anthropomorphism *n* the attribution of human behaviour, feelings and beliefs to animals, gods, objects, etc. — *adj* **anthropomorphic**. [**anthropo-** + Gr *morphe*, form]

anthropomorphous *adj* human in form.

anti *n* & *adj* (a person who is) opposed to something. [Gr, against]

anti- *comb fm* **1** opposed to; against: *anti-aircraft*. **2** opposite to: *anticlockwise*, *anticlimax*. [Gr *anti*, against]

anti-aircraft *adj* (of a gun or missile) used to attack enemy aircraft.

antibiotic *n* any substance, e.g. medicine, which is used to kill the bacteria that cause disease. — *adj* of or relating to antibiotics. [**anti-** (sense **1**) + Gr *bios*, life]

antibody *n* **-ies** a protein produced by the blood in response to the presence of harmful bacteria.

Antichrist *n* **1** an enemy of Christ. **2** in the Christian Church, the great enemy of Christ who is expected to appear before the end of the world. [Gr *anti*, against + *Christos*, Christ]

anticipate *v* (*tr*) **1** to see what will be needed or wanted in the future and do what is necessary in advance. **2** to expect. **3** to look forward to. **4** to mention (part of a story, what a person thinks, etc.) before the proper time. **5** to spend (e.g. one's salary) before receiving it. — *n* **anticipation**. — *adj* **anticipatory**. [Lat *anticipare*, from *ante*, before + *capere*, to take]

anticlerical *adj* opposed to public and political power being held by members of the clergy. — *n* **anticlericalism**.

anticlimax *n* a dull or disappointing end to a series of events, play, etc. which one thought would end with a climax. — *adj* **anticlimactic**.

anticlockwise *adv* & *adj* in the opposite direction to that in which the hands of a clock move.

anticoagulant *n* a drug that stops the blood from clotting.

antics *n* (*pl*) odd, silly or foolish behaviour. [Ital *antico*, grotesque]

anticyclone *n* a system of winds circling outwards from an area of high air pressure, usu. producing good weather.

antidepressant *n* & *adj* (a drug) used or able to treat depression.

antidote *n* **1** a medicine given to stop the harmful effects of a poison. **2** anything that prevents or counteracts something bad. [Gr *anti*, against + *didonai*, to give]

antifreeze *n* a substance which is added to a liquid to stop it from freezing, esp. to the water in a car radiator.

antigen *n* any substance, usu. poisonous, which causes the body to produce antibodies. [**anti-** + Gr *genes*, born, produced]

antihero *n* **-*oes*** a principal character in a book, play, film, etc. who has no noble qualities but is just like an ordinary person.

antihistamine *n* a medicine which is used to treat allergic reactions such as hay fever.

antiknock *n* a substance added to motor fuel to slow down the rate of combustion and so prevent a knocking sound in the engine.

anti-lock *adj* (of a braking system) designed to prevent the wheels of a vehicle locking when the brakes are applied.

antilog *abbrev* antilogarithm.

antilogarithm *n* (*math*) the number of which a given number is the logarithm.

antimacassar *n* a covering for the back of a chair to stop it getting dirty. [**anti-** (sense **1**) + *macassar*, an oil once used on hair]

antimatter *n* hypothetical particles of matter with the opposite electrical charge to those forming the Earth.

antimony *n* a silvery metallic element (symbol **Sb**), added to alloys to make them stronger. [Lat *antimonium*]

antinomian *n* & *adj* (a person) believing that Christians do not have to observe moral law. [Lat *Antinomi*, the name of a sect believing this, from **anti-** (sense **1**) + Gr *nomos*, law]

antinomy *n* **-*ies*** a contradiction between two laws or beliefs that are reasonable in themselves. [Gr *anti*, against + *nomos*, law]

antinovel *n* a novel in which all the accepted elements of novel-writing are ignored or avoided.

antinuclear *adj* opposed to the use of nuclear power or nuclear weapons.

antipasto *n* **-*ti*** or **-*tos*** food served at the beginning of a meal to sharpen the appetite. [Ital]

antipathy *n* **-*ies*** strong dislike or hostility. — *adj* **antipathetic**. — *adv* **antipathetically**.

anti-personnel *adj* (of weapons and bombs) designed to attack and destroy people rather than buildings and other weapons.

antiperspirant *n* a substance applied to the skin to help stop sweating.

antiphon *n* a hymn or psalm sung alternately by two groups of singers. [Lat *antiphona*, from Gr *anti*, in return + *phone*, voice]

antipodes *n* (*pl*; also *cap*) places on the Earth's surface exactly opposite each other, esp. Australia and New Zealand as being opposite Europe. — *adj* **antipodean**. [Gr, from *antipous*, having the feet opposite]

antipope *n* a pope elected in opposition to one already elected.

antipyretic *n* & *adj* (a drug used for) reducing fever. [**anti-** (sense **1**) + Gr *pyretos*, fever]

antiquary *n* **-*ies*** a person who collects, studies or deals in antiques and antiquities. [Lat *antiquarius*, from *antiquus*, ancient]

antiquarian *adj* of or dealing in antiques and rare books. — *n* an antiquary.

antiquated *adj* old and out of date; old-fashioned. [Lat *antiquare*, to make old]

antique *n* a piece of furniture, china, etc. which is very old, usu. very valuable, and often much sought after by collectors. — *adj* **1** old and usu. valuable. **2** (*coll*) old-fashioned. [Lat *antiquus*, ancient]

antiquity *n* **-*ies*** **1** ancient times, esp. before the end of the Roman Empire in AD 476. **2** great age. **3** (in *pl*) works of art or buildings surviving from ancient times. [Lat *antiquitas*, from *antiquus*, ancient]

antirrhinum *n* a plant with white, red or yellow two-lipped flowers; a snapdragon. [Gr *antirrinon*, from *anti*, mimicking + *rhis*, nose]

antiscorbutic *n* & *adj* (a drug used for) preventing or curing scurvy.

anti-semitic *adj* disliking or prejudiced against Jews. — *n* **anti-semite**. — *n* **anti-semitism**.

antiseptic *n* & *adj* (of) a substance or drug that kills germs and so prevents infection or disease.

antiserum *n* **-*ra*** a blood serum containing particular antibodies, used to treat or prevent a particular disease. [**antibody** + **serum**]

antisocial *adj* **1** unwilling to mix socially with other people. **2** (of behaviour) harmful or annoying. — *adv* **antisocially**.

antistatic *adj* reducing the effects of static electricity.

antitank *adj* (of weapons) designed to destroy military tanks.

antithesis *n* ***-eses*** **1** a direct opposite. **2** the placing together of contrasting ideas, words or themes in any oral or written argument, esp. to produce an effect. — *adj* **antithetic** or **antithetical**. — *adv* **antithetically**. [Gr *antitithenai*, to set against]
antitoxin *n* any substance which acts against a poison in the body.
antitrades *n* (*pl*) winds blowing above, and in the opposite direction to, trade winds.
anti-trust *adj* (esp. *US*) (of a law) protecting small companies and trade from domination by monopolies.
anti-vivisection *n* opposition to scientific experiments on living animals. — *n* **anti-vivisectionist**.
antler *n* either of the two branched horns on the head of a stag. [Fr *antoillier*]
antonym *n* a word opposite in meaning to another word. — *adj* **antonymous**. — *n* **antonymy**. [Gr *anti*, opposite + *onyma* or *onoma*, name]
antrum *n* ***-ra*** (*anat*) a natural cavity in the body, esp. in a bone. [Gr *antron*, cave]
anus *n* the opening at the end of the alimentary canal between the buttocks, through which faeces leave the bowels. — *adj* **anal**. [Lat, ring]
anvil *n* a heavy iron block on which metal objects can be hammered into shape. [OE *anfilt*]
anxious *adj* **1** worried, nervous or fearful about what will or may happen. **2** causing worry, fear or uncertainty. **3** very eager: *anxious to do well*. — *n* **anxiety**, ***-ies***. — *adv* **anxiously**. — *n* **anxiousness**. [Lat *anxius*, from *angere*, to press tightly]
any *adj* **1** one, no matter which: *can't find any answer*. **2** some, no matter which: *Have you any apples?* **3** a very small amount of: *won't tolerate any nonsense*. **4** large or indefinite: *have any number of dresses*. **5** whichever or whatever: *Any child could tell you*. — *pron* any one or any amount. — *adv* (in questions and negative sentences) in any way whatever: *It isn't any better*. [OE *ænig*]
anybody *pron* **1** any person, no matter which. **2** (in questions and negative sentences) an important person.
anyhow *adv* **1** in spite of what has been said, done, etc.; anyway. **2** carelessly; in an untidy state.
anyone same as **anybody**.
anyplace (*US*) same as **anywhere**.
anything *pron* a thing of any kind; a thing, no matter which. — *adv* in any way; to any extent: *She isn't anything like her sister*. — **anything but** not at all. — **like anything** (*coll*) with great speed or enthusiasm.
anyway *adv* **1** nevertheless; in spite of what has been said, done, etc. **2** in any way or manner.
anywhere *adv* in, at or to any place. — *pron* any place.
Anzac *n* a soldier in the *A*ustralian and *N*ew *Z*ealand *A*rmy *C*orps during the First World War.
Anzac Day *n* 25 April, a public holiday in Australia and New Zealand in memory of the Anzac landing in Gallipoli in 1915.
AOB or **AOCB** *abbrev* any other business or competent business, the last item on the agenda for a meeting, when any matter not already dealt with may be raised.
aorta *n* the main artery in the body, carrying blood from the heart. [Gr *aorte*]
apace *adv* (*literary*) quickly. [MidE; **a**[3] (sense **3**) + **pace**[1]]
apart *adv* **1** in or into pieces: *come apart*. **2** separated by a certain distance or time. **3** to or on one side. **4** (after a noun) leaving aside: *joking apart*. — **apart from** except for. [OFr *a part*, to one side]
apartheid *n* in S Africa, the official policy of keeping people of different races apart. [Afrikaans *apart*, apart + *-heid*, -hood]
apartment *n* **1** a large room. **2** (esp. *NAm*) a flat. **3** (in *pl*) a set of rooms used for accommodation, usu. in a large building. [Fr *appartement*, from Ital *appartare*, to separate]
apathy *n* lack of interest or enthusiasm. — *adj* **apathetic**. — *adv* **apathetically**. [Gr *a*, without + *pathos*, feeling]
ape *n* **1** an animal related to human beings and monkeys, with little or no tail. **2** an ugly, stupid or clumsy person. — *v* (*tr*) to imitate (someone's behavior, speech, etc.). — *adj* **apish**. — **go ape** (*US slang*) to go crazy. [OE *apa*]
apeman *n* any of several extinct apes thought to be the forerunners of human beings.
aperient *n* & *adj* (a medicine) having a mild laxative effect. [Lat *aperire*, to open]
aperitif *n* an alcoholic drink taken before a meal to stimulate the appetite. [Fr, from Lat *aperire*, to open]
aperture *n* **1** a small hole or opening. **2** a small opening in a camera lens which controls the amount of light going in. [Lat *apertura*, from *aperire*, to open]
APEX *abbrev* advance purchase excursion, a reduced fare for journeys booked a certain period in advance.
apex *n* ***apexes*** or ***apices*** the highest point or tip. [Lat]
aphasia *n* the loss of, or a reduction in, the ability to speak or understand speech, usu. because of brain damage. [Gr *a*, not + *phanai*, to speak]
aphelion *n* ***-ia*** the point in a planet's orbit when it is furthest from the sun. ◇ See also **perihelion**. [Gr *apo*, from + *helios*, sun]
aphid or **aphis** *n* ***aphids*** or ***aphides*** a small insect which feeds by sucking the juices from plants, e.g. a greenfly.
aphorism *n* a short, often clever or humorous saying expressing some well-known truth. — *adj* **aphoristic**. [Gr *aphorizein*, to define]

aphrodisiac *n* & *adj* (any food, drug, etc.) increasing sexual desire or excitement. [Gr *aphrodisiakos*, from *Aphrodite*, the goddess of love]

apiary *n* **-ies** a place where bees are kept. [Lat *apiarum*, from *apis*, bee]

apiarist *n* a bee-keeper.

apical *adj* of, at or forming an apex. [**apex**]

apiculture *n* bee-keeping. [Lat *apis*, bee]

apiece *adv* to, for, by or from each one. [MidE; **a** + **piece**]

apish. See **ape**.

aplomb *n* calm self-assurance and poise. [Fr *à plomb*, straight up and down]

apocalypse *n* **1** (*cap*) the last book of the New Testament, also called the Revelation of St John, which describes the end of the world. **2** any revelation of the future, esp. future destruction or violence. — *adj* **apocalyptic**. [Gr *apocalypsis*, uncovering]

Apocrypha *n* the books included in the ancient Greek and Latin versions of the Old Testament but not in the Hebrew version, excluded from modern Protestant Bibles but included in Roman Catholic and Orthodox Bibles. [Gr *apocryphos*, hidden]

apocryphal *adj* (of a story, etc.) unlikely to be true.

apogee *n* **1** the point in the moon's or a satellite's orbit when it is farthest from the Earth. ◇ See also **perigee**. **2** the highest point. [Gr *apo*, away + *gaia*, Earth]

apolitical *adj* not interested or active in politics. — *adv* **apolitically**. [**a-**[1] + **political**]

apology *n* **-ies 1** an expression of regret for a mistake, failure or wrong-doing. **2** a formal defence of a belief or cause. — **an apology for** a poor example of. [Gr *apologia*, from *apologeisthai*, to speak in defence]

apologetic *adj* showing or expressing regret for a fault, etc. — *adv* **apologetically**.

apologia *n* a formal statement in defence of a belief or cause.

apologise or **-ize** *v* (*intr*) to say one is sorry for some mistake, etc.

apologist *n* a person who formally defends a belief or cause.

apophthegm *n* a short saying expressing some general truth. [Gr *apophthegma*, from *apo*, forth + *phthengesthai*, to speak]

apoplexy *n* a sudden loss of the power to feel, move, etc., due to a stroke. [Gr *apoplexia*, being struck down]

apoplectic *adj* **1** of or relating to apoplexy. **2** (*coll*) red-faced and very angry. — *adv* **apoplectically**.

apostasy *n* **-ies** the giving up of one's religion, principles, or political party. [Gr *apo*, away + *stasis*, standing]

apostate *n* & *adj* (a person who is) guilty of apostasy.

a posteriori *adj* & *adv* (of an argument or reasoning) based on observation or experience. ◇ See also **a priori**. [Lat, from what comes after]

apostle *n* **1** (often *cap*) a person sent out to preach about Christ in the early Christian church, esp. one of his twelve original disciples. **2** an enthusiastic champion or supporter of a cause, belief, etc. [Gr *apostolos*, from *apo*, away + *stellein*, to send]

apostolic *adj* **1** of or relating to the apostles in the early Christian church or their teaching. **2** of or relating to the pope: *the Apostolic See*. — *adv* **apostolically**.

apostrophe *n* **1** the mark ('), used to show the omission of a letter or letters, e.g. *I'm* for *I am*, and possession, e.g. *Anne's book*. **2** a passage in a speech, poem, etc. which turns away from its course to address a person (esp. dead or absent) or thing. [Gr *apostrephein*, to turn away]

apostrophise or **-ize** *v* (*tr*) to speak an apostrophe to.

apothecary *n* **-ies** (*old*) a chemist licensed to dispense drugs. [Gr *apotheke*, storehouse]

apotheosis *n* **-oses 1** a raising to the rank of god. **2** a perfect example. [Gr *apo*, completely + *theos*, god]

appal *v* **-ll-** (*tr*) to shock or horrify. [Fr *appallir*, to grow pale]

appalling *adj* **1** causing feelings of shock or horror. **2** (*coll*) extremely bad. — *adv* **appallingly**.

apparatus *n* **-ses** or **-tus 1** the equipment needed for a particular purpose. **2** an organisation or system made up of many different parts. [Lat, from *apparare*, to prepare for]

apparel *n* (*old* or *formal*) clothing. [Fr *apareillier*, to make fit]

apparent *adj* **1** easy to see or understand. **2** seeming to be real but perhaps not actually so. — *adv* **apparently**. ◇ See also **heir**. [Lat *apparere*, to appear]

apparition *n* **1** a sudden, unexpected appearance, esp. of a ghost. **2** a ghost. [Lat *apparitio*]

appeal *v* (*intr*) **1** (**for, to**) to make an urgent or formal request. **2** (**to**) to be pleasing, interesting or attractive. **3** (esp. *legal*; **against, to**) to request a higher authority or law court to review or change a decision given by a lower one. **4** (**to**) to call on for support: *appeal to her better nature*. **5** (*cricket*) to ask the umpire whether a batsman is out or not. — *n* **1** (**for, to**) an urgent or formal request for help, money, etc. **2** (esp. *legal*; **against, to**) a request to a higher authority or law court for a review or change of a decision taken by a lower one. **3** the quality of attracting, interesting or pleasing. [Lat *appellare*, to address by name]

appealing *adj* **1** pleasing, attractive or interesting. **2** arousing sympathy. — *adv* **appealingly**.

appear *v* (*intr*) **1** to become visible or come into sight. **2** to seem. **3** to present oneself formally or in public, e.g. on stage. **4** to be present in a law court as either accused or counsel. **5** to be published. [Lat *apparere*]
appearance *n* **1** an act or instance of appearing. **2** how a person or thing looks. **3** how someone or something looks, if different from how he, she or it really is. — **keep up appearances** to keep up an outward show of happiness, wealth, etc. when this is really lacking. — **put in an appearance** to attend (a meeting, party, etc.) only briefly. — **to all appearances** so far as it can be seen.

appease *v* (*tr*) **1** to calm or pacify, esp. by agreeing to demands made on one. **2** to satisfy (an appetite or doubt). — *n* **appeasement**. [Fr *apeser*, from *a*, to + *pes*, peace]

appellant *n* a person who makes an appeal to a higher court to review or change the decision of a lower one. — *adj* of an appeal or appellant. [Lat *appellare*, to address by name]

appellate *adj* (*legal*) (esp. of a court) concerned with appeals. [Lat *appellare*, to address by name]

appellation *n* a name or title. [Lat *appellare*, to address by name]

append *v* (*tr*) to add or attach, esp. as a supplement to a document. [Lat *appendere*, to hang]
appendage *n* anything added or attached to a larger or more important part.

appendectomy or **appendicectomy** *n* ***-ies*** a surgical operation to remove a diseased appendix from the body. [**appendix** + **-ectomy**]

appendicitis *n* inflammation of the appendix. [**appendix** + **-itis**]

appendix *n* ***-xes*** or ***-dices*** **1** a section containing extra information, notes, etc. at the end of a book or document. **2** a small, tube-like sac attached to the lower end of the large intestine. [Lat *appendere*, to hang]

appertain *v* (*intr*; **to**) to belong or relate. [Lat *ad*, to + *pertinere*, to belong]

appetite *n* **1** a natural physical desire, esp. for food. **2** (**for**) a liking or willingness. [Lat *appetitus*, from *appetere*, to seek after]
appetiser or **-z-** *n* a small amount of food or drink eaten before a meal to increase the appetite.
appetising or **-z-** *adj* increasing the appetite, esp. by looking or smelling delicious. — *adv* **appetisingly**.

applaud *v* **1** (*tr* & *intr*) to praise or show approval by clapping. **2** (*tr*) to express approval of. [Lat *applaudere*, to clap]
applause *n* praise or approval shown by clapping.

apple *n* **1** a firm, round, edible fruit with a green, red or yellow skin and white flesh. **2** the tree bearing this fruit. — **apple of one's eye** a person or thing one loves a lot. — **in apple-pie order** very neat and tidy. — **upset the apple cart** to upset carefully made plans. [OE *æppel*]
apple-pie bed *n* a bed made with the sheets doubled up so that one cannot stretch out one's legs, usu. for a joke.

appliance *n* a machine, instrument or tool used for a particular job. [**apply**]

applicable *adj* (**to**) that may be applied; suitable; appropriate. [Lat *applicare*, to apply]

applicant *n* (**for**) a person applying for a job, a university place, a grant, etc. [Lat *applicare*, to apply]

application *n* **1** (**for**) a formal request, e.g. for a job. **2** the act of putting something on to a surface; the thing put on to a surface. **3** the act of using something for a particular purpose. **4** hard work and effort. **5** (**to**) relevance. **6** (*comput*) a program designed to perform a particular function as a complement to other software. [Lat *applicare*, to apply]
applications package *n* (*comput*) a set of programs forming a single package designed to perform a particular function or set of functions, such as the creation of graphics.

applicator *n* a device for putting something on to a surface, esp. the skin. [Lat *applicare*, to apply]

appliqué *n* decoration for clothes, fabric, etc., in which material is cut into shapes which are sewn on to the clothes, etc. to make patterns and designs. [Fr, applied]

apply *v* ***-ies***, ***-ied*** **1** (*intr*; **for**) to make a formal request (for e.g. a job). **2** (*tr*; **to**) to put or spread on a surface. **3** (*intr*; **to**) to be relevant or suitable. **4** (*tr*; **to**) to put (a skill, rule, theory, etc.) to practical use. — **apply oneself** (**to**) to give one's full attention or energy (to a task, etc.). [Lat *applicare*, to attach]
applied *adj* (of a skill, theory, etc.) put to practical use: *applied science*.

appoint *v* (*tr*) **1** (**to**) to give (a person) a job or position. **2** to fix or agree on (a date, time or place). **3** to equip or furnish: *well-appointed rooms*. [Fr *apointer*, from *à*, to + *point*, point]
appointee *n* a person appointed.
appointment *n* **1** an arrangement to meet someone. **2** (**as**, **to**) the act of giving someone a job or position. **3** the job or position a person is given. **4** the person given a job or position. **5** (in *pl*; *formal*) equipment and furnishings.

apportion *v* (*tr*) to share out fairly. [Lat *apportionare*]

apposite *adj* (**to**) suitable; well chosen. — *adv* **appositely**. — *n* **appositeness**. [Lat *appositus*, from *apponere*, to put to]

apposition *n* a grammatical construction in which two or more nouns, or phrases including nouns, are put together without being linked by *and*, *but*, *or*, etc., e.g. *his wife the doctor*. [Lat *appositio*, from *apponere*, to put to]

appraise *v* (*tr*) **1** to decide the value or quality of (a person's skills, ability, etc.). **2** to put a price on, esp. officially. — *n* **appraisal**. — *n* **appraiser**. [OFr *aprisier*, from *a*, to + *prisier*, to price or prize]

appreciable *adj* noticeable; significant. — *adv* **appreciably**. [Lat *appretiare*, to appreciate]

appreciate *v* **1** (*tr*) to be grateful or thankful for. **2** (*tr*) to be aware of the value, quality, etc. of. **3** (*tr*) to understand or be aware of. **4** (*intr* & *tr*) to increase in value. [Lat *appretiare*, from *ad*, to + *pretium*, price]

appreciation *n* **1** gratitude or thanks. **2** sensitive understanding and enjoyment of the value or quality of something: *an appreciation of good music*. **3** the state of knowing or being aware of. **4** an increase in value.

appreciative *adj* feeling or expressing appreciation. — *adv* **appreciatively**.

apprehend *v* (*tr*) **1** to arrest. **2** to understand. [Lat *apprehendere*, to seize]

apprehension *n* **1** fear or anxiety about the future. **2** the act of arresting. **3** understanding. [Lat *apprehendere*, to seize]

apprehensive *adj* anxious or worried about the future. — *adv* **apprehensively**.

apprentice *n* a usu. young person who works for a skilled person for an agreed period of time in order to learn his or her trade. — *v* (*tr*; **to**) to give as an apprentice. — *n* **apprenticeship**. [Fr *apprentiz*, from Lat *apprehendere*, to lay hold of]

apprise or **-ize** *v* (*tr*; **of**) to inform or make aware. [Fr *appris*, learnt]

appro: **on appro** *abbrev* (*coll*) on approval.

approach *v* **1** (*tr* & *intr*) to come near or nearer in space or time. **2** (*tr*) to suggest or propose something to. **3** (*tr*) to begin to deal with (a problem, subject, etc.). **4** (*tr*) to be like or similar to: *Nothing approaches this for quality*. — *n* **1** the act of coming near. **2** a way to, or means of reaching, a place. **3** a request for help, support, etc.; a suggestion or proposal. **4** a way of considering or dealing with, e.g. a problem: *a new approach*. **5** the course followed by an aircraft as it comes in to land. **6** an approximation. [Lat *appropriare*, from *ad*, to + *prope*, near]

approachable *adj* **1** friendly and ready to listen and help. **2** that can be reached.

approbation *n* approval; consent. [Lat *approbatio*, from *approbare*, to approve of]

appropriate *adj* suitable or proper. — *v* (*tr*) **1** to take (something) as one's own, esp. without permission. **2** to put (money) aside for a particular purpose. — *adv* **appropriately**. — *n* **appropriateness**. — *n* **appropriation**. [Lat *appropriare*, from *ad*, to + *proprius*, one's own]

approve *v* **1** (*tr*) to agree to or permit. **2** (*intr*; **of**) to be pleased with or think well of. — *adj* **approving**. — *adv* **approvingly**. [Lat *approbare*, to approve of]

approval *n* **1** a favourable opinion. **2** official permission. — **on approval** (of goods for sale) that may be returned to the shop if not satisfactory.

approx. *abbrev* approximate.

approximate *adj* almost exact or accurate. — *v* (*tr* & *intr*; **to**) to come close to in value, quality, accuracy, etc. — *adv* **approximately**. [Lat *approximare*, from *ad*, to + *proximus*, nearest]

approximation *n* **1** a figure, answer, etc. which is almost exact. **2** the process of estimating a figure, etc.

appurtenance *n* (usu. in *pl*) an accessory to, or minor detail of, something larger, such as duties or rights connected with owning property. [Fr *apertenance*, from Lat *appertinere*, to belong]

APR *abbrev* annual percentage rate.

Apr. *abbrev* April.

après-ski *n* evening social activities after a day's skiing. — *adj* (of clothes, etc.) suitable for such activities. [Fr]

apricot *n* a small, round, pale-orange fruit with a soft furry skin, related to the peach and plum. — *adj* apricot-coloured or apricot-flavoured. [Port *albricoque*, from Lat *praecox*, early-ripening]

April *n* the fourth month of the year, following March. [Lat *Aprilis*]

April fool *n* a victim of a trick or joke played on 1 April, April Fools' Day.

a priori *adj* & *adv* (of an argument or reasoning) working from cause to effect or from general principles to particular cases. ◇ See also **a posteriori**. [Lat, from what is before]

apron *n* **1** a piece of cloth, plastic, etc. worn over the front of the clothes for protection from dirt. **2** a hard-surface area at an airport where aircraft are loaded. **3** the part of a theatre stage in front of the curtain. — **tied to his mother's** or **wife's apron strings** (of a man or boy) completely dominated by and dependent on his mother or wife. [MidE *napron*, from OFr *naperon*; *a napron* came to be understood as *an apron*]

apropos *adj* (of remarks) suitable or to the point. — *prep* (**of**) in reference to. — *adv* by the way; appropriately. [Fr *à propos*, to the purpose]

apse *n* the arched, domed east end of a church. [Gr *hapsis*, arch]

apsis *n* ***apsides*** either of the points in the orbit of a planet or satellite furthest from and nearest to the body it is orbiting. [Gr *hapsis*, arch]

apt *adj* **1** suitable. **2** (**to**) likely. **3** (**at**) clever or quick to learn. — *adv* **aptly**. — *n* **aptness**. [Lat *aptus*, fit]

apteryx *n* a kiwi. [Gr *a*, without + *pteryx*, wing]

aptitude *n* **1** (**for**) a natural skill or talent. **2** ability or fitness. [Lat *aptitudo*]

aqua- *comb fm* water: *aqualung*.

aqua fortis *n* (*old*) nitric acid. [Lat, strong water]

aqualung *n* an apparatus consisting of air cyclinders worn by divers on their backs, with tubes leading to the mouth, allowing them to breathe under water.

aquamarine *n* **1** a bluish-green precious stone. **2** its colour. — *adj* of this stone or its colour. [Lat *aqua marina*, sea water]

aquaplane *n* a thin board which a person stands on to be towed very fast by a motor boat. — *v* (*intr*) **1** to ride on an aquaplane. **2** (of a car, etc.) to slide along out of control on a thin film of water.

aqua regia *n* a mixture of acids used to dissolve gold and platinum. [Lat, royal water]

aquarium *n* **-iums** or **-ia** a glass tank, or a building containing several such tanks (e.g. in a zoo), for keeping fish and other water animals. [Lat *aquarius*, of water]

Aquarius *n* **1** a constellation and the eleventh sign of the zodiac, the Water-carrier. **2** a person born between 21 January and 19 February, under this sign. — *n & adj* **Aquarian**. [Lat *aquarius*, water-carrier]

aquatic *adj* **1** living or growing in water. **2** (of sports) taking place in water. — *n* **1** an aquatic animal or plant. **2** (in *pl*) water sports. [Lat *aquaticus*, from *aqua*, water]

aquatint *n* a picture produced by printing with a copper plate that has been etched using acid and wax. [Ital *aqua tinta*, dyed water]

aqua vitae *n* a strong alcoholic drink, esp. brandy. [Lat, water of life]

aqueduct *n* a channel or canal carrying water, esp. in the form of a tall bridge across a valley. [Lat *aqua*, water + *ducere*, to lead]

aqueous *adj* of, like or produced by water; watery. [Lat *aqua*, water]

aqueous humour *n* (*physiol*) the clear liquid in the eyeball.

aquiline *adj* **1** of or like an eagle. **2** (of a nose) curved like an eagle's beak. [Lat *aquila*, eagle]

AR *abbrev* Arkansas.

Ar *symbol* (*chem*) argon.

Arab *n* **1** one of the Semitic people living in the Middle East and N Africa. **2** a breed of horse famous for its grace and speed. — *adj* of Arabs or Arabia. [Gr *Araps*]

Arabian *adj* of Arabia or the Arabs. — *n* (*old*) an Arab.

Arabic *n* the Semitic language of the Arabs. — *adj* of the Arabs, their language or culture.

Arabic numeral *n* any of the numbers 0, 1, 2, 3, 4, 5, 6, 7, 8 or 9, brought to Europe from India by the Arabs.

arabesque *n* **1** (*ballet*) a position in which the dancer stands with one leg stretched out backwards and the body bent forwards from the hips. **2** a complex design of leaves, flowers, etc. woven together. **3** a short, ornate piece of music. [Ital *arabesco*, in the Arabian style]

arable *adj* (of land) suitable or used for growing crops. [Lat *arare*, to plough]

arachnid *n* any of a class of eight-legged insect-like creatures, such as spiders and scorpions. [Gr *arachne*, spider]

arachnoid *adj* like a cobweb. — *n* (*anat*) (also **arachnoid membrane**) the membrane between the dura mater and the pia mater.

arak. Same as **arrack**.

Aramaic *n* any of a group of Semitic languages, including the language spoken by Christ and modern forms spoken in parts of Syria. — *adj* of or in Aramaic. [Gr *Aramaios*]

arbiter *n* **1** a person with the authority or influence to settle arguments between other people. **2** a person with great influence in matters of style, taste, etc. [Lat]

arbitrary *adj* **1** based on personal or random choice, not rules, etc. **2** (of a person) dictatorial; despotic. — *adv* **arbitrarily**. — *n* **arbitrariness**. [Lat *arbitrarius*]

arbitrate *v* (*tr* & *intr*; **between**) to act as a judge in a quarrel or disagreement. — *n* **arbitrator**. [Lat *arbitrari*, to judge]

arbitration *n* the settling of a quarrel or disagreement between two groups by a person not involved in their quarrel.

arbor *n* a shaft or axle on which a piece of machinery revolves. [Lat, tree]

arboreal *adj* of or living in trees. [Lat *arboreus*, from *arbor*, tree]

arboretum *n* **-ta** a botanical garden where rare trees and shrubs are grown. [Lat *arbor*, tree]

arboriculture *n* the cultivation of trees and shrubs. [Lat *arbor*, tree]

arbour *n* a shady area in a garden formed by trees or climbing plants, usu. with a seat. [Lat *herba*, grass, influenced by Lat *arbor*, tree]

ARC *abbrev* AIDS-related complex.

arc *n* **1** a part of the line which forms a circle or other curve. **2** a curve of bright light formed by a strong electric current passing across a space between two electrodes. — *v* **-cing**, **-ced** (*intr*) to form an arc. [Lat *arcus*, bow]

arc lamp or **light** *n* a lamp in which the source of light is an electric arc.

arc welding *n* the joining of two pieces of metal using arc electricity to melt them.

arcade *n* **1** a covered walk or passage, usu. lined with shops. **2** a row of arches supporting a roof, wall, etc. [Ital *arcata*]

Arcadia *n* a district in Ancient Greece, whose inhabitants enjoyed innocent, simple, rural pleasures, such as dancing and singing. — *adj* **Arcadian**. [Gr]

arcana. See **tarot**.

arcane *n* & *adj* (anything which is) mysterious, secret, and understood by only the select few. [Lat *arcanus*, shut]

arch[1] *n* **1** a curved structure forming an opening, supporting a roof, bridge, etc., or as an ornament. **2** anything shaped like an arch, esp. a monument. **3** the raised part of the sole of the foot, between the heel

and the toes. — *v* (*tr* & *intr*) to (cause to) form an arch. — *adj* **arched**. [Lat *arcus*, bow]
archway *n* a passage or entrance under an arch or arches.
arch[2] *adj* self-consciously playful or cunning. — *adv* **archly**. [**arch-**]
arch- or **archi-** *comb fm* chief; most important: *archangel*; *archduke*. [OE *arce-*, from Gr *archos*, chief]
archaeology *n* the study of the history and culture of ancient civilisations through studying physical remains, e.g. tools, pots, etc., dug up from the ground. — *adj* **archaeological**. — *n* **archaeologist**. [Gr *archaiologia*, ancient history]
archaeopteryx *n* an ancient fossil bird, with sharp teeth, feathers, and a long bony tail. [Gr *archaios*, ancient + *pteryx*, wing]
archaic *adj* **1** ancient; of or from a much earlier period. **2** out of date; old-fashioned. **3** (of a word, phrase, etc.) no longer in general use. — *adv* **archaically**. [Gr *archaikos*, from *archaios*, ancient]
archaism *n* **1** an archaic word or expression. **2** the deliberate use of archaic words or expressions.
archangel *n* an angel of the highest order. [Gr *archos*, chief + *angelos*, messenger]
archbishop *n* a chief bishop, in charge of all the other bishops, clergy and churches in a particular area. [OE *arcebiscop*; see etys. for **arch-** + **bishop**]
archbishopric *n* the office or diocese of an archbishop.
archdeacon *n* in the Church of England, a member of the clergy ranking just below a bishop. ◇ See also **archidiaconal**. [OE *arcediacon*; see etys. for **arch-** + **deacon**]
archdeaconry *n* **-ies** the office or residence of an archdeacon.
archdiocese *n* in the Church of England, an area under the control of an archbishop.
archduke *n* the title of some princes, esp. (*hist*) the Emperor's son in the Austrian royal family.
archduchess *n* **1** (*hist*) a princess in the Austrian royal family. **2** the wife of an archduke.
archduchy *n* **-ies** the area ruled by an archduke.
archeology (*US*). Same as **archaeology**.
archenemy *n* **-ies** **1** a chief enemy. **2** the Devil.
archer *n* **1** a person who shoots with a bow and arrows. **2** (*cap* with **the**) the constellation and sign of the zodiac Sagittarius. [Lat *arcus*, bow]
archery *n* the art or sport of shooting with a bow.
archetype *n* **1** **1** an original model; a prototype. **2** a perfect example. — *adj* **archetypal**. — *adv* **archetypally**. [Gr *arche*, beginning + *typos*, model]
archfiend *n* the Devil.
archidiaconal *adj* of an archdeacon or archdeaconry. [Gr *archidiakonos*]
archiepiscopal *adj* of an archbishop or an archbishopric. [Gr *archiepiskopos*]
archimandrite *n* in the Greek church, a priest in charge of a group of monks. [Gr *archos*, chief + *mandra*, monastery]
archipelago *n* **-os** **1** a group of islands. **2** an area of sea with many islands. [Ital *arcipelago*, from Gr *archi-*, chief + *pelagos*, sea]
architect *n* **1** a person qualified to design buildings and other large structures. **2** a person responsible for creating something: *the architect of the European Community*. [Gr *archi-*, chief + *tekton*, builder]
architecture *n* **1** the art of designing and constructing buildings. **2** a particular historical, regional, etc. style of building: *Victorian architecture*. **3** the buildings built in any particular style. — *adj* **architectural**. — *adv* **architecturally**.
architrave *n* **1** a beam that rests on top of a row of columns. **2** a moulded frame around a door or window. [Fr, from Gr *archi-*, chief + *trabs*, beam]
archive *n* (usu. in *pl*) **1** a collection of old public documents, records, etc. **2** a place where such documents are kept. [Gr *archeion*, public office]
archivist *n* a person in charge of archives.
Arctic *n* (**the**) the area round the North Pole. — *adj* **1** of the area round the North Pole. **2** (without *cap*; *coll*) very cold. [Gr *arktikos*, from *arktos*, (the constellation of the) bear]
Arctic Circle *n* an imaginary line drawn around the Earth at a latitude of 66° 32' N, marking the limits of the Arctic.
ardent *adj* **1** enthusiastic; eager. **2** burning; passionate. — *adv* **ardently**. [Lat *ardere*, to burn]
ardour *n* a great enthusiasm or passion. [Lat *ardor*, from *ardere*, to burn]
arduous *adj* **1** difficult; needing hard work or a lot of energy. **2** steep. — *adv* **arduously**. — *n* **arduousness**. [Lat *arduus*, steep]
are[1]. See **be**.
are[2] *n* a unit of land measure equal to 100 m^2. [Fr, from Lat *area*, open space]
area *n* **1** the extent or size of a flat surface. **2** a region or part. **3** any space set aside for a particular purpose. **4** the range of a subject, activity or topic. **5** (*US*) a sunken space in front of a building's basement. [Lat, open space]
arena *n* **1** an area surrounded by seats, for public shows, sports contests, etc. **2** a place of great activity, esp. conflict: *the political arena*. **3** the open area in the middle of an amphitheatre. [Lat, sanded area for combats]
aren't *v* (*aux*) **1** are not. **2** (in questions) am not.
areola *n* **-lae** a faintly coloured circular area, esp. that around the nipple. [Lat, dimin. of *area*, open space]

argon *n* an element (symbol **Ar**), an odourless gas forming 1% of the Earth's atmosphere. [Gr, inactive, from *a*, without + *ergon*, work]

argot *n* slang used and understood only by a particular group of people. [Fr]

argue *v* **1** (*intr*; **with**, **about**, **over**) to exchange views with someone, esp. heatedly or angrily. **2** (*tr* & *intr*; **for**, **against**) to suggest reasons for or against (something), esp. clearly and in a proper order: *argue the point*. **3** (*tr*; **into**, **out of**) to persuade. **4** (*tr*) to show or be evidence for. — *adj* **arguable**. — *adv* **arguably**. [Lat *arguere*, to show, accuse]

argument *n* **1** a quarrel or unfriendly discussion. **2** a reason for or against an idea, etc. **3** the use of reason in making decisions. **4** a summary of the theme or subject of a book, etc. [Lat *argumentum*, from *arguere*, to show, accuse]

argumentation *n* sensible and methodical reasoning.

argumentative *adj* fond of arguing; always ready to quarrel. — *adv* **argumentatively**.

aria *n* a long accompanied song for one voice, e.g. in an opera. [Ital]

Arian. See **Arianism** and **Aries**.

Arianism *n* the doctrine of *Arius* of Alexandria (died AD 336), who denied that Christ was God. — *n* & *adj* **Arian**.

arid *adj* **1** dry; having very little water. **2** boring; dull. — *n* **aridity**. — *n* **aridness**. [Lat *aridus*]

Aries *n* **1** a constellation and the first sign of the zodiac, the Ram. **2** a person born between 21 March and 20 April, under this sign. — *n* & *adj* **Arian**. [Lat, ram]

aright *adv* (*old*) correctly. [OE *ariht*]

arise *v* ***arose***, ***arisen*** (*intr*) **1** to come into being. **2** (**from**, **out of**) to result or be caused. **3** to get up or stand up. **4** to come to one's notice. [OE *arisan*]

aristocracy *n* ***-ies*** **1** the highest social class, usu. owning land and having titles. **2** government by this class. **3** people considered to be the best representatives of something. [Gr *aristos*, best + *kratos*, power]

aristocrat *n* a member of the aristocracy.

aristocratic *adj* **1** of the aristocracy. **2** proud and noble-looking. — *adv* **aristocratically**.

Aristotelian *adj* of or relating to the Greek philosopher *Aristotle* (died 322 BC) or his ideas. — *n* a student or follower of Aristotle.

arithmetic *n* **1** (the science of) adding, subtracting, multiplying and dividing numbers. **2** ability or skill at this: *My arithmetic is poor*. — *adj* (also **arithmetical**) of arithmetic. — *adv* **arithmetically**. — *n* **arithmetician**. [Gr *arithmetike*, of numbers, from *arithmos*, number]

arithmetic mean *n* the average of two or more numbers, given as their sum divided by their number, e.g. the arithmetic mean of 1 and 5 is (1 + 5) ÷ 2, i.e. 3.

arithmetic progression *n* a sequence of numbers in which each differs from the preceding and following ones by a set amount, e.g. 2, 4, 6, 8, 10.

Ariz. *abbrev* Arizona.

Ark. *abbrev* Arkansas.

ark *n* **1** (*Bible*) the vessel built by Noah in which his family and animals survived the Flood. **2** (*cap*) a chest or cupboard in a synagogue in which the law scrolls are kept. [OE *arc*, from Lat *arca*, chest]

Ark of the Covenant *n* a chest containing two stone tablets inscribed with the Ten Commandments given to Moses by God, now lost.

arm[1] *n* **1** either of the two upper limbs of the body, from the shoulders to the hands. **2** anything shaped like or similar to this: *an arm of the sea*. **3** the sleeve of a garment. **4** the part of a chair, etc. that supports an arm. **5** a section or division of a larger group, e.g. of the army, etc. **6** power and influence: *the long arm of the law*. — **arm in arm** with arms linked together. — **at arm's length** at a distance, esp. to avoid becoming too friendly. — **with open arms** with a very friendly welcome. [OE *earm*]

armband *n* a strip of cloth worn round the arm, usu. to show one is in an official position or in mourning.

armchair *n* a comfortable chair with arms at each side. — *adj* taking no active part.

armful *n* ***-fuls*** the amount that can be held in one's arms.

armhole *n* the opening at the shoulder of a garment through which the arm is put.

armlet *n* a band or bracelet worn round the arm.

armpit *n* the hollow under the arm at the shoulder.

arm[2] *n* **1** (usu. in *pl* or *in cmpds*) a weapon: *carry arms*; *a sidearm*. **2** a branch of a military force. **3** (in *pl*) fighting; soldiering. **4** (in *pl*) the heraldic design which is the symbol of a family, school, country, etc. — *v* **1** (*tr*) to equip with weapons. **2** (*intr*) to equip oneself with weapons. **3** (*tr*; **with**) to supply with whatever is needed. **4** (*tr*) to prepare (a bomb) for use. — *adj* **armed**. — **bear arms** to serve as a soldier. — **lay down one's arms** to stop fighting. — **take up arms** to begin fighting. — **under arms** armed and ready to fight. — **up in arms** very angry and protesting strongly. [Lat *arma*]

armed forces or **services** *n* (*pl*) the military forces of a country, such as the army and navy.

arms race *n* a contest between countries for superiority in weapons.

armada *n* **1** a fleet of ships. **2** (*cap*; *hist*) the fleet of Spanish ships sent to attack England in 1588. [Span, from Lat *armata*, armed forces]

armadillo *n* **-os** a small S American burrowing animal covered with a hard bony shell. [Span, from *armado*, armed]

Armageddon *n* a large-scale and bloody battle, esp. the final battle between good and evil before the Day of Judgement. [Hebr *Megiddo*, a place in northern Palestine]

armament *n* **1** (usu. in *pl*) arms, weapons and military equipment. **2** preparation for war. [Lat *armamenta*]

armature *n* **1** the moving part of a generator, dynamo, etc. wound with wire carrying the current. **2** a soft iron bar placed across the two poles of a horseshoe magnet to preserve its power. **3** a wire framework around which a sculpture is modelled. [Lat *armatura*, armour]

armistice *n* a stopping of hostilities; a truce. [Lat *armistitium*, from *arma*, arms + *sistere*, to stop]

Armistice Day *n* the anniversary of the day (11 November 1918) when fighting ended in World War I; replaced after World War II by Remembrance Day.

armorial *adj* of heraldry or coats of arms. [Lat *arma*, arms]

armour *n* **1** (*hist*) a metal suit or covering worn by men or horses as a protection against injury in battle. **2** metal covering to protect ships, tanks, etc. against damage from weapons. **3** armoured fighting vehicles as a group. **4** a protective covering on some animals and plants. **5** heraldic designs and symbols. [Fr *armure*, from Lat *armatura*, armour]

armoured *adj* **1** protected by armour. **2** (*mil*) made up of armoured vehicles.

armourer *n* **1** a person who makes or repairs arms and armour. **2** a person in charge of a regiment's arms.

armour-plate *n* strong metal or steel for protecting ships, tanks, etc. — *adj* **armour-plated**.

armoury *n* **-ies 1** a place where arms are kept. **2** a collection of arms and weapons.

army *n* **-ies 1** a large number of people armed and organised for fighting on land. **2** the military profession. **3** a large number. **4** a group of people organised for a particular cause: *Salvation Army*. [Fr *armee*, from Lat *armare*, to arm]

aroma *n* **1** a distinctive, usu. pleasant smell that a substance has or gives off. **2** a subtle quality or charm. [Gr, spice]

aromatherapy *n* a method of treating ailments using oils from plants and flowers. — *n* **aromatherapist**.

aromatic *adj* **1** having a strong, but sweet or pleasant smell. **2** (*chem*) (of organic compounds) with carbon atoms in one or more rings rather than open chains. ◇ See also **aliphatic**. — *adv* **aromatically**.

arose. See **arise**.

around *adv* **1** on every side. **2** here and there; in different directions or to different places. **3** in existence. **4** near at hand. — *prep* **1** on all sides of. **2** at or to different points in. **3** somewhere in or near. **4** approximately in or at; about. **5** (esp. *US*) round. — **have been around** (*coll*) to have a great deal of experience of life. [MidE; **a**[3] + **round**[1]]

arouse *v* (*tr*) **1** to cause or produce (an emotion, reaction, sexual desire, etc.). **2** to cause to become awake or active. — *n* **arousal**. [*a*, up + **rouse**]

arpeggio *n* **-os** a chord whose notes are played one at a time in rapid succession. [Ital *arpeggiare*, to play the harp]

arquebus *n* (*hist*) an early type of portable gun. [Dut *hakebusse*, from *hake*, hook + *busse*, gun]

arr. *abbrev* **1** arrival; arrives. **2** (*mus*) arranged by.

arrack *n* an alcoholic drink made from grain or rice. [Arabic *'araq*, sweat]

arraign *v* (*tr*) **1** to bring into a court of law, usu. to face serious charges. **2** to find fault with. — *n* **arraignment**. [Fr *aresnier*]

arrange *v* **1** (*tr*) to put into the proper order. **2** (*tr* & *intr*; **for**) to plan in advance. **3** (*intr*; **with**, **for**) to come to an agreement: *arrange with him for you to get time off.* **4** (*tr*) to make (a piece of music) suitable for particular voices or instruments. [OFr *arangier*, from *a*, to + *rangier*, to put in a row]

arrangement *n* **1** (usu. in *pl*) a plan or preparation for some future event. **2** the act of putting things into a proper order or pattern. **3** the order, pattern, etc. which results from things being arranged. **4** (**with**) an agreement. **5** a piece of music which has been made suitable for particular voices or instruments.

arrant *adj* out-and-out; notorious: *an arrant liar*. [MidE variant of **errant**]

arras *n* a tapestry for hanging on a wall or concealing an alcove. [*Arras*, town in N France]

array *n* **1** a large and impressive number or collection. **2** a well-ordered arrangement: *troops in battle array*. **3** an arrangement of numbers, figures and symbols in rows and columns. **4** (*comput*) an arrangement of individual elements of data, each of which has a reference number allowing it to be found. **5** (*poetic*) fine clothes. — *v* (*tr*) **1** to put in order, e.g. for battle. **2** to dress (someone or oneself) in fine clothes. [OFr *areer*, to arrange]

arrears *n* (*pl*) that which still needs to be done or paid back. — **in arrears** late in paying money owed or doing the required work. [OFr *arere*, from Lat *ad*, to + *retro*, back, behind]

arrest *v* (*tr*) **1** to take (a person) into custody. **2** to stop or slow the development of (a disease, etc.). **3** to catch or attract (a person's attention). — *n* **1** the act of taking, or being taken, into custody, esp. by the police. **2** a stopping: *cardiac arrest*. — **under arrest** having been arrested by the police. [OFr *arester*, from Lat *ad*, to + *restare*, to stand still]

arresting *adj* **1** attractive. **2** (of a police officer) making an arrest.

arrive *v* (*intr*) **1** to reach a place or destination. **2** (**at**) to come to a conclusion, decision, etc. **3** (*coll*) to be successful. **4** (of a child) to be born. **5** (of a thing) to be brought. **6** (of a time) to occur. [Fr *ariver*, from Lat *ad*, to + *ripa*, shore]

arrival *n* **1** the act of arriving. **2** a person or thing that has arrived, esp. a newborn baby.

arrogant *adj* extremely proud; having or showing too high an opinion of one's own abilities or importance. — *n* **arrogance**. — *adv* **arrogantly**. [Lat *arrogare*, to arrogate]

arrogate *v* (*tr*; **to**) to claim (a responsibility, power, etc.) for someone or oneself without having any legal right to it. — *n* **arrogation**. [Lat *ad*, to + *rogare*, to ask]

arrow *n* **1** a thin, straight stick with a point at one end and feathers at the other, fired from a bow. **2** an arrow-shaped sign, e.g. one showing the way to go or the position of something. [OE *arwe*]

arrowhead *n* the sharp, pointed, usu. metal or (*hist*) stone tip of an arrow.

arrowroot *n* a starch, obtained from a W Indian plant, used in foods and medicines and, formerly, to treat wounds made by poisoned arrows.

arse *n* (*vulg*) the buttocks. [OE *ears*]

arsehole *n* (*vulg*) **1** the anus. **2** a stupid person.

arsenal *n* **1** a factory or store for weapons, explosives, etc. **2** the weapons, etc. that a country or group has. [Arabic *dar sina'ah*, workshop]

arsenic *n* **1** a semi-metallic element (symbol **As**), used in alloys and poisons. **2** a powerful poison, an oxide of arsenic, usu. found in the form of a white powder, used in insecticides. — *adj* of, containing or using arsenic. [Gr *arsenikon*, yellow arsenic]

arson *n* the crime of deliberately setting fire to a building, etc. — *n* **arsonist**. [Lat *arsio*, from *ardere*, to burn]

art[1] *n* **1** the creation of works of beauty. **2** (in *pl*) the different branches of creative activity, e.g. music, painting and literature, as a group. **3** one of these branches. **4** (in *pl*) the branches of learning linked to creative skills, e.g. languages, literature and history: *Faculty of Arts*. **5** human skill and work as opposed to nature. **6** a skill, esp. gained through practice. **7** (in *pl*; *coll*) cunning schemes. [Lat *ars*]

art deco *n* a style of art and decoration popular in Europe and America in the 1920s and 1930s, based on geometric shapes and strong colours.

art form *n* a recognised form for music or literature, e.g. the novel or the sonnet.

artful *adj* **1** cunning; able to get what one wants, by lying and dishonesty. **2** skilful. — *adv* **artfully**. — *n* **artfulness**.

artless *adj* **1** simple and natural in manner. **2** honest, not deceitful. — *adv* **artlessly**. — *n* **artlessness**.

art nouveau *n* a style of art and decoration popular in Europe and America at the end of the nineteenth century, based on plant patterns, etc.

arty *adj* **-ier**, **-iest** (*coll*) trying to appear artistic to other people. — *n* **artiness**.

art[2] *v* (*aux*; *old*) the form of the present tense of the verb *be* used with *thou*. [OE]

artefact *n* an object made by man, e.g. a tool, esp. with historical or archaeological interest. [Lat *arte*, by art + *factum*, made]

arterial. See **artery**.

arteriosclerosis *n* ***-oses*** a disease in which the artery walls become hard, making the arteries less able to carry blood around the body. [**artery** + **sclerosis**]

artery *n* **-ies** **1** a tube that carries blood rich in oxygen from the heart through the body. **2** a main road, railway or shipping lane. [Gr *arteria*, windpipe]

arterial *adj* **1** of or like an artery. **2** (of a road, etc.) important.

artesian well *n* a well in which water is pumped out of the ground by natural pressure. [*Artesian*, of Artois, in N France, where such wells were common]

artful. See **art**.

arthritis *n* inflammation of a joint or joints, causing pain and great difficulty in moving. — *n* & *adj* **arthritic**. [Gr *arthron*, joint + **-itis**]

arthropod *n* a creature with a body in segments, jointed limbs, and its skeleton on the outside, such as a spider or crab. [Gr *arthron*, joint + *pous*, foot]

artichoke *n* (also **globe artichoke**) a plant with large, thistle-like flower-heads, parts of which can be eaten when cooked. [Arabic *al-kharshuf*]

Jerusalem artichoke *n* a plant related to the sunflower, whose potato-like roots can be eaten as a vegetable. [**Jerusalem** a corruption of Ital *girasole*, sunflower]

article *n* **1** a thing or object. **2** a usu. short written composition in a newspaper or magazine. **3** a clause or paragraph in a document, legal agreement, etc. **4** (*gram*) *the* (the **definite article**) or *a* or *an* (the **indefinite article**), or any equivalent word in other languages. [Lat *articulus*, little joint]

articled *adj* (of a lawyer, accountant, etc.) bound by a legal contract while working in an office to learn the job.

articular *adj* of a relating to the joints. [Lat *articularis*, from *articulus*, little joint]

articulate *v* **1** (*tr* & *intr*) to pronounce (words) or speak clearly and distinctly. **2** (*tr*) to express (one's thoughts, feelings, ideas, etc.) clearly. — *adj* **1** able to express one's thoughts clearly. **2** (of speech) pronounced clearly and distinctly so that each sound can be heard. **3** having joints. — *adj* **articulated**. — *adv* **articulately**. — *n*

articulateness. [Lat *articulare*, to divide into distinct parts]

articulated lorry *n* a lorry in two parts, the front section of which can turn at an angle to the main part, making it easier to turn corners.

articulation *n* **1** the act of speaking or expressing an idea in words. **2** the word, idea, etc. expressed. **3** the state of being jointed together. **4** a joint.

artifact. Same as **artefact**.

artifice *n* **1** a clever trick. **2** clever skill and tricks; cunning. [Lat *artificium*, from *ars*, arts + *facere*, to make]

artificer *n* a skilled craftsman, esp. a mechanic in the army or navy.

artificial *adj* **1** made by man; not occurring naturally. **2** made in imitation of a natural product. **3** (of a person, behaviour, etc.) not genuine or sincere. — *n* **artificiality**. — *adv* **artificially**. [Lat *artificialis*, from *ars*, art + *facere*, to make]

artificial insemination *n* the putting of semen into a womb using some form of instrument, rather than naturally.

artificial intelligence *n* a branch of computer science which studies ways of making computers learn, understand, make judgements, etc. like people do.

artificial respiration *n* the process of forcing air into and out of the lungs of a person who has stopped breathing, to try to make him or her start breathing naturally again.

artillery *n* **-ies** **1** large guns for use on land. **2** the part of an army equipped with such guns. [Fr *artillier*, to arm]

artisan *n* a person who does skilled work with his or her hands. [Fr, from Lat *artitus*, trained in arts and crafts]

artist *n* **1** a person who produces works of art, esp. paintings. **2** a person who is skilled at some particular thing. **3** an artiste. [Lat *ars*, art]

artistic *adj* **1** liking or skilled in painting, music, etc. **2** made or done with skill and good taste. — *adv* **artistically**.

artistry *n* artistic skill and imagination.

artiste *n* a professional performer, esp. a singer or dancer, in a theatre, circus, etc. [Fr]

arty. See **art**.

arum *n* a tall plant with arrow-shaped leaves and white flowers enclosed in bracts. [Gr *aron*]

arum lily *n* a plant with spikes of yellow flowers enclosed in white bracts.

-ary *sfx* forming adjectives or nouns meaning of or connected with: *budgetary*; *dignitary*. [Lat *-arius*]

Aryan *n* **1** a member of the peoples speaking any of the Indo-European languages, now esp. the Indo-Iranian languages. **2** (*hist*) (in Nazi Germany) a Caucasian, esp. of northern European type. — *adj* of the Aryans or Aryan languages. [Sanskrit *arya*, noble]

As *symbol* (*chem*) arsenic.

as[1] *conj* **1** when; while; during. **2** because; since. **3** in the manner which: *behave as one likes*. **4** that which; what: *do as one's told*. **5** although: *Try as he might, he still couldn't reach*. **6** for instance: *large books, as this one for example*. — *prep* in the role of: *speaking as her friend*. — *adv* to whatever extent or amount. — *pron* **1** that, who, or which also: *She is a singer, as is her husband*. **2** (after **so**) for the reason that: *Come early so as to avoid the rush*. **3** a fact that: *She'll be late, as you know*. — **as for** or **to** with regard to; concerning. — **as from** or **of** starting at (a particular time). — **as if** or **though** as it would be if. — **as it were** in a way; to some extent. — **as well** also. — **as yet** until now. [OE *eallswa*, just as]

as[2] *n* **asses** an ancient Roman copper coin. [Lat, unit]

ASA *abbrev* American Standards Association, used e.g. in labelling photographic film speeds.

asafoetida *n* a plant resin with an unpleasant smell, used in medicine and Indian cooking. [Persian *aza*, gum + Lat *foetida*, fetid]

ASAP or **asap** *abbrev* as soon as possible.

asbestos *n* a fibrous mineral that can be woven into fireproof cloth. [Gr, from *a*, not + *sbestos*, extinguished]

asbestosis *n* a lung disease caused by breathing in asbestos dust.

ascend *v* (*tr* & *intr*) to climb, go, or rise up. — **ascend the throne** to become king or queen. [Lat *ascendere*]

ascendancy or **ascendency** *n* **(over, in)** controlling or dominating power.

ascendant or **ascendent** *adj* **1** having more influence or power. **2** (*astrol*) rising over the eastern horizon. — *n* **1** increasing influence or power. **2** (*astrol*) the sign of the zodiac rising over the eastern horizon at the time of an event, esp. birth.

ascending *adj* from the lowest to the highest, the least to the greatest, or the worst to the best.

ascension *n* **1** an ascent. **2** (*cap*) Christ's ascent to heaven on the fortieth day after the Resurrection. [Lat *ascensio*, from *ascendere*, to ascend]

Ascension Day *n* the Thursday ten days before Whit Sunday, on which Christ's Ascension is commemorated.

ascent *n* **1** the act of climbing, going up or rising. **2** an upward slope. **[ascend]**

ascertain *v* (*tr*) to find out; to discover (the truth, etc.). — *adj* **ascertainable**. [OFr *acertener*]

ascetic *n* a person who avoids all physical comfort and pleasure, esp. as a way of achieving holiness. — *adj* avoiding physical pleasure and comfort; self-denying. — *adv* **ascetically**. — *n* **asceticism**. [Gr *asketikos*, from *askein*, to practise, train]

ASCII *abbrev* American Standard Code for Information Interchange, a system for representing letters and numbers which allows information to be sent between computers, etc.

ascorbic acid *n* vitamin C. [**a-**[1] + **scorbutic**]

ascribe *v* (*tr*) to think of (something) as done, made or caused by (someone or something): *ascribe her success to hard work.* — *adj* **ascribable**. [Lat *ascribere*]

aseptic *adj* free from harmful bacteria; sterile. [**a-**[1] + Gr *sepein*, to cause to decay]

asexual *adj* **1** (of reproduction) without involving sexual activity. **2** without sex or sexual organs. **3** not sexually attracted to others. — *n* **asexuality**. — *adv* **asexually**. [**a-**[1] + **sexual**]

ash[1] *n* **1** the dust that remains after something is burnt. **2** (in *pl*) the remains of a human body after cremation. [OE *asce*]

ashcan *n* (*US*) a dustbin.

ashen *adj* (of someone's face) grey or very pale, usu. through shock.

the Ashes *n* (*pl*) the trophy which goes to the team winning the regular series of cricket matches played by England and Australia. [From a newspaper announcement after Australia defeated England in 1882 that the ashes of English cricket were to be taken to Australia]

ashtray *n* a dish or other container for the ash from cigarettes.

Ash Wednesday *n* the first day of Lent.

ashy *adj* **-ier**, **-iest** **1** covered in ash. **2** grey; ashen.

ash[2] *n* (the hard, pale wood from) a forest tree with silver-grey bark. [OE *æsc*]

ashamed *adj* **1** feeling shame or embarrassment. **2** (**to**) hesitant or reluctant through shame or a fear of being wrong. — *adv* **ashamedly**. [OE *ascamian*, to feel shame]

ashen. See **ash**[1].

ashlar or **ashler** *n* **1** a large stone cut square, used for building or facing walls. **2** masonry made of ashlars. [OFr *aiseler*, from Lat *axilla*, small plank]

ashore *adv* on or on to the shore or land (from water). [**a**[3] + **shore**]

ashram *n* a place for periods of study and prayer for Hindus. [Sanskrit *asrama*]

Asian *n* **1** a person born and living in Asia. **2** a person of Asian descent. — *adj* of Asia, its people, languages and culture. [Gr *Asianos*]

Asiatic *adj* Asian. [Gr *Asiatikos*]

aside *adv* **1** on or to one side. **2** (**from**) apart. — *n* **1** words said by a character in a play which the audience hears, but the other characters do not. **2** a remark unrelated to the main subject of a conversation. [MidE; **a**[3] + **side**]

asinine *adj* of or like an ass, esp. in being stupid and stubborn. [Lat *asininus*, from *asinus*, ass]

ask *v* **1** (*tr* & *intr*) to put a question to (someone) or call for an answer to (a question). **2** (*tr*) to inquire about: *ask the way.* **3** (*tr* & *intr*; **for**) to make a request; to seek. **4** (*tr*) to invite. **5** (*intr*; **of**) to expect: *ask too much of her.* — **ask after** to ask for news of (esp. a person). — **ask for it** or **for trouble** (*coll*) to behave in a way that is likely to bring trouble on oneself. [OE *ascian*]

asking price *n* the price of an object suggested by the seller.

askance *adv* sideways. — **look askance at** to look at or consider with suspicion or disapproval.

askew *adv* & *adj* not properly straight or level; awry. [**a**[3] + **skew**]

asleep *adj* & *adv* **1** in or into a sleeping state: *fall asleep.* **2** (*coll*) not paying attention. **3** (of limbs) numb. [OE *on slæpe*]

asp *n* a small poisonous snake of various kinds, found in S Europe, N Africa and Arabia. [Gr *aspis*]

asparagus *n* **1** a plant related to the lily. **2** the young shoots of this plant, which can be cooked and eaten. [Gr *asparagos*]

aspect *n* **1** a particular or distinct part or element (of a problem, subject, etc.). **2** a particular way of considering a matter. **3** look or appearance. **4** the direction in which a building faces. **5** (*astron*) the situation of one planet with respect to another. [Lat *aspectus*, from *ad*, to + *specere*, to look]

aspen *n* a poplar tree with flat leaves that make a lot of noise in the wind. [OE *æspe*]

asperity *n* **-ies** roughness, bitterness or harshness, esp. of temper. [Lat *asper*, rough]

aspersion : **cast aspersions on** to make damaging or spiteful remarks about. [Lat *aspersio*, sprinkling, slander]

asphalt *n* a black, tar-like substance used as a surface for roads, roofs, etc. — *v* (*tr*) to cover with asphalt. [Gr *asphaltos*]

asphyxia *n* unconsciousness or death caused by a lack of oxygen in the blood. [Gr, *a*, without + *sphyxis*, pulse]

asphyxiate *v* (*tr* & *intr*) to stop or cause to stop breathing. — *n* **asphyxiation**.

aspic *n* a savoury jelly, made from meat or fish, used as a glaze, or to make a mould for fish, eggs, etc. [Fr]

aspidistra *n* a house plant with long, broad leaves. [Gr *aspis*, shield]

aspirant. See **aspire**.

aspirate *n* the sound represented in English and several other languages by the letter *h*. — *v* **1** (*tr* & *intr*) to pronounce (a word, etc.) with a breath at the beginning. **2** (*tr*) to remove (liquid or gas) out of a hole by sucking. — *n* **aspiration**. [Lat *aspirare*, from *ad*, to + *spirare*, to breathe]

aspirator *n* an apparatus for sucking gas, liquid, etc. out of a hole, esp. in the body.

aspiration. See **aspirate** and **aspire**.

aspire *v* (*intr*; **to, after**) to have a strong desire to achieve or reach (e.g. an ambition): *aspire to greatness.* — *n* **aspiration**. — *adj* **aspiring**. [Lat *aspirare*, from *ad*, to + *spirare*, to breathe]

aspirant *n* a person who aspires to something.

aspirin *n* (a tablet of) a drug widely used for relieving pain and fever. [Orig. a German trademark]

ass[1] *n* **1** an animal like a horse but smaller and with longer ears. **2** (*coll*) a stupid person. [OE *assa*]

ass[2] (*US*). Same as **arse**.

assagai. See **assegai**.

assail *v* (*tr*) **1** to make a strong physical or verbal attack on. **2** to make a determined start on (a task). [Lat *ad*, to + *salire*, to leap]

assailant *n* an attacker.

assassin *n* a person who murders someone, esp. for political reasons or a reward. [Arabic *hashshashin*, hashish-eaters]

assassinate *v* (*tr*) **1** to murder, esp. for political reasons or a reward. **2** to destroy a (person's) good reputation. — *n* **assassination**.

assault *n* **1** a violent physical or verbal attack. **2** (*euph*) rape. — *v* (*tr*) to make an assault on. [Fr *asaut*, from Lat *ad*, to + *saltus*, leap]

assault and battery *n* (*legal*) the crime of threatening to attack someone followed by actually attacking him or her.

assault course *n* an obstacle course with walls, pools, nets, etc., used for training soldiers.

assay *v* (*tr*) to analyse and assess the quality of (a metal or ore). — *n* an assaying of metal or ore. [OFr *assaier*]

assegai or **assagai** *n* a thin, light, iron-tipped wooden spear used in southern Africa. [Arabic *az-zagayah*, the spear]

assemble *v* **1** (*tr* & *intr*) to gather or collect together. **2** (*tr*) to put together the parts of (a machine, etc.). [OFr *asembler*, from Lat *ad*, to + *simul*, together]

assemblage *n* **1** a collection of people or things. **2** a gathering together.

assembler *n* a computer program which converts a program in an assembly language to a code that the computer can understand.

assembly *n* **-ies** **1** a group of people gathered together, esp. for a meeting. **2** the act of assembling.

assembly language *n* a language used for writing computer programs, which are then translated by an assembler into a code the computer can understand.

assembly line *n* a continuous series of machines and workers along which an article, product, etc. passes in the stages of its manufacture.

assent *n* consent or approval, esp. official. — *v* (*intr*; **to**) to agree. [Lat *assentari*]

royal assent *n* in the UK, formal permission given by the King or Queen for a parliamentary act to become law.

assert *v* (*tr*) **1** to state firmly. **2** to insist on or defend (one's rights, opinions, etc.). — **assert oneself** to state one's wishes, defend one's opinions, etc. confidently and vigorously. [Lat *asserere*]

assertion *n* (the act of making) a strong statement or claim.

assertive *adj* expressing one's opinions in a strong and confident manner. — *adv* **assertively**. — *n* **assertiveness**.

assess *v* (*tr*) **1** to judge the quality or importance of. **2** to estimate the cost, value, etc. of. **3** (**at**) to fine or tax by an amount stated: *assess at £500*. — *n* **assessment**. [Lat *assidere*, to sit as a judge]

assessor *n* **1** a person who assesses the value of property, etc. for taxation. **2** a person who advises a judge, etc. on technical matters. **3** a person who assesses the importance or quality of e.g. a job.

asset *n* **1** a valuable skill, quality or person. **2** (in *pl*) the total value of the property and possessions of a person or company, esp. as able to cover debts. [OFr *asez*, enough]

asset-stripping *n* the practice of buying an unsuccessful company at a low price and selling off its assets separately for a profit. — *n* **asset-stripper**.

asseverate *v* (*tr*) to state solemnly. [Lat *asseverare*]

assiduous *adj* **1** hard-working. **2** done carefully and exactly. — *adv* **assiduously**. — *n* **assiduousness**. [Lat *assiduus*, persistent]

assiduity *n* **-ies** constant care and attention to a person, or to what one is doing.

assign *v* (*tr*) **1** (**to**) to give (a task, etc.) to someone or appoint (someone) to a position or task. **2** to fix (a time, place, etc.) for a purpose. **3** (*legal*; **to**) to give (one's title, property, interest, etc.) to someone else by contract. [Lat *assignare*, to mark out]

assignation *n* a secret appointment to meet, esp. between lovers.

assignee *n* (*legal*) a person to whom property, interest, etc. is given by contract.

assignment *n* **1** a task or duty assigned to someone. **2** the act of assigning. **3** (*legal*) a transfer of property, interest, etc. to someone else.

assignor *n* (*legal*) a person who gives property, interest, etc. by contract.

assimilate *v* **1** (*tr*) to become familiar with and understand (facts, information, etc.) completely. **2** (*tr* & *intr*) to become part of, or make (people) part of, a larger group, esp. of a different race or culture. **3** (*tr*) to take in and digest (food). **4** (*tr*) to cause to resemble, esp. to make (a sound) like another. — *adj* **assimilable**. — *n* **assimilation**. [Lat *ad*, to + *similis*, like]

assist *v* **1** (*tr* & *intr*; **in, with**) to help. **2** (*intr*) to take part in a ceremony, etc. [Lat *assistere*, to take a stand beside]

assistance *n* help.

assistant *n* **1** a person employed to help someone of higher rank, position, etc. **2** a person who serves customers in a shop.

assizes *n* (*pl*; *hist*) a court sitting at regular intervals in each county in England and Wales. [Lat *assidere*, to sit as a judge]

assoc. *abbrev* **1** associated. **2** association.

associate *v* **(with) 1** (*tr*) to connect in the mind: *associate lambs with spring.* **2** (*intr*) to mix socially: *don't associate with him.* **3** (*tr*) to involve (oneself) in a group because of shared views or aims. **4** (*intr*) to join with people for a common purpose. — *n* **1** a business partner. **2** a colleague or friend. **3** a person admitted to a society without full membership. — *adj* **1** joined with another, esp. in a business: *an associate director.* **2** not having full membership of a society. [Lat *associare*, from *ad*, to + *socius*, companion]

associated *adj* (usu. *cap*) used in the name of a company to show that it has been formed from several smaller companies.

association *n* **1** an organisation or club. **2** a friendship or partnership. **3** a connection in the mind. **4** the act of associating.

Association football *n* same as **soccer**.

associative *adj* (*math*) (of sums involving multiplication and addition) always giving the same answer even when the brackets are in different positions, e.g. $(1 + 2) + 3 = 6$ and $1 + (2 + 3) = 6$.

assonance *n* (*poetry*) **1** the rhyming of vowel sounds but not consonants, as in *load* and *cold.* **2** the use of a consonant or consonants with different vowel sounds, as in *milled* and *mulled.* [Lat *assonare*, to sound]

assorted *adj* **1** mixed; of or containing various different kinds. **2** arranged in sorts; classified. [Lat *ad*, to + *sors*, lot]

assortment *n* a mixed collection.

assuage *v* (*tr*) to make (a pain, sorrow, hunger, etc.) less severe. [Lat *ad*, to + *suavis*, mild, sweet]

assume *v* (*tr*) **1** to accept (something), though without proof; to take for granted. **2** to take upon oneself (a responsibility, duty, etc.). **3** to take on or adopt (an appearance, quality, etc.): *an issue assuming immense importance.* **4** to pretend to have or feel. [Lat *assumere*, to take to oneself]

assumed *adj* **1** false; not genuine. **2** accepted as true before proof is available.

assuming *adj* (of a person) arrogant. — **assuming that** taking it as true that.

assumption *n* **1** something accepted as true without proof. **2** the act of accepting something as true without proof. **3** the act of assuming. **4** (*cap*) the taking up of the Virgin Mary bodily into heaven. [Lat *assumptio*, from *assumere*, to take to oneself]

assure *v* (*tr*) **1** to state positively and confidently. **2 (of)** to convince or make (someone) sure: *assure her of my innocence.* **3** to make (an event, etc.) certain: *assure her success.* **4** (*Br*) to insure, esp. one's life. [Lat *ad*, to + *securus*, safe]

assurance *n* **1** a promise, guarantee or statement that a thing is true. **2** confidence. **3** (*Br*) insurance, esp. of one's life.

assured *adj* **1** (of a person) confident. **2** certain to happen.

assuredly *adv* certainly.

Assyrian (*hist*) *n* **1** an inhabitant of Assyria, an ancient kingdom in Mesopotamia. **2** the Semitic language of Assyria. — *adj* of Assyria, its people, language and culture. [Gr *Assyrios*]

astatine *n* a radioactive chemical element (symbol **At**), occurring naturally and also produced artificially. [Gr *astatos*, unstable]

aster *n* a garden plant with small pink, white, blue or purple daisy-like flowers. [Gr, star]

asterisk *n* a star-shaped mark (*) used in printing and writing, to mark esp. a reference to a note or an omission. — *v* (*tr*) to mark with an asterisk. [Gr *asteriskos*, small star]

astern *adv* & *adj* **1** in or towards the stern. **2** backwards. **3** behind. [**a**[3] + **stern**]

asteroid *n* any of the small planets moving round the sun, mainly between Jupiter and Mars. [Gr *asteroeides*, star-like]

asthma *n* an illness, usu. caused by an allergy, which makes breathing difficult. [Gr, from *aazein*, to breathe hard]

asthmatic *adj* of or suffering from asthma. — *n* a person who suffers from asthma. — *adv* **asthmatically**.

astigmatism *n* a defect in a lens, esp. in the eye, in which light rays fail to meet at a common point, resulting in blurred vision. — *adj* **astigmatic**. [Gr *a*, without + *stigma*, point]

astir *adj* & *adv* **1** awake and out of bed. **2** in a state of motion or excitement. [OE; **a**[3] + **stir**]

astonish *v* (*tr*) to surprise greatly. — *adj* **astonished**. — *adj* **astonishing**. — *adv* **astonishingly**. — *n* **astonishment**. [OFr *estoner*, from Lat *ex*, out + *tonare*, to thunder]

astound *v* (*tr*) to greatly amaze or shock. — *adj* **astounded**. — *adj* **astounding**. — *adv* **astoundingly**. [From the obsolete word *astone*, to astonish]

astrakhan *n* dark, tightly curled wool from lambs, used to make cloth. [*Astrakhan*, city in the USSR]

astral *adj* of or like the stars. [Lat *astralis*, from *astrum*, star]

astray *adj* & *adv* out of the right or expected way. — **go astray** to get lost. [MidE; **a**[3] + **stray**]

astride *adv* **1** with a leg on each side. **2** with legs apart. — *prep* **1** with a leg on each side of. **2** stretching across. [**a**[3] + **stride**]

astringent *adj* **1** severe and harsh. **2** making body tissues draw together, e.g. to stop blood flowing or tone the skin. — *n* an astringent liquid or drug. — *n* **astringency**. — *adv* **astringently**. [Lat *astringere*, to draw tight]

astro- *comb fm* of stars or space. [Gr *astron*, star]

astrology *n* the study of the movements of the stars and planets and their influence on people's lives. — *n* **astrologer**. — *adj* **astrological**. — *adv* **astrologically**. [Gr *astron*, star + *logos*, discourse]

astronaut *n* a person trained for space-travel. [**astro-** + Lat *nautes*, sailor]

astronautics *n* (*sing*) the science of space travel.

astronomy *n* the scientific study of the stars and planets, etc. — *n* **astronomer**. [Gr *astron*, star + *nomos*, law]

astronomical or **astronomic** *adj* **1** (of numbers, amounts, etc.) very large. **2** of astronomy. — *adv* **astronomically**.

astrophysics *n* (*sing*) the scientific study of the chemical and physical properties of stars and planets, etc. — *adj* **astrophysical**. — *n* **astrophysicist**. [**astro-** + **physics**]

astute *adj* able to judge quickly and act to one's own advantage. — *adv* **astutely**. — *n* **astuteness**. [Lat *astutus*, from *astus*, craft]

asunder *adv* apart or into pieces. [OE *onsundran*]

asylum *n* **1** (a place of) safety or protection. **2** (*hist*) a mental hospital. [Gr *asylon*, from *a*, not + *sylon*, right of seizure]

political asylum *n* protection given by a country to political refugees from a foreign country.

asymmetry *n* a lack of symmetry. — *adj* **asymmetric** or **asymmetrical**. — *adv* **asymmetrically**. [Gr *a*, not + *symmetria*, symmetry]

At *symbol* (*chem*) astatine.

at *prep* expressing **1** position or location. **2** direction: *look at the book*. **3** position in time. **4** state or occupation: *children at play*. **5** time during which: *work at night*. **6** rate or level: *work at speed*. **7** cost: *sell at £5 each*. **8** cause: *shocked at his behaviour*. — **at that 1** at that point. **2** as well. [OE *æt*]

atavism *n* **1** a resemblance to one's ancestors rather than one's parents. **2** reversion to an earlier, esp. more primitive, type. — *adj* **atavistic**. [Lat *atavus*, great-great-great-grandfather]

ataxia *n* the loss of the ability to control muscle movements. [Gr, disorder]

ate. See **eat**.

-ate *sfx* **1** forming verbs meaning cause to be: *hyphenate*. **2** forming nouns meaning rank, profession, or group: *doctorate*; *magistrate*; *electorate*. **3** forming nouns denoting a salt: *carbonate*. ◇ See also **-ide** and **-ite**. **4** forming adjectives meaning having, showing features of, like or related to: *passionate*; *fortunate*.

atheism *n* the belief that there is no god. — *n* **atheist**. — *adj* **atheistic** or **atheistical**. — *adv* **atheistically**. [Gr *a*, without + *theos*, god]

atherosclerosis *n* **-oses** a disease in which the artery walls become thick and hard with fat. — *adj* **atheroslerotic**. [Gr *athere*, gruel + **sclerosis**]

athlete *n* **1** a person who is good at sport, esp. track and field events such as running. **2** a healthy person with athletic ability. [Gr *athlos*, contest]

athlete's foot *n* a disease which damages the skin between the toes, caused by a fungus.

athletic *adj* **1** (of people) physically fit and strong. **2** of athletics.

athletics *n* (*sing*) track and field events such as running, shot-putting, etc.

athwart *adv* & *prep* across, from side to side (of). [MidE; **a**[3] + **thwart**]

-ation *sfx* forming nouns meaning the process or result of: *expectation*; *mechanisation*; *representation*.

-ative *sfx* forming adjectives meaning having a particular feature or tendency: *authoritative*; *talkative*.

Atlantic *n* (with **the**) the Atlantic Ocean, which separates Europe and Africa from America. — *adj* of or bordering on the Atlantic Ocean. [Gr *Atlantikos*, from *Atlas*, so-called because it lay beyond the Atlas mountains; see ety. at **atlas**]

atlas *n* **atlases** a book of maps and geographical charts. [Gr *Atlas*, the Titan in Greek mythology who bore the heavens on his shoulders and was turned into the Atlas mountains in N Africa; his picture used to appear on the title-pages of early atlases]

atmosphere *n* **1** the gases surrounding a planet. **2** the air in a particular place. **3** the mood of a place, book, etc. or the general impression one has of it. **4** a unit of atmospheric pressure, equal to normal air pressure at sea level. [Gr *atmos*, vapour + *sphaira*, ball]

atmospheric *adj* **1** of a planet's atmosphere. **2** (of a place) giving a strong impression of a mood. — *adv* **atmospherically**.

atmospherics *n* (*pl*) noises caused by electrical disturbances in the air, esp. when interfering with radio broadcasts.

atoll *n* a ring-shaped coral reef surrounding a lagoon. [*Atolu*, native name in the Maldive Islands]

atom *n* **1** the smallest particle of an element that can take part in a chemical reaction. **2** this particle as a source of nuclear energy. **3** a small amount. [Gr *atomos*, undivided]

atom bomb or **atomic bomb** *n* a bomb which uses nuclear energy produced by splitting atoms.

atomic *adj* **1** using atomic energy or atom bombs. **2** of atoms. — *adv* **atomically**.

atomic energy *n* nuclear energy.

atomic mass unit *n* a unit of mass equal to one twelfth of the mass of an atom of a particular isotope of carbon (carbon-12).

atomic number *n* the number of protons in the nucleus of an atom.

atomic weight *n* (also called **relative atomic mass**) the ratio of the weight of one atom of a substance to the atomic mass unit (see above).

atomise or **-ize** *v* (*tr*) **1** to reduce to atoms or small particles. **2** to reduce (a liquid or solid) to small particles or a fine spray.

atomiser or **-izer** *n* a container from which liquid can be released as a fine spray.

atonal *adj* (*mus*) not written in any key. — *n* **atonality**. [Gr *atonos*, toneless]

atone *v* (*intr*; **for**) to do something in order to make up for something bad that has been done. [MidE; orig. to 'make at one', to reconcile]

atonement *n* **1** an act of atoning. **2** (*cap*) the reconciliation of God and man through the death of Christ.

atrium *n* **-ia** or **-iums 1** a central court or entrance hall in an ancient Roman house. **2** either of the two upper parts of the heart that receive blood from the veins. — *adj* **atrial**. [Lat]

atrocious *adj* **1** (*coll*) very bad. **2** extremely cruel or wicked. — *n* **atrociousness**. [Lat *atrox*, cruel]

atrocity *n* **-ies 1** wicked or cruel behaviour. **2** (usu. in *pl*) an act of wickedness or cruelty.

atrophy *v* **-ies**, **-ied** (*tr* & *intr*) to make or become weak and thin through lack of use or nourishment. — *n* the process of atrophying. [Gr *a*, not + *trophe*, nourishment]

atropine *n* a poison found in deadly nightshade, used in medicine. [Gr *Atropos*, the Fate that cut the thread of life]

attach *v* **1** (*tr*) to fasten or join. **2** (*tr*) to associate (oneself) with or join. **3** (*tr*) to attribute or assign: *attach great importance to detail*. **4** (*intr*; **to**) to be connected with or form part of: *Certain conditions attach to the offer*. **5** (*tr*; *legal*) to arrest (a person) or seize (property) by legal authority. — *adj* **attached**. — **attached to** very fond of. [Fr *atachier*]

attachment *n* **1** an act or means of fastening. **2** liking or affection. **3** an extra part that can be fitted to a machine to change its function slightly. **4** a legal seizure of a person or property. **5** a temporary period of working with a different group.

attaché *n* a junior official in an embassy. [Fr, attached]

attaché-case *n* a small, rigid leather case for documents, etc.

attack *v* **1** (*tr*) to make a sudden, violent attempt to hurt, damage or capture. **2** (*tr*) to criticise strongly in speech or writing. **3** (*intr*) to make an attack. **4** (*tr*) to begin to do (something) with enthusiasm or determination. **5** (*tr*) to begin to damage. **6** (*intr*) to take the initiative in a game, contest, etc. to attempt to score points. — *n* **1** an act or the action of attacking. **2** a sudden spell of illness. — *n* **attacker**. [Ital *attaccare*]

attain *v* (*tr*) **1** to complete successfully or accomplish. **2** to reach. — *adj* **attainable**. — *n* **attainment**. [Lat *ad*, to + *tangere*, to touch]

attar *n* a fragrant oil made from rose petals. [Persian]

attempt *v* (*tr*) **1** to try. **2** to try to climb or master (a mountain, problem, etc.). — *n* (**at**) an endeavour to achieve something. — **an attempt on someone's life** an attempt to kill someone. [Lat *attemptare*, to test]

attend *v* **1** (*tr* & *intr*) to be present (at). **2** (*tr*) to go regularly to (e.g. a school). **3** (*intr* with **to**) to give attention to or take action about. **4** (*tr*; *formal*) to accompany or escort. **5** (*tr*; *formal*; **on**, **upon**) to follow as a result of. **6** (*tr*) to serve or wait on. [Lat *attendere*, to direct one's attention to]

attendance *n* **1** the act of attending. **2** the number of people attending. **3** regularity of attending.

attendance allowance *n* (*Br*) money paid by the government to severely disabled people to pay for a nurse, etc. to help them.

attendant *n* a person employed to help, esp. the public. — *adj* **1** giving attendance. **2** accompanying.

attention *n* **1** the act of concentrating or directing the mind. **2** special care and consideration. **3** (in *pl*) an act of politeness or courtship. **4** (*mil*, etc.) a position in which one stands rigidly erect with heels together and hands by one's sides. [Lat *attentio*]

attentive *adj* **1** concentrating. **2** polite and courteous. — *adv* **attentively**. — *n* **attentiveness**. [**attend**]

attenuate *v* **1** (*tr* & *intr*) to make or become thin and weak. **2** (*tr*) to reduce the strength or value of. — *adj* **attenuated**. — *n* **attenuation**. [Lat *attenuare*]

attest *v* **1** (*tr*) to affirm or be proof of the truth or validity of. **2** (*tr* & *intr*; **to**) to witness or bear witness to. — *n* **attestation**. [Lat *attestari*, from *ad*, to + *testare*, to witness]

attested *adj* (*Br*) (of cattle) officially certified free from disease, esp. tuberculosis.

Attic *adj* **1** of or relating to ancient Athens or Attica, or the Greek spoken there. **2** elegant. — *n* the dialect of ancient Greek spoken in Athens. [Gr *Attikos*]

attic *n* a space or room at the top of a house under the roof. [**Attic**, such a structure being supposedly in the Athenian style]

attire *n* clothing, esp. formal or elegant. [Fr *atirier*, to put in order]

attired *adj* dressed, esp. formally or elegantly.

attitude *n* **1** a way of thinking or behaving. **2** a position of the body. **3** a pose, esp. adopted for dramatic effect: *strike an attitude*. **4** the angle of an aircraft relative to the direction of the air flowing round it or to the horizontal plane, or of a spacecraft relative to its direction of movement. [Fr, from Lat *aptitudo*, suitability]

attitudinise or **-ize** *v* (*intr*) to adopt an opinion or position for effect.

atto- *comb fm* a million million millionth, 10^{-18} [Dan or Norw *atten*, eighteen]

attorney *n* **-eys 1** a person able to act for another in legal or business matters. **2** (*US*) a lawyer. — **power of attorney** the right to act for another person in legal and business matters. [Fr *atourner*, to turn over to]

Attorney General *n* ***Attorneys General*** or ***Attorney Generals*** the principal law officer in England, the US, and several other countries.

attract *v* (*tr*) **1** to cause to come close or stay close. **2** to arouse or draw to oneself. **3** to arouse liking or admiration; to be attractive to. [Lat *ad*, to + *trahere*, to draw]

attraction *n* **1** the act or power of attracting. **2** a person or thing that attracts. **3** (*physics*) the force by which bodies attract or approach each other.

attractive *adj* **1** capable of attracting attention; appealing. **2** good-looking. — *adv* **attractively**. — *n* **attractiveness**.

attribute *v* (*tr*; **to**) to think of as being written, made, said, or caused by. — *n* a quality, characteristic or feature. — *adj* **attributable**. — *n* **attribution**. [Lat *attribuere*, to assign to]

attributive *adj* (*gram*) **1** (of an adjective or noun) placed before the noun to which it refers, e.g. in *the young girl* and *a buffet car*. — *adv* **attributively**. ◇ See also **predicative**.

attrition *n* **1** a rubbing together; friction. **2** a wearing away or making weaker, esp. by continual friction or attacks: *a war of attrition*. [Lat *attritio*, from *atterere*, to rub]

attune *v* (*tr*) **1** to adjust to or prepare for (a situation, etc.) **2** to put (a musical instrument, an orchestra, etc.) into tune. [Lat *ad*, to + **tune**]

atypical *adj* not typical. [**a-**[1] + **typical**]

Au *symbol* (*chem*) gold. [Lat *aurum*]

aubergine *n* a tropical plant which produces a dark purple fruit which can be cooked and eaten as a vegetable. [Sanskrit *vatinganah*]

aubrietia *n* a small, trailing rock plant with pink or purple flowers. [Claude *Aubriet* (1665–1742), French botanist]

auburn *adj* (esp. of hair) reddish-brown. [Lat *alburnus*, whitish, from *albus*, white]

auction *n* a public sale in which each item is sold to the person who offers the most money. — *v* (*tr*; **off**) to sell in this way. [Lat *auctio*, an increase]

auctioneer *n* a person who conducts an auction.

audacious *adj* **1** bold and daring. **2** disrespectful; impudent. — *adv* **audaciously**. — *n* **audacity**. [Lat *audax*, bold]

audible *adj* loud enough to be heard. — *n* **audibility**. — *adv* **audibly**. [Lat *audire*, to hear]

audience *n* **1** a group of people watching a performance. **2** the people reached by a film, radio broadcast, book, magazine, etc. **3** a formal interview with an important person. [Lat *audientia*, from *audire*, to hear]

audio *adj* & *comb fm* of sound, hearing, or the recording and broadcasting of sound. [Lat *audire*, to hear]

audio frequency *n* a radio frequency which can be heard by the human ear.

audio-typist *n* a person who types letters, etc. which have been recorded on a dictation machine. — *n* **audio-typing**.

audiovisual *adj* (of teaching aids, etc.) using both sound and vision.

audit *n* an official inspection of an organisation's accounts by an accountant. — *v* **-t-** (*tr*) to examine accounts officially. — *n* **auditor**. [Lat *audire*, to hear]

audition *n* a short performance as a test of the ability of an actor, singer, musician, etc. and of his or her suitability for a particular part or role. — *v* **-n-** (*tr* & *intr*) to test or be tested for one's ability or suitability for a part or role. [Lat *auditio*, from *audire*, to hear]

auditor. See **audit**.

auditorium *n* **-iums** or **-ia** the part of a theatre, hall, etc. where the audience sits. [Lat, a lecture-room, court, etc.]

auditory *adj* of or relating to hearing. [Lat *audire*, to hear]

au fait *adj* (**with**) well informed or familiar. [Fr]

Aug. *abbrev* August.

Augean *adj* extremely dirty. [Gr *Augeas*, a king in Greek mythology whose stables were cleaned by Hercules]

auger *n* a hand-tool with a corkscrew-like point for boring holes in wood. [OE *nafogar*; in MidE, *a nauger* was understood as *an auger*]

aught *pron* (*old*) anything. [OE *awiht*]

augment *v* (*tr* & *intr*) to make or become greater in size, number, strength, amount, etc. — *n* **augmentation**. [Lat *augere*, to increase]

augmentative *adj* tending to augment or increase.

augmented *adj* **1** having become or been made greater in size, etc. **2** (*mus*) increased by a semitone.

au gratin *adj* (of food) covered and cooked with breadcrumbs and often with grated cheese. [Fr]

augur: **augur well** or **ill (for)** to be a good or bad sign for the future. [Lat, soothsayer]

augury *n* **-ies 1** a sign or omen. **2** the practice of predicting the future.

August *n* the eighth month of the year. [Lat *Augustus*, the first Roman emperor]

august *adj* noble; imposing. — *adv* **augustly**. — *n* **augustness**. [Lat *augustus*, grand]

auk *n* a seabird with a heavy body, short wings and black and white feathers. [Norse *alka*]

auld lang syne *n* (*Scot*) days of long ago. [Scot, old long since]

aunt *n* **1** the sister of one's father or mother, or the wife of one's uncle. **2** a close female friend of a child's parents. [Lat *amita*, father's sister]

auntie or **aunty** *n* **-ies** (*coll*) an aunt.

Aunt Sally *n* **-ies 1** a game in which sticks or balls are thrown at a dummy. **2** any target of abuse.

au pair *n* a young person from abroad, usu. a woman, who lives with a family and helps with housework, looking after children, etc. in return for board and lodging. [Fr]

aura *n* **-ras** or **-rae 1** a distinctive character or quality around a person or in a place. **2** a fine substance coming out of something, esp. that supposedly coming from and surrounding the body, which many mystics claim is visible as a faint light. [Gr, breeze]

aural *adj* of the sense of hearing or the ears. — *adv* **aurally**. [Lat *auris*, ear]

aureate *adj* **1** golden. **2** very ornamental. [Lat *aurum*, gold]

aureole or **aureola** *n* **1** (in painting) a bright light surrounding the head or body of a holy figure. **2** a circle of light round the sun or moon. [Lat *aureolus*, golden]

au revoir *interj* goodbye; until we meet again. [Fr]

auricle *n* (*anat*) **1** the outer part of the ear. **2** a small muscle on the wall of the atrium; the atrium itself. — *adj* **auricular**. [Lat *auricula*, little ear]

auriferous *adj* containing gold. [Lat *aurum*, gold]

aurochs *n* **-rochs** an extinct wild ox. [Ger *urohso*]

aurora *n* **-ras** or **-rae 1** the appearance of bands of moving, coloured lights in the night sky, called the **aurora borealis** when it occurs above the North Pole, and the **aurora australis** when it occurs above the South Pole. **2** (*poetic*) the dawn. [Lat, dawn]

auscultation *n* the practice of listening, usu. with a stethoscope, to the sounds made by the organs of the body, as a way of diagnosing illness. [Lat *ascultare*, to listen]

auspices *n* (*pl*): **under the auspices of** arranged or supported by (a person, society, etc.). [Lat *auspicium*, foretelling the future by watching birds]

auspicious *adj* promising future success; favourable. — *adv* **auspiciously**. — *n* **auspiciousness**. [See ety. for **auspices**]

Aussie *n* & *adj* (*coll*) Australian.

austere *adj* **1** severely simple and plain. **2** serious; severe; stern. **3** severe in self-discipline. — *adv* **austerely**. [Gr *austeros*, strict, rigorous]

austerity *n* **-ies 1** the state of being austere; strictness or harshness. **2** severity and extreme simplicity of dress, etc. **3** a period of economic depression.

austral *adj* southern. [Lat *Auster*, the south wind]

Australasian *adj* of or relating to Australia, New Zealand, and the nearby Pacific islands.

Australian *adj* of or relating to Australia. — *n* a person born or living in Australia. [Lat *australis*, southern]

Australia Day *n* a public holiday in Australia, 26 January or the first Monday after that, celebrating the landing of the British in 1788.

Australian rules football *n* a type of football played by two teams with eighteen players each, with a rugby ball on an oval pitch.

autarchy *n* **-ies** government of a country by a ruler who has absolute power. [Gr *autos*, self + *archein*, to rule]

autarky *n* **-ies** economic self-sufficiency. [Gr *autos*, self + *arkeein*, to suffice]

authentic *adj* **1** genuine. **2** reliable; trustworthy. — *adv* **authentically**. — *n* **authenticity**. [Gr *authentikos*]

authenticate *v* (*tr*) to prove to be true or genuine. — *n* **authentication**.

author *n* **1** the writer of a book, article, play, etc. **2** the creator or originator of an idea, event, etc. [Lat *auctor*]

authorship *n* **1** the origin, i.e. the name of the author, of a particular piece of writing. **2** the profession of writing.

authorise or **-ize** *v* (*tr*) **1** to give (someone) the power or right to do something. **2** to give permission for. — *n* **authorisation** or **-z-**. [Lat *auctorizare*, from *auctor*, author]

Authorised Version *n* the English translation of the Bible completed in 1611.

authoritarian *adj* in favour of, or insisting on, strict authority. — *n* an authoritarian person. — *n* **authoritarianism**. [**authority**]

authoritative *adj* **1** accepted as a reliable source of knowledge. **2** having authority; official. — *adv* **authoritatively**. — *n* **authoritativeness**. [**authority**]

authority *n* **-ies 1** the power or right to control or judge others. **2** (often in *pl*) the person or people who have power, esp. political or administrative. **3** a position which has such a power or right: *be in authority*. **4** the ability to influence others, usu. as a result of knowledge or expertise. **5 (on)** an expert. **6** a passage in a book used to support a statement. [Lat *auctoritas*, from *auctor*, author]

autism *n* a severe mental illness in which sufferers are absorbed in their own minds and imaginations, with limited ability to communicate with others. — *adj* **autistic**. — *adv* **autistically**. [Gr *autos*, self]

auto *n* **-os** (*US coll*) a car. [Abbrev. of **automobile**]

auto- *comb fm* of or by oneself or itself. [Gr *autos*, self]
autobahn *n* a motorway in Austria, Switzerland or Germany. [Ger *Auto*, car + *Bahn*, road]
autobiography *n* **-ies 1** the story of a person's life written by that person. **2** this as a literary form. — *n* **autobiographer**. — *adj* **autobiographical** . — *adv* **autobiographically**.
autoclave *n* an apparatus for sterilising objects using steam under high pressure. [Gr *autos*, self + Lat *clavis*, key or *clavus*, nail]
autocracy *n* **-ies** absolute government by one person; dictatorship. [Gr *autos*, self + *kratos*, power]
autocrat *n* **1** a ruler with absolute power. **2** an authoritarian person. — *adj* **autocratic**. — *adv* **autocratically**.
autocross *n* motor-racing on a rough grass track.
Autocue® *n* a screen, unseen by an audience, which displays a speaker's script, so that he or she may speak without being seen to be reading.
auto-da-fé *n* ***autos-da-fé*** **1** (*hist*) the ceremonial passing of sentence on heretics by the Spanish Inquisition. **2** the public burning of a heretic. [Port, act of the faith]
autogiro or **autogyro** *n* **-os** a helicopter-like aircraft with large horizontal rotating blades turned by the forward motion of the aircraft and so keeping the machine in the air. [Orig. Span trademark, from Gr *autos*, self + *gyros*, circle]
autograph *n* **1** a person's signature, esp. a famous person's, kept as a souvenir. **2** a manuscript in the author's handwriting. — *v* (*tr*) to sign (a photograph, etc). [Gr *autos*, self + *graphein*, to write]
automat *n* (*US*) a vending machine. [**automatic**]
automate. See **automation**.
automatic *adj* **1** (of a machine) working by itself, with little or no control by people. **2** (of an action) done without thinking; unconscious; spontaneous. **3** happening as a necessary and inevitable result: *conviction bringing automatic disqualification.* **4** (of a firearm) able to reload itself and so able to fire continuously. **5** (of a motor vehicle) having gears which change by themselves according to the speed of the vehicle, and which do not have to be changed by the driver. — *n* **1** an automatic firearm. **2** a vehicle with an automatic gearbox. — *adv* **automatically**. [Gr *automatos*, self-moving]
automatic pilot *n* a device that keeps an aircraft on a preset course whilst the pilot is resting, etc. — **on automatic pilot** (*coll*) doing one's work, etc. without thinking.
automatic transmission *n* the system for controlling the automatic gears in road vehicles.
automation *n* the use of automatic machines and equipment to control production in manufacturing. [**automatic**]
automate *v* (*tr*) to convert (a factory, etc.) to automation. — *adj* **automated**. [**automatic**]
automaton *n* **-ons** or **-ta 1** a machine with a usu. hidden electronic or clockwork control which makes it move. **2** a person who acts like a machine, according to routine and without thinking. [**automatic**]
automobile *n* (esp. *US*) a car. [Fr, from Gr *autos*, self + Lat *mobilis*, mobile]
automotive *adj* of motor vehicles. [Gr *autos*, self + Lat *motivus*, causing to move]
autonomy *n* **-ies 1** the power or right of self-government. **2** personal freedom. [Gr *autos*, self + *nomos*, law]
autonomous *adj* **1** having self-governing. **2** independent of others. — *adv* **autonomously**.
autopilot *n*. Same as **automatic pilot**.
autopsy *n* **-ies** an examination of a dead body to find out the cause of death. [Gr *autos*, self + *opsis*, sight]
autoroute *n* a motorway in France. [Fr, *auto*, car + *route*, road]
autostrada *n* a motorway in Italy. [Ital, *auto*, car + *strada*, road]
auto-suggestion *n* the process of making suggestions to oneself, esp. subconsciously, which change one's behaviour. — *adj* **auto-suggestive**.
autumn *n* **1** the season of the year, between summer and winter, when leaves change colour and fall. **2** a period of maturity before decay. — *adj* **autumnal**. — *adv* **autumnally**. [Lat *autumnus*]
auxiliary *adj* **1** helping or supporting. **2** additional or extra. — *n* **-ies 1** a helper. **2** (in *pl*) foreign troops helping another nation at war. **3** (*gram*) an auxiliary verb. [Lat *auxiliarius*, from *auxilium*, help]
auxiliary verb *n* a verb which shows the tense, voice or mood of the main verb in a phrase, e.g. *should*, *will*, *can*.
AV *abbrev* Authorised Version.
avail *v* (*tr* & *intr*) to help or be of use. — *n* use; advantage: *of no avail.* — **avail oneself of** to make use of. [Lat *valere*, to be worth]
available *adj* able or ready to be obtained or used. — *adj* **availability**. — *adv* **availably**. [**avail**]
avalanche *n* **1** a sudden, huge fall of snow and ice down a mountain. **2** a sudden appearance of a large number of people or things. [Fr]
avant-garde *n* those writers, painters, musicians, etc. whose ideas and techniques are the most modern or advanced. — *adj* (of a work of art, idea, etc.) using or supporting the most modern and advanced ideas in literature, art, music, etc. [Fr, vanguard]

avarice *n* a great desire for money, possessions, etc. [Lat *avaritia*, from *avere*, to crave]
avaricious *n* greedy for money, possessions, etc. — *adv* **avariciously**. [**avarice**]
avatar *n* the appearance of a Hindu god in human or animal form. [Sanskrit *ava*, down + *tar-*, pass over]
Ave or **Ave Maria** *n* a prayer to the Virgin Mary. ◇ See also **hail Mary**. [Lat; the opening words of the angel's greeting to Mary in Luke i. 28]
Ave. *abbrev* avenue.
avenge *v* (*tr*) to punish (someone) in return for (harm they have done to someone). — *n* **avenger**. — *adj* **avenging**. [OFr *avengier*, from Lat *vindicare*, to claim]
avenue *n* **1** a broad road or street, often with trees along the sides. **2** a tree-lined approach to a house. **3** a means or way: *explored several avenues before deciding on a plan.* [Lat *advenire*, to come to]
aver *v* **-rr-** (*tr*) to state firmly. [Lat *ad*, to + *verus*, true]
average *n* **1** the usual or typical amount or number. **2** the result obtained by adding together a group of numbers and dividing the total by the number of numbers in the group; e.g. the average of 1 and 3 is $(1+3)\div 2$, i.e. 2. — *adj* **1** usual or ordinary. **2** estimated by taking an average. **3** mediocre. — *v* (*tr*) **1** to obtain the numerical average of. **2** to amount to on average. — *v* **average out** (*intr*; **at**) to result in an average or balance. — **on average** usually; normally. [Arabic *awariya*, damaged goods]
law of averages *n* the theory that if something happens, its opposite is likely to happen too, so that balance may be maintained.
averse *adj* (**to**) reluctant or opposed: *not averse to helping*. [Lat *aversus*]
aversion *n* **1** a strong dislike. **2** an object of strong dislike. [Lat *aversio*, from *aversus*, averse]
aversion therapy *n* treatment which changes part of a person's behaviour by associating it with an unpleasant feeling.
avert *v* (*tr*) **1** to turn away: *avert one's eyes.* **2** to prevent (esp. danger). [Lat *ab*, from + *vertere*, to turn]
Avesta *n* the sacred Zoroastrian writings. ◇ See also **Zend-Avesta**.
aviary *n* **-ies** a large, enclosed area in which birds are kept. [Lat *aviarium*, from *avis*, bird]
aviation *n* **1** the science or practice of flying in aircraft. **2** the aircraft industry. [Lat *avis*, bird]
aviator *n* (*old*) an aircraft pilot. [Lat *avis*, bird]
avid *adj* **1** enthusiastic. **2** (**for**) eagerly wanting. — *n* **avidity**. — *adv* **avidly**. [Lat *avidus*, from *avere*, to crave]
avocado *n* **-os** (also **avocado pear**) a pear-shaped tropical fruit with leathery green skin, a large stone, and creamy, light green flesh. [Aztec *ahuacatl*]
avocation *n* (*old*) **1** a diversion or distraction from one's main job; a hobby. **2** (*coll*) a vocation. [Lat *avocatio*, from *ab*, from + *vocare*, to call]
avocet *n* a wading bird with long legs, black and white feathers, and a long, thin beak curving up at the end. [Fr]
avoid *v* (*tr*) **1** to keep away from (a place, person, action, etc.). **2** to stop, prevent, manage not to, or escape. — *adj* **avoidable**. — *adv* **avoidably**. — *n* **avoidance**. [Fr *avoidier*]
avoirdupois *n* a system of weights based on a pound weighing 16 ounces. [Fr, to have weight]
avow *v* (*tr*) to state openly; to declare; to admit. — *n* **avowal**. — *adj* **avowed**. — *adv* **avowedly** . [Lat *advocare*]
avuncular *adj* of or like an uncle, esp. in being kind and caring. [Lat *avunculus*, maternal uncle]
await *v* (*tr*) **1** to wait for. **2** to be certain to happen (to someone) in the future. [Fr *awaitier*]
awake *v* ***awoke***, ***awoken*** (*intr* & *tr*) **1** to (cause to) stop sleeping. **2** to (cause to) become active. — *adj* **1** not sleeping. **2** alert or aware. [OE *awæcnian* & *awacian*]
awaken *v* **-n-** (*tr* & *intr*) **1** to awake. **2** to (cause to) start feeling or be aware of. — *n* **awakening**.
award *v* (*tr*) to give (someone something) esp. as a payment or prize. — *n* **1** a payment, prize, etc. awarded. **2** a legal judgement. [Fr *awarder*]
aware *adj* **1** (**of**) knowing about or conscious of something. **2** well informed. — *n* **awareness**. [OE *gewær*]
awash *adj* **1** covered or flooded by water. **2** (**with**) covered by a large amount of. [**a**[3] + **wash**]
away *adv* **1** (**from**) showing distance or movement from a particular place, position, person or time. **2** in or to another, usual or proper place: *put the books away.* **3** gradually into nothing: *fade away*. **4** continuously: *work away*. **5** as one wishes: *ask away*. **6** (of a sporting event) at the opponent's ground. — *adj* **1** (**from**) not present. **2** (**from**) distant: *not far away*. **3** (of a sporting event) played on the opponent's ground. — *n* a match won by a team playing on their opponent's ground. [OE *aweg*, *onweg*]
awe *n* admiration, fear and wonder. — *v* (*tr*) to fill with awe. [Norse *agi*]
awe-inspiring *adj* causing awe.
awesome *adj* causing awe; dreaded.
awestricken or **awestruck** *adj* filled with awe.
aweigh *adv* (of an anchor) in the process of being raised from the bottom of the sea. [**a**[3] + **weigh**]

awful *adj* **1** (*coll*) very bad. **2** (*coll*) very great: *an awful shame*. **3** awe-inspiring, terrible or shocking. — *adv* (*coll*) very. — *n* **awfulness**. [**awe**]

awfully *adv* **1** very badly. **2** very.

awhile *adv* for a short time. [OE *æne hwil*, a while]

awkward *adj* **1** clumsy and ungraceful. **2** embarrassed or embarrassing. **3** difficult, dangerous or inconvenient to deal with: *an awkward customer*; *make things awkward for him*. — *adv* **awkwardly**. — *n* **awkwardness**. [Norse *ofugr*, turned the wrong way + **-ward**]

awl *n* a pointed tool for making small holes, esp. in leather. [OE *æl*]

awn *n* a small bristle growing from the head of barley and other grasses. [Norse *ogn*]

awning *n* a soft plastic or canvas covering above the entrance to a shop, hotel, etc. which can be extended to give shelter from the sun or rain.

awoke, **awoken**. See **awake**.

AWOL *abbrev* absent without leave, absent from one's place of duty without official permission.

awry *adj* & *adv* **1** twisted to one side; crooked(ly). **2** wrong; amiss. [MidE; **a**[3] + **wry**]

axe *n* **1** a tool with a long handle and a heavy metal blade, for cutting down trees, chopping wood, etc. **2** a severe cut in spending or staff. — *v* (*tr*) **1** to get rid of or dismiss. **2** to reduce (costs, services, etc.). — **have an axe to grind** to have a personal, often selfish, reason for being involved in something. [OE *æcs*]

axial *adj* of, forming, or placed along an axis. — *n* **axiality**. [**axis**]

axil *n* the upper angle between a leaf and the stem from which it grows. [Lat *axilla*, armpit]

axiom *n* **1** a fact or principle which is generally accepted as true. **2** a self-evident statement. [Gr *axios*, worthy]

axiomatic *adj* **1** obvious; self-evident. **2** containing or based on axioms. — *adv* **axiomatically**.

axis *n* ***axes*** **1** an imaginary line around which an object, e.g. a planet, rotates. **2** the real or imaginary line which divides a flat geometrical shape into two identical halves. **3** one of two or three fixed lines used as a reference on a map or a graph. [Lat, axle, pivot]

the Axis *n* an alliance formed by Germany and Italy during the Second World War, later extended to include Japan.

axle *n* a rod on which a wheel or pair of wheels turns. [Norse *öxull*]

axolotl *n* a newt-like salamander which lives in Mexican lakes. [Aztec, from *atl*, water + *xolotl*, servant]

ayah *n* a native maid, esp. one who looks after children, esp. formerly in India and some other parts of the British Empire. [Hindi *aya*, from Lat *avia*, grandmother]

ayatollah *n* a Shi'ite religious leader in Iran. [Arabic, sign of God]

aye[1] or **ay** *interj* (*dialect*) yes. — *n* a vote in favour. [Equivalent to *I*, expressing agreement]

aye[2] *adv* (*old* or *poetic*) always. [Norse]

AZ *abbrev* Arizona.

azalea *n* a garden shrub related to the rhododendron, with pink or purple flowers. [Gr *azaleos*, dry]

azimuth *n* the angle between the horizon running from north to south, and a vertical plane containing the line of a planet or star, as seen from a point on Earth. [Arabic *al*, the + *sumut*, directions]

Aztec *n* **1** a member of a Mexican Indian people whose great empire was overthrown by the Spanish in the 16th century. **2** the language spoken by this people, also called **Nahuatl**. — *adj* of the Aztec people, their language and culture. [Aztec, *aztecatl*, men of the north]

azure *n* & *adj* (of) a deep, sky-blue colour. [Persian *lajward*, lapis lazuli]

B

B[1] or **b** *n* ***Bs*** or ***B's***, ***b's*** **1** the second letter of the English alphabet. **2** (usu. **B**) (a mark indicating) the second highest grade or quality. **3** (only **B**; *mus*) the seventh note in the scale of C major. **4** (only **B**) a musical key with the note B as its base.

B-movie *n* a film, usu. second-rate, made to support the main film at a cinema.

B-road *n* in Britain, a road of secondary importance.

B-side *n* the less important side of a record.

B[2] *abbrev* **1** Bachelor. **2** bass. **3** (*chess*) bishop. **4** (on pencils) black.

B[3] *symbol* (*chem*) boron.

b. *abbrev* **1** born. **2** (*cricket*) bowled.

BA *abbrev* **1** Bachelor of Arts. **2** British Airways.

Ba *symbol* (*chem*) barium.

baa *n* the cry of a sheep or lamb. — *v* ***baaed*** (*intr*) to make this cry. [Imit.]

baba or **rum baba** *n* a type of small sponge cake soaked in a rum-flavoured syrup. [Fr, from Pol]

babble *v* **1** (*tr & intr*) to talk or say quickly, esp. in a way that is hard to understand. **2** (*intr*; *coll*) to talk foolishly. **3** (*intr*; *formal* or *literary*) (esp. of a brook) to make a low murmuring sound. **4** (*tr*) to give away (a secret) carelessly. — *adj* **babbling**. [Prob. imit.]

babe *n* **1** (*coll*; esp. *US*; often used as a term of affection) a girl or young woman. **2** (*old* or *literary*) a baby. [Prob. imit. of the sound made by a baby]

babel *n* **1** a confused sound of voices. **2** a scene of noise and confusion. [Hebr *Babel*, the place where, according to the Book of Genesis, God caused people to speak different languages]

baboon *n* **1** a large African monkey with a dog-like face and tail. **2** (*derog*) a clumsy or stupid person. [OFr *babuin*]

baby *n* ***-ies*** **1** a newborn or very young child or animal. **2** an unborn child. **3** the youngest member of a group. **4** (*derog*) a very childish person. **5** (*coll*) a person's own particular project, responsibility, etc. **6** (*coll*; esp. *US*) a term of affection. — *v* ***-ies***, ***-ied*** (*tr*) to treat as a baby. — *n* **babyhood**. — *adj* **babyish** (*derog*). — **be left holding the baby** (*coll*) to be left with the responsibility for something. — **throw out the baby with the bathwater** (*coll*) to give up or throw away the important part of something when getting rid of an unwanted part. [Prob. imit. of the sound a baby makes]

baby-sit *v* (*intr*) to look after a child (usu. in its own home) while its parents are out. — *n* **baby-sitter**. — *n* **baby-sitting**.

baby-walker *n* a frame with a seat and wheels in which a baby can sit while learning to walk.

baccalaureate *n* **1** (*formal*) a Bachelor's degree. **2** a diploma of a lower status than a degree. [Fr]

baccarat *n* a card game in which players bet money against the banker. [Fr]

bacchanal *n* **1** (*literary*) a noisy and drunken party. **2** a follower of *Bacchus*, the god of wine and pleasure in ancient Greece and Rome. — *adj* **bacchanalian**. [Lat]

baccy *n* ***-ies*** *coll* shortening of **tobacco**.

bachelor *n* **1** an unmarried man. **2** (*cap*) (a person who has taken) a first university degree: *Bachelor of Arts*. ◇ See also **master**. — *n* **bachelorhood**. [OFr *bacheler*]

bacillus *n* ***-lli*** (*tech*) a rod-shaped bacterium, esp. one which causes disease. [Lat, little stick]

back *n* **1** the rear part of the human body from the neck to the bottom of the backbone. **2** the upper part of an animal's body. **3** the part of an object that is opposite to or furthest from the front. **4** the side of an object that is not normally seen or used. **5** the upright part of a chair. **6** (*football*, *hockey*, etc.) a player whose job is to defend. — *adj* **1** situated, etc. behind or at the back. **2** of or from an earlier date: *back pay*. **3** away from or behind (esp. something more important): *back roads*. — *adv* **1** to or towards the rear; away from the front. **2** in or into an original position or condition. **3** in return or in response: *hit back*. **4** in or into the past: *look back to happier days*. — *v* **1** (*tr*) to help or support, usu. with money. **2** (*tr & intr*; **away**, **out**, **out of**, etc.) to (cause to) move backwards. **3** (*tr*) to bet on the success of (a horse, etc.). **4** (*tr*) to provide a back or support for. **5** (*tr*) to accompany (a singer) with music. **6** (*tr*) to lie at the back of. **7** (*intr*; *naut*) (of the wind) to change direction anticlockwise. — *adj* **backless**. — *v* **back down** (*intr*) to give up one's claim, change one's opinion, etc. — *v* **back off** (*intr*) **1** to move backwards or retreat. **2** to back down. — *v* **back on to** (*tr*) (of a building, etc.) to have its back next to or facing (something). — *v* **back out** (*intr*; **of**) to withdraw (from a promise or agreement, etc.) — **back to front 1** with the back where the front should be. **2** in the wrong order. — *v* **back up 1** (*tr*) to support or assist (*n* **backup**). **2** (*tr & intr*) to copy information kept on a computer on to a disk or tape (*n* **backup**). — **get off someone's back** (*coll*) to stop annoying or troubling someone. — **have one's back to the wall**

(*coll*) to be in a very difficult or desperate situation. — **put one's back into** (*coll*) to do (something) with all one's strength. — **put someone's back up** (*coll*) to make someone angry. — **see the back of** (*coll*) to be rid of or finished with (someone or something unpleasant, annoying or difficult). [OE *bæc*]
backache *n* a pain in the back.
backbencher *n* in the UK, Australia, etc., a Member of Parliament who does not hold an official position in either the government or the opposition. ◇ See also **frontbencher**. — *adj* **backbench**.
backbite *v* (*intr*; *coll*) to speak unkindly about a person who is absent. — *n* **backbiting**.
backbone *n* **1** the spine. **2** the main support. **3** firmness and strength of character.
backbreaking *adj* (of a task, etc.) extremely hard or tiring.
backchat *n* (*Br*) (the act of making) impertinent replies.
back-cloth or **backdrop** *n* the painted cloth at the back of a stage, forming part of the scenery.
backcomb *v* (*tr*) to comb (the hair) towards the roots to make it look thicker.
backdate *v* (*tr*) **1** to put an earlier date on. **2** to make effective from a date in the past.
back-door *adj* secret, and often dishonest.
backdrop see **back-cloth**.
backer *n* a person who gives financial support to a project, etc.
backfire *v* (*intr*) **1** (of an engine or vehicle) to make a loud bang as the result of an explosion of unburnt gases in the exhaust system. **2** (of a plan, etc.) to go wrong.
back-formation *n* (*gram*) **1** the making of a new word on the mistaken assumption that it is the root of an existing word. **2** a word made in this way, e.g. *laze* from *lazy*.
background *n* **1** the space behind the main figures of a picture. **2** a less noticeable or less public position: *stay in the background*. **3** the events or circumstances that precede and help to explain an event, etc. **4** a person's social origins, education, etc.
backhand *n* **1** (*tennis*, etc.) a stroke made with the back of the hand turned towards the ball. ◇ See also **forehand**. **2** handwriting with the letters sloping backwards.
backhanded *adj* **1** made with or as a backhand. **2** apparently but not really complimentary: *a backhanded compliment*.
backhander *n* (*coll*) a bribe.
backing *n* **1** support, esp. financial. **2** material, etc. that supports the back of something. **3** music accompanying a pop singer.
backlash *n* **1** a sudden violent reaction to an action, situation, etc. **2** a jarring or recoil between parts of a machine that do not fit together properly.
backlog *n* a pile of uncompleted work.
back number *n* **1** an out-of-date copy or issue of a newspaper or magazine. **2** (*coll*) a person or thing that is out of date or no longer useful.
backpack *n* (*US*) a rucksack. — *v* (*intr*) to go hiking with a pack on the back. — *n* **backpacker**. — *n* **backpacking**.
back passage *n* the rectum.
back-pedal *v* (*intr*) **1** to turn the pedals on a bicycle backwards. **2** to reverse one's previous opinion or course of action.
backroom *adj* doing important work behind the scenes, esp. in secret.
back seat *n* an inferior or unimportant position.
back-seat driver *n* a person, e.g. a passenger in a car, who gives unwanted advice.
back shift *n* **1** a group of workers whose working period comes between the night shift and the day shift. **2** this period. ◇ See also **day shift** and **night shift**.
backside *n* (*coll*) the buttocks.
backslide *v* (*intr*) to relapse into former bad behaviour, immorality, etc. — *n* **backslider**. — *n* **backsliding**.
backspace *v* (*intr*) to move the carriage of a typewriter or a computer cursor back one or more spaces. — *n* the key on a typewriter or computer keyboard used for backspacing.
backspin *n* (*sport*) the spinning of a ball in the opposite direction to the way it is travelling, reducing its speed on hitting a surface. ◇ See also **sidespin** and **topspin**.
backstage *adj* & *adv* **1** behind a theatre stage. **2** not seen by the public.
backstroke *n* a stroke made by a swimmer lying on his or her back.
backtrack *v* (*intr*) **1** to return the way one came. **2** to reverse one's previous opinion or course of action.
backstreet *n* a street away from a town's main streets. — *adj* illegal or secret: *a backstreet abortion*.
backup see **back up** above.
backwash *n* **1** waves washed backwards by the movement of a ship, oars, etc. through the water. **2** a repercussion.
backwater *n* **1** a pool of stagnant water connected to a river. **2** (usu. *derog*) an isolated place, not affected by what is happening in the world outside.
backwoods *n* (*pl*) **1** remote, uncleared forest. **2** a remote region. — *n* **backwoodsman**.

backgammon *n* a game for two people, played on a board, with pieces moved according to the throws of a dice. [**back** + MidE *gamen*, play]

backward *adj* **1** directed behind or towards the back. **2** less advanced than normal in mental, physical or intellectual development. **3** reluctant or shy. — *adv* **backwardly**. — *n* **backwardness**. [**back** + **-ward**]
backwards *adv* **1** towards the back or rear. **2** with one's back facing the direction one is going. **3** in reverse order. **4** in or into a worse state. — **backwards and forwards** first in one direction, and then in

the opposite direction. — **bend, fall** or **lean over backwards** (*coll*) to try extremely hard (to please someone). — **know backwards** to know thoroughly.

bacon *n* meat from the back and sides of a pig, usu. salted or smoked. [OFr]

bacteria *n* (*pl* — *sing* **bacterium**; *tech*) a group of microscopic single-celled organisms, often causing diseases. — *adj* **bacterial**. [Gr *bakterion*, little stick]

bacteriology *n* the scientific study of bacteria. — *adj* **bacteriological**. — *n* **bacteriologist**. [**bacteria + -logy**]

Bactrian camel *n* a camel with two humps, native to central Asia. ◇ See also **dromedary.** [*Bactria* in N Afghanistan]

bad *adj* ***worse***, ***worst*** **1** not good. **2** wicked; immoral. **3** naughty. **4** (**at**) not skilled or clever. **5** (**for**) harmful. **6** unpleasant; unwelcome. **7** rotten; decayed. **8** serious; severe. **9** unhealthy; injured; painful. **10** sorry, upset or ashamed. **11** not valid; worthless. **12** (*slang*) very good. — *n* **1** unpleasant events: *take the good with the bad.* **2** evil; badness. — *n* **badness**. — **go to the bad** to become morally bad. — **in a bad way** very ill or in serious trouble. — **not bad** (*coll*) quite good. — **too bad** (*coll*) unfortunate. [MidE *badde*]

bad blood or **bad feeling** *n* angry or bitter feelings.

baddy *n* ***-ies*** (*coll*) a criminal or villain, esp. in films, etc.

bad feeling see **bad blood** above.

bad language *n* swearing.

badly *adv* ***worse***, ***worst*** **1** poorly; inefficiently. **2** unfavourably. **3** severely. — **badly off** poor.

bad-tempered *adj* easily annoyed or made angry.

bade. See **bid**.

badge *n* **1** a small emblem or mark worn to show rank, membership of a society, etc. **2** any distinguishing feature or mark. [MidE *bage*]

badger *n* an animal with a grey coat and black and white stripes on its head, which lives underground and is active at night. — *v* (*tr*) to pester or worry. [Prob. **badge**, from the white mark on its forehead]

badminton *n* a game for two or four players played with rackets and a shuttlecock which is hit across a high net. [*Badminton* in Gloucester]

baffle *v* (*tr*) **1** to confuse or puzzle. **2** to hinder. — *n* a device for controlling the flow of gas, liquid or sound through an opening. — *n* **bafflement**. — *adj* **baffling**. — *adv* **bafflingly**. [Perhaps Scot, perhaps related to OFr *befe*, mockery]

BAFTA *abbrev* British Academy of Film and Television Arts.

bag *n* **1** a container made of cloth, animal skin, plastic, paper, etc., open or openable at the top, for carrying things. **2** (also **bagful**, ***-fuls***) the amount a bag contains. **3** the amount of fish or game caught. **4** (*coll offensive*) an ugly, scruffy or immoral woman. **5** (in *pl*) loose, wide-legged trousers. — *v* ***-gg-*** **1** (*tr* & *intr*; **up**) to put (something) into a bag. **2** (*tr*) to kill (game). **3** (*tr*; *coll*) to obtain or reserve (a seat, etc.). **4** (*intr*) (esp. of clothes) to hang loosely or bulge. — **bag and baggage** completely: *clear out bag and baggage*. — **bags of** (*coll*) lots of. — **in the bag** (*coll*) as good as secured or done. [MidE *bagge*]

baggy *adj* ***-ier***, ***-iest*** hanging loose or bulging. — *adv* **baggily**. — *n* **bagginess**.

bag lady *n* a homeless woman who carries all her belongings around with her in bags.

bagatelle *n* **1** a game played on a board with holes into which balls are rolled. **2** an unimportant thing. **3** a short piece of music. [Fr, from Ital *bagatella*, trick, trifle]

bagel or **beigel** *n* a hard, ring-shaped bread roll. [Yiddish *beygel*]

baggage *n* **1** a traveller's luggage. **2** the portable equipment of an army. [OFr *bagage*]

bagpipes *n* (*pl*) an instrument consisting of a bag into which air is blown through a pipe and from which air flows through other pipes to make music. — *n* **bagpiper**.

baguette *n* a long narrow French loaf. [Fr]

bah *interj* expressing displeasure or disgust.

bail[1] *n* money given to a law court to obtain a person's release, as a guarantee that he or she will return to court for trial. — *v* **bail out** (*tr*) to provide bail for. — **forfeit** or (*coll*) **jump bail** to fail to return for trial after being released on bail. — **on bail** released once bail money has been given to the court. — **put up**, **stand** or **go bail** to provide bail (for a prisoner). [OFr *bail*, custody]

bail[2] or **bale** *v* (*tr* & *intr*; **out**) to remove (water) from a (boat) with a bucket. — *v* **bail** or **bale out** (*intr*) to escape from an aeroplane by jumping out. [Fr *baille*, bucket]

bail[3] *n* one of the cross pieces laid on top of the stumps in cricket.

bailey *n* ***-eys*** the outer wall of a castle, or a courtyard within the wall. [OFr *baille*, enclosure]

Bailey bridge *n* a temporary bridge built from pieces which can be assembled quickly. [From the designer, Sir Donald *Bailey* (1901–85)]

bailiff *n* **1** esp. in England and Wales, an officer of a law court, esp. one who seizes the property of a person who has not paid money owed to the court. **2** a person who looks after property for its owner. [OFr *baillier*, to control, hand over]

bain-marie *n* a pan filled with hot water in which a container of food can be cooked gently or kept warm. [Fr, bath of Mary, prob. from the name of a supposed alchemist]

bairn *n* (*dialect*) a child. [OE *bearn*, to bear]

bait *n* **1** food put on a hook or in a trap to attract fish or animals. **2** anything intended to attract or tempt. — *v* (*tr*) **1** to put food on or in (a hook or trap). **2** to annoy, harass or tease. **3** to set dogs on (another animal). [Norse *beita*, to cause to bite]

baize *n* a usu. green woollen cloth, used e.g. on snooker tables. [OFr *baies*, chestnut-coloured]

bake *v* **1** (*tr* & *intr*) to cook (cakes, bread, vegetables, etc.) using dry heat in an oven. **2** (*tr* & *intr*) to dry or harden by heat from the sun or a fire. **3** (*intr*; *coll*) to be extremely hot. — *n* **baker**. — *n* **baking**. [OE *bacan*]

baked beans *n* (*pl*) haricot beans baked in tomato sauce.

bakehouse *n* (*old*) a bakery.

baker's dozen *n* thirteen.

bakery *n* **-ies** a place where bread, cakes, etc. are made or sold.

baking powder *n* a powder containing sodium bicarbonate, used to make cakes, etc. rise.

baking soda *n* sodium bicarbonate, used e.g. in baking powder.

Bakelite® *n* a type of hard plastic used, esp. formerly, to make dishes, buttons, etc. [L H *Baekeland* (1863–1944), its inventor]

baksheesh *n* (in some eastern countries) money given as a tip or present. [Persian]

balaclava *n* a warm knitted hat that covers the head and neck, with an opening for the face. [*Balaklava*, in the Crimea, in southern Ukraine]

balalaika *n* a Russian musical instrument with a triangular body, a neck like a guitar and usu. three strings. [Russ]

balance *n* **1** an instrument for weighing, usu. with two dishes hanging from a bar supported in the middle. **2** a state of physical stability in which the weight of a body is evenly distributed. **3** a state of mental or emotional stability. **4** a state existing when two opposite forces are equal. **5** something that is needed to create such equality. **6** the amount by which the two sides of an account (money spent and money received) differ. **7** an amount left over. **8** a device which regulates the speed of a clock or watch. — *v* **1** (*tr* & *intr*) to be or put into a state of physical balance. **2** (*tr*) to compare two or more things in one's mind. **3** (*tr*) to find the difference between money put into an account and money taken out of it, and to make them equal: *balance the books*. **4** (*intr*; **out**) to be or become equal in amount. — **in the balance** not decided. — **on balance** having taken all the advantages and disadvantages into consideration. [Lat *bilanx*, having two scales]

balanced *adj* **1** in a state of balance. **2** fair; considering all sides of an argument, etc. **3** (of a person) calm and sensible.

balance of payments *n* the difference between the amount of money coming into a country and the amount going out of it, over a period of time.

balance of power *n* the equal distribution of political or military power, with no one nation or group having supremacy. — **hold the balance of power** to be in a position where either of two equal and opposed groups, etc. can be made more powerful than the other through one's support.

balance of trade *n* the difference in value of a country's imports and exports.

balance sheet *n* a summary and balance of financial accounts.

balcony *n* **-ies** **1** a platform surrounded by a wall or railing, projecting from the wall of a building. **2** an upper tier in a theatre or cinema. [Ital *balcone*]

bald *adj* **1** (of people) having little or no hair on the head. **2** (of birds or animals) without feathers or fur. **3** bare or plain. — *n* **baldness**. [Perhaps MidE *balled*, rounded]

balding *adj* becoming bald.

baldly *adv* in a plain and often hurtful way.

balderdash *n* (*old*) nonsense.

bale[1] *n* a large bundle of cloth, hay, etc. tied with rope, etc. — *v* (*tr*) to make into bales. [OFr]

bale[2]. See **bail**[2].

baleen *n* whalebone. [Lat *balaena*, whale]

baleful *adj* **1** evil; harmful. **2** threatening; gloomy. — *adv* **balefully**. — *n* **balefulness**. [OE *bealu*, evil]

balk or **baulk** *v* **1** (*intr*; **at**) to hesitate or refuse to go on. *2* (*tr*) to check or block. [OE *balca*, ridge]

Balkan *adj* **1** of the peninsula in SE Europe, surrounded by the Adriatic, Aegean and Black seas. **2** of its peoples or countries. — *n* (in *pl*) the Balkan countries.

balkanise or **-ize** *v* (*tr*) to divide (a large country) into smaller countries which then fight against each other. — *n* **balkanisation** or **-z-**.

ball[1] *n* **1** a round or roundish object used in some sports. **2** anything round or nearly round in shape: *a snowball*. **3** the act of throwing a ball, or the way a ball is thrown. **4** a rounded, fleshy part of the body: *the ball of the foot*. **5** (usu. in *pl*; *vulg*) a testicle. ◇ See also **balls** below. — *v* (*tr* & *intr*) to form or gather into a ball. — **have the ball at one's feet** to have the opportunity to do something. **on the ball** (*coll*) well-informed; alert. — **play ball** (*coll*) to co-operate. — **start** or **set**, or **keep, the ball rolling** to begin, or continue, an activity, conversation, etc. [MidE *bal*]

ball-and-socket joint *n* a joint, esp. in the body, in which the ball-shaped end of one part fits into the cup-shaped end of the other part.

ball-bearing *n* **1** an arrangement of small steel balls between the moving parts of some machines, to help reduce friction. **2** one of these balls.

ballcock *n* a floating ball attached to a hinged rod, which controls the flow of water in e.g. a toilet's tank or cistern.

ball game *n* **1** (*NAm*) a baseball game. **2** (*coll*) a situation: *a whole new ball game*.

ballpoint or **ballpoint pen** *n* a pen with a tiny ball as the writing point.

balls *n* (*sing*; *vulg*) **1** (esp. *US*) courage or bravery. **2** (also *interj*) rubbish or nonsense. — *v* **balls up** (*tr* & *intr*; *Br vulg slang*) to make a complete mess (of something) (*n* **balls-up**).

ball[2] *n* **1** a formal social meeting for dancing. **2** (*coll*) an enjoyable time: *have a ball*. [Fr *bal*]

ballroom *n* a large hall where balls are held.

ballroom dancing *n* a formal kind of dancing, where couples dance to music with a strict rhythm.

ballad *n* **1** a slow, usu. romantic, song. **2** a poem or song with short verses, which tells a popular story. [Provençal *balada*, dance]

ballade *n* a poem consisting of verses grouped in threes, with a repeated refrain, and a final short concluding verse (an envoy). [Earlier form of **ballad**]

ballast *n* **1** heavy material used to keep a balloon or a ship without cargo steady. **2** broken rocks or stones used as a base for roads and railway lines. [Prob. OSwed *bar*, bare + *last*, load]

ballerina *n* a female ballet-dancer, esp. one taking leading roles. [Ital]

ballet *n* (a performance of) a classical style of dancing and mime, using set steps and body movements. — *n* **ballet-dancer**. [Fr, dimin. of *bal*, dance]

balletic *adj* of or like (a) ballet. — *adv* **balletically**.

ballistics *n* (*sing*) the scientific study of the flight of objects through the air, esp. bullets. — *adj* **ballistic**. [Lat *ballista*, military machine for throwing large rocks at buildings, etc.]

ballistic missile *n* a type of missile which is guided towards its target but which then drops on it under gravity.

balloon *n* **1** a small rubber bag filled with air or other gas, used e.g. as a toy. **2** a large bag, made of light material and filled with a light gas or hot air, designed to float in the air carrying people in a basket underneath. **3** an outline containing the words or thoughts of characters in a cartoon. — *v* (*intr*) **1** to swell out like a balloon. **2** to travel by balloon. — *n* **ballooning**. — *n* **balloonist**. — **go down like a lead balloon** (*coll*) (of something said or done) to be very unsuccessful or unpopular. — **when the balloon goes up** when the trouble starts. [Ital *ballone*]

ballot *n* **1** the method or act of voting, usu. in secret, by putting e.g. a marked piece of paper into a box or other container. **2** the total number of votes recorded in an election. **3** a piece of paper, etc. used in voting. — *v* **-t- 1** (*intr*) to vote by ballot. **2** (*tr*) to take a ballot of: *ballot the members*. [Ital *ballotta*, little ball]

ballot-box *n* **1** the box into which voters put their marked ballot-papers. **2** the system of voting in secret by ballot, esp. as a sign of political freedom.

ballot-paper *n* a piece of paper used for voting in a ballot.

bally *adj* (*Br old coll*) a euphemism for **bloody** (sense **4**).

ballyhoo *n* (*coll*) **1** a noisy, confused situation. **2** noisy or sensational publicity or advertising.

balm *n* **1** an oil with a pleasant smell, obtained from some trees, used in healing or reducing pain. **2** something comforting to either the body or the spirit. [OFr *basme*]

balmy[1] *adj* **-ier**, **-iest** (of the air) warm and soft. — *adv* **balmily**. — *n* **balminess**. [OFr *basme*, balm]

balmy[2] . Same as **barmy**.

baloney or **boloney** *n* (*slang*) nonsense. [Perhaps from *Bologna*, a type of sausage]

balsa *n* **1** a tropical American tree. **2** (also **balsa-wood**) the very light wood of this tree. [Span, raft]

balsam *n* **1** a pleasant-smelling, thick, sticky substance obtained from some trees and plants, used to make medicines and perfumes. **2** a tree or plant from which this substance is obtained. [Lat *balsamum*]

baluster *n* any of a series of posts or pillars supporting a rail. [Fr *balustre*]

balustrade *n* a row of posts or pillars, joined by a rail, on the edge of a balcony, staircase, bridge, etc. [Fr, from *balustre*, baluster]

bamboo *n* **1** a tall, tropical grass with hollow, jointed, woody stems. **2** the stem, used for making furniture, etc. or for food. [Prob. Malay *bambu*]

bamboozle *v* (*tr*; *coll*) **1** to trick or cheat. **2** to confuse. — *n* **bamboozlement**.

ban *n* (**on**) an official order that something may not be done. — *v* **-nn-** (*tr*) to forbid or prevent, esp. officially or formally. [OE *bannan*, to summon]

banal *adj* not original or interesting; boring. — *n* **banality**. [Fr]

banana *n* **1** a long curved fruit, yellow when ripe. **2** the large tropical tree-like plant which this fruit grows on. [From the native name in Guinea]

banana republic *n* (*derog*) a poor country whose economy is dependent on foreign money.

band[1] *n* **1** a flat, narrow strip of cloth, metal, paper, etc. used to hold things together or as a decoration. **2** a stripe of colour or strip of material different from its background or surroundings. **3** a belt for driving machinery. **4** a group or range of radio frequencies between two limits: *waveband*. **5** a range of values between two limits. — *v* (*tr*) to fasten or mark with a band. [OFr *bande*]

bandbox *n* a light, round box for holding hats.

banded *adj* marked with a stripe or stripes of a different colour.

band-saw *n* a saw which consists of a blade with teeth attached to a metal band which moves very fast around two wheels.

band[2] *n* **1** a group of people with a common purpose or interest. **2** a group of musicians who play music other than classical music: *a rock band*. — *v* (*intr* & *tr*; **together**) to unite to work for a common purpose. [OFr *bande*]

bandmaster *n* the conductor of a musical, esp. brass, band.

bandsman *n* a member of a musical, esp. brass, band.

bandstand *n* a platform with a roof, usu. in a park, where bands play music.

bandwagon: **jump** or **climb on the bandwagon** to join or show interest in a popular movement only because it is fashionable and likely to succeed.

bandage *n* a strip of cloth for winding round a wound or a broken limb. — *v* (*tr*; **up**) to wrap (a wound or a broken limb) in a bandage. [Fr]

bandana or **bandanna** *n* a large, brightly coloured cotton or silk square, folded and worn around the neck or head. [Hindi *ba(n)dhnu*, a type of dyeing]

B and B, **B & B** or **b & b** *abbrev* bed and breakfast.

bandeau *n* **-*eaux*** a narrow band of soft material worn around the head. [Fr]

banderole *n* **1** a long, narrow flag, usu. with a forked end. **2** a flat, ribbon-like band carved into a stone wall, etc. with writing on it. [Fr]

bandicoot *n* **1** a large rat-like animal found in Australia. **2** the largest type of rat, found in India and Sri Lanka. [Telugu (Indian language) *pandikokku*]

bandit *n* an armed robber, esp. a member of a gang which attacks travellers. [Ital *bandito*, outlaw]

bandoleer or **bandolier** *n* a leather shoulder belt, esp. for carrying bullets. [OFr *bandouillere*]

bandy[1] *v* **-*ies***, **-*ied*** (*tr*) **1** (**about** or **around**) to pass (a story, information, etc.) from one person to another. **2** (**about**) to mention (someone's name) in rumour: *Her name is being bandied about*. **3** (**with**) to exchange (cross words, insults, blows, etc.) with: *Don't bandy words with me!*

bandy[2] *adj* **-*ier***, **-*iest*** (of legs) curved or bending wide apart at the knee. — *adj* **bandy-legged**.

bane *n* the cause of worry, trouble or evil: *the bane of my life*. [OE *bana*, murderer]

baneful *adj* evil; causing harm.

bang[1] *n* **1** a sudden loud noise. **2** a heavy blow. **3** (*vulg slang*) an act of sexual intercourse. **4** (*slang*) an injection of an illegal drug. — *v* (*tr* & *intr*) **1** to make a loud noise by hitting, dropping, closing violently, etc. **2** (**against**, **on**, etc.) to hit sharply, esp. by accident. **3** to (cause to) make the sound of an explosion. **4** (*vulg slang*) to have sexual intercourse with (someone). — *adv* (*coll*) **1** exactly: *bang on time*. **2** suddenly. — *v* **bang away** (*intr*; *coll*) **1** to make a continual noise. **2** (**at**) to work very hard. — **go (off) with a bang** to be a great success. [Norse *banga*, to hammer]

banger *n* **1** (*coll*) a sausage. **2** (*coll*) an old car, usu. in poor condition and often noisy. **3** a loud firework.

bang[2] *n* (*US*; usu. in *pl*) hair cut in a straight line across the forehead.

bangle *n* a piece of jewellery in the form of a solid band, worn round the arm or leg. [Hindi *bangri*, glass ring]

banian. See **banyan**.

banish *v* (*tr*) **1** to send (someone) away from a place, usu. his or her own country. **2** to put (thoughts, etc.) out of one's mind. — *n* **banishment**. [OFr *bannir*]

banister or **bannister** *n* (usu. in *pl*) a row of posts and the hand-rail they support, running up the side of a staircase. [**baluster**]

banjo *n* **-*os*** or **-*oes*** a stringed musical instrument with a long neck and a round body, played like a guitar. — *n* **banjoist**. [Prob. of African origin]

bank[1] *n* **1** a long raised pile of earth, snow, etc. **2** the side or slope of a hill. **3** the ground at the edge of a river, lake, etc. **4** a raised area of sand under the sea. **5** a mass (of cloud, mist or fog). — *v* **1** (*tr* & *intr*; **up**) to form into a bank or banks. **2** (*tr*; **up**) to cover (a fire) with a large amount of coal to keep it burning. **3** (*intr* & *tr*) (of an aircraft) to (cause to) move in a curve, with one wing higher than the other. [MidE *banke*]

bank[2] *n* **1** (the building used by) an organisation which keeps money in accounts for its clients, lends money, etc. **2** a box in which money can be saved, esp. by children. **3** a place where something is stored or collected for later use: *blood bank*. **4** in some games, a stock of money controlled by one of the players (the banker). — *v* **1** (*tr*) to put (money) into a bank. **2** (*intr*; **with**) to have a bank account. **3** (*intr* with **on**) to rely on or expect. [Fr *banque*]

bank account *n* an arrangement by which a person or company keeps money in a bank and takes it out when needed.

bank book *n* a book recording the amounts of money put into, or taken out of, a bank account.

bank card or **banker's card** same as **cheque card**.

bank draft *n* a written order sent from a bank to another bank for paying money to a customer.

banker *n* **1** a person who owns or manages a bank. **2** a person in charge of the bank in some games.

banker's order see **standing order**.

bank holiday *n* (in Britain) any one of several days in the year on which banks are closed, observed as a public holiday in England and Wales.
banking *n* the business done by a bank.
banknote *n* a piece of paper money issued by a bank.

bank[3] *n* a collection of similar things arranged in rows. [OFr *banc*, bench]

bankrupt *n* a person who is legally recognised as not being able to pay his or her debts. — *adj* **1** not having money to pay one's debts. **2 (of)** without; lacking: *bankrupt of ideas*. — *v (tr)* to make bankrupt. — *n* **bankruptcy**, **-*ies***. [Fr *banqueroute*, altered under the influence of Lat *banca rupta*, bank broken]

banner *n* **1** a large piece of cloth or cardboard, with a design, slogan, etc. carried e.g. at public meetings and parades. **2** a military flag. [OFr *baniere*]
banner headline *n* a newspaper headline written in large letters across the whole width of the page.

bannock *n (dialect)* a small, flat, round cake usu. made from oatmeal. [OE *bannuc*]

banns *n (pl)* a public announcement in church of two people's intention to marry. [OE *bannan*, to summon]

banquet *n* **1** a sumptuous formal dinner. **2** a sumptuous meal. — *v* **-*t*-** *(tr & intr)* to entertain with or take part in a banquet. [Fr]

banshee *n* esp. in Irish and Scottish stories, a female spirit whose sad cries outside a house warn that a member of the family will die. [Irish Gaelic *bean sidhe*, woman of the fairies]

bantam *n* **1** a small breed of farm chicken. **2** a small but forceful person. [Prob. *Bantam* in Java, from where such chickens may have been first imported]
bantamweight *n* **1** a class for boxers, wrestlers and weight-lifters of not more than a specified weight (53·5 kg in professional boxing, slightly more in the other sports). **2** a boxer, etc. of this weight. — *n adj* (for contestants) of this weight.

banter *n* friendly, joking talk. — *v* **-*r*-** *(intr)* to tease or joke. — *adj & n* **bantering**.

Bantu *n* **1** a group of languages spoken in southern and central Africa. **2** *(pl)* the group of peoples who speak these languages. **3** *(offensive)* (esp. in S Africa) a Black speaker of one of these languages. — *adj* of the Bantu languages or Bantu-speaking people. [Bantu, people]

Bantustan *n* (often considered *offensive*) any of the partially self-governing regions reserved for Black South Africans. [**Bantu** + *-stan* as in Hindustan]

banyan or **banian** *n* an Indian fruit tree with branches from which shoots grow down into the ground and take root. [Port *banian*, from Gujarati (Indian language) *vaniyo*, man of the trading caste]

baobab *n* a huge tropical African tree with a very thick trunk and large, round, soft fruit. [Prob. from an African language]

baptise or **-ize** *v (tr)* **1** to dip in or sprinkle with water as a sign of having become a member of the Christian church; in the case of babies, usu. accompanied by name-giving. **2** to give a name to. [Gr *baptizein*, to immerse]
baptism *n* the religious ceremony of baptising a person. — *adj* **baptismal**. —
baptism of fire *n* **1** a soldier's first experience of battle. **2** a difficult or frightening first experience of something.
baptist *n* **1** a person who baptises, esp. *(cap)* John the Baptist. **2** *(cap)* a member of a Christian group which believes that only people who are able to profess their religious beliefs should be baptised into the church, and that they should be completely dipped in water.
baptistery or **baptistry** *n* **-*ies*** **1** the part of a church where baptisms are carried out. **2** a tank of water for baptisms in a Baptist church.

bar[1] *n* **1** a block of some solid substance: *bar of soap*. **2** a rod or long piece of a strong rigid material: *bars on the windows to prevent burglary*; *a five-bar gate*. **3 (to)** anything that prevents or hinders: *a bar to progress*. **4** a line or band of colour, light, etc., esp. a stripe on a shield. **5** a room or counter in a restaurant, hotel, etc., or a separate establishment, where alcoholic drinks are sold and drunk. **6** *(in cmpds)* a small café where drinks and snacks are served: *a coffee bar*. **7** *(in cmpds)* a counter where some special service is available: *a heel bar*. **8** a vertical line marked on music, dividing it into sections of equal value; one of these sections. **9** the rail in a law court where the accused person stands. **10** *(cap* with **the)** (the profession of) barristers and advocates. **11** a raised area of sand, mud, stones, etc. at the mouth of a river or harbour. **12** an addition to a medal, usu. to show that it has been won twice: *DSO and bar*. — *v* **-*rr*-** *(tr)* **1** to fasten with a bar. **2 (from)** to forbid (someone) to enter. **3** to prevent (progress). **4** to mark with a stripe or bar. — *prep* except. — **be called to the Bar** to be made a barrister. — **behind bars** in prison. [OFr *barre*]
barbell *n* a bar with heavy metal weights at each end, used for exercising one's muscles.
bar chart or **bar graph** *n* a graph which shows values or amounts by means of vertical bars. ◇ See also **pie chart**.
bar code *n* an arrangement of thick and thin lines on the cover or wrapping of products in shops, containing information on price, size, etc. which can be read by a computer.
barmaid, **barman** or **barperson** (*US* **bartender**) *n* a person who serves drinks in a bar.
barred *adj* **1** having bars. **2** closed off; blocked.

barring *prep* except for; leaving out of consideration: *barring accidents.*

bar[2] *n* a unit of (esp. atmospheric) pressure, 10^5 newtons per square metre. ◇ See also **millibar**. [Gr *baros*, weight]

barb *n* **1** a point on a hook facing in the opposite direction to the main point, which makes it difficult to pull the hook out. **2** a humorous but hurtful remark. — *v* (*tr*) to fit with barbs. — *adj* **barbed.** [Lat *barba*, beard]

barbed wire *n* wire with short, sharp points twisted on at intervals, used for making fences, etc.

barbarian *n* & *adj* **1** (a person who is) coarse, cruel, rough and wild in behaviour. **2** (a person who is) uncivilised and uncultured. [Gr *barbaros*, foreign]

barbaric *adj* **1** cruel and brutal. **2** coarse and rude. — *adv* **barbarically.**

barbarism *n* **1** the state of being uncivilised, coarse, etc. **2** a coarse or ignorant act. **3** something said which is considered coarse or not grammatically correct.

barbarity *n* **-ies 1** the state of being cruel, coarse, uncivilised, rude, etc. **2** a cruel, coarse, uncivilised or rude act.

barbarous *adj* **1** uncultured and uncivilised. **2** extremely cruel or brutal. **3** coarse or rude. — *adv* **barbarously.** — *n* **barbarousness.**

barbecue *n* **1** a metal frame, etc. on which food is grilled over an open fire. **2** food cooked in this way. **3** a party held out of doors at which food is cooked on a barbecue. — *v* (*tr*) to cook on a barbecue. [Arawak (S American language) *barbacòa*, framework of sticks]

barbel *n* **1** a long beard-like growth at the mouth of some fishes. **2** a type of fish with such growths. [Lat *barba*, beard]

barbell. See **bar.**

barber *n* a person who cuts and styles men's hair, and shaves their beards. [OFr *barbeor*, from Lat *barba*, beard]

barbershop *n* a type of singing in which four men sing in close harmony without musical accompaniment.

barberry *n* **-ies** a bushy plant or shrub with thorns, yellow flowers and red berries. [Lat *berberis*]

barbican *n* a tower over the outer gate of a castle or town, allowing the gate to be defended. [OFr *barbacane*]

barbiturate *n* a drug used to calm one's nerves or make one sleep.

barcarole or **barcarolle** *n* a gondolier's song, or a piece of music with the same rhythm as one. [Ital *barcarola*, boat-song]

bard *n* **1** (*literary*) a poet. **2** a poet who has won a prize at the Eisteddfod in Wales. — *adj* **bardic.** [Scots Gaelic *bàrd* and Irish Gaelic *bard*, poet]

bare *adj* **1** not covered by clothes; naked. **2** without the usual or natural covering: *bare trees.* **3** empty: *The cupboard was bare.* **4** simple; plain: *the bare facts.* **5** basic; essential: *the bare necessities.* — *v* (*tr*) to uncover. — *n* **bareness.** — **bare one's heart** or **soul** to make known one's private thoughts and feelings. — **lay bare** to make known (a secret, etc.). — **with one's bare hands** without weapons or tools. [OE *bær*]

bareback *adv* & *adj* on a horse without a saddle.

bare bones *n* (*pl*) the basic, essential facts.

barefaced *adj* without shame or regret. — *adv* **barefacedly.**

barefoot and **barefooted** *adj* & *adv* not wearing shoes or socks.

bareheaded *adj* & *adv* not wearing a hat.

barelegged *adj* & *adv* with the legs not covered by trousers, tights or socks.

barely *adv* **1** scarcely or only just: *barely enough.* **2** plainly, simply: *barely furnished.*

bargain *n* **1** an agreement made between people buying and selling things, offering and accepting services, etc.: *strike a bargain.* **2** something offered for sale, or bought, at a low price. — *v* (*intr*; **with, for**) to discuss the terms for buying or selling, etc. — *n* **bargainer.** — *v* **bargain for** (*tr*) to expect or be prepared for. — *v* **bargain on** (*tr*) to rely on or expect. — **drive a hard bargain** to enter into an agreement only after bargaining hard to achieve the greatest benefit to oneself. — **into the bargain** in addition; besides. [OFr *bargaine*]

barge *n* **1** a long, flat-bottomed boat used on rivers and canals. **2** a large boat, often decorated, used in ceremonies, celebrations, etc. — *v* **1** (*intr*; **about, around**) to move in a clumsy, ungraceful way. **2** (*intr* with **in, into**) to hit or knock. **3** (*intr* & *tr*; **past, through**) to make (one's way) rudely or roughly. **4** (*intr* with **in, into**) to interrupt a conversation, esp. rudely or awkwardly. [OFr, from Lat *barga*]

bargee *n* a person in charge of a barge.

bargepole *n* a long pole used to move or guide a barge. — **not touch with a bargepole** (*coll*) to refuse to have anything to do with (a person or a thing).

baritone *n* **1** the second lowest male singing voice, between bass and tenor. **2** a singer with such a voice. **3** in music, a part written for such a voice. [Gr *barytonos*, deep-sounding]

barium *n* an element (symbol **Ba**), a soft, silver-coloured metal. [Gr *barys*, heavy]

barium meal *n* a mixture containing barium sulphate which a person drinks before having an x-ray taken of his or her stomach, intestines, etc., to make the x-ray clearer.

bark[1] *n* the short, sharp cry of a dog, fox, etc. — *v* **1** (*intr*) to make this sound. **2** (*tr* & *intr*; **out**) to say or speak loudly and sharply: *bark out commands.* — **bark up the wrong tree** (*coll*) to have the wrong idea. [OE *beorcan*]

barker *n* a person outside a circus, show, etc. who shouts to attract customers.

bark[2] *n* the tough covering of the trunk and branches of a tree. — *v (tr)* **1** to scrape or rub off the skin from (one's leg). **2** to strip or remove the bark from (a tree, etc.). [Norse *börkr*]

bark[3]. See **barque**.

barley *n* **1** a tall, grass-like plant, grown for its grain. **2** (also **barleycorn**) the grain of this plant, used for food and for making beer and whisky. [OE *bærlic*, of barley]

barley sugar *n* a kind of hard, orange-coloured sweet, made by melting and cooling sugar.

barley water *n* a drink made from water in which barley has been boiled, usu. with orange or lemon juice added.

pearl barley *n* grains of barley without the outer husk.

bar mitzvah *n* **1** a Jewish ceremony in which a usu. thirteen-year-old boy formally accepts full religious responsibilities. **2** a boy for whom this ceremony is conducted. [Hebr, son of the law]

barmy *adj* **-ier**, **-iest** (*coll*) crazy. [Orig. bubbling or fermenting, from OE *beorma*, froth on fermenting liquor]

barn *n* **1** a building in which grain, hay, etc. is stored, or for cattle, etc. **2** a large, bare building. [OE *bere*, barley + *ærn*, house]

barn dance *n* **1** a kind of party at which there is music and country dancing, orig. held in a barn. **2** a particular kind of country dance.

barnyard *n* the area around a barn.

barnacle *n* a small shellfish that sticks to rocks and ships' bottoms. [OFr *bernaque*]

barney *n* **-eys** (*coll*) a rough, noisy quarrel.

barnstorm *v* (*intr*) **1** to tour a country, stopping briefly in each town to give theatrical performances. **2** (*NAm*) to travel about the country making political speeches just before an election. — *n* **barnstormer**.

barograph *n* a type of barometer which keeps a printed record of the changes in the pressure of the atmosphere. [Gr *baros*, weight + *graphein*, to write]

barometer *n* **1** an instrument which measures the pressure of the atmosphere, used to predict likely changes in the weather. **2** anything that indicates a change: *a barometer of public opinion*. — *adj* **barometric**. — *adv* **barometrically**. [Gr *baros*, weight + *metron*, measure]

baron *n* **1** a man holding the lowest rank of nobility. **2** a powerful businessman: *an oil baron*. — *adj* **baronial**. [Lat *baro*, man]

baroness *n* **1** a baron's wife. **2** a woman holding the title of baron in her own right.

barony *n* **-ies** the rank of, or land belonging to, a baron.

baronet *n* in the UK, (a man holding) a title below that of baron. [Dimin. of **baron**]

baronetcy *n* **-ies** the rank or title of a baronet.

baroque *n* a bold, complex, decorative style of architecture, art, decoration and music, popular in Europe from the late 16th to the early 18th century. — *adj* in such a style. [Fr, from Port *barroco*, irregularly shaped pearl]

barque or **bark** *n* **1** a small sailing ship with three masts. **2** (*literary*) any boat or small ship. [Fr *barque*, from Lat *barca*, small boat]

barrack[1] *n* (usu. in *pl*) a building or buildings for housing soldiers. — *v* (*tr*) to house soldiers in barracks. [Fr *baraque*]

barrack[2] *v* (*tr & intr*) to shout and laugh rudely at (a speaker, sports team, etc.). — *n* **barracking**.

barracuda *n* **-da** or **-das** a large tropical sea fish which feeds on other fish and sometimes attacks people. [Span]

barrage *n* **1** a long burst of gunfire which keeps an enemy back while soldiers move forward. **2** a large number (of questions, criticisms, etc.) coming in quickly one after the other. **3** a man-made barrier across a river. [Fr, from *barrer*, to block]

barrage balloon *n* a large balloon, attached to the ground by a cable and often with a net hanging from it, used to prevent attack by low-flying aircraft.

barre *n* a rail, fixed to a wall at waist level, which ballet dancers use to balance themselves while exercising. [Fr]

barrel *n* **1** a large round container, with a flat top and bottom and curving out in the middle, usu. made of planks of wood held together with metal bands. **2** (also **barrelful**, **-fuls**) the amount a barrel will hold. **3** a measure of capacity, esp. of industrial oil. **4** the long, hollow, tube-shaped part of a gun, pen, etc. — *v* **-ll-** (*tr*) to put in barrels. — **have someone over a barrel** to be in a position to get whatever one wants from someone. [OFr *baril*]

barrel-chested *adj* (of a person) with a large, round chest.

barrel organ *n* a large instrument which plays music when a handle is turned.

barren *adj* **1** (of women) not able to have children. **2** not able to produce crops, fruit, etc: *barren land*. **3** not producing results. **4** dull. — *n* **barrenness**. [OFr *brahaigne*]

barricade *n* a barrier made of anything which can be piled up quickly, e.g. to block a street. — *v* (*tr*) **1** to block or defend with a barricade. **2** (**in**) to shut (e.g. oneself) away behind a barrier. [Fr *barricade*, from *barrique*, barrel; barricades were often made from barrels]

barrier *n* **1** a fence, gate, bar, etc. put up to defend, block, protect, separate, etc. **2** any thing, circumstance, etc. that separates things, people, etc.: *a language barrier*. [OFr *barriere*]

barrier cream *n* cream used to protect the skin, esp. on the hands, from damage or infection.

barrier reef *n* a long, narrow, coral reef separated from the shore by a deep channel of water.

barrister *n* in England and Wales, a lawyer qualified to act for someone in the higher law courts. ◇ See also **advocate**, **solicitor**. [Lat *barra*, bar]

barrow[1] *n* **1** a small one-wheeled cart used to carry tools, earth, etc. **2** a larger cart, with two or four wheels, from which goods are often sold in the street. [OE *bearwe*, bier]

barrow boy *n* a man who sells goods from a barrow.

barrow[2] *n* (*archaeol*) a large pile of earth over an ancient grave. [OE *beorg*, hill]

Bart *abbrev* Baronet.

barter *v* (*tr* & *intr*) to trade or exchange (goods or services) without using money. — *n* trade by exchanging goods rather than selling them for money. — *n* **barterer**. [OFr *barater*, to trick or cheat]

baryon *n* (*physics*) one of the particles which makes up the internal structure of an atom, and which decays into a proton. [Gr *barys*, heavy]

basal *adj* of, at or forming a base.

basalt *n* a dark-coloured, volcanic rock. — *adj* **basaltic**. [Gr *basanites*]

base[1] *n* **1** the lowest part or bottom; the part which supports something or on which something stands. **2** the origin, root, or foundation (of something). **3** the headquarters or centre of activity or operations. **4** a starting point. **5** the main part of a mixture: *Rice is the base of this dish.* **6** (*chem*) a substance which combines with an acid to form a salt. **7** (*baseball*, etc.) one of several fixed points which players run between. **8** the number which is the starting point for a system of counting: *The base of the decimal system is ten.* **9** (*geom*) the side a figure is regarded as standing on. — *v* (*tr*) **1** (with **on**, **upon**) to make or use as the base. **2** to give as a headquarters or centre of operations: *troops based in France*. [Lat *basis*, pedestal]

baseball *n* **1** a game played with a bat and ball by two teams of nine people, in which the person batting may score a point (or run) by running round a pitch marked with four bases. **2** the ball used in this game.

baseless *adj* having no cause or foundation: *baseless fears*.

baseline *n* **1** one of the two lines which mark the ends of a tennis court. **2** an amount or value taken as a basis for comparison.

base rate *n* the rate used by a bank to fix its charges for lending money to customers.

base[2] *adj* **1** lacking morals; wicked. **2** not pure. **3** low in value. — *adv* **basely**. — *n* **baseness**. [Lat *bassus*, low, short]

base metal *n* any metal other than the precious metals, e.g. iron, tin, copper.

basement *n* the lowest floor of a building, usu. below ground level.

bases. *pl* of **base**[1] and of **basis**.

bash *v* (*coll*) **1** (*tr*) to strike or smash bluntly. **2** (*tr*; **up**) to attack violently. **3** (*tr*; **down**, **in**) to damage or break by striking very hard. **4** (*intr* with **into**) to crash into. — *n* **1** a heavy blow or knock. **2** a mark caused by a heavy blow. **3** (*coll*; **at**) an attempt: *have a bash at singing*. **4** (*slang*) a noisy party.

-bashing *in cmpds* (*coll*) **1** making strong, and usu. unjustified, physical or verbal attacks on a person or group of people one dislikes: *union-bashing*. **2** any of various other activities: *Bible-bashing* (i.e. enthusiastic evangelical Christian preaching); *spud-bashing* (i.e. potato-peeling).

bashful *adj* lacking confidence; shy. — *adv* **bashfully**. — *n* **bashfulness**. [OFr *abaissier*, to bring low]

BASIC *n* a computer programming language which uses everyday words. [*B*eginner's *A*ll-purpose *S*ymbolic *I*nstruction *C*ode]

basic *adj* **1** of, or forming, the base or basis. **2** of or at a very simple or low level. **3** without additions: *basic pay*. — *n* (usu. in *pl*) the essential part(s) or facts or the simplest principle(s). [Lat *basis*, pedestal]

basically *adv* mostly, essentially; described in simple or general terms.

basil *n* a small, sweet-smelling herb, used in cooking. [OFr *basile*, from Gr *basilikon*, royal]

basilica *n* **1** an ancient Roman public hall, with a rounded wall at one end and a row of stone pillars along each side, used as a lawcourt. **2** a church shaped like this. [Gr *basilike*, hall]

basilisk *n* **1** in legends, a snake which can kill people by breathing on them or looking at them. **2** a type of lizard found in S America. [Gr *basiliskos*, prince]

basin *n* **1** a wide, open dish, esp. for holding water. **2** a bowl or sink in a bathroom, etc. for washing oneself in. **3** (also **basinful**, **-*fuls***) the amount a basin holds. **4** a valley or area of land drained by a river, or streams running into a river. **5** the deep part of a harbour. [Lat *bacinum*, water vessel]

basis *n* ***bases*** **1** a principle on which an idea, theory, etc. is based. **2** a starting point: *a basis for discussion*. **3** the main part of a mixture. [Lat *basis*, pedestal]

bask *v* (*intr*) **1** to lie (in warmth or sunshine). **2** to enjoy and take great pleasure: *basking in her approval*. [Norse *bathask*, to bathe]

basket *n* **1** a container made of strips of wood or cane, woven together. **2** (also **basketful**, **-*fuls***) the amount contained by a basket. **3** one of two nets into which the ball is thrown in basketball. **4** a goal scored in basketball.

basketball *n* **1** a game in which two teams of five players score by throwing a ball into a net on a high post at each end of the court. **2** the ball used in this game.

basket chair *n* a chair made from strips of wood or cane woven together.

basketwork *n* (the art of making) articles made of strips of wood or cane woven together.
basketry *n* the art of making baskets.

Basque *n* **1** a member of a people living in the western Pyrenees, in Spain and France. **2** the language spoken by these people. — *adj* of the Basque people or their language. [Fr]

basque *n* a tight-fitting garment for women, covering the body between the shoulders and the hips.

bas-relief *n* a technique of cutting and shaping stone or wood so that the figures on it are only slightly raised from the background. [Ital *basso rilievo*, low relief]

bass[1] *n* **1** the lowest male singing voice. **2** a singer with such a voice. **3** in music, a part written for such a voice or for an instrument of the lowest range. **4** (*coll*) a double bass or bass guitar. [Lat *bassus*, low]
bass clef *n* a sign at the beginning of a piece of written music which places the note F below middle C on the fourth line of the staff.
bass drum *n* a large drum that produces a very low sound.
bass guitar *n* (also **bass**) in popular music, an electric guitar which plays the bass part.
bassist *n* a person who plays a bass guitar or double bass.

bass[2] *n* ***bass*** or (*rare*) ***basses*** a type of fish found in rivers and seas, often used as food. [OE *bærs*, perch]

basset or **basset hound** *n* a type of dog with a long body, smooth hair, short legs, and very long ears. [Fr *bas*, low]

bassinet *n* a baby's basket-like bed or pram, usu. covered at one end. [Dimin. of Fr *bassin*, basin]

bassoon *n* a woodwind instrument which produces a very low sound. — *n* **bassoonist**. [Ital *basso*, low]

bast *n* threads of the soft inner bark of some trees, woven together and used to make ropes, mats, etc. [OE *bæst*]

bastard *n* **1** (usu. considered *offensive*) a child born of parents not married to each other. **2** (*vulg*) a very unpleasant (usu. male) person. **3** (*vulg slang*) any (usu. male) person for whom one feels sympathy or affection. **4** (*vulg slang*) something annoying or difficult. — *adj* **1** born to parents not married to each other. **2** not genuine, standard, original or pure. [Lat *bastardus*]
bastardise or **-ize** *v* (*tr*) to make less genuine or pure. — *n* **bastardisation** or **-z-**. — *adj* **bastardised** or **-z-**.
bastardy *n* the state of being a bastard.

baste[1] *v* (*tr*) to pour hot fat or butter over (esp. roasting meat).

baste[2] *v* (*tr*) to sew with temporary, loose, long stitches. [Ger *basten*, to sew]

bastinado *n* ***-oes*** beating of the soles of the feet with a stick as torture or punishment. — *v* ***-oes***, ***-oed*** (*tr*) to beat on the soles of the feet with a stick. [Span *bastonada*, from *bastón*, stick]

bastion *n* **1** a kind of tower which sticks out at an angle from a castle wall. **2** a person, place or thing regarded as a defender of a principle, etc. [Ital *bastire*, to build]

bat[1] *n* **1** a shaped piece of wood, with a flat or curved surface, for hitting the ball in cricket, baseball, table-tennis, etc. ◇ See also **racket**. **2** a batsman, esp. in cricket. — *v* ***-tt-*** **1** (*intr*) to take a turn at hitting a ball with a bat in cricket, baseball, etc. **2** (*tr*) to hit with, or as if with, a bat. — **off one's own bat 1** without help. **2** without being prompted by anyone else. [OE *batt*]
batman see separate entry.
batsman or **batswoman** *n* a man, or woman, who bats, esp. in cricket. ◇ See also **batter** below.
batter *n* a person who bats, esp. in baseball. ◇ See also **batsman** above.

bat[2] *n* a mouse-like animal with wings, active at night. — **have bats in the belfry** (*coll*) to be crazy or slightly mad. ◇ See also **bats** and **batty**. — **like a bat out of hell** (*coll*) very fast. [MidE *bakke*]

bat[3] *v* ***-tt-*** (*tr*) to open and close (one's eyelids) very quickly, usu. to attract sympathy or admiration. — **not bat an eye** or **eyelid** (*coll*) to show no surprise or emotion. [MidE *baten*, to flap]

batch *n* a number of things or people prepared, delivered, dealt with, etc. at the same time. — *v* (*tr*) to arrange in batches. [MidE *bache*, from OE *bacan*, to bake]
batch processing *n* a computer system which allows several batches of similar information to be processed by a single computer at the same time.

bated : **with bated breath** feeling anxiety, excitement or fear. [**abate**]

Bath: **Bath bun** *n* a small, sweet cake. [*Bath*, city in Avon]
Bath chair *n* (esp. *formerly*) a kind of chair with three wheels in which an invalid can be pushed.

bath *n* **1** a large open container for water, in which to wash the whole body. **2** an act of washing the body in a bath. **3** the water filling a bath: *run a bath*. **4** (in *pl*) a public swimming pool. **5** (a container of) a liquid in which something is washed, etc., usu. as part of a technical process such as developing photographs. — *v* (*tr & intr*) to wash in a bath. [OE *bæth*]
bathcube *n* a small block of bath salts.
bathrobe *n* a loose towelling coat.
bathroom *n* **1** a room in a house which contains a bath. **2** a toilet.
bath salts *n* (*pl*) a sweet-smelling substance in the form of large grains, which perfumes and softens the water in a bath.

bathe *v* **1** (*intr*) to swim in the sea, etc. for pleasure. **2** (*intr*; esp. *US*) to have a bath. **3** (*tr*) to wash or treat (part of the body) with water, a liquid, etc. to clean it or to lessen pain. **4** (*tr*; **in**) to cover and surround (e.g. in light). — *n* an act of swimming in the sea, etc. — *n* **bather**. [OE *bathian*, to wash]

bathing cap *n* a tight rubber cap worn to keep one's hair dry when swimming.

bathing costume *n* a swimming costume or swimsuit.

bathos *n* (*literary*) in speech or writing, a sudden change from very important, serious or beautiful ideas to very ordinary or silly ones. — *adj* **bathetic**. [Gr, depth]

bathyscaphe *n* a vessel for deep-sea diving. [Gr *bathys*, deep + *skaphos*, ship]

bathysphere *n* a large, round, steel container, lowered deep into the sea to allow a person to observe sea animals, plants, etc. [Gr *bathys*, deep + **sphere**]

batik *n* **1** a way of printing coloured patterns on cloth, where those parts not to be coloured or dyed are covered with wax. **2** cloth coloured in this way. [Malay]

batman *n* **-*men*** an officer's personal servant in the armed forces. [Fr *bat*, pack-saddle]

baton *n* **1** a light, thin stick used by the conductor of an orchestra. **2** a short, heavy stick, carried by a policeman as a weapon. ◇ See also **truncheon. 3** a short stick passed from one runner to another in a relay race. **4** a stick carried by a person at the head of a marching band. [Fr *bâton*, stick]

bats *adj* (*coll*) crazy. [From the phrase *have bats in the belfry*]

batsman, batswoman. See **bat**[1].

battalion *n* an army unit made up of several smaller units (companies), and forming part of a larger unit (a brigade). [Fr *bataillon*, from Ital *battaglione*, squadron of soldiers]

batten *n* **1** a long, flat piece of wood used for keeping other pieces in place. **2** a strip of wood used to fasten the covers over the hatches in a ship's deck, etc. — *v* (*tr*) to fasten or shut with battens. — **batten down the hatches** to prepare for a crisis. [OFr *batre*, to beat]

batter[1] *v* ***-r-*** **1** (*tr* & *intr*) to strike or hit hard and often, or continuously: *wind battering against the door*. **2** (*tr* with **down, in**) to break down or to destroy by battering. **3** (*tr*) to damage or wear through continual use. — *n* **battering**. [OFr *batre*, to beat]

battered *adj* (of a person) frequently severely beaten by another person: *battered baby/wife*.

battering-ram *n* a large wooden beam with a metal head used, esp. formerly, in war for breaking down walls or gates.

batter[2] *n* eggs, flour and usu. either milk or water, beaten together and used in cooking. [OFr *bateure*, beating]

batter[3]. See **bat**[1].

battery *n* ***-ies*** **1** a small container (cell) holding chemicals which produce or store electricity, or a container of two or more such cells. **2** a number of similar things: *a battery of questions*. **3** a long line of small cages in which e.g. hens are kept. **4** (*legal*) a physical attack on a person. ◇ See also **assault and battery**. **5** a group of heavy guns and the place where they are mounted. [Fr *batterie*, from *battre*, to strike]

battle *n* **1** a fight between opposing armies or people. **2** a competition between opposing groups or people: *a battle of wits*. **3** a long or difficult struggle: *a battle for equality*. — *v* (*intr*) **1** to fight. **2** (**against, for, through, with**, etc.) to struggle. — **do battle** to fight. — **fight a losing battle** to try to do something which is sure to fail. — **half the battle** something that takes one well on the way to success. — **join battle** to begin to fight. [Fr *bataille*]

battle-axe *n* **1** an axe used, esp. formerly, in war. **2** (*coll*) a severe, unfriendly, bossy woman.

battle-cruiser *n* a large warship, the same size as a battleship but faster and with fewer guns.

battle-cry *n* **1** a shout given by soldiers charging into battle. **2** a slogan.

battledress *n* a soldier's ordinary uniform.

battle or **combat fatigue** *n* a usu. temporary mental disorder caused by the anxiety of fighting for a long time.

battleship *n* the largest type of warship.

battlement *n* a low wall around the top of a castle, etc. with gaps for shooting through. [OFr *bataillier*, to provide with ramparts]

batty *adj* ***-ier, -iest*** (*coll*) crazy. — *n* **battiness**. [**bat**[2]]

bauble *n* a small, cheap ornament or piece of jewellery. [OFr *babel*, a child's toy]

baulk. See **balk**.

bauxite *n* a substance like clay, the main source of aluminium. [*Les Baux* in southern France, where it was first found]

bawdy *adj* ***-ier, -iest*** (of language, writing, etc.) containing coarse but usu. humorous references to sex. — *adv* **bawdily**. — *n* **bawdiness**. [OFr *baude*, dissolute]

bawl *v* (*intr* & *tr*; **out**) to cry or shout loudly. — *v* **bawl out** (*tr*; *coll*) to scold angrily. [Lat *baulare*, to bark]

bay[1] *n* (the sea in) a wide inward bend of a coastline. [OFr *baie*]

bay[2] *n* **1** a small area of a room set back into a wall. **2** an area for parking, or loading and unloading, vehicles. **3** a compartment for storing or carrying. **4** an enclosed or partly enclosed area within a building for storage or some other purpose. [OFr *baer*, to gape]

bay window *n* a three-sided or rounded window that sticks out from the wall of a building. ◇ See also **bow window**.

bay[3] *adj* (of a horse) reddish-brown in colour. — *n* a bay-coloured horse. [OFr *bai*, chestnut-coloured]

bay[4] *n* **1** a type of laurel tree, with dark green shiny leaves. **2** (usu. in *pl*) a wreath of bay leaves, usu. worn on the head by champions in some competitions, etc. [OFr *baie*]

bay[5] *v (intr) & n* (of a dog) (to make) a deep bark or cry, esp. when hunting. — **at bay 1** not able to escape, forced to face an attacker. **2** at a distance: *keep poverty at bay*. — **bring to bay** to trap. [OFr *abai*, barking]

bayonet *n* a steel knife fixed to the end of a soldier's rifle. — *v* **-t-** *(tr)* to stab with a bayonet. [Fr *baïonnette*, from *Bayonne* in SW France, where bayonets were first made]

bayou *n* in the US, a marshy offshoot of a lake or river. [Louisiana Fr]

bazaar *n* **1** (in Eastern countries) a market place. **2** a sale of goods, etc., usu. in order to raise money for a particular organisation or purpose. [Persian *bazar*, market]

bazooka *n* a gun which fires small rockets, esp. at tanks. [From the name of a toy wind-instrument]

BB *abbrev* **1** Boys' Brigade. **2** (on pencils) very black.

BBC *abbrev* British Broadcasting Corporation.

BC or **B.C.** *abbrev* **1** before (the birth of) Christ. ◇ See also **AD**. **2** British Columbia.

BCG or **bcg** *abbrev* bacillus Calmette-Guérin, the vaccine given to a person to prevent him or her catching tuberculosis.

BCom. or **BComm**. *abbrev* Bachelor of Commerce.

BD *abbrev* Bachelor of Divinity.

Be *symbol (chem)* beryllium.

be *v present tense* ***am***, ***are***, ***is***; *past tense* ***was***, ***were***; *past participle* **been** *(intr)* **1** to exist or live: *I think, therefore I am*. **2** to occur or take place: *Lunch is in an hour*. **3** to occupy a position in space: *She is at home*. **4** (in past tense) to go: *He's never been to Italy*. **5** to remain or continue without change: *Let it be*. **6** used to link a subject and what is said about it: *She is a doctor. He is ill.* **7** *(intr)* used with the infinitive form of a verb to express a possibility, command, intention, outcome, etc.: *if it were to rain. We are to come tomorrow. It was not to be.* — *v (aux)* **1** used with the past participle of a verb to form a passive: *The film was shown last night*. **2** used with a present participle to form the continuous tenses: *He was running*. — **the be-all and end-all** the only thing of importance. — **be that as it may** although that may be true. [Present tense from OE *beon*, to live or exist; past tense from OE *weran*, to be]

being *n* **1** existence; life. **2** any living person or thing.

-to-be *in cmpds* of the future: *a mother-to-be*.

be- *pfx* **1** all over or all around; thoroughly or completely: *beset*; *bedazzle*. **2** considering as or causing to be: *befriend*; *benumb*. **3** having or covered with; affected by: *bejewelled*. **4** affecting (someone or something) by an action: *bereave*. [OE]

beach *n* the sandy or stony shore of a sea or lake. — *v (tr)* to push or pull (a boat) on to a beach.

beachcomber *n* a person who searches beaches for things of interest or value. — *n* **beachcombing**.

beachhead *n* an area of shore, captured from the enemy, on which an army can land men and equipment.

beacon *n* **1** a fire on a hill or mountain, lit as a signal. **2** *(Br)* (esp. in place names) a hill, etc. on which a beacon could be lit. **3** a warning or guiding device for aircraft or ships, e.g. a lighthouse or (also **radio beacon**) a radio transmitter that broadcasts signals. [OE *beacen*]

Belisha beacon see **Belisha**.

bead *n* **1** a small, usu. round, ball of glass, stone, etc. strung with others, e.g. in a necklace. **2** (in *pl*) a string of beads worn as jewellery, or one used when praying (a rosary). **3** a small drop (of liquid): *beads of sweat*. — *v (tr)* to decorate with beads. — *adj* **beaded**. — **draw a bead on** *(coll)* to aim a gun at. [OE *biddan*, to pray]

beading *n* thin strips of patterned wood used to decorate the edges of furniture, walls, etc. **[bead]**

beadle *n* **1** a person who leads formal processions in church or some old British universities. **2** in Scotland, a church officer. **3** formerly in England, a minor parish official who had the power to punish minor offences. [OE *bydel*, from *beodan*, to proclaim]

beady *adj* ***-ier***, ***-iest*** (often *derog*) (of eyes) small, round and bright. **[bead]**

beagle *n* a type of small hunting-dog with a short coat. — *v (intr)* to hunt with beagles. — *n* **beagling**. [OFr *baer*, to gape + *goule*, throat, mouth]

beak *n* **1** the hard pointed or hooked part of a bird's mouth. **2** *(coll facet)* a nose, esp. if big and pointed. **3** *(Br old slang)* a headmaster, judge or magistrate. — *adj* **beaked**. [OFr *bec*]

beaker *n* **1** a large drinking-glass, or a large (often plastic) cup without a handle. **2** a deep glass container with a lip, used in chemistry. **3** (also **beakerful**, ***-fuls***) the amount contained in a beaker. [Norse *bikarr*]

beam *n* **1** a long, straight, thick piece of wood, used e.g. in a building. **2** the widest part of a ship or boat. **3** a ray (of light). **4** the part of a set of scales from which the weighing-pans hang. **5** a narrow wooden bar on which gymnasts perform balancing exercises. — *v* **1** *(intr)* to smile broadly with pleasure. **2** *(intr)* to shine. **3** *(tr)* to send out (rays of light, radio waves, etc). — **off beam** *(coll)* wrong. — **on the beam** *(coll)* on the right track. — **on one's beam ends** *(Br coll)* with only a very small amount of money left. — **on the port**, or **starboard**, **beam** *(naut)* on the left, or right, side of a ship. [OE *beam*, tree]

bean *n* **1** any of several kinds of climbing plant which produce edible seeds in long thin pods. **2** a seed or young pod of the plant, used as food. **3** the bean-like seed of other plants. — **full of beans** (*coll*) full of energy; very cheerful. [OE]

bean bag *n* **1** a small cloth bag filled with dried beans, or something similar, thrown like a ball in children's games. **2** a very large floor cushion.

beanfeast *n* (*Br coll*) a party or celebration.

beansprout or **beanshoot** *n* a young shoot of a bean plant, esp. of the mung bean, used as food.

beanstalk *n* the stem of a bean plant.

bear[1] *v* ***bore***, ***borne*** or, in sense **4**, ***born*** **1** (*tr*) to carry, bring or take: *bear gifts*. **2** (*tr*) to support (a weight). **3** (*tr*) to produce: *bear fruit*. **4** (*tr*; **born** is used with the passive, except where the verb is followed by **by** and a name) to give birth to: *Has she borne children? a child borne by Mary*; *He was born in 1960*. **5** (*tr*) to take or accept: *bear the blame*. **6** (*tr*) to put up with or like. **7** (*tr*) to show or be marked by: *bear the traces of tears*. **8** (*tr*) to carry in thought or memory: *bear a grudge*. **9** (*intr*) to turn slightly in a given direction: *bear left*. **10** (*tr*) to have: *bear no resemblance to*. **11** (*tr*) to behave: *bear oneself well*. — *v* **bear down on** (*tr*) to move towards as if to attack. — *v* **bear on** (*tr*) to affect or concern. — *v* **bear out** (*tr*) to support or confirm: *The evidence bears him out*. — *v* **bear up** (*intr*) to remain strong, brave, etc. under strain. — *v* **bear with** (*tr*) to be patient with. — **bring to bear** to apply (pressure or influence). [OE *beran*]

bearable *adj* able to be suffered or put up with. — *adv* **bearably**.

bearer *n* **1** a person or thing that bears or carries. **2** a person who helps carry equipment on an expedition. **3** a person who has a banknote, cheque, or other money order which can be exchanged for money.

bearing *n* **1** the way a person stands, walks, etc. **2** (with **on, upon**) a relation or effect: *have no bearing on the situation*. **3** (a calculation of) angular direction or position relative to a known point. **4** (often in *pl*) (a calculation of) position: *the ship's bearings*. **5** (in *pl*; *coll*) a sense or knowledge of one's own position: *lose one's bearings in the fog*. **6** a part of a machine which supports another moving part. ◇ See also **ball-bearing** at **ball**[1].

bear[2] *n* **1** a large, heavily built, four-legged animal with thick fur. **2** a rough, ill-mannered person. **3** (*stock exchange*) a person who sells shares, hoping to buy them back later at a much lower price. [OE *bera*]

bear hug *n* (*coll*) a rough, tight squeeze with one's arms.

bearish *adj* **1** (of a person) bad-tempered. **2** (*stock exchange*) causing or linked with a fall in prices. — *adv* **bearishly**. — *n* **bearishness**.

bearskin *n* **1** the skin of a bear. **2** a tall fur cap worn as part of some military uniforms.

beard *n* **1** the hair that grows on a man's chin and neck. **2** a beard-like growth on some animals, esp. goats. **3** a hair-like growth on an ear of corn, grass, etc. — *v* (*tr*) to face or oppose openly or boldly. — *adj* **bearded**. —*adj* **beardless**. [OE]

beast *n* **1** any large, esp. four-footed, wild animal. **2** (*coll*) a cruel, brutal person. **3** (*coll*) a difficult or unpleasant person or thing. [OFr *beste*]

beastly *adj* ***-ier***, ***-iest*** **1** like a beast in actions or behaviour. **2** (*coll*) unpleasant. — *adv* extremely and unpleasantly: *beastly hot*. — *n* **beastliness**. ◇ See also **bestial**.

beat *v* ***beat***, ***beaten*** **1** (*tr*) to hit violently and repeatedly, esp. to harm or punish. **2** (*tr*) to strike repeatedly, e.g. to remove dust or make a sound. **3** (*intr* with **against**, **at**, **on**, etc.) to knock repeatedly: *waves beating against the shore*. **4** (*tr*) to defeat; to do something better, sooner or quicker than. **5** (*tr*) to be too difficult to be solved or understood by: *The puzzle had me beaten*. **6** (*tr*) to mix or stir thoroughly: *beat eggs*. **7** (*tr*; **out**) to make or shape by striking. **8** (*intr*) to move in a regular pattern of strokes, etc.: *a beating heart*. **9** (*tr*; **out**) to mark or show musical time. **10** (*tr* & *intr*) to move rhythmically up and down. **11** (*tr* with **back**, **down**, **off**, etc.) to push, drive or force. **12** (*tr* & *intr*) to strike (bushes, trees, etc.) to force birds or animals into the open for shooting. — *n* **1** a regular stroke, or its sound: *the beat of a heart*. **2** the main accent in music. **3** a regular or usual course or journey, esp. one made by a policeman or policewoman. — *n* **beating**. — **beat about the bush** to talk about a subject without coming to the main point. — *v* **beat down 1** (*intr*) (of the sun) to give out great heat. **2** (*tr*) to force (a person) to reduce (the price of something) by bargaining. — **beat a hasty retreat** to go away in a hurry. — **beat it** (*slang*) to go away immediately and quickly. — *v* **beat off** (*tr*) to succeed in overcoming; to stop: *beat off an attack*. — *v* **beat up** (*tr*) to punch, kick or hit severely and repeatedly. — **dead beat** (*coll*) very tired. — **off the beaten track** away from main roads and towns; isolated. [OE *beatan*]

beater *n* **1** a person who forces animals into the open for shooting. **2** an instrument used for beating: *an egg-beater*.

beat-up *adj* (*coll*) old and worn; in very bad condition.

beatific *adj* **1** showing great happiness: *a beatific smile*. **2** making blessed. [Lat *beatus*, blessed + *facere*, to make]

beatify *v* ***-ies***, ***-ied*** (*tr*) **1** in the Roman Catholic church, to declare formally that (a dead person) is blessed by God, usu. as the first step towards making that person a saint. **2** to make extremely happy. — *n* **beatification**. [Lat *beatus*, blessed + *facere*, to make]

beatitude *n* **1** a state of extreme happiness, blessing and peace. **2** (in *pl* with *cap*) the statements made by Jesus, during the Sermon on the Mount (in Matthew 5: 3–11), about the kinds of people who receive God's blessing. [Lat *beatitudo*, from *beatus*, blessed]

beatnik *n* a young person, esp. in the 1950s, who rejected Western social and political ideas and wore unconventional clothes, long hair, etc. [**beat** + **-nik**]

beau *n* ***beaux*** (*old*) **1** a boyfriend or (male) lover. **2** a man who thinks a lot about his clothes and appearance. [Fr *beau*, beautiful]

Beaufort scale *n* an international scale of wind speeds, from 0 for calm to 12 for hurricane, devised by Sir Francis *Beaufort* (1774–1857).

beauteous *adj* (*poetic*) beautiful. — *adv* **beauteously**. — *n* **beauteousness**. [**beauty** + **-ous**]

beautician *n* a person who styles women's hair, treats their skin, applies their make-up, etc., esp. in a beauty parlour. [**beauty**]

beautiful *adj* **1** with an appearance or qualities which please the senses. **2** pleasing or enjoyable. — *adv* **beautifully**. [**beauty** + **-ful**]

beautify *v* ***-ies, -ied*** (*tr*) to make beautiful, often by decorating. — *n* **beautification**. [**beauty** + **-fy**]

beauty *n* ***-ies*** **1** a quality pleasing to the senses, esp. the eye or ear. **2** a beautiful woman or girl. **3** (*coll*) an excellent example of something. **4** a benefit: *the beauty of the plan*. [OFr *biaute*]

beauty contest *n* a competition in which usu. young women are judged by the beauty of their faces and bodies.

beauty parlour or **salon** *n* a place which offers hairdressing, make-up, massage, etc. to women.

beauty queen *n* a usu. young woman who is voted the most beautiful in a beauty contest.

beauty spot *n* **1** a place of great natural beauty. **2** a small dark-coloured, sometimes artificial, mark on the face, considered to be a sign of beauty.

beaver *n* **1** a large, rat-like animal, with thick, soft fur, strong front teeth and a large flat tail, which builds dams in rivers and streams. **2** its fur. **3** a hat made of beaver fur. — *v* **beaver away** ***-r-*** (*intr*; *coll*; **at**) to work very hard. [OE *befer*]

becalmed *adj* (of a sailing ship) unable to move because of lack of wind. [**be-** (sense 2) + **calm**]

became. See **become**.

because *conj* for the reason that. — **because of** on account of; by reason of. [**by** + **cause**]

beck[1]: **at someone's beck and call** having to be always ready to carry out someone's orders or wishes. [OE *biecnan*, to beckon]

beck[2] *n* a stream. [Norse *bekkr*]

beckon *v* ***-n-*** (*tr* & *intr*) to call (someone) towards oneself, esp. by making a sign with the hand. [OE *biecnan*]

become *v* ***became***, ***become*** **1** (*intr*) to come or grow to be. **2** (*intr* with **of**) to happen to: *What became of him?* **3** (*tr*) to suit, or look good on: *That hat becomes you*. [OE *becuman*, to come, approach]

becoming *adj* **1** attractive. **2** suitable or proper: *Such behaviour is not becoming*. — *adv* **becomingly**.

becquerel *n* the unit used to measure radioactivity; symbol **Bq**. [A H *Becquerel* (1852–1908), French physicist]

BEd. *abbrev* Bachelor of Education.

bed *n* **1** a piece of furniture for sleeping on. **2** the bottom of a river, lake or sea. **3** an area of ground in a garden, for growing plants: *flower-bed*. **4** a support or foundation. **5** a layer, esp. of rock. — *v* ***-dd-*** **1** (*tr* & *intr*; **down**) to put or go to bed or a place to sleep: *bed down on the sofa*. **2** (*tr*; *coll*) to have sexual intercourse with. **3** (*tr*; **out**) to plant in a garden. **4** (*tr*) to place or fix firmly. **5** (*tr* & *intr*) to arrange in, or form, layers. — **bed and board** lodgings and food. — **bed of roses** an easy or comfortable place, job or situation. — **go to bed with** (*coll*) to have sexual intercourse with. — **make the bed** to make the bedclothes tidy after one has slept in the bed. [OE *bedd*]

bedbath *n* a complete wash of the body of a person who cannot get out of bed.

bedbug *n* a very small, wingless insect, found in dirty houses and esp. beds, that bites people and feeds on their blood.

bedclothes *n* (*pl*) the sheets, blankets, etc. used to cover a bed.

bedcover *n* a top cover for a bed.

bedding *n* **1** mattresses, blankets, etc. **2** straw, etc. for animals to sleep on.

bedfellow *n* **1** a person with whom one shares a bed. **2** a partner or associate.

bed linen *n* the sheets and pillowcases used on a bed.

bedpan *n* a wide, shallow pan used as a toilet by people who cannot get out of bed.

bedridden *adj* not able to get out of bed, e.g. because of old age or sickness.

bedrock *n* **1** the solid rock forming the lowest layer under soil and rock fragments. **2** the basic principle, idea, etc. on which something rests.

bedroom *n* a room for sleeping in. — *adj* of or referring to sexual relations: *bedroom comedy*.

bedside *n* the place or position next to a bed, esp. of a sick person: *a doctor's bedside manner*.

bedsitting room, or (*coll*) **bedsit** or **bedsitter** *n* a single room for both eating and sleeping in.

bedsore *n* an ulcer on a person's skin, caused by lying in bed for long periods.

bedspread *n* a top cover for a bed.
bedstead *n* the frame of a bed.
bed-wetting *n* accidental urination in bed at night. ◇ See also **incontinence**.
bedazzle *v* (*tr*) **1** to impress greatly. **2** to confuse. — *adj* **bedazzled**. — *n* **bedazzlement**. [**be-** (sense **1**) + **dazzle**]
bedeck *v* (*tr*; **with**) to cover (with decorations). [**be-** (sense **1**) + **deck**]
bedevil *v* **-ll-** (*tr*) **1** to cause continual difficulties, problems or trouble to. **2** to confuse. — *n* **bedevilment**. [**be-** (sense **3**) + **devil**]
bedlam *n* (*coll*) a noisy, confused place or situation. [From the hospital of St Mary of *Bethlehem*, a lunatic asylum in London]
Bedouin *n* ***Bedouin*** or ***Bedouins*** a member of a wandering Arab tribe that lives in the deserts of the Middle East. [Arabic *badawi*, desert-dweller]
bedraggled *adj* (of people and animals) very wet and untidy. [**be-** (sense **2**) + **draggle**]
Beds. *abbrev* Bedfordshire.
bee *n* **1** a type of four-winged, stinging insect, some species of which live in large groups and make honey. **2** (esp. *US*) a meeting of friends or neighbours to work or for enjoyment. **3** (*old*) a friendly competition. — **a bee in one's bonnet** an idea which has become an obsession. — **the bee's knees** (*Br coll*) a person or thing considered to be extremely good. [OE *beo*]
beehive *n* **1** a box or hut in which bees are kept, and where they store their honey. **2** a place where a lot of people are working hard. — *adj* shaped like an old-fashioned beehive with a rounded roof: *beehive hairstyle*.
beekeeper *n* a person who keeps bees for their honey. — *n* **beekeeping**.
beeline *n* a straight line between two places. — **make a beeline for** to go directly to.
beeswax *n* the solid yellowish substance produced by bees for making the cells in which they live, used as a polish.
beech *n* **1** (also **beech tree**) a kind of forest tree with smooth silvery bark and small nuts. **2** the hard wood of this tree. — *adj* made from the wood of the beech tree. [OE *bece*]
beech mast *n* the nuts of the beech tree.
beef *n* **1** the flesh of a bull, cow or ox, used as food. **2** (*coll*) muscle, strength. **3** (*coll*) a complaint. — *v* (*intr*; **about**) to complain. — *v* **beef up** (*tr*; *coll*) **1** to make stronger or heavier. **2** to make more interesting or exciting. [OFr *boef*, ox]
beefburger *n* a piece of finely chopped beef, made into a flat, round shape, grilled or fried
beefcake *n* (*coll*; often *derog*) very muscular men displayed in photographs. ◇ See also **cheesecake**.
beefeater *n* a guard at the Tower of London.
beefsteak *n* a thick slice of beef for grilling or frying.
beef tea *n* the juice of chopped beef, sometimes taken by people who are ill.
beefy *adj* **-ier**, **-iest** **1** of or like beef. **2** (*coll*) having a lot of fat or muscle. — *adv* **beefily**. — *n* **beefiness**.
been. See **be**.
beep *n* a short, high sound, e.g. made by a car horn. — *v* (*intr* & *tr*) to produce a beep (on or for something): *beep a horn*. — *n* **beeper**. [Imit.]
beer *n* **1** a type of alcoholic drink made from malt, barley, sugar, hops and water. **2** a glass, can or bottle of beer. **3** a similar, usu. non-alcoholic, drink: *ginger beer*. — **beer and skittles** (*Br*) pleasure. [OE *beor*]
beer garden *n* a garden, usu. attached to a pub, where beer and other refreshments can be drunk.
beery *adj* **-ier**, **-iest** **1** of or like beer. **2** (*coll*) affected by drinking beer.
small beer *n* (*coll*) a thing or things of little importance or value.
beet *n* any of several types of plant with large round or carrot-shaped roots, used as food or for making sugar. ◇ See also **beetroot** and **sugar beet**. [OE *bete*]
beetle[1] *n* an insect with four wings, the front pair being hard and forming a cover for the back pair. — *v* (*intr*; with **about**, **around**, **away**, etc.; *Br*) to move quickly or as if in a hurry. [OE *bitela*]
beetle[2] *n* a tool with a heavy head, for crushing, beating, etc. [OE *bietle*]
beetle[3] *v* (*intr*) to project, to overhang. — *adj* **beetling**.
beetle-browed *adj* with bushy eyebrows.
beetroot *n* a type of plant with a round, red root which is cooked and used as a vegetable. ◇ See also **beet**. [OE *bete*, beet]
befall *v* ***befell***, ***befallen*** (*intr* & *tr*; *old* or *literary*) to happen (to). [OE *befeallan*]
befit *v* **-tt-** (*tr*; *formal*) to be suitable or right for. — *adj* **befitting**. — *adv* **befittingly**. [**be-** (sense **2**) + **fit**]
before *prep* **1** earlier than: *before noon*. **2** ahead of; in front of: *stand before the table*. **3** in the presence of; for the attention of: *the question before us*. **4** (*formal* or *literary*) in the face of: *draw back before the blast*. **5** rather than; in preference to: *put money before friendship*. — *conj* **1** earlier than the time when: *Do it before you forget*. **2** rather than; in preference to: *I'd die before I'd surrender*. — *adv* **1** (*formal*) in front of; ahead of: *go before*. **2** previously; in the past: *Haven't we met before?* [OE *beforan*]
beforehand *adv* in advance; in preparation.
befriend *v* (*tr*) to become the friend of. [**be-** (sense **2**) + **friend**]
befuddle *v* (*tr*) to confuse, esp. with alcohol. — *adj* **befuddled**. [**be-** (sense **4**) + **fuddle**]
beg *v* **-gg-** (*intr* & *tr*; **for**) **1** to ask for (money, food, etc.). **2** to ask earnestly or humbly. — **beg the question** to assume

in an argument the truth of something which is (part of) what is to be proved. — **beg to differ** to disagree. — **go begging** to be unused or unwanted. ◇ See also **beggar**. [OE *bedecian*]

began. See **begin**.

beget *v* ***-tt-***, ***begot*** or (*old*) ***begat***, ***begotten*** (*tr*) **1** (*old*) to be the father of. **2** to cause. [OE *begietan*]

beggar *n* **1** a person who lives by begging. **2** (*coll*) a person: *cheeky beggar*. — **beggar description**, **belief**, etc. to be impossible to describe, believe, etc. [**beg** + **-ar**]

beggarly *adj* extremely small or poor. — *n* **beggarliness**.

begin *v* ***-nn-***, ***began***, ***begun*** **1** (*tr* & *intr*) to start. **2** (*tr* & *intr*) to bring or come into being. **3** (*intr*) to start speaking. **4** (*intr*) to be the first, or take the first step. **5** (*intr* with **with**) to deal with first. **6** (*intr*; *coll*) to have the ability or possibility: *I can't even begin to understand*. — *n* **beginning**. — **to begin with 1** at first. **2** firstly. [OE *beginnan*]

beginner *n* someone who is just learning how to do something.

begone *interj* (*old* or *poetic*) go away. [**be** + **gone**]

begonia *n* a kind of tropical plant with brightly coloured, waxy flowers and unevenly shaped leaves. [Michel *Bégon* (1638–1710), French patron of botany]

begot, **begotten**. See **beget**.

begrudge *v* (*tr*) **1** to do, give, allow unwillingly or with regret. **2** to envy (someone) for having (something). [**be-** (sense **1**) + **grudge**]

beguile *v* (*tr*) **1** to charm. **2** (**of**, **out of**, **into**) to cheat, trick, or deceive. **3** (**away**) to pass (time) pleasantly. — *n* **beguilement**. — *adj* **beguiling**. — *adv* **beguilingly**. [**be-** (sense **1**) + *guile*, to deceive]

begun. See **begin**.

behalf: **on behalf of 1** of, for or in the interests of. **2** as a representative of. [OE *be*, by + *healfe*, side]

behave *v* **1** (*intr*) to act in a stated way: *behave well*. **2** (*intr* & *tr*) to act or conduct (oneself) in a suitable, polite or orderly way: *Behave yourself at the party*. [**be-** (sense **1**) + **have**]

behaviour *n* **1** way of behaving; manners: *good behaviour*. **2** (*psychol*) a response to a stimulus. — **be on one's best behaviour** to behave as well as one can. [**behave**]

behavioural *adj* of or related to behaviour. — *adv* **behaviourally**.

behaviourism *n* (*psychol*) the belief that the only valid theories are those based on the scientific study of how people and animals behave. — *n* & *adj* **behaviourist**.

behead *v* (*tr*) to cut off the head of, usu. as punishment for a crime. — *n* **beheading**. [OE *beheafdian*]

beheld. See **behold**.

behest *n* (*old* or *formal*) a command or request: *at his behest*. [OE *behæs*, vow]

behind *prep* **1** at or towards the back of or the far side of. **2** later or slower than; after in time: *behind schedule*. **3** supporting: *We're all behind you*. **4** in the past with respect to: *Those problems are all behind me now*. **5** not as far advanced as. **6** being the cause of: *reasons behind the decision*. — *adv* **1** in or to the back or far side of. **2** remaining: *leave something behind*. **3** following: *run behind*. — *adj* (**with**) **1** not up to date; late: *behind with the payments*. **2** not having progressed enough: *get behind with one's work*. — *n* the part of the body a person sits on. — **behind someone's back** without someone's knowledge or permission. — **put something behind one** to (try to) forget something unpleasant. [OE *behindan*]

behindhand *adj* **1** late. **2** (**with**) not up to date; in arrears.

behold (*old* or *literary*) *v* **beheld** (*tr*) to see; to look at. — *interj* look. — *n* **beholder**. [OE *behealdan*, to hold, observe]

beholden *adj* (with **to**; *formal*) owing a debt or favour to; grateful to. [OE *behealdan*, to hold, observe]

behove *v* (*tr*; *old*) to be necessary or fitting on the part of: *It behoves me to tell you the truth*. [OE *behofian*, to have need of]

beige *adj* & *n* (of) a pale pinkish-yellow colour. [Fr]

beigel. See **bagel**.

bejewelled *adj* wearing or decorated with a lot of jewels. [**be-** (sense **3**) + **jewel**]

bel *n* a unit of measurement for comparing noises, electrical currents, etc., equal to 10 decibels. [From A G *Bell* (1847–1922), the inventor of the telephone]

belabour *v* (*tr*; *old*) **1** to beat thoroughly. **2** to argue (about) or discuss at too great length. [**be-** (sense **4**) + **labour**]

belated *adj* happening or coming late or too late. — *adv* **belatedly**. [**be-** (sense **2**) + **late**]

belay *v* (*tr*) **1** (*mountaineering*) to make (a climber) safe by tying his or her rope to a rock or pin. **2** (*naut*) to make (a rope) secure by winding it round a hook, peg, etc. — *n* **1** an act of belaying. **2** a piece of rock used for belaying. [OE *belecgan*]

belch *v* **1** (*intr*) to give out air noisily from the stomach through the mouth. **2** (*tr*; **out**) (of a chimney, volcano, etc.) to send out (smoke, etc.). — *n* an act of belching. [OE *bealcan*]

beleaguer *v* ***-r-*** (*tr*) **1** to surround with an army and lay seige to. **2** to cause (someone) bother or worry. — *adj* **beleaguered**. [Dut *belegeren*, to beseige]

belfry *n* ***-ies*** a tower for a bell or bells, or the part of it containing the bell or bells. — **have bats in the belfry** see **bat**[2]. [Fr *berfroi*, watch tower]

belie *v* ***belying*** (*tr*) **1** to show to be untrue or false. **2** to give a false idea or impression of. **3** to fail to fulfil or justify (a hope, etc.). [OE *beleogan*, to deceive by lying]

belief *n* **1** (**in**) a principle, idea, etc. accepted as true, esp. without proof: *belief in the afterlife*. **2** (**in**) trust or confidence. **3** a person's religious faith. **4** a firm opinion. — **beyond belief** incredible. — **to the best of one's belief** as far as one knows. [OE *geleafa*]

believe *v* **1** (*tr*) to accept as true. **2** (*tr*) to accept what is said by (a person) as true. **3** (*tr*) to think, assume, or suppose. **4** (*intr*; **in**) to have religious faith. **5** (*intr* with **in**) to be convinced of the existence of. **6** (*intr* with **in**) to have trust or confidence. **7** (*intr* with **in**) to consider right or good: *believe in telling the truth*. — *adj* **believable**. — *n* **believer**. — **not be able to believe one's ears** or **eyes** (*coll*) to find it very hard to believe in what one is hearing or seeing. [OE *belyfan*]

Belisha beacon *n* in the UK, esp. formerly, a tall black and white post with a flashing orange light on the top, marking a pedestrian crossing on a road. [L Hore-*Belisha*, the Minister of Transport who introduced them in 1934]

belittle *v* (*tr*) to treat as or cause to seem unimportant. — *n* **belittlement**. — *adj* **belittling**. [**be-** (sense **2**) + **little**]

bell *n* **1** a deep, hollow, usu. metal, object, rounded at one end and wide and open at the other, with a small hammer or clapper inside, which gives a ringing sound when struck. **2** the sound made by such an object. **3** any other device which makes a ringing sound. **4** anything shaped like a bell. **5** the ringing of a bell on board ship to tell the time. **6** (*Br coll*) a telephone call. — **bell the cat** to do something very daring and dangerous. — **ring a bell** (*Br coll*) to sound familiar; to remind one of something. — **sound as a bell** (*Br coll*) in very good condition or health. [OE *belle*]

bell-bottoms *n* (*pl*) trousers with legs which are much wider at the bottom than at the top. — *adj* **bell-bottomed**.

bell-boy or (*US*) **bell-hop** *n* a man or boy who works in a hotel, carrying guests' bags, delivering messages, etc.

bell jar *n* a bell-shaped glass cover put over instruments, experiments, etc. in a laboratory, to stop gases escaping.

bell-pull *n* a handle or cord which operates a bell.

bell-push *n* a button which, when pressed, operates an electric bell.

bell-ringer *n* a person who rings a bell in a church, or who plays tunes with hand-held bells. — *n* **bell-ringing**.

bellwether *n* the leading sheep in a flock, with a bell on its neck.

belladonna *n* **1** a poisonous plant, deadly nightshade. **2** a drug obtained from this plant, used in medicine. [Ital, beautiful lady, so called because the drug was formerly used as a cosmetic]

belle *n* (*old*) a beautiful woman, esp. the most beautiful woman at a dance: *belle of the ball*. [Fr, beautiful, fine]

belles-lettres *n* (*pl*) works of literature, esp. poetry and essays, valued for their style rather than their content. [Fr, beautiful letters]

bellicose *adj* (*literary*) likely or wanting to cause an argument or war. [Lat *bellicosus*]

belligerent *adj* **1** aggressive and unfriendly. **2** fighting a war. — *n* a person or country fighting a war. — *n* **belligerence** or **-ency**. — *adj* **belligerently**. [Lat *belligerare*, to wage war]

bellow *v* **1** (*intr*) to make a loud, deep cry like that of a bull. **2** (*tr*) to shout loudly or angrily. — *n* **1** the loud roar of a bull. **2** a deep loud sound or cry. [OE *bylgan*]

bellows *n* (*sing* or *pl*) **1** a device consisting of or containing a bag-like or box-like part with folds in it which is squeezed to create a current of air. **2** on some cameras, a sleeve with bellows-like folds connecting the body of the camera to the lens. [OE *belg*, bag]

belly *n* **-ies 1** the part of the body below the chest containing the organs used for digesting food. **2** the stomach. **3** the lower or under part of an animal's body, which contains the stomach and other organs. **4** a part of a structure shaped like a belly. — *v* **-ies**, **-ied** (*intr*; **out**) to swell out. [OE *belg*, bag]

bellyache *n* a pain in the belly. — *v* (*intr*; *slang*) to complain noisily or repeatedly.

belly button *n* (*coll*) the navel.

belly-dance *n* an Eastern dance performed by women in which the belly and hips are moved around, often very fast. — *n* **belly-dancer**.

belly-flop *n* a dive in which the body accidentally hits the water flat, instead of at an angle.

bellyful *n* **-fuls** enough to eat. — **have had a bellyful of** (*slang*) to have had more of than one can bear.

belly-landing *n* the landing of an aeroplane without using its wheels, e.g. because they are broken.

belly laugh *n* a loud, deep laugh.

belong *v* (*intr*) **1** (with **to**) to be the property or right of. **2** (with **to**) to be a native of, member of a group, etc. **3** (**with**, **in**, etc.) to have a proper place; to go together with; to have the right qualities to fit in. [MidE *belongen*]

belongings *n* (*pl*) personal possessions.

beloved *adj* much loved. — *n* a much loved person. [From the old verb *belove*, to love]

below *prep* **1** lower in position, rank, amount, etc. **2** not worthy of. — *adv* **1** at, to or in a lower place, point or level. **2** further on in a book, etc. [MidE *bilooghe*]

belt *n* **1** a long, narrow piece of leather or cloth worn around the waist to keep clothing in place or for decoration. **2** a strap passed across the body, to secure a person in a seat: *a seat-belt*. **3** an area, usu. relatively long and narrow: *a belt of rain*. **4** a band of rubber, etc. moving the wheels, or round the wheels, of a machine: *a conveyor belt*. **5** (*slang*) a hard blow. — *v* **1** (*tr*) to put a belt round. **2** (*tr*; **on**) to fasten with a belt. **3** (*tr*) to beat with a belt. **4** (*tr* & *intr*; *coll*; **into**, etc.) to hit. **5** (*intr*; *coll*; **along**, etc.) to move very fast. — **below the belt** (*coll*) unfair; unfairly. — *v* **belt out** (*tr*; *coll*) to sing or say very loudly. — *v* **belt up** (*intr*) **1** to attach a seat-belt. **2** (*coll*) to stop talking. — **tighten one's belt** (*coll*) to begin to spend less than before. — **under one's belt** (*coll*) as part of one's experience: *have a good education under one's belt*. [OE, from Lat *balteus*]

belted *adj* **1** having or wearing a belt. **2** (of an animal, etc.) marked with a band of different colour.

beluga *n* **1** a kind of large sturgeon. **2** caviar from this type of sturgeon. **3** a white whale. [Russ, from *beliy*, white]

bemoan *v* (*tr*) to express great sadness or regret about (something). [**be-** (sense **4**) + **moan**]

bemuse *v* (*tr*) to puzzle or confuse. — *adj* **bemused**. [**be-** (sense **1**) + **muse**]

ben *n* (*Scot*; in place names) a mountain. [Gaelic *beann*]

bench *n* **1** a long wooden or stone seat. **2** a work-table for a carpenter, scientist, etc. **3** (with **the**) a judge's seat in court. **4** (with **the**) judges and magistrates as a group. ◇ See also **Queen's Bench**. **5** a seat in the House of Commons. ◇ See also **backbench** and **frontbench**. — **raise (someone) to the bench** to make (someone) a judge or a bishop. [OE *benc*]

benchmark *n* **1** a mark on a post, etc. giving the height above sea level of the land at that exact spot, used when measuring land and making maps. **2** anything used as a standard or point of reference.

bend *v* ***bent*** **1** (*tr* & *intr*) to make or become angled or curved. **2** (*intr*) to move or stretch in a curve: *a road bending to the left*. **3** (*intr*; **down**, **over**, etc.) to move the body to form a curve: *bend down to pick something up*. **4** (*tr*) to modify or change unofficially: *bend the rules*. **5** (*tr* & *intr*; **to**) to (force to) submit: *bent her to his will*. — *n* **1** a curve or bent part. **2** the act of curving or bending. — **bend over backwards** (*Br*) to try very hard to be helpful. — **round the bend** (*coll*) mad. [OE *bendan*]

bends *n* (*sing* or *pl*; with **the**) decompression sickness.

bendy *adj* ***-ier***, ***-iest*** **1** having a lot of bends or curves. **2** able to bend easily.

bent *adj* **1** not straight. **2** (**on**) with one's attention or energy directed on: *bent on revenge*. **3** (*Br slang*) dishonest. **4** (*Br slang derog*) homosexual. — *n* (**for**) a natural liking or ability.

beneath *prep* **1** under; below. **2** not worthy of. — *adv* below, underneath. [OE *beneothan*]

Benedictine *n* **1** a member of the Christian community that follows the teachings of St Benedict (480–543). **2** a strong greenish-yellow alcoholic drink first made by Benedictine monks in France in the 16th century. — *adj* of the community or St Benedict.

benediction *n* **1** a prayer giving blessing, esp. at the end of a religious service. **2** in the Roman Catholic church, a short service in which the congregation is blessed. — *adj* **benedictory**. [Lat *benedictio*]

benefactor or **benefactress** *n* a man, or a woman, who gives help, often in the form of money. — *n* **benefaction**. — *adj* **benefactory**. [Lat *bene*, good + *facere*, to do]

benefice *n* a position as priest or a church office, and the income (from land, buildings, etc.) which goes with it. — *adj* **beneficed**. [Lat *beneficium*, favour]

beneficent *adj* good, kind, and generous. — *n* **beneficence**. — *adv* **beneficently**. [Lat *beneficium*, favour]

beneficial *adj* having good results or benefits. — *adv* **beneficially**. [Lat *beneficialis*, generous]

beneficiary *n* ***-ies*** **1** a person who benefits from something. **2** (*legal*) a person who receives land, money, etc., usu. in a will. [Lat *beneficiarius*]

benefit *n* **1** something good gained or received. **2** advantage or sake: *for your benefit*. **3** (often in *pl*) a payment made by a government or company insurance scheme, usu. to someone who is ill or out of work: *social security benefit*. **4** a game, performance at a theatre, etc. from which the profits are given to a person or people in need. — *v* ***-t-*** **1** (*intr*; **from**, **by**) to gain an advantage or receive something good. **2** (*tr*) to do good to. — **give someone the benefit of the doubt** to assume that someone is innocent or is telling the truth because there is not enough evidence to the contrary. [OFr *benfet*, from Lat *benefactum*, good deed]

benefit society *n* a society to which people pay money, which they will receive back when they are ill or old.

Benelux *n* the economic union between *Be*lgium, the *Ne*therlands and *Lux*embourg.

benevolence *n* **1** the desire to do good; kindness; generosity. **2** an act of kindness or generosity. — *adj* **benevolent**. — *adv* **benevolently**. [Fr *benivolence*, from Lat *bene*, good + *volens*, wishing]

Bengali *n* **1** a member of a people living in Bangladesh and the state of West Bengal in India. **2** the language of this people. — *adj* of or relating to this people or their language.

benighted *adj* lacking intelligence or a sense of morality. — *adv* **benightedly**. [**be-** (sense **3**) + **night**]

benign *adj* **1** kind; gentle. **2** favourable. **3** (of a disease, growth, etc.) not fatal. — *n* **benignity**, ***-ies***. — *adv* **benignly**. [Lat *benignus*]

benignant *adj* **1** kind. **2** favourable. **3** (of a disease, growth, etc.) not fatal. **[benign]**

bent. See **bend**.

benumb *v* (*tr*) to make numb. **[be-** (sense **2**) + **numb]**

benzene *n* a colourless, poisonous liquid obtained by heating coal, used in the manufacture of numerous chemical products. **[benzoin]**

benzine *n* a motor fuel obtained from petroleum. **[benzoin]**

benzoin *n* a thick liquid obtained from a tree native to Java and Sumatra, used to make perfumes. [Arabic *luban jawa*, incense of Java]

bequeath *v* (*tr*) to leave (personal belongings) in a will. [OE *becwethan*]

bequest *n* **1** an act of leaving (personal belongings) in a will. **2** anything left or bequeathed in someone's will. [OE *becwethan*, to bequeath]

berate *v* (*tr*) to scold severely. **[be-** (sense **1**) + **rate**[2]**]**

Berber *n* **1** a person belonging to a Muslim race of North Africa. **2** the language spoken by these people. — *adj* of the Berber people or language. [Arabic *barbar*]

bereaved *adj* having recently suffered the death of a close friend or relative. — *n* **bereavement**. [OE *bereafian*]

bereft *adj* **(of)** having had something taken away. [Past tense of *bereave*; see **bereaved]**

beret *n* a round, flat cap made of soft material. [Fr *béret*, cap]

bergamot *n* a fruit related to the orange and lemon, from which an oil is obtained which is used in perfumes and for flavouring food. [*Bergamo* in northern Italy]

beribboned *adj* decorated with ribbons. **[be-** (sense **3**) + **ribbon]**

beriberi *n* a disease, caused by lack of vitamin B_1, which affects the nerves and often causes permanent loss of movement or paralysis in some limbs. [Sinhalese (language of Sri Lanka) *beri*, weakness]

berk or **burk** *n* (*Br slang*) a fool. [Short for *Berkeley Hunt*, Cockney rhyming slang for **cunt]**

berkelium *n* an artificial radioactive metallic element, symbol **Bk**, made by firing particles of high energy at another element, americium. [From *Berkeley*, California, where it was first made]

Berks. *abbrev* Berkshire.

Bermuda shorts or **Bermudas** *n* (*pl*) close-fitting shorts reaching almost to the knee. [*Bermuda*, in the west Atlantic]

berry *n* **-ies 1** a small round juicy fruit without a stone, various kinds of which are used as food, such as the strawberry. **2** (*bot*) a fruit with seeds enclosed in the flesh or pulp, such as the tomato. [OE *berie*]

berserk *adj* violently angry; wild and destructive. [Norse *berserkr*, prob. from *bern*, bear + *serkr*, coat]

berth *n* **1** a sleeping-place in a ship, train, etc. **2** a place in a port where a ship or boat can be tied up. **3** enough room for a ship to be able to turn round in. — *v* **1** (*tr*) to tie up (a ship) in its berth. **2** (*intr*) (of a ship) to arrive at its berth. **3** (*tr*) to provide a sleeping-place for. — **give a wide berth to** to stay well away from.

beryl *n* a hard mineral, used as a source of beryllium and as a precious stone (e.g. emerald and aquamarine). [Gr *beryllos*]

beryllium *n* a metallic element, symbol **Be**, used to control reactions in the production of nuclear power, and to harden some alloys in industry. [From **beryl]**

beseech *v* ***beseeched*** or ***besought*** (*tr*; *old* or *literary*) to ask desperately; to beg. — *adj* **beseeching**. — *adv* **beseechingly**. [From **be-** (sense **1**) + *secan*, to seek]

beset *v* ***-tt-***, ***beset*** (*tr*; with **with**, **by**; *literary*) to attack on all sides; to worry: *beset by problems*. [OE *besettan*]

beside *prep* **1** next to, by the side of or near. **2** compared with. **3** not relevant to: *beside the point*. — **beside oneself (with)** in a state of very great, uncontrolled anger, excitement or other emotion: *beside oneself with worry*. [OE *be*, by + *sidan*, side]

besides *prep* in addition to; as well as. — *adv* also; as well. [OE *be*, by + *sidan*, side]

besiege *v* (*tr*) **1** to surround (a town, etc.) with an army in order to force it to surrender. **2** to gather round in a huge crowd. **3** (with **with**) to bother; to annoy constantly: *beseiged with questions*. **[be-** (sense **1**) + **siege]**

besmirch *v* (*tr*; *formal*) **1** to make dirty. **2** to spoil (the reputation of). **[be-** (sense **1**) + **smirch]**

besom *n* a large brush made from sticks tied to a long wooden handle. [OE *besma*]

besotted *adj* **(with) 1** so much in love that one appears ridiculous or foolish. **2** confused, esp. through having drunk too much alcohol. — *adv* **besottedly**. **[be-** (sense **2**) + **sot]**

besought. See **beseech**.

bespangle *v* (*tr*) to decorate with objects which shine or sparkle. **[be-** (sense **3**) + **spangle]**

bespatter *v* ***-r-*** (*tr*; **with**) to cover with spots, splashes, large drops, etc. **[be-** (sense **1**) + **spatter]**

bespeak *v* ***bespoke*** , ***bespoken*** (*tr*; *formal*) **1** to claim in advance. **2** to show or be evidence of. **[be-** (sense **1**) + **speak]**

bespoke *adj* **1** (of clothes) made to fit a particular person. **2** (of a tailor) making clothes to fit individual people.

best *adj* **1** most excellent, suitable or desirable. **2 (at)** most successful, clever, etc. **3** the greatest or most: *the best part of an hour*. — *adv* **1** most successfully, etc.: *do best in the exam*. **2** more than all others: *I like her best*. — *n* **1** the most excellent or suitable person or thing, most desirable quality, etc.: *the best of the bunch*; *bring out the best in her*. **2** the greatest effort: *do one's best*. **3** a person's finest clothes: *Sunday* *best*. **4** victory or success: *get the best of an argument*. — *v* (*tr*) to beat, defeat. — **as best one can** as well as one can. — **at best** considered in the most favourable way; in the best circumstances. — **at the best of times** in the most favourable circumstances. — **for the best** likely or intended to have the best results possible. — **had best** would find it wisest to. — **make the best of a bad job** or **of it** to do as well as possible in an unfavourable situation. — **put one's best foot forward** to make the best attempt possible. — **to the best of one's knowledge, belief** or **ability** as far as one knows, believes or can. ◇ See also **good, well** and **better**. [OE *betst*]

best man *n* a bridegroom's main male attendant at a wedding.

best-seller *n* **1** a book or other item which sells in large numbers. **2** a person whose books, etc. have been sold in large quantities. — *adj* **best-selling**.

bestial *adj* **1** of or like an animal. **2** (*derog*) cruel.— *adv* **bestially**. [Lat *bestia*, animal]

bestiality *n* **1** disgusting or cruel behaviour. **2** sexual intercourse between a human and an animal.

bestiary *n* ***-ies*** a kind of book popular in Europe in the Middle Ages, containing pictures and descriptions of animals, often intended as morals. [Lat *bestia*, animal]

bestir *v* ***-rr-*** (*tr*) to cause (oneself) to become active, start moving, etc. [**be-** (sense **1**) + **stir**]

bestow *v* (*tr*; *formal*; **on, upon**) to give (a title, award, quality, etc.) to. — *n* **bestowal**. [**be-** (sense **1**) + OE *stow*, spot or position]

bestrewn *adj* (*formal* or *literary*; with **with**) covered loosely, usu. with things which have been thrown or scattered: *a beach bestrewn with shells*. [OE *bestreowian*, to strew]

bestride *v* **bestrode** , **bestridden** (*tr*; *formal* or *literary*) to sit or stand across (something) with one leg on each side. [OE *bestridan*]

bet *v* ***-tt-***, ***bet*** or ***betted*** **1** (*intr* & *tr*; **on, against**) to risk (money, etc.) by guessing at the outcome or result of a future event, winning extra money, etc. if the guess is right and losing one's money, etc. if it is wrong: *bet £10 on a race*. **2** (*tr*; *coll*) to feel sure or confident (that): *I bet she'll be late*. — *n* **1** an act of betting. **2** a sum of money betted. **3** (*coll*) an opinion. — *n* **betting**. — **an even bet** an equal chance (that something will happen or not). — **you bet** (esp. *US*; *slang*) certainly; definitely; of course.

best bet *n* the wisest action to take.

better or **bettor** *n* a person who bets.

betting shop *n* (*Br*) a place where one can go to bet money on races, etc.

beta *n* **1** the second letter of the Greek alphabet (Β, β). **2** (a mark indicating) the second highest grade or quality.

beta-blocker *n* a kind of drug that calms the nerves and slows down the heart, used to reduce high blood pressure.

beta particle *n* a particle given off by radioactive substances.

betake *v* ***betook*** , ***betaken*** (*tr*; *literary*) to take (oneself); to go somewhere. [**be-** (sense **1**) + **take**]

betel *n* an Asian climbing plant whose leaves are wrapped around the seeds of the plant and chewed. [Malayalam (S Indian language) *vettila*]

betel nut *n* the seed of the betel plant.

bête noire *n* ***bêtes noires*** a person or thing that bothers, annoys or frightens one more than anything else. [Fr, black beast]

betide: **woe betide** see **woe**. [OE *tidan*, to befall]

betoken *v* ***-n-*** (*tr*; *formal*) to be evidence or a sign of. [OE *betacnian*]

betook. See **betake**.

betray *v* (*tr*) **1** to hand over (a friend, one's nation, etc.) to the enemy. **2** to give away (a secret, etc.). **3** to break (a promise, etc.) or be unfaithful to: *betray a trust*. **4** to be evidence of: *Her face betrayed her unhappiness*. — *n* **betrayal**. — *n* **betrayer**. [Lat *tradere*, to hand over]

betroth *v* (*tr; old*) to promise to marry. — *n* **betrothal**. — *n* & *adj* **betrothed**. [MidE *betrouth*, from **be-** (sense **4**) + *treuth*, truth]

better[1] *adj* **1** good to a greater extent; more excellent, suitable, desirable, etc. **2** (**at**) more successful, etc. at. **3** partly or fully recovered from illness. **4** greater: *the better part of a day*. — *adv* **1** more excellently, successfully, etc. **2** in or to a greater degree. — *n* (often in *pl*) a person superior in quality, rank, etc.: *one's elders and betters*. — *v* ***-r-*** **1** (*tr*) to beat; to improve on. **2** (*tr* & *intr*) to make or become better. **3** (*tr*) to achieve a higher social standing for (oneself): *better oneself through education*. — **all the better for** very much better as a result of. — **better off 1** richer. **2** happier in some way. — **a change for the better** an improvement. — **for better or for worse** no matter what happens. — **get the better of** to gain the advantage over. — **go one better than** to do, offer, etc. something better or more than. — **had better** ought to: *We'd better hurry or we'll be late*. — **so much the better** that is, or would be, preferable. ◇ See also **best, good** and **well**. [OE *betera*]

betterment *n* improvement; advancement.

better[2] or **bettor**, **betting-shop**. See **bet**.

between *prep* **1** in, to, through or across the space dividing (two people, places, times, etc.) **2** to and from: *a regular bus service between Leeds and Bradford*. **3** in combination; acting together: *They bought the car between them*. **4** shared out among: *divide the money between them*. **5** involving choice: *choose between right and wrong*. **6** including; involving: *a fight between her* *and her sister.* — *adv* (also **in between**) in, into the middle (of two points in space, time, etc.): *time for a quick lunch (in) between.* — **between you and me** or **between ourselves** this is a secret; don't tell anyone else. [OE *betweonum*]

betweentimes *adv* (also **in betweentimes**) at intervals between other events.

betwixt *prep* & *adv* (*old*) between.

betwixt and between undecided; in a middle position. [OE *betweox*]

bevel *n* **1** a sloping edge. **2** a tool which makes a sloping edge on a piece of wood or stone. — *v* ***-ll-*** **1** (*tr*) to give a bevel or slant to. **2** (*intr*) to slope at an angle. — *adj* **bevelled**. [OFr *baif*, from *baer*, to gape]

beverage *n* any liquid for drinking except water, esp. tea, coffee, hot milk, etc. [OFr *beuvrage*, from Lat *bibere*, to drink]

bevy *n* ***-ies*** **1** a group (of women or girls). **2** a flock (of larks, quails or swans).

bewail *v* (*tr*; *literary*) to express great sorrow or be very sad about: *bewail the dead.* — *n* & *adj* **bewailing**. [**be-** (sense **4**) + **wail**]

beware *v* **1** (*intr*; **of, that** or **lest**) to be careful; to be on one's guard. **2** (*tr*; *old* or *literary*) to be on one's guard against. [OE *bewarenian*, to be on one's guard]

bewilder *v* ***-r-*** (*tr*) to confuse or puzzle. — *adj* **bewildered**. — *adj* **bewildering**. — *adv* **bewilderingly**. — *n* **bewilderment**. [**be-** (sense **1**) + *wilder*, to lose one's way]

bewitch *v* (*tr*) **1** to cast a spell on. **2** to charm. [**be-** (sense **1**) + OE *wiccian*, to use witchcraft]

bewitching *adj* charming. — *adv* **bewitchingly**.

bey *n* (*hist*) a title given to a Turkish governor. [Turk]

beyond *prep* **1** on the far side of: *beyond the hills.* **2** farther on than (something) in time or place. **3** out of the range, reach, power, understanding, possibility, etc. of: *It's beyond me. beyond recognition.* **4** greater or better than in amount, size, or level. **5** other than; apart from: *unable to help beyond giving money.* — *adv* farther away; to or on the far side of. — **the back of beyond** a lonely, isolated place. — **the beyond** the unknown, esp. life after death. — **beyond a joke** too extreme, annoying, etc. to be funny. [OE *begeondan*]

bezique *n* a card game for two, three or four people played with two packs of cards from which all cards of a value below seven have been removed. [Fr *bésigue*]

b.f. *abbrev* (in accounts, etc.) brought forward.

BFPO *abbrev* British Forces Post Office (written on mail sent to a British soldier, etc. abroad, along with the number or name of the military unit to which the soldier, etc. belongs).

bhp *abbrev* brake horsepower, the power of an engine measured by the force needed to stop it.

Bi *symbol* (*chem*) bismuth.

bi- *pfx* **1** having, involving, etc. two: *bifocal.* **2** happening twice in every one, or once in every two: *bi-monthly.* **3** on or from both sides: *bilateral.* **4** (*chem*) indicating a salt which contains hydrogen: *sodium bicarbonate* ($NaHCO_3$, as opposed to sodium carbonate Na_2CO_3). [Lat *bis*, twice]

biannual *adj* happening twice a year. — *adv* **biannually**. [**bi-** (sense **2**) + **annual**]

bias *n* **1** (**towards, against**) a prejudice. **2** a tendency, or principal quality of a person's character. **3** a weight on or in an object, such as a bowl in the game of bowls, which makes it move in a particular direction. **4** in statistics, etc. a lack of balance in a result. **5** a line cut across the grain of fabric. — *v* ***-s-*** or ***-ss-*** (*tr*) **1** to influence or prejudice. **2** to give a bias to. [Fr *biais*]

biased or **biassed** *adj* favouring one side rather than another.

bias binding *n* a long narrow strip of cloth sewn into or on to the edges or corners of garments to make them strong.

biathlon *n* an outdoor sporting event in which competitors cross a 20 km course on skis, stopping at intervals to shoot at targets with rifles. [**bi-** (sense **1**) + Gr *athlon*, contest]

bib *n* **1** a piece of cloth or plastic fastened under a child's chin to protect its clothes while eating. **2** the top part of an apron or overalls, covering the chest.

Bible *n* **1** the sacred writings of the Christian Church, consisting of the Old and New Testaments. **2** (also **bible**) a copy of these. **3** (also **bible**) a highly-detailed book, regarded as an authority. [Fr, from Lat *biblia*, from Gr *biblos*, papyrus]

biblical or **Biblical** *adj* of, like, or according to the Bible.

bibliography *n* ***-ies*** **1** a list of books by one author or on one subject. **2** a list of books used as the sources of a book and usu. given in a list at the back of it. — *n* **bibliographer**. — *adj* **bibliographic** or **bibliographical**. [Gr *biblion*, book + *graphein*, to write]

bibliophile *n* a lover or collector of books. [Gr *biblion*, book + *philos*, friend]

bibulous *adj* (usu. *humorous*) liking alcohol too much, or drinking too much of it. [Lat *bibulus*, drinking freely]

bicameral *n* (of a law-making institution) made up of two parts, such as the House of Commons and the House of Lords in the British parliament. [**bi-** (sense **1**) + Lat *camera*, a chamber]

bicarb. See **bicarbonate**.

bicarbonate *n* a salt of carbonic acid (H_2CO_3) in which only one of the hydrogen atoms has been replaced, as in sodium bicarbonate ($NaHCO_3$). [**bi-** (sense **5**) + **carbonate**]

bicarbonate of soda or (*coll*) **bicarb** *n* sodium bicarbonate, a white powder used in baking, as a cure for indigestion, and in some types of fire extinguishers. ◇ See also **baking soda**.

bicentenary *n* **-*ies*** **1** a day or year exactly two hundred years after some event: *the bicentenary of the founding of the school.* **2** a celebration of this. — *adj* of or concerning a bicentenary. [**bi-** (sense **2**) + **centenary**]

bicentennial *n* (esp. *US*) a bicentenary. — *adj* **bicentennial**. [**bi-** (sense **2**) + **centennial**]

biceps *n* ***biceps*** a muscle with two heads or attachments, such as the muscle in the arm which bends the elbow. [**bi-** (sense **1**) + Lat *caput*, head]

bicker *v* **-r-** (*intr*; **about, over, with**; *coll*) to argue or quarrel, usu. about unimportant things. — *n* **bickering**. [MidE **biker**]

bicuspid *adj* having two points. — *n* an adult's tooth with two points. [**bi-** (sense **1**) + **cusp**]

bicycle *n* a vehicle consisting of a metal frame with two wheels, one behind the other, and a seat, which is driven by the rider turning pedals with his or her feet. — *v* (*intr*) to ride a bicycle. — *n* **bicyclist**. [**bi-** (sense **1**) + Gr *kyklos*, circle, wheel]

bicycle chain *n* a metal chain connecting the pedals to the back wheel of a bicycle, making it move when the pedals are turned.

bicycle clip *n* a metal clip worn around the bottoms of a cyclist's trousers, keeping them close to the leg so that they do not touch the chain and become dirty or entangled.

bicycle pump *n* a long thin pump for blowing up bicycle tyres.

bid[1] *v* **-*dd-*, *bid*** **1** (*tr* & *intr*; **for, against**) to offer (an amount of money) when trying to buy something, esp. at an auction: *bid against two other people.* **2** (*intr* & *tr*; *cards*) to state in advance (the number of tricks one will try to win). **3** (*intr*; **for**) to state a price one will charge for work to be done. — *n* **1** an offer of a price, esp. at an auction. **2** (*cards*) a statement of how many tricks one hopes to win. **3** an attempt (to obtain): *make a bid for freedom.* — *n* **bidder**. — **bid fair** (*formal*) to seem likely. [OE *beodan*, to command, summon]

biddable *adj* obedient.

bidding *n* **1** a command, request or invitation. **2** the offers at an auction. **3** (*cards*) the act of making bids. — **be at** or **do someone's bidding** to be ready to carry out someone's orders or commands.

bid[2] *v* **-*dd-*, *bade*, *bidden*** (*tr*; *formal*) **1** to command. **2** to invite: *bid her to start.* **3** to express a wish, greeting, etc.: *bid him welcome.* [OE *biddan*, to beg, pray]

bide *v* ***bode*, *bided*** (*intr*; *old*) to wait or to stay. — **bide one's time** to wait patiently for a good opportunity. [OE *bidan*]

bidet *n* a small low basin with taps, on which one sits to wash one's sexual organs, etc. [Fr, pony]

biennial *adj* **1** happening once in every two years. **2** lasting two years. — *n* a plant which takes two years to grow and flower, and which then dies. — *adv* **biennially**. [**bi-** (senses **2** & **3**) + Lat *annus*, year]

bier *n* a movable stand on which a coffin rests or is transported. [OE *bær*]

biff *v* (*tr*; *slang*) to hit very hard. — *n* a blow.

bifocal *adj* (of a lens) having two different parts, allowing both near and distant vision. [**bi-** (sense **1**) + **focal**]

bifocals *n* (*pl*) a pair of glasses with bifocal lenses, which allow the wearer to look at distant objects through the top part of the lens, and to read through the bottom part of it.

bifurcate *v* (*intr*) (of roads, etc.) to divide into two parts; to fork. — *adj* **bifurcated**. — *n* **bifurcation**. [Lat *bifurcus*, two-forked]

big *adj* **-*gg-*** **1** large or largest in size, weight or number: *the big toe.* **2** significant, important (to someone): *his big day.* **3** important, powerful, successful: *the big four.* **4** older or adult: *my big sister.* **5** (with **of**; often *ironic*) generous: *That's big of him.* **6** boastful; extravagant; ambitious: *big ideas.* **7** (*old*; with **with**) in an advanced stage of pregnancy: *big with child.* — *adv* (*coll*) **1** boastfully: *talk big.* **2** on a big scale: *think big.* — *adj* **biggish**. — *n* **bigness**. — **big deal** (*slang*) I don't care; I'm not impressed. — **make it big** (*coll*) to become successful and famous. — **too big for one's boots** (*coll*) considering oneself to be better or more important than one really is.

Big Bang *n* **1** according to some scientists, the explosion about 10 000 million years ago of a small dense quantity of matter, from which the universe was created. **2** (*Br coll*) the change, in 1986, of the rules controlling the British Stock Exchange.

Big Brother *n* an all-powerful government or its leader, that keeps complete control over its citizens.

big business *n* **1** powerful commercial and industrial organisations, esp. considered as a group. **2** an activity or object on which people spend a lot of money: *The diet industry is big business.*

big cat *n* a large member of the cat family, such as the lion or tiger.

big dipper *n* **1** a roller coaster. **2** (*caps*) a group of seven bright stars in the Great Bear constellation; the Plough.

big end *n* (*Br*) the larger end of a main connecting rod in a car engine.

big game *n* large animals, such as lions, tigers, etc. that are hunted for sport.

big guns *n* (*pl*; *coll*) the most important or powerful people in an organisation.

bighead *n* (*coll derog*) a person who has a very high opinion of his or her own importance, abilities, etc. — *adj* **big-headed**. — *n* **big-headedness**.

big-hearted *adj* thoughtful, kind, and generous. — **big-heartedness**.

big mouth *n* (*coll*) a person who often tells secrets or boasts about his or her own abilities, etc.
big time *n* (*coll*) success in any activity or profession, but esp. in show business: *hit the big time*.
big top *n* a large, round tent in which a circus gives its performances.
bigwig *n* (*coll*; often *derog*) an important person.
bigamy *n* **-ies** the crime of being married to two wives or two husbands at the same time. — *n* **bigamist**. — *adj* **bigamous**. — *adv* **bigamously**. ◇ See also **monogamy** and **polygamy**. [From **bi-** (sense **1**) + Gr *gamos*, marriage]
bight *n* **1** a stretch of gently curving coastline. **2** a loose curve or loop in a length of rope. [OE *byht*]
bigot *n* a person who has very fixed opinions, esp. about religion, politics, or race, and who refuses to tolerate the opinions of other people. — *adj* **bigoted**. — *n* **bigotry**. [OFr]
bijou *n* a small, delicate jewel or object. — *adj* (often *facet*) small and elegant. [Fr]
bike *n* (*coll*) a bicycle or motorcycle. [**bicycle**]
biker *n* (*coll*) a person who rides a motorcycle.
bikini *n* a small two-piece swimming costume for women. [From *Bikini*, an atoll in the Marshall Islands in the Pacific where atom-bomb experiments were held; the bikini's effect on men was supposed to be similarly 'explosive']
bilabial *n* & *adj* (a consonant, such as *b*) made with both lips touching, or almost touching, each other. [**bi-** (sense **1**) + Lat *labium*, lip]
bilateral *adj* **1** of or on two sides. **2** affecting, or signed or agreed by, two countries, groups, etc.: *a bilateral agreement*. — *adv* **bilaterally**. [**bi-** (sense **4**) + Lat *latus*, side]
bilateralism *n* equality, esp. in the value of trade between two countries.
bilberry *n* **-ies** **1** a small bushy plant or shrub with dark blue edible berries. **2** one of its berries.
bile *n* **1** a yellowish or greenish thick bitter liquid produced by the liver to help digest fats in food. **2** (*literary*) anger or bad temper. ◇ See also **bilious**. [Lat *bilis*]
bilge *n* **1** the broadest part of a ship's bottom. **2** (also **bilge-water**) the dirty water that collects in a ship's bilge. **3** (*coll*) rubbish or nonsense. [Prob. variant of **bulge**]
bilingual *adj* **1** written or spoken in two languages. **2** speaking two languages very well. — *n* **bilingualism**. — *n* **bilinguist**. [**bi-** (sense **1**) and Lat *lingua*, tongue]
bilious *adj* **1** sick. **2** (*derog*) (of some colours) unpleasant, making one feel sick. **3** (*literary*) bad-tempered. — *adv* **biliously**. — *n* **biliousness**. ◇ See also **bile**. [Lat *biliosus*, from *bilis*, bile]
bilk *v* (*tr*) **1** to avoid paying (someone) money one owes. **2** (with **out of**) to cheat or trick. [A term in cribbage]
bill[1] *n* **1** a piece of paper stating the amount of money owed for goods or services received. **2** a written plan for a proposed law. **3** (*US*) a banknote. **4** an advertising poster. **5** a list of items, events, performers, etc. — *v* (*tr*) **1** to send a bill to, requesting payment for goods, etc. **2** to advertise or announce (a person or event) in a poster, etc. — **fit** or **fill the bill** (*coll*) to be suitable or what is required. [Lat *bulla*, seal, document bearing a seal]
billboard *n* a large board on which advertising posters are displayed.
billing *n* the importance of a performer in a play or concert (esp. as shown by the position of his or her name on the poster advertising the performance): *top billing*.
bill of exchange *n* a written order to a person to pay a certain sum of money to some other person on a certain date or when payment is asked for.
bill of fare *n* a menu.
bill of lading *n* a receipt for goods transported by ship.
Bill of Rights *n* a written declaration of the rights of the citizens of a country.
bill of sale *n* in English law, a formal legal paper stating that something has been sold by one person to another.
billposter or **billsticker** *n* a person who puts up advertising posters.
clean bill of health *n* a declaration that a person is healthy, or that a machine or organisation is working satisfactorily.
double or **triple bill** *n* two or three films or plays presented as a single entertainment, one after the other.
bill[2] *n* **1** a bird's beak. **2** a long thin piece of land that sticks out into the sea. — **bill and coo** (*coll*; often *derog*) to kiss and whisper affectionately. [OE *bile*]
bill[3] *n* (*hist*) a weapon with a long handle and a hook-shaped blade. [OE]
billabong *n* (*Austr*) **1** a pool of water left when most of a river or stream has become dry. **2** a branch of a river which comes to an end without flowing into a sea, lake, or other river. [Wiradhuri (Australian Aboriginal language) *billa*, river + *bung*, dead]
billet[1] *n* **1** a formal order to provide lodgings for a soldier. **2** a house, often a private home, where soldiers are given food and lodging temporarily. — *v* **-t-** (*tr*) to give lodging to (soldiers, etc). [OFr *billette*]
billet[2] *n* **1** a small log of wood. **2** a bar of metal. [OFr *billette*]
billet-doux *n* ***billets-doux*** (*old*) a love-letter. [Fr *billet*, letter + *doux*, sweet]
billiards *n* (*sing*) a game played on a cloth-covered table with pockets at the sides and corners, into which balls must be struck with long thin sticks called cues. ◇ See also **snooker** and **pool**. [Fr *billard*, from *bille*, narrow stick]

billion *n* **1** in Britain and Europe, a million millions. **2** in the US, and increasingly in Britain and Europe, a thousand millions. — *n & adj* **billionth**. [**bi-** (sense **1**) + **million**]

billionaire or **billionairess** *n* a man, or a woman, who has money and property worth a billion pounds, dollars, etc.

billions *n* (*pl*; *coll*) very many; lots.

billow *n* **1** a large wave. **2** an upward-moving mass (of smoke, mist, etc.). — *v* (*intr*) **1** to move in great waves or clouds. **2** (**out**) to swell or bulge like a sail in the wind. — *n* **billowing**. — *adj* **billowy**. [Norse *bylgja*]

billy, **-ies** or **billycan** *n* (*esp. Br & Austr*) a metal container used for cooking in or for eating and drinking from, esp. when camping.

billy goat *n* a male goat. ◇ See also **nanny goat**. [From the name *Billy*]

billy-o or **billy-oh** : **like billy-o** or **-oh** (*Br old slang*) quickly, powerfully, or forcefully: *raining like billy-oh*.

bimbo *n* **-os** (*slang*, usu. *derog*) a person, esp. a young woman, who is physically attractive but empty-headed. [Ital *bimbo*, baby, small child]

bimetallic *adj* made of or using two metals. [**bi-** (sense **1**) + **metallic**]

bimonthly *adj* **1** happening once in every two months. **2** happening twice a month. — *adv* **1** every two months. **2** twice a month. [**bi-** (sense **2**) + **monthly**]

bin *n* **1** a large container for rubbish, often with a lid, kept inside or outside a house, and in a street. **2** a container for storing some kinds of food: *a bread bin*. **3** a large industrial container for storing things in large quantities. **4** a stand or case with sections in, for storing bottles of wine. [OE *binn*]

bin-liner *n* a plastic bag kept inside a rubbish bin, which can be removed and thrown away when it is full.

binary *adj* **1** consisting of two. **2** relating to the binary system .— *n* **-ies** a thing made up of two parts. [Lat *binarius*]

binary star *n* two stars sharing and revolving round the same centre of gravity.

binary system *n* the system of calculating, used esp. in computers, with a base of 2 (instead of 10) and which uses only the numbers 0 and 1.

bind *v* **bound 1** (*tr*; **to, on, together**) to tie or fasten tightly. **2** (*tr*; **up**) to tie or pass strips of cloth, bandage, etc. around. **3** (*tr*) to control or prevent from moving. ◇ See also **bound**[1]. **4** (*tr*) to make (someone) promise (to do something). **5** (*tr*) to require or oblige (to do something): *legally bound to reply*. **6** (*tr*) to fasten together and put a cover on (the separate pages of a book). **7** (*tr*) to put a strip of cloth on the edge of (something) to strengthen it. **8** (*tr*) to cause dry ingredients to stick together. **9** (*intr*) to stick together. — *n* (*coll*) a difficult or boring situation. — *v* **bind over** (*tr*) to make (a person) legally obliged to do a particular thing, e.g. to keep the peace and not cause a disturbance. [*bindan*]

binder *n* **1** a person who binds books. **2** a hard, book-like cover in which loose pieces of paper can be kept in order. **3** a machine used for harvesting grain that binds it as it cuts it.

bindery *n* **-ies** a place where books are bound.

binding *n* **1** the part of a book cover on to which the pages are stuck. **2** cloth, etc. used to bind something. — *adj* formally or legally obliging (someone) to do (something).

bindweed *n* a type of wild plant that attaches itself to other plants. ◇ See also **convolvulus**.

binge (*coll*) *n* a period of uncontrolled drinking (of alcohol) or eating. — *v* (*intr*) to spend a period of time eating or drinking too much. — *n* **binger**.

bingo *n* a game of chance in which players have a card with different numbers on, which they cross off as another person calls numbers out at random, the winner being the first person to cross off all the numbers on his or her card. — *interj* **1** the word shouted by the winner of a game of bingo. **2** an expression of success or sudden pleasure.

binnacle *n* a case for a ship's compass. [Earlier *bittacle*, from Lat *habitaculum*, habitation]

binoculars *n* (*pl*) an instrument with lenses for making distant objects look nearer, like two small telescopes joined together. [Lat *bini*, two by two + *oculus*, eye]

binocular *adj* with or suitable for two eyes.

binocular vision *n* the ability to adjust both eyes in order to see an object clearly and to judge its distance from oneself.

binomial *n* a mathematical expression made up of two sets of numbers or letters, e.g. $6x-3y$. — *adj* consisting of two sets of numbers or letters. [**bi-** (sense **1**) + Lat *nomen*, name]

binomial theorem *n* a formula for finding any power of a binomial without lengthy multiplication, e.g. $(a + b)^2 = (a^2 + 2ab + b^2)$.

bio- *comb fm* life or living things: *biology*. [Gr *bios*, life]

biochemistry *n* a branch of chemistry which studies the chemicals and chemical changes in living organisms. — *adj* **biochemical**. — *n* **biochemist**.

biocontrol *n* biological control.

biodegradable *adj* able to be broken down by bacteria and other living organisms, and so decay naturally. ◇ See also **photodegradable**. [**bio-** + **degrade** (sense **3**)]

bioengineering or **biological engineering** *n* the manufacture of mechanical or electronic aids for parts of the body which don't work properly.

bioflavonoid *n* vitamin P. [**bio-**]
biography *n* **-*ies*** **1** a written account by someone of another person's life. **2** the art of writing such accounts. — *n* **biographer**. — *adj* **biographic** or **biographical**. — *adv* **biographically**. [**bio-** + Gr *graphein*, to write]
biology *n* the science and study of living things. — *adj* **biological** . — *adv* **biologically**. — *n* **biologist**. [**bio-** + **-logy** (sense **1**)]
biological clock *n* a supposed natural mechanism inside one's body which controls the body's functions.
biological control *n* a method of reducing the numbers of a pest (plant, animal or parasite) by introducing or encouraging one of its natural enemies (a predator, parasite or disease), as opposed to the use of chemical pesticides.
biological engineering see **bioengineering**.
biological warfare *n* the use of diseases as a weapon in war.
bionics *n* (*sing*) **1** the study of how living organisms function and the application of the principles observed to develop computers and other machines which work in similar ways. **2** the replacement of damaged parts of the body, such as limbs and heart valves, by electronic devices. [**bio-** + **electronics**]
bionic *adj* **1** of or using bionics. **2** (*coll*) having extraordinary powers of speed, strength, etc.
biophysics *n* (*sing*) the application of the laws of physics to biology. — *n* **biophysicist**.
biopsy *n* **-*ies*** examination of a sample of cells or liquids from a sick person's body to discover what disease they have. [**bio-** + Gr *opsis*, sight or appearance]
biorhythms *n* (*pl*) patterns of biological changes in the body which are supposed to affect how a person feels and behaves.
biosphere *n* the parts of the Earth's surface and atmosphere where living things exist.
biosynthesis *n* the production of complex chemical substances by living organisms.
biotechnology *n* the use of living organisms to produce chemicals and other substances for industry.
biotin *n* one of the members of the vitamin B group. [Gr *bios*, life]
bipartisan *adj* of, supported by, or consisting of, the members of two groups or political parties. [**bi-** (sense **1**) + **partisan**]
bipartite *adj* **1** consisting of two parts. **2** involving, or agreed by, two parties: *a bipartite agreement*. [**bi-** (sense **1**) + Lat *partire*, to divide]
biped *n* an animal with two feet, e.g. man. — *adj* (also **bipedal**) having two feet. [**bi-** (sense **1**) + Lat *pes*, foot]
biplane *n* an aeroplane with two sets of wings, one above the other. [**bi-** (sense **1**) + **plane**[2]]
bipolar *adj* have two poles or extremes. [**bi-** (sense **1**) + **polar**]
birch *n* **1** a small tree with pointed leaves and smooth bark, valued for its wood. **2** the hard wood of this tree. **3** a bundle of birch branches, formerly used as an instrument of punishment. — *adj* made of birch wood. [OE *beorc*]
bird *n* **1** a two-legged, egg-laying creature with feathers, a beak and two wings. **2** (*Br slang*; often considered *offensive*) a girl or woman. **3** (*old coll*) a person, esp. a strange or unusual one. — **the birds and the bees** (*coll euph* or *humorous*) information about sex and reproduction. — **birds of a feather** (*Br coll*) people who are like each other, share the same ideas, the same way of life, etc. — **do bird** (*Br slang*) to serve a prison sentence. — **give (someone)**, or **get, the bird** (*coll*) to criticise or be criticised, esp. loudly. — **kill two birds with one stone** (*coll*) to achieve two things with a single action. — **strictly for the birds** (*coll*) worthless; unimportant. [OE *bridd*, young bird]
birdie *n* **1** a child's word for a little bird. **2** (*golf*) a score of one stroke less than the fixed standard number of strokes (par) for a particular hole on a course. — *v* **-*dying*** (*tr*) (*golf*) to complete a hole with a birdie score.
bird-lime *n* a sticky substance put on the branches of trees to catch small birds.
bird of paradise *n* any of various brightly-coloured birds found in and around New Guinea.
bird of passage *n* **1** a bird that flies to different parts of the world as the seasons change. **2** a person who moves around a lot and never settles in one place.
bird of prey *n* any of several types of bird (e.g. the owl) that kill animals and birds for food.
bird's-eye view *n* **1** a general view from above. **2** a general impression.
bird strike *n* a crash between a bird or birds and the engine of an aeroplane.
bird-watcher *n* someone who studies birds by observing them closely, usu. as a hobby. — *n* **bird-watching**.
biretta *n* a stiff, square cap worn by Roman Catholic clergy, which may be black (worn by priests), purple (worn by bishops) or red (worn by cardinals). [Ital *berretta*]
biriani or **biryani** *n* a type of highly seasoned Indian dish consisting mainly of rice, with meat or fish. [Urdu]
Biro® *n* **-*os*** a type of pen which writes using a small ball. [L *Biró* (1899–1985), the inventor]
birth *n* **1** the act or process of being born or of bearing children. **2** family history or origin: *of humble birth*. **3** beginning; origins: *the birth of socialism*. — **give birth to 1** (of a mother) to bear or produce (a baby). **2** to produce or be the cause of: *give birth to a new idea*. [Norse *byrthr*]

birth certificate *n* an official form stating the time and place of a person's birth, his or her parents, etc.

birth control *n* the prevention of pregnancy, e.g. by means of contraception.

birthday *n* **1** the anniversary of the day on which a person was born. **2** the day on which one was born.

birthday honours *n* (*pl*) in the UK, titles or medals awarded to people on the official birthday of the king or queen.

birthday suit *n* (*coll humorous*) one's naked body.

birthmark *n* a permanent dark mark on a person's skin at or from birth.

birthplace *n* the place where a person was born or where something began.

birthrate *n* a number of births in a particular area within a particular period, compared to the number of people living there.

birthright *n* the rights a person may claim by being born into a particular family, social class, etc.

biryani. See **biriani**.

biscuit *n* **1** a crisp, flat cake. **2** (also **biscuitware**) objects made from baked clay that have not been glazed. **3** a pale brown colour. — *adj* pale brown in colour. — **take the biscuit** (*coll*) to be worse than everything else that has happened. [OFr *bescoit*, from Lat *bis*, twice + *coquere*, to cook]

bisect *v* (*tr*) to divide into two strictly equal parts. — *n* **bisection**. [**bi-** (sense **1**) + Lat *secare*, to cut]

bisexual *adj* **1** sexually attracted to both males and females. **2** having the sexual organs of both male and female. ◇ See also **unisexual**. — *n* a bisexual person. — *n* **bisexuality** — *adv* **bisexually**. [**bi-** (sense **1**) + **sexual**]

bishop *n* **1** a senior Christian priest or minister in the Roman Catholic, Anglican, Orthodox, etc. churches, in charge of a group of churches in an area, or diocese. **2** a piece in the game of chess, which may only be moved diagonally across the board. [OE *bisceop*, from Gr *episkopos*, overseer]

bishopric *n* **1** the post or position of bishop. **2** the area under the charge of a bishop.

bismuth *n* a reddish-white metallic element, symbol **Bi**, used in alloys and in medicine. [Ger *Wismut*]

bison *n* ***bison*** either of two species of shaggy wild cattle with large heads, short horns, heavy front bodies and humps on their backs. [Lat, from Germanic]

bisque[1] *n* a thick, rich soup, usu. made from shellfish, cream and wine. [Fr]

bisque[2] *n* a type of baked clay or china, which has not been glazed. [See **biscuit** (sense **3**)]

bistro *n* ***-os*** a small bar or informal restaurant. [Fr]

bit[1] *n* a small piece. — **a bit** (*coll*) **1** a short time or distance: *wait a bit*. **2** a little; slightly; rather: *a bit of a fool*. **3** a lot: *takes a bit of doing*. — **a bit much, thick** or **rich** (*coll*) (behaviour that is) unacceptable, unreasonable, or unfair. — **a bit off** (*Br coll*) bad manners, taste, or behaviour. — **bit by bit** gradually. — **do one's bit** to do one's fair share. [OE *bita*]

bit-part *n* a small acting part in a play or film.

bits and pieces or **bobs** *n* (*pl*; *Br coll*) small objects or possessions.

bitty *adj* **-ier**, **-iest** (*coll*) made up of small, unrelated pieces. — *n* **bittiness**.

bit[2]. See **bite**.

bit[3] *n* **1** a small metal bar which a horse holds in its mouth as part of the bridle with which it is controlled. **2** a tool with a cutting edge which can be fitted into a drill and turned at high speed. **3** the part of a key which connects with the lever in a lock. — **take the bit between one's teeth** to begin to deal with a problem, etc. in a serious and determined way. [**bite**]

bit[4] *n* a unit of information stored in a computer, expressed as a choice between 0 and 1. [**binary** + **digit**]

bitch *n* **1** a female of the dog family. **2** (*coll derog offensive*) a bad-tempered, unpleasant, spiteful woman. **3** (*slang*) a difficult or unpleasant thing. [OE *bicce*]

bitchy *adj* **-ier**, **-iest** (*coll derog*) spiteful. — *adv* **bitchily**. — *n* **bitchiness**.

bite *v* ***biting, bit, bitten*** **1** (*tr* & *intr*; **away**, **off**, **out**, etc.) to grasp, seize or tear with the teeth. **2** (*tr* & *intr*) (of insects and snakes) to make a hole in (a person's) skin and suck blood. **3** (*intr*) (of fish) to get caught on the hook on a fishing line. **4** (*intr*) to have an effect, usu. bad: *The rise in the cost of petrol is really beginning to bite*. **5** (*intr*) (of a wheel, screw, etc.) to grip firmly. **6** (*tr*; *coll*) to annoy or worry: *What's biting him?* — *n* **1** an act of biting. **2** a wound caused by biting. **3** a small amount of food: *a bite to eat*. **4** strength, sharpness or bitterness of taste. — *v* **bite back** (*tr*; *coll*) to stop oneself from saying (something) that one had almost begun to say. — **bite someone's head off** (*coll*) to shout at (someone) suddenly and very angrily, often in answer to a question. — **bite one's tongue** to stop oneself saying something one very much wants to say. [OE *bitan*]

biting *adj* **1** cold and causing pain or discomfort: *a biting wind*. **2** sharp and hurtful.

bitter *adj* **1** having a sharp, acid and often unpleasant taste. **2** feeling or causing sadness or pain: *bitter memories*. **3** difficult to accept: *a bitter disappointment*. **4** showing a lot of dislike, hatred, or opposition: *bitter criticism*. **5** (of the weather, etc.) very cold. — *n* (*Br*) a type of beer with a slightly bitter taste, strongly flavoured with hops. — *adj* **bitterly**. — *n* **bitterness**. — **a bitter pill to swallow** something difficult to accept. — **until, till** or **to the bitter end** up to the very end, however unpleasant, and in spite of difficulties. [OE *biter*]

bitters *n* (*pl*) a liquid made from bitter herbs or roots, used to help digestion or to flavour certain alcoholic drinks.

bittersweet *adj* pleasant and unpleasant, or bitter and sweet, at the same time.

bittern *n* a long-legged European bird that lives on or near water and makes a very loud, deep sound. [OFr *butor*]

bitumen *n* a brown or black sticky substance obtained from petroleum and used for surfacing roads, etc. [Lat]

bituminous *adj* containing bitumen.

bituminous coal *n* a type of coal which burns with a smoky flame.

bivalent *adj* (*chem*) divalent. [**bi**-]

bivalve *n* & *adj* (any of several kinds of shellfish, such as an oyster) with a shell made up of two parts held together by a type of hinge. [**bi**- (sense **1**) + **valve**]

bivouac *n* a temporary camp without tents, esp. used by soldiers and mountaineers. — *v* **-ck-** (*intr*) to camp out temporarily at night without a tent. [Fr, from Swiss Ger *Beiwacht*, an additional guard at night]

bizarre *adj* odd or very strange. — *adv* **bizarrely**. — *n* **bizarreness**. [Span *bizarro*, gallant or brave]

Bk *symbol* (*chem*) berkelium.

BL *abbrev* **1** Bachelor of Law. **2** British Library.

blab *v* **-bb-** **1** (*intr* & *tr*; **out**) to tell (a secret, etc.). **2** (*intr*) to chatter foolishly. [MidE *blabbe*]

blabber *v* (*intr*; **on**) to talk nonsense, esp. without stopping.

blabbermouth *n* a person who gives away secrets.

black *adj* **1** of the colour of coal, the night sky, etc. **2** without light. **3** (also *cap*) (of people) dark-skinned, esp. of African, West Indian, or Australian Aboriginal origin. **4** (also *cap*) belonging or relating to black people: *black rights*. **5** dirty. **6** (of drinks) without milk: *black coffee*. **6** angry, threatening: *black looks*. **7** sad, gloomy or depressed: *a black mood*. **8** promising trouble; likely to be bad in some way: *The future looks black*. **9** evil, wicked or sinister: *black-hearted*. **10** amusing, but also sinister: *black comedy*. **11** (of goods, etc.) not allowed by a trade union to be handled, usu. during a strike. — *n* **1** the colour of coal, the night sky, etc. **2** anything which is black in colour. **3** (also *cap*) a person of African, West Indian or Australian Aboriginal origin. **4** black clothes worn when in mourning. — *v* (*tr*) **1** to make black. **2** to clean with black polish. **3** to forbid work to be done on or with (certain goods). — *n* **blackness**. — **black and blue** (*coll*) covered in bruises. — *v* **black out 1** (*tr*) to cause to be without light (*n* **blackout**). **2** (*intr*) to lose consciousness (*n* **blackout**). **3** (*tr*) to prevent (news, etc.) from being broadcast or published (*n* **blackout**). — **black and white 1** (of television, photographs, etc.) having no colours except black, white and shades of grey. **2** either good or bad, right or wrong, etc. with no compromise. **3** writing or print: *see it in black and white*. — **in the black** with money on the credit side of an account. [OE *blæc*]

Black Africa *n* the part of Africa south of the Sahara desert, where the population is mainly black.

blackamoor *n* (*old*; usu. *derog*) a dark-skinned or black person.

black art same as **black magic**.

blackball *v* (*tr*) **1** to vote against (esp. a person who wants to join a club or society of which one is a member). **2** to refuse to see or speak to (someone).

black belt *n* **1** (in judo, karate, etc.) a belt showing the wearer has reached the highest possible level of skill. **2** a person who has won and is allowed to wear a black belt.

blackberry *n* a very dark purple-coloured fruit growing on a thorny bush.

blackbird *n* **1** a small European bird, the male of which is black with a yellow beak. **2** any of various similar N American birds.

blackboard *n* a dark-coloured board for writing on with chalk, esp. used in schools.

black box *n* a small machine in an aeroplane which automatically records the details of the aeroplane's flight.

blackcap *n* a small songbird, the male of which has a black-topped head.

blackcock *n* the male of the black grouse.

Black Country *n* the industrialised West Midlands region of England.

blackcurrant *n* **1** a garden bush grown for its small, round black fruit. **2** its fruit.

Black Death *n* a form of bubonic plague, which killed over 50 million people in Europe and Asia in the 14th century.

black economy *n* unofficial business, trade, etc. which is not declared to the government in order to avoid paying tax.

blacken *v* **-n-** **1** (*tr* & *intr*) to make or become black or very dark in colour. **2** (*tr*) to speak evil or badly of: *blacken his name*.

black eye *n* an eye with darkened swollen skin around it, usu. from being hit.

blackguard *n* (*old*) a rogue or villain. — *adj* **blackguardly**.

blackhead *n* a small black spot on the skin caused by sweat blocking one of the skin's tiny pores.

black hole *n* an area in space which pulls matter into itself, thought to exist where a star has collapsed.

black ice *n* a type of ice which cannot be seen, and which makes roads dangerous to drive on.

blacking *n* (*old*) black polish, esp. for shoes.

blackjack *n* **1** pontoon or a similar card-game. **2** (*NAm*) a length of hard, flexible leather, esp. used for hitting people.
black lead same as **graphite**.
blackleg *n* (*derog*) a person willing to work when his or her fellow-workers are on strike. — *v* **-gg-** (*intr*) to refuse to join a strike.
blacklist *n* a list of people convicted or suspected of something, or not approved of. — *v* (*tr*) to put (a person, etc.) on such a list.
blackly *adv* in an angry or threatening way.
black magic *n* magic which calls up the power of the devil to perform evil.
blackmail *v* (*tr*; **into**) **1** to obtain money illegally from (a person) by threatening to make known something which he or she wants to keep secret. **2** to try to influence (a person) using unfair pressure. — *n* the act of blackmailing someone. — *n* **blackmailer**.
Black Maria *n* (*coll*) a van for taking criminals to prison.
black mark *n* an indication of disapproval or criticism.
black market *n* the illegal buying and selling, at high prices, of goods which are scarce or in great demand. — *n* **black=marketeer**.
black mass *n* a ceremony like a Christian mass, performed by people who worship the devil.
blackout see **black out** above.
black pepper *n* pepper produced by grinding the dried fruits of the pepper plant, or peppercorns, without removing their dark outer covering.
Black Power *n* a movement seeking political and social rights for black people.
black pudding *n* a dark sausage made from pig's blood and fat.
Black Rod *n* in Britain, the chief usher in the House of Lords.
black sheep *n* a member of a family or group who is disapproved of in some way.
Blackshirt *n* a member of the Italian Fascist Party before and during the Second World War.
blacksmith *n* a person who makes and repairs by hand things made of iron, such as horseshoes.
black spot *n* (*Br*) **1** a dangerous part of a road where accidents often occur. **2** an area where a particular social condition is very bad: *an unemployment black spot*.
blackthorn *n* a shrub with black twigs and white flowers, which produces sour, plum-like fruit called sloes.
black-tie *n* a black bow-tie. — *adj* (of a celebration, party, etc.) very formal, at which men are expected to wear a dinner jacket and a bow-tie, and women an evening dress.
black widow *n* a very poisonous kind of spider.
bladder *n* **1** the bag-like organ in the body in which urine collects. **2** a hollow bag made of leather, etc. stretched by filling with air or liquid. **3** a small, air-filled pouch in certain plants, e.g. seaweed. [OE *blædre*, blister, pimple]
blade *n* **1** the cutting part of a knife, sword, etc. **2** the flat, usu. long and narrow part of a leaf or petal. **3** the wide flat part of an oar, bat, etc. **4** a flat bone, esp. in the shoulder: *shoulder blade*. [OE *blæd*]
blame *v* (*tr*; **for, on**) **1** to consider (a person or thing) as responsible for (something bad or wrong). **2** to find fault with (a person). — *n* (**for**) responsibility (for something bad or wrong). — **be to blame (for)** to be the cause (of something bad or wrong). [OFr *blasmer*, from Lat *blasphemare*, to blaspheme]
blameless *adj* innocent; free from blame. — *adv* **blamelessly**. — *n* **blamelessness**.
blameworthy *adj* deserving blame. — *n* **blameworthiness**.
blanch *v* **1** (*tr*) to make white by removing the colour. **2** (*intr* & *tr*) to make or become white, esp. through fear. **3** (*tr*) to prepare (vegetables or meat) for cooking or freezing by boiling in water for a few seconds. **4** (*tr*) to remove the skins (from almonds, etc.) by soaking in boiling water for a few seconds. [OFr *blanchir*]
blancmange *n* a cold, sweet, jelly-like pudding made with milk. [OFr *blanc*, white + *manger*, food]
bland *adj* (usu. *derog*) **1** (of food) almost without taste. **2** (of people or their actions) mild or gentle; showing no strong emotions. **3** boring, uninteresting: *a bland appearance*. — *adv* **blandly**. — *n* **blandness**. [Lat *blandus*, soft, smooth]
blandish *v* (*tr*) to persuade by gentle flattery. [OFr *blandir*]
blandishments *n* (*pl*) flattery intended to persuade.
blank *adj* **1** (of paper) not written or printed on. **2** (of magnetic tape, video tape, etc.) with no sound or pictures recorded on it. **3** with spaces left for details, information, a signature, etc.: *a blank form*. **4** not filled in; empty. **5** showing no expression or interest: *a blank look*. **6** having no thoughts or ideas: *Her mind went blank*. **7** without a break or ornament: *a blank wall*. — *n* **1** an empty space. **2** an empty space left (on forms, etc.) to be filled in with particular information. **3** a printed form with blank spaces. **4** a state of having no thoughts or ideas: *My mind went a complete blank*. **5** a dash written in place of a word. **6** a blank cartridge. — *v* (*tr*; **off, out**) to hide or form a screen in front (of): *clouds blanking out the sun*. — *adv* **blankly**. — *n* **blankness**. — **draw a blank** to get no results; to fail. [Fr *blanc*]
blank cartridge *n* a cartridge containing an explosive but no bullet.

blank cheque *n* **1** a cheque which has been signed but on which the amount to be paid has been left blank. **2** complete freedom or authority.

blank verse *n* poetry which does not rhyme.

blanket *n* **1** a thick, warm covering, usu. made of wool, used to cover beds, or for wrapping people, etc. in. **2** something which covers (something) thickly: *a blanket of fog*. — *adj* general; applying to or covering all cases, etc.: *a blanket rule*. — *v* **-t-** (*tr*) **1** to cover with, or as if with, a blanket. **2** to keep quiet or suppress. [OFr *blankete*, from *blanc*, white]

blanket bath *n* the washing of a sick person in his or her bed.

blanquette *n* a dish made with white meat such as chicken or veal, cooked in a white sauce. [Fr]

blare *v* **1** (*intr*) to make a sound like a trumpet. **2** (*intr* & *tr*) to sound or say loudly and harshly. — *n* a loud, harsh sound. [MidE *blaren*]

blarney *n* flattering words used to persuade or deceive. — *v* **-neyed** (*tr*) to persuade using flattery. [From *Blarney* Castle, near Cork in Ireland, where a stone that is difficult to reach is said to give the gift of persuasive talk to those who kiss it]

blasé *adj* bored or without enthusiasm, usu. through over-familiarity. [Fr]

blaspheme *v* **1** (*intr* & *tr*) to speak disrespectfully or rudely about (God or sacred matters). **2** (*intr*) to use the name of God as a swear word. — *n* **blasphemer**. [Lat *blasphemare*]

blasphemy *n* **-ies** speaking about God or sacred matters in a disrespectful or rude way. — *adj* **blasphemous**. — *adv* **blasphemously**.

blast *n* **1** an explosion, or the strong wave of air spreading out from it. **2** a strong, sudden stream or gust (of air, wind, etc.). **3** a sudden loud sound of a trumpet, car horn, etc. **4** a sudden and violent outburst of anger or criticism. — *v* **1** (*tr*) to blow up (a tunnel, rock, etc.) with explosives. **2** (*tr*) to destroy: *blast his hopes*. **3** (*tr*) to wither or cause to shrivel up. **4** (*intr*; **away, out**) to make a loud or explosive noise: *music blasting out from the radio*. **5** (*tr*; **out**) to cause to make or send out a loud or explosive noise: *a radio blasting out music*. **6** (*tr*) to criticise severely. — *interj* (*coll*) an expression of annoyance, etc. — *n* **blasting**. — **at full blast** at full power, speed, etc. — *v* **blast off** (*intr*) (of a spacecraft) to be launched (*n* **blast-off**). [OE *blæst*]

blasted *adj* (*coll*) annoying. — *adv* (*coll*) extremely: *blasted cold*.

blast furnace *n* a furnace for melting iron, into which blasts of hot air are blown.

blatant *adj* **1** very obvious and without shame: *a blatant lie*. **2** very noticeable and obtrusive. — *adv* **blatantly**.

blather. See **blether**.

blaze[1] *n* **1** a bright, strong fire or flame. **2** a sudden and sharp bursting out (of emotion). **3** a brilliant display. **4** (in *pl* in phrases; *coll*) hell: *Go to blazes!* — *v* (*intr*) **1** (**away**) to burn or shine brightly. **2** to show great emotion, esp. anger. — *v* **blaze away** (*intr*; **at**) **1** to fire a gun rapidly and without stopping. **2** (*coll*) to work very hard. — *v* **blaze up** (*intr*) **1** to suddenly burn much more brightly. **2** to become very angry. — **like blazes** (*coll*) quickly or with great energy. [OE *blæse*, torch]

blazing *adj* **1** burning brightly. **2** (*coll*) extremely angry.

blaze[2] *n* **1** a white mark on an animal's face. **2** a mark made on the bark of a tree, esp. to show a route or path. — *v* (*tr*) to mark (a tree, path, etc.) with blazes. — **blaze a trail** to be the first to do, study, discover, etc. something. [Perhaps related to Norse *blesi*]

blaze[3] *v* (*tr*; **abroad**) to make (news or information) widely known. [Related to Norse *blasa*, to blow]

blazer *n* a light jacket, often in the colours of a school or club and sometimes worn as part of a uniform. [**blaze**[1]]

blazon *v* **-n-** (*tr*) **1** to make public. **2** to describe (a coat of arms) in technical terms. **3** to paint names, designs, etc. on (a coat of arms). — *n* a shield or coat of arms. [OFr *blason*, shield]

bleach *v* (*tr* & *intr*) to make or become white or without colour, through exposure to the sun or by chemicals. — *n* **1** a liquid chemical used to bleach clothes, etc. **2** the process of bleaching. [OE *blæcan*]

bleaching powder *n* a white powder used in bleaching, a compound of calcium, chlorine and oxygen.

bleak *adj* **1** exposed and desolate. **2** cold and not welcoming. **3** offering little or no hope. — *adj* **bleakly**. — *n* **bleakness**. [OE *blac*, pale]

bleary *adj* **-ier, -iest** **1** (of eyes) red and dim, usu. because of tiredness or through crying. **2** blurred, indistinct and unclear. — *adv* **blearily**.

bleat *v* **1** (*intr*) to cry like a sheep, goat or calf. **2** (*intr* & *tr*; **out**) to speak or say (something) foolishly and in a weak, high voice. [OE *blætan*]

bleed *v* **bled** **1** (*intr*) to lose or let out blood. **2** (*tr*) to remove or take blood from. **3** (*intr*) (of plants, etc.) to lose juice or sap. **4** (*tr*) to empty liquid or air from (a machine, radiator, etc.). **5** (*tr*; *coll*) to obtain money from (someone), usu. illegally. **6** (*intr*) to be very sad: *My heart bleeds for her*. **7** (*intr*) (of dye) to come out in water. [OE *bledan*]

bleeding *adj* & *adv* (*vulg slang*) expressing anger or disgust: *a bleeding fool*; *He's bleeding lying*.

bleep *n* **1** a short, high burst of sound, usu. made by an electronic machine. **2** same as **bleeper**. — *v* **1** (*intr*) to give out a short, high sound. **2** (*tr*) to call (someone) using a bleeper. [Prob. imit.]

bleeper *n* a small, portable radio receiver which makes a bleeping sound when it picks up a signal, used esp. to call a doctor in a hospital.

blemish *n* a stain, mark or fault. — *v* (*tr*) to stain or spoil the beauty of. [OFr *blesmir*]

blench *v* (*intr*) to start back or move away, esp. in fear. [OE *blencan*]

blend *v* **1** (*tr*) to mix (different sorts or varieties) into one. **2** (*intr*; **in**, **with**) to form a mixture or harmonious combination; to go well together. **3** (*tr*; **with**) to mix together. **4** (*intr*; **into**) (esp. of colours) to shade gradually into: *sea blending into the sky*. — *n* a mixture or combination. [MidE *blenden*]

blender *n* a machine for mixing food or making it into a liquid.

blende *n* a mineral containing zinc sulphide. [Ger *blenden*, to deceive]

blenny *n* **-ies** a type of small fish with a scaleless, slimy skin. [Gr *blennos*, mucus]

bless *v* ***blessed*** or ***blest*** (*tr*) **1** to ask God to show favour to or protect. **2** to make or pronounce holy; to consecrate. **3** to praise; to give honour or glory to. **4** (**with**) to give (great happiness, beauty, etc.) to: *blessed with good health*. **5** to thank or be thankful for: *I bless the day I met him*. — **bless me** or **bless my soul** an expression of surprise, pleasure, dismay, etc. — **bless you!** said to a person who has just sneezed. [OE *bletsian*]

blessed *adj* **1** holy. **2** (in the Roman Catholic Church) pronounced holy by the Pope, usu. as the first stage of becoming a saint. **3** (*coll euph*) damned. — *adv* **blessedly**. — *n* **blessedness**.

blessing *n* **1** a wish or prayer for happiness or success. **2** a cause of happiness; a benefit or advantage. **3** approval or good wishes. **4** a short prayer said before or after a meal. — **a blessing in disguise** something that has proved to be fortunate after seeming unfortunate. — **count one's blessings** to remember what is good in one's life instead of complaining.

blether or **blather** *v* **-r-** (*intr*; esp. *Scot*) to talk foolishly. [Norse *blathra*]

blew. See **blow**[1].

blight *n* **1** a disease that causes plants to wither and die. **2** an insect, etc. that causes blight. **3** a person or thing that causes decay or destruction, or spoils things. — *v* (*tr*) **1** to affect with blight. **2** to harm or destroy. **3** to disappoint or frustrate: *blighted hopes*.

blighter *n* (*old coll*) **1** a person one dislikes. **2** a person one feels some sympathy for or envy of: *poor old blighter*. [**blight**]

blimey *interj* (*Br slang*) used to express surprise or annoyance. [*gorblimey*, God blind me]

Blimp or **blimp** *n* a very conservative, old-fashioned, reactionary person. — *adj* **blimpish**. [From the fat, pompous cartoon character Colonel *Blimp*, used in anti-German and anti-government cartoons during the Second World War]

blimp *n* **1** a type of large balloon or airship, used for publicity, observation or defence. **2** a soundproof cover for a camera used to shoot films.

blind *adj* **1** not able to see. **2** (**to**) unable or unwilling to understand or appreciate: *blind to his faults*. **3** without preparation or previous knowledge. **4** unthinking, without reason or purpose: *blind hatred*. **5** hidden from sight: *a blind entrance*. **6** not allowing sight of what is beyond: *a blind summit*. **7** (in flying) using instruments only. **8** having no openings: *a blind wall*. **9** closed at one end. **10** (of pies, pastry cases, etc.) cooked without a filling. **11** (of plants) failing to produce flowers. **12** (*coll*) for people who are blind. — *adv* blindly: *flying blind*. — *n* **1** a screen to stop light coming through a window. **2** a person, action or thing which hides the truth or deceives. **3** anything which prevents sight or blocks out light. **4** (with **the**) people who cannot see. — *v* (*tr*) **1** to make blind. **2** to make unreasonable, foolish, etc.: *blinded by anger*. **3** (**with**) to confuse or dazzle: *blind him with science*. — *n* & *adj* **blinding**. — *adv* **blindly**. — *n* **blindness**. — **blind drunk** (*coll*) completely drunk. — **swear blind** (*coll*) to state with certainty. — **turn a blind eye to** to pretend not to notice. [OE]

blind alley *n* **1** a very narrow road with an opening at one end only. **2** a situation, etc. which is leading nowhere.

blind date *n* **1** a date with a person of the opposite sex whom one has not met before, organised by a third person. **2** the person met on such a date.

blindfold *n* a piece of cloth used to cover the eyes to prevent a person from seeing. — *adj* & *adv* with one's eyes covered. — *v* (*tr*) to cover (someone's) eyes to prevent him or her from seeing.

blindman's-buff *n* a children's game in which one child wears a blindfold and tries to catch the other children.

blind spot *n* **1** a small area on the retina at the back of the eye which is not sensitive to light and has no vision. **2** a place where sight or vision is obscured because something is in the way: *a motorist's blind spot*. **3** any subject which a person either cannot understand, or refuses to even try to understand.

blindworm *n* same as **slow-worm**.

blink *v* **1** (*intr*) to open and shut the eyes very quickly. **2** (*tr*) to open and shut (an eyelid or an eye) very quickly. **3** (*intr*) (of a light) to flash on and off or shine unsteadily. **4** (*intr* with **at**) to refuse to recognise or accept (esp. something unpleasant). — *n* **1** an act of blinking. **2** a brief period (of sunshine, etc.). — **in the blink of an eye** very quickly. — **on the blink** (*coll*) not working properly. [MidE *blinken*]

blinker *n* (usu. in *pl*) one of two small, flat pieces of leather attached to a horse's bridle to prevent it from seeing sideways. — *v* **-r-** (*tr*) **1** to provide a horse with blinkers. **2** to limit or obscure sight or awareness. [**blink**]

blinkered *adj* **1** (of a horse) wearing blinkers. **2** (*derog*) (of a person) unable or unwilling to understand the opinions of others.

blinking (*coll*) *adj* used to express mild annoyance or disapproval: *broke the blinking thing.* — *adv* very. [**blink**]

blip *n* **1** a sudden, sharp sound produced by a machine. **2** a spot of light on a screen showing the position of an object. — *v* **-pp-** (*intr*) to make a blip. [Imit.]

bliss *n* **1** very great happiness. **2** the special happiness of heaven. — *adj* **blissful**. — *adv* **blissfully**. [OE *bliths*]

blister *n* **1** a thin bubble on the skin containing liquid, caused by something rubbing or burning the skin. **2** a similar swelling on any other surface. — *v* **-r- 1** (*tr*) to cause a blister on. **2** (*intr*) to come up in blisters. **3** (*tr*) to criticise or attack sharply. — *adj* **blistered**. [Norse *blastr*]

blistering *adj* **1** very hot. **2** full of anger and intended to hurt (someone): *blistering criticism.* — *adv* **blisteringly**.

blister pack see **bubble pack**.

blithe *adj* **1** happy, without worries or cares. **2** (*derog*) done without serious thought; casual. — *adv* **blithely**. [OE]

blithering *adj* (*coll*) stupid. [*blither*, a form of **blether**]

BLitt *abbrev* for *Baccalaureus Litterarum*, Bachelor of Letters.

blitz *n* **1** a sudden, strong attack, or period of such attacks, esp. from the air. **2** (*cap* with **the**) the German air raids on Britain in 1940. **3** a period of hard work, etc. to get something finished. — *v* (*tr*) **1** to attack, damage or destroy as if by a blitz or air raid. **2** to work hard at for a short period. [Ger *Blitzkrieg*, lightning war, a sudden and intensive attack to win a quick victory in war]

blizzard *n* a lot of snow falling and being blown by the wind.

bloat *v* **1** (*tr* & *intr*) to (cause to) swell or puff out, with air, pride, etc. **2** (*tr*) to prepare (fish, esp. herring) by salting and half drying in smoke. — *adj* **bloated**. [Norse *blautr*, wet, soft]

bloater *n* a fish, esp. a herring, which has been salted and half dried in smoke.

blob *n* **1** a small, soft, round mass of something: *a blob of jam.* **2** a small drop of liquid. [Imit. of the sound of dripping]

bloc *n* a group of countries, people, etc. who have a common interest, purpose or policy. [Fr, block]

block *n* **1** a mass of solid wood, stone, ice, etc., usu. with flat sides. **2** a piece of wood, stone, etc. used for chopping and cutting food, etc. on. **3** (usu. in *pl*) a wooden or plastic cube, used as a child's toy. **4** a large building containing offices, flats, etc. **5** a group of buildings with roads on all four sides. **6** a group of seats, tickets, etc. thought of as a single unit: *a block booking.* **7** (something which causes) a stopping of movement, thought, etc.: *a road block.* **8** a piece of wood or metal which has been cut to be used in printing. **9** a series of ropes and wheels for lifting things, or pulleys, mounted in a case. ◇ See also **block and tackle** below. **10** (*slang*) a person's head. — *v* (*tr*) **1** (**up**) to make (progress) difficult or impossible; to obstruct. **2** (**off**) to restrict or limit the use of: *block off the street.* **3** to print (a design, title, etc.) on (the cover of a book, piece of material, etc.). **4** (*cricket*) to stop (a ball) with one's bat resting upright on the ground. — *adj* **blocked**. — *v* **block in** (*tr*) **1** to prevent a person or thing from moving or from getting out; to confine. **2** to draw or sketch roughly. — *v* **block out** (*tr*) **1** to shut out (ideas, light, etc.). **2** to draw or sketch roughly. — *v* **block up** (*tr*) **1** to block completely. **2** to fill (a window, doorway, etc.) with (bricks, etc.). [Fr *bloc*]

blockade *n* the closing off of a port, region, etc. by surrounding it with soldiers, ships, etc. to stop people, goods, etc. from passing in and out. — *v* (*tr*) to put a blockade round (a port, etc.).

blockage *n* **1** anything causing a pipe, etc. to be blocked. **2** the state of being blocked.

block and tackle *n* a series of ropes and wheels used for lifting heavy things. ◇ See also **block** (sense **9**).

blockbuster *n* (*coll*) **1** a very popular and successful film, book, etc. **2** an extremely large bomb.

block capital or **letter** *n* a capital letter written in imitation of printed type.

blockhead *n* (*coll*) a stupid person.

blockhouse *n* **1** a small shelter made from very strong concrete, used for watching battles, spacecraft take off, etc. **2** a small, temporary fort.

block letter see **block capital** above.

block vote *n* a vote by a person in a conference, etc., counted as the total number of people he or she represents.

bloke *n* (*Br coll*) a man.

blond (of a woman, usu. **blonde**) *adj* **1** having pale yellow hair and light-coloured or pale skin. **2** (of hair) pale yellow. [Lat *blondus*, yellow]

blonde *n* a woman with pale yellow hair.

blood *n* **1** the red liquid pumped through the body by the heart. **2** the taking of life; murder. **3** relationship through belonging to the same family, race, etc.; descent: *of royal blood.* **4** near family: *my own flesh and blood.* **5** temper; passion. **6** a group of people seen as adding new strength to an existing group: *new blood in the teaching profession.* **7** a man who is interested in fashion, etc. and thinks a lot about his appearance. — *v* (*tr*) **1** to give a (young hunting dog) its first taste of a freshly killed animal. **2** to give (a person, etc.) the first experience of (war, battle, etc.). — **after** or **out for someone's blood** to be extremely angry with a person and to want revenge, to fight him or her, etc. — **in cold blood** deliberately, cruelly, showing no concern or passion. — **make one's blood boil** to make one extremely angry. — **make someone's blood run cold** to frighten or horrify (someone). — **sweat blood** to work very hard. [OE *blod*]

blood-and-thunder *adj* (of a film, etc.) with a lot of drama, excitement, violent action, etc.

blood bank *n* a place where human blood is kept until it is needed for people who are ill.

bloodbath *n* a massacre.

blood brother *n* a man or boy who has promised to treat another as his brother, usu. in a ceremony in which some of their blood has mixed.

blood count *n* a medical examination to count the red or white blood cells in a person's blood.

bloodcurdling *adj* causing great fear.

blood donor *n* a person who gives blood for use by a person who is ill, in operations, etc.

blood group or **type** *n* any one of the four types into which human blood is classified, A, B, AB and O.

blood heat *n* the normal temperature of human blood, about 37°C, 98·4°F.

bloodhound *n* a large dog with a very good sense of smell, used for tracking.

bloodless *adj* **1** without violence or anybody being killed. **2** pale and lifeless. **3** dull and boring. — *adv* **bloodlessly**. — *n* **bloodlessness**.

bloodletting *n* **1** killing. **2** the treating, esp. formerly, of sick people by removing some of their blood.

blood-money *n* **1** money paid for committing murder. **2** money paid in compensation to the relatives of a murdered person.

blood orange *n* a type of orange with red flesh.

blood-poisoning *n* an infection of the blood.

blood relation *n* a person related to one by birth rather than by marriage.

bloodshed *n* the shedding of blood or killing of people.

bloodshot *adj* (said of the eyes) sore and red with blood.

blood sports *n* (*pl*) those sports involving the killing of animals.

bloodstained *adj* stained with blood.

bloodstock *n* horses that have been bred specially for racing.

bloodstream *n* the blood flowing through the body.

bloodsucker *n* **1** an animal that sucks blood, e.g. the leech. **2** (*coll*) a person who forces another to give him or her money; an extortioner. — *adj* **bloodsucking**.

blood test *n* a medical examination of a small amount of blood, usu. to diagnose illness, etc.

bloodthirsty *adj* **1** eager to kill people. **2** (said of a film, etc.) with a lot of violence and killing. — *adv* **bloodthirstily**. — *n* **bloodthirstiness**.

blood transfusion *n* the process of giving a sick person blood which has been donated by another person.

blood type see **blood group** above.

blood-vessel *n* any of the tubes, arteries, veins, etc. in the body, through which blood flows.

bloody *adj* **-ier**, **-iest** **1** stained or covered with blood. **2** involving or including a lot of killing. **3** cruel. **4** (*slang*) used to express annoyance, etc.: *a bloody fool*. — *adv* (*slang*) extremely. — *v* **-ies**, **-ied** (*tr*) to stain or cover with blood. — *adv* **bloodily**. — *n* **bloodiness**.

bloody Mary *n* a drink made from vodka and tomato juice.

bloody-minded *adj* (*derog*) awkward or not willing to help; making things harder for other people on purpose. — *n* **bloody-mindedness**.

bloom *n* **1** a flower, esp. on a plant valued for its flowers. **2** the state of flowering: *in bloom*. **3** a state of perfection or great beauty: *in full bloom*. **4** a glow or flush on the skin. **5** a fine white powder on leaves, fruit, etc. — *v* (*intr*) **1** to be in flower. **2** to be in or achieve a state of great beauty or perfection. **3** to be healthy; to be growing well; to flourish. [Norse *blom*]

blooming *adj* **1** flowering. **2** bright; beautiful. **3** very healthy; flourishing. **4** (*slang*) used as an expression of annoyance, etc.: *a blooming idiot*. — *adv* (*slang*) very.

bloomer *n* (*coll*) a silly mistake. [**blooming**]

bloomers *n* (*pl*) **1** (*formerly*) short loose trousers gathered at the knee, worn by women. **2** (*old coll*) women's underpants or knickers. [From Amelia *Bloomer* (1818–94), an American social reformer who believed women should dress in short full skirts and bloomers]

blossom *n* **1** a flower or mass of flowers, esp. on a fruit tree. **2** the state of flowering: *in blossom*. — *v* **-m-** (*intr*) **1** to develop flowers. **2** (**into**, **out**) to grow well or develop (into): *blossom into an accomplished dancer*. — *adj* **blossoming**. [OE *blostm*]

blot *n* **1** a spot or stain, esp. of ink. **2** a spot or blemish which spoils the beauty of something. **3** a stain on a person's good reputation or character. — *v* **-tt-** (*tr*) **1** to make a spot or stain on, esp. with ink. **2** to dry with blotting-paper. — **blot one's copybook** to spoil one's good reputation, etc., esp. through a small mistake. — *v* **blot out** (*tr*) **1** to hide from sight: *blot out the writing*. **2** to refuse to think about or remember (a painful memory). [MidE *blotte*]

blotter *n* a large sheet or pad of blotting-paper with a hard backing.

blotting-paper *n* soft, thick paper used for drying wet ink when writing.

blotch *n* a large coloured or sore spot or mark on the skin, etc. — *v (tr)* to cover or mark with blotches. — *adj* **blotchy**, ***-ier***, ***-iest***. [Perhaps **blot**]

blouse *n* **1** a woman's shirt-like garment. **2** a loose jacket gathered in at the waist, part of a soldier's uniform. — *v (tr)* to arrange in loose folds. [Fr]

blouson *n* a loose jacket fitting tightly at the waist. [Fr]

blow[1] *v* ***blew***, ***blown*** **1** *(intr & tr)* (of a current of air, wind, etc.) to be moving, esp. rapidly. **2** *(intr & tr*; **along**, **down**, etc.) to move or be moved by a current of air, wind, etc. **3** *(intr & tr)* to send (air, etc.) from esp. the mouth. **4** *(tr)* to form or shape by blowing air from the mouth: *blow bubbles*; *blow glass*. **5** *(tr*; **off**, etc.) to move or destroy by an explosion: *The blast blew the chimney off the roof*. **6** *(tr & intr)* to (cause to) produce a sound by blowing: *blow a whistle*. **7** *(tr*; **away**, **off**, etc.) to remove by blowing. **8** *(intr)* to breathe heavily. **9** *(tr)* to clear by blowing through: *blow one's nose*. **10** *(tr & intr)* to (cause to) melt or explode: *blow the fuse*. **11** *(tr)* to break into using explosives: *blow a safe*. **12** *(tr; slang)* to lose, waste: *blow one's chances*. **13** *(tr; coll*; **on**) to spend a lot of money (on). **14** *(intr & tr; slang)* to leave (a place) quickly and suddenly. **15** *(intr)* (of a whale) to send out air and water through a hole in the top of its head. — *n* **1** an act or example of blowing. **2** an exposure to fresh air: *go for a blow on the cliffs*. — *interj* an expression of annoyance. — *v* **blow away** *(tr; US slang)* to murder with a gun. — *v* **blow-dry** *(tr)* to dry (hair) in a particular style with a hair-drier. — *n* an act of blow-drying. — **blow hot and cold** *(coll)* to keep changing one's mind. — *v* **blow out** *(tr)* **1** to put (a flame, etc.) out by blowing. **2** to send outwards through an explosion. ◇ See also **blow-out** below. — *v* **blow over** *(intr)* to pass by without having an (esp. bad) effect. — **blow one's own trumpet** *(coll)* to praise oneself and one's abilities, etc. — **blow sky-high** to destroy completely. — **blow one's top** *(coll)* to lose one's temper. — *v* **blow up 1** *(intr & tr)* to (cause to) explode (*n* **blow-up**). **2** *(tr & intr)* to fill up or swell up with air or gas. **3** *(tr)* to make (a photograph, etc.) bigger (*n* **blow-up**). **4** *(intr; coll)* to lose one's temper. **5** *(tr; slang)* to scold (someone) angrily. **6** *(tr; coll)* to make (something) seem more serious or important than it really is. — **blow the whistle on** *(slang)* **1** to bring to an end. **2** to inform on. [OE *blawan*]

blower *n* **1** a device for blowing. **2** *(coll)* a telephone.

blowfly *n* a type of fly that lays its eggs on meat or in wounds.

blowhole *n* **1** a hole in ice through which animals (such as seals) can breathe. **2** a hole on top of a whale's head through which it blows (sense **15**).

blowlamp or **blowtorch** *n* a device for producing and directing a very hot flame at a particular spot, used for burning paint off, etc.

blow-out *n (coll)* **1** the bursting of a car tyre. **2** a violent escape of gas, etc., on e.g. an oil rig. **3** a very large meal. ◇ See also **blow out** above.

blowpipe *n* **1** a tube through which small, sometimes poisonous, arrows are blown. **2** a tube for blowing air into a flame to make its heat greater, esp. when blowing glass.

blowtorch see **blowlamp**.

blow-up see **blow up** above.

blowy *adj* ***-ier***, ***-iest*** windy.

blow[2] *n* **1** a stroke or knock with the hand or a weapon. **2** a sudden shock or misfortune. — **come to blows** to end up fighting.

blow-by-blow *adj* (of a description, etc.) giving all the details in the right order.

blown. See **blow**[1].

blowzy or **blowsy** *adj* ***-ier***, ***-iest*** *(coll derog)* (of a woman) **1** fat and red-faced. **2** dirty and untidy. [*blowze*, beggar's woman]

blubber *n* the fat of sea animals such as the whale. — *v* ***-r-*** *(coll derog)* **1** *(intr)* to weep noisily. **2** *(tr)* to try to say (words, etc.) while weeping. [Imit.]

bludgeon *n* a stick or club with a heavy end. — *v* ***-n-*** *(tr)* **1** to hit with, or as if with, a bludgeon. **2** to force or bully into doing something.

blue *adj* **1** of the colour of a clear, cloudless sky. **2** sad or depressed. ◇ See also **blues** below. **3** sexual in a way many people find offensive; indecent. **4** politically conservative. **5** with a skin which is pale blue or purple because of the cold. — *n* **1** the colour of a clear, cloudless sky. **2** blue paint, or dye. **3** blue material or clothes: *dressed in blue*. **4** (the status of) a person who represents, or has represented, his or her college or university, esp. Oxford or Cambridge, at sport. **5** *(Br coll)* a supporter of the Conservative Party. — *v* ***bluing*** or ***blueing*** *(tr)* **1** to make blue. **2** *(coll)* to waste. — *n* **blueness**. — **do (something) till one is blue in the face** to do (something) repeatedly but without success. — **once in a blue moon** hardly ever. — **out of the blue** without warning; unexpectedly. [OFr *bleu*]

blue baby *n* a baby whose skin is a pale blue colour when it is born, due to a fault in its heart.

bluebell *n* a small wild flower which has blue bell-shaped flowers.

blueberry *n* a dark blue berry from a bush common in N America.

bluebird *n* a small blue-backed N American songbird.

blue blood *n* royal or noble blood or descent.

bluebottle *n* a large fly with a blue body.

blue cheese *n* cheese with thin lines of blue mould running through it.

blue-chip *adj* used to describe a company, etc. in which people can invest safely.

blue-collar *adj* (of workers) working with the hands in a factory, etc., not in an office. ◇ See also **white-collar**.

blue-eyed boy *n* (*coll*; sometimes *derog*) a favourite.

bluegrass or **bluefunk** *n* a simple style of country music popular in southern states of America.

blue-pencil *v* *-ll-* (*tr*) to correct, edit, or cut parts out of (a piece of writing).

Blue Peter *n* a blue flag with a white square, flown on a ship which is about to sail.

blueprint *n* **1** a photographic print of plans, designs, etc., consisting of white lines on a blue background. **2** a detailed plan of work to be done.

blues *n* (usu. with **the**) **1** a feeling of sadness or depression. **2** (usu. *sing*) slow, sad jazz music of Black American origin.

bluestocking *n* (often *derog*) a highly educated woman who is interested in serious academic subjects.

blue tit *n* a small bird with blue wings and tail and blue on its head, common in Britain.

bluish *adj* quite blue; close to blue.

bluff[1] *v* **1** (*intr*) to try to deceive someone by pretending to be stronger, cleverer, etc. than one really is. **2** (*tr*; **into**) to trick by bluffing: *bluff him into doing all the work*. — *n* an act of bluffing. — **call someone's bluff** to challenge another person's bluff. [Dut *bluffen*, to play a trick at cards]

bluff[2] *n* a steep cliff or bank of ground. — *adj* **1** (of a cliff or the bow of a ship) steep and upright. **2** rough, cheerful and honest in manner. — *adv* **bluffly**. — *n* **bluffness**.

bluish. See **blue**.

blunder *v* *-r-* (*intr*) **1** to make a stupid, clumsy and usu. serious mistake. **2** (**about**, **into**, etc.) to move about awkwardly and clumsily.— *n* a stupid, clumsy and usu. serious mistake. — *n* **blunderer**. — *adj* **blundering**. — *adv* **blunderingly**. [MidE *blunderen*, from Norse *blunda*, to shut one's eyes]

blunderbuss *n* (*hist*) a type of shotgun with a short, wide barrel. [Dut *donderbus*, from *donder*, thunder + *bus*, gun]

blunt *adj* **1** having no point or sharp edge. **2** not sharp. **3** honest and direct in a rough way. — *v* (*tr*) to make less sharp or blunt. — *adv* **bluntly**. — *n* **bluntness**.

blur *n* **1** a thing not clearly seen or heard. **2** a smear or smudge. — *v* ***-rr-*** **1** (*tr* & *intr*) to make or become less clear or distinct. **2** (*tr*) to rub over and smudge. **3** (*tr*) to make (one's memory, judgement, etc.) less clear. — *adj* **blurred** or **blurry**, ***-ier***, ***-iest***.

blurb *n* a brief description of what a book is about, printed on the back cover, etc. [Invented by Gelett Burgess, an American author (d. 1951)]

blurt *v* (*tr*; **out**) to say suddenly or without thinking of the effect or result.

blush *n* **1** a red or pink glow on the skin of the face, caused by shame, embarrassment, etc. **2** a pink, rosy glow. — *v* (*intr*) **1** to become red or pink in the face because of shame, embarrassment, etc. **2** to feel ashamed or embarrassed: *blush when one thinks of past mistakes*. — *adj* **blushing**. — *adv* **blushingly**. [OE *blyscan*]

blusher *n* a pink or pale orange cream or powder used to give colour to the cheeks.

bluster *v* *-r-* (*intr*) **1** to speak in a boasting, angry or threatening way, often to hide fear. **2** (of the wind, waves, etc.) to blow or move roughly. — *n* **1** boasting, angry, threatening, etc. speech. **2** the roaring noise of the wind or sea on a rough day. — *n* **blusterer**. — *adj* **blustery**. [Prob. German dialect *blustern*, to blow violently]

blvd *abbrev* boulevard.

BM *abbrev* **1** Bachelor of Medicine. **2** British Museum.

BMA *abbrev* British Medical Association.

B-movie. See **B**.

BMus *abbrev* Bachelor of Music.

BMW *abbrev* for *Bayerische Motoren Werke*, Bavarian motor works.

BMX *n* **1** bicycle riding and racing over a rough track with obstacles. **2** a bicycle designed for this. [Abbrev. of *bi*cycle *moto-cross*]

BO *abbrev* (*coll*) body odour.

boa *n* **1** (also **boa constrictor**) a large S American snake that kills by winding itself round its prey and crushing it. **2** a woman's long thin scarf, usu. made of feathers or fur. [Lat *boa*, a kind of snake]

boar *n* **1** (also **wild boar**) a wild pig. **2** a male pig kept for breeding. **3** its flesh. [OE *bar*]

board *n* **1** a long flat strip of wood. **2** a piece of material resembling this, made from fibres compressed together: *chipboard*. **3** a flat piece of wood, etc. for a stated purpose: *notice board*; *chessboard*. **4** thick, stiff card used e.g. for binding books. **5** a person's meals, provided in return for money: *bed and board*. **6** an official group of people controlling or managing an organisation, etc., or examining or interviewing candidates: *a board of examiners*. **7** (in *pl*) a theatre stage: *tread the boards*. **8** (*naut*) the side of a ship. — *v* **1** (*tr*) to enter or get on to (a ship, aeroplane, bus, etc.). **2** (*intr*) to receive accommodation and meals in someone else's house, in return for payment. **3** (*tr*) to provide (someone) with accommodation and meals in return for payment. **4** (*tr* with **out**) to arrange for (someone) to receive accommodation and meals away from home. **5** (*tr* with **up**) to cover (a hole, etc.) with boards. — **across the board** see

across. — **go by the board** (*coll*) to be given up or ignored. — **on board** on or into a ship, aeroplane, etc. — **sweep the board** to win everything. — **take on board** to understand or accept (new ideas, responsibilities, etc.) completely. [OE *bord*]

boarder *n* **1** a person who receives accommodation and meals in someone else's house, in return for payment. **2** a pupil who lives at school during term time.

board game *n* a game played with pieces to be moved on a board, e.g. chess.

boarding *n* **1** a collection of wooden boards laid next to each other. **2** the act of boarding a ship, aeroplane, etc.

boarding-house *n* a house where people live and take meals as paying guests.

boarding-pass or **boarding-card** *n* a card or piece of paper which allows a person to board an aeroplane, etc.

boarding-school *n* a school where pupils may live during term time.

boardroom *n* **1** a room in which the directors of a company meet. **2** the highest level of management of a company.

boast *v* **1** (*intr*; **about, of**, etc.) to talk with too much pride (about one's own abilities, achievements, etc.). **2** (*tr*) to own or have (something it is right to be proud of): *The hotel boasts magnificent views across the valley*. — *n* **1** an act of boasting. **2** a thing one is proud of. — *n* **boasting**. [MidE *bost*]

boastful *adj* (*derog*) **1** given to boasting about oneself. **2** showing or characterised by boasting. — *adv* **boastfully**. — *n* **boastfulness**.

boat *n* **1** a small vessel for travelling over water. **2** (*coll* or *loosely*) a larger vessel; a ship. **3** a boat-shaped dish, for serving sauce, etc. — *v* (*intr*) to sail in a boat for pleasure. — **in the same boat** in the same difficult circumstances. — **miss the boat** or **bus** to lose a good opportunity. — **rock the boat** to disturb the balance or calmness of a situation. [OE *bat*]

boater *n* **1** a person who sails in a boat, usu. for pleasure. **2** a straw hat with a flat top and a brim.

boathook *n* a metal hook fixed to a pole, for pulling or pushing a boat.

boathouse *n* a building where boats are stored.

boating *n* the sailing of boats for pleasure.

boatman *n* a man in charge of a small boat which carries passengers.

boat people *n* (*pl*) refugees who have fled their country by boat.

boatswain see separate entry.

boat train *n* a train which takes passengers to or from a ship.

boater. See **boat**.

boatswain, bosun, bo'sun or **bo's'n** *n* a ship's officer in charge of the lifeboats, ropes, sails, etc. and crew. [OE *batswegen*, boatman]

bob[1] *v* **-bb- 1** (*intr*) to move up and down quickly. **2** (*intr*) to curtsy. **3** (*tr*) to move (the head) up and down, usu. as a greeting. — *n* **1** an up-and-down bouncing movement. **2** a curtsy. — *v* **bob up** (*intr*) to appear or reappear suddenly. [MidE *bobben*]

bob[2] *n* **1** a short hairstyle for women and children, with the hair cut square across the face and evenly all round the head. **2** a hanging weight on a clock's pendulum. **3** a bobsleigh. — *v* **-bb- 1** (*tr*) to cut (hair) in a bob. **2** (*intr*) to ride on a bobsleigh. [MidE *bobbe*, spray, cluster]

bobsleigh or **bobsled** *n* a sleigh with metal runners used in crossing, and sometimes racing on, snow and ice.

bobtail *n* (an animal with) a short or cut tail. — *adj* **bobtailed**.

bob[3] *n* **bob** (*old coll*) a shilling.

bob[4]: **bob's your uncle** (*Br coll*) an expression used to show that something should follow as a matter of course: *Just turn the knob and bob's your uncle!* [The name *Bob*]

bobbin *n* a small cylindrical object on which thread is wound, used in sewing and weaving machines. [Fr *bobine*]

bobble *n* a small ball, often made of wool, used to decorate clothes. [**bob**[1]]

bobby *n* **-ies** (*Br coll*) a policeman. [The name *Bob*, after Sir Robert Peel (1788–1850), who founded the Metropolitan Police in 1828]

bobsled, bobsleigh. See **bob**[2].

bobtail, bobtailed. See **bob**[2].

Boche *n* (*hist derog slang*) (esp. during the First World War) a German, esp. a German soldier. [Fr]

bod *n* (*coll*) a person. [Short for **body**]

bode[1] *v* (*tr*) to be a sign of. — **bode ill** or **well** to be a bad or good sign for the future. [OE *bodian*, to announce]

bode[2]. See **bide**.

bodge *v* (*intr* & *tr*; *coll*) to make a mess of (something); to do (something) badly or carelessly. [**botch**]

bodice *n* **1** the part of a dress covering the upper part of the body. **2** a woman's close-fitting outer garment, worn over a blouse. **3** (*formerly*) a similar close-fitting under-garment. [From *bodies*, plural of **body**]

bodied, bodily. See **body**.

bodkin *n* a large blunt needle. [MidE *badeken*]

body *n* **-ies 1** the whole physical structure of a person or animal. **2** the physical structure of a person or animal excluding the head and limbs. **3** a corpse. **4** the main or central part of anything. **5** a person's physical needs and desires as opposed to his or her spirit. **6** a section, group or (with **the**) majority: *the body of opinion*. **7** a group of people thought of as a single unit. **8** a quantity: *a body of water*. **9** a piece of matter: *a heavenly body*. **10** (of wine, music, etc.) a full or strong quality or tone. **11** (*coll*) a person. **12** thickness; substantial quality. — *v* ***-ies, -ied*** (*tr*) to give body or form to. — **keep body and soul together** to manage to survive. — **over my dead body** (*coll*) not if I can prevent it. [OE *bodig*]

bodily *adj* of or concerning the body. — *adv* **1** as a whole. **2** in person.

body-building *n* physical exercise which makes one's muscles bigger and stronger. — *n* **body-builder**.

bodyguard *n* a person or group of people guarding an important person, etc.

body politic *n* all the people of a nation in their political capacity.

body-snatcher *n* (*hist*) a person who robs graves of their dead bodies.

body stocking *n* a garment worn next to the skin, covering all of the body and often the arms and legs as well.

bodysuit *n* a close-fitting one-piece garment for women, worn esp. during exercise and sporting activities.

bodywork *n* the outer painted structure of a motor vehicle.

Boer *n* a descendant of the early Dutch settlers in S Africa. — *adj* of or relating to the Boers. [Dut]

boffin *n* (*Br coll*) a scientist.

bog *n* **1** an area of very wet, spongy ground. **2** (*Br vulg slang*) a toilet. — *v* **bog down** ***-gg-*** (*tr*) to prevent from progressing: *get bogged down in difficulties*. — *adj* **boggy**, ***-ier, -iest***. [Gaelic *bogach*, from *bog*, soft]

bogey[1] or **bogy** *n* ***-eys*** or ***-ies*** **1** an evil or mischievous spirit. **2** something specially feared.

bogeyman or **bogyman** *n* a cruel or frightening person, existing or imaginary, used in threats to children.

bogey[2] *n* ***-eys*** (*golf*) a standard score for a hole or a course, formerly par but now usu. a score of one stroke more than par for each hole. [Perhaps from the name of an imaginary player]

boggle *v* (*intr*; *coll*) **1** to be amazed at, or unable to understand or imagine: *the mind boggles*. **2** (**at**) to hesitate.

bogie *n* a frame with four or six wheels which supports part of a long vehicle, such as a railway carriage.

bogus *adj* false; not genuine.

bogy. See **bogey**[1].

bohemian *n* **1** (*cap*) a person from Bohemia, formerly a kingdom, now in Czechoslovakia. **2** a person, esp. a writer or an artist, who lives in a way which ignores standard customs and rules of social behaviour. — *adj* **1** (*cap*) of or from Bohemia. **2** ignoring standard customs and rules of social behaviour. [Fr *bohémien*, Bohemian, gypsy]

boil[1] *v* **1** (*intr*) (of liquids) to start to bubble and turn from liquid to gas when heated. **2** (*intr*) to contain a liquid which is boiling: *The kettle is boiling*. **3** (*tr*) to bring (a liquid or container holding a liquid) to a heat at which the liquid boils. **4** (*tr* & *intr*) (of food) to cook or be cooked by boiling. **5** (*intr*; *coll*) to be very hot. **6** (*tr*) to treat with boiling water, esp. to clean. **7** (*intr*) to be angry. **8** (*intr*) (of the sea, etc.) to move and bubble as if boiling. — *n* the act or point of boiling. — *v* **boil away** (*tr* & *intr*) to lose or remove (a liquid), or be lost or removed, by boiling. — *v* **boil down** (*tr*) to reduce the amount of (a liquid), or be reduced in amount, by boiling. — *v* **boil down to** (*tr*; *coll*) to mean; to have as the most important part. — *v* **boil over** (*intr*) **1** to boil and flow over the edge of the container. **2** to let one's anger burst out. — *v* **boil up 1** (*tr*) to heat (a liquid) until it boils. **2** (*intr*) to come to a dangerous level. [OFr *boillir*, from Lat *bullire*, to bubble]

boiler *n* **1** an apparatus for heating a building's hot water supply. **2** an apparatus in which water is heated until it turns into steam. **3** a metal vessel, tub, etc. for boiling and washing clothes in.

boiler suit *n* a garment worn over one's clothes to protect them while working.

boiling-point *n* **1** the temperature at which a liquid, esp. water, boils. **2** a point of great anger, high excitement, etc. at which emotions can no longer be controlled.

boil[2] *n* a painful red pus-filled swelling on the skin. [OE *byl*]

boisterous *adj* **1** very lively, noisy and cheerful. **2** (of the sea, etc.) rough and stormy. — *adv* **boisterously**. — *n* **boisterousness**. [MidE *boistous*]

bold *adj* **1** daring or brave. **2** not showing respect; impudent. **3** striking and clearly marked. **4** (*printing*) printed in boldface. — *adv* **boldly**. — *n* **boldness**. [OE *beald*]

boldface *n* (*printing*) thicker stronger letters, as used in the word **boldface**.

bole *n* the trunk of a tree. [Norse *bolr*]

bolero *n* ***-os*** **1** a traditional Spanish dance, or the music for it. **2** a short open jacket reaching not quite to the waist. [Span]

boll *n* that part of a cotton plant, etc. which contains the seeds. [OE *bolla*, bowl]

boll-weevil *n* an insect which attacks cotton bolls.

bollard *n* **1** (esp. *Br*) a small post used to mark a traffic island or to keep traffic away from a certain area. **2** a short but strong post on a ship, quay, etc. round which ropes are fastened. [Prob. **bole**]

bollocks *n* (*vulg slang*) **1** (*pl*) the testicles. **2** (*sing*) rubbish, nonsense. [OE *beallucas*, testicles]

boloney. See **baloney**.

Bolshevik *n* **1** (*hist*) a member of the radical faction of the Russian socialist party, which became the Communist Party in 1918. **2** a Russian communist. **3** (*coll*; *derog*; often without *cap*) any radical socialist. — *adj* **1** of the Bolsheviks. **2** communist. — *n* **Bolshevism**. — *n* & *adj* **Bolshevist**. [Russ, from *bolshe*, greater, because they were in the majority at the 1903 party congress or because they favoured more extreme measures]

bolshie or **bolshy** (*slang derog*) *adj* **-ier**, **-iest 1** bad-tempered and unco-operative. **2** left-wing. — *n* **-ies** a Bolshevik. [**Bolshevik**]

bolster *n* **1** a long narrow pillow. **2** any pad or support. — *v* **-r-** (*tr*; **up**) to support, make stronger or hold up. [OE]

bolt[1] *n* **1** a bar to fasten a door, gate, etc. **2** a small, thick, round bar of metal, with a screw thread, used with a nut to fasten things together. **3** a flash of lightning. **4** a sudden movement or dash away, esp. to escape: *make a bolt for it*. **5** a roll (of cloth). **6** a short arrow fired from a crossbow. — *v* **1** (*tr*) to fasten (a door, window, etc.) with a bolt. **2** (*tr*) to eat very quickly. **3** (*intr*; **away**, etc.) to run or dash away suddenly and quickly. **4** (*intr*; **away**, etc.) (of a horse) to run away out of control. **5** (*tr*) to fasten together with bolts. **6** (*intr*) (of plants) to flower and produce seeds too early, and so be useless. — **a bolt from the blue** a sudden, unexpected and usu. unpleasant event. — **bolt upright** very straight and stiffly. — **have shot one's bolt** to have made a last attempt to do something but to have failed. [OE]

bolthole *n* a refuge from danger or means of escape.

bolt[2] or **boult** *v* (*tr*) **1** to pass (flour, etc.) through a sieve. **2** to examine or investigate. [OFr *bulter*]

bolthole. See **bolt**[1].

bomb *n* **1** a hollow case or other device containing substances capable of causing explosions, fires, etc. **2** (with **the** and often *cap*) the atomic bomb, esp. seen as the most powerful destructive weapon. **3** (*Br coll*) a lot of money: *cost a bomb*. **4** (*NAm coll*) a failure: *The film was a bomb*. — *v* **1** (*tr*) to attack, damage, etc. with a bomb or bombs. **2** (*intr*; *coll*; **along**, **off**, etc.) to move or drive quickly: *bombing along the road*. **3** (*intr*; *coll*, esp. *NAm*) to fail badly. — *n* **bombing**. — **go like a bomb** (*coll*) **1** to move very quickly. **2** to sell extremely well; to be very successful. [Fr *bombe*, from Gr *bombos*, humming sound]

bomb disposal *n* the act of making unexploded bombs harmless.

bomber *n* **1** an aeroplane built for bombing. **2** a person who bombs something.

bomber jacket *n* a short jacket gathered tightly at the waist.

bombshell *n* **1** a piece of surprising and usu. disappointing news. **2** (*coll*) a very attractive woman.

bombsite *n* an area in a town where a bomb has exploded and left only ruins.

bombard *v* (*tr*) **1** to attack with large, heavy guns or bombs. **2** to direct questions or abuse at (someone) very quickly and without stopping. **3** (*physics*) to direct a stream of high-speed particles at (a substance). — *n* **bombardment**. [Fr *bombarder*, from *bombarde*, machine for throwing stones]

bombardier *n* **1** (*Br*) a noncommissioned officer in the Royal Artillery. **2** (*US*) the member of an aircraft's crew who releases the bombs. [**bombard**]

bombast *n* important-sounding, boastful or insincere words with little real force or meaning. — *adj* **bombastic**. — *adv* **bombastically**. [MidE, cotton padding]

bona fide *adj* genuine or sincere. — *adv* genuinely or sincerely. [Lat]

bonanza *n* **1** a usu. unexpected and sudden source of good luck or wealth. **2** a large amount, esp. of gold from a mine. [Span *bonanza*, good weather at sea]

bonbon *n* a sweet. [Fr]

bond *n* **1** something used for tying, binding or holding. **2** (usu. in *pl*) something which restrains or imprisons (a person): *break one's bonds*. **3** something that unites or joins people together: *a bond of friendship*. **4** a binding agreement or promise. **5** a certificate issued by a government or a company, which promises to pay back money borrowed at a fixed rate of interest at a stated time. **6** (*legal*) a written agreement to pay money or carry out the terms of a contract. **7** (*chem*) a way of combining atoms in a molecule. — *v* **1** (*tr*) to join or tie together. **2** (*intr*) to hold or stick together. **3** (*tr*) to put (goods) into a bonded warehouse. — **in** or **out of bond** (of goods) in or out of a bonded warehouse. [Norse *band*]

bonded warehouse *n* a building where goods are kept until customs or other duty on them is paid.

bond paper *n* a type of very good quality paper.

bondage *n* **1** slavery. **2** the state of being confined, imprisoned, etc. **3** a sexual practice where one partner is tied up. [Lat *bondagium*]

bone *n* **1** any of the pieces of hard tissue forming the skeleton. **2** the hard tissue forming these pieces. **3** (in *pl*) the skeleton. **4** (in *pl*) the body as the place where feelings come from: *feel it in one's bones*. **5** a substance similar to human bone, such as ivory, whalebone, etc. **6** (in *pl*) the basic or essential part: *the bare bones*. — *v* (*tr*) **1** to take bone out of (meat, etc.). **2** to make (a piece of clothing) stiff by adding pieces of bone or some other hard substance. — *adj* **boneless**. — **a bone of contention** something which causes arguments or disagreement. — *v* **bone up on** (*tr*; *coll*) to learn or study (something). — **have a bone to pick with** to have a reason to argue about something with (someone). — **make no bones about 1** to admit or allow without fuss or bother. **2** to be quite willing to say or do openly. — **near**, or **close to**, **the bone** (*coll*) **1** offensively or indecently sexual. **2** upsettingly critical. — **to the bone 1** thoroughly and completely. **2** to the minimum. — **work one's fingers to the bone** to work very hard, usu. for little or no thanks. [OE *ban*]

bone china *n* a type of fine china made from clay mixed with ash from burnt bones.
bone-dry *adj* completely dry.
bonehead *n* (*slang*) a stupid person. — *adj* **bone-headed**.
bone idle *adj* (*coll*) very lazy.
bone meal *n* ground bones, used as fertiliser and in animal feed.
boneshaker *n* (*coll*) an old, uncomfortable and unsteady vehicle, esp. a bicycle.
bony *adj* **-ier**, **-iest** **1** of or like bone. **2** full of bones. **3** thin.

bonfire *n* a large, outdoor fire, often burned to celebrate something. [MidE *bonefire*, from **bone** (formerly used as fuel) + **fire**]

bong *n* & *v* (*intr* & *tr*) (to make) a long, deep sound such as is made by a large bell. [Imit.]

bongo *n* **-os** or **-oes** (also **bongo drum**) one of a pair of small drums held between the knees and played with the hands. [Span *bongó*]

bonhomie *n* an easy, friendly nature. [Fr, from *bonhomme*, good fellow]

bonk *v* (*tr* & *intr*) **1** to bang or hit. **2** (*vulg slang*) to have sexual intercourse with (someone). — *n* **1** the act of banging. **2** (*vulg slang*) the act of having sex. [Imit.]

bonkers *adj* (*slang*) mad, crazy.

bon mot *n* ***bons mots*** a short, clever remark. [Fr]

bonnet *n* **1** a type of hat fastened under the chin with ribbon, formerly worn by women but now worn esp. by babies. **2** (*Br*) the hinged cover over a motor vehicle's engine. **3** a soft Scottish cap. [OFr *bonet*]

bonny *adj* **-ier**, **-iest** **1** (esp. Scot) pretty. **2** looking very healthy and attractive.

bonsai *n* ***bonsai*** **1** a very small ornamental tree kept small by being grown in a pot. **2** the art of growing such trees. [Jap, from *bon*, tray, bowl + *sai*, cultivation]

bonus *n* **1** an extra sum of money given on top of what is due as interest or wages. **2** an unexpected extra benefit. [Lat, good]

bon vivant or **viveur** *n* ***bons*** (or ***bon***) ***vivants***, ***bons*** (or ***bon***) ***viveurs*** a person who enjoys good food and wine. [Fr]

bon voyage *interj* have a pleasant journey. [Fr]

bony. See **bone**.

boo *interj* & *n* a sound expressing disapproval or made when trying to frighten or surprise someone. — *v* (*intr* & *tr*) to shout boo (at someone) to express disapproval. — **one couldn't** or **wouldn't say boo to a goose** one is very shy or easily frightened. [Imit.]

boob[1] *n* (*coll*) **1** (also **booboo**) a stupid or foolish mistake. **2** a stupid or foolish person. — *v* (*intr*; *coll*) to make a stupid or foolish mistake. [**booby**]

boob[2] *n* (*slang*) a woman's breast.

booby *n* **-ies** **1** (*old coll*) a stupid or foolish person. **2** a type of sea-bird related to the gannet.
booby prize *n* a prize for the lowest score, the person coming last, etc. in a competition.
booby trap *n* **1** a bomb or mine which is disguised so that it is set off by the victim. **2** something placed as a trap, e.g. a bucket of water put above a door so as to fall on the person who opens the door. — *v* **booby-trap** (*tr*) to put a booby trap in or on.

boodle *n* (*old slang*) money, esp. when gained dishonestly or as a bribe. [Dut *boedel*, possessions]

boogie (*coll*) *v* ***boogieing*** or ***boogying*** (*intr*) to dance to pop or jazz music. — *n* a dance to pop or jazz music.

book *n* **1** a number of printed pages bound together along one edge and protected by covers. **2** a piece of written work which the author hopes will be published. **3** a number of sheets of blank paper bound together: *a notebook*. **4** (usu. in *pl*) a record of the business done by a company, a society, etc. **5** a major division of a very long literary work. **6** a number of stamps, matches, cheques, etc. bound together. **7** the words of an opera or musical; a libretto. **8** a record of bets. **9** a telephone directory: *She isn't in the book*. — *v* **1** (*tr* & *intr*) to reserve (a ticket, seat, etc.) or engage (a person's services) in advance. **2** (*tr*) to enter (a person's name, etc.) in a book or list. **3** (*tr*) to take the details of (a person who has done something wrong) so that he or she may be charged with an offence. — *adj* **bookable**. — *n* **booking**. — **be in someone's good**, or **bad**, **books** to be in, or out of, favour with someone. — *v* **book in** (*intr*) **1** to sign one's name on the list of guests at a hotel, etc. **2** (*tr*) to reserve a place for (someone) in a hotel, etc. — *v* **book up** (*intr* & *tr*) to buy (a ticket, a holiday, etc.) in advance. (**booked up** **1** having bought tickets, etc. in advance. **2** with no more places, etc. available.) — **bring to book** to make (a person) explain, or punish (a person) for, his or her behaviour. — **by the book** strictly according to the rules. — **in my book** in my opinion. — **suit one's book** to be what one wants or likes. — **take a leaf out of someone's book** to profit or benefit from someone's example or experience. — **throw the book at someone** (*coll*) to charge (someone) with as many offences as possible or punish (him or her) as severely as possible. [OE *boc*]
bookbinder *n* a person whose job is to bind books. — *n* **bookbinding**.
bookcase *n* a set of shelves for books.
book club *n* a club which sells books to its members at reduced prices.
book end *n* (usu. in *pl*) one of a pair of supports used to keep a row of books standing upright.
bookie *n* (*coll*) a bookmaker.
bookish *adj* **1** very fond of reading. **2** (sometimes *derog*) with knowledge or

opinions based on books rather than practical experience. — *n* **bookishness**.
bookkeeping *n* the keeping of financial accounts. — *n* **bookkeeper**.
booklet *n* a small, thin book with a paper cover.
bookmaker *n* a person who takes people's bets on races, etc. and pays money to the people who bet successfully.
bookmark *n* a strip of leather, card, etc. put in a book to mark a particular page, esp. the reader's place.
bookplate *n* a piece of decorated paper with a person's name on, stuck into the front of a book he or she owns.
bookstall *n* a small shop in a station, etc. where books, newspapers, magazines, etc. are sold.
book token *n* (a card containing) a paper token worth a certain amount of money which can be used to buy books.
bookworm *n* **1** (*coll*) a person devoted to reading. **2** a type of small insect which feeds on the paper and glue used in books.

boom[1] *n* a loud, deep, resounding sound, like that make by a large drum or gun. — *v* **1** (*intr*) to make a loud, deep, resounding sound. **2** (*tr*; **out**) to say with a booming sound. [Prob. imit.]

boom[2] *n* a sudden increase or growth in business, prosperity, etc. — *v* (*intr*) to prosper rapidly. [Perhaps **boom**[1]]

boom[3] *n* **1** a pole to which the bottom of a ship's sail is attached, keeping the sail stretched tight. **2** a heavy pole or chain, etc. across the entrance to a harbour. **3** a long pole with a microphone attached to one end, allowing the microphone to be held above the heads of people being filmed. [Dut *boom*, beam]

boomerang *n* **1** a piece of flat, curved wood used by Australian Aborigines for hunting, often so balanced that, when thrown to a distance, it returns to the thrower. **2** a malicious act or statement which harms the perpetrator rather than the intended victim. — *v* (*intr*) (of an act, statement, etc.) to go wrong and harm the perpetrator rather than the intended victim. [Dharuk (Australian Aboriginal language) *bumariny*]

boon[1] *n* **1** an advantage, benefit or blessing. **2** (*old*) a gift or favour. [Norse *bon*, prayer]

boon[2] *adj* close, intimate, or favourite: *boon companion*. [OFr *bon*, good]

boor *n* (*derog*) a coarse person with bad manners. — *adj* **boorish**. — *adv* **boorishly**. — *n* **boorishness**. [Dut *boer*, farmer, peasant]

boost *v* (*tr*) **1** to improve or encourage: *boost the spirits*. **2** to make greater or increase: *boost profits*. **3** to promote by advertising. — *n* **1** a piece of help or encouragement, etc. **2** a push upwards. **3** a rise or increase.
booster *n* **1** a person or thing that boosts. **2** a dose of a drug or vaccine given to increase the power or effectiveness of an earlier dose. **3** the engine in a rocket which provides the power for the first stage of a flight. **4** a device for increasing electrical power, e.g. in a radio to strengthen signals.

boot[1] *n* **1** a usu. leather covering for the foot and lower part of the leg. **2** a place for luggage in a car. **3** (*coll*) a hard kick. **4** (*coll*) dismissal from a job: *get the boot*. — *v* (*tr*) **1** to kick. **2** (with **out**) to throw out or remove with force. **3** (with **out**) to dismiss. **4** (*comput*; **up**) to start (a computer) by loading the programs which control its basic functions. — **the boot is on the other foot** or **leg** (*coll*) the situation is now the reverse of what it was before. — **lick someone's boots** (*coll derog*) to try to win a person's favour by flattery, excessive obedience, etc. [OFr *bote*]
bootee *n* a soft knitted boot for a baby.
bootlace *n* a piece of string, ribbon, etc. used to fasten boots.
bootleg *v* **-gg-** (*tr*) to make or transport alcoholic drinks illegally. — *adj* (of alcoholic drinks) illegally produced or transported. — *n* **bootlegger**. — *n* **bootlegging**.
bootlicker *n* (*coll*) a person who tries to gain the favour of someone in authority by flattery, excessive obedience, etc.
boots *n* (*old*) a person in a hotel who carries guests' bags and cleans their shoes.

boot[2]: **to boot** as well; in addition. [OE *bot*, help, advantage]

bootee. See **boot**[1].

booth *n* **1** a small temporary roofed structure, or a tent, esp. at a fair. **2** a small building or structure for a stated purpose: *a polling booth*. [Norse *buth*]

bootleg, **bootlicker**. See **boot**[1].

booty *n* **-ies** valuable goods taken in wartime or by force. [MidE *botye*]

booze (*slang*) *n* **1** alcoholic drink. **2** the drinking of alcohol: *on the booze*. — *v* (*intr*) to drink a lot of, or too much, alcohol. [ODut *busen*, to drink in excess]
boozer *n* (*slang*) **1** a person who drinks a lot of alcohol. **2** a public house.
booze-up *n* (*slang*) an occasion when a lot of alcohol is drunk.
boozy *adj* **-ier**, **-iest** (*slang*) **1** given to drinking a lot of alcohol. **2** drunken.

bop[1] *v* **-pp-** (*intr*; *coll*) to dance to popular music. — *n* (*coll*) a dance. — *n* **bopper**. [*bebop*, a type of 1940s' jazz music]

bop[2] *v* **-pp-** (*tr*; *coll*) to hit lightly. [Imit.]

borage *n* a plant with blue flowers, the leaves of which are used in salads or as a herb. [OFr *bourache*]

borax *n* a mineral salt, usu. found in white powder or crystal form, used in glass-making and antiseptics, and as a source of boron. [Lat *borax*, from Arabic *buraq*]
boracic *adj* **1** of or containing borax. **2** of or containing boron.
boracic acid same as **boric acid**.

border *n* **1** a band or margin along the edge of something. **2** the boundary of a country.

3 the land on either side of a country's border. ◇ See also **the Borders**. **4** a narrow strip of ground planted with flowers, surrounding a small area of grass. **5** any decorated or ornamental edge. — *v* **1** (*tr*) to provide with a border. **2** (*tr*) to be a border to or on the border of. **3** (*intr* with **on**) to be nearly the same as: *actions bordering on stupidity*. — *adj* **bordered**. [MidE *bordure*]

borderer *n* a person who lives on the border of a country.

borderland *n* **1** land at or near the country's border. **2** a condition between two states, e.g. between sleeping and waking.

borderline *n* **1** the border between one thing, country, etc. and another. **2** a line dividing two opposing or extreme conditions: *the borderline between passing and failing*. — *adj* on the border between one thing, state, etc. and another.

the Borders *n* (*pl*) the area of land lying either side of the border between Scotland and England.

bore[1] *v* (*tr*) **1** to make (a hole) in (something) by drilling. **2** to produce (a tunnel, mine, etc.) by drilling. — *n* **1** the hollow barrel of a gun. **2** the diameter of the hollow barrel of a gun, esp. to show which size bullets the gun requires. **3** same as **borehole**. — *n* **borer**. [OE *borian*]

borehole *n* a deep, narrow hole made by boring, esp. one made in the earth to find oil, water, etc.

bore[2] *v* (*tr*) to make (someone) feel tired and uninterested, by being dull, uninteresting, unimaginative, etc. — *n* a dull, uninteresting, tedious person or thing. — *adj* **bored**. — *adj* **boring**. — *adv* **boringly**.

boredom *n* the state of being bored.

bore[3] *n* a high wave, caused by the sea's tides, which moves quickly up certain rivers. [Norse *bara*, wave]

bore[4]. See **bear**[1].

boredom. See **bore**[2].

boric *adj* of or containing boron. **[borax]**

boric acid *n* an acid, usu. in the form of a white powder, obtained from borax, used as a mild antiseptic, in glass-making, and as a source of boron.

born *adj* **1** brought into being by birth. **2** having a natural quality or ability: *a born leader*. **3** (with **to**) destined to (do something stated): *born to lead men*. **4** having a stated given status by birth: *Scots-born*. — **in all one's born days** (*coll*) in all one's lifetime or experience. — **not born yesterday** not a fool. ◇ See also **bear**[1] (sense 4). **[bear**[1]**]**

born-again *adj* **1** having been converted to a strong Christian faith. **2** (*coll*) showing a new and strong enthusiasm for something: *a born-again vegetarian*.

borne see **bear**[1]. — *in cmpds* carried or transported by: *seaborne*. **[bear**[1]**]**

boron *n* a hard, non-metallic element, symbol **B**, obtained from borax and boric acid, and used for making steel hard. ◇ See also **borax** and **boric**. **[borax + carbon]**

borough *n* **1** in Britain, a town or urban area which sends a member to Parliament. **2** (*hist*) in Britain, a town with special rights granted by royal charter. **3** a division of a large town, esp. of London or New York. [OE *burg*]

borrow *v* **1** (*tr*) to take (something) temporarily, usu. with permission and with the intention of returning it. **2** (*intr*) to get money in this way. **3** (*tr*) to take, adopt or copy (words, ideas, etc.) from another language, person, etc. — *n* **borrower**. — **live on borrowed time** to live longer than expected. [OE *borgian*, from *borg*, pledge]

borrowing *n* a thing borrowed, esp. a word taken from one language into another.

borstal *n* (*Br hist*) an institution which was both a prison and a school, to which young criminals were formerly sent; now replaced by **detention centres** and **youth custody centres**. [*Borstal* in Kent, where the first of these was established]

borzoi *n* a large dog, orig. used for hunting, with a narrow head and a long, soft coat. [Russ *borzii*, swift]

bosh *n* & *interj* (*coll*) nonsense. [Turk *boş*, worthless, empty]

bo's'n. See **boatswain**.

bosom *n* **1** a person's, esp. a woman's, chest or breast. **2** (*coll*; sometimes in *pl*) a woman's breasts. **3** the part of a dress covering the breasts and chest. **4** a loving or protective centre: *the bosom of one's family*. **5** the seat of emotions and feelings. [OE *bosm*]

bosom friend *n* a very close, dear friend.

boss[1] *n* (*coll*) a person who employs or who is in charge of others. — *v* (*tr*; **about**, **around**; *coll*) to give orders to in a domineering way. [Dut *baas*, master]

bossy *adj* **-ier**, **-iest** (*coll*) liking to give orders and commands to others. — *adv* **bossily**. — *n* **bossiness**.

bossy-boots *n* (*coll*) a very bossy, domineering person.

boss[2] *n* **1** a round, raised knob for decoration, on a shield, etc. **2** a round, raised, decorative knob, found where the ribs meet in a vaulted ceiling. ◇ See also **emboss**. [OFr *boce*]

bossa nova *n* **1** a dance like the samba, which originated in Brazil. **2** music for this dance. [Port *bossa*, trend + *nova*, new]

boss-eyed *adj* (*Br coll*) **1** having only one good eye. **2** cross-eyed. **3** crooked, squint.

bosun or **bo'sun**. See **boatswain**.

botany *n* the scientific study of plants. — *adj* **botanic** or **botanical**. — *n* **botanist**. [Gr *botane*, plant]

botanic or **botanical gardens** *n* (*pl*) a public park where both native and foreign plants are grown and often studied.

botch (*coll*) *v* (*tr*; **up**) **1** to do badly and without skill. **2** to repair carelessly or badly. — *n* (also **botch-up**) a badly or carelessly done piece of work, repair, etc. — *adj* **botched**. — *n* **botcher**.

both *adj* & *pron* the two — *adv* as well: *She both works and runs a family*. [Norse *bathir*]

bother *v* **-r-** **1** (*tr*) to annoy, worry or trouble. **2** (*intr*; **about**, **with**) to take the time or trouble. **3** (*intr*; **about**) to worry. — *n* **1** a minor trouble or worry. **2** a person or thing that causes bother. — *interj* an exclamation of slight annoyance or impatience.

botheration *n* & *interj* (*coll*) same as **bother**.

bothersome *adj* causing bother or annoyance.

bottle *n* **1** a hollow, usu. glass or plastic container with a narrow neck, for holding liquids. **2** (also **bottleful**, **-fuls**) the amount contained in a bottle. **3** a baby's feeding bottle, or the liquid in it: *give the baby her bottle*. **4** (*slang*) courage, nerve or confidence. **5** (usu. with **the**; *slang*) drinking of alcohol, esp. to excess: *hit the bottle*. — *v* (*tr*) **1** to put into or store in bottles. **2** (**up**) to restrain or hide (feelings): *bottle up one's sadness*. — *v* **bottle out** (*intr*; *slang*) to lose one's courage and decide not to do something. [OFr *botele*, from Lat *buttis*, cask]

bottle bank *n* a large container, usu. in the street or a public place, where people can put empty bottles so that the glass can be used again.

bottle-feed *v* (*tr*) to feed (a baby) with milk from a bottle. — *n* **bottle-feeding**.

bottle-green *n* & *adj* (of or in) a very dark green colour.

bottleneck *n* any place or thing which stops progress or slows it down, esp. a narrow part of a road which becomes very crowded with traffic.

bottom *n* **1** the lowest position or part. **2** the point farthest away from the front, top, most important or most successful part: *the bottom of the garden*; *bottom of the class*. **3** the part of the body on which a person sits. **4** the base on which something stands. **5** the seat of a chair. **6** the ground underneath a sea, river or lake. **7** the part of a ship which is under the water. — *adj* lowest or last. — *v* **-m-** **1** (*tr*) to put a bottom on. **2** (*intr*) (of a ship) to reach or touch the bottom. **3** (*intr* with **out**) to reach the lowest level and begin to rise again: *Prices are expected to bottom out soon*. — **at bottom** in reality. — **be at the bottom of** to be the basic cause of. — **bet one's bottom dollar** (*coll*) to bet all one has because one is very certain. — **get to the bottom of** to discover the real cause of (a mystery, etc.). [OE *botm*]

bottom drawer *n* (*Br*) the sheets, cups and saucers, plates, etc. that a woman collects ready for when she gets married and has her own home.

bottomless *adj* very deep.

bottom line *n* **1** the last line of a financial statement showing profit or loss. **2** (*coll*) the essential or most important part of a situation.

botulism *n* serious food poisoning caused by eating food infected with a particular type of bacteria. [Lat *botulus*, sausage, from the shape of the bacteria]

bouclé *n* (a material made from) a type of wool with curled or looped threads. [Fr, curled, looped]

boudoir *n* (*old*) a woman's private sitting-room or bedroom. [Fr, from *bouder*, to sulk]

bouffant *adj* (of a hairstyle or dress, etc.) very full and puffed out. [Fr]

bougainvillaea *n* a tropical climbing plant whose bracts (modified leaves) are red and purple and hide the flowers. [Louis Antoine de *Bougainville* (1729–1811), the first Frenchman to sail round the world]

bough *n* a branch of a tree. [OE *bog*, arm, shoulder]

bought. See **buy**.

bouillabaisse *n* a thick, spicy, fish soup from Provence. [Fr]

bouillon *n* a thin, clear soup made by boiling meat and vegetables in water, often used as a basis for thicker soups. [Fr, from *bouillir*, to boil]

boulder *n* a large rock or stone, rounded and worn smooth by the weather. [MidE *bulderston*]

boules *n* (*sing*) a game popular in France, played on rough ground, in which the players try to hit a small metal ball, the jack, with larger balls. [Fr *boule*, bowl[2]]

boulevard *n* a broad, tree-lined street. [Fr, from Ger *Bollwerk*, bulwark; orig. used of roads built on a town's demolished fortifications]

bounce *v* **1** (*intr*; **back**, **off**, etc.) (of a ball, etc.) to spring or jump back from a solid surface. **2** (*tr*) to make (a ball, etc.) spring or jump back from a solid surface. **3** (*intr* with **about**, **up**, etc.) to move or spring suddenly: *bounce about the room*. **4** (*intr* with **in**, **into**, **out**, etc.) to rush noisily, angrily, with a lot of energy, etc.: *bounce out in a temper*. **5** (*intr*; *coll*) (of a cheque) to be sent back without being paid, because of lack of money in a bank account. — *n* **1** the act of springing back from a solid surface. **2** the ability to spring back or bounce well. **3** a jump or leap. **4** (*coll*) energy and liveliness. — *v* **bounce back** (*intr*) to recover one's health, a former good position, etc. after a period of bad health, bad luck, etc. [Dut *bonzen*, to thump]

bouncer *n* (*coll*) a strong person employed by clubs and restaurants, etc. to stop unwanted guests entering and to throw out people who cause trouble.

bouncing *adj* (esp. of a baby) strong and lively.

bouncy *adj* **-ier**, **-iest** **1** able to bounce well. **2** (of a person) full of energy and very lively. — *adv* **bouncily**. — *n* **bounciness**.

bound[1] *adj* **1** tied with, or as if with, a rope, etc. **2** (*in cmpds*) restricted to or by: *housebound*; *snowbound*. **3** certain: *bound to happen*. **4** obliged: *duty bound to help*. **5** (of a book) having been put into a cover. — **bound up with** very closely linked with. ◇ See also **bind**. [Past participle of **bind**]

bound[2] *adj* (**for**) going to or towards: *southbound*. [Norse *bua*, to get ready]

bound[3] *n* (often in *pl*) **1** a limit or boundary. **2** a limitation or restriction. — *v* (*tr*) **1** to form a boundary of. **2** to set limits to; to restrict. — **out of bounds** outside the permitted area or limits. [OFr *bonde*]

boundless *adj* very great; having no limit. — *adv* **boundlessly**. — *n* **boundlessness**.

bound[4] *n* **1** a jump or leap upwards. **2** a bounce back from a solid surface. — *v* (*intr*; **down**, **up**, etc.) **1** to spring or leap: *bound down the stairs*. **2** to move with leaps. **3** (of a ball) to bounce back from a solid surface. [Fr *bondir*, to spring]

boundary *n* **-ies 1** a line marking the farthest limit of an area, etc. **2** the marked limits of a cricket field. **3** (*cricket*) a stroke that hits the ball across the boundary line, scoring four or six runs. [**bound**[3]]

bounden *adj* (*old*) which must be done; obligatory. ◇ See also **bind**. [Old past participle of **bind**]

bounder *n* (*old coll*) a man whose behaviour is unacceptable, usu. because it is considered morally wrong.

boundless. See **bound**[3].

bounteous *adj* **1** generous. **2** freely given. — *adv* **bounteously**. — *n* **bounteousness**. [**bounty** + **-ous**]

bountiful *adj* **1** generous. **2** in plenty. — *adv* **bountifully**. — *n* **bountifulness**. [**bounty** + **-ful**]

bounty *n* **-ies 1** the giving of things generously; generosity. **2** a generous gift. **3** a reward given, esp. by a government, as encouragement e.g. to kill or capture dangerous animals, criminals, etc. [OFr *bonte*, goodness, from Lat *bonus*, good]

bouquet *n* **1** a bunch of flowers arranged in an artistic way, given as a gift, carried by a bride, etc. **2** the delicate smell of wine. [Fr, from *bois*, a wood]

bouquet garni *n* a bunch or small packet of mixed herbs used to add flavour to food, usu. removed before serving. [Fr *garnir*, to garnish]

bourbon *n* a type of whisky made from maize and rye, popular in the US. [From *Bourbon* county, Kentucky, where it was first made]

bourgeois *n* ***bourgeois*** (usu. derog) a member of the middle class, esp. seen as politically conservative and only interested in his or her social position or wealth. — *adj* of or like the middle class or bourgeois people. [Fr]

the bourgeoisie *n* (usu. *derog*) the middle classes, esp. seen as politically conservative and interested only in social position and money.

bourn[1] *n* a small stream. [A form of **burn**[2]]

bourn[2] *n* (*old*) a boundary or limit. [OFr *bodne*, boundary]

bout *n* **1** a period or turn (of doing something): *a drinking bout*. **2** a period of illness: *a bout of flu*. **3** a boxing or wrestling match. [A form of the obsolete word *bought*, bend, turn]

boutique *n* a small shop, esp. one selling fashionable clothes. [Fr]

bouzouki *n* a Greek musical instrument with a long neck and metal strings, related to the mandolin. [Gr]

bovine *adj* **1** of or like cattle. **2** (*derog*) (of people) dull or stupid. [Lat *bos*, ox]

bovine spongiform encephalopathy *n* a serious and usu. fatal disease of the brain and nervous system in cattle.

bow[1] *v* **1** (*intr*) to bend the head or the upper part of the body forwards and downwards, usu. as a sign of greeting, respect, shame, etc. or to acknowledge applause. **2** (*tr*) to bend (the head or the upper part of the body) forwards and downwards: *bow one's head*. **3** (*intr* with **to**) to accept or submit to, esp. unwillingly: *bow to the inevitable*. — *n* an act of bowing (sense **1**). — **bow and scrape** (*derog*) to behave towards (someone) with excessive politeness. — *v* **bow down** (*intr*) to submit to or agree to obey: *bow down to one's enemies*. — *v* **bow out** (*intr*) to stop taking part; to withdraw: *bow out of the contest*. — **take a bow** to acknowledge applause. [OE *bugan*]

bow[2] *n* **1** a knot with a double loop. **2** a weapon made of a piece of curved wood, bent by a string attached to each end, for shooting arrows. **3** a long thin piece of wood with horsehair stretched along its length, for playing the violin, cello, etc. **4** anything which is curved or bent in shape. — *v* (*tr*) to use a bow on (a violin, cello, etc.). [OE *boga*, arch]

bow-legged *adj* (of a person) with legs which curve out.

bowshot *n* the distance which an arrow can be shot from a bow.

bowstring *n* the string on a bow which allows arrows to be shot.

bow tie *n* a tie which is tied in a double loop.

bow window *n* a window which is curved out. ◇ See also **bay window**.

bow[3] *n* **1** (often in *pl*) the front part of a ship or boat. **2** (*rowing*) the rower nearest the bow. [Ger dialect *boog* or Dut *boeg*, a ship's bow]

bowdlerise or **-ize** *v* (*tr*) to remove potentially offensive passages or words from (a book, play, etc.), esp. when it is unnecessary to do so. — *n* **bowdlerisation** or **-z**. — *adj* **bowdlerised** or **-z**. [Dr T *Bowdler* (1754–1825), who published an expurgated Shakespeare in ten volumes in 1818]

bowel *n* **1** the organs for digesting food next after the stomach; the intestines. **2** (usu. in *pl*) the depths or innermost part of something, esp. when deep or mysterious: *the bowels of the earth.* [OFr *buel*, from Lat *botellus*, sausage]

bower *n* **1** a place in a garden which is shaded from the sun by plants and trees. **2** (*literary*) a lady's private room. [OE *bur*, chamber]

bowerbird *n* any of various species of Australian birds, the males of which build bowers decorated with feathers, leaves, shells, etc. during courtship.

bowl[1] *n* **1** a round, deep dish for mixing or serving food, for holding liquids or flowers, etc. **2** (also **bowlful**, ***-fuls***) the amount a bowl will hold; the contents of a bowl. **3** the round, hollow part of an object, such as a spoon or pipe. [OE *bolla*]

bowl[2] *n* a wooden ball designed to run in a curve, used in the game of bowls; a similar metal ball used in boules. — *v* **1** (*tr*) to roll (a ball, hoop, etc.) smoothly along the ground. **2** (*intr*) to play bowls. **3** (*intr* & *tr*; *cricket*, etc.) to throw (a ball) towards the person batting. **4** (*tr*; *cricket*, etc.; **out**) to put (the person batting in cricket) out by hitting the wicket with the ball. **5** (*intr* with **along**) to move smoothly and quickly: *a carriage bowling along the road.* — *v* **bowl over** (*tr*) **1** to knock (someone) over. **2** (*coll*) to surprise or impress greatly. [Fr *boule*]

bowler *n* **1** a person who bowls the ball in cricket, etc. **2** a person who plays bowls or goes bowling.

bowling *n* **1** the game of bowls. **2** a game played indoors in which a ball is rolled at a group of skittles in order to knock them down: *go bowling*.

bowling-alley *n* **1** a long narrow channel made of wooden boards used in bowling (sense **2**). **2** a building containing several of these.

bowling-green *n* an area of smooth grass set aside for the game of bowls.

bowls *n* (*sing*) a game played on smooth grass with bowls, the object of the game being to get one's bowl as close as possible to a smaller ball called the jack.

bowler[1]. See **bowl**[2].

bowler[2] *n* (also **bowler hat**) a man's hard, round, usu. black, felt hat with a narrow brim. [From *Bowler*, a nineteenth-century hatter]

bowline *n* **1** a rope used to keep a sail taut against the wind. **2** a knot which makes a loop that will not slip at the end of a piece of rope. [OGer dialect *boline*]

bowls. See **bowl**[2].

bowsprit *n* a pole projecting from the front of a ship, with ropes from the sails fastened to it. [OGer dialect *boch*, bow[3] + *spret*, pole]

bow-wow *n* a child's word for a dog. — *interj* an imitation of a dog's bark. [Imit.]

box[1] *n* **1** a usu. square or rectangular container made from wood, cardboard, plastic, etc. and with a lid, for holding things. **2** (also **boxful**, ***-fuls***) the amount contained in a box. **3** a separate compartment for a particular purpose, e.g. for a group of people in a theatre, for a horse in a stable or vehicle, or a witness in a lawcourt. **4** a small enclosed area for a particular purpose: *a telephone box*. **5** a section on a piece of paper, field, road, etc. marked out by straight lines: *a penalty box*. **6** a newspaper office or agency which collects mail and sends it on to the person it is intended for: *a post-office box*; *a box number*. **7** (*Br coll*; with **the**) the television. **8** a raised seat for the driver on a carriage. **9** a small country house, used as a base for some sports: *a shooting-box*. **10** a gift of money given to tradesmen and, formerly, servants: *a Christmas box*. — *v* (*tr*) **1** (**up**) to put into or provide with a box or boxes. **2** (with **in**, **up**) to stop from moving, confine or enclose. — *adj* **boxed**. — **box the compass** to name all the 32 points of the compass in their correct order. [Lat *buxis*]

box girder *n* a hollow, square or rectangular girder.

Boxing Day *n* **1** 26 December, the day after Christmas Day. **2** the first weekday after Christmas, a public holiday in the UK.

box junction *n* (*Br*) an area at a road junction marked by yellow lines painted on the ground, which a car may enter only if its exit is clear.

box-kite *n* a kite in the form of a box with open ends.

box office *n* **1** an office which sells theatre tickets. **2** the ability of an actor, performer, etc. to attract an audience and so make money.

box pleat *n* on a skirt or dress, a large double pleat formed by folding the material in two pleats facing in opposite directions.

boxroom *n* (*Br*) a very small room in a house, used to store bags, boxes, etc. or as a bedroom.

box[2] *v* **1** (*tr* & *intr*) to fight with one's hands formed into fists and protected by thick leather gloves, esp. as a sport. **2** (*tr*) to hit (esp. a person's ears) with the fist. — *n* a punch with the fist, esp. on the ears: *a box on the ears*. — *n* **boxing**. [MidE *box*, blow]

boxer *n* **1** a person who boxes, esp. as a sport. **2** a medium-sized breed of dog with a short, smooth coat.

boxer shorts *n* (*pl*) loose shorts worn by men as underpants.

boxing-glove *n* either of a pair of thick leather gloves worn by boxers.

box[3] *n* **1** (also **boxtree**) a small evergreen tree or shrub, with dark shiny leaves, often used for hedges. **2** (also **boxwood**) its wood. [OE, from Lat *buxus*]

boxer, **boxing**. See **box**[2].

Boxing Day. See **box**[1].
boy *n* **1** a male child. **2** a son. **3** a young man, esp. thought of as not being very mature. **4** (in *pl*; *coll*) a group of men with whom a man is friendly: *go out with the boys*. **5** (*offensive*) a black male servant. — *interj* (also **oh boy**) an expression of excitement, surprise or pleasure. — *n* **boyhood**.
boyish *adj* like a boy in appearance or behaviour: *boyish good looks*. — *adv* **boyishly**. — *n* **boyishness**.
boyfriend *n* the man or boy with whom a woman or girl has her closest friendship or sexual relationship.
Boys' Brigade *n* an organisation for boys which encourages discipline, self-respect, etc.
Boy Scout see **Scout**.
boycott *v* (*tr*) **1** to refuse to have any business or social dealings with (a company, a country, etc.) because one disapproves of something it is doing. **2** to refuse to handle, buy, etc. (goods) because one disapproves of something the producer is doing. — *n* an act of boycotting. [Captain C C *Boycott* (1832–97), so treated by his neighbours in 1880]
BP *abbrev* **1** blood pressure. **2** British Petroleum. **3** British Pharmacopoeia.
Bq *symbol* becquerel.
BR *abbrev* British Rail.
Br[1] *abbrev* **1** brother. **2** British. **3** Britain.
Br[2] *symbol* (*chem*) bromine.
bra or **brassière** *n* an undergarment worn by a woman to support her breasts. — *adj* **braless**. [Fr *brassière*, baby's vest]
brace *n* **1** a device, usu. made from metal, which supports, makes stronger, or holds two things together. **2** (in *pl*; *Br*) straps worn over the shoulders, for holding trousers up. **3** a wire device worn on the teeth to straighten them. **4** ***brace*** a pair or couple, esp. of game birds: *four brace of pheasants*. **5** in printing, either of two symbols, { or }, used to show that lines, figures, parts of text, etc. are connected. **6** a rope attached to a ship's yard, used for adjusting the sails. — *v* (*tr*) **1** to make tight or stronger, usu. by supporting in some way. **2** to prepare (oneself) for a blow, a shock, etc. [OFr *brace*, two arms, from Lat *bracchium*, arm]
brace and bit *n* a hand tool for drilling holes.
bracing *adj* (of the wind, air, etc.) cold and fresh but also refreshing and stimulating.
bracelet *n* **1** a band or chain worn as a piece of jewellery round the arm or wrist. **2** (in *pl*; *slang*) handcuffs. [OFr, little arm]
brachiopod *n* a sea animal like a worm, which lives in a shell, and which has two arm-like growths for wafting food into its mouth. [Gr *brachion*, arm + *podos*, foot]
bracken *n* a type of fern common in Britain, growing on hills and in woods. [MidE *braken*]
bracket *n* **1** either one of a pair of symbols, [], (), < > or {}, used to group together or enclose words, figures, etc. ◇ See also **brace** (sense **5**) and **parenthesis**. **2** a group or category falling within a certain range: *out of my price bracket*. **3** a usu. L-shaped piece of metal or strong plastic, used for attaching shelves, etc. to walls. — *v* **-t- 1** to enclose or group together (words, etc.) in brackets. **2** to put (people, things, etc.) into a group or category.
brackish *adj* (of water) tasting slightly salty. — *n* **brackishness**. [Dut *brak*, salty]
bract *n* a usu. small, scaly, and often brightly coloured leaf growing at the base of a flower. [Lat *bractea*, thin plate of metal or gold-leaf]
brad *n* a thin, flat nail with a small head. [Norse *broddr*, spike]
bradawl *n* a small hand tool for making holes in wood, leather, etc.
brae *n* (*Scot*) a slope on a hill. [Norse *bra*, brow]
brag *v* **-gg-** (*intr*) to talk boastfully or too proudly about oneself, what one has done, etc. — *n* **1** a boastful statement or boastful talk. **2** a card game like poker. — *adv* **braggingly**. [MidE *brag*, arrogance]
braggart *n* a person who brags a lot. [Fr *bragard*, vain, bragging]
Brahman or **Brahmin** *n* a Hindu who belongs to the highest, priestly caste. [From **Brahma**, the creator of the universe in Hindu belief]
braid *n* **1** a band or tape, often made from threads of gold and silver twisted together, used as a decoration on uniforms, etc. **2** a length of hair consisting of several lengths which have been twisted together. — *v* (*tr*) **1** to twist (several lengths of thread, hair) together. **2** to decorate with braid. — *adj* **braided**. — *n* **braiding**. [OE *bregdan*, to weave]
Braille *n* a system of printing using raised dots, which blind people can feel with their fingers and so read what is printed. [Louis *Braille* (1809–52), its inventor]
brain *n* **1** the soft grey organ inside the head which controls thought, sight, etc. **2** (in *pl*; *coll*) cleverness, intelligence. **3** (*coll*) a very clever person. **4** (usu. in *pl* but treated as *sing*; *coll*) a person who thinks up and controls a plan, etc.: *the brains behind the idea*. — *v* (*tr*; *coll*) to hit hard on the head. — **have (something) on the brain** (*coll*) to be unable to stop thinking about (something). [OE *brægen*]
brainchild *n* a person's particular theory, idea or plan.
brain-dead *adj* with the brain not functioning at all but with the heart still working.
brain death *n* the stopping of the functioning of the brain even though the heart is still working.
brain drain *n* (*coll*) the loss of scientists, academics, professionals, etc. to another country, usu. to one where they can earn more money.

brainless *adj* (*coll*) stupid, silly. — *adv* **brainlessly**.

brainstorm *n* **1** a sudden loss of the ability to think clearly and act properly. **2** (*NAm*; *coll*) same as **brainwave** (sense **1**).

brainstorming *n* (esp. *US*) the practice of trying to solve problems or come up with new ideas, etc. by group discussions at which as many suggestions as possible are made but none discussed in depth.

brainteaser *n* a difficult exercise or puzzle.

brainwash *v* (*tr*) to force (someone) to change his or her beliefs, ideas, etc. by continually applying mental pressure. — *n* **brainwashing**.

brainwave *n* **1** (*coll*) a sudden bright or clever idea. **2** an electrical current produced by the brain.

brainy *adj* **-ier**, **-iest** (*coll*) clever, intelligent. — *n* **braininess**.

braise *v* (*tr*) to cook (meat, etc.) slowly with a small amount of liquid in a closed dish. — *adj* **braised**. [Fr *braiser*, from *braise*, live coals]

brake[1] *n* **1** a device on a vehicle for making it slow down or stop. **2** anything which makes something stop, prevents progress, etc.: *a brake on public spending*. **3** a toothed instrument for crushing flax or hemp. **4** a type of harrow for breaking up large lumps of hard earth. — *v* **1** (*intr*) to apply or use a brake. **2** (*tr*) to use a brake to make (a vehicle) slow down or stop. **3** (*tr*) to crush (flax or hemp) by beating.

brake drum *n* the round device in a wheel which is pressed by the brake shoe when the brake is applied.

brake horsepower *n* the power of a motor, measured by the amount of power needed to brake it.

brake light *n* either of the red lights at the back of a vehicle, etc. which light up when the driver applies the brakes.

brake shoe *n* a long curved piece of metal that presses on the brake drum when the brake is applied.

brake[2] *n* **1** an area of wild, rough ground covered with low bushes, etc. **2** a thicket. [OGer dialect, thicket]

bramble *n* **1** a common wild prickly bush which produces blackberries. **2** (*Scot*) a blackberry. [OE *bremel*]

brambling *n* a small orange-breasted bird related to the chaffinch. [**broom** + **-ling**]

bran *n* the outer covering of grain separated from flour. [OFr]

bran tub *n* (*Br*) a tub filled with bran, paper, wood shavings, etc. with presents hidden in it for a lucky dip.

branch *n* **1** a shoot or stem growing out like an arm from the main body of a tree. **2** a main division of a railway line, river, road or mountain range: *a branch line on the railway*. **3** a division in a family, subject, group of languages, etc. **4** a local office of a large company or organisation. — *v* (*intr*; **off**) **1** to send out branches. **2** to divide from the main part: *a road branching off to the left*. — *v* **branch out** (*intr*) to develop different interests, projects, etc. — *adj* **branched**. — *n* & *adj* **branching**. — *adj* **branchless**. [OFr *branche*, from Lat *branca*, paw]

brand *n* **1** a maker's name or trademark. **2** a variety or type: *her brand of humour*. **3** an identifying mark on cattle, etc., usu. burned on with a hot iron. **4** (also **branding-iron**) an iron used for burning identifying marks on cattle, etc. **5** a sign of disgrace or shame. **6** a piece of burning or smouldering wood. **7** (*literary*) a torch. **8** (*literary*) a sword. — *v* (*tr*) **1** to mark (cattle, etc.) with a hot iron. **2** to make a permanent impression on (someone). **3** to give (someone) a bad name or reputation: *branded him a liar*. [OE, fire, flame]

brand-new *adj* completely new.

brandish *v* (*tr*) to wave (a weapon, etc.) as a threat or display. [OFr *brandir*]

brandy *n* **-ies** a strong alcoholic drink made from wine or fermented fruit juice. [Dut *brandewijn*, from *branden*, to burn or distil + *wijn*, wine]

brandy-snap *n* a very thin biscuit in the form of a hollow tube, flavoured with ginger and usu. served filled with cream.

brash *adj* **1** very loud or showy. **2** rude, impudent. — *adv* **brashly**. — *n* **brashness**.

brass *n* **1** a hard yellowish metal, a mixture of copper and zinc. **2** objects, tools, etc. made of brass. **3** wind instruments made of brass, such as the trumpet. **4** the people who play brass instruments in an orchestra. **5** a piece of flat brass with a figure, design, name, etc. on it, usu. found in a church, in memory of some dead person. **6** a small, flat, brass ornament with a design on it, for a horse's harness. **7** (also **top brass**; *coll*) people in authority or of high military rank. **8** (also **brass neck**; *coll*) confidence, nerve, and a complete lack of shame. **9** (*coll*, esp. *North of England*) money. — *adj* made of brass. — **brassed off** (*coll*) fed up; annoyed. ◇ See also **brazier**[2]. [OE *bræs*]

brass band *n* a band in which most people play brass wind instruments, such as the trumpet.

brass hat *n* (*slang*) a high-ranking military officer.

brass rubbing *n* **1** a copy of the design on a brass (sense **5**) made by putting paper on top of it and rubbing with coloured wax or charcoal. **2** the making of such a copy.

brass tacks *n* (*pl*; *coll*) the essential details: *get down to brass tacks*.

brassy *adj* **-ier**, **-iest** **1** like brass in appearance, esp. in colour. **2** like a brass musical instrument in sound. **3** (*coll*) loudly confident and rude. **4** flashy or showy. — *adv* **brassily**. — *n* **brassiness**.

brasserie *n* a small and usu. quite cheap restaurant, esp. one serving French food, and orig. beer. [Fr, brewery]

brassica *n* a plant belonging to the cabbage and turnip family. [Lat, cabbage]
brassière. See **bra**.
brat *n* a child, esp. a rude or badly behaved one.
bravado *n* a (sometimes boastful and insincere) display of courage, confidence, daring, etc. [Span *bravada*]
brave *adj* **1** without fear of danger, pain, etc. **2** fine, excellent. — *v* (*tr*; **out**) to meet or face (danger, pain, etc.) boldly and without fear: *brave the storm*. — *n* (*formerly* or *films*) a warrior from a N American Indian tribe. — *adv* **bravely**. — *n* **bravery**. [OFr, from Lat *barbarus*, barbarous]
bravo[1] *interj* well done! excellent! — *n* ***-os*** a cry of 'bravo'. [Ital]
bravo[2] *n* ***-os*** or ***-oes*** a hired killer. [Ital]
bravura *n* **1** a display of great spirit or daring. **2** a piece of music, esp. to be sung, which is very complicated and requires great technical ability. [Ital]
brawl *n* a noisy quarrel or fight, usu. in public. — *v* (*intr*) to quarrel or fight noisily. — *n* **brawler**. — *n* & *adj* **brawling**. [MidE *bralle*]
brawn *n* **1** muscle or physical strength. **2** boiled, jellied meat from the head of a pig. [OFr *braon*, meat]
brawny *adj* ***-ier***, ***-iest*** muscular; strong. — *n* **brawniness**.
bray *n* the loud, harsh sound made by an ass or donkey. — *v* **1** (*intr*) (of an ass or donkey) to make such a noise. **2** (*intr*) (of people) to make a loud, harsh sound. **3** (*tr*) to say in a loud, harsh voice. [OFr *braire*]
braze *v* (*tr*) to join (two pieces of metal) with a mixture of brass and zinc. [Fr *braser*, from *braise*, live coals]
brazen *adj* **1** (also **brazen-faced**) bold, impudent and without shame. **2** of or like brass, esp. in sound or colour. — *v* ***-n-*** (*tr*; **out**) to face (an embarrassing or difficult situation) boldly and without shame. — *adv* **brazenly**. — *n* **brazenness**. [OE *bræsen*, from *bræs*, brass]
brazier[1] *n* a metal frame or container for holding burning coal, esp. used by people who have to work outside in cold weather. [Fr *brasier*, from *braise*, live coals]
brazier[2] *n* a worker in brass. [**brass**]
Brazil or **brazil** *n* **1** a type of red wood from any of several tropical trees. **2** (also **Brazil nut**) a type of long, three-sided, edible white nut from a tropical American tree. [*Brazil* in S America, the country itself being so named from the similarity of the red wood found there to that found in the East and known as *brasil*]
breach *n* **1** a breaking (of a law, promise, etc.) or failure to carry out (a duty). **2** a serious disagreement. **3** a gap, break or hole. — *v* (*tr*) **1** to break (a promise, etc.) or fail to carry out (a duty). **2** to make an opening or hole in. — **in breach of** not following or agreeing with (a law, etc.). — **step into the breach** to take responsibility, or an absent person's place, in a crisis. [OE *bryce*]
breach of confidence *n* a failure to keep the secrets, etc. told to one.
breach of the peace *n* a fight, riot, etc., which upsets the public peace.
breach of promise *n* the breaking of a promise, esp. of a promise to marry someone.
bread *n* **1** a food made from flour, water and yeast, baked in an oven. **2** food and other things one needs to live: *earn one's bread*. **3** (*slang*) money. — *v* (*tr*) to cover (food) with breadcrumbs. — *adj* **breaded**. — **know which side one's bread is buttered** to know how to act for one's own best interests. [OE]
bread and butter *n* **1** sliced, buttered bread. **2** one's way of earning a living.
bread basket *n* **1** a basket for holding bread. **2** an area which produces a lot of grain which it sends to other areas. **3** (*slang*) the stomach.
breadboard *n* **1** a wooden board on which bread, etc. is cut. **2** a board on which it is possible to make models of electric circuits.
breadcrumbs *n* (*pl*) very tiny pieces of bread.
breadfruit *n* the fruit of a tree found in the S Pacific islands, which looks like bread when it is roasted.
breadline: **on the breadline** with hardly enough food and money to live on.
breadwinner *n* the person who earns money to support a family.
breadth *n* **1** the measurement from one side to the other. **2** openness and willingness to understand and respect other people's opinions, beliefs, etc.: *breadth of vision*. — *adv* **breadthways** and **breadthwise**. [OE *bræd*]
break *v* ***broke***, ***broken*** **1** (*tr* & *intr*) to divide or become divided into two or more parts by force. **2** (*tr* & *intr*) to damage or become damaged, so as to no longer work and be in need of repair. **3** (*tr*) to fracture a bone in (a limb, etc.): *break one's leg*. **4** (*tr*) to burst or cut (the skin) or the skin of (the head). **5** (*tr*) to do something not allowed by (a law, agreement, promise, etc.). **6** (*tr*) to interrupt (a journey). **7** (*intr*) to stop work, etc. for a short period of time: *break for tea*. **8** (*tr*) to do better than (a sporting record, etc.). **9** (*tr* & *intr*) (of news, etc.) to make or become known. **10** (*intr* with **with**) to stop associating with: *broke with his former friends*. **11** (*intr*) (of the weather) to change suddenly, esp. after a fine spell. **12** (*tr* & *intr*) to make or become weaker: *break his spirit*. **13** (*tr*) to defeat or destroy: *break a strike*. **14** (*tr*) to make (the force of something) less: *break her fall*. **15** (*tr*) to decipher: *break a code*. **16** (*tr* with **of**) to make (someone) give up (a bad habit, etc.): *break him of smoking*. **17** (*intr*) to come into being: *day breaking over the hills*. **18** (*intr*) (of a storm) to begin

violently. **19** (*intr*) to cut or burst through: *sun breaking through the clouds.* **20** (*intr* with **into**) to begin (to do something), esp. suddenly: *break into song.* **21** (*intr*) (of the voice of a boy becoming an adult) to become lower in tone. **22** (*tr*) to disprove (an alibi, etc.). **23** (*tr*) to interrupt the flow of electricity in (a circuit). **24** (*tr*) to open with explosives: *break a safe.* **25** (*intr*) (of waves, etc.) to collapse into foam. **26** (*tr*) to lose or disrupt the order or form of: *break ranks.* **27** (*intr*; *snooker*, etc.) to take the first shot at the beginning of a game. **28** (*tr*; *tennis*) to win (an opponent's service game): *break his service.* **29** (*intr*; *boxing*, etc.) to come out of a clinch. **30** (*intr*; *cricket*) (of a ball) to change direction on hitting the ground. — *n* **1** an act of or result of breaking. **2** a brief pause in work, lessons, etc. **3** a change: *a break in the weather.* **4** a sudden rush, esp. to escape: *make a break for it.* **5** (*coll*) an opportunity to show how good one is. **6** (*coll*) a piece of good or bad luck: *a bad break.* **7** (*snooker*, etc.) a series of successful shots played one after the other. **8** (*snooker*, etc.) the opening shot of a game. **9** an interruption in the electricity flowing through a circuit. **10** (*mus*) a short, improvised, solo passage in jazz. — *v* **break away** (*intr*) **1** to escape from control. **2** to put an end to one's connection with a group, etc. (*n* & *adj* **breakaway**). — **break the back of** to complete the heaviest or most difficult part of (a job, etc.). — **break camp** to pack up tents, etc. — **break cover** to come out of hiding. — *v* **break down 1** (*tr*) to use force to knock down (a door, etc.). **2** (*intr*) to stop working properly (*n* **breakdown**). **3** (*intr*) (of human relationships) to be unsuccessful and so come to an end (*n* **breakdown**). **4** (*intr*; **in**) to give way to one's emotions: *break down in tears.* **5** (*tr*) to divide into parts and analyse (*n* **breakdown**). **6** (*intr*) to fail in mental health (*n* **breakdown**). — **break even** to make neither a profit nor a loss. — **break free** see **break loose** below. — **break fresh ground** see **break new ground** below. — *v* **break in 1** (*intr*) to enter (a building) by force, esp. to steal things inside (*n* **break-in**). **2** (*intr*) to interrupt (a conversation, etc.). **3** (*tr*) to train (a horse) to carry a saddle and a rider. **4** (*tr*) to wear (new shoes, boots, etc.) so that they lose their stiffness. — **break loose** or **free 1** to escape from control. **2** to become detached: *The boat broke loose from its mooring.* — **break new** or **fresh ground** to do something no one has done before. — *v* **break off 1** (*tr* & *intr*) to remove or be removed by breaking. **2** (*intr* & *tr*) to come or be brought to an end suddenly. **3** (*intr*) to stop talking. — **break open** to open (a box, door, etc.) by force. — *v* **break out 1** (*intr*) to escape from (a prison, etc.) using force (*n* **breakout**). **2** (*intr*) to begin suddenly and usu. violently: *war broke out* (*n* **outbreak**). **3** (*intr*; **in**) to become suddenly covered (in spots, a rash, etc.). **4** (*intr*) to say loudly or exclaim. **5** (*tr*) to remove from a container. — **break step** (of soldiers, etc.) to stop marching in time. — *v* **break through 1** (*tr* & *intr*) to force a way through (*n* **breakthrough**). **2** (*intr*) to make a new discovery or be successful, esp. after a period of problems or lack of success (*n* **breakthrough**). — *v* **break up 1** (*intr* & *tr*) to divide or break into pieces (*n* **break-up**). **2** (*intr* & *tr*) to (cause to) finish or come to an end (*n* **break-up**). **3** (*intr*) (of people) to end a relationship or marriage: *His parents have broken up* (*n* **break-up**). **4** (*intr*) (of a relationship, marriage, etc.) to come to an end: *Their marriage has broken up* (*n* **break-up**). **5** (*intr*) (of a school or pupil) to begin the holidays. **6** (*tr*; *US coll*) to make (someone) laugh a lot. — **break wind** to let gas out from the bowels through the anus. [OE *brecan*]

breakable *adj* able to be broken. — *n* (usu. in *pl*) a breakable thing.

breakage *n* **1** the act of breaking. **2** a broken thing; damage caused by breaking.

breakaway see **break away** above.

breakdancing *n* an energetic style of dancing which involves complicated jumps and twists, etc., orig. developed by young black Americans.

break of day *n* (*literary*) dawn.

breakdown *n* see **break down** above. — *adj* (of a van, lorry, etc.) used to give assistance after a vehicle breakdown.

breaker *n* **1** a person or thing that breaks (something). **2** a large wave which breaks on rocks or the beach.

break-in see **break in** above.

breaking and entering *n* the act of breaking into someone's house to rob it.

breaking-point *n* a point at which a person or thing can no longer stand the strain of a situation.

breakneck *adj* (of speed) extremely fast.

breakout see **break out** above.

breakthrough see **break through** above.

break-up see **break up** above.

breakwater *n* a wall built on a beach to break the force of the waves.

breakfast *n* the first meal of the day. ◇ See also **wedding breakfast**. — *v* (*intr*) to have breakfast. [**break** + **fast**[2]]

bream *n* ***bream*** **1** a type of freshwater fish. **2** (also **sea bream**) a similar sea fish. [OFr *bresme*]

breast *n* **1** either of the two fleshy parts on the front of a woman's body which produce milk. **2** the front part of the body between the neck and stomach. **3** the source or seat of emotions. **4** the part of a garment covering the breast. — *v* (*tr*) **1** to face or oppose: *breast the wind.* **2** to come to the top of (a hill, etc.). **3** (*athletics*) to touch (the tape at the end of the race) with the chest. — **make a clean breast of it**

to tell the truth about something one has done, feels or thinks, etc. [OE *breost*]

breastbone *n* the thin, flat bone running down the front of the chest.

breastfeed *v* (*tr* & *intr*) to feed (a baby) with milk from the breast. — *adj* **breastfed**. — *n* **breastfeeding**.

breastplate *n* a piece of armour which protects the chest.

breaststroke *n* a style of swimming in which the arms are pushed out in front and then pulled backwards together.

breastwork *n* a temporary wall built from earth for defence, reaching up to a person's chest.

breath *n* **1** the air drawn into and sent out from the lungs. **2** an act of breathing air in. **3** a faint breeze. **4** a slight trace (of perfume, etc.). **5** a slight hint, suggestion or rumour (esp. of scandal). — **catch one's breath** to stop breathing for a moment, from fear, amazement, pain, etc. — **draw breath** to breathe. — **get one's breath back** to begin to start breathing normally again, e.g. after exercise. — **hold one's breath** to stop breathing, usu. because of worry or to avoid being heard. — **out of** or **short of breath** breathless, esp. because of exercise. — **take someone's breath away** to so surprise, shock, please, excite (someone) that he or she cannot speak. ◇ See also **breathtaking**. — **under one's breath** in a whisper. — **waste one's breath** (*coll*) to say something to someone which he or she takes no notice of. [OE *bræth*]

Breathalyser® or **-z-** *n* a small piece of equipment used to test the amount of alcohol on a driver's breath. — *v* **breathalyse** or **-z-** (*tr*).

breathless *adj* **1** having difficulty in breathing normally, either from illness or from hurrying, etc. **2** very eager or excited. **3** with no wind or fresh air. — *adv* **breathlessly**. — *n* **breathlessness**.

breathtaking *adj* very surprising, exciting or impressive. — *adv* **breathtakingly**.

breath test *n* (*Br*) a test given to drivers to check the amount of alcohol in their blood.

breathy *adj* **-ier**, **-iest** (of a voice) producing a sound of breathing when speaking. — *adv* **breathily**.

breathe *v* **1** (*intr*; **in, out**) to draw air into, and force it out of, the lungs. **2** (*tr*; **in, out**) to draw (air, smoke, etc.) into, or force it out of, the lungs: *breathe fresh air*. **3** (*tr* & *intr*) to say, speak or sound quietly. **4** (*tr*) to show or express: *breathe defiance*. **5** (*intr*) to take breath or pause. **6** (*intr*) to blow softly. **7** (*intr*) (of wine) to develop flavour when exposed to the air. — *n* **breathing**. — **breathe again, easily** or **freely** to feel safe or relaxed after a period of worry or fear. — **breathe down someone's neck** to watch someone so closely that he or she feels uncomfortable. — **breathe fire** (*coll*) to speak very angrily. — **breathe one's last** to die. [**breath**]

breather *n* (*coll*) a short rest or break from work.

breathing-space *n* a short time allowed for rest.

bred. See **breed**.

breech *n* **1** the back part of a gun barrel, where it is loaded. **2** (*old*) the buttocks or bottom. [OE *brec*]

breech birth or **delivery** *n* the birth of a baby bottom first instead of head first.

breeches *n* (*pl*) **1** short trousers fastened below the knee. **2** (*coll humorous*) trousers.

breeches buoy *n* a pair of canvas breeches on a rope, used for rescuing people esp. from ships.

breed *v* ***bred*** **1** (*intr*) (usu. of animals) to produce young. **2** (*tr*) to keep (animals or plants) for the purpose of producing more, or developing new types. **3** (*tr*) to train, bring up or educate: *well-bred children*. **4** (*tr*) to cause or produce (usu. something bad): *Dirt breeds disease*. **5** (*tr*; *physics*) to create (atoms which can be split, etc.) by nuclear reaction. ◇ See also **breeder reactor** below. — *n* **1** a group of animals within a species which all share some characteristics: *Spaniels are a breed of dog*. **2** a race or lineage. **3** a kind or type. — *n* **breeder**. [OE *bredan*, to produce, cherish]

breeder reactor *n* a type of nuclear power station which is capable of creating more atoms that can be split, etc. than it uses.

breeding *n* **1** the act of producing animals or plants, esp. for sale. **2** the result of a good education and training: *show good breeding*.

breeding-ground *n* **1** a place where animals, birds, etc. go to produce their young. **2** a place, situation, etc. which encourages the development of (something, usu. regarded as bad): *a breeding-ground for communism*.

breeze[1] *n* **1** a gentle wind. **2** (*coll*) any job, etc. which is easily done. — *v* (*intr*; *coll*) **1** (**along, into, out**, etc.) to move quite quickly in a cheerful, casual, confident manner: *breeze into the room*. **2** (with **through**) to do (something) easily and without any difficulty: *breeze through the exam*. [Prob. OSpan *briza*, north-east wind]

breezy *adj* **-ier**, **-iest** **1** slightly windy. **2** (of people, etc.) lively, confident and casual. — *adv* **breezily**. — *n* **breeziness**.

breeze[2] *n* ashes from coal, coke or charcoal. [Fr *braise*, live coals]

breezeblock *n* a type of brick made from breeze and cement, used for building houses, etc.

bren gun *n* (also *cap* **B**) a light, quick-firing machine-gun used during the Second World War. [*Br*no in Czechoslovakia (where it was orig. made) + *En*field in England (where it was later made)]

brethren. See **brother**.

Breton *n* **1** a person from Brittany in France. **2** the Celtic language spoken in Brittany. — *adj* of Brittany, its people or language. [Fr]

breve *n* **1** (*mus*) a note (rarely used) twice as long as a semibreve. **2** a mark (˘) sometimes put over a vowel to show that it is short in length. ◇ See also **macron**. [Lat *brevis*, short]

breviary *n* **-ies** a book containing the hymns, prayers and psalms which form the daily service in the Roman Catholic church. [Lat *breviarum*, summary]

brevity *n* **1** conciseness. **2** shortness of time. [OFr *brievete*, from Lat *brevis*, short]

brew *v* **1** (*tr*) to make (beer) by mixing, boiling and fermenting. **2** (*tr & intr*; **up**) to make (tea, coffee, etc.) by mixing the leaves, grains, etc. with boiling water. **3** (*intr*) to be prepared by brewing: *The tea is brewing*. **4** (*intr*; **up**) to get stronger and threaten: *There's a storm brewing*. **5** (*tr*; **up**) to plan or prepare: *brew up trouble*. — *n* **1** a drink produced by brewing, esp. tea or beer. **2** an amount (esp. of beer) produced by brewing: *last year's brew*. **3** the quality of what is brewed: *a good strong brew*. — *n* **brewing**. [OE *breowan*]

brewer *n* a person or company that brews and sells beer.

brewer's yeast *n* a type of yeast used in brewing beer, causing the sugar in the beer to change into alcohol, or as a source of the B vitamins.

brewery *n* **-ies** a place where beer, etc. is brewed.

briar[1] or **brier** *n* any prickly bush, esp. a wild rose bush. [OE *brer*]

briar[2] or **brier** *n* **1** a shrub with a hard, woody root, found in southern Europe. **2** a tobacco pipe made from the root. [Fr *bruyère*, heath]

bribe *n* a gift, usu. money, offered to someone to persuade him or her to do something. — *v* (*tr*) to give, offer or promise money, etc. to (a person) to persuade him or her to do something. — *n* **bribery**. [OFr *briber*]

bric-à-brac *n* small objects of little value kept as decorations or ornaments. [Fr]

brick *n* **1** a rectangular block of baked clay used for building. **2** the material used for making bricks. **3** a child's usu. plastic or wooden rectangular, cylindrical, etc. toy for building. **4** something in the shape of a brick: *a brick of ice-cream*. **5** (*Br old coll*) a trusted and helpful person. — *adj* made of, or the colour of, bricks. — *v* (*tr*; **in**, **up**, etc.) to close or fill in with bricks: *brick up the window*. — **drop a brick** (*Br coll*) to do or say something embarrassing or insulting without realising that it is. — **like banging** or **knocking one's head against a brick wall** (*coll*) a waste of time and effort. — **make bricks without straw** to do a job without having the proper materials for it. [ODut *bricke*]

brickbat *n* **1** an insult or criticism. **2** a piece of brick, or anything hard, thrown at someone.

bricklayer *n* a person who builds with bricks. — *n* **bricklaying**.

brickwork that part of a building, e.g. the walls, that is made of brick.

brickyard *n* a place where bricks are made.

bridal *adj* of a wedding or a bride. [OE *brydeala*, wedding feast, from *bryd*, bride + *ealu*, ale]

bride *n* (esp. on the wedding day) a woman who has just been, or is about to be, married. [OE *bryd*]

bridegroom *n* (esp. on the wedding day) a man who has just been, or is about to be, married.

bridesmaid *n* a girl or usu. unmarried woman attending the bride at a wedding.

bridge[1] *n* **1** a structure joining the two sides of a road, railway, river, etc. to allow people, vehicles, etc. to cross. **2** anything joining or connecting two separate things. **3** the narrow raised platform from which the captain of a ship directs its course. **4** the hard, bony, upper part of the nose. **5** a small piece of wood on a violin, guitar, etc. which keeps the strings stretched tight. **6** (also **bridgework**) a plate with false teeth, which is connected to the real teeth on either side of it. — *v* (*tr*) **1** to build a bridge over. **2** to make a connection, close a gap, etc. — **cross a bridge when one comes to it** to deal with a problem when it arises and not before. [OE *brycg*]

bridge-builder *n* **1** a person who builds bridges. **2** a person who tries to settle a dispute between two other people.

bridgehead *n* a position well into enemy land from which an attack can be made.

bridgework see **bridge** (sense **6**) above.

bridging loan *n* a loan of money, usu. from a bank, to cover the period between buying one house and selling another.

bridge[2] *n* a card game for four people playing in pairs, in which the partner of the person declaring trumps lays down his or her cards face upwards for them to be played by the declarer.

bridle *n* **1** the leather straps on a horse's head which help the rider control the horse. **2** anything which controls, keeps back or restrains. — *v* **1** (*tr*) to put a bridle on (a horse). **2** (*tr*) to bring under control: *bridle one's anger*. **3** (*intr*; **up**) to show anger or resentment by moving the head upwards proudly. [OE *bridel*]

bridle path, **road** or **way** *n* a path for riders and horses.

Brie *n* a French soft cheese. [*Brie*, in NE France, where it is made]

brief *adj* **1** lasting only a short time. **2** short or small. **3** (of writing or speech) using few words; concise. — *n* **1** (in *pl*) a woman's or man's underpants without legs. **2** (*legal*) a summary of the facts and legal points of a case, prepared for the barrister who will be dealing with the case in court. **3** (*legal*) a case taken by a barrister. **4** instructions given for a job or task. **5** in the Roman Catholic Church, a letter from the Pope on discipline. **6** (*slang*) a barrister — *v* (*tr*; **on**) **1** to prepare (a person) by giving him or her instructions in advance: *brief him on the procedure*. **2** (*legal*) to tell (a barrister) about a case by brief. — *adv* **briefly**. — *n* **briefness**. — **hold no brief for** to not support or be in favour of. [OFr *brief*, from Lat *brevis*, short]

briefcase *n* a light, usu. flat case for carrying papers, etc.

briefing *n* **1** a meeting at which instructions and information are given. **2** the instructions or information given at a meeting.

brier. See **briar**[1,2].

Brig. *abbrev* brigadier.

brig *n* a type of sailing ship with two masts and square sails. **[brigantine]**

brigade *n* **1** one of the divisions in the army, usu. commanded by a brigadier. **2** a group of people organised for a particular purpose: *the fire brigade*. [Fr, from OItal *brigata*, company of soldiers]

brigadier *n* **1** an officer commanding a brigade. **2** a staff officer of similar rank, above a colonel but below a major-general. **[brigade]**

brigadier general *n* in the US army, an officer ranking above a colonel.

brigand *n* a member of a band of robbers, esp. one operating in quiet, mountain areas. [Fr, from OItal *brigante*, member of an armed band]

brigantine *n* a type of sailing ship with two masts, with square sails on the main mast, and sails set lengthwise on the second mast. [OItal *brigantino*, armed escort ship.]

bright *adj* **1** giving out or shining with much light. **2** (of a colour) strong, light and clear. **3** lively, cheerful. **4** (**at**) clever and quick at learning. **5** full of hope or promise: *a bright future*. — *adv* brightly: *a fire burning bright*. — *adv* **brightly**. — *n* **brightness**. — **bright and early** very early in the morning. — **look on the bright side** to be cheerful and full of hope in spite of problems. [OE *beorht*]

brighten *v* (*tr* & *intr*; **up**) **1** to make or become bright or brighter. **2** to make or become happier or more cheerful.

the bright lights *n* (*pl*) a big city seen as a place of entertainment, excitement and fun.

bright spark *n* a lively, intelligent person, esp. one who is young or who has lots of new ideas.

brill *n* ***brill*** or ***brills*** a European flatfish with white spots, related to the turbot.

brilliant *adj* **1** very bright and sparkling. **2** (of a colour) bright and vivid. **3** of outstanding intelligence or talent. **4** making a great display or show: *a brilliant display of flowers*. **5** (*coll*) excellent. — *n* a diamond cut to have a lot of facets so that it sparkles brightly. — *n* **brilliance** or **brilliancy**. — *adv* **brilliantly**. [Fr *briller*, to shine]

brilliantine *n* (*old*) a perfumed oil used by men to make the hair shiny. [Fr *brillantine*, from *brillant*, shining]

brim *n* **1** the top edge or lip of a cup, glass, bowl, etc. **2** the projecting edge of a hat. — *v* ***-mm-*** (*intr*; **with**) to be full to the brim: *eyes brimming with tears*. — *adj* **brimless**. — *v* **brim over** (*intr*; **with**) to become full and begin to overflow. [MidE *brymme*]

brimful or **brim-full** *adj* full to the brim.

brimstone *n* (*old*) sulphur. [OE *bryne*, burning + **stone**]

brimstone butterfly *n* a common yellow butterfly.

fire and brimstone see **fire**.

brindled *adj* (of animals) brown or grey marked with stripes of a darker colour. [MidE *brended*, from *brend*, burnt]

brine *n* **1** very salty water, used for preserving food. **2** (*literary*) the sea. [OE *bryne*]

briny *adj* ***-ier***, ***-iest*** (of water) very salty. — *n* (with **the**; *coll*) the sea.

bring *v* ***brought*** (*tr*) **1** to carry or take (something or someone) to a stated or implied place or person. **2** to cause or result in: *War brings misery*. **3** to cause to be in or reach a certain state: *bring him to his senses*; *bring into effect*. **4** to make or force (oneself): *I can't bring myself to tell her*. **5** to be sold for; to produce as income. **6** to make (a charge) against someone: *bring a case against him*. **7** to give (evidence) to a court, etc. — *v* **bring about** (*tr*) to cause to happen. — *v* **bring along** (*tr*) **1** to bring or convey with one. **2** to help (something) develop. — *v* **bring back** (*tr*) to cause (a person, thing, memories, etc.) to return. — *v* **bring down** (*tr*) **1** to cause to fall. **2** to make sad, disappointed, etc. — *v* **bring forth** (*tr*; *formal*) to give birth to or produce. — *v* **bring forward** (*tr*) **1** to move to an earlier date or time. **2** to draw attention to. — **bring home (to)** to prove or show (something) clearly. — **bring the house down** (of an actor, performer, etc.) to get a lot of applause. — *v* **bring in** (*tr*) **1** to introduce. **2** to produce as profit. **3** to pronounce or give a decision on (someone) in court: *bring him in guilty*. — *v* **bring off** (*tr*; *coll*) to succeed in doing (something difficult). — *v* **bring on** (*tr*) **1** to cause to appear. **2** to help to develop. — *v* **bring out** (*tr*) **1** to make clear, cause to be seen, emphasise. **2** to publish. **3** (**in**) to cause to be covered (with spots, a rash, etc.): *Cats bring me out in spots*. — *v* **bring over** (*tr*) to convert (a person) to one's own opinion, etc. — *v* **bring round** (*tr*) **1** to cause (someone unconscious) to wake up. **2** to convince (someone) that one's own opinions, etc. are right. — *v* **bring to** (*tr*) to cause (someone unconscious) to wake up. — **bring to mind** to cause to be remembered or thought about. — *v* **bring**

up (*tr*) **1** to care for and educate (a child, etc.). **2** to introduce (a subject) for discussion. **3** to vomit. — **bring up the rear** to come last or behind. — **bring up short** to cause to stop suddenly. [OE *bringan*]

brink *n* **1** the edge or border of a steep, dangerous place or of a river. **2** the point immediately before the start of something dangerous, unknown, exciting, etc: *on the brink of new discoveries.* [Norse]

brinkmanship *n* (*coll*) the art of going to the very edge of a dangerous situation before moving back or withdrawing.

briny. See **brine**.

brioche *n* a type of bread-like cake made with a yeast dough, eggs and butter. [Fr]

briquette *n* a brick-shaped block made from coal dust, used for fuel. [Fr, little brick]

brisk *adj* **1** lively, active or quick: *a brisk walk.* **2** (of the weather) pleasantly cold and fresh. — *adv* **briskly**. — *n* **briskness**.

brisket *n* the breast of an animal, esp. of a bull or cow, when eaten as food. [MidE *brusket*]

brisling *n* a small herring or sprat. [Norw]

bristle *n* **1** a short, stiff hair on or from an animal's back. **2** something like this but man-made, used e.g. for brushes. — *v* **1** (*intr* & *tr*) (of hair) to (cause to) stand upright. **2** (*intr*) to show anger, rage, etc. **3** (*intr*; **with**) to be covered with or full of: *a room bristling with people.* [OE *byrst*]

bristling *adj* (of a beard, eyebrows, etc.) very thick and rough.

bristly *adj* **-ier**, **-iest** **1** having bristles; rough. **2** likely to be or quickly get angry.

Brit *n* (*coll*) a British person.

Brit. *abbrev* **1** Britain. **2** British.

Britannia *n* a female warrior wearing a helmet and carrying a shield and a trident, used as an image or personification of Britain. [Lat, Britain]

Britannia metal *n* a silvery metal made from tin, copper and antimony.

Britannic *adj* (*formal*) of Britain: *His Britannic Majesty.* [Lat *britannicus*, from *Britannia*, Britain]

British *adj* of Great Britain or its people. — *n* (with **the**) people from Great Britain. [OE *Bryttisc*, from *Bryt*, Briton]

British Summer Time *n* the system of time used in Britain in the summer to give extra daylight in the evenings, one hour ahead of Greenwich Mean Time used the rest of the year.

Briton *n* **1** one of the Celtic people living in S Britain before the Roman conquest. **2** a British person. [OFr *breton*, from Lat *britto*]

brittle *adj* **1** hard but easily broken or likely to break. **2** sharp or hard in quality: *a brittle laugh.*— *adv* **brittlely** or **brittly**. — *n* **brittleness**. [OE *breotan*, to break in pieces]

brittle bone disease *n* a disease in which a person's bones are very brittle and likely to break easily.

broach *v* (*tr*) **1** to raise (a subject, esp. one likely to cause arguments or problems) for discussion. **2** to open (a bottle or barrel, etc.) to remove liquid. **3** to open and start using the contents of: *broach a new bottle.* — *n* **1** a tool for making holes. **2** a roasting-spit. [MidE *broche*]

broad *adj* **1** large in extent from one side to the other. **2** wide and open; spacious. **3** general, not detailed: *a broad inquiry.* **4** clear: *in broad daylight.* **5** strong; obvious: *a broad hint.* **6** main: *the broad facts.* **7** tolerant or liberal: *take a broad view.* **8** (of an accent or speech) strongly marked by local features: *broad Scots.* **9** (esp. of jokes, stories, etc.) rather rude and vulgar. — *n* **1** the broad part of anything. **2** (*US offensive slang*) a woman. **3** (in *pl* with *cap*) a series of low-lying, shallow lakes connected by rivers in E Anglia. — *n* **broadness**. [OE *brad*]

broad-based *adj* including a wide range of opinions, people, political groups, etc.

broad bean *n* a large flat green bean which contains large flat white seeds that can be eaten.

broadcloth *n* a thick cloth of good quality made from wool, cotton or silk.

broaden *v* **-n-** (*tr* & *intr*; **out**) to make or become broad or broader.

broad gauge *n* a railway track wider than the standard size.

broadloom *adj* (esp. of a carpet) woven on a wide loom to give broad widths.

broadly *adv* widely; generally: *broadly speaking.*

broad-minded *adj* tolerant of others' opinions, etc. — *adv* **broad-mindedly**. — *n* **broad-mindedness**.

broadsheet *n* **1** a large sheet of paper usu. printed on one side only, for advertisements, etc. **2** a newspaper printed on large sheets of paper. ◇ See also **tabloid**.

broadside *n* **1** the firing of all the guns on one side of a warship. **2** a strong verbal attack. — **broadside on** sideways.

broadsword *n* a heavy sword with a broad blade, used for cutting rather than stabbing.

broadcast *v* ***broadcast*** **1** (*tr* & *intr*) to send out (a programme) by radio or television. **2** (*tr*) to make (something) widely known. **3** (*tr*) to scatter (seed) by hand. — *n* a television or radio programme. — *adv* **1** communicated or sent out by radio or television. **2** widely known or scattered. — *n* **broadcaster**. — *n* **broadcasting**. **[broad + cast]**

brocade *n* a heavy silk material with a raised design on it. [Ital or Span *broccato*, from *brocco*, twisted thread or spike]

brocaded *adj* (of material) woven with a brocade design on it.

broccoli *n* a variety of cauliflower with green or purple flower-like heads growing on thick branches. [Ital, sprouts]

brochure *n* a short book or pamphlet giving information about holidays, products, etc. [Fr *brocher*, to stitch]

broderie anglaise *n* a way of decorating cotton and linen by making patterns from tiny holes and stitches. [Fr, English embroidery]

brogue[1] *n* a type of strong outdoor shoe. [Gaelic *bròg*, shoe]

brogue[2] *n* a strong but gentle accent, esp. of the Irish speaking English.

broil *v* (*tr*; esp. *NAm*) to grill (food). [OFr *bruiller*, to burn]

broiler *n* **1** a small chicken suitable for broiling. **2** (*NAm*) a grill. **3** (*coll*) a very hot day.

broke *adj* (*coll*) completely without money. — **go for broke** (*coll*) to take a very dangerous or the most extreme piece of action in a last attempt at success. ◇ See also **break**. **[break]**

broken *adj* **1** smashed, fractured. **2** disturbed or interrupted: *broken sleep*. **3** not working properly. **4** (used of a promise, agreement, etc.) not kept. **5** (of language) not perfect or fluent. **6** weak or tired, esp. through illness. — *adv* **brokenly**. — *n* **brokenness**. ◇ See also **break**. **[break]**

broken chord *n* an arpeggio.

broken-down *adj* **1** not in working order. **2** not in good condition or good health.

broken-hearted *adj* extremely sad. — *adv* **broken-heartedly**.

broken home *n* the home of children whose parents are divorced.

broken-in *adj* **1** (of an animal) made tame through training. **2** (of shoes, etc.) made comfortable by being worn.

broker *n* **1** a person employed to buy and sell esp. shares, for others. ◇ See also **stockbroker**. **2** a person who buys and sells secondhand goods. [OFr *brocour*]

brokerage *n* the profit or fee charged by a broker.

broking *n* the trade or business of a broker.

brolly *n* **-ies** (*Br coll*) an umbrella. **[umbrella]**

bromide *n* **1** a compound of bromine, esp. one used to calm a person down. **2** a much-used and now meaningless statement or phrase. **[bromine + -ide]**

bromide paper *n* a type of paper with a surface which has been coated with silver bromide to make it sensitive to light, used for printing photographs.

bromine *n* a non-metallic, liquid element with an extremely unpleasant smell, used to make chemicals used in photography and medicine; symbol **Br**. [Gr *bromos*, stink]

bronchial *adj* of or relating to the two large air tubes, the bronchi, in the lungs, or the smaller tubes they divide into. **[bronchus]**

bronchitis *n* an infection of the two large air tubes, the bronchi, in the lungs, causing coughing, difficulty in breathing, etc. — *adj* & *n* **bronchitic**. **[bronchus + -itis]**

bronchus *n* ***-chi*** either of the two main divisions of the windpipe carrying air to and from the lungs. [Gr *bronchus*, windpipe]

bronco *n* ***-os*** a wild or half-tamed horse from the western US. [Span *bronco*, rough]

brontosaurus *n* a large, plant-eating dinosaur, with a long tail and a very small head on a long neck. [Gr *bronte*, thunder + *sauros*, lizard]

bronze *n* **1** a mixture of copper and tin. **2** the dark red-brown colour of bronze. **3** a work of art made of bronze. — *adj* **1** made of bronze. **2** of the colour of bronze. — *v* **1** (*tr*) to give a bronze colour or surface to: *sun bronzing the skin*. **2** (*intr*) to become the colour of bronze. — *adj* **bronzed**. [Fr]

the Bronze Age *n* the period in the history of mankind when tools, weapons, etc. were made out of bronze, between about 3000 and 1000 BC.

bronze medal *n* a medal given to the person who comes third in a race, etc.

brooch *n* a decoration or piece of jewellery, fastened to clothes by a pin. [MidE *broche*]

brood *n* **1** a number of young animals, esp. birds, born or hatched at the same time. **2** (often *humorous*) all the children in a family. — *v* (*intr*) **1** (of birds) to sit on eggs until the young are born. **2** (**about, on, over**, etc.) to think anxiously or resentfully for a period of time. **3** (**over**) to hang over as a threat. — *adj* **brooding**. — *adv* **broodingly**. [OE *brod*]

broody *adj* ***-ier, -iest*** **1** (of birds) ready and wanting to brood. **2** deep in anxious thought. **3** (*coll*) (of women) badly wanting to have children. — *adv* **broodily**. — *n* **broodiness**.

brook[1] *n* a small stream. [OE *broc*]

brook[2] *v* (*tr*) to tolerate or accept: *brook no criticism*. [OE *brucan*, to enjoy]

broom *n* **1** a brush with a long handle for sweeping the floor. **2** a wild shrub of the pea family, with yellow flowers. [OE *brom*]

broomstick *n* the long handle of a broom.

Bros. *abbrev* Brothers, esp. in the name of a company.

broth *n* a thin, clear soup made by boiling meat, fish or vegetables. [OE *broth*]

brothel *n* a house where men pay money for sexual intercourse with women. [MidE, worthless man or prostitute]

brother *n* ***brothers***, or, in sense **3**, ***brethren*** **1** a boy or man with the same parents as another person or people. **2** a man belonging to the same group, society, church, trade union, etc. as another or others. **3** a man who is a member of a religious group, esp. a monk. [OE *brothor*]

brotherhood *n* **1** the state of being a brother. **2** friendliness felt towards people one has something in common with. **3** an association of men for a particular, esp. religious, purpose.

brother-in-law *n* ***brothers-in-law*** **1** the brother of one's husband or wife. **2** the husband of one's sister. **3** the husband of the sister of one's own wife or husband.

brotherly *adj* like, or of, a brother; kind, affectionate.

brougham *n* a type of light closed carriage pulled by four horses, with a raised open seat for the driver. [Named after Lord *Brougham* (1778–1868)]

brought. See **bring**.

brouhaha *n* noisy, excited and confused activity. [Fr]

brow *n* **1** (usu. in *pl*) an eyebrow. **2** the forehead. **3** the top (of a hill, road, pass, etc.). **4** the edge (of a cliff, etc.). [OE *bru*]

browbeat *v* ***browbeat***, ***browbeaten*** (*tr*) to frighten (someone) by speaking angrily or looking fierce; to bully.

browbeaten *adj* quiet, shy and frightened because of having been continually bullied.

brown *adj* **1** having a colour similar to that of bark, tanned skin, coffee, etc. **2** (of bread) brown in colour, usu. because of the wholemeal flour used. **3** with a dark skin or complexion. **4** with a skin tanned from being in the sun. — *n* **1** any of various dark colours similar to bark, tanned skin, coffee, etc. **2** brown paint, dye, material or clothes. — *v* (*tr* & *intr*) to make or become brown by cooking, burning in the sun, etc. — *adj* **brownish**. — *n* **brownness**. — **browned off** (*coll*) **1** bored; fed up. **2** discouraged. [OE *brun*]

browning *n* (*Br*) a substance used to turn gravy brown.

brown owl *n* **1** the tawny owl. **2** (*caps*) same as **Brownie Guider**.

brown paper *n* very thick brown-coloured paper used e.g. for wrapping up parcels sent through the post.

brown rice *n* rice which has not had its outer covering removed.

Brownshirt *n* **1** (in Nazi Germany) a member of the Nazi political militia. **2** a member of any fascist organisation.

brown study *n* **1** deep thought. **2** absent-mindedness.

brown sugar *n* sugar which has not been completely refined and which has kept some of its original brown colour.

brownie *n* **1** (*folklore*) a friendly fairy. **2** (*cap*; also **Brownie Guide**) a young member of the Girl Guides in Britain or of the Girl Scouts in the US. **3** (esp. *US*) a small, square, sweet chocolate-and-nut cake. [**brown**]

Brownie Guider *n* (also **Brown Owl**) a woman in charge of a group of Brownie Guides.

brownie point *n* (*coll*) a mark of approval earned by doing something good, useful, etc.

browse *v* **1** (*intr* & *tr*; **through**) to look through (a book, group of books, etc.) casually, reading only bits and pieces. **2** (*intr* & *tr*; **on**) (of animals) to feed by nibbling on (plants). — *n* **1** an act of browsing. **2** young shoots, twigs, leaves, etc. used as food for cattle. [OFr *brost*, new shoot]

brucellosis *n* a serious disease which causes female cattle to lose any young they may be carrying, and which can be caught by people. [*Brucella*, the name of the bacteria causing the disease + **-osis**]

bruise *n* an injury caused by a blow, turning the skin a dark colour but not breaking it. — *v* **1** (*tr*) to cause a bruise on (the skin, etc.). **2** (*intr*) to develop bruises. **3** (*tr* & *intr*) to hurt or be hurt emotionally or mentally. — *adj* **bruised**. [OE *brysan*, to crush + OFr *bruiser*, to break]

bruiser *n* (*coll*) a big strong person, esp. one who likes fighting.

bruising *n* the dark-coloured marks which show on bruised skin.

bruit *v* (*tr*; **about, abroad**; *old*) to spread or report (news, rumours, etc.). [Fr, noise]

brûlé *adj* (of food) with brown sugar on top and cooked so that the sugar melts. [Fr, burnt]

brunch *n* (*coll*) a meal eaten late in the morning combining breakfast and lunch. [*br*eakfast + l*unch*]

brunette *n* a woman with brown or dark hair and a fair skin. [Fr, from *brun*, brown]

brunt *n* the main force or shock (of a blow, attack, etc.): *bear the brunt of his anger*. [MidE]

brush *n* **1** a tool with lengths of stiff nylon, wire, hair, bristles, etc., for tidying the hair, cleaning, painting, etc. **2** an act of brushing. **3** a short fight or disagreement: *a brush with the law*. **4** a fox's brush-like tail. **5** a piece of metal or carbon, bunch of wires, etc. which conducts electricity to a moving part of a machine. **6** brushwood. — *v* **1** (*tr*; **down**) to rub with a brush or other object to remove dirt, dust, etc. **2** (*tr*; **away, on,** etc.) to remove or apply with a brush or brushing movement. **3** (*tr* & *intr*; **against,** etc.) to touch lightly in passing. — *v* **brush aside** (*tr*) to pay no attention to; to dismiss. — *v* **brush off** (*tr*) to refuse to listen to; to ignore (*n* **brush-off**: *get the brush-off*). — *v* **brush up 1** (*tr* & *intr*; **on**) to improve or refresh one's knowledge of (a language, etc.): *brush up one's Spanish* or *on one's Spanish* (*n* **brush-up**). **2** (*intr*) to make oneself clean, tidy one's appearance, etc. (*n* **brush-up**). [OFr *brosse*, brushwood]

brushed *adj* (of material) treated by a brushing process so that it feels soft and warm: *brushed cotton*.

brush fire *n* a fire of dead and dry bushes and trees, which usu. spreads quickly.

brushwood *n* **1** dead and broken branches, etc. from trees and bushes. **2** small trees and bushes on rough land. **3** rough land covered by such trees and bushes.

brushwork *n* the particular way a painter has of putting paint on to canvas.

brusque *adj* blunt, rough and often impolite in manner. — *adv* **brusquely**. — *n* **brusqueness**. [Fr, from Ital *brusco*, sour]

Brussels sprout *n* (usu. in *pl*) a small, round, cabbage-like bud, eaten as a vegetable. [First grown near *Brussels*, capital of Belgium]

brutal *adj* very cruel, severe or violent. — *n* **brutality**, **-ies**. — *adv* **brutally**. [Lat *brutalis*]

brutalise or **-ize** *v* (*tr*) **1** to make brutal. **2** to treat brutally. — *n* **brutalisation** or **-z-**.

brute *n* **1** an animal other than man. **2** a cruel, violent person. — *adj* **1** not able to use reason or intelligence. **2** coarse and animal-like. [Lat *brutus*, heavy, irrational]

brute force *n* sheer physical strength, with no thought or skill.

brutish *adj* of, or like, a brute. — *adv* **brutishly**. — *n* **brutishness**.

bryony *n* **-ies** a climbing plant with green-white flowers and either red or black berries, usu. found in hedges. [Lat *bryonia*]

BS *abbrev* **1** British Standard(s); found on manufactured goods as a sign they are of good quality or are safe to use. **2** Bachelor of Surgery.

BSc. *abbrev* Bachelor of Science.

BSE *abbrev* bovine spongiform encephalopathy.

BSI *abbrev* British Standards Institution, an organisation which controls the quality and safety of manufactured goods, etc.

B-side. See **B**.

BST *abbrev* British Summer Time.

BT *abbrev* British Telecom.

Bt. *abbrev* Baronet.

bubble **1** a thin film of liquid forming a ball round air or gas, esp. one which floats in liquid: *soap bubbles*. **2** a ball of air or gas which has formed in a solid: *an air bubble in glass*. **3** a dome made of clear plastic or glass. **4** a plan, idea, scheme, etc. which is not likely to be successful. — *v* (*intr*) **1** to form or rise in bubbles. **2** (**away**) to make the sound of bubbling liquid: *water bubbling away in the pan*. — *v* **bubble over** (*intr*) **1** to boil over. **2** (**with**) to be full of happiness, excitement, enthusiasm, good ideas, etc. [MidE *bobel*]

bubble and squeak *n* (*Br*) cold cooked cabbage and potatoes mixed together and then fried.

bubble bath *n* a scented liquid which is put into bath water to make bubbles.

bubble gum *n* a type of chewing gum which can be blown into bubbles.

bubble memory *n* a type of computer memory in which information is stored in magnetic bubbles which move through a layer of magnetised material.

bubble or **blister pack** *n* a clear plastic bubble, usu. on cardboard, in which goods for sale are packed.

bubbly *adj* **-ier**, **-iest** **1** having or being like bubbles. **2** very lively and cheerful and full of high spirits. — *n* (*coll*) champagne.

bubo *n* **-oes** an inflamed swelling, esp. in the armpit or groin. [Lat]

bubonic plague *n* an often fatal infectious disease which causes buboes, and which is spread by fleas from rats to people.

buccaneer *n* a pirate, esp. one who attacked Spanish ships in the Caribbean during the 17th century. — *n* & *adj* **buccaneering**. [Fr *boucanier*]

buck[1] *n* **1** the male of some animals, esp. the rabbit, hare, or deer. **2** a lively young man. **3** an act of bucking. — *v* **1** (*intr*) (of a horse) to make a series of rapid jumps into the air, with the back arched and legs held stiff, esp. in an attempt to throw a rider. **2** (*tr*; **off**) (of a horse) to throw (a rider) from its back in this way. **3** (*tr*; *coll*) to oppose or resist (an idea, etc.). **4** (*tr*; **up**) to improve (one's ways, ideas, etc.). **5** (*tr* & *intr*; **up**) to make or become more cheerful. **6** (*intr* with **up**) to hurry. [OE *bucca*]

bucked *adj* (*Br coll*) pleased and encouraged.

buckshot *n* large lead shot used in hunting.

buckskin *n* **1** the skin of a deer. **2** a soft leather made from deer-skin.

buckthorn *n* a thorny shrub with berries which supply a green dye used by painters.

bucktooth *n* a tooth which sticks out in front. — *adj* **bucktoothed**.

buck[2] *n* (esp. *NAm coll*) a dollar. — **make a fast** or **quick buck** to make money quickly, easily and often dishonestly. [Perhaps from **buckskin**, deer-skins being used as a unit of exchange by Indians and frontiersmen in the 19th century in the US]

buck[3] *n* **1** an item placed before the person who is to deal next in poker. **2** (*coll*) the responsibility, esp. to deal with a problem: *pass the buck*. [From *buckhorn knife*, an item which used to be used as a buck in poker]

bucket *n* **1** a round, open-topped container for holding or carrying liquids, sand, etc. **2** (also **bucketful**, **-fuls**) the amount a bucket will hold. **3** (in *pl*) a large quantity of liquid: *weep buckets of tears*. **4** the scoop of a machine for dredging. — *v* **-t-** (*intr*; *coll*; **down**) (of rain) to pour down heavily. — **kick the bucket** (*slang*) to die. [OE *buc*]

bucket seat *n* a small seat with a round back, for one person, e.g. in a car.

bucket shop *n* **1** (*Br coll*) a travel agent which sells cheap airline tickets. **2** an office where one may deal in shares, gamble on the money market, etc.

buckle *n* a flat piece of metal attached to one end of a strap or belt, with a pin in the middle which goes through a hole in the other end of the strap or belt to fasten it. — *v* **1** (*tr* & *intr*) to fasten or be fastened with a buckle. **2** (*tr* & *intr*) (of metal) to bend or become bent out of shape, usu. as a result of great heat or force. — *adj* **buckled**. — *v* **buckle down** (*intr*; *coll*; **to**) to begin working seriously (at something):

buckle down to work. — *v* **buckle to** (*intr*; *coll*) to begin to work seriously. — *v* **buckle under** (*intr*) to collapse under strain. [OFr *boucle*, from Lat *buccula*, cheek-strap of a helmet]

buckler *n* a small round shield. [OFr *bocler*, from *bocle*, boss[2]]

buckram *n* stiffened cotton or linen, used to line clothes or cover books. [MidE *bukeram*, perhaps from *Bukhara*, a town in central Asia once noted for its textiles]

Bucks *abbrev* Buckinghamshire.

buckshee *adj & adv* (*slang*) free of charge. [**baksheesh**]

buckshot, buckskin, buckthorn, buck-tooth. See **buck**[1].

buckwheat *n* a type of small black grain used for feeding animals or made into flour. [Dut *boekweit*, beech wheat, from the shape of the seeds]

bucolic *adj* of or to do with the countryside or people living there; pastoral. — *n* (often in *pl*) a poem about the countryside. — *adv* **bucolically**. [Gr *boukolos*, herdsman]

bud *n* **1** a small swelling on the stem of a tree or plant which will develop into leaves or a flower. **2** a partly opened flower: *rose-buds*. **3** (*biol*) a small bud-like growth which will develop as a new individual. — *v* **-dd-** (*intr*) **1** to put out buds. — **in bud** producing buds. — **nip in the bud** to put a stop to at a very early stage. [MidE *budde*]

budding *adj* developing; beginning to show talent: *a budding pianist*.

Buddhism *n* the religion founded by the *Buddha*, Gautama, in the 6th century BC, which teaches spiritual purity and freedom from human concerns. — *n & adj* **Buddhist**. [Sanskrit *budh*, to awaken, notice or understand]

buddleia *n* a shrub with long spikes of purple, white or yellow flowers, attractive to butterflies. [Named after Adam *Buddle* (d. 1715), English botanist]

buddy *n* **-ies 1** (esp. *NAm coll*) a friend or companion. **2** a volunteer who helps care for a person suffering from AIDS. — *v* **-ies, -ied 1** (*intr*; *coll*; **up**) to become friendly. **2** (*tr*) to help care for (someone suffering from AIDS). [Perhaps *butty*, companion]

budge *v* (*intr & tr*) **1** (**from, off**, etc.) to move or cause to move. **2** to change or cause to change one's mind or opinions: *Nothing you say will make her budge*. [OFr *bouger*]

budgerigar *n* a type of small parrot native to Australia, often kept as a pet. [Yuwaalaraay (Australian Aboriginal language) *gijirrigaa*]

budget *n* **1** any plan, esp. for a particular period of time, showing how money coming in will be spent. **2** (*cap* with **the**) a plan issued by the government telling people how much money it intends to raise in taxes and how it intends to spend it. **3** the amount of money set aside for a particular purpose. — *adj* cheap: *a budget holiday*. — *v* **-t- 1** (*intr*) to calculate how much money one is earning and spending, so that one does not spend more than one has. **2** (*intr* with **for**) to allow for in a budget: *budget for a new car*. **3** (*tr*) to provide (an amount of money) in a budget: *budget £600 for a holiday*. — *adj* **budgetary**. — *n* **budgeting**. [OFr *bougette*, dimin. of *bouge*, pouch]

budget account *n* an account with a bank or shop into which one pays money regularly so that regular bills can be paid.

budgie *n* (*coll*) a budgerigar.

buff *n* **1** a dull yellow colour. **2** a soft, undyed leather. **3** (*coll*) a person who is enthusiastic about and knows a lot about a certain subject: *an opera buff*. — *adj* dull yellow in colour. — *v* (*tr*) **1** (**up**) to polish with a buff or piece of soft material: *buff up one's shoes*. **2** to make (leather) soft like buff. — *n* **buffer**. — **in the buff** (*Br coll*) naked. [Fr *buffle*, buffalo]

buffalo *n* ***buffalo*** or ***-oes*** **1** a kind of large wild cow with long curved horns, several varieties of which are found in Asia and Africa. **2** the American bison. [Port *bufalo*]

buffer[1] *n* **1** an apparatus, esp. one using springs, on railway carriages, etc., or a cushion of rope on a ship, which takes the shock when the carriage or ship hits something. **2** a person or thing which protects from harm or shock. **3** a temporary memory in a computer for storing information which is waiting to be printed or transferred to another computer system. — *adj* **buffered**. [MidE *buffe*, blow]

buffer state *n* a usu. neutral country situated between two larger countries which are hostile, or potentially hostile, towards each other, making war less likely.

buffer stock *n* stock held in reserve to try and control prices.

buffer[2] *n* (*Br coll*) a rather foolish or dull person, esp. a man: *old buffer*.

buffer[3]. See **buff**.

buffet[1] *n* **1** a place where light meals and drinks may be bought and eaten. **2** a usu. cold meal set out on tables from which people help themselves. **3** a sideboard or cupboard for holding china, glasses, etc. [OFr]

buffet car *n* a carriage in a train where light meals and drinks may be bought.

buffet[2] *n* a blow with the hand. — *v* **-t-** (*tr*) **1** to strike or knock with the fist. **2** to knock about: *a ship buffeted by the waves*. — *n* **buffeting**. [OFr *buffe*, blow]

buffoon *n* (often *derog*) a person who does amusing or foolish things. — *n* **buffoonery**. [Fr *bouffon*, from Ital *buffone*]

bug *n* **1** any insect with a flat body and a mouth which can suck blood. **2** an insect thought of as dirty and living in dirty houses, etc. **3** (*NAm*) any small insect. **4** (*coll*) any germ or virus causing infection or illness: *a stomach bug*. **5** (*coll*) a small, hidden microphone. **6** (*coll*) a fault in a machine or computer program which stops it from working properly. **7** (*coll*) an obsession or craze: *get the skiing bug*. — *v* **-gg-** (*tr*) **1** (*coll*) to hide a microphone in (a room, etc.) so that one can listen to any conversations carried on there. **2** (*slang*) to annoy or worry. [OE *budda*, beetle]

bug-eyed *adj* with eyes that stick out from the face, esp. with astonishment.

bugaboo *n* an imaginary thing which causes fear.

bugbear *n* a thing which causes fear, worry or hate. [MidE *bugge*, perhaps from Welsh *bwg*, hobgoblin, + **bear**[2]]

bugger *n* **1** (*vulg slang*) a person or thing considered unpleasant, annoying, difficult or offensive. **2** (*slang*, sometimes thought *vulg*) a person one feels affection or pity for: *poor old bugger*. **3** (sometimes thought *vulg*) a person who practices anal sex. — *v* **-r-** (*tr*) **1** (*vulg*) to practise anal sex with. **2** (**up**; *vulg coll*) to spoil or ruin. **3** (*vulg coll*) to tire or exhaust. — *interj* (*vulg coll*; sometimes with **it**) an expression of annoyance. — *v* **bugger about** or **around** (*vulg coll*) **1** (*intr*) to waste time or not do something seriously. **2** (*tr*) to cause (someone) problems. — **bugger all** (*vulg slang*) nothing at all. — *v* **bugger off** (*intr*; *vulg slang*) to go away. [OFr *bougre*, from Lat *Bulgarus*, a heretic (literally, a Bulgarian), from the large number of heretical beliefs, including deviant sexual practices, thought in the Middle Ages to have come from the Balkans]

buggery *n* anal sex.

buggy *n* **-ies** **1** a light open carriage pulled by one horse. **2** (*US*) a pram.

bugle *n* a brass instrument like a small trumpet, used mainly for military signals. — *v* **1** (*intr*) to sound a bugle. **2** (*tr*) to sound (a call) on a bugle. — *n* **bugler**. [OFr, from Lat *bos*, ox]

build *v* ***built*** (*tr*) **1** to make or construct from parts. **2** to develop gradually. **3** to make in a particular way or for a particular purpose. — *n* physical form, esp. of the human body: *a slim build*. — *v* **build in** or **into** (*tr*) to make (something) so that it is a permanent part of (something larger). — *v* **build on** (*tr*) **1** to add on by building. **2** to use (a previous success, etc.) as a basis from which to develop: *build on previous experience*. **3** to base (hopes), achieve (success), etc. on: *success built on a popular product*. **4** to depend on. — *v* **build up** **1** (*tr* & *intr*) to increase gradually in size, strength, amount, etc. **2** (*tr*) to build in stages. **3** (*tr*) to speak with great enthusiasm about. ◇ See also **build-up** below. [OE *byldan*]

builder *n* **1** a person who builds, or organises the building of, houses, etc. **2** anything which helps to develop or build something.

building *n* **1** the business of constructing houses, etc. **2** a structure with walls and a roof, such as a house.

building-block *n* any of the separate parts out of which something is built.

building society *n* a business firm that lends people money for buying or improving houses and with which one can bank one's money in order to earn interest.

build-up *n* **1** a gradual increase. **2** a gradual approach to a conclusion or climax. **3** publicity or praise of something or someone given in advance of its, his or her appearance. ◇ See also **build up** above.

built-up *adj* **1** (of land, etc.) covered with buildings, esp. houses. **2** increased in height by additions. **3** made up of separate parts. ◇ See also **build up** above.

bulb *n* **1** the onion-shaped part of the stem of certain plants from which the roots grow. **2** a flower grown from a bulb, e.g. a daffodil or hyacinth. **3** (also **light-bulb**) a pear-shaped glass and metal device from which electric light is produced. **4** anything which is shaped like a pear. [Lat *bulbus*, from Gr *bolbos*, onion]

bulbous *adj* **1** like a bulb in shape; fat or bulging. **2** having or growing from a bulb.

bulge *n* **1** a swelling, esp. where one would expect to see something flat. **2** a sudden and usu. temporary increase, e.g. in population. — *v* (*intr*) to swell outwards. — *n* **bulginess**. — *adj* **bulging**. — *adj* **bulgy**. [OFr *boulge*, from Lat *bulga*, knapsack]

bulimia nervosa *n* an illness in which the sufferer overeats and then makes himself or herself vomit to get rid of the food eaten; often caused by an obsession about weight or by emotional problems. [Gr *boulimia*, great hunger + Lat *nervosus*, nervous]

bulk *n* **1** size, esp. when large. **2** the greater or main part of: *The bulk of the applicants are women*. **3** a large body, shape or person. **4** a large quantity: *buy in bulk*; *bulk buying*. **5** roughage. — **bulk large** to be or seem important: *an issue which bulks large in his mind*. [Norse *bulki*, cargo]

bulk carrier *n* any ship which carries dry goods such as grain, in bulk and unpackaged.

bulky *adj* **-ier**, **-iest** large in size and awkward to carry or move. — *adv* **bulkily**.— *n* **bulkiness**.

bulkhead *n* a wall in a ship or aircraft which separates one section from another, so that if one section is damaged, the rest is not affected. [MidE *bulk*, stall + **head**]

bull[1] *n* **1** the uncastrated male of animals in the cattle family. **2** the male elephant, whale and other large animals. **3** (*cap* with **the**) the constellation and sign of the zodiac Taurus. **4** a person who buys shares hoping to sell them at a higher price at a later date. **5** same as **bull's-eye** (sense **1**). — **a bull in a china shop** a person who acts in a rough and careless way and is likely to break things. — **take the bull by the horns** to face a difficulty boldly. [MidE *bole*]

bulldog *n* a small, fierce, heavily built dog with a large head.

bulldog clip *n* a clip with a spring, used to hold papers together or on to a board.

bullfight *n* a public show, popular esp. in Spain, in which men on horseback and on foot torment and then kill a bull. — *n* **bullfighter**. — *n* **bullfighting**.

bullfinch *n* a small European bird with a red breast, black head and a strong beak.

bullfrog *n* a large frog with a loud croak, found in the US.

bullish *adj* **1** like a bull, esp. in temper. **2** (*stock exchange*) tending to cause or hoping for rising prices. **3** very confident about the future. — *adv* **bullishly**. — *n* **bullishness**.

bull-mastiff *n* a type of dog, a cross between a mastiff and a bulldog.

bull-necked *adj* (of a person) having a short, thick, strong neck.

bullock *n* a castrated bull.

bullring *n* an arena where bullfights take place.

bull's-eye *n* **1** the small circular centre of a target used in shooting, darts, etc. **2** a shot hitting this. **3** (*coll*) anything which hits its target or achieves its aim, etc. **4** a large, hard, round peppermint sweet. **5** a thick, round disc of glass forming a window, esp. on a ship. **6** a thick, round boss in a sheet of glass. **7** a round lens in a lantern, or a lantern with such a lens.

bullshit *n* (*vulg slang*) nonsense. — *v* **-tt-** (*intr*; *vulg slang*) to talk bullshit.

bull terrier *n* a terrier with a short smooth coat and strong body, orig. a cross between a bulldog and a terrier.

bull[2] *n* an official letter or written instruction from the Pope. [OFr *bulle*, from Lat *bulla*, seal]

bull[3] *n* **1** an illogical, nonsensical statement, e.g. 'If you don't receive this card, you must write and tell me.' **2** (*slang*) nonsense. **3** boring and sometimes unnecessary routine tasks.

bulldog. See **bull**[1].

bulldoze *v* (*tr*) **1** to use a bulldozer to move, flatten or demolish. **2** (**into**) to force (someone) to do something he or she does not want to do: *bulldoze him into taking part*.

bulldozer *n* a large, powerful tractor with a vertical blade at the front, for pushing heavy objects, clearing the ground or making it level.

bullet *n* a small metal cylinder with a pointed end, for firing from small guns and rifles. [Fr *boulette*, little ball]

bullet-proof *adj* (of a material, etc.) strong enough to prevent bullets passing through.

bulletin *n* **1** a short official statement of news issued as soon as the news is known. **2** a short printed newspaper or leaflet, esp. one produced regularly by a group or organisation. [Fr, from Ital *bullettino*]

bulletin-board *n* (esp. *US*) a notice-board.

bullfight, bullfinch, bullfrog. See **bull**[1].

bullion *n* gold or silver in large bars. [OFr *bouillon*, boiling]

bullock, bullshit. See **bull**[1].

bully[1] *n* **-ies** a person who hurts or frightens weaker or smaller people. — *v* **-ies**, **-ied** (*tr*) **1** to act like a bully towards. **2** (**into**) to force (someone) to do something he or she doesn't want to do: *bully him into helping*. — *adj* excellent; very good. — *n* **bullying**. [ODut *boele*, lover]

bully-boy *n* (*coll*) a rough person employed to bully and threaten people.

bully[2] or **bully beef** *n* corned beef. [Fr *bouilli*, boiled beef]

bully[3] *v* **-ies**, **-ied** (*intr*; **off**) to begin a game, e.g. hockey, by hitting one's stick three times against an opponent's before trying to beat him or her to the ball (*n* **bully-off**).

bulrush *n* **1** a tall strong grass-like water plant. **2** (*Bible*) a papyrus plant. [Perhaps **bull**[1] + **rush**[2]]

bulwark *n* **1** a wall built as a defence, often made of earth. **2** a thing or person that defends a cause, way of life, etc. **3** (usu. in *pl*) the side of a ship projecting above the deck. [ODut *bolwerc*]

bum[1] *n* (*Br coll*) the buttocks. [MidE *bom*]

bumbag *n* a small bag on a belt.

bum[2] (*coll*, esp. *NAm*) *n* **1** a person who lives by begging. **2** a person who is lazy and shows no sense of responsibility. — *v* **-mm-** (*tr*) to get by begging, borrowing or cadging: *bum a lift*. — *v* **bum around** or **about** (*intr*) to travel around or spend one's time doing nothing in particular. [Perhaps Ger *Bummler*, loafer]

bummer *n* **1** a person who is lazy or who does nothing in particular with his or her time. **2** (*coll*) a difficult or unpleasant thing.

bumble *v* (*intr*) **1** to speak in a confused or confusing way. **2** to move or do something in an awkward, clumsy way. — *adj* **bumbling**.

bumblebee *n* a large, hairy bee which makes a loud hum. [MidE *bomblen*, to boom or buzz + **bee**]

bumf or **bumph** *n* (*Br coll*; usu. *derog*) leaflets, documents, etc. one finds useless or boring. [Short for *bum-fodder*]

bump *v* **1** (*tr* & *intr*; **against**, **into**) to knock or hit (something). ◇ See also **bump into**. **2** (*tr*; **against**, **on**) to hurt or damage by hitting. **3** (*intr*; **together**) (of two moving objects) to collide. **4** (*intr*; **along**) to move or travel with jerky or bumpy movements: *bump along the road*. — *n* **1** a knock, jolt or collision. **2** a dull sound caused by a knock, collision, etc. **3** a lump or swelling on the body, esp. one caused by a blow. **4** a lump on a road surface. — *v* **bump into** (*tr*; *coll*) to meet by chance. — *v* **bump off** (*tr*; *slang*) to kill or murder. — *v* **bump up** (*tr*; *coll*) to increase: *bump up production*. [Imit.]

bumper *n* **1** (*Br*) a bar on the front or back of a motor vehicle which lessens the shock or damage if it hits anything. **2** an exceptionally good or large example. **3** a large, full glass. — *adj* exceptionally good or large: *a bumper crop.*

bumpy *adj* **-*ier*, -*iest*** **1** having a lot of bumps: *a bumpy road.* **2** affected by bumps: *a bumpy ride.* — *adv* **bumpily**. — *n* **bumpiness**.

bumph. See **bumf**.

bumpkin *n* (*coll*) an awkward, simple or stupid person, esp. one from the country. [ODut *bommekijn*, little barrel]

bumptious *adj* offensively or irritatingly conceited. — *adv* **bumptiously**. — *n* **bumptiousness**. [**bump** + **fractious**]

bun *n* **1** a small, round, sweetened roll, often containing currants, etc. **2** a mass of hair fastened in a round shape on the back of the head. [MidE *bunne*]

bun fight *n* (*Br coll*) a noisy tea party.

bunch *n* **1** a number of things fastened or growing together. **2** (in *pl*) long hair divided into two pieces and tied separately at each side or the back of the head. **3** (*coll*) a group or collection. **4** (*coll*) a group of people; a gang. — *v* (*tr* & *intr*) to group together in or form a bunch or bunches. — *n* **bunching**. — *adj* **bunchy -*ier*, -*iest***. [MidE *bunche*]

bunch of fives *n* (*Br slang*) a fist; a blow with a fist.

bundle *n* **1** a number of things loosely fastened or tied together. **2** a loose parcel, esp. one made from cloth. **3** (*biol*) a strand of nerve or muscle fibres. **4** (*slang*) a large amount of money. — *v* (*tr*) **1** (**up, together**) to make into a bundle, esp. quickly and untidily. **2** (**away, off, out, into**, etc.) to put quickly and roughly or untidily: *bundled him into the taxi. bundled the papers into the drawer.* — **be a bundle of nerves** to be extremely nervous. — **go a bundle on** (*slang*) to like. [MidE *bundel*]

bung *n* a small round piece of wood, rubber, cork, etc., which closes a hole in the bottom of a barrel, a small boat, etc. — *v* (*tr*) **1** to block (a hole) with a bung. **2** (*coll*; **up**) to block (something). **3** (*slang*) to throw or put in a careless way. [ODut *bonge*, stopper]

bunghole *n* a hole by which a barrel, etc. is emptied or filled.

bungalow *n* a single-storey house. [Gujarati *bangalo*, from Hindi *bangla*, in the style of Bengal]

bungee jumping *n* the sport of jumping from a height with strong rubber ropes or cables attached to the ankles to ensure that the jumper bounces up before reaching the ground or whatever surface is below him or her.

bungle *v* (*tr* & *intr*) to do (something) carelessly or badly. — *n* carelessly or badly done work; a mistake. — *adj* **bungled**. — *n* **bungler**. — *n* & *adj* **bungling**.

bunion *n* a painful swelling on the first joint of the big toe. [Perhaps OFr *buigne*, bump on the head]

bunk[1] *n* a narrow bed attached to the wall in a cabin in a ship, caravan, etc. — *v* (*intr*; *coll*; **down**) to lie down and go to sleep, esp. somewhere other than on a bed.

bunk bed *n* one of a pair of narrow beds fixed one on top of the other.

bunkhouse *n* a building with many beds, usu. for workers.

bunk[2]. See **bunkum**.

bunk[3] (*Br slang*) *n* the act of running away: *do a bunk.* — *v* **bunk off** (*intr*) to stay away from school or work when one ought to be there.

bunker *n* **1** a large container or cupboard for storing coal. **2** an obstacle on a golf course consisting of a hollow containing sand. **3** an underground shelter. [Scots *bonker*, box or chest]

bunkum or **bunk** *n* (*coll*) nonsense, foolish talk. [*Buncombe*, a county in N Carolina, whose congressman is said to have excused a long, stupid speech in Congress on the grounds that he was only speaking for Buncombe]

bunny *n* **-*ies*** (also **bunny rabbit**) a child's word for rabbit. [*bun*, rabbit, from Scots Gaelic *bun*, bottom.]

bunny girl *n* a club hostess or waitress whose costume includes false rabbit's ears and tail.

Bunsen burner *n* a gas burner which produces a very hot flame but no smoke, used in laboratories. [From the inventor R W *Bunsen* (1811–99), German chemist]

bunting[1] *n* **1** a row of small cloth or paper flags and other decorations. **2** thin, loosely woven cotton used to make flags, esp. for ships.

bunting[2] *n* any of various small birds related to finches and sparrows.

buoy *n* a brightly coloured floating object fastened to the bottom of the sea by an anchor, to warn ships of rocks, etc. or to mark channels, etc. — *v* (*tr*) **1** (**up**) to keep afloat. **2** (**up**) to raise the spirits of. **3** to mark with a buoy or buoys. [MidE *boye*, float]

buoyant *adj* **1** (of an object) able to float in a liquid. **2** (of a liquid or gas) able to keep an object afloat. **3** cheerful. **4** (of sales, profits, etc.) increasing. **5** (of a firm, etc.) having increasing trade, rising profits, etc. — *n* **buoyancy**. — *adv* **buoyantly**. [**buoy**]

BUPA *abbrev* British United Provident Association, a private medical insurance scheme.

bur or **burr** *n* **1** the rough, prickly seed-case or flower of some plants, which sticks readily to things it touches. **2** any plant which produces burs. [MidE *burre*]

burble *v* **1** (*intr*) to speak at length but with little meaning. **2** (*intr*) (of a stream, etc.) to make a bubbling, murmuring sound. **3** (*tr*) to say (something) in a way that is hard to understand. [Prob. imit.]

burbot *n* ***burbot*** or **-*bots*** an eel-like, freshwater fish. [OFr *bourbotte*]

burden[1] *n* **1** something to be carried; a load. **2** a duty, obligation, etc. which is difficult, time-consuming, costly, etc. **3** the carrying of loads: *a beast of burden.* **4** (also **burthen**) the amount a ship can carry. — *v* **-n-** (*tr*) to load with a burden, difficulty, problem, etc. — **the burden of proof** the responsibility for proving something, esp. in a law court. [OE *byrthen*]

burdensome *adj* difficult to carry, support or bear.

burden[2] *n* **1** the main theme (of a book, speech, etc.). **2** a line repeated at the end of each verse of a song; a refrain. [OFr *bourdon*, droning sound]

burdock *n* a weed with prickly flowers and broad leaves. [**bur** + **dock**[3]]

bureau *n* **-eaux** or **-eaus** **1** (esp. *Br*) a desk for writing at, with drawers and usu. a front flap which opens downwards to provide the writing surface. **2** (esp. *US*) a chest of drawers. **3** an office or department for business, esp. for collecting and supplying information. **4** (esp. *US*) a government or newspaper department. [OFr *burel*, dark red cloth]

bureau de change *n* a place where one can change money from one currency to another.

bureaucracy *n* **-ies** **1** a system of government by officials who are responsible to their department heads and are not elected. **2** these officials as a group, esp. when seen as oppressive. **3** a country governed by officials. **4** any system of administration in which matters are complicated by minor rules and take longer than they need to. [**bureau** + Gr *kratos*, power]

bureaucrat *n* **1** a government official. **2** an official who follows rules rigidly, so creating delays and difficulties. — *adj* **bureaucratic**. — *adv* **bureaucratically**.

bureau de change. See **bureau**.

burette *n* a glass tube with a tap at one end, for measuring small quantities of liquid in experiments, etc. [Fr]

burgeon *v* (*intr*) to grow or develop quickly; to flourish. — *adj* **burgeoning**. [OFr *burjon*, bud, shoot]

burger *n* **1** a hamburger. **2** a hamburger covered or flavoured with something: *a cheeseburger*. **3** an item of food shaped like a hamburger but made of something different: *a nutburger*. [Short for **hamburger**]

burgess *n* **1** (in England) an inhabitant of a town or borough, esp. a person who has the right to elect people to government. **2** (*Br hist*) a Member of Parliament for a borough, a town with a municipal corporation or a university. [OFr *burgeis*, from Lat *burgus*, borough]

burgh *n* (in Scotland until 1975) a town or borough with a certain amount of self-government under a town council. [Scots form of **borough**]

burgher *n* a citizen of a town or borough, esp. on the Continent. [OGer *burger*, from *burg*, borough]

burglar *n* a person who enters a building, etc. illegally to steal. [OFr *burgler*]

burglar alarm *n* an alarm with a loud bell that starts to ring if someone tries to enter a building illegally.

burglary *n* **-ies** the crime of entering a building, etc. illegally to steal.

burgle *v* **1** (*tr*) to enter (a building, etc.) illegally and steal from it; to steal from (a person). **2** (*intr*) to commit burglary.

burgomaster *n* a mayor of a town in Germany, Belgium, the Netherlands and Austria. [Dut *burgemeester*, from *burg*, borough + *meester*, master]

burial *n* **1** the burying of a dead body in a grave. **2** (*archaeol*) a grave and the remains found in it. [OE *byrgels*, tomb]

burin *n* a steel tool for engraving copper, wood, etc. [Fr]

burk. See **berk**.

burlesque *n* **1** a piece of literature, acting, etc. which exaggerates and mocks a serious subject or art form. **2** (esp. *US*) a type of theatrical entertainment involving humorous sketches, songs and usu. strip-tease. — *adj* of or like a burlesque. — *v* (*tr*) to make fun of (something) using burlesque. [Ital *burlesco*, from *burla*, jest]

burly *adj* **-ier**, **-iest** (of a person) big, strong and heavy in build. — *n* **burliness**. [MidE *borli*]

burn[1] *v* ***burned*** or ***burnt*** **1** (*tr* & *intr*) to be or set on fire. **2** (*tr* & *intr*; **away, down, off,** etc.) to destroy or be destroyed by fire. ◇ See also **burn up** below. **3** (*tr* & *intr*) to damage or injure, or be damaged or injured, by fire or heat. **4** (*tr*) to use as fuel. **5** (*tr*) to make (a hole, etc.) by or as if by fire, heat, etc.: *Acid can burn holes in material*. **6** (*tr* & *intr*) to (cause to) die by fire. **7** (*intr*) to be or feel hot: *My face is burning*. **8** (*intr* & *tr*) to (cause to) feel a stinging pain: *Vodka burns my throat*. **9** (*intr*; **with**) to feel strong emotion: *burn with shame*. **10** (*intr*; *coll*) to want to do something very much: *burning to be revenged*. **11** (*tr* & *intr*) to char or scorch or become charred or scorched. — *n* **1** an injury or mark caused by fire, heat, acid, etc. **2** an act of burning. **3** an act of firing the engines of a space rocket. — **burn one's boats** or **bridges** (*coll*) to destroy all chance of escape or retreat. — **burn the candle at both ends** **1** to work from early in the morning till late at night. **2** to get extremely tired by trying to do too many things and not getting enough rest. — **burn one's fingers** or **get one's fingers burnt** (*coll*) to get involved in something foolish, dangerous, etc. and suffer as a result of it. — **burn the midnight oil** to work late into the night. — *v* **burn out** **1** (*intr*) to be no longer burning as there is nothing left to burn. **2** (*intr* & *tr*) to stop or cause to stop working because of too much use or heat. **3** (*intr* & *tr*; esp. *US*) to become or make (oneself) extremely tired or ill through too much work or exercise (*n* **burn-out**). **4** (*intr*) (of an engine in a space rocket, etc.) to use all the fuel and stop working (*n* **burn-out**). — *v* **burn up** **1** (*tr* & *intr*) to destroy or be destroyed by fire, heat, acid, etc. **2** (*tr*) to use a lot of (fuel). **3** (*intr* & *tr*; *US slang*) to become or make very angry. [OE *biernan*, to be on fire, & *bærnan*, to cause to burn]

burner *n* the part of a gas lamp, stove, etc. which produces the flame. — **put on the back burner** (*coll*) to delay doing (something) until later.

burning *adj* **1** on fire. **2** feeling extremely hot. **3** very strong or intense: *a burning desire*. **4** very important or urgent: *a burning issue*.

burn-out see **burn out** above.

burnt ochre or **burnt sienna** *n* a natural, reddish-brown pigment made dark by being burnt.

burn² *n* (esp. *Scot*) a small stream. [OE *burna*, brook.]

burnish *v* (*tr*) to make (metal) bright by polishing. — *adj* **burnished**. — *n* **burnishing**. [OFr *brunir*, from *brun*, brown]

burnous *n* a long cloak with a hood, worn by Arabs. [Arabic *burnus*]

burnt. See **burn**.

burp (*coll*) *v* **1** (*intr*) to let air escape noisily from one's stomach through one's mouth. **2** (*tr*) to rub or pat (a baby) on the back to help get rid of air in its stomach. — *n* a belch. [Imit.]

burr¹. See **bur**.

burr² *n* **1** in some accents of English, a rough 'r' sound pronounced at the back of the throat. **2** a continual humming sound. **3** a rough edge on metal or paper. **4** a small drill used esp. by a dentist or surgeon. — *v* **1** (*intr*) to make a burring sound. **2** (*tr*) to pronounce with a burr.

burrow *n* a hole or tunnel dug by rabbits and other small animals for shelter. — *v* **1** (*intr* & *tr*; **in**, **into**, etc.) to make (a hole or tunnel) in, under, etc. (something). **2** (*intr*) to live in a burrow. **3** (*intr*) (of people) to hide or keep warm as if in a burrow. **4** (*intr*; **into**) to search or investigate something: *burrow into one's pockets*. [MidE *berg*, refuge]

bursar *n* **1** a treasurer in a school, college or university. **2** a student or pupil who has a bursary. [Lat *bursa*, bag, purse]

bursary *n* **-ies** **1** an award or grant of money made to a student; a scholarship. **2** the bursar's room in a school, college, etc.

burst *v* ***burst*** **1** (*intr* & *tr*; **down**, etc.) to (cause to) break open or into pieces, usu. suddenly and violently: *the balloon burst*; *burst the door down*. **2** (*intr*; **into, through**, **out**, etc.) to make one's way suddenly or violently: *burst into the room*. **3** (*intr*; **on to**, **upon**, etc.) to appear suddenly and be immediately important or noteworthy: *burst on to the political scene*. **4** (*intr*) to be full. **5** (*tr*) to break open, overflow, etc. **6** (*intr* with **with**) to be full of (a strong emotion): *bursting with anger*. **7** (*intr* with **into, out**) to begin to do something suddenly and noisily: *burst into tears*; *burst out laughing*. — *n* **1** an instance of, or the place of, bursting or breaking open. **2** a sudden brief period of: *a burst of speed*; *a burst of gunfire*. — **burst open** to open suddenly and violently. [OE *berstan*]

bursting *adj* (*coll*) **1** very eager (to do something): *bursting to tell you the news*. **2** (with **with**) very full of: *bursting with pride*. **3** needing very badly to urinate.

burthen. See **burden**.

burton: **gone for a burton** (*Br slang*) lost, broken, dead, no longer in existence, etc.

bury *v* ***-ies***, ***-ied*** (*tr*) **1** to place (a dead body) in a grave, the sea, etc. **2** to hide in the ground: *a dog burying a bone*. **3** to put out of sight; to cover: *bury one's face in one's hands*. **4** to lose by death: *bury her husband*. **5** to occupy (oneself) with: *bury oneself in one's work*. — **bury the hatchet** to stop quarrelling and become friends again. — **bury one's head in the sand** to refuse to think about or accept something unpleasant. [OE *byrgan*]

bus *n* **1** a usu. large road vehicle which carries passengers to and from established stopping points along a fixed route for payment. **2** (*coll*) a car or aeroplane, esp. one which is old and shaky. **3** a number of conductors forming a link between different parts of a computer system or network, which allow information to be passed from one part to another. — *v* ***busing*** or ***-ss-***, ***bused*** or ***-ss-*** **1** (*intr* & *tr*) to go or take by bus. **2** (*tr*; *US*) to transport (children) by bus to a school in a different area, as a way of promoting racial integration. — **miss the bus** see **miss the boat** at **boat**. [Short for **omnibus**]

bus conductor *n* a person on a bus who collects the fares from passengers and gives out tickets.

busman's holiday *n* free time or a holiday spent in doing exactly the same thing that one normally does at work.

busby *n* ***-ies*** a tall fur hat worn as part of the uniform of some British soldiers.

bush *n* **1** a thick, woody plant with many branches, smaller than a tree. **2** a dense group of such plants. **3** a thing like a bush, esp. in thickness or density: *a bush of hair*. **4** (usu. with **the**) wild, uncultivated country, covered with shrubs, and sometimes trees, esp. in Australia, New Zealand and Africa. [MidE *busshe*; some uses are from Dut *bosch*]

bush-baby *n* a small, furry, tree-living African animal with big eyes and a long tail.

bushed *adj* (*coll*) extremely tired.

bush jacket see **bush shirt**.

bushman *n* **1** a person who lives or travels in the bush in Australia or New Zealand. **2** (*cap*) a member of an aboriginal tribe in S Africa. **3** (*cap*) the language spoken by this tribe.

bushranger *n* (*Austr hist*) a robber or criminal living in the bush.

bush shirt or **jacket** *n* a light cotton jacket with four pockets and a belt.

bush telegraph *n* the rapid spreading of information, rumours, etc., usu. by word of mouth.

bushwhack *v* (*intr*) to travel through woods or bush clearing it. — *n* **bushwhacker**. — *n* **bushwhacking**.

bushy *adj* **-ier**, **-iest 1** covered in bushes. **2** (of hair, etc.) thick and spreading. — *adv* **bushily**. — *n* **bushiness**.

bush[2] *n* a sheet of thin metal lining a cylinder in which an axle revolves. — *v* (*tr*) to provide with a bush. [ODut *bussche*, box]

bushel *n* a unit of measurement used for weighing grains, fruit, liquid, etc., equivalent to 8 gallons (36·4 litres). — **hide one's light under a bushel** to keep one's good qualities or abilities hidden from other people. [OFr *boissiel*]

business *n* **1** the buying and selling of goods and services. **2** a shop, firm, commercial company, etc. **3** one's regular occupation, trade or profession. **4** the things that are one's proper or rightful concern: *mind one's own business.* **5** serious work or activity: *get down to business.* **6** an affair, matter: *a nasty business.* **7** (*coll*) a difficult or complicated problem; a bother or nuisance: *It's a real business filling in this form.* — **like nobody's business** (*coll*) very fast, very well or very efficiently. — **mean business** (*coll*) to be very serious about something. — **on business** in the process of doing business or something official. — **out of business** no longer able to function as a business. — **send someone about his** or **her business** to dismiss or send a person away. [OE *bisig*, busy + *-nes*, -ness]

business card *n* a card carried by businessmen and businesswomen showing their name, the name and address of the company they work for, and their position in that company.

business class *n* on an aeroplane, etc., seats between the standard and first classes in price and quality.

business end *n* (*coll*) the part of something which does the work the thing is made for.

businesslike *adj* practical and efficient.

businessman or **businesswoman** *n* a man or woman who works in trade or commerce, esp. at quite a senior level.

business park *n* an area, usu. just outside a town, specially designed to accommodate business offices and small factories.

busk *v* (*intr*) to sing, play music, etc. in the street for money. — *n* **busker**. — *n* **busking**. [Prob. Span *buscar*, to seek]

bust[1] *n* **1** the upper front part of a woman's body. **2** a sculpture of a person's head, shoulders and chest. [Fr *buste*]

busty *adj* **-ier**, **-iest** (*coll*) (of a woman) having large breasts.

bust[2] *v* ***busted*** or ***bust*** **1** (*tr* & *intr*; *coll*) to break or burst. **2** (*tr*; *slang*) to arrest. **3** (*tr*; *slang*) to raid or search. — *n* (*slang*) **1** a police raid. **2** a drinking bout; a spree. — *adj* (*coll*) **1** broken or burst. **2** having no money left; bankrupt. — **go bust** (*coll*) to go bankrupt. [**burst**]

buster *n* (esp. *US slang*) a form of address used for a man or boy.

bust-up *n* (*coll*) **1** a quarrel; the ending of a relationship or partnership. **2** an explosion or collapse.

bustard *n* a medium-sized long-legged quick-running bird. [OFr *bistarde*, from Lat *avis tarda*, slow bird (although it is not slow)]

bustle[1] *v* **1** (*intr*; **about**) to busy oneself noisily and energetically. **2** (*tr*) to make (someone) hurry, work hard, etc.: *bustle her out of the room.* — *n* hurried, noisy and excited activity. — *n* **bustler**. [MidE *bustelen*, to hurry along aimlessly]

bustling *adj* very lively and busy.

bustle[2] *n* (*hist*) a frame or pad for holding a skirt out from the back of the waist.

busy *adj* **-ier**, **-iest 1** fully occupied, with a lot of work to do. **2** full of activity: *a busy day*; *a busy street.* **3** (esp. *US*) (of a telephone line) engaged. **4** always working or occupied. **5** fussy and tending to interfere in the affairs of others. — *v* **-ies**, **-ied** (*tr*; **with**) to occupy (someone, oneself). — *adv* **busily**. — *n* **busyness**. [OE *bisig*]

busybody *n* a person who is always interfering in other people's affairs.

busy Lizzie *n* a popular house-plant with usu. pink or white flowers.

but *conj* **1** contrary to expectation: *She fell down but didn't hurt herself.* **2** in contrast: *You've been to Spain but I haven't.* **3** other than: *You can't do anything but wait.* — *prep* except: *They are all here but him.* — *adv* only: *I can but try.* — *n* an objection or doubt: *no buts about it.* — **but for** were it not for; without: *I couldn't have managed but for your help.* — **the last but one** the one before the last. [OE *butan*, outside of, without]

butane *n* a colourless gas obtained from petrol and used as fuel. [Lat *butyrum*, butter]

butch *adj* (*slang*) (of a woman or a man) aggressive, tough and strong-looking. [A boy's nickname in the US]

butcher *n* **1** a person or shop that sells meat. **2** a person who kills animals for food. **3** a person who kills people needlessly and savagely. — *v* (*tr*) **1** to kill and prepare (an animal) for sale as food. **2** to kill cruelly. **3** to ruin or spoil. [OE *bouchier*, person who kills and sells he-goats]

butchery *n* **1** the preparing of meat for sale as food. **2** senseless or cruel killing.

butler *n* the head male servant in a house, in charge of the wine cellar, dining table, etc. [OFr *bouteillier*, from *botele*, bottle]

butt[1] *v* (*tr* & *intr*) **1** to push or hit hard or roughly with the head like a ram or goat.

2 to join or be joined end to end. — *n* **1** a blow with the head or horns. **2** the place where two edges join. — *v* **butt in** (*intr*; *coll*) to interrupt or interfere. [OFr *boter*, to push or strike]

butt[2] *n* a large barrel for beer, rain, etc. [OFr *bout*, from Lat *buttis*, cask]

butt[3] *n* **1** a person who is often a target (of jokes, ridicule, criticism, etc.). **2** a mound of earth behind a target on a shooting range. [Fr *but*, goal]

butt[4] *n* **1** the thick, heavy or bottom end of a tool or weapon. **2** the unused end of a finished cigar, cigarette, etc. **3** (*NAm coll*) the buttocks. [MidE *bott*, from OE *butt*, tree stump]

butter *n* **1** a pale yellow solid fat made from cream or milk, which is spread on bread, etc. and used in cooking. **2** any substance which is thick and creamy like butter: *peanut butter*. — *v* **-r-** (*tr*) to put butter on or in. — *adj* **buttered**. — *adj* **buttery**. — *v* **butter up** (*tr*; *coll*) to flatter (usu. in order to gain a favour). [OE *butere* from Gr *boutyron*, prob. meaning 'ox-cheese']

butter bean *n* a large, flat, cream-coloured bean.

buttercup *n* a wild plant with small yellow cup-shaped flowers.

butterfingers *n* (*coll*) a person who often drops things, or who does not manage to catch things.

butter-knife *n* a blunt knife for spreading butter.

buttermilk *n* the slightly sharp-tasting liquid left after all the butter has been removed from milk.

butter muslin *n* a loosely woven cloth, orig. used for wrapping butter.

butterpat *n* **1** a small lump of butter. **2** a piece of wood used for shaping butter.

butterscotch *n* a kind of hard sweet made from butter and sugar.

butterfly *n* **-ies** **1** a type of insect with large, delicate, and usu. brightly coloured wings. **2** a not very serious person, only interested in pleasure: *a social butterfly*. **3** (in *pl*) a nervous feeling in the stomach. **4** same as **butterfly stroke**. [OE *buter-fleoge*, butter-fly]

butterfly nut *n* a screw or nut with two flat projections which allow it to be turned with the fingers.

butterfly stroke *n* a swimming stroke where both arms are brought out of the water and over the head at the same time.

buttery[1]. See **butter**.

buttery[2] *n* **-ies** a room, esp. in a college or university, where food is kept and supplied to students. [OFr *boterie*, place for storing butts (**butt**[2])]

buttock *n* **1** (usu in *pl*) either one of the fleshy parts of the body between the back and the legs. **2** the similar part of some animals. [Prob. **butt**[4]]

button *n* **1** a small usu. round piece of metal, plastic, etc. sewn on to clothes, which fastens them by being passed through a slit or hole. **2** a small round disc pressed to operate a door, bell, etc. **3** a small round object worn as decoration or a badge. **4** any small round object more or less like a button: *chocolate buttons*; *a button nose*. — *v* **1** (*tr*; **up**) to fasten using a button or buttons: *button one's coat*. **2** (*intr* with **up**; *slang*) to stop talking. **3** (*tr* with **up**) to bring to a successful conclusion. — **on the button** (*coll*) exactly right or correct. [OFr *bouton*]

button cell or **button cell battery** *n* a small, flat, circular battery used to power a watch, etc.

buttonhole *n* **1** a small slit or hole through which a button is passed to fasten a garment. **2** a flower or flowers worn in a buttonhole or pinned to a lapel. — *v* (*tr*) to stop and force conversation on (a usu. reluctant person).

button mushroom *n* a small mushroom which has not opened out.

buttress *n* **1** a support built on to the outside of a wall. **2** any support or prop. — *v* (*tr*) **1** to support (a wall, etc.) with buttresses. **2** to support or encourage (an argument, etc.). [OFr *bouterez*, thrusting]

butty *n* **-ies** (*Br coll*) a sandwich. [**butter**]

buxom *adj* (of a woman) plump, healthy-looking and attractive. [MidE *buhsum*, pliant]

buy *v* ***bought*** **1** (*tr* & *intr*) to get (something) by paying a sum of money for it. **2** (*tr*) to be a means of obtaining (something): *Money can't buy love*. **3** (*tr*) to obtain by giving up or sacrificing something: *success bought at the expense of happiness*. **4** (*tr*; *coll*) to believe or accept as true. **5** (*tr*) to bribe (someone). — *n* a thing bought: *a good buy*. — *v* **buy in** (*tr*) to buy a stock or supply of. — *v* **buy into** (*tr*) to buy shares in (a company, etc.). — *v* **buy off** (*tr*) to get rid of (a claim, threatening person, etc.) by paying. — *v* **buy out** (*tr*) **1** to buy all the shares held by (someone) in a company (*n* **buy-out**). **2** to pay to obtain the release of (usu. oneself) from the armed forces. — **buy time** (*coll*) to do something in order to get more time before e.g. a decision, action, etc. is taken. — *v* **buy up** (*tr*) to buy the whole stock of. — **have bought it** (*slang*) to have been killed. [OE *bycgan*]

buyer *n* **1** a person who buys; a customer. **2** a person employed by a large shop or firm to buy goods on its behalf.

buyer's market *n* a situation where there are more goods for sale than people wanting to buy them, so keeping prices low.

buy-out see **buy out** above.

buzz *v* **1** (*intr*) to make a continuous humming or rapidly vibrating sound. **2** (*intr*; **with**) to be filled with activity or excitement: *buzzing with activity*. **3** (*tr*; *coll*) to call (someone) on the telephone. **4** (*tr*; *coll*) to call (someone) using a buzzer. **5** (*tr*;

coll) (of an aircraft) to fly very low over or very close to (another aircraft, a building, etc.). — *n* **1** a humming or rapidly vibrating sound, e.g. as made by a bee. **2** a low murmuring sound e.g. as made by many people talking. **3** (*coll*) a telephone call. **4** (*coll*) a sense of activity, excitement, etc. **5** (*coll*) a rumour. — *v* **buzz about** or **around** (*intr*) to move quickly or excitedly. — *v* **buzz off** (*intr*; *slang*) to go away. [Imit.]

buzzer *n* an electrical device which makes a buzzing sound.

buzz word *n* (*coll*) a word or expression from a particular subject or field, used by people who may not understand it in an attempt to appear fashionable and up to date.

buzzard *n* a large eagle-like bird which hunts small animals for food. [OFr *busard*]

bwana *n* (often used as a form of address in E Africa) master; sir. [Swahili]

by *prep* **1** next to, beside, near. **2** past: *drive by the house*. **3** through, along, or across: *enter by the window*. **4** used to show the person or thing that does, causes, produces, etc. something: *bitten by a dog*; *a play by Shakespeare*. **5** used to show method or means: *travel by air*. **6** not later than: *be home by 10 pm*. **7** during: *escape by night*. **8** used to show extent or amount: *bigger by six feet*. **9** used in stating rates of payment, etc.: *paid by the hour*. **10** according to: *by my watch*. **11** used in giving measurements, compass directions, etc.: *a room measuring six feet by ten*; *north-north-east by north*. **12** used to show the number which must perform a mathematical operation on another: *divide six by two*; *multiply three by four*. **13** with regard to: *do his duty by them*. — *adv* **1** near: *live close by*. **2** past: *drive by without stopping*. **3** aside; away; in reserve: *put money by*. — *n* ***byes*** same as **bye**[1]. — **by and by** after a short time. — **by the by** or **bye** (*coll*) while I think of it; incidentally. — **by and large** generally; all things considered. — **by oneself 1** alone. **2** without anyone else's help. [OE *be*]

by-election *n* an election during the sitting of parliament to fill a seat which has become empty because the member has died or resigned.

bygone *adj* past, former. — *n* (esp. in *pl*) a past event or argument. — **let bygones be bygones** to agree to forget past quarrels.

byline *n* a line under the title of a newspaper or magazine article which has the author's name on it.

bypass *n* **1** a road which avoids a busy area or town. **2** a channel, pipe, etc. which carries gas, electricity, etc. when the main channel is blocked. **3** a tube inserted into a blood vessel to provide an alternative route for the blood flow, either temporarily during an operation or permanently to get round a blockage in the blood vessel. — *v* (*tr*) **1** to avoid (a place) by taking a road which goes around it or avoids it. **2** to leave out (a step in a process) or ignore and not discuss something with (a person). **3** to provide with a bypass.

by-play *n* less important action happening at the same time as the main action.

by-product *n* **1** a substance or product obtained or formed during the making of something else. **2** an unexpected, extra result; a side effect.

byroad or **byway** *n* a minor road.

bystander *n* a person who watches but does not take part in what is happening.

byway see **byroad**.

byword *n* a person or thing well known as an example of something: *Their name is a byword for luxury*.

bye[1] *n* **1** a pass to the next round of a competition given to a competitor or team that has not been given an opponent in the current round. **2** (*cricket*) a run scored from a ball which the batsman has not hit or touched. — **by the bye** see **by the by**. [**by**]

bye-law see **by-law**.

bye[2] or **bye-bye** *interj* (*coll*) goodbye. [Short form of **goodbye**]

by-law or **bye-law** *n* a law or rule made by a local authority. [Norse *byjar-log*, town law]

byre *n* (esp. *Scot*) a cowshed. [OE *byre*, stall, shed]

byte *n* a group of eight binary digits forming a unit of memory in a computer.

Byzantine *adj* **1** of *Byzantium* (now Istanbul in Turkey) or the eastern part of the Roman Empire from AD 395 to 1453. **2** of the style of architecture or painting developed by the Byzantine Empire, with domes, arches, mosaics, etc. **3** secret, difficult to understand and extremely complicated. — *n* an inhabitant of Byzantium. [Lat *byzantinus*]

C

C[1] or **c** *n* **Cs** or **C's**, **c's** **1** the third letter of the English alphabet. **2** (usu. **C**) (a mark indicating) the third highest grade or quality. **3** (only **C**; *mus*) the note on which the Western system of music is based. **4** a musical key with the note C as its base.
C[2] *abbrev* **1** Celsius. **2** centigrade. **3** century: *C19*.
C[3] *symbol* **1** the Roman numeral for 100. **2** (*chem*) carbon.
c *abbrev* **1** centi-. **2** cubic. **3** (*physics*) the speed of light.
c. *abbrev* **1** cent. **2** century. **3** chapter. **4** (*cricket*) caught.
c. *abbrev* for *circa* (Lat), approximately.
© *symbol* copyright.
¢ *symbol* cent.
CA *abbrev* **1** Chartered Accountant. **2** California.
Ca *symbol* (*chem*) calcium.
ca. *abbrev* for *circa* (Lat), approximately.
cab *n* **1** a taxi. **2** the driver's compartment in a lorry, railway engine, etc. **3** (*hist*) a carriage for hire, pulled by a horse. [Short for **cabriolet**]
C.A.B. *abbrev* (*Br*) Citizens' Advice Bureau, an office to which people can go for free advice.
cabal *n* **1** a small group formed within a larger body, for secret, esp. political, discussion, planning, etc. **2** a political plot or conspiracy. [Fr *cabale*, from Hebr *qabbalah*, tradition]
cabaret *n* **1** an entertainment with songs, dancing, etc. at a restaurant or nightclub. **2** a restaurant or nightclub providing this. [Fr, tavern]
cabbage *n* **1** a vegetable with green or red edible leaves usu. forming a large round head. **2** (*derog*) a dull, inactive person. **3** (*offensive*) a person so severely brain-damaged or mentally subnormal as to be completely dependent on other people for survival. [Fr *caboche*, head]
cabby or **cabbie** *n* ***-ies*** (*coll*) a taxi-driver. [**cab**]
caber *n* (*athletics*) in the contest of **tossing the caber**, a heavy wooden pole that must be carried upright and then tipped end over end. [Gaelic *cabar*, pole]
cabin *n* **1** a small house, esp. made of wood. **2** a small room on a ship for living, sleeping or working in. **3** the passenger section of a plane. **4** the section at the front of a plane for pilot and crew. **5** the driving compartment of a (usu. large) lorry. [Fr *cabane*, cabin]
cabin boy *n* (*hist*) a boy who serves officers and passengers on board ship.
cabin cruiser *n* a large, esp. luxurious, power-driven boat with living and sleeping accommodation.
cabinet *n* **1** a piece of furniture with shelves and doors, for storing or displaying things. **2** the casing round a television set, music centre, etc. **3** (often *cap*) the group of ministers in charge of the various departments of government who meet regularly for discussion with the prime minister. [Dimin. of **cabin**]
cabinet-maker *n* a skilled maker and repairer of fine furniture. — *n* **cabinet=making**.
cable *n* **1** a very strong thick rope made of hemp or metal wire, used e.g. on ships. **2** an enclosed set of wires carrying telephone signals or electricity. **3** (*naut*) a measure of length or depth, about 600 ft (220 m). **4** (also **cablegram**) a telegram sent by cable. **5** (also **cable stitch**) a pattern in knitting that looks like twisted cable. — *v* (*intr* & *tr*) to send a cable, or send (a message) to (a person) by cable. [Lat *caplum*, halter]
cable car *n* a small box-shaped vehicle suspended from a continuous moving cable, for carrying passengers up or down a steep mountain, across a valley, etc.
cable television, cable tv or **cablevision** *n* a service by which television programmes are transmitted by cable, rather than broadcast over radio waves, to viewers who pay the supplier directly.
caboodle: **the whole caboodle** (*coll*) the whole lot; everything. [Orig. US; perhaps from *boodle*, collection]
caboose *n* **1** (*NAm*) a guard's van on a railway train. **2** (*naut*) a ship's galley or kitchen. [Dut *cabuse*, ship's galley]
cabriole *n* & *adj* (a furniture leg) ornamentally curved to resemble an animal's leg. [Fr, goat-like leap]
cabriolet *n* **1** (*hist*) a light two-wheeled carriage drawn by one horse. **2** a car with a folding roof. [Fr, from *cabriole*, goat-like leap]
cacao *n* **1** a tropical American tree whose seeds are roasted and crushed to produce chocolate and cocoa. **2** the seeds of this tree. [Span, from Aztec *cacauatl*, cacao tree]
cache **1** a hiding-place, e.g. for weapons. **2** a collection of hidden things. — *v* (*tr*) to put or collect in a cache. [Fr, from *cacher*, to hide]
cachet **1** something that brings one respect or admiration; a distinction. **2** a distinguishing mark. **3** an official seal. **4** a special commemorative postmark. **5** (*old med*) a small edible container for a pill, etc. [Fr, something compressed]
cack-handed *adj* (*coll*) **1** clumsy; awkward. **2** left-handed. [Dialect *cack*, excrement]

cackle *n* **1** the sound that a hen or goose makes. **2** (*derog*) a laugh like this. **3** shrill, silly chatter. — *v* (*intr*) **1** to laugh with a hen-like sound. **2** to chatter shrilly. — **cut the cackle** (*coll*) to stop talking unproductively and come to the point. [Imit.]

cacophony *n* a disagreeable combination of loud noises. — *adj* **cacophonous**. [Gr *kakos*, bad + *phone*, sound]

cactus *n* **-*ti*** or **-*tuses*** any of many prickly desert plants whose thick stems store water. [Gr *kaktos*, prickly plant in Sicily]

cad *n* (*old derog*) a man who behaves discourteously or dishonourably. — *adj* **caddish**. [Short for *caddie*, odd-job man]

cadaver *n* a dead body, esp. a human one. [Lat]

cadaverous *adj* corpse-like in appearance; pale and gaunt.

CAD *abbrev* computer-aided design.

caddie or **caddy** *n* **-*ies*** a person whose job is to carry the golf clubs for a golf-player. — *v* **-*dies***, **-*dying***, **-*died*** (*intr*; **for**) to act as caddy. [Scot, from Fr *cadet*, cadet]

caddis fly *n* a small hairy-winged insect whose larvae live in water and build round themselves a protective cylinder of sand, gravel, etc.

caddy[1] *n* **-*ies*** a small container for tea leaves. [Malay *kati*, a unit of weight]

caddy[2]. See **caddie**.

cadence *n* **1** a fall of pitch in the voice. **2** the rising and falling of the voice in speaking. **3** rhythm or beat. **4** a pattern of notes that closes a musical passage. [Fr, from Lat *cadere*, to fall]

cadenza *n* an elaborate variation played by a solo musician at the end of a concerto movement, etc. [Ital, from Lat *cadere*, to fall]

cadet *n* **1** a student at a military, naval or police training school. **2** a schoolboy training in a cadet corps. [Fr dialect *capdet*, chief]

cadet corps *n* in some schools, a group of pupils organised into a unit for military training.

cadge *v* (*tr* & *intr*; *derog*; **from**, **off**) to get (something) from someone by begging or scrounging. — *n* **cadger**.

cadi or **kadi** *n* a judge in Muslim countries. [Arabic *qadi*, judge]

cadmium *n* an element (symbol **Cd**), a soft bluish-white metal used in magnets, metal-plating and as a control in nuclear reactors. [Gr *kadmeia*, calamine]

cadre *n* **1** a basic, highly trained military unit that can be expanded in emergencies. **2** an inner group of politically active people, e.g. within the Communist party. **3** a member of a cadre. [Fr, framework]

caecum *n* **-*ca*** (*anat*) the bag-like part of the large intestine from which the appendix projects, at the point where the small intestine joins it. — *adj* **caecal**. [Lat *intestinum caecum*, blind-ended intestine]

Caenozoic. Same as **Cainozoic**.

caesarean or **caesarian** *n* (*med*) (also **caesarean section**) a surgical operation to cut open a woman's abdomen to remove a baby from the womb, when birth through the vagina would be dangerous. [The Roman name *Caesar*, said to be from Lat *caedere*, to cut, the first holder of the name having been delivered by this method]

caesium *n* an element (symbol **Cs**), a soft silvery-white metal used esp. in photo-electric cells (devices that discharge electrons in response to light, used in apparatuses such as burglar alarms). [Lat *caesius*, bluish-grey]

caesura *n* a pause in a line of poetry, usu. in the middle of it. [Lat *caedere*, to cut]

café or **cafe** *n* a usu. small restaurant serving meals or snacks. [Fr, coffee, coffee house]

cafeteria *n* a self-service restaurant. [Span, coffee shop]

caffeine *n* the stimulant that is present in coffee and tea. [Fr *caféine*, from *café*, coffee]

caftan or **kaftan** *n* **1** a long loose-fitting garment worn by men in Middle Eastern countries. **2** a similarly shaped garment worn as a dress by Western women or (esp. formerly) as a shirt or jacket by men. [Turk *qaftan*]

cage *n* **1** a container with bars, etc., in which to keep captive birds or animals. **2** a lift for taking mineworkers up and down a shaft in a mine. **3** any structure or framework something like a bird's or animal's cage: *the ribcage*. — *v* (*tr*) to put in a cage. — *v* **cage in** (*tr*) **1** to imprison or confine. **2** to limit the freedom of action of; to inhibit. [Fr, from Lat *cavea*, hollow place

cagebird *n* a bird, e.g. a canary, suitable for keeping in a cage.

caged *adj* kept in a cage.

cagey *adj* **-*ier***, **-*iest*** (*coll*) not speaking frankly and openly; secretive and cautious. — *adv* **cagily**. — *n* **caginess**. [Poss. from **cage**]

cagoule *n* a light waterproof hooded outer garment, esp. one that is made of thin nylon, is pulled on over the head, and reaches down to the knees. [Fr, hood]

cahoots: in cahoots (**with**; *coll*, usu. *derog*) working in close partnership (with someone), esp. in the planning of something unlawful.

caiman. See **cayman**.

Cain: raise Cain (*coll*) to cause a great disturbance, esp. deliberately, e.g. from anger. [*Cain*, the first son of Adam and Eve according to the Bible, who killed his brother]

Cainozoic *adj* & *n* (*geol*) Tertiary and Quaternary together. [Gr *kainos*, new + *zoe*, life]

cairn[1] *n* a heap of stones piled up to mark e.g. a grave or pathway. [Gaelic *carn*]

cairn[2] or **cairn terrier** *n* a small short-legged breed of dog with a rough coat, orig. from Scotland. [Gaelic *carn*, cairn; the dogs were believed to come from rocky areas]

cairngorm *n* a yellowish or brownish variety of quartz, found on *Cairngorm*, a Scottish mountain, and used as a gemstone. [Gaelic *carn gorm*, blue cairn]

caisson *n* a watertight chamber inside which construction work can be carried out underwater. [Fr, large box]

caisson disease *n* decompression sickness.

cajole *v* (*tr*; **into**) to use flattery, promises, etc. to persuade (someone) to do something — *n* **cajolery**. [Fr *cajoler*, to coax]

cake *n* **1** a solid food made by baking a mixture of flour, fat, eggs, sugar, etc. **2** an individually baked portion of this food. **3** a portion of some other food pressed into a particular shape. **4** a solid block (of soap, etc.) — *v* **1** (*intr*) to dry as a thick hard crust. **2** (*tr*; **in, with**) to cover in a thick crust: *skin caked with blood*. — **a piece of cake** (*coll*) a very easy task. — **one can't have one's cake and eat it** one can't enjoy the advantages of both alternatives, since each excludes the other. — **sell** or **go like hot cakes** to be bought enthusiastically in large numbers. [Norse *kaka*]

cakehole *n* (*slang*) the mouth.

Cal. *abbrev*. California.

cal. *abbrev* calorie.

calabash *n* **1** a tropical American tree that bears large round gourd-like fruits. **2** the dried, hollowed-out shell of one of these fruits used as a bowl. [Fr *calebasse*]

calaboose *n* (*US slang*) a small local prison. [Span *calabozo*, dungeon]

calabrese *n* a kind of broccoli. [Ital, Calabrian]

calamine *n* zinc carbonate, or sometimes zinc oxide, in the form of a pink powder, used in lotions and creams for soothing stings and bites, reducing itching, etc. [Lat *calamina*]

calamity *n* **-ies** a catastrophe, disaster or serious misfortune, causing great loss or damage. — *adj* **calamitous**. — *adv* **calamitously**. — *n* **calamitousness**. [Lat *calamitas*, harm]

calcareous *adj* containing, or relating to, calcium carbonate; chalky. [Lat *calcarius*, from *calx*, lime]

calciferol *n* vitamin D_2 [*calciferous*, calcium-carrying. as it increases the absorption of calcium]

calcify *v* **-ies, -ied** (*tr* & *intr*) **1** to harden as a result of the deposit of calcium salts. **2** to change or be changed into lime. — *n* **calcification**. [**calcium** + **-ify**]

calcite *n* a crystalline form of calcium carbonate, of which marble is chiefly composed. [Lat *calx*, lime]

calcium *n* an element (symbol **Ca**), a soft silvery metal, compounds of which are found in the ground and in bones and teeth. [Lat *calx*, lime]

calcium carbonate *n* the white solid substance of which chalk, limestone and marble are composed.

calculate *v* **1** (*tr*) to work out, find out or estimate, esp. by mathematical means. **2** (*intr* with **on**) to make plans that depend on or take into consideration (some probability or possibility). — *adj* **calculable**. — *adv* **calculably**. — **calculated to** designed to, intended to, or likely to. [Lat *calculare*, to calculate]

calculated *adj* intentional; deliberate: *a calculated insult*.

calculated risk *n* a possibility of failure that has been taken into consideration before some action is taken.

calculating *adj* (*derog*) inclined to see other people, or situations, in terms of how one can use them to benefit oneself. — *adv* **calculatingly**.

calculation *n* **1** the act or process of calculating. **2** something estimated or calculated. **3** (*derog*) the cold and deliberate use of people or situations to benefit oneself.

calculator *n* a small electronic machine for doing mathematical calculations.

calculus *n* **1** a system of mathematical calculation for dealing with quantities that change constantly, such as the speed of something falling, **differential calculus** dealing with the rate of such change, and **integral calculus** with the cumulative increase in the quantities. **2** (*med*) a small stone in the bladder, kidney, etc. [Lat, pebble (formerly used in counting)]

Caledonian *adj* belonging to Scotland. — *n* (esp. *facet*) a Scot. [Lat *Caledonia*, Scotland]

calendar *n* **1** a booklet or chart, or an adjustable device, that shows the months and days of the year. **2** any system by which the beginning, length and divisions of the year are fixed: *the Julian calendar*. **3** a timetable or list of important dates, events, appointments, etc. [Lat *calendrium*, account book]

calender *n* a machine with heated rollers for pressing, smoothing and giving a shiny surface to cloth or paper. — *v* **-r-** (*tr*) to press (cloth or paper) in a calender. [Fr *calandre*, from Gr *kylindros*, cylinder, roller]

calends *n* (*pl*) in the Roman calendar, the first day of the month. [Lat *calendae*]

calf[1] *n* ***calves*** **1** the young of a cow, and of several other animals, e.g. the elephant, whale and the larger deer. **2** (also **calfskin**) leather made from the skin of a calf. — **in calf** pregnant with a calf. [OE *cælf*]

calf love *n* romantic love between adolescents, or the love of an adolescent for an older person.

calve *v* (*intr*) to give birth to a calf.

calf[2] *n* ***calves*** the thick fleshy back part of the leg below the knee. [Norse *kálfi*]

calibrate *v* (*tr*) **1** to mark the scale on (a measuring instrument). **2** to correct or adjust (the scale or instrument) **[calibre]**
calibration *n* **1** the act of calibrating. **2** one of the marks showing the scale on a measuring instrument.

calibre *n* **1** the inner diameter of the barrel of a gun or of any tube. **2** the diameter of a bullet or shell. **3** quality; standard; ability. [Fr, from Arabic *qalib*, mould]

calico *n* **-oes** a kind of cotton cloth, usu. plain white or in its natural, unbleached state. [*Calicut* in India, from where the cloth was first brought]

Calif. *abbrev* California.

californium *n* an element (symbol **Cf**), an artificially produced radioactive metal. [*California*, where the element was first made]

caliph or **khalif** *n* a Muslim civil and religious leader. [Arabic *khalifah*, successor (of Mohammed)]
caliphate *n* the rank of, or area ruled by, a caliph.

call *v* **1** (*tr* & *intr*; **out**) to shout or speak loudly in order to attract attention or in announcing something. **2** (*tr*) to ask (someone) to come, esp. with a shout. **3** (*tr*) to ask for a professional visit from. **4** (*tr*) to summon or invite. **5** (*tr* & *intr*) to telephone. **6** (*tr*) to waken. **7** (*intr*; **at**, **round**) to make a visit: *call at the grocer's*. **8** (*intr* with **at**) to stop at (a place) during a journey. **9** (*tr*) to give a name to. **10** (*tr*) to regard or consider (something) as. **11** (*tr*) to say or imply that (someone) is (something unpleasant). **12** (*tr*) to summon or assemble people for (a meeting). **13** (*tr*) to announce or declare: *call an election*. **14** (*intr* with **for**) to make a demand or appeal for. **15** (*tr* & *intr*) to make a bid, or choose (a suit for trumps), in a card game. **16** (*tr*) (of an umpire, etc.) to judge (a ball) to be in or out of play. **17** (*intr*) (of a bird, etc.) to make its typical or characteristic sound. — *n* **1** a shout or cry. **2** the cry of a bird or animal. **3** an invitation; a summons. **4** (with **for**) a demand, request or appeal. **5** (with **on**) a claim or demand: *too many calls on my time*. **6** a brief visit. **7** an act of contacting someone by telephone; a telephone conversation. **8** (**for**) a need or reason: *not much call for Latin teachers*. **9** an act of waking someone usu. by arrangement. **10** a signal blown on a bugle, etc. **11** a feeling that one has been chosen to do a particular job; a vocation. **12** a player's turn to bid or choose trumps in a card game. **13** the decision of a referee, etc. on whether a ball is in or out of play. **14** an instrument that imitates a bird's call. — *v* **call back 1** (*intr*) to visit again. **2** (*intr* & *tr*) to telephone again. — **call collect** (*US*) to have the telephone call one is making charged to the receiver of the call; to reverse the charges. — *v* **call down** (*tr*; with **on**) to try to bring down (as if) from heaven. — *v* **call for** (*tr*) **1** to require. **2** to collect; to fetch. — *v* **call forth** (*tr*) to bring into action. — *v* **call in 1** (*tr*) to invite or request the help of. **2** (*tr*) to request the return of (e.g. library books, a batch of faulty products, etc.). **3** (*intr*; **on**, **at**) to visit. — **call into question** to suggest reasons for doubting (something). — **call it a day** to decide to finish work, etc. — *v* **call off** (*tr*) **1** to cancel (something). **2** to order (a dog) to stop attacking (someone). **3** to give orders for (something) to be stopped: *call off the search*. — *v* **call on** or **upon** (*tr*) **1** to visit. **2** to appeal to. **3** to request or invite: *call on the secretary to read the minutes*. **4** to gather or summon up (one's strength, etc.). — *v* **call out** (*tr*) **1** to instruct (workers) to strike. **2** to summon (e.g. the fire brigade, the army, etc.) to help with an emergency, etc. — **call to mind 1** to remember. **2** to remind one of (something). — *v* **call up** (*tr*) **1** to order (a person) to join the armed forces (*n* **call-up**). **2** to cause (memories, images, etc.) to come into the mind. **3** (*coll*) to telephone (someone). — **have first call on** to have the right to (someone's help, attention, etc.) before anyone else. — **on call** (of e.g. a doctor) available if needed, e.g. to deal with an emergency. — **within call** close enough to hear if called. [OE *ceallian*]
call box *n* a public telephone box.
caller *n* a person visiting or making a telephone call.
call girl *n* a prostitute with whom appointments are made by telephone.
calling *n* **1** a trade or profession. **2** an urge to follow a particular profession, esp. one involving the care of other people.
calling-card *n* **1** (esp. *NAm*) a card bearing one's name, etc. that one leaves when calling at someone's house; a visiting-card. **2** an unmistakable and usu. disagreeable sign, esp. deliberately left, that a particular person has been present.
call sign or **call signal** *n* a word, letter, or number that identifies a ship, plane, etc. when communicating with another by radio.

calligraphy *n* **1** handwriting as an art. **2** beautiful, decorative handwriting. — *n* **calligrapher** or **calligraphist**. [Gr *kallos*, beauty + *graphein*, to write]

calliper *n* **1** (in *pl*) a small instrument consisting of a pair of hinged legs, used to measure the inside or outside diameter of objects, distances on maps, etc. **2** a metal frame or splint fitted to an injured or weak leg, to support it in walking. [Another form of **calibre**]

callisthenics *n* (a system of) physical exercises for increasing the body's strength and grace. — *adj* **callisthenic**. [Gr *kallos*, beauty + *sthenos*, strength]

callosity *n* **-ies** an area of skin that has become hardened and thickened as a result of pressure or friction. [Lat *callositas*]

callous[1] *adj* lacking any concern for others; unfeeling; coldly and deliberately cruel. — *adv* **callously**. — *n* **callousness**. [Lat *callosus*, thick-skinned]

callous[2]. See **callus**.

callow *adj* (*derog*) young and inexperienced. [OE *calu*, bald]

callus or **callous** *n* an area of hard thick skin, e.g. on the hand or foot, caused by constant pressure or rubbing. [Lat *callus*, hardened skin or tissue]

calm *adj* **1** relaxed and in control; not anxious, upset, angry, etc. **2** (of weather, etc.) still, quiet, peaceful; not rough or stormy. — *n* **1** peace, quiet, tranquillity. **2** stillness of weather. **3** a lack of sufficient wind for sailing. — *v* (*tr* or *intr*; **down**) to make or become calmer. — *adv* **calmly**. — *n* **calmness**. [Fr *calme*, from Gr *kauma*, (a rest during) the heat of noon]

Calor gas® *n* the gas butane stored under pressure in liquid form in metal containers, used as a fuel. [Lat *calor*, heat]

calorie *n* **1** (also **small calorie**) a unit representing the amount of heat required to raise the temperature of one gram of water by 1° Celsius. **2** (also **large calorie**) a unit representing the amount of heat required to raise the temperature of one kilogram of water by 1° Celsius, used as a unit of the energy-producing value of various types of food. [Fr, from Lat *calor*, heat]

calorific *adj* relating to, or producing, heat. [Lat *calorificus*, warming]

calorimeter *n* an instrument for measuring amount of heat. [Lat *calor*, heat + **-meter**]

calumny *n* **-ies** (the act of uttering) an untrue, malicious spoken statement about a person; slander. — *n* **calumniator**. — *adj* **calumnious**. [Lat *calumnia*, false accusation]

calumniate (*tr*) to utter a calumny against.

Calvary *n* **-ies 1** the name of the place where Jesus was crucified. **2** (sometimes without *cap*) a model or representation of the scene of the Crucifixion.

calve. See **calf**[1].

calves. Plural of **calf**[1] and **calf**[2].

Calvinism *n* the teachings of the 16th-cent. Christian reformer John *Calvin*, laying emphasis on mankind's inability to repent and believe in Christ without God's help, and on predestination (God's deciding in advance who will go to heaven and who will not). — *n* **Calvinist**. — *adj* **Calvinistic**.

calx *n* **calces** or **calxes** the powdery remains of a metal or mineral after strong heating. [Lat, lime]

calypso *n* **-os** a type of popular song invented in the West Indies, usu. dealing with current happenings in an amusing way, and often made up by the singer as he or she goes along.

calyx *n* **calyces** or **calyxes** (*bot*) a cup-shaped group of leaves, called sepals, which protect an unopened flower, and provide support under the flower once it has opened. [Gr *calyx*, covering, husk]

cam *n* (*engin*) a projection on a wheel that converts circular movement into movement backwards and forwards or side to side. [Dut *kam*, comb]

camshaft *n* (*engin*) a rod in an engine bearing one or more cams.

camaraderie *n* a feeling of friendship and cheerful support for one another within a group or team of people. [Fr]

camber *n* a slight curve across the surface of a road, etc. that makes water run off it, down to the sides. [Fr *cambre*]

Cambrian *adj* & *n* (of) the geological period lasting from 590 to 505 million years ago. [Lat *Cambria*, from Welsh *Cymru*, Wales]

cambric *n* a fine white cotton or linen cloth. [*Cambrai*, in N France, where the cloth was first made]

Cambs. *abbrev* Cambridgeshire.

came. See **come**.

camel *n* **1** an animal with a long neck and either one hump (the **Arabian camel** or **dromedary**) or two (the **Bactrian camel**), that stores fat in its hump(s) as a source of energy, can survive long periods in the desert without food or water and is used for carrying loads or for riding. **2** the pale brown colour of this animal. [Gr *kamelos*, from a Semitic source]

camelhair *n* **1** a soft usu. pale brown cloth made from camels' hair. **2** hair from a squirrel's tail used to make paintbrushes.

camellia *n* **1** a tall, evergreen, shiny-leaved shrub from eastern Asia that bears large white, red or pink flowers. **2** one of these flowers. [Josef *Kamel*, 17th-cent. plant-collector]

Camembert *n* a kind of soft white French cheese with a strong flavour and smell. [*Camembert* in N France, where orig. made]

cameo *n* **-os 1** a smooth rounded gemstone with a raised design, esp. a head in profile, carved on it. ◇ See also **intaglio**. **2** a piece of jewellery containing such a gemstone. **3** the design itself. **4** (also **cameo role**) a small part in a play or film performed by a well-known actor. **5** a short descriptive piece of writing. [Ital *cammeo* or *cameo*]

camera[1] *n* **1** an apparatus for taking still photographs or making moving films, with a lens through which light passes to form an image on light-sensitive film. **2** an apparatus that receives the image of a scene and converts it into electrical signals for transmission as television pictures. — **on camera** in front of the camera; being filmed. [Lat, vaulted chamber]

cameraman *n* a person who operates a camera in television or film-making.

camera-shy *adj* having a dislike of being photographed.

camera[2]: **in camera**. See **in camera**.

camera obscura *n* a darkened room with an opening through which the scene outside can be projected on to a screen. [Lat, dark chamber]

camiknickers *n* (*pl*) **1** loose-legged knickers for women, usu. of a silky material. **2** a woman's undergarment consisting of a camisole and knickers combined. [**camisole** and **knickers**]

camisole *n* a woman's loose undergarment for the top half of the body with narrow shoulder straps. [Fr]

camomile *n* **1** a plant with white or yellow sweet-smelling flowers. **2** the crushed flowers and leaves of this plant, used in drinks, etc., e.g. for medicinal purposes. [Gr *chamaimelon*, literally 'earth apple' (from its smell)]

camouflage *n* colouring used on military equipment, vehicles or buildings, or for soldiers' uniforms, that imitates the colours of nature and so makes them difficult for an enemy to see. **2** covering, consisting e.g. of tree branches or undergrowth, used to disguise military equipment, etc. **3** colouring on an animal or bird that blends with the animal's or bird's natural surroundings and makes it difficult to see. **4** devices of any kind used to disguise identity or make someone or something less distinguishable in particular surroundings. — *v* (*tr*) to disguise or conceal with some kind of camouflage. [Fr, from *camoufler*, to disguise]

camp[1] *n* **1** a piece of ground on which tents have been erected. **2** a collection of buildings, huts, tents, etc. used as temporary accommodation or for short stays for a particular purpose. **3** a permanent site where troops are housed or trained. **4** (*archaeol*) an ancient fortified site. **5** a party or side in a dispute, etc.; a group having a particular set of opinions, beliefs, etc. — *v* (*intr*) to stay in a tent or tents, cooking meals in the open, etc. — *n* **camping**. — **break camp** to take down tents, etc. when leaving a campsite. — *v* **camp out** (*intr*) **1** to live and sleep in the open, with or without a tent. **2** to stay in temporary accommodation with a minimum of furniture, equipment, etc. [Lat *campus*, field]

camp bed *n* a light folding bed consisting of a metal or wooden frame with canvas stretched across it.

camper *n* **1** a person who camps. **2** a motor vehicle equipped for sleeping in, with cooking and washing facilities, etc.

camp-follower *n* **1** (*derog*) a person who supports a particular group, party, etc. only because it is fashionable. **2** a person who travels about with an army or other moving group in order to earn money e.g. as a prostitute or by doing odd jobs for them.

campsite *n* a piece of land for camping on.

camp[2] (*coll derog*) *adj* **1** (of a man or his behaviour) using mannerisms that are typically associated with women, esp. in a deliberate, exaggerated or theatrical way. **2** (of a man) homosexual. **3** theatrical and exaggerated, esp. amusingly so. — *n* camp behaviour or style. — *v* **1** (*intr*) to behave in a camp way. **2** (*tr*; **up**) to make (something) camp. — **camp it up** to behave in an exaggerated, theatrical way; to overact.

campaign *n* **1** an organised series of actions to gain support for or build up opposition to a particular practice, group, etc. **2** the operations of an army while fighting in a particular area or to achieve a particular goal or objective. — *v* (*intr*; **for, against**) to organise, or take part in, a campaign in support of or against something. — *n* **campaigner**. [Fr *campagne*, countryside, campaign]

campanile *n* a bell tower standing by itself, i.e. not attached to a church, etc., found esp. in Italy. [Ital, from Lat *campana*, bell]

campanology *n* **1** the art of bell-ringing. **2** the study of bells. — *n* **campanologist**. [Lat *campana*, bell + **-logy**]

campanula *n* a tall plant with bell-shaped white or blue flowers. [Dimin. of Lat *campana*, bell]

camphor *n* a strong-smelling oil in solid form obtained from a type of laurel tree or made artificially, used in ointments, etc. and in industry, e.g. in manufacturing celluloid. [Lat *camphora*]

camphorated *adj* containing camphor.

campion *n* a wild plant with small red, pink, or white flowers with notched petals. [Old form of **champion**, translating *stephanomatikos*, part of the Gr name meaning 'for making champions' wreaths']

campus *n* **1** the grounds of a college or university. **2** a university, or the university as an institution. **3** the academic world. — **on campus** within university premises or grounds. [Lat, field]

CAMRA *abbrev* Campaign for Real Ale.

can[1] *v* (*aux*) **1** to be able to: *Can you lift that?* **2** to know how to: *Can he swim yet?* **3** to feel able to; to feel it right to: *How can you believe that?* **4** used to express surprise: *Can it really be that late?* **5** used to express a possibility: *The weather can change so quickly in the mountains.* **6** to have permission to: *Can I take an apple?* **7** used when asking for help, etc.: *Can you give me the time?* ◇ See also **cannot, can't, could** and **couldn't**. [OE *cunnan*, to know]

can[2] *n* **1** a sealed metal container in which food and drink can be preserved for sale. **2** a large container made of metal or another material, for holding liquids. **3** (also **canful**, ***-fuls***) the amount contained in a can. **4** (*slang*) prison. **5** (*US slang*) a toilet. — *v* ***-nn-*** (*tr*) to put (food or drink) into cans to preserve it.— **carry the can**

(*coll*) to take the blame. — **in the can** (*coll*) completed; finished. [OE *canne*, pot, can]
canned *adj* **1** contained or preserved in cans. **2** (*slang*) drunk. **3** (*coll*) previously recorded.
cannery *n* **-ies** a factory where goods are canned.
can-opener *n* a small tool for opening cans.

Can. *abbrev* **1** Canada. **2** Canadian.

canal *n* **1** an artificial channel or waterway for ships, barges, etc., or for bringing water into a particular area, irrigating land, etc. **2** (*anat*) a tube-shaped passage in the body. [Lat *canalis*, water pipe, channel]
canalise or **-ize** *v* (*tr*) **1** to deepen, widen or straighten (a river) to stop it flooding or to allow shipping along it. **2** (**into**) to guide or direct into a useful, practical or profitable course. — *n* **canalisation** or **-z-**.
canal boat *n* a barge.

canapé *n* a type of food served at parties, etc. consisting of a small piece of bread or toast spread or topped with something savoury. [Fr]

canard *n* an untrue report or piece of news; a rumour, hoax, etc. [Fr, duck]

canary *n* **-ies** a small yellow singing bird of the finch family, often kept in a cage as a domestic pet. [*Canary* Islands, where the birds came from]

canasta *n* a card game played with two packs of cards, in which the aim is to collect sets of cards of the same value. [Span *canasta*, basket, into which rejected cards were thrown]

cancan *n* a lively dance orig. from Paris, usu. performed in the theatre by dancing girls, who execute high kicks, raising their skirts to reveal their petticoats, etc. [Fr]

cancel *v* **-ll- 1** (*tr*) to stop (something already arranged) from taking place, by an official announcement, etc. **2** (*tr*) to stop (something in progress) from continuing. **3** (*intr*) to withdraw from an engagement, etc. **4** (*tr*) to tell a supplier that one no longer wants (something). **5** (*tr*) to put an end to (an existing arrangement, rule, law, etc.). **6** (*tr*) to cross out, delete. **7** (*tr*) to put an official stamp on (e.g. a cheque or postage stamp) so that it cannot be re-used. **8** (*tr*; *math*) to strike out (factors common to both numbers) from the numbers above the line (numerator) and below the line (denominator) of a fraction, or take out (equal quantities) from either side of an equation. — *v* **cancel out** (*tr*) to remove the effect of, by having an exactly opposite effect. — *n* **cancellation**. [Lat *cancellare*, to cross out]

cancer *n* **1** an illness in which there are one or more diseased areas (tumours) in the body consisting of new cells growing in an irregular, uncontrolled way, which expand and multiply and may cause death. **2** one of these diseased areas. **3** an evil within an organisation, community, etc. that is gradually destroying it. — *adj* **cancerous**. [Lat, crab, cancerous growth]

Cancer *n* **1** the Crab, the name of a constellation (group of stars) and the fourth sign of the zodiac. **2** a person born between 22 June and 22 July, under the sign of Cancer. — *n* & *adj* **Cancerian**. [Lat, crab]
Tropic of Cancer see **tropic**.

candela *n* a unit of measurement of the strength or intensity of a source of light. [Lat, candle]

candelabrum *n* ***candelabra*** (sometimes used as a singular) or ***-brums*** a decorative candle-holder with branches for several candles. [Lat *candela*, candle]

candid *adj* **1** saying honestly and openly what one thinks; outspoken. **2** (of a photograph; *coll*) taken of someone without his or her knowledge so as to catch him or her unawares in an informal situation. — *adv* **candidly**. — *n* **candidness**. ◇ See also **candour**. [Lat *candidus*, shining white, pure, honest]

candidate *n* **1** a person who is competing with others for a job, prize, parliamentary seat, etc. **2** a person taking an examination. **3** (**for**) a person or thing considered suitable for a particular purpose or likely to suffer a particular fate. — *n* **candidacy**, **-ies** or **candidature**. [Lat *candidatus*; Roman candidates always wore white (Lat *candidus*)]

candle *n* a stick or block of wax or (esp. formerly) tallow, usu. long and cylindrical in shape but sometimes more ornamental, containing a wick that is burnt to provide light. — **burn the candle at both ends** to exhaust oneself with work or activity from early morning till late in the night; to try to do too many things. — **not fit** or **able to hold a candle to** to be very inferior to. — **not worth the candle** (of a task, etc.) not worth the trouble and effort it would take. [Lat *candela*]
candlelight *n* the light given by a candle or candles.
candlelit *adj* lit by candles.
candlestick *n* a holder for a candle.

Candlemas *n* a festival of the Christian church on 2 February celebrating the purification of the Virgin Mary after childbirth, at which candles are carried in procession. [OE *Cændelmæsse*, candle mass]

candlewick *n* a cotton fabric with a tufted surface formed by cut loops of thread, used for bedcovers, etc. [From the similarity of the thread used to a candle's wick]

candour *n* the quality of being candid; frankness and honesty. [Lat *candor*, purity, sincerity]

candy *n* **-ies** (*NAm*) **1** a sweet. **2** sweets or confectionery. — *v* (*tr*) **1** to reduce (sugar) to a crystalline form by boiling and evaporating slowly. **2** to preserve (fruit, peel, etc.) by boiling in sugar or syrup. **3** to coat or encrust with sugar or candied sugar. — *adj* **candied**. [OFr (*sucre*) *candi*, candied sugar, from Persian *qandi*, sugar]

candyfloss *n* a fluffy mass of spun sugar usu. coloured and served on a stick.

candy-striped *adj* having a pattern of (esp. pink or red) stripes on a white background.

candytuft *n* an evergreen plant with narrow leaves and white, pink or purple flowers. [*Candia*, in Crete, from where the plant was brought + **tuft**]

cane *n* **1** the hollow stem of any of several large plants of the grass or reed families, e.g. bamboo, or of one of the small palms. **2** short for **sugar cane**. **3** the stem of a raspberry plant. **4** thin stems or strips cut from stems, e.g. of rattan, for weaving into baskets, etc. **5** a walking-stick. **6** a long slim stick for beating people as a punishment, or for supporting plants. — *v* (*tr*) **1** to beat with a cane. **2** to construct or mend with cane. — *n* **caning**. [Gr *kanna*, reed]

canine *adj* **1** relating to, belonging to, or like, a dog. **2** relating to the dog family in general, including wolves and foxes. — *n* **1** an animal of the dog family. **2** a canine tooth. [Lat *canis*, dog]

canine tooth *n* any of the four sharp-pointed teeth situated one on each side of the front four top and bottom teeth in the human mouth.

canister *n* **1** a metal or plastic container for tea or other dry foods. **2** (*mil*) a metal cylinder filled with gas or metal shot, which explodes when thrown or fired. [Lat *canistrum*, basket]

canker *n* **1** a fungus that grows on trees and plants. **2** an ulcer that forms on the lips. **3** an ulcer inside a dog's or cat's ear. **4** a disease of horses' hooves that makes them soft and spongy. **5** an evil, destructive influence, etc. — *adj* **cankerous**. [OE, from Lat *cancer*, crab, ulcer]

cannabis *n* **1** a drug obtained from the dried leaves and flowers of the Indian hemp plant, that has a brief relaxing and elating effect. **2** the hemp plant itself. [Gr *kannabis*, hemp]

cannabis resin *n* the drug prepared for sale in solid form.

cannelloni *n* a kind of pasta in the form of large tubes, served with a filling of meat, cheese, etc. [Ital, from *cannello*, tube]

cannibal *n* **1** a person who eats human flesh. **2** an animal that eats others of its own kind. — *n* **cannibalism**. — *adj* **cannibalistic**. [Span *canibal*, from *Caribes*, the Caribs of the W Indies, once believed to be cannibals]

cannibalise or **-ize** *v* (*tr*; *coll*) to take parts from (a machine, vehicle, etc.) for use in repairing another.

cannon *n* ***cannon*** or ***cannons*** **1** (*hist*) a large gun mounted on wheels. **2** a rapid-firing gun fitted to an aircraft or ship. **3** a stroke in billiards in which the cue ball strikes the other balls one after the other; a similar stroke in other related games. — *v* **1** (with **into**) to hit or collide with while moving at speed. **2** (with **off**) to hit with force and bounce off (something). [OFr *canon*, from Ital *cannone*, from *canna*, tube]

cannonball *n* (*hist*) a ball, usu. of iron, for shooting from a cannon.

cannon fodder *n* (*coll*) soldiers regarded merely as material to be sacrificed in war.

cannonade *n* a continuous bombardment by heavy guns. [Fr *canonnade*, from Ital *cannonata*, cannon shot]

cannot *v* (*aux*) can not. ◇ See also **can't**. — **cannot but** see **can't**.

canny *adj* ***-ier***, ***-iest*** **1** wise, clever and alert, esp. in business matters; shrewd. **2** careful; cautious. **3** (*dialect*) (of a person) nice; good. — *adv* **cannily**. — *n* **canniness**. [**can**[1], in the sense of 'to know how']

canoe *n* a light narrow boat propelled by one or more single- or double-bladed paddles by an occupant or occupants facing the direction of travel. — *v* ***canoeing*** (*intr*) to travel by canoe. — *n* **canoeing**. — *n* **canoeist**. — **paddle one's own canoe** (*coll*) **1** to manage without other people's help. **2** to look after one's own affairs; to mind one's own business. [Span *canoa*]

canon[1] *n* **1** a basic law, rule, or principle. **2** an officially accepted collection of e.g. religious writings, or of works considered to be by a particular writer. **3** in the Christian church, a list of saints. **4** a section of the Roman Catholic mass. **5** a piece of music similar to a round, in which a particular sequence is repeated, with a regular overlapping pattern, by different voices or instruments. — *adj* **canonical**. [Gr *kanon*, rod, rule]

canonical hours *n* (*pl*) set hours for prayer. ◇ See also **compline, lauds, matins, none**[2]**, sext, terce, vespers**.

canonise or **-ize** *v* (*tr*) to declare (someone) officially to be a saint. — *n* **canonisation** or **-z-**.

canon law *n* the law of the Christian church.

canon[2] *n* a member of the clergy attached to a cathedral or, in the Church of England, a member of the clergy having special rights with regard to the election of bishops. — *adj* **canonical**. [OE *canonic*, from Lat *canonicus*, person under a monastic rule; see **canon**[1]]

canoodle *v* (*intr*; *coll*, slightly *humorous*) to hug and kiss; to cuddle.

canopy *n* ***-ies*** **1** a covering hung or held up over something or someone for shelter or ornament, or ceremonially. **2** a wide overhead covering. **3** (*archit*) a roof-like structure over an altar, recess, etc. **4** a transparent cover over the cockpit of an aeroplane. **5** the upper layer of cover provided by the topmost leaves and branches in a forest, etc. **6** the fabric part of a parachute, that opens like an umbrella. — *adj* **canopied**. [Lat *conopeum*, mosquito net]

canst (*old*) the form of the verb **can** used in the 2nd person singular with **thou**.

cant[1] *n* **1** (*derog*) insincere talk, esp. with a false display of moral or religious principles. **2** the special slang or jargon of a particular group of people, e.g. thieves. — *v* (*intr*) to talk in a preaching way. — *adj* **canting**. — *adv* **cantingly**. [Lat *cantare*, to chant]

cant[2] *n* **1** a slope. **2** a jerk or toss that makes something tilt. **3** a sloping or tilting position or plane. — *v* (*tr* & *intr*) to tilt, slope or tip up. [MidE, border, side]

can't short for **cannot**. — **can't but** or **cannot but** must; have to: *You can't but admire her perseverance.*

Cantab. *abbrev* for *Cantabrigiensis* (Lat), belonging to Cambridge.

cantabile *adj* (*mus*) in an easy, flowing, melodious style. [Ital, suitable for singing]

cantaloup or **cantaloupe** *n* a large melon with a thick, ridged skin and orange-coloured flesh. [Fr *cantaloup*, prob. from *Cantaluppi* in Italy, where first cultivated in Europe]

cantankerous *adj* bad-tempered; irritable. — *adv* **cantankerously**. — *n* **cantankerousness**.

cantata *n* a sung musical work, esp. on a religious theme, with parts for chorus and soloists. [Ital *cantata* (*aria*), sung (air)]

canteen *n* **1** a restaurant, esp. a cafeteria, attached to a factory, office, etc. for the use of employees. **2** a shop selling food and drink in an army camp, etc. **3** a case containing cutlery; a full set of knives, forks, spoons, etc. **4** a flask for water, etc. carried by soldiers or campers. [Fr *cantine*, a shop in a barracks, etc.]

canter *n* a horse-riding pace between trotting and galloping. — *v* ***-r-*** (*intr* & *tr*) to (cause to) move at this pace. [Orig. *Canterbury gallop*, the pace used by the pilgrims riding to Canterbury in the Middle Ages]

canticle *n* a hymn or chant with a text taken from the Bible. [Lat *canticulum*, dimin. of *canticum*, song]

cantilever *n* **1** a beam or other support projecting from a wall to support a balcony, staircase, etc. **2** a beam or girder that is fixed at one end only. [Poss. **cant**[2] + **lever**]

cantilever bridge *n* a bridge consisting of two cantilever supports that are joined in the middle.

canto *n* ***-os*** a section of a long poem. [Ital, song]

canton *n* a division of a country, esp. one of the separately governed regions of Switzerland. [OFr]

Cantonese *n* **1** the dialect of Chinese used in the Canton area of China. **2** (*sing* or *pl*) a person, or the people, belonging to Canton. — *adj* belonging to Canton.

cantonment *n* (*hist*) a permanent military station in India.

cantor *n* **1** a man who chants the liturgy and leads the congregation in prayer in a synagogue. **2** a person who leads the choir in a Christian church service. [Lat, singer]

canvas *n* **1** a thick heavy coarse cloth used for sails, tents, etc. and for painting pictures on. **2** a painting done on canvas, or a piece of canvas prepared for painting. **3** the sails of a ship. — **under canvas 1** in tents. **2** (*naut*) with sails spread. [OE *canevas*, from Lat *cannabis*, hemp]

canvass *v* **1** (*tr* & *intr*; **for**) to ask for votes or support from (someone) for a person or proposal. **2** (*tr*) to find out the opinions of, on a particular matter. **3** to discuss or examine (a question) in detail. — *n* **canvasser**. [From **canvas** in an old sense, to toss in a sheet, or to criticise severely]

canyon *n* a deep valley with steep sides; a gorge. [Span *cañón*, tube, hollow]

CAP *abbrev* Common Agricultural Policy.

cap *n* **1** a hat with a flat or rounded crown and a peak, of any of various types, some worn as part of a uniform or issued to members of a team. **2** a small hat of any of various shapes, many worn as an indication of occupation, rank, etc. **3** (usu. *in cmpds*) a close-fitting hat of various sorts. **4** a lid, cover or top, e.g. for a bottle or pen. **5** (also **percussion cap**) a little metal or paper case containing a small amount of gunpowder, that explodes when struck, used e.g. to make a noise in toy guns. **6** a protective covering fitted over a damaged or decayed tooth. **7** a covering or top layer: *icecap*. **8** the top or top part. **9** a person chosen for a team representing a country, etc., or the fact of being chosen for such a team. **10** (also **diaphragm** or **Dutch cap**) a contraceptive device consisting of a rubber cover that fits tightly over the woman's cervix (opening into the womb) and prevents the male sperm entering. — *v* ***-pp-*** (*tr*) **1** to put a cap on, or cover the top or end of, with a cap. **2** to be or form the top of. **3** to choose for a team by awarding a cap to. **3** to do better than, improve on or outdo: *cap someone's achievement*. **4** to set an upper limit to (a tax), or to the tax-gathering powers of (a local authority). — **cap in hand** humbly. — **if the cap fits, wear it** (*coll*) you can take the general criticism, etc. personally if you think it applies to you. — **set one's cap at** (*old coll*) (of a woman) to make obvious efforts to attract (a particular man). — **to cap it all** (*coll*) as a final blow; to make matters worse. [OE *cæppe*, from Lat *cappa*, hooded cloak]

cap. *abbrev* capital (letter).

capable *adj* **1** (with **of**) having the ability or the personality for: *capable of murder*. **2** clever; able; efficient. — *adv* **capably**. [Fr, from Lat *capabilis*]

capability *n* ***-ies*** **1** ability or efficiency. **2** a power or ability, often one that has not yet been made full use of.

capacious *adj* (*formal*) having plenty of room for holding things; large; roomy. —

adv **capaciously**. — *n* **capaciousness**. [Lat *capax*]

capacitance *n* (*electr*) (a measurement of) the ability of a system to store electric charge. [**capacity**]

capacitor *n* (*electr*) a device with a large capacitance. [**capacity**]

capacity *n* **-ies** **1** the amount that something can hold. **2** the amount that a factory, etc. can produce. **3** (with **for**) ability; power. **4** function; role. [Lat *capacitas*, from *capax*, capable, roomy]

caparison *n* **1** (*hist*) a decorative covering, harness, etc. for a horse. **2** (*formal*) a fine set of clothes. — *v* (*tr*) **-n-** **1** to put a caparison on. **2** (*formal* or *facet*) to dress up. [Span *caparazón*, saddle cloth]

cape[1] *n* **1** a short cloak. **2** an extra layer of cloth attached to the shoulders of a coat, etc. [Lat *cappa*, hooded cloak]

cape[2] *n* a part of the coast that projects into the sea. [MidE *cap*, from Lat *caput*, head]

the Cape **1** the Cape of Good Hope, the most southerly part of Africa. **2** Cape Province in S Africa.

caper[1] *v* **-r-** (*intr*) to jump or dance about playfully. — *n* **1** a playful jump. **2** (*old*) a playful trick or joke. **3** (*derog*) a scheme, activity, etc., esp. something dishonest or illegal. [Lat *caper*, goat, or short for **capriole**, goat-like leap]

caper[2] *n* **1** a prickly shrub of southern Europe. **2** one of its flower buds pickled for use as flavouring. [From the earlier form *capers* (mistaken as a plural), from Gr *kapparis*]

capercailzie or **capercaillie** *n* a large European grouse. [Gaelic *capull coille*, horse of the wood]

capillary *n* **-ies** **1** a tube with a very small diameter. **2** one of the very small blood vessels in the body that connect arteries with veins. — *adj* **1** (of a tube) having a very small diameter. **2** relating to capillarity. **3** hair-like.

capillarity *n* (also called **capillary attraction** or **repulsion**) the effect that causes liquids to rise up narrow tubes, and spread through, or be repelled by, solids. [Lat *capillus*, hair]

capita see **per capita** under **per**.

capital[1] *n* **1** the chief city of a country, usu. where the government is based. **2** a capital letter. **3** the total amount of money or wealth possessed by a person or business, etc., esp. when used to produce more wealth. — *adj* **1** principal; chief. **2** (of a letter of the alphabet) in its large form, as used e.g. at the beginnings of names and sentences. ◇ See also **upper case** under **case**[1] and **upper-case**. **3** (of a crime) punished by death. **4** (*Br old coll*) excellent. — *adv* **capitally** (*Br old coll*). — **make capital out of** to use (a situation or circumstance) to one's advantage. — **with a capital A, B, C**, etc. in a very real or genuine sense: *poverty with a capital P*. [Lat *capitalis*, from *caput*, head]

capitalise or **-ize** *v* **1** (*tr*) to write with a capital letter or in capital letters. **2** (*tr*) to sell (property, etc.) in order to raise money. **3** (*tr*) to supply (a business, etc.) with needed capital. **4** (*intr* with **on**) to use to one's advantage. — *n* **capitalisation** or **-z-**.

capital assets *n* (*pl*) the things a person or company owns that could be sold to raise capital.

capital expenditure *n* the money that a company, etc. uses to buy equipment, buildings, etc.

capital gains *n* (*pl*) money obtained from selling possessions.

capital-intensive *adj* (of an industry, etc.) needing a lot of capital to keep it going. ◇ See also **labour-intensive**.

capitalism *n* an economic system based on private rather than state ownership of businesses, factories, transport services, etc., with free competition and profit-making.

capitalist *n* **1** a person who believes in capitalism. **2** (*derog*) a wealthy person, esp. one who is obviously making a great deal of personal profit from business, etc. — *adj* believing in capitalism. — *adj* **capitalistic**.

capital punishment *n* punishment of a crime by death.

capital sum *n* a sum of money paid all at once, e.g. to someone insured.

capital transfer tax *n* in the UK, a tax on money or property that one gives to other people.

working capital *n* money used to keep a business, etc. going.

capital[2] *n* (*archit*) the slab of stone, etc., usu. ornamentally carved, that forms the top section of a column or pillar. [Lat *capitellum*, dimin. of *caput*, head]

capitation *n* a tax of so much paid per person. [Lat *capitatio*, poll tax, from *caput*, head]

capitulate *v* (*intr*) **1** to surrender formally, usu. on agreed conditions. **2** to give in to argument or persuasion. — *n* **capitulation**. [Lat *capitulare*, to set out (conditions) under headings]

capon *n* a male chicken that has had its sex organs removed and been fattened for eating. [Lat *capo*]

cappuccino *n* **-os** coffee with frothy hot milk and usu. chocolate powder on top. [Ital]

caprice *n* **1** a sudden change of mind for no good or obvious reason. **2** a sudden strange wish or desire. **3** the tendency to have caprices. **4** (*mus*) a lively composition in an original style. [Ital *capriccio*, fancy]

capricious *adj* often changing one's mind for no good reason; changeable in behaviour, mood or opinion. — *adv* **capriciously**. — *n* **capriciousness**. [Ital *capriccioso*, wayward, fanciful]

Capricorn *n* **1** the Goat, the name of a constellation (group of stars) and the tenth sign of the zodiac. **2** a person born between 23 December and 19 January, under the sign of Capricorn.— *n & adj* **Capricornian**. [Lat *caper*, goat + *cornu*, horn]
Tropic of Capricorn see **tropic**.

caps. *abbrev* capital letters.

capsicum *n* **1** a plant of tropical America bearing hollow seedy fruits. **2** the hot-tasting red, green or yellow fruit of this plant, called a pepper, used as a vegetable or flavouring. [Prob. from Lat *capsa*, box, case]

capsize *v* **1** (*intr*) (esp. of a boat) to tip over completely; to overturn. **2** (*tr*) to cause (a boat) to capsize. — *adj* **capsizable**.

capstan *n* **1** a cylinder-shaped apparatus that is turned to wind a heavy rope or cable, e.g. that of a ship's anchor. **2** one of a pair of shafts or spindles in a tape-recorder, round which the tape winds. [Provençal *cabestan*]

capsule *n* **1** a small container holding a dose of medicine, that is swallowed whole and dissolves to release its contents. **2** (also **space capsule**) a part of a spacecraft designed to separate and travel independently. **3** (*anat*) a thin-walled hollow structure enclosing a bodily organ. **4** (*bot*) a dry seed-case that splits to release the seeds. — *adj* **capsular**. [Lat *capsula*, dimin. of *capsa*, box]
capsulise or **-ize** *v* (*tr*) to present (information) in a very concise form. — *n* **capsulisation** or **-z-**.

Capt. *abbrev* Captain.

captain *n* **1** a leader, chief. **2** the commander of a ship. **3** the commander of a company of troops. **4** a naval officer below a commodore and above a commander in rank. **5** an army officer of the rank below major and above lieutenant. **6** the chief pilot of a civil aircraft. **7** the leader of a team or side, or chief member of a club. — *v* (*tr*) to be captain of. — *n* **captaincy**, ***-ies***. [OFr *capitain*, from Lat *capitaneus*, chief]

caption *n* **1** the words that accompany a photograph, cartoon, etc. to explain it. **2** a heading given to a chapter, article, etc. **3** wording appearing on a television or cinema screen as part of a film or broadcast. — *v* ***-n-*** (*tr*) to provide with a caption or heading. [Lat *captio*, act of seizing]

captious *adj* inclined to criticise and find fault. — *adv* **captiously**. — *n* **captiousness**. [Lat *captiosus*, arguing falsely]

captivate *v* (*tr*) to delight, charm or fascinate. — *adj* **captivating**. — *adv* **captivatingly**. — *n* **captivation**. [Lat *captivare*, to take captive]

captive *n* a person or animal that has been caught or taken prisoner. — *adj* **1** kept prisoner. **2** held so as to be unable to get away. **3** forced into a certain state or role. — *n* **captivity**. [Lat *captivus*, prisoner]

captor *n* the capturer of a person or animal. [Lat]

capture *v* (*tr*) **1** to catch, take prisoner. **2** to gain possession or control of. **3** to succeed in recording (a subtle quality, etc.): *The camera captured her smile.* — *n* **1** the capturing of someone or something. **2** the person or thing captured. — *n* **capturer**. [Lat *captura*]

Capuchin *n* **1** a monk belonging to one of the Franciscan orders. **2** (without *cap*) a S American monkey with thick hair resembling a hood. [OFr, from Ital *cappuccio*, hood]

car *n* **1** a motor vehicle, usu. four-wheeled, for carrying a small number of people. **2** (esp. *NAm* or *in cmpds*) a railway carriage or van. **3** a passenger compartment in e.g. a balloon, airship, lift or cable railway. [MidE *carre*, from Lat *carrum*, cart]
car park *n* a building or piece of land where cars can be parked.
car phone *n* a portable telephone for use in a car, operating by cellular radio. ◇ See **cellular radio** under **cellular**.
carport *n* a roofed shelter for a car, attached to the side of a house.
car-sick *adj* feeling sick as a result of travelling in a car. — *n* **car-sickness**.
car wash *n* a place at a petrol station, etc. fitted with automatic equipment for washing cars.

carafe *n* a wide-necked bottle or flask for wine, etc., for use on the table. [Fr, from Span *garrafa*]

carambola *n* a SE Asian tree, the fruit of which is known as star fruit. [Span]

caramel *n* **1** sugar boiled till slightly burnt, used for colouring or flavouring food. **2** a sweet made with sugar and butter. **3** a pale yellowish brown colour. [Fr, from Span *caramelo*]
caramelise or **-ize** *v* **1** (*tr*) to change (sugar) into caramel. **2** (*intr*) to turn into caramel. — *n* **caramelisation** or **-z-**.

carapace *n* **1** (*zool*) the thick shell that encloses the body of certain creatures such as the tortoise and lobster. **2** a layer of heat-resistant tiles covering a spacecraft. [Span *carapacho*, shell]

carat *n* **1** a unit of weight used for precious stones, equal to 0·2 grams. **2** a measure of the purity of gold, pure gold being 24 carats. [Arabic *qirat*, 4-grain weight, from Gr *keration*, carob bean, 3⅓-grain weight]

caravan *n* **1** a large vehicle fitted for living in, designed for towing by a motor vehicle or, esp. formerly, a horse. **2** (esp. *hist*) a group of travellers, merchants, etc. usu. with camels, crossing the desert in company for safety. — *v* ***-nn-*** (*intr*) to go travelling with, or stay in, a caravan. — *n* **caravanning**. [Persian *karwan*, company of travellers]
caravanette *n* (also **camper**) a motor vehicle equipped for living in.

caravan site *n* a place where caravans may be parked, permanently or temporarily, usu. with showers and toilets, a shop, etc.

caravanserai *n* in some Eastern countries, an inn with a central courtyard, for receiving caravans crossing the desert, etc. [Persian *karwansarai*, caravan inn]

caraway *n* a plant of Europe and Asia with small white flowers. [Arabic *karawiya*]

caraway seed *n* the small, strong-flavoured fruit of this plant, used in baking.

carbide *n* (*chem*) a compound of carbon with a metal. [**carbon** + **-ide**]

carbine *n* a short light rifle. [Fr *carabine*]

carbohydrate *n* any of a group of compounds of carbon with hydrogen and oxygen, esp. the sugars and starches which form the main source of energy in food. [**carbon** + **hydrate**]

carbolic acid *n* phenol, an acid obtained from coal, used as a disinfectant. [**carbon**]

carbolic soap *n* soap containing carbolic acid.

carbon *n* **1** an element (symbol **C**) that occurs naturally as diamond, graphite and charcoal, and is present in all organic matter. **2** a sheet of carbon paper. **3** a carbon copy. [Fr *carbone*, from Lat *carbo*, charcoal]

carbonaceous *adj* containing, or like, carbon.

carbonate *n* (*chem*) a salt of carbonic acid.

carbonated *adj* (of a drink) made fizzy by being filled with carbon dioxide.

carbon copy *n* **1** a copy of typewritten matter, etc. made using carbon paper. **2** (*coll*) a person or thing that looks exactly like someone or something else.

carbon dating *n* (*archaeol*) a scientific method of calculating the age of ancient articles by measuring the amount of one type of carbon (the radioactive isotope carbon-14) they contain.

carbon dioxide *n* a gas (CO_2) present in the air, breathed out by man and animals and used by plants in photosynthesis.

carbonic *adj* relating to carbon.

carbonic acid *n* a weak acid formed from carbon dioxide and water.

carbonise or **-ize 1** (*tr* & *intr*) to turn into or reduce to carbon, by heating. **2** (*tr*) to coat with carbon. — *n* **carbonisation** or **-z-**.

carbon monoxide *n* a poisonous gas (CO) with neither smell nor colour, formed by the incomplete burning of carbon compounds.

carbon paper *n* paper coated on one side with an ink-like substance containing carbon, placed between two or more sheets of paper e.g. on a typewriter so that a copy is made on the lower sheets of what is typed on the top sheet.

carboniferous *adj* **1** producing carbon or coal. **2** (*cap*; *geol*) relating to the period between 360 and 286 million years ago, when coal was formed. — *n* (*cap*; with **the**) the Carboniferous period. [**carbon** + **-ferous**]

carborundum® *n* silicon carbide, a very hard material made from sand and coke, used for grinding and cutting. [**carbon** and **corundum**]

carboy *n* a large round glass or plastic bottle used for storing dangerous acids, usu. with an outer case made of basketwork, etc. [Persian *qaraba*, glass flagon]

carbuncle *n* **1** a very large kind of pimple or boil on the skin. **2** a round red gem, a garnet in uncut form. [Lat *carbunculus*, dimin. of *carbo*, coal]

carburettor *n* a device that mixes petrol with air and controls the amount of this mixture that is taken into an engine. [Old word *carburet*, carbide]

carcase or **carcass** *n* **1** the dead body of an animal. **2** (*coll*, esp. *derog*) a living person's body. **3** the rotting remains of something, e.g. a ship. [OFr *carcasse*]

carcinogen *n* (*med*) a substance that tends to cause cancer. — *adj* **carcinogenic**. [Gr *karkinos*, crab, cancer + **-gen**]

carcinoma *n* (*med*) a diseased area in the body where there is an irregular growth of cells; a cancer; a tumour. [Gr *karkinos*, crab, cancer]

card[1] *n* **1** a thick stiff kind of paper or thin cardboard. **2** (also **playing card**) a rectangular piece of card bearing a design, usu. one of a set of 52, for playing games with. **3** a small rectangular piece of card or plastic, showing e.g. one's identity, job, membership of an organisation, etc. **4** a small rectangular piece of stiff plastic issued by a bank, etc. to a customer, used instead of cash or a cheque when making payments, as a guarantee for a cheque, for operating a cash machine, etc. **5** (*comput*) a piece of card on which information is stored in the form of punched holes or magnetic codes. **6** a piece of card, usu. folded double, bearing a design and message, sent to someone on a special occasion. **7** a postcard. **8** (*old coll*) an amusing person. **9** (*horse-racing*; also **racecard**) a programme of events at a race meeting. **10** (in *pl*) games played with playing cards. **11** (in *pl*) an employee's personal documents held by his or her employer. — **the card's are stacked against** (*coll*) the circumstances do not favour (someone or something) — **get one's cards** (*coll*) to be dismissed from one's job. — **have a card up one's sleeve** in an argument or contest, to have something to one's advantage that one's opponent is not aware of and that one can still make use of. — **hold all the cards** (*coll*) to have the stronger or strongest position of opposing parties; to have all the advantages. — **lay** or **put one's cards on the table** (*coll*) to announce one's intentions, reveal one's thoughts, etc. openly. —

on the cards (*coll*) likely to happen. — **play one's best, strongest** or **trump card** (*coll*) to make use of one's strongest advantage. — **play one's cards close to one's chest** to be secretive about one's intentions. — **play one's cards right** (*coll*) to make good use of one's opportunities and advantages. [Fr *carte*]

card-carrying *adj* **1** officially registered as a member of a political party, etc. and openly supporting it. **2** strongly supporting.

cardphone *n* a payphone in which calls are paid for with a phonecard. ◇ See also **cashphone.**

card-sharp or **card-sharper** *n* (*derog*) a person who makes a business of cheating at card games played for money.

card table *n* a small folding table, usu. covered with green cloth, for playing card games on.

card vote *n* (*Br*) a vote by representatives of bodies, each vote counting in proportion to the number of members represented.

card[2] *n* a comb-like device with sharp teeth for removing knots and tangles from sheep's wool, etc. before spinning, or for pulling across the surface of cloth to make it fluffy. — *v* (*tr*) to treat with a card. [MidE *carde*, teasel head]

cardamom, **cardamum** or **cardamon** *n* the seeds of a tropical SE Asian plant, used as a spice. [Gr *kardamomum*]

cardboard *n* a stiff material manufactured from pulped waste paper, used for making boxes, card, etc. — *adj* **1** made of cardboard. **2** (*derog*) (of e.g. characters in a play, etc.) not realistic or life-like. [**card**[1] + **board**]

cardiac *adj* relating to the heart. [Gr *kardia*, heart]

cardiac arrest *n* the sudden stopping of the heart.

cardiac massage *n* manual pressure applied over the heart with the rhythm of a heartbeat, to start the heart again after cardiac arrest.

cardigan *n* a long-sleeved knitted jacket that fastens down the front. [After the first wearer, the 7th Earl of *Cardigan*, 1797–1868]

cardinal *n* **1** one of a group of leading clergy in the Roman Catholic Church, who elect the pope and advise him, their official dress being bright red. **2** a cardinal number. **3** a N American songbird of which the male is bright red. **4** (also **cardinal red**) a bright red colour. — *adj* of the highest importance; principal or fundamental. [Lat *cardinalis*, principal]

cardinalate *n* **1** the rank or office of a cardinal. **2** the cardinals as a body.

cardinal number *n* a number expressing quantity, such as one, two or three, as distinct from a number expressing order, such as first, second or third. ◇ See also **ordinal number** under **ordinal.**

cardinal point *n* any of the four main points of the compass — north, south, east and west.

cardinal virtue *n* any of the most important virtues, usu. listed as justice, prudence, temperance, fortitude, faith, hope and charity.

cardio- *comb fm* belonging or relating to the heart. [Gr *kardia*, heart]

cardiogram *n* a reading obtained from a cardiograph, showing the movement of a heart. [**cardio-** + **-gram**]

cardiograph *n* an instrument for recording the movements of the heart. — *n* **cardiographer.** — *n* **cardiography.** [**cardio-** + **-graph**]

cardiology *n* the study of the structure, function, and diseases of the heart. — *n* **cardiologist.** [**cardio-** + **-logy**]

cardiovascular *adj* relating to both the heart and the blood vessels. [**cardio-** + **vascular**]

care *n* **1** attention and thoroughness. **2** caution; gentleness; regard for safety. **3** the activity of looking after someone or something, or the state of being looked after. **4** worry or anxiety. **5** a cause for worry; a responsibility. — *v* (*intr*) **1** to mind or be upset by something, or the possibility of something. **2** (**about**, **for**) to concern oneself about or be interested in. **3** (with **for**) to have a wish or desire for: *Would you care for a drink?* **4** to wish or be willing: *Would you care to come?* — **as if I**, etc. **care** or **cared** (*coll*) it doesn't matter to me, etc. — *v* **care for** (*tr*) **1** to look after (someone). **2** to be fond of or love (someone). **3** to like or approve of: *I don't care for mushrooms.* — **care of** (written **c/o**) written on letters, etc. addressed to a person at someone else's address. — **for all I**, etc. **care** (*coll*) without upsetting me, etc. in the least. — **have a care!** (*old*) be more careful, considerate, etc. — **I**, etc. **couldn't care less** (*coll*) it doesn't matter to me, etc. in the least. — **in care** being looked after by a local authority, etc., or in a hospital, etc., instead of at home. — **take care** to be cautious, watchful or thorough. — **take care of 1** to look after. **2** to attend to or organise. [OE *caru*, anxiety, sorrow]

carefree *adj* having few worries; cheerful.

careful *adj* **1** giving or showing care and attention; thorough. **2** (**with**) gentle; watchful or mindful; cautious. **3** (**of**) taking care (to avoid harm or damage). **4** (with **of**) protective. — *adj* **carefully.** — *n* **carefulness.**

careless *adj* **1** not careful or thorough enough; inattentive. **2** (**with**) lacking, or showing a lack of, a sense of responsibility. **3** effortless: *careless charm.* — *adv* **carelessly.** — *n* **carelessness.**

carer *n* the person who has the responsibility for looking after an ill, disabled or otherwise helpless person.

caretaker *n* a person employed to look after a public building, e.g. a school, or a house, e.g. if the owner is away. — *adj* taking temporary responsibility.

careworn *adj* worn out with, or marked by, worry and anxiety.

caring *adj* showing concern for others; sympathetic and helpful.

caring profession *n* a job that involves looking after people socially or medically.

careen *v* **1** (*tr*) to turn (a boat) over on its side for cleaning, etc. **2** (*intr*) (of a ship) to lean over to one side; to heel over. **3** (*intr*; *US*) (of a vehicle, etc.) to swerve or lurch violently from side to side. [Lat *carina*, keel]

career *n* **1** one's professional life; one's progress in one's job. **2** a job, occupation or profession. **3** one's progress through life generally. **4** a swift or headlong course. — *v* (*intr*; *coll*) to rush in an uncontrolled or headlong way. [Fr *carrière*, racecourse, career]

careerist *n* (*derog*) a person who is chiefly interested in his or her own advancement or promotion. — *n* **careerism**.

careers adviser or **officer** *n* in schools, etc., a person whose job is to help young people to choose a suitable career.

caress *v* (*tr*) to touch or stroke gently and lovingly. — *n* a gentle, loving touch; a gentle embrace. [Ital *carezza*]

caret *n* a mark (^) made on written or printed material to show where a missing word, letter, etc. should be inserted. [Lat, there is missing]

cargo *n* **-oes** the goods carried by a ship, aircraft or other vehicle. [Span, burden]

Caribbean *adj* relating or belonging to the West Indies, to the **Caribs** and other native people of this area, or to the sea (**Caribbean (Sea)**) between the West Indies and Central and S America. [Span *Caribe*, from the Arawak language of the W Indies]

caribou *n* **-bous** or **-bou** a type of reindeer found in N America. [Canadian Fr, from an American Indian language]

caricature *n* **1** a representation, esp. a drawing, of someone, with his or her most noticeable and distinctive features exaggerated for comic effect. **2** a ridiculously poor attempt at something. — *v* (*tr*) to make or give a caricature of. — *n* **caricaturist**. [Ital *caricatura*, from *caricare*, to distort]

caries *n* the gradual decay or rotting of teeth or bones. [Lat, decay]

carillon *n* **1** a set of bells hung usu. in a tower and played by means of a keyboard or mechanically. **2** a tune played on such bells. [Fr, from Lat *quaternio*, prob. a set of four bells]

carmine *n* **1** a deep red colour; crimson. **2** a red colouring substance obtained from the cochineal insect. [Fr]

carnage *n* great slaughter. [Fr, from Lat *carnaticum*, payment in meat]

carnal *adj* **1** belonging to the body or the flesh, as opposed to the spirit or intellect. **2** sexual. — *n* **carnality**. — *adv* **carnally**. [Lat *caro*, flesh]

carnation *n* **1** a plant with sweet-smelling red, white or pink flowers. **2** a deep pink colour. [Lat *carnatio*, flesh colour, from *caro*, flesh]

carnelian. See **cornelian**.

carnival *n* **1** a period of public festivity with e.g. street processions, colourful costumes, and singing and dancing. **2** a circus or fair. [Lat *carnelevarium*, prob. from *caro*, flesh + *levare*, to remove, the original carnival being Shrove Tuesday, the day before the start of the Lent fast]

carnivore *n* **1** any of a group of animals, including cats and dogs, with teeth specialised for eating flesh. **2** any flesh-eating animal or plant. — *adj* **carnivorous**. ◇ See also **herbivore**. [Lat *carnivorus*, flesh-eating]

carob *n* **1** an evergreen Mediterranean tree. **2** its edible brown pod. **3** the pod ground for use as a substitute for chocolate. [Fr *carobe*]

carol *n* a religious song, esp. one sung at Christmas in honour of Christ's birth. — *v* **-ll-** (*intr*) **1** to sing carols. **2** to sing joyfully. [OFr *carole*]

carol-singer *n* a person who sings carols, esp. in the streets at Christmas.

carotid or **carotid artery** *n* one of two large blood vessels in the neck that carry blood to the head. [Gr *karotides*, from *karos*, stupor, pressure on these arteries causing unconsciousness]

carouse *v* (*intr*) to take part in a noisy drinking party. — *n* **carousal**. [Ger *gar aus*, all out, i.e. completely emptying the glass]

carousel *n* **1** a revolving belt in an airport, etc. on to which luggage is unloaded so that passengers can collect it as it passes by. **2** a revolving case for holding photographic transparencies, for use in a projector. **3** (*NAm*) a merry-go-round. [Ital *carusello*, kind of ball game]

carp[1] *n* **carp** or **carps** a large edible fish of lakes and rivers. [MidE *carpe*]

carp[2] *v* (*intr*; **at**, **about**) to complain about, find fault with or criticise, esp. unnecessarily. — *n* **carper**. — *adj* **carping**. — *adv* **carpingly**. [Norse *karpa*, to boast, dispute]

carpal (*anat*) *adj* relating to the wrist. — *n* any of the group of bones in the wrist. ◇ See also **carpus**. [Gr *karpos*, wrist]

carpel *n* (*bot*) the female reproductive part of a flowering plant. [Gr *karpos*, fruit]

carpenter *n* a skilled workman in wood, e.g. in building houses, etc. or in making and repairing fine furniture. — *n* **carpentry** the work or skill of a carpenter. [Lat *carpentarius*, person who builds wagons]

carpet *n* **1** a covering for floors and stairs, made of heavy, usu. woven and tufted, fabric. **2** something that covers a surface like a carpet does. — *v* (*tr*) **1** to cover with, or as if with, a carpet. **2** (*coll*) to reprimand or scold. — **on the carpet** (*coll*) being scolded or reprimanded. [MidE *carpete*, from Ital *carpita*, woollen bed-covering]

carpet-bag *n* an old-fashioned travelling-bag made of carpeting.

carpetbagger *n* (*derog*) a politician seeking election in a place where he or she is a stranger; orig. a northerner in the southern US after the Civil War of 1861–5.

carpeting *n* **1** fabric for making carpets. **2** carpets generally.

carpet slippers *n* (*pl*) slippers, esp. men's, with the upper part made of carpeting or a fabric resembling it.

carpet-sweeper *n* a long-handled device fitted with a revolving brush, that picks up dust, etc. from carpets as it is pushed along.

carpus *n* **-pi** (*anat*) (the set of bones in) the wrist. ◇ See also **carpal**. [Gr *karpos*, wrist]

carrel or **carrell** *n* a small compartment or desk in a library, for private study. [MidE *carole*, enclosure for study in a cloister]

carriage *n* **1** a four-wheeled horse-drawn passenger vehicle. **2** a railway coach for carrying passengers. **3** the process or cost of transporting goods. **4** a moving section of a machine, e.g. a typewriter, that carries some part into the required position. **5** the way one holds oneself in standing or walking. [MidE *cariage*, from OFr *carier*, to carry]

carriage clock *n* a small ornamental clock with a handle on top, orig. used by travellers.

carriageway *n* the part of a road used by vehicles, or a part used by vehicles travelling in one direction.

carrion *n* dead and rotting animal flesh. [OFr *charogne*, from Lat *caro*, flesh]

carrot *n* **1** a usu. long and pointed orange-coloured root vegetable. **2** (*coll*) something offered as an incentive. [OFr *carrotte*]

carroty *adj* (*derog*) (of hair) of a strong reddish colour.

carry *v* **-ies -ied 1** (*tr*) to hold in one's hands, have in a pocket, bag etc., or support the weight of on one's body, while moving from one place to another. **2** (*tr*) to bring, take or convey. **3** (*tr*) to have on one's person. **4** (*tr*) to be the means of spreading (a disease, etc.). **5** (*tr*) to support: *The walls carry the roof.* **6** (*tr*) to be pregnant with. **7** (*tr*) to hold (oneself or a part of one's body) in a certain way: *carry oneself well.* **8** (*tr*) to bear (responsibilities, etc.). **9** (*tr*) to bear the burden or expense of: *We can't carry unprofitable enterprises.* **10** (*tr*) to do the work of (someone who is not doing enough) in addition to one's own. **11** (*tr*) to print or broadcast. **12** (*tr*) to stock or sell. **13** (*tr*) to have, involve, etc.: *a crime carrying the death penalty.* **14** (*intr*) (of a sound or something making a sound) to be able to be heard a distance away. **15** (*tr*) to pass or agree to by majority vote. **16** (*tr*) to win the support of (voters, an audience, etc.). **17** (*tr*) to bear the effects of: *He carries his age well.* **18** (*tr*) to take to a certain point: *carry politeness too far.* **19** (*tr*; *math*) to transfer (a figure) in a calculation from one column to the next. **20** (*intr*) (of a golf ball, etc.) to travel (a certain distance). **21** (*tr*; *mil*) to capture (a town, etc.). — **be** or **get carried away** (*coll*) to become over-excited or over-enthusiastic. — *v* **carry forward** (*tr*) to transfer (a number, amount, etc.) to the next column, page or financial period. — *v* **carry off** (*tr*) **1** to manage (an awkward situation, etc.) well. **2** to win (a prize, etc.). **3** to take away by force. — *v* **carry on 1** (*tr* & *intr*) to continue; to keep going. **2** (*tr*) to conduct or engage in (business, etc.). **3** (*intr*; *coll*) to make a noisy or unnecessary fuss (*n*, esp. *Br*, **carry-on**). **4** (*intr*; *coll*; **with**) to have a love affair (with). — *v* **carry out** (*tr*) to accomplish successfully. — *v* **carry over** (*tr*) **1** to continue on the following page, etc.; to carry forward. **2** to postpone. — *v* **carry through** (*tr*) **1** to help (someone) to survive a difficult period, etc. **2** to complete or accomplish. [OFr *carier*, from Lat *carricare*, to cart]

carrier *n* **1** a person or thing that carries. **2** a person or firm that transports goods. **3** a person or animal infected by a disease in such a way as to be able to pass it on to others without actually suffering from it. **4** a carrier bag.

carrier bag *n* a plastic or paper bag with handles, supplied to shop customers for carrying purchased goods.

carrier pigeon *n* a pigeon that carries messages.

carrycot *n* a light, box-like cot for a baby, with handles for carrying it.

carrying *adj* (of a voice) easily heard at a distance.

carry-on see **carry on** above.

carry-out *n* (*coll*) **1** (*US* & *Scot*) cooked food bought at a restaurant, etc. for eating elsewhere. **2** (*US* & *Scot*) a shop or restaurant supplying such food. **3** (*Scot*) (an) alcoholic drink bought in a shop or pub for drinking elsewhere.

cart *n* **1** a two- or four-wheeled, horse-drawn vehicle for carrying goods or passengers. **2** a light vehicle pushed or pulled by hand. — *v* (*tr*) **1** to carry in a cart. **2** (**around**, **off**, etc.; *coll*) to carry or convey. — **in the cart** (*coll*) in difficulties. — **put the cart before the horse** to reverse the normal or logical order of doing things. [Related to Norse *cartr*]

carthorse *n* a large strong horse bred for heavy work on farms, etc.

cartwheel *n* **1** the wheel of a cart. **2** an acrobatic movement in which one throws one's body sideways with the turning action of a wheel, putting one's weight on each hand and foot in turn. — *v* (*intr*) to perform a cartwheel.

carte blanche *n* freedom to do or organise things as one thinks best. [Fr, blank paper]

cartel *n* a group of firms that agree, esp. illegally, on similar fixed prices for their products, so as to reduce competition and keep profits high. [Fr, from Ital *cartello*, letter of defiance]

cartilage *n* a tough flexible substance found in the body, e.g. round the ends of the bones at joints and between the vertebrae in the backbone. — *adj* **cartilaginous**. [Fr, from Lat *cartilago*]

cartography *n* the art or science of making maps. — *n* **cartographer**. — *adj* **cartographic**. [Fr *carte*, chart + **-graphy**]

carton *n* **1** a plastic or cardboard container in which food of various types is packaged for sale. **2** a cardboard box. [Fr, pasteboard, from Ital *cartone*, strong paper]

cartoon *n* **1** a humorous drawing in a newspaper, etc., often ridiculing someone or something. **2** (also **animated cartoon**) a film made by photographing a series of drawings, each showing the subjects in a slightly altered position, giving the impression of movement when the film is run at normal speed. **3** (also **strip cartoon**) a strip of drawings in a newspaper, etc. showing a sequence of often humorous events. **4** a preparatory drawing of a subject done by an artist before attempting a large painting of it. [Ital *cartone*, strong paper, or a drawing on it]

cartoonist *n* an artist who draws cartoons for newspapers, etc.

cartridge *n* **1** a small case containing the explosive charge and bullet for a gun (a **blank cartridge** or **blank** containing the charge only, for use in practice). **2** the part of the pick-up arm of a record-player that contains the needle or stylus. **3** a tube containing ink for loading into a fountain pen. **4** a plastic case containing sound-recording tape, larger and more efficient than a cassette. **5** a plastic case containing photographic film, for loading directly into the camera. [From the earlier form *cartage*, a variant of *cartouche*, from Fr, cartridge]

cartridge belt *n* a wide belt with a row of loops or pockets for gun cartridges.

cartridge paper *n* thick rough-surfaced paper for drawing on.

carve *v* **1** (*tr*) to cut (wood, stone, etc.) into a shape. **2** (*tr*) to make (something) from wood or stone by cutting into it. **3** (*tr*) to produce (a design, inscription, etc.) in wood or stone. **4** (*tr*) to cut (meat) into slices; to cut (a slice) of meat. **5** (*intr*) to cut meat into slices. **6** (*tr;* **out**) to establish or create for oneself through personal effort: *carve out a career*. — **carve up** *v* **1** (*tr*) to cut up. **2** (*tr*; *coll*) to divide up or share out, esp. in an insensitive or brutal fashion (*n* **carve-up**). **3** (*tr; slang*) to attack and cut (a person) with a knife. — *n* **carving**. [OE *ceorfan*, to cut]

carver *n* **1** a person who carves. **2** a carving-knife.

carvery *n* **-ies** a restaurant where meat is carved from a joint for customers on request.

carving-fork *n* a large fork with two long prongs, for holding meat steady during carving.

carving-knife *n* a long sharp knife for carving meat.

carvel-built *adj* (of a boat) built with planks laid flush, not overlapping. ◇ See also **clinker-built**. [*carvel*, a type of ship]

caryatid *n* ***-atids*** or ***-atides*** (*archit*) a carved female figure used as a support for a roof, etc., instead of a column or pillar. [Gr *Karyatides*, priestesses of the goddess Artemis at Caryae in S Greece, or columns in the form of women]

Casanova *n* (usu. *derog*) a man with a reputation for having a lot of love affairs. [Giacomo *Casanova* (1725–98), an Italian famous for his success with women]

cascade *n* **1** a waterfall or series of waterfalls. **2** something resembling a waterfall in appearance or manner of falling. — *v* (*intr*) to fall like a waterfall. [Fr, from Ital *cascare*, to fall]

case[1] *n* **1** a box, container or cover, for storage, protection, carrying, etc. **2** a suitcase or briefcase. **3** (*printing*) a tray with compartments for type, the terms **lower case** for small letters and **upper case** for capital letters resulting from the traditional positioning of the trays containing those letters. — *v* (*tr*) **1** to put in a case. **2** (*slang*) to have a good look at (a house, etc.) with the intention of breaking into it and stealing. ◇ See also **case the joint** under **joint**. [Lat *capsa*, case for holding a scroll]

case-harden *v* (*tr*) **1** (*metall*) to harden the surface of (iron, etc.). **2** (usu. in *passive*) to make (someone) insensitive or callous.

casing *n* a protective covering, e.g. of rubber for electricity cables.

case[2] *n* **1** a particular occasion, situation or set of circumstances. **2** an example, instance or occurrence. **3** a person receiving some sort of treatment or care. **4** a matter requiring investigation: *The police are looking into the case*. **5** a matter to be decided in a law court. **6** (**for, against**) the argument for or against something, with the relevant facts fully presented. **7** (*gram*) the relationship of a noun, pronoun or adjective to other words in a sentence, or the form the noun, etc. takes which shows this relationship. **8** an odd character. — **as the case may be** according to how things turn out. — **be the case** to be true. — **a case in point** a good example, relevant to the present discussion. — **in any case** whatever happens; no matter what happens. — **in case** so as to be prepared or safe (if a certain thing should happen). — **in case of** if (a certain occurrence) happens. — **in that case** if that

happens, since that has happened, etc. [Fr *cas*, from Lat *casus*, fall]
casebook *n* a written record of cases dealt with by a doctor, etc.
case history *n* a record of relevant details from a person's past kept by a doctor, social worker, etc.
case law *n* law based on decisions made about similar cases in the past, as distinct from statute law established by the government.
case load *n* the number of cases a doctor, etc. has to deal with at any particular time.
casework *n* social work with individuals, in which family background and environment are closely studied.

casement or **casement window** *n* a window that opens outwards like a door. [MidE, from **case**[1]]

cash *n* **1** coins or paper money, as distinct from cheques, credit cards, etc. **2** (*coll*) money in any form. — *v* (*tr*) to obtain or give cash in return for (a cheque, traveller's cheque, postal order, etc.). — **cash down** (*colloq*) with payment immediately on purchase. — *v* **cash in** (*tr*) to exchange (tokens, vouchers, etc.) for money. — *v* **cash in on** (*tr*; *coll*) to make money, or profit in some other way, by taking advantage of (a situation, etc.). — **cash on delivery** (*abbrev* **c.o.d.**) with payment for goods immediately on delivery. — *v* **cash up** (*intr*; *Br coll*) (of a shopkeeper, etc.) to count up the money taken, usu. at the end of the day. [Back-formation from **cashier**]
cash-and-carry *n* a large shop where customers pay for goods in cash and take them away immediately. — *adj* (of a business, etc.) using this system.
cash book *n* a written record of all money paid out and received by a business, etc.
cash box *n* a box, usu. metal and with a lock, for keeping cash in.
cash card *n* a card, issued by a bank, etc., with which one can obtain money from a cash machine.
cash crop *n* a crop grown for sale, not for use by the grower.
cash desk *n* a desk in a shop, etc. at which one pays for goods.
cash flow *n* the amount of money coming into, and going out of, a business, etc.
cashless *adj* using payment by credit card or electronic transfer of money, rather than by cash or cheque.
cash machine or **cash dispenser** *n* an electronic machine, e.g. fitted into the outside wall of a bank, from which one can obtain cash using one's personal cash card.
cashphone *n* a coin-operated payphone, as opposed to a **cardphone**.
cash point *n* **1** the place in a supermarket, etc. where money is taken for goods purchased. **2** a cash machine.
cash register *n* a machine in a shop, etc. that calculates and records the amount of each sale and from which change and a receipt are usu. given.

cashew *n* **1** a small kidney-shaped nut. **2** the evergreen tropical American tree on which it grows. [Port *cajú*, from Tupí (S American Indian language)]

cashier[1] *n* the person in a business firm, etc. who receives, pays out, and generally deals with, the cash. [OFr *caissier*, from *caisse*, cash box]

cashier[2] *v* **-r-** (*tr*) to dismiss (an officer) from the armed forces in disgrace. [ODut *kasseren*]

cashmere *n* **1** very fine soft wool from a long-haired Asian goat. **2** a fabric made from this. [*Kashmir*, in N India, where shawls were woven from this wool]

casino *n* **-*os*** a public building or room for gambling. [Ital dimin. of *casa*, house]

cask *n* **1** a barrel for holding liquids, esp. alcoholic liquids. **2** the amount contained by a cask. [Back-formation from **casket**, the ending **-et** having been understood as a diminutive suffix]

casket *n* **1** a small case for holding jewels, etc. **2** (*NAm*) a coffin. [MidE]

cassava *n* a plant, orig. from tropical America. **2** flour or starch made from the roots of this plant, used in tapioca. [Span *cazabe*, from Taino (W Indian language)]

casserole *n* a dish with a lid, in which meat, vegetables, etc. can be cooked and served. **2** the food produced in such a dish. — *v* (*tr*) to cook in a casserole. [Fr]

cassette *n* **1** a small sealed plastic case containing magnetic recording tape, for use in a cassette-recorder or video equipment. **2** a small plastic case containing a photographic film, designed for quick loading into the camera. [Fr, from Ital *cassetta*, dimin. of *cassa*, box]
cassette recorder or **cassette-player** *n* a machine that records or plays material on cassette.

cassock *n* a long black or red garment worn in church by clergymen and male members of a church choir. [OFr *casaque*, type of coat]

cassowary *n* **-*ies*** a large flightless bird of NE Australia and New Guinea. [Malay *kasuari*]

cast *v* ***cast*** **1** (*tr*; esp. *old*) to throw. **2** (*tr*) to turn, direct, shed or cause to fall or arise: *cast doubt on*; *cast a shadow*; *cast one's eye over*; *cast a spell*. **3** (*tr* & *intr*) to throw (a fishing-line) out into the water. **4** (*tr*) to let down (an anchor). **5** (*tr*) to release from a secured state: *cast adrift*. **5** (*tr*) (of animals) to get rid of or shed (a skin, horns, etc.). **6** (*tr*; **off**, **aside**, **away** or **out**) to throw off or away; to get rid of. **7** (*tr*) to give (an actor) a part in a play or film; to distribute the parts in (a film, play, etc.). **8** (*tr*) to shape (metal, plastic, plaster, etc.) by pouring it in a molten or liquid state into a mould; to create (an object) by this means. **9** (*tr*) to give or record (one's vote). **10** (*tr*) to work out (a horoscope). **11** (*tr*; **up**) to add up (figures). **12** (*tr*) to present (work, facts, etc.) in a certain way. — *n* **1**

a throw; an act of throwing (dice, a fishing-line, etc.). **2** an object shaped by pouring metal, plastic, plaster, etc. in molten or liquid form into a mould. **3** (also **plaster cast**) a covering of plaster moulded, when wet, round a broken limb, etc. to support it while it heals. **4** the set of actors or performers in a play, opera, etc. **5** (*formal*) type, form, shape or appearance: *an analytical cast of mind.* **6** a slight tinge; a faint colour. **7** the slight turning inwards of an eye; a squint. **8** a coiled heap of earth or sand thrown up by a burrowing worm, etc. — *v* **cast about** or **around** (*intr*; **for**) to look about for, or try to think of: *cast about for ideas.* — *v* **cast away** (*tr*; usu. in *passive*) to cause (someone) to be abandoned on a remote piece of land after shipwreck, etc. — *v* **cast down** (*tr*; usu. in *passive*) to depress or discourage. — **cast one's mind back** to think about something in the past. — *v* **cast off** (*tr* & *intr*) **1** to untie (a boat) ready to sail away. **2** to finish off and remove (knitting) from the needles. — *v* **cast on** (*tr* & *intr*) to form (stitches, knitting) by looping and securing the wool, etc. over the needles. — *v* **cast up** (*tr*) **1** to mention (a person's past faults, etc.) to them, as a reproach. **2** (usu. in *passive*) to throw (a body, etc.) up on to a beach. [Norse *kasta*, to throw]

castaway *n* a person who has been shipwrecked.

casting *n* an object that has been cast from molten material.

casting vote *n* the deciding vote of a chairperson when the votes taken at a meeting, etc. are equally divided.

cast iron *n* iron that has been shaped in a mould when molten because its carbon content makes it too brittle to bend into shape. ◇ See also **wrought iron**. — *adj* (**cast-iron**) **1** made of cast iron. **2** very strong. **3** (of a rule or decision) very firm; not to be altered. **4** (of an argument, etc.) with no flaws, loopholes, etc.

cast-off *n* something, esp. a garment, discarded or no longer wanted. — *adj* no longer needed; discarded.

castanets *n* (*pl*) a musical instrument consisting of two small hollow pieces of wood or plastic attached to each other by string, held in the palm and struck together rhythmically, used esp. by Spanish dancers to accompany their movements. [Span *castañeta*, from *castaña*, chestnut, the wood used]

castaway. See **cast**.

caste *n* **1** any of the four hereditary social classes into which Hindus are divided. **2** this system of division into classes, or any system of social division based on inherited rank or wealth. — **lose caste** to drop to a lower social class. [Port *casta*, breed, race]

castellated *adj* (of a building) having turrets and battlements like a castle's. — *n* **castellation**. [Lat *castellare*, to fortify]

caster[1]. See **castor**[2].

caster[2] or **castor** *n* a closed container with holes in its lid, through which to sprinkle the contents, e.g. sugar or flour, over food. [**cast**]

caster sugar *n* finely crushed white sugar used in baking, etc.

castigate *v* (*tr*) to criticise or punish severely. — *n* **castigation**. [Lat *castigare*, to whip]

castle *n* **1** a large fortified, esp. mediaeval, building with battlements and towers. **2** (also **rook**; *chess*) a piece that can be moved any number of squares forwards, backwards or sideways. — *v* (*intr*; *chess*) to move the king two squares sideways towards either castle, and place the castle on the square the king has passed over. [Lat *castellum*]

castles in the air or **in Spain** *n* (*pl*) grand but impossible schemes; daydreams.

castor[1]. See **caster**[2].

castor[2] or **caster** *n* a small swivelling wheel fitted to the legs or underside of a piece of furniture so that it can be moved easily. [**cast**]

castor oil *n* oil from the seeds of a tropical plant, used as a lubricant and medicinally as a laxative.

castrate *v* (*tr*) **1** to remove the testicles of. **2** to deprive of masculinity or strength. — *adj* **castrated**. — *n* **castration**. [Lat *castrare*]

casual *adj* **1** happening by chance. **2** careless; showing no particular interest or concern. **3** without serious purpose or intention. **4** (of clothes) informal. **5** (of work, etc.) occasional; not permanent or regular. — *adv* **casually**. — *n* **casualness**. [Lat *casualis*, accidental]

casualty *n* **-ies** **1** a person who is killed or hurt in an accident or war. **2** (without **the** and often *cap*) the casualty department of a hospital. **3** something that is lost, destroyed, sacrificed, etc. as a result of some event. [**casual**]

casualty department or **ward** *n* the part of a hospital where casualties from an accident, etc. are attended to.

casuist *n* a person who uses cleverly misleading arguments, esp. to make things that are really morally wrong seem acceptable. — *adj* **casuistic**. — *n* **casuistry**. [Fr *casuiste*, from Lat *casus*, case]

cat[1] *n* **1** any member of a family of four-legged furry carnivores with claws and whiskers. **2** a small animal belonging to this family, kept as a domestic pet. **3** (also **big cat**) any of the larger members of this family, e.g. the tiger, lion and leopard. **4** (*derog coll*) a person, esp. a woman, with a spiteful tongue. **5** (*slang*) a person. **6** short for **cat-o'-nine-tails**. — **the cat's whiskers** or **pyjamas** (*coll*; usu. *ironic*) absolutely the greatest thing. — **fight like cat and dog** (*coll*) to quarrel ferociously. — **let the cat out of the bag** (*coll*) to give away a secret unintentionally. — **like a cat on a hot tin roof** or **on hot bricks** (*coll*) very nervous or uneasy. — **like something the cat brought in** (*coll*) messy, dirty, untidy or bedraggled in appearance. — **no room to swing a cat** far too little room. — **not have a cat in hell's chance** (*coll*) to have absolutely no chance. — **play cat and mouse with** to keep chasing and almost catching; to tease cruelly. — **put** or **set the cat among the pigeons** to do or say something that upsets everyone, causes a fuss, etc. — **rain cats and dogs** (*coll*) to rain very heavily. — **see which way the cat jumps** (*coll*) to wait and see how a situation develops before deciding how to react oneself. [Lat *cattus*]

cat burglar *n* a burglar who breaks into buildings by climbing walls, water pipes, etc.

catcall *n* a long shrill whistle expressing disagreement or disapproval.

catfish *n* a large fish with whisker-like growths round its mouth.

catgut *n* a string-like material produced from the dried intestines of sheep, etc., used in surgery for stitching, and for stringing violins and (now rarely) tennis racquets.

catnap *n* a short sleep. — *v* ***-pp-*** (*intr*) to doze; to sleep briefly, esp. without lying down.

cat-o'-nine-tails *n* (*hist*) a whip with nine knotted rope lashes, used as an instrument of punishment in the navy.

cat's cradle *n* a game with a long piece of string, which is looped over the fingers and passed from person to person in a series of changing patterns.

cat's eye *n* **1** (*cap*; ®) a small glass reflecting device, set into the road surface to guide drivers. **2** a type of precious stone.

cat's paw *n* a person used by someone else to perform an unpleasant job.

catsuit *n* a woman's close-fitting garment, combining trousers and top.

catwalk *n* **1** a narrow walkway, usu. at a high level, e.g. alongside a bridge. **2** the narrow raised stage along which models walk at a fashion show.

cat^2 *n* (*coll*) a *cat*alytic converter.

cataclysm *n* **1** an event causing tremendous change or upheaval. **2** a terrible flood or other disaster. — *adj* **cataclysmic**. [Gr *kataklysmos*, flood]

catacomb *n* (usu. in *pl*) a system of underground tunnels containing burial places. [Lat *catacumbas*]

catafalque *n* a platform on which the coffin of a king or other important person is placed for the lying-in-state or funeral. [Fr, from Ital *catafalco*]

catalepsy *n* a state of unconsciousness with complete rigidity of the body, as in a hypnotic trance or severe mental illness. — *adj* **cataleptic**. [Gr *katalepsis*, seizing]

catalogue *n* **1** a list of items arranged in a systematic order, esp. alphabetically. **2** a brochure, booklet, etc. containing a list of goods for sale. **3** a list or index of all the books in a library. **4** a series of things mentioned one by one as though in a list: *the catalogue of his faults*. — *v* (*tr*) **1** to make a catalogue of (a library, books, etc.). **2** to enter (an item) in a catalogue. **3** to list or mention one by one: *He catalogued her virtues*. — *n* **cataloguer**. [Gr *katalegein*, to reckon up]

catalysis *n* the speeding up of a chemical reaction by use of a catalyst. — *adj* **catalytic**. [Gr, breaking up]

catalyse or **catalyze** *v* (*tr*) to speed up (a chemical reaction) by catalysis; to act on by catalysis.

catalyst *n* **1** a substance that causes or speeds up a chemical reaction without going through a chemical change itself. **2** something or someone that causes, or speeds up the pace of, change.

catalytic converter *n* (*coll abbrev* **cat**) a device fitted to the exhaust of a motor vehicle, containing a catalyst that converts exhaust gases into compounds thought to be less harmful to the environment.

catalytic cracker *n* an industrial plant in which the breaking down of petroleum is speeded up by the use of a catalyst.

catamaran *n* **1** a sailing-boat with two hulls lying parallel to each other, joined across the top by the deck. **2** a raft made of logs or boats lashed together. [Tamil *kattumaram*, tied wood]

cataplexy *n* a sudden temporary paralysis, caused by severe shock. — *adj* **cataplectic**. [Gr *kataplexis*, astonishment]

catapult *n* **1** a Y-shaped stick with an elastic or rubber band fitted between its prongs, used esp. by children for firing stones, etc. **2** (*hist*) a weapon of war designed to fire boulders. **3** an apparatus on an aircraft-carrier for launching aircraft. — *v* **1** (*tr*) to fire or send flying with, or as if with, a catapult. **2** (*intr*) to be sent flying as if from a catapult. [Gr *kata*, against + *pallein*, to throw]

cataract *n* **1** a condition of the eye in which the lens becomes progressively clouded, eventually causing blindness. **2** the clouded area on the lens. **3** a huge, spectacular waterfall. **4** a cascade or downpour. [Gr *katarraktes*, waterfall]

catarrh *n* inflammation of the lining of the nose and throat, causing a discharge of thick mucus. — *adj* **catarrhal**. [Gr *kata*, down + *rheein*, to flow]

catastrophe *n* **1** a terrible blow or calamity. **2** a great disaster, causing destruction, loss of life, etc. **3** a disastrous ending or conclusion. **4** a violent event in the geological history of the earth. — *adj* **catastrophic**. — *adv* **catastrophically**. [Gr, overturning, conclusion]

catatonia *n* a form of the mental illness schizophrenia with periods both of rigid immobility and violent activity. — *adj* **catatonic**. [Gr *kata*, down + *tonos*, tension]

catch *v* ***caught*** **1** (*tr*) to stop (a moving object) and hold it. **2** (*tr*) to manage to get hold of or trap, esp. after a hunt or chase. **3** (*tr*) to be in time to get, reach, see, etc.: *catch the last post*. **4** (*tr*) to overtake or draw level with. **5** (*tr*) to discover so as to prevent, or to encourage, the development of: *The disease can be cured if caught early. Catch children young for athletic training.* **6** (*tr*) to surprise (someone) doing something wrong or embarrassing. **7** (*tr*) to trick or trap. **8** (*tr*) to become infected with. **9** (*tr* & *intr*) to (cause to) get accidentally attached or held: *My dress caught on a nail.* **10** (*tr*) to hit. **11** (*tr*) to manage to hear, see or understand. **12** (*tr*) to attract (attention, etc.): *catch her eye*. **13** (*intr*) to start burning. **14** (*tr*) to succeed in recording (a subtle quality, etc.): *The artist perfectly caught her expression.* **15** (*tr*; *cricket*; usu. in *passive*) to put (a batsman) out by catching the ball he has struck before it touches the ground. — *n* **1** an act of catching. **2** a small device for keeping a lid, door, etc. closed. **3** something caught. **4** the total amount of e.g. fish caught. **4** a hidden problem or disadvantage; a snag; some unsuspected trick in a question, etc. **5** something or someone that it would be advantageous to get hold of, e.g. a certain person as a husband or wife. **6** a slight breaking sound in one's voice, caused by emotion. **7** a children's game of throwing and catching a ball. **8** (*mus*) a humorous round sung by two or three people. — **be caught short** see **short**. — **be** or **get caught up in** to be or get involved in, esp. unintentionally. — **catch me**, etc. or **you won't catch me**, etc. (*coll*) there's no likelihood of me, etc. (doing a certain thing). — *v* **catch at** (*tr*) to try to catch or hold; to hold on to briefly. — **catch fire** to start burning. — **catch hold of** to grasp or grab. — **you'll**, etc. **catch it** (*coll*) you'll, etc. be scolded, punished, etc. — *v* **catch on** (*intr*; *coll*) **1** to become popular. **2** (**to**) to understand. — *v* **catch out** (*tr*) **1** to trick into making a mistake. **2** to discover or take unawares in embarrassing circumstances. — **catch sight of** or **a glimpse of** to see only for a brief moment. — *v* **catch up 1** (*intr* & *tr*; **with**, **on**) to pursue and draw level with. **2** (*intr*; **on**) to bring oneself up to date with (one's work, the latest news, etc.). **3** (*tr*) to pick up or grab hastily. [OFr *cachier*, from Lat *captiare*, to try to catch]

catch-all *adj* (of a phrase in an agreement, etc.) covering all possibilities.

catch crop *n* a small, fast-growing crop, planted between the rows of, or the periods of growth of, a main crop.

catcher *n* (*baseball*) the fielder who stands behind the batter.

catching *adj* infectious.

catchment *n* **1** the collection of rainwater; the rainwater collected. **2** the population within the catchment area of a school, hospital, etc.

catchment area *n* **1** the area served by a particular school, hospital, etc., to which people within the area are expected to go. **2** the area of land whose rainfall feeds a particular river, lake or reservoir.

catchpenny *adj* (*derog*) poor in quality but designed to appeal to the eye and sell quickly.

catchphrase *n* a frequently used popular and fashionable phrase or slogan.

catch-22 *n* a set of circumstances by which one is permanently frustrated and from which one cannot escape, all possible courses of action either having undesirable consequences or leading inevitably to further frustration of one's aims.

catchword *n* **1** a much-repeated, well-known word or phrase. **2** either of the two words — the first and last on a page — printed in the top corners of e.g. a dictionary page as a guide. **3** a word — the first on a page — printed at the bottom of the previous page.

catchy *adj* ***-ier***, ***-iest*** (of a song, etc.) tuneful and easily remembered. — *n* **catchiness**.

catechise or **-ize** *v* (*tr*) **1** to teach by means of a catechism, or using a question-and-answer method. **2** to question (a person) very thoroughly. [Gr *katechizein*, to instruct orally]

catechism *n* **1** a series of questions and answers about the Christian religion, or a book containing this, used for instruction. **2** any long series of difficult questions, e.g. in an interview.

categorical *adj* (of a statement, refusal, denial, etc.) absolute or definite; making no exceptions and giving no room for doubt or argument. — *adv* **categorically**. [Gr *kategorikos*; see ety. for **category**]

categorise or **-ize** *v* (*tr*) to put into a category or categories; to classify. — *n* **categorisation** or **-z-**. [**category** + **-ise**]

category *n* ***-ies*** a group of things, people or concepts classed together because of some quality or qualities that they all have. [Gr *kategoria*, statement, affirmation]

cater *v* ***-r-*** (*intr*) **1** (with **for**) to supply food, accommodation or entertainment for. **2** (with **for**) to provide something for. **3** (with **to**) to indulge (esp. unworthy desires, etc.): *cater to the public's desire for sensation*. [MidE *acatour*, buyer, from OFr]

caterer *n* a person whose job is to provide food, etc. for social occasions.

catering *n* the job of a caterer.

caterpillar *n* **1** the many-legged worm-like larva of a butterfly or moth. **2** (usu. *cap*; ®; also **Caterpillar track**®) a continuous band or track made up of metal plates, driven by cogs, used instead of wheels on heavy vehicles for travelling over rough surfaces. **3** (usu. *cap*; ®) a vehicle fitted with such tracks. [Prob. OFr *chatepelose*, hairy cat]

caterwaul *v* (*intr*) **1** (of a cat) to make a loud high wailing noise. **2** to wail or shriek in this way.— *n* a loud high wail. — *n* **caterwauling**. [Formed from **cat**[1]]

Cath. *abbrev* Catholic.

catharsis *n* **-arses 1** the emotional relief that results either from allowing repressed feelings to surface, as in psychoanalysis, or from an intensely dramatic experience, esp. orig. a stage tragedy that inspires acute fear and pity in the onlooker. **2** (*med*) the clearing out or purging of the bowels. — *adj* **cathartic**. [Gr *kathairein*, to purify]

cathedral *n* the principal church of a diocese (the area presided over by a bishop), in which the bishop has his throne. [Gr *kathedra*, seat]

Catherine wheel *n* a wheel-like firework which is fixed to a post, etc. and which whirls round when set off. [After St *Catherine*, who escaped being martyred on a spiked wheel]

catheter *n* (*med*) a long narrow flexible tube inserted into a part of the body, esp. the bladder, to drain off fluids. [Gr *kathienai*, to send down]

cathode *n* **1** the negative electrode in an electrolytic cell, from which positive ions are discharged. **2** the positive terminal of a battery. ◇ See also **anode**. [Gr *kathodos*, downward way]

cathode rays *n* (*pl*) streams of negatively charged electrons issuing from the cathode of a vacuum tube.

cathode ray tube *n* a vacuum tube in which the electrons are made to act on a fluorescent screen (e.g. that of a television set) to produce an image.

catholic *adj* **1** (*cap*) relating to the Roman Catholic Church. **2** (*cap*) relating to the whole Christian church, or to the church before the East-West split of 1054, or to the Western church before the split caused by the Reformation. **3** (esp. of a person's interests and tastes) broad; wide-ranging. — *n* (*cap*) a member of the Roman Catholic Church. — *n* **catholicity**. [Gr *katholikos*, universal]

cation *n* (*electr*) a positively charged ion. ◇ See also **anion**. [Gr *kateinai*, to go down]

catkin *n* a silky or velvety spike of tiny flowers, growing on a birch, willow or hazel tree. [ODut *kateken*, kitten]

CAT scanner *abbrev* computer-assisted tomography scanner, an X-ray machine producing a three-dimensional picture on a computer screen.

cattery *n* **-ies** a place where cats are bred or looked after. [**cat**[1]]

cattle *n* (*pl*) cows, bulls and oxen. [OFr *catel*, property]

cattle cake *n* blocks of concentrated food for cattle.

cattle grid *n* a trench covered by a grid, taking up the width of a road, that can be crossed by wheeled vehicles, but not by cattle and sheep.

catty *adj* **-ier, -iest** inclined to talk spitefully about other people. — *adv* **cattily**. — *n* **cattiness**. [**cat**[1]]

Caucasian *adj* **1** relating to the *Caucasus*, a mountain range between the Black Sea and the Caspian Sea, representing the boundary between Europe and Asia. **2** (also **Caucasoid**) belonging to one of the light-skinned or white races of mankind. — *n* **1** (also **Caucasoid**) an inhabitant or native of the Caucasus. **2** a white-skinned person.

caucus *n* **-ses 1** (usu. *derog*) (a meeting of) a small dominant group of people taking independent decisions within a larger organisation. **2** (*US*) a group of members of a political party, or a meeting of such a group for some purpose.

caudal *adj* **1** (*anat*) relating to the area of the buttocks. **2** (*zool*) relating to, or like, a tail. [Lat *cauda*, tail]

caudate *adj* (*zool*) having a tail. [Lat *caudatus*, from *cauda*, tail]

caught. See **catch**.

caul *n* **1** the membrane in which the foetus is enclosed. **2** part of this sometimes found over a baby's head at birth. [OFr *cale*, little cap]

cauldron *n* a very large bowl-shaped metal pot for boiling or heating liquids. [OFr *cauderon*]

cauliflower *n* a variety of cabbage with an edible white flower, used as a vegetable. [From the earlier *colieflorie*, with spelling influenced by Lat *caulis*, cabbage, and **flower**]

cauliflower ear *n* an ear permanently swollen and misshapen by injury, esp. from repeated blows.

caulk *v* (*tr*) to fill up (the seams or joints of a boat) with tarred rope, called oakum; to make (a boat) watertight by this means. [Lat *calcare*, to trample]

causal *adj* **1** relating to, or being, a cause. **2** relating to cause and effect. — *adv* **causally**. [Lat *causalis*]

causality *n* **1** the relationship between cause and effect. **2** the principle that everything has a cause. **3** the process at work in the causing of something.

causation *n* **1** the relationship of cause and effect; causality. **2** the process of causing. [Lat *causatio*]

causative *adj* **1** making something happen; producing an effect. **2** (*gram*) expressing the action of causing. — *n* a causative verb. — *adv* **causatively**. [Lat *causativus*]

cause *n* **1** something which produces an effect; the person or thing through which something happens. **2** (**for**) a reason or justification. **3** an ideal, principle, aim, etc., that people support and work for. **4** a matter that is to be settled by a lawsuit; the lawsuit itself. — *v* (*tr*) to produce as an effect; to bring about. — **make common**

cause with to co-operate with, so as to achieve a common aim. [Lat *causa*]

'cause *conj* (*coll*) short for **because**.

cause célèbre *n* ***causes célèbres*** a legal case, or some other matter, that attracts a lot of attention and causes much controversy. [Fr, famous case]

causeway *n* **1** a raised roadway crossing low-lying, marshy ground or shallow water. **2** a stone-paved pathway. [OFr *caucie*, from Lat (*via*) *calciata*, limestone-paved (way)]

caustic *adj* **1** (*chem*) having a burning or corroding effect. **2** (of remarks, etc.) sarcastic; cutting; bitter. — *n* a caustic substance. — *adv* **caustically**. — *n* **causticity**. [Gr *kaustikos*, capable of burning]

caustic soda *n* sodium hydroxide, used in making soap and paper.

cauterise or **-ize** *v* (*tr*) to burn away (infected or damaged tissue in the body) using a caustic substance or hot iron. — *n* **cauterisation** or **-z-**. [Lat *cauterizare*, from Gr *kauter*, branding-iron]

caution 1 care in avoiding danger; prudent wariness. **2** a warning. **3** a reprimand or scolding for an offence, accompanied by a warning not to repeat it. **4** (*legal*) a warning from the police to someone suspected of an offence, that anything he or she says may be used as evidence. **5** (*old coll*) an amusing person or thing. — *v* ***-n-*** **1** (*tr* & *intr*; **against**) to warn. **2** (*tr*) to give (someone) a caution. [Lat *cautio*]

cautionary *adj* giving, or acting as, a warning: *cautionary remarks*.

cautious *adj* having or showing caution; careful; wary. — *adv* **cautiously**. — *n* **cautiousness**. **[caution]**

cavalcade *n* a ceremonial procession of cars, horseback riders, etc. [Fr, from Ital *cavalcata*, raid on horseback]

cavalier *n* **1** (*old*) a horseman or knight. **2** (*old*) a courtly gentleman. **3** (now *facet*) a man acting as escort to a lady. **4** (*cap*; *hist*) a supporter of King Charles I during the 17th-cent. English Civil War. — *adj* (*derog*) (of a person's behaviour, attitude, etc.) thoughtless, offhand, casual or disrespectful. — *adv* **cavalierly**. [Ital *cavaliere*, from Lat *caballarius*, horseman]

cavalry *n* ***-ies*** (*pl* or *sing*) **1** (esp. *hist*) (the part of an army consisting of) soldiers on horseback. **2** (the part of an army consisting of) soldiers in armoured vehicles. — *n* **cavalryman**. [Fr *cavallerie*, from Lat *caballarius*, horseman]

cave *n* a large natural hollow in a cliff or hillside, or underground. — *v* **cave in** (*intr*) **1** (of walls, a roof, etc.) to collapse inwards (*n* **cave-in**). **2** (*coll*) to give way to persuasion. [Lat *cavus*, hollow]

caveman *n* **1** (also **cave-dweller**) a person of prehistoric times, living in caves. **2** (*derog*) a man of crude, brutish behaviour.

caver *n* a person whose pastime is exploring caves.

caving *n* the sport of exploring caves.

caveat *n* **1** a warning. **2** (*legal*) an official request that a court should not take some particular action without warning the person who is making the request. [Lat, let him beware]

cavern *n* a large dark cave. [Lat *caverna*, from *cavus*, hollow]

cavernous *adj* **1** (of a hole or space) deep and vast. **2** (of rocks) full of caverns. — *adv* **cavernously**.

caviare or **caviar** *n* the roe of the sturgeon, a spiny fish of the northern hemisphere, used as food and considered a delicacy. [Perhaps Turk *havyar*]

cavil *v* ***-ll-*** (*intr*; **at, about**) to object to, or find fault with, unnecessarily; to complain about (trivial details). — *n* a trivial objection. — *n* **caviller**. [Lat *cavillari*, to scoff]

cavity *n* ***-ies*** **1** a hollow or hole. **2** a hole in a tooth, caused by decay. [Lat *cavitas*, hollowness]

cavity wall *n* a wall of a building constructed in two separate layers or partitions with a space between them.

cavort *v* (*intr*; often *humorous* or *derog*) to jump, prance or caper about.

caw *v* (*intr*) & *n* (to make) the loud harsh cry of a crow or rook. [Imit.]

cay. See **key**[2].

cayenne or **cayenne pepper** *n* a hot spice made from the seeds of certain types of capsicum, a tropical American vegetable. [Formerly *cayan*, from Tupí (S American language), changed by association with *Cayenne* in French Guiana]

cayman or **caiman** *n* ***-mans*** a S American reptile similar to an alligator. [Span *caimán*, from Carib, a W Indian language]

CB *abbrev* **1** Citizens' Band. **2** Companion of (the Order of) the Bath.

CBE *abbrev* Commander of (the Order of) the British Empire.

CBI *abbrev* Confederation of British Industry (an association of UK employers that researches and reports to the government on the needs, problems and plans of business organisations).

CBS *abbrev* Columbia Broadcasting System.

cc *abbrev* **1** cubic centimetre. **2** carbon copy.

CCTV *abbrev* closed-circuit television.

CD *abbrev* **1** compact disc. **2** civil defence, or Civil Defence (Corps), a voluntary organisation of civilians, active esp. in World War II, trained to cope with the effects of enemy attack. **3** *Corps Diplomatique*, (Fr) Diplomatic Corps, the body of diplomats in the service of any country.

Cd *symbol* (*chem*) cadmium.

cd *abbrev* candela.

Cdr *abbrev* Commander.

CD-ROM *abbrev* (*comput*) compact disc read-only memory, a facility allowing examination, but not alteration, of a text on compact disc.

CDT *abbrev* craft, design, technology.

Ce *symbol* (*chem*) cerium.

cease *v* (*tr* & *intr*) to bring or come to an end. — **without cease** (*formal*) continuously. [OFr *cesser*]

cease-fire *n* **1** a break in the fighting during a war, agreed to by both sides. **2** the order to stop firing.

ceaseless *adj* continuous; going on without a pause or break. — *adv* **ceaselessly**.

cedar *n* **1** a tall evergreen tree with spreading branches, needle-like leaves, and cones. **2** (also **cedarwood**) its hard, sweet-smelling wood. [Gr *kedros*]

cede *v* **1** (*tr*) to hand over or give up formally. **2** (*intr* with **to**) to yield or give way to: *cede to a higher authority*. [Lat *cedere*, to yield]

cedilla *n* **1** in French and Portuguese, a mark put under *c* in some words (e.g. *façade*) to show that it is to be pronounced like *s*, not like *k*. **2** the same mark used under other letters in other languages to indicate various sounds. [Span, a variant of *zedilla*, dimin. of *zeda*, z]

Ceefax® *n* a television information service provided by the BBC. **[see + facts]**

ceilidh *n* orig. in Scotland and Ireland, an informal gathering, esp. with entertainment in the form of songs, storytelling, instrumental music and dancing. [Gaelic, visit]

ceiling *n* **1** the inner roof of a room, etc. **2** an upper limit. **3** the maximum height that a particular aircraft can reach. **4** the height above the ground of the base of the cloud-layer. [MidE *celen*, to panel]

celandine *n* a small wild plant with glossy yellow flowers, similar to a buttercup. [Gr *chelidonion*, from *chelidon*, swallow, the flowering of the plant coinciding with the arrival of the swallows in spring]

celebrate *v* **1** (*tr*) to mark (e.g. a success or other happy occasion, a birthday or other anniversary) with festivities. **2** (*intr*) to do something enjoyable to mark a happy occasion, anniversary, etc. **3** (*tr*) to give public praise or recognition to, e.g. in the form of a poem. **4** (*tr*) to conduct (a religious ceremony, e.g. a marriage or Mass). — *n* **celebration**. — *n* **celebrator**. — *adj* **celebratory**. [Lat *celebrare*, to honour]

celebrant *n* a person who performs a religious ceremony.

celebrated *adj* famous.

celebrity *n* **-ies** **1** a famous person. **2** fame. [Lat *celebritas*, fame]

celeriac *n* a variety of celery whose turnip-like root is eaten as a vegetable. **[celery]**

celerity *n* (*formal*) quickness. [Lat *celeritas*]

celery *n* a plant with crisp juicy stalks eaten as a vegetable. [Fr *céleri*, from Gr *selinon*, parsley]

celestial *adj* belonging to, or relating to, the sky: *celestial bodies*. **2** belonging to heaven; heavenly; divine: *celestial voices*. [Lat *celestialis*, from *caelum*, the heavens]

celestial equator *n* (*astron*) the circle, lying in the same plane as the earth's equator, that intersects the celestial sphere.

celestial sphere *n* the apparent sphere of the heavens, on which the stars are seen as points.

celiac *adj* & *n* (esp. *US*). Same as **coeliac**.

celibate *adj* **1** unmarried, esp. in obedience to a religious vow. **2** having no sexual relations with anyone. — *n* a person who is unmarried, esp. because of a religious vow. — *n* **celibacy**. [Lat *caelebs*, unmarried]

cell *n* **1** a small room for an inmate in a prison or monastery. **2** (*biol*) the smallest unit of living matter, consisting of protoplasm (i.e. a nucleus surrounded by cytoplasm or 'cell plasm', covered by a thin skin or membrane). **3** (*electr*) a device containing electrodes and an electrolyte for producing electricity by chemical action; a battery. **4** one of the cavities or compartments in a honeycomb or in a structure similarly divided. **5** (*radio telecomm*) one of the small geographical areas into which a country may be divided for coverage by cellular radio, or a transmitter serving it. **6** a small group of people (esp. spies or terrorists) conducting their own operation within a larger organisation. **7** (*hist*) a tiny one-roomed dwelling used by a hermit. [Lat *cella*, room, small apartment]

cellar *n* **1** a room, usu. underground, for storage, e.g. of wine. **2** a stock of wines. — *v* **-r-** (*tr*) to store in a cellar. [Lat *cellarium*, storeroom, pantry]

cellarage *n* **1** the volume of cellar space in a building. **2** the cost of storing goods in a cellar.

cello *n* **-os** a stringed musical instrument similar to a violin but much larger, played sitting, with the instrument's neck against the player's shoulder. — *n* **cellist**. [Short for **violoncello**]

cellophane® *n* a thin transparent wrapping material. **[cellulose** + Gr *phainein*, to shine or appear]

cellular *adj* **1** composed of cells, or divided into cell-like compartments. **2** containing many cavities or holes; porous. **3** knitted with an open pattern. [Lat *cellula*, tiny cell or room]

cellular radio *n* a system of radio communication used esp. for car phones, based on a network of small geographical areas or 'cells', each served by a transmitter.

cellule *n* a very small cell. [Lat *cellula*, tiny cell or room]

cellulite *n* a type of body fat that has a dimpling effect on the skin, and is claimed to be difficult to get rid of by dieting. [Fr, cellulitis, the formation of fatty deposits under the skin]

celluloid *n* **1** a flammable type of plastic made from camphor and cellulose nitrate, used formerly in the manufacture of cinema film and X-ray film. **2** cinema film. [**cellulose** + **-oid**]

cellulose *n* the substance of which the cell walls of plants chiefly consist, an important ingredient in paper and used in the manufacture of synthetic fibres. [Fr *cellule*, tiny cell]

cellulose acetate *n* a cellulose compound, one form of rayon, also used in making modern cinema film.

cellulose nitrate *n* a cellulose compound, nitrocellulose, used e.g. in explosives.

Celsius *adj* according to, or relating to, the scale on a centigrade thermometer, in which the freezing-point of water is 0° and its boiling-point 100°. [Anders *Celsius* (1701–44), Swedish astronomer and inventor of the centigrade thermometer]

Celt *n* a member of one of the ancient peoples that inhabited most parts of Europe in pre-Roman and Roman times, or of the peoples descended from them, e.g. in Scotland, Wales and Ireland. [Gr *Keltoi*, Celts]

Celtic *adj* relating to the Celts or their languages. — *n* the group of languages spoken by the Celts, including Gaelic, Irish, Manx, Welsh, Cornish and Breton.

cement *n* **1** a grey powder consisting of clay and lime, to which sand and water are added to produce mortar or concrete. **2** any of various types of glue that set hard. **3** a material used by dentists to fill holes in teeth. — *v* (*tr*) **1** to stick together with cement. **2** to cover with cement. **3** to bind or make firm (e.g. a friendship). [OFr *ciment*, from Lat *caementum*, quarried stone]

cemetery *n* **-ies** a burial ground for the dead, esp. one that is not attached to a church. [Gr *koimeterion*, sleeping-room, burial place]

cenotaph *n* a tomb-like monument in honour of a person or people buried elsewhere, esp. soldiers killed in war. [Gr *kenos*, empty + *taphos*, tomb]

censer *n* a container in which incense is burnt, used e.g. in some churches. [Lat *incensarium*]

censor *n* an offical who examines books, films, newspaper articles, etc. and has the power to cut out any parts thought undesirable (e.g. because containing information a government wants kept secret) or offensive (e.g. because over-violent or sexually too explicit), and to forbid publication or showing altogether. — *v* (*tr*) to alter or cut out parts of, or forbid publication, showing or delivery of. — *adj* **censorial**. [Lat, a Roman official empowered to punish moral and political offences]

censorship *n* **1** the practice of censoring. **2** the job of a censor.

censorious *adj* inclined to find fault; severely critical. — *adv* **censoriously**. — *n* **censoriousness**. [Lat *censorius*, relating to a censor, hence severe]

censure *n* severe criticism or disapproval. — *v* (*tr*) to criticise severely or express strong disapproval of. — *adj* **censurable**. [Fr, from Lat *censura*, the job of a censor, hence judgement, esp. severe]

census *n* **1** an official count, carried out at intervals, of a population, covering information such as sex, age, job, etc. **2** an official count made of something else, e.g. vehicles using a particular road. [Lat, from *censere*, to assess]

cent *n* (a coin worth) a hundredth fraction of the standard currency unit of several countries, e.g. the US dollar. [Lat *centum*, a hundred]

cent. *abbrev* **1** century. **2** centigrade. **3** central.

centaur *n* (*Gr mythol*) a creature with a man's head, arms and trunk joined to the four-legged body of a horse. [Gr *kentauros*]

centenarian *n* a person who is 100 years old or more. — *adj* **1** 100 years old or more. **2** relating to a centenarian. [Lat *centenarius*, composed of 100]

centenary *n* **-ies** the 100th anniversary of some event, or the celebration of it. — *adj* **1** occurring every 100 years. **2** relating to a period of 100 years. [Lat *centenarius*, composed of 100]

centennial *n* (esp. *NAm*) a centenary. — *adj* **1** relating to a period of 100 years. **2** occurring every 100 years. **3** lasting 100 years. [Lat *centum*, 100 + *-ennial* as in **biennial**]

centi- *comb fm* 100. [Lat *centum*, 100]

centigrade *adj* **1** (of a scale) having or based on 100 degrees. **2** same as **Celsius**. [Lat *centum*, 100 + *gradus*, step]

centime *n* (a coin worth) a 100th part of the standard currency unit of several countries, e.g. the French franc. [OFr *centiesme*, from Lat *centesimum*, a 100th]

centimetre *n* the 100th part of a metre.

centipede *n* a small insect-like creature with a long, many-sectioned body, each section having a pair of legs. [**centi-** + Lat *pes*, foot]

central *adj* **1** at, or forming, the centre of something. **2** near the centre of a city, etc.; easy to reach. **3** principal or most important. — *n* **centrality**. — *adv* **centrally**. [Lat *centralis*, from *centrum*, centre]

central bank *n* a national bank acting as banker to the government, issuing currency and having control over interest rates.

central government *n* the government that has power over a whole country, as distinct from local government.

central heating *n* a system for heating a whole building, by means of pipes, radiators, etc. connected to a central source of heat. — *adj* **centrally-heated**.

centralise or **-ize** *v* (*tr* & *intr*) to bring under central control. — *n* **centralisation** or **-z-**.

centralism *n* the policy of bringing the administration of a country under central control, with a decrease in local administrative power. — *n* & *adj* **centralist**.

central nervous system *n* the brain and the spinal cord.

central processing unit *n* the part of a computer that performs arithmetical and logical operations on data, and controls the other units contained in the system.

central reservation *n* (*Br*) a narrow strip of grass, concrete, etc. dividing the two sides of a dual carriageway, esp. a motorway.

centre *n* **1** a part at the middle of something: *chocolates with soft centres.* **2** a point inside a circle or sphere that is an equal distance from all points on the circumference or surface, or a point on a line at an equal distance from either end. **3** a point or axis round which a body revolves or rotates. **4** a central area. **5** a place where a particular activity is concentrated or particular facilities, information, etc. are available: *a sports centre.* **6** something that acts as a focus: *the centre of attraction.* **7** a point from which activities radiate and are controlled: *the centre of operations.* **8** a position that is at neither extreme, esp. in politics. **9** in some playing-field sports, a position in the middle of the field, or a player in this position. — *adj* at the centre; central. — *v* **1** (*tr*) to place in or at the centre; to position centrally or symmetrically. **2** (*tr*) to adjust or focus (e.g. one's thoughts). **3** (*intr* & *tr* with **on, upon**) to concentrate on. [Lat *centrum*, from Gr *kentron*, sharp point, the point round which a circle is drawn]

centreboard *n* in a sailing boat or dinghy, a movable plate that can be let down through the keel to prevent sideways drift.

centrefold *n* (also **centre spread**) the sheet that forms the two central facing pages of a magazine, etc., or a picture, etc. occupying it.

centre-forward and **centre-half** *n* in some playing-field sports, the positions in the centre of the front line and of the half-back line respectively, or the players in these positions.

centre of gravity *n* the point on a body at which it balances.

centrepiece *n* **1** a central or most important item. **2** an ornament or decoration for the centre of a table.

centri- *comb fm* centre, middle. [Lat *centrum*, centre]

-centric *comb fm* having a stated centre, focus, basis, etc.

centrifugal *adj* **1** tending to move away from a centre, used esp. of the force that appears to keep a circling body away from the centre it is revolving round. **2** (of a machine, etc.) operating by means of centrifugal force. [**centri-** + Lat *fugere*, to flee]

centrifuge *n* a machine that uses centrifugal force to separate e.g. the liquid and solid contents of a mixture by spinning it very fast. [**centri-** + Lat *fugere*, to flee]

centripetal *adj* tending to move towards a centre. [**centri-** + Lat *petere*, to seek]

centrist *n* & *adj* (a person) having moderate, non-extreme political opinions. — *n* **centrism**. [**centre** + **-ist**]

centurion *n* (*hist*) in the army of ancient Rome, an officer in charge of a century. [Lat *centurio*, from *centum*, a hundred]

century *n* ***-ies*** **1** any of the 100-year periods counted forwards or backwards from an important event, esp. the birth of Christ. **2** a period of 100 years. **3** in the game of cricket, 100 runs made by a batsman in a single innings. **4** (*hist*) in the army of ancient Rome, a company of (orig.) 100 foot soldiers. Lat *centuria*, unit of 100 parts]

cephalic *adj* relating to the head. [Gr *kephale*, head]

cephalopod *n* any of a group of sea creatures, including the octopus, squid and cuttlefish, consisting of a head and a ring of tentacles equipped with suckers. [Gr *kephale*, head + *pous*, foot]

ceramic *adj* relating to or made of pottery. [Gr *keramos*, potter's clay]

ceramics *n* **1** (*sing*) the art of making pottery. **2** (*pl*) articles made of pottery.

cereal *n* **1** any plant that yields an edible grain. **2** the grain produced. **3** a breakfast food prepared from grain. — *adj* relating to edible grains. [Lat *Cerealis*, relating to *Ceres*, goddess of agriculture]

cerebellum *n* ***-ums*** or ***-a*** the smaller section of the brain at the back of the skull, by which voluntary movement is controlled. — *adj* **cerebellar**. [Lat, dimin. of *cerebrum*, brain]

cerebral *adj* **1** relating to the brain. **2** (esp. *facet*) requiring the use of, or using, the brain, esp. too much: *a cerebral play.* [**cerebrum**]

cerebral haemorrhage *n* bleeding in the brain from a burst blood vessel.

cerebral hemisphere *n* either of the two halves of the cerebrum.

cerebral palsy *n* weakness in or poor control over muscles, caused by brain damage before or during birth.

cerebrate *v* (*intr*; *facet*) to think; to use one's brain. — *n* **cerebration**. [**cerebrum**]

cerebrum *n* ***-brums*** or ***-bra*** the brain, esp. the larger, front section, which controls thinking, emotions and personality. [Lat]

ceremonial *adj* relating to, used for, or involving a ceremony. — *adv* **ceremonially**. [Lat *caerimonia*, rite]

ceremonious *adj* elaborately formal. — *adv* **ceremoniously**. [Lat *caeremoniosus*, full of religious rites]

ceremony *n* ***-ies*** **1** a ritual performed to mark a particular, esp. public or religious, occasion. **2** formal politeness. — **stand on**

ceremony to insist on behaving formally. — **without ceremony** in a hasty, informal way. [Lat *caerimonia*, rite]

cerise *n* cherry-red. — *adj* of this colour. [Fr, cherry]

cerium *n* a metallic element, symbol **Ce**. [Named after the asteroid *Ceres*]

cert *n* (*coll*) a certainty.

cert. *abbrev* **1** certificate. **2** certified.

certain *adj* **1** proved or known beyond doubt. **2** (**about**, **of**) having no doubt; absolutely sure. **3** (used with reference to the future; **of**) definitely going to happen, etc.; able to rely on or be relied on. **4** particular, and, though known, not named or specified: *a certain friend of yours*. **5** used before a person's name to indicate either their obscurity or one's own unfamiliarity with them: *a certain Mrs Seaton*. **6** (of a quality) undeniably present without being clearly definable: *The beard gave his face a certain authority*. **7** some, though not much: *That's true to a certain extent*. — *pron* some. — **for certain** definitely; without doubt. — **make certain** (**of**) to take action so as to ensure or be sure. [OFr, from Lat *certus*, sure]

certainly *adv* **1** without any doubt. **2** definitely. **3** (in giving permission) of course.

certainty *n* **-ies 1** something that cannot be doubted or is bound to happen. **2** freedom from doubt; the state of being sure. **3** the state of being bound to happen: *the certainty of death*.

certificate *n* an official document that formally acknowledges or witnesses a fact (e.g. *a marriage certificate*), an achievement or qualification (e.g. *a First-Aid certificate*), or one's condition (e.g. *a doctor's certificate*). — *v* (*tr*) to provide with a certificate. — *n* **certification**. ◇ See also under **certify**. [Lat *certificare*, to certify]

certificated *adj* qualified by a particular course of training.

certify *v* **-ies**, **-ied** (*tr*) **1** to declare or confirm officially. **2** to declare (someone) insane. **3** to declare to have reached a required standard, passed certain tests, etc. — *adj* **certifiable**. — *n* **certification**. ◇ See also under **certificate**. — *adj* **certified**. [Lat *certificare*]

certitude *n* a feeling of certainty. [Lat *certitudo*, from *certus*, sure]

cervix *n* **1** the opening from the vagina into the womb. **2** (*anat*) the neck. — *adj* **cervical**. [Lat, neck]

cervical smear *n* the procedure of taking a tiny sample of tissue from the cervix of the womb to test for cancer.

cesium. Same as **caesium**.

cessation *n* stopping or ceasing; a pause. [Lat *cessare*, to cease]

cession *n* the giving up or yielding of territories, rights, etc. to someone else. [Lat *cessio*, from *cedere*, to yield]

cesspit or **cesspool** *n* a pool, pit or tank for the collection and storage of sewage and waste water. [Ital *cesso*, latrine]

cetacean *n* any of a group of animals that includes the whale, dolphin and porpoise. — *adj* relating to this group. [Gr *ketos*, whale]

cetane *n* a hydrocarbon present in diesel fuel, in amounts indicated by a **cetane number**, used for grading the fuel. [Gr *ketos*, whale, cetane also being obtainable from *cetyl* compounds found in spermaceti]

Cf *symbol* (*chem*) californium.

cf. *abbrev* for *confer* (Lat), compare.

CFC *abbrev* chlorofluorocarbon.

CH *abbrev* Companion of Honour, a British title awarded to people who have given particular service to the nation.

ch. *abbrev* **1** chapter. **2** church. **3** (*chess*) check.

cha-cha or **cha-cha-cha** *n* a Latin American dance, or music for it. [American Span]

chador, **chadar** or **chuddar** *n* a thick veil worn by Muslim women covering the head and body. [Persian]

chafe *v* **1** (*tr* & *intr*) to make or become sore or worn by rubbing. **2** (*tr*) to make warm by rubbing. **3** (*intr* with **at**, **under**) to become angry or impatient at: *chafe at the rules*. [OFr *chaufer*, to heat]

chafer *n* any of several large, slow-moving beetles. [OE *ceafor*]

chaff[1] *n* **1** the husks or shells separated from grain during threshing. **2** chopped hay and straw used to feed cattle. **3** worthless material. **4** strips of metal foil dropped by aircraft to confuse enemy radar. [OE *ceaf*]

chaff[2] *n* light-hearted joking or teasing. — *v* (*tr*) to tease or make fun of.

chaffinch *n* a songbird of the finch family, the male having a pinkish body and grey head. [OE *ceaffinc*, chaff finch]

chagrin *n* acute annoyance or disappointment. [Fr]

chain *n* **1** a series of connected links or rings, esp. of metal, used for fastening, binding, holding, supporting, transmitting motion or, e.g. in jewellery, for ornament. **2** a series or progression: *a chain of events*. **3** a number of shops, hotels, etc. under common ownership or management. **4** (in *pl*) something that restricts or frustrates. **5** (*chem*) a number of atoms linked in a series to form a molecule, etc. **6** an old measure of length equal to 22 yards (about 20m). — *v* (*tr*) to fasten, bind or restrict with, or as if with, chains. — **in chains** bound by chains, as a prisoner or slave. [OFr *chaeine*, from Lat *catena*]

chain gang *n* a group of prisoners chained together for working outside the prison.

chain letter *n* a letter copied to a large number of people, esp. with a request for and promise of something (e.g. money), each recipient being asked to copy the letter to a stated number of acquaintances.

chainmail same as **mail**[2].

chain of office *n* a heavy ornamental chain worn round the neck as a symbol of office, e.g. by a mayor.

chain reaction *n* **1** (*chem*) a process involving a series of chemical or nuclear reactions, each reaction causing a further similar reaction. **2** a series of events, each causing the next.

chainsaw *n* a power-driven saw, the blade of which is a fast-revolving chain composed of metal teeth.

chain smoker *n* a person who smokes cigarettes continually. — *v* (*tr* & *intr*) **chain-smoke**.

chain store *n* one of a series of shops, esp. department stores, owned by the same company and selling the same goods.

chair *n* **1** a seat for one person, with a back-support and usu. four legs. **2** the office of chairman or chairwoman at a meeting, etc., or the person holding this office. **3** a professorship. **4** (*hist*) a sedan chair. — *v* (*tr*) **1** to control or conduct (a meeting) as chairman or chairwoman. **2** to lift up and carry (a victor, etc.) in triumph. **3** to place (someone) in a seat of authority. — **the chair** (*coll*; esp. *US*) the electric chair as a means of capital punishment. — **in the chair** acting as chairman. — **take the chair** to be chairman or chairwoman. [OFr *chaiere*, from Gr *kathedra*, seat]

chairlift *n* a series of seats suspended from a moving cable, for carrying skiers, etc. up a mountain.

chairman, chairwoman or **chairperson** *n* **1** a person who conducts or controls a meeting or debate. **2** a person who presides over a committee, a board of directors, etc.

chaise *n* (*hist*) a light open two-wheeled horse-drawn carriage. [Fr, chair]

chaise longue *n* ***chaises longues*** a long seat with a back and one arm-rest, on which one can recline at full length. [Fr, long chair]

chalcedony *n* a type of quartz, several varieties of which, e.g. jasper and onyx, are used as gemstones. [Gr *chalkedon*]

chalet *n* **1** a style of house typical of snowy Alpine regions, built of wood, with window-shutters and a heavy, sloping, wide-eaved roof. **2** a small cabin for holiday accommodation, esp. one of a number at a holiday camp, etc. **3** a wooden villa. [Swiss Fr]

chalice *n* **1** (*poetic*) a wine cup; a goblet. **2** in the Christian Church, the cup used for serving the wine at Communion or Mass. [OFr, from Lat *calix*, cup]

chalk *n* **1** a soft white rock composed of calcium carbonate. **2** a material similar to this, or a stick of it, often coloured, used for writing and drawing, esp. on a blackboard. — *v* (*tr*) to write or mark in chalk. — *v* **chalk up** (*tr*) **1** to add (an item) to one's list of successes or experiences. **2** (**to**) to add (something) to the account of money owed by or to (someone). — **as different** (or **as like**) **as chalk and cheese** (*coll*) completely different. — **by a long chalk** (*coll*) by a considerable amount. — **not by a long chalk** (*coll*) not at all. [OE *cealc*, from Lat *calx*, limestone]

chalkboard *n* (esp. *US*) a blackboard.

chalky *adj* **-ier, -iest** **1** like, or consisting of, chalk. **2** (of e.g. a face) very pale. — *n* **chalkiness**.

challenge *v* (*tr*) **1** to call on (someone) to settle a matter by any sort of contest: *challenge him to a duel*. **2** to cast doubt on or call in question: *challenge her right to dismiss staff*. **3** to test, esp. in a stimulating way: *a task that challenges you*. **4** (of a guard or sentry) to order (someone) to stop and show official proof of identity, etc. **5** (*legal*) to object to the inclusion of (a person) on a jury. — *n* **1** an invitation to a contest. **2** the questioning or doubting of something. **3** a problem or task that stimulates effort and interest. **4** an order from a guard or sentry to stop and prove identity. **5** (*legal*) an objection to the inclusion of (someone) on a jury. — *n* **challenger**. — *adj* **challenging**. — *adv* **challengingly**. [OFr *chalenge*]

chamber *n* **1** (*old*) a room, esp. a bedroom. **2** a hall for the meeting of an assembly, esp. a legislative or judicial body. **3** one of the houses of which a parliament consists. **4** (in *pl*) a suite of rooms used by e.g. a judge or lawyer. **5** an enclosed space or hollow; a cavity. **6** the compartment in a gun into which the bullet or cartridge is loaded. **7** a room or compartment with a particular function: *a decompression chamber*. [OFr *chambre*, from Lat *camera*, room]

chambermaid *n* a woman in a hotel, etc. who cleans bedrooms.

chamber music *n* music composed for a small group of players, suitable for performing in a room rather than a large hall.

chamber of commerce *n* (sometimes *caps*) a group of business people working to promote local trade.

chamber orchestra *n* a small orchestra that plays classical music.

chamberpot *n* a receptacle for urine, etc. for use in a bedroom.

chamberlain *n* **1** a person who manages a royal or noble household. ◇ See also **Lord Chamberlain**. **2** the treasurer of a corporation, etc. [OFr *chambrelenc*, from Lat *camera*, room]

chameleon *n* **1** a type of lizard that changes colour so as to blend with its surroundings. **2** someone who readily adapts to any new environment. **3** (*derog*) a changeable, unreliable person. [Gr *chamai*, on the ground + *leon*, lion]

chamfer *v* **-r-** (*tr*) to give a smooth rounded shape to (an edge or corner). —

n a rounded or bevelled edge. [OFr *chamfrein*, from *chant*, edge + *fraindre*, to break]

chamois *n* ***chamois*** **1** a small goat-like antelope of mountainous regions of Europe and SW Asia. **2** soft suede leather made from its skin or from that of sheep and goats. **3** (also **shammy**, or **shammy leather**) a piece of this used as a polishing cloth for glass, etc. [Fr]

champ[1] *v* (*tr* & *intr*) to munch noisily. — *n* the sound of munching. — **champ at the bit** to be impatient to act. [Imit.]

champ[2] *n* (*coll*) a champion.

champagne *n* **1** a sparkling white French wine traditionally drunk at celebrations. **2** a pale pinkish-yellow colour. [*Champagne*, the French district where the wine was orig. made]

champers *n* (*coll*) champagne.

champion *n* **1** in games, competitions, etc., a competitor that has defeated all others. **2** the supporter or defender of a person or cause. — *adj* & *adv* (*dialect*) fine. — *v* (*tr*) to strongly support or defend (a person or cause). [OFr, from Lat *campio*, from *campus*, battlefield, place for exercise]

championship *n* **1** a contest held to find the champion. **2** the title or position of champion. **3** the strong defending or supporting of a cause or person.

chance *n* **1** the way that things happen unplanned and unforeseen; fate or luck as causing this to happen, or something that happens in this way. **2** an unforeseen, unexpected occurrence. **3** a possibility or probability. **4** a possible or probable success: *not stand a chance*. **5** an opportunity: *your big chance*. **6** risk, or a risk: *take a chance*. — *v* **1** (*tr*) to risk. **2** (*intr*) to do or happen by chance: *I chanced to meet her*. — **be in with a chance** to have some hope of success. — **a chance in a million 1** the faintest possibility. **2** (also **chance of a lifetime**) an opportunity not to be missed. — **chance it, chance one's luck** or **one's arm** to take a risk. — *v* **chance on** or **upon** (*tr*) to meet or find by accident. — **(the) chances are** it is likely that. — **an eye to the main chance** a tendency to act from motives of personal advantage rather than consideration for others. — **on the off chance** in hope rather than expectation. — **an outside chance** a very faint possibility. — **take a chance on** to act in the hope of (something being the case). — **take one's chance** or **chances** to make the most of whatever opportunities arise. [OFr *cheance*, from Lat *cadere*, to fall]

chancer *n* (*coll derog*) a person inclined to take any opportunity to profit, whether honestly or dishonestly.

chancy *adj* ***-ier***, ***-iest*** risky; uncertain. — *n* **chanciness**.

chancel *n* the eastern part of a church, where the altar is, formerly separated from the nave by a screen. [Lat *cancelli*, lattice, grating]

chancellery. See **chancellor**.

chancellor *n* **1** the head of the government in certain European countries. **2** a state or legal official of various kinds. ◇ See also **Lord Chancellor**. **3** in the UK, the honorary head of a university. **4** in the US, the president of a university or college. — *n* **chancellorship**. [Lat *cancellarius*, court usher]

chancellery *n* ***-ies*** **1** the rank of a chancellor. **2** a chancellor's department or staff. **3** (also **chancery**) the offices or residence of a chancellor. **4** (also **chancery**) the office of an embassy or consulate.

Chancellor of the Exchequer *n* the chief minister of finance in the British government.

chancery *n* ***-ies*** **1** (usu. *cap*) a division of the High Court of Justice. **2** a record office containing public archives. **3** (also **chancellery**) the premises occupied by a chancellor. **4** (also **chancellery**) the office of an embassy or consulate. — **in chancery 1** (of a legal case) being heard in a court of chancery. **2** in the charge of a lord chancellor. **3** in a very difficult situation. [A contracted form of **chancellery**]

chancre *n* (*med*) a small hard sore, a sign of syphilis. — *adj* **chancrous**. [OFr]

chancy. See **chance**.

chandelier *n* an ornamental light-fitting hanging from the ceiling, with branching holders for candles or light-bulbs. [OFr, candle-holder]

chandler *n* **1** a dealer in ship's supplies and equipment. **2** a dealer in certain other goods: *corn chandler*. **3** (*old*) a grocer. **4** (*old*) a dealer in candles, oil, etc. — *n* **chandlery**, ***-ies***. [OFr *chandelier*, dealer in candles]

change *v* **1** (*tr* & *intr*; **from, to**) to make or become different. **2** (*tr*; **for**) to give, leave or substitute (one thing) for another. **3** (*tr*) to exchange (usu. one's position) with another person, etc.: *change places*. **4** (*tr* & *intr*; **into, out of**) to remove (clothes, etc.) and replace them with clean or different ones. **5** (*tr*) to put a fresh nappy or clothes on (a baby), or clean sheets on (a bed). **6** (*tr* & *intr* with **into**) to make into or become (something different). **7** (*tr*; **for, into**) to obtain or supply another kind of money for. **8** (*intr* & *tr*) on a journey, to leave (one vehicle) and get into another. **9** (*intr* & *tr* with **into**) to put a vehicle engine into (another gear). — *n* **1** the process of changing or an instance of it. **2** the replacement of one thing with another; the leaving of one thing for another. **3** a variation, esp. a welcome one, from one's regular habit, etc.: *eat out for a change*. **4** the leaving of one vehicle for another during a journey. **5** a fresh set (of clothes) for changing into. **6** (also **small** or **loose change**) coins as distinct from notes. **7** coins or notes given in exchange for ones of higher value. **8**

money left over or returned from the amount given in payment. **9** (usu. in *pl*) any of the various orders in which a set of church bells can be rung. **10** (also **change of life**; *coll*) the menopause. — *v* **change down** (*intr*) to change to a lower gear. — **change hands** to pass into different ownership. — **change one's mind** to alter one's intentions or opinion. — *v* **change over** (*intr*) **1** (**from**, **to**) to change from one preference, system, etc. to another (*n* **change-over**). **2** to make an exchange (of jobs, etc.): *He drove for two hours, then we changed over*. (*n* **change-over**). — *v* **change up** (*intr*) to change to a higher gear. — **get no change out of** (*coll*) to get no help from (someone). [Fr *changer*]

changeable *adj* **1** inclined or liable to change often. **2** able to be changed. — *n* **changeability** or **changeableness**. — *adv* **changeably**.

changeless *adj* never-changing. — *adv* **changelessly**. — *n* **changelessness**.

changing-room *n* a room in a sports centre, etc. where one can change one's clothes.

changeling *n* in folklore, a child substituted by the fairies for an unbaptised human baby. [**change**]

channel *n* **1** a natural water course, such as the bed of a stream. **2** an artificially constructed course for water, etc., e.g. for irrigation. **3** the deeper part of a river, through which ships can sail. **4** a narrow stretch of water joining two seas. **5** a groove, furrow or any long narrow cut, esp. one along which something moves. **6** a set of frequencies on which television or radio programmes are received or radio messages are sent. **7** (*electr & comput*) a path for the transmission of an electrical signal or data. **8** (in *pl*) a means by which information, etc. is communicated, obtained or received. **9** a course, project, etc. into which some resource may be directed: *a channel for one's energies*. **10** (*cap* with **the**) the English Channel, the stretch of sea between England and France. — *v* **-ll-** (*tr*) **1** to make a channel or channels in. **2** to convey (a liquid, information, etc.) through a channel. **3** to direct (a resource, e.g. talent, energy, money) into a course, project, etc. [OFr *chanel*]

chant *v* (*tr & intr*) **1** to recite in a singing voice. **2** to keep repeating, esp. loudly and rhythmically. — *n* **1** a type of singing used in religious services for passages in prose, with a simple melody and several words sung on one note. **2** a phrase or slogan constantly repeated, esp. loudly and rhythmically. — *n* **chanting**. [OFr *chant*, song, and *chanter*, to sing]

chanter *n* **1** the pipe on which the melody is played on a set of bagpipes. **2** this pipe adapted for separate use as a practice instrument. **3** someone who chants. [OFr *chanteor*, singer]

chanterelle *n* an edible yellow fungus with a trumpet-shaped cap. [Fr, from Lat *cantharellus*, dimin. of *cantharus*, tankard]

chantry *n* **-ies** a chapel, or a sum of money, provided for the chanting of masses. [OFr *chanter*, sing]

chanty. See **shanty**[2].

Chanukkah. Same as **Hanukkah**.

chaos *n* **1** complete confusion; utter disorder. **2** the supposed formless, haphazard state of matter before it was organised to form the universe. — *adj* **chaotic**. — *adv* **chaotically**. [Gr]

chap[1] *n* (*coll*) a man or boy; a fellow. [Formerly, a customer; shortened from **chapman**]

chap[2] *v* **-pp-** (*tr & intr*) (of skin) to make or become roughened, sore and red from rubbing or exposure to cold. — *n* (usu. in *pl*) a sore, red, roughened patch on the skin. — *adj* **chapped**. [MidE *chappen*]

chap. *abbrev* **chapter**.

chaparral *n* an area of dense undergrowth, shrubs and small trees. [Span, from *chapparro*, evergreen oak]

chapati or **chapatti** *n* in Indian cooking, a thin flat portion of unleavened bread. [Hindi *capati*]

chapel *n* **1** a recess within a church or cathedral, with its own altar. **2** a place of worship attached to a house, school, etc. **3** (esp. in England and Wales) a place of Nonconformist worship, or the services held there. **4** (a meeting of) an association of workers in a newspaper office, or a printing- or publishing-house. [Lat *cappella*, cloak, i.e. the cloak of St Martin, which was kept in a shrine, to which the word became attached]

chaperone or **chaperon** *n* **1** (esp. *formerly*) an older woman accompanying a younger unmarried one on social occasions, for respectability's sake. **2** an older person accompanying and supervising a group of young people. — *v* (*tr*) to act as chaperone to. [OFr, hood]

chaplain *n* a clergyman or -woman attached to a chapel, to a school, hospital or other institution, or to the armed forces. — *n* **chaplaincy**, **-ies**. [Lat *cappellanus*, custodian of St Martin's cloak; see ety. for **chapel**]

chaplet *n* **1** a wreath of flowers or a band of gold, etc. for the head. **2** a string of beads, esp. one used by Roman Catholics as a short version of the rosary. [OFr *chapel*, wreath, hat]

chapman *n* **-men** (*hist*) a travelling dealer; a pedlar. [OE *ceapman*, from *ceap*, trading]

chappie *n* (*coll*) dimin. of **chap**[1].

chaps *n* (*pl*) a cowboy's protective leather riding leggings, worn over the trousers. [Span *chaparejos*]

chapter *n* **1** one of the numbered or titled sections into which a book is divided. **2** a period associated with certain happenings: *an unfortunate chapter in my life*. **3** a sequence or series: *a chapter of accidents*.

4 (esp. *US*) (a meeting of) a branch of a society. **5** the body, or a meeting, of canons of a cathedral, or of the members of a religious order. — **chapter and verse** an exact reference, description of circumstances, etc. quoted in justification of a statement, etc. [OFr *chapitre*, from Lat *caput*, head]

chapter house *n* the building used for the meetings of a chapter.

char[1] *v* **-rr-** (*tr* & *intr*) **1** to blacken by burning. **2** (of wood) to turn into charcoal by partial burning. [Shortened from **charcoal**]

char[2] *v* **-rr-** (*intr*) to do paid cleaning work in someone's house, an office, etc. — *n* (*coll*) a charwoman. [OE *cierran*, to turn; later, as *chare*, to accomplish (a task)]

charwoman or **charlady** *n* a woman employed to clean a house, office, etc.

char[3] *n* (*old coll*) tea. [Hindi *ca* and Chinese *ch'a*]

char[4] or **charr** *n* **char**, **charr**, **chars** or ***charrs*** a small fish of the salmon family found in cold northern lakes, rivers or seas.

charabanc *n* (*old*) a single-decker bus for tours, sightseeing, etc.; a coach. [Fr *char à bancs*, carriage with seats]

character *n* **1** the combination of qualities that makes up a person's nature or personality. **2** the combination of qualities that typifies anything. **3** type or kind. **4** strong, admirable qualities such as determination, courage and honesty. **5** interesting qualities that make for individuality: *a house with character*. **6** a person in a story or play. **7** an odd or amusing person. **8** (*coll*) a person. **9** reputation: *blacken someone's character*. **10** a letter, number or other written or printed symbol. — **in** (or **out of**) **character** typical (or untypical) of a person's nature. [Gr *charakter*, engraving tool, branding-iron, hence a distinctive mark impressed on something]

character actor *n* an actor who specialises in character parts.

characterise or **-ize** *v* (*tr*) **1** to describe, give the chief qualities of. **2** to be a distinctive and typical feature of.

characterisation or **-z-** *n* **1** characterising. **2** the process by which a writer builds up the characters in a story or play so that their individual personalities emerge. **3** the art of an actor in giving a convincing performance as a particular character.

characteristic *adj* **1** typical. **2** distinctive. — *n* (*math*) in a logarithm, the figure which precedes the decimal point. ◇ See also **mantissa**. — *adv* **characteristically**.

characterless *adj* (*derog*) dull; uninteresting; lacking individuality.

character part *n* a colourful part in a play or film, giving good opportunities for characterisation.

character sketch *n* a quick description of someone, mentioning his or her chief qualities.

charade *n* (*derog*) a ridiculous pretence; a farce. [Fr, from Provençal *charrado*, entertainment]

charades *n* (usu. *sing*) a party game in which players act out each syllable of a word, or each word of a book title, etc. in successive scenes, while the watching players try to guess the complete word or title.

charcoal *n* **1** a black material, a form of carbon, produced by partially burning wood, used for drawing and as a fuel. **2** a drawing done in charcoal. **3** (also **charcoal grey**) a dark grey colour. [MidE *charcole*]

charge *v* **1** (*tr* & *intr*; **for**) to ask for (an amount) as the price of (something); to ask (someone) for an amount as payment. **2** (*tr* with **to**) to record as a debt against: *Charge the breakages to me*. **3** (*tr*; **with**) to accuse officially: *charged with manslaughter*. **4** (*tr* & *intr*) to rush at in attack. **5** (*intr*) to rush. **6** (*tr*; *formal*) to order officially: *She was charged to appear in court*. **7** (*tr*; *formal*; **with**) to give a task to: *He was charged with looking after the books*. **8** (*tr*) to load (a gun, etc.). **9** (*tr*; *old* or *formal*) to fill up: *Charge your glasses*. **10** (*tr*; **up**) (of a battery, etc.) to store up, or cause to store up, electricity. **11** (*tr*) to load or saturate: *The liquid is made fizzy by charging it with carbon dioxide*. **12** (*tr*) to fill: *The moment was charged with emotion*. — *n* **1** (**for**) a price, cost or fee. **2** (**of**) control, care, responsibility, supervision or guardianship: *in charge of repairs*; *The police arrived and took charge*. **3** (*formal* or *humorous*) something or someone, e.g. a child, that is in one's care. **4** (**of**) something of which one is accused: *a charge of murder*. **5** a rushing attack. **6** an amount of electricity carried by something, or stored in a device such as a battery. **7** a quantity of material appropriate for filling something. **8** an amount of explosive for loading into a gun, etc.; a cartridge or shell. **9** an order. **10** a task, duty or burden: *undertake a difficult charge*. — **press** or **prefer charges** to charge someone officially with a crime, etc. [OFr *chargier* or *charger*, from Lat *carricare*, to load a vehicle]

chargeable *adj* **1** (with **to**) (of costs, etc.) that may or should be charged to someone. **2** permitted or liable to be charged: *A fee is chargeable for missed appointments*. **3** incurring tax or duty: *chargeable assets*. **4** (of an offence) serious enough to justify a legal charge by the police.

charge card *n* a small card entitling one to make purchases on credit, supplied to one by a shop with which one has a credit account.

charged *adj* filled with excitement or other strong emotion: *the charged atmosphere in the room.*

charge hand *n* the deputy to a foreman in a factory, etc.

charge nurse *n* a nurse in charge of a hospital ward, esp. if a male; the equivalent of a sister.

charger *n* (*hist*) a strong horse used by a knight in battle, etc.

chargé d'affaires *n* ***chargés d'affaires*** *n* a deputy to, or substitute for, an ambassador. [Fr, person in charge of affairs]

chariot *n* (*hist*) a two-wheeled vehicle pulled by horses, used in ancient times for warfare or racing. [Dimin. of OFr *char*, carriage]

charioteer *n* a chariot-driver.

charisma *n* ***charismata*** **1** a strong ability to attract people, and inspire loyalty and admiration. **2** (*relig*) a divinely bestowed talent or power. — *adj* **charismatic**. [Gr, grace]

charismatic movement *n* a movement within Christianity that emphasises the power of the Holy Spirit at work within individuals, manifesting itself as an ability to heal, a talent for prophecy, etc.

charitable *adj* **1** kind and understanding in one's attitude to others. **2** generous in assisting people in need. **3** relating to, belonging to, or in the nature of, a charity: *charitable institutions.* — *n* **charitableness**. — *adv* **charitably**. [OFr, from *charite*, charity]

charity *n* **-*ies*** **1** assistance given to those in need. **2** an organisation established to provide such assistance. **3** kindness and understanding in one's attitude towards, or judgement of, other people. **4** (*Bible*) compassionate love for others. [OFr *charite*, from Lat *caritas*, love]

charlady. See **char**[2].

charlatan *n* (*derog*) a person posing as an expert in some profession, e.g. medicine. — *n* **charlatanism**. [OFr, from Ital *ciarlare*, to chatter]

Charleston *n* a vigorous dance popular in the 1920s, its characteristic step being a pivot on one leg with a side-kick of the other from the knee. [*Charleston*, town in US]

charlie *n* (*Br coll*) a fool.

charm *n* **1** the power of delighting, attracting or fascinating. **2** (in *pl*) delightful qualities possessed by a person, place, thing, etc. **3** an object believed to have magical powers. **4** a magical saying or spell. **5** a small ornament, esp. of silver, worn on a bracelet. — *v* (*tr*) **1** to delight, attract or fascinate. **2** (**into**, **out of**) to influence or persuade by charm. **3** to control by, or as if by, magic: *charm snakes.* — *adj* **charmless**. — *adv* **charmlessly**. — **work like a charm** to produce the desired result as if by magic. [OFr *charme*, from Lat *carmen*, song, spell]

charmed *adj* seeming to be protected by magic: *lead a charmed life.*

charmer *n* **1** (*coll*) a person with an attractive, winning manner. **2** (usu. *in cmpds*) a person who can charm animals: *a snake-charmer.*

charming *adj* delightful; pleasing; attractive; enchanting. — *adv* **charmingly**.

charnel house *n* (*hist*) a building where dead bodies or bones are stored. [OFr *charnel*, burial place]

chart *n* **1** a map, esp. one designed as an aid to navigation by sea or air, or one on which weather developments are shown. **2** a sheet of information presented as a table, graph or diagram. **3** (in *pl*; *coll*) the weekly lists of top-selling pop records. — *v* **1** (*tr*) to make a chart of (e.g. part of the sea). **2** (*tr*) to plot the course or progress of. **3** (*intr*; *coll*) to appear in the record charts. [OFr *charte*, from Lat *charta*, leaf of paper]

charter *n* **1** a document guaranteeing the rights and privileges of subjects, issued by a sovereign or government. **2** a document in which the constitution and principles of an organisation are presented. **3** a document creating a borough. **4** the hire of aircraft or ships for private use, or a contract for this. — *v* **-*r-*** **1** to hire (an aircraft, etc.) for private use. **2** to grant a charter to. — *n* **charterer**. [OFr *chartre*, from Lat *charta*, paper]

chartered *adj* **1** qualified according to the rules of a professional body that has a royal charter: *chartered accountant.* **2** having been granted a charter.

charter flight *n* a flight in a chartered aircraft.

Chartism *n* a mid-19th century working-class movement in Great Britain, seeking e.g. voting rights for all male citizens and the abolition of the property qualification for members of parliament. — *n & adj* **Chartist**. [From 'The People's *Charter*', published 1838]

chartreuse *n* a green or yellow liqueur made from brandy and herbs. [*Chartreuse*, monastery in SE France, where the liqueur is produced]

charwoman. See **char**[2].

chary *adj* **-*ier***, **-*iest*** (**of**) **1** cautious; wary: *chary of lending money.* **2** sparing; rather mean: *chary of praise.* — *adv* **charily**. — *n* **chariness**. [OE *cearig*, sorrowful, anxious]

Charybdis. See **Scylla**.

chase[1] *v* **1** (*tr* & *intr*; **after**) to go after in an attempt to catch. **2** (*tr* with **away**, **off**, etc.) to drive or force away, out, etc. **3** (*intr*) to rush; to hurry. **4** (*tr*; *coll*) to try to obtain: *too many applicants chasing too few jobs.* **5** (*tr*) to pursue a particular matter urgently with: *chase the post office about the missing parcel.* — *n* **1** a pursuit. **2** (with **the**) the hunting of animals, e.g. foxes. **3** a large area of open land, orig. where wild animals were kept for hunting. — *v* **chase up** (*tr*) **1** to inquire about (a matter) or seek out (information). **2** to speak to (the person responsible) in order to get something done. — **give chase** to rush off in pursuit. [OFr *chasser*, from Lat *captare*, to try to catch]

chaser *n* **1** (*coll*) a drink taken after one of a different kind, e.g. beer after spirits. **2** a person, animal, etc. that chases. **3** a horse for steeplechasing.

chase[2] *v* (*tr*) to decorate (metal) with engraved or embossed work. [Short for *enchase*, to engrave or emboss]

chase[3] *n* (*printing*) a metal frame that holds assembled type in position for printing. [OFr *chas*, from a variant of Lat *capsa*, case]

chasm *n* **1** a deep crack in the ground, found e.g. close to a cliff edge. **2** a very wide difference in opinion, feeling, etc. [Gr *chasma*]

chassé *n* a gliding step used in ballroom dancing, etc. — *v* ***chasséd*** (*intr*) to perform this step. [Fr]

chassis *n* ***chassis*** **1** the central structure of a vehicle, on which wheels, bodywork, etc. are mounted. **2** any rigid basic structure, e.g. that of a radio or television, on which electronic parts, etc. are mounted. **3** an aeroplane's landing-gear. [Fr *châssis*, frame]

chaste *adj* **1** sexually virtuous or pure; refraining either from sex outside marriage or from sex with anyone. **2** (of behaviour, etc.) modest; decent. **3** (of clothes, jewellery, style, etc.) simple; plain; unadorned. — *adv* **chastely**. — *n* **chasteness**. ◇ See also **chastity**. [OFr]

chasten *v* (*tr*) to produce in (someone) a feeling of guilt and a resolve to improve. [OFr *chastier*, to punish]

chastise *v* (*tr*) **1** to punish severely, esp. by beating. **2** to scold. — *n* **chastisement**. [Lat *castigare*, to punish]

chastity *n* **1** the state of refraining entirely from sexual intercourse or from from sex outside marriage; chasteness. **2** simplicity or plainness of style. [OFr *chastete*]

chastity belt *n* (esp. *hist*) a leather garment covering the genitals in such a way as to prevent sexual intercourse, into which e.g. crusaders were said to lock their wives to ensure chastity in their absence.

chasuble *n* a long sleeveless garment, usu. elaborately embroidered, worn by a priest when celebrating Mass or Communion. [Fr, from Lat *casubla*, variant of *casula*, hooded cloak]

chat[1] *v* ***-tt-*** (*intr*) to talk or converse in a friendly, informal way. — *n* informal, familiar talk; a friendly conversation. — *v* **chat up** (*tr*; *coll*) to chat to in a flirtatious way, or in the hope of extracting some favour. [Shortened from **chatter**]

chat show *n* a television or radio programme in which well-known people are interviewed informally.

chatty *adj* ***-ier***, ***-iest*** (*coll*) **1** given to friendly chatting. **2** friendly and informal in style. — *adv* **chattily**. — *n* **chattiness**.

chat[2] *n* any of several small birds of the thrush family. [Imit.]

château *n* ***-eaux*** **1** a large French castle or country seat. **2** a vineyard estate around a castle or house. [Fr]

châtelaine *n* **1** (esp. *hist*) the mistress of a large house. **2** (*hist*) a chain or set of chains for attaching keys to, worn hanging from the belt by women. [Fr]

chattel *n* (usu. in *pl*) a moveable possession, esp. in the expression **goods and chattels**. [OFr *chatel*, from Lat *capitale*, wealth]

chatter *v* ***-r-*** (*intr*) **1** to talk rapidly, noisily, unceasingly and heedlessly, usu. about trivial matters. **2** (of the teeth) to keep knocking together as a result of cold or fear. **3** (of e.g. monkeys and birds) to make high-pitched noises similar to chattering. — *n* chattering talk or a sound similar to it. — *n* **chatterer**. [Imit.]

chatterbox *n* (usu. *derog*) a person who is inclined to chatter.

chatty. See **chat**[1].

chauffeur *n* a person employed to drive a car for someone else. — *v* (*tr*) to act as a driver for (someone). [Fr, stoker]

chauffeuse *n* a female chauffeur.

chauvinism *n* (*derog*) an unreasonable belief, esp. if aggressively expressed, in the superiority of one's own nation, sex, etc. — *n* **chauvinist**. — *adj* **chauvinistic**. — *adv* **chauvinistically**. [Nicolas *Chauvin*, a fanatically patriotic soldier under Napoleon]

ChB *abbrev* for *Chirurgiae Baccalaureus* (Lat), Bachelor of Surgery.

cheap *adj* **1** low in price; being, or charging, less than the usual price; being, or offering, good value for money. **2** low in price but of poor quality: *cheap plastic jewellery*. **3** of little worth; valueless: *War makes human life seem cheap*. **4** mean; unfair; unpleasant; nasty. — *adv* (*coll*) cheaply: *Good houses don't come cheap*. — *adv* **cheaply**. — *n* **cheapness**. — **on the cheap** cheaply. [OE *ceap*, trade, price, bargain]

cheapen *v* ***-n-*** **1** (*tr*) to cause to appear cheap or not very respectable. **2** (*tr* & *intr*) to make or become cheaper.

cheapjack *n* (*derog*) a seller of cheap, poor-quality goods. — *adj* of poor quality.

cheapskate *n* (*coll derog*) a mean, miserly person.

cheat *v* **1** (*tr*) to trick, deceive, swindle. **2** (*tr*; **of, out of**) to deprive of something by deceit or trickery. **3** (*intr*; **at**) to act dishonestly so as to gain an advantage: *cheat at cards*. **4** (*intr* with **on**; *coll*) to break one's promise to be faithful to (one's husband, wife, etc.), by having sex with another person. **5** (*tr*) to escape (something unpleasant) by luck or skill. — *n* **1** a person who cheats. **2** a dishonest trick. [Shortened from **escheat**]

check *v* **1** (*tr* & *intr*; **against, for, on, up, up on, with**) to make sure about (something), or that (something) is as it should be or (someone) is doing what they should be, e.g. by inspecting or investigating it. **2** (*tr*) to hold back, prevent, stop: *He nearly swore, but checked himself*. **3** (*tr*; *NAm*) to mark (something correct, etc.) with a tick. **4** (*tr*; *NAm*) to hand over or deposit for safekeeping. **5** (*tr*; **in, through**) to get (luggage) accepted for air transport: *bags checked through to Singapore*. **6** (*intr*; **with, out**; esp. *NAm*) (of information, etc.) to be consistent; to agree (with): *That checks with the other boy's story. The stories check out*. **7** (*tr*; *chess*) to put (one's opponent's king) under attack. — *n* **1** (**on**) an inspection or investigation made to find out about something or to ensure that something is as it should be. **2** a standard or test by means of which to check something. **3** a stoppage in, or control on, progress or development. **4** a pattern of squares: *cotton with a purple check*. **5** (*US*) a tick marked against something. **6** (*US*) a cheque. **7** (esp. *NAm*) a restaurant bill. **8** (*NAm*) a ticket or token for claiming something left in safekeeping. **9** (*chess*) the position of a king under attack. — *adj* **checkable**. — *n* **checker**. — *v* **check in 1** (*intr*; **at, to**) to report one's arrival at an air terminal or hotel. **2** (*tr*) to register or record the arrival of (esp. guests at a hotel or passengers at an air terminal). **3** (*tr*) to hand in (luggage for weighing and loading) at an air terminal. ◇ See also **check-in**. — *v* **check off** (*tr*) to mark (items on a list) as dealt with. — *v* **check out 1** (*intr*) to register one's departure, esp. from a hotel as one pays the bill. **2** (*tr*; esp. *NAm*) to investigate thoroughly. ◇ See also **check** (sense **6**). [OFr *eschec*, check in chess, from Persian *shah*, king]

checked *adj* having a squared pattern: *purple-checked cotton*.

check-in *n* at an air terminal, the desk at which passengers' tickets are checked and luggage weighed and accepted for loading.

checklist *n* a list of things to be done or systematically checked.

checkout *n* the pay desk in a supermarket.

checkpoint *n* a place, e.g. at a frontier, where vehicles are stopped and travel documents checked.

check-up *n* a thorough examination, esp. a medical one.

checker[1]. See **check**.

checker[2]. See **chequer** and **chequers**.

checkmate *n* **1** (*chess*; also **mate**) a winning position, putting one's opponent's king under inescapable attack. **2** frustration or defeat. — *v* (*tr*) **1** (*chess*; also **mate**) to put (one's opponent's king) into checkmate. **2** to foil or outwit. [Persian *shah mata*, the king is checked]

Cheddar *n* any of various types of hard yellow, orange or white cheese. [*Cheddar* in Somerset, where the cheese was first made]

cheek *n* **1** either side of the face below the eye. **2** impudent speech or behaviour. **3** (usu. in *pl*; *coll*) either of the buttocks. — **cheek by jowl** very close together. — **turn the other cheek** to refuse to retaliate. [OE *ceace* or *cece*]

cheekbone *n* the bone that projects below the eye.

cheeky *adj* **-ier, -iest** impudent; disrespectful. — *adv* **cheekily**. — *n* **cheekiness**.

cheep *v* (*intr*) (esp. of baby birds) to make high-pitched little noises. — *n* a sound of this sort. [Imit.]

cheer *n* **1** a shout of approval or encouragement. **2** (*old*) mood; spirits: *be of good cheer*. **3** (*old*) merriment. **4** (*old*) food and drink: *Christmas cheer*. — *v* **1** (*intr* & *tr*) to give approval or encouragement by shouting. **2** (*tr* with **on**) to encourage by shouting: *cheer her on*. — *v* **cheer up** (*tr* & *intr*) to make or become more cheerful. [OFr *chere*, face]

cheerful *adj* **1** happy; optimistic. **2** in a good mood. **3** bright and cheering. **4** willing; glad; ungrudging. — *adv* **cheerfully**. — *n* **cheerfulness**.

cheering *adj* bringing comfort; making one feel glad or happier.

cheerleader *n* (esp. in US) a person who leads organised cheering, esp. at sports events.

cheerless *adj* dismal, depressing, dreary or dull. — *adv* **cheerlessly**. — *n* **cheerlessness**.

cheery *adj* **-ier, -iest** cheerful; lively; jovial. — *adv* **cheerily**. — *n* **cheeriness**.

cheerio *interj* (esp. *Br*; *coll*) **1** goodbye. **2** cheers (sense **1**). [**cheer**]

cheers *interj* (esp. *Br*; *coll*) **1** used as a toast before drinking. **2** thank you. **3** goodbye. [**cheer**]

cheese[1] *n* **1** a soft or hard food made from the curds of milk. **2** a large, usu. round block of firm cheese. **3** a conserve for spreading, with the consistency of soft cheese: *lemon cheese*. — *adj* **cheesy, -ier, -iest**. — **cheesed off** (*Br slang*; **with**) bored or annoyed. — **hard cheese** (*Br old slang*) bad luck. [OE *cyse*, from Lat *caseus*]

cheese board *n* **1** a board on which to serve cheese. **2** the selection of cheeses served.

cheeseburger *n* a hamburger served with a slice of cheese, usu. in a bread roll.

cheesecake *n* a sweet food made with soft cheese. **2** (*coll; often derog*) photographs of partially clothed women, esp. used to add sex appeal in advertising. ◇ See also **beefcake**.

cheesecloth *n* **1** a type of thin cloth used for pressing cheese. **2** a loosely woven cloth used for shirts, etc.

cheeseparing *adj* (*derog*) mean with money.

cheese straw *n* a long thin light cheese-flavoured biscuit.

cheese[2] *n* (*slang*; also **big cheese**) an important person. [Perhaps from Urdu *chiz*, thing]

cheetah *n* a large long-legged spotted animal of the cat family found in Africa and SW Asia, the fastest-running of all mammals. [Hindi *cita*]

chef *n* the chief cook, usu. male, in a restaurant, etc. [Fr, chief]

chef d'oeuvre *n* ***chefs d'oeuvre*** an artist's or writer's masterpiece. [Fr]

cheiromancy. See **chiromancy**.

chemin de fer *n* a variation of the card game baccarat. [Fr, railway]

chemise *n* a woman's shirt or loose-fitting dress. [OFr, from Lat *camisa*, shirt]

chemical *adj* relating to, or made using, chemistry or chemicals. — *n* a substance produced by or used in chemistry. — *adv* **chemically**. [From the earlier *chemic*, relating to alchemy or chemistry]

chemical engineering *n* the design and operation of equipment for chemical processes in industry.

chemical toilet *n* a toilet in which human waste is treated with chemicals, used where running water is not available.

chemical warfare *n* the use of poison gas and other harmful chemicals as weapons in war.

chemist *n* **1** a scientist specialising in chemistry. **2** a person qualified to dispense medicines; a pharmacist. **3** (also **chemist's**) a shop dealing in medicines, toiletries, cosmetics, etc. [Earlier *chymist*, from Lat *alchimista*, alchemist]

chemistry *n* **1** the science of elements and compounds and the ways in they which act on, or combine with, each other. **2** (*coll*) emotional and psychological interaction experienced in a relationship.

chemotherapy *n* the use of chemical substances to treat diseases, esp. cancer. — *adj* **chemotherapeutic**. — *adv* **chemotherapeutically**. [*chemo-*, combining form meaning chemical, + **therapy**]

chenille *n* a soft shiny velvety fabric. [Fr, caterpillar]

cheque *n* a printed form on which to fill in instructions to one's bank to pay a certain person, etc. a certain amount of money from one's account, used in place of cash. [**check** (sense 1)]

blank cheque see **blank**.

chequebook *n* a book of cheques ready for use, printed with one's own name and that of the bank issuing it.

chequebook journalism *n* (*derog*) the practice of paying enormous prices for exclusive rights to esp. sensational material for newspaper stories.

cheque card *n* a card issued to customers by a bank, guaranteeing payment of their cheques up to a stated amount.

chequer or, in N America, **checker** *n* **1** a pattern of squares alternating in colour as on a chessboard. **2** one of the pieces used in the game of Chinese chequers. **3** (*NAm*) one of the round pieces used in the game of draughts. [OFr *escheker*, chessboard, from *eschec*, check in chess; see ety. for **check**]

chequered *adj* **1** patterned with squares or patches of alternating colour. **2** (of a person's life, career, etc.) eventful, with alternations of good and bad fortune.

chequered flag *n* a black-and-white-checked flag waved in front of the winner and subsequent finishers in a motor race.

chequers or, in N America, **checkers** *n* (*sing*) the game of draughts.

cherish *v* (*tr*) **1** to care for lovingly. **2** to take great care to keep (a tradition, etc.) alive. **3** to cling fondly to (a hope, belief or memory). [OFr *cherir*, from *cher*, dear]

cheroot *n* a cigar that is cut square at both ends. [Fr *cheroute*, from Tamil *curuttu*, roll]

cherry *n* ***-ies*** **1** a small round red, yellow or dark purple fruit with a stone. **2** the tree bearing this fruit, or its wood. **3** (also **cherry-red**) a bright red colour. — **two bites**, or **another** or **a second bite, at the cherry** (*coll*) the luxury of a second chance. [OE *ciris* (mistaken for a plural), from Gr *kerasion*]

cherry brandy *n* a liqueur made with brandy in which cherries have been steeped.

cherub *n* ***cherubs*** or (for sense **1**) ***cherubim*** **1** an angel, represented in painting and sculpture as a winged child. **2** a sweet, innocent and beautiful child. — *adj* **cherubic**. — *adv* **cherubically**. [Hebr *k'rubh*, plural *k'rubhim*]

chervil *n* a herb whose aniseed-flavoured leaves are used in salads, etc. [OE *cherfelle*, from Gr *chairephyllon*]

Ches. *abbrev* Cheshire.

Cheshire cat : **grin like a Cheshire cat** to smile broadly and knowingly.

chess *n* a board game for two people each with 16 playing-pieces, the most important pieces being the kings, and the object of the game to trap one's opponent's king. [OFr *esches*, plural of *eschec*, check in chess, from Persian *shah*, king]

chessboard *n* the board, divided into alternating black (or brown) and white squares, on which chess is played.

chessman *n* one of the 32 figures used as playing-pieces in chess.

chest[1] *n* **1** the part of the body between the neck and the waist that contains the heart and lungs, or the front part of this. **2** a big, strong, esp. wooden box used for storage or transport. **3** a small cabinet, e.g. for medicines. — **get (something) off one's chest** (*coll*) to get release from anxiety about (something that is troubling one) by talking openly about it. — [OE *cist*, *cest* or *cyst*, box, from Lat *cista*]

chest of drawers *n* a piece of furniture fitted with drawers, esp. for holding clothes.

chesty *adj* **-ier**, **-iest** (*coll*) **1** (*Br*) liable to, suffering from, or caused by, illness affecting the lungs. **2** (of a woman) having large breasts. — *adv* **chestily**. — *n* **chestiness**.

chesterfield *n* a heavily padded leather-covered sofa with arms and back of the same height. [Named after a 19th-cent. Earl of *Chesterfield*]

chestnut *n* **1** either of two shiny reddish-brown nuts — the edible **sweet chestnut** and the **horse chestnut** (or 'conker'). **2** either of the two trees bearing the nuts, or their wood. **3** a reddish-brown colour, esp. of hair. **4** a reddish-brown horse. **5** an often-repeated joke or anecdote. — **pull someone's chestnuts out of the fire** (*coll*) to rescue someone from difficulties. [From the earlier *chesten nut*, from Lat *castanea*, chestnut tree]

cheval glass *n* a full-length mirror mounted on a stand with swivelling hinges that allow it to be positioned at any angle. [Fr *cheval*, horse, support]

chevalier *n* **1** in France, a member of a modern order such as the Legion of Honour, or of one of the historical knighthood orders. **2** (*old*) a knight; a chivalrous man. [Fr, from Lat *caballarius*, horseman]

chevron *n* a V-shaped mark or symbol, e.g. one worn on a military uniform to indicate rank. [OFr, rafter]

chew *v* **1** (*tr* & *intr*) to use the teeth to break up (food) inside the mouth before swallowing. **2** (*tr* & *intr*; **at, on**) to keep biting or nibbling. **3** (*tr* with **up**) to crush, damage, destroy, etc. by chewing, or as if by chewing. — *n* **1** an act of chewing. **2** something for chewing, e.g. a chewy sweet. — *v* **chew over** or **on** (*tr*; *coll*) to consider or discuss at length. [OE *ceowan*]

chewing-gum *n* a sticky sweet-flavoured substance for chewing without swallowing.

chewy *adj* **-ier**, **-iest** (*coll*) needing a lot of chewing. — *n* **chewiness**.

Chianti *n* a dry, usu. red, Italian wine. [*Chianti* in Italy, where the wine was first produced]

chiaroscuro *n* (*art*) an orig. Italian painting style in which strong highlighting and deep shadow are used to give figures their shape. [Ital, light-dark]

chic *adj* appealingly elegant or fashionable. — *n* stylishness; elegance. — *adv* **chicly**. [Fr]

chicane *n* **1** an obstacle, e.g. a series of sharp bends, on a motor-racing circuit. **2** trickery; chicanery. — *v* **1** (*tr*; **into, out of**) to cheat. **2** (*intr*) to use trickery or chicanery. [Fr, quibble]

chicanery *n* **-ies 1** clever talk intended to mislead. **2** a dishonest argument. **3** trickery; deception. [Fr, from *chicane*, quibble]

chick *n* **1** a baby bird. **2** (*old slang*) a young woman. [MidE *chike*, variant of *chiken*, chicken]

chicken *n* **1** the domestic or farmyard fowl, esp. a young one, bred for its eggs and flesh. **2** its flesh used as food. **3** (*coll derog*) a cowardly person. **4** (*slang*) a youthful person: *He's no chicken*. — *adj* (*coll derog*) cowardly. — *v* **chicken out** **-n-** (*intr*; **of**) to avoid doing, or withdraw from, something out of cowardice. [MidE *chiken*]

chicken-and-egg situation *n* a situation where one cannot tell which of two happenings is cause and which effect.

chickenfeed *n* **1** food for poultry. **2** something small and insignificant, esp. a paltry sum of money.

chicken-hearted or **chicken-livered** *adj* (*coll derog*) cowardly.

chickenpox *n* an infectious disease, esp. of childhood, with a fever and a rash of raised itchy spots.

chicken run *n* a small strip of ground usu. enclosed with wire netting, for keeping chickens in.

chicken wire *n* wire netting.

chickpea *n* a plant of the pea family with yellow wrinkled pea-like seeds used as a vegetable. [From earlier *chich pea*, from Fr *chiche*]

chickweed *n* a common weed with small white flowers. [**chick** + **weed**, the leaves and seeds being enjoyed by birds]

chicory *n* **1** a blue-flowered plant of the daisy family. **2** its carrot-like root, ground down as a flavouring, or substitute, for coffee. **3** its leaves, esp. used raw in salads. [Gr *kichorion*]

chide *v* ***chided*** or (*old*) ***chid***; ***chided*** or (*old*) ***chidden*** (*tr*) to scold, rebuke. — *n* **chiding**. [OE *cidan*]

chief *n* **1** the head of a tribe, clan, etc. **2** a leader. **3** the person in charge of any group, organisation, department, etc. — *adj* **1** (used in titles, etc.) first in rank; leading. **2** main; most important; principal. — **in chief** mainly; especially; most of all. [OFr *chef*, from Lat *caput*, head]

chief constable *n* in the UK, the officer in charge of the police force of a county or region.

chief executive *n* the director of a business, organisation, etc.

chiefly *adv* **1** mainly. **2** especially; above all.

chief of staff *n* ***chiefs of staff*** the senior officer of each of the armed forces.

chief petty officer *n* a senior non-commissioned officer in the Royal Navy and the navies of some other countries.

-in-chief *in cmpds* highest in rank; supreme: *commander-in-chief*.

chieftain *n* **1** the head of a tribe or clan. **2** a leader or commander. — *n* **chieftaincy**, **-ies** or **chieftainship**. [OFr *chevetaine*, from Lat *capitaneus*, captain]

chiffon *n* **1** a very fine transparent silk or nylon fabric. **2** (*cookery*) a light silkily frothy mixture, made with beaten whites of eggs. [Fr, rag]

chiffonier or **chiffonnier** *n* **1** a tall elegant chest of drawers. **2** a low wide cabinet with an open or grille front. [Fr, a container for *chiffons*, scraps of fabric]

chigger or **chigoe** *n* a tropical flea of Africa, India and America that burrows into the skin, esp. beneath the toenail. [Carib (a W Indian language) *chigo*]

chignon *n* a soft bun or coil of hair worn at the back of the neck. [Fr, from OFr *chaignon*, nape of the neck]

chigoe. See **chigger**.

chihuahua *n* a type of very small dog, with a smooth or long-haired coat. [*Chihuahua* in Mexico]

chilblain *n* a painful itchy red swelling usu. on the fingers or toes, caused by the cold. [**chill** + *blain*, blister]

child *n* ***children*** **1** a boy or girl between birth and physical maturity. **2** one's son or daughter. **3** someone lacking experience or understanding in something: *an absolute child in financial matters*. **4** (*derog*) an innocent or naive person. **5** a person seen as a typical product of a particular historical period, movement, etc.: *He was a child of his time*. — **child's play** (*coll*) a very simple task. — **with child** (*old*) pregnant. [OE *cild*]

child abuse *n* physical or mental cruelty to, or neglect of, a child, esp. by a parent or guardian.

childbearing *n* the process of giving birth to a child.

child benefit *n* a regular Government allowance to parents for the upbringing of children below a certain age.

childbirth *n* the process of giving birth to a child.

childhood *n* the state or time of being a child.

childish *adj* **1** (*derog*) silly; immature. **2** relating to children or childhood; like a child. — *adv* **childishly**. — *n* **childishness**.

childless *adj* having no children.

childlike *adj* like a child; innocent.

childminder *n* a person, usu. officially registered, who looks after children for payment, e.g. for working parents.

child-proof or **child-resistant** *adj* designed so as not to be able to be opened, operated, damaged, etc. by a child.

child welfare *n* care of children's health and living conditions, as a branch of social work.

chili. See **chilli**.

chill *n* **1** a feeling of coldness: *a wintry chill in the air*. **2** a feverish cold. **3** a feeling, esp. sudden, of depression or fear. **4** a coldness of manner; hostility. — *v* **1** (*tr* & *intr*) to make or become cold. **2** (*tr*) to cause to feel cold. **3** (*tr*) to scare, depress or discourage. **4** (*tr*) to harden (molten metal) quickly by putting it into a water-cooled mould. — *adj* **chilled**. — **take the chill off** to warm slightly. [OE *ciele*, cold]

chill factor *n* the degree by which weather conditions, e.g. wind, increase the effect of cold temperatures.

chilling *adj* frightening. — *adv* **chillingly**.

chilly *adj* ***-ier***, ***-iest*** **1** rather cold. **2** (*coll*) unfriendly; hostile. — *n* **chilliness**.

chilli or **chili** *n* ***-is*** or ***-ies*** **1** the hot-tasting seed-case of a type of pepper or capsicum, often used in dried, powdered form as a flavouring. **2** short for **chilli con carne**, a hot Mexican dish of minced meat and beans flavoured with chilli powder. [Aztec *chilli*]

chimaera. See **chimera**.

chime *n* **1** a set of tuned bells; the sound made by them. **2** (in *pl*) a percussion instrument consisting of hanging metal tubes that are struck with a hammer. — *v* **1** (*intr*) (of bells) to ring. **2** (*intr* & *tr*) (of a clock) to indicate (the time) by chiming. **3** (*intr* with **with**) to agree with: *That chimes with what others say*. — *v* **chime in** (*intr*; ***with***) **1** to break into a conversation, esp. repeating or agreeing with something. **2** to agree with, or fit in. [Earlier *chymbe belle*, prob. from OE *cimbal*, cymbal]

chimera or **chimaera** *n* **1** (*Gr mythol*) a creature with a lion's head, goat's body and serpent's tail. **2** a wild, impossible idea. — *adj* **chimerical**. [Gr *chimaira*, she-goat]

chimney *n* ***-eys*** **1** a narrow vertical shaft for the escape of smoke from a fire or furnace; the top part of this, rising from a roof. **2** an outlet for steam from an engine. **3** the outlet of a volcano. **4** a glass funnel protecting the flame of a lamp. **5** a narrow vertical cleft in a rock face. [OFr *cheminee*, from Lat *camera caminata*, room with a fireplace]

chimney breast *n* a projecting part of a wall built round the base of a chimney.

chimneypot *n* a short hollow rounded fitting, usu. made of pottery, that sits in the opening at the top of a chimney.

chimney stack *n* **1** a stone or brick structure rising from a roof, usu. carrying several chimneys. **2** a very tall factory chimney.

chimney-sweep *n* (also **sweep**) a person who cleans soot out of chimneys.

chimp *n* (*coll*) a chimpanzee.

chimpanzee *n* a small W African ape, the most similar to man of all animals. [From a W African language]

chin *n* the front central part of the lower jaw. — **keep one's chin up** (*coll*) to stay cheerful in spite of misfortune. — **take it on the chin** (*coll*) to accept a blow or misfortune bravely. [OE *cinn*]

chinless *adj* (*derog*) **1** having a small, weak, backwards-sloping chin. **2** having a weak, indecisive character.

chinstrap *n* a helmet strap, worn under the chin.

chinwag *n* (*coll*) a chat.

china *n* **1** (articles made from) a fine translucent earthenware, orig. from China. **2** (articles made from) similar materials. — *adj* made of china. [Persian *chini*, Chinese]

china clay *n* kaolin, a fine white clay used for making porcelain.

Chinaman *n* **-men** **1** (*old derog*) a Chinese man. **2** (*cricket*) a ball, spinning from the off to the leg side, bowled by a left-handed bowler to a right-handed batsman.

China tea *n* a kind of smoke-cured tea grown in China.

Chinatown *n* in any city outside China, a district where most of the inhabitants are Chinese.

chinchilla *n* **1** a small rodent of S America, much valued for its soft grey fur. **2** the fur itself. **3** a breed of cats or of rabbits with grey fur. [Span]

chine[1] *n* **1** the backbone. **2** a cut, esp. of pork, consisting of part of the backbone and adjoining parts. **3** a steep-sided ridge. — *v* (*tr*) to cut (the carcass of an animal) along the backbone. [OFr *eschine*]

chine[2] *n* a deep ravine, esp. in S England. [OE *cinu*, crevice]

Chinese *n* ***Chinese*** **1** a native or citizen of China, or a member of the main ethnic group of China. **2** the language of the main ethnic group of China. — *adj* belonging or relating to China, its people or language.

Chinese cabbage *n* (also **Chinese leaves**) a green lettuce-like vegetable used raw in salads.

Chinese chequers *n* (*sing*) a game played by moving pegs or marbles on a star-shaped board.

Chinese gooseberry *n* the kiwi fruit.

Chinese lantern *n* **1** a collapsible paper lantern that folds concertina-fashion. **2** a plant with bright orange papery calyxes resembling lanterns.

Chinese puzzle *n* **1** a very difficult wooden puzzle, esp. consisting of a series of boxes that fit one inside the next. **2** any highly complicated puzzle or problem.

chink[1] *n* **1** a small slit or crack. **2** a narrow beam of light shining through such a crack. [Related to **chine**[2]]

chink[2] *n* a faint, short ringing noise; a clink. — *v* (*intr* & *tr*) to make or cause to make this noise. [Imit.]

Chink, or **Chinkie** or **Chinky**, **-ies** (*coll offensive*) *n* a Chinese person. — *adj* (also without *cap*) Chinese. [Fr]

chintz *n* a shiny cotton material orig. imported from India, usu. printed in bright colours on a light background, used esp. for soft furnishings. [*chints*, plural of *chint*, from Gujarati (an Indian language) *chi(n)t*]

chintzy *adj* **-ier**, **-iest** (*derog*) sentimentally or quaintly showy.

chip *v* **-pp-** **1** (*tr* & *intr*; **off**, **away**, **at**) to knock or strike small pieces off a hard object or material; to be broken off in small pieces; to have small pieces broken off. **2** (*tr*) to shape by chipping: *chip a design into the stone.* **3** to cut (potatoes) into strips for frying. **4** (*tr* & *intr*; *golf*, *football*, etc.) to strike with, or play, a chip shot. — *n* **1** a small piece chipped off. **2** a place from which a piece has been chipped off: *a big chip in the rim.* **3** (*Br*: usu. in *pl*) a strip of potato, fried or for frying. **4** (*NAm*; also **potato chip**) a potato crisp. **5** a plastic counter used as a money token in gambling. **6** (*comput*; also **microchip** or **silicon chip**) a very small piece of silicon, on which a large amount of information can be stored electronically. **7** a small piece of stone. — *adj* **chipped**. — *v* **chip in** (*intr*; **with**; *coll*) **1** to interrupt: *chip in with a suggestion.* **2** (*tr* & *intr*) to contribute. — **a chip off the old block** (*coll*) a person very like one or other parent in personality or appearance. — **have a chip on one's shoulder** (*coll*) to feel resentful about something, esp. unreasonably. — **have had one's chips** (*coll*) to have lost one's chance; to have failed or been killed. — **when the chips are down** (*coll*) at the moment of crisis; when it comes to the point. [OE *cipp*, log, ploughshare, beam]

chipboard *n* solid board made from compressed wood chips.

chip shop *n* a shop selling chips, fish and other fried foods, for taking away to eat.

chip shot *n* (*golf*, *football*, etc.) a short, high shot or kick.

chipmunk *n* a black-and-white-striped American squirrel with a large bushy tail. [Earlier *chitmunk*, from Ojibwa, a N American Indian language]

chipolata *n* a small sausage. [Fr, from Ital *cipollata*, onion dish]

Chippendale *adj* (*furniture*) made by, or imitating the style of, the 18th-cent. designer Thomas *Chippendale*, with graceful, elegant lines and detailed carving.

chipper *adj* (*US coll*) (of a person) cheerful and lively. [Perhaps from N English dialect]

chippy *n* **-ies** (*Br coll*) **1** a chip shop **2** a carpenter or joiner.

chiromancy or **cheiromancy** *n* palmistry. [Gr *cheir*, hand + *manteia*, divination]

chiropodist *n* a person who treats minor disorders of the feet, e.g. corns. — *n* **chiropody**. [Gr *cheir*, hand + *pous*, foot; the original practitioners treated hands as well as feet]

chiropractic *n* a method of treating pain by manual adjustment of the spinal column, etc. so as to release pressure on the nerves. [Gr *cheir*, hand + *prattein*, to do]

chirp *v* **1** (*intr*) (of birds, grasshoppers, etc.) to produce a short high unmusical sound. **2** (*tr* & *intr*) to chatter, or say (something), merrily. — *n* a chirping sound. [Imit.]

chirpy *adj* **-ier**, **-iest** (*coll*) cheerful and lively. — *adv* **chirpily**. — *n* **chirpiness**.

chirrup *v* **-p-** (*intr*) to chirp, esp. in little bursts. — *n* a burst of chirping. — *adj* **chirrupy**. [Imit.]

chisel *n* a tool with a strong metal blade with a cutting edge at the tip, used for cutting and shaping wood or stone. — *v* **-ll-** (*tr*) **1** to cut or shape (wood or stone) with a chisel. **2** (*slang*) to cheat. [OFr *cisel*]

chit[1] *n* (*coll*; also **chitty**, **-ies**) a short note, esp. an officially signed one, recording money owed or paid, an order for goods, etc. [Hindi *citthi*]

chit[2] *n* (*derog*) a cheeky young girl; a mere child. [Related to *kitten*]

chitchat (*derog*) *n* chatter; gossip. — *v* **-tt-** (*intr*) to gossip idly. [Reduplicated form of **chat**]

chitin *n* (*biol*) the tough material that forms the hard covering of lobsters and other crustaceans, insects, spiders, etc. — *adj* **chitinous**. [Fr *chitine*, from Gr *chiton*, tunic]

chitterlings *n* (*pl*) a pig's or other animal's intestines, prepared as a food. [MidE *chet-erling*]

chitty. See **chit**[1].

chivalry *n* courtesy and protectiveness shown to the weak, or to women by men. **2** (*hist*) a code of moral and religious behaviour followed by mediaeval knights; the mediaeval system of knighthood. [OFr *chevalerie*, from *chevalier*, knight]

chivalrous *adj* **1** showing chivalry; courteous towards, and concerned for, those weaker than oneself. **2** relating to mediaeval chivalry. — *adv* **chivalrously**. — *n* **chivalrousness**.

chive *n* a plant of the onion family with purple flowers and long thin hollow leaves used as a flavouring or garnish. [OFr *cive*]

chivvy or **chivy** *v* **-ies**, **-ied** (*tr*) to keep urging on or nagging (someone), esp. to hurry or to get some task done. [Perhaps from the ballad *Chevy Chase*]

chlor- or **chloro-** *comb fm* **1** green. **2** chlorine. [Gr *chloros*, green]

chloral or **chloral hydrate** *n* (*med*) a colourless crystalline compound used as a sedative. [**chlorine** + **alcohol**]

chlorate *n* (*chem*) a salt of chloric acid ($HClO_3$). [**chlorine** + **-ate**]

chloric *adj* (*chem*) relating to, containing, or obtained from, chlorine: *chloric acid*. [**chlorine** + **-ic**]

chloride *n* **1** (*chem*) a compound of chlorine with another element or radical (group of atoms); a salt of hydrochloric acid (HCl). **2** chloride of lime, a bleaching agent. [**chlorine** + **-ide**]

chlorine *n* an element (symbol **Cl**), a poisonous strong-smelling yellowish-green gas used as a water-purifying agent, and in bleaches and disinfectants.

chlorinate *v* (*tr*) to treat (e.g. water) with, or cause (a substance) to combine with, chlorine. — *adj* **chlorinated**. — *n* **chlorination**. [Gr *chloros*, green]

chloro-. See **chlor-**.

chlorofluorocarbon *n* (also **CFC**) any of various compound gases containing chlorine, fluorine, hydrogen and carbon, used e.g. as refrigerating agents and propellants in aerosols, some causing the ozone in the atmosphere to break down.

chloroform *n* a strong-smelling liquid now used mainly as a solvent; formerly used as an anaesthetic, its vapour being inhaled to produce unconsciousness. — *v* (*tr*) to anaesthetise with chloroform. [**chlorine** + **formic**]

chlorophyll *n* (*bot*) the green colouring matter in plants that absorbs the energy from the sun needed for the process of photosynthesis. [**chlor-** + Gr *phyllon*, leaf]

chloroplast *n* (*biol*) one of the chlorophyll-containing particles in a plant in which photosynthesis takes place. [**chlor-** + Gr *plastos*, moulded]

choc *n* (*coll*) chocolate.

chock *n* a heavy block or wedge used to prevent movement of a wheel, etc. — *v* (*tr*) to wedge or immobilise with chocks.

chock-a-block *adj* **1** tightly jammed. **2** (**with**) crammed.

chock-full *adj* absolutely full.

chocolate *n* **1** the roasted and ground seeds of the cacao tree, used, usu. sweetened, in the form of a powder, paste or solid block. **2** a sweet made from, or coated with, chocolate. **3** a drink prepared with chocolate powder. **4** a dark-brown colour. — *adj* **1** made from, or coated with, chocolate. **2** dark brown.— *adj* **chocolaty**. [Aztec *chocolatl*]

chocolate-box *adj* (*derog*) over-pretty or sentimental, like the designs on boxes of chocolates.

choice *n* **1** the act or process of choosing. **2** the right, power or opportunity to choose: *have no choice*. **3** something or someone chosen: *a good choice*. **4** a variety of things available for choosing between: *a wide choice*. — *adj* of specially good quality. — *n* **choiceness**. — **from choice 1** willingly. **2** if given a choice.— **of one's choice** selected according to one's own preference. — **take one's choice** to choose whatever one wants. [OFr *chois*]

choir *n* **1** an organised group of trained singers, esp. one that performs in church. **2** esp. in a cathedral or large church; the area occupied by the choir; the chancel. [OFr *cuer*, from Lat *chorus*]

choirboy or **choirgirl** *n* a young boy or girl who sings in a church choir.

choirmaster or **choirmistress** *n* the trainer of a choir.

choir stalls *n* (*pl*) fixed wooden seats for the choir in the chancel of a church.

choke *v* **1** (*tr* & *intr*; **on**) to prevent, or be prevented, wholly or partially, from breathing: *choke on a piece of food*. **2** (*tr* & *intr*; **with**) to make or become speechless from emotion: *choking with rage*. **3** (*tr*; **with**) to fill up, block or restrict. **4** (*tr*) to restrict the growth or development of: *plants choked by weeds*. — *n* **1** a device in a carburettor that helps to start an engine when cold by restricting the amount of air mixing with the petrol, so as to produce a richer mixture. **2** (*electronics*) a device for controlling the surges in an electric current. — *v* **choke back** (*tr*) to suppress (tears, laughter or anger). — *v* **choke off** (*tr*) **1** to put a stop to; to prevent. **2** to prevent (someone) from continuing to speak. [OE *aceocian*, to suffocate]

choker *n* a close-fitting necklace or broad band of velvet, etc. worn round the neck.

cholecalciferol *n* vitamin D_3. [Gr *chole*, bile + **calciferol**]

choler *n* (*old*) anger; irritability. [Earlier meaning, bile; Gr *chole*, bile]

choleric *adj* irritable; bad-tempered.

cholera *n* a highly infectious, often fatal, intestinal disease with severe diarrhoea, caused by bacteria in drinking water or food. [Gr, from *chole*, bile]

choleric. See **choler**.

cholesterol *n* a fatty alcohol found in body tissues and fluids, and in animal fats, thought to cause fatty deposits in the blood vessels that narrow and harden them. [Gr *chole*, bile + *stereos*, solid]

chomp *v* (*tr* and *intr*) to munch noisily. — *n* an act of chomping. [Variant of **champ**]

choose *v* ***chose***, ***chosen*** **1** (*tr* & *intr*; **from, between**) to take or select (one or more things or persons) from a larger number, according to one's own preference or judgement. **2** (*tr*) to decide; to think fit. — **nothing to choose between** with little difference in quality, value, etc. between. [OE *ceosan*]

choosy *adj* ***-ier***, ***-iest*** (*coll*) difficult to please; fussy.

chosen few *n* a select, privileged group of people.

chop[1] *v* ***-pp-*** **1** (*tr* & *intr*; **off, up, at,** etc.) to cut with a vigorous downwards or sideways slicing action, with an axe, knife, etc. **2** (*tr*) to hit (a ball) with a sharp downwards stroke. **3** (*tr*; *coll*) to reduce or completely withdraw (funding, etc.). — *n* **1** a slice of pork, lamb or mutton containing a bone, esp. a rib. **2** a chopping action or stroke. **3** a sharp downward stroke given to a ball. **4** a short sharp blow. **5** (*coll with* **the**) dismissal from a job: *get the chop*. **6** the sudden stopping or closing down of something: *Our project got the chop*. [Variant of **chap**[2]]

chophouse *n* (*coll*) a restaurant specialising in steak and chops.

chopper *n* **1** (*coll*) a helicopter. **2** (*coll*) a motorcycle with high handlebars. **3** a short-handled axe-like tool. **4** (in *pl*; *coll*) the teeth.

chopping-board *n* a board for chopping up vegetables, etc. on.

choppy *adj* ***-ier***, ***-iest*** (of the sea, etc.) rather rough, with small irregular waves. — *adv* **choppily**. — *n* **choppiness**.

chop[2] : **chop and change** to keep changing one's mind, plans, etc. — **chop logic** to use over-subtle or complicated and confusing arguments. [OE *ceapian*, to bargain or trade]

chops *n* (*pl*) the jaws or mouth, esp. an animal's. — **lick one's chops** (*coll*) to look forward to some pleasure with relish. [*chap*, the lower half of the cheek]

chopsticks *n* (*pl*) a pair of slender wooden, plastic or ivory sticks, operated in one hand like pincers, used for eating with in several Oriental countries. [Pidgin English *chop*, quick + **stick**]

chop suey *n* a Chinese dish of chopped meat and vegetables fried in a sauce, usu. served with rice. [Chin dialect *jaahp seui*, mixed bits]

choral *adj* relating to, or to be sung by, a choir or chorus: *choral music*. — *adv* **chorally**. [Lat *choralis*, from *chorus*, choir]

choral society *n* a group that meets regularly to practise and perform choral music.

chorale *n* **1** a hymn tune with a slow, dignified rhythm and strong harmonisation. **2** (*US*) a choir or choral society. [Ger *Choral*, short for *Choralgesang*, choral singing]

chord[1] *n* (*mus*) a combination of musical notes played together. [Earlier *cord*, shortened from **accord**]

chord[2] *n* **1** (*poetic*) a string of a musical instrument. **2** (*anat*) another spelling of **cord**. **3** (*math*) a straight line joining two points on a curve or curved surface. — **strike a chord** to prompt a feeling of recognition or familiarity. — **touch the right chord** to get the desired emotional or sympathetic response from someone. [Gr *chorde*, string, gut]

chore *n* a piece of housework or other boring and laborious task. [**char**[2]]

chorea *n* (*med*) a disease of the nervous system, causing continuous involuntary and jerky movements. [Gr *choreia*, dance]

choreography *n* the arrangement of the sequence and pattern of movements in dancing. — *n* **choreographer**. — *adj* **choreographic**. [Gr *choreia*, dance + **-graphy**]

choreograph *v* (*tr*) to plan the choreography for (a dance, ballet, etc.).

chorister *n* a singer in a choir, esp. a choirboy in a church or cathedral choir. [MidE *queristre*, from *quer*, choir, influenced by Lat *chorista*, singer in a choir]

chortle *v* (*intr*) to give a half-suppressed, amused or triumphant laugh. [Word invented by Lewis Carroll in *Through the Looking-glass*, combining **snort** and **chuckle**]

chorus *n* **1** a set of lines in a song, sung after each verse. **2** a large choir. **3** a piece of music for such a choir. **4** the group of singers and dancers supporting the soloists in an opera or musical show: *a chorus girl*. **5** something uttered by a number of people at the same time: *a chorus of 'No's'*. **6**

(*drama*) an actor who delivers an introductory or concluding passage to a play. **7** (*Gr drama*) a group of actors, always on stage, who comment on the developments in the plot. — *v* **-s-** (*tr*) to say, sing or utter together. — **in chorus** all together; in unison. [Lat, choir]

chose, chosen. See **choose**.

chough *n* a red-legged black bird of the crow family.

choux pastry *n* a very light pastry made with eggs. [Fr *pâte choux*, cabbage pastry]

chow[1] *n* a breed of dog, orig. Chinese, with thick fur, a curled tail, and a blue tongue. [Prob. from a Chinese dialect]

chow[2] *n* (esp. *US*; *slang*) food. [Pidgin English *chow-chow*, mixed fruit preserve]

chowder *n* (esp. *NAm*) a thick soup containing clams or fish and vegetables, often made with milk. [Fr *chaudière*, kettle]

chow mein *n* a Chinese dish of chopped meat and vegetables served with fried noodles. [Chin, fried noodles]

chrism *n* **1** holy oil used in the Roman Catholic and Orthodox Churches for anointing. **2** (*relig*) confirmation. [Gr *chrisma*, anointing]

Christ *n* **1** the Messiah or 'anointed one' whose coming is prophesied in the Old Testament. **2** Jesus of Nazareth, or Jesus Christ, believed by Christians to be the Messiah. **3** a figure or picture of Jesus. — *interj* (*offensive* to many) expressing surprise, anger, etc. [Gr *christos*, anointed]

christen *v* **-n-** (*tr*) **1** to give (a person, esp. a baby) a name, as part of the religious ceremony of receiving him or her into the Christian church. **2** to give a name or nickname to. **3** (*humorous*) to use for the first time: *christen the new wine glasses*. — *n* **christening**. [OE *cristnian*, from *cristen*, Christian]

Christendom *n* **1** all Christians. **2** the parts of the world in which Christianity is the recognised religion. [OE, from *cristen*, Christian + **-dom**]

Christian *n* **1** a person who believes in, and follows the teachings and example of, Jesus Christ. **2** (*coll*) a person of Christian qualities. — *adj* **1** relating to Jesus Christ, the Christian religion, or Christians. **2** (*coll*) showing virtues associated with Christians, such as kindness, patience, tolerance and generosity. [Lat *Christianus*]

Christian era *n* the period of time from the birth of Jesus Christ to the present.

Christianity *n* **1** the religious faith based on the teachings of Jesus Christ. **2** the spirit, beliefs, principles and practices of this faith. **3** Christendom.

christian name *n* **1** the personal name given to a Christian at baptism. **2** anyone's first or given name; a forename.

Christian Science *n* a system of religion in which spiritual or divine power is relied on for healing, rather than medicines or surgery. — *n* **Christian Scientist**.

Christmas *n* **1** the annual Christian festival commemorating the birth of Christ, held on 25 December. **2** the period of celebration surrounding this date. — *adj* **Christmassy**. [OE *Cristesmæsse*, Christ's Mass]

Christmas box *n* a small gift of money given at Christmas to a postman or tradesman providing regular services.

Christmas cake *n* a large rich iced fruitcake, eaten at Christmas.

Christmas Day *n* 25 December.

Christmas Eve *n* 24 December, or the evening of this day.

Christmas pudding *n* a rich steamed pudding containing dried fruit, spices, etc., eaten esp. at Christmas.

Christmas rose *n* an evergreen plant with white or pink flowers that bloom in the winter.

Christmas stocking *n* a long sock, traditionally hung up by children on Christmas Eve to be filled with presents.

Christmas tree *n* a small fir tree, sometimes artificial, on which decorations, lights and presents are hung at Christmas.

chromatic *adj* **1** relating to colours; coloured. **2** (*mus*) relating to, or using notes from, the 12-note form of scale (**chromatic scale**) that includes semitones. ◇ See also **diatonic**. — *adv* **chromatically**. [Gr *chromatikos*, from *chroma*, colour]

chromatin *n* the substance in a cell nucleus that contains the chromosomes, and can be easily stained so as to enable cell-division to be seen under the microscope. [Gr *chroma*, colour]

chromato-. See **chromo-**.

chromatography *n* a method of separating the substances that make up a liquid or gas mixture by passing it over or through materials that attract, or adsorb, the different substances to a greater or lesser extent, so as to produce a **chromatogram**, typically a column of coloured bands, as an analysis of the substances present. [Gr *chroma*, colour + **-graphy**]

chrome *n* a non-technical word for chromium, esp. when used as a silvery plating for other metals. [Gr *chroma*, colour]

chrome yellow *n* a yellow colouring matter obtained from a lead compound of chromium.

chromite *n* a brownish mineral containing chromium and iron oxides, the usual source of chromium. [**chromium** + **-ite**]

chromium *n* an element (symbol **Cr**), a hard shiny metal used in alloys, esp. with steel, and to plate other metals to prevent rust. [**chrome**]

chromo- or **chromato-** *comb fm* colour. [Gr *chroma*, colour]

chromosome *n* a microscopic rod-like structure found in pairs in the cell nuclei of animals and plants during cell-division, carrying the genes that control growth, physical appearance, etc. — *adj* **chromosomal**. [Gr *chroma*, colour + *soma*, body]

chron- or **chrono-** *comb fm* time. [Gr *chronos*, time]

chronic *adj* **1** (of a condition or illness) always present or frequently recurring. ◇ See also **acute**. **2** (of a person) suffering from this type of illness: *a chronic bronchitic*. **3** (*Br coll*) very bad; severe; grave. **4** habitual. — *adv* **chronically**. — *n* **chronicity**. [Gr *chronikos*, relating to time]

chronicle *n* (often in *pl*) a record of esp. historical events in the order in which they happened. — *v* (*tr*) to record (a happening) in a chronicle. — *n* **chronicler**. [Dimin. of OFr *chronique*, from Gr *chronika*, annals]

chrono-. See **chron-**.

chronology *n* **-ies 1** the study or science of determining the correct order of historical events. **2** the arrangement of events in order of occurrence. **3** a table or list showing events in order of occurrence. — *n* **chronologist**. **[chron- + -logy]**

chronological *adj* **1** according to order of occurrence: *in chronological order*. **2** relating to chronology. — *adv* **chronologically**.

chronometer *n* a very accurate type of watch or clock designed to keep accurate time in all conditions, used esp. at sea. **[chron- + -meter]**

chrysalis *n* the pupa of a butterfly or moth, enclosed in a case or cocoon. [Gr *chrysallis*, from *chrysos*, gold]

chrysanthemum *n* a garden plant of the daisy family, with large bushy flowers, pale yellow to deep gold. [Gr *chrysos*, gold + *anthemon*, flower]

chrysoberyl *n* a greenish-yellow or golden mineral, used as a gemstone. [Gr *chrysos*, gold + *beryllos*, beryl]

chrysolite *n* a yellow or green precious stone. [Gr *chrysos*, gold + *lithos*, stone]

chrysoprase *n* an apple-green mineral used as a gemstone, a variety of chalcedony. [Gr *chrysos*, gold + *prason*, leek]

chub *n* a small fat river-fish of the carp family.

chubby *adj* **-ier**, **-iest** plump, esp. in a childishly attractive way. — *adv* **chubbily**. — *n* **chubbiness**. [Perhaps from **chub**]

chuck[1] *v* (*tr*) **1** (*coll*) to throw or fling. **2** to give (a child, etc.) an affectionate tap under the chin. **3** (*slang*; **up**) to give up, abandon or reject. — *n* **1** (*coll*) a toss, fling or throw. **2** (with **the**; *slang*) dismissal; rejection: *gave her boyfriend the chuck*. **3** an affectionate tap under the chin. — *v* **chuck out** (*tr*; *coll*) **1** to order (someone) to leave a place. **2** to get rid of or reject.

chuck[2] *n* (also **chuck steak**) beef cut from the area between the neck and shoulder. [Variant of **chock**]

chuck[3] *n* a device for holding a piece of work in a lathe, or for holding the blade or bit in a drill. [Variant of **chock**]

chuckle *v* **1** (*intr*) to laugh quietly, esp. in a half-suppressed private way. **2** (*tr*) to utter with a little laugh. — *n* an amused little laugh. [From an old word *chuck*, to cluck like a hen]

chuff *v* (*intr*) (of steam trains) to progress with regular puffing noises. [Imit.]

chuffed *adj* (*Br coll*) very pleased. [Dialect *chuff*, plump, swollen with pride]

chug *v* **-gg-** (*intr*) (of a motor boat, motor car, etc.) to progress while making the typical quiet thudding noise of an unsophisticated engine. — *n* this noise. [Imit.]

chukker or **chukka** *n* one of the six seven-and-a-half-minute periods of play in the game of polo. [Hindi *cakkar*, round]

chukka boot *n* a leather ankle boot.

chum *n* (*coll*) a close friend. — *v* **chum up** **-mm-** (*intr*; **with**) to make friends. [Perhaps from *chamber fellow*, a fellow student, etc. sharing one's room.]

chummy *adj* **-ier**, **-iest** (*coll*) friendly.

chump *n* **1** (*coll*) an idiot; a fool. **2** the thick end of a loin cut of lamb or mutton: *a chump chop*. **3** a short thick heavy block of wood. — **off one's chump** (*Br coll*) crazy; insane. [Perhaps a combination of **chunk** and **lump**]

chunk *n* **1** a thick, esp. irregularly shaped, piece. **2** (*coll*) a large or considerable amount. [Variant of **chuck**[3]]

chunky *adj* **-ier**, **-iest 1** thick-set; stockily or strongly built. **2** (of clothes, fabrics, etc.) thick; bulky. **3** solid and strong. **4** containing chunks: *chunky marmalade*.

church *n* **1** a building for public Christian worship. **2** the religious services held in a church: *go to church*. **3** (*cap*) the profession of a clergyman: *enter the Church*. **4** (*cap*) the clergy considered as an esp. political group: *quarrels between Church and State*. **5** (*cap*) any of many branches of Christians with their own doctrines, style of worship, etc.: *the Methodist Church*. **6** the whole Christian establishment: *studying church history*. [OE *cirice*, from Gr *kyriakon* (*doma*), the house of the Lord, from *kyrios*, lord]

churchgoer *n* a person who attends church services, esp. regularly.

churchman or **churchwoman** *n* a member of the clergy or of a church.

Church of England *n* the official state church in England, which has the Sovereign as its head, allows its priests to marry, and does not recognise the authority of the Pope.

church officer *n* in some churches, a person acting as church caretaker, with certain other duties.

Church of Scotland *n* the largest Presbyterian church in Scotland, formerly the established state church.

churchwarden *n* **1** in the Church of England, one of two lay members of a congregation elected to look after the church's property, money, etc. **2** an old-fashioned long clay pipe.

churchyard *n* the burial ground round a church.

churlish *adj* bad-tempered; rude; ill-mannered. — *adv* **churlishly**. — *n* **churlishness**. [*churl*, surly person, peasant]

churn *n* **1** a machine in which milk is shaken about to make butter. **2** a large milk can. — *v* **1** (*tr*) to make (butter) in a churn, or to turn (milk) into butter in a churn. **2** (*intr* & *tr*; **up**) to move about violently. — *v* **churn out** (*tr*; usu. *derog*) to keep producing (esp. things of boring similarity) in great quantities: *churn out novels*. [OE *cirin* or *cyrn*]

chute[1] *n* **1** a sloping channel down which to send water, rubbish, etc. **2** a slide in a children's playground or swimming-pool. [Fr, fall]

chute[2] *n* (*coll*) a parachute.

chutney *n* an Indian type of pickle made with fruit, vinegar, spices, sugar, etc. [Hindi *catni*]

chutzpah *n* (*coll*; esp. *US*) self-assurance bordering on impudence; audacity; effrontery; nerve. [Yiddish]

chyle *n* (*physiol*) a milky fluid produced in the small intestine during digestion, composed of lymph and food fats. [Gr *chylos*, juice]

chyme *n* (*physiol*) the thick fluid mass of partially digested food that enters the small intestine from the stomach. [Gr *chymos*, juice]

CI *abbrev* Channel Islands.

Ci *symbol* curie.

CIA *abbrev* Central Intelligence Agency, a department in the US government responsible for security and espionage. ◇ See also **FBI**.

cicada *n* a large insect of warm climates, the male of which makes a loud chirping sound by means of a pair of drum-like organs in its abdomen. [Lat]

cicatrice *n* **-*trices*** (*pathol*; also **cicatrix**, **-*trices*** or **-*trixes***) a scar left by a wound after healing. [Lat *cicatrix*]

cicely *n* (also **sweet cicely**) a plant with a strong smell of aniseed, used as a flavouring. [Gr *seselis*, with spelling influenced by the name *Cicely*]

CID *abbrev* Criminal Investigation Department, the detective branch of the British police force.

-cide *comb fm* **1** the act of killing; murder: *homicide*. **2** a person, substance or thing that kills: *He's a potential suicide*. — *adj comb fm* **-cidal**. [Lat *-cida*, -killer, and *-cidium*, -killing]

cider *n* an alcoholic drink made from apples. [Fr *cidre*]

cigar *n* a long slender roll of tobacco leaves for smoking. [Span *cigarro*]

cigar-shaped *adj* having an elongated oval shape with pointed ends.

cigarette *n* a tube of finely cut tobacco rolled in thin paper, for smoking. [Fr, dimin. of *cigare*, cigar]

cigarette end or **cigarette butt** *n* the unsmoked stub of a cigarette.

cigarette-holder *n* a long slim mouthpiece into which a cigarette can be fitted for smoking.

cigarette-lighter *n* a petrol- or gas-fuelled device with a flint, for lighting cigarettes.

C-in-C *abbrev* Commander-in-Chief.

cinch *n* (*coll*) **1** an easily accomplished task. **2** a certainty. [Span *cincha*, saddle girth]

cincture *n* (*literary*) a belt or girdle. [Lat *cinctura*]

cinder *n* **1** a piece of burnt coal or wood. **2** (in *pl*) ashes. — *adj* **cindery**. [OE *sinder*, slag]

Cinderella *n* someone or something whose charms or merits go unnoticed; a neglected member of a set or group. [From the fairy-tale character]

cine *adj* or *comb fm* relating to moving pictures: *a cinecamera*; *a cine projector*. [Shortened from *cinema*]

cinema *n* **1** a theatre in which motion pictures are shown. **2** cinemas in general: *don't go to the cinema much*. **3** (sometimes with **the**) motion pictures or films generally. **4** the art or business of making films. — *adj* **cinematic**. [**cinematograph**]

cinematography *n* the art of making motion pictures. — *n* **cinematographer**. — *adj* **cinematographic**.

cinematograph *n* an apparatus for taking and projecting moving pictures, i.e. a series of still photographs each representing an instant of time, in rapid succession. [Gr *kinema*, motion + **-graphy**]

cineraria *n* a plant with brightly coloured daisy-like flowers and leaves with a thick white down. [Lat *cinerarius*, relating to ashes]

cinerary *adj* relating to ashes; for holding ashes: *a cinerary urn*. [Lat *cinerarius*, relating to ashes]

cinnabar *n* **1** sulphide of mercury, a red mineral from which mercury and the colouring matter vermilion are obtained. **2** vermilion, a reddish-orange colour. **3** a moth with red and black wings. [Gr *kinnabari*, from Persian]

cinnamon *n* **1** a spice obtained from the inner bark of a SE Asian tree. **2** a brownish-orange colour. [Gr *kinnamon*]

cinquefoil *n* **1** a plant of the rose family with five-petalled flowers and leaves divided into five sections. **2** (*heraldry*) a five-petalled flower. **3** (*archit*) a design composed of five petal-like arcs, found at the top of an arch, in a circular window, etc. [OFr *cincfoille*, from Lat *quinquefolium*, five-leaved plant]

cipher *n* **1** a secret code. **2** something written in code. **3** the key to a code. **4** an interlaced set of initials; a monogram. **5** (*arith*; *old*) the symbol **0**, used to fill blanks in writing numbers, but of no value itself. **6** a person or thing of little importance. **7** any Arabic numeral. — *v* **-r-** (*tr*) to write (a message, etc.) in code. [Lat *ciphra*, from Arabic *sifr*, empty, zero]

circa *prep* (used esp. with dates) about; approximately: *circa 1250*. [Lat]

circadian *adj* (*biol*) relating to the body's daily biological rhythms, including e.g. the times of highest and lowest activity for any bodily process within the 24-hour period. [**circa** + Lat *dies*, day]

circle *n* **1** a line evenly and continuously curved so as to form a round figure, with every point on it an equal distance from the centre; the area enclosed within the line. **2** anything in the form of a circle. **3** a circular route, e.g. the orbit of a planet, etc. **4** a curved upper floor of seats in a theatre, etc. **5** a series of events, steps or developments, ending at the point where it began. ◇ See also **vicious circle**. **6** a group of people associated in some way: *his circle of acquaintances*. — *v* **1** (*tr* & *intr*) to move in a circle; to move in a circle round. **2** (*tr*) to draw a circle round. — **come full circle 1** to complete a full cycle. **2** to reach or arrive back at the starting-point. — **go round in circles** to be trapped in an endless and frustrating cycle of repetitive discussion or activity. — **run round in circles** to rush around frantically, making little progress. [OE *circul*, from Lat *circulus*]

circlet *n* **1** a simple band or hoop of gold, silver, etc. worn on the head. **2** a small circle. [OFr *cerclet*, dimin. of *cercle*, circle]

circuit *n* **1** a complete course, journey or route round something. **2** a race track, running-track, etc. **3** the path of an electric current and the parts it passes through. ◇ See also **short circuit** and **closed circuit**. **4** the places or venues visited in turn and regularly by entertainers, etc. **5** a round of places made by a travelling judge. **6** a group of cinemas, theatres, etc. under common control, with shows moving on from one to the next. [Fr, from Lat *circuitus*, round trip, revolution]

circuit-breaker *n* a device that automatically interrupts an electric current when a fault occurs.

circuitous *adj* taking a long complicated route; indirect; roundabout. — *adv* **circuitously**. — *n* **circuitousness**.

circuitry *n* **-ies** (*electr*) **1** a plan or system of circuits. **2** the equipment or components making up such a system.

circuit training *n* athletic training in the form of a repeated series of exercises.

circular *adj* **1** having the form of a circle. **2** moving or going round in a circle, leading back to the starting-point. **3** (of reasoning, etc.) containing a fallacy, the truth of the conclusion depending on a point that depends on the conclusion being true. **4** (of a letter, etc.) addressed and copied to a number of people. — *n* a circular letter or notice. — *n* **circularity, -ies**. — *adv* **circularly**. [Lat *circularis*]

circularise *v* (*tr*) to send circulars to.

circular saw *n* a power-driven saw with a rotating disc-shaped toothed blade.

circulate *v* **1** (*tr* & *intr*) to move or cause to move round freely, esp. in a fixed route: *traffic circulating through the town centre*. **2** (*tr* & *intr*) to spread; to pass round: *circulate the report*. **3** (*intr*) to move around talking to different people, e.g. at a party. [Lat *circulare*, to encircle]

circulation *n* **1** the act or process of circulating. **2** the flow of blood round the body, from the heart through the arteries and veins back to the heart. **3** the distribution of a newspaper or magazine, or the number of copies of it that are sold. — **in**, or **out of**, **circulation 1** (of money) being, or not being, used by the public. **2** taking part, or not taking part, in one's usual social activities.

circulatory *adj* relating to circulation, esp. of the blood.

circum- *comb fm* round about. [Lat *circum*, about]

circumcise *v* **1** (*tr*) to cut away the foreskin of (a male), as a religious rite or medical necessity. **2** to cut away the clitoris of (a woman), or the skin covering it, for the same reasons. — *n* **circumcision**. [Lat *circum*, around + *caedere*, to cut round]

circumference *n* **1** the outer edge of a circle. **2** a path round a globe or other round object, esp. at its widest point. **3** the boundary of an area of any shape. **4** the distance represented by any of these. — *adj* **circumferential**. [Lat *circum*, around + *ferre*, to carry]

circumflex *n* a mark (ˆ) placed above a vowel in some languages as an indication of pronunciation, length, or the omission of a letter. [Lat *circumflexus*, arch]

circumlocution *n* an unnecessarily long or indirect way of saying something. — *adj* **circumlocutory**. [Lat *circum*, around + *loqui*, to speak]

circumnavigate *v* (*tr*) to sail or fly round (esp. the world). — *n* **circumnavigation**. — *n* **circumnavigator**. [Lat *circum*, around + *navigare*, to sail]

circumscribe *v* (*tr*) **1** to put a line or boundary round. **2** to limit or restrict. **3** (*geom*) to draw a figure round (another figure) so that they touch without intersecting. ◇ See also **inscribe** — *n* **circumscription**. [Lat *circum*, around + *scribere*, to write]

circumspect *adj* cautious; prudent; wary. — *n* **circumspection**. — *adv* **circumspectly**. [Lat *circum*, around + *specere*, to look]

circumstance *n* **1** a fact, incident, occurrence or condition, esp. (in *pl*) when relating to an act or event: *died in mysterious circumstances*. **2** (in *pl*) one's financial situation: *living in reduced circumstances* (i.e. poverty). **3** events that one cannot control; fate: *a victim of circumstance*. **4** ceremony: *pomp and circumstance*. — **in** or **under no circumstances** never, not for any reason

at all. — **in** or **under the circumstances** the situation being what it is or was. [Lat *circum*, around + *stare*, to stand]
circumstantial *adj* (of an account of an event) full of detailed description, etc. — *adv* **circumstantially**.
circumstantial evidence *n* (*legal*) details or facts that give a statement, etc. the appearance of truth, but do not prove it.
circumvent *v* (*tr*) **1** to find a way of getting round or evading (a rule, law, etc.). **2** to outwit or frustrate (someone). — *n* **circumvention**. [Lat *circum*, around + *venire*, to come]
circus *n* **1** a travelling company of performers including acrobats, clowns, and often trained animals, etc.; a performance by such a company, traditionally in a circular tent. **2** (*coll*) a scene of noisy confusion. **3** a travelling group of professional sportspeople, etc. who put on displays. **4** (esp. in place names, with *cap*) an open space, esp. one roughly circular, at the junction of a number of streets; a circular terrace of houses. **5** in ancient Rome, an esp. oval open-air stadium for chariot-racing and other competitive sports. [Lat, circle, ring, stadium]
cirque *n* (*geog*) a bowl-shaped hollow in the side of a mountain or at a valley-head, scooped out by ice. [Fr, circus]
cirrhosis *n* (*med*) a progressive disease of the liver, caused esp. by persistent excessive drinking of alcohol, with a wasting away of normal tissue, and an overgrowth of abnormal lumpy tissue. [Gr *kirrhos*, tawny, from the colour of the diseased liver + **-osis**]
cirriped or **cirripede** *n* (*zool*) any of the class of sea creatures that includes barnacles. [Lat *cirrus*, curl + *pes*, foot]
cirrus *n* **-ri 1** (*meteorol*) a thin wispy cloud high in the sky. **2** (*bot*) the tendril of a plant. **3** (*zool*) a slender tentacle. [Lat, curl]
cirrocumulus *n* **-li** a high cloud forming small white masses.
cirrostratus *n* **-ti** a high cloud forming a thin white sheet.
CIS *abbrev* Commonwealth of Independent States, an association formed by many of the now-independent states of the former USSR.
cissy. See **sissy**.
cist *n* (*archaeol*) a grave lined and covered with slabs of stone. [Welsh, chest, from Lat *cista*]
cistern *n* **1** a tank storing water, usu. in the roof-space of a house, or serving a flushing toilet. **2** (*archaeol*, etc.) an underground reservoir. [Lat *cisterna*, reservoir]
citadel *n* a stronghold or fortress close to, or dominating the centre of, a city, built for its protection and as a place of refuge. [Ital *cittadella*, dimin. of *città*, city]
cite *v* (*tr*) **1** to quote (a book, its author or a passage from it) as an example or proof. **2** to mention as an example or illustration. **3** (*legal*) to summon (a person) to appear in court; to name (a person) as being involved in a case. **4** (**for**) to mention (someone) in an official report by way of commendation: *cited for bravery*. [OFr *citer*, to summon]
citation *n* **1** the quoting or citing of something as example or proof. **2** a passage quoted from a book, etc. **3** (*legal*) an order to appear in court. **4** (**for**) a special official commendation or award for merit, bravery, etc., or a list of the reasons for such an award.
citizen *n* **1** an inhabitant of a city or town. **2** a native of a country or state, or a naturalised member of it. [MidE *citesein*, from OFr *citeain*, from *cite*, city]
citizenry *n* the citizens of a town, country, etc.
citizen's arrest *n* an arrest, allowable in some countries, made by a member of the public.
citizens' charter *n* a set of proposals drawn up by the government, or other body such as a local authority, outlining e.g. the minimum acceptable standards of service in health care, education, etc., people's rights with regard to public bodies, compensation for unacceptable poor service, etc.
Citizens' Band *n* a set of radio frequencies that members of the public may use for sending messages to each other.
citizenship *n* **1** the status or position of a citizen. **2** the rights and duties of a citizen.
citrate *n* (*chem*) a salt of citric acid.
citric *adj* relating to, or obtained from, citrus fruits or citric acid. **[citrus]**
citric acid *n* the sharp-tasting acid present in lemons and other citrus fruits, used as a flavouring, perfume, etc.
citrin *n* vitamin P. [*citrus*]
citron *n* **1** a fruit like a large lemon, with a thick sweet-smelling yellow rind. **2** the candied rind of this fruit, used for flavouring or decorating cakes, etc. **3** the Asian tree bearing the fruit. [Ital *citrone*, from Lat *citrus*, the citron tree]
citrus *n* any tree of the group that includes the lemon, orange and citron, bearing thick-skinned, sharp-tasting fruits. — *adj* (also **citrous**) relating or belonging to this type of tree: *citrus fruits*. [Lat, citron tree]
city *n* **-ies 1** any large town; in the UK, a town with a royal charter, and usu. a cathedral. **2** the body of inhabitants of a city. **3** (*cap* with **the**) the business centre of a city, esp. London. [OFr *cite*, from Lat *civitas*, state]
city desk *n* in a newspaper office, the department of the **city editor**, dealing with financial news.
city fathers *n* (*pl*) the magistrates of a city, or members of its council.
city hall *n* (often *caps*) (the building housing) the local government of a city.
city state *n* (esp. *hist*) a city that has the status of an independent state.

civet *n* **1** (also **civet cat**) a small spotted cat-like animal, found in Asia and Africa. **2** a strong-smelling fluid produced by the animal's glands, used in perfumes to make their scent last. **3** the fur of the animal. [Fr *civette*]

civic *adj* relating to a city, citizen or citizenship. — *adv* **civically**. [Lat *civicus*, from *civis*, citizen]

civic centre *n* a place, often a specially designed complex, where the administrative offices and chief public buildings of a city are grouped.

civics *n* (*sing*) the study of local government and of the rights and duties of citizenship.

civil *adj* **1** relating to the community: *civil affairs*. **2** relating to or occurring between citizens: *civil disturbances*. **3** relating to ordinary citizens; not military, legal or religious. **4** (*legal*) relating to cases about individual rights, etc., not criminal cases. **5** polite; not discourteous. — *adv* **civilly**. [Lat *civilis*, relating to citizens, from *civis*, citizen]

civil defence *n* **1** the organisation and training of ordinary citizens to assist the armed forces in wartime, esp. during enemy attack. **2** the body of people involved in this.

civil disobedience *n* the refusal to obey regulations, pay taxes, etc., as a form of non-violent protest.

civil engineer *n* an engineer who designs and builds roads, bridges, tunnels, etc.

civil law *n* the part of a country's law that deals with its citizens' rights, etc., not with crimes.

civil liberty *n* (often in *pl*) personal freedom of thought, word, action, etc.

civil list *n* in the UK, the annual Parliamentary allowance to the sovereign and the Royal family for household expenses.

civil rights *n* (*pl*) the personal rights of any citizen of a country, esp. to freedom and equality regardless of race, religion, sex or sexuality.

civil servant *n* a person employed in the civil service.

civil service *n* the body of officials employed by a government to administer the affairs of a country.

civil war *n* a war between citizens of the same state.

civilian *n* anyone who is not a member of the armed forces or the police force. — *adj* relating to civilians. [OFr *civilien*, relating to civil law]

civilise or **-ize** *v* (*tr*) **1** to lead out of a state of barbarity to a more advanced stage of social development. **2** to educate and enlighten morally, intellectually and spiritually. [Fr *civiliser*, from Lat *civilis*, relating to political life]

civilisation or **-z-** *n* **1** the state of being, or process of becoming, civilised; the act of civilising. **2** a stage of development in human society that is socially, politically, culturally and technologically advanced. **3** the parts of the world that have reached such a stage. **4** (esp. *history*) a people, their society and culture: *the Minoan civilisation*. **5** built-up areas as opposed to wild, uncultivated or sparsely populated parts. **6** intellectual or spiritual enlightenment, as opposed to brutishness or coarseness.

civilised or **-z-** *adj* **1** socially, politically and technologically advanced. **2** agreeably refined, sophisticated or comfortable. **3** (*facet*) trained to behave and speak politely.

civility *n* ***-ies*** **1** politeness. **2** an act of politeness; a polite remark or gesture. [OFr *civilite*]

civvies *n* (*pl*; *coll*) ordinary civilian clothes as opposed to a military uniform.

civvy street *n* (*coll*) ordinary civilian life outside the armed forces.

Cl *symbol* (*chem*) chlorine.

clack *n* a sharp noise made by one hard object striking another. — *v* **1** (*tr* & *intr*) to make or cause to make this kind of noise. **2** (*intr*) to talk noisily. [Imit.]

clad *adj* or *in cmpds* **1** (**in**) wearing. **2** covered with a layer of. — *v* ***-dd-***, ***clad*** (*tr*) to cover (one material) with another, as protection, etc. [A past tense & past participle of **clothe**]

cladding *n* material for covering and protecting a surface: *steel cladding*.

cladistics *n* (*sing*; *biol*) a system of animal and plant classification by analysis of common characteristics. [Gr *klados*, branch]

claim *v* **1** (*tr*) to state (something) firmly, insisting on its truth. **2** (*tr*) to declare oneself (to be, to have done, etc.). **3** to assert that one has. **4** (*tr* & *intr*; **for**, **on**) to demand as a right: *claim on one's insurance*. **5** (*tr*) to take, use up. **6** (*tr*) to need; to deserve; to have a right to. **7** (*tr*) to declare that one is the owner of. **8** (*tr*) to identify oneself as having (responsibility). — *n* **1** a statement one insists on the truth of. **2** (**to**, **on**) a demand, esp. for something that one has, or believes one has, a right to: *lay claim to the throne*; *stake one's claim*; *make claims on someone's time*. **3** (**to**) a right to or reason for: *a claim to fame*. **4** something one has claimed, e.g. a piece of land or a sum of money. — **jump a claim** to claim land containing gold, oil, etc. which already belongs to someone else (*n* **claim-jumper**). [Lat *clamare*, to cry out]

claimant *n* a person who makes a claim.

no-claims bonus *n* a reduction in the fee one pays for insurance if one has made no claim for payment over a particular period.

clairvoyance *n* the ability, claimed by some, to see into the future, or know things that cannot be discovered through the normal range of senses. — *adj* & *n* **clairvoyant**. [Fr, from *clair*, clear + *voir*, to see]

clam *n* **1** a shellfish whose shell is in two halves that close together firmly. **2** (*coll*) an uncommunicative person. — *v* **clam up -*mm*-** (*intr*; *coll*) to stop talking suddenly; to refuse to speak, answer questions, etc. [Shortened from *clamshell*, from *clam*, an old word related to **clamp**]

clamber *v* (*intr*) to climb, esp. using hands as well as feet. — *n* an act of clambering. [Related to **climb**]

clammy *adj* **-*ier*, -*iest*** moist or damp, esp. unpleasantly so. — *adv* **clammily**. — *n* **clamminess**. [OE *clæman*, to smear]

clamour *n* **1** a noise of shouting or loud talking. **2** an outcry; loud protesting or loud demands. **3** any loud noise. — *v* (*intr* with **for**) to demand noisily. — *adj* **clamorous**. — *adv* **clamorously**. — *n* **clamorousness**. [Lat *clamor*, shout]

clamp[1] *n* **1** a tool with adjustable jaws for gripping things firmly or pressing parts together. **2** a reinforcing or fastening device, used in woodwork, etc. **3** (also **wheel clamp**) a heavy metal device that can be fitted to the wheels of a car to prevent it being moved. — *v* (*tr*) **1** to fasten together or hold with a clamp. **2** to fit a clamp to a wheel of (a parked car) to stop it being moved. **3** to hold, grip, shut or press tightly. — *v* **clamp down on** (*tr*) to put a stop to or control strictly (*n* **clampdown**). [ODut *clampe*]

clamp[2] *n* a mound of dug potatoes or other root crop, covered with earth and straw as protection against cold. [ODut *clamp*, heap]

clan *n* **1** a group of families, in Scotland or of Scots origin, generally with the same surname, and (esp. *formerly*) led by a chief. **2** (*humorous*) one's family or relations. **3** a group of people who have similar interests, concerns, etc. **4** a division of a tribe. [Gaelic *clann*, children]

clannish *adj* (*derog*) (of a group of people) closely united, with little interest or trust in people not belonging to the group. — *adv* **clannishly**. — *n* **clannishness**.

clansman or **clanswoman** *n* a member of a clan (sense **1**).

clandestine *adj* **1** concealed; kept secret. **2** furtive; sly; surreptitious. — *adv* **clandestinely**. [Lat *clandestinus*, from *clam*, secretly]

clang *v* (*intr* & *tr*) to (cause to) make a loud deep ringing sound. — *n* this sound. [Lat *clangere*, to clang, resound]

clanger *n* (*coll*) a tactless, embarrassing and all too obvious blunder: *drop a clanger*.

clangour *n* (*poetic*) a continuous loud confused and intrusive noise. [Lat *clangor*, noise]

clank *v* (*intr* & *tr*) to (cause to) make a sharp sound of metal striking metal or some other hard surface. — *n* this sound. [Imit.]

clannish, **clansman**, **clanswoman**. See **clan**.

clap[1] *v* **-*pp*- 1** (*intr* & *tr*) to strike (esp. the palms of one's hands) together with a loud noise, to applaud (someone), mark (a rhythm), gain attention, etc. **2** (*tr*) to strike (someone) with the palm of the hand, usu. as a friendly gesture. **3** (*tr*; **on**, **over**) to place forcefully. **4** (*tr*; *coll*) to put suddenly (into prison, chains, etc.). — *n* **1** an act of clapping. **2** the sudden loud explosion of noise that thunder makes. — **clap eyes on** (*coll*) to see. — **clapped out** (*coll*) **1** (of a machine, etc.) old, worn out, and no longer working properly. **2** (of a person) exhausted. [OE *clæppan*]

clapper *n* **1** the dangling piece of metal inside a bell that strikes against the side to make it ring. **2** a device that produces a loud clattering noise, for scaring birds from crops, etc. — **like the clappers** (*coll*) very quickly.

clapperboard *n* a pair of hinged boards clapped together in front of the camera before and after shooting a piece of film, so as to help synchronise sound and vision.

clap[2] *n* (*vulg slang*; with **the**) venereal disease, esp. gonorrhoea. [Related to OFr *clapier*, brothel]

clapper, **clapperboard**. See **clap**[1].

claptrap *n* meaningless, insincere or pompous talk. [**clap**[1] + **trap**]

claque *n* **1** a group of people paid to applaud a speaker at a meeting or performer in a theatre, etc. **2** a circle of flatterers or admirers. [Fr *claquer*, to clap]

claret *n* **1** a French red wine, esp. from the Bordeaux district. **2** the deep reddish-purple colour of this wine. [OFr *clare*, spiced wine]

clarify *v* **-*ies*, -*ied*** (*tr* & *intr*) **1** to make or become clearer or easier to understand. **2** (of butter, fat, etc.) to make or become clear by heating. — *n* **clarification**. [Lat *clarus*, clear + *facere*, to make]

clarinet *n* a woodwind instrument with keys and a single reed. — *n* **clarinettist**. [Fr *clarinette*, dimin. of OFr *clarin*, clarion]

clarion *n* an old kind of trumpet with a shrill sound, used to call men to arms, etc.: *a clarion call*. [Lat *clario*, from *clarus*, clear]

clarity *n* **1** the quality of being clear and pure. **2** the quality of being easy to see, hear or understand. **3** clearness and accuracy of thought, reasoning and expression. [Lat *claritas*]

clarsach *n* a small harp strung with wire, played in Scotland and Ireland. [Gaelic]

clash *n* **1** a loud noise, like that of metal objects striking each other. **2** (**with**) a serious disagreement; a quarrel or argument. **3** (**with**) a fight, battle or match. **4** the coinciding in one's timetable of two or more events, both or all of which one ought to or would like to attend. — *v* **1** (*intr* & *tr*) (of metal objects, etc.) to strike against each other noisily. **2** (*intr*; **with**) to fight, have a battle. **3** (*intr*; **with**) to disagree violently. **4** (*intr*; **with**) (of two or more events that one ought to or would like to attend) to be planned for the same time. **5** (*intr*; **with**) (of colours, styles, etc.) to be unpleasing to look at when placed side by side. [Imit.]

clasp *n* **1** a fastening on jewellery, a bag, etc. made of two parts that link together. **2** a firm grip, or act of gripping. — *v* (*tr*) **1** to hold, or take hold of, firmly. **2** to fasten or secure with a clasp.

clasp knife *n* a folding pocket knife, orig. one held open by a catch.

class *n* **1** a lesson or lecture. **2** a number of pupils taught together. **3** the body of students that begin or finish university or school in the same year. **4** a category, kind or type. **5** a grade or standard. **6** any of the social groupings into which people fall according to their job, wealth, etc. **7** the system by which society is divided into these groups. **8** (*coll*) stylishness in dress, behaviour, etc.; good quality. — *v* (*tr*; **as**) to regard as belonging to a certain class; to put into a category. — **in a class of its own** outstanding; with no equal. [Lat *classis*, rank, class, division]

class-conscious *adj* (usu. *derog*) aware of one's own and other people's social class. — *n* **class-consciousness**.

classless *adj* **1** (of a community) not divided up into social classes. **2** not belonging to any particular social class. — *n* **classlessness**.

classmate *n* a fellow pupil or student in one's class at school or college.

classroom *n* a room in a school or college where classes are taught.

classy *adj* **-ier**, **-iest** (*coll*) stylish; fashionable; superior.

classic *adj* **1** of the highest quality; established as the best. **2** entirely typical. **3** simple, neat and elegant, esp. in a traditional style: *a classic black suit*. — *n* **1** an established work of literature. **2** an outstanding example of its type. **3** something, e.g. an item of clothing, always approved of and essential to have: *the little black dress, a classic of the 50s*. **4** a celebrated annual sporting event, esp. (also **classic race**) a horse race. — *adv* **classically**. [Lat *classicus*, relating to classes, esp. the best]

classical *adj* **1** (of literature, art, etc.) of ancient Greece and Rome. **2** (of architecture or the other arts) showing the influence of ancient Greece and Rome: *a classical façade*. **3** (of music and arts related to it) having an established, traditional and somewhat formal style and form: *classical music*. **4** (of procedures, etc.) following the well-known traditional pattern: *the classical method*. **5** (of shape, design, etc.) simple; pure; without complicated decoration. **6** (of a language) being the older, literary form — *n* (*coll*) classical music. — *adv* **classically**. — *n* **classicalness**.

classicism *n* in art, architecture, prose and poetry, a simple, elegant style typical in 18th- and early 19th-century Europe.

classicist *n* someone who has studied classics, esp. as a university subject.

classics *n* (*sing*; often *cap*) the study of Latin and Greek and the literature and history of ancient Greece and Rome.

classify *v* **-ies**, **-ied** (*tr*) **1** to put into a particular class or group. **2** to declare (information) secret, and not for publication. — *adj* **classifiable**. [Lat *classis*, class, division + *facere*, to make]

classification *n* **1** the arrangement and division of things and people into classes. **2** a group or class into which a thing or person is put.

classified *adj* **1** arranged in groups or classes. **2** (of information) kept secret by the government. **3** (of a road) classed as a motorway, A-road or B-road.

classified ad *n* a small advertisement in a newspaper offering something for sale, advertising a job, etc.

clatter *n* a loud noise made by hard objects striking each other, or falling on to a hard surface. — *v* **-r-** (*intr* & *tr*) to (cause to) make this noise. [Imit.]

clause *n* **1** (*gram*) part of a sentence that has its own subject, verb, object, etc. **2** (*legal*) a paragraph or section in a contract, will, or act of parliament. [Lat *clausa*]

claustrophobia *n* **1** fear felt in, or fear of being in, confined spaces. **2** an uncomfortable feeling of being shut in or confined. — *adj* **claustrophobic**. [Lat *claustrum*, bolt, barrier + **-phobia**]

clavichord *n* an early keyboard instrument with a soft tone. [Lat *clavis*, key + *chorda*, string]

clavicle *n* (*anat*) either of two short slender bones linking the shoulder-blades with the top of the breastbone. [Lat *clavicula*, dimin. of *clavis*, key]

claw *n* **1** one of the sharply-pointed hooked nails of an animal or bird. **2** the foot of an animal or bird with claws. **3** either of the feet of a crab or lobster which ends in pincers. **4** something with the shape or action of a claw, e.g. part of a mechanical device. — *v* (*tr* & *intr*; **at**) to tear or scratch with claws, nails or fingers. — *v* **claw back** (*tr*) **1** (of the government) to get back (money given in the form of benefits and allowances) by imposing a new tax (*n* **clawback**). **2** to regain (a commercial advantage, etc.) with difficulty (*n* **clawback**). [OE *clawu*]

claw hammer *n* a hammer with two points on one side of its head, that can be used for pulling out nails.

clay *n* **1** soft sticky earth that can be formed into pottery, bricks, etc. and baked hard. **2** earth or soil generally. **3** (*tennis*) the hard surface of clay courts. **4** (*poetic*) the substance of which the human body is formed. — *adj* **clayey**. — **have feet of clay** to have a character weakness that remains unsuspected till a crisis exposes it. [OE *clæg*]

clay court *n* a tennis court with a hard surface of clay or a similar substance.

clay pigeon *n* a clay disc that is thrown up mechanically as a target in the sport of **clay-pigeon shooting**.

clay pipe *n* a tobacco pipe made of baked clay.

claymore *n* (*hist*) a two-edged broadsword used by Scottish highlanders. [Gaelic *claidheamh mór*, large sword]

clean *adj* **1** free from dirt. **2** not containing anything harmful to health; pure. **3** pleasantly fresh: *a clean taste*. **4** hygienic in habits: *a clean animal*. **5** unused; unmarked: *a clean sheet of paper*. **6** neat and even: *a clean cut*. **7** simple and elegant: *a ship with good clean lines*. **8** clear of legal offences: *a clean driving licence*. **9** morally pure; innocent. **10** (of humour, etc.) not offensive or obscene. **11** fair: *a clean fight*. **12** (*slang*) not carrying drugs or offensive weapons. **13** (of nuclear installations, etc.) not producing a harmful level of radioactivity. **14** (*relig*) (of certain animals) allowed for people to eat. **15** (of musical sounds) pure and accurate. **16** absolute; complete: *make a clean break*. — *adv* **1** (*coll* before a verb) completely: *get clean away*; *I clean forgot*. **2** straight; directly; encountering no obstruction: *sailed clean through the window*. — *v* **1** (*tr* & *intr*) to make or become free from dirt. **2** (*tr* & *intr*) to dry-clean or be dry-cleaned. **3** (*intr*) to dust, polish floors and furniture, etc. in a house or office, esp. as a job. **4** (*tr*) to prepare (vegetables, etc.) for cooking or eating by cutting away the inedible bits. — *n* **1** an act of cleaning. **2** (*weight-lifting*) a lift of the weight as far as the shoulders. — *adv* **cleanly**. — *n* **cleanness**. — **clean bill of health** a medical certificate or report confirming that one is in good health, esp. after being ill. — *v* **clean out** (*tr*) **1** to clean (a cupboard, etc.) thoroughly (*n* **clean-out**). **2** (*slang*) to deprive of cash (*n* **clean-out**). — *v* **clean up 1** (*tr* & *intr*) to make (a dirty place or person) clean; to get rid of (a mess) (*n* **clean-up**). **2** (*intr*; *slang*) to make a huge profit. — *v* **clean up after** (*tr*) to clean up a mess, etc. left by (someone). — **come clean** (*coll*) to admit or tell the truth about something that one has previously concealed or lied about. — **have clean hands** (*coll*) to have no connection with the crime, etc. in question. — **make a clean sweep (of) 1** to replace or make great changes in (methods, staff, etc.). **2** to win all the prizes at a sporting event, etc. — **with a clean slate** or **sheet** with a fresh start, as though from the beginning again, esp. after an error or misdeed. [OE *clæne*]

clean-cut *adj* **1** pleasingly regular in outline or shape: *clean-cut features*. **2** neat; respectable.

cleaner *n* **1** a person employed to clean inside buildings, offices, etc. **2** a machine or substance used for cleaning.

cleaner's *n* (also **dry-cleaner's**) a shop where clothes, etc. can be taken to. — **take to the cleaner's** (*coll*) to obtain a lot of money from (someone) through the law courts or by a dishonest deal.

cleaning lady or **woman** *n* a woman whose job is to clean inside a house, factory, office, etc.

clean-limbed *adj* having a tall slim shapely body.

clean-living *adj* leading a decent, healthy existence.

cleanly[1] *adv* **1** smoothly and easily. **2** fairly.

cleanly[2] *adj* (*old*) hygienic in one's personal habits. — *n* **cleanliness**.

clean-shaven *adj* without a beard or moustache.

cleanse *v* (*tr*; **of, from**) **1** to clean or get rid of dirt from. **2** to purify; to remove sin or guilt from. [OE *clænsian*]

cleanser *n* a substance that cleans, e.g. a cream or liquid for cleaning the face.

cleansing department *n* the local-government department responsible for cleaning the streets and collecting rubbish.

clear *adj* **1** transparent; easy to see through. **2** (of weather, etc.) not misty or cloudy. **3** (of the skin) healthy; unblemished by spots, etc. **4** easy to see, hear or understand. **5** bright; sharp; well-defined; *a clear photograph*. **6** (of vision) able to see well. **7** (of musical sounds) pure and accurate. **8** (**about**) certain; convinced; having no doubts or confusion. **9** definite; free of doubt, ambiguity or confusion. **10** capable of, or resulting from, accurate observation, logical thinking, etc. **11** evident; obvious. **12** (**of**) free (of obstruction). **13** (**of**) well away from; out of range of or contact with: *well clear of the rocks*. **14** (**of**) free (of); no longer affected (by). **15** remaining after all charges, taxes, expenses, etc. have been paid. **16** (of the conscience, etc.) free from guilt, etc. **17** entire; without interruption: *need a clear week to finish*. **18** free of appointments, etc. — *adv* **1** in a clear manner. **2** completely: *get clear away*. **3** (with **to**; esp. *NAm*) all the way to: *see clear to the hills*. **4** (**of**) well away from; out of the way of: *keep* or *steer clear of trouble*; *stand clear*. — *v* **1** (*tr* & *intr*; **of**) to make or become clear, free of obstruction, etc. **2** (*tr*; **away, from**) to remove or move out of the way. **3** (*tr*; **of**) to prove or declare to be innocent. **4** (*tr*) to get over or past without touching: *clear the fence*. **5** (*tr*) to make as profit or over expenses. **6** (*tr*) to pass inspection by (customs). **7** (*tr*) to give or get official permission for (a plan, etc.). **8** (*tr*) to approve (someone) for a special assignment, access to secret information, etc. **9** (*tr* & *intr*) to pass (a cheque), or (of a cheque) to pass from one bank to another through a clearing-house. **10** (*tr*) to decode. **11** (*tr*) to pay (a debt). — *n* **clearness**. — **clear the air** (*coll*) to get rid of bad feeling, suspicion or tension, esp. by frank discussion. — **clear the decks** see **deck**. — *v* **clear off 1** (*tr*) to finish paying (one's debts). **2** (*intr*; *coll*) to go away. — *v* **clear out 1** (*tr*) to get rid of (rubbish, etc.) from (*n* **clear-out**). **2** (*intr*; *coll*) to go away. — *v* **clear up 1** (*tr*) to tidy up (a mess, room, etc.) (*n* **clear-up**). **2** (*tr*) to solve (a mystery, etc.). **3** (*tr*) to make or get better. — **in the clear** no longer under suspicion, in difficulties or in danger. [OFr *cler*]

clearance *n* **1** the act of clearing. **2** the distance between one object and another passing beside or under it. **3** (a certificate giving) permission. **4** (also **security clearance**) official acknowledgement that one can be trusted not to pass secrets to an enemy.

clear-cut *adj* clear; sharp.

clear-headed *adj* capable of, or showing, clear, logical thought. — *adv* **clear-headedly**.

clearing *n* an area in a forest, etc. that has been cleared of trees, etc.

clearing bank *n* a bank using the services of a central clearing-house.

clearing-house *n* **1** an establishment that deals with transactions between its member banks. **2** a central agency that collects, organises and distributes information.

clearly *adv* **1** in a clear manner. **2** obviously: *Clearly, he's wrong*.

clear-sighted *adj* capable of, or showing, accurate observation and good judgement. — *adj* **clear-sightedly**. — *n* **clear-sightedness**.

clearway *n* a stretch of road on which cars may not stop except in an emergency.

cleavage *n* **1** a splitting or division. **2** (*coll*) the hollow between a woman's breasts, esp. as revealed by a dress with a low neck. [**cleave**[1]]

cleave[1] *v* ***cleft***, ***cleaved*** or ***clove***; ***cleft***, ***cleaved*** or ***cloven*** (*tr* & *intr*; *formal* or *literary*) **1** to split or divide. **2** to cut or slice: *cleave a way through the undergrowth*, ◇ See also **cloven**. [OE *cleofan*]

cleave[2] *v* ***cleaved*** (*intr* with **to**) to cling or stick to. [OE *cleofian*]

cleaver *n* a knife with a large square blade, used by butchers for chopping meat. [**cleave**[1]]

clef *n* (*mus*) any of three symbols placed on the stave (the *treble clef* or *G clef* on the second line up, the *bass* or *F clef* on the second line down, and the *alto clef* or *C clef* on the middle line) to show pitch. [Fr, key]

cleft[1] *n* a split, fissure, wide crack or deep indentation. [Related to **cleave**[1]]

cleft[2] *adj* split; divided. — **in a cleft stick** in a difficult or awkward situation. [Past participle of **cleave**[1]]

cleft palate *n* a split in the roof of the mouth, present from birth, usu. causing speech difficulties.

clematis *n* a garden climbing plant of the buttercup family, with purple, yellow or white flowers. [Gr, periwinkle, convolvulus or traveller's joy]

clement *adj* **1** (of weather) mild; not harsh or severe. **2** merciful. — *n* **clemency**. — *adv* **clemently**. [Lat *clemens*, mild, calm, merciful]

clementine *n* a citrus fruit like a small tangerine. [Fr]

clench *v* (*tr*) **1** to close (one's teeth or one's fists) tightly, esp. in anger. **2** to hold or grip firmly. — *n* **1** the action of clenching. **2** a very tight grasp. [OE *beclencan*, to hold fast]

clerestory or **clearstory** *n* **-*ies*** (*archit*) in a church, an upper row of windows in the nave wall, above the roof of the aisle. [**clear** (in reference to the windows) + **storey**]

clergy *n* **-*ies*** (*pl* or, sometimes, *sing*) the ordained ministers of the Christian church, or the priests of any religion. [Fr *clergé*]

clergyman or **clergywoman** *n* a member of the clergy.

cleric *n* a clergyman. [Lat *clericus*, priest]

clerical *adj* **1** relating to the clergy. **2** relating to clerks, office workers or office work.

clerical collar *n* the stiff white collar, fastening at the back, worn by clergymen.

clerihew *n* a humorous poem four lines long, esp. about a famous person. [From the inventor, E *Clerihew* Bentley]

clerk *n* **1** a person in an office or bank who deals with letters, accounts, records, files, etc. **2** in a law court, a person who keeps records or accounts. **3** a public official in charge of the records and business affairs of the town council. **4** an unordained or lay minister of the church. **5** (*NAm*) a shop assistant or hotel receptionist. **6** (*old*) a scholar or clergyman. [OE *clerc*, variant of **cleric**]

clerkess *n* a female clerk.

clerk of works *n* the person in charge of the construction and care of a building.

clever *adj* **1** good or quick at learning and understanding. **2** skilful, dexterous, nimble or adroit. **3** well thought out; ingenious. — *adv* **cleverly**. — *n* **cleverness**. [MidE *cliver*, related to OE *clifer*, claw]

clever dick *n* (*coll derog*) a person who is over-sure of his or her cleverness.

clew *n* **1** (*naut*) the corner of a ship's sail. **2** (*old*) a ball of thread. **3** the arrangement of cords by which a hammock is suspended. — *v* (*tr* with **up, down**) to haul up or let down (a sail). [OE *cliewen*, ball of thread]

cliché *n* (usu. *derog*) **1** a phrase or combination of words that was striking and effective when first used, but has become stale and feeble through repetition. **2** a too-frequently used idea or image; a stereotype. — *adj* **clichéd**. [Fr, a stereotype plate or stencil]

click *n* **1** a short sharp sound like that made by two parts of a mechanism locking into place. **2** (*mech*) a catch in a piece of machinery. **3** in some African languages, a click-like speech sound produced by a sucking action with the tongue. — *v* **1** (*tr* & *intr*) to (cause to) make a click. **2** (*intr*; *coll*) to meet with approval. **3** (*intr*; *coll*) to become clear or understood. **4** (*intr*; *coll*; **with**) to become friendly. [Imit.]

client *n* **1** a person using the professional services of e.g. a lawyer, bank manager, architect, etc. **2** a customer. [Lat *cliens*, dependant]

clientèle *n* the clients of a professional person, customers of a shopkeeper, etc., or people habitually attending a theatre. [Fr]

cliff *n* a high steep rock face, esp. on the coast. [OE *clif*]

cliffhanger *n* **1** a story that keeps one in suspense up to the end. **2** the ending of an episode of a serial story which leaves the audience in suspense, as if with the hero clinging to a cliff edge. **3** an exciting situation, esp. a contest, of which the conclusion is in doubt until the very last minute. — *adj* **cliffhanging**.

climacteric *n* a time of life when the body undergoes a major change, esp. in women the menopause and in men a reduction in fertility and desire for sex. [Gr *klimakter*, rung of a ladder]

climactic. See **climax**.

climate *n* **1** the typical weather conditions of a particular part of the world. **2** a part of the world considered from the point of view of its weather conditions: *move to a warmer climate*. **3** a current trend in general feeling, opinion, policies, etc. — *adj* **climatic**. — *adv* **climatically**. [Gr *klima*, latitude, region]

climatology *n* the scientific study of climates. — *adj* **climatological**. — *n* **climatologist**. [**climate** and **-logy**]

climax *n* **1** the high point or culmination of a series of events or of an experience. **2** a sexual orgasm. — *v* (*intr* & *tr*) to come or bring to a climax. — *adj* **climactic**. — *adv* **climactically**. [Gr, ladder, climax]

climb *v* **1** (*tr* & *intr*; **up**) to go towards the top of (a hill, ladder, etc.). **2** (*intr*; **down**, **in**, **out**, etc.) to get somewhere using hands and feet. **3** (*intr*) to rise or go up. **4** (*intr*) to increase. — *n* **1** an act of climbing. **2** a slope to be climbed. — *adj* **climbable**. — *v* **climb down** (*intr*) to give up one's position on some issue, etc., esp. with an admission that one has been wrong (*n* **climb-down**). [OE *climban*]

climber *n* **1** a climbing plant. **2** a mountaineer. **3** (*derog*) a person who is too obviously trying to rise through the social ranks.

climbing *n* the sport of climbing rock faces, esp. with the help of ropes and other devices.

climbing-frame *n* a strong framework of metal or wooden bars for children to climb around on.

clime *n* (*poetic* or *humorous*) a part of the world: *foreign climes*. [Gr *klima*, region, latitude]

clinch *v* **1** (*tr*) to settle (an argument or bargain) finally and decisively. **2** (*intr*; *boxing* & *wrestling*) (of contestants) to hold each other in a firm grip. **3** (*intr*; *coll*) to embrace. **4** (*tr*; *joinery*) to bend over and hammer down the projecting point of (a nail or rivet that has been driven through a piece of wood, etc.). — *n* **1** an act of clinching. **2** (*boxing* & *wrestling*) an act of clinging to each other to prevent further blows, create a breathing space, etc. **3** (*coll*) an embrace. [Variant of **clench**]

clincher *n* a point, argument or circumstance that finally settles or decides a matter.

cline *n* the range of variations between members of a related group of things, e.g. members of the same biological species, presented as a gradually sloping scale. [Gr *klinein*, to lean]

cling *v* ***clung*** (*intr*; **to**, **on**) **1** to hold firmly or tightly; to stick. **2** (*derog*) to be emotionally too dependent: *still clinging to his mother*. **3** to refuse to drop or let go. — *adj* (also **clingstone**) (of e.g. peaches) having a stone that sticks to the flesh. — *n* **clinger**. [OE *clingan*]

clingfilm *n* a thin, clear plastic material that adheres to itself, used for wrapping food, covering containers, etc.

clingy *adj* ***-ier***, ***-iest*** inclined to cling. — *n* **clinginess**.

clinic *n* **1** a department of a hospital where outpatients receive treatment or advice. **2** a session for giving treatment or advice. **3** a private hospital or nursing-home. **4** a specialised hospital. **5** instruction given to medical students at the patients' bedside. **6** a session in which an expert is available for consultation. [Gr *klinikos*, relating to the sickbed]

clinical *adj* **1** relating to, or like, a clinic or hospital. **2** (of medical studies) based on, or relating to, direct observation and treatment of the patient, as distinct from theoretical or experimental work. **3** (of manner, behaviour, etc.) cold; impersonal; unemotional; detached. **4** (of surroundings, etc.) severely plain and simple, with no personal touches. — *adv* **clinically**.

clinical death *n* the state of the body in which the brain has ceased to function, though artificial means can be used to maintain the action of the heart, lungs, etc.

clinical thermometer *n* a thermometer used for finding the temperature of the body.

clinician *n* a doctor who works directly with patients, in a clinic, etc.

clink[1] *n* a short sharp ringing sound. — *v* (*intr* & *tr*) to (cause to) make a clink. [Perhaps ODut *klinken*, to ring]

clink[2] *n* (*slang*) prison. [Orig. the name of a prison in Southwark]

clinker *n* **1** a mass of fused ash or slag left unburnt in a furnace. **2** the cindery crust on a lava flow. [Dut *klinker*, hard brick]

clinker-built *adj* (of a boat) with a hull each of whose planks overlaps the one below it on the outside. ◇ See also **carvel-built**. [*clink*, a form of **clinch**, from the use of clinched nails]

clip[1] *v* **-pp-** (*tr*) **1** to cut (hair, wool, etc.). **2** to trim or cut off the hair, wool or fur of. **3** to punch out a piece from (a ticket) to show that it has been used. **4** to cut (an article, etc.) from a newspaper, etc. **5** (*coll*) to hit or strike sharply. **6** to cut (a small amount) from something. — *n* **1** an act of clipping. **2** a short sequence extracted from a film. **3** (*coll*) a sharp blow. **4** (*coll*) speed; rapid speed: *going at a fair clip*. **5** (esp. *Austr* & *NZ*) the total amount of wool shorn from sheep, at one time, place, etc. — **clip someone's wings** to reduce someone's power or scope for activity. [Norse *klippa*, to cut]

clip joint *n* (*slang*) a bar, restaurant or nightclub charging excessively high prices.

clipped *adj* **1** (of the form of a word) shortened, as, e.g., *sec* from *second*. **2** (of speaking style) tending to shorten vowels, omit syllables, etc.

clippers *n* (*pl*; often *in cmpds*) a clipping instrument.

clipping *n* **1** a piece clipped off: *hair clippings*. **2** a cutting from a newspaper, etc.

clip[2] *n* **1** (often *in cmpds*) any of various usu. small devices for holding things together or in position. **2** (also **cartridge clip**) a container for bullets attached to a gun, that feeds bullets directly into it. **3** a piece of jewellery in the form of a clip, for attaching to clothing. — *v* **-pp-** (*tr* & *intr*; **on, together**, etc.) to fasten with a clip. [OE *clyppan*, to embrace, clasp]

clipboard *n* a board serving as a portable writing surface, with a clip at the top for holding paper, forms, etc.

clip-on *adj* (of e.g. earrings) fastening with a clip.

clipper *n* (*hist*) a fast sailing ship with large sails. [**clip**[1]]

clique *n* (*derog*) a group of friends, professional colleagues, etc. who stick together and are hostile towards outsiders. — *adj* **cliquey** or **cliquy**, **-ier**, **-iest**, or **cliquish**. — *n* **cliquiness** or **cliquishness**. [Fr]

clitoris *n* a small highly sensitive organ forming part of the female genitals. — *adj* **clitoral**. [Gr *kleitoris*]

Cllr *abbrev* Councillor.

cloak *n* **1** a loose outdoor garment, usu. sleeveless, fastened at the neck so as to hang from the shoulders. **2** a covering: *a cloak of mist*. **3** a concealment or disguise: *use one's job as a cloak for spying activities*. — *v* (*tr* with **in**) to cover up or conceal: *cloaked in mystery*. [OFr *cloke*, from Lat *clocca*, bell, bell-shaped cape]

cloak-and-dagger *adj* (of stories, situations, etc.) full of adventure, mystery, plots, spying, etc.

cloakroom *n* **1** a room in a theatre, restaurant, etc. where coats, hats, etc. may be left. **2** a toilet, esp. in a public building.

clobber[1] *v* **-r-** (*tr*; *coll*) **1** to hit. **2** to defeat completely. **3** to criticise severely.

clobber[2] *n* (*slang*) **1** clothing. **2** personal belongings, equipment, etc.

cloche *n* **1** a covering of glass or transparent plastic for protecting young plants. **2** a woman's close-fitting dome-shaped hat. [Fr, bell, bell jar, from Lat *clocca*, bell]

clock[1] *n* **1** an instrument for measuring and showing time by means of pointers on a dial or displayed figures. **2** any clock-like measuring instrument. **3** a device in a vehicle for showing distance travelled or speed travelled at. **4** (also **time clock**) an instrument for recording employees' times of arrival and departure. **5** the downy seed-head of a dandelion. **6** (*slang*) the face. — *v* (*tr*) **1** to record with a stopwatch the time taken by (a racer, etc.) to complete a distance, etc. **2** (*coll*) to travel at (a speed as shown on a speedometer). **3** (*slang*) to hit (someone). — **against the clock** very fast, because of lack of time. — **beat the clock** to finish before the set time limit or deadline. — *v* **clock in** or **on**, and **clock out** or **off** (*intr*) to record one's time respectively of arriving at, and leaving, one's place of work. — *v* **clock up** (*tr*) to reach (a particular speed), cover (a particular distance), or achieve (a particular score, etc.). — **put back the clock** to return to the conditions of an earlier period. — **round the clock** throughout the day and night. — **watch the clock** to be less concerned with one's work than with making sure one leaves it punctually (*n* **clockwatcher**; *n* **clockwatching**). [ODut *clocke*, bell, clock]

clock tower *n* a four-walled tower with a clock face on each wall.

clockwise *adj* & *adv* (moving, etc.) in the same direction as that in which the hands of a clock move.

clockwork *n* a mechanism like that of a clock, working by means of gears and a spring that must be wound periodically. — *adj* operated by clockwork. — **like clockwork** smoothly and successfully; without difficulties.

clock[2] *n* a decoration on the side of a sock.

clod *n* **1** a lump of earth, clay, etc. **2** (*coll*) a stupid person. — *adj* **cloddish**. — *adv* **cloddishly**. — *n* **cloddishness**. [MidE *clodde*]

clodhopper *n* (*coll*) **1** a clumsy person. **2** a large, heavy boot or shoe. — *adj* **clodhopping**. [**clod** + **hop**]

clog *n* a shoe carved entirely from wood, or having a thick wooden sole. — *v* **-gg-** (*tr* & *intr*; **up, with**) to obstruct or become obstructed so that movement is difficult or impossible. [MidE]

cloisonné *n* a form of decoration for vases, etc., the pattern being formed in wire and filled in with coloured enamel. [Fr, compartmented]

cloister *n* **1** a covered walk built against the wall of a church, college, etc. with arches along its other side that open on to a garden, quadrangle, etc. **2** a place of religious retreat, e.g. a monastery or convent; the quiet secluded life of such a place. — *v* **-r-** (*tr*) to keep (someone) away from the problems of normal life in the world. — *adj* **cloistral**. [OFr *cloistre*]

cloistered *adj* cut off or protected from the life of the world: *a cloistered existence*.

clone *n* **1** (any one of) a group of identical organisms reproduced by a non-sexual process from a single cell of the parent. **2** (*coll*) a person or thing that looks like a replica of someone or something else. — *v* (*tr* & *intr*) to (cause to) produce a clone. — *adj* **clonal**. [Gr *klon*, twig]

clonk *n* a noise of a heavy, esp. metal, object striking something. — *v* (*intr* & *tr*) to (cause to) make this noise. [Imit.]

clop *n* the hollow sound of a horse's hooves on hard ground. — *v* **-pp-** (*intr*) (of a horse) to walk along making this noise. [Imit.]

close[1] *adj* **1** (**to, by**) near in space or time; at a short distance: *at close range*. **2** (**to**) near in relationship, friendship or connection. **3** touching or almost touching. **4** tight, not loose; dense or compact; with little space between. **5** near to the surface: *a close haircut*. **6** thorough; searching. **7** (of a contest, etc.) with little difference between entrants, etc. **8** (**to**) about to happen, do something, etc.: *close to tears*. **9** (**to**) similar to the original, or to something else: *a close translation*; *a close resemblance*. **10** uncomfortably warm; stuffy. **11** (**about**) secretive. **12** (with **with**; *derog*) mean. **13** heavily guarded: *under close arrest*. **14** (esp. *old*) shut; closed; confined. **15** (of an organisation, etc.) restricted in membership. — *adv* **1** (sometimes *in cmpds*) in a close manner; closely: *close-fitting*; *follow close behind*. **2** (with **up** or **to**) at close range. **3** (with **on** or **to**) nearly. — *adv* **closely**. — *n* **closeness**. — **at close quarters 1** at close range; near to. **2** (of fighting) hand-to-hand, one individual fighting another. — **close at**, or **to, hand** close by; easily available. — **a close call** or **shave** a narrow or lucky escape. — **a close thing 1** a narrow escape. **2** something only just managed or achieved. — **close to home** uncomfortably close to the truth, or to a sensitive matter. — [OFr *clos*, closed, from Lat *claudere*, to close]

close-fisted *adj* (*coll*) mean; miserly.

close harmony *n* a style of singing in harmony with the voice parts nearly coinciding.

close-hauled *adj* (*naut*) with sails set for sailing as nearly into the wind as possible.

close-knit *adj* (of a group, community, etc.) closely bound together.

close season *n* the time of year when it is illegal to kill certain birds, animals or fish for sport.

close-up *n* **1** a photograph, television shot, etc. taken at close range. **2** a detailed look at, or examination of, something.

close[2] *v* **1** (*tr* & *intr*) to shut. **2** (*tr*) to block (a road, etc.) so as to prevent use. **3** (*tr* & *intr*) (of shops, etc.) to (cause to) stop being open to the public for a period of time. **4** (*tr* & *intr*) (of a factory, business, etc.) to (cause to) permanently stop operating. **5** (*tr* & *intr*) to finish; to come or bring to an end; to stop discussion, etc. of. **6** (*tr* & *intr*) to join up or come together; to cause edges, etc. of to come together. **7** (*tr*) to settle or agree on: *close a deal*. **8** (*intr*; *econ*) (of currency, shares, etc.) to be worth at the end of a period of trading. **9** (*intr*; **on**) to catch up: *The police were closing on him*. — *n* an end or conclusion. — *v* **close down** (*intr* & *tr*) **1** (of a business) to close permanently. **2** (of a television or radio station, etc.) to stop broadcasting at the end of the day (*n* **close-down**). — **close one's eyes to** to pretend not to notice. — *v* **close in 1** (*intr*; **on**) to come nearer and surround: *The enemy closed in on them*. **2** (of days) to become shorter in winter, while nights get longer. — *v* **close up** (*intr* & *tr*) to bring or get closer together; to bring edges, etc. of together: *close up the gaps*. — *v* **close with** (*tr*) **1** (*old*) to begin fighting with. **2** to strike a bargain with; to agree to (an offer, etc.). [Lat *claudere*, to close]

closed *adj* **1** shut; blocked. **2** (of a community or society) with membership restricted to a chosen few. — **behind closed doors** privately, the public being excluded.

closed book *n* a person or subject which one cannot understand.

closed circuit *n* a complete electrical circuit, able to carry electricity.

closed-circuit television *n* a television system serving a limited number of receivers, e.g. within a building, the signal being transmitted by wires.

closed shop *n* a factory, etc. in which only members of a trade union are employed. ◇ See also **open shop**.

closed syllable *n* a syllable ending in a consonant.

closing-time *n* the time when pubs must stop serving drinks and close.

close[3] *n* **1** in Scotland, a narrow passage leading from the street to the stair of a tenement building. **2** (*cap*) used as the name of a street, usu. one closed to traffic at one end. **3** the land and buildings surrounding and belonging to a cathedral; a quadrangle. [MidE *clos*, enclosure, from Lat *claudere*, to close]

closet *n* **1** a cupboard. **2** (*old*) a small private room. **3** (*old*) short for **water closet**. — *adj* secret, not openly declared. — *v* **-t-** (*tr*; **together**, **with**) to shut (oneself) away in private, e.g. for confidential discussion. [OFr dimin. of *clos*, enclosed place]

closure *n* **1** the act of closing something, e.g. a business or a transport route. **2** a device for closing or sealing something. **3** a parliamentary procedure for cutting short a debate and taking an immediate vote. — *v* (*tr*) to use this procedure for ending (a debate). [Lat *clausura*, from *claudere*, to close]

clot *n* **1** a soft mass, esp. of solidified liquid matter such as blood. **2** (*coll*) a fool. — *v* **-tt-** (*intr* & *tr*) to form into clots. [OE *clott*, lump, mass]

clotted cream *n* thick cream made by slowly heating milk and taking the cream from the top.

cloth *n* **1** woven, knitted or felted material. **2** (often *in cmpds*) a piece of fabric for a special use: *tablecloth*. **3** (with **the**) the clergy. [OE *clath*]

cloth cap *n* a flat cap, esp. made of tweed, with a stiff brim.

cloth of gold *n* a silk or woollen fabric interwoven with gold thread.

clothe *v* ***clothed*** or (esp. *old*) ***clad*** (*tr*) **1** to cover or provide with clothes. **2** (**in**) to dress. **3** (with **in**) to cover, conceal or disguise: *hills clothed in mist*. ◇ See also **clad**. [OE *clathian*]

clothes *n* (*pl*) **1** articles of dress for covering the body, for warmth, decoration, etc. **2** (usu. **bedclothes**) the sheets and blankets on a bed. [OE *clathas*, plural of *clath*, cloth]

clothes horse *n* a hinged frame on which to dry or air clothes indoors.

clothesline *n* a rope suspended usu. outdoors, on which to hang clothes to dry.

clothes peg *n* a small clip-like or forked device for securing clothes to a clothesline.

clothes pole *n* a fixed vertical pole for tying a clothesline to.

clothier *n* (*old*) a person who makes, sells or deals in cloth or esp. men's clothing. [MidE, altered from *clother*, from **cloth**]

clothing *n* **1** clothes. **2** something forming a covering: *a clothing of snow*. [**clothe**]

cloud *n* **1** a grey or white mass floating in the sky, composed of particles of water or ice. **2** a mass of dust, smoke or moving insects in the air. **3** a dark or dull spot. **4** a circumstance that causes anxiety. **5** a state of gloom, depression or suspicion: *He left the firm under a cloud*. — *v* **1** (*intr* with **over**) to become overcast with clouds. **2** (*tr* & *intr*; **over**) to make or become misty or cloudy. **3** (*intr*; **over**) to develop a troubled expression: *His face clouded*. **4** (*tr*) to make dull or confused. **5** (*tr*) to spoil, mar. — *adj* **cloudless**. — **(up) in the clouds** (*coll*) not in touch with reality. — **on cloud nine** (*coll*) extremely happy. — **with one's head in the clouds** (*coll*) too concerned with one's own thoughts and theories to take in the real situation. [OE *clud*, hill, mass of rock]

cloud base *n* the height above sea level of the under surface of the clouds.

cloudburst *n* a sudden downpour of rain.

cloud-cuckoo-land *n* a place where everything goes well, the apparent dwelling-place of over-optimistic people who refuse to see the problems of the real world.

cloudy *adj* **-ier**, **-iest** **1** full of clouds; overcast. **2** (of e.g. a liquid) not clear; milky. **3** confused; muddled. — *adv* **cloudily**. — *n* **cloudiness**.

clout *n* **1** a blow. **2** (*coll*) influence or power. **3** (*dialect*) a piece of clothing. — *v* (*tr*; *coll*) to hit. [OE *clut*, piece of cloth]

clove[1] *n* the strong-smelling dried flower-bud of a tropical Asian tree, used as a spice. [Fr *clou*, nail, from its shape]

clove[2] *n* one of the sections into which a bulb naturally splits. [OE *clufu*, bulb]

clove[3]. See **cleave**[1].

cloven *adj* (*old* or *poetic*) split; divided. [Past participle of **cleave**[1]]

cloven hoof *n* the partly split hoof of cattle, sheep or goats, and, in folklore, etc., of the Devil.

clover *n* a plant grown as cattle fodder, with leaves divided into usu. three parts and pink, purple or white flowers. — **in clover** (*coll*) in great comfort and luxury. [OE *clæfre*]

cloverleaf *n* an arrangement of curving roads at the junction of two motorways, etc., having, from the air, the shape of a four-leaved clover.

clown *n* **1** a comic performer in a circus or pantomime, usu. wearing ridiculous clothes and make-up. **2** someone who behaves comically. **3** (*derog*) a fool. — *v* (*intr*; **about**, **around**) to behave ridiculously. — *adj* **clownish**. — *adv* **clownishly**. — *n* **clownishness**.

cloy *v* (*intr*) to become distasteful through excess, esp. of sweetness. — *adj* **cloying**. [Variant of earlier *acloy*, orig. meaning to nail, from Lat *clavus*, nail]

club *n* **1** a stick, usu. thicker at one end, used as a weapon. **2** a stick with a specially shaped head, for playing golf or putting with. **3** (also **Indian club**) a bottle-shaped wooden object for swinging and throwing, for exercise. **4** a society or association. **5** the place where such a group meets. **6** a building with dining, reading and sleeping facilities for members. **7** (also **nightclub**) a place offering night-time entertainment, dancing, etc. **8** any playing-card of the suit **clubs**, bearing a black cloverleaf-shaped symbol. — *v* **-bb-** (*tr*) **1** to beat or strike with a club. **2** (with **together**) to contribute money jointly for a special purpose. — **in the club** or **pudding club** (*coll*) pregnant. — **join the club** (*coll*) I'm

in the same situation as you. [Norse *klubba*, cudgel]
clubbable *adj* friendly; able to mix well socially.
clubbed *adj* (of the fingers) thickened at the tips.
club foot *n* a deformity in which the foot is turned inwards.
clubhouse *n* a building where a club meets, esp. the premises of a sports club.
cluck *n* the sound that a hen makes. — *v* (*intr*) **1** (of a hen) to make clucks. **2** to express disapproval by making a similar sound with the tongue. [Imit.]
clue *n* **1** a fact or circumstance the discovery of which helps one to solve a mystery or to make progress in investigating something, e.g. a crime. **2** a word or words representing, in a more or less disguised form, something to be entered in a crossword. — **not have a clue** (*coll*) to be completely ignorant about something. — *v* ***cluing*** (*tr* & *intr* with **in**, **up on**; *coll*) to inform or become informed (*adj* **clued-in** or **clued-up**). [Variant of **clew**, ball of thread, from its use in finding the way out of a maze]
clueless *adj* (*derog*) stupid, incompetent or ignorant.
clump *n* **1** a group of e.g. trees, plants or people standing close together. **2** a dull heavy sound, e.g. of treading feet. — *v* **1** (*intr*) to walk with a heavy tread. **2** (*tr* & *intr*) to form into clumps. [Related to Dut *klompe*, lump, mass]
clumpy *adj* ***-ier***, ***-iest*** **1** large and heavy: *clumpy shoes*. **2** clumping. — *n* **clumpiness**.
clumsy *adj* ***-ier***, ***-iest*** **1** unskilful with the hands or awkward and ungainly in movement. **2** badly or awkwardly made. — *adv* **clumsily**. — *n* **clumsiness**. [MidE *clumse*, to be numb with cold]
clung. See **cling**.
clunk *n* the sound of a heavy, esp. metal, object striking something. — *v* (*intr* & *tr*) to (cause to) make this sound. [Imit.]
cluster *n* **1** a small group or gathering. **2** a number of flowers growing together on one stem. — *v* ***-r-*** (*tr* & *intr*) to form into a cluster or clusters. [OE *clyster*, bunch]
clutch[1] *v* **1** (*tr*) to grasp tightly. **2** (*intr*; **at**) to try to grasp. — *n* **1** (usu. in *pl*) control or power. **2** a device in a motor vehicle that connects or disconnects two revolving shafts, thereby passing, or preventing the passing of, the driving force from engine to gearbox. **3** the pedal operating this device. — **clutch at straws** to try anything, however unlikely, in one's desperation. [OE *clyccan*]
clutch bag *n* a small handbag without handles, held in the hand or under the arm.
clutch[2] *n* **1** a number of eggs laid at the same time. **2** a brood of chickens. [Norse *klekja*, to hatch]
clutter *n* an untidy accumulation of objects, or the confused, overcrowded state caused by it. — *v* ***-r-*** (*tr*; **up**) to overcrowd or make untidy with accumulated objects. [Variant of earlier *clotter*, from **clot**]
Cm *symbol* (*chem*) curium.
cm *abbrev* centimetre.
CMG *abbrev* Companion of (the Order of) St Michael and St George.
CND *abbrev* Campaign for Nuclear Disarmament.
CNAA *abbrev* Council for National Academic Awards.
CO *abbrev* **1** Commanding Officer. **2** Colorado.
Co[1] *abbrev* **1** Company. **2** County.
Co[2] *symbol* (*chem*) cobalt.
co- *pfx* with: *co-author*; *co-star*; *co-exist*; *co-operate*. ◇ See also **con-**.
c/o *abbrev* care of (see **care**).
coach *n* **1** a railway carriage. **2** a bus designed for long-distance travel. **3** (esp. *hist*) a closed horse-drawn carriage. **4** a trainer or instructor in a sport, etc., or a private tutor, esp. one who prepares pupils for examinations. — *v* **1** (*tr* & *intr*) to train in a sport, etc., or teach privately. — *n* **coaching**. — **drive a coach and horses through** (*coll*) to ignore and therefore make nonsense of (laws, regulations, existing arrangements, etc.). [OFr *coche*, from Hung *kocsi*, from *Kocs* in Hungary]
coachbuilder *n* a person who builds the bodies of motor vehicles.
coachman *n* (*hist*) the driver of a horse-drawn coach.
coachwork *n* the painted outer bodywork of a motor or rail vehicle.
coagulate *v* (*intr* & *tr*) to (cause to) pass from a liquid state to a semi-solid one; to curdle or clot. — *n* **coagulation**. [Lat *coagulare*]
coagulant *n* a substance that causes coagulation.
coal *n* **1** a hard black mineral composed of carbon formed by decayed and compressed plants, mined and used as a fuel. **2** a piece of this. — **coals to Newcastle** something brought to a place where it is already in plentiful supply. — **haul over the coals** (*coll*) to scold severely. — **heap coals of fire on someone's head** to make someone feel guilty by repaying evil with good. [OE *col*]
coalface *n* **1** the exposed face in a coalmine from which coal is being cut. **2** the area where the essential practical work is carried on in any particular field of activity.
coalfield *n* an area where there is coal underground.
coal-fired *adj* fuelled by coal.
coal gas *n* the mixture of gases obtained from coal, used for cooking and heating.
coalmine *n* a place where coal is mined.
coal tar *n* a thick black liquid substance produced when gas is obtained from coal, used in the manufacture of drugs, etc.
coal tit *n* a small grey bird with a black head.

coalesce *v* (*intr*) to come together so as to form a single mass. — *n* **coalescence**. — *adj* **coalescent**. [Lat *co-*, together + *alescere*, to grow]

coalition *n* a combination or temporary alliance, esp. between political parties. [Lat *coalitio*]

coaming *n* (*naut*) the raised edging round the hatches on a ship, to keep out water.

coarse *adj* **1** rough or open in texture. **2** rough or crude; not refined. **3** (of behaviour, speech, etc.) rude or offensive. — *adv* **coarsely**. — *n* **coarseness**.

coarsen *v* **-n-** (*tr* & *intr*) to make or become coarse.

coarse fish *n* freshwater fish, other than trout and salmon. — *n* **coarse fishing**.

coast *n* the edge of the land, alongside the sea; the seaside or seashore. — *v* (*intr*) **1** to travel downhill, e.g. on a bicycle or in a motor vehicle, using no kind of propelling power, relying on gravity or momentum. **2** to progress smoothly and satisfactorily without much effort. — *adj* **coastal**. — **the coast is clear** (*coll*) there is no danger of being spotted or caught. [OFr *coste*]

coastguard *n* a person stationed on the coast to watch for ships or swimmers in difficulties, and to give help.

coastline *n* the shape of the coast, esp. as seen on a map, or from the sea.

coaster *n* **1** a vessel that sails along the coast taking goods to coastal ports. **2** a small mat or tray for slipping under a glass, bottle, decanter, etc. to protect the table surface. **[coast]**

coat *n* **1** an outer garment with long sleeves, typically reaching to the knees. **2** a jacket. **3** the hair, fur or wool of an animal. **4** a covering or application (of something, e.g. paint, dust, sugar, etc.). — *v* (*tr*; **in, with**) to cover with a layer of something. — *n* **coating**. [OFr *cote*]

coat-hanger *n* a shaped piece of wood, plastic or metal, with a hook, on which to hang garments.

coat of arms *n* a heraldic design consisting of a shield bearing the special symbols of a particular person, family, organisation or town.

coat of mail *n* (*hist*) a protective garment made of interlinked metal rings, worn by soldiers.

coat tails *n* (*pl*) the two long pieces that hang down at the back of a man's tailcoat. — **on someone's coat-tails** enjoying undeserved success as a result of someone else's achievement.

co-author *n* one's fellow author. — *v* (*tr*) to write (a book, etc.) with one or more others.

coax *v* (*tr*) **1 (into, out of)** to persuade using e.g. flattery, promises, kind words, etc. **2** to get by coaxing. — *adv* **coaxingly**. [From earlier *cokes*, fool]

coaxial *adj* **1** having a common axis. **2** (*electr*) (of a cable) consisting of two conductors arranged concentrically and insulated from each other. **[co- + axis]**

cob *n* **1** a strong horse with short legs. **2** a male swan. **3** a hazelnut or hazel tree. **4** a corncob. **5** a loaf with a rounded top.

cobalt *n* **1** a silvery white metallic element (symbol **Co**) used e.g. in making certain types of steel. **2** (also **cobalt blue**) a compound of cobalt used as a blue colouring substance, or its deep colour. — *adj* **cobaltic**. [Ger *Kobold*, goblin, the name given to the material by frustrated miners looking for silver]

cobber *n* (*Austr* & *NZ coll*; often used as a form of address) a pal.

cobble[1] *n* (also **cobblestone**) a rounded stone used esp. formerly to surface streets. — *adj* **cobbled**. **[cob]**

cobble[2] *v* **1** (*tr* & *intr*) to mend (shoes). **2** (*tr* with **together**) to construct roughly or unskilfully. [Back-formation from **cobbler**]

cobbler *n* a person who mends shoes.

cobblers *n* (*slang*) nonsense. [Rhyming slang: *cobblers' awls*, i.e. *balls*]

COBOL *n* short for *C*ommon *B*usiness-*O*riented *L*anguage, a computer programming language used in commerce, based on English.

cobra *n* a poisonous Indian and African snake that can expand the skin at the back of its head to give it a threatening appearance. [Port, from Lat *colubra*, snake]

cobweb *n* **1** a web formed of fine sticky threads spun by a spider. **2** a single thread from this. — *adj* **cobwebby**. [MidE *coppeweb*, from OE *atorcoppe*, spider]

coca *n* a S American shrub, or its leaves, which contain cocaine and are chewed as a stimulant. [Span, from Quechua *kuka*]

cocaine *n* an addictive narcotic drug, used also as a local anaesthetic. **[coca]**

coccyx *n* ***-xes*** or ***coccyges*** (*anat*) a small triangular tail-like bone at the base of the human spine. [Gr, cuckoo, from its triangular beak]

cochineal *n* **1** a red insect of Mexico. **2** a bright red colouring substance used in food, got from the dried body of this insect. [Span *cochinilla*]

cochlea *n* ***cochleae*** (*anat*) a spiral cavity in the inner ear. — *adj* **cochlear**. [Gr *cochlias*, snail with spiral shell]

cock[1] *n* **1** a male bird, esp. an adult male chicken. **2** a stopcock for controlling the flow of liquid, gas, etc. **3** the hammer of a gun, raised and let go by the trigger. **4** (*vulg*) the penis. **5** (*vulg slang*) nonsense. **6** (*slang*) a pal, usu. used as a form of address. — *v* **1** (*tr* & *intr*) to lift; to stick up. **2** (*tr*) to turn in a particular direction: *cock an ear towards the door*. **3** (*tr*) to draw back the hammer of (a gun). **4** (*tr*) to set (one's hat) at an angle. — **go off at half cock** to begin too soon, without being fully prepared. [OE *cocc*]

cock-and-bull story *n* (*coll*) an unlikely story, esp. one used as an excuse or explanation.
cock-crow *n* dawn; early morning.
cockfight *n* a fight between cocks armed with sharp metal spurs. — *n* **cockfighting**.

cock[2] *n* a small pile of hay, etc. [Related to Norse *kökkr*, lump]

cockade *n* (*hist*) a feather or a rosette of ribbon worn on the hat as a badge. [**cock**[1]]

cock-a-hoop *adj* (*coll*) jubilant; exultant.

cock-a-leekie *n* soup made from chicken boiled with leeks. [**cock**[1] + **leek**]

cockatoo *n* a large pale-coloured crested parrot of Australia and the E Indies. [Malay *kakatua*]

cockatrice *n* **1** (*mythol*) a monster with the head, wings and legs of a cock and the body and tail of a serpent. **2** (*Bible*) a poisonous snake. [OFr *cocatris*]

cockchafer *n* a large greyish-brown beetle. [**cock**[1] + *chafer*, beetle]

cocked hat *n* (*hist*) a three-cornered hat with upturned brim. — **knock into a cocked hat** (*coll*) to surpass spectacularly or defeat utterly. [**cock**[1], *v*]

cocker *n* (also **cocker spaniel**) a small, esp. copper-coloured, spaniel. [From **woodcock**, which it was bred to hunt]

cockerel *n* a young cock. [Dimin. of **cock**[1]]

cock-eyed *adj* **1** crooked; lopsided. **2** senseless; crazy; impractical. [**cock**[1]]

cockle *n* an edible shellfish with a rounded, ribbed, hinged shell in two equal halves. — **warm the cockles of one's heart** (*coll*) to delight and gladden one. [Fr *coquille*, shell]
cockleshell *n* **1** the shell of the cockle. **2** any tiny insubstantial boat.

cockney *n* **-eys** **1** (often *cap*) a native of London, esp. of the East End. **2** the dialect used by Cockneys. — *adj* relating to Cockneys or their dialect. [MidE *cokeney*, a cock's egg (i.e. a misshapen egg), contemptuous name for a town-dweller]

cockpit *n* **1** the compartment for the pilot and crew aboard an aircraft. **2** the driver's seat in a racing-car. **3** the part of a small yacht, etc. containing the wheel and tiller. **4** (*hist*) a pit into which cocks were put to fight each other. **5** any scene of prolonged conflict, esp. in war. [**cock**[1] + **pit**[1]]

cockroach *n* a large black or brown beetle-like insect found esp. in dirty kitchens. [Span *cucaracha*]

cockscomb *n* **1** the fleshy red crest on a cock's head. **2** (*old derog*; also **coxcomb**) a conceited fellow. [**cock's comb**]

cocksure *adj* foolishly over-confident. [**cock**[1]]

cocktail *n* **1** a mixed drink of spirits and other liquors. **2** a mixed dish esp. of seafood and mayonnaise. **3** a mixture of different things.
cocktail stick *n* a short thin pointed wooden stick on which to impale small items of food for serving at parties, etc.

cock-up *n* (*slang*) a mess or muddle resulting from incompetence. [**cock**[1]]

cocky *adj* **-ier**, **-iest** (*derog*) cheekily self-confident. — *adv* **cockily**. — *n* **cockiness**. [**cock**[1]]

coco. See **coconut**.

cocoa *n* **1** a powder made from the roasted and ground seeds of the cacao tree. **2** a hot drink made with the powder. [**cacao**]
cocoa bean *n* the seed of the cacao tree.
cocoa butter *n* a fat obtained from cocoa beans.

coconut *n* the large oval fruit of the **coconut palm** or **coco**, having a hard hairy brown shell filled with solid edible white flesh and a clear, sweet-tasting liquid (**coconut milk**). [Port *coco*, grimace or ugly face, from the face-like markings on a coconut]
coconut shy *n* a stall at a fair where contestants throw balls to knock coconuts off stands.

cocoon *n* the silky casing spun round itself by an insect larva, inside which it undergoes transformation into its adult form. — *v* (*tr*) **1** to wrap up as if in a cocoon. **2** to protect from the problems of everyday life. [Provençal *coucoun*, eggshell]

cocotte *n* a small lidded pot for oven and table use, esp. intended for an individual portion. [Fr]

cod[1] *n* ***cod*** a large edible white fish found in northern seas.
codfish *n* a cod.
cod-liver oil *n* a medicinal oil obtained from cods' livers, rich in vitamins A and D.

cod[2] (*slang*) *n* **1** a hoax. **2** a parody. — *v* ***-dd-*** **1** (*intr* & *tr*) to hoax (someone). **2** (*tr*) to parody.

cod[3] *n* (*slang*) nonsense. [**codswallop**]

coda *n* (*mus*) a passage added at the end of a movement or piece, to bring it to a satisfying conclusion. [Ital, tail]

coddle *v* (*tr*) **1** to cook (eggs) gently in hot, rather than boiling, water. **2** to pamper, mollycoddle or over-protect. [Variant of *caudle*, spiced egg drink for an invalid, from Lat *calidus*, warm]

code *n* **1** a system of words, letters, or symbols, used in place of those really intended, for secrecy's or brevity's sake. **2** a set of signals for sending messages, etc. **3** (*comput*) a set of programming instructions. **4** a group of numbers and letters used as means of identification. **5** a set of principles of behaviour. **6** a systematically organised set of laws. — *v* (*tr*) to put (a message, etc.) into a code. [OFr, from Lat *codex*, book]
code word *n* a word or phrase of special and secret significance, agreed on by its users for a purpose.
dialling code *n* the part of a telephone number that represents a town or area.

postal code or **postcode** see under **post**[3].
codeine *n* an opium-based pain-killing and sleep-inducing drug. [Gr *kodeia*, poppy head]
codex *n* ***codices*** an ancient manuscript bound in book form. [Lat, set of tablets, book]
codger *n* (*coll*; sometimes *derog*) a man, esp. an old one. [Perhaps a variant of **cadger**]
codicil *n* (*legal*) a short addition to a will, added after the will has been written. [Lat *codicillus*, dimin. of *codex*, book]
codify *v* ***-ies***, ***-ied*** (*tr*) to arrange (laws, etc.) into a systematic code. — *n* **codification**. [**code** + **-ify** as in *magnify*]
codling[1] *n* a kind of cooking-apple. [MidE *querdling*]
codling[2] *n* the young of the cod.
codpiece *n* (*hist*) a flap of material attached to a man's breeches, covering his genitals. [From earlier *cod*, scrotum]
codswallop *n* (*slang*) nonsense.
co-ed *abbrev* (*coll*) co-education or co-educational. — *n* (*US*) a female student in a co-educational school or college.
co-education *n* education of pupils of both sexes in the same school or college. — *adj* **co-educational**.
coefficient *n* **1** (*math*) a number placed before, and multiplying, another quantity, as, e.g. *5* in the term $5x$ or $3a^2$ in $3a^2b$. **2** (*physics*) a number used to measure a particular property in any material: *the coefficient of expansion*. [**co-**]
coelacanth *n* a primitive bony fish believed extinct till a live specimen was found in 1938. [Gr *koilos*, hollow + *akantha*, spine]
coelenterate *n* any of a group of simple invertebrate creatures including jellyfish, with a single body cavity and single opening. [Gr *koilos*, hollow + *enteron*, intestine]
coeliac *adj* **1** relating to the abdomen. **2** relating to coeliac disease. — *n* a person suffering from coeliac disease. [Gr *koilia*, belly]
coeliac disease *n* a condition of the intestines in which they are sensitive to the gluten in wheat, and become unable to absorb nutrients properly.
coenobite *n* a member of a monastic community. — *adj* **coenobitic**. [Gr *koinos*, common + *bios*, life]
coerce *v* (*tr*; **into**) to force or compel, using threats, etc. — *adj* **coercible**. — *n* **coercion**. — *adj* **coercive**. [Lat *coercere*, to restrain]
coeval (*formal*) *adj* (with **with**) of the same age or period of time. — *n* someone of the same age or period of time. [Lat *co-*, with + *aevum*, age]
co-exist *v* (*intr*) **1** to exist together, or simultaneously. **2** to live peacefully side by side in spite of differences, etc. — *n* **co-existence**. — *adj* **co-existent**.
co-extensive *adj* covering the same distance or time.
C of E *abbrev* Church of England.
coffee *n* **1** a tropical shrub whose roasted and ground seeds are used to make a drink. **2** the seeds of this plant, ground or whole. **3** a drink made from the ground seeds. **4** the brown colour of the drink when mixed with milk. [Turk *kahveh*, from Arabic *qahwah*, coffee or wine]
coffee bar *n* a place where coffee and snacks are sold at a counter.
coffee bean *n* the seed of the coffee plant.
coffee break *n* a pause for a cup of coffee during working hours.
coffee house *n* (*hist*) an establishment serving coffee, used by fashionable people esp. in the 18th century.
coffee mill *n* a machine for grinding coffee beans.
coffee table *n* a small low table.
coffee-table book *n* (slightly *derog*) a large expensive highly illustrated book, suitable for visitors to browse through.
coffer *n* **1** a large chest for holding valuables. **2** (in *pl*) a treasury or supply of funds. **3** (*archit*) a hollow or sunken section in the elaborate panelling or plasterwork of a ceiling. [OFr *cofre*, from Gr *kophinos*, basket]
cofferdam *n* a caisson.
coffin *n* a box in which to bury or cremate a corpse. [OFr *cofin*, from Gr *kophinos*, basket]
cog *n* **1** one of a series of teeth on the edge of a wheel or bar which engage with another series of teeth to bring about motion. **2** a person unimportant in, though necessary to, a process or organisation. [MidE *cogge*]
cogwheel *n* a wheel with cogs.
cogent *adj* (of arguments, reasons, etc.) strong; persuasive; convincing. — *n* **cogency**. — *adv* **cogently**. [Lat *cogere*, to drive]
cogitate *v* (*intr*) to think deeply; to ponder. — *n* **cogitation**. — *adj* **cogitative**. [Lat *cogitare*, to think]
cognac *n* a high-quality French brandy from *Cognac* in SW France.
cognate *adj* (**with**) **1** descended from or related to a common ancestor. **2** (of words or languages) derived from the same original form. **3** related; akin. — *n* **cognateness**. [Lat *co-*, with + *gnasci*, to be born]
cognition *n* the process of learning by such means as observation and reasoning. — *adj* **cognitive**. — *adv* **cognitively**. [Lat *cognitio*, study, knowledge]
cognisance or **cognizance** *n* **1** knowledge; understanding; perception; awareness. **2** the range or scope of one's awareness or knowledge. **3** (*legal*) the right of a court to deal with a particular matter. **4** (*heraldry*) a distinctive mark or sign. — **take cognisance of** to take into consideration. [OFr *conoisance*, from Lat

cognoscere, to know; *g* added later under the influence of Latin]

cognisant *adj* (with **of**) aware of.

cognomen *n* **1** (*Roman hist*) a Roman's third name, often in origin an epithet or nickname. **2** a nickname or surname. [Lat, from *co-*, with + *nomen*, name]

cognoscenti *n* (*pl*) people in the know; connoisseurs. [Ital, from Lat *cognoscere*, to know]

cohabit *v* **-t-** (*intr*; **with**) to live together as, or as if, husband and wife. — *n* **cohabitation**. — *n* **cohabiter** or **cohabitee**. [Lat *cohabitare*, to live together]

cohere *v* (*intr*) **1** to stick together. **2** to be consistent; to have a clear logical connection or development. [Lat *cohaerere*, to be connected]

coherent *adj* **1** (of a description or argument) logically and clearly developed; consistent. **2** speaking intelligibly. **3** sticking together; cohering. **4** (*physics*) (of radiating waves) having the same frequency and a constant phase difference. — *n* **coherence**. — *adv* **coherently**. [Lat *cohaerere*, to be connected]

cohesion *n* **1** the process or state of sticking together. **2** the tendency to stick together. **3** (*physics*) the force with which the particles of a liquid or solid stick together. — *adj* **cohesive**. [Lat *cohaerere*, to stick together]

cohort *n* **1** (*hist*) in the ancient Roman army, one of the ten divisions of a legion. **2** a band of warriors. **3** a group of people sharing a common quality or belief. **4** (*coll*) a follower, supporter or companion. [Lat *cohors*]

coif[1] *n* a close-fitting cap worn esp. by women in mediaeval times or by nuns under a veil. [OFr *coiffe*]

coif[2] *n* a hairstyle. — *v* **-ff-** (*tr*) to dress (hair); to dress the hair of. [Prob. from **coiffure**]

coiffeur *n* a male hairdresser. [Fr]

coiffeuse *n* a female hairdresser.

coiffure *n* a hairstyle. — *v* (*tr*) to dress (hair); to dress the hair of. [Fr]

coil[1] *v* (*tr* & *intr*; **up**) to wind round and round in loops to form rings or a spiral. — *n* **1** something looped into rings or a spiral. **2** a single loop in such an arrangement. **3** a wound length of wire for conducting electricity. **4** a piece of plastic-covered wire inserted into the womb to prevent pregnancy. [OFr *cuillir*, to gather together]

coil[2] *n* (*old*) trouble and tumult: *this mortal coil* (i.e. the troubles of the world).

coin *n* **1** a small metal disc stamped for use as money. **2** coins generally. — *v* (*tr*) **1** to manufacture (coins) from metal; to make (metal) into coins. **2** to invent (a new word or phrase). — **coin it, coin it in** or **coin money** (*coll*) to be making a lot of money. — **the other side of the coin** the opposite way of looking at the issue under consideration. — **pay someone back in his own coin** to respond to someone's discourteous or unfair treatment with similar behaviour. — **to coin a phrase** (*ironic*) used to introduce an over-used expression. [OFr *coin*, wedge, die]

coinage *n* **1** the process of coining. **2** coins. **3** a newly invented word or phrase. **4** the official currency of a country.

coin-operated *adj* (of a machine) operating on the insertion of a coin.

coincide *v* (*intr*; **with**) **1** to happen at the same time. **2** to be the same; to agree. **3** to occupy the same position. [Lat *co-*, together + *incidere*, to happen]

coincidence *n* **1** the occurrence of events together or in sequence in a startling way, without any causal connection. **2** the fact of being the same.

coincident *adj* **1** coinciding in space or time. **2** (with **with**) in agreement with.

coincidental *adj* happening by coincidence. — *adv* **coincidentally**.

coir *n* fibre from coconut shells, used for making ropes, matting, etc. [Malayalam (a SW Indian language) *kayaru*, cord]

coition or **coitus** *n* sexual intercourse. — *adj* **coital**. [Lat *coire*, to unite]

coke[1] *n* the solid fuel left after gases have been extracted from coal. — *v* (*tr* & *intr*) to turn into coke. [Dialect *colk*, core]

coke[2] *n* (*coll*) cocaine.

Col. *abbrev* **1** Colonel. **2** Colorado.

col *n* a dip in a mountain ridge between two peaks. [Fr, neck]

col. *abbrev* **1** column. **2** colour.

col-. See **con-**.

cola or **kola** *n* **1** *n* a W African tree from whose nuts is obtained an extract used as a tonic and in soft drinks. **2** a fizzy drink flavoured with this. [Malinke (a W African language) *kolo*, nut]

colander *n* a perforated metal or plastic bowl in which to drain the water from cooked vegetables, etc. [Lat *colare*, to strain]

cold *adj* **1** low in temperature; not hot or warm. **2** lower in temperature than is normal, comfortable or pleasant. **3** (of food) cooked, but not eaten hot: *cold meat*. **4** unfriendly. **5** comfortless; depressing. **6** (*coll*) unenthusiastic: *His suggestion left me cold*. **7** without warmth or emotion: *a cold, calculating person*. **8** sexually unresponsive. **9** (of colours) producing a feeling of coldness rather than warmth. **10** (*coll*) unconscious, usu. after a blow, fall, etc.: *out cold*. **11** dead. **12** (in trying to guess or find something) far from the answer or the hidden object. **13** (of a trail or scent) not fresh; too old to follow. — *adv* without preparation or rehearsal. — *n* **1** lack of heat or warmth; cold weather. **2** an illness of the nose and throat, with running nose, sneezing, coughing, etc.: *catch a cold*. — *adv* **coldly**. — *n* **coldness**. — **catch cold** to become ill (**catch one's death of cold**, die) as a result of exposure to cold. — **get cold feet** (*coll*) to lose courage; to become reluctant to carry something out. — **give**

(someone) the cold shoulder (*coll*) to respond coldly to; to rebuff or snub. — **in cold blood** deliberately and unemotionally. — **make someone's blood run cold** to terrify or horrify someone. — **out in the cold** (*coll*) ignored, disregarded and neglected by others. — **pour** or **throw cold water on** (*coll*) to be discouraging or unenthusiastic about. [OE *cald*]

cold-blooded *adj* **1** (of fish, reptiles, etc.) having a body temperature that varies with that of the environment. **2** lacking emotion; callous; cruel. — *adv* **cold-bloodedly**. — *n* **cold-bloodedness**.

cold chisel *n* a chisel for cutting cold metal, stone, etc.

cold comfort *n* no comfort at all.

cold cream *n* face cream for cleaning the skin and keeping it soft.

cold frame *n* a glass-covered frame for protecting young plants growing outdoors.

cold front *n* (*meteorol*) the edge of a mass of cold air pushing against a mass of warm air.

cold-hearted *adj* unkind. — *adv* **cold-heartedly**. — *n* **cold-heartedness**.

cold-shoulder *v* (*tr*) to give (someone) the cold shoulder (see above).

cold sore *n* a patch of small blister-like spots around or near the mouth, caused by a virus.

cold storage *n* **1** the storage of food, etc. under refrigeration. **2** the state of being put aside or saved till another time; postponement; abeyance.

cold sweat *n* sweating from fear or nervousness.

cold turkey *n* (*slang*) the acute discomfort felt by someone withdrawing from an addictive drug.

cold war *n* a state of hostility and antagonism between nations, without actual warfare.

cole *n* any of various vegetables of the cabbage type. [OE *cawl*, from Lat *caulis*]

coleslaw *n* a salad made with finely-cut raw cabbage and carrots. [Dut *koolsla*, cabbage salad]

coley *n* **-*eys*** a large edible fish of the cod family, found in the N Atlantic, with white or grey flesh.

colic *n* severe pains in the abdomen or bowels. — *adj* **colicky**. [Gr *kolikos*, from *kolon*, colon (**colon**[2])]

coliseum *n* (*hist*) a large stadium or amphitheatre for sports and other entertainment. [Lat variant of *Colosseum*, the largest Roman amphitheatre]

colitis *n* (*med*) inflammation of the lining of the large intestine. [**colon**[2] + **-itis**]

collaborate *v* (*intr*) (**with**) **1** to work together with another or others on something. **2** (*derog*) to co-operate with or help (an enemy occupying one's country). — *n* **collaboration**. — *adj* **collaborative**. — *adv* **collaboratively**. — *n* **collaborator**. [Lat *com-*, together + *laborare*, to work]

collaborationist *n* (*derog*) a collaborator with an enemy. — *n* **collaborationism**.

collage *n* **1** a design or picture made up of pieces of paper or cloth, or parts of photographs, etc. fixed to a background surface. **2** the art of producing such works. [Fr, pasting, gluing]

collagen *n* (*biol*) a substance found in bones, cartilage, etc. that can be boiled to produce gelatin. [Gr *kolla*, glue + **-gen**]

collapse *v* **1** (*intr*) to fall, give way or cave in. **2** (*intr;* **with**) to drop unconscious; to faint; to drop exhausted or helpless. **3** (*intr*) to break down emotionally. **4** (*intr*) to fail suddenly: *Several firms collapsed.* **5** (*intr* & *tr*) to fold up compactly for storage or space-saving. **6** (*intr* & *tr*) (of the lungs or blood vessels, etc.) to (cause to) become flattened. **7** (*intr*; *stock exchange*) to suffer a sudden steep drop in value. — *n* the process of collapsing. — *n* **collapsibility**. — *adj* **collapsible**. [Lat *collabi*, to slide, fall]

collar *n* **1** a band or flap of any of various shapes, folded over or standing up round the neck of a garment; the neck of a garment generally. **2** something worn round the neck. **3** a band of leather, etc. worn round the neck by a dog, etc. **4** a padded leather object, shaped to fit round a horse's neck, to ease the strain of pulling a vehicle. **5** a distinctively coloured ring of fur or feathers round an animal's or bird's neck. **6** a cut of meat from the neck of an animal. **7** a ring-shaped fitting for joining two pipes, etc. together. **8** any collar-like part. — *v* **-*r*-** (*tr*) **1** to seize by the collar. **2** (*coll*) to catch or capture. **3** (*coll*) to grab for oneself. — *adj* **collarless**. — **get hot under the collar** (*coll*) to become angry or embarrassed. [OFr *colier*, from Lat *collum*, neck]

collarbone *n* either of two bones, the clavicles, linking the shoulder-blades with the top of the breastbone.

collate *v* (*tr*) **1** to examine and compare (texts, evidence, etc.). **2** to check and arrange in order (sheets of paper, pages of a book, etc.) ready for fastening together. — *n* **collator**. [Lat *collatus*, past participle of *conferre*, to put together, compare]

collation *n* **1** the act of collating. **2** a light meal.

collateral *adj* **1** descended from a common ancestor, but through a different branch of the family. **2** additional; secondary in importance; subsidiary. — *n* (also **collateral security**) property, etc. that one promises to a person giving one a loan, as guarantee of its repayment. — *adv* **collaterally**. [Lat *collateralis*, from Lat *com-*, with + *latus*, side]

collation. See **collate**.

colleague *n* a fellow-worker, esp. in a profession. [Lat *collega*, partner, colleague]

collect *v* **1** (*tr* & *intr*; **up**) to bring or come together; to gather; to accumulate. **2** (*tr*) to build up an assortment of (things of a particular type) out of enthusiasm for them: *collect stamps.* **3** (*tr*) to call for; to fetch; to pick up. **4** (*tr* & *intr*; **for**) to get (e.g. money owed or voluntary contributions) from people. **5** (*tr*) to calm or control (oneself); to get (one's thoughts, etc.) under control. — *adj* (*US*) (of a telephone call) paid for by the person receiving it. — *adv* (*US*) reversing the charges. — *adj* **collectable**. [Lat *colligere*, to gather]

collected *adj* **1** (of a writer's works) all published together in a single volume or a uniform set of volumes. **2** cool; calm; self-possessed. — *adv* **collectedly**. — *n* **collectedness**.

collection *n* **1** the act of collecting. **2** an accumulated assortment of things of a particular type. **3** an amount of money collected. **4** the removal of mail from a postbox at scheduled times.

collective *adj* of, belonging to or involving all the members of a group. — *adv* **collectively**.

collective bargaining *n* talks between a trade union and a company's management to settle questions of pay and working conditions.

collective farm *n* a large state-controlled farm composed of a number of small farms, run by the farmers on co-operative principles.

collective noun *n* a noun standing for a group of people, animals, etc., usu. taking a singular verb, e.g. *swarm*, *herd*, *gang*, *committee*.

collectivise or **-ize** *v* (*tr*) to group (farms, factories, etc.) into larger units and bring under state control and ownership. — *n* **collectivisation** or **-z-**. — *n* **collectivism**.

collector *n* (often *in cmpds*) a person who collects, as a job or hobby.

collector's item *n* something that is a good specimen of its type and would interest a collector.

colleen *n* (*Irish*) a girl. [Irish *cailin*, girl]

college *n* **1** an institution (not a university) providing higher education, further education or professional training. **2** one of a number of self-governing establishments that make up certain universities. **3** the staff and students of a college. **4** (with *cap*) a name used by some larger secondary schools. **5** a body of people with particular duties and rights: *the College of Cardinals* (i.e. all the cardinals as a group). **6** an official body of members of a profession, concerned with maintaining standards, etc. [Lat *collegium*, group of associates, fellowship]

collegiate *adj* **1** of, relating to, or belonging to a college. **2** having the form of a college. **3** (of a university) consisting of individual colleges. [Lat *collegiatus*, from *collegium*, fellowship]

collegiate church *n* **1** in Scotland, a church served by two clergymen of equal rank. **2** a church having a chapter of canons attached to it.

collide *v* (*intr*; **with**) **1** to crash together, or crash into. **2** (of people) to disagree or clash. [Lat *collidere*, from *com-*, with + *laedere*, to strike]

collie *n* a usu. long-haired black- or tan-and-white dog used for herding sheep, etc. [Perhaps from Scot *colle*, coal, the breed having once been black]

collier *n* **1** a coal-miner. **2** a coal-transporting ship. [MidE *coliere*, from OE *col*, coal]

colliery *n* **-ies** a coalmine with its buildings.

collision *n* **1** the violent meeting of objects; a crash. **2** a disagreement, conflict or clash. [Lat *collisio*]

collision course *n* a direction taken, or course of action begun, that is bound to result in collision with something or someone.

collocate *v* (*intr* with **with**; *gram*) (of a word) to occur frequently alongside (another word): *'Close' collocates with 'friend', but 'near' doesn't.* — *n* **collocation**. [Lat *collocare*, to place together]

colloquial *adj* (of language or vocabulary) informal; used in conversation rather than in formal speech or writing. — *adv* **colloquially**. [Lat *colloquium*, conversation]

colloquialism *n* a colloquial expression.

colloquium *n* **-ia** an academic conference; a seminar. [Lat, conversation]

colloquy *n* **-ies** a conversation; talk. [Lat *colloquium*, conversation]

collusion *n* secret and illegal co-operation for the purpose of fraud or other criminal activity, etc. — *adj* **collusive**. [Lat *collusio*]

collywobbles *n* (*pl*; *coll*) **1** pain or discomfort in the abdomen. **2** nervousness; apprehensiveness. [Prob. from **colic** + **wobble**]

Colo. *abbrev* Colorado.

cologne *n* eau-de-Cologne. [*Cologne*, Germany, the place of manufacture]

colon[1] *n* a punctuation mark (:), properly used to introduce a list, an example, or an explanation. [Gr, clause]

colon[2] *n* the large intestine, extending from the caecum to the rectum. — *adj* **colonic**. [Gr, large intestine]

colonel *n* a senior army officer, in charge of a regiment, below a brigadier in rank. — *n* **colonelcy**, **-ies**. [Ital *colonello*, leader of a column]

Colonel Blimp see **Blimp**.

colonel-in-chief *n* in the British army, an honorary rank and title often held by a member of the Royal family.

colonial *adj* **1** relating to, belonging to, or living in a colony or colonies. **2** possessing colonies: *colonial powers.* — *n* an inhabitant of a colony. — *adv* **colonially**. [**colony**]

colonialism *n* (often *derog*) the policy of acquiring colonies, esp. as a source of profit. — *n* **colonialist**.

colonise or **-ize** *v* (*tr*) to establish a colony in, establish as a colony, or settle as a colonist in (an area or country). — *n* **colonisation** or **-z-**. [**colony**]

colonnade *n* a row of columns, usu. supporting a roof. — *adj* **colonnaded**. [Fr, from Lat *columna*, column]

colony *n* **-ies 1** a settlement abroad controlled by the founding country; the settlers living there; the territory they occupy. **2** a group of the same nationality or occupation forming a distinctive community within a city, etc. **3** a group of animals, birds, etc. of one type living together. [Lat *colonia*, farm, colony]

colophon *n* **1** an inscription at the end of a printed book or manuscript giving the name of writer, printer, etc. and place and date of production. **2** a publisher's ornamental mark or device. [Gr, summit, finishing touch]

colorant *n* a substance used for colouring. [Lat *color*, colour]

coloration *n* arrangement or combination of colours; colouring. [Lat *colorare*, to colour]

coloratura *n* **1** an elaborate and intricate passage or style in singing. **2** a soprano specialising in such singing. [Ital, colouring]

colossal *adj* **1** huge; vast. **2** (*coll*) splendid; marvellous. — *adv* **colossally**. [**colossus**]

colossus *n* **-lossi** or **-uses 1** a gigantic statue. **2** an overwhelmingly powerful person or organisation. [Gr *kolossos*]

colostomy *n* **-ies** (*surg*) an operation to construct an opening in the colon through which it can be emptied, when emptying through the anus is not possible. [**colon**[2] + Gr *stoma*, mouth]

colostrum *n* a mammal's first milk after giving birth. [Lat]

colour *n* **1** a property that surfaces have when light falls on them, arising from their capacity to reflect or absorb light waves, variations in wavelength producing perceived variations of shade. **2** any of these variations or colours, often with the addition of black and white. **3** (*photography*, *art*, etc.) the use of some or all colours, as distinct from black and white only: *in full colour*. **4** a colouring substance, esp. paint. **5** the shade of a person's skin, as related to race; the darker skin shades. **6** pinkness of the face or cheeks. **7** lively or convincing detail: *add local colour to the story*. **8** richness of quality in music, or its mood and quality generally. — *v* **1** (*tr*) to put colour on; to paint or dye. **2** (*tr*; **in**) to fill in (an outlined area) or (a black and white picture) with colour. **3** (*tr*) to influence: *allow one's feelings to colour one's judgement*. **4** (*intr*) to blush. — **off colour** (*coll*) unwell. ◇ See also **colours** below. [OFr *color*]

colour bar *n* discrimination against coloured people.

colour-blind *adj* unable to distinguish certain colours. — *n* **colour-blindness**.

colour coding *n* the systematic use of colour as a means of identification or classification, as in electrical wiring. — *adj* **colour-coded**.

coloured *adj* **1** (sometimes *in cmpds*) having colour: *lemon-coloured*. **2** belonging to a dark-skinned race; non-white. **3** (*cap*; *SAfr*) of mixed white and non-white descent. — *n* **1** a person of dark-skinned race. **2** (*cap*; *SAfr*) a person of mixed white and non-white descent.

colour-fast *adj* (of fabrics) dyed with colours that will not run when washed.

colourful *adj* **1** full of esp. bright colour. **2** lively; vivid; full of interest or character. — *adv* **colourfully**.

colouring *n* **1** a substance used to give colour, e.g. to food. **2** the applying of colour. **3** arrangement or combination of colour. **4** facial complexion, or this in combination with eye and hair colour.

colourist *n* someone skilled in the use of colour; an artist.

colourless *adj* **1** without, or lacking, colour. **2** uninteresting; dull; lifeless. **3** pale. — *adv* **colourlessly**. — *n* **colourlessness**.

colours *n* (*pl*) **1** (sometimes in *sing*) the flag of a nation, regiment or ship: *the regimental colours*. **2** the coloured uniform or other distinguishing badge awarded to team-members in certain games. **3** a badge of ribbons in colours representing a particular party, etc., worn to show support for it. **4** the coloured dress of a jockey and horse, identifying the horse's owner. — **in one's true colours** as one really is. — **nail one's colours to the mast** to announce openly one's support for something or someone. — **with flying colours** with great success.

colour scheme *n* a choice or combination of colours in house decoration, etc.

colour sergeant *n* a sergeant who carries the company's colours.

colour supplement *n* an illustrated magazine accompanying a newspaper.

colourway *n* a combination of colours in patterned material, etc.

Colt *n* a type of small pistol. [Samuel *Colt*, the inventor]

colt *n* **1** a young male horse. **2** an inexperienced young team-player or member of a junior team. [OE]

coltish *adj* youthfully awkward in movement or behaviour. — *adv* **coltishly**.

coltsfoot *n* a wild plant with bright yellow flowers.

columbine *n* a wild flower related to the buttercup, with spurred petals that look like a group of pigeons. [Lat *columba*, dove, pigeon]

column *n* **1** (*archit*) a usu. cylindrical pillar with a base and capital. **2** something similarly shaped; a long more or less cylindrical mass. **3** a vertical row of numbers. **4** a vertical strip of print on a newspaper page, etc. **5** a regular section in a newspaper concerned with a particular topic, or by a regular writer. **6** a troop of soldiers or vehicles standing or moving a few abreast. — *adj* **columnar**. [Lat *columna*, pillar]

columnist *n* a person writing a regular section of a newspaper.

com-. See **con-**.

coma *n* a state of long-continuing deep unconsciousness caused by e.g. injury, illness or drugs. [Gr *koma*, deep sleep]

comatose *adj* **1** in a coma. **2** (*facet*) sleepy; asleep. [Gr *koma*, deep sleep]

comb *n* **1** a rigid toothed device for tidying and arranging the hair, sometimes worn in the hair to keep it in place. **2** a toothed tool for disentangling and cleaning strands of wool or cotton. **3** an act of combing. **4** a honeycomb. **5** the fleshy crest on the head of the male chicken or other cock bird. — *v* (*tr*) **1** to arrange, smooth or clean with a comb. **2** (**for**) to search (a place) thoroughly. — *v* **comb out** (*tr*) **1** to remove (dirt, etc.) by combing. **2** to find and get rid of (unwanted elements). [OE *camb*]

combat *n* fighting; a struggle or contest: *single combat*. — *v* ***-t-*** to fight against; to oppose. [Fr]

combatant *n* & *adj* (a person) participating in a fight.

combative *adj* inclined to fight or argue.

combine *v* **1** (*tr* & *intr*; **with**) to join together; to unite. **2** (*tr*; **with**) to possess (two contrasting qualities, etc.); to manage or achieve (two different things) at the same time. — *n* **1** a group of people or businesses associated for a common purpose. **2** (*coll*) a combine harvester. — *adj* **combinatory**. [Lat *combinare*, from *com-*, with + *bini*, two each]

combination *n* **1** the process of combining or state of being combined. **2** two or more things, people, etc. combined; the resulting mixture or union. **3** a set of numbers or letters for opening a combination lock. **4** a motorcycle with sidecar. **5** (*math*) any of a number of groups into which a set can be arranged, regardless of order within the group. **6** (in *pl*) an old-fashioned one-piece undergarment combining long-sleeved vest and long underpants.

combination lock *n* a lock with a numbered dial or rotating sections, that must be turned so as to register or line up a particular combination of numbers before it will open.

combine harvester *n* an agricultural vehicle equipped both to reap and thresh a crop.

combining form *n* (*gram*) a word form that occurs in combinations or compounds, e.g. *Anglo-* as in *Anglo-American* or *-lysis* in *electrolysis*.

combinatory. See **combine**.

combo *n* ***-os*** (*coll*) a small jazz dance band. [**combination**]

combustible *adj* **1** easily catching fire; burning readily; capable of being burnt as fuel. **2** easily exploding into violent passion. — *n* a combustible material. — *n* **combustibility**. [Lat *combustibilis*]

combustion *n* **1** the process of catching fire and burning. **2** the chemical process by which heat and light are produced when oxygen combines with other substances. [Lat *combustio*]

come *v* ***came***, ***come*** **1** (*intr*) to move in the direction of speaker or hearer. **2** (*intr*) to reach a place; to arrive. **3** (*intr* with **to**) to form (an opinion, etc.). **4** (*intr*; **to, into**) to reach (a certain stage); to pass into (a certain state): *come to power*. **5** (*intr* with **to**) to meet with: *come to harm*. **6** (*intr* with **up to**) to extend to or reach (a level, standard, etc.). **7** (*intr* with **to**) to total. **8** (*tr*) to travel or traverse (a distance, etc.). **9** (*intr* with **from**) to have as a source or place of origin. **10** (*intr*) to happen: *How did he come to hurt himself?* (*coll*) *How come you didn't know?* **11** (*intr*) to enter one's consciousness or perception: *come into view*. **12** (*intr*) to occupy a specific place in order, etc.: *In 'ceiling', 'e' comes before 'i'*. **13** (*intr*) to be available; to exist or be found: *come in several sizes*. **14** (*intr*) to become: *come undone*. **15** (*intr*) to turn out; *come true*. **16** (*intr* with **to**) to be a case of: *When it comes to hard work, Jim's your man*. **17** (*intr* with **of**) to descend or result from: *come of healthy stock*; *This is what comes of being indulgent*. **18** (*tr*; **over, with**) to act like; to pretend to be: *Don't come the innocent*. **19** (*intr*; *coll*) to have a sexual orgasm. **20** (*intr*) on the arrival of (a particular point in time): *Come next Tuesday I'll be free*. — *interj* used to reassure or admonish: *Oh, come now, don't exaggerate*. — *v* **come about** (*intr*) **1** to happen. **2** (*naut*) to change direction. — *v* **come across 1** (*tr*) to discover; to encounter. **2** (*intr*) to make a certain impression: *His speech came across well*. **3** (*intr*; *slang*; **with**) to provide (the required money, etc.). — **come again?** (*coll*) could you repeat that? — *v* **come along** (*intr*) **1** to progress; to improve. **2** to arrive. **3** to hurry up. — **come and go** to reappear from time to time. — **come apart** to fall to pieces. — *v* **come at** (*tr*) **1** to attack. **2** to approach: *come at a solution*. — *v* **come away** (*intr*) to become detached. — *v* **come back** (*intr*) **1** (**to**) to be recalled to mind: *It's all coming back to me now*. **2** (**in**) to become fashionable again. **3** (**at**) to answer rudely. — *v* **come between** (*tr*) to interfere or cause trouble between. — *v* **come by** (*tr*) to get: *How did you come by that cut?* — *v* **come down** (*intr*) **1** to lose one's social position: *come down in the world* (*n* **comedown**). **2**

to be inherited. **3** (**from**) to leave university. **4** to decide. **5** (with **on**) to punish severely; to be very disapproving of: *come down heavily on bullying*. **6** (with **to**) to be, in simple terms: *It comes down to this*. **7** (with **with**) to develop (an illness). — *v* **come for** (*tr*) **1** to attack. **2** to call for: *came for our subscription*. — *v* **come forward** (*intr*) to offer oneself: *Several witnesses came forward*. — *v* **come in** (*intr*) **1** to arrive; to be received. **2** to have a particular role, function or use: *This is where you come in*; *come in useful*. **3** (of the tide) to rise. **4** to become fashionable. **5** (with **for**) to earn; to incur. — *v* **come into** (*tr*) to inherit (money, etc.). — **come into one's own** to have the opportunity to display one's talents. — **come it** (**over**, **with**; *slang*) to put on an act: *Don't come it over me*. — *v* **come off** (*intr*) **1** to become detached. **2** to succeed. **3** to take place. — **come off it!** (*coll*) stop talking nonsense! — *v* **come on** (*intr*) **1** to start. **2** to hurry up, cheer up, not talk nonsense. — **come one's way** to crop up. — *v* **come out** (*intr*) **1** (of the sun or stars) to appear. **2** to become known. **3** to fade in the wash: *The mark won't come out*. **4** to strike: *come out in sympathy*. **5** to declare one's opinion openly: *come out in favour of the plan*. **6** to work out: *can't get the sum to come out*. **7** to emerge in a certain position or state: *come out well from the affair*. **8** (of a photograph) to be developed: *come out nice and clear*. **9** (*coll*) to declare openly that one is a homosexual. **10** (*old*) (of a girl) to be launched in society. **11** (with **in**) to develop (a rash, etc.): *come out in spots*. **12** (with **with**) to make (a remark, etc.): *What will she come out with next?* — *v* **come over 1** (*intr*) to change one's opinion or side: *come over to our side*. **2** (*intr*) to make a certain impression: *comes over well on television*. **3** (*tr*) to affect: *What's come over you?* **4** (*intr*; *coll*) to feel or become: *come over a bit faint*. — *v* **come round** (*intr*) **1** to regain consciousness. **2** to regain one's temper; to calm down. **3** to change one's opinion: *came round to our opinion*. **4** to recur in order or routine. — *v* **come through** (*tr & intr*) to survive. — *v* **come to** (*intr*) to regain consciousness. — **come to nothing** to fail. — **come to oneself 1** to regain consciousness. **2** to calm down; to regain one's self-control. — *v* **come under** (*tr*) **1** to belong to (a category). **2** to be the responsibility of: *Swimming-pools come under the local authority*. — *v* **come up** (*intr*) **1** (**to**) to approach. **2** to occur; to happen: *I'll contact you if anything comes up*. **3** to be considered or discussed: *The question didn't come up*. **4** to rise socially: *come up in the world*. **5** (with **against**) to encounter: *come up against prejudice*. **6** (with **with**) to offer; to put forward: *come up with an idea*. — *v* **come upon** (*tr*) to discover. — **have it coming to one** (*coll*) to deserve whatever unpleasant fate befalls one. — **not know whether one is coming or going** to be in a dazed or bewildered state. [OE *cuman*]

comeback 1 *n* a return to former success, or to the stage, etc. after a period of retirement or obscurity: *stage a comeback*. **2** a retort. **3** an opportunity for redress or retaliation.

comedown *n* **1** a fall in status. **2** an anticlimax.

come-hither *adj* (*coll*) flirtatious: *a come-hither look*.

comer *n* (often *in cmpds*) a person who comes: *latecomers*; *a newcomer*; *challenge all comers*.

coming *n* an arrival; an approach: *await their coming*. — *adj* **1** (*coll*) looking like a winner: *the coming man*. **2** approaching: *in the coming months*. — **comings and goings** bustle; activity; movement.

come-on *n* (*coll*) sexual encouragement: *give someone the come-on*.

come-uppance *n* (*coll*) a well-deserved punishment: *get one's come-uppance*.

Comecon *abbrev* the *Co*uncil for *M*utual *Econ*omic Aid or Assistance, the economic league of the former Communist countries of eastern Europe.

comedian *n* **1** an entertainer who tells jokes, performs comic sketches, etc. **2** an actor in comedy. [**comedy**]

comedienne *n* a female comedian.

comedo *n* **-os** (*med*) a blackhead in the skin. [Lat, glutton]

comedy *n* **-ies 1** a light, amusing play or film. **2** drama of this type generally. **3** in earlier literature, a play with a fortunate outcome. **4** funny incidents or situations. [Gr *komoidia*, from *komos*, comic chorus + *aoidos*, singer]

comely *adj* **-ier**, **-iest** (usu. of women) wholesomely attractive. — *n* **comeliness**. [OE *cymlic*, beautiful]

comestible *n* (usu. in *pl*) something to eat. [Fr, from Lat *comedere*, to eat up]

comet *n* a body with a frozen nucleus and tail-like trail, travelling round the sun. [Gr *kometes*, literally 'longhaired', from *kome*, hair]

comfit *n* (*hist*) an old type of sweet, usu. a sugar-coated nut, etc. [Fr *confit*]

comfort *n* **1** a state of physical and mental contentedness or wellbeing. **2** relief from suffering, or consolation in grief. **3** a person or thing that provides such relief or consolation. **4** (usu. in *pl*) something that makes for ease and physical wellbeing. — *v* (*tr*) to relieve from suffering; to console or soothe. [Fr *conforter*]

comforter *n* **1** a person who comforts. **2** (*old*) a warm scarf. **3** (*old*) a baby's dummy. **4** (*US*) a quilt.

comfortable *adj* **1** in a state of esp. physical wellbeing; at ease. **2** providing comfort. **3** (*coll*) fairly well off financially. **4** (of a hospital patient, etc.) in a stable, more or less pain-free condition. **5** quite large: *win* *by a comfortable margin.* — *adv* **comfortably**. — **comfortably off** (*coll*) having enough money to live in comfort. [Fr *confortable*]

comfrey *n* a bristly plant of the borage family, with bell-shaped blue flowers, formerly used medicinally. [Lat *conferva*, healing water plant]

comfy *adj* **-ier**, **-iest** (*coll*) comfortable.

comic *adj* **1** relating to comedy; intended to amuse. **2** funny. — *n* **1** a comedian. **2** a periodical containing stories told through a series of pictures. [Gr *komikos*, from *komos*, comic chorus]

comical *adj* funny; amusing; humorous; ludicrous. — *n* **comicality**. — *adv* **comically**.

comic opera *n* a lighthearted opera with spoken dialogue as well as singing.

comic strip *n* a brief story or episode told through a short series of pictures, in a newspaper, etc.

comity *n* civility; politeness; courtesy. [Lat *comitas*, from *comis*, friendly]

comity of nations *n* mutual respect between nations for one another's laws and customs.

comma *n* a punctuation mark (,) indicating a slight pause or break made for clarity's sake, etc. [Gr, clause]

command *v* (*tr*) **1** to order formally. **2** to have authority over or be in control of. **3** to have at one's disposal. **4** to deserve or be entitled to. **5** to look down over: *The window commands a view of the bay.* — *n* **1** an order. **2** control; charge; *second in command.* **3** knowledge of and ability to use. **4** a military unit, or a district, under one's command. **5** a specialised section of an army, air force, etc.: *Bomber Command.* **6** a group of high-ranking army officers, etc.: *the British High Command.* **7** an instruction to a computer to carry out some operation. [Fr *commander*]

commanding *adj* **1** powerful; leading; controlling. **2** in charge. **3** inspiring respect or awe. **4** giving good views all round: *a house with a commanding position.*

commandment *n* a divine command, esp. (with *cap*) one of ten given to Moses, listed in the Bible in Exodus, chapter 20.

command module *n* the section of a spacecraft from which operations are directed, serving also as living quarters.

command paper *n* a government document presenting a report on some matter or outlining government policy. ◇ See also **Green Paper**, **White Paper**.

command performance *n* a special performance of a play, etc. given at the request, and in the presence, of the head of state.

command post *n* a temporary military headquarters.

commandant *n* a commanding officer, esp. of a prisoner-of-war camp or a military training establishment. [Fr, present participle of *commander*, to command]

commandeer *v* (*tr*) **1** to seize (e.g. property) for military use in wartime, official use in an emergency, etc. **2** to seize without justification. [Afrikaans, from Fr *commander*, to command]

commander *n* **1** a person who commands. **2** in the British navy, an officer just below captain in rank. **3** a high-ranking police officer. **4** (also **knight commander**) a senior member in some orders of knighthood. **[command]**

commander-in-chief *n* **-ders-in-chief** the officer in supreme command of a nation's forces.

commandment. See **command**.

commando *n* **-os** (a member of) a unit of soldiers specially trained to carry out dangerous and difficult attacks or raids. [Afrikaans, orig. Port, from *commandar*, to command]

commedia dell'arte *n* an Italian 16th-century form of comedy with certain stock characters and plots full of intrigue. [Ital, comedy of the arts]

commemorate *v* (*tr*) **1** to honour the memory of (a person or event) with a ceremony, etc. **2** to be a memorial to. — *n* **commemoration**. — *adj* **commemorative**. [Lat *commemorare*, to keep in mind]

commence *v* (*tr* & *intr*) to begin. [OFr *commencier*, from Lat *initiare*, to begin]

commencement *n* **1** a beginning. **2** (*NAm*) a graduation ceremony.

commend *v* (*tr*) **1** to praise. **2** **(to)** to entrust (someone or something) to someone. **3** **(to)** to recommend: *if the idea commends itself to you* (i.e. is acceptable). — *adj* **commendatory**. [Lat *commendare*]

commendable *adj* praiseworthy; creditable. — *adv* **commendably**.

commendation *n* **1** praise; approval. **2** an award or honour.

commensurable *adj* **(with, to)** **1** (*math*) having a common factor; divisible by a common unit with an integer or whole number as a result. **2** measurable by a common standard. [Lat *com-*, with + *mensurare*, to measure]

commensurate *adj* **(with)** **1** in proportion to; appropriate to. **2** equal to in extent, quantity, etc. — *adv* **commensurately**. [Lat *com-*, with + *mensurare*, to measure]

comment *n* **1** a remark or observation, esp. a critical one. **2** talk, discussion or gossip. **3** an explanatory or analytical note on a passage of text. — *v* (*tr* & *intr*; **on**) to make observations. — **no comment** I decline to comment. [Lat *commentum*, commentary]

commentary *n* **-ies** **1** a continuous, esp. broadcast, report on an event, match, etc. as it actually takes place. **2** an explanation accompanying a film, etc. **3** a set of notes explaining or interpreting points in a text, etc. [Lat *commentarium*, notebook]

commentator *n* **1** a broadcaster giving a commentary on a match, event, etc. **2** the writer of a textual commentary. — *v* **commentate** (*intr*; **on**). [Lat, interpreter]

commerce *n* **1** the buying and selling of commodities and services; trade, including banking, insurance, etc. **2** (*old*) social dealings or communication. [Fr, from Lat *commercium*, trade]

commercial *adj* **1** relating to, engaged in or used for commerce. **2** profitable; having profit as chief aim; exploited or exploitable for profit. **3** paid for by advertising.— *n* a radio or television advertisement. — *n* **commerciality**. — *adv* **commercially**. [Lat *commercium*, trade]

commercialise or **-ize** *v* (*tr*) **1** to exploit for profit, esp. by sacrificing quality. **2** to make commercial. — *n* **commercialisation** or **-z-**.

commercialism *n* **1** commercial attitudes and aims. **2** undue emphasis on profit-making.

commercial traveller *n* a person who travels around the country representing a business firm and selling their goods.

commie *n* & *adj* (*coll derog*) (a person who is a) communist.

comminute *v* (*tr*; *tech*) **1** to crush (e.g. minerals) into tiny pieces. **2** to reduce to small portions. — *n* **comminution**. [Lat *comminuere*]

commis or **commis chef** *n* ***commis*** or ***commis chefs*** an assistant or trainee waiter or chef. [Fr]

commiserate *v* (*intr*; **with**) to express sympathy. — *n* **commiseration**. [Lat *com-*, with + *miserari*, to lament]

commissar *n* **1** (*formerly*) the head of a government department in the Soviet Union. **2** (*formerly*) in the Soviet Union, a Communist Party official responsible for the political education of military units. [Russ *komisar*, from Lat *commissarius*, officer in charge]

commissariat *n* **1** a department in the army responsible for food supplies. **2** (*formerly*) a government department in the Soviet Union. [Fr & Russ, from Lat *commissarius*, officer in charge]

commissary *n* ***-ies*** **1** an officer responsible for supplies and provisions in the army. **2** (*NAm*) a store supplying provisions and equipment to a military force. **3** (orig. *US*) a canteen serving a film studio, etc. — *adj* **commissarial**. [Lat *commissarius*, officer in charge]

commission *n* **1** a formal or official request to someone to perform a task or duty; the authority to perform it; the task or duty. **2** (a document conferring) military rank above a certain level. **3** an order for a piece of work, esp. a work of art. **4** a board or committee entrusted with a particular task. **5** a fee or percentage given to the agent arranging a sale. **6** the act of committing, e.g. a crime. — *v* (*tr*) **1** to give a commission or authority to. **2** to grant military rank above a certain level to. **3** to request (someone to do something). **4** to place an order for (a work of art, etc.). **5** to prepare (a ship) for active service. — **in**, or **out of**, **commission** in, or not in, use or working condition. [Lat *commissio*, entrusting]

commissioned officer *n* a military officer holding a commission. ◇ See also **non-commissioned officer**.

commissionaire *n* a uniformed attendant at the door of a cinema, theatre, office or hotel. [Fr]

commissioner *n* **1** a representative of the government in a district, department, etc. **2** a member of a commission. — *n* **commissionership**. **[commission]**

commit *v* ***-tt-*** (*tr*) **1** to carry out or perpetrate (a crime, offence, error, etc.). **2** to have (someone) put in prison or a mental institution. **3** to promise or engage (esp. oneself) for some undertaking, etc. **4** to dedicate (oneself) to a cause, etc. from a sense of conviction: *a committed Christian*. **5** (**to**) to entrust or give; *commit facts to memory* (i.e. memorise them); *commit thoughts to paper* (i.e. write them down). **6** to send (a person) for trial in a higher court. — **commit oneself** to make a definite decision. [Lat *committere*, to give, entrust or perpetrate]

commitment *n* **1** the act of committing (e.g. oneself); the state of being committed. **2** dedication or devotion; strong conviction. **3** an undertaking or responsibility: *taking on too many commitments*.

committal *n* the action of committing (esp. someone to prison).

committee *n* (*sing* or *pl*) **1** a group of people selected by, and from, a larger body, e.g. a club, to undertake esp. administrative work on its behalf. **2** a body specially appointed to undertake an investigation, enquiry, etc. [Earlier *committen*, to entrust + **-ee**]

committee stage *n* the stage between the second and third readings of a parliamentary bill, when it is examined in detail by members sitting in committee.

commode *n* **1** a chair with a hinged seat covering a chamber pot. **2** a chest of drawers. [Fr, from Lat *commodus*, convenient]

commodious *adj* comfortably spacious. — *adv* **commodiously**. — *n* **commodiousness**. [Lat *commodus*, convenient]

commodity *n* ***-ies*** **1** something that is bought and sold, esp. a manufactured product or raw material. **2** something, e.g. a quality, from the point of view of its value in society: *Courtesy is a scarce commodity*. [Lat *commoditas*, benefit]

commodore *n* **1** in the British navy, an officer just below a rear admiral in rank. **2** the president of a yacht club. **3** the senior captain in charge of a fleet of merchant ships. [Perhaps through Dut from Fr *commandeur*, commander]

common *adj* **1** often met with; frequent; familiar. **2** (**to**) shared by two or more people, things, etc.: *characteristics common to both animals*. **3** publicly owned. **4** of a standard one has a right to expect: *common decency*. **5** widespread: *common knowledge*. **6** (*derog*) lacking taste or refinement; vulgar. **7** of the ordinary type: *the common cold*. **8** not of high rank or class: *the common people*. **9** (*math*) shared by two or more numbers: *highest common factor*. — *n* **1** a piece of land that is publicly owned or available for public use. **2** (*legal*) a right to something, or to do something, on someone else's land. **3** (*slang*) common sense. ◇ See also **commons** below. — *adv* **commonly**. — *n* **commonness**. — **the common touch** an ability, in someone distinguished by accomplishment or rank, to relate sociably to ordinary people. — **in common 1** (of interests, etc.) shared: *have nothing in common with someone*. **2** in joint use or ownership: *a garden owned in common by the residents*. — **make common cause** to co-operate to achieve a common aim. [Lat *communis*]

commoner *n* a person who is not a member of the nobility.

common gender *n* (*gram*) the gender of such nouns as *doctor*, *scientist* or *baby*, that can refer to either sex.

common ground *n* an area of agreement between people, as a starting-point for discussion.

common law *n* in England, law based on custom and decisions by judges, as distinct from written law. — *adj* (**common-law**) so called because of long cohabitation: *common-law wife, marriage*.

Common Market *n* the European Community.

common noun *n* (*gram*) a noun that is not a proper name and which can refer to any member of a class of things, e.g. *car*, *table*, *girl* as opposed to *Paris* or *John*. ◇ See also **proper noun**.

common-or-garden *adj* of the ordinary, everyday kind.

common room *n* in a college, school, etc. a sitting-room for general use by students or staff.

commons *n* **1** (*pl*; *hist*; with **the**) the ordinary people. **2** (*cap*; *pl* or *sing*; with **the**) the House of Commons. **3** (*old* or *facet*) shared food rations. — **on short commons** having reduced rations.

common sense *n* practical good sense. — *adj* **common-sense** or **common-sensical**.

common time *n* (*mus*) a rhythm with two or four beats to the bar.

commonplace *adj* **1** ordinary; everyday. **2** (*derog*) unoriginal; lacking individuality; trite. — *n* **1** (*derog*) a trite comment; a cliché. **2** an everyday occurrence. [Translation of Lat *locus communis*, an argument widely used]

commonwealth *n* **1** a country or state. **2** an association of states that have joined together for their common good. **3** (*cap*; with **the**) (also **Commonwealth of Nations** or **British Commonwealth**) an association consisting of Great Britain and a number of independent states that were formerly its colonies and dominions. **4** a title used by certain U.S. states. **5** (*cap*) the republican form of government in Britain from 1649 to 1660. [**common** + **wealth**]

commotion *n* **1** a disturbance; an upheaval; tumult. **2** noisy confusion; uproar; din. [Lat *commotio*, from *movere*, to move]

communal *adj* **1** relating to, or belonging to, a community. **2** shared; owned in common. **3** relating to a commune or communes. — *adv* **communally**. [Lat *communalis*, from *communis*, common]

commune[1] *n* **1** a number of unrelated families and individuals living as a mutually supportive community, with shared accommodation, supplies, responsibilities, etc. **2** in some European countries, the smallest local administrative unit. [Lat *communa*, from *communis*, common]

commune[2] *v* (*intr*; **with**) **1** to communicate intimately or confidentially with. **2** to get close to or relate spiritually to (e.g. nature). [Fr *communer*, to share]

communicable *adj* **1** capable of being communicated. **2** (of a disease) passed on easily. [Lat *communicabilis*, from *communicare*, to share or impart]

communicant *n* **1** a person who receives Communion. **2** an informant. [Lat *communicare*, to partake, impart]

communicate *v* **1** (*tr* & *intr*) to impart (information, ideas, etc.); to make (something) known or understood; to get in touch. **2** (*tr*) to pass on or transmit (a disease, feeling, etc.) to. **3** (*intr*; **with**) to understand one another; to relate in an easy, natural way. **4** (*intr*; **with**) (of rooms, etc.) to be connected: *a communicating door*. **5** (*intr*) in the Christian church, to receive Communion. [Lat *communicare*, to share]

communication *n* **1** the process or act of communicating; the exchanging or imparting of ideas and information, etc. **2** a piece of information, a letter or a message. **3** social contact. **4** (in *pl*) the systems involved in transmission of information, etc. esp. by electronic means or radio waves. **5** (in *pl*) means or routes used for moving troops or supplies. **6** (in *pl*) the science and activity of transmitting information, etc.

communication cord *n* (*Br*) a chain or cord fitted in a railway carriage, to be pulled in an emergency to stop the train.

communicative *adj* **1** sociable; talkative. **2** relating to communication: *communicative skills.* — *adv* **communicatively**.

communion *n* **1** the sharing of thoughts, beliefs and feelings. **2** a group of people sharing the same religious beliefs. **3** (*cap*; also **Holy Communion**) in the Christian Church, (participation in) the service at which bread and wine are taken as symbols of Christ's body and blood; the consecrated bread and wine. [Lat *communio*, mutual participation]

communiqué *n* an official bulletin, communication or announcement. [Fr, something communicated]

communism *n* **1** a political theory whereby society should be classless, private property abolished, and land, factories, etc. collectively owned and controlled by the people. **2** (*cap*) a political movement founded on the principles of communism set out by Karl Marx. **3** the political and social system established on these principles in e.g. the former Soviet Union. — *n & adj* **communist**. — *adj* **communistic**. [Fr *communisme*, from *commun*, common]

community *n* **-ies 1** the group of people living in a particular locality. **2** a group of people bonded together by a common religion, nationality or occupation. **3** a religious or spiritual fellowship of people living together. **4** the quality or fact of being shared or common: *community of interests*. **5** a group of states with common interests. **6** the public; society in general. **7** the mutually dependent plants and animals of an area. [Lat *communitas*, fellowship]

community centre *n* a place where members of a community may meet for social, sporting or educational activities.

community charge *n* a tax levied on individuals to pay for local services; the poll tax. ◇ See also **rate**[1] (sense **6**), **council tax**.

community home *n* an institution in which young offenders are accommodated.

community service *n* work of benefit to the local community, sometimes prescribed for offenders in place of a prison sentence.

community singing *n* organised singing at a large gathering, with everyone taking part.

community work *n* work that serves the social and economic needs of members of a community. — *n* **community worker**.

commute *v* **1** (*intr*) to travel regularly between two places, esp. between home and work in a city, etc. **2** (*tr*) to alter (a criminal sentence) to one less severe. **3** (*tr*; **for**, **into**) to substitute; to convert. **4** (*tr*) to exchange (a pension, etc.) for another form of payment, esp. a lump sum. — *adj* **commutable**. — *n* **commutation**. — *n* **commuter**. [Lat *commutare*, to alter or exchange]

commutative *adj* (*math*) (of e.g. addition) coming to the same result whatever the order of the numbers, etc. operated on.

commutator *n* an apparatus for reversing an electric current.

compact[1] *adj* **1** firm and dense in form or texture. **2** small, but with all essentials neatly contained. **3** neatly concise. — *v* (*tr*) to compress. — *n* **1** a small case for women's face powder, usu. including a mirror. — *n* **compaction**. — *adv* **compactly**. — *n* **compactness**. [Lat *compactus*, put together]

compact disc *n* an aluminium-coated plastic disc containing digitally stored information, readable by laser beam, esp. one for recording sound, played on a machine (**compact-disc player**) equipped with a laser beam.

compact[2] *n* a contract or agreement. [Lat *com-*, with + *pacisci*, to, agree]

companion[1] *n* **1** a friend, comrade or frequent associate. **2** someone who accompanies one on a journey. **3** (esp. *hist*) a woman paid to live or travel with, and be company for, another. **4** (esp. as a title) a book of advice; a handbook or guide. **5** one of a pair of matching objects. **6** (*cap*) an honourable title denoting a low-ranking member of any of various orders of knighthood. — *n* **companionship**. [Fr *compagnon*, from Lat *companio*, lit. food-sharer, from *panis*, bread]

companionable *adj* friendly; sociable; comfortable as a companion. — *adv* **companionably**.

companion[2] *n* (*naut*) a hatch admitting light to a cabin or lower deck. [Dut *kompanje*, quarterdeck]

companionway *n* a staircase between decks.

company *n* **-ies 1** the presence of another person or other people; companionship. **2** (the presence of) guests or visitors. **3** one's friends, companions or associates: *get into bad company*. **4** a business organisation. **5** a troop of actors or entertainers. **6** a military unit of about 120 men. **7** a ship's crew. **8** a gathering of people, at a social function, etc. — **be good**, or **bad**, **company** to be an entertaining, or dreary, companion. — **be in good company** to be not the only one in a situation. — **in company with** together with; along with: *in company with other reasons.* — **keep someone company** to act as companion to someone. — **part company (with) 1** to separate. **2** to disagree. [OFr *compaignie*, from the same root as **companion**]

company secretary *n* a senior member of a business organisation, in charge of financial and legal matters.

comparable *adj* **1** of the same or equivalent kind. **2** able to be compared; similar enough to allow comparison. — *n* **comparability**. — *adv* **comparably**. [Lat *comparabilis*]

comparative *adj* **1** judged by comparison; as compared with others. **2** relating to, or using the method of, comparison. **3** as observed by comparing one another: *their comparative strengths*. **4** (*gram*) (of adjectives and adverbs) in the form (using the suffix *-er* or the word *more*) denoting a greater degree of the quality in question. — *n* (*gram*) **1** a comparative adjective or adverb. **2** the comparative form of a word. — *adv* **comparatively**. [Lat *comparare*, to match]

compare *v* **1** (*tr*; **with**) to examine (things of the same kind) to see what differences there are between them. **2** (*tr*; **to**) to liken: *compare her to a summer's day*. **3** (*intr*; **with**) to stand comparison with; to be comparable with: *He can't compare with his predecessor in ability*. — **beyond** or **without compare** (*formal*) without equal; incomparable. — **compare notes** to exchange ideas and opinions. [Lat *comparare*, to match]

comparison *n* **1** (**between**, **with**, **to**) the process of, an act of, or a reasonable basis for, comparing: *doesn't bear* or *stand comparison with her*; *can be no comparison between them* (i.e. one is far better than the other); *I was lucky by comparison* (i.e. with the unlucky person in question). **2** (*gram*) the positive, comparative and superlative forms of adjective and adverbs: *the degrees of comparison*. [Fr *comparaison*]

compartment *n* **1** a separated-off or enclosed section. **2** any of several enclosed sections into which a railway carriage is divided. — *adj* **compartmental**. [Fr *compartiment*]

compartmentalise or **-ize** *v* (*tr*) to divide, distribute or force into categories. — *n* **compartmentalisation** or **-z-**.

compass *n* **1** a direction-finding instrument containing a dial (**compass card**) marked with 32 points, with a magnetised needle that always points to magnetic north. **2** (often in *pl*; also **pair of compasses**) an instrument consisting of two hinged legs, for drawing circles, measuring distances on maps, etc. **3** range or scope. **4** (*mus*) the range, from highest to lowest possible note, of a voice or instrument. [Fr *compas*, from *compasser*, to measure]

compassion *n* a feeling of sorrow and pity for someone in trouble, usu. inclining one to help, show mercy, etc. — *adj* **compassionate**. — *adv* **compassionately**. [Lat *compassio*]

compassionate leave *n* special leave granted in cases of bereavement.

compatible *adj* (**with**) **1** able to associate or coexist agreeably. **2** (of two pieces of e.g. electronic machinery) able to be used in conjunction. — *n* **compatibility**. — *adv* **compatibly**. [Lat *compatibilis*]

compatriot *n* someone from one's own country; a fellow-citizen. [Lat *compatriota*, from *com-* with + *patria*, one's country]

compeer *n* an equal; a companion or comrade. [Fr *comper*, from Lat *com-* with + *par*, equal]

compel *v* **-ll-** (*tr*) **1** to force; to drive. **2** to arouse; to draw forth: *Their plight compels sympathy*. [Lat *compellere*, to force]

compelling *adj* **1** powerful; forcing one to agree, etc. **2** irresistibly fascinating. — *adv* **compellingly**.

compendium *n* **-diums** or **-dia** **1** a concise summary; an abridgement. **2** a collection of boardgames, puzzles, etc. in a single container. [Lat, from *com-*, together + *pendere*, to weigh]

compendious *adj* concise but comprehensive. — *adv* **compendiously**. [Lat *compendiosus*, from *compendium*, summary]

compensate *v* **1** (*tr*; **for**) to make amends to (someone) for loss, injury or wrong, esp. by a suitable payment. **2** (*intr*; **for**) to make up for (a disadvantage, loss, etc.). — *adj* **compensatory**. [Lat *compensare*]

compensation *n* **1** the process of compensating. **2** something that compensates. **3** a sum of money given to make up for loss, injury, etc.

compère *n* a person who presents a radio or television show, introduces performers, etc. — *v* (*tr*) to act as compère for (a show). [Fr, godfather]

compete *v* (*intr*; **with**, **against**, **for**) **1** to take part in a contest **2** to strive or struggle: *compete with other firms*. **3** (of a product, firm, etc.) to give good value, be reasonably cheap, etc. when compared to market rivals. [Lat *competere*, to coincide, ask for, seek]

competent *adj* **1** efficient. **2** having sufficient skill or training (to do something). **3** legally capable. — *adv* **competently**. [Lat *competere*, to meet, be sufficient]

competence *n* (also **competency**) **1** capability; efficiency. **2** legal authority or capability. **3** (*old*) sufficient income to live comfortably.

competition *n* **1** an event in which people compete. **2** the process or fact of competing. **3** one's rivals, e.g. in business, or their products. [Lat *competitio*, meeting together]

competitive *adj* **1** involving rivalry. **2** enjoying rivalry; aggressive; ambitious. **3** (of a price or product) reasonably cheap; comparing well with those of market rivals. — *adv* **competitively**. — *n* **competitiveness**. [Lat *competere*, to meet together]

competitor *n* a person, team, firm or product that competes; a rival. [Lat, from *competere*, to meet]

compile *v* (*tr*) **1** to collect and organise (information, etc.); to produce (a list, reference book, etc.) from information collected. **2** (*comput*) to devise (a set of instructions) from a programming

language by means of a compiler. [Lat *compilare*, to plunder]
compilation *n* **1** the process of compiling. **2** the book, etc. compiled.
compiler *n* **1** a person who compiles information, etc. **2** (*comput*) a program for converting a programming language into a language usable with a particular computer.
complacent *adj* **1** self-satisfied; smug. **2** too easily satisfied; disinclined to worry. — *n* **complacence** or **complacency**. — *adv* **complacently**. [Lat *complacere*, to be pleasing]
complain *v* (*intr*; **about, at**) **1** to express one's dissatisfaction or displeasure. **2** (with **of**) to say that one is suffering from. — *n* **complainer**. [OFr *complaindre*, to pity]
complainant *n* (*legal*) a plaintiff.
complaint *n* **1** the act of complaining. **2** an expression of dissatisfaction; a cause for this. **3** a disorder, illness, etc.
complaisant *adj* wanting to please; obliging; amenable. — *n* **complaisance**. — *adv* **complaisantly**. [Fr, from *complaire*, to please]
complement *n* **1** (**to**) something that completes or perfects; something that provides a needed balance or contrast: *Use as a complement to spicy dishes*. **2** the number or quantity required to fill something: *a ship with a full complement of men*. **3** (*gram*) a word or phrase added to a verb to complete the predicate of a sentence, e.g. *dark* in *It grew dark*. **4** (*math*) the angle that must be added to a given angle to make 90°. — *v* (*tr*) to be a complement to. [Lat *complementum*, from *complere*, to fill]
complementary *adj* **1** serving as a complement to something. **2** complementing each other. **3** (*physics*) (of two colours) producing white when combined. — *adv* **complementarily**.
complete *adj* **1** whole; finished; with nothing missing. **2** thorough; utter; absolute; total. — *v* (*tr*) **1** to finish; to make complete or perfect. **2** to fill in (a form). — *adv* **completely**. — *n* **completeness**. — *n* **completion**. — **complete with** having the additional feature of. [Lat *complere*, to fill up]
complex *adj* **1** composed of many interrelated parts. **2** complicated; involved; tangled. **3** (*math*) (of a number) being the sum of a real and an imaginary number; (of a fraction) with either the numerator or denominator, or both, containing a fraction. — *n* **1** something made of interrelating parts, e.g. a multi-purpose building: *a leisure complex*. **2** a set of repressed ideas, emotions, etc. that have a distorting affect on one's personality and behaviour; (*coll*) an obsession or phobia. [Lat, closely connected]
complexity *n* **-ies 1** the quality of being complex. **2** a complication; an intricacy.
complex sentence *n* a sentence comprising a main clause and one or more subordinate clauses. ◇ See also **compound sentence, simple sentence**.
complexion *n* **1** the colour or appearance of the skin, esp. of the face. **2** character or appearance: *That puts a different complexion on the whole thing*. [Lat *complexio*, combination]
compliant *adj* (too) inclined to give in to the wishes of others; obedient; submissive. — *n* **compliance**. — *adv* **compliantly**. **[comply]**
complicate *v* (*tr*) to add difficulties or intricacies to; to make complex or involved. [Lat *com-*, + *plicare*, to fold]
complicated *adj* **1** difficult to understand or deal with. **2** intricate; complex. **3** (of a fracture in a bone) accompanied by damage to blood vessels, nerves or organs.
complication *n* **1** the process of becoming complicated. **2** a circumstance that causes difficulties. **2** a development in an illness, etc. that causes the patient's condition to worsen.
complicity *n* participation in a crime or wrongdoing. [Lat *complex*, closely connected]
compliment *n* **1** an expression of praise, admiration or approval. **2** a gesture implying approval: *paid her the compliment of dancing with her*. **3** (in *pl*) formal regards accompanying a gift, etc. — *v* (*tr*; **on**) to congratulate; to pay a compliment to. [Fr, from Ital *complimento*]
complimentary *adj* **1** paying a compliment; admiring or approving. **2** given free.
compline *n* in Roman Catholic liturgy, the seventh and last service of the day, at 9 pm, completing the set hours for prayer. ◇ See also **lauds, matins, none**[2], **sext, terce, vespers**. [Fr *complie*, from Lat *completa* (*hora*), complete hour]
comply *v* **-ies, -ied** (*intr*; **with**) to act in obedience to an order, command, request, etc.: *comply with his wishes*. [Ital *complire*, to fulfil]
component *n* any of the parts that make up a machine, engine, instrument, etc. — *adj* being one of the parts of something. [Lat *componere*, to assemble into a whole]
comport *v* **1** (*tr*) to behave (oneself) in some way. **2** (*intr* with **with**) to suit or be appropriate to. — *n* **comportment**. [Lat *com-*, together + *portare*, to carry]
compose *v* **1** (*tr & intr*) to create (music). **2** (*tr*) to write (a poem, letter, article, etc.). **3** (*tr*) to make up or constitute. **4** (*tr*) to arrange as a balanced, artistic whole: *compose a painting*. **5** (*tr*) to calm (oneself); to get (one's thoughts, etc.) under control. **6** (*tr*) to settle (differences between people in dispute). **7** (*tr*; *printing*) to arrange (type) or set (a page, etc.) in type ready for printing. [Fr *composer*, from Lat *pausare*, to rest; confused with words from *ponere*, to put]
composed *adj* (of people) calm; controlled. — *adv* **composedly**.

composer *n* someone who composes, esp. music.

composite *adj* **1** made up of different parts, materials or styles. **2** (*bot*) (of a plant) of the same family as the daisy, with flower heads composed of many small flowers. — *n* a composite thing or plant. [Lat *com-*, together + *ponere*, to put]

composition *n* **1** something composed, esp. a musical or literary work. **2** the process of composing. **3** (*art*, etc.) arrangement, esp. with regard to balance and visual effect: *photographic composition*. **4** (*old*) a school essay. **5** what something consists of. **6** a synthetic material of any of various kinds. **7** (*printing*) the arrangement of pages of type ready for printing. [Lat *com-*, together + *ponere*, to put]

compositor *n* (*printing*) a person who sets or arranges pages of type ready for printing. [Lat *com-*, together + *ponere*, to put]

compos mentis *adj* (*legal* or *facet*) being of sound mind; perfectly rational. [Lat, in control of one's mind]

compost *n* rotting vegetable matter, etc. kept for mixing into soil to enrich it and to nourish plants. [Lat *com-* , together + *ponere*, to put]

composure *n* mental and emotional calmness; self-control. [**compose**]

compound[1] *n* **1** (*chem*) a substance composed of the atoms of two or more elements, bound together in fixed proportions. **2** something composed of two or more ingredients or parts. **3** a word made up of two or more words, e.g. *tablecloth*. ◇ See also **derivative**. — *adj* composed of a number of parts or ingredients. — *v* **1** (*tr*) to make (esp. something bad) a lot worse; to complicate or add to (a difficulty, error, etc.). **2** (*tr*) to mix or combine (ingredients); to make up (a mixture, etc.) by doing this. **3** (*tr*; *legal*) to agree to overlook (an offence, etc.) in return for payment. **4** (*intr* with **with**) to come to an esp. financial agreement with. [Fr *compoundre*, from Lat *componere*, to put together]

compound fracture *n* a break in a bone accompanied by an open wound.

compound interest *n* interest on the original sum and on any interest already accumulated. ◇ See also **simple interest**.

compound sentence *n* a sentence comprising more than one main clause. ◇ See also **complex sentence**, **simple sentence**.

compound time *n* (*mus*) with three, or a multiple of three, beats to a bar.

compound[2] *n* **1** in China, India, etc., an area enclosed by a wall or fence and containing a house or factory. **2** (in a prison) an enclosed area used for a particular purpose. **3** in S Africa, an enclosure in which labourers are housed. [Malay *kampong*]

comprehend *v* (*tr*) **1** to understand; to envisage. **2** to include. [Lat *comprehendere*, to seize, understand]

comprehensible *adj* capable of being understood. — *n* **comprehensibility**. — *adv* **comprehensibly**. [Lat *comprehensibilis*]

comprehension *n* **1** the process or power of understanding; the scope or range of one's knowledge or understanding. **2** a school exercise for testing students' understanding of a passage of text, [Lat *comprehensio*]

comprehensive *adj* **1** covering or including everything or a great deal. **2** (of a school or education) providing teaching for children of all abilities between the ages of 11 and 18. — *n* a comprehensive school. — adv **comprehensively**. — *n* **comprehensiveness**. [Lat *comprehendere*, to comprise, include]

compress *v* (*tr*) **1** to press together, squeeze or squash. **2** to reduce in bulk; to condense. — *n* a pad pressed against a part of the body to reduce swelling, stop bleeding, etc. — *n* **compressibility**. — *adj* **compressible**. [Lat *compressare*, to squeeze together]

compression *n* **1** the process of compressing or state of being compressed. **2** reduction in volume of, and increase in the pressure on, the fuel mixture in internal combustion engines before ignition.

compressor *n* something that compresses, esp. a device in an engine for compressing gases.

comprise *v* (*tr*) **1** to contain, include or consist of. **2** to go together to make up. [Fr *compris*, included]

compromise *n* something agreed on after concessions have been made on each side. — *v* **1** (*intr*) to make concessions; to reach a compromise. **2** (*tr*) to endanger, or expose to scandal, by acting indiscreetly. **3** (*tr*) to settle (a dispute) by making concessions; to relax (one's principles, etc.). [Lat *compromittere*, to promise reciprocally]

compulsion *n* **1** the act of compelling or condition of being compelled. **2** a strong or irresistible urge to do something, esp. absurd or irrational. [Lat *compulsio*]

compulsive *adj* **1** (of an action) resulting from a compulsion; (of a person) acting on compulsion. **2** (of a book, film, etc.) holding one's attention. — *adv* **compulsively**. [Lat *compulsivus*]

compulsory *adj* required by the rules, law, etc.; obligatory. — *adv* **compulsorily**. [Lat *compulsorius*]

compulsory purchase *n* the purchase, against the will of the owner, of property or land needed for some public project, etc. by a local authority.

compunction *n* a feeling of guilt, remorse or regret; scruples or misgivings. [Lat *compungere*, to puncture]

compute *v* (*tr* & *intr*) to calculate, estimate or reckon, with or without the help of a computer. — *adj* **computable**. [Lat *computare*, to reckon]

computation *n* the process or art, or a system, of calculating or computing; a result calculated or computed. — *adj* **computational**.

computer *n* an electronic machine that processes, stores, analyses and retrieves data, or is programmed to control some mechanical operation. [**compute**]

computerise or **-ize** *v* (*tr*) to transfer (a procedure, operation, system, etc.) to control by computer; to organise (information) by computer; to equip with computers. — *n* **computerisation** or **-z-**.

computer science *n* the study of the use and application of computers. — *n* **computer scientist**.

comrade *n* **1** a friend or companion; an associate, fellow worker, etc. **2** a fellow communist or socialist. — *adj* **comradely**. — *n* **comradeship**. [Span *camarada*, the soldiers sharing a billet, a room-mate, from Lat *camera*, room]

comrade-in-arms *n* a fellow soldier or campaigner.

comsat *abbrev* communications satellite.

con[1] (*coll*) *n* a confidence trick; a deception, trick or bluff. — *v* **-nn-** (*tr*) to swindle or trick (someone), esp. after winning his or her trust. [**confidence trick**]

con man *n* (*coll*) a swindler using confidence tricks.

con trick *n* (*coll*) a confidence trick.

con[2] *v* **-nn-** (*tr* & *intr*; *old*) to read over and learn by heart. [**can**[1]]

con[3] *v* **-nn-** (*tr*; *naut*) to direct the steering of (a ship). [Earlier *cond*, from Fr *conduire*, to conduct]

con- or (before a vowel) **co-**, (before *l*) **col-**, (before *b*, *m* or *p*) **com-**, (before *r*) **cor-** *pfx* (found usu. in words derived from Latin) with or together; sometimes used with emphatic or intensifying effect. [Lat *com-*, form of *cum*, with]

conc. *abbrev* concentrated.

concatenate *v* (*tr*) to link up into a connected series. [Lat *con-*, with + *catena*, chain]

concatenation *n* a series of things, e.g. events, each linked to the one before in chain-like fashion.

concave *adj* (of a surface or shape) inward-curving, like the inside of a bowl. — *n* **concavity, -ies**. ◇ See also **convex**. [Lat *concavus*, vaulted, from *cavus*, hollow]

conceal *v* (*tr*) **1** to hide; to place out of sight. **2** to keep secret. — *n* **concealment**. [Lat *concelare*]

concede *v* (*tr*) **1** to admit to be true or correct. **2** to give or grant. **3** to yield or give up. **4** to admit defeat in (a contest) before, or without continuing to, the end. — **concede defeat** to admit that one is beaten. [Lat *concedere*, from, to yield]

conceit *n* **1** too good an opinion of oneself; vanity. **2** (*old*) a witty, fanciful or (over-) ingenious thought or idea. [**conceive**]

conceited *adj* having too good an opinion of oneself. — *adv* **conceitedly**.

conceive *v* **1** (*tr* or *intr*) to become pregnant; to begin to form (a baby). **2** (*tr*) to form (an idea, etc.). **3** (*tr* & *intr*; **of**) to think of or imagine. [Fr *concever*, from Lat *concipere*, to conceive or perceive]

conceivable *adj* imaginable; possible: *try every conceivable method*. — *n* **conceivability**.

conceivably *adv* possibly; perhaps.

concentrate *v* **1** (*intr*; **on**) to give all one's attention and energy to something. **2** (*tr*) to focus: *concentrate our efforts*. **3** (*tr* or *intr*) to bring or come together in one place. **4** (*tr*) to make (a liquid) stronger by removing water or other diluting substance from it. — *n* a concentrated liquid. — *adj* **concentrated**. [Lat *con-*, together + *centrum*, centre]

concentration *n* **1** intensive mental effort. **2** the act of concentration, or state of being concentrated. **3** the proportion in which a substance is present in a solution, etc. **4** a concentrate.

concentration camp *n* a prison camp for civilians who are not tolerated by the authorities.

concentric *adj* (of circles) having a common centre. — *adv* **concentrically**. — *n* **concentricity**. [Lat *con-*, same + *centrum*, centre]

concept *n* a notion; an abstract or general idea. [Lat *conceptum*]

conception *n* **1** an idea; a notion. **2** origin; start: *the whole project, from conception to completion*. **3** the fertilisation in the womb of a female egg by the male sperm. [Lat *concipere*, to conceive]

conceptual *adj* relating to concepts or conceptions. — *adv* **conceptually**. [**concept**]

conceptualise or **-ize** *v* (*tr*) to form a concept of. — *n* **conceptualisation** or **-z-**.

concern *v* (*tr*) **1** to have to do with; to be about: *It concerns your son*. **2** (**about, for, with**) to worry, bother or interest. **3** to affect; to involve: *a perfectionist where food is concerned*. — *n* **1** (a cause of) worry; (a subject of) interest. **2** one's business or responsibility: *no concern of yours*. **3** an organisation; a company or business. — *n* **concernment**. [Lat *concernere*, to distinguish or relate to]

concerned *adj* worried. — *adv* **concernedly**. — *n* **concernedness**. — **concerned with** about; having to do with.

concerning *prep* about; regarding.

concert *n* a musical performance given before an audience by singers or players. — **in concert 1** jointly; in co-operation. **2** (of singers, etc.) in a live performance. [Fr, from Ital *concerto*, from *concertare*, to organise]

concerted *adj* planned and carried out jointly.

concert pitch *n* (*mus*) the standard pitch that instruments are tuned to for concert performances.

concertina *n* a musical instrument like a small accordion. — *v* ***-naed*** (*intr* & *tr*) to fold or collapse like a concertina. [Made up by inventor]

concerto *n* ***-tos*** or ***-ti*** a musical composition for one or more solo instruments and orchestra. [Ital, from *concertare*, to organise]

concession *n* **1** the act of conceding. **2** something conceded or allowed. **3** the right, granted under government licence, to extract minerals, etc. in an area; the right to conduct a business from within a larger concern. **4** a reduction in price, fare, etc. for categories such as students, the elderly, the disabled, the unemployed. — *adj* **concessionary**. [Lat *concessio*, yielding]

concessionaire *n* the holder of a mining or trading concession.

concessive *adj* (*gram*) expressing concession, esp. by means of words such as *although*, *though*, and *even if*. [Lat *concessivus*]

conch *n* (the large spiral shell of) any of several similar shellfish. [Gr *konche*]

conchology *n* the study of shells and shellfish. — *n* **conchologist**.

conciliate *v* (*tr*) **1** to win over; to overcome the hostility of; to placate. **2** to reconcile (people in dispute, etc.). — *n* **conciliation**. — *n* **conciliator**. — *adj* **conciliatory**. [Lat *conciliare*, to unite in friendship]

concise *adj* brief, but covering essential points. — *adv* **concisely**. — *n* **conciseness** or **concision**. [Lat *concisus*, cut short]

conclave *n* **1** a private or secret meeting. **2** in the RC Church, the body of cardinals gathered to elect a new pope; their meeting-place. [Lat, a room that can be locked, from *clavis*, key]

conclude *v* **1** (*tr* & *intr*) to come or bring to an end. **2** (*tr*) to reach an opinion based on reasoning. **3** (*tr*; **with**) to settle or arrange: *conclude a treaty with a neighbour state*. [Lat *concludere*, from *claudere*, to close]

conclusion *n* **1** an end. **2** a reasoned judgement; an opinion based on reasoning: *come to* or *draw a conclusion*. **3** the settling (of terms, an agreement, etc). — **in conclusion** finally; lastly. — **jump to conclusions** to presume something with too little evidence. [Lat *conclusio*, from *concludere*, to end]

conclusive *adj* (of evidence, proof, etc.) convincing; decisive; leaving no room for doubt. — *adv* **conclusively**. — *n* **conclusiveness**. [Lat *conclusivus*]

concoct *v* (*tr*) **1** to make, esp. ingeniously from a variety of ingredients. **2** to invent (a story, excuse, etc.). — *n* **concoction**. [Lat *concoctus*, cooked together]

concomitant *adj* accompanying: *fever with concomitant headache, sore throat, etc.* — *n* something that is concomitant. — *adv* **concomitantly**. [Lat *concomitare*, to accompany]

concord *n* **1** agreement; peace or harmony. **2** (*gram*) agreement between words, esp. in number and gender, e.g. between verb and subject. **3** (*mus*) a chord with a harmonious sound, the opposite of a *discord*. **4** a treaty; a pact. — *adj* **concordant**. [Lat *concordia*, agreement]

concordance *n* **1** a state of harmony. **2** an alphabetical index of words used by an author or in a book, giving the reference and usu. meaning. [Lat *concordantia*, from Lat *concordare*, to agree]

concordat *n* an agreement, esp. between church and state. [Fr, from Lat *concordare*, to agree]

concourse *n* **1** a large open area for people, in a railway station, airport, etc. **2** a throng; a gathering. [Fr *concours*, from Lat *concursus*, assembly]

concrete *n* a building material composed of cement, sand and gravel mixed with water. — *adj* **1** made of concrete. **2** able to be felt, touched, seen, etc., as opposed to abstract: *concrete objects*. **3** definite or positive, as opposed to vague or general: *concrete evidence*. **4** (*gram*) (of nouns) denoting a thing rather than a quality, condition or action. **5** (of music) produced from sounds and music already recorded. **6** (of poetry) relying partly for its effect on the physical arrangement of words on the page. — *v* **1** (*tr*; **over**, **in**, etc.) to cover with or embed in concrete. **2** (*tr* & *intr*) to solidify. — *adv* **concretely**. — *n* **concreteness**. [Lat *concretus*, from *con-*, together + *crescere*, to grow]

concretion *n* **1** a hard, solid mass. **2** the process of fusing and solidifying into a mass. [Lat *concretio*, from *con-*, together + *crescere*, to grow]

concubine *n* (esp. *old*, or in Eastern societies) a woman who lives with, and has sexual intercourse with, a man, but is not married to him. — *n* **concubinage**. [Lat *concubina*, from *con-*, together + *cumbere*, to lie]

concupiscence *n* strong sexual desire. — *adj* **concupiscent**. [Lat *concupiscere*, to long for]

concur *v* ***-rr-*** **1** (*tr*; **with**) to agree. **2** to happen at the same time; to coincide. [Lat *con-*, together + *currere*, to run]

concurrent *adj* **1** running parallel; happening or taking place simultaneously. **2** (of lines) meeting or intersecting. **3** in agreement. — *adv* **concurrently**. [Lat *con-*, together + *currere*, to run]

concurrence *n* **1** agreement; consent. **2** the coinciding of events, etc.

concuss *v* (*tr*) to cause concussion in. [Lat *concutere*, to shake together]

concussion *n* **1** temporary injury to the brain caused by a blow or fall, usu. producing unconsciousness. **2** violent shaking or jarring.

condemn *v* (*tr*) **1** to declare to be wrong or evil. **2** to find guilty; to convict. **3** (**to**) to sentence (to a punishment). **4** to betray the guilt of; to give away: *His obvious nervousness condemned him.* **5** to declare (a building) unfit to be used or lived in. **6** (**to**) to be the cause of someone's disagreeable fate: *condemned to a friendless existence by his own ill-temper.* — *n* **condemnation**. — *adj* **condemnatory**. [Lat *condemnare*, to condemn]

condense *v* **1** (*tr*) to concentrate or compress; to make denser. **2** (*tr* & *intr*) to turn from gas or vapour to liquid or solid. **3** (*tr*) to express more briefly; to summarise. [Lat *condensare*, to compress]

condensation *n* **1** the process of condensing. **2** condensed water vapour, on cold glass, etc.

condenser *n* **1** (*electr*) a capacitor. **2** an apparatus for turning gas or vapour into liquid or solid form. **3** a lens for concentrating light.

condensed milk *n* milk thickened by evaporation and sweetened.

condescend *v* (*intr*) **1** to act in a gracious manner to (those one considers) one's inferiors. **2** to be gracious enough (to do something), esp. as though it were a favour. — *adj* **condescending**. — *adv* **condescendingly**. — *n* **condescension**. [Lat *condescendere*, from *descendere*, to descend]

condign *adj* (of praise, reward, punishment, etc.) well-deserved. [Lat *condignus*, from *dignus*, worthy]

condiment *n* a seasoning, e.g. salt, pepper, mustard, etc., used at table to give flavour to food. [Lat *condimentum*]

condition *n* **1** a particular state. **2** a state of health, fitness, or suitability for use: *out of condition.* **3** an ailment or disorder: *a heart condition.* **4** (in *pl*) circumstances: *poor working conditions.* **5** a requirement or qualification: *a necessary condition for membership.* — *v* **-n-** (*tr*) **1** to accustom or train to behave or react in a particular way; to influence. **2** to affect or control; to determine. **3** to get (an animal, one's hair, skin, etc.) into good condition. — *n* **conditioning**. — **on condition that** only if: *will go on condition that you go too.* — **on no condition** absolutely not. [Lat *conditio*, from *condicere*, to agree]

conditional *adj* **1** (**on**) dependent on a particular condition, etc. — *adv* **conditionally**.

conditioned reflex *n* an automatic response to something developed through training.

conditioner *n* (often *in cmpds*) a substance for improving the condition of something.

condole *v* (*intr* with **with**) to express one's sympathy to. [Lat *con-*, with + *dolere*, to grieve]

condolence *n* (usu. in *pl*) (an expression of) sympathy: *offer condolences.*

condom *n* a thin rubber sheath worn on the penis during sexual intercourse, to prevent the release of sperm into the vagina and so avoid pregnancy, and to prevent the spread of disease.

condominium *n* **1** (*NAm*) (a flat in) a block of individually owned flats. **2** joint control of a state by two or more other states. [Lat *con-*, with + *dominium*, dominion, rule]

condone *v* (*tr*) to pardon or overlook (an offence or wrong). — *adj* **condonable**. [Lat *condonare*, to present, overlook]

condor *n* a large S American vulture. [Span, from Quechua *kuntur*]

conduce *v* (*intr* with **to**) to help or tend towards (esp. a desirable result). [Lat *con-*, together + *ducere*, to lead]

conducive *adj* (**to**) likely to help or encourage (something desirable).

conduct *v* **1** (*tr*) to lead or guide. **2** (*tr*) to manage; to control: *conduct the firm's business.* **3** (*tr* & *intr*) to direct the performance of (an orchestra or choir) by movements of the hands or a baton. **4** (*tr*) to transmit (heat or electricity) by conduction: *Metal conducts heat.* **5** (*tr*) to direct, channel or convey: *hot air conducted through pipes.* **6** (*tr*) to behave (oneself). — *n* **1** behaviour. **2** the managing or organising of something: *the conduct of the war.* [Lat *conductus*, guide]

conductance *n* the power of any particular material or body to conduct electricity.

conduction *n* the process by which heat or electricity is transmitted through a material, body, etc.

conductivity *n* the property or power of conducting heat, electricity, etc.

conductor *n* **1** the director of a choir's or orchestra's performance. **2** a material, etc. that conducts heat or electricity. **3** a person who collects the fares from passengers on a bus, etc.

conductress *n* a woman who collects fares on a bus, etc.

conduit *n* a channel, trough or pipe carrying water or electric cables. [Fr, from Lat *conductus*, channel]

cone *n* **1** (*geom*) a solid figure that has a circular base and terminates in a point. **2** something similar to this in shape, e.g. a pointed holder for ice cream, made of wafer biscuit, or a plastic object used to mark off temporary lanes for traffic, etc. **3** the pointed oval fruit of a fir, pine or other coniferous tree, made up of overlapping woody scales. — *v* **cone off** (*tr*) to close off (part of a road) with a line of traffic cones. [Gr *konos*]

confab (*coll*) *n* a confabulation. — *v* **-bb-** (*intr*) to confabulate.

confabulate *v* (*intr*; *formal*) to talk, discuss or confer. — *n* **confabulation**. [Lat *confabulari*, to converse]

confection *n* **1** any sweet food, e.g. a cake, sweet, biscuit, pudding. **2** (*old* or *facet*) a fancy or elaborate garment, e.g. a hat. [Lat *confectio*, making]

confectioner *n* a person who makes or sells sweets or cakes.

confectionery *n* **1** sweets, biscuits and cakes. **2** the art or business of a confectioner.

confederacy *n* **-*ies*** **1** a league or alliance of states. **2** (*hist*; *cap*) the union of eleven states in the southern US that broke away from the USA, so causing the American Civil War. **3** a conspiracy; an association formed for illegal purposes. [Lat *confoederatio*, league]

confederate *n* **1** a member of a confederacy. **2** a friend or ally; an accomplice or fellow conspirator. **3** (*hist*; *cap*) a supporter of the Confederacy. — *adj* **1** allied; united. **2** (*hist*; *cap*) belonging to the Confederacy. — *v* (*tr*) to unite into a confederacy. [Lat *confoederatus*, united in a league]

confederation *n* **1** the uniting of states into a league. **2** the league so formed.

confer *v* **-*rr*-** **1** (*intr*; **with**) to consult together. **2** (*tr*; **on**) to bestow (an honour) on someone. [Lat *con-*, together + *ferre*, to bring]

conferment *n* the bestowing of honours.

conference *n* **1** a formally organised gathering for the discussion of matters of common interest or concern. **2** consultation; the formal exchanging of views: *in conference with the Prime Minister*. **3** an assembly of representatives of an association, church denomination, etc. [Lat *conferentia*, from *con-*, together + *ferre*, to bring]

confess *v* **1** (*tr* & *intr*) to own up to (a fault, wrongdoing, etc.); to admit (a disagreeable fact, etc.) reluctantly. **2** (*tr* & *intr*) to recount (one's sins) to a priest, in order to gain absolution. **3** (*tr*) (of a priest) to hear the confession of (someone). [Lat *confiteri*, to admit]

confessed *adj* having openly admitted a weakness: *a confessed alcoholic*. — *adv* **confessedly**.

confession *n* **1** the admission of a sin, fault, crime, distasteful or shocking fact, etc. **2** the formal act of confessing one's sins to a priest. **3** a declaration of one's religious faith or principles: *a confession of faith*. **4** a religious body with its own creed or set of beliefs.

confessional *n* the small enclosed stall in a church where a priest sits when hearing confessions.

confessor *n* **1** a priest, esp. one to whom one goes regularly, who hears confessions and gives spiritual advice. **2** (*hist*) a person whose holy life serves as a demonstration of his or her religious faith: *Edward the Confessor*. [Lat, martyr, witness]

confetti *n* tiny pieces of coloured paper traditionally thrown at the bride and groom by wedding guests. [Ital, pl. of *confetto*, sweetmeat]

confidant or **confidante** *n* respectively a male or female friend with whom one discusses personal matters. [Fr *confident(e)*, from Lat *confidere*, to trust]

confide *v* **1** (*intr* with **in**) to speak freely about personal matters (to someone one trusts). **2** (*tr*) to tell (a secret, etc.) to someone. **3** (*tr*) to entrust to someone's care. [Lat *confidere*, to trust]

confiding *adj* trustful; not suspicious. — *adv* **confidingly**.

confidence *n* **1** (**in**) trust in, or reliance on, a person or thing. **2** faith in one's own ability; self-assurance. **3** a secret, etc. confided to someone. **4** a relationship of mutual trust: *took her into his confidence*. — **in confidence** in secret; confidentially. [Lat *confidentia*]

confidence trick *n* a form of swindle in which the swindler first wins the trust of the victim. — *n* **confidence trickster**.

confident *adj* **1** (**of**) certain; sure: *confident of success*. **2** self-assured.

vote of confidence, or **of no confidence** *n* a vote taken on a motion that the voters have, or do not have, faith in the leader, controlling group, etc. in question.

confidential *adj* **1** secret; not to be divulged: *confidential information*. **2** trusted with private matters: *a confidential secretary*. **3** used for privacy's sake: *a confidential whisper*. — *n* **confidentiality**. — *adv* **confidentially**. [Lat *confidentia*, confidence]

configuration *n* **1** the positioning of the parts of something with relation to each other. **2** an outline or external shape. **3** (*psychol*) an organised whole. [Lat *configurare*, to form, fashion]

confine *v* (*tr*) **1** (**to**) to restrict; to limit. **2** to prevent the spread of: *confined the fire*. **3** to keep prisoner or keep from moving. **4** (*old*) to keep (a woman about to give birth) indoors or in bed. [Lat *confinis*, border]

confined *adj* narrow; restricted.

confinement *n* **1** the state of being shut up or kept in an enclosed space. **2** the period surrounding childbirth: *her fourth confinement*.

confines *n* (*pl*) limits; boundaries; restrictions.

confirm *v* (*tr*) **1** to prove correct. **2** to support or prove: *refused to confirm or deny the rumour*. **3** to finalise or make definite (a booking, arrangement etc.). **4** (**in**) to make (someone) more convinced about something: *I was confirmed in my suspicion that he was cheating us*. **5** (**in**) to give formal approval to; to establish officially: *confirm someone in his appointment*. **6** to accept (someone) formally into full membership of the Christian church. — *adj* **confirmatory**. [Lat *confirmare*]

confirmation *n* **1** the act of confirming.

2 proof or support. **3** finalisation. **4** the religious ceremony in which a person is admitted to full membership of the church.

confirmed *adj* so settled into the state or condition mentioned as to be unlikely to change.

confiscate *v* (*tr*) to take away (something) from someone, as a penalty. — *n* **confiscation.** [Lat *confiscare*, to transfer to the state treasury]

conflagration *n* a fierce and destructive blaze. [Lat *conflagrare*]

conflate *v* (*tr*) to blend or combine (e.g. two different versions of a text, story, etc.) into a single whole. — *n* **conflation**. [Lat *conflare*, to smelt or fuse]

conflict *n* **1** (**between, with**) disagreement; fierce argument; a quarrel. **2** (**between**) a clash (between different aims, interests, ideas, etc.) **3** a struggle, fight, battle or war. — *v* (*intr*; **with**) to be incompatible or in opposition: *The demands of a career often conflict with those of family life.* [Lat *confligere*, to dash together, clash]

confluence *n* the place where one river flows into another. — *adj* **confluent**. [Lat *con-*, together + *fluere*, to flow]

conform *v* (*intr*) **1** to behave, dress, etc. in obedience to some standard considered normal by the majority. **2** (with **to**) to obey (rules, etc.); to meet or comply with (standards, etc.). **3** (with **to, with**) to be in agreement with; to match or correspond to. [Lat *conformare*, to shape]

conformable *adj* **1** (**to**) corresponding or matching. **2** compliant; agreeable. **3** (*geol*) (of rock layers) still lying as originally laid down.

conformation *n* a shape, structure or arrangement.

conformist *n* a person who conforms to the norm, obeys rules, does the expected thing, etc.

conformity *n* **1** obedience to rules, normal standards, etc. **2** accordance; compliance: *in conformity with safety standards.*

confound *v* (*tr*) **1** to puzzle; to baffle. **2** to defeat or thwart (one's enemies or their schemes). **3** to mix up or confuse (one thing with another). — **confound it, her, them,** etc.! Damn it, her, them, etc.! [Lat *confundere*, to pour together, throw into disorder, overthrow]

confounded *adj* used to indicate annoyance: *a confounded nuisance.* — *adv* **confoundedly**.

confrère *n* a fellow member of one's profession, etc.; a colleague. [OFr, from Latin *con-*, with + *frater*, brother]

confront *v* (*tr*) **1** to face, esp. defiantly or accusingly: *He confronted his accusers.* **2** to prepare to deal firmly with: *confront the problem.* **3** (with **with**) to bring (someone) face to face with (something that condemns him or her): *confront him with his error.* **4** (of an unpleasant prospect) to present itself to: *Certain death confronted him.* [Lat *confrontari*, from *frons*, forehead, brow]

confrontation *n* (**between**) an act of confronting; a hostile meeting or exchange of words.

Confucianism *n* the teachings of the Chinese philosopher Confucius (551–479 BC), with emphasis on morality, consideration for others, obedience, and good education. — *n* & *adj* **Confucian**. — *n* **Confucianist**.

confuse *v* (*tr*) **1** to put into a muddle or mess. **2** (**with**) to fail to distinguish; to mix up: *confuse 'ascetic' with 'aesthetic'.* **3** to puzzle, bewilder, or muddle. **4** to complicate. **5** to embarrass. — *adj* **confused**. — *adv* **confusedly**. — *adj* **confusing**. — *adv* **confusingly**. [Lat *confundere*, to mix]

confusion *n* **1** the act of confusing or state of being confused. **2** disorder; muddle. **3** mental bewilderment. [Lat *confusio*, from *confundere*, to mix]

confute *v* (*tr*) to prove (a person) wrong, or (a theory, etc.) false. — *n* **confutation**. [Lat *confutare*, to pour cold water on]

conga *n* **1** an orig. Cuban dance performed in single file, with three steps followed by a kick. **2** a large drum beaten with the fingers. — *v* ***-gaed*** (*intr*) to dance the conga. [Span]

congé *n* **1** permission to depart. **2** abrupt dismissal. [Fr]

congeal *v* (*tr* & *intr*) (of liquid) to thicken, coagulate or solidify, esp. through cooling. — *n* **congealment** or **congelation.** [Lat *congelare*, to freeze completely]

congener *n* something of the same kind or nature, e.g. a plant or animal of the same genus. [Lat *con-*, same + *genus*, kind]

congenial *adj* **1** companionable; having a personality and interests that fit well with one's own. **2** (**to**) pleasant or agreeable. — *n* **congeniality**. — *adv* **congenially**. [Lat *con-*, same + *genius*, spirit]

congenital *adj* **1** (of bodily and mental disorders) present since birth. **2** affected since birth by a particular condition: *a congenital idiot.* — *adv* **congenitally**. [*con-*, with + *gignere*, to give birth to]

conger *n* (also **conger eel**) a large sea eel. [Gr *gongros*]

congeries *n* ***-ries*** a miscellaneous accumulation; a confused heap. [Lat, heap]

congested *adj* (**with**) **1** crowded; too full; obstructed. **2** (*pathol*) (of a part of the body) over-full of blood. **3** (of the nose or air passages) obstructed with mucus. — *n* **congestion**. [Lat *congerere*, to heap together]

conglomerate *n* **1** a mass formed from things of different kinds. **2** a kind of rock composed of rounded pebbles embedded in clay. **3** a business group composed of a large number of firms merged together. — *adj* composed of things of different kinds formed into a mass. — *v* (*intr*) to accumulate to form a mass. — *n* **conglomeration**. [Lat *con-*, together + *glomus*, ball of yarn]

congrats *n* (*pl*; often as *interj*; *coll*) congratulations.
congratulate *v* (*tr*; **on**) **1** to express one's pleasure to (someone) at his or her success, good fortune, happiness, etc. **2** to consider (oneself) lucky or clever to have managed something: *congratulated herself on her narrow escape*. — *n* **congratulation**. — *adj* **congratulatory**. [Lat *congratulari*, to wish one another joy]
congratulations *n* (*pl*; often as *interj*; **on**) an expression used to congratulate.
congregate *v* (*tr* & *intr*) to gather together into a crowd. [Lat *congregare*, from *grex*, herd]
congregation *n* **1** a gathering or assembly of people, esp. for worship in church. **2** the people regularly attending a particular church.
congregational *adj* **1** of, run by, etc. a congregation or separate congregations. **2** (*cap*) belonging to a Protestant denomination in which the affairs of each individual church are run by its own congregation. — *n* **Congregationalism**. — *n* **Congregationalist**.
congress **1** a large, esp. international assembly of delegates, gathered for discussion. **2** a name used for the law-making body in some countries, esp. (*cap*) that of the US. — *adj* **congressional**. [Lat *congredi*, to meet]
congressman and **congresswoman** *n* respectively a male and female member of a congress.
congruent **1** *adj* (*geom*) (of two or more figures) identical in size and shape. **2** (with **with**) suitable or appropriate to. — *n* **congruence** or **congruency**. — *adv* **congruently**. [Lat *congruere*, to meet together]
congruous *adj* (**with**) fitting; suitable; proper. — *n* **congruity**. — *adv* **congruously**. [Lat *congruus*, from *congruere*, to meet together]
conic *adj* (*geom*) relating to a cone. [Gr *konikos*, from *konos*, cone]
conic section *n* (*geom*) a figure formed by a flat surface intersecting a cone.
conical *adj* cone-shaped. [Gr *konikos*, cone-shaped]
conifer *n* a tree that bears cones, such as the pine, fir and larch. [Lat, *conus*, cone + *ferre*, to carry]
coniferous *adj* (of trees) bearing cones.
conj *abbrev* (*gram*) conjunction.
conjecture *n* an opinion based on incomplete evidence; a guess; the process of guessing. — *v* (*intr*) to make a conjecture. [Lat *conjectura*, conclusion]
conjectural *adj* based on guesswork. — *adv* **conjecturally**.
conjoin *v* (*tr* & *intr*) to join together, combine or unite. [Fr *conjoindre*, to join together]
conjoint *adj* joint; associated; united. — *adv* **conjointly**.
conjugal *adj* relating to marriage, or to the relationship between husband and wife. — *adv* **conjugally**. — *n* **conjugality**. [Lat *conjugalis*, from *con-*, together + *jugum*, yoke]
conjugate (*tr* & *intr*) **1** (*gram*) to give the inflected parts of (a verb), indicating number, person, tense, voice and mood, or (of a verb) to have inflected parts. ◇ See also **decline**. **2** (*biol* & *biochem*) to unite or fuse together. — *adj* **1** joined, connected or coupled. **2** (*bot*) occurring in pairs. **3** (*math*) related reciprocally. **4** (of words) having a common origin. — *n* a conjugate word or thing. [Lat *con-*, with + *jugum*, yoke]
conjugation *n* **1** (*gram*) the inflection of a verb to indicate number, person, tense, voice and mood, or a particular class of verbs having the same set of inflections. ◇ See also **declension**. **2** a uniting, joining or fusing.
conjunction *n* **1** (*gram*) a word used to link sentences, clauses or words, e.g. *and*, *but*, *if*, *or*, *because*. **2** a joining together; combination. **3** the coinciding of two or more events. **4** (*astrol*) the apparent meeting or passing of two or more heavenly bodies. — **in conjunction (with)** together (with). [Lat *con-*, with + *jungere*, to join]
conjunctiva *n* ***-vas*** or ***-vae*** *n* (*anat*) the membrane that covers the eyeball and the inside of the eyelid. — *adj* **conjunctival**. [Lat *membrana conjunctiva*, conjunctive membrane]
conjunctivitis *n* inflammation of the conjunctiva.
conjunctive *adj* connecting; linking. — *adj* & *n* (*gram*) (a word or phrase) used as a conjunction. — *adv* **conjunctively**. [Lat *conjunctivus*, connecting]
conjunctivitis. See **conjunctiva**.
conjuncture *n* a combination of circumstances, esp. one leading to a crisis. [Lat *conjungere*, to join]
conjure *v* **1** (*intr*) to practise conjuring. **2** (*tr*) to summon (a spirit, demon, etc.) to appear. **3** (*tr*; *old*) to beg (someone) earnestly (to do something). — *v* **conjure up** (*tr*) **1** to produce as though from nothing. **2** to call up, evoke or stir (images, memories, etc.). — **a name to conjure with** a name of great importance or significance. [Lat *conjurare*, to swear together]
conjuring *n* the performing of tricks that deceive the eye or seem to defy nature, esp. by adroit use of the hands.
conjurer or **conjuror** *n* an entertainer who performs conjuring tricks.
conk[1] *n* (*slang*) the nose.
conk[2] *v* (*tr*; *slang*) to hit (someone) on the head.
conk[3]: **conk out** *v* (*intr*) **1** (of a machine, etc.) to break down. **2** (of a person) to collapse with fatigue, etc.
conker *n* (*coll*) the nut of the horse chestnut tree. [Either dialect *conker*, snail shell,

orig. used in the game, or a form of **conquer**]
conkers *n* (*sing*) a children's game played with conkers on strings, in which players try to shatter each other's conkers by hitting them with their own.

Conn. *abbrev* Connecticut.

connect *v* **1** (*tr* & *intr*; **to, with, up**) to join; to link. **2** (*tr*; **with**) to associate or involve: *connected with advertising*. **3** (*tr*; **with**) to associate or relate mentally. **4** (*tr*) to join by telephone. **5** (*tr*; **with**) to relate by marriage or birth. **6** (*intr*; **with**) (of aeroplanes, trains, buses, etc.) to be timed so as to allow transfer from one to another. **7** (*intr*; **with**; *humorous*) (of the fist, etc.) to strike. **8** (*intr*; *coll*) to make sense. — *adj* **connectable** or **connectible**. — *n* **connecter** or **connector**. — **well connected** with important or aristocratic relatives. [Lat *con-*, together + *nectere*, to fasten]
connecting-rod *n* the metal rod connecting the piston to the crankshaft in a motor vehicle.
connection or **connexion** *n* **1** the act of connecting or state of being connected. **2** (**with**) something that connects; a link. **3** a relationship through marriage or birth. **4** an esp. influential person whom one meets through one's job, etc.; a contact. **5** a train, bus, etc. timed so as allow transfer to it from another passenger service; the transfer from one vehicle to another: — **in connection with** about; concerning. — **in this connection** while we are considering this matter.
connective *adj* serving to connect. — *adj* & *n* (*gram*) (a word) linking two sentences, clauses, etc.
connective tissue *n* the fibrous elastic body tissue that fills the spaces between, and supports, organs, and forms cartilage and ligaments.

conning-tower *n* **1** the raised part of a submarine containing the periscope. **2** the wheelhouse of a warship. [**con**[3]]

connive *v* (*intr*) **1** (with **at**) to pretend not to notice, and thereby encourage (wrongdoing). **2** (**with**) to conspire. — *n* **connivance**. — *n* **conniver**. [Lat *connivere*, to blink]

connoisseur *n* a person who is knowledgeable about, and a good judge of, e.g. the arts, wine, food, etc. [Fr, from *connaître*, to know]

connote *v* (*tr; formal*) **1** (of a word) to suggest, in addition to its literal meaning: *'Portly' somehow connotes pomposity*. **2** to mean; to imply. — *n* **connotation**. — *adj* **connotative**. [Lat *connotare*, to mark in addition]

connubial *adj* of or relating to marriage or to relations between a husband and wife. — *adv* **connubially**. [Lat *connubium*, marriage]

conquer *v* **-r- 1** (*tr*) to gain possession or dominion over (territory) by force. **2** (*tr*) to defeat. **3** (*tr*) to overcome or put an end to (a failing, difficulty, evil, etc.). **4** (*tr*) to succeed in climbing, reaching, traversing, etc. **5** (*tr*) to become a celebrity in: *the singer who conquered America*. **6** (*intr*) to win; to succeed. — *adj* **conquering**. — *n* **conqueror**. [Lat *conquirere*, to go in search of]

conquest *n* **1** the act of conquering. **2** a conquered territory. **3** something won by effort or force. **4** a person whose affection or admiration one has won. [Fr *conqueste*, from Lat *conquirere*, to seek out]

conquistador *n* ***-dores*** , ***-dors*** *n* any of the 16th-century Spanish conquerors of Peru and Mexico. [Span, conqueror]

consanguineous *adj* descended from a common ancestor. — *n* **consanguinity**. [Lat *con-*, same + *sanguis*, blood]

conscience *n* the sense of right and wrong that guides one's behaviour: *have a guilty*, or *clear*, *conscience*. — **in all conscience** by any normal standard of fairness. — **on one's conscience** making one feel guilty. [Lat *conscientia*]
conscience-stricken *adj* feeling guilty over something one has done.
freedom of conscience *n* the right to hold religious or other beliefs without persecution.
prisoner of conscience *n* a person imprisoned for his or her political beliefs.

conscientious *adj* **1** careful; thorough; painstaking. **2** guided by conscience. — *adv* **conscientiously**. — *n* **conscientiousness**. [Lat *conscientiosus*]
conscientious objector *n* a person who refuses on moral grounds to serve in the armed forces.

conscious *adj* **1** awake and aware of one's surroundings: *half-conscious*. **2** (**of**) aware. **3** deliberate: *a conscious effort to be polite*. **4** (often *in cmpds*) concerned, esp. too concerned, with: *class-conscious*. — *n* the conscious part of the mind. — *adv* **consciously**. [Lat *conscius*, from *scire*, to know]
consciousness *n* **1** the state of being conscious. **2** awareness. **3** (*psychol*) the thoughts, feelings, etc. that one is aware of having, as distinct from the processes of the unconscious mind.

conscript *v* (*tr*) to enrol for compulsory military service. — *n* a person who has been conscripted. — *n* **conscription**. [Lat *conscribere*, to enlist]

consecrate *v* (*tr*) **1** to set apart for a holy use; to make sacred; to dedicate to God. **2** to devote to a special use. — *n* **consecration**. [Lat *consecrare*, from *sacer*, sacred]

consecutive *adj* **1** following one after the other: *consecutive numbers*. **2** (*gram*) expressing result or consequence. — *adv* **consecutively**. [Lat *consequi*, to follow]

consensus *n* general feeling or opinion; agreement; a majority view. [Lat, agreement, from *con-*, same + *sensus*, feeling]

consent *v* **1** (*intr*; **to**) to give one's permission; to agree. **2** (*tr*) to agree (to do something). — *n* agreement; assent; permission: *give one's consent*. — **by common consent** as is generally agreed. [Lat *consentire*, to agree]

age of consent *n* the age at which sexual intercourse becomes permissible by law.

consequence *n* **1** something that follows from, or is caused by, an action or set of circumstances. **2** a conclusion reached from reasoning. **3** importance: *of no consequence*. — **in consequence (of)** as a result. — **take the consequences** to accept whatever results from one's decision or action. [Lat *consequi*, to follow]

consequent *adj* (**on, upon**) resulting.

consequently *adv* as a result; therefore.

consequential *adj* **1** important. **2** (of people) self-important; pompous. **3** following as a result. [Lat *consequentia*, consequence]

conservancy *n* **1** a body controlling a port or river. **2** (an area under the protection of) a body concerned with environmental conservation. **3** conservation. [Lat *conservare*, to preserve]

conservation *n* **1** the act of conserving; the state of being conserved. **2** the preservation and protection of wildlife and the environment. — **conservation of energy, mass**, etc. (*physics*) the theory that the energy, or mass, or whatever, within a system that is isolated from external forces will remain constant. [Lat *conservare*, to save]

conservationist *n* a supporter of environmental conservation.

conservatism *n* **1** the inclination to preserve the existing state of affairs and avoid esp. sudden or radical change. **2** (*cap*) the policies and principles of a Conservative Party. [**conservative**]

conservative *adj* **1** favouring the keeping of what is established or traditional; disliking change. **2** (of an estimate) deliberately low, for the sake of caution. **3** (of tastes, clothing, etc.) restrained; not flamboyant. **4** (*cap*) of or relating to the Conservative Party, the right-wing political party in the UK, supporting private ownership of industry, or any other Conservative Party. — *n* **1** a traditionalist. **2** (*cap*) a member or supporter of a Conservative Party. — *adv* **conservatively**. [Lat *conservare*, to preserve]

conservatoire *n* a school specialising in music or any of the fine arts. [Fr, from Ital *conservatorio*, orig. an orphanage]

conservatory *n* **-ies 1** a greenhouse for plants, or a similar room used as a lounge, attached to, and entered from, the house. **2** a conservatoire. [Lat *conservare*, to conserve]

conserve *v* (*tr*) to keep safe from damage, deterioration, loss or undesirable change. — *n* a jam made esp. from fresh fruit. — *adj* **conservable**. [Lat *conservare*, to save]

consider *v* **-r- 1** (*tr*) to go over in one's mind. **2** (*tr*) to look at thoughtfully. **3** (*tr*) to call to mind for comparison, etc. **4** (*tr*; **for**) to assess with regard to employing, using, etc.: *consider someone for a job*. **5** (*tr*) to contemplate (doing something). **6** (*tr*) to regard as. **7** (*tr*) to think; to have as one's opinion. **8** (*tr*) to take into account; to make allowances for. **9** (*intr*) to think carefully. — **all things considered** taking all the circumstances into account. [Lat *considerare*, to examine]

considered *adj* **1** carefully thought about: *my considered opinion*. **2** (with *adv*) thought of or valued: *highly considered*.

considering *conj* taking into account: *still very active, considering her age*. — *adv* taking the circumstances into account: *pretty good, considering*.

considerable *adj* **1** large; great. **2** having many admirable qualities: *a considerable person*. — *adv* **considerably**. [Lat *considerabilis*]

considerate *adj* careful not to hurt or inconvenience others. — *adv* **considerately**. — *n* **considerateness**. [Lat *consideratus*, careful]

consideration *n* **1** thoughtfulness on behalf of others. **2** careful thought. **3** a fact, circumstance, etc. to be taken into account. **4** a payment, reward or recompense. — **in consideration of** in return for: *a small fee in consideration of your efforts*. — **take into consideration** to allow for. — **under consideration** being considered. [Lat *considerare*, to consider]

consign *v* (*tr*) **1** (**to**) to hand over; to entrust. **2** to send, commit or deliver. **3** to send (goods). [Lat *consignare*, to put one's seal to]

consignee *n* the addressee or recipient of goods, etc.

consignment *n* **1** a load of goods, etc. sent or delivered. **2** the act of consigning. — **on consignment** (of goods ordered for stock by a shop, etc.) to be paid for only if sold, and returned if unsold.

consignor *n* the sender or deliverer of goods.

consist *v* (*intr*) **1** (with **of**) to be composed or made up of. **2** (with **in, of**) to have as an essential feature. [Lat *consistere*, to stand firm]

consistency[1] *n* **-ies** the texture or composition of something, with regard to density, thickness, firmness, solidity, etc. [Lat *consistere*, to stand together]

consistency[2]. See **consistent**.

consistent *adj* **1** (**with**) in agreement; in keeping: *injuries consistent with a fall from a height*. **2** unchanging, reliable, regular, steady. — *n* **consistency**. — *adv* **consistently**. [Lat *consistere*, to stand firm]

consistory *n* **-ies** an ecclesiastical council, esp. one composed of the pope and cardinals. [Lat *consistorium*, meeting-place]

console[1] *v* (*tr*) to comfort, in distress, grief or disappointment. — *adj* **consolable.** — *adj* **consolatory**. [Lat *consolari*, to comfort]

consolation *n* **1** a circumstance or person that brings one comfort. **2** the act of consoling.

consolation prize *n* a prize given to someone who just fails to win a major prize.

console[2] *n* **1** (*mus*) the part of an organ with the keys, pedals and panels of stops. **2** a panel of dials, switches, etc. for operating an electronic machine. **3** a free-standing cabinet for audio or video equipment. **4** an ornamental bracket for a shelf, etc. [Fr, from *consolateur*, comforter, supporter]

consolidate *v* (*tr* & *intr*) **1** to make or become solid or strong. **2** (of businesses, etc.) to combine or merge. — *n* **consolidation**. — *n* **consolidator**. [Lat *consolidare*]

consols *n* (*pl*; *Br*) government securities. [*consol*idated annuitie*s*]

consommé *n* thin clear soup made from meat stock. [Fr, finished]

consonant[1] *n* (a letter representing) a speech sound produced by obstructing the passage of the breath in any of several ways. — *adj* **consonantal**. [Lat *consonans litera*, letter having the same sound]

consonant[2] *adj* (with **with**) in harmony or agreement (with). [Lat *consonare*, to sound together]

consonance *n* **1** the state of agreement. **2** (*mus*) a pleasant-sounding combination of musical notes.

consort[1] *n* **1** a wife or husband, esp. of a reigning sovereign. **2** (*naut*) an accompanying ship. — *v* (*intr* with **with**) to associate with (esp. undesirable people). [Lat *consors*, sharer]

consort[2] *n* a group of players, singers or instruments, esp. specialising in early music. [Variant of **concert**]

consortium *n* ***-ia*** or ***-iums*** an association or combination of several banks, businesses, etc. [Lat *consortium*, partnership]

conspectus *n* a survey or report; a summary. [Lat, view, survey]

conspicuous *adj* **1** very noticeable or obvious. **2** notable; striking; glaring. — *adv* **conspicuously**. — *n* **conspicuousness**. [Lat *conspicuus*, visible]

conspiracy *n* ***-ies*** **1** the activity of conspiring. **2** a plot. **3** a group of conspirators. [Lat *conspiratio*, plot]

conspiracy of silence *n* an agreement to keep quiet about something.

conspirator *n* someone who plots, or joins a conspiracy. — *adj* **conspiratorial**. — *adv* **conspiratorially**. [Lat, from *conspirare*, to plot]

conspire *v* (*intr*) **1** to plot secretly together esp. for an unlawful purpose. **2** (of events) to seem to gang up esp. to thwart one: *Everything conspired to make me miss my train.* [Lat *conspirare*]

constable *n* **1** a policeman or policewoman of the most junior rank. **2** (*hist*) the chief officer of a royal household. **3** the governor of a royal castle. [Fr *conestable*, from Lat *comes stabuli*, count of the stable]

constabulary *n* ***-ies*** the police force of a district or county. — *adj* of or relating to constables or the police. [Lat *constabularius*, from MidE *constablerie*, from Fr *conestable*, constable]

constant *adj* **1** never stopping. **2** frequently recurring. **3** unchanging. **4** faithful; loyal. — *n* **constancy**. — *adv* **constantly**. [Lat *constare*, to be unchanging or steadfast]

constellation *n* **1** a group of stars having a name, often one relating to the distinctive shape they seem to form. **2** a group of associated people or things. [Lat *constellatio*, from *stella*, star]

consternation *n* dismay, alarm, agitation or anxiety. [Lat *consternatio*]

constipate *v* (*tr*) to cause constipation in. — *adj* **constipated**. [Lat *con-*, together + *stipare*, to press]

constipation *n* a condition in which the faeces become hard and difficult to pass from the bowels.

constituency *n* ***-ies*** **1** the district represented by a member of parliament or other representative in a legislative body. **2** the voters in that district. [**constituent**]

constituent *adj* **1** forming part of a whole. **2** having the power to create or alter a constitution: *a constituent assembly*. **3** having the power to elect. — *n* **1** a necessary part; a component. **2** a resident in a constituency. [Lat *constituere*, to establish]

constitute *v* (*tr*) **1** to be; to go together to make. **2** to establish; to appoint: *the recently constituted board of enquiry*. [Lat *constituere*, to establish]

constitution *n* **1** a set of rules governing an organisation; the supreme laws and rights of a country's people, etc. **2** the way in which something is formed or made up. **3** one's physical make-up, health, etc. **4** the act of forming or constituting. [Lat *constitutio*, arrangement, physical make-up]

constitutional *adj* **1** legal according to a given constitution. **2** relating to, or controlled by, the law of the land. **3** relating to one's physical make-up, health, etc. — *n* (*old*) a regular walk taken for the sake of one's health. — *adv* **constitutionally**.

constrain *v* **1** (*tr*; usu. in *passive*) to force; to compel: *feel constrained to tell the truth.* **2** to limit the freedom, scope or range of. [Fr *constraindre*]

constrained *adj* awkward; embarrassed; forced.

constraint *n* **1** (**on**) a limit or restriction. **2** force; compulsion. **3** awkwardness, unnaturalness, embarrassment or inhibition.

constrict *v* (*tr*) **1** to squeeze or compress; to enclose tightly, esp. too tightly; to cause to tighten. **2** to inhibit. — *n* **constriction**. — *adj* **constrictive**. [Lat *constringere*, to bind]

constrictor *n* **1** a snake that kills by coiling itself round its prey and squeezing. **2** (*anat*) a muscle that narrows an opening.

construct *v* (*tr*) **1** to build. **2** to form, compose or put together. **3** (*geom*) to draw (a figure). — *n* **1** something constructed, esp. in the mind. **2** a mental image constructed from a number of sense-impressions. — *n* **constructor**. [Lat *construere*, to build, pile together]

construction *n* **1** the process of building or constructing. **2** something built or constructed; a building. **3** (*gram*) the arrangement of words in a particular grammatical relationship, to form a sentence, clause, etc. **4** interpretation: *put a wrong construction on someone's words*. — *adj* **constructional**.

constructive *adj* **1** helping towards progress or development; useful. **2** (*legal*) (of facts) realised from what has been stated, rather than actually stated themselves. **3** relating to construction. — *adv* **constructively**. — *n* **constructiveness**.

construe *v* (*tr*) **1** to interpret or explain. **2** (*gram*) to analyse the grammatical structure of (a sentence, etc.). **3** (*gram*; **with**) to combine (a word) grammatically with another. **4** (*gram*) to translate word for word. **5** to deduce; to infer. [Lat *construere*, to construct]

consul *n* **1** an official repesentative of a state, stationed in a foreign country to look after e.g. the interests of fellow citizens living there. **2** (*hist*) either of the two joint chief magistrates in ancient Rome. — *adj* **consular**. — *n* **consulship**. [Lat]

consulate *n* the post or official residence of a consul (sense **1**).

consult *v* **1** (*tr*) to ask the advice of: *consult a lawyer*. **2** (*tr*) to refer to (a map, book, etc.). **3** (*tr*) to consider (wishes, feelings, etc.). **4** (*intr*; **with**) to have discussions. **5** (*intr*) to give advice as a consultant: *the doctor's consulting hours*. [Lat *consultare*]

consultant *n* **1** a person who gives professional advice. **2** a senior hospital doctor usu. specialising in a particular branch of medicine. — *n* **consultancy**.

consultation *n* **1** the act or process of consulting. **2** a meeting for the obtaining of advice or for discussion.

consultative *adj* available for consultation; advisory: *a consultative committee*.

consulting *adj* acting as an adviser: *a consulting architect*.

consulting room *n* the room in which a doctor sees patients.

consume *v* (*tr*) **1** to eat or drink. **2** to use up. **3** to destroy. **4** (**with**) to obsess or possess: *consumed with jealousy*. — *adj* **consumable**. [Lat *consumere*]

consumer *n* **1** the person who uses a product; any member of the public buying and using goods and services. **2** someone or something that consumes.

consumer durables *n* (*pl*) goods that do not need frequent replacement, e.g. furniture, television sets, etc.

consumer goods *n* (*pl*) goods bought to satisfy personal needs, as distinct from e.g. machinery and other equipment used in the production of goods.

consumerism *n* **1** the protection of the interests of consumers. **2** the economic policy of encouraging spending and consuming.

consumer research *n* the study of the needs and preferences of consumers.

consuming *adj* (of an enthusiasm, etc.) obsessive; overwhelming: *a consuming passion for beetles*.

consummate *v* (*tr*) **1** to finish, perfect or complete. **2** to make (a marriage) into a marriage in its full legal sense through the act of sexual intercourse. — *adj* **1** supreme; very great; very skilled. **2** complete; utter: *a consummate idiot*. — *adv* **consummately**. — *n* **consummation**. [Lat *consummare*, to complete, perfect]

consumption *n* **1** the act or process of consuming. **2** the amount consumed. **3** the buying and using of goods. **4** (*old*) tuberculosis of the lungs. [Lat *consumptio*]

consumptive *adj* **1** relating to consumption; wasteful or destructive. **2** suffering from tuberculosis of the lungs. — *n* a person suffering from tuberculosis of the lungs.

cont. *abbrev* continued.

contact *n* **1** the condition of touching physically. **2** (a means of) communication. **3** an acquaintance whose influence or knowledge may prove useful to one, esp. in business. **4** an electrical connection, allowing passage of a current. **5** a person who has been exposed to an infectious disease through being near a person who has it. — *v* (*tr*) to get in touch with; to communicate with. — *adv* **contactable**. [Lat *contactus*, touching]

contact lens *n* a small plastic lens worn on the eyeball, instead of spectacles.

contagion *n* **1** the spreading of disease by physical contact. **2** (esp. *old*) an infectious disease. **3** a spreading social evil; a corrupting influence. [Lat *contagio*, touching, contact]

contagious *adj* **1** (of a disease) spread by bodily contact. **2** (of a person) in an infectious condition; likely to infect others. **3** (of a mood, laughter, etc.) spreading from person to person; affecting everyone in the vicinity.

contain *v* (*tr*) **1** to hold or have; to have in or inside; to consist of. **2** to control, limit, check, or prevent the spread of. **3** to control (oneself or one's feelings). **4** to enclose or surround. **5** (*math*) to be divisible by (a number) without a remainder. —

adj **containable**. [Lat *continere*, to contain, restrain]

container *n* **1** an object designed for holding or storing, such as a box, tin, carton, etc. **2** a huge sealed metal box of standard size and design for carrying goods by lorry or ship.

containerise or **-ize** *v* (*tr*) to put (cargo) into containers. — *n* **containerisation** or **-z-**.

containment *n* the action of preventing the expansion of a hostile power.

contaminate *v* (*tr*) **1** to make impure; to pollute or infect. **2** to make radioactive. — *n* **contaminant**. — *n* **contamination**. [Lat *contaminare*]

contd *abbrev* continued.

contemn *v* (*tr*; *literary*) to despise, disdain or scorn. [Lat *contemnere*]

contemplate *v* **1** (*tr* & *intr*) to think about; to go over (something) mentally; to meditate. **2** (*tr*) to look thoughtfully at. **3** (*tr*) to consider as a possibility. — *n* **contemplation**. [Lat *contemplari*, to survey, look at carefully]

contemplative *adj* **1** thoughtful; meditative. **2** relating to religious contemplation. — *n* a person whose life is spent in religious contemplation. — *adv* **contemplatively**.

contemporaneous *adj* (**with**) existing or happening at the same time or period. — *n* **contemporaneity**. — *adv* **contemporaneously**. [Lat *contemporaneus*, from *con-*, same + *tempus*, time]

contemporary *adj* **1** (**with**) belonging to the same period or time. **2** (**with**) of the same age. **3** modern. — *n* ***-ies*** **1** a person who lives or lived, or thing that exists or existed, at the same time as another. **2** a person of about the same age as another. [Lat *con-*, same + *tempus*, time]

contempt *n* **1** scorn. **2** (*legal*) disregard of, disrespect for, or disobedience to the rules of a court of law. — **hold in contempt** to despise. [Lat *contemnere*, to scorn]

contemptible *adj* **1** despicable; disgusting; vile. **2** worthless; paltry. — *adv* **contemptibly**.

contemptuous *adj* (**of**) scornful. — *adv* **contemptuously**. [Lat *contemnere*, to scorn]

contend *v* **1** (*intr*; **with, for**) to struggle, strive, fight, or compete. **2** (*intr*) to argue earnestly. **3** (*tr*) to say, maintain or assert. [Lat *contendere*, to strive]

contender *n* a contestant or competitor.

content[1] *adj* (**with**) satisfied; happy; uncomplaining. — *v* (*tr*) **1** to satisfy. **2** (**with**) to limit (oneself) to: *contented herself with writing to her MP*. — *n* peaceful satisfaction; peace of mind. — *n* **contentment**. [Lat *contentus*]

contented *adj* peacefully happy or satisfied. — *adv* **contentedly**. — *n* **contentedness**.

content[2] *n* **1** the subject-matter of a book, speech, etc. **2** the proportion in which a particular ingredient is present in something: *a diet with a high starch content*. **3** (in *pl*) the things contained in something. **4** (in *pl*) (a list of) the chapters, etc. in a book. [Lat *continere*, to contain]

contention *n* **1** a point that one asserts or maintains in an argument. **2** argument or debate. [Lat *contentio*, strife, controversy]

bone of contention *n* a point over which there is much disagreement.

contentious *adj* **1** likely to cause argument or quarrelling. **2** quarrelsome or argumentative. — *adv* **contentiously**. [Lat *contendere*, to strive]

contest *n* **1** a competition. **2** a struggle. — *v* (*tr*) **1** to enter the competition or struggle for. **2** to dispute (a claim, someone's will, etc.). — *adj* **contestable**. [Lat *contestari*, to call to witness]

contestant *n* a person who takes part in a contest; a competitor.

context *n* **1** the passage in a text or speech within which a particular word, statement, etc. occurs. **2** circumstances, background or setting. — *adj* **contextual**. — **out of context** without reference to context. [Lat *contextus*, connection]

contiguous *adj* (**with, to**) **1** touching; neighbouring; adjacent. **2** near or next in order or time. — *n* **contiguity**. — *adv* **contiguously**. [Lat *contiguus*, touching]

continence *n* **1** the ability to control one's bowels and bladder. **2** self-control; control over one's appetites and passions. — *adj* **continent**. [Lat *continentia*, self-control]

continent[1]. See **continence**.

continent[2] *n* **1** any of the large land masses of the world—Europe, Asia, Africa, America, Australia and Antarctica. **2** (*cap*) the mainland of Europe, seen as separate from the British Isles. [Lat *continere*, to contain]

continental *adj* **1** belonging or relating to the mainland of the continent of Europe. **2** relating to any of the continents of the world. — *n* (*old*) an inhabitant of the mainland of Europe.

continental breakfast *n* a light breakfast of e.g. rolls and coffee.

continental drift *n* (the theory of) the gradual drifting of large land masses across the Earth's surface, as a result of the instability of its molten interior.

continental quilt *n* a duvet.

continental shelf *n* the sea bed forming a projecting edge to a continent, under relatively shallow water.

contingent *n* **1** a body of troops. **2** any identifiable body of people: *There were boos from the Welsh contingent*. — *adj* **1** (with **on, upon**) dependent on (some uncertain circumstance). **2** liable, but not certain, to occur; accidental. [Lat *contingere*, to touch, happen]

contingency *n* ***-ies*** **1** something liable, but not certain, to occur; a chance happening. **2** something dependent on a chance future happening.

contingency plans *n* (*pl*) plans made in case a certain situation should arise.

continual *adj* **1** constantly happening or done; frequent. **2** constant; never ceasing. — *adv* **continually**. [Lat *continualis*, from *continuus*, uninterrupted]

continuance *n* **1** the act or state of continuing. **2** duration. [Lat *continuare*, to make continuous]

continue *v* **1** (*tr* & *intr*) to go on; not to stop. **2** (*tr* & *intr*) to (cause to) last. **3** (*tr* & *intr*) to carry on or start again after a break. **4** (*intr* with **with**) to keep on with. **5** (*intr*) to keep moving in the same direction: *continue up the hill*. [Lat *continuare*]

continuation *n* **1** the act or process of continuing, often after a break or pause. **2** that which adds to something or carries it on, e.g. a further episode of or sequel to a story.

continuity *n* **1** the state of being continuous, unbroken or consistent. **2** (*television*, *cinema*, etc.) the arrangement of scenes so that one progresses smoothly from another. [Lat *continuitas*, from *continuus*, unbroken]

continuo *n* **-os** (*mus*) a bass part for a keyboard or stringed instrument; the instrument(s) playing this. [Ital, continuous]

continuous *adj* **1** never ceasing. **2** unbroken; uninterrupted. **3** (*gram*) (of tense) formed with the verb *be* + present participle, and representing continuing action. — *adv* **continuously**. [Lat *continuus*, unbroken]

continuous assessment *n* (*education*) the judging of pupils' progress by means of frequent tests throughout the year, as an alternative to occasional examinations.

continuum *n* **-ua** or **-uums** a continuous sequence; an unbroken progression. [Lat *continuus*, unbroken]

contort *v* (*tr* & *intr*) to twist violently out of shape. — *n* **contortion**. [Lat *contorquere*, to twist]

contortionist *n* an entertainer who is able to twist his body into spectacularly unnatural positions.

contour *n* **1** (usu. in *pl*) the distinctive outline of something **2** (also **contour line**) a line on a map joining points of the same height or depth. — *v* (*tr*) **1** to shape the contour of, or shape so as to fit a contour. **2** to mark the contour lines on (a map). [Fr, from Ital *contornare*, to outline]

contra- *pfx* **1** against: *contraception*. **2** opposite: *contraflow*. **3** contrasting: *contradistinction*. **4** (*mus*) lower in pitch: *contrabass*. [Lat]

contraband *n* (the smuggling of) goods prohibited from being imported or exported; smuggled goods. — *adj* prohibited from being imported or exported; smuggled. [Span *contrabanda*, from Lat *contra-* + *bandum*, ban]

contrabass *n* another name for the double bass. [**contra-** (sense **4**)]

contraception *n* the prevention of pregnancy; birth-control. [**contra-** (sense **1**) + **conception**]

contraceptive *n* & *adj* (a drug or device) that prevents pregnancy.

contract *n* **1** an agreement, esp. a legally binding one. **2** a document setting out the terms of such an agreement. — *v* **1** (*intr* & *tr*) to make or become smaller. **2** (*intr* & *tr*) (of muscles) to make or become shorter, so as to bend a joint, etc. **3** (*intr* & *tr*) (of the brows) to draw together into a frown. **4** (*tr*) to catch (a disease). **5** (*tr*) to enter into (an alliance or marriage). **6** (*tr*) to incur or accumulate (a debt). **7** (*tr* & *intr*) (of a word, phrase, etc.) to reduce to a short form: *'Am not' is contracted to 'aren't'*. **8** (*intr* & *tr*; **with**) to promise, bind or arrange by legal agreement: *contract with someone to supply goods*. — *v* **contract in** or **out** (*intr*) to arrange to participate, or not to participate, e.g. in a pension scheme. — *v* **contract out** (*tr*) (also **put out to contract**) (of a business company, etc.) to arrange for (part of a job) to be done by another company. [Lat *contractus*, contraction, agreement]

breach of contract *n* failure to fulfil the terms of a contract: *He's in breach of contract*.

contractable *adj* (of e.g. a disease or habit) liable to be contracted.

contract bridge *n* the usual form of the card game bridge, in which only tricks bid and won count in one's score.

contractible *adj* (of e.g. muscles) capable of being contracted.

contraction *n* **1** the process of contracting or state of being contracted. **2** a tightening of a muscle or set of muscles, esp. those of the abdomen in childbirth. **3** a shortened form of a word or phrase: *'Aren't' is a contraction of 'are not'*.

contractor *n* a person or firm that undertakes work on contract, esp. connected with building, installation of equipment, or the transportation of goods.

contractual *adj* relating to a contract or binding agreement. — *adv* **contractually**.

contradict *v* (*tr*) **1** to assert the opposite of or deny (a statement, etc.) made by (a person). **2** (of a statement, etc.) to disagree or be inconsistent with (another): *Her two accounts contradict each other*. — *n* **contradiction**. — *adj* **contradictory**. [Lat *contra-*, opposite + *dicere*, to say]

contradistinction *n* a distinction made in terms of a contrast between qualities, properties, etc. [**contra-** (sense **3**)]

contraflow *n* a form of traffic diversion used on dual carriageways, with vehicles moving in opposite directions sharing the same carriageway. [**contra-** (sense **2**)]

contraindicate *v* (*tr*) to be a reason for not using (a treatment, operation, etc.). — *n* **contraindication**. [**contra-** (sense **1**)]

contralto *n* **-os** **1** the female singing voice that is lowest in pitch. **2** a singer with this voice. **3** a part to be sung by this voice. [Ital, lower than alto]

contraption *n* (*humorous coll*) a machine or apparatus.

contrapuntal *adj* (*mus*) relating to, or arranged as, counterpoint. — *adv* **contrapuntally**. [Ital *contrappunto*, counterpoint]

contrariwise *adv* reversing the situation; the opposite way round. [**contrary** + **-wise**]

contrary *adj* **1** (**to**) opposite; quite different; opposed. **2** (of a wind) blowing against one; unfavourable. **3** obstinate, perverse, self-willed or wayward. — *n* **-ies** **1** an extreme opposite. **2** either of a pair of opposites. **3** (*logic*) either of two propositions that cannot both be true of the same thing. — *n* **contrariety** or **contrariness**. — *adv* **contrarily**. — **contrary to** in opposition or contrast to. — **on the contrary** in opposition or contrast to what has just been said. — **to the contrary** to the opposite effect; giving the contrasting position. [Lat *contrarius*, from *contra*, opposite]

contrast *n* **1** (**between, with, to**) difference or dissimilarity between things or people that are being compared: *It snowed yesterday — today is warm by contrast. These figures look pretty good in contrast to last year's*. **2** (**to**) a person or thing that is strikingly different from another. **3** the degree of difference in tone between the colours, or the light and dark parts, of a photograph or television picture. — *v* **1** (*tr*) to compare so as to reveal contrasts. **2** (*intr*; **with**) to show a contrast. [Lat *contra*, against + *stare*, to stand]

contravene *v* (*tr*) to break or disobey (a law or rule). — *n* **contravention**. — **in contravention of** in the position of disobeying (a law, etc.) [Lat *contra-*, against + *venire*, to come]

contretemps *n* **1** an awkward or embarrassing moment, happening, etc. **2** a slight disagreement. [Fr, from *contre*, against + *temps*, time]

contribute *v* **1** (*tr & intr*; **to**) to give for some joint purpose **2** (*intr* with **to**) to be one of the causes of. **3** (*tr*) to supply (an article, etc.) for publication in a magazine, etc. — *n* **contributor**. — *adj* **contributory**. [Lat *contribuere*, to bring together]

contribution *n* **1** the act of contributing. **2** something contributed, e.g. money, or an article for a magazine.

contrite *adj* sorry for something one has done. — *adv* **contritely**. — *n* **contrition**. [Lat *contritus*, crushed]

contrive *v* (*tr*) **1** to manage or succeed. **2** to bring about: *contrive one's escape*. **3** to make or construct, esp. with difficulty. [OFr *controver*, to find]

contrivance *n* **1** the act or power of contriving. **2** a device or apparatus. **3** a scheme; a piece of cunning.

contrived *adj* forced or artificial: *a contrived ending to a play*.

control *n* **1** authority or charge; power to influence or guide: *in control*; *take control*; *under control*; *out of control*. **2** (a method of) limitation: *impose strict controls on spending*. **3** (in *pl*) the levers, switches, etc. by which a machine, etc. is operated. **4** the people in control of some operation: *mission control*. **5** the place where something is checked: *go through passport control*. **6** something used as a standard against which to check the results of an experiment. **7** (*spiritualism*) a dead person guiding a medium. — *v* ***-ll-*** (*tr*) **1** to have or exercise control over. **2** to regulate. **3** to limit. **4** to check or verify against a standard: *a controlled experiment*. — *n* **controllability**. — *adj* ***controllable***. [OFr *contrerolle*, duplicate account or register]

controller *n* **1** a person or thing that controls. **2** an official in charge of public finance. **3** a person in charge of the finances of an enterprise, etc.

control tower *n* a tall building at an airport from which take-off and landing instructions are given.

controversy *n* ***-ies*** a usu. long-standing disagreement or dispute. — *adj* **controversial**. — *adv* **controversially**. [Lat *contra-*, against + *vertere*, to turn]

contumacy *n* (*formal*) obstinate refusal to obey; resistance to authority. — *adj* **contumacious**. — *adv* **contumaciously**. [Lat *contumacia*, stubbornness]

contumely *n* ***-ies*** (*formal*) scornful or insulting treatment or words. — *adj* **contumelious**. [Lat *contumelia*, outrage, insult]

contuse *v* (*tr*; *med*) to bruise. — *n* **contusion**. [Lat *contundere*, to beat, bruise]

conundrum *n* **1** a confusing problem. **2** a riddle, esp. involving a pun.

conurbation *n* an extensive built-up area, consisting of several towns whose outskirts have merged. [**con-** + Lat *urbs*, city]

convalesce *v* (*intr*) to recover one's strength after an illness, operation or injury, esp. by resting. [Lat *convalescere*, to recover]

convalescent *n* & *adj* (a person who is) recovering from an illness. — *n* **convalescence**.

convection *n* the transmission of heat through liquids or gases by means of currents that begin to circulate as heated particles rise from the cooler and denser areas to the warmer, less dense areas. [Lat *con-*, together + *vehere*, to carry]

convector *n* a heating apparatus that circulates warm air by convection. [Lat *con-* together + *vehere*, to carry]

convene *v* (*tr* & *intr*) to (cause to) assemble: *convene a meeting*. [Lat *con-*, together + *venire*, to come]

convener or **convenor** *n* a person who convenes or chairs a meeting.

convenient *adj* **1** **(for, to)** fitting in with one's plans, etc.; not causing trouble or difficulty. **2** useful; handy; saving time and trouble. **3** available; at hand. — *adv* **conveniently**. [Lat *convenire*, to fit, be suitable]

convenience *n* **1** the quality of being convenient. **2** something useful or advantageous. **3** a lavatory, esp. a public one. — **at one's convenience** when and where it suits one.

convenience food *n* food (partly) prepared before sale, so as to be (nearly) ready for serving.

flag of convenience see **flag**.

marriage of convenience see **marriage**.

convent *n* **1** a community of nuns, or the building they occupy. **2** a school where the teaching is done by nuns. [Lat *conventus*, assembly]

conventicle *n* (esp. *hist*) a secret, esp. unlawful, religious meeting. [Lat *conventiculum*, assembly]

convention *n* **1** a large and formal conference or assembly. **2** a formal treaty or agreement. **3** a custom or generally accepted practice, esp. in social behaviour. [Lat *conventio*, meeting, agreement]

conventional *adj* **1** traditional; normal; customary. **2** conservative or unoriginal: *conventional attitudes*. **3** (of weapons or war) non-nuclear. — *v* (*tr*) **conventionalise** or **-ize**. — *n* **conventionality**. — *adv* **conventionally**.

converge *v* (*intr*) **1** **(on, upon)** to move towards or meet at one point. **2** (of e.g. opinions) to tend towards one another; to coincide — *n* **convergence**. — *adj* **convergent**. [Lat *con-*, together + *vergere*, to turn, incline]

conversant *adj* **(with)** having a thorough knowledge of. [Lat *conversari*, to associate with]

conversation *n* informal talk between people. [Lat *conversatio*]

conversational *adj* **1** relating to conversation. **2** used in conversation rather than formal language. **3** communicative; talkative.

conversationalist *n* a person fond of, or skilled in, conversation.

conversation piece *n* **1** a striking object that stimulates conversation. **2** a group portrait, e.g. showing members of a family engaged in characteristic activities in their usual setting.

converse[1] *v* (*intr*; **with**) to hold a conversation; to talk. [Lat *conversari*, to associate with]

converse[2] *adj* reverse; opposite. — *n* opposite. — *adj* **conversely**. [Lat *conversus*, opposite]

conversion *n* **1** the act of converting. **2** something converted to another use. **3** (*Rugby*) the scoring of one or two further points after a try by kicking the ball over the goal.

convert *v* **1** (*tr* & *intr*; **into**) to change in form or function. **2** (*tr* & *intr*; **to**) to win over, or be won over, to another religion, opinion, etc. **3** (*tr*; **into, to**) to change into another measuring system or currency. **4** (*tr*; *Rugby*) to achieve a conversion after (a try). — *n* **converter** or **convertor**. — *adj* **convertible**. [Lat *convertere*, to change]

convex *adj* (of a surface or shape) outward-curving, like the surface of the eye. — *n* **convexity, -ies**. ◇ See also **concave**. [Lat *convexus*, arched]

convey *v* (*tr*) **1** to carry; to transport. **2** to communicate: *difficult to convey exactly what I mean*. **3** (*legal*) to transfer the ownership of (property). — *adj* **conveyable**. — *n* **conveyer** or **conveyor**. [OFr *conveier*, from Lat *via*, way]

conveyance *n* **1** the process of conveying. **2** a vehicle of any kind. **3** (*legal*) the transfer of the ownership of property. — *n* **conveyancer**. — *n* **conveyancing**.

conveyor belt *n* an endless moving rubber or metal belt for conveying articles, e.g. in a factory.

convict *v* (*tr*; **of**) to prove or declare (someone) guilty of a crime. — *n* a person serving a prison sentence. [Lat *convincere*]

conviction *n* **1** the act of convicting; an instance of being convicted. **2** the state of being convinced; a strong belief. — **carry conviction** to be convincing. [Lat *convincere*, to overcome, convict]

convince *v* (*tr*; **of**) to persuade; to cause to believe. — *adj* **convincing**. — *adv* **convincingly**. [Lat *convincere*, to overcome]

convinced *adj* firm in one's belief: *a convinced atheist*.

convivial *adj* **1** lively, jovial, sociable and cheerful. **2** festive. — *n* **conviviality**. — *adv* **convivially**. [Lat *convivialis*, from *convivium*, feast]

convocation *n* **1** the act of summoning together. **2** an assembly. **3** the synod or assembly of Anglican bishops and clergy. **4** a formal assembly of graduates of a college or university. [Lat *convocatio*, summoning together]

convoke *v* (*tr*) to call together; to assemble: *convoke the committee*. [Lat *convocare*]

convoluted *adj* **1** coiled and twisted. **2** complicated: *convoluted reasoning*. — *n* **convolution**. [Lat *convolvere*, to roll together]

convolvulus *n* the bindweed, or other twining plant of the same family. [Lat *convolvere*, to roll up]

convoy *n* a group of vehicles or merchant ships travelling together, or under escort. — *v* (*tr*) to accompany for protection. [OFr *convoier*, from Lat *con-*, with + *via*, way]

convulse *v* (*tr* & *intr*) to jerk or distort violently (as if) by a powerful spasm. — *adj* **convulsive**. — *adv* **convulsively**. [Lat *convellere*, to pull violently]

convulsion *n* **1** the state of being convulsed. **2** (often in *pl*) a sudden jerking movement caused by involuntary contraction of the muscles. **3** (in *pl*; *coll*) spasms of laughter. [Lat *convulsio*]

cony *n* **-ies** **1** a rabbit. **2** its fur used for clothing, etc. [OFr *conil*]

coo[1] *n* the soft murmuring call of a dove. — *v* **cooed** **1** (*intr*) to make this sound. **2** (*intr* & *tr*) to murmur affectionately. — *adj* **cooing**. — *adv* **cooingly**. [Imit.]

coo[2] *interj* (*coll*) used to express amazement.

cooee *interj* used to attract attention. — *v* **-eed** (*intr*) to call 'cooee'. [From an Australian Aboriginal language]

cook *v* **1** (*tr* & *intr*) to prepare or be prepared by heating. **2** (*tr*; *coll*) to alter (accounts, etc.) dishonestly. — *n* a person who cooks or prepares food. — **cook up** (*coll*) to invent: *cook up an excuse*. — **what's cooking?** (*coll*) what's up?; what's the plan? [OE *coc*, from Lat *coquus*]

cooker *n* **1** an apparatus, or special pot, for cooking food. **2** (*coll*; also **cooking-apple**) an apple for cooking rather than eating raw.

cookery *n* the art or practice of cooking food.

cookery book or **cookbook** *n* a book of recipes.

cookie *n* **1** (*NAm*) a biscuit. **2** (*Scot*) a bun. **3** (*coll*) a person: *a smart cookie*. — **that's the way the cookie crumbles** (*coll*) **1** that's what you'd expect. **2** that's how it is. [Dut *koekje*, little cake]

cool *adj* **1** between cold and warm; fairly cold. **2** pleasantly fresh; free of heat: *a cool breeze*. **3** calm: *keep a cool head*. **4** lacking enthusiasm; unfriendly: *a cool response*. **5** impudent; audacious; brazen. **6** (of a large sum) at least: *made a cool million*. **7** (*coll*) admirable; excellent. **8** (of colours) suggestive of coolness — typically pale and containing blue. — *n* **1** a cool part or period; coolness: *in the cool of the evening*. **2** (*coll*) self-control; composure: *lose* or *keep one's cool*. — *v* (*tr* & *intr*; **down, off**) to make or become cool. — *adv* **coolly**. — *n* **coolness**. — **cool it** (*coll*) to calm down. — *v* **cool off** **1** (*tr* & *intr*; also **cool down**) to calm down. **2** (*intr*) to lose one's enthusiasm. — **cool one's heels** to be kept waiting. — **play it cool** to deal with a situation calmly but warily. [OE *col*]

coolant *n* a liquid or gas used as a cooling agent, esp. a fluid used to remove heat from a working engine.

cooler *n* **1** a container or device for cooling things. **2** (*slang*) prison.

cooling-off period *n* an interval for reflection and negotiation before (otherwise over-hasty) action.

cooling-tower *n* a large structure in which water heated in an industrial process is cooled for re-use.

coolie *n* (*offensive*) **1** an unskilled native labourer in Eastern countries. **2** (*SAfr*) an Indian. [Tamil *kuli*, hired person]

coomb *n* a hollow in a hillside, or a short valley. [OE *cumb*, valley]

coon *n* **1** (*offensive slang*) a black person. **2** (*US coll*) a raccoon.

coop *n* a cage for hens. — *v* **coop up** (*tr*) to shut into a small place. [Related to OE *cypa*, basket]

co-op *n* (*coll*) a co-operative society, or a shop run by one.

cooper *n* a person who makes or repairs barrels. [Lat *cuparius*, from *cupa*, cask]

co-operate *v* (*intr*) **1** (**with**) to work together. **2** to be helpful, or willing to fit in with others' plans. — *n* **co-operation**. — *n* **co-operator**. [**co-** + **operate**]

co-operative *adj* **1** relating to, or giving, co-operation. **2** helpful; willing to fit in with others' plans, etc. **3** (of a business or farm) jointly owned by workers, with profits shared equally. — *n* a co-operative business or farm. — *adv* **co-operatively**.

co-operative society *n* a profit-sharing association for the cheaper purchase of goods.

co-opt *v* (*tr*) (of the members of a body, etc.) to choose as an additional member. — *n* **co-option**. — *adj* **co-optive**. [Lat *cooptare*, to appoint, admit as member]

co-ordinate *v* (*tr*) **1** to combine, integrate and adjust (a number of different parts or processes) so as to relate smoothly one to another. **2** to bring (one's limbs or bodily movements) into a smoothly functioning relationship. — *adj* **1** relating to, or involving, co-ordination or co-ordinates. **2** (*gram*) (of clauses) equal in status, as when joined by *and* or *but*. — *n* **1** (*math* or *geog*) either of a pair of numbers taken from a vertical and horizontal axis which together establish the position of a fixed point, e.g. on a map. **2** (in *pl*) garments designed to be worn together. — *n* **co-ordination**. — *n* **co-ordinator**. [**co-** + **subordinate**]

coot *n* **1** a water bird with a white patch above the beak. **2** (*old coll*) a fool. [MidE *cote*]

cop[1] *n* (*slang*) a policeman. [**copper**[2]]

cop[2] *v* **-pp-** (*tr*; *slang*) **1** to catch. **2** to grab; to seize. **3** to suffer (a punishment, etc.). — **cop it** (*slang*) to be punished. — *v* **cop out** (*intr*; *coll*) to escape or withdraw, esp. through cowardice (*n* **cop-out**). — **not much cop** (*coll*) of little use or interest. [OFr *caper*, to seize]

cope[1] *v* (*intr*) **1** (with **with**) to deal with (problems, etc.) successfully. **2** to manage; to get by. [OFr *couper*, to hit]

cope[2] *n* a long sleeveless cape worn by clergy on ceremonial occasions. [Lat *capa*]

coping *n* the top row of stones in a wall. [Related to **cope**[2]]

coping-stone *n* one of the stones forming the top row in a wall, etc.

co-pilot *n* the assistant pilot of an aircraft.

copious *adj* plentiful. — *adv* **copiously**. [Lat *copiosus*]

copper[1] *n* **1** an element (symbol **Cu**), a brownish-red metal. **2** any coin of low value made of copper or bronze. **3** a large metal vessel for boiling water in. — *adj* of the brownish-red colour of copper. — *adj* **coppery**. [Lat *cuprum*, from *cyprium aes*, brass of Cyprus]

copper-bottomed *adj* **1** (of e.g. ships or pans) having the bottom protected by a layer of copper. **2** (*coll*) reliable, esp. financially.

copperhead *n* a poisonous Australian or American snake with a copper-coloured head.

copperplate *n* **1** (*printing*) a copper plate used for engraving or etching, or a print made from it. **2** fine regular handwriting of the style formerly taught in schools and used on copperplates.

copper[2] *n* (*slang*) a policeman. [**cop**[2]]

coppice *n* a small wood of low-growing trees and bushes, with thick undergrowth, for periodic cutting. [OFr *copeiz*]

copra *n* the dried kernel of the coconut, yielding coconut oil. [Port, from Malayalam (Indian language) *koppara*]

copse *n* a coppice.

Copt *n* **1** a member of the **Coptic Church**, a branch of the Christian Church found in Egypt. **2** an Egyptian descended from the ancient Egyptians.

Coptic *adj* **1** relating to the Copts. — *n* & *adj* (of or in) the language of the Copts, now used only in the Coptic Church. [Gr *Aigyptios*, Egyptian]

copula *n* (*gram*) a verb that links subject and complement, e.g. *is* in *She is a doctor*. [Lat, bond]

copulate *v* (*intr*; **with**) to have sexual intercourse. — *n* **copulation**. [Lat *copulare*, to bind, couple]

copy *n* **-*ies*** **1** an imitation or reproduction. **2** one of the many specimens of a book, or of a particular issue of a magazine, newspaper, etc. **3** written material for printing, esp. as distinct from illustrations, etc. **4** the wording of an advertisement. **5** material suitable for a newspaper article. — *v* **-*ies***, **-*ied*** **1** (*tr*) to imitate. **2** (*tr*) to make a copy of. **3** (*tr* & *intr*) to reproduce; to photocopy. **4** (*tr* & *intr*) to make a copy of another's work, pretending that it is one's own. **5** (*tr*) to give a copy to. — *n* **copier**. [Lat *copia*, transcript]

copybook *n* a book of handwriting examples for copying. — *adj* **1** (*derog*) unoriginal. **2** faultless; perfect. — **blot one's copybook** to spoil one's good record by misbehaviour or error.

copycat *n* (*derog*) a mere imitator.

copyist *n* **1** a person who makes copies in writing. **2** an imitator.

copyright *n* the sole right to print, publish, translate, perform, film or record a literary, dramatic, musical or artistic work.

copywriter *n* a person who writes advertising copy.

coquette *n* a flirtatious woman. — *n* **coquetry**. — *adj* **coquettish**. — *adv* **coquettishly**. — *n* **coquettishness**. [Fr *coquet*, dimin. of *coq*, cock]

cor-. See **con-**.

coracle *n* a small oval rowing-boat made of wickerwork covered with hides or other waterproof material. [Welsh *corwgl*]

coral *n* **1** a hard pink, red or white material made up of the skeletons of polyps, tiny tubular sea creatures, and much used in jewellery. **2** a pinkish-orange colour. — *adj* pinkish-orange in colour. — *adj* **coralline**. [Gr *korallion*]

coral island or **reef** *n* an island or reef formed by the accumulation of coral deposits on the sea bed.

cor anglais n ***cors anglais*** a woodwind musical instrument similar to, but lower in pitch than, the oboe. [Fr, English horn]

corbel *n* (*archit*) a stone or timber projecting from a wall, taking the weight of e.g. a parapet, arch or bracket. — *adj* **corbelled**. — *n* **corbelling**. [OFr, crow]

cord *n* **1** (a piece of) thin rope or thick string. **2** (*anat*) a string-like bodily organ. **3** the cable of an electrical appliance. **4** a ribbed fabric, esp. corduroy. **5** (in *pl*) corduroy trousers. **6** a unit of measurement for cut wood equal to 128 cubic ft. (3.63 m^3). [Gr *chorde*, string]

corded *adj* (of fabric) ribbed.

cordless *adj* (of an electrical appliance) operating without a cord.

cordial *adj* **1** warm and affectionate. **2** heartfelt; profound: *a cordial dislike*. — *n* a fruit-flavoured drink. — *n* **cordiality**. — *adv* **cordially**. [Lat *cordialis*, from *cor*, heart]

cordite *n* a smokeless explosive, stringy in appearance, used in guns and bombs. [**cord**]

cordon *n* **1** a line of police or soldiers, or a system of road blocks, encircling an area so as to prevent or control passage into or out of it. **2** a ribbon bestowed as a mark of honour. **3** a fruit tree trained to grow as a single stem. — *v* **cordon off** (*tr*) to close off with a cordon. [Fr, dimin. of *corde*, cord]

cordon bleu *adj* (of a cook or cookery) of the highest standard. — *n* ***cordons bleus*** a cook of the highest standard. [Fr, blue ribbon]

corduroy *n* **1** a thick ribbed cotton fabric. **2** (in *pl*) trousers made of corduroy. **3** (*NAm*; also **corduroy road**) a road made of logs lying side by side.

core *n* **1** the fibrous case at the centre of an apple, pear, etc., containing the seeds. **2** the innermost, central, essential or unchanging part. **3** (*geol*) the inner part of the earth. **4** (*archaeol*) the lump of stone left after flakes have been struck off it for shaping into tools. **5** the part of a nuclear reactor containing the fissionable material. **6** (*electr*) a piece of magnetic material that concentrates the magnetic field produced as an electric current passes through a surrounding coil. **7** a ring-shaped piece of magnetisable material formerly used in a computer memory. **8** a computer memory. **9** the inner part of an electric cable. **10** a cylindrical portion of rock or soil removed with a hollow tubular drill. — *v* (*tr*) to remove the core of (an apple, etc.).

corer *n* a knife with a hollow cylindrical blade for coring fruit.

co-respondent *n* (*legal*) in divorce cases, a person said to have committed adultery with the partner (called the *respondent*) against whom the case is being brought.

corgi *n* a short-legged dog with a thick coat and fox-like head. [Welsh *cor*, dwarf + *ci*, dog]

coriander *n* a European plant whose strong-smelling leaves and seeds are used as a flavouring. [Gr *koriannon*]

Corinthian *adj* **1** belonging to Corinth in Greece. **2** (*archit*) denoting a style of column with a heavily carved capital with a distinctive acanthus-leaf design. ◇ See also **Doric** and **Ionic**.

cork *n* **1** the light outer bark of a Mediterranean tree, the cork oak. **2** a piece of this used as a stopper for a bottle, etc. — *v* **1** (*tr*; **up**) to stop (a bottle, etc.) with a cork. **2** (*tr*; **up**) to suppress (one's feelings, etc.). **3** (*intr* with **up**; *slang*) to be quiet. [Arabic *qurq*, from Lat *quercus*, oak]

corkage *n* the fee charged by a restaurant for serving to customers wine that they have bought elsewhere.

corked *adj* (of wine) spoilt as a result of having a faulty cork.

corkscrew *n* a tool with a spiral spike for screwing into bottle corks to remove them. — *adj* shaped like a corkscrew. — *v* (*intr*) to move spirally.

corker *n* (*old slang*) something or someone marvellous.

corm *n* the bulb-like underground stem of certain plants. [Gr *kormos*, lopped tree trunk]

cormorant *n* a large black seabird. [Fr, from Lat *corvus marinus*, sea raven]

corn[1] *n* **1** cereal plants, esp. in Britain wheat, oats or barley and in N America maize. **2** the seeds of these plants; grain. **3** (*slang*) something stale or old-fashioned. [OE]

corncob *n* the core part of an ear of maize, to which the grains are attached (**corn on the cob** a corncob cooked and served as a vegetable).

corn dolly *n* a figure made of plaited straw.

cornflakes *n* (*pl*) toasted maize flakes, eaten as a breakfast cereal.

cornflour *n* finely ground flour, usu. made from maize.

cornflower *n* a plant with deep blue flowers that grows in cornfields.

corn[2] *n* a small patch of hardened skin, esp. on a toe. — **tread on someone's corns** (*coll*) to hurt someone's feelings. [Lat *cornu*, horn]

Corn. *abbrev* Cornwall.

corncrake *n* a bird with a harsh grating cry, that inhabits cornfields. [**corn**[1] + *crake*, from Norse *krakr*, crow]

cornea *n* the transparent covering of the eyeball. — *adj* **corneal**. [Lat *cornea* (*tela*), horny (tissue)]

corned *adj* (of beef) salted, cooked and canned. [**corn**[1]]

cornelian or **carnelian** *n* a gemstone, a translucent red quartz. [OFr *corneline*]

corner *n* **1** a point or place where lines or surface-edges meet; the inside or outside of the angle so formed. **2** an intersection between roads. **3** a quiet or remote place. **4** an awkward situation: *in a tight corner*. **5** (*econ*) control of a particular market gained by buying up the total stocks of a commodity, to re-sell at one's own price. **6** (*boxing*) either of the angles of the ring used as a base between bouts by contestants. **7** (*football*) a free kick from a corner of the field. — *v* **-r-** **1** (*tr*) to force into a place or position from which escape is difficult. **2** (*tr*) to gain control of (a market) by buying up total stocks of a commodity. **3** (*intr*) (of a driver or vehicle) to turn a corner. — **cut corners** to spend less money, effort, time, etc. on something than one should. — **take a corner** to corner: *took the corner too fast*. — **turn the corner 1** to go round a corner. **2** to get past the most dangerous stage, e.g. of an illness. [OFr *corne*, corner, horn]

cornerstone *n* **1** a stone built into the corner of the foundation of a building. **2** a crucial or indispensable part; a basis: *the cornerstone of his argument*.

cornet *n* **1** a brass musical instrument similar to the trumpet. **2** a cone-shaped edible holder for ice cream; an ice-cream cone. — *n* **cornetist** or **cornettist**. [OFr, dimin. of Lat *cornu*, horn]

cornice *n* **1** a decorative border of moulded plaster round a ceiling. **2** (*archit*) the lower section of the horizontal layer of masonry surmounting a row of columns. **3** (*archit*) a projecting moulding at the top of an external wall. **4** (*art*) the projecting top part of a pedestal. **5** (*mountaineering*) an overhang formed of snow or ice. [Ital, crow]

Cornish *adj* belonging to Cornwall, its people, or language. — *n* the Celtic language once spoken in Cornwall, related to Welsh.

Cornish pasty *n* a semicircular folded pastry case containing meat and vegetables.

cornucopia *n* (*art*) a horn full to overflowing with fruit and other produce, used as a symbol of abundance. — *adj* **cornucopian**. [Lat *cornu*, horn + *copia*, abundance]

corny *adj* **-ier**, **-iest** (*coll*) **1** (of a joke) old and stale. **2** embarrassingly old-fashioned or sentimental. — *adv* **cornily**. — *n* **corniness**. [**corn**[1]]

corolla *n* (*bot*) a flower's circle of petals. [Lat, garland]

corollary *n* **-*ies* 1** something that follows from another thing that has been proved. **2** a natural or obvious consequence. [Lat *corollarium*, gift of money, orig. for a garland, from *corolla*, garland]

corona *n* **-*ae*** or **-*as* 1** a ring of light round the sun or moon. **2** the edge of the sun's gassy atmosphere, visible when the sun is in total eclipse behind the moon. **3** (*anat*) the name of any of several more or less crown-shaped bodily parts. **4** (*bot*) a crown-like structure on top of a seed or inside the corolla. **6** (*electr*) a glow surrounding a conductor. [Lat, crown]

coronary *adj* (*physiol*) denoting the arteries supplying blood to the heart muscle. — *n* **-*ies*** a coronary thrombosis. [Lat *coronarius*, encircling (the heart) like a wreath, from *corona*, wreath]

coronary thrombosis *n* the formation of an obstructive blood clot in a coronary artery, causing acute pain and the death of part of the heart muscle.

coronation *n* the ceremony of crowning a king, queen or consort. [Lat *coronatio*, from *corona*, crown]

coroner *n* **1** an official who inquires into sudden or accidental deaths, and investigates cases of treasure trove. **2** the principal officer of one of the six ancient divisions of the Isle of Man. [OFr *corouner*, supervisor of the Crown's pleas]

coronet *n* **1** a small crown. **2** a circlet of jewels for the head. [OFr, dimin. of *corone*, crown]

corp. *abbrev* **1** (*cap*) corporal. **2** corporation.

corpora. See **corpus**.

corporal[1] *n* an officer in the army or air force just below a sergeant in rank. [Ital *caporale*, from *capo*, head]

corporal[2] *adj* relating to the human body. [Lat *corporalis*, from *corpus*, body]

corporal punishment *n* physical punishment such as beating or caning.

corporate *adj* **1** shared by members of a group; joint. **2** belonging, or relating, to a corporation: *corporate finance*. **3** formed into a corporation: *a corporate body*. — *adv* **corporately**. [Lat *corporare*, to form into a body]

corporation *n* **1** a body of people acting jointly e.g. for administration or business purposes. **2** the council of a town or city. **3** (*facet*) a paunch. [Lat *corporatio*, trade guild]

corporation tax *n* a tax paid by companies on the profits they make.

corporeal *adj* relating to the body as distinct from the soul; bodily; physical; material. — *n* **corporeality** — *adv* **corporeally**. [Lat *corpus*, body]

corps *n* ***corps*** **1** a military body or division: *the intelligence corps*. **2** a body of people engaged in particular work: *the diplomatic corps*. [Fr, body]

corps de ballet *n* a company of ballet dancers, e.g. at a theatre. [Fr]

corpse *n* the dead body of a human being. [Lat *corpus*, body]

corpus *n* ***corpora*** **1** a body of writings, e.g. by a particular author. **2** a body of written and/or spoken material for language research. **3** (*anat*) the name of any of various structures within the body. [Lat, body]

corpulent *adj* fat; fleshy; obese. — *n* **corpulence**. [Lat *corpulentus*]

corpuscle *n* (*physiol*) a red or white blood cell. — *adj* **corpuscular**. [Lat *corpusculum*, dimin. of *corpus*, body]

corral (esp. *NAm*) *n* an enclosure for driving horses or cattle into. — *v* **-*ll*-** (*tr*) to herd or pen into a corral. [Span]

correct *v* (*tr*) **1** to set or put right; to remove errors from. **2** to mark the errors in. **3** to adjust or make better. **4** (*old*) to rebuke or punish. — *adj* **1** free from error; accurate; not mistaken. **2** right; proper; appropriate. **3** conforming to accepted standards: *very correct in his behaviour*. — *adv* **correctly**. — *n* **correctness**. — *n* **corrector**. — **I stand corrected** I acknowledge my mistake. [Lat *corrigere*]

correcting fluid *n* a thick, usu. white, liquid for covering up errors in writing or typing.

correction *n* **1** the act of correcting. **2** an alteration that corrects something. **3** (*old*) punishment.

corrective *adj* having the effect of correcting or adjusting. — *n* something that has this effect.

correlate *v* **1** (*intr* & *tr*; **with**) to link up; to relate one to another: *Smoking in pregnancy correlates with low birth weight*. **2** to combine, compare, show relationships between (information, reports, etc). — *n* **correlation**. [Lat *cor-*, with + *relatio*, carrying back]

correlative *adj* **1** mutually linked. **2** (*gram*) (of words) used as an inter-related pair, like *either* and *or*.

correspond *v* (*intr*) **1** (**to**) to be similar or equivalent: *an increase in wages followed by a corresponding increase in prices*. **2** (**with, to**) to be in agreement; to match. **3** (**with**) to exchange letters. [Lat *cor-*, with + *respondere*, to answer]

correspondence *n* **1** similarity; equivalence. **2** agreement. **3** communication by letters; letters received or sent.

correspondence course *n* a course of study conducted by post.

correspondent *n* **1** a person with whom one exchanges letters. **2** a person employed by a newspaper to write reports from a particular part of the world, or on a particular topic.

corridor *n* **1** a passageway, esp. one off which rooms open or, on a train, one giving access to compartments. **2** a strip

of land through foreign territory, giving access e.g. to a port. **3** a restricted route through the air that air traffic must follow. [Ital *corridore*, corridor, place for running]
corridors of power *n* (*pl*) places where the people who make the important decisions are to be found.

corrie *n* in the Highlands of Scotland, a hollow in the side of a hill. [Gaelic *coire*, pot]

corrigendum *n* **-da** an error for correction, e.g. in a book. [Lat, something to be corrected]

corroborate *v* (*tr*) to confirm (e.g. someone's statement): *corroborating evidence*. — *n* **corroboration**. — *adj* **corroborative**. — *n* **corroborator**. [Lat *corroborare*, to strengthen]

corroboree *n* (*Austr*) **1** a ceremonial or warlike dance. **2** a noisy gathering. [From an Australian Aboriginal language]

corrode *v* **1** (*tr* & *intr*) (of e.g. rust or chemicals) to eat away (a material or object) little by little, or (of a material or object) to be gradually eaten away. **2** (*tr*) to destroy gradually: *a relationship corroded by mutual ill feeling*. [Lat *corrodere*, to gnaw to pieces]

corrosion *n* **1** the process of corroding. **2** a corroded part or patch. — *adj* **corrosive**. [Lat *corrodere*, to gnaw to pieces]

corrugate *v* (*tr*) to fold into parallel ridges, so as to make stronger: *corrugated iron*. — *n* **corrugation**. [Lat *corrugare*, to wrinkle]

corrupt *v* **1** (*tr* & *intr*) to change for the worse, esp. morally. **2** (*tr*) to spoil, deform or make impure. **3** (*tr*) to bribe. **4** (*intr*) to decay or deteriorate. — *adj* **1** morally evil. **2** accepting bribes. **3** dishonest. **4** (of a text) so full of errors and alterations as to be unreliable. **5** (*comput*) (of a program or data) containing errors arising e.g. from a fault in the hardware or software. — *n* **corruptibility**.— *adj* **corruptible**. — *adj* **corruptive**. — *adv* **corruptly**. [Lat *corrumpere*, to spoil]
corruption *n* **1** the process of corrupting or condition of being corrupt. **2** a deformed form of a word or phrase: *'Santa Claus' is a corruption of 'Saint Nicholas'*.

corsage *n* a small spray of flowers for pinning to the bodice of a dress. [OFr, bodily shape, later bodice, from Lat *corpus*]

corsair *n* (*old*) **1** a pirate or pirate ship. **2** a privately owned warship. [OFr *corsaire*]

corselet *n* **1** (also **corslet**; *hist*) a protective garment or piece of armour for the upper part of the body. **2** (also **corselette**) a woman's undergarment combining girdle and brassière. [OFr dimin. of *cors*, body, bodice]

corset *n* **1** a tightly fitting undergarment stiffened by strips of bone or plastic, for shaping, controlling or supporting the figure. **2** (*finance*) government restrictions on the lending power of banks. — *v* **-t-** (*tr*) **1** to put a corset on. **2** to restrict. — *n* **corsetry**. [OFr dimin. of *cors*, body, bodice]

cortège *n* a procession, esp. at a funeral. [Fr, from Ital *corteggio*, retinue]

cortex *n* **-tices** (*anat*) the outer layer of an organ, e.g. the brain. — *adj* **cortical**. [Lat *cortex*, tree bark]

cortisone *n* a steroid hormone used medicinally to control allergies, skin diseases and inflammation. [*Corti*co*s*ter*one*, hormone secreted by the cortex of the adrenal gland]

corundum *n* a very hard mineral composed of aluminium oxide, used as an abrasive and occurring also in the form of rubies and sapphires. [Tamil *kuruntam*]

coruscate *v* (*intr*) to sparkle. — *n* **coruscation**. [Lat *coruscare*, to sparkle]

corvette *n* **1** a small warship for escorting larger vessels. **2** (*hist*) a sailing warship with one tier of guns. [Dut *corver*, pursuit vessel]

cos[1] *n* (also **cos lettuce**) a lettuce with slim crisp leaves. [*Cos*, Greek island of origin]

cos[2] *abbrev* cosine.

cosec. *abbrev* cosecant.

cosecant *n* (*math*) in a right-angled triangle, the ratio of the hypotenuse to the side opposite a given angle. ◇ See also **secant, sine, cotangent [co-]**

cosh *n* a club, esp. a rubber one filled with metal, used as a weapon. — *v* (*tr*; *coll*) to hit with a cosh or something heavy. [Perhaps Romany *koshter*, stick]

cosine *n* (*math*) in a right-angled triangle, the ratio of a side adjacent to a given angle to the hypotenuse. ◇ See also **secant, sine, tangent [co-]**

cosmetic *adj* **1** used to beautify the face, body or hair. **2** improving superficially, for the sake of appearance only. — *n* a cosmetic application, esp. for the face. — *adv* **cosmetically**. [Gr *kosmetikos*, of adornment]

cosmic *adj* **1** relating to the whole cosmos; universal. **2** coming from outer space: *cosmic rays*. **3** (*coll*) large or significant. — *adv* **cosmically**. [Gr *kosmikos*, from *kosmos*, universe]

cosmogony *n* **-ies** (a theory about) the way the universe was formed. [Gr *kosmos*, universe + *-gonia*, giving birth to]

cosmology *n* the science dealing with the nature of the universe. — *adj* **cosmological**. — *n* **cosmologist**. [Gr *kosmos*, universe + **-logy**]

cosmonaut *n* a Russian astronaut. [Gr *kosmos*, universe + *nautes*, sailor]

cosmopolitan *adj* **1** belonging to, or representative of, all parts of the world. **2** free of national prejudices; international in experience and outlook. — *n* a person of this type; a citizen of the world. — *n* **cosmopolitanism**. [Gr *kosmos*, universe + *polites*, citizen]

cosmos *n* the universe seen as an ordered system. [Gr *kosmos*, world order, universe]

Cossack *n* a member of a people of SE Russia famous as horsemen. — *adj* belonging, or relating, to this people. [Ukrainian (the language of the Ukraine) *kozak*, orig. freebooter]

cosset *v* **-t-** (*tr*) to treat too kindly; to pamper. [Perhaps OE *kossetung*, kissing]

cost *v* ***cost*** **1** (*tr*) to be obtainable at a certain price. **2** (*tr*) to involve the loss or sacrifice of. **3** (*tr*; ***costed***) to estimate or decide the cost of. **4** (*tr* & *intr*; *coll*) to put (someone) to some expense. — *n* **1** what something costs. **2** loss or sacrifice. **3** (in *pl*; *legal*) the expenses of a case. — **at all costs** no matter what the risk or effort may be. — **cost someone dear** to prove costly to someone. — **count the cost 1** to consider all the risks before taking action. **2** to realise the bad effects of something done. — **to one's cost** with some loss or disadvantage. [Lat *constare*, to cost]

cost-effective *adj* giving acceptable value for money.

cost of living *n* the cost to the individual of ordinary necessities such as food and clothing.

cost price *n* the price paid for something by the retailer, before resale at a profit.

costal *adj* (*anat*) relating to the ribs. [Lat *costa*, rib]

co-star *n* a fellow star in a film, play, etc. — *v* **-rr-** (*intr*) **1** (of an actor) to appear alongside another star. **2** (of a production) to feature as fellow stars: *co-starred Gielgud and Olivier*. [**co-**]

costermonger *n* (*Br*; also **coster**) a person who sells fruit and vegetables from a barrow. [*costard*, an apple + **-monger**]

costive *adj* (*old*) constipated. [OFr *costivé*]

costly *adj* ***-lier***, ***-liest*** **1** expensive. **2** lavish; sumptuous. **3** involving big losses or sacrifices. — *n* **costliness**. [**cost**]

costume *n* **1** (a set of) clothing of a special kind, esp. of a particular historical period or particular country. **2** a garment or outfit for a special activity: *a swimming-costume*. **3** (*old*) a woman's suit. [Ital, habit, dress]

costume jewellery *n* jewellery made of inexpensive or artificial materials.

costumier *n* a person who makes or supplies costumes.

cosy *adj* ***-ier***, ***-iest*** **1** warm and comfortable. **2** friendly, intimate and confidential. — *n* ***-ies*** a warm cover for a teapot (also **tea-cosy**) or a boiled egg (also **egg-cosy**). — *adv* **cosily**. — *n* **cosiness**.

cot[1] *n* **1** a small bed with high sides for a child. **2** (*US*) a camp bed. [Hindi *khat*, bedstead]

cot death *n* the sudden, unexplained death of a baby during sleep.

cot[2] *n* **1** (*poetic*) a cottage. **2** a cote. [OE]

cot[3] *abbrev* cotangent.

cotangent *n* (*math*) the ratio of the side adjacent to a given angle to the side opposite. ◇ See also **cosecant**, **secant**, **tangent** [**co-**]

cote *n* (esp. *in cmpds*) a small shelter for birds or animals. [OE]

coterie *n* a small exclusive group of people with interests in common. [OFr, group of tenant farmers]

coterminous *adj* having the same boundaries, duration or range. [Lat *con-*, same + *terminus*, boundary]

cotoneaster *n* a garden shrub with red or orange berries. [Lat *cotonea*, quince]

cottage *n* a small house, esp. an old stone one, in a village or the countryside. [**cot**[2]]

cottage cheese *n* a type of soft white cheese made from sour milk.

cottage industry *n* a craft industry such as knitting or weaving, employing workers in their own homes.

cottage loaf *n* a loaf consisting of a round piece of dough with a smaller round piece on top of it.

cottager *n* a person who lives in a cottage.

cottar or **cotter** *n* (*hist* or *Scot*) a farm labourer occupying a cottage rent-free. [**cot**[2]]

cotton *n* the soft downy fibres that cover the seeds of the cotton plant. **2** the plant itself, grown in warm climates. **3** thread or cloth made from the fibres. — *adj* **cottony**. — *v* **cotton on**, ***-n-*** (*intr*; **to**; *coll*) to understand. [OFr *coton*, from Arabic *qutun*]

cotton gin *n* a machine for separating the seeds from the cotton.

cottonwool *n* soft fluffy wadding used in treating injuries, applying cosmetics, etc., orig. made from cotton fibre.

cotyledon *n* (*bot*) the first leaf produced by a plant embryo. [Gr, from *kotyle*, cup]

couch[1] *n* **1** a sofa or settee. **2** a bed-like seat with a headrest, e.g. for patients to lie on when being examined or treated by a doctor or psychiatrist. **3** (*poetic*) a bed. — *v* (*tr*) to express in words of a certain kind. [Fr *coucher*, to lay down]

couch[2] *n* (also **couch grass**) a grass of the wheat family, with creeping roots. [OE *cwice*]

couchette *n* a sleeping-berth on a ship or train, converted from ordinary seating; a railway carriage with such berths. [Fr, dimin. of *couche*, bed]

cougar *n* (esp. *NAm*) a puma. [Fr *couguar*, from a S American Indian word]

cough *v* (*intr*) **1** to expel air, mucus, etc. from the throat or lungs with a rough sharp noise. **2** (of an engine, etc.) to make a similar noise. — *n* **1** an act or sound of coughing. **2** a condition of lungs or throat causing coughing. — *v* **cough up 1** (*tr*) to bring up (mucus, phlegm, blood, etc.) by coughing. **2** (*tr*; *slang*) to part with (information). **3** (*tr* & *intr*; *slang*) to part with (money). [Imit.]

cough mixture *n* a liquid medicine for relieving coughing.

could *v* (*aux*) **1** *past tense* of **can**: *I found I could lift it*. **2** used to express a possibility or a possible course: *You could try telephoning her*. **3** used in making requests: *Could you help me?* **4** to feel like (doing something) or able to (do something): *I could have strangled him. I could not allow that*. — **could be** (*coll*) that may be the case.

couldn't short for **could not**.

couldst *v* (aux) the form of **could** used with the pronoun **thou**.

coulomb *n* a unit of measurement of electric charge. [C A *Coulomb* (1736–1806), French physicist]

council *n* **1** a body of people whose function is to advise, administer, organise, discuss or legislate. **2** the elected body of people that directs the affairs of a town, district, region, etc. [OFr *concile*, from Lat *concilium*]

council house *n* a house owned and rented out by a local council.

councillor *n* a member of a council, esp. of a town, etc.

council tax *n* a proposed replacement for the community charge, based on property values.

counsel *n* **1** advice. **2** consultation, discussion or deliberation: *take counsel with one's supporters*. **3** a lawyer or group of lawyers that gives legal advice and fights cases in court. — *v* **-ll-** (*tr*) to advise. — **keep one's own counsel** to keep one's opinions and intentions to oneself. [OFr *conseil*, from Lat *consilium*, advice]

counsellor *n* **1** an adviser. **2** (*US*; **counselor**) a lawyer.

count[1] *v* **1** (*intr*) to say numbers in order: *count to five*. **2** (*tr*) to find the total amount of, by adding up item by item. **3** (*tr*) to include. **4** (*intr*) to be important; to matter; to have an effect or value. — *n* **1** an act of counting. **2** the number counted. **3** a charge brought against an accused person. — *adj* **countable**. — *v* **count in** (*tr*) to include. — **count me in** (or **out**) I'm willing (or not willing) to be included. — *v* **count on** (*tr*) to rely on. — *v* **count out** (*tr*) **1** to declare (a floored boxer) to have lost the match if he is unable to get up within a count of ten seconds. **2** to lay down one at a time while counting: *counted out five pounds each*. — **keep** (or **lose**) **count** to keep (or fail to keep) a note of the running total. — **out for the count 1** (of a boxer) unable to rise to his feet within a count of ten. **2** unconscious; (*facet*) fast asleep. [OFr *cunter*, from Lat *computare*]

countdown *n* a count backwards, with zero as the moment for action, used e.g. in launching a rocket.

count[2] *n* a European nobleman equal in rank to a British earl. [Lat *comes*, companion]

countenance *n* face; expression or appearance. — *v* (*tr*) to allow; to tolerate. — **give countenance to** to support (a proposal, etc.). — **keep one's countenance** to remained composed, not burst out laughing, etc. [OFr *contenance*, from Lat *continentia*, self-control]

counter[1] *n* **1** the long flat-topped fitting in a shop, cafeteria, bank, etc. over which goods are sold, food is served or business transacted. **2** a small flat disc used as a playing-piece in various board games. **3** a disc-shaped token used as a substitute coin. **4** a device for counting something. — **over the counter** by the normal method of sale in a shop, etc. (*adj* **over-the-counter**). — **under the counter** by secret, illegal sale or unlawful means (*adj* **under-the-counter**). [Lat *computare*, to reckon]

counter[2] *v* **-r-** (*tr* & *intr*) to oppose, act against, or hit back. — *adv* (with **to**) in the opposite direction to; in contradiction of: *Results ran counter to expectations*. — *n* **1** a return blow; an opposing move. **2** an opposite or contrary. **3** something that can be used to one's advantage in negotiating or bargaining. **4** (*naut*) the curved, overhanging part of a ship's stern. [OFr *contre*, against]

counter- *pfx* **1** against: *counter-attack*. **2** in competition or rivalry: *counter-attraction*. **3** matching or corresponding: *counterpart*. [OFr *contre*, against]

counteract *v* (*tr*) to reduce or prevent the effect of. — *n* **counteraction**. — *adj* **counteractive**.

counter-attack *n* an attack in response to an attack. — *v* (*intr*) to attack in return.

counter-attraction *n* a rival attraction.

counterbalance *n* a weight, force or circumstance that balances another and cancels it out. — *v* (*tr*) to act as a counterbalance to; to neutralise or cancel out.

counterblast *n* a vigorous and indignant verbal or written response.

counter-charge *n* an accusation made in response to one made against oneself.

counter-claim *n* a claim or assertion made in opposition to one made by someone else.

counter-clockwise *adj* & *adv* anticlockwise.

counter-espionage *n* activities undertaken to frustrate spying by an enemy or rival.

counterfeit *adj* **1** made in imitation of a genuine article, esp. with the purpose of deceiving; forged. **2** not genuine; insincere. — *v* (*tr*) **1** to copy for a dishonest purpose; to forge. **2** to pretend: *counterfeit friendship*. [OFr *contrefait*, copied, from Lat *contra-*, against + *facere*, to make]

counterfoil *n* the section of a cheque, receipt, ticket, etc. retained as a record by the person who issues it. [Lat *folium*, leaf]

counter-insurgency *n* military action taken against insurgents or rebels.

counter-intelligence *n* counter-espionage.

countermand *v* (*tr*) to cancel (an order or command). [OFr *contremander*, from Lat *contra-*, against + *mandare*, to order]

counter-measure *n* an action taken to counteract a threat, dangerous development or move.

counter-offensive *n* an aggressive move made in response to an initial attack.

counterpane *n* a coverlet; a bedspread. [OFr *coitepoint*, quilt, from Lat *culcita puncta*, quilted mattress]

counterpart *n* the matching or corresponding person or thing elsewhere.

counterpoint *n* (*mus*) **1** the combining of two or more melodies sung or played simultaneously into a harmonious whole. **2** a part or melody combined with another. ◇ See also **contrapuntal**.

counterpoise *n* **1** a state of balance between two weights. **2** something that counterbalances.

counter-productive *adj* tending to undermine productiveness and efficiency; having the opposite effect to that intended.

counter-revolution *n* a revolution to overthrow a system of government established by a previous revolution. — *adj & n* **counter-revolutionary**.

countersign *v* (*tr*) to sign (a document, etc. already signed by someone else) by way of confirmation. — *n* a password or signal used in response to a sentry's challenge. — *n* **counter-signature**.

countersink *v* **-sank**, **-sunk** (*tr*) **1** to widen the upper part of (a screw hole) so that the top of the screw when inserted will be level with the surrounding surface. **2** to insert (a screw) into such a hole.

counter-tenor *n* an adult male singer who sings falsetto, using the same range as a female alto.

counterweight *n* a counterbalancing weight.

countess *n* **1** the wife or widow of an earl or count. **2** a woman with the rank of earl or count. [OFr *contesse*, from Lat *comitissa*, fem. of *comes*, companion]

countless *adj* a very great many; numberless. [**count**[1]]

country *n* **-ies** **1** the land of any of the nations of the world. **2** the population of such land. **3** one's native land. **4** open land, with moors, woods, hills, fields, etc., as distinct from towns, etc. **5** land having a certain character or connection: *Burns country*. **6** an area of knowledge or experience: *back in the familiar country of simple addition and subtraction*. — **across country** not keeping to roads. — **go to the country** to dissolve parliament and hold a general election. [Lat *contrata* (*terra*), (land) lying in front of one]

countrified *adj* rural; rustic in appearance or style.

country-and-western *adj & n* (folk music or songs) of a style popular amongst white people of the Southern US.

country club *n* a club in a rural area with facilities for sport and recreation.

country dance *n* a traditional British dance in which partners face each other in parallel lines. — *n* **country dancing**.

country house or **seat** *n* a landowner's large house in the country.

countryman or **countrywoman** *n* **1** a man or woman who lives in a rural area. **2** a man or woman belonging to the same country as oneself.

countryside *n* land outside or away from towns.

countrywide *adj* all over the country.

county *n* **-ies** **1** any of the geographical divisions within England, Wales and Ireland that form the larger units of local government. **2** in the US, the main administrative subdivision within a state. — *adj* (*coll derog*) typical of the landed gentry. [OFr *conte*]

county town *n* the chief town of a county, acting as its seat of administration.

county court *n* a local court for non-criminal cases.

coup *n* **1** a successful move. **2** a coup d'état. [Fr, stroke or blow]

coup de grâce *n* a final decisive blow. [Fr, blow of mercy]

coup d'état *n* ***coups d'état*** the sudden, usu. violent, overthrow of a government. [Fr, stroke involving the state]

coupe *n* a dessert made with fruit and ice cream. [Fr, glass, cup]

coupé *n* a four-seated two-door car with a sloping rear. [Fr, from *couper*, to cut]

couple *n* **1** a man and wife, boyfriend and girlfriend, or other pair of people romantically attached. **2** a pair of partners, e.g. for dancing. **3** two, or a few. — *v* **1** (*tr*; **together, with**) to link; to connect. **2** (*intr*; **with**) to have sexual intercourse.

coupling *n* **1** a link for joining things together. **2** (usu. *derog*) the act of having sex.

couplet *n* a pair of consecutive lines of verse, esp. rhyming. [Dimin. of **couple**]

coupon *n* **1** a slip of paper entitling one to something, e.g. a discount. **2** a detachable order form, competition entry form, etc. printed on packaging, etc. **3** a betting form for football pools. [OFr *colpon*, piece cut off]

courage *n* **1** bravery. **2** cheerfulness or resolution in coping with setbacks. — **have the courage of one's convictions** to be brave enough to act in accordance with one's beliefs. — **pluck up courage**, or **take one's courage in both hands** to become resolved to meet a challenge. — **take courage** to cheer up. [OFr *corage*, from Lat *cor*, heart]

courageous *adj* having or showing courage. — *adv* **courageously**. — *n* **courageousness**.

courgette *n* a long green vegetable, a type of small marrow. [Fr]

courier *n* **1** a guide who travels with, and looks after, parties of tourists. **2** a messenger. [OFr, from Lat *currere*, to run]

course *n* **1** the path that anything moves in. **2** a direction taken or planned: *go off course*. **3** the channel of a river, etc. **4** the normal progress of something. **5** the passage of a period of time: *in the course of the next hour*. **6** a line of action: *Your best course is to wait*. **7** a series of lessons, etc. **8** a prescribed treatment, e.g. medicine to be taken, over a period. **9** any of the successive parts of a meal. **10** (often in *cmpds*) the ground over which a game is played or a race run. **11** (*building*) a single row of bricks or stones in a wall, etc. — *v* **1** (*intr*) to move or flow. **2** (*tr*) to hunt (hares, etc.) using dogs. — *n* **coursing**. — **in the course of** while (doing something); during. — **in the course of time** eventually. —**in due course** at the appropriate or expected time. — **a matter of course** a natural or expected action or result. — **of course 1** as expected. **2** naturally; certainly; without doubt. **3** admittedly. — **stay the course** to endure to the end. [OFr *cours*, from Lat *currere*, to run]

coursebook *n* a book to accompany a course of instruction.

courser *n* **1** a person who courses hares, etc., or a hound used for this. **2** (*poetic*) a swift horse. **3** any of several swiftly running birds of Asia or Africa.

court *n* **1** the judge, law officials and members of the jury gathered to hear and decide on a legal case. **2** the room (also **courtroom**) or building (also **courthouse**) used for such a hearing. **3** an area marked out for a particular game, or a division of this. **4** an open space or square surrounded by houses or by sections of a building. **5** (*cap*) a name used for a group of houses so arranged, or for a block of flats or for a country mansion. **6** the palace, household, attendants and advisers of a sovereign. — *v* **1** (*tr* & *intr*; *old*) to try to win the love of. **2** (*tr*) to try to win the favour of. **3** (*tr*) to seek (popularity, etc.). **4** (*tr*) to risk or invite: *court danger*. — **the ball is in his**, **your**, etc. **court** he, you, etc. must make the next move. — **go to court** to take legal action. — **hold court** to be surrounded by a circle of admirers. — **out of court** without legal action being taken: *settle out of court*. — **pay court to** to pay flattering attention to. — **put** or **rule out of court** to prevent from being listened to or considered. — **take to court** to bring a legal case against. [OFr *cort*, from Lat *cohors* or *cors*, yard]

court card *n* (*cards*) the king, queen or jack.

courtly *adj* having fine manners. — *n* **courtliness**.

court-martial *n* ***courts-martial***, (*coll*) ***court-martials*** a trial, by a group of officers, of a member of the armed forces, for a breach of military law. — *v* (*tr*) to try by court-martial.

courtship *n* the courting or wooing of an intended spouse; the period for which this lasts.

court shoe *n* a woman's shoe in a plain, low-cut style.

courtyard *n* an open space surrounded by buildings or walls.

courteous *adj* polite; considerate; respectful. — *adj* **courteously**. — *n* **courteousness**. ◇ See also **courtesy**. [OFr *corteis*, from *cort*, court]

courtesan *n* (esp. *hist*) a prostitute with wealthy or noble clients. [OFr *courtisane*, from Ital *cortigiana*, woman of the court]

courtesy *n* ***-ies*** **1** courteous behaviour; politeness. **2** a courteous act. — **(by) courtesy of 1** by permission of. **2** (*coll*) from. [OFr *corteisie*, from *corteis*, courteous]

courtesy title *n* a frequently used but legally invalid title, e.g. 'Lord' before the first name of a peer's younger son.

courtier *n* **1** a person in attendance at a royal court. **2** an elegant flatterer. [OFr *courteiour*, attendant at court]

courtly. See **court**.

couscous *n* a N African dish of crushed wheat steamed and served e.g. with meat. [Fr, from Arabic *kuskus*]

cousin *n* (also **first cousin**) a son or daughter of one's uncle or aunt. [OFr *cosin*, from Lat *con-*, with + *sobrinus*, cousin]

(first) cousin once removed *n* a son or daughter of one's cousin.

second cousin *n* a child of one's parent's first cousin.

couture *n* the designing, making and selling of fashionable clothes for women. [Fr, sewing]

couturier *n* a fashion designer.

couturière *n* a female fashion designer.

cove[1] *n* a small bay or inlet of the sea. [OE *cofa*, room]

cove[2] *n* (*old coll*) a fellow.

coven *n* a gathering of witches. [OFr *covin*, from Lat *convenire*, to meet]

covenant *n* **1** a formal written promise to pay a sum of money regularly, e.g. to a charity. **2** (*legal*) a formal sealed agreement. **3** (*Bible*) God's agreement with the Israelites. — *v* (*tr*; **with**) to agree by covenant (to do something).

covenanter *n* **1** a person who covenants. **2** (*cap*; *hist*) an adherent of either of two 17th-century religious covenants defending Presbyterianism in Scotland. [OFr *covenir*, to agree]

Coventry: **send (someone) to Coventry** to punish someone by refusing to speak to him or her. [Perhaps from the imprisonment of Royalists in Coventry during the Civil War]

cover *v* ***-r-*** (*tr*) **1** to form a layer over. **2** to protect or conceal by putting something over. **3 (up)** to clothe. **4** to extend over. **5** to strew, sprinkle, spatter, mark all over, etc. **6** (usu. in *passive*) (of an emotion, etc.)

to overwhelm: *covered with embarrassment*. **7** to deal with (a subject). **8** (of a reporter, etc.) to investigate or report on. **9** to have as one's area of responsibility. **10** to travel (a distance). **11** to be adequate to pay: *cover one's expenses*. **12** to insure; to insure against. **13** to threaten by aiming a gun at. **14** to keep (a building, its exits, etc.) under armed watch. **15** to shield with a firearm at the ready or with actual fire. **16**. (*sport*) to protect (a fellow team-member) or obstruct (an opponent). **17** (of a stallion, bull, etc.) to mate with. **18** (of a bird) to sit on (eggs). — *n* **1** something that covers. **2** a lid, top, protective casing, etc. **3** the covering of something: *plants that give good ground cover*. **4** (in *pl*) the sheets and blankets on a bed. **5** the paper or board binding of a book, magazine, etc.; one side of this. **6** an envelope: *a first-day cover*. **7** shelter or protection: *take cover*. **8** insurance. **9** service: *Dr Brown will provide emergency cover*. **10** a pretence; a screen; a false identity: *His cover as a salesman was blown*. **11** armed protection; protective fire. **12** (*cricket*) cover point. **13** in restaurants, etc., a place setting at table. — *v* **cover for** (*tr*) to take over the duties of (an absent colleague, etc.). — *n* & *adj* **covering**. — *v* **cover up 1** (*tr*) to conceal (a dishonest act, a mistake, etc.) (*n* **cover-up**). **2** (*intr* with **for**) to protect (e.g. an inefficient colleague). — **under cover 1** in secret. **2** within shelter. — **under cover of** using the protection or pretence of. — **under plain cover** in a plain envelope without tradename, etc. — **under separate cover** in a separate envelope or parcel. [OFr *covrir*]

coverage *n* an amount covered; the fullness of treatment of a news item in any of the media, etc.

coverall *n* (in *pl*) a one-piece protective garment worn over one's clothes.

cover charge *n* a service charge made per person in a restaurant, etc.

cover girl *n* a girl or woman whose photograph is shown on a magazine cover.

covering letter *n* a letter accompanying and explaining documents or goods.

cover note *n* a temporary certificate of insurance.

cover point *n* (*cricket*) the fielding position forward and to the right of the batsman.

cover version *n* an artist's version of a song, etc. already recorded by someone else.

coverlet *n* a thin top cover for a bed; a bedspread or counterpane. [OFr *cuver-lit*, cover-bed]

covert *adj* secret; secretive; stealthy. — *n* **1** a thicket providing cover for game. **2** (*biol*) a feather covering the base of a wing or tail feather. — *adv* **covertly**. [OFr, past participle of *covrir*, to cover]

covet *v* **-t-** (*tr*) to long to possess (something belonging to someone else). — *adj* **covetous**. — *adv* **covetously**. — *n* **covetousness**. [OFr *coveitier*, from Lat *cupiditas*, longing, greed]

covey *n* **-eys 1** a small flock of grouse or partridge. **2** a small group of people. [OFr *covee*, from *cover*, to hatch]

cow[1] *n* **1** the female of any species of cattle. **2** the female of other large animals, e.g. the elephant, whale, seal and moose. **3** a term of abuse for a woman. — **till the cows come home** (*coll*) for an unforeseeably long time. [OE *cu*]

cowbell *n* a bell hanging from a cow's neck.

cowboy *n* **1** in the western US, a man in charge of cattle, esp. as a character in films of the Wild West. **2** (*derog*) someone who undertakes building or other work without proper training or qualifications; a dishonest businessman or entrepreneur.

cowcatcher *n* a concave metal fender on the front of a railway engine for clearing cattle and other obstacles from the line.

cowgirl, **cowhand**, **cowherd** or **cowman** *n* workers assisting with, or having charge of, cattle.

cowhide *n* a cow's hide made into leather.

cowlick *n* a lock of hair standing up stiffly from the forehead.

cowpat *n* a flat circular deposit of cow dung.

cowpox *n* a disease of cows transmissible to humans, related to, and giving protection from, smallpox.

cowshed or **cowhouse** *n* a building for housing cattle.

cow[2] *v* (*tr*) to frighten into submission. [ON *kuga*, to subdue]

coward *n* **1** someone easily frightened, or lacking courage to face danger or difficulty. **2** someone who acts brutally towards the weak or undefended. — *n* **cowardice** or **cowardliness**. — *adj* **cowardly**. [OFr *couard*, from Lat *cauda*, tail]

cower *v* **-r-** (*intr*) to shrink away in fear. [MidE *couren*]

cowl *n* **1** a monk's large loose hood or hooded habit. **2** a revolving cover for a chimney-pot for improving ventilation. **3** a cowling. [OE *cugele*, from Lat *cucullus*, hood]

cowling *n* a removable metal covering for the engine of a vehicle or aircraft. [**cowl**]

co-worker *n* a fellow worker; a colleague.

cowrie *n* **1** a large tropical shellfish. **2** its brightly coloured shell, in primitive societies used as money or prized for magic qualities. [Hindi *kauri*]

cowslip *n* a wild plant with yellow sweet-smelling flowers. [OE *cuslyppe*, cow dung]

cox *n* short for **coxswain**. — *v* (*tr* & *intr*) to act as cox of (a boat).

coxcomb *n* (*old derog*) a foolishly vain or conceited man. [**cock's comb**; orig. applied to jesters from their comb-like headgear]

coxswain *n* **1** the person who steers a small boat. **2** a petty officer in a small ship. [*cock*, ship's boat + **swain**]

coy *adj* **1** shy; modest; affectedly bashful. **2** irritatingly uncommunicative about something. — *adv* **coyly**. — *n* **coyness**. [OFr *coi*, calm, from Lat *quietus*, quiet]

coyote *n* ***coyote*** or **-*tes*** a small N American wolf. [Aztec *coyotl*]

coypu *n* ***coypu*** or **-*pus*** a S American rodent similar to a beaver, bred for its fur. [From a S American Indian language]

CPO *abbrev* Chief Petty Officer.

CPU *abbrev* (*comput*) central processing unit.

Cr *symbol* (*chem*) chromium.

crab *n* **1** an edible shellfish with a wide flat shell and five pairs of legs, the front pair taking the form of pincers. **2** (*cap* with **the**) the sign of the zodiac and constellation Cancer. **3** the crab louse; (in *pl*) infestation by this. — **catch a crab** in rowing, either to sink the oar too deeply or to miss the water, and fall backwards as a result. [OE *crabba*]

crab louse *n* a crab-like louse that infests the hair of the pubis.

crabwise *adj* & *adv* (moving) sideways.

crab apple *n* a small sour wild apple. [MidE *crabbe*]

crabbed *adj* **1** bad-tempered. **2** (of handwriting) cramped and hard to decipher. — *adv* **crabbedly**. — *n* **crabbedness**. [**crab**]

crabby *adj* **-*ier***, **-*iest*** (*coll*) bad-tempered. [**crab**]

crack *v* **1** (*tr* & *intr*) to fracture partially without falling to pieces. **2** (*tr* & *intr*) to split. **3** (*tr* & *intr*) to (cause to) make a sudden sharp noise. **4** (*tr* & *intr*) to strike sharply. **5** (*tr* & *intr*) to (cause to) give way: *crack someone's resistance*. **6** (*tr*) to force open (a safe). **7** (*tr*) to solve (a code or problem). **8** (*tr*) to tell (a joke). **9** (*intr*) (of the voice) to change pitch or tone suddenly and unintentionally. **10** (*tr* & *intr*) (of petroleum) to break into simpler molecules. — *n* **1** a sudden sharp sound. **2** a partial fracture. **3** a narrow opening. **4** a resounding blow. **5** (*coll*) a joke. **6** a highly addictive form of cocaine. — *adj* (*coll*) expert: *a crack shot*. — **at the crack of dawn** (*coll*) at daybreak; very early. — *v* **crack down on** (*tr*; *coll*) to take firm action against (*n* **crackdown**). — *v* **crack up 1** (*intr*) to go to pieces emotionally. **2** (*tr*; *coll*) to praise (**not all it's cracked up to be** not as good as it's said to be). — **a fair crack of the whip** a fair opportunity. — **get cracking** (*coll*) to get moving quickly. — **have a crack at** (*coll*) to attempt. [OE *cracian*, to resound]

crackbrained *adj* (*coll*) mad; crazy.

cracked *adj* **1** (*coll*) crazy; mad. **2** (of a voice) harsh; uneven in tone.

cracker *n* **1** a thin crisp unsweetened biscuit. **2** a small noisy firework. **3** a party toy in the form of a gaudy paper tube usu. containing a paper hat, gift and motto, that pulls apart with an explosive bang.

crackers *adj* (*coll*) mad.

cracking (*coll*) *adj* **1** very good. **2** very fast: *a cracking pace*. — *adv* used for emphasis: *a cracking good story*.

crackpot (*coll*) *n* & *adj* (someone who is) crazy.

crackle *v* (*intr*) to make a faint continuous cracking or popping sound. — *n* this kind of sound. — *adj* **crackly**. [**crack**]

crackling *n* the crisp skin of roast pork. [**crack**]

cracknel *n* **1** a light brittle biscuit. **2** a hard nutty filling for chocolates. **3** (in *pl*; *NAm*) crisply fried pieces of fat pork. [MidE *krakenelle*]

-cracy *comb fm* rule, government or domination by a particular group, etc.: *democracy*. — *adj comb fm* **-cratic**. — *adv comb fm* **-cratically**. [Gr *kratos*, power]

cradle *n* **1** a cot for a small baby, esp. one that can be rocked. **2** (**of**) a place of origin; the home (of something): *the city of Ur, cradle of civilisation*. **3** a suspended platform or cage for workmen engaged in the construction, repair or painting of a ship or building. **4** the support for the receiver on an old-style telephone. — *v* (*tr*) to rock or hold gently: *cradle a baby in one's arms*. — **from the cradle to the grave** throughout one's life. [OE *kradol*]

cradle-snatcher *n* (*derog*) someone who chooses a much younger person as lover or marriage partner.

craft *n* **1** (sometimes *in cmpds*) a skill or occupation, esp. one requiring the use of the hands: *crafts such as weaving and pottery*. **2** skilled ability. **3** cunning. **4** ***craft*** (often *in cmpds*) a boat or ship, or an air or space vehicle. — *v* (*tr*) to make skilfully. [OE *cræft*]

craftsman or **craftswoman** *n* a man or woman skilled at a craft. — *n* **craftsmanship**.

crafty *adj* **-*ier***, **-*iest*** clever, shrewd, cunning or sly. — *adv* **craftily**. — *n* **craftiness**.

crag *n* a rocky peak or jagged outcrop of rock. — *n* **cragginess**. — *adj* **craggy**, **-*ier***, **-*iest***. [Celtic, related to Welsh *craig* and Gaelic *creag*]

cram *v* **-*mm*- 1** (*tr*) to stuff full. **2** (*tr*; **in**, **together**) to push or pack. **3** (*intr* & *tr*) to study intensively, or prepare (someone) rapidly for, an examination. [OE *crammian*, to stuff full]

cram-full *adj* full to bursting.

crammer *n* a person or school that prepares pupils for examinations.

cramp[1] *n* **1** the painful involuntary contraction of a muscle. **2** (in *pl*) severe abdominal pain. — *v* (*tr*) to restrict tiresomely. — **cramp someone's style** to restrict someone's scope for creativity or individuality. [OFr *crampe*]

cramped *adj* **1** (of a space) too small; overcrowded. **2** (of handwriting) small and closely written.

cramp² *n* (also **cramp-iron**) a clamp for holding stone or timbers together. — *v* (*tr*) to fasten with a cramp. [ODut *crampe*, hook]

crampon *n* a spiked iron attachment for climbing boots, to improve grip on ice or rock. [Fr]

cranberry *n* **-*ies*** (an evergreen shrub bearing) a red acid berry. [Ger dialect *kraanbeere*, crane berry]

crane *n* **1** a machine for lifting heavy weights, having a long arm from which lifting gear is suspended. **2** any of various large, long-legged, long-necked birds. — *v* (*tr* & *intr*) to stretch (one's neck), or lean forward, in order to see better. [OE *cran*]

cranefly *n* a long-legged two-winged insect, the daddy-long-legs.

cranium *n* **-*ia*** or **-*iums*** **1** the dome of the skull, enclosing the brain. **2** the skull. — *adj* **cranial**. [Gr *kranion*]

crank *n* **1** a right-angled bend in, or an arm projecting at right angles from, a shaft, for communicating motion to or from the shaft. **2** a tool bent at right angles for starting an engine by hand. **3** (*derog*) an eccentric person. — *v* (*tr*; **up**) to start (an engine) with a crank. [OE *crancstæf*, weaving implement]

crankshaft *n* a shaft driving, or driven by, a crank, e.g. in a vehicle engine.

cranky *adj* **-*ier***, **-*iest*** (*coll*) eccentric or faddy.

cranny *n* **-*ies*** **1** a narrow opening; a cleft or crevice. **2** an out-of-the-way corner. — *adj* **crannied**. [MidE *crany*]

crap (*vulg*) *n* **1** faeces. **2** nonsense. — *v* **-*pp-*** (*intr*) to defecate. [MidE, chaff]

crape. See **crêpe**.

craps *n* (*sing*) a gambling game in which the player rolls two dice.

crapulence *n* (sickness caused by) excessive drinking. — *adj* **crapulent** or **crapulous**. [Lat *crapula*, drunkenness]

crash *v* **1** (*tr* & *intr*) to fall or strike with a banging or smashing noise. **2** (*tr* & *intr*; **into**) to (cause to) collide; (of an aircraft) to (cause to) hit something destructively on landing. **3** (*intr*) to make a deafening noise. **4** (*intr*) to move noisily. **5** (*intr*) (of a business or the stock exchange) to collapse. **6** (*intr*) (of a computer or program) to fail completely, because of a malfunction, etc. **7** (*tr*; *slang*) to gatecrash. **8** (*intr*; *slang*; **out**) to fall asleep; to sleep the night. — *n* **1** (the sound of) a violent impact or breakage. **2** a deafening noise. **3** a traffic or aircraft accident; a collision. **4** the collapse of a business or the stock exchange. **5** the failure of a computer or program. — *adj* concentrated or intensive, so as to produce results in minimum time: *a crash diet*. [Imit.]

crash barrier *n* a protective metal barrier along the edge of a road or carriageway.

crash dive *n* a rapid emergency dive by a submarine. — *v* (*intr*) **crash-dive**.

crash helmet *n* a protective helmet worn e.g. by motor-cyclists.

crashing *adj* (*coll*) utter; great: *a crashing bore*.

crash-land *v* (*tr* & *intr*) (of an aircraft) to land in an emergency, with the risk of damage. — *n* **crash-landing**.

crass *adj* **1** gross; downright. **2** colossally stupid. **3** utterly tactless or insensitive. — *adv* **crassly**. — *n* **crassness**. [Lat *crassus*, thick, stupid]

-crat. See **-cracy**.

crate *n* **1** a strong wooden, plastic or metal case with partitions, for carrying breakable or perishable goods. **2** (*slang derog*) a decrepit vehicle or aircraft. — *v* (*tr*) to pack in a crate. [Lat *cratis*, wickerwork barrier]

crater *n* **1** the bowl-shaped mouth of a volcano. **2** a hole left in the ground where a meteorite has landed or a bomb or mine has exploded. **3** a circular rimmed depression in the surface of the moon. [Gr *krater*, mixing-bowl]

-cratic. See **-cracy**.

cravat *n* a formal style of neckerchief worn by men instead of a tie. [Fr *cravate*, an imitation of the neckwear of the *Cravates* (Croatians)]

crave *v* **1** (*tr* or *intr*; **for**, **after**) to long for; to desire overwhelmingly. **2** (*old formal*) to ask for politely; to beg. [OE *crafian*]

craving *n* an intense longing; an overwhelming desire.

craven (*old derog*) *adj* cowardly; cringing. — *n* a coward. — *adv* **cravenly**. — *n* **cravenness**. [MidE *cravant*, defeated]

craw *n* **1** the crop of a bird or insect. **2** the stomach of an animal. — **stick in one's craw** (*coll*) to be difficult for one to swallow or accept. [MidE *crawe*]

crawfish *n* **-*fish*** same as **crayfish**.

crawl *v* (*intr*) **1** (of insects, worms, etc.) to move along the ground. **2** to move along on hands and knees, esp. as a stage before learning to walk. **3** (of e.g. traffic) to progress very slowly. **4** to be, or feel as if, covered with crawling insects. **5** (*coll derog*; **to**) to behave in an over-humble way (to someone whose approval one wants). — *n* **1** a crawling motion. **2** a very slow pace. **2** a swimming-stroke with an alternate overarm action.

crawler *n* (*coll derog*) someone who behaves in an over-humble, ingratiating way to those in senior positions.

crayfish *n* **-*fish*** an edible shellfish similar to a lobster. [OFr *crevice*, from OGer *krebiz*, crab]

crayon *n* a coloured pencil, or stick of coloured wax or chalk. — *v* **-*n-*** (*tr* & *intr*) to draw or colour with a crayon. [Fr, from *craie*, chalk]

craze *n* an intense but passing enthusiasm or fashion. — *v* **1** (*tr*) to make crazy: *a crazed look*. **2** (*tr* & *intr*) (of e.g. a glazed or varnished surface) to (cause to) develop a network of fine cracks. [Prob. Norse]

crazy *adj* **-*ier***, **-*iest*** **1** mad; insane. **2** foolish; absurd; foolhardy. **3** (**about**) madly enthusiastic. — *adv* **crazily**. — *n* **craziness**. — **like crazy** (*coll*) keenly; fast and furious.

crazy paving *n* paving made up of irregularly shaped slabs of stone or concrete.

creak *n* the squeaking noise made typically by an unoiled hinge or loose floorboard. — *v* (*intr*) **1** to make this noise. **2** (*facet*) to be in an unreliable or infirm condition. — *adv* **creakily**. — *n* **creakiness**. — *adj* **creaky**, **-*ier***, **-*iest***. [Imit.]

cream *n* **1** the yellowish-white fatty substance that forms on the top of milk, from which butter and cheese are made. **2** a food made with, or similar to, cream. **3** any of many cosmetic preparations similar to cream in texture. **4** the best part of something; the pick. **5** a yellowish-white colour. — *v* **1** (*tr*) to beat (e.g. butter and sugar) till creamy. **2** (*tr*) to remove the cream from (milk). **3** (*tr*; **off**) to select or take away (the best part). — *adj* **creamy**, **-*ier***, **-*iest***. [OFr *cresme*]

creamer *n* **1** a powdered milk substitute, used in coffee. **2** (*antiq* or *US*) a cream jug. **3** a device for separating cream from milk.

creamery *n* **-*ies*** a place where dairy products are made or sold.

cream of tartar *n* purified tartar, a white powder used in cooking.

crease *n* **1** a line made by folding, pressing or crushing. **2** (*cricket*) a line marking the position of batsman or bowler. — *v* (*tr* & *intr*) to make a crease or creases in; to develop creases. — *v* **crease up** (*tr* & *intr*; *coll*) to double up with laughter, pain or exhaustion. [MidE *creeste*, connected with **crest**]

create *v* **1** (*tr*) to form from nothing: *create the universe*. **2** (*tr*) to bring into existence; to introduce: *create a system*. **3** (*tr*) to cause. **4** (*tr*) to produce or contrive. **5** (*tr* & *intr*) (of an artist, etc.) to use one's imagination to make. **6** (*intr*; *coll*) to make a fuss. **7** (*tr*) (of an actor) to be the first to play (a certain role). **8** (*tr*) to raise to an honourable rank: *was created a peer*. [Lat *creare*]

creation *n* **1** the act of creating. **2** something created. **3** the universe; all created things.

creative *adj* having or showing the ability to create; inventive or imaginative. — *adv* **creatively**. — *n* **creativity**.

creator *n* **1** a person who creates. **2** (*cap* with **the**) God.

creature *n* **1** a bird, beast or fish. **2** a person: *a wretched creature*. **3** the slavish underling or puppet of someone. [Lat *creatura*, act of creating]

creature comforts *n* (*pl*) comforts such as food, clothes, warmth, etc.

creature of habit *n* **1** an animal with fixed, esp. seasonal, behaviour patterns. **2** a person of unchanging routines.

crèche *n* a nursery where babies can be left and cared for while their parents are at work, shopping, exercising, etc. [Fr, manger]

credence *n* faith or belief placed in something: *give their claims no credence*. [Lat *credentia*]

credentials *n* (*pl*) personal qualifications and achievements that one can quote in evidence of one's trustworthiness; (papers giving) proof of these. [Lat *credentia*, belief]

credible *adj* **1** capable of being believed. **2** reliable; trustworthy. — *n* **credibility**. — *adv* **credibly**. [Lat *credibilis*]

credibility gap *n* in politics, the discrepancy between what is claimed and what is actually, or is likely to be, the case.

credit *n* **1** faith placed in something. **2** (a cause of) honour: *To her credit, she didn't say anything. Your loyalty does you credit.* **3** acknowledgement, recognition or praise: *give him credit for trying*; *take credit for someone else's hard work*. **4** (in *pl*) a list of acknowledgements to those who have helped in the preparation of a book or (also **credit titles**) film. **5** trust given to someone promising to pay later for goods already supplied: *buy goods on credit*. **6** one's financial reliability, esp. as a basis for such trust. **7** the amount of money available to one at one's bank. **8** an entry in a bank account acknowledging a payment. **9** the side of an account on which such entries are made. ◇ See also **debit**. **10** a certificate of completion of a course of instruction; a distinction awarded for performance on such a course. — *v* **-*t*-** (*tr*) **1** to believe; to place faith in. **2** (**to, with**) to enter (a sum) as a credit on someone's account, or allow (someone) a sum as credit. **3** (**with**) to attribute a quality or achievement to: *credited you with more sense*. [OFr *crédit*, from Lat *creditum*, loan]

creditable *adj* praiseworthy; laudable. — *adv* **creditably**.

credit account *n* a financial arrangement with a shop that allows one to purchase goods on credit.

credit card *n* a card authorising one to purchase goods or services on credit.

credit note *n* a form entitling one to a certain sum as credit, e.g. in place of returned or faulty goods.

creditor *n* a person to whom one owes money. ◇ See also **debtor**.

credit rating *n* (an assessment of) a person's creditworthiness.

credit squeeze *n* restrictions on borrowing imposed by the government.

credit transfer *n* payment made directly from one bank account to another.

creditworthy *adj* judged as deserving financial credit on the basis of earning ability and previous promptness in repaying debts. — *n* **creditworthiness**.

credo *n* **-*os*** a creed. [Lat, I believe]

credulous *adj* too trusting; too ready to believe. — *adv* **credulously**. — *n* **credulity**. [Lat *credulus*, trustful]

creed *n* **1** (*cap*) a statement of the main points of Christian belief. **2** any set of beliefs or principles, personal or religious. [OE *creda*, from Lat *credo*, I believe]

creek *n* **1** a narrow coastal inlet. **2** (*NAm*, *Austr* & *NZ*) a small river or tributary. — **up the creek** (*coll*) in desperate difficulties. [ON *kriki*, nook]

creel *n* a large basket for carrying fish. [MidE *crele*]

creep *v* ***crept*** (*intr*) **1** to move slowly, with stealth or caution. **2** to move with the body close to the ground; to crawl. **3** (of plants) to grow along the ground, up a wall, etc. **4** to enter barely noticeably: *Anxiety crept into her voice*. **5** to develop little by little: *creeping inflation*. **6** (esp. of the flesh) to feel as if covered with crawling insects, as a response to fear or disgust. — *n* **1** an unpleasantly sly person; a generally abusive term, esp. for a man. **2** the gradual change in shape of metal or other material caused by pressure, prolonged heating, etc. — **give one the creeps** (*coll*) to disgust or repel one. [OE *creopan*]

creeper *n* a creeping plant.

creepers *n* (*pl*) shoes with thick quiet soles.

creepy *adj* ***-ier***, ***-iest*** (*coll*) slightly scary; spooky; eerie. — *adv* **creepily**. — *n* **creepiness**.

creepy-crawly *n* ***-lies*** (*coll*) a small creeping insect.

cremate *v* (*tr*) to burn (a corpse) to ashes, as an alternative to burial. — *n* **cremation**. [Lat *cremare*, to burn]

crematorium *n* ***-ia*** or ***-iums*** a place where corpses are cremated.

crème *n* **1** cream, or a creamy food. **2** a liqueur. [Fr, cream]

crème caramel *n* an egg custard baked in a dish lined with caramel.

crème de la crème *n* the cream of the cream; the very best.

crème de menthe *n* a green peppermint-flavoured liqueur.

crenellated *adj* (of a castle, wall, etc.) having battlements. [Fr *crenel*, the notch or space in battlements]

creole *n* **1** a pidgin language that has become the accepted language of a region. **2** (*cap*) the French-based creole spoken in the US states of the Caribbean Gulf. **3** (*cap*) a native-born West Indian or Latin American of mixed European and Negro blood; a French or Spanish native of the US Gulf states. [Fr, from Port *crioulo*, native]

creosote *n* **1** a dark brown oil distilled from coal tar, used for preserving wood. **2** a transparent oil distilled from wood tar, used as an antiseptic. [Literally 'flesh-preserver', from Gr *kreas*, flesh + *soter*, saviour]

crêpe or **crepe** *n* **1** (also **crape**) a thin, finely-wrinkled silk fabric, dyed black for mourning wear; a mourning armband made of this. **2** rubber with a wrinkled surface, used for shoe soles. **3** a thin pancake. — *adj* **crepy**, ***-ier***, ***-iest***. [Fr, from Lat *crispus*, crisp]

crêpe paper *n* paper with a wrinkled, elastic texture, used for making decorations, etc.

crept. See **creep**.

crepuscular *adj* **1** of, or relating to, twilight; dim. **2** (of animals) appearing, or active, during twilight hours. [Lat *crepusculum*, twilight]

Cres. *abbrev* Crescent.

crescendo *n* ***-os*** **1** a gradual increase in loudness; a musical passage of increasing loudness. **2** (an approach to) a high point or climax. — *adv* & *adj* (*mus*) (played) with increasing loudness. ◇ See also **diminuendo**. [Ital, from Lat *crescere*, to grow]

crescent *n* **1** the moon in its first quarter — the new moon; loosely, the moon in its first or last quarter. **2** something similar in shape to this, e.g. a semicircular row of houses. [Lat *crescere*, to grow]

cress *n* any of several plants whose sharp-tasting leaves are used in salads, etc. [OE *cressa* or *cærse*]

crest *n* **1** a comb, vertical tuft of feathers, or ridge-like projection on the head of certain birds or animals. **2** a plume on a helmet. **3** (*heraldry*) the part of a coat of arms that appears above the shield. **4** the topmost ridge of a mountain. **5** the foaming edge of a wave. — *adj* **crested**. [Lat *crista*]

crestfallen *adj* dejected as a result of a blow to one's pride or ambitions. [**crest**]

Cretaceous *adj* & *n* (of) a geological period between 144 and 65 million years ago. [Lat *creta*, chalk]

cretin *n* **1** a person who is mentally retarded and physically deformed as the result of a congenital malfunction of the thyroid gland, a disorder formerly common in alpine districts. **2** (*offensive*) an idiot. — *n* **cretinism**. — *adj* **cretinous**. [Fr dialect *crestin*, from Lat *christianus*, Christian, human creature]

cretonne *n* a strong cotton material used for curtains, chair-covers, etc. [Fr, from *Creton* in Normandy]

crevasse *n* a deep wide-mouthed crack, esp. in a glacier. [Fr, from OFr *crevace*, crevice]

crevice *n* a crack; a narrow opening; a cleft or cranny. [OFr *crevace*, from Lat *crepare*, to crack]

crew[1] *n* **1** the team of people manning a ship, aircraft, train, bus, etc. **2** a ship's company excluding the officers. **3** a team engaged in some operation: *camera crew*. **4** (*coll*, usu. *derog*) a bunch of people: *a strange crew*. — *v* (*intr*; **for**) to serve as a crew member on a yacht, etc. [MidE *creue*, reinforcements, from OFr *creu*, increase]

crewcut *n* a closely cropped hairstyle for men.
crew neck *n* a firm round neckline on a sweater. — *adj* **crew-necked**.

crew[2]. See **crow**.

crewel *n* thin, loosely twisted yarn for tapestry or embroidery. — *n* **crewelwork**.

crib *n* **1** a baby's cot or cradle. **2** a manger. **3** a model of the nativity, with the infant Christ in a manger. **4** a literal translation of a text, used as an aid by students. **5** something copied or plagiarised from another's work. **6** the discarded cards in cribbage, used by the dealer in scoring. — *v* **-bb-** (*tr & intr*) to copy or plagiarise. [OE *cribb*, stall, manger]

cribbage *n* a card game for two to four players, who each try to be first to score a certain number of points. [**crib**, the discarded cards in the game]

crick (*coll*) *n* a painful spasm or stiffness, esp. in the neck. — *v* (*tr*) to wrench (e.g. one's neck or back).

cricket[1] *n* an outdoor game played with a ball, bats and wickets, between two sides of eleven players. — *n* **cricketer**. — **not cricket** (*coll*) unfair; unsporting.

cricket[2] *n* a grasshopper-like insect, the male of which makes a chirping noise by rubbing its forewings together. [Imit.]

cri de coeur *n* a cry from the heart; a sincere appeal. [Fr]

crikey *interj* (*old slang*) an expression of astonishment. [Altered form of **Christ**]

crime *n* **1** an illegal act; an act punishable by law. **2** such acts collectively. **3** an act gravely wrong morally. **4** (*coll*) a deplorable act; a shame. [Lat *crimen*, charge, crime]

criminal *n* a person guilty of a crime. — *adj* **1** against the law: *criminal activities*. **2** of, or relating to, crime or criminals or their punishment. **3** (*coll*) very wrong; wicked. — *n* **criminality**. — *adv* **criminally**. [Lat *criminalis*, from *crimen*, crime]

criminology *n* the study of crime and criminals. — *n* **criminologist**. [Lat *crimen*, crime + **-logy**]

crimp *v* (*tr*) **1** to press into small regular ridges; to corrugate. **2** to wave or curl (hair) with curling-tongs. **3** to roll the edge of (sheet metal). **4** to seal by pinching together. [OE *crympan*, to curl]

Crimplene® *n* (a crease-resistant man-made clothing material made from) a thick polyester yarn.

crimson *n & adj* (of) a deep purplish red colour. — *v* **1** (*tr*) to dye crimson. **2** (*intr*) to become crimson; to blush. [OFr *cramoisin*, from Arabic *qirmizi*, a dye made from a Mediterranean insect]

cringe *v* (*intr*) **1** to cower away in fear. **2** (*derog*) to behave in a submissive, over-humble way. **3** (*loosely*) to wince in embarrassment, etc. — *n* **cringer**. [OE *cringan*, to fall in battle]

crinkle *v* (*tr & intr*) to wrinkle or crease. — *n* a wrinkle or crease; a wave. — *adj* **crinkly, -ier, -iest**. [Related to OE *crincan*, to yield]

crinoline *n* (*hist*) a hooped petticoat for making skirts stand out. [Orig. a stiff horsehair fabric, from Lat *crinis*, hair + *linum*, flax]

cripple *v* (*tr*) **1** to make lame; to disable. **2** to damage, weaken or undermine. — *n* **1** a person who is lame or badly disabled. **2** a person damaged psychologically: *an emotional cripple*. [OE *crypel*]

crisis *n* **crises** **1** a crucial or decisive moment. **2** a turning-point, e.g. in a disease. **3** a time of difficulty or distress. **4** an emergency. [Gr *krisis*, decision, judgement]

crisp *adj* **1** dry and brittle: *crisp biscuits*. **2** (of vegetables or fruit) firm and fresh. **3** (of weather) fresh; bracing. **4** (of manner or speech) firm; decisive; brisk. **5** (of fabric, etc.) clean; starched. **6** (of hair) springy. — *n* (esp. in *pl*; also **potato crisp**) a thin deep-fried slice of potato, sold in packets as a snack. — *adv* **crisply**. — *adj* **crispy, -ier, -iest**. — **to a crisp** (*facet*) (burnt) till black and brittle. [Lat *crispus*, curly]
crispbread *n* a brittle unsweetened rye or wheat biscuit.

criss-cross *adj* (of lines) crossing one another in different directions; (of a pattern, etc.) consisting of criss-cross lines. — *adv* running or lying across one another. — *n* a pattern of criss-cross lines. — *v* (*tr & intr*) to form, mark with, or move in, a criss-cross pattern. [*Christ-Cross*, a decorative cross introducing the alphabet in old learning-books]

criterion *n* **-ia** a standard or principle on which to base a judgement. [Gr *kriterion*, from *krites*, judge]

critic *n* **1** a professional reviewer of literature, art, drama or music. **2** a person who finds fault with or disapproves of something. [Gr *kritikos*, discerning, from *krites*, judge]
critical *adj* **1** fault-finding; disapproving. **2** relating to a critic or criticism. **3** involving analysis and assessment. **4** relating to a crisis; decisive; crucial. **5** (*physics*) (of e.g. a measurement) marking the point of transition between one state and another. **5** (*nuc*) having reached the point at which which a nuclear chain reaction will sustain itself. — *adv* **critically**.
critical path analysis *n* the working out of the sequence of operations that must be followed to complete a complex task in minimum time.
criticise or **-ize** *v* (*tr & intr*) **1** to find fault; to express disapproval of. **2** to analyse and assess.
criticism *n* **1** fault-finding. **2** reasoned analysis and assessment, esp. of art, literature, music or drama; the art of such assessment. **3** a critical comment or piece of writing.

critique *n* a critical analysis; a criticism. [Fr, from Gr *kritike*, the art of criticism]

croak *n* the harsh throaty noise typically made by a frog or crow. — *v* **1** (*intr*) to make this sound. **2** (*tr*) to utter with a croak. **3** (*intr & tr*; *slang*) to die or kill. [Imit.]

crochet *n* decorative work consisting of intertwined loops, made with wool or thread and a hooked needle. — *v* **-t-** (*intr* & *tr*) to work in crochet. [Fr, dimin. of *croche*, hook]

crock[1] *n* (*coll*) an old decrepit person, vehicle, etc.: *poor old crock*. [MidE *crok*, old ewe]

crock[2] *n* an earthenware pot. [OE *crocc*, pot]

crockery *n* earthenware or china dishes; plates, cups, etc.

crocodile *n* **1** a large, thick-scaled, long-tailed tropical reptile with huge pointed jaws. **2** leather made from its skin. **3** a line of schoolchildren walking in twos. [Gr *krokodeilos*]

crocodile tears *n* (*pl*) a show of pretended grief.

crocus *n* **-cuses** a spring-flowering plant that grows from a bulb, with brilliant yellow, purple or white flowers. [Gr *krokos*, saffron]

croft *n* esp. in the Scottish Highlands, a small piece of enclosed farmland attached to a house. — *v* (*intr*) to farm a croft. — *n* **crofter**. [OE]

croissant *n* a crescent-shaped bread roll, made with a high proportion of fat, and flaky in consistency. [Fr, crescent]

cromlech *n* (*archaeol*) a prehistoric circle of standing stones. **2** (*loosely*) a dolmen. [Welsh *crom*, curved + *llech*, stone]

crone *n* (*offensive*) an old woman. [ODut *croonie*, old ewe, from OFr *caronie*, carrion]

crony *n* **-ies** a close friend. [Gr *chronios*, long-lasting]

crook *n* **1** a bend or curve: *carried it in the crook of his arm*. **2** a shepherd's or bishop's hooked staff. **3** any of various hooked fittings, e.g. on woodwind instruments. **4** (*coll*) a thief or swindler; a professional criminal. — *adj* (*Austr & NZ coll*) **1** ill. **2** not working properly. **3** nasty; unpleasant. — *v* (*tr*) to bend or curve. [ON *kraka*, hook]

crooked *adj* **1** bent, curved, angled or twisted. **2** not straight; tipped at an angle. **3** (*coll*) dishonest. — *adv* **crookedly**. — *n* **crookedness**.

croon *v* (*intr* & *tr*) to sing in a subdued tone and reflective or sentimental style. — *n* this style of singing. — *n* **crooner**. [ODut *cronen*, to lament]

crop *n* **1** a cereal or other plant cultivated for its produce; the season's yield from such a plant. **2** a batch; a bunch: *this year's crop of graduates*. **3** a short style of haircut. **4** a whip handle; a horserider's short whip. **5** a pouch projecting from the neck of certain birds, in which food is prepared for digestion. — *v* **-pp-** **1** (*tr*) to trim; to cut short. **2** (*tr*) (of animals) to feed on (grass, etc.). **3** (*tr*) to harvest or reap. **4** (*tr*) to grow (a plant for its produce). **5** (*tr*) to sow (land). **6** (*intr*) (of land) to produce a crop. — *v* **crop up** (*intr*; *coll*) to occur or appear unexpectedly. [OE *cropp*]

crop circle *n* a (not always circular) area or pattern of flattened crops in a crop field, of as yet unknown cause.

cropper: **come a cropper** (*coll*) **1** to fall heavily. **2** to fail disastrously.

croquet *n* a game played on a lawn, in which mallets are used to drive wooden balls through hoops. [Fr, dimin. of *croc*, hook]

croquette *n* a ball or roll of e.g. minced meat, fish or potato, coated in breadcrumbs and fried. [Fr, from *croquer*, to crunch]

crosier or **crozier** *n* a bishop's hooked staff, carried as a symbol of office. [MidE *crocer* or *croser*, staff-bearer, from OFr *croce*, hooked staff]

cross *n* **1** a mark, structure or symbol composed of two lines, one crossing the other in the form + or ×; the mark × indicating a mistake or cancellation, as distinct from a tick. **2** a vertical post with a horizontal bar fixed to it, on which criminals were crucified in antiquity; (*cap*) the one on which Christ suffered, or a representation of it; this as a symbol of Christianity. **3** a burden or affliction: *have one's own cross to bear*. **4** a monument, not necessarily in the form of a cross; (as a place name) the site of such a monument. **5** a medal in the form of a cross. **6** an intermingling between breeds or species; the resulting hybrid. **7** a mixture or compromise: *a cross between a dictionary and an encyclopaedia*. **8** a movement across, e.g. of a football from wing to centre. — *v* **1** (*tr* & *intr*; **over**) to move, pass, or get across. **2** (*tr*) to place one across the other: *cross one's legs*. **3** (*intr*) to meet; to intersect. **4** (*intr*) (of letters between two correspondents) to be in transit simultaneously. **5** (*tr*) to make the sign of the Cross over (oneself). **6** (*tr*) to draw a line across: *cross one's t's*. **7** (*tr*) to make (a cheque) payable only through a bank by drawing two parallel lines across it. **8** (*tr*; **out**, **off**, **through**) to delete or cancel by drawing a line through. **9** (*tr*) to interbreed: *cross a sheep with a goat*. **10** (*tr*) to frustrate or thwart: *wouldn't risk crossing him*. **11** (*tr*) to cause unwanted connections between (telephone lines). — *adj* **1** (**with**) angry; in a bad temper. **2** (usu. *in cmpds*) across, as in *cross-Channel ferries* and *cross-country running*; intersecting or at right angles, as in *crossbar*; contrary, as in *cross purposes*; intermingling, as in *cross-breeding*. — **be at cross purposes** (of two people) to misunderstand or clash with each other. — **cross one's fingers** or **keep one's fingers crossed** to cross one's middle finger over one's index finger to ensure good luck; to hope for something even without performing this action. — **cross one's heart** to make a crossing gesture over one's heart as an indication of one's earnestness in promising or asserting something. — **cross someone's mind** to occur to someone. — **cross someone's palm** to put a coin in someone's hand. — **cross someone's path** to encounter someone. — **cross swords with** to have a disagreement or argument with. — **make the sign of the Cross** to make a gesture representing Christ's cross. [OE *cros*, from Lat *crux*]

crossbar *n* **1** a horizontal bar, esp. between upright posts. **2** the horizontal bar on a man's bicycle.

crossbench *n* a seat in parliament for members not belonging to the government or opposition. — *n* **crossbencher**.

crossbill *n* a finch with a beak in which the points cross instead of meeting.

crossbones *n* (*pl*) a pair of crossed femurs appearing beneath the skull in the skull-and-crossbones symbol e.g. used on pirate flags or gravestones.

crossbow *n* a bow placed crosswise on a stock, with a crank to pull back the bow, and a trigger to release arrows.

cross-breed *v* (*tr*) to interbreed (different species). — *n* an animal bred from two different species.

cross-check *v* (*tr*) to check (information) from an independent source. — *n* **cross-check**.

cross-country *adj* across fields, etc. rather than on roads.

cross cut *n* a transverse or diagonal cut.

cross-examine *v* (*tr*) to question (esp. a witness for the opposing side in a law case) so as to develop or throw doubt on his or her statement. — *n* **cross-examination**. — *n* **cross-examiner**.

cross-eyed *adj* having one or both eyes turned inward; squinting.

cross-fertilisation or **-z-** *n* **1** fertilisation of plants or animals from the pollen or sperm of a different individual. **2** the fruitful interaction of ideas from different cultures, etc. — *v* (*tr* & *intr*) **cross-fertilise** or **-ize**.

crossfire *n* **1** gunfire coming from different directions. **2** a bitter or excited exchange of opinions, arguments, etc.

cross-grained *adj* **1** (of wood) having the grain or fibres crossing or intertwined. **2** (of a person) perverse; awkward to deal with.

crosshatch *v* (*tr* & *intr*; *art*) to shade with intersecting lines.

crossing *n* **1** a place for crossing a river, road, etc. **2** a journey across water: *a rough crossing*.

cross-legged *adj* & *adv* (sitting) with ankles crossed and knees wide apart.

crosspatch *n* (*coll*) a bad-tempered person.

cross-ply *adj* (of a tyre) with the cords in the outer casing lying crosswise to strengthen the tread. ◇ See also **radial**.

cross-question *v* (*tr*) to cross-examine.

cross-refer *v* (*intr* & *tr*; **to, from**) to direct (the reader) to refer from one part of a text to another.

cross-reference *n* a reference from one part of a text to another. — *v* (*tr*) to supply with cross-references.

crossroads *n* (*sing*) **1** the point where two or more roads cross or meet. **2** a point at which an important choice has to be made.

cross section *n* **1** (a diagram, etc. of) the surface revealed when a solid object is sliced through, esp. at right angles to its length. **2** a representative sample. — *adj* **cross-sectional**.

cross-stitch *n* an embroidery stitch made by two crossing stitches.

cross-talk *n* **1** unwanted interference between communication channels. **2** fast and clever conversation; repartee.

crosswind *n* a wind blowing across the path of a vehicle or aircraft.

crosswise *adj* & *adv* (lying or moving) across, or so as to cross.

crossword *n* a puzzle in which clues yield words that cross vertically and horizontally within a grid of squares.

crosse *n* a lacrosse stick. [Fr, hooked stick]

crotch *n* the place where the body or a pair of trousers forks into the two legs. [Variant of **crutch**]

crotchet *n* (*mus*) a note equal to two quavers or half a minim in length. [OFr *crochet*, hooked staff]

crotchety *adj* (*coll*) irritable; peevish. — *n* **crotchetiness**. [**crotchet**, in the sense of an odd fancy]

crouch *v* (*intr*; **down**) **1** to bend low or squat with legs close to the chest and often also with one's hands on the ground. **2** (of animals) to lie close to the ground ready to spring up. — *n* a crouching position or action.

croup[1] *n* inflammation of the trachea and larynx in children, causing difficulty in breathing and a hoarse cough. — *adj* **croupy, -*ier*, -*iest***. [Imit.]

croup[2] *n* the rump of a horse. [OFr *crope*, related to **crop**]

croupier *n* the person who presides over a gaming-table, collecting the stakes and paying the winners. [Fr, pillion passenger on a horse]

croûton *n* a small cube of fried or toasted bread, served in soup, etc. [Fr, dimin. of *croûte*, crust]

crow *n* **1** a large black bird (the **carrion crow**) or any of several related large birds including the rook, raven, jackdaw and magpie. **2** the shrill, long-drawn-out cry of a cock. — *v* (*intr*) **1** ***crew*** (of a cock) to cry shrilly. **2** (of a baby) to make happy inarticulate sounds. **3** (**over**) to triumph gleefully; to gloat: *crow over one's defeated* *opponent*. — **as the crow flies** in a straight line. [OE *crawa*]

crowbar *n* a heavy iron bar with a bent, flattened end, used as a lever.

crow's feet *n* (*pl*) the wrinkles at the outer corner of the eye.

crow's nest *n* a platform for a lookout, fixed to the top of a ship's mast.

crowd *n* **1** a large number of people gathered together. **2** the spectators or audience at an event. **3** (esp. in *pl*; *coll*) a lot (of people). **4** a set or group of people. **5** the general mass of people: *don't just follow the crowd*. — *v* **1** (*intr*; **into**, **round**, etc.) to gather or move in a large, usu. tightly-packed, group. **2** (*tr*) to fill: *crowded streets*. **3** (*tr*) to pack; to cram. **4** (*tr*) to press round, or supervise (someone) too closely. — *adj* **crowded**. — *v* **crowd out** (*tr*) **1** to overwhelm and force out: *Big businesses crowd out the small ones*. **2** to fill completely: *The concert hall was crowded out*. [OE *crudan*, to press]

crown *n* **1** the circular, usu. jewelled gold headdress of a sovereign. **2** (*cap*) the sovereign as head of state; the authority or jurisdiction of a sovereign or of the government representing a sovereign. **3** a wreath for the head, or other honour, awarded for victory or success. **4** a highest point of achievement; a summit or climax: *the crown of one's career*. **5** the top, esp. of something rounded. **6** the part of a tooth projecting from the gum; an artificial replacement for this. **7** a representation of a royal crown used as an emblem, symbol, etc. **8** a British coin worth 25 pence (formerly 5 shillings). **9** the junction of the root and stem of a plant. **10** a UK paper size, 385 × 505 mm. — *v* (*tr*) **1** to place a crown ceremonially on the head of; to make king or queen. **2** to be on or round the top of. **3** to reward; to make complete or perfect: *efforts crowned with success*. **4** to put an artificial crown on (a tooth). **5** (*coll*) to hit on the head. **6** (*draughts*) to give (a piece) the status of king. — **to crown it all** (*coll*) as the finishing touch to a series of esp. unfortunate events. [OFr *coroune*, from Lat *corona*, wreath, crown]

crown colony *n* a colony under the direct control of the British government.

Crown Court *n* (*legal*) a court of criminal jurisdiction in England and Wales.

crowning *adj* highest; greatest: *her crowning achievement*.

crown jewels *n* (*pl*) the crown, sceptre and other ceremonial regalia of a sovereign.

crown prince *n* the male heir to a throne.

crown princess *n* **1** the wife of a crown prince. **2** the female heir to a throne.

crozier. See **crosier**.

CRT *abbrev* cathode ray tube.

cruces. See **crux**.

crucial *adj* **1** decisive; critical. **2** (**to**, **for**) very important; essential. **3** (*slang*) very good; great. — *adv* **crucially**. [Lat *crux*, cross]

crucible *n* an earthenware pot in which to heat metals or other substances. [Lat *crucibulum*, lamp]

crucifix *n* a representation, esp. a model, of Christ on the cross. [Lat *crucifixus*, man fixed to a cross]

crucifixion *n* **1** execution by crucifying. **2** (*cap*) (a representation of) the crucifying of Christ. [Lat *crucifixio*, from *crux*, cross + *figere*, to fix]

cruciform *adj* cross-shaped. [Lat *crux*, cross]

crucify *v* **-ies**, **-ied** (*tr*) **1** to put to death by fastening to a cross by the hands and feet. **2** to torment, torture or persecute. **3** (*slang*) to defeat or humiliate utterly. [OFr *crucifier*, from Lat *crux*, cross + *figere*, to fix]

crude *adj* **1** in its natural, unrefined state: *crude oil*. **2** rough or undeveloped: *a crude sketch*. **3** vulgar; tasteless. — *adv* **crudely** *adv*. — *n* **crudity**. [Lat *crudus*, raw]

cruel *adj* **1** deliberately and pitilessly causing pain or suffering. **2** painful; distressful. — *adv* **cruelly**. — *n* **cruelty**, ***-ies***. [Fr]

cruet *n* **1** a small container for salt, pepper, mustard, vinegar, etc., for use at table. **2** a stand for a set of such jars. [OFr, dimin. of *cruye*, jar]

cruise *v* (*intr*) **1** to sail about for pleasure, calling at a succession of places. **2** (of e.g. a vehicle or aircraft) to go at a steady, comfortable speed. [Dut *kruisen*, to cross]

cruise missile *n* a low-flying, long-distance, computer-controlled winged missile.

cruiser *n* **1** a large fast warship. **2** (also **cabin-cruiser**) a motor boat with living quarters.

cruiserweight *n* & *adj* light heavyweight.

crumb *n* **1** a particle of dry food, esp. bread. **2** a small amount: *a crumb of comfort*. **3** the soft interior of a loaf of bread. **4** (*slang*) an obnoxious person. — *v* (*tr*) to coat in breadcrumbs. — *adj* **crumby**, ***-ier***, ***-iest***. [OE *cruma*]

crumble *v* **1** (*tr* & *intr*) to break into crumbs or powdery fragments. **2** (*intr*) to collapse, decay or disintegrate. — *n* a dish of cooked fruit covered with a crumbled mixture of sugar, butter and flour. — *adj* **crumbly**, ***-ier***, ***-iest***. [MidE *kremelen*, from OE *gecrymian*]

crumbs *interj* (*coll*) an expression of surprise, dismay, etc. [Altered form of **Christ**]

crummy *adj* ***-ier***, ***-iest*** (*coll derog*) shoddy, dingy, dirty or generally inferior. — *n* **crumminess**. [Variant of **crumby**]

crumpet *n* **1** a thick round cake made of soft light dough, eaten toasted and buttered. **2** in Scotland, a type of large thin pancake. **3** (*offensive male slang*) a girl; female company generally.

crumple *v* **1** (*tr* & *intr*) to make or become creased or crushed. **2** (*intr*) (of a face or features) to pucker in distress. **3** (*intr*) to collapse; to give away. [OE *crump*, crooked]

crunch *v* **1** (*tr* & *intr*) to crush or grind noisily between the teeth or under the foot. **2** (*intr*) to produce a crunching sound. **3** (*intr* & *tr*; *comput*; *coll*) to key or process at speed. — *n* **1** a crunching action or sound. **2** (*coll*) the moment of decision or crisis: *when it comes to the crunch*. — *adj* **crunchy, *-ier*, *-iest***. [Imit.]

crusade *n* **1** (*hist*) any of a number of Christian military expeditions in mediaeval times to regain the Holy Land from the Muslims. **2** (**against**, **for**) a strenuous campaign in aid of a cause. — *v* (*intr*; **for**, **against**) to engage in a crusade; to campaign. — *n* **crusader**. [Fr *croisade* & Span *cruzada*, from Lat *crux*, cross]

crush *v* **1** (*tr*) to break, damage, bruise, injure or distort by compressing violently. **2** (*tr*) to grind or pound into powder, crumbs, etc. **3** (*tr* & *intr*) to crumple or crease. **4** (*tr*) to defeat, subdue or humiliate. — *n* **1** violent compression. **2** a dense crowd. **3** a drink made from the juice of crushed fruit. **4** (*coll*; **on**) an amorous passion, usu. unsuitable; an infatuation. — *n* **crusher**. [OFr *cruisir*]

crush barrier *n* a barrier for separating a crowd, e.g. of spectators, into sections to prevent crushing.

crust *n* **1** the hard-baked outer surface of a loaf of bread; a piece of this; a dried-up piece of bread. **2** the pastry covering a pie, etc. **3** a crisp or brittle covering. **4** the solidified outer surface of the earth. — *v* (*tr* & *intr*) to cover with, or form, a crust.

crusty *adj* ***-ier*, *-iest*** **1** having a crisp crust. **2** irritable, snappy or cantankerous. — *adv* **crustily**. [Lat *crusta*, shell, rind]

crustacean *n* any of a large group of mainly aquatic creatures with hard shells, e.g. crabs, lobsters, crayfish, shrimps, etc. — *adj* of or relating to these creatures. [Lat *crusta*, shell]

crutch *n* **1** a stick, usu. one of a pair, used as a support by a lame person, with a bar fitting under the armpit or a grip for the elbow. **2** a support, help or aid. **3** same as **crotch**. [OE *crycc*]

crux *n* **cruxes** or **cruces** **1** a decisive, essential or crucial point. **2** a problem or difficulty. [Lat, cross]

cry *v* ***-ies*, *-ied*** **1** (*intr*) to shed tears; to weep. **2** (*intr*; **out**) to shout or shriek, e.g. in pain or fear, or to get attention or help. **3** (*tr*) to exclaim. **4** (*intr*) (of an animal or bird) to utter its characteristic noise. **5** (*tr*; *old*) (of a street trader) to proclaim (one's wares). — *n* ***-ies*** **1** a shout or shriek. **2** an excited utterance or exclamation. **3** (**for**) an appeal or demand. **4** a rallying call or slogan. **5** a bout of weeping. **6** the characteristic utterance of an animal or bird. **7** a street trader's call: *street cries*. — *v* **cry down** (*tr*) to be critical of; to scorn. — **cry one's eyes** or **heart out** to weep long and bitterly. — *v* **cry off** (*tr* & *intr*) to cancel (an engagement or agreement). — *v* **cry out for** (*tr*) to call out or appeal for; to demand: *an abuse crying out for justice*. — *v* **cry up** (*tr*) to praise. — **for crying out loud** (*coll*) an expression of impatience or annoyance. — **in full cry** in keen pursuit of something.

crier *n* (*hist*) an official who announces news by shouting it out in public.

crybaby *n* (*coll derog*) a person who weeps at the slightest upset.

crying *adj* demanding urgent attention: *a crying need*.

cryogenics *n* (*sing*) the branch of physics dealing with very low temperatures and their effects. [Gr *kryos*, frost + **-genic**]

crypt *n* an underground chamber or vault, esp. one beneath a church used for burials. [Gr *krypte*, from *kryptein*, to hide]

cryptic *adj* **1** puzzling, mysterious, obscure or enigmatic. **2** (of a crossword) with clues in the form not of synonyms but of riddles, puns, anagrams, etc. — *adv* **cryptically**. [Gr *kryptikos*, from *kryptein*, to hide]

crypto- *comb fm* **1** hidden or obscure: *cryptogram*. **2** secret or undeclared: *crypto-fascist*. [Gr *kryptein*, to hide]

cryptogam *n* (*bot*) a plant such as a seaweed, moss, fern or fungus, that reproduces by spore rather than seed. [**crypto-** + Gr *gamos*, marriage]

cryptogram *n* something written in a code or cipher. [**crypto-** + **-gram**]

cryptography *n* the study of, or art of writing in and deciphering, codes. — *n* **cryptographer**. — *adj* **cryptographic**. [**crypto-** + **-graphy**]

crystal *n* **1** (also **rock crystal**) a mineral, colourless transparent quartz. **2** (also **crystal ball**) a globe of rock crystal or glass used for crystal-gazing. **3** a brilliant, highly transparent glass used for cut glass; cut-glass articles. **4** (*chem*) a solid substance that has a regularly occurring internal atomic structure, and an external structure of symmetrically arranged facets. **5** (*electr*) a crystalline element functioning e.g. as a transducer or oscillator. — *adj* like crystal in brilliance and clarity. — **crystal clear** as clear or obvious as can be. [Gr *krystallos*, ice]

crystal-gazing *n* **1** a fortune-teller's practice of gazing into a crystal ball long and hard enough to conjure up a vision, for interpreting as appropriate. **2** (*derog*) guesswork about the future. — *n* **crystal-gazer**.

crystalline *adj* **1** having the clarity and brilliance of crystal. **2** (*chem*) taking the form of crystals.

crystallise or **-ize** *v* **1** (*tr* & *intr*) to form into crystals. **2** (*tr*) to coat or preserve (fruit) in sugar. **3** (*tr* & *intr*) (of plans, ideas, etc.) to make or become clear and definite. — *n* **crystallisation** or **-z-**.

crystallography *n* the study of the structure of crystals. — *n* **crystallographer**. [**crystal** + **-graphy**]

crystalloid *n* a substance that when dissolved will pass through a membrane. [**crystal** + **-oid**]

Cs *symbol* (*chem*) caesium.

c/s *abbrev* cycles per second.

CSE *abbrev* Certificate of Secondary Education (replaced in 1988 by **GCSE**).

CS gas *n* a gas that irritates the air passages and eyes, used against rioters, etc. [Invented in the US in 1928 by B *C*arson & R *S*taughton]

CSYS *abbrev* Certificate of Sixth Year Studies.

CT and **Ct.** *abbrev* Connecticut.

Cu *symbol* (*chem*) copper. [Lat *cuprum*]

cu. *abbrev* cubic.

cub *n* **1** the young of certain animals, e.g. the fox, bear, lion and wolf. **2** (*cap*; also **Cub Scout**) a member of the junior branch of the Scout Association. **3** (*old derog*) an impudent young man. **4** (*coll*) a beginner; a novice: *a cub reporter*. — *v* ***-bb-*** (*intr*) to give birth to cubs.

cubbyhole *n* (*coll*) **1** a tiny room. **2** a cupboard, nook or recess in which to accumulate miscellaneous objects. [Dialect *cub*, stall, pen]

cube *n* **1** a solid body having six equal square faces. **2** a block of this shape. **3** (*math*) the product of a number multiplied by itself twice. — *v* (*tr*) **1** to calculate the cube of (a number). **2** to form or cut into cubes. [Fr, from Gr *kybos*, dice]

cube root *n* the number of which a given number is the cube.

cubic *adj* **1** shaped like a cube. **2** having three dimensions. **3** (of a unit of measurement) indicating a volume equivalent to a cube with the unit as its edge measurement: *a cubic metre*. — *adj* **cubical**.

cubicle *n* a small compartment for sleeping or undressing in, screened for privacy. [Lat *cubiculum*, from *cubare*, to lie down]

cubism *n* an early-20th-century movement in painting, with objects represented as geometrical shapes. — *n* & *adj* **cubist**. [**cube**]

cubit *n* an old measure, equal to the length of the forearm from the elbow to the tip of the middle finger. [Lat *cubitum*, elbow]

cuckold *n* (*old*) a man whose wife is unfaithful. — *v* (*tr*) to make a cuckold of. — *n* **cuckoldry**. [MidE *cokkewold*, from OFr *cocu*, cuckoo]

cuckoo *n* a bird known for its distinctive two-note call, that lays its eggs in the nests of other, smaller birds. — *adj* (*coll*) insane; crazy. [Imit.]

cuckoo clock *n* a clock from which a model cuckoo springs on the hour, uttering the appropriate number of cries.

cuckoopint *n* a plant, the wild arum.

cuckoo spit *n* a white froth discharged by the larvae of certain insects on leaves and stems.

cucumber *n* a long green vegetable with juicy white flesh, used in salads. — **cool as a cucumber** (*coll*) calm and composed. [Lat *cucumis*]

cud *n* the half-digested food that a cow or other ruminating animal brings back into the mouth from the stomach to chew again. — **chew the cud** (*coll*) to meditate, ponder or reflect. [OE *cwudu*]

cuddle *v* **1** (*tr* & *intr*) to hug or embrace affectionately. **2** (*intr*; **in**, **up**) to lie close and snug; to nestle. — *n* an affectionate hug. — *adj* **cuddlesome** — *adj* **cuddly**, ***-ier***, ***-iest***.

cudgel *n* a heavy stick or club used as a weapon. — *v* ***-ll-*** (*tr*) to beat with a cudgel. — **cudgel one's brains** to struggle to remember or solve something. — **take up the cudgels for** to fight for or defend. [OE *cycgel*]

cue[1] *n* **1** the final words of an actor's speech, or something else said or done by a performer, that serves as a prompt for another to say or do something. **2** anything that serves as a signal or hint to do something. — *v* ***cueing*** (*tr*) to give a cue to. — **on cue** at precisely the right moment. — **take one's cue from** to follow the lead of, in a matter of behaviour, etc. [Perh. from *q* for *quando* (Lat, when), formerly written in actors' scripts]

cue[2] *n* **1** a stick tapering to a point, used to strike the ball in billiards, snooker and pool. **2** (*old*) a tail of hair or plait at the back of the head. — *v* ***cueing*** (*tr*) to strike (a ball) with the cue. [Fr *queue*, tail]

cuff[1] *n* **1** (a band or folded-back part at) the lower end of a sleeve, usu. at the wrist. **2** (*NAm*) the turned-up part of a trouser leg. **3** (in *pl*; *slang*) handcuffs. — **off the cuff** (*coll*) without preparation or previous thought. [MidE *cuffe*, mitten]

cufflink *n* one of a pair of decorative fasteners for shirt cuffs.

cuff[2] *n* a blow with the open hand. — *v* (*tr*) to hit with an open hand. [Prob. Norse]

cuirass *n* (*hist*) a piece of armour, a breastplate with or without a back plate attached to it. [Fr *cuirasse*]

cuisine *n* **1** a style of cooking. **2** the range of food served at a restaurant, etc. [Fr, kitchen]

cul-de-sac *n* ***culs-de-sac*** a street closed at one end. [Fr, sack-bottom]

culinary *adj* relating to cookery or the kitchen. [Lat *culina*, kitchen]

cull *v* (*tr*) **1** to gather or pick up (information or ideas). **2** to select and kill (weak or surplus animals) from (a herd, etc.). — *n* an act of culling. [OFr *cuillir*, to gather]

culminate *v* (*intr*; **in**) to reach the highest point or climax. — *n* **culmination**. [Lat *culmen*, top, summit]

culottes *n* (*pl*) flared trousers for women, looking like a skirt. [Fr, breeches]

culpable *adj* deserving blame. — *n* **culpability**. — *adv* **culpably**. [Lat *culpare*, to blame]

culprit *n* **1** a person guilty of a misdeed or offence. **2** (*legal*) a person accused of a crime. [Said to be OFr *cul*pable, guilty + *prest*, ready]

cult *n* **1** a system of religious belief; the sect of people following such a system. **2** an esp. extravagant admiration for a person, idea, etc. **3** a fashion, craze or fad. [Lat *cultus*, from *colere*, to worship]

cultivate *v* (*tr*) **1** to prepare and use (land or soil) for crops. **2** to grow (a crop, plant, etc.). **3** to develop or improve: *cultivate one's mind, a taste for literature*. **4** to try to develop a friendship with (someone), esp. for personal advantage. [Lat *cultivare*]

cultivated *adj* **1** well bred and knowledgeable. **2** (of plants) not wild; grown in a garden, etc.

cultivation *n* **1** the act of cultivating. **2** education, breeding and culture.

cultivator *n* **1** a machine for breaking up ground. **2** a person who cultivates.

culture *n* **1** (the customs, ideas, art, etc. of) a particular civilisation, society, or social group. **2** (appreciation of) art, music, literature, etc. **3** improvement and development through care and training: *beauty culture*. **4** (also *in cmpds*) the cultivation of e.g. plants, trees, bees, etc., esp. for commercial purposes: *silkworm culture*; *apiculture*. **5** a crop of bacteria grown for study. — *v* (*tr*) to grow (bacteria) for study. — *adj* **cultural**. — *adv* **culturally**. [Lat *cultura*, from *colere*, to cherish, practise]

cultured *adj* **1** well-educated; having refined tastes and manners. **2** (of a pearl) formed by an oyster round a foreign body deliberately inserted into its shell.

culvert *n* a covered drain or channel carrying water under a road or railway.

-cum- *in cmpds* combined with; also used as: *a kitchen-cum-dining-room*. [Lat, with]

cumbersome *adj* heavy, awkward, unwieldy, clumsy or unmanageable. [MidE *cummyrsum*]

cumin *n* a Mediterranean herb whose seeds are used as flavouring. [Gr *kyminon*]

cummerbund *n* a wide sash, esp. one worn with a dinner jacket. [Hindi *kamarband*, loin band]

cumulative *adj* increasing in amount, effect or strength with each successive addition. — *adv* **cumulatively**. [Lat *cumulare*, to pile up]

cumulus *n* **-li** a white or grey cloud consisting of rounded masses on a darker horizontal base. [Lat, heap, mass]

cuneiform *adj* of, or in, any of several ancient Middle-Eastern scripts with impressed wedge-shaped characters. — *n* cuneiform writing. [Lat *cuneus*, wedge]

cunnilingus *n* the stimulation of a woman's genitals by licking, etc. [Lat *cunnus*, vulva + *lingere*, to lick]

cunning *adj* **1** clever, wily, sly, crafty or artful. **2** ingenious, skilful or subtle. — *n* **1** slyness; wiliness. **2** skill; expertise. — *adv* **cunningly**. [OE *cunnan*, to know]

cunt *n* (*vulg*) **1** the female genitals. **2** (*offensive slang*) used as an abusive term for a person. [MidE *cunte*]

cup *n* **1** a small round container with a handle, from which to drink esp. hot liquids, e.g. tea or coffee. **2** (also **cupful**, **-fuls**) the amount contained in a cup, sometimes used as a measure in cookery. **3** a container or something else shaped like a cup: *egg cups*; *bra cups*. **4** an ornamental, usu. silver, vessel awarded as a prize in sports competitions, etc. **5** a competition in which the prize is a cup. **6** a drink based on wine, with added fruit juice, etc.: *claret cup*. **7** (*literary*) something that one undergoes or experiences: *one's own cup of woe*. — *v* **-pp-** (*tr*) **1** to form (one's hands) into a cup shape. **2** to hold (something) in one's cupped hands. — **one's cup of tea** (*coll*) one's personal preference. [OE *cuppe*, from Lat *cupa*, cask]

cup final *n* the final match in a football contest or other competition for a cup.

cup tie *n* one of a series of knockout matches in a competition for a cup.

cupboard *n* a piece of furniture, or a recess, fitted with doors, shelves, etc., for storing provisions or personal effects. [OE *cuppe-bord*, table for crockery]

cupboard love *n* an insincere show of affection towards someone from whom one wants something.

cupidity *n* greed for wealth and possessions. [Lat *cupiditas*]

Cupid *n* **1** the Roman god of love, represented as a naked winged boy with a bow and arrows. **2** (without *cap*) a figure of Cupid in art or sculpture. [Lat *cupido*, desire, love]

cupola *n* **1** a small dome or turret on a roof; a domed roof or ceiling. **2** an armoured revolving gun turret. **3** a furnace used in iron foundries. [Ital, from Lat *cupula*, dimin. of *cupa*, cask]

cuppa *n* (*coll*) a cup of tea. [Altered form of *cup of*]

cupreous *adj* of, like, or containing, copper. [Lat *cupreus*, from *cuprum*, copper]

cupric *adj* of, or containing, copper, esp. in the bivalent state.

cupro-nickel *n* an alloy of copper with nickel.

cur *n* (*old derog*) **1** a surly mongrel dog. **2** a surly fellow; a scoundrel. [MidE *curdogge*, related to Norse *kurra*, to grumble]

curable. See **cure**.

curare *n* a paralysing poison smeared on arrow-tips by S American Indian hunters, with medicinal uses as a muscle relaxant. [Carib (S American Indian language) *kurari*]

curate *n* a clergyman who acts as assistant to a vicar or rector in the Church of

England. — *n* **curacy**. [Lat *curatus*, from *cura*, care]

curative *adj* able, or tending, to cure. — *n* a substance that cures. [Lat *curativus*, from *cura*, healing]

curator *n* a person who has responsibility for a museum or other collection. [Lat, keeper, from *cura*, care]

curb *n* **1** something that restrains or controls. **2** a chain or strap passing under a horse's jaw, attached at the sides to the bit; a bit with such a fitting. **3** a raised edge or border. **4** (esp. *NAm*) a kerb. — *v* (*tr*) **1** to restrain or control. **2** to put a curb on (a horse). [OFr *courb*, curved]

curd *n* **1** (often in *pl*) milk thickened or coagulated by acid; the solid parts of this, as distinct from the liquid whey, used in making cheese. **2** any of several substances of similar consistency. [MidE *curden*, to congeal]

curdle *v* (*tr* & *intr*) to turn into curds. — **make someone's blood curdle** to horrify or petrify someone. [**curd**]

cure *v* (*tr*) **1** (**of**) to restore to health or normality; to heal. **2** to get rid of (an illness, harmful habit, or other evil). **3** to preserve (meat, fish, etc.) by salting, smoking, etc., or (leather, tobacco, etc.) by drying. **4** to vulcanise (rubber). — *n* **1** something that cures or remedies. **2** restoration to health. **3** a course of healing or remedial treatment. **4** (*relig*) the responsibility of a minister for the souls of his parishioners. — *n* **curability**. — *adj* **curable**. [Lat *curare*, to care for, heal, and *cura*, healing]

cure-all *n* a universal remedy; a panacea.

curette or **curet** *n* a surgeon's instrument for scraping the walls of body cavities free of dead tissue, etc. — *v* ***-tt-*** (*tr*) to scrape with this. — *n* **curettage**. [Fr, from *curer*, to clean, clear]

curfew *n* **1** an order forbidding people to be in the streets after a certain hour. **2** the time at which such an order applies. **3** (*hist*) the ringing of a bell as a signal to put out fires and lights. [OFr *covrefeu*, literally 'covers the fire']

curie *n* a unit of radioactivity. [Marie & Pierre *Curie*, Nobel prizewinners for physics, 1903]

curio *n* ***-os*** an article valued for its rarity or unusualness. [**curiosity**]

curiosity *n* ***-ies*** **1** eagerness to know; inquisitiveness. **2** something strange, odd, rare, exotic or unusual. [Lat *curiositas*]

curious *adj* **1** strange; odd. **2** eager or interested: *curious to see what happens*. **3** inquisitive. — *adv* **curiously**. [Lat *curiosus*, careful, inquisitive]

curl *v* **1** (*tr* & *intr*) to twist, roll or wind (hair) into coils or ringlets; to grow in coils or ringlets. **2** (*intr* & *tr*) to move in, or form into, a spiral, coil or curve. **3** (*intr*) to take part in the game of curling. — *n* **1** a small coil or ringlet of hair. **2** the tendency of hair to curl. **3** a twist, spiral, coil or curve. — *adj* **curly**, ***-ier***, ***-iest***. — *n* **curliness**. — *v* **curl up** (*intr*) **1** to sit or lie with the legs tucked up. **2** (*coll*) to writhe in embarrassment, etc. [MidE *crull*, curly]

curler *n* a device for curling the hair.

curlew *n* a long-legged wading bird with a long curved beak. [OFr *corleu*, perhaps imit.]

curlicue *n* a fancy twist or curl; a flourish made with a pen. [**curly** + **cue**[2]]

curling *n* a team game played on ice with smooth heavy stones with handles, that are slid towards a circular target marked on the ice. [**curl**]

curmudgeon *n* a bad-tempered or mean person. — *adj* **curmudgeonly**.

currant *n* **1** a small dried seedless grape. **2** (*in cmpds*) any of several small soft berries. [OFr (*raisins de*) *Corinthe*, (grapes of) Corinth (the place of export)]

currency *n* ***-ies*** **1** the system of money, or the coins and notes, in use in a country. **2** general acceptance or popularity, esp. of an idea, theory, etc. **3** modernity; up-to-dateness. [Lat *currere*, to run]

current *adj* **1** generally accepted: *according to the current view*. **2** of or belonging to the present: *current affairs*. — *n* **1** a continuous flow of water or air in a particular direction. **2** the flow of electricity through a circuit or wire. **3** a popular trend or tendency: *currents of opinion*.

current account *n* a bank account from which one may draw money without giving notice, but on which no interest is paid.

currently *adv* at the present time.

curriculum *n* ***-la*** a course, esp. of study at school or university. [Lat, course, from *currere*, to run]

curriculum vitae *n* ***curricula vitae*** a written summary of one's personal details and the main events of one's education and career, produced to accompany job applications, etc. [Lat *vita*, life]

curry[1] *n* ***-ies*** a dish, orig. Indian, of meat, fish, or vegetables cooked with usu. hot spices. [Tamil *kari*, sauce]

curry powder *n* a selection of ground spices used in making curry.

curry[2] *v* (*tr*) **1** to groom (a horse). **2** to treat (tanned leather) so as to improve its flexibility, strength and waterproof quality. — **curry favour** (**with**) to use flattery to gain approval; to ingratiate oneself with (someone). [OFr *correier*, to make ready]

curse *n* **1** a blasphemous or obscene expression, usu. of anger; an oath. **2** (**on**) an appeal to God or other divine power to harm someone. **3** the resulting harm suffered by someone: *under a curse*. **4** (**to**) an evil; a cause of harm: *the curse of drugs*. **5** (*coll*; **the**) menstruation; one's period. — *v* **1** (*tr*) to utter a curse against; to revile with curses. **2** (*intr*) to use violent language; to swear. — **be cursed with** to be burdened or afflicted with. [OE *curs*]

cursed *adj* **1** under a curse. **2** (*offensive*) damnable; hateful.

cursive *adj* (of writing) with letters joined up, not printed separately. — *n* cursive writing. — *adv* **cursively**. [Lat *cursivus*, from *currere*, to run]

cursor *n* **1** a flashing marker on a computer screen indicating the current position of the operator in the content. **2** the transparent movable part of a slide rule or other measuring instrument. [Lat, runner]

cursory *adj* hasty; superficial, not thorough. — *adv* **cursorily**. [Lat *cursorius*]

curt *adj* rudely brief; dismissive; abrupt. — *adv* **curtly**. — *n* **curtness**. [Lat *curtus*, short]

curtail *v* (*tr*) to reduce; to cut short; to restrict. — *n* **curtailment**. [Orig. *curtal*, (something) docked or shortened, from Lat *curtus*, short]

curtain *n* **1** a hanging cloth over a window, round a bed, etc. for privacy or to exclude light, or in front of a stage to screen it from the auditorium. **2** the rise of the curtain at the beginning, or fall of the curtain at the end, of a stage performance, act, scene, etc. **3** something resembling a curtain: *a curtain of thick dark hair*. **4** (in *pl*; *coll*) the end; death. — *v* (*tr*) **1** (**off**) to surround or enclose with a curtain. **2** to supply (windows, etc.) with curtains. [OFr *cortine*, from Lat *cortina*]

curtain call *n* an audience's demand for performers to appear in front of the curtain after it has fallen, to receive further applause.

curtain-raiser *n* **1** a short play, etc. before the main performance. **2** any introductory event.

curtain wall *n* **1** (*building*) a wall that is not load-bearing. **2** (*fort*) a wall between two towers or bastions.

curtsy *n* **-ies** a slight bend of the knees with one leg behind the other, performed as a formal gesture of respect by women. — *v* **-ies**, **-ied** (*intr*; **to**) to perform a curtsy. [Variant of **courtesy**]

curvaceous *adj* (*coll*) (of a woman) having a shapely figure. [**curve**]

curvature *n* the condition of being curved; the degree of curvedness. [Lat *curvatura*]

curve *n* **1** a line no part of which is straight, or a surface no part of which is flat. **2** any smoothly arched line or shape, like part of a circle or sphere. **3** (in *pl*; *coll*) the roundnesses of a woman's body. **4** (a line on) a graph. **5** (*math*) a line representing an equation. — *v* (*intr* & *tr*) to form, or form into, a curve; to move in a curve. — *adj* **curvy**, **-ier**, **-iest**. [Lat *curvus*, crooked]

curvilinear *adj* consisting of, or bounded by, a curved line. [**curve** + **rectilinear**]

cushion *n* **1** a stuffed fabric case used for making a seat comfortable, for kneeling on, etc. **2** a thick pad, or something having a similar function. **3** something that gives protection from shock, reduces unpleasant effects, etc. **4** the resilient inner rim of a billiard table. — *v* (*tr*) **1** to reduce the unpleasant or violent effect of. **2** to protect from shock, injury or the extremes of distress. **3** to provide with cushions. [OFr *cuissin*, from Lat *coxa*, hip]

cushy *adj* **-ier**, **-iest** (*coll*) comfortable; easy; undemanding. — *n* **cushiness**. [Hindi *khush*, pleasant]

cusp *n* **1** a point formed by the meeting of two curves. **2** either point of a crescent moon. **3** a point on the grinding surface of a tooth. **4** (*astrol*) the point of transition between one sign of the zodiac and the next. [Lat *cuspis*, a point]

cuss (*old coll*) *n* **1** a curse. **2** a person or animal, esp. if stubborn. — *v* (*intr* & *tr*) to curse. [**curse**]

cussed *adj* **1** obstinate, stubborn, awkward or perverse. **2** cursed. — *adv* **cussedly**. — *n* **cussedness**.

custard *n* **1** a sweet sauce made with milk and cornflour. **2** (also **egg custard**) a dish or sauce of baked eggs and milk. [Formerly *custade*, altered from MidE *crustade*, pie with a crust]

custodian *n* a person who has care of something, e.g. a public building or ancient monument; a guardian or curator. — *n* **custodianship**. [Lat *custodia*, watch, watchman]

custody *n* **1** protective care; the guardianship of a child, awarded to someone by a court of law. **2** the condition of being held by the police; arrest or imprisonment. — *adj* **custodial**. — **take into custody** to arrest. [Lat *custodia*, watch, vigil]

custom *n* **1** a traditional activity or practice. **2** a personal habit. **3** the body of established practices of a community; convention. **4** an established practice having the force of a law. **5** the trade or business that one gives to a shop, etc. by regular purchases.

customary *adj* usual; traditional; according to custom. — *adv* **customarily**.

custom-built or **custom-made** *adj* built or made to an individual customer's requirements.

customer *n* **1** a person who purchases goods from a shop, uses the services of a business, etc. **2** (*coll*) a person with whom one has to deal: *an awkward customer*. [**custom**]

customs *n* **1** (*pl*) taxes or duties paid on imports. **2** (*sing*) the government department that collects these taxes. **3** (*sing*) the place at a port, airport, frontier, etc. where baggage is inspected for goods on which duty must be paid. [**custom**]

customs house *n* the office at a port, etc. where customs duties are paid or collected.

cut *v* **-tt-**, ***cut*** **1** (*tr* & *intr*; **off**, **out**, etc.) (of a sharp-edged instrument or person using it) to slit, pierce, slice or sever; to be so slit, pierced, etc. **2** (*tr*; **up**) to divide by cutting. **3** (*tr*) to trim (hair, nails, etc.), reap (corn), mow (grass) or detach (flowers). **4**

(*tr*; **out**) to make or form by cutting. **5** (*tr*) to shape the surface of (a gem) into facets, or decorate (glass), by cutting. **6** (*tr*) to shape the pieces of (a garment): *badly cut clothes*. **7** (*tr*) to bring out (a record or disc). **8** (*tr*) to injure or wound with a sharp edge or instrument. **9** (*tr*) to hurt: *cut someone to the heart*. **10** (*tr*) to reduce (e.g. prices, wages, interest rates, working hours, etc.). **11** (*tr*) to shorten (e.g. a book or play). **12** (*tr*) to delete or omit. **13** (*tr*) to edit (a film). **14** (*intr*) to stop filming. **15** (*intr* with **to**; *films*) to go straight to (another shot, etc). **16** (*tr*; *math*) to cross or intersect. **17** (*tr*) to reject or renounce: *cut one's links with one's family*. **18** (*tr*) to ignore or pretend not to recognise (a person). **19** (*tr*) to stop: *cut drinking*. **20** (*tr*) to absent oneself from: *cut classes*. **21** (*tr*) to switch off (an engine, etc.). **22** (*tr*; *cricket*, etc.) to hit (a ball) with a slicing action, causing it to spin or swerve. **23** (*tr*) (of a baby) to grow (teeth). **24** (*intr*; **across, through**, etc.) to go off in a certain direction; to take a short route. **25** (*tr*) to dilute (e.g. an alcoholic drink) or adulterate (a drug). **26** (*tr*) to divide; to partition: *a room cut in half by a bookcase*. — *n* **1** an act of cutting; a cutting movement or stroke. **2** a slit, incision or injury made by cutting. **3** a reduction. **4** a deleted passage in a play, etc. **5** the stoppage of an electricity supply, etc. **6** (*slang*) one's share of the profits. **7** a piece of meat cut from an animal. **8** the style in which clothes or hair are cut. **9** a sarcastic remark. **10** a refusal to recognise someone; a snub. **11** a short cut. **12** a channel, passage or canal. — *n* **cutter**. — **a cut above** (*coll*) superior to. — *v* **cut across** (*tr*) **1** to go against (normal procedure, etc.). **2** (of an issue, etc.) to be more important than, or transcend (the barriers or divisions between parties, etc.). — **cut and dried** decided; definite; settled beforehand. — **cut and run** (*coll*) to escape smartly. — **cut and thrust** aggressive competition; quick verbal exchange or repartee. — *v* **cut back** (*tr* or *intr*; **on**) to reduce (spending, etc.) (*n* **cutback**). — **cut both ways** to have advantages and disadvantages; to bear out both sides of an argument. — **cut dead** to ignore (a person) completely. — *v* **cut down 1** (*tr*) to fell (a tree). **2** (*tr* or *intr*; **on**) to reduce; to do less of: *cut down on drinking*. — *v* **cut in** (*intr*) **1** to interrupt. **2** (of a vehicle) to overtake and squeeze in front of another vehicle. — **cut it fine** (*coll*) to leave barely enough time or space for something. — **cut it out** (*slang*) to stop (doing something bad or undesirable). — *v* **cut off** (*tr*) **1** to separate or isolate. **2** to stop the supply of (gas, electricity, etc.). **3** to stop or cut short (*n* **cut-off point** a limit). **4** to disconnect (people conversing on the telephone). — *v* **cut out 1** (*tr*) to remove or delete. **2** (*tr*) to clip (pictures, etc.) out of a magazine, etc. (*n* **cut-out**). **3** (*tr*) (*coll*) to stop. **4** (*tr*) to exclude. **5** (*tr*) to block out (the light or view). **6** (*intr*) (of an engine, etc.) to stop working (*n* **cut-out**). — **(not) cut out for, to be**, etc. (not) having the right qualities for, to be, etc. — **cut short 1** to cut down or shorten (**to cut a long story short** to come straight to the point). **2** to silence by interrupting. — **cut up** (*coll*) distressed; upset. — **cut up rough** (*coll*) to get angry and violent. [MidE *cutten*]

cutaway *adj* **1** (of a diagram, etc.) having outer parts omitted so as to show the interior. **2** (of a coat) with the front part cut away below the waist.

cut glass *n* glass with patterns cut into its surface.

cut-throat *adj* **1** (of competition, etc.) very keen and aggressive. **2** (of a card game) played by three people. — *n* **1** a murderer. **2** a long-bladed razor with a handle.

cutting *n* **1** an extract, article or picture cut from a newspaper, etc. **2** a piece cut from a plant for rooting or grafting. **3** a narrow excavation made through high ground for a road or railway. — *adj* hurtful; sarcastic.

cutwater *n* **1** the sharp vertical front edge of a ship's prow. **2** a pointed projection at the base of a bridge support.

cute *adj* (*coll*) **1** attractive; pretty. **2** clever; cunning; shrewd. — *adv* **cutely**. — *n* **cuteness**. **[acute]**

cuticle *n* **1** the hardened skin forming a rim at the base of a fingernail or toenail. **2** the outer skin; the epidermis. [Lat *cuticula*, skin]

cutlass *n* (*hist*) a short, broad, slightly curved sword with one cutting edge. [Fr *coutelas*, from Lat *cultellus*, little knife]

cutler *n* a person who manufactures cutlery. [Fr *coutelier*, from Lat *culter*, knife]

cutlery *n* knives, forks and spoons for table use.

cutlet *n* **1** a small piece of meat with a bone attached; a rib or neck chop. **2** a slice of veal. **3** a rissole of minced meat or flaked fish. [OFr *costelette*, little rib, from Lat *costa*, rib]

cutter[1]. See **cut**.

cutter[2] *n* **1** a small, single-masted sailing ship. **2** a ship's boat. **3** a motor launch sometimes armed. **[cut]**

cuttlefish *n* ***-fish*** or ***-fishes*** a 10-armed sea creature related to the squid and octopus, that squirts inky fluid. [OE *cudele*]

CV *abbrev* curriculum vitae.

cwm *n* **1** in Wales, a valley. **2** (*geog*) a cirque. [Welsh]

cwt *abbrev* hundredweight. [Lat *centum*, hundred + *wt*, weight]

cyanide *n* a salt of hydrocyanic acid (HCN), esp. the highly poisonous potassium salt (KCN) used e.g. in extracting gold and silver. [Gr *kyanos*, blue (hydrocyanic acid having been first obtained from Prussian blue, a blue dye)]

cyanocobalamin *n* vitamin B_{12}. [**cyanide + cobalt + vitamin**]

cyanosis *n* (*pathol*) blueness of the skin caused by lack of oxygen in the blood. — *adj* **cyanosed**. [Gr *kyanos*, blue + **-osis**]

cybernetics *n* the comparative study of the automatic systems of communication and control in animals and electronic machines. — *adj* **cybernetic**. [Gr *kybernetes*, steersman]

cyclamate *n* any of a number of sweet chemical compounds formerly used as sweetening agents. [Made-up chemical name]

cyclamen *n* a plant with white, pink or red flowers with turned-back petals. [Gr *kuklaminos*]

cycle *n* **1** a constantly repeating series of events or processes. **2** (*electr*; *radio*) one complete oscillation, vibration, or other repeated phenomenon. **3** a series of poems, songs, plays, etc. centred on a particular person or happening. **4** a bicycle or motor cycle. — *v* (*intr*) **1** to ride a bicycle. **2** to happen in cycles. [Gr *kyklos*, circle]

cyclic or **cyclical** *adj* **1** occurring in cycles. **2** (*chem*) (of a compound) having atoms forming a closed ring. — *adv* **cyclically**.

cyclist *n* the rider of a bicycle or motor cycle.

cyclo- *comb fm* **1** circle; ring; cycle. **2** (*chem*) cyclic compound. **3** bicycle. [Gr *kyklos*, circle]

cyclo-cross *n* a cross-country bicycle race in the course of which bicycles have to be carried over natural obstacles.

cyclometer *n* a device for recording the revolutions of a wheel, used on a bicycle to measure the distance travelled. [**cyclo- + -meter**]

cyclone *n* **1** (*meteorol*) a system of winds blowing spirally inward towards a centre of low pressure; a depression. **2** a violent wind storm; a hurricane. — *adj* **cyclonic**. [Gr *kyklon*, a whirling round]

cyclopaedia or **cyclopedia** *n* an encyclopaedia. [**encyclopaedia**]

Cyclops *n* **-*opses*** or **-*lopes*** (*Gr mythol*) one of a race of giants with a single eye in the centre of their foreheads. [Gr, round-eyed]

cyclostyle *n* a duplicating machine that reproduces from a stencil. — *v* (*tr*) to reproduce by means of a cyclostyle. [**cyclo-** + Lat *stylus*, writing tool]

cyclotron *n* (*physics*) an apparatus for accelerating charged atomic particles in a magnetic field. [**cyclo-** + *-tron*, denoting particle accelerator]

cygnet *n* a young swan. [Gr *kyknos*, swan]

cylinder *n* **1** (*math*) a solid or hollow body with a circular top and base and a single straight side curving to follow the circle of the top and base. **2** a container, machine part, or other object of this shape. **3** in an internal-combustion engine, the chamber inside which the piston moves. — *adj* **cylindrical**. [Gr *kylindros*, roller]

cymbal *n* a plate-like brass percussion instrument, either beaten with a drumstick, or used as one of a pair that are struck together to produce a ringing clash. — *n* **cymbalist**. [Gr *kymbalon*]

cyme *n* (*bot*) a spike of flowers in which the stems all terminate in a flower. — *adj* **cymose**. [Gr *kyma*, wave]

Cymric *adj* of or belonging to Wales, its people or language. — *n* the Welsh language. [Welsh *Cymru*, Wales]

cynic *n* **1** a person who has no belief in human unselfishness. **2** (*cap*) one of a group of philosophers of ancient Greece who despised wealth, learning and all pleasures. — *adj* **cynical**. — *adv* **cynically**. — *n* **cynicism**. [Gr *kyon*, dog]

cynosure *n* the focus of attention; the centre of attraction. [Gr *Kynosoura*, dog's tail, i.e. the Little Bear constellation, used as a guide by sailors]

cypher. Another spelling of **cipher**.

cypress *n* a slim, dark green coniferous tree, sometimes associated with death and mourning. [Gr *kyparissos*]

Cypriot *n* **1** a native of Cyprus, an E Mediterranean island. **2** the dialect of Greek spoken in Cyprus. — *adj* of or belonging to Cyprus, its people or language.

Cyrillic *adj* of or in the alphabet used for Russian, Bulgarian and related languages, said to have been invented by St *Cyril*.

cyst *n* **1** (*pathol*) a sac growing in the body or on the skin, containing diseased matter, etc. **2** (*anat*) a bladder or bag-like organ. — *adj* **cystic**. [Gr *kystis*, bladder, pouch]

cystic fibrosis *n* an inherited disease of children causing the formation of cysts, fibrous matter and excess mucus in the body, which interfere with breathing and digestion.

cystitis *n* inflammation of the bladder.

-cyte *comb fm* a cell: *an erythrocyte*. [Gr *kytos*, vessel]

cytology *n* the study of plant and animal cells. — *adj* **cytological** . — *n* **cytologist**. [Gr *kytos*, vessel + **-logy**]

cytoplasm *n* the protoplasm of a cell, not including the nucleus. [**cyto-** + Gr *plasma*, body]

czar, **czarevitch** and **czarina**. See **tsar**.

Czech *n* **1** a native of Czechoslovakia, or of Bohemia or Moravia. **2** one of the two official languages of Czechoslovakia (the other being Slovak). — *adj* of or relating to the Czechs or their language. [Polish]

D

D[1] or **d** *n* ***Ds*** or ***D's***, or ***d's*** **1** the fourth letter of the English alphabet. **2** (usu. **D**) (a mark indicating) the fourth highest grade or quality. **3** (only **D**; *mus*) the second note in the scale of C major. **4** (only **D**) a musical key with the note D as its base. **5** (only **D**) the D-shaped mark on a billiards table.

D[2] *abbrev* **1** (*cards*) diamonds. **2** (*US*) Democrat. ◇ See also **3-D**.

D-Day *n* **1** the opening day (6 June 1944) of the invasion of Europe by the Allied (i.e. British, American, etc.) forces in World War II. **2** the day on which something important is to happen or begin. [*Day*-day]

D-notice *n* a notice sent by the government to newspapers asking them not to publish certain information for reasons of security. [*d*efence notice]

D[3] *symbol* **1** the Roman numeral for 500. **2** (*chem*) deuterium.

3-D *abbrev* three-dimensional.

d[1] *abbrev* **1** deci-. **2** a penny or pence (in the UK before 1971) [Lat *denarius*]. ◇ See also **s**.

d. *abbrev* **1** died. **2** daughter.

'd *short form* **1** would: *I'd go.* **2** had: *he'd gone.* **3** (*coll*) did: *Where'd he go?*

DA *abbrev* ***DAs*** or ***DA's*** (*US*) District Attorney.

da *abbrev* deca-.

dab[1] *v* ***-bb-*** **1** (*intr* & *tr*; **at**) to touch lightly and usu. repeatedly with a cloth, etc. **2** (*tr*; **on, off**) to spread on or remove with light touches of a cloth, etc. — *n* **1** a small amount of something creamy or liquid. **2** a light, gentle touch. **3** a gentle blow. **4** (in *pl*; *slang*) fingerprints. [MidE *dabben*; prob. imit.]

dab[2] *n* a small brown European flatfish with rough scales. [OFr *dabbe*]

dab[3]: **a dab hand** (with **at**) an expert.

dabble *v* **1** (*tr* & *intr*) to move or shake (one's hand, foot, etc.) about in water, esp. playfully. **2** (*intr*; **at, in, with**) to do or study something without serious effort. — *n* **dabbler**. [**dab**[1] or Dut *dabbelen*]

dabchick *n* a small duck-like bird, the little grebe.

da capo (*mus*) an indication to the performer to go back to the beginning of the piece. [Ital, from the beginning]

dace *n* ***dace*** or ***daces*** a small European river fish. [OFr *dars*, dart]

dachshund *n* a breed of small dog with a long body and very short legs. [Ger *Dachs*, badger + *Hund*, dog]

dactyl *n* (*poetry*) a foot consisting of one long or stressed syllable followed by two short or unstressed ones: *'Think of her / mournfully' consists of two dactyls.* — *adj* **dactylic**. [Gr **daktylos**, finger, from the similarity between the lengths of the syllables in a dactyl and the lengths of the bones in a finger (one long and two short)]

dad *n* (*coll*) a father. [From the sound *da da* made by a baby]

Dada or **Dadaism** *n* a movement in art and literature in the early 20th century which turned away from all traditional forms and styles. [Fr *dada*, hobby-horse]

daddy *n* ***-ies*** (*coll*) **1** a father. **2** the oldest, biggest, best, worst, etc. example (of something). [**dad**]

daddy-long-legs *n* (*Br coll*) a cranefly.

dado *n* ***-oes*** or ***-os*** **1** the lower part of the wall of a room when decorated differently from the upper part. **2** (*archit*) the plain square part of the base of a column or pedestal. [Ital, dice]

daemon *n* **1** a spirit occupying a position halfway between gods and men. **2** a spirit which guards a place or takes care of or helps a person. ◇ See also **demon**. [Gr *daimon*]

daffodil *n* **1** a plant which grows from a bulb, with a yellow trumpet-shaped flower on a long stem. **2** the flower of the plant. **3** a pale yellow. — *adj* pale yellow. [MidE *affodille*; the initial *d* is unexplained]

daft *adj* (esp. *Br*; *coll*) **1** silly or foolish. **2** insane or mad. **3** (with **about, on**) enthusiastic about or keen on; in love with. — *adv* **daftly**. — *n* **daftness**. [OE *gedæfte*, meek, mild]

dagger *n* **1** (esp. *hist*) a knife or short sword with a pointed end, used for stabbing. **2** (in books, etc.) the symbol †, used as a reference mark. — **at daggers drawn** openly showing anger or dislike and almost fighting. — **look daggers at** to look angrily at.

dago *n* ***-oes*** (*offensive*) a person of Spanish, Portuguese, Italian or S American origin. [Prob. Span *Diego*, James]

daguerreotype *n* **1** an early type of photography which used mercury vapour to develop an exposure of silver iodide on a copper plate. **2** a photograph made by this method. [Fr, from its inventor, Louis *Daguerre* (1789–1851)]

dahl. See **dal**.

dahlia *n* a garden plant with large brightly-coloured flowers, some varieties having ball-like heads with many petals. [Anders *Dahl*, 18th-century Swedish botanist]

Dáil or **Dáil Éireann** *n* the lower house of the parliament of the Republic of Ireland. [Irish, assembly of Ireland]

daily *adj* **1** happening, appearing, etc. every day, or every day except Sunday, or (now often) every day except Saturday and Sunday. **2** relating to a single day. — *adv* every day. — *n* **-ies 1** a newspaper published every day except Sunday. **2** (*Br coll*) a person, usu. a woman, who is paid to clean and tidy a house regularly, but not necessarily every day. [**day**]

daily bread *n* the money, food, etc. one needs to live.

daily dozen *n* (*old*) physical exercises performed every day for the sake of one's health.

dainty *adj* **-ier**, **-iest 1** small and pretty, and usu. delicate. **2** small and neat. **3** (of food) particularly nice to eat. **4** (often *derog*) very, or excessively, careful and sensitive about what one does or says. — *n* **-ies** (usu. in *pl*) something small and nice to eat, esp. a small cake or sweet. — *adv* **daintily**. — *n* **daintiness**. [OFr *daintie*, worthiness]

daiquiri *n* a drink made with rum, lime juice and sugar. [*Daiquiri* in Cuba]

dairy *n* **-ies 1** a shop where milk, butter, cheese, etc. are sold. **2** the building on a farm where milk is kept and butter and cheese are made, or a factory where milk, cream, etc. are processed and bottled or packaged. **3** a company which processes and supplies milk, cream, butter, etc. [MidE *daierie*, from *daie*, dairymaid]

dairy cattle *n* cattle kept to produce milk rather than meat.

dairy farm *n* a farm which specialises in producing milk, etc. — *n* **dairy farmer**.

dairymaid *n* (esp. *hist*) a milkmaid.

dairyman or **dairywoman** *n* a person who looks after the cows on a farm.

dais *n* a raised platform in a hall, e.g. for speakers at a meeting. [OFr *deis*]

daisy *n* **-ies 1** a common small flower with a yellow centre and usu. white petals. **2** any of various plants like the common daisy. [OE *dæges eage*, day's eye]

daisy-wheel *n* in a typewriter, etc., a metal disc divided into separate spokes, each with a letter of the alphabet at the end, the disc rotating so that the letter printed corresponds to the letter struck on the keyboard.

dal, **dahl** or **dhal** *n* **1** any of various edible dried split pea-like seeds. **2** a cooked dish made of any of these seeds. [Hindi *dal*, to split]

Dalai Lama *n* the head of the Buddhist religion in Tibet. [Mongolian *dalai*, ocean + Tibetan *lama*, high priest]

dale *n* a valley, esp. in the N of England. [OE *dæl*]

dally *v* **-ies**, **-ied** (*intr*) **1** to waste time by going slowly or doing silly and unnecessary things. **2** (*old derog*; with **with**) to have a love relationship with (someone) which is not serious although it may seem to be. — *n* **dalliance**. [OFr *dalier*, to chat]

Dalmatian *n* a large short-haired dog, white with dark spots. [*Dalmatia* in Yugoslavia]

dal segno (*mus*) an indication that the performer must go back to the sign 𝄋. [Ital, from the sign]

dam[1] *n* **1** a wall built across a river, etc. to hold back the water. **2** the water held back in this way, often forming a lake. — *v* **-mm-** (*tr*; **up**) to hold back with a dam. [Prob. from OGer dialect]

dam[2] *n* (of e.g. horses, cattle and sheep) a female parent. [**dame**]

damage *n* **1** harm or injury, or loss caused by injury. **2** (in *pl*; *legal*) payment due for loss or injury caused by another person, organisation, etc. — *v* (*tr*) to cause harm, injury or loss to. — *adj* **damaged**. [OFr, from Lat *damnum*, loss]

damaging *adj* having a bad effect e.g. on a person's reputation.

damask *n* a type of cloth, orig. silk, now usu. linen, with a pattern woven into it, often used for tablecloths, curtains, etc. — *adj* greyish-pink or greyish-red. [*Damascus* in Syria, where such cloth was made]

damask rose *n* a sweet-smelling pink or red variety of rose.

dame *n* **1** (the status or title of) a lady who has been awarded the highest or second highest class of distinction in any of four British orders of chivalry (= honours for service or merit awarded by the Queen or the Government). ◇ See also **knight**. **2** (*NAm slang*) a woman. **3** a comic female character in a pantomime, usu. played by a man. [OFr, from Lat *domina*, lady]

damn *v* (*tr*) **1** (*relig*) to sentence to never-ending punishment in hell. **2** to declare to be useless or worthless. **3** to suggest or prove the guiltiness of. — *interj* (also **damn it**) an expression of annoyance or disappointment. — *adj* (often used *coll* for mere emphasis) annoying; hateful. — *adv* (*coll*) used for emphasis. — **as near as damn it** (*coll*) as accurately, closely, etc. as possible; acceptably accurate, etc.; very nearly. — **be damned if** (*coll*) **1** to refuse (to do something). **2** not to do (something) at all. — **damn all** (*coll*) nothing at all. — **damn with faint praise** to praise so unenthusiastically that one is in effect condemning (someone or something). — **not give a damn** (*coll*) not to care at all. [Lat *damnare*, to condemn]

damnable *adj* **1** hateful; awful; deserving to be condemned. **2** annoying.

damnably *adv* annoyingly; very.

damnation *n* (*relig*) **1** never-ending punishment in hell. **2** the act of condemning or state of being condemned to such punishment. — *interj* an expression of annoyance or disappointment.

damned *adj* **1** (*relig*) sentenced to damnation. **2** (*coll*) annoying, hateful, etc. — *adv* (*coll*) very. — **do one's damnedest** (*coll*) to do one's best.

damning *adj* **1** very critical. **2** proving or suggesting guilt.

damp *adj* slightly wet. — *n* slight wetness, e.g. in walls or the air, esp. if cold and unpleasant. — *v* (*tr*) **1** to make slightly wet. **2** (**down**) to make (emotions, interest, etc.) less strong. **3** (**down**) to make (a fire) burn more slowly. **4** (*mus*) to press (the strings, or a string, of an instrument) to stop or lessen vibration. — *adv* **damply**. — *n* **dampness**. [MidE, harmful vapour]

damp-course or **damp-proof course** *n* a layer of material in a wall of a building, usu. near the ground, which stops wetness (rising damp) rising up through the bricks.

dampen *v* **-*n*-** **1** (*tr*) to make slightly wet. **2** (*tr* & *intr*; **down**) (of emotions, interest, etc.) to make or become less strong. **3** (*tr*; **down**) to make (a fire) burn more slowly. — *n* **dampener**.

damper *n* **1** something which lessens enthusiasm, interest, etc. **2** a movable plate which allows the flow of air to a fire, etc. to be controlled so that the amount of heat may be altered. — **put a damper on** to lessen (enthusiasm for, interest in, etc.).

damp-proof *adj* (of a material or substance) not allowing wetness to get through.

damp-proof course see **damp-course** above.

damp squib *n* an event which one expects to be exciting or interesting, but which turns out to be disappointing.

rising damp *n* wetness which rises up through the bricks of a wall.

damsel *n* (*old* or *literary*) a girl or young woman. [OFr *dameisele*]

damson *n* **1** a small purple plum. **2** the tree it grows on. [Lat *Damascenus*, of Damascus in Syria]

Dan. *abbrev* Danish.

dan *n* any of the grades of black belt awarded for particular levels of skill in judo, karate, etc. [Jap]

dance *v* **1** (*intr*) to make a usu. repeated series of rhythmic steps or movements (usu. in time to music). **2** (*tr*) to perform (a particular series of such steps or movements): *dance a waltz*. **3** (*intr*; **about**, **around**, etc.) to move or jump quickly up and down or from side to side. **4** (*tr*) to bounce (a baby), usu. on one's knee. — *n* **1** a series of fixed steps, usu. made in time to music. **2** a social gathering at which people dance. **3** a piece of music played for dancing. — *n* **dancer**. — *n* **dancing**. — **dance attendance on** (usu. *derog*) to follow (someone) and do whatever he or she wants. — **dance to someone's tune** to do what someone wants or expects. — **lead (someone) a (merry) dance** (*Br*) to involve (someone) in unnecessary difficulties and exertions. [OFr *danser*, to dance]

dandelion *n* a common wild plant with indented leaves, yellow flowers and round fluffy seed-heads. [Fr *dent de lion*, lion's tooth]

dander: **get one's**, or **someone's**, **dander up** (*coll*) to (cause to) become angry.

dandle *v* (*tr*) to bounce (usu. a small child) on one's knee.

dandruff *n* small pieces of dead skin on or from the head under the hair.

dandy *n* **-*ies*** a man who pays a lot of attention to his appearance, dressing very fashionably or elegantly. — *adj* (*coll*) **-*ier*, -*iest*** good; fine.

Dane *n* **1** a person born in Denmark or a citizen of Denmark. **2** (*hist*) any of the Vikings from Scandinavia who invaded Britain in the 9th to 11th centuries. ◇ See also **Danish**. [Dan *Daner*, Danes]

Danegeld *n* a tax imposed in England in the 10th century, to pay for the defence of the country against the invading Danes or to pay them to go away. [OE *Dene*, Danes + *geld*, payment]

Danelaw *n* the part of England occupied by the Danes in the 9th to 11th centuries. [OE *Dena lagu*, Danes' law]

danger *n* **1** a situation or state in which someone or something may suffer harm, an injury or a loss: *in danger of falling*. **2** something that may cause harm, injury or loss. **3** a possibility (of something unpleasant happening). — **on the danger list** (*med*) so ill or seriously injured that there is a high risk of death. [OFr *dangier*, power (therefore power to harm)]

danger money *n* extra money paid to a person for doing a dangerous job.

dangerous *adj* likely to or able to cause harm or injury. — *adv* **dangerously**.

dangle *v* **1** (*intr* & *tr*) to (cause or allow to) hang loosely. **2** (*tr*) to offer or present (an idea, a possible reward, etc.) to someone.

Danish *adj* **1** of Denmark or its inhabitants. **2** of the language spoken in Denmark. — *n* **1** the language spoken in Denmark. **2** (*pl*; with **the**) the people of Denmark. ◇ See also **Dane**. [OFr *daneis*]

Danish blue *n* a type of strong-tasting cheese, white with streaks of bluish mould through it.

Danish pastry *n* a flat cake of rich, light pastry, with any of various types of sweet filling on the top.

dank *adj* (usu. of a place) unpleasantly wet and cold. — *n* **dankness**.

dapper *adj* (usu. used of small men) neat and smart in appearance and lively in movement. [Dut, brave]

dappled *adj* marked with spots or rounded patches of a different, usu. darker, colour.

dapple-grey *adj* & *n* (a horse) of a pale grey colour with darker spots.

Darby and Joan *n* (*pl*) an old man and old woman who have been happily married for many years. [Characters in an 18th-century song]

Darby and Joan club *n* a social club for elderly men and women.

dare *v* **1** (*aux* & *intr*) to be brave enough (to do something frightening, difficult or dangerous): *He wouldn't dare to leave. Dare I tell him?* **2** (*tr*) to challenge (someone to do something frightening, difficult, dangerous, etc.). **3** (*tr*) to be brave enough to risk facing: *dare his father's anger*. — *n* a challenge (to do something dangerous, etc.). — **how dare you!** an expression used when one is very angry or upset at something someone has said or done. — **I daresay** or **I dare say** probably; I suppose. [OE *durran*]

dare-devil *n* a person who does dangerous or adventurous things without worrying about the risks involved. — *adj* (of actions, etc.) daring and dangerous.

daring *adj* **1** bold, courageous or adventurous. **2** designed or intended to shock or surprise. — *adv* **daringly**.

dark *adj* **1** without light. **2** (of a colour) not light or pale; closer to black than white. **3** (of a person or the colour of his or her skin or hair) not light or fair. **4** sad or gloomy. **5** evil or sinister: *dark powers*. **6** mysterious and unknown: *a dark secret*. — *n* **1** (usu. with **the**) the absence of light. **2** the time of day when night begins and there is no more light: *after dark*. **3** a dark colour. — *n* **darkness**. — **in the dark** not knowing or aware. — **keep it dark** to keep (something) secret. [OE *deorc*, dark]

the Dark Ages *n* (*pl*) in European history, the period of time from about the 5th to the 11th centuries.

darken *v* (*tr* & *intr*) to make or become dark or darker. — *adj* **darkened**.

dark horse *n* a person about whom little is known.

darkly *adv* in a mysterious, gloomy, sinister or threatening way or tone of voice.

darkroom *n* a room into which no ordinary light is allowed, used for developing photographs.

darky or **darkie** *n* (*very offensive*) a person with black or brown skin, esp. a Black.

darling *n* **1** a dearly loved person (often used as a term of affection). **2** a lovable person or thing. — *adj* **1** well loved. **2** (*coll*) delightful.

darn[1] *v* (*tr*) to mend by sewing with rows of stitches which cross each other.

darning *n* **1** the work of darning (clothes, etc.). **2** clothes, etc. which need to be darned or which have been darned.

darn[2] *interj* a less offensive or emphatic substitute for **damn**.

darned *adj* irritating; disliked.

dart *n* **1** a narrow, pointed weapon that can be thrown or fired. **2** a small sharp-pointed missile used in the game of darts. **3** a sudden, quick movement. **4** a fold sewn into a piece of clothing to make it fit more neatly. — *v* **1** (*intr*) to move suddenly and quickly. **2** (*tr*) to send or give (a look or glance) quickly. — *adj* **darting**. [OFr]

darts *n* (*sing*) a game in which darts (sense **2**) are thrown at a circular target (**dartboard**) divided into numbered sections, points being scored according to where one's darts land on the board.

Darwinism *n* the theory of the development of the various species of plants and animals by evolution, proposed by Charles *Darwin* (1809–82).

dash[1] *v* **1** (*intr*) to run quickly; to rush. **2** (*intr*) to crash or smash. **3** (*tr*) to (cause to) hit violently. **4** (*tr*) to destroy or put an end to (hopes, etc.) — *n* **1** a quick run or sudden rush. **2** a small amount of something added, esp. a liquid. **3** a patch of colour. **4** a short line (—) used in writing to show a break in a sentence, etc. **5** in Morse code, the longer of the two lengths of signal element, written as a short line. ◇ See also **dot**. **6** confidence, enthusiasm and stylishness. **7** (esp. *NAm sport*) a short race for fast runners. [MidE *daschen* or *dassen*, to rush or strike violently]

dashing *adj* **1** smart; stylish. **2** lively and enthusiastic. — *adv* **dashingly**.

dash[2] *interj* a milder and less offensive substitute for **damn**. [**dash**[1]]

dashboard *n* (*Br*) a panel with dials, switches and instruments in front of the driver's seat in a motor vehicle, boat, etc. [**dash**[1]; orig. a board protecting the driver of a horse-drawn coach from splashes of mud]

dastardly *adj* (*old*) cowardly, mean and cruel. [Prob. connected with **dazed**]

dat. *abbrev* dative.

data *n* (orig. *pl* but now usu. treated as *sing*. ◇ See also **datum**) **1** facts or information. **2** information given to, stored in and operated on by a computer. [Lat, things given]

data-bank *n* **1** a usu. large organised store of information. **2** a data-base.

data-base *n* a large amount of information stored in a computer, from which any particular piece of information can be obtained quickly and easily.

data capture *n* any process of changing information from its original form into a form which can be fed into a computer.

data processing *n* the operations carried out by a computer on the information fed into it.

date[1] *n* **1** the day of the month, and/or the year, in which something happened, is happening or is going to happen. **2** a statement on a letter, document, etc. giving usu. the day, the month and the year when it was written, sent, etc. **3** a particular period of time in history: *costumes of an earlier date*. **4** (*coll*) a planned meeting or social outing, usu. with a person of the opposite sex. **5** (*NAm coll*) a person of the opposite sex whom one is meeting or going out with. **6** (*coll*) an agreed time and place of performance. — *v* **1** (*tr*) to put a date on. **2** (*tr*) to find, decide on or guess the date of. **3** (with **back to** or **from**) to have begun at (an earlier time). **4** (*tr*) to show the age of; to make (esp. a person) seem old. **5** (*intr*) to become old-fashioned. **6** (*tr* & *intr*; *coll*) to go out with (a person of the opposite sex), esp. regularly. — **to date** up to the present time. [OFr, from Lat *datum*, given]

closing date *n* the last possible date on which something can be done, sent in, etc.

dated *adj* old-fashioned.

dateline *n* a line, usu. at the top of a newspaper article, which gives the date and place of writing.

date line *n* a line which more or less corresponds to the line running from north to south 180° east or west of Greenwich, on the east side of which the date is one day earlier than on the west side.

date-stamp *n* **1** a device, usu. a rubber stamp, for printing the date on something. **2** the date printed by this.

date[2] *n* the fruit of the date-palm, brown, sticky and sweet-tasting when dried. [Fr *datte*, from Gr *daktylos*, finger, date]

date-palm *n* a tall tree with long spreading leaves which grows in hot countries.

dative *n* (*gram*) in some languages, a case which is mostly used to show that a noun or pronoun is the indirect object of a verb. — *adj* (*gram*) of or in this case. [Lat *dativus*, from *dare*, to give]

datum *n* ***data*** a piece of information. ◇ See also **data**. [Lat *datum*, something given]

daub *v* **1** (*tr*; **on**) to spread (something) carelessly, roughly or unevenly on to or over. **2** (*tr* with **with**) to cover with a soft sticky substance or liquid. **3** (*tr* & *intr*; *derog*) to paint carelessly or without skill. — *n* **1** soft, sticky material such as clay, often used as a covering for walls. ◇ See also **wattle and daub**. **2** (*coll derog*) an unskilful or carelessly done painting. — *n* **dauber**. [OFr *dauber*, from Lat *dealbare*, to whitewash]

daughter *n* **1** a female child considered in relation to her parents. **2** a woman closely associated with, involved with or influenced by a person, thing, or place: *a faithful daughter of the Church*. — *adj* derived by some process from and thought of as being like a daughter of: *French is a daughter language of Latin*. — *adj* **daughterly**. [OE *dohtor*]

daughter-in-law *n* ***daughters-in-law*** a son's wife.

daunt *v* (*tr*) to frighten, worry or discourage. — *adj* **daunting**. — *adv* **dauntingly**. — **nothing daunted** not at all discouraged or less enthusiastic. [OFr *danter*]

dauntless *adj* fearless; not easily discouraged. — *adv* **dauntlessly**. — *n* **dauntlessness**.

dauphin *n* (*hist*) the eldest son of the king of France (between 1349 and 1830). [OFr *daulphin*, from *Delphinus*, family name of the lords of the territory around Vienne in western France]

dauphine *n* the wife of a dauphin.

davenport *n* **1** (*Br*) a type of desk. **2** (*NAm*) a large sofa.

davit *n* a curved device used as a crane on a ship, esp. either one of a pair of such devices from which a lifeboat is hung and by means of which it can be lowered over the side of the ship. [From a form of the name *David*]

Davy Jones's locker *n* the bottom of the sea, esp. as the place where the bodies of drowned sailors lie. [*Davy Jones*, a sailors' name for the evil spirit of the sea]

Davy lamp *n* a miner's safety-lamp, invented by Sir Humphry *Davy* (1778–1829).

dawdle *v* (*intr*) **1** to walk more slowly than necessary or desirable. **2** to waste time, esp. by taking longer than necessary to do something. — *n* **dawdler**.

dawn or (*literary*) **dawning** *n* **1** the time of day when light first appears as the sun rises. **2** the beginning of (a new period of time, etc.). — **at (the) break of dawn** at the first light of day when the sun rises. — *v* **dawn on** (*tr*) to be realised or understood by. [Related to **day**]

dawn chorus *n* the singing of birds at dawn.

day *n* **1** the period of twenty-four hours from one midnight to the next. **2** the period of time from sunrise to sunset. **3** the period of time in any twenty-four hours normally spent doing something, esp. working: *the working day*. **4** (in *pl*) a particular period of time. — **all in a**, or **the, day's work** a normal or acceptable part of one's job. — **carry the day** see **win the day** below. — **day by day** as each day passes. — **day in, day out** (usu. *derog*) every day without change. — **from day to day 1** thinking only of the problems, etc. of each day as it comes. **2** as each day passes. — **have had one's day** to have passed the time of one's greatest success, influence, popularity, etc. — **in someone's day** during the time in the past when someone was young or active. — **in this day and age** nowadays; in modern times. — **make someone's day** to make (someone) very happy. — **one of these days** at some time in the future. — **one of those days** (*coll*) a day when things have gone wrong. — **that will be the day** (*coll*) that is very unlikely to happen. — **those were the days** that was a good or happy time. — **win** or **carry the day** to win a victory. [OE *dæg*]

daybreak *n* the time in the morning when light first appears in the sky; dawn.

day care *n* supervision and care given by trained nurses or other staff to young children or elderly handicapped people during the day.

day centre or **day care centre** *n* a place which provides supervision and care, and/or social activities, during the day for the elderly, the handicapped, people who have just left prison, etc.

daydream *n* pleasant thoughts which take one's attention away from what one is, or should be, doing. — *v* (*intr*) to be engrossed in daydreams. — *n* **daydreamer**.

daylight *n* **1** the light given by the sun; natural light as opposed to electric light, etc. **2** the time in the morning when light first appears in the sky; dawn. — **beat**, etc. **the living daylights out of** (*coll*) to beat, etc. severely. — **in broad daylight** (talking of a shocking or criminal act) **1** during the day. **2** openly, with no attempt to hide one's actions. — **scare**, etc. **the living daylights out of** (*coll*) to frighten greatly. — **see daylight 1** to begin to understand. **2** to know that one has nearly completed a difficult or long task.

daylight robbery *n* (*coll*) greatly overcharging for something.

day nursery *n* a place where young children are looked after during the day, e.g. while their parents are at work.

day of reckoning *n* a time when mistakes, failures, bad deeds, etc. are punished.

day-release *n* (*Br*) a system by which employees are given time off work (usu. one day a week) to study at college, etc.

day return *n* (*Br*) a reduced bus or train fare for a journey to somewhere and back again on the same day.

day shift *n* **1** a period of working during the day. **2** the people who work during this period. ◇ See also **back shift** and **night shift**.

daytime *n* the time when there is daylight, between sunrise and sunset.

daze *v* (*tr*) to make (someone) feel confused or unable to think clearly (e.g. by a blow or shock). — *n* a confused, forgetful or inattentive state of mind. — *adj* **dazed**. [Norse *dasask*, to be weary]

dazzle *v* (*tr*) **1** to cause to be unable to see properly, with or because of a strong light. **2** to impress greatly by one's beauty, charm, skill, etc. — *adj* **dazzling**. — *adv* **dazzlingly**. **[daze]**

dB *abbrev* decibel.

DBE *abbrev* Dame (Commander of the Order) of the British Empire.

DBS *abbrev* direct broadcasting by satellite.

DC *abbrev* **1** District of Columbia. **2** District Commissioner. **3** (*mus*) da capo. **4** direct current.

DD *abbrev* for *Divinitatis Doctor* (Lat), Doctor of Divinity.

DDR *abbrev* for *Deutsche Demokratische Republik* (Ger), the former German Democratic Republic (East Germany).

DDT *abbrev* dichlorodiphenyltrichloroethane, a chemical used, esp. formerly, to kill insects.

DE *abbrev* Delaware.

de- *pfx* **1** down or away. **2** reversal or removal. **3** completely. [Senses **1** and **3** from Lat *de*, off, from; sense **2** from OFr *des-*, from Lat *dis-* (see **dis-**)]

deacon *n* **1** a member of the lowest rank of clergy in the Roman Catholic and Anglican churches. **2** in some other churches, a member of the church with certain duties such as looking after the church's financial affairs. ◇ See also **diaconate**. [Gr *diakonos*, servant]

deaconess *n* **1** in some churches, a woman who has similar duties to those of a deacon. **2** in some churches, a woman whose duties are similar to those of a minister and who acts as an assistant to the minister.

deactivate *v* (*tr*) to remove or lessen the capacity of (something such as a bomb) to function or work. — *n* **deactivation**. **[de-** (sense **2**) + **activate]**

dead *adj* **1** no longer living. **2** not alive. **3** no longer in existence; extinct. **4** with nothing living or growing in or on it. **5** not, or no longer, functioning; not connected to a source of power. **6** no longer burning. **7** no longer in use: *a dead language*. **8** no longer of interest or importance: *a dead issue*. **9** having little or no excitement or activity; boring. **10** without feeling; numb. **11** complete; absolute. **12** (of a sound) dull. **13** (*sport*) (of a ball) in a position where it cannot be played until brought back into the game. — *n* (with **the**) **1** (*pl*) dead people. **2** the middle (of night, when it is very still and dark, or of winter, when it is very cold). — *adv* (*slang*) quite; very. — *n* **deadness**. — **dead against** or **dead set against** completely opposed to. — **dead from the neck up** (*coll derog*) very stupid or of little intelligence. — **dead set on** very determined or keen to. — **dead to** incapable of understanding; not affected by. — **dead to the world** (*coll*) fast asleep. — **stop dead** to stop quickly and completely. — **one wouldn't be seen dead** (*coll*) one would not ever, for any reason, be (with someone, doing something, etc.). [OE]

dead-beat *n* (*coll*) a useless person. ◇ See also under **beat**.

dead duck *n* (*coll*) someone or something with no chance of success or survival.

deaden *v* (*tr*) to lessen, weaken or make less sharp, strong, etc.

dead end *n* **1** a road closed off at one end. **2** a situation or activity with no possibility of further progress or movement. — *adj* **dead-end** allowing no progress.

dead-head *v* (*tr*) to remove withered or dead flowers from (plants).

dead heat *n* in a race, competition, etc., the result when two or more competitors produce equally good performances.

dead letter *n* a rule or law no longer obeyed or in force.

deadline *n* a time by which something must be done, produced or finished.

deadlock *n* a situation in which no further progress towards an agreement is possible. — *v* (*tr* & *intr*) to cause or come to such a situation.

dead loss *n* (*coll*) someone or something that is totally useless.

deadly *adj* **1** causing or likely to cause death. **2** (*coll*) very dull or uninteresting. **3**

very great: *in deadly earnest*. — *adv* very; absolutely. — *n* **deadliness**.

deadly nightshade *n* a plant with bell-shaped purple flowers and poisonous black berries from which a drug, belladonna, is obtained.

dead man's handle or **pedal** *n* a device on a machine, e.g. a railway engine, which must be kept pressed down for the machine to operate and which stops the machine if the pressure is released.

dead-nettle *n* a plant like a nettle but which has no sting.

deadpan *adj* (of someone's expression, etc.) showing no emotion or feeling, esp. when joking but pretending to be serious.

dead reckoning *n* the estimating of the position of a ship, aircraft, etc. from the distance and direction travelled, without looking at the position of the stars, sun or moon.

deadweight *n* **1** a heavy load. **2** (*tech*; **dead weight**) the difference in the weight of a ship when unloaded and loaded.

dead wood *n* (*coll*) someone or something that is no longer useful or needed.

deaf *adj* **1** unable to hear at all or to hear well. **2** (with **to**) not willing to listen to (advice, criticism, etc.). — *n* (*pl*; with **the**) deaf people. — *n* **deafness**. — **turn a deaf ear to** to ignore or refuse to pay any attention to. [OE]

deaf-aid *n* (*Br*) a hearing-aid.

deafen *v* (*tr*) to make deaf or temporarily unable to hear. — *adj* **deafening**. — *adv* **deafeningly**.

deaf-mute *n* (considered *offensive* by some people) a person who is both deaf and unable to speak.

deal[1] *n* **1** a bargain, agreement or arrangement, esp. in business or politics. **2** treatment. **3** the act of, the way of, or a player's turn of sharing out cards among the players in a card game. — *v* ***dealt*** **1** (*intr* with **in**) to buy and sell. **2** (*tr* & *intr*; **out**) to divide (the cards) among the players in a card game. **3** (*intr* & *tr*; **out**) to give (something) out to a number of people, etc. — *n* **dealer**. — **deal (someone) a blow** to hit or strike (someone). — *v* **deal with** (*tr*) **1** to take action on. **2** to be about or concerned with. — **a good** or **great deal 1** a large quantity. **2** very much. [OE *dæl*, part]

dealership *n* **1** a business which buys and sells things. **2** a business licensed to sell a particular product by its manufacturer.

dealings *n* (*pl*) business, etc. contacts.

deal[2] *n* a plank, or planks, of fir or pine wood, or other soft wood, used for making e.g. furniture. [OGer dialect *dele*]

dealt. See **deal**[1].

dean *n* **1** a senior clergyman in an Anglican cathedral. **2** a senior official in a university or college, sometimes with responsibility for student discipline. **3** the head of a university or college faculty. [OFr *deien*]

deanery *n* **-*ies*** **1** the house or office of a dean. **2** a group of parishes for which a rural dean has responsibility.

rural dean *n* in the Church of England, a clergyman with responsibility over a group of parishes.

dear *adj* **1** high in price; charging high prices. **2** lovable; attractive. **3** used in addressing someone at the start of a letter. **4** (**to**) greatly loved. **5** (with **to**) very important or precious. — *n* **1** a charming or lovable person. **2** (used esp. as a form of address) a person one loves or likes. — *interj* an expression of dismay, etc. — *n* **dearness**. — **cost (someone) dear** to cause or result in a lot of trouble or suffering. — **dear knows** (*coll*) no one knows. [OE *deore*]

dearly *adv* **1** very much. **2** at a high price or cost. — **pay dearly** to be made to suffer.

dearth *n* a scarceness or lack (of something). [**dear** + **-th**[2]]

death *n* **1** the time, act or manner of dying, or the state of being dead. **2** the fact that people, etc. die. **3** something which causes one to die: *be the death of someone*. **4** the end or destruction of something. **5** (*cap*) the figure of a skeleton, as a symbol of death. — **at death's door** almost dead. — **in at the death 1** present when a hunted animal, e.g. a fox, is killed. **2** present at the end or destruction (of something). — **like death warmed up** or **over** (*coll*) very ill. — **like grim death** very hard or tightly. — **put to death** to kill or cause to be killed; to execute. — **to death** very much. — **to the death** until dead or until one's opponent is dead. [OE]

death-bed *n* the bed in which a person dies or is about to die.

death blow *n* an action, decision, etc. which puts an end to or destroys (hopes, plans, etc.).

death cell *n* a prison cell in which a prisoner who is condemned to death is kept before the sentence is carried out.

death certificate *n* a certificate, signed by a doctor, stating the time and cause of someone's death.

death duty *n* (*Br*) formerly, a tax paid on the value of property left by a person after he or she has died (now replaced by **inheritance tax**).

death-knell *n* **1** the ringing of a bell when someone has died. **2** an action, announcement, etc. that heralds the end or destruction of (hopes, plans, etc.).

deathless *adj* (often *ironic*) immortal; unforgettable; *deathless prose*.

deathly *adj* & *adv* like in death.

death-mask *n* a mask made of a person's face after he or she has died.

the death penalty *n* punishment of a crime by death.

death-rate *n* the number of deaths as a proportion of the total population, usu. calculated as a percentage or rate per thousand.

death row *n* (*US*) part of a prison where people who have been sentenced to death are kept.

death's-head *n* a human skull, or a picture, mask, etc. representing one.

deathtrap *n* a building, vehicle, etc. which is unsafe and likely to cause serious or fatal accidents.

death-warrant *n* an official order that a death sentence is to be carried out.

deathwatch beetle *n* a type of beetle which makes a ticking or tapping sound that used to be thought to mean that someone in the building was going to die.

death wish *n* a desire to die, or that someone else should die.

deb *n* (*coll*) a debutante.

debacle or **débâcle** *n* total disorder, defeat, collapse of organisation, etc. [Fr]

debar *v* **-rr-** (*tr*) to stop (someone) from joining, taking part in, doing, etc. something. — *n* **debarment**. [**de-** (sense **3**) + **bar**]

debase *v* (*tr*) **1** to lower the value, quality or status (of something). **2** to lower the value of (a coin) by adding metal of a lower value. — *adj* **debased**. — *n* **debasement**. [**de-** (sense **1**) + **base**[2]]

debate *n* **1** a formal discussion, often in front of an audience, in which two or more people put forward opposing views on a particular subject. **2** any general discussion on a subject, not necessarily in one place or at one time. — *v* (*tr* & *intr*) **1** to hold or take part in a formal discussion (about something), often in front of an audience. **2** to consider the arguments for or against (something). — *n* **debater**. — *n* **debating**. — **open to debate** not certain or agreed; in doubt. [OFr *debatre*, to discuss]

debatable or **debateable** *adj* doubtful; which could be argued about; uncertain.

debauch *v* (*tr*) to corrupt; to cause or persuade (someone) to take part in immoral (esp. sexual) activities or excessive drinking. — *n* a period of debauched behaviour. — *adj* **debauched**. — *n* **debauchee**. — *n* **debauchery**, ***-ies***. — *n* **debauchment**. [OFr *desbaucher*, to corrupt]

debenture *n* **1** a type of loan to a company or government agency which is usu. made for a set period of time and carries a fixed rate of interest. **2** the document or bond acknowledging this loan. [Lat *debentur*, there are due or owed]

debilitate *v* (*tr*) to make weak or weaker. — *n* **debilitation**. — *adj* **debilitating**. [Lat *debilis*, weak]

debility *n* weakness of the body or mind, esp. as a result of illness or disease.

debit *n* **1** an entry in an account recording what is owed or has been spent. **2** a sum taken from a bank, etc. account. **3** a deduction made from a bill or account. ◇ See also **credit**. — *v* **-t-** (*tr*) **1** to take from (an account, etc.). **2** (**against, to, with**) to record in a debit entry: *debited £150 against her; debited her with £150*. [Lat *debitum*, what is due]

debonair *adj* (esp. of a man) cheerful, charming and of elegant appearance and good manners. — *adv* **debonairly**. — *n* **debonairness**. [OFr *de bon aire*, of good manners]

debouch *v* (*intr*; *tech*) (of troops or a river, etc.) to come out of a narrow place or opening into a wider or more open place. — *n* **debouchment**. [Fr *déboucher*, from *de*, from + *bouche*, mouth]

debrief *v* (*tr*) to gather information from (a diplomat, astronaut, soldier, etc.) after a battle, event, mission, etc. — *n* **debriefing**. [**de-** (sense **2**) + **brief**]

debris or **débris** *n* **1** what remains of something crushed, smashed, destroyed, etc. **2** rubbish. **3** small pieces of rock. [Fr]

debt *n* **1** something which is owed. **2** the state of owing something. [OFr *dette*, from Lat *debitum*, what is owed]

bad debt *n* a debt which will never be paid.

debt of honour *n* a debt one is morally but not legally obliged to pay.

debtor *n* someone owing money. ◇ See also **creditor**.

national debt see **national**.

debug *v* **-gg-** (*tr*) **1** to remove secret microphones from (a room, etc.). **2** to look for and remove faults in (a computer program). [**de-** (sense **2**) + **bug**]

debunk *v* (*tr*) to show (a person's claims, good reputation, etc.) to be false or unjustified. [**de-** (sense **2**) + **bunk**[2]]

début or **debut** *n* the first public appearance of a performer. [Fr]

débutante *n* a young woman making her first formal appearance as an adult in upper-class society, usu. at a ball. [Fr, from *débuter*, to start off]

Dec. *abbrev* **December**.

deca- *comb fm* ten: *decahedron*. [Gr *deka*, ten]

decade *n* **1** a period of ten years. **2** a group or series of ten things, etc. [Gr *deka*, ten]

decadence *n* **1** a falling from high to low standards in morals, art, etc. **2** the state of having low or immoral standards of behaviour, etc. — *adj* **decadent**. — *adv* **decadently**. [Fr *décadence*, from Lat *de*, from + *cadere*, to fall]

decaffeinate *v* (*tr*) to remove all or part of the caffeine from. — *adj* **decaffeinated**. [**de-** (sense **2**) + **caffeine**]

decagon *n* (*geom*) a polygon with ten sides and ten angles. — *adj* **decagonal**. [Gr *deka*, ten + *gonia*, angle]

decahedron *n* a solid figure with ten faces. — *adj* **decahedral**. [**deca-** + Gr *hedra*, seat]

Decalogue *n* (*Bible*; with **the**) the Ten Commandments given by God to Moses. [Gr *deka*, ten + *logos*, word]

decamp *v* (*intr*) to go away suddenly, esp. secretly. [Fr *décamper*]

decant *v* (*tr*) **1** to pour (wine, etc.) from one bottle or container to another, leaving any sediment behind. **2** to remove (people) from where they usually live to some other place. [Fr *décanter*, from Lat *de*, from + *canthus*, spout]

decanter *n* an ornamental bottle for wine, sherry, whisky, etc.

decapitate *v* (*tr*) to cut off the head of. — *n* **decapitation**. [Lat *de*, from + *caput*, head]

decapod *n* **1** any of a group of sea animals which have ten feet (including the pincers), e.g. a crab or lobster. **2** any of a group of sea animals with ten tentacles, e.g. a squid or cuttlefish. [Gr *deka*, ten + *pous*, foot]

decarbonise or **-ize** *v* (*tr*) to remove carbon from (an internal-combustion engine). — *n* **decarbonisation** or **-z-**. [**de-** (sense **2**) + **carbon**]

decathlon *n* an athletic competition (usu. for men) in which competitors take part in ten different events over two days. — *n* **decathlete**. [Gr *deka*, ten + *athlon*, contest]

decay *v* **1** (*tr* & *intr*) to make or become rotten, ruined, weaker in health or power, etc. **2** (*intr*; *physics*) (of radioactive substances) to lose radioactivity. — *n* **1** the state or process of rotting; being or becoming ruined. **2** a gradual decrease in health, power, quality, etc. **3** rotten matter in a tooth, etc. [OFr *decair*]

decease *n* (*formal* or *legal*) death. [OFr *deces*]

deceased (*formal* or *legal*) *adj* dead. — *n* (with **the**) a dead person or dead people.

deceit *n* **1** (an act of) deceiving or misleading. **2** dishonesty; deceitfulness; willingness to deceive. [OFr *deceite*]

deceitful *adj* **1** deceiving, esp. as a general habit. **2** intended to deceive. — *adv* **deceitfully**. — *n* **deceitfulness**.

deceive *v* (*tr*) **1** to mislead or lie to. **2** to convince (oneself) that something is true when it is not. — *n* **deceiver**. ◇ See also **deception**. [OFr *deceivre*]

decelerate *v* (*tr* & *intr*) to (cause to) slow down (esp. a vehicle, machine, etc.) — *n* **deceleration**. [Lat *de-*, down + **accelerate**]

December *n* the twelfth month of the year. [Lat, from *decem*, ten (because it was at one time the tenth month of the Roman year)]

decency. See **decent**.

decennial *adj* **1** happening every ten years. **2** consisting of ten years. [Lat *decem*, ten + *annus*, year]

decent *adj* **1** respectable; suitable; modest, not vulgar or immoral. **2** kind, tolerant or likeable. **3** fairly good; adequate. — *adv* **decently**. [Lat *decere*, to be fitting]

decency *n* **-ies** **1** decent behaviour or character. **2** (in *pl*) the generally accepted rules of respectable or moral behaviour.

decentralise or **-ize** *v* (*tr* & *intr*) (of a part of government, industry, etc.) to alter or be altered by the transfer of organisation, etc. from one main central place to several smaller, less central positions. — *n* **decentralisation** or **-z-**. [**de-** (sense **2**) + **centralise**]

deception *n* **1** an act of deceiving or the state of being deceived. **2** something which deceives or misleads. [Lat *decipere*, to deceive]

deceptive *adj* deceiving; misleading. — *adv* **deceptively**. — *n* **deceptiveness**.

deci- *comb fm* one-tenth: *decilitre*. [Lat *decimus*, tenth]

decibel *n* a unit of measurement of the loudness of a sound. [**deci-** + **bel**]

decide *v* **1** (*tr* & *intr*; **on, against**, etc.) to (cause or help) to reach a decision. **2** (*tr*) to settle (something); to make the final result of (something) certain. **3** (*intr* with **for, against, in favour of**, etc.) to make a formal judgement. [Lat *decidere*, to cut down, settle]

decided *adj* **1** clear and definite; unmistakeable. **2** determined; showing no doubt. — *adv* **decidedly**.

decider *n* **1** someone or something that decides. **2** something that decides the result of something.

deciduous *adj* (*biol*) **1** (of trees or shrubs) having leaves that fall off in autumn. ◇ See also **evergreen**. **2** (of horns, teeth, wings, etc.) falling off or out after a certain period. [Lat *decidere*, to fall down]

decilitre *n* a tenth of a litre. [**deci-** + **litre**]

decimal *adj* **1** based on the number ten. **2** (of a system of measurement, etc.) with units that are each ten times greater than the next smallest unit. — *n* a decimal fraction. [Lat *decimalis*, of tenths]

decimal currency *n* a system of money in which each coin or note is either a tenth of or ten times another in value.

decimal fraction *n* a fraction in which tenths, hundredths, thousandths, etc. are written in figures after a dot (decimal point) which follows the figure or figures expressing whole numbers: $0{\cdot}5 = \frac{5}{10}$ *or* $\frac{1}{2}$; $1{\cdot}125 = 1\frac{125}{1000}$ *or* $1\frac{1}{8}$. ◇ See also **vulgar fraction**.

decimalise or **-ize** *v* (*tr*) to convert (numbers, a currency, etc.) from a non-decimal to a decimal form. — *n* **decimalisation** or **-z-**.

decimate *v* (*tr*) to reduce greatly in number; to destroy a large part or number of. — *n* **decimation**. [Lat *decimare*, to take a tenth person or thing, from *decem*, ten]

decipher *v* **-r-** (*tr*) **1** to translate (a message or text in code or in an unfamiliar or strange form of writing) into ordinary, understandable language. **2** to work out the meaning of (something obscure or difficult to read). — *adj* **decipherable**. — *n* **decipherment**. [**de-** (sense **2**) + **cipher**]

decision *n* **1** the act of deciding. **2** something decided. **3** the ability to make decisions and act on them firmly. [Lat *decisio*, cutting off]

decisive *adj* **1** putting an end to doubt or dispute. **2** willing and able to make decisions quickly and with firmness. — *adv* **decisively**. — *n* **decisiveness**.

deck[1] *n* **1** a platform extending from one side of a ship to the other, and forming a floor or covering. **2** a floor in a bus, etc. **3** (esp. *US*) a pack of playing-cards. **4** the platform which supports and includes the turntable on a record-player, or (tape deck) the part of a tape-recorder in which the magnetic tapes are placed. — **clear the decks** (*coll*) to clear away obstacles or deal with preliminary jobs in preparation for further activity. — **hit the deck** (*coll*) to lie or fall down suddenly and quickly on the ground or floor. [ODut *dec*, roof, covering]

deck-chair *n* (*Br*) a light folding chair made of wood and canvas or other heavy fabric, usu. used for sitting outside.

-decker *comb fm* having (a certain number of) decks.

deck hand *n* a person who does general work on the deck of a ship.

deck[2] *v* (*tr*; **out**) to decorate. [Dut *dekken*, to cover]

decko. See **dekko**.

declaim *v* **1** (*tr* & *intr*) to make (a speech) in an impressive and dramatic manner. **2** (*intr* with **against**) to protest about (something) loudly and passionately. [Lat *declamare*]

declamation *n* an impressive or emotional speech, usu. made in protest or condemnation. — *adj* **declamatory**. [Lat *declamare*, to declaim]

declare *v* **1** (*tr*) to announce publicly or formally: *declare war*. **2** (*tr*) to say firmly or emphatically. **3** (*tr*) to make known (goods on which duty must be paid, income on which tax should be paid, etc.). **4** (*intr*; *cricket*) to end an innings before ten wickets have fallen. **5** (*intr*; **for**, **against**) to state one's support or opposition. **6** (*tr* & *intr*; *cards*) to state or show that one is holding (certain cards). — *n* **declaration**. [Lat *declarare*, from *clarus*, clear]

declarative *adj* (*gram*) making a statement.

declassify *v* **-ies**, **-ied** (*tr*) to take (an official document, etc.) off the list of secret information and allow the general public access to it. — *n* **declassification**. [**de-** (sense **2**) + **classify**]

declension *n* (*gram*) **1** in certain languages, such as Latin, any of various sets of different forms taken by nouns, adjectives or pronouns to indicate case, number and gender. **2** the act of stating these forms. ◇ See also **conjugation** and **decline**. **3** any group of nouns or adjectives showing the same pattern of forms. [Lat *declinatio*, bending aside]

declination *n* **1** (*tech*) the angle of a compass needle east or west of true north. **2** (*astron*) the angular distance of a star or planet from the celestial equator. [Lat *declinatio*, bending aside]

decline *v* **1** (*tr*) to refuse (an invitation, etc.), esp. politely. **2** (*intr*) to become less strong or less healthy. **3** (*intr*) to become less in quality or quantity. **4** (*tr*; *gram*) to state the pattern of forms representing the various cases of (a noun, adjective or pronoun). ◇ See also **conjugate** and **declension**. — *n* a lessening of strength, health, quality, quantity, etc. [Lat *declinare*, to bend aside]

declivity *n* **-ies** (*formal*) a downward slope. ◇ See also **acclivity**. [Lat *de*, down + *clivus*, sloping]

declutch *v* (*intr*) to release the clutch of (a motor vehicle). [**de-** (sense **2**) + **clutch**]

decoction *n* a liquid obtained by boiling something in water, e.g. to extract its flavour. [Lat *decoctio*, from *coquere*, to cook or boil]

decode *v* (*tr*) to translate (a coded message) into ordinary language. — *n* **decoder**. [**de-** (sense **2**) + **code**]

décolleté or **décolletée** *adj* **1** (of a woman's dress, etc.) having the neckline cut low at the front. **2** (of a woman) wearing such a dress, etc. [Fr *décolleter*, to bare the neck and shoulders]

décolletage *n* a low-cut neckline on a woman's dress, etc.

decommission *v* **-n-** (*tr*) to take (e.g. a warship or atomic reactor) out of use or operation. [**de-** (sense **2**) + **commission**]

decompose *v* **1** (*intr*) to decay or rot. **2** (*tr* & *intr*; *tech*) to separate into smaller or simpler parts or elements. — *n* **decomposition** . [Fr *décomposer*]

decompress *v* (*tr*; *tech*) to decrease the pressure on. — *n* **decompression**. [**de-** (sense **2**) + **compress**]

decompression chamber *n* a sealed room in which the air pressure can be varied, used esp. to enable deep-sea divers to return gradually and safely to normal air pressure after a dive.

decompression sickness *n* a painful, and sometimes fatal, condition affecting divers and others who are exposed to a sudden lowering of atmospheric pressure, caused by bubbles forming in the blood; the bends.

decongestant *n* a medicine which helps to reduce blocking of the nose, e.g. during a cold. [**de-** (sense **2**) + **congestion**]

decontaminate *v* (*tr*) to make (something) safe by removing poisons, radioactivity, etc. — *n* **decontamination**. [**de-** (sense **2**) + **contaminate**]

décor *n* the style of decoration, furnishings, etc. in a room or house. [Fr, decoration]

decorate *v* (*tr*) **1** to beautify with ornaments, etc. **2** to put paint or wallpaper on. **3** to give a medal or badge to as a mark of honour. — *n* **decoratoring**. — *n* **decorator**. [Lat *decorare*, to beautify]

decoration *n* **1** something used to decorate. **2** the act of decorating. **3** a medal or badge given as a mark of honour.

decorative *adj* ornamental or beautiful (esp. if not useful).

decorous *adj* (of behaviour or appearance) correct or socially acceptable; showing proper respect. — *adv* **decorously**. — *n* **decorousness**. [Lat *decorus*, becoming, fitting]

decorum *n* correct or socially acceptable behaviour. [Lat *decorus*, becoming or fitting]

decoy *v* (*tr*) to lead or lure into a trap. — *n* someone or something used to lead or lure (a person or animal) into a trap. [Prob. from Dut *de kooi*, the cage]

decrease *v* (*tr* & *intr*) to make or become less. — *n* a lessening or loss. — *adj* **decreasing**. — *adv* **decreasingly**. [Lat *decrescere*]

decree *n* **1** a formal order or ruling made by someone in high authority (e.g. a king) and which becomes law. **2** (*legal*) a ruling made in a law court. — *v* (*tr*) to order or decide (something) formally or officially. [Lat *decretum*]

decree absolute *n* (*legal*) a decree issued by a court in divorce proceedings which officially ends a marriage.

decree nisi *n* (*legal*) a decree issued by a court in divorce proceedings which will become a decree absolute after a period of time unless some reason is shown why it should not. [Lat *nisi*, unless]

decrepit *adj* **1** weak or worn out because of old age. **2** in a very poor state because of age or long use. — *n* **decrepitness** or **decrepitude**. [Lat *decrepitus*, very old]

decretal *n* a papal decree. [Lat *decretalis*, of a decree]

decry *v* ***-ies***, ***-ied*** (*tr*) to express disapproval of; to criticise as worthless or unsuitable. [Fr *décrier*]

dedicate *v* (*tr*) **1** (with **to**) to give or devote (oneself or one's time, money, etc.) wholly or chiefly to. **2** (with **to**) to name a person as a token of one's love or respect or as a greeting, e.g. at the front of a book or when having a record played for them on the radio. **3** (**to**) to set apart for some sacred purpose. — *n* **dedicator**. — *adj* **dedicatory**. [Lat *dedicare*, to declare, dedicate]

dedicated *adj* **1** working very hard at or spending a great deal of one's time and energy on something. **2** (*tech*) (esp. of a computer) designed to carry out one particular function. — *adv* **dedicatedly**.

dedication *n* **1** the quality of being dedicated. **2** the act of dedicating. **3** the words dedicating a book, etc. to someone.

deduce *v* (*tr*) to think out or judge on the basis of what one knows or assumes to be fact. — *n* **deducibility**— *adj* **deducible**. ◇ See also **deduction**. [Lat *de*, from + *ducere*, to lead]

deduct *v* (*tr*) to take away (a number, amount, etc.). — *n* **deductibility** — *adj* **deductible**. ◇ See also **deduction**. [Lat *de*, from + *ducere*, to lead]

deduction *n* **1** the act or process of deducting. **2** something, esp. money, which has been or will be deducted. **3** the act or process of deducing, esp. of deducing a particular fact from what one knows or thinks to be generally true. ◇ See also **induction**. **4** something that has been deduced. [Lat *de*, from + *ducere*, to lead]

deductive *adj* (of a logical process of thought) deducing or involving deduction of particular facts from general truths. ◇ See also **inductive**.

deed *n* **1** something someone has done. **2** a brave action or notable achievement. **3** (*legal*) a signed statement which records the terms of an agreement, esp. about a change in ownership of a house or other property. [OE *dæd* or *ded*]

deed poll *n* (*Br legal*) a deed made and signed by one person only, esp. when changing his or her name.

dee-jay or **deejay** *n* (*coll*) a disc jockey. [From the initials *DJ*]

deem *v* (*tr*; *formal* or *old*) to judge, think or consider. [OE *deman*, to form a judgement]

deep *adj* **1** far down from the top or surface; with a relatively great distance from the top or surface to the bottom. **2** going or being far in from the outside surface or edge. **3** (usu. *in compds*) going or being far down by a specified amount: *knee-deep in mud*. **4** in a specified number of rows or layers: *lined up four deep*. **5** coming from or going far down; long and full: *a deep sigh*; *a deep breath*. **6** very great; serious: *deep trouble*. **7** (of a colour) strong and relatively dark; not light or pale. **8** (with **in**) occupied or involved to a great extent: *deep in thought*. **9** low in pitch. **10** (of emotions, etc.) very strongly felt. **11** obscure; hard to understand: *deep thoughts*. **12** (of a person) mysterious; keeping secret thoughts. **13** (*cricket*) not close to the wickets. **14** (*football*) well behind one's team's front line of players. — *adv* **1** deeply. **2** far down or into. **3** late on in or well into (a period of time). — *n* **1** (with **the**) the ocean. **2** (sometimes in *pl*; *old*) a place far below the surface of the ground or the sea. ◇ See also **depth**. — **deep down** in reality although not in appearance. — **go off (at) the deep end** (*coll*) to lose one's temper suddenly and violently. — **in** or **into deep water** (*coll*) in or into trouble or difficulties. — **jump**, **dive**, or **be thrown**, **in at the deep end** (*coll*) to begin, or be forced to begin, a (usu. difficult) job or activity with little or no experience or preparation. [OE *deop*]

deepen *v* ***-n-*** (*tr* & *intr*) to make or become deeper, greater, more intense, etc.

deep-freeze *n* a freezer. — *v* (*tr*) to freeze and keep (food) in a freezer.

deep-fry *v* (*tr*) to fry (something completely submerged in hot fat or oil).

deeply *adv* very greatly.

deep-rooted, deeply-rooted or **deep-seated** *adj* (of ideas, habits, etc.) deeply and firmly established in a person or group of people and not easily removed or changed.

deep-sea *adj* of, for, working, etc. in, the deeper parts of the sea.

deep-seated see **deep-rooted**.

deep-set *adj* (of the eyes) in relatively deep sockets.

the Deep South *n* the south-east part of the USA, roughly the states of S Carolina, Georgia, Louisiana, Mississippi and Alabama.

deep space *n* outer space, understood by some people as the area of space well outside the earth's atmosphere or beyond the moon's orbit, by others as the area outside the solar system.

deer *n* ***deer*** any member of a family of usu. large, four-footed, hoofed animals, the male of which often has antlers. [OE *deor*, animal, deer]

deerskin *n* leather made from the skin of a deer.

deerstalker *n* a kind of hat with peaks at the front and back and flaps at the side to cover the ears.

deface *v* (*tr*) to deliberately spoil the appearance of (e.g. by marking or cutting). — *n* **defacement**. [OFr *desfacier*]

de facto actual or actually, though not necessarily legally so. ◇ See also **de jure**. [Lat, in fact]

defame *v* (*tr*) to attack the good reputation of (someone) by saying something bad and untrue about him or her. — *n* **defamation**. — *adj* **defamatory**. [Lat *diffamare*, to spread bad reports about]

default *v* (*intr*; **on**) to fail to do what one should do, esp. to fail to pay what is due. — *n* **1** a failure to do or pay what one should. **2** (*comput*) a preset option which will always be followed unless the operator enters a command to the contrary. — *n* **defaulter**. — **by default** because of someone's failure to do something which would have prevented or altered the situation. [OFr *defaillir*, to fail]

defeat *v* (*tr*) **1** to beat, win a victory over, e.g. in a war, competition, game or argument. **2** to cause (plans, etc.) to fail. — *n* the act of defeating or state of being defeated. [OFr *desfait*, from *desfaire*, to ruin, undo]

defeatism *n* a state of mind in which one too readily expects or accepts defeat. — *n* & *adj* **defeatist**.

defecate *v* (*intr*; *formal* or *tech*) to empty the bowels of waste matter. — *n* **defecation**. ◇ See also **faeces**. [Lat *defaecare*]

defect *n* a flaw, fault or imperfection. — *v* (*intr*) to leave one's country, political party or group, esp. to support or join an opposing one. — *n* **defection**. — *n* **defector**. [Lat *deficere*, to fail]

defective *adj* imperfect; having a defect or defects.

defence *n* **1** the act of defending against attack. **2** the method, means, equipment or (often in *pl*) fortifications used to guard or protect against attack or when attacked. **3** the armed forces of a country. **4** a person's answer to an accusation, justifying or denying what he or she has been accused of. **5** (with **the**) in a law-court, the person or people on trial and the lawyer or lawyers acting for them. **6** (*sport*; with **the**) the players in a team whose main task is to prevent their opponents from scoring. ◇ See also **defend** and **defensive**. [Lat *defendere*, to defend]

defenceless *adj* unable to defend oneself if attacked. — *adv* **defencelessly**. — *n* **defencelessness**.

defence mechanism *n* (*psychol*) a (usu. subconscious) method of blocking out of one's mind a feeling or memory one finds painful.

defend *v* **1** (*tr*) to guard or protect against attack or when attacked. **2** (*tr*) to explain, justify, or argue in support of, the actions of (someone accused of doing wrong). **3** (*tr* & *intr*) to be the lawyer acting on behalf of (the accused) in a trial. **4** (*tr* & *intr*; *sport*) to try to prevent one's opponents from scoring. **5** (*tr*; *sport*) to take part in a contest against a challenger for (a title, medal, etc. one holds). — *n* **defender**. [Lat *defendere*]

defendant *n* a person against whom a charge is brought in a law-court. ◇ See also **plaintiff**.

defensible *adj* able to be defended or justified. — *adv* **defensibly**. [Lat *defensibilis*]

defensive *adj* **1** defending or ready to defend. **2** attempting to justify one's actions when criticised or when expecting criticism. — *adv* **defensively**. — *n* **defensiveness**. — **on the defensive** defending oneself or prepared to defend oneself against attack or criticism. [Lat *defensivus*]

defer[1] *v* **-rr-** (*tr*) to put off or leave until a later time. — *n* **deferment** or **deferral**. [Lat *differre*, to delay, postpone]

deferred payment *n* payment for goods one has received by small sums of money over a period of time.

defer[2] *v* **-rr-** (*intr* with **to**) to give in to the wishes, opinions or orders of. [Fr *déférer*]

deference *n* **1** willingness to consider or respect the wishes, etc. of others. **2** the act of deferring. — **in deference to** deferring to; showing recognition of or respect for.

deferential *adj* showing deference or respect. — *adv* **deferentially**.

defiance *n* open disobedience; challenging or opposition, esp. in a way that shows lack of respect. — *adj* **defiant**. — *adv* **defiantly**. [**defy** + **-ance**]

deficient *adj* (**in**) not good enough; not having all that is needed. [Lat *deficere*, to fail or be lacking]

deficiency *n* **-ies 1** a shortage or lack in quality or amount. **2** the thing or amount lacking.

deficit *n* the amount by which some quantity (esp. a sum of money) is less than what is required (e.g. the amount by which expenditure is greater than income). [Lat *deficere*, to fail or be lacking]

defile[1] *v* (*tr*) **1** to make dirty or polluted. **2** to take away or spoil the goodness, purity, holiness, etc. of. — *n* **defilement**. — *n* **defiler**. [OFr *defouler*, to trample or violate; altered under the influence of the old word *befile*, from OE *befylan*, to make foul]

defile[2] *n* a narrow valley or passage between mountains. [Fr *défilé*, from *défiler*, to march in file]

define *v* (*tr*) **1** to fix or state the exact meaning of (a word, etc.). **2** to fix, describe or explain (opinions, duties, the qualities or limits of, etc.). **3** to make clear the outline or shape of: *an ill-defined splodge on the canvas*. — *adj* **definable**. ◇ See also **definition**. [Lat *definire*, to set boundaries to]

definite *adj* **1** fixed or firm; not liable to change. **2** sure; certain. **3** clear and precise. **4** having clear outlines. — *n* **definiteness**. [Lat *definire*, to set boundaries to]

definite article *n* (*gram*) the word **the**. ◇ See also **indefinite article**.

definitely *adv* clearly or certainly.

definition *n* **1** a statement of the meaning of a word or phrase. **2** the act of defining a word or phrase. **3** the quality of having clear, precise limits or form. **4** the degree of clearness and preciseness of limits or form. — **by definition** because of what it, he, etc. is. [Lat *definitio*]

definitive *adj* **1** final and settling a matter once and for all. **2** most complete or authoritative. — *adv* **definitively**. — *n* **definitiveness**. [Lat *definitivus*]

deflate *v* **1** (*tr* & *intr*) to (cause to) collapse or grow smaller by letting out gas. **2** (*tr*) to reduce or take away the hopes, excitement, feelings of importance or self-confidence, etc. of. **3** (*tr* & *intr*; *econ*) to cause or undergo deflation. ◇ See also **inflate** and **reflate**. — *adj* **deflated**. [**de-** (sense **2**) + **inflate**]

deflation *n* **1** the act of deflating or the process of being deflated. **2** the state of being or feeling deflated. **3** (*econ*) a reduction in the amount of money available in a country, resulting in lower levels of economic activity, industrial output and employment, and a lower rate of increase in wages and prices. ◇ See also **inflation** and **reflation**. — *adj* **deflationary**.

deflect *v* (*tr* & *intr*) to turn aside (from the correct or intended course or direction). — *n* **deflection**. [Lat *deflectere*]

deflower *v* (*tr*; *literary*) to have sexual intercourse with (a woman who has not had sexual intercourse before). [Lat *deflorare*, from *de*, from + *flos*, flower]

defoliate *v* (*tr; tech*) to cause leaves to fall off (trees, etc.). — *n* **defoliation**. [Lat *defoliare*, from *de*, off + *folium*, leaf]

defoliant *n* (*tech*) a chemical substance which causes the leaves to fall off trees, etc.

deforest *v* (*tr*) to clear (an area) of trees. — *n* **deforestation**. [**de-** (sense **2**) + **forest**]

deform *v* (*tr*) to change the shape of (something) without breaking it, so that it looks ugly, unpleasant, unnatural or spoiled. — *adj* **deformed**. — *n* **deformity**, **-ies**. [Lat *deformis*, ugly]

defraud *v* (*tr*; **of**) to prevent (someone) getting or keeping something which belongs to them or to which they have a right, by cheating, lies, dishonesty, etc. [Lat *defraudare*]

defray *v* (*tr*; *formal*) to provide the money to pay (someone's costs or expenses). — *n* **defrayal** or **defrayment**. [OFr *deffroier*, to pay costs]

defrock *v* (*tr*) to remove (a priest) from his or her position in the church, e.g. because of unacceptable behaviour or beliefs. [**de-** (sense **2**) + **frock** (sense **2**)]

defrost *v* (*tr* & *intr*) **1** to remove ice from or have the ice removed from; to unfreeze. **2** (of frozen food, etc.) to make or become no longer frozen. [**de-** (sense **2**) + **frost**]

deft *adj* skilful, quick and neat. — *adv* **deftly**. — *n* **deftness**. [OE *gedæfte*, meek]

defunct *adj* (*facet* or *formal*) no longer living, existing, active, usable or in use. [Lat *defungi*, to finish]

defuse *v* (*tr*) **1** to remove the fuse from (a bomb, etc.). **2** to make (a situation, etc.) harmless or less dangerous. [**de-** (sense **2**) + **fuse**]

defy *v* **-ies**, **-ied** (*tr*) **1** to resist or disobey boldly and openly. **2** to dare or challenge (someone). **3** (*formal*) to make impossible or unsuccessful. ◇ See also **defiance**. [OFr *defier*, from Lat *diffidare*, to renounce one's faith]

degenerate *adj* **1** physically, morally or intellectually worse than before. **2** (*biol*) having lost former qualities, structure or characteristics. — *n* a degenerate person or animal. — *v* (*intr*) **1** to go from a better, more moral, etc. state to a worse one. **2** (*biol*) to lose former qualities, structure or characteristics. — *n* **degeneracy**. [Lat *degenerare*, to become unlike one's kind]

degeneration *n* **1** the process or act of degenerating. **2** (*biol*) a breaking down or decay of animal or plant tissue.

degenerative *adj* (*tech*) (of a condition or disease) which steadily destroys or damages (a part of) the body.

degrade *v* **1** (*tr*) to disgrace or humiliate. **2** (*tr*) to reduce in rank, status, etc. **3** (*tr* & *intr*; *chem*) to change or be converted into a substance with a simpler structure. — *n* **degradation**. — *adj* **degrading**. [OFr *degrader*, from Lat *de*, down + *gradus*, step]

degradable *adj* (*tech*) capable of being broken down or destroyed chemically or biologically.

degree *n* **1** amount; extent. **2** (*symbol* °) a unit of temperature. **3** (*symbol* °) a unit by which angles are measured, one 360th part of a complete revolution. **4** an award or title given by a university or college, either earned by examination or research or given as a mark of honour. **5** a comparative amount of severity or seriousness. **6** any of the three categories of comparison (*positive*, *comparative* and *superlative*) of an adjective or adverb. — **by degrees** gradually. — **to a degree 1** to a certain extent or small extent. **2** to a great extent. [OFr *degre*, from Lat *de*, down + *gradus*, step]

first-, **second-** and **third-degree** *adj* **1** of the three levels of seriousness of a burn, third-degree burns being the most serious. **2** (*NAm*) of the three levels of seriousness of a murder, first-degree murder being the most serious.

third degree *n* severe, sometimes brutal, questioning to get information or a confession.

dehiscent *adj* (*bot*) (of a seed pod, etc.) bursting open by itself. [Lat *dehiscere*, to gape, split open]

dehumanise or **-ize** *v* (*tr*) to remove the human qualities from. [**de-** (sense **2**) + **humanise**]

dehydrate *v* **1** (*tr*) to remove water or moisture from (esp. foodstuffs) as a means of preservation or storage. **2** (*tr* & *intr*) to (cause to) lose too much water or moisture from the body. — *adj* **dehydrated**. — *n* **dehydration**. [**de-** (sense **2**) + Gr *hydor*, water]

de-ice *v* (*tr*) to remove ice from; to make or keep free of ice. [**de-** (sense **2**) + **ice**]

de-icer *n* **1** a mechanical device for preventing the formation of ice, e.g. on an aircraft wing. **2** a chemical used to remove ice, e.g. from a car windscreen.

deify *v* **-ies**, **-ied** (*tr*) to make a god of (something or someone); to treat as an object of worship. — *n* **deification**. [OFr *deifier*, from Lat *deus*, god + *facere*, to make]

deign *v* (*intr*) to do something reluctantly and in a way that shows that one considers the matter hardly important or beneath one's dignity: *didn't even deign to reply*. [OFr *daigner*, from Lat *dignari*, to consider worthy]

deism *n* belief in the existence of God without acceptance of any religion or message revealed by God to man. — *n* **deist**. ◇ See also **theism**. [Lat *deus*, god + **-ism**]

deity *n* **-ies** (*formal*) **1** a god or goddess. **2** the state of being divine. **3** (*cap* with **the**) God. [Lat *deitas*, from *deus*, god]

déjà vu *n* the feeling or illusion that one has experienced something before although one is actually experiencing it for the first time. [Fr, already seen]

dejected *adj* sad; miserable. — *adv* **dejectedly**. — *n* **dejection**. [Lat *deicere*, to throw down, disappoint]

de jure (*legal*) according to law; by right. ◇ See also **de facto**. [Lat, by law]

dekko : **have** or **take a dekko** or **decko** (*Br slang*) to take a look. [Hindi *dekhna*, to see]

Del. *abbrev* Delaware.

delay *v* **delayed 1** (*tr*) to slow down or cause to be late. **2** (*tr*) to put off to a later time. **3** (*intr*) to be slow in doing something; to linger. — *n* **1** the act of delaying or state of being delayed. **2** the amount of time by which someone or something is delayed. [OFr *delaier*]

delayed action *n* the operation of e.g. the switch on a camera or detonator on a bomb some time after the setting of the operating mechanism.

delectable *adj* (esp. of food) delightful or enjoyable; delicious. — *adv* **delectably**. [Lat *delectare*, to delight]

delectation *n* (*formal*) delight, enjoyment or amusement.

delegate *v* (*tr*) **1** to give (part of one's work, power, etc.) to someone else. **2** to send or name (a person) as a representative, as the one to do a job, etc. — *n* someone chosen to be the representative for another person or group of people, e.g. at a conference or meeting. [Lat *de*, away + *legare*, to send as ambassador]

delegation *n* **1** a group of delegates. **2** the act of delegating or the state of being delegated.

delete *v* (*tr*) to rub out, score out or remove (esp. from something written or printed). — *n* **deletion**. [Lat *delere*, to blot out]

deleterious *adj* (*formal*) harmful or destructive. — *adv* **deleteriously**. [Gr *deleterios*]

delf or **delph** or **delft** *n* a kind of earthenware orig. made at *Delft* in the Netherlands, typically with a blue design on a white background.

deliberate *adj* **1** done on purpose; not accidental. **2** slow and careful. — *v* (*tr* & *intr*) to think about something carefully. — *adv* **deliberately**. [Lat *deliberare*, to consider carefully]

deliberation *n* **1** careful thought. **2** (in *pl*) formal and thorough thought and discussion. **3** slowness and carefulness.

delicacy *n* **-ies 1** the state or quality of being delicate. **2** something considered particularly delicious to eat. [**delicate**]

delicate *adj* **1** easily damaged or broken. **2** not strong or healthy. **3** of fine texture or workmanship. **4** dainty; small and attractive. **5** small, neat and careful: *delicate movements*. **6** requiring tact and careful handling: *a delicate situation*. **7** (**in**) careful about what one says or does, so as not to offend others. **8** (of colours, flavours, etc.) light; not strong. — *adv* **delicately**. [Lat *delicatus*]

delicatessen *n* a shop selling foods prepared ready for the table, esp. cooked meats, cheeses and unusual or imported foods. [Ger *Delikatessen*, from Fr *délicatesse*, delicacy]

delicious *adj* **1** with a very pleasing taste or smell. **2** giving great pleasure. — *adv* **deliciously**. — *n* **deliciousness**. [OFr *delicious*, from Lat *deliciae*, delight]

delight *v* **1** (*tr*) to please greatly. **2** (*intr* with **in**) to take great pleasure from. — *n* **1** great pleasure. **2** something or someone that gives great pleasure. — *adj* **delighted**. — *adv* **delightedly**. [OFr *deliter*, from Lat *delectare*; spelling influenced by **light**]

delightful *adj* giving great pleasure. — *adv* **delightfully**.

delimit *v* **-t-** (*tr*) to mark or fix the limits or boundaries of (powers, etc.). — *n* **delimitation**. — *adj* **delimitative**. [Lat *delimitare*]

delineate *v* (*tr*) to show by drawing or by describing in words. — *n* **delineation**. [Lat *delineare*, to sketch out]

delinquent *n* & *adj* (someone, esp. a young person) guilty of a minor criminal offence or of disruptive behaviour in public. — *n* **delinquency**. [Lat *delinquere*, to fail in one's duty]

deliquesce *v* (*intr*; *chem*) (esp. of salts) to dissolve slowly in water absorbed from the air. — *n* **deliquescence**. — *adj* **deliquescent**. [Lat *deliquescere*, to dissolve]

delirious *adj* **1** affected by delirium, usu. as a result of fever or other illness. **2** very excited or happy. — *adv* **deliriously**. [Lat *delirus*, from *delirare*, to rave, orig. to go off a straight furrow, from *de*, from + *lira*, furrow]

delirium *n* **1** a state of madness or mental confusion and excitement, often caused by fever or other illness, drugs, etc. **2** extreme excitement or joy. [Lat, from *delirare*; see ety. at **delirious**]

delirium tremens *n* (*coll abbrev* **DT's** or **dt's**) delirium caused by habitual and persistent drinking of too much alcohol, inducing hallucinations, anxiety, confusion and trembling in the sufferer. [Lat *tremere*, to tremble]

deliver *v* **-r-** **1** (*tr* & *intr*) to carry (goods, letters, etc.) to a person or place. **2** (*tr*; *formal*; **up**) to hand over. **3** (*tr*) to give or make (a speech, etc.). **4** (*tr*; *formal* or *old*; **from**) to set free or rescue. **5** (*tr*) to help (a woman) at the birth of (a child). **6** (*tr* & *intr*; *coll*) to keep or fulfil (a promise or undertaking). **7** (*tr*; *formal*) to aim or direct (a blow, criticism, etc.) towards someone or something. — *n* **deliverer**. — **deliver the goods** (*coll*) to do something one has promised.

deliverance *n* (*formal* or *old*) the act of rescuing, freeing or saving from danger or harm, or the state of being rescued, freed or saved.

delivery *n* **-ies** **1** the carrying of (goods, letters, etc.) to a person or place. **2** the thing or things being delivered. **3** the process or manner of giving birth to a child. **4** the act of making, or one's manner of making, a speech, etc. **5** the act or manner of throwing a ball, esp. in some sports.

dell *n* a small valley or hollow, usu. with trees. [OE]

delphinium *n* **-iums** or **-ia** a garden plant with tall spikes of usu. blue flowers. [Gr *delphis*, dolphin (from the shape of the flowers)]

delta *n* **1** a roughly triangular area of land at the mouth of a river whose main stream has split into several channels. **2** the fourth letter of the Greek alphabet (Δ, δ). [Gr]

delude *v* (*tr*) to deceive or mislead. ◇ See also **delusion**. [Lat *deludere*, to cheat]

deluge *n* **1** a flood. **2** a downpour of rain. **3** a great quantity of anything coming or pouring in. — *v* (*tr*) **1** (usu. in *passive*; with **with**) to overwhelm. **2** (*formal*) to flood; to cover in water. [OFr, from Lat *diluvium*, flood]

delusion *n* **1** the act of deluding or being deluded. **2** a false or mistaken belief, esp. because of mental illness. [Lat *delusio*]

delusions of grandeur *n* (*pl*) a false belief in one's own importance.

delusive or **delusory** *adj* deluding or likely to delude.

de luxe or **deluxe** *adj* very luxurious or elegant; with special features or qualities. [Fr, of luxury]

delve *v* (*intr*) **1** (**into**) to search for information (about something). **2** (with **through**, etc.) to search through, among, etc. [OE *delfan*, to dig]

Dem. *abbrev* **Democrat** and **Democratic**.

demagnetise or **-ize** *v* (*tr*) to take away the magnetic properties of. [**de-** (sense **2**) + **magnetise**]

demagogue *n* (usu. *derog*) a person who tries to win political power or support by appealing to people's emotions and prejudices. — *adj* **demagogic**. — *n* **demagoguery** or **demagogy**. [Gr *demos*, people + *agogos*, leading]

demand *v* (*tr*) **1** to ask or ask for firmly, forcefully or urgently. **2** to require or need. **3** to claim as a right. — *n* **1** a forceful request or order. **2** (with **on**) an urgent claim for action or attention: *makes great demands on one's time*. **3** (**for**) people's desire or ability to buy or obtain (goods, etc.) — **in demand** very popular; frequently asked for. — **on demand** when asked for. [OFr *demander*, to ask]

demanding *adj* **1** requiring a lot of effort, ability, etc.: *a demanding job*. **2** needing or expecting a lot of attention: *a demanding child*.

demarcation *n* **1** the marking out of limits or boundaries. **2** the strict separation of the areas or types of work to be done by the members of the various trade unions in a factory, etc.: *a demarcation dispute*. —

v **demarcate** (*tr*). [Span *demarcar*, to mark the boundaries of]

demean *v* (*tr*) to lower the dignity of or lessen respect for (someone, esp. oneself). — *adj* **demeaning**. [**mean**[1]]

demeanour *n* manner of behaving; behaviour towards others. [OFr *demener*, to treat]

demented *adj* mad; out of one's mind. — *adv* **dementedly**. — *n* **dementedness**. [Lat *de*, from + *mens*, mind]

dementia *n* (*psychol*) a loss or severe lessening of normal mental ability and functioning, occurring esp. in the elderly. ◇ See also **senile dementia**. [Lat *de*, from + *mens*, mind]

demerara or **demerara sugar** *n* a form of brown sugar. [*Demerara* in Guyana, S America]

demerit *n* (*formal*) a fault or failing. [Lat *demereri*, to deserve]

demi- *comb fm* half or partly: *demigod.* [Fr *demi*, half]

demigod *n* (*mythol*) a person who is part human and part god. [**demi-** + **god**]

demijohn *n* a large bottle with a short narrow neck and one or two small handles, used e.g. for storing wine. [Fr *dame-jeanne*, Dame Jane, influenced by **demi-** and the name *John*]

demilitarise or **-ize** *v* (*tr*) to remove armed forces from or not allow any military activity in (an area). — *n* **demilitarisation** or **-z-**. [**de-** + **military** + **-ise**]

demise *n* **1** (*formal*) death. **2** a failure or end. [OFr *demise*, from *desmettre*, to lay down]

demisemiquaver *n* (*mus*) a note equal in time to half a semiquaver. [**demi-** + **semiquaver**]

demist *v* (*tr*) to free (a vehicle's windscreen) from condensation or frost by blowing warm air over it. — *n* **demister**. [**de-** + **mist**]

demo *n* **-os** short for **demonstration**.

demob (*Br coll*) *v* **-bb-** (*tr*) short for **demobilise**. — *n* short for **demobilisation**.

demobilise or **-ize** *v* (*tr*) to release from service in the armed forces, e.g. after a war. — *n* **demobilisation** or **-z-**. [**de-** (sense **2**) + **mobilise**]

democracy *n* **-ies 1** a form of government in which the people govern themselves or elect representatives to govern them. **2** a country, state or other body with such a form of government. [Gr *demos*, people + *kratos*, strength]

democrat *n* **1** a person who believes in democracy as a principle. **2** (*cap*) a member or supporter of the Democratic Party in the US, or of any political party with *Democratic* in its title. ◇ See also **republican**.

democratic *adj* **1** concerned with or following the principles of democracy. **2** believing in or providing equal rights and privileges for all. **3** (*cap*) relating to or belonging to the **Democratic Party**, one of the two chief political parties of the US. — *adv* **democratically**.

demodulation *n* (*tech*) the inverse of modulation, the process by which an output radio wave is obtained that has the same characteristics as the original modulating wave. — *v* **demodulate** (*tr*). — **demodulator**. [**de-** (sense **2**)]

demography *n* (*tech*) the scientific study of population statistics (births, deaths, etc.). — *n* **demographer**. — *adj* **demographic**. [Gr *demos*, people + *graphein*, to write]

demolish *v* (*tr*) **1** to pull or tear down (a building, etc.). **2** to destroy (an argument, etc.). **3** (*facet*) to eat up. [Lat *demoliri*, to throw down]

demolition *n* the act of demolishing.

demon *n* **1** an evil spirit. **2** a cruel or evil person. **3** (**at**, **for**) a person who has great energy, enthusiasm, or skill. **4** (also **daemon**) a good or friendly spirit. [Gr *daimon*, spirit]

demoniac or **demoniacal** *adj* **1** of or like a demon or demons. **2** influenced or as if influenced by demons; frenzied or very energetic. — *adv* **demoniacally**.

demonic *adj* **1** of or like a demon or demons. **2** possessed or as if possessed by a demon or demons; evil. — *adv* **demonically**.

demonstrate *v* **1** (*tr*) to show or prove by reasoning or providing evidence. **2** (*tr* & *intr*) to show (how something is done, operates, etc.) **3** (*intr* & *tr*) to show (one's support, opposition, etc.) by protesting, marching, etc. in public. — *adj* **demonstrable**. — *adv* **demonstrably**. — *n* **demonstration**. — *n* **demonstrator**. [Lat *demonstrare*, to show, indicate]

demonstrative *adj* **1** showing one's feelings openly. **2** (**of**) showing or proving. — *adv* **demonstratively**. — *n* **demonstrativeness**.

demonstrative pronoun and **adjective** *n* (*gram*) a word indicating the person or thing referred to, i.e. *this*, *that*, *these* and *those*.

demoralise or **-ize** *v* (*tr*) to take away the confidence, courage or enthusiasm of; to dishearten. — *n* **demoralisation** or **-z-**. ◇ See also **morale**. [Fr *démoraliser*]

demote *v* (*tr*) to reduce to a lower rank or grade. — *n* **demotion**. [**de-** (sense **2**) + **promote**]

demotic *adj* (esp. of a language) used by ordinary people; colloquial. — *n* **1** colloquial language. **2** (*cap*) a form of the modern Greek language based on colloquial speech. **3** a simplified form of the ancient Egyptian writing. [Gr *demotikos*, from *demos*, people]

demur *v* **-rr-** (*intr*; **at**) to object mildly to or be reluctant to do. — *n* **demurral**. — **without demur** without objecting. [OFr *demorer*, to wait]

demure *adj* (esp. of young women) quiet, modest and well-behaved. — *adv* **demurely**. — *n* **demureness**. [OFr *demorer*, to wait, influenced by *meur*, ripe]

demystify *v* **-ies**, **-ied** (*tr*) to remove the mystery from. — *n* **demystification**. [**de-** (sense **2**) + **mystify**]

den *n* **1** a wild animal's home. **2** a centre (often secret) of illegal or immoral activity. **3** a room in a house or a hut outside it, used as a place to work or play. [OE *denn*, cave, lair]

denarius *n* **-ii** an ancient Roman silver coin. [Lat *denarius*, containing ten, because orig. equal to ten asses]

denationalise or **-ize** *v* (*tr*) to return or transfer (an industry) to private ownership from state ownership. — *n* **denationalisation** or **-z-**. [**de-** (sense **2**) + **nationalise**]

denature *v* (*tr*) **1** to change the nature or properties of. **2** to add something to (e.g. alcohol) to prevent its misuse. [**de-** (sense **2**) + **nature** (sense **2**)]

dendrology *n* the scientific study of trees. — *n* **dendrologist**. [Gr *dendron*, tree + **-logy**]

denial *n* **1** an act of declaring something not to be true. **2** an act of refusing something to someone. **3** an act of refusing to acknowledge connections with somebody or something. ◇ See also **deny**. [**deny** + **-al**]

denier *n* the unit of weight of silk, rayon or nylon thread, usu. used as a measure of the fineness of stockings or tights. [Fr; orig. a small coin, from **denarius**]

denigrate *v* (*tr*) to scorn or criticise; to attack or belittle the reputation, character or worth of. — *n* **denigration**. — *n* **denigrator**. [Lat *denigrare*, to blacken]

denim *n* **1** a kind of hard-wearing, usually blue, cotton cloth used for making jeans, overalls, etc. **2** (in *pl*) trousers or jeans made of denim. [Fr *de Nîmes*, of Nîmes (in France)]

denizen *n* **1** (*literary*, *formal* or *facet*) an inhabitant (human or animal). **2** (*biol*) a species of animal or plant which has become well established in a place to which it is not native and into which it has been introduced. [OFr *deinzein*, from *deinz*, within]

denominate *v* (*tr*; *formal*) to give a specific name or title to (something). [Lat *denominare*, to name]

denomination *n* **1** a religious group with its own particular beliefs, organisation and practices. **2** a particular unit of value of a postage stamp, coin or banknote, etc. — *adj* **denominational**.

denominator *n* (*math*) in a vulgar fraction, the number shown below the line, indicating the units into which the fraction is dividing the whole, e.g. '5' in the fraction $\frac{3}{5}$. ◇ See also **numerator**.

common denominator *n* **1** (*math*) a number that is a multiple of each of the denominators of a set of fractions, e.g. 15 (3 × 5) is a common denominator of $\frac{1}{3}$ and $\frac{3}{5}$. **2** something that enables comparison, agreement, etc. between people or things.

denote *v* (*tr*) **1** to mean; to be the name of or sign for. **2** to be a sign, mark or indication of. — *n* **denotation**. [Lat *denotare*, to mark out]

dénouement *n* the final part of a story or plot (esp. in a play or book) in which what has until then been unclear is explained and previously unresolved problems and mysteries are solved. [Fr, from *dénouer*, to untie a knot]

denounce *v* (*tr*) **1** (**as**) to inform against or accuse publicly (someone who is, or one thinks is, guilty of a crime). **2** to condemn (an action, proposal, idea, etc.) strongly and openly. ◇ See also **denunciation**. [OFr *dénoncier*, from Lat *denuntiare*, to announce]

dense *adj* **1** closely packed or crowded together. **2** thick. **3** (*coll*) very stupid; slow to understand. — *adv* **densely**. — *n* **denseness**. [Lat *densus*]

density *n* **-ies** **1** the state of being dense or the degree of denseness. **2** the number or quantity of something in a given unit of area or volume.

dent *n* a hollow in the surface of something, esp. something hard, made by pressure or a blow. — *v* **1** (*tr*) to make a dent in. **2** (*intr*) to become dented. [OE *dynt*, blow]

dental *adj* concerned with or for the teeth. [Lat *dentalis*, from *dens*, tooth]

dental floss *n* a soft thread used for cleaning between the teeth.

dental surgeon *n* a dentist.

dentate *adj* (*tech*) with a tooth-like notched pattern round the edge.

dentifrice *n* paste or powder for cleaning the teeth. [Fr, from Lat *dens*, tooth + *fricare*, to rub]

dentine *n* the type of hard tissue which forms the main part of a tooth. [Lat *dens*, tooth]

dentist *n* a person qualified to repair or remove decayed teeth, fit false teeth, etc. [Fr *dentiste*, from *dent*, tooth]

dentistry *n* the branch of medicine which specialises in the care and repair of the teeth.

dentition *n* (*tech*) the number, arrangement and type of teeth in a human or animal. [Lat *dentitio*, teething]

denture *n* (usu. in *pl*) a false tooth or set of false teeth. [Fr, from *dent*, tooth]

denude *v* (*tr*) to make completely bare; to strip. — *n* **denudation**. [Lat *denudare*, to lay bare, uncover]

denunciation *n* a public condemnation or accusation. ◇ See also **denounce**. [Lat *denuntiare*, to announce]

deny *v* **-ies**, **-ied** (*tr*) **1** to declare (something) not to be true. **2** to refuse to give or allow to (someone). **3** to refuse to acknowledge a connection with. — **deny oneself** to do without (things that one desires or needs). ◇ See also **denial**. [OFr *denier*, from Lat *denegare*]

deodorant *n* a substance that prevents or conceals unpleasant smells, esp. the smell of stale sweat on the human body. [**de-** (sense **2**) + **odour**]

deodorise or **-ize** *v* (*tr*) to remove, conceal or absorb the unpleasant smell of. — *n* **deodorisation** or **-z-**.

deoxyribonucleic acid or **DNA** *n* an acid present in the chromosomes of all plant and animal cells, by means of which hereditary characteristics are passed from parent to offspring. [*deoxy-*, containing less oxygen than + **ribonucleic acid**]

depart *v* (*intr*) **1** (**from**, **for**) to leave. **2** (with **from**) to stop following or not follow (a planned or usual course of action). [OFr *departir*]

departed (*formal* or *euph*) *adj* dead. — *n* (with **the**) the person who has or people who have (recently) died.

departure *n* **1** (**from**, **for**) (an act of) going away or leaving. **2** (with **from**) a change from a planned or usual course of action. **3** a new activity, different from what one has been doing or normally does.

department *n* **1** a section of an organisation (a government or other administration, a university, an office or a shop), with responsibility for one particular aspect or part of the organisation's work. **2** a subject or activity which is someone's special skill or particular responsibility. [Fr *département*]

departmental *adj* **1** of or concerning a department or departments. **2** divided into departments.

department store *n* a large shop with many different departments selling a wide variety of goods.

departure. See **depart**.

depend *v* (*intr*) **1** (with **on**, **upon**) to rely on; to be able to trust. **2** (with **on** or **upon**) to rely on financial or other support from. **3** (**on**, **upon**) to be decided by or vary according to (something else). [OFr *dependre*, from Lat *dependere*, to hang down]

dependable *adj* trustworthy or reliable. — *n* **dependability**. — *adv* **dependably**.

dependant *n* a person who is kept or supported financially by another.

dependence *n* (**on**, **upon**) **1** the state of being dependent. **2** trust and reliance.

dependency *n* **-ies 1** a country governed or controlled by another. **2** addiction (to drugs, etc.).

dependent *adj* (with **on** or **upon**) **1** relying on for financial or other support. **2** to be decided or influenced by.

dependent clause *n* same as **subordinate clause**.

depict *v* (*tr*) **1** to paint or draw. **2** to describe. — *n* **depiction**. [Lat *depingere*, to paint]

depilatory (*tech*) *n* **-ies** a chemical substance used to remove unwanted hair from the body. — *adj* able to remove hair. [Lat *depilare*, to remove hair]

deplete *v* (*tr*) to reduce greatly in number, quantity, etc.; to use up (supplies, money, energy, resources, etc.). — *n* **depletion**. [Lat *deplere*, to empty]

deplore *v* (*tr*) to feel or express great disapproval of or regret for. [Fr *déplorer*, from Lat *deplorare*, to weep for]

deplorable *adj* very bad, shocking or regrettable. — *adv* **deplorably**.

deploy *v* (*tr*) **1** to spread out and position (troops) ready for battle. **2** to organise and bring into use (resources, arguments, etc.). — *n* **deployment**. [Fr *déployer*]

depopulate *v* (*tr*) to reduce greatly the number of people living in (an area, country, etc.). — *adj* **depopulated**. — *n* **depopulation**. [Lat *depopulari*, to lay waste, later understood as meaning to deprive of people]

deport[1] *v* (*tr*) to legally remove or expel (a person) from a country. — *n* **deportation**. — *n* **deportee**. [Lat *deportare*, to carry away]

deport[2] *v* (*tr*; *formal*) to behave (oneself) in a particular way. [Lat *deportare*, to carry away]

deportment *n* **1** the way one holds or carries oneself; one's bearing. **2** behaviour.

depose *v* (*tr*) to remove from a high office or powerful position. [OFr *deposer*, to put down or away]

deposit *v* **-t-** (*tr*) **1** to put or leave. **2** to put (money, etc.) in a bank, etc., for safekeeping or to earn interest. **3** to give (a sum of money) as the first part of the payment for something, so guaranteeing that one can complete the purchase later. **4** to pay (a sum of money) as a guarantee against loss or damage. — *n* **1** a sum of money, etc. deposited in a bank, etc. **2** a sum of money given as part payment for something or paid as a guarantee against loss or damage. **3** solid matter that has settled at the bottom of a liquid, or is left behind by a liquid. **4** a layer (of coal, oil, minerals, etc.) occurring naturally in rock. [Lat *depositum*, from *deponere*, to put down]

deposit account *n* a bank account on which one is paid interest and which cannot be used for the transfer of money to other people by e.g. cheque or standing order.

depositary *n* **-ies** (*formal*) a person, etc. to whom something is given for safekeeping.

depositor *n* a person who deposits money in a bank.

depository *n* **-ies 1** a place where things such as furniture are stored. **2** a depositary.

deposition *n* **1** the act of deposing or process of being deposed. **2** the act of depositing or process of being deposited. **3** (*legal*) a written statement made under oath and used as evidence in a court of law when the witness cannot be present. [Lat *depositio*, putting down]

depot *n* **1** a storehouse or warehouse. **2** a place where buses, trains and certain types of vehicles are kept and repaired. **3** (*NAm*) a bus or railway station. **4** a military headquarters, or military post where stores are kept and recruits trained. [Fr *dépôt*, from Lat *deponere*, to put down]

deprave *v* (*tr*) to make evil or morally corrupt. — *adj* **depraved**. [Lat *depravare*, to pervert, distort]

depravity *n* **-ies** (an act of) wickedness, evil or corruption.

deprecate *v* (*tr*) to express disapproval of; to allow, but with disapproval. — *adj* **deprecating**. — *adv* **deprecatingly**. — *n* **deprecation**. [Lat *deprecari*, to try to avert]

deprecatory *adj* **1** showing or expressing disapproval. **2** apologetic; trying to avoid disapproval.

depreciate *v* **1** (*tr* & *intr*) to (cause to) fall in value. **2** (*tr*) to be contemptuous of the worth of; to belittle. — *adj* **depreciatory**. [Lat *depretiare*, to lower the price of]

depreciation *n* **1** (*econ*) a fall in value of a currency against the value of other currencies. **2** the reduction in the value of fixed assets such as buildings and equipment through use or age. **3** the act of depreciating.

depredation *n* (often in *pl*) damage, destruction or robbery. [Lat *depraedatio*, from *praedari*, to plunder]

depress *v* (*tr*) **1** to make sad and gloomy. **2** (*formal*) to make lower. **3** (*formal*) to press down. — *adj* **depressing**. — *adv* **depressingly**. [OFr *depresser*]

depressant *n* & *adj* (*med*) (a drug which is) able to reduce mental or physical activity. ◇ See also **antidepressant**.

depressed *adj* **1** sad and gloomy. **2** (*psychol*) suffering from a mental illness which causes feelings of sadness, inadequacy, tiredness, etc. **3** suffering from high unemployment and low standards of living: *a depressed area*.

depression *n* **1** (*psychol*) a state of being depressed (sense **2**). **2** a period of low business and industrial activity accompanied by a rise in unemployment. **3** (*cap* with **the**) the period of worldwide economic depression from 1929 to 1934. **4** an area of low pressure in the atmosphere. **5** a hollow, esp. in the ground.

depressive *n* a person who suffers frequently from depression.

deprive *v* (*tr*; **of**) to take or keep from; to prevent from using or enjoying. [Lat *deprivare*, to degrade]

deprivation *n* **1** hardship, etc. caused by being deprived of necessities, rights, etc. **2** the act of depriving or state of being deprived.

deprived *adj* **1** (with **of**) having had (something) kept or taken from one. **2** (of a person) suffering from hardship through lack of money, reasonable living conditions, etc. **3** (of a district, etc.) lacking good housing, schools, medical facilities, etc.

dept. *abbrev* department.

depth *n* **1** deepness; the distance from the top downwards, from the front to the back or from the surface inwards. **2** (of feelings or colours) intensity or strength. **3** extensiveness: *the depth of one's knowledge*. **4** (in *pl* with **the**) somewhere far from the surface or edge of: *the depths of the ocean, of the country*. **5** (in *pl* with **the**) an extreme feeling (of despair, sadness, etc.) or great degree (of deprivation, etc.). **6** (often in *pl* with **the**) the middle and severest part of (winter, etc.). **7** (in *pl*) serious aspects of a person's character that are not immediately obvious. **8** (of sound) lowness of pitch. — **in depth** deeply and thoroughly (*adj* **in-depth**). — **out of one's depth 1** in water so deep that one would be below the surface even when standing up. **2** not able to understand information or an explanation, or in a situation which is too difficult for one to deal with. [OE *deop*, deep + **-th**[2]]

depth charge *n* a type of bomb dropped from a ship which explodes underwater and is used to attack submarines.

deputation *n* a group of people appointed to represent and speak on behalf of others. [Lat *deputare*, to select]

depute *v* (*tr*; *formal*) **1** to appoint (someone) to do something. **2** (with **to**) to give (one's work, etc., or part of it) to someone else to do. [OFr *deputer*, from Lat *deputare*, to select]

deputy *n* **-ies 1** a person appointed to act on behalf of or as an assistant to someone else. **2** in some countries, a person elected to the lower house of parliament. — *adj* in some organisations, next in rank to the head and having the authority to act on his or her behalf. [OFr *deputer*, to appoint, from Lat *deputare*, to select]

deputise or **-ize** *v* **1** (*intr*; **for**) to act as a deputy. **2** (*tr*) to appoint as a deputy.

derail *v* (*tr* & *intr*) to (cause to) leave the rails. — *n* **derailment**. [**de-** (sense **2**) + **rail**[1]]

derange *v* (*tr*) **1** to make insane. **2** to disrupt or throw into disorder or confusion. — *adj* **deranged**. — *n* **derangement**. [Fr *déranger*, to disturb]

derby[1] *n* **-ies 1** *n* (*cap* with **the**) a horse race held annually at Epsom Downs. **2** a race or a sporting event or contest, esp. (**local derby**) a contest between teams from the same area. [The Earl of *Derby*, one of the founders of the race in 1780]

derby[2] *n* **-ies** (*NAm*) a bowler hat. [**derby**[1]]

Derbys. *abbrev* Derbyshire.

deregulate *v* (*tr*) to remove controls and regulations from (a business or business activity). — *n* **deregulation**. [**de-** (sense **2**) + **regulate**]

derelict *adj* abandoned and falling in ruins. — *n* a tramp; a person with no home or money. — *n* **dereliction**. [Lat *derelinquere*, to abandon]

dereliction of duty *n* (*formal*) failure to do what one ought to do.

derestrict *v* (*tr*) to remove a restriction from (something), esp. a speed limit from (a road). — *n* **derestriction**. [**de-** (sense **2**) + **restrict**]

deride *v* (*tr*) to laugh at or make fun of. ◇ See also **derision**. [Lat *deridere*]

de rigueur required by fashion, custom or the rules of politeness. [Fr, of strictness]

derision *n* the act of deriding; scornful laughter. [Lat *derisio*]

derisive *adj* scornful; mocking. — *adv* **derisively**. [**derision**]

derisory *adj* **1** ridiculous and insulting, esp. ridiculously small. **2** derisive. — *adv* **derisorily**. [Lat *derisorius*]

derive *v* (with **from**) **1** (*intr*) to come or arise from; to have as a source. **2** (*tr*) to obtain or produce from. **3** (*tr*) to trace back to a source or origin.

derivation *n* **1** the act of deriving or the state or process of being derived. **2** the source or origin (esp. of a word). **3** (*gram*) the process of forming a word by adding one or more prefixes or suffixes to another word. ◇ See also **inflection**, **root** and **stem**. [OFr *deriver*, from Lat *de*, from + *rivus*, stream]

derivative *adj* not original; derived from or copying something else (esp. someone else's work). — *n* **1** something which is derived from something else. **2** (*gram*) a word formed by adding one or more prefixes or suffixes to another word, such as *happily* from *happy* and *decarbonise* from *carbon*. ◇ See also **compound** and **inflection**.

dermatitis *n* (*med*) inflammation of the skin. [**dermat-** + **-itis**]

dermato- or **dermat-**, and **-derm** *comb fm* of the skin, as in **dermatitis** and **ectoderm**. [Gr *derma*, skin]

dermatology *n* the branch of medical science concerned with the study of the skin and treatment of its diseases. — *n* **dermatologist**. [**dermato-** + **-logy**]

derogate *v* (*intr* & *tr*; **from**; *formal*) to cause to appear inferior; to show one's low opinion of (something). — *n* **derogation**. [Lat *derogare*, to detract from]

derogatory *adj* showing, or intended to show, disapproval, dislike, scorn or lack of respect. — *adv* **derogatorily**. [Lat *derogatorius*]

derrick *n* **1** a type of crane with a movable arm. **2** a framework built over an oil-well, used for raising and lowering the drill. [*Derrick*, 17th-century hangman]

derring-do *n* (*old* or *literary*) daring deeds. [From a wrong understanding by Spenser, the 16th-century poet, of the phrase *derrynge do* (= daring to do) in the work of an earlier poet]

derris *n* **1** a climbing plant related to peas and beans. **2** an insecticide made from its roots. [Gr *derris*, leather jacket]

derv *n* (*Br*) diesel oil used as a fuel for road vehicles. [*d*iesel-*e*ngine *r*oad *v*ehicle]

dervish *n* a member of any of various Muslim religious groups vowed to poverty, some of whom perform spinning dances as part of their religious ritual. [Turkish *derviş*, from Persian *darvish*, poor man, dervish]

DES *abbrev* Department of Education and Science.

desalinate *v* (*tr*; *tech*) to remove salt from (esp. sea-water). — *n* **desalination**. [**de-** (sense **2**) + **saline**]

descant (*mus*) *n* a melody played or harmony sung above the main tune. — *adj* (of a musical instrument) having a higher pitch than others of the same type. [OFr, from Lat *dis-*, apart + *cantus*, song]

descend *v* **1** (*tr* & *intr*) to go or move down from a higher to a lower place or position. **2** (*intr*) to lead or slope downwards. **3** (*intr* with **on, upon**) to invade or attack. **4** (*intr*; **from, to**) (of titles, property, etc.) to pass by inheritance. — **be descended from** to have as one's ancestor. — **descend to** to lower oneself to (behaviour which is considered bad or unworthy). [OFr *descendre*]

descendant *n* a person, animal, etc. that is the child, grandchild, great-grandchild, etc. of another.

descending *adj* from the highest to the lowest, the greatest to the least, or the best to the worst.

descent *n* **1** the act or process of coming or going down. **2** a slope downwards. **3** family origins or ancestry; the fact of being descended from someone. **4** a sudden invasion or attack. [OFr *descente*]

describe *v* (*tr*) **1** to say what (someone or something) is like. **2** (with **as**) to call (oneself), or claim to be, something. **3** (*tech* or *geom*) to draw or form. **4** (*formal*) to move in the shape of: *skaters describing circles on the ice*. [Lat *describere*]

description *n* **1** the act of describing. **2** a statement of what someone or something is like. **3** (*coll*) a sort, type or kind: *toys of every description*. [Lat *descriptio*]

descriptive *adj* describing, esp. describing well or vividly. — *adv* **descriptively**. — *n* **descriptiveness**. [Lat *descriptivus*]

descry *v* **-ies**, **-ied** (*tr*; *formal*) **1** to see or catch sight of. **2** to see or discover by looking carefully. [OFr *descrier*, to announce & *descrire*, to describe]

desecrate *v* (*tr*) to treat or use (a sacred object) or behave in (a holy place) in a way that shows a lack of respect or causes damage. — *n* **desecration**. — *n* **desecrator**. [**de-** (sense **2**) + **consecrate**]

desegregate *v* (*tr*) to end esp. racial segregation in (public places, schools, transport systems, etc.). — *n* **desegregation**. [**de-** (sense **2**) + **segregate**]

deselect *v* (*tr*; *Br*) **1** (of a branch of a political party) to reject (the existing Member of Parliament or local councillor) as a candidate for the next election. **2** (of a selection committee, etc.) not to re-select (e.g. an athlete) for a place on a team, etc. — *n* **deselection**. [**de-** (sense **2**) + **select**]

desensitise or **-ize** *v* (*tr*) to make less sensitive to light, pain, suffering, etc. — *n* **desensitisation** or **-z-**. [**de-** (sense **2**) + **sensitise**]

desert[1] *v* **1** (*tr*) to leave or abandon (a place or person), intending not to return. **2** (*intr*) to leave, esp. a branch of the armed forces, without permission. **3** (*tr*) to take away one's support from (a person, cause, etc.). [Fr *déserter*]

deserted *adj* (of a building, etc.) empty or abandoned.

deserter *n* a person who deserts from military service.

desertion *n* the act of or an instance of deserting (esp. deserting one's husband or wife or deserting from military service).

desert[2] *n* an area of land where there is little water or rainfall, with few plants and often covered with sand. [OFr, from Lat *deserere*, to abandon]

desertification or **desertisation** (or **-z-**) *n* the process of land becoming a desert, usu. due to farming methods or soil erosion.

deserts: **get one's (just) deserts** to get what one deserves (esp. something bad). [OFr *desert*, from *deservir*, to deserve]

deserve *v* (*tr*) to have earned, be entitled to, or be worthy of (something good) or to merit (something bad) because of one's actions, character, etc. [OFr *deservir*]

deservedly *adv* as one rightly deserves.

deserving *adj* **1** worthy or suitable (to be given support, a reward, etc.). **2** (*formal*; with **of**) worthy of; meriting.

déshabillé *adj* the state of being only partly dressed. [Fr, undressed]

desiccate *v* (*tr*) to dry or remove the moisture from (something, esp. food in order to preserve it). — *adj* **desiccated**. — *n* **desiccation**. [Lat *desiccare*, to dry up]

desideratum *n* **-ta** (*formal*) something wanted or required. [Lat *desiderare*, to long for]

design *v* (*tr*) **1** to develop or prepare a plan, drawing or model of (something) before it is built or made. **2** (*formal*; **for**) to plan, intend or develop for a particular purpose. — *n* **1** a plan, drawing, or model showing how something is to be made. **2** the art or job of making such drawings, plans, etc. **3** the way in which something has been made. **4** a picture, pattern, arrangement of shapes, etc. used e.g. as decoration. **5** one's plan, purpose or intention: *put there by design*. — **have designs on** to have plans to get (usu. something belonging to somebody else). [Fr *désigner*]

designedly *adv* intentionally; on purpose.

designer *n* a person whose job it is to make designs, plans, patterns, drawings, etc. — *adj* **1** designed by and bearing the name of a famous fashion designer. **2** (*coll*) following current fashion.

designer drug *n* a synthesised drug which is not illegal but which has the same narcotic effect as some illegal drug; any narcotic taken for non-medical purposes whose chemical structure has been altered in some way.

designing *adj* (*derog*) prepared to use cunning and deceit to get what one wants.

designate *v* (*tr*) **1** (**as**) to name, choose or specify for a particular purpose or duty. **2** to mark or indicate. **3** to be a name or label for. — *adj* (used after a noun) having been appointed to some official position but not yet in it. [Lat *designare*, to plan or mark out]

designation *n* **1** a name or title. **2** (**as**) the act of designating or state of being designated.

desire *n* **1** (**for**) **1** a longing or wish. **2** strong sexual interest and attraction. — *v* (*tr*) **1** (*formal*) to want. **2** to long for or feel sexual desire for. **3** (*old* or *formal*) to ask or command. [OFr *desirer*]

desirable *adj* **1** pleasing; worth having. **2** sexually attractive. — *n* **desirability**. — *adv* **desirably**.

desirous *adj* (*formal* or *facet*; with **of**) wanting (something).

desist *v* (*intr*; *formal*; **from**) to stop (doing something). [OFr *desister*]

desk *n* **1** a sloping or flat table, often with drawers, for sitting at while writing, reading, etc. **2** a place or counter in a public building where a service is provided. **3** a section of a newspaper, etc. office with responsibility for a particular subject. [Lat *discus*, disc, table]

desk-top *adj* small enough to fit on the top of a desk.

desolate *adj* **1** (of a place) deserted, barren and lonely. **2** (of a person) very sad; in despair. **3** lacking pleasure or comfort: *a pretty desolate life*. **4** lonely; alone. — *v* (*tr*) **1** to make very sad. **2** to make deserted or barren; to lay waste. — *adj* **desolated**. — *n* **desolation**. [Lat *desolare*, to forsake]

despair *v* (*intr*; **of**) to be without or lose hope. — *n* **1** the state of having lost hope. **2** (with **the**) someone or something that causes worry and despair: *He's the despair of his parents*. — *adj* **despairing**. — *adv* **despairingly**. [OFr *desperer*]

despatch. See **dispatch**.

desperado *n* **-os** or **-oes** (esp. in the western USA in the 19th century) a bandit or outlaw. [Prob. a pretend Spanish word formed from **desperate**]

desperate *adj* **1** extremely anxious, fearful or despairing. **2** willing to take risks fearlessly because of hopelessness and despair. **3** very serious, difficult, dangerous and almost hopeless: *a desperate situation*. **4**

dangerous and likely to be violent: *a desperate criminal.* **5** extreme and carried out as a last resort because of the seriousness or hopelessness of the situation: *desperate measures.* **6** very great: *desperate need.* **7** (**for**) in great or urgent need: *desperate for supplies.* **8** very anxious or eager: *desperate to go to the concert.* — *n* **desperation.** [Lat *desperare*, to despair]

desperately *adv* **1** in a despairing or desperate manner. **2** very hard. **3** extremely.

despicable *adj* deserving one's contempt; mean. — *n* **despicableness**. — *adv* **despicably**. [Lat *despicabilis*]

despise *v* (*tr*) to look down on with scorn and contempt. [OFr *despire*, from Lat *despicere*]

despite *prep* in spite of. [OFr *despit*, from Lat *despicere*, to despise]

despoil *v* (*tr*; *formal* or *literary*; **of**) to rob or steal everything valuable from (a place). — *n* **despoiler**. — *n* **despoliation**. [OFr *despoiller*, from Lat *spolium*, plunder]

despondent *adj* sad; disheartened. — *n* **despondency**. — *adv* **despondently**. [Lat *despondere*, to lose heart]

despot *n* a person who has very great or total power, esp. one who uses such power in a cruel or oppressive way. — *adj* **despotic**. — *adv* **despotically**. [Gr *despotes*, master]

despotism *n* absolute power; tyranny.

dessert *n* **1** a sweet food served after the main course of a meal. **2** the course at or near the end of a meal, when such food is served. [OFr, from *desservir*, to clear the table]

dessertspoon *n* **1** a medium-sized spoon, about half the size of a tablespoon and twice the size of a teaspoon. **2** (also **dessertspoonful**, **-*fuls***) the amount held by a dessertspoon.

destabilise or **-ize** *v* (*tr*) to make (a country, economy, etc.) less stable. — *n* **destabilisation** or **-z-**. [**de-** (sense **2**) + **stabilise**]

destination *n* the place to which someone or something is going or being sent. [Lat *destinatio*, purpose]

destine *v* (*tr*; *formal*; **for**) to have a purpose arranged for; to intend: *destined to be a politician*, *for a career in politics.* [OFr *destiner*]

destiny *n* **-*ies*** **1** one's purpose or future as arranged by fate or God. **2** (also *cap*) fate; the power which appears or is believed to control events. [OFr *destinee*, from Lat *destinare*, to appoint]

destitute *adj* **1** lacking money, food, shelter, etc.; extremely poor. **2** (*formal*; with **of**) completely lacking in (something necessary or desirable). — *n* **destitution**. [Lat *destitutus*]

destroy *v* (*tr*) **1** to knock down, break into pieces, completely ruin, etc. **2** to put an end to. **3** to defeat totally. **4** to ruin or seriously damage the reputation, health, financial position, etc. of. **5** to kill (a dangerous, injured or unwanted animal). [OFr *destruire*, from Lat *de*, down + *struere*, to build]

destroyer *n* **1** a person or thing that destroys or causes destruction. **2** a type of small, fast warship.

destruction *n* **1** the act or process of destroying or being destroyed. **2** something that destroys. [Lat *destruere*, to destroy, from *de*, down + *struere*, to build]

destruct *v* (*tr* & *intr*; esp. *US*) (of equipment, esp. a missile in flight) to destroy or be destroyed, esp. for safety reasons.

destructible *adj* able to be destroyed. — *n* **destructibility**.

destructive *adj* **1** causing destruction or serious damage. **2** (of criticism, etc.) pointing out faults, etc. without suggesting improvements. — *adv* **destructively**. — *n* **destructiveness**.

desultory *adj* jumping from one thing to another with no plan, purpose or logical connection. — *adv* **desultorily**. — *n* **desultoriness**. [Lat *desultorius*, from *desultor*, circus performer who jumped from horse to horse]

Det. *abbrev* Detective.

detach *v* (*tr*; **from**) **1** to unfasten or separate. **2** (*mil*) to select and separate (a group of soldiers, etc.) from a larger group, esp. to carry out a special task. — *adj* **detachable**. [OFr *destachier*, from *des-*, **dis-** + *atachier*, to attach]

detached *adj* **1** (of a building) not joined to another on either side. ◇ See also **semi-detached**. **2** (of a person) feeling no personal or emotional involvement; showing no prejudice or bias. — *adv* **detachedly**.

detachment *n* **1** the state of being emotionally detached or free from prejudice. **2** a group (e.g. of soldiers) detached from a larger group for a special purpose. **3** the act of detaching or state or process of being detached.

detail *n* **1** a small feature, fact or item. **2** something considered unimportant. **3** all the small features and parts (of something) considered as a whole: *an artist's eye for detail.* **4** a part of a painting, map, photograph, etc. considered separately, often enlarged to show small features. **5** (*mil*) a group of e.g. soldiers given a special task or duty. — *v* (*tr*) **1** to describe or list fully. **2** to appoint (someone) to do a particular task. — **in detail** giving or looking at all the details. [OFr *detailler*, to cut up]

detailed *adj* having or giving many details; thorough.

detain *v* (*tr*) **1** to stop, hold back, keep waiting or delay. **2** (of the police, etc.) to keep (someone) in a cell, prison, or elsewhere, esp. before trial. ◇ See also **detention**. [OFr *detenir*, to hold]

detainee *n* a person held under guard e.g. by the police, esp. for political reasons.

detect *v* (*tr*) **1** to see or notice. **2** to discover, and usu. indicate, the presence or existence of (something which should not be there or whose presence is not obvious). — *adj* **detectable** or **detectible**. [Lat *detegere*, to uncover]

detection *n* **1** the act or process of detecting or state of being detected. **2** the work of a detective, investigating and solving crime.

detective *n* a police officer whose job is to solve crime by observation and gathering evidence. ◇ See also **private detective**.

detective story *n* a story whose main theme is the solving of a crime.

detector *n* an instrument or device used for detecting the presence of something.

détente *n* a lessening of tension, esp. in the relationships between countries. [Fr]

detention *n* **1** the act of detaining or the state of being detained, esp. in prison or police custody. **2** a punishment in which a pupil is kept in school after the other pupils have gone home. [Lat *detinere*, to detain]

detention centre *n* a place where young criminals are kept for a short time by order of a court.

deter *v* **-rr-** (*tr*; **from**) to discourage or prevent (someone) from doing (something) because of fear of unpleasant consequences. [Lat *deterrere*, to frighten off]

deterrent *n* something which deters, esp. a weapon intended to deter attack. — *n* **deterrence**.

detergent *n* a chemical substance used for cleaning, esp. one which is not a soap. — *adj* having the power to clean. [Lat *detergere*, to wipe off]

deteriorate *v* (*intr*) to grow worse. — *n* **deterioration**. [Lat *deterior*, worse]

determine *v* **1** (*tr*) to fix or settle the exact limits or nature of. **2** (*tr*) to find out or reach a conclusion about by gathering facts, making measurements, etc. **3** (*tr* & *intr*) to decide or cause (someone) to decide. **4** (*tr*) to be the main influence on; to control. [OFr *determiner*, from Lat *determinare*, to fix the limits of]

determinant *n* **1** a determining factor or circumstance. **2** (*math*) the sum of the products of the elements in a block of quantities (matrix) calculated according to certain rules. **3** (*math*) the matrix itself.

determinate *adj* having definite, fixed limits, etc.

determination *n* **1** firmness or strength of will, purpose or character. **2** the act of determining or process of being determined.

determinative *adj* having the power to limit or determine.

determined *adj* **1** (**to**) having firmly decided. **2** having or showing a strong will.

determiner *n* (*gram*) a word that comes before a noun or noun phrase, and limits its meaning in some way, e.g. *a*, *the*, *this*, *every*, *some*.

determinism *n* (*philos*) the doctrine that all things are caused and determined by previous events, and that there is no such thing as free will. — *n* **determinist**.

deterrence, **deterrent**. See **deter**.

detest *v* (*tr*) to dislike intensely; to hate. [OFr *detester*]

detestable *adj* hateful. — *adv* **detestably**.

detestation *n* great dislike; hatred.

dethrone *v* (*tr*) **1** to remove (e.g. a king or queen) from his or her position as ruler. **2** to remove from a position of power, influence or authority. — *n* **dethronement**. [**de-** (sense **2**) + **throne**]

detonate *v* (*tr* & *intr*) to (cause to) explode. — *n* **detonation**. [Lat *detonare*, to thunder down]

detonator *n* an explosive substance or a device used to make a bomb, etc. explode.

detour *n* (a journey deliberately made on) a route away from and longer than a planned or more direct route. — *v* (*intr*) to make or go by a detour. [Fr *détour*]

detoxify *v* **-ies**, **-ied** (*tr*) to remove poison, drugs, or harmful substances from (a patient). — *n* **detoxification**. [**de-** (sense **2**) + **toxic** + **-ify**]

detract *v* (*intr*; with **from**) to take away from or lessen. — *n* **detraction**. [Lat *detrahere*, to pull away]

detractor *n* a person who criticises or belittles (someone, or someone's beliefs, achievements, etc.), esp. unfairly.

detriment *n* harm or loss: *to the detriment of her health*. [Lat *detrimentum*]

detrimental *adj* (**to**) harmful; damaging. — *adv* **detrimentally**.

detritus *n* **1** a loose mass of stones, sand, etc. produced by the breaking up or wearing away of rocks. **2** bits and pieces of rubbish left over from something. [Lat *deterere*, to rub away]

de trop not wanted; in the way. [Fr]

deuce[1] *n* **1** (*tennis*) a score of forty points each in a game or five games each in a match. **2** a card, dice throw, etc. of the value two. [OFr *deus*, two]

deuce[2] *n* (*old euph*; with **the**, in exclamations) the devil. [Perh. from **deuce**[1], two being an unlucky throw in dice]

deuterium *n* an isotope of hydrogen with a mass double that of the usual isotope. [Gr *deuteros*, second]

deuterium oxide *n* a compound of deuterium and oxygen; heavy water.

Deutschmark or **Deutsche Mark** *n* (also **mark**: *abbrev* **DM**) the standard unit of currency in Germany, equal to 100 pfennigs. [Ger]

devalue or **devaluate** *v* **1** (*tr* & *intr*) to reduce the value of (a currency) in relation to the values of other currencies. **2** (*tr*) to make (a person, action, etc.) seem less valuable or important. — *n* **devaluation**. [**de-** (sense **2**) + **value**]

devastate *v* (*tr*) **1** to cause great destruction in or to. **2** to overwhelm with grief; to shock greatly. — *adj* **devastated**. — *n* **devastation**. [Lat *devastare*, to lay waste]

devastating *adj* **1** completely destructive. **2** shocking; overwhelming. **3** (*coll*) very good or impressive; extremely attractive. — *adv* **devastatingly**.

develop *v* **-p- 1** (*tr* & *intr*; **from, into**) to make or become more mature, more advanced, more complete, more organised, more detailed, etc. **2** (*tr*) to begin to have; to have an increasing amount of: *develop an interest in politics*. **3** (*intr* & *tr*) to appear and grow, or to have or suffer from something which has appeared and grown: *be developing a cold*. **4** (*tr*) to make the picture on (a photographic film) become visible and permanent by a chemical process. **5** (*tr*) to bring into fuller use (the natural resources, etc. of a country or region). **6** (*tr*) to build on (land) or prepare (land) for being built on. [Fr *développer*]

developer *n* **1** a chemical used to develop photographic film. **2** a person who builds on land or improves and increases the value of buildings.

developing *adj* (of a country) relatively poor, but growing or trying to grow industrially or economically.

development *n* **1** (**from, into**) the act of developing or the process of being developed. **2** a new stage, event or situation. **3** (**from**) result. **4** land which has been or is being developed, or the buildings built or being built on it. — *adj* **developmental**. — *adv* **developmentally**.

development area *n* (*Br*) an area of high unemployment into which the government encourages businesses and industry to move e.g. by offering grants.

deviant *adj* not following the normal patterns, accepted standards, etc. — *n* a person who does not behave in a normal or acceptable fashion, esp. sexually. — *n* **deviance**. [Lat *deviare*; see ety. at **deviate**]

deviate *v* (*intr*; **from**) to turn aside or move away from what is considered a correct or normal course, standard of behaviour, way of thinking, etc. [Lat *deviare*, to turn from the road, from *de*, from + *via*, road]

deviation *n* **1** the act of deviating. **2** (*geog*) the existence of or the amount of a difference between north as shown on a compass and true north, caused by the magnetism of objects near the compass, etc.

deviationist *n* a person who disagrees with some aspects of a (usu. political) belief or ideology. — *n* **deviationism**.

device *n* **1** something made for a special purpose, e.g. a tool or instrument. **2** a plan or scheme for doing something, sometimes involving trickery or deceit. **3** a sign, pattern or symbol used e.g. on a crest or shield. ◇ See also **devise**. — **leave to one's own devices** to leave alone and without supervision, support or help. [OFr *devis* and *devise*, from Lat *divisa*, mark, device]

devil *n* **1** (*cap* with **the**) the most powerful evil spirit; Satan. **2** any evil or wicked spirit. **3** (*coll*) a mischievous or bad person. **4** (*coll*) a person of a stated type: *lucky devil*. **5** someone or something difficult to deal with. **6** a person who excels at something. **7** (with **the**) used for emphasis in mild oaths and exclamations: *What the devil is she doing?* — *v* **-ll-** (*tr*) to prepare or cook with a spicy seasoning. — **be a devil** (*coll*; usu. *humorous*) said to encourage someone to do something he or she is hesitating to do. — **between the devil and the deep blue sea** in a situation where the alternatives are equally undesirable. — **devil take the hindmost** one should take care of one's own success, safety, etc. with no thought for others. — **the devil to pay** serious trouble as a consequence of an action, etc. — **give the devil his due** to admit the good points of a person one dislikes. — **go to the devil 1** to be ruined. **2** (usu. as a command, in anger) to go away. — **like the devil** (*coll*) very hard. — **speak** or **talk of the devil** said at the arrival of someone one has just been talking about. [OE *deofol*, from Gr *diabolos*, slanderer]

devilish *adj* **1** of or like a devil; as if from, produced by, etc. a devil. **2** very wicked. **3** (*coll*) very great or very difficult. — *adv* (*old*) very.

devilishly *adv* (*old*) very; terribly.

devil-may-care *adj* cheerfully heedless of danger, consequences, etc.

devilment *n* mischievous fun.

devilry *n* **-ies 1** mischievous fun. **2** wickedness or cruelty. **3** witchcraft; black magic.

devil's advocate *n* a person who argues for or against something simply to encourage discussion or argument.

devious *adj* **1** not totally open or honest; deceitful. **2** cunning; able to think up clever and usu. deceitful ways of achieving things, etc. **3** not direct: *came by a devious route*. — *adv* **deviously**. — *n* **deviousness**. [Lat *devius*, from *de*, from + *via*, road]

devise *v* (*tr*) **1** to invent, make up or put together (a plan, etc.) in one's mind. **2** (*legal*) to leave (property such as land or buildings) to someone in a will. ◇ See also **bequeath**. [OFr *deviser*, from Lat *divisa*, division of goods]

devoid *adj* (with **of**) free from, lacking, or empty of. [OFr *devoidier*, to take away]

devolution *n* the act of devolving, esp. the giving of certain powers to a regional government by a central government. — *n* **devolutionist**. [Lat *devolutio*, from *devolvere*, to roll down]

devolve *v* (with **to, on, upon**) **1** (*tr* & *intr*) (of duties, power, etc.) to (cause or allow to) be transferred to someone else. **2** (*intr*; *legal*) to pass by succession: *On his death, the title will devolve on his nephew*. [Lat *devolvere*, to roll down]

Devonian *adj* & *n* (of) a geological period lasting between 408 and 360 million years ago, when the first insects appeared. [*Devon* in England]

devote *v* (*tr* with **to**) to give up wholly to or use entirely for. [Lat *devovere*, to consecrate]
devoted *adj* **1** (**to**) loving and loyal. **2** (with **to**) given up to; totally occupied by. — *adv* **devotedly**. — *n* **devotedness**.
devotee *n* **1** a keen follower or enthusiastic supporter. **2** a keen believer in a religion or follower of a god.
devotion *n* **1** (**to**) great love or loyalty; enthusiasm for or willingness to do what is required by. **2** the act of devoting or of being devoted. **3** religious enthusiasm and piety. **4** (in *pl*) worship and prayers. — *adj* **devotional**.
devour *v* (*tr*) **1** to eat up greedily. **2** to destroy thoroughly. **3** to read eagerly. **4** to look at with obvious pleasure. **5** (esp. in *passive*) to take over totally: *devoured by guilt*. — *adj* **devouring**. [Lat *devorare*, to gulp down]
devout *adj* **1** sincerely religious in thought and behaviour. **2** deeply-felt; earnest. — *adv* **devoutly**. — *n* **devoutness**. [Lat *devovere*, to consecrate]
dew *n* tiny drops of moisture coming from the air as it cools, esp. at night, and forming on leaves, etc. [OE *deaw*]
dewclaw *n* a small functionless toe or claw on the leg of some dogs and other animals.
dewdrop *n* a drop of dew.
dewy *adj* **-ier**, **-iest** covered in dew.
dewy-eyed *adj* naïve and too trusting.
mountain dew *n* whisky, esp. when made illicitly.
dewlap *n* a flap of loose skin hanging down from the throat of certain cattle, dogs, and other animals. [Prob. **dew** + OE *læppa*, loose hanging piece]
dexter *adj* (*heraldry*) on the right-hand side of a shield considered from the point of view of the person carrying it, i.e. the left as seen by someone looking at it. ◇ See also **sinister**. [Lat, right]
dexterity *n* **1** skill in using one's hands. **2** quickness of mind. [Fr *dextérité*, from Lat *dexter*, right, skilful]
dexterous or **dextrous** *adj* having, showing or done with dexterity. — *adv* **dexterously** or **dextrously**.
dextrin or **dextrine** *n* a gummy substance obtained from starch, used as a thickener in foods and in adhesives. [Fr *dextrine*]
dextrose *n* a form of glucose found in fruit and honey. [Lat *dexter*, right]
DF *abbrev* Defender of the Faith.
DFC *abbrev* Distinguished Flying Cross.
DFM *abbrev* Distinguished Flying Medal.
DG *abbrev* **1** Director General. **2** *Dei gratia*, (Lat) by the grace of God. **3** *Deo gratias*, (Lat) thanks be to God.
dhal. See **dal**.
dharma *n* **1** (*Buddhism*) truth. **2** (*Hinduism*) the universal laws, esp. the moral laws to be followed by each individual. [Sanskrit]
dhoti *n* a garment worn by some Hindu men, consisting of a long strip of cloth wrapped around the waist and between the legs. [Hindi]
dhow *n* a type of ship with one or more sails, used in countries around the Indian Ocean.
DHSS *abbrev* Department of Health and Social Security (now, since 1989, the Department of Social Services).
di- *pfx* **1** two or double: *dicotyledon*. **2** (*chem*) containing two atoms of the same type: *dioxide*. [Gr *dis*, twice]
diabetes *n* any of several disorders characterised by excessive production of urine, esp. **diabetes mellitus** in which the body fails to absorb sugar and starch properly from the blood due to a deficiency of insulin, with, consequently, an excess of sugar in the blood and urine. [Gr *diabetes*, siphon]
diabetic *n* a person suffering from diabetes. — *adj* **1** relating to or suffering from diabetes. **2** especially for people who have diabetes.
diabolic *adj* **1** of or like a devil; devilish. **2** very wicked or cruel. — *adv* **diabolically**. [Gr *diabolos*, slanderer, devil]
diabolical *adj* (esp. *Br coll*) very shocking, annoying, bad, etc. — *adv* **diabolically**.
diabolism *n* the worship of the Devil or devils; witchcraft; black magic. [Gr *diabolos*, devil + **-ism**]
diaconate *n* **1** the position of deacon. **2** one's period of time as a deacon. **3** deacons as a group. [Lat *diaconus*, deacon]
diacritic *n* a mark written or printed over, under or through a letter to show that that letter has a particular sound, as in *é*, *è*, *ç* and *ñ*. — *adj* **diacritic** or **diacritical**. [Gr *diakritikos*, able to distinguish]
diadem *n* **1** a crown or jewelled head-band, worn by a royal person. **2** royal power or authority. [OFr *diademe*, from Gr *dia*, around + *deein*, to bind]
diaeresis *n* **-eses** a mark (¨) placed over a vowel to show that it is to be pronounced separately from the vowel before it, as in *naïve*. [Gr *diairesis*, separation]
diagnosis *n* **-oses** **1** the identification of a disease from a consideration of the patient's symptoms. **2** a statement of the results of this. [Gr, from *diagignoskein*, to distinguish]
diagnose *v* (*tr*) **1** to identify (an illness) from a consideration of its symptoms. **2** to identify (a fault).
diagnostic *adj* relating to or useful in diagnosis.
diagonal *adj* **1** (*math*) (of a straight line) joining any two non-adjacent corners of a polygon or any two vertices not on the same face in a polyhedron. **2** sloping or slanting. — *n* a diagonal line. — *adv* **diagonally**. [Gr *dia*, through + *gonia*, angle]
diagram *n* a simple line drawing, not drawn to show the actual appearance of what it represents but only the structure of it or how it operates. [Gr *diagramma*, from *dia*, round + *graphein*, to write]

diagrammatic *adj* in the form of a diagram. — *adv* **diagrammatically**.

dial *n* **1** a disc or plate on a clock, radio, meter, etc. with numbers or other scales or measurements marked on it and a movable pointer or indicator, used to indicate e.g. measurements of speed, time, etc. or selected settings of time, temperature, radio frequency, etc. **2** the round numbered plate on some telephones and the movable disc fitted over it. — *v* **-ll-** (*tr* & *intr*) to use a telephone dial to call (a number). [Lat *dialis*, daily]

dialect *n* a form of a language spoken in a particular region or by a certain class of people, differing from other forms in pronunciation, grammar and vocabulary. — *adj* **dialectal**. [Gr *dialektos*, manner of speech]

dialectic *n* (*philos*) **1** (also **dialectics** *n sing*) the art or practice of establishing truth by discussion. **2** (also **dialectics** *n sing*) a debate which aims to resolve the conflict between two opposing theories rather than to disprove either of them. **3** the art of reasoning and arguing logically. [Gr *dialektike* (*techne*), (the art) of debating]

dialectical *adj* (*philos*) of or by dialectic; depending on or proceeding by the resolving of the conflict between opposing factors, theories, etc.

dialogue *n* **1** a conversation, esp. a formal one. **2** the words spoken by the characters in a play, book, etc. **3** a discussion or exchange of ideas and opinions, esp. between two groups, with a view to resolving conflict or achieving agreement. [Gr *dialogos*, conversation]

dialysis *n* **-yses 1** (*tech*) a process by which solids are separated from a liquid by passing through a membrane into another liquid. **2** (*med*) the removal by this process of harmful wastes from the blood of people suffering from kidney failure. [Gr *dialysis*, separation]

diamanté *adj* & *n* (a fabric) decorated with small sparkling ornaments. [Fr, decorated with diamonds]

diameter *n* **1** a straight line drawn from one side of a circle, sphere, etc. to the other side and passing through its centre. **2** the length of such a line. [Gr *dia*, across + *metron*, measure]

diametric or **diametrical** *adj* **1** of or along a diameter. **2** (of opinions, etc.) directly opposed; very far apart. — *adv* **diametrically**.

diamond *n* **1** a usu. colourless transparent precious stone, a crystallised form of carbon, the hardest of all minerals. **2** a piece of (often artificial) diamond, used for cutting glass, as a record-player needle, etc. **3** a shape or figure with four equal straight sides and angles which are not right angles. **4** (in *pl*) one of the four suits of playing-cards with red symbols of this shape. **5** one of the playing-cards of this suit. **6** a baseball pitch, or the part of it between the bases. — *adj* (of a wedding or other anniversary) 60th. [OFr *diamant*, from Lat and Gr *adamas*, steel, diamond]

rough diamond see **rough**.

dianthus *n* any plant of the genus (*Dianthus*) of flowers to which carnations and pinks belong. [Lat, from Gr *Dios anthos*, Zeus's flower]

diaper *n* **1** a type of linen or cotton cloth with a pattern of small diamond or square shapes. **2** (*NAm*) a baby's nappy. [OFr *diaspre*]

diaphanous *adj* (of cloth) very light, fine and almost transparent. [Gr *dia*, through + *phanein*, to show]

diaphragm *n* **1** the wall of muscle which separates the chest from the abdomen in the bodies of mammals. **2** a device, e.g. a metal plate with a central hole or an adjustable circle of thin plates, by means of which the light entering an optical instrument such as a camera may be controlled. **3** a thin vibrating disc of metal or other material, e.g. in a telephone, which converts electrical signals to sound-waves or sound-waves to electrical signals. **4** a thin rubber or plastic cap fitted over the neck of the womb before sexual intercourse in order to prevent pregnancy. [Gr *diaphragma*, partition]

diarist. See **diary**.

diarrhoea *n* a condition in which the bowels are emptied more frequently than usual and the faeces are very soft or liquid. — *adj* **diarrhoeal** or **diarrhoeic**. [Gr *dia*, through + *rhoia*, flow]

diary *n* **-ies 1** (a book containing) a written record of daily events in a person's life. **2** (*Br*) a book with separate spaces or pages for each day of the year in which appointments, daily notes and reminders may be written. [Lat *diarium*, from *dies*, day]

diarist *n* a person who writes a diary, esp. one which is published.

Diaspora *n* (with **the**) **1** the scattering of the Jewish people to various countries following their exile in Babylon in the 6th century BC. **2** the new communities of Jews which arose in various countries as a result. **3** the Jews who do not live in the modern state of Israel. [Gr *dia*, through + *speirein*, to scatter]

diastase *n* an enzyme which converts starch to sugar. [Gr *diastasis*, division]

diastole *n* (*med*) the rhythmic expansion of the chambers of the heart during which they fill with blood. ◇ See also **systole**. — *adj* **diastolic**. [Gr *dia*, apart + *stellein*, to place]

diatom *n* any plant of a class of microscopic one-celled algae which have hard shells in two halves which fit together like a box and its lid. [Gr *diatomos*, cut through]

diatomic *adj* (*tech*) **1** consisting of two atoms. **2** having two replaceable atoms or groups. [**di-** + **atom**]

diatonic *adj* (*mus*) (of a scale, etc.) consisting of or involving only the basic notes proper to a particular key, with no additional sharps, flats or naturals. ◇ See also **chromatic**. [Gr *dia*, through + *tonos*, tone]
diatribe *n* (**against**) a bitter or abusive critical attack in speech or writing. [Gr *diatribe*, discourse]
dibasic *adj* (*chem*) (of an acid) containing two replaceable hydrogen atoms. [**di-** + **basic**]
dibble or **dibber** *n* a short pointed hand-tool used for making holes in the ground for seeds, young plants, etc.
dice *n* ***dice*** **1** a small cube with a different number of spots, from 1 to 6, on each of its sides or faces, used in certain games of chance. **2** a game of chance played with one or more dice. ◇ See also **die**[2]. — *v* **1** (*tr*) to cut (vegetables, etc.) into small cubes. **2** (*intr*) to play or gamble with dice. — **dice with death** to take a great risk. — **no dice** (*coll*) used to indicate a negative answer or unsuccessful outcome. [Orig. *pl* of **die**[3]]
dicey *adj* ***-ier***, ***-iest*** (*coll*) risky.
dichotomy *n* ***-ies*** a division or separation into two groups or parts, esp. when these are sharply opposed or contrasted. — *adj* **dichotomous**. [Gr *dicha*, in two + *tome*, cut]
dick *n* **1** (*vulgar slang*) the penis. **2** (*slang*) a detective. [From the name *Dick*]
clever Dick *n* (*coll*) a know-all.
dickens *n* (*coll*; with **the**) the devil, used esp. for emphasis. [From the name *Dickon* or *Dicken*, from *Richard*]
Dickensian *adj* of or like the very bad living or working conditions or the odd or amusing characters described in the novels of Charles *Dickens* (1812-70).
dicker *v* (*intr*) to argue about the price or cost of something.
dicky[1], **dickie** or **dickey** *n* ***-ies***, ***-eys*** a false shirt front, esp. when worn with evening dress.
dicky[2] *adj* ***-ier***, ***-iest*** (*coll*) not in good condition.
dicky-bird *n* a child's word for a small bird. [From the name *Dicky*, for *Richard*]
dicotyledon *n* (*bot*) a plant which has two tiny leaves when it first grows from the seed. ◇ See also **cotyledon** and **monocotyledon**. [**di-** + **cotyledon**]
dicta. See **dictum**.
Dictaphone® *n* a small tape-recorder for use esp. when dictating letters.
dictate *v* **1** (*tr* & *intr*) to say or read out (something) for someone else to write down. **2** (*tr*) to state or lay down (rules, terms, etc.) forcefully or with authority. **3** (*tr* & *intr*; *derog*) to give orders to or try to impose one's wishes on (someone). — *n* **dictate** (usu. in *pl*) **1** an order or instruction. **2** a guiding principle. [Lat *dictare*]
dictation *n* **1** something read for another to write down. **2** the act of dictating.
dictator *n* **1** a ruler with complete and unrestricted power. **2** a person who behaves in a dictatorial manner. **3** in ancient Rome, a person given complete authority in the state for a period of six months at a time of crisis. — *n* **dictatorship**.
dictatorial *adj* **1** of, like or suggesting a dictator; fond of using one's power and authority and imposing one's wishes on or giving orders to other people. — *adv* **dictatorially**.
diction *n* **1** the way in which one speaks. **2** one's choice or use of words to express meaning. [Lat *dicere*, to say]
dictionary *n* ***-ies*** **1** a book containing the words of a language arranged alphabetically with their meanings. **2** an alphabetically arranged book of information. [Lat *dictionarium*]
dictum *n* ***-tums*** or ***-ta*** **1** a formal or authoritative statement of opinion. **2** a popular saying or maxim. [Lat]
did. See **do**[1].
didactic *adj* **1** intended to teach or instruct. **2** (*derog*) too eager or too obviously intended to instruct, in a way resented by the reader, listener, etc. — *adv* **didactically**. — *n* **didacticism**. [Gr *didaskein*, to teach]
diddle *v* (*tr*; *coll*) to cheat or swindle. — *n* **diddler**. [Prob. from Jeremy *Diddler*, character in a 19th-century play]
didgeridoo *n* an Australian Aborigine wind instrument, consisting of a long wooden or bamboo tube which when blown into produces a low droning sound. [From an Australian Aborigine language]
didn't did not.
didst the form of **did** used with the pronoun *thou*.
die[1] *v* ***dying*** (*intr*) **1** to stop living; to cease to be alive. **2** to cease to exist, come to an end or fade away. **3** (of an engine, etc.) to stop working suddenly and unexpectedly. **4** (with **of**) to suffer or be overcome by the effects of: *die of boredom*. — **be dying** (*coll*; **for**) to have a strong desire or need for or to do something. — *v* **die away** (*intr*) **1** to fade away from sight or hearing until gone. **2** to become steadily weaker and finally stop. — *v* **die back** (*intr*) (of a plant's soft shoots) to die or wither from the tip back to the hard wood. — *v* **die down** (*intr*) **1** to lose strength or force. **2** (of a plant or its soft shoots) to wither back to the root without completely dying. — **die hard** to be difficult to change or remove. — *v* **die off** (*intr*) to die one after another. — *v* **die out** (*intr*) to cease to exist anywhere; to become extinct. — **never say die** never give up or give in. [MidE *dien*, from Norse *deyja*]
diehard *n* a person who stubbornly refuses to accept new ideas or changes.
dying *adj* **1** occurring immediately before death: *recorded his dying words*. **2** of or relating to death. **3** last; final.

die[2] *n* ***dies*** (sense **1**), ***dice*** (sense **2**) **1** a metal tool or stamp for cutting or shaping metal or making designs on coins, etc. **2** a dice. — **the die is cast** a decision has been made or an action taken which cannot be changed or gone back on. — **straight as a die 1** completely straight. **2** completely honest. [OFr *de*, from Lat *datum*, something given]

die-casting *n* **1** the process of shaping metal or plastic in a metal mould. **2** an object made in this way.

dieresis. *US* form of **diaeresis**.

diesel *n* **1** diesel oil. **2** a diesel engine. **3** a train, etc. driven by by a diesel engine. [Rudolph *Diesel* (1858–1913), German engineer who invented the engine]

diesel engine *n* an internal-combustion engine in which the fuel oil is ignited by the heat of the compressed air into which it is injected.

diesel oil *n* heavy oil used as fuel for a diesel engine.

diet[1] *n* **1** the sort of food normally eaten by a person or animal. **2** a limited variety or quantity of food that a person is allowed to eat, esp. in order to lose weight or because of illness. — *v* ***-t-*** (*intr*) to limit one's food to what is allowed by a prescribed diet, esp. in order to lose weight. — *n* **dieter**. [OFr *diete*, from Gr *diaita*, way of life]

dietary *adj* of or concerning a diet.

dietary fibre *n* fibrous substances in fruit, vegetables and cereals which keep bowel movements regular and are therefore thought to help prevent certain diseases.

dietetic *adj* **1** of or concerning diet. **2** for use in a special medical diet.

dietetics *n* (*sing*) the scientific study of diet and its relation to health.

dietician or **dietitian** *n* a person who is trained in dietetics.

diet[2] *n* **1** the legislative assembly of certain countries, e.g. Japan. **2** (*hist*) a conference held to discuss political or church affairs. [Lat *dieta*, public assembly, from Gr *diaita*, way of life]

differ *v* **-r-** (*intr*) **1** (**from**) to be different, unlike or of more than one kind. **2** (**with, from**) to disagree. [OFr *differer*]

difference *n* **1** (**between**) what makes one thing or person unlike another. **2** the state of being unlike. **3** a change from an earlier state, etc. **4** the amount by which one quantity or number is greater or less than another. **5** a quarrel or disagreement. — **make a, no,** etc. **difference** to have some, no, etc. effect (on a situation). [Lat *differentia*]

different *adj* **1** (**from, to** or, esp. *US*, **than**) not the same. **2** separate; distinct; various. **3** (*coll*) unusual. — *adv* **differently**.

differential *adj* **1** of, showing or based on a difference. **2** (*math*) involving very small differences. — *n* **1** (also **wage differential**) a difference in the rate of pay between one category of worker and another in the same industry or company. **2** (*math*) a very small difference. **3** a differential gear. [Lat *differentialis*]

differential calculus see **calculus**.

differential coefficient *n* (*math*) the ratio of the rate of change of a function to that of its independent variable.

differential gear *n* an arrangement of gears which allows one of the driving wheels of a vehicle to turn at a different speed from the other when the vehicle is going round a corner.

differentiate *v* **1** (*intr* & *tr*; **between, from**) to see a difference between; to be able to distinguish (one from another). **2** (*tr*; **from**) to show or be the difference between. **3** (*intr*; **between**) to treat one person, etc. differently from another. **4** (*intr*) to become different. **5** (*tr*; *math*) to find the differential coefficient of. — *n* **differentiation**. [Lat *differentiare*]

difficult *adj* **1** requiring great skill, intelligence or effort. **2** not easy to please. **3** unco-operative. **4** (of a problem, situation, etc.) potentially embarrassing; hard to resolve or get out of. [Lat *difficultas*, difficulty]

difficulty *n* ***-ies*** **1** the state or quality of being difficult. **2** a difficult thing to do or understand. **3** a problem, obstacle or objection. **4** (usu. in *pl*) trouble or embarrassment, esp. financial.

diffident *adj* lacking in confidence; too modest or shy. — *n* **diffidence**. — *adv* **diffidently**. [Lat *diffidere*, to distrust]

diffract *v* (*tr*; *physics*) to cause diffraction in. — *adj* **diffractive**. [Lat *diffringere*, to shatter]

diffraction *n* (*physics*) the breaking-up of a beam of light into dark and light bands or into coloured bands, e.g. when passed through a narrow opening.

diffuse *v* (*tr* & *intr*) to spread or send out in all directions. — *adj* **1** widely spread; not concentrated. **2** (of a style of writing or speaking) using too many words; not concise. — *adj* **diffused**. — *adv* **diffusely**. — *n* **diffuseness**. [Lat *diffundere*, to pour out in various directions]

diffusion *n* **1** the act of diffusing or state of being diffused. **2** (*physics*) the mixing together of gases or liquids in contact with each other.

dig *v* ***-gg-***, ***dug*** **1** (*tr* & *intr*) to turn up or move (earth, etc.), esp. with a spade. **2** (*tr*) to make (a hole, etc.) by digging. **3** (*tr* & *intr*; **in, into**) to poke. **4** (*tr*; *old slang*) to appreciate. **5** (*tr* & *intr*; *old slang*) to understand. — *n* **1** a remark intended to irritate, criticise or make fun of. **2** a place where archaeologists are digging, e.g. to uncover ancient ruins. **3** a poke. **4** an act of digging. **5** (in *pl*; *Br coll*) lodgings. — *v* **dig in 1** (*intr*; *coll*) to start to eat. **2** (*tr*) to mix into the soil, etc. by digging. **3** (*tr* & *intr*) to make a protected place for oneself. **4** (*tr*) to establish (oneself) in a position, job, etc. — *v* **dig into** (*tr*) **1** to thrust or push (something) into. **2** (*coll*) to examine or search through for information. — **dig in one's heels** or **dig one's heels in** to refuse to change one's mind. — **dig one's own grave** to be the cause of one's own failure or downfall. — *v* **dig out** (*tr*) **1** to get (something or someone) out by digging. **2** (*coll*) to find by searching. — *v* **dig up** (*tr*) **1** to remove from the ground by digging. **2** to find or reveal (something buried or hidden) by digging. **3** (*coll*) to search for and find (information, etc.). [MidE *diggen*]

digger *n* **1** a machine used for digging and excavating. **2** a person who digs, esp. a gold-miner. **3** (*coll*) an Australian or New Zealander, esp. a soldier.

diggings *n* (*pl*) **1** a place where people dig, esp. for gold or precious stones. **2** (*Br old coll*) lodgings. ◇ See also **dig** (*n* sense **5**).

digest[1] *v* **1** (*tr* & *intr*) to break down (food), or (of food) to be broken down, in the stomach, intestine, etc. into a form which the body can use. **2** (*tr*) to take in and think over the meaning and implications of (information). [Lat *digerere*, to dissolve]

digestible *adj* able to be digested. — *n* **digestibility**.

digestion *n* **1** the act of digesting food or information. **2** the ability to digest food.

digestive *adj* of or for digestion. — *n* (*Br*) (also **digestive biscuit**) a type of plain slightly sweetened biscuit made from wholemeal flour.

digest[2] *n* **1** a usu. regularly published collection of summaries or shortened versions (of news stories or current literature). **2** a summary or shortened version. **3** a systematically arranged collection of laws. [Lat *digerere*, to arrange]

digit *n* **1** any of the ten figures 0 to 9. **2** (*tech*) a finger or toe. [Lat *digitus*, finger, toe]

digital *adj* **1** showing quantity, time, etc. by means of numbers rather than by a pointer on a scale, dial, etc. **2** processing information which is in the form of a series of digits, generally in binary notation: *a digital computer*. **3** (of sound reproduction or storage) involving the conversion of sound to information in the form of series of digits. **4** of or involving digits in any way. ◇ See also **analogue**.

digitise or **-ize** *v* (*tr*) to convert (data, etc.) into numbers. — *n* **digitisation** or **-z-**. — *n* **digitiser** or **-z-**.

digitalis *n* a drug prepared from dried foxglove leaves, used as a heart stimulant. [Lat name of the foxglove genus]

dignify *v* **-ies**, **-ied** (*tr*) **1** to make (something) impressive or dignified. **2** to make (something) seem more important or impressive than it is: *tried to dignify his scribblings by calling them free verse.* [Lat *dignus*, worthy + *facere*, to make]

dignified *adj* stately, serious or showing dignity.

dignitary *n* **-ies** a person of high rank or position, esp. in public life. [**dignity** + **-ary**]

dignity *n* **1** stateliness, seriousness and formality of manner and appearance. **2** goodness and nobility of character. **3** calmness and self-control. **4** high rank or position. — **beneath one's dignity** not worthy or fit to be done by as important, respectable or noble a person as one considers oneself to be. — **stand on one's dignity** to demand to be treated with proper respect, esp. to do so arrogantly. [Lat *dignitas*, from *dignus*, worthy]

digraph *n* a pair of letters that represent a single sound, as in the *ph* of *digraph*. [Gr *di-*, twice + *graphe*, mark, character]

digress *v* (intr; **from**) to wander from the point, or from the main subject in speaking or writing. — *n* **digression**. [Lat *digredi*, to move away, digress]

dihedral *adj* (*geom*) formed or bounded by two planes. [Gr *di-*, twice + *hedra*, seat]

dike. Same as **dyke**.

diktat *n* **1** a forceful, sometimes unreasonable, order which must be obeyed. **2** a harsh settlement forced on the defeated or powerless. [Ger, something dictated]

dilapidated *adj* (of furniture, buildings, etc.) falling to pieces because of neglect or age; in great need of repair. — *n* **dilapidation**. [Lat *dilapidare*, to demolish]

dilate *v* **1** (*tr* & *intr*) (esp. of an opening in the body) to (cause to) become larger, wider or further open. **2** (*intr*; *formal*; with **on**) to speak or write at great length about. — *n* **dilation** or **dilatation**. [Lat *dilatare*, to spread out]

dilatory *adj* slow (in doing things); inclined to or causing delay. — *adv* **dilatorily**. — *n* **dilatoriness**. [Lat *dilatorius*]

dildo *n* **-os** a object shaped like an erect penis, used for sexual pleasure.

dilemma *n* **1** a situation in which one must choose between two (or more than two) courses of action, both (or all) equally undesirable. **2** (*coll*) a problem or difficult situation. [Gr *di-*, twice + *lemma*, assumption]

dilettante *n* **-tes** or **-ti** (sometimes *derog*) a person who has an interest in a subject, esp. art, literature or science, but does not study it very seriously or in depth. — *n* **dilettantism**. [Ital, from *dilettare*, to delight]

diligent *adj* **1** hard-working and careful. **2** showing or done with care and serious effort. — *n* **diligence**. — *adv* **diligently**. [Lat *diligens*, careful]

dill *n* a European herb the fruit of which is used in flavouring, esp. pickles. [OE *dile*]

dilly-dally *v* **-dallies**, **-dallied** (*intr*; *coll*) **1** to be slow or waste time. **2** to be unable to make up one's mind. [From **dally**.]

dilute *v* (*tr*) **1** to make (a liquid) thinner or weaker by mixing with water or another liquid. **2** to reduce the strength, influence or effect of (something). — *adj* (esp. *chem*) diluted. — *n* **dilution**. [Lat *diluere*, to wash away]

diluvial or **diluvian** *adj* **1** of or pertaining to a flood, esp. the flood mentioned in the Book of Genesis in the Bible. **2** caused by a flood. [Lat *diluvium*, flood]

dim *adj* **-mm- 1** not bright or distinct. **2** lacking enough light to see clearly. **3** faint; not clearly remembered: *a dim memory*. **4** (*coll*) not very intelligent. **5** (of eyes) not able to see well. **6** (*coll*) not good; not hopeful: *dim prospects*. — *v* **-mm-** (*tr* & *intr*) to make or become dim. — *adv* **dimly**. — *n* **dimness**. — **take a dim view of** (*coll*) to disapprove of. [OE *dimm*]

dimmer or **dimmer switch** *n* a switch used to reduce the brightness of a light.

dimwit *n* (*coll*) a stupid person. — *adj* **dim-witted**.

dime *n* a coin of the US and Canada worth ten cents or one tenth of a dollar. [OFr *disme*, from Lat *decima*, tenth]

dimension *n* **1** a measurement of length, breadth, height, etc. **2** (often in *pl*) size or extent. **3** a particular aspect (of a problem, situation, etc.). [OFr, from Lat *dimensio*, measuring]

-dimensional *in cmpds* having (a certain number of) dimensions: *a two-dimensional drawing of a three-dimensional building*.

fourth dimension *n* (usu. with **the**) **1** time, as a dimension in addition to length, breadth and height. **2** a dimension attributed to space in addition to length, breadth and height.

dimin. *abbrev*. diminutive.

diminish *v* **1** (*tr* & *intr*) to make or become less or smaller. **2** (*tr*) to cause to seem less important, valuable or satisfactory. [From an obsolete word *minish* combined with MidE *diminue*, from Lat *deminuere*, to make less]

diminished *adj* **1** having become less, smaller, less important, etc. **2** (*mus*) reduced by a semitone.

diminuendo (*mus*) *n* **-os 1** a gradual lessening of sound. **2** a musical passage with gradually lessening sound. — *adj* & *adv* with gradually lessening sound. ◇ See also **crescendo**. [Ital, from Lat *deminuere*, to make less]

diminution *n* a lessening or decrease. [Lat *diminutio*]

diminutive *adj* very small. — *n* (*gram*) **1** (also **diminutive suffix**) an ending added to a word to indicate smallness, e.g. *-let* in *booklet*. **2** a word formed in this way. [Lat *deminuere*, to make less]

dimple *n* a small hollow, esp. in the skin of the cheeks, chin or, in babies, at the knees and elbows.

dimpled *adj* having slight hollows on the surface.

dimwit. See **dim**.

din *n* a loud, continuous and unpleasant noise. — *v* **-nn-** (*tr* with **into**) to repeat (something) forcefully to someone over and over again so that it will be remembered. [OE *dyne*]

dinar *n* the standard unit of currency in Yugoslavia and several Arab countries. [Arabic & Persian]

dine *v* (*intr*; *formal*) **1** to eat dinner. **2** (with **off, on, upon**) to eat (something) for one's dinner. — *v* **dine out** (*intr*; *formal*) to have dinner somewhere other than one's own house, e.g. in a restaurant. [OFr *disner*, from Lat *dis-*, **dis-** + *jejunare*, to fast]

diner *n* **1** a person who dines. **2** a dining-car on a train. **3** (*NAm*) a small, cheap restaurant.

dining-car *n* a carriage on a train in which meals are served.

dining-room *n* a room in a house used mainly for eating in.

ding *v* (*intr* & *tr*) & *n* (to make) a ringing sound. [Imit.]

ding-dong *n* **1** the sound of bells ringing. **2** (*coll*) a heated argument or fight. — *adj* (*coll*) (of a fight, argument, etc.) fierce or heated. [Imit.]

dinghy *n* **-ies 1** a small open boat propelled by oars, sails or an outboard motor. **2** a small collapsible rubber boat, esp. one kept for use in emergencies. [Hindi *dingi*, small boat]

dingo *n* **-oes** a species of wild dog found in Australia. [Dharuk (Australian Aborigine language) *dinggu*]

dingy *adj* **-ier, -iest 1** faded and dirty-looking: *dingy clothes*. **2** dark and rather dirty: *a dingy room*. — *n* **dinginess**.

dinkum *adj* (*Austr* & *NZ coll*) real; genuine; honest. [Dialect *dinkum*, fair share of work]

dinky *adj* **-ier, -iest** (*coll*) neat; dainty. [Scot *dink*, neat]

dinner *n* **1** the main meal of the day, eaten in the middle of the day or in the evening. **2** a formal meal, esp. in the evening, often held to honour a person or in celebration of an event. [Ety. same as **dine**]

dinner-dance *n* a social occasion consisting of a formal dinner followed by dancing.

dinner-jacket *n* a usu. black jacket worn by men at formal social gatherings, esp. in the evening.

dinner-service or **dinner-set** *n* a complete set of plates and dishes for serving dinner to several people.

dinosaur *n* any animal of the large number of species of extinct reptiles of the order *Dinosauria*, ranging in length from two to eighty feet. [Gr *deinos*, terrible + *sauros*, lizard]

dint *n* a hollow made by a blow; a dent. — **by dint of** by means of. [OE *dynt*, blow]

diocese *n* the district over which a bishop has authority. [Gr *dioikesis*, housekeeping]

diocesan *adj* relating to or concerning a diocese.

diode *n* **1** a type of valve with two electrodes which allows electric current to flow in only one direction and is used to convert alternating current to direct current. **2** a type of thermionic valve with two electrodes. [Gr *di-*, twice + *hodos*, way]

dioecious *adj* (*bot*) having male and female flowers on different plants. ◇ See also **monoecious**. [Gr *di-*, twice + *oikos*, house]

dioxide *n* (*chem*) a compound formed by combining two atoms of oxygen with one atom of another element. [Gr *di-*, twice + **oxide**]

dioxin *n* any of a group of highly toxic chemicals found in certain weedkillers, known to cause cancer and other disorders.

dip *v* *-pp-* **1** (*tr*) to put into a liquid for a short time. **2** (*intr*) to go briefly under the surface of a liquid. **3** (*intr*) to drop below a surface or level. **4** (*intr* & *tr*) to (cause to) go down briefly and then up again. **5** (*intr*) to slope downwards. **6** (*intr* & *tr* with **into**) to put (one's hand, etc.) into a dish, container, etc. and take out some of the contents. **7** (*intr* with **into**) to take something from or use part of. **8** (*intr* with **into**) to look briefly at (a book) or study (a subject) in a casual manner. **9** (*tr*) to immerse (an animal) in a bath of disinfectant chemical that kills parasitic insects. **10** (*tr*; *Br*) to lower the beam of (a vehicle's headlights). — *n* **1** an act of dipping. **2** a downward slope or hollow (esp. in a road). **3** a short swim or bathe. **4** a chemical liquid for dipping animals. **5** a type of thick sauce into which biscuits, raw vegetables, etc. are dipped. [OE *dyppan*]

dipper *n* **1** a type of ladle. **2** a small songbird which can swim under water and feeds on river-beds.

dip-stick *n* a stick used to measure the level of a liquid in a container, esp. the oil in a car engine.

dip-switch *n* a switch used to dip headlights.

Dip. *abbrev* Diploma, as in **Dip. Ed.** Diploma in Education.

diphtheria *n* a serious infectious disease of the throat which makes breathing and swallowing difficult. [Gr *diphthera*, leather (from the leathery covering formed in the throat)]

diphthong *n* (*gram*) **1** two vowel sounds pronounced as one syllable, as the sound represented by the *ou* in *sounds*. **2** a digraph. [Gr *di-*, twice + *phthongos*, sound]

diploma *n* a document certifying that one has passed a certain examination or completed a course of study. [Lat, official document, from Gr, letter folded over]

diplomat *n* **1** a government official or representative engaged in diplomacy. **2** a very tactful person. [Fr *diplomate*, from Lat *diploma*, official document]

diplomacy *n* **1** the art or profession of making agreements, treaties, etc. between countries, or of representing and looking after the affairs and interests of one's country in a foreign country. **2** skill and tact in dealing with people.

diplomatic *adj* **1** concerning or involved in diplomacy. **2** tactful. — *adv* **diplomatically**.

diplomatic bag *n* a bag or other container for official letters, packages, etc. sent to and from an embassy, not subject to customs inspection.

diplomatic corps *n* all the diplomats and embassy staff of all the embassies in the capital of a country.

diplomatic immunity *n* the privilege granted to members of the diplomatic corps by which they may not be taxed, arrested, etc. by the country in which they are working.

dipsomania *n* an occasional uncontrollable desire for alcoholic drink. — *n* **dipsomaniac**. [Gr *dipsa*, thirst + *mania*, madness]

diptych *n* a work of art, esp. on a church altar, consisting of a pair of pictures painted on hinged wooden panels which can be folded together like a book. ◇ See also **triptych**. [Gr *diptychos*, folded together]

dire *adj* **1** dreadful; terrible. **2** extreme; very serious; very difficult. [Lat *dirus*]

direct *adj* **1** straight; following the quickest and shortest path from beginning to end or to a destination. **2** (of a person's manner, etc.) open, straightforward and honest; going straight to the point. **3** with no other factors involved: *the direct cause of the accident*. **4** not working or communicating through other people, organisations, etc.: *This telephone allows direct communication with the Prime Minister*. **5** exact; complete: *a direct opposite*. **6** forming or being part of an unbroken line of descent from parent to child to grandchild, etc.: *a direct descendant of Sir Walter Raleigh*. — *v* **1** (*tr*) to point, aim or turn in a particular direction. **2** (*tr*) to show the way. **3** (*tr*) to order or instruct. **4** (*tr*) to control or manage; to be in charge of (something). **5** (*tr* & *intr*) to plan and supervise the production of (a play or film). **6** (*tr*; *formal*) to put a name and address on (a letter). — *adv* directly; by the quickest or shortest path. — *n* **directness**. [Lat *directus*]

direct current *n* electric current which flows in one direction. ◇ See also **alternating current**.

direct debit *n* an order to one's bank which allows someone else to withdraw sums of money from one's account, esp. in payment of bills.

directly *adv* **1** in a direct manner. **2** by a direct path. **3** at once; immediately. **4** very soon. **5** exactly: *directly opposite*.

direct object *n* (*gram*) the noun, noun phrase or pronoun which is directly affected by the action of a transitive verb, as *the dog* in *The boy kicked the dog*. ◇ See also **indirect object**.

direct speech *n* (*gram*) speech reported in the actual words of the speaker. ◇ See also **indirect speech**.

direct tax *n* a tax paid directly to the government by a person or organisation rather than one levied on goods and services (e.g. income tax as opposed to e.g. value-added tax). ◇ See also **indirect tax**.

direction *n* **1** the place or point towards which one is moving or facing. **2** the way in which someone or something is developing. **3** (usu. in *pl*) information, instructions or advice, e.g. on how to construct or operate a piece of equipment. **4** (in *pl*) instructions about the way to go to reach a place. **5** management or supervision. **6** the act, style, etc. of directing a play or film. [Lat *directio*]

directional *adj* of or relating to direction in space; able to trace the direction of e.g. signals or to receive e.g. signals from one direction only.

direction-finder *n* a device for detecting where radio signals are coming from, used esp. in navigation.

directive *n* an official instruction issued by a higher authority, e.g. a government. [Lat *directivus*]

director *n* **1** any of the most senior managers of a business firm. **2** the person in charge of a college, organisation, institution, or special activity. **3** the person directing a play, film, etc. — *adj* **directorial**. — *n* **directorship**. [**direct** + **-or**]

directorate *n* **1** the directors of a business firm. **2** the position or office of director.

directory *n* **-*ies*** a book with a (usu. alphabetical) list of names and addresses of people or organisations. [Lat *directorium*]

dirge *n* **1** a funeral song or hymn. **2** (sometimes *derog*) a slow sad song or piece of music. [Lat *dirige*, lead, the first word in a hymn sung in the Latin Office (religious service) for the Dead]

dirigible *n* (*tech*) an airship. [Lat *dirigere*, to direct]

dirk *n* a small knife or dagger. [Scots *durk*]

dirndl *n* **1** a traditional Alpine peasant-woman's dress, tight-fitting at the top and waist, and wide and loose at the bottom. **2** a skirt that is tight at the waist and wide at the bottom. [Ger dialect]

dirt *n* **1** any unclean substance, e.g. mud or dust. **2** soil; earth. **3** a mixture of earth and cinders used to make road surfaces. **4** (*euph*) excrement. **5** (*coll*) obscene speech or writing. **6** (*coll*) spiteful gossip; scandal: *got some dirt on him*. — **treat (someone) like dirt** to treat (someone) with no consideration or respect. [Norse *drit*, excrement]

dirt-cheap *adj* & *adv* (*coll*) very cheap or cheaply.

dirty *adj* **-*ier***, **-*iest*** **1** marked with dirt; soiled. **2** which involves one becoming soiled with dirt: *a dirty job*. **3** unfair; dishonest: *dirty tricks*. **4** obscene, lewd or pornographic: *dirty films*. **5** for the purposes of having sex in secret: *a dirty weekend*. **6** (of weather) rainy or stormy. **7** (of a colour) dull. **8** showing dislike or disapproval: *a dirty look*. **9** unsportingly rough or violent: *a dirty tackle*. — *v* **-*ies***, **-*ied*** (*tr*) to make dirty. — *adv* dirtily: *fight dirty*. — *adv* **dirtily**. — *n* **dirtiness**. — **do the dirty on** (*coll*) to cheat or trick.

dirty word *n* **1** an obscene word. **2** an unpopular concept or point of view.

dirty work *n* **1** work that makes one dirty. **2** (*coll*) unpleasant or dishonourable duties.

dis- *pfx* **1** not or un-; lack or opposition: *disagree*. **2** reversal: *disassemble*. **3** removal: *disrobe* [Lat]

disability *n* **-*ies*** **1** the state of being disabled. **2** a physical or mental handicap. [**dis-** (sense **1**)]

disable *v* (*tr*) **1** to deprive of a physical or mental ability. **2** to make (e.g. a machine) unable to work; to make useless. — *adj* **disabled**. — *n* **disablement**. [**dis-** (sense **1**)]

disabuse *v* (*tr*; **of**) to rid (someone) of (a mistaken idea or impression). [**dis-** (sense **1**)]

disadvantage *n* **1** a difficulty, drawback or weakness. **2** an unfavourable situation. — *v* (*tr*) to put at a disadvantage. — *adj* **disadvantageous**. [**dis-** (sense **1**)]

disadvantaged *adj* in an unfavourable position, esp. deprived of ordinary social or economic benefits.

disaffected *adj* dissatisfied and no longer loyal or committed. — *n* **disaffection**. [**dis-** (sense **2**)]

disagree *v* (*intr*) **1** (**with**) to have a different opinion; (of two or more people) to have conflicting opinions. **2** (**with**) to be opposed (to something). **3** to conflict with each other: *The two theories disagree*. **4** (*euph*) to quarrel. **5** (with **with**) to cause digestive problems. [OFr *desagreer*]

disagreeable *adj* **1** unpleasant. **2** bad-tempered; unfriendly. — *adv* **disagreeably**.

disagreement *n* **1** the state of disagreeing. **2** (*euph*) a quarrel.

disallow *v* (*tr*) to formally refuse to allow or accept; to judge to be invalid. — *n* **disallowance**. [OFr *desalouer*]

disappear *v* (*intr*) **1** to go out of sight; to vanish. **2** to cease to exist. **3** to go missing. — *n* **disappearance**. [**dis-** (sense **1**)]

disappoint *v* (*tr*) **1** to fail to fulfil the hopes or expectations of. **2** (*formal*) to prevent (e.g. a plan) from being carried out. — *adj* **disappointed**. — *adj* **disappointing**. [OFr *desapointer*]

disappointment *n* **1** the state of being disappointed. **2** something that disappoints.

disapprobation *n* (*formal*) disapproval, esp. on moral grounds. [**dis-** (sense **1**)]

disapprove *v* (*intr*; **of**) to have a low opinion of; to think bad or wrong. — *n* **disapproval**. — *adj* **disapproving**. [**dis-** (sense **1**)]

disarm *v* **1** (*tr*) to take weapons away from. **2** (*intr*) to reduce or destroy one's own military capability. **3** (*tr*) to take the fuse out of (a bomb). **4** (*tr*) to take away the anger or suspicions of. [OFr *desarmer*]

disarmament *n* the reduction or destruction by a nation of its own military forces.

disarming *adj* taking away anger or suspicion; quickly winning confidence or affection. — *adv* **disarmingly**.

disarrange *v* (*tr*) to make untidy or disordered. — *n* **disarrangement**. [**dis-** (sense **2**)]

disarray *n* & *v* (*tr*) (to throw into a state of) disorder, confusion or untidiness. [**dis-** (sense **1**)]

disassociate. Same as **dissociate**.

disaster *n* **1** an event causing great damage, injury or loss of life. **2** a total failure. **3** extremely bad luck: *Disaster struck*. — *adj* **disastrous**. [Orig. 'bad influence of the stars', from OFr *desastre*, from *des-*, **dis-** + *astre*, star]

disavow *v* (*tr*; *formal*) to deny knowledge of, a connection with, or responsibility for. — *n* **disavowal**. [OFr *desavouer*]

disband *v* (*tr* & *intr*) to (cause to) stop operating as a group; to break up. — *n* **disbandment**. [OFr *desbander*, to unbind]

disbelieve *v* (*tr*) **1** to believe to be false or lying. **2** (**in**) to believe to be non-existent: *disbelieve in God*. — *n* **disbelief**. [**dis-** (sense **1**)]

disburse *v* (*tr*) to pay out, esp. from a fund. — *n* **disbursement**. [OFr *desbourser*]

disc *n* **1** any flat thin circular object. **2** (*coll*) a gramophone record. **3** (*anat*) a layer of cartilage between vertebrae. **4** (*comput*) a disk. [Gr *diskos*]

disc brake *n* a brake in which pads are pressed against a metal disc attached to the vehicle's wheel.

disc jockey *n* a person who presents a programme of recorded popular music on the radio or at a disco.

discard *v* (*tr*) **1** to get rid of as useless or unwanted. **2** (*cards*) to put down (a card of little value) esp. when unable to follow suit. [**dis-** (sense **3**)]

discern *v* (*tr*) to perceive, notice, or make out; to judge. — *adj* **discernible**. [Lat *discernere*]

discerning *adj* having or showing good judgement.

discernment *n* good judgement.

discharge *v* **1** (*tr*; **from**) to allow to leave; to send away or dismiss, esp. from employment. **2** (*tr*) to perform or carry out (e.g. duties). **3** (*tr* & *intr*) to (cause to) flow out or be released. **4** (*tr*; *legal*) to release from custody. **5** (*tr* & *intr*) to fire (a gun). **6** (*tr*; *legal*) to pay off (a debt). **7** (*tr* & *intr*) to unload (a cargo). **8** (*tr* & *intr*; *tech*) to (cause a device to) lose some or all electrical charge. — *n* **1** the act of discharging. **2** something discharged. **3** (*formal* or *legal*) release or dismissal. **4** (*tech*) a flow of electric current through a gas. [OFr *descharger*]

disciple *n* **1** a person who believes in, and follows, the teachings of another. **2** one of the twelve close followers of Christ. [Lat *discipulus*, from *discere*, to learn]

discipline *n* **1** strict training, or the enforcing of rules, intended to produce ordered and controlled behaviour in oneself or others; the ordered behaviour resulting from this. **2** punishment designed to create obedience. **3** an area of learning, esp. a subject of academic study. — *v* (*tr*) **1** to train or force (oneself or others) to behave in an ordered and controlled way. **2** to punish. [Lat *disciplina*]

disciplinarian *n* a person who enforces strict discipline on others.

disciplinary *adj* of, relating to, or enforcing discipline; intended as punishment.

disclaim *v* (*tr*) **1** to deny (e.g. involvement with or knowledge of). **2** to give up a legal claim to. [OFr *desclaimer*]

disclaimer *n* **1** a written statement denying legal responsibility. **2** a denial.

disclose *v* (*tr*) to make known; to show or make visible. — *n* **disclosure**. [OFr *desclore*]

disco *n* **-os** **1** a discotheque. **2** a party with dancing to recorded music. **3** the mobile hi-fi and lighting equipment used for such a party. — *adj* suitable for, or designed for, discotheques.

discolour *v* (*tr* & *intr*) to stain or dirty; to (cause to) change colour. — *n* **discoloration** or **discolouration**. [OFr *descolorer*]

discomfit *v* **-t-** (*tr*) **1** to cause to feel embarrassed or uneasy; to perplex. **2** to frustrate the plans of. — *n* **discomfiture**. [OFr *desconfire*]

discomfort *n* (a cause of) slight physical pain or mental uneasiness. — *v* (*tr*) to make physically uncomfortable or mentally uneasy. [OFr *desconfort*]

discompose *v* (*tr*) to upset, worry or agitate. — *n* **discomposure**. [**dis-** (sense **2**)]

disconcert *v* (*tr*) to cause to feel anxious or uneasy; to fluster. — *adj* **disconcerting**. [Obsolete Fr *disconcerter*]

disconnect *v* (*tr*) **1** to break the connection between (esp. an electrical device and a power supply). **2** to stop the supply of (a public service such as the gas supply or the telephone) to (a building, etc.). — *n* **disconnection**. [**dis-** (sense **2**)]

disconnected *adj* **1** no longer connected. **2** (e.g. of speech) not correctly constructed, and often not making sense.

disconsolate *adj* deeply sad or disappointed; not able to be consoled. — *adv* **disconsolately**. [Lat *disconsolatus*]

discontent *n* dissatisfaction; lack of contentment. — *adj* **discontented**. [**dis-** (sense **1**)]

discontinue *v* **1** (*tr* & *intr*) to stop or cease. **2** (*tr*) to stop producing: *a discontinued line*. — *n* **discontinuance**. — *n* **discontinuation**. [OFr *discontinuer*]

discontinuous *adj* having breaks or interruptions. — *n* **discontinuity, -ies**.

discord *n* **1** disagreement; conflict; failure to get on. **2** (*mus*) an unpleasant-sounding combination of notes; lack of harmony. **3** uproarious noise. — *adj* **discordant**. [Lat *discordia*]

discotheque *n* a night-club with dancing to recorded pop music. [Fr]

discount *n* an amount deducted from the normal price, e.g. for prompt payment. — *v* (*tr*) **1** to disregard as unlikely, untrue or irrelevant. **2** to make a deduction from (a price). — **at a discount** for less than the usual price. [OFr *descompter*]

discourage *v* (*tr*) **1** to deprive of confidence, hope, or the will to continue. **2** (**from**) to seek to prevent (a person or an action) with advice or persuasion. — *n* **discouragement**. — *adj* **discouraging**. [OFr *descourager*]

discourse *n* **1** (**on, upon**) a formal speech or essay on a particular subject. **2** serious conversation. — *v* (*intr*; **on, upon**) to speak or write at length, formally or with authority. [Lat *discursus*]

discourteous *adj* showing a lack of courtesy; impolite. — *adv* **discourteously**. — *n* **discourteousness**. — *n* **discourtesy**. [**dis-** (sense **1**)]

discover *v* **-r-** (*tr*) **1** to be the first person to find. **2** to find by chance, esp. for the first time. **3** to learn of or become aware of for the first time. [OFr *descouvrir*]

discovery *n* **-ies** **1** the act of discovering. **2** a person or thing discovered.

discredit *n* (something that causes) loss of good reputation. — *v* **-t-** (*tr*) **1** to cause to be disbelieved or regarded with doubt or suspicion. **2** to damage the reputation of. [**dis-** (sense **1**)]

discreditable *adj* bringing discredit.

discreet *adj* **1** careful to prevent suspicion or embarrassment, esp. by keeping a secret. **2** avoiding notice; inconspicuous. ◇ See also **discretion**. [Lat *discretus*]

discrepancy *n* **-ies** (**in, between**) a failure (e.g. of sets of calculations) to correspond or be the same. — *adj* **discrepant**. [Lat *discrepare*, to differ in sound]

discrete *adj* separate; distinct. — *adv* **discretely**. — *n* **discreteness**. [Lat *discretus*]

discretion *n* **1** the quality of behaving in a discreet way. **2** the ability to make wise judgements. **3** the freedom or right to make decisions and do as one thinks best: *allowed to change the plans at our own discretion*. [Lat *discretio*]

discretionary *adj* made, done, given, etc. according to the wishes of a particular person or group; not compulsory or automatic.

discriminate *v* (*intr*) **1** (**between**) to recognise a difference. **2** (**against, in favour of**) to give different treatment to different people or groups in identical circumstances, usu. without justification. [Lat *discriminare*, to separate]

discriminating *adj* showing good judgement; able to recognise (even slight) differences.

discrimination *n* **1** unjustifiably different treatment given to different people or groups. **2** the ability to draw fine distinctions; good judgement, esp. in matters of taste.

discriminatory *adj* displaying or representing unfairly different treatment.

discursive *adj* **1** wandering from the main point. **2** (*philos*) based on argument or reason, rather than on intuition. — *n* **discursiveness**. [**discourse**]

discus *n* **1** a heavy metal disc, thicker at the centre than the edge, thrown in athletic competitions. **2** the competition itself. [Gr *diskos*]

discuss *v* (*tr*) to examine or consider in speech or writing. — *n* **discussion**. [Lat *discutere*, to shake to pieces]

disdain *n* dislike arising out of lack of respect; contempt. — *v* (*tr*) **1** to refuse or reject out of disdain. **2** to regard with disdain. — *adj* **disdainful**. — *adv* **disdainfully**. [OFr *desdaigner*, from Lat *dignus*, worthy]

disease *n* **1** illness or lack of health caused by infection rather than by an accident; any one such illness with characteristic symptoms. **2** any undesirable phenomenon. — *adj* **diseased**. [OFr *desaise*, unease]

diseconomy *n* **-ies** an economic disadvantage, such as lower efficiency or higher costs. [**dis-** (sense **1**)]

disembark *v* (*tr* & *intr*) to take or go from a ship on to land. — *n* **disembarkation**. [OFr *desembarquer*]

disembodied *adj* **1** (e.g. of a spirit or soul) separated from the body; having no physical existence. **2** seeming not to come from, or be connected to, a body: *a disembodied voice*. [**dis-** (sense **3**)]

disembowel *v* **-ll-** (*tr*) to remove the internal organs of, as a punishment, torture, etc. — *n* **disembowelment**. [**dis-** (sense **3**)]

disenchant *v* (*tr*) **1** to free from illusion. **2** to make dissatisfied or discontented. — *adj* **disenchanted**. — *n* **disenchantment**. [**dis-** (sense **2**)]

disenfranchise. See **disfranchise**.

disengage *v* **1** (*tr*; **from**) to release or detach from a connection. **2** (*tr* & *intr*) to withdraw (troops) from combat. — *n* **disengagement**. [OFr *desengager*]

disentangle *v* (*tr*) **1** (**from**) to free from complication, difficulty or confusion. **2** to take the knots or tangles out of (e.g.

hair). — *n* **disentanglement**. [**dis-** (sense **2**)]

disestablish *v* (*tr*) to take away the official status or authority of. — *n* **disestablishment**. [**dis-** (sense **2**)]

disfavour *n* **1** (**with**) the state of being disliked, unpopular, or disapproved of: *in disfavour with*. **2** dislike or disapproval. [**dis-** (sense **1**)]

disfigure *v* (*tr*) to spoil the beauty or general appearance of. — *n* **disfigurement**. [OFr *desfigurer*]

disfranchise or **disenfranchise** *v* (*tr*) to deprive of the right to vote. — *n* **disfranchisement** or **disenfranchisement**. [**dis-** (sense **2**)]

disgorge *v* (*tr*) **1** to vomit. **2** to discharge or pour out. **3** to give up or relinquish, esp. under pressure. [OFr *desgorger*, from *gorge*, throat]

disgrace *n* (something that brings, or ought to bring) shame or loss of favour or respect. — *v* (*tr*) to bring shame upon. — *adj* **disgraceful**. [Fr *disgrâce*]

disgruntled *adj* (**at**, **with**) annoyed and dissatisfied; in a bad mood. [**dis-** (sense **4**) + the old word *gruntle*, to complain]

disguise *v* (*tr*) to hide the identity of by a change of appearance. **2** to conceal the true nature of (e.g. intentions). — *n* **1** a disguised state: *in disguise*. **2** something, esp. a combination of clothes and make-up, intended to disguise. [OFr *desguiser*]

disgust *v* (*tr*) to sicken; to provoke intense dislike or disapproval in. — *n* intense dislike; loathing. — *adj* **disgusted**. — *adv* **disgusting**. [OFr *desgouster*]

dish *n* **1** any shallow, usu. roundish container in which food is served or cooked; its contents; the amount it can hold. **2** anything shaped like this: *an aerial dish*. **3** a particular kind of food. **4** (*pl*) any of the utensils needed to prepare or eat a meal. **5** a dish aerial. **6** (*coll*) a physically attractive person. — *v* (*tr*; *coll*) to ruin (esp. chances or hopes). — *v* **dish out** (*tr*; *coll*) **1** to distribute. **2** to give out. — *v* **dish up** (*tr*; *coll*) **1** to serve (food). **2** to offer or present (e.g. facts). [OE *disc*, plate, bowl, table]

dish aerial *n* a large dish-shaped aerial used to receive signals in radar, radio-telescopes and satellite broadcasting.

dishwasher *n* **1** a machine that washes and dries dishes. **2** a person employed to wash dishes, e.g. in a restaurant.

dishwater *n* water in which dirty dishes have been washed.

dishy *adj* **-ier**, **-iest** (*coll*) physically attractive.

dishabille. Same as **déshabillé**.

disharmony *n* disagreement; lack of harmony. — *adj* **disharmonious**. [**dis-** (sense **1**)]

dishearten *v* **-n-** (*tr*) to dampen the courage, hope or confidence of. — *adj* **disheartening**. — *n* **disheartenment**. [**dis-** (sense **1**)]

dishevelled *adj* (of clothes or hair) untidy; in a mess. — *n* **dishevelment**. [OFr *descheveler*]

dishonest *adj* not honest; likely to deceive or cheat; insincere. — *adv* **dishonestly**. — *n* **dishonesty**. [OFr *deshoneste*]

dishonour *n* (something that brings) shame; loss of honour. — *v* (*tr*) **1** to bring dishonour on. **2** to treat with no respect. **3** (*commerce*) to refuse to honour (a cheque). — *adj* **dishonourable**. [OFr *deshonneur*]

disillusion *v* **-n-** (*tr*) to correct the mistaken beliefs or illusions of. [**dis-** (sense **2**)]

disillusioned *adj* sad or disappointed at having discovered the unpleasant truth. — *n* **disillusionment**.

disincentive *n* something that discourages or deters. [**dis-** (sense **1**)]

disinclined *adj* unwilling. — *n* **disinclination**. [**dis-** (sense **1**)]

disinfect *v* (*tr*) to clean with a substance that kills germs. [**dis-** (sense **2**)]

disinfectant *n* a germ-killing substance.

disinformation *n* false information intended to deceive or mislead. [**dis-** (sense **1**)]

disingenuous *adj* not entirely sincere or open; creating a false impression of frankness. — *adv* **disingenuously**. — *n* **disingenuousness**. [**dis-** (sense **1**)]

disinherit *v* **-t-** (*tr*) to legally deprive of an inheritance. — *n* **disinheritance**. [**dis-** (sense **2**)]

disintegrate *v* (*tr* & *intr*) **1** to break into tiny pieces; to shatter or crumble. **2** to break up. **3** to (cause to) undergo nuclear fission. — *n* **disintegration**. [**dis-** (sense **1**)]

disinter *v* **-rr-** (*tr*) **1** to dig up (esp. a body from a grave). **2** to discover and make known. — *n* **disinterment**. [**dis-** (sense **2**)]

disinterested *adj* **1** unbiased; objective. **2** (*coll*) showing no interest; uninterested. — *n* **disinterest** or **disinterestedness**. [**dis-** (sense **1**)]

disjointed *adj* (of speech) not properly connected; incoherent. [OFr *desjoindre*]

disjunctive *adj* marked by breaks; discontinuous. [OFr *desjoindre*]

disk *n* (*comput*) **1** (also **floppy disk**) a flat plastic disc, coated with a magnetic substance, on to which data can be copied. **2** (also **hard disk**) a stack of flat metal disks on which data is stored inside a computer. [**disc**]

disk drive *n* the device that controls the transfer of information on to a floppy disk.

dislike *v* (*tr*) to consider unpleasant or unlikeable. — *n* **1** (**of**, **for**) mild hostility; aversion. **2** something disliked. [**dis-** (sense **1**)]

dislocate *v* (*tr*) **1** to put (a bone) out of joint. **2** to disturb the order of; to disrupt. — *n* **dislocation**. [Lat *dislocare*]

dislodge *v* (*tr*; **from**) **1** to force out of a fixed or established position: *dislodge a stone*. **2** to drive from a place of rest, hiding or defence. — *n* **dislodgement** or **dislodgment**. [OFr *desloger*]

disloyal *adj* (**to**) not loyal or faithful. — *n* **disloyalty**. [OFr *desloyal*]

dismal *adj* **1** not cheerful; causing or suggesting sadness. **2** (*coll*) third-rate; of poor quality. — *adv* **dismally**. [OFr, from Lat *dies mali*, unlucky days]

dismantle *v* (*tr*) **1** to take to pieces; to demolish. **2** to abolish or close down, esp. bit by bit. [OFr *desmanteller*]

dismay *n* & *v* (*tr*) (to fill with) a mixture of sadness and deep disappointment or discouragement. [OFr *desmaiier*]

dismember *v* **-r-** (*tr*) **1** to tear or cut the arms and legs from. **2** to divide up (esp. land). — *n* **dismemberment**. [OFr *desmembrer*]

dismiss *v* (*tr*) **1** to refuse to consider or accept. **2** to put out of one's employment. **3** to send away; to allow to leave. **4** to close (a court case). **5** (*cricket*) to bowl out. — *n* **dismissal**. [Lat *dis-*, from, away + *mittere*, to send]

dismissive *adj* (**of**) giving no consideration or respect; showing no willingness to believe.

dismount *v* **1** (*intr*; **from**) to get off a horse, bicycle, etc. **2** (*tr*) to force (someone) off a horse, bicycle, etc. **3** (*tr*) to remove from a stand or frame. [OFr *desmonter*]

disobedient *adj* refusing or failing to obey. — *n* **disobedience**. [**dis-** (sense **1**)]

disobey *v* (*tr* & *intr*) to act contrary to the orders of; to refuse to obey. [OFr *desobeir*]

disobliging *adj* unwilling to help; disregarding, or tending to disregard, wishes or requests. [**dis-** (sense **1**)]

disorder *n* **1** lack of order; confusion or disturbance. **2** unruly or riotous behaviour. **3** a disease or illness. — *adj* **disordered**. [OFr *desordre*]

disorderly *adj* **1** not neatly arranged; disorganised. **2** causing trouble in public.

disorganise or **-ize** *v* (*tr*) to disturb the order or arrangement of; to throw into confusion. — *n* **disorganisation** or **-z-**. [**dis-** (sense **1**)]

disorientate or **disorient** *v* (*tr*) to cause to lose all sense of position, direction or time. — *n* **disorientation**. [**dis-** (sense **2**)]

disown *v* (*tr*) to deny having any relationship to or connection with; to refuse to recognise or acknowledge. — *n* **disownment**. [**dis-** (sense **2**)]

disparage *v* (*tr*) to speak of with contempt. — *n* **disparagement**. — *adj* **disparaging**. [OFr *desparager*, to marry below one's class]

disparate *adj* completely different; too different to be compared. [Lat *disparare*, to separate]

disparity *n* **-ies** great or fundamental difference; inequality.

dispassionate *adj* **1** calm; unemotional. **2** not influenced by personal feelings; impartial. [**dis-** (sense **1**)]

dispatch or **despatch** *v* (*tr*) **1** to send to a place for a particular reason. **2** to finish off or deal with quickly: *dispatch a meal*. **3** (*euph*) to kill. — *n* **1** (often in *pl*) an official (esp. military or diplomatic) report. **2** a journalist's report sent to a newspaper. **3** the act of dispatching; the fact of being dispatched. **4** (*old*) speed or haste. [OFr *despeechier*, to set free]

dispatch rider *n* a person employed to deliver messages by motorcycle or, formerly, on horseback.

dispel *v* **-ll-** (*tr*) to drive away or banish (thoughts or feelings). [Lat *dispellere*]

dispensable *adj* that can be done without; expendable.

dispensary *n* **-ies** a place where medicines are given out or dispensed.

dispensation *n* **1** special exemption from a rule, obligation or (esp. religious) law. **2** the act of dispensing. **3** a religious or political system regarded as the chief governing force in a nation or during a particular time. **4** (*relig*) God's management of human affairs.

dispense *v* (*tr*) **1** to give out (e.g. advice). **2** to prepare and distribute (medicine). **3** to administer (e.g. the law). — *v* **dispense with** (*tr*) **1** to do without. **2** to do away with. [Lat *dispendere*, to weigh out]

disperse *v* (*tr* & *intr*) **1** to (cause to) spread out over a wide area. **2** to (cause e.g. a crowd at a gathering to) break up and leave. **3** to (cause to) vanish. **4** (*physics*) to (cause light to) break up into the colours of the spectrum. **5** (*physics*) to (cause particles to) become evenly distributed thoughout a liquid or gas. — *n* **dispersal** or **dispersion**. [Lat *dispergere*, to scatter widely]

dispirit *v* **-t-** (*tr*) to dishearten or discourage. [**dis-** (sense **3**)]

displace *v* (*tr*) **1** to put or take out of the usual place. **2** to take the place of. **3** to remove from a post. [OFr *desplacer*]

displaced person *n* a person forced to leave his or her own country through war or persecution.

displacement *n* **1** the act of displacing. **2** (*tech*) the quantity of liquid, gas, etc. displaced by an immersed object, esp. of water by a floating ship.

display *v* (*tr*) **1** to put on view. **2** to show or betray (e.g. feelings). — *n* **1** the act of displaying. **2** an exhibition; a show of talent; an arrangement of objects on view. **3** an electronic device presenting information visually. **4** a pattern of animal behaviour used in marking territory or attracting a mate. [OFr *despleier*]

displease *v* (*tr*) to annoy or offend. — *n* **displeasure**. [OFr *desplaisir*]

disport *v* (*tr* & *intr*; *literary*) to indulge (oneself) in lively amusement. [OFr *se desporter*, to carry oneself away]

dispose *v* **1** (*intr* with **of**) to get rid of; to deal with or settle. **2** (*tr*) to place in an arrangement or order. **3** (*tr*; **to, towards**) to cause to feel; to incline: *ill-disposed towards him*. [Lat *disponere*, to set out]
disposable *adj* **1** intended to be thrown away or destroyed after use. **2** (of income) left over after tax and bills are paid; (of assets, etc.) available for use when needed.
disposal *n* the act of getting rid of something. — **at the disposal of** available for use by.

disposition *n* **1** temperament; personality; a tendency. **2** arrangement; position; distribution. **3** (*legal*) the act of giving over (e.g. property).

dispossess *v* (*tr*; **of**) to take (esp. property) away from. — *n* **dispossession**. [**dis-** (sense **2**)]

disproof *n* the act of disproving; something that disproves.

disproportion *n* (**between**) lack of balance or equality; failure to be in proportion. [**dis-** (sense **1**)]
disproportionate *adj* (**to**) unreasonably large or small in comparison (with something else). — *adv* **disproportionately**.

disprove *v* (*tr*) to prove to be false or wrong. [OFr *desprover*]

dispute *v* **1** (*tr*) to question or deny the accuracy or validity of. **2** (*tr*) to quarrel over rights to or possession of: *disputed territory*. **3** (*tr* & *intr*) to argue about (something). — *n* an argument. — *adj* **disputable**. — *n* **disputation**. — *adj* **disputatious** . [Lat *disputare*, to discuss]

disqualify *v* **-ies**, **-ied** (*tr*) **1** to remove from a competition, esp. as punishment for breaking rules. **2** to make unsuitable or ineligible. — *n* **disqualification**. [**dis-** (sense **1**)]

disquiet *n* & *v* (*tr*) (to cause to feel) anxiety or uneasiness. — *adj* **disquieting**. — *n* **disquietude**. [**dis-** (sense **1**)]

disquisition *n* (*formal*) a long and detailed discussion of a subject in speech or writing. [Lat *disquisitio*]

disregard *v* (*tr*) to pay no attention to; to dismiss as unworthy of consideration. — *n* (**for**) dismissive lack of attention or concern. [**dis-** (sense **1**)]

disrepair *n* bad condition or working order owing to a need for repair. [**dis-** (sense **1**)]

disreputable *adj* suffering from, or leading to, a bad reputation. — *adv* **disreputably**.

disrepute *n* the state of having a bad reputation: *bring something into disrepute*. [**dis-** (sense **1**)]

disrespect *n* lack of respect; impoliteness; rudeness. — *adj* **disrespectful**. — *adv* **disrespectfully**. [**dis-** (sense **1**)]

disrobe *v* (*tr* & *intr*) **1** (*literary*) to undress. **2** to take ceremonial robes off. [**dis-** (sense **3**)]

disrupt *v* (*tr*) to disturb the order or peaceful progress of. — *n* **disruption**. — *adj* **disruptive**. [Lat *disrumpere*, to break into pieces]

dissatisfy *v* **-ies**, **-ied** (*tr*) to fail to satisfy; to make discontented. — *n* **dissatisfaction**. — *adj* **dissatisfied**. [**dis-** (sense **1**)]

dissect *v* (*tr*) **1** to cut open (a plant or dead body) for scientific or medical examination. **2** to examine in minute detail, esp. critically. — *n* **dissection**. [Lat *dissecare*, to cut into pieces]

dissemble *v* (*tr* & *intr*) to conceal or disguise (true feelings or motives); to assume a false appearance of (something). [Lat *dissimulare*]

disseminate *v* (*tr*) to cause (e.g. news or theories) to be widely circulated or diffused. — *n* **dissemination**. [Lat *disseminare*, to sow widely]

dissent *n* **1** disagreement, esp. open or hostile. **2** voluntary separation, esp. from an established church. — *v* (*intr*; **from**) **1** to differ in opinion; to disagree. **2** to break away, esp. from an established church. — *n* **dissension**. — *n* **dissenter**. — *adj* **dissenting**. [Lat *dissentire*, to disagree]
dissentient *n* & *adj* (*formal*) (a person) disagreeing with a majority or established view.

dissertation *n* **1** a long essay, esp. forming part of a higher education degree course. **2** a formal lecture on a particular subject. [Lat *disserere*, to discuss]

disservice *n* a wrong; a bad turn. [OFr *desservir*]

dissident *n* a person who disagrees publicly, esp. with a government. — *adj* disagreeing; dissenting. — *n* **dissidence**. [Lat *dissidere*, to sit apart]

dissimilar *adj* (**to, from**) unalike; different. — *n* **dissimilarity**. [**dis-** (sense **1**)]

dissimulate *v* (*tr* & *intr*) to hide or disguise (esp. feelings). — *n* **dissimulation**. [Lat *dissimulare*]

dissipate *v* **1** (*tr* & *intr*) to (cause to) separate and scatter. **2** (*tr*) to use up carelessly; to squander. [Lat *dissipare*]
dissipated *adj* over-indulging in pleasure and enjoyment; debauched.
dissipation *n* **1** the process of dissipating. **2** extravagant or debauched living.

dissociate *v* (*tr*; **from**) **1** to regard as separate. **2** to declare (someone or oneself) to be unconnected with. — *n* **dissociation**. [Lat *dissociare*]

dissoluble *adj* **1** able to be disconnected. **2** (*rare*) soluble. [Lat *dissolubilis*]

dissolute *adj* indulging in pleasures considered immoral; debauched. — *n* **dissoluteness**. [Lat *dissolutus*, lax, loose]

dissolution *n* **1** the breaking up of a meeting or assembly, e.g. Parliament; the ending of a formal or legal partnership, e.g. a marriage or business. **2** abolition, e.g. of the monarchy. **3** the process of breaking up into parts. [**dissolve**]

dissolve *v* **1** (*tr* & *intr*) to (cause to) break up and merge with a liquid. **2** (*tr*) to bring (an assembly, e.g. Parliament) to a close; to end (a legal partnership, e.g. a business). **3** (*tr* & *intr*) to (cause to) disappear: *Our support dissolved.* **4** (*intr*; **into**) to collapse emotionally: *dissolve into tears.* **5** (*intr*; *tech*) (of a film or television image) to fade out as a second image fades in. — *n* (*tech*) a fading out of one film or television image as a second is simultaneously faded in. [Lat *dissolvere*, to loosen]

dissonance *n* **1** (*mus*) an unpleasant combination of sounds or notes; lack of harmony. **2** disagreement; incompatibility. — *adj* **dissonant**. [Lat *dissonare*, to be discordant]

dissuade *v* (*tr*; **from**) to deter with advice or persuasion. — *n* **dissuasion**. [Lat *dissuadere*]

dissyllable. Same as **disyllable**.

distaff *n* the rod on which a bunch of wool, flax, etc. is held ready for spinning by hand. — **the distaff side** (*old*) the wife's or mother's side of the family. [OE *distæf*]

distance *n* **1** (the extent of) the separation between points in space or time; the fact of being apart. **2** any faraway point or place; the furthest visible area. **3** coldness of manner. — *v* (*tr*; **from**) **1** to declare (esp. oneself) to be unconnected or unsympathetic (to something): *distanced himself from government policy*. **2** to put at a distance. — **go the distance** (*coll*) to last out until the end, usu. of a sporting (esp. boxing) contest. — **keep one's distance** to stay safely away, esp. refusing involvement; to avoid friendship or familiarity. [Lat *distancia*]

distant *adj* **1** far away or far apart in space or time. **2** not closely related. **3** cold and unfriendly. **4** (showing that one is) lost in thought or daydreams. — *adv* **distantly**.

distaste *n* (**for**) dislike. [**dis-** (sense **1**)]

distasteful *adj* unpleasant or offensive. — *n* **distastefulness**.

distemper[1] *n* an infectious disease of animals, esp. dogs. [OFr *destemprer*, to derange]

distemper[2] *n* any water-based paint, esp. when mixed with glue or size and used for poster-painting or murals. — *v* **-r-** (*tr*) to paint with distemper. [Lat *distemperare*, to soak]

distend *v* (*tr* & *intr*) to (cause to) become swollen, inflated or stretched. — *adj* **distensible**. — *n* **distension**. [Lat *distendere*]

distil *v* **-ll-** (*tr*) **1** to purify (a liquid) by converting it to a vapour by heat, then cooling the vapour to liquid form again. **2** to produce (alcoholic spirit) from raw materials in this way. **3** to create a shortened version of. [Lat *destillare*, to drip down]

distillate *n* a concentrated extract, the product of distilling.

distillation *n* **1** the process of distilling. **2** a distillate.

distiller *n* a person or company that makes alcoholic spirits.

distillery *n* **-ies** a place where alcoholic spirits are distilled.

distinct *adj* **1** easily seen, heard or recognised; clear or obvious. **2** noticeably different or separate. [Lat *distinctus*, from *distinguere*, to distinguish]

distinction *n* **1** (an honour awarded in recognition of) exceptional ability or achievement. **2** the act of differentiating. **3** the state of being noticeably different. **4** a distinguishing feature.

distinctive *adj* easily recognised because very individual. — *n* **distinctiveness**.

distinctly *adv* clearly; unmistakably.

distinguish *v* **1** (*tr*; **from**) to mark or recognise as different. **2** (*intr*; **between**) to see the difference (between people or things). **3** (*tr*) to make out; to identify. **4** (*tr*) to cause (esp. oneself) to be considered outstanding. — *adj* **distinguishable**. [Lat *distinguere*]

distinguished *adj* **1** famous (and usu. well respected). **2** with a noble or dignified appearance.

distinguishing *adj* serving to identify.

distort *v* (*tr*) **1** to twist out of shape. **2** to change the meaning or tone of by inaccurate retelling. **3** to alter the quality of (sound). — *adj* **distorted**. — *n* **distortion**. [Lat *distorquere*]

distract *v* (*tr*) **1** (**from**) to divert the attention of. **2** to entertain or amuse. **3** to confuse, worry, or anger. — *adj* **distracted**. — *adj* **distracting**. [Lat *distrahere*, to draw apart]

distraction *n* **1** something that diverts the attention. **2** an amusement; recreation. **3** anxiety; anger. **4** madness.

distrain *v* (*tr*; *legal*) to seize (e.g. property) as, or in order to force, payment of a debt. — *n* **distraint**. [OFr *destraindre*]

distrait *adj* (*literary*) thinking of other things. [Fr]

distraught *adj* in an extremely troubled state of mind. [A form of **distract**]

distress *n* **1** mental or emotional pain. **2** financial difficulty; hardship. **3** great danger; peril: *in distress.* — *v* (*tr*) to cause distress to; to upset. — *adj* **distressing**. [OFr *destresse*]

distressed *adj* **1** suffering distress. **2** (of furniture or fabric) given an antique appearance; artificially aged.

distribute *v* (*tr*) **1** (**to, among**) to give out. **2** to supply or deliver (goods). **3** to spread out widely; to disperse. [Lat *distribuere*]

distribution *n* **1** the process of distributing or being distributed. **2** the location or pattern of things spread out.

distributive *adj* **1** relating to distribution. **2** (*gram*) (of a word) referring individually to all members of a group, as do the words *each* and *every*.

distributor *n* **1** a person or company that distributes goods. **2** a device in a petrol engine that sends electric current to the spark plugs.

district *n* an area or region, esp. one forming an administrative or geographical unit. [Lat *districtus*, jurisdiction]

district attorney *n* (*US*) a lawyer employed by a district to conduct prosecutions.

district nurse *n* a travelling nurse giving treatment to patients in their own homes.

distrust *v* (*tr*) to have no trust in; to doubt. — *n* suspicion; lack of trust. — *adj* **distrustful**. [**dis-** (sense **1**)]

disturb *v* (*tr*) **1** to interrupt. **2** to inconvenience. **3** to upset the arrangement or order of. **4** to upset the peace of mind of. — *adj* **disturbing**. [Lat *disturbare*]

disturbance *n* **1** an outburst of noisy or violent behaviour. **2** an interruption. **3** an act of disturbing or process of being disturbed.

disturbed *adj* (*psychol*) emotionally upset or confused.

disunite *v* (*tr*) to drive apart; to cause disagreement or conflict between or within. — *n* **disunity**. [**dis-** (sense **2**)]

disuse *n* the state of no longer being used, practised or observed; neglect. — *adj* **disused**. [**dis-** (sense **1**)]

disyllable *n* a word of two syllables. — *adj* **disyllabic**. [Gr *di-*, twice + **syllable**]

ditch *n* a narrow channel dug in the ground for drainage or irrigation, or as a boundary. — *v* (*tr*; *slang*) to get rid of; to abandon. [OE *dic*]

dither *v* **-r-** (*intr*) to act in a nervously uncertain manner; to waver. — *n* a state of nervous indecision. — *n* **ditherer**. — *adj* **dithery**. [MidE *didderen*]

ditto *n* **-os** *n* the same thing; the above; that which has just been said. — *adv* likewise; the same. [Lat *dictum*, said]

ditto marks *n* (*pl*) the marks („) written immediately below a word, etc. in a list to mean 'same as above'.

ditty *n* **-ies** a short simple song or poem. [Lat *dictare*, to dictate or compose]

diuretic *n* & *adj* (a medicine) increasing the flow of urine. [Gr *dia*, through + *ouron*, urine]

diurnal *adj* **1** daily. **2** daytime; (of animals) active, or (of flowers) open, during the day. — *adv* **diurnally**. [Lat *diurnus*]

diva *n* **-vas** or **-ve** a great female singer, esp. in opera. [Lat, goddess]

divalent *adj* (*chem*) (of an atom) able to combine with two atoms of hydrogen or the equivalent. [**di-** + **valency**]

divan *n* **1** a sofa with no back or sides. **2** a bed without a headboard or footboard. [Persian *diwan*, long seat]

dive[1] *v* (*intr*) **1** to leap head first into water. **2** to become submerged. **3** to fall steeply through the air. **4** to throw oneself to the side or to the ground. **5** to move quickly and suddenly out of sight. **6** (**into**) to plunge one's hands (e.g. into a bag). **7** (**into**) to involve oneself enthusiastically. — *n* **1** an act of diving. **2** (*slang*) any dirty or disreputable place, esp. a bar or club. **3** (*boxing slang*) a faked knockout: *take a dive*. — *n* **diving**. [OE *dyfan*]

dive-bomber *n* an aeroplane that releases a bomb while diving. — *v* **dive-bomb** (*tr* & *intr*). — *n* **dive-bombing**.

diver *n* **1** a person who dives. **2** a person who swims or works underwater.

diving-bell *n* a large hollow bottomless underwater container pumped full of air, to which an unequipped diver returns to take in oxygen.

diving-board *n* a narrow platform from which swimmers can dive into a pool, etc.

diving-suit *n* a diver's waterproof suit, esp. one with a helmet and heavy boots for walking on the sea-bottom, etc.

dive[2]. See **diva**.

diverge *v* (*intr*) **1** to separate and go in different directions. **2** (**from**) to differ. **3** (**from**) to depart or deviate (e.g. from a usual course). — *n* **divergence**. — *adj* **divergent**. [Lat *di-*, apart + *vergere*, to turn]

divers *adj* (*old* or *literary*) various; many different. [Ety. as for **diverse**]

diverse *adj* **1** various; assorted. **2** different; dissimilar. — *n* **diversity**. [Lat *diversus*, turned different ways]

diversify *v* **-ies**, **-ied** **1** (*tr* & *intr*) to make or become diverse. **2** (*intr*) to engage in new and different activities; to branch out. — *n* **diversification**.

diversion *n* **1** the act of diverting; the state of being diverted. **2** a detour from a usual route. **3** something intended to draw attention away. **4** amusement. [Lat *diversio*]

diversionary *adj* intended to cause a diversion.

divert *v* (*tr*) **1** (**from**, **to**) to cause to change direction. **2** to draw away (esp. attention). **3** to amuse. [Lat *divertere*, to turn aside]

divest *v* (*tr*) **1** to undress (oneself or another). **2** (**of**) to deprive. **3** (**of**) to free or unburden. — *n* **divestment**. [Lat *de-*, away from + *vestire*, to clothe]

divide *v* **1** (*tr* & *intr*; **in**, **into**, **from**) to split up or separate into parts. **2** (*tr*; **up**, **between**, **among**) to share. **3** (*tr* & *intr*) to determine how many times one number is contained in (another); (of a number) to be a number of times greater or smaller than another: *3 divides into 9*. **4** (*tr*) to cause disagreement among; to set at odds. **5** (*tr*) to serve as a boundary between. — *n* **1** a disagreement; a gap or split. **2** (esp. *US*) a ridge of high land between two rivers. [Lat *dividere*, to force apart]

dividers *n* (*pl*) a V-shaped device with movable arms, used in geometry, etc. for measuring.

dividend *n* **1** a portion of a company's profits paid to a shareholder. **2** a benefit: *Meeting her would pay dividends*. **3** (*math*) a number divided by another number. [Lat *dividendum*, what is to be divided]

divination *n* **1** the practice of foretelling the future (as if) by supernatural means. **2** insight. **3** a guess. **[divine]**

divine *adj* **1** of, from, or relating to God or a god. **2** (*coll*) extremely pleasant or beautiful; excellent. — *v* **1** (*tr*) to foretell; to learn of by intuition; to guess. **2** (*tr* & *intr*) to search for (underground water) with a divining-rod. — *n* a member of the clergy expert in theology. — *adv* **divinely**. [Lat *divinus*, from *divus*, a god]

divining-rod *n* a stick, esp. of hazel, held near the ground when divining for water, (allegedly) twitching when a discovery is made.

divinity *n* ***-ies*** **1** theology. **2** a god. **3** the state of being God or a god. **[divine]**

divisible *adj* able to be divided. — *n* **divisibility**.

division *n* **1** the act of dividing; the state of being divided. **2** something that divides or separates; a gap or barrier. **3** one of the parts into which something is divided; a major unit of an organisation, e.g. an army or police force. **4** the process of determining how many times one number is contained in another. **5** a formal vote in Parliament. — *adj* **divisional**.

division sign *n* the symbol ÷ representing division in calculations.

divisive *adj* tending to cause disagreement or conflict. — *n* **divisiveness**. **[divide]**

divisor *n* (*math*) a number by which another number is divided. [Lat, divider]

divorce *n* **1** the legal ending of a marriage. **2** a complete separation. — *v* **1** (*tr* & *intr*) to legally end marriage to (someone). **2** (*tr*) to separate. — *adj* **divorced**. [Lat *divortere*, to leave one's husband]

divorcé *n* a divorced man.

divorcée *n* a divorced woman.

divot *n* a clump of grass and earth removed, esp. by the blade of a golf club. [Scot]

divulge *v* (*tr*) to make known; to reveal. — *n* **divulgence**. [Lat *divulgare*, to publish widely]

divvy (*slang*) *n* ***-ies*** a dividend or share. — *v* ***-ies***, ***-ied*** (*tr*; **up**) to divide or share.

Diwali *n* the Hindu or Sikh festival of light, held in October or November. [Hindi *divali*]

Dixie *n* (also **Dixieland**) the southern states of the US, esp. with reference to the American Civil War.

Dixieland *n* early jazz music as played by small bands in New Orleans in the southern US.

dixie *n* a large metal cooking-pot or kettle. [Perhaps Hindi *degci*]

DIY *abbrev* do-it-yourself.

dizzy *adj* ***-ier***, ***-iest*** **1** experiencing or causing a spinning sensation causing loss of balance: *feel dizzy*; *dizzy heights*. **2** (*coll*) silly; not reliable or responsible. **3** (*coll*) bewildered. — *v* ***-ies***, ***-ied*** (*tr*) **1** to make dizzy. **2** to bewilder. — *adv* **dizzily**. — *n* **dizziness**. [OE *dysig*, foolish]

DJ *abbrev* **1** (*slang*) dinner jacket. **2** disc jockey.

djinn and **djinni**. See **jinni**.

dl *abbrev* decilitre.

DLitt or **DLit** *abbrev* for *Doctor litterarum* or *litteraturae* (Lat), Doctor of Letters or of Literature.

DM *abbrev* Deutschmark.

DMus *abbrev* Doctor of Music.

DNA *abbrev* deoxyribonucleic acid.

do[1] *v* ***does***, ***doing***, ***did***, ***done*** **1** (*tr*) to carry out, perform, or commit. **2** (*tr*) to finish or complete. **3** (*tr* & *intr*; **for**) to be enough or suitable. **4** (*tr*) to work at or study. **5** (*intr*) to be in a particular state: *Business is doing well*. **6** (*tr*) to put in order or arrange. **7** (*intr*) to act or behave. **8** (*tr*) to provide as a service: *do lunches*. **9** (*tr*) to bestow (honour, etc.). **10** (*tr*) to cause or produce. **11** (*tr*) to travel (a distance); to travel at (a speed). **12** (*tr*; *coll*; **for**) to improve to (a stated degree) the appearance (of): *This dress doesn't do much for my figure*. **13** (*tr*; *coll*) to cheat. **14** (*tr*; *coll*) to copy the behaviour of; to mimic. **15** (*tr*) to visit as a tourist. **16** (*tr*; *coll*) to ruin: *Now she's done it!* **17** (*tr*; *coll*) to assault or injure: *Tell me, or I'll do you*. **18** (*tr*; *coll*) to spend (time) in prison. **19** (*tr*; *coll*) to convict. **20** (*intr*; *coll*) to happen: *There was nothing doing*. **21** (*tr*; *slang*) to take (drugs). — *v* (*aux*) **1** used in questions and negative statements or commands: *Do you smoke? I don't like wine. Don't do that!* **2** used to avoid repetition of a verb: *She eats as much as I do*. **3** used for emphasis: *She does know you've arrived*. — *n* ***dos*** or ***do's*** (*coll*) **1** a party or other gathering. **2** something done as a rule or custom: *dos and don'ts*. **3** a violent scene; a fracas: *a bit of a do in the pub*. — *adj* **doable**. — *n* **doer**. — *v* **do away with** (*tr*) **1** to murder. **2** to abolish. — *v* **do down** (*tr*) to speak of as if unimportant or not very good. — *v* **do for** (*tr*; *coll*) **1** to kill; to bring the downfall of. **2** to do housework for. — *v* **do in** (*tr*; *coll*) **1** to kill. **2** to exhaust. — *v* **do out** (*tr*) to clear out; to decorate. — *v* **do out of** (*tr*) to deprive of, esp. by trickery. — *v* **do over** (*tr*; *slang*) **1** to rob. **2** to attack or injure. — *v* **do up** (*coll*) **1** (*tr*) to repair, clean, or improve the decoration of. **2** (*tr* & *intr*) to fasten; to tie or wrap up. **3** (*tr*) to dress or dress up. — *v* **do with** (*tr*) **1** (with **could**) to need. **2** (with **cannot**, etc.) to tolerate: *I can't be doing with people like her*. — *v* **do without** (*tr* & *intr*) to manage without (something). — **have** or **be to do with** to be related to or connected with; to be (partly) responsible for. [OE *don*]

do-gooder *n* (*coll*) an enthusiastically helpful person, esp. one whose help is unwanted or impractical.

doings *n* (*sing*; *coll*) the thing whose name cannot be remembered; a thingummy.

do-it-yourself *n* the practice of doing one's own household repairs, etc. without professional help.

done *adj* **1** finished. **2** (of food) fully cooked. **3** socially acceptable. **4** used up. **5** (*coll*) exhausted. — *interj* I agree!; it's a deal! — **be done with** (*coll*) to be no longer involved or associated with. — **done for** (*coll*) facing death or inescapable ruin or other unpleasantness. — **have done with** (*coll*) to finish dealing with; to get finished.

do[2]. Same as **doh**.

do. *abbrev* ditto.

Doberman pinscher or **Doberman** *n* a large breed of dog with a smooth black-and-tan coat. [*Dobermann*, breeder's name + Ger *Pinscher*, terrier]

doc *n* (*coll*) a doctor.

docile *adj* easy to manage or control; submissive. — *adv* **docilely**. — *n* **docility**. [Lat *docilis*, easily taught]

dock[1] *n* **1** a harbour where ships are loaded, unloaded, and repaired; (in *pl*) the area surrounding this. — *v* (*tr* & *intr*) **1** to bring or come into a dock. **2** to (cause space vehicles to) link up in space. — **in dock** being repaired. [ODut *docke*]

docker *n* a labourer who loads and unloads ships.

dockyard *n* a shipyard.

dock[2] *v* (*tr*) **1** to cut off all or part of (an animal's tail). **2** to make deductions from (esp. pay); to deduct (an amount). [MidE *dok*]

dock[3] *n* a weed with large broad leaves and a deep root. [OE *docce*]

dock[4] *n* the enclosure in a court of law where the accused sits or stands. [Flemish *dok*, cage, sty]

docket *n* any label or note accompanying a parcel, e.g. detailing contents or recording receipt. — *v* **-t-** (*tr*) to fix a label to; to record the contents or delivery of.

doctor *n* **1** a person trained and qualified to practise medicine. **2** a person holding a doctorate. — *v* **-r-** (*tr*) **1** to falsify (e.g. information); to tamper with; to drug (food or drink). **2** (*coll*) to sterilise or castrate (an animal). **3** (often *facet*) to give medical treatment to. [Lat, teacher]

doctoral *adj* relating to a doctorate.

doctorate *n* a high academic degree, awarded esp. for research.

doctrinaire *adj* (usu. *derog*) adhering rigidly to theories or principles without considering practicalities. [**doctrine**]

doctrine *n* a thing or things taught, esp. (any one of) a set of religious or political beliefs. — *adj* **doctrinal**. [Lat *doctrina*, teaching]

docudrama *n* a play or film based on real events and characters. [**documentary drama**]

document *n* any piece of writing of an official nature, e.g. a certificate. — *v* (*tr*) **1** to record, esp. in written form. **2** to provide written evidence to support or prove. [Lat *documentum*, lesson, proof]

documentary *n* **-ies** a film or television or radio programme presenting real people in real situations. — *adj* **1** connected with, or consisting of, documents. **2** of the nature of a documentary; undramatised.

documentation *n* (the preparation or presentation of) documents or documentary evidence.

dodder *v* **-r-** (*intr*) to move in an unsteady, trembling fashion as a result of old age. — *n* **dodderer**. — *adj* **doddery**. [Variant of old word *dadder*]

doddle *n* (*coll*) something easily done or achieved.

dodecagon *n* a flat geometric figure with twelve sides and angles. [Gr *dodeka*, twelve + *gonia*, angle]

dodecahedron *n* a solid geometric figure with twelve faces. [Gr *dodeka*, twelve + *hedra*, seat]

dodge *v* (*tr*) **1** to avoid by moving quickly away, esp. sideways. **2** to escape or avoid by cleverness or deceit. — *n* **1** a sudden movement aside. **2** a trick to escape or avoid something. — *n* **dodger**.

dodgy *adj* **-ier**, **-iest** (*coll*) **1** difficult or risky. **2** untrustworthy; dishonest, or dishonestly obtained. **3** unstable; slightly broken.

Dodgems® *n* a fairground amusement consisting of a rink in which drivers of small electric cars try to bump each other.

dodo *n* **-os** or **-oes** **1** a large grey flightless bird of Mauritius, extinct since the 17th century. **2** (*coll*) any old-fashioned person or thing. **3** (*coll*) a stupid person. — **as dead as a dodo** (*coll*) **1** extinct. **2** very out-of-date; completely forgotten about. [Port *doudo*, silly]

DOE *abbrev* Department of the Environment.

doe *n* ***does*** or ***doe*** an adult female rabbit, hare or small deer, e.g. the fallow deer. [OE *da*]

doer, does. See **do**[1].

doesn't does not.

doff *v* (*tr*; *old* or *literary*) to take off (a piece of clothing); to lift (one's hat) in greeting. [**do**[1] + **off**]

dog *n* **1** any of a family of four-legged mammals that includes the wolf and the fox, esp. a domesticated species of this family, of which numerous breeds exist. **2** the male of any such animal. **3** a mechanical gripping device. **4** (*offensive slang*) an unattractive woman. **5** (*coll*; esp. *old*) a fellow or rogue: *You filthy dog!* — *v* **-gg-** (*tr*) **1** to follow very closely; to track. **2** to trouble or plague. — **a dog's breakfast** or **dinner** (*coll*) an untidy mess; a shambles. — **a dog's life** a life of misery. — **like a dog's dinner** (*coll*) (dressed) smartly or showily. [OE *docga*]

dogcart *n* a two-wheeled horse-drawn passenger carriage with seats back-to-back.

dog-collar *n* **1** a collar for a dog. **2** (*coll*) a close-fitting white collar worn by members of the clergy.

dog days *n* (*pl*) the hottest period of the year, when the Dogstar rises and sets with the sun.
dog-eared *adj* (of a book) with pages turned down at the corners; shabby; scruffy.
dog-end *n* (*slang*) a cigarette end.
dogfight *n* **1** a battle at close quarters between two fighter aeroplanes. **2** a fight between dogs. **3** any violent fight. — *n* **dogfighting**.
dogfish *n* any of various kinds of small shark.
dogged *adj* determined; resolute. — *adv* **doggedly**. —*n* **doggedness**.
doggy *adj* **-ier**, **-iest** (*coll*) **1** of, like, or relating to dogs. **2** fond of dogs. — *n* **-ies** (also **doggie**) a child's word for a dog.
doggy-bag *n* a bag in which a restaurant customer can take home leftovers (ostensibly) for a pet.
doggy-paddle or **dog-paddle** *n* & *v* (*intr*) (to swim using) a basic swimming stroke with short paddling movements like a dog's.
doghouse: **in the doghouse** (*coll*) out of favour.
dog in the manger *n* a person who refuses to let others use something he or she possesses but has no use for. — *adj* **dog-in-the-manger**.
dogleg *n* a sharp bend, esp. on a golf course.
dog rose *n* a European wild rose with pink or white flowers.
the dogs *n* (*pl*; *coll*) greyhound racing. — **go to the dogs** (*coll*) to deteriorate greatly.
dogsbody *n* **-ies** (*coll*) a person who does menial tasks for someone else.
Dogstar *n* Sirius, the brightest star in the sky, part of the Greater Dog (or Canis Major) constellation.
dog-tired *adj* (*coll*) extremely tired.
dogtrot *n* a gentle trotting pace.
dogwood *n* a European shrub with small white flowers and purple berries.

doge *n* the chief magistrate in the former republics of Venice and Genoa. [Ital dialect, duke]

dogged. See **dog**.

doggerel *n* **1** badly written poetry. **2** poetry with an irregular rhyming pattern for comic effect. — *adj* of poor quality. [MidE *dogerel*, worthless]

doggo: **lie doggo** (*old coll*) to hide; to lie low. [Prob. **dog**]

doggy. See **dog**.

dogma *n* **1** a belief or principle laid down by an authority as unquestionably true; such beliefs or principles in general. **2** (*coll*) an opinion arrogantly stated. [Gr, opinion]
dogmatic *adj* **1** (of an opinion) forcefully (and arrogantly) stated as if unquestionable. **2** (of a person) tending to make such statements of opinion.
dogmatism *n* the quality of being, or the tendency to be, dogmatic. — *v* (*intr*) **dogmatise** or **-ize**. — *n* **dogmatist**.

doh *n* the first note of the scale in the sol-fa system of music notation.

doily, **-ies** or **doyley**, **-eys** *n* a small decorative napkin of lace or lace-like paper laid on plates under sandwiches, cakes, etc. [*Doily*, London draper]

Dolby® *n* a device, built into sound equipment, for reducing unwanted noise on broadcast or recorded sound. [R *Dolby* (1933–), its inventor]

doldrums *n* (*pl*; **the**) **1** a depressed mood; low spirits. **2** a state of inactivity. **3** areas of sea near the equator renowned for a lack of wind. [Old word *dold*, stupid]

dole *n* (*coll*; with **the**) unemployment benefit. — *v* (*intr* with **out**) to hand out or give out. — **on the dole** (*coll*) unemployed; receiving unemployment benefit. [OE *dal*, share]

doleful *adj* sad; expressing or suggesting sadness; mournful. — *adv* **dolefully**. — *n* **dolefulness**. [OFr *doel*, grief + **-ful**]

doll *n* **1** a toy in the form of a model of a human being, esp. a baby. **2** (*coll derog*) an over-dressed, appearance-conscious woman. **3** (*slang*; often *offensive*) any girl or woman, esp. when considered pretty. **4** (*coll*) a term of endearment, esp. for a girl. — *v* **doll up** (*tr* & *intr*) to dress smartly or showily. [From *Dolly*, dimin. of the name *Dorothy*]
dolly *n* **-ies** **1** a doll (sense **1**). **2** (*tech*) a frame with wheels on which a film or television camera is mounted for moving shots.

dollar *n* (*symbol* **$**) the standard unit of currency in the US, Canada, Australia and numerous other countries, divided into 100 cents. [Ger *Taler*]

dollop *n* (*coll*) a small shapeless mass of any semi-solid substance, esp. food.

dolmen *n* a simple prehistoric monument consisting of a large flat stone supported by several vertical stones. [Perhaps Breton *dol*, table + *men*, stone]

dolorous *adj* (*literary*) causing, involving, or suggesting sorrow or grief. [**dolour**]

dolour *n* (*poetic*) sorrow or grief. [Lat *dolor*, pain]

dolphin *n* a highly intelligent smooth-skinned marine mammal of the whale family. [Gr *delphinos*]

dolt *n* (*derog*) a stupid person. — *adj* **doltish**. [OE *dol*, stupid]

-dom *sfx* **1** a state or rank: *serfdom* or *dukedom*. **2** an area ruled or governed: *kingdom*. **3** a group of people with a specified characteristic: *officialdom*. [OE *dom*, judgement]

domain *n* **1** the scope of any subject or area of interest. **2** a territory owned or ruled by one person or government. [Fr *domaine*]

dome *n* **1** a roof in the shape of a hemisphere. **2** anything of similar shape. **3** (*coll*) a head. — *adj* **domed**. [Lat *domus*, house]

Domesday Book or **Doomsday Book** *n* a record of a survey of all lands in England, commissioned by William the Conqueror in 1086, detailing their value, ownership, etc. ◇ See also **doomsday** under **doom**. [OE *dom*, judgement]

domestic *adj* **1** of or relating to the home, the family, or private life. **2** (of animals) not wild; kept as a pet or farm animal. **3** within or relating to one's country; not foreign: *domestic sales and export sales*. **4** enjoying home life. — *n* a household servant. — *adv* **domestically**. [Lat *domesticus*, from *domus*, house]

domesticate *v* (*tr*) **1** to train (an animal) for life in the company of people. **2** (often *facet*) to make used to home life, esp. to train in cooking, housework, etc. — *n* **domestication**.

domesticity *n* home life, or a liking for it.

domestic science *n* training in household skills, esp. cooking; home economics.

domicile *n* **1** (*formal*) a house. **2** a legally recognised place of permanent residence. — *v* (*tr*; *legal*) to establish in a fixed residence. — *adj* **domiciliary**. [Lat *domicilium*, dwelling]

dominant *adj* **1** most important, evident, or active; foremost. **2** tending to (want to) command or influence others. **3** (e.g. of a house) overlooking others from an elevated position. **4** (*biol*) of or being a gene controlling a characteristic which will appear in all carriers regardless of other genes carried. ◇ See also **recessive**. — *n* the fifth note on a musical scale. — *n* **dominance**. **[dominate]**

dominate *v* (*tr & intr*) **1** to have command or influence over (someone). **2** to be the most important, evident, or active of (a group). **3** to enjoy an elevated position over (a place). — *adj* **dominating**. — *n* **domination**. [Lat *dominari*, to be master]

domineer *v* (*intr*) to behave in an arrogantly dominant way. — *adj* **domineering**. [Ety. as for **dominate**]

Dominican *n & adj* (a member) of a Christian order of friars and nuns founded by Saint Dominic in 1215.

dominion *n* **1** rule; power; influence. **2** a territory or country governed by a single ruler or government; formerly, a self-governing colony within the British Empire. [Lat *dominium*, ownership]

domino *n* **-oes** **1** any of a set of small rectangular tiles marked, in two halves, with a varying number of spots, tiles with matching halves laid end to end in the game of **dominoes**. **2** a black cloak with a hood and mask attached, worn at masked balls. [Perhaps Ital *domino!*, master!, the winner's cry in dominoes]

domino effect *n* the effect that, according to the **domino theory**, one (esp. political) event has of setting off a whole series of similar events, like a falling domino causing all others in a row to fall in turn.

Don *n* the Spanish equivalent of Mr. [Span, from Lat *dominus*, lord]

Don Juan *n* a man who is, or claims to be, a regular seducer of women.

don[1] *n* a university lecturer, esp. at Oxford or Cambridge. [Ety. as for **Don**]

donnish *adj* of, typical of, or resembling a don; intellectual or bookish.

don[2] *v* **-nn-** (*tr*) to put on (clothing). **[do**[1] **+ on]**

donate *v* (*tr*) to give, esp. to charity. — *n* **donation**. [Lat *donare*, to give]

done. See **do**[1].

doner kebab. See **kebab**.

dong[1] *v* (*intr & tr*) & *n* (to make) a deep ringing sound. [Imit.]

dong[2] *n* (*vulg slang*) a penis.

donjon *n* a heavily fortified central tower in a mediaeval castle. [Old variant of **dungeon]**

donkey *n* **-eys** **1** an animal of the horse family, smaller than a horse and with longer ears. **2** (*coll*) a stupid person.

donkey jacket *n* a workman's heavy jacket made of a thick (usu. black) woollen fabric.

donkey's years *n* (*pl*; *coll*) a very long time; ages.

donkey-work *n* **1** heavy manual work. **2** preparation; groundwork.

donor *n* **1** a person who donates. **2** a person who gives blood or an organ for use in the medical treatment of another. **[donate]**

donor card *n* a card indicating that its carrier is willing, in the event of sudden death, to have (usu. specified) healthy organs removed for transplant to others.

don't do not. — *n* (*coll*) something that must not be done: *dos and don'ts*.

don't-know *n* a person undecided, esp. as to whom to vote for.

donut . Same as **doughnut**.

doodah *n* (*coll*) a thing whose name one cannot remember.

doodle *v* (*intr*) to scrawl or scribble aimlessly and meaninglessly. — *n* a meaningless scribble.

doom *n* inescapable death, ruin or other unpleasant fate. — *v* (*tr*; **to**) to condemn (to death or some other horrible fate). [OE *dom*, judgement]

doomsday *n* the last day of the world; in Christianity, the day on which God will judge everyone. — **till doomsday** (*coll*) for ever.

Doomsday Book see **Domesday Book**.

door *n* **1** a movable barrier opening and closing an entrance, e.g. to a room, cupboard or vehicle. **2** an entrance. **3** a house: *three doors away*. **4** **(to)** a means of entry; an opportunity to gain access: *opened the door to stardom*. — **lay (something) at someone's door** to blame (something) on someone. [OE *duru*]

doorbell *n* a bell on or at a door, rung by visitors as a sign of arrival.

doorknocker see **knocker**.
doorman *n* a (usu. uniformed) man employed to guard the entrance to a hotel, restaurant, theatre, etc. and give assistance to guests or customers.
doormat *n* **1** a mat for wiping shoes on before entering. **2** (*coll*) a person easily submitting to unfair treatment by others.
doorstep *n* **1** a step just in front of a door. **2** (*slang*) a very thick sandwich or slice of bread. — **on one's doorstep** situated very close, esp. to one's home.
doorstop *n* a device, esp. a wedge, for holding a door open.
door-to-door *adj* & *adv* **1** going from house to house. **2** (e.g. of a journey time) between precise points of departure and arrival.
doorway *n* an entrance to a building or room; the space filled by a door.

dope *n* **1** (*coll*) a drug taken for pleasure, esp. cannabis. **2** (*coll*) a drug of any kind, esp. one given to athletes or horses to affect performance. **3** (*coll*) a stupid person. **4** (*slang*; with **the**) information, esp. when confidential. — *v* (*tr*) to give or apply drugs to, esp. dishonestly or furtively. [Dut *doop*, sauce]
dopey or **dopy** *adj* **-ier**, **-iest** (*coll*) **1** sleepy or inactive, as if drugged. **2** stupid. — *adv* **dopily**. — *n* **dopiness**.

doppelgänger *n* a person's ghostly double. [Ger, double-goer]

Doric *adj* (*archit*) of, like, or denoting the oldest style of classical Greek architecture, characterised by thick fluted columns. ◇ See also **Corinthian** and **Ionic**. [Gr *Dorikos*, from *Doris*, in ancient Greece]

dorm *n* (*coll*) a dormitory.

dormant *adj* temporarily quiet, inactive, or out of use; hibernating. — *n* **dormancy**. [Lat *dormire*, to sleep]

dormer or **dormer window** *n* a window fitted vertically into an extension built out from a sloping roof. [From **dormitory**, in which they were orig. fitted]

dormitory *n* **-ies** **1** a large bedroom for several people, esp. in a school. **2** (*US*) a hall of residence in a college or university. [Lat *dormitorium*, from *dormire*, to sleep]
dormitory town or **suburb** *n* a town or suburb from which most residents travel to work elsewhere.

Dormobile® *n* a van equipped for living and sleeping in. [**dormitory** + **automobile**]

dormouse *n* **-mice** a small forest animal, like a mouse with a squirrel's tail. [Connected with Lat *dormire*, to sleep, from its hibernating habits]

Dors. *abbrev* Dorset.

dorsal *adj* (*biol* or *physiol*) of or on the back: *dorsal fin*. [Lat *dorsum*, back]

dory *n* **-ies** a golden-yellow fish of the mackerel family. [Fr *dorée*, golden]

DOS *abbrev* (*comput*) disk operating system, a program for handling information on a disk.

dose *n* **1** a quantity of medicine taken at one time. **2** an amount of radiation received. **3** (*coll*; **of**) a bout: *a dose of the flu*. **4** (*slang*) any sexually transmitted disease, esp. gonorrhoea: *catch a dose*. — *v* (*tr*; **up**, **with**) to give medicine to. — *n* **dosage**. — **like a dose of salts** (*coll*) extremely quickly. [Gr *dosis*, giving]

dosh *n* (*slang*) money.

doss *v* (*intr*; *slang*; **down**) to sleep, esp. on an improvised bed. [Perhaps *doss*, dialect for **hassock**]
dosser *n* (*slang*) **1** a homeless person sleeping on the street or in a doss-house. **2** a lazy person.
doss-house *n* (*slang*) a very cheap lodging-house for homeless people.

dossier *n* a file of papers containing information on a person or subject. [Fr]

dost (*old*) the form of the verb **do** used with the pronoun *thou*.

dot *n* **1** a small round mark; a spot; a point. **2** in Morse code, the shorter of the two lengths of signal element, written as a point. ◇ See also **dash**. — *v* **-tt-** (*tr*) **1** to put a dot on. **2** to scatter; to cover with a scattering. — **dot the i's and cross the t's 1** to pay very close attention to detail. **2** to finish the last few details of something. — **on the dot** exactly (on time). — **the year dot** (*coll*) a very long time ago. [OE *dott*, head of a boil]
dot matrix printer *n* a computer printer using arrangements of pins from a matrix or set to form the printed characters.
dotty *adj* **-ier**, **-iest** (*coll*) **1** silly; crazy. **2** (**about**) infatuated. — *adv* **dottily**. — *n* **dottiness**.

dotage *n* a state of feeble-mindedness owing to old age; senility: *in one's dotage*. [Ety. as for **dote**]

dotard *n* a person in his or her dotage. [**dote**]

dote *v* (*intr* with **on**, **upon**) to show a foolishly excessive fondness for. — *adj* **doting**. [ODut *doten*, to be silly]

doth (*old*) does.

double *adj* **1** made up of two similar parts; paired; in pairs. **2** of twice the (usual) weight, size, etc. **3** for two people: *a double bed*. **4** ambiguous: *double meaning*. **5** (of a musical instrument) sounding an octave lower: *double bass*. — *adv* **1** twice. **2** with one half over the other: *folded double*. — *n* **1** a double quantity. **2** a duplicate or lookalike. **3** an actor's stand-in, used esp. in dangerous scenes. **4** a double measure of alcoholic spirit. **5** a racing bet in which any winnings from the first stake become a stake in a subsequent race. **6** a win in two events on the same racing programme. — *v* **1** (*tr* & *intr*) to (cause to) become twice as large in size, number, etc. **2** (*tr*; **over**) to fold one half of over the other. **3** (*intr* with **as**) to have a second use or function. **4** (*intr* with **for**) to act as a substitute. **5** (*intr*) to turn round sharply. — **at** or **on the double** very quickly. — *v* **double back**

(*intr*) to turn and go back, often by a different route. — *v* **double up 1** (*tr* & *intr*) to (cause to) bend sharply at the waist. **2** (*intr*; **with**) to share (esp. a bedroom). [Lat *duplus*]

double agent *n* a spy working for two governments with conflicting interests.

double-barrelled *adj* **1** (of a gun) having two barrels. **2** (of a surname) made up of two names.

double-breasted *adj* (of a coat or jacket) with overlapping front flaps.

double-check *v* (*tr* & *intr*) to check twice or again.

double chin *n* a chin with an area of loose flesh underneath.

double cream *n* thick cream with a high fat content.

double-cross *v* (*tr*) to cheat or deceive (a person on whose behalf one is deceiving another). — *n* such a deceit. — *n* **double-crosser**.

double-dealing *n* cheating; treachery. — *n* **double-dealer**.

double-decker *n* **1** a bus with two decks. **2** (*coll*) anything with two levels or layers: *double-decker sandwich*.

double Dutch *n* (*coll*) nonsense; incomprehensible jargon.

double-edged *adj* **1** having two cutting edges. **2** having two possible meanings or purposes.

double figures *n* (*pl*) the numbers between 10 and 99 inclusive, esp. the lower ones.

double-glazing *n* windows constructed with two panes separated by a vacuum, providing added heat insulation. — *adj* **double-glazed**.

double-jointed *adj* having extraordinarily flexible body joints.

double negative *n* an expression containing two negative words where only one is needed, as in *He hasn't never asked me*.

double-park *v* (*tr* & *intr*) to park at the side of another vehicle parked alongside the kerb.

double-quick *adj* & *adv* very quick or quickly.

doubles *n* (*sing*) a competition in tennis, etc. between two teams of two players each.

double standard *n* (often in *pl*) a principle or rule applied firmly to one person or group and loosely or not at all to another, esp. oneself.

double take *n* an initial inattentive reaction followed swiftly by a sudden full realisation, esp. used as a comic device: *do a double take*.

double-talk *n* ambiguous talk, or talk that seems relevant but is really meaningless, esp. as offered up by politicians.

doublethink *n* simultaneous belief in, or acceptance of, two opposing ideas or principles.

double time *n* a rate of pay equal to double the basic rate.

doubly *adv* **1** to twice the extent; very much more. **2** in two ways.

double entendre *n* a remark having two possible meanings, one of them usu. sexually suggestive; the use of such remarks. [Old Fr, double meaning]

doublet *n* **1** a close-fitting man's jacket, with or without sleeves, popular between the 14th and 17th centuries. **2** (one of) a pair of objects of any kind. [OFr]

doubloon *n* a former gold coin of Spain and S America. [Span *doblón*]

doubt *v* (*tr*) **1** to feel uncertain about; to be suspicious, or show mistrust, of. **2** to be inclined to disbelieve. — *n* **1** (a feeling of) uncertainty, suspicion, or mistrust. **2** an inclination to disbelieve; a reservation. — *n* **doubter**. — **no doubt** surely; probably. — **without (a) doubt** certainly. [Lat *dubitare*]

doubtful *adj* **1** feeling doubt. **2** uncertain; able to be doubted. **3** likely not to be the case. — *adv* **doubtfully**. — *n* **doubtfulness**.

doubtless *adv* probably; certainly.

douche *n* (an apparatus producing) a jet of water applied to the body for medical purposes; a treatment using water in this way. — *v* (*tr*) to apply a douche to. [Fr]

dough *n* **1** a mixture of flour, water and other ingredients, the basis of bread, pastry, etc. **2** (*slang*) money. — *adj* **doughy**, **-ier**, **-iest**. [OE *dah*]

doughnut *n* a spongy ring-shaped pastry, esp. filled with cream or jam, usu. with a hole in the middle.

doughty *adj* **-ier**, **-iest** (*old* or *poetic*) brave; stout-hearted. — *adv* **doughtily**. — *n* **doughtiness**. [OE *dyhtig*]

dour *adj* stern; sullen. [Lat *durus*, hard]

douse or **dowse** *v* (*tr*) **1** to throw water over; to plunge into water. **2** to extinguish (a light or fire).

dove *n* **1** a bird of the pigeon family, typically smaller than a pigeon. **2** (*politics*) a person favouring peace rather than hostility. ◇ See also **hawk**. [OE *dufe*]

dovecote or **dovecot** *n* a shed in which domestic pigeons are kept.

dovetail *n* (also **dovetail joint**) a corner joint, esp. in wood, made by fitting v-shaped pegs into v-shaped slots. — *v* (*tr* & *intr*) to fit or combine neatly.

dowager *n* **1** a title given to a nobleman's widow, to distinguish her from the wife of her husband's heir: *dowager duchess*. **2** (*coll*) a grand-looking old lady. [OFr *douagiere*, from Lat *dotare*, to endow]

dowdy *adj* **-ier**, **-iest** (esp. of a woman or her clothes) dull, plain and unfashionable. — *adv* **dowdily**. — *n* **dowdiness**. [MidE *dowd*, slut]

dowel *n* a thin cylindrical (esp. wooden) peg, esp. used to join two pieces by fitting into corresponding holes in each. [OGer *dovel*]

dower *n* a widow's share, for life, in her deceased husband's property. [OFr *douaire*, from Lat *dotare*, to endow]

dower house *n* a house smaller than, and within the grounds of, a large country house, orig. one forming part of a dower.

down[1] *adv* **1** towards or in a low or lower position, level or state; on or to the ground. **2** from a greater to a lesser size, amount or level: *scaled down*; *calm down*. **3** towards or in a more southerly place. **4** in writing; on paper: *take down notes*. **5** as a deposit: *put down five pounds*. **6** to an end stage or finished state: *hunt someone down*; *grind down*. **7** from earlier to later times: *handed down through generations*. **8** not vomited up: *keep food down*.— *prep* **1** in a lower position on. **2** along; at a further position on, by, or through: *down the road*. **3** from the top to, or towards, the bottom. **4** (*dialect*) to or in (a particular place): *going down the town*. — *adj* **1** sad; in low spirits. **2** going towards or reaching a lower position: *a down pipe*. **3** (**by**) with a deficit (of): *down by three goals*. **4** made as a deposit: *a down payment*. **5** reduced in price. **6** (**for**) noted; entered in a list, etc.: *Your name is down for the hurdles*. **7** (of a computer, etc.) not working properly. — *v* (*tr*) **1** to drink quickly, esp. in one gulp. **2** to force to the ground. — *n* **1** an unsuccessful or otherwise unpleasant period: *ups and downs*. **2** (*pl*) an area of rolling (esp. treeless) hills. — **down to the ground** (*coll*) completely; perfectly. — **down tools** (*coll*) to stop working, as a protest. — **down under** (*coll*) in or to Australia or New Zealand. — **down with...!** let us get rid of...! — **have a down on** (*coll*) to be ill-disposed towards. [OE *of dune*, from the hill]

down-and-out *n* & *adj* (a person who is) homeless and penniless, with no hope of earning a living.

down-at-heel *adj* shabby.

downbeat *adj* **1** pessimistic; cheerless. **2** calm; relaxed. — *n* (*mus*) the first beat of a bar.

downcast *adj* **1** glum; dispirited. **2** (of eyes) looking downwards.

downer *n* **1** (*coll*) a state of depression: *be on a downer*. **2** (*slang*) a tranquillising or depressant drug.

downfall *n* (the cause of) failure or ruin.

downgrade *v* (*tr*) to reduce to a lower grade.

downhearted *adj* dispirited; discouraged; dismayed.

downhill *adv* **1** downwards. **2** to or towards a worse condition. — *adj* **1** downwardly sloping. **2** becoming increasingly easier. **3** deteriorating.

down-in-the-mouth *adj* unhappy; depressed.

download *v* (*tr*) to transfer (data) from one computer to another, esp. smaller.

down-market *adj* cheap, poor quality, or lacking prestige.

down payment *n* a deposit.

downpour *n* a very heavy fall of rain.

downright *adj* & *adv* utter or utterly.

downside *n* **1** the lower or under side. **2** (*coll*) a negative aspect; a disadvantage.

downstage *adj* & *adv* (performed, etc.) at or towards the front of a theatre stage.

downstairs *adv* to or towards a lower floor; down the stairs. — *n* & *adj* (on) a lower or ground floor.

downstream *adj* & *adv* (lying) further along a river towards the sea; (flowing) with the current.

downtime *n* time during which work ceases because a machine, esp. a computer, is not working.

down-to-earth *adj* **1** sensible and practical. **2** not at all pretentious. **3** plain-speaking.

downtown *n*, *adj* & *adv* (in, to, or towards) the lower part of the city, or the city centre.

downtrodden *adj* oppressed; ruled or controlled tyrannically.

downturn *n* a decline in (esp. economic) activity.

downward *adj* leading or moving down; descending; declining. — *adv* **downwardly**.

downwards or **downward** *adv* to or towards a lower position or level.

downwind *adv* **1** in or towards the direction in which the wind is blowing; with the wind blowing from behind. **2** (**of**) behind in terms of wind direction; with the wind carrying one's scent away from (e.g. an animal one is stalking). — *adj* moving with, or sheltered from, the wind.

down[2] *n* soft fine feathers or hair. — *adj* **downy, *-ier*, *-iest***. [Norse *dunn*]

Downing Street *n* the British government or the office of the Prime Minister. [The London street in which the Prime Minister's official residence lies]

Down's Syndrome *n* a medical condition, caused by a genetic abnormality, whose symptoms are mental retardation and a broadening and flattening of the face. [J L H *Down* (1828–96), English physician]

dowry *n* ***-ies*** an amount of wealth handed over by a woman to her husband on marriage. [**dower**]

dowse[1] *v* (*intr*) to search for underground water with a divining-rod. — *n* **dowser**.

dowse[2]. See **douse**.

doxology *n* ***-ies*** a Christian hymn, verse, or fixed expression praising God. [Gr *doxa*, glory + *logos*, discourse]

doyen and **doyenne** *n* (*literary*; with **the**) the most senior and most respected male or female member, e.g. of a profession. [Fr]

doyley. See **doily**.

doz. *abbrev* dozen.

doze *v* (*intr*) to sleep lightly. — *n* a brief period of light sleeping. — *v* **doze off** (*intr*) to fall into a light sleep. [Norse *dus*, lull]

dozy *adj* ***-ier***, ***-iest*** **1** sleepy. **2** (*coll*) stupid; slow to understand; not alert. — *adv* **dozily**. — *n* **doziness**.

dozen *n* ***-zen*** or ***-zens*** a set of twelve. — *adj* **dozenth**. — **dozens of** (*coll*) very many. [Lat *duodecim*]

DPhil or **DPh** *abbrev* Doctor of Philosophy. ◇ See also **PhD**.

DPP *abbrev* Director of Public Prosecutions.

Dr *abbrev* **1** Doctor. **2** drachma. **3** Drive (in addresses).

drab *adj* ***-bb-*** **1** dull; dreary. **2** of a dull greenish-brown colour. — *adv* **drably**. — *n* **drabness**. [Perhaps Fr *drap*, cloth]

drachm *n* a measure equal to $\frac{1}{8}$ of an ounce or fluid ounce, formerly used by pharmacists. [Ety. as for **drachma**]

drachma *n* ***-mas*** or ***-mae*** (*symbol* **Dr**) the standard unit of currency in Greece, divided into 100 lepta. [Gr *drakhme*, handful]

draconian *adj* (of a law, etc.) severe; cruel. [*Draco*, magistrate in ancient Greece]

draft *n* **1** a written plan; a preliminary sketch. **2** a written order requesting a bank to pay out money, esp. to another bank. **3** a group of people drafted. **4** (*US*) conscription. — *v* (*tr*) **1** to set out in preliminary sketchy form. **2** to select and send off (personnel) to perform a specific task. **3** (*US*) to conscript. [A form of **draught**]

draft-dodger *n* (*coll*; *US*) a person who avoids conscription.

drag *v* ***-gg-*** **1** (*tr*) to pull roughly or violently; to pull along slowly and with force. **2** (*tr* & *intr*) to (cause to) move along scraping the ground. **3** (*tr*; *coll* with **away**) to force or persuade to come away. **4** (*tr*; **for**) to search (e.g. a lake) with a hook or dragnet. **5** (*intr*) (of time, etc.) to progress or move slowly. ◇ See also **drag on** below. — *n* **1** an act of dragging; a dragging effect. **2** a person or thing that makes progress slow. **3** (*coll*) a draw on a cigarette. **4** (*coll*) a dull or tedious person or thing. **5** (*coll*) women's clothes worn by a man. **6** an object's resistance to movement through air or water. — *v* **drag on** (*intr*; *coll*) to proceed or continue slowly and boringly. — **drag one's feet** or **heels** (*coll*) to delay; to be deliberately slow to take action. — *v* **drag out** (*tr*; *coll*) to make to last as long as possible. — *v* **drag up** (*tr*; *coll*) to mention (an unpleasant subject long forgotten). [OE *dragan*]

dragnet *n* a heavy net pulled along the bottom of a river, lake, etc. in a search for something.

drag race *n* a contest in acceleration between specially designed vehicles (**dragsters**) over a short course. — *n* **drag-racing**.

draggle *v* (*tr* & *intr*) to make or become wet and dirty (as if) through trailing along the ground. **[drag]**

dragon *n* **1** a large mythical fire-breathing reptile-like creature with wings and a long tail. **2** (*coll*) a frighteningly domineering woman. — **chase the dragon** (*slang*) to smoke heroin by heating it and inhaling the fumes. [Gr *drakon*]

dragonfly *n* ***-ies*** an insect with a long thin body and two sets of transparent wings.

dragoon *n* (*hist*) a heavily armed mounted soldier. — *v* (*tr*; **into**) to force or bully (into doing something). [Fr *dragon*]

drain *v* **1** (*tr*; **off**, **of**) to cause or allow (liquid) to escape; to empty (a container) in this way. **2** (*intr*; **off**, **from**) (of liquid, etc.) to escape; to flow away. **3** (*tr*) to drink the total contents of. **4** (*tr* & *intr*; **away**) to (cause to) disappear: *Our support drained away*. **5** (*tr*) to use up the strength, emotion, or resources of. **6** (*tr*) (of a river) to carry away surface water from (land). — *n* **1** any device, esp. a pipe, for carrying away liquid. **2** (**on**) anything that exhausts a supply. — **down the drain** (*coll*) wasted; lost. [OE *dreahnian*]

drainage *n* the process, method or system of draining.

draining-board *n* a sloping (esp. channelled) surface at the side of a sink allowing water from washed dishes to drain away.

drainpipe *n* **1** a pipe carrying water from a roof into a drain below ground. **2** (*pl*; *coll*) very narrow tight-fitting trousers.

drake *n* a male duck.

dram *n* **1** (*coll*) a small amount of alcoholic spirit, esp. whisky. **2** a measure of weight equal to $\frac{1}{16}$ of an ounce. [Ety. as for **drachma**]

drama *n* **1** a play; any work performed by actors. **2** plays in general, as an art form. **3** the art of producing, directing, and acting in plays. **4** (a situation full of) excitement and emotion. [Gr]

dramatic *adj* **1** of or relating to plays, the theatre, or acting in general. **2** exciting. **3** sudden and striking; drastic. **4** (of behaviour) flamboyantly emotional; (of a person) prone to such behaviour. — *adv* **dramatically**.

dramatics *n* (*sing*) **1** activities associated with the staging and performing of plays. **2** exaggeratedly emotional behaviour.

dramatise or **-ize** *v* (*tr*) **1** to make into a work for public performance. **2** to treat as, or cause to seem, more exciting or important. — *n* **dramatisation** or **-z-**.

dramatist *n* a writer of plays.

dramatis personae *n* (a list of) the characters in a play. [Lat]

drank. See **drink**.

drape *v* (*tr*) **1** to hang (cloth) loosely over (something). **2** to arrange or lay loosely. [OFr *draper*]

draper *n* a person who sells fabric.

drapery *n* ***-ies*** **1** fabric; textiles. **2** curtains and other hanging fabrics. **3** a draper's business or shop.

drapes *n* (*pl*; *US*) curtains.

drastic *adj* extreme; severe. — *adv* **drastically**. [Gr *drastikos*, from *draein*, to act]

drat *interj* (*coll*) expressing anger or annoyance. — *adj* **dratted**. [An alteration of *God rot*]

draught *n* **1** a current of air, esp. indoors. **2** a quantity of liquid swallowed in one go. **3** the amount of water required to float a ship. **4** any of the discs used in the game of draughts. **5** (*coll*) draught beer. **6** the act of pulling or drawing. **7** a dose of liquid medicine. — *adj* **1** (of beer) pumped direct from the cask to the glass. **2** (of an animal) used for pulling loads. — **on draught** (of beer) stored in casks from which it is served direct. [OE *draht*, from *dragan*, to draw]

draughts *n* (*sing*) a game for two people played with 24 discs on a chequered board.

draughtsman *n* **1** a person skilled in drawing. **2** a person employed to produce accurate and detailed technical drawings. **3** any of the discs used in the game of draughts. — *n* **draughtsmanship**.

draughty *adj* **-ier**, **-iest** prone to or suffering draughts of air. — *n* **draughtiness**.

draw *v* ***drew***, ***drawn*** **1** (*tr* & *intr*) to make a picture of (something or someone), esp. with a pencil. **2** (*tr*; **from, off**) to pull out, take out or extract: *draw water from a well*; *with swords drawn*. **3** (*intr*; **ahead, back, in**, etc.) to move or proceed: *draw nearer*. **4** (*tr*; **out, on**) to take from a fund or source: *draw on reserves of energy*. **5** (*tr*) to open or close (curtains). **6** (*tr*) to attract (e.g. attention or criticism). **7** (*tr* & *intr*; **with**) to end (e.g. a game) with neither side winning; to finish on equal terms (with an opponent). **8** (*tr*) to choose or be given as the result of random selection. **9** (*tr*; **on**) to persuade to talk or give information: *He refused to be drawn on his plans*. **10** (*tr*) to arrive at or infer (a conclusion). **11** (*intr*; **on**) to suck air (e.g. through a cigarette); (of a chimney) to cause air to flow through a fire, allowing burning. **12** (*tr*; *tech*) (of a ship) to require (a certain depth of water) to float. **13** (*intr*) (of tea) to brew or infuse. **14** (*tr*) to disembowel: *hanged, drawn and quartered*. — *n* **1** a result in which neither side is the winner; a tie. **2** the making of a random selection, e.g. of the winners of a competition; a competition with winners chosen at random. **3** (a person or thing with) the potential to attract many people. **4** the act of drawing a gun. — *v* **draw back** (*intr*; **from**) to refuse to become involved; to avoid commitment. ◇ See also **drawback** below. — *v* **draw in** (*intr*) (of nights) to start earlier, making days shorter. — **draw the line (at)** to fix a limit, e.g. on one's actions or tolerance. — *v* **draw out** (*tr*) **1** to make to last a long time or longer than necessary (*adj* **drawn-out**). **2** to encourage to be less shy or reserved. — *v* **draw up 1** (*intr*) to come to a halt. **2** (*tr*) to plan and set out in writing (e.g. a contract). **3** (*tr*) to lift (oneself) into an upright position. [OE *dragan*]

drawback *n* a disadvantage. ◇ See also **draw back** above.

drawbridge *n* a bridge that can be lifted to prevent access across, or to allow passage beneath.

drawing *n* any picture made up of lines, esp. one drawn in pencil.

drawing-board *n* a board to which paper is fixed for drawing. — **(go) back to the drawing-board** to return to the planning stage, to find a more successful approach.

drawing-pin *n* a pin with a broad flat head, used esp. for fastening paper to a board or wall.

drawing-room *n* a sitting-room or living-room.

drawn *adj* showing signs of mental strain or tiredness.

-drawn *in cmpds* pulled by: *horse-drawn*.

drawstring *n* a cord sewn inside a hem e.g. on a bag or piece of clothing, closing up the hem when pulled.

drawer *n* **1** a sliding lidless storage box fitted as part of a desk or other piece of furniture. **2** a person who draws. **3** (*pl*; *old*) knickers, esp. when large and roomy. — **out of the top drawer** (*coll*) of the very best quality or the highest standard. [Ety. as for **draw**]

drawl *v* (*tr* & *intr*) to speak or say in a slow lazy manner, esp. with prolonged vowel sounds. — *adj* **drawling**. [Connected with **draw**]

dray[1] *n* a low horse-drawn cart used for heavy loads. [OE *dræge*, from *dragan*, to draw]

dray[2]. Same as **drey**.

dread *v* (*tr*) & *n* (to look ahead to with) great fear or apprehension. — *adj* (*literary*) inspiring awe or great fear. [OE *ondrædan*]

dreaded *adj* **1** greatly feared. **2** (*loosely*) much disliked.

dreadful *adj* **1** inspiring great fear; terrible. **2** (*loosely*) very bad, unpleasant, or extreme. — *adv* **dreadfully**. — *n* **dreadfulness**.

dreadlocks *n* (*pl*) thin braids of hair tied tightly all over the head, esp. worn by Rastafarians.

dreadnought *n* **1** a heavily armed battleship. **2** a fearless person.

dream *n* **1** a series of thoughts and images occurring in the mind during sleep. **2** a state of complete engrossment in one's own thoughts. **3** a distant ambition, esp. unattainable. **4** (*coll*) an extremely pleasing person or thing. — *v* ***dreamt*** or ***dreamed*** **1** (*tr* & *intr*; **about**) to have thoughts and visions (of) during sleep. **2** (*intr*; **of**) to have a distant ambition or hope. **3** (*tr* & *intr*; **of**) to imagine; to conceive (of). **4** (*intr*) to have extravagant and unrealistic thoughts or plans. **5** (*intr*) to be lost in thought. — *adj* ideal. — *n* **dreamer**. — *v* **dream up** (*tr*) to invent (esp. something ridiculous). — **like a dream** (*coll*) extremely well, easily, or successfully. [MidE]

dreamboat *n* (*slang*) an ideal romantic partner.

dreamy *adj* **-ier**, **-iest** **1** unreal, like in a dream. **2** having or showing a wandering mind. **3** (*coll*) lovely. — *adv* **dreamily**. — *n* **dreaminess**.

dreary *adj* **-ier**, **-iest** **1** dull and depressing. **2** uninteresting. — *adv* **drearily**. — *n* **dreariness**. [OE *dreorig*, bloody, mournful]

dredge[1] *v* (*tr* & *intr*) to clear the bottom of or deepen (the sea or a river) by bringing up mud and waste. — *n* a machine for dredging, with a scooping or sucking action. — *v* **dredge up** (*tr*; *coll*) to mention or bring up (something long forgotten).

dredger *n* a barge or ship fitted with a dredge.

dredge[2] *v* (*tr*) to sprinkle (food), e.g. with sugar or flour. — *n* **dredger**. [OFr *dragie*, sugar-plum]

dregs *n* (*pl*) **1** solid particles in a liquid that settle at the bottom. **2** worthless or contemptible elements. [Norse *dregg*]

drench *v* (*tr*) **1** to make soaking wet. **2** to administer liquid medicine to (an animal). — *n* a dose of liquid medicine for an animal. [OE *drencan*, to cause to drink]

dress *v* **1** (*tr* & *intr*) to put clothes on; to (cause to) wear clothes (of a certain kind). **2** (*tr*) to treat and bandage (wounds). **3** (*tr*) to prepare, or add seasoning or a sauce to, (food). **4** (*tr*) to arrange a display in (a window): *window dressing*. **5** (*tr*) to shape and smooth (esp. stone). **6** (*intr*) to put on or have on formal evening wear. — *n* **1** a woman's garment with top and skirt in one piece. **2** clothing; wear: *in evening dress*. — *adj* formal; for wear in the evenings: *dress jacket*. — *v* **dress down** **1** (*tr*) to give a telling-off (*n* **dressing-down**). **2** (*intr*) to change into more informal clothes. — *v* **dress up** **1** (*tr* & *intr*; **as**, **in**) to (cause to) put on or wear fancy dress. **2** (*intr*) to dress in very smart or formal clothes. **3** (*tr*) to cause to appear more pleasant or acceptable by making additions or alterations. [OFr *dresser*, to prepare]

dress circle *n* a balcony in a theatre, esp. the first above the ground floor.

dresser *n* **1** a free-standing kitchen cupboard with shelves above, for storing and displaying dishes, etc. **2** a theatre assistant employed to help stage actors with their costumes. **3** a person who dresses in a particular way.

dressing *n* **1** any sauce added to food, esp. salad. **2** a covering for a wound. **3** fertiliser, e.g. manure, used on land.

dressing-down see **dress down**.

dressing-gown *n* a loose robe worn informally indoors, esp. over nightclothes.

dressing-table *n* a piece of bedroom furniture typically with drawers and a large mirror.

dressmaker *n* a person who makes women's clothes. — *n* **dressmaking**.

dress rehearsal *n* **1** the last rehearsal of a play, with full costumes, lighting and other effects. **2** a practice under real conditions, or an event considered as such in relation to another more important.

dressy *adj* **-ier**, **-iest** **1** dressed or dressing stylishly. **2** (of clothes) for formal wear; elegant. **3** (*coll*) fancy; over-decorated. — *adv* **dressily**. — *n* **dressiness**.

dressage *n* horses' training in, or performance of, set manoeuvres signalled by the rider. [Fr]

drew. see **draw**.

drey *n* a squirrel's nest.

dribble *v* **1** (*intr*) to fall or flow in drops. **2** (*intr*) to allow saliva to run slowly down from the mouth. **3** (*tr* & *intr*) to move along keeping (a ball) in close control with frequent short strokes. — *n* **1** a small quantity of liquid, esp. saliva. **2** an act of dribbling a ball. [Obsolete *drib*]

driblet *n* a very small amount, esp. of liquid. [Ety. as for **dribble**]

dribs and drabs *n* (*pl*) very small quantities at a time. [Ety. as for **dribble**]

drift *n* **1** a pile or mass formed by the wind or a current. **2** a general movement or tendency to move. **3** the movement of a stretch of sea in the direction of a prevailing wind: *North Atlantic Drift*. **4** degree of movement off course caused by wind or a current. **5** (overall) meaning. — *v* (*intr*) **1** to float or be blown along or into heaps. **2** to move aimlessly or passively from one place or occupation to another. **3** to move off course. [Norse, snowdrift]

drifter *n* **1** a fishing-boat that uses a drift-net. **2** a person who moves from place to place, settling in none.

drift-net *n* a large fishing-net allowed to drift with the tide.

driftwood *n* wood floating near, or washed up on, a shore.

drill[1] *n* **1** a tool for boring holes. **2** a training exercise, or a session of it. **3** (*coll*) correct procedure; routine. — *v* **1** (*tr* & *intr*) to make (a hole) with a drill; to make a hole in (something) with a drill. **2** (*tr*) to exercise or teach through repeated practice. [Prob. Dut *drillen*, to bore]

drill[2] *n* thick strong cotton cloth. [Ger *Drillich*, ticking]

drill[3] *n* **1** a shallow furrow in which seeds are sown; the seeds sown. **2** a machine for sowing seeds in rows. — *v* (*tr*) to sow in rows.

drill[4] *n* a W African baboon related to, but smaller than, the mandrill. [W African language]

drily. See **dry**.

drink *v* ***drank***, ***drunk*** **1** (*tr* & *intr*) to swallow (a liquid); to consume (a liquid) by swallowing. **2** (*intr*) to drink alcohol; to drink alcohol to excess. **3** (*tr*; **to**, **into**) to get (oneself) into a certain state by drinking alcohol. **4** (*tr* & *intr*; **to**) to drink a toast (to). — *n* **1** an act of drinking; a liquid suitable for drinking. **2** (a glass of) alcohol of any kind; the habit of drinking alcohol to excess. **3** (*coll*; with **the**) the sea. — *adj* **drinkable**. — *n* **drinker**. — *v* **drink in** (*tr*) to take in eagerly. [OE *drincan*]

drink-driving *n* & *adj* (relating to) the act or practice of driving while drunk. — *n* **drink-driver**.

drip *v* **-pp-** **1** (*tr* & *intr*) to (allow to) fall in drops. **2** (*intr*) to release a liquid in drops: *a dripping tap*. **3** (*tr* & *intr*; *coll*; **with**) to bear or contain an impressive or excessive amount (of): *a film dripping (with) sentimentality*. — *n* **1** the action or noise of dripping. **2** (also **drip-feed**) a device for passing a liquid slowly and continuously, esp. into a vein. ◇ See also **drip-feed** below. **3** (*coll derog*) a person lacking spirit or character. [OE *dryppan*]

drip-dry *adj* (of a garment) requiring little or no ironing if hung up to dry. — *v* (*tr* & *intr*) to dry in this way.

drip-feed *v* (*tr*) to feed with a liquid drop by drop, esp. intravenously. — *n* a drip.

dripping *n* fat from roasted meat, esp. when solidified.

drive *v* ***drove***, ***driven*** **1** (*tr* & *intr*) to control the movement of (a vehicle); to be legally qualified to do so. **2** (*intr*) to travel in a vehicle. **3** (*tr*) to take or transport in a vehicle. **4** (*tr*) to urge or force to move. **5** (*tr*) to (cause to) strike firmly. **6** (*tr*) to produce motion in; to cause to function. **7** (*tr*; **to**, **by**) to force or lead; to motivate. **8** (*tr*) to conduct or dictate: *drive a hard bargain*. — *n* **1** a (pleasure) trip in a vehicle; travel by road. **2** (also **driveway**) a path for vehicles, leading from a private residence to the road outside. **3** energy and enthusiasm. **4** an organised campaign; a group effort: *economy drive*. **5** (a device supplying) operating power. **6** a forceful strike of a ball in various sports. **7** a united movement forward, esp. by a military force. **8** a meeting to play a game, esp. cards. — *v* **drive at** (*tr*) to lead to as a meaning or conclusion: *What is he driving at?* — **drive (something) home** to make (something) clearly understood. [OE *drifan*]

drive-in *n* & *adj* (a cinema, restaurant, etc.) providing a service or facility for customers remaining seated in vehicles.

driver *n* **1** a person who drives a vehicle. **2** a large-headed golf club for hitting the ball from the tee.

driving *n* the act, practice, or way of driving vehicles. — *adj* **1** producing or transmitting operating power: *driving wheel*. **2** heavy and windblown: *driving rain*. **3** providing the motive for determined hard work.

driving seat: **in the driving seat** (*coll*) in a controlling or commanding position.

drivel *n* nonsense. — *v* **-ll-** (*intr*) **1** to talk nonsense. **2** to dribble or slaver. [OE *dreflian*, to dribble]

drizzle *n* fine light rain. — *v* (*intr*) to rain lightly. — *adj* **drizzly**. [OE *dreosan*, to fall]

droll *adj* oddly amusing or comical. — *n* **drollery**. — *n* **drollness**. — *adv* **drolly**. [Fr *drôle*]

dromedary *n* **-ies** a camel with a single hump. ◇ See also **Bactrian**. [Gr *dromados*, running]

drone *v* (*intr*) **1** to make a low humming noise. **2** (**on**) to talk at length in a monotonous voice, esp. boringly. — *n* **1** a deep humming sound. **2** a male honeybee. **3** a lazy person, esp. one living off others. [OE *dran*, bee]

drool *v* (*intr*) **1** to dribble or slaver. **2** (**over**) to show uncontrolled admiration (for) or pleasure (at the sight of). [Alteration of **drivel**]

droop *v* (*intr*) **1** to hang loosely; to sag. **2** to be weak with tiredness. — *n* drooping state. — *adj* **droopy**, ***-ier***, ***-iest***. [Norse *drupa*]

drop *v* **-pp-** **1** (*tr* & *intr*) to (allow to) fall. **2** (*tr* & *intr*; **down**, **off**) to (cause to) decline, lower, or weaken. **3** (*tr*) to give up or abandon (e.g. a friend or a habit); to stop doing temporarily. **4** (*tr*) to stop discussing. **5** (*tr*; **off**, **in**) to set down from a vehicle; to deliver or hand in. **6** (*tr*) to leave or take out: *dropped from the team*. **7** (*tr*) to mention casually: *drop a hint*. **8** (*tr*) to fail to pronounce: *drop one's h's*. **9** (*tr*; *coll*) to write informally: *drop me a line*. **10** (*intr* with **in**) to pay an unexpected (and usu. short) visit. **11** (*intr*; **back**, **behind**) to change to a position behind others in a group. **12** (*intr* with **into**) to pass idly or passively (into a habit, etc.). **13** (*tr* & *intr*; *vulg slang*) to give birth (to). **14** (*tr*; *slang*) to beat to the ground. — *n* **1** a small round or pear-shaped mass of liquid, esp. falling; a small amount (of liquid). **2** a descent; a fall. **3** a vertical distance. **4** a decline or decrease. **5** any small round or pear-shaped object, e.g. an earring or boiled sweet. **6** (*pl*) liquid medication administered in small amounts. **7** a delivery. — **at the drop of a hat** (*coll*) promptly; for the slightest reason. — *v* **drop off** (*intr*; *coll*) to fall asleep. — *v* **drop out** (*intr*; **of**) **1** to withdraw, e.g. from a school or a pre-arranged activity. **2** (*coll*) to adopt an alternative lifestyle as a reaction against traditional social values. ◇ See also **dropout** below. — **let drop** to make known (as if) by accident. [OE *droppian*]

drop-kick *n* (*rugby*) a kick in which the ball is released from the hands and struck as it hits the ground. — *v* (*tr*) to kick (a ball) in this way.

droplet *n* a tiny drop.

dropout *n* **1** a student who quits before completing a course of study. **2** a person whose alternative lifestyle is a reaction against traditional social values; (*loosely*) any unconventional person. ◇ See also **drop out** above.

dropper *n* a short narrow glass tube with a rubber bulb on one end, for applying liquid in drops.

droppings *n* (*pl*) animal faeces.

dropsy *n* the abnormal accumulation of watery liquid in body cavities or tissues. — *adj* **dropsical**. [Gr *hydrops*, from *hydor*, water]

dross *n* **1** waste coal. **2** scum that forms on molten metal. **3** (*coll derog*) rubbish; any worthless substance. [OE *dros*]

drought *n* (a prolonged period of) lack of rainfall. [OE *drugath*, dryness]

drove[1] past tense of **drive**.

drove[2] *n* **1** a moving herd of animals, esp. cattle. **2** a large moving crowd. [OE *draf*, herd]

drover *n* (*hist*) a person employed to drive farm animals to and from market.

drown *v* **1** (*tr* & *intr*) to kill or die by suffocating in a liquid. **2** (*tr*; **with**, **in**) to apply an excessive amount of liquid to; to soak or flood. **3** (*tr*; **out**) to block out (esp. one sound with a louder one). — **drown one's sorrows** (*coll*) to get drunk in order to forget one's troubles. [MidE *drounen*]

drowse *v* (*intr*) to sleep lightly for a short while; to be in a pleasantly sleepy state. [OE *drusian*, to be sluggish]

drowsy *adj* **-ier**, **-iest** **1** sleepy; causing sleepiness. **2** lethargic. **3** quiet and peaceful. — *adv* **drowsily**. — *n* **drowsiness**.

drub *v* ***-bb-*** (*tr*) **1** to defeat severely. **2** to beat (as if) with a stick. — *n* **drubbing**. [Arabic *daraba*, to beat]

drudge *v* (*intr*) to do hard, boring, or menial work. — *n* a servant; a labourer. — *n* **drudgery**.

drug *n* **1** any substance used in the treatment of disease. **2** any substance taken (esp. illegally) for its effect on the mind. **3** anything craved for. — *v* ***-gg-*** (*tr*) **1** to make sleepy or unconscious with a drug. **2** to poison (e.g. food) with a drug. — **a drug on the market** a commodity in plentiful supply but not in demand. [OFr *drogue*]

druggist *n* (*US*) a pharmacist.

drugstore *n* (esp. *US*) a chemist's shop, esp. one also selling refreshments.

drugget *n* thick coarse woollen fabric; a protective cover for a floor or carpet made from this. [OFr *droguet*, waste fabric]

druid *n* **1** a member of a Celtic order of priests in N Europe in pre-Christian times. **2** an eisteddfod official. — *adj* **druidic** or **druidical**. [Gaulish *druides*]

drum *n* **1** a percussion instrument consisting of a hollow frame with a skin or other membrane stretched tightly across its opening, sounding when struck. **2** any object (vaguely) resembling this in shape, esp. a cylindrical container. **3** an eardrum. — *v* ***-mm-*** **1** (*intr*) to beat a drum. **2** (*tr* & *intr*) to make continuous tapping or thumping sounds (with). — *n* **drummer**. — *v* **drum in** or **into** (*tr*) to force into the mind through constant repetition. — *v* **drum out** (*tr*; **of**) to expel. — *v* **drum up** (*tr*; *coll*) to attract by energetic persuasion. [Ger *Trommel*, orig. imit.]

drumhead *n* the part of a drum that is struck.

drum major *n* the leader of a marching (esp. military) band.

drum majorette see **majorette**.

drumstick *n* **1** a stick used for beating a drum. **2** the lower leg of a cooked fowl, esp. a chicken.

drunk *v* past participle of **drink**. — *adj* **1** lacking control in movement, speech, etc. through having drunk an excess of alcohol. **2** (**with**) overwhelmed; intoxicated: *drunk with self-pity*. — *n* a drunk person, esp. one regularly drunk.

drunkard *n* a person who is often drunk.

drunken *adj* **1** drunk. **2** relating to, or brought on by, alcoholic intoxication. — *adv* **drunkenly**. — *n* **drunkenness**.

drupe *n* any fruit with a centre stone, soft flesh and an outer covering, e.g. a cherry or peach. [Gr *dryppa*, olive]

dry *adj* **-ier**, **-iest** **1** free from moisture or wetness. **2** with little or no rainfall. **3** from which all the water has evaporated or been taken: *a dry well*. **4** thirsty. **5** (of an animal) no longer producing milk. **6** (of wine, etc.) not sweet. **7** not buttered. **8** (of humour) expressed in a quietly sarcastic or matter-of-fact way. **9** forbidding the sale and consumption of alcohol. **10** (of eyes) without tears. **11** dull; uninteresting. **12** lacking warmth of character. **13** (of a cough) not producing catarrh. — *v* ***-ies***, ***-ied*** **1** (*tr* & *intr*; **off**, **out**, **up**) to make or become dry. **2** to preserve (food) by removing all moisture. — *n* ***-ies*** (*coll*) a staunch right-wing Conservative politician. ◇ See also **wet**. — *adv* **drily**. — *n* **dryness**. — *v* **dry out** (*intr*; *coll*) to receive treatment to cure addiction to alcohol; to have one's addiction cured. — *v* **dry up** (*intr*) **1** (*coll*) (of a speaker) to run out of words; (of an actor) to fail to remember lines while on stage. **2** (*slang*) to shut up or be quiet. [OE *dryge*]

drier or **dryer** *n* a device or substance that dries (hair, paint, etc.).

dry battery *n* a battery consisting of dry cells.

dry cell *n* an electric cell whose conducting substance is a paste, rather than a liquid.

dry-clean *v* (*tr*) to clean (esp. clothes) with liquid chemicals, not with water. — *n* **dry-cleaner**. — *n* **dry-cleaning**.

dry dock *n* a dock from which the water can be pumped out to allow work on a ship's lower parts.

dryer see **drier** above.

dry ice *n* solid carbon dioxide used as a refrigerating agent.

dry land *n* land as opposed to sea or other water.

dry rot *n* wood decay in which the attacking fungus causes brittleness.

dry run *n* a rehearsal or practice.

dry-stone *adj* (of a wall) in which the stones are fixed without mortar.

dryad *n* (*Gr mythol*) a woodland nymph or fairy, often with demigod status. [Gr *dryados*]
DSC *abbrev* Distinguished Service Cross.
DSc *abbrev* Doctor of Science.
DSM *abbrev* Distinguished Service Medal.
DSO *abbrev* Distinguished Service Order.
DSS *abbrev* Department of Social Services.
DTh or **DTheol** *abbrev* Doctor of Theology.
DT's or **dt's** *abbrev* (*coll*) delirium tremens.
dual *adj* **1** consisting of or representing two separate parts. **2** double; twofold. — *n* **duality**. [Lat *duo*, two]
dual carriageway *n* a road on which traffic moving in opposite directions is separated by a central barrier or strip of land.
dualism *n* (*philos*) the belief that reality is made up of two separate parts, one spiritual and one physical, or influenced by two separate forces, one good and one bad.
dub[1] *v* **-bb-** (*tr*) **1** to give a name, esp. a nickname, to. **2** to confer the title of knight on by touching each shoulder with a sword. **3** to smear (leather) with grease. [OE *dubbian*]
dub[2] *v* **-bb-** (*tr*) **1** to add a new soundtrack to (e.g. a film), esp. one in a different language. **2** to add sound effects or music to (e.g. a film). [Contraction of **double**]
dubbin *n* a wax-like mixture of oil and tallow for softening and waterproofing leather. [**dub**[1]]
dubiety *n* (*formal*) dubiousness. [Lat *dubietas*]
dubious *adj* **1** (**about**) feeling doubt; unsure; uncertain. **2** arousing suspicion; potentially dishonest or dishonestly obtained. — *adv* **dubiously**. — *n* **dubiousness**. [Lat *dubium*, doubt]
ducal *adj* relating to a duke. [Lat *ducalis*]
ducat *n* a former European gold or silver coin of varying value. [Lat *ducatus*, duchy]
duchess *n* **1** the wife or widow of a duke. **2** a woman of the same rank as a duke in her own right. [OFr *duchesse*]
duchy *n* **-ies** the territory owned or ruled by a duke or duchess. [OFr *duché*]
duck[1] *n* **1** any of a family of water birds with short legs, webbed feet and a broad flat beak. **2** its flesh used as food. **3** the female of such a bird, as opposed to the male *drake*. **4** (*coll*) a likeable person; a term of endearment or (loosely) of address. **5** (*cricket*) a batsman's score of zero. — **break one's duck** (*coll*) to enjoy one's first success after several failures. — **like water off a duck's back** (*coll*) with no effect at all. [OE *duce*]
duck-billed platypus see **platypus**.
duckboard *n* a narrow board laid across muddy ground to form a path.
duckling *n* a young duck.
ducks and drakes *n* the game of skimming stones across the surface of water. — **play ducks and drakes with** (*coll*) to squander or waste.
duckweed *n* any of a family of plants whose broad flat leaves grow on the surface of water.
ducky (*coll*) *n* **-ies** a term of endearment. — *adj* **-ier**, **-iest** excellent; attractive or pleasing.
duck[2] *v* **1** (*intr*) to lower the head or body suddenly, to avoid notice or a blow. **2** (*tr*) to push briefly under water. **3** (*tr*; *coll*; also **duck out of**) to avoid (e.g. an unpleasant duty). — *n* **ducking**. [MidE *douken*]
ducking-stool *n* (*hist*) a chair on a long wooden pole, used for ducking offenders into water as punishment.
duck[3] *n* hard-wearing cotton fabric, used for tents, sails, etc. [Dut *doek*, linen cloth]
duct *n* **1** any tube in the body carrying liquids, e.g. tears. **2** a pipe or channel carrying liquids, protecting electric cables, etc. [Lat *ducere*, to lead]
ductile *adj* **1** (of metal) able to be stretched or pressed into shape without heating. **2** easily influenced by others. — *n* **ductility**. [Lat *ductilis*, from *ducere*, to lead]
dud (*coll*) *n* **1** a counterfeit article. **2** a bomb or other projectile that fails to go off. **3** any useless or ineffectual person or thing. **4** (in *pl*) clothes. — *adj* **1** useless. **2** counterfeit.
dude *n* (*coll*; *US*) **1** a man. **2** a city man, esp. an Easterner holidaying in the West. **3** a man preoccupied with dressing smartly.
dudgeon: **in high dudgeon** very angry, resentful or indignant.
due *adj* **1** owed; payable. **2** expected according to timetable or pre-arrangement. **3** proper. — *n* **1** what is owed; that which can be rightfully claimed or expected. **2** (in *pl*) subscription fees. — *adv* directly: *due north*. — **due to 1** caused by. **2** because of. — **give someone his** or **her due** to be fair to someone; to speak fairly of. [OFr *deü*, from *devoir*, to owe]
duel *n* **1** a pre-arranged fight to the death between two people, to settle a matter of honour. **2** any serious conflict between two people or groups. — *v* **-ll-** (*intr*) to fight a duel. — *n* **duellist**. [Lat *duellum*, variation of *bellum*, war]
duenna *n* an older woman acting as a chaperone to a girl or young woman (esp. formerly) in Spanish and Portuguese society. [Span *dueña*]
duet *n* a piece of music for two singers or players; a pair of musical performers. — *n* **duettist**. [Ital *duetto*, from Lat *duo*, two]
duff[1] *n* a heavy boiled or steamed pudding, esp. containing fruit. [Form of **dough**]
duff[2] *adj* (*coll*) useless; broken. [Perhaps from **duffer**]
duff[3]: **duff up** *v* (*tr*; *slang*) to beat up. [Perhaps from **duffer**]
duff[4] *v* (*tr*; *coll*) **1** to bungle. **2** to misplay or mishit (a shot, esp. in golf). — *adj* bungled. [**duffer**]
duffel or **duffle** *n* a thick coarse woollen fabric. [Dut, from *Duffel*, Belgian town]
duffel bag *n* a cylindrical canvas shoulder bag with a drawstring fastening.

duffel coat *n* a heavy (esp. hooded) coat made of duffel, typically with toggle fastenings.

duffer *n* (*coll*) a clumsy or incompetent person.

dug[1] past tense of **dig**.

dugout *n* **1** a canoe made from a hollowed-out log. **2** a soldier's rough shelter dug into a slope or bank or in a trench. **3** a covered shelter at the side of a sports field, for the trainer, substitutes, etc.

dug[2] *n* **1** an animal's udder or nipple. **2** (*vulg slang*) a woman's breast.

dugong *n* a whale-like plant-eating tropical sea mammal. [Malay *duyong*]

duke *n* **1** a nobleman of the highest rank outside the royal family. **2** the ruler of a small state or principality. **3** (*old slang*) a fist. — *n* **dukedom**. [Lat *dux*, leader]

dulcet *adj* (*literary*) (of sounds) sweet and pleasing to the ear. [Lat *dulcis*, sweet]

dulcimer *n* a musical instrument consisting of a flattish box with tuned strings stretched across, struck with small hammers. [Lat *dulce melos*, sweet song]

dull *adj* **1** (of colour or light) lacking brightness or clearness. **2** (of sounds) deep and low; muffled. **3** (of weather) cloudy; overcast. **4** (of pain) not sharp. **5** (of a person) slow to learn or understand. **6** uninteresting; lacking liveliness. **7** (of a blade) blunt. — *v* (*tr* & *intr*) to make or become dull. — *n* **dullness**. — *adv* **dully**. [OE *dol*, stupid]

dullard *n* (*old*) a dull person.

dulse *n* an edible red seaweed. [Gaelic *duileasg*]

duly *adv* **1** in the proper way. **2** at the proper time. **[due]**

dumb *adj* **1** not having the power of speech; (of animals) not having human speech. **2** temporarily deprived of the power of speech, e.g. by shock. **3** silent; not expressed in words. **4** (*coll*; esp. *US*) foolish; unintelligent. **5** performed without words: *dumb show*. — *adv* **dumbly**. — *n* **dumbness**. [OE]

dumbbell *n* **1** a weight used in pairs in muscle-developing exercises, consisting of a short metal bar with a heavy ball or disc on each end. **2** (*coll*; esp *US*) a stupid person.

dumbfound or **dumfound** *v* (*tr*) to astonish (into silence).

dumbstruck *adj* silent with astonishment or shock.

dumbwaiter *n* **1** a small lift for transporting laundry, dirty dishes, etc. between floors in a restaurant or hotel. **2** a movable shelved stand for food, placed near a table. **3** a revolving food tray set in the middle of a table.

dumbo *n* **-os** (*coll*) a stupid person. **[dumb]**

dumdum *n* a bullet that expands on impact, causing severe injury. [*Dum-Dum*, arsenal near Calcutta, India]

dumfound. See **dumbfound**.

dummy *n* **-ies 1** a life-size model of the human body, e.g. used for displaying clothes. **2** a realistic copy, esp. one misleadingly substituted for the genuine article. **3** (also **dummy tit**) a baby's rubber teat sucked for comfort. **4** (*coll*; esp. *US*) a stupid person. **5** (*sport*) an act of dummying with the ball. **6** a person or company acting seemingly independently, but really the agent of another. — *adj* false; sham; counterfeit. — *v* **-ies**, **-ied** (*tr* & *intr*; *sport*) to make as if to move one way before sharply moving the other, in order to deceive (an opponent). **[dumb]**

dummy run *n* a practice; a try-out.

dump *v* **1** (*tr*) to put down heavily or carelessly. **2** (*tr* & *intr*) to dispose of (rubbish), esp. improperly. **3** (*tr*; *coll*) to break off a romantic relationship with. **4** (*tr*; *econ*) to sell (goods unsaleable domestically) abroad at a much reduced price, usu. to keep the domestic price high. **5** (*tr*) to transfer (data from a computer's memory) to a disk or printed page. — *n* **1** a place where rubbish may be dumped. **2** a military store, e.g. of weapons or food. **3** (*coll*) a dirty or dilapidated place. [MidE]

dumpling *n* **1** a baked or boiled ball of dough served with meat. **2** a rich fruit pudding. **3** (*coll*) a plump person. [Obsolete *dump*, lump]

dumps: **down in the dumps** (*coll*) in low spirits; depressed. [Perhaps Ger *dumpf*, gloomy]

dumpy *adj* **-ier**, **-iest** short and plump. — *n* **dumpiness**. [Perhaps **dumpling**]

dun[1] *n* **1** a dark greyish brown colour. **2** a horse of this colour. [OE]

dun[2] *v* **-nn-** (*tr*) to press persistently for payment. — *n* a demand for payment.

dunce *n* a stupid person; a slow learner. [*Dunses*, followers of J *Duns* Scotus, 13th-century educationalist opposed to classical studies]

dunderhead *n* a stupid person. — *adj* **dunderheaded**.

dune *n* a low ridge of sand on a seashore or in a desert. [ODut *duna*]

dung *n* animal excrement. [OE]

dung-beetle *n* any of a number of beetles, including the scarab, which feed or breed in dung.

dungarees *n* (*pl*) loose trousers with a bib and shoulder straps attached, worn as casual wear or overalls. [Hindi *dungri*]

dungeon *n* a prison cell, esp. underground. [OFr *donjon*]

dunk *v* (*tr*) **1** to dip (e.g. a biscuit) into tea or a similar beverage. **2** to submerge. [OGer *dunkon*]

duo *n* **-os 1** a pair of musicians or other performers. **2** any two people considered a pair. [Lat, two]

duodecimal *adj* relating to the number twelve, or multiples of it; twelfth. [Lat *duodecim*, twelve]

duodenum *n* ***-na*** or ***-nums*** the first portion of the small intestine. — *adj* **duodenal**. [Lat, from *duodecim*, twelve, the portion being twelve fingers' breadth in length]

duologue *n* **1** a dialogue between two actors. **2** a play for two actors. [Lat *duo*, two + Gr *logos*, discourse]

dupe *v* (*tr*) to trick or deceive. — *n* a person who is deceived. [Fr]

duple *adj* **1** double; twofold. **2** (*mus*) having two beats in the bar. [Lat *duplus*]

duplex *n* **1** a flat on two floors. **2** a semi-detached house. — *adj* **1** double; twofold. **2** (of a computer circuit) allowing transmission of signals in both directions simultaneously. [Lat]

duplicate *adj* identical to another. — *n* **1** an exact (esp. printed) copy. **2** another of the same kind; a subsidiary or spare. — *v* (*tr*) **1** to make or be an exact copy or copies of. **2** to repeat. — *n* **duplication**. — *n* **duplicator**. — **in duplicate** in the form of two exact copies. [Lat *duplicare*, to fold in two]

duplicity *n* (*formal*) deception; trickery; double-dealing. — *adj* **duplicitous**. [Lat *duplicis*, double]

Dur. *abbrev* Durham.

durable *adj* **1** lasting a long time without breaking; sturdy. **2** long-lasting; enduring. — *n* a durable item, esp. one not frequently replaced. — *n* **durability**. — *adv* **durably**. [Lat *durare*, to last]

dura mater *n* (*anat*) the outer membrane of the brain and spinal column. ◇ See also **arachnoid**, **pia mater**. [Lat, hard mother]

duration *n* the length of time that something lasts or continues. [Lat *durare*, to last]

duress *n* the influence of force or threats; coercion. [Lat *duritia*, hardness]

during *prep* **1** throughout the time of. **2** in the course of. [Obsolete *dure*, to last, from Lat *durare*]

dusk *n* twilight, (the period of) half darkness before night. [OE *dox*, dark]

dusky *adj* ***-ier***, ***-iest*** **1** dark; shadowy. **2** dark-coloured; dark-skinned. — *n* **duskiness**.

dust *n* **1** earth, sand, or household dirt in the form of a fine powder. **2** a cloud of this. **3** any substance in powder form. **4** (*coll*) an angry complaint; a commotion: *kick up a dust*. **5** (*poetic*) human remains; a dead body. — *v* **1** (*tr & intr*) to remove dust from (furniture, etc.). **2** (*tr*) to sprinkle with a substance in powder form. — **let the dust settle** (*coll*) to wait until calm is restored (before acting). — **throw dust in someone's eyes** (*coll*) to deceive someone. [OE]

dustbin *n* a large (usu. cylindrical) lidded container for household rubbish, esp. one kept outside.

dustbowl *n* an exceptionally dry area prone to dust-storms.

dustcart *n* a vehicle in which household rubbish is collected.

dust cover *n* **1** a dust jacket. **2** a dust sheet.

duster *n* **1** a cloth for removing household dust. **2** a machine for spraying crops with fertiliser or other preparations.

dust jacket *n* a loose protective paper cover on a book, carrying the title and other information.

dustman *n* a person employed to collect household rubbish.

dustpan *n* a handled container into which dust is swept, like a flattish open-ended box with a shovel edge.

dust sheet *n* a cloth sheet used to protect unused furniture from dust.

dust-storm *n* a whirling mass of dust blown up by severe winds.

dust-up *n* (*coll*) an argument or fight.

dusty *adj* ***-ier***, ***-iest*** **1** covered with, or containing, dust. **2** (of a colour) dull. **3** old-fashioned; dated. **4** lacking liveliness; flat. **5** impolitely blunt. — *adv* **dustily**. — *n* **dustiness**.

Dutch *n* **1** the language of the Netherlands. **2** (with **the**) the people of the Netherlands. — *adj* of the Netherlands, its people or their language. — **go Dutch** (*coll*) to each pay his or her own share. [ODut *dutsch*]

Dutch auction *n* an auction at which the price is gradually lowered until someone agrees to buy.

Dutch barn *n* an open-sided barn with a curved roof.

Dutch cap *n* a cap (sense **10**)

Dutch courage *n* artificial courage gained by drinking alcohol.

Dutch elm disease *n* a fungal disease of elm trees.

Dutchman and **Dutchwoman** *n* a citizen of, or person from, the Netherlands.

Dutch oven *n* **1** an open-fronted metal box for cooking food in front of a fire. **2** a lidded earthenware or iron stewpot or casserole.

Dutch treat *n* an amusement where each person pays for himself or herself.

Dutch uncle *n* a person who openly criticises or reprimands where appropriate, without sparing one's feelings.

duteous *adj* (*literary*) dutiful. [**duty** + **-ous**]

dutiable *adj* (of goods) on which duty is payable. [**duty** + **-able**]

dutiful *adj* having or showing a sense of duty. — *adv* **dutifully**. [**duty** + **-ful**]

duty *n* ***-ties*** **1** something one is or feels obliged to do; a moral or legal responsibility, or the awareness of it. **2** a task to be performed, esp. in connection with a job. **3** tax on goods, esp. imports. **4** respect for elders or seniors. — **do duty for** to serve as; to act as a substitute for. — **on** or **off duty** working, or not working; liable or not liable to be called upon to go into action. [OFr *dueté*]

duty-bound *adj* obliged by one's sense of duty.

duty-free *adj* (of goods, esp. imports) non-taxable. — *n* (*coll*) a duty-free shop.

duty-free shop *n* a shop, esp. at an airport, where duty-free goods are sold.

duvet *n* a thick quilt filled with feathers or man-made fibres, for use on a bed instead of a sheet and blankets. [Fr]

dwarf *n* **-*fs*** or **-*ves*** **1** an unusually small person, esp. one with limbs out of proportion to the head. **2** an animal or plant (bred to be) much smaller than others of the species. **3** a mythical man-like creature with magic powers. — *v* (*tr*) **1** to cause to seem small or unimportant. **2** to stunt the growth of. — *adj* **dwarfish**. [OE *dweorg*]

dwell *v* ***dwelt*** or ***dwelled*** (*intr; formal* or *literary*) to reside. — *n* **dweller**. — **dwell on** or **upon** *v* (*tr*) to think or speak about at length. [OE *dwellan*, to delay or tarry]

dwelling *n* (*formal* or *literary*) a place of residence; a house.

dwindle *v* (*intr*) to shrink in size, number or intensity. [OE *dwinan*, to fade]

Dy *symbol* (*chem*) dysprosium.

dye *v* ***dyeing*** (*tr* & *intr*) to colour or stain permanently. — *n* **1** any colouring substance. **2** the colour produced by dyeing. — *n* **dyer**. [OE *deagian*]

dyed-in-the-wool *adj* of firmly fixed opinions; out-and-out.

dying *v* present participle of **die**[1]. — *adj* **1** expressed immediately before death. **2** final: *dying seconds of the match*.

dyke[1] *n* **1** a wall or earth embankment built to prevent flooding. **2** a channel dug to drain off water; a ditch. **3** (*Scot*) a wall, e.g. surrounding a field. — *v* (*tr*) to protect or drain with a dyke. [OE *dic*, ditch]

dyke[2] *n* (*offensive slang*) a lesbian.

dynamic *adj* **1** full of energy, enthusiasm, and new ideas. **2** relating to dynamics. — *adv* **dynamically**. [Gr *dynamis*, power]

dynamics *n* **1** (*sing*) the branch of physics dealing with motion and the forces causing it. **2** (*pl*) (the forces causing) movement or change in any sphere: *political dynamics*.

dynamism *n* limitless energy and enthusiasm.

dynamite *n* **1** an explosive consisting of an absorbent substance, e.g. porous silica, soaked in nitroglycerine, used in mining, etc. **2** (*coll*) a thrilling or dangerous person or thing. — *v* (*tr*) to blow up with dynamite. [Gr *dynamis*, power]

dynamo *n* **-*os*** a device that converts mechanical movement into electrical energy, esp. using magnets. **2** (*coll*) a tirelessly active person. [Gr *dynamis*, power]

dynamometer *n* an instrument for measuring mechanical power.

dynasty *n* **-*ies*** **1** a succession of rulers from the same family; their period of rule. **2** a succession of members of a powerful family or other connected group. — *adj* **dynastic**. [Gr *dynasteia*, power, dominion]

dyne *n* a unit of force, producing an acceleration of one centimetre per second per second on a mass of one gram. [Gr *dynamis*, force]

dysentery *n* any infection of the intestines causing severe diarrhoea, usu. mingled with blood and mucus. [Gr *dysenteria*, bad bowels]

dyslexia *n* abnormal difficulty in reading and spelling, unrelated to intelligence. — *adj* & *n* **dyslexic**. [Gr *dys-*, amiss + *lexis*, word]

dyspepsia *n* (*med*) indigestion. [Gr *dys-*, amiss + *pepsis*, digestion]

dyspeptic *adj* **1** suffering from dyspepsia. **2** (*coll*) bad-tempered; liverish.

dysprosium *n* an element (*symbol* **Dy**), a soft silvery-white metal used in the nuclear industry. [Gr *dysprositos*, difficult to reach]

dystrophy. See **muscular dystrophy**.

E

E[1] or **e** *n* ***Es*** or ***E's, e's*** **1** the fifth letter of the English alphabet. **2** (usu. **E**) (a mark indicating) the fifth highest grade or quality. **3** (only **E**; *mus*) the third note in the scale of C major. **4** (only **E**) a musical key with the note E as its base.

E[2] *abbrev* **1** East. **2** (*physics*) electromotive force. **3** (also **e**) electronic: *E-mail* (see **electronic mail** under **electronic**). **4** (*physics*) energy. **5** European: *E-number*. **6** Ecstasy.

E-number *n* any of several identification codes for food additives, consisting of the letter E followed by a number, required by EC law to be displayed on food packaging.

e[1] *abbrev*. See **E**[2] (sense **3**).

e[2] *symbol* used with a number to mark any of several standard sizes of pack as set out in EC law.

each *adj* every one of two or more (people, animals or things) considered separately. — *pron* every single one of two or more people, animals or things. — *adv* to, for or from each one: *give them one each*. — **each other** used as the object of a verb or preposition when an action takes place between two (or more than two) people, etc.: *They were talking to each other*. ◇ See also **one another**. — **each way** (of a bet) winning if the horse, dog, etc. on which the bet is risked finishes first, second or third in a race. [OE *ælc*]

eager *adj* (**for**) feeling or showing great desire or enthusiasm; keen (to do or get). — *adv* **eagerly**. — *n* **eagerness**. [OFr *aigre*]

eager beaver *n* (*coll*) a person who is exceptionally enthusiastic or willing.

eagle *n* **1** any of various kinds of large birds of prey. **2** a figure of an eagle, used as a national emblem by various countries. **3** (*golf*) a score of two under par. [OFr *aigle*, from Lat *aquila*]

bald eagle a kind of eagle with a white head, the US national emblem.

eagle eye *n* **1** exceptionally good eyesight. **2** careful supervision, with an ability to notice small details. — *adj* **eagle-eyed**.

eaglet *n* a young eagle.

EAK *abbrev* (on vehicles) Kenya (i.e. East Africa Kenya).

ear[1] *n* **1** one of the two parts of the head by means of which we hear. **2** the external part of the ear. **3** the sense or power of hearing, esp. the ability to hear the difference between sounds. **4** anything like an ear in shape or position. **5** (*formal* or *literary*) attention; the act of listening: *lend an ear*; *give ear to*. — **be all ears** (*coll*) to listen attentively or with great interest. — **have someone's ear** to have someone willing to listen or pay attention. — **have one's ear to the ground** to keep oneself well informed about what is happening around one. — **in one ear and out the other** (*coll*) listened to but immediately disregarded. — **make someone's ears burn** to talk (esp. unpleasantly) about someone in his or her absence. — **out on one's ear** (*coll*) dismissed swiftly and without politeness. — **play by ear 1** to play without the help of printed music. **2** (*coll*; usu. with **it**) to act without a fixed plan, according to the situation that arises. — **up to one's ears in** (*coll*) deeply involved in or occupied with. [OE *eare*]

earache *n* pain in the inner part of the ear.

eardrum *n* the small thin membrane inside the ear, which transmits vibrations made by sound waves to the inner ear.

earful *n* (*coll*; ***-fuls***; not usu. in *pl*) a long complaint or telling-off.

earlobe *n* the soft, loosely hanging piece of flesh which forms the lower part of the ear.

earmark *v* (*tr*) to set aside or intend (for a particular purpose).

earmuffs *n* (*pl*) coverings worn over the ears to protect them from cold or noise.

earphones. Same as **headphones**.

earpiece *n* the part of a telephone or hearing-aid which is placed at or in the ear.

ear-piercing *adj* (of a noise) loud and sharp. — *n* the piercing of the earlobe for the purpose of inserting an earring.

earplug *n* a piece of wax, rubber, etc. placed in the ear as a protection against noise, cold or water.

earring *n* a piece of jewellery worn attached to the ear, esp. to the earlobe.

earshot *n* the distance at which sound can be heard: *out of earshot*; *within earshot*.

ear-splitting *adj* (of a noise) extremely loud.

ear-trumpet *n* an old-fashioned hearing-aid consisting of a small trumpet held up to the ear.

ear[2] *n* the part of a cereal plant, such as wheat, that contains the seeds. [OE]

earl *n* a male member of the British nobility ranking below a marquess and above a viscount. — *n* **earldom**. ◇ See also **countess**. [OE *eorl*]

earlobe. See **ear**[1].

early *adv* & *adj* ***-ier***, ***-iest*** **1** (happening, existing, etc.) near the beginning of a period of time, period of development, etc. ◇ See also **early on** below. **2** (happening, arriving, etc.) sooner than others, sooner than usual, or sooner than expected or intended. **3** (happening, etc.) in the near future. **4** (happening, etc.) in the far-off past. — *n* **earliness**. — **at the earliest** not before, and probably later than. — **early on** at or near the beginning of a

period of time, etc. — **it's early days** (*coll*) it is too soon to be able to judge the outcome or expect a result. [OE *ærlice*]
early bird *n* (*coll*) **1** a person who gets out of bed early. **2** a person who arrives early.
early warning system *n* a radar system designed to give the earliest possible warning of attack from enemy aircraft or missiles.
earmark, earmuffs. See **ear**[1].
earn *v* **1** (*tr & intr*) to gain (money, wages, one's living) by working. **2** (*tr*) to gain. **3** (*tr*) to deserve. ◇ See also **well-earned**. [OE *earnian*]
earner *n* **1** a person who earns. **2** (*slang*) an easy and sometimes dishonest way of making money.
earnings *n* (*pl*) money earned.
earnest[1] *adj* **1** (sometimes *derog*) serious or over-serious. **2** showing determination, sincerity or strong feeling. — *adv* **earnestly**. — *n* **earnestness**. — **in earnest** serious or seriously. [OE *eornust*]
earnest[2] *n* (*literary* or *old*) **1** a part payment made in advance, esp. to confirm an agreement. **2** a sign or foretaste of what is to come. [MidE *ernes*, from OFr *erres*, pledges]
earpiece, earplug, earring, earshot. See **ear**[1].
earth *n* **1** (often *cap*; often with **the**) the planet on which we live, the third planet in order of distance from the Sun. **2** the world as opposed to heaven or hell. **3** the land and sea as opposed to the sky. **4** dry land; the land surface; the ground. **5** soil. **6** a hole in which an animal, esp. a badger or fox, lives. **7** (a wire that provides) an electrical connection with the ground. — v **1** (*tr & intr*; *elect*) to connect to the ground. **2** (*tr* with **up**) to heap soil around the lower part of (a plant), e.g. as a protection against frost. — **come back** or **down to earth** to become aware of the realities of life (again). — **cost the earth** (*coll*) to be extremely expensive.— **go to earth** (of an animal) to go into its hole or hiding-place. — **on earth** used for emphasis: *What on earth is that?* — **run to earth 1** to chase or hunt (an animal) to its hole or hiding-place. **2** to find after a long search. [OE *eorthe*]
earthbound *adj* **1** attached to the earth. **2** (of a spacecraft, etc.) moving towards the earth. **3** (sometimes *derog*) unable to think beyond what is known or familiar; lacking imagination.
earthen *adj* **1** (of a floor, etc.) made of earth. **2** (of a pot, etc.) made of baked clay.
earthenware *n* pottery made of a kind of baked clay which is rather coarse to the touch.
earthling *n* in science fiction, a native of the Earth.
earthly *adj* **1** (*literary*) of or belonging to this world; not spiritual. **2** (*coll*) used for emphasis: *have no earthly chance*. — **not have an earthly** (*coll*) **1** not to have the slightest chance of success. **2** not to have the faintest idea. ◇ See also **unearthly**.
earthquake *n* a shaking of the earth's surface caused by movements in the earth's crust.
earth science *n* any of the sciences broadly concerned with the earth, e.g. geology, meteorology.
earth-shattering or **earth-shaking** *adj* (*coll*) of great importance. — *adv* **earth-shatteringly** or **earth-shakingly**.
earth tremor *n* a slight earthquake.
earthwork *n* (*tech*; often in *pl*) a man-made bank of earth, used formerly as a fortification, or as a foundation in modern road-building.
earthworm *n* the common worm.
earthy *adj* **-ier**, **-iest 1** of or like earth or soil. **2** coarse or crude; lacking politeness. — *adv* **earthily**. — *n* **earthiness**.
earwig *n* an insect with pincers at the end of its body, once thought to crawl into a person's head through the ear. [OE *eare*, ear + *wicga*, insect]
ease *n* **1** freedom from pain or anxiety. **2** absence of difficulty. **3** freedom from embarrassment. **4** absence of restriction. — *v* **1** (*tr*) to free from pain, trouble or anxiety. **2** (*tr & intr*; **off, up**) to make or become less strong, less tight, less tense, etc. **3** (*tr*; **in, off**, etc.) to move (something heavy or awkward) gently or gradually in or out of position. — **at ease 1** relaxed; free from anxiety or embarrassment. **2** (*mil*; often in imperative) (standing) with legs apart and hands clasped behind the back. — **ill at ease** anxious or embarrassed. — **take one's ease** (*formal* or *facet*) to relax; to make oneself comfortable. [OFr *aise*]
easel *n* a stand for supporting a blackboard, an artist's canvas, etc. [Dut *ezel*, ass]
east *n* (sometimes *cap*; often with **the**) the direction from which the sun rises, or any part of the earth, a country, a town, etc. lying in that direction. ◇ See also **the East** below. — *adj* **1** in the east; on the side which is on or nearest the east. **2** coming from the direction of the east: *an east wind*. — *adv* towards the east. — **the East 1** the countries of Asia, east of Europe. ◇ See also **Far East, Middle East**. **2** (*politics*) the former USSR and the communist countries of eastern Europe. [OE]
eastbound *adj* going or leading towards the east.
East End *n* in the UK, the eastern part of a town or city (esp. London). — *n* **Eastender**.
easterly *adj* **1** (of a wind, etc.) coming from the east. **2** looking, lying, etc. towards the east. — *adv* to or towards the east. — *n* **-ies** an easterly wind.
eastern *adj* of the east or the East.
easterner *n* a person who lives in or comes from the east, esp. the eastern US.
easternmost *adj* situated furthest east.

eastward *adv* (also **eastwards**) & *adj* towards the east.

Easter *n* **1** a Christian religious festival, held on the Sunday after the first full moon in spring, celebrating the resurrection of Christ. **2** the period during which the festival takes place, thought of as running from Good Friday (the Friday before Easter Sunday) to the following Monday (Easter Monday). [OE *eastre*, perhaps from *Eostre*, a goddess associated with spring]

Easter Day *n* Easter Sunday

Easter egg *n* an egg, traditionally a painted hard-boiled egg, but now more commonly a chocolate egg, given as a present at Easter.

easy *adj* **-ier**, **-iest** **1** not difficult. **2** free from pain, trouble, anxiety, etc. **3** not stiff or formal; friendly. **4** not tense or strained; leisurely. **5** (*coll*) having no strong preference. — *adv* (*coll*) in a slow, calm or relaxed way: *take it easy*. — *n* **easiness**. — **easy does it!** be careful!; (in the performing of a physical task) don't strain yourself! — **easy on the eye** or **ear** pleasant to look at or listen to. — **go easy** (**with, on**) **1** to use, take, etc. not too much of: *Go easy on the wine*. **2** to handle, deal with, etc. gently or calmly. — **stand easy** (*mil*; often in *imperative*) to stand less stiffly than standing at ease. [OFr *aisie*, from *aisier*, to ease]

easily *adv* **1** without difficulty. **2** clearly; beyond doubt; by far. **3** very probably.

easy chair *n* a soft, comfortable chair, usu. with arms.

easy-going *adj* not strict; relaxed; tolerant.

easy street *n* (*coll*) a situation of comfort and financial well-being.

easy terms *n* (*pl*) payment in instalments rather than all at once.

eat *v* **ate**, **eaten** **1** (*tr* & *intr*) to bite, chew and swallow (food). **2** (*intr*) to take in food. **3** (*tr*) to take in as food. **4** (*tr* with **away**, **into**) to destroy the material, substance, form, etc. of, esp. by chemical action. **5** (*tr* with **into, through**) to use up gradually. **6** (*tr* & *intr* with **up**) to finish (one's food). **7** (*tr*; **up**; usu. in *passive*) (usu. of a bad feeling) to affect greatly, be felt intensely: *be eaten up with/by jealousy*. **8** (*tr*; *coll*) to trouble or worry: *What's eating you?* — **eat one's heart out** to suffer, esp. in silence, from some longing or anxiety, or from envy. — **eat humble pie** to lower oneself or lose dignity, e.g. by admitting a mistake. — *v* **eat in** (*intr*) to eat at home rather than in a restaurant. — *v* **eat out** (*intr*) to eat at a restaurant rather than at home. — **eat out of someone's hand** (*coll*) to be very willing to follow, obey or agree with someone. — **eat one's words** to suffer the humiliation of admitting one was wrong. [OE *etan*]

eatable *adj* fit to be eaten. — *n* (usu. in *pl*) an item of food. ◇ See also **edible.**

eater *n* **1** a person who eats: *a noisy eater*. **2** an eating apple, or any other fruit meant to be eaten raw.

eatery *n* **-ies** (*coll*) a small restaurant.

eating apple *n* an apple for eating raw.

eats *n* (*pl*; *coll*) food.

eau-de-cologne or **cologne** *n* a mild type of perfume, orig. made in Cologne in Germany. [Fr, water of Cologne]

eaves *n* (*pl*) the part of a roof that sticks out beyond the wall, or the underside of it. [OE *efes*, the clipped edge of thatch]

eavesdrop *v* **-pp-** (*intr*; **on**) to listen secretly to a private conversation. — *n* **eavesdropper**. — *n* **eavesdropping**. [OE *yfæsdrypæ*, eavesdropper, a person who stands under the eaves to listen to conversations]

ebb *v* (*intr*) **1** (of the tide) to move back from the land. **2** (**away**) to grow smaller or weaker. — *n* **1** the movement of the tide away from the land. **2** a growing smaller or weaker: *His health is on the ebb*. — **at a low ebb** in a poor or weak state (mentally or physically). [OE *ebba*]

ebony *n* **1** a type of hard, almost black wood. **2** the tropical tree from which it is obtained. — *adj* **1** made from this wood. **2** (*literary*) black. [Lat *ebeninus*]

ebullient *adj* (*formal*) very high-spirited; full of cheerfulness or enthusiasm. — *n* **ebullience** or **ebulliency**. — *adv* **ebulliently**. [Lat *ebullire*, to boil out]

EC *abbrev* **1** European Commission. **2** European Community.

eccentric *adj* **1** (of a person, behaviour, etc.) odd; unusual. **2** (*tech*) (of a wheel, etc.) not having the axis at the centre. **3** (*geom*) (of circles) not having a common centre; not concentric. **4** (of an orbit) not circular. — *n* **1** an eccentric person. **2** (*tech*) a device for converting rotating motion into motion backwards and forwards. — *adv* **eccentrically**. — *n* **eccentricity**, **-ies**. [Lat *eccentricus*, from Gr *ek*, out of + *kentros*, centre]

ecclesiastic *n* (*formal*) a clergyman. [Lat *ecclesiasticus*, from Gr *ekklesia*, church]

ecclesiastic or **ecclesiastical** *adj* of or relating to the church or the clergy. — *adv* **ecclesiastically**.

ECG *abbrev* electrocardiogram or electrocardiograph (see under **electro-**).

echelon *n* **1** (*formal*) a level or rank in an organisation, etc., or the people at that level. **2** (*tech*) a roughly V-shaped formation, used by ships, planes, birds in flight, etc. in which each member is in a position slightly to the outside of the one in front. [Fr *échelon*, from *échelle*, ladder]

echidna *n* the spiny anteater, an egg-laying mammal of Australia and New Guinea, with a long snout and long claws. [Gr, viper]

echinoderm *n* any sea animal of the family to which starfish and sea urchins belong. [Gr *echinos*, hedgehog, sea urchin + *derma*, skin]

echo *n* **-oes 1** the repeating of a sound caused by the sound waves striking a surface and coming back. **2** a sound repeated in this way. **3** (often *facet*) a person who imitates or repeats what others say or think. **4** an imitation or repetition (sometimes accidental). **5** (often in *pl*) a trace; something which brings to mind memories or thoughts of something else. **6** a reflected radio or radar beam, or the visual signal it produces on a screen. — *v* **-oes, -oed 1** (*intr*; **with, to**) to sound loudly with an echo. **2** (*tr*) to send back an echo of. **3** (*tr*) to repeat (a sound or a statement). **4** (*tr*) to imitate or in some way be similar to. [Gr, sound]

echoic *adj* **1** (*formal*) (of a sound) of or like an echo. **2** (of a word) imitating the sound it represents; onomatopoeic: *'Bump' is an echoic word.*

echo-sounding *n* a method used at sea, etc. for testing depth of water, by measuring the time taken for a signal sent out from the ship, etc. to return as an echo. — *n* **echo-sounder**.

éclair *n* a long cake of light pastry, with a cream filling and usu. chocolate (or sometimes coffee) icing. [Fr, flash of lightning, perhaps because it does not last very long]

éclat *n* (*formal* or *literary*) **1** striking effect. **2** splendid success. **3** applause; praise. [Fr]

eclectic *adj* (of a style of writing or art, or a set of beliefs) selecting material or ideas from a wide range of sources or authorities. — *adv* **eclectically**. — *n* **eclecticism**. [Gr *ek*, from + *legein*, to choose]

eclipse *n* **1** the total or partial obscuring of one planet or heavenly body by another, e.g. of the sun when the moon comes between it and the earth (a **solar eclipse**), or of the moon when the earth's shadow falls across it (a **lunar eclipse**). **2** a loss of fame or importance. — *v* (*tr*) **1** to cause an eclipse of. **2** to surpass or outshine. [Gr *ekleipsis*, failure to appear]

ecliptic *n* (with **the**) the course which the sun seems to follow in relation to the stars. — *adj* of or relating to an eclipse or the ecliptic.

eco- *comb fm* concerned with living things in relation to their environment, as in **ecology**. [Gr *oikos*, house]

eco-friendly *adj* not harmful to the environment. [**eco-**]

ecology *n* (the study of) the relationship between living things and their surroundings. — *adj* **ecological**. — *adv* **ecologically**. — *n* **ecologist**. [Gr *oikos*, house + *logos*, discourse]

econ. *abbrev* economic, economics or economy.

economic *adj* **1** of or concerned with the economy of a nation, etc. **2** (of a business practice, etc.) likely to bring a profit. **3** of economics. [**economy**]

economical *adj* not wasting money or resources. — *adv* **economically**.

economics *n* (*sing*) **1** the study of the production, distribution and consumption of money, goods and services. **2** financial aspects: *the economics of the situation.* ◇ See also **home economics.**

economise or **-ize** *v* (*intr*; **on**) to cut down on spending or waste. — *n* **economisation** or **-z-**.

economist *n* an expert in economics.

economy *n* **-ies 1** the organisation of money and resources within a nation, etc., esp. in terms of the production, distribution and consumption of goods and services. **2** a system in which these are organised in a particular way: *a socialist economy*. **3** careful management of money or other resources, avoiding waste and cutting down on spending. **4** (usu. in *pl*) an instance of economising; a saving. **5** efficient or sparing use: *economy of movement*. — *adj* **1** (of a class of travel, esp. air travel) of the cheapest kind. **2** (also **economy-size** or **economy-sized**) (of a packet of food, etc.) larger than the standard or basic size, and proportionally cheaper. [Gr *oikos*, house + *nomos*, law]

ecosphere *n* (*tech*) the parts of the universe, esp. of the earth, in which living things can exist. [**eco-**]

ecosystem *n* a community of living things and their relationships to their surroundings. [**eco-**]

ecstasy *n* **-ies 1** a feeling of immense joy. **2** (*psychol*) a trance-like state or any similar state. **3** (*slang*; often *cap*; also **Ecstasy**) a powerful hallucinatory drug, methylenedioxymethamphetamine. [Fr *extasie*, from Gr *ekstasis*, standing outside oneself]

ecstatic *adj* **1** of, showing, or causing ecstasy. **2** (*coll*) very happy or pleased. — *adv* **ecstatically**.

ECT *abbrev* electro-convulsive therapy (see under **electro-**).

ecto- *comb fm* outside. ◇ See also **endo-**, **ento-** and **exo-**. [Gr *ektos*, outside]

ectoplasm *n* **1** (*biol*) the outer layer of a cell's protoplasm, the material which makes up the living part. **2** the substance thought by some people to be given off by the body of a spiritualistic medium during a trance. [**ecto-** + Gr *plasma*, something moulded]

-ectomy *comb fm* **-ies** (*med*) removal by surgery: *hysterectomy*. [Gr *ektome*, from *ektemnein*, to cut out]

ecu *n* (also **ECU**) the *E*uropean *c*urrency *u*nit, a trading currency whose value is based on the combined values of several European currencies.

ecumenical *adj* **1** bringing together different branches of the Christian church. **2** working towards the unity of the Christian church. **3** of the whole Christian church: *an ecumenical council*. — *adv* **ecumenically**. — *n* **ecumenicalism** or **ecumenism**. [Gr *oikoumenikos*, of the inhabited world]

eczema *n* (*med*) a skin disorder in which red blisters form on the skin, usu. causing an itching or burning sensation. [Gr *ekzema*, from *ek*, out of + *zeein*, to boil]
ed. *abbrev* **1** edited. **2** edition. **3** editor. **4** educated. **5** education.
-ed *sfx* used to form past tenses and past participles: *walked*. **2** used to form adjectives from nouns: *bearded*; *bald-headed*.
Edam *n* a type of mild yellow cheese, usu. shaped into balls and covered with red wax. [*Edam*, near Amsterdam, where it was orig. made]
eddy *n* ***-ies*** **1** a current of water running back against the main stream or current, forming a small whirlpool. **2** a movement of air, smoke, fog, etc. similar to this. — *v* ***-ies***, ***-ied*** (*intr* & *tr*) to (cause to) move in this way.
edelweiss *n* ***edelweiss*** a small European mountain plant with white woolly leaves around the flower-heads. [Ger *edel*, noble + *weiss*, white]
Eden *n* **1** (also **Garden of Eden**) the garden where, according to the Bible, the first man and woman lived after being created. **2** a beautiful region; a place of delight. [Hebr *eden*, delight, pleasure]
edentate (*biol*) *adj* having few or no teeth. — *n* an edentate animal. [Lat *edentatus*, toothless]
edge *n* **1** the part farthest from the middle of something; a border or boundary. **2** the area beside a cliff or steep drop. **3** the cutting side of something sharp such as a knife. **4** (*geom*) the meeting point of two surfaces. **5** sharpness or severity: *a cold wind with an edge to it*. **6** bitterness: *There was an edge to his criticism*. — *v* **1** (*tr*; **with**) to form or make a border to. **2** (*tr*) to shape the edge or border of. **3** (*tr* & *intr*; **forward**, **in**, **out**, etc.) to move little by little. **4** (*tr*) to sharpen (a knife, etc.). — **have the edge on** or **over** to have an advantage over. — **on edge** uneasy; nervous; likely to become annoyed. — **take the edge off 1** to make less unpleasant or less difficult. **2** to weaken or diminish. [OE *ecg*]
edgeways or **edgewise** *adv* sideways. — **get a word in edgeways** to manage to add a comment, however brief, in a conversation.
edging *n* a decorative border.
edgy *adj* ***-ier***, ***-iest*** (*coll*) easily annoyed; nervous or tense. — *adv* **edgily**. — *n* **edginess**.
edible *adj* fit to be eaten; suitable to eat. — *n* **edibility**. [Lat *edibilis*]
edict *n* an order issued by a monarch or government. [Lat *edicere*, to proclaim]
edification. See **edify**.
edifice *n* (*formal*) **1** a building, esp. a large impressive one. **2** a large and complex organisation. [Fr *édifice*, from Lat *aedificare*, to build]
edify *v* ***-ies***, ***-ied*** (*tr*; *formal*) to improve the mind or morals of. — *n* **edification**. — *adj* **edifying**. [Fr *édifier*, from Lat *aedificare*, to build]
edit *v* ***-t-*** (*tr*) **1** to prepare (a book, newspaper, programme, film, etc.) for publication or broadcasting, esp. by making corrections or alterations. **2** to be in overall charge of the process of producing (a newspaper, etc.). **3** (with **out**) to remove (parts of a work) before printing, broadcasting, etc. **4** to prepare (a cinema film, or a television or radio programme) by putting together material previously photographed or recorded. **5** to prepare (data) for processing by a computer. — *n* a period or instance of editing. — *adj* **edited**. — *n* **editing**. [Fr *éditer*, from Lat *edere*, to bring forth]
edition *n* **1** a number of copies of a book, etc. printed at one time, or at different times without alteration. **2** the form in which a book, etc. is published: *paperback edition*.
editor *n* **1** a person who edits books, etc. **2** a person who is in charge of a newspaper, magazine or programme, or one section of it. **3** a person who puts together the various sections of a cinema film, etc. — *n* **editorship**.
editorial *adj* of or relating to editors or editing. — *n* an article written by or on behalf of the editor of a newspaper or magazine, usu. one offering an opinion on a current topic. — *adv* **editorially**.
editorialise or **-ize** *v* (*intr*) **1** to write an editorial. **2** (*derog*) in journalism, to introduce personal opinion into what is meant to be factual reporting.
EDP *abbrev* electronic data processing.
educate *v* (*tr*) **1** to train and teach. **2** to provide school instruction for. **3** to train and improve (one's taste, etc.). — *n* **educability**. — *adj* **educable** or **educatable**. — *adj* **educative**. — *n* **educator**. — *adj* **educatory**. [Lat *educare*, to bring up]
educated *adj* **1** having received an education, esp. to a level higher than average. **2** produced by or suggesting a (good) education. **3** based on experience or knowledge: *an educated guess*.
education *n* **1** the process of teaching. **2** the instruction received. **3** the process of training and improving (one's taste, etc.). — *adj* **educational**. — *adv* **educationally**.
educationalist or **educationist** *n* an expert in methods of education.
educe *v* (*tr*; *formal*) to bring out or develop. — *adj* **educible**. — *n* **eduction**. [Lat *e*, out + *ducere*, to lead]
Edwardian *adj* of, or characteristic of, Britain in the years 1901–10, the reign of King *Edward* VII.
-ee *sfx* **1** used to form nouns denoting the person who is the object of the action of the verb: *payee*; *employee*. **2** used to form nouns denoting a person in a stated condition: *absentee*; *escapee*; *refugee*. **3** used to form nouns denoting a person with a stated

association or connection: *bargee*. [Fr *-é* or *-ée*]

EEC *abbrev* European Economic Community, the former name of the European Community.

EEG *abbrev* electroencephalogram or electroencephalograph (see under **electro-**).

eel *n* any of several kinds of fish with a long smooth snake-like body and very small fins. [OE *æl*]

electric eel *n* an eel-like fish, which is able to deliver electric shocks by means of an organ in its tail.

e'en (*archaic* or *poetic*) *adv* even. — *n* evening.

-eer *sfx* **1** used to form nouns denoting a person concerned with or engaged in a stated activity: *auctioneer*; *mountaineer*. **2** used to form verbs denoting actions or behaviour associated with a stated activity: *electioneer*. [Fr *-ier*]

e'er *adv* (*archaic* or *poetic*) ever.

eerie *adj* **-ier**, **-iest** strange and disturbing or frightening. — *adv* **eerily**. — *n* **eeriness**. [Perhaps OE *earg*, cowardly]

efface *v* (*tr*) **1** to rub or wipe out. **2** to block out (a memory, etc.). **3** to avoid drawing attention to (oneself). ◇ See also **self-effacing**. **4** to surpass or outshine. — *n* **effacement**. [Fr *effacer*]

effect *n* **1** a result. **2** an impression given or produced. **3** operation; working state: *come, bring, put into effect*. **4** (*formal*; in *pl*) property. **5** (in *pl*) devices, esp. lighting and sound, used to create a particular impression in a film, on a stage, etc.: *special effects*. — *v* (*tr*; *formal*) to do, cause to happen or bring about. — **for effect** in order to make an impression on others. — **give effect to** (*formal*) to perform or bring into operation. — **in effect** in reality; practically speaking. — **take effect** to begin to work; to come into force. — **to the effect that** (*formal*) with the meaning or result that. — **to good, some, no**, etc. **effect** with much, some, no, etc. success. — **to that effect** (*formal*) with that meaning or intended result. — **with effect (from)** (*formal*) coming into operation or becoming valid (at the time stated): *with immediate effect*. [OFr, from Lat. *effectus*]

effective *adj* **1** having the power to produce, or producing, a desired result. **2** producing a pleasing effect. **3** in, or coming into, operation; working; active. **4** actual, rather than theoretical. — *n* **effectiveness**.

effectively *adv* **1** in an effective way. **2** in reality; for all practical purposes.

effectual *adj* **1** producing the intended result. **2** (of a document, etc.) valid. — *adv* **effectually**. [Lat *effectualis*]

effectuate *v* (*tr*; *formal*) to do; to carry out with success. — *n* **effectuation**. [Lat *effectuare*]

effeminate *adj* (sometimes *derog*) (of a man) having features of behaviour or appearance more typical of a woman. — *n* **effeminacy**. — *adv* **effeminately**. [Lat *effeminare*, to make like a woman]

efferent *adj* (*med*) (of a nerve) carrying impulses out from the brain. ◇ See also **afferent**. [Lat *efferre*, from *e*, from + *ferre*, to carry]

effervesce *v* (*intr*) **1** to give off bubbles of gas. **2** to behave in a lively, energetic way. — *n* **effervescence**. — *adj* **effervescent**. — *adv* **effervescently**. [Lat *effervescere*, to boil up]

effete *adj* (*derog*) **1** (of an institution, an organisation, etc.) lacking its original power or authority. **2** (of a person) lacking strength or energy; made weak by too much protection or refinement. **3** (of plants and animals) no longer able to reproduce. — *n* **effeteness**. [Lat *effetus*, weakened by having given birth]

efficacious *adj* (*formal*) producing, or certain to produce, the intended result. — *adv* **efficaciously**. — *n* **efficaciousness** or **efficacy**. [Lat *efficax*]

efficient *adj* **1** producing satisfactory results with an economy of effort and a minimum of waste. **2** (of a person) capable of competent (and fast) work. — *n* **efficiency**. — *adv* **efficiently**. [Lat *efficere*, to accomplish]

effigy *n* **-ies 1** a crude doll or model representing a person, on which hatred of or contempt for the person can be expressed, e.g. by burning. **2** (*formal*) a portrait or sculpture of a person used as an architectural ornament. [Lat *effigies*]

effloresce *v* (*intr*) **1** (*bot*) (of a plant) to produce flowers. **2** (*chem*) (of a chemical compound) to become powdery as a result of crystallisation or a loss of water to the atmosphere. — *adj* **efflorescent**. [Lat *efflorescere*, to blossom]

efflorescence *n* **1** the act of efflorescing. **2** (*chem*) a powdery substance formed as a result of crystallisation or loss of water. **3** (*bot*) the period during which a plant is producing flowers.

effluent *n* **1** industrial waste or sewage released into a river, the sea, etc. **2** (*geog*, etc.) a stream or river flowing from a larger body of water. — *adj* (*formal* or *tech*) flowing out. [Lat *effluere*, to flow out]

effluvium *n* **-ia** (*formal*) an unpleasant smell or vapour given off by something, e.g. decaying matter. [Lat, flowing out]

effort *n* **1** (something that requires) hard mental or physical work. **2** an act of trying hard. **3** the result of an attempt; an achievement. [OFr *esfort*, from Lat *fortis*, strong]

effortless *adj* done without effort or apparent effort. — *adv* **effortlessly**. — *n* **effortlessness**.

effrontery *n* **-ies** shameless rudeness; impudence. [Fr *effronterie*, from Lat *effrons*, shameless]

effulgent *adj* (*literary*) shining brightly; brilliant. — *n* **effulgence**. — *adv* **effulgently**. [Lat *effulgere*, to shine out]

effusion *n* **1** a pouring or flowing out. **2** (usu. *derog*) an uncontrolled flow of speech or writing. [Lat *effusio*, pouring out]

effusive *adj* (usu. *derog*) expressing feelings, esp. happiness or enthusiasm, in an excessive or very showy way. — *adv* **effusively**. — *n* **effusiveness**. [*effuse*, to pour out + **-ive**]

EFL *abbrev* English as a Foreign Language.

EFTA or **Efta** *abbrev* European Free Trade Association.

EFTPOS *abbrev* electronic funds transfer at point of sale (see under **electronic**).

e.g. *abbrev* for *exempli gratia* (Lat), for example.

egalitarian *adj* relating to, promoting, or believing in the principle that all human beings are equal and should enjoy the same rights. — *n* a person who upholds this principle. — *n* **egalitarianism**. [Fr *égalitaire*, from *égal*, equal]

egg[1] *n* **1** the reproductive cell produced by a female animal, bird, etc., from which the young one develops. **2** a reproductive cell or developing embryo produced and deposited in a hard shell by female birds, reptiles, and certain animals. **3** the hard shell of an egg. **4** a hen's egg, used as food. **5** anything with the shape of a hen's egg. — **have** or **put all one's eggs in** or **into one basket** to depend entirely on one plan, etc. — **have** or **get egg on one's face** (*coll*) to be made to look foolish. — **teach one's grandmother to suck eggs** (*coll*) to try to show someone more experienced than oneself how to do something he or she already knows how to do. [Norse]

egg-cup *n* a small cup-shaped container for holding a boiled egg while it is being eaten.

egg-flip see **eggnog**.

egg custard see **custard.**

egghead *n* (*coll*; sometimes *derog*) a very clever person; an intellectual.

eggnog or **egg-flip** *n* a drink made from raw eggs, milk, sugar and an alcoholic spirit, esp. rum or brandy.

eggplant *n* (*US*) an aubergine.

eggshell *n* the hard, thin covering of an egg. — *adj* **1** (of paint or varnish) having a slightly glossy finish. **2** (of articles of china) very thin and fragile.

egg-timer *n* a device consisting of a sealed glass tube narrowed in the middle, containing sand or salt which, by trickling slowly from the top to the bottom of the tube through the narrow part, indicates the approximate time required to boil an egg.

egg[2]: **egg on** *v* (*tr*; *coll*) to urge or encourage. [Norse *eggja*, edge]

eglantine *n* a fragrant species of wild rose, the sweet-brier. [Fr *églantine*]

ego *n* **-os** **1** personal pride. **2** (*psychol*) the part of a person that is conscious and thinks, as opposed to instinct and the subconscious mind. [Lat, I]

egocentric *adj* (*derog*) interested in oneself only. — *adv* **egocentrically**. — *n* **egocentricity**.

egoism *n* **1** (*philos*) the principle that self-interest is the basis of morality. **2** selfishness. **3** egotism. — *n* **egoist**. — *adj* **egoistic** or **egoistical**. — *adv* **egoistically**.

egomania *n* (*psychol*) extreme self-interest which prevents one from allowing other people to come between oneself and the achievement of one's desires. — *n* **egomaniac**.

egotism *n* (*derog*) **1** the habit of speaking too much about oneself. **2** the fact of having a very high opinion of oneself. — *n* **egotist**. — *adj* **egotistic** or **egotistical**. — *adv* **egotistically**.

ego trip *n* (*coll*) an action or actions carried out mainly to increase one's high opinion of oneself, or because one has a high opinion of oneself.

egregious *adj* (*formal*) outrageous; shockingly bad. — *adv* **egregiously**. — *n* **egregiousness**. [Lat *egregius*, standing out from the herd, from *e*, out of + *grex*, herd]

egress *n* (*formal* or *legal*) **1** the act of leaving, or the right to leave, a building or other enclosed place. **2** an exit. [Lat *egredi*, to go out]

egret *n* any of various white, long-legged wading birds similar to herons. [Fr *aigrette*]

Egyptian *adj* of or belonging to Egypt. — *n* **1** a citizen of Egypt. **2** the language of ancient Egypt.

Egyptology *n* the study of the language, culture and history of ancient Egypt. — *n* **Egyptologist**. [**Egypt** + **-logy**]

eider or **eider duck** *n* a large sea duck from northern countries. [Icelandic *æthr*]

eiderdown *n* **1** the down or soft feathers of the eider. **2** a quilt filled with this or some similar material.

eight *n* **1** the number or figure 8; any symbol representing this. **2** the age of 8. **3** something, esp. a garment, or a person, whose size is denoted by the number 8. **4** 8 o'clock. **5** a set of 8 people or things, e.g. the crew of an eight-oared boat. **6** a playing-card with 8 pips. **7** a score of 8 points. — *adj* **1** 8 in number. **2** aged 8. — *n, adj & adv* **eighth**. — *adv* **eighthly**. — **be** or **have had one over the eight** (*coll*) to be slightly drunk. [OE *æhta*]

eightfold *adj* **1** equal to eight times as much or as many. **2** divided into, or consisting of, eight parts. — *adv* by eight times as much.

eightsome reel *n* **1** a lively Scottish dance for eight people. **2** the music for this dance.

figure of eight *n* a pattern, movement, etc. in the shape of an 8.

pieces of eight *n* (*pl*) old Spanish coins each worth eight reals (see **real**[2]).

eighteen *n* **1** the number or figure 18; any symbol for this number. **2** the age of 18. **3** something, esp. a garment or a person, whose size is denoted by the number 18. **4** a set of 18 people or things. **5** a film classified as suitable for people aged 18 and over.— *adj* **1** 18 in number. **2** aged 18. — *n, adj & adv* **eighteenth**. [OE *æhtatene*]

eighty *n* **-ies 1** the number or figure 80; any symbol for this number. **2** the age of 80. **3** a set of 80 people or things. — *adj* **1** 80 in number. **2** aged 80. — *n, adj & adv* **eightieth**. [OE *æhtatig*]

eighties *n* (*pl*) **1** the period of time between one's eightieth and ninetieth birthdays. **2** the range of temperatures between eighty and ninety degrees. **3** the period of time between the eightieth and ninetieth years of a century.

einsteinium *n* an element (symbol **Es**) produced artificially from plutonium. [Named after Albert *Einstein*, American physicist, 1879–1955]

eisteddfod *n* **-fods** or **-fodau** an annual Welsh arts festival during which competitions are held to find the best poetry, drama, songs, etc. [Welsh, session]

either *adj* **1** any one of two. **2** each of two; both: *a garden with a fence on either side*. — *pron* any one of two things, people, etc. — *adv* **1** (used in negative statements) also; as well: *I thought him rather unpleasant, and I didn't like his wife either*. **2** (used after a negative phrase) what is more; besides: *She plays golf, and she's not bad, either*. — **either ... or** introducing two choices or possibilities. — **either way** or **in either case** in whichever of two cases. [OE *ægther*]

ejaculate *v* **1** (*intr* & *tr*) (of a man or male animal) to discharge (semen). **2** (*tr*) to exclaim. — *n* semen. — *n* **ejaculation**. — *adj* **ejaculatory**. [Lat *ejaculari*, to throw out]

eject *v* **1** (*tr*; **from**) to throw out with force. **2** (*tr*; **from**) to force to leave. **3** (*intr*) to leave a moving aircraft using an ejector seat. — *n* **ejection**. — *adj* **ejective**. — *n* **ejector**. [Lat *ejicere*, to throw out]

ejector seat *n* a type of seat designed to propel a pilot out of the cockpit at speed in case of emergency.

eke: **eke out** *v* (*tr*; **with**) **1** to make (a supply) last longer, e.g. by adding something else to it or by careful use. **2** to manage with difficulty to make (a living, etc.). [OE *eacan*, to increase]

elaborate *adj* **1** complicated in design; complex. **2** carefully planned or worked out. — *v* **1** (*intr*; **on, upon**) to add detail. **2** (*tr*) to work out in great detail. **3** (*tr*) to make more ornate. — *adv* **elaborately**. — *n* **elaborateness**. — *n* **elaboration**. [Lat *elaborare*]

élan *n* (*literary*) impressive and energetic style. [Fr]

eland *n* **elands** or **eland** a large African antelope with spiral horns. [Dut]

elapse *v* (*intr; formal*) (of time) to pass. [Lat *elabi*, to slide away]

elastic *adj* **1** (of a material or substance) able to return to its original shape or size after being pulled or pressed out of shape; (of a force) caused by, or causing, such an ability. **2** able to be changed; flexible. **3** made of elastic. **4** (of a person or feelings) able to recover quickly from a shock or upset. — *n* stretchable cord or fabric woven with strips of rubber. — *adv* **elastically**. — *n* **elasticity**. [Gr *elastikos*, from *elaunein*, to propel]

elasticated *adj* (of a fabric) having been made elastic by being interwoven with rubber.

elastic band *n* (also **rubber band**) a small thin loop of rubber for holding things together or in place.

elasticise or **-ize** *v* (*tr*) to make elastic.

elate *v* (*tr*) to make very happy or fill with optimism. — *adj* **elated**. — *adv* **elatedly**. — *n* **elation**. [Lat *elatus*, elevated, exalted]

elbow *n* **1** the joint where the human arm bends. **2** the part of a coat, jacket, etc. which covers this joint. **3** the corresponding joint in animals. **4** a sharp turn or bend, e.g. in a road or pipe. — *v* (*tr*) **1** to push or strike with the elbow. **2** to make (one's way through) by pushing with the elbows. — **at one's elbow** close to one. — **give** or **get the elbow** (*slang*) to dismiss or be dismissed. — **out at elbow** or **elbows 1** (of a garment) no longer smart; worn out. **2** (of a person) wearing worn-out clothes. [OE *elnboga*]

elbow-grease *n* (*coll*) hard work, esp. hard polishing.

elbow-room *n* **1** space enough for moving or doing something. **2** freedom; lack of constraint.

elder[1] *adj* **1** older. **2** (with **the**) used before or after a person's name to distinguish him or her from a younger person of the same name. — *n* **1** a person who is older. **2** (often in *pl*) an older person, esp. when regarded as having authority. **3** in some Protestant churches, a lay person who has some responsibility for administration. [OE *eldra*]

elderly *adj* rather old. — *n* (with **the**) old people. — *n* **elderliness**.

elder statesman *n* an old and very experienced member of a group, esp. a politician, whose opinions are respected.

elder[2] *n* a kind of bush or small tree with white flowers and purple-black or red berries. [OE *ellærn*]

elderberry *n* **-ies** the fruit of the elder.

eldest *adj* oldest. — *n* a person who is the oldest of three or more.

elec. *abbrev* electric or electricity.

elect *v* (*tr*) **1** to choose by vote. **2** to choose (to do something). — *adj* **1** (*following the noun*) elected to a position, but not yet formally occupying it. **2** specially chosen. **3** (*relig*) chosen by God for salvation. — *n* (with **the**) people chosen, for salvation or otherwise. — *n* **electability**. — *adj* **electable**. — *adj* **elected**. [Lat *eligere*, to choose]

election *n* the process or act of choosing people for (esp. political) office by taking a vote. ◇ See also **general election** under **general**.

electioneer *v* (*intr*) to take part in an (esp. political) election campaign. — *n* **electioneering**.

elective *adj* **1** (of a position, office, etc.) to which someone is appointed by election. **2** having the power to elect. **3** optional. — *adv* **electively**.

elector *n* **1** a person who has the right to vote at an election. **2** (*cap*; *hist*) a German prince or archbishop in the Holy Roman Empire who had the right to elect the emperor.

electoral *adj* of elections or electors. — *adv* **electorally**.

electoral college *n* in the US, the body of people who elect the President, having themselves been elected by popular vote.

electoral roll or **register** *n* the list of people in a particular area who are allowed to vote in local and general elections.

electorate *n* (with **the**) all the electors of a city, country, etc.

electric *adj* **1** of, produced by, worked by or generating electricity. **2** having or causing great excitement, tension or expectation. — *n* (in *pl*) **1** electrical appliances. **2** (*coll*) wiring. [Gr *elektron*, amber, which produces electricity when rubbed]

electrical *adj* related to or operated by electricity. — *adv* **electrically**.

electric chair *n* a chair used for executing criminals by sending a powerful electric current through them.

electric eel see **eel**.

electric eye *n* (*coll*) a photo-chemical cell, a light-sensitive device which, when the beam of light completing its circuit is broken, produces an electric current, e.g. in order to bring an alarm system into operation.

electric fence *n* a wire fence with an electric current passing through it.

electric field *n* a region surrounding an electrically charged particle, within which any other particles present will experience a force on them.

electric guitar *n* a guitar with an electrical amplifier.

electrician *n* a person whose job is to install and repair electrical equipment.

electricity *n* **1** the energy which exists in a negative form in electrons and in a positive form in protons, and also as a flowing current, usu. of electrons. **2** a supply of this energy to a household, etc., e.g. for heating and lighting. **3** excitement, tension or expectation.

electric shock therapy *n* (also **electro-convulsive therapy** or **ECT**) the treatment of mental illness by passing small electric currents through the brain.

electrify *v* **-ies**, **-ied** (*tr*) **1** to give an electric charge to. **2** to equip (e.g. a railway system) for the use of electricity as a power supply. **3** to cause great excitement in. — *n* **electrification**. [**electric** + **-ify**]

electrifying *adj* extremely exciting. — *adv* **electrifyingly**.

electro- *comb fm* of, relating to or caused by electricity.

electrocardiogram *n* (*med*; *abbrev* **ECG**) the diagram or tracing produced by an electrocardiograph. [**electro-** + **cardio-** + **-gram**]

electrocardiograph *n* (*med*; *abbrev* **ECG**) an apparatus which registers, as a diagram or tracing, the electrical changes of the beating heart.

electro-convulsive therapy. See **electric shock therapy** under **electric**.

electrocute *v* (*tr*) **1** to kill accidentally by electric shock. **2** to execute by means of electricity. — *n* **electrocution**. [**electro-** + **execute**]

electrode *n* (*tech*) either of the two conducting points by which electric current enters or leaves a battery or other electrical apparatus. [**electric** + Gr *hodos*, way]

electroencephalogram *n* (*med*; *abbrev* **EEG**) a diagram or tracing produced by an electroencephalograph. [**electro-** + **encephalo-** + **-gram**]

electroencephalograph *n* (*med*; *abbrev* **EEG**) an apparatus which registers, as a diagram or tracing, the electrical activity of the brain.

electrolysis *n* **1** (*chem*) the decomposition of a chemical in the form of a liquid or solution by passing an electric current through it. **2** the removal of tumours or hair roots by means of an electric current. [**electro-** + **-lysis**]

electrolyte *n* (*chem*) a solution of chemical salts which can conduct electricity, e.g. in a battery. — *adj* **electrolytic**. [**electro-** + Gr *lutos*, released]

electromagnet *n* (*physics*, etc.) a piece of soft metal, usu. iron, made magnetic by the passage of an electric current through a coil of wire wrapped around the metal. — *adj* **electromagnetic**. — *n* **electromagnetism**.

electromotive *adj* (*physics*, etc.) producing or tending to produce an electric current. [**electro-** + **motive**]

electromotive force *n* (*physics*, etc.) the energy which forces a current to flow in an electrical circuit.

electron *n* (*physics*, etc.) a particle, present in all atoms, which has a negative electric charge and is responsible for carrying electricity in solids. [**electric**]

electron microscope *n* a microscope which operates using a beam of electrons rather than a beam of light, and is capable of very high magnification.

electronvolt *n* (*physics*) a unit of energy equal to that acquired by an electron when accelerated by a potential of one volt.

electronic *adj* **1** operated by means of (usu. several) very small electrical circuits which handle very low levels of electric current. **2** produced, operated, etc. using electronic apparatus: *electronic music*. **3** of electronics. — *adv* **electronically**. [**electron + -ic**]

electronic funds transfer at point of sale *n* (usu. *abbrev* **EFTPOS**) a payment system in a shop, which allows the direct transfer of money from the customer's bank account to the shop's without the use of cash or cheques.

electronic mail *n* (usu. *abbrev* **E-mail**) messages transmitted electronically, e.g. from one computer to another.

electronic point of sale *n* (usu. *abbrev* **EPOS**) a computerised till system at shop checkouts which links tills with bar-code readers to a stock control system.

electronics *n* **1** (*sing*) the science that deals with the study of the behaviour of electronic circuits and their applications in machines, etc. **2** (*pl*) the electronic parts of a machine or system.

electronic tagging *n* the use of electronic tags (see **tag**[1] sense **2**).

electroplate *v* (*tr*) to coat an object with metal (esp. silver) by electrolysis. — *n* articles coated in this way. — *adj* **electroplated**. — *n* **electroplating**. [**electro- + plate**]

elegant *adj* **1** having or showing good taste in dress or style, combined with dignity and gracefulness. **2** (of a movement) graceful. **3** (of a plan, etc.) simple and ingenious. — *n* **elegance**. — *adv* **elegantly**. [Lat *elegans*]

elegiac *adj* (*formal* or *literary*) mournful or thoughtful; which is, or is like, an elegy. — *adv* **elegiacally**. [**elegy**]

elegy *n* a mournful or thoughtful song or poem, esp. one whose subject is death or loss. [Lat *elegia*, from Gr *elegos*, lament]

elegise or **-ize** *v* (*formal* or *literary*) **1** (*intr* & *tr*) to write an elegy (about). **2** (*intr*) to produce mournful or thoughtful writings or songs.

element *n* **1** a part of anything; a component or feature. **2** (*chem* & *physics*) any one of 105 known substances that cannot be split by chemical means into simpler substances. **3** (sometimes *derog*) a person or small group within a larger group. **4** a slight amount. **5** the wire coil through which an electric current is passed to produce heat in various electrical appliances. **6** any one of the four basic substances —earth, air, fire and water — from which, according to ancient philosophy, everything is formed. **7** (in *pl*) weather conditions, esp. when severe. **8** (in *pl*) basic facts or skills. **9** (*relig*; in *pl*) bread and wine as the representation of the body and blood of Christ in the Eucharist. — **in one's element** in the surroundings that one finds most natural and enjoyable. [Lat *elementum*]

elemental *adj* **1** basic or primitive; of the forces of nature, esp. the four elements earth, air, fire and water. **2** immense; of the power of a force of nature.

elementary *adj* dealing with simple or basic facts.

elementary particle *n* (*chem* & *physics*) any of the twenty or more particles (e.g. electrons, protons, neutrons) which make up an atom.

elementary school *n* (esp. *US*) primary school.

elephant *n* ***elephants*** or ***elephant*** the largest living land animal, with thick greyish skin, a nose in the form of a long hanging trunk, and two curved tusks. ◇ See also **white elephant**. [Lat *elephantus*, from Gr *elephas*]

elephantiasis *n* (*med*) a disease, esp. of tropical climates, in which the skin becomes thicker and the limbs become greatly enlarged.

elephantine *adj* **1** of or like an elephant. **2** huge. **3** (*derog*) large and awkward; not graceful.

elephant seal *n* any of the two largest species of seals, the males of which have large snouts.

elevate *v* (*tr*) **1** to raise or lift. **2** to give a higher rank or status to. **3** to improve (a person's mind, etc.) morally or intellectually. **4** to make more cheerful. — *adj* **elevatory**. [Lat *elevare*]

elevated *adj* **1** (of a rank, position, etc.) very high; important. **2** (of thoughts, ideas, etc.) intellectually advanced or very moral. **3** (of land or buildings) raised above the level of their surroundings. **4** cheerful; elated.

elevating *adj* improving the mind; morally uplifting.

elevation *n* **1** the act of elevating or state of being elevated. **2** (*tech*) height, e.g. of a place above sea-level. **3** (*tech*) a drawing or diagram of one side of a building, machine, etc. **4** (*formal*) a high place.

elevator *n* **1** (*US*) a lift. **2** (esp. *US*) a tall building in which grain is stored.

eleven *n* **1** the number or figure 11; any symbol for this number. **2** the age of 11. **3** something, esp. a garment, or a person, whose size is denoted by the number 11. **4** 11 o'clock. **5** a set of 11 people or things, esp. a team of eleven players. **6** a score of eleven points. — *adj* **1** 11 in number. **2** aged 11. — *n*, *adj* & *adv* **eleventh**. — **at the eleventh hour** at the last possible moment; only just in time. [OE *endleofan*]

eleven-plus (examination) *n* the examination, taken at 11 or 12, to determine, esp. formerly before the introduction of comprehensive education, which sort of secondary school a pupil will attend.

elevenses *n* (*coll*) a snack, usu. consisting of coffee, tea, biscuits, etc., taken at about eleven o'clock in the morning.

elf *n* ***elves*** **1** a tiny fairy with a tendency to play tricks. **2** a mischievous child. — *adj* **elfish** or **elvish**. [OE *ælf*]

elfin *adj* **1** (of physical features, etc.) small and delicate. **2** elfish; small and mischievous, but charming.

elicit *v* **-*t*-** (*tr*; **from**) **1** to succeed in getting (e.g. information from a person), usu. with difficulty. **2** to cause or bring out. — *n* **elicitation**. — *n* **elicitor**. [Lat *elicere*]

elide *v* (*tr*) **1** (*gram*) to omit (a vowel or syllable) at the beginning or end of a word. **2** to omit (a part of anything). ◇ See also **elision**. [Lat *elidere*, to strike out]

eligible *adj* (**for**) **1** suitable, or deserving to be chosen (for a job, as a husband, etc.). **2** having a right: *eligible for compensation*. — *n* **eligibility**. [Lat *eligere*, to elect]

eliminate *v* (*tr*) **1** (**from**) to get rid of or exclude. **2** (**from**) to exclude from a later part of a competition by defeat in an earlier part. **3** (*slang*) to murder. — *adj* **eliminable**. — *n* **elimination**. [Lat *eliminare*, to carry outside]

eliminator *n* someone or something that eliminates, e.g. the first round of a competition.

elision *n* (*gram*) the omission of a vowel or syllable, as in *I'm* and *we're*. ◇ See also **elide**. [Lat *elidere*, to strike out]

elite or **élite** *n* **1** the best, most important or most powerful people within society. **2** the best of a group or profession. **3** a size of letter in typewriting, twelve characters per inch. — *adj* best, most important or most powerful. [OFr *eslire*, to choose, from Lat *eligere*, to elect]

elitism or **élitism** *n* **1** the belief in the need for a powerful social elite. **2** the belief in the natural social superiority of some people. **3** (often *derog*) awareness of, or pride in, belonging to an elite group in society. — *n* and *adj* **elitist** or **élitist**.

elixir *n* **1** in medieval times, a liquid chemical preparation that supposedly had the power to give people everlasting life or turn base metals into gold. **2** any medical preparation which is claimed to cure all illnesses; a panacea. **3** a liquid solution containing medicine and something, esp. honey or alcohol, to hide the unpleasant taste. [Arabic *al-iksir*, the philosopher's stone]

Elizabethan *adj* of, typical of, or relating to the reign of Queen *Elizabeth* I of England (1558–1603). — *n* a person who lived during this time.

elk *n* ***elks*** or ***elk*** the largest of all deer, found in northern parts of Europe and Asia, and in N America, where it is called the moose. [Prob. OE *elh*]

ellipse *n* (*geom*) a regular oval, as formed by a diagonal cut through a cone above the base. [Lat *ellipsis*, from Gr *elleipsis*, omission]

ellipsis *n* ***ellipses*** **1** (*gram*) a figure of speech in which a word or words needed for the sense or grammar are omitted but understood. **2** a set of three dots that indicate the omission of a word or words, e.g. in a lengthy quotation. [Ety. as for **ellipse**]

ellipsoid *n* (*geom*) a surface or solid object of which every plane section is an ellipse or a circle. [**ellipse** + **-oid**]

elliptical or **elliptic** *adj* **1** (*math*) of or having the shape of an ellipse. **2** (of speech or writing) containing an ellipsis; so concise as to be unclear or ambiguous. — *adv* **elliptically**. [Gr *elleipsis*, omission]

elm *n* **1** (*also* **elm tree**) any of various tall trees with broad serrated leaves and clusters of small flowers. **2** the hard heavy wood of these trees. [OE]

elocution *n* the art of speaking clearly and effectively. — *adj* **elocutionary**. [Lat *eloqui*, to speak out]

elocutionist *n* a teacher of, or an expert in, elocution.

elongate *v* (*tr*) to lengthen or stretch out. — *n* **elongation**. [Lat *elongare*]

elongated *adj* (made) long and narrow.

elope *v* (*intr*; **with**) to run away secretly, esp. with a lover in order to get married. — *n* **elopement**. — *n* **eloper**. [OFr *aloper*, prob. from MidE *alopen*]

eloquence *n* **1** the art or power of using speech to impress, move or persuade. **2** fine and persuasive language. [Lat *eloqui*, to speak out]

eloquent *adj* having or showing eloquence. — *adv* **eloquently**.

else *adj* & *adv* different from or in addition to something or someone known or already mentioned: *Would you like something else? Where else can you buy it?* — **or else 1** or if not; otherwise: *Hurry up, or else you'll be late*. **2** (*coll*) or I will punish or harm you: *Give me the money, or else!* [OE *elles*]

elsewhere *adv* somewhere else.

ELT *abbrev* English Language Teaching.

elucidate *v* (*tr*) to make clear or explain; to shed light on. — *n* **elucidation**. — *adj* **elucidatory**. [Lat *elucidare*]

elude *v* (*tr*) **1** to escape or avoid by quickness or cleverness. **2** to fail to be understood by, discovered by, or found in the memory of. [Lat *eludere*]

elusive *adj* **1** difficult to find or catch. **2** difficult to remember. **3** avoiding the issue or the question. — *adv* **elusively**. — *n* **elusiveness**. [**elude** + **-ive**]

elver *n* a young eel. [old word *eelfare*, literally 'eel journey', a reference to the migration of young eels upstream]

elves, **elvish**. See **elf**.

Elysium *n* **1** the place, according to Greek mythology, where the blessed were supposed to rest after death. **2** (*poetic*) a state or place of perfect happiness. — *adj* **Elysian**. [Lat, from Gr *elysion*]

em- *pfx* a form of **en-** used before b, m and p.

'em *pron* (*coll*) them. [MidE *hem*, them]

emaciate *v* (*tr*) to make extremely thin (through illness, starvation, etc.). — *adj* **emaciated**. — *n* **emaciation**. [Lat *emaciare*]

emanate *v* (*intr*; **from**) **1** (of an idea, etc.) to come out (from); to originate. **2** (of light, gas, etc.) to flow; to issue. — *n* **emanation**. [Lat *emanare*, to flow out]

emancipate *v* (*tr*; **from**) to set free (from slavery, or from some other social or political restraint). — *adj* **emancipated**. — *n* **emancipation**. [Lat *emancipare*, to free]

emasculate *v* (*tr*) **1** to reduce the force, strength or effectiveness of. **2** to remove the testicles of; to take away the masculinity of. — *adj* **emasculated**. — *n* **emasculation**. — *adj* **emasculatory**. [Lat *e*, from + *masculus*, dimin. of *mas*, male]

embalm *v* (*tr*) to preserve (a dead body) from decay, orig. with oils and spices, but now by treatment with chemicals or drugs. — *n* **embalmer**. — *n* **embalmment**. [OFr *embaumer*]

embankment *n* **1** a bank or wall of earth made to enclose a waterway, or to carry a road or railway. **2** a slope of grass, earth, etc. which rises from either side of a road or railway. [**em-** + **bank**[1] + **-ment**]

embargo *n* **-*oes*** **1** an official order forbidding something, esp. trade with another country. **2** the resulting stoppage, esp. of trade. **3** any restriction or prohibition. — *v* **-*oes*, -*oed*** (*tr*) **1** to place under an embargo. **2** to take for use by the state. [Span *embargar*, to impede or restrain]

embark *v* **1** (*tr & intr*; **on, for**) to go, or put, on board ship: *embark (goods) on a ship*; *embark for America*. **2** (*intr* with **on**) to begin. — *n* **embarkation**. [Fr *embarquer*]

embarrass *v* **1** (*tr & intr*) to cause to feel, or to become, anxious, self-conscious or ashamed. **2** (*tr*; usu. in passive) to cause to be in financial difficulties. **3** (*tr*) to make more complicated. **4** (*tr*) to confuse or perplex. — *adj* **embarrassed**. — *adj* **embarrassing**. — *adv* **embarrassingly**. — *n* **embarrassment**. [Fr *embarrasser*]

embassy *n* **-*ies*** **1** the official residence of an ambassador. **2** an ambassador and his or her staff. **3** (the people undertaking) a mission, esp. diplomatic, to a foreign country. [OFr *ambassee*]

embattled *adj* **1** prepared for battle. **2** troubled by problems or difficulties. [OFr *embataillier*, to prepare or arm for battle]

embed *v* **-*dd*-** (*tr*) to set or fix firmly and deeply. [**em-** + **bed**]

embellish *v* (*tr*; **with**) **1** to make (a story, etc.) more interesting by adding details which may not be true. **2** to beautify with decoration. — *adj* **embellished**. — *n* **embellishment**. [OFr *embellir*, to make beautiful]

ember *n* (usu. in *pl*) **1** a piece of glowing or smouldering coal or wood in a dying fire. **2** (*literary*) what remains of a once strong feeling. [OE *æmyrge*]

embezzle *v* (*tr*) to take dishonestly (money with which one has been entrusted). — *n* **embezzlement**. — *n* **embezzler**. [OFr *embesiler*, to make away with]

embitter *v* **-*r*-** (*tr*) to cause (someone) to feel bitter. — *adj* **embittered**. — *adj* **embittering**. — *n* **embitterment**. [**em-** + **bitter**]

emblazon *v* **-*n*-** (*tr*; **on, with**) **1** to decorate with a coat of arms or some other bright design. **2** to display in a very obvious or striking way. — *n* **emblazonment**. [**em-** + *blazon*, from Fr *blason*, shield]

emblem *n* an object chosen to represent an idea, a quality, a country, etc. — *adj* **emblematic**. — *adv* **emblematically**. [Lat *emblema*]

embody *v* **-*ies*, -*ied*** (*tr*) **1** to be an expression or a representation of in words, actions or form; to typify or personify. **2** to include or incorporate. — *n* **embodiment**. [**em-** + **body**]

embolden *v* **-*n*-** (*tr*) to make bold. [**em-** + **bold** + **-en**]

embolism *n* (*med*) the blocking of a blood vessel by an air bubble or a blood clot. [Gr *embolismos*, from *emballein*, to insert]

embolus *n* **-*li*** (*med*) any obstruction in a blood vessel, esp. a blood clot.

emboss *v* (*tr*; **on, with**) to carve or mould (a raised design) on (a surface). — *adj* **embossed**. [OFr *embocer*]

embrace *v* **1** (*tr*) to hold closely in the arms, affectionately or as a greeting. **2** (*intr*) (of two people) to hold each other closely in the arms, affectionately or as a greeting. **3** (*tr*) to take (e.g. an opportunity) eagerly, or accept (e.g. a religion) wholeheartedly. **4** (*tr*) to include. — *n* **1** an act of embracing. **2** a loving hug. [OFr *embracer*, from Lat *in*, in + *bracchium*, arm]

all-embracing *adj* including everything; missing nothing out.

embrasure *n* **1** an opening in the wall of a castle, etc. for shooting through. **2** an opening in a thick wall for a door or window, with angled sides which make it narrower on the outside. **3** the sloping of these sides. [Fr *embraser*, to splay]

embrocation *n* **1** a lotion for rubbing into the skin as a treatment for sore or pulled muscles. **2** the act of rubbing in such lotion. [Gr *embroche*, lotion]

embroider *v* **-*r*-** **1** (*tr & intr*) to decorate (cloth) with sewn designs. **2** (*tr*) to make (a story, etc.) more interesting by adding details, usu. untrue. — *n* **embroiderer**. [OFr *embroder*]

embroidery *n* **1** the art or practice of sewing designs on to cloth. **2** articles decorated in this way. **3** (*derog*) gaudy decoration. **4** the addition of (usu. false) details to a story, etc.

embroil *v* (*tr*) **1** (**in**) to involve (a person) in a quarrel or in a difficult situation. **2**

to throw into a state of confusion. — *n* **embroilment**. [Fr *embrouiller*]

embryo *n* **-os 1** a human or animal in the earliest stages of development before birth, in humans usu. up to the end of the eighth week of the pregnancy. **2** a plant in its earliest stages of development. **3** anything in its earliest stages. [Gr *embryon*, from *en*, in + *bryein*, to swell]

embryology *n* the science of the formation and development of embryos. — *adj* **embryological**. — *n* **embryologist**.

embryonic *adj* in an early stage of development.

emend *v* (*tr*) to edit (a text), removing errors and making improvements. — *n* **emendation**. ◇ See also **amend**. [Lat *emendare*]

emerald *n* **1** a bright-green precious stone. **2** (also **emerald green**) its colour. [OFr *esmeralde*, from Gr *smaragdos*]

Emerald Isle *n* (*poetic*) Ireland, so called from its greenness.

emerge *v* (*intr*) **1** to come out (from hiding or into view). **2** to become known or apparent. **3** to survive a difficult or dangerous situation. — *n* **emergence**. — *adj* **emergent**. [Lat *emergere*]

emergency *n* **-ies 1** an unexpected and serious happening which calls for immediate and determined action. **2** (a patient with) a serious injury needing immediate medical treatment.

state of emergency *n* the suspension of normal law and order procedures and the introduction of strict control of the population by the military, in order to deal with a crisis, revolution or other trouble. [Lat *emergentia*]

emergent. See **emerge**.

emeritus *adj* retired, but retaining a former title as an honour: *emeritus professor* or *professor emeritus*. [Lat *mereri*, to earn]

emery *n* a very hard mineral used, usu. in powder form, for polishing. [Gr *smyris*, polishing powder]

emery board *n* a small flat strip of wood or card coated with emery powder or some other abrasive, used for filing one's nails.

emery paper or **cloth** *n* paper or cloth coated with emery, used for cleaning or polishing metal.

emetic *adj* & *n* (*med*) (a medicine) that causes vomiting. [Gr *emeein*, to vomit]

EMF *abbrev* **1** (also **emf**) electromotive force. **2** European Monetary Fund.

emigrant *n* a person who emigrates or who has emigrated. — *adj* emigrating or having emigrated. ◇ See also **immigrant**. [Lat *emigrare*, to move from a place]

emigrate *v* (*intr*) to leave one's native country and settle in another. — *n* **emigration**. ◇ See also **immigrate**. [Lat *emigrare*, to move from a place]

émigré *n* a person who has emigrated, usu. for political reasons. [Fr, from Lat *emigrare*, to move from a place]

eminence *n* **1** honour, distinction or prestige. **2** an area of high ground. **3** (*cap* with **Your** or **His**) a title of honour used in speaking to or about a cardinal. [Lat *eminere*, to stand out]

eminent *adj* famous and admired.

eminently *adv* **1** very. **2** obviously.

éminence grise *n* ***éminences grises*** a person who has great influence (over a king, government, etc.) without actually occupying an official position of power. [Fr, grey eminence, first applied to Cardinal Richelieu's private secretary, Father Joseph]

emir *n* a title given to various Muslim rulers, esp. in the Middle East or W Africa. [Arabic *amir*, ruler]

emirate *n* the position or authority of, or the territory ruled by, an emir.

emissary *n* **-ies 1** a person sent on a mission, esp. on behalf of a government. **2** a person sent with a message. [Lat *emissarius*]

emission *n* **1** the act of emitting. **2** something emitted, esp. heat, light or gas. — *adj* **emissive**. [Lat *emissio*, a sending out]

emit *v* **-tt-** (*tr*) to give out (light, heat, a sound, a smell, etc.). [Lat *emittere*, to send out]

Emmental or **Emmenthal** *n* a mild hard Swiss cheese with holes in it. [*Emmenthal*, valley in Switzerland]

emollient *adj* **1** (*med*) softening or soothing the skin. **2** (*formal*) advocating a calmer, more peaceful attitude. — *n* (*med*) a substance which softens or soothes the skin. [Lat *emollire*, to soften]

emolument *n* (*formal*; often in *pl*) any money earned or otherwise gained through a job or position, e.g. salary or fees. — *adj* **emolumentary**. [Lat *emolumentum*, a corn-grinder's fee, from *molere*, to grind]

emote *v* (*intr*; *coll derog*) to display exaggerated or insincere emotion. [Back-formation from **emotion**]

emotion *n* a strong feeling. — *adj* **emotionless**. — *adv* **emotionlessly**. [Lat *emovere*, to stir up, disturb]

emotional *adj* **1** of the emotions. **2** causing or expressing emotion. **3** (of a person) tending to express emotions easily or excessively. **4** (often *derog*) based on emotions, rather than rational thought: *an emotional response*. — *adv* **emotionally**.

emotionalism *n* (often *derog*) the tendency to be too easily affected or excited by the emotions. — *n* **emotionalist**.

emotive *adj* tending, or designed, to excite emotion. — *adv* **emotively**. [Lat *emovere*, to stir, disturb]

empanel *v* **-ll-** (*tr*) **1** to enter (the names of prospective jurors) on a list. **2** to select (a jury) from such a list. — *n* **empanelment**. [**em-** + **panel**]

empathy *n* the ability to share and understand another person's feelings. — *adj* **empathetic**. [Gr *empatheia*, passion, affection]

empathise or **-ize** *v* (*intr*; **with**) to have or feel empathy.

emperor *n* (the rank or position of) the male ruler of an empire or of a country which was once the centre of an empire. ◇ See also **empress**. [OFr *emperere*, from Lat *imperator*, commander]

emperor penguin *n* the largest species of penguin, found in the Antarctic.

emphasis *n* ***emphases*** **1** (**on**) importance or greatest attention. **2** greater force or loudness on certain words or parts of words to show that they are important or have a special meaning. **3** force or firmness of expression. [Gr, outward appearance, implied meaning]

emphasise or **-ize** *v* (*tr*) to put emphasis on.

emphatic *adj* **1** expressed with or expressing emphasis. **2** (of a person) expressing oneself firmly and forcefully. — *adv* **emphatically**. [Gr *emphatikos*]

emphysema *n* (*med*) **1** a condition in which the lungs become expanded with air, making breathing very difficult. **2** swelling of a part of the body caused by the presence of air. [Gr, from *emphysaein*, to swell]

empire *n* **1** a group of nations or states under the control of a single ruler or ruling power, esp. an emperor or empress. **2** the period of time during which such control is exercised. **3** a large commercial or industrial organisation controlling many separate firms, esp. one headed by one person. **4** (often *facet*) that part of an organisation, a company, etc. under the management of a particular person. **5** (*formal* or *literary*) supreme control or power. ◇ See also **emperor**, **empress** and **imperial**. [OFr, from Lat *imperium*, command, power]

empire-building *n* (*coll*; usu. *derog*) the practice of increasing one's power or authority, esp. within an organisation, usu. by needlessly acquiring extra staff. — *n* **empire-builder**.

empirical or **empiric** *adj* **1** based on experiment, observation or experience, rather than on theory. **2** regarding experiment and observation as more important than scientific law. — *adv* **empirically**. [Gr *empeiria*, experience]

empiricism *n* **1** (*philos*) the theory or philosophy stating that knowledge can only be gained through experiment and observation. **2** the application of empirical methods, e.g. to science. — *n* **empiricist**. [**empirical** + **-ism**]

emplacement *n* **1** (*mil*) a strongly defended position from which a field gun may be fired. **2** (*formal*) the act of putting, or the state of having been put, into place. [Fr]

employ *v* (*tr*) **1** to give (usu. paid) work to. **2** (usu. in *passive*; **in**) to occupy the time or attention of: *busily employed in writing letters*. **3** (**as**) to use. — *n* (*formal*) the state of being in paid work; employment. — *adj* **employable**. [Fr *employer*]

employed *adj* having a job; working.

employee *n* a person who works for another in return for payment.

employer *n* a person or company that employs workers.

employment *n* **1** the act of employing or the state of being employed. **2** an occupation, esp. regular paid work. ◇ See also **unemployment**.

employment agency *n* an organisation which finds jobs for people out of work, and workers for companies seeking them.

employment exchange *n* the former name for a job centre.

emporium *n* **-iums** or **-ia** (*formal* or *humorous*) a shop, esp. a large one selling a wide variety of goods. [Gr *emporion*, trading station]

empower *v* (*tr*; **to**) to give authority or official permission to. [**em-** + **power**]

empress *n* **1** (the rank or position of) the female ruler of an empire or of a country which was once the centre of an empire. **2** the wife or widow of an emperor. [OFr *emperesse*, from *emperere*, emperor]

empty *adj* ***-ier***, ***-iest*** **1** having nothing inside. **2** not occupied, inhabited or furnished. **3** not likely to be satisfied or carried out: *empty promises*. **4** (with **of**) completely without: *a life empty of meaning*. — *v* ***-ies***, ***-ied*** (*tr* & *intr*) **1** to make or become empty. **2** to tip, pour, or fall out of a container. — *n* ***-ies*** (*coll*) an empty container, esp. a bottle. — *adv* **emptily**. — *n* **emptiness**. [OE *æmetig*, unoccupied]

empty-handed *adj* **1** carrying nothing. **2** having gained or achieved nothing.

empty-headed *adj* foolish; having no capacity for serious thought.

empyrean *n* (*poetic*; usu. with **the**) the sky. — *adj* **empyreal**. [Lat *empyreus*, from Gr *empyros*, fiery]

EMS *abbrev* European Monetary System.

EMU *abbrev* Economic and Monetary Union (between EC countries).

emu *n* a large Australian flightless bird with grey or brown plumage. [Port. *ema*, ostrich]

emulate *v* (*tr*) **1** to try hard to equal or be better than. **2** to imitate. — *n* **emulation**. [Lat *aemulari*, to rival]

emulsify *v* ***-ies***, ***-ied*** (*tr* & *intr*) to make or become an emulsion. [**emulsion** + **-ify**]

emulsifier or **emulsifying agent** *n* a chemical which forms or preserves an emulsion, used esp. in the food industry.

emulsion *n* **1** a mixture of liquids, e.g. oil and water, which do not unite completely or form a solution of one in the other. **2** a light-sensitive compound for coating photographic plates or films. **3** emulsion paint. — *v* ***-n-*** (*tr*; *coll*) to apply emulsion paint to. [Lat *emulgere*, to drain out]

emulsion paint *n* water-based paint.

EN *abbrev* Enrolled Nurse.

en- *pfx* **1** forming verbs with the meaning 'put into, on or on to': *entrust*; *enthrone*. **2**

forming verbs with the meaning 'cause to be': *enrich*; *enfeeble*. **3** forming verbs with the meaning 'in, into' or with a meaning simply stronger than that of the base verb: *entangle*; *enliven*.

-en *sfx* **1** forming verbs with the meaning 'make or become (more)': *deepen*; *sadden*. **2** forming verbs with the meaning 'give, endow with': *strengthen*. **3** forming adjectives with the meaning 'made or consisting of': *wooden*.

enable *v* (*tr*) **1** to give the necessary means, power or authority to. **2** to make possible. [**en-** (sense **2**) + **able**]

enact *v* **1** to act or perform, not necessarily on stage. **2** to establish by law. [**en-** (sense **2**) + **act**]

enactment *n* (*formal*) **1** the act of passing, or the passing of, a parliamentary bill into law. **2** that which is enacted; a law.

enamel *n* **1** a hardened coloured glass-like substance applied as a decorative or protective covering to metal or glass. **2** any paint or varnish which gives a finish similar to this. **3** the hard white covering of the teeth. — *v* **-ll-** (*tr*) to cover or decorate with enamel. [OFr *enameler*, from *esmail*, enamel]

enamoured *adj* (**with**, **of**) **1** (*formal* or *literary*) in love with. **2** very fond of, pleased with or enthusiastic about. [OFr *enamourer*, from *amour*, love]

en bloc *adv* all together; as one unit. [Fr, in a block]

enc. *abbrev* **1** enclosed. **2** enclosure.

encamp *v* (*tr* & *intr*) to settle in a camp. — *n* **encampment**. [**en-** (sense **2**) + **camp**[1]]

encapsulate *v* (*tr*) **1** to express concisely the main points or ideas of, or capture the essence of. **2** to enclose in, or as if in, a capsule. — *n* **encapsulation**. [**en-** (sense **1**) + **capsule**]

encase *v* (*tr*) **1** to enclose in, or as if in, a case. **2** to surround or cover. — *n* **encasement**. [**en-** (sense **1**) + **case**]

encash *v* (*tr*) to convert into cash; to cash. — *n* **encashment**. [**en-** (sense **2**) + **cash**]

encaustic *adj* (of ceramics) decorated using pigments melted in wax and burnt into the clay. — *n* **1** the technique which uses pigments in this way. **2** a piece of pottery or any other article decorated using this technique. [Gr *enkaustikos*, from *enkaiein*, to burn in]

-ence *sfx* **1** forming nouns indicating a state or quality, or an action, etc. which shows a state or quality: *confidence*; *diligence*; *impertinence*. **2** forming nouns indicating an action: *reference*. [Fr, from Lat *-entia*]

encephalitis *n* (*med*) inflammation of the brain. [Gr *enkephalos*, brain + **-itis**]

encephalogram, **encephalograph**. Same as **electroencephalogram**, **electroencephalograph**.

enchain *v* (*tr*; *literary*) **1** to put in chains. **2** to hold or fix (attention, etc.). [Fr *enchaîner*]

enchant *v* (*tr*) **1** to charm or delight. **2** to put a magic spell on. — *adj* **enchanted**. [Fr *enchanter*, from Lat *incantare*, to sing a magic spell over]

enchanter or **enchantress** *n* **1** a person who casts spells. **2** a charming person, esp. one who sets out to be so.

enchanting *adj* charming; delightful. — *adv* **enchantingly**.

enchantment *n* **1** the act of enchanting or state of being enchanted. **2** a magic spell. **3** charm; attraction.

enchilada *n* a Mexican dish consisting of a flour tortilla with a meat filling, served with a chilli-flavoured sauce. [Span *enchilar*, to season with chilli]

encircle *v* (*tr*) to surround, form a circle round. — *n* **encirclement**. [**en-** (sense **1**) + **circle**]

encl. *abbrev* **1** enclosed. **2** enclosure.

enclave *n* **1** a small country or state entirely surrounded by foreign territory. **2** a distinct racial or cultural group isolated within a country. [Fr, from Lat *inclavare*, to lock up]

enclose *v* (*tr*) **1** to put inside a letter or its envelope. **2** to shut in or surround. — *adj* **enclosed**. [**en-** (sense **1**) + **close**[1]]

enclosure *n* **1** the act of enclosing or the state of being enclosed. **2** land surrounded by a fence or wall. **3** something put in along with a letter.

encode *v* (*tr*) to express in code. [**en-** (sense **1**) + **code**]

encomium *n* **-iums** or **-ia** (*formal*) a formal speech or piece of writing praising someone. — *adj* **encomiastic**. [Gr *enkomion*, song of praise]

encompass *v* (*tr*) **1** to include or contain, esp. contain a wide range or coverage of. **2** to surround. **3** to cause or bring about. — *n* **encompassment**. [**en-** (sense **1**) + **compass**]

encore *n* a repetition of a performance, or an additional performed item, after the end of a concert, etc. — *interj* an enthusiastic call from the audience for such a peformance. — *v* (*tr*) to call for an extra performance of or from. [Fr, again]

encounter *v* **-r-** (*tr*) **1** to meet, esp. unexpectedly. **2** to meet with (difficulties, etc.). **3** to meet in battle or conflict. — *n* **1** a chance meeting. **2** a fight or battle. [OFr *encontrer*, from Lat *contra*, against]

encounter group *n* (*psychol*) a group whose members are encouraged to discuss their problems and feelings openly in order to arrive at a better understanding of themselves and others.

encourage *v* (*tr*) **1** to give support, confidence or hope to. **2** to urge (to do something). **3** to promote or recommend. — *n* **encouragement**. — *adj* **encouraging**. — *adv* **encouragingly**. [Fr *encourager*]

encroach *v* (*intr*) **1** (**on, upon**) to intrude or extend gradually or stealthily (onto someone else's land, etc.). **2** (**on, upon**) to go beyond the fair limits (of a right, etc.). **3** to overstep proper or agreed limits. — *n* **encroachment**. [OFr *encrochier*, to seize]

encrust *v* (*tr*) to cover with a thick hard coating, e.g. of jewels or ice. — *n* **encrustation**. [Lat *incrustare*]

encumber *v* **-r-** (*tr*; **by, with**) **1** to prevent the free and easy movement of; to hamper or impede. **2** to burden (with a load or debt). [OFr *encombrer*, to block]

encumbrance *n* an impediment, hindrance or burden.

-ency *sfx* forming nouns indicating a state or quality, or something which shows a state or quality: *efficiency*; *inconsistency*. [Lat *-entia*]

encyclical *n* (*relig*) a letter sent by the Pope to all Roman Catholic bishops. — *adj* (*formal*) (of a letter) for general or wide circulation. [Gr *enkyklios*, from *en*, in + *kyklos*, circle]

encyclopaedia or **encyclopedia** *n* a reference work containing information on every branch of knowledge, or on one particular branch, usu. arranged in alphabetical order. [Gr *enkyklios paideia*, general education]

encyclopaedic or **encyclopedic** *adj* **1** (of knowledge) very full and detailed. **2** of, belonging to, or like an encyclopaedia.

end *n* **1** the point or part farthest from the beginning, or either of the points or parts farthest from the middle, where something stops. **2** a finish or conclusion: *come to an end*. **3** a piece left over: *a cigarette end*. **4** death or destruction: *meet one's end*. **5** an object or purpose: *The ends justify the means*. **6** (*sport*) one of the two halves of a pitch or court defended by a team, player, etc. **7** the part of a project, etc. for which one is responsible: *They've had a few problems at their end*. — *v* (*tr* & *intr*) to (cause to) finish, close, reach a conclusion or cease to exist. — *adj* **endless**. — *adv* **endlessly**. — *n* **endlessness**. — **at the end of the day** (*coll*) when everything has been taken into account. — **end it all** (*coll euph*) to kill oneself. — **the end of the road** the point beyond which one cannot continue or survive. — **end on** or **end to end** with ends touching. — *v* **end up** (*intr*; *coll*) **1** to arrive or find oneself eventually. **2** (**as**) to become in the end. — **in the end** finally; after much discussion, work, etc. — **keep** or **hold one's end up** (*coll*) to fulfil one's promises or obligations in spite of difficulties. — **make (both) ends meet** to live within one's income; to manage; not to get into debt. — **no end** (*coll*) very much; very many. — **on end 1** vertical; standing straight up. **2** continuously; without a pause. [OE *ende*]

ending *n* **1** the end, esp. of a story, poem, etc. **2** (*gram*) the end part of a word, esp. an inflection.

endmost *adj* farthest; nearest the end.

endpaper *n* one of the two leaves at the front or back of a hardback book, fixed with paste to the inside of the cover, to give strength to the binding.

end-product *n* the final product of a series of operations, esp. industrial processes.

end-user *n* the person, company, etc. that will actually use a product that is being sold.

endways *adv* **1** with the end forward or upward. **2** end to end.

endanger *v* **-r-** (*tr*) to put in danger; to expose to possible loss or injury. [**en-** (sense **2**) + **danger**]

endangered species *n* a species of animal threatened with extinction, usu. because of hunting or the destruction of its natural habitat.

endear *v* (*tr*; **to**) to cause to be beloved or liked. [**en-** (sense **2**) + **dear**]

endearing *adj* arousing feelings of affection. — *adv* **endearingly**.

endearment *n* **1** a word or phrase expressing affection. **2** affection or fondness.

endeavour *v* (*tr*) to try (to do something), esp. seriously and with effort. — *n* a determined attempt or effort. [MidE *endeveren*, to exert oneself, from Fr *devoir*, duty]

endemic *adj* (of a disease, etc.) regularly occurring in a particular area or among a particular group of people. [Gr *endemos*, native]

endive *n* a plant, related to chicory, whose crisp curly or broad leaves are used in salads. [Fr]

endo- *comb fm* internal; inside. ◇ See also **ecto-**, **ento-** and **exo-**. [Gr *endon*, within]

endocrine: **endocrine gland** *n* (*med*) a gland, such as the pituitary and thyroid glands, which releases hormones directly into the bloodstream. ◇ See also **exocrine**. [**endo-** + Gr *krinein*, to separate]

endorse *v* (*tr*) **1** to write one's signature on the back of (a document), esp. on the back of (a cheque) to specify oneself or another person as payee. **2** to make a note of an offence on (a driving licence). **3** to state one's approval of or support for. — *n* **endorsement**. [OFr *endosser*, to put on the back, from Lat *dorsum*, back]

endoscope *n* (*med*) a long, thin instrument through which the cavities of internal organs can be looked at. — *adj* **endoscopic**. — *n* **endoscopy**. [**endo-** + **-scope**]

endow *v* (*tr*; **with**) **1** to give a permanent income to (a hospital, place of learning, etc.). **2** to give a quality, ability, etc. to: *endowed with common sense*. — *n* **endowment**. [OFr *endouer*, from Lat *dos*, dowry]

endowment assurance or **insurance** *n* a form of insurance in which a set sum is paid at a certain date, or earlier in the event of death.

endue *v* (*tr*; **with**) to provide with a certain quality. [OFr *enduire*, from Lat *inducere*, to lead in]

endure *v* **1** (*tr*) to bear patiently, put up with. **2** (*intr; formal*) to continue to exist; to last. — *adj* **endurable**. [OFr *endurer*, from Lat *indurare*, to harden]

endurance *n* **1** the capacity for, or the state of, patient toleration. **2** the ability to withstand physical hardship or strain.

enduring *adj* lasting. — *adv* **enduringly**.

enema *n* (*med*) **1** the injection of a liquid into the rectum. **2** the liquid injected. [Gr *enienai*, to send in]

enemy *n* **-ies 1** a person who hates or dislikes, or who is hated or disliked. **2** a hostile nation or force, or a member of it. **3** an opponent or adversary. **4** (with **of**) a person, thing, etc. that opposes or acts against: *Cleanliness is the enemy of disease*. — *adj* hostile; belonging to a hostile nation or force. ◇ See also **enmity**. [OFr *enemi*, from Lat *inimicus*]

energetic *adj* having or displaying energy; forceful; vigorous. — *adv* **energetically**. [Gr *energetikos*]

energy *n* **-ies 1** (the capacity for) vigorous activity; liveliness or vitality. **2** force or forcefulness. **3** (*physics*) power; the capacity to do work. [Gr *energeia*, from *en*, in + *ergon*, work]

energise or **-ize** *v* (*tr*) **1** to stimulate, invigorate or enliven. **2** to provide energy for the operation of (a machine, etc.).

enervate *v* (*tr*) **1** to take energy or strength from. **2** to deprive of moral or mental vigour. — *adj* **enervating**. — *n* **enervation**. [Lat *enervare*, to weaken]

enfant terrible *n* ***enfants terribles*** a person with a reputation for rude or embarrassing behaviour in public. [Fr, dreadful child]

enfeeble *v* (*tr; formal*) to make weak. — *adj* **enfeebled**. — *n* **enfeeblement**. [**en-** (sense **2**) + **feeble**]

enfilade (*mil*) *n* a continuous burst of gunfire sweeping from end to end across a line of enemy soldiers. — *v* (*tr*) to direct an enfilade at. [Fr *enfiler*, to thread]

enfold *v* (*tr;* **in**) **1** to wrap up, enclose. **2** to embrace. [**en-** (sense **3**) + **fold**]

enforce *v* (*tr*) **1** to cause (a law or decision) to be carried out. **2** (**on**) to impose (one's will, etc.) on. **3** to strengthen (an argument). **4** to persist in (a demand). — *adj* **enforceable**. — *n* **enforcement**. [OFr *enforcer*]

enforced *adj* not voluntary or optional.

enfranchise or **-ize** *v* (*tr; formal*) **1** to give the right to vote in elections to. **2** to set free, esp. from slavery. **3** to give (a town) the right to be represented in parliament. — *n* **enfranchisement**. [OFr *enfranchir*, to set free]

engage *v* **1** (*tr*) to take on as a worker. **2** (*tr*) to book or reserve. **3** (*tr;* **in**) to involve or occupy: *engage someone in conversation*. **4** (*intr* & *tr; mil;* **with**) to come or bring into battle: *engage (with) the enemy*. **5** (*tr* & *intr*) to (cause part of a machine, etc. to) fit into and lock with another part: *engage a gear*. [Fr *engager*]

engaged *adj* **1** (**to**) bound by a promise to marry. **2** (**in**) busy; occupied (with). **3** not free or vacant; occupied; being used.

engagement *n* **1** the act of engaging or state of being engaged. **2** a firm agreement between two people to marry. **3** an arrangement made in advance; an appointment. **4** (*mil*) a battle.

engaging *adj* charming or attractive. — *adv* **engagingly**.

engagé *adj* having or showing a political or moral commitment. [Fr]

engender *v* **-r-** (*tr*) to produce or cause (esp. feelings or emotions). [Fr *engendrer*]

engine *n* **1** a piece of machinery which converts power into work, esp. one that produces motion. **2** a railway locomotive. **3** (*formal*) a device or instrument: *an engine of destruction*. [OFr *engin*, from Lat *ingenium*, device]

engine-driver *n* a person who drives a railway locomotive.

engineer *n* **1** a person who designs, makes or works with machinery. **2** (also **civil engineer**) a person who designs or constructs roads, railways, bridges, etc. **3** an officer in charge of a ship's engines. **4** a person, esp. a member of the armed forces, who designs and builds military apparatus. — *v* (*tr*) **1** (often *derog*) to arrange or bring about by skill or deviousness. **2** to design or contruct as an engineer. [**engine + -eer**]

engineering *n* **1** the profession or the activities of an engineer of any kind. **2** the application of certain scientific techniques and processes not connected with engineers: *genetic engineering*.

English *adj* **1** of England or its people. **2** (usu. *offensive* to the Scots and Welsh) of Great Britain or its inhabitants. **3** of or using the English language. — *n* **1** the main language of Britain, N America, a great part of the British Commonwealth and some other countries. **2** (*pl* with **the**) the people of England, or of Great Britain. — **Middle English** English as spoken and written between about 1150 and 1500. — **Old English** English as spoken and written until about 1150. [OE *Englisc*]

English horn same as **cor anglais**.

Englishman and **Englishwoman** *n* a native or citizen of England.

engorged *adj* **1** crammed full. **2** (*med*) blocked by blood. [**en-** (sense **3**) + **gorge**]

engrave *v* (*tr*) **1** to carve (letters or designs) on stone, wood, metal, etc. **2** (**with**) to decorate (stone, etc.) in this way. **3** to fix or impress deeply (on the mind, etc.). — *n* **engraver**. [**en-** (sense **3**) + old word *grave*, to carve]

engraving *n* **1** the art of carving designs on stone, etc. **2** a piece of stone, etc. decorated in this way. **3** a print taken from an engraved metal plate.

engross *v* (*tr*) to take up completely the attention and interest of. — *adj* **engrossed**. — *adj* **engrossing**. [OFr *engrosser*, from *en gros*, completely]

engulf *v* (*tr*; **in**) **1** to swallow up completely. **2** to overwhelm. [**en-** (sense **3**) + *gulf*, to swallow]

enhance *v* (*tr*) to improve or increase the value, quality or intensity of (often something already good). — *n* **enhancement**. [OFr *enhauncer*]

enigma *n* **1** a puzzle or riddle. **2** a mysterious person, thing or situation. — *adj* **enigmatic**. — *adv* **enigmatically**. [Gr *ainigma*]

enjoin *v* (*tr; formal*) **1** to order or command (someone) to do something. **2** (with **on**) to impose on or demand from someone (behaviour of a certain kind): *enjoin politeness on one's children*. **3** (*legal*; **from**) to forbid with an injunction. [Fr *enjoindre*]

enjoy *v* (*tr*) **1** to find pleasure in. **2** to have, experience, have the benefit of (something good): *The room enjoys sunlight all day*. — *adj* **enjoyable**. — *adv* **enjoyably**. — *n* **enjoyment**. — **enjoy oneself** to experience pleasure or happiness. [OFr *enjoir*]

enkindle *v* (*tr*; *literary*) **1** to set fire to. **2** to stir up (feelings), or arouse strong feelings in. [**en-** (sense **3**) + **kindle**]

enlarge *v* **1** (*tr* & *intr*) to make or become larger. **2** (*tr*) to reproduce (a photograph, etc.) in a larger form. **3** (*intr* with **on**, **upon**) to speak or write about at greater length or in greater detail. [**en-** (sense **2**) + **large**]

enlargement *n* **1** something enlarged, esp. a photographic print larger than the standard or original print. **2** the act of enlarging or the state of being enlarged.

enlighten *v* **-*n*-** (*tr*) **1** to give more information to. **2** to free from prejudice, superstition, ignorance or misunderstanding. — *adj* **enlightening**. [**en-** (sense **3**) + **lighten**]

enlightened *adj* having or showing awareness and understanding and a freedom from prejudice and superstition.

enlightenment *n* **1** the act of enlightening or the state of being enlightened. **2** (*cap* with **the**) in 18th-century Europe, the philosophical belief in the ability of science and reasoning to improve the human condition, with a questioning of beliefs passed down by tradition and authority.

enlist *v* **1** (*intr*; **in**) to join one of the armed forces. **2** (*tr*) to obtain the support and help of; to obtain (support and help). — *n* **enlistment**. [**en-** (sense **1**) + **list**]

enlisted man or **woman** *n* (*US*) a member of the armed forces below the rank of officer.

enliven *v* **-*n*-** (*tr*) to make (more) active, lively or cheerful. — *n* **enlivenment**. [**en-** (sense **3**) + **liven**]

en masse all together; as a mass or group. [Fr]

enmesh *v* (*tr*) to catch or trap in, or as if in, a net; to entangle. [**en-** (sense **1**) + **mesh**]

enmity *n* **1** the state or quality of being an enemy. **2** ill-will; hostility. [OFr *enemistie*, from Lat, from *inimicus*, enemy]

ennoble *v* (*tr*) **1** to make (something) noble or dignified. **2** to make (someone) a member of the nobility. — *n* **ennoblement**. [**en-** (sense **2**) + **noble**]

ennui *n* (*literary*) boredom or discontent caused by a lack of activity or excitement. [Fr, boredom]

enormity *n* **-*ies*** **1** outrageousness or wickedness. **2** an outrageous or wicked act. **3** enormousness. [**enormous**]

enormous *adj* extremely large; huge. — *adv* **enormously**. — *n* **enormousness**. [Lat *enormis*, unusual]

enough *adj* in the number or quantity needed: *enough food to eat*. — *adv* **1** to the necessary degree or extent. **2** fairly: *She's pretty enough*. **3** quite: *Oddly enough, I can't remember*. — *pron* the amount needed. — **have had enough (of)** to be able to tolerate no more (of). [OE *genoh*]

en passant in passing; by the way. [Fr, in passing]

enquire, **enquiry**. See **inquire**.

enrage *v* (*tr*) to make very angry. — *adj* **enraged**. [OFr *enrager*]

enrapture *v* (*tr*) to give intense pleasure or joy to. — *adj* **enraptured** or **enrapt**. [**en-** (sense **1**) + **rapture**]

enrich *v* (*tr*) **1** to make better or stronger in quality, intensity, value, flavour, etc. **2** to make wealthy or wealthier. — *adj* **enriched**. — *n* **enrichment**. [**en-** (sense **2**) + **rich**]

enrol *v* **-*ll*-** **1** (*tr*) to add the name of (a person) to a list or roll, e.g. of members; to secure the membership or participation of. **2** (*intr*) to add one's own name to such a list; to become a member. — *n* **enrolment**. [OFr *enroller*]

en route (to, for) on the way (to). [Fr]

ensconce *v* (*tr*; *literary* or *humorous*; esp. in *passive*) to settle comfortably or safely. [**en-** (sense **1**) + *sconce*, small fort]

ensemble *n* **1** a small group of (usu. classical) musicians who regularly perform together. **2** a passage in opera, ballet, etc. performed by all the singers, musicians or dancers together. **3** a set of items of clothing worn together; an outfit. **4** all the parts of a thing considered as a whole. [Fr, together]

enshrine *v* (*tr*) **1** to enter and protect (a right, idea, etc.) in the laws or constitution of a state, constitution of an organisation, etc. **2** to place in a shrine. [**en-** (sense **1**) + **shrine**]

enshroud *v* (*tr*) **1** to cover completely; to hide by covering up. **2** to cover in a shroud. [**en-** (sense **1**) + **shroud**]

ensign *n* **1** the flag of a nation or regiment. **2** a coloured flag with a smaller union flag in one corner, esp. the **White Ensign**, the flag of the Royal Navy and the Royal Yacht Squadron, or the **Red Ensign**, the flag of the Merchant Navy. **3** (*hist*) the lowest rank of officer in the infantry, or an officer of this rank. **4** (*US*) the lowest rank in the navy, or an officer of this rank. [OFr *enseigne*, from Lat *insignia*, from *signum*, sign]

ensilage. Same as **silage**.

enslave *v* (*tr*) **1** to make into a slave. **2** to subject to a dominating influence. — *n* **enslavement**. [**en-** (sense **1**) + **slave**]

ensnare *v* (*tr*; **in, into**) to catch in, or as if in, a trap; to trick or lead dishonestly (into doing something). [**en-** (sense **1**) + **snare**]

ensue *v* (*intr*; **from**) **1** to follow, happen after. **2** to result (from). [OFr *ensuer*, from Lat *sequi*, to follow]

ensuing *adj* **1** following. **2** happening as a result.

en suite forming, or attached as part of, a single unit or set. — *adj* **en-suite**. [Fr, in sequence]

ensure *v* (*tr*) **1** to make certain; to assure or guarantee. **2** to make safe and secure. [OFr *enseurer*, from Lat *securus*, safe]

ENT *abbrev* ear, nose and throat.

-ent *sfx* (a person or thing) performing the stated action or function: *resident*; *different*. [Lat]

entablature *n* in classical architecture, the part of a building directly supported by the columns, usu. with a frieze and a cornice. [Ital *intavolatura*]

entail *v* (*tr*) **1** to have as a necessary result or requirement. **2** (*legal*; **on, upon**) to bequeath (property) to one's descendants, not allowing them the option to sell it. — *n* (*legal*) **1** the practice of entailing (property). **2** property which has been entailed. **3** the successive heirs to property. — *n* **entailment**. [**en-** (sense **1**) + **tail**[2].]

entangle *v* (*tr*; **in, with**) **1** to cause to get caught in some obstacle, e.g. a net. **2** to involve in difficulties. **3** to make complicated or confused. — *n* **entanglement**. [**en-** (sense **1**) + **tangle**]

entente cordiale *n* a friendly agreement or relationship between nations or states. [Fr, cordial understanding]

enter *v* **-r- 1** (*intr* & *tr*) to go or come in or into. **2** (*tr* & *intr*) to register (another person, oneself, one's work, etc.) in a competition. **3** (*tr*) to record in a book, diary, etc. **4** (*tr*) to join (a profession, society, etc.). **5** (*tr*) to submit or present: *enter a complaint*. **6** (*intr* with **into**) to begin to take part in. **7** (*intr* with **into**) to agree to be associated in or bound by: *enter into an agreement*. **8** (*intr* with **on, upon**) to begin: *enter upon a new stage of life*. [OFr *entrer*]

enteric *adj* (*med*) of the intestines. [Gr *enteron*, intestine]

enteritis *n* (*med*) inflammation of the intestine. [**entero-** + **-itis**]

entero- or **enter-** *comb fm* intestine, as in **enteritis**. [Gr *enteron*, intestine]

enterprise *n* **1** a project, undertaking. **2** a project that requires boldness and initiative. **3** boldness and initiative. **4** a business firm. [OFr *entreprendre*, to undertake]

enterprising *adj* full of enterprise. — *adv* **enterprisingly**.

entertain *v* **1** (*tr*) to provide amusement or recreation for. **2** (*intr* & *tr*) to give hospitality to (a guest), esp. in the form of a meal. **3** (*tr*) to consider or be willing to adopt (an idea, suggestion, etc.). [Fr *entretenir*, to maintain, to hold together]

entertainer *n* a person who provides amusement, esp. professionally.

entertaining *adj* interesting and amusing. — *adv* **entertainingly**.

entertainment *n* **1** something that entertains, e.g. a theatrical show. **2** the act of entertaining. **3** amusement or recreation.

enthral *v* **-ll-** (*tr*) to fascinate; to hold the attention or grip the imagination of. — *adj* **enthralled**. — *adj* **enthralling**. — *n* **enthralment**. [**en-** (sense **1**) + **thrall**]

enthrone *v* (*tr*) to place on a throne. — *n* **enthronement**. [**en-** (sense **1**) + **throne**]

enthuse *v* (*intr* & *tr*; **over, about**) to (cause to) be enthusiastic. [Back-formation from **enthusiasm**]

enthusiasm *n* lively or passionate interest or eagerness. [Gr *enthousiasmos*, zeal inspired by a god, from *en*, in + *theos*, god]

enthusiast *n* a person filled with enthusiasm, esp. for a particular subject; a fan or devotee. — *adj* **enthusiastic**. — *adv* **enthusiastically**.

entice *v* (*tr*) to tempt or persuade, by arousing hopes or desires or by promising a reward. — *n* **enticement**. — *adj* **enticing**. — *adv* **enticingly**. [OFr *enticier*]

entire *adj* **1** whole, complete. **2** absolute; total. — *n* **entireness**. [OFr *entier*, from Lat *integer*, whole]

entirely *adv* **1** fully or absolutely. **2** solely.

entirety *n* **-ies** completeness; wholeness. — **in its entirety** totally; taken as a whole.

entitle *v* (*tr*) **1** (**to**) to give (someone) a right to have, or to do, something. **2** to give a title or name to (a book, etc.). — *n* **entitlement**. [OFr *entitler*]

entity *n* **-ies 1** something that has a physical existence, as opposed to a quality or mood. **2** the essential nature (of something). **3** (*philos*) the fact or quality of existing. [Lat *entitas*, from *ens*, thing that exists]

ento- *comb fm* inside. ◇ See also **ecto-**, **endo-** and **exo-**. [Gr *entos*, within]

entomb *v* (*tr*) **1** to put in a tomb. **2** to cover, bury or hide as if in a tomb. — *n* **entombment**. [OFr *entoumber*]

entomology *n* the scientific study of insects. — *adj* **entomological**. — *n* **entomologist**. [Gr *entomon*, insect (from *entomos*, cut into sections) + **-logy**]

entourage *n* a group of followers or assistants, esp. if accompanying a famous or high-ranking person. [Fr, from *entourer*, to surround]

entr'acte *n* **1** an interval between the acts of a play. **2** (esp. *formerly*) entertainment provided during this interval. [Fr, from *entre*, between + *acte*, act]

entrails *n* (*pl*) **1** the internal organs of a person or animal. **2** (*literary*) the inner parts of anything. [OFr *entrailles*, from Lat *intralia*, from *inter*, within]

entrance[1] *n* **1** a way in, e.g. a door. **2** (*formal*) the act of entering: *gain entrance*. **3** the right to enter. **[enter + -ance]**

entrance[2] *v* (*tr*) **1** to grip the attention and imagination of. **2** to put into a trance. — *n* **entrancement**. — *adj* **entrancing**. **[en-** (sense **1**) + **trance]**

entrant *n* a person who enters (esp. an examination, a competition or a profession). **[enter + -ant]**

entrap *v* **-pp-** (*tr*) **1** to catch in, or as if in, a trap. **2** (with **into**) to trick (into doing something). [OFr *entraper*]

entrapment *n* **1** the act of entrapping or process of being entrapped. **2** (*legal*) the act or process of deliberately inducing someone to commit a crime in order to provide a reason for arresting and prosecuting him or her.

entreat *v* (*tr*; **for**) to ask passionately or desperately; to beg. [OFr *entraiter*]

entreaty *n* **-ies** a passionate or desperate request.

entrecôte *n* a boneless steak cut from between two ribs. [Fr, from *entre*, between + *côte*, rib]

entrée *n* **1** a small dish served after the fish course and before the main course at a formal dinner. **2** a main course. **3** (*formal*) the right of admission or entry: *entrée into polite society*. [Fr, entrance]

entrench *v* (*tr*) **1** to fix or establish firmly, often too firmly: *deeply entrenched ideas*. **2** to fortify with trenches dug around. — *n* **entrenchment**. **[en-** (sense **1**) + **trench]**

entrepôt *n* a port through which goods are imported and exported, often without duty being paid on them. [Fr, warehouse]

entrepreneur *n* a person who starts up or manages a business, using his or her drive and initiative and usu. with some personal financial risk. — *adj* **entrepreneurial**. [Fr, one who undertakes]

entropy *n* **-ies** (*physics*) **1** the measure of the energy in a mechanical or chemical system which is not available to perform work because it exists as the internal motion of molecules. **2** the measure of loss of order or of decay in the universe. [Ger *Entropie*, from Gr *en*, in + *tropos*, turn, change]

entrust *v* (*tr*; **to, with**) to give (something) to (someone) to take care of or deal with: *entrust her with the money*. **[en-** (sense **1**) + **trust]**

entry *n* **-ies 1** the act of coming or going in. **2** the right to enter. **3** a place of entering such as a door or doorway. **4** a person, or the total number of people, entered for a competition, etc. **5** an item written on a list, in a book, etc., or the act of recording an item in this way. [OFr *entree*, from *entrer*, to enter]

entryism *n* (usu. *derog*) the practice of joining a political party in large enough numbers to gain power and change the party's policies. — *n* **entryist**.

Entryphone ® *n* an intercom system fitted at the entrance to a building, esp. a block of flats, by which visitors can identify themselves to specific occupants before being admitted to the building.

entwine *v* (*tr*) **1** (**round, around, together**, etc.) to wind or twist. **2** to make by winding or twisting something together. **[en-** (sense **3**) + **twine]**

E-number. See **E**[2].

enumerate *v* (*tr*) **1** to list one by one. **2** to count. — *n* **enumeration**. — *adj* **enumerative**. [Lat *enumerare*, to count up]

enunciate *v* **1** (*tr* & *intr*) to pronounce (words) clearly. **2** (*tr*) to state formally. — *n* **enunciation**. [Lat *enuntiare*, to announce]

enuresis *n* (*med*) involuntary urination, esp. during sleep. — *adj* **enuretic**. [Gr *en*, in + *ouresis*, urination]

envelop *v* **-p-** (*tr*) to cover, wrap, surround or conceal. — *n* **envelopment**. [OFr *envoloper*, from *en*, in + *voloper*, to wrap]

envelope *n* **1** a thin flat sealable paper packet or cover, esp. for a letter. **2** a cover or wrapper of any kind. **3** (*biol*) any plant or animal structure that contains or encloses something, e.g. a ring of petals or a shell. **4** (*tech*) the bag containing the gas in a balloon or airship. [Fr *enveloppe*, from *enveloper*; see ety. at **envelop]**

enviable *adj* causing envy; highly desirable. — *adv* **enviably**. **[envy + -able]**

envious *adj* feeling or showing envy. — *adv* **enviously**. **[envy + -ous]**

environment *n* **1** the surroundings or conditions within which something or someone exists. **2** (usu. with **the**) the natural conditions necessary for the healthy existence of all plants, animals and people. — *adj* **environmental**. — *adv* **environmentally**. [OFr *environnement*, from *environner*, to surround]

environmentalism *n* concern about the natural environment and its protection from pollution and other harmful influences. — *n* **environmentalist**.

environs *n* (*pl*) surrounding areas, esp. the outskirts of a town or city. [OFr *environ*, around]

envisage *v* (*tr*) **1** to picture in the mind. **2** to consider to be likely in the future. [Fr *envisager*, from *visage*, face]

envoy *n* **1** a diplomat ranking next below an ambassador. **2** a messenger or agent. [Fr *envoyer*, to send]

envy *n* **1** bitter or resentful feelings of desire for another person's better fortune, success, personal qualities or possessions.

2 the cause of such feelings. — *v* **-ies**, **-ied** (*tr*) to feel envy against (a person) about (his or her better fortune, etc.): *envy (her) her success*. [OFr *envie*]

enzyme *n* any of a large class of proteins produced by living cells, which act as catalysts in biochemical reactions. [Gr *en*, in + *zume*, leaven]

EOC *abbrev* Equal Opportunities Commission.

Eocene *adj & n* (of) a geological epoch of the early Tertiary. [Gr *eos*, dawn + *kainos*, recent]

eolian. Same as **aeolian**.

eolithic *adj* (also *cap*) of or relating to the early part of the Stone Age, when very crude stone implements were first used by man. [Gr *eos*, dawn + *lithos*, stone]

eon. See **aeon**.

EP *n* an *extended-play* gramophone record, the same size as a single but with about twice the playing-time.

epaulette or **epaulet** *n* a decoration on the shoulder of a garment, esp. a military uniform. [Fr *épaulette*, from *épaule*, shoulder]

épée *n* a sword with a narrow flexible blade, used formerly in duelling and, with a blunted end, in modern fencing. [Fr]

ephemeral *adj* **1** lasting a very short time. **2** (of insects and flowers) lasting for only a day or a few days. — *adv* **ephemerally**. [Gr *ephemeros*, living a day, from *epi*, for + *hemera*, day]

ephemera *n* (*pl*) short-lived, transitory things.

epi- *comb fm* above, over or upon, as in **epicentre**. [Gr *epi*, on, over]

epic *n* **1** a long narrative poem telling of heroic acts, the birth and death of nations, etc. **2** a long adventure story, film, etc. — *adj* of or like an epic, esp. large-scale and impressive. [Gr *epikos*, from *epos*, word, song]

epicene *adj* **1** having characteristics of both sexes, or of neither sex. **2** of, or for use by, both sexes. **3** effeminate. **4** (*gram*) (of a noun) referring to people or animals of either sex, e.g. 'driver', as opposed to 'waiter' and 'waitress'. [Gr *epikoinos*, common to many]

epicentre *n* the place on the earth's surface which is directly above the point of origin of an earthquake. [Gr *epi*, over + *kentron*, point]

epicure *n* a person who has refined taste, esp. one who enjoys good food and drink. [*Epicurus*, the ancient Greek philosopher who argued that pleasure is the highest good]

epicurean *adj* **1** given to luxury or to the tastes of an epicure. **2** (usu. *cap*) relating to the theories of Epicurus. — *n* **epicureanism** or **Epicureanism**.

epicurism *n* **1** the pursuit of pleasure, esp. as found in good food and drink. **2** the tendency to be critical and hard to please in matters of luxury.

epidemic *n* **1** a sudden and widespread outbreak of a disease. **2** the disease itself. **3** a sudden and extensive spread of anything undesirable. — *adj* of or like an epidemic. [Gr *epi*, among + *demos*, the people]

epidemiology *n* the branch of medicine dealing with the occurrence, distribution and control of epidemics. [**epidemic** + **-logy**]

epidermis *n* (*med*) the thin outer layer of the skin. — *adj* **epidermal**. [Gr *epi*, upon + *derma*, the skin]

epidural *adj* (*med*) situated on, or administered into, the dura mater, the membrane enveloping the brain and the spinal cord. — *n* (*med*) an epidural anaesthetic, administered esp. during childbirth to remove all sensation below the waist. [**epi-** + *dura* (*mater*)]

epiglottis *n* a flap of cartilage which hangs at the back of the tongue to prevent food and drink from entering the lungs. — *adj* **epiglottal**. [Gr *epi*, over + *glottis*, glottis]

epigram *n* a witty or sarcastic saying, or a short poem with such an ending. — *adj* **epigrammatic**. — *adv* **epigrammatically**. [Gr *epigramma*, from *epi*, upon + *gramma*, writing]

epigraph *n* **1** a quotation or motto at the beginning of a book or chapter. **2** an inscription on a building. [Gr *epigraphe*, from *epi*, upon + *graphein*, to write]

epilepsy *n* a disorder of the nervous system causing periodic loss of consciousness, usu. accompanied by violent convulsions. [Gr *epilepsia*, from *epilambanein*, to seize]

epileptic *adj* of or suffering from epilepsy. — *n* a person who suffers from epilepsy.

epilogue *n* **1** the closing section of a book, programme, etc. **2** a speech addressed to the audience at the end of a play. [Gr *epilogos*, from *epi*, upon + *logos*, speech]

epiphany *n* **-ies** **1** (usu. *cap*) the Christian festival on 6 January which, in the western churches, commemorates the showing of Christ to the three wise men, and, in the orthodox and other eastern churches, the baptism of Christ. **2** the sudden appearance of a god. **3** (*literary*) a sudden revelation or insight. [Gr *epiphaneia*, manifestation]

episcopacy *n* **-ies** **1** the government of the church by bishops. **2** bishops as a group. **3** the position or period of office of a bishop. [Gr *episkopos*, overseer]

episcopate *n* **1** the position or period of office of a bishop. **2** bishops as a group. **3** an area under the care of a bishop; a diocese or bishopric.

episcopal *adj* of, relating to, or governed by bishops. — *adv* **episcopally**. [Ety. as for **episcopacy**]

episcopalian *adj* **1** relating to or advocating church government by bishops. — *n* a member of an episcopal (esp. Anglican) church. — *n* **episcopalianism**.

episcopate. See **episcopacy**.

episiotomy *n* **-ies** (*med*) a surgical cut made at the opening of the vagina during childbirth, to assist the delivery of the baby. [Gr *epision*, pubic area + **-tomy**]

episode *n* **1** one of several events or distinct periods making up a longer sequence. **2** one of the separate parts in which a radio or television serial is broadcast or a serialised novel, etc. published. **3** (*literature*) any scene or incident forming part of a novel or narrative poem, often one providing a digression from the main story. [Gr *epeisodion*, from *epi*, upon + *eisodos*, a coming in]

episodic *adj* **1** consisting of several distinct periods. **2** occurring at intervals; sporadic. — *adv* **episodically**.

epistemology *n* the study or theory of how knowledge is obtained, how valid knowledge is, and what its limits are. — *adj* **epistemological**. — *adv* **epistemologically**. [Gr *episteme*, knowledge + **-logy**]

epistle *n* **1** (*literary* or *facet*) a letter, esp. a long one dealing with important matters. **2** a novel or poem written in the form of letters. **3** (usu. *cap*) any of the letters written by Christ's apostles which form part of the New Testament. **4** a reading from one of the Epistles as part of a religious service. [Lat *epistola*]

epistolary *adj* (*formal* or *literary*) relating to or consisting of letters. [Ety as for **epistle**]

epitaph *n* **1** an inscription on a gravestone. **2** a short commemorative speech or piece of writing in a similar style. [Gr *epitaphion*, from *epi*, upon + *taphos*, tomb]

epithelium *n* **-ia** (*biol*) the top layer of tissue covering all external and internal surfaces of a body. — *adj* **epithelial**. [Gr *epi*, upon + *thele*, nipple]

epithet *n* an adjective or short descriptive phrase which captures the particular quality of the person or thing it describes: *King Ethelred II was given the epithet 'The Unready'*. [Gr *epitheton*, from *epi*, on + *tithenai*, to place]

epitome *n* **1** a miniature representation of a larger or wider idea, issue, etc. **2** a person or thing that is the embodiment of or a perfect example of (a quality, etc.). **3** a summary of a written work. [Gr, abridgement]

epitomise or **-ize** *v* (*tr*) to be or make an epitome of.

EPNS *abbrev* electroplated nickel silver.

epoch *n* **1** (the start of) a particular period of history, a person's life, etc., usu. marked by some important event. **2** (*geol*) a division of a geological period, during which a single layer of rock is formed. — *adj* **epochal**. [Gr *epoche*, fixed point]

epoch-making *adj* (often *facet*) very significant.

eponym *n* a person after whom something is named, esp. the main character in a play, novel, etc. whose name provides its title. — *adj* **eponymous**. [Gr *epi*, upon + *onyma*, a name]

EPOS *abbrev* electronic point of sale.

epoxy *n* **-ies** (also **epoxy resin**) an industrially prepared chemical resin, used in laminates and as an adhesive. — *adj* (*chem*) containing an oxygen atom bonded to two carbon atoms. [Gr *epi*, upon + **oxygen**]

Epsom salts *n* (*sing* or *pl*) a bitter white powder, a preparation of magnesium sulphate, used as a medicine for clearing the bowels. [*Epsom* in Surrey, where it occurs naturally in spring water]

equable *adj* **1** (of a climate) never showing very great variations or extremes. **2** (of a person) even-tempered. — *n* **equability**. — *adv* **equably**. [Lat *aequabilis*, from *aequus*, equal]

equal *adj* **1** (**to**) the same in size, amount, value, etc. **2** evenly balanced; displaying no advantage or bias. **3** having the same status; having or entitled to the same rights. **4** (with **to**) having the necessary ability (for). — *n* a person or thing of the same age, rank, ability, worth, etc. — *v* **-ll-** (*tr*) **1** to be the same in amount, value, size, etc. as. **2** to be as good as; to match. **3** to achieve something which matches (a previous achievement or achiever). — *n* **equality**, **-ies**. — *adv* **equally**. [Lat *aequus*]

equalise or **-ize** *v* **1** (*tr* & *intr*) to make or become equal. **2** (*intr*) to reach the same score as an opponent, after being behind. — *n* **equalisation** or **-z-**.

equaliser or **-z-** *n* a person or thing that equalises, esp. a goal or point scored which makes one equal to one's opponent. ◇ See also **graphic equaliser** under **graph**.

equal opportunities *n* (*pl*) the principle of equal treatment of all employees or candidates for employment, irrespective of race, religion, sex, etc.

equanimity *n* calmness of temper; composure. [Lat *aequanimitas*, from *aequus*, equal + *animus*, mind]

equate *v* **1** (*tr*; **to, with**) to regard as equivalent. **2** (*intr*; **with**) to be equivalent. [Lat *aequare*, to make equal]

equation *n* **1** a mathematical statement of the equality of two quantities or groups. **2** a scientific formula expressing the reaction of chemical compounds. **3** the act of equating.

equator *n* (with **the**) an imaginary line (or one drawn on a map, etc.) passing round the Earth at an equal distance from the North and South poles. [Lat *aequator*, equaliser (of day and night)]

equatorial *adj* of or near the equator.

equerry *n* **-ies** an official who serves as a personal attendant to a member of a royal family. [OFr *esquierie*, company of squires, from *esquier*, squire]

equestrian *adj* **1** of horse-riding or horses. **2** on horseback. [Lat *equestris*, relating to horsemen]

equi- *comb fm* equal or equally, as in **equidistant**. [Lat *aequus*, equal]

equiangular *adj* having equal angles.

equidistant *adj* (**from**) equally distant. — *n* **equidistance**.

equilateral *adj* having all sides of equal length. [**equi-** + Lat *latus*, side]

equilibrium *n* **1** a state of balance between weights, forces, etc. **2** a calm and composed state of mind. [Lat *aequi librium*, from *aequus*, equal + *libra*, balance]

equine *adj* (*formal*) of, relating to or like a horse or horses. [Lat *equinus*, from *equus*, horse]

equinoctial *adj* happening on or near an equinox. — *n* **1** a storm or gale occurring about the time of an equinox. **2** (*astron*; also **equinoctial line**) the celestial equator, the imaginary line occurring where the plane of the earth's equator cuts the celestial sphere (the imaginary sphere to which the stars appear to be fixed).

equinox *n* either of the two occasions on which the sun crosses the equator, making night and day equal in length, the **vernal** or **spring equinox** occurring around 21 March and the **autumnal equinox** around 23 September. [Lat *a equi noctium*, from *aequus*, equal + *nox*, night]

equip *v* **-pp-** (*tr*; **for, with**) to fit out or provide with the necessary tools, supplies, abilities, etc. [Fr *équiper*, from OFr *eschiper*, to fit out a ship, prob. from Norse *skip*, ship]

equipment *n* **1** the clothes, machines, tools, instruments, etc. necessary for a particular kind of work or activity. **2** (*formal*) the act of equipping.

equipage *n* **1** a horse-drawn carriage with its footmen. **2** (esp. *formerly*) the equipment carried by a military unit. [**equip** + **-age**]

equipoise *n* (*formal*) **1** a state of balance. **2** a counterbalancing weight. [**equi-** + **poise**]

equitable *adj* **1** fair and just. **2** (*legal*) relating to, or valid according to, the concept of natural justice, or equity, as opposed to common law or statute law. [Fr *équitable*; see ety. for **equity**]

equitation *n* (*formal*) the art of riding a horse. [Lat *equitare*, to ride, from *equus*, horse]

equity *n* **-ies 1** fairness or justness. **2** (*legal*) the concept of natural justice, as opposed to common law or statute law, often invoked to support an interpretation, or the complete waiving, of a law. **3** (usu. in *pl*) an ordinary share in a company. [OFr *equite*, from Lat *aequitas*, equality]

equivalent *adj* equal in value, power, meaning, etc. — *n* an equivalent thing, amount, etc. — *n* **equivalence**. — *adv* **equivalently**. [Lat *aequus*, equal + *valere*, to be worth]

equivocal *adj* **1** ambiguous; of doubtful meaning. **2** of an uncertain nature. **3** questionable, suspicious or mysterious. — *adv* **equivocally**. [Lat *aequivocus*, from *aequus*, equal + *vox*, voice, word]

equivocate *v* (*intr*) to use ambiguous words in order to deceive or to avoid answering a question. — *n* **equivocation**. [Ety. as for **equivocal**]

ER *abbrev* **1** *Elizabeth Regina* (Lat), Queen Elizabeth. **2** *Edwardus Rex* (Lat), King Edward.

Er *symbol* (*chem*) erbium.

-er[1] *sfx* used to form the comparative of adjectives and some adverbs, as in **happier** and **sooner**. [OE *-ra* (*adj*), *-or* (*adv*)]

-er[2] *sfx* **1** used to form words meaning the person or thing performing the action of the stated verb, as in **driver** and **heater**. **2** used to form words meaning a person from the stated town or city, as in **Londoner** and **New Yorker**. [OE *-ere*]

era *n* **1** a distinct period in history marked by or beginning at an important event. **2** (*geol*) a main division of time. [Lat *aera*, number]

eradicate *v* (*tr*) to get rid of completely. — *n* **eradication**. [Lat *eradicare*, to root out]

erase *v* (*tr*) **1** to rub out (pencil marks, etc.). **2** to remove all trace of. [Lat *eradere*, to scratch out]

eraser *n* something that erases, esp. a rubber for removing pencil or ink marks.

erasure *n* **1** the act of rubbing out. **2** a place where something written has been erased.

erbium *n* an element (symbol **Er**), a soft silvery-white rare metal. [Ytt*erby* in Sweden, where it was first discovered]

ere *prep* & *conj* (*poetic*) before. [OE *ær*]

erect *adj* **1** upright; not bent or leaning. **2** (of the penis, clitoris or nipples) enlarged and rigid through being filled with blood, usu. as a result of sexual excitement. — *v* (*tr*) **1** to put up or to build. **2** to set or put (a pole, flag, etc.) in a vertical position. **3** to set up or establish. — *adv* **erectly**. — *n* **erectness**. [Lat *erigere*, to set upright]

erectile *adj* (*physiol*) (of an organ, etc.) capable of becoming erect.

erection *n* **1** the act of erecting or the state of being erected. **2** (sometimes *derog*) a building or structure. **3** (of a sexual organ, esp. the penis) the process of becoming erect or the state of being erect. **4** an erect sexual organ, esp. the penis.

erg *n* the unit of work or energy in the centimetre-gramme-second system of measurement. [Gr *ergon*, work]

ergo *adv* (*formal* or *logic*) therefore. [Lat]

ergonomics *n* the study of the relationship between people and the machines they work with and the environment they work in, with a view to increasing efficiency in work. — *adj* **ergonomic**. — *adv* **ergonomically**. — *n* **ergonomist**. [Gr *ergon*, work + *-nomics* as in **economics**]

ergot *n* **1** a disease of rye and other cereals, caused by a fungus. **2** the fungus itself, or a medical preparation of it, used esp. to ease contractions in childbirth. [Fr]

Erin *n* (*old* or *poetic*) Ireland. [OIrish *Erinn*]
ermine *n* **1** the stoat, esp. the northern breed whose winter coat is white. **2** this fur, used esp. to decorate the ceremonial robes of judges, etc. [OFr *hermine*, from Lat *Armenius* (*mus*), Armenian (mouse)]
Ernie *n* the computer which applies the laws of chance to pick the prize-winning numbers of premium bonds. [*E*lectronic *r*andom *n*umber *i*ndicator *e*quipment]
erode *v* (*tr* & *intr*) to wear away, destroy or be destroyed gradually. ◇ See also **erosion**. [Lat *erodere*, to gnaw away]
erogenous *adj* (of part of the body) sensitive to sexual stimulation. [Gr *eros*, love + *genes*, born]
erosion *n* the wearing away, or eroding, of rock, soil, etc. by the action of wind, water or ice. — *adj* **erosive**. [Ety. as for **erode**]
erotic *adj* of or arousing sexual desire, or giving sexual pleasure. — *adv* **erotically**. [Gr *erotikos*, from *eros*, love]
erotica *n* (*pl*) erotic literature, pictures, etc.
eroticism *n* **1** the erotic quality of a piece of writing, a picture, etc. **2** interest in, or pursuit of, sexual sensations. **3** the use of erotic images and symbols in art, literature, etc.
err *v* (*intr*) **1** to make a mistake, be wrong, or do wrong. **2** to sin. — **err on the side of** to be guilty of a fault, or of what might be seen as a fault, in order to avoid an opposite and greater fault: *err on the side of caution rather than rush in too quickly*. [OFr *errer*, from Lat *errare*, to stray]
errand *n* **1** a short journey made in order to get or do something, esp. for someone else. **2** the purpose of such a journey. [OE *ærende*, mission]
errant *adj* **1** (*formal* or *literary*) doing wrong; erring. **2** (*old* or *literary*) wandering in search of adventure: *a knight errant*. — *n* **errantry**. [OFr *errer*, in sense **1** from Lat *errare*, to stray, and in sense **2** from Lat *itinerare*, to make a journey]
errata. See **erratum**.
erratic *adj* **1** irregular; having no fixed pattern or course. **2** unpredictable in behaviour. — *adv* **erratically**. [Lat *errare*, to stray]
erratum *n* **-ta** (*formal*) an error in writing or printing. [Lat, from *errare*, to stray]
erroneous *adj* (of an impression, etc.; not of a person) wrong or mistaken. — *adv* **erroneously**. — *n* **erroneousness**. [Lat *erroneus*, straying]
error *n* **1** a mistake, inaccuracy or misapprehension. **2** the state of being mistaken. **3** the possible discrepancy between an estimate and an actual value or amount: *a margin of error*. [Lat, a wandering or straying, error]
ersatz (*derog*) *n* a cheaper substitute, often used because the genuine article is unavailable. — *adj* substitute; imitation. [Ger]
Erse *n* & *adj* Gaelic, formerly Scottish Gaelic, now usu. Irish Gaelic. [Lowland Scots *Erisch*, Irish]
erstwhile *adj* (*formal* or *old*) former; previous. [OE *ærest*, from *ær*, before]
eructation *n* (*formal*) **1** a belch or the act of belching. **2** the sending out of ash and gases from a volcano. [Lat *eructare*, to belch out]
erudite *adj* showing or having a great deal of knowledge; learned. — *adv* **eruditely**. — *n* **erudition**. [Lat *erudire*, to instruct]
erupt *v* (*intr*) **1** (of a volcano) to throw out lava, ash and gases. **2** to break out suddenly and violently. **3** (of a skin blemish) to appear suddenly and in a severe form. — *n* **eruption**. [Lat *erumpere*, to break out]
-ery or **-ry** *sfx* **1** indicating a place where work or an activity of the stated kind is carried out: *brewery*. **2** indicating a class, group or type of the stated kind: *greenery* and *weaponry*. **3** indicating an art, skill or practice of the stated kind: *dentistry*. **4** indicating behaviour of the stated kind: *bravery*. **5** indicating anything connected with the stated person or thing: *popery*. [Fr *-erie*, from Lat *-arius*]
erysipelas *n* an infectious disease of the skin, esp. of the face, producing deep red sore patches, accompanied by fever. [Gr, perhaps from *eruthros*, red + *pella*, skin]
erythrocyte *n* (*med*) a red blood corpuscle. [Gr *erythros*, red + *kytos*, hollow vessel]
Es *symbol* (*chem*) einsteinium.
-es[1,2]. See **-s**[1,2].
Esc. *abbrev* escudo.
escalate *v* (*intr* & *tr*) to increase or be increased rapidly in scale, degree, etc. — *n* **escalation**. [Back-formation from **escalator**]
escalator *n* a type of conveyor belt which forms a continuous moving staircase. [Orig. a trademark]
escallop *n*. Same as **scallop**.
escalope *n* a thin slice of boneless meat, esp. veal. [Fr]
escapade *n* a daring, adventurous or unlawful act. [Fr]
escape *v* **1** (*intr*) to gain freedom. **2** (*tr*) to manage to avoid (punishment, disease, etc.). **3** (*tr*) not to be noticed or remembered by: *Nothing escapes his notice*. **4** (*intr*) (of a gas, liquid, etc.) to leak out or get out. **5** (*tr*) (of words, etc.) to be uttered unintentionally by. — *n* **1** an act of escaping. **2** a means of escape. **3** the avoidance of danger or harm: *a narrow escape*. **4** a leak or release. **5** something providing a break or distraction. [OFr *escaper*, prob. from Lat *excappare*, to remove one's cape]
escape clause *n* a clause in a contract stating the conditions under which the contract may be broken.
escapee *n* a person who has escaped, esp. from prison.

escapement *n* the mechanism in a clock or watch which connects the moving parts to the balance.

escape road *n* a short side-road, e.g. at a bend on a hill, into which a driver can turn in order to stop if in difficulty.

escape velocity *n* (*tech*) the minimum velocity required for a space vehicle, etc. to escape from the gravity of a planet.

escapism *n* the means of escaping, or the tendency to escape, from unpleasant reality into day-dreams or fantasy. — *n* & *adj* **escapist**.

escapology *n* the art or practice of freeing oneself from chains and other constraints, esp. as theatrical entertainment. — *n* **escapologist**. [**escape** + **-logy**]

escarpment *n* the long steep side of a hill or rock face. [Fr *escarper*, to cut steeply]

eschatology *n* the branch of theology dealing with last things, e.g. death, divine judgement and life after death. — *adj* **eschatological**. [Gr *eschatos*, last + **-logy**]

escheat (*legal*) *n* **1** (*formerly*) the handing over of property to the state or a feudal lord in the absence of a legal heir. **2** property handed over in this way. — *v* **1** (*intr*) to be handed over in this way. **2** (*tr*) to hand over, or confiscate (property). [OFr *eschete*, from *escheoir*, to fall to someone]

eschew *v* (*tr*; *formal*) to avoid, keep away from, or abstain from. — *n* **eschewal**. [OFr *eschever*]

escort *n* **1** one or more people, vehicles, etc. accompanying another or others for protection, guidance, or as a mark of honour. **2** a person of the opposite sex asked or hired to accompany another at a social event. — *v* (*tr*) to accompany as an escort. [Fr *escorte*]

escritoire *n* a writing-desk, usu. ornamented and with drawers, compartments, etc. [Fr, from Lat *scriptorium*, writing-room]

escudo *n* **-os** (*abbrev* **Esc.**) the standard unit of currency in Portugal. [Port, from Lat *scutum*, shield]

esculent (*formal*) *adj* edible. — *n* any edible substance. [Lat *esculentus*, from *esca*, food]

escutcheon *n* **1** a shield decorated with a coat of arms. **2** a small metal plate around a keyhole or doorknob. — **a blot on the escutcheon** (usu. *facet*) a stain on one's good reputation. [OFr *escuchon*, from Lat *scutum*, shield]

-ese *sfx* **1** of a stated country or place, as in **Japanese** and **Viennese**. **2** indicating the people or language of a stated country, as in **Chinese**. **3** (often *derog*) the typical style or language of a stated profession, as in **journalese**. [OFr *-eis*, from Lat *-ensis*]

Eskimo *n* **-mos** or **-mo** **1** a member of any of several peoples who inhabit northern Canada, Greenland, Alaska and eastern Siberia. (Although **Eskimo** is the established English name for the people, the people themselves find it offensive and prefer to be known as **Inuit**.) **2** the family of languages spoken by these peoples. — *adj* of or relating to these peoples or their language. [Dan, from Abnaki (N American Indian language) *esquimantsic*, eaters of raw flesh]

Eskimo dog *n* a powerful breed of dog used by Eskimos to pull sledges.

ESL *abbrev* English as a second language.

ESN *abbrev* educationally subnormal.

esophagus. Same as **oesophagus**.

esoteric *adj* understood only by those few people who have the necessary special knowledge; secret; mysterious. — *adv* **esoterically**. [Gr *esoterikos*, from *eso*, within]

ESP *abbrev* **1** English for special purposes. **2** extra-sensory perception.

esp. *abbrev* especially.

espadrille *n* a light canvas shoe with a sole made of rope or other plaited fibre. [Fr, from Provençal *espardillo*, from *espart*, esparto grass]

espalier *n* **1** a trellis or arrangement of wires against which a shrub or fruit tree is trained to grow flat, e.g. against a wall. **2** such a shrub or tree. [Fr]

esparto or **esparto grass** *n* a tough coarse grass native to Spain and N Africa, used to make rope, etc. [Span, from Lat, from Gr *sparton*, kind of rope]

especial *adj* special. — *adv* **especially**. [OFr, from Lat *specialis*, individual]

Esperanto *n* a language invented for international use, published in 1887. [The pseudonym of its inventor, Dr Zamenhof, meaning 'the one who hopes']

espionage *n* the activity of spying, or the use of spies to gather information. [Fr *espionnage*, from *espion*, spy]

esplanade *n* a long wide pavement next to a beach. [Fr]

espouse *v* (*tr*) **1** (*formal*) to adopt or give one's support to (a cause, etc.). **2** (*old*) to marry, or to give (e.g. a daughter) in marriage. [OFr *espouser*, to marry]

espousal *n* **1** (*formal*) the act of espousing (a cause, etc.). **2** (*old*) a marriage or engagement.

espresso *n* **-os** **1** coffee made by forcing steam or boiling water through ground coffee beans. **2** the machine for making it. [Ital, pressed out]

esprit *n* (*formal* or *literary*) liveliness or wit. [Fr, spirit]

esprit de corps *n* (*formal* or *literary*) loyalty to, or concern for the honour of, a group or body to which one belongs. [Fr, group spirit]

espy *v* **-ies**, **-ied** (*tr*; *literary* or *humorous*) to catch sight of; to observe. [OFr *espier*]

Esq. *abbrev* esquire.

-esque *sfx* **1** in the style or fashion of: *Byronesque*. **2** like, or similar to: *picturesque*. [Fr]

esquire *n* **1** (usu. *abbrev* **Esq.**) a title used after a man's name when no other form of address, e.g. Mr, is used, esp. when addressing letters. **2** a squire. [OFr *esquier*, squire]

-ess *sfx* indicating a female of the type or class: *lioness* and *duchess*. [Fr *-esse*, from Lat *-issa*]

essay *n* **1** a short formal piece of writing, usu. dealing with a single subject. **2** (*formal*) an attempt. — *v* (*tr*; *formal*) to attempt. [Fr *essayer*, to try]

essayist *n* a writer of literary essays.

essence *n* **1** the basic distinctive part or quality of something, determining its nature or character. **2** a liquid obtained from a plant, drug, etc. and having its properties in concentrated form. — **in essence** basically or fundamentally. — **of the essence** absolutely necessary or extremely important. [Fr, from Lat *esse*, to be]

essential *adj* **1** absolutely necessary. **2** of the basic or inner nature, the essence, of something. — *n* **1** something necessary. **2** a basic or fundamental element, principle or piece of information. — *n* **essentiality**.

essentially *adv* **1** basically; most importantly. **2** necessarily.

essential oils *n* (*pl*) the oils which give plants their smell, used in food as flavourings, in perfumes, and in herbal medicine.

est. *abbrev* established.

-est[1] *sfx* forming the superlative of regular adjectives and some adverbs: *quickest* and *soonest*. [OE *-est* and *-ost*]

-est[2] or **-st** *sfx* forming the *old* second person singular forms of verbs (used with the pronoun *thou*): *knowest* and *canst*. [OE *-est*, *-ast*, *-st*]

est. *abbrev* **1** established. **2** estimated.

establish *v* (*tr*) **1** (**as, in**) to settle firmly (in a position, place, job, etc.). **2** to set up (e.g. a university or a business). **3** to find, show, or prove. **4** to cause people to accept (e.g. a custom or a claim). [OFr *establir*]

established *adj* **1** settled or accepted. **2** (of a church) recognised as the official church of a country.

establishment *n* **1** the act of establishing. **2** a business, its premises, or its staff. **3** a public or government institution: *a research establishment*. **4** (*cap* with **the**) the group of people in a country, society or community who hold power and exercise authority, regarded as being opposed to change.

estate *n* **1** a large piece of land owned by a person or group of people. **2** an area of land on which development of a particular kind has taken place, e.g. houses (a **housing estate**) or factories (an **industrial** or **trading estate**). **3** (*legal*) a person's total possessions (property, money, etc.), esp. at death. **4** a plantation. **5** (esp. *hist*) any of various groups or classes within the social structure of society, e.g. the **first estate** or lords spiritual (i.e. bishops and archbishops), the **second estate** or lords temporal (i.e. the nobility) and the **third estate** (the common people). **6** (*old*) a condition or state: *the holy estate of matrimony*. [OFr *estat*]

estate agent *n* **1** a person whose job is the buying, selling, leasing and valuation of houses and other property. **2** the manager of a private estate.

estate car *n* a car with a large area behind the rear seats for luggage, etc., and a rear door.

estate duty. Same as **death duty**.

esteem *v* (*tr*) **1** to value, respect or think highly of. **2** (*formal*) to consider to be. — *n* high regard or respect. [OFr *estimer*, from Lat *aestimare*, to estimate the value of]

ester *n* a chemical compound formed by the reaction of an acid with an alcohol. [Prob. a contraction of Ger *Essigäther*, acetic ether]

esthetic. Same as **aesthetic**.

estimable *adj* highly respected; worthy of respect. [Ety. as for **estimate**]

estimate *v* (*tr*) **1** (**at**) to judge or calculate (size, amount, value, etc.) roughly or without measuring. **2** to have or form an opinion (that); to think. **3** (**at**) to submit to a possible client a statement of (the likely cost) of carrying out (a job). — *n* **1** a rough assessment (of size, etc.). **2** a calculation of the probable cost of a job. — *n* **estimator**. [Lat *aestimare*, to estimate the value of]

estimation *n* **1** judgement; opinion. **2** the act of estimating.

estrange *v* (*tr*; **from**) to cause (someone) to break away from a previously friendly state or relationship. — *adj* **estranged**. — *n* **estrangement**. [OFr *estranger*, from Lat *extraneare*, to treat as a stranger]

estuary *n* **-ies** the widening lower tidal part of a river, the end of which flows into the sea. [Lat *aestus*, commotion, tide]

ETA *abbrev* estimated time of arrival.

et al. *abbrev* for *et alia* or *alii* (Lat), and other things or people.

etc. *abbrev* et cetera.

et cetera or **etcetera** (usu. **etc.** or **&c.**) (Lat) and the rest, and so on.

etceteras *n* (*pl*) additional things or people; extras.

etch *v* (**on, in**) **1** (*tr* & *intr*) to make (designs) on (metal, glass, etc.) using an acid to eat out the lines. **2** (*tr*) to make a deep or irremovable impression. — *n* **etcher**. [Ger *ätzen*, to etch, eat away with acid]

etching *n* **1** the act or art of making etched designs. **2** a print made from an etched plate.

ETD *abbrev* estimated time of departure.

eternal *adj* **1** without beginning or end; everlasting. **2** unchanging; valid for all time. **3** (*coll*) frequent, endless. — *adv* **eternally**. — **the Eternal** God. [OFr *eternel*, from Lat *aeternalis*]

eternal triangle *n* a relationship, involving love and jealousy, between two men and a woman, or two women and a man.

eternity *n* **-*ies*** **1** time regarded as having no end. **2** the state of being eternal. **3** (*relig*) a timeless existence after death. **4** (*coll*) an extremely long time. [OFr *eternite*]

eternity ring *n* a ring set with a circle of stones, as a symbol of lasting love.

ethane *n* a colourless, odourless hydrocarbon obtained from natural gas and petroleum, used as fuel. [**ether**]

ether *n* **1** a colourless sweet-smelling, volatile liquid, used as a solvent and an anaesthetic. **2** (also **aether**) a substance formerly believed to fill all space, and to be responsible for transmitting electromagnetic waves. **3** (*poetic*; also **aether**) the clear upper air or a clear sky. [Gr *aither*, the heavens]

ethereal *adj* **1** of an unreal lightness or delicateness; fairy-like. **2** heavenly or spiritual. — *adv* **ethereally**. [Ety. as for **ether**]

ethic *n* the moral system or set of principles particular to a certain person, community, group, etc. [Gr *ethikos*, from *ethos*, custom, character]

ethical *adj* **1** of or concerning morals, justice or duty. **2** morally right. **3** (of a medicine or drug) not advertised to the general public, and available only on prescription. — *adv* **ethically**.

ethics *n* **1** (*sing*) the study or the science of morals. **2** (*pl*) rules or principles of behaviour: *medical ethics*.

ethnic *adj* **1** relating to, or having, a common race or cultural tradition: *an ethnic group*. **2** associated with, or resembling, an exotic, esp. non-European, racial or tribal group: *ethnic clothes*. **3** from the point of view of race, rather than nationality: *ethnic Asians*. **4** between or involving different racial groups: *ethnic violence*. — *adv* **ethnically**. — *n* **ethnicity**. [Gr *ethnikos*, from *ethnos*, nation]

ethnocentric *adj* relating to, or holding, the belief that one's own cultural tradition or racial group is superior to all others. — *adv* **ethnocentrically**. — *n* **ethnocentricity** or **ethnocentrism**. [Gr *ethnos*, nation + **-centric**]

ethnology *n* the scientific study of different races and cultural traditions, and their relations with each other. — *adj* **ethnological**. — *adv* **ethnologically**. — *n* **ethnologist**. [Gr *ethnos*, nation + **-logy**]

ethos *n* the typical spirit, character or attitudes (of a group, community, etc.) [Gr, custom, culture]

ethyl *n* (*chem*) the radical (C_2H_5-) of **ethyl alcohol** (C_2H_5OH), the alcohol found in beer, wine, etc. [**ether** + Gr *hyle*, matter]

ethylene *n* a colourless flammable hydrocarbon gas used in the manufacture of polythene and other chemicals. [**ethyl**]

etiolate *v* (*tr*) **1** to cause (a plant) to become white through lack of sunlight. **2** (*formal* or *literary*) to make (a person) pale and weak. — *n* **etiolation**. [Fr *étioler*, to become pale]

etiology. Same as **aetiology**.

etiquette *n* **1** conventions of correct or polite social behaviour. **2** rules, usu. unwritten, regarding the behaviour of members of a particular profession, etc. towards each other. [Fr *étiquette*, label]

-ette *sfx* **1** indicating a female of the stated type: *usherette*. **2** indicating a small thing of the type: *cigarette* and *kitchenette*. **3** indicating an imitation: *leatherette*. [OFr *-ette*]

étude *n* (*mus*) a short piece written for a single instrument, intended as an exercise or a means of displaying talent. [Fr, study]

ety. *abbrev* etymology.

etymology *n* **-*ies*** **1** the study of the origin and development of words and their meanings. **2** an explanation of the history of a particular word. — *adj* **etymological**. — *adv* **etymologically**. — *n* **etymologist**. [Lat *etymologia*, from Gr *etymon*, the literal sense of a word, from *etymos*, true]

Eu *symbol* (*chem*) europium.

eucalyptus *n* **-*tuses*** or **-*ti*** **1** (also **eucalyptus tree**) a tall evergreen tree, native to Australia, yielding timber, gum and an oil widely used in medicine. **2** eucalyptus oil. [Gr *eu*, well + *kalyptos*, covered]

Eucharist *n* **1** the Christian ceremony commemorating Christ's Last Supper. **2** the bread and wine consumed during this ceremony. — *adj* **Eucharistic**. [Gr *eucharistia*, thanksgiving]

euchre *n* an American card-game for two, three or four players, played with 32 cards.

Euclidean or **Euclidian** *adj* of, or relating to, the geometrical system devised by *Euclid*, a Greek mathematician of the 3rd century BC.

eugenics *n* (*sing*) the science of improving the human race by systematically selecting for breeding people who are strong, healthy, intelligent, etc. — *adj* **eugenic**. — *adv* **eugenically**. [Gr *eugenes*, well-born, of good stock]

eulogy *n* **-*ies*** **1** a speech or piece of writing in praise of someone or something. **2** high praise. [Lat *eulogium*, from Gr *eu*, well + *logos*, discourse]

eulogise or **-ize** *v* (*tr*) to praise highly. — *adj* **eulogistic**. — *adv* **eulogistically**.

eunuch *n* **1** a man who has been castrated, esp. one formerly employed as a guard of a harem in Eastern countries. **2** (*derog*) a person who lacks power or effectiveness in some respect. [Gr *eunouchos*]

euphemism *n* (the use of) a mild or inoffensive term used in place of one considered offensive or unpleasantly direct, e.g. *pass on* instead of *die*. — *adj* **euphemistic**. — *adv* **euphemistically**. [Gr *eu*, well + *phanai*, to speak]

euphonious *adj* pleasing to the ear. — *adv* **euphoniously**. [Ety. as for **euphony**]

euphonium *n* a brass instrument of the tuba family. [Ety. as for **euphony**]

euphony *n* **-*ies*** **1** a pleasing sound, esp. in speech. **2** pleasantness of sound, esp. of pronunciation. [Gr *eu*, well + *phone*, sound]

euphoria *n* a strong feeling of wild happiness, esp. if exaggerated or unjustified. — *adj* **euphoric**. — *adv* **euphorically**. [Gr, ability to endure well]

euphuism *n* a pompous and affected style of writing. — *adj* **euphuistic**. — *adv* **euphuistically**. [From the style of John Lyly's romance *Euphues* (1579–80)]

Eur. *abbrev* Europe.

Eurasian *adj* **1** of mixed European and Asian descent. **2** of, or relating to, Europe and Asia. — *n* a person of mixed European and Asian descent.

Euratom *abbrev* European Atomic Energy Community.

eureka *interj* an exclamation of triumph at finding something, solving a problem, etc. [Gr *heureka*, I have found it]

Euro- *comb fm* Europe or European.

eurhythmics *n* (*sing*) the art or a system of exercising the body to music. — *adj* **eurhythmic**. [Gr *eu*, well + *rhythmos*, rhythm]

Eurocheque *n* a cheque which may be drawn on the user's own account and exchanged for cash, goods or services in a number of European (and non-European) countries.

Eurocrat *n* (sometimes *derog*) an official involved in the administration of any organisation in the European Community. [**Euro-** + **bureaucrat**]

Eurodollars *n* (*pl*) US currency held in European banks to assist trade.

European *adj* **1** of, or relating to, Europe. **2** showing or favouring a spirit of co-operation between the countries of Europe, esp. those of the European Community. — *n* **1** a native or inhabitant of Europe. **2** a person who favours close political and economic contact between the countries of Europe, esp. those of the European Community.

europium *n* an element (symbol **Eu**), a soft silvery metal. [**Europe**]

Eustachian tube *n* either of the two tubes which connect the middle ear to the pharynx, serving to equalise the pressure on the two sides of the eardrum. [B *Eustachio*, 16th-century Italian anatomist]

euthanasia *n* (the act or practice of bringing about) painless death, esp. to release someone from incurable illness or suffering. [Gr, from *eu*, well + *thanatos*, death]

eV *abbrev* electronvolt.

evacuate *v* (*tr*) **1** to leave (a place), esp. because of danger. **2** (usu. with **from**) to cause (people) to leave a place, esp. because of danger. **3** (*med*) to empty (the bowels). — *n* **evacuation**. [Lat *evacuare*, to empty out]

evacuee *n* an evacuated person.

evade *v* (*tr*) **1** to escape or avoid by trickery or skill. **2** to avoid answering (a question). ◇ See also **evasion**. [Lat *evadere*, to go out]

evaluate *v* (*tr*) **1** to form an idea or judgement about the worth of. **2** (*math*) to calculate the value of. — *n* **evaluation**. [Fr *évaluation*]

evanesce *v* (*intr*; *literary*) to disappear gradually; to fade from sight. [Lat *evanescere*, to vanish]

evanescent *adj* (*literary*) **1** quickly fading. **2** short-lived; transitory. — *n* **evanescence**.

evangelical *adj* **1** based on the gospel. **2** of or denoting any of various groups within the Protestant church stressing the authority of the Bible and claiming that personal acceptance of Christ as saviour is the only way to salvation. **3** enthusiastically advocating a particular cause, etc. — *n* a member of an evangelical sect, or a supporter of evangelical beliefs. — *n* **evangelicalism**. — *adv* **evangelically**. [Gr *eu*, well + *angellein*, to bring news]

evangelise or **-ize** *v* **1** (*tr*) to attempt to persuade (someone) to adopt Christianity. **2** (*intr*) to preach Christianity, esp. travelling from place to place to do so. **3** (*intr* & *tr*; often *facet*) to attempt to persuade (someone) to adopt a particular principle or cause. — *n* **evangelisation** or **-z-**. [Ety. as for **evangelical**]

evangelism *n* **1** the act or practice of evangelising. **2** evangelicalism. — *adj* **evangelistic**.

evangelist *n* **1** a person who preaches Christianity, esp. at large public meetings. **2** (usu. *cap*) any of the writers of the four Biblical Gospels, Matthew, Mark, Luke or John.

evaporate *v* (*tr* & *intr*) **1** to (cause to) change from a solid or liquid into gas. **2** to (cause to) lose liquid or moisture as gas. **3** to (cause to) disappear. — *n* **evaporation**. [Lat *evaporare*, from *vapor*, steam, vapour]

evaporated milk *n* milk which has been thickened by evaporation.

evasion *n* **1** the act of evading. **2** a trick or excuse used to evade (a question, etc.). [Lat *evasio*, from *evadere*, to go out]

evasive *adj* **1** having the purpose of evading, esp. trouble or danger. **2** not honest or open: *an evasive answer*. — *adv* **evasively**. — *n* **evasiveness**.

eve *n* **1** the evening or day before some notable event. **2** the period immediately before: *the eve of war*. [**even**[2]]

even[1] *adj* **1** smooth and flat. **2** constant or regular: *travelling at an even 50 mph*. **3** (of a number) divisible by 2, with nothing left over. **4** marked by such a number: *the even houses in the street*. **5** (**with**) level; on the same plane or at the same height. **6** (**with**) having no advantage or owing no debt. **7** (of temper, character, etc.) calm. **8** equal: *an even chance*. — *adv* **1** used with a comparative *adj* or *adv* to emphasise a comparison with something else: *He's good, but she's even better*. **2** used with an expression stronger than a previous one: *He looked sad, even depressed*. **3** used to introduce a surprising piece of information: *Even John was there!* **4** used to indicate a lower extreme in an implied comparison: *Even a child (let alone an educated adult) would have known that!* **5** (with **if**, **though**, etc.) used to emphasise that whether or not something is or might be true, the following or preceding statement is or would remain true: *He'd be unhappy even if he did get the job. Even though he got the job, he's still unhappy. He got the job but, even so, he's still unhappy.* — *v* **1** (*tr*; **out**, **up**) to make equal. **2** (*tr*; **out**, **up**) to make smooth or level. **3** (*intr* with **out**) to become level or regular. — *n* **1** (usu. in *pl.*) (something marked by) an even number. **2** (in *pl*) even money (see below). — *adv* **evenly**. — *n* **evenness**. — **even now** still; after all that has happened. — **even then** after all that had happened, will have happened or would have happened. — **get even (with)** to be revenged (on). [OE *efen*]

even-handed *adj* fair. — *adv* **even-handedly**. — *n* **even-handedness**.

even money *n* gambling odds with the potential to win the same as the amount gambled.

even[2] *n* (*old* or *poetic*) evening. [OE *æfen*]

evening *n* **1** the last part of the day, usu. from late afternoon until bedtime. **2** a party or other social gathering held at this time: *a poetry evening*. **3** (*poetic*) the latter part of anything: *the evening of his life*. — *adj* of or during the evening. [OE *æfnung*]

evening dress *n* clothes worn on formal occasions in the evening.

evening star *n* a planet, esp. Venus, clearly visible in the west just after sunset.

evensong *n* the service of evening prayer in the Anglican Church. [OE *æfensang*, evening song]

event *n* **1** something that happens; an incident, esp. an important one. **2** an item in a programme of sports, etc. — **at all events** or **in any event** in any case; whatever happens. — **in either event** no matter which (of two things, possibilities, etc.) happens. — **in the event** in the end; as it happened, happens, or may happen. — **in the event of** or **that** if (something) occurs. — **in that event** if that happens. [Lat *eventus*, result, event]

eventful *adj* full of important or exciting events. — *adv* **eventfully**. — *n* **eventfulness**.

eventing *n* the practice of taking part in horse-riding events, esp. the **three-day event**, a competition in jumping, cross-country riding and dressage. — *n* **eventer**.

eventide *n* (*poetic* or *old*) evening. [OE *æfentid*]

eventide home *n* a home for old people.

eventual *adj* happening after or at the end of a period of time, a process, etc. — *adv* **eventually**. [Fr *éventuel*, from Lat *eventus*, result, event]

eventuality *n* **-ies** a possible happening or result: *plan for every eventuality*.

eventuate *v* (*intr*; *formal* **in**) to result; to turn out. **[event]**

ever *adv* **1** at any time. **2** (*formal*) always; continually. **3** (*coll*) used for emphasis: *She's ever so beautiful!* [OE *æfre*]

ever- *in cmpds* always, continually, as in **ever-hopeful**.

evergreen *adj* **1** (of trees, etc.) having leaves all the year round. ◇ See also **deciduous**. **2** always popular. — *n* an evergreen tree or shrub.

everlasting *adj* **1** without end; continual. **2** lasting a long time, esp. so long as to become tiresome. — *n* **1** any of several kinds of flower that keep their shape and colour when dried. **2** eternity. — *adv* **everlastingly**.

evermore *adv* or **for evermore** for all time to come; eternally.

everglade *n* a large shallow lake or marsh, esp. (in *pl*) a huge expanse of these in southern Florida in the USA.

every *adj* **1** each single, omitting none. **2** the greatest or best possible: *We're making every effort to avoid war*. — *adv* at, in, at the end of, each (stated period of time, distance, etc.): *every fourth week*; *every six inches*. — **every now and then**, **every now and again** or **every so often** occasionally; from time to time. — **every other** or **every second** one of every two repeatedly (the first, third, fifth, etc. or second, fourth, sixth, etc.). [OE *æfre ælc*, ever each]

everybody *pron* every person.

everyday *adj* **1** happening, done, used, etc. daily, or on ordinary days, rather than on special occasions. **2** common or usual: *an everyday occurrence*.

Everyman *n* the ordinary or common person.

everyone *pron* every person.

everything *pron* **1** all things; all. **2** the most important thing: *Fitness is everything in sport*.

everywhere *adv* in or to every place.

evict *v* (*tr*; **from**) to put out of a house, etc. or off land by force of law. — *n* **eviction**. [Lat *evincere*, to overcome]

evidence *n* **1** information, etc. that gives grounds for belief; that which points to, reveals or suggests something. **2** written or spoken testimony used in a court of law. — *v* (*tr*; *formal*) to be evidence of; to prove. — **in evidence** easily seen; clearly displayed. [Lat *evidentia*, clearness of speech]

evident *adj* clear to see or understand; obvious; apparent. — *adv* **evidently**.

evidential *adj* (*formal*) relating to, based on, or providing evidence. — *adv* **evidentially**.

evil *adj* **1** morally bad or offensive. **2** harmful. **3** (*coll*) very unpleasant: *an evil stench*. — *n* **1** (a source of) wickedness or moral offensiveness. **2** (a source of) harm; a harmful influence. **3** anything bad or unpleasant, e.g. crime, disease, etc. — *adv* **evilly**. — *n* **evilness**. [OE *yfel*]

evildoer *n* a person who does evil things.
evil eye *n* (with **the**) **1** the supposed power of causing harm by a look. **2** a glare, superstitiously thought to cause harm.
evince *v* (*tr*; *formal*) to show or display (usu. a personal quality) clearly. [Lat *evincere*, to overcome]
eviscerate *v* (*tr*; *formal*) **1** to tear out the bowels of. **2** to take away the essential quality or meaning of. — *n* **evisceration**. [Lat *eviscerare*, to disembowel]
evoke *v* (*tr*) **1** to cause or produce (a response, a reaction, etc.). **2** to bring into the mind. — *n* **evocation**. — *adj* **evocative**. [Lat *evocare*, to call out]
evolution *n* **1** the process of evolving. **2** a gradual development. **3** (*biol*) the gradual development of present-day plants and animals, including human beings, from earlier, more primitive forms of life. **4** (*chem*, etc.) the giving off of e.g. heat or vapour. — *adj* **evolutionary**. [Lat *evolutio*, unrolling]
evolutionist *n* a person who believes in the theory of evolution (sense **3**).
evolve *v* **1** (*tr* & *intr*) to develop or produce gradually. **2** (*intr*) to develop from a primitive into a more complex or advanced form. **3** (*tr*; *chem*, etc.) to give off (heat, etc.). [Lat *evolvere*, to roll out, unroll]
ewe *n* a female sheep. [OE *eowu*]
ewer *n* a large water-jug with a wide mouth. [OFr *eviere*, from Lat *aquarius*, of water]
ex[1] *n* ***ex's*** or ***exes*** (*coll*) a person who is no longer what he or she was, esp. a former husband, wife or lover. [**ex-**]
ex[2] *prep* (*commerce*) **1** direct from: *ex warehouse*. **2** excluding: *ex dividend*. [Lat, out of]
ex- *pfx* **1** former: *ex-wife*. **2** outside: *ex-directory*. [Lat, out of]
exacerbate *v* (*tr*) to make (a bad situation, anger, pain, etc.) worse. — *n* **exacerbation**. [Lat *exacerbare*, to irritate]
exact *adj* **1** absolutely accurate or correct. **2** insisting on accuracy or precision in even the smallest details. **3** dealing with measurable quantities or values: *Psychology is not an exact science*. — *v* (*tr*) **1** (**from, of**) to demand (payment). **2** to insist on (a right, etc.). — *n* **exactness**. [Lat *exigere*, to demand]
exacting *adj* making difficult or excessive demands. — *adv* **exactingly**.
exaction *n* (*formal*) **1** the act of demanding payment, or the payment demanded. **2** illegal demands for money; extortion.
exactitude *n* (*formal*) accuracy or correctness.
exactly *adv* **1** just; quite; precisely; absolutely. **2** with accuracy; with attention to detail. **3** (as a reply) you are quite right.
exaggerate *v* **1** (*tr* & *intr*) to regard or describe (someone or something) as having more of a quality, being greater in extent, etc. than is really the case. **2** (*tr*) to emphasise or make more noticeable: *The tight skirt exaggerated her thick waist*. **3** (*tr*) to do in an excessive or affected way. — *n* **exaggeration**. — *n* **exaggerator**. [Lat *exaggerare*, to heap up]
exalt *v* (*tr*) **1** to praise highly. **2** to fill with great joy. **3** to give a higher rank or position to. [Lat *exaltare*, to raise]
exaltation *n* **1** the act of exalting or state of being exalted. **2** a strong feeling of happiness.
exalted *adj* **1** noble; very moral: *exalted ideals*. **2** exaggerated; too high: *an exalted opinion of one's own importance*. — *adv* **exaltedly**. — *n* **exaltedness**.
exam *n* (*coll*) an examination (sense **1**).
examination *n* **1** a set of tasks, esp. written, designed to test knowledge or ability. **2** an inspection of a person's state of health, carried out by a doctor. **3** the act of examining, or process of being examined. **4** (*legal*) formal questioning in a court of law. [Lat *examinatio*, from *examinare*; see ety. for **examine**]
examine *v* (*tr*) **1** to inspect, consider, or look into closely. **2** to check the health of. **3** (**on, in**) to test the knowledge or ability of (a person). **4** (*legal*; **on**) to question formally in a court of law. — *n* **examinee**. — *n* **examiner**. [Fr *examiner*, from Lat *examinare*, to weigh or test, from *examen*, the pointer on a set of scales]
example *n* **1** something or someone that is a typical specimen. **2** something that illustrates a fact or rule. **3** a person, pattern of behaviour, etc. as a model to be, or not to be, copied: *set a good example*. **4** a punishment given, or the person punished, as a warning to others: *make an example of someone*. — **for example** as an example or illustration. [OFr, from Lat *exemplum*]
exasperate *v* (*tr*) to make (someone) annoyed and frustrated. — *n* **exasperation**. [Lat *exasperare*, to make rough]
ex cathedra *adv* with authority, esp. the full authority of the Pope. — *adj* (**ex-cathedra**) **1** (of a papal pronouncement) stating an infallible doctrine. **2** made with, or as if with, authority. [Lat, from the chair]
excavate *v* (*tr*) **1** to dig up or uncover (esp. historical remains). **2** to dig up (a piece of ground, etc.) or to make (a hole) by doing this. — *n* **excavation**. — *n* **excavator**. [Lat *excavare*, to make hollow]
exceed *v* (*tr*) **1** to be greater than. **2** to go beyond; to do more than is required by. [OFr *exceder*]
exceedingly *adv* very; extremely.
excel *v* **-ll- 1** (*intr*; **in, at**) to be exceptionally good. **2** (*tr*) to be better than. — **excel oneself** (often *ironic*) to do better than usual or previously. [Lat *excellere*, to rise up]
excellence *n* great worth; very high or exceptional quality. — *adj* **excellent**. — *adv* **excellently**. [OFr, from Lat *excellentia*]

Excellency *n* **-*ies*** (usu. with **His, Your**, etc.) a title of honour given to certain people of high rank, e.g. ambassadors.

except *prep* leaving out; not including. — *v* (*tr*; **from**) to leave out or exclude: *present company excepted.* — **except for** apart from; not including or counting. [Lat *excipere*, to take out]

excepting *prep* leaving out; not including or counting.

exception *n* **1** a person or thing not included. **2** someone or something that does not, or is allowed not to, follow a general rule: *make an exception.* **3** an act of excluding. — **take exception to** to object to, be offended by. [Lat *excipere*, to take out]

exceptionable *adj* **1** likely to cause disapproval, offence or dislike. **2** open to objection.

exceptional *adj* **1** remarkable or outstanding. **2** being or making an exception. — *adv* **exceptionally**.

excerpt *n* a short passage or part taken from a book, film, etc. — *v* (*tr*) to select extracts from (a book, etc.). — *n* **excerption**. [Lat *excerptum*, from *excerpere*, to pick]

excess *n* **1** the act of going, or the state of being, beyond normal or suitable limits. **2** an amount or extent greater than is usual, necessary or wise. **3** the amount by which one quantity, etc. exceeds another; an amount left over. **4** (usu. in *pl*) an outrageous or offensive act. — *adj* **1** greater than is usual, necessary or permitted. **2** additional; required to make up for an amount lacking: *excess postage.* — **in excess of** going beyond; more than. [OFr *exces*, from Lat *excessus*, departure, going beyond]

excessive *adj* too great; beyond what is usual, right or appropriate. — *adv* **excessively**. — *n* **excessiveness**.

exchange *v* (*tr*) **1** (**for, with**) to give, or give up, in return for something else. **2** to give and receive in return: *The two leaders exchanged gifts.* — *n* **1** the giving and taking of one thing for another. **2** a thing exchanged. **3** a giving and receiving in return. **4** a conversation or argument, esp. when brief. **5** the act of exchanging the currency of one country for that of another. **6** a place where shares are traded, or international financial deals carried out. **7** (also **telephone exchange**) (a building containing) a central telephone system where lines are connected. — *adj* **exchangeable**. — **in exchange (for)** in return (for). [OFr *eschangier*, from Lat *excambiare*, from *ex*, from + *cambiare*, to barter.]

exchange rate or **rate of exchange** *n* the value of the currency of one country in relation to that of another country or countries.

exchequer *n* (often *cap*) the government department in charge of the financial affairs of a nation. [OFr *eschequier*, from Lat *scaccarium*, chessboard, from the practice of keeping accounts on a chequered cloth]

excise[1] *n* the tax on goods, etc. produced and sold within a country, and on certain licences. — *v* (*tr*) **1** to charge excise on (goods, etc.). **2** to force (a person) to pay excise. [ODut *excijs*, from OFr *acceis*, tax]

excise[2] *v* (*tr*) **1** to remove (e.g. a passage from a book). **2** to cut out or cut off by surgery. — *n* **excision**. [Lat *excidere*, to cut out]

excite *v* (*tr*) **1** to cause to feel lively expectation or a pleasant tension and thrill. **2** to arouse (feelings, emotions, sensations, etc.). **3** to provoke (e.g. action). **4** to arouse sexually. — *adj* **excited**. — *adv* **excitedly**. [OFr *exciter*]

excitable *adj* easily made excited, flustered, frantic, etc. — *n* **excitability**. — *adv* **excitably**.

excitement *n* **1** the state of being excited. **2** objects and events that produce such a state, or the quality they have which produces it: *the excitement of travel.* **3** behaviour, a happening, etc. which displays excitement.

exciting *adj* arousing a lively expectation or a pleasant tension and thrill. — *adv* **excitingly**.

exclaim *v* (*tr & intr*) to call or cry out suddenly and loudly, e.g. in surprise or anger. [Lat *exclamare*]

exclamation *n* **1** a word or expression uttered suddenly and loudly. **2** the act of exclaiming. [Lat *exclamatio*]

exclamation mark *n* the punctuation mark '!', used to indicate an exclamation.

exclamatory *adj* containing or expressing exclamation.

exclude *v* (*tr*) **1** (**from**) to prevent from sharing or taking part. **2** to shut out or keep out. **3** to omit or leave out of consideration. **4** to make impossible. [Lat *excludere*, to shut out]

excluding *prep* not counting; without including.

exclusion *n* the act of excluding, or the state of being excluded. — **to the exclusion of** so much as to leave out or make no time or room for. [Lat *exclusio*, from *excludere*, to shut out]

exclusive *adj* **1** involving the rejection or denial of something else or everything else: *mutually exclusive statements.* **2** (**to**) limited to, given to, found in, etc. only one place, group or person. **3** not including (something mentioned). **4** not readily accepting others into the group, esp. because of a feeling of superiority: *an exclusive club.* **5** fashionable and expensive: *an exclusive restaurant.* — *n* a report or story published in only one newspaper or magazine. — *adv* **exclusively**. — *n* **exclusiveness** or **exclusivity**. — **exclusive of** excluding. [Lat *exclusivus*]

excommunicate *v* (*tr*) to take away membership of the Church from, as punishment. — *n* **excommunication**. [Lat *excommunicare*, to exclude from the community]

excoriate *v* (*tr*) **1** to strip the skin from (a person or animal). **2** to criticise severely. — *n* **excoriation**. [Lat *excoriare*]

excrement *n* waste matter passed out of the body, esp. faeces. — *adj* **excremental**. [Lat *excrementum*]

excrescence *n* **1** an abnormal, esp. ugly, growth on a part of the body or a plant. **2** an unsightly addition. [Lat *excrescere*, to grow up]

excreta *n* (*formal*) excreted matter; faeces or urine. [Lat *excernere*, to sift out]

excrete *v* (*tr*) to pass (waste matter) from the body. — *n* **excretion**. — *adj* **excretory**. [Lat *excernere*, to sift out]

excruciating *adj* **1** causing great physical or mental pain. **2** (*coll*) extremely bad or irritating. — *adv* **excruciatingly**. [Lat *excruciare*, to torture]

exculpate *v* (*tr*; *formal*; **from**) to remove from suspicion or blame, prove not guilty. — *n* **exculpation**. [Lat *ex*, from, + *culpa*, fault, blame]

excursion *n* **1** a short trip, usu. one made for pleasure. **2** a brief change from the usual course or pattern: *a novelist making an excursion into journalism*. [Lat *excurrere*, to run out]

excursive *adj* (*formal*) tending to wander from the main point. [Lat *excursus*, a running out + **-ive**]

excuse *v* (*tr*) **1** (**for**) to pardon or forgive. **2** to offer justification for (a wrongdoing). **3** (**from**) to free (from an obligation, a duty, etc.). **4** to allow to leave (a room, etc.), e.g. (esp. in *passive*) in order to go to the lavatory. — *n* **1** an explanation for a wrongdoing, offered as an apology or justification. **2** (*derog*; with **for**) a very poor example (of): *You'll never sell this excuse for a painting!* — **excuse me** an expression of apology, or used to attract attention. — **excuse oneself** to leave after apologising or asking permission. — **make one's** or **someone's excuses** to apologise, on one's own behalf or someone else's, for leaving or not attending. — *adj* **excusable**. — *adv* **excusably**. [Lat *excusare*, from *ex*, from, + *causa*, cause, accusation]

ex-directory *adj* **1** (of a telephone number) left out of the directory at the request of the subscriber. **2** (of a telephone subscriber) having such a number. [**ex-** (sense **2**) + **directory**]

execrable *adj* **1** detestable. **2** dreadful; of very poor quality. — *adv* **execrably**. [Lat *exsecrabilis*, detestable]

execrate *v* (*tr*; *formal*) **1** to feel or express hatred or loathing of. **2** to curse. — *n* **execration**. [Lat *exsecrari*, to curse]

execute *v* (*tr*) **1** to put to death by order of the law. **2** to perform or carry out. **3** to produce, esp. according to a design. **4** (*legal*) to make valid by signing. **5** (*legal*) to carry out instructions contained in (a will or contract). ◇ See also **executor**. [OFr *executer*]

execution *n* **1** the act, or an instance, of putting to death by law. **2** the act of carrying out, or the state of being carried out.

executioner *n* a person who carries out a sentence of death.

executive *adj* **1** (in a business organisation, etc.) concerned with management or administration. **2** for the use of managers and senior staff. **3** (*coll*) expensive and sophisticated: *executive cars*. **4** (*legal* or *politics*) relating to the carrying out of laws: *executive powers*. — *n* **1** a person or body of people in an organisation, etc. having power to direct or manage. **2** (*legal* or *politics*; with **the**) the branch of government that puts laws into effect. [Lat *executivus*]

executor *n* (*legal*) a male or female person appointed to carry out instructions stated in a will. [**execute**]

executrix *n* **-trices** or **-trixes** (*legal*) a female executor.

exegesis *n* **-eses** a critical explanation of a text, esp. of the Bible. — *adj* **exegetic** or **exegetical**. [Gr, explanation]

exemplar *n* **1** a person or thing worth copying; a model. **2** a typical example. [Lat *exemplum*, example]

exemplary *adj* **1** worth following as an example. **2** serving as an illustration or warning. [Lat *exemplaris*, from *exemplum*, example]

exemplify *v* **-ies**, **-ied** (*tr*) **1** to be an example of. **2** to show an example of, show by means of an example. — *n* **exemplification**. [Lat *exemplum*, example + *facere*, to make]

exempt *v* (*tr*; **from**) to free (from a duty or obligation that applies to others). — *adj* (**from**) free (from), not liable (for). — *n* **exemption**. [Lat *eximere*, to take out]

exercise *n* **1** physical training or exertion for health or pleasure. **2** an activity intended to develop a skill. **3** a task designed to test ability. **4** (*formal*) the act of putting into practice or carrying out: *the exercise of one's duty*. **5** (usu. in *pl*; *mil*) training and practice for soldiers. — *v* **1** (*intr* & *tr*) to give exercise to (oneself, or someone or something else). **2** (*tr*) to use, bring into use: *exercise a skill/right*. **3** (*tr*) to trouble, concern, or occupy the thoughts of. [OFr *exercice*, from Lat *exercere*, to keep busy]

exert *v* (*tr*) **1** to bring into use or action forcefully: *exert one's authority*. **2** to force (oneself) to make a strenuous, esp. physical, effort. — *n* **exertion**. [Lat *exserere*, to thrust out]

exeunt *v* (*intr*) (as a stage direction) (they) leave the stage. — **exeunt omnes** all leave the stage. ◇ See also **exit**. [Lat *exire*, to go out; *omnis*, all, every]

ex gratia given as a favour, not in recognition of an (esp. legal) obligation: *an ex gratia payment*. [Lat, as a favour]

exhale *v* (*tr* & *intr*) **1** to breathe out. **2** to give off or be given off. — *n* **exhalation**. [OFr *exhaler*]

exhaust *v* (*tr*) **1** to make very tired. **2** to use up completely. **3** to say all that can be said about (a subject, etc.). **4** (*engin*) to empty (a container), or draw off (gas). — *n* **1** the escape of waste gases from an engine, etc. **2** the gases themselves. **3** the part or parts of an engine, etc. through which the waste gases escape. — *adj* **exhausted**. — *adj* **exhaustible**. — *adj* **exhausting**. — *n* **exhaustion**. [Lat *exhaurire*, to draw off, drain away]

exhaustive *adj* complete; very thorough. — *adv* **exhaustively**. — *n* **exhaustiveness**.

exhibit *v* **-t-** (*tr*) **1** to present or display for public appreciation. **2** to show or manifest (a quality, etc.). — *n* **1** an object displayed publicly, e.g. in a museum. **2** (*legal*) an object or article produced in court as part of the evidence. [Lat *exhibere*, to produce, show]

exhibitor *n* a person who provides an exhibit for a public display.

exhibition *n* **1** a display, e.g. of works of art, to the public. **2** the act, or an instance, of showing, e.g. a quality. **3** a scholarship awarded by a college or university. — **make an exhibition of oneself** to behave foolishly in public. [Lat *exhibere*, to show]

exhibitioner *n* a student receiving an educational exhibition.

exhibitionism *n* **1** (*derog*) the tendency to behave so as to attract attention to oneself. **2** (*psychol*) the compulsive desire to expose one's sexual organs publicly. — *n* **exhibitionist**. — *adj* **exhibitionistic**.

exhilarate *v* (*tr*) to fill with a lively cheerfulness. — *n* **exhilaration**. [Lat *exhilarare*, from *hilaris*, cheerful]

exhort *v* (*tr*) to urge or advise strongly and sincerely. — *n* **exhortation**. [Lat *exhortari*, to encourage]

exhume *v* (*tr*) to dig up (esp. a body from a grave). — *n* **exhumation**. [Fr *exhumer*, from Lat *ex*, out of + *humus*, the ground]

exigency *n* **-ies** (*formal*) **1** an urgent need. **2** an emergency. [Lat *exigere*, to drive out]

exigent *adj* (*formal*) **1** pressing; urgent. **2** demanding.

exiguous *adj* (*formal*) scarce; meagre; insufficient. — *n* **exiguity** or **exiguousness**. — *adv* **exiguously**. [Lat *exiguus*, small, meagre]

exile *n* **1** enforced or regretted absence from one's country or town, esp. for a long time, often as a punishment. **2** a person suffering such absence. — *v* (*tr*) to send into exile. [OFr *exil*, from Lat *exsilium*, banishment]

exist *v* (*intr*) **1** to be, esp. to be present in the real world or universe rather than in story or imagination. **2** to occur or be found. **3** to manage to stay alive; to live with only the most basic necessities of life. [Lat *exsistere*, to stand out]

existence *n* **1** the state of existing. **2** a life, or a way of living. **3** everything that exists.

existent *adj* having an actual being; existing.

existential *adj* **1** relating to human existence. **2** (*philos*) relating to existentialism.

existentialism *n* a philosophy emphasising freedom of choice and personal responsibility for one's own actions, which create one's own moral values and determine one's future. — *adj* & *n* **existentialist**.

exit *n* **1** a way out of a building, etc. **2** an act of going out or departing. **3** an actor's departure from the stage. **4** a place where vehicles can leave a motorway or main road. — *v* **-t-** (*intr*) **1** (*formal*) to go out, leave or depart. **2** (as a stage direction) (he or she) leaves the stage. ◇ See also **exeunt**. [Lat *exire*, to go out]

exo- *comb fm* out or outside. ◇ See also **ecto-**, **endo-** and **ento-**. [Gr *exo*, outside]

exocrine : **exocrine gland** *n* (*med*) a gland which secretes through a duct or ducts, such as the sweat and salivary glands. ◇ See also **endocrine**. [**exo-** + Gr *krinein*, to separate]

exodus *n* **1** a mass departure of people. **2** (*cap*) the departure of the Israelites from Egypt, prob. around the 13th century BC. **3** (*cap*) the Old Testament book which tells of this. [Gr *exodos*, from *ex*, out + *hodos*, way]

ex officio *adv* by virtue of one's official position. [Lat]

exonerate *v* (*tr*; **from**) to free from blame, or acquit of a criminal charge. — *n* **exoneration**. [Lat *ex*, from + *onus*, burden]

exorbitant *adj* (of prices or demands) very high, excessive or unfair. — *n* **exorbitance**. — *adv* **exorbitantly**. [Lat *ex*, out of + *orbita*, track]

exorcise or **-ize** *v* (*tr*) **1** to drive away (an evil spirit) with prayer or holy words. **2** to free (a person or place) from the influence of an evil spirit in this way. — *n* **exorcism**. — *n* **exorcist**. [Gr *exorkizein*]

exordium *n* **-iums** or **-ia** (*formal*) an introductory part, esp. of a formal speech or piece of writing. [Lat, beginning of a speech]

exoskeleton *n* (*biol*) the hard cover which protects and supports the bodies of some animals, esp. insects and shellfish. [**exo-**]

exotic *adj* **1** introduced from a foreign, esp. distant and tropical, country: *exotic plants*. **2** interestingly different or strange, esp. colourful and rich, and suggestive of a distant land. — *n* an exotic person or thing. — *adv* **exotically**. [Gr *exotikos*, from *exo*, outside]

exotica *n* (*pl*) strange or rare objects.

expand *v* **1** (*tr* & *intr*) to make or become greater in size, extent or importance. **2** (*intr*; **on, upon**) to give additional information; to enlarge (on a description, etc.).

3 (*intr*; *formal*) to become more at ease, more open and talkative. **4** (*intr* & *tr*; *formal*) to fold out flat or spread out. **5** (*tr*) to write out in full. **6** (*tr*; *math*) to multiply out (terms in brackets). — *adj* **expandable**. ◇ See also **expansible**, **expansion** and **expansive**. [Lat *expandere*, to spread out]

expanse *n* a wide area or space. [Lat *expansum*]

expansible *adj* able to expand or be expanded. [Lat *expandere*, to spread out + **-ible**]

expansion *n* **1** the act or state of expanding. **2** the amount by which something expands. **3** (*math*) the result of expanding (terms in brackets). [Lat *expandere*, to spread out]

expansionism *n* the act or practice of increasing territory or political influence or authority, usu. at the expense of other nations or bodies. — *n* & *adj* **expansionist**.

expansive *adj* **1** ready or eager to talk; open; effusive. **2** wide-ranging. **3** able or tending to expand. — *adv* **expansively**. — *n* **expansiveness**. [**expansion** + **-ive**]

expat *n* (*coll*) an expatriate.

expatiate *v* (*intr*; *formal*; **on, upon, about**) to talk or write at length or in detail. — *n* **expatiation**. [Lat *exspatiari*, to digress]

expatriate *adj* **1** living abroad, esp. for a long but limited period. **2** exiled. — *n* (often shortened to **expat**) a person living or working abroad. [Lat *ex*, out of + *patria*, native land]

expect *v* (*tr*) **1** to think of as likely to happen or come. **2** (**from, of**) to require, or regard as normal or reasonable. **3** (*coll*) to suppose. — **be expecting** (*coll*) to be pregnant. [Lat *exspectare*, to look out for]

expectation *n* **1** the state, or an attitude, of expecting. **2** (often in *pl*) something expected, whether good or bad. **3** (usu. in *pl*) money, property, etc. that one expects to gain, esp. by a will.

expectancy *n* **-ies** **1** the act or state of expecting. **2** a future chance or probability: *life expectancy*. [Lat *exspectare*, to look out for]

expectant *adj* **1** eagerly waiting; hopeful. **2** not yet, but expecting to be (esp. a mother or father). — *adv* **expectantly**.

expectorant (*med*) *n* & *adj* (a medicine) promoting the coughing up of phlegm. [Ety. as for **expectorate**]

expectorate *v* (*intr* & *tr*; *med*) to cough up and spit out (phlegm). [Lat *expectorare*, from *ex*, from + *pectus*, the chest]

expedience or **expediency** **-ies** *n* **1** suitability or convenience. **2** practical advantage or self-interest, esp. as opposed to moral correctness. [Ety. as for **expedite**]

expedient *adj* **1** suitable or appropriate. **2** practical or advantageous, rather than morally correct. — *n* a suitable method or solution, esp. one quickly thought of to meet an urgent need. — *adv* **expediently**.

expedite *v* (*tr*) **1** to speed up, or assist the progress of. **2** to carry out quickly. [Lat *expedire*, set free]

expedition *n* **1** an organised journey with a purpose, or the group making it. **2** (*formal*) speed, promptness. [Lat *expeditio*]

expeditionary *adj* of, forming, or for use on, an expedition.

expeditious *adj* (*formal*) carried out with speed and efficiency. — *adv* **expeditiously**. — *n* **expeditiousness**. [**expedition** + **-ous**]

expel *v* **-ll-** (*tr*; **from**) **1** to dismiss from or deprive of membership of (a club, school, etc.), usu. permanently and usu. as punishment for misconduct. **2** to get rid of; to force out. [Lat *expellere*, to drive out]

expend *v* (*tr*) to use or spend (time, supplies, effort, etc.). [Lat *expendere*, to weigh out]

expendable *adj* **1** that may be given up or sacrificed for some purpose or cause. **2** not valuable enough to be worth preserving.

expenditure *n* **1** the act of expending. **2** an amount expended, esp. of money.

expense *n* **1** the act of spending money, or money spent. **2** something on which money is spent. **3** (in *pl*) a sum of one's own money spent doing one's job, or this sum of money or an allowance paid by one's employer to make up for this. — **at the expense of** **1** with the loss or sacrifice of. **2** causing damage to the pride or reputation of. **3** with the cost paid by. [Lat *expensa*, from *expendere*, to weigh out]

expensive *adj* costing a great deal. — *adv* **expensively**. — *n* **expensiveness**. [**expense** + **-ive**]

experience *n* **1** practice in an activity. **2** knowledge or skill gained through practice. **3** wisdom in all matters, gained through long and varied observation of life. **4** an event which affects or involves one. — *v* (*tr*) **1** to have practical acquaintance with. **2** to feel or undergo. [Lat *experientia*, from *experiri*, to try]

experienced *adj* having knowledge or skill gained from experience.

experiential *adj* (*philos*) based on direct experience, rather than theoretical knowledge. — *adv* **experientially**.

experiment *n* **1** a trial carried out in order to test a theory, a machine's performance, etc. or to discover something unknown. **2** the carrying out of such trials. **3** an attempt at something original. — *v* (*intr*; **on, with**) to carry out such a trial. — *n* **experimentation**. — *n* **experimenter**. [Lat *experimentum*, from *experiri*, to try]

experimental *adj* **1** of the nature of an experiment. **2** relating to, or used in, experiments. **3** trying out new styles and techniques. — *adv* **experimentally**.

expert *n* (**at, in, on**) a person with great skill in, or extensive knowledge of, a particular subject. — *adj* **1** (**at, in**) highly skilled or extremely knowledgeable. **2** relating to or done by an expert or experts. — *adv* **expertly**. [Lat *expertus*, from *experiri*, to try]

expertise *n* special skill or knowledge.

expiate *v* (*tr*) to make up for (a wrongdoing). — *n* **expiation**. [Lat *expiare*, to atone for]

expire *v* (*intr*) **1** to come to an end, cease to be valid. **2** to breathe out. **3** to die. [Lat *exspirare*, to breathe out]

expiration *n* (*formal*) **1** expiry. **2** the act or process of breathing out.

expiry *n* **-ies** (**of**) the coming to an end; the ending of validity.

explain *v* **1** (*tr*) to make clear or easy to understand. **2** (*tr*) to give, or be, a reason for. **3** (*tr*) to justify (oneself or one's actions). — *v* **explain away** (*tr*) to dismiss, or lessen the importance of, by clever reasoning. [Lat *explanare*, to make flat]

explanation *n* **1** the act or process of explaining. **2** a statement or fact that explains.

explanatory *adj* serving to explain.

expletive *n* **1** a swear-word or curse. **2** a word added to fill a gap, e.g. in poetry. **3** a meaningless exclamation. — *adj* being or of the nature of such a word or exclamation. [Lat *explere*, to fill up]

explicable *adj* able to be explained.

explicate *v* (*tr*) to explain (esp. a literary work) in depth, with close analysis of particular points. — *n* **explication**. [Lat *explicare*, to fold out]

explicit *adj* **1** stated or shown fully and clearly. **2** speaking plainly and openly. — *adv* **explicitly**. — *n* **explicitness**. [Lat *explicitus*, straightforward]

explode *v* **1** (*tr & intr*) to (cause to) burst or shatter violently; to blow up. **2** (*intr*) (of a gas) to expand rapidly as a result of a release of internal energy. **3** (*intr*; **in, into, with**) to suddenly show a strong or violent emotion, esp. anger. **4** (*tr*) to prove (a theory, etc.) wrong. **5** (*intr*) (esp. of population) to increase rapidly. [Lat *explodere*, to force off stage by clapping]

exploded *adj* **1** blown up. **2** (of a theory, etc.) no longer accepted; proved false. **3** (of a diagram) showing the different parts (of something) relative to, but slightly separated from, each other.

exploit *n* (usu. in *pl*) an act or feat, esp. a bold or daring one. — *v* (*tr*) **1** to take unfair advantage of so as to achieve one's own aims. **2** to make good use of: *exploit oil resources*. — *n* **exploitation**. [OFr *exploiter*]

explore *v* (*tr*) **1** to search or travel through (a place) for the purpose of discovery. **2** to examine carefully: *explore every possibility*. — *n* **exploration**. — *adj* **exploratory**. — *n* **explorer**. [Lat *explorare*, to search out]

explosion *n* **1** a blowing up, or the noise caused by this. **2** the act of exploding. **3** a sudden display of strong feelings, etc. **4** a sudden great increase. [Lat *explodere*, to force off stage by clapping]

explosive *adj* **1** likely to, tending to, or able to explode. **2** likely to become marked by physical violence or emotional outbursts: *an explosive situation*. — *n* a substance capable of exploding. — *adv* **explosively**. — *n* **explosiveness**. [**explosion** + **-ive**]

expo *n* **-os** (*coll*) a large public exhibition. [**exposition**]

exponent *n* **1** a person able to perform some art or activity, esp. skilfully. **2** a person who explains and promotes (a theory, belief, etc.). **3** (*math*) a power or index, showing how many times a number is to be multiplied by itself.

exponential *adj* **1** (*math*) **1** of or indicated by an exponent. **2** (of an increase, etc.) very rapid. — *n* (*math*) a quantity with a variable exponent. — *adv* **exponentially**. [Lat *exponere*, to set out]

export *v* (*tr*) to send or take (goods, etc.) to another country, esp. for sale. — *n* **1** the act or business of exporting. **2** something exported. — *n* **exportation**. — *n* **exporter**. [Lat *exportare*, to carry away]

expose *v* (*tr*) **1** (**to**) to remove cover, protection or shelter from: *exposed to wind, to criticism*. **2** to discover or make known (e.g. a criminal or crime). **3** to allow light to fall on (a photographic film or paper) in taking or printing a photograph. **4** (usu. with **to**) to cause or allow to have experience of. — **expose oneself** (*euph*) to display one's sexual organs in public. [OFr *exposer*, to set out]

exposé *n* **1** a formal statement of facts, esp. one introducing an argument. **2** an article or programme which exposes a public scandal, crime, etc. [Fr, from *exposer*, to expose]

exposition *n* **1** an in-depth explanation or account (of a subject). **2** the act of presenting such an explanation, or a viewpoint. **3** a large public exhibition. [Lat *expositio*, a setting out]

expostulate *v* (*intr*; **with**) to argue or reason, esp. in protest or so as to dissuade. — *n* **expostulation**. [Lat *expostulare*, to demand]

exposure *n* **1** the act of exposing or the state of being exposed. **2** the harmful effects on the body of extreme cold. **3** the number or regularity of appearances in public, e.g. on television. **4** the act of exposing photographic film or paper to light. **5** the amount of light to which a film or paper is exposed, or the length of time for which it is exposed. **6** the amount of film exposed or to be exposed in order to produce one photograph. [**expose**]

expound *v* **1** (*tr*) to explain in depth. **2** (*intr*; **on**) to talk at length. [Lat *exponere*, to set out]

express *v* **1** (*tr*) to put into words. **2** (*tr*) to indicate or represent with looks, actions, symbols, etc. **3** (*tr*) to show or reveal. **4** (*tr*; **from, out of**) to press or squeeze out. **5** (*tr*) to send by fast delivery service. — *adj* **1** (of a train) travelling especially fast, with few stops. **2** of or sent by a fast delivery service. **3** clearly stated: *his express wish.* **4** particular; clear: *with the express purpose of.* — *n* **1** an express train. **2** an express delivery service. — *adv* by express delivery service. — *adj* **expressible**. — **express oneself** to put one's own thoughts into words. [Lat *exprimere*, to press out]

expression *n* **1** the act of expressing. **2** a look on the face that displays feelings. **3** a word or phrase. **4** the indication of feeling, e.g. in a manner of speaking or a way of playing music. **5** (*math*) a symbol or combination of symbols.

expressionism *n* the style of painting, writing or music which expresses inner feelings, dreams, etc., rather than representing external reality, nature, human actions, etc. — *n & adj* **expressionist**.

expressionless *adj* (of a face or voice) showing no feeling.

expressive *adj* **1** showing meaning or feeling in a clear or lively way. **2** (**of**) expressing: *words expressive of anger*. — *adv* **expressively**. — *n* **expressiveness**.

expressly *adv* **1** clearly and definitely. **2** particularly; specifically.

expropriate *v* (*tr*; *formal* or *legal*) to take (property, etc.) from its owner, esp. for use by the state. — *n* **expropriation**. — *n* **expropriator**. [Lat *expropriare*]

expulsion *n* **1** the act of expelling from school, a club, etc. **2** the act of forcing or driving out. — *adj* **expulsive**. [Lat *expulsio*, a forcing out]

expunge *v* (*tr*) **1** to cross out or delete (e.g. a passage from a book). **2** to cancel out or destroy. [Lat *expungere*, to mark for deletion]

expurgate *v* (*tr*) **1** to revise (a book) by removing objectionable or offensive words or passages. **2** to remove (such words or passages). — *n* **expurgation**. [Lat *expurgare*, to purify]

exquisite *adj* **1** extremely beautiful or skilfully produced. **2** able to exercise sensitive judgement; discriminating: *exquisite taste*. **3** (of pain, pleasure, etc.) extreme. — *adv* **exquisitely**. — *n* **exquisiteness**. [Lat *exquisitus*]

ex-serviceman and **ex-servicewoman** *n* **-*men***, **-*women*** a former male or female member of the armed forces.

ext. *abbrev* **1** extension. **2** exterior. **3** external or externally.

extant *adj* still existing. [Lat *exstare*, to stand out]

extemporaneous or **extemporary** *adj* **1** spoken, done, etc. without preparation; impromptu. **2** makeshift; improvised. — *adv* **extemporaneously** or **extemporarily**. — *n* **extemporaneousness** or **extemporariness**. [Lat *ex*, out of + *tempus*, time]

extempore *adv* & *adj* (done) without planning or preparation. [Lat, *ex*, out of + *tempus*, time]

extemporise or **-ize** *v* (*tr & intr*) to speak or perform without preparation. — *n* **extemporisation** or **-z-**. [**extempore** + **-ise**]

extend *v* **1** (*tr*) to make longer or larger. **2** (*intr & tr*; **to, for**) to reach or stretch in space or time. **3** (*tr*) to hold out or stretch out (a hand, etc.). **4** (*tr*; **to**) to offer (kindness, greetings, etc.). **5** (*tr*) to increase in scope. **6** (*intr* with **to**) to include or go as far as: *My kindness doesn't extend to doing your washing*. **7** (*tr*) to exert to the physical or mental limit: *extend oneself* — *n* **extendability** or **extendibility**. — *adj* **extendable** or **extendible**. [Lat *extendere*, to stretch out]

extended family *n* the family as a unit including all relatives. ◇ See also **nuclear family**.

extended-play record *n* (usu. *abbrev* **EP**) a gramophone record the same size as a single, but holding a longer recording.

extensible *adj* extendable. — *n* **extensibility**. [**extension** + **-ible**]

extension *n* **1** the process of extending, or the state of being extended. **2** an added part, making the original larger or longer. **3** a subsidiary or extra telephone, connected to the main line. **4** an extra period beyond an original time limit. **5** a scheme by which services, e.g. those of a university or library, are made available to non-members: *an extension course*. **6** range or extent. [Lat *extensio*]

extensive *adj* large in area, amount, range or effect. — *adv* **extensively**. [Lat *extensivus*, from *extendere*, to stretch out]

extensor *n* (*med*) any of various muscles that straighten out parts of the body. [Lat, from *extendere*, to stretch out]

extent *n* **1** the area over which something extends. **2** amount, scope or degree. [OFr *extente*, from Lat *extendere*, to stretch out]

extenuate *v* (*tr*) to reduce the apparent seriousness of (a crime, etc.) by giving an explanation that partly excuses it. — *adj* **extenuating**. — *n* **extenuation**. [Lat *extenuare*, to make thin, to lessen]

exterior *adj* **1** on, from, or for use on the outside. **2** foreign, or dealing with foreign nations. — *n* **1** an outside part or surface. **2** an outward appearance, esp. when intended to conceal or deceive. **3** an outdoor scene in a film, etc. [Lat, from *exterus*, on the outside]

exterminate *v* (*tr*) to get rid of or destroy completely. — *n* **extermination**. — *n* **exterminator**. [Lat *exterminare*, to drive away, from *ex*, out of + *terminus*, boundary]

external *adj* **1** of, for, from, or on, the outside. **2** of the world, as opposed to the mind: *external realities*. **3** foreign; involving foreign nations: *external affairs*. **4** (of a medicine) to be applied on the outside of the body, not swallowed, etc. **5** taking place, or coming from, outside one's school, university, etc.: *an external examination*. — *n* **1** (often in *pl*) an outward appearance or feature, esp. when superficial or insignificant. **2** (*coll*) an external examination or examiner. — *adv* **externally**. [Lat *externus*, from *exterus*, on the outside]

externalise or **-ize** *v* (*tr*) to express (thoughts, feelings, ideas, etc.) in words. — *n* **externalisation** or **-z-**.

extinct *adj* **1** (of a species of animal, etc.) no longer in existence. **2** (of a volcano) no longer active. **3** (*formal*) (of an emotion, etc.) no longer felt; dead. — *n* **extinction**. [Lat *exstinguere*, to extinguish]

extinguish *v* (*tr*) **1** to put out (a fire, etc.). **2** (*formal*) to kill off or destroy (e.g. passion). **3** (*legal*) to pay off (a debt). [Lat *exstinguere*]

extinguisher *n* **1** a person or thing that extinguishes. **2** (also **fire extinguisher**) an apparatus filled with water or chemicals for putting out fires.

extirpate *v* (*tr*) **1** (*formal*) to destroy completely. **2** (*formal*) to uproot. **3** to remove surgically. — *n* **extirpation**. [Lat *exstirpare*, to tear up by the roots]

extn. *abbrev* extension.

extol *v* **-ll-** (*tr*) to praise highly. — *n* **extolment**. [Lat *extollere*, to lift or raise up]

extort *v* (*tr*; **from**) to obtain (money, information, etc.) by threats or violence. — *n* **extortion**. — *n* **extortionist**. [Lat *extorquere*, to twist or wrench out]

extortionate *adj* **1** (of a price, demand, etc.) unreasonably high or great. **2** using extortion. — *adv* **extortionately**.

extra *adj* **1** additional; more than is usual, necessary or expected. **2** for which an additional charge is made. — *n* **1** an additional or unexpected thing. **2** (something for which there is) an extra charge. **3** an actor employed temporarily in a small, usu. non-speaking, part in a film. **4** a special edition of a newspaper containing later news. **5** (*cricket*) a run scored other than by hitting the ball with the bat. — *adv* unusually or exceptionally. [Prob. contraction of **extraordinary**]

extra- *pfx* outside or beyond: *extra-curricular*. [Lat *extra*, outside]

extract *v* (*tr*; **from**) **1** to pull or draw out, esp. by force or with effort. **2** to take out (e.g. juice or dye) by physical or chemical means. **3** to derive (e.g. pleasure). **4** to obtain (money, etc.) by threats or violence. **5** to select (passages from a book, etc.). — *n* **1** a passage selected from a book, etc. **2** a substance obtained by a physical or chemical process, esp. a substance in concentrated form. — *n* **extractor**. [Lat *extrahere*, to draw out]

extraction *n* **1** the act of extracting. **2** family origin; descent: *of Dutch extraction*.

extra-curricular *adj* not belonging to, or offered in addition to, the subjects studied in a school's, college's, etc. main teaching curriculum.

extradite *v* (*tr*) to send back (an alleged criminal) for trial in the country where the alleged crime was committed. — *adj* **extraditable**. — *n* **extradition**. [Lat *ex*, from + *tradere*, to deliver up]

extramarital *adj* (esp. of sexual relations) taking place outside marriage.

extramural *adj* **1** (of courses, etc.) for people who are not full-time students at a college, etc. **2** outside the scope of normal studies. [**extra-** + Lat *murus*, wall]

extraneous *adj* **1** not belonging; not relevant or related. **2** coming from outside. — *adv* **extraneously**. — *n* **extraneousness**. [Lat *extraneus*, external]

extraordinary *adj* **1** unusual; surprising; remarkable. **2** additional, not part of the regular pattern or routine: *extraordinary meeting*. **3** (*formal*; often following the noun) employed to do additional work, or for a particular occasion: *ambassador extraordinary*. — *adv* **extraordinarily**. [Lat *extra ordinem*, outside the usual order]

extrapolate *v* (*tr* & *intr*) **1** (*math*) to estimate (a value outside a known range) by extending known values according to known tendencies. **2** to make (estimates) or draw (conclusions) from known facts. — *n* **extrapolation**. [Lat *extra*, outside + **interpolate**]

extrasensory *adj* achieved using means other than the ordinary senses of sight, hearing, touch, taste and smell: *extrasensory perception*.

extraterrestrial *n* & *adj* (a being, creature, etc.) coming from outside the Earth or its atmosphere.

extravagant *adj* **1** using, spending, or costing too much. **2** unreasonably or unbelievably great: *extravagant claims/praise*. — *n* **extravagance**. — *adv* **extravagantly**. [Lat *extra*, beyond + *vagari*, to wander]

extravaganza *n* a spectacular display, performance or production. [Ital *estravaganza*, extravagance]

extravert. Same as **extrovert**.

extreme *adj* **1** very high, or highest, in degree or intensity. **2** very far, or furthest, in any direction, esp. out from the centre. **3** very violent or strong. **4** not moderate; severe: *extreme measures*. — *n* **1** either of two people or things as far, or as different, as possible from each other. **2** the highest limit; the greatest degree of any state or condition. — **go to extremes** to take action beyond what is thought to be reasonable. — **in the extreme** to the highest degree. — *adv* **extremely**. [Lat *extremus*, from *exterus*, on the outside]

extremist *n* a person who has extreme (esp. political) opinions. — *adj* relating to, or favouring, extreme measures. — *n* **extremism**.

extreme unction see **unction**.

extremity *n* **-ies 1** the farthest point. **2** an extreme degree; the quality of being extreme. **3** a situation of great danger. **4** (in *pl*) the hands and feet. [Lat *extremitas*, end, farthest point]

extricate *v* (*tr*) to free from difficulties; to disentangle. — *adj* **extricable**. — *n* **extrication**. [Lat *extricare*, from *ex*, from, + *tricae*, hindrances]

extrovert *n* & *adj* **1** (*psychol*) (a person) more interested in the outside world than with inner feelings. **2** (a person who is) sociable and outgoing. — *n* **extroversion**. — *adj* **extroverted**. [Lat *extra*, outwards + *vertere*, to turn]

extrude *v* (*tr*; **from**) **1** to squeeze or force out. **2** to shape (metal, plastic, etc.) by forcing it through a die. — *n* **extrusion**. [Lat *extrudere*, to push out]

exuberant *adj* **1** in very high spirits. **2** enthusiastic and energetic. **3** (of health, etc.) excellent. **4** (of plants, etc.) growing abundantly. — *n* **exuberance**. — *adv* **exuberantly**. [Lat *exuberans*, from *uber*, rich]

exude *v* **1** (*tr*) to give off or give out (a smell, sweat, etc.). **2** (*tr*) to show or convey by one's behaviour: *exude friendliness*. **3** (*intr*) to ooze out. — *n* **exudation**. [Lat *exsudare*, to sweat out]

exult *v* (*intr*) **1** (**in, at**) to be very joyful. **2** (**over**) to show or enjoy a feeling of triumph. — *adj* **exultant**. — *n* **exultation**. [Lat *exsultare*, to jump up and down]

eye *n* **1** the organ of sight in man and animals. **2** the coloured part of this, the iris. **3** the area around this organ. **4** (often in *pl*) sight; vision: *Surgeons need good eyes*. **5** attention, gaze or observation: *keep one's eyes on*; *catch someone's eye*; *in the public eye*. **6** (**for**) the ability to appreciate and judge: *an eye for beauty*. **7** judgement; opinion: *in the eyes of the law*. **8** a look or expression: *a hostile eye*. **9** a dark seed-bud on a potato. **10** an area of calm and low pressure at the centre of a tornado, etc. **11** any rounded thing, esp. when hollow, e.g. the hole in a needle or the small wire loop that a hook fits into. — *v* ***eyeing*** or ***eying***, ***eyed*** (*tr*) **1** to look at (carefully). **2** (*coll*; **up**) to assess the worth or sexual attractiveness of. — **be all eyes** (*coll*) to watch intently. — **cast** or **run an eye over** to examine quickly. — **clap, lay** or **set eyes on** (*coll*) to see, esp. for the first time. — **close** or **shut one's eyes to** to ignore or disregard. — **get** or **keep one's eye in 1** to regain or maintain one's proficiency (e.g. in a sport) through practice. **2** to become or remain used to existing conditions (e.g. of play in a sport). — **give an eye to** (*coll*) to attend to. — **give (someone) the eye** or **the glad eye** (*coll*) to look at in a sexually inviting way. — **have one's eye on** to be eager to have, get, obtain, etc. — **have eyes for** to be interested in. — **have an eye to** to have as a purpose. — **keep one's eyes skinned** or **peeled (for)** (*coll*) to watch out. — **make eyes at** (*coll*) to look at with sexual interest or admiration. — **more than meets the eye** something more complicated, difficult, etc. than appearances suggest. — **my eye!** (*coll*) nonsense! — **one in the eye for** (*coll*) a harsh disappointment or rebuff for. — **see eye to eye (with)** to be in agreement. — **be up to the** or **one's eyes (in** or **with)** to be very busy or deeply involved. — **with an eye to** having as an aim. [OE *eage*]

eyeball *n* the ball-shaped part of the eye, without the lids or lashes. — **eyeball to eyeball** (*coll*) face to face and close together in a threatening confrontation.

eyebrow *n* the arch of hair above each eye. — **raise one's eyebrows** or **an eyebrow** to show surprise, interest or disbelief.

eye-catching *adj* striking or drawing attention, esp. if attractive. — *n* **eye-catcher**.

eyeful *n* (*coll*) **1** an interesting or beautiful sight. **2** a look or view.

eyeglass *n* a single lens in a frame, to assist weak sight.

eyelash *n* any of the short hairs that grow on the edge of the eyelid.

eyelet see separate entry.

eyelid *n* either of the two folds of skin that can be moved to cover or open the eye.

eye-opener *n* (*coll*) a surprising or revealing sight, experience, etc.

eyepiece *n* the part of a telescope, etc. to which one puts one's eye.

eyesight *n* the ability to see.

eyesore *n* (*derog*) an ugly thing, esp. a building.

eye teeth *n* the two canine teeth in the upper jaw. — **give one's eye teeth for** to go to any lengths in order to obtain.

eyewash *n* **1** liquid for soothing sore eyes. **2** (*coll derog*) nonsense; insincere or deceptive talk.

eyewitness *n* a person who sees something happen, esp. a crime.

eyelet *n* a small hole through which a lace, etc. is passed, or the metal ring reinforcing it. [OFr *oillet*, dimin. of *oil*, eye]

eyrie *n* **1** the nest of an eagle or other bird of prey, built in a high inaccessible place. **2** any house, fortified place, etc. perched high up. [OFr *airie*]

F

F[1] or **f** *n* ***Fs*** or ***F's, f's*** **1** the sixth letter of the English alphabet. **2** (only **F**; *mus*) the fourth note in the scale of C major. **3** (only **F**) a musical key with this note as its base.
F[2] *abbrev* **1** Fahrenheit. **2** farad. **3** Fellow (of a society, etc.). **4** (on pencil leads) fine. **5** franc.
F[3] *symbol* **1** (*chem*) fluorine. **2** (*physics*) force.
f *abbrev* **1** (*mus*) forte. **2** frequency.
f. *abbrev* **1** fathom. **2** female. **3** feminine. **4** focal length. **5** folio. **6** following (page).
f-stop see **stop** (*n* sense **7**).
FA *abbrev* Football Association.
Fa. *abbrev* Florida.
fa. Same as **fah**.
Fabian *adj* **1** cautious; inclined to use delaying tactics. **2** of the Fabian Society, a body founded in 1884 for the gradual establishment of socialism. — *n* a member of this society. [Q *Fabius*, Roman general who wore down Hannibal by guerilla tactics, avoiding a pitched battle]
fable *n* **1** a story with a moral, usu. with animals as characters. **2** a lie; a false story. **3** a tale of wonder; myths and legends generally. [Lat *fabula*, story]
fabled *adj* made famous by legend.
fabric *n* **1** woven, knitted or felted cloth. **2** quality; texture. **3** the walls, floor and roof of a building. **4** orderly structure: *the fabric of society*. [Lat *fabrica*, craft]
fabricate *v* (*tr*) **1** to invent (a false story, etc.). **2** to make, esp. from whatever materials are available. **3** to forge (a document). — *n* **fabrication**. — *n* **fabricator**. [Lat *fabricari*, to construct]
fabulous *adj* **1** (*coll*) marvellous. **2** immense; amazing. **3** legendary; mythical. — *adv* **fabulously**. [Lat *fabulosus*]
façade or **facade** *n* **1** the front of a building. **2** a false appearance that hides the reality. [Fr]
face *n* **1** the front part of the head, from forehead to chin. **2** the features or facial expression. **3** a surface or side, e.g. of a mountain, gem, geometrical figure, etc. **4** the important or working side, e.g. of a golf-club head. **5** in a mine, the exposed surface from which coal, etc. is mined. **6** the dial of a clock, watch, etc. **7** the side of a playing-card marked with numbers, symbols, etc. **8** general look or appearance. **9** an aspect. **10** impudence; cheek. **11** (*literary*) someone's presence: *stand before his face*. **12** (*printing*) a typeface. — *v* **1** (*tr* & *intr*) to be opposite to; to (turn to) look at or look in some direction. **2** (*tr*) to have before one (something unpleasant): *face ruin*. **3** (*tr*) to confront, brave or cope with (problems, difficulties, etc.). **4** (*tr*) to accept (the unpleasant truth, etc.). **5** (*tr*) to present itself to: *the scene that faced us*. **6** (*tr*; **with**) to cover with a surface of. — *v* **face down** (*tr*) to confront (someone) boldly till he or she gives way, from embarrassment, shame, etc. — **face to face** facing or confronting each other (*adj* **face-to-face**). — *v* **face up to** (*tr*) to cope with bravely; to accept (an unpleasant fact, etc). — **fly in the face of** to act contrary to; to flout. — **in one's face** right in front of one. — **in the face of** in spite of. — **look in the face** to look straight at (someone) without shame or embarrassment. — **lose face** to suffer a loss of dignity or self-respect. — **make** or **pull a face** to grimace, scowl, frown, etc. — **on the face of it** at first glance. — **put a good** or **brave face on** to try to hide one's disappointment, fear, etc. concerning. — **save one's face** to avoid losing one's dignity or self-respect (*adj* & *n* **face-saving**). — **set one's face against** to oppose firmly. — **show one's face** to let oneself be seen. — **to someone's face** directly; openly, in someone's presence. ◇ See also **facial**. [Fr, from Lat *facies*]
face card *n* a court card.
facing *n* **1** an outer layer, e.g. of stone covering a brick wall. **2** a piece of material used to back and strengthen part of a garment. **3** (in *pl*) the collar and cuffs of a jacket, etc., esp. if in a contrasting colour.
faceless *adj* lacking identity; impersonal; anonymous.
facelift *n* **1** a surgical operation to remove facial wrinkles by tightening the skin. **2** a procedure for improving the appearance of something.
face pack *n* a liquid cosmetic preparation for cleaning the face, that hardens on the skin and is peeled off.
face value *n* **1** the stated value on a coin, stamp, etc. **2** the apparent meaning or implication, e.g. of a statement.
facer *n* (*coll*) a problem. [**face**]
facet *n* **1** any of the faces of a cut jewel. **2** an aspect, e.g. of a problem, topic, or personality. [Fr *facette*, dimin. of *face*, face]
facetious *adj* (intending or intended to be) amusing or witty, esp. unsuitably. — *adv* **facetiously**. — *n* **facetiousness**. [Lat *facetus*, witty]
facia. Another spelling of **fascia**.
facial *adj* of, relating to or belonging to, the face. [Lat *facies*, face]
facile *adj* **1** (*derog*) (of success, etc.) too easily achieved. **2** (*derog*) (of remarks, opinions, etc.) over-simple; showing a lack

of careful thought. **3** speaking or performing with fluency and ease. — *adv* **facilely**. [Lat *facilis*, easy]

facilitate *v* (*tr*) to ease (a process, etc.). — *n* **facilitation**. [**facility**]

facility *n* **-ies 1** (**for**) skill, talent or ability. **2** fluency; ease. **3** an arrangement, feature, attachment, etc. that enables something to do something. **4** (usu. in *pl*) a building, service or piece of equipment for a particular activity. [Lat *facilitas*, ease]

facsimile *n* **1** an exact copy made e.g. of a manuscript, picture, etc. **2** electronic copying and telegraphic transmission of material; fax. **3** a copy made by facsimile. [Lat *fac simile*, make the same]

fact *n* **1** a thing known to be true, to exist, or to have happened. **2** truth or reality, as distinct from mere statement or belief. **3** an assertion of fact; a piece of information. **4** (*legal*) a crime, as in *after*, or *before*, *the fact*. — **as a matter of fact, in actual fact, in fact**, or **in point of fact** actually. — **for a fact** with complete certainty. [Lat *factum*, something done]

fact of life *n* **1** an unavoidable truth, esp. if unpleasant. **2** (in *pl*) required information on sexual matters and reproduction.

faction[1] *n* **1** an active or trouble-making group within a larger organisation. **2** argument and fighting between members of a group. — *adj* **factional**. [Lat *factio*, party, side]

faction[2] *n* a docudrama. [**fact** + **fiction**]

factitious *adj* deliberately contrived rather than developing naturally. [Lat *facticius*]

factor *n* **1** a circumstance that contributes to a result. **2** (*math*) one of two or more numbers that when multiplied together produce a given number. **3** in Scotland, the manager of an estate. [Lat, person who acts]

factorial *n* (*math*) the number resulting when a number and all those below it are multiplied together. — *adj* relating to a factor or factorial.

factorise or **-ize** *v* (*tr*; *math*) to find the factors of (a number). — *n* **factorisation** or **-z-**.

factory *n* **-ies** a building or buildings with equipment for the large-scale manufacture of goods. [Lat *factoria*]

factory farm *n* (*derog*) a farm in which animals are reared by fast factory-like methods. — *n* **factory-farming**.

factotum *n* a person employed to do a large number of different jobs. [Lat *fac totum*, do all]

factual *adj* concerned with, or based on, facts. — *adv* **factually**. [**fact**]

faculty *n* **-ies 1** any of the range of mental or physical powers. **2** (**for**) a particular talent or aptitude for something. **3** a section of a university, comprising a number of departments. **4** (*NAm*) the staff of a college, school or university. [Lat *facultas*, capability]

fad *n* (*derog*) **1** a shortlived fashion; a craze. **2** an esp. unreasonable prejudice or dislike, usu. with regard to food. — *n* **faddiness** or **faddishness**. — *adj* **faddy** or **faddish**.

fade *v* (**away**) **1** (*tr* & *intr*) to (cause to) lose strength, freshness or colour. **2** (*intr*) (of a sound or image) to disappear gradually. — *v* **fade in** and **fade out** (*tr*; *films*, *television*, *radio*) respectively to cause (a sound or picture) gradually to become louder and more distinct, or to to become fainter and disappear (*n* **fade-in** and **fade-out**). [OFr *fade*, dull, pale]

faeces *n* (*pl*) the solid waste matter discharged from the body through the anus. — *adj* **faecal**. [Lat *faex*, dregs]

faff *v* (*intr*; *coll*; **about**) to act in a fussy, uncertain way; to dither.

fag[1] *n* **1** (*coll*) a cigarette. **2** (*coll*) a piece of drudgery; a bore. **3** in some schools, a young schoolboy who runs errands and does jobs for an older one. — *v* **-gg- 1** (*tr*) to tire out; to exhaust. **2** (*intr*) (of a schoolboy) to act as fag for an older boy. **3** (*intr*) to work hard; to toil.

fag end *n* (*coll*) **1** a cigarette end. **2** the last part (of something).

fag[2] *n* (*NAm offensive slang*) a male homosexual. [Short for **faggot**]

faggot *n* **1** a ball or roll of chopped liver mixed with bread and herbs. **2** a bundle of sticks. **3** (*offensive slang*) a male homosexual. **4** (*derog slang*) an old woman. [OFr *fagot*, bundle of sticks]

fah *n* in tonic sol-fa, the fourth note of the major scale. [From the first syllable of the word *famuli* in a mediaeval Latin hymn, certain syllables of which were used in naming the notes of the scale]

Fahrenheit *adj* & *n* (on or of) a scale of temperature on which water boils at 212° and freezes at 32°. [G D *Fahrenheit* (1686–1736), German physicist]

faience or **faïence** *n* glazed decorated pottery. [Fr, from *Faenza* in Italy, the place of manufacture]

fail *v* **1** (*intr* & *tr*; **in**) not to succeed; to be unsuccessful in. **2** (*tr*) to judge (a candidate) not good enough to pass a test, etc. **3** (*intr*) (of machinery, a bodily organ, etc.) to stop working or functioning. **4** (*intr*) not to manage (to do something). **5** (*tr*) not to bother (doing something). **6** (*tr*) to let (someone) down; to disappoint. **7** (*tr*) (of courage, strength, etc.) to desert (one) at the time of need. **8** (*intr*) to become gradually weaker. **9** (*intr*) (of a business, etc.) to collapse. — **fail to see** to be unable to understand. — **without fail** for certain; with complete regularity. [Lat *fallere*, to deceive, disappoint]

failing *n* a fault; a weakness.

fail-safe *adj* (of a mechanism) ensuring a return, or (of a machine) returning, to a safe condition when something goes wrong.

failure *n* **1** the act of failing; lack of success. **2** a person or thing that is unsuccessful. **3** a stoppage in functioning. **4** a poor result. **5** the non-doing of something: *failure to turn up*.

fain *adv* (*old*) gladly; willingly. [OE *fægen*]

faint *adj* **1** pale; dim; indistinct; slight. **2** physically weak; on the verge of losing consciousness. **3** feeble; timid; unenthusiastic. — *v* (*intr*) to lose consciousness; to collapse. — *n* a sudden loss of consciousness. — *adv* **faintly**. — *n* **faintness**. [OFr *faindre*, to feign]

faint-hearted *adj* timid; cowardly.

fair[1] *adj* **1** just; not using dishonest methods or discrimination. **2** in accordance with the rules. **3** (of hair and skin) light-coloured; having light-coloured hair and skin. **4** (*old*) beautiful. **5** quite good; reasonable. **6** sizeable; considerable. **7** (of weather) fine. **8** (of wind) favourable. **9** (of words) insincerely encouraging. — *adv* **1** in a fair way. **2** (*dialect*) completely. — *n* **fairness**. — **be fair game** to deserve to be attacked or criticised. — **by fair means or foul** using any possible means, even if dishonest. — **fair and square 1** absolutely; exactly. **2** honest and open. — **fair enough** all right. — **in a fair way to** likely to. — **in all fairness** or **to be fair** one ought to remember, if one is fair. [OE *fæger*, beautiful]

fair copy *n* a neat finished copy of a piece of writing.

fair dos or **do's** *n* (*pl*; *coll*) equal treatment for everyone.

fairly *adv* **1** justly; honestly. **2** quite; rather. **3** (*coll*) absolutely.

fair play *n* honourable behaviour; just treatment.

the fair sex *n* (*facet*) women.

fairway *n* **1** (*golf*) a broad strip of short grass extending from one tee to the next green. **2** a deep-water channel in a river, etc., used by shipping.

fair-weather friend *n* a friend who deserts one when one is in trouble.

fair[2] *n* **1** (also **funfair**) an assortment of sideshows, amusements, rides, etc. travelling round from place to place. **2** (*hist*) a market for the sale of produce, livestock, etc., with or without such sideshows. **3** an indoor exhibition of goods from different countries, firms, etc., held to promote trade. **4** a sale of goods to raise money for charity, etc. [OFr *feire*, from Lat *feriae*, holiday]

fairground *n* the piece of land on which sideshows and amusements are set up for a fair.

fairing *n* an external structure fitted to an aircraft or vehicle to improve streamlining and reduce drag. [*fair*, to make smooth, to streamline]

Fair Isle *n* a complex multicoloured type of knitting pattern. [*Fair Isle*, Shetland, where first developed]

fairy *n* **-ies 1** any of various supernatural beings with magical powers and more or less human shape, common in folklore. **2** (*derog*) a male homosexual.

fairy godmother *n* someone who comes unexpectedly or magically to one's aid.

fairyland *n* **1** the home of fairies. **2** an entrancing place.

fairy lights *n* (*pl*) small coloured lights used for decoration.

fairy ring *n* a ring of dark grass at the outer edge of a growth of fungi.

fairy tale or **fairy story** *n* **1** a story about fairies, magic, etc. **2** (*coll euph*) a lie.

fait accompli *n* ***faits accomplis*** something done and unalterable; an established fact. [Fr, accomplished fact]

faith *n* **1** (**in**) trust or confidence. **2** strong belief, e.g. in God. **3** a religion. **4** any set or system of beliefs. **5** loyalty to a promise, etc.; trust: *keep* or *break faith with someone*. — **in good faith** from good or sincere motives. [OFr *feid*]

bad faith *n* dishonesty; treachery.

faithful *adj* **1** having or showing faith. **2** (**to**) loyal and true. **3** accurate. **4** loyal to one's sexual partner. **5** reliable; constant. — *n* **1** (*pl*; with **the**) the believers in a particular religion; loyal supporters. **2** a supporter: *party faithfuls*. — *adv* **faithfully**. — *n* **faithfulness**. — **yours faithfully** formal wording for ending a letter.

faith healing *n* the curing of illness through religious faith rather than medical treatment. — *n* **faith healer**.

faithless *adj* **1** disloyal; treacherous. **2** having no religious faith. — *adv* **faithlessly**. — *n* **faithlessness**.

fake *n* a person, thing or act that is not genuine. — *adj* not genuine; false. — *v* **1** (*tr*) to alter dishonestly; to falsify or make up. **2** (*tr* & *intr*) to pretend to feel (an emotion) or have (an illness). — *n* **faker**. — *n* **fakery**.

fakir *n* **1** a wandering Hindu or Muslim holy man depending on begging for survival. **2** a member of any Muslim religious order. [Arabic *faqir*, poor man]

falcon *n* a type of bird of prey that can be trained to hunt small birds and animals. [Lat *falco*, hawk]

falconry *n* the breeding and training of falcons for hunting. — *n* **falconer**.

fall *v* ***fell***, ***fallen*** (*intr*) **1** to descend or drop by force of gravity, esp. accidentally. **2** (**over**, **down**) (of a person, or something upright) to drop to the ground after losing balance. **3** (of a building, bridge, etc.) to collapse. **4** (of rain, snow, etc.) to come down. **5** (of e.g. hair) to hang down. **6** (of land) to slope down. **7** (of a blow, glance, shadow, light, etc.) to land. **8** to go naturally or easily into position: *fell open at page 61*. **9** to throw oneself; to move hurriedly or ungracefully. **10** (of a government, etc.) to collapse. **11** (**to**) (of a stronghold) to be captured (by). **12** (of defences or barriers) to be lowered or broken down. **13** to die or be badly wounded in battle, etc. **14** to give in to temptation; to sin. **15** (of e.g. value, temperature, etc.) to become less. **16** (of sound) to diminish. **17** (of e.g. silence) to intervene. **18** (of darkness or night) to arrive. **19** to pass into a certain state: *fall asleep*. **20** to be grouped or classified in a certain way: *falls into two categories*. **21** to occur at a certain time or place: *The accent falls on the first syllable*. **22** (of someone's face) to show disappointment. — *n* **1** an act or way of falling. **2** something, or an amount, that falls. **3** (in *pl*) a waterfall. **4** a drop in e.g. quality, quantity, value, temperature, etc. **5** a defeat or collapse. **6** (*wrestling*) a manoeuvre by which one pins one's opponent's shoulders to the ground. **7** (*cap*; with **the**; *Bible*) the sinning of Adam and Eve. — **break someone's fall** to stop someone landing with the full impact of a free fall. — *v* **fall about** (*intr*; *coll*) to be helpless with laughter. — *v* **fall apart** (*intr*) **1** to break in pieces. **2** to fail; to collapse. — *v* **fall away** (*intr*) **1** (of land) to slope downwards. **2** to become fewer or less. **3** to disappear. — *v* **fall back** (*intr*) **1** to move back; to retreat. **2** (with **on**) to make use of in an emergency. — *v* **fall behind 1** (*intr* & *tr*) to fail to keep up (with). **2** (*intr* with **with**) to be late in paying (instalments) or doing (work). — *v* **fall down** (*intr*) **1** (of an argument, etc.) to collapse. **2** (with **on**) to perform badly. — *v* **fall for** (*tr*) **1** to be deceived or taken in by. **2** to fall in love with. — *v* **fall in** (*intr*) **1** (of e.g. a roof) to collapse. **2** (of a soldier, etc.) to take one's place in military formation. **3** (with **with**) to agree to; to support. **4** (with **with**) to chance to meet or coincide with. — *v* **fall into** (*tr*) to become involved in. — *v* **fall off** (*intr*) to decline, in quality or quantity (*n* **falling-off**). — *v* **fall on** or **upon** (*tr*) **1** to attack. **2** to embrace. — *v* **fall out** (*intr*) **1** (**with**) to quarrel. **2** (of soldiers) to come out of military formation. **3** to happen in the end; to turn out. — **fall over oneself** or **fall over backwards** (*coll*) to be eager (to please, etc.). — *v* **fall through** (of a plan, etc.) to fail; to come to nothing. — *v* **fall to 1** (*intr*) to begin eating. **2** (*tr*) to start: *fall to work*. **3** (*tr*) to become the job or duty of. — **fall to pieces** or **bits** to break up; to disintegrate. [OE *feallan*]

fallen *adj* **1** (esp. *old*) having lost one's virtue, honour or reputation. **2** killed in battle. **3** having dropped or overturned.

fall guy *n* (*coll*) **1** someone who is easily cheated. **2** someone who is left to take the blame for something.

falling star *n* a meteor.

fallout *n* a cloud of radioactive dust caused by a nuclear explosion.

fallacy *n* **-ies 1** a mistaken notion. **2** a mistake in reasoning that spoils a whole argument. — *adj* **fallacious**. — *adv* **fallaciously**. [Lat *fallax*, deceptive]

fallen. See **fall**.

fallible *adj* capable of making mistakes. [Lat *fallere*, to deceive]

Fallopian tubes *n* (*pl*) the two trumpet-shaped ducts through which eggs pass from a woman's ovaries into her womb. [G *Fallopius* (1523–62), Italian anatomist]

fallow *adj* (of land) left unplanted after ploughing, to recover its natural fertility. [OE *fealga*]

fallow deer *n* a small reddish-brown deer, white-spotted in summer. [OE *fealu*, tawny]

false *adj* **1** (of a statement, etc.) untrue. **2** (of an idea, etc.) mistaken. **3** artificial; not genuine. **4** (of words, promises, etc.) insincere. **5** (**to**) treacherous; disloyal. **6** (*bot*) (of a plant) resembling, but wrongly so called: *false acacia*. — *adv* **falsely**. — *n* **falseness** or **falsity**. — **play (someone) false** to cheat or deceive. — **under false pretences** by giving a deliberately misleading impression. [Lat *falsus*]

false alarm *n* an alarm given unnecessarily.

falsehood *n* **1** lying; dishonesty. **2** a lie.

false move *n* a careless or unwise action that puts one in danger.

false start *n* **1** a failed attempt to begin something. **2** an invalid start to a race, in which one competitor begins before the signal is given.

falsetto *n* **-os** an artificially high voice, esp. produced by a tenor above his normal range. [Ital]

falsify *v* **-ies**, **-ied** (*tr*) to alter dishonestly or make up, in order to deceive or mislead. — *n* **falsification**. [Lat *falsus*, false + *facere*, to make]

falter *v* **-r- 1** (*intr*) to move unsteadily; to stumble. **2** (*intr*) to start functioning unreliably. **3** (*intr*) to lose strength or conviction; to hesitate or break down in speaking. **4** (*tr*) to say hesitantly. — *adv* **falteringly**.

fame *n* **1** the condition of being famous. **2** (*old*) repute. [Lat *fama*, report, rumour]

famed *adj* famous.

familial *adj* belonging to, typical of, or occurring in, a family. [**family**]

familiar *adj* **1** (**to**) well known or recognisable. **2** frequently met with. **3** (with **with**) well acquainted with; having a thorough knowledge of. **4** friendly; close. **5** over-friendly; offensively informal. — *n* **1** a close friend. **2** a demon or spirit esp. in the shape of an animal, serving a witch. — *n* **familiarity**. — *adj* **familiarly**. [Lat *familiaris*, domestic, intimate]

familiarise or **-ize** *v* (*tr*) **1** (with **with**) to make (esp. oneself) familiar with something. **2** to make well known or familiar. — *n* **familiarisation** or **-z-**.

family *n* **-ies 1** a group consisting of a set of parents and children. **2** a set of relatives. **3** a person's children. **4** a household of people. **5** all those descended from a common ancestor. **6** a related group, e.g. of races, languages, words, etc. **7** a related group of plant or animal genera. — **in the family way** (*coll*) pregnant. [Lat *familia*, household, family]

family allowance *n* (*old*) child benefit.

family credit *n* an allowance paid to families with low incomes.

family doctor *n* a general practitioner.

family man *n* a married man with children, esp. one fond of home life.

family name *n* **1** a surname. **2** the family honour: *a stain on the family name*.

family planning *n* control over the number of children born in a family, esp. through use of contraceptives.

family tree *n* (a diagram showing) the relationships within a family throughout the generations.

famine *n* a severe or disastrous shortage of food. [OFr, from Lat *fames*, hunger]

famished or **famishing** *adj* very hungry; starving: *famished children*. [Lat *fames*, hunger]

famous *adj* **1** (**for**) well known; celebrated; renowned. **2** great; glorious: *a famous victory*. — *adv* **famously**. [Lat *famosus*, from *fama*, report, fame]

fan[1] *n* **1** a hand-held device made of paper, silk, etc., usu. semicircular and folding flat when not in use, for creating a current of air to cool the face. **2** something of a similar shape, with parts diverging from a central point. **3** a machine with revolving blades, for producing a current of air. **4** a device for winnowing grain. — *v* **-nn- 1** (*tr*) to cool by creating a current of air round (as if) with a fan. **2** (*tr*) to kindle or stir up (as if) with a current of air. **3** (*intr* & *tr* with **out**) to spread out in the shape of a fan. **4** (*tr*) to agitate (air) (as if) with a fan. **5** (*tr*) to winnow (grain). [OE *fann*]

fan belt *n* the rubber band that drives the cooling fan in a vehicle engine.

fanlight *n* a semicircular window over a door or window.

fantail *n* a pigeon with a fan-shaped tail.

fan[2] *n* an enthusiastic supporter or devoted admirer. [**fanatic**]

fan club *n* a club of admirers of a pop star, etc.

fan mail *n* the admiring letters received by a celebrity.

fanatic *n* someone with an extreme or excessive enthusiasm for something. — *adj* excessively enthusiastic. — *adj* **fanatical**. — *adv* **fanatically**. — *n* **fanaticism**. [Lat *fanaticus*, filled with a god, frenzied]

fancier *n* (esp. *in cmpds*) someone with a special interest in something, esp. a breeder or grower of a certain kind of bird, animal or plant. [**fancy**]

fanciful *adj* **1** indulging in fancies; (over-) imaginative. **2** existing in fancy only; imaginary. **3** designed in a curious or fantastic way. — *adv* **fancifully**. [**fancy**]

fancy *n* **-ies 1** one's imagination. **2** an image, idea or whim. **3** a sudden liking or desire. — *adj* **1** elaborate. **2** (*coll*) of special, unusual or superior quality. **3** (*coll facet*) (of prices) too high. — *v* **-ies**, **-ied 1** (*tr*) to think or believe. **2** (*tr*) to have a desire for. **3** (*tr*; *coll*) to be sexually attracted to. **4** (*tr*) to consider likely to win or do well. **5** (*tr* & *intr*) to take in mentally; to imagine: *Fancy him getting married at last!* **6** (*tr*; *coll*) to think too well of (oneself). — *adv* **fancily**. — **fancy the chances of** to predict success for. — **take a fancy to** to become fond of. — **take** or **tickle the fancy of** to appeal to; to intrigue or attract. [Contracted from **fantasy**]

fancy dress *n* clothes one dresses up in to represent a historical, fictional, etc. character.

fancy-free *adj* **1** not in love. **2** free to do as one pleases.

fancy goods *n* (*pl*) small gifts, souvenirs, etc.

fancy man or **woman** *n* (*old coll derog*) a lover.

fancywork *n* fine decorative needlework.

fandango *n* **-os** (a piece of music for) an energetic Spanish dance. [Span]

fanfare *n* a short piece of music played on trumpets to announce an important event or arrival. [Fr]

fang *n* **1** the pointed canine tooth of a carnivorous animal. **2** the tooth of a poisonous snake. **3** (one of the prongs of) the root of a tooth. [OE, something caught]

fanny *n* **-ies 1** (*vulgar slang*) a woman's genitals. **2** (*N Am slang*) the buttocks.

fantasia *n* **1** a musical composition that is free and unconventional in form. **2** a piece of music based on a selection of popular tunes. [Ital, imagination]

fantasise or **-ize** *v* (*intr*; **about**) to indulge in pleasurable fantasies or daydreams. [**fantasy**]

fantastic *adj* **1** (*coll*) splendid. **2** (*coll*) enormous; amazing. **3** (of a story) absurd; unlikely; incredible. **4** strange, weird or fanciful. — *adv* **fantastically**. [Gr *phantastikos*, presenting to the mind]

fantasy *n* **-ies 1** a pleasant daydream; a longed-for but unlikely happening. **2** a mistaken notion. **3** one's imaginings. **4** the activity of imagining. **5** a product of the imagination; a fanciful piece of writing, music, film-making, etc. [Gr *phantasia*, image in the mind, imagination]

far ***farther***, ***farthest*** or ***further***, ***furthest*** *adv* **1** at, to or from, a great distance in space. **2** to or by a great extent: *My guess wasn't far out*. **3** at or to a distant time. — *adj* **1** distant; remote. **2** the more distant of two. **3** extreme: *the far Right of the party*. — **as far as 1** up to (a certain place or point). **2** (also **so far as**) to the extent that. — **as** (or **so**) **far as I'm**, etc. **concerned** in my, etc. opinion. — **as** (or **so**) **far as it goes** in its own limited way. — **as** (or **so**) **far as that**, etc. **goes** or **is concerned** concerning that, etc. in particular. — **by far** or **far and away** very much. — **far and wide** extensively. — **far be it from me to** I'm reluctant to (criticise, etc.). — **a far cry from** greatly different from. — **far from 1** (also **so far from**) not only not, but: *So far from winning, she came second last*. **2** the opposite of; not at all. — **far gone** in an advanced state, e.g. of illness or drunkenness. — **go far** to achieve great things. — **go so** (or **as**) **far as to** to go to the extent of; to be prepared to. — **go too far** to behave, speak, etc. unreasonably. — **in so far as** to the extent that. [OE *feorr*]

faraway *adj* **1** distant. **2** (of a look or expression) dreamy; abstracted.

Far East *n* the countries of E and SE Asia. — *adj* **Far-Eastern**.

far-fetched *adj* unlikely; unconvincing.

far-flung *adj* **1** extensive. **2** distant.

far-off *adj* distant; remote.

far-out *adj* (*coll*) **1** strange; weird; outlandish. **2** excellent.

far-reaching *adj* having widespread effects.

far-sighted *adj* **1** (also **far-seeing**) wise; prudent; forward-looking. **2** long-sighted. — *n* **far-sightedness**.

farad *n* (*electr*) the unit of capacitance. [M *Faraday* (1791–1867), physicist]

farce *n* **1** a comedy involving a series of ridiculously unlikely turns of events; comedies of this type. **2** an absurd situation; something ludicrously badly organised. — *adj* **farcical**. — *adv* **farcically**. [OFr, stuffing]

fare *n* **1** the price paid by a passenger to travel on a bus, train, etc. **2** a taxi passenger. **3** (*old* or *formal*) food. — *v* (*intr*; *formal*) **1** to get on. **2** to be treated in a certain way. [OE *faran*]

fare stage *n* (a bus stop marking the end of) any of the sections into which a bus route is divided, for which there is a standard fare.

farewell *interj* (*old*) goodbye! — *n* an act of saying goodbye. [**fare** + **well**[2]]

farinaceous *adj* like or containing flour or starch. [Lat *farina*, flour, meal]

farm *n* **1** a piece of land with its buildings, used for growing crops or breeding and keeping livestock. **2** the farmer's house and the buildings round it. **3** a place specialising in the rearing of particular animals, etc.: *a fish farm*. — *v* **1** (*tr* & *intr*) to prepare and use (land) for crop-growing, animal-rearing, etc.; to be a farmer. **2** (*tr*) to collect and keep the proceeds from (taxes, etc.) in return for a fixed sum. **3** (*tr* with **out**) to give (some of one's work) to others to do; to hand over (one's children) temporarily to a carer. — *n* & *adj* **farming**. [MidE *ferme*, rented land]

farmer *n* a person who manages or owns a farm.

farm hand *n* a person employed to work on a farm.

farmhouse *n* the farmer's house on a farm.

farmstead *n* a farmhouse and the buildings round it.

farmyard *n* the central yard at a farm, surrounded by farm buildings.

farrago *n* **-os** or **-oes** a confused mixture; a hotchpotch. [Lat, mixed fodder]

farrier *n* **1** a person who shoes horses. **2** (*old*) a horse doctor. [OFr *ferrier*, from Lat *ferrarius*, smith]

farrow *n* a sow's litter of piglets. — *v* (*tr* & *intr*) (of a sow) to give birth to (pigs). [OE *fearh*]

fart (*vulg slang*) *v* (*intr*) **1** to emit gas from the anus, sometimes noisily. **2** (**about**, **around**) to fool about, waste time, etc. — *n* **1** an act of farting. **2** a term of abuse for a person. [MidE *farten*]

farther, **farthest**. See **far**.

farthing *n* (an old coin worth) one quarter of an old British penny. [OE *feortha*, quarter]

fasces *n* (*pl*; *Roman hist*) a bundle of rods with an axe in the middle, carried before magistrates as a symbol of authority. [Lat *fascis*, bundle]

fascia or **facia** *n* **1** the board above a shop entrance, bearing the shop name. **2** the dashboard of a motor vehicle. **3** (*archit*) a long flat band or surface. **4** (*anat*) tissue sheathing a muscle or organ. — *adj* **fascial** or **facial**. [Lat *fascia*, band]

fascinate *v* (*tr*) **1** to interest strongly; to intrigue. **2** (of a snake) to make unable to move, from fright. **3** to hold spellbound; to enchant irresistibly. — *adj* **fascinating**. — *adv* **fascinatingly**. — *n* **fascination**. [Lat *fascinare*, to bewitch]

fascism *n* **1** (an extreme right-wing movement in favour of) a political system in which there is, typically, state control of all aspects of society, a supreme dictator, suppression of democratic bodies such as trade unions, and emphasis on nationalism and militarism. **2** (*cap*) this system in force in Italy from 1922 to 1943. — *n* & *adj* **fascist** (also *cap*). [Ital *fascismo*]

fashion *n* **1** style, esp. the latest style, in clothes, etc. **2** a currently popular style or practice; a trend. **3** a manner of doing something. **4** the way something is made or constructed. — *v* (*tr*) **1** to form or shape, esp. with the hands. **2** to mould or influence. — **after a fashion** in a rather inexpert way. — **in** (or **out of**) **fashion** currently (or no longer) fashionable. [OFr *fachon*]

fashionable *adj* **1** (of clothes or people) following the latest fashion. **2** used by, or popular with, wealthy, fashionable people. — *adv* **fashionably**.

fast[1] *adj* **1** moving, or able to move, quickly. **2** taking a relatively short time. **3** (of a clock, etc.) showing a time in advance of the correct time. **4** allowing or intended for rapid movement: *the fast lane*. **5** (of a photographic film) requiring only brief exposure. **6** (*coll*) living a life of high excitement and expensive enjoyment. **7** (*coll*) tending to make sexual advances on rather brief acquaintance. **8** firmly fixed or caught. **9** (of friends) firm; close. **10** (of fabric colours) not liable to run or fade. — *adv* **1** quickly; rapidly. **2** in quick succession: *coming thick and fast.* **3** firmly; tight. **4** deeply; thoroughly: *fast asleep.* — **fast and furious** fast and lively; frenzied or frantic in pace. — **play fast and loose** to behave irresponsibly or unreliably. — **pull a fast one (on)** (*coll*) to cheat or deceive. [OE *fæst*, fixed, firm]

fast-breeder reactor *n* an apparatus for producing nuclear energy, which produces more fuel than it uses in the process.

fast food *n* food that is prepared and served quickly.

fastness *n* **1** the quality of being firmly fixed, or (of fabric colours) fast. **2** (*old*) a stronghold.

fast[2] *v* (*intr*) to go without food, esp. as a religious discipline. — *n* a period of fasting. [OE *fæstan*]

fasten *v* **-n-** (*tr* & *intr*; **up**) to make or become firmly closed or fixed. — *v* **fasten on** or **upon** (*tr*) to concentrate upon eagerly; to seize upon. [OE *fæstnian*]

fastener or **fastening** *n* a device that fastens something; a clasp or catch.

fastidious *adj* **1** (over-)particular in matters of taste; (too) careful over details. **2** easily disgusted. — *adv* **fastidiously**. — *n* **fastidiousness**. [Lat *fastidium*, disgust]

fat *n* **1** excess flesh on the body. **2** the solid greasy substance occurring in cells just below the skin in animals, that stores energy and generates warmth. **3** any of various greasy or oily substances got from animals or plants and used in liquid or esp. solid form as food or in cooking. — *adj* **-tt- 1** having too much fat on the body; plump; overweight. **2** containing a lot of fat. **3** thick or wide. **4** (*coll*) (of a fee, profit, etc.) large. **5** fertile; profitable. **6** (*slang facet*) none at all: *a fat lot of good.* — *v* **-tt-** (*tr*; *old*) to fatten. — *n* **fatness**. — **the fat's in the fire** that's done it; now there'll be trouble. — **grow fat on** to grow wealthy from the profits of. — **kill the fatted calf** to prepare a feast for a homecoming. — **live off the fat of the land** to live in luxury.

fathead *n* (*coll*; *offensive*) a fool. — *adj* **fat-headed**.

fatal *adj* **1** causing death; deadly. **2** bringing ruin; disastrous. **3** destined; unavoidable. — *adv* **fatally**. [Lat *fatalis*, from *fatum*, fate]

fatalism *n* the belief that fate controls everything, and humans cannot alter it. — *n* **fatalist**. — *adj* **fatalistic**. — *adv* **fatalistically**.

fatality *n* **-ies 1** an accidental or violent death. **2** the quality of being fatal. **3** the quality of being controlled by fate.

fate *n* **1** (sometimes *cap*) the apparent power that determines the course of events, over which humans have no control. **2** the individual destiny or fortune of a person or thing; what happens to someone or something. **3** death, downfall, destruction or doom. **4** (in *pl*; *cap*; *classical mythol*) the three goddesses who determine the birth, life and death of humans. — **a fate worse than death** (*facet*) a frightful fate, esp. (*old*) a woman's loss of virginity before marriage. [Lat *fatum*, fate]

fated *adj* **1** destined or intended by fate. **2** doomed.

fateful *adj* **1** (of a remark, etc.) prophetic. **2** decisive; critical; having significant results. **3** bringing calamity or disaster. — *adv* **fatefully**.

father *n* **1** a natural or adoptive male parent. **2** (in *pl*) one's ancestors. **3** a founder, inventor, originator, pioneer, or early leader. **4** (*cap*) a title, or form of address for a priest. **5** (*cap*) God. **6** (in *pl*) the leading, senior men of a city, etc. **7** (*cap*) used as a title in personifying something ancient or venerable: *Father Time.* — *v* (*tr*) **1** to be the father of. **2** to invent or originate. **3** (**on**) to claim that (someone) is the child of, or that (something) is the responsibility of. — *n* **fatherhood**. — *adj* **fatherless**. [OE *fæder*]

fatherly *adj* benevolent, protective and encouraging, like a father. — *n* **fatherliness**.

Father Christmas *n* a white-bearded old man in a red coat, traditionally supposed to deliver presents on Christmas Eve.

father figure *n* an older man to whom one turns for help, support, advice, etc.

father-in-law *n* ***fathers-in-law*** the father of one's wife or husband.

fatherland *n* one's native country.

fathom *n* a unit of measurement of the depth of water, equal to 6 ft (1·8 m). — *v* **-m-** (*tr*; **out**) **1** to work out (a problem); to get to the bottom of (a mystery). **2** to measure the depth of. [OE *fæthm*]

fathomless *adj* **1** too deep to be measured. **2** too difficult or mysterious to understand.

fatigue *n* **1** tiredness after work or effort; exhaustion. **2** weakness, esp. in metals, caused by variations in stress. **3** (*mil*) a domestic task performed by a soldier. **4** (in *pl*) uniform worn by soldiers in battle or for domestic tasks. — *v* (*tr* & *intr*) to exhaust or become exhausted. [Fr, from Lat *fatigare*, to weary]

fatten *v* **-n-** (*tr* & *intr*; **up**) to make or become fat. — *adj* **fattening**.

fatty *adj* **-ier, -iest 1** containing fat. **2** greasy; oily. **3** (of an acid) occurring in, derived from, or chemically related to, animal or vegetable fats. — *n* **-ies** (*coll derog*) a fat person. — *n* **fattiness**.

fatuous *adj* foolish, esp. in a self-satisfied way; empty-headed. — *n* **fatuity, -ies**. — *adv* **fatuously**. — *n* **fatuousness**. [Lat *fatuus*]

fatwa or **fatwah** *n* a formal legal opinion or decision issued by a Muslim authority. [Arabic]

faucet *n* **1** a tap fitted to a barrel. **2** (*NAm*) a tap on a washbasin, etc. [OFr *fausset*, peg]

fault *n* **1** a weakness or failing in character. **2** a flaw or defect in an object or structure. **3** responsibility for something wrong: *all my fault*. **4** (*geol*) a break or crack in the earth's crust, resulting in the slippage of a rock mass. **5** (*tennis*, etc.) an incorrectly placed or delivered serve. **6** (*showjumping*) a penalty for refusing or failing to clear a fence. — *adj* **faultless**. — *adv* **faultlessly**. — **at fault** blameworthy; to blame; wrong. — **find fault with** to criticise, esp. excessively or unfairly; to complain about. — **to a fault** to too great an extent. [OFr *faute*]

faulty *adj* **-ier, -iest** having a fault or faults; not working correctly.

faun *n* a mythical creature with a man's head and body and a goat's horns, hind legs and tail. [Lat *Faunus*, a rural god]

fauna *n* **-nas** or **-nae** the wild animals of a particular place or time. ◇ See also **flora**. [Lat *Fauna*, goddess of living creatures]

faux pas *n* ***faux pas*** an embarrassing, esp. social, blunder. [Fr, false step]

favour *n* **1** a kind or helpful action performed out of goodwill. **2** the liking, approval or goodwill of someone. **3** unfair preference. **4** a knot of ribbons worn as a badge of support for a particular team, political party, etc. **5** (esp. *hist*) something given or worn as a token of affection. **6** (in *pl*; *old euph*) a woman's consent to lovemaking or sexual liberties. — *v* (*tr*) **1** to regard with goodwill. **2** to treat with preference, or over-indulgently. **3** to prefer; to support. **4** (of circumstances) to give an advantage to. **5** (*old*) to look like (e.g. one's mother or father). **6** (*pompous*) to be wearing (a colour, etc.). — **in favour of 1** having a preference for. **2** to the benefit of. **3** in support or approval of. — **in** (or **out of**) **favour** (**with**) having gained (or lost) the approval (of). [Lat *favor*, from *favere*, to favour]

favourable *adj* **1** (**to**) showing or giving agreement or consent. **2** pleasing; likely to win approval. **3** (**to**) advantageous; helpful; suitable. **4** (of winds) following. — *adv* **favourably**.

favourite *adj* best-liked; preferred. — *n* **1** a favourite person or thing. **2** someone unfairly preferred or particularly indulged. **3** a horse or competitor expected to win. [OFr *favorit*]

favouritism *n* the practice of giving unfair preference, help or support to someone or something.

fawn[1] *n* **1** the young of one of the small types of deer. **2** the colour of a fawn, beige. [OFr *faon*]

fawn[2] *v* (*intr* with **on**) **1** (of dogs) to show affection for by licking, nuzzling, etc. **2** to flatter or behave over-humbly towards, in order to win approval. — *adj* **fawning**. — *adv* **fawningly**. [OE *fagnian*]

fax *n* **1** a machine that scans documents electronically and transmits a photographic image of the contents to a receiving machine by telephone line. **2** a copy so transmitted. — *v* (*tr*) **1** to transmit a photographic image of by this means. **2** to send a faxed communication to. [Contracted from **facsimile**]

fay *n* (*poetic*) a fairy. [OFr *fae*]

FBI *abbrev* Federal Bureau of Investigation, a police department in the US esp. investigating political or other activities that threaten state security. ◇ See also **CIA**.

FC *abbrev* football club.

FD *abbrev* (on coins) *Fidei Defensor* (Lat), Defender of the Faith.

Fe *symbol* (*chem*) iron. [Lat *ferrum*]

fealty *n* (*hist*) the loyalty sworn by a vassal or tenant to his feudal lord. [OFr *fealte*, from Lat *fidelitas*, loyalty]

fear *n* **1** anxiety and distress caused by the awareness of danger or expectation of pain. **2** a cause of this feeling. **3** religious awe or dread. **4** (*coll*) likelihood: *There's no fear of my getting the job*. — *v* **1** (*tr*) to be afraid of (someone or something). **2** (*intr*; **for**) to be frightened or anxious. **3** (*tr*) to think or expect with dread. **4** (*tr*) to regret; to be sorry to say. — **for fear of** or **that** because of the danger of or that. — **in fear of** frightened of. — **put the fear of God into** (*coll*) to terrify. — **without fear or favour** completely impartially. [OE *fær*, calamity]

fearful *adj* **1** afraid. **2** frightening. **3** (*coll*) very bad. — *adv* **fearfully**. — *n* **fearfulness**.

fearless *adj* without fear; brave. — *adv* **fearlessly**. — *n* **fearlessness**.

fearsome *adj* frightening.

feasible *adj* capable of being done or achieved. — *n* **feasibility**. — *adv* **feasibly**. [OFr *faisible*]

feast *n* **1** a large rich meal, e.g. to celebrate some occasion. **2** a pleasurable abundance of. **3** (*relig*) a festival or saint's day. — *v* **1** (*intr*; **on, upon**) to eat or experience with enjoyment. **2** (*tr*) to honour with a feast. — **feast one's eyes on** or **upon** to gaze at with pleasure. [OFr *feste*]

feat *n* a deed or achievement, esp. a remarkable one. [OFr *fait*]

feather *n* **1** any of the light growths that form the soft covering of a bird. **2** condition; spirits: *in fine feather*. — *v* **-r-** (*tr*) **1** to provide, cover or line with feathers. **2** to turn (one's oar) parallel to the water, to lessen air resistance. — *adj* **feathered**. — *adj* **feathery**. — **a feather in one's cap** something one can be proud of. — **feather one's (own) nest** to accumulate money for oneself, esp. dishonestly. — **make the feathers fly** (*coll*) to cause a commotion. [OE *fether*]

feather bed *n* a mattress stuffed with feathers. — *v* **feather-bed** (*tr*) to spoil or pamper.

feather-brained *adj* (*derog*) empty-headed.

feather duster *n* a dusting implement consisting of a stick with a head made of feathers.

featherweight *n* **1** a class for boxers, wrestlers and weight-lifters of not more than a specified weight (57 kg in professional boxing, similar weights in the other sports). **2** a boxer, etc. of this weight. **3** someone who weighs very little. **4** (*derog*) someone of little importance or influence. — *adj* (involving people) of the stated weight.

feature *n* **1** any of the parts of the face, e.g. eyes, nose, mouth, etc.; (in *pl*) the face. **2** a noticeable part or quality of something. **3** a non-news article in a newspaper. **4** a feature film. [OFr *faiture*]

feature film *n* a film that forms the main part of a cinema programme.

featureless *adj* dull; with no points of interest.

Feb. *abbrev* February.

febrile *adj* of or relating to fever; feverish. [Lat *febris*, fever]

February *n* **-ies** the second month of the year. [Lat *Februarius*, month of expiation]

feckless *adj* helpless; clueless. **2** irresponsible; aimless. — *adv* **fecklessly**. — *n* **fecklessness**. [Scot *feck* (from **effect**) + **-less**]

fecund *adj* fruitful; fertile; richly productive. — *n* **fecundity**. [Lat *fecundus*]

fed. See **feed**.

federal *adj* **1** consisting of a group of states independent in local matters but united under a central government for other purposes, e.g. defence. **2** relating to the central government of a federal union. **3** (*cap*; *hist*) supporting the union government during the American Civil War. — *v* **federalise** or **-ize** (*tr* & *intr*). — *n* **federalism**. — *n* **federalist**. [Lat *foedus*, treaty]

federate *v* (*tr* & *intr*) to unite to form a federation. — *adj* **federative**. [Lat *foedus*, treaty]

federation *n* **1** a federal union of states. **2** a union of business organisations, etc. **3** the act of uniting in a league.

fee *n* **1** a charge made for professional services, e.g. by a doctor or lawyer. **2** a charge for e.g. membership of a society, sitting an examination, entrance to a museum, etc. **3** (sometimes in *pl*) a payment for school or college education, or for a course of instruction. **4** a payment made to a football club for the transfer of one of its players. **5** (*legal*) an estate in the form of land that is inheritable with either restricted rights (**fee tail**) or unrestricted rights (**fee simple**). [OFr *fie*]

feeble *adj* **1** lacking strength; weak. **2** lacking power, influence, or effectiveness. — *n* **feebleness**. — *adv* **feebly**. [OFr *feible*, from Lat *flebilis*, lamentable]

feeble-minded *adj* **1** stupid. **2** mentally below normal. — *n* **feeble-mindedness**.

feed *v* ***fed*** **1** (*tr*; **on**, **with**) to give food to or prepare food for. **2** (*intr*; **on**) (esp. of animals) to eat. **3** (*intr* with **on**) to be fuelled by. **4** (*tr*) to give as food. **5** (*tr*) to supply with fuel or other material required for continued operation or processing. **6** (*tr*) to strengthen or encourage (a feeling, etc.). — *n* **1** an act or session of feeding. **2** food for animals or babies. **3** (*coll*) a meal, esp. a hearty one. **4** the channel or mechanism by which a machine is supplied with fuel, etc. — **fed up** (*coll*) bored and impatient. — *v* **feed up** (*tr*) to fatten up with nourishing food. [OE *fedan*]

feedback *n* **1** responses and reactions, e.g. customers' comments on a product or service, that provide guidelines for adjustment and development. **2** (*comput*) the process by which part of the output of a machine is reinserted into it, to show where self-adjustment is needed. **3** in a public-address system, etc. the partial return to the microphone of the sound output, producing a whistle or howl.

feeder *n* **1** a baby or animal with particular eating habits: *a poor feeder*. **2** a minor road, railway line, etc. leading to a main one.

feel *v* ***felt*** **1** (*tr*) to become aware of through the sense of touch. **2** (*tr* & *intr*) to have the sensation of; to sense. **3** (*tr* & *intr*) to find out or investigate with the hands, etc. **4** (*intr* & *tr*) to have (an emotion). **5** (*tr* & *intr*) to react (to) emotionally: *feels everything very deeply*. **6** (*intr*) to give the impression of being (soft, hard, rough, etc.) when touched. **7** (*intr*) to be or seem. **8** (*tr*) to think, be of the opinion or be under the impression (that). **9** (*tr* & *intr*) to seem to oneself to be: *feel a fool*. — *n* **1** a sensation or impression produced by touching. **2** an impression or atmosphere created by something. **3** an act of feeling with the fingers, etc. **4** (**for**) a natural ability for, or understanding of, an activity, etc. — *v* **feel around** (*intr*; **for**) to search with the fingers, etc. — *v* **feel for** (*tr*) **1** to feel sympathy for. **2** to try to find by feeling. — **feel like** to have an inclination for (a coffee, walk, etc.). — **feel oneself** to feel as well as normal. — **feel one's way** to make one's way cautiously. — *v* **feel up to** (*tr*) to feel fit enough to.— **get the feel of** to become familiar with or used to. [OE *felan*]

feeler *n* **1** an organ of touch found in certain creatures, esp. one of two thread-like projections on an insect's head. — **put out feelers** (*coll*) to test for possible reactions, before taking action.

feeling *n* **1** a sensation or emotion. **2** (in *pl*) one's attitude to something: *have strong feelings*. **3** emotion as distinct from reason. **4** strong emotion: *speak with feeling*. **5** a belief or opinion. **6** (**for**) a natural ability for, or understanding of, something. **7** affection. — *adj* sensitive; sympathetic.

feelingly *adv* with sincerity resulting from experience.

feet. See **foot**.

feign *v* (*tr*) to pretend to have (e.g. an illness) or feel (an emotion, etc.). — *adj* **feigned**. [Lat *fingere*, to contrive]

feint[1] *n* in boxing, fencing or other sports, a movement, e.g. a mock attack, intended to deceive or distract one's opponent.

feint[2] *adj* (of paper) ruled with faint lines. [Variant of **faint**]

feisty *adj* **-*ier***, **-*iest*** (*coll*) **1** spirited; lively. **2** irritable; quarrelsome. [US dialect *fist*, an aggressive small dog]

feldspar or **felspar** *n* a white or red mineral containing silicates, e.g. of aluminium. — *adj* **feldspathic** or **felspathic**. [Ger, from *Feld*, field + *Spat*, spar]

felicitate *v* (*tr*) to congratulate. — *n* **felicitation**. [Lat *felicitas*, happiness]

felicitations *n* (*pl*) congratulations.

felicitous *adj* **1** (of wording) elegantly apt. **2** pleasant; happy. — *adv* **felicitously**. — *n* **felicitousness**. [Lat *felicitas*, happiness]

felicity *n* **1** happiness. **2** elegance or aptness of wording. [Lat *felicitas*, happiness]

feline *adj* of or like a cat. [Lat *felis*, cat]

fell[1]. See **fall**.

fell[2] *v* (*tr*) **1** to cut down (a tree). **2** to knock down. **3** (*needlework*) to turn under and stitch down the edges of (a seam). [OE *fyllan*, to cause to fall]

fell[3] *n* (often in *pl*) a hill or moor. [Norse *fjall*]

fell[4] *adj* (*old*) destructive; deadly. — **at one fell swoop** at a single deadly blow; in one quick operation. [OFr *fel*, cruel]

fellatio *n* sexual stimulation of the penis by sucking or licking. [Lat *fellare*, to suck]

fellow *n* **1** a man or boy. **2** a companion or equal. **3** a person in the same situation or condition as oneself, or having the same status, etc.: *a fellow citizen*. **4** a senior member of a college or university. **5** a postgraduate research student financed by a fellowship. **6** a member of any of many learned societies. **7** (*coll*) a boyfriend. **8** one of a pair: *one sock on the chair, its fellow on the floor*. [OE *feolaga*, partner]

fellow feeling *n* sympathy for someone with experiences similar to one's own.

fellowship *n* **1** friendly companionship. **2** commonness or similarity of interests between people. **3** a society or association. **4** the status of a fellow of a college, society, etc.; a salary paid to a research fellow.

fellow traveller *n* someone who sympathises with a political party, esp. the Communist Party, without actually joining it.

felon *n* a person guilty of a serious crime. [OFr, from Lat *fello*, traitor]

felony n **-*ies*** (*legal*) a serious crime. — *adj* **felonious**.

felspar. See **feldspar**.

felt[1]. See **feel**.

felt[2] *n* a fabric formed by matting or pressing together wool fibres, etc. — *v* **1** (*tr* & *intr*) to form into felt; to mat. **2** (*tr*) to cover with felt. [OE]

felt-tip (or **-tipped**) **pen** *n* a pen with a point made of felt.

fem. *abbrev* **1** feminine. **2** female.

female *adj* **1** of the sex that gives birth to children, produces eggs, etc. **2** (of a plant) bearing seeds or fruit. **3** of, relating to, or belonging to, a woman. **4** (of a piece of machinery, etc.) having a hole or holes into which another part fits. — *n* **1** (sometimes *derog*) a woman or girl. **2** a female animal or plant. [Lat *femella*, dimin. of *femina*, woman]

feminine *adj* **1** of, or typically belonging to, a woman. **2** (having qualities) considered suitable for a woman. **3** (*gram*) (of nouns in certain languages) belonging to the gender into which most words for females fall. — *n* **femininity**. [Lat *feminina*, dimin. of *femina*, woman]

feminism *n* (a movement supporting) the attitude that women's rights and opportunities should be equal to those of men. — *n* **feminist**. [Lat *femina*, woman]

femme fatale *n* ***femmes fatales*** a woman whose irresistible charms fascinate and destroy people, usu. men. [Fr, fatal woman]

femto- *comb fm* a thousand million millionth (10^{-15}). [Dan or Norw *femten*, fifteen]

femur *n* the thigh bone. — *adj* **femoral**. [Lat, thigh]

fen *n* an area of low flat marshy or flooded land. [OE *fenn*]

fence *n* **1** a barrier e.g. of wood and/or wire, for enclosing or protecting land. **2** a barrier of any of various designs for a horse to jump. **3** (*slang*) a person who receives and disposes of stolen goods. **4** a guard to limit motion in a piece of machinery. **5** a guiding device on a circular saw or plane. — *v* **1** (*tr*; **in**, **off**) to enclose or separate (as if) with a fence. **2** (*intr*) to practise the sport of fencing. **3** (*intr*) to avoid answering directly. — *n* **fencer**. — **sit on the fence** to avoid supporting either side in a dispute, etc. [**defence**]

fencing *n* **1** the sport of fighting with swords. **2** material for constructing fences.

fend *v* **1** (*tr*; **off**) to defend oneself from (blows, questions, etc.). **2** (*intr* with **for**) to provide for (esp. oneself). [**defend**]

fender *n* **1** (*NAm*) the wing or mudguard of a car. **2** a low guard fitted round a fireplace to keep ash, coals, etc. within the hearth. **3** a bundle of rope or other object hanging from a ship's side to protect it when in contact with piers, etc. [**fend**]

fennel *n* a strong-smelling, yellow-flowered plant whose seeds, leaves and root are used in cooking. [OE *finol*]

fenugreek *n* a white-flowered plant with strong-smelling seeds used as flavouring. [Lat *fenum graecum*, Greek hay]

feoff *n*. Same as **fief**.

feral *adj* **1** (of animals) wild, esp. after escaping from captivity or domestication. **2** (of a plant) uncultivated; having run wild. [Lat *fera*, wild beast]

ferment *n* a substance that causes fermentation. **2** fermentation. **3** a state of agitation or excitement. — *v* **1** (*intr* & *tr*) to (cause to) undergo fermentation. **2** to (cause to) be in a state of excitement or instability. [Lat *fermentum*, yeast]

fermentation *n* a chemical change that takes place in a substance through the action of micro-organisms, as in the conversion of sugar into alcohol.

fermium *n* an artificially produced metallic radioactive element (symbol **Fm**). [E Fermi (1901–54), Italian physicist]

fern *n* any of a class of flowerless, usu. feathery-leaved plants that reproduce by spores rather than seeds. — *adj* **ferny**, **-*ier***, **-*iest***. [OE *fearn*]

ferocious *adj* fierce; cruel; savage. — *adv* **ferociously**. — *n* **ferocity** or **ferociousness**. [Lat *ferox*, wild]

-ferous *comb fm* bearing or containing: *carboniferous*. [Lat *ferre*, to carry]

ferret *n* **1** a small half-tame albino type of polecat, used for driving rabbits and rats from their holes. **2** an inquisitive and persistent investigator. — *v* **-*t*-** (*coll*) **1** (*intr*; **about**, **around**) to search busily; to rummage. **2** (*tr* with **out**) to find out through persistent investigation. [OFr *furet*, from Lat *fur*, thief]

ferric *adj* (*chem*) containing iron in its trivalent state. [Lat *ferrum*, iron]

Ferris wheel *n* a giant fairground wheel that turns vertically, with seats hanging from its rim. [G W G *Ferris* (1859–96), US engineer]

ferro- *comb fm* of, or containing, iron, as in *ferromagnetic* (having the high magnetism typical of iron) or *ferroconcrete* (reinforced concrete). [Lat *ferrum*, iron]

ferrous *adj* (*chem*) containing iron, esp. in its divalent form. [*ferrum*, iron]

ferrule *n* **1** a metal ring or cap for protecting the tip of a walking-stick or umbrella. **2** a cylindrical fitting, threaded internally like a screw, for joining pipes, etc. together. [Lat *viriola*, little bracelet]

ferry *n* **-*ies*** a boat that carries passengers and often cars across a river or strip of water, esp. as a regular service. — *v* **-*ies***, **-*ied*** (*tr* & *intr*) to transport or go by ferry. **2** (*tr*) to convey in a vehicle. — *n* **ferryman**. [OE *ferian*, to convey]

fertile *adj* **1** (of land, soil, etc.) producing abundant crops, plants, etc. **2** capable of producing babies, young or fruit. **3** (of an egg or seed) capable of developing into a new individual. **4** (of the mind) rich in ideas. **5** providing a wealth of possibilities: *fertile ground for research*. **6** (*physics*) (of material) capable of becoming fissile or fissionable. — *n* **fertility**. [Lat *fertilis*]

fertilise or **-ize** *v* **1** (*tr*) to introduce sperm into (an egg) or pollen into (a plant) so that reproduction results. **2** (*tr*) to add nutrients to (soil) to make it fertile and productive. — *n* **fertilisation** or **-z-**.

fertiliser or **-z-** *n* a natural or chemical substance dug into soil to make it more fertile.

fervent *adj* enthusiastic; earnest or ardent. — *adv* **fervently**. [Lat *fervere*, to boil]

fervid *adj* fervent; full of fiery passion or zeal. — *adv* **fervidly**. [Lat *fervidus*, fiery]

fervour *n* passionate enthusiasm; intense eagerness or sincerity. [Lat *fervor*, violent heat]

festal *adj* relating to a festival; festive. [Lat *festum*, holiday]

fester *v* **-*r*-** (*intr*) **1** to become infected; to go septic. **2** (of an evil) to continue unchecked or get worse. **3** to rot or decay. **4** (of resentment or anger) to smoulder; to become more bitter. **5** to be a continuing cause of resentment; to rankle. [OFr *festre*, from Lat *fistula*, kind of ulcer]

festival *n* **1** a day or period of celebration, esp. one kept traditionally. **2** (*relig*) a feast or saint's day. **3** a programme of musical, theatrical or other cultural events. [Lat *festivalis* (*dies*), festive day]

festive *adj* of, or suitable for, a celebration; lively and cheerful. [Lat *festivus*]

festivity *n* **-*ies*** **1** celebration; merrymaking. **2** (in *pl*) festive activities.

festoon *n* a decorative chain of flowers, ribbons, etc. looped between two points. — *v* (*tr*) to hang or decorate with festoons. [Ital *festone*, decoration for a feast]

fetal. *NAm* spelling of **foetal**.

fetch *v* (*tr*) **1** to go and get, and bring back. **2** to be sold for (a certain price). **3** to deal (someone a blow). **4** (*old*) to utter (a sigh or groan). **5** to bring forth (tears or blood). — *n* a trick or dodge. — **fetch and carry** to act as servant. — *v* **fetch up** (*coll*) **1** (*intr*) to arrive; to turn up; to end up. **2** (*tr*) to vomit (food). [OE *feccan*]

fetching *adj* (*coll*) charming; attractive. — *adv* **fetchingly**.

fête or **fete** *n* an outdoor entertainment with competitions, stalls, etc. usu. to raise money for a charitable or other purpose. — *v* (*tr*) to entertain or honour lavishly. [Fr, feast]

fetid or **foetid** *adj* having a disgusting smell. [Lat *fetere*, to stink]

fetish *n* **1** in primitive societies, an object worshipped for its magical powers. **2** a procedure or ritual followed obsessively, or an object of obsessive devotion. **3** an object that is handled or visualised as an aid to sexual stimulation; a person's attachment to such an object. — *n* **fetishism**. — *n* **fetishist**. — *adj* **fetishistic**. [Fr *fétiche*, from Port *feitiço*, magic]

fetlock *n* (the tuft of hair growing on) the projection on a horse's leg just above the hoof. [MidE *fetlak*]

fetter *n* **1** (usu. in *pl*) a chain or shackle fastened to a prisoner's ankle. **2** (in *pl*) tiresome restrictions. — *v* **-r-** (*tr*) **1** to put in fetters. **2** to restrict. [OE *fetor*]

fettle *n* spirits or condition: *in fine fettle.* [OE *fetel*, belt]

fetus. *NAm* spelling of **foetus**.

fetwa. Same as **fatwa**.

feud *n* a long-drawn-out bitter quarrel between families, tribes or individuals. — *v* (*intr*; **with**) to carry on a feud. [OFr *feide*]

feudal *adj* of or relating to the social system of mediaeval Europe, in which vassals or tenants were obliged to serve under their lord in battle, and were in return protected by him. — *n* **feudalism**. [Lat *feudum*, fee]

fever *n* **1** (an illness with) an abnormally high body temperature and racing pulse. **2** agitation or excitement. [Lat *febris*]

fevered *adj* feverish; affected with fever.

feverish *adj* **1** suffering from, or showing symptoms of, fever. **2** agitated or restless. — *adv* **feverishly**.

fever pitch *n* a state of high excitement.

few *adj* not many; hardly any. — *pron* hardly any things, people, etc. — **a few** a small number; some. — **as few as** no more than. — **few and far between** (*coll*) rare; scarce. — **a good few**, **quite a few** or **not a few** a fairly large number; several. — **have had a few** (*coll*) to have drunk a fair amount of alcohol. — **no fewer than** as many as. — **precious few** (*coll*) hardly any at all. — **the few** the minority, or the discerning people, as distinct from *the many*. [OE *feawa*]

fey *adj* **1** strangely fanciful. **2** able to foresee future events. **3** (*Scot*) doomed to die early. — *n* **feyness**. [OE *fæge*, doomed to die]

fez *n* **-zz-** a hat shaped like a flat-topped cone, with a tassel, worn by some Muslim men. [Turk *fes*, from *Fez*, Moroccan city]

ff *abbrev* (*mus*) fortissimo.

ff. *abbrev* and the following (pages, etc.).

fiancé or **fiancée** *n* respectively, a man or woman to whom one is engaged to be married. [OFr *fiancier*, to betroth]

fiasco *n* **-os** or **-oes 1** a ludicrous or humiliating failure. **2** a disgraceful or ludicrous affair. [Ital, bottle]

fiat *n* **1** an official command; a decree. **2** a formal authorisation for some procedure. [Lat, let it be done]

fib (*coll*) *n* a trivial lie. — *v* **-bb-** (*intr*) to tell fibs. — *n* **fibber**.

fibre *n* **1** a fine thread, or thread-like cell, of a natural or artificial substance. **2** a material composed of fibres. **3** the indigestible parts of edible plants or seeds, that help to move food quickly through the body. **4** character; stamina. [Lat *fibra*]

fibreboard *n* board made from compressed wood fibres.

fibreglass *n* **1** material consisting of fine, tangled fibres of glass, used for insulation. **2** a strong light plastic strengthened with glass fibres, for boat-building, etc.

fibre optics *n* (*sing*) the technique of using flexible glass fibres to carry information in the form of light signals. — *adj* **fibre-optic**.

fibril *n* a small fibre. [Lat *fibrilla*, dimin. of *fibra*, fibre]

fibrillate *v* (*intr*) (of the heart muscle) to twitch irregularly instead of contracting with the normal regular rhythm. — *n* **fibrillation**. [Lat *fibrilla*, fibril]

fibroid *adj* fibrous. — *n* a fibrous growth, e.g. in the uterus. [**fibre** + **-oid**]

fibrosis *n* the formation of an abnormal amount of fibrous tissue, e.g. in the lungs. [**fibre** + **-osis**]

fibrositis *n* inflammation of the fibrous tissue sheathing the muscles. [*fibrose*, fibrous + **-itis**]

fibrous *adj* consisting of, containing, or like, fibre. [**fibre**]

fibula *n* **-lae** or **-las** the outer and narrower of the two bones in the lower leg. [Lat, brooch]

fickle *adj* (*derog*) changeable, esp. in one's loyalties. — *n* **fickleness**. [OE *ficol*, cunning]

fiction *n* **1** literature concerning imaginary characters or events. **2** a pretence; a lie. **3** (esp. *legal*) a misrepresentation of the truth, accepted for convenience. — *adj* **fictional**. — *adv* **fictionally**. [Lat *fictio*, from *fingere*, to mould]

fictitious *adj* **1** imagined; invented; not real. **2** of, or occurring in, fiction. — *adv* **fictitiously**. [Lat *ficticius*]

fiddle *n* **1** (*coll*) a violin, esp. when used to play folk music or jazz. **2** (*coll*) a dishonest arrangement; a fraud. — *v* **1** (*intr*; **with**) to play about aimlessly; to tinker, toy or meddle. **2** (*intr*; **around, about**) to waste time. **3** (*tr* & *intr*) to falsify (accounts, etc.); to manage or manipulate dishonestly. **4** (*intr* & *tr*) to play a violin, or play (a tune) on one. — **(as) fit as a fiddle** in excellent health. — **fiddle while Rome burns** to ignore the current crisis and busy oneself with trifles. — **on the fiddle** (*coll*) making money dishonestly. — **play second fiddle to** to be subordinate to. [OE *fithele*]

fiddler *n* **1** a person who plays the fiddle. **2** a swindler. **3** a kind of small crab.

fiddlesticks *interj* nonsense.

fiddling *adj* unimportant; trifling.

fiddly *adj* **-ier**, **-iest** awkward to handle or do, esp. because requiring delicate finger movements.

fidelity *n* **1** faithfulness; loyalty. **2** accuracy in reporting, describing or copying something. **3** precision in sound reproduction. [Lat *fidelitas*]

fidget *v* **-t- 1** (*intr*) to move or fiddle restlessly. **2** (*tr*) to cause to feel nervous and uneasy. — *n* a person who fidgets. **2** (often in *pl*) nervous restlessness. — *n* **fidgety**. [Earlier *fidge*]

fiduciary (*legal*) *adj* held or given in trust. — *n* **-ies** a trustee. [Lat *fiducia*, trust]

fie *interj* (*old*) for shame!

fief *n* (*hist*) **1** under the feudal system, land granted to a vassal by his lord in return for military service, or on other conditions. **2** one's own area of operation or control. [OFr *fie*]

field *n* **1** a piece of land enclosed for crop-growing or pasturing animals. **2** a piece of open grassland. **3** an area marked off as a ground for a sport, etc. **4** (esp. *in cmpds*) an area rich in a particular mineral, etc.: *a coalfield*. **5** (esp. *in cmpds*) an expanse: *snowfields*. **6** an area of knowledge, interest or study. **7** the area included in something; the range over which a force, etc. extends: *field of vision*. **8** practical work or research away from the laboratory or place of study. **9** the contestants, or a particular contestant's rivals, in a race, competition, etc. **10** a place of battle: *fell on the field*. **11** (*cricket*, etc.) the fielding side. **12** the background to the design on a flag, coin, etc. — *v* **1** (*intr* & *tr*; *cricket*, etc.) to (be the team whose turn it is to) retrieve balls hit by the batting team; (of a fielder) to retrieve (the ball). **2** (*tr*) to put forward as (a team or player) for a match. **3** (*tr*) to deal with a succession of (inquiries, etc.). — **hold the field** to remain supreme. — **lead the field** to be in the foremost or winning position. — **play the field** (*coll*) to try out the range of possibilities before making a choice. — **take the field 1** (of a team) to go on to the pitch ready for a match. **2** to go into battle; to begin a campaign.

field day *n* **1** (*mil*) a day of exercises and manoeuvres. **2** (esp. *facet*) an occasion on which one has unusually wide scope for one's activities.

fielder *n* (*cricket*, etc.) a member of the fielding side.

field event *n* (*athletics*) a contest involving jumping, throwing, etc., as distinct from a track event. ◇ See also **track event**.

field glasses *n* (*pl*) binoculars.

field gun *n* a light cannon mounted on wheels.

field hockey *n* (*NAm*) ordinary hockey as distinct from ice hockey.

field marshal *n* an army officer of the highest rank.

fieldmouse *n* a small long-tailed mouse inhabiting fields, woods, etc.

field officer *n* an army officer between the ranks of captain and general.

field sports *n* (*pl*) the sports of hunting, shooting and line-fishing.

fieldwork *n* **1** work done in the field (sense **8**). **2** (*mil*) a temporary fortification. — *n* **fieldworker**.

fiend *n* **1** a devil; an evil spirit. **2** (*coll*) a spiteful person. **3** (*coll*) an enthusiast. — *adj* **fiendish**. — *adv* **fiendishly**. [OE *feond*]

fierce *adj* **1** violent and aggressive. **2** intense; strong; severe; extreme. — *adv* **fiercely**. — *n* **fierceness**. [OFr *fers*, from Lat *ferus*, savage]

fiery *adj* **-ier**, **-iest 1** consisting of fire; like fire. **2** easily enraged. **3** passionate; spirited; vigorous: *fiery oratory*. **4** (of food) hot-tasting; causing a burning sensation. — *adv* **fierily**. **[fire]**

fiesta *n* (esp. in Spain or Latin America) a religious festival, with dancing, singing, etc. [Span, feast]

fife *n* a small type of flute played in military bands. [OGer *pfifa*, pipe]

fifteen *n* **1** the number or figure 15; any symbol for this number. **2** the age of 15. **3** something, esp. a garment, or a person, whose size is denoted by the number 15. **4** a set of 15 things or people, e.g. a Rugby team. **5** (a film with) a certificate from the censors stating that the film is suitable for people aged 15 and over. — *adj* **1** 15 in number. **2** aged 15. — *n*, *adj* & *adv* **fifteenth**. [OE *fiftene*]

fifth. See **five**.

fifty *n* **-ies 1** the number or figure 50; any symbol for this number. **2** the age of 50. **3** a set of 50 people or things. — *adj* **1** 50 in number. **2** aged 50. — *n*, *adj* & *adv* **fiftieth**. [OE *fiftig*]

fifties *n* (*pl*) **1** the period of time between one's fiftieth and sixtieth birthdays. **2** the range of temperatures between fifty and sixty degrees. **3** the period of time between the fiftieth and sixtieth years of a century.

fifty-fifty *adj* (of a chance) equal either way. — *adv* & *adj* (divided) equally between two.

fig *n* **1** a soft fruit full of tiny seeds. **2** the tree bearing it. — **not give** or **care a fig** (*coll*) not to care in the least. [Lat *ficus*]

fig leaf *n* **1** a fig-tree leaf, in art the traditional covering for the genitals in representations of nude figures. **2** any device used to cover up something embarrassing.

fig. *abbrev* figure (sense **9**).

fight *v* ***fought* 1** (*tr* & *intr*) to attack or engage in combat. **2** (*intr*; **for**) to struggle. **3** (*intr*; **for**) to campaign. **4** (*tr*) to oppose vigorously. **5** (*intr*) to quarrel. **6** (*tr*) to take part in or conduct (a battle, campaign, etc.). **7** (*tr*) to make (one's way) with a struggle. — *n* **1** a battle; a physically violent struggle; a quarrel. **2** resistance. **3** the will or strength to resist: *lost all his fight*. **4** a contest. **5** a boxing-match. **6** a campaign or crusade: *the fight for freedom*. — *v* **fight back 1** (*intr*) to resist one's attacker. **2** (*tr*; also **fight down**) to try not to show (emotions, etc.). — **fighting fit** (*coll*) in vigorous health. — *v* **fight off** (*tr*) **1** to repulse (an attacker). **2** to get rid of or resist (an illness). — **fight it out** to fight over something until one side wins. — **fight shy of** to avoid. [OE *feohtan*, to fight]

fighter *n* **1** a person who fights; a professional boxer. **2** a person with determination. **3** an aircraft equipped to attack other aircraft.

fighting chance *n* a chance to succeed dependent chiefly on determination.

figment *n* something imagined or invented. [Lat *figmentum*]

figure *n* **1** an indistinctly seen or unidentified person. **2** the shape of one's body. **3** a symbol representing a number; a numeral. **4** a number representing an amount; a cost or price. **5** (in *pl*) arithmetical calculations; statistics. **6** a well-known person: *a public figure*. **7** the impression that one makes: *cut a poor figure*. **8** a representation of the human form. **9** a diagram or illustration. **10** an image, design or pattern. **11** a geometrical shape. **12** a set pattern of steps or movements in dancing or skating, or of notes in music. **13** a figure of speech. — *v* **1** (*intr*; **in**) to play a part in a story, incident, etc. **2** (*tr*; esp. *NAm*) to think; to reckon. **3** (*tr*) to imagine; to envisage. **4** (*tr* & *intr*; *old NAm*) to calculate. **5** (*intr*; *coll*) to be probable or predictable; to make sense: *That figures*. **6** (*tr*) to decorate (a surface) with a design; to add elaborations to (music). — *v* **figure on** (*tr*) **1** to intend (doing something). **2** to make plans that depend on (something happening). — *v* **figure out** (*tr*) to work out; to understand. — **keep**, or **lose, one's figure** respectively to remain slim or get fat. [Lat *figura*, from *fingere*, to mould]

figurehead *n* **1** a leader in name only, without real power. **2** (*hist*) a carved wooden figure fixed to a ship's prow.

figure of eight see **eight**.

figure of fun *n* someone whom others ridicule.

figure of speech *n* any of many devices such as metaphors, similes, etc. that enliven language.

figurative *adj* **1** metaphorical, not literal. **2** (of writing, etc.) full of figures of speech, esp. metaphor. **3** (of art) not abstract; showing things as they look; representational; pictorial. — *adv* **figuratively**. [**figure**]

figurine *n* a little statue. [Ital *figurina*, dimin. of *figura*, figure]

filament *n* **1** a fine thread or fibre. **2** (*electr*) a fine conducting wire, e.g. in a light bulb or thermionic valve. **3** (*bot*) the stem of a stamen. [Lat *filum*, thread]

filch *v* (*tr*) to steal (something small). [ME *filchen*, to take as booty]

file[1] *n* a steel tool with a rough surface for smoothing or rubbing away wood, metal, etc. [OE *fil*]

filings *n* (*pl*) pieces of wood, metal, etc. rubbed off with a file.

file[2] *n* **1** a folder or box in which to keep loose papers. **2** a collection of papers so kept, esp. dealing with a particular subject. **3** a body of data stored in a computer under one reference number or name. **4** a line of people or things moving one behind the other: *single file*. — *v* **1** (*tr*) to put (papers, etc.) into a file. **2** (*intr*; **for**) to make a formal application (e.g. for divorce) to a law court. **3** (*intr*) to move along one behind the other. **4** (*tr*) (of a reporter) to submit (a story) to a newspaper. — **on file** retained in a file for reference; on record. [Lat *filum*, a thread]

filing cabinet *n* a piece of furniture with drawers, etc. for holding files.

filial *adj* of, or suitable to, a son or daughter. [Lat *filius*, son, & *filia*, daughter]

filibuster *n* **1** the practice of making long speeches to delay the passing of laws. **2** a member of a law-making assembly who uses this practice. — *v* **-r-** (*intr*) to obstruct legislation in this way. [Span *filibustero*, freebooter]

filigree *n* delicate work in gold or silver wire, used in jewellery, etc. [Lat *filum*, thread + *granum*, grain]

fill *v* **1** (*tr*; **up, with**) to make full. **2** (*tr*; **with**) to take up the space in. **3** (*tr*; **with**) to (cause ideas, feelings, etc. to) flood into. **4** (*intr*; **up, with**) to become full. **5** (*tr*) to satisfy (a need); to perform (a role) satisfactorily. **6** (*tr*; **up, in**) to occupy (time). **7** (*tr*) to appoint someone to (a job). **8** (*tr*; **in, up**) to put material into (a hole, cavity, etc.) to level the surface. **9** (*intr*) (of a sail) to billow out in the wind. — *n* as much as satisfies one or as one can tolerate: *eat one's fill; had my fill of computers*. — *v* **fill in 1** (*tr*) to write information as required on to (a form). **2** (*tr*; **on**) to inform fully about something. **3** (*intr*; **for**) to take over the work of (someone) temporarily. **4** (*tr*; *slang*) to hit (someone). — *v* **fill out 1** (*intr* & *tr*) to (cause to) become plumper. **2** (*tr*) to enlarge satisfactorily; to amplify. **3** (*tr*) to fill in (a form). — *v* **fill up** (*tr*) to fill in (a form). [OE *fyllan*]

filler *n* a substance used for filling cracks or holes.

filling *n* **1** the material used to fill a hole in a tooth. **2** food put inside a pie, sandwich, etc.

filling-station *n* a place where one can get petrol for one's car.

fillet *n* **1** a boneless piece of meat or fish. **2** a broad ribbon or headband. **3** (*archit*) a narrow flat band. — *v* **-t-** (*tr*) to remove the bones from; to divide into fillets. [Lat *filum*, thread]

fillip *n* **1** something that has a stimulating or brightening effect; a boost. **2** a flick made with the nail of a finger. [MidE *philippe*]

filly *n* **-ies 1** a young female horse. **2** (*old coll*) a young girl. [Norse *fylja*]

film *n* **1** a strip of thin flexible plastic or other substance, coated so as to be light-sensitive and exposed inside a camera to produce still or moving pictures. **2** (the story or subject matter of) a motion picture for showing in the cinema, or on television or video. **3** (in *pl*) the cinema in general. **4** a fine skin or coating. — *v* **1** (*tr* & *intr*) to photograph with or operate a cine camera. **2** (*intr*; **over**) to become covered with a film. [OE *filmen*, membrane]

film star *n* a celebrated film actor or actress.

film strip *n* a series of photographs on a strip of film, for separate projection as slides.

filmy *adj* **-ier**, **-iest** (of a fabric) thin, light and transparent. — *n* **filminess**.

Filofax ® *n* a small loose-leaf filing system containing a diary and a selection of information, e.g. addresses, maps, to help the user organise his or her affairs.

filter *n* **1** (a device consisting of) a porous substance that allows liquid, gas, smoke, etc. through but traps solid matter, impurities, etc. **2** a transparent tinted disc used to reduce the strength of certain colour frequencies in the light entering a camera or emitted by a lamp. **3** (*electr*, *radio*, etc.) a device for suppressing the waves of unwanted frequencies. **4** a traffic signal at traffic lights that allows left- or right-turning vehicles to proceed while the main stream is halted. — *v* **-r- 1** (*tr* & *intr*) to pass through a filter. **2** (*intr*; **through**, **into**, etc.) to pass little by little. **3** (*intr*) (of vehicles) to proceed left or right at a filter. — *v* **filter out 1** (*tr*) to remove (impurities, etc.) by filtering. **2** (*intr*; also **filter through**) (of news) to leak out. ◇ See also **filtrate**. [Lat *filtrum*, felt used as a filter]

filter paper *n* (a piece of) paper used for filtering.

filter tip *n* (a cigarette with) a filter that traps some of the smoke's impurities before the smoker inhales it. — *adj* **filter-tipped**.

filth *n* **1** repulsive dirt; disgusting rubbish. **2** obscene vulgarity. [OE *fylth*]

filthy *adj* **-ier**, **-iest 1** extremely dirty. **2** obscenely vulgar. — *adv* (*coll*) used for emphasis, esp. showing disapproval: *filthy rich*. — *adv* **filthily**. — *n* **filthiness**.

filtrate *n* a substance that has been filtered. — *v* (*tr*) to filter. — *n* **filtration**. [Lat *filtrare*, to filter]

fin *n* **1** a thin wing-like projection on a fish's body, with which it balances, steers itself, etc. **2** anything that resembles a fin in appearance or function, e.g. the vertical projection in the tail of an aircraft. **3** a swimmer's flipper. [OE *finn*]

final *adj* **1** occurring at the end; last. **2** completed; finished. **3** (of a decision, etc.) definite; not to be altered; conclusive. — *n* **1** the last round of a competition, or (in *pl*) a round of deciding heats. **2** (in *pl*) the last, decisive examinations in a degree course, etc. — *n* **finality**. — *adv* **finally**. [Lat *finis*, end]

finalise or **-ize** *v* (*tr*) **1** to decide on, or agree to, finally. **2** to complete; to finish. — *n* **finalisation** or **-z-**.

finalist *n* a person who reaches the final round in a competition.

finale *n* the grand conclusion to a show, etc. [Ital, from Lat *finis*, end]

finance *n* **1** money affairs; their study or management. **2** the money needed or used to pay for something. **3** (in *pl*) one's financial state. — *v* (*tr*) to provide funds for. [OFr]

financial *adj* relating to finance. — *adv* **financially**. [**finance**]

financial year *n* the twelve-month period, in Britain starting 6 April, used in accounting, annual taxation, etc.

financier *n* **1** a person engaged in large financial transactions. **2** someone who finances an operation. [Fr]

finch *n* any of several small songbirds with short sturdy beaks adapted for seed-crushing. [OE *finc*]

find *v* ***found* 1** (*tr*) to discover through search, enquiry, mental effort or chance. **2** (*tr*) to seek out and provide: *I'll find you a plumber*. **3** (*tr*) to realise or discover. **4** (*tr*) to experience as being: *find it hard to express oneself*. **5** (*tr*) to get or experience: *find pleasure in reading*. **6** (*tr*) to consider; to think. **7** (*tr*) to become aware of: *found her beside him*. **8** (*tr*) to succeed in getting (time, courage, money, etc.) for something. **9** (*tr*; usu. in *passive*) to see or come across: *a bird found only in Madagascar*. **10** (*tr*) to reach: *find one's best form*. **11** (*tr* & *intr*; *legal*; **for**, **against**) (of a jury) to give a verdict; to declare (innocent or guilty). — *n* something or someone found; an important discovery. — *n* **finder**. — **all found** with food and housing provided. — **find it in oneself** or **in one's heart** to be prepared (to do something hurtful, etc.). — **find oneself 1** to discover that one is: *found herself agreeing*. **2** to find the role, etc. that satisfies one. — **find one's feet** to establish oneself in a new situation. — *v* **find out 1** (*tr* & *intr*; **about**) to discover; to ascertain; to get information. **2** (*tr*) to detect (someone) in wrongdoing; to discover the truth about. — **find one's way** to get somewhere: *find my own way out*. [OE *findan*]

finding *n* (usu. in *pl*) a conclusion reached as a result of an investigation, etc.

fine[1] *adj* **1** of high quality; excellent; splendid. **2** beautiful; handsome. **3** (*facet*) grand; superior: *her fine relations*. **4** (of weather) bright; not rainy. **5** well; healthy. **6** quite satisfactory. **7** pure; refined. **8** thin; delicate. **9** close-set in texture or arrangement. **10** consisting of tiny particles. **11** intricately detailed: *fine embroidery*. **12** slight; subtle: *fine adjustments*. — *adv* **1** (*coll*) satisfactorily. **2** finely; into fine pieces. — *adv* **finely**. — *n* **fineness**. — **cut** or **run it fine** (*coll*) to leave barely enough time for something. — *v* **fine down** (*tr*) to make more effective, efficient or economical by cutting out inessentials. — **get down to a fine art** to find the most efficient way of doing. — **not to put too fine a point on it** to speak honestly or bluntly. [OFr *fin*]

fine arts *n* (*pl*) painting, drawing, sculpture and architecture, the arts that appeal to the sense of beauty.

finery *n* splendid clothes, jewellery, etc.

finespun *adj* delicate; over-subtle.
fine-tooth comb *n* a comb with narrow, close-set teeth. — **go over with a fine-tooth comb** to search or examine exhaustively.
fine-tune *v* (*tr*) to make slight adjustments to (a machine, etc.) to make it work perfectly.
fine[2] *n* an amount of money to be paid as a penalty. — *v* (*tr*) to exact a fine from. — **in fine** in total; to sum up. [OFr *fin*]
fines herbes *n* (*pl*) a mixture of herbs for use in cooking. [Fr, fine herbs]
finesse *n* **1** skilful elegance or expertise. **2** tact and poise in handling situations. **3** (*cards*) an attempt by a player holding a high card to win a trick with a lower one. [OFr, fineness]
finger *n* **1** one of the five jointed extremities of the hand; any of the four of these other than the thumb. **2** the part of a glove that fits over a finger. **3** anything similar to a finger in shape. **4** a measure of alcoholic spirits in a glass, equal to the breadth of a finger. — *v* **-r-** (*tr*) **1** to touch or feel with the fingers. **2** to play (a musical instrument) with the fingers. **3** (*slang*) to identify (a criminal) to the police, etc. — **be all fingers and thumbs** (*coll*) to be clumsy in handling or holding things. — **get one's fingers burnt** (*coll*) to suffer for one's over-boldness or mistakes. — **have a finger in every pie** (*coll*) to have an interest, or be involved, in everything. — **not lay a finger on** (*coll*) not to touch or harm. — **not lift a finger** (*coll*) to make not the slightest effort. — **point the finger** (*coll*) to blame or accuse someone. — **pull** or **get one's finger out** (*slang*) to make an effort to work effectively. — **put one's finger on** (*coll*) to identify (a point, difficulty, etc.). — **put the finger on** (*slang*) to finger (a criminal, etc.). — **slip through someone's fingers** to manage to escape from someone. — **twist someone round one's little finger** (*coll*) to be able to get what one wants from someone. [OE]
fingerboard *n* the part of a violin, guitar, etc. against which the strings are pressed by the fingers to change the note.
fingerbowl *n* a small bowl of water for cleaning one's fingers at table.
fingering *n* the correct positioning of the fingers for playing a particular musical instrument or piece of music.
fingermark *n* a mark left on a surface by a finger.
fingernail *n* the nail at the tip of one's finger.
fingerprint 1 *n* a mark, unique to the individual, left on a surface by a fingertip, useful as a means of identification. **2** a unique identifying feature or characteristic. — *v* (*tr*) to make a record of the fingerprints of.
fingerstall *n* a sheath for an injured finger.
fingertip *n* the tip of one's finger. — **have at one's fingertips** to know (a subject) thoroughly. — **to one's fingertips** absolutely; in all ways.
finicky *adj* **-ier, -iest 1** too concerned with detail. **2** (of a task) intricate; tricky. **3** fussy; faddy. [*finical*, over-precise]
finish *v* **1** (*tr* & *intr*; **off**) to bring or come to an end; to stop. **2** (*tr*) to complete or perfect. **3** (*tr*; **off, up**) to use, eat, drink, etc. the last of. **4** (*intr*; **up**) to reach or end up in a certain position or situation. **5** (*tr*; **off**; *coll*) to exhaust; to defeat; to kill. **6** (*intr*; **with**) to end a relationship; to stop dealing with or needing. **7** (*tr*) to give a particular treatment to the surface of (cloth, wood, etc.). — *n* **1** the last stage; the end. **2** the last part of a race, etc. **3** perfecting touches put to a product. **4** the surface texture given to cloth, wood, etc. — *n* **finisher**. — **fight to the finish** to fight till one party is dead or too severely disabled to continue. [OFr *finir*]
finished *adj* **1** (*coll*) no longer useful, productive, creative, wanted or popular. **2** (of a performer) accomplished. **3** (**with**) having reached the end of one's need for or interest in (someone or something).
finishing-school *n* a private school where girls are taught social skills and graces.
finite *adj* **1** having an end or limit. **2** (*gram*) (of a verb) being of a form that reflects person, number, tense, etc., as distinct from being an infinitive or participle. [Lat *finire*, to finish]
Finn *n* a native or citizen of Finland. [OE *Finnas*, Finns]
Finnish *adj* of, belonging to, or relating to Finland, its inhabitants, or their language. — *n* the language of Finland.
finnan *n* haddock cured in the smoke from peat, turf or green wood. [Prob. *Findon*, Kincardineshire]
fiord. Another spelling of **fjord**.
fipple *n* the piece of wood, etc. that plugs the mouthpiece of a recorder or other similar wind instrument.
fir *n* a tall evergreen tree of the pine family, with cones and thin needle-like leaves. [OE *fyrh*]
fire *n* **1** flames coming from something that is burning. **2** an occurrence of destructive burning: *a warehouse fire*. **3** a pile of burning wood, coal or other fuel, used for warmth or cooking. **4** a gas or electric room-heater. **5** shooting from guns. **6** heat and light produced by something burning or some other source. **7** enthusiasm; passion; ardour. **8** fever; a burning sensation. **9** sparkle; brilliance (e.g. of a gem). — *v* **1** (*tr* & *intr*; **at, on**) to shoot (a gun); to send off (a bullet or other missile) from a gun, catapult, bow, etc. **2** (*tr*) to launch (a rocket). **3** (*tr*) to detonate (an explosive). **4** (*tr*; **at**) to direct (e.g. questions) in quick succession at someone. **5** (*tr*; *coll*) to dismiss from employment. **6** (*tr* & *intr*) to (cause to) start burning. **7** (*tr* & *intr*) to (cause to) glow. **8** (*intr*; of a vehicle engine) to start working when a spark

causes the fuel to burn. **9** (*tr*) to put fuel into (a furnace, etc.). **10** (*tr*) to inspire or stimulate. **11** (*tr*) to bake (pottery or bricks) in a kiln. — **catch fire** to begin to burn. — **cease fire** to stop fighting (*n* **cease-fire**). — **draw someone's fire** deliberately to divert someone's gunfire, criticism, etc. towards oneself. — *v* **fire away** (*intr*; *coll*) to say or ask what one wants to. — **fire and brimstone** (the flaming contents of) hell; eternal damnation. — **go through fire and water for** to suffer or undergo danger for the sake of. — **hold one's fire** to stop shooting. — **in the line of fire** between the guns and the target. — **on fire 1** burning. **2** filled with enthusiasm, love, etc. — **open fire (on)** to begin shooting (at). — **play with fire** (*coll*) to take stupid risks. — **pull something out of the fire** to rescue the situation at the last minute. — **return someone's fire** to shoot back at someone firing at one. — **set fire to** or **set on fire 1** to cause to begin burning. **2** to fill with enthusiasm, love, etc. — **under fire 1** being shot at. **2** being criticised or blamed.

fire alarm *n* a bell or other device activated to warn people of fire.

firearm *n* a gun, pistol, revolver or rifle.

fireball *n* **1** a mass of hot gases at the centre of a nuclear explosion. **2** (*coll*) a lively person. **3** a ball-shaped flash of lightning. **4** a brilliant meteor.

fire-bomb *n* an incendiary bomb.

firebrand *n* **1** a piece of burning wood. **2** someone who stirs up unrest; a trouble-maker.

firebreak *n* a cleared strip in a forest to stop the spread of a fire.

firebrick *n* a heat-resistant brick used in furnaces, fireplaces, etc.

fire brigade *n* a team of people trained to prevent and extinguish fires.

firebug *n* (*coll*) a person who deliberately sets fire to buildings, etc.

firecracker *n* a small firework that bangs repeatedly.

-fired (*in cmpds*) fuelled by: *gas-fired central heating*.

firedamp *n* an explosive mixture of the gas methane and air, found in coalmines.

firedog *n* an andiron.

fire drill *n* (a practice of) the routine to be followed in case of fire.

fire-eater *n* **1** a performer who pretends to swallow fire from flaming torches. **2** an aggressive or quarrelsome person.

fire engine *n* a vehicle carrying fire-fighting equipment.

fire escape *n* an external metal staircase or other device by which people can escape from a burning building.

fire-extinguisher *n* a cylinder containing water or chemicals for directing at fires to extinguish them.

fire-fighter *n* a fireman or other person who puts out large fires. — *n* **fire-fighting**.

firefly *n* a beetle that glows intermittently in the dark.

fireguard *n* a protective metal or wire-mesh screen for putting round an open fire.

fire hydrant same as **hydrant**.

fire irons *n* (*pl*) a set of tools for looking after a household fire, including a poker, tongs, brush and shovel.

firelighter *n* a block of flammable material used to help light a fire.

fireman *n* a male member of a fire brigade.

fireplace *n* a recess for a fire in a room, with a chimney above it; a hearth, grate, or the structure surrounding it.

fire-power *n* (*mil*) the destructive capacity of an artillery unit.

fireproof *adj* resistant to fire and fierce heat. — *v* (*tr*) to make fireproof.

fire-raising *n* arson. — *n* **fire-raiser**.

fireside *n* the area round a fireplace, esp. as a symbol of home.

fire station *n* a fire brigade's headquarters, housing its fire engines, etc.

firetrap *n* **1** a building without adequate escape routes in case of fire. **2** a building likely to burn easily.

firewater *n* (*coll*) alcoholic spirit.

firewood *n* wood for burning as fuel.

firework *n* **1** a device containing explosive chemicals that are ignited to produce bangs and spectacular flashes. **2** (in *pl*) a show at which these are let off for entertainment. **3** (in *pl*; *coll*) a show of anger or bad temper.

firing line *n* the front line of battle. — **in the firing line** in a prominent position, liable to get shot at or criticised.

firing squad *n* a detachment of soldiers with the job of shooting a condemned person.

firm[1] *adj* **1** strong; steady. **2** solid; not soft or yielding. **3** definite: *a firm offer*. **4** determined; resolute. **5** (of a mouth or chin) suggesting determination. — *adv* firmly: *hold firm to one's promise*. — *v* (*intr* & *tr*; **up**) to become or make firm or firmer. — *adv* **firmly**. — *n* **firmness**. [Lat *firmus*]

firm[2] *n* a business company. [Span *firma*, signature]

firmament *n* (*old literary*) the sky. [Lat *firmamentum*]

first *adj* **1** earliest in time or order. **2** foremost in importance: *first prize*. **3** basic: *first principles*. **4** (*mus*) having the higher part. **5** denoting the lowest forward gear in a motor vehicle. — *adv* **1** before anything or anyone else. **2** foremost: *got in feet first*. **3** before doing anything else: *First make sure of the facts*. **4** for the first time: *since I first saw her*. **5** rather; preferably: *I'd die first*. — *n* **1** a first person or thing. **2** a first occurrence of something; something never done before. **3** first-class honours in a university degree. **4** the beginning: *from first to last*. — **at first** at the beginning. — **at first hand** directly from the original source (*adj* **first-**

hand). — **be the first to** to be the most willing. — **first and last** essentially. — **first thing** (*coll*) early; before anything else. — **in the first place** firstly. — **not have the first idea** or **know the first thing (about)** (*coll*) to be completely ignorant. [OE *fyrest*]

first aid *n* immediate emergency treatment given to an injured or ill person.

first-born *n* & *adj* the eldest (child) in a family.

first class *n* **1** the highest grade, e.g. of travelling accommodation, of academic performance, etc. **2** the category of mail most speedily delivered. — *adj* (**first-class**) **1** of the first class. **2** excellent. — *adv* by first-class mail or transport.

first cousin see **cousin**.

first-day cover *n* a stamped envelope postmarked with the stamps' date of issue.

first-degree see **degree**.

first floor *n* **1** the floor above the ground floor. **2** (*NAm*) the ground floor.

first foot *n* the first person to enter one's house in the new year. — *v* **first-foot** (*tr* & *intr*) to visit as first foot.

first fruits *n* (*pl*) **1** the first produce of the season. **2** the first results or proceeds from an enterprise.

First Lady *n* (*US*) the wife of the American President.

first light *n* dawn.

firstly *adv* first; in the first place; to begin with.

first name *n* one's personal name as distinct from one's family name or surname. — **be on first-name terms** to be friendly enough to address one another by first names.

first night *n* the first public performance of a play, etc.

first offender *n* a person found guilty for the first time of a crime.

first officer or **first mate** *n* the officer second in command on a merchant ship.

first-past-the-post *adj* of an election system in which voters have one vote only and whoever gets most votes wins.

first person (*gram*) see **person**.

first-rate *adj* **1** of the highest quality. **2** splendid; fine.

first school *n* a primary school.

firth *n* esp. in Scotland, a river estuary or an inlet. [Norse *fjörthr*]

fiscal *adj* **1** relating to government finances or revenue. **2** relating to financial matters generally. — *n* (*Scot*) the procurator fiscal. — *adv* **fiscally**. [Lat *fiscus*, purse, state treasury]

fish *n* ***fish*** or ***fishes*** **1** a cold-blooded creature with a spine and fins, living in water and breathing through gills. **2** (*in cmpds*) any of various water-inhabiting creatures: *shellfish*; *jellyfish*. **3** the flesh of fish as food. **4** (*coll derog*) a person: *an odd*, *queer* or *cold fish*. **5** (in *pl*; *cap* with **the**) the constellation and sign of the zodiac Pisces — *v* **1** (*intr*; **for**) to try to catch fish. **2** (*tr*) to try to catch fish in (a river, etc.). **3** (*intr*; **for**) to search or grope: *fished in her bag for a pen*. **4** (*tr*; **out**) to retrieve. **5** (*intr* with **for**) to seek (information, compliments, etc.) by indirect means. — **drink like a fish** (*coll*) to be in the habit of drinking a lot of alcohol. — **have other fish to fry** (*coll*) to have other, more important, things to do. — **like a fish out of water** (*coll*) ill at ease in uncongenial company or surroundings. [OE *fisc*]

fishcake *n* a breadcrumb-coated flat round cake of cooked fish and potato.

fisher *n* **1** (*old*) a fisherman. **2** an animal that catches fish.

fisherman *n* a person who fishes as a job or hobby.

fishery *n* ***-ies*** **1** a stretch of sea where fishing is carried on. **2** the business of catching and marketing fish. **3** a place where fish are reared.

fish-eye lens *n* a convex camera lens giving a scope of nearly 180°.

fish finger *n* an oblong, breadcrumb-coated piece of fish.

fish hook *n* a hook with barbs for gripping the jaw of a fish taking the bait.

fishing *n* the sport or business of catching fish.

fishing-line *n* a strong nylon, etc. line with a fish hook.

fishing-rod *n* a long flexible rod to which a fishing-line is attached.

fishmonger *n* a dealer in fish.

fishnet *adj* having an open mesh like netting.

fish slice *n* a kitchen tool with a flat slotted head, for lifting and turning food in a frying-pan, etc.

fishwife *n* a woman who guts or sells fish, in tradition typically loud-voiced and coarse-mannered.

fishy *adj* ***-ier***, ***-iest*** **1** of or like a fish. **2** (*coll*) odd; suspicious. — *n* **fishiness**.

fissile *adj* capable of being split by nuclear fission. [Lat *fissilis*, that can be split]

fission *n* **1** a splitting or division. **2** (*biol*) the division of a cell during reproduction. **3** (usu. **nuclear fission**) the splitting of the nucleus of an atom, with a release of energy. — *adj* **fissionable**. [Lat *fissio*, splitting]

fissure *n* a crack, esp. in rock. [Lat *fissura*, split]

fist *n* **1** a clenched hand. **2** (*coll*) a hand. **3** (*coll*) a person's handwriting. [OE *fyst*]

fistful *n* ***-fuls*** an amount that can be held in a closed hand.

fisticuffs *n* (*pl*; *humorous*) fighting with fists. [*fisty*, of the fist + **cuff**[2]]

fistula *n* (*pathol*) a tube-like ulcer. [Lat, tube, ulcer]

fit[1] *v* ***-tt-*** **1** (*tr* & *intr*; **together**, **into**, etc.) to be, or be made, the right shape or size for. **2** (*intr* with **in**, **into**) to be small or few enough to go into. **3** (*tr*) to be suitable or appropriate for: *a punishment that fits the* *crime*. **4** (*tr* & *intr*) to be consistent or compatible with (something): *a theory that fits the facts*. **5** (*tr*; *together*, *in*, etc.) to insert or place in position. **6** (*tr*) to fix or install. **7** (*tr*; **with**) to equip. **8** (*tr*; **for**) to make suitable: *qualities that fit her for the job*. **9** (*tr*; **for**) to try clothes on (someone) to see where adjustment is needed. — *n* the way something fits: *a good*, *bad*, etc. *fit*. — *adj* **-*tt*- 1** (**for**) suitable; good enough. **2** healthy, esp. because of exercise; healthy enough. **3** about (to do something): *looked fit to drop*. — *adv* enough (to do something): *laughed fit to burst*. — *adv* **fitly**. — *n* **fitness**. — *v* **fit in 1** (*intr*; **with**) to behave in a suitable or accepted way. **2** (*tr*) to find time to deal with (someone or something). — *v* **fit out** (*tr*) to equip as necessary: *fit out the ship*. — *v* **fit up** (*tr*) **1** to fit out. **2** to frame (someone) for a crime. — **see** or **think fit** (usu. *ironic*) to choose (to do something, esp. unwise). [MidE *fitten*]

fitment *n* a fixed piece of equipment or furniture.

fitted *adj* **1** made to fit closely: *fitted sheets*. **2** (of a carpet) covering a floor entirely. **3** fixed; built-in: *fitted cupboards*. **4** (of a kitchen, etc.) with built-in shelves, cupboards, etc.

fitter *n* a person who installs, adjusts or repairs machinery, equipment, etc.

fitting *adj* suitable. — *n* **1** (usu. in *pl*) a piece of fitted furniture or equipment. **2** an act of trying on a garment being made for one, to see where adjustment is necessary. — *adv* **fittingly**.

fit[2] *n* **1** a sudden loss of consciousness with uncontrolled, convulsive movements, esp. in epilepsy. **2** a burst, spell or bout. — **by** or **in fits and starts** in irregular spells; spasmodically. — **in fits** (*coll*) laughing uncontrollably.

fitful *adj* irregular, spasmodic or intermittent; not continuous. — *adv* **fitfully**. [**fit**[2]]

fitment, **fitted**, **fitter**, **fitting**. See **fit**[1].

five *n* **1** the number or figure 5; any symbol for this number. **2** the age of 5. **3** something, esp. a garment, or a person, whose size is denoted by the number 5. **4** 5 o'clock. **5** a set of 5 people or things. **6** a playing-card with 5 pips. **7** a score of 5 points — *adj* **1** 5 in number. **2** aged 5. — *n*, *adj* & *adv* **fifth**. — *adv* **fifthly**. [OE *fif*]

fifth column *n* a body of citizens prepared to co-operate with an invading enemy. — *n* **fifth columnist**.

fivefold *adj* **1** equal to five times as much or many. **2** divided into, or consisting of, five parts. — *adv* by five times as much.

fiver *n* (*coll*) a five-pound note.

fives *n* (*sing*) a game like squash in which a gloved hand or a bat is used to hit the ball.

fix *v* (*tr*) **1** to attach or place firmly. **2** to mend or repair. **3** to direct; to concentrate: *fixed his eyes on her*. **4** to transfix: *fixed him with a stare*. **5** to arrange or agree (a time). **6** (*tr*) to establish (the time of an occurrence). **7** (*coll*) to arrange the result of (a race, trial, etc.) dishonestly. **8** (*coll*) to bribe or threaten into agreement. **9** (*coll*) to thwart, punish or kill. **10** to make (a dye) or the image in (a photograph) permanent by the use of chemicals. **11** (esp. *NAm*) to prepare (a meal, etc.). **12** (esp. *NAm*) to tidy. — *n* **1** (*coll*) a difficulty; a spot of trouble. **2** (*slang*) an act of injecting a narcotic drug, etc. **3** (**on**) a calculation of the position of a ship, etc. — *v* **fix on** (*tr*) to choose. — *v* **fix up** (*tr*) **1** to arrange (e.g. a meeting). **2** (**with**) to provide (what is needed by). **3** to get (a place) ready for some purpose. **4** to set up, esp. temporarily. [Lat *fixare*]

fixed *adj* **1** fastened; immovable. **2** unvarying; set or established: *fixed ideas*. **3** (of a gaze) steady; concentrated; (of an expression) rigid. **4** (of a point) stationary. **5** permanent: *a fixed address*. **6** (*coll*; **for**) supplied, esp. financially: *How are you fixed for cash?*

fixedly *adv* steadily.

fixed star *n* a distant star that seems almost stationary.

fixer *n* **1** (*photography*) a solution for fixing photographic images. **2** (*slang*) a person who arranges things, esp. illegally.

fixation *n* **1** something with which one is preoccupied or obsessed. **2** (*psychol*) an extreme attachment formed in early childhood, e.g. to one's mother. — *adj* **fixated**. [Lat *fixare*, to fix]

fixative *n* **1** a liquid sprayed on a drawing, painting or photograph to preserve and protect it. **2** a liquid used to hold e.g. dentures in place. **3** a substance added to perfume to stop it evaporating. [Lat *fixare*, to fix]

fixity *n* the quality of being fixed, steady, unchanging, unmoving or immovable. [**fix**]

fixture *n* **1** a permanently fixed piece of furniture or equipment. **2** a match or other event in a sports calendar; the date for this. [Lat *fixura*, from *figere*, to fasten]

fizz *v* (*intr*) **1** (of a liquid) to give off bubbles. **2** to hiss. — *n* **1** a fizzing sound or sensation; fizziness. **2** vivacity; high spirits. **3** (*old coll*) champagne. — *n* **fizziness**. — *adj* **fizzy**. [**fizzle**]

fizzle *v* (*intr*) **1** to make a faint hiss. **2** (with **out**) to come to a feeble end. [MidE *fysel*, to break wind]

fjord or **fiord** *n* a long narrow inlet in a high rocky coast, esp. in Norway. [Norse *fiörthr*]

FL or **Fla**. *abbrev* Florida.

flabbergast *v* (*tr*; *coll*) to amaze; to astonish.

flab *n* (*coll*) excess flesh or fat on the body. [**flabby**]

flabby *adj* **-*ier*, -*iest*** (*derog*) **1** (of flesh) sagging, not firm; (of a person) having excess or sagging flesh. **2** lacking vigour;

feeble; ineffective. — *adv* **flabbily**. — *n* **flabbiness**. [Altered form of **flappy**]

flaccid *adj* limp and soft, not firm. — *n* **flaccidity**. — *adv* **flaccidly**. [Lat *flaccidus*]

flag[1] *n* **1** a usu. rectangular piece of cloth with a distinctive design, flown from a pole to represent a country, party, etc., or used for signalling. **2** national identity represented by a flag. **3** a small paper emblem with a pin, e.g. to wear in exchange for supporting a charity, or fixed as a marker to a map, etc. **4** a marker generally. **5** an adjustable plate in a taxi, raised to show that the taxi is for hire. — *v* ***-gg-*** (*tr*) **1** to mark with flag, tag or symbol. **2** (**down**) to signal (a vehicle or driver) to stop. **3** to signal (a message) using flags. — **fly the flag** or **keep the flag flying** to maintain a show of support for one's country or other affiliation. — **with flags flying** with flying colours; triumphantly.

flag day *n* a day chosen by a charity for stationing collectors in the street who distribute flags or stickers in return for donations.

flag of convenience *n* the flag of a foreign country in which a ship is registered to avoid taxation, etc. in its real country of origin.

flag of truce *n* a white flag flown to show willingness to stop fighting.

flagpole or **flagstaff** *n* the pole from which a flag is flown.

flagship *n* **1** the ship that carries, and flies the flag of, the fleet commander. **2** the leading ship in a shipping-line. **3** a commercial company's leading product.

flag-waving *n* an excessive show of patriotic feeling.

flag[2] *v* ***-gg-*** (*intr*) to grow tired or feeble; to lose vigour or enthusiasm.

flag[3] *n* a flagstone. — *v* ***-gg-*** (*tr*) to pave with flagstones. [Norse *flaga*, slab]

flagstone *n* a large flat stone for paving.

flag[4] *n* any of several plants of the iris family, with long blade-like leaves.

flagellate *v* (*tr*) to whip, as a means of religious discipline or for sexual stimulation. — *adj* (*biol*) having flagella. — *n* **flagellant**. — *n* **flagellation**. [Lat *flagellum*, whip]

flagellum *n* ***-la*** **1** (*bot*) a creeping shoot or runner. **2** (*biol*) a whip-like limb. [Lat, whip]

flageolet *n* a high-pitched woodwind instrument similar to the recorder. [Fr]

flagon *n* a large bottle or jug with a narrow neck, usu. with a spout and handle. [OFr *flacon*]

flagrant *adj* (of something bad) undisguised; glaring; brazen or barefaced: *a flagrant lie*. — *n* **flagrance**. — *adv* **flagrantly**. [Lat *flagrare*, to blaze]

flail *n* a threshing tool consisting of a long handle with a wooden or metal bar loosely attached to the end. — *v* **1** (*intr*; **about**, **around**) to wave about violently. **2** (*tr*) to beat (as if) with a flail. [OE *fligel*]

flair *n* **1** (**for**) a natural ability or talent for something. **2** stylishness; dash. [Fr, sense of smell]

flak *n* **1** anti-aircraft fire. **2** (*coll*) unfriendly criticism. [Ger *F*lieger*a*bwehr*k*anone, flyer defence gun]

flak jacket *n* a metal-reinforced jacket worn for protection by police or soldiers.

flake *n* (often *in cmpds*) a small flat particle: *snowflakes*; *flakes of plaster*. — *v* **1** (*intr*) to come off in flakes: *flaking paint*. **2** (*tr*) to break (e.g. cooked fish) into flakes. — *adj* **flaky**, ***-ier***, ***-iest***. — *v* **flake out** (*tr*; *coll*) to faint or drop asleep from exhaustion.

flambé *adj* (of food) soaked in brandy and set alight before serving. — *v* ***-éing***, ***-éed*** (*tr*) to serve (food) in this way. [Fr *flamber*, to expose to flame]

flamboyant *adj* **1** (of a person or behaviour) dashing, colourful and exuberant. **2** (of clothing or colouring) bright, bold and striking. — *n* **flamboyance**. — *adv* **flamboyantly**. [Fr *flamboyer*, to blaze]

flame *n* **1** the luminous flickering mass of burning gases coming from something that is on fire; a tongue of this: *burst into flames*; *go up in flames*. **2** a strong passion: *the flame of love*. **3** a bright reddish-orange colour. — *v* (*intr*) **1** to burn with flames; to blaze. **2** to shine brightly. **3** to explode with anger. **4** to get red and hot: *flaming cheeks*. — **fan**, or **add fuel to, the flames** to stir up already existing feeling or unrest. [Lat *flamma*]

flameproof *adj* not easily damaged by fire or fierce heat.

flame-thrower *n* a gun that discharges a stream of burning liquid, used as a weapon or to clear plants from ground.

flaming *adj* **1** blazing. **2** bright; glowing. **3** (*coll*) very angry; furious; violent. **4** (*coll*) damned: *that flaming dog!*

flamenco *n* ***-os*** a rhythmical, emotionally stirring type of Spanish gypsy music; the dance performed to it. [Span, Flemish]

flamingo *n* ***-os*** or ***-oes*** *n* a large long-legged wading bird with a curved beak and pink plumage. [Perhaps Span, as for **flamenco**, or Provençal *flamenc*, flaming]

flammable *adj* liable to catch fire; inflammable. [Lat *flammare*, to blaze]

flan *n* an open pastry or sponge case with a savoury or fruit filling. [OFr *flaon*]

flange *n* a broad flat projecting rim, e.g. round a wheel, added for strength or for connecting with another object or part. [OFr *flanche*]

flank *n* **1** the side of an animal or human body, between ribs and hip. **2** the side of anything, esp. of a body of troops or a fleet drawn up in formation. — *v* (*tr*) to be or move beside. [Fr *flanc*]

flannel *n* **1** a soft woollen cloth used to make clothes. **2** (in *pl*) trousers made of flannel. **3** a small square of towelling for washing oneself with. **4** (*coll*) flattery, or meaningless talk intended to hide one's ignorance or true intentions. — *v* **-ll-** **1** (*intr & intr*) to flatter, persuade by flattery, or talk flannel. **2** (*tr*) to rub with a flannel. [Welsh *gwlanen*, from *gwlan*, wool]

flannelette *n* cotton cloth with a soft brushed surface.

flap *v* **-pp-** **1** (*tr & intr*) to wave up and down or backwards and forwards. **2** (*tr & intr*) (of a bird) to move (the wings) thus; to fly with pronounced wing movements. **3** (*intr; coll*) to get into a panic or flustered state. — *n* **1** a broad piece or part of something attached along one edge and hanging loosely: *pocket flaps*. **2** an act, sound or impact of flapping. **3** (*coll*) a panic; a flustered state. **4** a hinged section on an aircraft wing adjusted to control speed. — *adj* **flappy, -ier, -iest**. [Imit.]

flapper *n* **1** a fashionable and frivolous young woman of the 1920s. **2** something or someone that flaps.

flapjack *n* **1** a thick biscuit made with oats and syrup. **2** (*NAm*) a pancake. [**flap** + **jack**]

flare *v* (*intr*) **1** to burn with sudden brightness. **2** (*intr*) to explode into anger. **3** (*tr & intr*; **out**) to widen towards the edge or bottom: *flared jeans*. — *n* **1** a sudden blaze of bright light. **2** a device for producing a blaze of light, used as a distress signal or emergency illumination. **3** a device for burning off waste gas or oil. **4** a flared edge or bottom. **5** (in *pl*; *coll*) flared trousers. — *v* **flare up** (*intr*) **1** to blaze suddenly. **2** to explode into anger (*n* **flare-up**).

flash *n* **1** a sudden brief blaze (of light). **2** an instant. **3** a brief but intense occurrence: *a flash of inspiration*. **4** a fleeting look on a face. **5** a camera flashgun. **6** a brief news announcement on radio or television. **7** an emblem on a military uniform, etc. indicating one's unit. — *v* **1** (*intr & tr*) to shine briefly or intermittently. **2** (*intr & tr*) to (cause to) appear briefly; to move or pass quickly. **3** (*intr*) (of the eyes) to brighten with anger, etc. **4** (*tr*) to give (a smile or look) briefly. **5** (*tr*) to display briefly; to flourish, brandish or flaunt. **6** (*tr*) to send (a message) by radio, satellite, etc. **7** (*tr & intr*) to operate (a light) as a signal. **8** (*intr; coll*) (of a man) to expose the genitals. — *adj* **1** sudden and severe: *flash floods*. **2** quick: *flash freezing*. **3** (*coll*) smart and expensive. — **a flash in the pan** (*coll*) an impressive but untypical success, never repeated. [Imit.]

flashback *n* a return to the past, esp. as a scene in a film, etc.

flashbulb *n* a small light bulb used (esp. formerly) to produce a brief bright light in photography.

flasher *n* **1** a light that flashes; a device causing a light to do this. **2** (*coll*) a man who exposes his genitals in public.

flashgun *n* **1** a device that produces brief but brilliant illumination for indoor or night photography. **2** a device that holds and operates a flashbulb.

flashlight *n* (*NAm*) a torch.

flashpoint *n* **1** a stage in a tense situation at which people lose their tempers and become angry or violent. **2** an area of political unrest where violence is liable to break out. **3** the lowest temperature at which vapour from oil will ignite.

flashy *adj* **-ier, -iest** (*coll*) **1** ostentatiously smart. **2** cheap and showy. — *adv* **flashily**. — *n* **flashiness**.

flask *n* **1** (also **hip flask**) a small flat leather-cased pocket bottle for alcoholic spirits. **2** a vacuum flask. **3** a narrow-necked bottle used in chemical experiments, etc. [Lat *flasco*]

flat *adj* **-tt-** **1** level; horizontal; even. **2** without hollows or prominences. **3** lacking the usual prominence: *a flat nose*. **4** not bent or crumpled. **5** (of shoes) not having a raised heel. **6** bored; depressed. **7** dull; not lively. **8** toneless and expressionless. **9** (*coll*) definite; downright; emphatic: *a flat refusal*. **10** (of a tyre) having too little air in it. **11** (of a drink) having lost its fizziness. **12** (of a battery) having little or no electrical charge remaining. **13** (of a price, rate, fee, etc.) fixed; unvarying. **14** (*mus*) lower than the correct pitch. **15** (of paint) matt, not glossy. — *adv* **1** stretched out rather than curled up, etc. **2** into a flat compact shape: *folds flat for storage*. **3** exactly: *in two minutes flat*. **4** bluntly and emphatically: *I can tell you that flat*. **5** (*mus*) at lower than the correct pitch. — *n* **1** a set of rooms for living in, esp. all on one floor; an apartment. **2** something flat; a flat surface or part. **3** (in *pl*) an area of flat land. **4** (*coll*) a flat tyre. **5** (*mus*) a note lowered by a semitone; a sign (♭) indicating this. **6** a flat upright section of stage scenery. **7** (*cap*; with **the**; *horse-racing*) the season of flat racing. — *adv* **flatly**. — *n* **flatness**. — **fall flat** (*coll*) to fail to achieve the hoped-for effect. — **fall flat on one's face** (*coll*) to fail humiliatingly. — **flat broke** (*coll*) completely without money. — **flat out** (*coll*) with maximum speed and energy. — **that's flat** (*coll*) that's certain or final. [Norse *flatr*, flat]

flat feet *n* (*pl*) a condition of the feet in which the arches are low and the toes turned out.

flatfish *n* any of several flat-bodied fish with both eyes on one side, that lie on the sea bed.

flat-footed *adj* **1** having flat feet. **2** (*derog*) clumsy or tactless.

flatiron *n* (*hist*) a clothes-pressing iron heated on the fire or stove.

flatlet *n* a small flat.

flat race *n* a horse race over a course without jumps. — *n* **flat racing**.

flat spin *n* **1** uncontrolled horizontal spinning by an aircraft. **2** (*coll*) a state of agitated bustle.

flatten *v* **-n-** **1** (*tr* & *intr*; **out, down**) to make or become flat or flatter. **2** (*tr*; *coll*) to knock to the ground. **3** (*tr*; *coll*) to overcome, crush or subdue utterly.

flatworm *n* a tapeworm or other flat-bodied worm.

flatter *v* **-r-** (*tr*) **1** to compliment excessively or insincerely. **2** (of a picture or description) to represent (someone or something) over-favourably. **3** to show off well: *a dress that flatters the figure*. **4** to cause to feel honoured; to gratify. — *n* **flatterer**. — **flatter oneself** to feel pleased, usu. smugly and unjustifiably, about something concerning oneself. [MidE *flateren*, to fawn upon]

flattery *n* **-ies** excessive or insincere praise.

flatulence *n* an accumulation of gas in the stomach or intestines, causing discomfort. — *adj* **flatulent**. [Lat *flatus*, blowing]

flaunt *v* (*tr*) to display or parade, in the hope of being admired.

flautist *n* a flute-player. [Ital *flautista*, from *flauto*, flute]

flavour *n* **1** the taste of any particular food or drink. **2** a characteristic quality or atmosphere. — *adj* **flavourless**. — *adj* **flavoursome**. [OFr *flaour*]

flavouring *n* any substance used to give food flavour.

flaw *n* **1** a fault, defect, imperfection or blemish. **2** a mistake, e.g. in an argument. — *adj* **flawed**. — *adj* **flawless**. — *adv* **flawlessly**. [Norse *flaga*, stone flag]

flax *n* a blue-flowered plant whose stem yields a fibre used for making linen, and whose seeds are used to make linseed oil. [OE *fleax*]

flaxen *adj* (of hair) very fair.

flay *v* (*tr*) **1** to strip the skin from. **2** to whip or beat violently. **3** to criticise harshly. [OE *flean*]

flea *n* a tiny wingless jumping insect that sucks blood. — **a flea in one's ear** (*coll*) a severe scolding. [OE]

flea bite *n* **1** (an itchy swelling caused by) the bite of a flea. **2** a trivial inconvenience.

flea-bitten *adj* **1** bitten or infested with fleas. **2** dingy; squalid.

flea market *n* (*coll*) a street market selling second-hand goods or clothes.

flea pit *n* (*coll*) a drab cinema or other public building.

fleck *n* a spot or speck. — *adj* **flecked**. [Norse *flekkr*]

fled. See **flee**.

fledged *n* **1** (of a young bird) able to fly. **2** qualified; trained: *a fully fledged doctor*. [OE *flycge*, able to fly]

fledgling or **fledgeling** *n* a young bird learning to fly. [*fledge*, ready to fly + **-ling**]

flee *v* ***fled*** **1** (*tr*) to run away; to take to flight. **2** (*tr*) to escape from (danger or a dangerous place). **3** (*intr*; *poetic*; **away**) to vanish [OE *fleon*, to fly from]

fleece *n* **1** a sheep's woolly coat. **2** a sheep's wool cut from it at one shearing. **3** sheepskin or a fluffy fabric for lining garments, etc. — *v* (*tr*) **1** to cut wool from (sheep). **2** (*slang*) to rob, swindle or overcharge. — *adj* **fleecy**, **-ier**, **-iest**. [OE *flies*]

fleet[1] *n* **1** a number of ships under one command. **2** a navy. **3** a number of buses, taxis, under the same ownership or management. [OE *fleot*, ship]

fleet[2] *adj* (*poetic*) swift: *fleet of foot*. — *n* **fleetness**. [OE *fleotan*, to float]

fleeting *adj* passing swiftly; brief; short-lived. — *adv* **fleetingly**. [OE *fleotan*, to float]

Fleming *n* a native of Flanders or of the Flemish-speaking part of Belgium. [OE *Flæming*]

Flemish *adj* of, relating to, or belonging to, Flanders, the Flemings or their language. — *n* the language of the Flemings; Dutch. [ODut *vlaemsch*]

flesh *n* **1** the soft tissues covering the bones, consisting chiefly of muscle. **2** the meat of animals, as distinct from that of fish and, sometimes, birds. **3** the pulp of a fruit or vegetable. **4** the body as distinct from the soul or spirit; bodily needs. **5** (*poetic*) mankind. **6** excess fat; plumpness. **7** a yellowish-pink colour. — **flesh and blood** bodily or human nature (**one's flesh and blood** one's family or relations). — *v* **flesh out** (*tr*) to add descriptive detail to. — **in the flesh** in person. [OE *flæsc*]

flesh-coloured *adj* yellowish pink.

fleshly *adj* relating to the body as distinct from the soul; worldly.

fleshpots *n* (*pl*; *facet*) **1** luxurious living. **2** a place where bodily desires or lusts can be gratified.

flesh wound *n* a superficial wound, not deep enough to damage bone or a bodily organ.

fleshy *adj* **-ier**, **-iest** **1** plump. **2** of or like flesh. **3** (of leaves, etc.) thick and pulpy. — *n* **fleshiness**.

flew. See **fly**[2].

fleur-de-lis or **-lys** *n* ***fleurs-de-lis*** or ***-lys*** a stylised three-petal representation of a lily or iris, used as a heraldic design. [OFr *flour de lis*, lily flower]

flex[1] *v* (*tr*) **1** to bend (a limb or joint). **2** to contract or tighten (a muscle) so as to bend a joint. [Lat *flectere*, to bend]

flex[2] *n* flexible insulated electric cable. [**flexible**]

flexible *adj* **1** bending easily; pliable. **2** readily adaptable to suit circumstances. — *n* **flexibility**. — *adv* **flexibly**. [Lat *flexibilis*]

flexitime *n* a system of flexible working hours operated in some organisations whereby employees may choose their time of arrival and departure, provided they work the agreed number of hours. [**flexible**]

flibbertigibbet *n* a silly unreliable frivolous or over-talkative person.

flick *v* **1** (*tr* & *intr*; **off, over, out**, etc.) to move or touch with a quick light movement. **2** (*intr* with **through**) to look quickly through (a book, etc.). — *n* a flicking action. [Imit.]

flick knife *n* a knife whose blade is concealed in its handle and springs out at the touch of a button.

flicker *v* **-r- 1** (*intr*) to burn or shine unsteadily. **2** (*tr* & *intr*) to move lightly to and fro; to flutter. — *n* **1** a brief or unsteady light. **2** a fleeting appearance or occurrence. [OE *flicorian*, to flutter]

flicks *n* (*pl*; with **the**; *old coll*) the cinema. [**flick**]

flight[1] *n* **1** the action or power of flying. **2** the path taken by something flying. **3** a journey made by or in an aircraft. **4** a set of steps or stairs leading straight up or down. **5** a number of birds or aircraft flying in a group. **6** a rather extreme example (of fancy, imagination, etc.). **7** a feather or something similar attached to the end of a dart or arrow. — **in flight** flying. [OE *flyht*]

flight deck *n* **1** the upper deck of an aircraft carrier where planes take off or land. **2** the forward part of an aeroplane where the pilot and crew sit.

flightless *adj* (of birds or insects) unable to fly.

flight lieutenant *n* the rank next below squadron leader.

flight recorder *n* an electronic instrument on an aircraft recording information about its performance in flight.

flight[2] *n* the act of fleeing; escape. — **put to flight** to cause to flee. — **take flight** or **take to flight** to run away. [MidE]

flimsy *adj* **-ier, -iest 1** (of clothing, etc.) light and thin. **2** (of a structure) insubstantially made; frail. **3** (of an excuse, etc.) inadequate or unconvincing. — *adv* **flimsily**. — *n* **flimsiness**. [Perhaps altered from **film**]

flinch *v* (*intr*) **1** to start or jump in pain or fright. **2** (with **from**) to shrink from or avoid (a task, duty, etc).

fling *v* **flung 1** (*tr*) to throw, esp. violently or vigorously. **2** (*intr*; **off, out**) to rush angrily. — *n* **1** (*coll*) a spell of enjoyable self-indulgence. **2** a lively reel: *the Highland fling*. **3** (**at**) a try; a go. — *v* **fling out** (*tr*) to throw away or reject. [MidE]

flint *n* **1** a hard quartz found in limestone or chalk. **2** (*archaeol*) a trimmed piece of this used as a tool. **3** a piece of a hard metal alloy from which a spark can be struck, e.g. in a cigarette-lighter. — *adj* **flinty, -ier, -iest**. [OE]

flintlock *n* (*hist*) a gun in which the powder was lit by a spark from a flint.

flip *v* **-pp- 1** (*tr*) to toss (e.g. a coin) so that it turns over in mid air. **2** (*tr*; **over**) to toss or turn with a light flick. **3** (*intr*; *coll*) to go crazy. **4** (*intr* with **through**) to look quickly through (a magazine, etc.). — *n* **1** a flipping action. **2** a somersault, esp. performed in mid air. **3** an alcoholic drink made with beaten egg. **4** (*coll*) a short air trip. — *adj* (*coll*) flippant; over-smart. — **flip one's lid** (*coll*) to lose one's temper. [Imit.]

flip side *n* (*coll*) the side of a gramophone record not containing the principal item.

flip-flop *n* **1** (*coll*) a rubber or plastic sandal consisting of a sole held on to the foot by a strap that separates the big toe from the other toes. **2** (*electr, comput*) a device or circuit able to take on either of two stable states, usu. 'on' or 'off' [**flip**]

flippant *adj* not serious enough about grave matters; disrespectful; irreverent; frivolous. — *n* **flippancy**. — *adv* **flippantly**. [**flip**]

flipper *n* **1** a limb adapted for swimming, e.g. in the whale, seal, penguin, etc. **2** a rubber foot-covering imitating an animal flipper, worn for underwater swimming. [**flip**]

flipping *adj* & *adv* (*coll*) used to express annoyance: *that flipping cat!* [**flip**]

flirt *v* (*intr*) **1** (**with**) to behave amorously towards someone without serious intentions. **2** (with **with**) to take a fleeting interest in; to consider briefly; to play riskily with. — *n* someone who flirts. — *n* **flirtation**. — *adj* **flirtatious**.

flit *v* **-tt-** (*intr*) **1** to dart lightly from place to place. **2** (*Scot & N of England*) to move house. **3** (*Br coll*) to move house to avoid paying debts. — *n* an act of flitting. — *n* **flitting**. [Norse *flytja*, to carry]

flitch *n* a salted and cured side of pork. [OE *flicce*]

float *v* **1** (*tr* & *intr*) to (cause to) rest or move on the surface of a liquid. **2** (*intr*) to drift about or hover in the air. **3** (*intr*) to move about in an aimless or disorganised way. **4** (*tr*) to start up (a company, scheme, etc.). **5** (*tr*) to offer (stocks) for sale. **6** (*tr*) to allow (a currency) to vary in value in relation to other currencies. — *n* **1** a floating device fixed to a fishing-line, that moves to indicate a bite. **2** a low-powered delivery vehicle: *milk float*. **3** a vehicle decorated as an exhibit in a street parade. **4** an amount of money set aside for giving change, etc. [OE *flotian*]

floating *adj* **1** not fixed; moving about: *a floating population*. **2** (of a voter) not committed to supporting any one party. **3** (of a currency) varying in value in relation to other currencies. **4** (of a bodily organ, e.g. a kidney) moving about abnormally.

floatation. See **flotation**.

flock[1] *n* **1** a group of creatures, esp. birds or sheep. **2** a crowd of people. **3** a body of people under the spiritual charge of a priest. — *v* (*intr*) to gather or move in a crowd. [OE *flocc*]

flock[2] *n* **1** a tuft of wool, etc. **2** waste wool or cotton used for stuffing mattresses, etc. **3** fine particles of wool or nylon fibre applied to paper or cloth to give a velvety surface. [Lat *floccus*, tuft of wool]

floe *n* a floating ice sheet. [Norw *flo*, layer]

flog *v* **-gg-** (*tr*) **1** to beat; to whip. **2** (*coll*) to sell. — **flog a dead horse** (*coll*) to waste time and energy on a lost cause. — **flog to death** (*coll*) **1** to over-use (an idea, expression, etc.) so that it becomes tedious and ineffective. **2** to overwork. [Lat *flagellare*, to whip]

flood *n* **1** an overflow of water over dry land, e.g. (*cap*; *Bible*) the one from which Noah took refuge in the Ark. **2** any overwhelming flow or quantity. **3** the rising of the tide. **4** (*coll*) a floodlight. — *v* **1** (*tr*) to overflow or submerge (land). **2** (*tr*) to fill too full or to overflowing. **3** (*tr* with **out**) to force to leave a building, etc. because of floods. **4** (*tr*) to supply (a market) with too much of a certain kind of commodity. **5** (*tr*) to supply (an engine) with too much petrol so that it cannot start. **6** (*intr*) to (tend to) become flooded. **7** (*intr*) to move in a great mass: *crowds flooding through the gates*. **8** (*intr*) to flow or surge. — **in flood** overflowing. [OE *flod*]

floodgate *n* a gate for controlling the flow of a large amount of water. — **open the floodgates** to remove all restraints or controls.

floodlight *n* (a lamp giving) powerful light used to illuminate football pitches or the outside of buildings. — *v* (*tr*) to illuminate with floodlights. — *adj* **floodlit**.

floor *n* **1** the lower interior surface of a room or vehicle. **2** all the rooms on the same level in a building. **3** the ground in a forest or cave; the bed of the sea, etc. **4** the debating area in a parliamentary assembly; the right to speak there: *have the floor*. — *v* (*tr*) **1** to construct the floor of (a room, etc.). **2** (*coll*) to knock (someone) down. **3** (*coll*) to baffle completely. — **hold the floor** to be the person who is talking while others listen. — **take the floor 1** to rise to speak in a debate, etc. **2** to start dancing at a dance, etc. — **wipe the floor with** (*slang*) to defeat ignominiously; to humiliate utterly. [OE *flor*]

floorboard *n* one of the boards forming a wooden floor.

flooring *n* material for constructing floors.

floor show *n* a series of performances at a nightclub or restaurant.

floosie or **floozie** *n* (*coll derog*) a woman or girl, esp. a disreputable or immodestly dressed one.

flop *v* **-pp-** (*intr*) **1** to fall, drop, move or sit limply and heavily. **2** (of e.g. hair) to hang or sway about loosely. **3** (*coll*) (of a play, etc.) to fail. — *n* **1** a flopping movement or sound. **2** (*coll*) a failure. — *adv* with a flop. — *adv* **floppily**. — *n* **floppiness**. — *adj* **floppy**, **-ier**, **-iest**. [Variant of **flap**]

floppy disk *n* a flexible magnetic disk for storing data for use in a computer.

flora *n* **-as** or **-ae** the plants of a particular place or time. ◇ See also **fauna**. [Lat *Flora*, goddess of flowers]

floral *adj* **1** of or relating to flowers. **2** patterned with flowers: *floral material*. — *adv* **florally**. [Lat *floralis*]

florid *adj* **1** over-elaborate. **2** pink or ruddy in complexion. — *adv* **floridly**. [Lat *floridus*, blooming]

florist *n* a person who grows or sells flowers. [Lat *flos*, flower]

florin *n* a former name of the coin worth two shillings or 24 old pence, the equivalent of the modern ten-penny piece. [Ital *fiorino*, a former gold coin from Florence]

floss *n* **1** loose strands of fine silk, for embroidery, tooth-cleaning, etc. **2** the rough silk on the outside of a silkworm's cocoon. — *adj* **flossy**, **-ier**, **-iest**. [Prob OFr *flosche*, down]

flotation or **floatation** *n* the launching of a commercial company with a sale of shares to raise money. [**float**]

flotilla *n* a small fleet, or one of small ships. [Span, little fleet]

flotsam *n* goods lost by shipwreck and found floating on the sea. — **flotsam and jetsam 1** odds and ends. **2** homeless people; vagrants. [OFr *floteson*, from *floter*, to float]

flounce[1] *v* (*intr*) to move in a way expressive of impatience or indignation. — *n* a flouncing movement. [Perhaps related to Norse *flunsa*, to hurry]

flounce[2] *n* a deep frill on a dress, etc. [Altered from *frounce*, plait, curl]

flounder[1] *v* (*intr*) **-r- 1** to thrash about helplessly, as when caught in a bog. **2** to be in difficulties or at a loss, from embarrassment, etc. [Partly imit., partly a blend of **founder** + **blunder**]

flounder[2] *n* a type of edible flatfish. [OFr *flondre*]

flour *n* powder from ground grain, esp. wheat, used for baking, etc. — *v* (*tr*) to cover or sprinkle with flour. — *adj* **floury**, **-ier**, **-iest**. [MidE, flower, i.e. best part]

flourish *v* **1** (*intr*) to be strong and healthy; to grow well. **2** to do well; to develop and prosper. **3** (*intr*) to be at one's most productive, or at one's peak. **4** (*tr*) to wave or brandish. — *n* **1** a decorative twirl in handwriting. **2** an elegant sweep of the hand. **3** a showy piece of music; a fanfare. **4** a piece of fancy language. [OFr *florir*, to flower]

flout *v* (*tr*) to defy (an order, etc.) openly; to disrespect (authority, etc.). [MidE *flouten*, to play the flute]

flow *v* (*intr*) **1** to move along like water. **2** (of blood or electricity) to circulate. **3** to keep moving steadily. **4** (of hair) to hang or ripple in a loose shining mass. **5** (of words or ideas) to come readily to mind or in speech or writing. **6** (of the tide) to rise. — *n* **1** the action of flowing. **2** the rate of flowing. **3** a continuous stream or outpouring. **4** the rising of the tide. —

in full flow speaking energetically. [OE *flowan*]

flow chart or **diagram** *n* a diagram representing movement through the progressive stages of some process.

flower *n* **1** the usu. brightly coloured part of a plant or tree from which the fruit or seed grows. **2** a plant bearing flowers, esp. if cultivated for them. **3** the best part; the cream. — *v* **-r-** (*intr*) **1** to produce flowers; to bloom. **2** to reach a peak; to develop to full maturity. — **in flower** blooming or blossoming; with flowers fully out. [OFr *flour*]

flowerpot *n* a clay or plastic container for growing plants in.

flowery *adj* **1** decorated or patterned with flowers. **2** (of e.g. language or gestures) too elegant or elaborate.

flown. See **fly**[2].

fl. oz *abbrev* fluid ounce.

flu *n* (*coll*) influenza.

fluctuate *v* (*intr*) to vary in amount, value, level, etc.; to rise and fall. — *n* **fluctuation**. [Lat *fluctus*, wave]

flue *n* **1** an outlet for smoke or gas, e.g. through a chimney. **2** a pipe or duct for conveying heat.

fluent *adj* **1** (**in**) speaking or writing in an easy flowing style. **2** spoken or written with ease: *speaks fluent German*. — *n* **fluency**. — *adv* **fluently**. [Lat *fluere*, to flow]

fluff *n* **1** small bits of soft woolly or downy material. **2** (*coll*) a mistake, e.g. in speaking or reading aloud. — *v* **1** (*tr*; **out, up**) to shake or arrange into a soft mass. **2** (*tr* & *intr*) (of e.g. an actor) to make a mistake in (one's lines, etc.); to bungle (something). — *n* **fluffiness**. — *adj* **fluffy**, **-ier**, **-iest**. [Earlier *flue*, down]

fluid *n* a substance such as liquid or gas that can flow freely. — *adj* **1** able to flow like a liquid. **2** (of e.g. movements) smooth and graceful. **3** altering easily; adaptable. — *n* **fluidity**. [Lat *fluidus*, flowing]

fluid ounce *n* a unit of liquid measurement, equal to a twentieth of a British pint or a sixteenth of a US pint.

fluke[1] *n* a success achieved by accident. — *adj* **fluky**, **-ier**, **-iest**.

fluke[2] *n* **1** a flatworm infesting the liver of a sheep. **2** a flounder. [OE *floc*, plaice]

flume *n* a descending channel for water, used in industry, or as a chute for riding or sliding down. [OFr *flum*, from Lat *flumen*, river]

flummery *n* **-ies** **1** a jelly made with oatmeal, milk, egg and honey. **2** pompous nonsense; empty flattery. [Welsh *llymru*]

flummox *v* (*tr*; *coll*) to confuse; to bewilder.

flung. See **fling**.

flunk *v* (*NAm coll*) **1** (*tr* & *intr*) to fail (a test, examination, etc.). **2** (*tr*) (of an examiner) to fail (a candidate).

flunkey **-eys** or **flunky**, **-ies** *n* **1** a uniformed manservant. **2** (*derog*) a slavish follower. **3** (*NAm*) a person doing a humble or menial job.

fluor. See **fluorspar**.

fluoresce *v* (*intr*) to be or become fluorescent. [**fluor**]

fluorescent *adj* absorbing radiation and simultaneously giving out electromagnetic radiation at a lower frequency in the form of light. — *n* **fluorescence**.

fluorescent light or **lamp** *n* a type of electric light or lamp using gas-filled tubes lined with phosphor, the electrical discharge causing the phosphor to fluoresce.

fluoride *n* either of two sodium compounds of fluorine that, added to toothpaste or drinking-water, help to prevent tooth decay. [**fluorine**]

fluoridate, fluoridise or **-ize** *v* (*tr*) to add fluoride to (a water supply). — *n* **fluoridation, fluoridisation** or **-z-**.

fluorine *n* an element (symbol **F**), a pale greenish-yellow gas. [**fluor**]

fluorspar *n* (also **fluor** or **fluorite**) a crystalline form of the mineral calcium fluoride. [Lat *fluor*, flow (from the use of fluorspar as a flux) + **spar**[3]]

flurry *n* **-ies** **1** a sudden gust; a brief shower of rain, snow, etc. **2** (*coll*) a commotion; a bustle or rush. — *v* **-ies**, **-ied** (*tr*) to agitate or confuse. [Imit.]

flush[1] *v* **1** (*intr* & *tr*) to (cause to) blush or go red. **2** (*tr*) to clean out (esp. a lavatory pan) with a rush of water; to wash (something) down the lavatory. **3** (*tr*; **with**) to fill with pride or elation: *flushed with success*. — *n* **1** a redness or rosiness, esp. of the face; a blush. **2** (the mechanism that operates) a rush of water that cleans the lavatory pan. **3** high spirits: *in the first flush of enthusiasm*. **4** freshness; bloom; vigour: *in the first flush of youth*. [Perhaps **flush**[4]]

flush[2] *adj* **1** (**with**) level with an adjacent surface. **2** (*coll*) having plenty of money. — *adv* so as to be level with an adjacent surface. [Perhaps **flush**[1]]

flush[3] *n* (*cards*) a hand made up of cards from a single suit. [Lat *fluxus*, flow]

flush[4] *v* (*tr*) **1** (*hunting*, etc.) to startle (game birds) so that they rise from the ground. **2** (with **out**) to drive out of a hiding-place. [MidE *flusshen*]

fluster *n* a state of confused agitation. — *v* **-r-** (*tr*) to agitate or confuse. [Related to Norse *flaustr*, hurry]

flute *n* **1** a woodwind instrument that is held horizontally out to the side of the head. **2** (*archit*) a rounded groove in wood or stone. — *v* **1** (*intr* & *tr*) to speak or utter in high shrill tones. **2** (*intr* & *tr*) to play the flute or play (a tune, etc.) on it. **3** (*tr*; *archit*) to make grooves in (wood or stone). — *adj* **fluty**, **-ier**, **-iest**. ◇ See also **flautist**. [OFr *flahute*]

fluting *n* parallel grooves cut into wood or stone.

flutter *v* **-r-** **1** (*tr* & *intr*) to flap lightly and rapidly; to fly with a rapid wing movement or drift with a twirling motion. **2** (*intr*) to move about in a restless, aimless way. **3** (*tr*; *old*) to cause agitation in: *must have fluttered a few hearts in his time*. **4** (*intr*) (of the heart) to race, from excitement or some disorder. — *n* **1** agitation; excitement. **2** (*coll*) a small bet. **3** in a record-player, etc., a regularly recurring variation in loudness and pitch. [OE *floterian*, to flutter]

fluvial *adj* of, relating to or found in, rivers. [Lat *fluvialis*]

flux *n* **1** constant change; instability. **2** any of several substances mixed with metal and used in fusing metals. **3** (*old med*) a flow or discharge. **4** (*physics*) the rate of flow of e.g. particles, energy or fluid. [Lat *fluxus*, flow]

fly[1] *n* ***flies*** **1** a two-winged insect. **2** (*in cmpds*) any of various other flying insects: *mayfly*; *dragonfly*; *butterfly*. **3** a fish hook tied with colourful feathers to look like a fly. — **drop like flies** (*coll*) to fall ill or die in large numbers. — **a fly in the ointment** a drawback in an otherwise satisfactory state of affairs. — **a fly on the wall** the invisible observer that one would like to be on certain occasions. — **no flies on** (*coll*) no lack of alertness in. — **he**, etc. **wouldn't harm a fly** he, etc. has a gentle nature. [OE *fleoge*]

flyblown *n* **1** (of food) covered with blowfly eggs, so unfit to eat; contaminated. **2** shabby, dirty or dingy.

fly-fish *v* (*intr*) to fish using artificial flies. — *n* **fly-fishing**.

flypaper *n* a strip of paper with a sticky poisonous coating that attracts, traps and kills flies.

flyspray *n* a liquid poisonous to flies, sprayed from an aerosol can.

flyweight *n* **1** a class for boxers, wrestlers and weight-lifters of not more than a specified weight (50.8 kg in professional boxing, similar weights in the other sports). **2** a boxer, etc of this weight. — *adj* (for contestants) of the specified weight.

fly[2] *v* ***flies***, ***flew***, ***flown*** **1** (*intr*) (of a bird, bat or insect) to move through the air on wings; (of an aircraft or spacecraft) to travel through the air or through space. **2** (*intr* & *tr*) to travel or convey in an aircraft. **3** (*tr*) to operate and control (an aircraft, kite, etc.). **4** (*tr*) to cross (a stretch of water, etc.) in an aircraft. **5** (*tr* & *intr*) to raise (a flag), or (of a flag) to blow in the wind. **6** (*intr*) to move or pass rapidly: *fly into a temper*; *rumours flying around*. **7** (*intr*; *coll*) to depart quickly: *I must fly*. **8** (*intr* with **at, out at**) to attack angrily. **9** (*intr* & *tr*) to escape; to flee (a country, etc.). **10** (*intr*) to vanish: *Darkness has flown*. — *n* ***flies*** **1** (usu. in *pl*) (a flap of cloth concealing) the zip or buttons fastening a trouser front. **2** a flap covering the entrance to a tent. **3** (in *pl*) the space above a stage from which scenery is lowered. — **fly high** to be ambitious. — **let fly (at)** to attack. ◇ See also **flying**. [OE *fleogan*, to fly]

fly-by-night *adj* (*derog*) (of a business, etc.) not reliable or trustworthy.

flyer or **flier** *n* **1** a creature that flies; someone or something that moves fast; an aviator or pilot. **2** an advertising leaflet.

fly half *n* (*Rugby*) a stand-off half.

flyleaf *n* a blank page at the beginning or end of a book.

flyover *n* a bridge that takes a road or railway over another.

flypast *n* a ceremonial flight of military aircraft over a particular place.

flysheet *n* **1** a protective outer sheet for a tent. **2** a single-sheet leaflet.

flywheel *n* a heavy wheel on a revolving shaft that regulates the action of a machine.

fly[3] *adj* (*coll*) cunning; smart.

flying *n* **1** flight. **2** the activity of piloting, or travelling in, an aircraft. — *adj* **1** hasty; brief. **2** designed or organised for fast movement. **3** that flies; able to fly, or to make long gliding leaps. **4** (of e.g. hair or a flag) streaming; fluttering. — **send flying** to knock down or knock over with considerable force.

flying boat *n* a seaplane whose fuselage is shaped like a boat hull.

flying buttress *n* a structure supporting, and forming an arch against, the outside wall of a large building, esp. a church.

flying doctor *n* esp. in Australia, a doctor who travels by light aircraft to visit patients.

flying fish *n* a tropical fish with wing-like fins that can rise above the water.

flying fox *n* a fruit-eating bat.

flying leap *n* a jump from a running start.

flying officer *n* a Royal Air Force rank immediately below flight lieutenant.

flying picket *n* a picket travelling from place to place to support local pickets during any strike.

flying saucer *n* any of a number of unidentified circular flying objects reported in the sky from time to time, believed by some to be craft from outer space.

flying squad *n* a body of police specially trained for fast movement or action, or available for duty wherever the need arises.

flying start *n* a start to a race in which the contestants are already travelling at full speed when they cross the starting-line. — **get off to a flying start** to begin promisingly or with a special advantage.

FM *abbrev* frequency modulation.

Fm *symbol* (*chem*) fermium.

FO *abbrev* **1** Flying Officer. **2** (*hist*) Foreign Office.

foal *n* the young of a horse or of a related animal. — *v* (*intr*) to give birth to a foal. — **in foal** (of a mare) pregnant. [OE *fola*]

foam *n* **1** a mass of tiny bubbles forming on the surface of liquids. **2** a substance composed of tiny bubbles formed by passing gas through it. **3** frothy saliva or perspiration. **4** any of many light cellular materials produced by passing gas through, and then solidifying, a liquid. **5** (*poetic*) the sea. — *adj* **foamy**, *-ier*, *-iest*. — **foam at the mouth 1** to produce frothy saliva. **2** (*coll*) to be furiously angry. [OE *fam*]

fob[1] *v* ***-bb-*** (*tr* with **off**) **1** (with **with**) to provide (someone) with (something inferior, e.g. a poor substitute, inadequate explanation, etc.) in the hope that he or she will be satisfied. **2** (with **on**) to manage to sell or offload (something unwanted or inferior) on (someone); to foist: *fob a fake diamond off on an innocent buyer*. **3** to dismiss or ignore: *tried to fob off his critics*. [Related to Ger *foppen*, to delude]

fob[2] *n* **1** a chain attached to a watch. **2** a decorative attachment to a key ring or watch chain. **3** (*hist*) a small watch pocket in a waistcoat or trouser waistband. [Perhaps related to Ger dialect *fuppe*, pocket]

fob watch *n* a watch for keeping in a fob.

focal *adj* relating to, or at, a focus. [**focus**]

focal distance or **length** *n* the distance between the surface of a mirror or centre of a lens, and its focal point.

focal point *n* **1** the meeting-point of rays reflected by a mirror or passing through a lens. **2** a centre of attraction.

fo'c'sle *n* a spelling of **forecastle** suggested by its pronunciation.

focus *n* ***-cuses*** or ***-ci*** **1** the point at which rays of light or sound waves meet or from which they seem to diverge. **2** the point where an object must stand to appear as a clear image in a lens or mirror. **3** the adjustment of one's eye or the lens of an instrument, etc., to obtain a clear image. **4** a positioning that gives, or the state of having, a satisfactorily clear image: *in* or *out of focus*. **5** a centre (of interest or attention). **6** special attention paid to something: *a shift of focus*. — *v* ***-s-*** or ***-ss-*** **1** (*tr* & *intr*) to bring or be brought into focus; to (cause to) meet or converge at a focus. **2** (*tr*) to adjust the focus of (one's eye or an instrument). **3** (*tr* & *intr*; **on**) to concentrate (one's attention). [Lat *focus*, hearth, as the centre of the home]

fodder *n* **1** food, esp. hay and straw, for cattle and other farm animals. **2** (*coll*) something that is made use of to feed a constant need: *Any story about the Queen is fodder for the popular press*. [OE]

foe *n* (*old* or *poetic*) an enemy. [OE *fah*, hostile]

foetid. Another spelling of **fetid**.

foetus *n* the young creature growing in an egg or womb, esp. a human embryo of two or more months' development. — *adj* **foetal**. [Lat *fetus*, offspring]

fog *n* **1** a thick cloud of condensed watery vapour suspended in the air close to the earth's surface, reducing visibility; thick mist. **2** (*phot*) a blurred patch on a negative, print or transparency. **3** a blur; cloudiness. **4** a state of confusion or bewilderment. — *v* ***-gg-*** **1** (*tr* & *intr*) to obscure or become obscured (as if) with fog or condensation. **2** (*tr*) to confuse or perplex. — *adj* **foggy**, *-ier*, *-iest*. — **not have the foggiest idea** (*coll*) not to know at all. [Perhaps Norse]

fog bank *n* a thick cloud of fog.

fogbound *adj* brought to a standstill by fog.

foghorn *n* a horn that sounds a warning at regular intervals to ships in fog.

fog lamp *n* a powerful lamp used by vehicles in fog.

fogey, ***-eys*** or **fogy**, ***-ies*** *n* (*derog*) someone with boring, old-fashioned ideas.

foible *n* a slight personal weakness or eccentricity. [OFr, variant of *faible*, feeble]

foil[1] *v* (*tr*) to prevent, thwart or frustrate (a person or attempt). [OFr *fuler*, to trample or full cloth]

foil[2] *n* **1** metal beaten or rolled out into thin sheets. **2** a thing or person that acts as a contrast to, and brings out, the superior or different qualities of another. [OFr, leaf, from Lat *folium*]

foil[3] *n* a long slender sword with its point protected by a button, used in the sport of fencing.

foist *v* (*tr* with **on**) **1** to inflict (an unwanted thing or person) on (someone). **2** to palm off (something inferior) dishonestly on (someone). [Perhaps Dut *vuist*, fist]

fold[1] *v* **1** (*tr*; **over**, **back**, **down**, **up**) to double over so that one part lies on top of another: *fold the paper in two*; *fold up blankets*. **2** (*intr*) to (be able to) be folded: *folds away for storage*. **3** (*tr*) to intertwine (one's arms) across one's chest or bend up (one's legs). **4** (*tr*) to bring in (wings) close to the body. **5** (*intr*) (of flower petals) to close. **6** (*tr*; **in**) to wrap up. **7** (*tr*; **in**) to clasp (someone) in one's arms, etc. **8** (*tr*; **in** or **into**) to stir (an ingredient) gently into a mixture with an action like folding. **9** (*intr*; **up**; *coll*) (of a business, etc.) to collapse; to fail. — *n* **1** a doubling of one layer over another. **2** a rounded or sharp bend made by this; a crease. **3** a hollow in the landscape. **4** (*geol*) a curve in layers of stratified rocks caused by movement of the earth's crust. [OE *faldan*, to fold]

folder *n* a cardboard or plastic cover in which to keep loose papers.

fold[2] *n* **1** a walled or fenced enclosure for sheep or cattle. **2** (the body of believers within) the protection of a church. [OE *falod*]

-fold *sfx* **1** multiplied by a stated number: *increased threefold*. **2** having a certain number of parts: *a twofold benefit*. [OE *-feald*]

foliaceous *adj* **1** like leaves. **2** (*geol*) composed of thin layers; laminated. [Lat *foliaceus*, from *folium*, leaf]

foliage *n* the leaves on a tree or plant. [OFr *fueillage*, from *feuille*, leaf]

foliate *v* **1** (*tr*) to beat (metal) into foil. **2** (*intr* & *tr*) to split into layers. — *adj* leaf-like, or having leaves. [Lat *foliatus*, leafy]
foliation *n* **1** the process of beating or dividing into layers. **2** (*bot*) the production of leaves.

folic acid a vitamin of the vitamin B complex. [Lat *folium*, leaf]

folio *n* **-os 1** a leaf of a manuscript, etc., numbered on one side. **2** (*printing*) a page number in a book. **3** (*hist*) a sheet of paper folded once; a book of the largest size, composed of such sheets: *a folio edition*. **4** (*old*) a folder. [Lat *in folio*, on (a certain numbered) leaf]

folk *n* **1** (*pl*; often *in cmpds*; also *coll* **folks**) people. **2** (*pl*; also *coll* **folks**) one's family. **3** a people or tribe. **4** (*coll*) folk music. — *adj* traditional among a people; of popular origin: *folk music*; *a folksong*. [OE *folc*]
folklore *n* (the study of) the customs, beliefs, stories, traditions, etc. of particular peoples.
folksy *adj* **-ier, -iest** simple and homely, esp. in an over-sweet way.

follicle *n* a small sac or cavity in the body, esp. one containing a hair root. [Lat *folliculus*, dimin. of *follis*, bellows]

follow *v* **1** (*tr* & *intr*; **after**) to go or come after. **2** (*tr*) to accompany. **3** (*tr*) to pursue stealthily. **4** (*tr*) to accept as leader or authority. **5** (*intr*) to result; to be a consequence. **6** (*tr*) to go along (a road, etc.), alongside (a river, etc.) or on the path marked by (signs). **7** (*tr*) to watch (someone or something) as he, she or it moves: *Her eyes followed him up the street*. **8** (*tr*) to pass or practise: *follow a life of self-denial*; *follow a trade*. **9** (*tr*) to conform to: *follows a familiar pattern*. **10** (*tr*; **out**) to obey (advice, etc.). **11** (*tr* & *intr*) to copy: *follow her example*. **12** (*tr* & *intr*) to understand. **13** (*tr*) to read (a piece of writing or music) while listening to a performance of it. **14** (*tr* with **through, up**) to investigate or test out. **15** (*tr* & *intr*; **up**) to do something as the next step after (a particular procedure): *She followed up her investigations with a long newspaper article* (*n* **follow-up**). **16** (*tr*) to take a keen interest in (a sport, etc.). — *n* **follower**. — **as follows** as announced after this or shown below. — **followed by** with (someone or something) next. — *v* **follow on** (*intr*) **1** (**from**) to continue. **2** (*cricket*) to have to bat a second innings immediately after the first (*n* **follow-on**). — *v* **follow through** (*intr* & *tr*; *tennis*, *golf*, etc.) to complete (a stroke) after hitting the ball (*n* **follow-through**). [OE *folgian*]
following *n* a body of supporters. — *adj* **1** coming after; next. **2** about to be mentioned: *need to deal with the following points*. **3** (of a wind) blowing in the direction in which a ship, etc. is travelling. — *prep* after.

folly *n* **-ies 1** foolishness; a foolish act. **2** a mock temple, castle, etc. built as a romantic addition to a view. [OFr *folie*, madness]

foment *v* (*tr*) to encourage or foster (ill-feeling, etc.). — *n* **fomentation**. [Lat *fomentum*, poultice]

fond *adj* **1** (with **of**) having a liking for. **2** loving. **3** (of wishes, hopes, etc.) foolishly impractical. — *adv* **fondly**. — *n* **fondness**. [MidE *fonnen*, to act foolishly]

fondant *n* a soft sweet or paste made with sugar and water. [Fr, from *fondre*, to melt]

fondle *v* (*tr*) to touch, stroke, or caress affectionately. [From earlier *fond*, to handle]

fondue *n* **1** an orig. Swiss dish of hot cheese sauce into which bits of bread are dipped. **2** a steak dish, the pieces of meat being cooked at table by dipping briefly into hot oil. [Fr, from *fondre*, to melt]

font *n* the basin in a church that holds water for baptisms. [OE *fant*, from Lat *fons*, fountain]

fontanelle *n* a gap between the bones of the skull in a young child or animal. [OFr *fontanele*]

food *n* **1** a substance taken in, or absorbed, by a living thing, that provides energy or helps growth. **2** solid as distinct from liquid nourishment: *food and drink*. **3** something that provides stimulation: *food for thought*. [OE *foda*]
food chain *n* a series of living organisms, each of which is fed on by the next in the series.
food poisoning *n* illness caused by eating food contaminated with bacteria.
food processor *n* an electrical apparatus for chopping or blending food.
foodstuff *n* a substance used as food.
food value *n* the nourishment to be got from any particular food.

fool[1] *n* **1** a person lacking common sense or intelligence. **2** someone made to appear ridiculous. **3** (*hist*) a person employed by kings, nobles, etc. to amuse them; a jester. — *v* **1** (*tr*; **into, out of**) to deceive; to persuade by deception. **2** (*intr*; **about, around**) to behave stupidly or playfully. — **make a fool of** to trick, or cause to appear ridiculous. — **make a fool of oneself** to (allow oneself to) look foolish. — **nobody's fool** too wary to be tricked or deceived. — **play the fool** deliberately to act in a comically foolish manner. [OFr *fol*]
foolery *n* **-ies** stupid or ridiculous behaviour.
foolish *adj* **1** unwise; senseless. **2** ridiculous. — *adv* **foolishly**. — *n* **foolishness**.
foolproof *adj* **1** (of a plan, etc.) unable to go wrong. **2** (of a machine, etc.) unable to be misunderstood or misused; simple to use.
fool's errand *n* a pointless or unprofitable task or venture.
fool's paradise *n* a state of confidence based on false expectations.

fool[2] *n* a dessert of puréed fruit mixed with cream or custard. [Perhaps **fool**[1]]

foolhardy *adj* taking foolish risks; rash; reckless. — *n* **foolhardiness**. [OFr *fol hardi*, foolish-bold]

foolscap *n* a large size of printing- or writing-paper, measuring usu. 17 × 13½ in. (432 × 343 mm). [From the jester's cap used as a watermark]

foot *n* ***feet*** **1** the part of the leg on which a human being or animal stands or walks. **2** the part of a sock, stocking, etc. that fits over the foot. **3** the bottom or lower part of something. **4** the end of a bed where the feet go. **5** (*pl* also **foot**) a measure of length equal to twelve inches (30·48 cm). **6** a unit of rhythm in verse containing any of various combinations of stressed and unstressed syllables. **7** (*pl*; *old*) infantry. — **fall on one's feet** to be unexpectedly or undeservedly lucky. — **foot it 1** (*coll*) to walk. **2** (*old*) to dance. — **foot the bill** to pay the bill. — **get a foot in the door** to break into, or get accepted for the first time in, an organisation, profession or other set-up. — **get off on the wrong foot** to make a bad start. — **get** or **rise to one's feet** to stand up. — **have a foot in both camps** to be connected with both of two opposed parties. — **have one's feet on the ground** to have plenty of common sense. — **have one foot in the grave** (*coll*) to be very old or near death. — **my foot!** (*coll*) used to express derisive disbelief. — **not put a foot wrong**, or **right** to make no, or all possible, mistakes. — **on foot** walking. — **put one's best foot forward** to set off with determination. — **put one's feet up** to take a rest. — **put one's foot down** to be firm about something. — **put one's foot in it** (*coll*) to say or do something embarrassingly silly or tactless. — **set foot in** or **on** to arrive in or on. — **under foot** beneath one's feet. — **under one's feet** in one's way; hindering one.

footage *n* **1** measurement or payment by the foot. **2** the length of exposed cine film measured in feet.

foot-and-mouth disease *n* a contagious viral disease of sheep, cattle, etc. with blistering of the mouth and hoof.

football *n* **1** any of several team games played with a large ball that players try to kick or head into the opposing team's goal or carry across their opponents' goal line. **2** the ball used in the game.

footbridge *n* a bridge for pedestrians.

footfall *n* the sound of a footstep.

foothill *n* a lower hill on the approach to a high mountain or range.

foothold *n* a place to put one's foot when climbing.

footing *n* **1** the stability of one's feet on the ground: *lose one's footing*. **2** basis or status. **3** relationship: *on a friendly footing*.

footlights *n* (*pl*) in a theatre, a row of lights set along the front edge of a stage to illuminate it.

footloose *adj* free to go where, or do as, one likes.

footman *n* a uniformed male attendant.

footnote *n* a note at the bottom of a page.

footpath *n* **1** a path or track for walkers. **2** a pavement.

footplate *n* in a steam train, a platform for the driver and fireman.

footprint *n* the mark or impression of a foot or shoe.

footslog *v* (*intr* & *tr*) to go on foot; to trudge.

footsore *adj* having painful feet from prolonged walking.

footstep *n* **1** the sound of a step in walking. **2** a footprint. — **follow in the footsteps of** to do as was done earlier by; to copy or succeed.

footstool *n* a low stool for supporting the feet while sitting.

footway *n* a passage for pedestrians.

footwear *n* shoes, boots, socks, etc.

footwork *n* the agile use of the feet in dancing or sport.

footsie *n* (*coll*) secret foot-touching with someone under the table, etc., esp. as an indication of sexual interest. [**foot**]

fop *n* a man who is too consciously elegant in his dress and manners; a dandy. — *n* **foppery**, ***-ies*** or **foppishness**. — *adj* **foppish**.

for *prep* **1** intended to be given or sent to. **2** towards: *heading for home*. **3** throughout (a time or distance). **4** in order to have, get, etc.: *meet for a chat*; *fight for freedom*. **5** at a cost of. **6** as reward, payment or penalty appropriate to: *got seven months for stealing*; *charge for one's work*. **7** with a view to: *train for the race*. **8** representing; on behalf of: *the MP for Greenfield*; *speaking for myself*. **9** to the benefit of: *What can I do for you?* **10** in favour of: *for or against the proposal*. **11** proposing to oneself: *I'm for bed*. **12** because of: *couldn't see for tears*. **13** on account of: *famous for its confectionery*. **14** (intended as) suitable to the needs of: *books for children*. **15** having as function or purpose: *scissors for cutting hair*. **16** on the occasion of: *got it for my birthday*. **17** meaning: *the German word for 'lazy'*. **18** in place of; in exchange with: *replacements for the breakages*; *translated word for word*. **19** in proportion to: *one woman for every five men*. **20** up to: *It's for him to decide*. **21** as being: *took you for someone else*; *know for a fact*. **22** with regard to: *can't beat that for quality*. **23** considering what one would expect: *serious for his age*; *warm for winter*. **24** about; aimed at: *proposals for peace*; *a desire for revenge*. **25** in spite of: *quite nice for all his faults*. **26** available to be disposed of or dealt with by: *not for sale*. **27** at or on: *an appointment for 12.00 on Friday*. **28** so as to be starting by: *7.30 for 8.00*. — *conj* because. — **be for it** (*coll*) to be about to receive a punishment, etc. — **for ever** for all time. — **if it hadn't been for** had (someone or something) not intervened. — **O for** if only I had. [OE]

forage *n* **1** food for horses or cattle. **2** the activity of foraging. — *v* **1** (*intr*; **for**) to search around, esp. for food. **2** (*tr*) to gather forage or provisions from (an area). **3** (*tr*) to find by searching. [OFr *fourrage*]

forasmuch as *conj* (*old* or *legal*) since; seeing that.

foray *n* **1** a raid or attack. **2** (**into**) a venture; an attempt (at). [MidE *forrayen*, to pillage]

forbade. See **forbid**.

forbear[1] *v* **-bore**, **-borne** (*tr* & *intr*; **from**) to stop oneself going as far as; to refrain. [OE *forberan*]

forbearance *n* patience and self-control.

forbearing *adj* patient and tolerant.

forbear[2]. Another spelling of **forebear**.

forbid *v* **-dd-**, **-bade** or **-bad**, **-bidden** **1** (*tr*) to order (someone) not to do something. **2** (*tr*) to prohibit. **3** (*tr*) to refuse access to: *had forbidden them the orchard*; *forbidden territory*. **4** (*tr* & *intr*) to prevent or not allow: *Time forbids a longer stay*. [OE *forbeodan*]

forbidding *adj* threatening; grim. — *adv* **forbiddingly**.

forbore, **forborne**. See **forbear**.

force *n* **1** strength; power; impact or impetus. **2** compulsion, esp. with threats or violence. **3** military power. **4** passion or earnestness. **5** strength or validity: *the force of her argument*; *come into force*. **6** meaning. **7** influence: *by force of habit*. **8** a person or thing seen as an influence: *a force for good*. **9** (*physics*) a power causing movement, alteration, etc.: *the force of gravity*. **10** any irresistible power or agency: *the forces of nature*. **11** the term used in specifying wind speed: *a force-10 gale*. **12** a military body; (in *pl*; with **the**) a nation's armed services. **13** any organised body: *a workforce*. **14** (*cap*; with **the**) the police force. — (*tr*) **1** to make or compel. **2** (**back**, **out**, etc.) to drive, esp. meeting resistance. **3** to obtain by effort, strength, threats, violence, etc: *forced an admission from them*. **4** to make (one's way) by effort or ruthless determination. **5** to produce with an effort. **6** to inflict: *force one's opinions on people*. **7** to cause (a plant) to grow or (fruit) to ripen unnaturally quickly. **8** to strain: *force one's voice*. — **force someone's hand** to give someone no alternative. — **in force 1** (of a law, etc.) valid; effective. **2** in large numbers. — **join forces (with)** to come together or unite for a purpose. [OFr, from Lat *fortia*, strength]

forced *adj* **1** (of a smile, laugh, etc.) unnatural; unspontaneous. **2** done or provided under compulsion: *forced labour*. **3** carried out as an emergency: *a forced landing*. **4** done with great and long effort: *forced marches*.

force-feed *v* (*tr*) to force to swallow food.

forceful *adj* powerful; effective; influential. — *adv* **forcefully**. — *n* **forcefulness**.

forcemeat *n* a mixture of sausage meat, herbs, etc. used as stuffing. [From earlier *farce*, stuffing]

forceps *n* (*pl*) a surgical instrument like pincers, for gripping firmly. [Said to be from Lat *formus*, warm + *capere*, to take]

forcible *adj* **1** done by, or involving, force. **2** powerful: *a forcible reminder*. — *adv* **forcibly**. [OFr, from *force*, force]

ford *n* a shallow crossing-place in a river. — *v* (*tr*) to ride, drive or wade across (a stream, etc.). — *adj* **fordable**. [OE]

fore *adj* towards the front. — *n* the front part. — *interj* (*golf*) ball coming! — **fore and aft** at front and rear; at bow and stern; from bow to stern (*adj* **fore-and-aft** pointing to bow and stern). — **to the fore** at or to the front; prominent; conspicuous. [OE]

fore- *pfx* **1** before or beforehand: *forewarn*. **2** in front: *foreleg*. [OE]

forearm[1] *n* the lower part of the arm between wrist and elbow.

forearm[2] *v* (*tr*) to prepare or arm beforehand.

forebear or **forbear** *n* an ancestor. [**fore-** + **be** + **-er**]

forebode *v* (*tr*) to foretell; to be a sign of (esp. something bad).

foreboding *n* a feeling of approaching trouble.

forecast *v* **-cast** or **-casted** (*tr*) to give warning of; to predict; to gauge or estimate (weather, statistics, etc.) in advance. — *n* a warning, prediction or advance estimate. [**cast**[1] (sense **10**)]

forecastle *n* the bow section of a ship, formerly the quarters of the crew.

foreclose *v* (*intr*) (of a bank, etc.) to repossess a property because of failure to pay back the loan used. — *n* **foreclosure**.

forecourt *n* a courtyard or paved area in front of a building, e.g. a filling-station.

forefather *n* an ancestor.

forefinger *n* the finger next to the thumb; the index finger.

forefoot *n* either of the two front feet of a four-legged animal.

forefront *n* **1** the very front. **2** the most prominent or active position.

foregather *v* **-r-** (*intr*) to meet together; to assemble.

forego or **forgo** *v* **-went**, **-gone** (*tr*) to do without; to sacrifice or give up.

foregoing *n* & *adj* (the thing or person) just mentioned.

foregone *adj*: **foregone conclusion** a predictable result; a certainty.

foreground *n* **1** the part of a view or picture nearest to the viewer. **2** a position where one is noticeable.

forehand *n* (*tennis*, etc.) a stroke made with palm facing forward. ◇ See also **backhand** (sense **1**).

forehead *n* the part of the face between the eyebrows and hairline; the brow.

foreign *adj* **1** of, from, relating or belonging to, another country. **2** concerned with relations with other countries: *foreign affairs*. **3** not belonging where found: *a piece of grit or other foreign body in the eye*. **4 (to)** unfamiliar: *The technique was foreign to her*. **5 (to)** uncharacteristic: *Envy was foreign to his nature*.

foreigner *n* **1** a person from another country. **2** an unfamiliar person; a person who doesn't belong.

foreign minister or **secretary** *n* the government minister responsible for a country's foreign affairs.

foreign office *n* the department of a government dealing with foreign affairs.

foreknowledge *n* knowledge about something before it happens.

foreleg *n* either of the two front legs of a four-legged animal.

forelock *n* a lock of hair growing or falling over the brow.

foreman or **forewoman** *n* **1** a man or woman in charge of a body of fellow workers. **2** the spokesman or spokeswoman of a jury.

foremost *adj* leading; best. — *adv* leading; coming first. — **first and foremost** essentially; most importantly. [OE *formest*, from *forma*, first]

forenoon *n* (esp. *Scot*) the morning.

forensic *adj* **1** relating to or belonging to courts of law, or to the work of a lawyer in court. **2** concerned with the scientific side of legal investigations. — *adv* **forensically**. [Lat *forensis*, of the *forum*, where law courts were held in Rome]

foreordain *v* (*tr*) to determine (events, etc.) in advance; to destine.

foreplay *n* sexual stimulation leading up to sexual intercourse.

forerunner *n* **1** a person or thing that goes before; a predecessor; an earlier type or version. **2** a sign of what is to come. **3** an advance messenger or herald.

foresee *v* **-*saw***, **-*seen*** (*tr*) to see or know in advance. — *adj* **foreseeable**.

foreshadow *v* (*tr*) to be an advance sign or indication of.

foreshore *n* the space on the shore between the high and low tide marks.

foreshorten *v* **-*n*-** (*tr*) in photographic or artistic perspective, to give a shortening effect to: *foreshortened limbs*.

foresight *n* **1** the ability to foresee. **2** consideration taken or provision made for the future. **3** the front sight on a gun.

foreskin *n* the skin covering the penis.

forest *n* **1** a dense growth of trees extending over a large area. **2** a tract of country formerly owned, and used for hunting, by a sovereign. **3** a dense arrangement of objects. — *adj* **forested**. [Lat *forestis* (*silva*), unfenced (woodland)]

forestation *n* the planting of trees.

forester *n* a person in charge of a forest or trained in forestry.

forestry *n* **1** the management of forests. **2** the science of growing and caring for trees.

forestall *v* (*tr*) to prevent by acting in advance: *issue an announcement to forestall the inevitable questions*. [MidE *forstallen*, to waylay]

foretaste *n* a brief experience of what is to come.

foretell *v* **-*told*** (*tr*) to tell about beforehand; to predict or prophesy.

forethought *n* consideration taken, or provision made, for the future.

foretold. See **foretell**.

forever *adv* **1** always; eternally. **2** continually: *forever whining*.

forewarn *v* (*tr*) to warn beforehand.

forewoman. See **foreman**.

foreword *n* an introduction to a book, often by a writer other than the author.

forfeit *n* something that one must surrender as a penalty. — *adj* (liable to be) surrendered as a penalty. — *v* (*tr*) **1** to hand over as a penalty: *forfeit one's passport*. **2** to give up or do without voluntarily. — *n* **forfeiture**. [OFr *forfait*, from Lat *forisfactum*, penalty]

forgave. See **forgive**.

forge[1] *n* **1** a furnace for heating metals. **2** a workshop where metal is shaped into horseshoes, tools, etc. — *v* (*tr*) **1** to shape (metal or metal objects) by heating and hammering. **2** to make an imitation of (a signature, document, banknote, etc.) for a dishonest or fraudulent purpose. [OFr, from Lat *fabrica*, workshop]

forge[2] *v* (*intr*) to move steadily. — *v* **forge ahead** (*intr*) **1** to progress swiftly. **2** to take the lead.

forgery *n* **-*ies*** **1** (the crime of) imitating pictures, documents, signatures, etc. for a fraudulent purpose. **2** a copy made for such a purpose. [**forge**[1]]

forget *v* **-*tt*-**, **-*got***, **-*gotten*** **1** (*tr* & *intr*; **about**) to fail to or be unable to remember. **2** (*tr* & *intr*; **about**) to stop being aware of: *forgot his headache in his excitement*. **3** (*tr* & *intr*; **about**) to neglect or overlook (something). **4** (*tr*) to leave behind accidentally. **5** (*tr* & *intr*; **about**; *coll*) to dismiss from one's mind: *You can forget your proposed skiing trip*. **6** (*tr*) to lose control over (oneself). — **forget it** (*coll*) it doesn't matter. — **not forgetting** and also; including. [OE *forgietan*]

forgetful *adj* inclined to forget. — *adv* **forgetfully**. — *n* **forgetfulness**.

forget-me-not *n* a small plant with blue flowers. [Translating OFr *ne m'oubliez mye*]

forgive *v* **-*gave***, **-*given*** (*tr*) **1** to stop being angry with (someone who has done something wrong) or about (an offence). **2** to pardon. **3** to spare (someone) the paying of (a debt). — *adj* **forgivable**. — *adv* **forgivably**. [OE *forgiefan*]

forgiveness *n* **1** the act of forgiving or state of being forgiven. **2** readiness to forgive.

forgiving *adj* ready to forgive; patient and tolerant.

forgot, forgotten. See **forget**.

fork *n* **1** an eating or cooking implement with prongs, for spearing and lifting food. **2** a pronged digging or lifting tool. **3** the (point of) division of a road, etc. into two branches; one such branch. **4** something that divides similarly into two parts, e.g. the wheel support of a bicycle. — *v* **1** (*intr*) (of a road etc.) to divide into two branches. **2** (*intr*) (of a person or vehicle) to follow one such branch: *fork left*. **3** (*tr*) to lift or move with a fork. — *v* **fork out** or **up** (*tr* & *intr*; *coll*) to pay, under pressure rather than voluntarily. [OE *forca*, from Lat *furca*]

forked *adj* **1** dividing into two branches or parts. **2** (of lightning) zigzag.

fork-lift truck *n* a small vehicle equipped with two horizontal prongs that can be raised or lowered to move or stack goods.

forlorn *adj* **1** pathetically unhappy or alone. **2** deserted; forsaken. **3** desperate. — *adj* **forlornly**. — *n* **forlornness**. [OE *forloren*, lost]

forlorn hope 1 *n* a desperate but impractical hope. **2** a hopeless undertaking. [Dut *verloren hoop*, lost troop]

form *n* **1** shape. **2** figure or outward appearance. **3** kind, type, variety or manifestation. **4** a printed document with spaces for the insertion of information. **5** a way, esp. the correct way, of doing or saying something. **6** structure and organisation in a piece of writing or work of art. **7** one's potential level of performance, e.g. in sport: *soon find your form again*. **8** any of the ways that a word can be spelt or grammatically inflected. **9** a school class. **10** a bench. **11** (*slang*) a criminal record. **12** a hare's burrow. — *v* **1** (*tr*; **into**) to (join together to) organise or set up. **2** (*intr*) to come into existence; to take shape. **3** (*tr*) to shape; to make (a shape). **4** (*tr*) to take on the shape or function of. **5** (*tr*) to make up; to constitute. **6** (*tr*) to develop: *form a relationship*. **7** (*tr*) to influence or mould: *the environment that formed him*. **8** (*tr*) to construct, inflect grammatically, or pronounce (a word). — **good** (or **bad**) **form** polite (or impolite) social behaviour. — **in good form** in good spirits or health. — **a matter of form** a case of a procedure being gone through for the sake of legality or convention. — **on** (or **off**) **form** performing well (or badly). — **take form** to come into existence; to begin to have shape. — **true to form** in the usual, typical, or characteristic way. [Lat *forma*, shape, model]

formless *adj* lacking a clear shape or structure. — *adv* **formlessly**. — *n* **formlessness**.

-form *comb fm* **1** having the appearance or structure of: *cuneiform*. **2** in (so many) forms or varieties: *multiform*. [Lat *-formis*]

formal *adj* **1** relating to or involving etiquette, ceremony, or conventional procedure generally: *formal dress*. **2** stiffly polite rather than relaxed and friendly. **3** valid; official; explicit: *a formal agreement, proof*, etc. **4** (of language) strictly correct with regard to grammar, style and choice of words, as distinct from conversational. **5** organised and methodical: *the formal approach to teaching*. **6** precise and symmetrical in design: *a formal garden*. **7** relating to outward form as distinct from content. — *adv* **formally**. [Lat *formalis*]

formalise or **-ize** *v* (*tr*) to make official, e.g. by putting in writing, etc.; to give definite or legal form to. — *n* **formalisation** or **-z-**.

formalism *n* (too much) concern with outward form. — *n* **formalist**.

formality *n* ***-ies*** **1** a procedure gone through as a requirement of etiquette, ceremony, the law, etc. **2** a procedure gone through merely for the sake of correctness or legality: *The interview was a formality, as he knew he would be appointed*. **3** strict attention to the rules of social behaviour.

formaldehyde *n* a pungent, irritating gas used as a preservative and disinfectant. [**formic** + **aldehyde**]

formalin *n* a clear solution of formaldehyde used as a preservative and disinfectant. [**formaldehyde**; orig. a trademark]

format *n* **1** the size and shape of something, esp. a book or magazine. **2** the style in which a television programme etc. is organised and presented. **3** an arrangement of data to suit the input system of a computer. — *v* ***-tt-*** (*tr*) **1** to design, shape or organise in a particular way. **2** to organise (data) for input into a particular computer. **3** to prepare (a disk) so that it is receptive to such data. [Lat *formatus*, shaped (in a certain way)]

formation *n* **1** the process of forming, making, developing or establishing. **2** a particular arrangement, pattern or order. **3** a shape or structure. [Lat *formatio*, shape]

formative *adj* **1** relating to development or growth. **2** having an effect on development. [OFr *formatif*]

former *adj* **1** belonging to an earlier time. **2** previous; earlier. — **the former** the first of two things mentioned. [Comparative of OE *forma*, first, earliest]

formerly *adv* previously; in the past.

Formica® *n* a hard, heat-resistant plastic, used for making easy-to-clean work surfaces in kitchens, laboratories, etc.

formic acid *n* a colourless irritant and corrosive acid produced by ants. [Lat *formica*, ant]

formidable *adj* **1** awesomely impressive. **2** (of problems, etc.) enormous; difficult to overcome. — *adv* **formidably**. [Lat *formidabilis*, causing fear]

formula *n* **-las** or **-lae** **1** the make-up of a chemical compound expressed in symbols. **2** a mathematical rule expressed in figures and letters. **3** the combination of ingredients used in a product, etc. **4** a method or rule of procedure, esp. a successful one. **5** an established piece of wording used e.g. in religion or law. **6** a term used for classifying racing cars acccording to engine size: *Formula 1 racing*. **7** (*NAm*) powdered milk for babies. — *adj* **formulaic**. [Lat, dimin. of *forma*, form]

formulary *n* **-ies** a book or collection of esp. legal or religious formulas. [OFr *formulaire*]

formulate *v* (*tr*) **1** to express in terms of a formula. **2** to express precisely and clearly. — *n* **formulation**. **[formula]**

fornicate *v* (*intr*) to have sexual intercourse outside marriage. — *n* **fornication**. [Lat *fornicari*, from *fornix*, brothel]

forsake *v* **-sook**, **-saken** (*tr*) to desert; to abandon. [OE *forsacan*]

forswear *v* **-swore**, **-sworn** (*tr*; *old*) **1** to give up or renounce (one's foolish ways, etc.). **2** to perjure (oneself). [OE *forswerian*, to swear falsely]

forsythia *n* a shrub with bright yellow flowers that appear before the leaves. [W *Forsyth* (1737–1804), British botanist]

fort *n* a fortified military building, enclosure or position. — **hold the fort** to keep things running in the absence of the person normally in charge. [Lat *fortis*, strong]

forte[1] *n* something one is good at; a strong point. [Fr *fort*, strong]

forte[2] *adj* & *adv* (*mus*) (played) loudly. [Ital]

forth *adv* (mainly *old*) **1** into existence or view: *bring forth children*. **2** forwards: *swing back and forth*. **3** out: *set forth on a journey*. **4** onwards: *from this day forth*. — **and so forth** and so on. — **hold forth** to speak, esp. at length. [OE]

forthcoming *adj* **1** happening or appearing soon. **2** (of a person) willing to talk; communicative. **3** available on request.

forthright *adj* firm, frank, straightforward and decisive. — *n* **forthrightness**. [OE *forthriht*]

forthwith *adv* immediately. **[forth + with]**

fortification *n* **1** the process of fortifying. **2** (in *pl*) walls and other defensive structures built in preparation for an attack. **[fortify]**

fortify *v* **-ies**, **-ied** (*tr*) **1** to strengthen (a building, city, etc.) in preparation for an attack. **2** to add extra alcohol to (wine): *Sherry is a fortified wine*. [Lat *fortis*, strong + *facere*, to make]

fortissimo *adj* & *adv* (played) very loudly. [Ital]

fortitude *n* uncomplaining courage in pain or misfortune. [Lat *fortitudo*, strength]

fortnight *n* a period of 14 days. [OE *feowertiene niht*, fourteen nights]

fortnightly *adj* & *adv* (occurring, appearing, etc.) once every fortnight.

FORTRAN *n* a computer-programming language used in scientific work. **[Formula Translation]**

fortress *n* a fortified town, or large fort or castle. [OFr *forteresse*, from Lat *fortis*, strong]

fortuitous *adj* happening by chance; accidental. — *adv* **fortuitously**. — *n* **fortuitousness**. [Lat *fortuitus*]

fortunate *adj* **1** lucky; favoured by fate. **2** timely; opportune. — *adv* **fortunately**. [Lat *fortunatus*]

fortune *n* **1** chance as a force in human affairs; fate. **2** luck. **3** (in *pl*) unpredictable happenings that swing affairs this way or that: *the fortunes of war*. **4** (in *pl*) the state of one's luck. **5** one's destiny. **6** a large sum of money. — **make one's fortune** to become prosperous. — **a small fortune** a large amount of money. — **tell someone's fortune** to tell someone what his or her destiny is. [Lat *fortuna*]

fortune-teller *n* a person who claims to be able to tell people their destinies.

forty *n* **-ies** **1** the number or figure 40; any symbol for this number. **2** the age of 40. **3** a set of 40 people or things. — *adj* **1** 40 in number. **2** aged 40. — *n*, *adj* & *adv* **fortieth**. [OE *feowertig*]

forties *n* (*pl*) **1** the period of time between one's fortieth and fiftieth birthdays. **2** the range of temperatures between forty and fifty degrees. **3** the period of time between the fortieth and fiftieth years of a century. — **roaring forties** the area of stormy west winds south of latitude 40°S, or north of latitude 40° N in the Atlantic.

forty winks *n* (*pl*; *coll*) a short sleep.

forum *n* **1** (*hist*) a public square or market place, esp. that in ancient Rome where public business was conducted and law courts held. **2** a place, programme or publication where opinions can be aired and discussed. [Lat]

forward *adv* **1** (also **forwards**) in the direction in front or ahead of one. **2** (also **forwards**) progressing from first to last. **3** on or onward; to a later time: *put the clocks forward*. **4** to an earlier time: *bring the wedding forward a month*. **5** into view or public attention: *put forward suggestions*. — *adj* **1** in the direction in front or ahead of one. **2** at the front. **3** advanced in development: *How far forward are the plans?* **4** concerning the future: *forward planning*. **5** (*derog*) inclined to push oneself forward; over-bold in offering one's opinions. — *n* (*football*, *hockey*, etc.) a player whose task is to score rather than defend the goal. — *v* (*tr*) **1** to send (mail) on to another address. **2** to help the progress

of. — *adv* **forwardly**. — *n* **forwardness**. [OE *foreweard*]
forward-looking *adj* planning ahead; progressive, enterprising or go-ahead.

forwent. See **forego**.

fossil *n* **1** the calcified remains of, or the impression left by, an animal or vegetable in rock. **2** a relic of the past. **3** (*coll*) a curiously antiquated person. — *adj* **1** like, or in the form of, a fossil. **2** formed naturally through the decomposition of organic matter, and dug or otherwise got from the earth: *Coal and oil are fossil fuels*. [Lat *fossilis*, dug up]
fossilise or **-ize** *v* (*tr* & *intr*) to change into a fossil or curious relic. — *n* **fossilisation** or **-z-**.

foster *v* **-r-** (*tr*) **1** to bring up (a child that is not one's own). **2** to encourage the development of (ideas, feelings, etc.). — *adj* **1** concerned with, or offering, fostering. **2** (*in cmpds*) in a specified family relationship through fostering rather than by birth: *foster-mother*, *-brother*, etc. [OE *fostrian*, to feed]

fought. See **fight**.

foul *adj* **1** disgusting: *a foul smell*. **2** soiled; filthy. **3** contaminated: *foul air*. **4** (*coll*; **to**) very unkind or unpleasant. **5** (of language) offensive or obscene. **6** unfair or treacherous: *by fair means or foul*. **7** (of weather) stormy. **8** clogged. **9** entangled. — *n* (*sport*) a breach of the rules. — *v* **1** (*intr* & *tr*; *sport*) to commit a foul against (an opponent). **2** (*tr*) to make dirty. **3** (*tr*) to contaminate or pollute. **4** (*tr* & *intr*; **up**) to become entangled, or entangled with. **5** (*tr* with **up**; *coll*) to mess up; to bungle (*n* **foul-up**). **6** (*tr* & *intr*) to clog. — *n* **foulness**. — **fall foul of** to get into trouble or conflict with.
foul-mouthed *adj* using offensive or obscene language.
foul play *n* **1** treachery or criminal violence, esp. murder. **2** (*sport*) a breach of the rules.

found[1]. See **find**.

found[2] *v* **1** (*tr*) to start or establish (an organisation, institution, city, etc.), often with a provision for future funding. **2** (*tr*; **on**, **upon**) to base: *a well-founded argument*. **3** (*tr*) to lay the foundation of (a building). — *n* **founder**. [Lat *fundare*]
foundation *n* **1** the act of founding or establishing an institution, etc.; the institution, etc. founded or the fund providing for it. **2** (usu. in *pl*) the underground structure on which a building is supported. **3** the basis on which a theory, etc. rests or depends. **4** a cream, etc. smoothed into the skin as a base for additional cosmetics.
foundation course *n* an introductory course, usually as a preparation for more advanced studies.
foundation stone *n* a stone laid ceremonially as part of the foundations of a new building.

found[3] *v* **1** (*tr*) to cast (metal or glass) by melting and pouring into a mould. **2** (*tr*) to produce (articles) by this method. ◇ See also **foundry**. [Lat *fundere*, to pour]

founder[1]. See **found**[2].

founder[2] *v* **-r-** (*intr*) **1** (of a ship) to sink. **2** (of a vehicle, etc.) to get stuck in mud, etc. **3** (of a horse) to go lame. **4** (of a business, scheme, etc.) to fail. [OFr *fondrer*, to submerge]

foundling *n* an abandoned child of unknown parents. **[found**[1] + **-ling]**

foundry *n* **-ies** a place where metal or glass is melted and cast. **[found**[3]**]**

fount[1] *n* **1** a spring or fountain. **2** a source (of inspiration, etc.). **[fountain]**

fount[2] *n* (*printing*) a set of printing type of the same design and size. [OFr *fonte*, casting]

fountain *n* **1** (a structure producing) a jet or jets of water for drinking or for ornamental effect. **2** a spring of water. **3** a source (of wisdom, etc.). [OFr *fontaine*, from Lat *fons*, fountain]
fountainhead *n* **1** a spring from which a stream flows. **2** the principal source of something.
fountain pen *n* a metal-nibbed pen equipped with a reservoir of ink.

four *n* **1** the number or figure 4; any symbol for this number. **2** the age of 4. **3** something, esp. a garment, or a person, whose size is denoted by the number 4. **4** 4 o'clock. **5** a set of 4 things or people, e.g. the crew of a 4-oared boat. **6** a playing-card with 4 pips. **7** a score of 4 points. — *adj* **1** 4 in number. **2** aged 4. — *n*, *adj* & *adv* **fourth**. — *adv* **fourthly**. — **on all fours** on hands and knees. [OE *feower*]
fourfold *adj* **1** equal to four times as much. **2** divided into or consisting of four parts. — *adv* by four times as much.
four-letter word *n* any of several short words referring to sex or excretions, usu. considered offensive.
four-poster *n* a large bed with a post at each corner to support curtains and a canopy.
fourscore *adj* & *n* eighty.
foursome *n* **1** a set of four people. **2** (*golf*) a game between two pairs.
four-square *adj* **1** strong; steady; solidly based. **2** (of a building) square and solid-looking. — *adv* steadily; squarely.
fourth dimension *n* time, as opposed to the dimensions of length, breadth and height. **2** in science fiction, etc. a mysterious extra dimension.

fourteen *n* **1** the number or figure 14; any symbol for this number. **2** the age of 14. **3** something, esp. a garment, or a person, whose size is denoted by the number 14. **4** a set of 14 people or things. — *adj* **1** 14 in number. **2** aged 14. — *n*, *adj* & *adv* **fourteenth**. [OE *feowertiene*]

fowl *n* ***fowls*** or ***fowl*** **1** a farmyard bird, e.g. a chicken or turkey. **2** (*old* or *in cmpds*) any bird, esp. if eaten as meat or hunted as game: *wildfowl*. — *v* (*intr*) to hunt or trap wild birds. — *n* **fowler**. [OE *fugel*, bird]

fox *n* **1** a dog-like wild animal with a bushy tail, esp. the reddish-brown variety found in Europe and N America. **2** its fur. **3** (*coll*) a cunning person. — *v* **1** (*tr*) to puzzle, confuse or baffle. **2** (*tr*) to deceive, trick or outwit. **3** (*tr* & *intr*) to (cause paper to) become discoloured with brown spots. [OE]

foxglove *n* a tall wild plant with hanging purple or white thimble-shaped flowers.

foxhole *n* a hole in the ground from which a soldier may shoot while protected from the enemy's guns.

foxhound *n* a breed of dog trained to chase foxes.

foxhunting *n* the sport of hunting foxes on horseback, with a pack of foxhounds.

fox terrier *n* a breed of dog orig. trained to drive foxes out of their holes.

foxtrot *n* (a piece of music for) a ballroom dance with gliding steps, alternating between quick and slow. — *v* **-tt-** (*intr*) to perform this dance.

foxy *adj* **-ier**, **-iest** **1** like a fox. **2** (*NAm coll*) (of a woman) sexually attractive. **3** cunning; sly. — *adj* **foxily**. — *n* **foxiness**.

foyer *n* **1** the entrance hall of a theatre, hotel, etc. **2** (*NAm*) the hallway of a house or apartment. [Fr, *fireplace*]

FP *abbrev* **1** former pupil. **2** fire plug, i.e. a hydrant.

Fr[1] *abbrev* **1** Father, as the title of a priest. **2** (also **fr**) franc. **3** French. **4** Friday.

Fr[2] *symbol* (*chem*) francium.

fracas *n* **-cas** a noisy quarrel; a fight or brawl. [Fr]

fraction *n* **1** a numerical quantity that is not a whole number, e.g. 0·25 or $\frac{1}{4}$, or $\frac{22}{7}$. **2** a portion; a small part. **3** (*chem*) an ingredient separated from a mixture by distillation. — *adj* **fractional**. — *adv* **fractionally**. ◇ See also **improper**, **proper**, **vulgar**. [Lat *fractio*, breaking]

fractious *adj* inclined to quarrel and complain. — *adv* **fractiously**. — *n* **fractiousness**. [*fraction*, with its earlier meaning of rupture or dissension]

fracture *n* a break in anything hard, esp. bone. — *v* (*tr* & *intr*) to break. [Lat *fractura*]

fragile *adj* **1** easily broken. **2** easily damaged or destroyed. **3** delicate: *fragile beauty*. **4** in a weakened state of health. — *n* **fragility**. [Lat *fragilis*, breakable]

fragment *n* **1** a piece broken off; a small piece of something that has broken. **2** something incomplete; a small part remaining. — *v* (*tr* & *intr*) to break into pieces. — *n* **fragmentation**. [Lat *fragmentum*]

fragmentary *adj* consisting of small pieces, not usu. amounting to a complete whole. — *adv* **fragmentarily**. — *n* **fragmentariness**.

fragrant *adj* having a pleasant smell. — *adv* **fragrantly**. [Lat *fragrare*, to give out a smell]

fragrance *n* **1** sweetness of smell. **2** a scent or odour.

frail *adj* **1** easily broken or destroyed; delicate; fragile. **2** in poor health; weak. **3** morally weak; easily tempted.— *n* **frailness**. [OFr *fraile*, from Lat *fragilis*, fragile]

frailty *n* **-ies** **1** physical or moral weakness. **2** a moral failing or weakness.

frame *n* **1** a hard main structure round which something is built or to which other parts are added. **2** a structure that surrounds and supports. **3** something that surrounds: *her face with its frame of dark hair*. **4** a body, esp. a human one, as a structure of a certain size and shape: *eased his tall frame into the chair*. **5** one of the pictures that make up a strip of film. **6** a single television picture. **7** one of the pictures in a comic strip. **8** a glass structure for protecting young plants growing out of doors. **9** a framework of bars for some purpose. **10** (*snooker*) a triangular structure for confining the balls at the start of a round; a round. — *v* (*tr*) **1** to put a frame round. **2** to be a frame for. **3** to compose or design. **4** (*coll*) to dishonestly direct suspicion for a crime, etc. at (someone innocent). [OE *framian*, to benefit]

frame of mind *n* a mood.

frame of reference *n* **1** a set of facts, beliefs or principles on the basis of which one can form opinions, make decisions, etc. **2** (*math*) a set of three geometrical axes for defining position in space.

frame-up *n* (*coll*) a plot to make an innocent person appear guilty.

framework *n* **1** a basic supporting structure. **2** a basic plan or system. **3** a structure composed of horizontal and vertical bars or shafts.

franc *n* the standard unit of currency in France, Belgium, Switzerland and several other French-speaking countries. [OFr *Francorum rex*, king of the Franks, the inscription on the first such coins]

franchise *n* **1** the right to vote, esp. in a parliamentary election. **2** a right, privilege, exemption from a duty, etc., granted to a person or organisation. **3** an agreement by which a business company gives someone the right to market its products in an area; the area concerned. — *v* (*tr*) to grant a franchise to. [OFr *franchir*, to set free]

Franciscan *n* a member of a Christian order of nuns and friars founded by St Francis of Assisi. — *adj* of or relating to this order. [Lat *Franciscus*, Francis]

francium *n* a metallic, radioactive element (symbol **Fr**). [Discovered in *France*]

Franco- *comb fm* France and French people: *Franco-German*. [Lat *Francus*, Frank]

francophone *n* a French-speaking person, esp. in a country where other languages are spoken. [**Franco-** + Gr *phone*, voice]

Frank *n* a member of a Germanic people that invaded Gaul in the late 5th century AD. [OE *Franca*]

Frankish *adj* of the Franks or their language. — *n* the W Germanic language of the Franks.

frank *adj* **1** open and honest in speech or manner. **2** bluntly outspoken. **3** undisguised; openly visible. — *v* (*tr*) to mark (a letter) to show that postage has been paid. — *n* a franking mark. — *adv* **frankly**. — *n* **frankness**. [Lat *francus*, free]

Frankenstein *n* (also, correctly, **Frankenstein's monster**) a name for a creation or creature that destroys its creator. [Baron *Frankenstein* in Mary Shelley's novel, the creator of a destructive monster]

frankfurter *n* a type of spicy smoked sausage. [Ger *Frankfurter Wurst*, Frankfurt sausage]

frankincense *n* a resin obtained from E African or Arabian trees, burnt to produce a sweet smell, esp. during religious ceremonies. [OFr *franc encens*, pure incense]

Frankish. See **Frank**.

frantic *adj* **1** desperate, e.g. with fear or anxiety. **2** hurried; rushed: *a frantic rush to meet the deadline*. — *adv* **frantically**. [OFr *frenetique*, from Gr *phrenetikos*, mad]

fraternal *adj* **1** of, or relating to, a brother; brotherly. **2** (of twins) developed from separate ova; not identical. — *adv* **fraternally**. [Lat *fraternus*, from *frater*, brother]

fraternise or **-ize** *v* (*intr*; **with**) to meet or associate together as friends. — *n* **fraternisation** or **-z-**. [Lat *fraternus*, brotherly]

fraternity *n* **-ies** **1** a religious brotherhood. **2** a group of people with common interests. **3** the fact of being brothers; brotherly feeling. **4** (*NAm*) a social club for male students. ◇ See also **sorority**. [Lat *fraternitas*, from *frater*, brother]

fratricide *n* **1** the murder of a brother. **2** a person who murders his or her brother. — *adj* **fratricidal**. [Lat *frater*, brother + *caedere*, to kill]

fraud *n* **1** (an act of) deliberate deception. **2** someone who pretends to be something that he or she is not. [Lat *fraus*, trick]

fraudulent *adj* involving deliberate deception; intended to deceive. — *n* **fraudulence**. — *adv* **fraudulently**. [Lat *fraudulentus*, from *fraus*, trick]

fraught *adj* **1** (with **with**) full of (danger, difficulties, problems, etc.). **2** (*coll*) causing or feeling anxiety or worry. [Dut *vracht*, freight]

fray[1] *v* (*intr* & *tr*) **1** (of cloth or rope) to wear away along an edge or at a point of friction, so that the threads come loose. **2** (of tempers, nerves, etc.) to make or become edgy and strained. [Fr *frayer*, from Lat *fricare*, to rub]

fray[2] *n* **1** a fight, quarrel or argument. **2** any scene of lively action. [**affray**]

frazzle *n* a state of nervous and physical exhaustion. — *v* (*tr*) to tire out physically and emotionally.

freak *n* **1** a person or animal of abnormal shape. **2** someone or something odd or unusual. **3** someone highly enthusiastic about something. **4** a drug addict: *an acid freak*. **5** a whim or caprice: *a freak of fancy*. — *adj* abnormal. — *v* (*intr* & *tr*; **out**) to put, or get, into a state of esp. drug-induced mental excitement. — *adj* **freakish** or **freaky**, **-ier**, **-iest**.

freckle *n* a small brown mark on the skin, esp. of fair-skinned people. — *v* (*tr* & *intr*) to mark, or become marked, with freckles. — *adj* **freckly**, **-ier**, **-iest**. [Norse *freknur*, freckles]

free *adj* ***freer***, ***freest*** **1** allowed to move as one pleases; not shut in. **2** not tied or fastened. **3** allowed to do as one pleases; not restricted, controlled, or enslaved. **4** (of a country) independent. **5** costing nothing. **6** open or available to all. **7** not working, busy, engaged or having another appointment. **8** not occupied; not being used. **9** (**of**, **from**) without; not, or no longer, having or suffering (esp. something harmful, unpleasant or not wanted). **10** (**with**) generous, lavish or liberal. **11** (of a translation) not precisely literal. **12** smooth and easy: *free and relaxed body movement*. **13** without obstruction: *given free passage*. **14** (*derog*) (of manner) disrespectful, overfamiliar or presumptuous. **15** (*chem*) not combined with anything. — *adv* **1** without payment: *free of charge*. **2** without restriction: *wander free*. — *v* (*tr*; **of**, **from**) **1** to make free; to release. **2** to rid or relieve of something. — *adv* **freely**. — **feel free** you have permission (to do something). — **for free** (*coll*) without payment. — **free and easy** (**about**) cheerfully casual or tolerant. — **a free hand** scope to choose how best to act. — **it's a free country** (*coll*) there's no objection to acting in the way mentioned. — **make free with** to make too much, or unacceptable, use of (something not one's own). [OE *freo*]

freeboard *n* the distance between the top edge of the side of a boat and the surface of the water.

-free *in cmpds* **1** not paying: *rent-free*. **2** not having; not affected or troubled by: *fat-free*; *pain-free*.

freeborn *adj* born as a free citizen, not a slave.

freebooter see separate entry.

Free Church *n* any Protestant church in England and Wales other than the Church of England and the Church in Wales.

freedman or **-woman** *n* a freed slave.

freedom *n* **1** the condition of being free to act, move, etc. without restriction. **2** liberty or independence. **3** a right or liberty: *freedom of speech*. **4** (**from**) the state of being without, or exempt from, something: *freedom from pain*. **5** (**of**) unrestricted access to or use of: *give someone the* *freedom of one's house*. **6** honorary citizenship of a place, entitling one to certain privileges. **7** frankness; candour. **8** overfamiliarity; presumptuous behaviour.

free enterprise *n* business done without government interference or control.

free fall *n* **1** the fall of something acted on by gravity alone. **2** the part of a parachute jump before the parachute opens out. — *n* **free-falling**.

free-for-all *n* a fight, argument or discussion in which everybody feels free to join.

freehand *adj* & *adv* (of a drawing, etc.) (done) without the help of a ruler, compass, etc.

freehold *adj* (of land, property, etc.) belonging to the owner for life and without limitations. — *n* ownership of such land, property, etc. — *n* **freeholder**. ◇ See also **leasehold**.

free house *n* a hotel or bar not owned by a particular beer-producer and therefore free to sell a variety of beers.

free kick *n* (*football*) a kick allowed to one side with no tackling from the other, as a penalty to the latter.

freelance *n* a self-employed person offering his or her services where needed, not under contract to any single employer. — *adj* & *adv* of, or as, a freelance. — *v* (*intr*) to work as a freelance. — *n* **freelancer**. [Term for a mercenary mediaeval soldier, first used by Sir Walter Scott]

freeload *v* (*intr*; **off**, **on**) to eat, live, enjoy oneself, etc. at the expense of someone else. — *n* **freeloader**.

free love *n* the practice of having sexual relations with people regardless of marriage.

freeman *n* a respected person who has been granted the freedom of a city.

Freemason *n* (also **Mason**) a member of an international secret male society, having among its purposes mutual help and brotherly fellowship. — *n* **Freemasonry**.

free pardon *n* an unconditional pardon given, e.g. as a result of fresh evidence, to someone convicted of a crime.

free-range *adj* **1** (of hens) moving about freely; not kept in a battery. **2** (of eggs) laid by such hens.

free speech *n* the right to express any opinion freely.

free-standing *adj* not attached to, or supported by, a wall or other structure.

freestyle *n* & *adj* (a competition or race) allowing competitors freedom to choose their own style or programme. — *n* crawl, as the swimming-stroke commonly used in freestyle races.

freethinker *n* someone who forms his or her own, esp. religious, ideas, rather than accepting the view of an authority.

free trade *n* trade with foreign countries without customs, taxes, etc.

free verse *n* poetry with no regular pattern of rhyme, rhythm or line length.

freeway *n* (*US*) a motorway.

freewheel *v* (*intr*) **1** to travel, usu. downhill, on a bicycle, in a car, etc. without using mechanical power. **2** to act or drift about unhampered by responsibilities.

free will *n* **1** the power of making choices that humans are generally believed to have. **2** independent, unforced choice: *left of his own free will*.

Free World *n* (**the**) formerly, the name used by non-communist countries for themselves.

freebie *n* (*coll*) something given or provided without charge. [**free**]

freebooter *n* (*hist*) a pirate. [Dut *vrijbuiter*, from *vrij*, free + *buit*, booty]

freesia *n* a plant of the iris family, grown from bulbs, with sweet-smelling trumpet-shaped flowers. [F H T *Freese*, H T *Frees* (German physicians), or E M *Fries*, Swedish botanist]

freeze *v* ***froze***, ***frozen*** **1** (*tr* & *intr*) to turn into ice or solidify as a result of cold. **2** (*tr* & *intr*; **over**) to cover or become covered with ice. **3** (*intr* & *tr*; **up**) to become blocked up or stop operating because of frost or ice. **4** (*tr* & *intr* with **to**, **together**) to (cause to) be stuck together with, by frost. **5** (*intr*) (of the weather, temperature, etc.) to be at or below freezing-point. **6** (*tr* & *intr*; *coll*) to be or make very cold: *frozen hands*. **7** (*intr*) to die of cold: *freeze to death*. **8** (*tr* & *intr*) (of food) to preserve, or be suitable for preserving, by refrigeration at below freezing-point. **9** (*tr* & *intr*) to (cause to) become motionless or unable to move, because of fear, etc. **10** (*tr*) to fix (prices, wages, etc.) at a certain level. **11** (*tr*) to prevent (money, shares, etc.) from being used. **12** to stop (a moving film) at a certain frame. — *n* **1** (also **freeze-up**) a period of very cold weather with temperatures below freezing-point. **2** a period of government control of wages, prices, etc. — *v* **freeze out** (*tr*) to exclude (someone) from an activity, conversation, etc. by persistent unfriendliness or unresponsiveness. [OE *freosan*]

freezer *n* a refrigerated cabinet or compartment in which to preserve food at below freezing-point.

freeze-dry *v* (*tr*) to preserve (e.g. food) by freezing it and drying it quickly in a vacuum.

freezing-point *n* **1** (also **freezing**) the freezing-point of water. **2** the temperature at which any particular liquid becomes solid.

freight *n* **1** transport of goods by rail, road, sea or air. **2** the goods so transported. **3** the cost of such transport. — *v* (*tr*) **1** to transport (goods) by freight. **2** to load with goods for transport. [ODut *vrecht*]

freighter *n* a ship or aircraft that carries cargo rather than passengers.

freightliner *n* a train designed for the rapid transport of goods.

French *adj* **1** belonging to France or its inhabitants. **2** relating to the language French. — *n* **1** the Romance language spoken in France, parts of Belgium and Switzerland, and elsewhere. **2** (*pl*; with **the**) the people of France.
French bean *n* a kind of green bean of which the pod and its contents are eaten.
French bread *n* white bread in the form of long narrow loaves.
French Canadian *n* a native of the French-speaking part of Canada. — *adj* **French-Canadian**.
French chalk *n* a form of the mineral talc used to mark cloth or remove grease marks.
French dressing *n* a salad dressing made from oil, spices and lemon juice or vinegar.
French fries *n* (*pl*) chips.
French horn see **horn**.
French leave *n* leave taken without permission from work or duty.
French letter *n* (*slang*) a condom.
Frenchman or **Frenchwoman** *n* a man or woman of French nationality.
French polish *n* a varnish for furniture. — *v* **French-polish** (*tr*).
French windows *n* (*pl*) a pair of glass doors that open on to a garden, balcony, etc.

frenetic *adj* frantic, distracted, hectic or wildly energetic. — *adv* **frenetically**. [OFr *frenetique*, from Gr *phrenitis*, delirium]

frenzy *n* **-*ies*** **1** a state of violent mental disturbance. **2** wild agitation or excitement. **3** a frantic burst of activity. — *adj* **frenzied**. [Gr *phrenesis*, madness]

frequency *n* **-*ies*** **1** the condition of happening often. **2** the rate at which a happening, phenomenon, etc., recurs. **3** (*radio, electr*) the number of times a function such as a vibration, alternation or wave repeats itself in a given time. **4** (*radio*) the particular rate of waves per second at which a particular signal is sent out. [Lat *frequens*, happening often]
frequency distribution *n* (*statistics*) the arrangement of data to show the frequency of an occurrence, etc. in relation to e.g. density of population or other relevant statistic.
frequency modulation *n* (*radio*) the variation of the frequency of a signal-carrying wave in relation to the amplitude of the signal.
frequent *adj* **1** recurring at short intervals. **2** habitual. — *v* (*tr*) to visit or attend often. — *adv* **frequently**.

fresco *n* **-*oes*** or **-*os*** a picture painted on a wall, usu. while the plaster is still damp. [Ital, fresh]

fresh *adj* **1** newly made, gathered, etc. **2** (**from**) having just arrived from somewhere, just finished doing something or just had some experience, etc.: *fresh from university*. **3** other or another; different; clean: *a fresh sheet of paper*. **4** new; additional: *fresh supplies*. **5** original: *a fresh approach*. **6** (of fruit or vegetables) not tinned, frozen, preserved, etc. **7** not tired; bright and alert. **8** cool; refreshing: *a fresh breeze*. **9** (of air) cool and uncontaminated. **10** (of water) not salt. **11** (of the face or complexion) youthfully healthy; ruddy. **12** (*coll*) (of behaviour) offensively informal. — *adv* recently; newly: *fresh-baked bread*. — *adv* **freshly**. — *n* **freshness**. [OE *fersc*, fresh, not salt]
freshen *v* **-*n*-** **1** (*tr*) to make fresh or fresher. **2** (*intr* & *tr* with **up**) to get washed and tidy; to wash and tidy (oneself). **3** (*intr*) (of wind) to get stronger.
fresher or **freshman** *n* a first-year college or university student.
freshwater *adj* found in rivers or lakes, not in the sea.

freshet *n* **1** a stream of fresh water flowing into the sea. **2** the sudden overflow of a river. [Dimin., from **fresh**]

fret[1] *v* **-*tt*-** **1** (*intr*) to worry, esp. unnecessarily; to show or express anxiety. **2** (*tr*) to worry or agitate. **3** (*tr*) to wear away or consume by rubbing or erosion. [OE *fretan*, to gnaw]
fretful *adj* anxious and unhappy; tending to fret. — *adv* **fretfully**. — *n* **fretfulness**.

fret[2] *n* any of the narrow metal ridges across the neck of a guitar or similar musical instrument.

fret[3] *n* an ornamental repeated pattern used as a border, etc. — *v* **-*tt*-** (*tr*) to decorate with a fret, or carve with fretwork. [OFr *frete*, interlaced design]
fretsaw *n* a narrow-bladed saw for cutting designs in wood or metal.
fretwork *n* decorative carved openwork in wood or metal.

Freudian *adj* relating to the ideas of the Austrian psychoanalyst Sigmund *Freud* (1856–1939).
Freudian slip *n* a slip of the tongue taken as revealing an unexpressed thought.

Fri. *abbrev* Friday.

friable *adj* easily broken; easily reduced to powder. — *n* **friability**. [Lat *friare*, to crumble]

friar *n* a member of any of various religious orders who, esp. formerly, worked as teachers of the Christian religion and lived by begging. [OFr *frere*, brother]
friar's balsam *n* a strong-smelling compound of benzoin, used as an inhalant.
friary *n* **-*ies*** (*hist*) a building inhabited by a community of friars.

fricassee *n* a cooked dish usu. of pieces of meat or chicken served in a sauce. [OFr *fricasser*, to cook chopped food in its own juice]

fricative *adj* & *n* (being or denoting) a consonant produced partly by friction, the breath being forced through a narrowed opening. [Lat *fricare*, to rub]

friction *n* **1** the rubbing of one thing against another. **2** the resistance met with by an object that is moving against another or through liquid or gas. **3** quarrelling; disagreement; conflict. — *adj* **frictional**. [Lat *frictio*, from *fricare*, to rub]

Friday *n* the sixth day of the week. [OE *Frigedæg*, (the goddess) Frig's day]

fridge *n* (*coll*) a refrigerator.

friend *n* **1** someone whom one knows and likes. **2** (**to, of**) someone who gives support or help: *a friend of the poor*. **3** an ally as distinct from an enemy. **4** a person or thing already encountered or mentioned: *our old friend the woodworm*. **5** (*cap*) a member of the Religious Society of Friends; a Quaker. **6** a member of an organisation giving voluntary financial support to an institution, etc.: *Friends of the National Gallery*. — *adj* **friendless**. — **be** or **make friends (with)** to be, or become, a friend of. [OE *freond*]

friendly *adj* **-ier, -iest 1** (**to, towards**) kind; behaving as a friend. **2** (**with**) on close or affectionate terms. **3** relating to, or typical of, a friend. **4** being a colleague, helper, partner, etc. rather than an enemy: *friendly nations*. **5** (*sport*) (of a match, etc.) played as between friends rather than with the aim of gaining points, etc. — *n* **-ies** a friendly match. — *n* **friendliness**.

-friendly (*in cmpds*) made easy for (the person for whom it is intended, etc.): *user-friendly*.

friendly society *n* an organisation giving support to members in sickness and old age, in return for regular contributions.

friendship *n* **1** the having and keeping of friends. **2** a particular relationship between two friends.

frier. Another spelling of **fryer**.

Friesian *n* one of a breed of black and white cattle from Friesland in NW Netherlands. [Variant of **Frisian**]

frieze *n* **1** a decorative strip running along a wall. **2** (*archit*) a horizontal band between the cornice and capitals of a classical temple, or the sculpture filling it. [OFr *frise*]

frigate *n* **1** a naval escort vessel, smaller than a destroyer. **2** (*hist*) a small fast-moving sailing warship. [OFr *fregate*]

fright *n* **1** sudden fear; a shock. **2** (*coll*) a person or thing of ludicrous appearance. — **take fright** to become scared. [OE *fyrhto*]

frighten *v* (*tr*) **1** to make afraid. **2** (with **away, off**) to scare away. **3** (**into, out of**) to persuade by threats.

frightened *adj* (**of**) afraid.

frightful *adj* **1** ghastly; frightening. **2** (*coll*) bad; awful. **3** (*coll*) great; extreme. — *n* **frightfulness**.

frightfully *adv* (*coll*) very.

frigid *adj* **1** cold and unfriendly. **2** (of a woman) not sexually responsive, esp. to sexual intercourse. **3** (*geog*, etc.) intensely cold. — *n* **frigidity**. [Lat *frigidus*, cold]

frill *n* **1** a gathered or pleated strip of cloth attached along one edge to a garment, etc. as a trimming. **2** (usu. in *pl*) something extra serving no very useful purpose. — *adj* **frilly, -ier, -iest**.

fringe *n* **1** a border of loose threads on a carpet, tablecloth, garment, etc. **2** hair cut to hang down over the forehead. **3** the outer area; the edge; the part farthest from the main area or centre. **4** (the area of activity of) people who have moved away from the conventional practices of their group, profession, etc.: *fringe medicine*. — *v* (*tr*) **1** to decorate with a fringe. **2** to form a fringe round. [OFr *frenge*, from Lat *fimbriae*, threads, fringe]

fringe benefits *n* (*pl*) things that one gets from one's employer in addition to wages or salary, e.g. a house, a car, etc.

frippery *n* or **fripperies** *n* (*pl*) showy and unnecessary finery or adornment. [OFr *freperie*, from *frepe*, a rag]

Frisbee® *n* a light plastic saucer-shaped object that spins when thrown, used for playing games with. [Perhaps from the surname *Frisbie*]

Frisian *n* **1** the language of Friesland in NW Netherlands. **2** a native of Friesland. — *adj* belonging or relating to Friesland, its people or their language. ◇ See also **Friesian**. [Lat *Frisii*, a tribe of NW Germany]

frisk *v* **1** (*intr*) to jump or run about happily. **2** (*tr*; *slang*) to search (a person) for e.g. weapons or drugs. — *n* **1** a spell of prancing about. **2** an act of searching a person for weapons, etc. [OFr *frisque*, lively]

frisky *adj* **-ier, -iest** lively; playful. — *adv* **friskily**. — *n* **friskiness**.

frisson *n* a shiver (of fear or excitement). [Fr]

fritter[1] *n* a piece of meat, fruit, etc. coated in batter and fried. [Fr *friture*]

fritter[2] *v* **-r-** (*tr*; **away**) to waste (time, money, etc.) on trifles. [From earlier *fitter*, fragment]

frivolous *adj* **1** silly; not sufficiently serious. **2** trifling or unimportant, not useful and sensible. — *n* **frivolity**. — *adv* **frivolously**. [Lat *frivolus*]

frizz *n* a mass of tight curls. — *v* (*tr* & *intr*) to (cause to) form a frizz. — *adj* **frizzy, -ier, -iest**. [Fr *friser*, to curl, or from **frizzle**[2]]

frizzle[1] *v* (*tr* & *intr*) (of food) to fry till scorched and brittle.

frizzle[2] *v* (*tr*) to frizz (hair). — *n* **1** a curl. **2** a frizz. [Perhaps related to OE *fris*, curly]

fro *adv* (*old*) back or from, as in **to and fro**, forwards and backwards. [Norse *fra*, from]

frock *n* **1** a woman's or girl's dress. **2** a priest's or monk's long garment. **3** a loose smock. [OFr *froc*, monk's garment]

frock-coat *n* (*hist*) a man's knee-length coat, close-fitting round the waist.

frog[1] *n* **1** a small tailless web-footed amphibious animal with long powerful hind legs adapted for jumping. **2** (*offensive coll*) a French person. — **a frog in one's throat** an accumulation of phlegm on the vocal cords that interferes with one's speech. [OE *frogga*]

frogman *n* an underwater swimmer wearing a protective rubber suit and using breathing equipment.

frog-march *v* (*tr*) **1** to force (someone) forward, holding him or her firmly by the arms. **2** to carry in a face-downward position. — *n* a face-downward carrying position, with all four limbs held.

frogspawn *n* a mass of frog's eggs encased in protective jelly.

frog[2] *n* a decorative looped fastener on a garment.

frogging *n* a set of such fasteners e.g. on a military uniform.

frog[3] *n* a triangular horny pad in a horse's hoof.

frolic *v* **-ck-** (*intr*) to frisk or run about playfully. — *n* **1** a spell of happy playing or frisking. **2** something silly done as a joke. — *adj* **frolicsome**. [Dut *vrolijk*, merry]

from *prep* indicating **1** a starting-point in place or time: *from London to Glasgow*; *crippled from birth*. **2** a lower limit: *tickets from £12 upwards*. **3** repeated progression: *trail from shop to shop*. **4** movement out of: *took a letter from the drawer*. **5** distance away: *16 miles from Dover*. **6** a viewpoint: *can see the house from here*. **7** separation; removal: *took it away from her*. **8** point of attachment: *hanging from a nail*. **9** exclusion: *omitted from the sample*. **10** source or origin: *made from an old curtain*. **11** change of condition: *translate from French into English*; *From being a close friend, she turned into an enemy*. **12** cause: *ill from overwork*. **13** deduction as a result of observation: *see from her face she's angry*. **14** distinction: *can't tell one twin from the other*. **15** prevention, protection, exemption, immunity, release, escape, etc.: *safe from harm*; *excused from attending*; *exempted from tax*; *released from prison*. [OE *fram*]

frond *n* a long feathery leaf of a fern or palm. [Lat *frons*]

front *n* **1** the side or part of anything that is furthest forward or nearest to the viewer; the most important side or part, e.g. the side of a building where the main door is. **2** any side of a large or historic building. **3** the part of a vehicle or vessel that faces, or is closest to, the direction in which it moves. **4** the auditorium of a theatre, etc. **5** the cover or first pages of a book. **6** a road in a town that runs beside the sea. **7** in war, the area where the soldiers are nearest to the enemy. **8** a matter of concern or interest: *no progress on the job front*. **9** (*meteorol*) the leading edge of a mass of warm or cold air. **10** an outward appearance. **11** (usu. *cap*) a name given to some political movements. **12** (*slang*) an organisation or job used to hide illegal or secret activity. — *v* **1** (*tr* & *intr*; **on, on to, towards**) (of a building) to have its front facing or beside (e.g. a road). **2** (*tr*) to be the leader or representative of (a group, etc.). **3** (*tr*) to be the presenter of (a radio or television programme). **4** (*intr* with **for**) to provide a front (sense **12**) for. **5** (*tr*; usu. in *passive*; **with**) to cover the front of (a building, etc.): *fronted with grey stone*. — *adj* situated, formed, etc. at the front. — **in front** on the forward-facing side; ahead. — **in front of 1** at or beyond the front of. **2** to a place towards which a vehicle, etc. is moving: *ran in front of a car*. **3** ahead of: *pushed in front of her*. **4** confronting: *stand up in front of an audience*. **5** in the presence of: *daren't say so in front of my mother*. — **out front** (*coll*) in the audience, from the performer's standpoint. — **up front** (*coll*) (of money) paid before work is done or goods received, etc. [Lat *frons*, forehead]

frontbencher *n* in the UK, Australia, etc., a member of Parliament holding an official position in the government or the opposition. ◇ See also **backbencher**. — *adj* **frontbench**.

front line *n* **1** that area in any concern where the important pioneering work is going on. **2** in a war, the area where soldiers are closest to the enemy.

front man *n* **1** the leader or representative of an organisation. **2** the presenter of a radio or television programme.

front-page *adj* (important enough to be) on the front page of a newspaper.

front-runner *n* the person most likely to win a competition, etc.

frontage *n* the front of a building, esp. in relation to the street, etc. along which it extends. **[front]**

frontal *adj* **1** relating to the front. **2** aimed at the front; direct: *a frontal assault*. **3** (*anat*) relating to the forehead. **[front**; sense **3** from Lat *frontalis*, from *frons*, forehead]

frontal system *n* the leading edge of a weather front.

frontier *n* **1** a boundary between countries. **2** (in *pl*) limits: *the frontiers of knowledge*. **3** (esp. *NAm hist*) the furthest edge of civilisation, habitation or cultivation, beyond which the country is wild and deserted. [OFr, from *front*, opposite side]

frontispiece *n* a picture at the beginning of a book, facing the title page. [Lat *frons*, front + *specere*, to see]

frost *n* **1** frozen water vapour forming patterns on glass and a white powdery deposit on other surfaces. **2** an air temperature below freezing-point: *12 degrees of frost*. — *v* **1** (*tr* & *intr*; **over, up**) to cover, or become covered, with frost. **2** (*tr*) to damage (plants) with frost. [OE]

frostbite *n* the destruction of bodily tissues by freezing. — *adj* **frostbitten**.

frosted *adj* (of glass) patterned or roughened as though with frost, so as to be difficult to see through.

frosting *n* (*NAm*) cake icing.

frosty *adj* **-ier**, **-iest 1** covered with frost. **2** cold enough for frost to form. **3** (of behaviour or attitude) cold; unfriendly. — *adv* **frostily**. — *n* **frostiness**.

froth *n* **1** a mass of tiny bubbles forming e.g. on the surface of a liquid, or round the mouth in certain diseases. **2** writing, talk, etc. that has no serious content or purpose. **3** showy glamour. — *v* (*intr* & *tr*) to (cause to) produce froth. — *adj* **frothy**, **-ier**, **-iest**. [Norse *frotha*]

frown *v* (*intr*) **1** to wrinkle one's forehead and draw one's eyebrows together in worry, disapproval, deep thought, etc. **2** (with **on**, **at**) to disapprove of: *frown on smoking*. — *n* a disapproving expression or glance. — *adv* **frowningly**. [OFr *froignier*]

frowsty *adj* **-ier**, **-iest** stuffy; stale-smelling. — *n* **frowstiness**. **[frowsy]**

frowsy or **frowzy** *adj* **-ier**, **-iest 1** (of someone's appearance) untidy, dishevelled or slovenly. **2** (of atmosphere) stuffy; stale-smelling. — *n* **frowsiness** or **frowziness**.

froze, **frozen**. See **freeze**.

FRS *abbrev* Fellow of the Royal Society (for the Advancement of Science).

fructify *v* **-ies**, **-ied** (*intr* & *tr*) to (cause to) bear fruit. [Lat *fructus*, fruit + *facere*, to make]

fructose *n* sugar found in fruit and honey. [Lat *fructus*, fruit]

frugal *adj* **1** (**with**) thrifty; economical; not generous. **2** not large; costing little: *a frugal meal*. — *n* **frugality**. — *adv* **frugally**. [Lat *frugalis*]

fruit *n* **1** the seed-carrying product of a plant, esp. if it has edible flesh, is relatively sweet, and is used esp. as a dessert, thus distinguished from a **vegetable**, used esp. in salads or to accompany meat; these collectively. **2** (*bot*) the fertilised ovary of a flowering plant, e.g. a peapod, banana or acorn. **3** plant products generally: *the fruits of the land*. **4** (also in *pl*) whatever is gained as a result of hard work, etc. **5** offspring; young: *the fruit of her womb*. **6** (*old coll*) a person: *old fruit*. — *v* (*intr*) to bear fruit. — **bear fruit 1** to produce fruit. **2** to produce esp. good results. — **dried fruit** fruit such as currants, raisins, sultanas, preserved by drying in the sun to remove moisture. — **in fruit** (of a tree) having fruit on it. — **soft fruit** small fruits and berries such as blackcurrants, redcurrants, strawberries and raspberries. [OFr *fruict*, from Lat *fructus*]

fruitcake *n* **1** a cake containing dried fruits, nuts, etc. **2** (*coll*) a slightly mad person.

fruiterer *n* a person who sells fruit.

fruitful *adj* producing good or useful results. — *adv* **fruitfully**. — *n* **fruitfulness**.

fruitless *adj* useless; unsuccessful; done in vain. — *adv* **fruitlessly**. — *n* **fruitlessness**.

fruit machine *n* a coin-operated gambling-machine with symbols in the form of fruits, that may be made to appear in winning combinations.

fruit sugar *n* fructose.

fruity *adj* **-ier**, **-iest 1** of or like fruit. **2** (of a voice) deep and rich in tone. **3** (*coll*) (of a story, etc.) containing humorous and slightly shocking references to sexual matters. **4** (*coll*) sexually aroused. — *adv* **fruitily**. — *n* **fruitiness**.

fruition *n* **1** the achievement of something that has been aimed at and worked for. **2** the bearing of fruit. [OFr, from Lat *frui*, to enjoy]

frump *n* (*coll derog*) a woman who dresses in a dowdy, old-fashioned way. — *adj* **frumpish** or **frumpy**, **-ier**, **-iest**.

frustrate *v* (*tr*) **1** to prevent (someone) from doing or getting something; to thwart or foil (a plan, attempt, etc.). **2** to make (someone) feel disappointed, useless, lacking a purpose in life, etc. — *n* **frustration**. [Lat *frustrari*, to deceive or disappoint]

frustrated *adj* **1** disappointed; unhappy; dissatisfied. **2** unfulfilled in one's ambitions for oneself. **3** not sexually satisfied.

fry[1] *v* **-ies**, **-ied** (*tr* & *intr*) to cook in hot oil or fat. — *n* ***fries* 1** a dish of anything fried, e.g. the offal of a pig or lamb. **2** (*coll*; also **fry-up**) (the frying together of) a mixture of fried foods. [OFr *frire*]

fryer or **frier** *n* **1** a frying-pan. **2** a chicken for frying.

frying-pan or **fry-pan** *n* a shallow long-handled pan for frying food in. — **out of the frying-pan into the fire** from a bad situation into a worse one.

fry[2] *n* young or newly spawned fish. [MidE, seed or descendant]

small fry *n* (*pl*) **1** unimportant people or things. **2** children.

ft *abbrev* foot or feet.

fuchsia *n* a shrub with purple, red or white hanging flowers. [L *Fuchs*, German botanist (1501–66)]

fuck (*vulg*) *v* (*tr* & *intr*) to have sexual intercourse (with). — *n* an act of, or partner in, sexual intercourse. — *interj* an expression of anger, frustration, etc. — *v* **fuck about** or **around** (*intr*; *vulg*) to behave foolishly or waste time. — *v* **fuck off** (*intr*; *vulg offensive*) to go away. — *v* **fuck up** (*tr*; *vulg*) to ruin; to spoil (*n* **fuck-up**). — **fuck all** (*vulg*) nothing; no.

fucking *adj* & *adv* (*vulg*) damned; bloody.

fuddle *v* (*tr*) to muddle the wits of; to stupefy. — *n* a state of confusion or intoxication.

fuddy-duddy *n* & *adj* **-ies** (*derog coll*) (someone who is) boringly old-fashioned or prim.

fudge[1] *n* a soft toffee made from butter and sugar. **2** (*coll*) nonsense.

fudge[2] *v* (*coll*) **1** (*intr*; **on**) to avoid stating a clear opinion. **2** (*tr*; **up**) to invent or concoct (an excuse, etc.). **3** (*tr*) to distort or deliberately obscure (figures, etc.). **4** (*tr*) to dodge or evade. [Perhaps from earlier *fadge*, to succeed or turn out]

fuel *n* **1** a material for burning as a source of heat or power. **2** fissile material for a nuclear reactor. **3** food, as a source of energy and a means of maintaining bodily processes. **4** something that feeds or inflames passions, etc. — *v* **-ll-** **1** (*tr*) to fill or feed with fuel. **2** (*intr*) to take on fuel. **3** (*tr*) to inflame (anger or other passions). [OFr *feuaile*, from Lat *focus*, hearth]

fuel cell *n* a cell generating electricity as part of a chemical reaction.

fug *n* a stale-smelling stuffy atmosphere. — *adj* **fuggy**, **-ier**, **-iest**.

fugitive *n* a person who is fleeing someone or something. — *adj* **1** fleeing away. **2** lasting only briefly; fleeting: *a fugitive smile*. [Lat *fugitivus*]

fugue *n* (*mus*) a style of composition in which a theme is introduced in one part and developed as successive parts take it up. [Fr, from Ital *fuga*, flight]

-ful *sfx* **1** ***-fuls*** forming nouns, denoting an amount held by a container, or something thought of as one: *two mugfuls of coffee*; *an armful of books*. **2** forming adjectives meaning 'full of': *meaningful*; *eventful*; 'characterised by': *merciful*; *graceful*; 'having the qualities of': *youthful*; 'in accordance with': *lawful*; 'showing an inclination to': *forgetful*. [OE]

fulcrum *n* ***-crums*** or ***-cra*** the point on which a lever turns, balances or is supported. [Lat, prop]

fulfil *v* **-ll-** (*tr*) **1** to carry out or perform (a task, promise, etc.). **2** to satisfy (requirements). **3** to achieve (an aim, ambition, etc.). — *n* **fulfilment**. — **fulfil oneself** to realise one's potential through the full use of one's talents. [OE *fullfyllan*]

full[1] *adj* **1** (**of**) holding, containing or having as much as possible, or a large quantity. **2** complete: *do a full day's work*. **3** detailed; thorough; including everything necessary: *a full report*. **4** occupied: *My hands are full*. **5** having eaten till one wants no more. **6** plump; fleshy: *the fuller figure*; *full lips*. **7** (of clothes) made with a large amount of material: *a full skirt*. **8** rich and strong: *a full-flavoured wine*. **9** rich and varied: *a full life*. **10** having all possible rights, etc.: *a full member*. **11** (of the moon) at the stage when it is a complete disc. **12** (of a brother or sister) having the same parents or (of a cousin) the same grandparents, as oneself. — *adv* **1** completely; at maximum capacity: *Is the heater full on?* **2** exactly; directly; *hit him full on the nose*. — **full of** unable to talk about anything but. — **full of oneself** (*derog*) having too good an opinion of oneself and one's importance. — **full well** perfectly well. — **in full 1** completely. **2** at length; in detail: *reported in full*. — **to the full** to the greatest possible extent. [OE]

full back *n* (*hockey*, *football* & *rugby*) a defence player positioned towards the back of the field to protect the goal.

full-blooded *adj* **1** of pure breed, not mixed blood. **2** enthusiastic; wholehearted. — *n* **full-bloodedness**.

full-blown *adj* **1** having all the features of: *a full-blown war*. **2** (of a rose, etc.) completely open.

full board *n* the provision of all meals at a hotel, etc.

full-bodied *adj* having a rich flavour or quality: *a full-bodied wine*.

full dress *n* the style of dress to be worn on formal or ceremonial occasions. — *adj* **full-dress**.

full-frontal *adj* exposing the genitals completely to view.

full house *n* **1** an audience of maximum size. **2** (*cards*, e.g. *poker*) a set of three cards of one kind and two of another.

full-length *adj* **1** complete; of the usual or standard length. **2** showing the whole body: *a full-length mirror*. **3** of maximum length; long: *a full-length skirt*.

fullness *n* the condition of being full or complete. — **in the fullness of time** when the proper time has elapsed.

full-scale *adj* **1** (of a drawing, etc.) of the same size as the subject. **2** using all possible resources, means, etc.; complete or exhaustive.

full stop *n* a punctuation mark (.) showing the end of a sentence.

full time *n* the end of the time normally allowed for a football match, etc. — *adj* & *adv* (**full-time**) occupying one's working time completely.

fully *adv* **1** to the greatest possible extent. **2** completely: *fully qualified*. **3** in detail: *deal with it more fully next week*. **4** quite; at least: *stayed for fully one hour*.

fully-fashioned *adj* (of knitwear or stockings) shaped so as to give a close fit.

fully-fledged *adj* **1** completely qualified. **2** (of birds) old enough to have grown feathers.

full[2] *v* (*tr*) to shrink and beat (cloth) to thicken it. — *n* **fuller**. [Lat *fullo*, fuller]

fuller's earth *n* a kind of clay used in fulling cloth.

fulmar *n* a gull-like sea bird of cold regions. [Icelandic *ful*, foul, stinking + *mar*, gull]

fulminate *v* (*intr* with **at, against**) to utter angry criticism or condemnation of. — *n* **fulmination**. [Lat *fulminare*, to hurl lightning]

fulsome *adj* (*derog*) (of praise, compliments, etc.) so overdone as to be distasteful. — *adv* **fulsomely**. — *n* **fulsomeness**. [**full**[1]]

fumble *v* **1** (*intr*) to handle things, or grope, clumsily. **2** (*tr*) to fail to manage, because of clumsy handling: *The fielder fumbled the catch*. — *n* an act of fumbling.

fume *n* (in *pl*) smoke or vapour, esp. if strong-smelling or poisonous. — *v* **1** (*intr*) to be furious; to fret angrily. **2** (*intr*) to give off fumes; to rise in fumes. **3** (*tr*) to treat (e.g. wood) with fumes. [Lat *fumus*, smoke]

fumigate *v* (*tr*) to disinfect (a room, etc.) with fumes. — *n* **fumigation**. [Lat *fumigare*, to smoke]

fun *n* **1** enjoyment. **2** a source of amusement or entertainment. — *adj* (*coll*) intended for amusement. — **figure of fun** someone whom others ridicule. — **for fun** as a joke; for amusement. — **fun and games 1** amusement; excitement. **2** (*ironic*) trouble. — **in fun** as a joke; not seriously. — **make fun of** or **poke fun at** to laugh at, esp. unkindly; to tease or ridicule. [From earlier *fon*, to make a fool of]

funfair see **fair**[2].

fun run *n* a long-distance race that people run in for amusement, to raise money for a charity, etc.

function *n* **1** the special purpose or task of a machine, person, bodily part, etc. **2** an organised event such as a party, reception, meeting, etc. **3** (*math*) a value that varies in relation to another value. **4** a quality that varies in relation to another varying quality. **5** (*comput*) a series of tasks that a computer is programmed to perform at the touch of a single key. — *v* (*intr*) **1** to work; to operate. **2** (**as**) to serve or act (as).

functional *adj* **1** designed for efficiency rather than decorativeness; plain rather than elaborate. **2** in working order; operational. — *adv* **functionally**.

functionary *n* **-ies** (*derog*) a person who works as a minor official in the government, etc.

fund *n* **1** a sum of money for a special purpose. **2** a large store or supply: *a fund of jokes*. **3** (in *pl*; *coll*) money available for spending. — *v* (*tr*) **1** to provide money for: *fund the project*. **2** to make (a debt) permanent, with fixed interest. — **in funds** (*coll*) having plenty of cash. [Lat *fundus*, bottom]

fundamental *adj* **1** basic; underlying: *fundamental rules of physics*; *her fundamental honesty*. **2** large; important: *fundamental differences*. **3** (**to**) essential; necessary. — *n* **1** (usu. in *pl*) a basic principle or rule. **2** (*mus*) the lowest note of a chord. — *adv* **fundamentally**. [Lat *fundamentum*, foundation]

fundamentalism *n* in religion, politics, etc. unquestioning faith in the traditional teachings; esp., in the Protestant church, belief in the literal interpretation of the Bible. — *n* **fundamentalist**.

fundamental particle *n* (*physics*) an elementary particle.

funeral *n* **1** the ceremonial burial or cremation of a dead person. **2** (*coll*) one's own problem. — *adj* of or relating to funerals. [Lat *funeralia*, funeral rites]

funeral director *n* an undertaker.

funeral parlour *n* an undertaker's place of business.

funereal *adj* **1** of or relating to funerals. **2** mournful; dismal. **3** (*coll*) (of pace) dead slow. — *adv* **funereally**. [Lat *funereus*]

funerary *adj* belonging to or used for funerals. [Lat *funerarius*]

fungicide *n* a substance that kills fungus. — *adj* **fungicidal**. [**fungus** + **-cide**]

fungus *n* **-guses** or **-gi 1** any of a group of plants, including mushrooms, toadstools, moulds and yeasts, that reproduce by spores, not seeds, and have no roots or leaves. **2** a disease caused by the growth of a fungus. — *adj* **fungal** or **fungous**. [Lat, mushroom, fungus]

fungoid *adj* fungus-like. — *n* a fungus-like plant. [**fungus** + **-oid**]

funicular *adj* (of a mountain railway) operating by a machine-driven cable, with two cars, one of which descends while the other ascends. — *n* a funicular railway. [Lat *funiculus*, dimin. of *funis*, rope]

funk[1] *n* (*coll*) **1** (also **blue funk**) a state of fear or panic. **2** a coward. — *v* (*tr*) to avoid doing (something) from panic.

funk[2] *n* (*coll*) jazz music with a strong rhythm and repeating bass pattern. [Fr dialect *funquer*, to give off smoke]

funky *adj* **-ier, -iest** (*coll*) **1** (of jazz music) strongly rhythmical and emotionally stirring. **2** trendy; good. **3** earthy; smelly.

funnel *n* **1** a tube with a cone-shaped opening through which liquid, etc. can be poured into a narrow-necked container. **2** a chimney on a steamship or steam engine through which smoke escapes. — *v* **-ll- 1** (*intr*) to rush through a narrow space: *wind funnelling through the streets*. **2** (*tr*) to transfer (liquid, etc.) from one vessel to another using a funnel. [OProvençal *fonil*, from Lat *infundere*, to pour in]

funny *adj* **-ier, -iest 1** amusing; causing laughter. **2** strange; odd; mysterious. **3** (*coll*) dishonest; shady; involving trickery. **4** (*coll*) ill. **5** (*coll*) slightly crazy. — *adv* **funnily**. [**fun**]

funny bone *n* a place in the elbow joint where the nerve passes close to the skin.

funny farm *n* (*coll*) a mental hospital.

fur *n* **1** the thick fine soft coat of a hairy animal. **2** the skin of such an animal with the hair attached, used to make, line or trim garments; a synthetic imitation of this. **3** a coat, cape or jacket made of fur or an imitation of it. **4** a whitish coating on the tongue, generally a sign of illness. **5** a whitish coating that forms on the inside of water pipes and kettles in hard-water regions. — *v* **-rr-** (*intr* & *tr*; **up**) to coat or become coated with a fur-like deposit. — **make the fur fly** (*coll*) to cause a commotion; to upset people. [OFr *fuerre*, sheath]

furrier *n* a person who makes or sells furs.

furry *adj* **-ier, -iest 1** covered with fur. **2** made of, or like, fur.

furbelow *n* **1** a dress trimming in the form of a ruched or pleated strip, ruffle or flounce. **2** (in *pl*) fussy ornamentation. [Fr & Ital *falbala*]

furbish *v* (*tr*; **up**) to restore, decorate or clean. [Fr *fourbir*, to polish]

furcate *adj* forked. — *v* (*intr*) to fork or divide. — *n* **furcation**. [Lat *furca*, fork]

furious *adj* **1** violently or intensely angry. **2** raging; stormy: *furious winds*. **3** frenzied; frantic: *furious activity*. — *adv* **furiously**. [**fury**]

furl *v* (*tr* & *intr*) (of flags, sails or umbrellas) to roll up. [OFr *fer*, firm (from Lat *firmus*) + *lier*, to bind (from Lat *ligare*)]

furlong *n* a measure of distance used esp. in horse-racing, equal to one-eighth of a mile (201·2 metres). [OE *furh*, furrow + *lang*, long]

furlough *n* leave of absence, esp. from military duty abroad. [Dut *verlof*]

furnace *n* **1** an enclosed chamber in which heat is produced, for e.g. smelting metal, heating water or burning rubbish. **2** (*coll*) a very hot place. [Lat *fornax*, kiln, oven]

furnish *v* (*tr*) **1** to provide (a house, etc.) with furniture. **2** (**with**) to supply or equip (someone) with what he or she requires. **3** to supply (what is necessary). [OFr *furnir*, to provide]

furnishings *n* (*pl*) furniture, fittings, carpets, curtains, etc.

furniture *n* **1** movable household equipment such as tables, chairs, beds, etc. **2** the equipment needed on board ship or in a factory. **3** door fittings such as locks and handles. [Fr *fourniture*, from *fournir*, to provide]

furore *n* a general outburst of excitement or indignation in reaction to something. [Ital, from Lat *furor*, frenzy]

furrier. See **fur**.

furrow *n* **1** a groove or trench cut into the earth by a plough; a rut. **2** a wrinkle, e.g. in the forehead. — *v* **1** (*tr*) to plough (land) into furrows. **2** (*intr*) to become wrinkled. [OE *furh*]

furry. See **fur**.

further *adj* **1** more distant or remote. **2** more extended: *further delay*. **3** additional: *no further clues*. — *adv* **1** at or to a greater distance or more distant point. **2** to or at a more advanced point: *further developed*. **3** to a greater extent or degree: *modified even further*. **4** moreover; furthermore. **5** (with **to**) following on from. — *v* **-r-** (*tr*) to help the progress of. ◇ See also **farther**. [OE *furthra*]

furtherance *n* the furthering, advancement or continuation of something.

further education *n* education for school-leavers not in higher education at a university or polytechnic.

furthermore *adv* in addition; moreover.

furthermost *adj* most distant or remote; farthest.

furthest *adj* most distant or remote. — *adv* **1** at or to the greatest distance or most distant point. **2** at or to the most advanced point; to the greatest extent or degree. ◇ See also **farthest**. [Superl. of **farther**]

furtive *adj* secretive; stealthy; sly. — *adv* **furtively**. — *n* **furtiveness**. [Lat *furtivus*, stolen, clandestine]

fury *n* **-ies 1** violent or frenzied anger; an outburst of this. **2** violence: *the fury of the wind*. **3** a frenzy: *a fury of activity*. — **like fury** (*coll*) fast; eagerly; powerfully; like mad. [Fr *furie*, from Lat *furere*, to rage]

the Furies *n* (*pl*; *Gr mythol*) goddesses of vengeance.

furze *n* gorse. [OE *fyrs*]

fuse[1] *n* a safety device in an electrical plug or circuit, containing a wire that melts and so breaks the circuit when the current becomes too strong; the wire itself. — *v* **1** (*tr* & *intr*) to melt as a result of intense heat. **2** (*tr* & *intr*; **together**) to melt together; to blend or combine. **3** (*tr* & *intr*) (of an electrical circuit or appliance) to (cause to) stop working because of the melting of a fuse. **4** (*tr*) to fit (a plug or circuit) with a fuse. — **blow a fuse** (*coll*) to fly into a temper. [Lat *fusus*, melted]

fuse[2] *n* (a piece of combustible material contained within) a cord or cable, used for detonating a bomb or explosive charge. — *v* (*tr*) to fit with such a device. [Lat *fusus*, spindle]

fuselage *n* the main body of an aircraft, carrying crew and passengers. [Fr *fuselé*, spindle-shaped]

fusilier *n* **1** (*hist*) an infantryman armed with a *fusil* or light musket. **2** a member of any of several British regiments formerly armed with these. [Fr]

fusillade *n* **1** a simultaneous or continuous discharge of firearms. **2** an onslaught, e.g. of criticism. [Fr, from *fusiller*, to shoot]

fusion *n* **1** the process of melting together. **2** a blending. **3** (*nuc*) the combining of atomic nuclei with resultant release of energy. [Lat *fusio*, melting]

fuss *n* **1** agitation and excitement, esp. over something trivial. **2** a commotion, disturbance or bustle. — *v* (*intr*) **1** to worry needlessly. **2** to concern oneself too much with trivial matters. **3** (**over**) to display a fond concern for. **4** (*tr*) to agitate. — **make**, or (*coll*) **kick up**, **a fuss** to complain.— **make a fuss of** (*coll*) to pay a lot of attention to (someone).

fusspot *n* (*coll derog*) a person who worries excessively, esp. over trifles.

fussy *adj* **-ier**, **-iest 1** over-concerned with details or trifles. **2** choosy; discriminating. **3** bustling and officious. **4** (of clothes, etc.) over-elaborate. — *adv* **fussily**. — *n* **fussiness**. [**fuss**]

fusty *adj* **-ier**, **-iest 1** stale-smelling; old and musty. **2** old-fashioned. — *n* **fustiness**. [MidE *fust*, wine cask]

futile *adj* unproductive, unavailing, foolish, vain or pointless. — *adv* **futilely**. — *n* **futility**. [Lat *futilis*, easily pouring out, unreliable]

futon *n* a cloth-filled mattress designed to be used on the floor and rolled up when not in use. [Jap]

future *n* **1** the time to come; events that are still to occur. **2** (*gram*) (a verb in) the future tense. **3** prospects: *must think about one's future*. **4** likelihood of success: *no future in that*. **5** (in *pl*; *stock exchange*) commodities bought or sold at an agreed price, to be delivered at a later date. — *adj* **1** yet to come or happen. **2** about to become: *my future wife*. **3** (*gram*) (of the tense of a verb) indicating actions or events yet to happen. — **in future** from now on. [Lat *futurus*, about to be]

futurism *n* an early 20th-cent. movement in the arts, originating in Italy and expressive of the dynamism of the machine age. — *n* **futurist**.

futuristic *adj* **1** relating to futurism. **2** (of design, etc.) so exotically innovative as to have no relation to traditional forms. — *adv* **futuristically**.

futurity *n* **-*ies*** **1** the future. **2** a future event.

futurology *n* the forecasting of future events from present tendencies. [**future** + **-logy**]

fuzz[1] *n* a mass of fine fibres or hair.

fuzzy *adj* **-*ier*, -*iest*** **1** covered with fuzz. **2** forming a mass of tight curls. **3** indistinct; blurred. — *adv* **fuzzily**.

fuzz[2] *n* (*slang*) the police.

G

G[1] or **g** *n* ***G's*** or ***Gs***, ***g's*** **1** the seventh letter of the English alphabet. **2** (only **G**; *mus*) the fifth note on the scale of C major. **3** (only **G**) the musical key having this note as its base.

G-string or **gee-string** *n* an under-garment (usu. for women) barely covering the pubic area.

G-suit see **g-suit**.

G[2] *abbrev* **1** German. **2** (*US slang*) a grand, 1000 dollars.

g *abbrev* **1** gallon. **2** gram or gramme. **3** (acceleration due to) gravity.

g-suit or **G-suit** *n* a suit for astronauts and military pilots, with inflating parts which maintain the body's normal blood flow during high acceleration.

GA, **Ga.** *abbrev* Georgia.

Ga *symbol* (*chem*) gallium.

gab (*coll*) *n* idle talk; chat. — *v* ***-bb-*** (*intr*; **on, away**) to talk idly, esp. at length. — **the gift of the gab** (*coll*) the ability to speak with ease, esp. persuasively. [Prob. Irish Gaelic *gob*, beak, mouth]

gabardine *n* **1** a closely woven twill fabric, esp. of wool or cotton. **2** a coat or loose cloak made from this. [OFr *gauvardine*, pilgrim's garment]

gabble *v* (*intr* & *tr*) to talk or say quickly and unclearly. — *n* fast indistinct talk. [Du *gabbelen*]

gaberdine. Same as **gabardine**.

gable *n* **1** the triangular upper part of a side wall between the sloping parts of a roof. **2** a triangular canopy above a door or window. — *adj* **gabled**. [Norse *gafl*]

gad[1] *v* ***-dd-*** (*intr*; *coll*; **about, around**) to go from place to place busily, esp. in the pursuit of amusement or pleasure. [Back-formation from OE *gædeling*, companion]

gadabout *n* (*coll derog* or *humorous*) a person who gads about.

gad[2] *interj* (*old*) an expression of surprise or affirmation. [A form of *God*]

gadfly *n* ***-ies*** **1** a fly that bites horses and cattle. **2** (*old derog*) a person who deliberately and persistently annoys others. [OE *gad*, goad]

gadget *n* any small device or appliance, esp. one more ingenious than necessary. — *n* **gadgetry**.

gadolinium *n* an element (symbol **Gd**), a silvery-white metal. [Johan *Gadolin* (1760–1852), Finnish mineralogist]

gadwall *n* a northern duck related to the mallard.

Gael *n* a Gaelic-speaking person from the Scottish Highlands, Ireland or the Isle of Man. [Gaelic *Gaidheal*]

Gaelic *n* any of the closely related Celtic languages spoken in these parts. — *adj* **1** of or relating to these languages, the people who speak them, or their customs.

gaff[1] *n* **1** a long pole with a hook, for landing large fish. **2** a vertical spar to which the tops of certain types of sail are attached. — *v* (*tr*) to seize (a fish) with a gaff. [Provençal *gaf*, boathook]

gaff[2]: **blow the gaff** (*slang*) to give away a secret.

gaffe *n* a socially embarrassing action or remark. [Fr]

gaffer *n* **1** (*coll*) a boss or foreman. **2** the senior electrician on a film or television set. **3** (*dialect*) (often as a form of address) an old man. [Perhaps **godfather**]

gag[1] *v* ***-gg-*** **1** (*tr*) to silence (someone) by putting something in or over their mouth. **2** (*tr*) to deprive of free speech. **3** (*intr*) to retch. **4** (*intr*) to choke. — *n* something put into or over a person's mouth to impose silence. [MidE *gaggen*, to suffocate]

gag[2] (*coll*) *n* a joke or trick, esp. as used by a professional comedian. — *v* ***-gg-*** (*intr*) to tell jokes.

gaga *adj* (*coll*) **1** weak-minded through old age; senile. **2** silly; foolish. **3** (**about**) wildly enthusiastic. [Fr]

gage[1] *n* **1** an object given as security or a pledge. **2** (*hist*) something thrown down to signal a challenge, e.g. a glove. [OFr]

gage[2]. Same as **greengage**.

gaggle *n* **1** a flock (of geese). **2** (*coll*) a group of noisy people. [Imit.]

gaiety, **gaily**. See **gay**.

gain *v* **1** (*tr*) to get, obtain or earn. **2** (*intr*; **by, from**) to benefit or profit. **3** (*tr*) to have or experience an increase in: *gain speed*. **4** (*tr* & *intr*) (of a clock, etc.) to go too fast by (an amount of time). **5** (*tr*) to reach (a place), esp. after difficulties. **6** (*intr*; **on, upon**) to come closer (to); to catch up. — *n* **1** (often in *pl*) something gained, e.g. profit. **2** an increase (e.g. in weight). **3** an instance of gaining. — **gain ground** to make progress or win an advantage. — **gain time** to get extra time for something through a delay or postponement. [OFr *gaaignier*, to earn, gain, or till (land)]

gainful *adj* **1** profitable. **2** (of employment) paid. — *adv* **gainfully**.

gainsay *v* ***-said*** (*tr*; *formal*) to deny or contradict. [OE *gean*, against + *sayen*, to say]

gait *n* **1** a way of walking. **2** an animal's leg-movements at a particular speed, e.g. trotting. [Variation of obsolete *gate*, manner of doing]

gaiter *n* a leather or cloth covering for the lower leg and ankle, often with a strap fitting under the shoe. [Fr *guêtre*]

gal *n* (*old coll*) a girl.

gal. *abbrev* gallon.

gala *n* **1** an occasion of special entertainment or a public festivity of some kind, e.g. a carnival. **2** a meeting for sports, esp. swimming, competitions. [OFr *galer*, to make merry]

galactic *adj* of or relating to a galaxy or the Galaxy. **[galaxy]**

galantine *n* a dish of boneless cooked white meat or fish served cold in jelly. [OFr]

galaxy *n* **-ies 1** a group of stars and planets held together by gravitational attraction. **2** (*cap* with **the**) the spiral-shaped group containing our solar system. **3** a fabulous gathering or array, e.g. of famous people. [Gr *galaktos*, milk]

gale *n* **1** a very strong wind. **2** (usu. in *pl*) a sudden loud burst, e.g. of laughter.

gall[1] *n* **1** (*coll*) impudence; cheek. **2** bitterness or spitefulness. **3** something unpleasant. **4** (*old med*) a bitter liquid produced in the liver to aid digestion; bile. [OE *gealla*, bile]

gall-bladder *n* the organ in which bile is stored, attached to the liver.

gallstone *n* a small hard mass of cholesterol and salts formed in the gall-bladder.

gall[2] *n* a small round abnormal growth on trees and plants caused by insects or fungus. [Lat *galla*]

gall[3] *n* **1** a painful swelling or sore, esp. on horses, caused by chafing. **2** something annoying or irritating. **3** a state of being annoyed. — *v* (*tr*) **1** to chafe (skin). **2** to annoy. — *adj* **galling**. [OE *gealla*, sore on a horse]

gall. *abbrev* gallon.

gallant *adj* **1** brave. **2** (*old* or *literary*) splendid, grand or fine. **3** (of a man) very courteous and attentive to women. — *n* (*old*) **1** a woman's lover. **2** a handsome young man who pursues women. — *adv* **gallantly**. [OFr *galer*, to make merry]

gallantry *n* **-ies 1** bravery. **2** (*old*) politeness and attentiveness to women; an action or phrase demonstrating this.

galleon *n* a large three-masted Spanish ship used for war or trade from the 15th to the 18th century. [Span *galeón*]

gallery *n* **-ies 1** a room or building used to display works of art. **2** a balcony along an inside upper wall, e.g. of a church or hall, providing extra seating or reserved for musicians, etc.: *minstrels' gallery*. **3** the upper floor in a theatre, usu. containing the cheapest seats; the part of the audience seated there. **4** a long narrow room or corridor. **5** an underground passage in a mine or cave. **6** a covered walkway open on one or both sides. **7** the spectators in the stand at a golf, tennis, etc. tournament. — **play to the gallery** to seek mass approval or favour by appealing to popular taste, often using crude methods. [Lat *galeria*]

galley *n* **-eys 1** a long single-deck ship propelled by sails and oars. **2** the kitchen on a ship. **3** a rectangular tray holding arrangements of individual metal letters, from which a preliminary printing of part of a book, etc. is made. **4** a galley proof. [Gr *galaia*]

galley proof *n* a preliminary printing of part of a book, etc. in the form of a continuous sheet, on which corrections are marked.

galley slave *n* **1** a slave forced to row a galley. **2** (*coll*) a person given menial tasks; a drudge.

Gallic *adj* **1** (typically) French. **2** of ancient Gaul or the Gauls. [Lat *gallicus*, Gaulish]

Gallicism *n* a French word or expression used in another language.

gallinaceous *adj* (*biol*) of or relating to birds such as grouse, pheasants and domestic poultry. [Lat *gallus*, cock]

gallium *n* an element (symbol **Ga**), a silvery metal. [Lat *gallus*, cock, from the name of its French discoverer, Le*coq* de Boisbaudran (1838–1912)]

gallivant *v* (*intr*; *coll humorous* or *derog*) to spend time idly or in search of amusement. [Perhaps from **gallant**]

gallon *n* a measure of liquid equal to eight pints or, in the UK, 4·546 litres (an **imperial gallon**), and in the US, 3·785 litres. — **gallons of** (*coll*) a large amount of (liquid). [OFr *galon*]

gallop *n* **1** the fastest pace at which a horse moves, with all four legs leaving the ground together. **2** a period of riding at this pace. **3** an unusually fast speed. — *v* **-p- 1** (*intr*) (of a horse) to move at a gallop. **2** (*tr*) to cause (a horse) to move at a gallop. **3** (*intr*; *coll*) to move, progress or increase very quickly: *galloping inflation*. [OFr *galoper*]

gallows *n* (*sing*) **1** a wooden frame on which criminals are put to death by hanging. **2** (with **the**) death by hanging. [OE *gealga*]

gallows humour *n* humour derived from unpleasant subjects like death and illness; black humour.

gallstone. See **gall**[1].

Gallup poll *n* a survey of the views of a representative group of people, used to assess overall public opinion, esp. with regard to voting intentions. [G H *Gallup* (1901–84), statistician]

galop *n* (a piece of music for) a lively 19th-century dance for couples. **[gallop]**

galore *adv* in large amounts or numbers: *books galore*. [Irish Gaelic *go leór*, to sufficiency]

galosh *n* (also **golosh**; usu. in *pl*) a waterproof overshoe. [OFr *galoche*, from Lat *gallicula*, small Gaulish shoe]

galumph *v* (*intr*; *coll*) **1** to stride along triumphantly. **2** to walk in a heavy ungainly manner. [Coined by Lewis Carroll, perhaps from **gallop** + **triumph**]

galvanic *adj* **1** (*physics*) producing an electric current chemically; (of current) produced chemically. **2** (of behaviour, etc.) sudden, or startlingly energetic, as if the result of electric shock. **[galvanism]**

galvanism *n* the production of an electric current chemically, as in a battery. [Luigi *Galvani* (1738–98), Italian scientist]
galvanise or **-ize** *v* (*tr*) **1** (*tech*) to apply a thin coating of zinc to (iron or steel), to prevent rusting. **2** (**into**) to stimulate or rouse (e.g. into action). — *n* **galvanisation** or **-z-**. — *adj* **galvanised** or **-z-**. [**galvanism**]
galvanometer *n* an instrument for detecting or measuring small amounts of electric current. [**galvanism** + **-meter**]
gambit *n* **1** a chess move made early in a game, in which a pawn or other piece is sacrificed in order to gain an overall advantage. **2** an initial action or remark inviting others or establishing a point of view. **3** a piece of trickery; a stratagem. [Ital *gambetto*, a tripping up]
gamble *v* **1** (*tr* & *intr*) to bet (usu. money) on the result of a card game, horse-race, etc. **2** (*intr*; **on, with**) to take a chance or risk: *gamble on the weather being fine*. **3** (*tr*; **away**) to lose (money) through gambling. — *n* **1** an act of gambling; a bet. **2** a risk, or a situation involving risk: *take a gamble*. — *n* **gambler**. — *n* **gambling**. [OE *gamen*, to play]
gamboge *n* a gum resin obtained from various SE Asian trees, used as a yellow dye and a laxative. [*Cambodia* in SE Asia]
gambol *v* **-ll-** (*intr*) to jump around playfully. — *n* an act of leaping around playfully; a frolic. [Ital *gamba*, leg]
game[1] *n* **1** an amusement or pastime; the equipment used for this, e.g. a board, cards, dice, etc. **2** a competitive activity with rules, involving some form of skill. **3** an occasion on which individuals or teams compete at such an activity; a match. **4** in some sports, a division of a match. **5** (in *pl*) an event consisting of competitions in various (esp. sporting) activities. **6** (*coll*; often *derog*) a type of activity, profession or business: *the game of politics*. **7** a person's ability or way of playing: *her backhand game*. **8** (*derog*) an activity undertaken light-heartedly: *War is just a game to him*. **9** (the flesh of) certain birds and animals which are killed for sport. **10** (*coll*; *derog*) a scheme, trick or intention: *give the game away*; *What's your game?* **11** (*slang*; with **the**) prostitution: *be on the game*. — *adj* (*coll*) **1** (**for**) ready and willing: *game for a laugh*. **2** (*old*) having plenty of fighting spirit; plucky. — *v* (*intr*) to gamble. — *adv* **gamely**. — **make game of** (*old*) to make fun of or laugh at. — **play the game** to behave fairly. [OE *gamen*, to play]
gamecock *n* a cock trained for cock-fighting.
gamekeeper *n* a person employed to take care of wildlife, e.g. on a country estate.
gamesmanship *n* (*derog*) the art or practice of winning games by trying to disturb or upset one's opponent.
gamey see **gamy**.
game[2] *adj* (*old*) lame. [Perhaps Irish Gaelic *cam*, crooked]
gamete *n* (*biol*) a cell which can unite sexually with another for reproduction. [Gr *gamete*, wife]
gamey. See **gamy**.
gamine *n* a girl or young woman with a mischievous, boyish appearance. [Fr]
gamma *n* **1** the third letter of the Greek alphabet (Γ, γ). **2** (a mark indicating) the third highest grade or quality.
gamma rays *n* (*pl*; also **gamma radiation** *n*) a powerful form of radiation given off by some radioactive substances.
gammon *n* **1** cured meat from the upper leg and hindquarters of a pig, usu. cut into thick slices. **2** the back part of a side of bacon including the whole back leg and hindquarters. [OFr *gambon*, from *gambe*, leg]
gammy *adj* **-ier**, **-iest** (*old coll*) lame; permanently injured. [Ety. as for **game**[2]]
gamp *n* (*coll*) an umbrella. [Mrs *Gamp*, a character in Dickens's novel *Martin Chuzzlewit*]
gamut *n* **1** the whole range of anything, e.g. a person's emotions. **2** a scale of notes in music; the range of notes produced by a voice or instrument. [*gamma*, the lowest note on a mediaeval six-note scale + *ut*, the first note (now *doh*) of an early sol-fa notation system]
gamy or **gamey** *adj* **-ier**, **-iest** (of meat) having the strong taste or smell of game which has been kept for a long time. — *n* **gaminess**. [**game**[1]]
gander *n* **1** a male goose. **2** (*coll*) a look: *have a gander*. [OE *gandra*]
gang *n* **1** a group (of criminals, thieves or troublemakers). **2** a group of friends, esp. children. **3** an organised group of workers. **4** a set of tools arranged so as to be used together. — *v* (*tr*) to arrange (tools) for simultaneous use. — *v* **gang up** (*intr*) **1** (**on**) to act as a group against (someone). **2** (**with**) to join in or form a gang. [OE *gangan*, to go]
gang-bang *n* (*slang*) an occasion on which several men successively have sex with one woman, often against her will.
ganger *n* (*coll*) the foreman of a group of workers.
gangland *n* & *adj* (of) the world of organised crime.
gangplank *n* a gangway (sense **1**).
gangster *n* a member of a gang of usu. armed criminals.
gangway *n* **1** a small movable bridge used for getting on and off a ship; the opening on the side of a ship into which this fits. **2** a passage between rows of seats, e.g. on a plane or in a theatre. — *interj* make way!
gangling *adj* (also **gangly**, **-ier**, **-iest**) tall, thin and usu. awkward in movement. [OE *gangan*, to go]
ganglion *n* **-ia** or **-ions** **1** a group of nerve-cells in the central nervous system. **2** a growth or swelling on the tissue around a

tendon. **3** (*literary*) a centre of energy or activity. [Gr, cystic tumour]

gangrene *n* the decay of tissue on part of the body caused by the obstruction of its blood supply, resulting from illness or injury. — *adj* **gangrenous**. [Gr *gangraina*]

ganja *n* marijuana. [Hindi *ganjha*]

gannet *n* **1** a large white seabird that dives to catch fish. **2** (*coll derog*) a greedy person. [OE *ganot*, seabird]

gantry *n* ***-ies*** a large metal supporting framework, e.g. overhead for railway signals or a travelling crane, or at the side of a rocket's launch-pad.

gaol and **gaoler**. See **jail**.

gap *n* **1** a break or open space, e.g. in a fence. **2** a break in time; an interval. **3** a difference or disparity: *the generation gap*. **4** a ravine or gorge. — *adj* **gappy**, ***-ier***, ***-iest***. [Norse, chasm]

gape *v* (*intr*) **1** (**at**) to stare with the mouth open, esp. in surprise or wonder. **2** to be or become wide open. **3** to open the mouth wide. — *n* **1** a wide opening. **2** an open-mouthed stare. **3** the extent to which the mouth can be opened. — *adj* **gaping**. [Norse *gapa*, to open the mouth]

garage *n* **1** a building in which motor vehicles are kept. **2** an establishment where motor vehicles are bought, sold and repaired, often also selling petrol, etc. [OFr *garer*, to shelter]

garb (*literary*) *n* **1** clothing, esp. as worn by people in a particular job or position. **2** outward appearance. — *v* (*tr*; usu. in *passive* as *adj*) to dress or clothe. [Ital *garbo*, grace]

garbage *n* **1** (*US*) domestic waste; refuse. **2** (*derog*) worthless or poor quality articles or matter. **3** (*derog*) nonsense. **4** (*comput*) unwanted meaningless information mistakenly appearing on a screen or printout.

garble *v* (*tr*) **1** to unintentionally mix up the details of. **2** to deliberately distort the meaning of, e.g. by making important omissions. [Arabic *ghirbal*, sieve]

garçon *n* a waiter in a French restaurant or café. [Fr]

garda *n* ***-dai*** a police officer in the Irish Republic. [Irish Gaelic, guard]

garden *n* **1** a piece of ground attached to a house, on which flowers, vegetables, trees, etc. are grown. **2** (usu. in *pl*) a large area where plants are grown and displayed for public enjoyment: *botanical gardens*. **3** a similar smaller place where food and drinks are served outdoors: *tea garden*. **4** a fertile region. — *adj* **1** (of a plant) cultivated, not wild. **2** for use in a garden, or in gardening. — *v* (*intr*) ***-n-*** to work at the care of a garden and its plants, usu. as a hobby. — *n* **gardener**. — *n* **gardening**. — **lead up the garden path** (*coll*) to deliberately mislead or deceive. [OFr *gardin*]

garden centre *n* a place where plants, seeds and garden tools are sold.

garden city *n* a spacious modern town designed to have private gardens and numerous public parks.

garden party *n* a formal party held in a large private garden.

gardenia *n* a tropical shrub with large fragrant white or yellow flowers. [Dr Alexander *Garden* (1730–91), US botanist]

gargantuan *adj* enormous; colossal. [*Gargantua*, the greedy giant in Rabelais's novel *Gargantua and Pantagruel*]

gargle *v* (*intr* & *tr*) to cleanse the mouth and throat by blowing air from the lungs through (a liquid) held there. — *n* **1** an act of gargling, or the sound produced. **2** the liquid used. [OFr *gargouille*, throat]

gargoyle *n* a grotesque carved open-mouthed head or figure acting as a rain-water spout from a roof-gutter, esp. on a church. [OFr *gargouille*, throat]

garish *adj* (*derog*) unpleasantly bright or colourful; very gaudy. — *adv* **garishly**. — *n* **garishness**. [Obsolete *gaurish*, from *gaure*, to stare]

garland *n* **1** a circular arrangement of flowers or leaves worn round the head or neck, or hung up. **2** a collection of short poems or pieces of prose. — *v* (*tr*) to decorate with a garland. [OFr *garlande*]

garlic *n* **1** a plant of the onion family, whose strong-tasting bulb is used as a flavouring in cooking. **2** its bulb. — *adj* **garlicky**. [OE *gar*, spear + *leac*, leek]

garment *n* an article of clothing. [OFr *garniment*, from *garnir*, to furnish]

garner *v* ***-r-***(*tr*; *formal* or *literary*) to collect and usu. store (information, knowledge, etc.). [Lat *granarium*, granary]

garnet *n* any of various hard translucent minerals, esp. a deep red variety used as a gem. [Lat *granatum*, pomegranate]

garnish *v* (*tr*; **with**) to decorate (esp. food to be served). — *n* a decoration, esp. one added to food. [Fr *garnir*, to furnish]

garret *n* an attic room, often a dingy one. [OFr *garite*, refuge]

garrison *n* **1** a body of soldiers stationed in a town or fortress in order to defend it. **2** the building they occupy. [OFr *garison*, from *garir*, to protect]

garrotte *n* (also **garotte**) **1** a wire loop or metal collar tightened around the neck to cause strangulation. **2** this method of execution. — *v* (*tr*) to execute or kill with a garrotte. [Span *garrote*]

garrulous *adj* **1** tending to talk a lot, esp. about trivial things. **2** (*derog*) (of a speech, etc.) too long; wordy. — *n* **garrulousness** or **garrulity**. [Lat *garrire*, to chatter]

garter *n* **1** a band of tight material, usu. elastic, worn on the leg to hold up a stocking or sock. **2** (*cap*; with **the**) the highest order of British knighthood; membership of the order; the emblem of the order, a blue garter. [OFr *gartier*]

garter stitch *n* a plain stitch in knitting.

gas *n* **1** any freely moving substance which is neither solid nor liquid, esp. one in this state at ordinary temperatures. **2** any such substance used for heating, lighting or cooking. **3** a gas, esp. nitrous oxide, used as an anaesthetic. **4** firedamp, a mixture of gases naturally occurring in coalmines, explosive in contact with air. **5** a poisonous gas used as a weapon in war. **6** (*coll*; esp. *US*) gasoline; petrol. **7** (*coll*) an amusing or enjoyable event or situation: *The film was a real gas!* **8** (*coll derog*) foolish talk; boasting. — *v* **-ss- 1** (*tr*) to poison or kill with gas. **2** (*intr*; *coll derog*) to chat, esp. at length, boastfully or about trivial things. [Coined by J B van Helmont, Belgian chemist (1577–1644), after Gr *chaos*, atmosphere]

gasbag *n* (*coll derog*) a person who talks a lot or too much.

gas chamber *n* a sealed room which can be filled with poisonous gas, used for killing people or animals.

gaseous *adj* of the nature of, or like, gas.

gas holder *n* a huge expandable metal tank used for storing gas (sense **2**) for distribution to consumers.

gasify *v* **-ies**, **-ied** (*tr*) to convert into gas. — *n* **gasification**.

gaslight *n* a lamp powered by gas, or the light from it.

gas mask *n* a mask, covering the full face, which filters out poisonous gas, allowing the wearer to breathe clean air.

gas meter *n* an instrument which measures and records the amount of gas (sense **2**) used.

gasoline *n* (esp. *US*; also *coll* **gas**) petrol.

gasometer *n* a gas holder.

gassy *adj* **-ier**, **-iest 1** like gas; full of gas. **2** (*coll derog*) talking a lot, esp. about unimportant things. — *n* **gassiness**.

gasworks *n* (*sing*) a place where gas (sense **2**) is manufactured from coal.

gash *n* a deep open cut or wound. — *v* (*tr*) to make a gash in. [OFr *garser*, to scratch or wound]

gasket *n* a thin flat shaped ring or sheet of rubber or paper fitting tightly in the join between two metal surfaces to form an airtight seal. — **blow a gasket 1** (of an engine, etc.) to cause a gasket to burst or break. **2** (*coll*) to fly into a temper. [Perhaps Fr *garcette*, end of a rope]

gasp *v* **1** (*intr*) to take a sharp breath in, through surprise, sudden pain, etc. **2** (*intr*) to breathe in with difficulty, e.g. because of illness. **3** (*tr*; **out**) to say breathlessly. **4** (*intr* with **for**; *coll*) to want or need very much. — *n* a sharp intake of breath. [Norse *geispa*, to yawn]

gasteropod. Same as **gastropod**.

gastric *adj* of the stomach. [Gr *gaster*, belly]

gastric flu *n* (*coll*) a disorder of the intestine, of unknown cause.

gastric juices *n* (*pl*) fluid produced by the stomach to aid digestion.

gastro- or **gastr-** *comb fm* the stomach. [Gr *gaster*, belly]

gastroenteritis *n* inflammation of the lining of the stomach and the intestines. [**gastro-** + Gr *enteron*, intestine]

gastronome, **gastronomer** or **gastronomist** *n* a person who enjoys, and has developed a taste for, good food and wine. [**gastro-** + Gr *nomos*, law]

gastronomy *n* **1** the enjoyment of good food and wine. **2** the style of cooking typical of a particular country or region: *French gastronomy*. — *adj* **gastronomic**.

gastropod *n* (*biol*) any of a class of small molluscs that move using a long muscular foot, including snails, slugs and whelks. [**gastro-** + Gr *pous*, foot]

gate *n* **1** a usu. hinged door or barrier, moved to open or close an entrance in a wall, fence, etc. leading e.g. into a garden, field or city; the entrance itself. **2** any of the numbered exits at an airport from which passengers can board or leave a plane. **3** the total number of people attending a sports event or other entertainment. **4** (also **gate money**) the total money paid in admission fees. **5** any of the pairs of posts that a slalom skier passes through. **6** (*tech*) an electronic circuit whose output is controlled by the combination of signals at the input terminals. — *v* (*tr*) to confine (pupils) to school after hours. [OE *geat*, a way]

gatecrash *v* (*tr* & *intr*; *coll*) to gain entry to (a party, meeting, etc.) uninvited or without paying. — *n* **gatecrasher**.

gatehouse *n* a building at or above the gateway to a city, castle, etc., often occupied by the person who guards it.

gateway *n* **1** an entrance, esp. to a city, park, etc., with a gate across it. **2** (**to**) a way in or to. **3** (**to**) a means of acquiring: *the gateway to fame and fortune*.

gateau *n* **-teaux** or **-teaus** (also **gâteau**, **-teaux**) a large rich cake, esp. filled with cream and decorated with fruit, nuts, etc. [Fr]

gather *v* **-r- 1** (*tr* & *intr*; **together**, etc.) to (cause to) come together in one place. **2** (*tr*; **in**) to collect, pick or harvest. **3** (*tr*) to increase in (speed or force). **4** (*tr*) to accumulate or become covered with (e.g. dust). **5** (*tr*) to learn or understand from information received. **6** (*tr*) to pull, and often stitch, (material) into small folds. **7** (*tr*) to pull (a garment) closely round the body. **8** (*tr*) to embrace: *She gathered the child into her arms*. **9** (*tr*) to wrinkle (the brow). **10** (*tr*; **together**) to draw together or muster (strength, courage, etc.) in preparation for something. **11** (*intr*) (of a boil, etc.) to form a head. — *n* a small fold in material, often stitched. [OE *gaderian*]

gathering *n* **1** a meeting or assembly. **2** a series of gathers in material.

GATT *abbrev* General Agreement on Tariffs and Trade, an international treaty to promote trade and economic benefits, signed in 1947.

gauche *adj* ill-at-ease or awkward in social situations. — *adv* **gauchely**. [Fr, left, left-handed]

gaucherie *n* (an example of) social awkwardness.

gaucho *n* **-os** a modern cowboy of the S American plains. [Span]

gaudy *adj* **-ier**, **-iest** (*derog*) coarsely and brightly coloured or decorated. — *adv* **gaudily**. — *n* **gaudiness**. [MidE *gaude*, trinket]

gauge *v* (*tr*) **1** to measure very accurately. **2** to estimate or guess (a measurement, size, etc.). **3** to judge. — *n* **1** a measuring instrument: *pressure gauge*. **2** (one of) a series of standard (esp. diameter) sizes, e.g. of wire, bullets, knitting needles. **3** the distance between the rails of a railway line. **4** a standard against which other things are measured or judged. [OFr]

Gaul *n* an inhabitant of ancient Gaul, corresponding to modern France, Belgium and adjacent parts of Italy, Germany and the Netherlands. [Lat *Gallus*]

Gaulish *n* the language of the Gauls. — *adj* of the Gauls or their language.

gaunt *adj* **1** thin or thin-faced (as if) through hunger or illness. **2** (of a place) barren and desolate. — *n* **gauntness**.

gauntlet[1] *n* **1** a metal or metal-plated glove worn by mediaeval soldiers. **2** a heavy protective leather glove loosely covering the wrist. — **throw down**, or **take up, the gauntlet** to make, or accept, a challenge. [OFr *gantelet*, dimin. of *gant*, glove]

gauntlet[2]: **run the gauntlet 1** (*hist*) to suffer the military punishment of running between rows of men who strike one with sticks as one passes. **2** to expose oneself to, or suffer, hostile treatment, e.g. physical attacks or criticism. [Altered from *gantlope*, from Swed *gatlopp*, from *gata*, lane + *lopp*, course]

gauze *n* **1** thin transparent cloth, esp. cotton as used to dress wounds. **2** thin wire mesh. — *adj* **gauzy**, **-ier**, **-iest**. [Fr *gaze*]

gave. See **give**.

gavel *n* a small hammer used by a judge, auctioneer, etc. to call attention.

gavotte *n* (a piece of music for) an old lively French country dance. [Fr]

gawk (*coll*) *v* (*intr*; **at**) to stare blankly or stupidly; to gawp. — *n* (*derog*) an awkward, clumsy or stupid person. [Obsolete *gaw*, to stare]

gawky *adj* **-ier**, **-iest** (*coll derog*) awkward-looking, ungainly, and usu. tall and thin. — *n* **gawkiness**.

gawp *v* (*intr*; *coll*; **at**) to stare stupidly, esp. open-mouthed; to gape. [Obsolete *gaw*, to stare]

gay *adj* **1** happily carefree. **2** bright and attractive. **3** fun-loving or pleasure-seeking. **4** homosexual; of, frequented by, or intended for, homosexuals: *a gay bar*. — *n* a homosexual. [OFr *gai*]

gaiety *n* **1** the condition of being merry or gay. **2** attractively bright appearance. **3** fun; merry-making. [Fr *gaieté*]

gaily *adv* **1** in a light-hearted, merry way. **2** brightly; colourfully.

gayness *n* the state of being gay, esp. homosexual.

gaze *v* (*intr*; **at**) to stare fixedly, usu. for a long time. — *n* a fixed stare. [MidE *gasen*]

gazebo *n* **-os** or **-oes** a small summerhouse or open hut, esp. in a garden, from which a fine view can be admired. [Perhaps coined from **gaze**]

gazelle *n* ***gazelles*** or ***gazelle*** a small graceful antelope of Africa and Asia, usu. fawn-coloured. [Fr, from Arabic *ghazal*, wild goat]

gazette *n* **1** an official newspaper giving lists of government, military and legal notices. **2** (often *facet*) a newspaper. — *v* (*tr*; *formal*) to announce or publish in an official gazette. [Venetian dialect *gazeta*, from *gazet*, a small coin, the cost of an early news-sheet]

gazetteer *n* a dictionary of place-names, with descriptions of the places. [**gazette**]

gazpacho *n* a Spanish vegetable soup, served cold. [Span]

gazump *v* (*tr*; *coll*) to go back on a verbal agreement to sell one's house to (someone), accepting a later offer of more money from someone else. — *n* **gazumper**. — *n* **gazumping**. [Perhaps Yiddish *gezumph*, to swindle]

GB *abbrev* Great Britain.

GBE *abbrev* (Knight or Dame) Grand Cross of the British Empire.

gbh or **GBH** *abbrev* grievous bodily harm.

GC *abbrev* George Cross, an award for bravery.

GCB *abbrev* (Knight or Dame) Grand Cross of the (Order of the) Bath.

GCE *abbrev* General Certificate of Education (see under **general**). — *n* (a pass in) a subject in which an examination is taken at this level.

GCMG *abbrev* (Knight or Dame) Grand Cross of (the Order of) St Michael and St George.

GCSE *abbrev* General Certificate of Secondary Education (see under **general**). — *n* (a pass in) a subject in which an examination is taken at this level.

GCVO *abbrev* (Knight or Dame) Grand Cross of the (Royal) Victorian Order.

Gd *symbol* (*chem*) gadolinium.

Gdns *abbrev* Gardens, esp. in street names.

GDP *abbrev* gross domestic product.

GDR *abbrev* German Democratic Republic, the former republic of East Germany.

Ge *symbol* (*chem*) germanium.

gear *n* **1** (also **gearwheel**) one of a set of small wheels with interlocking teeth, which combine to change the speed or direction of motion in a machine. **2** a particular combination of these wheels: *second gear*; *change gear*. **3** (*coll*) the equipment or tools needed for a particular job, sport, etc. **4**

(*coll*) clothes. — *v* **1** (*tr* with **to, towards**) to adapt or design to suit a particular need. **2** (*tr*) to supply with, or connect by, gears. **3** (*tr & intr* with **up**) to make or become ready or prepared. — **in gear** (esp. of a motor vehicle) with a gear selected. — **out of gear 1** (of a motor vehicle) with no gear selected. **2** not working properly. [MidE *gere*, from Norse *gervi*]

gearbox *n* (the metal case enclosing) a set of gears, esp. in a motor vehicle.

gear lever or (*NAm*) **gear shift** *n* a lever used in a motor vehicle to change gear.

gecko *n* **-*os*** or **-*oes*** a small tropical lizard with adhesive pads on its feet. [Malay *gekoq*, imit. of its cry]

gee[1] *interj* (also **gee up**) used to encourage a horse to move, or go faster. — *v* **gee up** (*tr*; *coll*) to encourage to work or perform better, more quickly, etc.

gee-gee *n* (*coll*; used esp. to or by small children) a horse.

gee[2] *interj* (*coll*; also **gee whiz**) an expression of surprise, admiration or enthusiasm. [A form of *Jesus*]

geese . See **goose**.

geezer *n* (*coll*) a man, esp. an old man, often odd in some way. [Dialect pronunciation of *guiser*, masked actor in mime]

Geiger counter *n* an instrument for detecting and measuring radioactivity. [Hans *Geiger* (1882–1945), German physicist]

geisha *n* **-*sha*** or **-*shas*** (also **geisha girl**) a female companion for Japanese men, trained in music, dancing and the art of conversation. [Jap *gei*, art + *sha*, person]

gel *n* **1** any jelly-like substance formed by causing a solid to be dispersed through a liquid. **2** (also **hair gel**) such a substance used to fix the hair in place. — *v* **-*ll*- 1** (*intr & tr*) to (cause to) become a gel. **2** (*intr*) to take on a definite form; to jell. [**gelatine**]

gelatine or **gelatin** *n* a clear jelly-like substance made by boiling animal bones and hides, used in foods, glues and photographic materials. [Ital *gelatina*, jelly]

gelatinise or **-ize** *v* (*tr & intr*; *tech*) to make or become like gelatine or jelly.

gelatinous *adj* like gelatine or jelly.

geld *v* (*tr*) to remove the testicles of (esp. a horse). [Norse *geldr*, barren]

gelding *n* a gelded horse.

gelignite *n* a powerful explosive used esp. in mining. [**gelatine** + Lat *ignis*, fire]

gem *n* **1** (also **gemstone**) a precious stone, esp. one cut and polished for use in jewellery. **2** (*coll*) a person or thing that one values, admires or likes very much. [Lat *gemma*, bud, precious stone]

geminate (*tech*) *adj* (esp. of leaves) arranged in pairs. — *v* (*tr & intr*) to arrange, or be arranged, in pairs. — *n* **gemination**. [Lat *geminus*, twin]

Gemini *n* **1** a constellation and the third sign of the zodiac, the Twins. **2** a person born between 21 May and 20 June, under this sign. *n & adj* **Geminean**. [Lat *geminus*, twin]

Gen. *abbrev* General.

gen *n* (*coll*; with **the**) information. — *v* **gen up -*nn*-** (*intr* with **on, about**; *coll*) to acquire thorough knowledge. [*gen*eral information]

gen. *abbrev* genitive.

-gen *comb fm* something that causes or produces: *carcinogen*, a cancer-producing substance. — *adj comb fm* **-genic**. [Gr *-genes*, born]

gendarme *n* a member of an armed police force in France and other French-speaking countries. [Fr *gens d'armes*, armed people]

gender *n* **1** (*gram*) in some languages, the system of dividing nouns and pronouns into different classes. **2** (*gram*) any of these classes, usu. two or three (masculine, feminine and neuter) in European languages. **3** the condition of being male or female; sex. [Lat *genus*, kind]

gene *n* a basic component in cells responsible for passing hereditary characteristics from parents to children. [Ger *Gen*, from Gr *-genes*, born]

-gene. Same as **-gen**.

genealogy *n* **-*ies* 1** (a diagram or account of) a person's direct line of descent from an ancestor. **2** (the study of) the history of families. **3** (the study of) the development of plants and animals into present-day forms. — *adj* **genealogical** . — *n* **genealogist**. [Gr *genea*, race + *logos*, discourse]

genera. See **genus**.

general *adj* **1** of, involving, or applying to all or most parts, people or things; widespread, not specific, limited or localised: *the general opinion*; *general rule*. **2** not detailed or definite; rough; vague: *general description*; *in general terms*. **3** not specialised: *general knowledge*. **4** chief: *general manager*. — *n* **1** a senior army officer of the rank next below Field Marshal. **2** the commander of a whole army. **3** any (esp. competent) leader. **4** the head of a religious order, e.g. the Jesuits. — **in general** usually; mostly. [Lat *generalis*, from *genus*, race, kind]

General Certificate of Education *n* (usu. *abbrev* **GCE**) in England and Wales, a qualification obtainable by passing an examination in one or more subjects at (formerly) Ordinary or O level (after usu. five years of study), or (still) at Advanced or A level and Scholarship or S level (as a requirement for entry into higher education).

General Certificate of Secondary Education *n* (usu. *abbrev* **GCSE**) in England and Wales, a school-leaving qualification in one or more subjects, which replaced the GCE Ordinary level and CSE qualifications in 1988.

general election *n* a national election in which the voters of every constituency in the country elect a member of parliament.

generalise or **-ize** *v* **1** (*intr*) to speak in general terms or form general opinions, esp. too general to be applied to all individual cases. **2** (*tr*) to make more general, esp. applicable to a wider variety of cases: *generalise a law*. — *n* **generalisation** or **-z-**.

generality *n* **-ies 1** the quality of being general. **2** a general rule or principle. **3** the majority.

generally *adv* **1** usually. **2** without considering details; broadly. **3** as a whole; collectively.

general practitioner *n* (usu. *abbrev* **GP**) a community doctor providing basic treatment for all common illnesses, not specialising in any one area of medicine.

general staff *n* the officers assisting a military commander.

general strike *n* a strike by workers in all or most of the industries in a country at one time.

generalissimo *n* **-os** a supreme commander of the combined armed forces in some countries, often also having political power. [Ital, superlative of *generale*, general]

generate *v* (*tr*) to produce or create. [Lat *generare*, from *genus*, a kind]

generation *n* **1** the act of producing (e.g. electricity). **2** all people born and living at about the same time, considered as a group: *the younger generation*. **3** the average period between a person's birth and the birth of his or her children, considered to be between 25 and 30 years: *three generations ago*. **4** a single stage in a person's descent. **5** a particular stage in the development of something: *fourth-generation computers*.

generation gap *n* the difference in the ideas and ways of living of people from different (esp. successive) generations.

generative *adj* (*formal*) **1** able to produce or generate. **2** relating to production or creation.

generator *n* a machine which produces one form of energy (esp. electricity) from another.

generic *adj* **1** from, or relating to, a general class or type. **2** (esp. *US*) not sold as a specific brand: *generic aspirin*. **3** (*biol*) of a genus: *a generic name*. **[genus]**

generosity *n* **1** the quality of being generous. **2** a generous act. **[generous]**

generous *adj* **1** giving or willing to give (esp. money) unselfishly; (of e.g. a donation) large and given unselfishly. **2** large; ample; plentiful: *generous portions*. **3** kind; willing to forgive: *of generous spirit*. — *adv* **generously**. [Lat *generosus*, of noble birth]

genesis *n* **-eses 1** a beginning or origin. **2** (*cap*) the first book in the Old Testament, describing God's creation of the world. [Gr]

genetic *adj* **1** of genes or genetics; inherited: *a genetic defect*. **2** relating to origin: *a genetic study of American folk music*. — *adv* **genetically**. **[gene]**

genetic code *n* (*biol*) the arrangement of genes in a cell, which determines the transmission of hereditary characteristics from a parent to a child.

genetic engineering *n* the artificial alteration of the structure of genes, in order to correct defects or develop particular characteristics in future breeds of plants or animals.

genetic fingerprinting *n* the analysis, from a blood, saliva or tissue sample, of a person's unique gene structure, used as a means of identification.

genetics *n* (*sing*) the scientific study of the transmission of hereditary characteristics. — *n* **geneticist**.

genial *adj* **1** cheerful; friendly; sociable. **2** (of a climate) pleasantly warm or mild. — *n* **geniality**. — *adv* **genially**. [Lat *genialis*, from *genius*, guardian spirit or deity]

genie *n* **-nies** or **-nii** in fairy stories, a spirit with the power to grant wishes. [Fr *génie*]

genitals *n* (*pl*; also **genitalia**) the external sex organs. [Lat *genitalis*, from *gignere*, to beget]

genital *adj* of the genitals or sexual reproduction.

genitive (*gram*) *n* **1** the form, or case, of a noun, pronoun or adjective which shows possession or association, e.g. 'John's'. **2** a noun, etc. in this case. — *adj* of or belonging to this case. [Lat *genitivus*]

genius *n* **-uses** (senses **1** to **4**) or **-ii** (sense **5**) **1** a person of outstanding creative or intellectual ability. **2** such ability. **3** a person who exerts a powerful (good or bad) influence on another. **4** in Roman mythology, a guardian spirit. **5** (*formal*) a quality or attitude with which something (e.g. a country or a period of time) is identified or typically associated: *Rational inquiry was the genius of the century*. [Lat, guardian spirit or deity]

genocide *n* the deliberate killing of a whole nation or people. — *adj* **genocidal**. [Gr *genos*, race + Lat *caedere*, to kill]

genre *n* **1** a particular type or kind (of literature, music or other artistic work). **2** (*art*) a type of painting featuring scenes from everyday life. [Fr]

gent *n* (*coll*) a gentleman.

gents *n* (*sing*) a men's public toilet.

genteel *adj* **1** (*derog*) polite or refined in an artificial, affected way approaching snobbishness. **2** well-mannered. **3** (*old* or *facet*) of, or suitable for, the upper classes. — *adv* **genteelly**. [Fr *gentil*, well-bred]

gentian *n* a small plant of mountainous regions with bright (usu. blue) flowers. [Lat *gentiana*]

gentile *n* & *adj* (often *cap*) (a person who is) not Jewish. [Lat *gentilis*, from *gens*, nation, clan]

gentility *n* **1** good manners and respectability. **2** (*derog*) artificial politeness. **3** (*old*) noble birth; the people of the upper classes. [OFr *gentilite*]

gentle *adj* **1** mild-mannered, not stern, coarse or violent. **2** light and soft; not harsh, loud, strong, etc.: *a gentle caress; a gentle breeze*. **3** moderate; mild: *a gentle reprimand*. **4** (of hills, etc.) rising gradually. **5** (*old*) noble; of the upper classes. — *n* **gentleness**. — *adv* **gently**. [Fr *gentil*, well-bred]

gentlefolk *n* (*pl*; *old*) people of good breeding; members of the upper classes.

gentleman *n* **1** a polite name for a man, used esp. as a form of address. **2** a polite, well-mannered, respectable man. **3** a man from the upper classes, esp. one with enough private wealth to live on without working.

gentleman-at-arms *n* any of a group of men who guard the king or queen on important occasions.

gentlemanly *adj* **1** polite and well-mannered. **2** suitable for, or typical of, a gentleman.

gentleman's, or **gentlemen's**, **agreement** *n* an unwritten agreement to which each participant is bound only by his or her sense of honour.

gentlewoman *n* (*old*) **1** a woman from the upper classes. **2** her female servant or attendant.

gentrification *n* (usu. *derog*) the change in the character of a traditionally working-class area following an influx of new middle-class residents. — *v* (*tr*) **gentrify**, ***-ies***, ***-ied***. **[gentry]**

gentry *n* **1** rich people belonging to the class directly below the nobility. **2** (*pl*; *coll derog*) people (considered inferior). [OFr *genterise*, nobility]

genuflect *v* (*intr*) to bend the knee, esp. in worship or as a sign of respect. — *n* **genuflection** or **-flexion**. [Lat *genu*, knee + *flectere*, to bend]

genuine *adj* **1** authentic, not artificial or fake. **2** honest; sincere. — *adv* **genuinely**. — *n* **genuineness**. [Lat *genuinus*, natural]

genus *n* ***genera*** **1** (*biol*) in plant and animal classification, a group of related species with similar characteristics. **2** a class divided into several subordinate classes. [Lat, race or kind]

geo- *comb fm* of the earth. [Gr *ge*, earth]

geocentric *adj* having the earth as the centre; measured from the centre of the earth.

geode *n* (*geol*) a crystal-lined cavity within a rock, or the rock itself. [Gr *geodes*, earthy]

geodesy *n* the science concerned with determining the precise size and shape of the earth. **[geo-** + Gr *daisis*, division]

geodesic *adj* of, or determined by, geodesy. — *n* a geodesic line.

geodesic line *n* the shortest line between two points on a curved surface.

geog. *abbrev* geographical or geography.

geography *n* **1** the scientific study of the earth's surface, esp. its physical features, climate and population. **2** (*coll*) the layout of a place. — *n* **geographer**. — *adj* **geographical**. — *adv* **geographically**. [Gr *ge*, earth + *graphein*, to write]

geol. *abbrev* geological or geology.

geology *n* **1** the scientific study of the earth's structure, esp. its history and development as shown in the formation of rocks. **2** the features of a particular region which are relevant to such study. — *adj* **geological**. — *adv* **geologically**. — *n* **geologist**. **[geo- + -logy]**

geometry *n* the branch of mathematics dealing with lines, angles, shapes, etc. and their relationships. [Gr *ge*, earth + *metron*, a measure]

geometric or **geometrical** *adj* **1** relating to, or measured using, geometry. **2** using, or consisting of, the kinds of basic forms dealt with in geometry, e.g. lines, circles and triangles: *a geometrical design*.

geometric progression *n* (*math*) a series of quantities which have each been obtained by multiplying or dividing their predecessor by the same fixed amount, e.g. 1, 2, 4, 8.

Geordie (*coll*) *n* **1** a person from Tyneside. **2** the Tyneside dialect. — *adj* of or relating to Tyneside, its people, or their dialect. [Dimin. of the name *George*]

George Cross *n* (*abbrev* **GC**) an award for bravery, usu. given to civilians. [King *George* VI, who instituted it]

George Medal *n* (*abbrev* **GM**) an award for bravery given to civilians and to members of the armed forces.

georgette *n* a kind of thin silk material. [*Georgette* de la Plante, French dressmaker]

Georgian *adj* **1** (of architecture, painting or furniture) from the reign of King George I, II, III and IV, 1714–1830. **2** (of literature) from the reign of King George V, esp. 1910–20. **3** of the Asian republic of Georgia, its people, or their language. **4** of the US State of Georgia, or its people. — *n* **1** a native of, or the official language of, the Asian republic of Georgia. **2** a native of the US state of Georgia.

geostationary *adj* (*tech*) (esp. of a satellite) orbiting the earth so as to stay above the same point on the earth's surface.

geothermal *adj* (*tech*) relating to, or using, the internal heat of the earth.

Ger. *abbrev* German.

geranium *n* **1** any cultivated flower of the Pelargonium genus, with fragrant leaves and bright red, pink or white flowers. **2** (*bot*) a shrub or herb of the Geranium genus, with seed-pods shaped like a crane's bill. [Gr *geranos*, crane]

gerbil *n* a mouse-like desert animal with long hind legs, native to Africa and Asia. [Lat *gerbillus*, little jerboa]

geriatrics *n* the branch of medicine concerned with the diseases of old age. — *n* **geriatrician**. [Gr *geras*, old age + *iatros*, physician]

geriatric *adj* **1** for or dealing with the very old (and ill). **2** (*coll derog*) very old. — *n* (*coll derog*) a very old person.

germ *n* **1** any microscopic plant or creature, esp. one causing disease. **2** any arrangement of plant or animal cells which will develop into a complete organism: *wheatgerm*. **3** an origin or beginning: *the germ of a plan*. [Lat *germen*, bud, sprout]

germ warfare *n* the use of germs to inflict disease on an enemy in war.

German *n* **1** a native or inhabitant of Germany. **2** the official language of Germany, Austria and parts of Switzerland. — *adj* of Germany, its people or their language. [Lat *Germanus*]

Germanic *n* a branch of the Indo-European family of languages that includes German, English, Dutch, and the Scandinavian languages. — *adj* **1** of these languages. **2** typical of Germany or the Germans.

German measles *n* (*sing*) an infectious disease with symptoms similar to measles; rubella.

German shepherd (dog) *n* an Alsatian dog.

german *adj* (*following the noun*) **1** having the same parents as oneself: *brother german*. **2** having the same grandparents as oneself on one side of the family: *cousin german*. [Lat *germanus*, having the same parents]

germane *adj* **(to)** (of ideas, remarks, etc.) relevant; closely related. [Ety. as for **german**]

germanium *n* an element (symbol **Ge**), a hard grey metal used in electronics. [*Germany*, the native country of its discoverer, C A Winkler (1838–1904)]

germicide *n* a substance that kills germs. — *adj* **germicidal**. [**germ** + **-cide**]

germinal *adj* **1** (*tech*) of or relating to germs. **2** in the earliest stage of development. [Lat *germen*, bud, sprout]

germinate *v* (*tr & intr*) to (cause a seed, an idea, etc. to) begin to grow. — *n* **germination**. [Lat *germinare*]

gerontology *n* the scientific study of old age, the ageing process and the problems of elderly people. — *adj* **gerontological**. — *n* **gerontologist**. [Gr *geron*, old man + **-logy**]

gerrymander (*derog*) *v* **-r-** (*tr*) to arrange or change the boundaries of (an electoral constituency) so as to favour one political party. — *n* a constituency arranged in such a way. — *n* **gerrymandering**. [Massachusetts Governor Elbridge *Gerry* (1744–1814) and **salamander** (from the shape on the map of one of his electoral districts after manipulation)]

gerund *n* (*gram*) a noun formed from a verb, in English ending in -ing, and describing an action, e.g. 'the *baking* of bread' and '*Smoking* damages your health.' [Lat *gerundium*, from *gerere*, to bear]

gesso *n* plaster for sculpting with or painting on. [Ital, from Lat *gypsum*; see **gypsum**]

gestalt *n* **-stalts** or **-stalten** (*psychol*) a whole pattern or structure perceived as something greater than simply the sum of its separate parts. [Ger, form]

Gestalt psychology *n* psychology based on the idea that human feelings, thoughts, reactions, etc. are all interconnected and should not be analysed separately.

Gestapo *n* the secret police in Nazi Germany, known for its brutality. [Ger *Ge*heime *Sta*ats*po*lizei, secret state police]

gestate *v* (*tr & intr*) **1** to carry or be carried in the womb from conception to birth. **2** to develop (an idea, etc.) slowly in the mind. — *n* **gestation**. [Lat *gestare*, to carry]

gesticulate *v* **1** (*intr*) to make (bold) gestures, esp. when speaking. **2** (*tr*) to express in this way. — *n* **gesticulation**. [Lat *gesticulare*, from *gestus*, gesture]

gesture *n* **1** a movement of (a part of) the body as an expression of meaning, esp. when speaking. **2** something done to communicate (esp. friendly) feelings or intentions. **3** (usu. *derog*) something done simply as a formality: *Asking her opinion was merely a gesture —he had no intention of taking her advice*. — *v* **1** (*intr*) to make gestures. **2** (*tr*) to express with gestures. — *adj* **gestural**. [Lat *gestus*]

get *v* **-tt-**, ***got*** **1** (*tr*; **back**) to receive or obtain. **2** (*tr*) to have or possess. **3** (*intr & tr*; **across, away, to, through,** etc.) to (cause to) go, move, travel or arrive: *get past him*; *got him to bed*; *got to Paris on Friday*. **4** (*tr*; **down, in, out,** etc.) to fetch, take or bring: *get it down from the shelf*. **5** (*tr*) to put into a particular state or condition: *Don't get it wet*; *got him into trouble*. **6** (*intr*) to become: *got angry*. **7** (*tr*) to catch (a disease, etc.). **8** (*tr*) to order or persuade: *get him to help us*. **9** (*tr*; *coll*) to receive (a broadcast, etc.): *can't get Radio Forth from here*. **10** (*tr*; *coll*) to make contact with, esp. by telephone: *never get him at home*. **11** (*tr*; *coll*) to arrive at by calculation. **12** (*intr* with **to**; *coll*) to receive permission: *get to stay out late*. **13** (*tr*; *coll*) to prepare (a meal). **14** (*tr*; *coll*) to buy or pay for: *got her some flowers for her birthday*. **15** (*tr*; *coll*) to suffer: *got a broken arm*. **16** (*tr*; *coll*) to receive as punishment: *got ten years for armed robbery*. **17** (*tr*; *coll*; **back**) to attack, punish or otherwise cause harm to: *I'll get you back for that!* **18** (*tr & intr*; *coll*; **to**) to annoy: *You shouldn't let him get to you*. **19** (*tr*; *coll*) to understand. **20** (*tr*; *coll*) to hear: *I didn't quite get his name*. **21** (*tr*; *coll*) to affect emotionally. **22** (*tr*; *coll*) to baffle: *You've got me there.* ◇ See also **have got to**. — *n* (*slang derog*) a stupid or contemptible person; a git. — **be getting on for** (*coll*) to approach (a time or an age). — *v* **get about** or **around** (*intr*; *coll*) **1** to travel; to go from place to place. **2** (of a rumour, etc.) to circulate. — *v* **get across** (*tr* & *intr*) to (cause to) be understood. — *v* **get along** (*intr*; *coll*; **with**) to have a friendly relationship. — *v* **get at** (*tr*) **1** to reach or take hold of. **2** (*coll*) to suggest or imply: *What are you getting at?* **3** (*coll*) to persistently criticise or victimise. **4** (*coll*) to (attempt to) influence by dishonest means, e.g. bribery. — *v* **get away** (*intr*) **1** to (be able to) leave. **2** to escape (*n* & *adj* **getaway**). — *interj* (*coll*) an expression of disbelief. — *v* **get away with** (*tr*) to do (something bad) without being caught or punished. — *v* **get back at** (*tr*; *coll*) to take revenge on. — *v* **get by 1** (*intr*; *coll*) to manage to live. **2** (*intr*; *coll*) to be acceptable. — *v* **get down** (*tr*) **1** (*coll*) to make sad or depressed. **2** to (manage to) swallow. **3** to write down. — *v* **get down to** (*tr*) to begin working (seriously) at. — *v* **get in 1** (*intr*) (of a political party) to be elected to power. **2** (*intr*) to be accepted for entry or membership. **3** (*tr*) to gather or harvest. **4** (*tr*; *coll*) to succeed in doing or making: *get some work in before dinner.* — *v* **get in on** (*tr*; *coll*) to take part, or share, in. — *v* **get into** (*tr*; *coll*) **1** to develop a liking or enthusiasm for. **2** to possess or control the behaviour of: *What's got into him?* — *v* **get in with** (*tr*; *coll*) to become friendly with, often for selfish reasons. — **get it** (*slang*) to receive punishment. — **get it together** (*coll*) **1** to use one's energies and abilities effectively. **2** (**with**) to have sex. — **get nowhere** (*coll*) to make no progress, or produce no results. — *v* **get off** (*coll*) **1** (*intr* & *tr*; **with**) to (cause to) escape with no punishment, or with the stated punishment: *got off with a fine*; *get him off with two years.* **2** (*tr*) to stop discussing or dealing with: *get off this subject.* — *v* **get off on** (*tr*; *coll*) to get excitement from. — *v* **get off with** (*tr*; *coll*) to begin a (usu.) casual sexual relationship with. — *v* **get on 1** (*intr*; **in**) to make progress or be successful. **2** (*intr*; **with**) to have a friendly relationship. **3** (*intr*; *coll*) to grow old. **4** (*intr*; **with**) to continue working or coping. **5** (*intr*; *coll*) to grow late. — *v* **get on at** (*tr*; *coll*) to pester or criticise continually. — *v* **get on to** (*tr*) **1** to begin dealing with. **2** (*coll*) to criticise continually; to get on at. — *v* **get out 1** (*intr*) (of information) to become known. **2** (*tr*) to manage to say, usu. with difficulty. — *v* **get out of** (*tr*) to avoid doing. — *v* **get over** (*tr*) **1** to recover from (an illness, disappointment, etc.). **2** to no longer be emotionally affected by, or feel an attachment towards. **3** to make (something) understood; to get across. — *v* **get over with** (*tr*) to deal with (something unpleasant) as quickly as possible: *get the exam over with.* — **get one's own back** (*coll*) to have one's revenge. — *v* **get round 1** (*tr*; *coll*) to persuade, or (easily) win the approval or permission of. **2** (*tr*) to successfully pass by or negotiate (a problem, etc.). **3** (*intr*; *coll*) to become (widely) known. — *v* **get round to** (*tr*) to deal with eventually. — **get somewhere** (*coll*) to make progress. — **get there** (*coll*) to make progress towards, or achieve, one's final aim. — *v* **get through 1** (*tr*) to complete (work, etc.). **2** (*intr*; **to**) to make contact (with another person) by telephone. **3** (*tr*) to use up. **4** (*intr* & *tr* with **to**; *coll*) to make (someone) understand (something): *can't get through to him* (*how important this is*). **5** (*intr* & *tr*; *coll*) to pass (an examination, etc.). — *v* **get up 1** (*intr* & *tr*) to (cause to) get out of bed. **2** (*tr*) to increase (speed). **3** (*intr*) (of wind, etc.) to become strong. **4** (*tr*; *coll*) to arrange, organise or prepare: *get up a celebration.* — *v* **get up to** (*tr*; *coll*) to do or be involved in (something bad). [Norse *geta*, to obtain or beget]

get-at-able *adj* (*coll*) able to be easily reached.

getaway see **get away** above.

get-together *n* (*coll*) an informal meeting.

get-up *n* (*coll*; usu. *derog*) outfit or clothes, when considered strange.

get-up-and-go *n* (*coll*) energy.

gewgaw *n* (*old derog*) a brightly-coloured trinket.

geyser *n* **1** an underground spring spouting out hot water and steam from time to time. **2** a domestic appliance for heating water rapidly. [Icelandic *geysa*, from Norse *göysa*, to gush]

ghastly *adj* **-ier, -iest 1** extremely frightening; hideous; horrific. **2** (*coll*) very bad. **3** (*coll*) very ill. — *adv* (*coll*) extremely; unhealthily: *ghastly pale.* — *n* **ghastliness**. [MidE *gasten*, to terrify]

ghat *n* (*India* & *Pakistan*) **1** a mountain pass. **2** a set of steps leading down to a river. [Hindi, descent]

ghee *n* butter made from cow's or buffalo's milk, purified by heating, used in Indian cooking. [Hindi *ghi*]

gherkin *n* a small variety of cucumber, usu. pickled. [Dut *augurkje*]

ghetto *n* **-os** or **-oes 1** (usu. *derog*) a poor area densely populated by people from a deprived social group, esp. a racial minority. **2** (*hist*) a part of a European city to which Jews were formerly restricted. [Perhaps from Ital *ghetto*, foundry, after one on the site of the first Jewish ghetto, in Venice]

ghetto-blaster *n* (*coll*) a large portable radio-cassette recorder, esp. one playing pop music at high volume.

ghost *n* **1** the spirit of a dead person when visible in some form to a living person. **2** a suggestion, hint or trace. **3** a faint shadow attached to the image on a television screen. — *v* (*intr* & *tr*) to be a ghost writer for (someone), or of (some written work). — *adj* **ghostly**. — **give up the ghost** (*coll*) **1** to die. **2** (*humorous*) to stop working properly. [OE *gast*]

ghost town *n* a deserted town, esp. one formerly thriving.

ghost writer *n* a person who writes books, speeches, etc. on behalf of another person who is credited as their author.

ghoul *n* **1** in Arab mythology, a demon that robs graves and eats dead bodies. **2** a person interested in morbid or disgusting things. — *adj* **ghoulish**. [Arabic *ghul*]

GHQ *abbrev* General Headquarters.

ghyll. Same as **gill**[3].

GI *n* (*coll*) a soldier in the US army, esp. during World War II. [*G*overnment *I*ssue]

giant *n* **1** in fairy stories, a huge, extremely strong, often cruel creature of human form. **2** (*coll*) an unusually large person or animal. **3** a person, group, etc. of exceptional ability or importance: *literary giants*. — *adj* **1** (*coll*) huge: *giant portions*. **2** of a particularly large species, in implied contrast to smaller ones: *giant tortoise*. [Gr *gigas*]

giantess *n* a female giant.

giant-killer *n* (*coll*) a person or team that unexpectedly defeats a superior opponent.

gibber *v* **-r-** (*intr*) **1** to talk so fast that one can not be understood. **2** (*derog*) to talk foolishly. — *adj* **gibbering**. [Imit.]

gibberish *n* **1** fast unintelligible talk. **2** foolish talk; nonsense.

gibbet *n* (*hist*) **1** a gallows-like frame on which the bodies of executed criminals were hung as a public warning. **2** a gallows. — *v* **-t-** (*tr*) **1** (*hist*) to hang on a gibbet. **2** to expose to public ridicule. [Fr *gibet*, gallows]

gibbon *n* a small tailless tree-dwelling ape with very long arms, native to Asia. [Fr]

gibbous *adj* (*tech*) **1** (of the moon or other planet) between half- and fully-illuminated. **2** humpbacked. **3** swollen; bulging. [Lat *gibbus*, hump]

gibe or **jibe** *v* (*intr*; **at**) to mock, scoff or jeer. — *n* a jeer. [OFr *giber*, to treat roughly]

giblets *n* (*pl*) the heart, liver and other edible internal organs of a chicken or other fowl. [OFr *gibelet*, game stew, from *gibier*, game]

giddy *adj* **-*ier***, **-*iest*** **1** suffering an unbalancing spinning sensation. **2** causing such a sensation. **3** (*literary*) overwhelmed by feelings of excitement or pleasure. **4** light-hearted and carefree; frivolous. — *adv* **giddily**. — *n* **giddiness**. [OE *gidig*, insane]

gift *n* **1** something given; a present. **2** a natural ability. **3** the act of giving: *the gift of a book*. **4** (*coll*) something easily obtained, or made easily available. — *v* (*tr*; *formal*) to give (something) as a present to (someone). — **in someone's gift** (*formal*) able to be given away by someone if they wish. — **look a gift-horse in the mouth** to find fault with a gift or lucky opportunity. [Norse *gipt*]

gifted *adj* having a great natural ability.

gift-wrap *v* **-*pp*-** (*tr*) to wrap attractively, (as if) for presentation as a gift.

gig[1] *n* **1** (*hist*) a small open two-wheeled horse-drawn carriage. **2** a small rowing boat carried on a ship. **3** a long lightweight rowing boat used for racing. [MidE *gigge*, whirling thing]

gig[2] (*coll*) *n* **1** a pop concert. **2** a musician's booking to play, esp. for one night only. — *v* **-*gg*-** (*tr*) to play a gig or gigs.

giga- *pfx* **1** ten to the power of nine (10^9): *gigavolt*. **2** (*comput*) two to the power of thirty (2^{30}): *gigabyte*. [Gr *gigas*, giant]

gigantic *adj* huge; enormous. — *adv* **gigantically**. [Gr *gigantikos*, from *gigas*, giant]

giggle *v* (*intr*) to laugh quietly in short bursts or in a nervous or silly way. — *n* **1** such a laugh. **2** (*pl* with **the**) a fit of giggling. **3** (*coll*) a very funny person, situation or activity. — *adj* **giggly**, **-*ier***, **-*iest***. [Imit.]

gigolo *n* **-*os*** **1** (usu. *derog*) the paid male companion and lover of a rich (usu. older) woman. **2** a hired professional dancing partner. [Fr]

gigot *n* a leg of lamb or mutton. [Fr]

gild *v* ***gilded*** or ***gilt*** (*tr*) to cover with a thin coating of gold or something similar. — **gild the lily** to try to improve something which is already beautiful enough, often spoiling it. [OE *gyldan*, gold]

gilder. Same as **guilder**.

gill[1] *n* **1** the breathing organ of many sea animals, esp. this organ in a slit on either side of a fish's head. **2** any of the ribs on the underside of a mushroom. **3** (in *pl*; *coll*) the flesh under the ears and jaw. — **green about the gills** (*coll*) looking or feeling sick. [Perhaps Norse *gil*]

gill[2] *n* **1** a measure of liquid equal to a quarter of a pint. **2** (*coll*) an alcoholic drink. [OFr *gelle*]

gill[3] *n* **1** a deep wooded ravine. **2** a mountain stream. [Norse *gil*]

gillie *n* (also **ghillie**) a guide or assistant to a game-hunter or fisherman, esp. in Scotland. [Gaelic *gille*, boy]

gilt[1] *adj* covered with a thin coating of gold; gilded. — *n* **1** gold or a gold-like substance used in gilding. **2** (in *pl*) gilt-edged securities. [**gild**]

gilt-edged securities *n* (*pl*) government securities with a fixed rate of interest, able to be sold at face value.

gilt[2] *n* a young female pig. [Norse *gyltr*]

gimbals *n* (*pl*) an arrangement of pivoting rings keeping navigation instruments in a horizontal position at sea or in the air. [OFr *gemel*, double ring for a finger]

gimcrack *n* & *adj* (*derog*) (an article that is) cheap, badly made and often gaudy. [MidE *gibecrake*, little ornament]

gimlet *n* **1** a T-shaped hand-tool for boring holes in wood. **2** a cocktail of lime juice and gin or vodka. [OFr *guimbelet*]
gimlet-eyed *adj* having a piercing look or stare.

gimmick *n* (usu. *derog*) a scheme or object used to attract attention or publicity, esp. to bring in customers. — *n* **gimmickry**. — *adj* **gimmicky**.

gimp *n* a strip of silk with a wire core, used as a decoration in dressmaking, etc. [Fr *guimpe*]

gin[1] *n* an alcoholic spirit made from barley, rye or maize, flavoured with juniper berries. [Dut *genever*, juniper]
gin rummy *n* (*coll* **gin**) a version of rummy allowing a finish by a player whose unmatched cards total 10 points or less.
gin sling *n* an iced drink of sweetened gin.

gin[2] *n* **1** a wire noose laid as a trap for animals. **2** a lifting device consisting of wire coiled round a drum turned by hand. **3** a device which turns a vertical shaft using the power from horses pulling a horizontal bar in a circle, used esp. for separating seeds from raw cotton. — *v* ***-nn-*** (*tr*) **1** to trap with a gin. **2** to separate (cotton) with a gin. [OFr *engin*, engine]
gintrap *n* a powerful animal trap with teeth.

ginger *n* **1** a hot-tasting root used in medicine and as a spice in cooking. **2** the Asian plant from which it is taken. **3** a reddish-brown colour. **4** (*coll*) energy; liveliness. — *adj* **1** flavoured with ginger. **2** (usu. of hair) reddish-brown in colour. — *adj* **gingery**. — *v* **ginger up** ***-r-*** (*tr*; *coll*) to urge, persuade or force to become more lively, active or efficient. [Lat *zingiber*, from Sanskrit *srnga*, horn + *vera*, body, from the shape of the root]
ginger ale or **beer** *n* a non-alcoholic fizzy drink flavoured with ginger.
gingerbread *n* cake flavoured with treacle and ginger.
ginger group *n* a small group within a larger (esp. political) group, which urges stronger or more radical action.
ginger nut or **snap** *n* a ginger-flavoured biscuit.

gingerly *adv* & *adj* showing delicate caution. [Perhaps OFr *gensor*, delicate]

gingham *n* striped or checked cotton cloth. [Malay *ginggang*, striped]

gingivitis *n* inflammation of the gums. [Lat *gingiva*, gum + **-itis**]

ginormous *adj* (*coll*) exceptionally huge. [**gigantic** + **enormous**]

ginseng *n* (a plant from China and N America with) an aromatic root used in medicine for its energy-giving properties. [Chin *jen-shen*, image of man, from the shape of the root]

gintrap. See **gin**[2].

gip. Same as **gyp**.

gippy tummy *n* (*coll*) a severe stomach upset, thought of as a hazard of holidaying in hot countries. [**Egyptian**]

gipsy. Same as **gypsy**.

giraffe *n* a tall African mammal with a very long neck, long legs and a ginger-coloured coat with regular brown patches. [Arabic *zarafah*]

gird *v* ***girded*** or ***girt*** (*tr*; *old* or *literary*) to encircle or fasten with a belt or something similar. — **gird (up) one's loins** (*literary*) to prepare oneself for action. [OE *gyrdan*]

girder *n* a large beam of wood, iron or steel used to support a floor, wall, road or bridge. [OE *gyrdan*, to gird]

girdle[1] *n* **1** a woman's close-fitting undergarment worn to reshape the figure from waist to thigh. **2** a belt or cord worn round the waist. **3** a surrounding part, esp. such a part of the body: *pelvic girdle*. — *v* (*tr*) **1** to put a girdle on. **2** (*literary*) to surround. [OE *gyrdan*, to gird]

girdle[2]. Same as **griddle**.

girl *n* **1** a female child. **2** a daughter. **3** (often *offensive*) a young woman, esp. unmarried. **4** (often *offensive*) a woman of any age. **5** (*coll*) a woman's female friend or colleague. **6** a female employee, esp. (*old*) a maid. — *n* **girlhood**. — *adj* **girlish**. [MidE *gerle, girle* and *gurle*, child]
Girl Friday *n* a young woman who does general office work.
girlfriend *n* **1** a female sexual or romantic partner. **2** a female friend, esp. of a woman.
Girl Guide see **guide**.
girlie or **girly** *adj* (*coll euph*) (of magazines) featuring naked or nearly naked women, intended to sexually excite the reader.

giro *n* ***-os*** **1** a banking system by which money can be transferred from one account directly to another. **2** (*coll*) a social security benefit received in cheque form. [Ital, turn or transfer]

girt. See **gird**.

girth *n* **1** distance round something, e.g. a tree or a person's waist. **2** the strap round a horse's belly that holds a saddle in place. [Norse *gjörth*, belt]

gist *n* general meaning; main point. [OFr, from *gesir*, to lie, consist in or reside in]

git *n* (*slang derog*) a stupid or contemptible person. [Variant of **get**]

give *v* ***gave***, ***given*** **1** (*tr*; **to**) to transfer ownership of; to transfer possession of temporarily: *gave him my watch*; *give me your bags*. **2** (*tr*) to provide or administer: *give advice, medicine*. **3** (*tr*) to produce: *Cows give milk*. **4** (*tr*) to perform (an action, service, etc.): *give a smile, a lecture on beetles*. **5** (*tr*) to pay: *gave £20 for it*. **6** (*intr*) to make a donation: *Please give generously*. **7** (*tr*; **up**) to sacrifice: *give one's life*. **8** (*tr*) to be the cause or source of: *gives me pain*. **9** (*intr*) to yield or break: *give under pressure*. **10** (*tr*) to organise at one's own expense: *give a party*. **11** (*tr*) to have as a result: *Four into twenty gives five*. **12** (*tr*) to reward or punish by: *was given 20 years*. **13** (*tr*; *coll*) to agree to or admit: *I'll give you that*. **14** (*tr*) to offer a toast to. **15**

(*tr*) (*sport*, etc.) to declare to be: *gave him offside*. **16** (*intr*; with **on to**, **into**) to lead or be an opening: *a terrace giving on to the lawn*. **17** (*tr*; *coll*; in *imperative*) used to state a preference: *Give me jazz any day*. — *n* capacity to yield; flexibility. — **give as good as one gets** (*coll*) to respond to an attack with equal energy, force and effect. — *v* **give away** (*tr*) **1** to hand over as a gift. **2** to allow to become known, usu. by accident. **3** to present (a bride) to a bridegroom at a wedding ceremony. ◇ See also **give-away** below. — *v* **give in** (*intr*; **to**) to admit defeat; to yield. — *v* **give off** (*tr*) to produce or emit (e.g. a smell). — **give or take** (*coll*) allowing for a (stated) margin of error. — *v* **give out 1** (*tr*) to distribute. **2** (*tr*) to emit; to give off. **3** (*intr*; *coll*) to break down or come to an end: *Their resistance gave out*. **4** (*tr*; *formal*) to declare or make known. — *v* **give over 1** (*tr*) to transfer. **2** (*tr* with **to**) to set aside or devote: *The morning was given over to prayer*. **3** (*intr* & *tr*; *coll*) to stop (doing something). — *v* **give up 1** (*intr*) to admit defeat. **2** (*tr*) to stop making the effort (to): *gave up trying to talk sense to him*. **3** (*tr*) to renounce or quit (a habit, etc.): *give up smoking*. **4** (*tr*) to surrender (oneself) as a prisoner. **5** (*tr* with **to**) to devote (oneself): *gave himself up to charity work*. **6** (*tr*; *formal* with **to**) to allow (oneself) to be overwhelmed by (a feeling): *gave herself up to despair*. **7** (*tr*; **for**) to assume or declare to be, after abandoning hope: *had given you up for dead*. — **give way 1** (**to**) to give priority. **2** to collapse under pressure. **3** (**to**) to allow oneself to be affected by: *give way to tears*. — **what gives?** what is happening? [OE *gefan*]

give-and-take *n* **1** mutual willingness to accept the other's point of view. **2** a useful exchange of views.

give-away *n* (*coll*) **1** an act of accidentally revealing secrets, etc. **2** something obtained extremely easily or cheaply: *The goal was a give-away*. **3** a free gift.

given *adj* **1** stated or specified. **2** (with **to**) in the habit of; prone to: *given to smoking too much*. — *prep* accepting as a basis for discussion; assuming.

gizzard *n* **1** a bird's second stomach, with muscles that break down hard food. **2** (*coll*) the stomach. [OFr *guisier*, fowl's liver]

glacé *adj* **1** coated with a sugary glaze; candied: *glacé cherries*. **2** frozen, or covered with ice. [Fr]

glacial *adj* **1** (*geol* or *geog*) of or caused by ice or glaciers. **2** (*coll*) extremely cold. **3** hostile: *a glacial stare*. — *adv* **glacially**. [Lat *glacialis*, icy]

glacial period *n* any period during which large areas of the earth were covered with ice; an ice age.

glaciate *v* (*tr*; *geol* or *geog*) to cover with, or subject to the eroding action of, moving masses of ice. — *n* **glaciation**. [Lat *glaciare*, to freeze]

glacier *n* an enormous moving or expanding mass of ice, formed from an accumulation of snow. [Fr, from *glace*, ice]

glad *adj* **-dd- 1** (**about**) happy or pleased. **2** (with **of**) grateful. **3** very willing. **4** (*old* or *literary*) bringing happiness: *glad tidings*. — *adv* **gladly**. — *n* **gladness**. [OE *glæd*]

gladden *v* **-n-** (*tr*) to make happy or pleased.

glad eye *n* (*old slang*; with **the**) a sexually inviting look: *giving me the glad eye*.

glad rags *n* (*pl*; *coll*) one's best clothes, worn for special occasions.

glade *n* (*literary*) an open space in a wood or forest.

gladiator *n* in ancient Rome, a man trained to fight against other men or animals in an arena. — *adj* **gladiatorial**. [Lat, swordsman]

gladiolus *n* **-li** or **-luses** a garden plant with sword-shaped leaves and spiky clusters of brightly coloured flowers. [Lat dimin. of *gladius*, sword]

glair *n* egg-white, or a similar substance, used as a glaze or an adhesive. [OFr *glaire*, perhaps from Lat *clarus*, clear]

glamour *n* **1** the quality of being fascinatingly, if perhaps falsely, attractive. **2** great beauty or sexual charm, esp. created by make-up, clothes, etc. — *adj* **glamorous**. — *v* **glamorise** or **-ize** (*tr*). [Old Scottish variant of **grammar**; hence, spell, from the mediaeval association of magic with learning]

glance *v* (*intr*; **at**, **over**, etc.) **1** to look very quickly or indirectly. **2** (*intr* with **off**) to be deflected: *a glancing blow*. **3** (*literary*) to shine in flashes; to glint. — *n* **1** a brief look, often indirect. **2** a deflection. **3** (*literary*) a brief flash of light. — **at a glance** at once; from one brief look. [MidE *glenten*]

gland *n* **1** (*med*) an organ that produces substances to be used by, or excreted from, the body. **2** (*bot*) a cell in plants performing a similar function. [Lat *glans*, acorn]

glanders *n* (*sing*) an infectious, often fatal disease in horses, causing inflammation of the lungs and lymph glands. [Lat *glans*, acorn]

glandular *adj* of, produced by, or affecting a gland or glands. [Fr *glandulaire*]

glandular fever *n* an infectious disease causing prolonged fever and swelling of the lymph glands.

glare *v* (*intr*) **1** (**at**) to stare angrily. **2** to be unpleasantly bright or shiny. — *n* **1** an angry stare. **2** dazzling light. **3** brash colour or decoration. [ODut *glaren*, to gleam]

glaring *adj* **1** unpleasantly bright. **2** obvious. — *adv* **glaringly**.

glasnost *n* openness and willingness to provide information on the part of governments, esp. the Soviet government under Mikhail Gorbachev. [Russ, speaking aloud, openness]

glass *n* **1** a hard, brittle, usu. transparent substance made by melting together and then rapidly cooling a mixture of usu. silicon oxide and certain other compounds. **2** an article made from this, e.g. a mirror, a lens, or esp. a drinking cup. **3** the amount held by a drinking glass. **4** articles made of glass: *a collection of glass*. **5** (in *pl*) spectacles. — *adj* made of glass. — *v* (*tr*) to supply or cover with glass. [OE *glæs*]

glass-blowing *n* the process of shaping molten glass by blowing air into it through a tube. — *n* **glass-blower**.

glasshouse *n* **1** a greenhouse. **2** (*slang*) a military prison.

glasspaper *n* paper coated with finely ground glass, used as an abrasive.

glass wool *n* glass fibres in the form of a wool-like mass, used for insulation.

glassy *adj* **-ier**, **-iest** **1** like glass. **2** expressionless: *glassy eyes*.

Glaswegian *n* a native or citizen of Glasgow. — *adj* of Glasgow or its inhabitants. [After *Norwegian*]

glaucoma *n* an eye disease in which increasing pressure inside the eye causes gradual loss of vision. [Gr *glaukoma*, cataract]

glaucous *adj* **1** of a dull green or blue colour. **2** (*bot*) (of leaves, etc.) covered with a fine green or blue powdery growth. [Gr *glaukos*, bluish-green or grey]

glaze *v* **1** (*tr*) to fit glass panes into (a window, door, etc.). **2** (*tr*) to give a hard shiny transparent coating to (pottery). **3** (*intr*; **over**) (of eyes) to become dull and expressionless. **4** (*tr*) to apply a shiny coating of milk, eggs or sugar to (e.g. pastry). — *n* **1** a hard glassy coating on pottery. **2** a shiny coating of milk, eggs or sugar on food. — *adj* **glazed**. [Ety. as for **glass**]

glazier *n* a person employed to glaze windows, doors, etc.

GLC *abbrev* Greater London Council, abolished in 1986.

gleam *n* **1** a gentle glow. **2** a brief flash of (esp. reflected) light. **3** (**of**) a brief appearance or sign: *a gleam of excitement in his eyes*. — *v* (*intr*) **1** to glow gently. **2** to shine with brief flashes of light. **3** (of an emotion, etc.) to be shown briefly. — *adj* **gleaming**. [OE *glæm*]

glean *v* **1** (*tr*) to collect (information, etc.) bit by bit, often with difficulty. **2** (*tr & intr*) to collect (loose grain left on a field) after harvesting. [OFr *glener*]

gleanings *n* (*pl*) things gleaned, esp. bits of information.

glebe *n* **1** a piece of church-owned land providing income in rent, etc. for the resident minister. **2** (*poetic*) land; a field. [Lat *gleba*, clod]

glee *n* **1** great delight; joy. **2** a song with different parts for three or four unaccompanied (esp. male) voices. [OE *gleo*, mirth]

glee club *n* esp. in the US, a society of singers of glees.

gleeful *adj* joyful; merry. — *adv* **gleefully**.

glen *n* a long narrow valley, esp. in Scotland. [Gaelic *gleann*]

glengarry *n* **-ies** a narrow brimless cap creased along its middle and usu. with two ribbons hanging at the back. [*Glengarry* in Inverness-shire]

glib *adj* **-bb-** (*derog*) speaking or spoken readily and persuasively, but neither sincere nor reliable: *glib politicians, explanations*. — *adv* **glibly**. — *n* **glibness**. [OGer *glibberich*, slippery]

glide *v* (*intr*) **1** to move smoothly: *glide along the ice*. **2** (of birds) to sail through the air without beating the wings. **3** (of an aircraft) to fly without engine power. **4** to fly a glider. **5** to pass gradually: *glide into sleep*. — *n* **1** a gliding movement. **2** (*music*) movement from one note to another with no break in sound. [OE *glidan*, to slip]

glider *n* a small aeroplane with no engine, kept in flight by rising currents of warm air.

glimmer *v* **-r-** (*intr*) to glow faintly. — *n* **1** a faint glow; a twinkle. **2** a hint or trace: *a glimmer of hope*. [MidE *glemern*]

glimpse *n* a very brief look. — *v* (*tr*) to see momentarily. [MidE *glymsen*]

glint *v* (*intr*) to give off flashes of bright light. — *n* a brief flash of light. [MidE *glent*]

glissade *n* **1** a sliding ballet step. **2** (*mountaineering*) an act of sliding down a snowy or icy slope. — *v* (*intr*) to perform a glissade. [Fr, from *glisser*, to slide]

glisten *v* (*intr*) (usu. of something wet, icy, etc.) to give off faint flashes of light. [MidE *glistnen*]

glitch *n* (*coll*) a sudden brief irregularity or failure to function, esp. in electronic equipment. [Perhaps Yiddish *glitsh*, slip]

glitter *v* **-r-** (*intr*) **1** to shine with bright flashes of light; to sparkle. **2** (*coll*; **with**) to be sparklingly attractive or resplendent: *a party glittering with famous film stars*. — *n* **1** sparkle. **2** (*coll*) bright attractiveness, often superficial. **3** tiny pieces of shiny material, esp. silvery paper, used for decoration. — *adj* **glittering**. [MidE *gliteren*]

glitterati *n* (*pl*; *coll*) famous, fashionable and beautiful people. [After **literati**, + **glitter**]

glitzy *adj* **-ier**, **-iest** (*slang derog*) extravagantly showy; flashy. — *n* **glitz**. [Perhaps Ger *glitzern*, to glitter]

gloaming *n* (*poetic*) dusk; twilight. [OE *glomung*]

gloat *v* (*intr*; **over**) to feel or show smug satisfaction, e.g. in one's own success. — *n* an act of gloating. [Perhaps Norse *glotta*, to grin]

glob *n* (*coll*) a small amount of thick liquid; a blob or dollop. [Perhaps **blob**]

global *adj* **1** affecting the whole world. **2** total; including everything. **3** globe-shaped. — *adv* **globally**.

global warming *n* an increase in the temperature of the earth's atmosphere as a result of the greenhouse effect.

globe *n* **1** (**the**) the earth. **2** a sphere with a map of the world on it. **3** any ball-shaped object, e.g. a glass lampshade. [Lat *globus*]

globe artichoke *n* the rounded head of the artichoke plant, with edible leaves.

globeflower *n* a northern plant with pale (esp. yellow) globe-shaped flowers.

globetrotter *n* (*coll*) a person who travels all over the world. — *n* **globetrotting**.

globular *adj* **1** shaped like a globe or globule. **2** consisting of globules. [Lat *globulus*, dimin. of *globus*, globe]

globule *n* a small drop, esp. of liquid.

glockenspiel *n* a musical instrument consisting of tuned metal plates in a frame, played with two small hammers. [Ger *Glocke*, bell + *Spiel*, play]

gloom *n* **1** near-darkness. **2** sadness or despair. — *v* **1** (*intr*) (of the sky) to be dark and threatening. **2** (*intr*) to behave in a sad or depressed way. **3** (*tr*) to make dark. **4** (*tr*) to make depressed or depressing. — *adv* **gloomily**. — *adj* **gloomy**. [MidE *gloumbe*]

glorify *v* **-ies**, **-ied** (*tr*) **1** to exaggerate the beauty, importance, etc. of. **2** to praise or worship (God). **3** to make glorious. — *n* **glorification**. [Lat *gloria*, glory + *facere*, to make]

glorified *adj* (*derog*) given a fancy name or appearance.

glorious *adj* **1** having or bringing glory. **2** splendidly beautiful. **3** (*coll*) excellent. **4** (*coll facet*) very bad: *glorious mess*. — *adv* **gloriously**.

glory *n* **-ies 1** great honour and prestige. **2** great beauty or splendour. **3** praise and thanks given to God. **4** a greatly admired asset: *Patience is her crowning glory*. — *v* **-ies**, **-ied** (*intr*; **in**) to feel or show great delight or pride. [Lat *gloria*]

glory-hole *n* (*coll*) a room or cupboard where odds and ends are (untidily) kept. [Perhaps MidE *glory*, to defile]

Glos. *abbrev* Gloucestershire.

gloss[1] *n* **1** shiny brightness on a surface. **2** a superficial pleasantness or attractiveness. **3** (also **gloss paint**) paint which produces a shiny finish. **4** a substance which adds shine: *lip gloss*. — *v* (*tr*) **1** to give a shiny finish to. **2** to paint with gloss. — *v* **gloss over** (*tr*) to conceal, esp. by treating briefly and dismissively.

glossy *adj* **-ier**, **-iest 1** smooth and shiny. **2** superficially attractive. **3** (of a magazine) printed on shiny paper. — *adv* **glossily**. — *n* **glossiness**.

gloss[2] *n* a short explanation of a difficult word, phrase, etc. in a text, e.g. in the margin. — *v* (*tr*) to provide a gloss of (a word, etc.), or add glosses to (a text). [Lat *glossa*, word requiring explanation]

glossary *n* **-ies** a list of glosses, often at the end of a book.

glottis *n* **-tises** or (*med*) **-tides** the space between the vocal cords, at the entrance to the windpipe. [Lat *glotta*, tongue]

glottal *adj* (*tech*) of or produced by the glottis.

glottal stop *n* (*tech*) a sound produced when the glottis is closed and then opened sharply, e.g. the sound substituted for a 't' in words such as 'bottle' in some pronunciations of English.

glove *n* a covering for the hand, usu. with a separate sheath for each finger. ◇ See also **mitten**. — *v* (*tr*) to cover with a glove or gloves. — **fit like a glove** to fit perfectly. — **the gloves are off** (*coll*) the serious argument, fight, etc. is about to begin. [OE *glof*]

glover *n* a glove-maker.

glow *v* (*intr*) **1** to give out a steady heat or light without flames. **2** (**with**) to shine brightly, as if very hot: *cheeks glowing with health*. **3** (**with**) to feel or communicate a sensation of intense contentment or well-being: *glow with pride*. — *n* **1** a steady flameless heat or light. **2** bright, shiny appearance. **3** intensity of (esp. pleasant) feeling. [OE *glowan*]

glowing *adj* **1** which glows. **2** full of praise: *glowing report*.

glow-worm *n* a European beetle the female and larva of which have a luminous tail.

glower *v* **-r-** (*intr*; **at**) to stare angrily. — *n* an angry stare; a scowl.

glucose *n* **1** a sugar present in plant and animal tissue. **2** a starch-based syrup containing this, used in food. [Gr *glykys*, sweet]

glue *n* any natural or man-made adhesive. — *v* **glueing** or **gluing** (*tr*) **1** to join with glue. **2** (*coll* with **to**) to put or stay very close to; to fix on: *eyes glued to the window*. — *adj* **gluey**, **-ier**, **-iest**. [Lat *glus*]

glue-sniffing *n* the practice of breathing in fumes from some types of glue to produce hallucinatory or intoxicating effects. — *n* **glue-sniffer**.

glum *adj* **-mm-** in low spirits; sullen. — *adv* **glumly**. — *n* **glumness**. [MidE *glome*, to frown]

glut *n* **1** an excessive supply (of goods, etc.). **2** an act of eating an unreasonably or unnecessarily large amount of food. — *v* **-tt-** (*tr*) **1** to feed or supply to excess. **2** to block or choke up. [Lat *glutire*, to swallow]

gluten *n* a protein found in cereals, esp. wheat. [Lat *gluten*, glue]

glutinous *adj* like glue; sticky. [Lat *gluten*, glue]

glutton[1] *n* **1** (*derog*) a person who eats too much. **2** (with **for**) a person whose behaviour suggests an eagerness (for something unpleasant): *glutton for punishment*. — *adj* **gluttonous**. [Lat *gluttire*, to swallow]

gluttony *n* (*derog*) the habit or practice of eating too much.

glutton[2] . Same as **wolverine.**

glycerine or **glycerin** *n* (also **glycerol**) a sweet sticky colourless liquid, a by-product of soap manufacture, with various industrial uses. [Gr *glykeros*, sweet]

glycogen *n* a starch-like substance, the form in which carbohydrate is stored in the animal liver. — *adj* **glycogenic**. [Gr *glykys*, sweet + **-gen**]

GM *abbrev* George Medal.

gm *abbrev* gram or gramme.

GMT *abbrev* Greenwich Mean Time.

gnarled *adj* (also **gnarly**, **-*ier***, **-*iest***) (of trees, branches, etc.) twisted; with knots and lumps, usu. as a result of age. [MidE *knarre*, knob-like protuberance]

gnash *v* (*tr* & *intr*) to grind (the teeth) together, esp. in anger. [MidE *gnasten*]

gnashers *n* (*pl*; *humorous slang*) teeth.

gnat *n* any of various small biting (and often bloodsucking) flies, common near stagnant water. [OE *gnætt*]

gnaw *v* ***gnawed*** or ***gnawn*** **1** (*tr* & *intr*; **away, at**) to bite with a scraping action, causing a gradual wearing away. **2** (*tr*) to make (e.g. a hole) in this way. **3** (*tr* & *intr*; **at**) to persistently cause physical or mental pain. — *adj* **gnawing**. [OE *gnagan*]

gneiss *n* coarse-grained rock made up of quartz, feldspar and mica. [Ger *Gneis*]

gnome *n* **1** a fairy-tale creature, a small misshapen man, who lives underground, often guarding treasure. **2** a statue of such a creature, esp. as a garden ornament. **3** (*coll*) a person with a secret powerful influence, esp. in finance: *gnomes of Zurich*. — *adj* **gnomish**. [Lat *gnomus*, dwarf]

gnomic *adj* (*formal*) (of speech or writing) **1** expressing generally held views or principles. **2** (often *derog*) moralising. [Gr *gnome*, opinion]

gnostic *adj* **1** relating to knowledge, esp. mystical or religious knowledge. **2** (*cap*) relating to Gnosticism. — *n* (*cap*) an early Christian heretic believing in redemption of the soul from the world of matter through special religious knowledge. — *n* **Gnosticism**. [Gr *gnosis*, knowledge]

GNP *abbrev* gross national product.

gnu *n* ***gnus*** or ***gnu*** a type of large African deer with a buffalo-like head and horns. [Hottentot]

go[1] *v* ***goes***, ***went***, ***gone*** **1** (*tr* & *intr*; **about, by, down**, etc.) to walk, move or travel. **2** (*intr* & *tr*; **across, down**, etc.) to lead or extend: *a path going across the field*; *The road goes all the way to the farm.* **3** (*intr*; **to**) to visit or attend, once or regularly: *go to the cinema*; *go to school*. **4** (*intr*) to leave or move away. **5** (*intr*) to be destroyed or taken away; to disappear: *The old door had to go. The peaceful atmosphere has gone.* **6** (*intr*) to proceed or fare: *The scheme is going well.* **7** (*intr*; **on**) to be used up: *money going on drink*. **8** (*intr*; **for**) to be given or sold. **9** (*intr* with **for, on**, or a verb ending in **-ing**) to leave for the purpose of having or doing: *go for a ride*, *on holiday*; *gone fishing*. **10** (*intr* & *tr*) to perform (an action) or produce (a sound): *go like this*; *go bang*. **11** (*intr*) to break, break down or fail: *The old TV finally went. His eyes have gone.* **12** (*intr*) to work or be in working order: *get it going*. **13** (*intr*) to become; to pass (into a certain condition): *go mad*. **14** (*intr*) to belong: *Where does this go?* **15** (*intr*) to fit, or be contained: *My foot won't go into the shoe. Four into three won't go.* **16** (*intr*) to continue (in a certain state): *go hungry*. **17** (*intr*) (of time) to pass. **18** (*intr*) to run in words or notes: *as the story goes*. **19** (*intr* with **for**) to apply; to be valid or accepted: *The same goes for you. In this office, anything goes.* **20** (*intr*; *coll*) to carry authority: *What she says goes.* **21** (*intr*; **with**) (of colours, etc.) to match or blend. **22** (*intr* with **with**) to co-exist: *Goodness doesn't always go with beauty.* **23** (*intr* with **by**) to be guided: *Don't go by what he says.* **24** (*intr* with **to**) to subject oneself: *go to trouble*. **25** (*intr*) to adopt a system: *go metric*. **26** (*tr*) to bet, esp. at cards: *went five pounds*. **27** (*intr*; *coll*) to be in general, for the purpose of comparison: *As girls go, she's quite naughty*. **28** (*intr*) to exist or be on offer: *the best offer going at the moment*. **29** (*tr*; *coll*) to welcome or enjoy: *I could go a cup of tea*. **30** (*tr*; *coll*) to say. — *n* ***goes*** **1** a turn or spell: *It's my go*. **2** an attempt: *have a go*. **3** energy; liveliness: *She lacks go*. **4** a verbal attack: *really had a go at me*. **5** (*coll*) busy activity: *It's all go*. **6** (*coll*) a success: *make a go of it*. — *adj* (*coll*) working properly; in operation: *all systems go*. — **be going on for** (*coll*) to be approaching: *She's going on for 60*. — *v* **go about 1** (*tr*) to busy oneself with. **2** (*tr*) to attempt or tackle: *how to go about doing this*. **3** (*intr*) to circulate: *a rumour going about*. **4** (*intr*; *naut*) to change course. — *v* **go against** (*tr*) **1** to be contrary to. **2** to be decided unfavourably for: *The court case went against him*. — *v* **go ahead** (*intr*) to proceed. ◇ See also **go-ahead** below. — **go all out for** or **to** to make a great effort to obtain or achieve. — *v* **go along with** (*tr*) to agree with and support. — **go and** to be so stupid as to: *They've gone and got lost*. — *v* **go back on** (*tr*) to break (an agreement, etc.). — *v* **go down** (*intr*; *coll*) **1** (**with**) to be accepted or received: *The joke went down well*. **2** (with **with**) to contract (an illness). — *v* **go for** (*tr*; *coll*) **1** to attack. **2** to be attracted by. **3** to choose: *went for the red dress instead*. — *v* **go in for** (*tr*; *coll*) **1** to take up (a profession). **2** to enter (a contest). **3** to be interested or attracted by, as a rule. — *v* **go into** (*tr*) **1** to take up or join (a profession). **2** to discuss or investigate. — **go it alone** (*coll*) to (try to) manage without help, esp. in difficulties. — *v* **go off 1** (*intr*) to explode. **2** (*intr*) to become rotten. **3** (*tr*) to cease to like. **4** (*intr*) to proceed or pass off: *The party went off well*. — *v* **go on** (*intr*) **1** (**to**) to continue or proceed. **2** (*coll*) to talk too much. **3** (with **at**; *coll*) to criticise or complain to persistently. — *v* **go out** (*intr*) **1** to become extinguished. **2** to be broadcast. **3** (with **to**) to feel sympathy: *My heart went out to him.* **4** (**with**) to spend time with socially or esp. romantically. **5** to no longer be fashionable.— *v* **go over 1** (*tr*) to examine. **2** (*tr*) to revise or rehearse. **3** (*intr*) to pass off or be received: *The play went over well.* **4** (*intr* with **to**) to transfer support or allegiance: *go over to the enemy.* — *v* **go round** (*intr*) to be enough for all. — **go slow** to work slowly so as to encourage an employer to negotiate or meet a demand (*n* **go-slow**). — *v* **go through 1** (*tr*) to use up. **2** (*tr*) to revise or rehearse. **3** (*tr*) to examine. **4** (*tr*) to suffer. **5** (*tr*) to search. **6** (*intr*) to be approved. — *v* **go through with** (*tr*) to carry out to the end. — *v* **go under** (*intr*; *coll*) to fail or become ruined. — *v* **go up** (*intr*) **1** to increase. **2** (of a building, etc.) to be erected. **3** (*coll*) to be destroyed by fire or explosion. — *v* **go with** (*coll*) to have a close romantic friendship with. — *v* **go without** (*intr* & *tr*) to suffer a lack of (an essential thing or things). — **have going for one** (*coll*) to have as an attribute or advantage: *You have a lot going for you.* — **no go** (*coll*) not possible; in vain. — **on the go** (*coll*) busily active. — **to be going on with** (*coll*) for the moment: *enough to be going on with.* [OE *gan*]

go-ahead (*coll*) *adj* energetically ambitious and far-sighted. — *n* (with **the**) permission to start.

go-between *n* a messenger between two people or sides; an intermediary.

go-by: **give the go-by** (*coll*) to ignore or snub.

goer *n* **1** (*in cmpds*) a person who makes (esp. regular) visits: *cinema-goer*. **2** (*coll*) a sexually energetic person, esp. a woman. **3** (*coll*) something that travels fast, or makes fast progress.

go-getter *n* (*coll*) an ambitious, enterprising person. — *adj* **go-getting**.

going *n* **1** an act of leaving; a departure. **2** the condition of the track in horse-racing. **3** progress: *made good going.* **4** (*coll*) general situation or conditions: *when the going gets tough.* **5** (*in cmpds*) the act or practice of making (esp. regular) visits to: *theatre-going.* — *adj* **1** working, esp. bringing in business: *a going concern.* **2** usual or accepted: *the going rate.*

going-over *n* (*coll*) **1** a beating. **2** a close inspection.

goings-on *n* (*pl*; *coll*) events or happenings, esp. if strange or disapproved of.

go-kart *n* a low racing vehicle consisting of a frame with wheels, engine and steering gear.

go-slow see **go slow** above.

no-go area *n* an area of a city to which access is controlled by one of the groups involved in e.g. an armed conflict or civil war.

go^2 *n* a Japanese board game for two players. [Jap]

goad *v* (*tr*; **into**) to urge or provoke. — *n* **1** a sharp-pointed stick used for driving cattle, etc. **2** anything that provokes or incites. [OE *gad*]

goal *n* **1** (the space between, or the area around) the set of posts through which the ball is struck to score points in various games. **2** an act of scoring in this way; the point or points scored. **3** an aim or purpose. [Perhaps MidE *gol*, boundary]

goalie *n* (*coll*) a goalkeeper.

goalkeeper *n* the player guarding the goal in various sports, with the task of preventing the opposition from scoring.

goal-line *n* the line marking each end of the field of play in some games.

goalpost *n* one of two upright posts forming the goal in some games. — **move the goalposts** to change the accepted rules or aims of an activity during its course, to suit new conditions.

goat *n* **1** a sure-footed horned bearded animal of the sheep family, bred for its milk and wool. **2** (*coll derog*) a man, esp. if old, who makes unwanted sexual advances to women. **3** (*coll derog*) a foolish person. **4** (*cap* with **the**) the constellation and sign of the zodiac Capricorn. — *adj* **goatish**. — **get someone's goat** (*coll*) to annoy or irritate (someone). [OE *gat*]

goatee *n* a pointed beard growing on the front of the chin only, like a goat's.

goatherd *n* a person who looks after goats.

gob *n* **1** (*vulg slang*) the mouth. **2** a soft wet lump. **3** (*vulg slang*) spit. — *v* ***-bb-*** (*intr*; *vulg slang*) to spit. [OFr *gober*, to gulp down]

gobsmacked *adj* (*coll*) astonished; dumbfounded.

gobstopper *n* (*coll*) a large round sweet for sucking.

gobbet *n* **1** a lump or chunk. **2** (*coll*) an extract from a text. [OFr *gobet*, dimin. of *gobe*, mouthful]

gobble *v* **1** (*tr* & *intr*; **up, down**) to eat hurriedly and noisily. **2** (*intr*) (of turkeys) to make a loud swallowing noise in the throat. — *n* the gobbling sound made by a turkey. [OFr *gober*, to gulp down]

gobbler *n* (*US*) a male turkey.

gobbledygook or **gobbledegook** *n* (*coll*, usu. *derog*) **1** official jargon, meaningless to ordinary people. **2** nonsense; rubbish. [Imit., after **gobble**]

goblet *n* a drinking-cup with a base and stem but no handles, often made from metal or glass. [OFr *gobelet*, dimin. of *gobel*, cup]

goblin *n* in folk-tales, an evil or mischievous spirit in the form of a small man. [OFr *gobelin*, perhaps from Gr *kobalos*, mischievous spirit]

goby *n* **-*ies*** a small fish whose lower fins are joined to form a sucker. [Lat *gobius*, gudgeon]

god *n* **1** (*cap*) in the Christian and other monotheistic religions, the unique supreme being, creator and ruler of the universe. **2** in other religions, a superhuman masculine being with power over nature and man, an object of worship. **3** a man greatly admired, esp. for his fine physique or wide influence. **4** (often *derog*) an object of excessive worship or influence: *He made money his god.* — *adj* **godlike**. — **the gods** (the people in) the balcony or upper circle in a theatre. [OE]

godchild *n* a child for whom a godparent is responsible.

goddaughter *n* a female godchild.

goddess *n* **1** a superhuman feminine being with power over nature and man, an object of worship. **2** a woman greatly admired for her great beauty or wide influence.

godfather *n* **1** a male godparent. **2** the head of a criminal group, esp. in the Mafia.

God-fearing *adj* respectful of God's laws; pious.

God-forsaken *adj* (*derog*) remote and desolate.

Godhead *n* **1** the state of being God. **2** (with **the**) God.

godless *adj* **1** not religious; not believing in God. **2** wicked; immoral. — *n* **godlessness**.

godly *adj* **-*ier***, **-*iest*** religious; pious. — *n* **godliness**.

godmother *n* a female godparent.

godparent *n* a person with responsibility for the religious education of another, esp. a child, or, loosely, for a child's upbringing in the event of the death of its parents.

godsend *n* a person or thing whose arrival is unexpected but very welcome.

godson *n* a male godchild.

Godspeed *interj* (*old*) an expression of wishes for a person's safety on a journey.

godwit *n* a large wading bird of northern regions, with an upturned bill.

goer. See **go**[1].

gofer *n* (esp. *US*) an office junior who runs errands. [**go for**]

goggle *v* **1** (*intr*; **at**) to look with wide staring eyes. **2** (*tr*) to roll (the eyes). **3** (*intr*) (of eyes) to stick out. — *n* a wide-eyed stare. [Perhaps MidE *gogelen*, to look aside]

goggle-box *n* (*coll*) a television set.

goggles *n* (*pl*) protective spectacles with edges fitting closely against the face.

go-go dancer *n* a female erotic dancer, esp. in a club or bar. [Fr *à gogo*, galore, aplenty]

goitre *n* enlargement of the thyroid gland, caused by its production of too much or too little hormone, resulting in (often massive) swelling in the neck. [Fr *goître*, from Lat *guttur*, throat]

gold *n* **1** an element (symbol **Au**), a soft yellow precious metal used for making jewellery, coins, etc. **2** articles made from it, esp. jewellery and coins. **3** its value, used as a standard for the value of currency. **4** its deep yellow colour. **5** (*coll*) a gold medal. **6** precious or noble quality: *heart of gold.* **7** monetary wealth. — *adj* **1** made of gold. **2** gold-coloured. [OE]

gold-digger *n* **1** a person who digs for gold. **2** (*slang derog*) a person who starts love affairs with rich people in order to get at their money.

gold dust *n* gold in the form of a very fine powder.

golden *adj* **1** gold-coloured. **2** made of or containing gold. **3** happy; prosperous or thriving: *golden years, age*. **4** excellent; extremely valuable: *golden opportunity*. **5** greatly admired or favoured: *golden girl*. **6** (of an anniversary) 50th.

golden eagle *n* a large northern mountain eagle with golden-brown plumage.

golden handshake *n* (*coll*) a large sum received from an employer on retirement, or in compensation for compulsory redundancy.

golden jubilee *n* a 50th anniversary.

golden mean *n* the midpoint between two extremes.

goldenrod *n* a plant with a rod-like stem and spikes of yellow flowers.

golden rule *n* **1** any essential principle or rule. **2** Christ's instruction to treat others as one would wish to be treated by them.

golden syrup *n* light golden-coloured treacle.

goldfield *n* an area where gold is mined.

goldfinch *n* a small European songbird the male of which has a yellow band across each wing.

goldfish *n* **-*fishes*** or **-*fish*** a small deep-orange Eurasian freshwater fish, often kept in aquariums.

gold leaf *n* gold rolled or beaten into very thin sheets, used to decorate books, etc.

gold medal *n* a medal awarded to the winner of a sporting contest, or in recognition of excellence, e.g. of a wine.

gold mine *n* **1** a place where gold is mined. **2** (*coll*) a source of great wealth.

gold plate *n* **1** a thin coating of gold, esp. on silver. **2** articles, e.g. spoons and dishes, made of gold. — *v* (*tr*) **gold-plate**. — *adj* **gold-plated**.

gold rush *n* a frantic settlement of masses of people in a newly-discovered goldfield.

goldsmith *n* a person who makes articles out of gold.

golf *n* a game played on a large outdoor course, the object being to hit a small ball into each of a series of (nine or eighteen) holes using a set of long-handled clubs, taking as few strokes as possible. — *v* (*intr*) to play this game. — *n* **golfer**. [Perhaps ODut *colf*, club]

golf club *n* **1** any of the set of long-handled clubs used to play golf. **2** an association of players of golf, or its premises with a golf course attached.

golf links *n* a golf course, esp. by the sea.

goliath *n* (*coll*) **1** an unusually large or tall person. **2** a person or organisation of great importance or influence. [*Goliath*, the Old Testament Philistine giant killed by David]

golliwog or **gollywog** *n* a child's cloth doll with a black face and fuzzy hair. [A character in children's books in the US]

golly[1] *interj* (*old*) an expression of surprise or admiration. [A euph. form of *God*]

golly[2] *n* **-ies** (*coll*) a golliwog.

golosh. See **galosh**.

-gon *comb fm* (*math*) a shape with a given number of sides: *polygon*. [Gr *gonia*, angle]

gonad *n* (*med*) an organ which produces reproductive cells, esp. the testis or ovary. [Gr *gone*, generation]

gondola *n* **1** a long narrow flat-bottomed boat with pointed upturned ends, used on the canals of Venice. **2** the passenger cabin suspended from an airship, balloon or cable-railway. [Venetian dialect]

gondolier *n* a person who rows a gondola on a canal.

gone *v* past participle of **go**. — *adj* **1** departed. **2** lost. **3** dead. **4** (*coll*) pregnant: *four months gone*. **5** (*coll*) in ecstasy. **6** (*coll*; with **on**) in love (with); fanatical (about).

goner *n* (*coll*) a person or thing beyond hope of recovery.

gonfalon *n* a banner hung from a horizontal bar. [Ital *gonfalone*, from OGer *gund*, battle + *fano*, flag]

gong *n* **1** a hanging metal plate which sounds when struck. **2** (*slang*) a medal. [Malay]

gonorrhoea *n* a sexually transmitted disease of the genitals, causing inflammation, a discharge, and a severe burning pain when urinating. [Gr *gonos*, seed, semen + *rheein*, to flow]

goo *n* (*coll*) **1** any sticky substance. **2** (*derog*) excessive sentimentality. — *adj* **gooey**, ***-ier***, ***-iest***.

good *adj* ***better***, ***best*** **1** having desirable or necessary (positive) qualities; admirable. **2** (**at**) competent; talented; well-made. **3** morally correct; virtuous. **4** (**for**) beneficial. **5** (**of**) kind and generous. **6** bringing happiness or pleasure: *good news*. **7** well-behaved. **8** wise; advisable: *a good buy*. **9** thorough. **10** finest among others: *my good cups*. **11** adequate; satisfactory: *a good supply*. **12** enjoyable: *having a good time*. **13** valid. **14** well-respected. **15** (**for**) sound; giving use; serviceable: *The roof is good for another winter*. **16** considerable; at least: *waited a good while*; *last a good month*. **17** (**for**) certain to provide the desired result: *good for a laugh*, *for a few pounds*. — *n* **1** moral correctness; virtue. **2** benefit; advantage: *do you good*; *£20 to the good*. **3** (*pl*; with **the**) good people. — *interj* an expression of approval or satisfaction. — *adv* (*coll*; esp. *US*) well. — **as good as** almost; virtually. — **for good (and all)** for ever; permanently. — **good and...** (*coll*) very; completely or absolutely: *good and ready*. — **good for** or **on you**, **him**, etc. (sometimes *ironic*) an expression of approval or congratulation. — **good morning**, **afternoon**, etc. expressions of farewell or esp. greeting. — **make good 1** to repair. **2** to be successful. **3** to carry out or fulfil. [OE *god*]

goodbye *interj* an expression of farewell. — *n* an act of saying goodbye.

good-for-nothing *n* & *adj* (a person who is) lazy and irresponsible.

Good Friday *n* a Christian festival on the Friday before Easter, in memory of Christ's crucifixion.

goodies *n* (*pl*; *coll*) things considered pleasant or desirable. ◇ See also **goody** below.

goodly *adj* ***-ier***, ***-iest*** (*old*) **1** quite large. **2** physically attractive; fine. — *n* **goodliness**.

goodness *n* **1** the state or quality of being good; generosity; kindness; moral correctness. **2** (*euph*) (used in exclamations) God: *goodness knows*. **3** nourishing quality: *all the goodness of the grain*. — *interj* an expression of surprise or relief.

goods *n* (*pl*) **1** articles for sale; merchandise. **2** freight: *goods train*. **3** (*coll*) the required result: *deliver the goods*. **4** (*old*) personal possessions. — **have the goods on** (*coll*) to have proof of wrongdoings or crimes committed by.

goodwill *n* **1** a feeling of kindness towards others. **2** the good reputation of an established business, seen as having an actual value.

goody (*coll*) *n* **-ies** a hero in a film, book, etc. ◇ See also **goodies** above.

goody-goody *n* & *adj* (*coll*) (a person who is) virtuous in a proud or self-satisfied way.

goof (*coll*; esp. *US*) *n* **1** a silly or foolish person. **2** a stupid mistake. — *v* (*intr*) **1** to make a stupid mistake. **2** (with **around**) to spend time idly or foolishly. [Perhaps OFr *goffe*, clumsy]

goofy *adj* ***-ier***, ***-iest*** (*coll*) silly; crazy.

googly *n* **-ies** (*cricket*) a ball bowled so as to change direction unexpectedly after bouncing.

goon *n* **1** (*coll*) a silly person. **2** (*slang*) a hired thug. [US cartoon character Alice the *Goon*, created by E C Segar (1894–1938)]

goosander *n* a large duck with a serrated bill, native to Europe and N America. [Perhaps **goose** + Norse *ander*, plural of *önd*, duck]

goose *n* ***geese*** (senses **1** to **4**), ***gooses*** (sense **5**) **1** a long-necked, web-footed bird like a large duck. **2** the female, as opposed to the gander, the male. **3** the flesh of a goose cooked as food. **4** (*old coll*) a silly person. **5** (*coll*) a poke or pinch on the buttocks. — *v* (*tr*; *coll*) to poke or pinch (someone) on the buttocks. — **cook**

someone's goose (*coll*) to ruin someone's plans or chances. [OE *gos*]
goosepimples *n* (*pl*; also *n* **goose flesh** and *n* (*pl*) **goosebumps**) a condition in which tiny raised lumps appear on the skin and body hair becomes erect, caused by cold, fear, excitement, etc.
goose-step *n* a military marching step in which the legs are kept rigid and swung very high. — *v* **goose-step** (*intr*).

gooseberry *n* **-ies 1** (the thorny shrub that produces) a small round edible berry, yellowish-green or reddish-purple. **2** (*coll*) a person whose presence with two others, esp. lovers, is (presumed to be) unwanted. — **play gooseberry** (*coll*) to be an unwanted third person.

gopher *n* **1** any of various burrowing rat-like animals found in Europe, Asia and N and Central America. **2** a burrowing N American tortoise.

Gordian: **cut the Gordian knot** (*literary*) to solve a difficult problem by forceful, decisive action. [*Gordius*, king of the ancient Asian country of Phrygia, who tied a complicated knot that no one could untie; Alexander the Great solved the problem by cutting the knot with a sword]

gore[1] *n* blood from a wound, esp. when clotted. [OE *gor*, filth]

gore[2] *v* (*tr*) to pierce with horn or tusk. [OE *gar*, spear]

gore[3] *n* a triangular piece of material, e.g. a section of an umbrella or a tapering piece in a garment. — *v* (*tr*) to construct from, or shape with, gores. — *adj* **gored**. [OE *gara*, triangular piece of land]

gorge *n* **1** a deep narrow valley, usu. containing a river. **2** the contents of the stomach. **3** a spell of greedy eating. **4** (*arch*) the throat or gullet. — *v* **1** (*intr* & *tr*) to eat or swallow greedily. **2** (*tr*; **on**) to stuff (oneself) with (food). — **make one's gorge rise** to disgust or sicken one; to fill one with resentment. [OFr *gorge*, throat]

gorgeous *adj* **1** extremely beautiful or attractive; magnificent. **2** (*coll*) excellent; extremely pleasant. — *adv* **gorgeously**. — *n* **gorgeousness**. [OFr *gorgias*, fine, elegant]

gorgon *n* **1** (*cap*; *mythol*) any of three monstrous sisters with live snakes for hair, capable of turning people to stone. **2** (*coll derog*) a fierce, frightening or very ugly woman. [Gr *gorgos*, terrible]

Gorgonzola *n* a blue-veined Italian cheese with a sharp flavour. [*Gorgonzola*, a town near Milan]

gorilla *n* **1** a powerfully built dark brown ape, the largest of all apes, native to W Africa. **2** (*coll*) a brutal-looking man, esp. a hired thug. [Gr *Gorillai*, a tribe of hairy African women]

gormless *adj* (*coll derog*) stupid; dim. — *adv* **gormlessly**. [Variant of obsolete *gaumless*, from *gaum*, understanding]

gorse *n* a wild thorny evergreen shrub with yellow flowers. — *adj* **gorsy**. [OE *gorst*]

gory *adj* **-ier**, **-iest 1** causing or involving bloodshed. **2** (*coll*) unpleasant: *gory details*. **3** covered in gore. [**gore**]

gosh *interj* (*coll*) a mild expression of surprise. [Euph. form of **God**]

goshawk *n* a large bluish-grey hawk native to Europe, Asia and N America. [OE *gos*, goose + *hafoc*, hawk]

gosling *n* a young goose. [OE *gos*, goose + **-ling**]

gospel *n* **1** the life and teachings of Christ: *preach the gospel*. **2** (*cap*) (the record of these in) any of the New Testament books ascribed to Matthew, Mark, Luke and John. **3** (*coll*; also **gospel truth**) the absolute truth. **4** a set of closely followed principles or rules. **5** (also **gospel music**) lively religious music of Black American origin. [OE *godspel*, from *god*, good + *spel*, story]

gossamer *n* **1** fine filmy spider-woven threads seen on hedges or floating in the air. **2** any soft fine material. [MidE *gossomer*, goose summer, a period in November when goose was traditionally eaten, and these cobwebs often seen]

gossip *n* **1** (usu. *derog*) talk or writing about the private affairs of others, often spiteful and untrue. **2** (*derog*) a person who engages in or spreads such talk. **3** (a) casual and friendly chat. — *v* **-pp-** (*intr*) **1** to engage in, or pass on, malicious gossip. **2** to chat. — *adj* **gossipy**. [OE *godsibb*, godparent, hence a familiar friend one chats to]

got. See **get**.

Goth *n* **1** a member of a Scandinavian people who invaded various parts of the Roman Empire between the third and fifth centuries. **2** a rude or uncivilised person. [OE *Gotan*]
Gothic *adj* **1** of the Goths or their language. **2** of a style of architecture featuring high pointed arches, popular in Europe between the 12th and 16th centuries. **3** of a type of literature dealing with mysterious or supernatural events in an eerie setting, popular in the 18th century. **4** (also **gothick**) of a modern style of literature, films, etc. which imitates this. **5** of various styles of heavy black printed letter. — *n* **1** Gothic architecture or literature. **2** Gothic lettering. **3** the extinct Germanic language of the Goths.

gotten (*US*) past participle of **get**.

gouache *n* **1** (a painting technique using) a blend of watercolour and a glue-like substance, giving an opaque matt surface. **2** a painting done in this way. [Fr]

Gouda *n* a flat round mild Dutch cheese. [*Gouda* in Holland]

gouge *n* **1** a chisel with a rounded hollow blade, used for cutting grooves or holes in wood. **2** a groove or hole made using this. — *v* (*tr*) **1** (**out**) to cut out (as if) with a gouge. **2** (with **out**) to press out: *gouged his eye out*. [OFr, from Lat *gubia*, chisel]

goulash *n* a thick meat stew heavily seasoned with paprika, orig. from Hungary. [Hungarian *gulyas hus*, herdsman's meat]

gourd *n* **1** (any of various plants related to the cucumber which bear) a large hard-skinned fruit similar to a marrow. **2** the hollowed-out skin of the fruit, dried and used esp. as a water container. [OFr *gourde*]

gourmand *n* **1** a greedy eater; a glutton. **2** a gourmet. — *n* **gourmandise** or **gourmandism**. [Fr]

gourmet *n* a person with expert knowledge of, and a passion for, good food and wine. [Fr]

gout *n* a disease of the blood which causes painful swelling of the joints, esp. of the toes. — *adj* **gouty**. [OFr *goute*, a drop, the disease having formerly been thought of as caused by drops of humours]

Gov. or **gov.** *abbrev* **1** government. **2** governor.

govern *v* **1** (*tr* & *intr*) to control and direct the affairs of (a country, state or organisation). **2** (*tr*) to guide or influence; to control or restrain: *govern his temper*. **3** (*tr*; *gram*) to determine the form, or case, taken by (a word). — *adj* **governable**. — *adj* **governing**. [Lat *gubernare*, from Gr *kybernaein*, to steer]

governance *n* (*formal*) **1** the act or state of governing. **2** the system of government. **3** authority or control.

governess *n* (esp. *hist*) a woman employed to teach, and perhaps look after, children, usu. resident in their home.

government *n* **1** (often *cap* with **the**) a body of people, usu. elected, with the power to control the affairs of a country or state. **2** the way in which this is done; the particular system used. **3** the act or practice of ruling. **4** (*gram*) the power of one word to determine the form, or case, of another. — *adj* **governmental**.

governor *n* **1** (often *cap*) the elected head of a US state. **2** the head of an institution, e.g. a prison. **3** a member of a governing body of a school, hospital, college, etc. **4** (often *cap*) the head of a colony or province, esp. the monarch's representative. **5** (*coll*; usu. **guvnor** or **guv'nor** , or **guv**) one's boss or father; a respectful form of address used to any man.

Governor-General *n* ***Governors-General*** or ***Governor-Generals*** *n* the official representative of the British monarch in a Commonwealth country or British colony.

Govt. *abbrev* Government.

gown *n* **1** a woman's long formal dress. **2** an official robe worn by clergymen, lawyers and academics. **3** a surgeon's protective overall. **4** (*formal*) the members of a university, esp. as opposed to *town*, the residents of the university town. [Lat *gunna*, garment made of fur or leather]

goy *n* ***goys*** or ***goyim*** (*slang*) a Jewish word for a non-Jewish person. [Hebr, people, nation]

GP *abbrev* **1** Gallup poll. **2** general practitioner.

GPO *abbrev* general post office.

Gr *abbrev* Greek.

gr. *abbrev* **1** grain. **2** gram or gramme. **3** gross.

grab *v* **-*bb-*** **1** (*tr* & *intr*; **at**) to seize suddenly and often with violence. **2** (*tr*) to take greedily. **3** (*tr*) to take hurriedly or without hesitation: *grab a snack*, *an opportunity*. **4** (*tr*; *coll*) to impress or interest: *How does that grab you?* — *n* **1** an act of taking suddenly or greedily. **2** a mechanical device with scooping jaws, used e.g. for excavation. — **up for grabs** (*coll*) available, esp. easily or cheaply. [OGer dialect or ODut *grabben*]

grace *n* **1** elegance and beauty of form or movement. **2** decency; politeness: *had the grace to offer*. **3** a short prayer of thanks to God said before or after a meal. **4** a delay allowed, esp. to a debtor, as a favour. **5** a pleasing or attractive characteristic: *social graces*; *a saving grace*. **6** (*relig*) the mercy and favour shown by God to mankind. **7** (*relig*) (of a person's soul) the condition of being made free from sin and evil by God. **8** (*cap*; with **His**, **Your**, etc.) a title used of or to a duke, duchess or archbishop. — *v* (*tr*) **1** (often *facet*) to honour (e.g. with one's presence). **2** to add beauty or charm to. — **airs and graces** behaviour meant to impress others or to show that one considers oneself superior to them. — **with (a) good** or **(a) bad grace** willingly or unwillingly. [Lat *gratia*, favour]

grace-and-favour *adj* (of a property) owned by the monarch and let rent-free.

graceful *adj* having or showing elegance and beauty of form or movement. — *adv* **gracefully**. — *n* **gracefulness**.

graceless *adj* **1** awkward in form or movement. **2** bad-mannered. — *adv* **gracelessly**. — *n* **gracelessness**.

the Graces *n* (*pl*; *Gr mythol*) the three sister goddesses with the power to grant beauty, charm and happiness.

gracious *adj* **1** kind and polite. **2** (of God) merciful. **3** having qualities of luxury, elegance, comfort and leisure. **4** (*formal*) used out of polite custom to describe a royal person or their actions. — *interj* an expression of surprise. — *adv* **graciously**. — *n* **graciousness**. [Lat *gratiosus*]

gradation *n* **1** (one stage or degree in) a series of gradual and successive stages or degrees. **2** the act or process of forming grades or stages. **3** the gradual change or movement from one state, musical note, colour, etc. to another. — *v* (*tr*) **gradate**. — *adj* **gradational**. [**grade**]

grade *n* **1** a stage or level on a scale of quality, rank, size, etc. **2** a mark indicating this. **3** (esp. *US*) (the pupils, or the level of work taught, in) a particular class or year in school. **4** slope or gradient. — *v* (*tr*) **1** to arrange in different grades. **2** to award a mark indicating grade to. **3** to produce a gradual blending or merging of (esp. colours). — **make the grade** (*coll*) to succeed; to reach the required or expected standard. [Lat *gradus*, step]

gradient *n* **1** the steepness of a slope. **2** (*formal*) a slope. **3** (*tech*) a measure of a gradual change, e.g. in the angle of a curve, over a specified distance. [Lat *gradiens*, stepping]

gradual *adj* **1** developing or happening slowly, by degrees. **2** (of a slope) not steep; gentle. — *adv* **gradually**. [Lat *gradualis*, from *gradus*, step]

gradualism *n* the process of, or support for, gradual progress or change, esp. in politics. — *n* & *adj* **gradualist**.

graduand *n* a person who is about to be awarded a higher-education degree. [Lat *graduare*, to take a degree]

graduate *v* **1** (*intr*; **in, from**) to receive an academic degree from a higher-education institution. **2** (*intr*; *NAm*) to receive a diploma at the end of one's course of study at a high school. **3** (*intr*) to move up from a lower to a higher level, often in stages. **4** (*tr*) to mark (e.g. a thermometer) with units of measurement or other divisions. **5** (*tr*) to arrange into regular groups, according to size, type, etc. — *n* a person with a higher-education degree or (*NAm*) a high-school diploma. [Lat *graduare*, to take a degree, from *gradus*, step]

graduation *n* **1** the act of receiving a higher-education degree or (*NAm*) a high-school diploma. **2** the ceremony marking this. **3** a unit of measurement or other division marked on a ruler, thermometer, etc.; the process of marking such divisions.

Graeco- *comb fm* of Greece; Greek: *Graeco-Roman*.

graffiti *n* (*pl*; *sing* **graffito**) words or drawings, usu. of a humorous, rude or political nature, scratched or painted on walls, etc. in public places. [Ital]

graft[1] *n* **1** a living plant shoot inserted into another to form a new growth. **2** a piece of skin or bone from one part of the body used to replace an unhealthy piece in another part. **3** a transplanted organ. — *v* **1** (*tr*; **in, into, on, together**) to attach a graft in; to attach as a graft. **2** (*intr*) to attach grafts. [OFr *graffe*, from Gr *graphein*, to write]

graft[2] *n* **1** (*coll*) hard work. **2** (*slang*) the use of illegal or unfair means to gain profit, esp. by people in the public eye; the profit gained. — *v* (*intr*) **1** (*coll*) to work hard. **2** (*slang*) to gain profit through corruption.

grafter *n* (*coll*) a hard worker.

Grail. See **Holy Grail** at **holy**.

grain *n* **1** a single seed of a cereal plant. **2** cereal plants or their seeds as a whole. **3** a small hard particle of anything. **4** a very small amount: *a grain of truth*. **5** a small unit of weight, equal to 0·065 grams. **6** the direction or arrangement of the lines of fibre in wood, paper or leather, or of the layers in rock; the pattern they form. **7** (any of) the tiny light and dark particles which form the image on a photograph. — *v* **1** (*tr* & *intr*) to (cause to) form into grains. **2** (*tr*) to give a rough appearance or texture to. **3** (*tr*) to paint or stain with a pattern like the grain of wood or leather. — **go against the grain** to be against one's principles or natural character. [Lat *granum*, seed]

grainy *adj* **-ier**, **-iest** (of a photograph) having a large grain size, and therefore not sharp or distinct.

gram or **gramme** *n* the basic unit of weight in the metric system, one thousandth of a kilogram, equal to 0·035 ounces. [Gr *gramma*, small weight]

gram. *abbrev* grammar or grammatical.

-gram *sfx* something written or recorded (in the stated way): *diagram*; *telegram*. [Gr *gramma*, letter]

grammar *n* **1** (the branch of language study dealing with) the accepted rules by which words are formed and combined into sentences. **2** a description of these rules as applied to a particular language; a book containing this. **3** a person's understanding or use of these rules: *bad grammar*. [Gr *gramma*, letter]

grammarian *n* an expert on grammar.

grammar school *n* esp. formerly, a secondary school emphasising the study of academic rather than technical subjects.

grammatical *adj* **1** relating to grammar. **2** correct according to the rules of grammar. — *adv* **grammatically**. [Gr *grammatikos*, from *gramma*, letter]

gramme. See **gram**.

gramophone *n* a record-player, esp. an old-fashioned one. [Gr *gramma*, letter or record + *phone*, sound]

grampus *n* **1** a grey blunt-nosed dolphin that blows out air and water noisily. **2** a killer whale. **3** a person who breathes heavily. [OFr *graspois*, from *gras*, fat + *pois*, fish]

gran *n* (*coll*) a grandmother.

granary *n* **-ies** **1** a building where grain is stored. **2** a region that produces large quantities of grain. — *adj* (of bread) containing whole grains of wheat. [Lat *granarium*, from *granum*, grain]

grand *adj* **1** large or impressive in size, appearance or style. **2** (sometimes *derog*) dignified; self-important. **3** intended to impress or gain attention: *a grand gesture*. **4** complete; in full: *grand total*. **5** (*coll*) very pleasant; excellent. **6** greatest; highest ranking: *Grand Master*. **7** highly respected: *grand old man*. **8** main; principal: *the grand entrance*. — *n* **1** ***grand*** (*slang*) a thousand dollars or pounds. **2** (*coll*) a grand piano. — *adv* **grandly**. [Fr, from Lat *grandis*, great]

grand duchess *n* **1** the wife or widow of a grand duke. **2** a high-ranking noblewoman who rules a grand duchy.

grand duchy *n* a small European country or state having a grand duke or grand duchess as its sovereign.

grand duke *n* a high-ranking nobleman who rules a grand duchy.

grand jury *n* in the US, a jury which decides whether there is enough evidence for a person to be brought to trial.

the Grand National *n* a steeplechase held annually at Aintree racecourse in Liverpool, famous for its high and difficult fences.

grand opera *n* serious opera in which all the dialogue is sung.

grand piano *n* a large piano in which the strings are arranged horizontally, used esp. for concerts.

grand slam *n* **1** (*sport*) the winning in one season of every part of a competition, or of all major competitions. **2** (*cards*) esp. in bridge, the winning of all thirteen tricks by one player or side, or the contract to do so.

grandstand *n* the largest covered stand at a sports ground, providing the best view.

grand tour *n* **1** a tour of the major cities of Europe, considered essential to the education of a rich young person, esp. in the 18th century. **2** (*coll*) any extended tour or inspection.

grand- *in cmpds* indicating a family relationship that is one generation more remote than that of the base word. [Ety. as for **grand**]

grandad *n* (*coll*) **1** a grandfather. **2** (*offensive*) an old man.

grandchild, **-daughter**, **-son** *n* a child, daughter, son, of one's son or daughter.

grandfather, **-mother**, **-parent** *n* the father, mother, parent, of one's father or mother.

grandfather clock *n* a clock built into a tall free-standing wooden case, operated by a long pendulum.

grandma (*coll*) a grandmother.

grandpa *n* (*coll*) a grandfather.

grandee *n* **1** a Spanish or Portuguese nobleman of the highest rank. **2** any well-respected or high-ranking person. [Span *grande*]

grandeur *n* **1** greatness of character, esp. dignity or nobility. **2** impressive beauty; magnificence. **3** (*derog*) self-importance; pretentiousness. [Fr]

grandiloquent *adj* (*derog*) speaking, or spoken or written, in a pompous, self-important style. — *n* **grandiloquence**. — *adv* **grandiloquently**. [Lat *grandis*, great + *loqui*, to speak]

grandiose *adj* **1** splendid; magnificent; impressive. **2** (*derog*) exaggeratedly impressive or imposing, esp. on a ridiculously large scale. [Ital *grandioso*, from *grande*, great]

grand mal *n* (*med*) the most violent form of epilepsy, resulting in prolonged loss of consciousness. [Fr, great illness]

grand prix *n* ***grands prix*** any of a series of races held annually in various countries to decide the motor racing championship of the world. [Fr, great prize]

grange *n* a country house with farm buildings attached. [OFr, barn]

granite *n* a hard coarse-grained grey or red rock composed of feldspar and quartz, used for building. [Ital *granito*, grained]

granny or **grannie** *n* ***-ies*** (*coll*) a grandmother.

granny flat *n* (*coll*) a flat for an elderly relative or parent, built on to or contained in a house.

granny knot *n* a reef knot with the ends crossed the wrong way, allowing it to slip or undo easily.

Granny Smith *n* a crisp green variety of (orig. Australian) eating apple.

grant *v* (*tr*) **1** to give, allow or fulfil. **2** to admit to be true. — *n* **1** something granted, esp. an amount of money from a public fund for a specific purpose. **2** (*legal*) the transfer of property by deed. — **granted** I admit that is true; I agree with that. — **take for granted 1** to assume to be true. **2** to treat casually, without appreciation. [OFr *granter* or *greanter*, variant of *creanter*, to promise]

Granth *n* (also **Granth Sahib**) the sacred scripture of the Sikh religion. [Hindi, book]

granular *adj* (*tech*) **1** made of, or containing, tiny particles or granules. **2** (of appearance or texture) rough. — *n* **granularity**. [Ety. as for **granule**]

granulate *v* (*tr*) **1** to break down into small particles or grains. **2** to give a rough appearance or texture to. — *n* **granulation**. [Ety. as for **granule**]

granule *n* a very small particle or grain. [Lat *granulum*, dimin. of *granum*, grain]

grape *n* **1** a berry, usu. green (**green** or **white grape**) or dark purple (**black grape**), growing in clusters on vines, eaten as a fruit, pressed to make wine, and dried to make currants, raisins and sultanas. **2** (*literary* or *pompous*; with **the**) wine. [OFr, bunch of grapes]

grapefruit *n* ***-fruit*** or ***-fruits*** a large round citrus fruit with thick yellow skin and slightly sour flesh.

grapeshot *n* ammunition in the form of small iron balls, spreading when fired in bunches from a cannon.

grapevine *n* **1** a vine on which grapes grow. **2** (*coll*; with **the**) informal chat between people, seen as a network through which information is reliably spread.

graph *n* a diagram which shows changes or comparisons in value, quantity, etc. by means of printed dots, lines or blocks. — *v* (*tr*) to represent with a graph. [Short for *graphic formula*, from Gr *graphein*, to write]

graphic *adj* **1** described or shown vividly and in detail. **2** of the branch of the arts concerned with drawing, printing and lettering: *graphic design*. **3** relating to graphs; shown using a graph. — *adv* **graphically**.

graphic equaliser *n* a device for boosting or cutting frequencies of an audio signal using a type of sliding control.

graphic novel *n* a full-length story, esp. of science fiction or a similar form of fantasy, told in comic-strip form and published as a book.

graphics *n* **1** (*sing*) the art or science of drawing according to mathematical rules. **2** (*pl*) the photographs and illustrations used in a magazine; the non-acted visual parts of a film or television programme, e.g. the credits.

graph paper *n* paper covered in small squares, used for drawing graphs.

-graph *comb fm* **1** an instrument that writes or records: *telegraph*. **2** something written or recorded: *autograph*. — *adj comb fm* **-graphic** or **-graphical**. [Gr *graphein*, to write]

graphite *n* a black soft form of carbon with various industrial and commercial uses, esp. as the 'lead' in pencils. [Gr *graphein*, to write + **-ite**]

graphology *n* the study of handwriting, esp. as a way of analysing the writer's character. — *n* **graphologist**. [Gr *graphein*, to write + **-logy**]

-graphy *comb fm* **1** a type of writing or method of representing: *biography*; *lithography*. 2 a descriptive science or art: *geography*; *choreography*. [Gr *graphein*, to write]

grapnel *n* **1** a large multi-pointed hook on the end of a rope, used for securing a heavy object on the other end. **2** a light anchor for small boats. [OFr *grapin*, dimin. of *grape*, hook]

grapple *v* **1** (*intr*; **with**) to grasp and struggle or fight. **2** (*intr*; **with**) to struggle mentally (with a difficult problem). **3** (*tr*) to secure with a hook, etc. — *n* **1** a hook or other device for securing. **2** an act of gripping, as in wrestling; a way of gripping. [OFr *grappelle*, dimin. of *grape*, hook]

grappling-iron or **-hook** *n* a grapnel.

grasp *v* **1** (*tr*) to take a firm hold of; to clutch. **2** (*intr*; **at**) to make a seizing movement. **3** (*tr*) to understand. — *n* **1** a grip or hold. **2** power or control; ability to reach, achieve or obtain: *in one's grasp*. **3** ability to understand: *beyond their grasp*. [MidE *graspen*]

grasping *adj* (*derog*) greedy, esp. for wealth.

grass *n* **1** any of numerous wild plants with (esp. green) blade-like leaves, covering the ground in fields, lawns, etc., and eaten by various animals. **2** any of a family of plants with long stems and thin leaves, including cereals and bamboo. **3** lawn or pasture. **4** (*slang*) marijuana. **5** (*slang*) a person who betrays others, esp. to the police. — *v* **1** (*tr*) to plant with grass or turf. **2** (*tr*) to feed with grass; to provide pasture for. **3** (*intr*; *slang*; **on**) to inform, esp. to the police. — *adj* **grassy**, ***-ier***, ***-iest***. — **let the grass grow under one's feet** to delay or waste time. — **put out to grass 1** to give a life of grazing to (e.g. an old racehorse). **2** (*coll*) to put (e.g. a worker) into retirement. [OE *gærs*, *græs*]

grasshopper *n* a jumping insect that makes a chirping noise by rubbing its long back legs against its wings.

grass roots *n* (*pl*) **1** ordinary people, as opposed to those in a position of (esp. political) power. **2** bare essentials; fundamental principles. — *adj* **grass-roots**.

grass snake *n* a small harmless European snake with a brownish-green body.

grass widow or **widower** *n* a person whose husband or wife is absent from home for long periods of time.

grate[1] *n* **1** a framework of iron bars for holding coal, etc. in a fireplace or furnace. **2** the fireplace or furnace itself. [Lat *grata*]

grate[2] *v* **1** (*tr*) to cut into shreds by rubbing against a rough surface. **2** (*tr* & *intr*) to (cause to) make a harsh grinding sound by rubbing. **3** (*intr* with **on**, **upon**) to irritate or annoy. [OFr *grater*, to scrape]

grater *n* a (usu. metal) device with a rough surface for grating food.

grateful *adj* **1** feeling thankful; showing or giving thanks. **2** (*formal*) pleasant and welcome: *grateful sleep*. — *adv* **gratefully**. ◇ See also **gratitude**. [Lat *gratus*, pleasing, thankful]

gratify *v* ***-ies***, ***-ied*** (*tr*) **1** to please. **2** to satisfy or indulge (e.g. a desire). — *n* **gratification**. [Lat *gratus*, pleasing, thankful + *facere*, to make]

grating[1] *n* a framework of metal bars fixed into a wall e.g. over a window, or into a pavement e.g. over a drain. [Ety. as for **grate**[1]]

grating[2] *adj* **1** (of sounds, etc.) harsh. **2** irritating. — *n* a grating sound. [Ety. as for **grate**[2]]

gratis *adv* & *adj* free; without charge. [Lat, from *gratia*, favour]

gratitude *n* the state or feeling of being grateful; thankfulness. [Lat *gratus*, thankful]

gratuitous *adj* **1** done without good reason; unnecessary or unjustified. **2** given or received without charge; voluntary. — *adv* **gratuitously**. [Lat *gratuitas*, from *gratia*, favour]

gratuity *n* ***-ies*** **1** a sum of money given as a reward for good service; a tip. **2** a sum of money given to a soldier, etc. on retirement, in recognition of long service. [Lat *gratus*, thankful]

grave[1] *n* **1** a hole dug in the ground for burying a dead body in. **2** the site of an individual tomb. **3** (*literary*; with **the**) death. — **dig one's own grave** to be the cause of one's own downfall. — **turn in one's grave** (often *humorous*) (of one's spirit after death) to be disturbed by events or actions which would have distressed one when alive. [OE *græf*, grave or trench, from *grafan*, to dig]

gravestone *n* a stone marking a grave, usu. having the dead person's name and dates of birth and death engraved.

graveyard *n* a burial place; a cemetery.

grave[2] *adj* **1** giving cause for great concern; very dangerous. **2** very important; serious. **3** solemn and serious in manner. — *adv* **gravely**. [Lat *gravis*]

grave[3] *n* (also **grave accent**) a sign placed above a vowel in some languages, e.g. *à* and *è* in French, to indicate a particular pronunciation or extended length of the vowel. [Fr]

gravel *n* **1** a mixture of small stones and coarse sand, used for the surface of paths and roads. **2** (*med*) stone-like masses of mineral salts in the kidneys or bladder. — *v* **-ll-** (*tr*) to cover (e.g. a path) with gravel. [OFr *gravele*]

gravelly *adj* **1** full of, or containing, small stones. **2** (of a voice) rough and usu. deep.

graven *adj* **1** (*old*) carved or engraved. **2** firmly fixed in the mind. [Old word *grave*, to carve or engrave]

graven image *n* (*Bible*) a carved idol used in worship.

gravid *adj* (*med*) pregnant. [Lat *gravis*, heavy]

gravimeter *n* an instrument for measuring variations in gravity at different points on the earth's surface. [Lat *gravis*, heavy + Gr *metron*, measure]

gravimetry *n* (*tech*) measurement of weight. — *adj* **gravimetric**.

gravitas *n* (*literary*) seriousness of manner; solemnity. [Lat]

gravitate *v* (*intr*) **1** to fall or be drawn under the force of gravity. **2 (to, towards)** to move or be drawn gradually, as if attracted by some force. [**gravity**[1]]

gravitation *n* **1** the force of attraction existing between two objects; gravity. **2** the process of moving or being drawn, either by this force or some other attracting influence. — *adj* **gravitational**.

gravity[1] *n* **1** the natural force which causes objects to be drawn towards each other, esp. the force which attracts things towards the Earth, causing them to fall to or stay on the ground. **2** the quality of having weight. [Lat *gravitas*, heaviness]

gravity[2] *n* **1** seriousness; dangerous nature. **2** serious attitude; solemnity. [Lat *gravitas*, seriousness]

gravy *n* **-ies 1** the juices released by meat as it is cooking. **2** a sauce made by thickening and seasoning these juices; a similar sauce made with an artificial substitute. **3** (*slang*) easily obtained money. [Perhaps Fr *gravé*, mistaken reading of *grané*, cooking spice]

gravy boat *n* a small boat-shaped container with a handle, for serving gravy and other sauces.

gravy train *n* (*slang*) a job or scheme from which a lot of money is gained for little effort.

gray (esp. *US*). Same as **grey**.

grayling *n* **-ing** or **-ings** a silver-grey freshwater fish of the salmon family. [**grey**]

graze[1] *v* **1** (*intr*) (of animals) to eat grass. **2** (*tr*) to feed (animals) on grass. [OE *grasian*, from *græs*, grass]

grazing *n* land with grass for animals to feed on; pasture.

graze[2] *v* (*tr*) **1** to suffer a break in the skin of (e.g. a limb), through scraping against a hard rough surface. **2** to brush against lightly in passing. — *n* **1** an area of grazed skin. **2** the action of grazing skin.

grease *n* **1** animal fat softened by melting or cooking. **2** any thick oily substance, esp. a lubricant for the moving parts of machinery. — *v* (*tr*) **1** to lubricate or dirty with grease. **2** to ease the progress of. — **grease the palm** or **hand of** (*coll*) to bribe. — **grease the wheels** (*coll*) to make progress easier. [OFr *graisse*]

greasepaint *n* waxy make-up used by actors.

greaser *n* **1** a person whose job it is to grease machinery. **2** (*slang*) a member of a gang of usu. long-haired motorcyclists. **3** (*US offensive slang*) a Mexican or Spanish American.

greasy *adj* **-ier**, **-iest 1** containing, or covered in, grease. **2** having an oily appearance or texture. **3** slippery, as if covered in grease. **4** (*coll*) insincerely friendly or flattering. — *n* **greasiness**.

great *adj* **1** outstandingly talented, and much admired and respected. **2** very large in size, quantity, intensity or extent. **3** (*biol*, etc.; also **greater**) larger in size than others of the same kind. **4** (*coll*) very enjoyable; excellent or splendid. **5** (*coll*; **at**) clever; talented. **6** (*coll*; **for**) very suitable or useful. **7** most important: *the great advantage of it*. **8** enthusiastic; keen: *a great reader*. **9** (*coll*) used to emphasise other adjectives describing size, esp. **big**. **10** (*cap*) in names and titles, indicating an importance or reputation of the highest degree: *Alfred the Great*. **11** (*old*) used in various expressions of surprise: *Great Scott!* — *n* a person who has achieved lasting fame, deservedly or not: *all-time greats*. — *adv* **greatly**. — *n* **greatness**. [OE]

the Great Bear *n* Ursa Major, a constellation of stars in the N hemisphere, whose seven brightest stars form the Plough.

Great Britain *n* the largest island in Europe, containing England, Wales and Scotland, and forming, together with Northern Ireland, the United Kingdom.

greatcoat *n* a heavy overcoat.

Great Dane *n* a very large breed of smooth-haired dog.

the Great War *n* the First World War, 1914–18.

great- *in cmpds* indicating a family relationship that is one generation more remote than that of the base word: *great-grandmother*. [OE]

great-aunt, **-uncle** *n* an aunt or uncle of one's father or mother.

great-grandchild, **-granddaughter**, **-grandson** *n* a child, daughter or son of one's grandchild.

great-nephew, **-niece** *n* a son or daughter of one's nephew or niece.

greave *n* (usu. in *pl*) a piece of armour for the leg below the knee. [OFr *greve*, shin]

grebe *n* a long-necked freshwater diving bird with a very short tail and webless feet. [Fr *grèbe*]

Grecian *adj* (of design, etc.) in the style of ancient Greece. [Lat *Graecus*, Greek]

Grecian nose *n* an uncurved nose forming a straight line with the forehead.

Greco-. Same as **Graeco-**.

greed *n* **1** an excessive desire for, or consumption of, food. **2** selfish desire in general, e.g. for money. [Back-formation from **greedy**, from OE *grædig*]

greedy *adj* ***-ier***, ***-iest*** filled with greed. — *adv* **greedily**.

Greek *n* **1** the official language of Greece. **2** a native or inhabitant of Greece. **3** (*coll*) any language, jargon or subject one cannot understand. — *adj* **1** of Greece, its people, or their language. [Lat *Graecus*]

green *adj* **1** of the colour between yellow and blue in the spectrum, the colour of the leaves of most plants. **2** covered with grass, bushes, etc.: *green areas of the city*. **3** consisting mainly of leaves: *green salad*. **4** (of fruit) not yet ripe. **5** (*coll*) (of people) young, inexperienced or easily fooled. **6** showing concern for, or designed to be harmless to, the environment. **7** (of a person's face) pale; showing signs of nausea. **8** not dried or dry: *green bacon*; *green timber*. **9** extremely jealous or envious. **10** healthy, vigorous or flourishing: *green old age*. — *n* **1** (any shade of) the colour of the leaves of most plants, between yellow and blue in the spectrum. **2** something of this colour. **3** an area of grass, esp. in a public place. **4** an area of specially prepared turf: *bowling-green*. **5** (in *pl*) vegetables with edible green leaves and stems. **6** a person who supports actions or political policies designed to benefit the environment, esp. (*cap*) one belonging to or supporting a **Green Party** (any of a number of political parties concerned with the protection of the environment). — *v* (*tr* & *intr*) to make or become green. [OE *grene*]

green bean *n* any variety of bean of which the unripe pod and contents are eaten whole.

green belt *n* open land surrounding a town or city, where building or development is strictly controlled.

greenery *n* (the leaves of) green plants, either when growing or cut for decoration.

green-eyed *adj* (*coll*) jealous or envious.

green fingers *n* (*pl*; *coll*) natural skill at growing plants successfully.

greenfly *n* ***-fly*** or ***-flies*** a small green insect which feeds on garden plants and crops.

greengage *n* a type of greenish-yellow plum; the tree that bears it.

greengrocer *n* a person or shop selling fruit and vegetables. — *n* **greengrocery**.

greenhorn *n* (*coll*) an inexperienced person; a novice.

greenhouse *n* a building with walls and a roof made of glass, used for growing plants which need special protection or conditions.

greenhouse effect *n* the blanketing effect of masses of man-made carbon dioxide and other gases in the atmosphere, preventing the escape of the sun's heat reflected by the earth's surface, causing warming of the Earth's atmosphere.

greenhouse gas *n* any of the gases such as carbon dioxide, methane and ozone that contribute to the greenhouse effect.

greenkeeper *n* a person responsible for the maintenance of a golf course or bowling-green.

green light *n* **1** a signal to move forward. **2** (*coll*; with **the**) permission to proceed: *give the green light to*.

green paper *n* (often *cap*) in the UK, a written statement of the government's proposed policy on a particular issue, for discussion by Parliament. ◇ See also **command paper**, **white paper**.

green pepper *n* a green unripe sweet pepper, eaten as a vegetable. ◇ See also **red pepper**.

green pound *n* the pound's value compared with that of the other European currencies used in trading EC farm produce.

greenroom *n* (esp. formerly) a backstage room in a theatre where actors can relax and receive visitors.

green tea *n* a sharp-tasting light-coloured tea made from leaves that have been dried quickly without fermenting.

Greenwich Mean Time *n* (*abbrev* **GMT**) the local time at the line of 0° longitude, passing through Greenwich in England, used to calculate times in most other parts of the world.

greet[1] *v* (*tr*) **1** to address or welcome, esp. in a friendly way. **2** (**with**) to react to in a certain way: *remarks greeted with dismay*. **3** to be immediately noticeable to: *Kitchen smells greeted me*. [OE *gretan*]

greeting *n* **1** a friendly expression or gesture used on meeting or welcoming someone. **2** (usu. in *pl*) a good or fond wish; a friendly message.

greetings card *n* a decorated card used to send greetings.

greet[2] (*Scot & N of England dialect*) *v* (*intr*) ***grat***, etc., ***grutten***, etc. to cry. — *n* a spell of crying. [OE *gretan*]

gregarious *adj* **1** liking the company of other people; sociable. **2** (of animals) living in groups. — *n* **gregariousness**. [Lat *gregarius*, from *grex*, flock]

Gregorian calendar *n* the system introduced by Pope *Gregory* XIII in 1582, and still widely in use, in which an ordinary year is divided into twelve months or 365 days, with a leap year of 366 days every four years. ◇ See also **Julian calendar**.

Gregorian chant *n* a type of plainsong used in Roman Catholic religious ceremonies, introduced by Pope *Gregory* I (540–604).

gremlin *n* an imaginary mischievous creature blamed for faults in machinery or electronic equipment.

grenade *n* a small bomb thrown by hand or fired from a rifle. [Span *granada*, pomegranate]

grenadier *n* a member of a regiment of soldiers formerly trained in the use of grenades. [Ety. as for **grenade**]

grenadine *n* a syrup made from pomegranate juice, used to flavour (esp. alcoholic) drinks. [Ety. as for **grenade**]

grew. See **grow**.

grey *adj* **1** of a colour between black and white, the colour of ash and slate. **2** (of weather) dull and cloudy. **3** (of hair) turning white; (of a person) having such hair. **4** (*derog*) anonymous or uninteresting; having no distinguishing features: *a grey character*. **5** (*literary*) aged, mature or experienced. — *n* **1** (any shade of) a colour between black and white. **2** something grey in colour: *dressed in grey*. **3** dull light. **4** an animal, esp. a horse, that is grey or whitish in colour. — *v* (*tr* & *intr*) to make or become grey. — *n* **greyness**. [OE *græg*]

grey area *n* an unclear situation or subject, often with no distinct limits or identifiable characteristics.

Grey Friar *n* a Franciscan friar.

greylag *n* a large grey Eurasian goose.

grey matter *n* **1** the grey-coloured tissue of the brain and spinal cord. **2** (*coll*) intelligence or common sense.

grey squirrel *n* a grey-furred squirrel native to America and now the most common squirrel in Britain.

greyhound *n* a tall thin sharp-sighted breed of dog capable of great speed. [OE *grighund*, prob. bitch-dog]

grid *n* **1** a set of numbered squares on a map, etc. by which precise points are located. **2** a network of cables, pipes, etc. bringing a supply to a large area. **3** a framework of metal bars, esp. one covering the opening to a drain. **4** an arrangement of lines marking the starting-points on a motor racing track. **5** (*tech*) a fine wire mesh controlling the flow of electrons between the electrodes in an electronic valve. [Back-formation from **gridiron**]

griddle *n* (also **girdle**) a flat iron plate, either loose with a handle or set into the top of a stove, heated for baking or frying. [OFr *gridil*]

gridiron *n* **1** a frame of iron bars used for grilling food over a fire. **2** the field of play in American football. [MidE *gredire*]

grief *n* **1** great sorrow and unhappiness, esp. at a person's death. **2** an event causing this. **3** (*coll*) trouble or bother. — **come to grief** (*coll*) to end in failure; to have an accident. [OFr, from *grever*, to grieve]

grievance *n* **1** a real or perceived cause for complaint, esp. unfair treatment at work. **2** a formal complaint, esp. made in the workplace. [OFr *grevance*]

grieve *v* **1** (*intr*) to feel grief, esp. at a death. **2** (*tr*) to upset or distress. [OFr *grever*, from Lat *gravare*, to burden]

grievous *adj* **1** very severe or painful. **2** causing or likely to cause grief. **3** showing grief. **4** extremely serious or evil. [OFr *grevos*]

grievous bodily harm *n* (*legal*; *abbrev* **gbh** or **GBH**) severe injury caused by a physical attack; the criminal charge of causing such injury.

griffin *n* (also **gryphon**) (*mythol*) a winged monster with an eagle's head and a lion's body. [OFr *grifon*]

griffon *n* **1** a small coarse-haired terrier-like dog. **2** a large pale-coloured vulture with black wings. [Variant of **griffin**]

grill *v* (*tr*) **1** to cook under radiated heat. **2** (*coll*) to interrogate, esp. at length. — *n* **1** a device on a cooker which radiates heat downwards. **2** a metal frame for cooking food over a fire; a gridiron. **3** a dish of grilled food. **4** (also **grillroom**) (a part of) a restaurant specialising in grilled food. [Fr *griller*, to grill]

grilling *n* (*coll*) an interrogation.

grille or **grill** *n* a protective framework of metal bars or wires, e.g. over a window or a car radiator. [Fr *gril*]

grilse *n* ***grilse*** or ***grilses*** a young salmon returned to fresh water after its first journey to the sea.

grim *adj* ***-mm-*** **1** stern and unsmiling. **2** terrible; horrifying. **3** resolute; dogged: *grim determination*. **4** depressing; gloomy. **5** (*coll*) unpleasant. **6** (*coll*) ill. — *adv* **grimly**. — *n* **grimness**. [OE *grimm*]

grimace *n* an ugly twisting of the face, expressing pain or disgust, or for amusement. — *v* (*intr*) to make a grimace. [Fr]

grime *n* thick ingrained dirt or soot. — *v* (*tr*) to soil heavily; to make filthy. — *n* **griminess**. — *adj* **grimy**, ***-ier***, ***-iest***. [MidE]

grin *v* ***-nn-*** **1** (*intr*) to smile broadly, showing the teeth. **2** (*tr*) to express (e.g. pleasure) in this way. — *n* a broad toothy smile. — *adv* **grinningly**. — **grin and bear it** (*coll*) to endure something unpleasant without complaining. [OE *grennian*]

grind *v* ***ground*** **1** (*tr*) to crush into small particles or powder between two hard surfaces. **2** (*tr*) to sharpen or polish by rubbing against a hard surface. **3** (*tr* & *intr*) to (cause to) rub together with a jarring noise. **4** (*tr*) to press hard with a twisting action: *ground his heel into the dirt*. **5** (*tr*) to operate by turning a handle: *organ-grinding*. **6** (*tr*; **down**) to crush the spirit of; to oppress. — *n* **1** (*coll*) steady, dull and laborious routine. **2** the act or sound of grinding. **3** the size or texture of crushed particles. **4** (*coll*) an erotic circling movement of the hips in dancing. — *v* **grind out** (*tr*) to produce routinely and disinterestedly. — **grind to a halt** to stop completely and abruptly. [OE *grindan*]

grinder *n* **1** a person or machine that grinds. **2** a molar tooth.

grindstone *n* a revolving stone wheel used for sharpening and polishing. — **have** or **keep one's nose to the grindstone** (*coll*) to work hard and with commitment.

gringo *n* **-os** (usu. *derog*) an English-speaking foreigner in Latin America, esp. Mexico. [Sp, from *griego*, a Greek, a foreigner]

grip *v* **-pp-** (*tr*) **1** to take or keep a firm hold of. **2** to capture the imagination or attention of. — *n* **1** (the action of taking) a firm hold. **2** a way of gripping. **3** a handle or part that can be gripped. **4** a U-shaped wire pin for keeping the hair in place. **5** (esp. *US*) a holdall. **6** (*coll*) understanding. **7** (*coll*) control; mastery: *lose one's grip of the situation*. **8** (*tech*) a stagehand who moves scenery. **9** (*tech*) a person who manoeuvres a film camera. — **get to grips with** to begin to deal successfully with. [OE *gripe*, a grasp]

gripping *adj* holding the attention.

gripe *v* **1** (*intr*; *coll*) to complain persistently. **2** (*tr* & *intr*) to (cause to) feel intense stomach pain. — *n* **1** (*coll*) a complaint. **2** (usu. in *pl*; *old coll*) a severe stomach pain. [OE *gripan*]

gripe water *n* medicine given to babies to relieve colic.

grisly *adj* **-ier**, **-iest** horrible; ghastly; gruesome. — *n* **grisliness**. [OE *grislic*]

grist *n* grain that is to be, or that has been, ground into flour. — **grist to the mill** anything useful or profitable; a useful contribution. [OE]

gristle *n* cartilage, esp. in meat. — *adj* **gristly**. [OE]

grit *n* **1** small hard particles of a hard material, esp. of stone or sand. **2** (*coll*) courage and determination. — *v* **-tt-** (*tr*) **1** to spread grit on (icy roads, etc.). **2** to clench (the teeth), e.g. to overcome pain. — *adj* **gritty**, **-ier**, **-iest**. [OE *greot*]

grits *n* **1** (*pl*) coarsely ground grain, esp. oats, with the husks removed. **2** (*sing*) a dish of these, boiled and eaten for breakfast in the southern US. [OE *grytta*]

grizzle *v* (*intr*; *coll*) **1** (esp. of babies) to cry fretfully. **2** to sulk or complain.

grizzled *adj* (*literary*) (of hair) grey or greying; (of a person) having such hair. [MidE *grisel*, from OFr *gris*, grey]

grizzly *adj* **-ier**, **-iest** grey or greying; grizzled. — *n* **-ies** (*coll*) a grizzly bear. [Ety. as for **grizzled**]

grizzly bear *n* a large fierce greyish-brown N American bear.

groan *v* **1** (*intr* & *tr*) to make, or utter with, a long deep sound in the back of the throat, expressing pain, distress, disapproval, etc. **2** (*intr*) to creak loudly. **3** (*intr*) to be weighed down or almost breaking: *a table groaning under heaps of food*; *a system groaning under inefficiency*. — *n* an act, or the sound, of groaning. [OE *granian*]

groat *n* an obsolete British silver coin worth four old pennies. [ODut *groot*, thick]

groats *n* (*pl*) crushed grain, esp. oats, with the husks removed. [OE *grot*, particle]

grocer *n* **1** a person selling food and general household goods. **2** a grocer's shop. [MidE *grosser*, wholesale merchant, from Fr *grossier*; see **gross**]

grocery *n* **-ies 1** the trade or premises of a grocer. **2** (in *pl*) merchandise, esp. food, sold in a grocer's shop.

grog *n* **1** a mixture of alcoholic spirit, esp. rum, and water, as formerly drunk by sailors. **2** (*Austr* & *NZ coll*) any alcoholic drink. [Old *Grog*, nickname of British admiral Edward Vernon, who in 1740 issued the naval ration of rum diluted with water]

groggy *adj* **-ier**, **-iest** (*coll*) weak, dizzy and unsteady on the feet, e.g. from the effects of illness or alcohol. — *adv* **groggily**. — *n* **grogginess**.

grogram *n* a coarse fabric made from a mix of silk and wool or mohair. [OFr *gros grain*, coarse grain]

groin *n* **1** the part of the body where the lower abdomen joins the upper thigh. **2** (*euph*) the male sex organs. **3** (*archit*) the edge formed by the joining of two vaults in a roof. — *v* (*tr*; *archit*) to build with groins. [Perhaps OE *grynde*, abyss]

grommet. Same as **grummet**.

groom *n* **1** a person who looks after horses and cleans stables. **2** a bridegroom. **3** a title given to various officers in a royal household. — *v* (*tr*) **1** to clean, brush and generally smarten (animals, esp. horses). **2** to keep (a person) clean and neat, esp. regarding clothes and hair. **3** to train or prepare for a specific purpose or job. [MidE *grom*, manservant]

groove *n* **1** a long narrow channel, esp. cut with a tool. **2** the long spiral cut in a gramophone record. **3** (*coll*) a set (esp. monotonous) routine. **4** (*coll*) a state of performing excellently; top form: *The champion is really in the groove*. — *v* **1** (*tr*) to cut a groove in. **2** (*intr*; *old slang*) to enjoy oneself. [Obsolete Dut *groeve*, furrow]

groovy *adj* **-ier**, **-iest 1** (*old slang*) excellent, attractive or fashionable. **2** (*slang*) no longer fashionable; dated.

grope *v* **1** (*intr*; **for**) to search by feeling about with the hands, e.g. in the dark. **2** (*intr*; **for**) to search uncertainly or with difficulty: *groping for answers.* **3** (*tr*) to find (one's way) by feeling. **4** (*tr*; *coll*) to touch or fondle (someone) in a sexual way. — *n* (*coll*) an act of sexual fondling. [OE *grapian*]

grosbeak *n* any of various finches with a strong thick beak. [Fr *grosbec*, thick beak]

gross *adj* **1** total, with no deductions, as opposed to *net*: *gross weight.* **2** very great; flagrant; glaring: *gross negligence.* **3** (*derog*) vulgar; coarse. **4** (*derog*) unattractively fat. **5** (*coll derog*; esp. *US*) very unpleasant. **6** dense; lush: *gross vegetation.* **7** (*derog*) dull; lacking sensitivity or judgement. **8** solid; tangible; concrete; not spiritual or abstract. — *n* **1** ***gross*** twelve dozen, 144. **2** ***grosses*** the total amount or weight, without deductions. — *v* (*tr*) to earn as a gross income or profit, before tax is deducted. [Fr *gros*, large, fat]

gross domestic product *n* (*abbrev* **GDP**) the total value of all goods produced and all services provided by a nation in one year.

grossly *adv* extremely and flagrantly.

gross national product *n* (*abbrev* **GNP**) gross domestic product plus the value of income from investments abroad.

grossness *n* extreme rudeness or vulgarity.

grotesque *adj* **1** very unnatural or strange-looking, so as to cause fear or laughter. **2** exaggerated; ridiculous; absurd. — *n* **1** (with **the**) a 16th-century style in art which features animals, plants and people mixed together in a strange or fantastic manner. **2** a work of art in this style. — *adv* **grotesquely**. — *n* **grotesqueness**. [Ital (*pittura*) *grottesca*, cave painting, from *grotta*, cave]

grotto *n* ***-os*** or ***-oes*** **1** a cave, esp. small and picturesque. **2** a man-made cave-like structure, esp. in a garden or park. [Ital *grotta*, cave]

grotty *adj* ***-ier***, ***-iest*** (*coll*) **1** (*derog*) unpleasantly dirty or shabby. **2** ill. — *n* **grottiness**. [Short form of **grotesque**]

grouch (*coll*) *v* (*intr*) to grumble or complain. — *n* **1** a complaining person. **2** a bad-tempered complaint; the cause of it. — *adj* **grouchy, *-ier*, *-iest***. [OFr *grouchier*, to complain]

ground[1] *n* **1** (any part of) the solid surface of the earth; soil; land. **2** (often in *pl*) an (esp. large) area of land attached to or surrounding a building. **3** an area of land used for a specific purpose: *football ground.* **4** the substance of discussion: *cover a lot of ground.* **5** a position or standpoint, e.g. in an argument: *stand* or *shift one's ground.* **6** progress relative to that made by an opponent; advantage: *lose* or *gain ground.* **7** (usu. in *pl*; **for**) a reason or justification. **8** background colour in a painting. **9** (in *pl*) sediment or dregs, esp. of coffee. **10** the bottom of the sea. — *v* **1** (*tr*; **on**) to base (an argument, complaint, etc.). **2** (*tr*; **in**) to give basic instruction to. **3** (*tr* & *intr*) to (cause a ship to) hit the seabed or shore and remain stuck. **4** (*tr*) to refuse to allow (a pilot or aeroplane) to fly. **5** (*tr*) to lay (e.g. weapons) on the ground. — *adj* on or relating to the ground: *ground forces.* — **cut** or **take the ground from under someone's feet** to act in anticipation of someone's plan, etc., destroying its effect. — **down to the ground** (*coll*) absolutely; completely: *suits me down to the ground.* — **get (something) off the ground** to get (something) started. — **go to ground 1** (of an animal) to go into a burrow to escape from hunters. **2** to go into hiding, e.g. from the police. — **into the ground** to the point of exhaustion; to a position of total defeat. — **on the ground** amongst ordinary people: *opinion on the ground.* [OE *grund*]

ground bait *n* bait which drops to the river bed, attracting fish to a general area.

ground bass *n* (*mus*) a short bass part constantly repeated throughout a changing melody.

ground control *n* the people or equipment on the ground that direct and monitor the flight of an aircraft or spacecraft.

ground floor *n* the floor of a building at or nearest to the level of the ground outside. — **be** or **get in on the ground floor** (*coll*) to be or become involved at the beginning (e.g. of a business venture).

grounding *n* a foundation of basic knowledge or instruction.

groundless *adj* having no reason or justification.

groundling *n* **1** a fish that lives close to the bottom of a river, etc. **2** a low-growing plant. **3** (*coll*) a person who lives or works on the ground, as opposed to a pilot, etc. **4** (*hist*) a person standing in the pit, the cheapest area, of an Elizabethan theatre. **5** (*derog*) a person of inferior tastes.

groundnut *n* **1** a fleshy rounded edible underground stem, or tuber, of a N American climbing plant. **2** a peanut.

ground plan *n* **1** a plan of the ground floor of a building. **2** any general, undetailed plan.

ground rent *n* rent paid to the owner of land leased for building on.

ground rule *n* a basic principle.

groundsheet *n* a waterproof sheet spread on the ground, e.g. in a tent, to give protection against damp.

groundsman *n* a person who maintains a sports field.

ground squirrel *n* (also **gopher**) any of various small burrowing rodents resembling rats or squirrels, e.g. the chipmunk.

groundswell *n* **1** a spell of forceful but smooth waves at sea caused by a distant storm or earth tremor. **2** a sudden and rapid growth, esp. of public opinion.

groundwork *n* essential preparatory work.

ground[2]. See **grind**.

groundsel *n* a weed with small yellow flowers. [OE *gundeswilge*, from *gund*, pus + *swelgan*, to swallow, from its use in poultices]

group *n* **1** a number of people or things gathered, placed or classed together. **2** (sometimes *cap*) a number of business companies under single ownership and central control. **3** a band of musicians and singers, esp. playing pop music. **4** a subdivision of an air force, consisting of two or more wings. **5** a set of chemical elements with similar properties. — *v* (*tr* & *intr*) to (cause to) form a group. [Fr *groupe*]

group captain *n* an air force officer of the rank above wing commander and below air commodore, equivalent to an army colonel.

groupie *n* (*coll* often *derog*) an ardent (esp. female) follower of a touring pop star or other celebrity, often eager for a sexual relationship with the idol.

group therapy *n* treatment of (esp. psychological) illness through discussion amongst similarly affected patients, to encourage mutual understanding and support.

grouse[1] *n* ***grouse*** or ***grouses*** a small plump brown game bird with feathered legs and feet.

grouse[2] (*coll*) *v* (*intr*) to complain. — *n* a complaint or spell of complaining.

grout *n* thin mortar applied to the joints between bricks or esp. ceramic tiles, as a decorative finish. — *v* (*tr*) to apply grout to the joints of. [OE *grut*]

grove *n* **1** (*literary*) a small group of trees. **2** an area planted with fruit trees. [OE *graf*]

grovel *v* ***-ll-*** (*intr*) **1** to act with exaggerated (and usu. insincere) respect or humility, esp. to gain the favour of a superior. **2** to lie or crawl face down, in fear or respect. — *n* **groveller**. [Back-formation from MidE *groveling*, prone]

grow *v* ***grew***, ***grown*** **1** (*intr*) (of a living thing) to develop into a larger, more mature form. **2** (*intr* & *tr*) (of hair, nails, etc.) to (allow to) increase in length or develop. **3** (*intr*) to increase in size, intensity or extent. **4** (*tr*) to cultivate (plants). **5** (*intr* with **into**) to develop. **6** (*tr*) to become gradually. **7** (*intr* with **to**) to come gradually: *grew to hate him.* **8** (*intr* with **from** or **out of**) to originate: *The scheme grew from an idea he'd had at school.* ◇ See also **grow out of** below. — *v* **grow into** (*tr*) to become big enough to wear (clothes). — *v* **grow on** (*tr*) to gradually come to be liked by (someone). — *v* **grow out of** (*tr*) **1** to become too big to wear (clothes). **2** to lose a liking for, or the habit of, with age: *grew out of (reading) comics.* ◇ See also **grow** (sense **8** above). — *v* **grow up** (*intr*) **1** to become, or be in the process of becoming, an adult. **2** to behave in an adult way. **3** to come into existence; to develop. [OE *growan*]

growing pains *n* (*pl*) **1** muscular pains, esp. in the legs, sometimes experienced by growing children. **2** (temporary) problems or difficulties in the early stages of anything.

grown *adj* **1** mature: *grown woman.* **2** developed (to a certain degree): *fully grown.*

grown-up *n* & *adj* (*coll*) (an) adult.

growth *n* **1** the process or rate of growing. **2** an increase. **3** an increase in economic activity or profitability: *a growth industry.* **4** something that has grown, e.g. on a plant: *cut off the tree's old growth.* **5** an area of abnormal tissue in the body, e.g. a tumour.

growl *v* **1** (*intr*) (of animals) to make a deep rough sound in the throat, showing hostility. **2** (*intr* & *tr*) (of people) to make a similar sound showing anger or displeasure; to speak or say angrily. — *n* an act, or the sound, of growling. [OFr *groulier*, to grumble]

groyne *n* a low broad wall built like a pier from a shore to reduce the force of waves and so check land erosion. [OFr *groign*, snout]

grub *n* **1** the worm-like larva of an insect, esp. a beetle. **2** (*coll*) food. — *v* ***-bb-*** **1** (*intr*; **about**, **up**, etc.) to dig or search in the soil. **2** (*intr*) to search generally. **3** (*tr*) to clear (ground) by digging up roots and stumps. [MidE *grobe*]

Grub Street *n* (*slang*) the profession, lifestyle or standards of writers of low-grade literature.

grubby *adj* ***-ier***, ***-iest*** (*coll*) dirty. — *adv* **grubbily**. — *n* **grubbiness**. **[grub]**

grudge *v* (*tr*) **1** to feel a sense of unfairness or resentment at. **2** to be unwilling to do or give; to do or give unwillingly. — *n* a long-standing feeling of resentment: *bear a grudge.* — *adj* **grudging**. — *adv* **grudgingly**. [OFr *grouchier*, to grumble]

gruel *n* thin porridge. [OFr, groats]

gruelling *adj* exhausting; punishing. [Old word *gruel*, to punish]

gruesome *adj* inspiring horror or disgust; sickening; macabre. [Dialect *grue*, shiver, shudder + **-some**]

gruff *adj* **1** (of a voice) deep and rough. **2** rough, unfriendly or surly in manner. — *adv* **gruffly**. — *n* **gruffness**. [Dut *grof*, coarse]

grumble *v* (*intr*) **1** to complain in a bad-tempered way. **2** to make a low rumbling sound. — *n* **1** a complaint. **2** a rumbling sound. — *n* **grumbler**. [OGer *grommelen*]

grumbling *adj* (of the human appendix) intermittently painful.

grummet *n* a rubber or plastic ring around a hole in metal, to protect a tube or insulate a wire passing through. [Perhaps OFr *grommette*, jaw strap on a bridle]

grumpy *adj* **-ier**, **-iest** bad-tempered; surly. — *adv* **grumpily**. — *n* **grumpiness**. [Old word *grump*, surly remark]

grump *n* (*coll*) **1** a grumpy person. **2** a fit of bad temper or sulking.

grunt *v* **1** (*intr*) (of animals, esp. pigs) to make a low rough sound in the back of the throat. **2** (*intr*) (of people) to make a similar sound, e.g. indicating disgust or unwillingness to speak fully. **3** (*tr*) to express with this sound. — *n* an act, or the sound, of grunting. [OE *grunian*]

Gruyère *n* a pale yellow cheese with holes, orig. made in *Gruyère*, in Switzerland.

gryphon. See **griffin**.

G-string. See **G**.

g-suit. See **g**.

GT *n* a name given to certain fast but comfortable sports cars. [Abbrev. of Ital *gran turismo*, grand touring]

Gt *abbrev* (in place-names) Great.

guacamole *n* a traditional Mexican dish of mashed avocado, tomatoes and onions, eaten cold. [Aztec *ahuacatl*, avocado + *molli*, sauce]

guano *n* **-nos 1** the dung of (fish-eating) sea-birds, used as fertiliser. **2** artificial fertiliser, esp. made from fish. [Span, from Quechua *huanu*, dung]

guarantee *n* **1** a formal (usu. written) promise, esp. by a manufacturer to repair or replace an article found to be faulty within a stated period of time. **2** (also **guaranty**) an agreement, esp. written, to take on another person's responsibility or debt if they neglect it. **3** a person making such an agreement; a guarantor. **4** (also **guaranty**) something undertaken to be handed over if a contract or agreement is broken; a security or pledge. — *v* (*tr*) **1** to act as, or give, a guarantee for. **2** to promise; to state as unquestionably true. **3** to ensure. [OFr *garantie*, from *garant*, warrant]

guarantor *n* a person who gives a guarantee.

guaranty *n* a guarantee (senses **2** and **4**). [Ety. as for **guarantee**]

guard *v* **1** (*tr*) to protect from danger or attack. **2** (*tr*) to prevent from escaping. **3** (*intr* with **against**) to take precautions to prevent. **4** (*tr*) to control or check: *guard your tongue*. — *n* **1** a person or group whose job is to provide protection, e.g. from danger or attack, or to prevent escape. **2** a person in charge of a railway train. **3** a state of readiness to give protection or prevent escape: *on guard*; *keep guard*. **4** on alert or in a wary state: *on one's guard against thieves*; *caught you off guard*. **5** a defensive position, e.g. in boxing or cricket. **6** (esp. *in cmpds*) anything that gives protection from something: *fire-guard*. **7** the act or duty of protecting. **8** (often *cap*) a soldier in any of certain army regiments orig. formed to protect the sovereign. — **stand guard** to act as a guard or sentry. [OFr *garder*, to protect]

guarded *adj* cautious. — *adv* **guardedly**. — *n* **guardedness**.

guardhouse or **guardroom** *n* a building or room for guards on duty, esp. at the gate of a military camp, often also housing prisoners.

guardsman *n* **1** a member of a regiment of guards. **2** a guard.

guardian *n* **1** a person legally responsible for the care of another, esp. an orphaned child. **2** a guard, defender or protector. — *n* **guardianship**. [OFr *gardein*]

guava *n* (a tropical American tree which bears) a pear-shaped fruit with yellow skin and pink edible flesh. [Span *guayaba*]

gubbins *n* (*sing*; *coll*) **1** (*derog*) a worthless object. **2** a device or gadget. **3** (*derog*) rubbish. [Old word *gobbon*, portion]

gubernatorial *adj* (*formal*) of or relating to a governor. [Lat *gubernator*, steersman]

gudgeon[1] *n* **1** a small European freshwater fish often used as bait by anglers. **2** (*coll*) a gullible person. [OFr *goujon*]

gudgeon[2] *n* **1** a pivot or pin of any kind. **2** the socket part of a hinge or rudder, into which the pin part fits. [OFr *goujon*, pin of a pulley]

guelder rose *n* a deciduous shrub producing bunches of white flowers. [*Gelderland*, province of the Netherlands]

guernsey *n* **-eys 1** a tight-fitting woollen pullover, esp. worn by sailors. **2** (*cap*) a breed of dairy cattle, producing creamy milk. [*Guernsey* in the Channel Islands]

guerrilla or **guerilla** *n* a member of a small, independent, often politically motivated armed force making surprise attacks, e.g. against government troops. [Span *guerrilla*, dimin. of *guerra*, war]

guess *v* **1** (*tr* & *intr*) to make an estimate (of) or form an opinion (about), based on little or no information. **2** (*tr*) to estimate correctly. **3** (*tr*; esp. *US*) to think or suppose. — *n* an estimate based on little or no information. — **anybody's guess** (*coll*) impossible to know for sure. [MidE *gessen*]

guesswork *n* the process or result of guessing.

guesstimate (*coll*) *n* a very rough estimate, based on scant knowledge. — *v* (*tr*) to make such an estimate of. [**guess** + **estimate**]

guest *n* **1** a person who receives hospitality in the home of, or at the expense of, another. **2** a person staying at a hotel, boarding-house, etc. **3** a person specially invited to take part: *guest star, speaker*. — *v* (*intr*) to appear as a guest, e.g. on a television show. [OE *gest*]

guesthouse *n* a private home offering accommodation to paying guests; a boarding-house.

guff *n* (*coll derog*) nonsense.

guffaw *v* (*intr*) & *n* (to utter) a loud coarse laugh. [Imit.]

guidance *n* **1** help, advice or counselling. **2** direction or leadership. **3** the process of directing a missile to its target: *guidance system*. [**guide**]

guide *v* (*tr*) **1** to lead, direct, or show the way to. **2** to control or direct the movement or course of: *guided missile*. **3** to advise or influence: *Be guided by your parents*. — *n* **1** a person who leads the way for e.g. tourists or mountaineers. **2** any device used to direct movement. **3** (also **guidebook**) a book containing information on a particular subject or place. **4** (*cap*; also **Girl Guide**) a member of a worldwide youth organisation for girls. **5** a person or thing, esp. a quality, which influences another person's decisions or behaviour: *Let truth be your guide*. [OFr *guider*]

guide dog *n* a dog specially trained to guide a blind person safely.

guideline *n* (often in *pl*) an indication of what future action is required or recommended.

guild *n* **1** a mediaeval association of merchants or craftsmen, maintaining standards and providing mutual support. **2** a name used by various modern societies, clubs and associations. [OE *gield*]

guildhall *n* **1** a hall where members of a guild or other association meet. **2** a town hall.

guilder *n* **1** ***-der*** or ***-ders*** the standard unit of currency of the Netherlands, divided into 100 cents. **2** ***-ders*** an old German and Dutch gold coin. [Dut *gulden*]

guile *n* the ability to deceive or trick; craftiness or cunning. — *adj* **guileful**. — *adj* **guileless**. [OFr, deceit]

guillemot *n* a northern diving sea-bird with black and white plumage and a long bill. [Fr *Guillaume*, William, perhaps from Breton *gwelan*, gull]

guillotine *n* **1** an instrument for beheading, consisting of a large heavy blade sliding rapidly down between two upright posts. **2** a device with a large blade moved lever-like to cut paper or metal. **3** a time limit set to speed up discussion of, and voting on, a parliamentary bill. — *v* (*tr*) to behead, cut, or speed up progress of, with a guillotine. [French physician Joseph *Guillotin* (1738–1814), who proposed beheading by guillotine in the French Revolution]

guilt *n* **1** (shame or remorse resulting from) an awareness of having done wrong. **2** the state of having done wrong or having broken a law. **3** blame. — *adj* **guiltless**. [OE *gylt*]

guilty *adj* ***-ier***, ***-iest*** **1** (**of**) (judged to be) responsible for a crime or wrongdoing. **2** feeling, showing or involving guilt: *a guilty look*. **3** (with **of**) able to be justly accused of: *guilty of working too hard*. — *adv* **guiltily**. — *n* **guiltiness**.

guinea *n* **1** an obsolete British gold coin worth 21 shillings (£1.05). **2** its value, still used as a monetary unit in some professions, esp. horse-racing. [*Guinea*, W Africa, where the gold for the coin was found]

guinea fowl *n* ***fowl*** an orig. African but now widely domesticated bird somewhat like a plump pheasant, dark grey with white speckles.

guinea pig *n* **1** a small tailless S American rodent, widely kept as a pet and used in scientific experiments. **2** (also **human guinea pig**) a person used as the subject of an experiment.

guipure *n* heavy lace having a large open pattern with no background. [Fr, from *guiper*, to cover with cloth]

guise *n* **1** assumed appearance; pretence: *under the guise of friendship*. **2** external appearance in general. [OFr]

guiser *n* (esp. *Scot*) a person, esp. a child, who goes from house to house in disguise, esp. at Hallowe'en, entertaining with songs, etc. and receiving small gifts in return. [**guise**]

guitar *n* a musical instrument with a body generally shaped like a figure of eight, a long neck, and (usu. six) strings that are plucked or strummed. — *n* **guitarist**. [Fr *guitare*]

gulag *n* **1** (one of) a network of political prisons or labour camps that once existed in the former Soviet Union. **2** the government department responsible for their administration. [Russ *g*(lavnoe) *u*(pravlenie ispravitelno-trudovykh) *lag*(erei), main administration for corrective labour camps]

gulch *n* (esp. *US*) a narrow rocky ravine with a fast-flowing stream running through it.

gulden. Same as **guilder**.

gulf *n* **1** a stretch of sea with land on most sides; a huge bay. **2** a vast difference or separation, e.g. between viewpoints. **3** a deep hollow in the ground; a chasm. [OFr *golfe*, from Gr *kolpos*, bosom]

Gulf States *n* (*pl*) **1** the oil-producing countries around the Persian Gulf, i.e. Iran, Iraq, Kuwait, Bahrain, Saudi Arabia, Oman, Qatar and the United Arab Emirates. **2** the US states around the Gulf of Mexico, i.e. Florida, Texas, Alabama, Mississippi and Louisiana.

Gulf Stream *n* (also **North Atlantic Drift**) a warm ocean current flowing from the Gulf of Mexico towards NE Europe.

gull[1] *n* any of various species of sea-bird with predominantly white plumage. [Prob. Welsh *gwylan*]

gull[2] (*old*) *v* (*tr*) to cheat or deceive. — *n* an easily fooled person. [Perhaps dialect, unfledged bird]

gullet *n* the tube by which food passes from the mouth to the stomach; the oesophagus. [OFr *goule*, throat, from Lat *gula*]

gullible *adj* easily tricked or fooled. — *n* **gullibility**. [**gull**[2]]

gully, **-*ies*** or **gulley**, **-*eys*** *n* **1** a channel worn by running water, e.g. on a mountainside. **2** in cricket, (a fielder in) a position around 10 yards from the batsman and at a level slightly behind the wicket.

gulp *v* **1** (*tr & intr*; **down**) to swallow (food, drink, etc.) eagerly or in large mouthfuls. **2** (*intr*) to make a swallowing motion, e.g. because of fear. **3** (*tr* with **back** or **down**) to stifle (tears, etc.). — *n* **1** a swallowing motion. **2** an amount swallowed at once; a mouthful. [ODut *gulpen*]

gum[1] *n* the firm flesh around the roots of the teeth. [OE *goma*, palate]

gumboil *n* a small abscess on the gum.

gummy *adj* **-*ier***, **-*iest*** toothless.

gum[2] *n* **1** a sticky substance obtained from the trunks and stems of certain trees and plants. **2** this or any similar substance used as glue. **3** (also **gumdrop**) a sweet made from transparent hard jelly. **4** (*coll*) chewing-gum. — *v* **-*mm-*** (*tr*) to glue with gum. — **gum up the works** (*coll*) to prevent a machine, scheme, etc. from working properly. [OFr *gomme*, from Lat *gummi*]

gum arabic *n* gum produced by some acacia plants, used in foods, pharmaceuticals and inks.

gumboot *n* a long rubber waterproof boot, a wellington boot.

gummy[2] *adj* **-*ier***, **-*iest*** **1** sticky. **2** producing gum.

gumshoe *n* **1** a rubber overshoe, a galosh. **2** (*slang*) a (private) detective.

gum tree *n* any gum-producing tree, esp. eucalyptus. — **up a gum tree** (*coll*) in a difficult position, esp. with no chance of escape.

gumbo *n* **-*os*** **1** a thick soup or stew made from meat or fish, okra and other vegetables. **2** okra. [Louisiana Fr *gombo*, from a Bantu language]

gumption *n* (*coll*) **1** common sense; initiative. **2** courage.

gun *n* **1** any weapon which fires bullets or shells from a metal tube. **2** any instrument which forces something out under pressure: *spray gun*. **3** (*coll*) a gunman. **4** a member of a party of hunters. **5** the signal to start, e.g. a race. — *v* **-*nn-*** (*tr* with **down**) to shoot (a person) with a gun. — **go great guns** (*coll*) to function or be carried out with great speed or success. — *v* **gun for** (*tr*) **1** to search for in order to attack or kill. **2** (*coll*) to pursue eagerly: *gunning for a pay rise*. — **jump the gun** to do something before the proper time. — **stick to one's guns** to maintain one's position firmly, in an argument, etc. [MidE *gonne*]

gunboat *n* a small warship with large mounted guns.

gunboat diplomacy *n* diplomacy consisting of threats of military attack.

gun cotton *n* a highly explosive cellulose material containing nitric acid.

gun dog *n* a dog specially trained to find and retrieve birds or small animals shot by hunters.

gunfire *n* **1** the act of firing guns. **2** the bullets fired. **3** the sound of firing.

gunman *n* **1** an armed criminal. **2** an assassin.

gunmetal *n* **1** an alloy of copper, zinc and tin, orig. used to make cannons. **2** any similar metal, esp. one formerly used to make toys. **3** a dark grey colour.

gunner *n* **1** any member of an armed force who operates a heavy gun. **2** a soldier in an artillery regiment.

gunnery *n* **1** the use of guns. **2** the science of designing guns.

gunpoint: **at gunpoint** threatening, or being threatened, with a gun.

gunpowder *n* an explosive mixture of saltpetre, sulphur and charcoal.

gunrunning *n* the act of smuggling arms into a country, often to help terrorists, etc. — *n* **gunrunner**.

gunshot *n* **1** bullets fired from a gun. **2** the distance over which a gun can fire a bullet: *within gunshot*. **3** a sound of firing.

gunslinger *n* (*slang*) an armed fighter in the lawless days of the American West.

gunge (*coll*) *n* any messy, slimy or sticky substance. — *v* (*tr* with **up**) to cover or block with gunge. — *adj* **gungy**, **-*ier***, **-*iest***. [Perhaps **goo** + **sponge**]

gung-ho *adj* (*derog*) excessively or foolishly eager, esp. to attack an enemy. [Chin *gong*, work + *he*, together]

gunk *n* (*coll*) any slimy oily (esp. semi-solid) substance. [Orig. a trademark of a grease-solvent]

gunnel. See **gunwale**.

gunny *n* **-*ies*** **1** thick coarse jute cloth, used esp. for sacking. **2** a sack made from this. [Hindi *goni*]

gunwale or **gunnel** *n* the upper edge of a ship's side. — **full to the gunwales** completely full. [**gun wale**]

guppy *n* **-*ies*** a small brightly-coloured W Indian freshwater fish, often kept in aquariums. [R J L *Guppy*, who sent the first specimens to the British Museum in the 19th century]

gurgle *v* **1** (*intr*) (of water) to make a bubbling noise when flowing. **2** (*intr & tr*) to make, or express with, a bubbling noise in the throat. — *n* the sound of gurgling. [Lat *gurgulare*]

Gurkha *n* a member of a Hindu people of Nepal, from whom whole regiments in the British and Indian armies are formed.

Gurkhali *n* the Indo-European language spoken by Gurkhas.

guru *n* **1** a Hindu or Sikh spiritual leader or teacher. **2** (sometimes *facet*) any greatly respected and influential leader or adviser. [Hindi, from Sanskrit, venerable]

gush *v* **1** (*intr & tr*) to (cause liquid to) flood out suddenly and violently. **2** (*intr*; *coll derog*) to speak or act in a false, over-emotional or over-enthusiastic way. — *n*

1 a sudden violent flooding-out. **2** (*coll derog*) exaggerated emotion or enthusiasm. — *adj* **gushing**. [MidE *gosshe* or *gusche*]
gusher *n* an oil-well from which oil flows without the use of pumps.
gusset *n* a piece of material sewn into a garment for added strength, or to allow for freedom of movement, e.g. at the crotch. [OFr *gousset*]
gust *n* **1** a sudden blast or rush, e.g. of wind or smoke. **2** an emotional outburst. — *v* (*intr*) (of wind) to blow in gusts. — *adj* **gusty**, **-*ier***, **-*iest***. [Norse *gustr*, blast]
gusto *n* enthusiastic enjoyment; zest; vigour. [Ital, from Lat *gustus*, taste]
gut *n* **1** the intestine. **2** (in *pl*; *coll*) the insides of a person or animal. **3** (*coll*) the stomach or abdomen. **4** (*coll*) a fat stomach; a paunch. **5** (in *pl*; *coll*) courage or determination. **6** (in *pl*; *coll*) the inner or essential parts: *the guts of the scheme*. **7** a strong thread made from animal intestines, used for violin and racket strings; catgut. — *v* **-*tt*-** (*tr*) **1** to take the guts out of (esp. fish). **2** to destroy the insides of; to reduce to a shell: *fire gutted the building*. — *adj* **1** based on instinct and emotion, not reason: *a gut reaction*. **2** essential; basic: *the gut problem*. — **hate someone's guts** (*coll*) to have a violent dislike for someone. — **work**, **sweat**, **slave**, etc. **one's guts out** (*coll*) to work extremely hard. [OE *gutt*]
gutless *adj* (*derog*) cowardly; lacking determination.
gutsy *adj* **-*ier***, **-*iest*** (*coll*) **1** courageous and determined. **2** gluttonous.
gutted *adj* (*coll*) extremely shocked or disappointed.
gutta-percha *n* a white rubber-like substance obtained from Malaysian trees, used as insulation for electrical cables, and in dentistry. [Malay *getah*, gum + *percha*, the tree producing it]
gutter *n* **1** a channel for carrying away rainwater, fixed to the edge of a roof or built between a pavement and a road. **2** (with **the**) a state of poverty and social deprivation, or of coarse and degraded living. **3** (*printing*) the inner margins between two facing pages. — *v* **-*r*-** **1** (*intr*) (of a candle) to melt away with wax forming channels down the side. **2** (*tr*) to wear away channels in. **3** (*intr*) to trickle. [OFr *goutiere*, from *goute*, drop]
guttering *n* **1** gutters collectively. **2** material for making roof-gutters.
gutter press *n* (*derog*) newspapers dealing largely with scandal and gossip reported in a sensational style.
guttersnipe *n* (*old derog*) a raggedly dressed or ill-mannered person, esp. a child.
guttural *adj* **1** (of sounds) produced deep in the throat. **2** (of a language or a style of speech) having or using such sounds; harsh-sounding. — *adv* **gutturally**. [Lat *guttur*, throat]
guv, **guvnor** and **guv'nor**. See **governor** under **govern**.
guy[1] *n* **1** (*coll*) a man or boy. **2** a crude model of Guy Fawkes, burnt on a bonfire on Guy Fawkes Day. — *v* (*tr*) to make fun of. [*Guy* Fawkes]
Guy Fawkes Day *n* 5 November, the anniversary of the discovery of the Gunpowder Plot, a plot to blow up Parliament in 1605 of which Guy Fawkes was the leader, celebrated with firework displays.
guy[2] *n* a rope or wire used to hold something, esp. a tent, firm or steady. — *v* (*tr*) to secure with guys. [OFr *guie*, guide]
guzzle *v* (*tr* & *intr*) to eat or drink greedily. — *n* **guzzler**. [Perhaps Fr *gosier*, throat]
gybe *v* (*tr* & *intr*; *naut*; also **gibe**) **1** to (cause a sail to) swing over from one side of a boat to the other. **2** to (cause a boat to) change course in this way. — *n* an act of gybing. [**jib**]
gym *n* (*coll*) **1** gymnastics. **2** a gymnasium.
gym shoe *n* a light, canvas, usu. rubber-soled, shoe.
gym slip *n* a belted sleeveless dress or tunic, worn (esp. formerly) by schoolgirls as part of their uniform.
gymkhana *n* **1** a local public event consisting of competitions in various sports, esp. horse-riding. **2** formerly, in India under British rule, an athletics meeting, or a public place providing athletics facilities. [Hindi *gend-khana*, racket-court, remodelled on **gymnasium**]
gymnasium *n* **-*iums*** or **-*ia*** **1** a building or room with equipment for physical exercise. **2** in various European countries, a top-grade secondary school preparing pupils for university. [Gr *gymnasion*, from *gymnazein*, to exercise naked]
gymnast *n* a person skilled in gymnastics. [Gr *gymnastes*, trainer of athletes]
gymnastics *n* (*sing*) **1** physical exercises designed to strengthen the body and improve agility, usu. using special equipment. **2** difficult exercises that test or demonstrate ability of any kind: *mental gymnastics*. — *adj* **gymnastic**.
gynaecology *n* the branch of medicine dealing with diseases and disorders of the female body, esp. the reproductive system. — *adj* **gynaecological**. — *n* **gynaecologist**. [Gr *gyne*, woman + **-logy**]
gyp[1]: **give someone gyp** (*slang*) to cause someone pain. [Possibly a contraction of **gee up**]
gyp[2] (*slang*) *v* **-*pp*-** (*tr*) to cheat or swindle. — *n* a cheat. [Back-formation from **gypsy**]
gypsum *n* a soft chalk-like mineral used to make plaster of Paris, cement and fertiliser. [Lat, from Gr *gypsos*, chalk]
gypsy *n* **-*ies*** a member of a dark-skinned travelling people, orig. from NW India, now scattered throughout Europe and N

America. [E*gyp*t, where they were orig. thought to have come from]

gyrate *v* (*intr*) to move with a circular or spiralling motion. — *n* **gyration**. [Gr *gyros*, circle]

gyrfalcon *n* a large rare northern and arctic falcon. [OFr *gerfaucon*]

gyrocompass *n* a non-magnetic compass operated by means of a motor-driven gyroscope.

gyroscope *n* an apparatus consisting of a circular frame containing a disc spinning rapidly around a free-moving axis, the axis keeping the same position regardless of any movement of the frame, used in ship's stabilisers and compasses. — *adj* **gyroscopic**. [Gr *gyros*, circle + **-scope**]

H

H[1] or **h** *n* ***Hs*** or ***H's, h's*** the eighth letter of the English alphabet.
H[2] *abbrev* **1** hospital. **2** (on a pencil) hard.
H[3] *symbol* (*chem*) hydrogen.
H-bomb *n* a hydrogen bomb.
h *abbrev* **1** hecto-. **2** height.
ha! *interj* an expression of surprise, happiness, triumph, etc.
ha. *abbrev* hectare.
habeas corpus *n* (*legal*) a writ requiring a prisoner to be brought into court for a judge to decide if his or her imprisonment is legal. [Lat, have the body (brought before the judge)]
haberdasher *n* a person who deals in small items used for sewing, such as ribbons, needles, buttons, etc. [OFr *hapertas*]
haberdashery *n* ***-ies*** **1** a haberdasher's shop, business or department. **2** the ribbons, etc. sold by a haberdasher.
habit *n* **1** a usual or regular practice or tendency. **2** a practice, often bad, which is hard to give up. **3** mental attitude or constitution: *habit of mind*. **4** a long loose garment worn by monks and nuns. [Lat *habitus*, practice]
habit-forming *adj* (of a drug, activity, etc.) likely to become a habit or addiction.
habitable *adj* suitable for living in. — *n* **habitability**. [Lat *habitabilis*]
habitat *n* the natural home of an animal or plant. [Lat, it inhabits]
habitation *n* **1** the act of living in (a building, etc.). **2** a house or home. [Lat *habitatio*]
habitual *adj* **1** seen, done, etc. regularly. **2** done, or doing something, by habit. — *adv* **habitually**. [Lat *habitualis*, from *habitus*, habit]
habituate *v* (*tr*; **to**) to make (someone) used to something. — *n* **habituation**. [Lat *habituare*]
habitué *n* a regular or frequent visitor to a place, e.g. a restaurant. [Fr]
hachure *n* **1** (also **hachures**) an area shaded with short lines on a map to show the steepness of a hill —the closer the lines, the steeper the land. **2** any of these lines. [Fr]
hacienda *n* (in Spanish-speaking countries) a ranch or large estate with a house on it. [Span]
hack[1] *v* **1** (*tr*; **down, up, out, away**) to cut or chop roughly. **2** (*tr*; **out**) to cut (a path, etc.) roughly. **3** (*intr* & *tr*; *coll*; **into**) to get access to (a computer's files) without permission. **4** (*tr*; *slang*) to be able to bear or suffer. **5** (*intr*) to cough. **6** (*tr*) to kick (an opponent) on the shins, esp. in football. — *n* **1** a kick on the shins. **2** a wound or rough cut, esp. from a kick. **3** a miner's pick. [OE *tohaccian*]
hacker *n* **1** a person who gains access to computer files without permission. **2** a computer enthusiast.
hacking *n* the act of gaining access to computer files without permission. — *adj* (of a cough) rough and dry.
hacksaw *n* a saw for cutting metals.
hack[2] *n* **1** a horse kept for general riding, esp. one for hire. **2** a ride on horseback. **3** a writer, journalist, etc. who produces dull, mediocre or routine work. — *v* (*intr*) to travel on horseback at a leisurely pace, usu. for pleasure. [Abbrev. of **hackney**]
hacking jacket *n* a tweed jacket with slits at the sides, worn when hacking.
hackles *n* (*pl*) the hairs or feathers on the back of the neck of some animals and birds, raised when they are angry. — **make someone's hackles rise** to make someone very angry. [MidE *hechele*]
hackney *n* ***-eys*** a horse for general riding. [*Hackney*, in E London, where horses used to be pastured]
hackney cab or **carriage 1** (*hist*) a horse-drawn carriage for public hire. **2** (*formal*) a taxi.
hackneyed *adj* (of a word, phrase, etc.) meaningless and trite through too much use. [From **hackney**, in the sense of 'for general use']
hacksaw. See **hack**.
had. See **have**.
haddock *n* ***haddock*** a small, N Atlantic sea-fish used as food. [MidE *haddok*]
Hades *n* (*Gr mythol*) the underworld, where the souls of the dead live. [Gr *Haides*, another name for Pluto, god of the underworld]
hadj, hadji. Same as **hajj, hajji**.
hadn't had not.
hadst *v* (*aux* & *tr*; *old*) the form of the past tense of the verb *have* used with *thou*.
haem- , **haemato-** or **haemo-** *comb fm* blood. [Gr *haima*, blood]
haematology *n* the study of blood. [**haemato-** + **-logy**]
haemoglobin *n* the substance in red blood cells that carries oxygen round the body. [**haemo-** + Lat *globus*, ball]
haemophilia *n* a hereditary disease, usu. only affecting men, in which the blood fails to clot so that cuts, etc. continue bleeding for a long time. — *n* & *adj* **haemophiliac**. [**haemo-** + Gr *philia*, friendship]
haemorrhage *n* an escape of large amounts of blood, esp. from a ruptured blood vessel. — *v* (*intr*) to suffer a haemorrhage. [Gr *haimo*, blood + *rhegnynai*, to burst]
haemorrhoid *n* (usu. in *pl*) a swollen vein in the wall of the anus. [Gr *haima*, blood + *rheein*, to flow]

hafnium *n* a metallic element (symbol **Hf**), used e.g. in electrodes. [Lat *Hafnia*, Copenhagen, where it was discovered]

haft *n* a handle of a knife, sword, axe, etc. [OE *hæft*]

hag *n* **1** (*offensive*) an ugly old woman. **2** a witch. — *adj* **haggish**. [OE *hægtes*]

hag-ridden *adj* troubled or unhappy, as if cursed by a witch.

haggard *adj* looking very tired and thin-faced, because of pain, worry, etc. [OFr *hagard*]

haggis *n* a Scottish dish made from sheep's or calf's offal mixed with suet, oatmeal and seasonings and then boiled in a bag made from the animal's stomach, or something similar. [OScot *haggeis*]

haggle *v* (*intr*; **over**, **about**) to bargain over or argue about (a price, etc.). — *n* **haggler**. [Norse *höggva*, to hew]

hagiography *n* ***-ies*** the writing of the stories of saints' lives. — *n* **hagiographer**. [Gr *hagios*, holy + **-graphy**]

hagiology *n* ***-ies*** literature about the lives of, and legends about, saints. [Gr *hagios*, holy + **-logy**]

ha-ha[1] or **ha ha** *interj* a standardised way of representing the sound of laughter. [Imit.]

ha-ha[2] *n* a ditch, often with a low wall inside it, which divides areas of land without interrupting the view. [Fr]

haiku *n* ***-ku*** a Japanese poem with three lines of three, five and three syllables. [Jap]

hail[1] *n* **1** grains of ice falling from the clouds. **2** a large number or amount (of words, questions, missiles, etc.). — *v* **1** (*intr*) (of hail) to fall from the clouds. **2** (*intr* & *tr*) to shower with (words, questions, missiles, etc.) or come down on in great numbers. [OE *hagol*]

hailstone *n* a single grain of hail.

hailstorm *n* a storm during which hail falls heavily.

hail[2] *v* (*tr*) **1** to call out to in order to attract attention, e.g. to signal to (a taxi) to stop. **2** to greet. **3** (**as**) to recognise or describe as being or representing. — *interj* (*old*) expressing greeting. — *v* **hail from** (*intr*) to come from or belong to (a place). — **within hail** or **within hailing distance** close enough to hear when shouted at. [Norse *heill*, healthy]

hail-fellow-well-met *adj* overpoweringly hearty and friendly.

hail Mary *n* a prayer to the Virgin Mary, the English version of the **Ave Maria**.

hair *n* **1** a thread-like object growing from the skin of animals. **2** a mass of these, esp. on a person's head. **3** anything resembling a hair. **4** a thread-like cell growing from the surface of a plant. **5** a hair's-breadth. — *adj* **hairless**. — **get in someone's hair** (*coll*) to annoy someone. — **a hair of the dog** (*coll*) an alcoholic drink taken as a cure for a hangover. — **keep one's hair on** (*coll*) to remain calm and not get angry. — **let one's hair down** (*coll*) to enjoy onself without restraint. — **make someone's hair curl** (*coll*) to shock someone. — **make someone's hair stand on end** (*coll*) to frighten someone. — **not turn a hair** to remain calm. — **split hairs** to make small, unimportant distinctions or quibbles. [OE *hær*]

hairbrush *n* a brush for smoothing and arranging one's hair.

haircut *n* the cutting of a person's hair; the shape or style in which it is cut.

hair-do *n* ***-dos*** (*coll*) a woman's haircut.

hairdresser *n* **1** a person who cuts, washes and styles hair. **2** a hairdresser's shop. — *n* **hairdressing**.

hairdrier or **-dryer** *n* an electrical apparatus which dries a person's hair by blowing hot air over it.

hair-grip *n* a small wire clasp for holding the hair in place.

hairline *n* the line along the forehead where the hair begins to grow.

hair-piece *n* a piece of false hair worn over a bald area on one's head, or to make one's own hair appear thicker.

hairpin *n* a thin, flat, U-shaped piece of wire for keeping the hair in place. — *adj* (of a bend, esp. on a mountain road) very sharp and U-shaped.

hair-raising *adj* extremely frightening.

hair's-breadth *n* a very small distance or margin.

hair shirt *n* a shirt made of a thick, coarse, uncomfortable cloth woven from hair, worn by religious people as a penance.

hair-slide *n* a small metal or plastic clip, used to keep the hair in place.

hair-splitting *n* the act of insisting on considering small, unimportant distinctions.

hairspray *n* liquid sprayed from a can as a fine mist, used to keep the hair in place.

hair-spring *n* a very small spring which regulates a watch.

hairstyle *n* the way in which a person's hair is cut or shaped.

hairy *adj* ***-ier***, ***-iest*** **1** covered in hair. **2** (*coll*) dangerous, frightening and exciting. — *n* **hairiness**.

hajj *n* a pilgrimage made by a Muslim to Mecca. [Arabic, pilgrimage]

hajji *n* a Muslim who has been on pilgrimage to Mecca.

hake *n* ***hake*** or ***hakes*** a sea-fish like cod, used for food.

halal *n* meat from an animal which has been killed in a way approved of by Muslim holy law. [Arabic, lawful]

halberd *n* (*hist*) a long spear with an axe-blade and a pick at one end. [OGer *helm*, handle + *barde*, hatchet]

halcyon *adj* peaceful, calm and happy: *halcyon days*. [Gr *halkyon*, kingfisher (from the ancient belief that it nested on the sea and that the sea remained calm while it did so)]

hale *adj* strong and healthy: *hale and hearty*. [OE *hal*]

half *n* ***halves*** **1** one of two equal parts which together form a whole. **2** the fraction equal to one divided by two. **3** (*coll*) a half pint, esp. of beer. **4** one of two equal periods of play in a match. **5** a half-price ticket, esp. for a child or old person. — *adj* forming or equal to half. — *adv* **1** to the extent or amount of one half: *half finished*. **2** almost; partly; to some extent: *half dead with exhaustion*. **3** thirty minutes past the hour stated. — **and a half** (*coll*) very good: *a singer and a half*. — **by half** (*coll*) excessively: *too clever by half*. — **by halves** without being thorough. — **go halves** to share the cost or expenses. — **not half** (*coll*) very; very much. — **one's better half** (*coll*) one's husband, wife, or partner. [OE *healf*]

half-and-half *adv* & *adj* in equal parts.

halfback *n* in football, hockey, etc., a player or position immediately behind the forwards.

half-baked *adj* (*coll*) (of an idea, etc.) stupid.

half-board *n* (*Br*) (in hotels, etc.) the provision of a bed, breakfast, and evening meal.

half-breed or **half-caste** *n* & *adj* (*offensive*) (a person) having parents of different races, esp. one black parent and one white.

half-brother or **half-sister** *n* a brother or sister with whom one has only one parent in common.

half-caste see **half-breed**.

half-crown or **half-a-crown** *n* (*hist*) a British coin worth two shillings and sixpence ($12\frac{1}{2}$p).

half-cut *adj* (*slang*) drunk.

half-day *n* a day on which one only works, etc. in the morning or in the afternoon.

half-hearted *adj* not eager; without enthusiasm. — *adv* **half-heartedly**. — *n* **half-heartedness**.

half-hitch *n* a simple knot or noose formed by passing the end of the rope through a loop made in the rope.

half-hour *n* a period of thirty minutes.

half-hourly *adj* & *adv* done, occurring, etc. every half-hour.

half-life *n* the time it takes for a radioactive substance to lose half its radioactivity.

half-light *n* dull light, esp. at dawn or dusk.

half mast *n* the position half way up a flagpole, where flags are flown as a mark of respect for a dead person.

half measures *n* (*pl*) actions which are not sufficient or thorough enough to deal with a problem.

half-moon *n* **1** the moon when only half of it can be seen from the Earth. **2** the time when this occurs. **3** anything shaped like a half-moon.

half nelson *n* a hold in wrestling in which one puts one's arm under one's opponent's arm from behind, and pushes on the back of his or her neck with one's palm.

halfpenny or **ha'penny** *n* (*hist*) a British coin worth half a penny.

halfpennyworth or **hap'orth** *n* (*Br*) **1** (*hist*) an amount of something costing a halfpenny. **2** (*coll*) a very small amount: *not make a hap'orth of difference*.

half-price *adj* & *adv* at half the usual price.

half-sister see **half-brother**.

half-term *n* (*Br*) a short holiday halfway through a school term.

half-timbered *adj* (of a house, etc.) built with a timber frame with brick or plaster filling.

half-time *n* an interval between the two halves of a match.

half-tone *n* a photograph produced using a method of printing in which black and white dots of different sizes create various shades of grey.

half-track *n* a usu. military vehicle with wheels in front and caterpillar tracks behind.

half-truth *n* a statement which is only partly true.

half volley *n* (*cricket*, *tennis*, etc.) a stroke in which the ball is hit immediately after it bounces or as it bounces.

halfway *adj* & *adv* **1** of, at or to a point equally far from two others: *halfway between France and England*. **2** in, of or into an incomplete manner. — **meet someone halfway** to compromise with someone.

halfway house *n* **1** (esp. *hist*) an inn where one can rest halfway through a journey. **2** (*coll*) something which is between two extremes, and which has some features of each. **3** a home where former prisoners or patients with mental illnesses stay so they may get used to life outside the prison or hospital.

halfwit *n* a foolish or stupid person. — *adj* **halfwitted**. — *adv* **halfwittedly**.

half-yearly *adj* & *adv* done, occurring, etc. every six months.

halibut *n* ***halibut*** a kind of large, flat, sea fish used for food. [MidE *halybutte*, from *haly*, holy + *butt*, flat fish, so-called because it was eaten on holy days]

halitosis *n* unpleasant-smelling breath. [Lat *halitus*, breath + **-osis**]

hall *n* **1** a room or passage just inside the entrance to a house, usu. allowing access to other rooms and the stairs. **2** a building or large room, used for concerts, public meetings, etc. **3** a large country house. **4** (*Br*; also **hall of residence**) a building where university or college students live. **5** (*Br*) the dining-room in a college or university; dinner in such a dining-room. [OE *heall*]

hallmark *n* **1** an official mark on a gold and silver article guaranteeing its quality. **2** a typical or distinctive feature, esp. of quality. — *v* (*tr*) to stamp with a hallmark.

hallstand *n* a piece of furniture in the hall of a house, on which coats, hats, etc. are hung.

hallway *n* an entrance hall.
hallelujah. See **alleluia**.
halliard. See **halyard**.
hallo. See **hello**.
halloo *n & interj* a cry encouraging hunting dogs or calling for attention. — *v (intr)* to cry halloo, esp. to dogs at a hunt. [Imit.]
hallow *v (tr)* to make or regard as holy. — *n (old)* a saint (see **Hallowe'en**). — *adj* **hallowed**. [OE *halgian*]
Hallowe'en *n* the evening of 31 October, the eve of All Saints' Day. [*all hallow even*, all saints' eve]
hallucinate *v (intr)* to seem to see or hear something which does not really exist. — *n* **hallucination**. — *adj* **hallucinatory**. [Lat *hallucinari*, to wander in the mind]
hallucinogen *n* a drug that causes hallucinations. — *adj* **hallucinogenic**. [**hallucinate** + **-gen**]
halo *n* ***-os*** or ***-oes*** **1** a ring of light around the head of a saint, angel, etc. in paintings, etc. **2** the glory or glamour attaching to a person or thing. **3** a ring of light which can be seen around the sun or moon in certain weather. — *v* ***-oes***, ***-oed*** *(tr)* to put a halo round. [Gr, circular threshing floor]
halogen *n* any of the non-metallic elements fluorine, chlorine, bromine, iodine and astatine which form salts when in union with metals. [Gr *hals*, salt + **-gen**]
halt *n* **1** a short or temporary stop. **2** *(Br)* a small railway station without a building. — *v (intr & tr)* to stop or cause to stop. — **call a halt to** to put an end to. [Ger *Halt*, stoppage]
halter *n* a rope or strap for holding and leading a horse by its head. — *v (tr)* to put a halter on. [OE *hælfter*]
halterneck *n* a woman's top or dress held in place by a strap which goes round her neck, leaving the shoulders and back bare.
halting *adj* pausing a lot; hesitant. — *adv* **haltingly**. [OE *healt*, lame]
halve *v (tr)* **1** to divide into two equal parts. **2** to reduce (costs, problems, etc.) by half. **3** *(golf)* to draw a hole or match with one's opponent. [**half**]
halves. See **half**.
halyard or **halliard** *n* a rope for raising or lowering a sail or flag on a ship. [MidE *halier*]
ham[1] *n* **1** the top part of the back leg of a pig, salted and smoked and used as food. **2** the back of the thigh. [OE *hamm*]
ham-fisted or **ham-handed** *adj (coll)* clumsy.
ham[2] *(coll) n* **1** a bad actor, esp. one who overacts and exaggerates. **2** an amateur radio operator. — *v* ***-mm-*** *(intr & tr;* **up***)* to overact or exaggerate. [*hamfatter*, a third-rate minstrel]
hamadryad *n (Gr & Rom mythol)* a nymph who lives in a tree and dies when it dies. [Gr *hama*, together + *drys*, oak tree]
hamburger *n* a flat, round cake of finely chopped beef, usu. fried and served in a soft roll. [Ger, of *Hamburg* in Germany]
Hamitic *n & adj* (of) a group of N African languages, including ancient Egyptian and Berber. [*Ham*, one of Noah's sons, supposed founder of a race of people in N Africa]
hamlet *n* a small village. [OFr *hamelet*]
hammer *n* **1** a tool with a heavy metal head on the end of a handle, used for driving nails into wood, breaking hard substances, etc. **2** the part of a bell, piano, clock, etc. that hits against some other part, making a noise. **3** the part of a gun, attached to the trigger, which causes the bullet to be fired. **4** a metal ball on a long, flexible steel chain, thrown in competitions; the sport of throwing this. **5** an auctioneer's gavel. — *v* ***-r-*** **1** *(tr & intr)* to hit with a hammer. **2** *(tr & intr;* **at, on***)* to strike loudly and repeatedly. **3** *(tr;* **in***)* to drive or force in with, or as if with, a hammer. **4** *(tr; Br coll)* to criticise or beat severely. **5** *(tr; coll)* to defeat. **6** *(intr;* **away at, at***)* to work constantly at: *hammer away at the problem*. — **come** or **go under the hammer** to be sold at auction. — **hammer and tongs** *(coll)* with a lot of noise and violence. — *v* **hammer out** *(tr)* to produce (an agreement, etc.) with a great deal of effort and discussion. [OE *hamor*]
hammer and sickle *n* the sign of a hammer and a sickle laid across each other, used as a symbol of communism.
hammerhead *n* a shark with a hammer-shaped head.
hammering *n (Br coll)* a severe beating.
hammer-toe *n* a condition in which a toe is permanently bent.
hammock *n* a piece of canvas or a net hung by the corners and used as a bed, e.g. in a ship. [Span *hamaca*]
hamper[1] ***-r-*** *v (tr)* to hinder the progress or movement of. [MidE *hampren*]
hamper[2] *n* **1** a large basket with a lid, used esp. for carrying food. **2** *(Br)* the food and drink packed in such a basket. [MidE *hanypere*, wicker basket]
hamster *n* a small, mouse-like animal with a short tail and pouches in its mouth for storing food, often kept as a pet. [OGer *hamstra*, weevil]
hamstring *n* a tendon at the back of the knee. — *v* ***-stringed*** or ***-strung*** *(tr)* **1** to make powerless or hinder. **2** to lame by cutting the hamstring. [**ham**[1]]
hand *n* **1** the part of the body at the end of each arm, with a thumb, four fingers and a palm. **2** (often in *pl*) control, agency or influence. **3** help; assistance. **4** a part or influence (in an activity): *had a hand in the victory*. **5** a needle or pointer on a clock, watch, or gauge. **6** *(coll)* applause. **7** a manual worker or assistant, esp. in a factory, on a farm, or on board ship. **8** a person skilful in some activity: *a dab hand at baking*. **9** a way of doing something: *have a light hand at pastry*. **10** the cards dealt to a player in one round of a card game. **11** one round of a card game. **12** a

position in relation to an object or (*in cmpds*) point in time: *on the right hand*; *behindhand with the work*. **13** a source of information considered in terms of closeness to the original source: *hear the news at first*, *second*, etc. *hand*. **14** a person's handwriting or its style. **15** a promise or agreement to marry: *ask for her hand*. **16** a unit of measurement, equal to four inches, used for measuring the height of horses. — *v* (*tr*; **back**, **in**, **out**, **round**, etc.) to deliver or give using the hands. — **at hand** near by; about to happen. — **by hand 1** with a person's hand or tools held in the hands. **2** delivered by messenger, not by post. — **from hand to mouth** with only enough money and food for one's immediate needs. — **get one's hands on** (*coll*) to catch or find (someone) or obtain (something). — *v* **hand down** (*tr*) to pass (an heirloom, tradition, etc.) on to the next generation. — **hand in glove** very closely associated. — **hand in hand 1** holding a person's hand. **2** in close association. — **hand it to** (*coll*) to give credit to. — *v* **hand on** (*tr*) to give (something) to the next person in succession. — *v* **hand over** (*tr*) to give possession (of something) to someone else. — **hand over fist** (*coll*) in large amounts and very quickly. — **have one's hands full** (*coll*) to be very busy. — **in hand 1** under control. **2** being done or prepared. — **keep one's hand in** (*coll*) to practise a skill, etc. so as to remain good at it. — **off hand** without thought or calculation. — **off one's hands** (*coll*) no longer one's responsibility. — **on hand** near; available for use. — **on one's hands 1** (*coll*) left over; not sold or used. **2** remaining as one's responsibility. — **on one's hands and knees 1** in a position with one's hands knees and feet on the ground. **2** begging. — **on the one hand ... on the other hand** from one point of view ... from another point of view. — **out of hand 1** unable to be controlled. **2** immediately and without thinking. — **to hand** within reach. [OE]

handbag *n* a woman's small bag, often with a strap for carrying, for money, make-up, etc.

handball *n* a game in which players hit a small ball with their hands.

handbill *n* a small printed notice or advertisement given out by hand.

handbook *n* a short manual or guidebook.

handbrake *n* a brake on a motor vehicle which is operated by the driver's hand.

handcart *n* a small light cart which can be moved by hand.

handclap *n* a clap of the hands.

handcrafted *adj* made by handicraft.

handcuff *v* (*tr*) to put handcuffs on (a person). — *n* (in *pl*) a pair of steel rings, joined by a short chain, for locking round the wrists of prisoners.

handful *n* **-*fuls*** **1** as much as can be held in one hand. **2** a small amount or number. **3** (*coll*) a person who is difficult to control; a difficult task.

hand-grenade *n* a grenade to be thrown by hand.

handless *adj* (*old*) awkward or clumsy.

handmade *adj* made with a person's hands or with tools held in the hands, not by machine.

handmaiden or **handmaid** *n* (*old*) a female servant.

hand-me-down *n* (*coll*) a second-hand garment, toy, etc.

handout *n* **1** money, food, etc. given to people who need it. **2** a leaflet, statement containing information, etc., given e.g. to students before a lecture, to newspaper reporters, etc.

handover *n* the transfer of power from one person or group of people to another.

hand-pick *v* (*tr*) to choose carefully, esp. for a particular purpose. — *adj* **hand-picked**.

handrail *n* a narrow rail running along stairs, etc. for support.

handset *n* a telephone mouthpiece and earpiece together in a single unit.

handshake *n* the act of holding or shaking a person's hand, esp. as a greeting.

hands-off *adj* not touched or operated by the hands.

hands-on *adj* involving practical experience rather than just information or theory.

handspring *n* a somersault or cartwheel in which one lands first on one's hands and then on one's feet.

handstand *n* an act of balancing one's body upside down on one's hands.

hand-to-hand *adj* (of fighting) in actual physical contact with the enemy.

handwriting *n* **1** writing with a pen or pencil. **2** the characteristic way a person writes.

handwritten *adj* written using a pen or pencil, not printed or typed.

handicap *n* **1** a physical, mental or social disability. **2** a disadvantage given to a superior competitor in a contest, race, etc. so that everyone has an equal chance of winning. **3** a race or competition in which some competitors are given a handicap. **4** the number of strokes by which a golfer usu. exceeds par for the course. — *v* **-*pp-*** (*tr*) **1** to give a handicap to. **2** to make something difficult for (someone). [*hand i' cap*, an old sporting lottery]

handicapped *adj* physically or mentally disabled. — *n* (*pl*) handicapped people.

handicraft *n* **1** an activity which requires skilful use of the hands, e.g. pottery, model-making. **2** (usu. in *pl*) any object produced by such craft. [OE *handcræft*]

handiwork *n* **1** work, esp. skilful, done by the hands. **2** something bad done or caused by a particular person. [OE *handgeweorc*]

handkerchief *n* **-*chiefs*** or **-*chieves*** a small, usu. square piece of cloth or soft paper used for wiping one's nose, face, etc. [**hand** + **kerchief**]

handle *n* **1** the part of an object by which it is held so that it may be used or operated. **2** an advantage or opening given to an opponent. **3** (*slang*) a person's name. — *v* **1** (*tr*) to touch, hold, move or operate with the hands. **2** (*tr*) to deal with or manage, esp. successfully or in the correct way. **3** (*tr*) to buy, sell, or deal in (goods). **4** (*tr*) to write about or discuss (a subject). **5** (*intr*) to respond to control in the way stated. — *n* **handling**. — **fly off the handle** (*coll*) to become extremely angry very suddenly. [OE]

handlebars *n* (*pl*) a usu. curved metal bar with handles at each end, for steering a bicycle or motorcycle.

handlebar moustache *n* a wide, thick moustache which curls up at the ends.

handler *n* **1** a person who trains and controls an animal, esp. a dog. **2** a person who handles something: *a baggage handler*.

handsome *adj* **1** (of a man) good-looking. **2** (of a woman) attractive in a strong, healthy, imposing way. **3** (of a building) large and imposing. **4** generous: *a handsome donation*. — *adv* **handsomely**. — *n* **handsomeness**. [**hand** + **-some**; orig. meaning easy to handle]

handy *adj* **-ier**, **-iest** **1** ready to use and conveniently placed. **2** easy to use or handle. **3** clever with one's hands. — *adv* **handily**. — *n* **handiness**. [**hand**]

handyman *n* a person skilled at, or employed to do, odd jobs around the house.

hang *v* ***hung*** (except for sense **3** which usu. has ***hanged*** for its past tenses and sense **12** which always has) **1** (*tr* & *intr*; **up**, **on**, **on to**, etc.) to fasten or be fastened from above. **2** (*tr* & *intr*) (of e.g. a door) to fasten or be fastened e.g. by hinges so that it can move freely. **3** (*tr* & *intr*) to suspend or be suspended by a rope or something similar around the neck until dead. **4** (*intr*; **over**) to remain without moving, esp. in the air or in a threatening way. **5** (*tr* & *intr*; **down**) to (cause to) droop: *hang one's head in shame*. **6** (*tr*) to fix (wallpaper) to a wall. **7** (*tr* & *intr*) (of a painting, etc.) to place or be placed in an exhibition. **8** (*tr* with **with**) to decorate (with pictures, etc.). **9** (*tr* with **on**; *coll*) to blame someone for (something); to assign (blame for something) to. **10** (*intr* with **on**) to depend. **11** (*intr* with **on**) to listen closely to: *hanging on her every word*. **12** (*tr* & *intr*; *coll*) to damn. **13** (*intr*) (of a piece of clothing) to sit in a stated way when worn: *a coat which hangs well*. **14** (*tr*) to suspend (game) from a hook until it is mature. — *n* the way something hangs, falls or droops. — **get the hang of** (*coll*) to learn or begin to understand how to do (something). — *v* **hang about** or **around** (*intr*; *coll*) **1** to stand around doing nothing. **2** (**with**) to spend a lot of time (with someone). — *v* **hang back** (*intr*) to be unwilling or reluctant to do something. — **hang fire** **1** to delay taking action. **2** to cease to develop or progress. — **hang in the balance** to be uncertain or in doubt. — **hang loose** (esp. *US coll*) to stay calm and in control of oneself. — *v* **hang on** **1** (*tr* & *intr*; **to**) to keep holding (something). **2** (*intr*; *coll*) to wait. **3** (*intr*) to carry on bravely, in spite of problems or difficulties. — *v* **hang out** (*intr*) **1** to lean or bend out of. **2** (*coll*) to spend a lot of time in a place (*n* **hang-out**). — *v* **hang together** (*intr*) **1** to be united and support each other. **2** (of ideas, etc.) to be consistent. — *v* **hang up** **1** (*tr*) to hang on a hook or hanger. **2** (*intr*) to finish a telephone conversation by replacing the receiver. — **let it all hang out** (*coll*) to be totally uninhibited and relaxed. [OE *hangian*]

hangdog *adj* ashamed or guilty.

hanger *n* **1** a metal, wooden or plastic frame on which jackets, dresses, etc. are hung up to keep their shape. **2** a person who hangs something.

hanger-on *n* ***hangers-on*** a fan or follower, esp. one who is not wanted.

hang-glider *n* **1** a large, light, metal frame with cloth stretched across it, which flies using air currents, with a harness hanging below it for the pilot. **2** the pilot. — *n* **hang-gliding**.

hanging *n* **1** the execution of a criminal by hanging (sense **3**). **2** (usu. in *pl*) curtains, tapestries, etc. hung on walls for decoration.

hangman *n* an official who hangs criminals.

hang-out see **hang out** above.

hangover *n* **1** severe sickness and headaches caused by having drunk too much alcohol. **2** something which remains from an earlier time.

hang-up *n* (*coll*) an emotional or psychological problem.

hangar *n* a large shed in which aircraft are kept. [Fr]

hangnail *n* a piece of loose skin that has been partly torn away from the base or side of a fingernail.

hank *n* a length of wool, string, rope, etc. gathered in a loop. [Norse]

hanker *v* **-r-** (*intr*; **after**, **for**) to long for or crave. — *n* **hankering**.

hankie or **hanky** *n* **-ies** (*coll*) a handkerchief. [Abbrev. of **handkerchief**]

hanky-panky *n* (*coll*) **1** slightly improper sexual behaviour. **2** dishonest dealing.

Hanoverian *adj* of British sovereigns from George I (1714) to Victoria (1901), George I being also the Elector of *Hanover*, N Germany.

Hansard *n* an official printed daily report of what has happened in the British parliament. [Luke *Hansard* (1752–1828), the first compiler and printer of such reports]

Hanseatic League *n* an organisation of N German commercial cities, formed in the 14th century to protect trade. [OGer *hansa*, a band of men]

hansom or **hansom cab** *n* (*hist*) a small, two-wheeled, horse-drawn carriage with a fixed roof and the driver's seat high up at the back, used as a taxi. [J A *Hansom* (1803–82), its inventor]

Hants *abbrev* Hampshire.

Hanukkah *n* the Jewish festival of lights, commemorating the re-dedication of the temple in Jerusalem in 165 BC. [Hebr, consecration]

ha'penny see **halfpenny** at **half**.

haphazard *adj* done by chance; random. — *adv* at random. — *adv* **haphazardly**. [Norse *happ*, good luck + **hazard**]

hapless *adj* unlucky; unfortunate. [Norse *happ*, good luck]

hap'orth see **halfpennyworth** at **half**.

happen *v* **-n-** (*intr*) **1** to take place or occur. **2** (**to**) (esp. of something bad) to be done to (someone). **3** to have the good or bad luck to: *happened to meet him on the way*. **4** (with **on**) to discover, esp. by chance. — *adv* (*dialect*) perhaps. [Norse *happ*, good luck]

happening *n* **1** an event. **2** a public performance, esp. one which takes place in the street, which has not been fully planned, and in which the audience is invited to take part.

happy *adj* **-ier**, **-iest** **1** feeling or showing pleasure or contentment: *a happy smile*. **2** causing pleasure: *a happy day for the company*. **3** suitable; fortunate: *a happy coincidence*. — *n* **happiness**. [Norse *happ*, good luck]

happily *adv* **1** in a happy way. **2** luckily.

happy event *n* (*euph*) the birth of a child.

happy-go-lucky *adj* carefree.

happy medium *n* a reasonable middle course between two extreme positions.

hara-kiri *n* ritual suicide by cutting one's belly open with a sword, formerly practised in Japan to avoid dishonour. [Jap *hara*, belly + *kiri*, cut]

harangue *n* a loud, forceful speech either to attack people or to try to persuade them to do something. — *v* (*tr*) to address such a speech to. [OFr *arenge*]

harass *v* (*tr*) **1** to annoy or trouble (a person) constantly or frequently. **2** to make frequent sudden attacks on (an enemy). — *adj* **harassed**. — *n* **harassment**. [OFr *harasser*, to harry]

harbinger *n* a person or thing which is a sign of something that is to come. [OFr *herbergere*, host]

harbour *n* **1** a place of shelter for ships. **2** a refuge. — *v* (*tr*) **1** to give shelter or protection to (e.g. a criminal). **2** to have (thoughts) in one's head: *harbour a grudge*. [OE *herebeorg*, lodgings]

harbour master *n* a person officially in charge of a harbour.

hard *adj* **1** firm or solid. **2** difficult to do, understand, solve or explain. **3** using, needing, or done with a great deal of effort. **4** harsh; cruel. **5** (of weather) severe. **6** causing or suffering hardship: *hard times*. **7** harsh and unpleasant to the senses: *a hard light*. **8** (of information, etc.) proven and reliable. **9** (of water) containing mineral salts which stop soap from lathering. **10** (of a drug) highly addictive. **11** (of an alcoholic drink) very strong; which is a spirit rather than beer or wine. **12** politically extreme: *hard right*. **13** (of the sounds of certain letters) produced as a stop rather than a fricative, as e.g. the *c* in *cat* and the *g* in *got*. **14** (of currency) with a stable value and exchange rate. **15** (of pornography) sexually explicit. — *adv* **1** with great effort or energy: *work hard*. **2** with difficulty; as a result of great effort: *a hard-won victory*; *hard-earned results*. — *n* **hardness**. — **be hard going** to be difficult to do. — **be hard put to** to have difficulty (doing). — **go hard with** to be unpleasant or difficult for. — **hard at it** working hard. — **hard by** close by. — **hard done by** (*coll*) unfairly treated. — **hard of hearing** partially deaf. — **hard on** close behind. — **hard up** (*coll*) short of something, esp. money. [OE *heard*]

hard-and-fast *adj* (of rules) that can never be changed.

hardback *n* a book with a hard cover. — *adj* having a hard cover.

hard-bitten *adj* (*coll*) (of people) tough and ruthless, esp. through difficult experience.

hardboard *n* light, strong board made by compressing wood pulp.

hard-boiled *adj* **1** (of eggs) boiled until the yolk is solid. **2** (of a person) tough; cynical.

hard case *n* (*coll*) a tough, often violent person.

hard cash *n* coins and bank-notes, as opposed to cheques and credit cards.

hard copy *n* information from a computer printed on paper.

hardcore *n* **1** pieces of broken brick, stone, etc. used as a base for a road. **2** (**hard core**) the central, most important group within an organisation.

hard-core *adj* **1** having long-lasting, strong, unchanging beliefs. **2** (of pornography) sexually explicit.

hard disk or **disc** *n* a metal disk with a magnetic coating, used for storing information in a computer.

harden *v* **-n-** **1** (*tr* & *intr*) to make or become hard or harder. **2** (*tr* & *intr*) to become or make less sympathetic or understanding: *hardened his heart to her tears*. **3** (*intr*) (of prices) to stop falling.

hardened *adj* toughened through experience and not likely to change: *a hardened criminal*.

hardening of the arteries same as **arteriosclerosis**.

hard-headed *adj* clever and not influenced by emotion.

hard-hearted *adj* feeling no pity or kindness. — *adv* **hard-heartedly**. — *n* **hard-heartedness**.
hard-hitting *adj* direct; frankly critical.
hard labour *n* heavy physical work, e.g. breaking rocks, esp. as a punishment in prison.
hard line *n* a strong opinion, decision, or policy which is not likely to be changed. — *adj* **hardline**. — *n* **hardliner**.
hard-nosed *adj* (*coll*) determined; influenced by reason, not emotion.
hard nut *n* (*coll*) a person or thing that is tough or difficult to deal with.
hard-on *n* (*vulg slang*) an erection of the penis.
hardpad *n* a symptom of distemper in dogs, causing hardness of the pads of the feet.
hard palate *n* the hard, bony part at the front of the roof of the mouth.
hard-pressed or **-pushed** *adj* having problems; in difficulties.
the hard sell *n* an aggressive and insistent way of promoting, selling or advertising.
hardship *n* (something which causes) severe suffering and pain.
hard shoulder *n* a hard verge along the side of a motorway, on which vehicles can stop if in trouble.
hardtack *n* hard biscuits formerly given to sailors as food on long journeys.
hardware *n* **1** metal goods such as pots, cutlery, tools, etc. **2** the mechanical and electronic equipment used in computing. ◇ See also **software**. **3** heavy military equipment, e.g. tanks.
hard-wearing *adj* that will last a long time and stay in good condition.
hard-wired *adj* (of circuits in computers) built-in, and with functions that cannot be changed.
hardwood *n* wood from a slow-growing deciduous tree, such as the oak or ash.

hardihood. See **hardy**.

hardly *adv* **1** only with difficulty; scarcely: *could hardly keep her eyes open.* **2** probably not: *She'll hardly come now.* **3** harshly. **[hard]**

hardy *adj* **-ier**, **-iest** **1** tough; strong; able to bear difficult conditions. **2** (of a plant) able to live outside in winter. — *n* **hardiness**. [OFr *hardi*, made bold]
hardihood *n* courage and daring.

hare *n* an animal like a rabbit but slightly larger and with longer legs and ears, and which can run very fast. — *v* (*intr*; *coll*) to run very fast. [OE *hara*]
harebell *n* a wild plant with violet-blue, bell-shaped flowers.
hare-brained *adj* (of people, actions, etc.) foolish; done without considering the consequences.
hare lip *n* a split in a top lip, present from before birth. — *adj* **hare-lipped**.

harem *n* **1** a separate part of a traditional Muslim house in which the women live. **2** the women living in this. [Arabic *harim*, forbidden]

haricot or **haricot bean** *n* a small, white, dried bean, used as food. [Fr]

hark *v* (*intr*; *old, literary* or *facet*; **at**, **to**) to listen attentively. — **hark back (to)** to remind one of, or refer to (something that has already happened): *hark back to one's childhood.* [OE *heorcnian*, to hearken]

harken. Same as **hearken**.

harlequin *n* (*cap*) a humorous character from traditional Italian plays who wears a black mask and a brightly coloured, diamond-patterned costume. — *adj* in varied bright colours. [OFr]

harlot *n* (*old*) a prostitute. — *adj* **harlotry**. [OFr *herlot*, rascal]

harm *n* physical, mental or moral injury or damage. — *v* (*tr*) to cause harm to. — **out of harm's way** in a safe place, not able to be harmed or cause harm. [OE *hearm*]
harmful *adj* causing harm. — *adv* **harmfully**. — *n* **harmfulness**.
harmless *adj* not able or likely to cause harm. — *adv* **harmlessly**. — *n* **harmlessness**.

harmonic *adj* of or relating to harmony; harmonious. — *n* a note produced on a stringed instrument by touching one of the strings lightly at one of the points which divide the string into exact fractions. [Gr *harmonikos*, from *harmos*, joint]
harmonics *n* (*sing*) the science of musical sounds.

harmonica *n* a small, rectangular, musical instrument with metal reeds along one side, played by being held against the mouth, blown down, and moved from side to side to change the notes. **[harmonic]**

harmonious *adj* **1** pleasant-sounding and tuneful. **2** forming a pleasing whole: *a harmonious arrangement of colours.* **3** without disagreement or bad feeling. — *adv* **harmoniously**. — *n* **harmoniousness**. **[harmony]**

harmonium *n* a musical instrument with a keyboard, in which air from bellows pumped by the feet makes the reeds vibrate to produce sound. **[harmony]**

harmony *n* **-ies** **1** (*mus*) a pleasing combination of notes or sounds produced simultaneously. **2** a pleasing arrangement of parts or things: *harmony of colour.* **3** agreement in opinions and feelings. [Gr *harmonia*, from *harmos*, joint]
harmonise or **-ize** *v* **1** (*intr* & *tr*) to be or bring into musical harmony. **2** (*intr* & *tr*) to form or be made to form a pleasing whole. **3** (*tr*) to add notes to (a simple tune) to form harmonies. — *n* **harmonisation** or **-z-**.

harness *n* **1** a set of leather straps used to attach a cart to a horse, and to control the horse's movements. **2** a similar set of straps for attaching to a person's body, e.g. to hold a child who is just learning to walk. — *v* (*tr*) **1** to put a harness on (a horse, person, etc.). **2** to control and make use of (esp.

natural resources), esp. to produce power. — **in harness** occupied with one's daily work or routine. [OFr *herneis*, equipment]

harp *n* a large, three-sided musical instrument with a series of strings stretched vertically across it, played by plucking the strings with the fingers. — *n* **harpist**. — *v* **harp on** or **on about** (*intr*; *coll*) to talk or write repeatedly and boringly about something. [OE *hearpe*]

harpoon *n* a barbed spear fastened to a rope, used for catching whales. — *v* (*tr*) to strike (a whale, etc.) with a harpoon. [Gr *harpe*, hook]

harpsichord *n* a keyboard instrument in which the strings are plucked mechanically (rather than hit with small hammers) when the player presses the keys. [Lat *harpa*, harp + *chorda*, string]

harpy *n* **-ies 1** (*Gr mythol*) an evil creature with the head and body of a woman and the wings and feet of a bird. **2** a cruel, grasping woman. [Gr *harpyia*, snatcher]

harridan *n* a bad-tempered, scolding old woman.

harrier[1] *n* **1** a cross-country runner. **2** a hound used orig. for hunting hares. [**hare**]

harrier[2] *n* **1** a bird of prey with long wings. **2** any person or thing which harries. [**harry**]

harrow *n* a heavy metal frame with teeth, used to break up clods of soil and cover seed. — *v* (*tr*) **1** to pull a harrow over. **2** to distress greatly. [MidE *harwe*]

harrowing *adj* distressing.

harry *v* **-ies, -ied** (*tr*) **1** to ravage or destroy. **2** to annoy or worry (a person). ◇ See also **harrier**[2]. [OE *hergian*]

harsh *adj* **1** rough; grating; unpleasant to the senses. **2** strict, cruel or severe. — *adv* **harshly**. — *n* **harshness**. [MidE *harsk*]

hart *n* a male deer, esp. one over five years old, when the antlers begin to appear. [OE *heorot*]

hartebeest *n* a large African antelope with curved horns. [Afrikaans, hart beast]

harum-scarum *adj* wild and thoughtless; reckless. — *adv* recklessly. — *n* a wild, thoughtless person.

harvest *n* **1** the gathering in of ripened crops, usu. in late summer or early autumn. **2** the season when this takes place. **3** the crops gathered. **4** the product or result of some action. — *v* (*tr & intr*) to gather as a harvest; to reap. [OE *hærfest*]

harvester *n* a person or machine that harvests corn.

harvest festival or **harvest thanksgiving** *n* a Christian religious service to thank God for the crops gathered in the harvest.

harvest moon *n* the full moon nearest to the autumnal equinox, usu. 22 or 23 September.

harvest mouse *n* a very small mouse that nests in the stalks of corn.

has. See **have**.

has-been *n* (*coll*) a person who is no longer successful, important or influential.

hash *n* **1** a dish of cooked meat and vegetables chopped up together and recooked. **2** a re-using of old material. **3** (*coll*) a mess: *make a hash of something*. — *v* (*tr*) to make into a hash. — **settle someone's hash** (*coll*) to silence or subdue someone. [OFr *hacher*, to chop]

hash browns *n* a dish of pieces of potato mixed with onions, fried and eaten hot.

hash[2] *n* (*slang*) hashish. [Abbrev.]

hashish *n* a drug in the form of a resin, made from the dried leaves and flowers of hemp, smoked or chewed for its intoxicating effects. [Arabic, dry leaves]

hasn't has not.

hasp *n* a metal fastening for a door, box, etc. consisting of a flat metal strip with a narrow slit in it, which fits over a small curved metal bar and is held shut by a pin or padlock fastened through the bar. [OE *hæpse*]

hassle (*coll*) *n* **1** (a cause of) trouble, annoyance and inconvenience. **2** a fight or argument. — *v* **1** (*tr*) to annoy or bother, esp. repeatedly. **2** (*intr*) to argue or fight.

hassock *n* **1** a firm cushion for kneeling on in church. **2** a tuft of grass. [OE *hassuc*]

hast *v* (*aux & tr*; *old*) the form of the present tense of the verb *have* used with *thou*.

haste *n* **1** urgency of movement. **2** too much speed. — **in haste** in a hurry; quickly. — **make haste** to hurry. [OFr]

hasten *v* **1** (*tr & intr*) to (cause to) move with speed. **2** (*intr*) to do immediately: *I hasten to say ...*

hasty *adj* **-ier, -iest 1** hurried; done or acting too quickly. **2** done without enough thought or preparation. — *adv* **hastily**. — *n* **hastiness**.

hat *n* **1** a covering for the head, usu. worn out of doors. **2** (*coll*) a role or capacity: *wearing her vet's hat*. — **keep (something) under one's hat** (*coll*) to keep (something) secret. — **old hat** (*coll*) so well-known, familiar, etc. as to be boring. — **pass the hat round** to collect money for a cause. — **take one's hat off to** (*coll*) to admire or praise. — **talk through one's hat** (*coll*) to talk nonsense. [OE *hæt*]

hatband *n* a band of cloth or ribbon around a hat just above the brim.

hatbox *n* a large, rounded, cardboard box for storing or carrying hats.

hatpin *n* a long metal pin, often decorated, pushed through a woman's hat and hair to keep the hat in place.

hatstand *n* a piece of furniture with pegs for hanging hats, coats, umbrellas, etc. on.

hatter *n* a person who makes or sells hats. — **mad as a hatter** mad or eccentric.

hat trick *n* **1** the taking of three wickets in cricket with three balls following each other. **2** the scoring of three points, goals, etc. in a single period of time or match. **3** the winning of three victories in a row.

hatch[1] *n* **1** a door covering an opening in a ship's deck. **2** a hatchway. **3** a door in an aircraft or spacecraft. **4** an opening in a wall between a kitchen and dining-room, used esp. for serving food. [OE *hæc*]

hatchback *n* (a car with) a sloping door at the back which opens upwards, allowing access to the boot, etc.

hatchway *n* an opening in a ship's deck for loading cargo through.

hatch[2] *v* **1** (*intr*; **out**) (of an animal or bird) to break out of an egg. **2** (*intr*) (of an egg) to break open, allowing young animals or birds to be born. **3** (*tr*) to produce (young animals or birds) from (eggs). **4** (*tr*; **up**) to plan or devise (a plot, etc.), esp. in secret. — *n* **1** an act of hatching. **2** a brood hatched. [MidE *hacchen*]

hatchery *n* **-ies** a place where eggs, esp. fish eggs, are hatched in controlled conditions.

hatch[3] *v* (*tr*) to shade (e.g. the surface of a map, drawing or engraving) with close parallel or crossed lines. — *n* **hatching**. [OFr *hacher*, to chop]

hatchet *n* a small axe held in one hand. [OFr *hachette*, from *hacher*, to chop]

hatchet-faced *adj* with a long thin face and sharp profile.

hatchet job *n* (*coll*) a severe written or spoken critical attack on a person or his or her good reputation.

hatchet man *n* (*coll*) a person employed to injure, kill, or ruin a person, his or her reputation, or some thing.

hatchway. See **hatch**[1].

hate *v* (*tr*) **1** to dislike very much. **2** (*coll*) to regret: *I hate to bother you.* — *n* **1** great dislike. **2** (*coll*) a greatly disliked person or thing. [OE *hatian*]

hateful *adj* causing or deserving great dislike. — *adv* **hatefully**. — *n* **hatefulness**.

hatred *n* great dislike or ill-will. [MidE]

hatter. See **hat**.

hauberk *n* (*hist*) a long coat of chain-mail. [OFr *hauberc*]

haughty *adj* **-ier**, **-iest** very proud; arrogant. — *adv* **haughtily**. — *n* **haughtiness**. [Lat *altus*, high]

haul *v* **1** (*tr & intr*) to pull with great effort or difficulty. **2** (*tr*) to transport by road, e.g. in a lorry. — *n* **1** the distance to be travelled: *a short haul.* **2** the act of pulling with effort or difficulty. **3** an amount gained at any one time, e.g. of fish caught in a single net or of something stolen. [OFr *haler*, to drag]

haulage *n* **1** the business of transporting goods by road, esp. in lorries. **2** the money charged for this.

haulier *n* a person or company which transports goods by road, esp. in lorries.

haulm *n* the stalks of potatoes, peas, beans, etc. [OE *healm*]

haunch *n* **1** the fleshy part of the buttock or thigh. **2** the leg and loin, esp. of a deer, as a cut of meat. [OFr *hanche*]

haunt *v* (*tr*) **1** (of a ghost) to live in (a place) or visit (a person or place) regularly. **2** (of unpleasant thoughts, etc.) to keep coming back to a person's mind: *haunted by the memory of his death.* **3** (*coll*) to visit (a place) frequently. — *adj* **haunted**. [OFr *hanter*]

haunting *adj* (of a place, memory, piece of music, etc.) making a very strong and moving impression. — *adv* **hauntingly**.

hautboy *n* (*old*) an oboe. [Fr *haut*, high + *bois*, wood]

haute couture *n* the most expensive and fashionable clothes available; the leading fashion designers or their products. [Fr]

haute cuisine *n* cookery (esp. French) of a very high standard. [Fr]

hauteur *n* haughtiness; arrogance. [Fr]

have *v* ***have***, ***has***, ***had*** (*tr*) **1** to possess. **2** to receive, obtain or take: *have a drink, a look.* **3** to think of or hold in the mind: *have an idea.* **4** to experience, enjoy or suffer: *have a good time, a headache; had my car stolen.* **5** to be in a state: *have a page missing.* **6** to take part in or hold: *have a party.* **7** to cause, order or invite (to do or be done): *have your hair cut; had him fired.* **8** (**to**) to be required to: *had to run fast.* **9** to eat or drink. **10** to gain an advantage over: *You have me on that point.* **11** (*coll*) to cheat or deceive: *You've been had.* **12** to show or feel: *have pity; have the goodness to leave.* **13** to accept or tolerate: *I won't have any of that!* **14** to receive as a guest: *have people to dinner.* **15** to be pregnant with or give birth to: *be having a baby.* **16** (*vulg slang*) to have sexual intercourse with. — *v* (*aux*) used with past participles of verbs to show that an action has been completed. — *n* (in *pl*; *coll*) people who have wealth and the security it brings: *the haves and the have-nots.* — **have had it** (*coll*) **1** to be dead, ruined or exhausted. **2** to have missed one's opportunity. — **have it coming** (*coll*) to deserve the bad luck, punishment, etc. that one will get. — **have it in for** (*coll*) to feel hostile towards (someone). — **have it off** or **away** (*vulg slang*; **with**) to have sexual intercourse. — *v* **have on** (*tr*) **1** to wear. **2** to have as an engagement or appointment. **3** (*coll*) to trick or tease. **4** to have (information) about someone, esp. proving he or she was involved in a crime. — **have it out** to settle a disagreement by arguing or discussing it frankly. — *v* **have up** (*tr*; **for**; *Br coll*) to make (a person) appear in court to answer a charge. — **have what it takes** (*coll*) to have the required qualities or ability. [OE *habban*]

haven *n* **1** a place of safety or rest. **2** a harbour. [OE *hæfen*]

haven't have not.

haversack *n* a canvas bag carried over one shoulder or on the back. [Ger *Habersack*, from *Haber*, oats + *Sack*, bag]

havoc *n* **1** great destruction or damage. **2** (*coll*) chaos. — **play havoc with** to cause a lot of damage or confusion to. [OFr *havot*, plunder]

haw[1]: **hum and haw**. See **hum**.

haw[2] *n* a hawthorn berry. [OE *haga*]

hawfinch *n* a type of finch with a large beak.

hawk[1] *n* **1** a bird of prey with short, rounded wings, and which is believed to have very good eyesight: *watch him like a hawk*. **2** (*politics*) a person favouring force and aggression rather than peaceful means of settling disputes. ◇ See also **dove**. — *v* (*intr*) to hunt with a hawk. — *n* **hawker**. — *adj* **hawkish**. — *n* **hawkishness**. [OE *hafoc*]

hawk-eyed *adj* having very keen eyesight.

hawk[2] *v* (*tr*) to carry (goods) round, usu. from door to door, trying to sell them. — *n* **hawker**. [OGer *haker*, retail dealer]

hawk[3] *v* **1** (*intr*) to clear the throat noisily. **2** (*tr*) to bring (phlegm) up from the throat. [Imit.]

hawser *n* a thick rope or a steel cable for tying ships to the quayside. [OFr *haucier*]

hawthorn *n* a thorny tree or shrub with pink or white flowers and red berries. [OE *haguthorn*]

hay *n* grass which has been cut and dried, used as food for cattle. — **hit the hay** (*slang*) to go to bed. — **make hay while the sun shines** to take advantage of an opportunity while one has the chance. [OE *hieg*]

haycock *n* a small, cone-shaped pile of hay in a field.

hay fever *n* an allergic reaction to pollen, which causes sneezing, breathing problems, and sore eyes.

hayfork *n* a long-handled long-pronged fork for tossing and lifting hay.

haystack or **hayrick** *n* a large, firm pile of hay built in a field. — **look for a needle in a haystack** to try to find something which is lost or hidden in a pile of things and so is almost impossible to find.

haywire *adj* (*coll*) out of order; in a state of confusion.

hazard *n* **1** a risk of harm or danger. **2** something which is likely to cause harm or danger. **3** an obstacle on a golfcourse. — *v* (*tr*) **1** to put forward (a guess or suggestion). **2** to risk. [OFr *hasard*]

hazardous *adj* dangerous. — *adv* **hazardously**. — *n* **hazardousness**.

haze *n* **1** a thin mist, vapour or shimmer which obscures visibility. **2** a feeling of confusion or not understanding. — *v* (*intr*; **over**) to become covered in a thin mist.

hazy *adj* **-ier**, **-iest** **1** misty. **2** (**about**) vague; not clear. — *adv* **hazily**. — *n* **haziness**.

hazel *n* a small tree or shrub on which nuts grow; its wood. — *adj* of a greenish-brown colour. [OE *hæsel*]

hazelnut *n* the edible nut of the hazel, with a smooth, shiny shell.

HB *abbrev* (on a pencil) hard black.

H-bomb. See **H**[3].

HE *abbrev* **1** His or Her Excellency. **2** His Eminence. **3** high explosive.

He *symbol* (*chem*) helium.

he *pron* **1** a male person or animal already referred to. **2** a person or animal of unknown or unstated sex. — *n* ***hes*** a male person or animal: *a he-goat*. [OE]

he-man *n* (*coll*) a very strong, virile man.

head *n* **1** the top or front part of a body, containing the eyes, nose, mouth, brain and ears. **2** the head thought of as the seat of intelligence, imagination, ability, etc.: *use your head*; *a good head for heights*. **3** something like a head in form or function, e.g. the top of a tool. **4** the person with the most authority in an organisation, country, etc. **5** the position of being in charge. **6** (*coll*) a headmaster, headmistress or head teacher. **7** the top or upper part of something, e.g. a table or bed. **8** the front or forward part of something, e.g. a queue. **9** the foam on top of a glass of beer. **10** the top part of a plant which produces leaves or flowers. **11** a crisis: *come to a head*. **12** the pus-filled top of a boil or spot. **13** ***head*** a person, animal or individual considered as a unit: *600 head of cattle*. **14** (*coll*) a headache. **15** the source of a river, lake, etc. **16** the height or length of a head, used as a measurement: *win by a head*. **17** a headland: *Beachy Head*. **18** the amount of pressure produced by water or steam in an enclosed space. **19** the part of a tape recorder which records sound or video on to the tape. **20** the side of a coin bearing the head of a monarch, etc. **21** a headline. — *v* **1** (*tr*) to be at the front of or top of: *head the queue*. **2** (*tr*) to be in charge of. **3** (*intr*; **for**) to move in a certain direction. **4** (*tr*) to put or write (a title or headline) at the beginning of a chapter, top of a letter, etc. **5** (*tr*) (*football*, etc.) to hit (the ball) with the head. — *adj* **headless**. — **above one's head** too difficult for one to understand. — **give someone his** or **her head** to allow someone to act freely and without restraint. — **go to one's head 1** (of alcoholic drinks) to make one slightly drunk. **2** (of praise, success, etc.) to make one conceited. — **have one's head in the clouds 1** to not be listening to what is said. **2** to have thoughts, ideas, etc. which are not practical. — *v* **head off** (*tr*) to get ahead of so as to intercept and turn back. — **head over heels 1** rolling over completely with the head first. **2** completely. — **head and shoulders above** very much better, cleverer, etc. than. — **keep one's head** to remain calm and sensible in a crisis. — **lose one's head** to become angry, excited, or act foolishly in a crisis. — **not make head or tail of** to not understand. — **off one's head** (*coll*) mad. — **off the top of one's head** (*coll*) without much thought or calculation. — **on your**, etc. **own head be it** you, etc. will bear the full responsibility for your, etc. actions. — **over one's head 1** to a higher authority. **2** too difficult for one to understand. — **put (our, your,** etc.) **heads together** to consult together. — **take it into one's head 1** to decide to do something, usu. foolish. **2** to come to believe something, usu. wrongly. — **turn someone's head** to make someone vain and conceited. [OE *heafod*]

headache *n* **1** a continuous pain in the head. **2** (*coll*) any person or thing that causes worry or annoyance. — *adj* **headachy**.

headband *n* a band worn round the head, esp. for decoration.

headbanger *n* (*slang*) **1** a person who shakes his or her head violently to the beat of music. **2** a stupid, foolish or fanatical person.

headboard *n* a board at the top end of a bed.

head cold *n* a cold which affects one's eyes, nose and head, rather than one's throat and chest.

head count *n* a count of people present.

headdress *n* a covering for the head, esp. one which is highly decorative and is used in ceremonies.

headed *adj* having a heading: *headed notepaper*.

header *n* **1** (*coll*) a fall or dive forwards. **2** (*football*) the hitting of the ball with the head.

headfirst *adv* **1** moving esp. quickly with one's head in front or bent forward. **2** without thinking; rashly.

headgear *n* anything worn on the head.

headhunting *n* **1** the practice of taking the heads of one's dead enemies as trophies. **2** the practice of trying to attract people away from their present jobs to work for one's own company, by offering them more money. — *n* **headhunter**.

heading *n* **1** a title at the top of a page, letter, section of a report, etc. **2** a horizontal tunnel in a mine.

headlamp same as **headlight**.

headland *n* a strip of land which sticks out into the sea.

headlight *n* a powerful light on the front of a vehicle.

headline *n* **1** a title of a newspaper article, written above the article in large letters. **2** (in *pl*) the most important points in a television or radio news broadcast. — **hit the headlines** (*coll*) to be a very prominent, shocking or exciting piece of news.

headlong *adj* & *adv* **1** moving esp. quickly with one's head in front or bent forward. **2** quickly and usu. without thinking.

headman *n* a tribal chief or leader.

headmaster or **headmistress** *n* the principal teacher in charge of a school.

head-on *adv* & *adj* **1** head to head; with the front of one vehicle hitting the front of another: *a head-on crash*. **2** in direct confrontation.

headphones or **earphones** *n* (*pl*) an apparatus, consisting of two small sound receivers which are held over the ears by a metal strap passed over the head, which can be connected to a radio or record-player so that the sound is heard only by the person wearing the headphones.

headquarters *n* (*sing* or *pl*) the centre of an organisation or group, e.g. in the army, from which activities are controlled.

headrest *n* a cushion which supports the head, fitted to the top of a car seat, etc.

headroom *n* the space between the top of a vehicle and the underside of a bridge.

headscarf *n* a scarf worn over the head and tied under the chin.

headset *n* a pair of headphones, often with a microphone attached.

headship *n* the position of, or time of being, head or leader of an organisation, esp. a school.

headshrinker *n* (*coll*) a psychiatrist.

headstall *n* the part of a bridle which fits round a horse's head.

head start *n* an advantage at the beginning of a race or competition.

headstone *n* an inscribed stone at the head of a grave.

headstrong *adj* (of people) difficult to persuade; determined; obstinate.

head teacher *n* a headmaster or headmistress.

headwaters *n* (*pl*) the small streams flowing from a river's source.

headway *n* **1** progress: *make no headway with the backlog*. **2** a ship's movement forwards. **3** same as **headroom**.

headwind *n* a wind which is blowing towards one, in the opposite direction to which one is travelling.

headword *n* a word forming a heading, esp. for a dictionary or encyclopaedia entry.

heady *adj* **-ier, -iest 1** tending to make one drunk quickly. **2** very exciting. **3** rash; impetuous.

heal *v* **1** (*intr*; **up, over**) (of wounds) to become healthy again. **2** (*tr*) to cause (a wound, person, etc.) to become healthy again. **3** (*tr*) to make (sorrow) less painful. **4** (*tr*) to settle or put right (disputes, etc.). — *n* **healer**. — *n* **healing**. [OE *hælan*]

health *n* **1** the state of being physically and mentally fit and free from illness. **2** a person's general mental or physical condition: *be in poor health*. **3** the soundness, esp. financial, of an organisation, country, etc.: *the economic health of the nation*. [OE *hælth*]

health centre *n* a centre where a group of doctors and nurses provide health care for a community.

health farm *n* a place, usu. in the country, where people go to improve their health through diet and exercise.

health food *n* food thought to be particularly good for one's health, esp. because it has been grown, prepared, etc. without the use of man-made fertilisers and pesticides.

healthful *adj* causing or bringing good health.

health service *n* a public service providing medical care, usu. without charge.

health visitor *n* a nurse who makes regular visits to people, e.g. the elderly and mothers with new babies, at home.

healthy *adj* **-*ier***, **-*iest*** **1** having or showing good health. **2** causing good health. **3** in a good state: *a healthy economy*. **4** wise: *a healthy respect for authority*. — *adv* **healthily**. — *n* **healthiness**.

heap *n* **1** a collection of things in an untidy pile or mass. **2** (usu. in *pl*; *coll*) a large amount or number. **3** (*coll*) something, esp. a motor vehicle, that is very old and not working properly. — *v* **1** (*tr* & *intr*; **up**) to collect or be collected together in a heap. **2** (*tr*; **on**) to give in large amounts. [OE]

heaped *adj* (of a spoonful) forming a rounded heap on the spoon.

heaps *adv* (*coll*) very much: *heaps better*.

hear *v* ***heard*** **1** (*tr* & *intr*) to perceive (sounds) with the ear. **2** (*tr*) to listen to. **3** (*intr*; **about**, **of**) to be told about or informed of: *heard about his problems*. **4** (*intr*; **from**) to be contacted by (someone), esp. by letter or telephone. **5** (*intr* with **of**) to allow: *I won't hear of it*. **6** (*tr*) (of a judge) to listen to and judge (a case). — *n* **hearer**. — **hear! hear!** an expression of agreement or approval. — *v* **hear out** (*tr*) to allow (someone) to finish saying what he or she wants to say. [OE *hieran*]

hearing *n* **1** the sense by which sound is perceived. **2** the distance within which something can be heard. **3** an opportunity to state one's case: *give him a hearing*. **4** a court case.

hearing-aid *n* a small electrical device for making sounds louder, which fits into the ear and helps people who are partially deaf hear more clearly.

hearsay *n* rumour; gossip.

hearken *v* (*intr*; **to**; *old*) to listen or pay attention. [OE *heorcnian*]

hearsay. See **hear**.

hearse *n* a car used for carrying a coffin at a funeral. [Lat *hirpex*, harrow]

heart *n* **1** the hollow, muscular organ inside the chest, which pumps blood around the body. **2** this organ considered as the centre of a person's thoughts, emotions, conscience, etc. **3** ability to feel tenderness or pity: *have no heart*. **4** courage and enthusiasm: *take heart*; *lose heart*. **5** the central or most important part: *the heart of the problem*. **6** the breast: *hold her to her heart*. **7** the compact inner part of some vegetables, e.g. cabbages and lettuces. **8** a usu. red symbol representing the heart, with two rounded lobes at the top curving down to meet in a point at the bottom. **9** a playing-card with a red symbol of such a shape on it. **10** (in *pl*) the suit of cards with such shapes on them. — **at heart** really; basically. — **break someone's heart** to cause (someone) great sorrow. — **by heart** by or from memory. — **change of heart** a change of decision, attitude, etc., usu. to a kinder one. — **have one's heart in one's mouth** to be very frightened, worried, or anxious. — **heart and soul** completely; with all one's attention and energy. — **lose heart** to become discouraged. — **lose one's heart to** to fall in love with. — **not have the heart (to do something)** to be too kind (to do something unpleasant). — **set one's heart on** to want very much. — **take heart** to become encouraged or more confident. — **take to heart** to pay great attention to or be very affected by. — **to one's heart's content** as much as one wants. — **wear one's heart on one's sleeve** to show one's deepest feelings openly. — **with all one's heart** very willingly or sincerely. [OE *heorte*]

heartache *n* great sadness or mental suffering.

heart attack *n* a sudden failure of the heart to work properly, causing severe pain and often death.

heartbeat *n* **1** the sound of the heart pumping blood. **2** a single pumping action of the heart.

heartbreak *n* very great sorrow or grief. — *adj* **heartbreaking**. — *adj* **heartbroken**.

heartburn *n* a feeling of burning in the chest caused by indigestion.

hearten *v* **-*n*-** (*tr* & *intr*) to make or become happier, more cheerful or encouraged. — *adj* **heartening**. — *adv* **hearteningly**.

heart failure *n* a condition in which the heart gradually stops working properly, often causing death.

heartfelt *adj* sincere.

heartland *n* a central or vitally important area or region.

heartless *adj* cruel; very unkind. — *adv* **heartlessly**. — *n* **heartlessness**.

heart-rending *adj* causing great sorrow or pity. — *adv* **heart-rendingly**.

heart-searching *n* the close examination of one's deepest feelings and conscience.

heartsick *adj* very sad or disappointed.

heartstrings *n* (*pl*) deepest feelings of love, sympathy or pity: *tug at her heartstrings*.

heart-throb *n* (*coll*) a person whom a lot of people find very attractive, esp. a male actor or singer.

heart-to-heart *adj* (of a conversation) intimate, sincere, and candid. — *n* an intimate and candid conversation.

heart-warming *adj* pleasing; emotionally moving.

heartwood *n* the hard wood from the centre of a tree.

hearty *adj* **-*ier***, **-*iest*** **1** very friendly and warm in manner. **2** strong, vigorous or enthusiastic: *hale and hearty*. **3** (of meals, or an appetite) large. — *adv* **heartily**. — *n* **heartiness**.

hearth *n* **1** the floor of a fireplace, or the area surrounding it. **2** the home. [OE *heorth*]

hearthrug *n* a rug placed on the floor in front of the hearth.

hearty. See **heart**.

heat *n* **1** the state of being hot. **2** the usu. high temperature produced by something. **3** hot weather. **4** warmth of feeling, esp. anger or excitement: *the heat of the argument*. **5** the most intense part of: *in the heat of the battle*. **6** in a sports competition, etc., a preliminary race or contest which eliminates competitors. **7** a period of sexual activity in animals, esp. female animals: *on heat*. **8** redness of the skin, esp. when sore, with a feeling of heat: *prickly heat*. — *v* (*tr* & *intr*) to make or become hot or warm. [OE *hætu*]

heated *adj* **1** having been made hot or warm. **2** angry or excited. — *adv* **heatedly**. — *n* **heatedness**.

heater *n* an apparatus for heating a room, building, water in a tank, etc.

heating *n* the system of heaters, etc. which heat a room, building, etc.

heat-seeking *adj* (of a missile, etc.) able to detect heat from its target and use this as a guide to it.

heat shield *n* an apparatus or substance which protects a spacecraft from the extreme heat it experiences when returning to the Earth's atmosphere.

heatstroke *n* same as **sunstroke**.

heatwave *n* a period of unusually hot weather.

heath *n* **1** an area of open, common, flat land with poor soil, often covered with bushes. **2** a heather or heather-like plant. [OE *hæth*]

heathen *n* **1** a person who is not a Christian, Jew or Muslim, but who follows another religion, esp. one with many gods. **2** (*coll*) an ignorant or uncivilised person. — *adj* of heathens; having no religion. — *adj* **heathenish**. [OE *hæthen*]

the heathen *n* (*pl*) heathens as a group.

heather *n* a low shrub with small pinkish-purple or white bell-shaped flowers, which grows esp. on open land with poor soil. [MidE *hathir*]

Heath-Robinson *adj* (of a mechanical apparatus, etc.) unnecessarily complicated in design given its simple function. [William *Heath Robinson* (1872–1944), the cartoonist who drew such machines]

heave *v* ***heaved*** (but ***hove*** in sense **6** and for **heave to**) **1** (*tr*) to lift or pull with great effort. **2** (*tr*; *coll*) to throw (something heavy). **3** (*tr*) to utter: *heave a sigh*. **4** (*intr*) to rise and fall heavily or rhythmically. **5** (*intr*) to retch or vomit. **6** (*intr*) (of a ship) to move: *heave into sight*. — *n* an act of heaving. — **give someone** or **get the heave** (*coll*) to dismiss (someone) or be dismissed, esp. from a job. — **heave to** to stop (a ship) while at sea; (of a ship) to stop at sea. [OE *hebban*]

heaven *n* **1** the place believed to be the abode of God, angels, and the righteous after death. **2** (usu. in *pl*) the sky. **3** great happiness or bliss. **4** (often used in exclamations) God or Providence: *heaven forbid*. [OE *heofon*]

heavenly *adj* **1** (*coll*) very pleasant; beautiful. **2** of or from heaven or the sky. — *n* **heavenliness**.

heavenly bodies *n* (*pl*) the sun, moon, planets, stars, etc.

heavens *interj* an expression of surprise, anger, dismay, etc.

heaven-sent *adj* very lucky or convenient; timely.

heavy *adj* **-*ier***, **-*iest*** **1** having great weight. **2** having a great or relatively high density: *a heavy metal*. **3** great in size, amount, force, power, etc.: *heavy traffic*; *a heavy crop*. **4** severe, intense or excessive: *heavy fighting*; *a heavy sleep*. **5** hard to bear or endure: *a heavy fate*. **6** (of the sky) dark and cloudy. **7** needing a lot of physical or mental effort. **8** (of literature) serious in tone and content. **9** (of food) difficult to digest. **10** (of breathing) loud, because of excitement, exhaustion, etc. **11** striking or falling with force; powerful: *heavy rain*; *a heavy sea*. **12** sad or dejected: *with a heavy heart*. **13** ungraceful and coarse: *heavy features*. **14** physically and mentally slow. **15** fat; solid. **16** (of soil) wet and soft because containing a lot of clay. **17** (*coll*) strict: *Don't be heavy on him*. **18** (of guns) large and powerful. **19** (of cakes and bread) dense through not having risen enough. — *n* ***heavies*** **1** (*slang*) a large, violent, and usu. not very intelligent man. **2** a villain in a play, film, etc. **3** (*Scot*) a beer like bitter but darker in colour and gassier. **4** (usu. in *pl*) a serious newspaper. — *adv* heavily: *Time hangs heavy on my hands*. — *adv* **heavily**. — *n* **heaviness**. — **heavy going** difficult or slow progress. — **make heavy weather of** to exaggerate the difficulties of. [OE *hefig*]

heavy-duty *adj* made to resist very hard wear or use.

heavy-handed *adj* **1** clumsy. **2** too severe or strict. — *adv* **heavy-handedly**. — *n* **heavy-handedness**.

heavy-hearted *adj* sad.

heavy hydrogen same as **deuterium**.

heavy industry *n* an industry or the industries involving the use of large or heavy machines or producing large or heavy products, such as coal-mining, ship-building, etc.

heavy metal *n* **1** loud, repetitive rock music with a strong beat. **2** large guns.

heavy water *n* same as **deuterium oxide**.

heavyweight *n* **1** the class for the heaviest competitors in boxing, wrestling and weight-lifting (**light heavyweight** a class between heavyweight and middleweight). **2** a boxer, etc. of this weight. **3** (*coll*) an important, powerful, or influential person.

4 a person who is heavier than average — *adj* (for contestants) of the specified weight.
hebdomadal *adj* weekly. — *adv* **hebdomadally.** [Gr *hebdomas*, week]
Hebraic *adj* of Hebrews or the Hebrew language. [Gr *hebraikos*]
Hebrew *n* **1** the ancient Semitic language of the Hebrews, revived and spoken in a modern form by Jews in Israel. **2** a member of an ancient Semitic people, orig. based in Palestine. — *adj* of the Hebrew language or people. [Gr *Hebraios*, from Aramaic *Ibhraij*, one from the other side of the river]
heck *interj* (*coll*) a mild exclamation of anger, annoyance, surprise, etc.; hell.
heckle *v* (*tr* & *intr*) to interrupt (a speaker) with loud, critical, and often rude comments, esp. at a political meeting. — *n* **heckler**. [MidE *hekelen*]
hectare *n* a metric unit of land measurement, equivalent to 100 ares, or 10 000 square metres. [**hecto-** + **are**[2]]
hectic *adj* very busy, confused and excited. — *adv* **hectically**. [Gr *hektikos*, habitual]
hecto- *comb fm* one hundred: *hectometre*. [Gr *hekaton*, one hundred]
hector *v* **-r-** (*tr*) to bully, intimidate or threaten. — *n* a bully. [Gr *Hektor*, the Trojan hero in Homer's *Iliad*]
he'd 1 he had. **2** he would.
hedge *n* **1** a fence or boundary formed by bushes and shrubs planted close together. **2** a barrier or protection against loss, criticism, etc. — *v* **1** (*intr*) to avoid making a decision or giving a clear answer. **2** (*tr*) to enclose (an area of land) with a hedge. **3** (*tr*) to protect oneself from possible loss or criticism (e.g. in a bet or argument) by backing both sides: *hedge one's bets*. [OE *hecg*]
hedgehog *n* a small brown insect-eating animal with a thick coat covered with spines.
hedge-hop *v* **-pp-** (*intr*) to fly at a very low altitude, e.g. when crop-spraying.
hedgerow *n* a row of bushes forming a hedge.
hedge-sparrow *n* a small, grey-brown song-bird.
hedonism *n* the belief that pleasure is the most important aim in life. — *n* **hedonist**. — *adj* **hedonistic**. [Gr *hedone*, pleasure]
heebie-jeebies *n* (*pl*; *coll*) feelings of nervousness or anxiety. [Coined by W De Beck (1890–1942), American cartoonist]
heed *v* (*tr*) to pay attention to or take notice of (advice, a warning, etc.). — *n* attention; notice: *take heed of what she says*.
heedful *adj* (**of**) careful, paying attention to (a warning, etc.).
heedless *adj* (**of**) careless; taking no notice of (a warning, etc.). — *adv* **heedlessly**. — *n* **heedlessness**. [OE *hedan*]
hee-haw *n* the bray of a donkey. — *v* (*intr*) to bray. [Imit.]
heel[1] *n* **1** the rounded back part of the foot. **2** the part of a sock, stocking, etc. that covers the heel. **3** the part of a shoe, boot, etc. which supports the heel. **4** anything shaped or functioning like the heel, e.g. that part of the palm near the wrist. **5** (*slang*) a person very much disliked, or not considered trustworthy. — *v* **1** (*tr*) to put a new heel on (a shoe, etc.). **2** (*intr*; *rugby*) to kick the ball backwards with the heel. **3** (*intr*) (of dogs) to walk at, or go to, a person's side. **4** (*intr*) to touch the ground with the heel, e.g. in dancing. — **cool** or **kick one's heels** to be kept waiting for some time. — **dig one's heels in** to behave stubbornly. — **down at heel** untidy; in poor condition. — **lay** or **set by the heels** (*old coll*) to put in prison. — **on the heels of** following close behind. — **take to one's heels** to run away. — **to heel** close behind; under control. — **turn on one's heel** to turn round suddenly or sharply. [OE *hela*]
heelball *n* a black waxy substance used for blacking the heels and soles of shoes and doing brass rubbings.
well-heeled *adj* wealthy.
heel[2] *v* (*intr*; **over**) (of a ship) to lean over to one side. [OE *hieldan*, to slope]
hefty *adj* **-ier**, **-iest** (*coll*) **1** (of people) big and strong. **2** (of an object, blow, etc.) large, heavy or powerful. **3** large in amount: *a hefty sum of money*. — *adv* **heftily**. — *n* **heftiness**. [**heave**]
hegemony *n* **-ies** leadership or control by one state within a group of states or alliance. [Gr *hegemonia*, from *hegemon*, leader]
Hegira *n* Mohammed's escape from Mecca to Medina in 622 AD, taken as the beginning of the history of the Muslim people. [Arabic *hijrah*, flight]
heifer *n* a young cow, esp. one that has not yet had a calf. [OE *heahfore*]
height *n* **1** the distance from the bottom of something to the top. **2** a distance above the ground from a recognised point, esp. above sea-level. **3** relatively great altitude. **4** a high place or rising ground. **5** the highest point; the summit. **6** the most intense part: *the height of battle*. **7** a very good, bad or serious example: *the height of stupidity*. [OE *hiehthu*]
heighten *v* **-n-** (*tr* & *intr*) to make or become higher, greater, stronger, brighter, etc.
heinous *adj* very evil or wicked. — *adv* **heinously**. — *n* **heinousness**. [OFr *haineus*, from *hair*, to hate]
heir *n* a person who by law receives wealth, a title, etc. when the owner or holder dies. [Lat *heres*]
heir apparent *n* ***heirs apparent*** **1** (*legal*) an heir whose claim cannot be set aside by the birth of another heir. **2** (*coll*) the probable next leader of an organisation, esp. a political party.

heiress *n* a female heir, esp. a woman who has inherited or will inherit great wealth when some person dies.

heirloom *n* an object that has been handed down in a family from parents to children over many years.

heir presumptive *n* ***heirs presumptive*** (*legal*) an heir whose claim can be set aside by the birth of another heir whose claim is more valid.

heist *n* (*US slang*) a robbery. [Variant of **hoist**]

Hejira. Same as **Hegira**.

held. See **hold**.

helical *adj* of or like a helix; coiled. [**helix**]

helicopter *n* an aircraft, lifted and propelled by rotating blades, which takes off and lands vertically, and can hover above the ground. [Gr *helix*, screw + *pteron*, wing]

heliograph *n* an instrument which uses mirrors to reflect light from the sun in flashes, as a way of sending messages in Morse code. [Gr *helios*, sun + **-graph**]

heliotrope *n* **1** a garden plant with small, fragrant, lilac-blue flowers which grow towards the sun. **2** the colour of these flowers. [Gr *helios*, sun + *trepein*, to turn]

heliport *n* a place where helicopters take off and land. [**helicopter airport**]

helium *n* a light gas (symbol **He**) which does not burn, used in balloons and airships. [Gr *helios*, sun, so-called because it was first identified in the sun's atmosphere]

helix *n* ***helices*** or ***helixes*** a spiral. [Gr]

hell *n* **1** the abode of evil spirits and the place or state of punishment for the wicked after death. **2** the abode of the dead. **3** any place or state which causes pain and misery. — *interj* (*coll*) an exclamation of annoyance. — **beat** or **knock the hell out of** (*coll*) to beat severely. — **come hell or high water** (*coll*) in spite of whatever problems or difficulties may arise. — **for the hell of it** (*coll*) just for fun. — **give someone hell** (*coll*) **1** to scold or punish someone severely. **2** to make things extremely difficult for someone. — **hell for leather** (*coll*) extremely fast. — **hell of a** (*coll*) very great: *one hell of a row*. [OE]

hell-bent *adj* (*coll*; **on**) determined.

hell-fire *n* the fire of, or punishment in, hell.

hellish *adj* (*coll*) very bad; very unpleasant. — *adv* **hellishly**. — *n* **hellishness**.

hell's angel *n* a member of a motorcycle gang, esp. one whose behaviour is violent and anti-social.

he'll he will.

hellebore *n* a plant with white, greenish-white or purplish flowers. [Gr *helleboros*]

Hellene *n* a Greek. — *adj* **Hellenic**. [Gr *Hellen*]

Hellenism *n* the Greek character or culture, esp. in ancient Greece between 323 BC and 30 BC.

Hellenist *n* an admirer of, or expert in, the Greek language and culture.

Hellenistic *adj* **1** of or relating to the people, language or culture of ancient Greece between 323 BC and 30 BC. **2** of Hellenists.

hello, **hallo** or **hullo** *interj* a word used as a greeting, to attract attention, to start a telephone conversation, or to express surprise.

helm *n* the wheel or tiller by which a ship is steered. — **at the helm** in a controlling position. [OE *helma*]

helmsman *n* a person who steers a ship.

helmet *n* a hard, protective covering for the head. [OE *helm*]

helot *n* a serf, esp. in ancient Sparta. [Gr *heilotes*, inhabitants of *Helos*, a town in ancient Laconia (the area around Sparta)]

help *v* **1** (*tr* & *intr*) to assist. **2** (*tr* & *intr*) to contribute towards making (difficulties, pain, etc.) less severe; to improve (a situation). **3** (*tr* & *intr*) to refrain from: *couldn't help laughing*. **4** (*tr*) to prevent or control: *I can't help the bad weather*. **5** (*tr*; **to**) to serve (a person): *help him to potatoes*. — *n* **1** an act of helping. **2** a person or thing that helps. **3** a domestic servant; servants in general. **4** a remedy or relief. — *n* **helper**. — **could not help oneself** was not able to refrain from (doing something). — **help oneself (to) 1** to take (food, drink, etc.) for oneself, without being served. **2** to take (something) without permission. — *v* **help out** (*tr* & *intr*) to help (a person), usu. for a short time, and esp. by sharing a burden or the cost of something. [OE *helpan*]

helpful *adj* giving help; useful. — *adv* **helpfully**. — *n* **helpfulness**.

helping *n* a single portion of food.

helpless *adj* **1** unable to do anything for oneself. **2** weak and defenceless. — *adv* **helplessly**. — *n* **helplessness**.

helpmate *n* a friend or partner, esp. a husband or wife.

helter-skelter *adj* careless and confused. — *adv* in a careless and confused manner. — *n* (*Br*) a spiral slide down the outside of a tower in an amusement park.

hem[1] *n* a bottom edge of a piece of clothing, folded over and sewn down. — *v* ***-mm-*** (*tr*) to make a hem on. — *v* **hem in** (*tr*) to surround closely, preventing movement. [OE]

hemline *n* the level at which the bottom of a garment or its hem hangs.

hemstitch *n* a decorative stitch used when sewing hems.

hem[2] *interj* a slight clearing of the throat or coughing to show hesitation or call for attention. — *n* such a sound. — *v* ***-mm-*** (*intr*) to clear the throat or cough slightly. [Imit.]

hem-, **hemat-** or **hemo-** (*US*). Same as **haem-**, **haemat-** or **haemo-**.

hemi- *comb fm* half: *hemisphere*. [Gr]

hemipterous *adj* of an order of insects which have mouth-parts designed for sucking or piercing, sometimes with wings which are half leathery and half transparent. [**hemi-** + Gr *pteron*, wing]

hemisphere *n* **1** one half of a sphere. **2** one half of the Earth's sphere, esp. where it is divided by the equator into the **Northern hemisphere** and the **Southern hemisphere**. 3 one of the two divisions of the brain. — *adj* **hemispherical**. [**hemi-** + **sphere**]

hemlock *n* (a poisonous drug made from) a poisonous plant with small white flowers and a spotted stem. [OE *hymlic*]

hemp *n* **1** a plant yielding coarse fibre and a drug. **2** the intoxicating drug made from the leaves and flowers of this plant. **3** the coarse fibre obtained from this plant, used to make rope and strong fabrics. [OE *hænep*]

hen *n* a female bird of any kind, esp. of the domestic fowl. [OE *henn*]

hen party *n* a party for a group of women only, esp. one to celebrate the future marriage of one woman in the group.

henpecked *adj* (*coll*) (of a man) dominated and ruled over by a nagging wife, girlfriend, etc.

henbane *n* a poisonous wild plant with hairy leaves, light green flowers and an unpleasant smell. [**hen** + **bane**, so-called because it is especially poisonous to domestic fowl]

hence *adv* **1** for this reason. **2** from this time. **3** (*old*) from this place. [MidE *hennes*]

henceforth or **henceforward** *adv* from now on.

henchman *n* ***-men*** a faithful supporter, esp. one who obeys without question. [OE *hengest*, horse + *man*, man]

henge *n* a circular, prehistoric monument consisting of large upright stones or wooden posts. [From *Stonehenge*, a famous stone circle in S England]

henna *n* reddish-brown dye obtained from a tropical shrub, used for colouring the hair and decorating the skin. — *v* (*tr*) **hennaed** to dye or stain using henna. [Arabic *hinna*]

henry *n* ***-ies*** the unit of inductance, e.g. of electrical circuits. [J *Henry* (1797–1878), American physicist]

hepatic *adj* of the liver. [Gr *hepar*, liver]

hepatitis *n* a serious disease in which the liver becomes inflamed. [Gr *hepar*, liver + **-itis**]

hepta- *comb fm* seven. [Gr *hepta*, seven]

heptagon *n* a plane figure with seven sides. — *adj* **heptagonal**. [Gr *hepta*, seven + *gonia*, angle]

heptathlon *n* an athletic contest consisting of seven events, 100 metres hurdles, shot-put, javelin, high jump, long jump, and races over 200 and 800 metres. [**hepta-** + Gr *athlon*, contest]

her *pron* & *adj* (of or belonging to) a female person or animal, or a thing personified or thought of as female, e.g. a ship. — **be her** (*coll*) to be suited to her: *that hat isn't her at all*. [OE *hire*]

herald *n* **1** a person who announces important news. **2** a person or thing that is a sign of what is to come. **3** (*hist*) an officer responsible for keeping a record of the genealogies and coats of arms of noble families. — *v* (*tr*) to be a sign of the approach of; to proclaim: *dark clouds heralding a storm*. [OFr *herault*]

heraldic *adj* of or concerning heraldry.

heraldry *n* the art of recording genealogies and studying and preparing coats of arms.

herb *n* **1** a plant with a soft stem, which dies back at the end of the growing season. **2** a plant used to flavour food or to make medicines, e.g. parsley, rosemary or thyme. [Lat *herba*, grass, green plant]

herbaceous *adj* (of plants) with a stem which is soft, not hard and woody. [Lat *herba*, grass, green plant]

herbaceous border *n* a garden border containing mainly perennial plants and flowers.

herbage *n* green plants in general, esp. those on which cattle graze. [Lat *herba*, grass, green plant]

herbal *adj* of herbs. — *n* a book describing the different uses of herbs. [Lat *herbalis*]

herbalist *n* a person who grows, sells or specialises in the use of herbs as medicine.

herbicide *n* a chemical for killing plants, esp. one which does not kill them all but only those which are not wanted. [Lat *herba*, grass, green crops + **-cide**]

herbivore *n* an animal which eats only plants, and not other animals. — *adj* **herbivorous**. [Lat *herba*, grass, green plant + *vorare*, to swallow]

herculean *adj* having, showing or needing great strength or effort: *a herculean task*. [Gr *Herakles* (in Lat *Hercules*), mythical Greek hero famous for his great strength]

herd *n* **1** a large group of animals, esp. cattle, which live and feed together. **2** a large group of people, esp. when behaving noisily. **3** (with **the**) the mass of people in general when seen as behaving in an unthinkingly conventional way. — *v* **1** (*tr* & *intr*) to gather or be gathered together in a group or herd. **2** (*tr*) to look after (sheep, cattle, etc.). [OE *heord*]

herd instinct *n* the instinct to associate with and act like a group of similar people or animals.

herdsman *n* a person who looks after a herd of animals.

here *adv* **1** at, in or to this place. **2** at this time; at this point in an argument. **3** used after a noun for emphasis: *this book here*. **4** (*coll* & *dialect*) used between a noun and *this*, *that*, etc. for emphasis: *this here book*. — *n* this place. — *interj* **1** calling for someone's attention. **2** calling attention to one's own presence. — **here and now** at this time; immediately. — **here and there** in, or to, various places. — **here goes!** I'm starting or going to do (something) now. — **here's to** (when drinking alcohol) I raise my glass to toast. — **neither here nor there** of no importance. [OE *her*]

hereabouts or **hereabout** *adv* near this place.

hereafter *adv* (*legal* or *formal*) after this; from now on. — *n* (with **the**) the future; life after death.

hereby *adv* (*formal*) by means of; as a result of this.

herein *adv* (*legal* or *formal*) in this place, document or matter.

hereinafter *adv* (*legal* or *formal*) from this point on.

hereof *adv* (*legal* or *formal*) of or concerning this.

hereto *adv* (*legal* or *formal*) to this place, document or matter.

heretofore *adv* (*legal* or *formal*) before this time; formerly.

hereupon *adv* (*legal* or *formal*) after or as a result of this.

herewith *adv* (*legal* or *formal*) with this; enclosed with this letter.

hereditable *adj* that may be inherited. [Lat *hereditas*, inheritance]

hereditary *adj* **1** able to be passed on from parents to children. **2** descending to one's children and grandchildren, etc. by inheritance. — *adv* **hereditarily**. — *n* **hereditariness**. [Lat *hereditas*, inheritance]

heredity *n* **-ies 1** the passing on of physical and mental characteristics from parents to children. **2** the characteristics passed on in this way. [Lat *hereditas*]

heresy *n* **-ies 1** an opinion or belief which is contrary to official doctrine held by the religious community to which one belongs. **2** an opinion contrary to that which is normally accepted. [Gr *hairesis*, choice]

heretic *n* a person who is guilty of esp. religious heresy.

heretical *adj* of heresy or heretics.

heritable *adj* **1** (of property) that may be passed on from parent to child. **2** (of people) able to inherit property. [OFr *heriter*, to inherit]

heritage *n* **1** that which is inherited. **2** the characteristics, qualities, property, etc. that one inherits at birth. **3** a nation's historic buildings, countryside, cultural traditions, etc. seen as the nation's wealth to be passed on to future generations. [OFr]

hermaphrodite *n* a person, animal or plant that has both male and female sexual organs. — *adj* having the characteristics of both male and female. — *adj* **hermaphroditic**. [Gr *Hermaphroditos*, in Greek mythology the son of *Hermes* and *Aphrodite*, who grew into one person with the nymph Salmacis]

hermetic *adj* closed very tightly so that no air gets in or out. — *adv* **hermetically**. [Gr *Hermes*, in Greek mythology the god of science, esp. alchemy]

hermit *n* a person who lives alone, esp. for religious reasons. [Gr *eremos*, solitary]

hermitage *n* **1** the place where a hermit lives. **2** any retreat or secluded place.

hermit crab *n* a small crab that lives in another sea-creature's cast-off shell.

hernia *n* a medical condition in which an organ (esp. part of the bowel) sticks out through an opening or weak spot in the wall of its surroundings. [Lat]

hero *n* **-oes 1** a person who is admired for his or her bravery, courage, noble qualities, etc. **2** the main male character in a story, play, etc. ◇ See also **heroine**. [Gr *heros*]

heroic *adj* **1** very brave. **2** of or about heroes or heroines. — *n* (in *pl*) over-dramatic speech or behaviour. — *adv* **heroically**.

heroism *n* the qualities of a hero, esp. great bravery.

hero-worship *n* very great, usu. too great, admiration for a person.

heroin *n* a powerful, habit-forming drug formed from morphine, used in medicine to stop pain, and illegally for pleasure. [Ger *Heroin*, from Gr *heros*, hero]

heroine *n* **1** a woman admired for her bravery, courage, noble abilities, etc. **2** the main female character in a play, story, etc. [Gr, from *heros*, hero]

heron *n* **1** a large wading bird, with grey and white feathers, long legs and a long neck. **2** any of a number of related birds. [OFr *hairon*]

herpes *n* any of several infectious skin diseases caused by a virus, which causes watery blisters. [Gr *herpein*, to creep]

herring *n* **-ing** or **-ings** a small sea fish with a long, silvery body, valued as food. [OE *hæring*]

herringbone *n* a zigzag pattern woven into cloth.

herring gull *n* a large gull with white feathers and black-tipped grey wings.

hers *pron* the one or ones belonging to her. — **of hers** of or belonging to her.

herself *pron* **1** the reflexive form of **her** and **she**: *She made herself a dress*. **2** used for emphasis: *She did it herself*. **3** her normal self: *She isn't feeling herself*. **4** (also **by herself**) alone; without help. [OE *hire self*]

Herts *abbrev* Hertfordshire.

hertz *n* ***hertz*** a unit of frequency of one cycle per second, used to measure radio waves. [Heinrich *Hertz* (1857–94), German physicist]

he's 1 he is. **2** he has.

hesitant *adj* uncertain; holding back; hesitating. — *n* **hesitance** or **hesitancy**. — *adv* **hesitantly**. **[hesitate]**

hesitate *v* (*intr*) **1** to be slow in speaking or acting, esp. because of uncertainty. **2** to be unwilling (to do or say something), e.g. because one is not sure it is right. — *n* **hesitation**. [Lat *haesitare*, to remain stuck]

hessian *n* & *adj* (of) a coarse cloth similar to sacking, made from jute. [*Hesse*, in Germany]
het: **het up** (*coll*) angry; over-anxious; over-excited. [Dialect for *heated*]
hetero- *comb fm* other; different: *heterosexual*. [Gr *heteros*, other]
heterodox *adj* having a (usu. religious) belief that is different from the one commonly accepted. [Gr *heteros*, other + *doxa*, opinion]
heterogeneous *adj* made up of parts, people, things, etc. of very different kinds. — *n* **heterogeneity**. [Gr *heteros*, other + *genos*, sort]
heteromorphic *adj* **1** of or having different forms. **2** (of insects) having different forms at different stages of life. — *n* **heteromorphism**. [**hetero-** + Gr *morphe*, form]
heterosexual *adj* **1** sexually attracted to people of the opposite sex. **2** (of a relationship) between a man and a woman. — *n* a heterosexual person. — *n* **heterosexuality**. [**hetero-** + **sexual**]
heuristic *adj* **1** (of a teaching method) encouraging learners to find their own solutions. **2** (*comput*) proceeding through trial and error. — *adv* **heuristically**. [Gr *heuriskein*, to find]
hew *v* ***hewed***, ***hewn*** **1** (*tr* & *intr*) to cut or hit (a person or thing) with an axe, sword, etc. **2** (*tr*) to carve or shape (figures, etc.) out of wood or stone. [OE *heawan*]
hexa- *comb fm* six. [Gr *hex*, six]
hexadecimal *adj* (esp. *comput*) relating to or using a number system with a base of 16. [**hexa-** + **decimal**]
hexagon *n* a plane figure with six sides. — *adj* **hexagonal**. [Gr *hex*, six + *gonia*, angle]
hexagram *n* a star-shaped figure formed by extending the lines of a hexagon until they meet at six points. [**hexa-** + Gr *gramma*, line]
hexameter *n* (*poetry*) a line or verse with six measures or feet. [Gr *hex*, six + *metron*, measure]
hey *interj* (*coll*) a shout expressing joy, surprise, a question, dismay, or used to attract attention. — **hey presto!** a conjuror's phrase, usu. used at the successful completion of a trick. [MidE *hei*]
heyday *n* a time of most success, power, importance, strength, popularity, etc. [OGer *heida*, hey there]
Hf *symbol* (*chem*) hafnium.
Hg *symbol* (*chem*) mercury. [Lat *hydrargyrum*]
HGV *abbrev* heavy goods vehicle.
HH *abbrev* **1** His or Her Highness. **2** His Holiness. **3** (on a pencil) double hard.
HI *abbrev* Hawaii.
hi *interj* a word used as a greeting or to attract attention. [**hey**]
hiatus *n* ***-uses*** **1** a break or gap in something which should be continuous. **2** a break between two vowels coming together but not in the same syllable. [Lat *hiare*, to gape]
hibernate *v* (*intr*) (of certain animals) to pass the winter in a sleep-like state. — *n* **hibernation**. [Lat *hibernare*, from *hibernus*, wintry]
Hibernia *n* (*poetic*) Ireland. [Lat]
Hibernian *adj* of Ireland. — *n* a native of Ireland.
hibiscus *n* ***-uses*** a usu. tropical tree or shrub with large, brightly coloured flowers. [Gr *hibiskos*, marsh-mallow]
hiccup or **hiccough** *n* **1** (the sound caused by) a sudden breathing in of air caused by a spasm in the diaphragm. **2** (in *pl*) the frequent repetition of this, at intervals of a few seconds. **3** (*coll*) a minor problem or interruption. — *v* ***-p-*** **1** (*intr*) to make a hiccup or hiccups. **2** (*tr*) to say with a hiccup. [Imit.]
hick *n* (*coll*, esp. *NAm*) an unsophisticated person from the country. [A familiar form of *Richard*]
hickory *n* ***-ies*** (the tough, heavy wood of) a N American tree related to the walnut, with edible nuts. [From an American Indian language]
hide[1] *v* ***hid***, ***hidden*** **1** (*tr*) to put (a person, thing, etc.) in a place where one cannot easily see or find him, it, etc. **2** (*intr*) to go to or be in a place where one cannot be seen or easily found. **3** (*tr*) to keep (information, feelings, etc.) secret. **4** (*tr*) to make (something) difficult to see; to obscure: *trees hiding the house*. — *n* a concealed shelter used for watching birds and wild animals. [OE *hydan*]
hidden *adj* difficult to see or find.
hidden agenda *n* a set of motives or goals kept secret from those who might object to them or until it is too late to object.
hide-and-seek *n* a children's game in which one child searches for the others who have hidden themselves.
hideaway or **hideout** *n* a hiding-place or refuge.
hiding *n* the state of being hidden or concealed.
hiding-place *n* a place of concealment.
hide[2] *n* **1** the skin of an animal, either raw or tanned. **2** (*coll*) the human skin. — **(not) hide nor hair** (not) the slightest trace. [OE *hyd*]
hidebound *adj* unwilling to accept new ideas or opinions, esp. because of a petty or conservative attitude. [**hide**[2] + **bound**[1]]
hideous *adj* (of a person or thing) extremely ugly or unpleasant. — *adv* **hideously**. — *n* **hideousness**. [OFr *hideus*]
hiding *n* (*coll*) a severe beating. [**hide**[2]]
hie *v* ***hieing*** or ***hying*** (*intr*; *old*) to go quickly. [OE *higian*]
hierarchy *n* ***-ies*** **1** an arrangement (esp. of people or things in a group) in order of rank or importance. **2** the people who control an organisation. — *adj* **hierarchical**. [Gr *hieros*, sacred + *archein*, to rule]

hieroglyph *n* a picture or symbol used to represent a word, syllable or sound, esp. in ancient Egyptian. [Gr *hieros*, sacred + *glyphein*, to carve]

hieroglyphic *adj* of or relating to hieroglyphs or hieroglyphics.

hieroglyphics *n* (*pl*) **1** a form of writing using hieroglyphs, used in ancient Egypt. **2** (*coll*) writing that is difficult to read.

hi-fi *adj* (*coll*) high fidelity. — *n* equipment, e.g. a record player, which reproduces sound accurately. [Abbrev. of **high fidelity**]

higgledy-piggledy *adv* & *adj* (*coll*) in confusion; in a muddle.

high *adj* **1** reaching up to a relatively great distance from the bottom: *high buildings*. **2** of a particular height: *three feet high*. **3** situated at a relatively great distance from the ground or from sea level: *a high branch*. **4** great; intense: *a high wind*. **5** greater than average height: *a high-necked sweater*. **6** at its peak: *high summer*. **7** very important or exalted: *high art*. **8** (of sound) acute in pitch. **9** extremely emotional: *high drama*. **10** (of meat) beginning to go bad. **11** elated. **12** (*coll*) under the influence of drugs or alcohol. — *adv* at or to a height; in or into a raised position. — *n* **1** a high point. **2** an area of high pressure; an anticyclone. **3** (*coll*) a state of great excitement or happiness, often produced by drugs or alcohol: *on a high*. — **high and dry** (of boats) out of the water; stranded or helpless. — **high and low 1** everywhere. **2** everyone, rich and poor alike. — **high and mighty** (*coll*) arrogant. — **on high** at or to a high place or position; in or to heaven. — **on one's high horse** (*coll*) behaving arrogantly or with great dignity. [OE *heah*]

highball *n* (*NAm*) an alcoholic drink of spirits and soda served with ice in a long glass.

high-born *adj* of noble birth.

highbrow (often *derog*) *n* an intellectual or cultured person. — *adj* (of art, literature, etc.) intellectual or cultured.

high-chair *n* a baby's or young child's tall chair, used esp. at mealtimes.

High Church *n* & *adj* (of or relating to) a section of the Church of England which places great importance on ceremony and priestly authority.

high-class *adj* of high quality or high social class.

High Commission *n* an embassy from one member of the Commonwealth to another.

High Commissioner *n* the senior diplomat at the head of such an embassy.

High Court *n* the supreme court for civil cases in England and Wales.

Higher *n* (also **Higher grade**) in Scotland, (a pass in) an examination generally taken at the end of the fifth year of secondary education.

higher education *n* education beyond secondary-school level, e.g. at university or college.

high explosive *n* a very powerful explosive, such as dynamite. — *adj* exploding with very great effect.

high-falutin or **-faluting** *adj* (*coll*) pompous or pretentious.

high fidelity *n* the reproduction of sound with great accuracy.

high-flier or **-flyer** *n* **1** an ambitious person who is likely to be successful. **2** a person with great ability in his or her career. — *adj* **high-flying**.

high-flown *adj* (usu. of language) sounding grand but lacking in real importance; extravagant.

high frequency *n* a radio frequency between 3 and 30 megahertz.

High German *n* the standard form of the German language.

high-handed *adj* acting or done without thought or consideration for others. — *adv* **high-handedly**. — *n* **high-handedness**.

highjack same as **hijack**.

high jump *n* **1** an athletic event in which competitors jump over a bar which is raised higher as the event progresses. **2** (*coll*) a severe punishment: *be for the high jump*.

highland *n* **1** (often in *pl*) a high, mountainous area. **2** (*cap*; in *pl*) the mountainous area of northern and western Scotland. — *adj* of highlands or (*cap*) the Highlands.

highlander *n* a person who comes from a mountainous area, esp. (*cap*) that of Scotland.

Highland cattle *n* a Scottish breed of cattle with a long, shaggy coat and long horns.

Highland fling *n* a lively solo dance from the Scottish highlands.

Highland games *n* (*pl*) an event at which people compete in sports such as tossing the caber, and in Scottish dancing, etc.

high-level *adj* involving important people.

high-level language *n* a computer language very like natural language and needing to be changed into machine code by the compiler. ◇ See also **low-level language**.

highlight *n* **1** the best or most memorable event, experience, part of something, etc. **2** a lighter patch in one's hair, usu. made artificially. **3** the brightest part of a photograph. — *v* (*tr*) to draw attention to or emphasise.

highly *adv* **1** very: *highly gratified*. **2** with approval: *speak highly of her*.

highly-strung *adj* very nervous and easily upset or excited.

High Mass *n* (esp. in the Roman Catholic Church) (a) formal, elaborate and solemn mass.

high-minded *adj* having or showing noble ideals and principles, etc. — *n* **high-mindedness**.

highness *n* **1** (*cap*) a title used when addressing, or speaking about, a member of a royal family: *Your Highness*. **2** the state or quality of being high.

high-pitched *adj* **1** (of sounds, voices, etc.) high in tone. **2** (of a roof) steep.

high point *n* the best state reached.

high-powered *adj* very powerful or energetic; very efficient.

high-pressure *adj* **1** having, using, etc. air, water, etc. at a high pressure. **2** (*coll*) very forceful and persuasive.

high priest or **priestess** *n* the priest or priestess who is the head of a cult.

high-rise *adj* (of a building) with many storeys.

high-risk *adj* dangerous: *high-risk sports*.

high road *n* a main road.

high school *n* a secondary school.

high seas *n* (*pl*) the open sea not under the control of any country.

high season *n* the busiest time of year at a holiday resort.

high-sounding *adj* pretentious; pompous.

high-spirited *adj* lively, cheerful and vivacious.

high street *n* the main shopping street of a town.

high tea *n* (*Br*) a meal consisting usu. of cooked food with bread, cakes and tea, served in the late afternoon.

high-tech or **hi-tech** *adj* (*coll*) **1** involving or using advanced, esp. electronic equipment. **2** (of interior decoration, designs, etc.) based on styles or elements found in industry.

high-tension *adj* carrying high-voltage electrical currents.

high tide *n* the time when the tide is farthest up the shore; the highest level reached by the water at this time.

high time *n* (*coll*) the time by which something ought to have been done.

high treason *n* treason against one's sovereign or country.

high water *n* the time at which the tide, river, etc. is at its fullest.

high-water mark *n* the highest level reached by a tide, river, etc.

highway *n* (esp. *NAm*) a public road that everyone may use, esp. a large or main road.

Highway Code *n* (*Br*) (a booklet containing) a set of official rules for road-users.

highwayman *n* (*hist*) a robber, usu. on horseback, who attacks and robs people travelling on public roads.

high wire *n* a tightrope high above the ground.

hijack *v* (*tr*) **1** to take control of (a vehicle) while it is moving and force it to go to a place chosen by the hijacker. **2** to stop and rob (a vehicle). **3** to steal (goods) in transit. **4** (*coll*) to seize control of (an organisation, event, etc.). — *n* **hijacker**. — *n* **hijacking**.

hike *n* a long walk, usu. in the country, often carrying equipment on one's back. — *v* **1** (*intr*) to go on a hike. **2** (*tr*; **up**) to pull up or raise with a jerk. **3** (*tr*) to increase (prices) suddenly. — *n* **hiker**.

hilarious *adj* very funny. — *adv* **hilariously**. — *n* **hilariousness**. — *n* **hilarity**. [Gr *hilaros*, cheerful]

hill *n* **1** a piece of high land, smaller than a mountain. **2** a slope on a road. **3** a heap or mound. — **over the hill** (*coll*) past one's best; (too) old. [OE *hyll*]

hillbilly *n* **-ies** (*US*) **1** (usu. *derog*) an unsophisticated person from a remote, mountainous country area. **2** country and western music.

hillock *n* a small hill.

hillside *n* the sloping side of a hill.

hilly *adj* **-ier**, **-iest** having many hills. — *n* **hilliness**.

hilt *n* the handle of a sword, dagger, knife, etc. — **up to the hilt** completely; thoroughly. [OE *hilte*]

hilum *n* **-la** (*bot*) a scar on a seed where it was joined to the stalk or pod. [Lat, a little thing]

him *pron* a male person or animal, the object form of **he**. — **be him** (*coll*) to be suited to him: *that jacket isn't really him*. [OE]

himself *pron* **1** the reflexive form of **him** and **he**: *He taught himself to dance*. **2** used for emphasis: *He did it himself*. **3** his normal self: *be feeling himself again after the operation*. **4** (also **by himself**) alone; without help.

hind[1] *n* a female deer, esp. a red deer, usu. after three years of age. [OE]

hind[2] *adj* at the back: *hind legs*. [MidE *hinde*]

hindmost *adj* last; farthest behind.

hindquarters *n* (*pl*) the back legs and buttocks of a four-legged animal.

hindsight *n* wisdom or knowledge after the event.

hinder[1] *v* **-r-** (*tr*) to delay or keep back; to prevent progress. [OE *hindrian*]

hinder[2] *adj* at the back: *the hinder part*. [**hind**[2]]

Hindi *n* **1** one of the main languages of India, a literary form of Hindustani. **2** a group of languages spoken in N India, including Hindustani. [Persian *Hind*, India]

hindmost, **hindquarters**. See **hind**[2].

hindrance *n* **1** a person or thing that hinders. **2** the act of hindering. [**hinder**[1]]

hindsight. See **hind**[2].

Hindu *n* a person who practises Hinduism. — *adj* of Hindus or Hinduism. [Persian *Hind*, India]

Hinduism *n* the main religion of India, which includes worship of many gods, a belief in reincarnation, and the arrangement of people in society in social castes.

Hindustani *n* a form of Hindi with elements from Arabic and Persian, used as a lingua franca in much of India.

hinge *n* the movable joint by means of which a door is fastened to a door-frame, a lid is fastened to a box, etc. and on which the door, lid, etc. turns when it opens or closes. **2** a principle or fact on which anything depends. — *v* **1** (*intr*) to hang or turn on. **2** (*intr* with **on**) to depend on. **3** (*tr*) to fit with a hinge. — *adj* **hinged**. [MidE *henge*]

hinny *n* **-*ies*** the offspring of a stallion and a female donkey or ass. [Gr *hinnos*, mule]

hint *n* **1** a statement that passes on information without giving it openly or directly. **2** a helpful piece of advice. **3** a very small amount; a slight impression or suggestion of: *a hint of perfume*. — *v* (*intr*; **at**) to suggest, esp. slightly or indirectly. — **take a hint** (*coll*) to understand what a person is hinting at, and do what that person wants. [OE *hentan*, to seize]

hinterland *n* **1** the district lying inland from the coast or the banks of a river. **2** an area dependent on a nearby port, commercial centre, etc. [Ger *hinter*, behind + *Land*, land]

hip[1] *n* the upper, fleshy part of the thigh just below the waist. [OE *hype*]

hip bath *n* a portable bath for sitting in.

hip[2] *n* the red, berry-like fruit of some kinds of (esp. wild) rose. [OE *heope*]

hip[3] *interj* an exclamation used to call for a united cheer: *hip, hip hooray!*

hip[4] *adj* **-*pp*-** (*coll*) interested in, knowing about and following current fashions in music, fashion, etc.

hippie or **hippy** *n* **-*ies*** (*coll*) (esp. during the 1960s) a usu. young person who does not wish to live by the normal rules of society and who shows his or her rejection of these rules by wearing brightly coloured, unconvential clothes, very long hair, etc.

hippo *n* **-*os*** (*coll*) a hippopotamus. [Abbrev.]

Hippocratic oath *n* an oath taken by doctors by which they agree to observe a code of medical ethics. [*Hippocrates*, Greek physician (born *c*. 460 BC)]

hippodrome *n* **1** a variety theatre or circus. **2** (in ancient Greece and Rome) an open-air racecourse for horses and chariots. [Gr *hippos*, horse + *dromos*, course]

hippopotamus *n* **-*muses*** or **-*mi*** a large African mammal with very thick, wrinkled skin and short legs, living in or near rivers and lakes. [Gr *hippos*, horse + *potamos*, river]

hippy. See **hip**[4].

hipsters *n* (*pl*) trousers which hang from the hips rather than the waist. [**hip**[1]]

hire *v* (*tr*) **1** (**from**) to get the temporary use of (something which belongs to someone else) in exchange for money. **2** (**out**) to give someone the use of (something) in exchange for money. **3** to employ (a servant, workman, etc.) for wages. — *n* **1** an act of hiring. **2** payment for hiring something. — **for hire** ready for hiring. — **on hire** hired out. [OE *hyr*]

hire-purchase *n* (*Br*) a way of buying an article by paying for it in several weekly or monthly parts after one has taken possession of it.

hireling *n* (usu. *derog*) a person who works for another for payment. [OE *hyrling*]

hirsute *adj* hairy; shaggy. [Lat *hirsutus*]

his *adj* of or belonging to a male person or animal. — *pron* the one or ones belonging to him. [OE]

Hispanic *adj* of Spain, the Spanish, or other Spanish-speaking countries and peoples, e.g. Mexican. — *n* (*US*) a Spanish-speaking American of Latin-American descent. [Lat *Hispania*, Spain]

hiss *n* a sharp sound like that of a long *s*. — *v* **1** (*intr*) (of snakes, geese, people, etc.) to make a hiss, esp. as a sign of disapproval or anger. **2** (*tr*) to show one's disapproval (of a person, etc.) by hissing. [Imit.]

histamine *n* a chemical compound present in the body tissues which is released into the blood during allergic reactions. [Gr *histos*, web + **amine**]

histogram *n* a chart consisting of vertical rectangles of differing sizes, each rectangle representing the amount or frequency of a given variable. [Gr *histos*, web + **-gram**]

histology *n* the study of the structure of plant or animal tissues and organs. [Gr *histos*, web + **-logy**]

historian *n* a person who studies or writes about history. [**history**]

historic *adj* famous or important in history; significant. [**history**]

historical *adj* **1** of or about history; of or about people or events from history. **2** (of the study of a subject) based on its development over a period of time. **3** that actually happened or existed; authentic. — *adv* **historically**.

historicism *n* **1** the belief that historical events are governed by natural laws. **2** too much emphasis on or respect for the past, past styles, etc.

historicity *n* historical truth or authenticity.

historiography *n* the study of the writing of history. [**history** + **-graphy**]

historiographer *n* a writer of history, esp. the official historian of a group.

history *n* **-*ies*** **1** the study of events, etc. that happened in the past. **2** a record or account of past events and developments: *a history of the computer*. **3** everything that is known about past events connected with a particular nation, the world, a person, etc.: *Castles are part of the history of our country*. **4** a past full of events and of more than usual interest: *a house with an interesting history*. **5** a play which represents historical events. — **make history** to do something very important or memorable, esp. to be the first person to achieve something. [Gr *historia*, from *histor*, knowing]

histrionic *adj* **1** (of behaviour, etc.) theatrical; showing too much emotion. **2** of actors or acting. — *n* (in *pl*) theatrical or dramatic behaviour which shows too much emotion and is insincere. — *adv* **histrionically**. [Lat *histrionicus*, from *histrio*, actor]

hit *v* **-*tt*-**, ***hit*** **1** (*tr*) to strike (a person or thing) with a blow, missile, etc. **2** (*tr*; **on**, etc.) to knock (something) against something, esp. hard or violently: *hit one's head on the door*. **3** (*tr*) to cause to suffer or affect badly: *The bad news hit her hard*. **4** (*intr*; **at, against**) to direct a blow; to strike: *Hit as hard as you can*. **5** (*tr*; *coll*) to find (esp. an answer) by chance: *You've hit it!* **6** (*tr*) to reach or arrive at: *hit an all-time low*. **7** (*tr*) to drive (a ball) with a stroke of a bat, etc. — *n* **1** a blow, stroke or shot. **2** a shot that is successful. **3** (*coll*) something which is popular or successful. — *v* **hit back** (*intr*) to retaliate. — **hit it off (with)** to get on well (with someone). — *v* **hit on** or **upon** (*tr*) to think of (an idea) or find (an answer, etc.) by chance. — *v* **hit out** (*intr*; **against, at**) to attack physically or verbally. — **make** or **score a hit (with)** to be successful or popular (with someone). [OE *hittan*]

hit-and-miss or **hit-or-miss** *adj* (*coll*) without any system, planning or care; random.

hit-and-run *adj* (of a motor vehicle accident) in which the driver leaves the scene immediately, without stopping, reporting the accident, or helping the victim.

hit list *n* (*coll*) a list of people, organisations, etc. to be killed, closed down, etc.

hit man *n* (*coll*) a hired assassin.

hit parade *n* the best-selling records.

hitch *v* **1** (*tr*) to fasten with a piece of rope, etc.; to tether. **2** (*tr* with **up**) to pull up with a jerk: *hitched up his trousers*. **3** (*intr* & *tr*; *coll*) to hitchhike; to obtain (a lift) by hitchhiking: *hitch a ride*. — *n* **1** a minor, temporary delay or difficulty. **2** a slight jerk. **3** a knot for attaching two pieces of rope together. — **get hitched** (*coll*) to get married. [MidE *hytchen*]

hitchhike *v* (*intr*) to travel by means of free rides in other people's vehicles. — *n* **hitchhiker**. [**hitch + hike**]

hi-tech. See **high-tech**.

hither *adv* (*old*) to this place. — **hither and thither** (*old*) in different directions. [OE *hider*]

hitherto *adv* up to this or that time.

HIV *abbrev* human immunodeficiency virus, any of several types of virus which cause AIDS.

hive *n* **1** a box for housing bees. **2** the bees that live in such a place. **3** a place where people are working very busily: *a hive of activity*. — *v* **hive off** (*tr*) **1** to separate (a company, etc.) from a larger group or organisation. **2** to transfer (the assets, esp. of a nationalised company) to other ownership, esp. private ownership. **3** to give (work) to another, subsidiary, company. [OE *hyf*]

hives *n* (*pl*) sore, itchy skin caused by contact with certain plants; nettlerash.

HM *abbrev* Her or His Majesty or Majesty's, used in the titles of some British government organisations.

HMI *abbrev* Her or His Majesty's Inspector, a British government official who checks on schools.

HMS *abbrev* Her or His Majesty's Ship.

HMSO *abbrev* Her or His Majesty's Stationery Office.

HNC *abbrev* Higher National Certificate, a qualification in a technical subject recognised by many professional institutions.

HND *abbrev* Higher National Diploma, a qualification in a technical subject recognised by many professional institutions as equivalent to a degree.

Ho *symbol* (*chem*) holmium.

hoar *adj* white or greyish-white, esp. with age. [OE *har*]

hoar-frost *n* the white frost on grass, leaves, etc. in the morning after a cold night.

hoary *adj* **-*ier*, -*iest*** **1** white or grey with age. **2** ancient. — *n* **hoariness**.

hoard *n* an often secret store of money, food, treasure, usu. hidden away for use in the future. — *v* (*tr* & *intr*; **up**) to store (food, money, etc.), often in secret and esp. for use in the future. — *n* **hoarder**. [OE *hord*]

hoarding *n* **1** a temporary fence of light boards, esp. round a building site. **2** a large, flat, wooden surface on which advertisements, posters, etc. are displayed. [OFr *hourd*, palisade]

hoarse *adj* **1** (of the voice) rough and croaking, esp. because of a sore throat or too much shouting. **2** (of people) having a hoarse voice. — *adv* **hoarsely**. — *n* **hoarseness**. [OE *has*]

hoary. See **hoar**.

hoax *n* a trick played to deceive people, done either humorously or spitefully. — *v* (*tr*) to trick or deceive with a hoax. — *n* **hoaxer**. [Prob. from *hocus*, to trick]

hob *n* **1** the flat surface for heating pots, etc. on top of a cooker. **2** a small shelf next to a fireplace on which pots, etc. may be kept hot.

hobble *v* **1** (*intr*) to walk with difficulty, taking short, unsteady steps. **2** (*tr*) to tie the legs of (a horse) together loosely, to stop it straying. [MidE *hobelen*]

hobby *n* **-*ies*** an activity or occupation done in one's spare time for pleasure or relaxation. [MidE *hobyn*, a pet form of the name *Robin*]

hobby-horse *n* **1** a child's toy consisting of a long stick with a horse's head at one end. **2** a figure of a horse used in Morris dancing. **3** a subject which a person talks about frequently.

hobgoblin *n* a mischievous or evil spirit. [MidE *Hob*, pet form of *Robin* + **goblin**]

hobnail *n* a short nail with a heavy head for protecting the soles of boots and shoes: *hobnail boots*. — *adj* **hobnailed**. [From an old meaning of **hob**, peg or pin]

hobnob *v* ***-bb-*** (*intr*; **with**) to spend time with socially. [From the phrase *hab or nab*, have or have not]

hobo *n* ***-os*** or ***-oes*** (esp. *NAm*) a tramp; a wandering worker.

Hobson's choice *n* the choice of taking what is offered, or nothing at all. [Thomas *Hobson* (died 1631), a Cambridge carrier who hired out his horses on the basis that customers had to take the one nearest the door]

hock[1] *n* a joint on the back leg of an animal, between the knee and the fetlock. [OE *hoh*, heel]

hock[2] *n* a German white wine from the Rhine valley. [Ger *Hochheimer*, from *Hochheim*, a town on the Main]

hock[3] *v* (*tr*; *coll*) to pawn. — **in hock** (*coll*) **1** in pawn. **2** in debt. **3** in prison. [Dut *hok*, prison, debt]

hockey *n* **1** a game for two teams of eleven players in which each team tries to score goals, played with long clubs which are bent at one end and a small, hard ball. **2** (*NAm*) same as **ice hockey**.

hocus-pocus *n* (*coll*) trickery; words, actions, etc. which are intended to deceive or mislead; a formula used in conjuring. [Sham Lat]

hod *n* **1** a V-shaped box on a pole, used for carrying bricks. **2** a container for coal used in the home, usu. near a fireplace. [MidE *hot*, basket]

hodgepodge *n* (*NAm*). Same as **hotch-potch**.

Hodgkin's disease *n* a disease in which the lymph nodes, spleen and liver become enlarged, causing progressive anaemia. [Thomas *Hodgkin* (1798–1866), English pathologist who first described the disease]

hoe *n* a long-handled tool with a metal blade at one end, used for loosening soil, removing weeds, etc. — *v* **1** (*tr*) to remove weeds from (crops, flower-beds, etc.) or loosen (soil). **2** (*intr*) to use a hoe. [OFr *houe*]

hog *n* **1** a castrated male pig. **2** (*US*) a pig. **3** (*coll*) a greedy, and often bad-mannered or dirty person. — *v* ***-gg-*** (*tr*; *coll*) to take, use or occupy selfishly. [OE *hogg*]

hogshead *n* a large cask.

hogwash *n* (*coll*) nonsense.

Hogmanay *n* New Year's Eve in Scotland. [Prob. from OFr *aguillanneuf*, a gift for New Year]

ho! ho! *interj* an expression used to show amusement or disbelief.

hoi. Same as **hoy**.

hoick *v* (*tr*; *coll*) to lift up sharply.

hoi polloi *n* (with **the**) the masses; the common people. [Gr]

hoist *v* (*tr*) **1** to lift or heave up (esp. something heavy). **2** to raise or lift using ropes and pulleys. — *n* **1** equipment for hoisting heavy objects. **2** (*coll*) an act of hoisting. — **hoist with one's own petard** caught in the trap one set to catch someone else. [Past tense of the old verb *hoise*, to hoist; *petard*, small bomb]

hoity-toity *adj* (*coll*) arrogant; haughty. [From old word *hoit*, to romp]

hokum *n* (*US slang*) **1** nonsense. **2** over-sentimental and over-sensational material in a play, film, etc. [Prob. **hocus-pocus** + **bunkum**]

hold[1] *v* ***held*** **1** (*tr*; **in**, **with**, etc.) to have or keep in one's hand, or in something else stated. **2** (*tr*; **down**, **up**, etc.) to support or keep in a particular position. **3** (*tr* & *intr*) to keep or stay in a particular state: *hold firm*. **4** (*intr*) to remain in position, fixed and unbroken, esp. when under pressure. **5** (*tr*) to detain or restrain. **6** (*tr*) to contain or be able to contain: *a bottle holding three pints*. **7** (*tr*) to cause to take place; to conduct: *hold a conversation, a meeting*. **8** (*tr*) to have (a position of responsibility, job, etc.): *hold office*. **9** (*tr*) to have or possess: *hold the world record*. **10** (*tr*) to keep (a person's attention). **11** (*intr*) (of good weather) to continue. **12** (*tr*) to consider to be; to think or believe. **13** (*intr*) to continue to be valid or apply. **14** (*tr*; **to**) to force (a person) to keep a promise, etc.: *hold him to his word*. **15** (*tr*) to defend from the enemy. **16** (*tr*) to be able to drink (alcohol) without feeling any bad effects. **17** (*tr*) to stop: *hold fire*. **18** (*tr*) to continue to sing or play (a musical note). **19** (*intr*) (of a person who is making a telephone call) to wait without hanging up while the person being called comes to the telephone. **20** (*tr* & *intr*) (of the future) to be going to bring. — *n* **1** the act of holding; a grasp. **2** power; influence: *have a hold over him*. **3** a way of holding someone, esp. in certain sports. **4** a thing to hold on to. — *n* **holder**. — **get hold of** (*coll*) **1** to manage to speak to (someone). **2** to get, buy or obtain. — **hold (something) against (someone)** to regard (something) as to (someone's) discredit. — **hold back 1** to restrain (from doing something); to prevent from happening. **2** to hesitate. **3** to keep in reserve. — **hold court** to be surrounded by a group of admirers. — *v* **hold down** (*tr*) **1** to manage to keep: *hold down a job*. **2** to strictly control the freedom (of people); to repress. — **hold forth** to give one's opinions about something, usu. loudly and at great length. — **hold good** or **true** to be true or valid; to apply. — *v* **hold in** (*tr*) to restrain or check. — *v* **hold off 1** (*tr*) to keep (an attacker) at a distance. **2** (*intr* & *tr*) to delay or not begin: *hope the rain holds off*; *hold off making a start*. — *v* **hold on** (*intr*) **1** (**to**) to keep. **2** (**to**) to keep a firm hold on. **3** (*coll*) (esp. when telephoning) to wait. — *v* **hold out 1** (*intr*) to continue to stand firm, resist difficulties, etc.: *hold out against the enemy*. **2** (*intr*) to last. **3** (*tr*) to offer. **4** (with **for**) to continue to demand or fight for (something). **5** (with **on**; *coll*) to keep back money, information, etc. from. — *v* **hold**

over (*tr*) to postpone or delay. — *v* **hold up** (*tr*) **1** to support. **2** to delay or hinder (*n* **hold-up**). **3** to stop and rob (*n* **hold-up**). **4** (**as**) to show or exhibit, esp. as an example. — *v* **hold with** (*tr*) to approve of. — **keep hold of** to continue to hold on to. — **no holds barred** not observing any rules; with no restrictions. [OE *healdan*]

holdall *n* a large, strong bag for carrying clothes, etc. when travelling.

holding *n* **1** land held by lease. **2** the amount of land, shares, etc. which a person or company owns.

holding company *n* a company which owns and controls all or part of at least one other company.

hold-up see **hold up** above.

hold[2] *n* the place where cargo is stored in ships and aeroplanes. [Variant of **hole**]

hole *n* **1** an opening or gap in or through something: *a hole in the wall*. **2** a hollow area in something solid. **3** an animal's burrow. **4** (*coll*) an unpleasant or gloomy place. **5** (*coll*) an awkward or difficult situation. **6** (*coll*) a fault or mistake: *a hole in the argument*. **7** (*golf*) (the distance or ground from the tee to) the round can-shaped hollow in the middle of the green into which the ball is hit; any of the usu. 18 such sections of a golf course. — *v* (*tr*) **1** to make a hole in. **2** to hit (a ball, etc.) into a hole. — *adj* **holey**, ***-ier***, ***-iest***. — *v* **hole up** (*intr*; *coll*) to hide. — **make a hole in** (*coll*) to use a lot of (esp. a supply of money). — **pick holes in** to find fault with. [OE *hol*]

hole-and-corner *adj* secretive; underhand.

hole in the heart *n* a congenital defect in the heart in which there is an opening in the wall between the left and right sides.

holiday *n* **1** (often in *pl*) a period of time taken as a break from work, etc. and during which one may go away from home. **2** a day when one does not have to work, e.g. a religious festival. — *v* (*intr*) to spend a holiday. [OE *haligdæg*, holy day]

holiday camp *n* a place, usu. near the sea, which organises games and other activities for the people staying there on holiday.

holidaymaker *n* a person who is on holiday away from home.

holistic *adj* (of a method of treating disease) considering a person as a whole and taking social and psychological factors into account as well as the physical symptoms. — *adv* **holistically**. [Gr *holos*, whole]

holland *n* a smooth, hard-wearing linen cloth, usu. unbleached or dyed brown. [Orig. made in *Holland*]

holler *v* ***-r-*** (*intr* & *tr*; *coll*) to shout or cry loudly. — *n* a shout. [Fr *holà*, stop!]

hollow *adj* **1** containing an empty space; not solid. **2** sunken: *hollow cheeks*. **3** (of sounds) echoing as if made in a hollow place. **4** worthless; insincere. — *n* **1** hollow or sunken space in something. **2** a small valley or depression in the land. — *adv* (*coll*) completely: *beat the other team hollow*. — *v* (*tr*; **out**) to make a hole or hollow in; to form by making a hollow. — *adv* **hollowly**. — *n* **hollowness**. [OE *holh*]

hollow-eyed *adj* having sunken eyes, usu. because of tiredness.

holly *n* ***-ies*** a tree or shrub with dark, shiny evergreen leaves, usu. with prickly edges, and red berries, used for Christmas decorations. [OE *holen*]

hollyhock *n* a tall garden plant with colourful flowers. [MidE *holi*, holy + *hoc*, mallow]

holmium *n* a soft, silver-white metallic element (symbol **Ho**). [Lat *Holmia*, Stockholm]

holocaust *n* **1** large-scale destruction and loss of life. **2** (*cap*) the mass murder of Jews by the Nazis during the Second World War. [Gr *holos*, whole + *kaustos*, burnt]

hologram *n* a kind of photograph which shows objects in three dimensions when lit with special lighting. [Gr *holos*, whole + **-gram**]

holograph *adj* (of a document) completely in the handwriting of the author. — *n* a holograph document. — *v* (*tr*) to make a hologram of. — *adj* **holographic**. — *adv* **holographically**. [Gr *holos*, whole + *graphein*, to write]

holography *n* the science of making or using holograms.

hols *n* (*pl*) (*coll*) holidays. [Abbrev.]

holster *n* a leather case for a pistol, usu. worn attached to a belt round a person's hips. [Dut]

holt *n* an otter's den. [**hold**[1]]

holy *adj* ***-ier***, ***-iest*** **1** belonging to or associated with God or gods; sacred. **2** morally pure and perfect; saintly. — *adv* **holily**. [OE *halig*]

holiness *n* **1** the state of being holy. **2** (*cap*) a title of the Pope and certain other religious leaders.

holier-than-thou *adj* (*derog*) thinking oneself to be morally superior.

Holy Communion see **Communion**.

Holy Ghost see **Holy Spirit**.

Holy Grail *n* (in mediaeval legend) the bowl used by Christ at the Last Supper.

the Holy Land *n* W Palestine, esp. Judaea.

holy of holies *n* **1** the sacred inner chamber in a Jewish temple, hidden by a screen. **2** any place or thing regarded as especially holy.

holy orders see **order**.

Holy See *n* the see of Rome, the Pope's see.

Holy Spirit or **Holy Ghost** *n* the third person of the Trinity.

Holy Week *n* the week before Easter Sunday.

Holy Writ *n* holy writings, esp. the Bible.

homage *n* **1** a display of great respect towards someone or something. **2** (*hist*) a vassal's formal public acknowledgement that he is his feudal lord's servant. [OFr]

home *n* **1** the place where one lives. **2** the country or area one originally comes from. **3** a place where a thing first occurred or was first invented. **4** an institution where people who need care or rest live, e.g. orphans, the aged, etc. **5** a match won by a team playing on their own ground. **6** the finishing point in some games and races. — *adj* **1** of one's home, country, or family. **2** made or done at home or in one's own country. **3** (of a sports contest) played on one's own ground rather than the opponent's. — *adv* **1** at or to a person's home. **2** to the place, position, etc. aimed at: *hit the point home*. **3** as far as possible: *hammer the nail home*. **4** at one's own ground, stadium, etc. — *v* (*intr*) **1** (of a bird) to return home safely. **2 (in on)** to be directed accurately towards (a target). — **at home 1** in one's home, country, sports ground, etc. **2** feeling at ease or familiar with a place. **3** prepared to receive visitors. — **bring home to** to make quite obvious to. — **home and dry** having arrived home or achieved one's goal. — **home from home** a place where one feels as comfortable, relaxed and happy as one feels at home. — **make oneself at home** to behave as one would in one's own home. — **nothing to write home about** (*coll*) not very exciting or attractive. [OE *ham*]

home-coming *n* the return home of a person who has been away for a long time.

Home Counties *n* (*pl*) the counties which surround London.

home economics *n* (*sing* or *pl*) the study of skills needed to run a home.

home farm *n* a farm, usu. one of several on a large estate, set aside to produce food, etc. for the owner of the estate.

Home Guard *n* (*Br hist*) a volunteer army formed to defend the country from invasion during the Second World War.

home help *n* (*Br*) a person who is paid, often by the local authority, to help people who are ill or old with their cleaning, cooking, etc.

homeland *n* **1** the country where a person is born, or from where his or her ancestors come. **2** in S Africa, land set aside by the government for the native black population.

homeless *n* (*pl*) people without a place to live. — *adj* (of people) having nowhere to live. — *n* **homelessness**.

homely *adj* **-ier**, **-iest 1** simple but pleasant. **2** making someone feel at home. **3** (*US*) (of a person) unattractive. — *n* **homeliness.**

home-made *adj* (of food, clothes, etc.) made at home.

Home Office *n* (*Br*) the government department which deals with law and order within the country, immigration, etc.

home rule *n* government of a country by its own citizens.

Home Secretary *n* (*Br*) the government minister in charge of the Home Office.

homesick *adj* sad and depressed at being away from one's home and family. — *n* **homesickness**.

homespun *adj* **1** (of advice, thinking, etc.) simple and straightforward. **2** (*old*) (of cloth) woven at home.

homestead *n* **1** a house, esp. a farmhouse, with the land and other buildings which belong to it. **2** (*US*) an area of land (usu. 160 acres) granted to a settler for development as a farm.

home straight or **stretch** *n* the last part of a racecourse just before the finish.

home truth *n* (usu. in *pl*) an unpleasant fact about a person said directly to his or her face.

homeward *adj* going home. — *adv* (also **homewards**) towards home.

homework *n* work or study done at home, esp. by school pupils.

homing *adj* **1** (of a pigeon) able to find its way home after being released a long way away. **2** (of a missile) able to guide itself to the place aimed at.

homy *adj* **-ier**, **-iest** like a home, esp. in being warm and comfortable.

homeopathy. Same as **homoeopathy**.

Homeric *adj* **1** of or relating to the Greek epic poet Homer (*c.* 850 BC), or his poems. **2** of Bronze Age Greece. [Gr *homerikos*]

homicide *n* **1** the killing of one person by another. **2** a person who kills another person. [Lat *homo*, man + **-cide**]

homicidal *adj* (of a person) likely to commit murder.

homily *n* **-ies 1** a sermon. **2** a long, boring talk, usu. telling someone how to behave. — *adj* **homiletic**. [Gr *homilia*, assembly, sermon]

hominid *n* & *adj* (any animal) of the family to which modern man and his ancestors belong. [Lat *homo*, man]

hominoid *adj* of man; manlike. — *n* any animal resembling man. [Lat *homo*, man + **-oid**]

hominy *n* (esp. *US*) coarsely ground maize, boiled with milk or water to make porridge. [An American Indian word]

homo- *comb fm* same: *homosexual*. [Gr *homos*, same]

homoeopathy *n* the system of medicine in which an illness is treated by giving the patient very small doses of drugs which induce the same symptoms as the disease. — *adj* **homoeopathic**. — *adv* **homoeopathically**. [Gr *homoios*, similar + *patheia*, suffering]

homoeopath *n* a person who practises homoeopathy.

homogeneous *adj* made of parts that are all of the same kind. — *n* **homogeneity**. — *adv* **homogeneously**. [Gr *homos*, same + *genos*, kind]

homogenise or **-ize** *v* (*tr*) **1** to treat (milk) so that the fat droplets are evenly distributed and the cream does not separate out. **2** to make homogeneous. [Gr *homos*, same + *genos*, kind]

homogeny *n* a likeness owing to common descent or origin. — *adj* **homogenous**. [Gr *homos*, same + *genos*, kind]

homograph *n* a word with the same spelling as another, but with a different meaning and origin, e.g. *like* (similar) and *like* (be fond of). [Gr *homos*, same + **-graph**]

homologous *adj* **1** having a related or similar function or position. **2** (*biol*) (of parts of the body) having the same origins but having developed different forms and functions, such as a bird's wing and a man's arm. [Gr *homos*, same + *logos*, proportion]

homology *n* the state of being homologous.

homonym *n* a word having the same sound and spelling as another word, but a different meaning, e.g. *kind* (helpful) and *kind* (sort). [Gr *homos*, same + *onoma*, name]

homophobia *n* an intense dislike or fear of homosexuals. [**homosexual** + **phobia**]

homophone *n* a word which has the same sound as another word but has a different spelling and meaning, e.g. *bear* and *bare*. [Gr *homos*, same + *phone*, voice]

Homo sapiens *n* the species of modern man. [Lat, wise man]

homosexual *n* a person who is sexually attracted to people of the same sex. — *adj* of or concerning a homosexual or homosexuals. — *n* **homosexuality**. [Gr *homos*, same]

homy. See **home**.

Hon. *abbrev* Honourable.

hone *n* a smooth stone for sharpening tools and knives. — *v* (*tr*) to sharpen with or as if with a hone. [OE *han*]

honest *adj* **1** truthful; trustworthy; not likely to steal, cheat or lie. **2** just or fair: *an honest wage*. **3** sincere and respectable: *an honest attempt*. **4** ordinary and undistinguished: *an honest wine*. — *adv* (*coll*) honestly: *I do like it, honest*. [Lat *honestus*]

honestly *adv* **1** in an honest way. **2** truly.

honesty *n* **1** the state of being honest and truthful. **2** a common garden plant with silvery leaf-like pods.

honey *n* **-eys** **1** the edible, thick, sweet substance made by bees. **2** the dark, dull yellow colour of honey. **3** (esp. *NAm coll*) a word used when speaking to a person one loves. **4** (*coll*) a person or thing which is excellent of its kind. [OE *hunig*]

honey-bee *n* any of the varieties of bee which live in hives and produce honey.

honeycomb *n* **1** the structure formed by the rows of wax cells in which bees store honey. **2** anything like a honeycomb.

honeyed *adj* (of someone's voice, words, etc.) pleasing, flattering, or soothing.

honeymoon *n* **1** a holiday taken by a newly married couple. **2** a period of goodwill and enthusiasm at the beginning, e.g. of a new business relationship. — *v* (*intr*) to spend a honeymoon. — *n* **honeymooner**.

honeysuckle *n* a climbing garden shrub with sweet-smelling white, pale yellow or pink flowers. [OE *hunigsuge*]

honk *n* **1** the sound made by a car horn. **2** the cry of a wild goose. — *v* (*tr* & *intr*) to make or cause to make a honking noise. [Imit.]

honky or **honkie** *n* **-ies** (*US Black slang*) a white person.

honky-tonk *n* (*coll*) **1** a style of popular piano music based on ragtime. **2** a cheap, seedy nightclub.

honorarium *n* **-iums** or **-ia** a gift, usu. money, given to someone in return for professional services which would normally be free. [Lat, honorary]

honorary *adj* **1** given to a person as a mark of respect, and without the usual functions, etc. **2** (of an official position) not having any payment. [Lat *honorarius*]

honorific *adj* showing or giving respect. [Lat *honor*, honour + *facere*, to do]

honour *n* **1** great respect or public regard. **2** the quality of doing what is right and having a high standard of moral behaviour. **3** fame or glory; distinction for bravery, etc. **4** a source of fame, glory or distinction (for one's country, etc.). **5** a pleasure or privilege. **6** (*old*) a woman's chastity or her reputation for this. **7** (in *pl*) (of a university degree) a higher grade of distinction for specialised or advanced work. **8** (*cap*) a title of respect given to judges, mayors, etc. **9** (in *pl*) a mark of respect, esp. at a funeral. **10** in some card games, any of the top four or five cards. **11** (*golf*) the right to play from the tee first. — *v* (*tr*) **1** to respect greatly. **2** to give (someone) an award, title, or honour as a mark of respect for (an ability or achievement, etc.). **3** to pay (a bill, debt, etc.) when it falls due. **4** to keep (a promise). — **do the honours** to perform the task of host towards one's guests, e.g. offering them drinks, etc. — **on one's honour** under a moral obligation. — **word of honour** a solemn promise. [Lat *honor*]

honourable *adj* **1** deserving or worthy of honour. **2** having high moral principles. **3** (*cap*) a courtesy title, given to some high officials, the children of some peers, and MPs. ◇ See also **Right Honourable**. — *adv* **honourably**.

honour-bound *adj* obliged (to do something) not by law, but by duty or because one knows it is right.

hooch *n* (*US coll*) strong alcoholic drink, esp. when distilled illegally. [From an Alaskan Indian word]

hood[1] *n* **1** a usu. loose covering for the whole head, often attached to a coat at the collar. **2** a folding, usu. removable, roof or cover on a car, cooker, push-chair, etc. **3**

(*NAm*) a car bonnet. **4** a piece of cloth worn as part of academic dress. — *adj* **hooded**. [OE *hod*]

hooded crow *n* a crow with a grey body and black head.

hood[2] *n* (*slang*) a hoodlum.

-hood *sfx* **1** a state or condition: *manhood*. **2** a collection or group: *priesthood*. [OE *-had*]

hoodlum *n* **1** (esp. *US*) a criminal. **2** a young, violent, destructive or badly behaved person.

hoodoo *n* **1** voodoo. **2** bad luck, or the thing or person which brings it. — *v* (*tr*) to bring bad luck to. [Variant of **voodoo**]

hoodwink *v* (*tr*; **into**) to trick or deceive. [**hood**[1] + **wink**]

hooey *n* (*slang*) nonsense.

hoof *n* ***hoofs*** or ***hooves*** the horny part at the end of the feet of horses, cows, etc. — **hoof it** (*slang*) to go on foot. — **on the hoof** (of cattle, horses, etc.) alive.

hoo-ha *n* (*coll*) excited and noisy talk; a commotion. [Prob. Yiddish *hu-ha*, uproar]

hook *n* **1** a small piece of metal, etc. shaped like a J, used for catching and holding things. **2** a curved tool for cutting grain, branches, etc. **3** a sharp bend or curve, e.g. in land or a river. **4** (*boxing*) a swinging punch with the elbow bent. **5** (*cricket, golf*) a shot that sends the ball to the right-handed player's left. — *v* **1** (*tr*) to catch with or as if with a hook. **2** (*tr* & *intr*; **up**) to fasten or be fastened to something else by means of a hook or hooks. **3** (*tr*) (*golf, cricket*) to hit (the ball) out round the other side of one's body, i.e. to the left if one is right-handed. **4** (*tr*) in a rugby scrum, to catch (the ball) with the foot and kick it backwards. **5** (*tr*) to make into the shape of a hook. — **by hook or by crook** by some means or another. — **hook and eye** a small metal hook and the loop it fits into, used to fasten clothes. — **hook, line and sinker** (*coll*) completely. — **off the hook** **1** (*coll*) no longer in trouble; excused of the blame for something. **2** (of a telephone receiver) not on its rest so not able to receive incoming calls. [OE *hoc*]

hooked *adj* **1** curved like a hook. **2** (*coll*; **on**) addicted (to a drug or activity); extremely interested (in something).

hooker *n* **1** (*coll*) a prostitute. **2** (*rugby*) the forward whose job is to hook the ball out of a scrum.

hook-up *n* a temporary linking up of different broadcasting stations, esp. the radio and a television channel, for a special broadcast.

hookworm *n* a parasitic worm with hook-like parts in its mouth, which affects animals and humans and causes a type of anaemia.

hookah *n* an oriental tobacco-pipe consisting of a tube which passes through water, used for cooling the smoke before it is drawn into the mouth. [Arabic *huqqah*, bowl]

hookey or **hooky**: **play hookey** (*US coll*) to be absent from school without permission.

hooligan *n* a violent, destructive or badly-behaved young person. — *n* **hooliganism**.

hoop *n* **1** a thin ring of metal, wood, etc., esp. those used round casks. **2** a large ring, esp. one made of light wood or plastic, rolled along the ground as a toy, whirled round the body, or for circus performers, etc. to jump through. **3** an iron arch that the ball is hit through in croquet. — *v* (*tr*) to bind or surround with a hoop or hoops. — **go** or **be put through the hoops** (*coll*) to undergo a thorough and difficult test. [OE *hop*]

hoop-la *n* a fairground game in which small rings are thrown at objects, with the thrower winning any objects he or she manages to throw a hoop over.

hoopoe *n* a bird with salmon-coloured feathers, black and white striped wings and fan-like feathers on top of its head. [Lat *upupa*, imit. of its cry]

hooray or **hoorah**. Same as **hurrah**.

Hooray Henry *n* (*slang*) a young middle- or upper-class man with a loud voice and immature and ineffectual manner.

hoot *n* **1** the call of an owl. **2** the sound of a car horn, siren, steam whistle, etc. **3** a loud shout of laughter, scorn or disapproval. **4** (*coll*) an amusing person, event or thing. — *v* **1** (*intr*) to make a hoot. **2** (*tr*) to sound (a car horn, etc.). **3** (*intr*) to shout or laugh loudly expressing disapproval, scorn, etc. **4** (*tr*) to force (a performer) off stage by hooting. — **not care** or **give a hoot** or **two hoots** (*coll*) not to care at all. [MidE *houten*, perhaps imit.]

hooter *n* **1** an instrument which makes a hooting sound. **2** (*Br coll*) a nose.

Hoover® *n* a vacuum cleaner. — *v* ***-r-*** (*tr* & *intr*) to clean (a carpet, etc.) with a vacuum cleaner.

hooves. See **hoof**.

hop[1] *v* ***-pp-*** **1** (*intr*) (of people) to jump on one leg. **2** (*intr*) (of certain small birds, animals and insects) to jump on both or all legs. **3** (*tr*) to jump over. **4** (*intr*; **in, into, out of**, etc.; *coll*) to move in a lively way. **5** (*intr*; with **over**; *coll*) to make a short journey, esp. by air. — *n* **1** an act of hopping; a short jump. **2** (*coll*) a distance travelled in an aeroplane without landing; a short journey by air. **3** (*coll old*) an informal dance. — **catch someone on the hop** (*coll*) to catch someone unprepared or unawares. — **hop it** (*Br coll*) to go away. — **hopping mad** (*coll*) very angry.— **keep someone on the hop** to keep someone busy, active or alert. [OE *hoppian*, to dance]

hopper *n* **1** a person, animal or insect which hops. **2** a large container used for feeding grain or other material through a hole in the bottom into another container, etc. below it.

hopscotch *n* a children's game in which players take turns at throwing a stone into one of a series of squares drawn on the ground and hopping in the others around it.

hop[2] *n* **1** a tall climbing plant. **2** (usu. in *pl*) the dried fruit of this plant, used for flavouring beer. — *v* ***-pp-*** **1** (*intr*) to pick hops. **2** (*tr*) to flavour (beer) with hops. [MidE *hoppe*]

hopper *n* a person or machine that picks hops.

hope *n* **1** a desire for something, with some confidence of obtaining it. **2** a person, thing, or event that one is relying on for help, or that gives one a good reason for hope. **3** a reason for believing that the thing desired will still happen. **4** that which is desired or hoped for. — *v* **1** (*tr* & *intr*; **for**) to wish or desire (that something may happen), esp. with some reason to believe that it will. **2** (*intr*; *old*) to have confidence. — **hope against hope** to continue hoping when all reason for it has gone. — **some hope** (*coll*) no hope at all. [OE *hopa*]

hopeful *adj* **1** feeling hope. **2** giving a reason for hope; likely to succeed. — *n* a (usu. young) person who is ambitious or expected to do well. — *n* **hopefulness**.

hopefully *adv* **1** in a hopeful way. **2** (*coll*) it is to be hoped.

hopeless *adj* **1** not likely to be successful. **2** (*coll*; **at**) not good. **3** unable to be stopped or cured. — *adv* **hopelessly**. — *n* **hopelessness**.

hopper. See **hop**[1] and **hop**[2].

hopscotch. See **hop**[1].

horde *n* **1** (often *derog*) a crowd or large group, esp. one which is noisy. **2** a group of nomads. [Turk *ordu*, camp]

horizon *n* **1** the line at which the earth and the sky seem to meet. **2** the limit of a person's knowledge, interests or experience. [Gr *horizein*, to limit]

horizontal *adj* **1** at right angles to vertical; parallel to the horizon; level or flat. **2** applying equally to all members of a group or aspects of a situation. — *n* a horizontal line or position. — *adv* **horizontally**.

hormone *n* **1** a chemical produced by some part of a plant or animal body, and which has a specific effect on that body. **2** a synthetic chemical which has the same effects as some natural hormone. — *adj* **hormonal**. [Gr *horman*, to stimulate]

horn *n* **1** either of a pair of hard, bony objects which grow on the heads of cows, sheep, etc.; a deer's antlers. **2** the bone-like substance of which horns are made. **3** a horn-like part projecting from the heads of other animals, e.g. a snail's tentacles. **4** something which looks like a horn in shape. **5** a musical wind instrument orig. made from horn but now usu. made of brass. **6** (also **French horn**) a coiled brass wind instrument. **7** an apparatus for making a warning sound, esp. on a vehicle. — *v* (*tr*) **1** to fit with a horn or horns. **2** to injure or gore with horns. — **horn of plenty** cornucopia. — **on the horns of a dilemma** having to make a choice between two equally unpleasant alternatives. — *adj* **horned**. [OE]

horny *adj* ***-ier***, ***-iest*** **1** of or like horn, esp. in being hard. **2** (*slang*) sexually excited.

hornbeam *n* a tree with hard, tough wood.

hornbill *n* a tropical bird with a horn-like growth on its beak.

hornblende *n* a black or green mineral, a constituent of some kinds of rock, e.g. granite. [Ger]

hornet *n* a large wasp which can sting severely. — **stir up a hornet's nest** to cause a strong, hostile reaction. [OE *hyrnet*]

hornpipe *n* **1** a lively, solo, sailor's jig. **2** the music for this dance.

horology *n* the art of measuring time or making clocks and watches. — *adj* **horological** . — *n* **horologist**. [Gr *hora*, hour + **-logy**]

horoscope *n* **1** a description of a person's future based on the position of the stars and planets at the time of his or her birth. **2** a diagram showing the positions of the stars and planets at a particular moment in time, e.g. at the time of a person's birth. [Gr *hora*, hour + *skopein*, to observe]

horrendous *adj* causing great shock, fear or terror; horrifying. — *adv* **horrendously**. — *n* **horrendousness**. [Lat *horrere*, to shudder]

horrible *adj* **1** causing horror, dread or fear. **2** (*coll*) unpleasant. — *adv* **horribly**. [Lat *horribilis*]

horrid *adj* **1** revolting; detestable. **2** (*coll*) unpleasant; disagreeable. — *adv* **horridly**. — *n* **horridness**. [Lat *horridus*]

horrific *adj* **1** causing fear, disgust or horror; terrible. **2** (*coll*) very bad. — *adv* **horrifically**. [Lat *horror*, horror + *facere*, to make]

horrify *v* ***-fies***, ***-fied*** (*tr*) to shock greatly. — *adj* **horrifying**. — *adv* **horrifyingly**. [Lat *horror*, horror + *facere*, to make]

horror *n* **1** great fear, loathing or disgust. **2** great dislike. **3** a person or thing causing horror. **4** (*coll*) a bad or ridiculous person or thing. — *adj* (of a film, etc.) very violent and frightening. — **the horrors** (*coll*) a fit of anxiety and fear. [Lat, a shudder with fear]

horror-stricken or **-struck** *adj* shocked; horrified.

hors d'oeuvre *n* a savoury appetiser served at the beginning of a meal. [Fr]

horse *n* **1** a large, four-legged animal with a long mane and tail, used e.g. to pull carts or carry people. **2** an adult male horse. **3** cavalry. **4** a piece of apparatus used for vaulting over and other gymnastic exercises. **5** (also **clothes-horse**) a frame on which clothes, etc. are hung to dry. — *v* **horse about** or **around** (*intr*; *coll*) to fool about. — **straight from the horse's mouth** directly from a well-informed and reliable source. [OE *hors*]

horseback: **on horseback** on the back of a horse.

horse-box *n* a closed trailer fixed to or pulled by a motor vehicle and used for carrying horses.

horse chestnut see **chestnut**.

horseflesh *n* **1** the meat of a horse. **2** horses as a group.

horsefly *n* a large fly that bites horses and cattle.

Horse Guards *n* in Britain, a section of the army that acts as a mounted guard for the sovereign, esp. on ceremonial occasions.

horse laugh *n* a loud, coarse laugh.

horseman or **horsewoman** *n* **1** a rider. **2** a skilled rider.

horsemanship *n* the art of riding, training and managing horses.

horseplay *n* rough and noisy play.

horsepower *n* a unit for measuring the power of an engine, equivalent to 745·7 watts.

horseradish *n* a plant with a long, white, sharp-tasting root which is used to make a sauce usu. eaten with beef.

horse sense *n* plain good sense.

horseshoe *n* **1** a piece of curved iron nailed to the bottom of a horse's hoof to protect the foot. **2** something in the shape of a horseshoe, esp. as a symbol of good luck.

horsetail *n* **1** the tail of a horse. **2** a plant resembling a horse's tail.

horse-trading *n* hard bargaining.

horsewhip *n* a whip for encouraging horses. — *v* ***-pp-*** (*tr*) to whip, esp. severely, and usu. as a punishment.

horsewoman see **horseman**.

horsey or **horsy** *adj* ***-ier***, ***-iest*** **1** of or relating to horses. **2** like a horse. **3** (*Br coll*) very interested in or devoted to horses.

hortative or **hortatory** *adj* encouraging. [Lat *hortari*, to incite to action]

horticulture *n* the science and art of gardening. — *adj* **horticultural**. [Lat *hortus*, garden + *cultura*, cultivation]

horticulturist *n* an expert gardener.

hosanna *n* & *interj* a shout of adoration or praise to God. [Hebr *hoshiah nna*, save now, I pray]

hose *n* **1** (also **hosepipe**) a flexible tube for directing water, e.g. for watering plants. **2** (*pl*) stockings, socks and tights. **3** (*hist*) breeches. — *v* (*tr*; **down**) to direct water at or clean with a hose. [OE *hosa*]

hosiery *n* stockings, socks, tights and knitted underwear. [**hose**]

hosier *n* a person who makes or sells hosiery.

hospice *n* **1** a home which cares for people suffering from incurable diseases or people who are destitute. **2** (*old*) a house offering lodging for travellers, esp. one kept by a religious order. [Lat *hospes*, guest]

hospitable *adj* showing kindness to guests or strangers. — *n* **hospitableness**. — *adv* **hospitably**. [Lat *hospes*, guest]

hospital *n* an institution where people who are physically or mentally ill receive medical or surgical care and nursing. [Lat *hospes*, guest]

hospitalise or **-ize** *v* (*tr*) to take or admit (a person) to hospital for treatment. — *n* **hospitalisation** or **-z-**.

hospitality *n* a friendly welcome for guests or strangers, which usu. includes offering them food and drink. [Lat *hospes*, guest]

hospitaller *n* a member of a religious order which does a lot of work for charity, esp. in hospitals. [Lat *hospes*, guest]

host[1] *n* **1** a person who receives and entertains guests or strangers in his or her own home. **2** (*old*) an innkeeper. **3** an animal or plant on which another, usu. lower, form lives and feeds. **4** a person who introduces performers, etc. on a television or radio show. **5** a person who has received a transplanted organ or tissue. — *v* (*tr*) to act as a host (to people) or be the host of (an event or programme). [Lat *hospes*, guest]

hostess *n* **1** a female host. **2** a woman employed to act as a man's companion for the evening at a night club. **3** an air hostess.

host[2] *n* **1** a very large number. **2** (*old*) an army. [Lat *hostis*, enemy]

host[3] *n* the bread or wafer used in a Holy Communion service. [Lat *hostia*, victim]

hostage *n* a person who is held prisoner as a guarantee that demands, the conditions of an agreement, etc. will be carried out. [Lat *obses*]

hostel *n* **1** a building which provides overnight accommodation as a charity, esp. for the homeless. **2** a residence for students or nurses. **3** a youth hostel. **4** (*old*) an inn. [OFr, from Lat *hospes*, guest]

hostelry *n* ***-ies*** (*old* or *facet*) an inn or public house.

hostess. See **host**[1].

hostile *adj* **1** unfriendly; aggressive. **2** of or belonging to an enemy. **3** (**to**) opposed. [Lat *hostis*, enemy]

hostility *n* ***-ies*** **1** unfriendliness; opposition; aggression. **2** (in *pl*) acts of war; battles.

hot *adj* ***-tt-*** **1** having or producing a great deal of heat. **2** having a higher temperature than is normal or desirable. **3** (of food) spicy; causing a burning sensation on the tongue. **4** easily made angry; excitable. **5** feeling intense emotion or sexual desire. **6** (of a contest or fight) intense; animated. **7** (of news) recent; fresh. **8** strongly favoured: *a hot favourite*. **9** (of music) with strong and exciting rhythms. **10** (of colours with red in them) bright and fiery. **11** (*slang*) (of goods) stolen. **12** (of a scent in hunting) fresh and strong, suggesting the quarry is not far ahead. **13** (*slang*) (of information) up to date and reliable: *a hot tip*. **14** (*coll*) (of a situation) difficult, unpleasant or dangerous: *make life hot for him*. **15** (*slang*) radioactive. **16** (in a game etc.) very close to guessing correctly or finding the thing sought.— *adv* hotly. — *adv* **hotly**. — **have** or **get the hots for** (*vulg slang*) to have a strong sexual desire for. — **hot and bothered** (*coll*) anxious, confused and unable to think clearly. — **hot on** very interested in or well informed about. — *v* **hot up -tt-** (*intr*) to become gradually hotter, more exciting, more dangerous, etc. — **in hot pursuit** chasing (a person) as fast as one can. [OE *hat*]

hot air *n* (*coll*) empty or boastful talk, promises that will not be kept, etc.

hotbed *n* a place which allows something, esp. something bad, to grow quickly: *a hotbed of discontent*.

hot-blooded *adj* having strong, esp. sexual, feelings.

hot cross bun *n* a fruit bun marked with a cross on top, traditionally eaten on Good Friday.

hot dog *n* a hot sausage in a long, soft, bread roll.

hotfoot *adv* (*coll*) in haste. — **hotfoot it** (*coll*) to rush.

hothead *n* a person who is easily made angry. — *adj* **hotheaded**. — *n* **hotheadedness**.

hothouse *n* a greenhouse which is kept warm for growing tender or tropical plants in. — *adj* (of a plant) able to grow only in a greenhouse.

hot line *n* **1** a direct telephone line between two (usu. important) people. **2** an emergency telephone number for inquiries about a particular incident or accident.

hot money *n* money transferred from one country to another to take advantage of exchange rates and trading conditions, and make a quick profit.

hotplate *n* **1** the flat top surface of a cooker on which food is cooked and kept warm. **2** a portable heated metal surface for keeping food, dishes, etc. hot.

hotpot *n* meat and vegetables, with a layer of sliced potato on top, cooked slowly in a closed pot.

hot potato *n* (*coll*) a difficult problem or situation.

hot rod *n* a motor car modified to have extra speed.

hot seat *n* **1** (*coll*) an uncomfortable or difficult position. **2** (*US slang*) the electric chair.

hot spot *n* **1** (*coll*) an area where there is likely to be trouble, esp. political or military. **2** an area where there is evidence of volcanic activity occurring underground.

hot stuff *n* (*coll*) **1** a person who has outstanding ability. **2** a person who is sexually exciting.

hot-tempered *adj* quick to get angry.

hotting *n* (*slang*) the performing of stunts and skilful manoeuvres at high speed in a stolen car. — *n* **hotter**.

hot water *n* (*coll*) trouble; bother: *get into hot water*.

hot-water bottle *n* a rubber container for hot water, used to warm beds.

hotchpotch *n* **1** a confused mass or jumble. **2** a mutton stew with many different vegetables in it. [OFr *hochepot*, from *hocher*, to shake + *pot*, pot]

hotel *n* a large house or building where travellers or holidaymakers receive food and lodging in return for payment. [OFr *hostel*, hostel, from Lat *hospes*, guest]

hotelier *n* a person who owns or manages a hotel.

Hottentot *n* **1** a member of a pale-brown-skinned race of people in SW Africa. **2** the language spoken by this people. [Afrikaans]

hound *n* **1** (esp. *in cmpds*) a hunting-dog: *wolfhound*. **2** (in *pl*) a pack of foxhounds. **3** (*coll*) a man one despises or feels contempt for. — *v* (*tr*) to chase or bother relentlessly. [OE *hund*]

hour *n* **1** sixty minutes, a twenty-fourth part of a day. **2** any of the points on a clock or watch that shows the hour. **3** a point in time: *an early hour*. **4** the time allowed or fixed for some activity: *office hours*. **5** the distance travelled in an hour: *two hours away from the airport*. **6** a special occasion: *his finest hour*. **7** a time for action: *the hour has come*. **8** (in *pl*; *relig*; also **canonical hours**) (prayers to be said at) seven set times during the day and night. — **after hours** after closing-time. — **at all hours** at irregular times, esp. late at night. — **out of hours** before or after usual working hours. [Gr *hora*]

hourglass *n* an instrument that measures time in hours, consisting of one glass container on top of and joined to another by a narrow glass tube, filled with as much sand as will pass from one container into the other in the space of one hour. — *adj* curving in at the waist or middle like an hourglass.

hourly *adj* **1** happening or done every hour. **2** measured by the hour. **3** frequent; continual: *live in hourly fear of discovery*. — *adv* **1** every hour. **2** at any hour: *expect news hourly*. **3** by the hour. **4** frequently.

houri *n* a beautiful young woman, esp. in the Muslim Paradise. [Arabic *haura*, gazelle-eyed]

house *n* **1** a building in which people, esp. a single family, live. **2** the people living in such a building. **3** (esp. *in cmpds*) a building used for a particular purpose: *an opera-house*. **4** (*cap*) the body of people who govern a country and make laws, or the place where they meet. **5** a business firm: *a publishing house*. **6** the audience in a theatre, a theatre, or a performance given there. **7** a family, esp. an important or noble one: *house of Stuart*. **8** (*astrol*) one of the twelve divisions of the heavens. **9** (*Br*) one of several divisions of pupils at a large school. **10** a building in which students or members of religious community live. — *v* (*tr*) **1** to provide with a house or similar shelter. **2** to store. **3** to protect (a part) by covering. — **bring the house down** (*coll*) to produce loud applause in a theatre. — **keep house** to manage a household. — **like a house on fire** (*coll*) **1** very well. **2** very quickly. — **on the house** (of food, drink, etc.) free; paid for by the manager or owner. — **put** or **set one's house in order** to organise or settle one's affairs, esp. by improving one's behaviour. [OE *hus*]

house agent *n* a person who arranges the buying, selling or renting of houses.

house arrest *n* confinement in one's own home rather than prison.

houseboat *n* a boat, usu. with a flat bottom and usu. stationary, which is built to be lived in.

housebound *adj* unable to leave one's house because of illness, young children, etc.

housebreaking *n* unlawful breaking into a building to steal. — *n* **housebreaker**.

housecoat *n* a woman's long, loose garment like a dressing-gown, worn at home.

housefly *n* a common fly, often found in houses.

household *n* the people who live together in a house and make up a family. — *adj* of the house or family living there.

householder *n* **1** the person who owns a house or pays the rent for it. **2** the head of a family.

household name or **word** *n* a name or saying known to everyone.

house husband *n* a husband who does the work usu. done by a housewife.

housekeeper *n* a person who is paid to look after the management of a usu. large house and household.

housekeeping *n* **1** the management of a house and household. **2** money set aside to pay for the expenses of running a house.

house lights *n* (*pl*) the lights in the part of a cinema, theatre, etc. where people sit.

housemaid *n* a maid employed to keep a house clean and tidy.

housemaid's knee *n* inflammation of the knee, caused by prolonged kneeling.

houseman *n* a recently qualified doctor who is living in a hospital while working there to complete his or her training.

house martin *n* a black and white bird with a short forked tail, that builds nests on house walls.

housemaster or **housemistress** *n* in Britain, a teacher in charge of a house in a school, esp. a boarding-school.

House of Commons *n* (in Britain) the lower, elected assembly in parliament, or the building where this meets.

House of Keys *n* (in the Isle of Man) the elected chamber of the Manx parliament, the Tynwald.

House of Lords *n* (in Britain) the upper assembly in parliament, made up of peers and bishops.

house party *n* a group of guests staying in a country house for several days.

house-proud *adj* taking a lot of, often too much, pride in the condition and appearance of one's house.

housetops *n* (*pl*): **shout something from the housetops** to announce something publicly.

housetrain *v* (*tr*) to train (a pet) to be clean in the house and to urinate and defecate outside or in a special tray, etc.

house-warming *n* a party given to celebrate moving into a new house.

housewife *n* **1** a woman who looks after her house, her husband and her family, and who sometimes does not have a job outside the home. **2** a pocket sewing-kit. — *adj* **housewifely**.

housework *n* the work of keeping a house clean and tidy.

housing *n* **1** houses as a group. **2** the act or job of providing housing for people. **3** the hard cover round a machine.

hove. See **heave**.

hovel *n* a small, dirty, dismal dwelling. [MidE *hovell*]

hover *v* *-r-* (*intr*) **1** (of a bird, helicopter, etc.) to remain in the air without moving in any direction. **2** to move around while still remaining near a person or thing. **3** (**between**) to be undecided. — *n* an act or state of hovering or waiting to make a decision. [MidE *hoveren*]

hovercraft *n* a vehicle which is able to move over land or water, supported by a cushion of air.

how *adv* **1** in what way; by what means: *How did it happen?* **2** to what extent: *How old is he?* **3** in what condition, esp. of health: *How is she feeling now?* **4** to what extent (is something) good, successful, etc.: *How was your holiday?* **5** using whatever means are necessary: *do it how best you can.* — *conj* (*coll*) that: *told me how he'd done it on his own.* — *n* a manner or means of doing something: *the how and why.* — **and how** (*coll*) very much indeed. — **how about** would you like?; what do you think of?: *How about another piece of cake?* — **how come** (*coll*) for what reason? — **how do you do?** a formal greeting, esp. to a person one is meeting for the first time. — **how's that? 1** what is your opinion of that. **2** (also **howzat**) an appeal to the umpire in cricket to give the batsman out. [OE *hu*]

howdah *n* a seat, usu. with a sun-shade, used for riding on an elephant's back. [Arabic *hawdaj*]

howdy *interj* (*US slang*) hello. [A corrupt form of **how do you do?**]

however *adv* **1** in spite of that; nevertheless. **2** (*coll*; esp. to show surprise) in what way?; by what means?: *However did you do that?* **3** by whatever means: *Do it* *however you want to*. **4** to no matter what extent: *You must finish this however long it takes*. [MidE]

howitzer *n* a short heavy gun which fires shells high in the air. [Czech *houfnice*, sling, catapult]

howl *n* **1** the long, loud, sad cry of a wolf or dog. **2** a long, loud cry made e.g. by the wind. **3** a cry of pain or distress. **4** a loud yell of laughter. — *v* **1** (*intr*) to make a long, loud, sad cry or similar wailing noise. **2** (*intr*) to cry or laugh loudly. **3** (*tr*) to shout or shriek (instructions, orders, etc.). — *v* **howl down** (*tr*) to stop (a speaker) from being heard by shouting loudly and angrily. [MidE *houlen*]

howler *n* (*coll*) a glaring mistake.

howling *adj* (*coll*) very great.

howsoever *adv* in whatever way; to whatever extent. [MidE]

howzat. See **how's that** (sense **2**).

hoy *interj* a word used to attract someone's attention. [A variant of **hey**]

hoyden *n* a wild, lively girl. — *adj* **hoydenish**. [Dut *heyden*, boor]

HP or **hp** *abbrev* **1** horsepower. **2** (*Br*) hire purchase. **3** high pressure.

HQ or **hq** *abbrev* headquarters.

hr *abbrev* hour.

HRH *abbrev* His or Her Royal Highness.

HRT *abbrev* hormone replacement therapy.

hub *n* **1** the centre of a wheel. **2** the main point of activity, interest, etc. [Perhaps a variant of **hob**]

hub-cap *n* the metal cover over the hub of a wheel.

hubble-bubble *n* **1** a bubbling sound. **2** confusion; confused talk. **3** a simple type of hookah. [**bubble**]

hubbub *n* **1** a confused noise of many sounds, esp. voices. **2** uproar. [Prob. of Irish origin]

hubby *n* **-ies** (*coll*) a husband. [Abbrev.]

hubris *n* arrogance or over-confidence, esp. when likely to end in disaster or ruin. [Gr *hybris*]

huckster *n* **1** (*old*) a street trader. **2** an aggressive seller. [MidE *huccstere*]

huddle *v* **1** (*tr* & *intr*; **together**, **up**) to heap or crowd together closely. **2** (*intr*) to sit curled up. **3** (*tr*) to curl (oneself) up. — *n* **1** a confused mass or crowd. **2** a secret or private conference: *go into a huddle*. [Prob. related to **hide**[1]]

hue[1] *n* **1** a colour or shade. **2** the feature of a colour which makes it different from other colours. **3** aspect. [OE *hiw*]

hue[2]: **hue and cry** a loud public protest. [OFr, outcry]

huff *n* a fit of anger or annoyance: *in a huff*. — *v* **1** (*intr*) to blow or puff loudly. **2** (*tr* & *intr*) to give or take offence. **3** (*tr*; *draughts*) to remove an opponent's man for failing to capture one's own man. — **huffing and puffing** loud, empty threats. [Imit.]

huffy, **-ier**, **-iest** or **huffish** *adj* **1** offended. **2** easily offended; touchy. — *adv* **huffily**. — *n* **huffiness**.

hug *v* **-gg-** (*tr*) **1** to hold tightly in one's arms, esp. to show love. **2** to keep close to: *a ship hugging the shore*. **3** to hold (a belief, etc.) very firmly. — *n* a tight grasp with the arms, esp. to show love. [Perhaps Norse *hugga*, to soothe]

huge *adj* very large. — *n* **hugeness**. [OFr *ahuge*]

hugely *adv* very; very much.

hugger-mugger *n* **1** secrecy. **2** confusion. — *adj* & *adv* **1** (in) secret. **2** confused; in confusion or disorder. [MidE *hokeren*, to hoard]

Huguenot *n* (*hist*) a French Protestant. [Fr]

huh *interj* (*coll*) an expression of disgust, disbelief or inquiry. [Imit.]

hula *n* a Hawaiian dance in which the dancer sways his or her hips and moves his or her arms gracefully. [Hawaiian]

hulk *n* **1** the body of an old ship from which everything has been taken away. **2** a ship which is or looks difficult to steer. **3** (*coll derog*) a large, awkward person or thing. **4** (*hist*) the body of an old ship used as a prison. [OE *hulc*]

hulking *adj* (*coll derog*) large and awkward.

hull[1] *n* the frame or body of a ship or airship. — *v* (*tr*) to pierce the hull of. [Perhaps from **hull**[2]]

hull[2] *n* the outer covering of certain fruit and vegetables, esp. the pod of beans and peas and the green leaves and stem at the bottom of a strawberry. — *v* (*tr*) to remove the hulls from (fruit and vegetables). [OE *hulu*, husk]

hullabaloo *n* (*coll*) an uproar. [Scots *baloo*, lullaby]

hullo. See **hello**.

hum *v* **-mm-** **1** (*intr*) to make a low, steady murmuring sound like a bee. **2** (*tr* & *intr*) to sing (a tune) with one's mouth shut. **3** (*intr*) to speak indistinctly or stammer, esp. through embarrassment. **4** (*intr*; *coll*) to be full of activity. **5** (*intr*; *slang*) to give off an unpleasant smell. — *n* **1** a humming sound. **2** (*slang*) a bad smell. — *interj* an expression of hesitation. — **hum and haw** to make sounds which express doubt, uncertainty or hesitation; to hesitate.

humming-bird *n* a small, brightly-coloured tropical bird which makes a humming sound with its wings.

human *adj* **1** of or belonging to people. **2** having or showing the qualities, esp. the weaknesses, of people as opposed to God, animals or machines. **3** having the better qualities of people, e.g. in being kind, thoughtful, etc. — *n* a human being. [Lat *humanus*, from *homo*, man]

human being *n* a person.

humanise or **-ize** *v* (*tr*) to make more caring, more thoughtful, less brutal, etc. — *n* **humanisation** or **-z-**.

humankind *n* human beings as a race.
humanly *adv* within human power.
human rights *n* (*pl*) the rights of every person to justice and freedom.
humane *adj* **1** kind; sympathetic. **2** (of a killing) done with as little pain and suffering as possible. **3** (of a branch of learning) likely to civilise or make more elegant. — *adv* **humanely**. — *n* **humaneness**. [A variant of **human**]
humanism *n* a non-religious system of thought which holds that man is a responsible, intelligent being capable by himself of solving the problems of mankind and deciding what is or is not correct moral behaviour.
humanist *n* **1** a follower of humanism. **2** (*hist*) a student of Greek and Roman culture during the Renaissance. — *adj* of humanism or humanists. — *adj* **humanistic**.
humanitarian *adj* concerned about improving, or likely to improve, people's lives: *humanitarian aid for the war-zone*. — *n* a person who tries to improve the quality of people's lives by means of reform, charity, etc. — *n* **humanitarianism**. [**human**]
humanity *n* **-ies 1** the human race. **2** the nature of human beings. **3** the qualities of human beings, esp. in being kind or showing mercy. **4** (in *pl*) subjects allowing the study of human culture, esp. language, literature and philosophy, and esp. Latin and Greek. [**human**]
humanoid *n* an animal or machine with human characteristics. — *adj* (of an animal or machine) having human characteristics. [**human** + **-oid**, from Gr *eidos*, form]
humble[1] *adj* **1** having a low opinion of oneself and one's abilities, etc.; not proud. **2** having a low position in society. **3** lowly; modest. — *v* (*tr*) to make humble, modest or of less importance. — *n* **humbleness**. — *adv* **humbly**. ◇ See also **humility**. [Lat *humilis*, low]
humble[2]: **eat humble pie** to be forced to make a humble apology. [A variant of *numbles*, the offal of a deer]
humbug *n* **1** a trick; something done to deceive. **2** nonsense; rubbish. **3** a person who pretends to be something he or she is not. **4** (*Br*) a hard, stripy, peppermint-flavoured sweet.
humdinger *n* (*slang*) an exceptionally good person or thing. [**hum** + **ding**]
humdrum *adj* dull; ordinary. [Prob. from **hum**]
humerus *n* **-ri** the bone in the upper part of the arm. — *adj* **humeral**. [Lat *umerus*, shoulder]
humid *adj* damp; moist. [Lat *humidus*]
humidifier *n* an apparatus for maintaining or increasing the humidity of a room, etc.
humidify *v* **-ies, -ied** (*tr*) to make (the air or atmosphere) damp or humid.
humidity *n* **1** the amount of moisture in the air. **2** dampness.
humiliate *v* (*tr*) to make (someone) feel ashamed or look foolish in front of another person. — *adj* **humiliating**. — *adv* **humiliatingly**. — *n* **humiliation**. [Lat *humilis*, humble]
humility *n* **1** the state or quality of being humble. **2** lowliness of mind; modesty. [Lat *humilis*, humble]
hummock *n* a low hill.
humorist *n* a person who writes or tells amusing stories, jokes, etc. [**humour**]
humorous *adj* funny; amusing. — *adv* **humorously**. — *n* **humorousness**. [**humour**]
humour *n* **1** the quality of being amusing. **2** the ability to amuse or be amused. **3** a state of mind: *good humour*. **4** writing, plays, speech, etc. that are amusing or funny. **5** any of various fluids in the body. **6** (*hist*) any of the four bodily fluids (blood, choler, melancholy and phlegm) which were formerly believed to govern a person's physical health and character. — *v* (*tr*) to please (someone) by doing what he or she wishes. — *adj* **humourless**. [Lat *humor*]
hump *n* **1** a large, rounded lump on the back of an animal, e.g. a camel. **2** a lump on a person's back caused by an abnormality of the spine. **3** a rounded lump on a road. **4** (*Br coll*; with **the**) a feeling of unhappiness or annoyance. — *v* **1** (*tr*; **about**, **around**) to carry (esp. something heavy) with difficulty. **2** (*tr* & *intr*) (*vulg slang*) to have sexual intercourse with (someone).
humpback *n* **1** a back with a hump. **2** a hunchback. **3** a whale with a fin on its back which forms a hump. — *adj* (also **humpbacked**) rising and falling in the shape of a hump; having a hump.
humpback bridge *n* a bridge with steep slopes on either side.
humph *interj* an expression of doubt or displeasure. [Imit.]
humus *n* a substance like earth found in soil, made of decayed plants, leaves, animal matter, etc. [Lat, soil]
Hun *n* **1** (*hist*) a member of a powerful and warlike people who invaded Europe in the 4th and 5th centuries. **2** (*offensive coll*) a German. [OE *Hune*]
hunch *n* **1** an idea or belief based on one's feelings, suspicions or intuition rather than on clear evidence. **2** a hump. — *v* **1** (*tr*) to bend or arch. **2** (*intr*; **up**) to sit with one's body curled up or bent.
hunchback *n* a person with a large rounded lump on his or her back, usu. caused by a problem with the spine. — *adj* **hunchbacked**.
hundred *n* **-dreds** or (after another number) **-dred 1** the number which is ten times ten. **2** a numeral, figure or symbol representing this, e.g. *100*, *C*. **3** a set of 100 people or things: *one hundred pounds*. **4** a

score of 100 points. **5** (usu. in *pl*; *coll*) very many: *hundreds of people*. **6** (in *pl*; *in cmpds*) the hundred years of a particular century: *the thirteen-hundreds*. **7** (*hist*) a division of an English county. — *adj* totalling one hundred. — *n* & *adj* **hundredth**. [OE]

hundredfold *n*, *adj* & *adv* (an amount which is) one hundred times as much or as great.

hundreds and thousands *n* (*pl*) tiny balls of coloured sugar used to decorate cakes.

hundredweight *n* **-*weight*** or **-*weights*** **1** (also **long hundredweight**) (*Br*) a measure of weight equal to 112 pounds (50·8 kilograms). **2** (also **short hundredweight**) (*NAm*) a measure of weight equal to 100 pounds (45·4 kilograms). **3** (also **metric hundredweight**) a metric measure of weight equal to 50 kilograms.

hung *v* see **hang**. — *adj* (of a parliament or jury) with no one side having a majority. — **hung over** (*coll*) suffering from a hangover. — **hung up** (*coll*) extremely worried about something, often for no good reason. [**hang**]

Hung. *abbrev* Hungarian.

Hungarian *adj* of Hungary or its official language. — *n* **1** a citizen of or person from Hungary. **2** the official language of Hungary.

hunger *n* **1** the desire or need, esp. very great, for food. **2** a strong desire: *hunger for affection*. — *v* (*intr*; **for, after**) to have a strong desire; to need or want food. [OE *hungor*]

hunger strike *n* a prolonged refusal to eat, usu. by a prisoner as a form of protest. — *n* **hunger striker**.

hungry *adj* **-*ier***, **-*iest*** **1** wanting or needing food. **2** (**for**) having a great desire. **3** greedy; eager: *hungry eyes*. — *adv* **hungrily**. — *n* **hungriness**. [OE *hungrig*]

hunk *n* **1** a lump broken or cut off from a larger piece. **2** (*coll*) a strong, muscular, sexually attractive man. [Perhaps a variant of **haunch**]

hunky *adj* **-*ier***, **-*iest*** (*coll*) (of a man) strong, muscular and sexually attractive.

hunky-dory *adj* (*coll*) (of a situation) quite satifactory; excellent.

hunt *v* **1** (*tr* & *intr*) to chase and kill (animals) for food or for sport. **2** (*intr*; *Br*) to hunt foxes using hounds, and on horseback. **3** (*intr*; **for**) to search: *hunt for a new house*. **4** (*tr*; **down, out**) to search for and find or capture. — *n* **1** an act or instance of hunting. **2** a group of people meeting together on horses to hunt foxes. **3** the area where such a group of people hunts. — *n* **hunting**. [OE *huntian*]

hunter *n* **1** a person who hunts. **2** an animal that hunts, usu. other animals for food. **3** a horse used in hunting, esp. fox-hunting. **4** a watch with a hinged metal cover to protect the glass over its face.

huntress *n* a female hunter (sense **1**).

huntsman *n* **1** a person who hunts. **2** an official who manages the hounds during a fox-hunt.

hurdle *n* **1** one of a series of light frames or hedges to be jumped in a race. **2** (in *pl*) such a race. **3** a problem or difficulty. **4** a light frame with bars or wire across it, used as a temporary fence. — *v* (*tr* & *intr*) to jump (hurdles) in a race. — *n* **hurdling**. [OE *hyrdel*]

hurdler *n* **1** a person or horse that runs hurdle races. **2** a person who makes hurdles.

hurdy-gurdy *n* **-*ies*** a musical instrument with strings which make a droning sound when they are sounded by a wheel turned by a handle. [A variant of Scots *hirdy-girdy*, uproar]

hurl *v* (*tr*) **1** to throw violently. **2** to speak (esp. words of abuse or insults) with force and spite. [MidE *hurlen*]

hurling or **hurley** *n* a traditional Irish game resembling hockey, played by two teams with 15 players each. [**hurl**]

hurly-burly *n* the noisy activity of crowds of people; uproar. [From obsolete *hurling*, uproar]

hurrah *n* & *interj* a shout of joy, enthusiasm or victory. [Ger *hurra*]

hurricane *n* a violent storm, esp. one with winds blowing at over 75 miles (120 km) per hour. [Native West Indian *hurakán*]

hurricane lamp *n* an oil lamp in which the flame is enclosed in glass to protect it from the wind.

hurry *v* **-*ies***, **-*ied*** **1** (*intr* & *tr*) to (cause to) move or act quickly. **2** (*tr*) to cause to move or progress too quickly. — *n* **1** great haste or speed. **2** the need for haste or speed. **3** eagerness. — *v* **hurry up** (*tr* & *intr*) to (cause to) move more quickly than before. — **in a hurry 1** hurrying; rushed. **2** easily: *He won't beat her in a hurry*. **3** willingly; eagerly: *won't do that again in a hurry*. [Prob. imit.]

hurried *adj* done or forced to act quickly, esp. too quickly. — *adv* **hurriedly**. — *n* **hurriedness**.

hurt *v* ***hurt*** **1** (*tr*) to injure or cause physical pain to. **2** (*tr*) to upset or cause mental or emotional pain to. **3** (*intr*) to be injured or painful. — *n* **1** an injury or wound. **2** mental pain or suffering. — *adj* **1** injured. **2** upset; distressed. [OFr *hurter*, to knock against]

hurtful *adj* causing mental or emotional pain. — *adv* **hurtfully**. — *n* **hurtfulness**.

hurtle *v* (*tr* & *intr*) to move or throw very quickly and violently. [MidE *hurtlen*]

husband *n* a man to whom a woman is married. — *v* (*tr*) to use (money, resources, etc.) wisely and with economy. [OE *husbonda*]

husbandry *n* **1** farming. **2** the management, esp. careful, of one's money and resources.

hush *interj* be quiet; be still. — *n* silence, esp. after noise. — *v* (*tr* & *intr*) to make or become quiet, calm or still. — *adj* **hushed**. — *v* **hush up** (*tr*) to prevent (something) becoming known; to keep secret. [Imit.]

hush-hush *adj* (*coll*) secret.

hush money *n* (*coll*) money paid to someone in return for his or her agreeing to keep certain facts secret.

husk *n* the thin, dry covering of certain fruits and seeds. — *v* (*tr*) to remove the husk of. [MidE *huske*]

husky[1] *adj* **-ier, -iest** **1** (of a voice) rough and dry in sound. **2** (*coll*) (usu. of a man) big and strong. — *adv* **huskily**. — *n* **huskiness**. [**husk**]

husky[2] *n* **-ies** a medium-sized, thick-set dog with a thick coat and curled tail, used as sled dog in the Arctic. [Inuit]

hussar *n* a soldier in a cavalry regiment who carries only light weapons. [Hung *huszar*]

hussy *n* **-ies** (*derog*) a shameless or immodest girl or woman. [A contraction of **housewife**]

hustings *n* (*pl*) **1** the platform, etc. from which speeches are made during a political election campaign. **2** the speeches, etc. made during an election campaign. [OE *husting*, tribunal, from *hus*, house + *thing*, assembly]

hustle *v* **1** (*tr*) to push quickly and roughly; to jostle. **2** (*tr*; **into, out of, through, etc.**; *coll*) to force (someone) to act or deal with (something) quickly. **3** (*intr*; *slang*) to work as a prostitute. — *n* **1** lively activity. **2** (*slang*) a swindle. [Dut *huselen*, to shake]

hustler *n* (*slang*) **1** a swindler. **2** a prostitute.

hut *n* a small house or shelter, usu. made of wood. [OGer *hutta*]

hutch *n* a box with a wire front in which small animals, e.g. rabbits, are kept. [OFr *huche*]

hyacinth *n* a plant which grows from a bulb and has sweet-smelling flowers, grown either in the garden or in pots indoors. [Gr *Hyakinthos*, in the Greek myths, a youth from whose blood sprang a blue flower when he was killed by Apollo]

hyaena. Same as **hyena**.

hybrid *n* **1** an animal or plant produced by crossing different species or varieties. **2** anything produced by combining elements from different sources. — *adj* produced by combining elements from different species, varieties, etc. — *n* **hybridism**.

hybridise or **-ize** *v* **1** (*tr*) to cause (different species, etc.) to breed together. **2** (*intr*) to produce hybrids. — *n* **hybridisation** or **-z-**.

hydr-. See **hydro-**.

hydra *n* **1** a freshwater polyp with a tube-like body and tentacles round the mouth. **2** anything which it is hard to finish, get rid of or destroy. [Gr, in the Greek myths, a water-snake with many heads which grew again when they were cut off]

hydrangea *n* a garden shrub with clusters of pink or blue flowers. [**hydr-** + Gr *angeion*, vessel]

hydrant *n* a pipe connected to the main water supply esp. in a street, with a nozzle for attaching a hose when fighting fires. [Gr *hydor*, water]

hydrate *n* a chemical compound of water and another compound or an element. — *v* (*tr*) **1** to combine (a chemical) with water. **2** to cause to absorb water. — *n* **hydration**. [Gr *hydor*, water]

hydraulic *adj* **1** worked by the pressure of water or some other liquid carried in pipes: *hydraulic brakes*. **2** relating to hydraulics. — *adv* **hydraulically**. [Gr *hydor*, water + *aulos*, pipe]

hydraulics *n* (*sing*) the study of the behaviour of moving liquids (e.g. of water in pipes) and of how to use them, esp. for power.

hydride *n* a chemical compound of hydrogen plus another element, esp. a metal. [Gr *hydor*, water]

hydro[1] *n* **-os** (*old*) a hotel or clinic providing hydropathic treatment. [**hydropathic**]

hydro[2] *n* **-os** a plant producing hydroelectric power. [**hydroelectric**]

hydro- or **hydr-** *comb fm* **1** of or by means of water: *hydroelectricity*. **2** combined with hydrogen. [Gr *hydor*, water]

hydrocarbon *n* a compound of hydrogen and carbon.

hydrocephalus *n* the condition of having an abnormal amount of liquid in the brain, causing the head to become enlarged. — *adj* **hydrocephalic**. [Gr *hydor*, water + *kephale*, head]

hydrochloric acid *n* a solution of the gas hydrogen chloride in water, a powerful acid used in industry.

hydrodynamics *n* (*sing*) the science of the movement and power of liquids.

hydroelectricity *n* electricity produced by means of water-power. — *adj* **hydroelectric**. — *adv* **hydroelectrically**.

hydrofoil *n* **1** a device on a boat which lifts it out of the water as its speed accelerates. **2** a boat fitted with such a device. [**hydro-** + **aerofoil**]

hydrogen *n* a gas (symbol **H**), the lightest element known, which produces water when combined with oxygen. — *adj* **hydrogenous**. [Gr *hydor*, water + *gennaein*, to produce]

hydrogenate *v* (*tr*) to combine (a substance) with hydrogen. — *n* **hydrogenation**.

hydrogen bomb *n* a very powerful bomb in which the explosion is caused by the fusion of nuclei.

hydrogen peroxide *n* an oily, liquid chemical used as a bleach.

hydrography *n* the science of charting seas, rivers and lakes. — *n* **hydrographer**. — *adj* **hydrographic**. [**hydro-** + **-graphy**]

hydrology *n* the study of the water resources on earth, and the movement of water in relation to land. [**hydro-** + **-logy**]
hydrolysis *n* the decomposition of organic compounds by the action of water. [**hydro-** + Gr *lysis*, a loosening]
hydrometer *n* a floating instrument for measuring the density of liquids. [**hydro-** + **-meter**]
hydropathy *n* a way of treating disease or illness using water both internally and externally. — *adj* **hydropathic**. [**hydro-** + Gr *patheia*, suffering]
hydrophobia *n* **1** the fear of water. **2** the inability to swallow water, esp. as a symptom of rabies. **3** rabies. — *adj* **hydrophobic**. [**hydro-** + **phobia**]
hydroplane *n* **1** a light, flat-bottomed motorboat which, at high speeds, skims along the surface of the water. **2** a fin-like device on a submarine which allows it to rise and fall in the water.
hydroponics *n* (*sing*) the art or science of growing plants in water, or in sand or gravel through which water is pumped, rather than in soil. — *adj* **hydroponic**. [**hydro-** + Gr *ponos*, work]
hydrosphere *n* the water, e.g. seas and rivers, on the surface of the earth. [**hydro-** + **sphere**]
hydrostatics *n* (*sing*) the science of the behaviour and power of liquids which are not moving. — *adj* **hydrostatic**. [**hydro-** + Gr *-states*, causing to stand]
hydrotherapy *n* the treatment of illness and disability by bathing and exercising in water.
hydrous *adj* (of substances) containing water. [Gr *hydor*, water]
hydroxide *n* (*chem*) a compound containing one or more hydroxyl groups. [**hydroxyl** + **-ide**]
hydroxyl *n* one atom of oxygen and one atom of hydrogen forming a compound together. [**hydrogen** + **oxygen** + Gr *hyle*, matter]
hyena *n* a dog-like animal with a shrill cry which sounds like human laughter. [Gr *hys*, pig]
hygiene *n* the practice or study of staying healthy and preventing the spread of disease, esp. by keeping oneself and one's surroundings clean. — *adj* **hygienic**. — *adv* **hygienically**. [Gr *hygieia*, health]
hygrometer *n* an instrument for measuring the humidity of the air or other gases. [Gr *hygros*, wet + **-meter**]
hygroscope *n* an instrument which can show changes in air humidity without measuring it. [Gr *hygros*, wet + **-scope**]
hygroscopic *adj* **1** of a hygroscope. **2** (of a substance) able to absorb moisture from the air.
hymen *n* a thin piece of skin that partially closes the vagina and is usu. broken the first time a woman has sexual intercourse. [Gr, membrane]
hymenopterous *adj* of an order of insects which have four transparent wings, e.g. ants, bees and wasps. [Gr *hymen*, membrane + *pteron*, wing]
hymn *n* a song of praise, esp. to God. [Gr *hymnos*]
hymnal or **hymnary**, *-ies* *n* a book containing hymns.
hymnody *n* **1** the writing of hymns. **2** hymns as a group.
hymnology *n* the study or writing of hymns. — *n* **hymnologist**.
hype[1] (*coll*) *n* intensive, exaggerated and usu. misleading publicity or advertising of something. — *v* (*tr*; **up**) to advertise intensively.
hype[2] *v* (*intr*; **up**; *slang*) to inject oneself with a drug. — **hyped up** (*slang*) highly excited, esp. as if by drugs. [Abbrev. of **hypodermic**]
hyper *adj* (*coll*) (of a person) over-excited; over-active. [Abbrev. of **hyperactive**]
hyper- *comb fm* over; beyond; more than normal: *hyperactive*. [Gr *hyper*, over]
hyperactive *adj* (esp. of a child) more active than is normal.
hyperbola *n* *-as* or *-ae* (*geom*) a plane curve produced when a section is cut in a cone at a steeper angle to its base than its side. — *adj* **hyperbolic** or **hyperbolical**. [Gr *hyperbole*, excess]
hyperbole *n* the use of an overstatement or exaggeration to produce an effect. — *adj* **hyperbolic** or **hyperbolical**. [Gr, excess]
hypercritical *adj* over-critical. — *adv* **hypercritically**.
hyperglycaemia *n* the condition of having too much sugar in the blood. [**hyper-** + Gr *glykys*, sweet]
hypermarket *n* a very large supermarket. [Fr *hypermarché*]
hypersensitive *adj* very sensitive, or more sensitive than is normal. — *n* **hypersensitivity**.
hypersonic *adj* having a speed more than five times the speed of sound. [**hyper-** + **supersonic**]
hypertension *n* abnormally high blood pressure.
hypertrophy *n* *-ies* an abnormal enlargement of an organ or cell. [**hyper-** + Gr *-trophia*, nutrition]
hyperventilation *n* an abnormal increase in the speed and depth of breathing.
hyphen *n* a punctuation mark (-) used to join two words as a compound (*barrel-chested*) or two parts of a word split over the end of one line and the beginning of the following one. — *v* *-n-* (*tr*) to hyphenate. [Gr *hypo*, under + *hen*, one]
hyphenate *v* *-n-* (*tr*) to join (two words or parts of words) with a hyphen. — *n* **hyphenation**.
hypnosis *n* *-oses* a sleep-like state in which the subject is totally relaxed and acts only on the suggestion of another person. [Gr *hypnos*, sleep]

hypnotic *adj* **1** of, causing, or caused by, hypnosis. **2** causing sleepiness. — *n* **1** a drug that produces sleep or hypnosis. **2** a person in a state of hypnosis. — *adv* **hypnotically**.

hypnotise or **-ize** *v (tr)* **1** to put (someone) in a state of hypnosis. **2** to fascinate or bewitch.

hypnotism *n* the science or practice of hypnosis. — *n* **hypnotist**.

hypnotherapy *n* the treatment of illness or habits such as smoking by hypnosis. [*hypno-*, of hypnosis]

hypo *n* **-os** *(coll)* a hypodermic syringe or injection. [Abbrev. of **hypodermic**]

hypo- *comb fm* under; beneath; inadequate: *hypotension.* [Gr *hypo*, under]

hypocaust *n* a hollow space under a floor or between double walls in ancient Roman houses, into which hot air was passed as a form of heating. [Lat *hypocaustum*, from Gr *hypo*, under + *kaiein*, to burn]

hypochondria *n* excessive worry about one's health. [Gr *hypochondrion*, abdomen, formerly believed to be the source of melancholy]

hypochondriac *n* a person suffering from hypochondria. — *adj* of or relating to hypochondria or hypochondriacs. — *adj* **hypochondriacal**.

hypocrisy *n* **-ies** the act or state of pretending to have feelings or beliefs which one does not actually have, or of hiding one's true character. [Gr *hypokrisis*, play-acting]

hypocrite *n* a person who pretends to have feelings or beliefs he or she does not actually hold, or who hides his or her true character. — *adj* **hypocritical**. — *adv* **hypocritically**.

hypodermic *adj* (of an instrument or drug) for injecting under the skin. — *n* **1** a hypodermic syringe. **2** an injection of a drug under the skin. [**hypo-** + Lat *dermis*, skin]

hypodermic syringe *n* a syringe with a fine hollow needle, used for injecting drugs under the skin or taking blood samples.

hypotension *n* abnormally low blood-pressure.

hypotenuse *n* *(math)* the longest side of a right-angled triangle, opposite the right angle. [Gr *hypoteinousa*, subtending]

hypothermia *n* a medical condition, caused by exposure to cold, in which the body temperature falls below normal. [**hypo-** + Gr *therme*, heat]

hypothesis *n* **-eses** a statement or proposition assumed to be true and on which an argument, etc. may be based. [Gr, supposition]

hypothesise or **-ize** *v* **1** *(intr)* to form a hypothesis. **2** *(tr)* to assume as a hypothesis.

hypothetical *adj* based on hypothesis; assumed. — *adv* **hypothetically**.

hysterectomy *n* **-ies** the surgical removal of a woman's womb. [Gr *hystera*, womb + **-ectomy**]

hysteria *n* **1** a mental disorder caused by a disturbance in the nervous system, with symptoms which often include emotional outbursts such as uncontrolled crying. **2** any wild or uncontrolled emotional state, esp. excessive laughing or crying. [Gr *hystera*, womb, from the former belief that disturbances in the womb caused emotional imbalance]

hysteric *n* a person suffering from hysteria.

hysterical *adj* **1** of or suffering from hysteria. **2** *(coll)* very funny. — *adv* **hysterically**.

hysterics *n (pl)* **1** a fit of hysteria. **2** *(coll)* uncontrollable laughter.

Hz *abbrev* hertz.

I

I[1] or **i** *n* ***I's*** or ***Is***, ***i's*** the ninth letter of the English alphabet.

I[2] *pron* used by the speaker or writer to refer to himself or herself as the subject of an actual or implied verb. [OE *ic*]

I[3] *abbrev* **1** Isle. **2** Island. **3** Institute.

I[4] *symbol* **1** (*chem*) iodine. **2** the Roman numeral for one.

IA or **Ia** *abbrev* Iowa.

-ial *sfx* **1** forming adjectives meaning 'of, relating to': *managerial*. **2** forming nouns meaning 'the action of': *tutorial*. [Lat *-ialis*]

iambus *n* ***-buses*** or ***-bi*** (also **iamb**) (*poetry*) a metrical foot containing one short or unstressed syllable followed by one long or stressed one. [Gr *iambos*, from *iaptein*, to lampoon, this verse form being first used by satirists]

iambic *adj* of or using iambuses. — *n* an iambus.

-ian *sfx* **1** forming adjectives meaning 'relating to, similar to': *Dickensian*. **2** forming nouns meaning 'a person interested or skilled in': *historian*.

ib. *abbrev* ibidem.

IBA *abbrev* (*Br*) Independent Broadcasting Authority.

Iberian *adj* of the Iberian Peninsula (now divided into Spain and Portugal), its inhabitants, languages, culture and history. — *n* a person from the Iberian Peninsula; a Spaniard or Portuguese. [Lat *Iberia*]

ibex *n* ***ibex***, ***ibexes*** or ***ibices*** a wild mountain goat with large, ridged, backward-curving horns, found in Europe, N Africa and Asia. [Lat]

ibid. *abbrev* ibidem.

ibidem *adv* in the same place in a book, article, passage, etc. previously mentioned or cited. [Lat, in the same place]

-ibility. See **-ible**.

ibis *n* ***ibis*** or ***ibises*** a wading bird with a long, slender, downward-curving beak. [Egyptian *hb*]

-ible *sfx* forming adjectives meaning 'that may be or is capable of being': *inexpressible*. — *n sfx* **-ibility**. — *adv sfx* **-ibly**. ◇ See also **-able**. [Lat *-ibilis*]

-ic *sfx* **1** (also **-ical**, though often with some difference in meaning) relating to: *historic*, *historical*; *photographic*; *political*. **2** (*chem*) formed with an element in its higher valency: *sulphuric*. ◇ See also **-ous**. — *adv sfx* **-ically**. ◇ See also **-ics**. [Fr *-ique*]

ICBM *abbrev* intercontinental ballistic missile.

ice *n* **1** frozen water. **2** a sheet of this, e.g. lying on the surface of water or a road. **3** (a portion of) ice-cream or water ice. **4** (*slang*) diamonds. **5** coldness of manner; reserve. — *v* **1** (*tr*) to cool with ice. **2** (*intr*; **over**, **up**) to become covered with ice; to freeze. **3** (*tr*) to cover (a cake) with icing. — *adj* **iced**. — **break the ice** to relax feelings of reserve, shyness or formality, esp. between strangers. — **cut no ice** to count for nothing. — **on ice** in readiness or reserve, either to be used later, or awaiting further attention. — **(skate) on thin ice** (to be) in a difficult, delicate or potentially embarrassing situation. [OE *is*]

ice age *n* a period of time during which large areas of the earth's surface are covered with ice, esp. (often *caps* with **the**) the Pleistocene epoch.

ice-axe *n* an axe used by mountain-climbers to cut holes in the ice for their hands and feet.

iceberg *n* a huge mass of ice floating in the sea, most of which lies hidden beneath the water. — **the tip of the iceberg** the small visible or perceived part of a much larger problem, most of which is unknown.

iceberg lettuce *n* a crisp, light-green type of lettuce.

icebox *n* **1** a refrigerator compartment where food is kept frozen and ice is made. **2** a container packed with ice, for keeping food cold. **3** (*NAm*) a refrigerator.

icebreaker *n* a ship designed to cut channels through floating ice.

ice-bucket *n* a small bucket for ice cubes, used for keeping bottles of wine cold.

icecap *n* a permanent covering of ice, e.g. on top of a mountain, or at the North or South Poles.

ice cream *n* a sweet, creamy frozen dessert, made either from cream or a substitute, and flavoured.

ice cube *n* a small block of ice used for cooling drinks, etc.

ice field *n* a large area covered with ice, esp. floating ice.

ice floe *n* a large sheet of ice floating on the sea.

ice hockey *n* a form of hockey played on ice by skaters, and with a puck instead of a ball.

ice lolly *n* (*Br coll*) flavoured water or ice-cream, frozen on a small stick.

ice pack *n* **1** a bag packed with crushed ice, used in medicine e.g. to reduce a swelling or to reduce a patient's temperature. **2** an area of pack ice.

ice pick *n* **1** a tool with a pointed end used by rock and mountain climbers for splitting ice. **2** a similar smaller tool for breaking ice into small pieces for drinks.

ice skate *n* a skate with a metal blade for use on ice.

ice-skate *v* (*intr*) to skate on ice. — *n* **ice-skater**. — *n* **ice-skating**.

icing *n* **1** a mixture of sugar, egg whites, water and sometimes lemon juice or other flavouring, used to form a hard coating on cakes. **2** the forming of ice on a ship or aircraft. — **the icing on the cake** (*coll*) a desirable although unnecessary addition to something which is already satisfactory.

icing sugar *n* sugar in the form of a very fine powder used to make icing, sweets, etc.

icy *adj* **-ier**, **-iest 1** very cold. **2** covered with ice. **3** (of someone's manner, behaviour, etc.) unfriendly; hostile. — *adv* **icily**. — *n* **iciness**.

Icelandic *adj* of Iceland or the Germanic language spoken in Iceland. — *n* the Icelandic language.

ichneumon *n* **1** any of several winged insects which lay their larvae in or on the larvae of other insects, esp. caterpillars. **2** a mongoose, esp. the Egyptian species which destroys crocodile eggs. [Gr, tracker]

ichthyology *n* the study of fishes. — *adj* **ichthyological**. — *n* **ichthyologist**. [Gr *ichthys*, fish + **-logy**]

icicle *n* a long hanging spike of ice, formed by water freezing as it drops. [OE *isgicel*]

icon or **ikon** *n* **1** an image of Christ, the Virgin Mary or a saint, usu. painted on wood or done as a mosaic, esp. in the Orthodox church. **2** a picture, image or representation. **3** (*comput*) an image on a computer screen which represents a function, operation, file, etc. which is available, and which may be selected using the cursor rather than a typed command. [Gr *eikon*, image]

iconoclast *n* **1** a person who destroys religious images and is opposed to their use in worship. **2** a person who is opposed to and attacks traditional and cherished beliefs and superstitions. — *n* **iconoclasm**. — *adj* **iconoclastic**. [Gr *eikon*, image + *klastes*, breaker]

icosahedron *n* **-rons** or **-ra** a solid figure with twenty faces. [Gr *eikosi*, twenty + *hedra*, seat]

-ics *sfx* denoting (in *sing*) a science or (in *pl*) something related to or the subject of that science: *acoustics*; *mathematics*. [Fr *-iques*, from Gr *-ika*]

icy. See **ice**.

ID *abbrev* **1** identification. **2** (also **Id**.) Idaho.

I'd 1 I had. **2** I would.

id *n* (*psychol*) the part of the unconscious mind which contains a person's inherited instincts, desires and needs which govern much of that person's (unconscious) behaviour. [Lat, it]

Id al-Adha *n* the Muslim 'Feast of Sacrifice' celebrating Abraham's faith in being willing to sacrifice his son. [Arabic]

Id al-Fitr *n* the Muslim 'Feast of Breaking Fast', celebrated on the first day after Ramadan. [Arabic]

-ide *sfx* (*chem*) denoting a compound of an element with some other element, etc., e.g. *chloride*, a compound of chlorine. ◇ See also **-ate** and **-ite**.

idea *n* **1** a thought, image, notion or concept formed by the mind. **2** a plan or intention. **3** a main aim, purpose or feature: *The idea of the game is to win as many cards as possible*. **4** an opinion or belief: *He's got the idea that no one likes him*. **5** a vague notion or fancy: *have no idea of the work required*. **6** a person's conception of what is the best or perfect example of something: *not my idea of fun*. **7** in Plato's philosophy, a universal model of which all existing examples are imperfect copies. — **get ideas** (*coll*) to have ideas which are either overambitious or undesirable. — **put ideas into someone's head** to cause someone to have overambitious or impractical ideas. [Lat, from Gr, form, pattern]

ideal *adj* **1** perfect; highest and best possible. **2** existing only in the mind; imaginary; visionary. — *n* **1** the highest standard of behaviour, perfection, beauty, etc. **2** a person or thing considered to be perfect. — *adv* **ideally**. [Lat *idealis*]

idealise or **-ize** *v* **1** (*tr*) to regard or treat (a person, etc.) as perfect or ideal. **2** (*intr*) to form ideas. — *n* **idealisation** or **-z-**.

idealism *n* **1** a tendency to show or present things in an ideal or idealised form rather than as they really are. **2** the practice of forming, and living according to, ideals. **3** (*philos*) the theory that material objects and the external world do not really exist but are products of the mind. ◇ See also **realism**. — *adj* **idealistic**. — *adv* **idealistically**.

idealist *n* **1** a person who lives or tries to live according to ideals. **2** an impractical person. **3** (*philos*) a believer in idealism.

idée fixe *n* ***idées fixes*** an idea which dominates the mind; an obsession. [Fr, fixed idea]

idem *adv* & *pron* (in) the same author, place, etc. as previously mentioned. [Lat, the same]

identical *adj* **1** being very similar or exactly alike in every respect. **2** being the very same. **3** (of twins) developed from a single egg and therefore of the same sex and practically indistinguishable in appearance. — *adv* **identically**. — *n* **identicalness**. [Lat *identicus*, from *idem*, the same]

identify *v* **-ies**, **-ied 1** (*tr*) to recognise (someone or something) as being a particular person or thing; to establish the identity of. **2** (*tr*; **with**) to associate (one person, thing or group) with another. **3** (*intr*; **with**) to feel sympathy and understanding for (a person, character in a novel, etc.) because one thinks of oneself as having personal characteristics or experiences in common with him or her. **4** (*tr*) to see clearly or pinpoint (a problem, method, solution, etc.). — *adj* **identifiable**. [Lat *idem*, the same + *facere*, to make]

identification *n* **1** an act of identifying or process of being identified. **2** something which allows a person or thing to be identified.

identification parade *n* (*Br*) a line of people containing one person who is suspected of a crime and others who are innocent of it, from which a witness will try to identify the criminal.

Identikit® *n* a series of transparent strips, each one showing a different typical facial feature, from which an impression or rough picture of a criminal or suspect can be put together from witnesses' descriptions.

identity *n* **-ies 1** the state or quality of being a specified person or thing; who or what a person or thing is: *The winner's identity is not yet known.* **2** the individual characteristics by which a person or thing can be identified; individuality; personality. **3** the state of being exactly the same. **4** (in full **identity element**; *math*) a member of a set which does not change another member of that set when combined with it: *The identity element for the multiplication of numbers is 1.* **5** (*math*) an equation which remains true whichever way it is written or expressed, and whichever values are substituted for the letters used. [Lat *identitas*, from *idem*, the same]

identity card *n* a card bearing information about, and often a photograph of, the holder, taken as proof of a person's identity.

identity crisis *n* (*psychol*) mental confusion and distress caused by an inability to control or bring together different elements of one's personality.

identity element *n* (*math*) an element which when combined with another element in a certain mathematical operation gives that second element as the product of the operation, *0* in addition (as $a + 0 = a$) and *1* in multiplication (as $a \times 1 = a$).

identity parade *n* same as **identification parade.**

ideogram *n* a written character or symbol that stands for the thing or concept it represents directly, rather than for a sequence of sounds forming a word, e.g. number symbols, the £ and $ signs, some Chinese and Japanese characters and some ancient Egyptian hieroglyphics. — *adj* **ideogramic, ideogrammic** or **ideogrammatic.** [Gr *idea*, idea + *gramma*, drawing]

ideograph *n* an ideogram. — *adj* **ideographic.** — *adv* **ideographically.** [Gr *idea*, idea + *graphein*, to write]

ideology *n* **-ies 1** the body of ideas and beliefs which form the basis for a social, economic or political system: *Thatcherite ideology.* **2** the opinions, beliefs and way of thinking characteristic of a particular person, group of people or nation. — *adj* **ideological.** — *adv* **ideologically.** — *n* **ideologist.** [Gr *idea*, idea + **-logy**]

Ides *n* (*pl*) (in the ancient Roman calendar) the fifteenth day of March, May, July and October and the thirteenth day of the other months. [Lat *idus*]

idiocy *n* **-ies 1** the state of being an idiot or extremely retarded mentally. **2** a foolish action or foolish behaviour. [**idiot**]

idiolect *n* an person's individual and distinctive way of speaking. [Gr *idios*, own + dia*lect*]

idiom *n* **1** an expression with a meaning which cannot be guessed at or derived from the meanings of the individual words which form it. **2** the syntax, grammar and forms of expression peculiar to a language or a variety of language. **3** the language, vocabulary, forms of expression, etc. used by a particular person or group of people. **4** the characteristic style or forms of expression of a particular artist, musician, artistic or musical school, etc. — *adj* **idiomatic.** — *adv* **idiomatically.** [Gr *idios*, own]

idiosyncrasy *n* **-ies** any personal way of behaving, reacting or thinking; a personal peculiarity or eccentricity. — *adj* **idiosyncratic.** — *adv* **idiosyncratically.** [Gr *idios*, own + *syn*, together + *krasis*, mixing]

idiot *n* **1** (*coll*) a foolish or stupid person. **2** a person who is severely mentally retarded. — *adj* **idiotic.** — *adv* **idiotically.** [Gr *idiotes*, person lacking skill or expertise]

idle *adj* **1** not in use; not being used; unoccupied. **2** not wanting to work; lazy; indolent. **3** having no effect, result, purpose or value: *idle gossip.* **4** without cause, basis or good reason; unnecessary: *idle rumour.* — *v* **1** (*tr*; **away**) to spend (time) doing nothing or being idle. **2** (*intr*) to do nothing or be idle. **3** (*intr*) (of an engine, machinery, etc.) to run gently without doing any work. **4** (*tr*) to cause (an engine, etc.) to idle. — *n* **idleness.** — *n* **idler.** — *adv* **idly.** [OE *idel*, worthless]

idol *n* **1** an image or symbol, esp. of a god, used as an object of worship. **2** an object of excessive love, honour or devotion. [Gr *eidolon*]

idolise or **-ize** *v* (*tr*) **1** to love, honour, admire, etc. (a person) too much. **2** to make an idol of. — *n* **idoliser** or **-z-.** — *n* **idolisation** or **-z-.**

idolater or **idolatress** *n* **1** a man or woman who worships idols. **2** a man or woman who is a passionate and devoted admirer (of someone or something).

idolatry *n* **-ies 1** the worship of idols. **2** excessive, love, honour, admiration or devotion. — *adj* **idolatrous.** — *adv* **idolatrously.**

idyll or **idyl** *n* **1** a short poem or prose work describing a simple, pleasant, usu. rural or pastoral scene. **2** a story, episode or scene suitable for such a work, e.g. one of happy innocence or love. — *adj* **idyllic.** — *adv* **idyllically.** [Gr *eidyllion*]

i.e. *abbrev* for *id est* (Lat), that is to say.

if *conj* **1** in the event that; on condition that; supposing that. **2** although; even though. **3** whenever. **4** whether. **5** used to express a wish: *If only it would stop raining*. **6** used to make a polite request or suggestion: *If you wouldn't mind stopping just a minute*. **7** used to express surprise or annoyance: *Well, if it isn't that book I'd thought I'd lost!* — *n* a condition or supposition: *too many ifs and buts*. — **if anything** perhaps; on the contrary. [OE *gif*]

iffy *adj* **-ier**, **-iest** (*coll*) uncertain; doubtful; dubious.

igloo *n* a dome-shaped Inuit house built with blocks of snow and ice. [Inuit *iglu*, house]

igneous *adj* **1** of or like fire. **2** (of rocks) formed by molten rock from the earth's core becoming hard. [Lat *ignis*, fire]

ignis fatuus *n* ***ignes fatui*** a will-o'-the-wisp. [Lat, foolish fire]

ignite *v* **1** (*tr*) to set fire to. **2** (*intr*) to catch fire. **3** (*tr*) to heat to the point at which combustion occurs. **4** (*tr*) to excite (feelings, emotions, etc.). — *adj* **ignitable** or **ignitible**. [Lat *ignis*, fire]

ignition *n* **1** the system or mechanism (e.g. an electric spark) used to ignite the fuel in an internal combustion engine. **2** the act or process of igniting.

ignoble *adj* **1** causing shame; dishonourable; mean. **2** of humble or low birth. — *adv* **ignobly**. — *n* **ignobility** or **ignobleness**. [Lat *ignobilis*]

ignominy *n* **1** public shame, disgrace or dishonour. **2** dishonourable conduct. [Lat *ignominia*]

ignominious *adj* causing shame or dishonour; humiliating. — *adv* **ignominiously**. — *n* **ignominiousness**.

ignoramus *n* **-ses** an ignorant person. [Lat, we do not know]

ignorant *adj* **1** knowing very little; uneducated. **2** (with **of**) knowing little or nothing (about). **3** rude; ill-mannered. — *adv* **ignorantly**. — *n* **ignorance**. [Lat *ignorare*, not to know]

ignore *v* (*tr*) to take no notice of deliberately; to refuse to pay attention to. [Lat *ignorare*, not to know]

iguana *n* ***-nas*** or ***-na*** a large grey-green tree-dwelling lizard with a row of spines along the back. [Carib (S American Indian language) *iwana*]

ikebana *n* the Japanese art of flower arranging. [Jap]

ikon. See **icon**.

IL *abbrev* Illinois.

il-. See **in-**[1,2].

ileum *n* ***ilea*** the lower part of the small intestine leading into the large intestine. [Lat *ilia*, groin, guts]

ilium *n* ***ilia*** the uppermost and largest of the three bones forming either side of the pelvis. — *adj* **iliac**. [Lat *ilia*, groin, guts]

ilk *n* type; kind; class. — *adj* (*Scot*) same. — **of that ilk 1** of that type or kind. **2** (*Scot*) of that same, i.e. of the estate or place of the same name (as the person's family name). [OE *ilca*]

ill *adj* ***worse***, ***worst*** **1** not in good health; sick. **2** (of health) not good. **3** bad or harmful: *ill effects*; *ill-treatment*. **4** hostile; unfriendly: *ill-will*. **5** causing bad luck: *an ill omen*. **6** (of manners) incorrect; improper. — *adv* ***worse***, ***worst*** **1** not easily; with difficulty. **2** hardly, scarcely: *be ill able to afford the money*. **3** badly; wrongly: *ill-matched*. **4** unfavourably: *It went ill with them*. **5** harshly: *speak ill of someone*. — *n* **1** evil; harm. **2** injury; ailment. — **ill at ease** uneasy; embarrassed. — **ill become one** to do one no credit; not to be to one's advantage. — **take it ill** to be offended. [Norse *illr*]

ill-advised *adj* foolish; done, or doing things, with little thought or consideration.

ill-assorted *adj* badly matched; not going well together.

ill-bred *adj* badly brought up or educated; rude.

ill-considered *adj* badly thought out; not well planned.

ill-disposed *adj* **(towards)** unfriendly; unsympathetic; unwilling to support or help.

ill-equipped *adj* poorly provided (with the necessary tools, abilities, etc.).

ill-fated *adj* ending in or bringing bad luck or ruin.

ill-favoured *adj* not attractive, esp. in appearance; objectionable.

ill-feeling *n* bad or hostile feeling; animosity.

ill-founded *adj* (of an argument, theory, suspicion, etc.) without basis or reason.

ill-gotten *adj* obtained dishonestly: *ill-gotten gains*.

ill-humoured *adj* bad-tempered; quick-tempered.

ill-informed *adj* lacking knowledge or information.

ill-judged *adj* poorly advised; done without proper consideration.

ill-mannered *adj* having bad manners; rude; uncouth.

ill-natured *adj* spiteful; mean; surly.

illness *n* **1** a disease. **2** the state of being sick or unwell.

ill-omened *adj* (of a plan, course of action, etc.) likely to end badly.

ill-starred *adj* marked by bad luck; bound to fail.

ill-tempered *adj* bad-tempered; spiteful and surly.

ill-timed *adj* said or done at an unsuitable time; inopportune.

ill-treat *v* (*tr*) to treat badly or cruelly; to abuse. — *n* **ill-treatment**.

ill-will *n* bad or unfriendly feeling; the urge or wish to do harm: *bear him no ill-will*.

Ill. *abbrev* Illinois.

I'll I will or I shall.

illegal *adj* against the law; not legal. — *n* **illegality**, **-ies**. — *adv* **illegally**. [Lat *illegalis*]
illegible *adj* difficult or impossible to read. — *n* **illegibility** . — *adv* **illegibly**. [**il-** (see **in-**[1]) + **legible**]
illegitimate *adj* **1** born of parents not married to each other at the time of birth. **2** unacceptable or not allowed, esp. illegal. **3** (*logic*) not properly inferred or reasoned. **4** improper. — *n* **illegitimacy**. — *adv* **illegitimately**. [**il-** (see **in-**[1]) + **legitimate**]
illiberal *adj* **1** having strict opinions about morality, behaviour, etc; narrow-minded; prejudiced. **2** not generous; mean. **3** uncultured; unrefined. — *n* **illiberality** . — *adv* **illiberally**. [Lat *illiberalis*]
illicit *adj* not permitted by law or by social custom. — *adv* **illicitly**. — *n* **illicitness**. [Lat *illicitus*]
illiterate *adj* **1** unable to read and write. **2** uneducated or ignorant, esp. in a particular field or subject. — *n* an illiterate person. — *n* **illiteracy**. — *adv* **illiterately**. [Lat *illiteratus*]
illogical *adj* **1** not based on careful thinking or reason. **2** not following the principles of logic. — *n* **illogicality**, **-ies**. — *adv* **illogically**. [**il-** (see **in-**[1]) + **logical**]
illuminant *n* something that gives off light. — *adj* giving off light. [Lat *illuminare*, from *lumen*, light]
illuminate *v* (*tr*) **1** to light up or make bright. **2** to decorate with lights. **3** to decorate (a manuscript) with elaborate designs and initial letters in gold, silver or bright colours. **4** to make clearer and more easily understood. **5** to enlighten spiritually or intellectually. — *adj* **illuminating**. — *adj* **illuminative**. [Lat *illuminare*, from *lumen*, light]
illumination *n* **1** the act of illuminating or state of being illuminated. **2** any source of light; lighting. **3** (in *pl*) coloured, decorative lights hung in streets and towns. **4** the art or skill of decorating manuscripts with elaborate designs and initial letters in gold, silver and bright colours. **5** such a design or initial letter in a manuscript.
illumine *v* (*tr*; *poetic* or *literary*) to illuminate. [OFr *illuminer*]
illusion *n* **1** a deceptive or misleading appearance. **2** a false or misleading impression, idea, belief or understanding; delusion. **3** (*psychol*) the state of forming false impressions of objects, or perceiving them wrongly; an object which is falsely perceived. [Lat *illusio*, irony, mocking]
illusionist *n* a conjurer who plays tricks on the eyes.
illusive or **illusory** *adj* **1** seeming to be or having the characteristics of an illusion. **2** deceptive; unreal.
illustrate *v* (*tr*) **1** to provide (a book, text, lecture, etc.) with pictures and diagrams. **2** to make (a statement, etc.) clearer, esp. by providing examples. **3** to be an example of. — *adj* **illustrated**. — *n* **illustrator**. [Lat *illustrare*, to light up]
illustration *n* **1** a picture or diagram that helps make a text, book, lecture, etc. clearer, or decorates it. **2** an example which makes something clear. **3** the act of illustrating or state of being illustrated.
illustrative *adj* being or acting as an illustration, explanation or example. — *adv* **illustratively**.
illustrious *adj* distinguished; renowned; celebrated; noble. — *adv* **illustriously**. — *n* **illustriousness**. [Lat *illustris*, bright, lustrous]
im-. See **in-**[1,2].
I'm I am.
image *n* **1** a likeness of a person or thing, esp. in the form of a portrait or statue. **2** a person or thing that resembles another person or thing closely. **3** an idea or picture in the mind. **4** an optical reproduction of an object formed by light reflected in a mirror or refracted through a lens. **5** (in full **public image**) the impression that people in general have of someone's character, behaviour, etc. **6** a typical example or embodiment. **7** a simile or metaphor. — *v* (*tr*) **1** to form an image of. **2** to form a likeness of in the mind; to imagine. **3** to mirror. **4** to be a typical example of. [Lat *imago*]
imagery *n* **-ies** **1** (the use of) figures of speech in a piece of literature, etc. **2** the making of images, esp. in the mind. **3** mental images. **4** statues, carvings, etc.
imagine *v* **1** (*tr* & *intr*) to form a mental picture (of something). **2** (*tr*) to see or hear, etc. something which is not true or does not exist: *imagine things*. **3** (*tr*) to think, suppose or guess: *I can't imagine where she's got to*. **4** (*intr*) to use the imagination. **5** (*intr* & *tr*; usu. as *interj*) used to express surprise: *Imagine that!* — *adj* **imaginable**. [Lat *imaginari*, from *imago*, image]
imaginary *adj* **1** existing only in the mind or imagination; not real. **2** (*math*) relating to or being the square root of a number less than 0.
imagination *n* **1** (the part of the mind responsible for) the ability to form or act of forming mental images of things, etc. one has not seen or of which one has no direct perception or knowledge. **2** the creative ability of the mind. **3** the ability to cope resourcefully with unexpected events or problems.
imaginative *adj* **1** showing, done with or created by imagination. **2** having a lively imagination. — *adv* **imaginatively**. — *n* **imaginativeness**.
imaginings *n* (*pl*) things seen or heard which do not exist; fancies; fantasies.
imago *n* **-gos**, **-goes** or **-gines** the last stage in an insect's development, when it is perfect and fully mature. [Lat, image]
imam *n* **1** a leader of prayers in a Mosque. **2** (*cap*) a title given to various Muslim leaders, e.g. a Shiite religious leader

believed to be a direct successor of the prophet Mohammed, or a learned Muslim theologian. [Arabic, chief, leader]

imbalance *n* a lack of balance or proportion; inequality. [**im-** (see **in-**[1]) + **balance**]

imbecile *n* **1** a person of very low intelligence, esp. someone who is capable only of keeping himself or herself out of danger and of performing simple tasks under supervision. **2** a stupid person; a fool. — *adj* mentally weak; stupid; foolish. — *n* **imbecility**. [Lat *imbecillus*]

imbed *v* **-*dd*-**. Same as **embed**.

imbibe *v* **1** (*tr* & *intr*) to drink (esp. alcoholic drinks). **2** (*tr*) to take in or absorb (ideas, etc.). [Lat *imbibere*]

imbroglio *n* **-*os*** **1** a confused mass or heap. **2** a confused and complicated situation. **3** a misunderstanding or disagreement. [Ital, confusion]

imbue *v* (*tr*; **with**) **1** to fill or inspire, esp. with ideals or principles. **2** to soak or saturate, esp. with dye. [Lat *imbuere*, to saturate]

IMF *abbrev* International Monetary Fund.

imitate *v* (*tr*) **1** to copy the behaviour, manners, appearance, etc. of; to take as a model. **2** to mimic. **3** to make a copy of; to reproduce or duplicate. — *adj* **imitable**. — *n* **imitator**. [Lat *imitari*]

imitation *n* **1** an act of imitating. **2** that which is produced by imitating; a copy or counterfeit. **3** (*mus*) the repeating of a passage, phrase, theme, etc. which has already been heard, often at a different pitch or in a different voice. — *adj* cheaply made to look or function like something which is more expensive.

imitative *adj* **1** imitating, copying or mimicking. **2** copying a more expensive original. **3** (of a word) imitating the sound (e.g. *sizzle*) or trying to represent the appearance, movement or general impression (e.g. *flash*) of a thing or action. — *adv* **imitatively**. — *n* **imitativeness**.

immaculate *adj* **1** perfectly clean and neat; perfectly groomed. **2** free from blemish, flaw or error; pure. — *adv* **immaculately**. [Lat *in-*, not + *macula*, spot, stain]

the Immaculate Conception *n* the Roman Catholic dogma that the Virgin Mary was conceived free from original sin.

immanent *adj* **1** existing or remaining within; inherent. **2** (of a supreme being or power, esp. God) present everywhere. — *n* **immanence** or **immanency**. [Lat *in*, in + *manere*, to remain]

immaterial *adj* **1** not important. **2** not formed of matter. [Lat *immaterialis*]

immature *adj* **1** not fully grown or developed; not ripe. **2** not fully developed emotionally or intellectually and therefore childish. — *adv* **immaturely**. — *n* **immaturity**. [Lat *immaturus*]

immeasurable *adj* too great to be measured; very great; immense. — *adv* **immeasurably**. [**im-** (see **in-**[1]) + **measurable**]

immediate *adj* **1** happening or done at once and without delay. **2** nearest or next in space, time or relationship: *the immediate family; the immediate vicinity*. **3** of the current time; urgent: *deal with the immediate problems first*. **4** having a direct effect and without anything coming in between: *the immediate cause of death*. — *n* **immediateness**. [Lat *immediatus*]

immediacy *n* **-*ies*** **1** the quality of being immediate or appealing directly to the emotions, understanding, etc. **2** an immediate problem, requirement or necessity.

immediately *adjv* at once or without delay; without anything coming in between. — *conj* as soon as.

immemorial *adj* extending far back in time beyond anyone's memory or written records: *a custom since time immemorial*. — *adv* **immemorially**. [Lat *immemorialis*]

immense *adj* **1** very or unusually large or great. **2** (*coll*) very good. — *adv* **immensely**. — *n* **immenseness** or **immensity**, **-*ies***. [Lat *immensus*, immeasurable]

immerse *v* (*tr*) **1** (**in**) to dip into or under the surface of a liquid completely. **2** to baptise by submerging the whole body in water. **3** (**in**) to engage or involve deeply; to absorb: *immersed in the book*. — *adj* **immersible**. — *n* **immersion**. [Lat *immergere*, to dip]

immersion heater *n* an electric water-heater which is immersed directly in a tank of water.

immigrate *v* (*intr*) to move into a foreign country with the intention of settling in it. ◇ See also **emigrate**. — *n* **immigration**. [Lat *immigrare*]

immigrant *n* **1** a person who immigrates. ◇ See also **emigrant**. **2** (*biol*) an animal or plant which becomes established in an area where it was previously not found. — *adj* of or being an immigrant.

imminent *adj* (esp. of something unpleasant) likely to happen very soon. — *n* **imminence**. [Lat *imminere*, to project over]

immobile *adj* **1** not able to move or be moved. **2** not moving; motionless. — *n* **immobility**. [Lat *immobilis*]

immobilise or **-ize** *v* (*tr*) to make or keep immobile. — *n* **immobilisation** or **-z-**.

immoderate *adj* going far beyond normal or reasonable limits; extreme; excessive. — *n* **immoderacy** — *adv* **immoderately**. — *n* **immoderateness**. [Lat *immoderatus*]

immodest *adj* **1** lacking modesty; shameful; indecent; improper. **2** boastful and conceited; forward. — *adv* **immodestly**. — *n* **immodesty**. [Lat *immodestus*]

immolate *v* (*tr*) to kill or offer in sacrifice. — *n* **immolation**. [Lat *immolare*, to sprinkle with meal before sacrificing]

immoral *adj* **1** morally wrong or bad; evil. **2** not conforming to the sexual standards of society; promiscuous. — *n* **immorality**, *-ies*. — *adv* **immorally**. ◇ See also **amoral**. [**im-** (see **in-**[1]) + **moral**]

immortal *adj* **1** living forever and never dying. **2** lasting forever; perpetual. — *n* **1** a person who will live forever, or who will always be remembered. **2** (in *pl*) the ancient Greek and Roman gods. — *n* **immortality**. [Lat *immortalis*]

immortalise or **-ize** *v* (*tr*) to make (a person, event, etc.) famous forever, e.g. by including him, her or it in a work of art, esp. literature.

immovable *adj* **1** impossible to move; not meant to be moved. **2** steadfast; unyielding. **3** incapable of feeling or showing emotion, esp. sorrow or pity. **4** (*legal*) (of property) consisting of land or houses. — *n* **immovability** or **immovableness**. — *adv* **immovably**. [**im-** (see **in-**[1]) + **movable**]

immune *adj* **1** (**to**) protected by inoculation from, or having a natural resistance to, a particular disease. **2** (**from**) free, exempt or protected from. — *n* **immunity**, *-ies*. [Lat *immunis*]

immunise or **-ize** *v* (*tr*; **against**) to make immune, esp. to a disease, and esp. by inoculation with antigens which cause the body to produce anitbodies. — *n* **immunisation** or **-z-**.

immunodeficiency *n* *-ies* a deficiency or breakdown in the body's ability to fight infection. [**immune** + **deficiency**]

immunology *n* the scientific study of resistance to, and protection against, infection. — *adj* **immunological**. — *n* **immunologist**. [**immune** + **-logy**]

immure *v* (*tr*) **1** to enclose or imprison within, or as if within, walls. **2** to shut (someone or oneself) away. [Lat *in*, in + *murus*, wall]

immutable *adj* that cannot be changed or will not change. — *n* **immutability**. — *adv* **immutably**. [Lat *immutabilis*]

imp *n* **1** a small mischievous or evil spirit. **2** a mischievous or annoying child. — *adj* **impish**. — *adv* **impishly**. — *n* **impishness**. [OE *impa*, shoot]

impact *n* **1** the act of an object hitting or colliding with another object; a collision. **2** the force of such a collision. **3** a strong effect or impression. — *v* **1** (*tr*) to press (two objects) together with force or to force (one object) into (another). **2** (*intr*) to come into contact with force. [Lat *impingere*, to strike against]

impacted *adj* **1** (of a tooth) unable to grow because of being wedged between the jawbone and another tooth. **2** (of a fracture) with the two broken ends of bone crushed together.

impair *v* (*tr*) to damage or weaken, esp. in quality or strength. — *n* **impairment**. [OFr *empeirer*]

impala *n* *-las* or *-la* *n* a graceful African antelope with lyre-shaped horns, capable of long high leaps. [Zulu]

impale *v* (*tr*) **1** (**on, upon, with**) to pierce with or as if with a long pointed object or weapon. **2** to put (two coats-of-arms) on a shield divided vertically into two. — *n* **impalement**. [Lat *in*, in + *palus*, stake]

impalpable *adj* **1** not able to be felt or perceived by touch. **2** difficult to understand or grasp. — *n* **impalpability**. — *adv* **impalpably**. [Lat *impalpabilis*]

impanel *v* *-ll-* Same as **empanel**.

impart *v* (*tr*) **1** to make (information, knowledge, etc.) known; to communicate (news, etc.). **2** to give or transmit (a particular quality). — *n* **impartation**. [Lat *impartire*]

impartial *adj* not favouring one person, etc. more than another; fair and unbiased. — *n* **impartiality**. — *adv* **impartially**. [**im-** (see **in-**[1]) + **partial**]

impassable *adj* not able to be passed through or travelled along. — *n* **impassability** or **impassableness**. — *adv* **impassably**. [**im-** (see **in-**[1]) + **passable**]

impasse *n* a situation in which progress is impossible and from which there is no way out. [Fr]

impassion *v* *-n-* (*tr*) to move with or fill with passion. [Ital *impassionare*]

impassioned *adj* moved by or showing very strong feelings.

impassive *adj* **1** incapable of feeling and expressing emotion. **2** showing no feeling or emotion. — *adv* **impassively**. — *n* **impassiveness** or **impassivity**. [**im-** (see **in-**[1]) + **passive**]

impasto *n* in painting and pottery, the technique of laying the paint or pigment on thickly. [Ital]

impatient *adj* **1** unwilling to wait or delay. **2** intolerant. **3** restlessly eager and anxious. — *n* **impatience**. — *adv* **impatiently**. [Lat *impatiens*]

impeach *v* (*tr*) **1** (*Br*) to charge with a serious crime, esp. a crime against the state or treason. **2** (esp. *NAm*) to accuse (a public or government official) with misconduct while in office. **3** to call into question; to cast doubt upon (e.g. a person's honesty). — *adj* **impeachable**. — *n* **impeachment**. [Lat *impedicare*, to fetter]

impeccable *adj* **1** free from fault or error. **2** not liable to sin. — *adv* **impeccably**. [Lat *impeccabilis*]

impecunious *adj* having little or no money; poor; penniless. — *adv* **impecuniously**. — *n* **impecuniousness**. [**im-** (see **in-**[1]) + obsolete *pecunious*, wealthy]

impede *v* (*tr*) to prevent or delay the start or progress of (an activity, etc.); to obstruct or hinder. [Lat *impedire*, to snare the foot]

impedance *n* **1** anything that impedes. **2** (*electr*) a seeming increase of resistance to the flow of an alternating current in an electrical circuit.

impediment *n* **1** a thing or person that delays or prevents the start or progress of something; an obstacle or hindrance. **2** a minor defect in a person's speech, e.g. a lisp. [Lat *impedimentum*]
impedimenta *n* (*pl*) any objects which impede progress or movement, esp. military baggage and equipment.

impel *v* **-ll-** (*tr*) **1** to push, drive or urge forward; to propel. **2** to force or urge into action. [Lat *impellare*]

impend *v* (*intr*) **1** to be about to happen. **2** (**over**) (of a danger, etc.) to threaten; to hover threateningly. — *adj* **impending**. [Lat *impendere*, to hang over]

impenetrable *adj* **1** incapable of being entered or passed through. **2** not capable of receiving or being touched by intellectual ideas and influences. — *adv* **impenetrably**. — *n* **impenetrability**. [Lat *impenetrabilis*]

impenitent *adj* not sorry for having done something wrong; unrepentant. — *n* **impenitence**. — *adv* **impenitently**. [Lat *impaenitens*]

imperative *adj* **1** absolutely essential; urgent. **2** having or showing authority; commanding. **3** (*gram*) of or being the mood of a verb used to give orders. — *n* **1** (*gram*) (a verb in) the imperative mood. **2** that which is imperative, esp. a command or order. — *adv* **imperatively**. [Lat *imperativus*, from *imperare*, to command]

imperceptible *adj* **1** too small or slight to be seen, heard, noticed, etc. **2** not able to be perceived by the senses. — *n* **imperceptibility**. — *adv* **imperceptibly**. [Lat *imperceptibilis*]

imperfect *adj* **1** having faults; spoilt; not perfect. **2** lacking the full number of parts; incomplete. **3** (*gram*) of or being the verb tense expressing a continuing state or incomplete action, usu. in the past. — *n* (*gram*) (a verb in) the imperfect tense. — *adv* **imperfectly**. [Lat *imperfectus*]
imperfection *n* **1** the state of being imperfect. **2** a fault, weakness or blemish.

imperial *adj* **1** of or suitable for an empire, emperor or empress. **2** having supreme authority. **3** commanding; august. **4** regal; magnificent. **5** (*Br*) (of a non-metric weight or measurement, or a system of these) conforming to standards fixed by parliament. — *adv* **imperially**. [Lat *imperialis*]
imperialism *n* **1** rule by an emperor or empress. **2** the policy or principle of having and extending control over the territory of other nations, or of extending one's country's influence through trade and diplomacy, etc. — *n & adj* **imperialist**. — *adj* **imperialistic**. — *adv* **imperially**.

imperil *v* **-ll-** (*tr*) to put in danger. — *n* **imperilment**. [**im-** (see **in-**[2]) + **peril**]

imperious *adj* arrogant, haughty and domineering. — *adv* **imperiously**. — *n* **imperiousness**. [Lat *imperiosus*]

imperishable *adj* which will not decay and will last forever. [**im-** (see **in-**[1]) + **perishable**]

impermanent *adj* not lasting or remaining; transient. — *n* **impermanence** or **impermanency**. [**im-** (see **in-**[1]) + **permanent**]

impermeable *adj* not allowing esp. liquids to pass through or penetrate. — *n* **impermeability**. [Lat *impermeabilis*]

impermissible *adj* not permitted or allowed. [**im-** (see **in-**[1]) + **permissible**]

impersonal *adj* **1** having no reference to any particular person; objective. **2** without or unaffected by personal or human feelings, warmth, sympathy, etc.; cold. **3** without personality. **4** (*gram*) (of a verb) used without a subject, or with a formal one, usu. *it*, as in *it's snowing*. **5** (*gram*) (of a pronoun) not referring to a definite person; indefinite. — *n* **impersonality**. — *adv* **impersonally**. [Lat *impersonalis*]

impersonate *v* (*tr*) to pretend to be, or copy the behaviour and appearance of, (another person), esp. to entertain or deceive. — *n* **impersonation**. — *n* **impersonator**. [Lat *in*, in + *persona*, person]

impertinent *adj* **1** rude; not showing respect where it is due; insolent. **2** (*archaic* or *legal*) not relevant. — *n* **impertinence**. — *adv* **impertinently**. [Lat *impertinens*]

imperturbable *adj* not easily worried or upset; always calm. — *n* **imperturbability**. — *adv* **imperturbably**. [Lat *imperturbabilis*]

impervious *adj* (**to**) **1** not allowing e.g. liquids to pass through or penetrate. **2** not influenced or affected (by). — *adv* **imperviously**. — *n* **imperviousness**. [Lat *impervius*]

impetigo *n* a contagious skin disease causing pustules and yellow sores. [Lat, from *impetere*, to attack]

impetuous *adj* **1** acting or done hurriedly and without thinking. **2** moving or acting forcefully or with great energy. — *n* **impetuosity** or **impetuousness**. — *adv* **impetuously**. [Lat *impetuosus*]

impetus *n* **-ses 1** the force or energy with which something moves. **2** a driving force. **3** an incentive or encouragement. [Lat, attack]

impi *n* **-is** or **-ies** a group of Zulu warriors. [Zulu]

impiety *n* **-ies** (an act showing) lack of piety or respect for religion. [Lat *impietas*]

impinge *v* (*intr*; **against, on, upon**) **1** to interfere (with) or encroach (on). **2** to come into contact (with). **3** to make an impression (on). — *n* **impingement**. [Lat *impingere*]

impious *adj* lacking respect or proper reverence for (e.g. God). — *adv* **impiously**. — *n* **impiousness**. [Lat *impius*]

implacable *adj* not able to be calmed, satisfied or appeased. — *n* **implacability** or **implacableness**. — *adv* **implacably**. [Lat *implacabilis*]

implant *v* (*tr*) **1** to fix or plant securely. **2** to fix (ideas, beliefs, etc.) permanently in a person's mind. **3** to put (tissue, hormones, etc.) permanently into the body. — *n* anything implanted, esp. tissue, a capsule containing a hormone, etc. in the body. — *n* **implantation**. [**im-** (see **in-**[2]) + **plant**]

implausible *adj* not easy to believe; not likely to be true. — *n* **implausibility**. — *adv* **implausibly**. [**im-** (see **in-**[1]) + **plausible**]

implement *n* a tool or utensil; a necessary piece of equipment. — *v* (*tr*) to carry out, fulfil or perform. — *n* **implementation**. [Lat *implementum*]

implicate *v* (*tr*) **1** to show or suggest that (a person) is involved, esp. in a crime. **2** to imply. [Lat *implicare*, to interweave]

implication *n* **1** the act of implicating or state of being implicated. **2** the act of implying or state of being implied. **3** that which is implied. — **by implication** by suggestion and without being stated directly.

implicit *adj* **1** implied or meant, although not stated directly. **2** (**in**) present, although not out in the open or visible: *be aware of the disappointment implicit in her words*. **3** unquestioning; complete. — *adv* **implicitly**. — *n* **implicitness**. [Lat *implicitus*, involved]

implode *v* (*intr* & *tr*) to (cause to) collapse inwards. — *n* **implosion**. — *adj* **implosive**. [**im-** (see **in-**[2]) + **explode**]

implore *v* (*tr*) **1** to entreat or beg (a person). **2** to beg for earnestly. — *adj* **imploring**. — *adv* **imploringly**. [Lat *implorare*]

imply *v* **-ies**, **-ied** (*tr*) **1** to suggest or express indirectly; to hint at. **2** to suggest or involve as a necessary result or consequence. — *adj* **implied**. ◇ See also **implication**. [Lat *implicare*, to interweave]

impolite *adj* not polite; rude. — *adv* **impolitely**. — *n* **impoliteness**. [**im-** (see **in-**[1]) + **polite**]

impolitic *adj* unwise; not to be advised. [**im-** (see **in-**[1]) + **politic**]

imponderable *n* & *adj* (something) having an influence or importance which is difficult or impossible to measure or estimate. [Lat *imponderabilis*]

import *v* (*tr*) **1** to bring (goods, etc.) in from another country. **2** to signify, imply or portend. — *n* **1** something imported. **2** the act or business of importing goods. **3** importance. **4** meaning. — *n* **importation**. — *n* **importer**. [Lat *importare*]

important *adj* **1** having great value, influence or effect. **2** (**to**) of great significance or value (to): *Her happiness is important to me*. **3** of high social rank or status; eminent. **4** pompous. — *n* **importance**. — *adv* **importantly**. [Lat *importare*, to be of consequence]

importunate *adj* **1** persistent or excessively demanding. **2** extremely urgent. — *adv* **importunately**. [Lat *importunus*, inconvenient]

importune *v* (*tr* & *intr*) **1** to make persistent and usu. annoying requests (of someone). **2** to solicit for immoral purposes, e.g. prostitution. — *n* **importunity**, **-ies**. [Lat *importunus*, inconvenient]

impose *v* **1** (*tr*; **on**, **upon**) to make (payment of a tax, fine, etc. or performance of a duty) compulsory; to enforce. **2** (*tr*; **on, upon**) to force (oneself, one's opinions and company, etc.) on. **3** (*intr*; **on, upon**) to take advantage (of); to set unfair burdens or tasks (on): *impose on his good nature*. **4** (*tr*; **on, upon**) to palm (something) off on someone dishonestly. **5** (*tr*) to arrange (pages) in the proper order for printing. [OFr *imposer*]

imposing *adj* impressive, esp. because of large size, dignity, handsome appearance, etc. — *adv* **imposingly.**

imposition *n* **1** the act of imposing or process of being imposed. **2** something imposed, esp. a tax, or an unfair or excessive demand or requirement. **3** (*Br*) work given as a punishment at school. **4** the arranging of pages in the proper order for printing. [Lat *impositio*]

impossible *adj* **1** that cannot be done or cannot happen. **2** that cannot be true; difficult to believe. **3** (*coll*) unacceptable, unsuitable, or difficult to bear; intolerable. — *adv* **impossibly**. [Lat *impossibilis*]

impossibility *n* **-ies 1** the state of being impossible. **2** something which is impossible.

impostor or **imposter** *n* a person who pretends to be someone else in order to deceive others. [Lat *imponere*, to impose]

imposture *n* (an act of) deceiving someone, esp. by pretending to be someone else.

impotent *adj* **1** powerless; lacking the necessary strength. **2** (of men) unable to maintain an erection and therefore unable to perform sexual intercourse. — *n* **impotence**. — *adv* **impotently**. [Lat *impotentia*, lack of self-control]

impound *v* (*tr*) **1** to shut (e.g. an animal) up in, or as if in, a pound; to confine. **2** to take legal possession of; to confiscate. **3** (of a reservoir, dam, etc.) to collect and hold (water). [**im-** (see **in-**[2]) + **pound**[2]]

impoverish *v* (*tr*) **1** to make poor. **2** to reduce the quality or fertility of (e.g. soil). — *adj* **impoverished**. — *n* **impoverishment**. [MidE *empoverishen*]

impracticable *adj* not able to be done, put into practice or used. — *n* **impracticability**. — *adv* **impracticably**. [**im-** (see **in-**[1]) + **practicable**]

impractical *adj* lacking common sense; not practical. ◇ See also **unpractical**. — *n* **impracticality**, **-ies**. — *adv* **impractically**. [**im-** (see **in-**[1]) + **practical**]

imprecate *v* (*tr*; *formal*) **1** to call down by prayer (esp. something evil). **2** (**upon**) to call down evil upon (someone); to curse. —

n **imprecation**. — *adv* **imprecatory**. [Lat *imprecari*, to pray to or for]

imprecise *adj* not precise; inaccurate. — *n* **imprecision**. [**im-** (see **in-**[1]) + **precise**]

impregnable *adj* **1** not able to be seized, defeated or taken by force. **2** not able to be affected by criticism, doubts, etc. — *n* **impregnability**. — *adv* **impregnably**. [MidE]

impregnate *v* (*tr*) **1** (**with**) to permeate completely or saturate. **2** (**with**) to fill or imbue. **3** to make pregnant or fertilise. — *n* **impregnation**. [Lat *impraegnare*, to fertilise]

impresario *n* **-os** an organiser of public entertainments, e.g. concerts, or the manager of an opera or theatre company. [Ital]

impress *v* **1** (*tr* & *intr*) to produce a strong, lasting and usu. favourable impression on (someone). **2** (*tr*; **on, upon**) to make very clear or emphasise (to). **3** (*tr*) to make or stamp (a mark) on by applying pressure. **4** (*tr*; **on, upon**) to fix (a fact, etc.) firmly in the mind or memory. — *n* **1** the act of impressing. **2** that which is made by impressing or being impressed, such as a mark or impression. [Lat *imprimere*, to press into or on]

impression *n* **1** an (esp. favourable) idea or effect produced in the mind or made on the senses. **2** a vague or uncertain idea, notion or belief. **3** an act of or the process of impressing. **4** a mark or stamp produced by, or as if by, impressing or pressure. **5** an imitation, esp. a caricature, of a person, or an imitation of a sound, done for entertainment. **6** the number of copies of a book, newspaper, etc. printed at one time. **7** (a copy made by) the pressing of a prepared inked plate or type on to the paper, etc. being printed.

impressionable *adj* easily impressed or influenced. — *n* **impressionability**. — *adv* **impressionably**.

impressionism *n* (also *cap*) **1** a 19th-century movement in painting which aimed to represent nature, esp. the play of light on objects, exactly as seen by the artist, without regard for the classical rules of composition, colouring, etc. **2** a style of music or writing which aims to give a general impression of feelings and events rather than a detailed description of them. — *n* & *adj* **impressionist** (also *cap*).

impressionistic *adj* based on impressions or personal observation as distinct from definite facts or particular knowledge. — *adv* **impressionistically**.

impressive *adj* capable of making a deep impression on a person's mind, feelings, etc.; causing admiration, wonder or approval. — *adv* **impressively**. — *n* **impressiveness**.

imprimatur *n* **1** a licence or permission to print or publish a book, granted esp. by the Roman Catholic church. **2** approval; permission. [Lat, let it be printed]

imprint *n* **1** a mark or impression made by pressure. **2** a permanent effect, e.g. on the mind, produced by some experience or event. **3** a publisher's name and address, printed at the bottom of a book's title page. — *v* (*tr*) **1** to mark or print an impression of (something). **2** to fix firmly in the mind. [**im-** (see **in-**[2]) + **print**]

imprison *v* **-n-** (*tr*) to put in prison. — *n* **imprisonment**. [**im-** (see **in-**[2]) + **prison**]

improbable *adj* **1** unlikely to happen or exist; not probable. **2** hard to believe. — *n* **improbability**, **-ies**. — *adv* **improbably**. [**im-** (see **in-**[1]) + **probable**]

improbity *n* **-ies** dishonesty; wickedness. [**im-** (see **in-**[1]) + **probity**]

impromptu *adj* & *adv* (made or done) without preparation; improvised; spontaneous(ly). — *n* **1** something that is impromptu. **2** a piece of music which suggests improvisation. [Lat *in promptu*, in readiness]

improper *adj* **1** not confroming to accepted standards of modesty and moral behaviour; unseemly; indecent. **2** not correct; wrong. **3** not suitable. — *adv* **improperly**. [Lat *improprius*]

improper fraction *n* a fraction in which the numerator has a value which is equal to or higher than that of the denominator, e.g. $\frac{5}{4}$. ◇ See also **proper fraction**.

impropriety *n* **-ies** **1** an improper act or improper use of a word. **2** the state of being improper; indecency. [Lat *improprietas*]

improve *v* **1** (*tr* & *intr*) to make or become better, of higher quality or value; to (cause to) make progress. **2** (*intr* with **on, upon**) to produce something better, of higher quality or value than (a previous example). **3** (*tr*) to increase the value or beauty of (land or property) by cultivation, laying out gardens, building, etc. [OFr *emprower*, from *prou*, profit]

improvement *n* **1** the act of improving or state of being improved. **2** something that adds beauty, quality, value, etc. **3** something which has been improved.

improvident *adj* **1** not considering or providing for likely future needs; lacking foresight. **2** careless; thoughtless. — *n* **improvidence**. — *adv* **improvidently**. [**im-** (see **in-**[1]) + **provident**]

improvise *v* **1** (*tr* & *intr*) to compose, recite or perform (music, verse, etc.) without preparing it in advance. **2** (*tr*) to make or provide quickly, without preparing in advance and using whatever materials are to hand. — *n* **improviser**. — *n* **improvisation**. [Lat *improvisus*, not foreseen]

imprudent *adj* not having or showing good sense or caution; rash; heedless. — *n* **imprudence**. — *adv* **imprudently**. [Lat *imprudens*, rash]

impudent *adj* rude, insolent or impertinent. — *n* **impudence**. — *adv* **impudently**. [Lat *impudens*, shameless]

impugn *v* (*tr*) to call into question or raise doubts about (a person's honesty, integrity, a claim, etc.); to criticise. — *adj* **impugnable**. — *n* **impugnment**. [Lat *impugnare*, to attack]

impulse *n* **1** a sudden push forwards; a force producing sudden movement forwards. **2** the motion or movement produced by such a force or push. **3** a sudden desire or urge to do something without thinking of the consequences: *bought the dress on impulse*. **4** an instinctive or natural tendency. **5** (*physiol*; also **nerve impulse**) an electrical stimulus in a nerve or muscle. **6** (*physics*) the product of the force produced when two objects or bodies collide and the time such a force lasts. **7** (*physics*) a change in an object's momentum caused by such a force. [Lat *impulsus*, pressure]

impulse buying *n* the buying of goods because one has a sudden desire or whim to do so, and not because such a purchase is planned.

impulsion *n* **1** an act of urging, forcing or pushing forwards, into motion or into action, or the state of being so urged. **2** a force which urges, etc. forwards, into motion, etc. **3** a sudden desire or urge.

impulsive *adj* **1** likely to act suddenly and without considering the consequences. **2** done without such consideration. **3** having the power to urge or push forwards, into motion or into action. — *adv* **impulsively**. — *n* **impulsiveness**.

impunity *n* freedom or exemption from punishment, injury, loss, or other ill consequences. — **with impunity** without having to suffer the normal ill consequences. [Lat *impunitas*]

impure *adj* **1** mixed with something else; adulterated. **2** dirty. **3** immoral; not chaste. **4** ritually unclean. [Lat *impurus*]

impurity *n* **-*ies*** **1** the state of being impure. **2** an impure or unclean thing or constituent.

impute *v* (*tr* with **to**) **1** to regard (usu. something bad, a crime, etc.) as being brought about by. **2** to believe (something) to be caused by (a person or thing): *imputed his failure to lack of work*. — *n* **imputation**. [Lat *imputare*, to bring into the reckoning]

IN *abbrev* Indiana.

In *symbol* (*chem*) indium.

in *prep* **1** used to express the position of a person or thing with regard to what encloses, surrounds or includes it, him, etc. **2** into: *get in the car*. **3** after (a period of time): *come back in an hour*. **4** during; while: *lost in transit*. **5** used to express arrangement or shape: *in a square*; *in alphabetical order*. **6** from; out of: *two in every eight*. **7** by the medium or means of; using: *sung in Italian*; *in code*. **8** wearing. **9** used to describe a state or manner: *in a hurry*. **10** used to state an occupation: *a job in local government*. **11** used to state a purpose: *a party in his honour*. **12** (of some animals) pregnant with: *in calf*. — *adv* **1** to or towards the inside; indoors. **2** at home or work. **3** so as to be added or included: *beat in the eggs*. **4** so as to enclose or conceal, or be enclosed or concealed. **5** in or into political power or office. **6** in or into fashion. **7** in a good position; in favour. **8** (in certain games) batting. **9** into a proper, required or efficient state: *run a new car in*. **10** (of the tide) at its highest point; as close to the shore as it gets. **11** (*in cmpds*) expressing prolonged activity, esp. by large numbers of people: *a sit-in*. — *adj* **1** internal; inside; inwards. **2** fashionable. **3** in power or office. **4** used for receiving things coming in: *an in-tray*. **5** (also *in cmpds*) shared by a group of people: *an in-joke*. — **have (got) it in for** (*coll*) to dislike and try to make life difficult for. — **in as far as, in so far as** or **insofar as** to the degree that. — **inasmuch as** or **in as much as** because; considering that. — **in for it** (*coll*) certain to experience trouble or difficulty. — **in on** (*coll*) knowing about and sharing in. — **ins and outs** the complex and detailed facts of a matter. — **insomuch (as) 1** to such an extent. **2** given that; because of the fact that. — **in with** very friendly with. [OE]

in-between *adj* coming between in space, time, style, etc.; neither one thing nor the other.

in-fighting *n* fighting or competition between members of the same group, company or organisation.

in-flight *adj* provided during an aircraft flight.

in-patient *n* a patient temporarily living in hospital while receiving treatment there.

in-service *adj* carried on while a person is employed.

in. *abbrev* inch.

in-[1] *pfx* (also **il-** before words beginning with **l**, **im-** before **b**, **m** and **p** and **ir-** before **r**) not; non-; lack of: *inhospitable*; *irrelevant*. [Lat]

in-[2] *pfx* (also **il-** before words or word-elements beginning with **l**, **im-** before **b**, **m** and **p** and **ir-** before **r**) in; into; towards; within: *intrude*; *imprison*. [Lat *in-*, OFr *en-*, in, into]

inability *n* **-*ies*** the lack of sufficient power, means or ability. [Lat *inhabilitas*]

in absentia *adv* in (his, her or their) absence. [Lat]

inaccessible *adj* **1** difficult or impossible to approach, reach or obtain. **2** (of a person) difficult to understand or influence; unapproachable. — *adv* **inaccessibly**. — *n* **inaccessibility**. [Lat *inaccessibilis*]

inaccurate *adj* containing errors; not correct or accurate. — *adv* **inaccurately**. [**in-**[1] + **accurate**]

inaccuracy *n* **-*ies*** **1** the state of not being inaccurate. **2** a mistake or error.

inaction *n* lack of action; sluggishness. [**in-**[1] + **action**]

inactive *adj* **1** taking little or no exercise; idle. **2** no longer operating or functioning. **3** (of members of a group, esp. members of the armed forces) not taking part in or available for e.g. military duties. **4** (*chem*) showing little or no reaction. — *adv* **inactively**. — *n* **inactivity**.

inadequate *adj* **1** not sufficient or adequate. **2** (of a person) not able to cope; not competent or capable. — *n* **inadequacy**, **-ies**. — *adv* **inadequately**. **[in-**[1] **+ adequate]**

inadmissible *adj* not allowable or able to be accepted. — *adv* **inadmissibly**. — *n* **inadmissibility** . **[in-**[1] **+ admissible]**

inadvertent *adj* **1** (of an act) not done on purpose; unintentional. **2** not paying proper attention; heedless. — *n* **inadvertence**. — *adv* **inadvertently**. [Lat *inadvertentia*, inadvertence]

inadvisable *adj* not wise; not to be advised. — *n* **inadvisability**. **[in-**[1] **+ advisable]**

inalienable *adj* not capable of being taken or given away (e.g. to another person). **[in-**[1] **+ alienable]**

inamorata *n* **-as** a woman who is in love or who is beloved. [Ital, from *innamorare*, to inflame with love]

inamorato *n* **-os** a man who is in love or who is beloved.

inane *adj* without meaning or point; silly. — *adv* **inanely**. [Lat *inanis*]

inanity *n* **-ies 1** the state of being inane. **2** an inane remark, action, etc.

inanimate *adj* **1** without life; not living: *inanimate objects*. **2** dull; spiritless. [Lat *inanimatus*]

inanition *n* emptiness or exhaustion, esp. physical from lack of food. [Lat *inanitio*]

inapplicable *adj* not applicable or suitable. — *n* **inapplicability**. — *adv* **inapplicably**. **[in-**[1]**+ applicable]**

inapposite *adj* not suitable or appropriate; out of place. — *adv* **inappositely**. — *n* **inappositeness**. **[in-**[1] **+ apposite]**

inappropriate *adj* **(to, for)** not suitable or appropriate. — *adv* **inappropriately**. — *n* **inappropriateness**. **[in-**[1] **+ appropriate]**

inapt *adj* **1** not suitable or appropriate. **2** lacking skill; unqualified. — *adv* **inaptly**. — *n* **inaptness**. **[in-**[1] **+ apt]**

inarticulate *adj* **1** unable to express oneself clearly or to speak distinctly. **2** badly expressed; not spoken or pronounced clearly. **3** not jointed or hinged. — *adv* **inarticulately**. — *n* **inarticulateness**. [Lat *inarticulatus*]

inartistic *adj* **1** not following the rules or principles of art. **2** not able to appreciate art. — *adv* **inartistically**. **[in-**[1] **+ artistic]**

inasmuch as. See **in**.

inattentive *adj* not paying proper attention; neglectful. — *n* **inattention**. — *adv* **inattentively**. — *n* **inattentiveness**. **[in-**[1] **+ attentive]**

inaudible *adj* not loud enough to be heard. — *n* **inaudibility**. — *adv* **inaudibly**. **[in-**[1] **+ audible]**

inaugural *adj* **1** relating to or describing a ceremony officially marking the beginning of something. **2** (of a speech, lecture, etc.) given by a person on taking office. — *n* an inaugural speech or lecture. [Lat *inaugurare*, to inaugurate]

inaugurate *v* (*tr*) **1** to place (a person) in office with a formal ceremony. **2** to mark the beginning of (some activity) with a formal ceremony. **3** to mark the opening of (a new building or service), esp. by being the first person to try it out. — *n* **inauguration**. — *n* **inaugurator**. [Lat *inaugurare*]

inauspicious *adj* not promising future success; not auspicious; unlucky. — *adv* **inauspiciously**. — *n* **inauspiciousness**. **[in-**[1] **+ auspicious]**

inboard *adj* & *adv* **1** (of a boat's motor or engine) (situated) inside the hull. **2** (situated) within or close to an aircraft's fuselage. ◇ See also **outboard**. **[in + board]**

inborn *adj* rooted in a person's nature; (seeming to have been) possessed by a person from birth; innate or hereditary. **[in + born]**

inbound *adj* (of a vehicle, passenger flight, etc.) coming in towards its destination; arriving. **[in + bound]**

inbreed *v* ***inbred*** (*tr*) to breed from closely related parents. — *n* **inbreeding**. **[in-**[2] **+ breed]**

inbred *adj* **1** inborn. **2** bred from closely related parents.

Inc. *abbrev* (esp. *US*) Incorporated.

incalculable *adj* **1** not able to be estimated or reckoned in advance; unpredictable. **2** too great to be measured. — *n* **incalculability**. — *adv* **incalculably**. **[in-**[1] **+ calculable]**

in camera *adv* **1** (*law*) in a judge's private room. **2** in secret; in private. [Lat, in a chamber]

incandescent *adj* **1** white or glowing with intense heat. **2** shining brightly. **3** of, relating to or being light produced by heating a substance until it glows white with intense heat. — *n* **incandescence**. — *adv* **incandescently**. [Lat *incandescere*, to glow]

incandesce *v* (*tr* & *intr*) to (cause to) glow white with intense heat.

incandescent lamp *n* a lamp with a filament which is heated until it glows white with intense heat.

incantation *n* **1** words said or sung as a spell; a magical formula. **2** the use of spells and magical formulae. — *adj* **incantatory**. [Lat *incantare*, to put a spell on]

incapable *adj* **(of) 1** not capable. **2** lacking the necessary ability (to do something). **3** unable or unfit to do anything, esp. look after one's own affairs. — *n* **incapability**. — *adv* **incapably**. [Lat *incapabilis*]

incapacitate *v* (*tr*) **1** to take away (a person's) strength, power or ability; to make (someone) unfit (for). **2** to disqualify legally. — *adj* **incapacitated**. — *n* **incapacitation**. **[incapacity]**

incapacity *n* **-ies 1** a lack of the necessary strength, power or ability. **2** legal disqualification. [Lat *incapacitas*]

incapsulate. Same as **encapsulate**.

incarcerate *v* (*tr*) to shut in or keep in prison. — *n* **incarceration**. [Lat *incarcerare*]

incarnate *adj* **1** in bodily, esp. human, form: *God incarnate*. **2** personified; typified. — *v* (*tr*) **1** to give bodily, esp. human, form to. **2** to personify or typify. [Lat *incarnare*, to make flesh]

incarnation *n* **1** the bodily, esp. human, form taken by a spirit or god. **2** (*cap*) the human form taken by Christ. **3** a person who personifies, or thing that typifies, a quality or idea. **4** the taking of bodily, esp. human, form by a spirit or god. **5** any of a succession of periods spent in a particular bodily form or state.

incautious *adj* acting or done without thinking; heedless. — *adv* **incautiously**. — *n* **incautiousness**. **[in-**[1] **+ cautious]**

incendiary *adj* **1** of or relating to the deliberate and illegal burning of property or goods. **2** (of e.g. a bomb) designed to start fires. **3** tending to cause trouble or violence. — *n* **-ies 1** a person who deliberately and illegally sets fire to buildings or property. **2** a device, e.g. a bomb, for starting fires. **3** a person who stirs up trouble or violence. — *n* **incendiarism**. [Lat *incendere*, to kindle]

incense[1] *n* **1** a spice or other substance which gives off a pleasant odour when burned, used esp. during religious services. **2** the odour or smoke given off by burning spices, etc. — *v* (*tr*) **1** to offer incense to (a god). **2** to perfume or fumigate with incense. [Lat *incensum*, thing burnt, from *incendere*, to kindle]

incense[2] *v* (*tr*) to make very angry. [Lat *incendere*, to kindle]

incentive *n* something that motivates or encourages an action, work, etc., such as extra money paid to workers to increase output. — *adj* serving to motivate or encourage. [Lat *incentivus*, provocative]

inception *n* a beginning. [Lat *incipere*, to begin]

incertitude *n* uncertainty; doubt. [Lat *incertitudo*]

incessant *adj* going on without stopping; continual. — *adv* **incessantly**. [Lat *in-*, not + *cessare*, to cease]

incest *n* (the crime of) sexual intercourse between people who are too closely related to be allowed to marry, e.g. between brother and sister. [Lat *incestum*, from *in-*, not + *castus*, chaste]

incestuous *adj* **1** of, guilty of or involving incest. **2** (of a relationship or group of people) too closed to outside influences or other people. — *adv* **incestuously**. — *n* **incestuousness**.

inch *n* **1** a measure of length equal to one twelfth of a foot (2·54 centimetres). **2** the amount of rain or snow that will cover a surface to the depth of one inch. **3** a small amount or distance. **4** (in *pl*) stature. — *v* (*tr* & *intr*) to move or be moved slowly, carefully and by degrees. — **every inch** completely; in every way. — **inch by inch** gradually; by small degrees. — **within an inch of** almost as far as. — **within an inch of one's life** almost as far as death; thoroughly: *beat him within an inch of his life*. [OE *ynce*]

inchoate *adj* **1** at the earliest stage of development; just beginning. **2** not fully developed; unfinished; rudimentary. — *adv* **inchoately**. — *n* **inchoateness**. [Lat *inchoare*, to begin]

incidence *n* **1** the frequency with which something happens or the extent of its influence. **2** the way in which something moving in a line, e.g. a ray of light, comes into contact with a surface. [Lat *incidentia*]

incident *n* **1** an event or occurrence. **2** an event or occurrence which is dependent on, related to or a consequence of something else. **3** a relatively minor event or occurrence which might have serious consequences. **4** a brief violent conflict or disturbance, e.g. a bomb explosion. — *adj* **1** (**to**) belonging naturally (to) or being a natural consequence (of). **2** (*legal*; **to**) dependent (on). **3** (*physics*) (of light rays, etc.) falling (on) or striking. [Lat *incidens*, from *in*, on + *cadere*, to fall]

incidental *adj* **1** happening, etc. by chance in connection with something else, and of secondary or minor importance: *incidental expenses*. **2** occurring or likely to occur as a minor consequence. — *n* **1** anything that occurs incidentally. **2** (in *pl*) minor expenses.

incidentally *adv* **1** by the way; parenthetically. **2** in an incidental manner.

incidental music *n* music which accompanies the action of a film, play, etc.

incinerate *v* (*tr*) to burn to ashes. — *n* **incineration**. [Lat *in*, in + *cinis*, ashes]

incinerator *n* a furnace or machine for burning rubbish, etc. to ashes.

incipient *adj* beginning to exist; in an early stage. — *n* **incipience** or **incipiency**. — *adv* **incipiently**. [Lat *incipere*, to begin]

incise *v* (*tr*) **1** to cut into. **2** to engrave (an inscription, stone, etc.). [Lat *incidere*, to cut into]

incision *n* **1** a cut, esp. one made by a surgeon. **2** an act of cutting, esp. by a surgeon.

incisive *adj* clear and sharp; to the point; acute. — *n* **incisiveness**. — *adv* **incisively**.

incisor *n* one of the eight (in humans) sharp cutting teeth in the front of the mouth.

incite *v* (*tr*; **to**) to stir up or provoke, e.g. to action. — *n* **incitement**. [Lat *incitare*, to urge forward]

incivility *n* **-ies 1** rudeness. **2** a rude act or remark. [Lat *incivilitas*]

incl. *abbrev* **1** including. **2** included. **3** inclusive.

inclement *adj* (of weather) stormy or severe; harsh. — *n* **inclemency, -ies**. [Lat *inclemens*]

incline *v* **1** (*tr* & *intr*; **to, towards**) to lean or cause to lean towards a particular opinion or conduct; to make or be disposed towards. **2** (*tr* & *intr*) to slope or cause to slope from a horizontal or vertical line or direction. **3** (*tr*) to bow or bend (the head, one's body) forwards or downwards. [Lat *inclinare*, to bend towards]

inclination *n* **1** a particular tendency or disposition, esp. a liking. **2** an act of inclining or bowing (the head, etc.); a bow or nod. **3** a slope. **4** the degree at which an object slopes away from a horizontal or vertical line or plane.

inclined plane *n* a plane surface at an angle to a horizontal surface, used esp. as a mechanism for lessening the force needed to raise or lower heavy objects.

include *v* (*tr*) **1** to take in or consider along with others as part of a group. **2** to contain or be made up of. [Lat *includere*]

inclusion *n* **1** the act of including or state of being included. **2** something which is included.

inclusive *adj* **1** comprehensive; including everything. **2** including the stated limits: *March to August inclusive*. — *adv* **inclusively**.

incognisant or **incognizant** *adj* **(of)** not aware (of); not knowing. — *n* **incognisance** or **-z-**. [**in-**[1] + **cognisant**]

incognito *adv* & *adj* keeping one's identity a secret, e.g. using a disguise and a false name. — *n* **-os 1** a person who is incognito. **2** the disguise and false name of a person who wishes to keep his or her identity secret. [Lat *incognitus*, unknown]

incoherent *adj* **1** (of speech or writing) not expressed clearly or logically; difficult to understand and follow. **2** (of a person) unable to speak clearly and logically. — *n* **incoherence**. — *adv* **incoherently**. [**in-**[1] + **coherent**]

incombustible *adj* incapable of being set alight or burned. [Lat *incombustibilis*]

income *n* money received over a period of time as payment for work, etc. or as interest or profit from shares or investment. [MidE, that which has come in]

income support *n* a state benefit paid to people on low incomes.

income tax *n* a personal tax levied on income over a certain amount.

incomer *n* a person who comes to live in a place, not having been born there. [**in** + **come**]

incoming *adj* **1** which is coming in; approaching. **2** next or following.

incommensurable *adj* (**with**) having no common standard or basis and not able to be compared. — *n* **incommensurability**. [Lat *incommensurabilis*]

incommensurate *adj* **1** (**with, to**) out of proportion (to); inadequate. **2** incommensurable. — *adv* **incommensurately**. — *n* **incommensurateness**. [**in-**[1] + **commensurate**]

incommode *v* (*tr*) to cause bother, trouble or inconvenience to. [Lat *incommodare*]

incommodious *adj* inconvenient or uncomfortable, esp. because too small. — *adv* **incommodiously**. — *n* **incommodiousness**. [Lat *incommodus*]

incommunicado *adv* & *adj* not allowed to communicate with other people, esp. because of being in solitary confinement. [Span *incomunicado*]

incomparable *adj* **1** without equal. **2** not to be compared. — *n* **incomparability**.— *adv* **incomparably**. — *n* **incomparableness**. [Lat *incomparabilis*]

incompatible *adj* **1** (of people) unable to live and work together in harmony. **2** (**with**) (of statements, etc.) not in agreement; inconsistent. **3** (e.g. of drugs) not able to be combined; mutually intolerant. — *n* **incompatibility**. — *adv* **incompatibly**. [Lat *incompatibilis*]

incompetent *adj* **1** lacking (the necessary) skill, ability or qualifications. **2** not legally qualified. — *n* **incompetence**. — *adv* **incompetently**. [Lat *incompetens*]

incomplete *adj* not complete or finished. — *adv* **incompletely**. — *n* **incompleteness**. [Lat *incompletus*]

incomprehensible *adj* difficult or impossible to understand. — *n* **incomprehensibility**. — *adv* **incomprehensibly**. [Lat *incomprehensibilis*]

incomprehension *n* inability or failure to understand.

inconceivable *adj* unable to be imagined, believed or conceived by the mind. — *n* **inconceivability**. — *adv* **inconceivably**. [**in-**[1] + **conceivable**]

inconclusive *adj* not leading to a definite conclusion, result or decision. — *adv* **inconclusively**. — *n* **inconclusiveness**. [**in-**[1] + **conclusive**]

incongruous *adj* out of place; unsuitable; inappropriate. — *adv* **incongruously**. — *n* **incongruousness**. [Lat *incongruus*]

incongruity *n* **-ies 1** the state of being incongruous. **2** something which is incongruous.

inconsequent *adj* **1** not following logically or reasonably; illogical. **2** irrelevant. **3** not connected or related. [Lat *inconsequens*]

inconsequential *adj* **1** of no importance or value. **2** illogical. — *n* **inconsequentiality, -ies**. — *adv* **inconsequentially**.

inconsiderable *adj* not worth considering; small in amount, value, etc. — *adv* **inconsiderably**. [Lat *inconsiderabilis*]

inconsiderate *adj* thoughtless, esp. in not considering the feelings, rights, etc. of others. — *adv* **inconsiderately**. — *n* **inconsiderateness** or **inconsideration**. [Lat *inconsideratus*]

inconsistent *adj* **1** (**with**) not in agreement or accordance (with). **2** (of a single thing) having contradictory or incompatible elements. **3** (of a person) not always thinking, speaking, behaving, etc. in accordance with the same principles; not consistent in thought, speech, behaviour, etc. — *n* **inconsistency**, **-ies**. — *adv* **inconsistently**. [**in-**[1] + **consistent**]

inconsolable *adj* not able to be comforted. — *adv* **inconsolably**. [Lat *inconsolabilis*]

inconspicuous *adj* not easily noticed; attracting little attention. — *adv* **inconspicuously**. — *n* **inconspicuousness**. [Lat *inconspicuus*]

inconstant *adj* **1** (of a person) having feelings which change frequently; fickle; unfaithful. **2** subject to frequent change; variable. — *n* **inconstancy**. [Lat *inconstans*]

incontestable *adj* too clear or definite to be disputed. — *n* **incontestability**. — *adv* **incontestably**. [Lat *incontestabilis*]

incontinent *adj* **1** unable to control one's bowels or bladder or both. **2** unable to control oneself, esp. one's sexual desires. **3** (**of**) lacking control (over). — *n* **incontinence** or **incontinency**. [Lat *incontinens*]

incontrovertible *adj* not able to be disputed or doubted. — *adv* **incontrovertibly**. [**in-**[1] + *controvert*, to oppose]

inconvenience *n* (something which causes) trouble or difficulty. — *v* (*tr*) to cause trouble or difficulty to. [Lat *inconvenientia*]

inconvenient *adj* not convenient, esp. causing trouble or difficulty. — *adv* **inconveniently**.

incorporate *v* **1** (*tr*) to contain as part of a whole. **2** (*tr* & *intr*) to include or be included as part of a whole. **3** (*tr* & *intr*) to combine or be united thoroughly in a single mass. **4** (*tr*) to admit to membership of a legal corporation. **5** (*tr*) to form into a legal corporation. **6** (*intr*) to form a legal corporation. — *adj* (also **incorporated**) **1** united in one body or as a single whole. **2** forming or formed into a legal corporation. — *n* **incorporation**. [Lat *incorporare*, from *in*, in + *corpus*, body]

incorporeal *adj* **1** without bodily or material form or substance. **2** (*legal*) having no material existence or value in itself, but attached as a right or profit to something else. — *adv* **incorporeally**. — *n* **incorporeity**. [Lat *incorporeus*, from *in-*, not + *corpus*, body]

incorrect *adj* **1** not accurate; wrong. **2** not in accordance with normal or accepted standards; improper. — *adv* **incorrectly**. — *n* **incorrectness**. [Lat *incorrectus*]

incorrigible *adj* (of a person, behaviour or habit) not able to be improved, corrected or reformed, usu. because too bad. — *n* **incorrigibility**. — *adv* **incorrigibly**. [Lat *incorrigibilis*]

incorruptible *adj* **1** incapable of being bribed or morally corrupted. **2** that cannot decay. — *n* **incorruptibility**. — *adv* **incorruptibly**. [Lat *incorruptibilis*]

increase *v* (*tr* & *intr*) to make or become greater in size, intensity or number. — *n* **1** the act or process of increasing or becoming increased; growth. **2** the amount by which something increases or is increased. — *adv* **increasingly**. — **on the increase** increasing in number, size or frequency. [Lat *increscere*, to grow]

incredible *adj* **1** difficult or impossible to believe. **2** (*coll*) amazing; unusually good. — *n* **incredibility**. — *adv* **incredibly**. [Lat *incredibilis*]

incredulous *adj* **1** unwilling to believe or accept something as true. **2** showing or expressing disbelief. — *n* **incredulity**. — *adv* **incredulously**. — *n* **incredulousness**. [Lat *incredulus*]

increment *n* **1** an increase, esp. of one point or level on a fixed scale, e.g. a regular increase in salary. **2** the amount by which something is increased. **3** (*math*) a small increase in the value of a variable quantity. — *adj* **incremental**. — *adv* **incrementally**. [Lat *incrementum*]

incriminate *v* (*tr*) **1** to show that (someone) was involved in esp. a crime. **2** to involve in esp. a crime. **3** to charge with a crime or fault. — *adj* **incriminating** or **incriminatory**. — *n* **incrimination**. [Lat *incriminare*, to accuse of a crime]

incrust. Same as **encrust**.

incubate *v* **1** (*tr* & *intr*) (of birds) to hatch (eggs) by sitting on them to keep them warm. **2** (*tr*) to cause (germs, bacteria, etc.) to develop by creating favourable and controlled conditions, e.g. in a laboratory. **3** (*intr*) (of germs, bacteria, etc.) to develop gradually and slowly before signs of disease begin to appear. — *adj* **incubative** or **incubatory**. [Lat *incubare*, to lie on]

incubation *n* **1** an act of incubating. **2** the period between infection with bacteria, germs, etc. and the appearance of the actual disease these cause.

incubator *n* **1** a heated box-like apparatus used to care for premature or sick babies. **2** a heated apparatus for hatching eggs or growing bacteria, etc.

incubus *n* **-ses** or **-bi** **1** an evil male spirit which is supposed to have sexual intercourse with sleeping women. ◇ See also **succubus**. **2** something which oppresses or weighs heavily upon one, esp. a nightmare. [Lat, nightmare]

inculcate *v* (*tr*; **in**, **upon**) to teach or fix (ideas, habits, a warning, etc.) firmly in a person's mind by constant repetition. — *n* **inculcation**. [Lat *inculcare*, to tread in]

inculpate *v* (*tr*) to blame or show to be guilty of a crime; to incriminate. [Lat *inculpare*, to blame]

incumbent *adj* **1** (**on, upon**) imposed as a duty. **2** occupying a specified position. — *n* a holder of an office, esp. a church office or benefice. [Lat *incumbere*, to lie on]

incumbency *n* **-*ies*** the period of office of an incumbent.

incunabulum *n* **-*la*** an early printed book, esp. one printed before 1501. [Lat *incunabula*, swaddling-clothes]

incur *v* **-*rr-*** (*tr*) to bring (something unpleasant) upon oneself; to become liable for (debts, etc.). [Lat *incurrere*, to run into]

incurable *adj* & *n* (someone or something) that cannot be cured or corrected. — *n* **incurability**. — *adv* **incurably**. [Lat *incurabilis*]

incurious *adj* showing no interest; lacking a normal curiosity; indifferent. — *adv* **incuriously**.

incursion *n* **1** a brief or sudden attack made into enemy territory. **2** a using up of something: *unexpected expenses which made an incursion into their savings*. — *adj* **incursive**. [Lat *incursio*]

Ind. *abbrev* **1** Independent. **2** India; Indian. **3** Indiana.

indaba *n* **1** an important conference or discussion between members of S African tribes. **2** (*coll*) a concern or problem for discussion. [Zulu, affair]

indebted *adj* **1** (**to**) having reason to be grateful (to). **2** owing money. — *n* **indebtedness**. [**in**[2] + **debt**]

indecent *adj* **1** offensive against accepted standards of morality or sexual behaviour. **2** in bad taste; improper; unseemly. — *n* **indecency, -*ies***. — *adv* **indecently**. [Lat *indecens*]

indecent assault *n* a sexual attack which falls short of being rape.

indecent exposure *n* the crime of indecently showing parts of one's body, esp. one's sexual organs, in public.

indecipherable *adj* that cannot be read or understood. — *n* **indecipherability**. — *adv* **indecipherably**. [**in-**[1] + **decipherable**]

indecision *n* the state of not being able to decide; uncertainty. [**in-**[1] + **decision**]

indecisive *adj* **1** not producing a clear or definite decision or result. **2** unable to make a firm decision; hesitating. — *adv* **indecisively**. — *n* **indecisiveness**. [**in-**[1] + **decisive**]

indecorous *adj* not decorous; in bad taste; improper. — *adv* **indecorously**. — *n* **indecorousness**. [Lat *indecorus*]

indecorum *n* improper or unseemly behaviour; lack of decorum.

indeed *adv* **1** without any question; in truth. **2** in fact; actually. **3** used for emphasis: *very wet indeed*. — *interj* an expression of irony, surprise, disbelief, etc. or acknowledgement. [MidE]

indefatigable *adj* **1** never becoming tired. **2** never stopping; unremitting. — *adv* **indefatigably**. [Lat *indefatigabilis*]

indefensible *adj* that cannot be defended or justified. — *n* **indefensibility**. — *adv* **indefensibly**. [**in-**[1] + **defensible**]

indefinable *adj* that cannot be clearly, fully or exactly defined or described. — *adv* **indefinably**. [**in-**[1] + **definable**]

indefinite *adj* **1** without fixed or exact limits. **2** uncertain; vague; imprecise. — *adv* **indefinitely**. — *n* **indefiniteness**. [Lat *indefinitus*]

indefinite article *n* either of the words **a** or **an**, which describe an unspecified, indefinite or unidentified person or thing.

indelible *adj* (making marks) that cannot be removed or rubbed out. — *adv* **indelibly**. [Lat *indelebilis*]

indelicate *adj* **1** tending to embarrass or offend; in poor taste; immodest. **2** slightly coarse; rough. — *n* **indelicacy, -*ies***. — *adv* **indelicately**. [**in-**[1] + **delicate**]

indemnify *v* **-*ies*, -*ied*** (*tr*) **1** (**against**) to secure (someone) e.g. against loss or damage; to insure. **2** (**for**) to pay money to (someone) in compensation (for esp. loss or damage); to reimburse. — *n* **indemnification**. [Lat *indemnis*, without loss, unhurt]

indemnity *n* **-*ies*** **1** (money paid as) compensation for loss or damage. **2** security from loss or damage. **3** legal exemption from liabilities or penalties incurred.

indent[1] *v* **1** (*tr* & *intr*) to begin (a line or paragraph) in from the margin. **2** (*tr*) to divide (a document drawn up in duplicate in two columns) along a zigzag line. **3** (*tr*) to draw up (a document, deed, etc.) in duplicate. **4** (*tr* & *intr*; **for**; *Br*) to make out a written order (for esp. foreign goods). **5** (*tr*) to indenture as an apprentice. **6** (*tr*) to make a notch in. — *n* **1** (*Br*) a written order for esp. foreign goods. **2** an indented line or paragraph. **3** a notch. **4** an indenture. [Lat *indentatus*]

indentation *n* **1** a cut or notch. **2** a deep inward curve or recess, e.g. in a coastline. **3** the act of indenting.

indention *n* **1** the indenting of a line or paragraph. **2** the blank space at the beginning of a line caused by indenting a line or paragraph.

indenture *n* **1** (usu. in *pl*) a contract binding an apprentice to his or her master. **2** an indented document, agreement or contract. — *v* (*tr*) to bind (e.g. an apprentice) by indentures or by an indented contract or agreement.

indent[2] *v* (*tr*) to form a dent in or mark with dents. [**in**[2] + **dent**]

independent *adj* **1** not under the control or authority of others, esp. (of a country or state) self-governing. **2** not relying on others for financial support, care, help or guidance. **3** thinking and acting for oneself and not under an obligation to others. **4** not dependent on something else for value, purpose or function. **5** (of two or more people or things) not related to or affected by the others. **6** (of private income or resources) large enough to make having to work for a living unnecessary: *independent means*. **7** not belonging to a political party. **8** (of a school or broadcasting company) not paid for with public money. — *n* **independence**. — *adv* **independently**. [**in-**[1] + **dependent**]

Independence Day *n* a public holiday celebrating the anniversary of a country's declaration of independence, e.g. held on 4 July in the US.

independent clause *n* (*gram*) a clause which is grammatically correct and complete and has meaning even when it is taken out of the sentence in which it is found, e.g. *she picked it up* in *she picked it up and ran off*; a main clause.

indescribable *adj* that cannot be described, often because too extreme or too vague. — *adv* **indescribably**. [**in-**[1] + **describable**]

indestructible *adj* that cannot be destroyed. — *n* **indestructibility**. — *adv* **indestructibly**. [**in-**[1] + **destructible**]

indeterminable *adj* **1** that cannot be fixed, decided or measured. **2** (of an argument, etc.) that cannot be settled. — *adv* **indeterminably**. [Lat *indeterminabilis*]

indeterminate *adj* **1** not precisely or exactly fixed, determined or settled. **2** doubtful; vague. **3** (*math*) not having a fixed or definite value. — *n* **indeterminacy**. — *adv* **indeterminately**. — *n* **indeterminateness**. [Lat *indeterminatus*]

index *n* ***indexes*** or (esp. *tech*) ***indices*** **1** an alphabetical list of names, subjects, etc. dealt with in a book, usu. given at the end of that book, and with the page numbers on which each item appears. **2** a catalogue or set of reference cards, e.g. in a library, which lists each book, magazine, etc. alphabetically, usu. by author or title, and gives details of where it is shelved. **3** anything which points to, identifies or highlights a particular trend or condition. **4** a scale of numbers which shows changes in price, wages, rates of interest, etc: *retail price index*. **5** a hand, needle or pointer on a dial or scale. **6** a superscript figure or symbol which indicates the number of times a value is to be multiplied by itself. **7** (*cap*; *RC hist*) a list of books that Roman Catholics were forbidden to read. — *v* (*tr*) **1** to provide (a book) with an index. **2** to list in an index. **3** to relate (prices, wages, etc.) to the cost-of-living index, so that they may rise or fall accordingly. — *n* **indexer**. [Lat, informer]

indexation or **indexing** *n* the linking of prices, wages, rates of interest, etc. to changes in an index showing the cost of living.

index finger *n* the finger next to the thumb; the forefinger.

index-linked *adj* (of prices, wages, rates of interest, etc.) calculated so as to rise or fall by the same amount as the cost of living.

Indiaman *n* ***-men*** (*hist*) a merchant ship trading with India or the East Indies.

Indian *n* **1** a person born in or a citizen of India. **2** a person whose ancestors were born in India. **3** a member of any of the various native peoples of N, Central and S America (but not including the Inuit). **4** any of the languages spoken by the native peoples of America. — *adj* **1** of or relating to India or the Indian subcontinent (India, Bangladesh and Pakistan), its inhabitants, languages and culture. **2** of or relating to the native peoples of America, their languages and culture. [Gr *India*, from *Indos*, the Indus river]

Indian club *n* one of a pair of heavy, bottle-shaped clubs swung to develop the arm muscles.

Indian corn *n* maize.

Indian file *n* single file.

Indian hemp. Same as **hemp** (sense **1**).

Indian ink *n* (also esp. *NAm* **India ink**) black ink made from lampblack.

Indian summer *n* **1** a period of unusually warm, dry weather in late autumn or early winter. **2** a period of happiness and success towards the end of a person's life.

India paper *n* **1** a thin, soft, absorbent paper orig. made in China and Japan. **2** a very thin, strong, opaque paper, used e.g. for printing Bibles.

India rubber *n* same as **rubber**[1] (sense **2**).

Indic *adj* of the Indian branch of the Indo-European languages, made up of Sanskrit, and modern languages such as Hindi, Gujarati and Urdu. — *n* the languages forming this group. [Gr *Indikos*, Indian]

indicate *v* (*tr*) **1** to point out or show. **2** to be a sign or symptom of. **3** (of a gauge, dial, etc.) to show as a reading. **4** to state briefly. **5** to point to as a suitable treatment or desirable or required course. [Lat *indicare*]

indication *n* **1** an act of indicating. **2** something which serves to indicate; a sign. **3** something which is indicated. **4** a reading on a gauge, dial, etc.

indicative *adj* **1** **(of)** being a sign or suggesting the existence (of). **2** (*gram*) being the mood, or in the mood, used to state facts, describe events or ask questions. — *n* (a verb in) the indicative mood.

indicator *n* **1** an instrument, or a needle or pointer on a device, that shows the level of temperature, fuel, pressure, etc. **2** any of the flashing lights on a motor vehicle which show that the vehicle is about to change direction. **3** any sign, condition, situation, etc. which shows or illustrates something. **4** a board or diagram giving information, e.g. in a railway station. **5** (*chem*) a substance (e.g. litmus paper) which changes colour to show the condition of a solution. — *adj* **indicatory**.

indices. See **index**.

indict *v* (*tr*) to accuse of or charge formally with a crime, esp. in writing. — *adj* **indictable**. [OFr *enditer*, with spelling influenced by Lat *indicere*, to announce]

indictment *n* **1** a formal written accusation or charge. **2** an act of indicting. **3** something which deserves severe criticism or censure.

indie *n* (*coll*) a small, independent and usu. non-commercial record or film company. [Abbrev. of **independent**]

indifferent *adj* **1** (**to**) showing no interest (in) or concern (for). **2** neither good nor bad; average; mediocre. **3** fairly bad; inferior. **4** without importance. **5** neutral. — *n* **indifference**. — *adv* **indifferently**. [Lat *indifferens*]

indigenous *adj* (**to**) belonging naturally to or occurring naturally in a country or area; native. — *adv* **indigenously**. [Lat *indigena*, original inhabitant]

indigent *adj* very poor; needy. — *n* **indigence**. [Lat *indigens*]

indigestible *adj* **1** (of food) difficult or impossible to digest. **2** not easily understood; complicated. — *n* **indigestibility**. — *adv* **indigestibly**. [Lat *indigestibilis*]

indigestion *n* (discomfort or pain in the stomach or chest caused by) difficulty in digesting food.

indignant *adj* feeling or showing anger or a sense of ill-treatment. — *adv* **indignantly**. [Lat *indignans*]

indignation *n* anger caused by a feeling of having been ill-treated.

indignity *n* **-ies** **1** any act or treatment which causes someone to feel shame; disgrace or dishonour. **2** a feeling of shame, disgrace or dishonour. [Lat *indignitas*]

indigo *n* **-os** or **-oes** **1** a violet-blue dye either obtained naturally from a plant or made synthetically. **2** any of several leguminous plants whose leaves yield a violet-blue dye. **3** the violet-blue colour of this dye. — *adj* violet-blue. [Gr *indikon*, Indian]

indirect *adj* **1** (of a route, course, line, etc.) not straight or direct. **2** not going straight to the point; devious. **3** not directly aimed at or intended: *indirect consequences*. — *adv* **indirectly**. — *n* **indirectness**. [Lat *indirectus*]

indirect object *n* (*gram*) a noun, noun phrase or pronoun which is affected indirectly by the action of a verb, usu. standing for the person or thing to whom something is given or for whom something is done, e.g. *him* in *give him a kiss*. ◇ See also **direct object**.

indirect speech *n* (*gram*) a speaker's words reported by another person with changes of person and tense, e.g. '*I will come*' becomes '*She said she would come*' in indirect speech. ◇ See also **direct speech**.

indirect tax *n* a tax levied on goods and services as opposed to a person's income. — *n* **indirect taxation**. ◇ See also **direct tax**.

indiscernible *adj* that cannot be noticed or recognised as being distinct, esp. because too small: *indiscernible differences*. [**in-**[1] + **discernible**]

indiscipline *n* lack of discipline. — *adj* **indisciplined**. [**in-**[1] + **discipline**]

indiscreet *adj* **1** giving away too many secrets or too much information; not discreet. **2** not wise or cautious; injudicious. — *adv* **indiscreetly**. [Lat *indiscretus*]

indiscretion *n* (an act or remark showing) lack of discretion or caution; rashness.

indiscriminate *adj* **1** making no distinctions; not making or showing careful choice and discrimination. **2** confused; not differentiated. — *adv* **indiscriminately**. — *n* **indiscriminateness**. [**in-**[1] + **discriminate**]

indispensable *adj* necessary; essential; that cannot be done without. — *n* **indispensability**. — *adv* **indispensably**. [Lat *indispensabilis*]

indisposed *adj* **1** slightly ill. **2** (**to**) unwilling. — *n* **indisposition**. [**in-**[1] + **dispose**]

indisputable *adj* certainly true; beyond doubt. — *adv* **indisputably**. [**in-**[1] + **disputable**]

indissoluble *adj* incapable of being dissolved or broken; permanent; lasting. — *n* **indissolubility**. — *adv* **indissolubly**. [Lat *indissolubilis*]

indistinct *adj* not clear to a person's eye, ear or mind; confused; dim. — *adv* **indistinctly**. — *n* **indistinctness**. [Lat *indistinctus*]

indistinguishable *adj* not able to be told apart. — *adv* **indistinguishably**. [**in-**[1] + **distinguishable**]

indium *n* a rare, soft, silver-white metallic element (symbol **In**), used in semiconductors. [Lat *indicium*, indigo, because of the indigo-coloured lines in its spectrum]

individual *adj* **1** intended for or relating to a single person or thing. **2** particular to one person; showing or having a particular person's unique qualities or characteristics. **3** separate; single. — *n* **1** a particular person, animal or thing, esp. in contrast to the group to which it belongs. **2** (*coll*) a person: *a most offensive individual*. — *adv* **individually**. [Lat *individualis*, from *individuus*, indivisible]

individualise or **-ize** (*tr*) **1** to give a distinctive character or personality. **2** to make suitable for a particular person, thing or situation. — *n* **individualisation** or **-z-**.

individualism *n* **1** behaviour governed by the belief that individual people should lead their lives as they want and should be independent. **2** the theory that the state should in no way control the actions of the individual. **3** self-centredness; egoism.

individualist *n* **1** a person who thinks and acts with independence or great individuality, sometimes for the sake of being different. **2** a person who supports individualism. — *adj* (also **individualistic**) of individualists or individualism. — *adv* **individualistically**.

individuality *n* **-*ies*** **1** the qualities and character which distinguish one person or thing from others. **2** a separate and distinct existence.

indivisible *adj* **1** not able to be divided or separated. **2** (*math*) leaving a remainder. — *n* **indivisibility**. — *adv* **indivisibly**. [Lat *indivisibilis*]

Indo- *comb fm* Indian; India: *Indo-European*. [Gr *Indos*]

indoctrinate *v* (*tr*) to teach (an individual or group) to accept and believe a particular teaching or set of beliefs uncritically. — *n* **indoctrination**. [Lat *indoctrinare*, to teach]

Indo-European *adj* of the family of languages which are spoken throughout Europe and in many parts of Asia, including most of the European languages and many Asian ones, such as Hindi and Persian. — *n* **1** the languages forming this family. **2** the hypothetical language which all of the languages in the Indo-European family come from.

indolent *adj* **1** lazy; disliking and avoiding work and exercise. **2** (*med*) causing no pain. — *n* **indolence**. — *adv* **indolently**. [Lat *indolens*, not suffering pain]

indomitable *adj* that cannot be conquered or defeated. — *n* **indomitability**. — *adv* **indomitably**. [Lat *indomitabilis*]

Indonesian *n* **1** a person born in or a national of Indonesia or the Malay archipelago. **2** the languages spoken in the Malay archipelago, esp. the official language of the Republic of Indonesia. — *adj* of Indonesia, its people, languages and culture. [Gr *Indos*, Indian + *nesos*, island]

indoor *adj* used, belonging, done, happening, etc. inside a building. [Earlier *withindoor*]

indoors *adv* in or into a building.

indorse. Same as **endorse**.

indrawn *adj* **1** (esp. of breath) drawn or pulled in. **2** aloof. [**in** + **drawn**]

indubitable *adj* that cannot be doubted; certain. — *adv* **indubitably**. [Lat *indubitabilis*]

induce *v* (*tr*) **1** to persuade, influence or cause to do. **2** to cause to happen or appear. **3** (*med*) to cause (labour) to begin, esp. by the use of drugs; to cause labour in (a pregnant woman). **4** to produce or transmit (an electrical current or magnetism) by induction. **5** (*logic*) to infer or come to (e.g. a general conclusion) from particular cases. — *adj* **induced** (also *in cmpds*). — *adj* **inducible**. [Lat *inducere*, to lead in]

inducement *n* that which induces, esp. something which is persuasive or which influences or encourages certain behaviour.

induct *v* (*tr*; **into**; **to**) **1** to place (e.g. a priest) formally and often ceremonially in an official position. **2** to initiate as a member of e.g. a society or profession. **3** (*US*) to enrol for military service or training. [Lat *inducere*, to lead in]

inductance *n* the property of an electric circuit which produces an electromotive force by changing the current.

induction *n* **1** the act or process of inducting or being inducted, esp. into office. **2** the act or process of causing the onset of labour using drugs. **3** (*logic*) the process of forming or coming to a general conclusion from particular cases. ◇ See also **deduction**. **4** the production of an electrified or magnetic state in an object caused by that object's close proximity to another, already electrified or magnetic, object. **5** the drawing in of the fuel and air mixture from the carburettor into the cylinders in an internal combustion engine.

induction coil *n* an electrical device which produces a high voltage from a low one.

inductive *adj* **1** (*logic*) of or using induction. **2** of electric or magnetic induction. — *adv* **inductively**. ◇ See also **deductive**.

indue. Same as **endue**.

indulge *v* **1** (*tr* & *intr*; **in**) to allow (oneself) pleasure or the particular pleasure (of). **2** (*tr*) to allow (someone) to have anything he or she wants; to pamper or spoil. **3** (*tr*) not to restrain or ignore (a desire, taste, wish, etc.): *indulge a whim*. **4** (*intr*; *coll*) to drink alcohol, esp. freely or without restraint. [Lat *indulgere*, to be kind or indulgent to]

indulgence *n* **1** an act of indulging a person, desire, etc. **2** the state of being indulgent; generosity; favourable or tolerant treatment. **3** a pleasure that is indulged in. **4** in the Roman Catholic church, remission from the punishment which remains due after the sin has been absolved.

indulgent *adj* too quick to overlook or forgive faults or gratify the wishes of others; too tolerant or generous. — *adv* **indulgently**.

industry *n* **-*ies*** **1** the business of producing goods; all branches of manufacturing and trade. **2** a branch of manufacturing and trade which produces a particular product: *the coal industry*. **3** organised commercial exploitation or use of natural or national assets, such as historical buildings, famous people, etc.: *the tourist industry*. **4** hard work or effort; diligence. [Lat *industria*]

industrial *adj* **1** of, relating to or concerned with industry. **2** used in industry. **3** (of a country, city, etc.) having highly developed industry. — *adv* **industrially**.

industrial action *n* (*Br*) action, e.g. strikes, taken by workers as a protest.

industrial estate *n* an area in a town which is developed for industry and business.

industrial relations *n* (*pl*) the relationship between management and the workers esp. in a factory.

industrial revolution *n* a rapid development of a country's industry characterised by a change from small-scale production in the home to increased mechanisation and mass production in factories, esp. in 18th-century Britain.

industrialise or **-ize** *v* (*tr & intr*) to (cause to) become industrially developed; to introduce industry, or have industry introduced. — *n* **industrialisation** or **-z-**.

industrialism *n* a social system in which industry (rather than agriculture) is dominant and forms the basis of commerce and the economy.

industrialist *n* a person who owns a large industrial organisation or who is involved in its management at a senior level.

industrious *adj* busy and hard-working; diligent. — *adv* **industriously**. — *n* **industriousness**.

-ine *sfx* like; relating to: *crystalline*; *Alpine*. [Lat *-inus*]

inebriate *v* (*tr*) **1** to make drunk. **2** to exhilarate greatly. — *adj* drunk, esp. habitually. — *n* a person who is drunk, esp. habitually. — *n* **inebriation** or **inebriety**. [Lat *inebriare*]

inedible *adj* not fit or suitable to be eaten; not edible. — *n* **inedibility**. — *adv* **inedibly**. **[in-**[1] **+ edible]**

ineducable *adj* not capable of being educated, esp. because mentally retarded. — *n* **ineducability**. — *adv* **ineducably**. **[in-**[1] **+ educable]**

ineffable *adj* **1** that is too great to be described or expressed in words. **2** that should not be said or uttered. — *n* **ineffability**. — *adv* **ineffably**. [Lat *ineffabilis*]

ineffective *adj* **1** having no effect; not producing a result or the result intended. **2** (of a person) incapable of achieving results. — *adv* **ineffectively**. — *n* **ineffectiveness**. **[in-**[1] **+ effective]**

ineffectual *adj* **1** not producing any result or the intended result. **2** (of a person) lacking the ability and confidence needed to achieve results; weak. — *adv* **ineffectually**. — *n* **ineffectualness**. [Lat *ineffectualis*]

inefficacious *adj* (esp. of a medicine) not having the desired or intended effect. — *adv* **inefficaciously**. — *n* **inefficacy**. **[in-**[1] **+ efficacious]**

inefficient *adj* not working or producing the required results, etc. in the best way, thus wasting time, energy, resources, etc.; not efficient. — *n* **inefficiency, *-ies***. — *adv* **inefficiently**. **[in-**[1] **+ efficient]**

inelegant *adj* not graceful; awkward; lacking elegance or good taste. — *n* **inelegance**. — *adv* **inelegantly**. [Lat *inelegans*]

ineligible *adj* **(for)** not qualified, not worthy or not allowed. — *n* **ineligibility**.

ineluctable *adj* that cannot be avoided, resisted or escaped from. — *adv* **ineluctably**. [Lat *ineluctabilis*]

inept *adj* **1** awkward; done without, or not having, skill. **2** not suitable or fitting; out of place. **3** silly; foolish. — *n* **ineptitude** or **ineptness**. — *adv* **ineptly**. [Lat *ineptus*]

inequable *adj* not fair or just. [Lat *inaequabilis*, uneven]

inequality *n* ***-ies*** **1** a lack of equality, fairness or evenness. **2** an instance of this. **3** any dissimilarity or disparity. **4** (*math*) a statement that two quantities or expressions are not equal. [Lat *inaequalitas*]

inequitable *adj* not fair or just. — *adv* **inequitably**. — *n* **inequity, *-ies***. **[in-**[1] **+ equitable]**

ineradicable *adj* not able to be removed completely or rooted out. — *adv* **ineradicably**. **[in-**[1] + Lat *eradicare*, to root out]

inert *adj* **1** without the power to move. **2** not wanting to move, act or think; indolent; sluggish. **3** without active chemical, biological, etc. properties. — *adv* **inertly**. — *n* **inertness**. [Lat *iners*, unskilled, idle]

inertia *n* **1** the property of matter of continuing in its existing state of movement or rest, or in its current position, unless a force is applied to it. **2** the state of not wanting to move, act or think; indolence; sluggishness. — *adj* **inertial**. [Lat *iners*, unskilled, idle]

inertia-reel seat belt *n* a vehicle seat belt on a reel which allows the wearer to move freely in normal conditions but which locks tight under impact or sudden movement.

inertia selling *n* (esp. *Br*) the illegal practice of sending unrequested goods to people followed by a bill if the goods are not returned.

inescapable *adj* that cannot be avoided. — *adv* **inescapably**. **[in-**[1] **+ escape]**

inessential *adj* not essential or necessary. — *n* an inessential thing. **[in-**[1] **+ essential]**

inestimable *adj* too great, or of too great value, to be estimated, measured or fully appreciated. — *adv* **inestimably**. [Lat *inaestimabilis*]

inevitable *adj* **1** that cannot be avoided; certain to happen. **2** (*coll*) tiresomely regular or predictable. — *n* that which is certain to happen and is unavoidable. — *n* **inevitability**. — *adv* **inevitably**. [Lat *inevitabilis*]

inexact *adj* not quite correct, exact or true. — *n* **inexactitude** or **inexactness**. — *adv* **inexactly**. **[in-**[1] **+ exact]**

inexcusable *adj* too bad to be excused, justified or tolerated. — *adv* **inexcusably**. [Lat *inexcusabilis*]

inexhaustible *adj* incapable of being used up (esp. because too big) or exhausted. — *n* **inexhaustibility**. — *adv* **inexhaustibly**. [Lat *inexhaustus*, not exhausted]

inexorable *adj* **1** that cannot be moved by entreaty or persuasion; unrelenting. **2** that cannot be altered or avoided. — *n* **inexorability**. — *adv* **inexorably**. [Lat *inexorabilis*]

inexpedient *adj* not wise, suitable or appropriate. — *n* **inexpedience** or **inexpediency**. [**in-**[1] + **expedient**]

inexpensive *adj* not costing much; cheap. — *adv* **inexpensively**. — *n* **inexpensiveness**. [**in-**[1] + **expensive**]

inexperience *n* lack of experience, or of skill or knowledge gained from experience. — *adj* **inexperienced**. [Lat *inexperientia*]

inexpert *adj* not skilled; not expert. — *adv* **inexpertly**. — *n* **inexpertness**. [Lat *inexpertus*]

inexplicable *adj* impossible to explain, understand or account for. — *n* **inexplicability**. — *adv* **inexplicably**. [Lat *inexplicabilis*]

inexplicit *adj* not clearly and exactly stated. — *adv* **inexplicitly**. — *n* **inexplicitness**. [Lat *inexplicitus*, not straightforward]

inexpressible *adj* that cannot be expressed or described, esp. because too strong. — *n* **inexpressibility**. — *adv* **inexpressibly**. [**in-**[1] + **expressible**]

inexpressive *adj* (often of a person's face) expressing little or no emotion. [**in-**[1] + **expressive**]

inextinguishable *adj* that cannot be put out or destroyed. [**in-**[1] + **extinguish**]

in extremis *adv* in desperate or extreme circumstances, esp. at or as if at the point of death. [Lat]

inextricable *adj* **1** that cannot be escaped from. **2** that cannot be disentangled or untied. — *adv* **inextricably**. [Lat *inextricabilis*]

infallible *adj* **1** (of a person) never making a mistake; incapable of error; (of the Pope) never making a mistake when pronouncing on dogma. **2** always successful; not likely to fail. — *n* **infallibility**. — *adv* **infallibly**. [Lat *infallibilis*]

infamous *adj* **1** having a very bad reputation; notoriously bad. **2** evil; vile. — *adv* **infamously**. [Lat *infamis*]

infamy *n* **-ies 1** bad reputation; notoriety; shame. **2** an infamous act.

infant *n* **1** a very young child in the first period of life. **2** (*legal*) a person who is under the legal age of maturity (in Britain, eighteen for most things). **3** (*Br*) a schoolchild under the age of seven or eight. [Lat *infans*, from *in*, not + *fari*, to speak]

infancy *n* **-ies 1** the state or time of being an infant. **2** an early period of existence, growth and development. **3** (*legal*) the state of being under the legal age of maturity (in Britain, eighteen for most things).

infant school *n* (*Br*) a school for children aged between five and seven or eight.

infante *n* (*hist*) a son of the king of Spain or Portugal who is not heir to the throne. [Span & Port, from Lat *infans*, infant]

infanta *n* (*hist*) **1** the eldest daughter of the king of Spain or Portugal. **2** the wife of an infante.

infanticide *n* **1** the murder of a young child or infant. **2** a person who murders a young child or infant. [Lat *infans*, infant + *caedere*, to kill]

infantile *adj* **1** of infants or infancy. **2** very childish; immature. [Lat *infantilis*]

infantile paralysis *n* (*old med*) poliomyelitis.

infantilism *n* the presence of childish characteristics in an adult or older child.

infantry *n* **-ies** (the part of an army consisting of) soldiers who are trained and equipped to fight on foot. — *adj* of, relating to or for the infantry. [Ital *infanteria*]

infantryman *n* a soldier in the infantry.

infarction *n* (*med*) (a case of) the cutting off of the blood supply to a part of the body. [Lat *infarcire*, to stuff]

infatuate *v* (*tr*) to cause to feel a passionate, foolish and unreasonable love or admiration. — *adj* **infatuated (with)**. — *n* **infatuation**. [Lat *infatuare*]

infect *v* (*tr*; **with**) **1** to fill (a person or thing) with germs, viruses or the disease they cause; to contaminate. **2** to pass esp. an adverse or negative feeling or opinion to (someone). [Lat *inficere*, to stain]

infection *n* **1** the process of infecting or state of being infected. **2** something which infects a person or thing. **3** an infectious or contagious disease. **4** the passing on of feelings, opinions, etc.

infectious *adj* **1** (of a disease) capable of being transmitted by air, water, etc. **2** causing infection. **3** (of a feeling, opinion, etc.) likely to be passed on to others. — *adv* **infectiously**. — *n* **infectiousness**.

infectious mononucleosis *n* same as **glandular fever**.

infelicity *n* **-ies 1** bad luck; misfortune; unhappiness. **2** something, esp. an expression, phrase, choice of word, etc, that is not suitable or fitting. [Lat *infelicitas*]

infelicitous *adj* **1** not happy, fortunate or lucky. **2** not suitable, fitting or apt.

infer *v* **-rr-** (*tr*) **1** to conclude or judge from facts, observation and careful thought. **2** (*coll*) to imply or suggest. — *adj* **inferable** or **inferrable**. [Lat *inferre*, to bring in]

inference *n* **1** an act of inferring, esp. of reaching a conclusion from facts, observation and careful thought. **2** that which is inferred, esp. a conclusion.

inferential *adj* of or based on inference. — *adv* **inferentially**.

inferior *adj* **1** (**to**) poor or poorer in quality. **2** (**to**) low or lower in value, rank or status. **3** (**to**) low or lower in position. **4** (of letters or figures) printed or written

slightly below the line. **5** (of a planet) revolving within the earth's orbit; nearer the sun. — *n* a person who is inferior in some way to another. [Lat, lower]
inferiority *n* the state of being inferior.
inferiority complex *n* (*psychol*) a constant feeling that one is not as good as others in some way, which may lead to shyness or, in an attempt to compensate for this feeling, aggressive behaviour.
infernal *adj* **1** of hell. **2** wicked; evil. **3** (*coll*) extremely annoying or unpleasant. — *adv* **infernally**. [Lat *infernalis*, from *inferus*, low]
inferno *n* **-os** **1** (often *cap*) hell. **2** a place or situation of horror and confusion. **3** a raging fire. [Ital, from Lat *infernus*, hell]
infertile *adj* **1** (of soil, etc.) not fertile or producing good crops. **2** (of people or animals) unable to have young. — *n* **infertility**. [Lat *infertilis*]
infest *v* (*tr*; **with**) (of something harmful, e.g. vermin) to be present in, cover or fill in large numbers. — *n* **infestation**. [Lat *infestare*, to disturb]
infidel *n* **1** a person who rejects a particular religion, esp. Christianity or Islam. **2** a person who rejects all religions; an unbeliever. **3** a person who rejects a theory. — *adj* of unbelievers; unbelieving. [Lat *infidelis*]
infidelity *n* **-ies** **1** unfaithfulness to someone, esp. a husband, wife or partner. **2** an instance of this. **3** lack of belief in a religion. [Lat *infidelitas*]
infield *n* **1** (*cricket*) (the players who stand in) the area of the field close to wicket. **2** (*baseball*) (the players who stand at the four bases surrounding) the diamond-shaped area of the pitch formed by four bases. ◇ See also **outfield**. [**in** + **field**]
infielder *n* a player who stands in the infield.
infill *n* (also **infilling**) **1** the act of filling or closing gaps, holes, etc. **2** the material used to fill a gap, hole, etc. — *v* (*tr*) to fill in (a gap, hole, etc.). [**in** + **fill**]
infiltrate *v* **1** (*tr* & *intr*) (of troops, agents, etc.) to pass into (territory or an organisation held by the enemy or rivals) secretly, to gain influence, control or information. **2** (*tr*) to filter (e.g. liquid or gas) through (a substance). **3** (*intr*) (of e.g. liquid or gas) to filter in. **4** (*tr* & *intr*) to permeate gradually in (a substance). — *n* **infiltration**. — *n* **infiltrator**. [**in**[2] + **filtrate**]
infinite *adj* **1** having no boundaries or limits in size, extent, time or space. **2** too great to be measured or counted. **3** very great; vast. **4** (*math*) having an unlimited number of elements, digits or terms. — *n* anything which has no limits, boundaries, etc., esp. (*cap* with **the**) God. — *adv* **infinitely**. — *n* **infiniteness**. [Lat *infinitus*]
infinitesimal *adj* **1** infinitely small; with a value close to zero. **2** (*coll*) extremely small. — *n* an infinitesimal amount. — *adv* **infinitesimally**. [Lat *infinitesimus*]
infinitive *n* (*gram*) a verb form which expresses an action but which does not refer to a particular subject or time, in English often used with *to*, e.g. *tell him to go*, but used without *to* after certain verbs, e.g. *let her go*. — *adj* (of a verb) having this form. [Lat *infinitivus*]
infinitude *n* **1** the state or quality of being infinite. **2** something infinite, esp. an infinite quantity, degree, amount. [**infinite** + **magnitude**]
infinity *n* **1** the quality or state of being infinite. **2** space, time, distance or quantity that is without limit or boundaries, or (*loosely*) is too great to be measured. **3** (*math*) a countless or indefinite number or amount, often represented by the symbol ∞. [Lat *infinitas*]
infirm *adj* (of a person) weak or ill, esp. from old age. [Lat *infirmus*]
infirmity *n* **-ies** **1** the state or quality of being sick, weak or infirm. **2** a disease or illness.
infirmary *n* **-ies** **1** a hospital. **2** a room or ward where the sick and injured are treated, esp. in a school or monastery. [Lat *infirmaria*]
infix *v* (*tr*) **1** to fix firmly in (something, the mind, etc.). **2** (*gram*) to insert (an affix) into the main part of a word as opposed to adding it as a prefix or suffix. — *n* an affix inserted into the main part of a word, as opposed to a prefix or suffix. — *n* **infixation**. [Lat *infigere*]
in flagrante delicto *adv* in the very act of committing the crime. [Lat, in the blazing crime]
inflame *v* **1** (*tr*) to arouse strong or violent emotion in. **2** (*intr*) to begin to feel strong or violent emotion; to become excited or angry. **3** (*tr* & *intr*) to burst or cause to burst into flames. **4** (*tr*) to make more heated or intense; to exacerbate. **5** (*tr* & *intr*) to cause (part of the body) to become, or (of part of the body) to become, affected by inflammation. [Lat *inflammare*, to kindle]
inflammable *adj* **1** easily set on fire. **2** easily excited or angered. — *n* an inflammable substance. — *n* **inflammability**. [Lat *inflammabilis*]
inflammation *n* **1** (a place in the body showing) development of heat with pain, redness and swelling, usu. as a response to injury. **2** an act of inflaming or state of being inflamed. [Lat *inflammatio*]
inflammatory *adj* **1** likely to cause strong or violent emotion, esp. anger. **2** of, causing or caused by inflammation of part of the body. [Lat *inflammare*, to kindle]
inflate *v* **1** (*tr* & *intr*) to (cause to) swell or expand with air or gas. **2** (*tr*) to exaggerate the importance or value of. **3** (*tr*) to increase (prices generally) artificially or to

increase (the volume of money in circulation). ◇ See also **deflate, reflate**. [Lat *inflare*, to blow into]

inflatable *adj* (of a cushion, ball, etc.) that can be filled with air for use. — *n* an inflatable object.

inflated *adj* **1** (of prices) artificially increased to a high level. **2** (esp. of language or opinions) showing too great a sense of one's importance. **3** blown up or filled with air or gas; distended.

inflation *n* **1** the process of inflating or being inflated. **2** a general increase in the level of prices accompanied by a fall in the purchasing power of money, caused by an increase in the amount of money in circulation and credit available. ◇ See also **deflation, reflation, stagflation**. — *adj* **inflationary**.

inflect *v* **1** (*tr*; *gram*) to change the form of (a word) to show e.g. tense, number, gender, grammatical case, etc. **2** (*intr*; *gram*) (of a word) to change, or be able to be changed, to show tense, number, gender, grammatical case, etc. **3** (*tr*) to vary the tone or pitch of (the voice). **4** (*tr*) to bend inwards. [Lat *inflectere*, to curve]

inflection or **inflexion** *n* **1** an act of inflecting or state of being inflected. **2** (*gram*) the change in the form of a word which shows tense, number, gender, grammatical case, etc. ◇ See also **derivation, root, stem**. **3** (*gram*) an inflected form of a word. **4** (*gram*) a suffix which is added to a word to form an inflected form, e.g. *-s* and *-es*. **5** a change in the tone, pitch, etc, of the voice. **6** a change in a curve from being convex to concave, or vice versa. — *adj* **inflectional** or **inflexional**.

inflective *adj* (*gram*) of or subject to inflection.

inflexible *adj* **1** incapable of being bent; rigid. **2** (of a person) never giving way; unyielding; obstinate. **3** that cannot or may not be changed; fixed. — *n* **inflexibility** or **inflexibleness**. — *adv* **inflexibly**. [Lat *inflexibilis*]

inflexion, inflexional. See **inflect**.

inflict *v* (*tr*; **on, upon**) to impose on or cause to suffer (something unpleasant, e.g. a blow, defeat or pain). [Lat *infligere*, to strike against]

infliction *n* **1** an act of inflicting. **2** something that is inflicted.

inflorescence *n* **1** the complete flower-head of a plant, made up of stalks, stem and flowers. **2** the arrangement of flowers, stalks, etc. in a flower-head. **3** the process of flowering. [Lat *inflorescere*, to begin to blossom]

inflow *n* **1** the act or process of flowing in. **2** something that flows in. — *n* & *adj* **inflowing**. [**in** + **flow**]

influence *n* **1** (**on, upon, over**) the power that one person or thing has to effect another. **2** (**on, upon**) a person or thing that has such a power: *be a good influence on him*. **3** (**over, with**) power resulting from political or social position, wealth, ability, standards of behaviour, etc. — *v* (*tr*) to have an effect, esp. an indirect or unnoticed one, on (a person, events, etc.). — **under the influence** (*coll*) badly affected by alcohol; drunk. [Lat *influentia*, from *influere*, to flow into]

influential *adj* **1** having influence or power. **2** (**in**) playing an important part (in). — *adv* **influentially**.

influenza *n* an infectious illness caused by a virus, whose symptoms include headache, fever, a sore throat, catarrh and muscle pains. [Ital, influence, from the belief that stars caused epidemics]

influx *n* **1** a continual stream or arrival of large numbers of people or things. **2** a flowing in. [Lat *influere*, to flow into]

info *n* (*coll*) information. [Abbrev.]

inform *v* **1** (*tr* & *intr*; **about, of, on**) to give knowledge or information (to). **2** (*intr*; **against, on**) to give incriminating information (about someone) to esp. the police. **3** (*tr*) to animate, inspire or give life to. **4** (*tr*) to give an essential quality to. [Lat *informare*, to give form to]

informant *n* someone who informs, e.g. against another person, or who gives information.

information *n* **1** knowledge gained or given; facts; news. **2** the communicating or receiving of knowledge. **3** an accusation made before a court or magistrate. **4** a signal or character which represents data, esp. in telecommunications and computing. — *adj* **informational**.

information retrieval *n* the storing, sorting and finding of information stored esp. in a computer.

information technology *n* technology related to the gathering, storing and communicating of information using computers and microelectronics.

informative *adj* giving useful or interesting information; instructive. — *adv* **informatively**. — *n* **informativeness**.

informed *adj* having or showing knowledge, esp. in being educated and intelligent.

informer *n* a person who informs against another, esp. to the police and usu. for money or some other reward.

informal *adj* **1** without ceremony or formality; relaxed and friendly. **2** (of language, clothes, etc.) suitable for and used in relaxed, everyday situations. — *n* **informality**. — *adv* **informally**. [**in-**[1] + **formal**]

infra *adv* below; lower down on the page or further on in the book. [Lat]

infra- *comb fm* below; beneath. [Lat *infra*, below]

infraction *n* (a case of) the breaking of a law, rule, etc. [Lat *infringere*, to break]

infra dig (*coll*) abbrev. of Lat *infra dignitatem*, beneath one's dignity.

infrared *adj* of, using, producing or sensitive to radiation with a wavelength just beyond the red end of the visible spectrum, usu. felt as heat. — *n* infrared radiation. [**infra-** + **red**]

infrasonic *adj* of or having a frequency below the range which can normally be heard by the human ear. [**infra-** + **sonic**]

infrastructure *n* **1** the basic structure of a society, organisation or system. **2** the permanent services and equipment, e.g. the roads, railways, bridges, factories and schools, needed for a country to be able to function properly. **3** the permanent services and equipment, e.g. roads, railways and bridges, needed for military purposes. [**infra-** + **structure**]

infrequent *adj* not frequent; occurring rarely or only occasionally. — *n* **infrequency**. — *adv* **infrequently**. [Lat *infrequens*]

infringe *v* **1** (*tr*) to break or violate (e.g. a law or oath). **2** (*tr*) to interfere with (a person's rights). **3** (*intr*; **on, upon**) to affect a person's rights, freedom, etc. in such a way as to limit or reduce them; to encroach or trespass. — *n* **infringement**. [Lat *infringere*, to break]

infuriate *v* (*tr*) to make very angry. — *adj* **infuriating**. — *adv* **infuriatingly**. [Lat *infuriare*]

infuse *v* **1** (*tr*; **into, with**) to put or inspire (a positive feeling, quality, etc.) in (someone). **2** (*tr* & *intr*) to soak or cause (leaves, e.g. tea) to be soaked in hot water to release their flavour or other qualities. — *n* **infusion**. [Lat *infundere*, to pour into]

-ing[1] *sfx* used to form nouns, esp. from verbs, usu. expressing the action of the verb, its result or product, etc.: *building*; *driving*. [OE *-ing, -ung*]

-ing[2] *sfx* used to form the present participle of verbs: *charming*; *walking*. [OE *-ende*]

-ing[3] *sfx* used (esp. *formerly*) to form nouns meaning 'one belonging to' or 'one of the same kind of': *gelding*. [OE *-ing*]

ingenious *adj* marked by, showing or having skill, originality and inventive cleverness. — *adv* **ingeniously**. — *n* **ingeniousness**. [Lat *ingenium*, common sense, cleverness]

ingénue *n* **1** a naive, innocent, unsophisticated young woman. **2** (an actress playing) the role of an ingénue. [Fr, from Lat *ingenuus*, native]

ingenuity *n* inventive cleverness, skill or originality; ingeniousness. [Lat *ingenuitas*, ingenuousness]

ingenuous *adj* innocent and childlike, esp. in being frank, honest and incapable of deception. — *adv* **ingenuously**. — *n* **ingenuousness**. [Lat *ingenuus*, native]

ingest *v* (*tr*) **1** to take (e.g. food or liquid) into the body. **2** (of a jet engine) to suck in (an object, e.g. a bird). — *adj* **ingestible**. — *n* **ingestion**. [Lat *ingerere*, to carry in]

inglenook *n* (a seat or bench in) a corner or alcove in a large open fireplace. [Scots Gaelic *aingeal*, fire + **nook**]

inglorious *adj* **1** ordinary; not glorious or noble. **2** bringing shame. — *adv* **ingloriously**. — *n* **ingloriousness**. [Lat *inglorius*]

ingoing *adj* going in; entering. [**in** + **go**]

ingot *n* a brick-shaped mass of metal, esp. of gold or silver. [MidE, something poured in]

ingrained *adj* (also **engrained**) fixed firmly; difficult to remove or wipe off or out. [From the phrase *dyed in grain*]

ingrate *n* an ungrateful person. — *adj* ungrateful. [Lat *ingratus*]

ingratiate *v* (*tr*; **with**) to gain or try to gain favour or approval of (oneself) with someone. — *adj* **ingratiating**. — *adv* **ingratiatingly**. [Lat *in*, into + *gratia*, favour]

ingratitude *n* the quality of being ungrateful; lack of proper gratitude. [Lat *ingratitudo*]

ingredient *n* one of several things that goes into a mixture, esp. in cooking. [Lat *ingrediens*, going into]

ingress *n* the act of going in or entering, or power or right to do so. [Lat *ingredi*, to go into]

ingrowing *adj* growing inwards, esp. (of a toenail) growing into the flesh. — *adj* **ingrown**. [**in** + **grow**]

inhabit *v* **-t-** (*tr*) to live, dwell in or occupy (a place). [Lat *inhabitare*, to live in]

inhabitable *adj* fit to be lived in.

inhabitant *n* a person or animal that lives permanently in a place.

inhale *v* (*tr* & *intr*) to breathe in (air, gas, etc.). [Lat *inhalare*]

inhalant *n* a medicine (e.g. one for relieving congestion in the chest) which is inhaled.

inhalation *n* the act of breathing in, or that which is breathed in.

inhaler *n* a small portable device used for inhaling certain medicines.

inharmonious *adj* **1** not sounding well together; lacking harmony. **2** not agreeing or going well together; not compatible. — *adv* **inharmoniously**. — *n* **inharmoniousness**. [**in-**[1] + **harmonious**]

inhere *v* (*intr*; **in**) (of character, a quality, etc.) to be an essential or permanent part of. [Lat *inhaerere*, to stick in]

inherent *adj* (**in**) (of a quality, etc.) belonging naturally (to) or being an essential or permanent part (of). — *adv* **inherently**.

inherit *v* **-t-** **1** (*tr* & *intr*) to receive (property, a title, position, etc.) from a member of one's family on his or her death, or through legal descent from a predecessor. **2** (*tr*) to receive (physical or mental characteristics) genetically from one's parents and ancestors. — *adj* **inheritable**. — *n* **inheritor**. [Lat *inhereditare*]

inheritance *n* **1** something (e.g. property, a title, physical or mental characteristics) that is or may be inherited. **2** the act of inheriting or right to inherit.

inheritance tax *n* a tax levied on inheritors according to their relationship to the person from whom they have inherited.

inhibit *v* **-t-** (*tr*) **1** to hold back, restrain or prevent (an action, desire, progress, etc.). **2** to make (a person) feel nervous or frightened about acting freely or spontaneously, e.g. by causing him or her to doubt his or her abilities. **3** (**from**) to prohibit or forbid (someone from doing something). — *adj* **inhibited**. — *adv* **inhibitedly**. [Lat *inhibere*, to keep back]

inhibition *n* **1** a feeling of fear or embarrassment, caused by emotional or psychological factors, which prevent one from acting, thinking, etc. freely or spontaneously in some way: *sexual inhibitions*. **2** an act of inhibiting or process of being inhibited. **3** something which inhibits, prevents progress, holds back or forbids, etc. **4** a stopping, either complete or partial, of some chemical bodily function.

inhospitable *adj* **1** (of people) not friendly or welcoming. **2** (of a place) offering little shelter (e.g. from harsh weather); barren. — *n* **inhospitableness**. — *adv* **inhospitably**. [Lat *inhospitabilis*]

inhuman *adj* **1** without human feeling; cruel and unfeeling; brutal. **2** not human. — *adv* **inhumanly**. [Lat *inhumanus*]

inhumanity *n* **-ies 1** the state of being inhuman or inhumane; cruelty; lack of feeling or pity. **2** an inhuman, inhumane, cruel, etc. act.

inhumane *adj* showing no kindness, sympathy, or compassion; cruel; unfeeling. — *adv* **inhumanely**. [A variant of **inhuman**]

inimical *adj* (**to**) **1** tending to discourage; unfavourable. **2** not friendly; hostile. — *adv* **inimically**. [Lat *inimicalis*]

inimitable *adj* too good, skilful, etc. to be satisfactorily imitated by others; unique. — *adv* **inimitably**. [Lat *inimitabilis*]

iniquity *n* **-ies 1** the state of being unfair, unjust, wicked or sinful. **2** an unfair, unjust, wicked or sinful act. — *adj* **iniquitous**. — *adv* **iniquitously**. [Lat *iniquitas*]

initial *adj* of or at the beginning. — *n* the first letter of a word, esp. of a proper name. — *v* **-ll-** (*tr*) to mark or sign with the initials of one's name, esp. as a sign of approval. — *adv* **initially**. [Lat *initialis*]

initiate *v* (*tr*) **1** to cause to begin. **2** (**into**) to accept (a new member) into a society, organisation, etc., esp. with secret ceremonies. **3** (**in, into**) to give (someone) instruction in the basics or rudiments of a skill, science, etc. — *n* a person who has recently been or is soon to be initiated. — *adj* having been recently initiated or soon to be initiated. — *n* **initiation**. — *n* **initiator**. [Lat *initiare*]

initiative *n* **1** the ability or skill to initiate things, take decisions or act resourcefully. **2** a first step or move towards an end or aim. **3** the right or power to begin something. **4** the right of voters to originate legislation. — *adj* serving to begin; introductory. — **on one's own initiative** without needing or waiting to be told to do so by someone else. [**initiate**]

inject *v* (*tr*) **1** to introduce (a liquid, e.g. medicine) into the body of (a person or animal) using a hypodermic syringe. **2** to force (fuel) into an engine. **3** to introduce (a quality, element, etc.): *inject a note of optimism*. [Lat *injicere*, to throw in]

injection *n* **1** an act of injecting or forcing in or the process of being injected. **2** that which is injected, e.g. a liquid medicine.

injudicious *adj* not wise; showing poor judgement. — *adv* **injudiciously**. — *n* **injudiciousness**. [**in-**[1] + **judicious**]

injunction *n* **1** (*legal*) an official order from a court forbidding something, or commanding that something should be done. **2** any authoritative order or warning. — *adj* **injunctive**. [Lat *in jungere*, to enjoin]

injure *v* (*tr*) **1** to do physical harm or damage to. **2** to harm, spoil or weaken. **3** to do an injustice or wrong to. — *n* (with **the**) & *adj* **injured**. [Lat *injuria*, injury]

injurious *adj* (**to**) harmful; causing injury, damage or harm. — *adv* **injuriously**.

injury *n* **-ies 1** physical harm or damage. **2** a wound. **3** a wrong or injustice.

injury time *n* playing time added to the end of a football, rugby, etc. match to make up for time taken to treat injured players during the match.

injustice *n* **1** unfairness or lack of justice. **2** an unfair or unjust act. — **do (someone) an injustice** to judge (someone) unfairly. [Lat *injustitia*]

ink *n* **1** a coloured liquid used in writing, printing and drawing. **2** a black or dark brown liquid squirted out by a cuttlefish, octopus, etc. to confuse a predator or its own prey. — *v* (*tr*) **1** to mark with ink. **2** to cover (a surface to be printed) with ink. — *v* **ink in** (*tr*) to write over (a rough design in pencil) using ink. [OFr *enque*]

inkblot test *n* same as **Rorschach test**.

inkpad *n* a pad of inked cloth inside a box, used for putting ink on rubber stamps.

inkstand *n* a container for ink bottles and pens on a desk.

inkwell *n* a small container for ink, esp. one which fits into a hole in a desk.

inky *adj* **-ier, -iest 1** covered with ink. **2** like ink, esp. in being black or very dark. — *n* **inkiness**.

inkling *n* a hint; a vague or slight idea or suspicion. [MidE *inclen*, to hint]

inlaid. See **inlay**.

inland *adj* **1** of or in that part of a country which is not beside the sea. **2** (esp. *Br*) done, operating, etc. inside one country and not abroad; domestic. — *n* those parts of a country that are not beside the sea. — *adv* in or towards the inner regions of a country away from the sea. [OE, domain]

Inland Revenue *n* (*Br*) the government department responsible for assessing and collecting taxes.

in-law *n* **-*laws*** (*coll*) a relative by marriage.

inlay *v* ***inlaid*** (*tr*) **1** to set in or embed (e.g. pieces of wood, metal, etc. in another material) so that the surfaces are flat. **2** (**with**) to decorate (e.g. a piece of furniture) by setting flat pieces of different coloured wood, ivory, metal, etc. in the surface. — *n* **1** a decoration or design made by inlaying. **2** the pieces used to create an inlaid design. **3** a filling shaped to fit a cavity in a tooth. — *adj* **inlaid**. [**in** + **lay**]

inlet *n* **1** a narrow arm of water running inland from a sea-coast or lake-shore, or forming a passage between two islands. **2** a place of entry, e.g. for liquid or gas in a machine. **3** an extra piece of material sewn into a garment to make it larger. [MidE]

in loco parentis *adv* (said esp. of teachers) in the place of a parent. [Lat]

inmate *n* any of several people living in an institution, esp. a prison or a hospital. [**in** + **mate**]

inmost *adj* **1** farthest in; most in towards the centre. **2** most secret or private. [MidE]

inn *n* a public house or small hotel providing food and accommodation, esp. (*hist*) one for travellers. [OE, dwelling]

Inn of Court *n* (*Eng law*) **1** any of the four societies which have the exclusive right of calling lawyers to the bar. **2** any of the sets of buildings that these societies occupy.

innkeeper *n* a person who owns or manages an inn.

innards *n* (*pl*; *coll*) **1** the inner organs of a person or animal, esp. the stomach. **2** the inner workings of a machine. [A variant of **inwards**]

innate *adj* belonging to or existing in a person from birth; natural rather than learnt or acquired; inherent. — *adv* **innately**. — *n* **innateness**. [Lat *innatus*]

inner *adj* **1** further in; situated inside or close to the centre. **2** (of thoughts, feelings, etc.) secret, hidden and profound. [OE *innera*]

inner city *n* the central area of a city, often densely populated and very poor, with bad housing, roads, etc.

inner man or **woman** *n* **1** the mind or soul. **2** (*humorous*) the stomach.

innermost *adj* **1** furthest within. **2** most secret or hidden.

inner tube *n* an inflatable rubber tube inside a tyre.

inning *n* (*US*) a division of a baseball match during which each team has an opportunity to bat. [See ety. for **innings**]

innings *n* (*pl*) **1** (*cricket*) a team's or a player's turn at batting. **2** (*cricket*) the runs scored, or the quality of batting, during such a turn. **3** (esp. *Br*) a period during which a person has an opportunity for action or achievement. — **have a good innings** (*coll*) to have a long life. [OE *innung*, contents]

innocent *adj* **1** free from sin; pure. **2** not guilty (e.g. of a crime). **3** not intending to cause or not causing harm. **4** (**of**) lacking, free or deprived (of). **5** simple, trusting and naive; guileless; artless. — *n* an innocent person, esp. a young child or rather simple and trusting adult. — *n* **innocence**. — *adv* **innocently**. [Lat *innocens*, harmless]

innocuous *adj* harmless; inoffensive. — *adv* **innocuously**. — *n* **innocuousness**. [Lat *innocuus*]

innovate *v* **1** (*intr*) to make changes; to introduce new ideas, methods, etc. **2** (*tr*) to introduce (something) as new. — *adj* **innovative** or **innovatory**. — *n* **innovator**. [Lat *innovare*, to renew]

innovation *n* **1** an act of innovating. **2** something new which is introduced.

innuendo *n* **-*os*** or **-*oes*** **1** an indirect, and usu. slightly unpleasant, critical, spiteful or rude remark, esp. about someone's reputation or character; an oblique allusion or insinuation. **2** the act of making such remarks. [Lat, by nodding at]

Innuit. Same as **Inuit**.

innumerable *adj* too many to be counted; a great many. — *adv* **innumerably**. [Lat *innumerabilis*]

innumerate *adj* having no knowledge or understanding of mathematics or science. — *n* **innumeracy**. [Coined in 1959 by Sir Geoffrey Crowther on the analogy of *illiterate*, from **in-**[1] + **numerate**]

inoculate *v* (*tr*) **1** to give (a person or animal) a vaccine against or mild form of a disease to create immunity against that disease, usu. by injection. **2** to introduce (e.g. a virus or bacteria) into (a person, animal or culture). **3** to imbue or instil (someone) with ideas. — *n* **inoculation**. [Lat *inoculare*, to graft a tree bud]

inoffensive *adj* harmless; not likely to offend. — *adv* **inoffensively**. — *n* **inoffensiveness**. [**in-**[1] + **offensive**]

inoperable *adj* **1** which cannot be removed by surgery or operated on successfully. **2** (of a plan, idea, etc.) not workable. [**in-**[1] + **operable**]

inoperative *adj* not working or functioning; having no effect. [**in-**[1] + **operative**]

inopportune *adj* not suitable or convenient; badly timed. — *adv* **inopportunely**. [Lat *inopportunus*]

inordinate *adj* greater than is reasonable; beyond acceptable limits. — *adv* **inordinately**. [Lat *inordinatus*]

inorganic *adj* **1** not made of or found in living (i.e. animal or plant) material; mineral. **2** not caused by natural growth. **3** not produced naturally. — *adv* **inorganically**. [**in-**[1] + **organic**]

inorganic chemistry *n* chemistry which deals with inorganic chemicals, i.e. those derived from or occurring in sources other than plants and animals, and containing elements other than carbon (though certain carbon compounds are included in inorganic chemistry). ◇ See also **organic chemistry**.

input *n* **1** the information put into a computer. **2** something which is put or taken in, e.g. a contribution to a discussion. **3** an act or process of putting something in. **4** the money, power, materials, labour, etc. required to produce something, esp. the power put into a machine. — *v* **-tt-** (*tr*) to put (information, data) into a computer. **[in + put]**

inquest *n* **1** an official investigation into an incident, esp. an inquiry into a sudden and unexpected death in a coroner's court before a jury. **2** (*coll*) any discussion after an event, game, etc., esp. one which analyses its result and discusses mistakes made. [Lat *inquesta*]

inquietude *n* physical or mental restlessness or uneasiness. [Lat *inquietudo*]

inquire or **enquire** *v* **1** (*tr* & *intr*; **about**) to ask for information (about). **2** (*intr*; **after**) to ask about the health or happiness of (a person). **3** (*intr*; **for**) to ask to see or talk to (someone). **4** (*intr*; **for**) to ask for (goods, a service, etc.). **5** (*intr*; **into**) to try to discover the facts of (a crime, etc.) esp. formally. **6** (*intr*; **of**) to ask (someone) for information. — *n* **inquirer** or **enquirer**. [Lat *inquirere*]

inquiring *adj* **1** eager to discover or learn things. **2** (of e.g. a look) which seems to be asking a question. — *adv* **inquiringly**.

inquiry or **enquiry** *n* **-ies** **1** an act of asking for information or inquiring. **2** an investigation, esp. a formal one.

inquisition *n* **1** a searching or intensive inquiry or investigation. **2** an official or judicial inquiry. **3** (*cap*; *hist*; also **Spanish Inquisition**) a greatly feared Roman Catholic tribunal founded to suppress and punish heresy, famous for doing so through torture and execution. — *adj* **inquisitional**. [Lat *inquisitio*]

inquisitive *adj* **1** over-eager to find out things, esp. about other people's affairs. **2** eager for knowledge or information. — *adv* **inquisitively**. — *n* **inquisitiveness**. [Lat *inquisitivus*]

inquisitor *n* **1** a person carrying out an inquisition or inquiry, esp. harshly or intensively. **2** (*cap*) a member of the Inquisition. [Lat]

inquisitorial *adj* **1** of or like an inquisitor. **2** unnecessarily or offensively curious about other people's affairs. **3** (*legal*) (of a trial or legal system) in which the judge is also the prosecutor. — *adv* **inquisitorially**.

in re *prep* in the matter of; about. [Lat]

inroad *n* **1** (in *pl*; **into, on**) a large or significant using up or consumption: *make inroads into my savings*. **2** a hostile attack or raid. **[in + road]**

inrush *n* a sudden crowding or rushing in. **[in + rush]**

insalubrious *adj* (of a place) unhealthy; sordid. [Lat *insalubris*]

insane *adj* **1** not of sound mind; mentally ill. **2** extremely foolish; stupid. **3** of or for the mentally ill. — *n* people who are insane. — *adv* **insanely**. [Lat *insanus*]

insanity *n* **-ies** **1** the state of being insane. **2** extreme folly or stupidity.

insanitary *adj* so dirty as to be dangerous to health. — *n* **insanitariness**. **[in-**[1] **+ sanitary]**

insanity. See **insane**.

insatiable *adj* not able to be satisfied; extremely greedy. — *n* **insatiability**. — *adv* **insatiably**. [Lat *insatiabilis*]

inscribe *v* (*tr*) **1** to write, print or engrave (words) on (paper, metal, stone, etc.), often as a lasting record. **2** to enter (a name) on a list or in a book; to enrol. **3** (**to**) to dedicate or address (a book, etc.) to (someone), usu. by writing in the front of it. **4** (*geom*) to draw (a figure) within another figure so as to touch all or some of its sides or faces. ◇ See also **circumscribe**. [Lat *in*, on + *scribere*, to write]

inscription *n* **1** words written, printed or engraved, e.g. as a dedication in the front of a book or as an epitaph on a gravestone. **2** the act of inscribing, esp. of writing a dedication in the front of a book or of entering a name on a list. — *adj* **inscriptional** or **inscriptive**. [Lat *inscriptio*, from *inscribere*, to inscribe]

inscrutable *adj* hard to understand or explain; mysterious; enigmatic. — *n* **inscrutability** or **inscrutableness**. — *adv* **inscrutably**. [Lat *inscrutabilis*]

insect *n* **1** any of many kinds of small invertebrates with a body consisting of a head, thorax and abdomen, three pairs of legs and usu. one or two pairs of wings. **2** (*loosely*) any other small invertebrate, e.g. a spider. **3** an insignificant or worthless person. [Lat *insectum*, cut, notched]

insecticide *n* a substance for killing insects. — *adj* **insecticidal**. **[insect + -cide]**

insectivore *n* **1** any of several small mammals which feed mainly on invertebrates and are mostly nocturnal, including hedgehogs, moles and shrews. **2** any animal or plant that feeds on insects. — *adj* **insectivorous**. [Lat *insectum*, insect + *vorare*, to devour]

insecure *adj* **1** (of a person) lacking confidence; anxious about possible loss or danger. **2** under threat or in danger or likely to be so. **3** not firmly fixed; unstable. — *n* **insecurity**, **-ies**. — *adv* **insecurely**. [Lat *insecurus*]

inseminate *v* (*tr*) **1** to introduce semen into (a female) by a natural or artificial method. **2** to sow (seeds, ideas, etc.). — *n* **insemination**. [Lat *inseminare*]

insensate *adj* **1** not able to perceive physical sensations or experience consciousness;

inanimate. **2** insensitive and unfeeling. **3** having little or no good sense; stupid. — *adv* **insensately**. — *n* **insensateness**. [Lat *insensatus*]

insensible *adj* **1** (**to**) not able to feel pain or experience consciousness; unconscious. **2** (**of, to**) unaware (of); not caring (about). **3** not capable of feeling emotion; callous. **4** too small or slight to be noticed; imperceptible. — *n* **insensibility**. — *adv* **insensibly**. [Lat *insensibilis*]

insensitive *adj* (**to**) **1** not aware (of) or incapable of responding sympathetically (to), esp. other people's feelings. **2** not reacting to stimulation, e.g. touch or light. — *n* **insensitivity**. — *adv* **insensitively**. [**in-**[1] + **sensitive**]

inseparable *adj* **1** incapable of being separated. **2** (of friends, siblings, etc.) unwilling to be apart and constantly together. — *n* **inseparability**. — *adv* **inseparably**. [Lat *inseparabilis*]

insert *v* (*tr*; **between, in, into**) **1** to put, place or fit (something) inside something else. **2** to introduce (text, words, etc.) into the body of other text, words, etc. — *n* something inserted, esp. a loose sheet in a book or magazine, or piece of material in a garment. [Lat *inserere*]

insertion *n* **1** an act of inserting. **2** something inserted, esp. a piece of lace or embroidery inserted in a garment or an advertisement in a newspaper. **3** (*med*) the place where, or the way in which, a muscle is attached to a bone.

inset *n* **1** something set in or inserted, e.g. a piece of lace or cloth set into a garment, or a leaf or leaves set in into a book. **2** a small map or picture put in the corner of a larger one. — *v* **-tt-**, ***inset*** (*tr*) to put in, add or insert. [**in** + **set**]

inshore *adv* & *adj* in or on the water but near or towards the shore. [**in** + **shore**]

inside *n* **1** the inner side, surface or part of something. **2** the part of a path away from the road. **3** the lower part of a double-decker bus. **4** the lane of a running track that is nearest the centre; the equivalent part of any racetrack. **5** (in *pl*; *coll*) the inner organs, esp. the stomach and bowels. **6** (*coll*) a position which gains one the confidence of and otherwise secret information from people in authority. — *adj* **1** being on, near, towards or from the inside. **2** (*coll*) coming from, provided by or organised by a person within an organisation: *The robbery was an inside job.* — *adv* **1** to, in or on the inside or interior. **2** indoors. **3** (*coll*) in or into prison. — *prep* (also *coll* **inside of**) **1** to or on the side of; within. **2** in less than: *be back inside an hour.* — **inside out 1** with the inside surface turned out. **2** (*coll*) thoroughly. [MidE]

insider *n* a recognised or accepted member of an organisation or group who has access to secret information about it.

insider dealing or **trading** *n* the illegal buying and selling of shares by people who work on the stock exchange, based on their having access to information which has not been made public.

inside track *n* **1** the inside lane of a race track, slightly shorter than the other lanes because of the curve. **2** a position of strength, power or advantage.

insidious *adj* **1** developing gradually without being noticed but causing very great harm. **2** attractive but harmful; treacherous. — *adv* **insidiously**. — *n* **insidiousness**. [Lat *insidiae*, ambush]

insight *n* (**into**) **1** the ability to gain a relatively rapid, clear and deep understanding of the real, often hidden and usu. complex nature of a situation, problem, etc. **2** an instance or example of this. — *adj* **insightful**. [MidE]

insignia *n* **-ia** or **-ias** badges or emblems of office, honour or membership. [Lat, badges]

insignificant *adj* **1** of little or no meaning, value, or importance. **2** relatively small in size or amount. — *n* **insignificance**. — *adv* **insignificantly**. [**in-**[1] + **significant**]

insincere *adj* not sincere or genuine; false; hypocritical. — *n* **insincerity**. — *adv* **insincerely**. [Lat *insincerus*]

insinuate *v* (*tr*) **1** to suggest or hint (something unpleasant) indirectly. **2** (**into**) to introduce (e.g. an idea) in an indirect, subtle or devious way. **3** (**into**) to gain acceptance or favour for (esp. oneself) by gradual, careful and often cunning means. — *adv* **insinuatingly**. [Lat *insinuare*]

insinuation *n* **1** an unpleasant, devious or indirect suggestion, reference or hint. **2** an act of insinuating.

insipid *adj* **1** without interest or liveliness; boring. **2** without taste or flavour. — *adv* **insipidly**. — *n* **insipidness**. [Lat *insipidus*]

insist *v* **1** (*intr* & *tr*; **on, upon**) to maintain, state or believe very firmly. **2** (*intr* with **on, upon**) to demand firmly: *insist on one's rights.* [Lat *insistere*]

insistent *adj* **1** making continual, forceful demands; insisting. **2** demanding attention; compelling. — *n* **insistence**. — *adv* **insistently**.

in situ *adv* & *adj* (done, carried out, etc.) while remaining in place; in the natural or original position. [Lat, in the place]

insofar as. See **in**.

insole *n* **1** a loose inner sole which can be put in a shoe or boot for extra warmth, or to make it slightly smaller. **2** a fixed inner sole in a shoe or boot. [**in** + **sole**]

insolent *adj* rude or insulting; showing a lack of respect. — *n* **insolence**. — *adv* **insolently**. [Lat *insolens*, departing from custom]

insoluble *adj* **1** not dissolving in liquid, esp. water. **2** (of a problem) not able to be solved. — *n* **insolubility**. [Lat *insolubilis*]

insolvent *adj* **1** not having enough money to pay one's debts. **2** of or relating to insolvent people or the state of being insolvent. — *n* an insolvent person. — *n* **insolvency**. [**in-**[1] + **solvent**]

insomnia *n* regular or habitual inability to sleep. — *n* & *adj* **insomniac**. [Lat, from *in-*, not + *somnus*, sleep]

insomuch as. See **in**.

insouciant *adj* without cares or worries; light-hearted. — *n* **insouciance**. [Fr, from *in*, not + *soucier*, to worry]

inspect *v* (*tr*) **1** to look at or examine closely, often to find faults or mistakes. **2** to look at or examine officially or ceremonially. — *n* **inspection**. [Lat *inspicere*, to look into]

inspector *n* **1** a person employed to inspect something, esp. officially. **2** (*Br*) a police officer below a superintendent and above a sergeant in rank.

inspectorate *n* **1** a body of inspectors. **2** the office or post of inspector.

inspire *v* **1** (*tr*) to stimulate (a person) to activity, esp. artistic or creative activity. **2** (*tr*) to fill (a person) with a feeling of confidence, encouragement and exaltation. **3** (*tr*; **with, in, into**) to create (a particular feeling) in (someone). **4** (*tr*) to be the origin or source of (a poem, piece of music, etc.). **5** (*tr*) (of supposed divine power or influence) to guide (someone). **6** (*tr* & *intr*) to breathe (air, etc.) in. — *adj* **inspiring**. — *adv* **inspiringly**. [Lat *inspirare*, to breathe into]

inspiration *n* **1** a supposed power which stimulates the mind, esp. to artistic activity or creativity. **2** a similar supposed divine power or influence which leads to the writing of Scripture. **3** a person or thing that inspires, or the state of being inspired. **4** a brilliant or inspired idea. **5** the act of drawing breath into the lungs, or a breath so taken. — *adj* **inspirational**.

inspired *adj* so good, skilful, accurate, etc. as to seem to be the result of inspiration, esp. divine inspiration.

inst *abbrev* instant (*adj* sense **4**).

instability *n* lack of physical or mental steadiness or stability. [Lat *instabilitas*]

install *v* (*tr*) **1** to put (equipment, machinery, etc.) in place and make it ready for use. **2** to place (a person) in office with a formal ceremony. **3** to place (something, oneself, etc.) in a particular position, condition or place. [Lat *installare*]

installation *n* **1** the act or process of installing. **2** a piece of equipment, machinery, etc. that has been installed ready for use. **3** a military base.

instalment *n* **1** one of a series of parts into which a debt is divided for payment. **2** one of several parts published, issued, broadcast, etc. at regular intervals. [OFr *estaler*, to fix, set, probably influenced by **install**]

instalment plan *n* payment for goods purchased by instalments; hire-purchase.

instance *n* **1** an example, esp. of a particular condition or circumstance. **2** a particular stage in a process or a particular situation: *in this instance*. **3** (*formal*) request; urging: *at the instance of*. **4** (*legal*) a process or suit. — **for instance** for example. [Lat *instantia*, from *instare*, to be present]

instant *adj* **1** immediate. **2** (of food, etc.) very quickly and easily prepared. **3** urgent; pressing. **4** of or occurring in the current month. **5** present; current. — *n* **1** a particular moment in time, esp. the present: *this instant*. **2** a very brief period of time. [Lat *instare*, to be present]

instantly *adv* at once; immediately.

instantaneous *adj* done, happening or occurring at once, very quickly or in an instant; immediate. — *adv* **instantaneously**. — *n* **instantaneousness**. [Lat *instantaneus*, from *instare*, to be present]

instead *adv* as a substitute or alternative; in place of something or someone. — **instead of** in place of or as an alternative to. [MidE *in stead*, in place]

instep *n* **1** the inside of the arched middle section of the human foot. **2** the part of a shoe, sock, etc. that covers this. [**in** + **step**]

instigate *v* (*tr*) **1** to urge on or incite (someone) esp. to do something wrong or evil. **2** to set in motion or intitiate (e.g. an inquiry). — *n* **instigation**. — *n* **instigator**. [Lat *instigare*, to goad on]

instil *v* **-ll-** (*tr*; **into**) **1** to put (ideas, feelings, etc.) gradually into a person's mind. **2** to pour (a liquid) into something drop by drop. — *n* **instillation** or **instilment**. — *n* **instiller**. [Lat *instillare*, to drip into]

instinct *n* **1** a natural and usu. fixed way of behaving to particular stimuli without having to think. **2** a natural, involuntary and usu. unconscious reaction, response or impulse. **3** intuition. [Lat *instinctus*, prompting]

instinctive *adj* prompted by instinct or intuition; involuntary; automatic. — *adv* **instinctively**.

institute *n* **1** a society or organisation which promotes research, education or a particular cause. **2** a building or group of buildings used by an institute. **3** an established law, principle, rule or custom. **4** (in *pl*) a book of laws or principles. — *v* (*tr*) **1** to set up, establish or organise. **2** to initiate or cause to begin. **3** to appoint to or install in a position or office. [Lat *instituere*, to establish]

institution *n* **1** an organisation or public body founded esp. for charitable or educational purposes, or as a hospital. **2** (*derog*) any organisation providing temporary residential care for people when considered as being a place which residents rarely manage to leave, and which robs them of their individuality and ability to cope with life, e.g. a long-stay hospital or prison. **3** a custom or tradition. **4** a familiar and well-known object or person. **5** the act of instituting or process of being instituted. [Lat *instituere*, to establish]

institutional *adj* of or like an institution, esp. in being dull or regimented. — *n* **institutionalism**.

institutionalise or **-ize** *v* (*tr*) **1** to place in an institution. **2** to cause (someone) to lose his or her individuality and ability to cope with life by keeping him or her in an institution (e.g. a long-stay hospital or prison) for too long. **3** to make into an institution.

instruct *v* (*tr*) **1** to teach or train (a person) in (a subject or skill). **2** to direct or order. **3** (*legal*) to give (a lawyer) the facts concerning a case. **4** (*legal*) to engage (a lawyer) to act in a case. [Lat *instruere*, to equip, train]

instruction *n* **1** (often in *pl*) a direction, order or command. **2** (in *pl*) (a book or manual giving) clear, detailed guidelines (e.g. on how to operate a machine or piece of equipment). **3** a command or code in a computer program that activates a particular function. **4** teaching.

instructive *adj* giving knowledge or information. — *adv* **instructively**. — *n* **instructiveness**.

instructor *n* **1** a person who gives instruction. **2** (*NAm*) a college or university teacher ranking below a professor.

instructress *n* a female instructor.

instrument *n* **1** a tool, esp. one used for delicate scientific work or measurement. **2** (also **musical instrument**) any of several devices which can be made to produce sounds and music. **3** any thing or person used as a means of achieving or doing something. **4** any of several devices inside a vehicle or aircraft which measure, show and control speed, temperature, direction, etc. **5** a formal or official legal document. — *v* (*tr*) **1** to arrange (music). **2** to equip with instruments for measuring, etc. [Lat *instrumentum*, equipment, tool]

instrumental *adj* **1** (**in, to**) being responsible (for) or an important factor (in). **2** performed by or written or arranged for musical instruments (as opposed to voices). **3** of or done with an instrument or tool. **4** (*gram*) of, in or being the grammatical case which shows how, or with what, an action is performed. — *n* **1** a piece of music performed by or written or arranged for musical instruments. **2** (*gram*) the instrumental case. — *adv* **instrumentally**.

instrumentalist *n* a person who plays a musical instrument.

instrumentation *n* **1** the particular way in which a piece of music is written or arranged to be played by instruments. **2** the instruments used to play a particular piece of music. **3** the use, design or provision of instruments or tools.

insubordinate *adj* disobedient; refusing to take orders. — *adv* **insubordinately**. — *n* **insubordination**. [**in-**[1] + **subordinate**]

insubstantial *adj* **1** not solid, strong, or satisfying; flimsy. **2** not made up of solid material; not real. — *n* **insubstantiality**. — *adv* **insubstantially**. [Lat *insubstantialis*]

insufferable *adj* too unpleasant, annoying, etc. to bear; intolerable. — *adv* **insufferably**. [**in-**[1] + **suffer**]

insufficient *adj* not enough or adequate; not sufficient. — *n* **insufficiency**. — *adv* **insufficiently**. [Lat *insufficientia*]

insular *adj* **1** of or belonging to an island or the inhabitants of an island. **2** (of a person, opinions, etc.) not influenced by or responsive to contact with other people, cultures, etc; narrow-minded; prejudiced. — *n* **insularity**. [Lat *insularis*, from *insula*, island]

insulate *v* (*tr*) **1** to prevent the passing of heat, sound, electricity, etc. from (a body), esp. by covering it with some special material. **2** to remove or set (someone or something) apart; to isolate. [Lat *insula*, island]

insulation *n* **1** material used in insulating, esp. material which does not conduct heat or electricity. **2** the process of insulating or being insulated.

insulating tape *n* adhesive tape used to cover bare or exposed electrical wires, to protect people from electric shocks.

insulator *n* a substance or device that provides insulation and is used esp. for insulating conductors.

insulin *n* a hormone produced in the pancreas which controls the amount of sugar in the blood, a lack of this hormone being the cause of diabetes. [Lat *insula*, island, because obtained from a part of the pancreas known as the Islands of Langerhans]

insult *v* (*tr*) to behave rudely or offensively to; to speak rudely or offensively to or about. — *n* **1** a rude, offensive remark or action. **2** an affront. **3** (*med*) (something that causes) injury or damage to the body. — *adj* **insulting**. — *adv* **insultingly**. — **add insult to injury** to make a bad situation, etc. even worse. [Lat *insultare*, to jump on]

insuperable *adj* too difficult to be overcome, defeated, or dealt with successfully. — *n* **insuperability**. — *adv* **insuperably**. [Lat *insuperabilis*]

insupportable *adj* **1** that is too unpleasant, severe, annoying, etc. to be tolerated. **2** that cannot be justified. [Lat *insupportabilis*]

insure *v* **1** (*tr* & *intr*; **against**) to arrange for the payment of an amount of money in the event of the loss or theft of or damage to (property) or injury to or the death of (someone), etc. by paying regular amounts of money to an insurance company. **2** (*tr*; **against**) to take measures to try to prevent (an event leading to loss, damage, difficulties, etc.). **3** (*intr*; esp. *NAm*) to provide insurance; to underwrite. — *adj* **insurable**. [OFr *enseurer*, to ensure]

insurance *n* **1** an agreement by which one party promises to pay another party money in the event of loss, theft or damage to property, personal injury or death, etc. **2** (also **insurance policy**) the contract for such an agreement. **3** the protection offered by such a contract. **4** money, usu. paid regularly, in return for such a contract; an insurance premium. **5** the sum which will be paid in the event of loss, theft or damage to property, personal injury or death, etc. **6** the business of providing such contracts for clients. **7** anything done, any measure taken, to try to prevent possible loss, disappointment, problems, etc. **8** an act or instance of insuring.

the insured *n* a person whose life, health or property is covered by insurance.

insurer *n* a person or company that provides insurance.

insurgent *adj* opposed to and fighting against the government of the country; rebellious. — *n* a rebel. — *n* **insurgence** or **insurgency**. [Lat *in surgere*, to rise up]

insurmountable *adj* too difficult to be dealt with successfully; impossible to overcome. — *n* **insurmountability**. [**in-**[1] + **surmountable**]

insurrection *n* an act of rebellion against authority. — *n* **insurrectionist**. [Lat *insurgere*, to rise up]

int. *abbrev* **1** internal. **2** interior. **3** international.

intact *adj* whole; not broken or damaged; untouched. [Lat *intactus*]

intaglio *n* **-lios** or **-li** **1** a stone or gem which has a design engraved in its surface (as opposed to a **cameo**). **2** a design which is engraved in the surface of a material. **3** the art or process of engraving designs into the surface of objects, esp. jewellery. [Ital, from *intagliare*, to cut into]

intake *n* **1** a thing or quantity taken in or accepted. **2** an opening through which liquid or gas enters a pipe, engine, etc. **3** an act of taking in. [**in** + **take**]

intangible *adj* **1** not able to be felt or perceived by touch. **2** difficult to understand or for the mind to grasp. **3** (of part of a business, e.g. an asset) not having a solid physical existence, but having some value or worth. — *n* **intangibility**. — *adv* **intangibly**. [Lat *intangibilis*]

integer *n* any whole number, e.g. *0, 8, −12*. [Lat, untouched]

integral *adj* **1** (**to**) being a necessary part (of a whole). **2** forming a whole; supplied or fitted as part of a whole. **3** whole; complete. **4** (*math*) of, being or involving integrals or integers. — *n* (*math*) the sum of a very large, definite or indefinite, number of very small quantities. [Lat *integralis*]

integral calculus see **calculus**.

integrand *n* (*math*) a function that is to be integrated. [Lat *integrandus*]

integrate *v* **1** (*tr*) to fit (parts) together to form a whole. **2** (*tr* & *intr*; **into, with**) to mix or cause to mix freely with other groups in society, etc. **3** (*tr*) to end racial segregation in. **4** (*tr*; *math*) to find the integral of. **5** (*tr*; *math*) to find the total or mean value of. — *n* **integration**. [Lat *integrare*, to renew]

integrated circuit *n* (esp. *comput*) a very small electronic circuit consisting of several separate semiconductor devices, such as transistors and resistors, printed into a single silicon chip.

integrity *n* **1** strict adherence to moral values and principles; uprightness. **2** the quality or state of being whole and unimpaired. [Lat *integritas*]

integument *n* any natural outer covering, e.g a shell, skin, husk, etc. — *adj* **integumental** or **integumentary**. [Lat *integumentum*]

intellect *n* **1** the ability to think, reason and understand, esp. when highly developed. **2** a particular person's ability to think, reason and understand. **3** a person who has a highly developed intellect and great mental ability. [Lat *intelligere*, to understand]

intellectual *adj* **1** of, involving or appealing to the intellect. **2** having a highly developed ability to think, reason and understand. — *n* a person with a highly developed intellect and great mental ability. — *adv* **intellectually**.

intellectualise or **-ize** *v* **1** (*tr*) to think about or analyse (e.g. a problem) intellectually or rationally. **2** (*intr*; **about**) to think rationally or intellectually; to philosophise.

intelligence *n* **1** the ability to learn, understand, apply knowledge and think rationally. **2** an act of understanding. **3** news or information. **4** the gathering of secret information about an enemy. **5** the government department or group of people, e.g. in the army, responsible for gathering such information. [Lat *intelligentia*, from *intelligere*, to understand]

intelligence quotient or **IQ** *n* a measure of a person's intelligence, given as a ratio of mental age to real age and usu. expressed as a percentage.

intelligent *adj* **1** having or showing highly developed mental ability; clever. **2** (of a machine, computer, weapon, etc.) able to vary its behaviour according to the situation. — *adv* **intelligently**.

intelligentsia *n* (usu. with **the**) the most highly educated and cultured people in a society, esp. when considered as a political class. [Russ]

intelligible *adj* **1** able to be understood; clear. **2** only able to be understood by the intellect and not by the senses or feelings. — *n* **intelligibility**. — *adv* **intelligibly**. [Lat *intelligibilis*]

intemperate *adj* **1** going beyond reasonable limits; not controlled or restrained. **2** habitually drinking too much alcohol. **3** (of a climate or region) having extreme and severe temperatures. ◇ See also **temperate**. — *n* **intemperance**. — *adv* **intemperately**. [Lat *intemperatus*]

intend *v* (*tr*) **1** to plan or have in mind as one's purpose or aim. **2** (**for**) to set aside (for) or destine (to some specified person or thing). **3** to mean. [Lat *intendere*, to stretch towards]

intended *adj* meant, done on purpose or planned. — *n* (*coll*) one's future husband or wife.

intense *adj* **1** very great or extreme. **2** feeling or expressing emotion deeply. **3** very deeply felt: *intense happiness*. — *adv* **intensely**. — *n* **intenseness**. [Lat *intendere*, to stretch towards]

intensify *v* (*tr* & *intr*) to make or become intense or more intense. — *n* **intensification**.

intensifier *n* (*gram*) an adverb or adjective which adds emphasis to or intensifies the word or phrase which follows it.

intensity *n* **-ies** **1** the quality or state of being intense. **2** (*physics*) the measurable amount of some force or quality, e.g. heat, light or sound.

intensive *adj* **1** (often *in cmpds*) using, done with or requiring considerable amounts of (thought, effort, time, etc.) within a relatively short period: *labour-intensive*. **2** thorough; concentrated; intense. **3** using large amounts of capital and labour (rather than more land or raw materials) to increase production. **4** (*gram*) (of an adverb or adjective) giving emphasis. — *n* (*gram*) an intensive adverb or adjective. — *adv* **intensively**. — *n* **intensiveness**. [Lat *intensivus*, from *intendere*, to stretch towards]

intensive care *n* (a hospital ward providing) medical treatment during which a patient's condition, temperature, blood pressure, heart, etc. is continually monitored.

intent *n* **1** something which is aimed at or intended; a purpose. **2** the purpose of committing a crime: *loitering with intent*. — *adj* **1** (**on, upon**) firmly determined (to do something). **2** (**on, upon**) having one's attention firmly fixed (on something); concentrating hard (on). **3** showing concentration; absorbed: *an intent look*. — *adv* **intently**. — *n* **intentness**. — **to all intents and purposes** in every important respect; virtually. [Lat *intendere*, to stretch towards]

intention *n* **1** that which one plans or intends to do; an aim or purpose. **2** (in *pl*; *coll*) someone's, esp. a man's, purpose with regard to marriage. **3** (*RC*; also **special** or **particular intention**) the purpose or reason for prayers being said or mass celebrated. [Lat *intendere*, to stretch towards]

intentional *adj* said, done, etc. on purpose; deliberate. — *adv* **intentionally**.

inter *v* **-rr-** (*tr*) to bury (a dead person, etc.) in the earth or a tomb. [Lat *in*, into + *terra*, earth]

interment *n* a burial.

inter- *comb fm* **1** between or among. **2** mutual(ly) or reciprocal(ly). [Lat *inter*, among]

interact *v* (*intr*) to act with or on one another. — *n* **interaction**. [**inter-** + **act**]

interactive *adj* **1** in which the people, things, etc. interact. **2** involving or allowing a continuous exchange of information between a computer and its user. — *adv* **interactively**.

inter alia *adv* among other things. [Lat]

interbreed *v* **-*bred*** (*intr* & *tr*; **with**) **1** to (cause to) breed with members of a different species or race. **2** to (cause to) breed with members of the same family or strain. — *n* **interbreeding**. [**inter-** + **breed**]

intercalary *adj* **1** (of a day) added to a calendar month to make the calendar year match the solar year, e.g. the day added to February every leap year. **2** (of a year) containing such a day or days. **3** coming between two layers; intervening. [Lat *intercalarius*]

intercede *v* (*intr*) **1** to act as a peacemaker between (two parties, countries, etc.). **2** (**for**) to plead or make an appeal on behalf of someone. ◇ See also **intercession**. [Lat *inter*, between + *cedere*, to move]

intercept *v* (*tr*) **1** to stop or catch (e.g. a person, missile, aircraft, etc.) on his, its, etc. way from one place to another; to prevent (a missile, etc.) from arriving at its destination, often by destroying it. **2** (*math*) to mark off (a space, line, curve, etc.) between two points. — *n* (*math*) that part of a line that is intercepted. — *n* **interception**. — *adv* **interceptive**. [Lat *inter*, between + *capere*, to seize]

interceptor *n* a person or thing that intercepts, esp. a small light aircraft used to intercept approaching enemy aircraft.

intercession *n* **1** an act of interceding or making an appeal on behalf of another. **2** (a prayer requesting) the asking of favour or forgiveness from God on behalf of someone else. — *adj* **intercessional**. — *n* **intercessor**. [Lat *intercessio*]

interchange *v* (*intr* & *tr*; **with**) to (cause to) change places (with). — *n* **1** an act of interchanging; an exchange. **2** a road junction, esp. leading to or from a motorway, consisting of a series of roads and bridges designed to prevent streams of traffic from directly crossing one another. — *n* **interchangeability**. — *adj* **interchangeable**. — *adv* **interchangeably**. [MidE *entrechaungen*]

intercity *adj* (*Br*) of or providing a fast service between major cities and not stopping at every station on the way. [**inter-** + **city**]

intercom *n* a system consisting of microphones and loudspeakers which allow communication within a building, aircraft, ship, etc. [Abbrev. of **intercommunication**]

intercommunicate *v* (*intr*) **1** to communicate mutually or together. **2** (of two rooms, etc.) to be joined by a connecting door; to interconnect. — *n* **intercommunication**. [Lat *intercommunicatus*, intercommunicating]

interconnect *v* (*tr* & *intr*; **with**) to connect (two things) or be connected together or with one another. — *n* **interconnection**. [**inter-** + **connect**]

intercontinental *adj* travelling between or connecting different continents. [**inter-** + **continental**]

intercontinental ballistic missile *n* a ballistic missile which can travel great distances and which can therefore be fired at a target in another continent.

intercourse *n* **1** sexual intercourse. **2** communication, connection or dealings between people, groups of people, countries, etc. **3** communion, e.g. between people and God. [Lat *intercursus*, a running between, communication]

interdenominational *adj* happening between or involving (members of) different religious denominations. [**inter-** + **denominational**]

interdepartmental *adj* happening between or involving (members of) different departments within a single organisation, etc. [**inter-** + **departmental**]

interdependent *adj* depending on one another. — *n* **interdependence**. — *adv* **interdependently**. [**inter-** + **dependent**]

interdict *n* **1** an official order forbidding someone to do something. **2** (*RC*) a sentence or punishment removing the right to most sacraments (including burial but not communion) from the people of a place or district. — *v* (*tr*) to place under an interdict; to forbid or prohibit. — *n* **interdiction**. — *adj* **interdictory**. [Lat *interdictum*, prohibition]

interdisciplinary *adj* involving two or more subjects of study. [**inter-** + **disciplinary**]

interest *n* **1** the desire to learn or know about someone or something; curiosity. **2** the power to attract a person's attention and curiosity. **3** something which arouses a person's attention and curiosity; a hobby or pastime. **4** money paid as a charge for borrowing money or using credit, usu. in the form of a percentage of what is borrowed or owed. **5** (often in *pl*) advantage, benefit or profit, esp. financial: *It is in your own best interests to be as quick as possible.* **6** a share or claim in a business and its profits, or a legal right to property. **7** (also **interest group**) a group of people or organisations with common, esp. financial, aims and concerns: *the banking interest*. — *v* (*tr*) **1** to attract the attention and curiosity of. **2** (**in**) to cause (someone or oneself) to take a part in or be concerned about some activity. — **in the interest(s) of** in order to achieve or help towards. [Lat, it concerns]

interested *adj* **1** (**in**) showing or having a concern or interest. **2** personally involved and therefore not impartial or disinterested. — *adv* **interestedly**. ◇ See also **disinterested** and **uninterested.**

interesting *adj* attracting interest; holding the attention. — *adv* **interestingly**.

interface *n* **1** a surface forming a common boundary between two regions, things, etc. which cannot be mixed, e.g. oil and water. **2** a common boundary or meeting-point between two different systems or processes. **3** a device, e.g. an electrical circuit, which allows two pieces of esp. computing equipment to be linked and operated together. — *v* (*tr* & *intr*; **with**) to connect (with another piece of equipment) by an interface. [**inter-** + **face**]

interfacing *n* a piece of stiff fabric sewn between two layers of material to give shape and stiffness. [**inter-** + **facing**]

interfere *v* (*intr*) **1** (**between**, **in**, **with**) to involve oneself in matters which do not concern one and where one is not wanted. **2** (with **with**) to get in the way of, slow down or hinder the progress of. **3** (with **with**; *euph*) to assault or molest sexually. **4** (*physics*) (of sound waves, rays of light, etc.) to combine together to cause disturbance or interference. — *adj* **interfering**. [OFr *s'entreferir*, to strike each other]

interference *n* **1** (**between**, **in**, **with**) the act of interfering. **2** the unwanted, confused noises and crackles which disturb radio or television reception, caused by the presence of unwanted signals and changes in the atmosphere. **3** (*physics*) the meeting of two or more waves of the same frequency to form a new wave in which the disturbance they produce is either neutralised or made stronger.

interferon *n* any of several proteins produced by the body to prevent the growth of a hostile virus. [**interfere**]

interfuse *v* **1** (*tr*) to mix (with something). **2** (*tr* & *intr*) to blend or fuse together. — *n* **interfusion**. [Lat *interfundere*, to pour between]

intergalactic *adj* happening or situated between different galaxies. [**inter-** + **galactic**]

interim *adj* temporary; not intended to be final or to last; provisional. — **in the interim** in the time between two events; in the meantime. [Lat, in the meantime]

interior *adj* **1** on, of, suitable for, happening or acting in, or coming from the inside; inner. **2** away from the shore or frontier; inland. **3** concerning the domestic or internal, rather than foreign, affairs of a country. **4** of or existing in the mind or spirit; of mental or spiritual life. — *n* **1** an internal or inner part; the inside. **2** the part of a country or continent that is furthest from the coast. **3** the internal or home affairs of a country. **4** a picture or representation of the inside of a room or building, esp. with reference to its decoration or style: *a typical southern French interior*. [Lat, further inward, from *inter*, inward]

interior angle *n* an angle between two adjacent sides of a polygon.

interior decoration or **design** *n* **1** the decoration, design and furnishings of a room or building. **2** the art or job of designing the insides of rooms, including selecting colours and furnishings. — *n* **interior decorator** or **designer**.

interj *abbrev* interjection.

interject *v* (*tr*) to say or add abruptly; to interrupt with. [Lat *interjicere*, to throw between]

interjection *n* **1** a word, phrase or sound used as an exclamation to express surprise, sudden disappointment, pain, etc. **2** an act of interjecting. — *adj* **interjectional**.

interlace *v* **1** (*tr* & *intr*; **with**) to join by lacing or by crossing over. **2** (*tr*; **with**) to mix or blend with: *a story interlaced with graphic descriptions*. — *n* **interlacement**. [MidE *entrelacen*]

interlard *v* (*tr*; **with**) to add foreign words, quotations, unusual phrases, etc. to (a speech or piece of writing), often excessively. [OFr *entrelarder*]

interleaf *n* **-ves** a usu. blank leaf of paper inserted between the leaves of a book. [**inter-** + **leaf**]

interleave *v* (*tr*) to insert a usu. blank leaf of paper between.

interleukin *n* a protein produced by white blood cells which fights infection. [**inter-** + **leucocyte**]

interline[1] *v* (*tr*) to insert (words) between the lines of (a document, book, etc.). — *n* **interlineation**. [Lat *interlineare*]

interlinear *adj* (of words) inserted between the lines of a document, book, etc.

interline[2] *v* (*tr*) to put an extra lining between the first lining and the fabric (of a garment), esp. for stiffness. [**inter-** + **line**[2]]

interlining *n* a piece of material used as an extra lining.

interlinear, **interlineation**. See **interline**[1].

interlink *v* (*tr* & *intr*) to join or connect together. [**inter-** + **link**]

interlock *v* (*tr* & *intr*) to fit, fasten or connect together, esp. by the means of teeth or parts which fit into each other. — *n* a device or mechanism that connects and coordinates the functions of different parts or components of e.g. a machine. — *adj* (of a fabric or garment) knitted with closely locking stitches. — *adj* **interlocking**. [**inter-** + **lock**]

interlocutor *n* a person who takes part in a conversation or dialogue. — *n* **interlocution**. [Lat *interloqui*, to speak between]

interlocutory *adj* **1** of conversation or dialogue. **2** (*legal*) (of a decree) given during legal proceedings and only provisional.

interloper *n* a person who meddles or interferes with other people's affairs, or goes to places where he or she has no right to be; an intruder.

interlude *n* **1** a short period of time between two events, or a short period of a different activity. **2** a short break between the acts of a play or opera, or between items of music. **3** a short piece of music, or short item of entertainment, played during such a break. [Lat *interludium*]

intermarry *v* **-ies**, **-ied** (*intr*) **1** (**with**) (of different races, social and religious groups, etc.) to become connected by marriage. **2** to marry someone from one's own family. — *n* **intermarriage**. [**inter-** + **marry**]

intermediary *n* **-ies** **1** a person who mediates between two people or groups, often to try to settle a dispute between them or bring them into agreement. **2** any intermediate person or thing. [Lat *intermedium*, intervening place]

intermediate *adj* in the middle; placed between two points, stages or extremes in place or time. — *n* **1** an intermediate thing. **2** any chemical compound which is manufactured from some material and which itself serves as the starting material for the manufacture of another product. — *v* (*intr*) to act as an intermediary. — *adv* **intermediately**. — *n* **intermediation**. [Lat *intermediatus*, from *intermedium*, intervening place]

interment. See **inter**.

intermezzo *n* **-zos** or **-zi** **1** a short piece of instrumental music played between two major sections in an extended piece of music such as an opera. **2** a short instrumental work performed on its own. [Ital, from Lat *intermedium*, intervening place]

interminable *adj* having or seeming to have no end, esp. because of being extremely dull and tedious. — *n* **interminableness**. — *adv* **interminably**. [Lat *interminabilis*]

intermingle *v* (*tr* & *intr*; **with**) to mingle or mix together. [**inter-** + **mingle**]

intermission *n* a short pause between two things, e.g. between two parts of a film, play, etc. or between two serious attacks of disease. [Lat *intermissio*, interruption]

intermittent *adj* happening occasionally; stopping for a while and then starting again; not continuous. — *n* **intermittence**. — *adj* **intermittently**. [Lat *intermittere*, to leave a space between]

intern[1] *v* (*tr*) to confine within a country, restricted area or prison, esp. during a war. — *n* **internment**. [Fr *interner*]

internee *n* a person who is interned.

intern[2] or **interne** *n* (*NAm*) an advanced student or graduate who is gaining practical professional experience by working, esp. a medical graduate working as an assistant physician or surgeon in a hospital. — *n* **internship**. [Lat *internus*, internal]

internal *adj* **1** of, on, in or suitable for the inside; inner. **2** of, on, in or suitable for the inside of the body. **3** of a nation's domestic affairs as opposed to its relations with foreign countries. **4** of, for or coming from within an organisation. **5** of the inner nature or feelings or of the mind or soul. — *adv* **internally**. [Lat *internalis*, from *internus*, inward]

internal combustion engine *n* an engine which produces power by burning a mixture of fuel and air within a cylinder, used e.g. in cars.

internalise or **-ize** *v* (*tr*) **1** to make (a type of behaviour, characteristic, etc.) part of one's personality. **2** to keep (an emotion) inside oneself rather than express it. — *n* **internalisation** or **-z-**.

international *adj* of, involving, affecting, used by or carried on between two or more nations. — *n* **1** a sports match between two national teams. **2** a player who takes part in, or has taken part in, such a match. **3** (usu. *cap*) any of four organisations (founded in 1864, 1889, 1919 and 1938) whose aim was to promote international socialism. — *n* **internationality**. — *adv* **internationally**. [**inter-** + **national**]

International Date Line *n* an imaginary line on the earth's surface running north to south across the middle of the Pacific Ocean, the date in countries on the west of it being one day ahead of the date in countries on the east.

internationalise or **-ize** *v* (*tr*) to make international, esp. to bring under the control of two or more countries. — *n* **internationalisation** or **-z-**.

internationalism *n* the view that the nations of the world should co-operate politically, economically, culturally, etc. and work towards greater mutual understanding. — *n* & *adj* **internationalist**.

International Monetary Fund *n* an international financial organisation set up to promote trade by keeping currencies stable and having a fund of money from which member states may borrow.

International Phonetic Alphabet *n* a system of signs and letters able to represent all of the speech sounds of every language.

Internationale *n* **1** an international socialist and communist song, with words orig. in French. **2** an international (sense **3**). [Fr, international]

interne. See **intern**[2].

internecine *adj* **1** (of a fight, war, etc.) destructive and damaging to both sides. **2** of, involving or being a conflict or struggle within a group or organisation: *an internecine feud.* [Lat *internecinus*, murderous]

internee, internment. See **intern**[1].

interpellate *v* (*tr*) to question (e.g. a government minister) about policy during the course of, and as an interruption to, a debate. — *n* **interpellation**. — *n* **interpellator**. [Lat *interpellare*, to disturb by speaking]

interpenetrate *v* **1** (*tr*) to penetrate thoroughly. **2** (*intr*) to penetrate mutually. — *n* **interpenetration**. [**inter-** + **penetrate**]

interpersonal *adj* of, concerning or involving the relationships between people. [**inter-** + **personal**]

interplanetary *adj* happening or existing between planets. [**inter-** + **planetary**]

interplay *n* the action and influence of two or more things on each other. [**inter-** + **play**]

Interpol *n* an international organisation through which police forces in different countries can communicate and co-operate with each other in fighting crime. [*Inter*national Criminal *Pol*ice Organisation]

interpolate *v* (*tr*; **in**) **1** to add (words) to a book or manuscript, esp. so as to make the text misleading or corrupt. **2** to alter (a text) in this way. **3** to interrupt a conversation, a person speaking, etc. with (a remark or comment). **4** (*math*) to estimate (values) from others in the same series which are already known. — *n* **interpolation**. [Lat *interpolare*, to refurbish or touch up]

interpose *v* **1** (*tr* & *intr*; **between**) to put (something), or come, between two other things. **2** (*tr*) to interrupt a conversation or argument with (a remark, comment, etc.). **3** (*intr*; **between**) to act as mediator; to intervene. — *n* **interposition**. [OFr *interposer*]

interpret *v* **-t- 1** (*tr*) to explain the meaning of (a foreign word, dream, etc.). **2** (*intr*) to act as an interpreter. **3** (*tr*; **as**) to consider or understand (behaviour, a remark, etc.): *interpret her silence as disapproval.* **4** (*tr*) to bring out one's idea of the meaning of (e.g. a dramatic role, piece of music) in one's performance. — *adj* **interpretative** or **interpretive**. — *adv* **interpretatively** or **interpretively**. [Lat *interpretari*]

interpretation *n* **1** an act of interpreting or the sense given as a result. **2** the representing of one's idea of the meaning of a dramatic role, piece of music, etc. in one's performance.

interpreter *n* **1** a person who translates speech in a foreign language as the words are spoken, relaying the translation orally as it is done. **2** a computer program that translates instructions one by one and executes them immediately.

interracial *adj* between different races of people. — *adv* **interracially**. [**inter-** + **racial**]

interregnum *n* **-nums** or **-na 1** the time between two reigns when the throne is unoccupied, e.g. between the death of one monarch and the coronation of the next. **2** the period between the end of rule by one government and the beginning of rule by the next. **3** any interval or pause in a continuous sequence of events. [Lat *inter*, between + *regnum*, reign]

interrelate *v* (*tr* & *intr*) to be in or be brought into a mutually dependent or reciprocal relationship. — *adj* **interrelated**. — *n* **interrelation**. — *n* **interrelationship**. [**inter-** + **relate**]

interrogate *v* (*tr*) **1** to question closely and thoroughly, or examine by asking questions and sometimes with threatening behaviour. **2** (of a radar set, etc.) to send out signals to (a radio beacon) to work out a position. — *n* **interrogation**. — *n* **interrogator**. [Lat *interrogare*]

interrogative *adj* **1** of, like, asking or seeming to ask a question. **2** (*gram*) (of an adjecive or pronoun) used to ask a question. — *n* an interrogative word, sentence or construction. — *adv* **interrogatively**. [Lat *interrogativus*]

interrogatory *adj* being or expressing a question. — *n* **-ies** a question or inquiry. [Lat *interrogatorius*]

interrupt *v* **1** (*tr* & *intr*) to break into (a conversation or monologue) by asking a question or making a comment. **2** (*tr*) to make a break in the continuous activity of (an event). **3** (*tr*) to destroy (a view e.g. of a clear sweep of land) by getting in the way. — *adj* **interruptive**. [Lat *interrumpere*, to break apart]

interrupter or **interruptor** *n* **1** a person who interrupts. **2** a device for interrupting, esp. for opening and closing an electric circuit.

interruption *n* **1** the act of interrupting or state of being interrupted. **2** something that interrupts, such as a question or remark. **3** a short pause or break.

intersect *v* **1** (*tr*) to divide (lines, an area, etc.) by passing or cutting through or across. **2** (*intr*) (esp. of lines, roads, etc.) to run through or cut across each other. [Lat *intersecare*, to cut through]

intersection *n* **1** a place where things meet or intersect, esp. a road junction. **2** the act of intersecting. **3** (*geom*) the point or line where two lines or plane surfaces intersect. **4** (*math*) the set of elements which two or more sets have in common. — *adj* **intersectional**.

interspace *n* a space between two things; an interval. — *v* (*tr*) to put a space or intervals between. [**inter-** + **space**]

intersperse *v* **1** (*tr*) to scatter or insert (something) here and there. **2** (*intr*) to diversify or change slightly with scattered things. — *n* **interspersion**. [Lat *interspergere*, to strew here and there]

interstate *adj* between two or more states, esp. in the USA or Australia. — *n* (*US*) a major road crossing a state boundary. [**inter-** + **state**]

interstellar *adj* between or among the stars. [**inter-** + **stellar**]

interstice *n* **1** a very small gap or space between two things. **2** (*physics*) any of the spaces between atoms in a crystal. [Lat *interstitium*]

intertwine *v* (*tr* & *intr*) to twist or be twisted together. [**inter-** + **twine**]

interval *n* **1** a period of time between two events. **2** a space or distance between two things. **3** (*Br*) a short break between the acts of a play or opera, or between parts of a concert or long film. **4** (*mus*) the difference in pitch between two notes or tones. — **at intervals 1** here and there; now and then. **2** (**of**) with a stated distance in time or space between. [Lat *intervallum*, space between pallisades]

intervene *v* (*intr*) **1** (**in**) to involve oneself (in something which is happening) in order to affect the outcome. **2** (**in, between**) to involve oneself or interfere (in a dispute between other people) in order to settle it or prevent more serious conflict. **3** to come or occur between two things in place or time. **4** (*legal*) to become involved in a lawsuit as a third party. [Lat *intervenire*, to come between]

intervention *n* an act of intervening, esp. in the affairs of other people or other countries.

interventionism *n* the belief that the government of a country should be allowed to interfere, or should interfere, in the economic affairs of the country or in the internal affairs of other countries or states. — *n* & *adj* **interventionist**.

interview *n* **1** a formal meeting and discussion with someone, esp. one at which an employer meets and judges a prospective employee. **2** a conversation or discussion which aims at obtaining information, esp. one in which a journalist asks questions of a famous or important person and which is broadcast or published. — *v* (*tr*) to hold an interview with. — *n* **interviewer**. [OFr *entrevue*, from *entrevoir*, to glimpse]

interviewee *n* a person who is interviewed.

interweave *v* **-wove**, **-woven** (*tr* & *intr*; **with**) to weave or be woven together. [**inter-** + **weave**]

intestate (*legal*) *adj* (of a person) dying without having made a valid will. — *n* a person who dies without making a valid will. — *n* **intestacy**. [Lat *intestatus*]

intestine *n* the tube-like part of the alimentary canal leading from the stomach to the anus, divided into the **small intestine** (comprising the duodenum, jejunum and ileum) and the **large intestine** (comprising the caecum, colon and rectum). — *adj* **intestinal** . [Lat *intestinus*, internal]

intifada *n* the uprising in 1987 and continuing resistance by Palestinians to Israeli occupation of the Gaza Strip and West Bank of the Jordan. [Arabic, shaking off]

intimate[1] *adj* **1** (**with**) marked by or sharing a close, warm and affectionate friendship. **2** very private or personal. **3** (of a place) small and quiet with a warm, friendly atmosphere promoting close personal relations. **4** (**with**) sharing a sexual relationship. **5** (of knowledge) deep and thorough. — *n* a close friend. [Lat *intimus*, innermost]

intimacy *n* **-ies 1** a warm, close personal friendship. **2** an intimate or personal remark. **3** sexual intercourse. **4** the state or quality of being intimate. — *adv* **intimately**.

intimate[2] *v* (*tr*) **1** to announce or make known. **2** to hint or suggest indirectly. — *n* **intimation**. [Lat *intimare*, to impress upon]

intimidate *v* (*tr*; **into**) to frighten (someone) into doing what one wants, esp. with threats. — *adj* **intimidating**. — *n* **intimidation**. [Lat *intimidare*, from *timidus*, frightened]

into *prep* **1** to or towards the inside or middle of. **2** against; into contact or collision with. **3** (expressing a change of state or condition) so as to be: *change into a suit*; *get into difficulties*; *form into groups*. **4** up to a certain point in time. **5** (*math*) used to express division: *divide four into twenty*. **6** (*coll*) involved with, interested in or enthusiastic about. [OE]

intolerable *adj* which is too bad, difficult, painful, etc. to be put up with. — *adv* **intolerably**. [Lat *intolerabilis*]

intolerant *adj* (**of**) refusing or unwilling to accept ideas, beliefs, behaviour, etc. different from one's own. — *n* **intolerance**. — *adv* **intolerantly**. [Lat *intolerans*, impatient]

intonate *v* (*tr* & *intr*) to intone. [Lat *intonare*, to intone]

intonation *n* **1** the rise and fall of the pitch of the voice in speech. **2** the opening phrase of a plainsong melody. **3** an act of intoning. **4** the correct pitching of musical notes.

intone *v* (*tr* & *intr*) **1** to recite (a prayer, etc.) in a solemn, monotonous voice or in singing tones. **2** to say (something) with a particular intonation or tone. [Lat *intonare*]

in toto *adv* totally; completely. [Lat]

intoxicant *n* something that causes intoxication, esp. an alcoholic drink. — *adj* intoxicating. [Lat *intoxicare*, to poison]

intoxicate *v* (*tr*) **1** to make drunk. **2** to excite or elate to the point at which self-control is lost. — *adj* **intoxicating**. — *n* **intoxication**.

intra- *pfx* within; inside; on the inside. [Lat *intra*, within]

intractable *adj* **1** (of a person) difficult to control or influence; obstinate. **2** (of a problem, illness, etc.) difficult to solve, cure or deal with. — *n* **intractableness** or **intractability**. — *adv* **intractably**. [Lat *intractabilis*]

intramural *adj* **1** within or amongst the people in an institution, esp. a school, college or university. **2** within the scope of normal studies. — *adv* **intramurally**. [**intra-** + **mural**]

intransigent *adj* holding firmly to one's (often extreme) beliefs and refusing to change or compromise; stubborn. — *n* an intransigent person. — *n* **intransigence**. — *adv* **intransigently**. [Span *intransigente*, from Lat *in-*, not + *transigere*, to come to an agreement]

intransitive *adj* (*gram*) (of a verb) that does not have a direct object, such as the verb *run* in the phrase *run as fast as you can*. — *adv* **intransitively**. ◇ See also **transitive**. [Lat *intransitivus*]

intrauterine *adj* within the uterus. [**intra-** + **uterine**]

intrauterine device *n* a small, usu. coiled length of plastic-covered wire inserted into the womb to prevent pregnancy.

intravenous *adj* in or into a vein or veins. — *adv* **intravenously**. [**intra-** + **venous**]

intrepid *adj* bold and daring; fearless; brave. — *n* **intrepidity**. — *adv* **intrepidly**. [Lat *intrepidus*]

intricate *adj* full of complicated, interrelating or tangled details or parts and therefore difficult to understand, analyse or sort out. — *n* **intricacy**, **-ies**. — *adv* **intricately**. [Lat *intricare*, to perplex]

intrigue *n* **1** secret plotting or underhand scheming. **2** a secret plot or plan. **3** a secret illicit love affair. — *v* **1** (*tr*) to excite the curiosity or interest of or fascinate. **2** (*intr*) to plot secretly. — *adj* **intriguing**. — *adv* **intriguingly**. [Fr]

intrinsic *adj* (**to**) **1** belonging to a thing as an inherent and essential part of its nature. **2** (of muscles) situated within (a part of the body). — *adv* **intrinsically**. [Lat *intrinsecus*, inwardly]

intro *n* **-os** (*coll*) an introduction. [Abbrev.]

intro- *pfx* within; into; inwards. [Lat *intro*, to the inside]

introduce *v* (*tr*) **1** (**to**) to make (a person) known by name to (another or others), esp. formally. **2** to announce or present (e.g. a radio or television programme) to an audience. **3** (**into**) to bring (esp. something new) into a place, situation, etc. for the first time. **4** to bring into operation, practice or use. **5** to put forward or propose (a possible law or bill) for attention, consideration or approval. **6** (**to**) to cause (a person) to experience or discover something for the first time. **7** (**with**) to start or preface: *introduce the play with a brief analysis of the plot*. **8** (**into**) to insert or put (something) into something else. — *adj* **introducible**. [Lat *introducere*]

introduction *n* **1** the act of introducing or process of being introduced. **2** a presentation of one person to another or others. **3** a section at the beginning of a book which explains briefly what it is about, why it was written, etc. **4** a book which outlines the basic principles of a subject. **5** a short passage of music beginning a piece or song, or leading up to a movement. **6** something which has been introduced.

introductory *adj* giving or serving as an introduction; preliminary. — *adv* **introductorily**.

introit *n* a hymn, psalm or anthem sung at the beginning of a service or (esp. *RC*) a psalm or anthem sung as the priest approaches the altar to celebrate Mass. [Lat *introitus*]

introspection *n* the (sometimes excessive or morbid) examination of one's own thoughts, feelings and intuitions, etc. — *adj* **introspective**. — *adv* **introspectively**. [Lat *introspicere*, to look within]

introvert *n* **1** a person who is more concerned with his or her thoughts and feelings than with other people and outside events. **2** a shy, quiet and withdrawn person. — *adj* (also **introverted**) concerned more with one's own thoughts and feelings than with other people and outside events. — *v* (*tr*) **1** to turn (one's thoughts) inward to concentrate on oneself. **2** to withdraw (e.g. a part of the body) into the main part, e.g. as a tortoise can withdraw its head into its shell. — *n* **introversion**. [Lat *intro*, within + *vertere*, to turn]

intrude *v* (*tr* & *intr*; **into, on, upon**) to force or impose (oneself, one's presence or the presence of something) where it is unwanted and unwelcome. [Lat *intrudere*, to thrust in]

intruder *n* a person who enters premises secretly or by force in order to commit a crime.

intrusion *n* **1** an act of intruding or process of being intruded, esp. on someone else's property. **2** the forcing of molten rocks through and into holes between layers of existing rock. **3** a mass of rock forced into such places while molten. [Lat *intrusio*, from *intrudere*, to thrust in]

intrusive *adj* **1** tending to intrude. **2** (of rock) being an intrusion. — *adv* **intrusively**. — *n* **intrusiveness**.

intrust. Same as **entrust**.

intuition *n* **1** the power of understanding or realising something without conscious rational thought or analysis. **2** something understood or realised in this way. **3** immediate, instinctive understanding or belief. [Lat *intuitio*, from *in*, in + *tueri*, to look]

intuit *v* **-t-** (*tr*) to become aware of (something) by intuition.

intuitive *adj* having, showing or based on intuition. — *adv* **intuitively**. — *n* **intuitiveness**.

Inuit *n* **-uit** or **-uits** **1** a member of any of several native peoples living in Greenland, Canada and N Alaska. (**Eskimo** is the established English name for these peoples but the people themselves find it offensive and prefer **Inuit**.) **2** the family of languages spoken by these peoples. [Inuit, people]

inundate *v* (*tr*) to overwhelm with or as if with water. [Lat *inundare*, to flow over]

inundation *n* **1** a flood. **2** an act of inundating.

inure *v* (*tr*; **to**) to accustom (someone or oneself) to something unpleasant. — *n* **inurement**. [OFr *en ure*, in use]

invade *v* **1** (*tr* & *intr*) to enter (a country) by force with an army. **2** (*tr* & *intr*) to attack or overrun. **3** (*tr*) to interfere with (a person's rights, privacy, etc.). — *n* **invader**. ◇ See also **invasion**. [Lat *invadere*]

invalid[1] *n* a person who is constantly ill or who is disabled. — *adj* of, suitable for or being an invalid. — *n* **invalidity**. — *v* **invalid out**, **-d-** (*tr*) to discharge (a soldier, etc.) from service because of illness. [Fr *invalide*, from Lat *invalidus*, weak]

invalid[2] *adj* **1** (of a document, agreement, etc.) having no legal force. **2** (of an argument, reasoning, etc.) based on false reasoning or a mistake and therefore not valid, correct or reliable. — *n* **invalidity**. — *adv* **invalidly**. [Lat *invalidus*, weak]

invalidate *v* (*tr*) to make (a document, agreement, argument, etc.) invalid. — *n* **invalidation**.

invaluable *adj* (**to**) whose value is too great to be measured. — *adv* **invaluably**. [**in-**[1] + **valuable**]

invariable *adj* which does not change and is always the same. — *adv* **invariably**. [Lat *invariabilis*]

invasion *n* an act of invading or process of being invaded, e.g. by a hostile country or by something harmful. — *adj* **invasive**. [Lat *invasio*]

invective *n* **1** angry attacking words, often including abuse and swearing. **2** an attack using such words. [Lat *invectivus*, abusive]

inveigh *v* (*intr*; **against**) to speak strongly, fiercely or violently against (someone or something), esp. in criticism or protest. [Lat *invehi*, to attack with words]

inveigle *v* (*tr*; **into**) to trick or deceive (someone) into doing something. — *n* **inveiglement**. [OFr *enveogler*, to blind]

invent *v* (*tr*) **1** to be the first person to make or use (a machine, game, method, etc.). **2** to think or make up (an excuse, false story, etc.). — *n* **inventor**. [Lat *invenire*, to find]

invention *n* **1** something invented, esp. a device, machine, etc. **2** the act of inventing. **3** the ability to create and invent things; inventiveness. **4** (*coll*) a lie. **5** (*mus*) a short piece of keyboard music based on a single, simple idea.

inventive *adj* good at inventing; creative; resourceful. — *n* **inventiveness**.

inventory *n* **-ies** **1** a formal and complete list of the articles, goods, etc. found in a particular place, e.g. of goods for sale in a shop, or of furniture and possessions in a house. **2** the items included in such a list. **3** the making of such a list of articles, goods, etc. — *v* ***-ies***, ***-ied*** (*tr*) to make an inventory of; to list in an inventory. [Lat *inventorium*, list of things found]

inverse *adj* opposite or reverse in order, sequence, direction, effect, etc. — *n* **1** a direct opposite. **2** the state of being directly opposite or reversed. **3** (*math*) a member of a set which, when combined with another element in the set, produces the identity element. — *adv* **inversely**. [Lat *inversus*, from *invertere*, to invert]

inversion *n* **1** the act of turning upside down or inside out, or otherwise inverting. **2** the state of being turned upside down, inside out, or otherwise inverted. **3** a reversal of position, order, direction, form, effect, etc. **4** something achieved by inverting. [Lat *inversio*]

invert *v* (*tr*) **1** to turn upside down or inside out. **2** to reverse in order, sequence, direction, effect, etc. **3** (*mus*) to change (e.g. a chord) by placing the lowest note an octave higher. [Lat *invertire*]

inverted comma *n* same as **quotation mark**.

invertebrate *n* an animal without a backbone. — *adj* **1** (of an animal) having no backbone. **2** having no strength of character. [Lat *in-*, no + *vertebra*, spinal joint]

invest *v* **1** (*tr* & *intr*; **in**) to put (money) into a company or business, e.g. by buying shares in it, in order to make a profit. **2** (*intr* with **in**; *coll*) to buy. **3** (*tr* & *intr*; **in**) to devote (time, effort, energy, etc.) to something, usu. for future gain. **4** (*tr*; **with**) to give (someone) (the symbols of) power, rights, rank, etc. officially. ◇ See also **investiture**. **5** (*tr*; **in**) to place (power, rank, a quality or feeling, etc.) in someone. **6** (*tr*; **with**) to clothe or adorn. — *n* **investor**. [Lat *investire*, to clothe]

investment *n* **1** a sum of money invested. **2** something, such as a business, house, etc. in which one invests money, time, effort, etc. **3** the act of investing.

investment trust *n* an organisation which invests money in different companies or financial concerns on behalf of its members.

investigate *v* (*tr* & *intr*) to carry out a thorough, detailed and often official inquiry into or examination of (something or someone). — *n* **investigation**. — *adj* **investigative** or **investigatory**. — *n* **investigator**. [Lat *investigare*, to track down]

investiture *n* a formal ceremony giving a rank or office to someone. ◇ See also **invest**. [Lat *investitura*]

inveterate *adj* **1** (of a habit, practice, etc.) firmly established. **2** (of a person) firmly fixed in a habit by long practice. — *adv* **inveterately**. [Lat *inveteratus*, long continued]

invidious *adj* likely to cause envy, resentment or indignation, esp. by being or seeming to be unfair. — *adv* **invidiously**. — *n* **invidiousness**. [Lat *invidia*, envy]

invigilate *v* (*tr* & *intr*; *Br*) to keep watch over people sitting (an examination), esp. to prevent cheating. — *n* **invigilation**. — *n* **invigilator**. [Lat *invigilare*, to keep watch over]

invigorate *v* (*tr*) to give fresh life, energy and health to; to strengthen or animate. — *adj* **invigorating**. — *n* **invigoration**. [Lat *in*, in + *vigor*, strength]

invincible *adj* that cannot be defeated. — *n* **invincibility** or **invincibleness**. — *adv* **invincibly**. [Lat *invincibilis*]

inviolable *adj* that must not be broken or violated; sacred. — *n* **inviolability**. — *adv* **inviolably**. [Lat *inviolabilis*]

inviolate *adj* which has not been broken, violated or injured. [Lat *inviolatus*, unhurt]

invisible *adj* **1** not able to be seen. **2** unseen. **3** (*econ*) relating to services (e.g. insurance, tourism) rather than goods: *invisible earnings, exports*. **4** not shown in regular statements: *invisible assets*. — *n* **invisibility**. — *adv* **invisibly**. [Lat *invisibilis*]

invite *v* (*tr*) **1** to request the presence of (someone) at one's house, at a party, etc., esp. formally or politely. **2** to ask politely or formally for (e.g. comments, advice, etc.). **3** to bring on or encourage (something unwanted or undesirable). **4** to attract or tempt. — *n* (*coll*) an invitation. [Lat *invitare*]

invitation *n* **1** a request to a person to come or go somewhere, e.g. to a party, meal, etc. **2** the form such a request takes, either verbally or written on a card. **3** an act of inviting. **4** encouragement; enticement; inducement.

inviting *adj* attractive or tempting. — *adv* **invitingly**.

in vitro *adv* & *adj* (*med*) (of biological processes) (performed or made to perform) outside the body of a person or animal in conditions created artificially by scientific equipment, esp. in a test tube: *in-vitro fertilisation*. ◇ See also **in vivo**. [Lat, in glass]

in vivo *adv* & *adj* (*med*) (of biological processes) (performed or made to perform) inside the body of a person or animal and not outside of it by artificial means. ◇ See also **in vitro**. [Lat, in a living thing]

invocation *n* **1** an act of invoking. **2** a prayer calling on God, a saint, etc. for blessing or help. **3** an opening prayer at the beginning of a public service or sermon. **4** any appeal to supernatural beings, spirits, etc, such as an appeal to a Muse for inspiration at the beginning of a poem. — *adj* **invocatory**. [Lat *invocatio*]

invoice *n* a list of goods supplied, delivered with the goods and giving details of price and quantity, usu. treated as a request for payment. — *v* (*tr*) **1** to send an invoice to (a customer). **2** to provide an invoice for (goods). [Obsolete *invoyes*, from OFr *envoyer*, to send]

invoke *v* (*tr*) **1** to make an appeal to (God, some deity, a Muse, authority, etc.) for help, support or inspiration. **2** to appeal to (a law, principle, etc.) as an authority or reason for e.g. one's behaviour. **3** to make an earnest appeal for (help, support, inspiration, etc.). **4** to conjure up (a spirit) by reciting a spell. **5** to put (a law, decision, etc.) into effect. ◇ See also **invocation**. [Lat *invocare*]

involuntary *adj* (of an action, movement, muscle action, etc.) done without being controlled by the will; not able to be controlled by the will; unintentional. — *adv* **involuntarily**. [Lat *involuntarius*]

involve *v* (*tr*) **1** to require as a necessary part. **2 (in)** to cause (someone) to take part or be implicated (in). **3** to have an effect on. **4 (in)** to make (oneself) emotionally concerned (in). **5** to complicate. — *adj* **involved**. — *n* **involvement**. [Lat *involvere*, to roll up]

invulnerable *adj* that cannot be hurt, damaged or attacked. — *n* **invulnerability**. — *adv* **invulnerably**. [Lat *invulnerabilis*]

inward *adj* **1** placed or being within. **2** moving towards the inside. **3** of or relating to the mind or soul. [OE *inweard*]

inwardly *adv* **1** on the inside; internally. **2** in one's thoughts; secretly.

inwards *adv* (also **inward**) **1** towards the inside or the centre. **2** into the mind, inner thoughts or soul.

IOC *abbrev* International Olympic Committee.

iodine *n* **1** a non-metallic element (symbol **I**), usu. occurring as dark blue or black crystals which give off a purple gas when heated, used in photography and medicine. **2** (*old med*; in full **tincture of iodine**) a solution of this in alcohol used as an antiseptic. [Gr *ioeides*, violet-coloured]

iodide *n* a chemical compound containing iodine.

iodise or **-ize** *v* (*tr*) to treat with iodine.

IOM *abbrev* Isle of Man.

ion *n* an atom or group of atoms given a positive electrical charge by the loss of one or more electrons or a negative charge by the addition of one or more electrons. [Gr, going]

ion exchange *n* the transfer of ions from a solution to a solid or another liquid, used in water-softening and other industrial processes.

ionic *adj* of, relating to or using ions.

ionise or **-ize** *v* (*tr* & *intr*) to (cause to) change completely or partially into ions. — *n* **ionisation** or **-z-**.

ioniser or **-z-** *n* a small machine which produces negatively charged ions in the air in rooms, houses, etc, considered to make the air healthier to breathe.

-ion *sfx* used to form nouns denoting a process, state, result, etc.: *completion*; *contrition*; *pollution*. ◇ See also **-ation**. [Fr *-ion*]

Ionic *adj* **1** of, like, or following that style of ancient Greek architecture characterised by spiral scrolls on the capitals. ◇ See also **Corinthian** and **Doric**. **2** of the Ionians (one of the main groups of ancient Greeks), their dialect of Greek or the area of ancient Greece in which they lived. [Gr *Ionikos*]

ionosphere *n* an area of the earth's atmosphere above the stratosphere stretching to about 1000 kilometres above the surface, which contains large quantities of ions and through which radio waves are carried. — *adj* **ionospheric**. [**ion** + **sphere**]

iota *n* **1** the ninth letter of the Greek alphabet (*I*, *ι*). **2** a very small amount. [Gr]

IOU *n* ***IOUs*** or ***IOU's*** (*coll*) a written and signed note of a debt. [Pronunciation of *I owe you*]

IOW *abbrev* Isle of Wight.

IPA *abbrev* International Phonetic Alphabet.

ipecacuanha *n* the dried root of several Latin American plants, used as a purgative or emetic. [Port, from Tupi (S American Indian language) *ipekaaguene*, from *ipeh*, low + *kaa*, leaves + *guene*, vomit]

ipso facto *adv* by or because of that very fact; thereby. [Lat]

IQ *n* ***IQs*** or ***IQ's*** (*coll*) intelligence *q*uotient.

Ir *symbol* (*chem*) iridium.

ir-. See **in-**[1] and **in-**[2].

IRA *abbrev* Irish Republican Army.

Iranian *n* **1** a person born, from or living in Iran. **2** a branch of the Indo-European family of languages which includes Persian. — *adj* of the Iranians, their language, history or culture.

irascible *adj* easily made angry; irritable. — *n* **irascibility**. — *adv* **irascibly**. [Lat *irascibilis*, from *ira*, anger]

irate *adj* very angry; enraged. — *adv* **irately**. — *n* **irateness**. [Lat *iratus*, from *ira*, anger]

ire *n* anger. — *adj* **ireful**. [Lat *ira*]

iridescent *adj* having many bright rainbow-like colours which seem to shimmer and change constantly. — *n* **iridescence**. — *adv* **iridescently**. [Gr *iris*, rainbow]

iridium *n* a hard, very heavy steel-grey metallic element (symbol **Ir**), which melts only at very high temperatures and has a high resistance to rust. [Gr *iris*, rainbow, from the colourful appearance of some solutions of its salts]

iris *n* **1** (*pl* also ***irides***) the coloured, central membrane in the eye which controls the size of the pupil. **2** a tall flower with long, sword-shaped leaves and blue, yellow, or white flowers. **3** (in full **iris diaphragm**) a series of thin plates which can be moved closer together or farther apart to adjust the size of the central hole, esp. in a camera for regulating the light entering the lens. [Gr, rainbow]

Irish *adj* **1** of Ireland, its inhabitants, history, culture, Celtic language or dialect of English. **2** (*coll*) amusingly contradictory or inconsistent. — *n* **1** (with **the**) the people of Ireland as a group. **2** (in full **Irish Gaelic**) the Celtic language of Ireland. **3** whiskey made in Ireland. — *n* **Irishman**. — *n* **Irishwoman**. [OE *Iras*, people of Ireland]

Irish coffee *n* coffee served with a dash of Irish whiskey and cream on top.

Irish moss *n* an edible red seaweed found in the N Atlantic, used for making soup.

Irish stew *n* a stew made from mutton, potatoes and onions.

irk *v* (*tr*) to annoy, irritate or bore. [MidE *irken*]

irksome *adj* annoying, irritating or boring. — *adv* **irksomely**.

iron *n* **1** a very common, heavy grey metallic element (symbol **Fe**), often used for making tools and in engineering. **2** a tool, weapon or other implement made of iron. **3** a triangular, flat-bottomed, now usu. electrical, household tool used for smoothing the creases out of and pressing clothes. **4** a golf club with an angled iron head. **5** (also **branding-iron**) a metal instrument with a long handle and shaped end which can be heated and used to mark animals for identification. **6** great physical or mental strength. **7** (in *pl*) chains; fetters. **8** (in *pl*) supports for a weak or lame leg or legs. — *adj* **1** made of iron. **2** like iron, esp. in being very strong, inflexible, unyielding, etc. — *v* **-*n*-** **1** (*tr*) to smooth the creases out of or press (e.g. clothes) with an iron. **2** (*tr*; **out**) to remove (creases) by ironing. **3** (*intr*) (of clothes or fabric) to react or respond in the way specified to being ironed: *shiny material which irons badly*. — *v* **iron out** (*tr*) to remove or put right (difficulties, problems, etc.) so that progress becomes easier. — **have several** or **too many irons in the fire** to have several or too many things, plans, etc. on the go at the same time. — **strike while the iron is hot** to act while the situation is to one's advantage. [OE *isen*]

Iron Age *n* the period in history following on from the Bronze Age when people made weapons and tools out of iron, from about 1000 BC.

ironclad *adj* covered with protective iron plates. — *n* (*hist*) a 19th-century warship covered with protective iron plates.

Iron Curtain *n* (*formerly*, until the late 20th century) a perceived barrier between countries in W Europe and the Communist countries of E Europe, which hindered trade and communications.

iron-grey *adj* dark grey.

iron hand see **velvet glove**.

ironing *n* clothes and household linen, etc. which need to be or have just been ironed.

ironing board *n* a collapsible, narrow wooden or metal table with a thick fitted cover, used for ironing clothes.

iron lung *n* an apparatus consisting of a long metal case which covers the body up to the neck and which by means of rhythmically varying air pressure helps the person in it to breathe.

ironmaster *n* the owner of an ironworks.

ironmonger *n* (*Br*) a person who sells articles made of metal, e.g. tools, locks, etc. and other household hardware.

ironmongery *n* **-*ies*** (*Br*) the business of, or the goods sold by, an ironmonger.

iron pyrites *n* a mineral compound of sulphur and iron, commonly found as shiny bright yellow streaks in rocks and often mistaken for gold.

iron rations *n* (*pl*) small quantities of food with a high energy value, carried for emergencies by climbers, walkers, military personnel, etc.

Ironsides *n* (*pl*; *hist*) Oliver Cromwell's cavalry during the English Civil War (1642–9).

ironstone *n* **1** rock containing considerable amounts or iron ore. **2** hard, white earthenware.

ironware *n* things made of iron, esp. household hardware.

ironwork *n* **1** things made of iron, esp. iron which has been specially shaped for decoration, such as gates and railings. **2** (in *pl*) a factory where iron is smelted and made into goods.

irony *n* **-*ies*** **1** a form of humour, or a way of expressing annoyance, in which one says the opposite of what is clearly true, with the intention of making someone appear ridiculous or of being sarcastic. **2** the fact of the odd circumstances of a situation making a person or his or her actions seem ridiculous. **3** a situation containing irony. [Gr *eironeia*, dissimulation]

ironic *adj* (also **ironical**) **1** containing, characterised by or expressing irony. **2** (of a person) using irony a lot. — *adv* **ironically**.

irradiate *v* **1** (*tr*) to treat with or subject to radiation or light rays. **2** (*tr*) to shed light on; to light up. **3** (*tr*) to make bright or clear intellectually or spiritually. **4** (*tr* & *intr*) to emit (heat, light or radiation) in rays; to radiate. — *n* **irradiation**. [Lat *irradiare*]

irrational *adj* **1** not the result of clear, logical thought. **2** not able to think logically and clearly. **3** (*math*) (of a root, expression, etc.) involving irrational numbers. — *n* an irrational number. — *n* **irrationality**. — *adv* **irrationally**. [Lat *irrationalis*]

irrational number *n* (*math*) a number which cannot be expressed in the form $\frac{a}{b}$ where *a* and *b* are whole numbers.

irreconcilable *adj* **1** (**with**) not agreeing or able to be brought into agreement; inconsistent; incompatible. **2** hostile and opposed; unwilling to be friendly. — *n* **irreconcilability**. — *adv* **irreconcilably**. [**ir-** (see **in-**[1]) + **reconcile**]

irrecoverable *adj* which cannot be recovered. — *adv* **irrecoverably**. [**ir-** (see **in**[1]) + **recoverable**]

irredeemable *adj* **1** (of a person) too evil to be saved; beyond help. **2** incapable of being recovered, repaired or cured. **3** (of shares, etc.) which the issuing company does not have the right to buy back from the shareholder for the sum originally paid. **4** (of paper money) which cannot be exchanged for coin. — *adv* **irredeemably**. [**ir-** (see **in-**[1]) + **redeemable**]

irredentist *n* a person, esp. in 19th-century Italy, who is in favour of his or her country recovering territory which belonged to it in the past. — *n* **irredentism**. [Ital (*Italia*) *irredenta*, unredeemed (Italy)]

irreducible *adj* **1** that cannot be reduced or made simpler. **2** (**to**) that cannot be brought from one state into another, usu. desired, state. — *adv* **irreducibly**. [**ir-** (see **in-**[1]) + **reducible**]

irrefutable *adj* not able to be denied or proved false. — *adv* **irrefutably**. [Lat *irrefutabilis*]

irregular *adj* **1** not happening or occurring at regular or equal intervals. **2** not smooth, even or balanced. **3** not conforming to rules, custom, accepted or normal behaviour or routine. **4** (*gram*) (of a word, esp. a verb or noun) not changing its form (e.g. to show tenses or plurals) according to the usual patterns in the language. **5** (of troops) not belonging to the regular army. — *n* an irregular soldier. — *n* **irregularity**, **-*ies***. — *adv* **irregularly**. [Lat *irregularis*]

irrelevant *adj* not connected with or applying to the subject in hand; not relevant. — *n* **irrelevance** or **irrelevancy**, **-*ies***. — *adv* **irrelevantly**. [**ir-** (see **in-**[1]) + **relevant**]

irreligious *adj* **1** lacking a religion. **2** lacking in respect for or hostile or opposed to religion. [Lat *irreligiosus*]

irreligion *n* **1** lack of religion. **2** lack of respect for or opposition or hostility towards religion.

irremediable *adj* which cannot be made better, cured or corrected. — *adv* **irremediably**. [Lat *irremediabilis*]

irremovable *adj* not able to be removed. — *adv* **irremovably**. [**ir-** (see **in-**[1]) + **removable**]

irreparable *adj* not able to be restored or put right. — *n* **irreparability**. — *adv* **irreparably**. [Lat *irreparabilis*]

irreplaceable *adj* not able to be replaced, esp. because too rare or valuable. — *adv* **irreplaceably**. [**ir-** (see **in-**[1]) + **replaceable**]

irrepressible *adj* not able to be controlled, restrained or repressed, esp. because of being too lively and full of energy or strength. — *n* **irrepressibility**. — *adv* **irrepressibly**. [**ir-** (see **in-**[1]) + **repress**]

irreproachable *adj* (esp. of someone's behaviour) free from faults; blameless. — *adv* **irreproachably**. [**ir-** (see **in-**[1]) + **reproach**]

irresistible *adj* too strong, tempting, or attractive to be resisted; overpowering. — *n* **irresistibility** or **irresistibleness**. — *adv* **irresistibly**. [Lat *irresistibilis*]

irresolute *adj* hesitating or doubtful; not able to take firm decisions; showing that no firm decision has been taken. — *adv* **irresolutely**. — *n* **irresoluteness** or **irresolution**. [**ir-** (see **in-**[1]) + **resolute**]

irrespective *adj* (**of**) without considering or taking into account. [**ir-** (see **in-**[1]) + **respective**]

irresponsible *adj* **1** done without or showing no concern for the consequences; reckless; careless. **2** not able to bear responsibility; not reliable or trustworthy. — *n* **irresponsibility**. — *adv* **irresponsibly**. [**ir-** (see **in-**[1]) + **responsible**]

irretrievable *adj* that cannot be recovered or put right. — *adv* **irretrievably**. [**ir-** (see **in-**[1]) + **retrievable**]

irreverent *adj* lacking respect or reverence (e.g. for things considered sacred or important people). — *n* **irreverence**. — *adv* **irreverently**. [Lat *irreverentia*]

irreversible *adj* unable to be changed back to a former or original state; permanent. — *adv* **irreversibly**. [**ir-** (see **in-**[1]) + **reversible**]

irrevocable *adj* that cannot be changed, stopped or undone. — *n* **irrevocability**. — *adv* **irrevocably**. [Lat *irrevocabilis*]

irrigate *v* (*tr*) **1** to supply water to (esp. farm land) through canals, ditches, etc. **2** (*med*) to wash out with or apply liquid to (a wound, etc.). — *adj* **irrigable**. — *n* **irrigation**. [Lat *irrigare*]

irritate *v* (*tr*) **1** to make angry or annoyed. **2** to make (part of the body, an organ, etc.) sore and swollen or itchy. **3** (*biol*) to stimulate (e.g. an organ) to respond. — *adj* **irritating**. — *adv* **irritatingly**. — *n* **irritation**. [Lat *irritare*]

irritable *adj* **1** easily annoyed, angered or excited. **2** extremely or excessively sensitive. **3** (*biol*) (of living organisms) able to respond to light, heat and touch. — *n* **irritability** or **irritableness**. — *adv* **irritably**.

irritant *n* something that causes irritation. — *adj* irritating.

irrupt *v* (*intr*; **into**) to burst (into) or enter suddenly with speed and violence. — *n* **irruption**. — *adj* **irruptive**. [Lat *irrumpere*]

is. See **be**. [OE]

-ise or **-ize** *sfx* forming verbs meaning **1** to make or become: *equalise*. **2** to treat or react to (in a stated way): *criticise*. **3** to engage in (a stated activity): *theorise*. — *n sfx* **-isation** or **-z-**. [Lat *-izare*]

ISBN *abbrev* International Standard Book Number.

-ish *sfx* forming adjectives meaning **1** slightly; fairly; having a trace of: *reddish*; *autumnish*. **2** like; having the qualities of: *childish*. **3** having as a nationality: *Swedish*. **4** approximately; about; roughly: *fiftyish*. [OE *-isc*]

isinglass *n* a form of gelatin made from the air-bladders of certain fish, e.g. sturgeons, and used in making jellies and glue. [ODut *huizenblas*, sturgeon's bladder]

Islam *n* **1** the Muslim religion, based on the worship of one god (Allah) and the teachings of his prophet Mohammed. **2** that part of the world where this religion is the dominant one. — *adj* **Islamic**. [Arabic, surrender (to God)]

Islamicise or **-ize** *v* (*tr*) to Islamise. — *n* **Islamicisation** or **-z-**.

Islamicist *adj* a person who studies Islam, Islamic law or Islamic culture.

Islamise or **-ize** *v* (*tr*) to cause to become a follower of or conform to Islam. — *n* **Islamisation** or **-z-**.

island *n* **1** a piece of land completely surrounded by water. **2** anything which is like an island, esp. in being isolated or detached. **3** (in full **traffic island**) a small, raised, traffic-free area in the middle of a street on which people may stand when crossing the road. [OE *iegland*, with the *s* from OFr *isle*]

islander *n* a person who lives on an island.

isle *n* a (usu. small) island. [OFr *isle*]

islet *n* **1** a small island. **2** a small area of tissue which has a different nature and structure to the tissue surrounding it.

ism *n* (*coll*, usu. *derog*) a distinctive and formal set of ideas, principles or beliefs. [**-ism**]

-ism *sfx* forming nouns meaning **1** a formal set of beliefs, ideas, principles, etc.: *feminism*. **2** a quality or state: *heroism*. **3** an activity or practice, or its result: *criticism*. **4** discrimination or prejudice on the grounds of: *ageism*. **5** an illness caused by, causing resemblance to or named after (something or someone stated): *alcoholism*; *dwarfism*. **6** a characteristic of (a specified language or type of language): *regionalism*. [Gr *-ismos* or *-isma*]

isn't is not.

iso- *comb fm* same; equal. [Gr *isos*, equal]

isobar *n* **1** a line on a weather map connecting areas which have the same atmospheric pressure at a particular time or as an average over a particular period of time. **2** (*physics*) either of two atoms of different elements which have the same mass number and approximately the same atomic mass. — *adj* **isobaric**. [Gr *isobares*, of equal weight]

isochronal or **isochronous** *adj* **1** having the same length of time. **2** performed or happening at the same time. **3** happening at equal or regular intervals. [Gr *isochronos*, equal in age or time]

isolate *v* (*tr*) **1** to separate from others; to cause to be alone. **2** to place in quarantine. **3** to separate or detach, esp. to allow closer examination: *isolate a problem*. **4** to separate so as to obtain in a pure or uncombined form. — *adj* **isolated**. — *n* **isolation**. [Ital *isolare*, from Lat *insula*, island]

isolationism *n* the policy of not joining with other countries in international political and economic affairs. — *n* & *adj* **isolationist**.

isomer *n* one of two or more chemical compounds with the same molecules but with them arranged differently. — *adj* **isomeric**. [Gr *isomeres*, having equal parts]

isometric *adj* **1** having equal size or measurements. **2** (of muscle movement) with the muscle tense and with an increase of muscle strength and tone but without the muscle being contracted or shortened (e.g. without causing a limb to bend). **3** (of a three-dimensional drawing) in which the three faces shown are drawn at the same angle to the drawing surface so that all of the lines are equally foreshortened. [**iso-** + Gr *metron*, measure]

isometrics *n* (*sing* or *pl*) a system of physical exercises for strengthening and toning the body in which the muscles are pushed either together or against an immovable object and are not contracted or flexed and or made to bend limbs.

isomorphism *n* **1** (*biol*) a similarity of form between individuals belonging to different races or species or to different generations of the same life-cycle. **2** (*chem*) a close resemblance in crystal structure of two or more different chemicals. **3** (*math*) a one-to-one correspondence between the elements of two or more sets and between the sums or products of the elements in the first set with the sums and products of the elements in the second. — *adj* **isomorphic** or **isomorphous**. [**iso-** + Gr *morphe*, from]

isomorph *n* an individual, chemical or set, etc. in an isomorphic relation with another.

isosceles *adj* (of a triangle) having two sides of equal length. [Gr *isos*, equal + *skelos*, leg]

isotherm *n* a line on a weather map connecting places where the temperature is the same at a particular time or where the average is the same for a particular period of time. [Gr *isos*, equal + *therme*, heat]

isotope *n* one of two or more atoms of the same element, which have the same atomic number and chemical properties but different atomic weights and nuclear properties. — *adj* **isotopic**. [**iso-** + Gr *topos*, place (i.e. on the periodic table)]

isotropic *adj* (of a substance, material, etc.) having physical properties (e.g. magnetism and elasticity) which do not vary with direction. [**iso-** + Gr *tropos*, turn]

Israeli *adj* of the modern state of Israel or its inhabitants. — *n* a person born or living in the modern state of Israel. [Hebr *Yisrael*, God perseveres]

Israelite *n* (*hist*) a person born or living in the ancient kingdom of Israel (922 BC to 721 BC), esp. a Jew claiming descent from Jacob. — *adj* of the ancient kingdom of Israel or its inhabitants.

issue *n* **1** the giving out, publishing or making available of something, e.g. stamps, a magazine, etc. **2** that which is given out, published or made available, e.g. stamps, a magazine, book, etc. **3** one item in a regular series: *the December issue of the magazine*. **4** a subject for discussion or argument. **5** a result or consequence. **6** (*formal*) children; offspring. **7** an act of going or flowing out. **8** a way out, outlet or outflow, e.g. where a stream begins. — *v* **1** (*tr*) to give or send out, distribute, publish or make available, esp. officially or formally. **2** (*tr*; **with**) to supply (with something required, e.g. an official document). **3** (*intr*; **from**, **forth**, **out**) to flow or come out. **4** (*intr*; **in**) to end or result (in). **5** (*intr*; **from**) to come or descend (from); to be produced (by). — **at issue 1** in dispute or disagreement. **2** under discussion. — **force the issue** to act so as to hasten or force a decision to be taken. — **join** or **take issue with** to disagree with. — **make an issue of** to make the subject of argument, disagreement or fuss. [OFr, from Lat *exitus*, exit]

-ist *sfx* **1** a believer in some formal system of ideas, principles or beliefs: *feminist*. **2** a person who carries out some activity or practises some art: *novelist*. [Gr *-istes*]

isthmus *n* ***-uses*** **1** a narrow strip of land joining two larger areas of land. **2** (*anat*) a narrow part of a structure connecting two larger parts. [Gr *isthmos*]

IT *abbrev* information technology.

it[1] *pron* **1** the thing, animal, small baby or group already mentioned. **2** the person in question: *Who is it?* **3** used as the subject with impersonal verbs and when describing the weather or distance or telling the time. **4** used as the grammatical subject of a sentence when the real subject comes later: *It's not a very good idea running away*. **5** used to refer to a general situation or state of affairs: *How's it going?* **6** used to emphasise a certain word or phrase in a sentence: *When is it her train is due to arrive?* **7** exactly what is needed, suitable or available: *That's it!* **8** used with many verbs and prepositions as an object with little meaning: *run for it*. — *n* **1** the person in a children's game who has to oppose all the others, e.g. by trying to catch them. **2** (*old coll*) sex appeal. **3** (*coll*) sexual intercourse. [OE *hit*]

it[2] *n* (*old coll*) Italian vermouth. [Abbrev.]

Italian *adj* of Italy, its inhabitants, culture, history, or the Romance language spoken there. — *n* **1** a person born or living in Italy. **2** the Romance language spoken in Italy and in parts of Switzerland. [Lat *Italianus*, from *Italia*, Italy]

Italianate *adj* of or in an Italian style, esp. of decoration, architecture or art.

italic *adj* **1** of or in a typeface with characters which slope upwards to the right. **2** (*cap*) of ancient Italy. — *n* (usu. in *pl*) a typeface, first used in Italy, with characters which slope upwards to the right or a letter printed or written in this typeface. [Gr *Italikos*]

italicise or **-ize** *v* (*tr*) to print or write in italics. — *n* **italicisation** or **-z-**.

Italo- *comb fm* of Italy, the Italians, etc.

ITC *abbrev* Independent Television Commission.

itch *n* **1** an unpleasant irritation on the surface of the skin which makes one want to scratch. **2** (*coll*) a strong or restless desire. **3** a skin disease or condition which causes a constant unpleasant irritation, esp. scabies. — *v* **1** (*intr*) to have an itch and want to scratch. **2** (*tr* & *intr*) to cause (someone) to feel an itch. **3** (*intr*; *coll*) to feel a strong or restless desire. — *n* **itchiness**. — *adj* **itchy**, ***-ier***, ***-iest***. [OE *giccan*]

itchy feet *n* (*coll*) the strong desire to leave, move, or travel.

an itchy or **itching palm** *n* greed for money.

it'd 1 it had. **2** it would.

-ite *sfx* forming nouns denoting **1** a place, origin or national group: *Israelite*. **2** a follower of or believer in: *pre-Raphaelite*; *anti-Semite*. **3** a fossil: *ammonite*. **4** a mineral: *graphite*. **5** a salt of a certain formula: *nitrite*. ◇ See also ***-ate***, ***-ide***. **6** an explosive: *dynamite*. [Gr *-ites*]

item *n* **1** a separate object or unit, esp. one on a list. **2** a separate piece of information or news. [Lat, likewise]

itemise or **-ize** *v* (*tr*) to list (things) separately, e.g. on a bill. — *n* **itemisation** or **-z-**.

iterate *v* (*tr*) to say or do again; to repeat. — *n* **iteration**. — *adj* **iterative**. [Lat *iterare*, from *iterim*, again]

itinerant *adj* travelling from place to place, e.g. on business. — *n* an itinerant person. [Lat *iter*, journey]

itinerary *n* ***-ies*** **1** a plan of one's route for a journey or trip. **2** a diary or record of a journey. **3** a guidebook. [Lat *iter*, journey]

-itis *comb fm* **1** (in the names of diseases) inflammation of: *appendicitis*. **2** (*coll*) distress or suffering caused by too much: *jazzitis*. [Gr]

it'll 1 it will. **2** it shall.

ITN *abbrev* Independent Television News.

its *adj* belonging to it. — *pron* the one or ones belonging to it. — **of its** of or belonging to it.

itself *pron* **1** the reflexive form of **it**. **2** used for emphasis. **3** its normal self: *not feeling itself today*. **4** (also *by itself*) alone; without help.

it's 1 it is. **2** it has.

itsy-bitsy *adj* (also esp. *NAm* **itty-bitty** ; *coll*) very small. [A rhyming compound based on *little bit*]

ITV *abbrev* (*Br*) Independent Television.
-ity *sfx* (an example of) a state or quality: *irregularity*. [Fr *-ité*]
IUD *abbrev* intrauterine device.
-ive *sfx* (a person or thing) having a quality, performing an action, etc.: *creative*; *detective*. [Fr *-if*]
I've I have.
IVF *abbrev* in-vitro fertilisation.
ivory *n* **1** the hard, bony, creamy-white substance which forms the tusks of elephants, hippopotamuses and walruses. **2** the creamy-white colour of this substance. **3** an article made from this substance. **4** (in *pl*; *coll*) the keys on a piano. — *adj* of or like ivory, esp. in colour. [Lat *ebur*]
ivory tower *n* a place where one can be secluded from the unpleasant realities of life.
ivy *n* **-ies 1** an evergreen shrub with dark leaves with five points which climbs on walls and trees. **2** any of several other climbing plants, such as poison ivy.
ixia *n* a plant of the iris family with large showy flowers, orig. found in S Africa. [Gr *ixos*, mistletoe]
-ize. See **-ise**.

J

J[1] or **j** *n* ***Js*** or ***J's, j's*** the tenth letter of the English alphabet.
J[2] *abbrev* joule.
jab *v* **-*bb*-** (*tr* or *intr*; **at**) to poke or prod. — *n* **1** a poke or prod. **2** (*coll*) an injection or inoculation. **3** (*boxing*) a short straight punch. [MidE *jobben*]
jabber *v* **-*r*-** (*intr* & *tr*) to talk or utter rapidly and indistinctly. — *n* rapid indistinct speech. [Imit.]
jabot *n* a lace ruffle for a shirt front, worn esp. with full Highland dress. [Fr]
jack *n* **1** a device for raising heavy objects off the ground. **2** (*cards*) (also **knave**) the court card of least value, bearing a picture of a page. **3** (*bowls*) the small white ball that players aim at. **4** a small national flag flown at the bows of a ship. **5** one of the playing-pieces used in the game of jacks. **6** (*telecomm*) (also **jack socket**) a socket whose connections are short-circuited till a single-pronged plug (**jack plug**) is inserted. **7** the male of certain animals, e.g. the donkey. — *v* (*tr*; **up**) to raise with a jack. — **before you can say Jack Robinson** in a trice. — **every man jack** everybody. — *v* **jack in** or **up** (*tr*; *slang*) to give up (a job, etc.). [From the name *Jack*]
Jack Frost *n* in story books, etc., a being personifying frost.
jack-in-office *n* (*derog*) a self-important minor official.
jack-in-the-box *n* **-*boxes*** a box containing a doll attached to a spring, that leaps out when the lid is opened.
jack-of-all-trades *n* ***jacks-*** a handyman used to a variety of jobs.
jack rabbit *n* a long-eared N American hare.
jacks *n sing* (also **jackstones**) a game in which playing-pieces (orig. small bones or pebbles) must be tossed and caught on the back of the hand.
Jack tar *n* (*old*) a sailor.
jackal *n* a long-legged, yellowish dog-like animal of Africa and Asia, that feeds on the remains of creatures killed by other animals. [Persian *shagual*]
jackanapes *n* (*old*) a mischievous or impertinent person. [MidE *Jakken apes*, or 'jack of the apes', i.e. the Duke of Suffolk (1396–1450), whose badge was an ape's ball and chain]
jackass *n* **1** a male ass. **2** (*coll*) a foolish person. [**jack** + **ass**]
laughing jackass *n* a kookaburra.
jackboot *n* a tall leather knee-high military boot, esp. as a symbol of oppressive military rule. [**jack**]
jackdaw *n* a bird of the crow family having a reputation for stealing bright objects. [**Jack** + old word *daw*, jackdaw]
jacket *n* **1** a short coat, esp. a long-sleeved hip-length one. **2** something worn over the top half of the body: *a life jacket*. **3** (also **dustjacket**) a loose paper cover for a hardback book. **4** an outer casing for a boiler, etc., for preventing heat loss; any protective casing. **5** the skin of a potato that has been cooked without being peeled. **6** an animal's natural coat. [OFr *jaquet*]
jackknife *n* **1** a large pocket knife with a folding blade. **2** a dive in which the body is bent double and then straightened before entering the water. — *v* (*intr*) (of an articulated vehicle) to go out of control in such a way that the trailer swings round against the cab. [**jack**]
jackpot *n* the maximum win, esp. consisting of the accumulated stakes, to be made in a lottery, card game, etc. — **hit the jackpot** (*coll*) to have a remarkable financial win or stroke of luck. [**jack**]
Jacobean *adj* **1** relating or belonging to the reign of James I of England (VI of Scotland) (1603–25). **2** (of furniture, drama, etc.) typical of the style current in his reign. [Lat *Jacobus*, James]
Jacobite *n* (*Brit hist*) a supporter of King James II after his abdication in 1688, or of his descendants, James and Charles Edward Stuart, in their attempts to regain the throne. [Lat *Jacobus*, James]
Jacuzzi® *n* (often without *cap*.) a large bath equipped with underwater jets that massage and invigorate the body.
jade[1] *n* **1** a hard, usu. green semi-precious stone. **2** the bluish green colour of jade. [Span *piedra de ijada*, colic(-curing) stone]
jade[2] *n* (*old*) **1** a disreputable or ill-natured woman. **2** a worn-out old horse.
jaded *adj* fatigued, dull and bored.
jag[1] *n* **1** a sharp projection. **2** (*Scot*) an injection or inoculation. — *v* **-*gg*-** (*tr*) to prick, sting or pierce.
jag[2] *n* (*slang*) **1** a bout of heavy drinking or drug-taking. **2** a bout of indulgence in anything.
jagged *adj* having a rough or sharp uneven edge. — *adv* **jaggedly**. — *n* **jaggedness**. [**jag**[1]]
jaguar *n* a large spotted S American animal of the cat family. [S American Indian (Tupí) *jaguara*]
jail or **gaol** *n* prison. — *v* (*tr*) to imprison. [OFr *gaole*]
jailbird or **gaolbird** *n* (*coll*) a person (frequently) in prison.
jailbreak or **gaolbreak** *n* an escape, esp. by several prisoners, from jail.
jailer or **gaoler** *n* a person who is in charge of prisoners in a jail.
jalopy *n* **-*ies*** (*coll*) a worn-out old car.

jam[1] *n* a thick sticky food made from fruit boiled with sugar, used as a spread on bread, etc. — **jam tomorrow** (*coll*) something agreeable constantly promised but never provided. — **money for jam** (*coll*) money easily made. — **want jam on it** (*coll*) to expect more than is reasonable. [Perhaps **jam**[2]]

jammy *adj* **-ier**, **-iest** **1** covered, or filled, with jam. **2** (*coll*) (of a person) lucky. **3** (*coll*) (of a job, etc.) profitable, esp. at little cost in effort.

jam[2] *v* **-mm-** **1** (*tr*; **up**) to fill (e.g. a street) so full that movement comes to a stop. **2** (*tr*) to push or shove; to cram, press or pack. **3** (*tr*) to stick or wedge. **4** (*tr* & *intr*) (of machinery, etc.) to (cause to) stick and stop working. **5** (*tr*) to cause interference to (a radio signal, etc.), esp. deliberately. **6** (*intr*; *coll*) to play jazz in a jam session. **7** (*tr* with **on**) to put on (a brake, switch, etc.) with sudden force. — *n* **1** a situation where vehicles, etc. are tightly crowded together and movement comes to a stop: *traffic jams*. **2** a stoppage of machinery, etc., caused by jamming. [Imit.]

jam-packed *adj* (*coll*) packed tight.

jam session *n* (*slang*) a session of live, esp. improvised, jazz or popular music.

jamb *n* the vertical post at the side of a door, window or fireplace. [OFr *jambe*, leg]

jamboree *n* **1** (*coll*) a large and lively gathering. **2** a large rally of Scouts, Guides, etc.

jammy. See **jam**[1].

Jan. *abbrev* January.

jangle *v* **1** (*tr* & *intr*) to (cause to) make a discordant ringing noise. **2** (*tr*) to upset or irritate. — *adj* **jangly**, **-ier**, **-iest**. [OFr *jangler*]

janissary or **janizary** *n* **-ies** (*hist*) a soldier of the Turkish sultan's personal guard. [Turk, *yeniçeri*, new troops]

janitor *n* **1** (*NAm* & *Scot*) a caretaker. **2** a doorkeeper. [Lat, from *janua*, door]

January *n* the first month of the year. [Lat *Januarius* (*mensis*), month of the god Janus]

japan *n* a hard glossy black lacquer, orig. from Japan, used to coat wood and metal. — *v* **-nn-** (*tr*) to lacquer with japan. [*Japan*]

Japanese *adj* relating or belonging to Japan, its people or language. — *n* **1** **-ese** a native or citizen of Japan. **2** the language of Japan.

jape *n* (*old*) a trick, prank or joke. [MidE *japen*]

japonica *n* **1** a red-flowered shrub of the quince family, orig. from Japan. **2** another name for the oriental plant camellia. [Lat *japonica*, Japanese]

jar[1] *n* **1** a wide-mouthed cylindrical container, usu. of glass; the contents of this. **2** (*coll*) a glass of beer. [OFr *jarre*, from Arabic *jarrah*, earthenware vessel]

jar[2] *v* **-rr-** **1** (*intr*; **on**) to have a harsh effect; to grate. **2** (*tr* & *intr*) to jolt or vibrate. **3** (*tr* & *intr*) to (cause to) make a harsh sound. **4** (*intr*; **with**) to clash or conflict: *buildings that jar with the environment*. — *n* a jarring sensation, shock or jolt. — *adj* **jarring**. — *adv* **jarringly**. [Imit.]

jardinière *n* **1** an ornamental pot or stand for flowers. **2** (*cookery*) an accompaniment of mixed vegetables for a meat dish. [Fr, fem. of *jardinier*, gardener]

jargon *n* **1** the specialised vocabulary of a particular trade, profession, group or activity. **2** (*derog*) confusing or meaningless talk. [OFr]

jasmine *n* a shrub or climbing plant with sweet-smelling yellow, white or red flowers. [Persian *yasmin*]

jasper *n* a brown, yellow, red or green semiprecious stone, a form of quartz, used for making jewellery and ornaments. [Gr *iaspis*]

jaundice *n* a condition in which there is an excess of bile in the blood, a pigment of which turns the skin and the whites of the eyes yellow. [OFr *jaunisse*, from *jaune*, yellow]

jaundiced *adj* **1** suffering from jaundice. **2** (of a person or attitude) bitter or resentful; cynical.

jaunt *n* a short journey for pleasure. — *v* (*intr*) to go for a jaunt.

jaunty *adj* **-ier**, **-iest** **1** (of manner or personality) breezy and exuberant. **2** (of dress, etc.) smart; stylish. — *adv* **jauntily**. — *n* **jauntiness**. [Fr *gentil*, noble, gentle]

javelin *n* **1** a light spear for throwing as a weapon or in sport. **2** (with **the**) throwing the javelin as an athletic event. [OFr *javeline*]

jaw *n* **1** either of the two hinged parts of the skull in which the teeth are set. **2** the lower part of the face round the mouth and chin. **3** (in *pl*) the mouth, esp. of an animal. **4** (in *pl*) a threshold, esp. of something fearful: *the jaws of death*. **5** (in *pl*) the gripping parts of a tool, etc. **6** (*coll*) a long conversation; a talking-to; talk; chatter. — *v* (*intr*; *coll*) to chatter, gossip or talk. [OFr *joue*, cheek]

jawbone *n* the bone that forms the lower jaw.

jay *n* a noisy bird of the crow family, with pinkish-brown plumage and blue, black and white bars on its wings. [OFr *jai*]

jaywalk *v* (*intr*) to cross streets carelessly, paying little attention to the traffic. — *n* **jaywalker**. — *n* **jaywalking**. [**jay**, with the meaning 'a fool']

jazz *n* **1** popular music of Black American origin, with strong, catchy rhythms, performed with much improvisation. **2** (*coll*) talk; nonsense; business, stuff, etc. — *v* (*tr*; **up**; *coll*) **1** to enliven or brighten up. **2** to give a jazzy rhythm to. — **and all that jazz** (*coll*) and all that sort of thing: *philosophy and all that jazz*.

jazzy *adj* **-ier**, **-iest** **1** in the style of, or like, jazz. **2** (*coll*) showy; flashy; stylish. — *adv* **jazzily**.

JCB *n* a vehicle or machine used in the building industry, with a hydraulic shovel at the front and a digging arm at the back. [*J*oseph *C*yril *B*amford, manufacturer]

jealous *adj* **1** **(of)** envious of someone else, his or her possessions, success, talents, etc. **2** suspicious and resentful of possible rivals; possessive. **3** **(of)** anxiously protective of something one has. **4** (*Bible*) (of God) intolerant of unfaithfulness. **5** caused by jealousy: *a jealous fury*. — *adv* **jealously**. [OFr *gelos*, from Gr *zelos*, rivalry, jealousy]

jealousy *n* **-ies** the emotion of envy or suspicious possessiveness; (in *pl*) an occurrence of this.

jeans *n* (*pl*) casual denim trousers, esp. blue. [*jean*, a strong cotton from *Gênes* (Fr, Genoa)]

jeep *n* (also *cap*) a light military vehicle capable of travelling over rough country. [*GP*, general-*p*urpose (vehicle)]

jeer *v* **1** (*tr*) to mock or deride (a speaker, performer, etc.). **2** (*intr*; **at**) to laugh unkindly: *jeered at his accent*. — *n* a taunt, insult, or hoot of derision.

jehad. See **jihad**.

Jehovah *n* the name used for God in the Old Testament. [Hebr *Yahweh*]

Jehovah's Witness *n* a member of a fundamentalist sect of Christians.

jejune *adj* (*derog*) (of writing, ideas, etc.) **1** dull, banal, unoriginal and empty of imagination. **2** childish; naïve. [Lat *jejunus*, hungry, empty]

jejunum *n* (*anat*) the part of the small intestine between the duodenum and the ileum. [Lat *jejunum* (*intestinum*) empty (intestine)]

Jekyll and Hyde *n* a person with (apparently) two distinct personalities, one good, the other evil. [The two manifestations of a character created by R L Stevenson]

jell or **gel** *v* **-ll-** (*intr*) **1** to become firm; to set. **2** to take definite shape. [*jelly*]

jelly *n* **-ies** **1** a wobbly, transparent, fruit-flavoured dessert set with gelatine. **2** a clear jam made by boiling and straining fruit. **3** meat stock or other savoury medium set with gelatine. **4** any jelly-like substance. [OFr *gelee*, from Lat *gelare*, to freeze]

jellied *adj* set in jelly: *jellied eels*.

jelly baby *n* a soft fruit-flavoured sweet in the shape of a baby, made with gelatine.

jellyfish *n* **-fish** or **-fishes** a sea creature with a translucent jelly-like body and trailing tentacles.

jemmy *n* **-ies** a small crowbar used by burglars for forcing open windows, etc. [From the name *James*]

jenny *n* **-ies** **1** a name given to the female of certain birds, e.g. the wren, or animals, e.g. the donkey. **2** a spinning-jenny. [From the name *Jenny*]

jeopardy *n* danger of harm, loss, or destruction. [OFr *jeu parti*, a divided or even (i.e. uncertain) game]

jeopardise or **-ize** *v* (*tr*) to put at risk of harm, loss or destruction.

jerbil. Another spelling of **gerbil**.

jerboa *n* a small rat-like animal of N Africa and Asia, with long hind legs adapted for jumping. [Arabic *yarbu*]

jeremiad *n* (*coll*) a lengthy and mournful tale of woe. [Fr *jérémiade*, from *The Lamentations of Jeremiah* in the Old Testament]

jerk *n* **1** a quick tug or pull. **2** a sudden movement; a jolt. **3** (*slang derog*) a stupid person. — *v* **1** (*tr*) to pull or tug with sharply. **2** (*intr*) to move with sharp suddenness. — *adv* **jerkily**. — *adj* **jerky**, **-ier**, **-iest**.

jerkin *n* a short close-fitting esp. sleeveless jacket.

jeroboam *n* a large wine bottle holding the equivalent of six standard bottles (or four of champagne). [*Jeroboam* in the Old Testament, I Kings xi. 28]

Jerry *n* **-ies** (*Brit World War II slang*) a German or German soldier; the Germans collectively. [Alteration of **German**]

jerry *n* **-ies** (*old coll*) a chamber pot. [**jeroboam**]

jerry-built *adj* (of buildings, etc.) built cheaply, hastily and incompetently. — *n* **jerry-builder**. — *n* **jerry-building**.

jerry can *n* a flat-sided can used for carrying water, petrol, etc. [**Jerry**]

jersey *n* **-eys** **1** a knitted garment worn on the upper part of the body, pulled on over the head; a pullover. **2** a fine knitted fabric used for clothing. **3** (*cap*) a breed of dairy cattle. [*Jersey* in the Channel Islands]

Jerusalem artichoke. See **artichoke**.

jest *n* a joke or prank. — *adv* **jestingly**. — **in jest** as a joke; not seriously. [OFr *geste*, deed, from Lat *gesta*, things done]

jester *n* (*hist*) a colourfully dressed professional clown employed by a king or noble to amuse the court. [MidE *gester*, from *gest*, exploit]

Jesuit *n* a member of the Society of Jesus, a Roman Catholic order founded by Ignatius Loyola in 1534. [**Jesus**]

jesuitical *adj* **1** (of an argument) over-subtle; cleverly misleading. **2** (of a plan) crafty; cunning. — *adv* **jesuitically**.

Jesus *n* (also **Jesus Christ**) the founder of Christianity, believed by Christians to be the son of God. — *interj* (*offensive*) used as an expression of surprise, anger, etc. [Hebr *Yeshua*]

jet[1] *n* a hard black mineral that takes a high polish and is used in jewellery, etc. [OFr *jaiet*]

jet-black *adj* deep glossy black.

jet[2] *n* **1** a strong fast stream (of liquid, gas, etc.), forced under pressure from a narrow opening. **2** the opening through which a jet is forced. **3** (also **jet aircraft**) an aircraft powered by a jet engine. — *v* **-tt-** **1** (*intr* & *tr*; *coll*) to travel or transport by jet aircraft. **2** (*intr*) to come out in a jet; to spurt. [Fr *jeter*, to throw]

jet engine *n* an engine using jet propulsion for forward thrust.

jet lag *n* the tiredness and lethargy that result from the body's inability to adjust to the rapid changes of time zone that go with high-speed, long-distance air travel. — *adj* **jet-lagged**.

jet plane *n* an aircraft powered by a jet engine.

jet-propelled *adj* **1** driven by jet propulsion. **2** (*coll*) fast.

jet propulsion *n* the forward thrust effected as air sucked into the front of an engine is forced out behind.

jet set *n* (*coll*; with **the**) wealthy people who lead a life of fast travel and expensive enjoyment. — *n* **jet-setter**. — *n* & *adj* **jet-setting**.

jetsam *n* goods jettisoned from a ship and washed up on the shore. ◇ See also **flotsam**. [Contracted from **jettison**]

jettison *v* (*tr*) **-*n*- 1** to throw (cargo) overboard to lighten a ship, aircraft, etc. in an emergency. **2** to abandon, reject or get rid of. [OFr *getaison*, from Lat *iactatio*, a tossing]

jetty *n* **-*ies* 1** a stone or wooden landing-stage. **2** a stone barrier built out into the sea to protect a harbour from currents and high waves. [OFr *jetee*, from *jeter*, to throw]

Jew *n* **1** a member of the Hebrew race. **2** someone who practises Judaism. **3** (*old offensive*) a miser; an unrelenting bargainer. [OFr *Juiu*, from Lat *Judaeus*]

Jewess *n* (*offensive*) a Jewish woman or girl.

Jewish *adj* relating or belonging to the Jews or to Judaism.

Jewry *n* (*old*) Jews collectively.

Jew's harp *n* a tiny lyre-shaped musical instrument held between the teeth, with a narrow metal tongue that is twanged with the finger.

jewel *n* **1** a precious stone. **2** a personal ornament made with precious stones and metals. **3** a gem used in the machinery of a watch. **4** someone or something greatly prized. — *adj* **jewelled**. [OFr *joel*]

jeweller *n* **1** a person who deals in, makes or repairs jewellery, watches, and objects of gold and silver.

jewellery or (esp. *US*) **jewelry** *n* articles worn for personal adornment, e.g. bracelets, necklaces, brooches, rings, etc.

Jezebel *n* (*derog*) a shameless or scheming woman. [Ahab's wife in the Old Testament, I Kings xxi; II Kings ix.30]

jib[1] *n* a small three-cornered sail in front of the mainsail of a yacht. — *v* **-*bb*- 1** (*intr* with **at**) (of a horse) to refuse (a jump, etc.). **2** (*intr* with **at**) to object to. **3** (*intr* & *tr*; *naut*) to gybe.

jib boom *n* (*naut*) an extension to the bowsprit on which the jib is spread.

jib[2] *n* the projecting arm of a crane from which the lifting gear hangs. [From **gibbet**]

jibe. Another spelling of **gibe** and **gybe**.

jiffy *n* **-*ies*** (*coll*; also **jiff**) a moment.

Jiffy bag® *n* a padded envelope.

jig *n* **1** a lively country dance or folk dance; music for this. **2** (*mech*) a device that holds a piece of work in position and guides the tools being used on it. — *v* **-*gg*- 1** (*intr*) to dance a jig. **2** (*intr*) to jump up and down. **3** (*tr*; *mech*) to work on (something under construction) using a jig.

jigger[1] *n* **1** (a glass for measuring) a small quantity of alcoholic spirits. **2** (*billiards*; *coll*) a cue rest. **3** (*golf*) an iron-headed club. **4** (*NAm coll*) an all-purpose term for any gadget whose name one has forgotten. [**jig**[1]]

jigger[2] *n* a variant of **chigger**.

jiggered *adj* (*coll*) exhausted. — **I'll be jiggered** (*coll*) an expression of astonishment. [Poss. euph. for *buggered*]

jiggery-pokery *n* (*coll*) trickery or deceit. [Scot *joukery-pawkery*, from *jouk*, to dodge + *pawk*, trick]

jiggle *n* (*tr* & *intr*) to (cause to) jump up and down or jerk about. — *n* a jiggling movement. [From **jig**]

jigsaw *n* **1** (also **jigsaw puzzle**) a picture mounted on wood or cardboard and sawn into irregularly shaped interlocking pieces, taken apart for later re-assembly into the picture. **2** a fine-bladed saw for cutting intricate patterns. [**jig** + **saw**[2]]

jihad or **jehad** *n* a holy war fought by Muslims as a duty on behalf of Islam. [Arabic, struggle]

jilt *v* (*tr*; *old*) to discard (a lover). [Contracted from *jillet*, a flirt]

Jim Crow *n* (*US slang*) **1** (*offensive*) a black person. **2** the policy of segregating blacks from whites. [From the title of a black minstrel song]

jimjams *n* (*pl*) **1** (*coll*) a state of nervous excitement. **2** (*slang*) delirium tremens. **3** (*coll*) pyjamas.

jingle *n* **1** a ringing or clinking sound, as of small bells, coins or keys. **2** a simple rhyming verse or song. — *v* (*tr* & *intr*) to (cause to) make a ringing or clinking sound. [Imit.]

jingoism *n* over-enthusiastic or aggressive patriotism. — *n* **jingoist**. — *adj* **jingoistic**. ['By *jingo*!' (i.e. by God!), from chauvinistic British song of 1878]

jink *v* (*intr* & *tr*) to dodge. — *n* a dodge. [Imit.]

high jinks *n* (*pl*) boisterous fun.

jinni, **jinnee** or **djinni** *n* ***jinn, djinn*** in Muslim folklore, a supernatural being able to take on human or animal form. [Arabic]

jinx *n* an evil spell or influence, held responsible for misfortune. — *v* (*tr*) to put a jinx on. [*jynx*, the wryneck, a bird used in spells; hence a spell or charm]

jitter (*coll*) *v* **-*r*-** (*intr*) to shake with nerves. — *n* (in *pl*) an attack of nervousness. — *adj* **jittery**. [Variant of *chitter*, to shiver]

jitterbug *n* **1** an energetic dance like jive, popular in the 1940s. **2** an alarmist or scaremonger. — *v* **-gg-** (*intr*) to dance the jitterbug. **[jitter]**

jive *n* a style of dancing to jazz popular in the 1940s and '50s, similar to the later rock-and-roll.

Jnr *abbrev* Junior.

job *n* **1** a person's regular paid employment. **2** a piece of work. **3** a completed task: *made a good job of the pruning*. **4** a function or responsibility. **5** (*coll*) a problem; difficulty: *had a job finding it*. **6** a crime, esp. a burglary: *an inside job*. **7** an underhand scheme: *a put-up job*. **8** (*coll*) a do, affair, business, etc.: *The wedding was a registry-office job*. **9** (*coll*) a surgical operation, usu. involving plastic surgery: *a nose job*. **10** (*coll*) a manufactured product, or other object: *Smart little jobs, these calculators*. — *v* **-bb-** **1** (*intr*) to do casual jobs. **2** (*tr & intr*) to buy and sell (stocks) as a stockjobber; to act as stockjobber. **3** (*tr & intr*) to bring about by, or practise, jobbery. **4** (*tr*) to hire or let out for a period or a job. — **do the job** to succeed in doing what is required. — **give up as a bad job** to abandon (a task, etc.) as impossible or not worthwhile. — **a good job** (*coll*) lucky. — **jobs for the boys** (*derog*) superfluous work created as employment for one's supporters and friends. — **just the job** exactly what is required. — **make the best of a bad job** to do one's best in difficult circumstances. — **more than one's job's worth** likely to lead to one's dismissal from one's job.

job centre or **Jobcentre** *n* (*Brit*) a government office displaying information on available jobs.

job club or **Jobclub** *n* an association aimed at helping the jobless find work through learning and using the necessary skills of presentation, etc.

jobless *n* & *adj* (people) having no paid employment.

job lot *n* a mixed collection of objects sold as one item at an auction, etc.

job-sharing *n* the practice of sharing the tasks of one full-time job between two or more part-time workers.

jobber *n* (*stock exchange*) a stockjobber. **[job]**

jobbery *n* the abuse of public office for private gain. **[job]**

Job's comforter *n* a person whose attempts at sympathy have the effect of adding to one's distress. [From *Job* in the Old Testament]

Jock *n* (*coll*) a Scotsman, esp. a soldier. [Scots form of *Jack*]

jockey *n* **-eys** a rider, esp. professional, in horse races. — *v* **1** (*tr*) to ride (a horse) in a race. **2** (*tr & intr*; with **into, out of, for,** etc.) to manoeuvre deviously. [Dimin. of **Jock**]

jockstrap *n* a garment for supporting the genitals, worn by male athletes. [*jock*, penis]

jocose *adj* playful; humorous. — *adj* **jocosely**. — *n* **jocosity** . [Lat *jocosus*]

jocular *adj* **1** given to joking; good-humoured. **2** (of a remark) intended as a joke. — *n* **jocularity**. — *adv* **jocularly**. [Lat *joculus*, a little joke]

jocund *adj* cheerful; merry; good-humoured. — *n* **jocundity**. [Lat *jocundus*, agreeable]

jodhpurs *n* (*pl*) riding-breeches that are loose-fitting over the buttocks and thighs and tight-fitting from knee to calf. [*Jodhpur* in India]

jog *v* **-gg-** **1** (*tr*) to knock or nudge slightly. **2** (*tr*) to prompt (the memory). **3** (*intr*; **along**) to progress slowly and steadily; to plod. **4** (*intr*) to run at a gentle, steady pace, for exercise. — *n* **1** a spell of jogging. **2** a nudge, knock or jolt. — *n* **jogger**. — *n* **jogging**. [Variant of *shog*, to shake]

jog pants, **joggers** or **jogging bottoms** *n* (*pl*) loose trousers of a warm material, fitting tightly round the waist and ankles.

jog-trot *n* an easy pace like that of a horse between walking and trotting.

joggle *v* (*tr* & *intr*) to jolt, shake or wobble. — *n* a shake or jolt **[jog]**

john *n* (*NAm coll euph*; with **the**) a lavatory. [From the name]

John Bull *n* (*old*) **1** a typical Englishman. **2** a personification of the English nation. [Name orig. used in 18th-cent. satire]

johnny *n* **-ies** (*coll*) a chap; a fellow. [Dimin. of *John*]

joie de vivre *n* enthusiasm for being alive; exuberant spirits. [Fr, *joy of life*]

join *v* **1** (*tr*; **up, on, to**) to connect, attach, link or unite. **2** (*tr & intr*) to become a member of (a society, firm, etc.). **3** (*intr & tr*) (of roads, rivers, etc.) to meet. **4** (*tr*) to come together with; to enter the company of: *joined them for supper*. **5** (*tr* or *intr*; **on**) to add oneself (to): *join the queue*. **6** (*tr*) to take part in. **7** (*tr*) to do the same as, for companionship: *Who'll join me in a drink?* — *n* a seam or joint. — *v* **join in** (*tr & intr*) to participate in; to take part. — *v* **join up** (*intr*) **1** to enlist as a member of an armed service. **2** (**with**) to come together for joint action, etc. [OFr *joindre*]

joiner *n* **1** a craftsman who makes and fits wooden doors, window frames, stairs, shelves, etc. **2** (*coll*) a sociable person who likes joining clubs and being a member of a group.

joinery *n* the trade or work of a joiner.

joint *n* **1** the place where two or more pieces join. **2** a part of the skeleton, such as the knee or elbow, where two bones meet and interlock with a certain range of movement. **3** a piece of meat, usu. containing a bone, for cooking or roasting. **4** (*slang*) a cheap, shabby cafe, bar, night-club, etc. **5** (*slang*) a cannabis cigarette. **6** (*geol*) a crack in a mass of rock. — *v* (*tr*) **1** to connect by joints. **2** to divide (a bird or animal) into, or at, the joints, for cooking. — *adj* **1** owned, done, etc. in common; shared. **2** working together. — *adv* **jointly**. — **case the joint** (*slang*) to make a preliminary investigation of premises one intends to burgle. — **out of joint 1** (of a bone) dislocated. **2** in disorder. [OFr *joint(e)*, from *joindre*, to join]

joint-stock company *n* a business whose capital is owned jointly by the shareholders.

jointure *n* property settled on a woman by her husband for her use after his death. — *v* (*tr*) to provide with a jointure. [OFr, from Lat *junctura*, joining]

joist *n* any of the beams supporting a floor or ceiling. [OFr *giste*, from *gesir*, to lie]

jojoba *n* a N American shrub whose seeds contain a wax similar to spermaceti and which is used as a substitute for it in cosmetics, etc. [Mexican Span]

joke *n* **1** a humorous story: *crack a joke*. **2** anything said or done in jest. **3** an amusing situation. **4** something or someone ludicrous. — *v* (*intr*; **about, with**) **1** to make jokes. **2** to speak in jest, not in earnest. — *adj* **jokey**. — *n* **jokiness**. — *adv* **jokingly**. — **the joke's on him**, etc. (*coll*) he, etc. has become the victim of his own joke. — **joking apart** or **aside** to be serious; seriously. — **no joke** (*coll*) a serious matter. — **play a joke on** to play a trick on. — **see the joke** (*coll*) to see the funny side. — **take a joke** to be able to laugh at a joke played on one. [Lat *jocus*, joke]

joker *n* **1** (*cards*) an extra card in a pack, usu. bearing a picture of a jester, used in certain games. **2** a cheerful person, always full of jokes. **3** (*coll*) an irresponsible or incompetent person. **4** (*coll*) a person. — **joker in the pack** a person or thing whose effect on a situation is unpredictable.

jollification *n* **1** merriment; fun. **2** (in *pl*) cheerful celebrations. [**jolly**]

jollity *n* **-ies 1** merriment. **2** (in *pl*) festivities. [MidE *jolite*, from OFr *jolif*, pretty, merry]

jolly *adj* **-ier**, **-iest 1** good-humoured; cheerful. **2** happy; enjoyable; convivial. — *adv* (*Brit coll*) very. — *v* **-ies**, **-ied** (*tr*) **1** (with **up**) to make more cheerful. **2** (**into, out of**) to coax or cajole. **3** (**along**) to keep (someone) cheerful and co-operative. — *n* **jolliness**. — **jolly well** (*Brit coll*) used for emphasis: *You jolly well deserved it*. [Fr *jolif*, pretty, merry]

jollyboat *n* a small boat carried on a larger ship.

Jolly Roger *n* (*hist*) the black flag of a pirate ship bearing a white skull-and-crossbones.

jolt *v* **1** (*intr*) to move along jerkily. **2** (*tr*) to shake, jog or jar. — *n* **1** a jarring shake. **2** an emotional shock. [Blend of dialect *jot* & *joll*, to bump]

Jonah *n* a person who seems to bring bad luck. [*Jonah* in the Old Testament, who almost brought disaster on the ship on which he was sailing]

jonquil *n* a European and Asian plant of the narcissus family, with sweet-smelling white or yellow flowers. [Fr *jonquille*]

josh (*N Am coll*) *v* (*tr* & *intr*) to tease. — *n* a bit of teasing.

joss-stick *n* a stick of dried scented paste, burnt as incense. [*joss* (pidgin Chinese), household god, from Port *deos*, god]

jostle *v* **1** (*intr* & *tr*) to push and shove; to push against (someone) roughly. **2** (*intr* with **for**) to compete aggressively. [Formed from **joust**]

jot *n* (usu. with *not*) the least bit: *not a jot of sympathy*. — *v* **-tt-** (*tr*; **down**) to write down hastily. [*iota*, the Gr letter *i*]

jotter *n* (*Scot*) a school notebook for rough work and notes.

jotting *n* (usu. in *pl*) something jotted down.

joule *n* (*physics*) a unit of energy or work. [J *Joule* (1818–89), English physicist]

journal *n* **1** a magazine or periodical, e.g. one dealing with a specialised subject. **2** a diary in which one recounts one's daily activities. **3** (*mech*) the part of an axle or rotating shaft within the bearing. [Lat *diurnalis*, daily]

journalese *n* (*derog*) the language, typically shallow and full of clichés and jargon, used by less able journalists.

journalism *n* the profession of writing for newspapers and magazines, or for radio and television. — *n* **journalist**. — *adj* **journalistic**.

journey *n* **-eys 1** a process of travelling from one place to another. **2** the distance covered by, or time taken for, a journey. — *v* **-eys**, **-eyed** (*intr*) to make a journey. [OFr *journee*, day]

journeyman *n* **-men 1** a craftsman qualified in a particular trade and working for an employer. **2** an experienced and competent but not outstanding worker. [**journey** in the old sense of a day's work]

joust *n* (*hist*) a contest between two knights on horseback armed with lances. — *v* (**with, against**) to take part in a joust. [Fr *jouster*, to joust, from Lat *juxta*, near]

Jove: **by Jove!** (*Brit old coll*) an exclamation of surprise or emphasis. [Another name for the Roman god Jupiter]

jovial *adj* good-humoured; merry; cheerful. — *n* **joviality**. — *adv* **jovially**. [Lat *jovialis*, of the planet Jupiter, believed to be a lucky influence]

jowl[1] *n* **1** the lower jaw. **2** the cheek. [OE *ceafl*, jaw]

jowl[2] *n* (usu. in *pl*) **1** loose flesh under the chin; a heavy double chin. **2** (in an animal) a dewlap. [OE *ceole*, throat]

joy *n* **1** a feeling of happiness. **2** a cause of this. **3** (*Brit coll*) satisfaction; success: *Any joy at the enquiry desk?* — *adj* **joyless**. [OFr *joie*]

joyful *adj* **1** happy; full of joy. **2** expressing or causing joy. — *adv* **joyfully**.

joyous *adj* filled with, causing or showing joy. — *adv* **joyously**. — *n* **joyousness**.

joyride *n* a jaunt, esp. a reckless drive in a stolen vehicle. — *v* (*intr*) to go for such a jaunt. — *n* **joy-rider**.

joystick *n* (*coll*) a controlling lever, e.g. for a computer or an aircraft.

JP *abbrev* Justice of the Peace.

Jr *abbrev* Junior.

jubilant *adj* showing and expressing triumphant joy. — *adj* **jubilantly**. [Lat *jubilare*, to shout for joy]

jubilation *n* **1** triumphant rejoicing. **2** (in *pl*) celebrations. [Lat *jubilatio*]

jubilee *n* a special anniversary, esp the 25th, 50th or 60th (respectively a **silver**, **golden**, and **diamond jubilee**) of a significant event, e.g. the succession of the monarch. [OFr *jubile*, from Lat *jubilaeus*, of the Jewish jubilee, from Hebr *yobhel*, (ram's horn or trumpet announcing) a year of debt-cancellation, slave-emancipation and land-restoration]

Judaeo- or (*US*) **Judeo-** *comb fm* Jewish, or Jewish and: *Judaeo-Hispanic*.

Judaism *n* **1** the religion of the Jews, having its basis in the Old Testament and the Talmud. **2** the traditional religious and cultural practices of the Jews. — *adj* **Judaic**. [Lat *Juda*, a son of Jacob]

Judas *n* a traitor, esp. to one's friends. [The disciple *Judas* Iscariot, who betrayed Jesus]

judder *v* **-r-** (*intr*) (of a vehicle) to jolt, shake, shudder or vibrate. — *n* a shuddering vibration. [Perhaps **shudder** + **jar**[2]]

judge *n* **1** a public officer who hears and decides cases in a law court. **2** a person appointed to decide the winner of a contest. **3** someone who assesses something; a connoisseur: *a good judge of character*, *wine*, etc. **4** the person who decides or assesses: *Let me be the judge of that*. — *v* **1** (*tr*) to try (a legal case) in a law court as judge. **2** (*tr*) to decide the winner of (a contest). **3** (*intr*) to act as judge or adjudicator. **3** (*tr* & *intr*) to assess; to form an opinion. **4** (*tr*) to estimate. **5** (*tr*) to consider or state: *judged her fit to travel*. **6** (*tr*) to criticise, esp. severely; to condemn. [OFr *juge*]

judgement or **judgment** *n* **1** the decision of a judge in a court of law. **2** the act or process of judging. **3** the ability to make wise or sensible decisions; good sense. **4** an opinion: *in my judgement*. **5** (esp. *old*; **on**) punishment sent by God: *His sickness was a judgement on him*. — *adj* **judgemental** or **judgmental**. — **against one's better judgement** contrary to what one believes to be the sensible course. — **pass judgement 1** (**on**) to give a judgement or verdict. **2** (with **on**) to condemn. — **reserve judgement** to postpone one's verdict. — **sit in judgement on** to assume the responsibility of judging (another person). [OFr *jugement*]

(the Day of) Judgement or **the Last Judgement** *n* the time, when the world ends, when God will judge all mankind.

judicature *n* **1** the administration of justice by legal trial. **2** the office of judge. **3** a body of judges. **4** a court or system of courts. [Lat *judicare*, to judge]

judicial *adj* of, or relating to, a court of law, judges, or their decisions. — *adv* **judicially**. [Lat *judicialis*, from *judicium*, judgement]

judiciary *n* **-ies** *n* **1** the branch of government concerned with the legal system and the administration of justice. **2** a country's body of judges. [Lat *judiciarius*, of the law courts]

judicious *adj* shrewd, sensible, wise or tactful. — *adv* **judiciously**. — *n* **judiciousness**. [Lat *judicium*, judgement]

judo *n* a Japanese form of wrestling using minimum physical effort, developed from jujitsu. [Jap *ju*, gentleness + *do*, art]

jug *n* **1** a deep container for liquids with a handle and a shaped lip for pouring. **2** the amount that a jug can hold. **3** (*slang*) prison. — *v* **-gg-** (*tr*) to stew (hare) in an earthenware container.

juggernaut *n* **1** a mighty force sweeping away and destroying everything in its path. **2** (*coll*) a very large lorry. [From the gigantic chariot of the god *Jagannath*, at his festivals in Puri, India]

juggle *v* **1** (*intr*) to keep several objects simultaneously in the air by skilful throwing and catching. **2** (*tr*, or *intr* with **with**) to adjust (facts or figures) to create a misleading impression. — *n* **juggler**. [OFr *jogler*, to act as jester]

jugular *adj* relating to the neck or throat. — *n* (also **jugular vein**) one of two large veins on either side of the neck conveying blood from the head to the heart. [Lat *jugulum*, throat]

juice *n* **1** liquid from fruit or vegetables. **2** (esp. in *pl*) the body's natural fluids: *digestive juices*. **3** (*slang*) power or fuel, esp. electricity or petrol. [OFr *jus*]

juicy *adj* **-ier**, **-iest 1** full of juice; rich and succulent. **2** (*coll*) (of a problem, etc.) challenging; meaty. **3** (*coll*) (of gossip) intriguing; spicy. **4** (*coll*) profitable; lucrative. — *n* **juiciness**.

jujitsu *n* a system of unarmed self-defence, developed in Japan. [Jap *ju*, gentleness, *jutsu*, art]

juju *n* **1** a charm or fetish used by W African tribes. **2** the magic contained in such a charm. [Hausa (W African language) *djudju*, fetish]

jujube *n* **1** a soft fruit-flavoured sweet made with gelatine. **2** (*hist*) the fruit of a spiny shrub of the buckthorn family, dried and eaten as a sweet. [Lat *jujuba*, from Gr *zizyphon*]

jukebox *n* a coin-operated machine that plays whatever gramophone record one selects. [Gullah (W African language) *juke*, disorderly]

Jul. *abbrev* July.

julep *n* esp. in N America, an iced drink of spirits and sugar, flavoured esp. with mint. [Persian *gulab*, rosewater]

Julian calendar *n* the calendar introduced by Julius Caesar in 46 BC, with a year of 365 days and 366 every leap year or centenary year. ◇ See also **Gregorian calendar**.

July *n* the seventh month of the year. [*Julius* (*mensis*), (the month) of Julius (Caesar)]

jumble *v* (*tr*; **up, together**) **1** to mix or confuse. **2** to throw together untidily. — *n* **1** a confused mass. **2** unwanted possessions collected, or suitable, for a jumble sale.

jumble sale *n* a sale of unwanted possessions, e.g. used clothing, usu. to raise money for charity.

jumbo (*coll*) *adj* extra-large. — *n* **-os** a jumbo jet. [Name of an elephant exhibited by P T Barnum in 1882]

jumbo jet *n* (*coll*) the largest size of passenger jet airliner.

jump *v* **1** (*intr*) to spring off the ground, pushing off with the feet. **2** (*intr*) to leap or bound. **3** (*tr*) to get over or across by jumping. **4** (*tr*) to make (esp. a horse) leap. **5** (*intr*) (of prices, levels, etc.) to rise abruptly. **6** (*intr*) to make a startled movement. **7** (*intr*) to twitch, jerk or bounce. **8** (*intr*) to pass directly from one point to another, omitting intermediate matter or essential steps: *jump straight to the mad scene*; *jump to conclusions*. **9** (*tr*) to omit; to skip: *jump the next chapter*. **10** (*tr*; *coll*) to pounce on. **11** (*tr*; *NAm coll*) to board and travel on (esp. a train) without paying. — *n* **1** an act of jumping. **2** an obstacle to be jumped, esp. a fence by a horse. **3** the height or distance jumped. **4** a jumping contest: *the high jump*; *the long jump*. **5** a sudden rise in amount, cost, or value. **6** an abrupt change or move. **7** a startled movement; a start: *gave a jump of surprise*. — **be** or **stay one jump ahead of** (*coll*) to anticipate the moves of, and so maintain an advantage over (rivals, etc.). — **have the jump on** (*coll*) to have an advantage over. — *v* **jump at** (*tr*) to take or accept eagerly. — **jump down someone's throat** (*coll*) to snap at someone impatiently. — *v* **jump on** (*tr*) to attack physically or verbally. — **jump to it** to hurry up.

jumped-up *adj* (*coll derog*) being no better than one's humble origins in spite of one's rise in status: *just a jumped-up office clerk*.

jumper *n* **1** a person or animal that jumps. **2** (*electr*) a wire used to make a temporary connection.

jump jet *n* a jet aircraft that can take off and land vertically.

jump lead *n* one of the two electric cables used to recharge one battery from another.

jump-off *n* (*showjumping*) an extra round held in the event of a tie.

jump-start *v* (*tr*) to start (a motor vehicle) by engaging gear while it is freewheeling. — *n* **jump start**.

jumpsuit *n* a one-piece garment combining trousers and top.

jumpy *adj* **-ier, -iest 1** nervy; anxious. **2** moving jerkily. — *adv* **jumpily**. — *n* **jumpiness**.

jumper[1] *n* **1** a knitted garment for the top half of the body. **2** (*NAm*) a pinafore dress. [Old word *jump*, a short coat]

jumper[2], **jumpy**. See **jump**.

Jun. *abbrev* **1** June. **2** Junior.

junction *n* **1** a place where roads or railway lines meet; an intersection. **2** a point of exit from, and access to, a motorway. **3** (*electr*) a point at which wires or cables are connected. **4** the process, an instance, or a point, of joining. [Lat *junctio*, joining]

junction box *n* the casing for an electrical junction.

juncture *n* a point in time, esp. if critical. [Lat *junctura*, connection]

June *n* the sixth month of the year. [*Junius* (*mensis*), (the month) of the goddess Juno]

jungle *n* **1** dense tropical forest. **2** any dense, overgrown mass of vegetation. **3** a mass of complexities difficult to penetrate: *the jungle of building regulations*. **4** a hostile environment where toughness is needed for survival: *the blackboard jungle* (i.e. the world of a teacher). — *adj* **jungly, -lier, -liest**. [Hindi *jangal*]

law of the jungle *n* the principle that one should help oneself rather than others.

junior *adj* **1** (**to**) low, or lower, in rank. **2** of or for schoolchildren aged between 7 and 11: *junior schools*. **3** (**to**) younger (than). **4** (*US*) of third-year college or university students. **5** younger; used after the name of a person with the same name as his or her parent. — *n* **1** a person of low, or lower, rank in a profession, organisation, etc. **2** a pupil in a junior school. **3** (*US*) a third-year college or high-school student. **4** a person younger than the one in question: *She's three years his junior*. **5** (*cap*) a name sometimes used for referring to the son of a family. [Lat, younger]

juniper *n* an evergreen shrub of northern regions with purple berries used as a medicine and for flavouring gin. [Lat *juniperus*]

junk[1] *n* (*coll*) **1** worthless or rejected material; rubbish. **2** old or second-hand articles sold cheaply: *a junk shop*. **3** nonsense. **4** (*slang*) narcotic drugs, esp. heroin. — *adj* cheap and worthless: *junk jewellery*. [MidE *jonke*, pieces of old rope]

junk food *n* food with little nutritional value.

junk[2] *n* a Far-Eastern flat-bottomed square-sailed boat. [Port *junco*, from Malay *jong*]

junket 1 *n* a dessert made from sweetened and curdled milk. **2** a feast or celebration. **3** a trip made by a government official and paid for out of public funds. — *v* **-t-** (*intr*) to feast, celebrate or make merry. [OFr *jonquette*, a rush basket (holding cheeses, etc.)]

junkie or **junky** *n* **-*ies*** (*slang*) a drug addict or drug-pusher. [**junk**]

junta *n* (*derog*) a group, clique or faction, usu. of army officers, in control of a country after a coup d'état. [Span, meeting]

Jurassic *adj* & *n* (*geol*) (of or denoting) a period between 213 and 144 million years ago, characterised by limestone formation, during which dinosaurs dominated over primitive birds and mammals. [*Jura*, limestone mountain range in E France]

juridical *adj* of or relating to the law or the administration of justice. [Lat *juridicus*, of justice]

jurisdiction *n* **1** the right or authority to apply laws and administer justice. **2** the district or area over which this authority extends. **3** authority generally. [Lat *jurisdictio*, administration of justice]

jurisprudence *n* **1** the science and philosophy of law. **2** a specialty within law: *medical jurisprudence*. — *adj* **jurisprudential**. [Lat *jurisprudentia*, from *jus*, law + *prudentia*, wisdom]

jurist *n* an expert in law. — *adj* **juristic**. [Fr *juriste*]

juror *n* **1** a member of a jury in a court of law. **2** a person taking an oath. [Lat *jurare*, to swear]

jury[1] *n* **-*ies*** **1** a body of usu. 12 people sworn to give an honest verdict on the evidence presented to a court of law on a particular case. **2** a group of people selected to judge a contest. [OFr *juree*, something sworn]

jury-box *n* the enclosure in which the jury sit in a law court.

jury[2] *adj* (*naut*) makeshift; temporary: *a jury mast*.

just[1] *adj* **1** fair; impartial. **2** reasonable; based on justice. **3** deserved. — *adv* **justly**. — *n* **justness**. [Lat *justus*, just, upright, equitable]

just[2] *adv* **1** exactly; precisely. **2** a short time before: *He had just gone*. **3** at this or that very moment: *was just leaving*. **4** and no earlier, more, etc.: *only just enough*. **5** barely; narrowly: *just missed his ear*. **6** only; merely; simply: *just a brief note*. **7** (*coll*) used for emphasis: *just not true*. **8** (*coll*) absolutely: *just marvellous*. — **just about** **1** almost. **2** on the point of going (to do something). — **just as well** **1** lucky. **2** advisable. — **just in case** as a precaution. — **just a minute, second**, etc. wait a minute, second, etc. — **just now** at this particular moment. — **just so** **1** I quite agree. **2** neat and tidy. — **just then** **1** at that particular moment. **2** in the next moment. — **just the same** nevertheless. — **not just yet** not immediately, but soon. [Lat *justus*, right, proper]

justice *n* **1** the quality of being just; just treatment; fairness. **2** the quality of being reasonable. **3** (administration of, or conformity to) the law: *a miscarriage of justice*. **4** (*cap*) the title of a judge. **5** a justice of the peace. **6** (*US*) a judge. — **bring to justice** to arrest, try and sentence (a criminal). — **do (someone or something) justice** or **do justice to** **1** to treat fairly or properly. **2** to show the full merit, etc. of. **3** (with **oneself**) to fulfil one's potential. **4** (*facet*) to eat (a meal, etc.) with hearty appreciation. — **in justice to** to be fair to. [Lat *justitia*, from *justus*, just]

justice of the peace *n* ***justices*** a person authorised to judge minor criminal cases.

justiciary *n* **-*ies*** an administrator of justice; a judge. [Lat *justiciarius*]

justify *v* **-*ies***, **-*ied*** (*tr*) **1** to prove or show to be right, just or reasonable. **2** (*printing*) to arrange (text) so that the margins are even-edged. — *adj* **justifiable**. — *adv* **justifiably**. — *n* **justification**. [Lat *justus*, just + *facere*, to make]

jut *v* **-*tt*-** (*intr*; **out**) to stick out; to project. [Variant of **jet**[2]]

Jute *n* a member of a Germanic people from Jutland who invaded southern Britain in the fifth century AD and settled in Kent and the Isle of Wight. [OE *Iotas*, the Jutes]

jute *n* fibre from certain tropical barks used for making sacking, ropes, etc. [Bengali *jhuta*]

juvenile *adj* **1** young; youthful. **2** suitable for young people. **3** (*derog*) childish; immature. — *n* **1** a young person. **2** a young animal. **3** an actor playing youthful parts. [Lat *juvenilis*, youthful]

juvenile delinquent *n* a young person who is guilty of a crime. — *n* **juvenile delinquency**.

juvenilia *n* (*pl*) the works produced by a writer or artist during his or her youth. [Lat *juvenilis*, youthful]

juxtapose *v* (*tr*) to place side by side. — *n* **juxtaposition**. [Lat *juxta*, beside + **position**]

K

K[1] or **k** *n* ***Ks*** or ***K's, k's*** the eleventh letter of the English alphabet.

K[2] *n* ***K* 1** (*coll*) one thousand, esp. £1000. **2** (*comput*) a unit of memory equal to 1024 bits, bytes or words. [**kilo-**]

K[3] *abbrev* **1** kilo-. **2** kelvin. **3** (*chess & cards*) king. **4** (*knitting instructions*) knit (a plain stitch). **5** krona, króna, or krone.

K[4] *symbol* (*chem*) potassium. [Lat *kalium*]

Kaaba, **Ka'ba**, or **Ka'bah** *n* a cube-shaped building at Mecca, into whose eastern wall is built a meteorite, the Black Stone, towards which Muslims symbolically turn when praying. [Arabic *ka'bah*, from *ka'b*, cube]

kabuki *n* a traditional form of Japanese drama with men playing both male and female parts. [Jap]

Kaffir *n* **1** (*SAfr offensive*) a black African. **2** (*old*) the Xhosa language, a Bantu language of South Africa. [Arabic *kafir*, unbeliever]

kaftan. See **caftan**.

kaiser *n* (*hist*) the emperor of Germany, Austria or the Holy Roman Empire. [Ger, from *Caesar*, family name of the earliest Roman emperors]

kalashnikov *n* a type of submachine-gun manufactured in the Soviet Union. [Russ; the name of the inventor]

kale *n* **1** a crinkly-leaved type of cabbage. **2** (*Scot*) cabbage. [OE *cawl*]

kaleyard *n* (*Scot*) a vegetable garden.

kaleidoscope *n* **1** a tubular device inside which loose fragments of coloured glass, etc. are reflected in mirrors, usu. two set at 45° or 60°, so as to form constantly changing symmetrical patterns as the tube is shaken or rotated. **2** any colourful and constantly changing scene or succession of events. — *adv* **kaleidoscopic**. — *adv* **kaleidoscopically**. [Gr *kalos*, beautiful, *eidos*, form + **-scope**]

kalends. Another spelling of **calends**.

kamikaze *n* in World War II, a Japanese plane loaded with explosives deliberately crashed by its pilot on an enemy target; the pilot himself. — *adj* (*coll*) (of exploits, missions, etc.) suicidally dangerous. [Jap, divine wind]

Kan. *abbrev* Kansas.

kangaroo *n* an Australian marsupial animal with large powerful hind legs adapted for leaping. [*gangurru* in an Australian Aboriginal language]

kangaroo court *n* an unofficial court of e.g. strikers to try strikebreakers, or prisoners to try fellow prisoners.

Kans. *abbrev* Kansas.

kaolin *n* china clay, a fine white clay used for making pottery, and medically in poultices and medicines. [Chin *Kao-ling* or *Gaoling* ('high ridge'), a mountain where it was mined]

kapok *n* a light cotton-like fibre got from a tropical tree and used as padding or as stuffing for toys, etc. [Malay *kapoq*]

kaput *adj* (*coll*) **1** broken. **2** ruined; destroyed. [Ger]

karakul *n* an Asian sheep whose lambs have a dark curly fleece; fur made from, or in imitation of, this fleece. [*Kara Kul*, lake in Tadzhik, central Asia, near which the sheep were orig. bred]

karaoke *n* the orig. Japanese form of entertainment in which amateur performers sing pop songs to the accompaniment of prerecorded music from a **karaoke machine**. [Jap, empty orchestra]

karate *n* an orig. Japanese system of unarmed self-defence, using blows and kicks. [Jap, empty hand]

karate chop *n* a sharp downward blow with the side of the hand.

karma *n* (*Buddhism & Hinduism*) one's lifetime's actions, seen as governing one's fate in one's next life. [Sanskrit, act, deed]

kart *n* (*coll*) a go-kart.

katydid *n* a large N American grasshopper. [Imit.]

kauri *n* a coniferous tree of New Zealand grown for its wood and resin. [Maori]

kayak *n* **1** a sealskin-covered canoe used by the Inuit. **2** a similar canvas-covered or fibreglass craft used in the sport of canoeing. [Inuit *qayaq*]

kazoo *n* a crude wind instrument consisting of a short metal tube into which one hums, causing a strip of parchment, etc. stretched across a hole in its upper surface, to vibrate with a buzzing effect. [Imit.]

KB *abbrev* King's Bench.

KBE *abbrev* Knight Commander of the British Empire.

KC *abbrev* King's Counsel.

kebab *n* a dish of small pieces of meat and vegetable, esp. (**shish kebab**) grilled on a skewer. [Arabic *kabab*; Turk *şiş*, skewer]

doner kebab *n* thin slices cut from a block of minced and seasoned lamb grilled on a spit and eaten on unleavened bread. [Turk *döner*, rotating]

kedge *v* (*tr & intr*) (of a ship) to manoeuvre by means of a hawser attached to a light anchor. — *n* a light anchor used for kedging. [Related to MidE *caggen*, to fasten]

kedgeree *n* an orig. E Indian dish, now usu. a mixture of rice, fish and eggs. [Hindi *khichri*]

keek *v* (*intr*) & *n* (*Scot*) (to take) a peep. [MidE *kiken*]

keel *n* the timber or metal strut extending from stem to stern along the base of a ship, from which the hull is built up. — *v* **keel over** (*intr*) **1** (of a ship) to tip over sideways. **2** (*coll*) to fall over, e.g. in a faint. — **on an even keel** calm and steady. [MidE *kele*, from ODut *kiel*, ship]

keelhaul *v* (*tr*) to drag (someone) under the keel of a ship as a punishment.

keelson. A variant of **kelson**.

keen[1] *adj* **1** eager; willing. **2** (with **on**) enthusiastic about; fond of. **3** (of competition, rivalry, etc.) fierce. **4** (of wind) bitter. **5** (of a blade, etc.) sharp. **6** (of the mind or senses) quick; acute. **7** (of prices) low; competitive. — *adv* **keenly**. — *n* **keenness**. [OE *cene*, bold, fierce]

keen[2] *v* (*intr* & *tr*) esp. in Ireland, to lament or mourn in a loud wailing voice. — *n* a lament for the dead. [Irish *caoine*, lament]

keep[1] *v* ***kept*** **1** (*tr*) to have; to possess. **2** (*tr*) to continue to have; not to part with; to save. **3** (*tr*) to maintain or retain: *keep one's temper*. **4** (*tr*) to store. **5** (*tr* & *intr*) to (cause to) remain in a certain state, position, place, etc. **6** (*intr*) to continue or be frequently (doing something): *keep smiling*; *kept fainting*. **7** (*tr*) (of a shopkeeper, etc.) to stock. **8** (*tr*) to own (an animal, etc.) for use or pleasure: *keep hens*. **9** (*tr*) to own or run (a shop, boarding-house, etc.). **10** (*tr*) to look after: *keep house*; *keep this for me*. **11** (*intr*) (of food) to remain fit to be eaten. **12** (*tr*) to maintain (a record, diary, accounts, etc.). **13** (*tr*; **from**) to hold back or delay. **14** (*tr*) to obey (the law, etc.). **15** (*tr*) to preserve (a secret). **16** (*tr*) to stick to (a promise or appointment). **17** (*tr*) to celebrate (a festival, etc.) in the traditional way; to follow (a custom). **18** (*tr*) to support financially. **19** (*tr*; **from**) to protect: *keep them from harm*. **20** (*tr*) to guard (the goal) in football or (the wicket) in cricket. **21** (*tr*) to remain firm on: *managed to keep his feet despite the strong wind*. — *n* the cost of one's food and other daily expenses: *earn one's keep*. — **for keeps** (*coll*) permanently; for good. — *v* **keep at** (*tr*) to persevere at or persist in. — *v* **keep back** (*tr*) **1** not to reveal (information, etc.). **2** to suppress (laughter, tears, etc.). — *v* **keep down** (*tr*) **1** to control, limit or keep low (prices, etc.). **2** to manage not to vomit (food, etc). **3** (*tr*) to oppress; to prevent the development, progress, etc. of. — *v* **keep from** (*tr*) **1** to prevent from, or succeed in not (doing something). **2** to prevent from reaching (someone): *keep the news from him*. — **keep going 1** to persevere in spite of problems. **2** to help (someone) survive difficulties, etc. — *v* **keep in with** (*tr*) to remain on good terms with, esp. for selfish reasons. — *v* **keep off** (*tr*) to avoid (a harmful food, awkward topic, etc.). — *v* **keep on 1** (*intr*) to continue (doing something). **2** (*tr*) to continue to employ, rent, etc. **3** (*intr*; **about**) to talk continually and repetitively. **4** (*intr*; **at**) to nag. — *v* **keep to** (*tr*) **1** not to leave: *keep to the path*. **2** to stick to, or make (someone) stick to (a decision, etc.): *I'll keep you to that*. — **keep to oneself 1** to avoid the company of others. **2** to keep (something) secret. — *v* **keep under** (*tr*) to subdue, repress or crush. — *v* **keep up 1** (*tr*) to prevent (e.g. spirits, morale, etc.) from falling. **2** (*tr*) to maintain (a habit, friendship, pace, etc.). **3** (*tr*) to go on making (payments, etc.). **4** (*tr*) to maintain (a house, garden, etc.) in good condition. **5** (*intr*; **with**) not to be left behind; to maintain the pace or standard set by (someone else). — **keep up with the Joneses** (*coll*) to compete with one's neighbours in a display of material prosperity. [OE *cepan*, to guard, observe, watch]

keeper *n* **1** a person who looks after something, e.g. animals in a zoo or a collection in a museum. **2** (*coll*) a goalkeeper or wicketkeeper.

keep-fit *n* a series or system of exercises, esp. for women, intended to improve suppleness, stamina, etc.

keeping *n* care or charge. — **in**, or **out of, keeping with** in, or not in, harmony with.

kept woman or **man** *n* (*derog*) a woman or man supported financially by someone in return for being available for sexual relations.

keep[2] *n* the central tower or stronghold in a Norman castle. [**keep**[1]]

keepsake *n* something kept in memory of the giver. [**keep**[1] + **sake**[1]]

keg *n* a small barrel for transporting and storing beer. [ON *kaggi*]

kelp *n* a brown seaweed that is a source of potassium and iodine. [Variant of MidE *culp*]

kelpie *n* (*Scot folklore*) a malignant water spirit in the form of a horse.

kelson or **keelson** *n* a timber fixed along a ship's keel for strength. [OGer *kielswin*, keel swine]

Kelt. Another form of **Celt**.

kelt *n* a salmon or sea trout that has just spawned.

kelvin *n* (*physics*) a degree or unit on the **Kelvin scale**, a scale for measuring temperature with zero at absolute zero. [Sir W Thomson, Lord *Kelvin* (1824–1907), physicist]

Ken. *abbrev* Kentucky.

ken *v* ***-nn-***, ***kent*** or ***kenned*** (*tr*; *Scot* & *dialect*) to know. — *n* one's range of knowledge: *beyond* or *within one's ken*. [OE *cennan*]

kendo *n* a Japanese form of fencing using bamboo swords. [Jap, sword way]

kennel *n* **1** a small shelter for a dog. **2** (in *pl*) an establishment where dogs are boarded or bred. — *v* **-ll-** (*tr*) to put or keep in a kennel. [Lat *canis*, dog]

kepi *n* a French military cap with a flat circular crown and horizontal straight-edged peak. [Fr *képi*, from Swiss German *Käppi*, dimin. of Ger *Kappe*, cap]

kept. See **keep**.

kerb *n* the row of stones forming the edging of a pavement. [Variant of **curb**]

kerb-crawling *n* the practice of driving slowly alongside the kerb in order to lure potential sexual partners into one's car. — *n* **kerb-crawler**.

kerbstone *n* one of the stones forming a kerb.

kerchief *n* (*old*) **1** a cloth or scarf for wearing over the head or round the neck. **2** a handkerchief. [OFr *cuevrechief*, from *covrir*, to cover + *chef*, head]

kerfuffle *n* (*coll*) a commotion or fuss. [Gaelic pfx. *car-* + Scot *fuffle*, to disorder]

kernel *n* **1** a seed within a husk, the edible part of a nut, or the stone of a fruit such as a plum, peach, etc. **2** the important, essential part of anything. [OE *cyrnel*, dimin. of *corn*, a grain]

kerosene *n* **1** paraffin oil distilled from petroleum or obtained from coal or shale, used for heating and lighting, and as an aircraft fuel. **2** (*NAm*) paraffin. [Gr *keros*, wax]

kestrel *n* a small type of falcon. [OFr *quercerelle*]

ketch *n* a small two-masted sailing boat. [MidE *cache*, related to **catch**]

ketchup *n* a thick sauce made from tomatoes, vinegar, spices, etc. [Malay *kechap*]

ketone *n* (*chem*) one of a class of organic compounds that includes acetone. [Ger *Keton*, from *Aketon*, acetone]

kettle *n* a kitchen vessel with a spout, lid and handle, for boiling water in. — **a different kettle of fish** (*coll*) an entirely different situation. — **a pretty kettle of fish** (*coll*) an awkward situation. [OE *cetel*]

kettledrum *n* a large copper or brass cauldron-shaped drum mounted on a tripod.

key[1] *n* **1** an instrument designed to turn a lock, wind a clock, grip and turn a nut, etc. **2** one of a series of buttons or levers pressed to sound the notes on a musical instrument, or to print or display a character on a computer, typewriter, calculator, etc. **3** a system of musical notes related to one another in a scale. **4** pitch, tone or style: *spoke in a low key*. **5** something that provides an answer or solution. **6** a means of achievement: *the key to success*. **7** a set of answers, e.g. at the back of a book of puzzles, exercises, etc. **8** a table explaining signs and symbols used on a map, etc. **9** (*electr*) a switch for completing or breaking a circuit. **10** the winged seed of the sycamore or ash tree. **11** roughness given to a surface by sandpapering, etc., so as to take paint, etc. more readily. **12** a fret pattern. **13** a pin or wedge for fixing something. — *adj* centrally important: *key questions*. — *v* **1** (*tr*; **in, into**) to enter (data) into a computer by operating keys. **2** (*tr*) to fasten or fix with a key. **3** (*tr*; **to**) to adjust or harmonise. — **keyed up** (*coll*) excited; tense; anxious. — **under lock and key 1** safely stored. **2** in prison. [OE *cæg*]

keyboard *n* **1** the set of keys on a piano, etc. or the bank of keys for operating a typewriter or computer. **2** (esp. *jazz*) a musical instrument with a keyboard, e.g. a synthesiser. — *v* **1** (*intr*) to operate the keyboard of a computer. **2** (*tr*) to set (text) using a computer keyboard. — *n* **keyboarder**.

keyhole *n* the hole through which a key is inserted into a lock.

keynote *n* **1** the note on which a musical scale or key is based. **2** a central theme of a speech, feature of an occasion, etc.

key pad *n* a small panel of keys or buttons. e.g. for dialling a telephone number, operating a calculator, adjusting a television, etc.

key punch *n* a device operated by a keyboard for transferring data on to punched cards.

keyring *n* a ring for keeping keys on.

key signature *n* (*mus*) the sharps and flats shown on the stave at the start of a piece of music, indicating its key.

keystone *n* **1** the central supporting stone at the high point of an arch. **2** the point in a theory or argument on which the rest depends.

keystroke *n* a single press of a key on a typewriter, computer, etc.

keyword *n* a word that sums up or gives an indication of the nature of the passage in which it occurs.

key[2] or **cay** *n* a low island or reef. [Span *cayo*]

Keynesian *adj* relating to the economic theories of J M *Keynes* (1883–1946) advocating government funding of public works to maintain full employment.

KG *abbrev* Knight of (the Order of) the Garter.

kg *abbrev* kilogram.

KGB *abbrev* for *Komitet Gosudarstvennoi Bezopastnosti* (*Russ*), Committee of State Security — the Soviet secret police.

khaki *n* **1** a brownish-green colour. **2** cloth of this colour, or military uniforms made of it. [Urdu & Pers, dusty]

khalif. See **caliph**.

khan *n* **1** the title of a ruler or prince in central Asia. **2** in ancient Persia, a governor. [Related to Turkish *kagan*, ruler]

KHz *abbrev* kilohertz.

kibbutz *n* ***kibbutzim*** in Israel, a farm or other concern owned and run jointly by its workers. [Mod Hebr *kibus*]

kibosh *n*: **put the kibosh on** (*coll*) to put an end to; to ruin.

kick *v* **1** (*tr*) to hit (a person, etc.) or propel (a ball, etc.) with the foot. **2** (*intr* & *tr*) to swing or jerk (the leg) vigorously. **3** (*intr*) (of a gun) to recoil when fired. **4** (*intr* with **against**) to resist: *kick against discipline*. **5** (*tr*) to get rid of (a habit, etc). **6** (*tr*) to score (a goal) with a kick. — *n* **1** a blow with the foot. **2** a swing of the leg: *high kicks*. **3** (*swimming*) any of various leg movements. **4** the recoil of a gun after firing. **5** (*coll*) a thrill of excitement. **6** (*coll*) a strong effect; power: *a drink with quite a kick*. **7** (*coll*) a brief enthusiasm: *We're on a culture kick*. — *n* **kicker**. — *v* **kick about** or **around** (*coll*) **1** (*tr*) to treat badly or roughly. **2** (*intr*) to lie around unused. **3** (*intr*) to be idle; to go about aimlessly. **4** (*tr*) to discuss (an idea, etc.) informally. — **kick in the teeth** (*coll*) (to crush with) a humiliating snub. — *v* **kick off 1** (*intr*) to start a football game by kicking the ball away from the centre (*n* **kick-off**). **2** (*tr* & *intr*; *coll*) to begin, e.g. a discussion. — *v* **kick out** (*tr*) to dismiss or get rid of, esp. using force. — *v* **kick up** (*tr*) to make (a fuss). — **kick upstairs** (*coll*) to promote to a position of higher rank but less influence. [MidE *kiken*]

kickback *n* money paid for help or favours, esp. if illegally given.

kick pleat *n* a small pleat at the back of a skirt.

kick-start *n* **1** (also **kick-starter**) a pedal on a motor cycle that is kicked vigorously downwards to start the engine. **2** the starting of an engine with this. — *v* (*tr*) to start (a motor cycle) using this.

kid[1] *n* **1** (*coll*) a child; a young person. **2** a young goat. **3** soft leather made from its skin. — *adj* (*coll*) younger: *my kid sister*. — **handle with kid gloves** to treat with special care or caution. — *v* **-dd-** (*intr*) (of a goat) to give birth to young. [Related to Norse *kith*, young goat]

kid[2] *v* **-dd-** (*coll*) **1** (*intr*; **on**) to bluff; to pretend. **2** (*tr*; **on**) to fool or deceive, esp. for fun. **3** (*tr* & *intr*) to tease. **4** (*tr*) to convince (oneself) of something untrue: *kidding himself all was well*. — *n* **kidder**. [Perhaps **kid**[1]]

kiddie or **kiddy** *n* **-ies** (*coll*) a small child. [**kid**[1]]

kidnap *v* **-pp-** (*tr*) to seize and hold (someone) prisoner illegally, usu. demanding a ransom for his or her release. [**kid**[1] + *nap*, variant of **nab**]

kidney *n* **-eys 1** one of a pair of abdominal organs whose function is to filter waste products from the blood, which are then excreted in the urine. **2** animal kidneys as food.

kidney bean *n* a dark red kidney-shaped bean eaten as a vegetable.

kidney machine *n* a machine for taking over the function of a damaged kidney.

kill *v* **1** (*tr*) to cause the death of. **2** (*tr*; *coll*) to cause pain to: *My feet are killing me*. **3** (*tr*; *coll*) to cause to fail; to put an end to: *how to kill a conversation*. **4** (*tr*) to defeat (a parliamentary bill). **5** (*tr*; *coll*) to destroy the effect of: *That turquoise kills the green*. **6** (*tr*; *coll*) to deaden (pain, noise, etc.). **7** (*tr*) to pass (time), esp. aimlessly or wastefully, while waiting for some later event. **8** (*tr*; *coll*, esp. *ironic*) to exhaust or put a strain on: *Don't kill yourself*. — *n* **1** an act of killing. **2** the prey killed by any creature. — *n* **killer**. — **be in at the kill** (*coll*) to be present at someone's dramatic downfall, or some other kind of showdown. — **dressed to kill** (*facet*) captivatingly or impressively dressed. — *v* **kill off** (*tr*) to destroy completely, or on a large scale. — **kill oneself** (*coll*) to be reduced to helpless laughter. [MidE *cullen* or *killen*]

killer whale *n* a fierce toothed whale of the dolphin family.

killing (*coll*) *n* an act of slaying. — *adj* **1** exhausting. **2** highly amusing. — *adv* **killingly**. — **make a killing** (*coll*) to make a large amount of money suddenly.

killjoy *n* someone who spoils others' pleasure.

kiln *n* an oven for baking pottery or bricks or for drying grain. [OE *cylen*, from Lat *culina*, kitchen]

kilo *n* **-os** a kilogram or kilometre.

kilo- *comb fm* one thousand. [Gr *chilioi*, thousand]

kilobyte *n* (*comput*) a unit of 1024 bytes.

kilocalorie *n* a unit of heat or energy equal to 1000 calories; same as **Calorie** or **large calorie**.

kilocycle *n* (*old*) a kilohertz.

kilogram or **kilogramme** *n* a unit of weight equal to 1000 grams (2·2 pounds).

kilohertz *n* **-hertz** a unit of frequency of sound and radio waves equal to 1000 cycles per second.

kilolitre *n* a unit of liquid measure equal to 1000 litres (220 gallons).

kilometre *n* a unit of distance equal to 1000 metres (0·62 miles).

kiloton or **kilotonne** *n* a unit of explosive force equal to that of 1000 tons of TNT.

kilowatt *n* a unit of electrical power equal to 1000 watts.

kilowatt hour *n* the unit by which electricity charges are made to the customer, equal to the energy consumed by a load of one kilowatt in one hour of use.

kilt *n* a pleated tartan knee-length skirt, traditionally worn by men as part of Scottish Highland dress. — *adj* **kilted**. [Related to Dan *kilte*, to tuck up]

kimono *n* **-os 1** a long loose wide-sleeved Japanese garment fastened by a sash at the waist. **2** a dressing-gown imitating this. [Jap, clothing]

kin *n* one's relations. — *adj* (**to**) related: *kin to the duke*. — **next of kin** a person's nearest relative. [OE *cynn*]

kinsfolk *n* one's relations.

kinship *n* family relationship.

kinsman or **kinswoman** *n* one's male or female relation.

-kin *sfx* indicating a diminutive: *catkin*; *lambkin*. [ODut]

kind[1] *n* **1** a group, class, sort or type. **2** nature, character or distinguishing quality: *differ in kind*. — **a kind of** something like a: *a kind of magazine*. — **in kind 1** (of payment) in goods instead of money. **2** (of repayment or retaliation) in the same form as the treatment received. — **kind of** (*coll*) somewhat; slightly: *kind of old-fashioned*. — **nothing of the kind** not at all; completely the reverse. — **of a kind 1** of the same sort: *three of a kind*. **2** (*derog*) of doubtful worth: *an explanation of a kind*. [OE *gecynd*, nature]

kind[2] *adj* **1** (**to**) friendly, helpful, well-meaning, generous, benevolent or considerate. **2** warm; cordial: *kind regards*. — *n* **kindness**. — **be so kind as to** or **be kind enough to** please. [OE *gecynde*, natural]

kind-hearted *adj* kind; generous; good-natured. — *adv* **kind-heartedly**. — *n* **kind-heartedness**.

kindly *adv* **1** in a kind manner. **2** please. — *adj* **-ier**, **-iest** kind, friendly, generous or good-natured. — *n* **kindliness**. — **look kindly on** to approve of. — **take kindly to** (usu. with a *negative*) to be willing to put up with. — **think kindly of** to have a good opinion of.

kindergarten *n* a school for young children, usu. ones aged between 4 and 6. [Ger, lit. 'children's garden']

kindle *v* (*tr* & *intr*) **1** to (cause to) start burning. **2** (of feelings) to stir or be stirred. [Related to Norse *kyndill*, torch]

kindling *n* dry wood, leaves, etc. for starting a fire.

kindred *n* **1** one's relations. **2** relationship by blood. — *adj* **1** related. **2** having qualities in common: *kindred arts*. [OE *cynred*]

kindred spirit *n* someone who shares one's tastes, opinions, etc.

kine *n* (*pl*; *old*) cattle. [OE *cyna*, of cows]

kinematics *n* (*sing*) the science of pure motion, without consideration of mass or force. — *adj* **kinematic**. [Gr *kinema*, movement]

kinetic *adj* of or relating to motion. — *adv* **kinetically**. [Gr *kinetikos*, from *kineein*, to move]

kinetic art or **sculpture** *n* art or sculpture of which movement (produced by air currents, electricity, etc.) is an essential feature.

kinetic energy *n* the energy that a body has in relation to its motion.

kinetics *n* (*sing*) the science of the relationship between moving objects and the forces acting on them.

king *n* **1** a male, esp. hereditary, ruler of a nation. **2** a ruler or chief. **3** a creature considered supreme in strength, fierceness, etc.: *the lion, king of beasts*. **4** a large, or the largest, variety of something: *king penguins*; *king prawns*. **5** a leading or dominant figure in some field, e.g. a wealthy manufacturer or dealer: *the diamond king*. **6** (*cards*) the court card bearing a picture of a king. **7** (*chess*) the most important piece, which must be protected from checkmate. **8** (*draughts*) a piece that, having crossed the board safely, has been crowned, and may move both forwards and backwards. — *n* **kingliness**. — *adj* **kingly**, **-ier**, **-iest**. — *n* **kingship**. — **live like a king** (*coll*) to live in great luxury. [OE *cyning*]

King Charles spaniel *n* a small black and tan spaniel, made popular by Charles II.

kingcup *n* the marsh marigold.

kingdom *n* **1** a region ruled by a king or queen. **2** any of the three divisions of the natural world: *the animal*, *vegetable* or *mineral kingdoms*. **3** the domain of, or area associated with, something: *the kingdom of the imagination*. — **to**, or **till**, **kingdom come** (*coll*) into, or until the coming of, the next world: *blow them all to kingdom come*; *wait till kingdom come* (i.e. for ever).

King James Version *n* same as **Authorised Version**.

kingmaker *n* someone who has influence over the choice of people for high office.

king of, or **at**, **arms** *n* the most senior rank in heraldry; the chief herald.

kingpin *n* **1** the most important person in an organisation, team, etc. **2** (*mech*) a bolt serving as a pivot.

King's Bench, **Counsel**, **English**, **evidence** see **queen**.

King's evil *n* (*old*) scrofula, i.e. tuberculosis of the neck glands, once believed curable by the touch of a monarch.

king-size or **-sized** *adj* of a large, or larger-than-standard, size.

kingfisher *n* a bird with brilliant blue and orange plumage that dives for fish. [Orig. *king's fisher*]

kink *n* **1** a bend or twist in a string, rope, wire, etc. **2** (*coll*) an oddness of personality; an eccentricity; a strange sexual preference. — *v* (*tr* & *intr*) to (cause to) develop a kink. [Dut]

kinky *adj* **-ier**, **-iest** (*coll*) intriguingly odd or eccentric, esp. in some sexual way. — *n* **kinkiness**.

kinsfolk, **kinship**, **kinsman**, **kinswoman**. See **kin**.

kiosk *n* **1** a booth or stall for the sale of sweets, newspapers, etc. **2** a public telephone box. [Fr *kiosque*, stand in a public park, from Turk *köşk*, villa]

kip (*slang*) *n* **1** sleep or a sleep. **2** somewhere to sleep; a bed. — *v* **-pp-** (*intr*) **1** to sleep. **2** (**down**) to go to bed; to doss down. [Orig. 'brothel']

kipper *n* **1** a herring split open, salted and smoked. **2** a male salmon in the spawning season. — *v* **-r-** (*tr*) to cure (herring) by salting and smoking. [OE *cypera*, spawning salmon]

Kirbigrip® *n* a hair-grip. [*Kirby*, manufacturer's name]

kirk *n* (*Scot*) **1** a church. **2** (*cap*; with **the**) the Church of Scotland. [Norse *kirkja*]

kirk session *n* the governing body of a Presbyterian congregation, consisting of the minister and elders.

kirsch *n* a clear liqueur distilled from black cherries. [Ger *Kirschwasser*, cherry water]

kismet *n* **1** fate. **2** one's destiny. [Turk *qismet*]

kiss *v* **1** (*tr*) to touch with the lips, as a greeting or sign of affection. **2** (*intr*) to kiss each other on the lips. **3** (*tr*) to express by kissing: *kissed them goodbye*. **4** (*tr*; *poetic*) to pass over with a gentle touch; to caress: *sun-kissed peaches*. — *n* **1** an act of kissing. **2** a gentle touch. — *adj* **kissable**. — **kiss hands** to kiss the sovereign's hands on acceptance of high office. [OE *cyssan*]

kiss curl *n* a flat curl pressed against the cheek or forehead.

kisser *n* **1** one who kisses. **2** (*slang*) the mouth or face.

kiss of death *n* (*coll*) something that brings failure or ruin on some enterprise; a fatal move.

kiss of life *n* **1** in first aid, a mouth-to-mouth method of restoring the breathing. **2** a means of restoring vitality or vigour.

kissogram or **kissagram** *n* **1** a greetings service by means of which one may employ someone to deliver a kiss to someone else on a special occasion. **2** the kiss or greeting thus delivered. **3** the person delivering it. [**kiss** + **telegram**]

kit[1] *n* **1** a set of instruments, equipment, etc. needed for a purpose, esp. if kept in a container. **2** a set of special clothing and personal equipment, e.g. for a soldier, footballer, etc. **3** a set of parts ready for assembling. — *v* ***-tt-*** (*tr*; **out**) to provide with the clothes and equipment necessary for a particular occupation, assignment, etc. [ODut *kitte*, tankard]

kitbag *n* a soldier's or sailor's bag, usu. cylinder-shaped, for holding kit.

kit[2] *n* a kitten. [Shortened form]

kitchen *n* a room where food is prepared and cooked. [OE *cycene*, from Lat *coquina*]

kitchenette *n* a small kitchen, or a section of a room serving as a kitchen.

kitchen garden *n* a garden, or a section of one, where vegetables are grown.

kite *n* **1** a long-tailed bird of prey of the hawk family. **2** a light frame covered in paper or some other light material, with a long holding string attached to it, for flying in the air for fun, etc. — **fly a kite** to spread a rumour or suggestion intended to provoke reaction and so test public opinion. — **high as a kite** (*coll*) in an elated state brought on by drugs or alcohol. [OE *cyta*]

kith *n* friends, as in **kith and kin**, friends and relations. [OE *cythth*, from *cunnan*, to know]

kitsch *n* sentimental or vulgar tastelessness in art, design, writing, film-making, etc. — *adj* **kitschy**, ***-ier***, ***iest***. [Ger]

kitten *n* **1** a young cat. **2** the young of any of several small furry mammals, e.g. the rabbit. — *adj* **kittenish**. — **have kittens** (*coll*) to get agitated.

kittiwake *n* a long-winged type of seagull. [Imit. of its cry]

kitty[1] *n* ***-ies*** **1** a fund contributed to jointly, for communal use by a group of people. **2** (*cards*) a pool of money used in certain games.

kitty[2] *n* ***-ies*** an affectionate name for a cat or kitten.

kiwi *n* **1** a flightless, tailless, long-beaked bird native to New Zealand. **2** (*coll*) a New Zealander. [Maori]

kiwi fruit *n* an oval fruit of Asia, with fuzzy brown skin and dark green juicy flesh.

kJ *abbrev* kilojoule.

kl *abbrev* kilolitre.

klaxon *n* a loud horn used as a warning signal on ambulances, fire engines, etc. [Orig. a tradename]

kleptomania *n* (*psychol*) an overwhelming impulse to steal, esp. things that one has no need or use for. — *n* & *adj* **kleptomaniac**. [Gr *kleptein*, to steal + **-mania**]

km *abbrev* kilometre.

kn *abbrev* (*naut*) knot.

knack *n* (**of**) **1** the ability to do something with easy dexterity. **2** a habit or tendency. [MidE, trick]

knacker *n* a buyer of worn-out old horses for slaughter. — *v* ***-r-*** (*tr*; *coll*) to exhaust.

knapsack *n* a hiker's or traveller's canvas bag for food, clothes, etc., carried on the back or over the shoulder. [OGer *knappen*, eat + *sack*, bag]

knapweed *n* a plant of the daisy family, with purple thistle-like flowers. [MidE *knopwed*]

knave *n* (*old*) **1** (*cards*) the jack. **2** a mischievous young man; a scoundrel. — *adj* **knavish**. — *adv* **knavishly**. [OE *cnafa*]

knavery *n* ***-ies*** mischief; trickery.

knead *v* (*tr*) **1** to work (dough) with one's fingers and knuckles. **2** to massage (flesh) with firm finger movements. [OE *cnedan*]

knee *n* **1** the middle joint of the leg; the corresponding joint in an animal. **2** the upper surface of a sitting person's thigh; the lap: *sat with the child on her knee*. **3** the part of a garment covering the knee. — *v* ***kneed*** (*tr*) to strike or nudge with the knee. — **at one's mother's knee** (of truths, lessons, etc; learnt) in one's extreme youth. — **bring someone to his** or **her knees** to defeat, prostrate or ruin someone utterly. — **go weak at the knees** (*coll*) to be overcome by emotion. — **on one's knees** **1** kneeling. **2** exhausted; prostrated. [OE *cneow*]

knee-breeches *n* (*pl*) knee-length breeches.

kneecap *n* a triangular plate of bone covering the front of the knee joint. — *v* ***-pp-*** (*tr*) to shoot or otherwise damage the kneecap(s) of as a form of revenge or unofficial punishment. — *n* **kneecapping**.

knee-deep *adj* & *adv* (coming) up to the knees.

knee-high *adj* tall enough to reach the knees: *knee-high grass.*

knee-jerk *n* an involuntary kick of the lower leg, a reflex response to a tap on the tendon below the knee. — *adj* (of a response or reaction) automatic; unthinking.

knee-length *adj* coming down, or up, as far as the knees.

knees-up *n* (*coll*) a party or dance.

kneel *v* ***knelt*** or ***kneeled*** (*intr*; **down**) to support one's weight on, or lower oneself on to, one's knees. [OE *cneowlian*]

kneeler *n* a cushion for kneeling on, esp. in church.

knell *n* **1** the tolling of a bell announcing a death or funeral. **2** something that signals the end of anything. — *v* (*tr*) to announce or summon (as if) by tolling. [OE *cnyll*]

knelt. See **kneel**.

knew. See **know**.

knickerbockers *n* (*pl*) baggy trousers tied just below the knee or at the ankle. [Diedrich *Knickerbocker*, the supposed author of Washington Irving's *History of New York*, 1809]

knickers *n* (*pl*) an undergarment for women and girls, covering the lower abdomen and buttocks, with separate legs or leg holes. [Short for **knickerbockers**]

knick-knack *n* a little trinket or ornament. [From **knack** with the old meaning 'toy']

knife *n* ***knives*** a cutting instrument or weapon, typically in the form of a blade fitted into a handle. — *v* (*tr*) to stab or kill with a knife. — **have one's knife into** (*coll*) to be constantly spiteful to. — **the knives are out** (*coll*) the argument has taken a savage turn. — **twist the knife (in the wound)** to deliberately increase someone's distress or embarrassment by constant reminders of the circumstances that caused it. — **under the knife** (*coll*) having a surgical operation. [OE *cnif*]

knife-edge *n* the cutting edge of a knife. — **on a knife-edge** in a state of agonising uncertainty.

knife pleat *n* a flat narrow pleat.

knight *n* **1** (*hist*) a man-at-arms of high social standing, usu. mounted, serving a feudal lord. **2** (*hist*) the armed champion of a lady, devoted to her service. **3** (the status or title of) a man who has been awarded the highest or second highest class of distinction in any of the four British orders of chivalry (= honours for service or merit awarded by the Queen or the Government). ◇ See also **dame**. **4** (*chess*) a piece shaped like a horse's head. — *v* (*tr*) to confer a knighthood on. [OE *cniht*, boy, servant, warrior]

knighthood *n* the rank of a knight, just below that of a baronet, conferring the title 'Sir'.

knightly *adj* ***-ier***, ***-iest*** relating to, or befitting, a knight.

knight errant *n* ***knights errant*** (*hist*) a knight travelling about in search of opportunities for daring and chivalrous deeds.

knit *v* ***-tt-***, ***knitted*** or (*old*) ***knit*** **1** (*tr* & *intr*) to produce a fabric composed of interlocking loops of yarn, using a pair of knitting-needles or a machine; to make (garments, etc.) by this means. **2** (*tr*) to make (a stitch) in plain knitting. **3** (*tr*) to unite: *a close-knit family*; *a loosely-knit alliance*. **4** (*tr* & *intr*) (of broken bones) to (cause to) grow together again. **5** (*tr*) to draw (one's brows) together in a frown. **6** (*tr*; *poetic*) to intertwine. — *n* **knitter**. [OE *cnyttan*, to tie]

knitting *n* knitted work or the art of producing it.

knitting-needle *n* an implement like a long stout pin, made of wood, plastic or metal.

knitwear *n* knitted garments.

knives. See **knife**.

knob *n* **1** a hard rounded projection. **2** a handle, esp. rounded, on a door or drawer. **3** a button on mechanical or electrical equipment, pressed or rotated to operate it. **4** a small roundish lump: *a knob of butter*. — *adj* **knobby**, ***-ier***, ***-iest***. [OGer *knobbe*, knot in wood]

knobbly *adj* ***-ier***, ***-iest*** covered with knobs. [**knob**]

knock *v* **1** (*intr*) to tap or rap with the knuckles or some object. **2** (*tr*; **down**, **over**, etc.) to strike and so push, esp. accidentally. **3** (*tr*) to put into a certain condition by hitting: *knocked him senseless*. **4** (*tr*) to make by striking. **5** (*tr* & *intr*; **against**, **on**, **into**, etc.) to strike, bump or bang against. **6** (*tr*; *coll*) to find fault with or criticise, esp. unfairly. **7** (*intr*) (of a faulty vehicle engine) to make a detonating noise. — *n* **1** an act of knocking. **2** a tap or rap. **3** (*coll*) a personal misfortune, blow, setback, calamity, etc. **4** a detonating sound made by a faulty engine. — *v* **knock about** or **around** (*coll*) **1** (*tr*) to treat roughly; to hit or batter. **2** (*intr* & *tr*) to wander about in (a place) in a casual, aimless way; to lie about unused; to be idle: *knocking about the streets*. **3** (*intr* with **with**; *coll*) to associate or go about with. — *v* **knock back** (*coll*; *tr*) **1** to eat or drink with rapidity and relish. **2** to cost (someone). **3** to surprise, dismay or disappoint. — *v* **knock down** (*tr*) **1** to strike (someone) to the ground. **2** to demolish (a building). **3** (*coll*; **to**) to sell (goods) at auction. **4** (*coll*) to reduce (a price). — **knocking on** (*coll*) nearly: *must be knocking on 60 by now*. — *v* **knock into** (*tr*; *coll*) to teach (something) forcefully to: *has had some sense knocked into him*. — *v* **knock off** (*coll*) **1** (*intr* & *tr*) to stop. **2** (*tr*) to produce at speed or in quick succession: *knocks off several books a year*. **3** (*tr*) to deduct: *knocked £15 off*. **4** (*tr*) to kill. **5** (*tr*) to steal. — *v* **knock on** (*tr*; *Rugby*) to commit the foul of pushing (the ball) forward with the hand (*n* **knock-on**). — **knock on the head** (*coll*) to put an end to. — *v* **knock out** (*tr*) **1** to hit unconscious, or (*boxing*) render incapable of rising in the required time. ◇ See also **knockout**. **2** to defeat in a knockout competition. **3** (*coll*) to cause to stop functioning. **4** (*coll*) to amaze; to impress hugely. — **knock sideways** (*coll*) to come as a severe shock to. — *v* **knock together** (*tr*; *coll*) to make hurriedly. — *v* **knock up** **1** (*tr*; *coll*) to make hurriedly. **2** (*tr*) to wake (someone) by knocking. **3** (*tr*; *coll*) to exhaust. **4** (*tr*; *NAm vulg slang*) to make pregnant. **5** (*intr*; *tennis*) to exchange practice shots with one's opponent before a match. [OE *cnucian*]

knockabout *adj* (of comedy, etc.) boisterous; slapstick.

knockdown *adj* (*coll*) **1** low; cheap: *knockdown prices*. **2** (of furniture) able to be taken to pieces easily. **3** (of an argument) overwhelmingly strong.

knocker *n* **1** (also **doorknocker**) a heavy piece of metal, usu. of a decorative shape, fixed to a door by a hinge and used for knocking. **2** (in *pl*; *vulg slang*) a woman's breasts.

knock knees *adj* a condition of the legs in which the knees are close together but the feet splayed out. — *adj* **knock-kneed**.

knock-on effect *n* a secondary or indirect effect of some action, etc.

knockout *n* **1** (*coll*) someone or something stunning. **2** a competition in which the defeated competitors are dropped after each round. **3** (esp. *boxing*) the act of knocking out.

knoll *n* a small round hill. [OE *cnoll*]

knot *n* **1** a join or tie in string, etc. made by looping the ends around each other and pulling tight. **2** a bond or uniting link. **3** a coil or bun in the hair. **4** a decoratively tied ribbon, etc. **5** a tangle in hair, string, etc. **6** a difficulty or complexity. **7** a hard mass in a tree trunk where a branch has grown out from it; the resultant crossgrained patch in timber. **8** a small gathering or cluster of people, etc. **9** a unit of speed at sea, a nautical mile (1·85 km) an hour. **10** a tight feeling, e.g. in the belly, caused by nervousness. — *v* **-tt-** **1** (*tr*) to tie in a knot. **2** (*tr* & *intr*) to tangle. **3** (*intr*) to become tight with nervousness, etc. — **at a rate of knots** (*coll*) fast. — **get knotted** (*slang offensive*) an expression of angry disagreement, refusal or dismissiveness. — **tie in knots** to confuse or perplex. — **tie the knot** (*coll*) to get married. [OE *cnotta*]

knothole *n* a hole left in a piece of wood where a knot has fallen out.

knotty *adj* **-ier**, **-iest** **1** full of knots. **2** (of a problem, etc.) difficult, complex or intricate.

know *v* ***knew***, ***known*** **1** (*tr* & *intr*; **of**, **about**) to be aware of; to be certain. **2** (*tr*) to have learnt and remember. **3** (*tr*) to have an understanding or grasp of. **4** (*tr*) to be familiar with: *know her well*. **5** (*tr*) to (be able to) recognise or identify. **6** (*tr* with **from**, **apart**) to be able to distinguish or tell apart: *wouldn't know him from Adam*. **7** (*intr*) to have (enough) experience or training: *knew not to question him further*. **8** (*tr*; **as**, **for**) to think of as: *knew him as* or *for a kindly man*. **9** (*tr*) to experience or be subject to: *know poverty*; *happiness knew no bounds*. **10** (*tr*; *old*, e.g. *Bible*) to have sexual intercourse with. — *adj* **knowable**. — **Heaven** or **God knows** (*coll*) I've no idea. — **in the know** (*coll*) having information not known to most. — **know a thing or two** (*coll*) to be pretty shrewd. — *v* **know backwards** (*tr*; *coll*) to know thoroughly. — **known as** called. — **know what's what** to be shrewd, wise, or hard to deceive. — **let it be known** to reveal, esp. indirectly. — **make oneself known** to introduce oneself. — **there's no knowing** it's impossible to predict. — **what do you know?** (*coll*) an expression of surprise. — **you never know** it's not impossible. [OE *cnawan*]

knowing *adj* **1** shrewd; canny; clever. **2** (of a glance, etc.) signifying secret awareness. — *n* **knowingness**.

knowingly *adv* **1** in a knowing manner. **2** on purpose; deliberately.

know-all *n* (*derog*) a person who seems, or claims, to know more than others.

know-how *n* (*coll*) skill; ability; adroitness.

knowledge *n* **1** the fact of knowing; awareness; understanding. **2** what one knows; the information one has acquired through learning or experience. **3** learning; the sciences: *a branch of knowledge*. — **to (the best of) my**, etc. **knowledge** as far as I, etc. know. [MidE *knouleche*]

knowledgeable *adj* well-informed. — *adv* **knowledgeably**.

known. See **know**.

knuckle *n* **1** a joint of a finger, esp. the one at its base. **2** the knee or ankle joint of an animal, esp. with the surrounding flesh, as food. — *v* **knuckle down** (*intr*; **to**) to (begin to) work hard at. — *v* **knuckle under** (*coll*) to submit, yield or give way. — **near the knuckle** (*coll*) bordering on the indecent or obscene. [MidE *knokel*]

knuckle-duster *n* a set of metal links or other metal device worn over the knuckles as a weapon.

KO (*coll*) *abbrev* & *n* a knockout. — *v* ***KO's***, ***KO'ing***, ***KO'd*** (*tr*) to knock out.

koala *n* (also **koala bear**) an Australian tree-climbing marsupial animal with thick grey fur and large ears, that feeds on eucalyptus leaves. [Aboriginal *koolah*]

kohl *n* an oriental cosmetic in the form of a powder, used to darken the eyelids. [Arabic]

kohlrabi *n* a kind of cabbage whose thick turnip-like stem is eaten as a vegetable. [Ital *cavolrape*, cabbage turnip]

kola. See **cola**.

kolkhoz *n* a collective farm in the former Soviet Union. [Russ]

kook *n (NAm coll)* a crazy or eccentric person. — *adj* **kooky** or **kookie**, *-ier*, *-iest*. [Perhaps from **cuckoo**]

kookaburra *n* (also **laughing jackass**) a large Australian bird of the kingfisher family, with a cry like cackling laughter. [Wiradhuri (Australian Aboriginal language) *gugubarra*]

kopeck or **kopek** *n* a coin or unit of currency of the former Soviet Union worth a hundredth of a rouble. [Russ *kopeika*]

Koran *n* the holy book of Islam, believed by Muslims to be composed of the revelations of Allah to Mohammed. — *adj* **Koranic**. [Arabic *qur'an*, book]

kosher *adj* **1** in accordance with Jewish law. **2** (of food) prepared as prescribed by Jewish dietary laws. **3** (*coll*) genuine; legitimate. — *n* kosher food, or a shop selling it. [Yiddish, from Hebr *kasher*, right, fit]

kowtow *v* **1** (*intr* with **to**; *coll*) to defer to, esp. in an over-submissive or obsequious way. **2** to touch the forehead to the ground in a gesture of submission. — *n* an act of kowtowing. [Chin *k'o t'ou*, strike the head]

kph *abbrev* kilometres per hour.

Kr *symbol* (*chem*) krypton.

kraal *n* **1** in S Africa, a village of huts surrounded by a fence. **2** (*SAfr*) an enclosure for cattle, sheep, etc. [Afrikaans, from Port *curral*, pen]

kremlin 1 *n* the citadel of a Russian town, esp. (*cap*) that of Moscow. **2** (*cap*) the government of the former Soviet Union. [Russ *kreml*]

krill *n* a tiny shrimp-like shellfish, eaten by whales, etc. [Norw *kril*, fry, i.e. young fish]

kris *n* a Malay or Indonesian dagger with a wavy blade. [Malay]

krona *n* **1** ***kronor*** the standard unit of Swedish currency. **2** (**króna**) ***krónur*** the standard unit of Icelandic currency. [Swed & Icelandic, crown]

krone *n* ***kroner*** the standard unit of Danish and Norwegian currency. [Dan & Norw, crown]

krugerrand *n* a S African one-ounce (or 28-gram) gold coin bearing a portrait of Paul *Kruger*, Boer statesman. [**rand**]

krypton *n* an element (symbol **Kr**), an inert, colourless gas, used in fluorescent lighting and lasers. [Gr *kryptos*, hidden, secret]

KS or **Ks.** *abbrev* Kansas, US state.

KT *abbrev* Knight of the Thistle.

Kt *abbrev* Knight.

kudos *n* (*coll*) credit, honour or prestige. [Gr, glory]

Ku-Klux-Klan *n* a secret society of White Protestants of the southern US, formed after the civil war of 1861–65, using violence against Blacks, Jews and Catholics. [Prob. Gr *kyklos*, circle + *klan* as variant of **clan**]

kukri *n* a heavy curved knife or short sword used by Gurkhas. [Hindi]

kulak *n* (*hist*) a wealthy, property-owning Russian peasant. [Russ, lit. 'fist']

kümmel *n* a German liqueur flavoured with cumin and caraway seeds. [Ger, from *kumin*, cumin]

kumquat *n* a citrus fruit resembling a miniature orange. [Chin dialect *gamgwat*, golden citrus fruit]

kung fu *n* a Chinese martial art with similarities to karate and judo. [Chin]

kW *abbrev* kilowatt.

kwashiorkor *n* a disease of children caused by lack of protein in the diet. [Ghanaian name]

kWh *abbrev* kilowatt hour.

KWIC *abbrev* keyword in context.

KWOC *abbrev* keyword out of context.

KY or **Ky** *abbrev* Kentucky.

kyle *n* (*Scot*) a channel, strait or sound. [Gaelic *caol*, narrow]

L

L[1] or **l** *n* ***Ls*** or ***L's, l's*** the twelfth letter of the English alphabet.

L[2] *abbrev* **1** lake. **2** Liberal. **3** learner driver. **4** licentiate. **5** lira or lire.

L-plate *n* a small, square, white sign with a red letter *L* on it, displayed on cars being driven by learners.

L[3] *symbol* the Roman numeral for 50.

l *abbrev* **1** (*pl* ***ll***) line. **2** litre. **3** left. **4** length. **5** lira or lire.

LA *abbrev* **1** Los Angeles. **2** Louisiana.

La *symbol* (*chem*) lanthanum.

La. *abbrev* Louisiana.

la or **lah** *n* (*mus*) in tonic sol-fa, the sixth note of the major scale. [From the first syllable of the word *labii* in a mediaeval Latin hymn, certain syllables of which were used in naming the notes of the scale]

Lab *abbrev* Labour.

lab *n* (*coll*) a laboratory.

label *n* **1** a small written note attached to a parcel, object, etc. giving details of its contents, owner, destination, etc. **2** a word or short phrase which describes only part of a person's or thing's character but which comes to be used as a general description. **3** a small strip of material inside a garment, giving the maker's or designer's name. **4** a record company's trademark. — *v* ***-ll-*** (*tr*) **1** to attach a label to. **2** (**as**) to call by a certain name or describe in a certain way. [OFr, ribbon]

labial *adj* **1** of, or relating to, the lips. **2** (of a sound) made with the lips almost or completely closed. — *n* a sound made with the lips almost or completely closed, e.g. *b* and *m*. [Lat *labium*, lip]

labiate (*bot*) *n* any of various plants with petals in a form suggesting lips, e.g. rosemary and thyme. — *adj* **1** of this family of plants. **2** like a lip. [Lat *labium*, lip]

labium *n* ***-ia*** a lip or lip-like structure, esp. one of the folds of the vulva. [Lat, lip]

laboratory *n* ***-ies*** a room or building specially equipped for scientific experiments, research, the preparation of drugs, etc. [Lat *laborare*, to work]

laborious *adj* **1** requiring hard work or a lot of effort. **2** not looking or sounding natural; not fluent. — *adv* **laboriously**. — *n* **laboriousness**. [Lat *laboriosus*]

labour *n* **1** physical or mental work, esp. when hard. **2** workers as a group or class. **3** a difficult task or job. **4** the process of giving birth to a baby. **5** (*cap*) in the UK, the Labour Party. — *v* **1** (*intr*) to work hard or with difficulty. **2** (*intr*) to progress or move slowly and with difficulty. **3** (*intr* with **under**) to have (a wrong impression). **4** (*tr*) to deal with (a subject, etc.) at too much length, with too many details, or with too much repetition: *labour the point*. [Lat]

labour camp *n* a prison camp where prisoners are made to work hard.

Labour Day *n* a public holiday in honour of workers, often celebrated with marches, held on 1 May in many countries and on the first Monday in September in the US and Canada.

laboured *adj* **1** showing signs of effort or difficulty. **2** not natural or spontaneous.

labourer *n* a worker employed to do heavy physical work such as digging.

labour exchange *n* (*Br old*) a job centre.

labour force *n* **1** all the people in a country who are able to work. **2** all the people who work for a particular company.

labour-intensive *adj* (of an industry, etc.) requiring a lot of people as opposed to machinery, etc. ◇ See also **capital-intensive**.

labour of love *n* a job, etc. which one does for personal satisfaction or pleasure and not for money or profit.

Labour Party *n* **1** in the UK, the major left-wing political party which believes in an economy controlled by the state rather than by private individuals, and which represents the interests of the workers. **2** a similar political party in any other country.

labour-saving *adj* serving to reduce the amount of work or effort needed.

Labrador *n* a breed of large dog with a short black or golden coat. [*Labrador*, a region in Canada]

laburnum *n* a small garden tree of the pea family, with hanging yellow flowers and poisonous seeds. [Lat]

labyrinth *n* **1** a complicated network of passages which it is very difficult to find one's way through. **2** a complicated arrangement. **3** the complicated arrangement of bones and membranes which forms the inner ear. — *adj* **labyrinthine**. [Gr *labyrinthos*]

lac *n* a resinous substance produced by certain Asian insects, used in varnish. [Hindi *lakh*]

lace *n* **1** a delicate material made from fine thread woven into net-like patterns. **2** a string or cord drawn through holes, used for fastening shoes, etc. — *v* **1** (*tr & intr*; **up**) to fasten or be fastened with a lace or laces. **2** (*tr*; **with**) to flavour or strengthen with alcohol. **3** (*tr*) to trim with lace. **4** (*tr*) to weave in and out of; to intertwine. — *v* **lace into** (*intr*; *coll*) to attack someone physically or with words. [Lat *laqueus*, noose]

lace-up *n* a shoe fastened with a lace. — *adj* (of shoes) fastened with a lace or laces.

lacy *adj* **-ier**, **-iest** of or like lace, esp. in being fine and delicate.

lacerate *v* (*tr*) **1** to tear or cut (flesh) roughly. **2** to wound or hurt (the feelings). — *n* **laceration**. [Lat *lacerare*, to tear]

lachrymal *adj* of, relating to, or producing tears. [Lat *lacrima*, tear]

lachrymal gland *n* the tear-producing gland at the outer edge of the eye.

lachrymose *adj* **1** crying very easily and very often. **2** very sad; likely to make a person cry. [Lat *lacrima*, tear]

lack *n* something missing or in short supply; a deficiency or want. — *v* **1** (*tr*) to be completely without or to have too little of. **2** (*intr*; **for**) to be in need of: *not lack for money*. — *adj* **lacking**. — **no lack of** a lot of. [MidE *lak*]

lackadaisical *adj* **1** without energy, interest or enthusiasm. **2** sentimental in a weak, dreamy way. — *adv* **lackadaisically**. [From archaic *alack the day*, alas the day]

lackey *n* **-eys 1** (*derog*) a grovelling or servile follower. **2** (*old*) a male servant. [OFr *laquais*]

lacklustre *adj* lacking in energy or brightness; dull. [**lack** + **lustre**]

laconic *adj* using few words to express a meaning. — *adv* **laconically**. [Gr *lakonikos*, of Laconia or Sparta, from the Spartans' terse style of speech]

lacquer *n* **1** a usu. clear substance made by dissolving natural or man-made resins in alcohol, used to form a hard, shiny covering on wood and metal. **2** the sap from some trees, used as a varnish for wood. **3** a clear, sticky substance used to keep hair tidy and in place. — *v* **-r-** (*tr*) to cover with lacquer. [Port *laca*, lac]

lacrimal. Same as **lachrymal**.

lacrosse *n* a game in which two teams use long sticks with rigid triangular nets at one end (**lacrosse sticks**) to throw a small ball into their opponent's goal-net. [Fr *la*, the + *crosse*, hooked stick]

lactate *v* (*intr*) (of mammals) to produce milk to feed a baby or young. — *n* a salt or ester of lactic acid. [Lat *lac*, milk]

lactation *n* **1** the production of milk by the mammary glands. **2** the period of time that this lasts.

lactic *adj* of or derived from milk. [Lat *lac*, milk]

lactic acid *n* an acid which forms in sour milk, used as a preservative in food.

lactose *n* a sugar found in milk and used as a food for babies and sick people. [Lat *lac*, milk]

lacuna *n* **-nae** or **-nas** a gap or a space where something is missing, esp. in a book. [Lat, pool]

lacy. See **lace**.

lad *n* **1** a boy or a youth. **2** (esp. in *pl* with **the**; *coll*) any man, esp. a man's male friend. **3** a person working in stables, regardless of age or sex. [MidE *ladde*]

laddie *n* (*dialect*) a young boy or lad.

ladder *n* **1** a piece of equipment consisting of a set of horizontal rungs or steps between two long vertical supports, used for climbing up or down. **2** a long, narrow flaw, esp. in a stocking, where a row of stitches have broken. **3** a means or route of progress or advancement: *the social ladder*. **4** anything like a ladder in arrangement, e.g. a list of names of players in a competition on which names are moved up or down depending on whether the players win or lose. — *v* **-r- 1** (*intr*) (of stockings, etc.) to develop a ladder. **2** (*tr*) to cause a ladder in (stockings, etc.). [OE *hlæder*]

laden *adj* **1** (of a ship) loaded with cargo. **2** (**with**) (of a person, animal or vehicle) heavily loaded. **3** (**with**) (of one's conscience, etc.) oppressed (with guilt, worry, etc.). [OE *hladan*, to load]

la-di-da or **lah-di-dah** *adj* (*coll*) behaving or speaking in a way one thinks is superior and elegant but is in fact affected and snobbish. [Imit. of upper-class speech]

lading *n* **1** a cargo or load carried. **2** the act of loading cargo or goods. ◇ See also **bill of lading**. [OE *hladan*, to load]

ladle *n* a large spoon with a long handle and deep bowl, for serving or transferring liquid. — *v* (*tr*) to serve or transfer with a ladle. — *v* **ladle out** (*tr*) to serve or distribute (praise, blame, etc.) generously, sometimes too generously. [OE *hlædel*]

ladleful *n* **-fuls** the amount held in a ladle.

lady *n* **-ies 1** any woman with good manners and elegant or refined behaviour. **2** a polite word for a woman. **3** (esp. *hist*) a woman belonging to the upper classes by birth. **4** (*cap*) in the UK, a title of honour used for peeresses (but not duchesses), the wives and daughters of peers and knights, and for some women of importance, e.g. mayoresses. **5** a woman in a position of authority or control: *lady of the house*. — *adj* female: *a lady doctor*. — **Our Lady** the Virgin Mary. [OE *hlæfdige*, kneader of bread]

ladies *n* (*sing*) a women's public toilet.

ladybird *n* a small red beetle with black spots.

Lady Chapel *n* a chapel dedicated to the Virgin Mary.

Lady Day *n* 25 March, the feast of the Annunciation.

lady-in-waiting *n* **ladies-** a woman attending a queen or princess.

lady-killer *n* (*coll*) a man who is, or thinks he is, irresistible to women.

ladylike *adj* like a lady in manners, appearance or behaviour, esp. in being polite and elegant.

Ladyship *n* (*cap*; with **Your** or **Her**) a title used to address peeresses (but not duchesses) and the wives and daughters of peers and knights.

lady's-slipper *n* an orchid with a large, yellow, slipper-like lip.

lag[1] *v* **-gg-** (*intr*; **behind**) to move or progress too slowly and become left behind. —

n **1** a lagging behind or delay. **2** the amount by which one thing is delayed behind another.

laggard *n* a person or thing that lags behind.

lag[2] *v* **-gg-** (*tr*) to cover (a boiler, water pipes, etc.) with a thick covering to keep the heat in. — *n* (also **lagging**) an insulating cover for pipes, boilers, etc.

lag[3] *n* (*slang*) a convict or former convict.

lager *n* a light beer. [Ger *Lagerbier*, beer for storing]

laggard. See **lag**[1].

lagging. See **lag**[2].

lagoon *n* a shallow stretch of water separated from the sea by sandbanks, rocks, etc. [Ital *laguna*]

lah. See **la**.

laid *past participle* of **lay**[1]. — **laid back** (*coll*) relaxed. — **laid up 1** (*coll*) confined to bed because of illness. **2** (of a boat) in dock or on shore.

laid paper *n* paper with fine lines running across the surface.

lain. See **lie**[2].

lair *n* **1** a wild animal's den. **2** (*coll*) a place of refuge or hiding. [OE *leger*]

laird *n* (*Scot*) a landowner, esp. of a large estate.

laissez-faire or **laisser-faire** *n* a policy of not interfering in what others are doing. [Fr, let do]

laity *n* ordinary people who are not members of a particular profession, esp. people who are not members of the clergy. ◇ See also **lay**[3]. [**lay**[3]]

lake[1] *n* a large area of water surrounded by land. [MidE *lac*]

the Lake District *n* (also **the Lakes**) an area in Cumbria where there are many lakes and mountains.

lake[2] *n* **1** a reddish dye, orig. obtained from lac. **2** a substance made from dye and a mordant, used in dying fabrics to make the dye insoluble. [**lac**]

lam *v* **-mm-** (*tr*; *slang*) to beat or thrash. [Norse *lemja*, to beat until lame]

lama *n* a Buddhist priest or monk in Tibet or Mongolia. [Tibetan *blama*]

lamb *n* **1** a young sheep. **2** its flesh, or that of an older sheep, eaten as food. **3** a person who is kind, gentle and good. — *v* (*intr*) **1** (of a ewe) to give birth to a lamb or lambs. **2** (of a shepherd) to tend lambing ewes. — *n* **lambing**. [OE]

the Lamb (or **Lamb of God**) *n* a title used for Christ.

lambskin *n* the skin of a lamb, usu. with the wool left on it, used to make slippers, coats, etc.

lambswool *n* the fine wool obtained from a lamb.

lambaste or **lambast** *v* (*tr*) **1** to thrash or beat severely. **2** to scold severely. [**lam** + *baste*, to thrash]

lambent *adj* **1** (of a flame or light) flickering over a surface. **2** (of eyes, etc.) gently sparkling. **3** (of wit) light and brilliant. — *n* **lambency**. — *adv* **lambently**. [Lat *lambere*, to lick]

lame *adj* **1** not able to walk properly, esp. because of an injury or defect. **2** (of an excuse, etc.) not convincing; weak. — *v* (*tr*) to make lame. — *adv* **lamely**. — *n* **lameness**. [OE *lama*]

lame duck *n* **1** a person who can do nothing without the help of others. **2** a company with financial problems.

lamé *n* a fabric which has gold and silver threads woven into it. [Fr]

lament *v* (*tr* & *intr*) to feel or express regret or sadness. — *n* **1** an expression of sadness, grief, regret, etc. **2** a poem, song, etc. which expresses great grief, esp. for someone's death. [Lat *lamentum*]

lamentable *adj* very disappointing, bad or regrettable. — *adv* **lamentably**.

lamentation *n* an act of lamenting; a lament.

Lamentations *n* (*pl*) an Old Testament book, traditionally believed to have been written by Jeremiah, which laments the destruction of Jerusalem in the 6th century BC.

lamented *adj* (of a dead person) mourned for.

lamina *n* **-ae** a thin plate or layer, esp. of metal or bone. [Lat]

laminate *v* **1** (*tr*) to beat (metal) into thin plate. **2** (*tr*) to make by bonding thin sheets of material on top of each other. **3** (*tr*) to cover with a thin sheet of plastic or other material. **4** (*tr* & *intr*) to split or be split into layers. — *n* material or a structure made by bonding thin layers of material together. — *adj* in thin plates or layers. — *adj* **laminated**. — *n* **lamination**. [Lat *lamina*, thin plate]

Lammas *n* 1 August, an old feast celebrating the first crops from the harvest. [OE *hlafmæsse*, from *hlaf*, loaf + *mæsse*, mass]

lamp *n* **1** an appliance for producing a steady light, esp. in the form of bulb-holder and shade. **2** an appliance with a glass case covering a flame produced by burning oil, etc., as a source of light. **3** an appliance producing radiation for treating certain medical complaints. [Gr *lampe*, torch]

lampblack *n* soot obtained from burning carbon, used as a pigment.

lamppost *n* the post supporting a street-lamp.

lampshade *n* a shade placed over a lamp or light bulb to soften or direct the light coming from it.

lampoon *n* a cruel, personal satire. — *v* (*tr*) to attack or laugh at in lampoons. — *n* **lampooner** or **lampoonist**. [Fr *lampon*, thought to be from *lampons*, let us drink, the refrain of a drinking-song]

Lancastrian *n* **1** a person from Lancaster or Lancashire. **2** (*hist*) a supporter of the House of Lancaster in the Wars of the Roses. — *adj* of or relating to Lancaster,

Lancashire, or (*hist*) the House of Lancaster. ◇ See also **Yorkist**.

lance *n* a long spear with a hard, pointed head at one end, and sometimes with a small flag at the other, used by horsemen. — *v* (*tr*) **1** to cut open (a boil, etc.) with a lancet. **2** to pierce with, or as if with, a lance. [Lat *lancea*]

lance corporal *n* in the British army, a soldier holding the lowest rank of non-commissioned officer, between private and corporal.

lancer *n* (*hist*) a cavalry soldier belonging to a regiment armed with lances.

lancers *n* (*sing*) a set of quadrilles, or the music for it.

lanceolate *adj* shaped like a spearhead, being much longer than it is wide, and tapering to a point at each end. [Lat *lanceola*, small lance]

lancet *n* a small surgical knife with a point and both edges sharpened. [OFr *lancette*, a small lance]

Lancs. *abbrev* Lancashire.

land *n* **1** the part of the earth's surface not covered by water. **2** the ground or soil, esp. in terms of its use or quality: *building land*; *farmland*. **3** farmland: *work on the land*. **4** a country, state or region: *one's native land*. **5** (in *pl*) estates. — *v* **1** (*intr* & *tr*) to (cause to) come to rest on the ground or water, or in a particular place, after flight through the air. **2** (*tr*) to bring on to land from a ship. **3** (*tr*; *coll*) to put (someone) or find (oneself) in a given position or situation: *land oneself in trouble*. **4** (*tr*) to bring (a fish caught on a line) to land. **5** (*tr*; *coll*) to succeed in getting (a job, prize, etc.). **6** (*tr*; *coll*) to give (a blow) to (someone). — *v* **land up** (*intr*; *coll*) to come to be in a given position or situation. — *v* **land with** (*tr*; *coll*) to give or pass something unpleasant or unwanted to (someone): *land him with all the bills to pay*. — **see how the land lies** to find out exactly what the situation is, esp. before making a decision. [OE]

land agent *n* a person who manages a large estate for the owner.

landed *adj* **1** owning land or estates: *landed gentry*. **2** consisting of or derived from land: *landed estates*.

landfall *n* an approach to land, or the land approached, after a journey by sea or air.

land-girl *n* a woman who works on a farm, esp. during a war.

landing *n* **1** the process of coming to shore or to ground. **2** a place for disembarking, esp. from a ship. **3** the level part of a staircase between flights of steps, or at the very top.

landing-craft *n* **-craft** (*mil*) a small, low, open vessel for landing troops and equipment on beaches.

landing-gear *n* the wheels and supporting structure which allow an aircraft to land and take off.

landing-stage *n* a platform, either fixed or floating, for disembarking passengers and goods from a ship.

landlady or **landlord** *n* **1** a woman or man who owns property which she or he rents out as accommodation to others. **2** a woman or man who keeps a public house or hotel.

landlocked *adj* (of a country) almost or completely enclosed by land.

landlord see **landlady**.

landlubber *n* (*naut*; *derog*) a person who lives and works on the land and has no experience of the sea.

landmark *n* **1** a conspicuous or well-known object on land, esp. one that serves as a guide (e.g. to sailors). **2** an event of great importance: *a landmark in the history of computing*.

landmass *n* a large area of land unbroken by seas.

land mine *n* a mine laid on or near the surface of the ground, detonated when something passes over it.

landowner *n* a person who owns land, esp. a lot of land.

Landrover® *n* a strong motor vehicle used for driving over rough ground.

landscape *n* **1** the area and features of land that can be seen from a single point. **2** a picture showing a view of the countryside. **3** the art of painting such pictures.

landscape gardening *n* the art of planning and laying out gardens, parks, etc., esp. to resemble natural scenery. — *n* **landscape gardener**.

landslide *n* **1** (also **landslip**) a fall of land or rock down the side of a hill or cliff. **2** a victory in an election by a massive majority.

landward *adj* lying or facing toward the land. — *adv* (also **landwards**) towards land.

landau *n* a four-wheeled, horse-drawn carriage with a removable front cover and a back cover which folds down. [*Landau* in Germany, where such carriages were first made]

lane *n* **1** a narrow road or street. **2** a division of a road for a single line of traffic. **3** a regular course across the sea taken by ships, or through the air by aircraft. **4** a division of a track for a runner, or swimming pool for a swimmer, in races and competitions. **5** a passage through a crowd. [OE *lanu*]

language *n* **1** human speech. **2** the speech of a particular nation or group of people. **3** the ability to speak. **4** a style of speech or expression with words: *elegant language*. **5** any other way of communicating or expressing what one means: *sign language*. **6** professional or specialised vocabulary: *legal language*. **7** (also **bad language**) (use of) rude and offensive words: *mind one's language*. **8** a system of signs and symbols, with strict rules as to how they may be put together, used to write computer programs. — **speak the same language** to have the same way of thinking or similar tastes. [OFr *langage*]

language laboratory *n* a room in a school, etc. with separate cubicles equipped with tape recorders and pre-recorded tapes, in which students are taught languages.

languid *adj* **1** lacking in energy or vitality; listless. **2** slow-moving; sluggish. — *adv* **languidly**. [Lat *languere*, to languish]

languish *v* (*intr*) **1** to grow weak; to lose energy or vitality. **2** to look sad, sorrowful and sentimental. **3** (**for**) to pine. — *adj* **languishing**. [Lat *languere*, to be faint]

languor *n* **1** a feeling of dullness, weakness or tiredness. **2** tender softness or sentiment. **3** a stuffy, suffocating atmosphere or stillness. — *adj* **languorous**. [Lat]

lank *adj* **1** long and thin. **2** (of hair) long, straight and lifeless. — *n* **lankness**. [OE *hlanc*]

lanky *adj* **-ier**, **-iest** thin, tall, awkward and ungainly. — *n* **lankiness**.

lanolin *n* fat obtained from sheep's wool, used in ointments and cosmetics. [Lat *lana*, wool + *oleum*, oil]

lantern *n* **1** a clear case for holding or carrying a light, and shielding the flame from the wind. **2** the top part of a lighthouse, where the light is kept. **3** a structure with windows or open sides, built over an opening in the top of a roof or dome, for letting in light or air. [OFr *lanterne*]

lantern jaws *n* (*pl*) long, thin jaws giving the face a hollow, drawn appearance. — *adj* **lantern-jawed**.

lanthanide series *n* the 15 rare earth elements from lanthanum to lutetium, all of which have similar properties. [**lanthanum**]

lanthanum *n* a silver-white metallic element (symbol **La**), used for making alloys and glass. [Gr *lanthanein*, to escape notice, because it was hidden in rare minerals until 1839]

lanyard *n* **1** a cord for hanging a knife, whistle, etc. round the neck, worn esp. by sailors. **2** (*naut*) a short rope for fastening rigging, etc. [OFr *laniere*]

lap[1] *v* **-pp- 1** (*tr*) to drink (liquid) by scooping it up with the tongue. **2** (*tr*) (of water) to wash or flow against (e.g. a shore) with a light splashing sound. **3** (*intr*) (of water) to move with a light splashing sound. — *n* **1** the sound of waves gently splashing or lapping. **2** the act of lapping or the amount lapped up. — *v* **lap up** (*tr*) **1** to drink by lapping, esp. eagerly or greedily. **2** to listen eagerly to (praise, gossip, information, etc.). [OE *lapian*]

lap[2] *n* **1** the front part of the body, from waist to knees, when a person is sitting. **2** the part of clothing, esp. of a skirt or dress, which covers this part of the body. — **drop** or **land in someone's lap** to become, or cause to become, someone's responsibility. — **in the lap of the gods** (of a situation) out of human control. — **in the lap of luxury** in very luxurious conditions. [OE *læppa*]

lapdog *n* a small pet dog.

laptop *adj* (of a computer) small enough to be carried in a briefcase and used on a person's lap.

lap[3] *n* **1** one circuit of a racecourse or other track. **2** one section of a journey. **3** a part which overlaps or the amount it overlaps by. **4** the amount of thread, material, etc. wound once round a reel, etc. — *v* **-pp- 1** (*tr*) to get ahead of (a competitor) in a race by one or more laps. **2** (*tr*; **round**) to fold (a garment) round. **3** (*tr*; **in**) to wrap (a person, etc.) up in, esp. protectively. **4** (*tr*) to cause to overlap. **5** (*intr*) to lie with an overlap. [MidE *lappen*]

lap of honour *n* a circuit of a racecourse by the winner to acknowledge the applause of the audience.

lap joint *n* a joint formed by overlapping edges.

lapel *n* the part of a coat joined to the collar and folded back a little across the chest. [Dimin. of **lap**[2]]

lapidary *n* **-ies** a person who cuts and polishes gem-stones. — *adj* **1** of or relating to stones. **2** engraved on stone. **3** (of writing) concise and to the point. [Lat *lapis*, stone]

lapis lazuli *n* **1** a bright blue mineral used as a gem-stone. **2** its bright blue colour. [Lat *lapis*, stone + *lazuli*, azure]

Lapp *n* **1** (also **Lapplander**) a member of a nomadic people living in N Scandinavia. **2** (also **Lappish**) the language spoken by this people. — *adj* (also **Lappish**) of this people, their language or culture.

lappet *n* **1** a small flap or fold in material, a garment, etc. **2** a piece of loose, hanging flesh. [Dimin. of **lap**[2]]

lapse *n* **1** a slight mistake or failure in virtue, attention or memory. **2** a decline in standards of behaviour. **3** a passing away of time: *a lapse of two years*. **4** (*law*) the loss of a right or privilege by failing or forgetting to renew one's claim to it. — *v* (*intr*) **1** to fail to behave properly or with virtue. **2** (**into**) to pass, esp. gradually, into a different, usu. bad, worse or earlier, state. **3** (**from**) to turn away from a faith or belief. **4** (*law*) (of a right or privilege) to be no longer valid because the claim to it has not been renewed. [Lat *lapsus*, slip]

lapsed *adj* **1** having fallen into evil, error, or former bad ways. **2** no longer used or valid.

lapwing *n* a plover with greenish-black and white feathers and a crest. [OE *hleapewince*]

larceny *n* **-ies** (*law old*) theft of personal property. — *n* **larcenist**. [OFr *larcin*]

larch *n* **1** a coniferous tree with needle-like leaves and cones, which loses its leaves in the winter. **2** the wood of this tree. [Lat *larix*]

lard *n* soft, white fat from pigs, used in cooking. — *v* (*tr*) **1** to put lard on. **2** to stuff (meat) with bacon or pork. **3** **(with)** to fill (a piece of writing, etc.) with details, technical or elaborate words, etc. [Lat *laridum*, bacon fat]

larder *n* a cool room or cupboard for storing food. [OFr *lardier*, from Lat *laridum*, bacon fat]

large *adj* **1** great in size, extent or amount. **2** broad; wide-ranging. **3** generous. **4** in a big way; extensive. — *adv* importantly; prominently. — **at large 1** (of prisoners, etc.) free. **2** in general; as a whole: *people at large*. **3** at length and with full details. **4** without a particular target: *bombing the country at large*. — *n* **largeness**. [Lat *largus*, plentiful]

largely *adv* **1** mainly or chiefly. **2** to a great extent.

largesse or **largess** *n* **1** generosity. **2** gifts, money, etc. given generously. [OFr, from Lat *largus*, plentiful]

largo (*mus*) *adv* slowly and with dignity. — *adj* slow and dignified. — *n* **-os** a piece of music to be played in this way. [Ital, broad]

lariat *n* a lasso or a rope used for tethering animals. [Span *la reata*, the lasso]

lark[1] *n* any of several kinds of song-birds, esp. the skylark, which flies high into the air as it sings. [OE *lawerce*]

lark[2] *n* (*coll*) **1** a piece of fun or a joke. **2** (*Br*) a job or activity. — *v* **lark about** or **around** (*intr*; *coll*) to play about or have fun in a rough and usu. noisy manner.

larkspur *n* a plant with spur-like calyces and blue, white or pink flowers. [**lark**[1] + **spur**]

larva *n* **-ae** a developing insect in a state which is different from the adult, e.g. a caterpillar. — *adj* **larval**. [Lat, ghost, mask]

laryngeal *adj* of or relating to the larynx. [**larynx**]

laryngitis *n* inflammation of the larynx, causing pain and making it difficult to speak. [**larynx** + **-itis**]

larynx *n* a hollow organ in the throat, forming the upper end of the windpipe and containing the vocal cords. [Gr]

lasagne *n* **1** (*pl*) thin, wide, flat strips of pasta. **2** (*sing*) an Italian dish consisting of alternate layers of this pasta and a mixture of meat and tomatoes, with cheese sauce, baked in the oven. [Ital]

lascivious *adj* feeling, expressing or causing sexual desire. — *adv* **lasciviously**. — *n* **lasciviousness**. [Lat *lascivus*, playful]

laser *n* a device that produces a narrow and very intense beam of single-coloured light. [*l*ight *a*mplification by *s*imulated *e*mission of *r*adiation]

laser printer *n* a fast computer printer which produces high-quality print-out using a laser beam to form the characters on the paper.

lash[1] *n* **1** (usu. in *pl*) an eyelash. **2** a stroke or blow with a whip, esp. formerly as a punishment. **3** the flexible part of a whip. — *v* **1** (*tr*) to hit or beat with a lash, esp. formerly as a punishment. **2** (*tr*) (of waves or rain) to beat with great force on: *waves lashing the shore*. **3** (*intr*; **down**, **against**, etc.) (of waves or rain) to beat with great force. **4** (*intr*) to make a sudden whip-like movement (of or with a tail, etc.). **5** (*tr*) to move (a tail) with a sudden or restless movement. **6** (*tr*) to attack with harsh, scolding words or criticism. **7** (*tr*) to urge on as if with a whip.— *n* **lashing**. — *v* **lash out** (*intr*) **1** (**against**, **at**) to kick, hit or complain violently. **2** (**on**; *coll*) to spend money in large quantities. [MidE *lashe*]

lashings *n* (*pl*; *coll*) a large amount.

lash[2] *v* (*tr*; **down**, **together**) to fasten with a rope or cord. [MidE *lasschyn*]

lashing *n* a rope for tying things fast.

lass *n* a girl or young woman.

lassie *n* (*Scot*) a young girl.

lassitude *n* a feeling of being physically or mentally tired and of having no energy or enthusiasm. [Lat *lassus*, faint]

lasso *n* **-os** or **-oes** a long rope with a loop which tightens when the rope is pulled, used for catching animals, etc. — *v* **-oes**, **-oed** (*tr*) to catch with a lasso. — *n* **lassoer**. [Span *lazo*, from Lat *laqueus*, noose]

last[1] *adj* **1** coming at the end of a series. **2** most recent; next before the present: *last week*. **3** coming or remaining after all the others. **4** least likely or suitable: *the last person to expect help from*. **5** lowest in rank; worst. **6** (used for emphasis) single: *broke every last one of the plates*. — *adv* **1** after all others. **2** most recently. **3** lastly. — *n* **1** the person or thing that is last. **2** the end or last moment. **3** the final appearance or mention: *hear the last of him*. — **at (long) last** in the end, esp. after a long delay. — **last thing** after doing everything else, esp. before leaving or going to bed. — **on one's last legs** worn out; exhausted. — **to the last** until the very end, esp. until death. [OE *latost*, latest]

last-ditch *adj* done as a last resort.

the Last Judgement *n* in some religions, the day at the end of time when God will judge people.

lastly *adv* finally or at the end.

last-minute *adj* made, done or given at the latest possible moment.

last name *n* a surname.

the last rites *n* (*pl*) religious rites for a dying person.

the last straw *n* a small event or minor fact, etc. which, when added to all the other events, facts, etc. makes a situation finally impossible to bear.

the Last Supper *n* the supper eaten by Christ and his disciples on the day before the Crucifixion.

the last word *n* **1** the final or definitive remark in an argument or debate. **2** the final decision. **3** the most up to date or fashionable thing: *the last word in elegance.*

last[2] *v* **1** (*intr*) to continue to exist; to remain in being. **2** (*tr*) to be enough for the needs of: *enough water to last us two days.* **3** (*intr*) to remain in good condition: *This bread will only last one more day.* **4** (*tr* & *intr*; **out**) to survive until a given time or until the end of (a given time): *last the winter in Spain.* [OE *læstan*]

lasting *adj* existing or continuing for a long time or permanently.

last[3] *n* a foot-shaped piece of wood or metal on which shoes are made and repaired. — **stick to one's last** to not interfere in things which do not concern one. [OE *læste*]

lat. *abbrev* latitude.

Lat *abbrev* Latin.

latch *n* **1** a door catch consisting of a bar which is lowered or raised from its notch by a lever or string. **2** a door-lock by which a door may be opened from the inside using the handle, but from the outside only by using a key. — *v* (*tr* & *intr*) to fasten or be fastened with a latch. — *v* **latch on 1** (*tr*; **to**) to attach oneself to: *latch on to her and follow her everywhere.* **2** (*intr*) to understand: *took her a moment to latch on.* — **on the latch** shut but not locked; able to be opened by the latch. [OE *læccan*]

latchkey *n* a small key for an outer door with a latch.

latchkey child *n* a child whose parents are still out at work when he or she gets home from school.

late *adj* **1** coming, arriving, etc. after the expected or usual time. **2** far on in the day or night; nearly at the end: *late afternoon.* **3** occurring, ripening, etc. at a relatively advanced time in the season: *late potatoes.* **4** having died, esp. recently. **5** former: *the late prime minister.* **6** most recent. — *adv* **1** after the expected or usual time. **2** far on in the day or night. **3** at an advanced time: *flower late in the season.* **4** recently: *as late as this morning.* **5** formerly, but no longer: *late of Glasgow.* — *n* **lateness**. — **late in the day** at a late stage, esp. too late to be of any use. — **of late** lately; recently. [OE *læt*]

lately *adv* in the recent past; not long ago.

later *adj* & *adv* (following, occurring, etc.) at some time after.

latest *adj* most recent. — *n* (with **the**) the most recent news, occurrence, fashion, etc. — **at the latest** not later than (a time stated).

lateen *adj* (*naut*) (of a ship) having a triangular sail on a long, sloping yard. [Fr (*voile*) *latine*, Latin (sail), so-called because they are common on the Mediterranean]

latent *adj* present but hidden and not yet developed. — *n* **latency**. [Lat *latere*, to lie hidden]

lateral *adj* of, at, to or from the side. — *n* a lateral part. — *adv* **laterally**. [Lat *latus*, side]

lateral thinking *n* a way of solving problems, etc. by being able to think about them in different and unusual ways which provide new possibilities.

latex *n* **-*texes*** or **-*tices*** the milky juice of some plants, esp. rubber trees. [Lat, liquid]

lath *n* a thin narrow strip of wood, esp. one of a series used to support plaster. [OE *lætt*]

lathe *n* a machine for shaping wood, metal, etc., which turns the wood, etc. to be shaped against cutting tools which are held steady. [MidE, frame, stand]

lather *n* **1** a foam made by mixing water and soap. **2** (esp. of a horse) foamy sweat. **3** (*coll*) a state of excitement or worry. — *v* **-*r*- 1** (*intr*) to form a lather. **2** (*tr*) to cover with lather. **3** (*tr*; *coll*) to beat or thrash. — *adj* **lathery**. [OE *leathor*, soap]

Latin *n* **1** the language spoken in ancient Rome and its empire. **2** a person who speaks a Latin language. — *adj* **1** of, relating to or in the Latin language. **2** (of a language) derived from Latin, as for example Italian and Spanish are. **3** (of a person) having a passionate, excitable character. **4** of the Roman Catholic Church. [Lat *latinus*, of Latium, the area to the SE of ancient Rome]

Latin America *n* the countries of Central and South America, where the official language is either Spanish or Portuguese. — *n* & *adj* **Latin American**.

latitude *n* **1** a distance north or south of the equator, measured in degrees. **2** (usu. in *pl*) a region or area in terms of its distance from the equator or its climate: *warm latitudes.* **3** scope for freedom of action or choice. — *adj* **latitudinal**. — *adv* **latitudinally**. ◇ See also **longitude**. [Lat *latus*, broad]

latrine *n* a lavatory, esp. in a barracks. [Lat *lavatrina*, bath]

latter *adj* **1** nearer to the end: *the latter part of the holiday.* **2** being the second of two people, things, etc. mentioned. **3** recent; modern. — *n* the second of two people, things, etc. mentioned. [OE *lætra*]

latter-day *adj* recent or modern.

Latter-day Saints *n* (*pl*) Mormons.

latterly *adv* **1** recently. **2** towards the end.

lattice *n* **1** (also **lattice-work**) an open frame made from crossed narrow strips of wood or metal, used esp. for gates and fences. **2** (also **lattice window**) a window with small diamond-shaped panels of glass formed by strips of lead. **3** a regular pattern of atoms and molecules. — *adj* **latticed**. [OFr *lattis*, from *latte*, lath]

laud *v* (*tr*; *formal*, *old* or *relig*) to praise (esp. God). — *n* **1** (*formal*, *old* or *relig*) praise. **2** (*relig*; in *pl*) the first morning service in the Roman Catholic Church. ◇ See also **compline, matins, none**[2], **sext, terce, vespers**. [Lat *laus*, praise]

laudable *adj* worthy of praise. — *n* **laudability**. — *adv* **laudably**.

laudanum *n* a solution of morphine prepared from opium in alcohol. [Lat, used by Paracelsus, a 16th-century physician, for an expensive medicine containing opium]

laudatory *adj* containing or expressing praise. [Lat *laus*, praise]

laugh *v* **1** (*intr*) to make sounds with the voice as a sign of happiness, amusement, scorn, etc. **2** (*tr*) to bring or force (someone or oneself) into a certain state through laughing: *laugh oneself sick*. **3** (*tr*) to express by laughing. — *n* **1** an act or sound of laughing. **2** (*coll*) any person or thing that is amusing or causes laughter. — **have the last laugh** to win in the end or be finally proved right. — *v* **laugh at** (*tr*) to make fun of or ridicule. — *v* **laugh off** (*tr*) to treat (an injury, embarrassment, etc.) as if it were a joke. — **laugh up one's sleeve** to laugh secretly. [OE *hlæhhan*]

laughable *adj* **1** deserving to be laughed at; not very good. **2** amusing. — *adv* **laughably**.

laughing *n* laughter. — *adv* **laughingly**. — **no laughing matter** a very serious matter.

laughing gas *n* nitrous oxide, which may cause laughter when breathed in, used as an anaesthetic.

laughing-stock *n* someone who is laughed at or ridiculed.

laughter *n* the act or sound of laughing.

launch[1] *v* **1** (*tr*) to cause (a boat or ship) to slide into the water, esp. for the first time. **2** (*tr*) to send (a spacecraft, missile, etc.) into the air. **3** (*tr*) to start (a person, project, etc.) off on a course. **4** (*tr*) to introduce (a new product) on to the market. **5** (*tr & intr*; **into, out**) to throw (oneself) into or begin (a new project) enthusiastically: *launch oneself into a new job*. **6** (*intr*; **into**) to begin a usu. long story or speech. — *n* an act or instance of launching, esp. a ship or spacecraft. [Lat *lanceare*, to wield a lance]

launcher *n* a device used for launching a spacecraft, etc.

launching-pad or **launch pad** *n* a platform from which a spacecraft, etc. can be launched.

launch[2] *n* **1** a large motorboat. **2** (*hist*) the largest boat carried by a man-of-war. [Span *lancha*]

launder *v* **-r-** (*tr*) **1** to wash and iron (clothes or linen). **2** (*coll*) to transfer (money obtained illegally) through banks or legitimate businesses to hide its origins. [Lat *lavare*, to wash]

launderette or **laundrette** *n* a shop where customers may wash clothes in coin-operated washing-machines. [Orig. trademark]

laundress *n* a woman who washes and irons clothes and linen, esp. professionally. [**launder**]

laundry *n* **-ies 1** a place where clothes and linen are washed, esp. in return for payment. **2** clothes, etc. which have been, or are to be, washed. [**launder**]

laureate *adj* crowned with laurel leaves as a sign of honour or distinction. — *n* same as **poet laureate**. — *n* **laureateship**. [Lat *laureatus*, from *laurus*, laurel]

laurel *n* **1** a small evergreen tree with smooth, dark, shiny leaves used for flavouring in cooking. **2** a crown of laurel leaves worn as a symbol of victory or mark of honour. **3** (in *pl*) honour; praise. — **look to one's laurels** to be careful not to lose a high position or reputation due to better performances, etc. by one's rivals. — **rest on one's laurels** to be satisfied with one's past successes and not try to achieve anything more. [Lat *laurus*]

lav *n* (*coll*) a lavatory.

lava *n* **1** the molten rock and liquid which flows from a volcano, becoming solid as it cools. **2** the solid substance which it forms when cooled. [Ital, from Lat *labes*, a sliding down]

lavatory *n* **-ies 1** a piece of equipment for receiving urine and faeces, and with a mechanism for flushing this away into a sewer. **2** a room containing one or more of these. [Lat *lavare*, to wash]

lavatorial *adj* (esp. of humour) relating to lavatories and excretion.

lavender *n* **1** a plant or shrub with sweet-smelling pale bluish-purple flowers. **2** the dried flowers from this plant, used to perfume clothes or linen. **3** the pale bluish-purple colour of the flowers. [Lat *lavendula*]

lavender water *n* a light perfume containing lavender oil.

laver *n* any of several edible seaweeds. [Lat, water plant]

laver bread *n* a Welsh dish made from boiled laver dipped in oatmeal and fried.

lavish *adj* **1** (of a person) spending or giving generously. **2** gorgeous or luxurious: *lavish decoration*. **3** too generous; extravagant or excessive. — *v* (*tr*; **on**) to spend (money) or give (praise, etc.) very freely or generously. — *adv* **lavishly**. — *n* **lavishness**. [OFr *lavasse*, deluge of rain]

law *n* **1** a rule recognised as allowing or prohibiting certain actions. **2** a collection of such rules according to which people live or a country or state is governed. **3** the control which such rules exercise: *law and order*. **4** a controlling force: *Her word is law*. **5** a collection of such rules as a subject for study. **6** a group of such rules relating to a particular activity: *commercial law*. **7** the group of people who work professionally with these rules. **8** (*coll*) the police or a member of the police. **9** (in *pl*) jurisprudence. **10** a rule in science, philosophy, etc., based on practice or observation, which says that under certain conditions certain things will always happen. **11** (*cap* with **the**) the first five books of the Old Testament, which contain Jewish law. — **be a law unto oneself** to act as one wants and not according to laws or custom. — **have the law on** (*coll*) (usu. used as a threat) to make sure that legal action is taken against (someone). — **lay down the law** to state one's opinions and orders forcefully. — **take the law into one's own hands** to get justice in one's own way, without involving the law or the police. [OE *lagu*]

law-abiding *adj* obeying the law.

law centre *n* (*Br*) an office where legal advice and help is available free of charge.

lawcourt *n* (also **court of law**) a place where people accused of crimes are tried and legal disagreements settled.

lawful *adj* **1** allowed by or according to law. **2** just or rightful. — *adv* **lawfully**. — *n* **lawfulness**.

lawless *adj* **1** ignoring or breaking the law, esp. violently. **2** having no laws. — *adv* **lawlessly**. — *n* **lawlessness**.

Law Lord *n* **1** a peer in the House of Lords who holds or has held high legal office, and who sits in the highest court of appeal. **2** (*Scot*) a judge of the Court of Session.

lawsuit *n* an argument or disagreement taken to a court of law to be settled.

lawyer *n* a person whose work it is to know about the law, and give legal advice and help, esp. a solicitor.

lawn[1] *n* an area of smooth, mown grass, esp. as part of a garden. [MidE *launde*, glade]

lawn-mower *n* a machine for cutting grass on lawns.

lawn tennis *n* the usual form of tennis, played on grass-covered or hard courts. ◇ See also **real tennis**.

lawn[2] *n* fine linen or cotton. [Prob. from *Laon* in France, where linen-making was once important]

lawrencium *n* a man-made metallic element (symbol **Lr**). [E O *Lawrence* (1901–58), American physicist]

lawyer. See **law**.

lax *adj* **1** loose, slack or flabby. **2** not careful or strict in one's behaviour or morals. — *n* **laxity** or **laxness**. — *adv* **laxly**. [Lat *laxus*, loose]

laxative *n* & *adj* (a medicine) which makes it easier to pass faeces from the body. [Lat *laxare*, to loosen]

lay[1] *v* ***laid*** **1** (*tr*) to place, set or put on a surface, esp. horizontally. **2** (*tr*) to place, put or bring into the proper or stated position or condition. **3** (*tr*) to design, arrange or prepare: *lay plans for his escape*. **4** (*tr*) to put plates and cutlery, etc. on (a table) ready for a meal. **5** (*tr*) to prepare (a fire) by putting coal, etc. in the grate. **6** (*tr* & *intr*) to produce (eggs). **7** (*tr*) to present: *lay one's case before the judge*. **8** (*tr*) to deal with or remove: *lay a fear*. **9** (*tr*) to locate or attribute: *lay the blame on him*. **10** (*tr*; *coll*) to place (a bet). **11** (*tr*; *vulg slang*) to have sexual intercourse with. — *n* **1** the way or position in which something is lying. **2** (*vulg slang*) a partner in sexual intercourse. **3** (*vulg slang*) an act of sexual intercourse. — **lay about one** to strike blows in all directions. — *v* **lay aside** (*tr*) **1** to put to one side, esp. for use, or to be dealt with, in the future. **2** to discard or abandon. — **lay bare** to show clearly or explain. — *v* **lay by** (*tr*) to put away for future use. — *v* **lay down** (*tr*) **1** to put on the ground. **2** to give up or sacrifice: *lay down one's life*. **3** to formulate or devise: *lay down a plan*. **4** to store (wine) in a cellar. **5** to begin to build (a ship or railway). — **lay one's hands on** (*coll*) **1** to find or be able to get. **2** to catch. — *v* **lay in** (*tr*) to get and store a supply of. — *v* **lay into** (*tr*; *coll*) to attack or scold severely. — **lay low** **1** (of an illness) to affect severely. **2** to make humble. — *v* **lay off** **1** (*tr*) to dismiss (employees) when there is no work available (*n* **lay-off**). **2** (*tr* & *intr*; *coll*) to stop doing something, esp. annoying or teasing someone. — *v* **lay on** (*tr*) to provide (a supply of). — **lay it on thick** (*coll*) to exaggerate, esp. praise or flattery. — **lay open** **1** to uncover or reveal. **2** to cut or wound. **3** to expose (oneself) to criticism or attack. — *v* **lay out** (*tr*) **1** to arrange (land), esp. according to a plan: *lay out the new park*. **2** to spread out or display. **3** (*coll*) to knock unconscious. **4** to prepare (a dead body) for burial. **5** (*coll*) to spend (money). ◇ See also **layout** below. — **lay to rest** to bury (a dead body). — *v* **lay up** (*tr*) **1** to keep or store. **2** (*coll*) (of an illness) to force (someone) to stay in bed or at home. **3** to put (a ship) out of use, esp. for repairs. — **lay waste** to destroy or devastate completely. [OE *lecgan*]

layabout *n* a lazy person.

lay-by *n* ***lay-bys*** (*Br*) a small area at the side of a road where drivers may stop out of the way of the traffic.

layer *n* **1** a thickness or covering, esp. one of several on a surface. **2** a person or thing that lays: *carpet-layer*. **3** a hen regularly laying eggs. **4** a shoot from a plant which is fastened into the soil to root while still attached to the parent plant. — *v* (*tr*) **1** to arrange or cut in layers. **2** to produce (a new plant) by preparing a layer from the parent plant.

lay-off see **lay off** above.

layout *n* **1** an arrangement or plan of how land, buildings, pages, etc. are to be set out. **2** the things thus displayed or arranged. **3** the general appearance of a printed page.

lay[2]. See **lie**[2].

lay[3] *adj* **1** of, relating to or involving people who are not members of the clergy. **2** not having specialised or professional knowledge of a particular subject. [Gr *laos*, the people]

layman, **layperson** or **laywoman** *n* **1** a person who is not a member of the clergy. **2** a person who does not have specialised or professional knowledge of a particular subject. ◇ See also **laity**.

lay reader *n* an unordained person licensed to undertake some religious duties.

lay[4] *n* a short narrative or lyric poem, esp. one intended to be sung. [OFr *lai*]

layette *n* a complete set of clothes, blankets, etc. for a baby. [OFr *laiete*, small chest]

lay figure *n* **1** a jointed model of the human body used by painters for seeing how clothes, etc. hang. **2** a person or a character in a novel who lacks individuality or is unrealistic. [Dut *leeman*, from *led*, jointed + *man*, man]

laze *v* (*intr*) **1** to be idle or lazy. **2** (**around**) to spend one's time doing nothing. — *n* a period of time spent lazing. [A back-formation from **lazy**]

lazy *adj* **-ier**, **-iest** **1** not wanting to do anything or very much; not wanting to take exercise, work hard, etc.; idle. **2** of or causing idleness. **3** slow-moving, sluggish. — *adv* **lazily**. — *n* **laziness**.

lazy-bones *n* (*coll*) a lazy person.

lb *abbrev* pound (weight). [Lat *libra*]

lbw *abbrev* (*cricket*) leg before wicket.

lc *abbrev* **1** *loco citato* (Lat), in the place cited. **2** (*printing*) lower case.

LCD *abbrev* **1** liquid crystal display. **2** (also **lcd**) lowest common denominator.

LCM or **lcm** *abbrev* lowest common multiple.

L/Cpl *abbrev* Lance Corporal.

LEA *abbrev* Local Education Authority.

lea *n* (*poetic*) a field, meadow, piece of arable or pasture land. [OE *leah*]

leach *v* **1** (*tr*) to make (liquid) seep through something. **2** (*tr*) to make liquid seep through (bark, ash or soil) to remove certain substances from (the bark, etc.). **3** (*tr & intr*; **away, out**) to remove (soluble substances) or be removed by having liquid seep through. [Prob. OE *leccan*, to water]

lead[1] *v* **led** **1** (*tr & intr*) to guide by going in front. **2** (*tr*) to guide or cause to go in a certain direction by holding or pulling with the hand, etc. **3** (*tr & intr*) to direct or be in control (of). **4** (*tr*) to cause to act, feel or think in a certain way. **5** (*tr*) to pass or experience: *lead a miserable existence*. **6** (*tr & intr*; **to**) to go: *All roads lead to Rome*. **7** (*intr* with **to**) to have as an end or consequence: *lead to problems*. **8** (*tr & intr*) to be first (in); to be the most important or influential person (in a group) in a particular field: *lead the world in engineering*. **9** (*intr* with **with**) (of a newspaper) to have (a particular story) as its most important article. **10** (*Br*; *tr*) to play the principal violin in (an orchestra). **11** (*tr*) to conduct (liquid) along a channel or course. **12** (*tr & intr*) to begin a round of cards by playing (the first card, esp. of a particular suit). — *n* **1** the guidance given by leading; an example: *follow the first singer's lead*. **2** the first, leading or most prominent place; leadership. **3** the amount by which a person, etc. is in front of others in a race, contest, etc. **4** a strap or chain for leading or holding a dog, etc. **5** a small piece of information or clue, esp. at the beginning of an inquiry, which will help solve a problem, mystery, etc. **6** the principal part in a play, film, etc., or the actor playing this role. **7** the most important story in a newspaper. **8** an act of playing the first card in a card game, or the first card played. **9** a wire or conductor taking electricity from a source to an appliance. — *v* **lead off** (*intr & tr*) to begin. — *v* **lead on** (*tr*) **1** to persuade to go further than intended. **2** to deceive or mislead. — *v* **lead up to** (*tr*) to prepare (to do something, for something to happen, etc.) by gradual steps or stages; to be an underlying cause of (*n* **lead-up**). — **lead the way** to go first, esp. to guide others. [OE *lædan*]

leader *n* **1** a person, animal or thing that leads or guides others. **2** a person who organises or is in charge (of a group). **3** (*Br*) the principal violinist in an orchestra. **4** (*Br*; also **leading article**) an article in a newspaper, etc. written to express the opinions of the editor. **5** (*Br cap*; also **Leader of the House**) the member of the government responsible for beginning debates, etc. in Parliament. **6** a short blank strip at the beginning and end of a film or tape, used for loading the film or tape on to a spool. **7** a horse or dog in front place in a team or pair. **8** a long shoot growing from the stem or branch of a plant.

leadership *n* **1** the state of being a leader. **2** the ability to lead others. **3** leaders as a group.

lead-in *n* **1** an introduction to an article, discussion, piece of music, etc. **2** a cable connecting a television or radio with an outside aerial.

leading *adj* acting as leader; guiding; directing. — *n* guidance, leadership.

leading aircraftman or **aircraftwoman** *n* a man or woman with the rank above aircraftman or aircraftwoman.

leading article see **leader** (sense **4**).

leading light *n* a very important and influential person in a particular field or subject.

leading note *n* the seventh note of the diatonic scale in any key.

leading question *n* a question asked in such a way as to suggest the answer one wants.

lead-up see **lead up to**.

lead[2] *n* **1** a soft, heavy, bluish-grey metallic element (symbol **Pb**) used in alloys. **2** graphite. **3** a thin stick of graphite, or some other coloured substance, used in pencils.

4 a lump of lead used for measuring the depth of the water, esp. at sea. **5** (in *pl*) a sheet of lead for covering roofs; a roof covered with lead sheets. **6** a lead frame for a small window-pane, e.g. in stained glass windows. **7** a lead weight or piece of lead shot used at the end of a fishing line and in cartridges. **8** (also **leading**) a thin strip of metal used formerly in printing to produce a space between lines. — *adj* made of lead. — *v* (*tr*) to cover, weight, fit or surround with lead. [OE]

leaden *adj* **1** made of lead. **2** dull grey in colour. **3** heavy or slow. **4** depressing; dull.

lead pencil *n* a pencil with a thin stick of graphite in the middle.

lead poisoning *n* severe poisoning caused by taking lead into the body.

leaf *n* ***leaves*** **1** a thin, flat, usu. green part growing usu. from the stem of a plant. **2** anything like a leaf. **3** leaves as a group. **4** the condition of having leaves: *in leaf*. **5** a single sheet of paper forming two pages in a book. **6** a very thin sheet of metal: *gold leaf*. **7** a hinged or sliding extra part or flap on a table, door, etc. — *v* **1** (*tr* & *intr*; **through**) to turn the pages (of a book) quickly, and usu. only glancing at their contents. **2** (*intr*) (of plants) to produce leaves. — *adj* **leafless**. — **turn over a new leaf** to begin a new and better way of behaving or working. [OE]

leafage *n* the leaves of plants.

leaflet *n* **1** a single sheet of paper, or several sheets of paper folded together, giving information, advertising products, etc. **2** a small leaf. **3** a division of a leaf. — *v* ***-t-*** (*tr* & *intr*) to distribute leaflets (to).

leaf mould *n* earth formed from rotted leaves, used as a compost for plants.

leafy *adj* ***-ier***, ***-iest*** **1** having or covered with leaves. **2** like a leaf.

league[1] *n* **1** a union of persons, nations, etc. formed for the benefit of the members. **2** a group of sports clubs which compete over a period for a championship. **3** a class or group, considered in terms of ability, importance, etc.: *He just isn't in her league*. — *v* (*tr* & *intr*) to form or be formed into a league. — **in league with** having agreed to work with (someone), usu. for some bad purpose. [Lat *ligare*, to bind]

league[2] *n* (*old*) a unit for measuring distances, usu. about 3 miles (4·8 km). [Lat *leuga*, a Gaulish unit of distance]

leak *n* **1** an unwanted crack or hole which allows liquid or gas to pass in or out. **2** liquid or gas which has escaped through such a crack or hole. **3** a loss of electricity from a conductor, etc., usu. because of faulty insulation. **4** a usu. unauthorised making known of secret information. **5** (*slang*) an act of urinating. — *v* **1** (*intr*) (of liquid, gas, etc.) to pass accidentally in or out of an unwanted crack or hole. **2** (*tr*) to allow (liquid, gas, etc.) to pass in or out through a crack or hole. **3** (*tr*) to make known (secret information) without authorisation. **4** (*intr*) (of secret information) to become known. — *n* **leakiness**. — *adj* **leaky**, ***-ier***, ***-iest***. [OE *hlec*, leaky]

leakage *n* **1** an act or instance of leaking. **2** something that enters or escapes through a leak.

lean[1] *v* ***leant*** or ***leaned*** **1** (*intr* & *tr*; **against**, **back**, **over**, etc.) to slope or be placed in a sloping position. **2** (*intr* & *tr*) to rest or be rested against (something) for support. **3** (*intr*; **on**, **upon**) to rely on or be supported by. **4** (*intr*; **towards**) to have an inclination or preference for or tendency towards. — *n* an act or condition of leaning. — *v* **lean on** (*tr*; *coll*) to put pressure on (someone) to persuade him or her to act in a certain way. [OE *hlinian*]

leaning *n* a liking or preference.

lean-to *n* ***-tos*** a building, esp. a shed, built against another building or wall.

lean[2] *adj* **1** (of a person or animal) thin. **2** (of meat) not containing much fat. **3** producing very little (food, money, etc.); unfruitful: *lean years*. — *n* **leanness**. [OE *hlæne*]

leant. See **lean**[1].

leap *v* ***leapt*** or ***leaped*** **1** (*intr*) to jump suddenly or with force. **2** (*tr*) to jump over. **3** (*intr* with **at**) to accept eagerly. **4** (*intr*) (of prices) to go up suddenly and quickly. — *n* **1** an act of leaping or jumping. **2** the distance leaped. — **by leaps and bounds** extremely rapidly and successfully. — **a leap in the dark** an action, decision, etc. whose results cannot be guessed in advance. [OE *hleapan*]

leap-frog *n* a game in which one player bends over for another player to vault over. — *v* **1** (*intr*; **over**) to jump over a person's back in this way. **2** (*tr* & *intr*) (of two or more people, vehicles, etc.) to move forward by passing each other one after the other.

leap year *n* a year of 366 days, 29 February being the extra day.

learn *v* ***learnt*** or ***learned*** **1** (*tr*) to gain knowledge of or skill in through experience, study or being taught. **2** (*tr*) to get to know by heart; to memorise. **3** (*intr*) to gain knowledge or skill. **4** (*intr*; **of**, **about**) to be informed of: *learn of the problem too late*. **5** (*tr*; *old*, *dialect* or *slang*) to teach. [OE *leornian*]

learned *adj* **1** having great learning, esp. through years of study. **2** showing or needing great learning. **3** of or relating to learned people; scholarly. — *adv* **learnedly**.

learner *n* a person who is in the process of learning something.

learning *n* knowledge gained through study.

learning support *n* teaching intended to help pupils with learning difficulties. ◇ See also **remedial**.

lease *n* a contract by which the owner of a house, land, etc. agrees to let another person use it for a stated period of time in return for rent. — *v* (*tr*) to give or borrow (a building or land) on lease. — **a new lease of life** the prospect of renewed life, energy, health, etc., often after a rest or repair. [OFr *lais*]

leasehold *n* **1** the holding of land or buildings by lease. **2** the land or building held by lease. — *adj* held by lease. — *n* **leaseholder**. ◇ See also **freehold**.

leash *n* a strip of leather or chain used for leading or holding a dog or other animal. — *v* (*tr*) **1** to put a leash on. **2** to control or restrain. — **straining at the leash** impatient or eager to begin. [OFr *laisser*, to let a dog run on a leash]

least *adj* smallest; slightest. — *adv* in the smallest or lowest degree: *speak the least in class*. — *pron* the smallest amount. — **at least 1** at all events; anyway. **2** not less than. — **at the least** as a minimum. — **not in the least** or **not the least bit** not at all. [OE *læst*]

leather *n* **1** the skin of an animal made smooth by tanning. **2** a small piece of leather for polishing or cleaning. **3** the leather part of something. — *v* **-r-** (*tr*) **1** to cover or polish with leather. **2** (*coll*) to thrash. [OE *lether*]

leather-jacket *n* a grub of the crane-fly with a skin which is tough like leather.

leathery *adj* like leather, esp. in being tough.

leave[1] *v* ***left*** **1** (*tr* & *intr*) to go away (from); to move out (of). **2** (*tr*; **behind**) to go without taking; to cause to remain behind. **3** (*tr*) to allow to remain in a particular state or condition: *leave the window open*. **4** (*tr* & *intr*) to stop going to, belonging to or working at: *leave the company*. **5** (*tr*) to deliver to or deposit with: *leave the keys with a neighbour*. **6** (*tr*; **to**) to allow or cause someone to do (something) without help: *leave the cleaning to me*. **7** (*tr*) to have as a remainder: *Three minus one leaves two*. **8** (*tr*) to make a gift of (something) in one's will when one dies. **9** (*tr*) to cause: *leaves a scar*. — *v* **leave alone** (*tr*) to not disturb, upset, worry or interfere with. — *v* **leave off** (*intr* & *tr*) to stop (doing something); to come or bring to an end. — *v* **leave out** (*tr*) to not include. [OE *læfan*]

leavings *n* (*pl*; *coll*) things which are left; rubbish.

leave[2] *n* **1** permission to be absent, esp. from work or military duties. **2** the length of time this lasts. **3** permission to do something. — **on leave** officially absent from work. — **take one's leave (of)** to say goodbye (to). [OE *leaf*]

-leaved *in cmpds* having the stated type or number of leaves: *prickly-leaved*. [**leaf**]

leaven *n* (also **leavening**) **1** a substance, esp. yeast, added to dough to make it rise. **2** anything which is an influence and causes change. — *v* (*tr*) **1** to cause (dough) to rise with leaven. **2** to influence or cause change in. [Lat *levare*, to lift]

leaves. See **leaf**.

lecher *n* a lustful or lecherous man. [OFr *lecheor*, from *lechier*, to lick]

lecherous *adj* having or showing great or excessive sexual desire, esp. in ways which are offensive. — *adv* **lecherously**. — *n* **lecherousness**.

lechery *n* excessive sexual desire.

lecithin *n* a chemical compound found naturally in animals and some animal products, e.g. egg-yolk, used in foods and cosmetics. [Gr *lekithos*, egg-yolk]

lectern *n* a stand with a sloping surface for holding a book to be read from, esp. in a lecture-hall or in church. [Lat *legere*, to read]

lecture *n* **1** a formal talk on a particular subject given to an audience, e.g. at university. **2** a long and boring scolding or warning. — *v* **1** (*tr* & *intr*) to give or read a lecture (to a group of people). **2** (*tr*) to scold (someone) at length. [Lat *legere*, to read]

lecturer *n* a person who lectures, esp. to students at college or university. — *n* **lectureship**.

LED *abbrev* light-emitting diode, a semiconductor which gives out light when an electric current passes through it, used for digital clock faces, etc.

led. See **lead**[1].

ledge *n* a narrow, horizontal shelf or shelf-like part. [MidE *legge*, perhaps from *leggen*, to lay]

ledger *n* the chief book of accounts of an office or shop, in which details of all transactions are recorded. [Prob. MidE *leggen*, to lay]

ledger-line *n* a short line added above or below a musical stave on which to mark a note higher or lower than the stave allows for.

lee *n* **1** shelter given by a neighbouring object. **2** (also **lee side**) the sheltered side, away from the wind. [OE *hleo*, shelter]

leeward (*naut*) *adj* & *adv* in or towards the direction in which the wind blows. — *n* the sheltered side.

leeway *n* **1** (*naut*) a ship's drift sideways, away from its true course. **2** scope for freedom of movement or action. — **make up leeway** to make up for lost progress or time.

leech *n* **1** a blood-sucking worm, used esp. formerly by doctors to take blood from patients. **2** a person who befriends another in the hope of personal gain. [OE *læce*]

leek *n* a long, thin vegetable with broad, flat, dark green leaves and a white base, closely related to the onion, taken as the national emblem of Wales. [OE *leac*]

leer *n* a lecherous grin or sneer. — *v* (*intr*) to grin or sneer lecherously at someone. — *adj* **leering**. — *adv* **leeringly**. [OE *hleor*, face, cheek]

leery *adj* ***-ier***, ***-iest*** **1** sly; cunning. **2** (**of**) not having great trust (in); suspicious (of).

lees *n* (*pl*) the sediment that settles at the bottom of wine. [OFr *lie*]

leet *n* (*Scot*) a selected list of candidates for an office.

leeward and **leeway**. See **lee**.

left[1] *past participle* of **leave**[1].

left-luggage office *n* a place at a railway or coach station where travellers may leave luggage safely in return for a small fee.

leftover *n* (in *pl*) pieces of food that have not been eaten up at a meal. — *adj* **left-over** not used up, eaten, etc.

left[2] *adj* **1** on, for, or relating to the side of the body that in most people has the less skilful hand, or the side of a person or thing which is towards the west when that person or thing is facing north. **2** of or relating to the political left. — *adv* on or towards the left side. — *n* **1** the left side, part, direction, etc. **2** (*cap* with **the**) people, political parties, etc., in favour of socialism. **3** the members of any political party holding the most socialist views. **4** the left hand. **5** a blow with the left hand. [OE, weak]

left-hand *adj* **1** on or towards the left. **2** done with the left hand.

left-handed *adj* **1** having the left hand stronger and more skilful than the right. **2** for use by left-handed people, or the left hand. **3** awkward, clumsy. **4** (of compliments, etc.) dubious, ambiguous; seeming sincere but probably not so. — *adv* **left-handedly**. — *n* **left-handedness**. — *n* **left-hander**.

leftist *adj* & *n* (a supporter) of the political left. — *n* **leftism**.

left wing *n* **1** the members of any political party holding the most socialist opinions. **2** the left side of a football, etc. team on the pitch. **3** a player playing on this side. **4** the left side of an army.

left-wing *adj* of, relating to or supporting the political left. — *n* **left-winger**.

lefty *n* **-ies** (*coll*) a left-winger.

leg *n* **1** one of the limbs on which animals, birds and people walk and stand. **2** an animal's or bird's leg used as food. **3** the part of a garment that covers one of these limbs. **4** a long, narrow support of a table, chair, etc. **5** one stage in a journey. **6** a section of a competition or lap of a race. **7** (*cricket*) the side of the field that is to the left of a right-handed batsman facing the bowler or to the right of a left-handed batsman; a fielder on this side of the field. **8** a branch or limb of a forked object. — **a leg up** (*coll*) a piece of help in climbing up or over something. — **leg before wicket** (*cricket*) (of a batsman) given out because of stopping with any part of the body other than the hand a ball which would otherwise have hit the wicket. — **leg it -gg-** (*coll*) to walk or run quickly. — **not have a leg to stand on** (*coll*) to have no way of excusing one's behaviour or supporting one's arguments with facts. — **on one's last legs** near to being no longer usable; near to death or total collapse. — **pull someone's leg** (*coll*) to try to make someone believe something which is not true, esp. as a joke. — **shake a leg** (*coll*) to hurry up. [Norse *leggr*]

leggings *n* (*pl*) outer coverings for the lower legs.

leggy *adj* **-ier**, **-iest 1** having long slim legs. **2** (of a plant) having a long stem.— *n* **legginess**.

leg-pull *n* (*coll*) a joking attempt to make someone believe something which is not true.

leg-room *n* enough space for one's legs to be comfortable when seated.

legacy *n* **-ies 1** something left in a will. **2** something left by a past owner or predecessor: *a legacy of mismanagement*. [Lat *legare*, to leave by will]

legal *adj* **1** lawful; allowed by the law. **2** of or relating to the law or lawyers. — *n* **legality -ies**. — *adv* **legally**. [Lat *legalis*]

legal aid *n* financial assistance given to people who cannot afford to pay their legal fees.

legalise or **-ize** *v* (*tr*) to make legal or lawful. — *n* **legalisation** or **-z-**.

legalism *n* strict adherence to the law. — *n* **legalist**. — *adj* **legalistic**.

legal tender *n* currency which must be accepted in payment.

legate *n* an ambassador or representative, esp. from the Pope. [Lat *legare*, to send a commission]

legatee *n* a person who is left a legacy in someone's will. [Lat *legare*, to leave by will]

legation *n* **1** a diplomatic mission or group of delegates. **2** the official residence of such a mission or group. [Lat *legare*, to send a commission]

legato (*mus*) *adj* & *adv* smooth or smoothly, with all of the notes running into each other. — *n* **-os 1** a piece of music to be played like this. **2** a legato style of playing. [Ital, bound]

legend *n* **1** a traditional story which may or may not be true. **2** a collection of such stories. **3** a famous person about whom popular stories, which may or may not be true, are told: *a legend in her own lifetime*. **4** words accompanying a map or picture, etc., which explain the symbols used. **5** an inscription on a coin, medal or coat of arms. [Lat *legenda*, to be read]

legendary *adj* **1** of or related to legend. **2** described or spoken about in legend. **3** very famous.

legerdemain *n* **1** skill to deceive or conjure with the hands. **2** trickery. [Fr *léger*, light + *de*, of + *main*, hand]

leger line. Same as **ledger line**.

legible *adj* (of handwriting) clear enough to be read. — *n* **legibility**. — *adv* **legibly**. [Lat *legibilis*]

legion *n* **1** (*hist*) a unit in the ancient Roman army, containing between three thousand and six thousand soldiers. **2** a very great number. **3** the name of certain military forces: *the French Foreign Legion.* — *adj* great in number: *Books on this subject are legion.* [Lat *legere*, to choose]

legionary *n* **-ies** (*hist*) a soldier in an ancient Roman legion. — *adj* of or relating to legions.

legionnaire *n* a member of a legion, esp. of the French Foreign Legion.

Legionnaires' Disease *n* a serious and often fatal pneumonia-like disease.

legislate *v* (*intr*) to make laws. — *n* **legislator**. [Lat *lex*, law + *latio*, bringing, proposing]

legislation *n* **1** the act of legislating. **2** a group of laws.

legislative *adj* **1** of or relating to law-making. **2** having the power to make laws.

legislature *n* the part of the government which has the power to make laws.

legitimate *adj* **1** lawful. **2** born to parents who are married to each other. **3** (of an argument or conclusion, etc.) reasonable or logical. **4** (of a sovereign) ruling according to strict hereditary right. — *v* (*tr*) to make lawful or legitimate. — *n* **legitimacy**. — *adv* **legitimately**. [Lat *legitimus*]

legitimise or **-ize** *v* (*tr*) **1** to make lawful or legal. **2** to make an illegitimate child the legal heir to its parents. — *n* **legitimisation** or **-z-**.

Lego® *n* a toy consisting of small plastic bricks which can be fastened together, for building models, etc. [Dan *lege*, to play]

legume *n* **1** a pod bearing seeds, produced by some plants, e.g. beans. **2** the seed or pod from such a plant, valued as food, e.g. peas and lentils. **3** the plant itself. [Lat *legumen*, that which is picked by hand]

leguminous *adj* (of plants) producing fruit or seeds in pods.

lei *n* a garland of flowers worn round the neck. [Hawaiian]

Leics. *abbrev* Leicestershire.

leisure *n* time when one does not have to work. — **at leisure 1** not occupied. **2** without hurrying. — **at one's leisure** at a convenient time. [Lat *licere*, to be allowed]

leisure centre *n* a centre providing a wide variety of recreational facilities.

leisured *adj* having a lot of leisure time.

leisurely *adj* not hurried; relaxed. — *adv* without hurrying and taking plenty of time. — *n* **leisureliness**.

leitmotiv or **leitmotif** *n* a theme associated with a particular person, thing, etc. which recurs throughout a piece of music, novel, etc. [Ger, from *leiten*, to lead + *Motiv*, motif]

lemming *n* a northern and arctic rodent, known for rushing into the sea in large numbers and drowning. [Norw]

lemon *n* **1** an oval-shaped citrus fruit with pale yellow skin and very sour-tasting flesh. **2** the tree which produces such fruit. **3** a pale yellow colour. **4** (*coll*) a person or thing thought of as worthless. — *adj* **1** pale yellow in colour. **2** tasting of or flavoured with lemon. [Persian *limun*]

lemonade *n* a fizzy or still drink flavoured with or made from lemons.

lemon curd or **cheese** *n* a thick, creamy paste made from lemons, sugar, butter and egg.

lemon squash *n* a concentrated drink made from lemons.

lemon sole *n* a European flatfish valued as food. [Fr *limande*]

lemur *n* a nocturnal animal related to the monkeys, with a long tail, pointed snout and large eyes, common in Madagascar. [Lat *lemures*, ghosts]

lend *v* **lent** (*tr*) **1** to give (someone) the use of (something) on the understanding that it is to be returned. **2** to allow (someone) the use of (money), esp. in return for interest paid on it. **3** to give or add (interest, beauty, etc.) to (something or someone). — *n* **lender**. — **lend a hand** to help. — **lend an ear** to listen. — **lend itself to** to be suitable for. — **lend oneself to** to adapt oneself to. [OE *lænan*]

length *n* **1** the distance from one end of an object to the other. **2** the distance a thing extends: *at arm's length*. **3** a period of time. **4** the quality of being long. **5** a long piece of something or a stated amount of something long, e.g. cloth, hair or tubing. **6** (*racing*) the measurement from end to end of a horse, boat, etc. **7** trouble or effort; action taken: *go to great lengths*. **8** (*phon*) the amount of time a vowel, syllable, note, etc. sounds. — **at length 1** in detail. **2** at last. [OE *lengthu*]

lengthen *v* (*tr* & *intr*) to make or become longer.

lengthways or **lengthwise** *adv* & *adj* (going) in the direction of the length.

lengthy *adj* **-ier**, **-iest 1** of great, often excessive, length. **2** (of speech, etc.) long and boring. — *adv* **lengthily**. — *n* **lengthiness**.

lenient *adj* punishing only lightly; not severe. — *n* **lenience** or **leniency**. — *adv* **leniently**. [Lat *lenis*, soft]

lenity *n* **-ies** mildness; mercifulness. [Lat *lenis*, soft]

lens *n* **1** a piece of glass, clear plastic, etc. curved on one or both sides, used to concentrate or separate light rays in cameras, spectacles, etc. **2** a clear substance behind the iris in the eye which focuses light rays and images on the retina. [Lat, lentil (because of the shape)]

Lent *n* in the Christian religion, the time from Ash Wednesday to Easter Sunday, kept as a fast in remembrance of Christ's fast in the wilderness. — *adj* **Lenten**. [OE *lencten*, spring]

lent. See **lend**.

lentil *n* a small orange, brown or green seed from a pod-bearing plant, valued as food. [Lat *lens*]

lento (*mus*) *adj* slow. — *adv* slowly. — *n* ***-os*** a piece of music to be performed slowly. [Ital]

Leo *n* **1** a constellation and the fifth sign of the zodiac, the Lion. **2** a person born between 21 July and 22 August, under this sign. [Lat, lion]

leonine *adj* of or like a lion. [Lat *leo*, lion]

leopard *n* **1** a large animal of the cat family, with a yellowish-brown coat and black spots, found in Africa and Asia. **2** a male of the species. [Gr, *leon*, lion + *pardos*, panther]

leopardess *n* a female leopard.

leotard *n* a tight-fitting garment covering the body and not the limbs, worn (esp. by women) for dancing, exercise, etc. [Jules *Léotard* (1830–70), French trapeze artist]

leper *n* **1** a person who has leprosy. **2** a person who is avoided, esp. on moral grounds. [Gr *lepros*, scaly]

Lepidoptera *n* (*pl*) butterflies and moths. — *adj* **lepidopterous**. [Gr *lepis*, scale + *pteron*, wing]

lepidopterist *n* a person who studies butterflies and moths.

leprechaun *n* a small, mischievous elf in Irish folklore. [O Irish *lúchorpán*, from *lú*, small + *corp*, body]

leprosy *n* a severe skin disease which can be passed from one person to another, and which causes serious and permanent damage to the body, including loss of fingers, limbs, etc. affected. — *adj* **leprous**. [Ety. as for **leper**]

lepton *n* (*physics*) any particle which does not interact strongly with other particles. [Gr *leptos*, small, thin]

lesbian *n* a woman who is sexually attracted to other women. — *adj* of or related to lesbians. — *n* **lesbianism**. [*Lesbos*, the Aegean island where lived the poetess Sappho (born *c*. 650 BC), whose works deal with relationships between women]

lese-majesty *n* treason. [Fr *lèse-majesté*, from Lat *laesa majestas*, injured majesty]

lesion *n* **1** an injury or wound. **2** (*med*) a change in the structure of an organ or body tissue caused by disease or injury. [Lat *laesio*, from *laedere*, to injure]

less *adj* smaller in size, duration, etc. **2** (*coll*) fewer. — *adv* not so much; to a smaller extent. — *n* a smaller amount or number. — *prep* without; minus. [OE *læssa* (adj), *læs* (adv)]

lessen *v* (*tr* & *intr*) to make or become less.

lesser *adj* smaller in size, quantity or importance.

-less *sfx* **1** free from; lacking; without: *heartless*; *godless*. **2** not able to be —ed: *countless*. **3** never —ing: *ceaseless*. [OE *leas*]

lessee *n* a person granted the use of property by lease. [**lease**]

lesson *n* **1** an amount taught or learned at one time. **2** a period of teaching. **3** (in *pl*) instruction in a particular subject given over a period of time: *have singing lessons*. **4** an experience or example which one should take as a warning or encouragement: *Let his problems be a lesson to you.* **5** a passage from the Bible read during a church service. [Fr *leçon*, from Lat *legere*, to read]

lessor *n* a person who rents out property by lease. [**lease**]

lest *conj* (*formal*) **1** for fear that: *Speak quietly lest they hear us.* **2** that: *worried lest the car breaks down.* [OE *thy læs the*, the less that]

let[1] *v* ***-tt-***, ***let*** (*tr*) **1** to allow, permit or cause to. **2** (with **in, out**) to allow or cause to pass in or out. **3** to give the use of (rooms, a building or land) in return for payment. **4** (usu. in *imperative*) to give orders, requests, warnings, permission, etc. and to show assumptions: *Let him go. Let him just try! Let D be the distance travelled.* — **let alone** not to mention; without considering. — *v* **let alone** or **let be** (*tr*) to not disturb or worry. — *v* **let down** (*tr*) **1** to lower. **2** to disappoint or fail to help when necessary, etc. **3** to allow the air to escape from: *let down a tyre*. **4** to make longer: *let the hem down*. — *v* **let fall** (*tr*) **1** to drop. **2** (also **let drop**) to make (secret information, etc.) known, esp. unintentionally. — **let fly** to attack physically or verbally. — **let go (of)** to stop holding (something). — **let (someone) in for** (*coll*) to involve (someone) in (something difficult or unpleasant). — **let (someone) in on** (*coll*) to share (a secret, etc.) with (someone). — **let loose** to release. — *v* **let off** (*tr*) **1** to fire (a gun) or cause (a bomb, etc.) to explode. **2** to release (liquid or gas). **3** to allow to go without punishment, etc. **4** to release from (work, duties, etc.). — *v* **let up** (*intr*) **1** to become less strong or violent (*n* **let-up**). **2** to stop or relax (*n* **let-up**). — **to let** (of property) available for rent. [OE *lætan*, to permit]

let-down *n* a disappointment.

let[2] *n* (*tennis* or *squash*) an obstruction of the ball (e.g. by the net) which means that that ball must be played again. — **without let or hindrance** without anything hindering or preventing action or progress. [OE *lettan*, to hinder]

-let *sfx* a small or young example of the thing described: *piglet*.

lethal *adj* causing or enough to cause death. — *adv* **lethally**. [Lat *letum*, death]

lethargy *n* **1** lack of interest, enthusiasm or energy. **2** (*med*) unnatural heavy or prolonged sleep. — *adj* **lethargic**. — *adv* **lethargically**. [Gr *lethargos*, drowsy]

letter *n* **1** a conventional mark, usu. part of an alphabet, used to express a speech sound. **2** a written or printed message usu. sent by post in an envelope. **3** the strict, literal meaning of words: *the letter of the law*. **4** (in *pl*) literature; knowledge of books: *a woman of letters*. — *v* ***-r-*** (*tr*) to write or mark letters on. — **to the letter**

exactly; in every detail. [Lat *littera*, letter of the alphabet]

letter bomb *n* a device inside an envelope that explodes when the envelope is opened.

letter box *n* (esp. *Br*) **1** a slot in a door, sometimes with a box behind it, by which letters are delivered to a building. **2** a large metal box with a slot in the front, where people may post letters.

lettered *adj* **1** well educated; literary. **2** marked with letters.

letterhead *n* a printed heading on notepaper, giving a person's or company's name, address, etc.

lettering *n* **1** the act of forming letters or the way in which they are formed. **2** letters which have been drawn, painted or inscribed.

letter of credit *n* a letter authorising a bank to issue credit or money to the bearer.

letterpress *n* **1** the printed words in an illustrated book. **2** a way of printing in which ink on raised surfaces is pressed on to paper.

letters patent *n* (*pl*) an official document giving a patent to an inventor, etc.

lettuce *n* a green plant with large, edible leaves used as a salad vegetable. [Lat *lactuca*, from *lac*, milk, because of the milky juice from the leaves]

leucocyte *n* a large white blood cell. [Gr *leukos*, white + **-cyte**]

leukaemia *n* a very serious, sometimes fatal disease in which an abnormal number of white blood cells are produced. [Gr *leukos*, white + *haima*, blood]

Levant *n* the eastern Mediterranean, its islands and the countries surrounding it. [OFr *levaunt*, place where the sun rises]

Levantine *adj* of the Levant; (of ships) trading to the Levant.

levee[1] *n* **1** (*hist*) a sovereign's official meeting on rising from bed. **2** (*old*) an official reception of guests or visitors in the morning or relatively early in the day. [Fr *levée*, from *lever*, to raise]

levee[2] *n* **1** a river's natural embankment. **2** a man-made embankment against floods. **3** a quay. [Fr *levée*, raised, from *lever*, to raise]

level *n* **1** a horizontal plane or line. **2** a height, value or extent. **3** position, status or importance in a scale of values: *discussions at government level*. **4** a stage or degree of progress. **5** an instrument for checking whether a surface is horizontal or not. **6** aspect; way: *provide help on a practical level*. **7** a flat area of land. — *adj* **1** having a flat, smooth, even surface. **2** horizontal. **3** (**with**) having the same height (as something else): *a chair level with the bed*. **4** (**with**) having the same standard (as); equal (to). **5** steady; constant; regular: *keep one's body temperature level*. — *v* **-ll-** **1** (*tr*) to make flat, smooth or horizontal. **2** (*tr*) to make equal. **3** (*tr*; **at**) to point (a gun, etc.). **4** (*tr*) to pull down or demolish. **5** (*tr*; **at, against**) to direct (an accusation, criticism, etc.). **6** (*intr*; **with**; *coll*) to speak honestly. — *n* **levelness**. — **do one's level best** (*coll*) to make the greatest possible effort. — **find one's level** to find one's proper place, rank, etc. among others, or a comfortable rate of work, etc. — *v* **level off** (*tr* & *intr*) to make or become flat, even, steady, regular, etc. — *v* **level out** (*tr* & *intr*) to make or become level. — **level pegging** equality of scores and accomplishments among rivals. — **on the level** (*slang*) fair; honest; genuine. [Lat *libella*, little scale]

level crossing *n* (*Br*) a place where a road crosses a railway on the same level.

level-headed *adj* sensible; well-balanced.

lever *n* **1** a simple device for lifting and moving heavy loads, being a rigid bar resting on a fixed point, one end being raised by pushing down on the other. **2** a strong bar for moving heavy objects, prising things open, etc. **3** a handle for operating a machine. **4** anything that can be used to gain an advantage. — *v* **-r-** (*tr*) to move or open using a lever. [Lat *levare*, to raise]

leverage *n* **1** the mechanical power or advantage gained by using a lever. **2** the action of a lever. **3** power or advantage over someone.

leveret *n* a young hare. [Lat *lepus*, hare]

leviathan *n* **1** (*Bible*) a sea-monster. **2** anything which is large or powerful. [Hebr *liwyathan*]

Levis® *n* (*pl*) heavy, close-fitting jeans with points of particular strain made stronger by rivets.

levitate *v* (*tr* & *intr*) to (cause to) float in the air, esp. through supernatural power or spiritualism. — *n* **levitation**. [Lat *levis*, light, on the model of *gravitate*]

levity *n* lack of seriousness, esp. when this is necessary. [Lat *levitas*, lightness]

levy *v* **-ies, -ied** (*tr*) to raise or collect, esp. an army or a tax. — *n* **1** the act of levying. **2** soldiers or money collected by order. [Lat *levare*, to raise]

lewd *adj* feeling or expressing crude sexual desire or lust; obscene, indecent. — *adv* **lewdly**. — *n* **lewdness**. [OE *læwede*, unlearned]

lexical *adj* **1** of or relating to the words of a language. **2** of or relating to a lexicon. — *adv* **lexically**. [Gr *lexis*, word]

lexicography *n* the writing of dictionaries. — *n* **lexicographer**. — *adj* **lexicographic**. [Gr *lexis*, word]

lexicon *n* **1** a dictionary. **2** the vocabulary of an individual person, branch of knowledge or language. [Gr *lexikon*, from *lexis*, word]

Leyden jar *n* a glass jar coated inside and out with layers of metal foil, used as an early form of electricity condenser. [*Leyden* (now Leiden) in the Netherlands, where it was invented in the 18th century]

Li *symbol* (*chem*) lithium.

liability *n* **-ies** **1** (**for**) the state of being legally liable or responsible for something. **2** a debt or obligation. **3** a person or thing one is responsible for. **4** a person or thing which is or causes a problem. [**liable**]

liable *adj* **1** (**for**) legally bound or responsible. **2** (with **to**) likely to have, get, suffer from, etc. **3** (**to**) possibly or probably about to happen: *liable to snow heavily*. [OFr *lier*, to bind]

liaise *v* (*intr*; **between, with**) to have or establish a close working relationship with or between other people. [Back-formation from **liaison**]

liaison *n* **1** communication or co-operation between groups. **2** a sexual or romantic relationship which is kept secret and is usu. illicit, e.g. adulterous. [Fr]

liana *n* a climbing, twisting plant found in tropical forests. [Fr *liane*]

liar *n* a person who tells lies, esp. as a habit. [**lie**[1]]

Lib *abbrev* Liberal.

lib *n* (*coll*) liberation, used esp. in the names of movements, e.g. *gay lib*. [Abbrev.]

libation *n* **1** the pouring out of wine, etc. in honour of a god. **2** the drink so poured. [Lat *libare*, to pour]

libel *n* **1** (*legal*) the publication of a false statement which damages a person's good reputation. ◇ See also **slander**. **2** any false, damaging or unflattering description of a person. — *v* **-ll-** (*tr*) **1** (*legal*) to publish a libel against. **2** to accuse wrongly and spitefully. [Lat *libellus*, little book]

libellous *adj* containing or forming a libel. — *adv* **libellously**.

liberal *adj* **1** given or giving generously, freely or abundantly. **2** tolerant of different opinions; open-minded. **3** in favour of social and political reform. **4** (*cap*) of the Liberal Party. **5** (of an education) aiming at developing general cultural interests and broadening the mind. **6** free from restraint: *a liberal translation*. **7** free from dogma, etc. — *n* **1** a liberal person. **2** (*cap*) a member or supporter of the Liberal Party, a radical UK political party influential esp. in the 19th century and early years of the 20th century, which combined with the Social Democratic Party in 1988 to form the Social and Liberal Democratic Party (later the Liberal Democrats); a member or supporter of any other Liberal Party. — *adv* **liberally**. [Lat *liberalis*, from *liber*, free]

liberalise or **-ize** *v* (*tr* & *intr*) to make or become more liberal and less strict. — *n* **liberalisation** or **-z-**.

liberalism *n* liberal moral, religious or (often *cap*) political views.

liberality *n* **-ies** **1** the quality of being generous. **2** the quality of being open-minded and free from prejudice.

liberate *v* (*tr*) **1** to set free. **2** to free (a country) from enemy occupation. **3** (*chem*) to give off (a gas). — *n* **liberation**. — *n* **liberator**.

liberated *adj* **1** not bound by traditional ideas about sexuality and morality. **2** freed from enemy occupation.

liberation theology *n* a development of Christian doctrine which emphasises a commitment to liberation from social, political and economic oppression.

libertine *n* (*old*) a person, esp. a man, who leads a life not bound by the generally accepted rules of morality. — *adj* leading such a life; dissolute; promiscuous. [Lat *libertinus*, freed-man]

liberty *n* **-ies** **1** freedom from captivity or from slavery. **2** freedom to do, think, speak, etc. as one pleases. **3** (usu. in *pl*) a natural right or privilege. **4** an action, speech, etc. thought of as over-familiar, presumptuous or insolent. — **at liberty** **1** free from prison or control. **2** allowed or permitted (to). — **take liberties (with)** to treat (someone) with or behave with too much freedom or familiarity. — **take the liberty** to do or venture to do, usu. without permission. [Lat *libertas*]

libidinous *adj* lustful. [Lat *libido*, desire]

libido *n* **-os** a vital urge or impulse, esp. the sexual urge. — *adj* **libidinal**. [Lat, desire]

Libra *n* **1** a constellation and the seventh sign of the zodiac, the Scales. **2** a person born between 23 September and 22 October, under this sign. — *n* & *adj* **Libran**. [Lat, pound weight]

library *n* **-ies** **1** a collection of books, either for public or private use. **2** the room or rooms or building which house(s) such a collection. **3** a similar collection of films, records, etc., or the place where it is kept. **4** a group of books published as a series. **5** a collection of computer programs stored on disks. [Lat *librarium*, book-case]

librarian *n* a person who is employed in or in charge of a library. — *n* **librarianship**.

libretto *n* **-ti** or **-tos** the words or text of an opera, oratorio or musical. [Ital, little book]

librettist *n* a person who writes the words for operas, etc.

lice. See **louse**.

licence or (*US*) **license** *n* **1** (a document giving) official permission (to own a dog, gun, television, etc., or to do something such as sell alcohol). **2** permission or leave. **3** excessive freedom of action or speech. **4** a departure from a rule or convention, esp. by writers and artists, for effect: *poetic licence*. [Lat *licentia*, from *licere*, to be allowed]

license *v* (*tr*) to give a licence or permit for (something) or to (someone). [**licence**, altered by analogy with verbs that end in *-se*]

licensed *adj* (of a shop, hotel, etc.) legally allowed to sell alcohol to customers.

licensee *n* a person to whom a licence is given, esp. to sell alcohol.

licentiate *n* **1** a person who holds a certificate of competence allowing him or her to practise a profession. **2** a person licensed to preach in the Presbyterian church. [Lat *licentia*, licence]

licentious *adj* immoral or promiscuous. — *adv* **licentiously**. — *n* **licentiousness**. [Lat *licentia*, licence]

lichee. Same as **lychee**.

lichen *n* any of a large group of simple plants formed from fungi and algae, which grow in patches on stones, trees and soil. [Gr *leichen*]

lichgate *n* a gate with a roof over it in a wall around a church, where orig. a coffin would wait for the arrival of a member of the clergy. [OE *lic*, corpse + **gate**]

licit *adj* lawful; permitted. — *adv* **licitly**. [Lat *licitus*]

lick *v* (*tr*) **1** to pass the tongue over to moisten, taste or clean. **2** to flicker over or around. **3** (*coll*) to defeat. **4** (*coll*) to beat or hit repeatedly. — *n* **1** an act of licking with the tongue. **2** (*coll*) a small amount. **3** (*coll*) a quick speed: *at a lick*. **4** (*coll*) a sharp blow. — **a lick and a promise** (*coll*) a short and not very thorough wash. — **lick into shape** (*coll*) to make more efficient or satisfactory. — **lick one's wounds** to recover after having been thoroughly defeated or humiliated. [OE *liccian*]

licorice (*US*). Same as **liquorice**.

lid *n* **1** a removable or hinged cover for a pot, box, etc. **2** an eyelid. — *adj* **lidded**. [OE *hlid*, covering]

lido *n* **-os 1** a fashionable beach. **2** a public open-air swimming pool. [Ital *Lido*, an island in the Venice lagoon which has a fashionable beach]

lie[1] *n* **1** a false statement made with the intention of deceiving. **2** anything misleading; a fraud: *live a lie*. — *v* ***lying*** (*intr*) **1** to say things which are not true with the intention of deceiving. **2** to give a wrong or false impression: *The camera never lies*. — **give the lie to 1** to accuse (someone) of lying. **2** to show (a statement, etc.) to be false. ◇ See also **liar**. [OE *lyge*]

lie detector *n* a machine which is attached to a person's body during questioning to measure changes in blood pressure and pulse, both of which are thought to increase when one is lying.

lie[2] *v* ***lying***, ***lay***, ***lain*** (*intr*) **1** to be in or take on a flat or more or less horizontal position on a supporting surface. **2** (of subjects for discussion) to remain undiscussed: *let matters lie*. **3** to be or remain in a particular, esp. hidden, state: *lie dormant*. **4** (**with**) to exist or rest with: *The responsibility lies with you*. **5** to be situated. **6** to stretch or be spread out to view: *The harbour lay before us*. **7** (**in**) to consist in or have as an essential part: *Success lies in hard work*. — *n* **1** the way or direction in which something is lying. **2** an animal's or bird's hiding-place. — *v* **lie back** (*intr*) **1** to lean back on a support. **2** to rest, esp. after a period of hard work. — *v* **lie down** (*intr*) to take a flat or horizontal position, esp. to sleep or have a short rest (*n* **lie-down**). — *v* **lie in** (*intr*) **1** to stay in bed late in the morning (*n* **lie-in**). **2** (*old*) to be in bed giving birth to a child (*n* **lying-in**, ***lyings-in***). — **lie in wait (for)** to wait in ambush (for). — **lie low** to stay quiet or hidden. — **the lie of the land** the current state of affairs. — **see how the land lies** to find out all the facts before taking a decision which will affect one. — **take (something) lying down** to accept (a decision, insult, etc.) without protest. [OE *licgan*]

lie-down see **lie down** above.

lie-in see **lie in** above.

lieder *n* (*pl*) German songs, esp. romantic ones, for solo voice and piano. [Ger, songs]

liege (*hist*) *adj* **1** entitled to receive feudal service or homage from a vassal. **2** bound to give feudal service or homage to a superior. — *n* **1** (also **liege lord**) a feudal superior, lord or sovereign. **2** a feudal subject or vassal. [OFr *lige*]

lien *n* (*legal*) a right to keep another person's property until the owner pays a debt. [OFr *loien*, from Lat *ligamen*, bond]

lieu: **in lieu of** in place of or instead of. [Fr, place]

Lieut *abbrev* Lieutenant.

lieutenant *n* **1** a deputy acting for a superior. **2** an officer in the British army with the rank next below captain. **3** an officer in the British navy with the rank next below lieutenant commander. **4** (*US*) a police officer or fireman with the rank next below captain. — *n* **lieutenancy**, ***-ies***. [Fr, from *lieu*, place + *tenant*, holding]

lieutenant colonel, **commander** or **general** *n* an officer with the rank next below colonel, commander or general.

life *n* ***lives*** **1** the quality or state which distinguishes living animals and plants from dead ones and from matter such as rocks, stones, etc. which have never been alive, including the ability to grow, develop and change. **2** the period between birth and death, between birth and the present time or between the present time and death. **3** the length of time a thing exists or is able to function: *a battery with a long life*. **4** living things as a group: *marine life*. **5** the condition of being alive as a living person: *many lives lost in war*. **6** a way or manner of living: *a joyless life*. **7** an aspect of one's life: *one's love-life*. **8** liveliness; energy; high spirits: *full of life*. **9** a source of liveliness, energy or high spirits: *the life and soul of the party*. **10** a written account of a person's life. **11** (*coll*) a prison sentence for life, now usu. taken to mean about fifteen years. **12** any of a number of opportunities of remaining in a game: *Each player starts with four lives*. — **as large as life** (*coll*) in person; real and living. — **bring to life** to make lively or interesting. — **come to life** to become lively or interesting. — **for life**

until death. — **a matter of life and death** an extremely important or urgent matter. — **not on your life** (*coll*) on no account. — **take one's life in one's hands** to take a very important decision which will have serious consequences for oneself; to put one's life at risk. — **to the life** exactly like the original. [OE *lif*]

life-and-death *adj* extremely serious or critical, (as if) deciding whether someone will live or die.

life assurance or **insurance** *n* insurance which will be paid to the policy-holder on reaching a certain age, or to the policy-holder's dependants in the case of his or her death.

lifebelt *n* a ring or belt which floats in water, used to support people in danger of drowning.

lifeblood *n* **1** the blood necessary for life. **2** anything which is an essential part or factor.

lifeboat *n* **1** a boat for rescuing people in trouble at sea. **2** a small boat, usu. one of several, on a much larger ship, for use in emergencies.

lifebuoy *n* a float for supporting a person in the water until he or she can be rescued.

life-cycle *n* the various stages through which a living thing passes.

life expectancy *n* the length of time a person in a given society and at a particular time can expect to live.

lifeguard *n* an expert swimmer employed at a swimming-pool or beach to rescue people in danger of drowning.

Life Guards *n* (*pl*) a British army regiment which guards the monarch, esp. on ceremonial occasions.

life-jacket *n* an inflatable, sleeveless jacket for supporting a person in the water until he or she can be rescued.

lifeless *adj* **1** dead. **2** unconscious. **3** having no energy or vivacity; dull and boring. — *adv* **lifelessly**. — *n* **lifelessness**.

lifelike *adj* very like the person or thing represented.

lifeline *n* **1** a rope for support in dangerous operations or for saving lives. **2** a vital means of communication or support.

lifelong *adj* lasting the whole length of a life.

life peer or **peeress** *n* a peer whose title is not hereditary.

lifer *n* (*slang*) a person sent to prison for life.

life raft *n* a raft kept on a ship, for use in emergencies.

life-saving *n* the act or skill of rescuing people who are drowning. — *n* **life-saver**.

life sciences *n* (*pl*) sciences concerned with living animals, plants or organisms, such as biology and zoology.

life-size or **-sized** *adj* (of a copy, drawing, etc.) as large as the original.

lifestyle *n* a person's or group's way of living.

life-support *adj* (of equipment) allowing a person to live, e.g. in an unfavourable environment such as space, or when seriously ill.

lifetime *n* the length of time a person is alive.

lift *v* **1** (*tr* & *intr*) to raise or rise to a higher position. **2** (*tr*) to move (esp. one's eyes or face) upwards. **3** (*tr*) to take and carry away. **4** (*tr*) to raise to a better, happier, etc. level: *lift her spirits*. **5** (*intr*) (of cloud, fog, etc.) to clear. **6** (*tr*) to remove (a barrier or restriction). **7** (*tr*) to dig up (crops growing in the ground, e.g. potatoes). **8** (*tr*; *coll*) to plagiarise. — *n* **1** an act of lifting. **2** the upward force of the air on an aircraft, etc. **3** (*Br*) a compartment which moves up and down in a vertical shaft between the floors of a building transporting people and goods. **3** a ride in a person's car or other vehicle. **4** a boost to the spirits or sudden feeling of happiness. — *v* **lift off** (*intr*) (of a spacecraft) to rise, esp. vertically, from the ground (*n* **lift-off**). [Norse *lypta*]

ligament *n* (*anat*) a band of tough tissue that joins bones and cartilages together. [Lat *ligare*, to bind]

ligature *n* **1** anything that binds or ties. **2** a thread, etc. for tying, esp. blood vessels during surgery. **3** (*mus*) a smooth link between two or more notes. **4** (*printing*) a character formed from two or more characters joined together. — *v* (*tr*) to bind with a ligature. [Lat *ligare*, to bind]

light[1] *n* **1** the natural power, electromagnetic radiation, which makes sight possible and things visible. **2** any source of light, such as the sun, a lamp, a candle, etc. **3** an appearance of brightness; a shine or gleam: *see a light away in the distance*. **4** daylight; dawn. **5** a particular quality or amount of light: *a good light for taking photographs*. **6** (usu. in *pl*) a traffic light: *turn left at the lights*. **7** a flame or spark for igniting. **8** a means of producing a flame for igniting, such as a match. **9** a way in which something is thought of or regarded: *see the problem in a new light*. **10** a glow in the eyes or on the face as a sign of energy, liveliness, happiness or excitement. **11** sudden understanding or spiritual insight: *see the light*. **12** an eminent person: *a leading light*. **13** (in *pl*) a person's mental ability, knowledge or understanding: *act according to one's lights*. **14** an opening in a wall that lets in light, such as a window. — *adj* **1** having light; not dark. **2** (of a colour) pale; closer to white than black. — *v* ***lit*** or ***lighted*** **1** (*tr*) to bring light to: *light the stage*. **2** (*tr* & *intr*) to (cause to) begin to burn: *light the fire*. **3** (*tr*) to guide or show (someone) the way, or (someone's way), using a light or torch. — *n* **lightness**. — **bring to light** to make known or cause to be noticed. — **come to light** to be made known or discovered. — **in the light of** taking into consideration. — *v* **light up 1** (*tr* & *intr*) to (cause to) become bright: *light up the streets*. **2** (*tr* & *intr*) to make or become bright, sparkling with liveliness, happiness or excitement. **3** (*tr* & *intr*; *coll*) to light (a cigarette, etc.) and begin smoking. — **see the light of day 1** to be born, discovered or produced. **2** to come to public notice. — **shed** or **throw light on** to make clear or help to explain. [OE *leoht*]

light-bulb *n* a hollow, pear-shaped glass device that gives out light when an electric current passes through it.

light-emitting diode see **LED**.

lighten *v* **1** (*tr* & *intr*) to make or become brighter. **2** (*tr*) to cast light on. **3** (*intr*) to shine or glow.

lighter *n* a device for lighting cigarettes, etc.

lighthouse *n* a building on the coast with a flashing light to guide ships or warn them of rocks, etc.

lighting *n* **1** equipment for providing light. **2** the quality or type of light produced.

lighting-up time *n* the time of day at which vehicles must have their lights turned on.

light meter *n* a meter for measuring the amount of light present, used esp. when taking photographs.

light pen *n* (*comput*) a pen-like device that can change or add to the data displayed on a visual display unit.

lightship *n* a ship which acts as a lighthouse.

light-year *n* the distance light travels in a year, nearly six million million miles.

light[2] *adj* **1** of little weight; easy to lift or carry. **2** low in weight, amount or density: *light rain*. **3** easy to bear, suffer or do: *light work*. **4** of less weight than is correct or proper. **5** having only light weapons or equipment: *light infantry*. **6** without problems, sorrow, etc.; cheerful: *a light heart*. **7** graceful and quick; nimble: *a light skip*. **8** not serious or profound, but for amusement only: *light reading*. **9** thoughtless, silly and trivial: *a light remark*. **10** not thinking clearly or seriously; giddy: *a light head*. **11** (of food) easily digested. **12** (*tech*) (of wine) with an alcohol content of between 5·5% and 15% by volume. **13** (*loosely*) (of wine) with a delicate, fresh flavour. **14** (of cakes, etc.) spongy and well risen. **15** (of soil) loose and sandy. **16** (of a vehicle or ship) designed to carry light loads only. **17** (of a ship) unloaded. — *adv* **1** in a light manner. **2** with little luggage: *travel light*. — *adv* **lightly**. — *n* **lightness**. — **get off lightly** to escape without severe punishment. — **make light of** to treat as not important. [OE *leoht*]

lighten *v* **1** (*tr* & *intr*) to make or become less heavy. **2** (*tr* & *intr*) to make or become happier or more cheerful. **3** (*tr*) to make (a problem, unhappy mood, etc.) less: *lighten her sadness*.

lighter-than-air *adj* (of aircraft) weighing less than the air it displaces.

light-fingered *adj* likely to steal.

light-headed *adj* **1** with a head which feels as if it is spinning. **2** thoughtless and silly; frivolous. — *adv* **light-headedly**. — *n* **light-headedness**.

light-hearted *adj* **1** (of a person) happy and free from worry. **2** not serious; cheerful and amusing. — *adv* **light-heartedly**. — *n* **light-heartedness**.

lightweight *adj* **1** light in weight. **2** with little importance, influence or authority. — *n* **1** a person or thing with little importance, influence or authority. **2** any person or thing not weighing very much. **3** a class for boxers, wrestlers and weight-lifters of not more than a specified weight (61·2 kg in professional boxing, different but similar weights in amateur boxing and the other sports). **4** a boxer, etc. of this class. — *adj* (for contestants) of the prescribed weight.

light[3] *v* ***lit*** or ***lighted*** (*intr*) **1** (with **on**, **upon**) to come upon or find by chance. **2** (**on**) (esp. of birds) to come to rest after flight. [OE *lihtan*, to alight]

lighter[1]. See **light**[1].

lighter[2] *n* a large, open boat used for transferring goods between ships, or between a ship and a wharf. [OE *lihtan*, to relieve of a weight]

lightning *n* a flash of light caused by electricity between clouds or between a cloud and the earth, esp. during a storm. — *adj* very quick and sudden. **[light**[1]**]**

lightning-conductor *n* a metal rod attached to a building or a ship's mast, which channels lightning to the ground or into the sea, thus protecting the building or ship from lightning.

lights *n* (*pl*) the lungs of an animal, used for food. **[light**[2]**]**

ligneous *adj* of, relating to or like wood. [Lat *lignum*, wood]

lignite *n* a soft brown coal with a structure somewhere between peat and coal, used as fuel. [Lat *lignum*, wood]

like[1] *adj* **1** similar; resembling. **2** typical of: *It's just like him to forget*. **3** in the correct state or mood for: *feel like a drink*. — *prep* in the same manner as; to the same extent as: *run like a deer*. — *adv* **1** (*old* or *dialect*) likely: *She'll be on time, like as not*. **2** (*old*) in the same manner. — *conj* **1** (*coll*) as if: *look like you've been awake all night*. **2** as: *not pretty like you are*. — *n* the equal of a person or thing: *compare like with like*. — **the like** a thing or things of the same kind: *hills, mountains and the like*. — **the likes of** people or things such as. [OE *gelic*, alike]

-like *in cmpds* resembling, suitable for or characteristic of: *childlike*.

likelihood *n* probability. — **in all likelihood** very probably.

likely *adj* **1** probable. **2** suitable or useful for a particular purpose: *a likely spot for a picnic*. — *adv* probably. — *n* **likeliness**. —

as likely as not probably. — **not likely** (*coll*) absolutely not.

like-minded *adj* having similar opinions, tastes or purpose. — *n* **like-mindedness**.

liken *v* **-n-** (*tr*; **to**) to think or speak of (something) as being similar (to something else).

likeness *n* **1** a similarity. **2** a person or thing which is like someone or something else. **3** a portrait: *have one's likeness taken.*

likewise *adv* **1** in the same or a similar manner. **2** also.

like[2] *v* (*tr*) **1** to be pleased with; to find pleasant or agreeable. **2** to be fond of. **3** to prefer: *She likes her tea without sugar.* **4** to wish, or wish for: *Would you like to help?* — *n* (usu. in *pl*) a thing liked: *likes and dislikes.* [OE *lician*, to please]

likeable or **likable** *adj* easy to like; lovable; pleasant.

liking *n* **1** a taste or preference: *have a liking for chocolates.* **2** satisfaction.

lilac *n* a small tree or shrub which has bunches of white or pale pinkish-purple, sweet-smelling flowers. — *adj* pale pinkish-purple in colour. [Persian *nilak*, bluish, from *nil*, blue]

Lilliputian *n* a very small person or thing. — *adj* very small. [*Lilliput*, an imaginary country inhabited by tiny people in Swift's *Gulliver's Travels*]

Lilo® *n* an inflatable mattress.

lilt *n* **1** a light, graceful, swinging rhythm. **2** a tune, song or voice with such a rhythm. **3** a springing, swinging quality when walking. — *v* (*intr*) to speak, sing or move with a lilt. — *adj* **lilting**. [MidE *lulte*]

lily *n* **-ies 1** a plant grown from a bulb, with white or coloured trumpet-shaped flowers growing at the end of a tall stem. **2** any of several other flowering plants, such as the water lily. **3** any person or thing considered exceptionally pure. — *adj* pale; white. [Lat *lilium*]

lily-livered *adj* cowardly.

lily-of-the-valley *n* a spring plant with small, sweet-smelling, white bell-shaped flowers.

lily-white *adj* pure white; faultless.

lima bean *n* a flat, white edible bean from tropical America. [*Lima* in Peru]

limb[1] *n* **1** an arm, leg or wing. **2** a main branch on a tree. **3** a branch or section of a larger organisation. — *adj* **limbed**. — *adj* **limbless**. — **out on a limb** isolated, in a dangerous or hazardous position, usu. because of having ideas or opinions not accepted by others. [OE *lim*]

limb[2] *n* **1** the edge of the disk of the sun, moon or a planet. **2** (*bot*) the expanded, blade-like part of a leaf or petal. [Lat *limbus*, border]

limber[1] *adj* flexible and supple. — *v* **limber up -r-** (*tr* & *intr*) to stretch and warm up (oneself or a part of the body) before exercise. [Perhaps from **limb**[1]]

limber[2] *n* the detachable front part of a gun carriage, consisting of an axle, pole and two wheels. — *v* **-r-** (*tr*) to attach (a gun) to a limber. [MidE *lymour*, the pole of a vehicle]

limbo[1] *n* **-os 1** an area between heaven and hell, reserved for the unbaptised dead. **2** a state of waiting, either before a decision is taken or because one has been forgotten or ignored: *in limbo.* **3** a place of oblivion or neglect. [Lat *in limbo*, from *in*, in + *limbus*, border]

limbo[2] *n* **-os** a West Indian dance in which the dancer leans backwards to dance under a rope or bar which is moved lower and lower towards the floor. [Jamaican English *limba*, to bend]

lime[1] *n* a white substance, calcium oxide, produced by heating limestone and used for making cement and spreading on ground which is too acidic. — *v* (*tr*) to cover (land) with lime. — *adj* **limy**, **-ier**, **-iest**. [OE *lim*]

limekiln *n* a kiln for heating limestone to produce lime.

limelight *n* **1** a bright white light produced by heating a block of lime in a flame, used formerly in theatres. **2** the glare of publicity: *in the limelight.*

limestone *n* a rock made mainly of calcium.

lime[2] *n* **1** a small, round, sour-tasting, green citrus fruit. **2** (also **lime green**) the green colour of this fruit. — *adj* **limy**, **-ier**, **-iest**. [Persian *limun*]

lime[3] *n* **1** (also **lime-tree** and **linden**) a tree with rough bark, heart-shaped leaves and sweet-smelling yellow blossom. **2** the wood from this tree. [OE *lind*, linden]

limelight. See **lime**[1].

limerick *n* a humorous poem of five lines with an *aabba* rhyme-scheme. [Said to be from *Will you come up to Limerick?*, a refrain sung between comic verses at a party]

limey *n* **-eys** (*NAm slang*) a British person, orig. a British sailor or ship. [**lime**[2], because of the use of lime-juice on British navy ships to prevent scurvy]

limit *n* **1** a point, degree or amount beyond which something does not or may not pass. **2** (often in *pl*) the boundary or edge of an area. **3** the greatest or smallest extent, degree, etc. allowed. **4** (with **the**; *coll*) an intolerable or extremely annoying person or thing. — *v* **-t-** (*tr*) to be a limit or boundary to; to restrict. — *adj* **limitless**. — **within limits** with a moderate degree of freedom only. [Lat *limes*, boundary]

limitation *n* **1** an act of limiting or the condition of being limited. **2** (often in *pl*) a person's weakness, lack of ability, etc. which sets a limit on what he or she can achieve: *know one's limitations.* **3** (*legal*) a period of time within which an action must be brought.

limited *adj* **1** having a limit or limits. **2** not great: *limited understanding of the problem.*

limited (liability) company *n* a business company owned by shareholders who are responsible for its debts only to the extent of the money they have put into it.

limited edition *n* an edition of a book, art print, etc. of which only a certain number of copies are printed or made.

limo *n* **-os** (*coll*) a limousine. [Abbrev.]

limousine *n* a large, luxurious motor car, esp. one with a screen separating the driver and passengers. [Fr, orig. a cloak worn in *Limousin*, a province in France]

limp[1] *v* (*intr*) **1** to walk with an awkward or uneven step, because one leg is weak or injured. **2** (of a damaged ship or aircraft) to move with difficulty. — *n* a limping walk. — *n* & *adj* **limping**. — *adv* **limpingly**. [OE *lempheal**t*]

limp[2] *adj* **1** not stiff or firm; hanging loosely. **2** without energy or vitality; drooping. **3** (of a book) with a soft cover not stiffened by boards. — *adv* **limply**. — *n* **limpness**.

limpet *n* **1** a small shellfish with a cone-shaped shell, which fastens itself very firmly to rocks. **2** a person it is difficult to get rid of. [OE *lempedu*]

limpet mine *n* a mine which attaches itself to its target with a magnet.

limpid *adj* (of water, the air, eyes, etc.) clear. — *n* **limpidity** or **limpidness**. — *adv* **limpidly**. [Lat *limpidus*]

linage *n* **1** the number of lines to a page. **2** payment by the line. [**line**[1]]

linchpin *n* **1** a pin-shaped rod passed through an axle to keep a wheel on. **2** a person or thing essential to a business, plan, etc. [OE *lynis*]

Lincs. *abbrev* Lincolnshire.

linctus *n* **-uses** (*Br*) a syrup-like medicine which helps soothe a sore throat. [Lat, licking]

linden. See **lime**[3].

line[1] *n* **1** a long, narrow mark, streak or stripe. **2** the use of such lines in art. **3** (a length of) thread, rope, wire, etc., esp. for a particular purpose: *a fishing-line*. **4** a wrinkle or furrow, esp. on the skin. **5** the path which a moving object is considered to leave behind it, having length but no breadth. **6** (often in *pl*) an outline or shape, esp. as part of the design: *clean lines of a car*. **7** a row. **8** a row of words. **9** (in *pl*) the words of an actor's part. **10** (in *pl*) an amount of text to be written as a punishment at school. **11** any one of the five horizontal marks forming a musical stave. **12** a series of notes forming a melody. **13** (*coll*) a short letter or note: *drop him a line*. **14** a series or group of people which come one after the other, esp. in the same family or profession: *come from a long line of doctors*. **15** a field of activity, interest, study or work: *one's line of business*. **16** a course or way of acting, behaving, thinking or reasoning: *think along different lines*. **17** (the rules or limits of) acceptable behaviour: *toe the line*. **18** a group or class of goods for sale. **19** the manufacturing process: *a production line*. **20** (esp. *US*) a boundary: *the county line*. **21** a point of change or development: *the dividing line between genius and madness*. **22** one of several white marks showing a pitch, race-track, etc. on a field. **23** a single track for a railway or trams; a branch or route of a railway system. **24** a route, track or direction of movement: *line of fire*. **25** a continuous system, e.g. of telephone cables, connecting one place with another. **26** a telephone connection: *not be able to get a line to Kent*. **27** a company running regular services of ships, buses or aircraft between two or more places. **28** an arrangement of troops or ships side by side and ready to fight. **29** a connected series of military defences: *behind enemy lines*. **30** the regular army. **31** one of several narrow horizontal bands forming a television picture. **32** (*NAm*) a queue. **33** (in *pl*; also **marriage lines**) a marriage licence. — *v* (*tr*) **1** to mark or cover with lines. **2** to form a line along. — **all along the line** at every point. — **get a line on** (*coll*) to get information about. — **hard lines!** (*coll*) bad luck! — **in line for** likely to get: *in line for promotion*. — **lay it on the line** to speak frankly. — **lay** or **put (something) on the line** to risk (esp. one's reputation or career) on. — *v* **line up 1** (*tr* & *intr*) to bring into or form a line. **2** (*tr* & *intr*) to organise or be organised: *line herself up a new job*. **3** (*intr*; **for, against**) to make a stand in support of or against. — **read between the lines** to understand something from a piece of writing which is not actually stated. [OFr *ligne*, combined with OE *line*, rope]

lined *adj* having lines.

line drawing *n* a drawing in pen or pencil using lines only.

line printer *n* a printer attached to a computer which prints a line at a time rather than a character at a time.

liner *n* a large passenger ship or aircraft.

linesman *n* an official at a boundary line in some sports, e.g. soccer, whose job is to indicate when the ball has gone out of play.

line-up *n* **1** an arrangement of things or people in line. **2** a list of people selected for a sports team, or appearing in a show. **3** an identity parade.

line[2] *v* (*tr*; **with**) **1** to cover the inside of (a garment, box, etc.) with some other material. **2** to cover as if with a lining: *line the walls with books*. **3** (*coll*) to fill, esp. with large amounts. — *adj* **lined**. [OE *lin*, flax]

liner *n* something used for lining: *bin-liner*.

lining *n* a piece of material, etc. used to line garments, boxes, etc.

lineage *n* ancestry. [Lat *linea*, line[1]]

lineal *adj* **1** (of a member of a family) in a direct line of descent. **2** of or in lines. — *adv* **lineally**. [Lat *linealis*, from *linea*, line[1]]

lineament *n* (usu. in *pl*) a feature or distinguishing mark, esp. of the face. [Lat *linea*, line[1]]

linear *adj* **1** of, consisting of or like a line or lines. **2** relating to length. — *n* **linearity**. [Lat *linea*, line[1]]

lineation *n* **1** the act of marking with lines. **2** an arrangement of lines. [Lat *linea*, line[1]]

linen *n* **1** cloth made from flax. **2** household articles such as sheets, tablecloths, tea-towels, etc. orig. made from linen, now more likely to be made from cotton, nylon, etc. **3** underclothes, orig. made from linen. — *adj* of or like linen. — **wash one's dirty linen in public** to let one's most personal and intimate problems and quarrels become generally known. [OE, from *lin*, flax]

liner. See **line**[1] and **line**[2].

ling[1] *n* ***ling*** or ***lings*** a fish of the cod family with a long, slender body. [MidE]

ling[2] *n* heather. [Norse *lyng*]

-ling *sfx* **1** a young, small or minor person or thing: *duckling*; *princeling*. **2** (sometimes *derog*) a person: *weakling*; *earthling*; *underling*.

linger *v* ***-r-*** (*intr*) **1** to be slow to depart; to delay. **2** (of a dying person) to die very slowly. **3** (**over**) to spend a long time with or doing something. — *n* **lingerer**. — *adj* **lingering**. — *adv* **lingeringly**. [OE *lengan*, to lengthen]

lingerie *n* women's underwear and night-clothes. [Fr, from Lat *linum*, flax]

lingo *n* ***-oes*** (*coll*; often *derog*) **1** language. **2** the specialised vocabulary used by a particular group of people or profession: *medical lingo*. [Lat *lingua*, tongue, language]

lingua franca *n* ***lingua francas*** **1** a language, or often a simplified form of it, used as a means of mutual communication by speakers of other languages. **2** any system or set of conventions which are readily and easily understood. **3** (*hist*) Italian with a mixture of French, Spanish, Greek and Arabic words, used in the eastern part of the Mediterranean for trade. [Ital, Frankish language]

lingual *adj* **1** of or pronounced using the tongue. **2** of speech or languages. — *adv* **lingually**. [Lat *lingua*, tongue, language]

linguist *n* **1** a person who has a good knowledge of languages. **2** a person who studies linguistics. [Lat *lingua*, tongue, language]

linguistic *adj* of language or linguistics. — *adv* **linguistically**.

linguistics *n* (*sing*) the scientific study of language.

liniment *n* a kind of thin, oily cream for rubbing into the skin to ease muscle pain. [Lat *linimentum*]

link *n* **1** a ring of a chain. **2** any person or thing that connects. **3** a means of communication or travel. **4** a cuff-link. **5** a unit of measurement, equal to one hundredth of a surveyor's chain, 7·92 inches (*c.* 20 cm). — *v* **1** (*tr*) to connect or join. **2** (*intr*) to be or become connected. — *v* **link up** (*tr* & *intr*) to join or be joined closely or by a link. [Norse]

link-up *n* a connection or union, esp. of two different systems.

links *n* **1** (*pl*) a stretch of more or less flat ground along a shore near the sea. **2** (*sing* or *pl*) a golf course by the sea. [OE *hlinc*, ridge]

linnet *n* a small brown song-bird. [OFr *linette*, from Lat *linum*, flax, so called because it feeds on flax seeds]

lino *n* ***-os*** (*coll*) linoleum.

linocut *n* **1** a design cut in relief in linoleum. **2** a print made from this.

linoleum *n* a smooth, hard-wearing covering for floors, made of canvas coated with linseed oil and cork. [Lat *linum*, flax + *oleum*, oil]

linseed *n* the seed of flax. [OE *linsæd*]

linseed oil *n* oil made from this seed, used in industry, e.g. for making paint.

lint *n* **1** linen or cotton with a raised nap on one side, for dressing wounds. **2** fine, very small pieces of wool, cotton, etc.; fluff. [MidE *lynt*]

lintel *n* a horizontal wooden or stone beam placed over a doorway or window. [OFr, from Lat *limes*, boundary, border]

lion *n* **1** a large, flesh-eating animal of the cat family, with a tawny yellow coat. **2** the male of this species. **3** a brave or celebrated person. **4** (*cap* with **the**) the constellation and sign of the zodiac Leo. — **the lion's share** the largest share. [Gr *leon*]

lioness *n* **1** a female lion. **2** a brave or celebrated woman.

lion-hearted *adj* very brave.

lionise or **-ize** *v* (*tr*) to treat as a celebrity or hero. — *n* **lionisation** or **-z-**.

lip *n* **1** either of the folds of flesh which form the edge of the mouth. **2** the edge or rim of something, esp. a container for liquid. **3** (*slang*) insolence. — **bite one's lip** to control or smother one's feelings, tears, anger, etc. — **curl one's lip** to sneer scornfully. — **keep a stiff upper lip** to show no emotion or worry when faced with difficulties. — **lick** or **smack one's lips** to lick or part one's lips noisily as a sign of relish or in anticipation of pleasure. — *adj* **lipped**. [OE *lippa*]

lip-read *v* (*intr*) to understand what a person is saying despite being unable to hear them, by watching the movement of his or her lips. — *n* **lip-reader**. — *n* **lip-reading**.

lip-service: **pay lip-service to** to pretend to agree with (someone) or approve of (an idea, etc.) without really doing so.

lipstick *n* a stick of cosmetic colouring for the lips.

liposuction *n* a process for removing excess fat from the body by sucking it out mechanically through an incision in the skin. [Gr *lipos*, fat + **suction**]

liquefy *v* ***-ies***, ***-ied*** (*tr* & *intr*) to make or become liquid. — *n* **liquefaction**. [Lat *liquere*, to be liquid + *facere*, to make]

liqueur *n* any of several strong, sweet, heavily perfumed alcoholic drinks, drunk esp. at the end of a meal. [Fr, liquor]

liquid *n* **1** a substance in a water-like state. **2** (*phon*) the sound of *l* or *r*. — *adj* **1** (of a substance) able to flow and change shape; in a state between solid and gas, like water. **2** like water in appearance, esp. in being clear: *liquid blue eyes*. **3** flowing and smooth. **4** (of sounds) harmonious. **5** (of assets) able to be easily changed into cash. [Lat *liquidus*, liquid, clear]

liquid crystal *n* a liquid which, like a crystal, reflects light in different directions.

liquid crystal display *n* a display of numbers, e.g. in watches, produced by passing electrical currents through an arrangement of liquid crystals.

liquidise or **-ize** *v* (*tr*) to make (food, etc.) into a liquid or pureé.

liquidiser or **-z-** *n* a machine used in cookery to liquidise food.

liquidate *v* (*tr*) **1** to bring the trading of (a person or company) to an end, and have its debts and assets calculated. **2** to turn (assets) into cash. **3** to pay off (a debt). **4** (*slang*) to get rid of by violence; to kill. — *n* **liquidator**. [Lat *liquidare*, to make clear]

liquidation *n* **1** the bringing to an end of a company's, etc. trading. **2** (*slang*) killing. — **go into liquidation** (of a company, etc.) to stop trading and have its debts and assets calculated.

liquor *n* **1** strong alcoholic, esp. distilled, drink. **2** water or liquid produced in cooking. **3** a solution of a drug or chemical in water. [Lat, from *liquere*, to be liquid]

liquorice *n* **1** a Mediterranean plant with sweet roots used in medicine and confectionery. **2** a black, sticky sweet made from the juice of the roots of this plant. [Gr *glykys*, sweet + *rhiza*, root]

lira *n* ***lire*** or ***-ras*** the standard unit of currency in Italy and Turkey. [Ital, from Lat *libra*, pound]

lisle *n* fine, smooth cotton thread, used for making gloves, stockings and underwear. [*Lisle* (now Lille), a town in N France where it was first made]

lisp *v* **1** (*intr*) to pronounce *s* and *z* as *th*. **2** (*tr*) to say or pronounce in this way. — *n* the act or habit of lisping. — *adv* **lispingly**. [OE *wlisp*, lisping]

lissom or **lissome** *adj* graceful and supple in shape and movement. — *n* **lissomness**. [**lithe** + **-some**]

list[1] *n* **1** a series of names, numbers, prices, etc. written down or said one after the other: *shopping list*. **2** (in *pl*; *hist*) the barriers enclosing an area used for jousting and tournaments. **3** (in *pl*) any scene of combat or conflict. — *v* (*tr*) **1** to make a list of. **2** to add to a list. — **enter the lists** to give or accept a challenge; to start or become involved in a fight or controversy. [OE *liste*, border]

listed building *n* a building of particular architectural or historical interest, which may not be destroyed or changed.

list price *n* a price for an article recommended by the maker.

list[2] *v* (*intr*) (esp. of ships) to lean over to one side. — *n* the act of listing or a listing position.

listen *v* ***-n-*** (*intr*) **1** (**to, for, out**) to give attention so as to hear something. **2** (**to**) to follow advice: *I warned him but he wouldn't listen*. — *n* an act or period of listening. — *v* **listen in** (*intr*) **1** (**on**) to listen deliberately to a telephone conversation, radio message, etc. intended for someone else. **2** (*old*; **to**) to listen to a radio broadcast. [OE *hlysnan*]

listener *n* a person who listens, esp. to radio programmes.

listeria *n* a bacterium sometimes found in certain foods, e.g. chicken and soft cheese, which if not killed in cooking may cause the disease **listeriosis**, a serious disease which can cause death and miscarriage. [Joseph *Lister* (1872–1912), English surgeon and pioneer of antiseptics]

listless *adj* tired and without energy or interest. — *adv* **listlessly**. — *n* **listlessness**. [MidE *listen*, to please]

lit. See **light**[1,3].

litany *n* ***-ies*** **1** a series of prayers or supplications with a response which is repeated several times by the congregation. **2** a long, boring list: *a litany of jobs to be done*. [Gr *litaneia*, prayer]

litchi. Same as **lychee**.

liter (*US*). Same as **litre**.

literacy *n* the ability to read and write. [**literate**]

literal *adj* **1** following the exact meaning of words or a text (i.e. without allegorical or metaphorical interpretation). **2** exactly following the words of the original: *a literal translation*. **3** (of a person) unimaginative and matter-of-fact. **4** true; exact: *the literal truth*. — *n* (*printing*) a misprint of one letter. — *adv* **literally**. — *n* **literalness**. [Lat *literalis*, from *litera*, letter]

literalism *n* strict adherence to the literal meaning of words. — *n* **literalist**.

literary *adj* **1** of, relating to or concerned with literature or the writing of books. **2** (of a person) knowing a great deal about literature. **3** (of a word) formal; used in (esp. older) literature. — *n* **literariness**. [Lat *literarius*, from *litera*, letter]

literate *adj* **1** able to read and write. **2** (usu. *in cmpds*) competent and experienced in: *computer-literate*. — *n* an educated person. ◇ See also **literacy**. [Lat *literatus*, from *litera*, letter]

literati *n* (*pl*) learned people; those who know a lot about literature. [Lat *literatus*, literate]

literature *n* **1** written material of high quality, valued for its language and content, such as novels, poems and plays. **2** the whole body of written works of a particular country or period in time: *Elizabethan literature*. **3** (the whole body of) information published on a particular subject: *literature on growing tomatoes*. **4** the art or works produced by a writer. **5** (*coll*) any printed matter, esp. advertising leaflets. [Lat *literatura*, from *litera*, letter]

lithe *adj* bending easily; supple and flexible. — *adv* **lithely**. — *n* **litheness**. [OE, gentle, soft]

lithium *n* a silver-white metallic element (symbol **Li**), the lightest known metal, used in alloys. [Gr *lithos*, stone]

litho *n* **-os** lithograph or lithography. — *adj* lithographic. — *v* (*tr*) to lithograph.

lithography *n* a method of printing using a stone or metal plate which has been treated so that the ink adheres only to the design or image to be printed. — *adj* **lithographic**. — *adv* **lithographically**. [Gr *lithos*, stone + *graphein*, to write]

lithograph *n* a picture or print made using lithography. — *v* (*tr*) to print (images, etc.) using lithography. — *n* **lithographer**.

litigant *n* a person involved in a lawsuit. [**litigate**]

litigate *v* **1** (*intr*) to be involved in a lawsuit; to go to law. **2** (*tr*) to contest (a point, claim, etc.) in a lawsuit. — *n* **litigation**. [Lat *litigare*, from *lis*, lawsuit + *agere*, to do]

litigious *adj* **1** of or relating to litigation or lawsuits. **2** often taking arguments, problems, etc. to a court of law. **3** disputable in a court of law. — *adv* **litigiously**. — *n* **litigiousness**. [Lat *litigium*, quarrel]

litmus *n* a substance obtained from certain lichens, which is turned red by acids and blue by alkalis. [Norse *litmosi*, dyeing-moss]

litmus paper *n* paper treated with litmus, used to test liquids for acidity and alkalinity.

litotes *n* understatement used for effect, as in *not a little angry* meaning *furious*. [Gr, simplicity]

litre *n* a metric unit of capacity equal to one cubic decimetre, or about 1·75 pints. [Gr *litra*, pound]

litter *n* **1** a mess of paper, rubbish, etc. in a public place. **2** a scattered or confused collection of objects. **3** straw, hay, etc. used as bedding for animals. **4** a number of animals born to the same mother at the same time. **5** a framework consisting of cloth stretched tight between two long poles, used to carry the sick or wounded. **6** a framework consisting of a couch covered by curtains, with poles on either side, for transporting a single passenger. — *v* **-r- 1** (*tr*; **with**) to make (a place) untidy by spreading litter or objects: *litter the room with books*. **2** (*tr*) (of objects) to lie untidily around (a place): *books littering a room*. **3** (*tr* & *intr*) (of animals) to give birth to (a number of young). **4** (*tr*) to give bedding litter to (animals). [OFr *litiere*, from Lat *lectus*, bed]

litter-lout, *NAm* **litterbug** *n* (*coll*) a person who drops litter in public places.

little *adj* **1** small in size, extent or amount. **2** young: *a little girl*. **3** small in importance; trivial; petty: *funny little ways*. **4** small-minded or mean: *He's a little liar*. — *n* anything small in size, amount or extent: *do a little to help out*; *He'll be here in a little* (= 'soon'). — *adv* **1** (with **a**) to a small degree or extent: *run around a little to keep warm*. **2** not much or at all: *little understand the importance*. — **little by little** gradually or by degrees. — **make little of 1** to treat (something) as unimportant, not serious, etc. **2** to understand only a little of (something). — **think little of** to not have a very good opinion of. ◇ See also **least**, **less**, **lesser**. [OE *lytel*]

little end *n* the smaller end of a main connecting rod in a car engine.

little people *n* (*pl*) fairies.

little slam *n* (*cards*) esp. in bridge, the winning of all but one trick, or the contract to do so.

littoral *adj* of, on or near the shore of a sea or lake. — *n* an area of land on a shore or coast. [Lat *littoralis*, from *litus*, shore]

liturgy *n* **-ies 1** the standard form of service in a church. **2** the service of Holy Communion in the Eastern Orthodox Church. — *adj* **liturgical**. — *adv* **liturgically**. [Gr *leitourgia*, public service]

live[1] *v* **1** (*intr*) to have life; to be alive. **2** (*intr*) to continue to be alive; to survive or to escape death. **3** (*intr*; **on**) to continue or last: *The memory of the accident lives on*. **4** (*intr* with **with**) to continue to suffer from or be haunted by the memory of; to put up with: *live with the mistake for the rest of his life*. **5** (*intr*; **in**) to have one's home or dwelling. **6** (*intr*) to lead one's life in a certain way: *live well*. **7** (*intr*; **by**, **on**, **off**) to support one's life; to get a living. **8** (*tr*) to pass or spend: *live a happy life in the country*. **9** (*intr*) to enjoy life passionately or to the full: *really know how to live*. **10** (*tr*) to express in one's life or live according to: *live a lie*; *live one's religion*. — **live and let live** to be tolerant and expect toleration from others. — *v* **live down** (*tr*) to cause (a mistake, guilt, etc. in one's past) to be forgotten by living a normal and blameless life. — *v* **live in** (*intr*) to have one's home where one works. ◇ See also **live-in** below. — **live it up** (*coll*) to fill one's life with excitement and pleasure, often excessively. — **live together** (of an unmarried couple) to live as man and wife. — *v* **live up to** (*tr*) to behave in a manner worthy of: *live up to her expectations*. ◇ See also **living**. [OE *lifian*, *libban*]

liveable *adj* **1** (of a house, etc.) fit to live in. **2** (of a person) friendly and easy to live with. **3** (of life) worth living.

lived-in *adj* **1** (of a room, etc.) with a cosy, homely feeling. **2** (of a face) with wrinkles, etc. showing life's experiences.

live-in *adj* **1** (of a worker) living where one works. **2** (of a sexual partner) living in the same house, etc. as one's partner.

liver *n* a person who lives his or her life in the way stated: *a fast liver*.

live[2] *adj* **1** having life; not dead. **2** (of a radio or television broadcast) heard or seen as the event takes place and not from a recording. **3** (of a record, etc.) recorded during a performance. **4** (of a wire) connected to a source of electrical power. **5** (of coal, etc.) still glowing or burning. **6** (of a bomb, etc.) still capable of exploding. — *adv* at, during or as a live performance: *perform live on stage*. **[alive]**

livestock *n* domestic animals, esp. horses, cattle, sheep, and pigs.

live wire *n* (*coll*) a person who is full of energy and enthusiasm.

livelihood *n* a means of living, esp. of earning enough money to feed oneself, etc. [OE *liflad*, from *lif*, life + *lad*, course]

livelong *adj* (*poetic*) (of the day or night) in all its pleasant or boring length. [MidE *lief*, dear + *longe*, long]

lively *adj* **-ier**, **-iest** **1** active and full of life, energy and high spirits. **2** brisk. **3** vivid, bright. — *n* **liveliness**. [OE *liflic*]

liven *v* **-n-** (*tr* & *intr*; **up**) to make or become lively. **[live**[2]**]**

liver[1]. See **live**[1].

liver[2] *n* **1** a large organ in the body which carries out several important functions, including cleaning the blood. **2** this organ in certain animals used as food. — *adj* dark reddish-brown in colour. [OE *lifer*]

liverish *adj* **1** (*old*) suffering from a disordered liver. **2** easily annoyed or made angry.

liver sausage *n* a sausage containing liver.

Liverpudlian *n* a native or citizen of Liverpool. — *adj* of Liverpool or its inhabitants.

liverwort *n* a moss-like plant with liver-shaped leaves, growing in damp places. **[liver**[2] **+ wort]**

livery *n* **-ies** **1** a distinctive uniform worn by male servants belonging to a particular household or the members of a trade guild. **2** (*literary*) distinctive markings or outward appearance: *trees in their autumn livery*. **3** the distinctive colours and decoration used to identify all of the aircraft, buses, etc. belonging to a particular company. **4** the feeding, care, stabling and hiring out of horses for money. [OFr *livree*, from Lat *liberare*, to free]

liveried *adj* wearing or covered in livery.

livery company *n* any of several trade guilds in the City of London whose members formerly used to wear distinctive clothes.

liveryman *n* a member of a livery company.

livery stable *n* a place where people may keep their horses or where horses can be hired for money.

lives. See **life**.

livestock. See **live**[2].

livid *adj* **1** of the greyish colour of lead. **2** (of a bruise) black and blue. **3** white or very pale. **4** (*coll*) extremely angry. — *n* **lividness**. [Lat *lividus*, lead-coloured]

living *adj* **1** having life; alive. **2** currently in existence, use or activity. **3** (of a likeness) exact. — *n* **1** livelihood or means of subsisting. **2** a manner of life: *riotous living*. **3** in the Church of England, a position as a vicar or rector which has an income or property attached to it. **4** (with **the**) people who are alive. — **within living memory** within a period of time remembered by people who are still alive. **[live**[1]**]**

living-room *n* a room in a house, etc. for sitting and relaxing in.

living wage *n* a wage which can support a wage-earner and family.

lizard *n* a reptile with a long body and tail, four legs, and a scaly skin. [Lat *lacerta*]

ll *abbrev* lines.

'll *abbrev* shall; will.

llama *n* a domesticated S American mammal of the camel family, kept for its wool and used as a beast of burden. [Quechua]

LLB *abbrev* Bachelor of Laws. [Lat *legum baccalaureus*]

LLD *abbrev* Doctor of Laws. [Lat *legum doctor*]

lo *interj* (*old*) look, see. — **lo and behold** an expression indicating surprise, etc. at seeing or finding something unexpected. [OE *la*]

load *n* **1** that which is carried; a burden. **2** that which is or can be carried at one time: *a coach-load of children*. **3** (in *pl*; *coll*) a large amount: *have loads of money*. **4** work, duties, sadness, etc. which are oppressive and heavy to bear. **5** an amount or number of things to be dealt with at one time, esp. of clothes to be washed: *have several loads of washing to do*. **6** the power carried by an electric circuit. **7** the power produced by an engine. — *v* **1** (*tr*) to put (a load of something) on or in (a ship, vehicle, washing-machine, etc.). **2** (*intr*; **up**) to take or pick up a load. **3** (*tr*) to be a weight on or burden to; to oppress. **4** (*tr*; **with**) to give lavishly or in great amounts to. **5** (*tr*) to put (film, audio or video tape, etc.) into a (camera, tape or video recorder, etc.). **6** (*tr*; *comput*) to transfer (a program or data) to a main memory, so that it may be used. **7** (*tr*; *comput*) to put (a disk, computer tape, etc.) into a drive, so that it may be used. **8** (*tr*) to put (ammunition) into (a gun). **9** (*tr*) to give weight or bias to (dice, a roulette wheel, etc.). — *n* **loader**. — **get a load of** (*slang*) to pay attention to, listen to, or look at. — **load the dice against someone** to deprive someone of a fair chance. [OE *lad*, course, journey]

loaded *adj* **1** carrying a load; with a load in place. **2** (of a gun) containing bullets. **3** (of a camera) containing film. **4** (*coll*) very rich.

loaded question *n* a question intended to trick someone into saying, admitting or agreeing to something which he or she is unwilling to do.

loadstar, **loadstone**. Same as **lodestar**, **lodestone**.

loaf[1] *n* ***loaves*** **1** a mass of bread for baking or when baked. **2** a quantity of food formed into a usu. regular shape, e.g. meat or sugar. **3** (*slang*) the head or brains: *use one's loaf*. [OE *hlaf*]

loaf[2] *v* **1** (*intr*; **about**, **around**) to pass time or stand about idly. **2** (*tr*; **away**) to spend or pass idly: *loaf away one's life*.

loafer *n* **1** a person who loafs. **2** a light, casual shoe like a moccasin.

loam *n* rich soil containing sand, clay and decaying animal and vegetable matter. — *n* **loaminess**. — *adj* **loamy**, ***-ier***, ***-iest***. [OE *lam*]

loan *n* **1** anything lent, but esp. money lent at interest. **2** the act of lending or state of being lent. — *v* (*tr*) to lend (esp. money). — **on loan** given as a loan. [Norse *lan*]

loan shark *n* (*coll*) a person who lends money at enormous and unreasonable rates of interest.

loan-word *n* a word taken into one's own language from another language.

loath *adj* (**to**) not willing or reluctant. — **nothing loath** willing or willingly. [OE *lath*, hated]

loathe *v* (*tr*) to feel dislike or disgust for. [OE *lathian*, to hate]

loathing *n* great dislike or disgust.

loathsome *adj* causing great dislike or disgust. — *adv* **loathsomely**. — *n* **loathsomeness**.

loaves. See **loaf**[1].

lob *n* **1** (*tennis*) a ball hit in a high overhead path. **2** (*cricket*) a slow, high, underhand ball. — *v* ***-bb-*** (*tr*) to hit or throw (a ball) in this way. [OE *lobbe*, spider]

lobar *adj* of, relating to or affecting a lobe, esp. in the lungs. [**lobe**]

lobate *adj* having lobes. [**lobe**]

lobby *n* ***-ies*** **1** a small entrance-hall, passage or waiting-room from which several rooms open. **2** (*Br*) either of two corridors in the House of Commons which members pass into when they vote. **3** (*Br*) a hall in the House of Commons where members of the public may meet politicians. **4** a group of people who try to influence the Government, politicians, etc. in favour of a particular cause. — *v* ***-ies***, ***-ied*** (*tr*) to try to influence (the Government, politicians, etc.) in favour of a particular cause. [Lat *lobia*]

lobbyist *n* a person employed to lobby politicians, etc. on behalf of a particular cause.

lobe *n* **1** the soft, broad, lower part of the ear. **2** a division of an organ or gland in the body, esp. the lungs or brain. **3** a broad, usu. rounded division or projection of a larger object. — *adj* **lobed**. [Gr *lobos*]

lobelia *n* a garden plant with red, white, purple, blue or yellow flowers. [Matthias de *Lobel* (1538–1616), Flemish botanist]

lobotomy *n* ***-ies*** (*med*) the cutting into a lobe of an organ or gland, esp. the front lobes in the brain to cure certain severe mental disorders. [Gr *lobos*, lobe + *tomia*, cutting]

lobster *n* **1** a large, edible shellfish with large claws, which goes red when boiled. **2** its flesh as food. [OE *loppestre*]

lobster pot *n* a basket for catching lobsters.

local *adj* **1** of or belonging to a particular place. **2** of or belonging to one's home area or neighbourhood. **3** (of a train or bus) stopping at all the stations or stops in a neighbourhood or small area. **4** (*med*) of, affecting or confined to a small area or part: *a local anaesthetic*. — *n* **1** a person living in a particular area. **2** one's nearest, and often most regularly visited, public house. **3** a local bus or train. **4** an anaesthetic affecting only a particular part of the body. — *adv* **locally**. [Lat *localis*, from *locus*, place]

local authority *n* the elected local government body in an area.

local colour *n* details in a story, etc. which are characteristic of the time or place in which it is set.

local government *n* government of town or county affairs by people living in that town or county rather than by national or central government.

localise or **-ize** *v* (*tr*) **1** to restrict to a place or area. **2** to mark with the characteristics of a particular place. — *n* **localisation** or **-z-**. — *adj* **localised** or **-z-**.

locale *n* the scene of some event or occurrence. [Fr *local*, local]

locality *n* ***-ies*** **1** a district or neighbourhood. **2** the scene of an event. **3** the position of a thing. [Lat *localitas*, from *locus*, place]

locate *v* **1** (*tr*) to set in a particular place or position. **2** (*tr*) to find the exact position of. **3** (*tr*) to establish in its proper place or position. **4** (*tr*) to describe or state the position of (something). **5** (*intr*; *NAm*) to establish oneself in business or residence in an area. [Lat *locare*, from *locus*, place]

location *n* **1** a position or situation. **2** the act of locating or process of being located. **3** a place outside the studio for filming: *made on location in Spain*. **4** in S Africa, under apartheid, any of the townships or other areas where Black or Coloured people are obliged to live. **5** (*comput*) a position in a memory which can hold a unit of information.

loc. cit. *abbrev* for *loco citato* (Lat), in the passage just quoted.

loch *n* (*Scot*) **1** a lake. **2** (also **sea loch**) a long narrow arm of the sea surrounded by land on three sides. [Gaelic]

loci. See **locus**.

lock[1] *n* **1** a small device for fastening doors, lids, etc., which has a bolt which usu. needs a key to move it. **2** a closed part of a canal or river where the water level may be controlled, allowing boats to pass from a higher section of the canal or river to a lower one or vice versa. **3** a state of being jammed or locked together, and completely immovable. **4** the part of a gun which explodes the charge. **5** (*wrestling*) a tight hold which prevents one's opponent from moving. **6** the full amount by which the front wheels of a vehicle will turn. **7** (also **lock forward**) a Rugby player in the second row of a scrum. **8** an airlock. — *v* **1** (*tr*) to fasten (a door, box, bag, etc.) with a lock. **2** (*intr*) (of a door, etc.) to become or have the means of becoming locked. **3** (*tr*) to shut up or secure (a building) by locking all the doors and windows. **4** (*tr* & *intr*) to jam or cause to jam. **5** (*tr* & *intr*) to fasten or cause to be fastened so as to prevent movement. **6** (*tr*) to hold closely in an embrace or tussle. — *adj* **lockable**. — *v* **lock in** (*tr*) to prevent (someone) from getting out of a building or room by locking the doors while he or she is inside. — *v* **lock out** (*tr*) **1** to prevent (someone) from getting into a building or room by locking the doors while he or she is outside. **2** to prevent (employees) from entering a factory, etc. during industrial action, usu. as a means of forcing them to accept an employer's conditions (*n* **lockout**). — **lock, stock and barrel** completely; the whole thing. — *v* **lock up 1** (*tr*) to confine or prevent from leaving by locking in somewhere. **2** (*tr*) to lock (a building, etc.) securely. **3** (*intr*) to lock all the doors and windows. — **under lock and key** securely locked up; in prison. [OE *loc*]

locker *n* a small, lockable cupboard for personal, temporary use, e.g. for sports equipment.

lockjaw *n* a disease which makes the muscles of the jaw stiff or rigid.

lockout see **lock out** above.

locksmith *n* a person who makes and mends locks.

lockup *n* **1** a cell for locking up prisoners. **2** (*Br*) a small shop with no living quarters attached.

lock[2] *n* **1** a section or curl of hair. **2** (in *pl*) hair. [OE *locc*]

locket *n* a small, ornamented case for holding a person's photograph, a lock of hair, etc., worn on a chain round the neck. [OFr *loquet*, latch]

loco[1] *n* **-os** (*coll*) a locomotive. [Abbrev.]

loco[2] *adj* (*slang*) mad. [Span]

locomotion *n* the act or power of moving from place to place. [Lat *locus*, place + *motio*, motion]

locomotive *n* a railway engine for pulling trains. — *adj* of, relating to or causing locomotion.

locum *n* (in full **locum tenens** ***locum tenentes***) a person who temporarily takes the place of someone else, esp. a doctor or dentist. [Lat *locus*, place + *tenere*, to hold]

locus *n* ***loci*** **1** an exact place or location. **2** (*math*) a line, curve or surface formed by all the points fulfilling a particular condition, or by a point, line or curve moving according to certain conditions. [Lat, place]

locust *n* **1** any of several kinds of large insect related to the grasshopper, which travel in swarms and eat and destroy crops and vegetation. **2** (also **locust tree**) a N American tree with clusters of white flowers and reddish-brown seed pods. **3** any of several other types of tree, including the carob. **4** (also **locust bean**) a carob pod. [Lat *locusta*, lobster, locust]

locution *n* **1** a style of speech. **2** a word, phrase or sentence. [Lat *locutio*, from *loqui*, to speak]

lode *n* a thin band or strip of rock containing metallic ore. [OE *lad*, course, journey]

lodestar *n* **1** a star used as a guide by sailors and astronomers, esp. the Pole Star. **2** any guide or guiding principle.

lodestone *n* **1** a type of magnetic iron ore. **2** a piece of this used as a magnet. **3** any person or thing that attracts.

lodge *n* **1** a small house at the gate to the grounds of a large house. **2** a small house in the country for sportsmen: *a hunting-lodge*. **3** a porter's room in a university or college. **4** the meeting-place of a local branch of some societies, or the members of this branch. **5** the home of a beaver or otter. — *v* **1** (*intr*) to live in rented accommodation, esp. in someone else's home and usu. temporarily. **2** (*tr*) to provide with rented, usu. temporary accommodation, esp. in one's home. **3** (*tr*; **with**) to bring (a charge or accusation) against someone; to make (a complaint) officially. **4** (*tr*; **in**, **with**) to deposit (money, etc.) for safety. **5** (*tr* & *intr*) to (cause to) become firmly fixed: *a piece of bone lodged in one's throat*. **6** (*tr*; **in**) to give (power, authority, a talent, etc.) to (someone). [OFr *loge*, shelter]

lodger *n* a person who rents accommodation in someone else's home, often temporarily.

lodging *n* **1** (usu. in *pl*) a room or rooms rented in someone else's home. **2** temporary accommodation.

loess *n* a fine-grained, wind-blown soil found esp. in river valleys. [Swiss Ger *lösch*, loose]

loft *n* **1** a room or space under a roof. **2** a gallery in a church or hall. **3** a room used for storage, esp. one over a stable for storing hay. **4** a loft in a house used for keeping pigeons in. **5** a backward slope on the head of a golfclub. **6** a stroke that causes a golfball to rise up high. — *v* (*tr*) to strike, kick or throw (a ball, etc.) high up in the air. [OE, from Norse *lopt*, sky, upper room]

lofty *adj* **-ier**, **-iest** **1** of great or imposing height. **2** of high or noble character: *lofty ideals*. **3** haughty or proud. — *adv* **loftily**. — *n* **loftiness**.

log[1] *n* **1** (part of) a tree trunk or thick, bare branch, esp. when used as firewood. **2** a detailed record of events occurring during a ship's, aircraft's, etc. voyage. **3** a logbook. **4** a float attached by a line to a ship, used for measuring its speed. — *v* **-gg-** **1** (*tr*) to record (distances covered on a journey, events, etc.) in a book or logbook. **2** (*tr*) to cut (trees, etc.) into logs. **3** (*intr*) to cut logs. — *v* **log in** or **on** (*intr*) to gain access to a computer system by keying in a usu. personal code. — *v* **log out** or **off** (*intr*) to finish using and leave a computer system by keying in a closing command. — **sleep like a log** to sleep very soundly. [MidE *logge*]

logbook *n* **1** a book containing an official record of a ship's, aircraft's, etc. journey, including details of crew and any incidents which occur. **2** (*Br*) the registration documents of a motor vehicle.

logging *n* the work of cutting trees and preparing timber.

log jam *n* **1** a jam caused by logs being floated down a river. **2** a complete stopping of movement or progress.

log[2] *n* (*coll*) a logarithm.

loganberry *n* **-ies** **1** a large dark red berry eaten as a fruit. **2** the plant which produces it, thought to be a cross between a raspberry and a blackberry. [J H *Logan* (1841–1928), the American judge in whose garden it first grew]

logarithm *n* the number of times a base, usu. 10, must be multiplied by itself to produce a given number: *The logarithm of 1000 to the base 10 is 3, because 10 × 10 × 10 = 1000*. — *adj* **logarithmic**. — *adv* **logarithmically**. [Gr *logos*, ratio + *arithmos*, number]

loggerhead: **at loggerheads** arguing or disagreeing violently. [Poss. dialect *logger*, a block of wood for hobbling a horse + **head**]

loggia *n* a roofed gallery or arcade on the side of a building, open to the garden. [Ital, lodge]

logic *n* **1** the science of reasoning correctly. **2** correct or incorrect use of reasoning; the ability to reason soundly. **3** an individual, personal or particular way of reasoning: *feminine logic*. **4** the convincing and compelling force of a thing; the inevitability of a consequence of a thing: *there's no escaping the logic of the event*. **5** (*electronics* and *comput*) the arrangement of circuit elements which allows specified arithmetical functions to be performed. [Gr *logike techne*, logical art]

logical *adj* **1** of or according to logic. **2** correctly reasoned or thought out. **3** able to reason correctly. **4** following reasonably or necessarily from facts or events. — *adv* **logically**. — *n* **logicality**.

logician *n* a person who is skilled in or studies logic.

-logic, **-logical**. See **-logy**.

logistics *n* (*sing* or *pl*) **1** the art of moving and supplying troops and military equipment. **2** the organising of everything needed for any large-scale operation. — *adj* **logistic** or **logistical**. — *adv* **logistically**. [Fr *logistique*, quartermaster's work, from *loger*, to lodge]

logo *n* **-os** a small design used as the symbol of an organisation. [Abbrev. of *logotype*, from Gr *logos*, word]

-logy *comb fm* **1** the science or study of: *geology*. **2** writing or speech: *trilogy*. — *adj comb fm* **-logic** or **-logical**. [Gr *logos*, word, reason]

loin *n* **1** (in *pl*) the waist and lower back area, between the ribs and the hips. **2** (in *pl*; *poetic*) the genitals, esp. when thought of as the source of life: *fruit of one's loins*. **3** a cut from the lower back area of an animal. [OFr *loigne*]

loincloth *n* a piece of material worn round the hips.

loiter *v* **-r-** (*intr*) **1** to work slowly and idly. **2** to stand around or pass one's time doing nothing in particular. — *n* **loiterer**. [MidE *loteren*]

loll *v* (*intr*) **1** **(about)** to lie or sit about lazily; to lounge or sprawl. **2** (of the tongue) to hang down or out. [MidE *lollen*]

lollipop *n* a large, round boiled sweet on a stick. [Dialect *lolly*, tongue + **pop**[1]]

lollipop man or **lady** *n* a man or woman whose job it is to see children safely across busy roads, recognised by carrying a pole with a circular sign on it.

lollop *v* **-p-** (*intr*; *coll*) to move about in a lively, but uncontrolled and puppy-like manner. [Poss. from **loll**]

lolly *n* **-ies** (*coll*) **1** a lollipop. **2** (also **ice lolly**) a frozen ice cream or flavoured water ice on a stick. **3** money. [Abbrev. of **lollipop**]

London pride *n* a plant of the saxifrage family with pink flowers.

lone *adj* **1** (of a person) alone; without a companion. **2** (of a place) isolated and unfrequented. **[alone]**

loner *n* a person who prefers to be alone and who avoids close relationships.

lonesome *adj* (esp. *NAm*) **1** sad and lonely. **2** causing feelings of loneliness.

lone wolf *n* a loner.

lonely *adj* **-ier**, **-iest** **1** (of a person) sad because without companions or friends. **2** solitary and without companionship: *a lonely existence*. **3** (of a place) isolated and unfrequented. — *n* **loneliness**. **[alone]**

lonely heart *n* a lonely person, esp. one who is looking for a happy, loving relationship. — *adj* **lonely-hearts**: *a lonely-hearts club.*

long[1] *adj* **1** measuring a great distance from one end to the other in space or time. **2** measuring a stated amount in space or time: *six inches long*. **3** having a large number of items: *a long list*. **4** measuring more in space or time than the average or more than is expected or wanted. **5** greater in value, amount, etc. than is usual or expected: *a long dozen* (= 13). **6** lasting for an extended period of time. **7** (of a dress, trousers, curtains, etc.) reaching down to or close to the ground, floor, etc.; full-length. **8** (of a cold drink) large and thirst-quenching. **9** (of stocks) bought in large amounts in expectation of a rise in prices. **10** (*phonetics*) (of a vowel or syllable) having the greater of two recognised lengths, such as the *i* in *pile*, as opposed to the *i* in *pill*, which is **short**. **11** (of betting odds) showing a low level of probability. — *adv* **1** for, during or by a long period of time: *long ago*; *long-lasting*. **2** throughout the whole time: *all night long*. — *n* anything that is long, esp. a long period of time, or a long vowel or syllable. — **as** or **so long as 1** provided that. **2** while; during the time that. — **before long** soon. — **in the long run** in the end. — **long on** (*coll*) having a lot of: *He isn't long on brains*. — **the long and the short of it** the most important facts in a few words. — **no longer** not now as it was in the past. — **so long** (*coll*) goodbye. [OE *lang*]

longboat *n* the largest small boat carried by a ship.

longbow *n* a large bow drawn by hand.

long-distance *adj* covering, travelling, operating, etc. between or over long distances: *a long-distance runner*; *long-distance telephone calls*.

long division *n* a division of numbers in which the working is shown in full.

long-drawn-out *adj* taking a longer time than it should.

long face *n* a dismal or disappointed expression.

longhand *n* ordinary writing as opposed to shorthand.

long haul *n* **1** the carrying of cargo or passengers over a long distance. **2** any work requiring great effort or considerable time. — *adj* **long-haul**.

long johns *n* (*pl*; *coll*) long, warm underpants.

long jump *n* an athletics contest in which competitors jump as far as possible along the ground from a running start.

long-lived *adj* having a long life.

long-playing *adj* (of a record) with each side playing for 20 to 30 minutes.

long-range *adj* **1** (of a missile or vehicle) able to reach to remote or far-off targets or destinations. **2** (of a weather forecast) going well into the future.

longship *n* (*hist*) a long, narrow warship propelled by rowers, built by the Vikings.

long shot *n* (*coll*) a guess, attempt, etc. which is not very likely to be successful. — **not by a long shot** not by any means.

long-sighted *adj* **1** able to see clearly things far away, but not things close at hand. **2** having or showing the ability to guess what is going to happen in the future. — *n* **long-sightedness**.

long-standing *adj* having existed or continued for a long time.

long-suffering *adj* patiently putting up with trouble and problems.

long-term *adj* (of a plan, etc.) occurring in or concerned with the future.

longtime *adj* lasting for a long time; long-standing.

long wave *n* a radio wave using wavelengths over 1000 metres. — *adj* **long-wave**.

longways *adv* lengthways.

long-winded *adj* (of a speaker or speech) going on longer than necessary and usu. very boring. — *adv* **long-windedly**. — *n* **long-windedness**.

long[2] *v* (*intr*; **for**) to want very much. — *adv* **longingly**. [OE *langian*, to yearn after]

longing *n* (**for**) a great desire.

longevity *n* great length of life. [Lat *longus*, long + *aevum*, age]

longitude *n* a distance measured in degrees east or west of 0°, the imaginary line passing from north to south through Greenwich. ◇ See also **latitude**. [Lat *longus*, long]

longitudinal *adj* **1** of or relating to longitude. **2** lengthways. — *adv* **longitudinally**.

longshore *adj* found on or employed along the shore. [From the phrase *along shore*]

longshoreman *n* (*NAm*) a person who loads and unloads ships at a sea-port.

loo *n* (*Br coll*) a lavatory.

loofah or **loofa** *n* the long, thin, dried inner part of a tropical gourd-like fruit, used as a sponge. [Arabic *lufah*]

look *v* **1** (*intr*; **at**) to turn the eyes in a certain direction so as to see; to use one's sight. **2** (*intr* with **at**, **to**) to consider, examine or give attention to. **3** (*intr*) to seem to be or appear. **4** (*intr*) to face or be turned towards: *a window looking south*. **5** (*intr*; **for**) to search (for). **6** (*intr*; **for**) to rely (on) or turn or refer (to): *look to you for support*. **7** (*intr* with **into**) to investigate: *look into the matter for him*. **8** (*tr*) to direct one's sight towards in a particular way: *look her in the eyes*. **9** (*tr*) to express by a look: *to look daggers at him*. **10** (*tr*) to consider or realise: *Just look where your short cut has got us!* — *n* **1** an act of looking; a glance or view: *have a good look*. **2** the general appearance of a thing or person. **3** (in *pl*) beauty; attractiveness. — *interj* used to call for attention or to express protest. — **have a look of** to look like. —

v **look after** (*tr*) to attend to or take care of. — *v* **look ahead** (*intr*) to consider what will happen in the future. — *v* **look down on** (*intr*) to consider as not good enough or not as good as oneself. — **look down one's nose at** to look down on. — *v* **look forward to** (*intr*) to wait for or anticipate with pleasure. — **look here!** used to call for attention or to express protest. — *v* **look in** (*intr*; **on**) to visit briefly and often without invitation. ◇ See also **look-in** below. — *v* **look on 1** (*intr*) to watch without taking part (*n* **looker-on**). **2** (*tr*) to think of or consider: *look on it as a mistake*. — **look oneself** to appear one's normal, healthy self: *He's not looking himself yet after the operation*. — *v* **look out 1** (*intr*; **for**) to keep watch (for) and be careful. **2** (*tr*) to find by searching: *Look out all her old clothes*. ◇ See also **lookout** below. — *v* **look over** (*tr*) to examine. — **look sharp** (*coll*) to act quickly. — *v* **look up 1** (*intr*) to improve. **2** (*tr*; *coll*) to visit (someone). **3** (*tr*) to search for (an item of information) in a reference book. — *v* **look up to** (*tr*) to respect the behaviour, opinions, etc. of. — **never look back** to continue to make progress. [OE *locian*]

lookalike *n* a person who looks very much like someone else; a double.

looker *n* (*coll*) an attractive person.

looker-on see **look on** above.

look-in *n* **1** a chance of joining in, being included, or doing something: *never get a look-in*. **2** a short visit.

looking-glass *n* (*old*) a mirror.

lookout *n* **1** a careful watch. **2** a place from which such a watch can be kept. **3** a person set to watch, e.g. on board ship. **4** (*coll*) a personal concern or problem: *That's your lookout*. **5** prospect or outlook: *a dim lookout*.

look-see *n* (*slang*) a brief look around or inspection.

loom[1] *n* a machine for weaving thread into fabric. [OE *loma*, tool]

loom[2] *v* (*intr*) **1** (**up**) to appear indistinctly and usu. in some enlarged or threatening form. **2** (**over**) (of an event) to be imminent, esp. in some menacing or threatening way.

loon *n* (esp. *NAm*) a diving bird with a slender body and sharp beak; a diver. [Norse *lomr*]

loony (*slang*) *n* **-ies** a mad person; a lunatic. — *adj* **-ier**, **-iest** crazy; mad. [Abbrev. of **lunatic**]

loony-bin *n* (*slang*) a mental home or hospital.

loop *n* **1** the oval-shaped coil in a piece of rope, chain, etc. which forms as it crosses over itself. **2** any similar oval-shaped or U-shaped bend, e.g. in a river. **3** a manoeuvre in which an aircraft flies upwards, briefly upside down, then downwards, so describing a complete circle in the sky. **4** a strip of tape or film allowing the sound or images on it to be continually repeated. **5** (*electronics*) a closed ciruit which a signal can pass round. **6** (*comput*) a sequence of instructions in a program that are repeated all the time a given condition exists. **7** a branch of a railway, telegraph line, etc. that leaves the main line and then rejoins it. **8** a contraceptive coil. — *v* (*tr*) **1** to fasten with or enclose in a loop. **2** to form into a loop or loops. — **loop the loop** (of aircraft, etc.) to make a loop (sense **3**) in the sky. [MidE *loupe*, loop of cloth]

loophole *n* a means of avoiding obeying a rule or law or fulfilling a contract without actually breaking it. [MidE *loupe*, window + **hole**]

loopy *adj* **-ier**, **-iest** (*slang*) mad; crazy. [**loop**]

loose *adj* **1** not or no longer tied or held in confinement; free. **2** not tight or close-fitting. **3** not held together; not fastened or firmly fixed in place; not packeted. **4** not tightly-packed or compact: *loose soil*. **5** vague or inexact: *a loose translation*. **6** immoral or promiscuous. **7** indiscreet: *loose talk*. **8** (*sport*) (of a ball, etc.) in play but not under a player's control. — *adv* loosely. — *n* (*rugby*) the part of play where the players are not in scrums or close together round the ball. — *v* (*tr*) **1** to release or set free. **2** to unfasten or untie. **3** to make less tight, compact or dense. **4** to relax: *loose one's hold*. **5** to discharge (a gun, bullet, arrow, etc.). — *adv* **loosely**. — *n* **looseness**. — **at a loose end** with nothing to do. — **on the loose** free from confinement or control. [Norse *lauss*]

loose box *n* a part of a stable or horse-box where horses are kept untied.

loose change *n* coins kept in one's pocket or bag, for small expenses.

loose-leaf *adj* (of a folder, binder, etc.) having a cover which opens to allow pages to be taken out and inserted.

loosen *v* **-n-** (*tr* & *intr*) **1** to make or become loose or looser. **2** (**up**) to make or become less tense, rigid or stiff.

loot *n* **1** stolen goods, esp. those stolen from the enemy in wartime. **2** (*coll*) money. — *v* **1** (*tr*) to steal (money or goods) from (someone, esp. the enemy in wartime, or somewhere). **2** (*intr*) to rob and plunder. — *n* **looter**. — *n* **looting**. [Hindi *lut*]

lop[1] *v* **-pp-** (*tr*) **1** (**off**) to cut off (the top or ends of), esp. the branches of a tree. **2** (**off**, **away**) to cut away (the unnecessary or superfluous parts). [MidE *loppe*, parts cut off]

lop[2] *v* **-pp-** (*intr*) to hang down loosely.

lop-eared *adj* (of animals) having ears that droop.

lopsided *adj* **1** with one side smaller, lower or lighter than the other. **2** leaning over to one side; unbalanced.

lope *v* (*intr*) to run with long, bounding steps. — *n* a bounding leap. [Norse *hlaupa*]

loquacious *adj* talking a lot. — *adv* **loquaciously**. — *n* **loquaciousness** or

loquacity. [Lat *loquax*, from *loqui*, to speak]

lord *n* **1** a master or ruler. **2** (*hist*) a feudal superior. **3** (*Br*) a male member of the nobility. **4** (*cap*) a title used to address some noblemen, e.g. earls, viscounts, the younger sons of dukes. **5** (*cap*) God or Christ. — *interj* (*cap*) an expression of surprise or dismay. — **live like a lord** to live in luxury. — **lord it over** (*coll*) to act like a lord, esp. in being haughty, proud and domineering. — **the (House of) Lords** the upper, non-elected chamber of the British parliament, whose members include peers, bishops and judges. — **Our Lord** Christ. [OE *hlaford*, from *hlaf*, bread + *weard*, guardian]

Lord Chamberlain *n* the senior official of the British Royal household.

Lord (High) Chancellor *n* the highest judge in the United Kingdom, and Speaker of the House of Lords.

Lord Chief Justice *n* the second highest judge in the United Kingdom, presiding over the Queen's Bench.

Lord Lieutenant *n* **1** the representative of the Crown and the chief magistrate in each county of the United Kingdom. **2** (*hist*) the British viceroy of Ireland.

lordly *adj* ***-ier***, ***-iest*** like or suitable for a lord, esp. in being grand, proud or haughty. — *n* **lordliness**.

Lord Mayor *n* the title of the mayor in the City of London and some other cities.

Lord Privy Seal *n* a senior British cabinet minister without official duties.

Lord Provost *n* the title of the mayor of certain Scottish cities.

the Lord's Day *n* Sunday.

Lordship *n* (with **His, Your**, etc.) a title used to address bishops, judges, and all peers except for dukes.

the Lord's Prayer *n* the prayer that Christ taught his disciples.

lords spiritual *n* (*pl*) the archbishops and bishops in the House of Lords.

the Lord's Supper *n* Holy Communion.

lords temporal *n* (*pl*) those members of the House of Lords who are not archbishops or bishops.

lore *n* the whole body of knowledge, esp. traditional knowledge, on a subject. [OE *lar*]

lorgnette *n* eyeglasses or opera-glasses held on a long handle. [Fr, from *lorgner*, to peer at]

lorry *n* ***-ies*** a large, heavily built road vehicle for transporting heavy loads.

lose *v* ***lost*** **1** (*tr*) to stop having; to fail to keep or obtain, esp. through carelessness. **2** (*tr*) to suffer the loss of or be bereaved of (esp. a parent or unborn baby) through death. **3** (*tr*) to leave accidentally or be unable to find: *lose one's way*. **4** (*tr*) to fail to use or get; to miss: *lose a good opportunity*. **5** (*tr* & *intr*) to fail to win (a game, battle, etc.). **6** (*tr*) to fail or cease to hear, see or understand: *lost the thread of his argument*. **7** (*tr*) to waste (time, money, etc.); to use to no purpose. **8** (*tr*) to escape or get away from. **9** (*tr*) to prevent the gaining or achieving of. **10** (*tr* & *intr*) (of a clock or watch) to become slow (by a stated amount). **11** (*intr*) to be in a worse position or suffer as the result of something. **12** (*tr*) to cause to disappear or die. — **lose oneself in** to have all one's attention taken up by. — *v* **lose out** (*intr*; **on**; *coll*) **1** to suffer loss or be at a disadvantage. **2** to fail to get something one desires. [OE *losian*, to be lost]

loser *n* **1** a person who loses. **2** (*coll*) a person who seems likely to always fail and be unsuccessful.

losing *adj* failing; never likely to be successful: *a losing battle*. ◇ See also **lost**.

loss *n* **1** the act or fact of losing or being lost. **2** the thing, amount, etc. lost. **3** the disadvantage or detriment resulting from losing: *be a great loss to the company*. — **at a loss 1** puzzled and uncertain. **2** (of an article sold, etc.) for less than was paid for it originally. **3** (of a company, etc.) losing more money than it is making. [OE *los*]

loss-leader *n* an item sold for less money than it would normally be sold for to attract customers into the shop.

lost *past participle* of **lose**. — *adj* **1** missing; no longer to be found. **2** unable to find one's way. **3** confused, puzzled. **4** (**on**) wasted; not used, noticed or understood properly: *Good wine is lost on him*. **5** morally fallen: *lost women*. **6** damned: *lost souls*. — **be lost in** to have one's attention completely engrossed in. — **get lost** (*slang*) to go away and stay away. — **lost to 1** to be no longer capable of feeling. **2** to be no longer open or available to (a person).

lost cause *n* an aim, ideal, etc. which will never be successful.

lot *n* **1** (*coll*; often in *pl*) a great number or amount. **2** any of a set of objects, e.g. a slip of paper, drawn from among a group, as a way of reaching a decision by chance: *draw lots*; *cast lots*. **3** this way of making a decision. **4** a person's fortune or destiny. **5** a separate part. **6** an item or set of items for sale by auction. **7** (esp. *NAm*) an area of land: *a parking lot*. — **a bad lot** a person with a bad character or bad reputation. — **cast** or **throw in one's lot with** to decide to share the fortunes of. — **the lot** the total; the whole number or amount. [OE *hlot*, portion, choice]

loth. Same as **loath**.

lotion *n* a liquid for healing or cleaning the skin, as either a medicine or a cosmetic. [Lat *lotio*, from *lavare*, to wash]

lottery *n* ***-ies*** **1** a way of raising money by selling tickets and giving prizes for those tickets drawn at random. **2** anything which is thought of as being a matter of chance. [Dut *loterie*, related to **lot**]

lotto *n* a game like bingo. [Ital]

lotus *n* **1** any of several types of water-lily. **2** (*Gr mythol*) a fruit which causes the eater to enter a state of blissful and dreamy forgetfulness. **3** a representation of a water-lily in architecture or art, esp. symbolically in ancient Egyptian or Hindu art. [Gr *lotos*]

lotus-eater *n* a person who lives a lazy, blissful, dreamy life.

lotus position *n* (*yoga*) a seated position with the legs crossed and each foot resting on the opposite thigh.

loud *adj* **1** making a great sound; noisy. **2** capable of making a great sound: *a loud horn*. **3** shrill and insistent: *loud complaints*. **4** (of colours or a design) too bright; gaudy. **5** (of behaviour) noisy, aggressive, vulgar and usu. offensive. — *adv* in a loud manner. — *adv* **loudly**. — *n* **loudness**. — **out loud** aloud; loudly. [OE *hlud*]

loudhailer *n* a portable electronic device which makes the voice much louder.

loud-mouthed *adj* (*coll*) noisy, aggressive and boastful.

loudspeaker *n* **1** a device which converts electrical signals into sound in televisions, radios, hi-fi equipment, etc.

lough *n* (*Irish*). Same as **loch**. [Irish Gaelic *loch*, MidE *lough*]

lounge *v* **1** (*intr*; **around**) to lie or recline comfortably. **2** (*intr*; **around**) to be idle or lazy. **3** (*tr*; **away**) to pass (time) lazily. — *n* **1** a sitting-room in a private house. **2** a large room in a public building, e.g. in a hotel for sitting in, or in an airport for waiting in, usu. providing refreshment facilities. **3** (also **lounge bar**; *Br*) a smarter and more expensive bar in a public house. **4** an act or spell of lounging.

lounger *n* **1** a person who lounges. **2** a comfortable chair for lounging on. **3** a woman's loose garment, worn when relaxing at home.

lounge suit *n* (*Br*) a man's formal suit for ordinary everyday wear.

lour or **lower** *v* **-r-** (*intr*) (esp. of the sky, etc.) to become dark or threaten rain, bad weather, etc. — *adj* **louring** or **lowering**. [MidE *louren*, to frown]

louse *n* **1** ***lice*** a wingless insect with a flat body and short legs, which sucks the blood of the animal or person it is living on. **2** ***louses*** (*slang*) an unpleasant or contemptible person. — *v* (*tr*) to remove lice from. — *v* **louse up** (*tr*; *slang*) to spoil or ruin. [OE *lus*]

lousy *adj* **-ier**, **-iest** **1** having lice. **2** (*slang*) very bad, unpleasant or disgusting. **3** (**with**; *slang*) infested (with) or full (of). — *adv* **lousily**. — *n* **lousiness**.

lout *n* a bad-mannered, rough and aggressive boy or man. — *adj* **loutish**. — *n* **loutishness**.

louvre or **louver** *n* **1** any one of a set of horizontal, sloping, overlapping slats in a door, etc., which let air in but keep rain and light out. **2** a dome-like structure on a roof for letting smoke out and air in. — *adj* **louvred** or **louvered**. [OFr *lovier*]

lovage *n* a herb with small, greenish-yellow flowers, used for flavouring. [OFr *luvesche*]

love *n* **1** a feeling of great affection for, and devotion to, another person. **2** strong sexual attraction. **3** a strong liking for something. **4** sexual relations; a love-affair. **5** (often used as a term of address) a person one loves. **6** (*Br coll*) a term of address used for anyone regardless of affection. **7** (*tennis, squash*, etc.) no score. — *v* **1** (*tr* & *intr*) to feel great affection for. **2** (*tr*) to enjoy very much; to like. — **fall in love** (**with**) to develop feelings of love and sexual attraction (for). — **in love** (**with**) feeling love and sexual attraction (for). — **make love 1** (**to**) to have sexual intercourse (with). **2** (*old*; with **to**) to woo. — **not for love or money** in no way at all; under no circumstances. [OE *lufu*]

lovable or **loveable** *adj* worthy of or inspiring love or affection.

love affair *n* a romantic and sexual relationship, esp. a temporary one.

lovebird *n* a small African parrot strongly attached to its mate.

love-child *n* an illegitimate child.

love-in-a-mist *n* a garden plant with pale blue or white flowers and feathery leaves.

loveless *adj* without love.

love-letter *n* a letter expressing love.

love-lies-bleeding *n* a garden plant with drooping spikes of reddish-purple flowers.

love life *n* that part of a person's life concerning romantic and sexual attachments.

lovelorn *adj* left by or pining for the person one is in love with.

lovely *adj* **-ier**, **-iest** **1** beautiful; attractive. **2** (*coll*) delightful or pleasing. — *n* **-ies** (*coll*) a pretty woman. — *n* **loveliness**.

love-making *n* sexual play between lovers, often including intercourse.

love-match *n* a marriage for love.

lover *n* **1** a person in love with another, esp. a person having a romantic and sexual relationship with the person loved. **2** (in *pl*) two people who are in love or who are having a sexual relationship. **3** a person who enjoys or is fond of (something): *dog-lovers*.

lovesick *adj* sad or pining because of love.

lovey-dovey *adj* (*coll*) affectionate in a sentimental and open way.

loving *adj* feeling and showing affection or love. — *adv* **lovingly**. — *n* **lovingness**.

loving-cup *n* a large, two-handled cup passed round at the end of a feast for everyone to drink from.

low[1] *adj* **1** not reaching up to a high level; not tall. **2** situated close to the ground, sea-level or the horizon. **3** (**in**) of less than average amount, etc.: *low in fat*. **4** (of numbers) small or reduced in amount. **5** with little value or quality. **6** (**on**) not having much (of): *low on petrol*. **7** of humble rank or position; common. **8** (of clothes) cut so as to expose the neck and part of the chest. **9** making little sound; soft: *a low voice*. **10** (of sounds, notes, etc.) produced by slow vibrations and having a deep pitch. **11** not physically or mentally strong; weak; with no energy or vitality: *be feeling low after the operation*. **12** unfavourable: *a low opinion*. **13** coarse, rude and vulgar. **14** (of latitudes) near the equator. **15** (of a gear) giving a relatively slow engine speed. — *adv* **1** in or to a low position, state or manner. **2** in a small quantity or to a small degree. **3** with a low voice; quietly. **4** at or in a low pitch. — *n* **1** the position, level, etc. which is low or lowest: *hit a low*. **2** an area of low atmospheric pressure. — *n* **lowness**. [Norse *lagr*]

low-born *adj* of humble birth.

low-brow *n* & *adj* (a person who is) not intellectual.

Low Church *n* a group within the Church of England which puts little value on ceremony and the authority of priests and which stresses evangelical theology.

low comedy *n* comedy which borders on the farcical and absurd.

Low Countries *n* (*pl*) the Netherlands, Belgium and Luxembourg.

low-down (*coll*) *adj* mean and dishonourable. — *n* (**on**) information (about).

lower *adj* **1** not as high as something else in position, status, height, value, etc. **2** (of an animal or plant) less highly developed than other species. — *adv* in or to a lower position. — *v* **-r-** **1** (*tr* & *intr*) to make or become lower in amount, value, status, sound, etc.: *lower one's standards, the volume*. **2** (*tr*) to close; to pull or let down: *lower the blinds*.

lower case *n* (*printing*) small type as opposed to capitals. — *adj* **lower-case**.

lower class *n* the lowest social class. — *adj* **lower-class**.

lower house or **chamber** *n* the larger and usu. elected part of a parliament that has two chambers, such as the House of Commons in the United Kingdom.

lowest common denominator *n* (*math*) the smallest number which can be divided exactly by each denominator in a group of fractions.

lowest common multiple *n* (*math*) the smallest number which can be divided exactly by all of the numbers in a group.

low frequency *n* a radio frequency between 30 and 300 kilohertz.

low-key *adj* **1** controlled, restrained and subdued. **2** (of a person) not easily excited.

lowland *n* **1** (usu. in *pl*) land which is low-lying in comparison with other areas. **2** (*cap*; in *pl*) the less mountainous region of Scotland lying to the south and east of the Highlands. — *adj* of or relating to lowlands or (*cap*) the Scottish Lowlands.

Lowlander *n* a person who lives in lowlands, esp. the Scottish Lowlands.

low-level language *n* a computer-programming language which is very like the machine code understood by the computer, and very different from natural language. ◇ See also **high-level**.

lowly *adj* **-ier**, **-iest** **1** humble in rank, status or behaviour. **2** simple, modest and unpretentious. — *n* **lowliness**.

low-pitched *adj* **1** (of a sound) low in pitch. **2** (of a roof) with a slight slope.

low-pressure *adj* (of steam and steam-engines) using or creating little pressure.

low profile *n* the deliberate avoidance of publicity and hiding of one's intentions and feelings.

low-spirited *adj* sad or depressed. — *n* **low-spiritedness**.

low technology *n* (also *coll* **low tech**) the simple, unsophisticated technology used to make basic products.

low tide or **water** *n* **1** the time the tide or water is at its lowest level. **2** the lowest place a tide normally comes to.

low[2] *v* (*intr*) (of cattle) to make a low, gentle, mooing sound. — *n* (also **lowing**) the low, gentle mooing sound made by cattle. [OE *hlowan*]

lower[1]. See **low**[1].

lower[2]. See **lour**.

loyal *adj* **1** faithful and true. **2** personally devoted to a sovereign, government, leader, friend, etc. **3** expressing or showing loyalty: *the loyal toast to the Queen*. — *adv* **loyally**. [OFr *loial*]

loyalist *n* **1** a loyal supporter, esp. of a sovereign or an established government. **2** (*cap*) in Northern Ireland, a supporter of the British Government.

loyalty *n* **-ies** **1** the state or quality of being loyal. **2** (often in *pl*) a feeling of loyalty or duty towards someone.

lozenge *n* **1** a small sweet or tablet which dissolves in the mouth. **2** a rhombus. [OFr *losenge*]

LP *abbrev* long player, a record which plays for 20 to 30 minutes on each side.

L-plate. See **L**[2].

Lr *symbol* (*chem*) lawrencium.

LSD *abbrev* lysergic acid diethylamide, a drug which causes hallucinations, often taken illegally.

L.S.D., **l.s.d.** or **£.s.d.** *abbrev* pounds, shillings, pence. [Lat *librae, solidi, denarii*]

Lt *abbrev* Lieutenant.

Ltd *abbrev* Limited, used in the names of limited liability companies.

Lu *symbol* (*chem*) lutetium.

lubber *n* a big, awkward, clumsy person. — *adj* & *adv* **lubberly**. [MidE *lobre*]

lubricant *n* oil, grease, etc. used to reduce friction. — *adj* lubricating. [**lubricate**]

lubricate *v* (*tr*) **1** to cover with oil, grease or some other such substance, to reduce friction. **2** to make smooth, slippery or greasy. — *n* **lubrication**. — *n* **lubricator**. [Lat *lubricus*, slippery]

lubricious *adj* (*literary*) lewd. — *n* **lubricity**. [Lat *lubricus*, slippery]

lucerne *n* (*Br*). Same as **alfalfa**. [Fr *luzerne*]

lucid *adj* **1** easily understood; expressed, or expressing something, clearly. **2** (of a person's mind) sane and not confused, esp. between periods of insanity. **3** bright, shining. — *n* **lucidity**. — *adv* **lucidly**. [Lat *lucidus*, full of light]

Lucifer *n* Satan. [Lat, light-bringer]

luck *n* **1** chance, esp. when thought of as bringing good fortune. **2** good fortune. **3** events in life which cannot be controlled and seem to happen by chance: *bad luck*. — **down on one's luck** experiencing problems or suffering hardship. — **push one's luck** (*coll*) to risk total failure by trying to gain too much when one has already been reasonably successful. — **worse luck** unfortunately. [ODut *luc*]

luckless *adj* not lucky; unfortunate.

lucky *adj* **-ier**, **-iest** **1** having good luck. **2** bringing good luck. **3** fortunate: *a lucky coincidence*. — *adv* **luckily**. — *n* **luckiness**.

lucky dip *n* a tub or container full of paper, bran, etc., from which children draw prizes at random.

lucrative *adj* profitable. — *adv* **lucratively**. [Lat *lucrativus*]

lucre *n* (*derog*) profit or financial gain. [Lat *lucrum*, gain]

filthy lucre *n* (*humorous*) money.

Luddite *n* **1** (*Br hist*) a member of a band of artisans who believed that mechanisation would lead to unemployment, and who destroyed machinery in protest, between about 1812 and 1818. **2** any person opposed to new technology or industrial change. — *adj* of the Luddites. [Ned *Ludd*, an 18th-century Leicestershire worker who smashed machinery]

ludicrous *adj* completely ridiculous; laughable. — *adv* **ludicrously**. — *n* **ludicrousness**. [Lat *ludicrus*]

ludo *n* a simple game in which counters are moved on a board according to the numbers shown on a dice. [Lat, I play]

luff *v* **1** (*tr* & *intr*) to turn (a ship) towards the wind. **2** (*tr*) to move (the jib of a crane or derrick) in and out or up and down, in order to move a load. [OFr *lof*]

lug[1] *v* **-gg-** (*tr*) to pull or drag (esp. something heavy) with difficulty. [MidE *luggen*]

lug[2] *n* **1** (*dialect* or *coll*) an ear. **2** a projection on a thing, esp. one by which it may be carried or turned.

lughole *n* (*coll*) the ear.

luggage *n* the suitcases, bags, etc. of a traveller. [**lug**[1]]

lugger *n* a small vessel with square sails attached to yards hanging obliquely to the mast. [MidE *lugge*, pole]

lugubrious *adj* sad; mournful. — *adv* **lugubriously**. — *n* **lugubriousness**. [Lat *lugere*, to mourn]

lugworm *n* a worm which lives in the sand on a sea-shore, often used as bait.

lukewarm *adj* **1** moderately warm. **2** (of interest, supporters, etc.) not enthusiastic; indifferent. — *adv* **lukewarmly**. [MidE *luke*, tepid + *warme*, warm]

lull *v* **1** (*tr* & *intr*) to make or become calm or quiet. **2** (*tr*) to deceive (someone) into feeling something, esp. safe and not under threat. — *n* a period of calm and quiet. [MidE *lullen*, imit.]

lullaby *n* **-ies** a soothing song to lull children to sleep. [**lull**]

lumbago *n* rheumatic pain in the lower part of the back. [Lat, from *lumbus*, loin]

lumbar *adj* of or relating to the lower part of the back between the lowest ribs and the pelvis. [Lat *lumbus*, loin]

lumbar puncture *n* the process of inserting a needle into the lower part of the spinal cord to remove fluid or inject drugs.

lumber[1] *n* **1** useless and disused articles of furniture, etc. which have been stored away. **2** (esp. *NAm*) timber, esp. that which has been partly cut up ready for use. — *v* **1** (*tr*; **with**; *coll*) to burden (someone) with an unwanted or difficult responsibility or task. **2** (*tr*) to fill with lumber or other useless items. **3** (*intr*; esp. *NAm*) to fell trees and saw the wood up into timber for transporting. [**lumber**[2]]

lumberjack *n* a person employed to fell, saw up and move trees.

lumber[2] *v* (*intr*) to move about heavily and clumsily. — *adj* **lumbering**. [MidE *lomeren*]

luminary *n* **-ies** **1** a famous or prominent member of a group. **2** a person considered as an expert or authority, and thus able to enlighten or instruct others: *one of the luminaries of the British theatre*. **3** (*literary*) a source of light, such as the sun or moon. — *adj* of or relating to light or enlightenment. [Lat *luminaria*, lamp]

luminescence *n* the giving out of light by a substance not caused by that substance's high temperature, as, for example, with glow-worms, some deep-sea creatures, and some minerals. — *adj* **luminescent**. [Lat *lumen*, light]

luminous *adj* **1** full of or giving out light. **2** giving out light in the dark; phosphorescent. — *n* **luminosity**. — *adv* **luminously**. [Lat *lumen*, light]

lump[1] *n* **1** a small, solid, shapeless mass. **2** a swelling or tumour. **3** a feeling of tightening or swelling, esp. in the throat. **4** the total number of things taken as a single whole. **5** a considerable quantity or heap. **6** a heavy, dull, awkward person. **7** (*Br*; with **the**) self-employed casual workers esp. in the building trade, paid in lump sums to evade tax. — *v* **1** (*tr* & *intr*) to form or collect into a lump. **2** (*tr*; **together**) to treat or consider as a single whole, esp. without good reason. [MidE *lumpe*]

lumpish *adj* (of a person) heavy, dull or awkward.

lump sugar *n* sugar in small lumps or cubes.

lump sum *n* a large, single payment instead of several smaller ones spread out over a period of time.

lumpy *adj* **-ier**, **-iest** full of lumps. — *adv* **lumpily**. — *n* **lumpiness**.

lump[2] *v* (*tr*; *coll*) to accept or put up with: *like it or lump it*.

lumpectomy *n* **-ies** the surgical removal of a lump, usu. a cancerous tumour, from the breast. [**lump**[1] + Gr *tome*, a cutting]

lunacy *n* **-ies 1** insanity. **2** great foolishness or stupidity. [**lunatic**]

lunar *adj* of, like, for use on or caused by the moon. [Lat *luna*, moon]

lunatic *adj* **1** insane. **2** foolish, stupid or eccentric. — *n* a person who is insane, or who is foolish, stupid or eccentric. [Lat *lunaticus*, moonstruck, from *luna*, moon, from the belief that intermittent insanity was due to the phases of the moon]

lunatic asylum *n* (*hist*; now *offensive)* a home or hospital for people with mental illnesses.

lunatic fringe *n* the most extreme, fanatical or eccentric members of any group.

lunch *n* a meal eaten in the middle of the day between breakfast and dinner. — *v* (*intr*) to eat lunch. [A short form of **luncheon**]

luncheon *n* a lunch, esp. a formal one. [MidE *noneschench*, from *none*, noon + *schench*, drink]

luncheon-meat *n* a type of pre-cooked meat, processed and mixed with cereal, usu. bought tinned and served cold.

luncheon voucher *n* a ticket worth a specified amount of money, given to employees by their employers and used to pay for lunches.

lunchtime *n* the time set aside for lunch.

lung *n* an organ for breathing, usu. one of a pair as in man and other animals. [OE *lungen*]

lungfish *n* a fish that has a lung as well as gills.

lunge *n* **1** a sudden plunge forwards. **2** (*fencing*) a sudden thrust with a sword. — *v* (*intr*) to make a sudden strong or thrusting movement forwards, in fencing with a sword in one's hand. [Fr *allonger*, to lengthen]

lupin *n* a garden plant with long spikes of brightly coloured flowers. [Lat *lupinus*, wolfish]

lupine *adj* of, relating to or like a wolf. [Lat *lupinus*, from *lupus*, wolf]

lupus *n* a skin disease characterised by the formation of ulcers and lesions. [Lat, wolf (so called because it eats away the skin)]

lurch[1] *v* (*intr*) to move or stagger unsteadily, esp. rolling slightly to one side. — *n* a sudden roll to one side.

lurch[2]: **leave in the lurch** (*coll*) to leave (a person, etc.) in a difficult situation and without help. [OFr *lourche*, a game like backgammon]

lurcher *n* a cross-bred dog, usu. a cross between a sheepdog or a golden retriever and a greyhound, used for hunting. [MidE *lorchen*, to lurk]

lure *v* (*tr*; **away**, **into**) to tempt, attract or entice, often by offering some reward. — *n* **1** a person or thing which tempts, attracts or entices. **2** (**of**) the attractive or tempting qualities (of): *the lure of the chase*. **3** (*angling*) a metal or plastic bait with hooks attached. **4** a bunch of feathers to which meat may be attached, used by falconers to recall a hawk. [OFr *luere*, bait]

lurid *adj* **1** glaringly bright: *lurid colours*. **2** horrifying or sensational: *lurid details*. **3** pale or wan. — *adv* **luridly**. — *n* **luridness**. [Lat *luridus*, pale yellow, wan]

lurk *v* (*intr*) **1** (**about**, **in**, **under**) to lie in wait, esp. in ambush, with some criminal purpose in mind. **2** to linger unseen or furtively; to be latent: *a lurking suspicion*. [MidE *lurken*]

luscious *adj* **1** richly sweet; delicious. **2** attractive in a voluptuous way. — *adv* **lusciously**. — *n* **lusciousness**. [MidE *lucius*, perhaps a variant of **delicious**]

lush[1] *adj* **1** (of grass, etc.) green and growing abundantly. **2** luxurious. — *n* **lushness**. [MidE *lusch*, slack]

lush[2] *n* (*slang*, esp. *NAm*) a drunkard or alcoholic. [Perhaps from **lush**[1]]

lust *n* **1** strong sexual desire. **2** enthusiasm; relish: *a lust for life*. — *v* (*intr*; **after**, **for**) to have a strong, esp. sexual, desire (for). — *adj* **lustful**. — *adv* **lustfully**. — *n* **lustfulness**. [OE, desire, appetite]

lusty *adj* **-ier**, **-iest 1** vigorous or loud: *a baby's lusty cries*. **2** strong and healthy. — *adv* **lustily**. — *n* **lustiness**.

lustre *n* **1** the shiny appearance of a surface in reflected light. **2** shine, brightness or gloss. **3** splendour, glory and fame, for physical beauty or mental accomplishments. **4** a thin metallic glaze for pottery. — *adj* **lustrous**. — *adv* **lustrously**. [Lat *lustrare*, to light up]

lusty. See **lust**.

lute *n* an ancient guitar-like instrument with a pear-shaped body and a long neck. [Arabic *al ud*]

lutenist *n* a person who plays the lute.

lutetium *n* a silver-white metallic element (symbol **Lu**), one of the 15 rare earth elements. [Lat *Lutetia*, Paris, where it was discovered in 1907]

Lutheran *n* a follower of the German Protestant reformer Martin *Luther* (1483–1546), or a member of the Lutheran Church, based on his teaching. — *adj* of Martin Luther, Lutherans, or the Lutheran Church.

Lutine bell *n* a bell rung in Lloyd's, the London ship insurers, to announce the loss or safe arrival of a ship, now rung only on ceremonial occasions. [The frigate *Lutine*, lost in 1799, whose bell it was]

luxe. See **de luxe**.

luxuriant *adj* **1** (of plants, etc.) growing abundantly; lush. **2** very elaborate;

extravagant; flowery. — *n* **luxuriance**. — *adv* **luxuriantly**. [Lat *luxuria*, luxury]

luxuriate *v* (*intr*) **1** (**in**) to enjoy greatly or revel (in). **2** to live in great comfort or luxury. **3** to grow richly or abundantly. [Lat *luxuria*, luxury]

luxurious *adj* **1** supplied or furnished with luxuries. **2** enjoying or providing luxury. — *adv* **luxuriously**. — *n* **luxuriousness**. [Lat *luxuriosus*, from *luxus*, excess]

luxury *n* **-ies 1** expensive, rich, extremely comfortable surroundings and possessions. **2** habitual indulgence in or enjoyment of luxurious surroundings. **3** something pleasant, often expensive, but not necessary. — *adj* relating to or providing luxury: *a luxury hotel*. [Lat *luxuria*, from *luxus*, excess]

LV *abbrev* luncheon voucher.

Lw *symbol* (*chem*; *formerly*; now generally replaced by **Lr**) lawrencium.

-ly *sfx* **1** used to form adverbs: *cleverly*. **2** used to form adverbs and adjectives with the sense of 'at intervals of': *daily*. **3** used to form adjectives with the sense 'in the manner of, like': *brotherly*.

lyceum *n* **1** (*cap*) the garden in Athens where Aristotle taught. **2** a place or building devoted to teaching, esp. literature and philosophy. [Gr *Lykeion*]

lychee *n* a small fruit with a sweet, white, juicy flesh, orig. from China. [Chin *lichi*]

lychgate. Same as **lichgate**.

lye *n* **1** a caustic solution made by passing water through wood ash. **2** a strong solution of sodium or potassium hydroxide. [OE *leag*]

lying. See **lie**[1,2].

lymph *n* a colourless liquid containing white blood cells, found in the tissues in animal bodies. [Lat *lympha*, water]

lymphatic *adj* **1** of, relating to or carrying lymph. **2** lethargic and flabby.

lymphatic system *n* the network of vessels that carries lymph throughout the body.

lymph gland *n* any of the small masses of tissue in the lymphatic system in which lymph is purified and lymphocytes formed.

lymphocyte *n* a type of leucocyte.

lynch *v* (*tr*) to condemn and put to death without a legal trial. — *n* **lynching**. [William *Lynch* (1742–1820), who presided over self-instituted tribunals in Virginia, USA]

lynx *n* an animal of the cat family, with a grey-brown coat, long legs, a short tail and tufted ears. [Gr]

lynx-eyed *adj* sharp-sighted.

lyre *n* a U-shaped, harp-like instrument plucked with a plectrum, used, esp. in ancient Greece, to accompany poetry. [Gr *lyra*]

lyre-bird *n* either of two Australian pheasant-like birds, the male of which has lyre-shaped tail feathers displayed during courtship.

lyric *adj* **1** (of poems or poets) expressing personal, private or individual emotions. **2** having the form of a song, meant to be sung, orig. to the lyre. — *n* **1** a short lyric poem or a song. **2** (usu. in *pl*) the words of a song. [Gr *lyrikos*, from *lyra*, lyre]

lyrical *adj* **1** lyric; song-like. **2** full of enthusiastic praise. — *adv* **lyrically**.

lyricism *n* **1** the state or quality of being lyrical. **2** a pouring out of emotions.

lyricist *n* **1** a person who writes the words to songs. **2** a lyric poet.

lysergic acid diethylamide. See **LSD**.

M

M[1] or **m** *n* ***Ms*** or ***M's, m's*** the thirteenth letter of the English alphabet.

M *abbrev* **1** Majesty. **2** Master. **3** Motorway. **4** mark (German currency).

M *symbol* the Roman numeral for 1000.

m *abbrev* **1** male. **2** married. **3** masculine. **4** *meridiem* (Lat), noon. **5** metre. **6** mile. **7** million. **8** minute. **9** month.

'm *short form* am: *I'm going*.

MA *abbrev* **1** Massachusetts. **2** Master of Arts.

ma *n* (*coll*) a mother.

ma'am *n* madam, used as a polite form of address, e.g. to female royalty.

mac *n* (*coll*) a mackintosh.

macabre *adj* **1** dealing with death. **2** ghastly or horrific. [Fr]

macadam *n* (a road surface made of) layers of compacted broken stones, usu. (**tarmacadam**) bound with tar. — *v* (*tr*) **macadamise** or **-ize**. [John *McAdam* (1756–1836), Scottish engineer]

macaque *n* any of various short-tailed or tailless monkeys of Asia and Africa, with large cheek-pouches. [Fr, from Port *macaco*, monkey]

macaroni *n* ***-is*** or ***-ies*** **1** pasta in the form of short tubes. **2** in 18th-century Britain, a dandy. [Ital *maccaroni*]

macaroon *n* a sweet cake or biscuit made with sugar, eggs and crushed almonds or coconut. [Fr *macaron*]

macaw *n* a large, long-tailed, brightly coloured tropical American parrot. [Port *macao*]

mace[1] *n* **1** a heavy club, usu. with a spiked metal head, used as a weapon in mediaeval times. **2** a ceremonial rod carried as a symbol of authority. [OFr]

mace[2] *n* a spice ground from the dried fleshy covering around the nutmeg seed. [MidE *macis*]

macerate *v* (*tech*) **1** (*intr* & *tr*) to (cause to) break up or become soft by soaking. **2** (*intr*) to waste away as a result of fasting. — *n* **maceration**. [Lat *macerare*, to soak]

Mach *n* (also **Mach number**) a ratio of the speed of an aircraft to the speed of sound (Mach 2, for example, being twice the speed of sound). [Ernst *Mach* (1838–1916), Austrian physicist]

machete *n* a long, heavy, broad-bladed knife used as a weapon or cutting tool, esp. in S America and the W Indies. [Span]

Machiavellian *adj* crafty, amoral and opportunist; seeking power or advantage at any price. — *n* **Machiavellianism**. [Niccolo *Machiavelli* (1469–1527), Italian political philosopher and statesman]

machination *n* (*formal*; usu. in *pl*) a crafty scheme or plot, usu. sinister. — *v* (*intr*) **machinate**. [Lat *machinari*, from Gr *mechane*, contrivance]

machine *n* **1** any (usu. powered) device with moving parts, designed to perform a particular task. **2** a group of people or institutions, or a network of equipment, under a central control: *the party's political machine*. **3** (*coll*) a motor vehicle, esp. a motorcycle. **4** (*coll*) a person with no initiative, capable only of following orders; a tireless or mechanically efficient worker. — *v* (*tr*) **1** to make, shape, cut, etc. with a machine. **2** to stitch with a sewing-machine. [Lat *machina*, from Gr *mechane*, contrivance]

machine code or **language** *n* a numerical (e.g. binary) code used for writing instructions in a form which a computer can understand.

machine-gun *n* any of various portable guns mounted on stands, that fire a continuous stream of bullets. — *v* (*tr*) to shoot with a machine-gun.

machinery *n* **1** machines in general. **2** the working or moving parts of a machine. **3** the combination of processes, systems or people that keeps anything working.

machine tool *n* a power-driven machine that cuts, drills or otherwise shapes metal, wood or plastic.

machinist *n* **1** a person who operates a machine. **2** a person who makes or repairs machines.

machismo *n* exaggerated manliness. [**macho**]

macho *adj* exaggeratedly or aggressively manly. — *n* ***-os*** **1** (*coll*) a man of this type. **2** machismo. [Span, male]

macintosh. Same as **mackintosh**.

mack *n* (*coll*) a mackintosh.

mackerel *n* ***-rels*** or ***-rel*** **1** a N Atlantic sea fish with a silver underside and a bluish-green body with dark wavy stripes. **2** its oily edible flesh. [OFr *maquerel*]

mackintosh *n* **1** a waterproof raincoat. **2** material waterproofed with rubber. [Charles *Macintosh* (1766–1843), the Scottish chemist who patented the waterproofing process]

macramé *n* **1** the art of weaving and knotting string or coarse thread into patterns. **2** articles produced in this way. [Turkish *maqrama*, towel]

macro *n* ***-os*** (*comput*; also **macro-instruction**) a single instruction that brings a set of instructions into operation.

macro- or **macr-** *comb fm* **1** large, long or large-scale: *macroeconomics*. **2** (*pathol*) abnormally large or overdeveloped: *macrocephaly* (the condition of having an abnormally large head). [Gr *makros*, long or great]

macrobiotics *n* (*sing*) the science of devising diets using whole grains and organically-grown fruit and vegetables; the practice of following such a diet, thought to prolong life. — *adj* **macrobiotic**. [**macro-** + Gr *biotos*, life]

macrocosm *n* **1** (with **the**) the universe as a whole. **2** any large or complex system or structure made up of similar smaller systems or structures. [**macro-** + Gr *kosmos*, world]

macro-instruction. See **macro**.

macron *n* a mark (¯) placed over a letter to show it is a long vowel. ◇ See also **breve**. [Gr *makros*, long or great]

macroscopic *n* **1** large enough to be seen by the naked eye. **2** considered in terms of large units or elements. [**macro-** + **-scopic**]

macula *n* **-ae** (*tech*) a spot or blemish, e.g. a freckle or sunspot. [Lat]

mad *adj* **-dd- 1** mentally disturbed; insane. **2** foolish or senseless; extravagantly carefree. **3** (*coll*; **at, with**) very angry. **4** (*coll*; **about**) extremely enthusiastic; fanatical; infatuated. **5** marked by extreme confusion, haste or excitement: *a mad dash for the door*. **6** (of a dog) infected with rabies. — *n* **madness**. — **like mad** (*coll*) frantically; very energetically. [OE *gemæded*, made insane]

madcap *n* & *adj* (a person who is) foolish, impulsive or reckless.

mad cow disease *n* (*coll*) BSE.

madden *v* **-n-** (*tr*) to make mad, esp. to enrage. — *adj* **maddening**.

madhouse *n* **1** (*old*) a mental hospital. **2** (*coll*) a place of great confusion and noise.

madly *adv* **1** in a mad way. **2** (*coll*) passionately: *I love you madly*.

madman or **madwoman** *n* an insane or foolish man or woman.

madam *n* ***mesdames*** (def **1**) and ***madams* 1** a polite form of address to any woman. **2** a form of address to a woman in authority, often prefixed to an official title: *Madam Chairman*. **3** (*coll*) an arrogant or spoiled girl or young woman. **4** a woman who manages a brothel. [**Madame**]

Madame *n* ***Mesdames*** a title equivalent to Mrs, used esp. of a French or French-speaking (esp. married) woman. [Fr, orig. *ma*, my + *dame*, lady]

madder *n* **1** a Eurasian herbaceous plant with yellow flowers and a red root; any of various related plants. **2** a dark red dye, orig. made from the root of this plant. [OE *mæddre* or *mædere*]

made *past tense* & *past participle* of **make**. — *adj* **1** artificially produced: *made ground*. **2** composed of various ingredients put together: *made dish*. — **have it made** (*coll*) to enjoy, or be assured of, complete success or happiness. — **made for** ideally suited to or for.

-made *in cmpds* produced, constructed or formed in the stated way: *handmade*.

made-up *adj* **1** wearing make-up. **2** not true; invented. **3** (*slang*) extremely pleased.

Madeira *n* a strong white dessert wine made on the N Atlantic island of Madeira.

Madeira cake *n* a kind of rich sponge cake.

Madonna *n* **1** (with **the**) the Virgin Mary, mother of Christ. **2** a picture or statue of the Virgin Mary. [Ital, orig. *ma*, my + *donna*, lady]

madrigal *n* a 16th- or 17th-century unaccompanied song with different parts sung together, typically about love or nature. [Ital *madrigale*]

maelstrom *n* **1** a violent whirlpool. **2** (*literary*) a place or state of uncontrollable confusion, esp. one to which one is inevitably drawn. [Dut (now *maalstroom*), whirlpool]

maenad *n* **1** (*mythol*) a female participant in orgies and rites in honour of Bacchus or Dionysus, the god of wine. **2** (*literary*) a woman who behaves in a frenzied or uncontrolled way. — *adj* **maenadic**. [Gr *mainas*, raving]

maestro *n* ***-ros*** or ***-ri*** (a title given to) a man regarded as the master of an art, esp. a famous musical composer, conductor or teacher. [Ital, master]

Mae West *n* an inflatable life-jacket worn by pilots. [*Mae West* (1892–1980), an American actress famous for her large bust]

Mafia *n* **1** (with **the**) a secret international criminal organisation controlling numerous illegal activities worldwide, esp. in the US. **2** any group exerting a secret and powerful influence, esp. one operating unscrupulously. [Ital, hostility to the law]

Mafioso *n* ***-osi*** a member of the Mafia.

mag *n* (*coll*) a magazine (sense **1**).

magazine *n* **1** a paperback periodical publication containing articles, stories, etc. by various writers, usu. heavily illustrated. **2** a regular broadcast presenting reports on a variety of subjects. **3** a metal container for several cartridges, used in some automatic firearms. **4** a storeroom for ammunition, explosives, etc. **5** a container from which photographic slides are automatically fed through a projector. [Ital *magazzino*, from Arabic *makhzan*, storehouse]

magenta *n* & *adj* (of) a dark purplish-red colour. [*Magenta*, Italian town, scene of a bloody battle in 1859]

maggot *n* the worm-like larva of various flies, esp. the housefly. — *adj* **maggoty**. [MidE *maddok* or *mathek*]

magi. See **magus**.

magic *n* **1** (the art or practice of using) the power of supernatural forces to affect people, objects and events. **2** (the art or practice of performing) entertaining illusions and conjuring tricks. **3** the quality of being wonderful, charming or delightful. — *adj* **1** of, used in, or using sorcery or conjuring. **2** (*coll*) excellent. — *v* ***-ck-***

(*tr*; **away**, **up**, etc.) to produce, transform or otherwise affect using, or as if using, sorcery or conjuring. — **like magic 1** mysteriously. **2** suddenly and unexpectedly. **3** excellently. [Gr *magike*]

magical *adj* **1** relating to the art or practice of magic. **2** fascinating; wonderful; charming. — *adv* **magically**.

magic carpet *n* a mythical carpet that can carry people through the air.

magic eye *n* a light-sensitive electric switch; a photoelectric cell.

magician *n* **1** a performer of illusions; a conjurer. **2** a person with supernatural powers.

magic lantern *n* an early form of slide projector.

magisterial *adj* **1** of, or administered by, a magistrate. **2** authoritative; commanding; dictatorial. **3** of, or suitable to, a teacher, instructor or master. — *adv* **magisterially**. [Lat *magister*, master]

magistracy *n* **-*ies*** **1** the rank or position of a magistrate. **2** magistrates as a whole. [Lat *magister*, master]

magistrate *n* **1** a judge in a lower court of law dealing with minor offences; a justice of the peace. **2** any public official administering the law. [Lat *magister*, master]

maglev *n* a high-speed transport system in which magnetism is used to keep an electrically powered train gliding above a track. [**magnetic levitation**]

magma *n* ***magmas*** or ***magmata*** **1** molten rock beneath the earth's crust. **2** a pasty or doughy mass. [Gr, thick ointment]

magnanimous *adj* having or showing admirable generosity of spirit not spoiled by petty feelings. — *n* **magnanimity**. [Lat *magnus*, great + *animus*, mind]

magnate *n* a person of high rank or great power, esp. in industry. [Lat *magnas*, from *magnus*, great]

magnesia *n* **1** (*chem*) a white light powder, magnesium oxide. **2** magnesium carbonate, used as a remedy for indigestion. [*Magnesia*, in Greece]

magnesium *n* an element (symbol **Mg**), a light silvery-white metal that burns with a dazzling white flame. [Ety. as for **magnesia**]

magnet *n* **1** a piece of metal, esp. iron, with the power to attract and repel iron, and the tendency to point in an approximate north-south direction when freely suspended. **2** a person or thing that attracts. [Gr *magnetis lithos*, Magnesian stone, from *Magnesia*, in Greece]

magnetic *adj* **1** of, having the powers of, or operating by means of a magnet or magnetism. **2** able to be made into a magnet. **3** extremely charming or attractive. — *adv* **magnetically**.

magnetic field *n* the area around a magnet within which its power of attraction is felt.

magnetic mine *n* a mine detonated when it detects a magnetic field created by the presence of a large metal object, e.g. a ship.

magnetic north *n* the direction in which a compass's magnetic needle always points, slightly east or west of true north.

magnetic pole *n* either of two nearly opposite points on the earth's surface at which a magnetic needle points vertically downwards.

magnetic storm *n* a sudden, severe disturbance of the earth's magnetic field, caused by streams of particles from the sun.

magnetic tape *n* any of various kinds of thin plastic tape coated with magnetic material, on which sound, television images or computer data can be recorded.

magnetise or **-ize** *v* (*tr*) **1** to make magnetic. **2** to attract strongly. — *n* **magnetisation** or **-z-**.

magnetism *n* **1** (the science and study of) the properties of attraction possessed by magnets. **2** strong personal charm.

magneto *n* **-*os*** a device generating electricity using magnetism, esp. one producing sparks for the ignition of an internal-combustion engine. [Short for *magnetoelectric generator*]

magnificat *n* **1** (*cap*; *relig*) the Virgin Mary's hymn of praise to God, sung in services in certain branches of the Christian Church. **2** any song of praise. [The opening word of the hymn in the Latin New Testament (Luke i. 46–55)]

magnification *n* **1** the act or power of magnifying; the state of being magnified. **2** enlarged appearance (by a stated amount). [Lat *magnificare*, to magnify]

magnificent *adj* **1** splendidly impressive in size or extent. **2** (*coll*) excellent; admirable. — *n* **magnificence**. — *adv* **magnificently**. [Lat *magnificens*, doing great things]

magnify *v* **-*ies***, **-*ied*** (*tr*) **1** to cause to appear larger, e.g. using a microscope or telescope. **2** to exaggerate. — *n* **magnifier**. [Lat *magnus*, great + *facere*, to make]

magnifying glass *n* a convex (esp. hand-held) lens through which objects appear larger.

magniloquent *adj* speaking or spoken in a grand or pompous style. — *n* **magniloquence**. [Lat *magnus*, great + *loqui*, to speak]

magnitude *n* **1** importance or extent. **2** size; largeness. **3** (*astronomy*) the degree of brightness of a star. [Lat *magnitudo*, from *magnus*, great]

magnolia *n* **1** a tree or shrub with large sweet-smelling white or pink flowers; one of its flowers. **2** a pale pinkish-white colour. — *adj* of the colour magnolia. [Pierre *Magnol* (1638–1715), French botanist]

magnum *n* a wine bottle holding twice the normal amount, approximately 1·5 litres. [Lat, big]

magnum opus *n* (*literary*) a great work of art or literature, esp. the greatest produced by a particular artist or writer. [Lat, great work]

magpie *n* **1** a black-and-white bird of the crow family, known for its chattering call and its habit of collecting shiny objects. **2** a person who hoards things, esp. useless trinkets. **3** a chattering person. [*Mag*, dimin. of *Margaret* + *pie*, obsolete form of **magpie**]

magus *n* ***magi*** **1** an ancient Persian priest. **2** an ancient sorcerer or astrologer. **3** (*cap*) one of the three wise men from the east who brought gifts to the infant Jesus. [OPersian, magician]

Magyar *n* **1** a member of the predominant race of people in Hungary, also found in NW Siberia. **2** the Hungarian language. — *adj* of the Magyars or their language. [Magyar]

maharajah or **maharaja** *n* (a title given to) any of various Indian princes, esp. the former rulers of the states of India. [Hindi, from Sanskrit *mahat*, great + *rajan*, king]

maharani or **maharanee** *n* **1** (a title given to) the wife or widow of a maharajah. **2** (a title given to) a woman of the same rank as a maharajah in her own right. [Hindi, from Sanskrit *mahat*, great + *rani*, queen]

maharishi *n* a Hindu religious teacher or spiritual leader. [Hindi, from Sanskrit *mahat*, great + *rishi*, sage]

mahatma *n* a wise and holy Hindu leader. [Hindi, from Sanskrit *mahat*, great + *atman*, soul]

mah-jong or **mah-jongg** *n* an orig. Chinese game for four players, played with small patterned tiles of wood or bone, with rules similar to rummy. [Chin dialect, sparrows]

mahogany *n* ***-ies*** **1** a tropical American tree; any of various related African and Asian trees. **2** the hard wood of any of these trees, often used in making furniture. **3** the colour of the wood, a reddish-brown. — *adj* **1** made from this wood. **2** reddish-brown.

mahout *n* a person who drives, trains and looks after elephants, esp. in India. [Hindi *mahaut*]

maid *n* **1** a female servant. **2** (*old* or *literary*) an unmarried (esp. young) woman. [Short form of **maiden**]

maid of honour *n* ***maids*** **1** an unmarried female servant of a queen or princess. **2** the principal bridesmaid at a wedding, if unmarried. ◇ See also **matron of honour**.

maidservant *n* (*old*) a female servant.

maiden *n* **1** (*old* or *literary*) a young unmarried woman. **2** (*old* or *literary*) a virgin. **3** a horse that has never won a race. **4** (*cricket*) a maiden over. — *adj* **1** first ever: *maiden voyage*. **2** (*literary*) unused; fresh. **3** (of a horse race) open to maidens only. — *n* **maidenhood**. [OE *mægden*]

maidenhair *n* any of various tropical ferns with delicate fan-shaped leaves.

maidenhead *n* (*old* or *literary*) **1** virginity. **2** the hymen.

maiden name *n* a married woman's surname before her marriage.

maiden over *n* (*cricket*) an over from which no runs are scored.

mail[1] *n* **1** the postal system. **2** letters, parcels, etc. sent by post. **3** a single collection or delivery of letters, etc. **4** a vehicle carrying letters, etc. — *v* (*tr*) to send by post. [OFr *male*, bag or trunk]

mailbag *n* a large strong bag in which mail is carried.

mailing list *n* a list of the people to whom an organisation regularly sends information.

mail order *n* & *adv* (using) a system of buying and selling goods by post. — *adj* **mail-order**.

mailshot *n* an unrequested item of post, esp. a piece of advertising material.

mail[2] *n* flexible armour for the body, made of small linked metal rings. — *adj* **mailed**. [OFr *maille*, mesh]

maim *v* (*tr*) to wound seriously, esp. to disable or cripple. [OFr *mahaignier*, to wound]

main *adj* **1** most important; chief. **2** (*literary*) extreme; utmost: *main force*. — *n* **1** (also **mains**) the chief pipe or cable in a branching system. **2** (in *pl*) the network by which power, water, etc. is distributed. **3** (*old*) the open sea: *the Spanish main*. **4** (*old*) great strength, now esp. in the phrase **with might and main**. — **in the main** mostly; on the whole. [OE *mægen*, strength, and Norse *meginn*, strong]

mainbrace *n* (*naut*) the rope controlling the movement of a ship's mainsail.

main clause *n* (*gram*) a clause which can stand alone as a sentence.

mainframe *n* a large powerful computer, esp. one to which several smaller computers can be linked.

mainland *n* (with **the**) a country's principal mass of land, as distinct from a nearby island or islands forming part of the same country.

main line *n* the principal railway line between two places.

mainline *v* (*tr* & *intr*; *slang*) to inject (a drug) into a principal vein, so that it has the quickest possible effect. — *n* **mainliner**. — *n* **mainlining**.

mainly *adv* for the most part; largely.

mainsail *n* the largest and lowest sail on a sailing ship.

mainspring *n* **1** the chief spring in a watch or clock. **2** a chief motive, reason or cause.

mainstay *n* **1** (*naut*) a rope stretching forward and down from the top of the principal mast of a sailing ship. **2** the chief support.

mainstream *n* **1** the principal current of a river. **2** the chief trend, or direction of development, in any activity.

maintain *v* (*tr*) **1** to continue; to keep in existence. **2** to keep in good condition. **3**

to pay the expenses of; to support financially. **4** to continue to argue; to assert. [OFr *maintenir*, from Lat *manu tenere*, to hold in the hand]

maintenance *n* **1** the process of keeping something in good condition. **2** money paid by one person to support another, as ordered by a court of law, e.g. following a divorce. ◇ See also **alimony**. **3** the process of continuing something or keeping something in existence. [OFr]

maisonette or **maisonnette** *n* a flat within a larger house or block, esp. on two floors, usu. with its own separate entrance. [Fr dimin. of *maison*, house]

maître d'hôtel *n* ***maîtres d'hôtel*** **1** a head waiter. **2** the manager of a hotel or restaurant. [Fr, master of the hotel]

maize *n* **1** a tall cereal plant widely grown for its edible yellow grain which grows in large spikes (corncobs). **2** the grain, used for food and as a source of oil. [Span *maíz*, from Taino (extinct S American Indian language) *mahiz*]

Maj. *abbrev* Major.

majesty *n* ***-ies*** **1** great and impressive dignity. **2** splendour. **3** (*cap*; with **His**, **Your**, etc.) a title used when speaking to or of a king or queen. — *adj* **majestic**. — *adv* **majestically**. [Lat *majestas*]

majolica *n* colourfully glazed or enamelled earthenware, esp. popular in Italy from the 14th to the 16th century. [Ital, from Lat *Majorica*, Majorca, where it was orig. made]

major *adj* **1** great, or greater, in number, size, importance, etc. **2** (of a musical key or scale) having two full tones between the first and third notes. — *n* **1** (an army officer of) the rank above captain and below lieutenant-colonel. **2** a major key, chord or scale. **3** (*US*) a student's main subject of study; the student studying such a subject. **4** a person who has reached the age of full legal responsibility. — *v* ***-r-*** (*intr*; **in**) to specialise (in a particular subject of study). [Lat, comparative of *magnus*, great]

major-general *n* (an army officer of) the rank above brigadier and below lieutenant-general.

major-domo *n* ***-os*** a chief servant in charge of the management of a household. [Span *mayor-domo*]

majorette *n* (also **drum majorette**) one of a group of girls who march in parades performing elaborate displays of baton-twirling.

majority *n* ***-ies*** **1** the greater number; the largest group; the bulk. **2** the winning margin of votes in an election. **3** the age at which a person legally becomes an adult. — **in the majority** forming the larger group or greater part. [Lat *majoritas*]

make *v* ***made*** **1** (*tr*) to form, create, manufacture or produce by mixing, combining or shaping materials. **2** (*tr*) to cause to be or become. **3** (*tr*) to cause, bring about or create by one's actions. **4** (*tr*) to force, induce or cause. **5** (*tr*; **into**) to cause to change into; to transform or convert: *make a man of him*; *made the barn into a cottage*. **6** (*tr*) to be suitable for; to have or develop the appropriate qualities for: *This material will make a nice dress. He'll never make a singer*. **7** (*tr*) to appoint. **8** (*tr*) to cause to appear; to represent as being: *Long hair makes her look younger. The film makes him a hero*. **9** (*tr*) to gain, earn or acquire: *make a fortune*. **10** (*tr*) to add up to or amount to; to constitute: *4 and 4 makes 8. The book makes interesting reading*. **11** (*tr*) to calculate, judge or estimate to be: *I make it three o'clock*. **12** (*tr*) to arrive at or reach; to succeed in achieving, reaching or gaining. **13** (*tr*) to score (points). **14** (*tr*) to ensure the success of: *made my day*. **15** (*tr*) to propose: *make an offer*. **16** (*tr*) to engage in; to perform, carry out or produce: *make war*; *make a speech, a decision*. **17** (*tr*) to tidy (a bed) after use. **18** (*intr* with **to**) to show an intention (of doing); to make an attempt or start to: *made to stand up, then sat down again*. **19** (*tr*; *slang*) to succeed in having sexual intercourse with. — *n* **1** a manufacturer's brand. **2** the way in which something is made. — *v* **make away with** (*tr*) **1** to steal. **2** to kill. — **make believe** to pretend (*n* **make-believe**). — **make do 1** (**without**) to manage. **2** (**with**) to make the best use of (a poor-quality alternative to the real thing). — *v* **make for** (*tr*) **1** to move towards, esp. quickly. **2** to have as a result: *Fine weather made for an enjoyable holiday*. — **make it** (*coll*) **1** to be successful. **2** to survive. — **make like** (*coll*; esp. *US*) to act or behave as (if). — *v* **make of** (*tr*) to understand to mean. — *v* **make off** (*intr*) **1** to leave, esp. hurriedly or secretly. **2** (with **with**) to run off with; to steal. — **make or break** to bring the success or failure of (*adj* **make-or-break**). — *v* **make out 1** (*tr*) to see, hear or understand. **2** (*tr*) to cause to seem. **3** (*tr*) to write or fill in. **4** (*tr*) to pretend. **5** (*tr*) to propose, put forward or argue for. **6** (*intr*; *coll*; esp. *US*) to manage, succeed, or survive. — *v* **make over** (*tr*) **1** to transfer ownership of. **2** (esp. *US*) to convert. — *v* **make up 1** (*tr*) to fabricate or invent. **2** (*tr*) to prepare (by putting parts together). **3** (*tr*) to compose; to be the parts of. ◇ See also **make-up** below. **4** (*tr*) to complete: *another player to make up the team*. **5** (*tr*) to apply cosmetics to the face of. ◇ See also **make-up** below. **6** (*intr* & *tr*) to become friends again by settling (differences). **7** (*intr*; **for**) to compensate or serve as an apology. **8** (*intr* with **to**; *coll*) to try to win the friendship or favour of; to flirt with. — *v* **make with** (*tr*; *coll*; esp. *US*) to supply or produce quickly. — **on the make** (*coll*) making a (large or illegal) profit. [OE *macian*]

maker *n* **1** (usu. *in cmpds*) a person who makes. **2** (*cap*) God.

making *n* (esp. *in cmpds*) the process of producing or forming something. — **be the making of** to ensure the success of. — **have the makings of** to have the ability to become; to show signs of becoming. — **in the making** in the process of being made, formed or developed. — **of one's own making** caused by one's own actions.

makeshift *adj* serving as a temporary (often poor) substitute.

make-up *n* **1** cosmetics applied to the face, etc. **2** the combination of characteristics or ingredients that form something, e.g. a personality. ◇ See also **make up** above.

makeweight *n* **1** a small quantity added to a scale to get the required weight. **2** a person or thing of little value or importance, included only to make up for a deficiency.

mal. See **grand mal** and **petit mal**.

mal- *comb fm* **1** bad or badly: *maladapted*. **2** incorrect or incorrectly: *malfunction*. [Lat *male*, badly]

malachite *n* a green mineral, containing (and used as a source of) copper, polished to make ornaments, etc. [Gr *malakhe*, mallow, whose leaves are a similar shade of green]

maladjusted *adj* psychologically unable to deal with everyday situations and relationships, usu. as a result of an emotionally disturbing experience. — *n* **maladjustment**.

maladministration *n* incompetent or dishonest management, esp. of public affairs. — *v* **maladminister**, **-r-** (*tr*).

maladroit *adj* clumsy; tactless. — *adv* **maladroitly**. — *n* **maladroitness**. [Fr]

malady *n* **-ies** (*old* or *formal*) an illness or disease. [Fr *maladie*, from Lat *male habitus*, in bad condition]

malaise *n* **1** a feeling of uneasiness or discontent. **2** a general feeling of ill health, not attributable to any particular disease. [Fr, from *mal*, ill + *aise*, ease]

malapropism *n* the (esp. comic) misuse of a word through confusion with another which sounds similar but has a completely different meaning; a word misused in this way. [Mrs *Malaprop*, a character in Sheridan's play *The Rivals*, who misuses words in this way]

malaria *n* an infectious disease producing recurring bouts of fever, caused by the bite of a certain type of mosquito. — *adj* **malarial**. [Ital *mal' aria*, bad air, formerly thought to be the cause of the disease]

malarkey *n* (*coll*) nonsense; rubbish.

Malay *n* **1** a member of a race inhabiting Malaysia, Singapore and Indonesia. **2** their language, the official language of Malaysia. — *adj* of the Malays or their language. [Malay *malayu*]

malcontent *n* & *adj* (a person who is) dissatisfied and inclined to rebel. [OFr]

male *adj* **1** of the sex which has a sperm-producing or similar organ or organs, not of the sex which gives birth to young. **2** having flowers with stamens which can fertilise female flowers. **3** of or characteristic of men; masculine. **4** for or made up of men or boys. **5** (*tech*) (of electrical plugs, etc.) having a projecting part made to fit into a socket, etc. — *n* a male person, animal or plant. — *n* **maleness**. [OFr *masle*]

male chauvinist *n* (*derog*; also **male chauvinist pig**) a man who believes that men are superior to women. — *n* **male chauvinism**.

malediction *n* a curse; an act of cursing. — *adj* **maledictory**. [Lat *male*, ill + *dicere*, to speak]

malefactor *n* (*old* or *formal*) a criminal; an evil-doer; a wrongdoer. — *n* **malefaction**. [Lat *male*, evil + *facere*, to do]

malevolent *adj* wishing to do evil to others; malicious. — *n* **malevolence**. [Lat *male*, ill + *velle*, to wish]

malfeasance *n* (*legal*) an unlawful act, esp. committed by a public official. — *adj* **malfeasant**. [Fr *malfaisance*]

malformation *n* **1** the state or condition of being badly or wrongly formed or shaped. **2** a badly or wrongly formed part; a deformity. — *adj* **malformed**.

malfunction *n* the act or state of working imperfectly or not at all. — *v* (*intr*) to work imperfectly; to fail to work.

malice *n* **1** the desire or intention to harm or hurt others. **2** mischievousness. [Fr, from Lat *malus*, bad]

malice aforethought *n* (*legal*) a firm intention to commit a crime, esp. against a person.

malicious *adj* feeling, or motivated by, hatred or a desire to cause harm.

malign *v* (*tr*) to say or write unpleasant things about. — *adj* **1** evil in nature or influence; displaying ill-will. **2** (of a disease) harmful; malignant. — *n* **malignity**. [Lat *malignus*, of evil disposition]

malignant *adj* **1** feeling or showing hatred or the desire to do harm; malicious or malevolent. **2** (*med*) tending to cause death, esp. (of cancerous tumours) growing uncontrollably and resisting treatment. — *n* **malignancy**, **-ies**. [Lat *malignare*, to act maliciously]

malinger *v* **-r-** (*intr*) to pretend to be ill, esp. in order to avoid work. — *n* **malingerer**. [Fr *malingre*, sickly]

mall *n* **1** a public promenade, esp. tree-lined. **2** a shopping precinct closed to vehicles. [The *Mall*, a street in London]

mallard *n* **-ard** or **-ards** a wild duck, the male of which has a green head, common in northern countries. [OFr *mallart*]

malleable *adj* **1** (esp. of metal) able to be shaped easily, without breaking. **2** easily influenced. — *n* **malleability**. [Lat *malleabilis*, from *malleus*, hammer]

mallet *n* **1** a hammer with a large (esp. wooden) head. **2** a long-handled wooden hammer for playing croquet or polo. [OFr *maillet*, wooden hammer]

mallow *n* any of various European plants with pink, purple or white flowers and fine hairs on the leaves and stem. [OE *mealwe*]
malmsey *n* a strong sweet wine orig. from Greece, but now usu. from Madeira. [Lat *Malmasia*, from Gr *Monembasia*, Greek port from which it was shipped]
malnutrition *n* (ill health resulting from) general lack of food or a very unbalanced diet.
malodorous *adj* (*formal*) foul-smelling.
malpractice *n* **1** improper, careless or illegal professional conduct; an example of this. **2** any wrong or illegal act.
malt *n* **1** barley or other grain that has been soaked in water, allowed to sprout, and then dried in a kiln, used in brewing. **2** malt whisky. — *v* (*tr*) to make into malt; to treat or combine with malt. [OE *mealt*]
malt whisky *n* whisky made entirely from malted barley.
Maltese *n* **1** a native or inhabitant of the Mediterranean island of Malta. **2** the official language of Malta, a Semitic language with a strong Italian influence. — *adj* of Malta, its people, or their language. [Lat *Melita*]
Maltese cross *n* a cross with four arms of equal length tapering towards the centre, each with a V cut into the end.
Malthusian *adj* of or supporting the theory of economist Thomas *Malthus* (1776–1834), that population increases tend to overtake food supplies, and that there should therefore be restraint or control with regard to sexual activity. — *n* a supporter of this theory.
maltreat *v* (*tr*) to treat roughly or cruelly. — *n* **maltreatment**.
malversation *n* (*formal*; **of**) corruption in public affairs; illegal use (of public funds). [Fr, from Lat *male*, badly + *versari*, to occupy oneself]
mama *n* (also **mamma**) a child's word for mother. [Reduplication of a baby's babbled syllable *ma*]
mamba *n* a large poisonous black or green African snake. [Zulu *imamba*]
mambo *n* **-os** (a piece of music for) a Latin American rhythmic dance. [American Span]
mamma. See **mama**.
mammal *n* any warm-blooded vertebrate animal the female of which produces milk to feed the young. — *adj* (*biol*) **mammalian**. [Lat *mammalis*, of the breast, from *mamma*, breast]
mammary *adj* (*biol* or *med*) of the breasts or other milk-producing glands. [Lat *mamma*, breast]
mammary gland *n* a mammal's milk-producing gland, e.g. a woman's breast or a cow's udder.
mammon *n* wealth when considered a source of evil and immorality, personified (with *cap*) in the New Testament as a false god. [Aramaic *mamon*, wealth]
mammoth *n* any of various large hairy prehistoric elephants, some having long curved tusks. — *adj* huge. [ORuss *mammot*]
man *n* **men** **1** an adult male human being. **2** human beings as a whole; the human race. **3** an adult male human being displaying typical masculine qualities: *a real man*. **4** (*coll*) a husband or boyfriend. **5** an ordinary employee, worker or member of the armed forces, not a manager or officer. **6** one of the movable pieces in various board games. **7** a male member of a team. **8** (*old*) any male servant, esp. a valet. **9** (*coll*) used as a form of address in various contexts, e.g. indicating friendship or impatience: *Damn it, man!* — *v* **-nn-** (*tr*) **1** to provide with sufficient (esp. male) workers. **2** to operate: *man the pumps*. — *interj* (*coll*) used to intensify a following statement: *Man, is she gorgeous!* — **as one man** simultaneously; together. — **man and boy** from childhood to manhood. — **man to man** openly or frankly (*adj* **man-to-man**). — **to a man** without exception. [OE *mann*]
-man *in cmpds* **1** a man associated with a specified activity: *postman*. **2** a man who is a native of a specified country or place: *Yorkshireman*.
man-about-town *n* **men-** a fashionable and sophisticated male socialiser.
man-at-arms *n* **men-** (*hist*) a soldier, esp. heavily armed and mounted.
man-eater *n* **1** a wild animal that attacks, kills and eats people. **2** (*coll*) a woman who pursues men energetically.
man Friday *n* a junior male worker given various duties.
manful *adj* brave and determined; manly. — *n* **manfulness**.
manhandle *v* (*tr*) **1** to treat roughly. **2** to move or transport using manpower, not machinery.
manhole *n* an opening large enough to allow a person through, esp. in a road, leading to a sewer.
manhood *n* **1** the state of being an adult male. **2** manly qualities. **3** men collectively.
man-hour *n* a unit of work equal to the work done by one person in one hour.
manhunt *n* an organised (usu. large-scale) search for someone, esp. a criminal.
mankind *n* the human race as a whole.
manly *adj* **-ier**, **-iest** displaying qualities considered admirable in a man, usu. strength, determination, courage, etc.; suitable for a man. — *n* **manliness**.
man-made *adj* artificial or synthetic, not natural or naturally produced.
mannish *adj* (usu. of a woman) having an appearance that is, or qualities that are, more typical of a man.
man-of-war or **man-o'-war** *n* **men-** (*hist*) an armed sailing ship used as a warship.

manpower *n* **1** number of employees. **2** human effort, as opposed to mechanical power.
manservant *n* ***menservants*** (*old*) a male servant, esp. a valet.
manslaughter *n* the crime of killing someone without intending to do so.
menfolk *n* (*pl*) men collectively, esp. the male members of a family or group.

manacle *n* a handcuff. — *v* (*tr*) to handcuff. [Lat *manicula*, from *manus*, hand]

manage *v* **1** (*tr*) to be in overall control or charge of. **2** (*tr*) to deal with or handle successfully or competently: *manage my own affairs*. **3** (*tr* & *intr*) to succeed in doing or producing (something). **4** (*tr*) to have enough room, time, etc. for. **5** (*tr*) to handle (a tool or weapon). **6** (*tr*) to control (an animal). — *adj* **manageable**. [Ital *maneggiare*, from Lat *manus*, hand]
management *n* **1** the skill or practice of controlling something, esp. a commercial enterprise. **2** the managers of a company, etc., as a group.
manager *n* a person in overall charge, esp. of a commercial enterprise.
manageress *n* (sometimes *offensive*) a female manager.
managerial *adj* of a manager or management.

mañana *n* & *adv* (*coll*) tomorrow; (at) some later time. [Span, tomorrow]

manatee *n* a large plant-eating marine mammal of the tropical waters of America, Africa and the W Indies. [Span *manati*, from Carib (a W Indian language)]

Mancunian *n* & *adj* (a citizen) of Manchester, in NW England. [Lat *Mancunium*, Manchester]

mandala *n* (*Buddhism* & *Hinduism*) a circular symbol representing the universe. [Sanskrit]

mandarin *n* **1** (*cap*; also **Mandarin Chinese**) the official spoken language of China since 1917. **2** (*hist*) a senior official in the Chinese empire. **3** any high-ranking official, esp. one thought to be outside political control. **4** a person of great influence, esp. in the literary world. **5** a small citrus fruit similar to the tangerine; the tree that bears it. [Port *mandarim*, from Malay *mantri*, counsellor]

mandate *n* **1** a right given to a nation, person, or political party to act on behalf of others. **2** an order given by a superior. **3** (*hist*; also **mandated territory**) a territory administered by a country on behalf of the League of Nations (forerunner of the United Nations). — *v* (*tr*) **1** to give authority or power to. **2** to assign (territory) to a nation under a mandate. [Lat *mandare*, from *manus*, hand + *dare*, to give]

mandatory *adj* **1** not allowing any choice; compulsory. **2** of the nature of, or containing, a mandate.

mandible *n* (*biol*) **1** the (esp. lower) jaw in mammals and fish. **2** the upper or lower part of a bird's beak. **3** either of the jaw-like parts of insects and other invertebrates. [Lat *mandibula*, from *mandere*, to chew]

mandolin *n* (also **mandoline**) a musical instrument like a small guitar, but with four pairs of metal strings and a rounded back. [Ital *mandolino*, dimin. of *mandora*, lute]

mandrake *n* a Eurasian plant with purple flowers and a forked root, formerly thought to have magical powers; the root, formerly used to make sleep-inducing drugs. [Lat *mandragora*]

mandrel *n* (*tech*; also **mandril**) **1** the rotating shaft on a lathe, to which the object being worked on is fixed. **2** the axle of a circular saw or grinding wheel. [Fr *mandrin*, lathe]

mandrill *n* a large W African baboon with a red and blue muzzle and hindquarters. [Probably **man** + **drill**[4]]

mane *n* **1** the long hair growing from the neck of horses, lions, and other animals. **2** a long thick head of human hair. [OE *manu*]

manège or **manege** *n* (*tech*) **1** the skill or practice of training or handling horses; the movements taught to a horse. **2** a riding-school. [Fr, from Ital *maneggiare*, to manage]

manganese *n* an element (symbol **Mn**), a brittle greyish-white metal, used in making steel, glass and bronze. [Lat *magnesia*]

mange *n* a skin disease of hairy (esp. domestic) animals, causing itching and loss of hair. [OFr *mangeue*, itch]

mangel-wurzel *n* a variety of beet with a large yellow root, used as cattle food. [Ger *Mangold*, beet + *Wurzel*, root]

manger *n* (*old*) an open box or trough from which cattle or horses feed. [OFr *mangeoire*, from *mangier*, to eat]

mangetout *n* a variety of garden pea of which the whole pod is eaten. [Fr, eat-all]

mangle[1] *v* (*tr*) **1** to damage or destroy by cutting, crushing or tearing. **2** to spoil, ruin or bungle. [OFr *mangler*, from *mahaigner*, to maim]

mangle[2] *n* a hand-operated device with two large rollers between which wet laundry is drawn to be squeezed dry. — *v* (*tr*) to pass through a mangle. [Dut *mangel*]

mango *n* ***-os*** or ***-oes*** (a tropical Asian tree that bears) a yellowish-red juicy pear-shaped fruit. [Port *manga*]

mangrove *n* any tropical evergreen tree that produces roots from its branches and grows densely in swamps and along coasts. [Earlier *mangrow*, from Port *mangue*]

mangy *adj* ***-ier***, ***-iest*** **1** suffering from mange. **2** (*derog*) shabby; seedy. — *adv* **mangily**. — *n* **manginess**. **[mange]**

mania *n* **1** (*med*) a form of mental illness characterised by over-active, over-excited behaviour, and sometimes violence. **2** (**for**) a great desire or enthusiasm; a craze. [Lat, from Gr *mainomai*, to be mad]

-mania *comb fm* **1** (*med*) an abnormal or uncontrollable desire for. **2** great enthusiasm for.

maniac *n* **1** (*coll*) a person who behaves wildly. **2** an extremely keen enthusiast: *a video maniac*. **3** (*old med*) a person suffering from mania. — *adj* **maniacal**.

-maniac *comb fm* a person affected with an uncontrollable desire, or with great enthusiasm, for.

manic *adj* **1** (*med*) of, relating to, or suffering from mania. **2** (*coll*) very energetic or active.

manic-depressive *n* & *adj* (a person) suffering from an illness which produces alternating phases of extreme elation and severe depression.

manicure *n* a cosmetic treatment of the hands, esp. the fingernails, usu. carried out by a trained professional. — *v* (*tr*) to carry out a manicure on (a person or hand). — *n* **manicurist**. [Lat *manus*, hand + *cura*, care]

manifest *v* (*tr*) **1** to show or display clearly. **2** to be evidence or proof of. **3** to reveal or declare (itself). — *adj* easily seen; obvious. — *n* **1** a customs document giving details of a ship or aircraft, its cargo and its destination. **2** a passenger list. — *n* **manifestation**. — *adv* **manifestly**. [Lat *manifestare*]

manifesto *n* **-os** or **-oes** a (usu. written) public declaration of policies or intentions, esp. by a political party or candidate. [Ital, from Lat *manifestare*, to manifest]

manifold *adj* **1** many and various; of many different kinds. **2** having many different features or functions. — *n* **1** (*formal*) a thing with many different forms or functions. **2** (*tech*) a pipe with several inlets and outlets. [**many** + **-fold**]

manikin *n* (also **mannikin**) **1** (*old*) an abnormally small person; a dwarf. **2** a model of the human body, used in teaching art and anatomy. [Dut *manneken*, double dimin. of *man*, man]

manila or **manilla** *n* & *adj* (made of) a type of thick strong brown paper, orig. made from the fibre of a Philippine tree. [*Manila* in the Philippines]

manipulate *v* (*tr*) **1** to handle, esp. skilfully. **2** to control or influence cleverly and unscrupulously, esp. to one's own advantage. **3** to apply treatment with the hands to (a part of the body). — *n* **manipulation**. [Back-formation from **manipulation**, from Lat *manipulus*, handful]

manipulative *adj* tending, or attempting, to manipulate (sense **2**).

manky *adj* **-ier**, **-iest** (*coll*) **1** dirty. **2** of poor quality; shoddy. [Obsolete Scots *mank*, defective]

manna *n* **1** in the Old Testament, the food miraculously provided by God for the Israelites in the wilderness. **2** any unexpected gift or windfall: *manna from heaven*. [Aramaic, poss. from Hebr *man*, gift]

mannequin *n* **1** a fashion model. **2** a life-size dummy of the human body, used in the making or displaying of clothes. [Fr; see **manikin**]

manner *n* **1** way; fashion. **2** (in *pl*) behaviour towards others: *bad manners*. **3** (in *pl*) polite social behaviour: *have no manners*. **4** style: *dressed in the Chinese manner*. **5** kind or kinds: *all manner of things*. — **to the manner born** accustomed since birth (to a particular occupation, activity, etc.). — **by no manner of means** or **not by any manner of means** under no circumstances; certainly not. — **in a manner of speaking** in a way; to some degree; so to speak. [OFr *maniere*, from Lat *manuarius*, of the hand]

mannered *adj* (*formal*; usu. *derog*) unnatural and artificial; affected.

-mannered *in cmpds* having or displaying (a certain kind of) social behaviour: *bad-mannered*.

mannerism *n* **1** an individual characteristic, e.g. a gesture or facial expression. **2** (usu. *derog*) excessive use of an individual style in art or literature. **3** (*cap*) the 16th-century style of (esp. Italian) art in which the human body was represented in an ideal form, rather than naturally.

mannerly *adj* (*old*) polite. — *n* **mannerliness**.

mannikin. See **manikin**.

mannish. See **man**.

manoeuvre *n* **1** a movement requiring, or performed with, considerable skill. **2** a clever handling of affairs, often involving deception. **3** (in *pl*) military exercises, esp. on a large scale. — *v* **1** (*tr* & *intr*) to move (something) accurately and with skill: *manoeuvred* (*the car*) *into the space*. **2** (*tr* & *intr*) to use ingenuity, and perhaps deceit, in handling (something or someone). **3** (*intr*) to carry out military exercises. — *n* **manoeuvrability**. — *adj* **manoeuvrable**. [Fr, from Lat *manu*, by hand + *opera*, work]

manometer *n* an instrument for measuring pressure in liquids and gases. — *adj* **manometric**. [Gr *manos*, rare, thin + **-meter**]

manor *n* **1** in mediaeval Europe, an area of land under the control of a lord. **2** (also **manor-house**) the principal residence on a country estate, often the former home of a mediaeval lord. **3** (*slang*) the area in which a particular person or group, esp. a police unit or a criminal, operates. — *adj* **manorial**. [OFr *manoir*, from Lat *manere*, to stay]

manqué *adj* (*literary*; used following a noun) having once had the potential to be, but never having been: *an artist manqué*. [Fr, having missed]

mansard *n* (also **mansard roof**) a four-sided roof, each side of which is in two parts, the lower part sloping more steeply. [François *Mansart* (1598–1666), French architect]

manse *n* the house of a religious minister, esp. in Scotland. [Lat *mansus*, dwelling]

mansion *n* **1** a large (esp. luxurious) house. **2** a manor-house. **3** (in *pl*; *cap*) a word often used in the name of blocks of (luxury) flats. [Lat *mansio*, remaining]

mantel *n* (*old*) a mantelpiece or mantelshelf. [Ety. as for **mantle**]

mantelpiece *n* the ornamental frame around a fireplace, esp. the top part which forms a shelf.

mantelshelf *n* the shelf part of a mantelpiece.

mantilla *n* **1** a scarf of lace or silk, worn by women over the hair and shoulders, esp. in Spain and S America. **2** a short lightweight cape or cloak. [Span, dimin. of *manta*, from *manto*, cloak]

mantis *n* **-tises** or **-tes** (also **praying mantis**) an insect-eating insect with a long body, large eyes, and a tendency to carry its two front legs raised as if in prayer. [Gr, prophet]

mantissa *n* (*math*) the part of a logarithm comprising the decimal point and the figures following it. ◇ See also **characteristic**. [Lat, something added]

mantle *n* **1** a fireproof mesh round a gas or oil lamp that glows when the lamp is lit. **2** a cloak or loose outer garment. **3** (*literary*) a position of responsibility: *given the leader's mantle*. **4** (*literary*) a covering: *a mantle of snow*. **5** (*geol*) the part of the earth between the crust and the core. — *v* (*tr*; *literary*) to cover or conceal. [Lat *mantellum*, dimin. of *mantum*, cloak]

mantra *n* **1** a word or sound repeated as an aid to concentration when meditating. **2** any of the hymns of praise in the ancient sacred Hindu scriptures, the Vedas. [Sanskrit, instrument of thought]

manual *adj* **1** of the hand or hands. **2** using the body, rather than the mind; physical: *manual worker*. **3** worked, controlled or operated by hand; not automatic. — *n* **1** a book of instructions, e.g. for repairing a car. **2** an organ keyboard. — *adv* **manually**. [Lat *manualis*, from *manus*, hand]

manufacture *v* (*tr*) **1** to make from raw materials, esp. in large quantities using machinery. **2** to invent or fabricate: *manufacture evidence*. **3** (*derog*) to produce in a mechanical fashion. — *n* the practice or process of manufacturing. — *n* **manufacturer**. — *adj* & *n* **manufacturing**. [Lat *manu*, by hand + *facere*, to make]

manumit *v* **-tt-** (*tr*; *formal*) to release from slavery; to set free. — *n* **manumission**. [Lat *manu*, by hand + *mittere*, to send]

manure *n* any substance, esp. animal dung, used on soil as a fertiliser. — *v* (*tr*) to apply manure to. [OFr *manouvrer*, to work by hand]

manuscript *n* **1** an author's handwritten or typed version of a book, etc., before it has been printed. **2** a book or document written by hand. [Lat *manuscriptus*, written by hand]

Manx *adj* of the Isle of Man or its inhabitants. — *n* an almost extinct Celtic language formerly widely spoken on the Isle of Man. — *n* **Manxman**. — *n* **Manxwoman**. [Earlier form *Maniske*, Man-ish]

Manx cat *n* a breed of tailless cat, orig. from the Isle of Man.

many *adj* **1** great in number; numerous. **2** being one of numerous: *many a man*. — *pron* (**of**) a great number of people or things. — *n* (with **the**) the majority; ordinary people, not nobility or royalty. — **in as many** in the same number of. [OE *manig*]

Maoism *n* (support for) the policies and theories of *Mao* Zedong (or Tse-tung) (1893–1976), the first leader of Communist China. — *n* & *adj* **Maoist**.

Maori *n* **-ri** or **-ris** **1** a member of the aboriginal Polynesian people of New Zealand. **2** the language of this people. — *adj* of this people or its language. [Maori]

map *n* **1** a diagram of (any part of) the earth's surface, showing geographical and other features, e.g. the position of towns and roads. **2** a similar diagram of the surface of the moon or a planet. **3** a diagram showing the position of the stars in the sky. **4** a diagram of the layout of anything. — *v* **-pp-** (*tr*) to make a map of. — *v* **map out** (*tr*) to plan (a route, course of action, etc.) in detail. — **put on the map** (*coll*) to cause to become well-known or important. [Lat *mappa*, napkin, painted cloth]

maple *n* **1** (also **maple tree**) any of various broad-leaved deciduous trees of northern regions, whose seeds float by means of wing-like growths. **2** the hard light-coloured wood of these trees, used to make furniture, etc. [OE *mapul*]

maple syrup *n* syrup made from the sap of the sugar maple tree.

maquis *n* **-quis** **1** a type of thick shrubby vegetation found in coastal areas of the Mediterranean. **2** (with **the**; often *cap*) the French resistance movement that fought against German occupying forces during World War II; a member of it. [Fr, from Ital *macchia*, thicket]

Mar. *abbrev* March.

mar *v* **-rr-** (*tr*) **1** to spoil. **2** to injure or damage. [OE *merran*]

marabou *n* **1** a large black-and-white African stork. **2** its feathers, used to decorate clothes, trim hats, etc. [Arabic *murabit*, hermit, holy man, the stork being considered holy in Islam]

maraca *n* a musical instrument consisting of a hollow shell filled with beans, pebbles, etc., held by a handle and shaken, usu. in pairs, orig. used in Latin America. [Port]

maraschino *n* **-os** a liqueur made from cherries, with a taste like bitter almonds. [Ital, from *amarasca*, sour cherry]

maraschino cherry *n* a cherry preserved in this liqueur or something similar, used for decorating cocktails, cakes, etc.

marathon *n* **1** a long-distance race on foot, usu. 42·195 km (26 miles 385 yds). **2** any lengthy and difficult task. — *adj* **1** of or relating to a marathon race. **2** requiring or displaying great powers of endurance: *a marathon effort.* [*Marathon*, in Greece, from where a messenger ran to Athens with news of victory over the Persians in 490 BC]

maraud *v* (*intr*) to wander in search of people to attack and property to steal or destroy. — *n* **marauder**. — *adj* **marauding**. [Fr *marauder*, to prowl]

marble *n* **1** hard streaky-looking limestone rock that can be highly polished, used in building and sculpture. **2** a small hard ball orig. of this rock, now of glass, used in children's games. [OFr *marbre*]

marbled *adj* having irregular streaks of different colours, like marble.

marbles *n* **1** (*sing*) any of several children's games played with marbles. **2** (*pl*; *coll*) mental faculties; wits: *have all one's marbles*; *lose one's marbles*.

marc *n* (a kind of brandy made from) the leftover skins and stems of grapes used in wine-making. [Fr]

marcasite *n* **1** a pale yellow mineral, a compound of iron, used in jewellery. **2** a polished gemstone made from this or any similar mineral. [Lat *marcasita*]

March *n* the third month of the year. [Lat *Martius*, of Mars]

March hare *n* a hare during its breeding season in March, proverbially mad because of its excitable behaviour.

march[1] *v* **1** (*intr*) to walk in a stiff upright formal manner, usu. at a brisk pace and in step with others. **2** (*tr*) to force (esp. soldiers) to walk in this way. **3** (*intr*) to walk in a purposeful and determined way. **4** (*intr*) to advance or continue steadily: *Events marched on.* — *n* **1** an act of marching; a distance travelled by marching. **2** a brisk walking pace. **3** a procession of people (not necessarily marching). **4** a piece of music written (as if) for marching to. **5** unstoppable progress or movement: *the march of time.* — *n* **marcher**. — **steal a march on** to get an advantage over, esp. by trickery. [Fr *marcher*, to walk]

marching orders *n* (*pl*) **1** orders to march in a certain way, given to soldiers, etc. **2** (*coll*) dismissal from a job, etc.

march[2] *n* **1** a boundary or border. **2** a border district, esp. (in *pl*; *cap*) those around the English-Welsh and English-Scottish borders, fought over continuously from the 13th to the 16th century. [Fr *marche*]

marchioness *n* **1** the wife or widow of a marquis. **2** a woman of the same rank in her own right. [Lat *marchionissa*, from *marchio*, marquis]

Mardi Gras *n* **1** Shrove Tuesday, celebrated with a festival in some places, especially famously in Rio de Janeiro, Brazil. **2** the festival. [Fr, fat Tuesday]

mare[1] *n* an adult female horse or zebra. [OE *mere*]

mare's nest *n* a discovery that proves to be untrue or without value.

mare[2] *n* ***maria*** any of numerous large flat areas on the surface of the Moon or Mars, seen from Earth as dark patches and orig. thought to be seas. [Lat, sea]

marg or **marge** *n* (*coll*) margarine.

margarine *n* a butter-like substance made from vegetable oils or animal fats. [Fr, from Gr *margaron*, pearl]

margin *n* **1** the blank space around a page of writing or print. **2** any edge or border. **3** something extra, beyond what should be needed; an amount by which one thing exceeds another: *allow a margin for error*; *win by a large margin.* **4** an upper or lower limit, esp. beyond which it is impossible to exist or operate. [Lat *margo*, border]

marginal *adj* **1** small and unimportant. **2** appearing in the margin of a page of text. **3** (of a political constituency) of which the present representative was elected by only a small majority of votes. — *n* a marginal constituency. — *adv* **marginally**.

marguerite *n* any of various garden plants whose large flowers have pale yellow or white petals round a yellow centre. [Fr, daisy]

marigold *n* any of various garden plants with bright orange or yellow flowers and strongly scented leaves. [(the Virgin) *Mary* + *gold*, obsolete name for the plant]

marijuana or **marihuana** *n* **1** the dried leaves and flowers of the hemp plant, used as an intoxicating drug, esp. in cigarette form. **2** the hemp plant. [Mexican Span]

marimba *n* an orig. African type of xylophone consisting of a set of hardwood strips which, when struck with soft hammers, vibrate metal plates underneath, producing musical sound. [From a W African language]

marina *n* a harbour for private pleasure boats. [**marine**]

marinade *n* any liquid mixture in which food, esp. meat or fish, is soaked to add flavour before cooking. — *v* (*tr* & *intr*) to marinate. [Fr, from Span *marinar*, to pickle in brine]

marinate *v* (*tr* & *intr*) to soak in a marinade. [Span *marinar*, to pickle in brine]

marine *adj* **1** of, concerned with, or found in the sea. **2** of ships, shipping trade, or the navy. — *n* **1** a soldier trained to serve on land or at sea. **2** the merchant or naval ships of a nation collectively. [Lat *marinus*, from *mare*, sea]

mariner *n* (*old*) a seaman.

marionette *n* a puppet with jointed limbs moved by strings. [Fr, dimin. of *Marion*, woman's name]

marital *adj* of or relating to marriage. — *adv* **maritally**. [Lat *maritus*, married]

maritime *adj* **1** of the sea or ships. **2** (living or growing) near the sea. **3** (of climate) having relatively small temperature differences between summer and winter. [Lat *maritimus*, of the sea]

marjoram *n* a purple-flowered Mediterranean plant whose sweet-smelling leaves are used to season food. [OFr *marjorane*]

mark[1] *n* **1** a visible blemish, e.g. a scratch or stain. **2** a patch, stripe, spot, etc. forming part of a larger pattern. **3** (a number or letter used as) a grade of a student's, competitor's, etc. proficiency. **4** a sign or symbol: *a question mark*. **5** an indication or representation: *a mark of respect*. **6** the position from which a competitor starts in a race: *on your marks*. **7** an object or thing aimed at; a target: *wide of the mark*. **8** a required standard: *up to the mark*. **9** influence: *Your work bears his mark*. **10** a cross or other sign used instead of a signature. **11** (often *cap*) a type of design, or model, esp. of vehicles. — *v* **1** (*tr* & *intr*) to (cause to) become spoiled by a mark. **2** (*tr*) to award a grade to. **3** (*tr*) to show; to be a sign of: *X marks the spot. events marking a new era*. **4** (*tr*) to make a note of. **5** (*tr*) to pay close attention to: *mark my words*. **6** (*tr*; *sport*) to stay close to (an opposing player), limiting his or her influence on the game. **7** (*tr*) to characterise or label: *This incident marks him as a criminal*. — **leave** or **make one's mark** to make a strong or permanent impression. — *v* **mark down** (*tr*) **1** to note. **2** to reduce the price of (*n* **mark-down**). — *v* **mark off** or **out** (*tr*) to fix the boundaries or limits of. — **mark time 1** to move the feet up and down as if marching, but without going forward. **2** to merely keep things going while waiting to speed up or progress. — *v* **mark up** (*tr*) to add to the cost price of, to provide profit for the seller (*n* **mark-up**). [OE *merc*, boundary, limit]

mark-down see **mark down** above.

marked *adj* **1** obvious or noticeable. **2** watched with suspicion; selected as the target for an attack: *a marked man*.

markedly *adv* noticeably.

marker *n* **1** a person who takes notes, e.g. of the score in a game. **2** anything used to mark the position of something. **3** (also **marker pen**) a pen with a thick point, for writing signs, etc.

marking *n* (often in *pl*) a distinctive pattern of colours on an animal or plant.

marksman *n* a person able to shoot (esp. a gun) accurately, esp. a soldier or policeman trained to do so. — *n* **marksmanship**.

mark-up see **mark up** above.

mark[2] *n* **1** (also **Deutschmark** or **Deutsche Mark**) the standard unit of currency in Germany, formerly only of the old Federal Republic of Germany. **2** (also **Ostmark**) the standard unit of currency of the former German Democratic Republic (East Germany). [OE *marc*, unit of weight of precious metal]

market *n* **1** a periodic gathering of people to buy and sell various goods. **2** the building or other public place in which this takes place. **3** a particular region or section of the population considered as a potential customer: *the teenage market*. **4** a level of trading: *The market is slow*. **5** opportunity to trade; demand: *no market for these goods*. — *v* **-t- 1** (*tr*) to offer for sale; to promote. **2** (*intr*) to trade or deal. — *adj* **marketable**. — **be in the market for** to wish to buy. — **on the market** on sale; able to be bought. [OE, from Lat *mercatus*, trade, market]

market forces *n* the willingness of customers to buy goods or services that suppliers are willing to offer at a particular price; supply and demand.

market-garden *n* a (usu. large commercial) garden where fruit and vegetables are grown for sale to markets. — *n* **market-gardener**.

marketing *n* the business techniques or processes by which anything may be sold.

market-place *n* **1** the open space in a town in which a market is held. **2** (with **the**; also **marketplace**) the commercial world of buying and selling.

market price *n* the price at which a thing is being sold at a particular time.

market research *n* investigation of the habits, needs and preferences of customers.

market town *n* a town, often at the centre of a farming area, where a market is regularly held.

marksman. See **mark**[1].

marl *n* soil consisting of clay, lime and silt, used as a fertiliser. — *v* (*tr*) to apply marl to. — *adj* **marly**. [OFr *marle*]

marlin *n* **-lin** or **-lins** (also **spearfish**) a large fish of warm and tropical seas, with a long spear-like upper jaw. **[marlinspike]**

marlinspike or **marlinespike** *n* (*naut*) a pointed metal tool for separating the strands of rope to be spliced. [Dut *marlijn*, from *marren*, to tie + *lijn*, rope]

marmalade *n* jam made from any citrus fruit, esp. oranges. [Port *marmelada*, from *marmelo*, quince, from which it was orig. made]

marmoreal *adj* (*formal*) of or like marble. [Lat *marmor*, marble]

marmoset *n* any of various small S American monkeys with a long bushy tail and tufts of hair around the head and ears. [OFr *marmouset*, grotesque figure]

marmot *n* any of various stout coarse-haired burrowing rodents of Europe, Asia and N America. [Fr *marmotte*]

maroon[1] *n* & *adj* (of) a dark brownish- or purplish-red colour. [Fr *marron*, chestnut]

maroon[2] *v* (*tr*) **1** to leave in isolation in a deserted place, esp. on an island. **2** to leave helpless. [Mexican Spanish *cimarrón*, wild]

marque *n* a brand or make, esp. of car. [Fr]

marquee *n* a very large tent used for circuses, parties, etc. [Orig. an army officer's tent, coined from **marquise**, wrongly thought to be plural]

marquetry *n* (the art or practice of making) decorative arrangements of pieces of different woods, often set into the surface of wooden furniture. [Fr *marqueterie*, from *marqueter*, to inlay]

marquis *n* (also **marquess**) **1** in the UK, a nobleman above an earl and below a duke in rank. **2** in other countries, a nobleman next in rank above a count. [OFr *marchis*, from Lat *marchensis*, prefect of the marches; see **march**[2]]

marquise *n* in various countries, a marchioness. [Fr; see ety. for **marquis**]

marram *n* (also **marram grass**) a coarse grass that grows on sandy shores, often planted to stop sand erosion. [Norse *marr*, sea + *halmr*, haulm or stem]

marriage *n* **1** the state or relationship of being husband and wife. **2** the act of becoming husband and wife. **3** the ceremony within which this act is performed; a wedding. **4** a joining together; a union. [OFr *mariage*]

marriageable *adj* suitable, esp. at a legal age, for marriage. — *n* **marriageability** or **marriageableness**.

marriage certificate *n* an official piece of paper showing that two people are legally married.

marriage guidance *n* professional advice given to couples (married or not) having problems with their relationship.

marriage licence *n* a paper giving official permission for a marriage to take place.

marriage of convenience *n* a marriage entered into for the advantages it will bring, rather than for love.

married. See **marry**.

marrow *n* **1** (also **bone marrow**) the soft tissue in the hollow centre of human or animal bones. **2** (also **vegetable marrow**) a large oblong rounded vegetable with thick green skin and soft white flesh. **3** the innermost, essential or best part of anything. — **to the marrow** right through. [OE *mærg*]

marrowbone *n* a bone containing edible marrow.

marrowfat *n* (also **marrowfat pea**) a variety of large edible pea; the plant that bears it.

marry *v* **-ies**, **-ied** **1** (*tr*) to take as one's husband or wife. **2** (*tr*) to perform the ceremony of marriage between. **3** (*tr*) to give (a son or daughter) in marriage. **4** (*intr*) to become husband and wife. **5** (*tr*; *formal*; **up**) to assemble, join up or match correctly. — *v* **marry into** (*tr*) to become part of (a family, social class, etc.) by marriage. — *v* **marry off** (*tr*) to find a husband or wife for (esp. a son or daughter). [Lat *maritare*]

married *adj* **1** having a husband or wife. **2** of or relating to marriage: *married life*. **3** fixed together; joined. — *n* (esp. in *pl*) a married person.

Marsala *n* a dark sweet sherry-like wine made in *Marsala*, in Sicily.

Marseillaise *n* (with **the**) the French national anthem, orig. a revolutionary song. [First sung in Paris by revolutionary soldiers from *Marseilles* in SE France, although composed in Strasbourg for the Rhine army]

marsh *n* (an area of) soft, low-lying, permanently watery land. — *adj* **marshy**, **-ier**, **-iest**. [OE *mersc* or *merisc*]

marsh gas *n* methane.

marsh mallow *n* a pink-flowered plant that grows wild in coastal marshes.

marshmallow *n* a spongy pink or white sweet, orig. made from the root of the marsh mallow.

marsh marigold *n* a marsh plant with flowers like large buttercups.

marshal *n* **1** any of various high-ranking officers in the armed forces. **2** an official who organises parades, etc., or controls crowds at large public events. **3** (*US*) a chief police or fire officer in some states. — *v* **-ll-** (*tr*) **1** to arrange (facts, etc.) in order. **2** to direct, lead or show the way to. [OFr *mareschal*]

marshalling-yard *n* a place where railway wagons are arranged into trains.

marshmallow. See **marsh**.

marsupial *n* a class of mammals, including kangaroos and koala, whose young are born undeveloped and are carried in an external pouch on the mother's body until fully developed. — *adj* of or like a marsupial. [Lat *marsupium*, pouch]

mart *n* a trading place; a market. [Dut *markt*]

martello *n* **-os** (also **martello tower**) a small circular fortified tower used for coastal defence. [Cape *Mortella*, Corsica]

marten *n* **1** any of various small tree-dwelling predatory mammals with a long thin body and a bushy tail. **2** their highly valued soft black or brown fur. [Dut *martren*, from OFr *martre*]

martial *adj* of, relating to, or suitable for war or the military. [Lat *martialis*, of Mars, Roman god of war]

martial art *n* any of various fighting sports or self-defence techniques of Far Eastern origin, e.g. karate or judo.

martial law *n* law and order strictly enforced by the army when ordinary civil law has broken down, e.g. during a war or revolution.

Martian *n* & *adj* (a fictional inhabitant) of the planet Mars. [Lat *Martius*]

martin *n* any of various small birds of the swallow family, with a square or slightly forked tail. [The name *Martin*]

martinet *n* (usu. *derog*) a person who maintains strict discipline. [*Martinet*, one of Louis XIV's generals]

martini *n* **1** (*cap*; ®) an Italian brand of vermouth. **2** a cocktail of gin and vermouth.

Martinmas *n* Saint Martin's day, 11 November.

martyr *n* **1** a person who chooses to die rather than give up his or her (esp. religious) beliefs. **2** (**to**) a person who suffers greatly for any cause or reason: *a martyr to arthritis*. — *v* **-r-** (*tr*) to put to death as a martyr. [Lat, from Gr *martus*, witness]

martyrdom *n* the death or suffering of a martyr.

marvel *n* an astonishing or wonderful person or thing. — *v* **-ll-** (*intr*; **at**) to be filled with astonishment or wonder. [Fr *merveille*]

marvellous *adj* **1** so wonderful or astonishing as to be almost beyond belief. **2** (*coll*) excellent. — *adv* **marvellously**.

Marxism *n* the theories of Karl *Marx* (1818–83), German economist and political philosopher, stating that the struggle between different social classes is the main influence on political change, and that communism will eventually replace capitalism. — *n & adj* **Marxist**.

marzipan *n* a sweet paste of crushed almonds and sugar, used to decorate cakes, make sweets, etc. [Ital *marzapane*]

masc. *abbrev* masculine.

mascara *n* a cosmetic for darkening the eyelashes, applied with a brush. [Ital, mask]

mascot *n* a person, animal or thing thought to bring good luck. [Fr *mascotte*, from Provençal *mascotto*, charm]

masculine *adj* **1** of, typical of, or suitable for men. **2** (of a woman) mannish; unfeminine. **3** (*gram*) of, or referring to, one of the (usu. two or three) classes into which nouns are divided in many languages, the class including males. — *n* (*gram*; with **the**) the masculine gender. — *n* **masculinity**. [Lat *masculinus*, from *masculus*, male]

maser *n* a device for increasing the strength of microwaves, used in radar. [*M*icrowave *a*mplification by *s*timulated *e*mission of *r*adiation]

mash *v* (*tr*) **1** (**up**) to beat or crush into a pulpy mass. **2** to mix (malt) with hot water. — *n* **1** a boiled mixture of grain and water used to feed farm animals. **2** a mixture of crushed malt and hot water, used in brewing. **3** any soft mass. **4** (*coll*) mashed potatoes. [OE *masc*]

mask *n* **1** any covering for (part of) the face, worn for amusement, for protection, or as a disguise. **2** (*literary*) anything that disguises the truth, e.g. false behaviour: *a mask of light-heartedness*. — *v* (*tr*) **1** to put a mask on. **2** to disguise or conceal. — *adj* **masked**. [Arabic *maskharah*, clown]

masking tape *n* sticky paper tape used in painting to cover the edge of a surface to be left unpainted.

masochism *n* **1** the practice of deriving (esp. sexual) pleasure from pain or humiliation inflicted by another person. **2** (*coll*) a tendency to take pleasure in one's own suffering. — *n* **masochist**. — *adj* **masochistic**. [Leopold von Sacher *Masoch* (1836–95), Austrian novelist who described it]

mason *n* **1** (also **stonemason**) a person trained in the craft of working with, or building in, stone. **2** (often *cap*) a freemason. [OFr *masson*]

masonic *adj* (often *cap*) of or relating to freemasons.

masonry *n* **1** the part of a building built by a mason; stonework and brickwork. **2** the craft of a mason. **3** (often *cap*) freemasonry.

masque *n* a kind of dramatic entertainment performed to music by masked actors in 16th- and 17th-century English royal courts. [Fr, mask]

masquerade *n* **1** a pretence or show. **2** a formal dance at which the guests wear masks and costumes. — *v* (*intr*; **as**) to disguise oneself; to act, with the intention of deceiving. [Fr *mascarade*]

Mass. *abbrev* Massachusetts.

mass[1] *n* **1** a large (usu. shapeless) quantity gathered together; a lump. **2** (*coll*; often in *pl*) a large quantity or number. **3** majority; bulk. **4** (*tech*) a measure of the quantity of matter in a body. **5** (in *pl* with **the**) ordinary people. **6** an area of uniform colour or shading in art. — *adj* involving a large number of people: *a mass meeting*. — *v* (*intr & tr*) to (cause to) gather in large numbers. [Fr *masse*, from Lat *massa*, lump]

mass media *n* (*pl*) those forms of communication that reach large numbers of people, e.g. television and newspapers.

mass-produce *v* (*tr*) to produce in a standard form in great quantities, esp. using mechanisation. — *adj* **mass-produced**. — *n* **mass-production**.

mass[2] *n* (often *cap*) **1** (in the Roman Catholic and Orthodox Churches) the Eucharist, a celebration of Christ's last supper; the ceremony in which this occurs. **2** a part of the text of this ceremony set to music and sung by a choir or congregation. [OE *mæsse*]

massacre *n* **1** a cruel killing of large numbers of people or animals. **2** (*coll*) an overwhelming defeat. — *v* (*tr*) **1** to kill cruelly and in large numbers. **2** (*coll*) to defeat overwhelmingly. [OFr]

massage *n* a technique of easing pain or stiffness in the body, esp. the muscles, by rubbing, kneading and tapping with the hands; a body treatment using this technique. — *v* (*tr*) **1** to perform massage on. **2** to alter (e.g. statistics) to produce a more favourable result. [Fr, from Gr *massein*, to knead]

masseur and **masseuse** *n* respectively a male and a female person trained to carry out massage. [Fr; see ety. for **massage**]

massif *n* a mountain range formed from one mass of rock. [Fr; see ety. for **massive**]

massive *adj* **1** very big, solid and heavy. **2** (*coll*) very large: *a massive salary*. — *adv* **massively**. [Fr *massif*, from *masse*, mass]

mast[1] *n* any upright wooden or metal supporting pole, esp. one carrying the sails of a ship, or a radio or television aerial. — **before the mast** (*naut*) serving as an apprentice seaman. [OE *mæst*]

masthead *n* **1** the top of a ship's mast. **2** the title of a newspaper or periodical printed at the top of its front page.

mast[2] *n* the nuts of various forest trees, esp. beech, oak and chestnut, used as food for pigs. [OE *mæst*]

mastectomy *n* **-ies** the surgical removal of (part of) a woman's breast. [Gr *mastos*, breast + **-ectomy**]

master *n* **1** a person, esp. male, who commands or controls. **2** the owner, esp. male, of a dog, slave, etc. **3** a person with outstanding skill in a particular activity. **4** the commanding officer on a merchant ship. **5** a fully qualified craftsman, allowed to train others. **6** (esp. *old*) a male teacher. **7** (*cap*) a title for the heads of certain university colleges. **8** (also **master copy**) an original from which copies are made. **9** (*cap*) (a person who holds) a degree of the level above Bachelor: *Master of Arts*. **10** (*cap*) a title for a boy too young to be called Mr. — *adj* **1** fully qualified; highly skilled; expert. **2** main; principal: *master bedroom*. **3** controlling: *master switch*. — *v* (*tr*) **1** to overcome or defeat (e.g. feelings or an opponent). **2** to become skilled in. [Lat *magister*, from *magnus*, great]

master-at-arms *n* ***masters-*** a ship's officer responsible for maintaining discipline.

masterful *adj* showing the authority, skill or power of a master. — *adv* **masterfully**.

master key *n* a key which opens a number of locks, each of which has its own different key.

masterly *adj* showing the skill of a master. — *n* **masterliness**.

mastermind *n* **1** a person of great intellectual ability. **2** the person responsible for devising a complex scheme or plan. — *v* (*tr*) to be the mastermind of (a scheme, etc.).

master of ceremonies *n* an announcer, esp. of speakers at a formal dinner, or of performers in a stage entertainment.

masterpiece *n* (also **masterwork**) an extremely skilful piece of work, esp. the greatest work of an artist or writer.

masterstroke *n* a very clever or well-timed action.

mastery *n* **1** (**of**) great skill or knowledge. **2** (**over**) control.

mastic *n* **1** a gum obtained from a Mediterranean evergreen tree, used in making varnish. **2** any of various waterproof putty-like pastes used as joint-sealers in the building trade. [Gr *mastiche*]

masticate *v* (*tr* & *intr*; *formal* or *tech*) to chew (food). — *n* **mastication**. [Lat *masticare*]

mastiff *n* a large powerful short-haired breed of dog, formerly used in hunting. [OFr *mastin*, from Lat *mansuetus*, tame]

mastitis *n* inflammation of a breast or udder. [Gr *mastos*, breast + **-itis**]

mastodon *n* a prehistoric elephant-like mammal with nipple-shaped projections on its teeth. [Gr *mastos*, breast + *odontos*, tooth]

mastoid *adj* like a nipple or breast. — *n* the raised area of bone behind the ear. [Gr *mastoeides*, like a breast]

masturbate *v* (*intr* & *tr*) to rub or stroke the genitals of (oneself or someone else) so as to produce sexual arousal, usu. to the point of orgasm or ejaculation. — *n* **masturbation**. — *adj* **masturbatory**. [Lat *masturbari*]

mat[1] *n* **1** a flat piece of any of various materials in carpet-like form, used as a decorative or protective floor-covering, or for wiping shoes on to remove dirt. **2** a smaller piece of fabric, or a harder material, used under a plate, vase, etc. to protect a surface from heat or scratches. **3** a carpet-like covering, e.g. of vegetation or hair. — *v* **-tt-** (*tr* & *intr*) to (cause to) become tangled into a dense untidy mass. — *adj* **matted**. [OE *matt* or *matte*]

matting *n* material of rough woven fibres for making mats.

mat[2]. Same as **matt**.

matador *n* the principal toreador in a bull-fight, the man who kills the bull. [Span, from *matar*, to kill]

match[1] *n* **1** a short thin piece of wood or strip of card coated on the tip with a substance that ignites when rubbed against a rough surface, used to light fires, etc. **2** a slow-burning fuse used in cannons. [OFr *mesche*]

matchbox *n* a small cardboard box for holding matches.

matchstick *n* the stem of a (used) wooden match.

matchwood *n* **1** wood suitable for making matches. **2** splinters.

match[2] *n* **1** a contest or game. **2** (**for**) a person or thing that is similar or identical to, or combines well with, another. **3** (**for**) a person or thing able to equal, or surpass, another: *meet one's match*. **4** a partnership or pairing; a suitable partner, e.g. in marriage. — *v* **1** (*tr* & *intr*; **up**) to combine well; to be well suited or compatible; to put (matching people or things) together. **2** (*tr*) to set in competition; to hold up in comparison. **3** (*tr*) to be equal to; to make, produce, perform, etc. an equivalent to:

can't match that offer. [OE *gemæcca*, spouse]

matching *adj* similar; compatible; part of the same set.

matchless *adj* (*literary*) having no equal; superior to all.

matchmaker *n* a person who tries to arrange romantic partnerships between people. — *n* **matchmaking**.

match point *n* the stage in a game at which only one more point is needed by a player to win; the winning point.

mate[1] *n* **1** an animal's breeding partner. **2** (*coll*) a person's sexual partner, esp. a husband or wife. **3** (*coll*) a companion or friend, often used as a form of address, esp. to a man. **4** (*in cmpds*) a colleague; a person with whom one shares something: *workmate*; *flatmate*. **5** a tradesman's assistant. **6** one of a pair. **7** any officer below the rank of master on a merchant ship. — *v* **1** (*intr*) (of animals) to copulate. **2** (*tr*) to bring (animals) together for breeding. **3** (*intr* & *tr*) to marry. **4** (*tr*) to join as a pair. [Related to OE *gemetta*, guest at one's table]

matey or **maty** *adj* **-ier**, **-iest** (*coll*) friendly or familiar, often in an insincere way. — *adv* **matily**.

mate[2]. See **checkmate**.

maté *n* (also **mate**) **1** a S American species of holly tree. **2** a type of tea made from its dried leaves. [Quechua *mati*, a gourd (in which the tea is made)]

mater *n* (*humorous* or *old coll*) a mother, also used as a form of address. [Lat]

material *n* **1** any substance out of which something is, or may be, made. **2** cloth; fabric. **3** (in *pl*) instruments or tools needed for a particular activity. **4** information providing the substance from which a book, television programme, etc. is prepared. — *adj* **1** of, relating to, or consisting of solid matter; not abstract or spiritual. **2** relating to physical, not emotional, well-being: *material comforts*. **3** (*formal*; **to**) important; significant; relevant: *facts not material to the discussion*. [Lat *materia*, matter]

materialise or **-ize** *v* (*intr*) **1** to become real, visible or tangible; to appear. **2** to become fact; to happen. — *n* **materialisation** or **-z-**.

materialism *n* **1** (often *derog*) excessive interest in material possessions and financial success. **2** (*philos*) the theory stating that only material things exist, esp. denying the existence of a soul or spirit. — *n* & *adj* **materialist**. — *adj* **materialistic**.

materially *adv* **1** (*formal*) to an important or significant extent. **2** with regard to physical well-being.

maternal *adj* **1** of, typical of, or like a mother. **2** related on the mother's side of the family. — *adv* **maternally**. [Lat *maternus*, from *mater*, mother]

maternity *n* the state of being or becoming a mother. — *adj* relating to pregnancy or giving birth. [**maternal**]

matey. See **mate**[1].

mathematics *n* (*sing*) the science dealing with measurements, numbers, quantities and shapes, usu. expressed as symbols. [Gr *mathematike*, relating to learning, from *manthanein*, to learn]

mathematical *adj* **1** of, relating to or using mathematics. **2** very exact or accurate. — *adv* **mathematically**.

mathematician *n* a student of, or expert in, mathematics.

maths *n* (*sing*; *coll*) mathematics.

matinée or **matinee** *n* an afternoon performance of a play or showing of a film. [Fr, morning]

matinée jacket or **coat** *n* a baby's short jacket or coat.

matins *n* (*sing* or *pl*) **1** (*RC*) the first of the seven canonical hours, periods during the day set aside for formal prayer. ◇ See also **compline**, **lauds**, **none**[2], **sext**, **terce**, **vespers**. **2** (*C of E*) the service of morning prayer. [Lat *matutinus*, of the morning]

matri- *comb fm* of a woman or a mother: *matricide*. [Lat *mater*, mother]

matriarch *n* the female head of a family, community or tribe. [**matri-** + **patriarch**]

matriarchal *adj* of, ruled by, or resembling a matriarch.

matriarchy *n* **-ies** a social system in which women are the heads of families or tribes, and property and power passes from mother to daughter.

matric. See **matriculation**.

matrices. See **matrix**.

matricide *n* **1** the killing of a mother by her own child. **2** a person who kills his or her own mother. — *adj* **matricidal**. [**matri-** + **-cide**]

matriculate *v* (*tr* & *intr*) to admit or (become eligible to) be admitted as a member, esp. of a university or college. [Lat *matriculare*, to register]

matriculation *n* **1** the process of matriculating. **2** (*coll* **matric**) formerly, a university or college entrance examination taken at school.

matrimony *n* **-ies** **1** the state of being married. **2** the wedding ceremony. — *adj* **matrimonial**. [Lat *matrimonium*, wedlock]

matrix *n* **-trices** or **-trixes** **1** (*math*) an arrangement of interrelated symbols, numbers, etc. in rows and columns, regarded as a mathematical unit. **2** the place in which anything develops or is formed. **3** (*tech*) the rock in which a mineral or fossil is embedded. **4** (*tech*) a mould, esp. one from which printing type is produced. **5** (*old*) the womb. [Lat, womb]

matron *n* **1** the former title of the head of the nursing staff in a hospital (now usu. **senior nursing officer**). **2** a woman in charge of nursing and domestic arrangements in an institution, e.g. a school or old people's home. **3** any dignified or solemn middle-aged to elderly (esp. married) woman. [Fr *matrone*, from Lat *mater*, mother]

matronly *adj* **1** (of a woman) dignified; authoritative. **2** (*euph*) (of a woman) plump owing to middle-age.

matron of honour *n* ***matrons*** a married woman who is a bride's chief attendant at a wedding. ◇ See also **maid of honour**.

matt *adj* (also **mat, matte**) having a dull surface without gloss or shine. [Fr *mat*, dull colour or unpolished surface]

matter *n* **1** the substance from which all physical things are made; material. **2** material of a particular kind: *vegetable matter*. **3** (often in *pl*; **of**) a subject or topic; a concern, affair or question: *if it's a matter of money*. **4** content, not style or form. **5** (**of**) an approximate amount: *in a matter of minutes*. **6** pus. — *v* (*intr*) to be important or significant. — **as a matter of fact** in fact. — **be the matter** (**with**) to be the trouble, difficulty or thing that is wrong. — **for that matter** as far as that is concerned. — **no matter** it is not important. — **no matter...** regardless of: *no matter when she comes*. [Lat *materia*, subject or substance]

matter-of-fact *adj* calm and straightforward, not excited or emotional. — *adv* **matter-of-factly**. — *n* **matter-of-factness**.

mattock *n* a kind of pickaxe whose blade is flattened horizontally at one end, used for breaking up soil, etc. [OE *mattuc*]

mattress *n* a large flat fabric-covered pad, now usu. of foam rubber or feathers, used for sleeping on, by itself or on a supporting frame. [OFr *materas*, from Arabic *almatrah*, place where anything is thrown]

maturate *v* (*tr* & *intr*) **1** to make or become mature. **2** (*med*) to (cause to) discharge pus. — *n* **maturation**. [Lat *maturare*]

mature *adj* **1** fully grown or developed. **2** having or showing adult good sense. **3** (of cheese, wine, etc.) having a fully developed flavour. **4** (of bonds, insurance policies, etc.) paying out, or beginning to pay out, money to the holder. **5** (*formal*) carefully or thoroughly thought out. — *v* **1** (*tr* & *intr*) to make or become fully developed, or adult in outlook. **2** (*intr*) (of an insurance policy, etc.) to begin to produce a return. — *n* **maturity**. [Lat *maturus*, ripe]

maty. See **mate**[1].

maudlin *adj* foolishly sad or sentimental, esp. when drunk. [OE *Maudelein*, Mary Magdalene, often portrayed weeping]

maul *v* (*tr*) **1** to attack fiercely, usu. tearing flesh. **2** to handle roughly or clumsily. **3** to subject to fierce criticism. — *n* (*Rugby*) a quickly formed gathering of players from both teams around a player holding the ball. [Lat *malleus*, hammer]

maunder *v* ***-r-*** (*intr*) **1** (**on**) to talk in a rambling way. **2** to wander about, or behave, in an aimless way. [Perhaps from obsolete *maunder*, to beg]

Maundy Thursday *n* the day before Good Friday, on which the sovereign gives out specially minted silver coins (**Maundy money**) to the poor. [OFr *mande*, from Lat *mandatum*, command (from Jesus' command in John 23.34)]

mausoleum *n* a large impressive tomb, often with a monument. [Lat, from the magnificent tomb of the ancient Greek king *Mausolos*]

mauve *n* & *adj* (of) a pale purple colour. [Fr, from Lat *malva*, mallow]

maverick *n* **1** (esp. *US*) an unbranded stray animal, esp. a calf. **2** a determinedly independent person; a nonconformist. [Samuel *Maverick* (1803–70), Texas cattle-raiser]

maw *n* **1** the jaws, throat or stomach of an (esp. insatiably greedy) animal. **2** (*facet*) a greedy person's stomach. **3** something that seems to swallow things up. [OE *maga*]

mawkish *adj* weakly sentimental; sickly. [Norse *mathkr*, maggot]

max. *abbrev* maximum.

maxi- *comb fm* extra long or large: *maxicoat*. [**maximum**]

maxilla *n* ***-ae*** (*biol*) **1** the upper jaw or jawbone in animals. **2** the chewing organ or organs of an insect, just behind the mouth. — *adj* **maxillary**. [Lat]

maxim *n* **1** a saying expressing a general truth. **2** a general rule or principle. [Lat *maxima* (*propositio* or *sententia*), greatest (axiom or opinion)]

maximal *adj* of a maximum; of the greatest possible size, value, etc. [**maximum**]

maximise or **-ize** *v* (*tr*) to make as high, great, etc. as possible. — *n* **maximisation** or **-z-**. [**maximum**]

maximum *adj* greatest possible. — *n* the greatest possible number, quantity, degree, etc. [Lat, greatest]

May *n* the fifth month of the year. [*Maia*, in ancient Greek and Roman mythology the mother of the god Mercury]

May Day *n* the first day of May, a national holiday in many countries, traditionally a day of festivities.

mayfly *n* a short-lived insect with transparent wings, appearing briefly in spring.

maypole *n* a tall pole set up for dancing round on May Day.

May queen *n* a young woman, crowned with flowers, chosen to preside over May Day festivities.

may tree *n* (also **may**) any variety of hawthorn tree.

may[1] *v* ***might*** (*aux*) expressing: **1** permission: *You may go now*. **2** possibility: *I may well leave*. **3** ability or competence: *May I help you?* **4** (*formal*) a wish: *May you prosper!* **5** (*formal* or *old*) purpose: *Listen, so that you may learn*. **6** (*old pomp* or *facet*) a question: *Who may you be?* **7** used to introduce the first of a pair of statements, with the sense of 'although': *You may be rich, but you're not happy*. [OE *mæg*, present tense of *magan*, to be able]

may[2] *n* **1** a may tree. **2** the blossom (**may-blossom**) of this tree. [Ety. as for **May**]
maybe *adv* it is possible (that); perhaps. [**may + be**]
mayday *n* (often *cap*) the international radio distress signal sent out by ships and aircraft. [Fr *m'aider*, help me]
mayfly. See **May**.
mayhem *n* **1** a state of great confusion and disorder; chaos. **2** (*legal*) the crime of maiming someone. [OFr *mahaignier*, to wound]
mayn't (*coll*) may not.
mayonnaise *n* a cold creamy sauce made of egg yolk, oil, vinegar or lemon juice, and seasoning. [Fr]
mayor *n* the head of the local council in a city, town or borough in England, Wales and N Ireland, or of any of various communities in other countries. — *adj* **mayoral**. [Lat *major*, comparative of *magnus*, great]
mayoralty *n* **-ies** the position, or period of office, of a mayor.
mayoress *n* **1** a mayor's wife. **2** (*old*) a female mayor.
maypole. See **May**.
maze *n* **1** a confusing network of paths, each bordered by high walls or hedges, designed to test orientation abilities. **2** any confusingly complicated system, procedure, etc. [Ety. as for **amaze**]
mazurka *n* (a piece of music for) a lively Polish dance. [Polish, of *Mazur*, Polish province]
MB *abbrev* for *Medicinae Baccalaureus* (Lat), Bachelor of Medicine.
MBA *abbrev* Master of Business Administration.
MBE *abbrev* Member of (the Order of) the British Empire.
MC *abbrev* **1** master of ceremonies. **2** Military Cross.
MCC *abbrev* Marylebone Cricket Club.
McCoy: **the real McCoy** *n* (*coll*) the genuine article, not an imitation.
MCP *abbrev* male chauvinist pig (see **male**).
MD *abbrev* **1** *Medicinae Doctor* (Lat), Doctor of Medicine. **2** managing director. **3** Maryland.
Md[1] *abbrev* Maryland.
Md[2] *symbol* (*chem*) mendelevium.
ME *abbrev* **1** Maine. **2** myalgic encephalomyelitis, severe muscle weakness and general fatigue, often the long-term effect of a viral infection.
Me *abbrev* Maine.
me[1] *pron* **1** the object form of I, used by a speaker or writer to refer to himself or herself. **2** (after the verb *be* or when standing alone) I: *It's only me*. — **be me** (*coll*) to be suited to me: *This dress isn't really me*. [OE]
me[2]. Same as **mi**.
mea culpa (*literary* or *facet*) I am to blame. [Lat, my fault]
mead[1] *n* an alcoholic drink made by fermenting honey and water, usu. with spices added. [OE *meodu*]
mead[2] *n* (*old & poetic*) a meadow. [OE *mæd*]
meadow *n* **1** a low-lying field of grass, used for grazing animals or making hay. **2** any moist grassy area near a river. [OE *mædwe*]
meadowsweet *n* a European and Asian wild plant of the rose family, with fragrant cream-coloured flowers.
meagre *adj* **1** lacking in quality or quantity; inadequate; scanty. **2** (of a person) thin, esp. unhealthily so. [OFr *maigre*, thin]
meal[1] *n* **1** an occasion on which food is eaten. **2** an amount of food eaten on one occasion. — **make a meal of 1** to eat as a meal. **2** (*coll*) to exaggerate the importance of, e.g. by taking unnecessary time or trouble. [OE *mæl*, measure, portion of time]
meals-on-wheels *n* (*pl* or *sing*) a welfare service delivering cooked meals by car to the homes of old or sick people.
meal ticket *n* **1** (*US*) a luncheon voucher. **2** (*coll*) a person or situation providing a source of income or other means of living.
meal[2] *n* (often *in cmpds*) **1** the edible parts of any grain, usu. excluding wheat, ground to a coarse powder: *oatmeal*. **2** any other food substance in ground form: *bone meal*. [OE *melu* or *melo*]
mealy *adj* **-ier**, **-iest** containing meal; dry and powdery, like meal.
mealy-mouthed *adj* (*derog*) afraid to speak plainly or openly.
mealie *n* (*S Afr*) an ear of maize. [Afrikaans *mielie*, maize]
mealie meal *n* (*S Afr*) maize ground to a fine flour.
mealy. See **meal**[2].
mean[1] *v* ***meant*** (*tr*) **1** to (intend to) express, show or indicate. **2** to intend; to have as a purpose: *didn't mean any harm*. **3** to be serious or sincere about: *He means what he says*. **4** to be important to (the stated degree); to represent: *Your approval means a lot to me*. **5** to result in; to involve: *Lower profits mean redundancies*. **6** (**for**) to destine: *She was meant for stardom*. **7** to foretell or portend: *Cold cloudless evenings mean overnight frost*. — **mean well** to have good intentions. [OE *mænan*]
meaning *n* **1** the sense in which a statement, action, word, etc. is (intended to be) understood. **2** significance, importance or purpose, esp. when hidden or special. — *adj* intended to express special significance: *a meaning look*.
meaningful *adj* important or significant in some way.
meaningless *adj* without meaning or reason; of no importance; pointless.
mean[2] *adj* **1** not generous. **2** unkind; despicable. **3** poor; shabby; of inferior quality. **4** (*coll*) vicious; malicious. **5** (*coll*) good; skilful: *plays a mean guitar*. — *adv*

meanly. — *n* **meanness.** — **no mean** (*coll*) **1** an excellent: *no mean singer*. **2** not an easy; a very difficult: *no mean feat*. [OE *gemæne*]

meanie or **meany** *n* **-ies** (*coll*) a selfish or ungenerous person.

mean[3] *n* **1** a midway position, course, etc. between two extremes. **2** a mathematical average. — *adj* **1** midway; intermediate. **2** average. [OFr *meien*, from Lat *medius*, middle]

meander *v* **-r-** (*intr*; *formal*) **1** (of a river) to bend and curve. **2** (**about**) to wander randomly or aimlessly. — *n* (often in *pl*) a bend; a winding course. [Lat *Maeander*, winding river in Turkey (now *Menderes*)]

meanie. See **mean**[2].

means *n* **1** (*sing* or *pl*) the instrument or method used to achieve some object. **2** (in *pl*) wealth; resources. — **by all means** yes, of course. — **by any means** using any available method. — **by means of** using. — **by no means** or **not by any (manner of) means** not at all; definitely not. — **a means to an end** something treated merely as a way of achieving a desired result, considered unimportant in every other respect. [**mean**[3]]

means test *n* an official inquiry into a person's wealth or income to determine eligibility for financial benefit from the state. — *v* (*intr*) **means-test**.

meant. See **mean**[1].

meantime *n* & *adv* (in) the time or period between. [**mean**[3] + **time**]

meanwhile *adv* during the time in between; at the same time. [**mean**[3] + **while**]

meany. See **mean**[2].

measles *n* (*sing*) an infectious disease, common in children, producing fever and red spots on the skin. [MidE *maseles*]

measly *adj* **-ier**, **-iest 1** (*coll derog*) (of an amount or value) very small; miserable; paltry. **2** relating to, or suffering from, measles.

measure *n* **1** size, volume, etc. determined by comparison with something of known size, etc., usu. an instrument graded in standard units. **2** (often *in cmpds*) such an instrument: *a tape-measure*. **3** a standard unit of size, etc.; a system of such units; a standard amount: *metric measure*; *a measure of whisky*. **4** (usu. in *pl*) an action; a step: *drastic measures*. **5** a limited, or appropriate, amount or extent: *a measure of politeness*; *in some measure*; *had my measure of luck*. **6** (*mus*) time or rhythm; a bar. **7** (*poetry*) rhythm. **8** (usu. in *pl*) a layer of rock containing a particular mineral, etc.: *coal measures*. **9** (*old*) a dance. — *v* **1** (*tr* & *intr*) to determine the size, volume, etc. of, usu. with a specially made instrument. **2** (*intr*) to be a (stated) size. **3** (*tr*; **off, out**) to mark or divide into units of known size, etc. **4** (*tr*; *formal*) to set in competition (with): *measure his strength against mine*. — **beyond measure** (*literary*) exceptionally great; to an exceedingly great degree. — **for good measure** as something extra, or above the minimum necessary. — **get the measure of** to assess the character or abilities of (someone). — *v* **measure up** (*intr*) to be or reach the required or desired standard. [Lat *mensura*, measure]

measurable *adj* **1** able to be measured; of sufficient quantity to be measured. **2** noticeable; significant.

measured *adj* **1** slow and steady. **2** carefully chosen or considered: *a measured response*.

measurement *n* **1** (often in *pl*) a size, amount, etc. determined by measuring. **2** (often in *pl*) the size of a part of the body. **3** the act of measuring. **4** a standard system of measuring.

meat *n* **1** the flesh of animals, usu. not including fish, used as food. **2** the basic, most important part; the essence. **3** (*old*) food in general; a meal. — **meat and drink 1** a source of enjoyment. **2** one's basic means of support. [OE *mete*]

meatball *n* a small ball of minced meat mixed with breadcrumbs and herbs.

meaty *adj* **-ier**, **-iest 1** full of, or containing, animal flesh. **2** (tasting, smelling, etc.) like (esp. cooked) animal flesh. **3** full of interesting information or ideas: *a meaty article*. — *n* **meatiness**.

Mecca *n* (often without *cap*) any place of outstanding importance or significance, esp. much visited: *St Andrews, the mecca of golf*. [City in Saudi Arabia, the birthplace of Mohammed and a place of pilgrimage for all Muslims]

mechanic *n* a skilled worker who repairs or maintains machinery. [Gr *mechane*, contrivance]

mechanical *adj* **1** of or concerning machines. **2** worked by, or performed with, machinery. **3** done without or not requiring much thought. — *adv* **mechanically**.

mechanics *n* **1** (*sing*) the branch of applied mathematics dealing with the action of forces on objects. **2** (*sing*) the science of the construction and operation of machines. **3** (*pl*) the system, process or mechanism of working.

mechanise or **-ize** *v* (*tr*) **1** to cause to operate with, or be operated by, machines rather than people. **2** to supply (troops) with motor vehicles rather than horses. — *n* **mechanisation** or **-z-**. [**mechanic**]

mechanism *n* **1** a working part of a machine, or its system of working parts. **2** (*psychol*) an action serving some (often subconscious) purpose: *Laughter is a common defence mechanism*. — *adj* **mechanistic**. [**mechanic**]

MEd *abbrev* Master of Education.

Med *n* (*coll*; with **the**) the Mediterranean Sea.

med. *abbrev* **1** mediaeval. **2** medical. **3** medicine. **4** medium.

medal *n* a flat piece of metal decorated with a design or inscription and offered as an award for merit or bravery, or in celebration of a special occasion. [Fr *médaille*, from Lat *metallum*, metal]

medallist *n* a person awarded a medal, esp. for excellence in sport.

medallion *n* **1** a large medal-like piece of jewellery, usu. worn on a chain. **2** an oval or circular decorative feature in architecture or on textiles. **3** a thin circular cut of meat. [Fr *médaillon*; see ety. for **medal**]

meddle *v* (*intr*; *derog*) **1** (**in**) to interfere. **2** (**with**) to tamper. — *n* **meddler**. [OFr *medler*]

meddlesome *adj* (*derog*) fond of meddling.

media. See **medium**.

mediaeval or **medieval** *adj* of, typical of, or relating to the Middle Ages. [Lat *medius*, middle + *aevum*, age]

mediaevalist or **medievalist** *n* a student of, or expert in, any area or aspect of study of the mediaeval period.

medial *adj* of or situated in the middle; intermediate. — *adv* **medially**. [Lat *medialis*, from *medius*, middle]

median *n* **1** a middle point or part. **2** (*geom*) a straight line through the middle, e.g. joining any angle of a triangle with the middle of the opposite side. **3** (*statistics*) the middle value in a set of values. — *adj* of, situated in, or passing through the middle. [Lat *medianus*, from *medius*, middle]

mediate *v* **1** (*intr*; **between**, **in**) to act as the agent seeking to reconcile the two sides in a disagreement. **2** (*tr*) to (try to) settle (a dispute) in this way. **3** (*tr*) to convey or transmit (views, etc.) as an agent or intermediary. — *adj* **1** resulting from mediation. **2** indirectly related or connected, e.g. through some other person. — *n* **mediation**. — *n* **mediator**. [Lat *mediare*, to be in the middle]

medic *n* (*coll*) a doctor or medical student.

medical *adj* **1** of doctors or the science or practice of medicine. **2** concerned with medicine rather than surgery. — *n* a medical examination, to discover a person's physical health. — *adv* **medically**. [Lat *medicus*, physician, from *mederi*, to heal]

medical certificate *n* a certificate, provided by a doctor, outlining a person's state of health, esp. for employment purposes.

medicament *n* (*formal*) a medicine. [Lat *medicamentum*, from *medicare*, to cure]

medicate *v* (*tr*) **1** to treat with medicine. **2** to add a healing or health-giving substance to: *medicated shampoo*. [Lat *medicare*, to cure]

medication *n* (treatment by) medicine.

medicinal *adj* **1** having healing qualities; used as a medicine. **2** of or relating to healing. — *adv* **medicinally**.

medicine *n* **1** any substance used to treat or prevent disease or illness, esp. taken internally. **2** the science or practice of treating or preventing illness, esp. using prepared substances rather than surgery. — **get a taste** or **dose of one's own medicine** to suffer the same unpleasant treatment one has used on others. — **take one's medicine** to accept an unpleasant but deserved punishment. [Lat *medicina*]

medicine ball *n* a heavy, fabric-covered metal ball thrown from person to person as a form of exercise.

medicine man *n* among certain peoples, a person believed to have magic powers, used for healing or sorcery.

medico *n* **-os** (*coll*) a doctor or medical student.

medieval. See **mediaeval**.

mediocre *adj* (*derog*) only ordinary or average; rather inferior. [Lat *mediocris*, from *medius*, middle]

mediocrity *n* **-ies** (*derog*) **1** the quality of being mediocre. **2** a mediocre person or thing.

meditate *v* **1** (*intr*) to spend time in deep (esp. religious) thought, often with the mind in a practised state of emptiness. **2** (*tr* & *intr*; **on**) to think deeply and carefully. — *n* **meditation**. — *adj* **meditative**. [Lat *meditari*, to reflect upon]

Mediterranean *n* & *adj* (of or relating to) the Mediterranean Sea, or the countries of S Europe, N Africa and SW Asia surrounding it. [Lat *mediterraneus*, from *medius*, middle + *terra*, earth]

medium *n* ***media*** or ***mediums*** (except sense **2**) **1** something by or through which an effect is produced. **2** (usu. in *pl*; also **mass medium**) a means by which news, information, etc. is communicated to the public, usu. television, radio and the press collectively. **3** a person through whom the spirits of dead people (are said to) communicate with the living. **4** (*biol*) a substance in which specimens are preserved, bacteria are grown, etc. **5** a middle position, condition or course: *a happy medium*. **6** (*art*) a particular category of materials seen as a means of expression, e.g. watercolours, photography or clay. — *adj* **1** intermediate; midway; average. **2** moderate. [Lat *medius*, middle]

medium wave *n* a radio wave with a length between 200 and 1000 metres. — *adj* **medium-wave**.

medlar *n* **1** a small brown apple-like fruit eaten only when already decaying. **2** the small Eurasian tree that bears it. [OFr *medler*]

medley *n* **-eys 1** a piece of music made up of pieces from other songs, tunes, etc. **2** a mixture or miscellany. **3** a race in stages, each stage a different length or, in swimming, swum using a different stroke. [OFr *medler*, to mix]

medulla *n* **-lae** or **-las 1** (*anat*; also **medulla oblongata**) the stalk-like part of the brain that joins the spinal cord. **2** (*anat*) the innermost part of an organ. **3** (*anat*) bone marrow. **4** (*biol*) the pith in plant stems. [Lat, marrow]

meek *adj* **1** having a mild and gentle temperament. **2** submissive. — *adv* **meekly**. — *n* **meekness**. [Norse *mjukr*]

meerschaum *n* **1** a fine whitish clay-like mineral. **2** a tobacco pipe with a bowl made of this. [Ger *Meer*, sea + *Schaum*, foam]

meet[1] *v* ***met*** **1** (*tr* & *intr*; also **meet up (with)**) to come together (with) by chance or arrangement. **2** (*tr* & *intr*) to be introduced (to) for the first time. **3** (*tr*) to be present at the arrival of: *met the train.* **4** (*tr* & *intr*; **with**) to come into opposition (against). **5** (*tr* & *intr*) to join; to come into contact (with): *where the path meets the road.* **6** (*tr*) to satisfy: *meet your requirements.* **7** (*tr*) to pay: *meet costs.* **8** (*tr*) to come into the view, experience or presence of: *the sight that met my eyes.* **9** (*tr* & *intr*; **with**) to encounter or experience: *met his death.* **10** (*intr* with **with**) to receive: *suggestions met with approval.* **11** (*tr*) to answer or oppose: *meet force with greater force.* — *n* **1** a sporting event, esp. a series of athletics competitions. **2** the assembly of hounds and huntsmen and -women before a fox-hunt. — **more to this than meets the eye** this is more complicated, interesting, etc. than it appears. [OE *metan*, to meet]

meeting *n* **1** an act of coming together. **2** an assembly or gathering. **3** a sporting event, esp. in athletics or horse-racing.

meet[2] *adj* (*old*) proper, correct or suitable. — *adv* **meetly**. [OE *gemæte*]

mega *adj* (*slang*) excellent. [**mega-** (sense 3)]

mega- *comb fm* **1** a million: *megawatt.* **2** (also **megalo-**) large or great: *megacephalous* (= having an unusually large head). **3** (*coll*) great: *megastar*. [Gr, big]

megabyte *n* (*comput*) a unit of storage capacity equal to 2^{20} or 1,048,576 bytes.

megalith *n* a very large stone, esp. one forming part of a prehistoric monument. [**mega-** + Gr *lithos*, stone]

megalithic *adj* **1** (of a period of prehistory) characterised by the use of megaliths. **2** made of megaliths.

megalomania *n* **1** (*med*) a mental illness characterised by an exaggerated sense of power and self-importance. **2** (*coll*) greed for power. — *n* & *adj* **megalomaniac**. [**mega-** + **mania**]

megaphone *n* a funnel-shaped device which, when spoken through, amplifies the voice. [**mega-** + Gr *phone*, sound]

megaton *n* **1** a unit of weight equal to one million tons. **2** a unit of explosive power equal to one million tons of TNT.

meiosis *n* ***-oses*** **1** (*biol*) a process in which a single cell nucleus divides into four nuclei, each of which has half the number of chromosomes of the original nucleus. **2** litotes, or understatement used as a figure of speech. [Gr *meion*, less]

melamine *n* a colourless compound used to make synthetic resins for use in adhesives, plastics, etc. [Ger *Melamin*]

melancholia *n* (*old*) mental depression. [**melancholy**]

melancholy *n* **1** a tendency to be gloomy or depressed. **2** prolonged sadness. **3** a sad, pensive state of mind. — *adj* sad; causing or expressing sadness. — *adj* **melancholic**. [Gr *melas*, black + *chole*, bile]

melange or **mélange** *n* (*literary*) a mixture, esp. varied or confused. [Fr *mélange*]

melanin *n* the black or dark brown pigment found to varying degrees in the skin, hair and eyes of humans and animals. [Gr *melas*, black]

melanoma *n* ***-mas*** or ***-mata*** a cancerous skin tumour made up of dark-coloured cells. [**melanin** + Gr *-oma*, suffix denoting the result of the action of a verb, used in English to denote a tumour]

Melba toast *n* very thin crisp toast. [Named after opera singer Dame Nellie *Melba*]

melee or **mêlée** *n* (*literary*) **1** a riotous brawl involving large numbers of people. **2** any confused or muddled collection. [Fr, from *mêler*, to mix]

mellifluous *adj* (*literary*; also **mellifluent**) (of sounds, speech, etc.) having a smooth, sweet, flowing quality. — *adv* **mellifluously**. — *n* **mellifluousness**. [Lat *mel*, honey + *fluere*, to flow]

mellow *adj* **1** (of character) calm and relaxed with age or experience. **2** (of sound, colour, light, etc.) soft, rich and pure. **3** (of wine, cheese, etc.) fully flavoured with age. **4** (of fruit) sweet and ripe. **5** pleasantly relaxed or warm-hearted through being slightly drunk. — *v* (*tr* & *intr*) to make or become mellow. [Perhaps OE *mearu*, soft, tender]

melodic *adj* **1** relating to melody. **2** pleasant-sounding; tuneful; melodious. — *adv* **melodically**. [**melody**]

melodious *adj* **1** pleasant to listen to. **2** having a (pleasant) recognisable melody. — *n* **melodiousness**. [**melody**]

melodrama *n* **1** drama featuring simplified characters, sensational events and traditional justice, usu. in the form of a happy ending. **2** a play or film of this kind. **3** (*derog*) excessively dramatic behaviour. [Gr *melos*, song + *drama*, action]

melodramatic *adj* exaggerated or sensational in expressing emotion. — *n* (*pl*) **melodramatics**.

melody *n* ***-ies*** **1** the sequence of single notes forming the core of a tune, as opposed to the harmony, the blend of other notes around it. **2** pleasantness of sound; tuneful music. **3** pleasant arrangement or combination of sounds, esp. in poetry. [Gr *melodia*, from *melos*, song + *aoidein*, to sing]

melon *n* the large rounded edible fruit of any of various climbing plants, with a thick skin, sweet juicy flesh and many seeds. [Gr, apple]

melt *v* (*tr* & *intr*) **1** to (cause to) become soft or liquid, esp. through the action of heat; to dissolve. **2** to combine or fuse, causing a loss of distinctness. **3** (**away**) to (cause to) disappear or disperse: *Support for the scheme melted away*. **4** (*coll*) to (cause to) become emotionally or romantically tender or submissive. — *v* **melt down** (*intr*; *tech*) (of the core of a nuclear reactor) to overheat, causing radioactivity to escape (*n* **meltdown**). [OE *meltan*]

melting-point *n* the temperature at which a given solid melts.

melting-pot *n* a place or situation in which varying beliefs, ideas, cultures, etc. are mixed. — **in the melting-pot** in the process of changing and forming something new.

member *n* **1** a person belonging to a group or organisation; a plant or animal belonging to a class or group. **2** (often *cap*) an elected representative of a governing body, e.g. Parliament or a local council. **3** a part of a whole, esp. a limb or a petal. [Lat *membrum*, limb, part]

membership *n* **1** the state of being a member. **2** the members of an organisation collectively; the number of members.

membrane *n* **1** a thin film of tissue covering, connecting or lining organs or cells in plants or animals. **2** any thin flexible covering or lining. — *adj* **membranous**. [Lat *membrana*, skin of the body]

memento *n* **-os** or **-oes** a thing that serves as a reminder of the past; a souvenir. [Lat, from *meminisse*, to remember]

memento mori *n* ***memento mori*** an object intended as a reminder of the inevitability of death.

memo *n* **-os** a memorandum.

memoir *n* **1** a written record of events in the past, esp. based on personal experience. **2** (in *pl*) a person's written account of his or her own life; an autobiography. **3** a learned essay on any subject. [Fr *mémoire*, memory]

memorabilia *n* (*pl*) souvenirs of people or events. [Lat]

memorable *adj* worth remembering; easily remembered. — *adv* **memorably**. [Lat *memorare*, to remember]

memorandum *n* **-dums** or **-da** **1** a note of something to be remembered. **2** a written statement or record, esp. one circulated for the attention of colleagues. [Lat, thing to be remembered]

memorial *n* a thing that honours or commemorates a person or an event, e.g. a statue. — *adj* serving to preserve the memory of a person or an event. [Lat *memoriale*, reminder]

memorise or **-ize** *v* (*tr*) to learn thoroughly, so as to be able to reproduce exactly from memory. [**memory**]

memory *n* **-ies** **1** the power of the mind to remember: *recite it from memory*. **2** the mind's store of mental impressions of the past. **3** any such impression reproduced in the mind. **4** the limit in the past beyond which one's store of mental impressions does not extend: *not in living memory* (= the memory of any living person). **5** the act of remembering; commemoration: *in memory of*. **6** reputation after death. **7** the part of a computer in which information is stored. [Lat *memoria*]

memsahib *n* formerly, in India, a European married woman; also used as a polite form of address. [**ma'am** + **sahib**]

men. See **man**.

menace *n* **1** a source of threatening danger. **2** a threat; a show of hostility. — *v* (*tr*) to threaten; to show an intention to cause damage or harm to. — *adj* **menacing**. [Fr, from Lat *minari*, to threaten]

ménage *n* (*literary*) a group of people living together; a household. [Fr]

ménage à trois *n* ***ménages*** (*literary*) a household consisting of three people, esp. a husband, a wife and the lover of one of them. [Fr, household of three]

menagerie *n* **1** a collection of wild animals caged for exhibition; the place where they are kept. **2** a varied or confused mixture, esp. of people. [Fr, from **ménage**]

mend *v* **1** (*tr*) to repair. **2** (*intr*) to improve, esp. in health; to heal. **3** (*tr*) to improve or correct: *mend one's ways*. — *n* a repaired part or place. — **on the mend** getting better, esp. in health. [Shortened from **amend**]

mendacity *n* **-ies** (*formal*) **1** untruthfulness; the tendency to lie. **2** a lie. — *adj* **mendacious**. [Lat *mendax*, untruthful]

mendelevium *n* an element (symbol **Md**), a synthetically produced radioactive metal. [D I *Mendeleev* (1834–1904), Russian chemist]

Mendelian *adj* of or relating to the principles of heredity put forward by Austrian monk and botanist Gregor *Mendel* (1822–84).

mendicant *n* **1** (*formal*) a beggar. **2** a member of an order of monks entirely dependent on charity. — *adj* **1** (*formal*) begging. **2** dependent on charity. [Lat *mendicare*, to beg]

menfolk. See **man**.

menhir *n* a prehistoric monument in the form of a single standing stone. [Breton *men*, stone + *hir*, long]

menial *adj* (of work) unskilled, uninteresting, and of low status. — *n* (usu. *derog*) a domestic servant. [OFr *meinie*, household]

meninx *n* ***meninges*** any of the three membranes that envelop the brain and the spinal cord. [Gr, membrane]

meningitis *n* a serious bacterial disease causing inflammation of the meninges.

meniscus *n* **-uses** or **-sci** **1** the imperceptibly curved upper surface of any liquid formed whenever the liquid is contained in a tube. **2** a crescent-shaped piece of cartilage in certain joints, esp. the knee. **3** a lens convex on one side and concave on the other. [Gr *meniskos*, dimin. of *mene*, moon]

menopause *n* the end of menstruation, or the time in a woman's life when this occurs, usu. between the ages of 45 and 50. — *adj* **menopausal**. [Gr *men*, month + *pausis*, cessation]

male menopause *n* (*coll*; esp. *facet*) a dramatic change in a middle-aged man's normal behaviour, thought to be caused by fear of ageing.

menorah *n* a candlestick with seven branches used in Jewish worship and regarded as a symbol of Judaism. [Hebrew, candlestick]

menses *n* (*pl*; *med*) the fluids discharged from the womb during menstruation. [Lat *mensis*, month]

menstrual *adj* of menstruation.

menstruate *v* (*intr*) to discharge blood and other fluids from the womb through the vagina. [Lat *menstruare*, from *mensis*, month]

menstruation *n* **1** the process of menstruating. **2** the period during which this occurs in non-pregnant women, usu. lasting three or four days and occurring at approximate monthly intervals from puberty to age 45–50.

mensuration *n* **1** the application of geometric principles to the calculation of measurements such as length, volume and area. **2** (*formal*) the process of measuring. [Lat *mensurare*, to measure]

-ment *sfx* **1** a process, action or means of: *repayment*; *treatment*. **2** a quality, state or condition: *enjoyment*; *merriment*. [Lat *-mentum*]

mental *adj* **1** of, relating to, or done using the mind or intelligence: *a mental handicap*; *mental arithmetic*. **2** of, or suffering from, an illness or illnesses of the mind: *a mental patient*. **3** (*coll*) foolish; stupid. **4** (*coll*) ridiculous; unimaginable. — *adv* **mentally**. [Lat *mentalis*, from *mens*, the mind]

mentality *n* **-ies** **1** an outlook; a certain way of thinking. **2** intellectual ability.

menthol *n* a sharp-smelling substance obtained from peppermint oil, used as a decongestant and a painkiller. — *adj* **mentholated**. [Lat *mentha*, mint]

mention *v* **-n-** (*tr*) **1** to speak of or make reference to. **2** to remark on, usu. briefly or indirectly. — *n* **1** (**of**) a remark, usu. a brief reference (to): *make no mention of*. **2** a reference made to an individual's merit in an official (esp. military) report. — **don't mention it** no thanks are needed. — **not to mention**... without including (facts the speaker is nevertheless about to include, usu. for emphasis). [Lat *mentio*, a calling to mind]

mentor *n* (*formal* or *literary*) a trusted teacher or adviser. [*Mentor*, adviser to Telemachus in Greek mythology]

menu *n* **1** (a list of) the range of dishes available in a restaurant, etc.; (a list of) the dishes to be served at a particular meal: *the wedding menu*. **2** a list of optional computer functions displayed on a screen. [Fr, small and detailed (list)]

MEP *abbrev* Member of the European Parliament.

mercantile *adj* (*formal*) of trade or traders; commercial. [Ital, from *mercante*, merchant]

Mercator: **Mercator's projection** *n* a type of map of the world on which all lines of latitude are the same length as the equator, increasingly exaggerating the size of areas the nearer they are to the poles. [Gerardus *Mercator*, Latinised name of Gerhard Kremer (1512–94), German cartographer]

mercenary *adj* (usu. *derog*) (too strongly) influenced by the desire for personal gain, esp. money. — *n* **-ies** a soldier who hires his or her services to any country or group willing to pay. [Lat *mercenarius*, from *merces*, reward, hire]

mercerise or **-ize** *v* (*tr*) to treat (esp. cotton) with a substance which strengthens it and gives it a silky appearance. — *adj* **mercerised** or **-z-**. [John *Mercer* (1791—1866), English textile manufacturer]

merchandise *n* commercial goods. — *v* (*intr* & *tr*) to trade; to buy and sell. [**merchant**]

merchant *n* **1** a trader, esp. wholesale. **2** (esp. *US* & *Scot*) a shopkeeper. **3** (*slang*) a person who indulges in a particular (esp. undesirable) activity: *gossip merchant*. — *adj* used for trade; commercial: *merchant ship*. [Lat *mercari*, to trade]

merchant bank *n* a bank whose main activity is lending money to industry.

merchant navy *n* the commercial ships of a country, and their crews.

merciful, **merciless**. See **mercy**.

mercurial *adj* **1** of or containing mercury. **2** (*formal* or *literary*) (of a personality, mood, etc.) lively or active; tending to change suddenly and unpredictably. [The planet *Mercury*]

mercury *n* an element (symbol **Hg**), a heavy poisonous silvery-white metal that is liquid at ordinary temperatures, used in thermometers and barometers, and in dentistry. [Lat *Mercurius*, the Roman god Mercury]

mercy *n* **-ies** **1** kindness or forgiveness shown when punishment is possible or justified. **2** an act or circumstance in which these qualities are displayed, esp. by God. **3** a tendency to be forgiving. **4** a piece of good luck; a welcome happening: *grateful for small mercies*. — **at the mercy of** wholly in the power of; liable to be harmed by. [Lat *merces*, reward, favour]

merciful *adj* showing mercy; forgiving.

mercifully *adv* luckily; thankfully.

merciless *adj* without mercy; cruel; pitiless. — *adv* **mercilessly**.

mercy killing *n* an act of killing painlessly to relieve suffering; euthanasia.

mere[1] *adj* nothing more than; no better, more important or useful than. [Lat *merus*, unmixed]

merely *adv* simply; only.

mere[2] *n* (*old* or *poetic*) (often in place-names) a lake or pool. [OE]

meretricious *adj* **1** bright or attractive on the surface, but of no real value. **2** false and insincere. [Lat *meretrix*, prostitute]

merganser *n* any of various kinds of large diving duck of northern countries, with a long hooked serrated bill. [Lat *mergus*, diving bird + *anser*, goose]

merge *v* **1** (*tr* & *intr*; **with**) to (cause to) blend, combine or join (with). **2** (*intr* with **into**) to become part of a larger whole, and therefore impossible to distinguish. [Lat *mergere*, to plunge]

merger *n* a joining together (esp. of business firms).

meridian *n* **1** (*geog*) an imaginary line on the earth's surface passing through the poles at right angles to the equator; a line of longitude. **2** (*literary*) the peak, e.g. of success. [Lat *meridianus*, from *medius*, middle + *dies*, day]

meridional *adj* **1** (*tech*) of, relating to, or along a meridian. **2** (*literary*) of the south, esp. of Europe.

meringue *n* (a cake made from) a crisp cooked mixture of sugar and egg-whites. [Fr]

merino *n* **-os** **1** a type of sheep bred for its long fine wool. **2** fine yarn or fabric made from its wool. [Span]

merit *n* **1** worth, excellence or praiseworthiness. **2** (often in *pl*) a good point or quality. — *v* **-t-** (*tr*) to deserve; to be worthy of or entitled to. [Lat *meritum*, reward]

meritocracy *n* **-ies** (a social system based on) leadership by people of great talent or intelligence, rather than of wealth or noble birth.

meritorious *adj* deserving reward or praise.

merlin *n* a species of small dark-coloured falcon with a black-striped tail. [OFr *esmerillon*]

mermaid *n* a mythical sea creature with a woman's head and upper body, and a fish's tail. [OE *mere*, lake, sea + **maid**]

merman *n* the male equivalent of a mermaid.

merry *adj* **-ier**, **-iest** **1** cheerful and lively. **2** (*coll*) slightly drunk. — *adv* **merrily**. — *n* **merriment**. — **make merry** (*old*) to have fun; to celebrate. [OE *myrige*]

merry-go-round *n* a fairground amusement consisting of a revolving platform fitted with rising and falling seats in the form of horses or other figures.

merrymaking *n* cheerful celebration. — *n* **merrymaker**.

mésalliance *n* (*literary*) a marriage to someone of lower social status. [Fr, misalliance]

mescal *n* a globe-shaped cactus of Mexico and the southwestern US. [Aztec *mexcalli*]

mescalin or **mescaline** *n* a hallucinogenic drug obtained from the button-like top of the mescal cactus, esp. by chewing it.

mesdames. See **madam** and **Madame**.

mesh *n* **1** (a piece of) netting made of (esp. fine) wire or thread. **2** (one of) the openings between the threads of a net. **3** (esp. in *pl*) a network. — *v* (*intr*; **with**) **1** (*tech*) (of teeth on gear wheels) to engage. **2** to fit or work together. **3** to become entangled. [Perhaps ODut *maesche*]

mesmerise or **-ize** *v* (*tr*) **1** (*old*) to hypnotise. **2** to grip the attention of; to fascinate. — *adj* **mesmerising** or **-z-**. [F A *Mesmer* (1734–1815), Austrian physician]

mesmerism *n* (*old*) hypnotism. — *n* **mesmerist**.

mesolithic *adj* (also *cap*) of the middle period of the Stone Age, from about 12,000 to 3000 BC in Europe. [Gr *mesos*, middle + *lithos*, stone]

meson *n* (*physics*) a particle smaller in mass than a proton but larger than an electron. [Gr, from *mesos*, middle]

mesosphere *n* the layer of the atmosphere above the stratosphere and below the thermosphere, in which temperature rapidly decreases with height. [Gr *mesos*, middle + **sphere**]

Mesozoic *adj* & *n* (denoting) a geological era comprising the Triassic, Jurassic and Cretaceous periods. [Gr *mesos*, middle + *zoe*, life]

mess *n* **1** (something in) an untidy or dirty state. **2** (something in) a state of disorder or confusion. **3** (something in) a badly damaged state. **4** (*coll*) animal faeces. **5** a communal dining room, esp. in the armed forces. **6** (*old*) a portion of any pulpy food. — *v* **1** (*intr*; *coll*; **with**) to interfere or meddle. **2** (*tr*; **up**) to put into an untidy, dirty, confused or damaged state. **3** (*intr*; **with**) (of soldiers, etc.) to eat, or live, together. **4** (*intr* with **with**; *coll*) to become involved in argument or conflict. — *adv* **messily**. — *adj* **messy**, **-ier**, **-iest**. — *v* **mess about** or **around** (*coll*) **1** (*intr*; **with**) to behave in an annoyingly foolish way; to potter or tinker. **2** (*intr* with **with**) to meddle or interfere. **3** (*tr*) to treat roughly or unfairly. **4** (*intr* with **with**) to practise adultery. — **no messing** (*slang*) **1** without difficulty. **2** honestly; truthfully. [OFr *mes*, dish]

message *n* **1** a (spoken or written) communication sent from one person to another. **2** the instructive principle contained within a story, religious teaching, etc. **3** (in *pl*; esp. *Scot*) an errand; household shopping. — **get the message** (*coll*) to understand. [Lat *mittere*, to send]

messenger *n* a person who carries communications between people.

Messiah *n* (with **the**) **1** in Christianity, Jesus Christ. **2** in Judaism, the king of the Jews still to be sent by God to free them.

3 a person who sets free a country or a people. — *adj* **Messianic**. [Hebrew *mashiah*, anointed]

messrs. See **Mr**.

messy. See **mess**.

mestizo -*os* and **mestiza** *n* respectively a male or female person of mixed Spanish-American and American Indian parentage. [Span]

Met *n* (*coll*; with **the**) the London Metropolitan Police Force.

met. See **meet**.

meta- *comb fm* indicating **1** a change: *metabolism*. **2** an area of study related to another subject of study, but going beyond it in some way, e.g. by going beyond the normal limits of investigation in that subject or by the analysis of its theoretical concepts: *metalinguistics*. **3** a position behind or beyond: *metacarpal*. [Gr, among, with, beside, after]

metabolism *n* the system of chemical processes occurring in a living body, from which energy, growth, and waste matter are produced. — *adj* **metabolic**. [Gr *metabole*, change]

metabolise or **-ize** *v* (*tr* & *intr*; *biol*) to subject to, or be changed by, the metabolism.

metacarpus *n* **-*pi*** the set of five bones in the hand between the wrist and the knuckles. — *adj* **metacarpal**. [**meta-** (sense **3**) + Gr *karpus*, wrist]

metal *n* **1** any of a group of elements that usu. are solid at ordinary temperatures, can conduct heat and electricity, can be worked into different shapes, and typically have a shiny appearance; an alloy, a mixture of any of these. **2** road metal, small broken stones used to make and repair roads. **3** (in *pl*) the rails of a railway. — *v* **-*ll*-** (*tr*) **1** to fit with metal. **2** to make or mend (a road) with small broken stones. [Gr *metallon*, mine]

metallic *adj* **1** made of metal. **2** characteristic of metal, e.g. in sound or appearance.

metallise or **-ize** *v* (*tr*) **1** to give a metallic appearance to. **2** to apply a thin coating of metal to.

metalloid *n* a non-metallic element with some of the properties of metal, e.g. arsenic.

metallurgy *n* the scientific study of the nature and properties of metals and their extraction from the ground. — *n* **metallurgist**.

metalwork *n* **1** the craft or practice of shaping metal. **2** (esp. decorative) articles made of metal. — *n* **metalworker**.

metamorphosis *n* **-*oses*** **1** a complete change of form, appearance or character. **2** (*biol*) the change of physical form that occurs during the development into adulthood of some creatures, e.g. butterflies. [**meta-** (sense **1**) + Gr *morphe*, form]

metamorphic *adj* **1** of metamorphosis or metamorphism. **2** (*geol*) (of rock) changed considerably from its original structure by the earth's pressure, heat or other processes.

metamorphism *n* the transformation of the structure of rock by the action of the earth's crust.

metamorphose *v* (*intr* & *tr*; *formal* or *tech*) to (cause to) undergo metamorphosis.

metaphor *n* an expression in which the person, action or thing referred to is described as if it really were what it merely resembles, as when a rejection is referred to as 'a slap in the face'; such expressions in general, or their use. [Gr *metaphora*]

metaphorical *adj* not actual or literal, only in a figure of speech. — *adv* **metaphorically**.

mixed metaphor *n* a combination of (usu. two) metaphors which produces an odd mental image, as in 'a rotten apple who turned out to be a good egg'.

metaphysics *n* **1** the branch of philosophy dealing with the nature of existence and the basic principles of truth and knowledge. **2** (*coll*) any type of abstract discussion, writing or thinking. [Gr *ta meta ta physika*, the things after natural science, from the order of subjects dealt with in Aristotle's writings]

metaphysical *adj* **1** of metaphysics. **2** (*cap*) denoting any of a group of 17th-century poets who used elaborate images to express intense feelings and complex ideas. — *adv* **metaphysically**.

metastasis *n* **-*ases*** (*med*) the spread of a disease, esp. cancer, from one part of the body to another. [Gr, change of place]

metatarsus *n* **-*arsi*** the set of five long bones in the foot, between the ankle and the toes. — *adj* **metatarsal**. [**meta-** (sense **3**) + Gr *tarsos*, instep]

metazoan *n* any creature whose body is a complex structure of many cells, i.e. all except the most microscopic creatures. [**meta-** (sense **2**) + Gr *zoion*, animal]

mete: **mete out** *v* (*tr*; *formal*) to give out or dispense (esp. punishment). [OE *metan*, to measure]

meteor *n* any of countless small bodies travelling through space, which become visible as streaks of light as they enter the earth's atmosphere. [Gr *ta meteora*, things on high]

meteoric *adj* **1** of or relating to meteors. **2** (of success, etc.) very rapid; very short-lived. — *adv* **meteorically**.

meteorite *n* a meteor fallen to earth as a lump of rock or metal.

meteoroid *n* a meteor before it enters the earth's atmosphere.

meteorology *n* the study of changes in the earth's atmosphere and the patterns of weather they produce, esp. for weather-forecasting purposes. — *n* **meteorologist**. [Gr *ta meteora*, things on high + **-logy**]

meteorological *adj* of or relating to meteorology.

Meteorological Office see **Met Office**.

meter *n* **1** an instrument for measuring and recording, esp. quantities of electricity, gas, water, etc. used. **2** a parking-meter. — *v* **-r-** (*tr*) to measure and record using a meter. [OE *metan*, to measure]

-meter *comb fm* **1** an instrument for measuring: *thermometer*. **2** a line of poetry with a stated number of units of stress, or feet: *pentameter*. [Gr *metron*, measure]

methadone *n* a drug similar to morphine, but less addictive, used as a painkiller and as a heroin substitute for drug-addicts. [di*meth*yl*a*mino-*d*iphenyl-heptan*one*]

methane *n* a colourless odourless inflammable gas, naturally occurring in coalmines and marshes, and the main ingredient of natural gas. [**methyl**]

methanol *n* (also **methyl alcohol**) a colourless volatile liquid used as a fuel and a solvent. [**methane + alcohol**]

methinks *v* ***methought*** (*tr*; *old*) it seems to me (that).

method *n* **1** a way of doing something, esp. an ordered set of procedures. **2** good planning; efficient organisation. **3** (often in *pl*) a technique used in a particular activity: *farming methods*. **4** (often *cap*; with **the**) an approach to acting in which the actor tries to take on, as realistically as possible, the personality of the character being played. — **there is method in one's madness** there is reason or good sense underlying what seems an odd or chaotic situation or procedure. [Gr *methodos*]

methodical *adj* efficient and orderly; done in an orderly way. — *adv* **methodically**.

methodology *n* ***-ies*** **1** the system of methods and principles used in a particular activity. **2** the study of method and procedure. — *adj* **methodological**.

Methodism *n* the beliefs and practices of a branch of the Protestant Church founded by followers of John Wesley (1707–88), based on the need for high personal and social moral standards. — *n* & *adj* **Methodist**.

methought. See **methinks**.

meths *n* (*sing*; *coll*) methylated spirits.

methyl alcohol. See **methanol**.

methylated spirits or **spirit** *n* (*sing*) alcohol used as fuel in lamps and heaters, made undrinkable (and therefore exempt from tax) by the addition of methanol.

meticulous *adj* paying, or showing, very careful attention to detail. — *adv* **meticulousness**. [Lat *meticulosus*, frightened]

Met Office *n* (*coll*; with **the**) the Meteorological Office, the government department monitoring national weather conditions and producing weather forecasts.

metonymy *n* ***-ies*** the use of a word referring to an element or attribute of some related notion to mean the larger notion itself, as when 'the bottle' is used to mean 'the drinking of alcohol'. [**meta-** + Gr *onoma*, name]

metre[1] *n* the principal unit of length in the metric system, equal to 39.37 inches. [Gr *metron*, measure]

metre[2] *n* **1** (*poetry*) the arrangement of words and syllables in a rhythmic pattern according to their length and stress; a particular pattern. **2** tempo in music. [Gr *metron*, measure]

metric[1] *adj* of or based on the metre or the metric system. — *adv* **metrically**.

metricate *v* (*tr* & *intr*) to convert to units of the metric system. — *n* **metrication**.

metric system *n* a decimal system of weights and measures with the metre, kilogram and litre as its principal units.

metric[2] *adj* (*tech*; also **metrical**) of or in verse, not prose. — *adv* **metrically**.

-metric *comb fm* of or relating to scientific measurement: *thermometric*.

metro *n* ***-os*** an urban railway system, usu. mostly underground, esp. (with *cap*) the system in Paris. [Fr *métro*, abbrev. of *chemin de fer métropolitain*, metropolitan railway]

metronome *n* a device that indicates musical tempo by means of a ticking pendulum that can be set to move at different speeds. [Gr *metron*, measure + *nomos*, law]

metropolis *n* ***-ises*** (*formal*) a large city, esp. the capital city of a nation or region. [Gr, from *meter*, mother + *polis*, city]

metropolitan *adj* **1** of, typical of, or situated in a large city. **2** of or referring to a country's mainland, as opposed to its overseas territories. — *n* **1** in the Catholic and Orthodox Churches, a bishop (usu. an archbishop) with authority over all the bishops in a province. **2** an inhabitant of a metropolis.

-metry *comb fm* a science involving measurement: *geometry*. [Gr *metron*, measure]

mettle *n* (*literary*) **1** courage, determination and endurance. **2** character; personal qualities: *show one's mettle*. — **on one's mettle** (*literary*) encouraged or forced to make one's best effort. [Variation of **metal**]

mettlesome *adj* (*literary*) (esp. of horses) lively; high-spirited.

mew[1] *v* (*intr*) to make the cry of a cat; to miaow. — *n* a cat's cry. [Imit.]

mew[2] *n* a seagull. [OE *mæw*]

mews *n* ***mews*** or ***mewses*** a set of stables around a yard or square, esp. converted into garages or accomodation; also used in street-names. [From *mew*, cage for moulting hawks, orig. the cages for royal hawks, later stables, at Charing Cross, London]

Mex. *abbrev* **1** Mexican. **2** Mexico.

Mexican *n* a native or citizen of Mexico. — *adj* of or pertaining to Mexico.

Mexican wave *n* a rippling wave effect passing across e.g. the spectators in a stadium, as they stand up and raise their arms, then sit with lowered arms, in turn around the stadium. [First performed at the football World Cup in Mexico in 1986]

mezzanine *n* a small floor built balcony-like between two other floors in a building, usu. the ground and first floors. [Ital *mezzanino*, from *mezzano*, middle]

mezzo *adv* (*mus*) moderately, quite, rather, as in **mezzo-forte**, rather loud. [Ital, half]

mezzo-soprano *n* **-nos** (a female singer with) a singing voice with a range between soprano and contralto.

mezzotint *n* a method of engraving a metal plate by polishing and scraping to produce areas of light and shade; a print from a plate engraved in this way. [Ital *mezzotinto*, from *mezzo*, half + *tinto*, shade]

Mg *symbol* (*chem*) magnesium.

mg *abbrev* milligram.

Mgr *abbrev* **1** manager. **2** Monsignor.

MHz *abbrev* megahertz.

MI *abbrev* **1** Michigan. **2** Military Intelligence.

mi *n* in tonic sol-fa, the third note of the major scale. [From the first syllable of the word *Mira* in a mediaeval Latin hymn, certain syllables of which were used in naming the notes of the scale]

miaow *v* (*intr*) to make the cry of a cat. — *n* a cat's cry. [Imit.]

miasma *n* ***miasmata*** or ***miasmas*** (*literary*) **1** a thick foul-smelling vapour, esp. as given off by swamps, marshes, etc. **2** an evil influence or atmosphere. — *adj* **miasmal**. [Gr, pollution]

mica *n* any of a group of metallic minerals with a flaky, layered structure and a high resistance to electricity and heat. [Lat, crumb]

mice. See **mouse**.

Mich. *abbrev* **1** Michaelmas. **2** Michigan.

Michaelmas *n* a Christian festival in honour of St Michael, held on 29 September. [**Michael** + *mas*, from **mass**[2]]

Michaelmas daisy *n* ***daisies*** any of various garden plants of the aster family, with purple, pink or white flowers that bloom in autumn.

mick *n* (*offensive slang*) an Irishman. [The name *Michael*]

mickey: **take the mickey (out of)** (*coll*) to tease, make fun (of), or mock. [Ety. as for **mick**]

Mickey Finn *n* (*slang*) a drink, esp. alcoholic, with a stupefying drug secretly added.

Mickey Mouse *adj* (*coll derog*) **1** of the nature of a cheap imitation. **2** ridiculously simple or unprofessional.

micro *n* **-os** (*coll*) a microcomputer, microprocessor, or microwave oven.

micro- *comb fm* **1** very small: *microchip*. **2** one millionth part: *micrometre*. [Gr *mikros*, little]

microbe *n* any tiny organism invisible to the naked eye, esp. a germ or bacterium. — *adj* **microbial** or **microbic**. [Gr *mikros*, little + *bios*, life]

microbiology *n* the branch of biology dealing with the study of micro-organisms. — *adj* **microbiological**. — *n* **microbiologist**. [Ety. as for **microbe**]

microchip *n* (also **chip**) a tiny piece of silicon, or a similar material, carrying several electrical circuits, used in computers and electrical appliances.

microcircuit *n* an electronic circuit with components formed in one microchip.

microcomputer *n* a small computer in which information is processed by one or more microprocessors, often contained within some larger machine, tool, etc.

microcosm *n* **1** any structure or system which contains, in miniature, all the features of the larger structure or system that it is part of. **2** (*philos*) man regarded as a miniature universe. — *adj* **microcosmic**. — **in microcosm** on a small scale; in miniature. [**micro-** (sense **1**) + Gr *kosmos*, world]

microdot *n* a photograph, e.g. of secret documents, reduced to the size of a pinhead.

microelectronics *n* (*sing*) the branch of electronics dealing with the design and use of small-scale electrical circuits. — *adj* **microelectronic**.

microfiche *n* a postcard-sized sheet of film on which printed material is stored in miniaturised form, viewed through a special projector; the projector itself. [**micro-** (sense **1**) + Fr *fiche*, sheet of paper]

microfilm *n* thin film on which printed material is stored in miniaturised form.

microlight *n* a very lightweight small-engined aircraft, like a powered hang-glider.

micrometer *n* an instrument for accurately measuring very small distances, thicknesses or angles.

micron *n* a unit of length equal to one millionth of a metre. [Gr, from *mikros*, small]

micro-organism *n* any living thing too small to be seen with the naked eye, e.g. a bacterium or virus.

microphone *n* an instrument which picks up sounds to be recorded or broadcast, converting them into an electric current. [**micro-** (sense **1**) + Gr *phone*, voice]

microprocessor *n* (*comput*) a single circuit performing most of the basic functions of a central processing unit. [**micro-** (sense **1**)]

microscope *n* an instrument with a system of lenses for viewing objects too small to be seen with the naked eye. [**micro-** (sense **1**) + **-scope**]

microscopic *adj* **1** too small to be seen without the aid of a microscope. **2** extremely small. **3** of, or by means of, a microscope. — *adv* **microscopically**.

microsecond *n* a unit of time equal to one millionth part of a second.

microsurgery *n* intricate surgery performed on minute body structures, requiring the use of a microscope.

microwave *n* **1** an electromagnetic wave of very short wavelength, used in cooking and radar. **2** a microwave oven. — *v* (*tr*) to cook in a microwave oven.

microwave oven *n* an oven which cooks food quickly by passing microwaves through it.

micturate *v* (*intr*; *formal*) to urinate. — *n* **micturition.** [Lat *micturire*]

mid[1] *adj* (often *in cmpds*) being the part at or in the middle: *mid-March*; *in mid sentence*. [OE *midd*]

mid-air *n* any area or point above the ground.

midday *n* the middle of the day; twelve o'clock.

midland *adj* of the central inland part of a country.

the Midlands *n* (*pl*) the inland counties of central England.

midmost *adj* & *adv* (*literary*) (being) in the middle.

midnight *n* twelve o'clock at night. — *adj* of or at midnight. — **burn the midnight oil** to work until very late into the night. **[mid**[1]**]**

the midnight sun *n* the sun seen at midnight during the summer months in the polar regions.

mid-on and **mid-off** *n* (*cricket*) a fielder in a rough horizontal line with, but at some distance from, the non-striking batsman, on the on or off side.

midpoint *n* a point at or near the middle in distance or time.

midstream *n* the area of water in the middle of a river or stream, away from its banks. — **in midstream** before a sentence, action, etc. is finished.

midsummer *n* & *adj* (of, or occurring in) the period of time in the middle of summer, around 21 June. **[mid**[1]**]**

Midsummer's Day *n* (also **Midsummer Day**) 24 June.

midway *adj* & *adv* (being, coming, etc.) halfway between two points in distance or time.

midweek *n* & *adj* (being, happening, etc. in) the period of time in the middle of the week, esp. Wednesday.

the Midwest *n* the central northern states of the US. — *adj* **Midwestern.**

mid-wicket *n* (*cricket*) the area between the stumps on the on side, roughly midway between the wicket and the boundary.

midwinter *n* the period of time in the middle of winter, around 22 December.

mid[2] *prep* (*poetic*; also **'mid**) amid.

midden *n* **1** (*old* or *dialect*) a rubbish heap; a pile of dung. **2** (*dialect*) an untidy mess. [Scandinavian]

middle *adj* **1** at, or being, a point or position between two others, usu. two ends or extremes, and esp. the same distance from each. **2** intermediate, not senior or chief: *middle management*. **3** moderate, not extreme; done, etc. as a compromise: *a middle course*. **4** (*cap*) (esp. of languages) belonging to a period coming after the Old period and before the Modern: *Middle English*. — **1** the middle point, part or position. **2** (*coll*) the waist. — *v* (*tr*) **1** to place in the middle. **2** (*cricket*) to hit (the ball) with the middle of the bat, therefore firmly and accurately. — **be in the middle of** to be busy with, esp. if not nearly finished. — **in the middle of** during. [OE *middel* (*adj*)]

middle age *n* the years between youth and old age, usu. reckoned as between ages 40 and 60. — *adj* **middle-aged.**

middle-age or **-aged spread** *n* (*coll*) fat around the waist when considered a consequence of reaching middle age.

the Middle Ages *n* (*pl*) the period of European history between the 12th and 15th centuries; loosely, the period between the 5th and 15th centuries.

middlebrow (usu. *derog*) *adj* intended for, or appealing to, people with conventional tastes and (only) average intelligence. — *n* a middlebrow person.

the middle class *n*. the social class between the working class and the upper class, traditionally containing educated people with professional or business careers. — *adj* **middle-class.**

middle ear *n* the system of tiny bones which transmits sounds from the eardrum to the inner ear.

the Middle East *n* all the countries between, but not including, Tunisia and Pakistan. — *adj* **Middle Eastern.**

middleman *n* **1** a dealer who buys goods from a producer or manufacturer and sells them to shopkeepers or to the public. **2** any intermediary.

middle name *n* **1** a name which comes between a first name and a surname. **2** a quality or feature for which a person is well known.

middle-of-the-road *adj* (often *derog*) not extreme; of widespread appeal; boringly average or familiar.

middle school *n* a school for children between the ages of 8 or 9 and 12 or 13.

middleweight *n* **1** a class for boxers, wrestlers and weight-lifters of not more than a specified weight (73 kg in professional boxing, 70 kg for **light middleweight**, 77 kg for **super-middleweight**; similar but different weights in the other sports). **2** a boxer, etc. of this weight. — *adj* for contestants of the prescribed weight.

middling (*coll*) *adj* average; moderate; mediocre. — *adv* fairly good; moderately: *middling good*. — **fair to middling** not bad; fairly good. [Scots, from **mid**[1] + **-ling]**

midge *n* any of various kinds of small insect that gather near water, esp. the kinds that bite people. [OE *mycge*]

midget *n* **1** an unusually small person whose limbs and features are of normal proportions. **2** any small thing of its kind. [Ety. as for **midge**]

midi *in cmpds* of medium size or length: *midi-skirt*. — *n* (*coll*) a midi-skirt or -coat. [**mid**[1]]

midi system *n* a complete hi-fi system in the form of a single unit, compact but not portable.

midriff *n* the part of the body between the chest and the waist. [**mid**[1] + OE *hrif*, belly]

midshipman *n* **-men** a trainee naval officer, stationed on land. [Orig. in quarters **amidships**]

midships. See **amidships**.

midst: **in the midst of 1** among, or in the centre of. **2** at the same time as; during. — **in our**, **your** or **their midst** among, or in the same place as, us, you or them. [OE *in middes*, amidst]

midwife *n* **-wives** a nurse, esp. female, trained to supervise childbirth and provide care and advice before and after. — *n* **midwifery**. [OE *mid*, with + *wif*, woman]

mien *n* (*literary*) an appearance, expression or manner, esp. reflecting a mood. [Perhaps from obsolete *demean*, appearance]

miff (*coll*) *v* **1** (*tr*) to offend. **2** (*intr*) to be offended. — *n* **1** a quarrel. **2** a fit of sulking; a huff. — *adj* **miffed**. [Perhaps imit. of noise of disgust or disdain]

miffy *adj* **-ier**, **-iest** (*coll*) easily offended; touchy.

might[1] *v* (*aux*) **1** past tense of **may**: *He asked if he might be of assistance.* **2** used to express possibility: *He might win if he tries hard.* **3** used to request permission: *Might I speak to you a moment?* **4** used in suggesting that a person is not doing what he or she should: *You might carry these bags for me!* **5** (*old pomp* or *facet*) used in asking a question: *And who might you be?* **6** used to introduce the first of a pair of statements, with the sense of 'although': *You might be the boss, but you're still an idiot!* [OE *miht*]

might[2] *n* power or strength. — **with might and main** (*literary*) with great strength; with all one's strength. [OE *miht*]

mighty *adj* **-ier**, **-iest 1** having great strength or power. **2** very large. — *adv* (*coll*; esp. *US*) very: *mighty pretty*. — *adv* **mightily**. — *n* **mightiness**.

mightn't (*coll*) might not.

migraine *n* an extremely severe headache, usu. felt on one side of the head only, often accompanied by nausea and flashes before the eyes; the medical condition in which such headaches recur. [Gr *hemikrania*, half skull]

migrant *n* a person or animal that migrates. — *adj* regularly moving from one place to another. [Lat *migrare*, to migrate]

migrate *v* (*intr*) **1** (of animals, esp. birds) to travel from one region to another at certain times of the year. **2** to leave one place and settle in another, esp. another country, often regularly. — *n* **migration**. — *adj* **migratory**. [Lat *migrare*]

mikado *n* **-os** (often *cap*) (a title formerly given by foreigners to) an emperor of Japan. [Jap, exalted gate]

mike *n* (*coll*) a microphone.

mil *n* **1** a unit of length equal to one thousandth of an inch. **2** (*coll*) a millilitre or millimetre. [Lat *mille*, a thousand]

milady *n* **-ies** (a term formerly used to address) a rich, esp. aristocratic, English woman. [Fr, from **my lady**]

milch *adj* (of cattle) producing milk. [OE *milce*]

mild *adj* **1** gentle in temperament or behaviour. **2** not sharp or strong in flavour or effect. **3** not great or severe. **4** (of climate, etc.) not characterised by extremes; rather warm. — *n* (also **mild ale**) dark beer less flavoured with hops than bitter beer. [OE *milde*]

mild steel *n* steel that contains little carbon and is easily worked.

mildew *n* **1** (the disease caused by) a whitish growth of fungus on plants. **2** a similar greenish growth on substances kept in warm damp conditions; mould. — *v* (*tr* & *intr*) to affect or become affected by mildew. — *adj* **mildewed**. [OE *mildeaw*]

mile *n* **1** a unit of distance equal to 1760 yards (1·61 km). **2** a race over this distance, esp. on foot. **3** (*coll*) a great distance; a large margin: *miss by a mile*. [OE *mil*, from Lat *mille* (*passuum*), a thousand (paces)]

mileage *n* **1** the number of miles (to be) travelled. **2** the number of miles a motor vehicle will travel on a fixed amount of fuel. **3** (*coll*) use; benefit; advantage.

mileometer or **milometer** *n* an instrument in a motor vehicle for recording the total number of miles travelled.

miler *n* an athlete or horse that runs races of one mile.

miles *adv* **1** at a great distance: *miles away*. **2** (*coll*) very much: *miles better*.

milestone *n* **1** a stone pillar at a roadside showing distances in miles to various places. **2** a very important event.

milieu *n* **-lieux** or **-lieus** (*literary*) an (esp. social) environment or set of surroundings. [Fr]

militant *adj* **1** taking, or ready to take, strong or violent action; aggressively active. **2** (*formal*) engaged in warfare. — *n* **militancy**. [Lat *militare*, to serve as a soldier]

military *adj* **1** of, by, or for the armed forces. **2** characteristic of members of the armed forces: *military bearing*. — *n* (with **the**) the armed forces. — *adv* **militarily**. [Lat *militaris*, from *miles*, soldier]

militarise or **-ize** *v* (*tr*) **1** to provide with a military force. **2** to make military in nature or character. — *n* **militarisation** or **-z-**.

militarism *n* (often *derog*) an aggressive readiness to engage in warfare; the (over-enthusiastic) pursuit of military aims and ideals. — *n* **militarist**. — *adj* **militaristic**.

military police *n* a police force within an army, enforcing army rules.

militate *v* (*intr* with **for**, **against**) to act, or have a strong influence (in favour of or against). [Lat *militare*, to serve as a soldier]

militia *n* a civilian fighting force used to supplement a regular army in emergencies. — *n* **militiaman**. [Lat, military force]

milk *n* **1** a whitish liquid produced by female mammals as food for their young; this liquid produced by a cow or goat and taken by humans as food. **2** any similar liquid, esp. that produced by some plants, e.g. the coconut. — *v* (*tr*) **1** to take milk from (an animal). **2** (*coll*) to obtain money, information, or other benefit from, cleverly or relentlessly. — *n* **milkiness**. — *adj* **milky**, ***-ier***, ***-iest***. — **cry over spilt milk** to waste time grieving over a mistake that cannot be undone. — **milk and water** (*derog*) weak or weakly sentimental speech or writing (*adj* **milk-and-water**). — **milk and honey** comfort; luxury; plenty. [OE *milc*]

milk chocolate *n* chocolate containing milk.

milk float *n* a vehicle, usu. electrically-powered, used for delivering milk.

milkmaid *n* a woman who milks.

milkman *n* a man who delivers milk to individual houses.

milk round *n* a milkman's regular route from house to house.

milkshake *n* a drink consisting of a mixture of milk, flavouring, and sometimes ice-cream, whipped until creamy.

milksop *n* (*old derog*) a weak or ineffectual man or youth.

milk tooth *n* any of a baby's first set of teeth.

the Milky Way *n* **1** the line of faint white light in the sky at night, formed by millions of distant stars. **2** the Galaxy.

mill *n* **1** (a building containing) a large machine that grinds grain into flour. **2** any of various smaller machines or devices for grinding: *a pepper mill*. **3** a large machine that presses, rolls, or otherwise shapes; a factory containing one or more of these; any factory: *a woollen mill*. — *v* **1** (*tr*) to grind (grain, etc.). **2** (*tr*) to shape (e.g. metal) in a mill. **3** (*tr*) to cut grooves into the edge of (a coin). **4** (*intr*; *coll*; **about**, **around**) to move in an aimless or confused manner. — **go** or **put through the mill** to (cause to) undergo an unpleasant experience or difficult test. [OE *myln*, from Lat *molere*, to grind]

miller *n* (*hist*) a person who owns or operates a grain mill.

millpond *n* a pond containing water which is, or used to be, used for driving a grain mill.

millstone *n* **1** either of the large heavy stones between which grain is ground in a mill. **2** any heavy burden, e.g. a duty or responsibility.

millwheel *n* a wheel, esp. a waterwheel, driving a grain mill.

millenarian *n* a person who believes that the coming of the millennium is a certainty. — *n* **millenarianism**. [**millennium**]

millennium *n* ***-ia*** **1** a period of a thousand years. **2** (with **the**) a future period of a thousand years during which some Christians believe Christ will rule the world. **3** (with **the**) a future period of worldwide peace and happiness. — *adj* **millennial**. [Lat *mille*, a thousand + *annus*, year]

millepede. Same as **millipede**.

millesimal *adj* thousandth; consisting of thousandths. — *n* a thousandth part. [Lat *mille*, a thousand]

millet *n* an Indian cereal plant used as animal fodder; its small edible seeds. [Lat *milium*]

milli- *comb fm* a thousandth part: *millisecond*. [Lat *mille*, a thousand]

milliard *n* (*old*) a thousand million. [Fr, from Lat *mille*, a thousand]

millibar *n* a unit of air pressure, equal to one thousandth of a bar.

milligram *n* (also **milligramme**) a unit of weight, equal to one thousandth of a gram.

millilitre *n* a unit of volume, equal to one thousandth of a litre.

millimetre *n* a unit of length, equal to one thousandth of a metre.

milliner *n* a person who makes or sells women's hats. [Orig. *Milaner*, a trader in the fancy goods for which *Milan* was once famous]

millinery *n* the hats and trimmings made or sold by milliners; the craft of making them.

million *n* ***millions*** or (after another number) ***million*** **1** the number or quantity 10^6, a thousand thousands. **2** a numeral, figure or symbol representing this, e.g. 1,000,000. **3** (*coll*) a million pounds or dollars. **4** (*coll*; often in *pl*) a great number: *millions of books*. — *adj* 1,000,000 in number. — *n* & *adj* **millionth**. — **in a million** very rare of its kind, and therefore very valuable. [Lat *millionis*, from *mille*, a thousand]

millionaire *n* a person whose wealth amounts to a million pounds, dollars, etc. or more.

millionairess *n* (*old*) a female millionaire.

millipede *n* a small worm-like creature with a many-jointed body and numerous pairs of legs. [Lat *mille*, a thousand + *pedis*, foot]

milometer. See **mileometer** at **mile**.

milord *n* (a term formerly used on the continent to address) a rich, esp. aristocratic, English man. [Fr, from **my lord**]

milt *n* the testis, sperm or semen of a fish. [OE *milte*, spleen]

mime *n* **1** the theatrical art of acting using movements and gestures alone. **2** a play or dramatic sequence performed in this way. **3** (also **mime artist**) an actor who practises this art. — *v* (*tr* & *intr*) **1** to act (feelings, etc.) in this way. **2** to mouth the words to (a song) to match a recording, giving the illusion of singing. [Gr *mimos*, imitator]

mimeograph *n* a machine that produces copies of printed or handwritten material from a stencil; a copy produced in this way. — *v* (*tr*) to make a copy of in this way. [*Mimeograph*, orig. a trademark]

mimetic *adj* **1** of or relating to imitation; imitative. **2** (*biol*) displaying mimicry (sense **2**). [Gr *mimesis*, imitation]

mimic *v* **-ck-** (*tr*) **1** to imitate, esp. for comic effect. **2** to copy. **3** to simulate. **4** (*biol*) to resemble closely. — *n* **1** a person skilled in (esp. comic) imitations of others. **2** (*biol*) a plant or animal displaying mimicry. [Gr *mimikos*, from *mimos*, imitator]

mimicry *n* **1** the skill or practice of mimicking. **2** (*biol*) the close resemblance of one plant or animal species to another, or to its natural environment, seemingly to protect it from predators.

mimosa *n* any of various tropical shrubs or trees with clusters of (esp. yellow) flowers, and leaves that droop when touched. [Gr *mimos*, imitator, from the leaf's imitation of a cowering animal]

Min. *abbrev* **1** Minister. **2** Ministry.

min *n* (*coll*) a minute.

min. *abbrev* **1** minimum. **2** minute.

mina. Same as **myna**.

minaret *n* a tower on a mosque, from which Muslims are called to prayer. [Arabic *manarat*, lighthouse]

minatory *adj* (*formal*) threatening. [Lat *minari*, to threaten]

mince *v* **1** (*tr*) to cut or shred (esp. meat) into very small pieces. **2** (*tr*) to soften the impact of (one's words). **3** (*intr*; *derog*) to walk or speak with affected delicateness. — *n* minced meat, esp. beef. [OFr *mincier*]

mincemeat *n* a spiced mixture of dried fruits, used as a filling for pies. — **make mincemeat of** (*coll*) to defeat or destroy thoroughly.

mince pie *n* a pie filled with mincemeat or with minced meat.

mincing *adj* (*derog*) over-delicate and affected. — *adv* **mincingly**.

mind *n* **1** the power of thinking and understanding; the place where thoughts and feelings exist; the intelligence. **2** memory; recollection: *call something to mind.* **3** opinion; judgement: *to my mind.* **4** attention: *His mind wanders.* **5** wish; inclination: *have a mind to go*; *change one's mind.* **6** a very intelligent person. **7** right senses; sanity: *lose one's mind.* — *v* **1** (*tr*) to look after, care for, or keep safe. **2** (*tr* & *intr*) to be upset, bothered or concerned (by). **3** (*tr*) to be careful or wary of: *mind the traffic.* **4** (*tr*) to take notice of, or pay attention to: *Mind my advice. Mind your own business.* **5** (*tr*) to take care to control: *mind one's language.* **6** (*tr* & *intr*) to take care to protect: *Mind your jacket near this wet paint!* **7** (*tr*; *dialect*) to remember. — *interj* be careful; watch out! — **bear in mind** to remember. — **do you mind!** I find that offensive or annoying. — **in one's mind's eye** in one's imagination. — **in two minds** undecided. — **know one's own mind** to have firm opinions or intentions. — **make up one's mind** to decide. — **never mind** don't worry; it doesn't matter. — **on one's mind** being thought about, considered, worried about, etc. — **a piece of one's mind** a scolding or criticism. — **put one in mind of** to remind one of. [OE *gemynd*, from *munan*, to think]

mind-blowing *adj* (*coll*) very surprising, shocking, or exciting.

mind-boggling *adj* (*coll*) too difficult, large, strange, etc. to imagine or understand.

minded *adj* **1** having an intention or desire: *not minded to reply to your letter.* **2** (*in cmpds*) having a (certain kind of) mind: *open-minded.*

minder *n* **1** (*in cmpds*) a person who takes care of or supervises: *childminder.* **2** (*coll*) a bodyguard.

mindful *adj* (*formal*; **of**) keeping in mind; attentive. — *n* **mindfulness**.

mindless *adj* **1** (*derog*) senseless; done without a reason. **2** (*derog*) needing no effort of mind. **3** (*formal* with **of**) taking no account: *mindless of his responsibilities.* — *adv* **mindlessly**.

mind-reader *n* a person claiming to know other people's thoughts. — *n* **mind-reading**.

mine[1] *pron* **1** something or someone belonging to, or connected with, me; those belonging to me. **2** my family or people. — *adj* (*old & poetic*; used before a vowel sound or *h*) my. — **of mine** belonging to, or connected with, me. [OE *min*]

mine[2] *n* **1** (often *in cmpds*) a place from which coal, minerals, metal ores, or precious stones are dug up. **2** an exploding device, either floating in water or laid just beneath the surface of the ground, designed to destroy enemy ships, troops, etc. **3** a rich source: *a mine of information.* — *v* **1** (*tr* & *intr*) to dig for (minerals, etc.) in (an area). **2** (*tr*) to lay exploding mines in (land or water). **3** (*tr*) to destroy with exploding mines. — *n* **mining**. [Fr *miner*, to mine]

minefield *n* **1** an area of land or water in which exploding mines have been laid. **2** a subject or situation presenting many (hidden) problems or dangers.

miner *n* (often *in cmpds*) a person who works in a mine, esp. a coal mine.

minesweeper *n* a ship equipped to clear mines from an area.

mineral *n* **1** any solid inorganic substance naturally occurring in the earth. **2** any such substance obtained by mining, esp. a metal ore. **3** (usu. in *pl*) mineral water. — *adj* of the nature of a mineral; containing minerals. [Fr *minéral*, from *miner*, to mine]

mineralogy *n* the scientific study of minerals. — *adj* **mineralogical**. — *n* **mineralogist**.

mineral oil *n* any oil obtained from minerals, rather than from a plant or animal source.

mineral water *n* **1** water containing small quantities of dissolved minerals, esp. when occurring naturally in this state at a spring. **2** any fizzy non-alcoholic drink.

minestrone *n* thick soup containing vegetables and pasta. [Ital, from *minestrare*, to serve]

mingle *v* **(with) 1** (*intr* & *tr*) to (cause to) become blended or mixed; to associate or have dealings (with). **2** (*intr*) to move from person to person at a social engagement, briefly talking to each. [OE *mengan*, to mix]

mingy *adj* **-ier**, **-iest** (*coll derog*) ungenerous; mean; meagre. — *n* **minginess**. [Perhaps a blend of **mean**[2] and **stingy**]

mini (*coll*) *n* a small or short one of its kind, esp. a miniskirt. — *adj* small or short of its kind; miniature. **[mini-]**

mini- *pfx* smaller or shorter than the standard: *mini-submarine*. [From **miniature** or **minimum**]

miniature *n* **1** a small copy or model of anything. **2** a very small painting, esp. a portrait; the art of painting such pictures. — *adj* of the nature of a miniature; small-scale. — *v* (*tr*) **miniaturise** or **-ize**. — **in miniature** on a small scale. [Lat *miniatura*, from *miniare*, to paint red, to illustrate]

miniaturist *n* an artist who paints miniatures.

minibus *n* a small bus, usu. with between twelve and fifteen seats.

minicab *n* a taxi ordered by telephone from a private company, not stopped in the street.

minicomputer *n* a medium-sized computer, larger than a microcomputer but smaller than a mainframe computer.

minim *n* **1** (*mus*) a note half the length of a semibreve. **2** a unit of liquid volume, equal to $\frac{1}{60}$ of a fluid drachm (0·06 ml). [Lat *minimus*, smallest]

minimal *adj* of the nature of a minimum; very small indeed; negligible. — *adv* **minimally**. [Lat *minimus*, smallest]

minimalism *n* the policy of using the minimum means to achieve the desired result, esp. in art or music. — *n* & *adj* **minimalist**.

minimise or **-ize** *v* (*tr*) **1** to reduce to a minimum. **2** to treat as being of little importance or significance. [Lat *minimus*, smallest]

minimum *n* **-mums** or **-ma** the lowest possible number, value, quantity or degree, or the lowest reached or allowed. — *adj* of the nature of a minimum; lowest possible; lowest reached or allowed. [Lat *minimus*, smallest]

minimum wage *n* the lowest wage an employer is allowed to pay, by law or union agreement.

minion *n* (*derog*) **1** a subordinate. **2** an employee or follower, esp. when fawning or subservient. [Fr *mignon*, pretty, dainty]

miniskirt *n* a very short skirt, with a hemline well above the knee.

minister *n* **1** the political head of, or a senior politician with responsibilities in, a government department. **2** a member of the clergy in certain branches of the Christian church. **3** a high-ranking diplomat, esp. the next in rank below an ambassador. **4** (*formal*) a person acting as agent for another, esp. in business. — *v* **-r-** (*intr*) **1** (*formal* with **to**) to provide help or service (to). **2** to perform the duties of a religious minister. — *adj* **ministerial**. [Lat, servant]

Minister of the Crown *n* (*Br*) the political head of a government department, with a place in the Cabinet.

Minister of State *n* (*Br*) an assistant to a Minister of the Crown in a large government department, with no place in the Cabinet.

ministration *n* (*formal*) **1** the act of ministering. **2** (usu. in *pl*) help or service given.

ministry *n* **-ies 1** a government department, or its premises. **2** (with **the**) the profession, duties, or period of service of a religious minister; religious ministers collectively.

mink *n* **mink 1** a weasel-like mammal of Europe, Asia and N America. **2** its highly valued fur. **3** a garment made of this, esp. a coat. [Perhaps Swed *mänk*]

Minn. *abbrev* Minnesota.

minneola *n* an orange-like citrus fruit, a cross between a grapefruit and a tangerine. [Perhaps *Mineola*, in Texas, USA]

minnow *n* **1** any of several kinds of small freshwater fish of the carp family. **2** an insignificant person, group, etc. [OE]

Minoan *adj* of or relating to the Bronze Age civilisation of Crete and other Aegean islands, approximately 3000–1100 BC. [*Minos*, mythological king of Crete]

minor *adj* **1** not as great in importance or size; fairly small or insignificant. **2** below the age of legal majority or adulthood. **3** (*mus*) (of a scale) having a semitone between the second and third, fifth and sixth, and seventh and eighth notes; based on such a scale. — *n* **1** a person below the age of legal majority. **2** (*mus*) a minor key, chord or scale. [Lat, less]

minority *n* **-ies 1** a small number; the smaller of two groups. **2** a group of people who are different, esp. in terms of race or religion, from most of the people in a country, region, etc. **3** the state of being the smaller of two groups: *in a minority*. **4** the state of being below the age of legal majority. **[minor]**

minster *n* a large church or cathedral, esp. one orig. attached to a monastery. [OE *mynster*, from Lat *monasterium*, monastery]

minstrel *n* **1** a travelling singer in the Middle Ages. **2** any of a group of white-skinned entertainers made up to look black, performing song and dance superficially of Negro origin. [OFr *menestrel*]

minstrelsy *n* the art or occupation of a mediaeval minstrel.

mint[1] *n* **1** any of various herbs of northern regions with serrated aromatic purplish-green leaves widely used as a flavouring. **2** a sweet flavoured with an extract of these leaves, or a synthetic substitute. — *adj* **minty,** ***-ier***, ***-iest***. [OE *minte*, from Lat *mentha*]

mint[2] *n* **1** a place where coins are produced under government authority. **2** (*coll*) a large sum of money. — *v* (*tr*) **1** to manufacture (coins). **2** to invent or coin (a new word, phrase, etc.). — **in mint condition** **1** brand new; never used. **2** used, but in extremely good condition. [OE *mynet*, money]

minuet *n* (a piece of music for) a slow, formal, 17th- and 18th-century dance with short steps. [Fr *menuet*, from *menu*, small]

minus *prep* **1** made smaller by. **2** (*coll*) without. — *n* (also **minus sign**) **1** a sign (−) indicating a negative quantity, or indicating that a following quantity is to be subtracted. **2** (*coll*) a negative point; a disadvantage. — *adj* **1** negative or less than zero. **2** (*coll*) of the nature of a disadvantage. **3** (of a student's grade) at a level slightly below: *a B minus for my essay*. [Lat, from *minor*, less]

minuscule *adj* **1** extremely small. **2** (of a letter) lower-case, not upper-case or capital. — *n* a lower-case letter. [Lat (*littera*) *minuscula*, small (letter)]

minute[1] *n* **1** a sixtieth part of an hour; sixty seconds. **2** (*coll*) a short while: *wait a minute*. **3** a particular point in time: *at that minute*. **4** the distance that can be travelled in a minute: *a house five minutes away*. **5** (*geom*) a sixtieth part of a degree; sixty seconds. **6** (usu. in *pl*) the official written record of what is said at a formal meeting. **7** a written note or statement sent to a colleague; a memorandum. — *v* (*tr*) **1** to make an official written record of. **2** to send a memorandum to. — **up to the minute** very modern or recent (*adj* **up-to-the-minute**). [Ety. as for **minute**[2]]

minute steak *n* a thin steak that can be cooked quickly.

minute[2] *adj* **1** very small; tiny. **2** (*formal*) precise; detailed. **3** (*formal*) petty. — *adv* **minutely**. [Lat *minutus*, small]

minutia *n* ***-ae*** (*formal*; usu. in *pl*) a very small or unimportant detail. [Lat, smallness]

minx *n* (*old*) a cheeky, sly, or flirtatious (esp. young) woman.

Miocene *adj* & *n* (of) a geological epoch of the later Tertiary. (Gr *meion*, smaller + *kainos*, recent]

miracle *n* **1** an act or event breaking the laws of nature, and therefore thought to be the result of direct intervention by a supernatural force, esp. God. **2** (*coll*) a fortunate happening; an amazing event. **3** (*coll*; **of**) an amazing example or achievement (of): *a miracle of modern technology*. [Lat *miraculum*, from *mirari*, to wonder at]

miracle play. See **mystery play**.

miraculous *adj* **1** of the nature of a miracle. **2** (*coll*) wonderful; amazing; amazingly fortunate.

mirage *n* **1** an optical illusion, esp. in the form of a distant mass of water, created by the action of hot air on sunlight. **2** anything illusory or imaginary. [Fr, from *mirer*, to reflect]

mire (*literary*) *n* **1** deep mud; a boggy area. **2** trouble; difficulty; anything unpleasant. — *v* **1** (*tr* & *intr*) to (cause to) sink in a mire. **2** (*tr*) to soil with mud. [Norse *myrr*, bog]

mirror *n* **1** a glass surface coated with an alloy of mercury and other metals so as to produce true reflections; any reflecting surface. **2** (**of**) a faithful representation or reflection. — *v* ***-r-*** (*tr*) **1** to reflect as in a mirror. **2** to represent or depict faithfully. **3** to fit with a mirror or mirrors. [OFr *mireor*, from Lat *mirari*, to wonder at]

mirror image *n* **1** a reflected image as produced by a mirror, i.e. with right and left sides reversed. **2** an object that matches another as if it were its image as seen in a mirror, i.e. with features reversed.

mirth *n* laughter; merriment. — *adj* **mirthful**. — *adj* **mirthless**. — *adv* **mirthlessly**. [OE *myrgth*, from *myrige*, merry]

mis- *pfx* **1** wrong or wrongly; bad or badly: *misclassify*. **2** negative; lack of: *mistrust*. [OE; connected with **miss**[1]]

misadventure *n* **1** (*formal*) an unfortunate happening; bad luck. **2** (*legal*) an accident, with total absence of intent to commit crime: *death by misadventure*. [OF *mésaventure*, from *mésavenir*, to turn out badly]

misalliance *n* (*formal*) a relationship or alliance, esp. a marriage, in which the parties are not suited to each other. [Fr *mésalliance*]

misanthrope or **misanthropist** *n* a person who hates or distrusts all people. — *adj* **misanthropic**. — *n* **misanthropy**. [Gr *misanthropos*, from *miseein*, to hate + *anthropos*, man]

misapply *v* ***-ies***, ***-ied*** (*tr*) to use unwisely. — *n* **misapplication**.

misapprehend *v* (*tr*; *formal*) to misunderstand. — *n* **misapprehension**.

misappropriate *v* (*tr*; *formal* or *legal*) to take (esp. money) dishonestly for oneself; to put to a wrong use. — *n* **misappropriation**.

misbegotten *adj* **1** (*literary*) illegally obtained. **2** (*literary*) foolishly planned or thought out. **3** (*old*) illegitimate; bastard. [**mis-** (sense **1**)]

misbehave *v* (*intr*) to behave badly. — *n* **misbehaviour**.

miscalculate *v* (*tr* & *intr*) to calculate or estimate wrongly. — *n* **miscalculation**.

miscarriage *n* **1** an act of uncontrollably releasing a foetus from the womb too early for it to be able to live. **2** (*formal*) a failure to reach a desired goal: *a miscarriage of justice*.

miscarry *v* **-ies**, **-ied** (*intr*) **1** (of a woman) to have a miscarriage. **2** (*formal*) to fail.

miscast *v* ***miscast*** (*tr*) to give an unsuitable part to (an actor) or put an unsuitable actor in (a part).

miscegenation *n* (*formal*) marriage or breeding between people of different races, esp. of different skin colours. [Lat *miscere*, to mix + *genus*, race]

miscellaneous *adj* made up of various kinds; mixed. [Lat *miscellaneus*, from *miscere*, to mix]

miscellany *n* **-ies** (*formal*) a mixture of various kinds, esp. a collection of writings on different subjects, or by different authors. [See ety. for **miscellaneous**]

mischance *n* (a piece of) bad luck. [OFr *meschance*]

mischief *n* **1** behaviour that annoys or irritates but causes no serious harm: *make mischief*. **2** the desire to behave in this way: *full of mischief*. **3** (*old*) a person with a tendency to behave in this way. **4** damage or harm; an injury: *do oneself a mischief*. [OFr *meschief*, disaster]

mischievous *adj* **1** tending to make mischief; playfully troublesome. **2** (*old*) causing damage or harm. — *adv* **mischievously**. — *n* **mischievousness**.

miscible *adj* (*formal*; **with**) able to mix without separating: *miscible with water*. — *n* **miscibility**. [Lat *miscere*, to mix]

misconceive *v* **1** (*tr* & *intr*; **of**) to have the wrong idea or impression (about); to misunderstand. **2** (*tr*) to plan or think out badly. — *n* **misconception**.

misconduct *n* **1** improper or unethical behaviour. **2** bad management.

misconstrue *v* (*tr*) to interpret wrongly or mistakenly. — *n* **misconstruction**.

miscreant *n* (*literary* or *old*) a malicious person; a rogue or scoundrel. [OFr *mescreant*, unbelieving, heretical]

misdeed *n* (*literary*) an example of bad or criminal behaviour; a wrongdoing. [OE *misdæd*]

misdemeanour *n* **1** (*formal*) a wrongdoing; a misdeed. **2** (*old legal*) a crime less serious than a felony. [Obsolete *misdemean*, to misbehave]

misdirect *v* (*tr*) **1** (*formal*) to give wrong directions to; to send to the wrong place. **2** (*formal*) to use (esp. funds) for an unsuitable purpose. **3** (*legal*) (of a judge) to provide incorrect legal information to (a jury). — *n* **misdirection**.

mise-en-scène *n* **1** (*theatre*) the process of arranging, or the arrangement of, scenery and props. **2** (*films*) the use of long scenes during which the position of the camera does not change. **3** (*literary*) the surroundings in which an event takes place. [Fr, a putting-on-stage]

miser *n* a person who lives in poor conditions in order to store up wealth; any ungenerous person. — *n* **miserliness**. — *adj* **miserly**. [Lat, wretched]

miserable *adj* **1** very unhappy; habitually bad-tempered. **2** marked by great unhappiness: *a miserable life*. **3** causing unhappiness or discomfort: *miserable weather*. **4** marked by poverty or squalor: *miserable living conditions*. **5** (*dialect*) ungenerous; mean. — *adv* **miserably**. [Fr *misérable*, from Lat *miser*, wretched]

misericord *n* a ledge on the underside of a seat in the choir stalls of a church, used, when the seat is folded up, as a support for the standing person. [Lat *misericordia*, compassion]

misery *n* **-ies** **1** (a cause of) great unhappiness. **2** poverty or squalor. **3** (*coll*) a habitually sad or bad-tempered person. [Lat *miseria*]

misfire *v* (*intr*) **1** (of a gun) to fail to fire, or fail to fire properly. **2** (of an engine) to fail to ignite the fuel at the right times. **3** to be unsuccessful; to produce the wrong effect. — *n* an act of misfiring. [**miss**[1] + **fire**]

misfit *n* **1** a person not suited to a particular situation or environment. **2** something that fits badly or not at all.

misfortune *n* bad luck; an unfortunate incident.

misgiving *n* (often in *pl*) a feeling of uneasiness, doubt or suspicion.

misguided *adj* acting from, or showing, mistaken ideas or bad judgement. — *adv* **misguidedly**.

mishandle *v* (*tr*) **1** to deal with carelessly or without skill. **2** to handle roughly; to mistreat.

mishap *n* an unfortunate (esp. minor) accident; bad luck. [**mis-** (sense **1**) + old *hap*, luck, happening]

mishear *v* ***-heard*** (*tr*) to hear incorrectly.

mishit *v* **-tt-**, ***mishit*** (*tr*) to fail to hit cleanly or accurately. — *n* an act of mishitting.

mishmash *n* (*coll*) a disordered collection or mixture; a hotchpotch. [Reduplication of **mash**]

misinform *v* (*tr*) to give incorrect or misleading information to. — *n* **misinformation**.

misinterpret *v* **-t-** (*tr*) to understand or explain incorrectly or misleadingly. — *n* **misinterpretation**.

misjudge *v* (*tr*) to judge wrongly; to have an unfairly low opinion of (someone). — *n* **misjudgement** or **-judgment**.

mislay *v* **-*laid*** (*tr*) to lose (something), usu. temporarily, esp. by not remembering where it was put.

mislead *v* ***misled*** (*tr*) to cause to take a wrong or undesirable course of action; to cause to have a false impression or belief. — *adj* **misleading**.

mismanage *v* (*tr*) to manage or handle badly or carelessly. — *n* **mismanagement**.

mismatch *v* (*tr*) to match unsuitably or incorrectly. — *n* an unsuitable or incorrect match.

misname *v* (*tr*) **1** to give an unsuitable name to. **2** to call by the wrong name.

misnomer *n* a wrong or unsuitable name; an act of using it. [OFr *mesnommer*, to misname]

misogynist *n* a person who hates women. — *adj* **misogynous**. — *n* **misogyny**. [Gr *miseein*, to hate + *gyne*, woman]

misplace *v* (*tr*) **1** to lose (something), usu. temporarily, esp. by forgetting where it was put. **2** to give (trust, affection, etc.) unwisely or inappropriately. **3** to put in the wrong place.

misprint *n* a mistake in printing. — *v* (*tr*) to print wrongly.

misprison *n* (*legal*) a failure to inform the authorities of a serious crime; deliberate concealment of one's knowledge of a serious crime. [OFr *mesprision*, error]

mispronounce *v* (*tr*) to pronounce (words, etc.) incorrectly. — *n* **mispronunciation**.

misquote *v* (*tr*) to quote inaccurately, often with the intention of deceiving. — *n* **misquotation**.

misread *v* ***misread*** (*tr*) **1** to read incorrectly. **2** to misunderstand or misinterpret.

misrepresent *v* (*tr*) **1** to give a false or misleading account or impression of, often intentionally. — *n* **misrepresentation**.

misrule (*formal*) *n* **1** bad or unjust government. **2** civil disorder. — *v* (*tr*) to govern in a disorderly or unjust way.

Miss. *abbrev* Mississippi.

miss[1] *v* **1** (*tr* & *intr*) to fail to hit or catch (something). **2** (*tr*) to fail to arrive in time for. **3** (*tr*) to fail to take advantage of: *missed your chance*. **4** (*tr*) to regret the absence of. **5** (*tr*) to notice the absence of. **6** (*tr*) to fail to hear or see. **7** (*tr*) to refrain from going to (a place or an event): *I'll have to miss the next class*. **8** (*tr*) to avoid or escape: *just missed being run over*. **9** (*intr*) (of an engine) to fail to burn fuel at the right times. — *n* a failure to hit or catch something. — **give (something) a miss** (*coll*) to refrain from doing, accepting, attending, etc. (something). — *v* **miss out** **1** (*tr*) to fail to include; to leave out. **2** (*intr*; **on**) to fail to benefit (from) or participate (in). [OE *missan*]

missing *adj* **1** absent; lost; not able to be found. **2** not able to be located, but not known to be dead or destroyed.

the missing link *n* **1** any one thing needed to complete a series. **2** a hypothetical extinct creature at a supposed stage of evolutionary development between apes and humans.

miss[2] *n* **1** (*cap*) a term used to address an unmarried woman. **2** (*cap*) a term used to address a female school teacher, married or not. **3** (*cap*) a title given to a beauty queen from a stated country, region, etc.: *Miss France*. **4** (*coll*) a girl; an unmarried woman. [Short form of **mistress**]

missy *n* (*old coll*, usu. *facet* or *derog*) a term used to address a girl or young woman.

missal *n* (*RC Church*) a book containing all the texts used in Mass in a year. [Lat *missale*, from *missa*, mass]

missel-thrush. Same as **mistle-thrush**.

misshapen *adj* badly shaped; deformed.

missile *n* **1** a self-propelled flying bomb. **2** (*formal*) any weapon or object that is thrown or fired. [Lat *missilis*, from *mittere*, to send]

mission *n* **1** a purpose for which a person or group of people is sent. **2** (a group of people sent on) a journey made for a scientific, military, or religious purpose. **3** a group of people sent to have (esp. political) discussions. **4** the purpose for which (one feels) one was born; a calling. **5** (the premises of) a group of missionaries. [Lat *missionis*, from *mittere*, to send]

missionary *n* **-*ies*** a member of a religious organisation seeking to carry out charitable works and religious teaching, often combined.

missis. Same as **missus**.

missive *n* (*literary* or *legal*) a letter. [Lat *missivus*, from *mittere*, to send]

misspell *v* **-*spelt*** or **-*spelled*** (*tr*) to spell incorrectly.

misspend *v* **-*spent*** (*tr*) to spend foolishly or wastefully.

missus *n* (*coll*) **1** (esp. *humorous*) a wife. **2** (esp. *old*) a term used to address an adult female stranger. [Spoken form of **mistress** (sense **4**)]

missy. See **miss**[2].

mist *n* **1** (a cloud of) condensed water vapour in the air near the ground; thin fog or low cloud. **2** a mass of tiny droplets of liquid, e.g. forced under pressure from a container. **3** condensed water vapour on a surface. **4** (*literary*) a watery film: *a mist of tears*. **5** (*literary*) an obscuring influence: *the mists of time*. — *v* (*tr* & *intr*; **up**, **over**) to cover or become covered with mist. [OE]

misty *adj* **-*ier***, **-*iest*** **1** covered with, or obscured by, mist. **2** (*literary*) not clear; vague. **3** (of eyes) filled with tears. — *adv* **mistily**. — *n* **mistiness**.

mistake *v* ***mistook***, ***mistaken*** (*tr*) **1** (**for**) to identify incorrectly (as); to wrongly assume or understand (to be): *She mistook my silence for disapproval*. **2** to misinterpret. **3** to make the wrong choice of: *He mistook his road in the fog*. — *n* **1** an error.

2 a regrettable action. **3** an act of wrongly understanding or interpreting something. [Norse *mistaka*, to take wrongly]

mistaken *adj* **1** understood or identified wrongly. **2** guilty of, or displaying, a failure to understand or interpret correctly. — *adv* **mistakenly**.

mister *n* **1** (*cap*) the full form of the abbreviation **Mr**. **2** (*coll*) a term used to address an adult male stranger. **3** a man not belonging to the nobility; an untitled man. [Orig. a spoken form of **master**]

mistime *v* (*tr*) **1** to do or say at a wrong or unsuitable time. **2** (*sport*) to misjudge the timing of (a stroke) in relation to the speed of an approaching ball.

mistle-thrush *n* a large European thrush fond of mistletoe berries. [OE *mistel*, mistletoe]

mistletoe *n* a Eurasian evergreen shrub that grows as a parasite on trees and produces clusters of white berries in winter; a similar American plant. [OE *misteltan*]

mistook. See **mistake**.

mistral *n* (with **the**) a violent cold dry northerly wind that blows in S France. [Provençal, from Lat *magistralis*, masterful]

mistreat *v* (*tr*) to treat cruelly or without care. — *n* **mistreatment**.

mistress *n* **1** a woman in a commanding or controlling position; a female head or owner. **2** a female teacher. **3** the female lover of a man married to another woman. **4** (*old*) a term used to address any woman, esp. one in authority. [OFr *maistresse*]

mistrial *n* (*legal*) a trial not conducted properly according to the law, and declared invalid.

mistrust *v* (*tr*) to have no trust in; to be suspicious of. — *n* lack of trust. — *adj* **mistrustful**.

misty. See **mist**.

misunderstand *v* ***-understood*** (*tr* & *intr*) to fail to understand properly.

misunderstanding *n* **1** a failure to understand properly. **2** (*euph*) a disagreement.

misunderstood *adj* (of a person) whose character, feelings, intentions, etc. are not properly understood by others.

misuse *n* improper or inappropriate use: *the misuse of funds*. — *v* (*tr*) **1** to put to improper or inappropriate use. **2** (*formal*) to treat badly or cruelly.

mite[1] *n* any of various small spider-like creatures, some of which are parasites. [OE]

mite[2] *n* **1** any small person or animal, esp. a child that is pitied. **2** a small amount of anything, esp. money. — **a mite** (*coll*) rather; somewhat: *a mite jealous*. [ODut *mite*]

mitigate *v* (*tr*) **1** (*legal*) to partially excuse or make less serious: *mitigating circumstances*. **2** (*formal*) to make (pain, anger, etc.) less severe. [Lat *mitigare*, from *mitis*, mild + *agere*, to make]

mitosis *n* (*biol*) a division of a cell in which two new nuclei are produced, each containing the same number of chromosomes as the parent nucleus. [Gr *mitos*, fibre]

mitre[1] *n* the ceremonial headdress of a bishop or abbot, a tall pointed hat with front and back sections divided. [Fr, from Gr *mitra*, fillet]

mitre[2] *n* (also **mitre joint**) a corner joint between two lengths of wood, etc. made by fitting together two 45° sloping surfaces cut into their ends. — *v* (*tr*) to join with a mitre. [Ety. perhaps as for **mitre**[1]]

mitt *n* **1** a mitten. **2** (*coll*) a hand. **3** a padded leather glove worn in baseball. [From **mitten**]

mitten *n* **1** a glove with one covering for the thumb and a large covering for all the other fingers together. **2** a glove covering the hand and wrist but not (the ends of) the fingers. [Fr *mitaine*]

mix *v* **1** (*tr*; **with**, **up**) to put together or combine to form one mass. ◇ See also **mix up** below. **2** (*tr*; **up**) to prepare or make by doing this: *mix a cake*. ◇ See also **mix up** below. **3** (*intr*) to blend together to form one mass: *Water and oil do not mix*. **4** (*intr*) to meet with people socially; to feel at ease in social situations. **5** (*tr*; **with**) to do at the same time; to combine: *mix business with pleasure*. **6** (*tr*; *tech*) to adjust electronically (the sounds produced by individual musicians) to create an overall balance of sound. — *n* **1** a collection of people or things mixed together. **2** a collection of (usu. dried) ingredients from which something is prepared: *a cake mix*. — **mix it** (*slang*) to cause trouble, argument, a fight, etc. — *v* **mix up** (*tr*) **1** to confuse: *I always mix him up with his brother* (*n* **mix-up**). **2** (**in, with**) to involve, esp. illegally or undesirably. **3** (*coll*) to upset or put into a state of confusion (*adj* **mixed-up**). [Lat *miscere*, to mix]

mixed *adj* **1** consisting of different (often opposite) kinds: *mixed feelings*. **2** done, used, etc. by people of both sexes.

mixed bag *n* (*coll*) a collection of people or things of different kinds, standards, etc.

mixed blessing *n* something which has both advantages and disadvantages.

mixed doubles *n* (*sing*) a variety of tennis, table-tennis, or badminton played by two pairs, each consisting of a man and a woman.

mixed economy *n* an economic system with some elements state-owned and others privately owned.

mixed farming *n* farming of both crops and livestock.

mixed grill *n* a dish of different kinds of grilled meat, and usu. tomatoes and mushrooms.

mixed marriage *n* (an example of) marriage between people of different races or religions.

mixer *n* **1** a machine used for mixing. **2** a soft drink for mixing with alcoholic drinks.

3 (*coll*) a person considered in terms of his or her ability to mix socially: *a good mixer*.
mixture *n* **1** a blend of ingredients prepared for a particular purpose: *cough mixture*. **2** a combination: *a mixture of sadness and relief*. **3** the act of mixing.

mizzenmast *n* (on a ship with three or more masts) the third mast from the front of the ship. [Ital *mezzano*, middle + **mast**[1]]

Mk *abbrev* mark (= a type of design, or model, esp. of vehicles).

ml *abbrev* **1** mile. **2** millilitre.

MLitt *abbrev* for *magister litterarum* (Lat), Master of Letters, or of Literature.

mm *abbrev* millimetre.

MN *abbrev* Minnesota.

Mn *symbol* (*chem*) manganese.

mnemonic *n* & *adj* (something, often a short verse) used as an aid to memory. — *adv* **mnemonically**. [Gr *mneme*, memory]

MO *abbrev* **1** Medical Officer, i.e. an army doctor. **2** modus operandi. **3** money order. **4** Missouri.

Mo *abbrev* Missouri.

Mo *symbol* (*chem*) molybdenum.

mo *n* ***mos*** (*coll*) a short while; a moment. [Abbrev. of **moment**]

moa *n* an extinct flightless ostrich-like bird of New Zealand. [Maori]

moan *n* **1** a low prolonged sound expressing sadness, grief or pain. **2** any similar sound, e.g. made by the wind or an engine. **3** (*coll*) a complaint; a person who complains a lot. — *v* (*intr*) **1** to utter or produce a moan. **2** (*coll*) to complain, esp. without good reason. — *n* **moaner**. [OE *mænan*, to grieve over]

moat *n* a deep (usu. water-filled) trench round a castle, etc., providing extra defence. [OFr *mote*, mound]

mob *n* **1** a large disorderly crowd. **2** (*coll*) any group or gang. **3** (*coll* with **the**) ordinary people; the masses. **4** (*slang* with **the**; often *cap*) an organised gang of criminals, esp. the Mafia. — *v* ***-bb-*** (*tr*) **1** to attack as a mob. **2** to crowd round curiously or admiringly. [Shortening of Lat *mobile vulgus*, fickle masses]
mobster *n* (*slang*) a member of an organised group of criminals, esp. the Mafia.

mobile *adj* **1** able to be moved easily; not fixed. **2** set up inside a vehicle travelling from place to place: *a mobile shop*. **3** (of a face) frequently changing expression. **4** able, or willing, to move house or change jobs. **5** moving, or able to move, from one social class to another: *upwardly mobile*. **6** (*coll*) provided with transport and able to get around: *Now my car's fixed, I'm mobile again*. — *n* a hanging decoration moved around by air currents. — *n* **mobility**. [Lat *mobilis*, from *movere*, to move]

mobilise or **-ize** *v* **1** (*tr*) to organise or prepare for use. **2** (*tr* & *intr*) to assemble and make or become ready for war. — *n* **mobilisation** or **-z-**. [**mobile**]

moccasin *n* **1** a heelless deerskin shoe worn by N American Indians; any slipper or shoe (even vaguely) resembling this. **2** (also **water moccasin**) a large poisonous snake of the swamps of the southern US. [From a N American Indian language]

mocha *n* **1** dark brown coffee of fine quality. **2** a flavouring made from coffee and chocolate. [*Mocha*, port in the Yemen Arab Republic where the coffee was originally shipped from]

mock *v* **1** (*tr* & *intr*) to speak or behave disparagingly or contemptuously (towards). **2** (*tr*) to mimic. **3** (*tr*; *literary*) to cause to seem impossible or useless; to seem to defy or frustrate: *Violent winds mocked my attempt to pitch the tent*. — *adj* **1** false; sham: *mock sincerity*. **2** serving as practice for something similar coming later: *a mock examination*. — *n* (*coll*) a mock examination. — *adj* **mocking**. [OFr *mocquer*]
mockery *n* ***-ies*** **1** ridicule; contempt; the subject of ridicule or contempt: *make a mockery of*. **2** an imitation, esp. contemptible or insulting. **3** any ridiculously inadequate person, action or thing.
mockingbird *n* a grey American bird that copies the calls of other birds.
mock orange *n* the philadelphus.
mock turtle soup *n* soup made in the style of turtle soup, but using a calf's head.
mock-up *n* a full-size (often working) model, built for experimental purposes.

mockers: **put the mockers on** (*coll*) to end the chances of success of; to spoil. [Perhaps **mock**]

MOD or **MoD** *abbrev* Ministry of Defence.

mod (*coll*) *adj* (*old*) modern. — *n* (*cap*) a follower of a British teenage culture orig. of the 1960s, characterised by a liking for smart clothes and motor scooters and a dislike of Rockers. [Short form of **modern**]
mod cons *n* (*pl*; *coll*) modern household conveniences, e.g. central heating.

modal *adj* of mode or a mode. — *n* (*gram*; also **modal auxiliary** or **modal verb**) any verb used to express a particular mood, e.g. possibility, i.e. the English verbs **can**, **could**, **may**, **might**, **shall**, **should**, **will**, **would**, **must**, **ought to**, **used to**, **need**, and **dare**. [**mode**]

mode *n* **1** (*formal*) a way of doing, living, operating, etc. **2** a fashion or style, e.g. in clothes or art. **3** (*mus*) any of several systems according to which notes are arranged. [Lat *modus*, manner, measure]

model *n* **1** a small-scale representation serving as a guide to construction. **2** a small-scale replica. **3** one of several types or designs of manufactured article. **4** a person who displays clothes to potential buyers by wearing them. **5** a (usu. paid) human subject of the work of an artist, photographer, etc. **6** a thing from which something else is to be derived; a basis. **7** an excellent example; an example to be copied: *She's a model of loyalty. a model boss.* — *v* **-ll-** **1** (*tr* & *intr*) to display (clothes) by wearing them. **2** (*intr*) to work as a model for an artist, photographer, etc. **3** (*tr* & *intr*) to make models (of). **4** (*tr*) to shape into a particular form: *to model clay.* **5** (*tr* with **on**) to plan, build or create according to a model. — *n* **modelling**. [Fr *modelle*, from Lat *modulus*]

modem *n* (*comput*) an electronic device that transmits information from one computer to another along a telephone line, converting digital data into audio signals and back again. [**modulator demodulator**]

moderate *adj* **1** not extreme; not strong or violent. **2** average; middle rate: *moderate intelligence.* — *n* a person holding moderate (esp. political) views. — *v* **1** (*tr*) to make or become less extreme or less violent. **2** (*intr*) to act as a moderator. — *adj* **moderately**. [Lat *moderatus*, from *modus*, measure]

moderation *n* **1** the quality of being moderate. **2** an act of making or becoming less extreme. **3** lack of excess; self-control. — **in moderation** to a moderate degree; in moderate amounts.

moderator *n* **1** a minister presiding over a court or assembly in any Presbyterian church. **2** a settler of disputes; a mediator. **3** a substance used for slowing down neutrons in nuclear reactors.

moderato *adv*, *adj* (*mus*) (to be played) at a moderate speed, in a controlled way. [Ital]

modern *adj* **1** belonging to the present or to recent times; not old or ancient. **2** involving, using, or being the very latest available (techniques, equipment, styles, etc.): *modern transport.* **3** (often *cap*) (of a language) in the most recent stage of development; as used at present. — *n* a person living in modern times, esp. a follower of the latest trends. — *n* **modernity**. [Lat *modernus*]

modernise or **-ize** *v* **1** (*tr*) to bring up to modern standards. **2** (*intr*) to switch to more modern methods or techniques. — *n* **modernisation** or **-z-**.

modernism *n* (a belief in the need for) modern ideas, opinions or standards, esp. those reacting sharply against traditional values. — *n* **modernist**. — *adj* **modernistic**.

modest *adj* **1** not having or showing pride; humble; not pretentious or showy. **2** not large; moderate: *a modest income.* **3** (*old*) (esp. of clothes) reflecting chastity or moral decency, esp. by not showing much bare skin: *a modest dress.* — *adv* **modestly**. — *n* **modesty**. [Lat *modestus*, from *modus*, a measure]

modicum *n* (*formal* or *facet*) a small amount: *a modicum of decency.* [Lat, from *modicus*, moderate]

modifier *n* (*gram*) a word or phrase that pinpoints, or slightly changes, the meaning of another word, e.g. *in the green hat* in the phrase *the man in the green hat*, and *vaguely* in the phrase *he was vaguely embarrassed.*

modify *v* **-ies**, **-ied** (*tr*) **1** to change the form or quality of, usu. slightly. **2** (*gram*) to act as a modifier of. — *n* **modification**. [Lat *modificare*]

modish *adj* (*formal*) stylish; fashionable. [**mode**]

modiste *n* (*old formal*) a fashion designer. [**mode**]

modulate *v* (*tr*) **1** (*tech*) to alter the tone or volume of (a sound or one's voice). **2** (*formal*) to change or alter. **3** (*tech*) to make slight changes in the frequency or amplitude of (radio waves). — *n* **modulation**. — *n* **modulator**. [Lat *modulari*]

module *n* **1** a separate unit that combines with others to form a larger unit, structure or system. **2** a separate self-contained part of a space vehicle used for a particular purpose: *lunar module.* — *adj* **modular**. [Lat *modulus*, a small measure]

modus operandi *n* ***modi*** a way of working; the way something operates. [Lat, way of working]

modus vivendi *n* ***modi*** **1** an arrangement by which people or groups in conflict can work or exist together; a compromise. **2** (*pompous*) a way of living. [Lat, way of living]

moggy *n* **-ies** (*slang*; also **mog**) a cat.

mogul *n* **1** an important, powerful or influential person, esp. in business or the film industry. **2** (*cap*) a Muslim ruler of India between the 16th and 19th centuries. — *adj* (*cap*) of, typical of, or relating to the Moguls. [Persian *Mughul*, Mongol]

mohair *n* the long soft hair of the angora goat; a yarn or fabric made of this, pure or mixed with wool. [Arabic *mukhayyar*]

Mohammedan *n* & *adj* (*old*; often *offensive* to Muslims) Muslim. [The prophet *Mohammed* (?570–632), founder of Islam]

mohican *n* a hairstyle popular amongst punks, in which the head is partially shaved, leaving a central front-to-back band of hair, usu. coloured and formed into a spiky crest. [*Mohicans*, N American Indian tribe on whose hairstyle this is based]

moiety *n* **-ies** (*literary* or *legal*) a half; one of two parts or divisions. [OFr *moité*]

moire *n* fabric, esp. silk, with a pattern of glossy irregular waves. [Fr]

moiré *n* & *adj* (having) such a pattern.

moist *adj* **1** damp; slightly wet. **2** (of food, esp. cake) pleasantly soft and fresh, not dry. — *n* **moistness**. [OFr *moiste*]

moisten *v* (*tr* & *intr*) to make or become moist.

moisture *n* liquid in vapour or spray form, or condensed as droplets; moistness.

moisturise or **-ize** *v* (*tr*) to make less dry, esp. to add moisture to (the skin) by rubbing in a cream. — *n* **moisturiser** or **-z-**.

moke *n* (*slang*) a donkey.

molar *n & adj* (of) any of the large back teeth in humans and other mammals, used for chewing and grinding. [Lat *mola*, millstone]

molasses *n* (*sing*) the thickest kind of treacle, left over at the very end of the process of refining raw sugar. [Port *melaço*]

mole[1] *n* a raised dark permanent spot on the skin, caused by a concentration of melanin. [OE *mal*]

mole[2] *n* **1** a small burrowing insect-eating mammal with tiny eyes and soft dark fur. **2** (*coll*) a spy working inside an organisation and passing secret information to people outside it. [MidE *molle*]

molehill *n* a little pile of earth thrown up by a burrowing mole.

moleskin *n* **1** mole's fur. **2** heavy twilled cotton fabric with a short nap; (in *pl*) trousers made of this.

mole[3] *n* (*chem*) an amount of a substance that contains as many particles of a stated kind, e.g. atoms or molecules, as there are atoms in 12 grams of Carbon-12. [Ger, from *Molekül*, molecule]

mole[4] *n* a pier, causeway or breakwater made of stone; a harbour protected by any of these. [Lat *moles*, mass]

molecule *n* the smallest unit into which a chemical compound can be divided without losing its basic nature, consisting of two or more atoms. [Lat *molecula*, from *moles*, mass]

molecular *adj* of or relating to molecules.

molecular weight *n* the sum of the atomic weights of the atoms in a molecule.

molest *v* (*tr*) **1** to attack or interfere with sexually. **2** (*formal*) to attack, causing physical harm. **3** (*old*) to disturb or upset. — *n* **molestation**. [Lat *molestare*]

moll *n* (*old slang*) **1** a gangster's girlfriend. **2** a prostitute. [*Moll*, woman's name]

mollify *v* **-ies**, **-ied** (*tr*) **1** to make calmer or less angry. **2** to soothe or ease. — *n* **mollification**. [Lat *mollis*, soft + *facere*, to make]

mollusc *n* any of numerous limbless invertebrate creatures with a soft body and usu. a hard shell, including shellfish, snails and squid. [Lat *molluscus*]

mollycoddle *v* (*tr*; *coll*) to treat with fussy care and protection. [*Molly*, woman's name + **coddle**]

Molotov cocktail *n* a small crude bomb for throwing, consisting of a bottle filled with petrol, usu. with a burning cloth as a fuse. [V M *Molotov* (1890–1986), Soviet statesman]

molten *adj* in a melted state. [Old past participle of **melt**]

molto *adv* (*mus*) very. [Ital]

molybdenum *n* an element (symbol **Mo**), a hard silvery-white metal, used in alloys for its strengthening properties. [Gr *molybdaina*, lead-like substance]

mom *n* (*coll*; esp. *US*; also **mommy**, **-ies**) mother.

moment *n* **1** a short while. **2** a particular point in time: *at that moment*. **3** (*formal*) importance; significance: *a literary work of great moment*. **4** (*physics*) (a measure of) the turning motion created by a force. — **at the moment** at this particular time; now. — **have her, its,** etc. **moments** (*coll*) to experience periodic, if not regular, times of happiness, success, etc. — **of the moment** currently very popular, important, fashionable, etc. [Lat *momentum*, movement]

momentary *adj* lasting for only a moment. — *adv* **momentarily**.

the moment of truth *n* a very important or significant point in time, esp. when a person or thing is put to the test.

momentous *adj* of great importance or significance. — *n* **momentousness**.

momentum *n* **1** (*tech*) the amount or force of motion in a moving object. **2** continuous speed of progress; impetus: *The campaign gained momentum*. [Lat, movement]

mommy. See **mom**.

Mon. *abbrev* Monday.

mon-. See **mono-**.

monad *n* **1** (*philos*) any self-contained non-physical unit of being, e.g. a soul, God. **2** (*biol*) a single-celled organism. [Gr, from *monas*, unit]

monandrous *adj* **1** (*sociol*) having or allowing only one husband or male sexual partner at a time. **2** (*bot*) having only one stamen in each flower. — *n* **monandry**. ◇ See also **polyandrous**. [Gr *monos*, single + *andros*, man]

monarch *n* a king, queen, or other non-elected sovereign with a hereditary right to rule. — *adj* **monarchic** or **monarchical**. [Gr *monos*, single + *archein*, to rule]

monarchist *n* a person in favour of rule by a monarch. — *n* **monarchism**.

monarchy *n* **-ies** (a country, etc. that has) a form of government in which supreme power is held, often only nominally, by a monarch.

monastery *n* **-ies** the home of a community of monks, or sometimes nuns. [Gr *monasterion*, from *monazein*, to live alone]

monastic *adj* **1** of or relating to monasteries, monks or nuns. **2** marked by simplicity and self-discipline, like life in a monastery. — *adv* **monastically**. — *n* **monasticism**. [Gr *monastes*, monk]

Monday *n* the second day of the week. [OE *monandæg*, moon day]

monetarism *n* (economic policies based on) the theory that the best way to control an economy is by controlling the amount of money in circulation. — *n & adj* **monetarist**. [Lat *moneta*, money]

monetary *adj* of, or consisting of, money. [Lat *moneta*, money]

money *n* **1** coins or banknotes used as a means of buying things. **2** wealth in general. **3** (*coll*) a rich person; rich people: *marry money*. ◇ See also **moneys** below. — **be in the money** (*coll*) to be wealthy. — **for my, our,** etc. **money** (*coll*) in my, our, etc. opinion. — **get one's money's worth** to get full value for the money one has spent (or the time, effort, etc. one has contributed). [Lat *moneta*]

moneybags *n* (*coll*) a very rich person.

money-changer *n* a person whose business is exchanging currencies.

moneyed *adj* (also **monied**) wealthy.

money-grubber *n* (*coll derog*) a person who greedily acquires as much money as possible. — *adj* **money-grubbing**.

moneylender *n* a person whose business is lending money at (usu. high rates of) interest.

moneymaker *n* (*coll*) **1** (often *derog*) a person whose main interest in life is acquiring money. **2** a project, company, etc. that makes a large profit. — *adj* **money-making.**

money markets *n* (*pl*) the finance companies, banks, etc. of a country that borrow and lend money for short periods.

money order *n* a written order for the transfer of money from one person to another, through a post office or bank.

moneys *n* (*pl*; *finance* & *legal*; also **monies**) sums of money.

money-spinner *n* (*coll*) an idea or project that brings in large sums of money.

-monger *in cmpds* **1** a trader or dealer: *fishmonger*. **2** a person who spreads or promotes something undesirable or evil: *scandalmonger*. [Lat *mango*, dealer]

mongol *n* (*old*, now *offensive*) a person affected by Down's syndrome. — *n* **mongolism.** — *adj* **mongoloid**. [From the supposed physical likeness of Down's syndrome sufferers to members of the *Mongol* people of Asia]

Mongolian *n* **1** a native or citizen of Mongolia. **2** the main language of Mongolia. — *adj* of or pertaining to Mongolia, its people or the language.

mongoose *n* ***-gooses*** a long-tailed weasel-sized mammal of Africa and Asia that preys on snakes and rats. [Marathi (language of India) *mangus*]

mongrel *n* & *adj* (sometimes *derog*) **1** (an animal, esp. a dog) of mixed breeding. **2** (anything) of mixed origin or nature. [Perhaps OE *mengan*, to mix]

monied, monies. See **money**.

monism *n* (*philos*) the theory that reality exists in one form only, esp. that there is no difference in substance between body and soul. — *n* **monist**. — *adj* **monistic**. [Gr *monos*, single]

monition *n* (*formal*) a warning or telling-off. [Lat *monere*, to warn or remind]

monitor *n* **1** any instrument or person that checks, records or controls. **2** a small screen in a television studio showing the picture being broadcast. **3** (often *in cmpds*) a pupil who helps with (specific) tasks, or a senior pupil enforcing discipline over other pupils. **4** (also **monitor lizard**) any of various large predatory lizards of Africa, Asia and Australia. — *v* ***-r-*** (*tr*) to check, control or record; to observe. [Lat *monere*, to warn or advise]

monitory *adj* (*formal*) serving as a warning or telling-off. [Lat *monere*, to warn]

monk *n* a member of a religious community of men living disciplined, austere lives devoted to worship. — *adj* **monkish**. [Gr *monachos*, from *monos*, alone]

monkey *n* ***-eys*** **1** any of various kinds of ape, esp. the smaller long-tailed varieties. **2** (*coll*) a mischievous child. **3** (*slang*) £500 or $500. — *v* (*intr*; *coll*; **about, around, with**) to play, fool, interfere, etc. — **make a monkey out of** (*coll*) to cause to seem ridiculous; to make a fool of. — **not give a monkey's** (*vulg slang*) not to care at all. [Perhaps OGer dialect *moneke*]

monkey business *n* (*coll*) mischief; illegal activities.

monkey nut *n* a peanut.

monkey puzzle *n* (also **monkey puzzle tree**) a S American conifer with close-set prickly leaves.

monkey wrench *n* a spanner-like tool with movable jaws; an adjustable spanner.

monkshood. See **aconite**.

mono (*coll*) *adj* short for **monophonic**. — *n* monophonic sound reproduction.

mono- or **mon-** *comb fm* one or single: *monocle*. [Gr *monos*, single]

monochrome *adj* **1** (of television, photography) black-and-white. **2** (esp. of painting) using shades of one colour only. [Gr *monos*, single + *chroma*, colour]

monochromatic *adj* **1** (of light) having only one wavelength. **2** monochrome.

monocle *n* a lens for correcting sight in one eye only, held in place between the bones of the cheek and brow. [**mono-** + Lat *oculus*, eye]

monocotyledon *n* (*biol*) any flowering plant with a single cotyledon. ◇ See also **dicotyledon**.

monocular *adj* having one eye only; for the use of one eye. [**mono-** + Lat *oculus*, eye]

monody *n* ***-ies*** **1** a mournful song or speech performed by a single actor, esp. in Greek tragedy. **2** a song in which the melody is sung by one voice only, with other voices accompanying. — *adj* **monodic**. [Gr *monos*, single + *oide*, song]

monoecious *adj* (*biol*) **1** having male and female reproductive parts in separate flowers on the same plant. **2** (of an animal) having both male and female sexual organs; hermaphrodite. ◇ See also **dioecious**. [Gr *monos*, single + *oikos*, house]

monogamy *n* the state or practice of having only one husband or wife at any one time. — *adj* **monogamous**. ◇ See also **polygamy**. [Gr *monos*, single + *gamos*, marriage]

monogram *n* & *v* (*tr*) ***-mm-*** (to mark with) a design made up of interwoven letters, usu. a person's initials. [Gr *monos*, single + *gramma*, letter]

monograph *n* (*formal*) a book or essay dealing with one particular subject or aspect of it. [Gr *monos*, single + *graphein*, to write]
monolingual *adj* able to speak one language only; expressed in, or dealing with, a single language: *a monolingual dictionary*. [**mono-** + Lat *lingua*, language]
monolith *n* **1** a single tall block of stone, often shaped into a column or pillar. **2** anything resembling this in uniformity, immovability or massiveness. — *adj* **monolithic**. [Gr *monos*, single + *lithos*, stone]
monologue *n* **1** a long speech by one actor in a film or play; a (short) play with only one actor. **2** any long uninterrupted piece of speech preventing conversation. [Gr *monos*, single + *logos*, speech]
monomania *n* domination of the mind by a single subject or concern; an obsession. — *n* & *adj* **monomaniac**. [Gr *monos*, single + *mania*, madness]
mononucleosis *n* glandular fever.
monophonic *adj* recording or reproducing sound on one channel only, not splitting it into two, as with stereophonic systems. [Gr *monos*, single + *phone*, sound]
monoplane *n* an aeroplane with one set of wings.
monopolise or **-ize** *v* (*tr*) **1** to have exclusive control of trade in (a commodity or service). **2** to dominate (e.g. a conversation), excluding all others. — *n* **monopolisation** or **-z-**. [**monopoly**]
monopoly *n* **-ies 1** (**of, on**) the right to be, or the fact of being, the only supplier of a particular commodity or service. **2** a commodity or service controlled in this way. **3** (**of, on**) exclusive possession or control of anything: *You don't have a monopoly on the truth!* — *n* **monopolist**. — *adj* **monopolistic**. [Gr *monos*, single + *poleein*, to sell]
monorail *n* a railway system in which the trains run on, or suspended from, a single rail.
monosodium glutamate *n* a chemical substance used in the manufacture of some foods to improve flavour.
monosyllable *n* a word consisting of only one syllable.
monosyllabic *adj* **1** having one syllable. **2** using short words, esp. 'yes' and 'no': *a monosyllabic reply*.
monotheism *n* the belief that there is only one God. — *n* **monotheist**. — *adj* **monotheistic**. [Gr *monos*, single + *theos*, God]
monotone *n* **1** a single unvarying tone in speech or sound. **2** a sequence of sounds of the same tone. **3** sameness, esp. in colour. — *adj* lacking in variety; unchanging. [Gr *monos*, single + *tonos*, tone]
monotonous *adj* lacking in variety; tediously unchanging. — *adv* **monotonously**. — *n* **monotony** .
monovalent *adj* (*chem*) having a valency of one.
monoxide *n* a chemical compound containing one oxygen atom in each molecule. [**mono-** + **oxide**]
Monsignor *n* **-*signors*** or **-*signori*** a title given to various high-ranking male members of the Roman Catholic church. [Ital, from Fr *Monseigneur*, a title given to high-ranking clergy and nobility]
monsoon *n* **1** a S Asian wind that blows from the southwest in summer, bringing rain, and from the northeast in winter. **2** the rainy season brought by the summer wind. **3** (*coll*) any heavy fall of rain. [Arabic *mawsim*, season]
monster *n* **1** any large and frightening imaginary creature. **2** a cruel or evil person. **3** any unusually large thing. **4** (*old*) a deformed person, animal or plant. — *adj* huge; gigantic: *monster portions*. [Lat *monstrum*, evil omen]
monstrance *n* (*RC Church*) a large gold or silver cup in which the host, bread representing Christ's body, is displayed to the congregation during Mass. [Lat *monstrare*, to show]
monstrosity *n* **-ies 1** any ugly or outrageous thing. **2** the quality of being monstrous. [**monster**]
monstrous *adj* **1** huge. **2** outrageous; absurd. **3** extremely cruel; evil. **4** (*old*) deformed. — *adv* **monstrously**. [**monster**]
Mont. *abbrev* Montana.
montage *n* (*tech*) **1** the process of creating a picture by piecing together elements from other pictures, photographs, etc.; a picture made in this way. **2** the process of editing cinema film. **3** extensive use of changes in camera position to create an impression of movement or action in a filmed scene. ◇ See also **mise-en-scène**. **4** a film sequence made up of short clips, esp. used to condense events taking place over a long period. [Fr, from *monter*, to mount]
month *n* **1** any of the twelve named divisions of the year, varying in length between 28 and 31 days. **2** a period of roughly four weeks or 30 days; the period between identical dates in consecutive months. [OE *monath*, from *mona*, moon]
monthly *adj* happening, published, etc. once a month; lasting one month. — *adv* once a month. — *n* **-ies 1** a monthly periodical. **2** (*coll*) a menstrual period.
monument *n* **1** something, e.g. a statue, built to preserve the memory of a person or event. **2** any ancient building or structure preserved for its historical value. **3** (*formal* with **to, of**) something serving as clear evidence; an excellent example: *The painting is a monument to her artistic skill.* **4** (*formal*) a tombstone. [Lat *monumentum*, from *monere*, to remind]
monumental *adj* **1** of or being a monument. **2** like a monument, esp. huge and impressive. **3** (*coll*) very great; extreme:

monumental arrogance. **4** (*formal*) of tombstones: *monumental sculptor.*

moo *v* (*intr*) & *n* (to make) the low long sound of a cow. [Imit.]

mooch *v* (*coll*) **1** (*intr*; **about, around**) to wander aimlessly. **2** (*tr* & *intr*; **off, from**) to get (things) for free by asking directly; to cadge. [Perhaps OFr *muchier*, to hide or lurk]

mood[1] *n* **1** a state of mind at a particular time; a suitable or necessary state of mind: *not in the mood for dancing.* **2** a temporary grumpy state of mind. **3** an atmosphere: *the mood in the factory.* [OE *mod*, mind]

moody *adj* **-ier, -iest** tending to change mood often; frequently bad-tempered. — *adv* **moodily**. — *n* **moodiness**.

mood[2] *n* (*gram*) one category of the forms of a verb, indicating whether the verb is expressing a fact, a wish, possibility or doubt, or a command: *the imperative mood.* [Ety. as for **mood**[1]]

moon *n* **1** the heavenly body that moves once round the earth each month, often visible as a (partially) illuminated circle in the sky, esp. at night. **2** any similar smaller body circling another planet. **3** something impossible to obtain: *promised me the moon.* — *v* (*intr*) **1** (**about, around**) to wander aimlessly; to spend time idly. **2** (*slang*) to make a show of one's bare buttocks in public. — **over the moon** (*coll*) delighted. [OE *mona*]

moonbeam *n* a ray of sunlight reflected from the moon.

moonlight *n* & *adj* (illuminated by) sunlight reflected by the moon. — *v* **-lighted** (*intr*; *coll*) to work at a second job outside normal working hours, paying no tax on earnings. — *n* **moonlighter**. — *n* **moonlighting**.

moonlit *adj* illuminated by moonlight.

moonshine *n* (*coll*) **1** foolish talk; nonsense. **2** smuggled or illegally distilled alcoholic spirit.

moonstone *n* a pearl-like stone, a form of feldspar, often used in jewellery.

moonstruck *adj* (*coll*) behaving in an unusually wild or excited way, as if affected by the moon.

moony *adj* **-ier, -iest** (*coll*) in a dreamy mood.

Moor *n* a member of an Arab people of NW Africa, whose ancestors ruled parts of Spain between the 8th and 15th centuries. — *adj* **Moorish**. [Lat *Maurus*]

moor[1] *n* an area of high open unfarmed land, usu. stony and covered with coarse grass. [OE *mor*]

moorhen *n* a small black water-bird with a red beak.

moorland *n* a moor.

moor[2] *v* **1** (*tr*) to fasten (a ship or boat) by a rope, cable or anchor. **2** (*intr*) to be fastened in this way. [Perhaps ODut *maren*]

mooring *n* **1** a place where a boat is moored. **2** (in *pl*) the ropes, anchors, etc. used to moor a boat.

moose *n* ***moose*** a large N American deer with flat rounded antlers, also found in Europe and Asia, where it is called an elk. [Algonquian (a N American Indian language) *moos*]

moot *v* (*tr*) to suggest; to bring up for discussion. — *adj* open to argument; debatable: *a moot point.* — *n* a court or administrative assembly in Anglo-Saxon England. [OE *mot*, assembly]

mop *n* **1** a tool for washing or wiping floors, consisting of a large sponge or a set of thick threads on a long handle. **2** a similar smaller tool for washing dishes. **3** (*coll*) a thick mass of hair. — *v* **-pp-** (*tr*) **1** to wash or wipe with a mop. **2** to wipe or clean (e.g. a sweaty brow). — *v* **mop up** (*tr* & *intr*) **1** to clean up with a mop. **2** (*coll*) to capture or kill (remaining enemy troops) after a victory; to deal with or get rid of (anything remaining). [Perhaps Lat *mappa*, napkin]

mope *v* (*intr*) to behave in a depressed, sulky or aimless way. — *n* **1** a habitually sulky or depressed person. **2** (in *pl* with **the**) low spirits; depression.

moped *n* a small-engined motorcycle, esp. one started using pedals. [*mo*tor-assisted *ped*al-cycle]

moppet *n* a term of affection used to a small child. [Obsolete *mop*, rag doll]

moquette *n* thick velvety material used to make carpets and upholstery. [Fr]

moraine *n* a ridge of rock and earth that was formed by the gradual movement of a glacier down a valley. [Fr]

moral *adj* **1** of or relating to the principles of good and evil, or right and wrong. **2** conforming to what is considered by society to be good, right, or proper. **3** having a psychological effect: *moral support.* **4** considered in terms of psychological effect, rather than outward appearance: *a moral victory.* **5** capable of distinguishing between right and wrong. — *n* **1** a principle (to be) learned from a story or event. **2** (in *pl*) (a standard of behaviour based on) a sense of right and wrong, often in sexual matters: *have no morals; loose morals.*

moral certainty *n* something about which there is hardly any doubt.

moralise or **-ize** *v* **1** (*intr*; **about, on**) to write or speak (esp. critically) about moral standards. **2** (*tr*) to explain in terms of morals. — *n* **moraliser** or **-z-**.

moralist *n* **1** a person who lives according to strict moral principles. **2** a person who tends to lecture others on their low moral standards. — *adj* **moralistic**.

morality *n* **-ies 1** the quality of being right or wrong; behaviour in relation to accepted moral standards. **2** a particular system of moral standards.

morality play *n* an (esp. mediaeval) drama in which the characters represent good and evil.

morale *n* level of confidence or optimism; spirits. [Fr]

morass *n* **1** an area of marshy or swampy ground. **2** (*literary*) a dangerous or confused situation, esp. one that entraps. [OFr *maresc*]

moratorium *n* **-iums** or **-ia** (*formal*) **1** (**on**) an agreed temporary break in an activity. **2** a legally authorised postponement of payment of a debt. [Lat, from *mora*, delay]

moray *n* (also **moray eel**) a sharp-toothed eel of warm coastal waters. [Port *moreia*]

morbid *adj* **1** displaying an unhealthy interest in unpleasant things, esp. death. **2** (*med*) relating to, or indicating the presence of, disease. — *n* **morbidity**. [Lat *morbus*, disease]

mordant *adj* sharply sarcastic or critical; biting. — *n* **1** a chemical substance used to fix dyes. **2** a corroding liquid used to eat away metal on a printing plate. [Lat *mordere*, to bite]

more *adj* a greater, or additional, number or quantity of. — *adv* **1** used to form the comparative of many adjectives and adverbs, esp. those of two or more syllables. **2** to a greater degree; with a greater frequency. **3** again: *once more*. — *pron* a greater, or additional, number or quantity of people or things. — **more of** better described as; closer to being: *more of a painter than a writer*. — **more or less** **1** almost: *more or less finished*. **2** roughly: *more or less two hours*. [OE *mara*, greater]

moreover *adv* also; and what is more important.

morello *n* **-os** a bitter-tasting dark-red cherry. [Ital, blackish]

mores *n* (*pl*; *formal*) social customs reflecting the basic (moral) values of a particular society. [Lat, from *mos*, custom]

morganatic *adj* (*tech*) (of marriage) between a person of high social rank and one of low rank, and allowing neither the lower-ranking person nor any child from the marriage to inherit the title or property of the higher-ranking person. [Lat *morganaticam*, morning gift, the offering of which, after consummation, is the husband's only duty in such a marriage]

morgue *n* **1** a building where corpses are kept until buried or cremated. **2** any gloomy or depressing place. **3** a store of miscellaneous information for reference. [Fr]

MORI *abbrev* Market and Opinion Research Institute.

moribund *adj* **1** dying; near the end of existence. **2** lacking strength or vitality. [Lat *mori*, to die]

Mormon *n* & *adj* (a member) of the Church of Jesus Christ of Latter-Day Saints, established in the US in 1830, accepting as scripture both the Bible and the Book of Mormon (a book regarded as a record of certain ancient American prophets). — *n* **Mormonism**.

morn *n* (*poetic*) morning. [OE *morgen*]

mornay *adj* served in a cheese sauce: *cod mornay*. [Perhaps Philippe de *Mornay* (1549–1623), Huguenot leader]

morning *n* **1** the part of the day from sunrise to midday, or from midnight to midday. **2** sunrise; dawn. — *adj* taken, or taking place, in the morning: *morning coffee*. — **the morning after** (*coll humorous*) the nausea and headaches that are the after-effects of drinking too much alcohol. [MidE *morwening*]

morning coat *n* a man's tailed black or grey jacket worn as part of morning dress.

morning dress *n* men's formal dress for the daytime, consisting of morning coat, grey trousers, and usu. a top hat.

morning glory *n* a tropical climbing plant with blue, pink or white trumpet-shaped flowers that close in the afternoon.

mornings *adv* (*coll*) regularly in the morning; on every or any morning.

morning sickness *n* nausea in the mornings, often experienced during the early stages of pregnancy.

morning star *n* a planet, usu. Venus, seen in the eastern sky just before sunrise.

morocco *n* soft fine goatskin leather, orig. brought from *Morocco* in N Africa.

moron *n* **1** (*coll derog*) a very stupid person. **2** (*tech*) an adult with the intelligence of a young child. — *adj* **moronic**. [Gr *moros*, foolish]

morose *adj* silently gloomy or bad-tempered. — *n* **moroseness**. [Lat *morosus*, peevish]

morpheme *n* (*gram*) any of the units of meaning contained in or forming a word, not divisible into smaller units, e.g. *out*, *go*, and *-ing*, contained in *outgoing*. ◇ See also **morphology**. [Gr *morphe*, form]

morphine *n* a drug obtained from opium, used to induce sleep and reduce pain. [*Morpheus*, Greek god of sleep]

morphology *n* **1** the study of morphemes and the rules by which they combine to form words. **2** the scientific study of the structure of plants and animals. **3** (*formal*) the structure of anything. — *adj* **morphological**. [Gr *morphe*, form + *logos*, discourse]

morris dancing *n* traditional English country dancing, performed by men carrying sticks and wearing costumes with bells and ribbons attached. — *n* **morris dance**. — *n* **morris dancer**. [MidE *moreys*, Moorish; see **Moor**]

morrow *n* (*arch* or *poetic*; with **the**) **1** the following day; the time after an event. **2** the morning. [OE *morgen*, morning]

Morse code *n* a code used for sending messages, each letter of a word being represented as a series of short or long radio signals or flashes of light. [Samuel *Morse* (1791–1872), inventor]

morsel *n* a small piece, esp. of food. [OFr, from *mors*, bite]

mortal *adj* **1** certain to die at some future time. **2** of or causing death. **3** extreme: *mortal fear*. **4** characterised by intense hostility: *mortal enemies*. **5** (used for emphasis) conceivable; single: *every mortal thing*. — *n* a mortal (esp. human) being. [Lat *mortalis*, from *mori*, to die]

mortality *n* **1** the state of being mortal. **2** (also **mortality rate**) the number of deaths, e.g. in a war. **3** loss of life.

mortal sin *n* (esp. *RC Church*) a serious sin, for which there can be no forgiveness from God. ◇ See also **venial sin**.

mortar *n* **1** a mixture of sand, water, and cement or lime, used in building to bond bricks or stones. **2** the small dish in which substances are ground with a pestle. **3** a type of short-barrelled artillery gun for firing shells over short distances. — *v* (*tr*) **-r- 1** to fix (esp. bricks) in place with mortar. **2** to bombard using a mortar. [Lat *mortarium*]

mortarboard *n* **1** a flat board used by bricklayers to carry mortar, held horizontally by a handle underneath. **2** a black cap with a hard square flat top, worn by academics at formal occasions.

mortgage *n* **1** a legal agreement by which a financial institution grants a client a loan for the purpose of buying property, ownership of the property being held by the institution until the loan is repaid. **2** the money borrowed, or the regular amounts repaid. **3** any loan for which property is used as security. — *v* (*tr*) to give ownership of (property) as security for a loan. [Fr, from *mort*, dead + *gage*, pledge]

mortice. Same as **mortise**.

mortician *n* (esp. *US*) an undertaker. [Lat *mortis*, death]

mortify *v* **-ies**, **-ied 1** (*tr*) to cause to feel humiliated or ashamed. **2** (*tr*; *relig*) to control (physical desire) through self-discipline or self-inflicted hardship: *mortify the flesh*. **3** (*intr*) (of a limb) to suffer from gangrene. — *n* **mortification**. [Lat *mortificare*, to cause death to]

mortise *n* a hole cut in a piece of wood, into which a tenon, or shaped end of a second piece, fits to form a mortise and tenon joint. — *v* (*tr*) to cut a mortise in; to join with a mortise and tenon joint. [OFr *mortoise*]

mortise lock *n* a lock fitted into a hole cut in the side edge of a door, rather than on to the door's surface.

mortuary *n* **-ies** a building or room where corpses are kept until buried or cremated. [Lat *mortuarius*, of the dead]

Mosaic *adj* of or relating to *Moses*, the biblical Hebrew prophet.

mosaic *n* a design formed by fitting together small pieces of coloured stone or glass. [Fr *mosaïque*]

moselle or **mosel** *n* (often *cap*) a dry German white wine from the regions around the river *Moselle* or *Mosel*.

mosey *v* **moseys**, **moseying**, **moseyed** (*intr*; *coll*; **along**) to walk in a leisurely way; to saunter or amble.

Moslem. See **Muslim**.

mosque *n* a Muslim place of worship. [Arabic *masjid*]

mosquito *n* **-os** or **-oes** any of various small long-legged insects, the females of which suck blood from animals and people and pass on diseases. [Span, dimin. of *mosca*, fly]

mosquito net *n* a fine net designed to keep away mosquitos, esp. hung over a bed at night.

moss *n* **1** any variety of small flowerless plant growing as a thick mass on rocks or tree trunks in damp conditions. **2** (*dialect*) (an area of) boggy ground. — *adj* **mossy**, **-ier**, **-iest**. [OE *mos*, bog]

most *adj* (**the**) the greatest part, amount or number (of). — *adv* **1** (**the**) used to form the superlative of many adjectives and adverbs, esp. those of more than two syllables. **2** (**the**) to the greatest degree; with the greatest frequency. **3** extremely. — *pron* (**the**) the greatest number or quantity, or the majority of people or things. — **at (the) most** certainly not more than. — **for the most part** mostly. — **make the most of** to take the greatest possible advantage of. [OE *mast* or *mæst*]

-most *sfx* furthest (in a particular direction): *southernmost*.

mostly *adv* usually; mainly.

MOT *n* an official annual test of roadworthiness, required by the *M*inistry *o*f *T*ransport on all vehicles over three years old; the certificate supplied on successful completion of this.

mote *n* a speck, esp. of dust. [OE *mot*]

motel *n* an (esp. single-storey) hotel near a road, intended for motorists, esp. one consisting of separate units of accommodation. [*mo*tor ho*tel*]

motet *n* a piece of church music for several (esp. unaccompanied) voices singing different parts at the same time. [OFr, dimin. of *mot*, word]

moth *n* any of various (usu. nocturnal) butterfly-like insects with wide bodies and dull colouring, one variety of which (the **clothes moth**) breeds in cloth, on which its larvae feed. [OE *moththe*]

mothball *n* a small ball of camphor or naphthalene hung in wardrobes, etc. to keep away clothes moths.

moth-eaten *adj* **1** (of cloth) damaged by clothes moths. **2** (*coll*) old and worn.

mothproof *adj* (of cloth) treated with chemicals which resist attack by clothes moths. — *v* (*tr*) to treat in this way.

mother *n* **1** a female parent. **2** (*cap*; usu. **Mother Superior**) the head of a female religious (esp. Christian) community. **3** the cause or origin: *Necessity is the mother of* *invention*. — *adj* like a mother in being protective, or being a source from which others spring: *mother church*. — *v* (*tr*) **1** to give birth to; to give rise to. **2** to treat with (excessive) care and protection. — *n* **motherhood**. — *adj* **motherly**. [OE *modor*]

mother country *n* **1** (also **motherland**) a person's native country. **2** the country that pilgrims leave to settle elsewhere.

Mothering Sunday *n* Mother's Day.

mother-in-law *n* ***mothers***- the mother of one's husband or wife.

mother-of-pearl *n* a shiny hard smooth substance coating the inside of certain shells.

Mother's Day *n* a day on which children offer gifts of thanks to mothers, the fourth Sunday in Lent in the UK.

mother tongue *n* one's native language.

motif *n* **1** a shape repeated many times within a pattern; a single design or symbol, e.g. on clothing. **2** something often repeated throughout a work or works of art, e.g. a passage of music in a symphony, or a theme in a novel. [Fr, motive]

motion *n* **1** the act, state or way of moving. **2** a single (esp. body) movement. **3** the ability to move a part of the body. **4** a proposal for formal discussion at a meeting. **5** (*med*) an act of discharging faeces; (often in *pl*) faeces. — *v* ***-n-*** (*tr* & *intr*; **to**) to give a signal or direction. — *adj* **motionless**. — **go through the motions** to pretend; to perform a task mechanically or half-heartedly. — **in motion** moving. [Lat *motio*, from *movere*, to move]

motion picture *n* (esp. *US*) a cinema film.

motivate *v* (*tr*) to cause or stimulate (a person) to act; to be the underlying cause of (action). — *n* **motivation**. **[motive]**

motive *n* a reason for, or underlying cause of, action of a certain kind. — *adj* **1** causing motion: *motive power*. **2** stimulating action: *motive force*. [Lat *motivus*, from *movere*, to move]

motley *adj* **1** made up of many different kinds: *a motley crew*. **2** many-coloured. — *n* a jester's multicoloured costume. [Perhaps OE *mot*, speck]

motocross *n* the sport or practice of motorcycle racing on rough open land. **[motor + cross-country]**

motor *n* **1** any device for converting energy into movement. **2** (*coll*) a car. — *adj* **1** of or relating to cars or other road vehicles: *a motor show*. **2** driven by a motor: *a motor boat*. **3** (*anat*) producing or transmitting motion: *motor nerves*. — *v* ***-r-*** (*intr*) **1** to travel by car. **2** (*coll*) to move, work, etc. very fast. [Lat, from *movere*, to move]

motorbike *n* (*coll*) a motorcycle.

motorcade *n* a procession of cars carrying important (esp. political) figures.

motor car *n* a car.

motorcycle *n* any two-wheeled road vehicle powered by a petrol engine. — *n* **motorcyclist**.

motoring *n* travelling by car, esp. for pleasure.

motorise or **-ize** *v* (*tr*) **1** to fit a motor to. **2** to supply (e.g. soldiers) with motor vehicles.

motorist *n* a person who drives a car.

motorway *n* a major dual-carriageway road for fast-moving traffic, esp. one with three lanes per carriageway.

Motown *n* a style of music combining the styles of pop and rhythm and blues. [*Mo*tor *Town*, nickname for Detroit, US town where it originated in the early 1960s]

mottled *adj* with a pattern of different coloured blotches or streaks. **[motley]**

motto *n* ***-os*** or ***-oes*** **1** a phrase adopted as a principle of behaviour. **2** a printed phrase or verse contained in a paper cracker. **3** a quotation at the beginning of a book or chapter, hinting at what is to follow. [Ital, from Lat *muttum*, utterance]

mould[1] *n* a growth of fungus on substances in damp (esp. warm) conditions. [MidE *mowle*]

mouldy *adj* ***-ier***, ***-iest*** **1** covered with mould; old and stale. **2** (*coll derog*) a general term of dislike: *I don't want your mouldy advice*.

mould[2] *n* **1** a hollow shaped container into which a liquid substance is poured to take on the container's shape when it cools and sets. **2** food, e.g. a pudding, shaped in such a container. **3** nature, character or personality. **4** a framework on which certain manufactured objects are built up. — *v* **1** (*tr*) to shape using a mould. **2** (*tr*) to shape (a substance) with the hands; to form by shaping a substance with the hands. **3** (*intr* & *tr*) to (cause to) fit tightly. **4** (*tr*) to exercise a controlling influence over the development of. [Lat *modulus*, measure]

moulding *n* a shaped decorative strip, esp. of wood or plaster.

mould[3] *n* loose soft earth, esp. rich in decayed matter: *leaf mould*. [OE *molde*]

moulder *v* (*intr*; **away**) to become gradually rotten with age; to decay.

moult *v* (*intr*) (of animals) to shed feathers, hair or skin to make way for a new growth. — *n* the process of moulting, or the time taken to moult. [OE *mutian*, to exchange]

mound *n* **1** any small hill, or bank of earth or rock, natural or man-made. **2** a heap or pile.

mount[1] *v* **1** (*tr* & *intr*; *formal*) to go up: *mount stairs*. **2** (*tr* & *intr*) to get up on to (e.g. a horse). **3** (*intr*; **up**) to increase in level or intensity. **4** (*tr*) to put in a frame or on a background for display; to hang or put up on a stand or support. **5** (*tr*) to organise or hold (a campaign, etc.). **6** (*tr*) to carry out (e.g. an attack). — *n* **1** a support or backing on which a thing is placed for display. **2** (*formal*) a horse that is ridden. [OFr *monter*, to go up]

mounted *adj* **1** on horseback. **2** hung on a wall, or placed in a frame or on a background.

Mountie or **Mounty** *n* ***-ies*** (*coll*) a member of the Royal Canadian Mounted Police.

mount[2] *n* (*poetic* & in place-names with *cap*) a mountain. [Lat *montis*]

mountain *n* **1** a very high steep hill, often of bare rock. **2** (*coll*) a great quantity; a heap or mass. **3** a huge surplus of some commodity. — **make a mountain out of a molehill** to exaggerate the seriousness or importance of a trivial matter. [Lat *mons*]

mountain ash *n* the rowan, a tree of the rose family, with feather-shaped leaves and red berries.

mountain bike *n* a sturdy bicycle with thick deep-tread tyres and straight handlebars.

mountaineer *n* a person skilled in climbing mountains. — *v* (*intr*) to climb mountains. — *n* **mountaineering**.

mountain lion *n* a puma.

mountainous *adj* **1** containing many mountains. **2** huge.

mountain sickness *n* feelings of nausea and light-headedness as a result of breathing low-oxygen mountain air.

mountebank *n* (*literary derog*) **1** orig., a person who sells quack medicines from a public platform. **2** any person who swindles or deceives. [Ital *montimbanco*, person who mounts a bench]

mourn *v* (*tr* & *intr*; **for, over**) to feel or show deep sorrow at the death or loss of (a person or thing). — *n* **mourner**. [OE *murnan*]

mournful *adj* **1** feeling or expressing grief. **2** suggesting sadness or gloom. — *adv* **mournfully**.

mourning *n* **1** grief felt or shown over a death. **2** a symbol of grief, esp. a black costume or armband; a period of time during which such symbols are worn.

mouse *n* ***mice*** **1** any of numerous types of small furry long-tailed rodent. **2** (*coll*) a very shy quiet person. **3** a hand-held device connected by wire to a computer, used to control certain functions. — *v* (*intr*) (of an animal) to hunt mice. [OE *mus*]

mouser *n* a cat used for catching mice.

mousetrap *n* **1** a mechanical trap for catching (and often killing) mice. **2** (*old coll*) poor quality cheese.

mousy or **mousey** *adj* ***-ier***, ***-iest*** **1** of or like a mouse: *mousy smells.* **2** (of hair) of a dull light brown colour. **3** shy or quiet, esp. boringly so. — *n* **mousiness**.

moussaka *n* an oven-cooked dish of minced meat and vegetables covered with a cheese sauce, traditionally eaten in Greece. [Gr]

mousse *n* **1** a dessert made from a whipped mixture of cream, eggs and flavouring, eaten cold. **2** a similar meat or fish dish. **3** (also **styling mousse**) a frothy chemical preparation applied to hair to make styling easier. [Fr, froth]

moustache *n* a line of unshaved hair above a man's upper lip. [Fr, Ital *mostaccio*]

mouth *n* ***mouths*** **1** in humans, animals, etc., an opening in the head through which food is taken in and speech or sounds emitted; in other creatures, an opening with similar functions. **2** the lips; the outer visible parts of the mouth. **3** an opening, e.g. of a bottle. **4** the part of a river that widens to meet the sea. **5** a person considered as a consumer of food: *five mouths to feed.* **6** (*coll derog*) boastful talk. **7** backchat or cheek: *don't want any of your mouth.* **8** (*coll derog*) a person who talks too much, esp. indiscreetly. — *v* **1** (*tr*) to form (words) without actually speaking. **2** (*tr* & *intr*; *derog*) to speak (words) pompously or without sincerity. — **down in the mouth** (*coll*) unhappy. [OE *muth*]

-mouthed *in cmpds* **1** using a certain kind of language: *foul-mouthed.* **2** having a certain kind of mouth: *wide-mouthed.*

mouthful *n* ***-fuls*** **1** as much as fills the mouth. **2** a small quantity, esp. of food. **3** (*coll*) a word or phrase difficult to pronounce. **4** (*coll*) an outburst of forceful, often abusive language.

mouth organ *n* a harmonica.

mouthpiece *n* **1** the part of a musical instrument, telephone receiver, tobacco pipe, etc. held in or against the mouth. **2** a person or publication expressing the views of a group.

mouth-to-mouth *n* & *adj* (indicating) a method of resuscitation in which air is breathed directly into the mouth of the person to be revived.

mouthwash *n* an antiseptic liquid gargled to freshen the mouth.

mouthwatering *adj* **1** (of food) whose delicious appearance or smell creates the desire to eat. **2** (*coll*) highly desirable.

move *v* **1** (*tr* & *intr*) to (cause to) change position or go from one place to another. **2** (*intr*) to make progress of any kind: *move towards a political solution.* **3** (*tr* & *intr*; **on, out**) to change (one's place of living, working, operating, etc.): *move house.* **4** (*tr*) to affect the feelings or emotions of. **5** (*tr* & *intr*; **to**) to (cause to) act: *What moved him to say that?* **6** (*tr* & *intr*) to change the position of (a piece in a board game). **7** (*intr* & *tr*; *formal*; **for**) to propose or request formally. **8** (*intr*; **in**) to spend time; to associate with people: *move in fashionable circles.* ◇ See also **move in** below. **9** (*intr*; *coll*) to progress speedily. **10** (*tr* & *intr*; *coll*) to sell or be sold. **11** (*tr* & *intr*) (of bowels) to (cause to) be evacuated. — *n* **1** an act of moving (the body). **2** an act of moving a piece in a board game, or the rules governing how the pieces are moved; any of a series of actions taken as part of an overall strategy. **3** an act of changing homes. — *v* **move in** (*intr*) **1** to begin to occupy new premises. **2** **(on)** to make an attack on, with a view to taking over; to make an (esp. sexual) approach to. — *n* **mover**. — **get a move on** or **get moving** (*coll*) to hurry up. — **make a move 1 (towards)** to take a step; to begin to proceed. **2** (*coll*) to leave. — **move heaven and earth** to make strenuous efforts (to achieve something). — **on the move 1** moving from place to place. **2** advancing or making progress. [Lat *movere*]

movable or **moveable** *adj* **1** not fixed in one place; portable. **2** (of a religious festival) taking place on a different date each year: *Easter is a movable feast.*

movement *n* **1** (an act of) changing position or going from one point to another. **2** an organisation or association. **3** a general tendency. **4** the theatrical art of moving the body gracefully or with expression. **5** (in *pl*) a person's actions during a particular time. **6** the moving parts of a watch or clock. **7** (*med*) the act of evacuating the bowels; the waste matter evacuated. **8** a section of a large-scale piece of music, esp. a symphony.

moving *adj* **1** having an effect on the emotions; touching; stirring. **2** in motion; not static: *a moving staircase.*

movie *n* a cinema film. [*Mov*ing picture]

mow *v* ***mowed*** or ***mown*** (*tr*) to cut (grass or a crop) by hand or with a machine. — *n* **mower**. — *v* **mow down** (*tr*) to knock down or kill in large numbers. [OE *mawan*]

mozzarella *n* a soft white Italian cheese, esp. used as a topping for pizza. [Ital]

MP *abbrev* **1** Member of Parliament. **2** military police; military police officer. **3** mounted police.

mpg *abbrev* miles per gallon.

mph *abbrev* miles per hour.

MPhil *abbrev* Master of Philosophy.

Mr *n* ***Messrs*** the standard title given to a man, used before his surname; a title given to a man who holds an official position: *Mr Jones*; *Mr Chairman*. **[Mister]**

Mrs *n* the standard title given to a married woman, used before her family name. **[Mistress]**

MS *abbrev* **1** ***MSS*** (also **ms**, ***mss***) manuscript. **2** Mississippi. **3** multiple sclerosis.

Ms *n* the standard title given to a woman, married or not, used with her family name: *Ms Brown.*

MSc *abbrev* Master of Science.

MSDOS *abbrev* (*comput*) Microsoft® disk-operating system.

MSG *abbrev* monosodium glutamate.

Msgr *abbrev* Monsignor.

MT *abbrev* Montana.

Mt *abbrev* Mount.

much *adj* & *pron* ***more***, ***most*** a great amount or quantity (of something). — *adv* **1** by a great deal: *much prettier*. **2** to a great degree: *don't like her much*. — **a bit much** (*coll*) very unreasonable. — **make much of** to treat as very important. — **(as) much as** although: (*As*) *much as I would like to come, I can't*. — **not much of** (*coll*) not very good as: *not much of a singer*. — **not up to much** (*coll*) of a poor standard. [MidE *muche*, from OE *mycel*]

muchness: **much of a muchness** (*coll*) very similar; more or less the same.

mucilage *n* **1** a sticky carbohydrate mixture present in some plants. **2** any sticky substance, esp. an adhesive. — *adj* **mucilaginous**. [Lat *mucilago*, mouldy juice]

muck *n* **1** (*coll*) dirt. **2** animal dung; manure. **3** (*coll derog*) anything disgusting, or of very poor quality. — *v* **1** (*tr* & *intr*; **out**) to clear dung from (e.g. a cowshed). **2** (*tr*) to treat (soil) with manure. — **make a muck of** (*coll*) to do badly; to ruin or spoil. — *v* **muck about** or **around** (*coll*) **1** (*intr*) to behave foolishly. **2** (*tr*) to treat without consideration; to try the patience of. — *v* **muck in** (*intr*; *coll*) to take a share of work or responsibilities. — *v* **muck up** (*tr*; *coll*) **1** to make dirty. **2** to do badly or wrongly; to ruin or spoil. [MidE *muk*]

muck-raking *n* (*coll*) the practice of searching for and exposing scandal, esp. about famous people. — *v* (*intr*) **muck-rake**. — *n* **muck-raker**.

mucky *adj* ***-ier***, ***-iest*** (*coll*) **1** very dirty; like muck. **2** featuring explicit sex; pornographic: *mucky films.*

mucus *n* thick sticky liquid secreted by glands in the nose and other cavities of the body. [Lat, from *mungere*, to wipe away]

mucous *adj* of, like, or producing mucus.

mucous membrane *n* the mucus-secreting lining of any of various cavities of the body.

mud *n* **1** soft wet earth. **2** any semi-solid mixture resembling this. **3** (*coll*) insults; slanderous attacks: *throw mud at*. — **my, his**, etc. **name is mud** (*coll*) I am, he is, etc. disgraced or very much out of favour. [Probably OGer *mudde*]

mudbath *n* **1** a medical treatment in which the body is covered in (esp. hot) mud rich in minerals. **2** (*coll*) any outdoor event taking place in muddy conditions.

muddy *adj* ***-ier***, ***-iest*** **1** covered with or containing mud. **2** (of a colour, a liquid, etc.) dull or cloudy. **3** (of thoughts, etc.) not clear; vague. — *v* ***-ies***, ***-ied*** (*tr*) to make muddy, esp. unclear or difficult to understand. — *n* **muddiness**.

mudflat *n* (often in *pl*) an area of muddy coastal land covered with water only at high tide.

mudguard *n* a curved metal guard over (usu. the upper half of) the wheel of a bicycle or motorcycle to keep rain or mud from splashing up.

mudpack *n* a thick paste applied to the face as a skin cleanser.

mud-slinging *n* (*coll*) the making of slanderous personal attacks. — *n* **mud-slinger**.

muddle *v* (*tr*; **up**) **1** to put into a disordered, mixed-up state. **2** to confuse the mind of; to confuse (different things) in the mind. — *n* a state of disorder or mental confusion. — *adj* **muddled**. — *v* **muddle along** (*intr*; *coll*) to proceed in a disordered and disorganised way. — *v* **muddle through** (*intr*; *coll*) to succeed in spite of foolish mistakes and lack of organisation. [Perhaps ODut *moddelen*, to make muddy]

muddle-headed *adj* not capable of clear thinking; confused.

muesli *n* a mixture of crushed grain, nuts and dried fruit, eaten with milk, esp. for breakfast. [Swiss Ger]

muezzin *n* the Muslim official who calls worshippers to prayer, usu. from a minaret. [Arabic *mu'adhdhin*]

muff[1] *n* a wide fur tube, carried usu. by women, inside which the hands are placed, one at each end, for warmth. [Probably Dut *mof*]

muff[2] (*coll*) *v* (*tr*) **1** (*sport*) to miss (a catch); to perform (a stroke) awkwardly or unsuccessfully. **2** to miss (an opportunity, etc.). — *n* a failure, esp. to hold a catch.

muffin *n* a small round flat bread-like cake, usu. eaten hot with butter.

muffle *v* (*tr*) **1** to make quieter; to suppress (sound). **2** to prevent from saying something. **3** (**up**) to wrap up in a coat or scarf against the cold. [OFr *moufle*, thick glove]

muffler *n* a thick scarf.

mufti *n* (*old*) civilian clothes when worn by people who usu. wear a uniform. [Arabic]

mug[1] *n* **1** a tallish drinking-cup with a handle, used without a saucer. **2** (also **mugful**, ***-fuls***) the contents of, or the amount contained in, such a cup.

mug[2] *v* ***-gg-*** (*tr*) to attack and rob violently or under threat of violence. — *n* **mugger**. — *n* **mugging**.

mug[3] *n* (*coll*) a face or mouth.

mugshot *n* (*coll*) a photograph of a criminal's face, taken for police records.

mug[4] *n* (*coll*) an easily fooled person. — **a mug's game** (*coll*) a worthless or foolish activity.

mug[5]: **mug up** *v* ***-gg-*** (*tr* & *intr*; **on**) to study hard for an examination.

muggins *n* (*coll*) a foolish person, esp. used of oneself when taken advantage of by others. [**mug**[4]]

muggy *adj* ***-ier***, ***-iest*** (of weather) unpleasantly warm and damp; close. — *n* **mugginess**. [Perhaps Norse *mugga*, mist]

Muhammadan. Same as **Mohammedan**.

mulatto *n* ***-os*** or ***-oes*** (*old*; now usu. *offensive*) a person of mixed race, esp. with one black and one white parent. [Span *mulato*, young mule]

mulberry *n* ***-ies*** **1** (also **mulberry tree**) a deciduous tree of temperate regions, producing small purple edible berries. **2** such a berry. **3** a dark purple colour. [OGer *mulberi*]

mulch *n* (a layer of) straw, compost, or any of various man-made substances laid on the soil around plants to retain moisture and prevent the growth of weeds. — *v* (*tr*) to cover with mulch. [Obsolete *mulch*, soft]

mulct *n* a fine or penalty. — *v* (*tr*) **1** to fine. **2** (**of**) to deprive. **3** to swindle. [Lat *mulcta*, fine]

mule[1] *n* the offspring of an (esp. male) donkey and an (esp. female) horse, notoriously stubborn, used as a working animal in many countries. [Lat *mulus* or *mula*]

muleteer *n* a person who drives mules.

mulish *adj* stubborn; obstinate.

mule[2] *n* a shoe or slipper with no back part covering the heel. [Fr]

mulish. See **mule**[1].

mull[1]: **mull over** *v* (*tr*) to think about carefully; to ponder.

mull[2] *v* (*tr*) to spice, sweeten and warm (wine or beer). — *adj* **mulled**.

mull[3] *n* (*Scot*) a headland or promontory: *the Mull of Kintyre*. [Gaelic *maol*]

mullah *n* a Muslim scholar and adviser in Islamic religion and sacred law. [Arabic *maula*]

mullet *n* any of a family of thick-bodied edible marine fish. [Lat *mullus*]

mulligatawny *n* a thick curry-flavoured meat soup, orig. made in E India. [Tamil *milagu-tannir*, pepper-water]

mullion *n* (*archit*) a vertical bar or post separating the panes or casements of a window. — *adj* **mullioned**. [OFr *moinel*]

multi- *pfx* many: *multicoloured*. [Lat *multus*, much]

multicoloured *adj* having many colours.

multicultural *adj* of, for, or combining the cultures of several different races of people.

multifarious *adj* (*formal*) of many different kinds; very varied. [Lat *multifarius*, manifold]

multiform *adj* (*formal*) having many different forms or shapes.

multilateral *adj* **1** involving or affecting several people, groups or nations. **2** many-sided.

multilingual *adj* written or expressed in, or able to speak, several different languages.

multimillionaire *n* a person whose wealth is valued at several million pounds, dollars, etc.

multinational *n* & *adj* (a company or business) operating in several different countries.

multiparous *adj* (*biol*) producing several young at one birth. [Lat *multiparus*]

multiple *adj* having, involving or affecting many parts, esp. of the same kind; many, esp. more than several. [Lat *multiplus*]

multiple-choice *adj* for which the correct answer must be chosen from several possible answers provided.

multiple sclerosis *n* a disease that attacks the nervous system, causing a gradual deterioration of speech and sight, and varying degrees of paralysis.

multiplex *adj* (*formal*) having very many parts; complex. — *n* a large cinema building divided into several smaller cinemas. [Lat, from *plicare*, to fold]

multiplicand *n* (*math*) a number to be multiplied by a second number, the **multiplier**. [Lat *multiplicare*, to multiply]

multiplication *n* **1** a mathematical operation in which one number is added to itself as many times as is indicated by a second number; the process of performing this operation. **2** the process of increasing in number.

multiplication sign *n* the symbol ×, used between two numbers to indicate that they are to be multiplied.

multiplication table *n* a table listing the products of multiplying pairs of numbers, esp. all pairs from 1 to 12 inclusive.

multiplicity *n* **-ies** (*formal*) **1** a great number and variety. **2** the state of being many and various. [Lat *multiplex*, of many kinds]

multiply *v* **-ies**, **-ied** (*tr* & *intr*) **1** (**by**) to add (a number) to itself a given number of times; to combine (two numbers) in multiplication. **2** to (cause to) increase in number, esp. by breeding. [Lat *multiplicare*, from *multi*, much + *plicare*, to fold]

multiplier *n* (*math*) a number indicating by how many times another number, the **multiplicand**, to which it is attached by a multiplication sign is to be multiplied.

multipurpose *adj* having many uses.

multiracial *adj* of, for, or including people of many different races.

multistorey *adj* (of a building) having many floors. — *n* **-eys** (*coll*) a multistorey car-park.

multitude *n* **1** a great number. **2** a huge crowd of people. **3** (with **the**) ordinary people. — *adj* **multitudinous**. [Lat *multitudo*]

mum[1] *n* a mother; a term used to address one's own mother. [A child's word, derived from a baby's babbling]

mum[2] *adj* (*coll*) silent; not speaking. — **mum's the word!** (*coll*) please don't, or I promise not to, tell anyone else about this! [A sound produced with closed lips]

mumble *v* (*tr* & *intr*) to speak (words) unclearly, (as if) with the mouth partly closed. — *n* the sound of unclear or hushed speech. [MidE *momelen*, from **mum**[2]]

mumbo-jumbo *n* **-jumbos** (*coll derog*) **1** foolish talk, esp. of a religious or spiritual kind. **2** baffling jargon. **3** something, e.g. a statue, foolishly treated as an object of worship. [Malinke (a W African language) *Mama Dyanbo*, a tribal god]

mummer *n* **1** (*hist*) an actor in a traditional mimed folk play, usu. performed at Christmas. **2** a disguised child taking part in traditional merrymaking during religious festivals, esp. Hallowe'en; a guiser. — *n* **mumming**. [OFr *momer*, to mime]

mummery *n* **-ies** **1** (a performance of) mumming. **2** (*derog*) ridiculous or pretentious ceremony.

mummify. See **mummy**[2].

mummy[1] *n* **-ies** a child's word for mother. [Variant of **mum**[1]]

mummy[2] *n* **-ies** a human or animal corpse preserved with spices and bandaged, esp. in preparation for burial in ancient Egypt. [Arabic and Persian *mumiya*, from Persian *mum*, wax]

mummify *v* **-ies**, **-ied** (*tr*) to preserve (a corpse) as a mummy. — *n* **mummification**.

mumps *n* (**the**) a contagious disease causing painful swelling of the salivary glands near the ears. [Archaic *mump*, to grimace]

munch *v* (*tr* & *intr*; **on**) to chew with a steady movement of the jaws, esp. noisily. [Probably imit.]

mundane *adj* **1** ordinary; dull; everyday. **2** of this world, not some other spiritual world. [Lat *mundus*, world]

mung bean *n* (the E Asian plant producing) an edible green or yellow bean, the source of beansprouts. [Hindi *mung*]

municipal *adj* of, relating to, or controlled by the local government of a town or region. — *adv* **municipally**. [Lat *municipium*, free town]

municipality *n* **-ies** a town or region having its own local government; the local government itself.

munificent *adj* (*formal*) extremely generous. — *n* **munificence**. [Lat *munus*, gift + *facere*, to make]

muniments *n* (*pl*; *legal*) official papers proving ownership, esp. title deeds to property. [Lat *munimentum*, title deed]

munitions *n* (*pl*) military equipment, esp. ammunition and weapons. [Lat *munire*, to defend or fortify]

mural *n* a painting painted directly on to a wall. — *adj* (*formal*) of or relating to a wall or walls. [Lat *murus*, wall]

muralist *n* a painter of murals.

murder *n* **1** (an example of) the act of unlawfully and intentionally killing a person. **2** (*coll*) something, or a situation, which causes hardship or difficulty: *The traffic in town was murder.* — *v* **-r-** **1** (*tr* & *intr*) to kill unlawfully and intentionally. **2** (*tr*; *coll*) to spoil or ruin (e.g. a piece of music, by performing it very badly). **3** (*tr*; *coll*) to defeat easily and by a huge margin. — *n* **murderer**. — **get away with murder** (*coll*) to behave very badly or dishonestly and not be caught or punished. — **scream**, **shout** or **cry blue murder** (*coll*) to protest loudly or angrily. [OE *morthor*, from *morth*, death]

murderess *n* (*old*) a female murderer.

murderous *adj* intending, intended for, or capable of murder.

murk *n* (*literary*) darkness. [OE *mirce*]

murky *adj* **-ier**, **-iest** **1** dark; gloomy. **2** (of water) dark and dirty. **3** suspiciously vague or unknown; shady: *her murky past*. — *n* **murkiness**.

murmur *n* **1** a quiet continuous sound, e.g. of running water or low voices. **2** anything said in a low, indistinct voice. **3** a complaint. **4** (*med*) an abnormal rustling sound made by the heart, usu. indicating the presence of disease. — *v* **-r- 1** (*tr & intr*) to speak (words) softly and indistinctly. **2** (*intr*) to complain or grumble. — *adj* **murmurous**. [Lat]

Murphy's Law . Same as **Sod's law** (see under **sod**[2]).

murrain *n* any infectious cattle disease, esp. foot-and-mouth disease. [OFr *morine*, pestilence]

mus. *abbrev* music.

Muscadet *n* a white wine from the Loire region of France; the grape variety from which it is produced. [Fr]

MusB or **MusBac** *abbrev* for *Musicae Baccalaureus* (Lat), Bachelor of Music.

muscat *n* **1** a variety of white grape with a musky smell. **2** muscatel. [Provençal]

muscatel *n* (also **muscat** or **muscadel**) a sweet white wine made from muscat grapes.

muscle *n* **1** a structure in the body responsible for the movement of joints and organs, consisting of bundles of contractible tissue; such tissue. **2** bodily strength. **3** power or influence of any kind: *financial muscle*. — *v* **muscle in** (*intr*; *coll*; **on**) to force one's way in; to grab a share (of). [Lat *musculus*]

muscle-bound *adj* having over-enlarged muscles that are stiff and difficult to move.

muscleman *n* a man with very big muscles, esp. one employed to intimidate others.

muscular *adj* **1** of, relating to, or consisting of muscle. **2** having well-developed muscles; strong. — *n* **muscularity**.

muscular dystrophy *n* a hereditary disease which causes gradual wasting of all muscles.

musculature *n* the arrangement, or degree of development, of muscles in a body or organ.

Muscovite *n & adj* (a citizen) of Moscow.

MusD or **MusDoc** *abbrev* for *Musicae Doctor* (Lat), Doctor of Music.

Muse *n* any of the nine mythical Greek goddesses of the arts, said to be a source of creative inspiration to all artists, esp. poets. [Gr *Mousa*]

muse *v* **1** (*intr*; **on, upon**) to think, reflect or ponder. **2** (*tr*) to say in a reflective way. [OFr *muser*]

musings *n* (*pl*; *literary*) thoughts.

museum *n* a place where objects of artistic, scientific or historic interest are displayed to the public. [Gr *mouseion*, temple of the Muses]

museum-piece *n* **1** any article displayed in a museum. **2** (*coll humorous*) any very old or old-fashioned person or thing.

mush[1] *n* **1** a soft half-liquid mass of anything. **2** (*coll derog*) sloppy sentimentality. [Probably a variant of **mash**]

mushy *adj* **-ier, -iest 1** in a soft half-liquid state. **2** sentimental in a sickly way.

mush[2] *interj* (esp. to a team of dogs) go on!; go faster! — *v* (*intr*; *US*) to travel on a sledge pulled by dogs. [Probably Fr *marcher*, to walk]

mushroom *n* **1** any of several types of fast-growing fungus with an umbrella-shaped cap, many of which are edible. **2** anything resembling this in shape or in speed of growth or development. — *v* (*intr*) to develop or increase with alarming speed. ◇ See also **toadstool**. [OFr *mousseron*, perhaps from *mousse*, moss]

mushroom-cloud *n* a huge mushroom-shaped cloud of radioactive dust produced by a nuclear explosion.

music *n* **1** (the art of making) sound in a rhythmically organised harmonious form, either sung or produced with instruments and usu. communicating some idea or emotion. **2** such sound produced by instruments, rather than voices. **3** any written form in which such sound is expressed. — **face the music** (*coll*) to confront one's critics; to deal with the consequences of one's actions. — **music to one's ears** anything one is glad to hear. [Gr *mousike*, of the Muses]

musical *adj* **1** of or producing music. **2** pleasant to hear; melodious. **3** having a talent for playing music. — *n* a play or film featuring much singing and dancing. — *n* **musicality**. — *adv* **musically**.

musical chairs *n* (*sing*) a game in which players walk round a number of chairs while music is playing and rush to sit on the chairs when the music stops, those unable to find an empty chair to sit on being eliminated and the number of chairs available being reduced in each round until only one remains.

music box *n* (also **musical box**) a small box containing a device that plays music when the box is opened.

music centre *n* a hi-fi unit in which turntable, amplifier, cassette recorder and radio are combined.

music hall *n* **1** theatre entertainment including singers, dancers and comedians. **2** a theatre in which such entertainment can be seen.

musician *n* a person skilled in performing or composing music. — *n* **musicianship**.

musicology *n* the academic study of music in all its aspects. — *n* **musicologist**.

musk *n* **1** a strong-smelling substance secreted by the glands of various animals, esp. the male musk deer, much used in perfumes; any similar synthetic substance. **2** the smell of such substances. [Lat *muscus*]

musk deer *n* a small hornless central Asian mountain deer.

musk ox *n* a long-haired ox of Canada and Greenland, whose breath has a musky smell.

muskrat *n* **1** a large N American water rodent. **2** (also **musquash**) its highly prized thick brown fur, used to make clothes.

musk rose *n* a Mediterranean rambling rose whose flowers have a musky scent.

musky *adj* **-ier**, **-iest** of, or like the smell of, musk. — *n* **muskiness**.

musket *n* an early rifle-like gun loaded through the barrel and fired from the shoulder, used by soldiers between the 16th and 18th centuries. — *n* **musketeer** . — *n* **musketry**. [OFr *mousquet*]

Muslim or **Moslem** *n* & *adj* (a follower) of the religion of Islam. [Arabic, one who submits]

muslin *n* a fine cotton cloth with a gauze-like appearance. [Fr *mousseline*]

musquash *n* (also **muskrat**) the fur of the muskrat. [Algonquian (an American Indian language group)]

muss *v* (*tr*; esp. *US*; **up**) to make (esp. clothes or hair) untidy; to ruffle.

mussel *n* any of a family of small shellfish, esp. an edible variety with a dark elongated rounded hinged shell. [Lat *musculus*, dimin. of *mus*, mouse]

must[1] *v* (*aux*) expressing **1** need: *I must earn some extra money*. **2** duty or obligation: *You must help him*. **3** certainty: *You must be Charles*. **4** determination: *I must remember*. **5** probability: *She must be there by now*. **6** inevitability: *We must all die some time*. — *n* something essential: *Fitness is a must in professional sport*. [OE *moste*]

must[2] *n* the juice of grapes or other fruit before it is fermented to become wine. [Lat *mustum* (*vinum*), new (wine)]

mustachio *n* **-ios** (often in *pl*) an elaborately curly moustache. — *adj* **mustachioed**. [Ital *mostaccio*]

mustang *n* a small wild horse native to the plains of the western US. [Sp *mestengo*]

mustard *n* **1** any of several European and Asian plants of the cabbage family with yellow flowers and slender seed-pods; their strong-smelling seeds. **2** a thick strong-tasting yellow or brown paste made from the crushed seeds, used as a condiment. **3** a light yellow or brown colour. — **(as) keen as mustard** (*coll*) extremely enthusiastic. [OFr *moustarde*]

mustard and cress *n* a mixture of the seedlings of the mustard plant and cress, used as a salad vegetable.

mustard gas *n* the poisonous vapour produced from a mixture of ethylene and sulphur chloride, often used as a weapon, esp. during World War I.

muster *v* **1** (*tr* & *intr*) to gather (esp. soldiers) together, for duty or inspection. **2** (*tr*; **up**) to summon or gather (e.g. courage or energy). — *n* any assembly or gathering, esp. of troops for duty or inspection. — **pass muster** to be accepted as satisfactory. [Lat *monstrare*, to show]

mustn't (*coll*) must not.

musty *adj* **-ier**, **-iest 1** mouldy or damp. **2** smelling or tasting stale. — *n* **mustiness**. [Perhaps obsolete *moisty*, moist]

mutable *adj* subject to change; variable. — *n* **mutability**. **[mutate]**

mutant *n* an animal, plant, or other organism that has undergone mutation. — *adj* resulting from mutation. [Lat *mutare*, to change]

mutate *v* (*tr* & *intr*) **1** (*biol*) to (cause to) undergo mutation. **2** (*formal*) to change. [Back-formation from **mutation**]

mutation *n* **1** (*biol*) a change in the structure of cells in an animal or plant, often causing offspring to be markedly different from ancestors. **2** (*biol*) (a physical characteristic of) an animal or plant resulting from such a change. **3** (*formal*) a change of any kind. **4** (*linguistics*) a change in a speech sound, esp. a vowel, because of the nature of the sound next to it. [Lat *mutatio*, from *mutare*, to change]

mutatis mutandis *adv* (*formal*) allowing for respective differences of detail; with necessary adjustments made. [Lat, having changed what needs to be changed]

mute *adj* **1** not able to speak; dumb. **2** silent. **3** felt, but not expressed in words: *mute anger*. **4** (of a letter in a word) not pronounced. — *n* **1** a person who does not have the power of speech. **2** any of various devices that soften or deaden the sound of a musical instrument. **3** an unpronounced letter in a word. — *v* (*tr*) to soften or deaden the sound of (a musical instrument). [Lat *mutus*]

muted *adj* **1** (of sound or colour) not loud or harsh; soft. **2** (of feelings, etc.) mildly expressed; not outspoken: *muted criticism*.

mute swan *n* the commonest European swan.

mutilate *v* (*tr*) **1** to cause severe injury to, esp. by removing a limb or organ. **2** to severely damage, esp. to alter (a text) beyond recognition. — *n* **mutilation**. [Lat *mutilare*, to cut off]

mutiny *n* **-ies** (an act of) rebellion against established authority, esp. in the armed services. — *v* **-ies**, **-ied** (*intr*) to engage in mutiny. [OFr *mutin*, rebellious]

mutineer *n* a person who mutinies.

mutinous *adj* **1** having mutinied; likely to mutiny. **2** of or relating to mutiny.

mutt *n* (*coll*) **1** a dog, esp. a mongrel. **2** a foolish person. [Perhaps **muttonhead**]

mutter *v* **-r- 1** (*tr* & *intr*) to utter (words) in a quiet, barely audible voice. **2** (*intr*; **against**, **at**) to grumble or complain. — *n* **1** a soft, barely audible tone of voice. **2** a complaint. [MidE *moteren*]

mutton *n* the flesh of an adult sheep, used as food. — **mutton dressed as lamb** (*coll derog*) an older person, esp. a woman, dressed (esp. unbecomingly) in youthful clothes. [OFr *moton*, sheep]

muttonchops *n* (*pl*) men's long side whiskers, narrow at the ears and broad and rounded at the lower jaw.

muttonhead *n* (*coll derog*) a stupid person.

mutual *adj* **1** felt by each of two or more people about the other or others; reciprocal: *mutual admiration*. **2** of, to or towards each other: *mutual supporters*. **3** (*coll*) shared by each of two or more; common: *a mutual friend*. — *n* **mutuality**. — *adv* **mutually**. [Lat *mutuus*, borrowed or reciprocal]

Muzak® *n* light recorded music as typically played in restaurants, shops, lifts, etc.; the system on which it is played.

muzzle *n* **1** the projecting jaws and nose of an animal, e.g. a dog. **2** an arrangement of straps fitted round an animal's jaws to prevent it biting. **3** the open end of a gun barrel. — *v* (*tr*) **1** to put a muzzle on (e.g. a dog). **2** to prevent from speaking; to silence or gag. [OFr *musel*]

muzzy *adj* **-ier, -iest 1** not thinking clearly; confused. **2** blurred; hazy. — *adv* **muzzily**. — *n* **muzziness**.

MW *abbrev* **1** medium wave. **2** megawatt.

my *adj* **1** of or belonging to me. **2** used with nouns in various exclamations: *my goodness!*; *my foot!* — *interj* expressing surprise: *My, how grown-up you look!* [OE *min*]

myself *pron* **1** the form of *me* used when the speaker or writer is the object of an action he or she performs: *I did myself a favour. I said to myself*. **2** used to emphasise *I* or *me*. **3** my normal self: *I'm not myself today*. **4** (also **by myself**) alone; without help.

myalgic encephalomyelitis. See **ME**.

Mycenaean *adj* of or relating to the ancient civilisation of *Mycenae* in S Greece (1400–1100 BC).

mycology *n* the study of fungi. [Gr *mykes*, mushroom + **-logy**]

myelitis *n* inflammation of the bone marrow. [Gr *myelos*, marrow]

myna or **mynah** *n* any of various large SE Asian birds of the starling family, some of which can be taught to imitate human speech. [Hindi *maina*]

myocardium *n* **-ia** (*anat*) the muscular tissue of the heart. — *adj* **myocardiac**. — *adj* **myocardial**. [Gr *myos*, muscle + *kardia*, heart]

myopia *n* (*med*) the inability to see distant objects clearly; short-sightedness. — *adj* **myopic**. [Gr *myops*, short-sighted]

myriad *n* & *adj* an exceedingly great number (of): *a myriad of stars*; *her myriad admirers*. [Gr *myrias*, ten thousand]

myrmidon *n* (*literary*) **1** a hired thug; a henchman. **2** a follower. [The name of the followers of Achilles in Greek mythology]

myrrh *n* (any of various African and Asian trees and shrubs producing) a brown aromatic resin, used medicinally and in perfumes. [Gr *myrra*]

myrtle *n* a S European evergreen shrub with pink or white flowers and dark blue aromatic berries; any of various related shrubs. [Gr *myrtos*]

mysterious *adj* **1** difficult or impossible to understand or explain; deeply curious. **2** creating or suggesting mystery. — *adv* **mysteriously**.

mystery *n* **-ies 1** an event or phenomenon that cannot be, or has not been, explained. **2** the quality of being difficult or impossible to explain or understand, or of being odd or obscure and arousing curiosity. **3** a person about whom very little is known. **4** a story about a crime that is difficult to solve. **5** a religious rite, esp. the Eucharist. [Gr *mysterion*]

mystery play *n* (also **miracle play**) a mediaeval play based on the life of Christ, or of a saint.

mystery tour *n* a round trip to a destination not revealed in advance.

mystic *n* a person whose life is devoted to meditation or prayer in an attempt to achieve direct communication with God, regarded as the ultimate reality. — *adj* mystical. [Gr *mystikos*, from *mystes*, an initiate]

mystical *adj* **1** relating to or involving truths about the nature of God and reality revealed only to those people with a spiritually enlightened mind; esoteric. **2** mysterious. **3** wonderful or awe-inspiring.

mysticism *n* the practice of gaining direct communication with God through prayer and meditation; the belief in the existence of such a state as a reality hidden from ordinary human understanding.

mystify *v* **-ies, -ied** (*tr*) **1** to puzzle or bewilder. **2** to make mysterious. — *n* **mystification**. — *adj* **mystifying**. [Fr *mystifier*]

mystique *n* a mysterious quality possessed by a person or thing. [Fr]

myth *n* **1** an ancient story dealing with gods and heroes, esp. one explaining some natural phenomenon; such stories in general. **2** a commonly held false notion. **3** a non-existent person or thing. [Gr *mythos*]

mythical *adj* **1** relating to myth. **2** imaginary. — *adv* **mythically**.

mythology *n* **-ies 1** myths in general. **2** a collection of myths. — *adj* **mythological**.

myxomatosis *n* an infectious, usu. fatal disease in rabbits, causing skin tumours and swelling of the mucous membranes. [Gr *myxa*, mucus + *-oma*, tumour + **-osis**]

N

N[1] or **n** *n* ***Ns*** or ***N's***, ***n's*** the fourteenth letter of the English alphabet.

N[2] *abbrev* **1** National or Nationalist. **2** newton. **3** New. **4** North or Northern.

N[3] *symbol* **1** (*chem*) nitrogen. **2** (*chess*) knight.

n[1] *n* **1** (*math*) an indefinite number. **2** (*coll*) a large number. — *adj* of an indefinite or large number. — *adj* **nth**.

n[2] *abbrev* **1** noun. **2** neuter. **3** note. **4** nano-. **5** neutron.

'n' (*coll abbrev*) and.

Na *symbol* (*chem*) sodium. [Lat *natrium*]

NAAFI *abbrev* Navy, Army and Air Force Institutes. — *n* a canteen or shop run by the NAAFI.

nab *v* ***-bb-*** (*tr*; *coll*) **1** to catch in the act of doing wrong. **2** to arrest. **3** to grab or take.

nabob *n* **1** (*coll*) a wealthy, influential person. **2** (*old*) a European returned from India with a vast fortune. **3** (*hist*) a Muslim governor under the Mogul empire in India; a nawab. [Urdu *nawwab*]

nacre *n* mother-of-pearl.— *adj* **nacreous** . [Arabic *naqqarah*, drum]

nadir 1 (*astron*) the point in the heavens directly beneath one and opposite to the zenith. **2** the absolute depth, e.g. of despair or degradation. [Arabic *nazir-as-samt*, opposite the zenith]

naevus *n* ***-vi*** a birthmark or mole on the skin. [Lat]

naff *adj* (*slang*) **1** stupid; foolish. **2** tasteless; vulgar. **3** rubbishy; of poor quality.

nag[1] *n* **1** (*derog*) a broken-down old horse. **2** a small horse for riding. [MidE *nagge*]

nag[2] *v* ***-gg-*** **1** (*tr* & *intr*; **at**) to scold constantly; to keep finding fault (with someone). **2** (*tr*; **into**) to keep urging (someone) to do something. **3** (*intr*; **at**) to cause anxiety: *a nagging suspicion*. **4** (*intr*) (of pain) to persist. — *n* a person who nags. — *n* **nagger**. — *n* **nagging**. [Norse *nagga*, to rub, grumble or quarrel]

Nahuatl. See **Aztec**.

nail *n* **1** the small horny plate protecting the tip of a finger or toe. **2** a metal spike hammered into something e.g. to join two objects together or to serve as a hook. — *v* (*tr*; **together**, **down**, etc.) **1** to fasten with, or as if with, a nail or nails. **2** (*coll*) to catch, trap or corner. **3** to detect, identify or expose (a lie, deception, etc.). — **hit the nail on the head** to pinpoint (e.g. a problem) exactly; to describe something in terms that sum it up precisely. — *v* **nail down** (*tr*; *coll*) **1** to extract a definite decision or promise from. **2** to define or identify clearly. — **on the nail** (*coll*) immediately. [OE *nægl*]

naïve or **naive** *adj* **1** simple, innocent or unsophisticated. **2** (*derog*) too trusting; credulous; not worldly enough. — *adv* **naïvely** or **naively**. — *n* **naïvety** or **naivety**. [Fr, fem. of *naïf*, from Lat *nativus*, native]

naked *adj* **1** wearing no clothes. **2** without fur, feathers or foliage. **3** barren; blank; empty. **4** undisguised; blatant or flagrant: *naked greed*. **5** (of a light or flame) uncovered; exposed. **6** (of the eye) unaided by a telescope or microscope. **7** (*literary*) vulnerable; defenceless. — *adv* **nakedly**. — *n* **nakedness**. [OE *nacod*]

namby-pamby *adj* ***-pambier***, ***-iest*** (*derog*) **1** feebly sentimental; soppy. **2** prim; over-demure. [From scornful nickname of *Ambrose* Phillips, 17th-cent. poet]

name *n* **1** a word or words by which an individual person, place or thing is identified and referred to. **2** reputation: *get a bad name*; *clear one's name*. **3** a famous or important person, firm, etc.: *the big names in fashion*. — *v* (*tr*) **1** to give a name to. **2** to mention or identify by name: *name three French poets*. **3** to specify or decide on. **4** (**as**) to choose or appoint. — **call (someone) names** to insult or abuse (someone). — **in all but name** in practice, though not officially: *leader in all but name*. — **in the name of 1** by the authority of. **2** for the sake of; using as justification: *hundreds tortured in the name of religion*. — **in name only** officially, but not in practice: *ruler in name only*. — **make a name for oneself** to become famous. — *v* **name after** or (*NAm*) **name for** to call by the same name as, by way of commemoration, etc. — **name the day** to announce the date of one's wedding. — **name names** to identify, e.g. culprits, by name. — **the name of the game** (*coll*) the predominant or essential aspect or aim of some activity. — **to one's name** belonging to one. [OE *nama*]

name day *n* the feast day of the saint after whom one is named.

name-dropping *n* (*derog*) the practice of casually referring to well-known people as if they were friends, to impress one's hearers. — *n* **name-dropper**.

nameless *adj* **1** having no name. **2** unidentified: *The culprit shall remain nameless*. **3** too awful to specify; unmentionable.

namely *adv* used to introduce an expansion or explanation of what has just been mentioned: *her intention, namely to discredit the other candidates*.

nameplate *n* a plate on or beside a door, bearing the occupant's name, etc.

namesake *n* a person with the same name as oneself.

nan *n* a slightly leavened Indian bread, similar to pitta bread. [Hindi]

nana. See **nanny**.

nancy *n* ***-ies*** (also **nancy boy**; *coll derog*) an effeminate young man. [From *Nancy*, dimin. of *Ann*]

nanny *n* ***-ies*** **1** a children's nurse. **2** (*coll*; also **nana**, **nanna**) a child's name for a grandmother. — *v* ***-ies***, ***-ied*** (*tr*) to over-protect or over-supervise. [From *Nanny*, a form of *Ann*]

nanny goat *n* an adult female goat.

nano- *comb fm* a thousand millionth (10^{-9}). [Gr *nanos*, dwarf]

nap[1] *n* a short sleep. — *v* ***-pp-*** (*intr*) to have a nap. — **catch (someone) napping** (*coll*) to catch (someone) in an unprepared state. [OE *hnappian*, to sleep]

nap[2] *n* the raised surface on cloth such as velvet, corduroy, etc. [MidE *noppe*]

napalm *n* a petroleum jelly made from naphthalene and coconut oil, used in fire-bombs, etc. — *v* (*tr*) to attack with napalm. [*na*phthenate *palm*itate]

nape *n* the back of the neck. [MidE]

naphtha *n* any of several flammable liquids distilled from coal or petroleum, used as solvents. [Gr]

naphthalene *n* a white crystalline substance distilled from coal tar, used e.g. in mothballs and dyes. [**naphtha**]

napkin *n* **1** (also **table napkin**) a piece of cloth or paper for wiping one's mouth and fingers at mealtimes. **2** a baby's nappy. [Dimin. of OFr *nappe*, napkin, from Lat *mappa*]

nappy *n* ***-ies*** a piece of towelling, or other soft cloth, or a pad of paper, secured round a baby's bottom to absorb its urine and faeces. [Dimin. of **napkin**]

narcissism *n* too great admiration for oneself or one's appearance. — *adj* **narcissistic**. [*Narkissos*, in Greek mythology a youth who fell in love with his reflection]

narcissus *n* ***-cissuses*** or ***-cissi*** a plant similar to the daffodil, that grows from a bulb and has white or yellow flowers. [Gr *narkissos*, supposedly from *narke*, numbness, because of its narcotic properties]

narcosis *n* ***-oses*** a state of insensibility produced by a narcotic or anaesthetic. [Gr *narkosis*, a numbing, from *narke*, numbness]

narcotic *n* **1** a drug causing numbness and drowsiness, that deadens pain, produces a temporary sense of well-being and can be addictive. **2** (*loosely*) any addictive drug. — *adj* relating to narcotics or to narcosis. [Gr *narkotikos*, numbing]

nard *n* **1** an aromatic oil —same as **spikenard**. **2** an Indian plant of the valerian family, from which this is obtained. [Gr *nardos*]

nark *n* (*slang*) **1** a spy or informer esp. working for the police. **2** a habitual grumbler. — *v* (*coll*) **1** (*tr*) to annoy. **2** (*intr*) to grumble. [Perhaps Romany *nak*, nose]

narky *adj* ***-ier***, ***-iest*** (*coll*) irritable.

narrate *v* (*tr*) **1** to tell (a story); to relate. **2** to give a running commentary on (a film). — *n* **narration**. — *n* **narrator**. [Lat *narrare*, to relate]

narrative *n* **1** an account of events. **2** those parts of a book, etc. that recount events. — *adj* **1** telling a story; recounting events: *narrative poetry*. **2** relating to the telling of stories: *narrative skills*. [Lat *narrativus*, from *narrare*, to relate]

narrow *adj* **1** of little breadth, esp. in comparison with length. **2** (of interests or experience) restricted; limited. **3** (of attitudes or ideas) illiberal or unenlightened; intolerant or bigoted. **4** (of the use of a word) restricted to its precise or original meaning; strict. **5** close; only just achieved, etc.: *a narrow victory*. — *n* (in *pl*) a narrow part of a channel, river, etc. — *v* (*intr* & *tr*) **1** to make or become narrow. **2** (**down**) (of e.g. a range of possibilities) to (cause to) be reduced or limited. — *n* **narrowness**. [OE *nearu*]

narrow boat *n* a canal barge.

narrow-gauge *adj* (of a railway) less than 4 ft $8\frac{1}{2}$ in (1·4 m) in width.

narrowly *adv* **1** only just; barely. **2** with close attention: *eyed him narrowly*. **3** in a narrow or restricted way.

narrow-minded *adj* (*derog*) intolerant; prejudiced. — *n* **narrow-mindedness**.

narwhal *n* an arctic whale, the male of which has a long spiral tusk. [Danish *narhval*, from *hval*, whale]

NASA *abbrev* National Aeronautics and Space Administration (a US body).

nasal *adj* **1** relating to the nose. **2** (of a sound, or letter such as *m* or *n*) pronounced through, or partly through, the nose. **3** (of a voice, etc.) abnormally or exceptionally full of nasal sounds. — *adv* **nasally**. [Lat *nasus*, nose]

nasalise or **-ize** *v* (*tr* & *intr*) to pronounce or speak nasally.

nascent *adj* in the process of coming into being; in the early stages of development. [Lat *nasci*, to be born]

nasturtium *n* a climbing garden plant with flat round leaves and red, orange or yellow trumpet-like flowers. [Lat, cress, said to be from *nasus*, nose + *torquere*, to twist, from its pungency]

nasty *adj* ***-ier***, ***-iest*** **1** unpleasant; disgusting. **2** malicious; ill-natured. **3** worrying; serious: *a nasty wound*; *a nasty situation*. **4** (of weather) wet or stormy. — *n* ***-ies*** something unpleasant or disgusting: *video nasties*. — *adv* **nastily**. — *n* **nastiness**.

Nat. *abbrev* **1** National. **2** Nationalist.

nation *n* **1** the people living in, belonging to, and together forming, a single state. **2** a race of people of common descent, history, language, culture, etc. **3** an American Indian tribe, or federation of tribes. [Lat *natio*, tribe]

nationwide *adj* & *adv* (extending) throughout the whole nation.

national *adj* **1** belonging to a particular nation. **2** concerning or covering the whole nation. — *n* a citizen of a particular nation. — *adv* **nationally**. [Lat *natio*, tribe]

national anthem *n* a nation's official song.

national debt *n* the money borrowed by the government of a country and not yet repaid.

national grid *n* **1** the network of high-voltage electric power lines in Britain. **2** the system of vertical and horizontal lines, or co-ordinates, used in Ordnance Survey maps of Britain.

national insurance *n* (*Br*) (a system of) state insurance contributed to by employers and employees, to provide for the sick, unemployed and retired.

nationalise or **-ize** *v* (*tr*) to bring (e.g. an industry) under state ownership and control. — *n* **nationalisation** or **-z-**.

nationalism *n* **1** extreme pride in the history, culture, successes, etc. of one's nation; excessive patriotism. **2** a policy of, or movement aiming at, national unity or independence. — *n* **nationalist**. — *adj* **nationalistic**. — *adv* **nationalistically**.

nationality *n* **-ies** **1** the status of citizenship of a particular nation. **2** the racial or national group to which one belongs.

national park *n* an area of countryside, usu. important for its natural beauty, wildlife, etc., under the ownership and care of the nation.

national service *n* a period of compulsory service in the armed forces.

native *adj* **1** being or belonging to the place of one's upbringing. **2** born a citizen of a particular place: *a native Italian*. **3** (**to**) belonging naturally to one; inborn or innate: *native wit*. **4** having a particular language as one's first, or mother, tongue. **5** (**to**) originating in a particular place. **6** belonging to the original inhabitants of a country: *native Balinese music*. — *n* **1** a person born in a certain place. **2** a plant or animal originating in a particular place. **3** (rather *derog*) one of the original inhabitants of a place as distinct from later, esp. European, settlers. — **go native** (*coll*) (of a visitor or immigrant) to adopt the customs, dress, routines, etc. of the local people. [Lat *nativus*, natural, from *nasci*, to be born]

nativity *n* **-ies** **1** birth, advent or origin. **2** (*cap*) the birth of Christ. [Lat *nativitas*, birth]

NATO *abbrev* North Atlantic Treaty Organisation, an alliance between certain European nations, the United States and Canada for mutual security and defence.

natter *v* **-r-** (*intr*; *coll*) to chat busily. — *n* an intensive chat. [Imit.]

natterjack *n* a European toad with a yellow stripe down its spine and a rough green skin.

natty *adj* **-ier**, **-iest** (*coll*) **1** (of clothes) flashily smart. **2** clever; ingenious. — *adv* **nattily**. [Related to **neat**]

natural *adj* **1** normal; unsurprising. **2** instinctive; not learnt. **3** (**to**) born in one; innate: *a natural talent*; *Kindness was natural to her*. **4** being such because of inborn qualities: *a natural communicator*. **5** (of manner, etc.) simple, easy and direct; not artificial. **6** (of looks) not, or apparently not, improved on artificially. **7** relating to nature, or to parts of the physical world not made or altered by man: *natural sciences*; *areas of natural beauty*. **8** following the normal course of nature: *died a natural death*. **9** (of materials) derived from plants and animals as opposed to man-made: *natural fibres*. **10** wild; uncultivated or uncivilised. **11** related to one by blood: *one's natural parents*. **12** (*euph*) born out of wedlock; illegitimate: *his natural son*. **13** (*mus*) not sharp or flat. — *n* **1** (*coll*) a person with an inborn feel for something: *She's a natural when it comes to acting*. **2** (*mus*) (a sign (♮) indicating) a note that is not to be played sharp or flat. — *n* **naturalness**. [Lat *naturalis*, from *natura*, nature]

natural gas *n* a gas mixture, mainly methane, found under the ground or sea-bed, used as a fuel.

natural history *n* the study of plants and animals.

naturalise or **-ize** *v* (*tr*) **1** to confer citizenship on (a foreigner). **2** to admit (a word) into the language, or (a custom) among established traditions. **3** to cause (an introduced species of plant or animal) to adapt to the local environment. — *n* **naturalisation** or **-z-**.

naturalism *n* **1** a realistic, as opposed to idealistic, treatment of subjects in art, sculpture, etc. **2** the view that rejects supernatural explanations of phenomena, maintaining that all must be attributable to natural causes. — *n* **naturalistic**. — *adv* **naturalistically**.

naturalist *n* **1** a person who studies animal and plant life. **2** a follower of naturalism.

naturally *adv* **1** of course; not surprisingly. **2** in accordance with the normal course of things. **3** by nature; as a natural characteristic: *Sympathy came naturally to her*. **4** by means of a natural process, as opposed to being produced by an artificial man-made process: *gold, silver and other naturally occurring elements*. **5** in a relaxed or normal manner.

natural number *n* (*math*) any whole number greater than 0.

natural philosophy *n* physics.

natural resources *n* (*pl*) sources of energy and wealth that occur naturally in the earth.

natural selection *n* the process by which plant and animal species that adapt most successfully to their environment survive, while others die out.

natural wastage *n* (the reduction of staff by) non-replacement of employees that leave or retire.

nature *n* **1** (also *cap*) the physical world not made by man; the forces that have formed it and control it. **2** what something is, or consists of. **3** a fundamental tendency; essential character; attitude or outlook: *human nature*; *a claim unprovable by its very nature*; *quiet and retiring by nature*. **4** a kind, type, etc. — **be second nature (to)** to be instinctive. — **one's better nature** one's kinder or nobler side. — **call of nature** (*coll euph*) a need to urinate. — **in the nature of** with the characteristics of; like. [Lat *natura*]

nature study *n* the study of plants and animals.

nature trail *n* an organised walk providing opportunities for studying nature.

naturist *n* a nudist. — *n* **naturism.**

naught *n* **1** (*old*) nothing. **2** (esp. *US*) nought. — **come to naught** to fail. — **set at naught** (*old*) to despise. [OE *nawiht*, from *na*, no + *wiht*, thing]

naughty *adj* **-ier**, **-iest 1** mischievous; disobedient. **2** mildly shocking or indecent. — *adv* **naughtily**. — *n* **naughtiness**. [**naught**, from its earlier meaning 'wickedness']

nausea *n* **1** an inclination to vomit. **2** disgust; revulsion. [Lat, from Gr *nausia*, seasickness, from *naus*, ship]

nauseate *v* (*tr*) **1** to cause to feel nausea. **2** to disgust. — *adj* **nauseating**. — *adv* **nauseatingly**. [Lat *nauseare*, to be seasick]

nauseous *adj* **1** sickening; disgusting. **2** affected by nausea. [Lat *nauseosus*, from Gr *nausia*, seasickness]

nautical *adj* relating to ships or sailors. — *adv* **nautically**. [Gr *nautikos*, from *nautes*, sailor]

nautical mile *n* a measure of distance at sea equal to about 1·85 kilometres. ◇ See also **knot.**

nautilus *n* **-luses** or **-li** a sea creature related to the squid and octopus, with a spiral chambered shell pearly on its interior. [Gr *nautilos*, sailor]

naval *adj* relating to a navy or to ships generally. [Lat *navalis*, from *navis*, ship]

nave[1] *n* the main central part of a church, where the congregation sits. [Lat *navis*, ship, from its similarity to an inverted hull]

nave[2] *n* the hub of a wheel. [OE *nafu*]

navel *n* **1** the small hollow in the belly at the point where the umbilical cord was attached. **2** the central point of something. [OE *nafela*, dimin. of *nafu*, hub]

navel orange *n* a seedless orange with a navel-like pit on top.

navigable *adj* **1** (of a river, channel, etc.) able to be sailed along, through, etc. **2** (of a ship) seaworthy. **3** (of a balloon or other craft) steerable. — *n* **navigability**. [Lat *navigabilis*, from *navigare*, to sail]

navigate *v* **1** (*intr*) to direct the course of a ship, aircraft or other vehicle. **2** (*intr*) to find one's way and hold one's course. **3** (*tr*) to steer (a ship or aircraft). **4** (*tr*) to manage to sail along or through (a river, channel, etc.); generally, to find one's way through, along, over, across, etc. **5** (*intr*) as a vehicle passenger, to give the driver directions on the correct route. — *n* **navigator**. [Lat *navigare*, from *navis*, ship]

navigation *n* **1** the act, skill or science of navigating. **2** the movement of ships and aircraft. — *adj* **navigational.**

navvy *n* **-ies** a labourer, esp. one employed in road-building. [**navigation**, from its earlier meaning 'canal']

navy *n* **-ies 1** (the crew and officers of) the warships of a state; the organisation to which they belong, one of the three armed services. **2** a body or fleet of ships with their crews: *the merchant navy*. **3** (also **navy blue**) a dark blue colour, typically used for naval uniforms. [OFr *navie*, from Lat *navis*, ship]

nawab *n* (*hist*) a Muslim ruler or landowner in India. [Urdu *nawwab*, from Arabic *nuwwab*, pl. of *na'ib*, viceroy]

nay *interj* (*old*) **1** no. **2** rather; to put it more strongly: *a misfortune, nay, a tragedy*. — *n* the word 'no'. — **say someone nay** to contradict, or refuse something to, someone. [Norse *nei*]

Nazarene *adj* belonging to Nazareth. — *n* **1** a person of Nazareth. **2** (*hist*; with **the**) Jesus Christ. **3** (*hist*) a Christian. [Gr *Nazarenos*]

Nazi *n* a member of the German National Socialist party, which came to power in Germany in 1933 under Adolf Hitler. — *n* **Nazism**. [Ger *Nationalsozialist*]

NB *abbrev* **1** *nota bene* (Lat), note well. **2** Nebraska. **3** New Brunswick. **4** (*hist*) North Britain, i.e. Scotland.

Nb *symbol* (*chem*) niobium.

NBC *abbrev* **1** National Broadcasting Company (in the US). **2** (of weapons) *n*uclear, *b*iological and *c*hemical.

NBC suit *n* a suit that protects against such weapons.

NC or **N.C.** *abbrev* North Carolina.

NCO *n* ***NCOs*** or ***NCO's*** non-commissioned officer.

ND or **N.D.** *abbrev* North Dakota.

Nd *symbol* (*chem*) neodymium.

N. Dak. *abbrev* North Dakota.

NE *abbrev* **1** north-east or north-eastern. **2** Nebraska.

Ne *symbol* (*chem*) neon.

Neanderthal *adj* denoting a primitive type of man of the early Stone Age in Europe, with a receding forehead and prominent brow ridges. [*Neandertal*, valley in Germany]

neap *n* (also **neaptide**) a tide occurring at the first and last quarters of the moon, when there is the least variation between high and low water. [OE *nepflod* (i.e. neap flood)]

near *prep* **1** at a short distance from. **2** close to (in amount, etc.): *near tears*; *nearer 1000 than 500*. — *adv* **1** (**to**) close: *came near to hitting her*. **2** (*old* or *coll* except *in cmpds*) almost; nearly: *near-disastrous results*; *She damn near died*; *nowhere near enough*. — *adj* **1** being a short distance away; close. **2** closer of two: *the near side*. **3** similar; comparable: *the nearest thing to a screwdriver*. **4** closely related to one: *a near relative*. **5** almost amounting to, or almost turning into: *a near tragedy*. **6** (*old*) mean; miserly. — *v* (*tr* & *intr*) to approach. — *n* **nearness**. — **go near** (with a *negative*) to go to or visit. — **near at hand** conveniently close. [OE *near*, compar. of *neah*, nigh]

nearby *adj* & *adv* (being) a short distance away; close at hand.

nearly *adv* almost. — **not nearly** very far from; nothing like.

near miss *n* something not quite achieved or only just avoided.

nearside *n* & *adj* (relating to) the side of a horse or vehicle nearer the kerb, i.e., in the UK, the left side.

near-sighted *adj* short-sighted.

near thing *n* a narrow escape; a success only just achieved.

neat *adj* **1** tidy; clean; orderly. **2** pleasingly small or regular. **3** elegantly or cleverly simple: *a neat explanation*. **4** skilful or efficient: *Neat work!* **5** (*NAm*) excellent. **6** (of alcoholic drink) undiluted. — *adv* **neatly**. — *n* **neatness**. [Fr *net*, clean, tidy]

neaten *v* **-n-** (*tr*) to make neat.

Neb. or **Nebr**. *abbrev* Nebraska.

nebula *n* **-*lae*** or **-*las*** a luminous or dark patch in space representing a mass of dust or particles; the luminous mass of a remote star cluster. — *adj* **nebular**. [Lat, mist]

nebulous *adj* vague; hazy; lacking distinct shape, form or nature. — *adv* **nebulously**. [Lat *nebulosus*, from *nebula*, mist]

necessary *adj* **1** (**to**) needed; essential; indispensable; that must be done. **2** that must be; inevitable; inescapable: *a necessary evil*. **3** logically required or unavoidable. — *n* **-*ies*** (usu. in *pl*) something necessary. — *adv* **necessarily**. — **the necessary** (*coll humorous*) **1** money needed for a purpose. **2** action that must be taken. [Lat *necessarius*, from *necesse*, necessary]

necessitate *v* (*tr*) to make necessary or unavoidable. [Lat *necessitare*, from *necessitas*, necessity]

necessity *n* **-*ies*** **1** something necessary or essential: *food and other necessities*. **2** circumstances that make something necessary, obligatory or unavoidable: *from necessity rather than choice*; *must of necessity draw this conclusion*. **3** a pressing need: *no necessity to rush*. **4** poverty; want; need. [Lat *necessitas*]

neck *n* **1** the part of the body between the head and the shoulders. **2** the part of a garment at or covering the neck. **3** a narrow part; a narrow connecting part: *joined to the mainland by a neck of land*. **4** (*horse-racing*) a head-and-neck's length; a small margin: *won by a neck*. **5** the meat from the neck of an animal. — *v* (*intr* & *tr*; *slang*) to hug and kiss amorously. — **breathe down someone's neck** (*coll*) to supervise someone so closely as to inhibit them. — **get it in the neck** (*coll*) to be severely rebuked or punished. — **neck and neck** (of competitors in a race, etc.) exactly level. — **risk one's neck** to risk one's life or do something dangerous. — **save one's neck** to escape from danger, etc. without loss or harm. — **stick one's neck out** to put oneself at risk of being attacked, contradicted, etc. — **up to one's neck** (*coll*; **in**) deeply involved; busy; preoccupied. [OE *hnecca*]

neckband *n* a band or strip of material sewn round the neck of a garment.

neckline *n* (the shape of) the edge of a garment at the neck.

neck of the woods *n* (*humorous*) a neighbourhood or locality.

necktie *n* a man's tie.

neckerchief *n* **-*chiefs*** or **-*chieves*** a cloth for wearing round the neck. [**neck** + **kerchief**]

necklace *n* a string of beads or jewels, etc., or a chain, worn round the neck as jewellery. [**neck** + **lace** in sense 'cord', 'tie']

necromancy *n* divination or prophecy through communication with the dead; black magic; sorcery. — *n* **necromancer**. [Gr *nekros*, corpse + *mantis*, prophet]

necrophilia *n* obsessive interest, esp. of an erotic kind, in dead bodies. — *n* & *adj* **necrophiliac**. [Gr *nekros*, corpse + **-philia**]

necropolis *n* a cemetery. [Gr *nekros*, corpse + *polis*, city]

necrosis *n* **-*oses*** the death of living tissue or bone, esp. where the blood supply has been interrupted. — *adj* **necrotic**. [Gr, from *nekros*, corpse]

nectar *n* **1** the liquid collected from flowers by bees to make honey. **2** (*Gr mythol*) the special drink of the gods. **3** any delicious drink. **4** anything delightfully welcome to the senses. [Gr *nektar*]

nectarine *n* a peach-like fruit with a shiny, downless skin. [**nectar**]

née *adj* born; used in giving a woman's maiden name: *Jane Day, née Osborn*. [Fr, fem. of *né*, born]

need *v* **1** (*tr*) to require. **2** (*intr*) to be required or obliged (to): *Do you need to shout?* — *v* (*aux*; in *neg* and *interrog* without **to** and with *3rd person singular* **need**) to be required or obliged (to): *It needn't be expensive. Need you shout?* — *n* **1** something one requires. **2** (**of**, **for**) a condition of lacking or requiring something; an urge or desire: *in need of a wife*; *feel the need to talk*; *a need for mental stimulation*. **3** (**for**) necessity or justification. **4** poverty: *for children in need*. — **if need** or **needs be** if necessary. ◇ See also **needs**. [OE *nead* or *nied*]

needful *adj* necessary. — *n* (*coll facet*; with **the**) **1** whatever action is necessary. **2** money needed for a purpose.

needless *adj* unnecessary. — *adv* **needlessly**. ◇ See also **needy**.

needle *n* **1** a slender pointed steel sewing instrument with a hole for the thread. **2** a longer, thicker implement of metal, wood, bone, plastic, etc. without a hole, for knitting, crocheting, etc. **3** (the pointed end of) a hypodermic syringe. **4** a gramophone stylus. **5** the moving pointer on a compass or other instrument. **6** the needle-shaped leaf of a tree such as the pine or fir. — *n* (*coll*) provocation. — *v* (*tr*; *coll*) to provoke or irritate, esp. deliberately. [OE *nædl*]

needlecord *n* a finely ribbed corduroy.

needlepoint *n* **1** embroidery on canvas. **2** lace made over a paper pattern, with needles rather than bobbins.

needlewoman *n* a woman who sews; a seamstress.

needlework *n* sewing and embroidery.

needn't (*coll*) need not.

needs *adv* (*old*) of necessity; inevitably: *He needs must*, or *must needs, submit*. [OE *niedes*, genitive of *nied*, need]

needy *adj* **-ier, -iest** poverty-stricken; destitute. [**need**]

nefarious *adj* wicked; evil. [Lat *nefarius*, from *nefas*, wrong]

neg *abbrev* negative.

negate *v* (*tr*) **1** to cancel or destroy the effect of. **2** to deny the existence of. [Lat *negare*, to deny]

negation *n* **1** the act of negating. **2** the absence or opposite of something. **3** the denial of the existence of something.

negative *adj* **1** meaning or saying 'no'; expressing denial, refusal or prohibition. **2** (of people, attitudes, etc.) unenthusiastic, defeatist or pessimistic. **3** (*math*) less than zero. **4** contrary to, or cancelling the effect of, whatever is regarded as positive. **5** (*math*) measured in the opposite direction to that chosen as positive. **6** (*electr*) having the kind of electric charge produced by an excess of electrons. **7** (*photography*) (of film) having the light and shade of the actual image reversed, or complementary colours in place of actual ones. — *n* **1** (a word, statement or grammatical form expressing) denial: *replied in the negative*. **2** a photographic film with a negative image, from which prints are made. — *v* (*tr*) **1** to reject; to veto. **2** to deny. **3** to neutralise or cancel out. **4** to disprove or prove the contrary of. — *adv* **negatively**. ◇ See also **positive** and **affirmative**. [Lat *negativus*, from *negare*, to deny]

neglect *v* (*tr*) **1** not to give proper care and attention to. **2** to leave (duties, etc.) undone. **3** to fail or omit (to do something). — *n* **1** lack of proper care. **2** a state of disuse or decay: *fell into neglect*. [Lat *negligere*, to neglect]

neglectful *adj* inattentive or negligent; undutiful or unconscientious.

négligé or **negligee** *n* a woman's thin light dressing-gown. [Fr *négligé*, carelessness, undress, from *négliger*, to neglect]

negligence *n* lack of proper attention or care; carelessness. [Lat *negligentia*]

negligent *adj* **1** not giving proper care and attention. **2** careless or offhand.

negligible *adj* small or unimportant enough to ignore. — *adv* **negligibly**. [Lat *negligere*, to disregard]

negotiable *adj* **1** (of a cash order or other asset) that can legally be transferred to another person in exchange for its value in money. **2** open to discussion. **3** (of a hazard in one's way) able to be got past. [**negotiate**]

negotiate *v* **1** (*intr*; **with, for**) to bargain together so as to reach a mutually satisfactory arrangement. **2** (*tr*) to bring about (e.g. an agreement) or arrange (e.g. a treaty, price, etc.) through bargaining. **3** (*tr*) to pass safely (a hazard on one's way, etc.). — *n* **negotiation**. — *n* **negotiator**. [Lat *negotiari*, to trade, from *negotium*, business]

Negro *n* **-oes** (now rather *offensive*) a person belonging to one of the black-skinned races (orig.) from Africa. — *adj* of, belonging or relating to these races. [Span, from Lat *niger*, black]

Negress *n* (now rather *offensive*) a female Negro.

Negroid *adj* having the physical characteristics of the Negro races, e.g. full lips, broad nose, tightly curling hair. — *n* a Negroid person.

neigh *v* (*intr*) & *n* (to make) the cry of a horse. [OE *hnægan* to neigh]

neighbour *n* **1** a person living near or next door to one. **2** an adjacent territory, person, etc. **3** (*old*) any of one's fellow humans: *Love your neighbour*. [OE *neah*, near + *gebur*, dweller]

neighbourhood *n* **1** a district or locality. **2** the area near something or someone. — **in the neighbourhood of** roughly: *in the neighbourhood of £7000*.

neighbouring *adj* nearby.

neighbourly *adj* friendly. — *n* **neighbourliness**.

neither *adj* & *pron* not the one nor the other (thing or person): *Neither proposal*, or *neither of the proposals, is acceptable*. — *conj* (introducing the first of two or more alternatives; usu. paired with **nor**) not: *I neither know nor care*. — *adv* nor; also not: *If you won't, neither shall I*. — **neither here nor there** unimportant. [OE *nawther* or *nahwæther*]

nelly: **not on your nelly** (*old slang*) certainly not. [Perhaps 'not on your Nelly Duff' rhyming slang for 'puff', i.e. life]

nelson *n* (also **full nelson**) a wrestling hold in which one passes one's arms under and over one's opponent's, from behind, with the palms against the back of his or her neck. [From the name]

half nelson *n* this hold applied on one side only.

nematode *n* any of several long thin unsegmented cylindrical worms, occurring as parasites in plants and animals as well as in soil or sediment. [Gr *nema*, thread + *eidos*, form]

nem. con. *abbrev* for *nemine contradicente* (Lat), with no one disagreeing; unanimously.

nemesis *n* **-meses** (something that brings) retribution or just punishment. [*Nemesis*, Gr goddess of retribution]

neo- *comb fm* new, or a new form of; modern. [Gr *neos*, new]

neoclassical *adj* (of artistic or architectural style, esp. in the late 18th and early 19th centuries) imitating or adapting the styles of the ancient classical world.

neodymium *n* a silvery metallic element (symbol **Nd**), one of the rare earth elements. [**neo-** + *didymium*, name of a substance once thought to be an element]

neolithic *adj* (also *cap*) belonging or relating to the later Stone Age, in Europe lasting from about 40 000 to 2400 BC, characterised by the manufacture of polished stone tools. [**neo-** + Gr *lithos*, stone]

neologism *n* **1** a new word or expression. **2** a new meaning acquired by an existing word or expression. [**neo-** + Gr *logos*, word]

neon *n* an element (symbol **Ne**), a colourless gas that glows red when electricity is passed through it, used e.g. in illuminated signs and advertisements. [Gr, neuter form of *neos*, new]

neon lamp or **light** *n* **1** a neon-filled glass tube used for lighting. **2** (*loosely*) any similar tubular fluorescent light.

neonatal *adj* relating to newly born children. [Lat *neonatus*, from Gr *neos*, new + Lat *natus*, born]

neonate *n* (*formal*) a newly born child.

neophyte *n* **1** a beginner. **2** a new convert to a religious faith. **3** a novice in a religious order. [Gr *neophytos*, newly planted]

nephew *n* the son of one's brother or sister, or of one's brother- or sister-in-law. [OFr *neveu*]

nephritis *n* inflammation of a kidney. [Gr *nephros*, kidney + **-itis**]

nepotism *n* the practice, by someone in authority, of selecting his or her own relatives for high office; favouritism towards one's relations. — *adj* **nepotistic**. [Lat *nepos*, grandson or nephew]

neptunium *n* a metallic element (symbol **Np**) obtained in nuclear reactors during the production of plutonium. [Named after the planet *Neptune*]

nerd *n* (*slang derog*) a foolish or annoying person.

nerve *n* **1** one of the cords, consisting of a bundle of fibres, that carry instructions for movement and information on sensation between the brain or spinal cord and other parts of the body. **2** courage. **3** (*coll*) cheek; impudence. **4** (in *pl*; *coll*) nervousness; tension or stress: *calm one's nerves*. **5** (usu. in *pl*; *coll*) one's capacity to cope with stress or excitement. — *v* (*tr*; **for**) to prepare (oneself) for a challenge or ordeal. — **get on someone's nerves** (*coll*) to annoy someone. — **lose one's nerve** to lose courage in mid-task. — **strain every nerve** to strive one's utmost. [Lat *nervus*, sinew, tendon, nerve]

nerve cell *n* one of the specialised impulse-conducting cells that make up nerves; a neuron.

nerve centre *n* **1** a cluster of nerve cells responsible for a particular bodily function. **2** the centre of control within an organisation, etc.

nerve gas *n* a poisonous gas that acts on the nerves, esp. those of respiration, used as a war weapon.

nerveless *adj* **1** lacking feeling or strength; inert. **2** fearless. — *adv* **nervelessly**.

nerve-racking *adj* causing one to feel tense and anxious.

nervy *adj* **-ier**, **-iest** excitable. — *adv* **nervily**. — *n* **nerviness**.

nervous *adj* **1** timid; easily agitated. **2** apprehensive; uneasy. **3** relating to the nerves: *nervous illnesses*. **4** consisting of nerves. — *adv* **nervously**. — *n* **nervousness**. [Lat *nervosus*, sinewy, from *nervus*, sinew, nerve]

nervous breakdown *n* a mental illness attributed loosely to stress, with intense anxiety, low self-esteem and loss of concentration.

nervous system *n* the network of communication represented by the brain, nerves and spinal cord, controlling all one's mental and physical functions.

-ness *sfx* used to form nouns indicating a state, condition, or degree: *slowness*; *darkness*.

nest *n* **1** a structure built by birds or other creatures, e.g. rats, wasps, etc., in which to lay eggs or give birth to and look after young. **2** a cosy habitation or retreat. **3** a den or haunt (e.g. of thieves) or secret centre (of vice, crime, etc.). **4** a set of things that fit together or one inside the other. — *v* **1** (*intr*) to build and occupy a nest. **2** (*tr* & *intr*) to fit together compactly. **3** (*intr*) to go in search of birds' nests. [OE]

nest egg *n* **1** a real or artificial egg left in a nest to encourage laying. **2** (*coll*) a sum of money saved up for the future; one's savings.

nestle *v* (*intr*; **down**, **together**, etc.) to lie or settle snugly. [OE *nestlian*, to make a nest]

nestling *n* a young bird still unable to fly. [**nest** + **-ling**]

net[1] *n* **1** an openwork material made of thread, cord, etc. knotted, twisted or woven so as to form regularly shaped meshes. **2** a piece of this in any of various shapes or qualities appropriate to such uses as catching fish or insects, protecting fruit bushes, confining hair, etc. **3** a strip of net dividing a tennis or badminton court, etc. **4** the net-backed goal in hockey, football, etc. **5** a snare or trap: *managed to slip* (i.e. escape) *the net.* — *v* **-tt- 1** (*tr*) to catch in a net. **2** (*tr*) to cover with a net. **3** (*tr*) to hit, kick, etc. (the ball) into the net or goal. **4** (*intr*) to construct net from thread, cord, etc. **5** (*tr*; *hist*) to make (a purse, etc.) using a knotting and looping process. [OE *nett*]

netball *n* a game played by women or girls on an outdoor court between teams of seven, the aim being to throw the ball through a net hanging from a ring at the top of a pole.

netting *n* any material with meshes, made by knotting or twisting thread, cord, wire, etc.

network *n* **1** any system resembling a mass of criss-crossing lines: *a network of streets.* **2** any co-ordinated system involving large numbers of people, branches, etc.: *a telecommunications network.* **3** a group of radio or television stations that broadcast the same programmes at the same time. **4** (*comput*) a system of linked terminals capable of passing information to one another. **5** netting. — *v* **1** (*tr*) to broadcast on a network. **2** (*intr*; *comput*) (of computer users) to pass information to one another's machines.

net[2] *adj* (also *Br* **nett**) **1** (of profit) remaining after all expenses, etc. have been paid. **2** (of weight) not including packaging or container. — *v* **-tt-** (*tr*) to produce, or earn, as clear profit. [Fr *net*]

nether *adj* (*old*) lower or under. [OE *nither*, down]

nethermost *adj* (*old*) lowest.

nether world *n* or **nether regions** *n* (*pl*) the underworld; hell.

nett. See **net**[2].

netting. See **net**[1].

nettle *n* a plant covered with hairs that sting if touched. — *v* (*tr*) to offend or irritate. — **grasp the nettle** to deal boldly with a difficult situation. [OE *netele*]

nettle rash *n* an allergic skin reaction with raised red or white itchy patches.

network. See **net**[1].

neur-. See **neuro-**.

neural *adj* relating to the nerves or nervous system. [Gr *neuron*, nerve]

neuralgia *n* spasmodic pain along the course of a nerve. — *adj* **neuralgic**. [**neur-** + **-algia**]

neuritis *n* inflammation of a nerve or nerves, in some cases with defective functioning of the affected part. [**neur-** + **-itis**]

neuro- or **neur-** *comb fm* relating to the nerves: *neurosurgery*.

neuron or **neurone** *n* a nerve cell, i.e. a specialised cell for transmitting nerve impulses. [Gr *neuron*, nerve]

neurosis *n* **-oses** *n* **1** a mental disorder causing obsessive fears, depression and unreasonable behaviour. **2** an anxiety or obsession. [**neuro-** + **-osis**]

neurotic *adj* **1** relating to, or suffering from, a neurosis. **2** (*coll*) over-anxious, over-sensitive or obsessive. — *n* a person suffering from a neurosis.

neuter *adj* **1** (*gram*) denoting a gender of nouns that are neither masculine nor feminine. **2** (of plants) lacking pistils or stamens. **3** (of animals) sexually undeveloped or castrated. **4** (of insects) sexually undeveloped. — *n* **1** the neuter gender. **2** a neuter word. **3** a neuter plant, animal or insect, e.g. a worker bee or ant. — *v* **-r-** (*tr*) to castrate (usu. an animal). [Lat, from *ne*, not + *uter*, either]

neutral *adj* **1** not taking sides in a quarrel or war. **2** not belonging or relating to either side: *neutral ground.* **3** (of colours, esp. grey and fawn) indefinite enough to blend easily with brighter ones. **4** having no strong or noticeable qualities. **5** (*electr*) having no positive or negative electrical charge. **6** (*chem*) neither acidic nor alkaline. — *n* **1** a person or nation taking no part in a war or quarrel. **2** the disengaged position of an engine's gears, with no power being transmitted to the moving parts. — *n* **neutrality**. [Lat *neutralis*, from *neuter*, neither]

neutralise or **-ize** *v* (*tr*) **1** to cancel out the effect of; to make useless or harmless. **2** to declare (a country, etc.) neutral. — *n* **neutralisation** or **-z-**.

neutron *n* (*physics*) one of the electrically uncharged particles in the nucleus of an atom, similar in mass to a proton. [Lat *neuter*, neither]

neutron bomb *n* a type of bomb that destroys life by intense radiation, without the blast and heat effects that destroy buildings.

Nev *abbrev* Nevada.

never *adv* **1** not ever; at no time. **2** not: *I never realised that.* **3** emphatically not; *This will never do.* **4** surely not: *Those two are never twins!* — **never ever** absolutely never. — **well I never!** an expression of astonishment. [OE *ne*, not + *æfre*, ever]

nevermore *adv* never again.

nevertheless *adv* in spite of that.

new *adj* **1** recently made, bought, built, opened, etc. **2** recently discovered: *a new planet.* **3** never having existed before; just invented, etc.: *new techniques.* **4** fresh; additional; supplementary: *a new consignment.* **5** recently arrived, installed, etc.: *under new management.* **6 (to)** unfamiliar; experienced or experiencing for the first time: *a sensation new to me*; *She's new to the work.* **7** changed physically, mentally or morally for the better: *a new man since his operation.* **8** renewed: *gave us new hope.* **9** modern: *the new generation.* **10** used in naming a place just founded after an old-established one: *New York.* — *adv* only just, or freshly: *a newborn babe*; *new-baked bread.* — *n* **newness**. [OE *niwe*]

New Age *n* & *adj* (of or relating to) a modern cultural trend concerned with the union of mind, body and spirit and expressing itself in an interest in a variety of beliefs and disciplines such as mysticism, meditation, astrology and holistic medicine.

new blood *n* new people with fresh ideas introduced into an organisation, etc. to revitalise it.

new broom *n* a new person in charge, bent on making sweeping improvements.

newcomer *n* someone recently arrived.

newly *adv* **1** only just; recently: *newly-mown grass*. **2** again; anew: *newly awakened desire*.

newly-weds *n* (*pl*) a recently married couple.

new maths *n* (*sing*) an approach to teaching mathematics that is more concerned with creating an early understanding of basic concepts than with drilling in arithmetic.

new potatoes *n* (*pl*) the first-dug potatoes of the new crop.

New Style *n* the present method of dating, using the Gregorian calendar. ◇ See also **Old Style**.

New Testament *n* the part of the Bible concerned with the teachings of Christ and his earliest followers. ◇ See also **Old Testament**.

new town *n* a town planned and built by the government as a unit, to relieve congestion in nearby cities, and encourage development.

the New World *n* the American continent. ◇ See also **Old World**.

New Year *n* the first day of the year or the usu. festive days immediately following or preceding it.

New Year's Day *n* 1 January.

New Year's Eve *n* 31 December.

newel *n* **1** the central spindle round which a spiral stair winds. **2** (also **newel post**) a post at the top or bottom of a flight of stairs, supporting the handrail. [OFr *nouel*, nut kernel]

newfangled *adj* modern, esp. objectionably so. [MidE *newefangel*, eager for novelty]

news *n* (*sing*) **1** information about recent events, esp. as reported in newspapers or on radio or television. **2** (with **the**) a radio or television broadcast report of news. **3** any fresh interesting information. **4** a currently celebrated person, thing, or event: *He's big news in the States*. — **bad** (or **good**) **news** (*slang*) something or someone that spells trouble (or the opposite). — **that's news to me** (*coll*) no one told me about this. **[new]**

news agency *n* an agency that collects news stories and supplies them to newspapers, etc.

newsagent *n* a person selling newspapers, confectionery, etc.

newscast *n* a broadcast of news in a radio or television programme. — *n* **newscaster**.

news conference *n* a press conference.

newsdealer *n* a newsagent.

newsflash *n* a brief announcement of important news interrupting a radio or TV broadcast.

newshound *n* (*facet*) a newspaper reporter.

newsletter *n* a sheet containing news issued to members of a society or other organisation.

newsman *n* a male reporter for a newspaper or a broadcast news programme.

newsmonger *n* a gossip.

newspaper *n* **1** a daily or weekly publication composed of folded sheets, containing news, advertisements, topical articles, correspondence, etc. **2** the printed paper which makes up such a publication: *chips wrapped in newspaper*.

newsprint *n* **1** the paper on which newspapers are printed. **2** the ink used to print newspapers.

newsreader *n* a radio or television news announcer.

newsreel *n* a film of news events, once a regular cinema feature.

newsroom *n* an office in a newspaper office or broadcasting station where news stories are received and edited for publication or broadcasting.

news stand *n* a stall or kiosk selling newspapers, magazines, etc.

news-vendor *n* a person who sells newspapers.

newsworthy *adj* interesting or important enough to be reported as news.

newsy *adj* ***-sier***, ***-siest*** full of news.

newspeak *n* (*ironic*) the ambiguous language, full of the latest distortions and euphemisms, used by politicians and other persuaders. [*Newspeak*, a deliberately impoverished English used as an official language, in G Orwell's novel *1984*]

newsy. See **news**.

newt *n* a small amphibious animal with a long body and tail and short legs. [OE *efeta*; *an ewt* came to be understood as *a newt*]

newton *n* a unit of force equivalent to that which gives a one-kilogram mass an acceleration of one second per second. [Named after Sir Isaac *Newton* (1642–1727), English mathematician]

next *adj* **1** following in time or order: *the next on the list*; *the next day*. **2** following this one: *next week*. **3** adjoining; neighbouring: *in the next compartment*. **4** first, counting from now: *the very next person I meet*. — *n* someone or something that is next. — *adv* **1** immediately after that or this: *What happened next?* **2** on the next occasion: *when I next saw her*. **3** following, in order of degree: *the next longest river after the Amazon*. — **next door** in the neighbouring house (*adj* **next-door**). —

next to 1 beside. **2** after, in order of degree: *Next to swimming I like dancing*. **3** almost: *wearing next to no clothes*. [OE *nehst*, superl. of *neah*, near]

next of kin *n* one's closest relative.

nexus *n* **-us** or **-ses 1** a connected series or group. **2** a bond or link. [Lat *nectere*, to bind]

NF, Nfd or **Nld** *abbrev* Newfoundland.

NH or **N.H.** *abbrev* New Hampshire.

NHS *abbrev* the National Health Service.

NI *abbrev* **1** National Insurance. **2** Northern Ireland.

Ni *symbol* (*chem*) nickel.

niacin *n* nicotinic acid. [Contracted form]

nib *n* **1** (also **pen-nib**) the writing-point of a pen, esp. a metal one with a divided tip. **2** (in *pl*) crushed coffee or cocoa beans. [Perhaps a variant of *neb*, nose]

nibble *v* **1** (*tr* or *intr*; **at**) to take very small bites of. **2** to bite gently. **3** (*intr* with **to**; *coll*) to show cautious interest in (a proposal, etc.). — *n* **nibbler**.

nibs: **his** or **her nibs** (*facet*) a contemptuous mock title for an important or would-be important person.

nice *adj* **1** pleasant. **2** (sometimes *ironic*) good; satisfactory. **3** (*ironic*) nasty: *a nice mess*. **4** fine; subtle: *nice distinctions*. **5** exacting; particular: *nice in matters of etiquette*. — *adv* **nicely**. — *n* **niceness**. — **nice and** (*coll*) satisfactorily; commendably: *nice and firm*. [Orig. 'foolish', 'coy', 'exotic', from Lat *nescius*, ignorant, or unknown]

nicety *n* **-ies 1** precision. **2** a subtle point of detail. — **to a nicety** exactly.

niche *n* **1** a shallow recess in a wall, suitable for a lamp, ornament, statue, etc. **2** a position in life in which one feels fulfilled and/or at ease. [Fr, from Lat *nidus*, nest]

nick *n* **1** a small cut. **2** (*coll*) a prison or police station. — *v* (*tr*) **1** to make a small cut in; to cut slightly. **2** (*slang*) to arrest (a criminal). **3** (*slang*) to steal. — **in good nick** (*coll*) in good condition. — **in the nick of time** at the last possible moment; just in time.

nickel *n* **1** an element (symbol **Ni**), a greyish-white metal used esp. in alloys and for plating. **2** in the US and Canada, a coin worth five cents. [Ger *Küpfernickel*, copper devil, so called by miners mistaking it for copper]

nickel silver *n* an alloy of copper, zinc and nickel.

nicker *n* **-er** (*old slang*) a pound sterling.

nick-nack *n* same as **knick-knack**.

nickname *n* a name, usu. additional to the real one, given to a person or place in fun, affection or contempt. — *v* (*tr*) to give a nickname to. [MidE *eke*, addition, extra; *an ekename* came to be understood as *a nickname*]

nicotine *n* a poisonous alkaline substance contained in tobacco. [J *Nicot* (1530–1600), said to have introduced tobacco into France]

nicotinic acid or **niacin** *n* a vitamin of the vitamin B complex (see under **vitamin**).

niece *n* the daughter of one's sister or brother, or of one's sister- or brother-in-law. [Lat *neptis*, granddaughter or niece]

niff *n* (*slang*) a bad smell. — *v* (*intr*) to smell bad. — *adj* **niffy, -ier, -iest**.

nifty *adj* **-ier, -iest 1** clever; adroit; agile. **2** stylish.

niggard *n* a stingy person.

niggardly 1 stingy; miserly. **2** meagre: *niggardly praise*. — *n* **niggardliness**.

nigger *n* (*offensive*) a person of black African origin or race. [Fr *nègre*, from Span *negro*]

niggle *v* **1** (*intr*) to complain about unimportant details. **2** (*tr*) to bother, esp. slightly but continually. — *n* **1** a slight nagging worry. **2** a small complaint or criticism. — *n* **niggler**. — *adj* **niggling**.

nigh *adv* (*old* or *poetic*) near. — **nigh on** or **well nigh** nearly; almost. [OE *neah*]

night *n* **1** the time of darkness between sunset and sunrise, during which most people sleep. **2** nightfall. **3** (*poetic*) darkness. **4** the evening: *stayed at home last night*. **5** an evening on which a particular activity or event takes place: *my aerobics night*. — **make a night of it** (*coll*) to celebrate late into the night. [OE *niht*]

night blindness *n* abnormally reduced vision in dim light or darkness.

nightcap *n* **1** a cap formerly worn in bed at night. **2** a drink, esp. alcoholic, taken before going to bed.

nightclub *n* a club open at night for drinking, dancing, entertainment, etc.

nightdress *n* a loose garment worn in bed by women.

nightfall *n* the beginning of night; dusk.

nightlife *n* entertainment available in a city, etc. late into the night.

night light *n* a dim-shining lamp or slow-burning candle that can be left alight all night.

nightlong *adj* & *adv* (lasting) throughout the night.

nightly *adj* & *adv* (happening, etc.) every night.

night owl *n* a person who likes to stay up late at night.

night safe *n* a safe built into the outer wall of a bank, in which to deposit money when the bank is closed.

night school *n* (an institution providing) educational evening classes for people who are at work during the day.

night shift *n* **1** a session of work or duty during the night. **2** the staff working during this period. ◇ See also **back shift** and **day shift**.

nightshirt *n* a long shirt-like garment, esp. for men, worn in bed.

nights *adv* at night; most nights or every night: *chooses to work nights*.

night soil *n* (*old*) human excrement collected at night for use as a soil fertiliser.

night spot *n* a nightclub.

night stick *n* (*NAm*) a police truncheon.
night-time *n* the time of darkness between sunset and sunrise.
nightwatchman *n* **1** someone who looks after industrial, etc. premises at night. **2** (*cricket*) a batsman, not a high scorer, put in to defend a wicket till close of play.

nightie *n* **-ies** (*coll*) a nightdress.

nightingale *n* a small bird with a melodious song, heard esp. at night. [OE *nihtegale*]

nightjar *n* a nocturnal bird of the swift family with a harsh discordant cry. [**night** + **jar**[2]]

nightmare *n* **1** a frightening dream. **2** an unpleasant or frightening experience. — *adj* **nightmarish**. [**night** + OE *mare*, an incubus, or nightmare-producing monster]

nightshade *n* any of several wild plants, some with poisonous berries, including the belladonna or deadly nightshade. [OE *nihtscada*]

nihilism *n* **1** the rejection of moral and religious principles. **2** a 19th-century Russian movement aimed at overturning all social institutions. **3** the view that nothing has real existence; extreme scepticism. — *n* **nihilist**. — *adj* **nihilistic**. [Lat *nihil*, nothing]

-nik *sfx* (sometimes *derog*) used to form nouns denoting someone concerned or associated with a certain cause, activity, etc.: *peaceniks*; *refuseniks*. [Yiddish, from Slavic]

nil *n* in games, etc., (a score of) nothing; zero. [Lat]

nimble *adj* **1** quick and light in movement; agile. **2** (of wits) sharp; alert. — *n* **nimbleness**. — *adv* **nimbly**. [OE *næmel*, receptive & *numol*, quick to learn]

nimbus *n* **-buses** or **-bi** **1** a heavy dark type of cloud bringing rain or snow. **2** a luminous mist or halo surrounding a god or goddess. [Lat]

nincompoop *n* a fool; an idiot.

nine *n* **1** the number or figure 9; any symbol for this number. **2** the age of 9. **3** something, e.g. a garment or a person, whose size is denoted by the number 9. **4** 9 o'clock. **5** a set of 9 people or things. **6** a playing-card with 9 pips. **7** a score of 9 points. — *adj* **1** 9 in number. **2** aged 9. — *n, adj* & *adv* **ninth**. — *adv* **ninthly**. — **dressed up to the nines** (*coll*) wearing one's best clothes. [OE *nigon*]
ninefold *adj* **1** equal to nine times as much or many. **2** divided into, or consisting of, nine parts. — *adv* by nine times as much.
ninepins *n* (*sing*) a game similar to skittles, using a wooden ball and nine skittles arranged in a triangle.

nineteen *n* **1** the number or figure 19; any symbol for this number. **2** the age of 19. **3** something, e.g. a garment or a person, denoted by the number 19. **4** a set of 19 people or things. — *adj* **1** 19 in number. **2** aged 19. — *n, adj* & *adv* **nineteenth**. — **talk nineteen to the dozen** (*coll*) to chatter away animatedly. [OE *nigontiene*]

ninety *n* **-ies** **1** the number or figure 90; any symbol for this number. **2** the age of 90. **3** a set of 90 people or things. — *adj* **1** 90 in number. **2** aged 90. — *n, adj* & *adv* **ninetieth**. [OE *nigontig*]
nineties *n* (*pl*) **1** the period of time between one's 90th and 100th birthdays. **2** the range of temperatures between 90 and 100 degrees. **3** the period of time between the 90th and 100th years of a century.

ninja *n* **-ja** or **-jas** (also *cap*) esp. in mediaeval Japan, one of a body of professional assassins trained in martial arts and stealth. [Jap *nin-*, endure + *-ja*, person]

ninny *n* **-ies** a foolish person.

Nip *n* (*offensive slang*) a Japanese person. [short for *Nipponese*, Japanese]

nip[1] *v* **1** (*tr*) to pinch or squeeze sharply. **2** (*tr*) to give a sharp little bite to. **3** (*tr* & *intr*) to sting; to cause smarting. **4** (*intr*; *coll*; **off**, **away**, etc.) to go quickly: *nip round to the shop*. **5** (*tr*) to halt the growth or development of: *nip it in the bud*. — *n* **1** a pinch or squeeze. **2** a sharp little bite. **3** a sharp biting coldness, or stinging quality. [Norse *hnippa*, to poke]
nipper *n* **1** the claw of a crab, lobster, etc. **2** (in *pl*) pincers, tweezers, forceps, or other gripping or severing tool. **3** (*old coll*) a small child.
nippy *adj* **-ier**, **-iest** (*coll*) **1** cold; chilly. **2** quick-moving; nimble. — *n* **nippiness**.

nip[2] *n* a small quantity of alcoholic spirits: *a nip of brandy*. [Dut *nippen*, to sip]

nipple *n* **1** the deep-coloured pointed projection on a breast, in the female the outlet of the ducts from which the young suck milk. **2** (esp. *NAm*) the teat on a baby's feeding-bottle. **3** (*mech*) any small projection with a hole through which a flow is regulated or machine parts lubricated.

nippy. See **nip**[1].

nirvana *n* (also *cap*) **1** (*Buddhism* & *Hinduism*) the ultimate state of spiritual tranquillity attained through release from everyday concerns and extinction of individual passions. **2** (*coll*) a place or state of perfect bliss. [Sanskrit, extinction]

nisi *adj* (of a court order) to take effect on the date stated, unless in the meantime a reason is given why it should not. ◇ See also **decree nisi**. [Lat, unless]

Nissen hut *n* a corrugated-iron hut in the shape of a semi-cylinder lying lengthwise. [P N *Nissen* (1871–1930), the designer]

nit[1] *n* the egg or young of a louse, found e.g. in hair. [OE *hnitu*]
nit-picking *n* & *adj* (inclined to go in for) petty criticism or fault-finding over minor details. — *n* **nit-picker**.

nit[2] *n* (*slang*) an idiot. [**nitwit**]

nitrate (*chem*) *n* **1** a salt or ester of nitric acid. **2** sodium nitrate or potassium nitrate used as a soil fertiliser. — *v* **1** (*tr*) to treat with nitric acid or a nitrate. **2** (*tr* & *intr*) to convert into a nitrate. — *n* **nitration**. **[nitre]**

nitre *n* (*chem*) potassium nitrate; saltpetre. [Fr, from Gr *nitron*, sodium carbonate]

nitric *adj* (*chem*) of or containing nitrogen. **[nitre]**

nitric acid *n* a colourless, pungent, caustic and corrosive acid, used as an oxidising agent and for making explosives, fertilisers and dyes.

nitride *n* a compound of nitrogen with another, metallic, element. **[nitre]**

nitrify *v* **-ies**, **-ied** (*tr* & *intr*) (usu. of ammonia) to convert or be converted into nitrates or nitrites, through the action of bacteria. — *n* **nitrification**. **[nitre]**

nitrite *n* a salt or ester of nitrous acid. **[nitre]**

nitro- *comb fm* (*chem*) **1** of, made with, or containing nitrogen, nitric acid or nitre. **2** containing the group $-NO_2$. **[nitre]**

nitrogen *n* an element (symbol **N**), a gas making up four-fifths of the air we breathe. **[nitre + -gen]**

nitroglycerine *n* an explosive liquid compound, produced by treating glycerine with nitric and sulphuric acids.

nitrous *adj* (*chem*) of or containing nitrogen in a low valency. **[nitre]**

nitrous acid *n* a weak acid occurring only in solution or in nitrite salts.

nitrous oxide *n* a colourless gas used as an anaesthetic; laughing gas.

nitty-gritty *n* (*coll*; with **the**) the fundamental issue or essential part of any matter, situation, activity, etc. [Orig. US; perhaps rhyming compound of **grit**]

nitwit *n* a stupid person. [Ger dialect *nit*, variant of *nicht*, not + **wit**[1]]

nix *n* (*slang*) nothing. — *interj* (*NAm*) no. [Ger coll. for *nichts*, nothing]

NJ or **N.J.** *abbrev* New Jersey.

NM, **N.M.** or **N. Mex.** *abbrev* New Mexico.

NNE *abbrev* north-north-east.

NNW *abbrev* north-north-west.

No[1]. See **Noh**.

No[2] *symbol* (*chem*) nobelium.

No. or **no.** *abbrev* number.

no[1] *interj* used as **1** a negative reply, expressing denial, refusal or disagreement. **2** (*coll*) a question tag expecting agreement: *It's a deal, no?* **3** an astonished rejoinder: *No! You don't say!* — *adv* **1** (with *comparative*) not any: *no bigger than one's thumb*. **2** (used to indicate a negative alternative) not: *whether he's willing or no*. — *n* ***noes*** a negative reply or vote. [OE *na*, from *ne*, not + *a*, ever]

no-no *n* ***-nos***, ***-no's*** or ***-noes*** (*coll*) something which must not be done, said, etc.

no[2] *adj* **1** not any. **2** certainly not a; far from a: *He's no fool*; *no easy task*. **3** hardly any: *do it in no time*. **4** not allowed: *no smoking*. — **no go** (*coll*) impossible; no good. — **no way** (*coll*) no; definitely not. [MidE; a variant of **none**]

no-ball *n* (*cricket*, *baseball*, etc.) a ball bowled in a manner disallowed by the rules.

nobody *pron* no person; no one. — *n* ***-ies*** a person of no significance.

no-go area *n* an area to which access is restricted or forbidden, esp. a part of a town closed off by its inhabitants to the police and army.

nohow *n* (*dialect*) in no way.

no-man's-land *n* **1** unclaimed land; waste land. **2** neutral territory between opposing armies or between two countries with a common border. **3** a state or situation that is neither one thing nor another.

no-nonsense *adj* sensible; practical.

no one or **no-one** *n* nobody; no person.

nothing see separate entry.

nowhere *adv* in or to no place; not anywhere. — **from** or **out of nowhere** suddenly and inexplicably: *appear from nowhere*. — **get nowhere** to make no progress. — **in the middle of nowhere** (*coll*) isolated; remote from towns or cities, etc. — **nowhere near** (*coll*) not nearly; by no means. — **nowhere to be found** or **seen** lost.

no[3]. Another spelling of **Noh**.

no. See **No.**

nob *n* (*slang*) a person of wealth or high social rank.

nobble *v* (*tr*; *coll*) **1** (*horse-racing*) to drug or otherwise interfere with (a horse) to stop it winning. **2** to persuade by bribes or threats. **3** to obtain dishonestly. **4** to catch (a criminal). **5** to swindle. [*an hobbler*, a person who lames horses (later understood as *a nobbler*)]

nobelium *n* (*chem*) a radioactive element (symbol **No**) produced artificially from the element curium. [*Nobel* Institute, Stockholm, where first produced]

Nobel prize *n* any of the prizes, awarded annually for work in physics, chemistry, medicine, literature and the promotion of peace, instituted by Alfred *Nobel* (1833–96), Swedish discoverer of dynamite.

nobility *n* **1** the quality of being noble, in character, conduct or rank. **2** (**the**) the class of people of noble birth. [Lat *nobilitas*, from *nobilis*, noble]

noble *adj* **1** honourable. **2** generous. **3** of high birth or rank. **4** grand, splendid, or imposing in appearance. — *n* a person of noble rank. — *n* **nobleness**. — *adv* **nobly**. [Lat *nobilis*, orig. *gnobilis*, knowable, i.e. well-known]

noble gas *n* (*chem*) any of the inert gaseous elements — argon, helium, krypton, neon, radon and xenon.

nobleman *n* a male member of the nobility.

noble metal *n* a metal such as gold, silver or platinum, that does not easily tarnish on exposure to the air. ◇ See also **base metal**.

noble rot *n* a mould that forms on over-ripe grapes.

noblewoman *n* a female member of the nobility.
noblesse oblige (usu. *ironic*) it is the duty of those who are privileged to use their privilege to the benefit of the less fortunate. [Fr, nobility obliges]
nobody. See **no**[2].
nocturnal *adj* **1** (of animals, etc.) active at night. **2** happening at night. **3** of, belonging to or relating to the night. — *adv* **nocturnally**. [Lat *nocturnus*, from *nox*, night]
nocturne *n* **1** a dreamy piece of music, usu. for the piano. **2** (*painting*) a night or moonlight scene. [Fr, from Lat *nocturnus*, from *nox*, night]
nod *v* **-dd- 1** (*intr* & *tr*) to make a brief bowing gesture with the head, in agreement, greeting, etc.; to bow (the head) briefly. **2** (*intr*) to let the head droop with sleepiness; to become drowsy. **3** (*intr*) to make a mistake through momentary loss of concentration. **4** (*tr*) to indicate or direct by nodding: *nodded her approval*; *was nodded through the Customs*. **5** (*intr*) (of flowers, plumes, etc.) to sway or bob about. — **have a nodding acquaintance with** to have a slight knowledge of. — **the Land of Nod** the imaginary country to which sleepers go. — *v* **nod off** (*intr*) to fall asleep in a chair, etc. — **on the nod** (*coll*) (of the passing of a proposal, etc.) by general agreement, without the formality of a vote.
noddle *n* (*coll*) the head or brain.
noddy *n* **-ies 1** a tropical bird of the tern family, so unafraid as to seem stupid. **2** a simpleton. [Perhaps old adj *noddy*, silly]
node *n* **1** a knob, lump, swelling or knotty mass: *lymph nodes*. **2** (*bot*) a swelling where a leaf is attached to a stem. **3** (*geom*) the point where a curve crosses itself. **4** (*astron*) a point where the orbit of a body intersects the apparent path of the sun; a point where any two great circles of the celestial sphere (i.e. circles on the surface of the sphere whose centre is the centre of the sphere) intersect. **5** (*electr*) in a vibrating body, the point of least movement. — *adj* **nodal**. [Lat *nodus*, knot]
nodule *n* **1** a small round lump. **2** (*bot*) a swelling in a root, inhabited by bacteria converting nitrogen to the plant's use. — *adj* **nodular**. [Lat *nodulus*, dimin. of *nodus*, knot]
Noel *n* (*old*) Christmas. [OFr, from Lat *natalis*, birthday]
nog *n* an alcoholic drink made with whipped eggs; an egg nog.
noggin *n* **1** a small measure or quantity of alcoholic spirits. **2** a small mug or wooden cup. **3** (*coll*) one's head.
Noh or **No** *n* ***Noh*** or ***No*** (also without *cap*) Japanese drama in the traditional style, developed from religious dance. [Jap *no*, ability]
nohow. See **no**[2].
noise *n* **1** a sound. **2** a harsh, disagreeable sound; a din. **3** (*radio*, etc.) interference in a signal. **4** (*comput*) irrelevant or meaningless material appearing in output. **5** (*facet*) something one utters by way of conventional response, vague indication of inclinations, etc.: *make polite noises*. — *adj* **noiseless**. — *adv* **noiselessly**. — *n* **noiselessness**. — **noise abroad** to make generally known; to spread (a rumour, etc.). [OFr, from Lat *nausea*, sea-sickness]
noisy *adj* **-ier, -iest 1** making a lot of noise: *noisy children*. **2** full of noise: *noisy streets*. — *adv* **noisily**. — *n* **noisiness**.
noisome *adj* **1** disgusting; offensive; stinking. **2** harmful; poisonous: *noisome fumes*. [From earlier *noy*, a variant of **annoy**]
nom. *abbrev* (*gram*) nominative.
nomad *n* **1** a member of a people without permanent home, who travel from place to place seeking food and pasture. **2** a wanderer. — *adj* **nomadic**. — *adv* **nomadically**. [Gr *nomas*, from *nomos*, pasture]
nom-de-plume *n* ***noms-*** a pseudonym used by a writer; a pen name. [Fr, name of pen]
nomenclature *n* **1** a naming system, esp. in science; terminology. **2** a list or set of names. [Lat *nomenclatura*, from *nomen*, name + *calare*, to call]
nominal *adj* **1** in name only; so called, but actually not: *a nominal head of state*. **2** very small in comparison to actual cost or value: *a nominal rent*. **3** (*gram*) of, being, or relating to a noun. — *adv* **nominally**. [Lat *nominalis*, from *nomen*, name]
nominalism *n* (*philos*) the view that a general term such as 'book' is no more than a name, and does not refer to an actual entity.
nominal value *n* the stated or face value, on a bond, share certificate, etc.
nominate *v* (*tr*) **1** (**for**) to suggest (someone) formally as a candidate for election, for a job, etc. **2** (**to**) to appoint (someone) to a post or job. **3** to specify formally (e.g. a date). — *n* **nomination**. [Lat *nominare*, to name]
nominative (*gram*) *adj* denoting the case used, in inflected languages such as Latin, for the subject of the verb. — *n* **1** the nominative case. **2** a word in this case. [Lat *nominativus*, from *nominare*, to name]
nominee *n* a person who is nominated as a candidate, or for or to a job, etc. [Lat *nominare*, to name + **-ee**]
non- *pfx* **1** not; the opposite of: *non-essential*; *non-existent*. **2** (*ironic*) not deserving the name of: *a non-event*. **3** not belonging to the category of: *non-fiction*; *non-metals*. **4** not having the skill or desire to be: *non-swimmers*; *non-smokers*. **5** denoting rejection, avoidance or omission of: *non-cooperation*; *non-aggression*; *non-payment*. **6** not liable to: *non-shrink*; *non-drip*. **7** not requiring a certain treatment: *non-iron*. [Lat *non*, not]
nonage *n* (*legal*) the condition of being under age; one's minority or period of

immaturity. [OFr, from *non*, non- + *age*, age]

nonagenarian *n* someone between 90 and 99 years old. [Lat *nonagenarius*, containing or consisting of 90]

nonagon *n* (*geom*) a nine-sided figure. [Lat *nonus*, ninth + Gr *gonia*, angle]

non-aligned *adj* (of a country) not allied to any of the major power blocs in world politics. — *n* **non-alignment**.

non-belligerent *adj* taking no part in a war. — *n* a non-belligerent country.

nonce: **for the nonce** for the time being; for the present. [Orig. *for then ones*, for the once (*then once* coming to be understood as *the nonce*)]

nonce-word *n* a word coined for one particular occasion.

nonchalant *adj* coolly unconcerned. — *n* **nonchalance**. — *adv* **nonchalantly**. [Fr *nonchaloir*, to lack warmth]

non-combatant *n* a non-fighting member of the armed forces, e.g. a surgeon or chaplain.

non-commissioned officer *n* an officer such as a corporal or sergeant, appointed from the lower ranks of the armed forces, not by being given a commission.

non-committal *adj* avoiding expressing any definite opinion or preference. — *adv* **non-committally**.

non compos mentis *adj* (often *humorous*) not of sound mind. [Lat, not in command of one's mind]

non-conductor *n* a substance that does not conduct heat, electricity or sound.

nonconformist *n* **1** someone who refuses to conform to generally accepted practice. **2** (*cap*) in England, a member of a Protestant church separated from the Church of England. — *adj* of or relating to nonconformists. — *n* **nonconformism**.

nonconformity *n* **1** refusal to conform to established practice. **2** lack of correspondence or agreement between things.

non-contributory *adj* (of a pension scheme) paid for by the employer, without contributions from the employee.

non-custodial *adj* (of a criminal sentence) not involving imprisonment.

non-denominational *adj* not linked with any particular religious denomination; for the use or participation of members of all denominations.

nondescript *adj* having no strongly noticeable characteristics or distinctive features. [**non-** + Lat *descriptus*, past participle of *describere*, to describe]

none[1] *pron* (with *sing* or *pl* verb) **1** not any. **2** no one: *None were as kind as she*. — **none but** only: *none but the finest ingredients*. — **none of** I won't put up with: *none of your cheek*. — **none other than** (*formal*) the very (person or thing) already mentioned; (so-and-so) him- or herself: *It was none other than Bill*. — **none the** (followed by *compar*) not any: *none the worse for his adventure*. — **none too** by no means: *none too clean*. — **none the less** (also **nonetheless**) nevertheless; in spite of that. [OE *nan*, not one, no]

none[2] *n* (also **nones**) the fifth of the canonical hours. ◇ See also **compline**, **lauds**, **matins**, **sext**, **terce**, **vespers**. [Latin *nona* (*hora*), the ninth hour]

nonentity *n* **-ies** a person of no significance, character, ability, etc.

nones[1] *n* (*pl*) in the Roman calendar, the seventh day of March, May, July and October, the fifth day of other months. [Lat *nonae*, from *nonus*, ninth — the nones being the ninth day before the Ides (counting inclusively)]

nones[2]. See **none**[2].

nonetheless. See **none**.

non-event *n* an event one has been greatly looking forward to that turns out to be a disappointment.

non-ferrous *adj* (of metals) not iron or steel.

non-flammable *adj* not liable to catch fire or burn easily.

non-metal *n* (*chem*) any of the non-metallic elements.

non-observance *n* failure to observe a rule, etc.

nonpareil *adj* & *n* (a person or thing) having no equal. [Fr, from *non*, non- + *pareil*, equal]

non-person *n* a person, once prominent, who has slipped into obscurity.

nonplus *v* **-ss-** (*tr*) to puzzle; to disconcert. [Lat *non plus*, no further]

non-proliferation *n* the policy of limiting the production and ownership of nuclear or chemical weapons.

nonsense *n* **1** words or ideas that do not make sense. **2** foolishness; silly behaviour. — *interj* you're quite wrong. — *adj* **nonsensical**. — *adv* **nonsensically**. — **make a nonsense of** to destroy the effect of; to make pointless.

non sequitur *n* an illogical step in an argument; a conclusion that does not follow from the premisses. [Lat, *it does not follow*]

non-standard *adj* (of words, usage or pronunciation) not accepted as correct by educated speakers.

non-starter *n* a person, thing, idea, etc. that has no chance of success.

non-stick *adj* (of a pan, etc.) having a coating to which food does not stick during cooking.

non-stop *adj* & *adv* without a stop.

non-U *adj* (*Br coll*) (of behaviour, language, etc.) not acceptable among the upper classes. [**U**[2]]

non-union *adj* **1** not belonging to a trade union. **2** employing, or produced by, workers not belonging to a trade union.

non-voting *adj* (of shares) not giving the holder the right to vote on company decisions.

non-white *adj* & *n* (a person) not belonging to one of the white-skinned races.

noodle[1] *n* (usu. in *pl*) a thin strip of pasta, usu. made with egg.
noodle[2] *n* (*coll*) a simpleton.
nook *n* **1** a secluded retreat. **2** a corner or recess. — **every nook and cranny** everywhere.
noon *n* midday; twelve o'clock. [Lat, *nona* (*hora*), the ninth hour, orig. 3 pm]
noose *n* a loop made in the end of a rope, etc. with a sliding knot, used e.g. for killing by hanging. — **put one's head in a noose** to walk into danger. [OFr *nous*, from Lat *nodus*, knot]
nor *conj* **1** (used to introduce alternatives after **neither**) *neither knows nor cares*; *takes neither meat, nor fish, nor eggs*. **2** and not: *It didn't look appetising, nor was it*. — *adv* not either: *If you won't, nor shall I*. [Contraction of OE *nother*, from *ne*, not + *other*, either]
nor' *in cmpds* (esp. *naut*) north: *a nor'-wester*; *nor'-nor'-east*.
Nordic *adj* **1** of or belonging to Scandinavia or its inhabitants. **2** Germanic or Scandinavian in appearance, typically tall, blond and blue-eyed. **3** (no *cap*) denoting a type of competitive skiing with cross-country racing and ski-jumping. [Fr *nordique*, from *nord*, north]
Norf. *abbrev* Norfolk.
norm *n* **1** (with **the**) a typical pattern or situation. **2** an accepted way of behaving, etc.: *social norms*. **3** a standard, e.g. for achievement in industry: *production norms*. [Lat *norma*, carpenter's square, rule]
normal *adj* **1** usual; typical; not extraordinary. **2** mentally or physically sound: *a normal baby*. **3** (*geom*; **to**) perpendicular. — *n* **1** what is average or usual. **2** (*geom*; **to**) a perpendicular line. — *n* **normality** or **normalcy**. [Lat *normalis*, regulated by a carpenter's square, from *norma*, carpenter's square]
normalise or **-ize** *v* (*tr* & *intr*) to make or become normal or regular. — *n* **normalisation** or **-z-**.
normally *adv* **1** in an ordinary or natural way. **2** usually.
Norman *n* **1** a person from Normandy, esp. one of the Scandinavian settlers of N France who conquered England in 1066. **2** Norman French. — *adj* **1** of or belonging to the Normans, their language, etc. **2** (*archit*) relating to a building style typical in 11th- and 12th-century England, similar to Romanesque, with round arches and heavy, massive pillars. [OFr *Normant*, from Norse *Northmathr*]
Norman French *n* the dialect of Old French spoken by the Normans.
normative *adj* establishing a guiding standard or rules: *normative grammar*. [**norm**]
Norn *n* (*Scandinavian mythol*) any of three goddesses of destiny. [Norse]
Norse *adj* **1** of or belonging to ancient or mediaeval Scandinavia. **2** Norwegian. — *n* **1** (*pl*; esp. *hist*) the Scandinavians, esp. the Norwegians. **2** the Germanic language group of Scandinavia, esp. (also **Old Norse**) that used in mediaeval Norway and its colonies. [Perhaps ODut *noorsch*]
north *n* (sometimes *cap*; often with **the**) the direction to one's left when one faces the rising sun, or any part of the earth, a country, town, etc. lying in that direction. — *adj* **1** in the north; on the side that is on or nearest the north. **2** coming from the direction of the north: *a north wind*. — *adv* towards the north. [OE]
northbound *adj* going or leading towards the north.
north-east *n* (sometimes *caps*; often with **the**) the direction midway between north and east or any part of the earth, a country, etc. lying in that direction. — *adj* **1** in the north-east. **2** from the direction of the north-east: *a north-east wind*. — *adj*, *adv* & *n* **north-easterly**, ***-ies***. — *adj* **north-eastern**.
north-easter *n* a strong wind from the north-east.
northerly *adj* **1** (of a wind, etc.) coming from the north. **2** looking, lying, etc. towards the north. — *adv* to or towards the north. — *n* ***-ies*** a northerly wind.
northern *adj* of the north or the North.
northerner *n* a person who lives in or comes from the north.
northernmost *adj* situated furthest north.
the northern lights *n* (*pl*) the aurora borealis.
the North Pole *n* the point on the earth's surface representing the northern end of its axis.
northward *adv* (also **northwards**) & *adj* towards the north.
north-west *n* (sometimes *caps*; often with **the**) the direction midway between north and west or any part of the earth, a country, etc. lying in that direction. — *adj* **1** in the north-west. **2** from the direction of the north-west: *a north-west wind*. — *adj*, *adv* & *n* **north-westerly**, ***-ies***. — *adj* **north-western**.
north-wester *n* a strong wind from the north-west.
Northants. *abbrev* Northamptonshire.
Northumb. *abbrev* Northumberland.
Norwegian *adj* of or belonging to Norway, its inhabitants or their language. — *n* **1** a native of Norway. **2** the language of Norway. [Lat *Norvegia*, from Norse *northr*, north + *vegr*, way]
Nos. or **nos.** *abbrev* numbers.
nose *n* **1** the projecting organ above the mouth, with which one smells and breathes; an animal's snout or muzzle. **2** the sense of smell. **3** (**for**) a faculty for detecting or recognising something. **4** a scent or aroma, esp. a wine's bouquet. **5** the front or projecting part of anything, e.g. a motor vehicle. **6** the nose as a symbol of inquisitiveness or interference: *poke one's nose into*, or *keep one's nose out of*, *something*. — *v* **1** (*tr* & *intr*) to move carefully forward: *nosed* (*the car*) *out of the*

yard. **2** (*intr*; **around**; *coll*) to pry. **3** (*tr* with **out**) to discover by prying; to track down. **4** (*tr*) to detect by smelling. **5** (*tr*) (of an animal) to sniff at or nuzzle. — **blow one's nose** to clear one's nose of mucus by breathing sharply through it. — **by a nose** by a narrow margin. — **cut off one's nose to spite one's face** to act from resentment in a way that can only cause injury to oneself. — **follow one's nose** (*coll*) to go straight forward. — **get up someone's nose** (*coll*) to annoy someone. — **keep one's nose clean** (*coll*) to avoid doing anything that might get one into trouble. — **lead by the nose** to dominate completely. — **look down**, or **turn up, one's nose at** (*coll*) to show disdain for. — **nose to tail** (of cars) in a slow-moving queue with the front of one almost touching the rear of the one in front. — **pay through the nose** (*coll*) to pay an exorbitant price. — **powder one's nose** (*old euph*) (of a woman) to go to the toilet. — **put someone's nose out of joint** (*coll*) to affront someone by giving him or her insufficient attention. — **rub someone's nose in it** (*coll*) to humiliate someone by reminding him or her of a failure. — **under one's very nose** very obviously in front of one.

nosebag *n* a food bag for a horse, hung over its head.

nose band *n* the part of a bridle that goes over the horse's nose.

nosebleed *n* a flow of blood from the nose.

nose cone *n* the cone-shaped cap on the front of a rocket, etc.

nosedive *n* **1** a steep nose-downward plunge by an aircraft. **2** a sharp plunge or fall. **3** a sudden drop, e.g. in prices. — *v* (*intr*) to plunge or fall suddenly. ◇ See also **nosy**.

nosegay *n* a posy of flowers. [**nose** + **gay** in the obsolete sense 'ornament']

nosey. See **nosy**.

nosh (*slang*) *n* food. — *v* (*intr*) to eat. [Yiddish]

nosh-up *n* (*slang*) a hearty feed.

nostalgia *n* **1** a yearning for the past. **2** homesickness. — *adj* **nostalgic**. — *adv* **nostalgically**. [Gr *nostos*, homecoming + *algos*, pain]

nostril *n* either of the two openings in the nose, through which one breathes, smells, etc. [OE *nosthyrl*, from *nosu*, nose + *thyrel*, hole]

nostrum *n* **1** a patent medicine; a panacea or cure-all. **2** a pet solution or remedy, e.g. for political ills. [Lat, our own (make, brand, etc.)]

nosy or **nosey** *adj* ***-ier***, ***-iest*** (*derog*) inquisitive. [**nose**]

nosy parker *n* (*derog coll*) a nosy person; a busybody.

not *adv* (often shortened to **-n't**) **1** used to make a negative statement, etc.: *It's not fair* or *It isn't fair*. **2** used with verbs of opinion, intention, etc. to make the clause or infinitive following the verb negative: *I don't think he's right* (= I think he is not right). **3** used in place of a negative clause or predicate: *might be late, but I hope not*. **4** (indicating surprise, an expectation of agreement, etc.) surely it is the case that: *Haven't you heard? Lovely, isn't it?* **5** used to contrast the untrue with the true: *It's a cloud, not a mountain*. **6** barely: *with his face not two inches from mine*. **7** (with **a**) absolutely no: *not a sound*. **8** by no means: *not nearly enough*; *Not everyone would agree*. **9** used with **only**, **just**, etc. to introduce usu. the lesser of two points, etc: *not just his family, but his wider public*. — **not at all** don't mention it; it's a pleasure. — **not that** though it is not the case that: *not that I care*. [MidE variant of **nought**]

notable *adj* **1** worth noting; significant. **2** distinguished. **3** (**for**) famous. — *n* **notability**. — *adv* **notably**. [Lat *notabilis*, from *notare*, to note or observe]

notary *n* ***-ies*** (also **notary public**, ***-ies public***) a public officer with the legal power to draw up and witness official documents. — *adj* **notarial** . [Lat *notarius*, secretary, clerk]

notation *n* **1** the representation of quantities, numbers, musical sounds, movements, etc. by symbols. **2** any set of such symbols. [Lat *notatio*, marking]

notch *n* a small V-shaped cut. — *v* (*tr*) **1** to cut a notch in. 2 (with **up**) to record a score of; to achieve. [OFr *oche* (*an oche* coming to be understood as *a notch*)]

note *n* **1** (often in *pl*) a brief record made for later reference: *lecture notes*; *took a note of the number*. **2** a short informal letter. **3** a brief comment explaining a textual point, etc.: *a footnote*. **4** a short account or essay. **5** a banknote. **6** a formal, esp. diplomatic, communication. **7** attention; notice: *buildings worthy of note*; *take note of the warning*. **8** distinction; eminence: *women of note*. **9** a written symbol indicating the pitch and length of a musical sound; the sound itself. **10** (esp. *poetic*) the call or cry of a bird or animal. **11** an impression conveyed; feeling; mood: *with a note of panic in her voice*; *end on an optimistic note*. — *v* (*tr*) **1** (**down**) to write down. **2** to notice; to be aware of: *Note this*. — **compare notes** to exchange ideas and opinions. — **strike the right note** to act or speak appropriately. [Lat *nota*, mark, sign]

notebook *n* a small book in which to write notes.

notecase *n* a case for banknotes; a wallet.

noted *adj* (**for**) well known.

notelet *n* a folded piece of usu. decorated notepaper, for short letters.

notepad *n* a block of writing-paper for notes.

notepaper *n* paper for writing letters.

noteworthy *adj* worthy of notice; remarkable. — *n* **noteworthiness**.

nothing *n* **1** no thing; not anything. **2** very little; something of no importance or not very impressive. **3** the number 0. **4** absence of anything: *a shriek and then nothing*. — *adv* not at all: *nothing daunted*. — **be nothing to** to be much less than: *That's nothing to what he's capable of*. — **be nothing to do with 1** to be unconnected with. **2** to be no concern of. — **come to nothing** to fail. — **for nothing 1** free; without payment or personal effort. **2** for no good reason; in vain: *all that work for nothing*. — **have nothing on** (*coll*) to be not nearly as good, beautiful, etc. as. — **have nothing to do with 1** to avoid. **2** to be unconnected with. **3** to be no concern of. — **like nothing on earth** (*coll*) **1** grotesque. **2** frightful. — **make nothing of** not to understand. — **mean nothing to** to be incomprehensible to. — **nothing but** only; merely. — **nothing doing** (*coll*) **1** an expression of refusal. **2** no hope of success. — **nothing for it but** no alternative except. — **nothing if not** primarily; above all; very: *nothing if not keen*. — **nothing like 1** not at all like. **2** by no means: *nothing like enough*. — **nothing much** very little. — **nothing short of** or **nothing less than 1** downright; absolute. **2** only: *will accept nothing less than an apology*. — **nothing to** or **in it** easy. — **think nothing of** to regard as normal or easy. — **think nothing of it** it doesn't matter; there is no need for thanks. — **to say nothing of** as well as; not to mention.

nothingness *n* the state of being nothing or of not existing; emptiness.

notice *n* **1** an announcement displayed or delivered publicly. **2** attention: *came to*, *was brought to*, etc. *my notice*; *escaped my notice*. **3** a warning or notification given, e.g. before leaving, or dismissing someone from, a job: *give in one's notice*; *give notice of one's intentions*; *will continue until further notice*. **4** a review of a performance, book, etc. — *v* (*tr*) **1** to observe. **2** to remark on. — **at short notice** with little warning, time for preparation, etc. — **take notice 1** (**of**) to pay attention; to heed: *took no notice of her advice*. **2** to take interest in one's surroundings, etc.: *sit up and take notice*. [OFr, from Lat *notitia*, from *notus*, known]

noticeable *adj* easily seen; clearly apparent. — *adv* **noticeably**.

notice-board *n* a board on which notices are displayed.

notify *v* **-ies**, **-ied** (*tr*; **of**) to inform or warn. [Lat *notus*, known + *facere*, to make]

notifiable *adj* (of an infectious disease) cases of which must be reported to the public health authorities.

notification *n* **1** an announcement or warning. **2** the act of giving this.

notion *n* **1** an impression, conception or understanding. **2** a belief or principle. **3** an inclination, whim or fancy. **4** (in *pl*; *US*) pins, needles and other small items used in sewing. [Lat *notio*, idea, notion]

notional *adj* existing in imagination only; theoretical; hypothetical.

notorious *adj* well-known for a bad reason; infamous. — *n* **notoriety**. — *adv* **notoriously**. [Lat *notorius*, well known]

Notts. *abbrev* Nottinghamshire.

notwithstanding *prep* in spite of. — *adv* in spite of that.

nougat *n* a chewy sweet containing nuts, etc. [Fr, from Lat *nux*, nut]

nought *n* **1** the figure 0; zero. **2** (*old*) nothing; naught. [OE *noht*, from *nowiht*, from *ne*, not + *owiht*, aught]

noughts and crosses *n* (*sing*) a game in which the aim is to write a line of three noughts (or crosses) within a nine-square framework without being blocked by one's opponent.

noun *n* (*gram*) a word used as the name of a person, animal, thing, place or quality. [Lat *nomen*, name]

nourish *v* (*tr*) **1** to supply with food needed for survival and growth. **2** to encourage the growth of; to foster (an idea, etc.). — *adj* **nourishing**. [OFr *norir*]

nourishment *n* something that nourishes; food.

nous *n* **1** (*coll*) common sense. **2** (*philos*) the intellect. [Gr, mind]

nouveau riche *n* ***nouveaux riches*** (*derog*; usu. in *pl*) a person who has recently acquired wealth but lacks the upper-class breeding to go with it. [Fr, new rich]

nouvelle cuisine *n* a simple style of cookery characterised by much use of fresh produce and elegant presentation. [Fr, new cookery]

Nov. *abbrev* November.

nova *n* ***-ae*** or ***-as*** a normally faint star that suddenly flares into brightness, then fades again. [Lat *nova* (*stella*), new (star)]

novel [1] *n* a book-length fictional story usu. involving relationships between characters and events concerning them. [Ital *novella*, short story, from Lat *novellus*, new]

novelette *n* (*derog*) a short, esp. trite or sentimental novel.

novelist *n* the writer of a novel.

novel [2] *adj* new; original; unheard-of previously. [Lat *novellus*, new]

novella *n* a short story or short novel. [See ety. for **novel**[1]]

novelty *n* ***-ies*** **1** the quality of being new and intriguing. **2** something new and strange. **3** a small cheap toy or souvenir. [OFr *novelete*, from Lat *novellitas*, newness]

November *n* the eleventh month of the year. [Lat, the ninth month, from *novem*, nine]

novena *n* ***-ae*** or ***-as*** (*RC Church*) a series of special prayers and services held over a period of nine days. [Lat *noveni*, nine each, from *novem*, nine]

novice *n* **1** a beginner. **2** a person who has recently joined a religious community but not yet taken vows; a probationary member. [Lat *novicius*, from *novus*, new]

noviciate or **novitiate** *n* **1** the period of being a novice in a religious community. **2** the novices' quarters in such a community.

now *adv* **1** at the present time or moment. **2** immediately. **3** (in narrative) then: *He now turned from journalism to fiction.* **4** in these circumstances; as things are: *I planned to, but now I can't.* **5** up to the present: *has now been teaching 13 years.* **6** used conversationally to accompany explanations, warnings, commands, rebukes, words of comfort, etc.: *Now, this is what happened. Careful, now!* — *n* the present time. — *conj* (also **now that**) because at last; because at this time: *Now we're all here, we'll begin.* — **any day, moment** or **time now** soon. — **as of now** from this time onward. — **for now** until later; for the time being. — **just now 1** a moment ago. **2** at this very moment. — **now and then** or **again** sometimes; occasionally. — **now for** used in anticipation, or in turning from one thing to another: *Now for some fun! Now for your second point.* — **now ... now** one moment ... the next: *now crying, now laughing.* [OE *nu*]

nowadays *adv* in these present times. [**now** + *a*, on + OE *dæges*, of a day]

Nowell *n*. Another spelling of **Noel**.

nowhere. See **no**[2].

nowt *n* (*coll* or *dialect*) nothing. [Ety. as for **naught**]

noxious *adj* harmful; poisonous. — *adv* **noxiously**. [Lat *noxius*, harmful]

nozzle *n* a fitting attached as an outlet to the end of a hose, etc. [Dimin. of **nose**]

Np *symbol* (*chem*) neptunium.

nr *abbrev* near.

NSPCC *abbrev* the National Society for the Prevention of Cruelty to Children.

NSW *abbrev* New South Wales.

NT *abbrev* National Trust.

-n't. See **not**.

nth. See **n**[1].

nuance *n* a subtle variation in colour, meaning, expression, etc. [Fr, shade, hue]

nub *n* the central, most important issue; the crux. [OGer *knubbe*, knob]

nubile *n* (of a young woman) **1** physically mature and ready for marriage. **2** sexually attractive. [Lat *nubilis*, from *nubere*, to veil oneself, marry]

nuclear *adj* **1** having the nature of a nucleus: *the nuclear family*. **2** of or relating to atoms or their nuclei: *nuclear physics*; *nuclear fission*. **3** relating to or produced by the fission or fusion of atomic nuclei: *nuclear energy, power, weapons, war*. [**nucleus**]

nuclear disarmament *n* a country's act of giving up its nuclear weapons.

nuclear energy *n* energy produced through a nuclear reaction.

nuclear family *n* the family consisting of mother, father and children only. ◇ See also **extended family**.

nuclear fission *n* the splitting of an atomic nucleus.

nuclear-free *adj* where nuclear weapons and nuclear energy are banned: *nuclear-free zones*.

nuclear fuel *n* material such as uranium or plutonium consumed to produce nuclear energy.

nuclear fusion *n* the uniting of two atomic nuclei, with a release of energy.

nuclear reaction *n* a process of fusion or fission as atomic nuclei interact with each other or with another particle.

nuclear reactor *n* an apparatus for producing nuclear energy, e.g. to generate electricity, by means of a sustained and controlled nuclear reaction.

nuclear winter *n* a period without light, heat or growth, predicted as a likely after-effect of nuclear war.

nucleate *v* (*tr* & *intr*) to form, or form into, a nucleus. — *adj* having a nucleus.

nucleic acid *n* either of the acids DNA or RNA, found in all living cells. [**nucleus**]

nucleon *n* (*physics*) a proton or neutron. [**nucleus**]

nucleonics *n* (*sing*) the study of the uses of radioactivity and nuclear energy.

nucleus *n* **-lei 1** (*physics*) the positively charged central part of an atom, consisting of neutrons and protons and surrounded by electrons. **2** (*biol*) the central part of a plant or animal cell, containing the substances that control its development and characteristics. **3** (*chem*) a stable group of atoms in a molecule acting as a base for the formation of compounds. **4** a core round which things accumulate. [Lat, kernel]

nude *adj* wearing no clothes; naked. — *n* **1** a representation of a naked figure in painting, sculpture, etc. **2** someone naked. **3** the state of nakedness: *in the nude*. — *n* **nudity**. [Lat *nudus*, naked]

nudism *n* the practice of not wearing clothes from principle. — *n* **nudist**.

nudge *v* (*tr*) **1** to poke or push gently, esp. with the elbow, to get attention, etc. **2** to push slightly or little by little. — *n* a gentle prod.

nugatory *adj* (*formal*) **1** worthless; trifling; valueless. **2** ineffective; futile. **3** invalid. [Lat *nugæ*, trifles]

nugget *n* **1** a lump, esp. of gold. **2** a small piece of something precious: *nuggets of wisdom*.

nuisance *n* **1** an annoying or troublesome person, thing or circumstance. **2** (*legal*) something obnoxious to the community or an individual, that is disallowed by law. — **make a nuisance of oneself** to behave annoyingly. [OFr, from *nuire*, to injure]

nuke *v* (*tr*; *slang*) to attack with nuclear weapons. — *n* a nuclear weapon.

null *adj* **1** legally invalid: *declared null and void.* **2** (*math*) (of a set) with no members; empty. — *n* **nullity**. [Lat *nullus*, none]

nullify *v* **-ies, -ied** (*tr*) **1** to cause or declare to be legally invalid. **2** to make ineffective; to cancel out. — *n* **nullification**. [Lat *nullus*, of no account + *facere*, to make]

numb *adj* **1** deprived completely, or to some degree, of sensation. **2** too stunned to feel emotion; stupefied: *numb with shock.* — *adv* **numbly**. — *n* **numbness**. [MidE *nomen*, seized (i.e. with paralysis)]

numbskull see **numskull**.

number *n* **1** the means or system by which groups, sets, etc. of individual things, etc. are counted; a quantity calculated in units. **2** one or more arithmetical symbols representing such a quantity; a numeral or set of numerals. **3** a numeral or set of numerals identifying something or someone within a series: *telephone numbers.* **4** (with a numeral) the person, animal, vehicle, etc. bearing the numeral: *Number 21 is pulling ahead.* **5** a single issue of a magazine, etc. **6** a quantity of individuals. **7** an act or turn in a programme. **8** a piece of popular music or jazz. **9** (*coll*) an article or person considered appreciatively: *drives a white sports number.* **10** a group or set: *isn't one of our number.* **11** (in *pl*) numerical superiority: *by sheer weight of numbers.* **12** (*gram*) the property of expressing, or classification of word forms into, singular and plural. — *v* **-r-** (*tr*) **1** to give a number to; to mark with a number. **2** (**among, in, with**) to include: *I number her among my enemies.* **3** to amount to: *a crowd numbering about 500.* — **any number of** many. — **one's days are numbered** one is soon to suffer some annihilating fate, esp. death. — **have someone's number** (*coll*) to have someone sized up. — **one's number is up** (*coll*) one is due for some unpleasant fate, e.g. death. — **there is safety in numbers** in situations where there is a risk of harm, rejection, failure, etc., it is better to be one of a group or to involve oneself in a number of activities, approach a number of people, etc. — **without number** more than can be counted; countless. [Fr *nombre*, from Lat *numerus*]

number-crunching *n* (*coll*) the performing of vast and complex mathematical calculations on a computer.

numberless *adj* too many to count; innumerable.

number one *n* (*coll ironic*) oneself. — *adj* first; of primary importance: *give it number-one priority.*

number plate *n* one of the two plates at the front and rear of a motor vehicle, bearing its registration number.

Number Ten *n* (*Br coll*) 10 Downing Street, the official home of the Prime Minister.

numeral *n* an arithmetical symbol used to express a number; a figure. [Lat *numerus*, number]

numerate *adj* **1** able to perform arithmetical operations. **2** having some understanding of mathematics and science. — *n* **numeracy**. [Coined, from Lat *numerus*, number, in imitation of **literate**]

numeration *n* **1** the process of counting or numbering. **2** a system of numbering. [Lat *numerare*, to count]

numerator *n* the number above the line in a fraction. ◇ See also **denominator**. [Lat, numberer, from *numerare*, to count]

numerical *adj* relating to, using, or consisting of, numbers: *numerical superiority.* — *adv* **numerically**. [Lat *numerus*, number]

numerology *n* (*occult*) the study of numbers as an influence on human affairs. [Lat *numerus*, number + **-logy**]

numerous *adj* **1** many. **2** (of an assembly, body, etc.) containing a large number of people. — *adv* **numerously**. [Lat *numerosus*, from *numerus*, number]

numinous *adj* **1** mysterious; awe-inspiring. **2** characterised by the sense of a deity's presence. [Lat *numen*, deity]

numismatics *n* (*sing*) the study, or collecting, of coins and medals. — *adj* **numismatic**. — *n* **numismatist**. [Gr *nomisma*, coin]

numskull *n* (*coll*) (also **numbskull**) a stupid person. [**numb** + **skull**]

nun *n* a member of a female religious order living, in obedience to certain vows, in a community. [Lat *nonna*]

nunnery *n* **-ies** a house in which a group of nuns live.

nuncio *n* **-os** an ambassador from the pope. [Lat *nuntius*, messenger]

nunnery. See **nun**.

nuptial *adj* relating to marriage, or (*zool*) to mating. — *n* (usu. in *pl*) a marriage ceremony. [Lat *nuptialis*, from *nuptiae*, marriage]

nurse *n* **1** a person who looks after sick or injured people, esp. in hospital. **2** a person, esp. a woman, who looks after small children in a household. — *v* **1** (*tr*) to look after (sick or injured people) esp. in a hospital. **2** (*intr*) to follow the career of a nurse. **3** (*tr & intr*) to feed (a baby) at the breast, or (of a baby) to feed at the breast. **4** (*tr*) to hold with care: *gave him the bag of meringues to nurse.* **5** (*tr*) to tend with concern: *was at home nursing a cold.* **6** (*tr*) to encourage (a feeling) in oneself. — *n* **nursing**. [OFr *norrice*, from Lat *nutrire*, to nourish]

nursemaid *n* a children's nurse in a household.

nursing home *n* a small private hospital or home, e.g. for old people.

nursery *n* **-ies** **1** a place where children are looked after while their parents are at work, etc. **2** (esp. *old*) a room in a house reserved for young children and their nurse. **3** a place where plants are grown for sale. [**nurse**]

nurseryman *n* a person who grows plants for sale.

nursery rhyme *n* a short simple traditional rhyme for children.

nursery school *n* a school for children aged between three and five.

nursery slopes *n* (*pl*; *skiing*) the lower gentle slopes used for practice by beginners.

nurture *n* care, nourishment and encouragement given to a growing child, animal or plant. — *v* (*tr*) **1** to nourish and tend (a growing child, animal or plant). **2** (*tr*) to encourage the development of (a project, idea, feeling, etc.). [OFr *norriture*, from Lat *nutrire*, to nourish]

nut *n* **1** a fruit consisting of a kernel contained in a hard shell; the kernel itself. **2** a small usu. hexagonal piece of metal with a hole through it, for screwing on the end of a bolt. **3** (*coll*) a person's head. **4** (*coll*) a crazy person. **5** a small lump: *a nut of butter*. — **do one's nut** (*coll*) to be furious. — **for nuts** (*coll*) at all: *can't sing for nuts*. — **a hard** or **tough nut (to crack)** (*coll*) a difficult problem to solve or an awkward person to deal with. — **off one's nut** (*coll*) mad. [OE *hnutu*]

nutcase *n* (*coll*) a crazy person.

nutcrackers *n* (*pl*) a utensil for cracking nuts.

nuthouse *n* (*coll offensive*) a mental hospital.

nuts *adj* (*coll*) **1** insane; crazy. **2** (**about**, **on**) madly keen.

nuts and bolts *n* (*pl*) essential or practical details.

nutshell *n* the case containing the kernel of a nut. — **in a nutshell** concisely expressed.

nutter *n* (*coll*) a crazy person.

nutty *adj* ***-ier***, ***-iest*** **1** full of, or tasting of, nuts. **2** (*coll*) crazy. — *adv* **nuttily**. — *n* **nuttiness**.

nutmeg *n* the hard aromatic seed of the fruit of an E Indian tree, used ground or grated as a spice. [MidE *notemugge*]

nutrient *n* any nourishing substance. — *adj* nourishing. [Lat *nutrire*, to nourish]

nutriment *n* nourishment; food. [Lat *nutrimentum*, from *nutrire*, to nourish]

nutrition *n* **1** the process of nourishment. **2** the study of the body's dietary needs. **3** food. — *adj* **nutritional**. [Lat *nutrire*, to nourish]

nutritious *adj* nourishing; providing nutrition.

nutritive *adj* **1** nourishing. **2** relating to nutrition.

nux vomica *n* the seed of an E Indian tree, containing strychnine. [Lat, vomiting nut]

nuzzle *v* (*tr* or *intr*; **up, against**) (usu. of animals) to push or rub with the nose. [Related to **nose**]

NV *abbrev* Nevada.

NW *abbrev* north-west(ern).

NWT *abbrev* Northwest Territories.

NY or **N.Y.** *abbrev* New York.

nylon *n* **1** a synthetic material from which a wide variety of products are manufactured, including clothing, hosiery, ropes and brushes. **2** (in *pl*; *old*) a woman's nylon stockings. [Orig. a tradename]

nymph *n* **1** (*mythol*) a goddess inhabiting e.g. water or trees. **2** (*poetic*) a beautiful young woman. **3** (*biol*) an immature larval form of certain insects. [Gr *nymphe*, nymph, bride]

nymphet *n* (*facet*) a sexually attractive and precocious girl in early adolescence. [OFr *nymphette*, from Gr *nymphe*, nymph + fem. dimin. *-ette*]

nympho *n* ***-os*** (*coll*) a nymphomaniac.

nymphomania *n* uncontrollable sexual desire in women, usu. resulting in promiscuity. — *n* & *adj* **nymphomaniac**. [Gr *nympho-* relating to brides + **-mania**]

NZ *abbrev* New Zealand.

O

O[1] or **o** *n* ***O's*** or ***Os***, ***o's*** **1** the fifteenth letter of the English alphabet. **2** zero; nought.

O grade or **Ordinary grade** *n* (*formerly*) in Scotland, (a pass in) an examination in a subject usu. taken at the end of one's fourth year in secondary school.

O level or **Ordinary level** *n* (*formerly*) in England and Wales, (a pass in) an examination in a subject usu. taken at the end of one's fifth year in secondary school.

O[2] or **oh** *interj* **1** (usu. **oh**) used to express surprise, admiration, pleasure, anger, fear, etc. **2** used in addressing a person or thing, or in expressing a wish: *O God!*; *Oh for a bit of peace!*

O[3] *abbrev* **1** Old. **2** Ocean. **3** (also **o**) octavo.

O[4] *symbol* (*chem*) oxygen.

O. *abbrev* Ohio.

o' *prep* **1** of. ◇ See also **o'clock**. **2** on.

oaf *n* a stupid or awkward person. — *adj* **oafish**. — *adv* **oafishly**. — *n* **oafishness**. [Norse *alfr*, elf]

oak *n* **1** a large, acorn-bearing tree of the beech family, with lobed leaves. **2** its hard wood, used esp. for building furniture and ships. **3** (*cap*; in *pl* with **the**) a race for three-year-old fillies run annually at Epsom. [OE *ac*]

oak-apple, **-gall** or **-nut** *n* a ball-like growth on an oak caused esp. by the eggs of certain insects.

oaken *adj* (*old*) made of oak.

oakum *n* pieces of old rope untwisted and pulled apart, used to fill small holes and cracks in wooden boats and ships. [OE *acumba*, from *a-* away + *cemban*, to comb]

OAP *abbrev* (*Br*) old age pensioner.

oar *n* **1** a long pole with a broad, flat blade used for rowing a boat. **2** a rower. — **put** or **stick one's oar in** (*coll*) to interfere or meddle, esp. by offering one's own opinion when it is not wanted. [OE *ar*]

oarsman or **oarswoman** *n* a man or woman who rows.

oarsmanship *n* skill in rowing.

oasis *n* ***oases*** **1** a fertile area in a desert where water is found and plants grow. **2** any place of rest or pleasure in the middle of hard work, problems, or trouble. [Gr, from Egyptian]

oast *n* a kiln for drying hops. [OE *ast*, kiln]

oast-house *n* a building with a cone-shaped roof containing several such kilns.

oat *n* **1** a cereal plant grown for its seeds. **2** (in *pl*) the seeds of this plant, valued as food. — **off one's oats** (*coll*) having no appetite. — **sow one's (wild) oats** (*coll*) to indulge in adventures, excessive drinking, promiscuity, etc. during youth. [OE *ate*]

oatcake *n* a thin, hard, dry biscuit made from oatmeal.

oaten *adj* made of oats.

oatmeal *n* oats ground into meal.

oath *n* **1** a solemn promise to tell the truth, be loyal, etc., usu. naming God as a witness. **2** the form of words used to take an oath. **3** a swearword, obscenity or blasphemy. — **on** or **under oath** having sworn to tell the truth, e.g. in a court of law. [OE *ath*]

ob. *abbrev* for *obiit* (Lat), he or she died.

obbligato *n* ***-tos*** or ***-ti*** a musical accompaniment forming an essential part of a piece of music, esp. that played by a single instrument accompanying a voice. — *adj* to be played with an obbligato. [Ital, obligatory]

obdurate *adj* **1** hard-hearted. **2** hard to influence or change, esp. morally. — *n* **obduracy**. — *adv* **obdurately**. — *n* **obdurateness**. [Lat *ob*, against + *durus*, hard]

OBE *abbrev* (*Br*) (Officer of the) Order of the British Empire, an award given to honour personal or professional excellence or services to the country.

obedience *n* **1** the act or practice of obeying. **2** willingness to obey orders. — *adj* **obedient**. — *adv* **obediently**. [Lat *obedientia*]

obeisance *n* a bow, act or other expression of obedience or respect. [OFr *obeissance*]

obeli. See **obelus**.

obelisk *n* **1** a tapering, needle-like, usu. four-sided, stone pillar. **2** (*printing*) a dagger-shaped mark used esp. for referring to footnotes. [Gr *obeliskos*, small spit]

obelus *n* ***-li*** **1** (*printing*) a dagger-shaped mark used esp. for referring to footnotes. **2** a sign used in ancient texts to mark passages which may not be by the original author of the text. [Gr *obelos*, spit]

obese *adj* very fat. — *n* **obesity**. [Lat *obesus*, plump]

obey *v* ***-eys***, ***-eyed*** **1** (*tr*) to do what one is told to do by (someone). **2** (*tr*) to carry out (a command). **3** (*intr*) to do what one is told. **4** (*tr*) to be controlled by (a force, impulse, etc.). [Lat *obedire*, from *ob*, towards + *audire*, to hear]

obfuscate *v* (*tr*) to confuse or make difficult to understand; to bewilder. — *n* **obfuscation**. — *adv* **obfuscatory**. [Lat *ob*, completely + *fuscus*, dark]

obituary *n* ***-ies*** a notice or announcement of a person's death, often with a short account of his or her life. [Lat *obitus*, death]

obiter dictum *n* ***dicta*** a remark that is in some way related to, but not essential to, the main argument. [Lat *obiter*, by the way + *dictum*, thing said]

object[1] *n* **1** a thing that can be seen or touched. **2** an aim or purpose. **3** the person or thing to which action, feelings or thought are directed. **4** (*gram*) the noun, noun phrase or pronoun affected by the action of the verb, or a preposition. ◇ See also **subject**, **direct object** and **indirect object**. **5** (*philos*) a thing which is outside of, and can be perceived by, the mind. — *adj* **objectless**. — **be no object** not to be a difficulty or obstacle. [Lat *objectus*, a throwing before]

object glass *n* the lens in a camera, telescope, etc. which is nearest to the object being viewed.

object lesson *n* an experience, event, etc., which gives a practical example of esp. a principle or ideal.

object[2] *v* **1** (*intr*; **to**, less commonly **against**) to feel or express dislike or disapproval. **2** (*tr*) to give as a reason for opposing: *object that he is never on time*. — *n* **objector**. [Lat *ob*, in the way of + *jacere*, to throw]

objection *n* **1** an expression of disapproval. **2** (**against**, **to**) a reason for disapproving.

objectionable *adj* unpleasant; likely to cause offence. — *adv* **objectionably**.

objective *adj* **1** not depending on, or influenced by, personal opinions or prejudices. **2** (*philos*) having existence outside the mind; based on fact or reality. ◇ See also **subjective**. **3** (*gram*) (of a case or word) showing the object; in the relation of object to a verb or preposition. — *n* **1** a thing aimed at or wished for; a goal. **2** (*gram*) the object case. **3** an object glass. — *adj* **objectival** . — *adv* **objectively**. — *n* **objectivity**. [Lat *objectivus*, from *ob*, in the way of + *jacere*, to throw]

objet d'art *n* ***objets*** a small object of artistic value. [Fr, object of art]

oblate *adj* (*geom*) (of something approximately spherical) flattened at the poles, like the Earth. [Lat *oblatus*, lengthened]

oblation *n* **1** a sacrifice or religious offering. **2** the offering of the bread and wine to God at a Eucharist. [Lat *oblatio*]

obligate *v* (*tr*) to bind by contract, duty, or moral obligation. [Lat *ob*, down + *ligare*, to bind]

obligation *n* **1** a moral or legal duty or tie. **2** the binding power of such a duty or tie. **3** a debt of gratitude for a service: *be under obligation to her*.

obligatory *adj* legally or morally binding; compulsory. — *adv* **obligatorily**. — *n* **obligatoriness**.

oblige *v* **1** (*tr*) to bind morally, legally or by physical force. **2** (*tr*) to bind by a service or favour. **3** (*tr*) to please or do a favour for: *Please oblige me by leaving at once*. **4** (*intr*) to do something stated as a favour or contribution: *oblige with a song*. — *adj* **obliged**. [Lat *ob*, down + *ligare*, to bind]

obliging *adj* willing to help other people. — *adv* **obligingly**. — *n* **obligingness**.

oblique *adj* **1** sloping; not vertical or horizontal. **2** not straight or direct; roundabout; underhand. **3** (*geom*) (of lines, etc.) not at a right angle. **4** (*gram*) being, or in, any case other than the nominative or vocative. — *n* **1** an oblique line (/). **2** anything that is oblique. — *adv* **obliquely**. — *n* **obliqueness** and **obliquity**. [Lat *ob*, completely + *liquis*, slanting]

obliterate *v* (*tr*) **1** to destroy completely. **2** to cover and prevent from being seen. — *n* **obliteration**. [Lat *obliterare*, to blot out]

oblivion *n* **1** the state of having forgotten or being unconscious. **2** the state of being forgotten. [Lat *oblivio*, forgetfulness]

oblivious *adj* (**of**, **to**) unaware or forgetful. — *adv* **obliviously**. — *n* **obliviousness**.

oblong *adj* forming or being a rectangle which is longer than it is broad. — *n* a rectangle longer than it is broad; an oblong figure or object. [Lat *ob*, over + *longus*, long]

obloquy *n* ***-ies*** **1** abuse, blame or censure. **2** loss of honour, good name or reputation. [Lat *ob*, against + *loqui*, to speak]

obnoxious *adj* offensive; objectionable. — *adv* **obnoxiously**. — *n* **obnoxiousness**. [Lat *ob*, exposed to + *noxa*, harm]

oboe *n* a wind instrument with a double reed, treble pitch, and a penetrating tone. [Ital, from Fr *hautbois*, from *haut*, high + *bois*, wood]

oboist *n* a person who plays an oboe.

obscene *adj* **1** offensive to accepted standards of behaviour or morality, esp. sexual morality. **2** (*coll*) indecent; disgusting. **3** (*Br legal*) (of publications) tending to deprave or corrupt. — *adv* **obscenely**. [Lat *obscenus*, foul, indecent]

obscenity *n* ***-ies*** **1** the state or quality of being obscene. **2** an obscene act or word.

obscurantism *n* opposition to inquiry or the spreading or use of new knowledge, up-to-date scientific research, etc. — *n* & *adj* **obscurantist**. [Lat *obscurare*, to obscure]

obscure *adj* **1** dark; dim. **2** not clear; hidden; difficult to see. **3** not well known. **4** difficult to understand. — *v* (*tr*) to hide; to make dark, or difficult to see or understand. — *adv* **obscurely**. [Lat *obscurus*, dark]

obscurity *n* ***-ies*** **1** the state of being obscure. **2** something that is obscure.

obsequies *n* (*pl*) funeral rites. [Lat *obsequiae*]

obsequious *adj* submissively obedient; fawning. — *adv* **obsequiously**. — *n* **obsequiousness**. [Lat *obsequiosus*, compliant]

observance *n* **1** the act of obeying rules, keeping customs, etc. **2** a custom or religious rite observed. [Lat *observantia*, from *observare*, to observe]

observant *adj* **1** quick to notice. **2** carefully attentive. — *adv* **observantly**.

observation *n* **1** the act of noticing or watching; the state of being observed or watched. **2** the ability to observe; perception: *test her powers of observation.* **3** a remark or comment. **4** the noting of behaviour, symptoms, phenomena, etc. as they occur, esp. before analysis or diagnosis: *keep the patient under observation.* **5** the result of such observing. — **take an observation** to observe the position of the sun or stars in order to calculate one's geographical position. [Lat *observatio*]

observational *adj* **1** relating to or consisting of observing or noticing. **2** based on observation of behaviour, phenomena, etc. as opposed to experiments.

observation car *n* a railway carriage with large windows to allow passengers to view the scenery.

observatory *n* **-ies** a room or building specially equipped for observing and studying the stars and weather. [Lat *observatorium*]

observe *v* **1** (*tr*) to notice or become conscious of. **2** (*tr*) to watch carefully. **3** (*tr* & *intr*) to examine and note (behaviour, symptoms, phenomena, etc.). **4** (*tr*) to obey, follow or keep (a law, custom, religious rite, etc.). **5** (*tr* & *intr*) to make a remark or comment: *observed that he was late again.* — *adj* **observable**. — *adv* **observably**. [Lat *ob*, towards + *servare*, to keep]

observer *n* **1** a person who observes. **2** a person who goes to meetings, etc. to watch and listen but not take part.

obsess *v* (*tr*) to occupy, grip or haunt the mind of completely, persistently, or constantly: *be obsessed with winning*. [Lat *obsidere*, to besiege]

obsession *n* **1** a persistent or dominating idea. **2** (*psychiatry*) a morbid persistence of an idea in the mind, often associated with anxiety. — *adj* **obsessional**. — *adv* **obsessionally**.

obsessive *adj* of, relating to, having, or resulting from an obsession or obsessions. — *adv* **obsessively**. — *n* **obsessiveness**.

obsidian *n* a dark, glassy rock, formed from cooled, hardened lava. [Lat *obsidianus*]

obsolescent *adj* going out of use; becoming out of date. — *n* **obsolescence**. [Lat *obsolescere*, to become obsolete]

obsolete *adj* no longer in use; out of date. [Lat *obsoletus*]

obstacle *n* a person or thing that stands in a person's way or prevents progress. [Lat *obstaculum*, from *ob*, before + *stare*, to stand]

obstacle race *n* a race in which runners have to climb over, crawl through, etc. various obstacles.

obstetrics *n* (*sing*) the branch of medicine and surgery which deals with pregnancy, childbirth and the care of the mother. — *adj* **obstetric**. [Lat *obstetrix*, a midwife, from *ob*, before + *stare*, to stand]

obstetrician *n* a doctor specially qualified in obstetrics.

obstinate *adj* **1** refusing to change one's opinion or course of action; stubborn; inflexible. **2** difficult to defeat, remove, or treat; unyielding. — *n* **obstinacy**. — *adv* **obstinately**. [Lat *obstinatus*, from *ob*, in the way of + *stare*, to stand]

obstreperous *adj* noisy and hard to control; unruly. — *adv* **obstreperously**. — *n* **obstreperousness**. [Lat *ob*, before + *strepere*, to make a noise]

obstruct *v* (*tr*) **1** to block or close. **2** to prevent or hinder the movement or progress of. [Lat *ob*, in the way of + *struere*, to pile up]

obstruction *n* **1** a thing that obstructs or blocks. **2** the act of obstructing. **3** an act of hindering or unfairly getting in the way, e.g. in sport.

obstructionism *n* the practice of obstructing parliamentary or legal action. — *n* **obstructionist**.

obstructive *adj* causing or designed to cause an obstruction. — *adv* **obstructively**. — *n* **obstructiveness**.

obtain *v* **1** (*tr*) to get; to become the owner, or come into possession, of, often by effort or planning. **2** (*intr*) to be established, exist or hold good. — *adj* **obtainable**. [Lat *obtinere*, to lay hold of]

obtrude *v* **1** (*intr*) to be or become unpleasantly noticeable or prominent. **2** (*tr*; **on, upon**) to push (oneself, one's opinions, etc.) forward, esp. when they are unwelcome. — *n* **obtruder**. — *n* **obtruding**. [Lat *ob*, against + *trudere*, to thrust]

obtrusion *n* **1** an act of obtruding. **2** that which obtrudes.

obtrusive *adj* **1** unpleasantly noticeable or prominent: *an obtrusive new housing scheme on the edge of town.* **2** sticking out; protruding. — *adv* **obtrusively**. — *n* **obtrusiveness**.

obtuse *adj* **1** blunt; not pointed or sharp. **2** (*coll*) stupid and slow to understand. **3** (*geom*) (of an angle) between 90° and 180°. — *adv* **obtusely**. — *n* **obtuseness**. [Lat *obtusus*, dull]

obverse *n* **1** the side of a coin with the head or main design on it. ◇ See also **reverse**. **2** the face, side, etc. of anything which is normally on view. **3** an opposite or counterpart, e.g. of a fact or truth. [Lat *obversus*, turned against]

obviate *v* (*tr*) to prevent or remove (a potential difficulty, problem, etc.) in advance. [Lat *obviare*, to go to meet]

obvious *adj* easily seen or understood; evident. — *adv* **obviously**. — *n* **obviousness**. [Lat *obvius*, from *ob*, in the way of + *via*, way]

ocarina *n* a small, simple wind instrument with an egg-shaped body and projecting mouthpiece. [Ital, from *oca*, goose, so-called because of its shape]

occasion *n* **1** a particular event or happening or the time at which it occurs. **2** a special event or celebration. **3** a suitable opportunity. **4** a reason; grounds: *have no occasion to be angry*. **5** an event which determines the time at which something happens, but which is not the actual cause of it. — *v* (*tr*) to cause. — **on occasion** from time to time. — **rise to the occasion** to produce the extra energy or ability needed by unusual circumstances. [Lat *occasio*, from *ob*, in the way of + *cadere*, to fall]

occasional *adj* **1** happening irregularly and infrequently. **2** produced on or for a special occasion. — *adv* **occasionally**.

occasional table *n* a small, usu. decorated table with no regular use.

Occident *n* **1** (with **the**) the countries in the west, esp. Europe and America, as opposed to the **Orient**. **2** that part of the sky where the sun sets. [Lat *occidens*, from *occidere*, to go down]

occidental *adj* of, from or relating to the Occident; western. — *n* (*cap*) a person born in the Occident; a westerner.

occiput *n* (*anat*) the back of the head. — *adj* **occipital**. [Lat, from *ob*, over + *caput*, head]

occlude *v* (*tr*) **1** to block up or cover (e.g. a pore or some other opening). **2** (*chem*) to absorb and retain (e.g. a gas). **3** to shut in or out. — *n* **occlusion**. [Lat *occludere*, to shut up]

occluded front *n* (*meteorol*) an area of cold air which overtakes an area of warm air, drawing the warm air up so that it is no longer in contact with the earth's surface.

occult *adj* **1** involving, using or dealing with that which is magical, mystical or supernatural. **2** beyond ordinary understanding. **3** secret, hidden or esoteric. — *n* (with **the**) the knowledge and study of that which is magical, mystical or supernatural. — *n* **occultist**. [Lat *occultus*, hidden]

occult sciences *n* (*pl*) astrology, palmistry, tarot, etc.

occupancy *n* **-ies 1** the act of occupying (a house, etc.). **2** a period of time during which a house, etc. is occupied. [Lat *occupare*, to seize]

occupant *n* a person who occupies, has, or takes possession of, something — not always the owner.

occupation *n* **1** a person's job or profession. **2** an activity that occupies a person's attention, free time, etc. **3** the act of occupying or state of being occupied. **4** the period of time during which a town, house, etc. is occupied. **5** the act of taking and keeping control of a foreign country, using military power. [Lat *occupatio*, seizing]

occupational *adj* of, connected with or caused by a person's job: *occupational disease*. — *adv* **occupationally**.

occupational hazard *n* a risk or danger caused by the working conditions of a particular job.

occupational therapy *n* the treatment of a mental or physical illness or injury by giving the patient craft-work to do to help recovery. — *n* **occupational therapist**.

occupy *v* **-ies**, **-ied** (*tr*) **1** to have possession of or live in (a house, etc.). **2** to be in or fill (time, space, etc.). **3** to take possession of (a building, a foreign country, etc.) by force. **4** to keep (oneself, a person, one's mind, etc.) busy; to fill in (time). **5** to hold (a post or office). [Lat *occupare*, to seize]

occupier *n* a person who lives in a building, as either a tenant or owner.

occur *v* **-rr-** (*intr*) **1** to happen or take place. **2** (**to**) to come into the mind, esp. unexpectedly or by chance: *occurred to her that she could do better*. **3** to be found or exist. [Lat *occurrere*, to run towards]

occurrence *n* **1** anything which occurs; an event, esp. an unexpected one. **2** the act of occurring.

ocean *n* **1** the salt water that covers most of the earth's surface. **2** any one of its five main divisions, the Atlantic, Indian, Pacific, Arctic and Antarctic. **3** the sea. **4** (usu. in *pl*) a very large number or expanse: *oceans of people*. — *adj* **oceanic**. [Gr *Okeanos*, the stream supposed by the ancients to run round the earth]

ocean-going *adj* (of a ship) built to sail in the sea rather than in rivers, etc.

oceanography *n* the scientific study of oceans. — *n* **oceanographer**. — *adj* **oceanographic** .

ocelot *n* a medium-sized wild cat, found in the forests of Central and S America, which has dark yellow fur marked with spots and stripes. [Aztec *ocelotl*, jaguar]

och *interj* (*Scot* & *Irish*) an expression of surprise, impatience, disagreement, annoyance, regret, etc. [Gaelic]

ochre *n* **1** a kind of fine earth or clay, used as a yellow, red or brown dye. **2** a pale brownish-yellow. — *adj* **ochreous**. [Gr *ochros*, pale]

o'clock *adv* a phrase used in specifying the time. **[of the clock]**

OCR *abbrev* (*comput*) optical character recognition, or reader.

Oct. *abbrev* October.

oct-, octa-. See **octo-**.

octad *n* a group, series, set, etc. of eight things. [Gr *okto*, eight]

octagon *n* a flat figure with eight straight sides and eight angles. — *adj* **octagonal**. — *adv* **octagonally**. [Gr *okto*, eight + *gonia*, angle]

octahedron *n* **-dra** or **-drons** a solid figure with eight plane faces. — *adj* **octahedral**. [Gr *okto*, eight + *hedra*, seat]

octane *n* a hydrocarbon found in petroleum. [Gr *okto*, eight + *-ane* as in **methane**]

high-octane *adj* (of petrol) having good antiknock qualities.
octane number or **rating** *n* a figure indicating the antiknock quality of fuels, the higher the number, the higher the quality.
octant *n* (*math*) **1** one-eighth of the circumference of a circle. **2** a section, formed by drawing two straight lines from the centre to the circumference, of one-eighth of a circle. [Lat *octans*, eighth]
octave *n* **1** (*mus*) the range of sound, or the series of notes, between the first note and the eighth note on a major or minor scale, e.g. from C to the C above. **2** a musical note that is an eighth above or below another. **3** (*poetry*) a verse or stanza with eight lines. **4** the first eight lines of a sonnet. [Lat *octavus*, eighth]
octavo *n* **-os 1** a size of book or page produced by folding a standard-sized sheet of paper three times to give eight leaves. **2** a book of this size. [Lat *octavus*, eighth]
octet *n* **1** a group of eight, e.g. musicians, lines in a poem, etc. **2** a piece of music written for eight musicians or singers. **3** the first eight lines in a sonnet. [Lat *octo*, eight + **duet**]
octo-, **oct-** and **octa-** *comb fm* eight. [Gr *okto*, eight]
October *n* the tenth month of the year. [Lat, from *octo*, eight, so called because it was the eighth month in the Roman calendar]
Octobrist *n* a member of a Russian political party which supported the political changes proposed by Tsar Nicholas II in October 1905.
octogenarian *n* & *adj* (a person) between 80 and 89 years old. [Lat *octogenarius*, of eighty]
octopus *n* **-ses** a sea creature with a soft oval body and eight tentacles. [Gr *okto*, eight + *pous*, foot]
octoroon or **octaroon** *n* a person having one black African or Caribbean great-grandparent. [Lat *octo*, eight]
octosyllable *n* **1** a word with eight syllables. **2** a line of verse containing eight syllables. — *adj* **octosyllabic**. [Lat *octo*, eight + *syllaba*, syllable]
octuple *adj* eight times as large; eightfold. [Lat *octuplus*]
ocular *adj* of or related to the eyes or vision. [Lat *oculus*, eye]
oculist *n* an optician or ophthalmologist. [Lat *oculus*, eye]
OD (*slang*) *n* an overdose of drugs. — *v* ***OD'ing, OD'd*** (*intr*) to take a drug overdose. [Abbrev. of **overdose**]
odalisque or **odalisk** *n* (*hist*) a female slave or concubine in a harem, esp. that belonging to the Turkish Sultan. [Turk *odalik*, from *oda*, room]
odd *adj* **1** left over when others are put into groups or pairs. **2** not matching: *odd socks*. **3** not one of a complete set. **4** (*math*) not exactly divisible by two. **5** unusual; strange. **6** occasional; not regular: *odd jobs*. **7** (*in cmpds* with a number) a little more than the number stated: *twenty-odd replies*. **8** (of pages, etc. numbered consecutively) having an odd number: *put pictures on the odd pages*. **9** out of the way; standing apart. — *adv* **oddly**. — *n* **oddness**. — **odd man out 1** a person or thing that is different from, and often unwilling to be like, others. **2** a person or thing left over when teams, sets, etc. have been formed. [Norse *oddi*, odd number]
oddball *n* (*coll*) a strange or eccentric person.
oddity *n* **-ies 1** a strange person or thing. **2** the state of being strange or unusual.
oddments *n* (*pl*) pieces left over from something much larger.
odds *n* (*pl*; sometimes treated as *sing*) **1** the chance or probability, expressed as a ratio, that something will or will not happen: *The odds are 10–1 against*. **2** the difference between the amount placed as a bet and the money which might be won, expressed as a ratio: *offer odds of 2 to 1*. **3** an advantage that is thought to exist: *The odds are in her favour. It makes no odds how we go*. **4** likelihood: *The odds are he'll be late again*. — **against all the odds** in spite of great difficulty or disadvantage. — **at odds** in disagreement or dispute: *at odds with the management*. — **odds and ends** or **sods** (*coll*) small objects, of different kinds, and usu. of little value or importance. — **over the odds** more than is required, expected or necessary. — **what's the odds?** (*coll*) what difference does it make?; what does it matter?
odds-on *adj* (of a chance) better than even.
ode *n* a usu. long lyric poem, with lines of different lengths, addressed to a particular person or thing. [Gr *oide*, from *aeidein*, to sing]
odious *adj* hateful, extremely unpleasant or offensive. — *adv* **odiously**. — *n* **odiousness**. [Lat *odiosus*, from *odi*, to hate]
odium *n* hatred, strong dislike or disapproval of a person or thing, esp. when widespread. [Lat, hatred]
odometer *n* (esp. *NAm*) a mileometer. [Gr *hodos*, way + **-meter**]
odoriferous *adj* having or giving off a sweet or pleasant smell. [Lat *odorifer*, from *odor*, smell]
odour *n* **1** a (usu. distinctive) smell. **2** reputation; standing; relationship: *in bad odour with someone*. **3** a characteristic or quality. — *adj* **odourless**. [Lat *odor*]
odorous *adj* giving off an odour, esp. a sweet or pleasant one.
odyssey *n* **-eys** a long, often adventurous, journey. [Gr *Odysseia*, an epic poem attributed to Homer (*c*. 9th century BC) describing the adventures had by Odysseus (Ulysses) on his journey home from Troy]
oedema *n* **-mata** or **-mas** an abnormal build-up of fluid in the tissues in the body, causing swelling. — *adj* **oedematous**. [Gr *oidema*, swelling]

Oedipus complex *n* (*psychol*) (according to Freud) a boy's unconscious sexual attraction towards his mother, accompanied by hatred of or hostility towards his father. — *adj* **Oedipal**. [Gr *Oidipous*, a king of Thebes, who unwittingly killed his father and married his mother]

o'er *prep* & *adv* (*poetic* or *old*) over. [A shortened form of **over**]

oesophagus *n* **-gi** the tube by which food passes from the mouth to the stomach. — *adj* **oesophageal**. [Gr *oisophagos*]

oestrogen *n* a sex hormone which develops and controls the female sexual and reproductive organs, and prepares the body for pregnancy. [**oestrus** + Gr *genes*, born, produced]

oestrus *n* a regularly recurring period of fertility and sexual preparedness in many female mammals, when pregnancy is possible; heat. [Gr *oistros*, a gadfly noted for its frenzy]

of *prep* **1** used to show origin, cause or authorship: *people of Glasgow*; *die of hunger*; *poems of Keats*. **2** belonging to; connected with. **3** used to specify a component, ingredient, characteristic, etc.: *built of bricks*; *an area of marsh*; *a heart of gold*. **4** at a given distance or amount of time from: *two miles out of the city*; *within a minute of arriving*. **5** about; concerning: *tales of Rome*; *think of the children*. **6** belonging to or forming a part: *most of the story*. **7** existing, happening, etc. at, on, in or during: *battle of Hastings*; *He works of a night*. **8** used with words denoting loss, removal, separation, etc.: *cured of cancer*; *cheated of the money*. **9** used to show the connection between a verbal noun and the person who is performing, or who is the object of, the action stated: *the running of the deer*; *the eating of healthy food*. **10** (*US*) to; before (a stated hour): *a quarter of one*. [OE]

off *adv* **1** away; at or to a distance. **2** in or into a position which is not attached; loose; separate: *the handle came off*; *take your coat off*. **3** ahead in time: *Easter is a week off*. **4** in or into a state of no longer working or operating: *turn the radio off*. **5** in or into a state of being stopped or cancelled: *The match was rained off*. **6** in or into a state of sleep: *doze off*. **7** to the end, so as to be completely finished: *finish the work off*. **8** away from work or one's duties: *take an hour off*. **9** away from a course; aside: *turn off into a side street*. **10** not available as a choice, esp. on a menu: *peas are off*. **11** in or into a state of decay: *The milk has gone off*. **12** situated as regards money: *well off*. **13** in or into a state of being completely memorised: *have the speech off pat*. — *adj* **1** most distant; furthest away. **2** (of the side of a vehicle, etc.) nearest the centre of the road, on the right in Britain. **3** not good; not up to standard: *an off day*. **4** (*cricket*) on the side of the field towards which the batsman's feet are pointing, usu. the bowler's left. ◇ See also **on** (sense **6**). — *prep* **1** from; away from. **2** removed from; no longer attached to. **3** opening out of; leading from: *a side street off the main road*. **4** not wanting; no longer attracted by: *go off him*; *off one's food*. **5** no longer using: *be off the tablets*. **6** not up to the usual standard: *off one's game*. **7** out to sea from: *off the coast of Spain*. — *n* **1** the start, e.g. of a race or journey: *ready for the off*. **2** (*cricket*) the side of a field towards which the batsman's feet are pointing, usu. the bowler's left. ◇ See also **on**. — **a bit off** (*coll*) (of behaviour) unacceptable or unfair. — **off and on** now and then; occasionally. [OE *of*, away]

offbeat *adj* (*coll*) unusual; not conventional; eccentric.

off chance see **chance**.

off-colour *adj* **1** (esp. *Br*) unwell; not in good health. **2** (of jokes, etc.) rude; smutty.

offcut *n* a small piece left over from a larger piece of e.g. wood, cloth, or meat.

offhand or **offhanded** *adj* casual or careless, often with the result of being rude. — *adv* **offhandedly**. — *n* **offhandedness**.

offing *n* the more distant part of the sea that is visible from the shore. — **in the offing** not far off; likely to happen soon.

off-key *adj* & *adv* **1** out of tune. **2** not quite suitable.

off-licence *n* (*Br*) a shop licensed to sell alcohol to be drunk elsewhere.

off-limits *adj* not to be entered.

off-line *adj* (of e.g. a printer) not under the direct control of a computer, and therefore not ready for use. ◇ See also **on-line**.

offload *v* (*tr*) to get rid of (esp. something unpleasant) by giving it to someone else.

off-peak *adj* (of services) used at a time when there is little demand, and therefore usu. cheaper.

offprint *n* a copy of an article forming part of a larger magazine or periodical.

off-putting *adj* (*coll*) disturbing; unpleasant.

off-season *n* the less popular and less busy period.

offset *n* **1** a side-shoot on a plant, used for developing new plants. **2** a printing process in which an image is inked on to a rubber roller which then transfers it to paper, etc. **3** anything which compensates or is a counterbalance for something else. — *v* **-tt-**, **-set** (*tr*) **1** to counterbalance or compensate for (something): *price rises offset by tax cuts*. **2** to print (something) using an offset process.

offshoot *n* **1** a shoot growing from a plant's main stem. **2** anything which is a branch of, or has developed from, something else.

offshore *adv* & *adj* **1** situated in, at or on the sea, not far from the coast: *offshore industries*. **2** (of winds) blowing away from the coast, out to sea.

offside *adj & adv* (*football, Rugby*, etc.) in an illegal position between the ball and the opponents' goal. — *n* the side of a vehicle or horse nearest the centre of the road, in Britain the right side.

offspring *n* **-spring 1** a person's child. **2** the young of an animal. **3** a result or outcome.

off-stage *adj* & *adv* not on the stage, so unable to be seen by the audience.

off-street *adj* (of parking) not on a road.

off-white *adj* yellowish or greyish white. — *n* this colour, or anything which is this colour, e.g. paint.

offal *n* **1** the heart, brains, liver, kidneys, etc. of an animal, used as food. **2** rubbish, waste or refuse. [MidE, from *of*, off + *fal*, fall]

offence *n* **1** the breaking of a rule; a crime. **2** any cause of anger, annoyance, or displeasure. **3** displeasure, annoyance or resentment: *mean no offence*. **4** an attack or assault. — **give offence** to cause displeasure or annoyance. — **take offence (at)** to be offended (by). [Lat *offendere*, to strike against]

offend *v* **1** (*tr*) to cause (someone) to feel hurt or angry; to insult. **2** (*tr*) to be unpleasant or annoying to (someone). **3** (*intr*; **against**) to commit a sin or crime; to act in a way that is not in accordance with custom, etc. — *adj* **offended**. — *n* **offender**. — *adj* **offending**. [Lat *offendere*, to strike against]

offensive *adj* **1** giving or likely to give offence; insulting. **2** unpleasant, disgusting, repulsive, esp. to the senses. **3** used for attacking. — *n* **1** an aggressive action or attitude: *go on the offensive*. **2** an attack. **3** a great or aggressive effort to achieve something: *a peace offensive*. — *adv* **offensively**. — *n* **offensiveness**. [Lat *offendere*, to strike against]

offer *v* **-r- 1** (*tr*) to put forward (a gift, payment, suggestion, etc.) to be accepted, refused or considered. **2** (*tr*) to provide: *a hill offering the best view*. **3** (*intr*) to state one's willingness (to do something). **4** (*tr*) to present for sale. **5** (*tr*) (of a thing) to present for consideration, acceptance or refusal; to provide an opportunity for: *a job offering rapid promotion*. **6** (*intr*) to present itself; to occur: *if opportunity offers*. **7** (*tr* & *intr*; **for**) to propose (a sum) as payment (to someone): *offer him £250 for the car*. **8** (*tr*; **up**) to present (a prayer or sacrifice) to God. **9** (*tr*) to show (resistance, etc.). — *n* **1** an act of offering. **2** that which is offered, esp. an amount of money offered to buy something. **3** a proposal, esp. of marriage. — **on offer** for sale, esp. at a reduced price. — **under offer** (of a house that is up for sale) with a possible buyer who has made an offer, but still waiting for the contracts to be signed. [Lat *offerre*, from *ob*, towards + *ferre*, to bring]

offering *n* **1** anything offered, esp. a gift. **2** a gift of money given to a church, usu. during a religious service, used for charity, etc. **3** a sacrifice made to God.

offertory *n* **-ies** (*Christian relig*) **1** the offering of bread and wine to God during a Eucharist. **2** an anthem or hymn sung while this is happening. **3** money collected during a church service. [Lat *offerre*, to offer]

office *n* **1** the room, set of rooms or building in which the business of a firm is done. **2** a room or building used for a particular kind of business. **3** a local centre or department of a large business. **4** a position of authority, esp. in the government or in public service: *run for office*. **5** (of a political party) forming the government: *out of office*. **6** (*cap*) a government department: *the Home Office*. **7** the group of people working in an office. **8** a function or duty. **9** (usu. in *pl*) an act of kindness or service: *through her good offices*. **10** an authorised form of Christian worship or service, esp. one for the dead. [Lat *officium*, favour, duty, service]

officer *n* **1** a person in a position of authority and responsibility in the armed forces. **2** a person with a position of authority in an organisation, society or government department. **3** a policeman or policewoman. **4** a person in authority on a non-naval ship.

office-bearer or **-holder** *n* a person with an official duty in a society, church organisation, etc.

office-block *n* a large, multistorey building divided into offices.

official *adj* **1** of or relating to an office or position of authority. **2** given or authorised by a person in authority: *an official report*. **3** formal; suitable for or characteristic of a person holding office: *official dinners*. — *n* a person who holds office or who is in a position of authority. — *adv* **officially**. [Lat *officialis*]

officialdom *n* officials and bureaucrats as a group.

officialese *n* the language of the government, civil service, etc., which is unclear, wordy and pompous.

official receiver *n* a government officer appointed to deal with the affairs of a company, etc. which has gone bankrupt.

officiate *v* (*intr*) **1** to act in an official capacity; to perform official duties, esp. at a particular function. **2** to conduct a religious service. [Lat *officiare*, to serve]

officious *adj* **1** offering help, advice, etc. when this is not wanted; interfering. **2** (of a diplomatic agreement) informal; unofficial. — *adv* **officiously**. — *n* **officiousness**. [Lat *officiosus*, obliging]

oft *adv* (*old* or *poetic*) often. [OE]

often *adv* **1** many times; frequently. **2** in many cases. — **as often as not** quite often; in about half the cases. — **every so often** sometimes; now and then. — **more often than not** usually; in most of the cases. [MidE, from **oft**]

ogee *n* an S-shaped curve, line or moulding. [OFr *ogive*, a diagonal rib in a vault]

ogle *v* (*tr* & *intr*) to look or stare at (a person) expressing sexual desire with the eyes. [Perhaps Dut *oogen*, to make eyes at]

ogre or **ogress** *n* **1** in fairy stories, a frightening, cruel, ugly, man-eating male or female giant. **2** a cruel or frightening person. — *adj* **ogrish** or **ogreish**. [Fr]

oh. See **O**[2].

OH *abbrev* Ohio.

ohm *n* the standard unit of electrical resistance. [Georg Simon *Ohm* (1787–1854), German physicist]

OHMS *abbrev* (*Br*) On Her (or His) Majesty's Service, often written on mail from government departments.

oho *interj* (*old*) an expression of surprise or triumphant satisfaction.

-oholic. See **-aholic**.

-oid *sfx* (used to form nouns and adjectives) having the form of: *humanoid*; *rhomboid*. — *adj sfx* **-oidal**. [Gr *eidos*, shape]

oik *n* (*Br offensive slang*) a person thought of as inferior, esp. because of being rude, ignorant, badly educated, or lower class.

oil *n* **1** a usu. thick liquid which will not mix with water and which burns easily, obtained from plants, animals and minerals, and used as a fuel, lubricant, food, etc. **2** petroleum. **3** (often in *pl*) oil-paint. **4** a picture painted with oil-paints. — *v* (*tr*) to apply oil to, lubricate, or treat with oil. — *adj* **oiled**. — **oil the wheels** to do something in order to make things go more smoothly or successfully. — **pour oil on troubled waters** to soothe or calm a person or situation. [Lat *oleum*, from Gr *elaia*, olive-tree]

oil-cake *n* a cattle-food made from linseed which has had its oil removed.

oilcloth *n* canvas coated with oil to make it waterproof, used esp. formerly as a covering for tables, etc.

oil-colour *n* an oil-paint.

oilfield *n* an area with reserves of mineral oil under the ground.

oil-fired *adj* using oil as a fuel.

oil-paint *n* a paint made by mixing ground pigment with oil.

oil-painting *n* **1** a picture painted with oil-paints. **2** the activity or art of painting in oils. — **no oil-painting** (*coll*) not very beautiful.

oil-rig *n* a structure, plus all the equipment, machinery, etc. that it supports, used for drilling oil.

oilskin *n* **1** a cloth treated with oil to make it waterproof. **2** (often in *pl*) a garment made of this.

oil slick *n* a patch of oil, esp. one forming a film on water.

oil-tanker *n* a large ship for carrying oil in bulk.

oil well *n* a well bored in the ground or sea-bed to obtain petroleum.

oily *adj* **-ier**, **-iest** **1** of, containing or like oil. **2** covered with oil. **3** (*derog*) (of a person, behaviour, etc.) unpleasantly friendly or polite; servile and flattering. — *adv* **oilily**. — *n* **oiliness**.

oink *v* (*intr*) & *n* (to produce) the noise made by a pig. [Imit.]

ointment *n* any greasy substance rubbed on the skin to heal injuries or as a cosmetic. — **a fly in the ointment** a minor nuisance or irritation which disturbs one's enjoyment. [Lat *unguentum*, unguent]

OK[1] *abbrev* Oklahoma.

OK[2] or **okay** (*coll*) *adj* all right; satisfactory. — *adv* well; satisfactorily. — *interj* yes; I agree. — *n* ***OK's***, ***OKs*** or ***okays*** approval, sanction or agreement. — *v* ***OK'ing***, ***OKing*** or ***okaying***; ***OK'ed***, ***OKed*** or ***okayed*** (*tr*) to approve or pass as satisfactory. [Abbrev. of American English *oll korrect*, a facetious spelling of *all correct*]

okapi *n* ***-pis*** or ***-pi*** an animal from Central Africa, related to the giraffe but with a shorter neck, and with a reddish-brown coat, white stripes on the legs and small horns. [A native Central African word]

okey-dokey *adv*, *adj* & *interj* (*slang*) OK.

Okla. *abbrev* Oklahoma.

okra *n* a tropical plant which produces long, green, edible pods used as a vegetable. [A W African native word]

old *adj* **1** advanced in age; having existed for a long time. **2** having a stated age: *five years old*. **3** of or relating to the end period of a long life or existence: *old age*. **4** worn out or shabby through long use: *old shoes*. **5** no longer in use; out of date; old-fashioned. **6** belonging to the past. **7** former or earlier; earliest of two or more things: *Their old house didn't have a garden*. **8** of long standing or long existence: *an old member of the society*. **9** familiar, practised or skilled through long experience: *an old hand*; *the same old excuses*. **10** having the characteristics (e.g. experience, maturity or appearance) of age: *be old beyond one's years*. **11** (*coll*) used in expressions of affection or contempt: *good old Bill*; *silly old fool*. **12** (of a language) being the earliest form known: *Old English*. **13** (*coll*) used for emphasis: *come round any old time*. — *n* **1** an earlier time: *men of old*. **2** (*pl*; with **the**) old people. — **as old as the hills** (*coll*) very old. — **of old** formerly; a long time ago. [OE *eald*]

old age *n* the later part of life.

old age pension *n* a state pension paid to people who have retired from work.

old age pensioner *n* a person in receipt of such a pension.

the Old Bailey *n* the Central Criminal Court in London.

old boy or **girl** *n* **1** (*Br*) a former pupil of a school. **2** (**old boy**; *coll*) an elderly man or woman. **3** (**old boy**; *coll*) an affectionate or familiar form of address.

old boy network *n* (esp. *Br*) the system by which former members of the same public school secure advantages for each other in later life.

old country *n* the country of origin of immigrants.

old dear *n* (*slang*) **1** (often *derog*) an old woman. **2** one's mother.

olden *adj* (*old*) former; past: *in olden days*.

Old English see **English**.

old-fashioned *adj* **1** belonging to, or in a style common, some time ago; out of date. **2** in favour of or living and acting according to the habits and moral views of the past. — *n* **old-fashionedness**.

old flame *n* (*coll*) a person with whom one used to be in love.

old girl see **old boy**.

old guard *n* the original or most conservative members of a society, group or organisation.

old hat see **hat**.

oldie *n* (*coll*) an old person, song, story or thing.

old lady *n* (*slang*) a person's wife or mother.

old lag *n* (esp. *Br slang*) a habitual criminal.

old maid *n* (*coll derog*) **1** a woman who is not married and is thought of as being unlikely ever to marry. **2** a woman or man who is prim and fussy. — *adj* **old-maidish**.

old man *n* **1** (*slang*) a person's husband or father. **2** an affectionate form of address for a man or boy.

old man's beard *n* a wild plant with fluffy white hairs around the seeds.

old master *n* any great painter or painting from the period stretching from the Renaissance to about 1800.

old moon *n* the moon in its last quarter, before the new moon.

Old Nick *n* (*coll*) the devil.

old school *n* people with traditional or old-fashioned ways of thinking, ideas, beliefs, etc.

old school tie *n* **1** a tie with a characteristic pattern or colour worn by former members of a public school. **2** (esp. *Br*) the system by which former members of the same public school do favours for each other in later life.

oldster *n* (*coll*) an old person.

old story *n* something which one has heard before or which has happened before, esp. frequently.

Old Style *n* a method of dating, using the Julian calendar. ◇ See also **New Style**.

Old Testament *n* the first part of the Christian Bible, containing the Hebrew scriptures.

old-time *adj* belonging to or typical of the past.

old-timer *n* **1** a person who has been in a job, position, profession, etc. for a long time; a veteran. **2** (esp. *US coll*) (used esp. as a form of address) an old person.

old wives' tale *n* an ancient belief or theory considered foolish and unscientific.

old woman *n* (*slang*) **1** a person's wife or mother. **2** a person (esp. a man) who is nervous, timid or fussy. — *adj* **old-womanish**.

the Old World *n* the Eastern hemisphere, comprising Europe, Asia and Africa, which forms that part of the world known before the discovery of the Americas. ◇ See also **New World**.

old-world *adj* **1** belonging to earlier times, esp. in being considered quaint or charming; not modern. **2** (*cap*) of the Old World.

oleaginous *adj* of, like or producing oil. [Lat *oleaginus*, from *oleum*, oil]

oleander *n* a poisonous Mediterranean shrub with leathery, evergreen leaves and clusters of white, pink or purple flowers. [Lat]

O level. See **O**[1].

olfactory *adj* of or relating to the sense of smell. [Lat *olfacere*, to smell]

oligarchy *n* **-ies** **1** government by a small group of people. **2** a state or organisation governed by a small group of people. **3** a small group of people which forms a government. — *adj* **oligarchic** or **oligarchical**. [Gr *oligarchia*, from *oligos*, little, few + *archos*, leader]

oligarch *n* a member of an oligarchy.

Oligocene *adj* & *n* (*geol*) (denoting) an epoch of the Tertiary period between Eocene and Miocene. [Gr *oligos*, few + *kainos*, recent]

olive *n* **1** an evergreen Mediterranean tree. **2** the small, oval fruit of this tree, dull yellowish-green when unripe, black when ripe, eaten as a food or pressed to extract its oil. **3** (also **olive green**) the dull yellowish-green colour of unripe olives. **4** the wood of the olive tree. — *adj* **1** dull yellowish-green in colour. **2** (of a complexion) sallow. [Lat *oliva*]

olive branch *n* a sign of a wish for peace or a gesture towards peace or reconciliation.

olive drab *n* the dull grey-green colour of American army uniforms.

olive oil *n* the oil pressed from ripe olives, valued in cooking.

-ology, **-ologic**, **-ological** and **-ologist**. Same as **-logy**, **-logic**, **-logical** and **-logist**.

Olympiad *n* **1** a celebration of the modern Olympic Games. **2** a period of four years between Olympic Games, used by the ancient Greeks as a way of reckoning time. **3** an international contest in esp. chess or bridge. [Gr *Olympias*, of Olympus]

Olympian *n* **1** (*Gr mythol*) any of the twelve ancient Greek gods thought to live on Mount Olympus in N Greece. **2** a person who competes in the Olympic Games. — *adj* **1** (*Gr mythol*) of or relating to Mount Olympus or the ancient Greek gods thought to live there. **2** godlike, esp. in being superior or condescending in behaviour or manners. [Gr *Olympios*, from Gr *Olympos*, Olympus]

Olympic *adj* **1** of the Olympic Games. **2** of ancient Olympia. — *n* (in *pl*) the Olympic Games. [Gr *Olympikos*]

Olympic Games *n* (*pl*) **1** (*hist*) the games celebrated every four years in Olympia in ancient Greece, including athletic, musical and literary competitions. **2** a modern international sports competition held every four years.

OM *abbrev* (*Br*) Order of Merit, an honour awarded for outstanding achievement or for services to the country.

ombudsman *n* **-*men*** an official appointed to investigate complaints against public authorities, government departments, or the people who work for them. [Swedish, legal representative]

omega *n* **1** the last letter of the Greek alphabet (Ω, ω). **2** the last of a series; a conclusion. [Gr *o mega*, great O]

omelette or (esp. *US*) **omelet** *n* a dish of beaten eggs fried in a pan, often folded round a savoury or sweet filling such as cheese or jam. [OFr *alemette*, from *lemelle*, knife-blade]

omen *n* **1** a sign of a future event, either good or evil. **2** threatening or prophetic character: *bird of ill omen.* [Lat]

ominous *adj* threatening; containing a warning of something evil or bad that will happen. — *adv* **ominously**. — *n* **ominousness**. [Lat *ominosus*, from *omen*, omen]

omission *n* **1** something that has been left out or neglected. **2** the act of leaving something out or neglecting it. [Lat *omissio*, from *omittere*, to omit]

omit *v* **-*tt*-** (*tr*) **1** to leave out, either by mistake or on purpose. **2** to fail (to do something). [Lat *omittere*, from *ob*, in front + *mittere*, to send]

omni- *comb fm* all; every. [Lat *omnis*, all]

omnibus *n* **-*ses*** **1** (*old* or *formal*) a bus. **2** a book containing a number of novels or stories by a single author. **3** a television or radio broadcast which brings together a number of programmes originally broadcast separately. — *adj* **1** made up of or bringing together several different items or parts. **2** serving several different purposes at the same time. [Lat, for all]

omnipotent *adj* having very great or absolute power. — *n* **omnipotence**. — *adv* **omnipotently**. [Lat *omnis*, all + *potens*, powerful]

omnipresent *adj* (esp. of a god) present everywhere at the same time. — *n* **omnipresence**. [Lat *omnis*, all + *praesens*, present]

omniscient *adj* knowing everything. — *n* **omniscience**. — *adv* **omnisciently**. [Lat *omnis*, all + *scire*, to know]

omnivorous *adj* **1** eating any type of food, esp. both meat and vegetable matter. **2** taking in, reading, using, etc. everything. — *n* **omnivore**. — *adv* **omnivorously**. — *n* **omnivorousness**. [Lat *omnis*, all + *vorare*, to devour]

on *prep* **1** touching, supported by, attached to, covering or enclosing: *a chair on the floor*; *a dog on a lead*; *a sheet on a bed.* **2** in or into (a vehicle, etc.). **3** carried with: *I've got no money on me.* **4** very near to or along the side of: *a house on the shore.* **5** at or during (a certain day, time, etc.). **6** immediately after, at or before: *He found the letter on his return.* **7** within the (given) limits of: *a picture on page nine.* **8** about: *a book on Jane Austen.* **9** towards: *march on the town.* **10** through contact with; as a result of: *cut oneself on the broken bottle.* **11** in the state or process of: *on fire*; *on a journey.* **12** using as a means of transport. **13** using as a means or medium: *talk on the telephone*; *a tune on the piano.* **14** on the occasion of: *shoot on sight.* **15** having as a basis or source: *on good authority*; *arrested on suspicion.* **16** working for or being a member of: *on the committee*; *work on the case.* **17** at the expense of; to the disadvantage of: *treatment on the National Health*; *The joke's on him.* **18** supported by: *live on bread and cheese*, *on £60 a week.* **19** regularly taking or using: *on tranquillisers.* **20** in a specified manner: *on the cheap.* **21** staked as a bet: *put money on a horse.* **22** following: *disappointment on disappointment.* — *adv* **1** (esp. of clothes) covering; in contact with: *have no clothes on.* **2** ahead, forwards or towards in space or time: *go on home*; *later on.* **3** continuously; without interruption: *keep on about something.* **4** in or into operation or activity: *put the radio on.* — *adj* **1** working, broadcasting or performing: *You're on in two minutes.* **2** taking place: *Which films are on this week?* **3** (*coll*) possible, practicable or acceptable: *That just isn't on.* **4** (*coll*) talking continuously, esp. to complain or nag: *always on at him to try harder.* **5** in favour of a win: *odds of 3 to 4 on.* **6** (*cricket*) on the side of the field towards which the bat is facing, usu. the batsman's left and the bowler's right. ◇ See also **off** (sense **4**). — *n* (*cricket*) the side of the field towards which the bat is facing, usu. the batsman's left and the bowler's right. ◇ See also **off**. — **just on** almost exactly. — **on and off** now and then; occasionally. — **on and on** continually; at length. — **on time** promptly; at the right time. — **on to** or (*coll*) **onto** **1** to a position on or in. **2** (*coll*) having become aware of or having discovered: *be on to his cheating.* **3** in or into contact with: *get on to her about this.* [OE]

oncoming *adj* approaching; advancing. — *n* an approach.

ongoing *adj* continuing; in progress.

on-line *adj* (of e.g. a printer) under the direct control of a computer, and therefore ready for use. ◇ See also **off-line**.

onlooker *n* a person who watches and does not take part; an observer. — *n* **onlooking**.

on-off *adj* (of a switch) able to be set to either the 'on' position or the 'off' position.

onrush *n* a sudden and strong movement forward.

onscreen *adj* & *adv* (with or using an image or picture) shown on a television or computer screen.

onset *n* **1** a beginning, esp. of something unpleasant. **2** an attack.

onshore *adj* & *adv* **1** (of a wind, etc.) blowing or moving towards the shore. **2** on, on to, or near the shore.

onside *adj* & *adv* (*football*, *rugby*, etc.) in a position where the ball may legally be played.

on-stage *adj* & *adv* on the stage and able to be seen by the audience.

on-stream *adj* & *adv* (of an industrial plant, process, etc.) in operation or ready to go into operation.

onto see **on to** above.

onward *adj* moving forward in place or time. — *adv* (also **onwards**) **1** towards or at a place or time which is advanced or in front. **2** forward. **3** continuing to move forwards or progress.

onager *n* a wild ass found in central Asia. [Gr *onagros*]

onanism *n* **1** sexual intercourse where the penis is withdrawn from the vagina before ejaculation. **2** masturbation. [From *Onan*, a character in the Bible (Gen 38.9)]

ONC *abbrev* Ordinary National Certificate, a qualification in a technical subject, more or less equivalent to an A-level.

once *adv* **1** a single time; on one occasion. **2** at some time in the past. **3** ever; at any time: *if once you are late*. **4** by one degree of relationship: *a cousin once removed*. — *conj* as soon as. — *n* one time or occasion. — **all at once 1** suddenly. **2** all at the same time. — **at once** immediately; without any delay. — **(just) for once** on this one occasion only; as an exception. — **once again** or **more** one more time, as before. — **once (and) for all** for the last time; now and never again. — **once in a way** or **while** occasionally; rarely. — **once or twice** a few times. — **once upon a time** (used to begin fairy-tales) at a certain time in the past. [OE *ænes*]

once-over *n* (*coll*) a quick, often casual examination: *give the car the once-over*.

oncology *n* the study of tumours, esp. those which are cancerous. — *n* **oncologist**. [Gr *onkos*, mass, tumour + **-logy**]

OND *abbrev* Ordinary National Diploma, a qualification in a technical subject reached after a two-year full-time or sandwich course, recognised by many professional institutions.

one *adj* **1** being a single unit, number or thing. **2** being a particular person or thing, esp. as distinct from another or others of the same kind: *lift one leg and then the other*. **3** being a particular but unspecified instance or example: *visit him one day soon*. **4** being the only such: *the one woman who can beat her*. **5** same; identical: *of one mind*. **6** undivided; forming a single whole: *a choir singing with one voice*. **7** first: *page one*. **8** (*coll*) an exceptional example or instance of: *one hell of an argument*. **9** aged 1. — *n* **1** the number or figure 1; any symbol for this number. **2** the age of 1. **3** a unity or unit. **4** something, esp. a garment or a person whose size is denoted by the number 1. **5** 1 o'clock. **6** (*coll*) a story or joke: *Heard the one about the singing policeman?* **7** (*coll*; **for**) an enthusiast: *She's quite a one for chess*. **8** (*coll*) a drink, esp. an alcoholic one: *drop in for a quick one*. **9** (*coll*) a daring, remarkable or cheeky person: *You are a one!* **10** a score of 1 point. — *pron* **1** (often referring to a noun already mentioned or implied) an individual person, thing, example or instance: *buy the blue one*. **2** anybody: *One can't do better than that*. **3** I; me: *One doesn't like to pry*. — **all one** just the same; of no consequence. — **at one (with)** in agreement. — **be one up on** (*coll*) to have an advantage over (someone). — **for one** as one person: *I for one don't agree*. — **(all) in one 1** together; combined; as one unit, object etc. **2** in one go or attempt. — **just one of those things** an unfortunate event or situation that must be accepted. — **one and all** everyone. — **one and only** (used for emphasis) only. — **one another** used as the object of a verb when the action of that verb involves exchange between people: *love one another*; *refuse to speak to one another*. ◇ See also **each other**. — **one by one** one after the other; individually. — **one or two** (*coll*) a few. [OE *an*]

one-armed bandit *n* a fruit machine with a long handle at the side which is pulled down hard to make the machine work.

one-horse *adj* **1** using a single horse. **2** (*coll*) small, poor, and of little importance.

one-liner *n* (*coll*) a short, amusing remark or joke made in a single sentence.

one-man or **one-woman** *adj* done by one person.

oneness *n* **1** the state or quality of being one; singleness. **2** agreement. **3** the state of being the same. **4** the state of being unique.

one-night stand *n* **1** a performance given only once in any place, the next performance taking place somewhere else. **2** (*coll*) a romantic or sexual relationship which lasts for only one night.

one-off *n* & *adj* (*coll*, esp. *Br*) (something which is) made or happening on one occasion only.

one-parent family *n* a family consisting of a child or children and one parent, the other parent being dead or estranged.

one-piece *adj* made in a single piece as opposed to separate parts.

oneself *pron* **1** the reflexive of *one*: *not able to help oneself*. **2** used for emphasis. **3** one's normal self: *not be feeling oneself yet after the operation.*

one-sided *adj* **1** (of a competition) with one person or side having a great advantage over the other. **2** seeing, accepting, representing or favouring only one side of a subject; unfair; partial. — *adv* **one-sidedly**. — *n* **one-sidedness**.

one-time *adj* former.

one-to-one *adj* **1** with one person or thing exactly corresponding to or matching another. **2** in which a person is involved with only one other person: *one-to-one teaching*.

one-track mind *n* (*coll*) an obsession with one idea.

one-up *adj* having a particular advantage.

one-upmanship *n* the art of gaining pyschological, social or professional advantages over other people.

one-way *adj* **1** (of a road or street) in which traffic can move in one direction only. **2** (of a feeling or relationship) not returned or reciprocated. **3** (esp. *US*) (of a ticket) valid for travel in one direction only, not back again.

one-woman see **one-man**.

onerous *adj* heavy; hard to bear or do; demanding a lot of effort. — *adv* **onerously**. — *n* **onerousness**. [Lat *onerosus*, from *onus*, burden]

onion *n* a vegetable with an edible bulb which has a strong taste and smell. — *adj* **oniony**. — **know one's onions** (*coll*) to know one's subject or one's job well. [Lat *unio*, unity, large pearl, onion]

only *adj* **1** without any others of the same type. **2** (of a child) having no brothers or sisters. **3** (*coll*) best: *Flying is the only way to travel.* — *adv* **1** not more than; just. **2** alone; solely. **3** not longer ago than; not until: *only a minute ago*. **4** merely; with no other result than: *I arrived only to find he had already left.* — *conj* **1** but; however: *Come if you want to, only don't complain if you're bored.* **2** if it were not for the fact that: *I'd come with you on the boat only I know I'll be sick if I do.* — **if only** I wish: *If only you could be on time for once.* — **only too** very; extremely. [OE *anlic*]

o.n.o. *abbrev* (*Br*) or near(est) offer.

onomatopoeia *n* the formation or use of a word which imitates the sound or action represented, such as *boo*, *hiss* and *squelch*. — *adj* **onomatopoeic**. [Gr *onoma*, name + *poieein*, to make]

onslaught *n* a fierce attack. [ODut *aenslag*]

ontology *n* (*philos*) the science dealing with the nature of being. — *adj* **ontological**. — *adv* **ontologically**. [Gr *on*, being + **-logy**]

onus *n* **-ses** a responsibility or burden. [Lat, burden]

onyx *n* a precious stone with layers of different colours. [Gr, nail]

oodles *n* (*pl*; *coll*) lots.

ooh *interj* an expression of pleasure, surprise, excitement or pain.

oolite *n* limestone formed from fine grains of calcium carbonate which look like fish eggs. [Gr *oion*, egg + *lithos*, stone]

oompah *n* (*coll*) a common way of representing the deep sound made by a large, brass musical instrument. [Imit.]

oomph *n* (*coll*) **1** energy; enthusiasm. **2** personal attractiveness, esp. sex appeal.

oops *interj* (*coll*) an exclamation of surprise or apology made when a person makes a mistake, drops something, etc. — **oops-a-daisy** (*coll*) an expression used e.g. when helping up or encouraging a child who has had a slight accident, fallen over, etc.

ooze[1] *v* **1** (*intr*) to flow or leak out gently or slowly. **2** (*intr*) (of a substance) to give out moisture. **3** (*tr*) to give out (a liquid, etc.) slowly: *a wound oozing blood.* **4** (*tr*) to overflow with (a quality or feeling): *ooze charm.* — *n* **1** anything which oozes. **2** a slow, gentle leaking or oozing. **3** an infusion of bark and other vegetable matter used for tanning leather. — *adj* **oozy**. [OE *wos*, sap, juice]

ooze[2] *n* **1** soft mud or slime found at the bottom of a lake, river or estuary. **2** soft, boggy ground. — *adj* **oozy**, ***-ier***, ***-iest***. [OE *wase*, marsh, mire]

op[1] *abbrev* opus.

op[2] *n* (*coll*) a surgical or military operation. [Abbrev.]

opacity *n* ***-ies*** **1** opaqueness. **2** the state of having an obscure meaning and being difficult to understand. [Lat *opacitas*, from *opacus*, opaque]

opal *n* a blue-white or milk-white precious stone, which has pink and green iridescent reflections in it according to the surrounding light. [Prob. Sanskrit *upala*, precious stone]

opalescent *adj* reflecting different colours as the surrounding light changes, like an opal. — *n* **opalescence**.

opaque *adj* **1** not able to be seen through; not transparent. **2** difficult to understand. — *adv* **opaquely**. — *n* **opaqueness**. ◇ See also **opacity**. [Lat *opacus*]

op. cit. *abbrev* for *opere citato* (Lat), in the work already quoted.

OPEC *abbrev* Organisation of Petroleum Exporting Countries, a group of petroleum-producing countries who decide how much should be produced each year and how much it should be sold for.

open *adj* **1** allowing things or people to go in or out; not blocked, closed or locked. **2** (of a container) not sealed; with the inside visible. **3** not enclosed, confined or restricted: *the open sea*; *an open view*. **4** not covered, guarded or protected: *an open wound.* **5** spread out or unfolded: *an open book*. **6** (**to**) (of a shop, etc.) receiving customers; ready for business. **7** generally known; public: *an open secret*. **8** (**to**) able to be attacked or questioned: *leave oneself open to abuse*. **9** (**to**) not restricted, allowing anyone to compete or take part, esp.

both amateurs and professionals. **10** free from restraint or restrictions of any kind: *the open fishing season.* **11** not decided; still being discussed: *an open question.* **12** ready to consider new ideas; unprejudiced: *an open mind.* **13** ready and willing to talk honestly; candid. **14** (esp. *in cmpds*) eagerly attentive, surprised or alarmed: *open-mouthed disbelief*; *open-eyed.* **15** (of cloth, etc.) having a lot of small openings or gaps. **16** (*phon*) (of a vowel) produced with the tongue low in the mouth. **17** (*phon*) (of a syllable) ending in a vowel. **18** (*music*) (of a string) not stopped by a finger. **19** (*music*) (of a note) played on an open string, or without holes being covered by fingers. **20** (of a cheque) to be paid in cash to the person named on it; not crossed. — *v* **-n-** **1** (*tr* & *intr*) to make or become open or more open. **2** (*tr* & *intr*) to unfasten or become unfastened to allow access. **3** (*tr* & *intr*; **out**) to spread out or be spread out or unfolded, esp. so as to see or be seen. **4** (*tr* & *intr*) to start or begin working: *The shop opens at nine.* **5** (*tr*) to declare open with an official ceremony: *open the new hospital.* **6** (*tr* & *intr*; **with**) to begin or start speaking, writing, etc. **7** (*intr*; **into**, **on to**, etc.) to provide access into or on to: *a gate opening into the field.* **8** (*tr*; **up**, **to**) to reveal (the feelings in one's heart, thoughts in one's mind, etc.). **9** (*tr*) to arrange (a bank account), usu. by making one's first deposit. **10** (*tr* & *intr*; *cricket*) to begin (the batting) for one's team. **11** (*intr*) (of legal counsel) to make a preliminary statement about a case before beginning to call witnesses. — *n* **1** (with **the**) an area of open country; an area not obstructed by buildings, etc. **2** public notice or attention: *bring the issue out into the open.* **3** (*cap*) a sports contest which both amateurs and professionals may enter. — *n* **openness**. — **open and above board** thoroughly honest or legal. — *v* **open out** or **up** (*intr*) to begin to reveal one's feelings and thoughts or to behave with less restraint. — *v* **open up 1** (*intr*) to open the door. **2** (*tr*) to make more accessible or available: *roads opening up the more remote areas.* **3** (*intr*) to start firing. **4** (*intr*) (of a game, etc.) to become more interesting as it develops. **5** (*tr*) to accelerate (a car, throttle, etc.). [OE]

open air *n* unenclosed space outdoors. — *adj* (**open-air**) in the open air; outside.

open-and-shut *adj* easily proved, decided or solved.

open book *n* a person who keeps no secrets and is easily understood.

opencast *adj* (of mines or mining) done at or just below the earth's surface by removing the surface soil covering the mineral mined for, and not by excavation.

open day *n* a day when members of the public are allowed to visit a place which is usu. closed to them.

open-ended *adj* with no limits or restrictions, e.g. of time, set in advance.

opener *n* **1** (usu. *in cmpds*) a device for opening something: *bottle-opener.* **2** the first item on a programme. **3** (*cricket*) either of the two batsmen who begin the batting for their team. — **for openers** to start with.

open fire *n* a fireplace in a house where coal, coke or wood may be burnt.

open-handed *adj* generous. — *adv* **open-handedly**. — *n* **open-handedness**.

open-hearted *adj* **1** honest, direct and hiding nothing; candid. **2** kind; generous. — *adv* **open-heartedly**. — *n* **open-heartedness**.

open-heart surgery *n* surgery on the heart in which the circulation of the blood is temporarily taken over by a heart-lung machine so that the heart may be examined and treated.

open house *n* the state of being willing to welcome and entertain visitors at any time: *keep open house.*

opening *n* **1** a hole, gap. **2** the act of making or becoming open. **3** a beginning. **4** the first performance of a play, opera, etc. **5** (*chess*) a recognised sequence of moves played at the beginning of a game. **6** an opportunity or chance. **7** a preliminary statement about a legal case made by counsel before witnesses are called. — *adj* of, relating to or forming an opening; first: *opening night at the opera.*

opening time *n* the time at which a public house, bar, hotel etc. can begin to sell alcoholic drinks.

open letter *n* a letter, esp. one of protest, addressed to a person or organisation, etc. but intended also for publication in a newspaper or magazine.

openly *adv* without trying to hide anything; in a direct and honest manner.

open market *n* a market in which buyers and sellers are allowed to compete without restriction.

open-minded *adj* willing to consider or receive new ideas; unprejudiced. — *adv* **open-mindedly**. — *n* **open-mindedness**.

open-plan *adj* having few internal walls and large, undivided rooms.

open prison *n* a prison which allows prisoners who are neither dangerous nor violent considerably more freedom of movement than in normal prisons.

open sandwich *n* a sandwich without a top slice of bread.

open season *n* a period of the year in which particular animals, birds, fish, etc. may be legally killed for sport.

open sesame *n* a means of gaining access to something which is otherwise out of one's reach.

open shop *n* a firm, business, etc. which does not oblige its employees to belong to a trade union. ◇ See also **closed shop**.

Open University *n* (*Br*) a university with no fixed entrance requirements, which teaches mainly by correspondence and using television and radio broadcasts.

open verdict *n* a verdict given by the coroner's jury at the end of an inquest that death has occurred, but without giving details of whether it was suicide, accidental, murder, etc.

openwork *n* work in cloth, metal, wood, etc., so constructed to have gaps or holes in it, used esp. for decoration.

opera[1] *n* **1** a dramatic work set to music, in which the singers are usu. accompanied by an orchestra. **2** operas as an art-form. **3** a theatre where operas are performed. **4** a company which performs operas. [Ital, from Lat, work]

opera-glass *n* small binoculars used at the theatre or opera.

opera-hat *n* a man's collapsible top hat.

opera-house *n* a theatre specially built for the performance of operas.

operatic *adj* of or like an opera, esp. in being dramatic. — *adv* **operatically**.

opera[2]. See **opus**.

operable *adj* **1** (of a disease, injury, etc.) that can be treated by surgery. **2** that can be operated. — *n* **operability**. [Lat *operabilis*, from *opus*, work]

operate *v* **1** (*tr* & *intr*) to (cause to) function or work. **2** (*intr*) to produce an effect or have an influence. **3** (*tr*) to manage, control or direct (a business, etc.). **4** (*intr*; **for, on**) to perform surgery. **5** (*intr*) to perform military, naval, police, etc. operations. [Lat *operari*, to work]

operating system *n* a set of programs which control the basic functions of a computer.

operating table *n* a special table on which surgery is performed.

operating theatre or **room** *n* the specially equipped room in a hospital where surgery is performed.

operatic. See **opera**[1].

operation *n* **1** an act, method or process of working or operating. **2** the state of working or being active: *The factory is not yet in operation*. **3** an activity; something done. **4** an action or series of actions which have a particular effect. **5** an act of surgery to treat a part of the body that is diseased or damaged. **6** (often in *pl*) one of a series of military, naval, police, etc. actions performed as part of a much larger plan. **7** (*math*) a process, such as addition and subtraction, by which a number is derived from another number or numbers. **8** a financial transaction. [Lat *operatio*]

operational *adj* **1** of or relating to an operation. **2** able or ready to work. — *adv* **operationally**.

operational or **operations research** *n* the analysis of problems in business and industry in order to bring about more efficient work practices.

operative *adj* **1** working; in action; having an effect. **2** (of a word) especially important or significant: *'Must' is the operative word.* **3** of or relating to a surgical operation. — *n* **1** a worker, esp. one with special skills. **2** (*US*) a private detective. [Lat *operativus*, from *opus*, work]

operator *n* **1** a person who operates a machine or apparatus. **2** a person who operates a telephone switchboard, connecting calls, etc. **3** a person who runs a business. **4** any symbol or letter used in mathematics and logic to show that a particular process is to be applied, e.g. × in mathematics, which shows that two numbers are to be multiplied. **5** (*coll*) a calculating, shrewd and manipulative person. [**operate**]

operetta *n* a short, usu. romantic, amusing and light-hearted opera. [Ital, little opera]

ophthalmia *n* inflammation of the eye, esp. of the conjunctiva. [Gr *opthalmos*, eye]

ophthalmic *adj* of or relating to the eye. [Gr *ophthalmos*, eye]

ophthalmic optician *n* an optician qualified to test people's eyes and prescibe, make and sell glasses or contact lenses.

ophthalmology *n* the scientific study of the eye. — *n* **ophthalmologist**. [Gr *ophthalmos*, eye + **-logy**]

ophthalmoscope *n* an instrument for examining the inside of the eye. [Gr *ophthalmos*, eye + **-scope**]

opiate *n* **1** any drug containing opium, used to cause sleep or relieve pain. **2** anything that calms or dulls the mind or feelings. [**opium**]

opine *v* (*tr*) to suppose or express as an opinion. [Lat *opinari*, to think]

opinion *n* **1** a belief or judgement which seems likely to be true, but which is not based on proof. **2** (**on, about**) what one thinks about something. **3** a professional judgement given by an expert: *medical opinion*. **4** estimation or appreciation: *have a low opinion of his abilities*. — **a matter of opinion** a matter about which people have different opinions. — **be of the opinion that** to think or believe that. [Lat *opinio*, belief]

opinionated *adj* having very strong opinions which one refuses to change; stubborn.

opium *n* **1** an addictive drug made from juice from the seeds of a variety of poppy, used in medicine to cause sleep and relieve pain. **2** anything which has a soothing, calming or dulling effect on people's minds. [Gr *opion*, poppy-juice]

opossum *n* any of several small, tree-dwelling, American or Australian marsupials with thick fur and a strong tail for gripping. [From an American Indian language]

opp. *abbrev* opposite.

opponent *n* a person who belongs to the opposing side in an argument, contest or battle. [Lat *opponere*, to set before or against]

opportune *adj* **1** (of an action) happening at a time which is suitable, proper or correct. **2** (of a time) suitable; proper. — *adv* **opportunely**. — *n* **opportuneness**. [Lat *opportunus*, from *ob*, before + *portus*, harbour, used orig. of a wind blowing towards a harbour]

opportunist *n* a person who shapes his or her policies or conduct to take advantage of opportunities and circumstances, without bothering about principles or possible consequences. — *adj* of such behaviour; behaving in this way. — *n* **opportunism**. — *adj* **opportunistic**.

opportunity *n* **-ies 1** (**for**) an occasion offering a possibility; a chance. **2** favourable or advantageous conditions. [Lat *opportunitas*, from *opportunus*, opportune]

oppose *v* **1** (*tr*) to resist or fight against by force or argument. **2** (*intr*) to object. **3** (*intr*) to compete in a game, contest, etc. against another person or team. **4** (*tr*) to place opposite or in contrast to so as to counterbalance. — *adj* **opposed** (**to**). — *n* **opposer**. — *adj* **opposing**. — **as opposed to** in contrast to. [Lat *opponere*, to set before or against + Fr *poser*, to place]

opposite *adj* **1** being on the other side of, or at the other end of, a real or imaginary line or space. **2** facing in a directly different direction: *opposite sides of the coin*. **3** completely or diametrically different. **4** being the other of a matching or contrasting pair: *the opposite sex*. **5** (*bot*) (of leaves) growing in pairs with one leaf on each side of the stem. — *n* an opposite person or thing. — *adv* in or into an opposite position: *live opposite*. — *prep* **1** (to a position) across from and facing: *a house opposite the station*. **2** (of an actor) in a role which complements that taken by another actor; co-starring with: *play opposite Gielgud*. [Lat *oppositus*, from *ob*, against + *ponere*, to place]

opposite number *n* a person with an equivalent position or job in another company, country, etc.

opposition *n* **1** (**to**) the act of resisting or fighting against (someone or something) by force or argument. **2** the state of being hostile or in conflict. **3** a person or group of people who are opposed to something. **4** (*cap*) a political party which opposes the party in power. **5** an act of opposing or being placed opposite. **6** (*astron & astrol*) the position of a planet or star when it is directly opposite another, esp. the sun, as seen from the earth. [Lat *oppositio*]

oppress *v* (*tr*) **1** to govern with cruelty and injustice. **2** to worry, trouble or make anxious; to weigh heavily upon. — *n* **oppressor**. [Lat *oppressare*, from *ob*, against + *premere*, to press]

oppression *n* **1** the state of suffering cruelty and injustice. **2** worry or mental distress.

oppressive *adj* **1** cruel, tyrannical and unjust. **2** causing worry or mental distress; weighing heavily on the mind. **3** (of the weather) hot and sultry. — *adv* **oppressively**. — *n* **oppressiveness**.

opprobrious *adj* insulting, abusive or severely critical. — *adv* **opprobriously**. [Lat *opprobriosus*]

opprobrium *n* (anything which causes) public shame, disgrace or loss of favour. [Lat, from *ob*, against + *probrum*, reproach, disgrace]

oppugn *v* (*tr*) to call into question; to dispute. [Lat *ob*, against + *pugnare*, to fight]

ops *n* (*pl*; *mil*) operations.

opt *v* (*intr*; **for**) (where there is more than one possibility) to decide between or choose to do. — *v* **opt out** (*intr*; **of**) **1** to choose or decide not to take part in something. **2** (of a school or hospital) to leave local authority control. [Lat *optare*, to choose]

optic *adj* of or concerning the eye or vision. [Gr *optikos*]

optical *adj* **1** of or concerning sight or what one sees. **2** of or concerning light or optics. **3** (of a lens) designed to help sight. — *adv* **optically**.

optical character recognition *n* (*comput*) the scanning, identification and recording of printed characters by a photoelectric device attached to a computer.

optical fibre *n* a thin strand of glass through which light signals may be transmitted.

optical illusion *n* a thing which has an appearance which deceives the eye; misunderstanding caused by a deceptive appearance.

optics *n* (*sing*) the scientific study of light and vision.

optician *n* **1** a person who makes and sells glasses and contact lenses. **2** (*loosely*) an ophthalmic optician. **[optic]**

optimal *adj* the best or most favourable. [Lat *optimus*, best]

optimism *n* **1** a tendency to take a bright, hopeful view of things and expect the best possible outcome. **2** (*philos*) the belief that we live in the best of all possible worlds. **3** the theory that good will ultimately triumph over evil. — *n* **optimist**. — *adj* **optimistic**. — *adv* **optimistically**. [Lat *optimus*, best]

optimise or **-ize** *v* (*tr*) to make the most or best of; to make the most efficient use of. [Lat *optimus*, best + **-ise**]

optimum *n* **-ma** or **-mums** the most favourable condition or situation. — *adj* the best or most favourable. [Lat *optimus*, best]

option *n* **1** an act of choosing. **2** that which is or which may be chosen. **3** the power or right to choose: *You have no option*. **4** the exclusive right to buy or sell something, e.g. stocks, at a fixed price and within a specified time-limit. — **keep** or **leave one's options open** to avoid making a choice or committing oneself to a particular course of action. [Lat *optio*, from *optare*, to choose]

optional *adj* a matter of choice; not compulsory. — *adv* **optionally**.

soft option *n* a course of action which is chosen because it is easy or requires little effort.

opulent *adj* **1** rich; wealthy. **2** luxurious. **3** abundant. — *n* **opulence**. — *adv* **opulently**. [Lat *opulentus*]

opus *n* **-ses** or ***opera*** an artistic work, esp. a musical composition, often used with a number to show the order in which a composer's works were composed: *Two Rhapsodies, Brahms opus 21*. [Lat, work]

or[1] *conj* used to introduce: **1** alternatives: *red or pink or blue*. **2** a synonym or explanation: *a puppy or young dog*. **3** an afterthought: *She's laughing — or is she crying?* **4** the second part of an indirect question: *Ask her whether she thinks he'll come or not*. **5** because if not; or else: *run or you'll be late*. **6** and not: *never joins in or helps*. — **or else 1** otherwise. **2** (*coll*) expressing a threat or warning: *Give it to me or else!* — **or rather** or to be more accurate: *He went too, or rather I heard he did*. — **or so** about; roughly: *been there two hours or so*. [MidE *other*]

or[2] *n* (*heraldry*) a gold colour. [Fr, from Lat *aurum*, gold]

OR *abbrev* Oregon.

-or *sfx* used to form words meaning the person or thing performing the action: *actor*; *elevator*. [MidE, from OFr]

oracle *n* **1** a holy place in ancient Greece or Rome where a god was believed to give advice and prophecy. **2** a priest or priestess at an oracle, through whom the god was believed to speak. **3** the usu. mysterious or ambiguous advice or prophecy given at an oracle. **4** a person who is believed to have great wisdom or be capable of prophesying the future. **5** a statement made by such a person. **6** (*cap*; ®) a teletext service run by the Independent Broadcasting Authority. [Lat *oraculum*]

oracular *adj* **1** of or like an oracle. **2** difficult to interpret; mysterious and ambiguous. **3** prophetic.

oral *adj* **1** spoken or verbal; not written. **2** of or used in the mouth. **3** (esp. of a medicine) taken in through the mouth. **4** (*psychol*) of a supposed stage of infant development, when satisfaction is obtained through sucking. — *n* a spoken test or examination. — *adv* **orally**. [Lat *os*, mouth]

orange *n* **1** a round, juicy citrus fruit with a thick reddish-yellow skin and sharp, sweet taste. **2** the evergreen tree on which it grows. **3** the reddish-yellow colour of its skin. **4** (a glass of) an orange-flavoured drink. — *adj* orange-coloured or orange-flavoured. — *adj* **orangey**. [Sanskrit *naranga*]

orangeade *n* a usu. fizzy orange-flavoured drink.

orangery *n* **-ies** a greenhouse or building which allows orange trees to be grown in cool climates.

Orangeman *n* **-men** a member of a society founded in 1795 to support Protestantism in Ireland. [William of *Orange*, later William III of the United Kingdom]

orang-utan or **orang-outang** *n* a large ape with shaggy reddish-brown hair and long, strong arms, found in the forests of Borneo and Sumatra. [Malay *orang*, man + *hutan*, forest]

oration *n* a formal or ceremonial public speech in dignified language. [Lat *oratio*]

orator *n* **1** a person who is skilled in persuading, moving or exciting people through public speech. **2** a person who gives an oration. [Lat, from *orare*, to pray]

oratorial *adj* of an orator, an oratory or an oratorio.

oratorical *adj* **1** of an orator. **2** like oratory, esp. in using rhetoric. — *adv* **oratorically**.

oratory *n* **-ies 1** the art of speaking well in public, esp. using elegant rhetorical devices. **2** a small place or chapel for private prayer.

oratorio *n* **-os** a usu. Biblical or religious story set to music, sung by soloists and a chorus accompanied by an orchestra, but without scenery, costumes or acting. [Ital, from Lat *oratorium*, oratory (sense **2**), so called because it developed out of singing in religious services held in oratories]

orb *n* **1** a globe decorated with jewels and with a cross on top, carried by the monarch during important ceremonies. **2** anything in the shape of a globe. **3** (*poetic*) a star, the sun or a planet. **4** (*poetic*) the eyeball. [Lat *orbis*, circle]

orbit *n* **1** the curved path in which something, e.g. a moon or spacecraft, moves around a planet or star. **2** one complete passage round this path. **3** a sphere of influence or action. **4** (*anat*) the bony hollow in which the eyeball rests. — *v* **1** (*intr* & *tr*) to move in an orbit (round something). **2** (*tr*) to put (a spacecraft, etc.) into orbit. [Lat *orbitus*, from *orbis*, circle]

orbital *adj* **1** of or going round in an orbit. **2** (of a road) running in a complete circle or loop round a city.

Orcadian *adj* of the Orkney Islands. — *n* a person who lives or was born in the Orkney Islands. [Gr *Orkades*, Orkney]

orchard *n* a garden or piece of land where fruit trees are grown. [OE *ortgeard*]

orchestra *n* **1** a usu. large group of musicians who play a variety of different instruments as an ensemble, led by a conductor. **2** (also **orchestra pit**) that part of a theatre or opera-house where the orchestra sits, usu. in front of or under the stage.

3 in the ancient Greek theatre, a semicircular area in front of the stage where the chorus danced. [Gr, from *orcheisthai*, to dance]

orchestral *adj* of, for, or played by an orchestra.

orchestrate *v* (*tr*) **1** to arrange or compose (a piece of music) for an orchestra. **2** to organise or arrange (something) so as to get the desired or best result. — *n* **orchestration**. — *n* **orchestrator**.

orchid *n* any of several types of plant which usu. have brightly-coloured, showy flowers, with one lip-shaped petal which is much larger than the others. [Gr *orchis*, testicle, so called because of the shape of its root-tubers]

ordain *v* (*tr*) **1** to make (someone) a priest, vicar, etc. **2** to order or command formally. **3** to destine. — *adj* **ordained**. — *n* **ordainment**. ◇ See also **ordination**. [Lat *ordinare*, from *ordo*, order]

ordeal *n* **1** a difficult, painful or testing experience. **2** (*hist*) a method of trial in which the accused person was subjected to physical danger from fire, water, etc., survival of which was taken as a sign from God of that person's innocence. [OE *ordal*]

order *n* **1** a state in which everything is in its proper place; tidiness. **2** an arrangement of objects according to importance, value, position, etc. **3** a command, instruction or direction. **4** a state of peace and harmony in society, characterised by the absence of crime and the general obeying of laws. **5** the condition of being able to function properly: *out of order*. **6** a social class or rank making up a distinct social group: *the lower orders*. **7** a kind or sort. **8** an instruction to a manufacturer, supplier, waiter, etc. to provide something. **9** the goods, food, etc. supplied. **10** an established system of society: *a new world order*. **11** (*biol*) a category in the classification of animals and plants which is below a class and above a family. **12** (*banking*, etc.) a written instruction to pay money. **13** the usual procedure followed at esp. official meetings and during debates: *a point of order*. **14** (*cap*; also **religious order**) a religious community living according to a particular rule and bound by vows. **15** any of the different grades of the Christian ministry. **16** (often in *pl*; also **holy orders**) the office of an ordained member of the Christian clergy: *take holy orders* (= join the clergy). **17** the specified form of a religious service: *order of marriage*. **18** (*cap*) a group of people to which new members are admitted as a mark of honour or reward for services to the sovereign or country: *the Order of the Garter*. **19** any of the five classical styles of architecture characterised by the way a column and entablature are moulded and decorated. — *v* **-r- 1** (*tr*) to give a command to. **2** (*tr*) to command (someone) to go to a specified place: *order the regiment to Germany*. **3** (*tr*) to instruct a manufacturer, supplier, waiter to supply or provide (something). **4** (*tr*) to arrange or regulate: *order one's affairs*. **5** (*intr*) to give a command, request or order, esp. to a waiter for food. — *interj* (also **Order! Order!**) a call for quiet, calm, proper behaviour to be restored, esp. during a debate. — *adj* **ordered**. — **call to order 1** to request calm, peaceful behaviour. **2** to declare a formal meeting open. — **in order 1** in accordance with the rules; properly arranged. **2** suitable or appropriate: *Such behaviour just isn't in order*. **3** in the correct sequence. — **in the order of** approximately (the number stated). — **in order that** so that. — **in order to** so as to be able to. — **on order** (of goods) having been ordered but not yet supplied. — *v* **order about** or **around** (*tr*) to give orders to (someone) continually, esp. making him or her rush from place to place. — *v* **order off** (*tr*) (*sport*) to order (a player) to leave the field because of bad or illegal behaviour. — **out of order** not correct, proper or suitable: *Your behaviour is out of order*. — **a tall order** (*coll*) a difficult or demanding job or task. — **to order** according to a customer's particular or personal requirements. — **under orders** having been commanded or instructed (to do something). [Lat *ordo*]

orderly *adj* **1** in good order; well-arranged. **2** well-behaved; quiet. — *n* **-ies 1** an attendant, usu. without medical training, who does various jobs in a hospital, such as moving patients. **2** (*mil*) a soldier who carries an officer's orders and messages. — *n* **orderliness**.

order of battle *n* the positions adopted by soldiers or ships before a battle.

Order of Merit see **OM**.

Order of the British Empire see **OBE**.

order of the day *n* **1** an agenda, e.g. for a meeting or for business in parliament. **2** that which is necessary, normal or fashionable at a given time.

order paper *n* a programme showing the order of business, esp. in Parliament.

ordinal *n* **1** (also **ordinal number**) a number which shows a position in a sequence, e.g. *first, second, third*, etc. ◇ See also **cardinal number**. **2** a Roman Catholic service book, or a service book containing the services for the ordination of ministers. — *adj* of an ordinal number; of or relating to a position in a sequence. [Lat *ordinalis*, from *ordo*, order]

ordinance *n* **1** a law, order or ruling. **2** an authorised religious ceremony. [Lat *ordinare*, from *ordo*, order]

ordinand *n* a person who is training to become a minister of the church. [Lat *ordinare*, from *ordo*, order]

ordinary *adj* usual; normal; unexceptional; familiar. — *n* **-ies** (*cap*) those parts of the Mass which do not vary from day to day. — *adv* **ordinarily**. — *n* **ordinariness**. — **in the ordinary way** if things are as normal; usually. — **out of the ordinary** unusual; strange. [Lat *ordinarius*, from *ordo*, order]

Ordinary grade see **O grade** at **O**[1].

Ordinary level see **O level** at **O**[1].

ordinary seaman *n* **-men** a sailor of the lowest rank in the Royal Navy.

ordinate *n* (*math*) a co-ordinate which gives the position of a point measured along the vertical line of a graph. ◇ See also **abscissa**. **[ordinance]**

ordination *n* the act or ceremony of ordaining a priest or minister of the church. [Lat *ordinatio*, from *ordo*, order]

ordnance *n* **1** heavy guns and military supplies. **2** the government department responsible for military supplies. **[ordinance]**

Ordnance Survey *n* (*Br*) (a government department responsible for) the production of official, large-scale maps of the United Kingdom.

Ordovician *adj* & *n* (denoting) a geological period lasting from 505 to 438 million years ago. [Lat *Ordovices*, a British tribe]

ordure *n* waste matter from the bowels; excrement. [OFr *ord*, foul]

ore *n* a rock or mineral containing a metal or other valuable substance which can be removed from it, and for which it is mined. [OE *ora*, unwrought metal combined with OE *ar*, brass]

Ore. or **Oreg.** *abbrev* Oregon.

oregano *n* a sweet-smelling Mediterranean herb used as a flavouring in cooking. [Gr *origanon*]

organ *n* **1** a part of a body or plant which has a special function, e.g. a kidney or leaf. **2** a usu. large musical instrument with a keyboard and pedals, in which sound is produced by air being forced through pipes of different lengths. **3** any similar instrument without pipes, such as one producing sound electronically or with reeds. **4** a means of spreading information, such as a newspaper. **5** (*euph* or *jocular*) the penis. [Gr *organon*, tool]

organ-grinder *n* a musician who plays a barrel organ in the streets for money.

organic *adj* **1** of, relating to or produced by a bodily organ or organs. **2** (of a disease) affecting an organ. **3** (of food, crops, etc.) produced without being treated with artificial compounds or chemicals. **4** being an inherent or natural part. **5** systematically organised. **6** (of a chemical compound) containing carbon. — *adv* **organically** *adv*.

organic chemistry *n* the branch of chemistry dealing with compounds which contain carbon, carbon being found in all living things. ◇ See also **inorganic chemistry**.

organist *n* a person who plays the organ.

organdie *n* a very fine, thin cotton fabric which has been stiffened. [Fr *organdi*]

organise or **-ize** *v* **1** (*tr*) to give an orderly structure to: *organise the books into a neat pile*. **2** (*tr*) to arrange, provide or prepare: *organise a meal*. **3** (*tr*; **into**) to form or enrol (people or a person) into a society or organisation, esp. a trade union. **4** (*intr*) to form a society or organisation, esp. a trade union. — *adj* **organised** or **-z-**. [Lat *organizare*]

organisation or **-z-** *n* **1** a group of people formed into a society, union, or esp. business. **2** the act of organising. **3** the state of being organised. — *adj* **organisational** or **-z-**. — *adv* **organisationally** or **-z-**.

organiser or **-z-** *n* **1** someone or something that organises. **2** a small bag or wallet which has (often removable) sections in which personal notes and information may be kept; a similar electronic device.

organism *n* **1** a living structure consisting of a single cell or a small group of cells. **2** a living animal or plant. **3** any establishment, system, or whole made up of parts that depend on each other. [Fr *organisme*, from Lat *organizare*]

organza *n* a very fine, thin dress material made of silk or synthetic fibres.

orgasm *n* **1** the highest point of sexual excitement. **2** violent excitement. — *v* (*intr*) to experience an orgasm. — *adj* **orgasmic**. [Gr *orgasmos*, swelling]

orgy *n* **-ies** **1** a wild party or celebration involving excessive drinking and sexual activity. **2** any act of excessive or frenzied indulgence: *an orgy of shopping*. — *adj* **orgiastic** . [Gr *orgia*, secret rites]

oriel-window *n* (also **oriel**) a window which projects from the wall of a house, usu. at an upper storey, and which is held in place by brackets. [OFr *oriol*, gallery]

orient *n* **1** (*cap* with **the**) the countries in the east, esp. E Asia, as opposed to the **Occident**. **2** that part of the sky where the sun rises. — *v* (*tr*) **1** to place in a definite position in relation to the points of the compass or some other fixed or known point. **2** to acquaint (oneself or someone) with the position relative to points known, or with details of a situation. **3** to position so as to face east. **4** to build a church so that it runs from east to west. [Lat *oriens*, from *oriri*, to rise]

oriental *adj* of, from or relating to the Orient; eastern. — *n* (*cap*) a person born in the Orient; an Asiatic.

Orientalist *n* a person who studies, or is expert in, oriental culture, languages, etc.

orientate *v* **1** (*tr*) to orient. **2** (*intr*) to face the east; to be oriented.

orientated *adj* (**to, towards**) oriented.

orientation *n* **1** the act or an instance of orienting or being oriented. **2** a position relative to a fixed point. **3** a person's position or attitude relative to his or her situation or circumstances. **4** a meeting giving information or training needed for a new situation; a briefing.

oriented *adj* (**to, towards**) directed (towards) or interested (in).

orienteering *n* a sport in which contestants race over an unfamiliar, cross-country course, finding their way to official check points using a map and compass. [Swedish *orientering*]

orifice *n* an opening or hole, esp. in the body. [Lat *os*, mouth + *facere*, to make]

origami *n* the orig. Japanese art of folding paper into shapes and figures. [Jap *ori* folding + *kami*, paper]

origin *n* **1** a beginning or starting-point; a source. **2** (in *pl*) a person's family background or ancestors. **3** (*anat*) a place where a muscle is firmly attached to a bone. **4** (*math*) a fixed point from which a measurement is made. [Lat *origo*]

original *adj* **1** existing from the beginning; earliest; first. **2** (of an idea) never thought of before; fresh or new. **3** (of a person) creative or inventive. **4** being the first form from which copies, reproductions or translations are made. — *n* **1** the first example of something which is copied, reproduced or translated to produce others. **2** a model from which a painting, etc. is made. **3** an odd or eccentric person. — *n* **originality**. — *adv* **originally**.

original sin *n* the supposed sinfulness of the human race as a result of Adam's disobedience of God.

originate *v* (*tr* & *intr*) to bring or come into being; to start. — *n* **origination**. — *n* **originator**.

oriole *n* any of several song-birds, the common European species of which has bright yellow and black plumage. [Lat *aureolus*, from *aurum*, gold]

ormolu *n* a gold-coloured alloy, e.g. copper, zinc and sometimes tin, which is used to decorate furniture, make ornaments, etc. [Fr *or*, gold + *moulu*, ground]

ornament *n* **1** anything that decorates or adds grace or beauty to a person or thing. **2** a small, usu. decorative object. **3** a person whose talents add honour to the group, company, etc. to which he or she belongs. **4** (usu. in *pl*; *mus*) a note which embellishes or decorates the melody or harmony but does not belong to it. — *v* (*tr*) to decorate or be an ornament to. — *n* **ornamentation**. [Lat *ornare*, to adorn]

ornamental *adj* used for decoration. — *adv* **ornamentally**.

ornate *adj* **1** highly or excessively decorated. **2** (of language) not plain and simple; using many elaborate literary words or expressions. — *adv* **ornately**. — *n* **ornateness**. [Lat *ornare*, to adorn]

ornithology *n* the scientific study of birds and their behaviour. — *adj* **ornithological**. — *adv* **ornithologically**. — *n* **ornithologist**. [Gr *ornis*, bird + **-logy**]

orotund *adj* **1** (of the voice) full, loud and grand. **2** (of a manner of speaking or a speech) boastful or self-important; pompous. — *n* **orotundity**. [Lat *os*, mouth + *rotundus*, round]

orphan *n* a child who has lost both parents, or, more rarely, one parent. — *v* **-n-** (*tr*) to cause to be an orphan. [Gr *orphanos*]

orphanage *n* a home for orphans.

orrery *n* **-ies** a clockwork model of the sun and the planets which revolve around it. [Charles Boyle, Earl of *Orrery* (1676–1731), for whom one was made]

orris *n* an iris, esp. the Florentine iris. [A form of **iris**]

orris-root *n* the dried, sweet-smelling root of this plant, used in perfumes and formerly in medicines.

ortho- *comb fm* correct; straight; upright. [Gr *orthos*, straight]

orthodontics *n* (*sing*) dentistry which corrects irregularities in the teeth or jaws. — *adj* **orthodontic**. — *n* **orthodontist**. [**ortho-** + Gr *odous*, tooth]

orthodox *adj* **1** believing in, living according to or conforming with established or generally accepted opinions, esp. in religion or morals; conventional. **2** (*cap*) of the Orthodox Church. **3** (*cap*) of the branch of Judaism which keeps to strict, traditional interpretations of doctrine and scripture. [Gr *orthos*, straight + *doxa*, opinion]

Orthodox Church *n* the eastern Christian church which separated from the western church in the eleventh century, found esp. in the Balkans and Russia.

orthodoxy *n* **-ies** **1** the state of being orthodox or of having orthodox beliefs. **2** an orthodox belief or practice.

orthography *n* **-ies** **1** correct or standard spelling. **2** the study of spelling. — *adj* **orthographic** or **orthographical**. — *adv* **orthographically**. [Gr *orthos*, straight + *graphein*, to write]

orthopaedics *n* (*sing*) the branch of surgery and medicine concerned with curing diseases and correcting injuries of the bones, esp. in children. — *adj* **orthopaedic**. — *n* **orthopaedist**. [**ortho-** + Gr *pais*, child]

orthoptics *n* (*sing*) the science or practice of correcting weak eyesight, esp. through exercising the eye muscles. [**ortho-** + Gr *optikos*, of sight]

ortolan *n* a small European song-bird, eaten as a delicacy. [Lat *hortulus*, small garden]

-ory[1] *sfx* forming nouns meaning a place for: *dormitory*; *laboratory*. [Lat *-orium*]

-ory[2] *sfx* forming adjectives and occasionally nouns with the sense of relating to or involving the action of the verb: *depository*; *signatory*. [Lat *-orius*]

OS *abbrev* **1** Ordnance Survey. **2** outsize. **3** ordinary seaman.

Os *symbol* (*chem*) osmium.

Oscar *n* (*coll*) an Academy Award. [Possibly named after an Academy employee's uncle]

oscillate *v* **1** (*tr* & *intr*) to swing or cause to swing backwards and forwards like a pendulum. **2** (*intr*; **between**) to vary between opinions, choices, courses of action, etc. **3** (*intr*) (of an electrical current) to vary regularly in strength or direction between certain limits. — *n* **oscillation**. [Lat *oscillare*, to swing]

oscillator *n* **1** an apparatus for producing electrical oscillations. **2** a person or thing that oscillates.

oscillograph *n* an apparatus for recording (electrical) oscillations.

oscilloscope *n* an apparatus with which electrical oscillations, appearing as waves, are shown on the screen of a cathode-ray tube.

osier *n* **1** a willow tree whose branches and twigs are used for making baskets. **2** a flexible branch or twig from this tree. [OFr]

-osis *sfx* ***-oses*** **1** condition or process: *hypnosis*; *metamorphosis*. **2** a diseased or disordered state: *neurosis*. [Gr]

osmium *n* a hard, bluish-white metal (symbol **Os**), the heaviest known element. [Gr *osme*, smell, from the unpleasant smell of one of its forms]

osmosis *n* **1** the gradual passing of liquid through a membrane, sometimes so as to make the concentration of the solution on either side of the membrane equal. **2** a gradual process of absorption. — *adj* **osmotic**. — *adv* **osmotically**. [Gr *osmos*, impulse]

osprey *n* ***-eys*** **1** a large, fish-eating bird of prey, with a brown back and brown and white underparts. **2** a feather used for trimming women's hats. [Lat *ossifraga*, bone-breaker]

osseous *adj* of, like, containing or formed from bone. [Lat *os*, bone]

ossify *v* ***-ies***, ***-ied*** **1** (*intr* & *tr*) to (cause to) turn into bone. **2** (*intr*) (of one's opinions, etc.) to become rigid, fixed or inflexible. — *n* **ossification**. — *adj* **ossified**. [Lat *os*, bone + *facere*, to make]

ostensible *adj* (of reasons, etc.) stated or claimed, but not necessarily true; apparent. — *n* **ostensibility**. — *adv* **ostensibly**. [Lat *ostendere*, to show]

ostensive *adj* directly showing. [Lat *ostendere*, to show]

ostentation *n* pretentious display of wealth, knowledge, etc., esp. to attract attention or admiration. — *adj* **ostentatious**. — *adv* **ostentatiously**. — *n* **ostentatiousness**. [Lat *ostendere*, to show]

osteoarthritis *n* arthritis in which the bones forming joints are worn away, causing pain and stiffness. [Gr *osteon*, bone + **arthritis**]

osteopathy *n* the treatment of disease and injuries by manipulating and massaging bones and muscles. — *n* **osteopath**. — *adj* **osteopathic**. [Gr *osteon*, bone + *patheia*, suffering]

osteoporosis *n* a disease in which the bones become brittle and fragile, more common in women than in men. [Gr *osteon*, bone + *poros*, passage]

ostler *n* (*hist*) a person who attends to horses at an inn. [OFr *hostelier*]

Ostmark. See **mark**[2].

ostracise or **-ize** *v* (*tr*) to exclude (someone) from a group, society, etc.; to refuse to associate with. — *n* **ostracism**. [Gr *ostrakon*, a potsherd on which the name of the person to be ostracised used to be written in ancient Greece]

ostrich *n* **1** the largest living bird, able to run very quickly but not fly, and with beautiful feathers. **2** a person who refuses to face or accept unpleasant facts. [Lat *avis*, bird + *struthio*, ostrich]

OT *abbrev* Old Testament.

OTC *abbrev* (*Br*) Officers' Training Corps.

other *adj* **1** remaining from a group of two or more when one or some have been specified already: *close the other eye*; *the other children*. **2** different to the one or ones already mentioned, understood or implied: *other people*. **3** additional; further: *need to buy one other thing*. **4** far or opposite: *the other side of the garden*. — *pron* another person or thing. — *adv* (*coll*) otherwise; differently: *couldn't do other than hurry home*. — **every other** each alternate. — **other than 1** except; apart from. **2** different from. — **the other day** or **night** on an unspecified day or night not long past. [OE]

other ranks *n* (*pl*; esp. *Br*) members of the armed services not having the rank of officer.

otherwise *conj* or else; if not. — *adv* **1** in other respects: *He is good at languages but otherwise not very bright*. **2** in a different way: *couldn't act otherwise than as she did*. **3** under different circumstances: *might otherwise have been late*. — *adj* different: *The truth is otherwise*. — **or otherwise** or the opposite; or not: *check all cars, fast or otherwise*.

otherworldly *adj* concerned with spiritual or intellectual matters to the complete exclusion of practical matters. — *n* **otherworldliness**.

otic *adj* of or relating to the ear. [Gr *ous*, ear]

otiose *adj* serving no purpose; unnecessary; useless. [Lat *otiosus*, from *otium*, leisure]

OTT *abbrev* (*slang*) over the top.

otter *n* a small, fish-eating river animal with smooth dark fur, a slim body, and webbed feet with claws. [OE *otor*]

Ottoman *adj* of the Ottomans or the Ottoman Empire, which lasted from the 13th century until the end of World War I, and which was centred in what is now Turkey, but at different times reached into Europe and the Near East. — *n* ***-mans*** **1** an inhabitant of the Ottoman Empire; a Turk. **2** (without *cap*) a long, low seat, usu. without a back or arms, and often in the form of a padded and upholstered box.

[Arabic *uthman*, Othman (1259–1326), the founder of the Ottoman Empire]

OU *abbrev* **1** Open University. **2** Oxford University.

oubliette *n* (*hist*) a secret dungeon with a single often concealed opening at the top. [Fr, from *oublier*, to forget]

ouch *interj* an expression of sudden sharp pain. [Imit.]

ought *v* (*aux*) used to express **1** duty or obligation: *You ought to help if you can.* **2** advisability: *You ought to see a doctor.* **3** probability or expectation: *She ought to be here soon.* **4** shortcoming or failure: *He ought to have been here hours ago.* **5** enthusiastic desire on the part of the speaker: *You really ought to read this book.* **6** logical consequence: *The answer ought to be 'four'.* — **ought not** used to express moral disapproval: *You ought not to speak to him like that.* [OE *ahte*]

Ouija® (in full **Ouija Board**) *n* a board with the letters of the alphabet printed round the edge, used at séances with a glass, pointer or other object to spell out messages supposed to be from spirits. [Fr *oui*, yes + Ger *ja*, yes]

ounce[1] *n* **1** a unit of weight equal to one sixteenth of a pound (28·35 g. **2** a fluid ounce. **3** a small amount. [Lat *uncia*, twelfth part]

ounce[2] *n* a big cat native to Asia, with leopard-like markings on a thick, soft, cream-coloured coat. [OFr *once*, from Gr *lynx*, lynx]

our *adj* **1** of, belonging to, associated with or done by us: *our children.* **2** (*formal*) used by a sovereign to mean 'my': *our royal will.* [OE *ure*]

Our Father same as **the Lord's Prayer**.

Our Lady *n* the Virgin Mary.

ours *pron* the one or ones belonging to us. — **of ours** of or belonging to us.

ourselves *pron* **1** used as the reflexive form of **us** and **we**: *We helped ourselves to cakes.* **2** used for emphasis: *We ourselves know nothing about that.* **3** our normal self: *We can relax and be ourselves.* — **4** (also **by ourselves**) alone; without anyone else's help.

-ous *sfx* forming adjectives meaning **1** having the character, quality or nature of: *marvellous*; *venomous.* **2** (*chem*) formed with an element in its lower valency. ◇ See also **-ic**. [Lat *-osus*]

ousel. Same as **ouzel**.

oust *v* (*tr*) to force (someone) out of a position and usu. take (his or her) place. [OFr *ouster*]

out *adv & adj* **1** away from the inside; not in or at a place: *go out into the garden.* **2** not in one's home or place of work: *I called but you were out.* **3** to or at an end; to or into a state of being completely finished, exhausted, extinct, etc.: *The milk has run out*; *before the day is out*; *put the candle out.* **4** aloud: *cry out.* **5** with, or taking, care: *listen out for the baby*; *watch out.* **6** in all directions from a central point: *share out the sweets.* **7** to the fullest extent or amount: *spread the blanket out.* **8** to public attention or notice; revealed: *The secret is out.* **9** (*sport*) (of a person batting) no longer able to bat, e.g. because of having the ball caught by an opponent: *bowled out.* **10** in or into a state of being removed, omitted or forgotten: *miss him out*; *rub out the mistake.* **11** not to be considered; rejected: *That idea's out.* **12** removed; dislocated: *have a tooth out.* **13** not in authority; not having political power: *vote them out of office.* **14** into unconsciousness: *pass out in the heat.* **15** in error: *Your total is out by three.* **16** (*coll*) existing: *the best car out.* **17** (**for**; *coll*) determined (to do) or intent on (doing): *out for revenge.* **18** (of a flower) in bloom. **19** (of a book) published. **20** visible: *The moon's out.* **21** no longer in fashion. **22** (of workers) on strike: *call the men out.* **23** (of a jury) considering its verdict. **24** (*old*) (of a young woman) introduced into fashionable society. **25** (of a tide) at or to the lowest level of water. — *adj* **1** external. **2** directing or showing direction outwards: *the out tray.* — *prep* (esp. *US*) out of. — *interj* expressing **1** (*sport*) that the batsman is dismissed. **2** that a radio transmission has finished: *over and out.* — *n* a way out, a way of escape; an excuse. — *v* **1** (*intr*) to become publicly known: *murder will out.* **2** (*tr*) to make public the homosexuality of (a famous person who has been attempting to keep his or her homosexuality secret). — **out and about** active outside the house, esp. after an illness. — **out and away** by far; much. — **out of 1** from inside: *drive out of the garage.* **2** not in; not within: *be out of the house.* **3** no longer having: *be out of butter.* **4** from among: *two out of three cats.* **5** from (a material): *made out of wood.* **6** because of: *out of anger.* **7** beyond the range, scope or bounds of: *out of reach*; *out of the ordinary.* **8** excluded from: *leave him out of the team.* **9** no longer in a stated condition: *out of practice.* **10** at a stated distance from: *a mile out of town.* **11** without or so as to be without: *cheat him out of his money.* — **out of date** old-fashioned and no longer of use; obsolete. — **out of doors** in or into the open. — **out of it 1** (*coll*) not part of, or wanted in, a group, activity, etc. **2** (*slang*) unable to behave normally or control oneself, usu. because of drink or drugs. — **out of pocket** having spent more money than one can afford. — **out of the way 1** difficult to reach or arrive at. **2** unusual; uncommon. — **out with it!** say what you want to say or have to say. [OE *ut*]

out-and-out *adj* complete; thorough: *an out-and-out liar.*

out- *comb fm* **1** external; separate; from outside: *outpatient*; *outhouse.* **2** away from the inside, esp. as a result: *output*; *outpouring.* **3** going away or out of; outward:

outdoor; *outboard*. **4** so as to excel or surpass: *outrun*; *outmanoeuvre*.

outage *n* a period of time during which a power supply fails to operate. **[out + -age]**

outback *n* isolated, remote areas of a country, esp. Australia.

outbalance *v* (*tr*) to weigh more than or be more important than.

outbid *v* ***-dd-***, ***-bid*** (*tr*) to offer a higher price (than someone else), esp. at an auction.

outboard *adj* **1** (of a motor or engine) portable and designed to be attached to the outside of a boat's stern. **2** (of a boat) having such a motor or engine. — *adv* & *adj* of, nearer or towards the outside of a ship or aircraft. — *n* **1** an outboard motor or engine. **2** a boat with an outboard motor or engine. ◇ See also **inboard**.

outbound *adj* (of a vehicle or passenger) going away from home, a station, etc.; departing.

outbreak *n* a sudden, usu. violent beginning or occurrence, usu. of something unpleasant.

outbuilding *n* a building such as a barn, stable or garage, that is separate from the main house but within the grounds surrounding it.

outburst *n* **1** a sudden, violent expression of strong emotion, esp. anger. **2** a sudden period of great activity.

outcast *n* a person who has been rejected by his or her friends or society.

outcaste *n* **1** a Hindu who has lost his or her caste. **2** a person who has no caste.

outclass *v* (*tr*) to be much better than.

outcome *n* a result or consequence.

outcrop *n* **1** a rock or group of rocks which sticks out above the surface of the ground. **2** an appearance or occurrence.

outcry *n* ***-ies*** **(about, against)** a widespread and public show of anger or disapproval.

outdated *adj* no longer useful or in fashion.

outdistance *v* (*tr*) to leave (a competitor) far behind.

outdo *v* ***-does***, ***-did***, ***-done*** (*tr*) to do much better than.

outdoor *adj* **1** done, taking place, situated, for use, etc. in the open air. **2** preferring to be in the open air: *an outdoor person*.

outdoors *adv* in or into the open air; outside a building. — *n* (*sing*) the open air; the world outside buildings.

outer *adj* **1** external; belonging to or for the outside. **2** further from the centre or middle. — *n* (*archery*) **1** the outermost ring on a target. **2** a shot which hits this.

outermost *adj* nearest the edge, furthest from the centre.

outer space *n* space beyond the earth's atmosphere.

outface *v* (*tr*) **1** to stare at (someone) until he or she looks away. **2** to fight or deal with (someone) bravely.

outfall *n* the mouth of a river, sewer, etc. where it flows into the sea.

outfield *n* **1** (*cricket*) the area of the pitch far from the part where the stumps, etc. are laid out. **2** (*baseball*) the area of the field beyond the diamond-shaped pitch where the bases are laid out. **3** (*cricket* & *baseball*) the players who have positions in this area. ◇ See also **infield**.

outfielder *n* (*cricket* & *baseball*) a fielder in the outfield.

outfight *v* ***-fought*** (*tr*) to fight better than; to defeat.

outfit *n* **1** a set of clothes worn together, esp. for a particular occasion. **2** a set of articles, tools, equipment, etc. for a particular task. **3** (*coll*) a group of people working as a single unit or team. — *v* ***-tt-*** (*tr*) to provide with an outfit, esp. clothes.

outfitter *n* a person who provides outfits, esp. one who sells men's clothes.

outflank *v* (*tr*) **1** to go round the side or sides of an enemy's position and attack from behind. **2** to get the better of, esp. by a surprise action.

outflow *n* **1** a flowing out. **2** anything that flows out. **3** the amount that flows out.

outfox *v* (*tr*) to get the better of (someone) by being more cunning; to outwit.

outgoing *adj* **1** friendly and sociable. **2** leaving: *the outgoing president*; *the outgoing flight*. — *n* (in *pl*) money spent.

outgrow *v* ***-grew***, ***-grown*** (*tr*) **1** to grow too large for (one's clothes). **2** to become too old for (childish ailments, children's games, etc.). **3** to grow larger or faster than.

outgrowth *n* **1** a natural product. **2** anything which grows out of something else; a by-product.

outhouse *n* a usu. small building such as a shed, etc. built close to a house.

outing *n* a short pleasure trip.

outlandish *adj* (of appearance, manner, habit, etc.) very strange; odd; queer. — *adv* **outlandishly**. — *n* **outlandishness**.

outlast *v* (*tr*) to last or live longer than.

outlaw *n* a criminal who is a fugitive from, or deprived of the protection of, the law. — *v* (*tr*) **1** to make (someone) an outlaw. **2** to forbid officially. [OE *utlaga*]

outlawry *n* the state of being or act of making someone an outlaw.

outlay *n* money, or occasionally time, spent on something.

outlet *n* **1** a way or passage out, esp. for water or steam. **2** a way of releasing or using energy, talents, strong feeling, etc.: *an outlet for her frustrations*. **3** a market for, or a shop that sells, the goods produced by a particular manufacturer: *an outlet for free-range eggs*. **4** (*US*) an electrical power point.

outline *n* **1** a line forming or marking the outer edge of an object. **2** a drawing with only the outer lines and no shading. **3** the main points, etc. without the details. **4** (usu. in *pl*) the most important features of something. **5** a line representing a word in shorthand. — *v* (*tr*) **1** to draw the outline of. **2** to give a brief description of the main features of.

outlive *v* (*tr*) **1** to live or survive longer than. **2** to survive the effects of (a disease, etc.).

outlook *n* **1** a view from a particular place. **2** a person's mental attitude or point of view. **3** a prospect for the future.

outlying *adj* distant; away from (a city or central area).

outmanoeuvre *v* (*tr*) to gain an advantage over or defeat by more skilful manoeuvring.

outmoded *adj* no longer in fashion; out of date.

outnumber *v* **-*r*-** (*tr*) to be more in number than.

outpace *v* (*tr*) to walk faster than; to outstrip.

outpatient *n* a patient who visits a hospital for treatment but does not stay there overnight.

outplay *v* (*tr*) to defeat or play better than in a game or contest.

outpost *n* **1** a group of soldiers stationed at a distance from the main body, esp. to protect it from a surprise attack. **2** a distant or remote settlement or branch.

outpouring *n* **1** (usu. in *pl*) a powerful or violent show of emotion. **2** the amount that pours out.

output *n* **1** the quantity or amount produced. **2** information in either printed or coded form after it has been processed by a computer. **3** the power or energy produced by an electrical component or apparatus. — *v* **-*tt*-** (*tr*) to produce (information, power, etc.) as output.

outrage *n* **1** an act of great cruelty or violence. **2** an act which breaks accepted standards of morality, honour and decency. **3** great anger or resentment. — *v* (*tr*) **1** to insult, shock or anger greatly. **2** to do physical violence to, esp. (*euph*) to rape. [OFr *outrer*, to exceed]

outrageous *adj* **1** not moderate in behaviour; extravagant. **2** greatly offensive to accepted standards of morality, honour and decency. **3** (*coll*) terrible; shocking. — *adv* **outrageously**. — *n* **outrageousness**.

outrank *v* (*tr*) to have a higher rank than.

outré *adj* not conventional; eccentric; shocking. [Fr, from *outrer*, to exceed]

outride *v* **-*rode***, **-*ridden*** (*tr*) **1** to ride faster than. **2** (esp. of a ship) to come safely through (a storm).

outrider *n* an attendant or guard who rides a horse or motorcycle at the side or ahead of a carriage or car conveying an important person.

outrigger *n* **1** a beam or framework sticking out from the side of a boat to help balance the vessel and prevent it capsizing. **2** a boat that is fitted with this sort of structure.

outright *adv* **1** completely: *be proved outright*. **2** immediately; at once: *killed outright*. **3** openly; honestly: *ask outright*. — *adj* **1** complete: *an outright fool*. **2** clear: *the outright winner*. **3** open; honest: *outright disapproval*.

outrun *v* **-*nn*-**, **-*ran***, **-*run*** (*tr*) **1** to run faster or further than. **2** to do better than or exceed.

outsell *v* **-*sold*** (*tr*) to sell or be sold more quickly or in greater quantities than.

outset *n* a beginning or start.

outshine *v* **-*shone*** (*tr*) **1** to shine brighter than. **2** to be very much better than.

outside *n* **1** the outer surface; the external parts. **2** everything that is not inside or within the bounds or scope of something: *view the problem from the outside*. **3** the farthest limit. **4** the side of a pavement next to the road. — *adj* **1** of, on or near the outside. **2** not forming part of a group, organisation, one's regular job, etc.: *outside interests*. **3** unlikely; remote. **4** (of a guess, etc.) stating the highest possible amount. — *adv* **1** on or to the outside; outdoors. **2** (*slang*) not in prison. — *prep* **1** on or to the outside of. **2** beyond the limits of. **3** except; apart from. — **at the outside** at the most. — **get outside of** (*slang*) to eat or drink. — **outside in** same as **inside out**.

outside broadcast *n* a radio or television programme that is recorded or filmed somewhere other than in a studio.

outside left or **right** *n* (*Br*; *football*) (a player in) the position at the extreme left or right of the middle of the field.

outside line *n* a connection by telephone from a building to another place.

outsider *n* **1** a person who is not part of a group, etc. or who refuses to accept the general values of society. **2** (in a race, contest, etc.) a competitor who is not expected to win.

outsize *adj* (also **outsized**) over normal or standard size. — *n* anything which is larger than standard, esp. a garment.

outskirts *n* (*pl*) the outer parts or area, esp. of a town or city.

outsmart *v* (*tr*; *coll*) to get the better of by being more cunning or cleverer than; to outwit.

outspoken *adj* saying exactly what one thinks; frank. — *adv* **outspokenly**. — *n* **outspokenness**.

outspread *adj* (of arms, etc.) stretched or spread out widely or fully.

outstanding *adj* **1** excellent; superior; remarkable. **2** not yet paid, done, etc.: *outstanding debts*. — *adv* **outstandingly**.

outstation *n* a position, post or station in a remote or lonely area far from towns.

outstay *v* (*tr*) **1** to stay longer than the length of (one's invitation, etc.): *outstay one's welcome*. **2** to stay longer than (other people).

outstretch *v* (*tr*) to stretch or spread out. — *adj* **outstretched**.

outstrip *v* **-*pp*-** **1** to go faster than. **2** to leave behind; to surpass.

out-take *n* a unwanted length of film cut out during editing.

out-tray *n* a shallow basket used in offices for letters, etc. that are ready to be sent out.

outvote *v* (*tr*) to defeat by a majority of votes.

outward *adj* **1** on or towards the outside. **2** (of a journey) away from a place. **3** apparent or seeming: *outward appearances*.

outwardly *adv* in appearance; on the outside.

outwards *adv* (also **outward**) towards the outside; in an outward direction.

outweigh *v* (*tr*) to be greater than in weight, value or importance.

outwit *v* **-tt-** (*tr*) to get the better of or defeat by being cleverer than.

outwith *prep* (*Scot*) outside; beyond.

outwork *n* **1** (usu. in *pl*) a defence work that is outside the main line of fortifications. **2** work done for a company, factory or shop by employees who work at home. — *n* **outworker**.

outworn *adj* no longer useful or in fashion; out of date.

ouzel *n* **1** (**ring ouzel**) a thrush with a broad white band across its throat. **2** (**water ouzel**) a small, aquatic song-bird; the dipper.

ouzo *n* **-os** a Greek alcoholic drink, flavoured with aniseed and usu. diluted with water. [ModGr *ouzon*]

ova. See **ovum**.

oval *adj* shaped like an egg. — *n* any egg-shaped figure or object. [Lat *ovum*, egg]

ovary *n* **-ies** **1** either of the two female reproductive organs which produce eggs and hormones. **2** the female part of a plant that produces seeds. — *adj* **ovarian**. [Lat *ovum*, egg]

ovation *n* cheering or applause, etc. to express approval, welcome, etc. [Lat *ovare*, to exult]

oven *n* an enclosed compartment which may be heated for baking or roasting food, or drying clay, etc. [OE *ofen*]

ovenproof *adj* (of dishes, plates, etc.) that will not crack at a high temperature.

oven-ready *adj* (of food) prepared and only needing to be cooked.

ovenware *n* heat-resistant dishes for use in ovens.

over *adv* **1** above and across. **2** outwards and downwards: *knock him over*; *the kettle boiled over*. **3** across a space; to or on the other side: *fly over from Australia*. **4** from one person, side or condition to another: *win them over*; *turn the card over*. **5** through, from beginning to end, usu. with concentration: *read the letter over*; *think it over thoroughly*. **6** again; in repetition: *do it twice over*. **7** at an end. **8** so as to cover completely: *paper the cracks over*. **9** beyond a limit; in excess. **10** remaining: *left over*. **11** until a later time: *hold payment over until February*. — *prep* **1** in or to a position which is above or higher in place, importance, authority, value, number, etc. **2** above and from one side to another: *fly over the sea*. **3** so as to cover: *hair flopping over his eyes*. **4** out and down from: *fall over the edge*. **5** throughout the extent of: *read over that page again*. **6** during: *visit him sometime over the weekend*. **7** until after: *stay over Monday night*. **8** more than: *over a year ago*. **9** concerning; about: *argue over who would pay*. **10** while occupied with: *chat about it over coffee*. **11** occupying time with: *spend a day over the preparations*. **12** recovered from the effects of: *be over the accident*. **13** by means of: *hear about it over the radio*. **14** divided by. — *adj* **1** upper; higher. **2** outer. **3** excessive. ◇ See also **over-**. — *interj* used during two-way radio conversations to show that one has finished speaking and expects a reply. — *n* (*cricket*) **1** a series of six or eight balls bowled by the same bowler from the same end of the pitch. **2** play during such a series of balls. — **be all over (someone)** to make a great fuss of (someone), often in the hope of getting something from him or her. — **over again** once more. — **over against** opposite; in contrast with. — **over and above** in addition to. — **over and over (again)** repeatedly. — **over head and ears** completely submerged. — **over the top** (*slang*) excessive. [OE *ofer*]

overly *adv fml* too much; excessively.

over- *comb fm* **1** excessively: *overconfident*. **2** above; in a higher position or authority: *overlord*. **3** across the surface; covering: *overcoat*. **4** down; away from an upright position: *overturn*; *overhang*. **5** completely: *overwhelm*.

overact *v* (*intr* & *tr*) to act (a part) with too much expression or emotion.

overall *n* **1** (*Br*) a loose-fitting, coat-like garment worn over ordinary clothes to protect them. **2** (in *pl*) a one-pieced garment with trousers to cover the legs and either a dungaree-type top, or top with sleeves, worn to protect clothes. — *adj* **1** including everything: *the overall total*. **2** from end to end: *the overall length*. — *adv* as a whole; in general.

overarm *adj* & *adv* (bowled or thrown) with the hand and arm raised over and moving round the shoulder.

overawe *v* (*tr*) to make silent by filling with awe, fear or astonishment.

overbalance *v* (*intr* & *tr*) to (cause to) lose one's balance and fall.

overbearing *adj* **1** domineering; too powerful and proud. **2** of particularly great importance. — *adv* **overbearingly**.

overblown *adj* **1** self-important and pretentious. **2** (of flowers) past their best; beginning to die.

overboard *adv* over the side of a ship or boat into the water. — **go overboard** (*coll*) to be very or too enthusiastic. — **throw overboard** to abandon or get rid of.

overbook *v* (*tr* & *intr*) to make or allow more reservations (for an aircraft, restaurant, etc.) than there are seats available.

overburden *v* **-*n*-** (*tr*) to give (someone) too much to do, carry, or think about. — *adj* **overburdened**.

overcast *adj* (of the sky) cloudy.

overcharge *v* **1** (*tr* & *intr*) to charge too much. **2** (*tr*) to fill or load with too much.

overcloud *v* **1** (*tr* & *intr*) to cover, or become covered, with clouds. **2** (*tr*) to make sad or worried.

overcoat *n* a warm, heavy coat worn in winter.

overcome *v* **-*came*, -*come*** **1** (*tr*) to defeat; to succeed in a struggle against; to deal successfully with. **2** (*intr*) to be victorious. **3** (*tr*) to affect strongly; to overwhelm: *overcome with sleep*. [OE *ofercuman*]

overcrowd *v* (*tr*) to cause too many people or things to be in (a place). — *adj* **overcrowded.** — *n* **overcrowding**.

overdo *v* **-*does*, -*did*, -*done*** (*tr*) **1** to do too much; to exaggerate. **2** to cook for too long. **3** to use too much of. — **overdo it** to work too hard.

overdose *n* too great a dose (of some drug). — *v* (*intr*; **on**) to take an overdose (of).

overdraft *n* **1** a state in which one has taken more money out of one's bank account than was in it. **2** the excess of money taken from one's account over the sum that was in it.

overdraw *v* **-*drew*, -*drawn*** **1** (*tr* & *intr*) to draw more money from (one's bank account) than one has in it. **2** (*tr*) to exaggerate in describing. — *adj* **overdrawn**.

overdress *v* (*tr* & *intr*) to dress or be dressed in clothes that are too formal, smart or expensive for the occasion. — *adj* **overdressed**.

overdrive *n* an additional very high gear in a motor vehicle's gear box, which reduces wear on the engine and saves fuel when travelling at high speeds.

overdue *adj* (of bills, work, etc.) not yet paid, done, delivered, etc. although the date for doing this has passed.

overestimate *v* (*tr*) to estimate, judge, etc. too highly. — *n* too high an estimate. — *n* **overestimation**.

overexert *v* (*tr*) to force (oneself) to work too hard. — *n* **overexertion**.

overexpose *v* (*tr*) to expose to too much publicity. **2** to expose (photographic film) to too much light. — *n* **overexposure**.

overflow *v* **-*flowed*** **1** (*tr*) to flow over (a brim) or go beyond (the limits or edge of). **2** (*intr*) to be filled so full that the contents spill over or out. **3** (*intr*; **with**) to be full of: *overflowing with gratitude*. — *n* **1** that which overflows. **2** the act of flowing over. **3** a pipe or outlet for spare water. [OE *oferflowan*]

overgrown *adj* **1** (of a garden, etc.) dense with plants that have grown too large and thick. **2** grown too large.

overhand *adj* & *adv* (thrown, done, etc.) with the hand brought down from above the shoulder.

overhang *v* **-*hung*** **1** (*tr* & *intr*) to project or hang out over. **2** (*tr*) to threaten. — *n* **1** a piece of rock, part of a roof, etc. that overhangs. **2** the amount by which something overhangs.

overhaul *v* (*tr*) **1** to examine carefully and repair. **2** to catch up with and pass. — *n* a thorough examination and repair.

overhead *adv* & *adj* above; over one's head. — *n* (in *pl*) the regular costs of a business, such as rent, wages and electricity.

overhead projector *n* a projector which sits on the speaker's desk and projects images on a screen behind it.

overhear *v* **-*heard*** (*tr* & *intr*) to hear (someone or something) without the speaker knowing, either by accident or on purpose.

overheat *n* (*tr* & *intr*) to make or become too hot.

overheated *adj* (of an argument, discussion, etc.) angry and excited; passionate.

overjoyed *adj* very glad; elated.

overkill *n* **1** action, behaviour, treatment, etc. which is far in excess of what is required. **2** the capability to destroy an enemy using a larger force than is actually needed to win a victory.

overladen *adj* overloaded.

overland *adv* & *adj* (of a journey, etc.) across land.

overlap *v* **-*pp*-** **1** (*tr*) (of part of an object) to partly cover (another object). **2** (*intr*) (of two parts) to have one part partly covering the other. **3** (of two things) to have something in common; to partly coincide. — *n* an overlapping part.

overlay *v* **-*laid*** (*tr*; **with**) to cover with a usu. thin layer of something else, esp. for decoration. — *n* something that is laid over something else, esp. for decoration.

overleaf *adv* on the other side of the page.

overlie *v* **-*lying*, -*lay*, -*lain*** (*tr*) **1** to lie on. **2** to smother and kill (a baby or small animal) by lying on it.

overload *v* (*tr*) **1** to load too heavily. **2** to put too great an electric current through (a circuit). — *n* too great an electric current flowing through a circuit.

overlook *v* (*tr*) **1** to give a view of from a higher position. **2** to fail to see or notice. **3** to allow (a mistake, crime, etc.) to go unpunished. **4** to supervise.

overlord *n* a lord or ruler with supreme power.

overly. See **over**.

overmuch *adv* & *adj* too much.

overnice *adj* fussy, critical and hard to please.

overnight *adv* **1** during the night. **2** for the duration of the night. **3** suddenly. — *adj* **1** done or occurring in the night. **2** sudden: *an overnight success*. **3** for use overnight: *an overnight case*.

overpass *n* (esp. *US*). Same as **flyover**.

overplay *v* (*tr*) to exaggerate or overemphasise. — **overplay one's hand** to try to get more than one's talents, assets, etc. will produce; to overestimate one's talents, assets, etc.

overpower *v* **-r-** (*tr*) **1** to defeat by greater strength. **2** to weaken or reduce to helplessness. — *adj* **overpowering**. — *adv* **overpoweringly**.

overprint *v* (*tr*) to print over (something already printed, e.g. a stamp). — *n* extra material printed on top of something printed, e.g. a stamp.

overrate *v* (*tr*) to think too highly of.

overreach *v* **1** (*tr*) to defeat (oneself) by trying to do too much, be too clever, etc. **2** (*intr*) (of a horse) to strike the hind foot against the forefoot.

overreact *v* (*intr*; **to**) to react too strongly to. — *n* **overreaction**.

override *v* **-rode**, **-ridden** (*tr*) **1** to annul or set aside, esp. to cancel the functioning of (e.g. an automatic control). **2** to be of more importance than.

overriding *adj* dominant; most important: *overriding considerations*.

overrule *v* (*tr*) **1** to rule against or cancel (esp. a previous decision or judgement) by higher authority. **2** to impose a decision on (a person) by higher authority.

overrun *v* **-nn-**, **-ran**, **-run** **1** (*tr*) to spread over or through (something); to infest. **2** (*tr*) to invade and take possession of (another country) quickly and by force. **3** (*tr* & *intr*) to go beyond (a fixed limit): *overrun the budget for the job*. [OE *oferyrnan*]

overseas *adv* abroad. — *adj* (also **oversea**) across or from beyond the sea; foreign.

oversee *v* **-saw**, **-seen** (*tr*) to supervise. — *n* **overseer**.

oversell *v* **-sold** **1** (*tr* & *intr*) to sell at too high a price or in greater quantities than can be supplied. **2** (*tr*) to praise too highly.

oversew *v* **-sewed**; **-sewn** or **-sewed** (*tr*) to sew (two edges) with close stitches that pass over both edges.

oversexed *adj* having unusually strong sexual urges.

overshadow *v* (*tr*) **1** to seem much more important than. **2** to cast a shadow over; to make seem more gloomy. [OE *ofersceadian*]

overshoe *n* a shoe, usu. made of rubber or plastic, worn over normal shoes to protect them in wet weather.

overshoot *v* **-shot** (*tr*) to go farther than (a target aimed at). — **overshoot the mark** to make a mistake as a result of misjudging a situation.

oversight *n* a mistake made through a failure to notice something.

oversimplify *v* **-ies**, **-ied** (*tr* & *intr*) to simplify (something) so much as to cause a mistake or distortion. — *n* **oversimplification**.

oversleep *v* **-slept** (*intr*) to sleep longer than one intended.

overspend *v* **-spent** (*intr*) to spend too much money.

overspill *n* (esp. *Br*) the people leaving an overcrowded or derelict town area to live elsewhere.

overstate *v* (*tr*) to state too strongly or with unnecessary emphasis. — *n* **overstatement**.

overstay *v* (*tr*) to stay longer than the length of (one's invitation, etc.): *overstay one's welcome*.

oversteer *v* (*intr*) (of a vehicle) to turn more sharply than the driver intends.

overstep *v* **-pp-** (*tr*): **overstep the mark** to go beyond what is wise, reasonable, acceptable or proper.

overstretched *adj* stretched too far; extended to the limit.

overstrung *adj* too sensitive and nervous; tense.

oversubscribe *v* (*tr*) to apply for or try to purchase in larger quantities than are available. — *adj* **oversubscribed**.

overt *adj* not hidden or secret; open; public. — *adv* **overtly**. [OFr *ovrir*, to open]

overtake *v* **-took**, **-taken** **1** (*tr* & *intr*; esp. *Br*) to catch up with and go past (a car, a person, etc.) moving in the same direction. **2** to draw level with and begin to do better than. **3** (*tr*) to come upon (someone) suddenly or without warning: *overtaken by the bad weather*.

overtax *v* (*tr*) **1** to put too great a strain on (someone or oneself). **2** to demand too much tax from.

overthrow *v* **-threw**, **-thrown** (*tr*) **1** to defeat completely. **2** to upset or overturn. — *n* **1** a defeat or downfall. **2** (*cricket*) an inaccurate return of the ball by a fielder which often allows the batsman to score extra runs.

overtime *n* **1** time spent working at one's job beyond one's regular hours. **2** the money paid for this extra time. — *adv* in addition to one's regular hours.

overtone *n* **1** (usu. in *pl*) a subtle hint, quality or meaning: *political overtones*. **2** (*mus*) a tone that contributes towards the musical sound and adds to its quality. [Ger *Oberton*]

overture *n* **1** an orchestral introduction to an opera, oratorio or ballet. **2** (usu. *in pl*) a proposal or offer intended to open a discussion. [OFr, opening]

overturn *v* **1** (*tr* & *intr*) to turn or be turned over or upside down. **2** (*tr*) to bring down or destroy (a government). **3** (*tr*) to overrule or cancel (a previous legal decision).

overview *n* a brief, general account or description.

overweening *adj* **1** (of a person) arrogant. **2** (of pride) inflated and excessive.

overweight *adj* above the desired, required or usual weight.

overwhelm *v* (*tr*) **1** to crush mentally; to overpower (a person's) emotions, thoughts, etc. **2** to defeat by superior force or numbers. **3** to supply or offer something in great amounts to: *overwhelmed with offers of help*. — *adj* **overwhelming**. — *adv* **overwhelmingly**.

overwork *v* **1** (*intr*) to work too hard. **2** (*tr*) to make (someone) work too hard. **3** (*tr*) to make too much use of. — *n* the act of working too hard. — *adj* **overworked**.

overwrite *v* **-*wrote*, -*written*** (*tr*; *comput*) to write new information over (existing data), thereby destroying it.

overwrought *adj* very nervous or excited; over-emotional.

oviduct *n* the tube which carries the egg from the ovary. [Lat *ovum*, egg + *ducere*, to lead]

oviform *adj* egg-shaped. [Lat *ovum*, egg + **-form**]

ovine *adj* of or like sheep. [Lat *ovis*, sheep]

oviparous *adj* (of birds, fish, etc.) producing eggs which hatch outside the mother's body. ◇ See also **viviparous**. — *n* **oviparity** . — *adv* **oviparously**. [Lat *ovum*, egg + *parere*, to produce]

ovoid *n* & *adj* (an object that is) egg-shaped. [Lat *ovum*, egg + **-oid**]

ovulate *v* (*intr*) to produce eggs from the ovary. — *n* **ovulation**. [Lat *ovulum*, dimin. of *ovum*, egg]

ovule *n* the part of a plant that contains the egg-cell, and which becomes a seed when fertilised. [Lat *ovulum*, dimin. of *ovum*, egg]

ovum *n* ***ova*** (*biol*) an egg-cell which, when fertilised, can develop into a new individual. [Lat, egg]

ow *interj* used to express sudden, usu. mild, pain.

owe *v* **1** (*tr* & *intr*; **for**) to be under an obligation to pay (money) to (someone). **2** (*tr*) to feel required by duty or gratitude to do or give: *owe you an explanation*. **3** (*tr*) to have or enjoy as a result of: *owe her promotion to her hard work*. [OE *agan*, to own]

owing *adj* still to be paid; due. — **owing to** because of; on account of.

owl *n* a bird of prey with a large, broad head, flat face, large eyes, a short, hooked beak and a hooting cry, active at night. [OE *ule*]

owlet *n* a young owl.

owlish *adj* **1** like an owl. **2** solemn or wise. — *adv* **owlishly**. — *n* **owlishness**.

own *adj* (often used for emphasis) belonging to or for oneself or itself: *my own sister*. — *pron* one or something belonging to oneself or itself: *have a room of one's own*. — *v* **1** (*tr*) to have as a possession or property. **2** (*intr*; **to**, **up**, **up to**) to admit or confess: *own up to the robbery*. **3** (*tr*) to admit or acknowledge: *own one's guilt*. — **get one's own back** (*coll*; **on**) to get even; to have revenge. — **on one's own 1** alone. **2** without help. [OE *agen*]

owner *n* a person who owns something. — *n* **ownership**.

owner-occupier *n* a person who owns the property he or she is living in.

own goal *n* **1** a goal scored by mistake for the opposing side. **2** (*coll*) a move that turns out to be to the disadvantage of the person who took it.

ox *n* ***oxen*** **1** any common domestic cattle, both bulls and cows, used for pulling loads, or supplying meat and milk. **2** a castrated bull. [OE *oxa*]

oxeye daisy *n* a daisy with long white petals and a dark yellow centre.

oxtail *n* the tail of an ox, used esp. in soups and stews.

oxalic acid *n* a poisonous acid found in wood sorrel and many other plants, used for cleaning metals and as a bleach. [Gr *oxalis*, wood sorrel]

Oxbridge *n* & *adj* (*Br*) (of or from) the universities of *Ox*ford and Cam*bridge* considered together and usu. in contrast to other universities.

oxen. See **ox**.

Oxfam or **OXFAM** *abbrev* Oxford Committee for Famine Relief.

oxidation *n* the act of oxidising or becoming oxidised. [**oxide**]

oxide *n* (*chem*) a compound of oxygen and another element. [Fr, from *oxygène*, oxygen]

oxidise or **-ize** *v* (*tr* & *intr*; *chem*) **1** to combine with oxygen. **2** to make or become rusty. — *n* **oxidisation** or **-z-**.

Oxon *abbrev* **1** Oxfordshire. **2** (esp. in degree titles) Oxford University. [Lat *Oxoniensis*, of Oxford]

Oxonian *n* **1** an inhabitant of Oxford. **2** a student or graduate of Oxford University. — *adj* of Oxford or Oxford University. [Lat *Oxonia*, Oxford]

oxyacetylene *n* & *adj* (of or using) a mixture of oxygen and acetylene, which burns at a very high temperature, and is used for cutting and welding metals. [**oxygen** + **acetylene**]

oxygen *n* a colourless, odourless gas (symbol **O**) which forms part of the air and water and which is essential to life. [Gr *oxys*, sharp + *gennaein*, to generate, from the old belief that all acids contained oxygen]

oxygenate *v* (*tr*) **1** to supply (e.g. the blood) with oxygen. **2** to treat with oxygen. — *n* **oxygenation**.

oxygenator *n* an apparatus that oxygenates the blood, esp. while a patient is being operated on.

oxygen debt *n* a temporary loss of oxygen from the body during very active exercise.

oxygen mask *n* a mask through which oxygen is supplied from a tank.

oxygen tent *n* a tent-like apparatus erected over a patient's bed, into which oxygen can be pumped to help his or her breathing.

oxymoron *n* a figure of speech in which contradictory terms are used together: *holy cruel.* [Gr *oxymoros*, from *oxys*, sharp + *moros*, foolish]

oyez or **oyes** *interj* (esp. *hist*) a cry for silence and attention, usu. shouted three times by an official before a public announcement or in a court of law. [OFr *oir*, to hear]

oyster *n* **1** an edible shellfish which sometimes produces a pearl. **2** the pale greyish beige or pink colour of an oyster. — **the world is your**, etc. **oyster** you, etc. have everything you desire within your grasp. [Gr *ostreon*]

oyster bed *n* a place where oysters breed or are bred.

oystercatcher *n* a black and white wading bird with a long orange-red beak, that feeds on mussels and limpets (but not oysters).

oz *abbrev* ounce. [Ital *onza*, ounce]

ozone *n* **1** a type of oxygen with a powerful smell, used in bleaching, sterilising water and purifying air. **2** (*coll*) fresh, bracing sea air. [Gr *ozein*, to smell]

ozone-friendly *adj* not containing chemicals thought to harm the ozone layer.

ozone layer *n* the layer of ozone, high above the earth's surface, that protects the earth from harmful radiation from the sun.

P

P[1] or **p** *n* ***Ps*** or ***P's***, ***p's*** the 16th letter of the English alphabet. — **mind one's p's and q's** (*facet*) to behave politely; to remember to say 'please' and 'thank you'.
P[2] *abbrev* **1** (as a street sign) parking. **2** (*chess*) pawn. **3** (*knitting instructions*) purl.
P[3] *symbol* (*chem*) phosphorus.
p *abbrev* **1** penny or pence. **2** ***pp*** page.
PA *abbrev* **1** (also **Pa**) Pennsylvania. **2** personal assistant. **3** public-address (system).
Pa *symbol* (*chem*) protactinium.
p.a. *abbrev* for *per annum* (Lat), yearly; per year.
pace[1] *n* **1** a single step. **2** the distance covered by one step. **3** rate of movement or progress: *can't stand the pace*; *at one's own pace*. **4** a manner of walking or running. **5** any of the gaits used by a horse. — *v* **1** (*intr* & *tr*; **about**, **around**, etc.) to keep walking about (over): *pace the floor*. **2** (*intr*) to walk steadily. **3** (*tr*) to set the pace for (others) in a race, etc. **4** (*tr*; **out**) to measure out (a distance) in paces. — **keep pace with** to go as fast as. — **put someone through his** or **her paces**, or **go through**, or **show, one's paces** to make someone demonstrate his or her, or to demonstrate one's own, skills at something. — **set the pace** to be ahead of, and so set the rate for, others (*n* **pacesetter**). [Fr *pas*, step]
pacemaker *n* an electronic device fitted next to the heart to regularise its beat. **2** a pacesetter.
pace[2] *prep* with the permission of; with due respect to (someone with whom one is disagreeing). [Lat, ablative of *pax*, peace, pardon]
pachyderm *n* a large, thick-skinned animal, esp. a rhinoceros, elephant or hippopotamus. [Gr *pachys*, thick + *derma*, skin]
pacific *adj* tending to make peace or keep the peace; peaceful; peaceable. [Lat *pacificus*]
Pacific *adj* of, belonging or relating to, the **Pacific Ocean** between Asia and America. [**pacific**, because the ocean was calm when discovered by Magellan]
pacifist *n* someone who believes that violence is unjustified and who refuses to take part in making war. — *n* **pacifism**. [**pacific**]
pacify *v* ***-ies***, ***-ied*** (*tr*) **1** to calm, soothe or appease. **2** to restore to a peaceful condition. **3** (*euph*) to subdue. — *n* **pacification**. [Lat *pax*, peace + *facere*, to make]
pacifier *n* (*NAm*) a baby's dummy.
pack[1] *n* **1** things tied into a bundle for carrying. **2** a rucksack; a backpack. **3** a complete set of playing-cards. **4** a troop of animals hunting together, e.g. dogs or wolves. **5** a compact package, e.g. of equipment for a purpose: *a first-aid pack*. **6** (*derog*) a collection or bunch: *a pack of idiots, lies*, etc. **7** a troop of Brownie Guides or Cub Scouts. **8** (*Rugby*) the forwards in a team. **9** a medicinal or cosmetic skin preparation: *a face pack*. **10** pack ice. — *v* **1** (*tr*) to stow (goods, clothes, etc.) compactly in cases, boxes, etc. for transport or travel. **2** (*intr*) to put one's belongings into a travelling-bag, etc., ready for a journey. **3** (*tr*; **out, with, in**, etc.) to cram. **4** (*tr* with **off**) to send off hastily: *pack the children off to their aunt's*. **5** (*tr*) to be capable of giving (a punch) of some force. **6** (*tr*; *US coll*) to make a habit of carrying (a gun). **7** (*intr*) (of animals) to form a pack. — **pack it in** (*coll*) to give up or stop what one is doing. — *v* **pack up 1** (*intr*) to stop work, etc. **2** (*tr*) to stow away in the proper place. **3** (*intr*; *coll*) (of machinery, etc.) to break down. — **send packing** (*coll*) to dismiss unceremoniously.
packhorse *n* (*hist*) a horse used to carry luggage or goods for sale.
pack ice *n* pieces of floating ice driven together into a mass by wind and currents.
packing *n* materials used for padding or wrapping goods for transport, etc.
packing-case *n* a wooden crate in which to pack goods for transport or storage.
pack[2] *v* (*tr*) to fill (a jury, meeting, etc.) illicitly with people one can rely on to support one.
package *n* **1** something wrapped and secured with string, adhesive tape, etc.; a parcel. **2** a package deal. — *v* (*tr*) to wrap up in a parcel. [**pack**]
package deal *n* a deal covering a number of related proposals that must be accepted as a whole or not at all.
package holiday or **package tour** *n* a holiday or tour for which one pays a fixed price that includes travel, accommodation, meals, etc.
packaging *n* the wrappers or containers in which goods are packed.
packet *n* **1** a paper, cardboard or plastic bag, wrapper or container, with its contents. **2** a small pack or package. **3** (also **packet boat**) a mail boat also carrying cargo and passengers, plying a fixed route. **2** (*coll*) a large sum of money: *cost a packet*. [OFr *pacquet*]
pact *n* an agreement reached between two or more esp. opposing parties, states, etc. [Lat *pactum*]
pad[1] *n* a wad of material used to cushion, protect, shape or clean. **2** a leg-guard for a cricketer, etc. **3** a quantity of sheets of paper fixed together into a block. **4** a

rocket-launching platform. **5** the fleshy underside of an animal's paw. **6** a compactly laid out set of keys pressed to dial a telephone number, operate a television set, etc.: *a key pad*. **7** (*US*) a large water-lily leaf. **8** (*slang*) one's living quarters. — *v* **-*dd*-** (*tr*) **1** to cover, fill, stuff, cushion or shape with layers of soft material. **2** (**out**) to include unnecessary or irrelevant material in (a piece of writing, speech, etc.) for the sake of length.

padding *n* **1** material for cushioning, shaping or filling. **2** irrelevant or unnecessary matter in a speech or piece of writing.

pad[2] *v* **-*dd*- 1** (*intr*) to walk softly or with a muffled tread. **2** (*tr* & *intr*) to tramp along (a road); to travel on foot. [ODut *pad*, path]

paddle[1] *v* **1** (*intr*) to walk about barefoot in shallow water. **2** (*tr*) to trail or dabble (fingers, etc.) in water. — *n* a spell of paddling.

paddle[2] *n* **1** a short light oar with a blade at one or both ends, used to propel and steer a canoe, etc. **2** one of the slats fitted round the edge of a paddle wheel or mill wheel. — *v* (*tr* & *intr*) to propel (a canoe, etc.) with paddles. **2** (*intr*; **along**, etc.) to move through water using, or as if using, a paddle or paddles.

paddle steamer *n* a steamer driven by paddle wheels.

paddle wheel *n* a large engine-driven wheel at the side or back of a ship which propels the ship through the water as it turns.

paddock *n* **1** a small enclosed field for keeping a horse in. **2** (*horse-racing*) an enclosure beside a race track where horses are saddled and walked round before a race. [OE *pearroc*, fence, enclosure]

paddy[1] *n* **-*ies* 1** (also **paddy field**) a field in which rice is grown. **2** rice as a growing crop; harvested rice still in the husk. [Malay *padi*]

paddy[2] *n* **-*ies*** (*coll*) a fit of rage. [*Paddy*, colloquial name for an Irishman]

padlock *n* a detachable lock with a U-shaped bar that pivots at one side so that it can be passed through a ring or chain and locked in position. — *v* (*tr*) to fasten with a padlock.

padre *n* a chaplain in any of the armed services. [Port, Span & Ital, father (as a form of address to a priest)]

paean *n* a song of triumph, praise or thanksgiving. [Gr *Paian*, healer, used in hymns as a title of Apollo]

paed-. See **paedo-**.

paederast, paederasty. See **pederast**.

paediatrics *n* (*sing*) the branch of medicine dealing with children and their illnesses. — *adj* **paediatric**. [Gr *pais*, child + *iatrikos*, medical]

paediatrician *n* a doctor specialising in studying and treating children's illnesses.

paedo- or **paed-** *comb fm* child: *paedophile*; *paediatrics*. [Gr, *pais*, child]

paedophile *n* a person sexually attracted to children. — *n* **paedophilia**. [**paedo-** + **-phile**]

paella *n* a Spanish dish of rice, fish or chicken, vegetables and saffron. [Catalan (the language of Catalonia in NW Spain), from Lat *patella*, pan]

pagan *adj* **1** not a Christian, Jew or Muslim; of or following a religion in which a number of gods are worshipped. **2** without religious belief. — *n* a pagan person. — *n* **paganism**. [Lat *paganus*, rustic, peasant, civilian (i.e. not a soldier of Christ)]

page[1] *n* **1** one side of a leaf in a book, etc. **2** a leaf of a book, etc. **3** (*literary*) an episode or incident in history, one's life, etc. — *v* (*tr*) to paginate (a text). [Fr, from Lat *pagina*]

page[2] *n* **1** a boy who carries messages or luggage, etc. **2** (*hist*) a boy attendant serving a knight, and training for knighthood. **3** a boy attending the bride at a wedding. — *v* (*tr*) to summon through a public-address system or pager. [OFr, from OItal *paggio*]

pageboy *n* a page. — *adj* denoting a smooth jaw-length hairstyle with the ends curling under.

pager *n* an electronic communication system, e.g. in a hospital, by means of which personnel can be summoned through individually worn radio receivers or bleepers.

pageant *n* **1** a series of tableaux or dramatic scenes, usu. depicting historical events. **2** any colourful and varied spectacle. — *n* **pageantry**. [Lat *pagina*, page, scene, stage]

paginate *v* (*tr*) to give numbers to the pages of (a text) as part of the printing process. — *n* **pagination**. [Lat *pagina*, page]

pagoda *n* an oriental temple, esp. in the form of a tall tower, each storey having its own projecting roof with upturned eaves. [Port *pagode*, from Persian *butkada*, from *but*, idol + *kada*, temple]

paid. See **pay**.

pail *n* **1** a bucket. **2** the amount contained in a bucket. — *n* **pailful, -*fuls***. [OE *pægel*, gill (liquid measure), associated with OFr *paielle*, pan]

pain *n* **1** physical or emotional suffering. **2** (*coll derog*) (also **pain in the neck**) an irritating or otherwise troublesome person. **3** (in *pl*) trouble taken or efforts made in doing something. — *v* (*tr*) to cause distress to. — *adj* **painless**. — *adv* **painlessly**. — **be at pains** to be anxious (to do something) with due care and thoroughness. — **for one's pains** (esp. *ironic*) as a (poor) reward for the trouble one has gone to. — **on pain of** at the risk of incurring (something) as a punishment. — **take pains** to be careful (to do something) properly; to be thorough (over a task, etc.). [Lat *poena*, punishment]

pained *adj* expressing distress or disapproval: *a pained look*.

painful *adj* **1** causing pain: *a painful injury*. **2** affected by something which causes pain: *a painful finger*. **3** causing distress: *a painful duty*. **4** laborious: *painful progress*.

painkiller *n* a drug that reduces or gets rid of pain.

painstaking *adj* conscientious and thorough.

paint *n* **1** colouring matter in the form of a liquid, for applying to a surface; a dried coating of this. **2** a tube or tablet of colouring matter for creating pictures. **3** (*old*) face make-up; cosmetics. — *v* **1** (*tr*) to apply a coat of paint to (walls, woodwork, etc.) **2** (*tr*) to turn (something) a certain colour by this means: *paint the door yellow*. **3** (*tr* & *intr*) to make (pictures) using paint. **4** (*tr*) to depict (a person, place or thing) in paint. **5** (*tr* & *intr*; *old*) to put make-up on (one's face). [OFr *peint*, past participle of *peindre*, to paint]

paintball *n* a game in which participants stalk each other and fight battles with paint fired from compressed-air guns.

paintbox *n* a case of paints in a variety of colours, for painting pictures.

paintbrush *n* a brush used for applying paint.

painter *n* **1** a person who decorates houses internally or externally with paint. **2** an artist who paints pictures.

painting *n* **1** the art or process of applying paint to walls, etc. **2** the art of creating pictures in paint. **3** a painted picture.

painter[1] *n* (*naut*) a rope for fastening a boat.

painter[2]. See **paint**.

pair *n* **1** a set of two identical or corresponding things, e.g. shoes, gloves, etc., intended for use together. **2** something consisting of two joined, corresponding parts: *a pair of pants, glasses, pliers*, etc. **3** one of a matching pair: *Where's its pair?* **4** two people associated in a relationship. **5** two mating animals, birds, fishes, etc. **6** two horses harnessed together: *a coach and pair*. — *v* **1** (*tr* & *intr*; **off**) to divide into pairs. **2** (*intr*; **up (with)**) to join with another, or (of two) to join together, for some purpose. — **in pairs** in twos. [OFr *paire*]

pajamas. See **pyjamas**.

pal (*coll*) *n* a friend. — *v* **pal up** *-ll-* (*intr*; **with**) to make friends. [Romany, brother]

pally *adj* *-ier*, *-iest* (*coll*) friendly. — *n* **palliness**.

palace *n* **1** the official residence of a sovereign, bishop, archbishop or president. **2** a spacious and magnificent residence or other building. [OFr *paleis*, from Lat *Palatium*, the Roman emperors' residence on the Palatine Hill]

paladin *n* (*mediaeval hist*) **1** any of the twelve peers of Charlemagne's court. **2** a knight errant; a champion of a sovereign. [Ital *paladino*, from Lat *palatinus*, belonging to the palace]

palaeo- or **palae-** *comb fm* old. [Gr *palaios*, old]

Palaeocene *adj* & *n* (*geol*) (denoting) the earliest epoch of the Tertiary period, lasting from about 65 to 55 million years ago, during which giant reptiles died out and apes and monkeys appeared. [**palaeo-** + Gr *kainos*, new]

palaeography *n* the study of ancient writing and manuscripts. — *n* **palaeographer**. [**palaeo-** + **-graphy**]

palaeolithic *adj* (also *cap*) of, or belonging to, the early part of the Stone Age, during which chipped stones served as primitive tools. [**palaeo-** + Gr *lithos*, stone]

palaeontology *n* the study of creatures existing during the geological past through their fossil remains. — *adj* **palaeontologist**. [**palae-** + Gr *onta*, neuter pl. present participle of *einai*, to be + **-logy**]

Palaeozoic *adj* & *n* (*geol*) (denoting) an era in the history of the earth lasting from 250 to 600 million years ago, during which the first vertebrates appeared. [**palaeo-** + Gr *zoion*, animal]

palanquin or **palankeen** *n* (*hist*) a light portable bed used in the Orient, suspended from poles carried on the shoulders of four bearers. [Port *palanquim*]

palatable *adj* **1** having a pleasant taste; appetising. **2** acceptable; agreeable. [**palate**]

palate *n* **1** the roof of the mouth. **2** the sense of taste; an ability to discriminate between wines, etc. [Lat *palatum*]

palatial *adj* like a palace in magnificence, spaciousness, etc. [Lat *palatium*, palace]

palaver *n* **1** (*coll*) unnecessary fuss. **2** (*hist*) an act of conferring between European traders, settlers, etc. and native inhabitants. [Port *palavra*, from Lat *parabola*, speech]

pale[1] *adj* **1** (of a person, face, etc.) having less colour than normal, e.g. from illness, fear, shock, etc. **2** (of a colour) closer to white than black; light: *pale green*. **3** lacking brightness or vividness; subdued: *pale sunlight*. — *v* (*intr*) **1** to become pale. **2** to fade by comparison: *pale into insignificance*. — *adv* **palely**. — *n* **paleness**. [OFr *palle*, from Lat *pallidus*]

paleface *n* the term supposed to have been used by N American Indians for the white settlers.

pale[2] *n* **1** a post used for making fences. **2** a fence made of these; a boundary fence. — **beyond the pale** outside the limits of acceptable behaviour. [Lat *palus*, stake]

paleo- or **pale-**. Other spellings of **palaeo-** and **palae-**.

palette *n* **1** a hand-held board with a thumb hole, on which an artist mixes colours. **2** the assortment or range of colours used by a particular artist, in a particular picture, etc. [Fr, from Ital *paletta*, diminutive of *pala*, spade]

palette knife *n* **1** an artist's knife for mixing and applying paint. **2** a flexible-bladed, round-ended knife used for spreading butter, mixing ingredients, etc.

palimpsest *n* **1** a parchment or other writing surface re-used after the original content has been erased. **2** a monumental brass that has been turned over and inscribed on the reverse. [Gr *palin* again + *psaein*, to rub]

palindrome *n* a word or phrase that reads the same backwards and forwards, e.g. *eye*, *Hannah*, or *Able was I ere I saw Elba*. — *adj* **palindromic**. — *adv* **palindromically**. [Gr *palin*, back + *dromein*, to run]

paling *n* any of a row of wooden posts fixed edge to edge to form a solid fence; a fence of this kind. [Lat *palus*, stake]

palisade *n* a tall fence of pointed wooden stakes fixed edge to edge, for defence or protection. [Provençal *palissada*, from *palus*, stake]

pall[1] *n* **1** the cloth that covers a coffin at a funeral; the coffin itself. **2** anything spreading or hanging over: *a pall of smoke*. [OE *pæll*, robe, covering]

pall-bearer *n* one of those carrying the coffin or walking beside it at a funeral.

pall[2] *v* (*intr*; **on**) to begin to bore. [Variant of **appal**]

palladium *n* a metallic element, symbol **Pd**, similar to platinum, used in jewellery. [After the asteroid *Pallas*, discovered 1802]

pallet[1] *n* **1** a small wooden platform on which goods can be stacked for lifting and transporting by fork-lift truck. **2** a flat-bladed wooden tool used for shaping pottery. **[palette]**

pallet[2] **1** a straw mattress. **2** a small make-shift bed. [OFr *paillette*, from *paille*, straw]

palliasse *n* a straw mattress. [Fr *paillasse*, from *paille*, straw]

palliate *v* (*tr*) **1** to ease the symptoms of (a disease) without curing it. **2** to serve to lessen the gravity of (an offence, etc.); to excuse to some extent. **3** to reduce the effect of (anything disagreeable). [Lat *pallium*, cloak]

palliative *n* & *adj* (something) having a palliating effect.

pallid *adj* **1** pale, esp. unhealthily so. **2** lacking vigour or conviction. [Lat *pallidus*, pale]

pallor *n* paleness, esp. of complexion. [Lat]

pally. See **pal**.

palm[1] *n* **1** the inner surface of the hand between the wrist and the fingers. **2** the part of a glove covering this. — *v* (*tr*; esp. *conjuring*) to conceal in the palm. — *v* **palm off** (*tr*; *coll derog*) **1** (**on**) to give (something or someone unwanted or inferior) to someone else, esp. by trickery. **2** (**with**) to give (someone) something or someone inferior, esp. by trickery. [Lat *palma*]

palm[2] *n* **1** a maritime or tropical tree usu. with a single unbranching trunk terminating in a cluster of long blade-like leaves. **2** a leaf of this carried as a symbol of triumph or victory; the supreme prize. [Lat *palma*, orig. palm of the hand]

palm oil *n* oil obtained from the pulp of the fruit of certain palms.

Palm Sunday *n* the Sunday before Easter, on which Christ's triumphal palm-strewn progress into Jerusalem is commemorated.

palmate *adj* (*bot*) (of leaves) shaped like an open hand. [Lat *palmatus*, from *palma*, palm of the hand]

palmetto *n* **-os** a small palm tree with fan-like leaves. [Span *palmito*, dimin. of *palma*, palm]

palmy *adj* **-ier**, **-iest** (*coll facet*) characterised by effortless success and prosperity: *one's palmy days*. [**palm**[2], as symbol of triumph]

palomino *n* **-os** a golden or cream horse with a white tail and mane. [Span, dove-like]

palpable *adj* **1** easily detected; obvious. **2** (*med*) able to be felt. — *adv* **palpably**. [Lat *palpare*, to touch]

palpate *v* (*tr*; *med*) to examine by feeling. [Lat *palpare*, to touch]

palpitate *v* (*intr*) **1** (of the heart) to beat rapidly. **2** to tremble or throb. — *n* **palpitation** (often in *pl*). [Lat *palpitare*, to throb]

palsy *n* paralysis, or loss of control or feeling in a part of the body. — *v* **-ies**, **-ied** (*tr*) to affect with palsy; to paralyse. [OFr *paralisie*, from Lat & Gr *paralysis*]

paltry *adj* **-ier**, **-iest** worthless; trivial; meagre; insignificant; insultingly inadequate. — *n* **paltriness**. [Ger dialect *paltrig*, ragged]

pamper *v* **-r-** (*tr*) to treat over-indulgently and over-protectively; to cosset or spoil. [MidE, orig. Germanic]

pamphlet *n* a booklet or leaflet providing information or dealing with a current topic. [OFr *pamphilet*, from the title of the mediaeval Latin love poem, *Pamphilus, seu de Amore*]

pan[1] *n* a usu. metal pot used for cooking. **2** (often *in cmpds*) any of various usu. shallow vessels, with domestic, industrial or other uses: *a dustpan*, *bedpan*, etc. **3** the bowl of a lavatory. **4** either dish on a pair of scales. **5** a shallow hollow in the ground: *a salt pan*. **6** (*hist*) the hollow part of an old gun lock, holding the priming. — *v* **-nn-** **1** (*intr* & *tr*; **for**) to wash (river gravel) in a shallow metal vessel in search of gold. **2** (*tr*; *coll*) to criticise or review harshly.

pan[2] *v* **-nn-** (*tr* & *intr*) (of a film camera, etc.) to swing round so as to follow a moving object or show a panoramic view. — *n* a panning movement or shot. **[panorama]**

pan- *comb fm* all: *Pan-African*. [Gr, from *pas*, all]

panacea *n* a universal remedy; a cure-all for any ill, problem, etc. [Gr *pan-*, all + *akos*, remedy]

panache *n* flamboyant self-assurance. [Fr, plume]

panama *n* (also **panama hat**) a lightweight brimmed hat for men made from the plaited leaves of a palm-like Central American tree. [*Panama* in Central America]

panatella *n* a long slim cigar. [American Span, long thin biscuit]

pancake *n* a round of thin batter cooked on both sides in a frying-pan or on a griddle. [**pan**[1]]

Pancake Day *n* Shrove Tuesday, when pancakes are traditionally eaten.

pancake landing *n* an aircraft landing made in an emergency, with the wheels up and landing flat on the belly of the aircraft.

panchromatic *adj* (*photography*) (of a film) sensitive to all colours. [**pan-**]

pancreas *n* a gland lying behind the stomach, that produces insulin and discharges a digestive juice into the duodenum. [Gr *pan-* all + *kreas*, flesh]

panda *n* **1** (also **giant panda**) a large black and white bear-like animal of Tibet and China. **2** (also **lesser panda**) a raccoon-like animal of the Himalayas. [Nepali (language of Nepal) name]

panda car *n* in the UK, a small police patrol car, formerly white with black markings.

pandemonium *n* noise, chaos and confusion. [Milton's name for Hell's capital in *Paradise Lost*, from Gr *pan-*, all + *daimon*, demon]

pander *v* **-r-** (*intr* with **to**) to indulge or gratify (a person, or his or her depraved passions or tastes). — *n* a person who obtains a sexual partner for another. [*Pandarus*, in the *Iliad* the go-between who procured Cressida for Troilus]

Pandora's box *n* **1** a potential source of unlimited evils. **2** (*mythol*) the box given to Pandora, the first woman, by Zeus, from which all human ills escaped. [Name from Gr *pan-*, all + *doron*, gift]

pane *n* a sheet of glass, esp. one fitted into a window or door. [OFr *pan*, strip of cloth]

panegyric *n* a speech or piece of writing in praise of someone or something; a eulogy. [Gr *panegyrikos*, fit for a national festival]

panel *n* **1** a rectangular wooden board forming a section, esp. ornamentally sunken or raised, of a wall or door. **2** one of several strips of fabric making up a garment. **3** any of the metal sections forming the bodywork of a vehicle. **4** a board bearing the instruments and dials for controlling an aircraft, etc. **5** a team of people selected to judge a contest, or participate in a discussion, quiz or other game before an audience. **6** a list of jurors; the people serving on a jury. — *v* **-ll-** (*tr*) to fit (a wall or door) with wooden panels. [OFr, dimin. of *pan*, a strip of cloth, etc.]

panel-beating *n* the removal of dents from metal, esp. from the bodywork of a vehicle, using a soft-headed hammer. — *n* **panel-beater**.

panel game *n* one played by a panel of people.

panelling *n* (wood for making) panels in walls or doors.

panellist *n* a member of a panel (sense **5**).

panel pin *n* a small slender nail with a very small head.

pang *n* a painfully acute feeling (of hunger, remorse, etc.).

panic *n* a sudden overpowering fear, esp. one that grips a crowd or population. — *v* **-ck-** (*tr* & *intr*) to (cause to) feel panic. — *adj* **panicky**. [Gr *panikon*, baseless terror, caused by *Pan*, god of flocks and pastures]

panic-buy *v* (*intr* & *tr*) to buy (a commodity) in large quantities, in expectation of a shortage.

panic-stricken *adj* terrified.

panicle *n* (*bot*) a loose cluster of flowers. [Lat *panicula*, tuft]

panjandrum *n* (*humorous*) a pompous official. [From a string of nonsense composed by Samuel Foote (1720–77)]

pannier *n* **1** one of a pair of baskets carried on either side of a donkey's back; one of a pair of bags carried on either side of the rear wheel of a bicycle, etc. **2** (*hist*) a tucked-up arrangement of fabric on either side of a woman's skirt. [Fr *panier*, from Lat *panarium*, bread basket]

panoply *n* **-ies 1** the full splendid assemblage got together for a ceremony, etc.: *the full panoply of a society wedding*. **2** (*hist*) a full set of armour and weapons. [Gr *panoplia*, from *pan-*, all + *hopla*, weapons]

panorama *n* **1** an open and extensive or all-round view, e.g. of a landscape. **2** a view of something in all its range and variety: *the panorama of history*. — *adj* **panoramic**. — *adv* **panoramically**. [**pan-** + Gr *horama*, view]

panpipes *n* (*pl*) a musical instrument consisting of pipes of graded lengths bound together, played by blowing along their open ends. [Pan, Gr god of forests and pastures]

pansy *n* **-ies 1** a small garden plant of the violet family with multi-coloured broad-petalled flowers. **2** (*offensive slang*) an effeminate man or boy; a male homosexual. [OFr *pensée*, thought]

pant *v* **1** (*intr*) to breathe in gasps as a result of exertion. **2** (*tr*) to say breathlessly. **3** (*intr* with **for**) to be longing for: *panting for a drink*. — *n* a gasping breath. [OFr *pantaisier*, from Gr *phantasioun*, to hallucinate]

pantaloons *n* (*pl*) **1** baggy trousers gathered at the ankle. **2** tight-fitting trousers for men worn at the turn of the 19th cent. [*Pantalone*, a figure from Ital comedy, a skinny old man in tight hose]

pantechnicon *n* a large furniture-removal van. [Name of the premises of a London art-dealer (later a furniture warehouse), from **pan-** + Gr *techne*, art]

pantheism *n* **1** the belief that equates all the matter and forces in the universe with God. **2** readiness to believe in any god. — *n* **pantheist**. — *adj* **pantheistic**. [**pan-** + Gr *theos*, god]

pantheon *n* **1** all the gods of a particular people: *the ancient Greek pantheon*. **2** a temple sacred to all the gods. **3** a building in which the glorious dead of a nation have memorials or are buried. [Gr *pantheios*, of all the gods]

panther *n* **1** the name usu. given to a black leopard. **2** (*NAm*) a puma. [Gr, leopard]

panties *n* (*pl*) thin light knickers for women. [**pants**]

pantihose. See **panty hose**.

pantile *n* a roofing-tile with an S-shaped cross-section, laid so that the upward curve of one tile fits under the downward curve of the next. [**pan**[1] + **tile**]

panto *n* **-os** (*coll*) pantomime.

panto- or **pant-** *comb fm* all. [Gr, from *pas*, all]

pantograph *n* **1** a device consisting of jointed rods forming an adjustable parallelogram, for copying maps, plans, etc. to any scale. **2** a similarly shaped metal framework on the roof of an electric train, transmitting current from an overhead wire. [**panto-** + **-graph**]

pantomime *n* **1** a Christmas entertainment usu. based on a popular fairy tale, with songs, dancing, comedy acts, etc. **2** communication by gesture and facial expression; dumbshow. [Gr *pantomimos*, mime actor, literally 'imitator of all']

pantothenic acid *n* a vitamin of the vitamin B complex. [Gr *pantothen*, from every side, because of its wide occurrence]

pantry *n* **-ies** a room or cupboard for storing food in. [OFr *paneterie*, from Lat *panis*, bread]

pants *n* (*pl*) **1** an undergarment worn over the buttocks and genital area. **2** (*NAm*) trousers. — **caught with one's pants down** (*coll*) caught embarrassingly unprepared. — **since one was in short pants** (*coll NAm*) since one's childhood. — **wear the pants** (*coll*) to be the marriage partner who makes the decisons. [Short for **pantaloons**]

pant, or **pants, suit** *n* (*NAm*) a trouser suit.

panty hose or **pantihose** *n* (*pl*; *NAm*) women's tights. [**pants** + **hose**]

pap[1] *n* **1** soft semi-liquid food for babies and invalids. **2** (*derog*) trivial or worthless reading matter or entertainment.

pap[2] *n* **1** (*old*) a nipple or teat. **2** (*Scot*) in place names, a rounded hill.

papa *n* (*old*) a child's word for father. [Fr, & partly from Gr *pappas*, father]

papacy *n* **-ies 1** the position, power or period of office of a pope. **2** government by popes. [Lat *papatia*, from *papa*, pope]

papal *adj* of, or relating to, the pope or the papacy. [Lat *papalis*, from *papa*, pope]

paparazzo *n* **-zzi** a newspaper photographer who follows famous people about in the hope of photographing them in unguarded moments. [Name of photographer in the film *La Dolce Vita* (1959)]

papaya *n* (also **papaw** & **pawpaw**) a large yellow fruit with sweet orange flesh, from a tropical palm-like tree. [Span]

paper 1 a material manufactured in thin sheets from wood, rags, etc., used for writing and printing on, wrapping things, etc. **2** a loose piece of paper, e.g. a wrapper or printed sheet. **3** wallpaper. **4** a newspaper. **5** a set of questions on a certain subject for a written examination. **6** a written article dealing with a certain subject, esp. for reading to an audience. **7** (in *pl*) personal documents establishing one's identity, nationality, etc. **8** (in *pl*) a person's accumulated correspondence, diaries, etc. — *v* **-r-** (*tr*) to decorate with wallpaper: *paper the hall*. — **on paper 1** in theory as distinct from practice: *plans that look OK on paper*. **2** captured in written form: *get one's ideas down on paper*. — *v* **paper over** (*tr*) to cover or disguise. [OFr *papier*, from Gr *papyros*, papyrus]

paperback *n* a book with a paper binding.

paperboy or **papergirl** *n* a boy or girl who delivers or sells newspapers.

paper chase *n* a cross-country race in which runners follow a trail of dropped shreds of paper.

paper clip *n* **1** a metal clip formed from bent wire, for holding papers together. **2** (also **paper-fastener**) a round-headed brass device having two flexible legs that can be pushed through papers, then separated and folded back to secure them.

paper hanger *n* a person who puts up wallpaper.

paper knife *n* a knife for slitting open envelopes, etc.

paper mâché *n* papier-mâché.

paper money *n* bank notes.

paper tiger *n* something or someone more apparently threatening than actually dangerous.

paperweight *n* a heavy usu. ornamental object for holding papers down.

paperwork *n* routine written work, e.g. keeping files, writing letters and reports, etc.

papery *adj* like paper in texture.

papier-mâché *n* a light material consisting of pulped paper mixed with glue and sometimes other substances, moulded into shape while wet. [Fr, chewed paper]

papist *n* (*offensive*) a Roman Catholic. [Lat *papa*, pope]

papoose *n* a N American Indian baby or young child. [Narragansett (American Indian language) *papoos*]

paprika *n* a powdered seasoning for food, made from red peppers. [Hung]

papyrus *n* **-*ri*** or **-*ruses*** **1** a tall water plant native to N Africa, whose fibrous stems were used in the ancient world to make a paper-like material. **2** this material. **3** an ancient manuscript written on this material. [Gr *papyros*]

par *n* **1** a normal level or standard. **2** (*golf*) the standard number of strokes that a good golfer would take for a certain course or hole. **3** (*commerce & banking*; also **par of exchange**) the established value of the unit of one national currency against that of another. — **below**, or **not up to**, **par** (*coll*) **1** not up to the usual or required standard. **2** unwell. — **on a par with** equal to; the equivalent of. — **par for the course** (*coll*) only to be expected; predictable; typical. [Lat, equal]

par value *n* the value shown on a share certificate at time of issue; face value.

par. or **para.** *abbrev* paragraph.

par-. See **para-**[1].

para *n* (*coll*) a paratrooper.

para-[1] or (before vowels) **par-** *pfx* **1** alongside: *parathyroid*. **2** beyond: *parapsychology*. **3** resembling: *paramilitary*. **4** auxiliary to: *paramedical*. **5** abnormal: *paraesthesia*, i.e. abnormal sensation. [Gr]

para-[2] *comb fm* parachute: *paratrooper*.

parable *n* a story whose purpose is to convey a moral or religious lesson; an allegorical tale. [Gr *parabole*, analogy]

parabola *n* (*math*) the curve made by intersecting a cone with a plane parallel to its side; any curve of this shape. — *adj* **parabolic**. [Gr *parabole*, placing alongside]

paracetamol *n* a mild pain-relieving and fever-reducing drug. [From medical name *para-acetylaminophenol*]

parachute *n* an apparatus consisting of a loose umbrella of light fabric, with a harness for attaching to, and slowing the fall of, a person or package dropped from an aircraft. — *v* (*intr* & *tr*) to drop by parachute. — *n* **parachutist**. [Fr, *para-* (from Ital *parare*, to defend against) + *chute*, fall]

parade *n* **1** a ceremonial procession of people, vehicles, etc. **2** (of soldiers, etc.) the state of being drawn up in rank for formal marching or inspection; a body of soldiers, etc. drawn up in this way: *be on parade*. **3** a self-advertising display: *make a parade of one's generosity*. **4** used as a name for a promenade, shopping street, etc. — *v* **1** (*intr* & *tr*) to (cause to) walk or march in procession. **2** to display ostentatiously; to flaunt. [Fr, from Span *parada*, halt, stopping-place]

parade ground *n* the square or yard where soldiers assemble for inspection, marching practice, etc.

paradigm *n* **1** an example, model or pattern. **2** (*gram*) a table of the inflected forms of a word serving as a pattern for words of the same declension or conjugation; the words showing a particular pattern. — *adj* **paradigmatic**. [Gr *paradeigma*, pattern]

paradise *n* **1** heaven. **2** a place of utter bliss or delight. **3** the Garden of Eden. [Gr *paradeisos*, park]

paradox *n* **1** a statement that seems to contradict itself, as *'More haste, less speed'*. **2** a situation involving apparently contradictory elements. **3** (*logic*) a proposition that is essentially absurd or leads to an absurd conclusion. — *adj* **paradoxical**. — *adv* **paradoxically**. [Gr *paradoxos*, incredible, from *para*, against + *doxa*, opinion]

paradoxical sleep *n* a phase of sleep in which there is increased electrical activity in the brain, and, in humans, dreaming and rapid eye movement.

paraffin *n* **1** a fuel oil obtained from petroleum or coal and used in aircraft, domestic heaters, etc. **2** any of a range of unreactive, saturated hydrocarbons. [Lat *parum*, little + *affinis*, having an affinity, with reference to its unreactiveness]

paraffin wax *n* a white waxy substance obtained from petroleum, used e.g. to make candles.

paragon *n* someone who is a model of excellence or perfection. [OItal *paragone*, comparison]

paragraph *n* **1** a section of a piece of writing, starting on a fresh, often indented, line, and dealing with a distinct point or idea. **2** a short report in a newspaper. **3** (*printing*) the sign (¶), indicating the start of a new paragraph. — *v* (*tr*) to divide (text) into paragraphs. [Gr *paragraphe*, marked passage, from *para*, beside + *graphein*, to write]

parakeet *n* any of various small, long-tailed parrots. [OFr *paroquet*, parrot]

parallax *n* (*physics*) the apparent change in the position of an object that occurs as the observer changes position. [Gr *parallaxis*, change]

parallel *adj* (**to**) **1** (of lines or planes) being at every point the same distance apart. **2** similar; exactly equivalent; corresponding. — *adv* (**to**) alongside and at an unvarying distance from. — *n* **1** (*geom*) a line or plane parallel to another. **2** a corresponding or equivalent instance. **3** (also **parallel of latitude**) any of the lines of latitude circling the earth parallel to the equator and representing the angular degrees of distance from it. **4** (*printing*; in *pl*) the sign (‖) used as a reference mark. — *v* **-*l*-** **1** to equal. **2** to correspond to or be equivalent to. — *n* **parallelism**. — **in parallel 1** (of electrical appliances) so co-ordinated that terminals of the same polarity are connected. — **on a parallel with** corresponding to. — **without parallel** unequalled; unprecedented. [Gr *parallelos*, side by side]

parallel bars *n* (*pl*) two parallel shoulder-height rails fixed to upright posts, used by men for gymnastic exercises.

parallelogram *n* a four-sided geometrical figure with opposite sides parallel to each other.

paralyse *v* (*tr*) **1** to affect (a person or bodily part) with paralysis. **2** (of fear, etc.) to immobilise. **3** to disrupt or bring to a standstill. [Gr *paralyein*, to enfeeble]

paralysis *n* **1** loss of the power of motion or of sensation in any part of the body. **2** a state of immobility; a standstill.

paralytic *adj* **1** relating to, caused by or suffering from paralysis. **2** (*coll*) helplessly drunk. — *n* a person affected by paralysis. — *adv* **paralytically**.

paramedical *adj* (of personnel or services) supporting, and supplementary to, the work of the medical profession. — *n* **paramedic**. [**para-**[1] (sense **4**)]

parameter *n* **1** (*math*) a constant quantity that determines the form of a particular mathematical equation, etc. **2** (usu. in *pl*) a limiting factor that serves to define the scope of a task, project, discussion, etc. [Modern Lat *parametrum*, from Gr *para-*, beside + *metron*, measure]

paramilitary *adj* organised similarly to (and supplementing) a military force. [**para-**[1] (sense **3**)]

paramount *adj* foremost; supreme; of supreme importance. [OFr *par*, by + *amont*, above, upwards]

paranoia *n* **1** (*psychol*) a mental illness characterised by feelings of persecution or exaggerated notions of one's importance. **2** a tendency to be suspicious and distrustful of others. — *adj* & *n* **paranoiac** or **paranoid**. — *adv* **paranoiacally**. [Gr *paranoia*, from *para*, beside, beyond + *nous*, mind]

paranormal *adj* (of occurrences) unexplainable scientifically. — *n* paranormal occurrences. [**para-**[1] (sense **2**)]

parapet *n* **1** a low wall along the edge of a bridge, balcony, etc. **2** an embankment of earth or sandbags protecting the soldiers in a military trench. [Ital *parapetto*, from *parare*, to defend + *petto*, chest]

paraphernalia *n* (*pl* or *sing*) **1** the equipment and accessories associated with an activity, etc. **2** personal belongings. [Gr *parapherna*, a bride's personal effects, i.e. not part of her dowry, from *para*, beside + *pherne*, dowry]

paraphrase *n* a restatement of something giving its meaning in other words; a re-wording or re-phrasing. — *v* (*tr*) to express in other words. [Gr *para*, beyond + *phrazein*, to speak]

paraplegia *n* paralysis of the lower part of the body. — *adj* & *n* **paraplegic**. [Gr *paraplegia*, a one-sided stroke, from *para*, beside + *plege*, blow]

parapsychology *n* the study of those mental phenomena, e.g. telepathy and clairvoyance, that imply an acquisition of knowledge otherwise than through the known senses. — *adj* **parapsychological**. — *n* **parapsychologist**. [**para-**[1] (sense **2**)]

paraquat® *n* a weedkiller highly poisonous to humans. [From part of the technical description of the chemical]

parasite *n* **1** an animal or plant that lives on, and obtains its nourishment from, another. **2** (*derog*) a person who lives at others' expense, making no adequate contribution in return. — *adj* **parasitic** or **parasitical**. — *adv* **parasitically**. — *n* **parasitism**. [Gr *para*, beside + *sitos*, food]

parasol *n* a light umbrella used as a protection against the sun; a sunshade. [Fr, from Ital *parasole*, from *parare*, to ward off + *sole*, sun]

parathyroid *n* any of four small glands beside the thyroid, producing a hormone that controls the level of calcium in the blood. [**para-**[1] (sense **1**)]

paratroops *n* (*pl*) troops trained to parachute into enemy territory or a battle zone. [**para-**[2]]

paratrooper *n* a member of the paratroops.

paratyphoid *n* a disease similar to typhoid, with fever, abdominal pain, vomiting and diarrhoea, caused by the bacterium salmonella in contaminated food. [**para-**[1] (sense **2**)]

parboil *v* (*tr*) to boil until partially cooked. [OFr *parboillir*, from Lat *perbullire*, to boil thoroughly; meaning altered by confusion of *par-* with **part**]

parcel *n* **1** something wrapped in paper, etc. and secured with string or sticky tape. **2** a portion, e.g. of land. **3** a group of people, etc. **4** a lot or portion of goods for sale; a deal or transaction. — *v* **-ll-** (*tr*) **1** (**up**) to wrap up in a parcel. **2** (**out**) to divide into portions and share out. [OFr *parcelle*, from Lat *particula*, dimin. of *pars*, part]

parch *v* (*tr*) **1** to dry up; to deprive (soil, plants, etc.) of water. **2** to make thirsty. **3** to roast (peas) slightly. [MidE *perchen*]

parchment *n* **1** a material formerly used for bookbinding and for writing on, made from goatskin, calfskin or sheepskin; a piece of this, or a manuscript written on it. **2** stiff off-white writing-paper resembling this. [OFr *parchemin* from Lat *Pergamena* (*charta*) paper of Pergamum, influenced by OFr *parche*, leather]

pardon *v* **-n-** **1** (*tr*) to forgive or excuse (someone) for (a fault or offence). **2** to cancel the punishment of. — *n* **1** forgiveness. **2** the cancellation of a punishment. — *adj* **pardonable**. — *adv* **pardonably**. — **I beg your pardon** or **pardon me** I apologise; excuse me; I'm sorry. **2** (also **pardon?**) could you repeat that?; I didn't hear. [Fr *pardonner*, from Lat *perdonare*, to overlook]

pardoner *n* in the Middle Ages, a person licensed to sell pardons from the pope, freeing people from punishment for their sins.

pare *v* (*tr*) **1** (**away**) to trim off (skin, etc.) in layers. **2** to cut (finger- or toe-nails). **3** to peel (fruit). **4** (**down**) to reduce (expenses, funding, etc.) bit by bit, for economy's sake. [Fr *parer*, from Lat *parare*, to prepare]

parent *n* **1** a father or mother. **2** the adopter or guardian of a child. **3** an animal or plant that has produced offspring. **4** that from which anything is derived; a source or origin. — *v* (*intr* & *tr*) to be or act as a parent; to care for as a parent. — *adj* **parental**. — *adv* **parentally**. — *n* **parenthood**. [Lat *parens*, from *parere*, to bring forth]

parentage *n* family or ancestry.

parent company *n* a business company owning other, usu. smaller companies.

parenting *n* the activities and duties of a parent.

parent-teacher association *n* an association of the parents and teachers of children at a school, intended to improve co-operation and mutual understanding.

parenthesis *n* **-eses** **1** a word or phrase inserted into a sentence as a comment, usu. marked off by brackets or dashes. **2** (in *pl*) a pair of round brackets () used to enclose such a comment. — *adj* **parenthetic** or **parenthetical**. — *adv* **parenthetically**. [Gr, from *para*, beside + *en*, in + *thesis*, placing]

par excellence *adv* in the highest degree; in the truest sense of the word; beyond compare. [Fr, as an example of excellence]

pariah *n* **1** someone scorned and avoided by others; a social outcast. **2** in S India and Burma, a person of no, or low, caste. [Tamil *paraiyan*, literally a drummer]

parietal *adj* relating to, or forming, the wall of a bodily cavity, e.g. the skull: *the parietal bones*. [Lat *paries*, wall]

parish *n* **1** a district or area served by its own church and priest or minister. **2** (also **civil parish**) esp. in England, the smallest unit of local government. **3** the inhabitants of a parish. [OFr *paroisse*, from Gr *paroikia*, from *paroikos*, neighbour]

parish clerk *n* an official performing various duties connected with a parish church.

parish council *n* the administrative body of a civil parish. — *n* **parish councillor**.

parishioner *n* a member or inhabitant of a parish.

parish register *n* a book in which the christenings, marriages and deaths in a parish are recorded.

parity *n* **-ies** **1** equality, e.g. in pay. **2** precise equivalence; exact correspondence. **3** (*finance*) an established equivalence between a unit of national currency and an amount in another national currency. [Lat *paritas*, from *par*, equal]

park *n* **1** an area in a town with grass and trees, reserved for public recreation. **2** an area of land kept as a nature reserve, etc.: *a wild-life park*. **3** the woodland and pasture forming the estate of a large country house. **4** (*cap*) used as a street name. **5** (*NAm*) a sports field or stadium. **6** (with **the**; *coll*) the pitch in soccer. **7** a place where vehicles can be left temporarily. — *v* **1** (*tr* & *intr*) to (manoeuvre into position and) leave (a vehicle) temporarily. **2** (*tr*; *coll*) to lay, place, leave or dump (something) somewhere temporarily. **3** (*tr*; *coll*) to install or sit (oneself). [OFr *parc*]

parking-lot *n* (*NAm*) a car park.

parking-meter *n* a coin-operated meter in the street beside which a car may be parked for a limited period.

parking-ticket *n* an official notice of a fine served on a motorist for illegal parking.

parkland *n* pasture and woodland forming part of a country estate.

parka *n* **1** a hooded jacket made of skins, worn by the Inuit and Aleut people of the Arctic. **2** a windproof jacket, esp. quilted with a fur-trimmed hood; an anorak. [Aleut, skin, coat, from Russ, pelt, skin jacket]

parkin *n* a moist ginger-flavoured oatmeal cake made with treacle.

Parkinson's disease *n* (also **parkinsonism**) a disease of the central nervous system causing a loss of muscular co-ordination and involuntary shaking of the limbs. [J *Parkinson* (1755–1824), Eng physician]

Parkinson's law *n* (*ironic*) the observed truth that work expands to fill the time available for its completion. [C Northcote *Parkinson* (1909–), Eng political scientist]

parky *adj* **-ier**, **-iest** (*coll*) (of weather) chilly.

parlance *n* a particular style of using words: *in legal parlance*. [OFr, from *parler*, to talk]

parley *v* **-eys**, **-eyed** (*intr*; **with**) to discuss peace terms, etc. with an enemy. — *n* **-eys** a meeting with an enemy to discuss peace terms, etc. [OFr *parler*, to talk]

parliament *n* the highest law-making assembly of a nation; (*cap*) in Britain, the House of Commons and House of Lords. [OFr *parlement*, from *parler*, to talk]

member of parliament *n* (also *caps*) a person elected to represent the people of a district in parliament.

parliamentarian *n* **1** an expert in parliamentary procedure. **2** an experienced parliamentary debater. **3** (*hist*) a supporter of the Parliamentary party in the 17th-cent. English Civil War.

parliamentary *adj* **1** of, relating to, or issued by, a parliament. **2** (of conduct or procedure) in keeping with the rules of parliament. **3** (of language) admissible in parliament.

parlour *n* **1** a sitting-room for receiving visitors. **2** a shop or commercial premises providing particular goods or services: *an ice-cream parlour*, *beauty parlour*, *funeral* *parlour*, etc. [OFr *parlur*, from *parler*, to talk]

parlour game *n* a game such as charades, suitable for playing in the sitting-room.

parlous *adj* precarious; perilous; dire. [Variant of **perilous**]

Parmesan *n* a hard dry Italian cheese, esp. served grated with pasta dishes. [Ital *Parmegiano*, from Parma]

parochial *adj* **1** (*derog*) concerned only with local affairs; narrow, limited or provincial in outlook. **2** of, or relating to, a parish. — *n* **parochialism**. — *adv* **parochially**. [Lat *parochialis*, from *parochia*, parish]

parody *n* **-ies 1** a comic or satirical imitation of a work, or the style, of a particular writer, composer, etc. **2** a poor attempt at something; a mockery or travesty. — *v* **-ies, -ied** (*tr*) to ridicule through parody; to mimic satirically. — *n* **parodist**. [Gr *para*, beside + *oide*, song]

parole *n* **1** the release of a prisoner before the end of his or her sentence, on promise of good behaviour: *released on parole*. **2** the promise of a prisoner so released to behave well. — *v* (*tr*) to release or place (a prisoner) on parole. [Fr *parole* (*d'honneur*), word (of honour)]

paroxysm *n* a sharp attack, e.g. of pain; a violent fit or burst, e.g. of coughing, rage, laughter, etc. — *adj* **paroxysmal**. [Gr *paroxysmos*, a fit]

parquet *n* flooring composed of small inlaid blocks of wood arranged in a geometric pattern. — *n* **parquetry**. [OFr, dimin. of *parc*, enclosure]

parr *n* ***parr*** or ***parrs*** a young salmon aged up to two years.

parricide *n* the killing of, or a person who kills, a parent or near relative. — *adj* **parricidal**. [Lat *parricidium* (the killing) & *parricida* (the killer), probably from *pater*, father + *caedere*, to kill]

parrot *n* **1** a tropical, esp. S American, bird with a hooked beak and colourful plumage, some species of which can imitate human speech. **2** a person who merely echoes what others say. — *v* **-t-** (*tr*) to repeat or echo (another's words, etc.) mindlessly. [OFr *paroquet*, perhaps dimin. of *Pierre*]

parrot-fashion *adv* by mindless repetition.

parry *v* **-ies, -ied** (*tr*) **1** to fend off (a blow). **2** to sidestep (a question) adroitly. — *n* **-ies** an act of parrying. [Fr *parer*, to ward off]

parse *v* (*tr & intr*) **1** (*gram*) to analyse (a sentence) grammatically; to give the part of speech, and explain the grammatical role, of (a word). **2** (*comput*) to analyse (a string of input symbols) in terms of the computing language being used. — *n* **parser**. [Lat *pars* (*orationis*), part (of speech)]

parsec *n* (*astron*) a unit of distance in space equal to 3·26 light years or 19·2 million million miles. [**parallax** + **second**]

Parsee *n* one of the descendants of the ancient Zoroastrians, who fled from Persia to settle in the Bombay area of India in the 8th cent. AD. — *n* **Parseeism**. [Persian, Persian]

parsimonious *adj* too careful in spending money; stingy. — *adv* **parsimoniously**. — *n* **parsimony**. [Lat *parsimonia*, thrift]

parsley *n* a plant with curled feathery leaves used as a garnish and flavouring. [Gr *petroselinon*, from *petra*, rock + *selinon*, parsley]

parsnip *n* a pungent-tasting root vegetable that looks like a thick white carrot. [Lat *pastinacum* (from *pastinum*, dibble) + MidE *nepe*, turnip]

parson *n* **1** a parish priest in the Church of England. **2** any clergyman. [Lat *persona*, parish priest, person, personage, mask]

parsonage *n* the residence of a parson.

parson's nose (*coll*) the rump of a plucked fowl, esp. a turkey or chicken.

part *n* **1** a portion, piece or bit; some but not all. **2** one of a set of equal divisions or amounts that compose a whole: *in the proportion of five parts cement to two of sand*. **3** an essential piece; a component: *vehicle spare parts*. **4** a section of a book; any of the episodes of a story, etc. issued or broadcast as a serial. **5** a performer's role in a play, opera, etc.; the words, actions, etc. belonging to the role. **6** the melody, etc. given to a particular instrument or voice in a musical work. **7** one's share, responsibility or duty in something: *do one's part*; *want no part in* or *of it*. **8** (usu. in *pl*) a region: *foreign parts*. **9** (in *pl*) talents; abilities: *a woman of parts*. — *v* **1** (*tr*) to separate (e.g. curtains, combatants, etc.). **2** (*intr* with **from, with**) to leave (someone, etc.). **3** (*intr*) to leave one another, separate or diverge. **4** (*intr* with **with** or *tr* with **from**) to (force to) give up or hand over: *reluctant to part with*, or *be parted from, her money*. **5** (*tr*) to put a parting in (hair). — **for the most part 1** usually. **2** mostly or mainly. — **for my part** as far as I am concerned. — **in great** or **large part** mostly. — **in part** partly. — **on the part of 1** as done by. **2** so far as (someone) is concerned. — **part and parcel of** an essential part of. — **part company (with)** to separate; to leave one another. — **play a part** to be involved. — **take in good part** to take no offence at (a criticism, joke, etc. against one). — **take part (in)** to participate; to share. — **take someone's part** to support someone; to take someone's side. — **the better, best** or **greater part of** most of. [Lat *pars*, part]

part exchange *n* a purchase or sale made by exchanging used goods for part of the value of new goods.

parting *n* **1** the act of taking leave. **2** a divergence or separation: *a parting of the ways*. **3** a line of exposed scalp dividing hair brushed in opposite directions.
parting shot *n* a last hostile remark made on leaving. ◇ See also **Parthian shot**.
partly *adv* to a certain extent; not wholly; in some parts.
part of speech *n* (*gram*) any of the grammatical classes of words, e.g. noun, adjective, verb, preposition, etc.
part song *n* a song for singing in harmonised parts.
part-time *adj* & *adv* during only part of the full working day. — *n* **part-timer**.
partake *v* ***-took***, ***-taken*** (*intr*) **1** (with **in**) to participate in. **2** (**of**) to eat or drink. **3** (with **of**; *literary*) to have some of (a certain quality, etc.). [Formed from *partaking*, from MidE *part-taking*]
parterre *n* **1** a formal, ornamental flower garden laid out with lawns and paths. **2** the pit of a theatre. [Fr *par terre*, on the ground]
parthenogenesis *n* (*biol*) in some insects and plants, reproduction without fertilisation by the male. [Gr *parthenos*, maiden + **-genesis**]
Parthian shot *n* a final hostile remark made on departing. ◇ See also **parting shot**. [From the practice of the horsemen of ancient Parthia of turning to shoot arrows at following enemies as they rode off]
partial *adj* **1** incomplete; in part only. **2** (with **to**) having a liking for. **3** favouring one side or person unfairly; biased. — *n* **partiality**. [Lat *partialis*, from *pars*, part]
participate *v* (*intr*; **in**) to take part or be involved. — *n* **participant** or **participator**. — *n* **participation**. — *adj* **participatory**. [Lat *pars*, part + *capere*, to take]
participle *n* a word formed from a verb and used as an adjective or to form tenses, the **present participle** in English being formed with **-ing** (*cheering news*; *was going*) and the **past participle** generally with **-ed**, **-t** or **-en** (*broken biscuits*; *will be burnt*). — *adj* **participial**. — *adv* **participially**. [Lat *participium*, a sharing, participle, from *pars*, part + *capere*, to take (from its sharing features of both a verb and an adjective)]
particle *n* **1** (*physics*) a tiny unit of matter such as a molecule, atom or electron. **2** a tiny piece. **3** the least bit: *not a particle of sympathy*. **4** (*gram*) an uninflected word, e.g. a preposition, conjunction or interjection. **5** (*gram*) an affix, such as *un-* or *-ly*. [Lat *particula*, dimin. of *pars*, part]
particoloured *adj* partly one colour, partly another; variegated. [OFr *parti*, variegated]
particular *adj* **1** specific; single; individually known or referred to. **2** especial: *took particular care*. **3** (**about**, **over**) difficult to satisfy; fastidious; exacting. **4** exact; detailed. — *n* **1** a detail. **2** (in *pl*) personal details: *took down her particulars*. — **in particular** especially; specifically. [Lat *particularis*, from *particula*, dimin. of *pars*, part]
particularise or **-ize** *v* **1** (*tr*) to specify individually. **2** (*tr*) to give specific examples of. **3** (*intr*) to go into detail. — *n* **particularisation** or **-z-**.
particularly *adv* more than usually: *particularly good*. **2** specifically; especially: *particularly hates board games*.
partisan *n* **1** an enthusiastic supporter of a party, person, cause, etc. **2** a member of a resistance group in a country occupied by an enemy. — *adj* strongly loyal to one side, esp. blindly so; biased. — *n* **partisanship**. [Fr]
partition *n* **1** a screen or thin wall dividing a room. **2** the dividing of a country into two or more independent states. — *v* ***-n-*** (*tr*) **1** to divide (a country) into independent states. **2** (with **off**) to separate off with a partition. [Lat *partitio*, division]
partitive *n* & *adj* (a word) denoting a part of a whole, e.g. *some*, *any*, *most*. — *adv* **partitively**. [Lat *partire*, to divide]
partner *n* **1** one of two or more people jointly owning or running a business or other enterprise on an equal footing. **2** a person one dances with. **3** a person who is on the same side as oneself in a game of e.g. bridge, tennis, etc. **4** a person with whom one has an esp. long-term sexual relationship, e.g. one's husband or wife. — *v* ***-r-*** (*tr*) to act as a partner to. [MidE *partener*, from *parcener*, joint inheritor, influenced by **part**]
partnership *n* **1** a relationship in which two or more people or groups operate together as partners. **2** the status of a partner: *offered her a partnership*. **3** a business or other enterprise jointly owned or run by two or more people, etc.
partook. See **partake**.
partridge *n* a plump-bodied, grey-and-brown game bird. [OFr *perd(r)iz*, from Lat & Gr *perdix*]
parturient *adj* (*med*) giving birth. [Lat *parturire*, to give birth]
parturition *n* (*med*) the process of giving birth; childbirth.
party *n* ***-ies*** **1** a social gathering, esp. of invited guests, for enjoyment or celebration. **2** a group of people involved in a certain activity together. **3** an esp. national organisation of people united by a common, esp. political, aim. **4** (esp. *legal*) any of the (groups of) people concerned in a contract, agreement, lawsuit, etc.: *third-party insurance*. **5** (*old facet*) a person: *an elderly party*. — **be (a) party to** to be one of the people involved in (an agreement, decision, action, etc.). [OFr *partie*, past participle of *partir*, to divide]
party line *n* **1** a telephone line shared by two or more people. **2** the official opinion of a political party on any particular issue.

party piece *n* an act or turn that one can be called on to perform to entertain others, e.g. at a party.

party wall *n* a wall that divides two houses, etc., being the joint responsibility of both owners.

parvenu or **parvenue** *n* (*derog*) respectively a man or woman who has recently acquired substantial wealth but lacks the social refinement to go with it. [Fr, past participle of *parvenir*, to arrive]

pas *n* ***pas*** (*ballet*) a step. [Fr]

pas de deux *n* ***pas de deux*** a dance for two performers.

PASCAL *n* (*comput*) a programming language designed to encourage structured programming. [In honour of B *Pascal* (1623–62), Fr mathematician who designed a calculating machine in 1642]

pascal *n* an SI unit of pressure, equivalent to one newton of force on one square metre. [Ety. as for **PASCAL**]

paschal *adj* **1** relating to the Jewish festival of Passover. **2** relating to Easter. [Lat *paschalis*, from Gr *pascha*, from Hebr *pesah*, Passover]

pasha *n* (*hist*) a high-ranking Turkish official; placed after the name in titles. [Turk *paşa*]

pasqueflower *n* a purple-flowered anemone that blooms at Easter. [OFr *passefleur* (from *passer*, to surpass + *fleur*, flower), influenced by *pasques*, Easter]

pass 1 (*tr* & *intr*) to come alongside and progress beyond: *passed her on the stair*. **2** (*intr*) to run, flow, progress, etc.: *the blood passing through our veins*. **3** (*tr* & *intr*; **through, into,** etc.) to (cause to) go, penetrate, etc.: *pass through a filter*. **4** (*tr* & *intr*) to move lightly across, over, etc.: *pass a duster over the furniture*. **5** (*intr*) to move from one state or stage to another: *pass from the larval to the pupal stage*. **6** (*tr*) to exceed or surpass: *pass the target*. **7** (*tr* & *intr*) (of a vehicle) to overtake. **8** (*tr* & *intr*) to achieve the required standard in (a test, etc.); to award (a student, etc.) the marks required for success in a test, etc. **9** (*intr*) to take place: *what passed between them*. **10** (*intr* & *tr*) (of time) to go by; to use up (time) in some activity, etc. **11** (*tr* & *intr*; **round**, **on**, **out**) to hand or transfer; to be transferred; to circulate. **12** (*tr* & *intr*; **down**) to hand down; to be inherited. **13** (*tr* & *intr*; *sport*) to throw or kick (the ball, etc.) to another player in one's team. **14** (*tr* & *intr*) to agree to (a proposal or resolution), or be agreed to; to vote (a law) into effect. **15** (*tr*) (of a judge or law court) to pronounce (judgement). **16** (*intr*) to go away after a while: *Her nausea passed*. **17** (*intr*) to be accepted, tolerated or ignored: *let it pass*. **18** (*intr* with **as**, **for**) to be accepted as or mistaken for: *insults that pass for wit*. **19** (*intr*) to choose not to answer in a quiz, etc. or bid in a card game. **20** (*tr*) to make (a comment, etc.). **21** (*tr*) to discharge (urine or faeces). — *n* **1** a route through a gap in a mountain range. **2** an official card or document permitting one to enter somewhere, be absent from duty, etc. **3** a successful result in an examination, but usu. without distinction or honours. **4** (*sport*) a throw, kick, hit, etc. to another player in one's team. **5** a state of affairs: *reach a sorry* or *pretty pass*. **6** (**at**) an attempt at sexual familiarity: *made a pass at her*. **7** a decision not to answer in a quiz, etc., or not to bid in a card game. — **come** or **be brought to pass** to happen. — **in passing** while dealing with something else; casually; by allusion rather than directly. — *v* **pass away** or **on** (*intr*; *euph*) to die. — *v* **pass by 1** (*intr* & *tr*) to go past. **2** (*tr*) to overlook or ignore. — *v* **pass off 1** (*intr*) (of sickness, an emotion, etc.) to go away. **2** (*intr*) (of an arranged event) to go off (well, badly, etc.). **3** (*tr*; **as**) to represent as: *pass oneself off as a student*. — *v* **pass out** (*intr*; *coll*) **1** to faint. **2** to leave a military or police college having successfully completed one's training. — *v* **pass over** (*tr*) to overlook; to ignore. — *v* **pass up** (*tr*; *coll*) to neglect or sacrifice (an opportunity). [Lat *passus*, step, pace]

passable *adj* **1** barely adequate or (*coll*) pretty good. **2** (of a road, etc.) able to be travelled along, crossed, etc. — *adv* **passably**.

passbook *n* a book in which the amounts of money put into and taken out of a bank account, etc. are recorded.

passer-by *n* ***passers-by*** a person walking past.

passing *adj* **1** lasting only briefly. **2** casual: *a passing glance, reference*, etc.

passkey *n* a key designed to open a varied set of locks; a master key.

pass law *n* formerly in S Africa, a law restricting the movement of non-Whites, requiring them to carry identification at all times.

passage *n* **1** (also **passageway**) a route through; a corridor, narrow street or channel. **2** a tubular vessel in the body. **3** a piece of a text or musical composition. **4** the process of passing: *the passage of time*. **5** (the cost of) a journey by boat. **6** permission or freedom to pass through a territory, etc. **7** the voting of a law, etc. into effect. [OFr, from *passer*, to pass]

passé *adj* outmoded; old-fashioned; having faded out of popularity. [Fr, past participle of *passer*, to pass]

passenger *n* **1** a traveller in a vehicle, boat, aeroplane, etc. driven, sailed or piloted by someone else. **2** (*derog*) someone not doing his or her share of the work in a joint project, etc. [OFr *passagier*, from *passage*, with inserted *n* as in *messenger*]

passerine *adj* & *n* (*zool*) (a bird) belonging to the order of perching birds, including all British songbirds. [Lat *passer*, sparrow]

passim *adv* (of a word, etc.) occurring frequently throughout the literary or academic work in question. [Lat, here and there]

passion *n* **1** a violent emotion, e.g. hate, anger or envy. **2** a fit of anger. **3** sexual love or desire. **4** (**for**) an enthusiasm; something for which one has great enthusiasm. **5** (*cap*) the suffering and death of Christ; an account of this from one of the Gospels; a musical setting of one of these accounts. [OFr, from Latin *passio*, from *pati*, to suffer]

passionate *adj* **1** easily moved to passion; strongly emotional. **2** keen; enthusiastic. — *adv* **passionately**.

passion flower *n* any of several tropical climbing plants with large yellow or purple flowers, having features suggestive of the nails, crown of thorns and other emblems of Christ's Passion.

passion fruit *n* the edible fruit of the passion flower, egg-shaped, with a wrinkled brown skin.

passion play *n* a religious drama representing the suffering and death of Christ.

passive *adj* **1** lacking positive or assertive qualities; submissive. **2** lethargic; inert. **3** (*gram*) denoting the form of the verb used when the subject undergoes, rather than performs, the action of the verb. ◇ See also **active**. — *n* **1** (also **passive voice**) the passive form of a verb. **2** a verb in the passive. — *adv* **passively**. — *n* **passiveness** or **passivity**. [Lat *passivus*, from *pati*, to suffer]

passive resistance *n* the use of non-violent means, e.g. fasting, to resist authority.

passive smoking *n* the involuntary breathing in of others' tobacco smoke.

Passover *n* an eight-day Jewish spring festival celebrating the sparing of the first-born Israelite children in Egypt, and the subsequent liberation of the Israelites, as recounted in the Book of Exodus.

passport *n* an official document issued by the government, giving proof of the holder's identity and nationality, and permission to travel abroad with its protection. **2** an asset that guarantees one something: *A degree is your passport to a good job*.

past *adj* **1** of an earlier time; of long ago; bygone. **2** recently ended; just gone by: *the past year*. **3** over; finished. **4** former; previous: *past presidents*. **5** (*gram*) (of the tense of a verb) indicating a past action or condition. — *prep* **1** up to and beyond: *went past me*. **2** after in time or age. **3** beyond; farther away than. **4** having advanced too far for: *She's past playing with dolls*. **5** beyond the reach of: *past help, belief, description*, etc. — *adv* **1** so as to pass by: *go past*. **2** ago: *two months past*. — *n* **1** the time before the present; events, etc. belonging to this. **2** one's earlier life or career. **3** a disreputable episode earlier in one's life: *Who hasn't a past?* **4** (*gram*) the past tense. — **not put it past someone** (*coll*) to believe someone quite liable (to do a certain thing). — **past it** (*coll*) having lost the vigour of one's youth or prime. [Old past participle of **pass**]

past master *n* (**at**) an expert.

past participle see **participle**.

pasta *n* **1** a dough made with flour, water and eggs shaped in a variety of forms such as spaghetti, macaroni, lasagne, etc. **2** a cooked dish of this, usu. with a sauce. [Ital, from Lat, from Gr, barley porridge]

paste *n* **1** a stiff moist mixture usu. of powder and water, e.g. a mixture of flour and water used as an adhesive. **2** a spread for sandwiches, etc. made from ground meat or fish. **3** any fine dough-like mixture: *almond paste*. **4** a hard brilliant glass used in making imitation gems. — *v* (*tr*) **1** to stick with paste. **2** (*coll*) to thrash or beat soundly. **3** (**up**; *printing*) to mount (text, illustrations, etc.) on a backing for photographing, etc. (*n* **paste-up**). [OFr, from Lat *pasta*, paste, from Gr, barley porridge]

pasteboard *n* stiff board built up from thin sheets of paper pasted together.

pasting *n* (*coll*) a thrashing.

pastel *n* **1** a chalk-like crayon made from ground pigment. **2** a picture drawn with pastels. — *adj* (of colours) delicately pale. [Fr, from Ital *pastello*, from Lat *pastillus*, a ball or cake of something]

pastern *n* part of a horse's foot between the hoof and the fetlock. [OFr *pasturon*, from *pasture*, pasture, tether]

pasteurise or **-ize** *v* (*tr*) to kill bacteria in (milk, beer, etc.) by a special heating process. — *n* **pasteurisation** or **-z-**. [L *Pasteur* (1822–95), Fr chemist]

pastiche *n* a musical, artistic or literary work in someone else's style, or in a mixture of styles. [Fr, from Ital *pasticcio*, pie, bungle, pastiche]

pastille *n* **1** a small fruit-flavoured, esp. medicinal, sweet. **2** a cone of fragrant paste for scenting a room. [Fr, from Lat *pastillus*, a ball or cake of something]

pastime *n* a spare-time pursuit; a hobby. [**pass** + **time**]

pastor *n* a member of the clergy, esp. in churches other than Anglican and Catholic, having a congregation in his or her care. [Lat, shepherd]

pastoral *adj* **1** relating to, or (of a poem, painting, musical work, etc.) depicting, the countryside or country life. **2** relating to a member of the clergy and his or her work. **3** relating to a shepherd and his or her work. **4** (of land) used for pasture. — *n* **1** a pastoral poem or painting. **2** (also **pastorale** *-les*) a musical work evoking the countryside. **3** a letter from a bishop to the clergy and people of the diocese.

pastorate *n* **1** the (period of) office, or the residence, of a pastor. **2** a body of pastors.

pastrami *n* strongly spiced smoked beef. [Yiddish]

pastry *n* **-ies 1** dough made with flour, fat and water, used for pie-crusts. **2** a sweet baked article made with this; a pie, tart, etc. **[paste]**

pasture *n* **1** (also **pastureland**) (an area of) grassland suitable for the grazing of cattle, etc. **2** grass and other plants suitable as cattle food. **3** the feeding of cattle. — *v* **1** (*tr*) to put (animals) in pasture to graze. **2** (*intr*) (of animals) to graze. [OFr, from Lat *pastura*, from *pascere*, to feed]

pasturage *n* grassland suitable for grazing animals.

pasty[1] *adj* **-ier**, **-iest** (of the complexion) unhealthily pale. — *n* **pastiness**. **[paste]**

pasty[2] *n* **-ies** a pie consisting of pastry folded round a savoury or sweet filling. [OFr *pastée*]

pat *v* **-tt-** (*tr*) **1** to strike lightly or affectionately with the palm of one's hand. **2** to shape by striking lightly with the palm or a flat instrument: *pat it into shape*. — *n* **1** a light, esp. affectionate, blow with the palm of the hand. **2** a round flat mass. — *adv* immediately and fluently, as if memorised: *Her answers came pat*. — *adj* (of answers, etc.) quickly and easily supplied. — **have**, or **know**, **off pat** to have memorised and know perfectly. — **pat on the back** (to congratulate or praise by means of) an approving word or gesture. — **stand pat** (*NAm*) to stand firmly by one's opinion, decision, etc. [Imit.]

Pat. *abbrev* Patent.

patch *n* **1** a piece of material sewn on or applied so as to cover a hole or reinforce a worn patch. **2** a plot of earth: *a vegetable patch*. **3** a pad or cover worn as protection over an injured eye. **4** a small expanse contrasting with its surroundings: *patches of ice*. **5** (*hist*) a tiny piece of black silk worn on the face in imitation of a mole or beauty spot, to enhance the whiteness of the complexion. **6** a scrap or shred. **7** (*coll*) a phase or period: *go through a bad patch*. **8** (*slang*) the area patrolled by a policeman or covered by a particular police station. **9** (*comput*) a set of instructions added to a program to correct an error. — *v* (*tr*) **1** to mend (a hole or garment) by sewing patches on. **2** (**up**) to repair hastily. **3** (**up**; *coll*) to settle (a quarrel). **4** (**together**) to assemble hastily. **5** (*comput*) to make a temporary correction in (a program). — **not a patch on** (*coll*) not nearly as good as. [MidE *pacche*]

patch pocket *n* a pocket made by sewing a piece of fabric on the outside of a garment.

patchwork *n* **1** needlework done by sewing together pieces of contrastingly patterned fabric. **2** a variegated expanse: *a patchwork of fields*.

patchy *adj* **-ier**, **-iest 1** forming, or occurring in, patches. **2** uneven or variable in quality. — *adv* **patchily**. — *n* **patchiness**.

pate *n* (*old* or *facet*) the head or skull.

pâté *n* a spread made from ground or chopped meat or fish blended with herbs, spices, etc. [Fr, pasty]

pâté de foie gras *n* pâté made from the livers of specially fattened geese.

patella *n* **-lae** or **-las** the triangular plate of bone covering the front of the knee joint; the knee-cap. [Lat, dimin. of *patina*, dish]

paten *n* the plate used for the bread at Holy Communion. [OFr *patene*, from Lat *patina*, dish]

patent *n* **1** an official licence from the government granting a person or business the sole right, for a certain period, to make and sell a particular article. **2** the right so granted. **3** the invention so protected. — *v* (*tr*) to obtain a patent for (an invention, design, etc.). — *adj* **1** (**to**) very evident. **2** concerned with the granting of, or protection by, patents. **3** (of products) made or protected under patent. **4** (*coll*) ingenious; infallible; original. **5** open for inspection: *letters patent*. [Lat *patere*, to lie open]

patentee *n* the person obtaining or holding a patent.

patent leather *n* leather made glossy by varnishing.

patently *adv* obviously; clearly.

patent medicine *n* **1** (*tech*) a patented medicine which is available without prescription. **2** (*coll*) any proprietary medicine, esp. one claimed as an infallible cure.

Patent Office *n* the government department that issues patents.

pater *n* (*old slang*) father. [Lat]

paterfamilias *n* **patresfamilias** the father as head of the household. [Lat *pater*, father + *familias*, old genitive of *familia*, family]

paternal *adj* **1** of, relating to, or appropriate to, a father. **2** (of a relation or ancestor) related to one on one's father's side. — *adv* **paternally**. [Lat *paternalis*, from *pater*, father]

paternalism *n* governmental or managerial benevolence taken to the extreme of over-protectiveness and authoritarianism. — *n* **paternalistic**.

paternity *n* **1** fatherhood. **2** the identity of a child's father. **3** the authorship, source or origin of something. [Lat *paternitas*, from *pater*, father]

paternity suit *n* a lawsuit brought by the mother of a child to establish that a certain man is the father of her child and therefore liable for its financial support.

paternoster *n* the Lord's prayer, esp. in Latin. [Lat *Pater noster*, Our Father]

path *n* **1** (also **pathway**) a track trodden by, or specially surfaced for, walking. **2** the line along which something is travelling: *the path of Jupiter*. **3** a course of action: *the path to ruin*. — **beat a path to someone's door** (*coll*) to compete for someone's services. — **cross someone's path** to encounter someone. [OE *pæth*]

pathfinder *n* **1** an explorer who finds routes through unexplored territory. **2** someone who devises new methods of doing things.

path-. See **patho-**.

-path. See **-pathy**.

pathetic *adj* **1** moving one to pity; touching, heart-rending, poignant or pitiful. **2** (*coll derog*) hopelessly inadequate. — *adv* **pathetically**.

pathetic fallacy *n* esp. in literature, the transference of human qualities to inanimate things, as in *a frowning landscape*.

patho- or **path-** *comb fm* disease: *pathology*. [Gr *pathos*, experience, suffering]

pathogen *n* something causing disease, such as a bacterium or virus. — *adj* **pathogenic**. — *n* **pathogenicity**. [Gr **patho-** + **-gen**]

pathology *n* the branch of medicine concerned with the study of the nature and causes of diseases. — *n* **pathologist**. [**patho-** + **-logy**]

pathological *adj* **1** relating to pathology. **2** caused by, or relating to, illness: *a pathological fear of dirt*. **3** (*coll*) compulsive; habitual: *a pathological liar*. — *adv* **pathologically**.

pathos *n* a quality in a situation, etc. that moves one to pity. [Gr, feeling, suffering]

-pathy *comb fm* **1** feeling: *telepathy*. **2** disease or disorder: *psychopathy*. **3** a method of treating disease: *homoeopathy*. — *adj comb fm* **-pathic**. [Gr *pathos*, suffering]

-path *comb fm* **1** a sufferer from a disorder: *psychopath*. **2** a practitioner of a therapy: *homoeopath*; *osteopath*.

patience *n* **1** the ability to endure delay, trouble, pain or hardship calmly. **2** tolerance and forbearance. **3** perseverance. **4** (*cards*) a solo game in which the player, in turning each card over, has to fit it into a certain scheme. [Lat *patientia*]

patient *adj* having or showing patience. — *n* a person who is being treated by, or is registered with, a doctor, dentist, etc. — *adv* **patiently**.

patina *n* **1** a coating formed on a metal surface through oxidation, esp. the greenish coating of verdigris on bronze or copper. **2** a mature shine on wood resulting from continual polishing and handling. **3** any fine finish acquired with age. **4** (*archaeol*) a surface appearance that develops with prolonged exposure or burial. [Ital, coating, from Lat, dish]

patio *n* **-os** **1** an open paved area beside a house. **2** an inner courtyard in a Spanish or Spanish-American house. [Span]

patisserie *n* (a shop selling) fancy cakes, sweet pastries, etc. [Fr *pâtisserie*, from Lat *pasta*, dough]

patois *n* ***patois*** **1** the local dialect of a region, used usu. in informal everyday situations, as opposed to the language used in literature, education, etc. **2** jargon. [Fr]

patrial *n* (*formerly*) a person who, being a citizen of the UK, a British colony or the British Commonwealth, or the child or grandchild of someone born in the UK, has a legal right to live in the UK. — *n* **patriality**. [Lat *patria*, fatherland]

patriarch *n* **1** the male head of a family or tribe. **2** in the Eastern Orthodox Church, a high-ranking bishop. **3** in the Roman Catholic Church, the pope. **4** in the Old Testament, any of the ancestors of the human race or of the tribes of Israel, e.g. Adam, Abraham or Jacob. **5** a venerable old man, esp. the senior member of a community or group. — *adj* **patriarchal**. [Gr *patriarches*, senior bishop, father of a family]

patriarchate *n* the (period of) office, (area of) authority, or residence of a church patriarch.

patriarchy *n* ***-ies*** (any society organised according to) the system in which a male is head of the family and descent is traced through the male line.

patrician *n* **1** a member of the ancient Roman nobility; a descendant of one of the founding families of Rome. **2** an aristocrat. **3** a person of taste, culture and refinement. — *adj* **1** relating to the ancient Roman nobility. **2** aristocratic; noble; of refined tastes. [Lat *patricius*, patrician, noble]

patricide *n* **1** the act of killing one's father. **2** a person who commits this act. — *adj* **patricidal**. [Late variant of **parricide**, influenced by Lat *pater*, father]

patrimony *n* ***-ies*** **1** property inherited from one's father or ancestors. **2** something inherited; a heritage. **3** a church estate or revenue. — *adj* **patrimonial**. [Lat *patrimonium*, from *pater*, father]

patriot *n* someone who loves and serves his or her fatherland devotedly. — *adj* **patriotic**. — *adv* **patriotically**. — *n* **patriotism**. [Gr *patriotes*, fellow-countryman]

patrol *v* ***-ll-*** (*tr*) to make a regular systematic tour of (an area) to maintain security or surveillance. — *n* **1** a person or group of people, performing this duty. **2** the act of patrolling: *on patrol*. **3** any of the units of six or so into which a troop of Scouts or Guides is divided. [Fr *patrouiller*]

patrol car *n* a police car equipped with a radio telephone, used to patrol streets and motorways.

patrolman *n* **1** (*NAm*) the lowest-ranking police officer; a police officer on the beat. **2** a person employed by a motoring organisation to patrol a certain area and help motorists in difficulty.

patron *n* **1** a person who gives financial support and encouragement e.g. to an artist, the arts, a movement or charity. **2** a regular customer of a shop, attender at a theatre, etc. [Lat *patronus*, protector]

patronage *n* **1** the support given by a patron. **2** regular custom given to a shop, theatre, etc. **3** the power of bestowing, or recommending people for, offices.

patronise or **-ize** *v* (*tr*) **1** to treat condescendingly, or with benevolent superiority, esp. inappropriately. **2** to give esp. regular custom to (a shop, theatre, restaurant, etc.). — *adj* **patronising** or **-z-**. — *adv* **patronisingly** or **-z-**.

patron saint *n* the guardian saint of a country, profession, craft, etc.

patronymic *n* a name derived from one's father's or other male ancestor's name, usu. with a suffix or prefix, as in *Donaldson* or *Macdonald*. [Gr *pater*, father + *onyma*, name]

patten *n* (*hist*) an overshoe with a wooden or metal mount, for raising the wearer above mud or water. [OFr *patin*, clog]

patter[1] *v* **-r-** (*intr*) **1** (of rain, footsteps, etc.) to make a light rapid tapping noise. **2** to move with light rapid footsteps. — *n* the light rapid tapping of footsteps or rain. [**pat**]

patter[2] *n* **1** the fast persuasive talk of a salesman, or the quick speech of a comedian. **2** the jargon or speech of a particular group or area: *Glasgow patter*. — *v* **-r-** (*intr* & *tr*) to say or speak rapidly or glibly. [From Lat *paternoster*, Our Father, from the fast mumbling of the prayer]

pattern *n* **1** a model, guide or set of instructions for making something. **2** a decorative design e.g. on wallpaper or fabric. **3** a piece, e.g. of fabric, as a sample. **4** any excellent example suitable for imitation. **5** a coherent series of occurrences or set of features: *a pattern of events*, *symptoms*, etc. — *v* (*tr*; **on**, **upon**) to model. [OFr, from Lat *patronus*, example, defender]

patterned *adj* (of fabric, etc.) having a decorative design; not plain.

patty *n* **-ies** **1** (*NAm*) a flat round cake of minced meat, vegetables, etc. **2** a small meat pie. [Fr *pâté*, from Lat *pasta*, dough]

paucity *n* smallness of quantity; fewness; a scarcity or lack. [Lat *pauci*, few]

paunch *n* a protruding belly, esp. in a man. — *adj* **paunchy**, **-ier**, **-iest**. — *n* **paunchiness**.

pauper *n* **1** a poverty-stricken person. **2** (*hist*) someone living on public charity. — *n* **pauperism**. [Lat, poor]

pause *n* **1** a usu. short break (in some activity, etc.). **2** (*mus*) (a sign indicating) the prolonging of a note or rest beyond its normal duration. — *v* (*intr*) **1** to have a break; to stop briefly. **2** to hesitate. — **give pause** to cause to hesitate before acting. [Lat *pausa*]

pavan or **pavane** *n* (a piece of music for) a stately 16th- to 17th-cent. dance. [Span or Ital *pavana*, from Span *pavo*, peacock, or Ital *Padovana*, (dance) of Padua]

pave *v* (*tr*) to surface (a street, path, etc.) with stone slabs, cobbles, etc. — **pave the way for** to ease the introduction or development of. [Lat *pavire*, to ram or tread down]

paving *n* **1** (also **paving-stones**) stones or slabs used to pave a surface. **2** a paved surface.

pavement *n* **1** a raised paved footpath edging a road, etc. **2** a paved road or expanse: *a mosaic pavement*. **3** a road surface; road-surfacing material. [Lat *pavimentum*, hard floor]

pavilion *n* **1** a building in a sports ground in which players change their clothes and store equipment. **2** a light temporary building in which to display exhibits at a trade fair, etc. **3** a summerhouse or ornamental shelter. **4** a large ornamental building for public pleasure and entertainment. **5** a large and elaborate tent. [Fr *pavillon*, from Lat *papilio*, butterfly, tent]

pavlova *n* a dessert consisting of meringue topped with fruit and whipped cream. [After Anna *Pavlova* (1885–1931), ballerina]

paw *n* **1** the foot of a four-legged mammal. **2** (*coll*) a hand. — *v* **1** (*tr* or *intr*; **at**) (of an animal) to scrape or strike with a paw. **2** (*tr*; **about**, **around**) to finger or handle clumsily; to touch or caress (someone) with unwelcome familiarity. [OFr *poue*]

pawky *adj* **-ier**, **-iest** drily witty. — *adv* **pawkily**. — *n* **pawkiness**. [Scot *pawk*, a trick]

pawl *n* a catch that engages with the teeth of a ratchet wheel to limit its movement to one direction only.

pawn[1] *v* (*tr*) **1** to deposit (an article of value) with a pawnbroker as a pledge for a sum of money borrowed. **2** to pledge or stake. — *n* **1** the condition of being deposited as a pledge: *in pawn*. **2** an article so pledged. [OFr *pan*, pledge, surety]

pawnbroker *n* a person who lends money in exchange for pawned articles. — *n* **pawnbroking**.

pawnshop *n* a pawnbroker's place of business.

pawn[2] *n* **1** a chess piece of lowest value. **2** a person used and manipulated by others. [OFr *poun*, from Lat *pedones*, infantry]

pawpaw. See **papaya**.

pay *v* ***paid*** **1** (*tr* & *intr*; **for**) to give (money) to (someone) in exchange for goods, services, etc. **2** (*tr* & *intr*) to settle (a bill, debt, etc.). **3** (*tr* & *intr*) to give (wages or salary) to an employee. **4** (*tr* & *intr*) to make a profit, or make as profit: *businesses that don't pay*; *an investment that pays £500 per annum*. **5** (*intr* & *tr*) to benefit; to be worthwhile: *It pays (one) to be polite*; *Dishonesty doesn't pay*. **6** (*tr* & *intr*; **for**) to suffer (a penalty); to be punished: *pay dearly for one's crimes*; *pay the price of sin*; *paid with his life*. **7** (*tr*) to do (someone) the honour of (a visit or call); to offer (someone) (a compliment or one's respects). **8** (*tr*) to give (heed or attention). — *n* money given or received for work, etc.; wages; salary. — *n* **payer**. — **in the pay of** employed by, esp. for a secret or dishonest purpose. — *v* **pay back**

(*tr*) **1** to return (money owed). **2** to revenge oneself on. — *v* **pay in** (*tr*) to put (money, etc.) into a bank account. — *v* **pay off 1** (*tr*) to pay and make redundant (workers). **2** (*intr*) to have profitable results. **3** (*tr*) to finish paying (a debt, etc.). — *v* **pay out 1** (*tr* & *intr*) to spend or give (money), e.g. to pay bills, debts, etc. **2** (*tr*) to release or slacken (a rope, etc.) esp. by passing it little by little through one's hands. — *v* **pay up** (*tr* & *intr*; *coll*) to pay what is due, esp. reluctantly. — **pay one's way** to pay one's own debts and living expenses. — **put paid to** (*coll*) to put an end to. [Lat *pacare*, to pacify, settle (a debt)]

paid-up *adj* (of a society member, etc.) having paid one's membership fee.

payable *adj* that can or must be paid: *make cheques payable to me*; *payable by 1 July*.

pay-as-you-earn *n* a method of collecting income tax from employees by deducting it from the wages or salary due to be paid to them.

pay-bed *n* a bed in a National Health Service hospital reserved for patients paying for their own treatment.

pay day *n* the day when wages or salaries are paid.

payee *n* a person to whom money is paid or a cheque made out.

paying guest *n* a lodger.

payload *n* **1** the revenue-earning part of a vehicle's load. **2** the operating equipment carried by a spaceship or satellite. **3** the quantity and strength of the explosive carried by a missile. **4** the quantity of goods, passengers, etc. carried by an aircraft.

paymaster *n* an official in charge of the payment of wages and salaries.

payment *n* **1** a sum of money paid. **2** the act of paying or process of being paid. **3** a reward or punishment.

pay-off *n* (*coll*) **1** a fruitful result. **2** a bribe. **3** a final settling of accounts. **4** a climax, outcome or final resolution.

pay packet *n* (an envelope containing) an employee's weekly wages.

payphone *n* a telephone operated by coins or a phonecard, esp. a coin-operated one.

payroll *n* **1** a register of employees listing the wage or salary due to each. **2** the total amount of money required for employees' wages or salaries.

pay slip *n* a note of pay, showing deductions for tax or national insurance, supplied weekly or monthly to employees.

PAYE *abbrev* pay-as-you-earn.

payola *n* **1** a bribe for promoting a product, given to someone, e.g. a disc jockey, in a position to do this. **2** the practice of giving or receiving such bribes. [Facetious, from **pay** + sfx. *-ola*, of no precise meaning]

Pb *symbol* (*chem*) lead.

PC *abbrev* **1** Police Constable. **2** personal computer. **3** Privy Councillor.

pc *abbrev* **1** per cent. **2** (*coll*) postcard.

pcm *abbrev* per calendar month.

Pd *symbol* (*chem*) palladium.

pd *abbrev* paid.

Pde *abbrev* Parade, as a street name.

PDSA *abbrev* People's Dispensary for Sick Animals.

PE *abbrev* physical education.

pea *n* **1** the round green seed of a hardy annual climbing plant, growing in pods and eaten as a vegetable. **2** the plant itself. [A singular form coined from **pease**, which was mistaken for a plural]

pea green *n* bright green, or yellowish green. — *adj* **pea-green**.

pea-shooter *n* a short tube through which to fire dried peas by blowing.

pea soup *n* thick soup made from dried peas.

pea-souper *n* (*coll*) a thick yellowish fog.

peace *n* **1** freedom from war. **2** a treaty or agreement ending a war. **3** freedom from noise, disturbance or disorder; quietness or calm. **4** freedom from mental agitation; serenity: *peace of mind*. — **at peace 1** not at war; not fighting. **2** (**with**) in harmony or friendship. **3** in a calm or serene state. **4** freed from earthly worries; dead. — **hold one's peace** to remain silent. — **keep the peace 1** (*legal*) to preserve law and order. **2** to prevent, or refrain from, fighting or quarrelling. — **make peace** to end a war, quarrel, etc. (*n* **peacemaker**). — **make one's peace with** to be reconciled with. [OFr *pais*, from Lat *pax*]

peaceable *adj* peace-loving; mild; placid. — *adv* **peaceably**.

peaceful *adj* **1** calm and quiet. **2** unworried; serene. **3** free from war, violence, disturbance or disorder. — *adv* **peacefully**. — *n* **peacefulness**.

peacemaker see **make peace** above.

peace offering *n* something offered to end a quarrel or as an apology.

peace pipe *n* (also **pipe of peace**) a long ornate pipe smoked by N American Indians as a token of peace.

peacetime *n* periods that are free of war.

peach[1] *n* **1** a round fruit with velvety yellowish-pink skin, juicy yellow flesh and a large stone. **2** the yellowish-pink colour of this fruit. **3** (*coll*) something delightful: *a peach of a day*. **4** (*coll*) a lovely young woman. — *adj* **peachy**, ***-ier***, ***-iest***. [OFr *peche*, from Lat *persicum* (*malum*), Persian (apple)]

peach Melba *n* a dessert consisting of peaches, ice-cream and raspberry sauce.

peach[2] *v* (*intr* with **on**) to betray (one's accomplice); to inform on. [MidE *peche* from *apeche*, to hinder]

peacock *n* ***-cock*** or ***-cocks*** **1** (also **peafowl**, ***-fowl*** or ***-fowls***) a bird of the pheasant family, the male of which has magnificent tail feathers that it can spread out like a fan. **2** a male peacock. **3** (*derog*) a vain person. [OE *pea*, from Lat *pavo*, peacock + **cock**]

peacock blue *n* the rich greenish blue in a peacock's plumage.

peahen *n* a female peacock.

peak *n* **1** a pointed summit; a pointed mountain or hill. **2** a maximum, e.g. in consumer use: *electricity consumed at peak periods.* **3** a time of maximum achievement, etc. **4** the front projecting part of a cap. — *v* (*intr*) **1** to reach a maximum. **2** to reach the height of one's powers or popularity. [Perhaps related to **pick**]

peaky *adj* **-ier**, **-iest** pallid; ill-looking. — *n* **peakiness**.

peal *n* **1** the ringing of a bell or set of bells. **2** a set of bells, each with a different note. **3** a burst (of noise): *peals of laughter* or *thunder.* — *v* **1** (*intr*) to ring or resound. **2** (*tr*) to sound or signal (e.g. a welcome) by ringing. [MidE *pele*]

peanut *n* an edible nut that ripens underground in a pod-like shell. [**pea** + **nut**]

peanut butter *n* a spread made from ground roasted peanuts.

pear *n* **1** a greenish- or brownish-skinned fruit with white juicy flesh, rounded at its base and narrowing towards the stem. **2** the tree bearing it. [OE *peru*, from Lat *pirum*]

pearl *n* **1** a bead of hard bluish-white iridescent material formed by an oyster inside its shell, prized as a gem; an imitation of this. **2** (in *pl*) a necklace of pearls. **3** mother-of-pearl. **4** something resembling a pearl. **5** something valued or precious: *pearls of wisdom.* — *adj* **1** like a pearl in colour or shape. **2** made of or set with pearls or mother-of-pearl. — *v* **1** (*tr*) to set with, or as if with, pearls. **2** (*tr*) to grind down (barley) into small pearl-like grains. **3** (*intr*) to form pearl-like beads or drops. — *adj* **pearly**, **-ier**, **-iest**. [MidE *perle*, from a dimin. of Lat *perna*, sea mussel]

pearl barley *n* seeds of barley ground into round polished grains, used in soups and stews.

pearlies *n* (*pl*) the traditional costume of costermongers, sewn with pearl buttons.

pearly gates *n* (*pl*; *coll*) the gates of Heaven.

pearly king and queen *n* the London costermonger couple whose pearl-button-covered costumes are judged the most splendid.

peasant *n* **1** in poor agricultural societies, a farm worker or small farmer. **2** (*derog*) a rough, unmannerly or culturally ignorant person. [OFr *païsant*, from Lat *pagus*, country district]

peasantry *n* the peasant class.

pease pudding *n* a purée made from split peas soaked and then boiled. [OE *pise*, pea, from Lat *pisa*]

peat *n* **1** a material consisting of partly-rotted and compacted vegetable matter found in bogs and hilly areas and used dried as a fuel. **2** a cut block of this. — *adj* **peaty**, **-ier**, **-iest**.

pebble *n* **1** a small stone worn round and smooth by water. **2** (a lens made of) a colourless rock crystal. — *adj* **pebbly**, **-ier**, **-iest**. [OE *papol(stan)*, pebble(stone)]

pebbledash *n* cement or plaster with small stones embedded in it, used as a coating for exterior walls.

pecan *n* **1** an oval brown smooth-shelled oily nut. **2** the hickory tree of the southern US, bearing this nut. [Illinois (N American Indian language) *pakani*]

peccadillo *n* **-os** or **-oes** a minor misdeed. [Span *pecadillo*, dimin. of *pecado*, sin]

peccary *n* **-ies** a small wild pig of tropical America. [Carib (S American Indian language) *pakira*]

peck[1] *v* **1** (*tr* or *intr*; **at**) to strike, nip or pick up with the beak. **2** (*tr*) to poke (a hole) with the beak. **3** (*intr* with **at**) to nibble (food) without relish. **4** (*tr*) to kiss perfunctorily: *pecked her on the cheek.* — *n* **1** a tap or nip with the beak. **2** a perfunctory kiss. [Related to **pick**]

pecker *n* **1** that which pecks; a beak. **2** (*coll*) spirits: *keep one's pecker up.* **3** (*US vulg*) the penis.

pecking order *n* a scale of ascendancy noticeably operating in a flock of poultry, such that any bird may peck one of lesser importance but must submit to being pecked by those of greater importance; any social hierarchy or system of ranks and associated privileges.

peckish *adj* (*coll*) somewhat hungry.

peck[2] *n* an old measure of capacity of dry goods, esp. grain, equal to two gallons or a quarter of a bushel. [OFr *pek*]

pectin *n* a carbohydrate occurring in ripe fruit, used as a setting agent in jellies and jams. [Gr *pektos*, congealed]

pectoral *adj* **1** of or relating to the breast or chest. **2** worn on the breast. — *n* **1** a pectoral muscle or pectoral fin. **2** a neck ornament worn covering the chest. [Lat *pectoralis*, from *pectus*, chest]

pectoral fin *n* either of a pair of fins behind a fish's head that it uses to steer itself.

peculiar *adj* **1** strange; odd. **2** (with **to**) belonging exclusively or typically to: *habits peculiar to snails.* **3** special; individual: *own peculiar methods.* **4** especial; particular: *of peculiar interest.* — *adv* **peculiarly**. [Lat *peculium*, private property]

peculiarity *n* **-ies** **1** the quality of being strange or odd. **2** a distinctive feature, characteristic or trait. **3** an eccentricity or idiosyncrasy.

pecuniary *adj* of, concerning or consisting of money. [Lat *pecunia*, money, from *pecus*, flock]

ped-[1]. See **pedi-**.

ped-[2]. See **pedo-**.

-ped or **-pede** *comb fm* foot: *quadruped*; *millipede.* [Lat *pes*, foot]

pedagogy *n* the science, principles or work of teaching. — *adj* **pedagogic** or **pedagogical**. — *adv* **pedagogically**. [Gr *paidagogia*, tutorship, from *pais*, child + *agein*, to lead]

pedagogue *n* (*old derog*) a teacher, esp. a strict or pedantic one. [Gr *paidagogos*, a child's tutor]

pedal *n* a lever operated by the foot, e.g. on a machine, vehicle or musical instrument. — *v* **-ll-** (*tr* & *intr*) to move or operate by means of a pedal or pedals. [Lat *pedalis*, of the foot]

pedalo *n* **-os** a small pedal-operated pleasure boat. [**pedal**]

pedant *n* (*derog*) someone over-concerned with correctness of detail, esp. in academic matters. — *adj* **pedantic**. — *adv* **pedantically**. — *n* **pedantry**. [Ital *pedante*, teacher]

peddle *v* **1** (*tr* & *intr*) to go from place to place selling (small goods); to be a pedlar. **2** (*tr*; *coll*) to deal illegally in (narcotic drugs). **3** (*tr*; *coll*) to publicise and try to win acceptance for (ideas, theories, etc.). [Formed from **pedlar**]

peddler *n* **1** (*US*) a pedlar. **2** someone dealing illegally in narcotics: *a dope peddler*.

-pede. See **-ped**.

pederast or **paederast** *n* a man who is sexually attracted to or has sexual relations with boys. — *n* **pederasty** or **paederasty**. [Gr *pais*, child + *erastes*, lover]

pedestal *n* the base on which a statue or column is mounted. — **put on a pedestal** to admire or revere excessively; to idolise. [Ital *piedistallo*, foot of stall]

pedestrian *n* a person travelling on foot, esp. in a street; a walker. — *adj* of or for pedestrians. **2** dull; unimaginative: *a pedestrian rendering by the orchestra*. [Lat *pedester*, on foot]

pedestrian crossing *n* a specially marked crossing-place for pedestrians, where they have priority over traffic.

pedestrianise or **-ize** *v* (*tr*) to convert (a street, etc.) into an area for pedestrians only. — *n* **pedestrianisation** or **-z-**.

pedestrian precinct *n* a shopping street or area from which traffic is excluded.

pedi- or **ped-** *comb fm* foot: *pedicure*. [Lat *pes*, foot]

pediatrics. Another spelling of **paediatrics**.

pedicure *n* a medical or cosmetic treatment of the feet and toenails. [**pedi-** + Lat *curare*, to look after]

pedigree *n* **1** a person or animal's line of descent, esp. if long and distinguished, or proof of pure breeding. **2** a genealogical table showing this; a family tree. — *adj* (of an animal) pure-bred; descended from a long line of known ancestors of the same breed. [OFr *pie de grue*, crane's foot, from its similarity to a branching family tree]

pediment *n* (*archit*) a wide triangular gable set over a classical portico or the face of a building. [Earlier *periment*, thought a corruption of **pyramid**]

pedlar *n* a person who goes from place to place peddling small articles. [MidE *ped*, basket]

pedo- or **ped-**. Other spellings of **paedo-** & **paed-**.

pedometer *n* a device that measures distance walked by recording the number of steps taken. [**pedo-** + **-meter**]

peduncle *n* **1** (*bot*) a short stalk, e.g. one carrying a single flower head. **2** (*anat* or *pathol*) any stalk-like structure. [Lat *pedunculus*, dimin. of *pes*, foot]

pee (*coll*) *v* (*intr*) to urinate. — *n* an act of urinating. **2** urine. [Euph. for **piss**]

peek *v* (*intr*) to glance briefly and surreptitiously; to peep. — *n* a brief furtive glance. [MidE *piken*, to peek]

peel *v* **1** (*tr*) to strip the skin or rind off (a fruit or vegetable). **2** (*intr*) to be able to be peeled: *peel easily*. **3** (*tr* with **off**, **away**) to strip off (an outer layer). **4** (*intr*) (of a wall or other surface) to shed its outer coating in flaky strips. **5** (*intr*) (of skin, paint or other outer covering) to flake off in patches. **6** (*intr*) (of a person or part of the body) to shed skin in flaky layers after sunburn. — *n* the skin or rind of vegetables or fruit, esp. citrus fruit. — *n* **peeler**. — *v* **peel off** (*intr*) **1** (of an aircraft or vehicle) to veer away from the main group. **2** (*coll*) to undress.

peelings *n* (*pl*) strips of peel removed from a fruit or vegetable.

peep[1] *v* (*intr*) **1** to look quickly or covertly, e.g. through a narrow opening or from a place of concealment; to peek. **2** to emerge briefly or partially. — *n* **1** a quick covert look. **2** a first faint glimmering: *at peep of day*. [Variant of **peek**]

peepers *n* (*pl*; *old coll*) eyes.

peephole *n* **1** a hole, crack, etc. through which to peep. **2** a tiny aperture in a front door, fitted with a convex lens, through which one can check on callers before opening the door.

peeping Tom *n* a voyeur.

peepshow *n* a box with a peephole through which a series of moving pictures can be watched.

peep[2] *n* **1** the faint high-pitched cry of a baby bird, etc.; a cheep. **2** the least utterance: *Not another peep out of you!* — *v* (*intr*) **1** (of baby birds, etc.) to utter a high-pitched cry; to cheep. **2** (*coll*) to (cause to) sound: *peep the horn*. [Imit.]

peer[1] *n* **1** a member of the nobility, i.e., in Britain, a duke, marquess, earl, viscount or baron. **2** someone who is one's equal in age, rank, etc.; a contemporary, companion or fellow. [OFr *per*, from Lat *par*, equal]

peerage *n* **1** the title or rank of a peer: *granted a peerage*; *raised to the peerage*. **2** (*sing* or *pl*) the members of the nobility as a group. **3** a book containing a list of peers with details of their families and descent.

peeress *n* **1** the wife or widow of a peer (sense **1**). **2** a female peer (sense **1**) in her own right.

peer group *n* one's peers or companions as a group, esp. as an influence on one's attitude and aspirations.

peerless *adj* without equal; excelling all; matchless. — *adv* **peerlessly**. — *n* **peerlessness**.

peer of the realm *n* a member of the nobility with the right to sit in the House of Lords.

peer[2] *v* (*intr*; **at, through**, etc.) **1** to look hard, esp. through narrowed eyes, as if having difficulty in seeing. **2** to peep out or emerge briefly or partially.

peeve *v* (*tr*; *coll*) to irritate, annoy or offend. — *n* (a cause of) vexation or irritation. — *adj* **peeved**. [Back-formation from **peevish**]

peevish *adj* irritable; cantankerous; inclined to whine or complain. — *adv* **peevishly**. — *n* **peevishness**.

peewit *n* a lapwing. [Imit. of its cry]

peg *n* **1** a little shaft of wood, metal or plastic shaped for any of various fixing, fastening or marking uses. **2** a coat hook fixed to a wall, etc. **3** a wooden or plastic clip for fastening washed clothes to a line to dry; a clothes peg. **4** any of several wooden pins on a stringed instrument, turned to tune it. **5** a point of reference on which to base an argument, etc. **6** (*old coll*) a drink of spirits. — *v* **-gg-** (*tr*) **1** to insert a peg into. **2** to fasten with a peg or pegs. **3** to freeze (prices, incomes, etc.) at a certain level. — **off the peg** (of clothes) ready to wear; ready-made (*adj* **off-the-peg**). — *v* **peg away** (*intr*; **at**; *coll*) to work steadily. — *v* **peg out 1** (*tr*) to mark out (ground) with pegs. **2** (*intr*; *coll*) to die. — **a square peg in a round hole** a person who does not fit in well in his or her environment, job, etc. — **take (someone) down a peg (or two)** (*coll*) to humble (someone). [ODut *pegge*]

peg board *n* a board with holes for receiving pegs that are used for scoring in games, or for attaching matter for display.

peg leg *n* (*coll*) (a person with) an artificial leg.

peignoir *n* a woman's light dressing-gown. [Fr, from *peigner*, to comb]

pejorative *adj* (of a word or expression) disapproving, derogatory, disparaging or uncomplimentary. — *n* a word or affix with derogatory force. — *adv* **pejoratively**. [Lat *peiorare*, to make worse]

peke *n* (*coll*) a Pekinese.

Pekinese or **Pekingese** *n* **-ese** a small, short-legged, flat-faced, silky-coated, feathery-eared, curly-tailed dog, orig. a Chinese breed. [*Peking* (Beijing) in China]

pekoe *n* a high-quality black China tea. [Chin dialect *pek-ho*]

pelagic *adj* **1** (*tech*) relating to, or carried out on, the deep open sea. **2** (of fish) inhabiting the surface waters or middle depths of the sea. **3** (*geol*) (of deposits) built up from material that has sunk to the bottom of the sea from its surface. [Gr *pelagos*, sea]

pelargonium *n* any of a genus of plants of the geranium family, with red, pink or white flowers and strong-smelling leaves, often grown as house and garden plants under the name of geranium. [Gr *pelargos*, stork]

pelican *n* **-can** or **-cans** a large water bird with a pouched beak for holding fish. [Gr *pelekan*]

pelican crossing *n* a pedestrian crossing with pedestrian-controlled traffic lights. [Respelt from *pe*destrian *li*ght-*con*trolled *crossing*]

pellagra *n* a disease caused by lack of niacin (a B vitamin), characterised by scaliness of the skin, diarrhoea and in some cases insanity. [Ital, from Lat *pellis*, skin + Gr *agra*, seizure]

pellet *n* **1** a small rounded mass of compressed material, e.g. paper. **2** a piece of small shot for an airgun, etc. **3** a ball of undigested material regurgitated by an owl or hawk. [OFr *pelote*, from Lat *pila*, ball]

pell-mell *adv* headlong; in confused haste; helter-skelter. [OFr *pesle-mesle*, rhyming compound from *mesler*, to mix]

pellucid *adj* **1** transparent. **2** absolutely clear in expression and meaning. [Lat *per*, utterly + *lucidus*, clear]

pelmet *n* a strip of fabric or a narrow board fitted along the top of a window to conceal the curtain rail.

pelota *n* a Spanish and Latin American court game, in which the players use a basket strapped to their wrists to hit a ball against a specially marked wall. [Span, ball]

pelt[1] *v* **1** (*tr*; **with**) to bombard with missiles: *was pelted with stones*. **2** (*intr*; **down**) (of rain, hail, etc.) to fall fast and heavily. **3** (*intr*) to rush along at top speed. — **at full pelt** as fast as possible.

pelt[2] *n* **1** the skin of a dead animal, esp. with the fur still on it. **2** the coat of a living animal. **3** a hide stripped of hair for tanning. [OFr *pelleterie*, animal skins, from Lat *pellis*, skin]

pelvis *n* **1** the basin-shaped bony cavity into which the base of the spine fits, enclosing the bowels, organs of reproduction, etc. **2** the bones themselves. — *adj* **pelvic**. [Lat *pelvis*, basin]

pemmican *n* **1** a N American Indian food of dried meat beaten to a paste and mixed with fat. **2** a similarly condensed and nutritious mixture of dried ingredients used as emergency rations. [Cree (N American Indian language) *pimekan*]

pen[1] *n* **1** a small enclosure for animals. **2** (often *in cmpds*) any small enclosure or area of confinement: *a playpen*. **3** a bomb-proof dock for submarines. — *v* **-nn-** (*tr*; **in, up**) to enclose or confine in, or as if in, a pen. [OE *penn*]

pen[2] *n* **1** a writing instrument that uses ink, formerly a quill, now any of various implements fitted with a nib, rotating ball, or felt or nylon point. **2** this as a symbol of the writing profession. — *v* ***-nn-*** to compose and write (a letter, poem, etc.) with a pen. [Lat *penna*, feather]

penfriend or **penpal** *n* a person, esp. foreign and otherwise unknown to one, with whom one regularly corresponds.

penknife *n* a pocket knife with blades that fold into the handle. [Orig. used for cutting quills]

penmanship *n* skill with the pen, whether calligraphic or literary.

pen name *n* a pseudonym used by a writer.

pen-pusher *n* a clerk or minor official whose job includes much tedious paperwork. — *n* **pen-pushing**.

pen[3] *n* (*NAm coll*) a penitentiary.

pen[4] *n* a female swan.

penal *adj* relating to punishment, esp. by law. — *adv* **penally**. [Lat *poenalis*, from *poena*, penalty]

penal code *n* a system of laws concerning the punishment of crime.

penalise or **-ize** *v* (*tr*) **1** to impose a penalty on, for wrongdoing, cheating, breaking a rule, committing a foul, etc. **2** to disadvantage: *income groups that are penalised by the new tax laws.* — *n* **penalisation** or **-z-**.

penal servitude *n* (*hist*) imprisonment with hard labour.

penalty *n* ***-ies*** **1** a punishment for wrongdoing, breaking a contract or rule, etc. **2** a punishment that one brings on oneself through ill-advised action: *pay the penalty for my error.* **3** (*sport & games*) a handicap imposed on a competitor or team for a foul or other infringement of the rules, in team games taking the form of an advantage awarded to the opposing side. [Lat *poenalitas*, from *poena*, punishment]

penalty area or **box** *n* (*football*) an area in front of either goal within which a foul by any player in the defending team is punished by a penalty awarded to the attacking team.

penalty kick *n* **1** (*Rugby*) a free kick. **2** (*football*) a free kick at goal from a distance of 12 yards, awarded to the attacking team for a foul committed in the penalty area by the defending team.

penance *n* **1** (**for**) (an act of) repentance or atonement for an offence or wrongdoing: *do penance.* **2** (*Roman Catholicism*) a sacrament involving confession, repentance, forgiveness and the performance of a penance suggested by one's confessor. [OFr *peneance*, from Lat *paenitentia*, penitence]

pence. See **penny**.

penchant *n* (**for**) a taste, liking, inclination or tendency: *a penchant for juvenile pranks.* [Fr, present participle of *pencher*, to lean]

pencil *n* **1** a writing and drawing instrument consisting of a wooden shaft containing a stick of graphite or other material, sharpened for use and making more or less erasable marks. **2** such material, esp. with regard to the alterability of marks made with it: *written in pencil.* **3** something with a similar function or shape: *an eyebrow pencil*; *a pencil of light.* — *v* ***-ll-*** (*tr*) to write, draw or mark with a pencil. — *v* **pencil in** (*tr*) to note down (a provisional appointment, etc.) in one's diary, not necessarily in pencil. [Lat *penicillus*, painter's brush, dimin. of *peniculus*, little tail]

pendant *n* **1** an ornament suspended from a neck chain, necklace, bracelet, etc.; a necklace with a pendant hanging from it. **2** any of several hanging articles, e.g. an earring, ceiling light, etc. **3** a companion piece, e.g. a painting or poem. [Lat *pendere*, to hang]

pendent *adj* **1** hanging; suspended; dangling. **2** projecting; jutting; overhanging. **3** undetermined or undecided; pending. [Lat *pendere*, to hang]

pending *adj* **1** waiting to be decided or dealt with. **2** (of a patent) about to come into effect; impending. — *prep* until; awaiting; during: *held in prison pending trial.* [Lat *pendere*, to hang]

pendulous *adj* hanging down loosely; drooping; swinging freely. — *adv* **pendulously**. [Lat *pendulus*, hanging]

pendulum *n* any weight hung from a fixed point so as to swing freely, e.g. the swinging weight that regulates the movement of a clock. [Lat, neuter of *pendulus*, hanging]

penetrate *v* **1** (*tr* or *intr*; **into**) to find a way in; to enter, esp. with difficulty. **2** (*tr*) to infiltrate (an organisation, etc.). **3** (*tr* or *intr*; **through**) to find a way (through); to pierce or permeate: *penetrate enemy lines*; *penetrated the silence.* **4** (*intr*) to come home to one: *The news didn't penetrate at first.* **5** (*tr*) to see through (a disguise). **6** (*tr*) to fathom, solve or understand (a mystery). **7** (*tr*) (of a man) to insert his penis into the vagina of (a woman). — *n* **penetrability**. — *adj* **penetrable**. [Lat *penetrare*, to penetrate]

penetrating *adj* **1** (of a voice, etc.) all too loud and clear; strident; carrying. **2** (of a mind) acute; discerning. **3** (of eyes or a look) piercing; probing.

penetration *n* **1** the process of penetrating or being penetrated. **2** mental acuteness; perspicacity; insight.

penguin *n* a black and white sea bird of the Antarctic and southern hemisphere, with webbed feet and wings adapted as flippers for swimming.

penicillin *n* an antibiotic extracted from moulds, used to treat bacterial infection. [Lat *penicillus*, hairy tuft, from the appearance of the mould]

peninsula *n* a piece of land almost surrounded by water or projecting into water from a larger land mass. — *adj* **peninsular**. [Lat *paene*, almost + *insula*, island]

penis *n* the male organ of copulation and, in mammals, urination. — *adj* **penile**. [Lat, orig. a tail]

penitent *adj* regretful for wrong one has done; repentant. — *n* a repentant person, esp. one doing penance on the instruction of a confessor. — *n* **penitence**. — *adv* **penitently**. [Lat *paenitens*, repentant]
penitential *adj* relating to penitence or penance.
penitentiary *n* **-ies** (*NAm*) a federal or state prison. — *adj* of or relating to punishment or penance. [Lat *paenitens*, repentant]
Penn. *abbrev* Pennsylvania.
pennant *n* a small narrow triangular flag, used on vessels for identification or for signalling. [Prob. **pennon** + **pendant**]
penniless. See **penny**.
pennon *n* **1** (*hist*) a long narrow flag with a tapering divided tip, e.g. borne on his lance by a knight. **2** a pennant. [Lat *penna*, feather]
penny *n* ***pence*** or ***pennies*** **1** (a bronze coin equal to) a hundredth part of £1. **2** before 1971, (a bronze coin equal to) $\frac{1}{12}$ of a shilling or $\frac{1}{240}$ of £1. **3** the least quantity of money: *won't cost a penny*. **4** (*NAm*) (a coin worth) one cent. **5** a coin of low value in certain other countries. — **in for a penny, in for a pound** once involved, one may as well do the thing properly. — **in penny numbers** (*coll*) in small quantities. — **the penny dropped** (*coll*) understanding came. — **a pretty penny** (*ironic*) a huge sum. — **spend a penny** (*coll euph*) to urinate. — **turn an honest penny** (*coll*) to earn one's living honestly. — **two** or **ten a penny** very common. [OE *pening*]
-pence *in cmpds* pennies (in value), esp. sense **1**: *threepence* .
penniless *adj* poverty-stricken.
-penny *in cmpds* pennies (in value): *a five-penny piece*.
penny dreadful *n* a cheap trivial novel or thriller.
penny-farthing *n* (*hist*) a bicycle with an enormous front wheel and tiny back wheel.
penny-halfpenny *n* (*hist*; also **three halfpence**) one and a half pence (sense **1**).
penny-in-the-slot *adj* (of a machine) coin-operated.
penny-pinching *adj* (*derog*) too careful with one's money; miserly; stingy. — *n* **penny-pincher**.
pennyworth *n* (*old*) an amount that can be bought for one penny.
penology *n* the study of crime and punishment. — *adj* **penological**. — *n* **penologist**. [Lat *poena*, punishment + **-logy**]
pension *n* a government allowance to a retired, disabled or widowed person; a regular payment by an employer to a retired employee. — *v* **-n-** (*tr*) to grant a pension to. — *v* **pension off** (*tr*) to put into retirement on a pension. [OFr, from Lat *pensio*, payment]
pensionable *adj* entitling one to a pension.
pensioner *n* a person in receipt of a pension.
pensive *adj* preoccupied with one's thoughts; thoughtful. — *adv* **pensively**. [OFr *pensif*, from *penser*, to think]
pent: **pent up** (of feelings, energy, etc.) repressed, stifled or bottled up; bursting to be released. [Old past participle of **pen**[1]]
penta- or **pent-** *comb fm* five: *pentatonic*. [Gr *pente*, five]
pentagon *n* **1** (*geom*) a two-dimensional figure with five sides and five angles. **2** (*cap* with **the**) the five-sided building in Washington DC that is the headquarters of the US Department of Defence. — *adj* **pentagonal**. [Gr *pente*, five + *gonia*, angle]
pentagram *n* a five-pointed star, esp. used as a magic symbol. [Gr *pente*, five + *gramma*, character, letter]
pentameter *n* a line of verse with five metrical feet. [Gr *pente*, five + *metron*, measure]
Pentateuch *n* the first five books of the Old Testament. — *adj* **Pentateuchal**. [Gr *pente*, five + *teuchos*, tool, scroll]
pentathlon *n* any of several athletic competitions composed of five events in all of which contestants must compete, the **modern pentathlon** comprising swimming, cross-country riding and running, fencing and pistol-shooting. [Gr, *pente*, five + *athlon*, contest]
pentatonic *adj* (*mus*) (of a scale) having five notes. [**penta-** + **tone**]
pentavalent *adj* (*chem*) having a valency of five. [**penta-**]
Pentecost *n* **1** (*Christianity*) a festival on Whit Sunday, the seventh Sunday after Easter, commemorating the descent of the Holy Spirit on the apostles. **2** (*Judaism*) Shabuoth or the Feast of Weeks. [Gr *pentecoste* (*hemera*), fiftieth (day)]
Pentecostal *adj* **1** denoting any of several fundamentalist Christian groups that put emphasis on God's gifts through the Holy Spirit. **2** relating to Pentecost.
penthouse *n* an apartment, esp. luxuriously appointed, built on to the roof of a tall building. [Earlier *pentice*, from OFr *appentis*, from Lat *appendicium*, appendage]
pent-up. See **pent**.
penultimate *adj* the last but one. [Lat *paene*, almost + *ultimus*, last]
penumbra *n* ***-rae*** or ***-ras*** **1** a rim of lighter shadow round the shadow proper of a body, e.g. the sun or moon during an eclipse; an area where dark and light blend. **2** a lighter border round the edge of a sunspot. — *adj* **penumbral** [Lat *paene*, almost + *umbra*, shadow]
penury *n* **1** extreme poverty. **2** lack; scarcity. [Lat *penuria*]
penurious *adj* **1** mean with money; miserly. **2** poor; impoverished. — *adv* **penuriously**.

peon *n* **1** in India and Ceylon, an office messenger; an attendant. **2** in Latin America, a farm labourer. [Span *peón*, from Lat *pedo*, foot soldier]

peony *n* **-ies** a garden plant or small shrub with large globular red, pink, yellow or white flowers. [Gr *paionia*, from *Paion*, the healer of the gods, from the plant's medicinal use]

people *n* **1** (*pl*) persons. **2** (*pl*) men and women in general. **3** (*pl*; **the**) ordinary citizens without special rank; the populace. **4** (*pl*; **the**) the voters as a body. **5** (*pl*) subjects. **6** a nation or race: *warlike people*. **7** (*pl*; *coll*) one's parents, or the wider circle of one's relations. — *v* (*tr*) **1** to fill or supply (a region) with people; to populate. **2** to inhabit. — **of all people** especially; more than anyone else. [OFr *poeple*]

PEP *abbrev* Personal Equity Plan.

pep *n* (*coll*) energy; vitality; go. — *v* **-pp-** **pep up** (*tr*) to enliven or invigorate. [Short for **pepper**]

pep pill *n* a pill containing a stimulant drug.

pep talk *n* a talking-to intended to encourage and inspire.

pepper *n* **1** a pungent seasoning prepared from the dried and crushed berries of a tropical climbing plant; the plant bearing these berries. **2** the red, yellow or green fruit of the capsicum, with a hollow seedy interior, eaten as a vegetable. **3** a seasoning prepared from varieties of this fruit: *cayenne pepper*. — *v* **-r-** (*tr*; **with**) **1** to bombard (with missiles). **2** to sprinkle liberally: *peppered with typing errors*. **3** to season with pepper. [OE *pipor*, from Lat *piper*]

peppercorn *n* the dried berry of the pepper plant (sense **1**).

peppermill *n* a device for grinding peppercorns.

peppermint *n* **1** a mint plant whose leaves yield a strong-tasting oil, used in flavouring sweets, etc. **2** this flavouring. **3** (also **mint**) a sweet flavoured with peppermint.

peppery *adj* **1** well seasoned with pepper; tasting of pepper; hot-tasting or pungent. **2** short-tempered; irascible.

pepsin *n* an enzyme produced in the stomach that, in combination with acid, breaks down proteins. [Gr *pepsis*, digestion]

peptic *adj* **1** relating to, or promoting, digestion. **2** relating to pepsin or the digestive juices. [Gr *peptikos*]

peptic ulcer *n* an ulcer of the stomach or duodenum.

per *prep* **1** out of every: *two per thousand*. **2** for every: *£5 per head*. **3** in every: *sixty miles per hour*; *100 accidents per week*. **4** through; by means of: *per post*. — **as per** according to: *proceed as per instructions*. — **as per usual** (*coll*) as always. [Lat, for each, by]

per- *pfx* **1** (*chem*) the highest degree of combination with oxygen or other element or radical. **2** (in words from Latin) through, beyond, thoroughly or utterly. [Lat *per-*, pfx.]

peradventure *adv* perhaps; by chance. [OFr *par aventure*, by chance]

perambulate *v* **1** (*tr*) to walk about (a place). **2** (*intr*) to stroll around. — *n* **perambulation**. [Lat *per*, through + *ambulare*, to walk]

perambulator *n* a pram.

per annum for each year; by the year. [Lat]

per capita for each person: *income per capita*. [Lat, by heads]

perceive *v* (*tr*) **1** to observe, notice or discern: *perceived a change*. **2** to understand, interpret or view: *how one perceives one's role*. — *adj* **perceivable**. [OFr *percever*, from Lat *percipere*]

per cent *adv* (symbol **%**) **1** in or for every 100. **2** on a scale of 1 to 100: *90 per cent certain*. — *n* (also **percent**) **1** a percentage or proportion. **2** (usu. in *pl*) a security yielding a certain rate of interest: *invest in four-percents*. **3** one part on every 100: *half a percent*. [Lat *per centum*, for every 100]

percentage *n* **1** an amount, number or rate stated as a proportion of one hundred. **2** a proportion: *What percentage of students fail?*

percentile *n* (*statistics*) (any of the groups formed by) one of the values or points into which a variable or range of data is divided to make 100 groups with equal frequencies.

perception *n* **1** the process of perceiving. **2** one's powers of observation; discernment; insight. **3** one's view or interpretation of something. [Lat *percipere*, to perceive]

perceptible *adj* able to be perceived; noticeable; detectable. — *n* **perceptibility**. — *adv* **perceptibly**.

perceptive *adj* quick to notice or discern; astute. — *adv* **perceptively**.

perch[1] *n* **1** a branch or other narrow support above ground for a bird to rest on. **2** any place selected, esp. temporarily, as a seat. **3** a high position or vantage point. **4** (also **rod** or **pole**) an old measure of length equal to 5·03 metres or $5\frac{1}{2}$ yards. — *v* **1** (*intr*) (of birds) to alight and rest on a perch. **2** (*intr*) to sit, esp. insecurely or temporarily. **3** (*intr* & *tr*) to sit or place high up. [OFr *perche*, from Lat *pertica*, rod]

perch[2] *n* ***perch*** or ***perches*** any of several edible, spiny-finned fish. [Gr *perke*]

perchance *adv* (*old*) **1** by chance. **2** perhaps. [OFr *par chance*, by chance]

percipient *adj* perceptive; acutely observant; discerning. [Lat *percipere*, to perceive]

percolate *v* **1** (*intr* & *tr*) to pass through a porous material; to ooze, trickle or filter. **2** (*intr*; *coll*) (of information or news) to trickle or spread slowly. **3** (*tr* & *intr*) (of coffee) to make or be made in a percolator. — *n* **percolation**. [Lat *percolare*, to filter through]

percolator *n* a pot for making coffee, in which boiling water is kept circulating up through a tube and down through ground coffee beans.

percussion *n* **1** the striking of one hard object against another. **2** musical instruments played by striking, e.g. drums, cymbals, xylophone, etc.; these as a section of an orchestra. — *adj* **percussive**. [Lat *percussio*, striking]

percussion cap *n* a metal case containing a material that explodes when struck, formerly used for firing rifles.

percussionist *n* a person who plays percussion instruments.

perdition *n* everlasting punishment after death; damnation; hell. [Lat *perditio*, from *perdere*, to lose utterly]

peregrinate *v* (*intr*) to travel, voyage or roam; to wander abroad. — *n* **peregrination** (usu. in *pl*). [Lat *peregrinari*, to roam, from *per*, through + *ager*, field]

peregrine *n* (also **peregrine falcon**) a small falcon with a dark back and streaked underparts, notable for its acrobatic flight. [Lat *peregrinus*, wandering abroad, the birds being captured during flight]

peremptory *adj* **1** (of orders) made in expectation of immediate compliance: *a peremptory summons*. **2** (of a tone or manner in making requests) arrogantly impatient. **3** (of a statement, conclusion, etc.) allowing no denial or discussion; dogmatic. — *adv* **peremptorily**. [Lat *peremptorius*, deadly]

perennial *adj* **1** (of a plant) living for at least two years. **2** lasting throughout the year. **3** constant; continual. — *n* a perennial plant. — *adv* **perennially**. [Lat *perennis*, from *per*, through + *annus*, year]

perestroika *n* a restructuring or reorganisation, specifically that of the economic and political system of the former USSR begun in the 1980s. [Russ, reconstruction]

perfect *adj* **1** complete in all essential elements. **2** faultless; flawless. **3** excellent; absolutely, or quite, satisfactory. **4** exact: *a perfect circle*. **5** (*coll*) absolute; utter: *perfect nonsense*. **6** (*gram*) (of the tense of a verb) denoting completed action. — *n* (*gram*) (a verb in) the perfect tense, in English formed with the auxiliary verb *have* and the past participle. — *v* (*tr*) **1** to improve to one's satisfaction: *perfect one's German*. **2** to finalise or complete. **3** to develop (a technique, etc.) to a reliable standard. — *n* **perfectibility**. — *adj* **perfectible**. — *adv* **perfectly**. [Lat *perficere*, to complete]

perfection *n* **1** the state of being perfect. **2** the process of making or being made perfect, complete, etc. **3** flawlessness. **4** (*coll*) an instance of absolute excellence: *The meal was perfection*. — **to perfection** perfectly.

perfectionist *n* a person inclined to be dissatisfied with standards of achievement, esp. his or her own, if they are not absolutely perfect. — *n* **perfectionism**.

perfect pitch see **pitch**[1].

perfidious *adj* treacherous, disloyal, or double-dealing. — *adv* **perfidiously**. — *n* **perfidy**, **-ies**. [Lat *perfidus*]

perforate *v* **1** (*tr*) to make a hole or holes in; to pierce. **2** (*tr*) to make a row of holes in, for ease of tearing. **3** (*intr*) (of an ulcer, diseased appendix, etc.) to develop a hole; to burst. [Lat *perforare*, to pierce]

perforation *n* **1** a hole made in something. **2** a row of small holes made in paper, a sheet of stamps, etc. for ease of tearing. **3** the process of perforating or being perforated.

perforce *adv* necessarily; inevitably or unavoidably. [OFr *par force*]

perform *v* **1** (*tr*) to carry out (a task, job, action, etc.); to do or accomplish. **2** (*tr*) to fulfil (a function) or provide (a service, etc.). **3** (*tr* & *intr*) to act, sing, play, dance, etc. to entertain an audience: *the performing arts* (i.e. music, dance and drama). **4** (*intr*) (of e.g. an engine) to function. **5** (*intr*) to conduct oneself, esp. when presenting oneself for assessment: *performs well in interviews*. **6** (*intr*) (of commercial products, shares, currencies, etc.) to fare in competition. — *n* **performer**. [OFr *parfournir*]

performance *n* **1** the performing of a play, part, dance, piece of music, etc. before an audience; a dramatic or artistic presentation or entertainment. **2** the act or process of performing a task, etc. **3** a level of achievement, success, or, in commerce, profitability. **4** manner or efficiency of functioning. **5** (*derog*) an instance of outrageous behaviour, esp. in public.

perfume *n* **1** a sweet smell; a scent or fragrance. **2** a fragrant liquid prepared from the extracts of flowers, etc., for applying to the skin or clothes; scent. — *v* (*tr*) to give a sweet smell to; to apply perfume to. — *n* **perfumery**. [OFr *parfum*, from Lat *per* through + *fumare*, to impregnate with smoke]

perfumer *n* a maker of or dealer in perfumes.

perfunctory *adj* done merely as a duty or routine, without genuine care or feeling. — *adv* **perfunctorily**. [Lat *perfunctorius*, slapdash]

pergola *n* a framework constructed from slender branches, for plants to climb up; a trellis. [Ital, from Lat *pergula*, shed]

perhaps *adv* possibly; maybe. [Earlier *perhappes*, from OFr *par*, by + Norse *happ*, fortune]

peri- *pfx* **1** around: *periscope*; *pericardium*. **2** near: *perinatal*; *perigee*. [Gr *peri*, round]

perianth *n* (*bot*) the outer part of a flower; the calyx and corolla. [**peri-** + Gr *anthos*, flower]

pericardium *n* **-ia** the sac enclosing the heart. [**peri-** + Gr *kardia*, heart]

pericarp *n* the wall of a fruit, developed from the wall of the plant ovary. [**peri-** + Gr *karpos*, fruit]

perigee *n* the point in the orbit of the moon or other satellite when it is closest to the earth. ◇ See also **apogee**. [Fr *perigée*, from Gr *perigeion*, from *peri*, near + *ge*, earth]

perihelion *n* **-*helia*** the point in a planet's orbit round the sun when it is closest to the sun. ◇ See also **aphelion**. [**peri-** + Gr *helios*, sun]

peril *n* **1** grave danger. **2** a hazard. — *adj* **perilous**. — *adv* **perilously**. — **at one's peril** at the risk of one's life. — [OFr, from Lat *periculum*, danger]

perimeter *n* **1** the boundary of an enclosed area. **2** (*geom*) the enclosing line or circumference of a two-dimensional figure; its length. [Gr *perimetros*, from *peri*, round + *metros*, measure]

perinatal *adj* relating to the period up to three months before, and up to one month after, birth. [**peri-** + **natal**]

period *n* **1** a portion of time. **2** a phase or stage in history, development, etc. **3** (*geol*) any of the phases in the earth's history characterised by some development, e.g. the formation of a certain type of rock: *the Cretaceous period*. **4** any of the sessions of equal length into which the school day is divided, and to which particular subjects or activities are assigned. **5** the punctuation mark (.), used e.g. at the end of a sentence; a full stop. **6** (*coll*) added to a statement to emphasise its finality: *You may not go, period*. **7** a woman's time of menstruation. **8** (*chem*) a series of elements represented in a horizontal row in the periodic table. **9** (*physics*) the time that elapses between recurrences of a cyclic phenomenon. — *adj* dating from, or designed in the style of, the historical period in question: *period costume* or *furniture*. [Gr *periodos*, from *peri*, round + *hodos*, way]

periodic *adj* happening at esp. regular intervals; occasional.

periodical *adj* periodic. — *n* a magazine published weekly, monthly, quarterly, etc. — *adv* **periodically**.

periodic function *n* (*math*) one whose values recur in a cycle as the variable increases.

periodicity *n* the fact of recurring, or tendency to recur, at intervals.

periodic law *n* (*chem*) the law that the properties of elements are periodic functions of their atomic numbers.

periodic table *n* (*chem*) a list of elements arranged in order of atomic number, horizontally in series and vertically in groups, showing how similar properties recur at regular intervals.

period piece *n* **1** a piece of furniture, etc. dating from, and in the distinctive style of, a certain historical period. **2** (*facet*) something quaintly old-fashioned.

peripatetic *adj* **1** travelling about from place to place. **2** (of a teacher) employed by several schools and so obliged to travel between them. **3** (also *cap*) denoting the school of philosophers founded by Aristotle, given to promenading while lecturing. — *n* a peripatetic teacher or philosopher. — *adv* **peripatetically**. [Gr *peri*, round + *pateein*, to tread]

periphery *n* **-*ies*** **1** the edge or boundary of something. **2** the external surface of something. [Gr *periphereia*, circumference, surface]

peripheral *adj* **1** relating to, or belonging to, the outer edge or outer surface: *peripheral nerves*. **2** (**to**) not central to the issue in hand; marginal. **3** (*comput*) supplementary; auxiliary. **4** relating to the outer edge of the field of vision. — *n* (*comput*) (also **peripheral device** or **unit**) a device with an auxiliary function, e.g. input, output or storage.

periphrasis *n* **-*ases*** **1** a roundabout way of saying something; a circumlocution. — *adj* **periphrastic**. — *adv* **periphrastically**. [Gr *peri*, round + *phrasis*, speech]

periscope *n* an optical instrument consisting of a shaft containing mirrors so angled as to allow one to see things not in one's unaided line of vision, used esp. in submerged submarines for scanning the water surface. — *adj* **periscopic**. [Gr *periskopeein*, to look around]

perish *v* **1** (*intr*) to die; to be destroyed or ruined. **2** (*tr* & *intr*) (of materials) to (cause to) decay or rot. [OFr *perir*]

perishable *adj* (of commodities, esp. food) liable to rot or go bad quickly. — *n* **perishability**.

perished *adj* (*coll*) feeling the cold severely.

perisher *n* (*old coll*) a mischievous child or other troublesome person.

perishing *adj* **1** (*coll*) very cold. **2** (*old coll*) damned, infernal or confounded. — *adv* **perishingly**.

peristalsis *n* (*physiol*) the contracting movement that passes with a wave-like progression along the alimentary canal, forcing its contents onward. — *adj* **peristaltic**. [Gr *peristellein*, to contract round]

peristyle *n* (*archit*) a colonnade round a courtyard or building. [Gr *peri*, round + *stylos*, column]

peritoneum *n* **-*nea*** or **-*neums*** the membrane that lines the abdominal cavity. — *adj* **peritoneal**. [Gr *peritonaion*, from *periteinein*, to stretch all round]

peritonitis *n* inflammation of the peritoneum. [**peritoneum** + **-itis**]

periwig *n* a man's wig of the 17th and 18th cent. [Variant of **peruke**]

periwinkle[1] *n* any of several evergreen plants with trailing stems and blue or white flowers. [OE *perwince*, from Lat *pervinca*]

periwinkle[2] *n* (also **winkle**) any one of several edible marine snails; its shell. [OE *pinewincle*]

perjure *v* (*tr*) to forswear (oneself) in a court of law, i.e. lie while under oath to tell the truth. — *n* **perjurer**. [Lat *perjurare*]

perjury *n* **-*ies*** the crime of lying while under oath in a court of law.

perk[1] *v* (*intr* & *tr* with **up**) **1** to become or make more lively and cheerful. **2** (of e.g. a dog's ears) to prick up. [MidE *perken*]

perk[2] *n* (*coll*) a perquisite (sense **1**).

perk[3] *v* (*intr* & *tr*; *coll*) to percolate.

perky *adj* **-*ier***, **-*iest*** lively and cheerful. — *adv* **perkily**. — *n* **perkiness**.

perm[1] *n* a hair treatment using chemicals that give a long-lasting wave or curl. — *v* (*tr*) to curl or wave (hair) with a perm. [**permanent wave**]

perm[2] (*coll*) *n* a permutation (sense **2**). — *v* (*tr*) to make a permutation of.

permafrost *n* permanently frozen subsoil in polar areas. [**permanent frost**]

permanent *adj* **1** lasting, or intended to last, indefinitely; not temporary. **2** (of a condition, etc.) unlikely to alter. — *n* **permanence** or **permanency**. — *adv* **permanently**. [Lat *permanere*, to remain]

permanent wave *n* a perm.

permanent way *n* a railway track, including the rails, sleepers and stones.

permanganate *n* any of the salts of **permanganic acid**, esp. **potassium permanganate**, used as an oxidising and bleaching agent and disinfectant. [**per**- (sense **1**) + **manganese**]

permeable *adj* (**by**) able to be permeated by liquids, gases, etc. — *n* **permeability**. [Lat *permeabilis*]

permeate *v* **1** (*tr* or *intr*; **through**) (of a liquid) to pass or seep through (a fine or porous material, a membrane, etc.). **2** (*tr* or *intr*; **throughout**, etc.) (of a smell, gas, etc.) to spread through (a room or other space); to fill or impregnate. — *n* **permeation**. [Lat *permeare*, to penetrate]

Permian *adj* & *n* (*geol*) (denoting) a period between 286 and 250 million years ago, when many marine invertebrates died out and reptiles grew in variety. [*Perm* in Russia]

permission *n* (**for**) consent, agreement, leave or authorisation. [Lat *permissio*]

permissible *adj* allowable; permitted. — *n* **permissibility**.

permissive *adj* allowing usu. excessive freedom, esp. in sexual matters; tolerant; liberal. — *adv* **permissively**. — *n* **permissiveness**.

permit *v* **-*tt*- 1** (*tr*) to consent to or give permission for. **2** (*tr*) to give (someone) leave or authorisation. **3** (*tr*) to allow (someone something): *permitted him access to his children*. **4** (*tr* & *intr*; **of**) to enable; to give scope or opportunity: *an outrage that permits of no excuse*. — *n* a document authorising something. [Lat *permittere*, to allow]

permute *v* (*tr*) (also **permutate**) to rearrange (a set of things) in different orders, esp. in every possible order in succession. — *n* **permutability**. — *adj* **permutable**. [Lat *permutare*, to interchange]

permutation *n* **1** the process of rearranging a set of things in every possible order in succession. **2** any of the resulting combinations. **3** a fixed combination in football pools for selecting the results of matches.

pernicious *adj* harmful; destructive; deadly. — *adv* **perniciously**. [Lat *perniciosus*, from *pernicies*, ruin, bane]

pernicious anaemia *n* anaemia caused by an inability to absorb vitamin B_2 leading to a reduction in red blood cells.

pernickety *adj* **1** over-particular about small details; fussy. **2** (of a task) tricky; intricate.

peroration *n* **1** the concluding section of a speech, in which the points made are summed up. **2** (*coll*) a long formal speech. [Lat *peroratio*]

peroxide *n* **1** (*chem*) an oxygen compound containing more oxygen than an oxide. **2** hydrogen peroxide (H_2O_2), used e.g. for bleaching hair. — *v* (*tr*) to bleach (hair) with hydrogen peroxide. [**per**- (sense **1**)]

perpendicular *adj* **1** vertical; upright. **2** at right angles. **3** (of e.g. a cliff) precipitous; steep. **4** (*archit*; usu. *cap*) denoting a 14th- to 16th-cent. style characterised by tall slender verticals. — *n* a perpendicular line, position or direction. — *n* **perpendicularity**. — *adv* **perpendicularly**. [Lat *perpendicularis*, from *perpendiculum*, a plumbline]

perpetrate *v* (*tr*) to commit, or be guilty of (a crime, misdeed, error, etc.). — *n* **perpetration**. — *n* **perpetrator**. [Lat *perpetrare*, to bring about, commit]

perpetual *adj* everlasting; eternal; continuous; permanent: *in perpetual bliss*. **2** continual: *perpetual quarrels*. [Lat *perpetualis*, from *perpetuus*, uninterrupted]

perpetual calendar *n* **1** a calendar for ascertaining on which day of the week any date falls. **2** a calendar that is usable for any year or for several years.

perpetual motion *n* the motion of a hypothetical machine that keeps going indefinitely without any external source of energy.

perpetuate *v* (*tr*) **1** to cause to last or continue: *perpetuate a feud*, *species*, etc. **2** to preserve the memory of (a name, etc.). **3** to repeat and pass on (an error, etc.). — *n* **perpetuation**. [Lat *perpetuare*, to make perpetual]

perpetuity *n* **-*ies* 1** the state of being perpetual. **2** eternity. **3** duration for an indefinite period. **4** something perpetual, e.g. an allowance to be paid indefinitely. — **in perpetuity** for ever. [Lat *perpetuitas*, from *perpetuus*, perpetual]

perplex *v* (*tr*) **1** to puzzle, confuse or baffle. **2** to complicate. — *adv* **perplexedly**. — *adj* **perplexing**. [Lat *per*-, thoroughly + *plexus*, entangled]

perplexity *n* **-*ies* 1** the state of being perplexed. **2** something baffling or confusing.

per pro. *abbrev* for *per procurationem*, by the agency of. [Lat]

perquisite *n* **1** a benefit, additional to one's wages, gained from one's employment, such as the use of a company car. **2** a tip expected on some occasions. **3** something regarded as due to one by right. [Lat *perquisitum*, something acquired]

perry *n* **-ies** an alcoholic drink made from fermented pear juice. [OFr *peré*, from Lat *pirum*, pear]

pers. *abbrev* person or personal.

per se in itself; intrinsically: *not valuable per se.* [Lat.]

persecute *v* (*tr*) **1** to ill-treat, oppress or torment, esp. on the grounds of religious or political beliefs. **2** to harass, pester or bother continually. — *n* **persecution**. — *n* **persecutor**. [Lat *persequi*, to pursue, ill-treat]

persevere *v* (*intr*; **in, with**) to keep on striving; to persist steadily. — *n* **perseverance**. [OFr *perseverer*]

Persian *adj* of Persia (modern Iran), its people or language. — *n* **1** a native or citizen of Persia. **2** the language of Persia or Iran.

Persian carpet *n* a distinctively patterned hand-woven woollen or silk carpet made in Persia or elsewhere in the Near East.

Persian cat *n* a breed of cat with long silky fur.

Persian lamb *n* **1** the black curly fur of the karakul lamb, used for coats and trimmings.

persiflage *n* banter, teasing, flippancy or frivolous talk. [Fr]

persimmon *n* a tropical plum-like fruit of America and Asia, or the tree that bears it. [From an Algonquian (N American Indian) language]

persist *v* **1** (*intr*; **in, with**) to continue in spite of resistance, discouragement, etc. **2** (of rain, etc.) to continue steadily. **3** (of e.g. a mistaken idea) to remain current. [Lat *persistere*, to stand firm]

persistent *adj* **1** continuing with determination in spite of discouragement; dogged. **2** constant; unrelenting: *persistent questions.* — *n* **persistence**. — *adv* **persistently**.

person *n* **1** ***persons*** (*formal*) or ***people*** an individual human being. **2** ***persons*** one's body: *drugs concealed on his person.* **3** ***persons*** (*gram*) one of the three classes into which pronouns and verb forms fall, **first person** denoting the speaker (or the speaker and others), **second person** the person addressed (with or without others) and **third person** the person(s) or thing(s) spoken of. **4** (*relig*; *cap*) in Christian doctrine, any of the three forms or manifestations of God (Father, Son and Holy Spirit) that together form the Trinity. — **be no respecter of persons** to make no allowances for rank. — **in person 1** actually present oneself: *was there in person.* **2** (doing something) oneself, not asking or allowing others to do it for one. [Lat *persona*, actor's mask]

-person *in cmpds* replacing *-man*, *-woman*, *-lady*, etc.: *chairperson.*

persona *n* ***-nae*** or ***-nas*** one's character as one presents it to other people. ◇ See also **persona non grata**. [Lat, actor's mask]

personable *adj* good-looking or likeable. — *adv* **personably**. **[person]**

personage *n* a well-known, important or distinguished person. [Lat *personagium*, from *persona*, person]

personal *adj* **1** coming from someone as an individual, not from a group or organisation: *my personal opinion.* **2** done, attended to, etc. by the individual person in question, not by a substitute: *give it my personal attention.* **3** relating to oneself in particular: *a personal triumph.* **4** relating to one's private concerns: *details of her personal life.* **5** (of remarks) referring insultingly to an individual's physical or other characteristics. **6** relating to the body: *personal hygiene.* [Lat *personalis*, from *persona*, person]

personal assistant *n* a secretary, esp. of a senior executive, manager, etc.

personal column *n* a newspaper column or section in which members of the public may place advertisements, enquiries, etc.

personal computer *n* a small desk computer used by an individual operator for word-processing, data storage, etc.

personal effects *n* (*pl*) one's belongings.

personalise or **-ize** *v* (*tr*) **1** to mark distinctively as the property of a particular person. **2** to focus (a discussion) etc. on personalities instead of the matter in hand. **3** to personify.

personally *adv* **1** as far as one is concerned: *Personally, I disapprove.* **2** in person. **3** as a person. **4** as directed against one: *take a remark personally.*

personal pronoun *n* (*gram*) any of the pronouns representing a person or thing, e.g. *I*, *you*, *he*, *him*, *she*, *it*, *they*, *us*.

personal property *n* everything one owns other than land or buildings. ◇ See also **real**[1] (sense **5**).

personal stereo *n* a small audio cassette player with earphones, that can be worn on one's person.

personify *v* ***-ies***, ***-ied*** (*tr*) **1** in literature, etc., to represent (an abstract quality, etc.) as a human or as having human qualities. **2** (of a figure in a work of art, etc.) to represent or symbolise (a quality, etc.). **3** to embody in human form; to be the perfect example of: *She's patience personified.* — *n* **personification**.

personality *n* ***-ies*** **1** a person's nature or disposition; the qualities that give one's character individuality. **2** strength or distinctiveness of character: *lots of personality.* **3** a well-known person; a celebrity. **4** (in *pl*) offensive personal remarks. [Lat *personalitas*, from *persona*, person]

persona non grata *n* ***-nae non gratae*** a person who is not wanted or welcome within a particular group. [Lat, person not welcome]

personnel *n* **1** (*pl*) the people employed in a business company, an armed service or other organisation. **2** a department within such an organisation dealing with matters concerning employees. [Fr, personal]

perspective *n* **1** the observer's view of objects in relation to one another, esp. with regard to the way they seem smaller the more distant they are. **2** the representation of this phenomenon in drawing and painting. **3** the balanced or objective view of a situation, in which all its elements assume their due importance: *get things into*, or *out of*, *perspective*. **4** an individual way of regarding a situation, e.g. one influenced by personal experience or considerations. [Lat (*ars*) *perspectiva*, optical (science)]

Perspex® *n* a tough transparent plastic, used for visors, etc.

perspicacious *adj* shrewd, astute, perceptive or discerning. — *adv* **perspicaciously**. — *n* **perspicacity**. [Lat *perspicax*]

perspicuous *adj* (of speech or writing) clearly expressed and easily understood. — *n* **perspicuity**. — *adv* **perspicuously**. [Lat *perspicuus*, transparent, manifest]

perspire *v* (*intr*) to sweat. [Lat *perspirare*, to breathe through, sweat]

perspiration *n* the salty moisture produced by the sweat glands of the skin.

persuade *v* (*tr*) **1** to urge successfully; to prevail on or induce. **2** (**of**) to convince. — *adj* **persuadable** or **persuasible**. — *n* **persuader**. — **put the persuaders on** (*slang*) to threaten with violence. [Lat *persuadere*]

persuasion *n* **1** the act of urging, coaxing or persuading. **2** a creed, conviction or set of beliefs, esp. that of a political group or religious sect.

persuasive *adj* having the power to persuade; convincing or plausible. — *adv* **persuasively**. — *n* **persuasiveness**.

pert *adj* **1** impudent; cheeky. **2** (of clothing or style) jaunty; saucy. — *adv* **pertly**. — *n* **pertness**. [OFr *apert*, open]

pertain *v* (*intr*) **1** (with **to**) to concern or relate to; to have to do with. **2** (with **to**) to belong to: *skills pertaining to the job*. **3** to be appropriate; to apply. [OFr *partenir*]

pertinacious *adj* determined in one's purpose; dogged; tenacious. — *adv* **pertinaciously**. — *n* **pertinacity**. [Lat *pertinax*]

pertinent *adj* (**to**) relating (to); concerned (with); relevant. — *n* **pertinence** or **pertinency**. [Lat *pertinere*, to relate]

perturb *v* (*tr*) to make anxious or agitated. — *n* **perturbation**. — *adj* **perturbed**. [Lat *perturbare*, to throw into confusion]

peruke *n* a 17th- to 18th-cent. style of wig, with side curls and a tail at the back. [OFr *perruque*, head of hair]

peruse *v* (*tr*) **1** to read through carefully. **2** to browse through casually. **3** to examine or study attentively. — *n* **perusal**. [**per-**, thoroughly + **use**[1]]

pervade *v* (*tr*) to spread or extend throughout; to affect throughout. [Lat *pervadere*]

pervasive *adj* tending to spread everywhere.

perverse *adj* deliberately departing from what is normal and reasonable; unreasonable, awkward, stubborn or wilful. — *adv* **perversely**. — *n* **perversity**, **-*ies***. [Lat *perversus*, from *pervertere*, to overturn]

perversion *n* **1** the process of perverting or condition of being perverted. **2** a distortion. **3** an abnormal sexual activity. [Lat *pervertere*, to corrupt]

pervert *v* (*tr*) **1** to divert illicitly from what is normal or right. **2** to lead into evil or unnatural behaviour; to corrupt. **3** to distort or misinterpret (words, etc.). — *n* someone who is morally or sexually perverted. [Lat *pervertere*, to corrupt]

peseta *n* **1** the standard unit of currency in Spain. [Span, dimin. of *pesa*, weight]

pesky *adj* **-*ier***, **-*iest*** (*NAm coll*) troublesome or infuriating. — *adv* **peskily**. [Prob. **pest**]

peso *n* **-*os*** the standard unit of currency in many Central and S American countries and the Philippines. [Span, weight]

pessary *n* **-*ies*** **1** a medicated dissolving tablet inserted into the vagina to treat an infection, etc.; a vaginal suppository. **2** a device worn in the vagina as a contraceptive, or as a support for the womb. [Lat *pessarium*, from Gr *pessos*, pebble, plug]

pessimism *n* **1** the tendency to emphasise the gloomiest aspects of anything, and to expect the worst to happen. **2** the belief that this is the worst of all possible worlds, and that evil is triumphing over good. — *n* **pessimist**. — *adj* **pessimistic**. — *adv* **pessimistically**. [*pessimus*, worst]

pest *n* **1** an insect or animal harmful to plants, food or livestock. **2** a person or thing that is a constant nuisance. [Lat *pestis*, plague]

pester *v* **-*r*-** (*tr*) **1** to annoy constantly. **2** to harass or hound with requests. [OFr *empestrer*, to entangle, influenced by **pest**]

pesticide *n* a chemical for killing insects or other pests. [**pest** + **-cide**]

pestilence *n* a deadly epidemic disease such as bubonic plague. [Lat *pestilentia*, from *pestis*, plague]

pestilent *adj* **1** deadly, harmful or destructive. **2** infuriating; troublesome. — *adv* **pestilently**. [Lat *pestilens*, from *pestis*, plague]

pestilential *adj* infuriating; troublesome.

pestle *n* a club-like utensil for pounding substances in a mortar. [OFr *pestel*]

pet[1] *n* **1** a tame animal or bird kept as a companion. **2** someone's favourite. **3** a darling or love. — *adj* **1** kept as a pet. **2** of or for pets. **3** favourite; own special. — *v* **-*tt*- 1** (*tr*) to pat or stroke (an animal, etc.)

2 (*tr*) to treat indulgently; to make a fuss of. **3** (*tr & intr*) to fondle and caress for erotic pleasure.

pet name *n* a special name used as an endearment.

pet[2] *n* a fit of bad temper or sulks. — *adj* **pettish**. — *adv* **pettishly**. — *n* **pettishness**.

petal *n* any of the group of coloured parts forming the head of a flower. [Gr *petalon*, leaf]

petard *n* (*hist*) a small bomb for blasting a hole in a wall, door, etc. — **hoist with one's own petard** blown up by one's own bomb, i.e. caught in one's own trap. [OFr, from *peter*, to break wind; obsolete *hoise*, to hoist]

peter: **peter out** *v* **-r-** (*intr*) to dwindle away to nothing. [Orig. US mining slang]

Peter Pan *n* someone who remains forever youthful. [Character created by J M Barrie (1860–1937)]

petersham *n* a stiff ribbed silk ribbon used for reinforcing waistbands, etc. [Lord *Petersham*, 19th-cent. English army officer]

pethidine *n* a synthetic pain-relieving drug widely used in childbirth.

petiole *n* (*bot*) the little stalk attaching a leaf to a plant. [Lat *petiolus*, little foot]

petit bourgeois *n* ***petits bourgeois*** a member of the lower middle class. — *n* **petite bourgeoisie** the lower middle class. [Fr]

petite *adj* (of women and girls) daintily built. [Fr, feminine of *petit*, small]

petit four *n* ***petits fours*** a small sweet biscuit, usu. decorated with icing. [Fr, little oven]

petition *n* **1** (**for, against**) a formal written request to an authority to take some action, signed by a large number of people. **2** (**for, against**) any appeal to a higher authority. **3** (*legal*; **for**) an application to a court for some procedure to be set in motion. — *v* **-n-** (*tr & intr*; **for, against**) to address a petition (to); to make an appeal or request (to). — *n* **petitioner**. [Lat *petitio*, from *petere*, to seek]

petit mal *n* a mild form of epilepsy characterised by brief lapses into unconsciousness. [Fr, little illness]

petit point *n* **1** a small diagonal stitch used for fine work in needlepoint. **2** needlework using this stitch. [Fr, small point]

petrel *n* any of several seabirds that live far from land, esp. the storm petrel. [Altered from earlier *pitteral*, perhaps by association with St *Peter's* walking on the water, as some species of storm petrel walk across the surface of the sea while feeding]

petrify *v* ***-ies, -ied*** **1** (*tr*) **1** to terrify; to paralyse with fright. **2** (*tr & intr*) (of organic material) to change into stone. **3** (*tr & intr*) to fix or become fixed in an inflexible mould. — *n* **petrifaction** or **petrification**. [Gr *petra*, stone]

petro- *comb fm* **1** of or relating to petroleum and its products: *petrochemical*. **2** of or concerning stone or rocks: *petrology*.

petrochemical *n* any chemical, e.g. ethyl alcohol or acetone, obtained from petroleum or natural gas. — *adv* **petrochemically**. — *n* **petrochemistry**.

petrodollar *n* the US dollar as representative of the foreign currency earned on a vast scale by oil-exporting countries.

petrol *n* a flammable liquid obtained from petroleum, used as fuel for motor vehicles, aircraft, etc. [OFr *petrole*, from Lat *petroleum*]

petrol bomb *n* a crude bomb consisting of a petrol-filled bottle stopped with rags that are set alight just as the bottle is thrown.

petrol station *n* a filling-station.

petrolatum *n* petroleum jelly. [Modern Lat]

petroleum *n* a dark-coloured mineral oil consisting of a mixture of hydrocarbons, found in sedimentary rock in the earth's upper strata and refined into a variety of products, esp. petrol and paraffin. [Lat, from Gr *petra*, rock + Lat *oleum*, oil]

petroleum jelly *n* a greasy jelly-like substance obtained from petroleum, used in ointments and as a lubricant.

petrology *n* the scientific study of rocks, their make-up, structure and origin. — *adj* **petrological**. — *n* **petrologist**.

petticoat *n* **1** a woman's underskirt. **2** (in *pl*; *hist*) skirts in general, those worn by boys in early childhood in particular. — *adj* (*facet*) (of e.g. tactics, administration, etc.) of or by women; feminine or female. [**petty** + **coat**]

pettifogger *n* **1** a lawyer dealing with unimportant cases, esp. somewhat deceitfully or quibblingly. **2** (*derog*) someone who argues over trivial details; a quibbler. — *v* **pettifog**, ***-gg-*** (*intr*). — *n* & *adj* **pettifogging**. [**petty** + German dialect *voger*, arranger]

pettish. See **pet**[2].

petty *adj* ***-ier, -iest*** **1** of minor importance; trivial. **2** small-minded or childishly spiteful. **3** of low or subordinate rank. [OFr *petit*, small]

petty cash *n* money kept for small everyday expenses in an office, etc.

petty officer *n* a non-commissioned officer in the navy.

petulant *adj* ill-tempered; peevish. — *adv* **petulantly**. — *n* **petulance**. [Lat *petulans*, from *petere*, to seek]

petunia *n* a plant native to tropical America, with white, pink or purple funnel-shaped flowers. [Fr *petun*, tobacco plant (from its similarity), from Guarani (S American Indian language) *pety*]

pew *n* **1** one of the long benches with backs used as seating in a church. **2** (*coll facet*) a seat: *Take a pew*. [OFr *puie*, from Lat *podium*, part of a choir stall]

pewter *n* **1** a metal, an alloy of tin and lead. **2** articles made of pewter. [OFr *peutre*]
peyote *n* the Mexican cactus mescal, or the intoxicant got from it. [Aztec *peyotl*]
pfennig *n* a German unit of currency worth a hundredth of a mark. [Ger; related to **penny**]
PG (*abbrev*) **1** (*coll*) paying guest. **2** (as a film classification) parental guidance, i.e. containing scenes possibly unsuitable for children.
pH *n* (also **pH value**) a measure of the alkinity or acidity of a solution. [Short for Ger *Potenz*, power, exponent + **H**, symbol for hydrogen]
phagocyte *n* a cell, esp. a white blood cell, that engulfs and absorbs micro-organisms such as bacteria. [Gr *phagein*, to eat + **-cyte**]
phalange. See **phalanx**.
phalanger *n* a tree-dwelling, thick-furred Australasian marsupial with webbed hind toes and a long prehensile tail. [Gr *phalangion*, spider's web, from its webbed toes]
phalanx *n* **1** (*hist*) in ancient Greece, a body of infantry in close-packed formation. **2** a solid body of people, esp. representing united support or opposition. **3** (also **phalange, *phalanges***) any of the bones of the finger or toe. [Gr, line of soldiers drawn up for battle]
phalarope *n* a wading bird of the sandpiper family, native to northern parts but wintering in the southern tropics. [Gr, *phalaris*, coot + *pous*, foot]
phallus *n* ***-luses*** or ***-li*** a representation or image of an erect penis, esp. as a symbol of male reproductive power. — *adj* **phallic**. [Gr *phallos*]
phantasm *n* **1** an illusion or fantasy. **2** a ghost or phantom. — *adj* **phantasmal**. [Gr *phantasma*, apparition]
phantasmagoria *n* a fantastic succession of real or illusory images seen as if in a dream. — *adj* **phantasmagoric** or **phantasmagorical**. [Gr *phantasma*, apparition + (perhaps) *agora*, assembly]
phantasy *n* ***-ies*** an old spelling of **fantasy**.
phantom *n* **1** a ghost or spectre. **2** an illusory image or vision. — *adj* of the nature of a phantom; spectral. **2** imaginary; fancied; not real. [OFr *fantosme*, from Gr *phantasma*, apparition]
pharaoh *n* the title of the kings of ancient Eygpt. [Gr *pharao*, from Hebr *par'oh*, from Egyptian *pr-'o*, great house]
Pharisee *n* **1** a member of an ancient Jewish sect who, because of their strict interpretation of the laws of Moses, became obsessed with rules governing the minor procedures of everyday life. ◇ See also **Sadducee**. **2** a self-righteous, sanctimonious or hypocritical person. — *adj* **Pharisaic**. [Gr *pharisaios*, from Hebr *parush*, separated]
pharmaceutical *adj* of or relating to the preparation of drugs and medicines. [Gr *pharmakeutikos*, from *pharmakon*, drug]
pharmaceutics *n* (*sing*) the preparation and dispensing of drugs and medicine.
pharmacist *n* a person trained to prepare and dispense drugs and medicines. [**pharmacy**]
pharmacology *n* the scientific study of medicines and drugs and their effects and uses. — *adj* **pharmacological**. — *n* **pharmacologist**. [Gr *pharmakon*, drug + **-logy**]
pharmacopoeia *n* a list of medicinal drugs with their uses, preparation, dosages, effects and side effects. [Gr *pharmakopoiia*, preparation of drugs]
pharmacy *n* ***-ies*** **1** the mixing and dispensing of drugs and medicines. **2** a dispensary in a hospital, etc. **3** a pharmacist's or chemist's shop. [Gr *pharmakeia*, use of drugs]
pharynx *n* ***-rynxes*** or ***-rynges*** the cavity in the head that lies behind the nose, throat and larynx. — *adj* **pharyngeal**. [Gr, throat]
pharyngitis *n* inflammation of the pharynx.
phase *n* **1** a stage or period in growth or development. **2** any of the series of shapes assumed by the moon or a planet according to how fully it is illuminated by the sun. **3** (*physics*) any of the stages in a recurring cycle of changes e.g. in an alternating current or light vibrations. — *v* (*tr*) to organise or carry out in stages. — **in** (or **out of**) **phase** coinciding (or failing to coincide) phase by phase throughout a series of changes. — *v* **phase in** (or **out**) (*tr*) to introduce (or get rid of) in stages. [Gr *phasis*, appearance]
phase difference *n* (*physics*) the amount by which one wave (sense **2**) is behind or ahead of another wave of the same frequency.
PhD *abbrev* for *philosophiae doctor* (Lat), Doctor of Philosophy. ◇ See also **DPhil**.
pheasant *n* ***pheasant*** or ***pheasants*** any of various species of game bird orig. from Asia, the male of which has colourful feathers and often a long tail. [OFr *fesan*, from Gr *phasianos* (*ornis*), (bird) of the Phasis river]
phenobarbitone *n* (also, esp. *US*, **phenobarbital**) a hypnotic and sedative drug used to treat epilepsy and insomnia.
phenol *n* carbolic acid. [*phene*, old name for benzene]
phenomenon *n* ***-ena*** **1** a happening perceived through the senses, esp. if something unusual or scientifically explainable. **2** an extraordinary or abnormal person or thing; a prodigy. **3** a feature of life, social existence, etc.: *stress as a work-related phenomenon*. [Gr *phainomenon*, neuter present participle of *phainesthai*, to appear]
phenomenal *adj* **1** of the nature of a phenomenon. **2** relating to phenomena. **3** remarkable; extraordinary; abnormal. — adv **phenomenally**.

phew *interj* used to express relief, astonishment or exhaustion. [Imit. of a whistle]

phial *n* a little medicine bottle. [Gr *phiale*, shallow dish]

Phil. *abbrev* **1** Philadelphia. **2** philosophy or (Lat) *philosophiae*, of philosophy.

phil- or **philo-** *comb fm* loving, liking or fond of. [Gr *philos*, loving]

-phil. See **-phile**.

philadelphus *n* any of a genus of tall deciduous shrubs with highly perfumed showy flowers, esp. the mock orange. [Gr *philadelphon*, loving one's brother]

philander *v* **-r-** (*intr*) to flirt, or have casual love affairs, with women. — *n* **philanderer**. [Gr *philandros*, loving men, used in Greek literature as a proper name for a lover]

philanthropy *n* charitable love for one's fellow human beings, esp. in the form of benevolence to those in need. — *adj* **philanthropic**. — *n* **philanthropist**. [Gr *philanthropia*, from *phil-*, loving + *anthropos*, man]

philately *n* the study and collecting of postage stamps. — *adj* **philatelic**. — *n* **philatelist**. [**phil-** + Gr *ateles*, untaxed (mail being delivered 'free' if prepaid by a stamp)]

-phile or **-phil** *comb fm* (a person, etc.) loving, attracted to, or having an affinity for: *bibliophile*; *paedophile*. — *n comb fm* **-philia** . — *adj* & *n comb fm* **-philiac**. [Gr *philos*, loving]

philharmonic *adj* (used in names of choirs and orchestras) dedicated to music. [**phil-** + Gr *harmonia*, harmony]

philippic *n* a speech making a bitter attack on someone or something. [From the orations of the Athenian Demosthenes (384–322 BC) against *Philip* of Macedon]

philistine *n* & *adj* (a person) having no interest in, or appreciation of, art, literature, music, etc., tending rather towards materialism. — *n* **philistinism**. [Orig. a member of a warlike people inhabiting SW Palestine, enemies of the Israelites]

philo-. See **phil-**.

philology *n* **1** the study of language, its history and development; the comparative study of related languages; linguistics. **2** the study of esp. older literary and non-literary texts. — *adj* **philological**. — *adv* **philologically**. — *n* **philologist**. [Gr *philologia*, love of argument, literature or learning, from *philo-*, loving + *logos*, reason, word]

philosophy *n* **-ies** **1** the search for truth and knowledge concerning the universe, human existence, perception and behaviour, pursued by means of reflection, reasoning and argument. **2** any particular system or set of beliefs established as a result of this. **3** a set of principles serving as a basis for making judgements and decisions: *one's philosophy of life*. [Gr *philosophia*, love of wisdom, from *philo-*, loving + *sophia*, wisdom]

philosopher *n* a person who studies philosophy, esp. one who develops a particular set of doctrines or theories.

philosopher's stone *n* (*hist*) a hypothetical substance able to turn any metal into gold, long sought by alchemists.

philosophical *adj* **1** of or relating to philosophy or philosophers. **2** calm and dispassionate in the face of adversity; resigned, stoical or patient. — *adv* **philosophically**.

philosophise or **-ize** *v* (*intr*) to form philosophical theories; to reason or speculate in the manner of a philosopher. — *n* **philosophiser** or **-z-**.

philtre *n* a magic potion for arousing sexual desire. [Gr *philtron*, love charm]

phlebitis *n* inflammation of a vein. [Gr *phleps*, vein + **-itis**]

phlegm *n* **1** a thick, yellowish substance produced by the mucous membrane lining the nose, throat and lungs, brought up by coughing. **2** calmness or impassiveness; stolidity or sluggishness of temperament. — *adj* **phlegmatic**. — *adv* **phlegmatically**. [Gr *phlegma*, flame, heat, phlegm (thought to be the result of heat), inflammation]

phloem *n* (*bot*) tissue made up of conducting cells, by which sap is transported from the leaves to other parts of a plant. [Gr *phloios*, bark]

phlox *n* a plant with clusters of variegated flowers in purple, red and white. [Gr, flame, wallflower]

phobia *n* (often as *comb fm*) a morbid fear or hatred of something: *a phobia about failing*; *claustrophobia*. — *adj* (also as *comb fm*) **phobic**. — *n comb fm* **-phobic** or **-phobe**. [Gr *phobos*, fear]

Phoenician *adj* of ancient Phoenicia on the coast of Syria, its people, colonies, language and arts. — *n* **1** one of the Phoenician people. **2** their Semitic language.

phoenix *n* in Arabian legend, a bird that every 500 years sets itself on fire and is reborn from its ashes to live a further 500 years. [Gr *phoinix*]

phone *n* a telephone. — *v* (*tr* & *intr*) to telephone. [**telephone**]

phonecard *n* a card obtainable from post offices, etc. and usable in place of cash to pay for calls from cardphones.

phone-in *n* a radio or television programme in which telephoned comments, etc. from listeners or viewers are invited and discussed live by an expert or panel in the studio. — *v* **phone in** (*intr* & *tr*).

-phone *comb fm* **1** an instrument transmitting or reproducing sound: *telephone*; *microphone*. **2** a musical instrument: *saxophone*. **3** a speech sound: *homophone*. — *adj* & *n comb fm* (a person) speaking a certain language: *Francophone*. — *adj comb fm* **-phonic**. [Gr *phone*, sound, voice]

phoneme *n* the smallest unit of speech in a language that has significance in distinguishing one word from another. — *adj*

phonemic. — *adv* **phonemically**. [Gr *phonema*, a sound uttered]
phonemics *n* (*sing*) **1** the study and analysis of phonemes. **2** the system or pattern of phonemes in a language.

phonetic *adj* **1** of or relating to the sounds of a spoken language. **2** (of e.g. a spelling) intended to represent the pronunciation. **3** denoting a pronunciation scheme using symbols that each represent one sound only. — *adv* **phonetically**. [Gr *phonetikos*, from *phoneein*, to speak]
phonetics *n* (*sing*) the branch of linguistics dealing with speech sounds, how they are produced and perceived.

phoney *adj* **-ier**, **-iest** **1** not genuine; fake, sham, bogus or insincere. — *n* ***phoneys*** someone or something bogus; a fake or humbug. — *n* **phoneyness**.

phonic *adj* **1** relating to esp. vocal sound. **2** denoting a method of learning to read by pronouncing each word letter by letter. — *adv* **phonically**. [Gr *phonikos*, from *phone*, sound, voice]

-phonic. See **-phone**.

phono- or **phon-** *comb fm* sound or voice: *phonology*; *phonograph*. [Gr *phone*, sound, voice]

phonograph *n* (*old US*) a record-player. [**phono-** + **-graph**]

phonology *n* **-ies** **1** the study of speech sounds, or of those in any particular language. **2** any particular system of speech sounds. — *adj* **phonological**. — *adv* **phonologically**. — *n* **phonologist**. [**phono-** + **-logy**]

phony (**-*ies***), **phoniness**. *US* spellings of **phoney**, **phoneyness**.

phooey *interj* (*coll*) an exclamation of scorn, contempt, disbelief, etc.

phosphate *n* a salt or ester of phosphoric acid, often used as a fertiliser. [**phosphorus**]

phosphor *n* **1** a general name for a luminescent substance. **2** (*electronics*) the fluorescent coating used on the screen of a cathode-ray tube. [Gr *phosphoros*; see ety. for **phosphorus**]

phosphorescence *n* **1** the emission of light resulting from, but prolonged after, bombardment by radiation. **2** light-emission without combustion or noticeable heat. — *v* (*intr*) **phosphoresce**. — *adj* **phosphorescent**. [**phosphorus**]

phosphorus *n* a poisonous flammable non-metallic element (symbol **P**), one form of it being a yellow wax-like substance luminous in the dark. [Gr *phosphoros*, light-bringer]
phosphoric and **phosphorous** *adj* relating to or containing phosphorus in, respectively, its pentavalent and trivalent state.

photo *n* **-*os*** (*coll*) a photograph.
photo finish *n* a race finish in which the runners are so close that the result must be decided by photograph.

photo- *comb fm* **1** of or relating to photography: *photomontage*. **2** (also **phot-**) of or relating to light: *photoelectric*. [Gr *phos*, light]

photocopy *n* **-*ies*** a photographic copy of a document, drawing, etc. — *v* **-*ies***, **-*ied*** (*tr*) to make a photographic copy of. [**photo-** (sense **1**)]
photocopier *n* a machine that makes photocopies.

photodegradable *adj* able to be broken down by the action of light, and so decay naturally. ◇ See also **biodegradable**. [**photo-** (sense **2**) + **degrade** (sense **3**)]

photoelectric *adj* relating to electric or electronic activity triggered by light or other electromagnetic radiation. — *n* **photoelectricity**. [**photo-** (sense **2**)]
photoelectric cell *n* (also **photocell**) a device activated by photoelectricity, used e.g. in burglar alarms.

Photofit® *n* **1** a system used by the police for building up a likeness of someone to fit a witness's description, similar to Identikit but using photographs rather than drawings of individual features. **2** a likeness so produced.

photogenic *adj* **1** having the quality of photographing well; looking attractive in photographs. **2** producing, or produced by, light. [**photo-** + **-genic**]

photograph *n* an image recorded by camera using the action of light on specially sensitised film. — *v* (*tr* & *intr*) to take a photograph of (a person, thing, etc.). [**photo-** (sense **2**) + **-graph**]
photographer *n* a person who takes photographs, esp. professionally.
photographic *adj* **1** of, relating or similar to photographs or photography. **2** (of someone's memory) retaining images in exact detail. — *adv* **photographically**.
photography *n* the art or process of taking photographs.

photogravure *n* **1** a method of engraving in which the design is photographed on to a metal plate, and then etched in. **2** a picture so produced. [**photo-** (sense **1**) + Fr *gravure*, engraving]

photolithography *n* a process of lithographic printing from a photographically produced plate. [**photo-** (sense **1**)]

photomontage *n* the process of combining several photographs or parts of photographs in a particular arrangement to convey a certain impression; a picture so put together. [**photo-** (sense **1**) + Fr *montage*, mounting]

photon *n* (*physics*) the quantum (basic particle or quantity) of light or other electromagnetic radiation. [Gr *phos*, light]

photosensitive *adj* reacting to light or other electromagnetic radiation. — *n* **photosensitivity**. [**photo-** (sense **2**)]

Photostat® *n* **1** (usu. without *cap*) a photographic apparatus for copying documents, drawings, etc. **2** a copy made by this. — *v* **-tt-** (without *cap*) to make a Photostat of.

photosynthesis *n* the manufacture by plants of complex compounds from carbon dioxide and water, using the energy from sunlight. — *v* **photosynthesise** or **-ize** (*intr* & *tr*). — *adj* **photosynthetic**. [**photo-** (sense **2**)]

phrase *n* **1** a set of words expressing a single idea, forming part of a sentence though not constituting a clause. **2** an idiomatic expression. **3** (*mus*) a run of notes making up an individually distinct part of a melody. — *v* (*tr*) **1** to express; to word: *a carefully phrased reply*. **2** (*mus*) to bring out the phrases in (music) as one plays. [Gr *phrasis*, expression, from *phrazein*, to tell]

phrasal *adj* relating to phrases; consisting of, or of the nature of, a phrase. — *adv* **phrasally**.

phrasal verb *n* a phrase consisting of a verb plus adverb or preposition, or a combination of these, frequently, as with *let on* or *come up with*, with a meaning or meanings that cannot be guessed from the meanings of the individual words.

phrase book *n* a book listing handy words and phrases in a foreign language, for the use of e.g. tourists.

turn of phrase *n* one's way of expressing oneself, esp. if distinctive; an instance of this: *has an amusing turn of phrase*.

phraseology *n* **1** one's choice of words and way of combining them, in expressing oneself. **2** the language belonging to a particular subject, group, etc.: *legal phraseology*. — *adj* **phraseological**. [**phrase** + **-logy**]

phrenology *n* the practice, popular in the 19th century but now discredited, of assessing a person's character and aptitudes by examining the shape of his or her skull. — *adj* **phrenological**. — *n* **phrenologist**. [Gr *phren*, mind + **-logy**]

phthisis *n* ***phthises*** any wasting disease, esp. tuberculosis. [Gr, emaciation, consumption]

phut (*coll*) *n* the noise of a small explosion. — **go phut 1** to break down or cease to function. **2** to go wrong. [Imit., or connected with Hindi & Urdu *phatna*, to burst]

phylactery *n* **-ies 1** either of two small boxes containing religious texts worn on the arm and forehead by Jewish men during prayers. **2** a charm or amulet. [Gr *phylakterion*, from *phylassein*, to guard]

phylum *n* ***-la*** (*biol*) one of the major classifications into which the animal and plant kingdoms are divided. [Gr *phylon*, race]

physic (*old*) *n* **1** the skill or art of healing. **2** a medicine. **3** anything with a curative or reinvigorating effect. — *v* **-ck-** (*tr*) to dose with medicine. [Gr *physike* (*episteme*), (knowledge) of nature]

physical *adj* **1** of the body rather than the mind; bodily: *physical strength, fitness, exercise*, etc. **2** relating to objects that can be seen or felt; material: *the physical world*. **3** relating to nature or to the laws of nature: *physical features*; *a physical impossibility*. **4** relating to physics. **5** involving bodily contact: *physical force*. — *n* **physicality**. — *adv* **physically**. [Gr *physikos*, of nature, from *physis*, nature]

physical education or **physical training** *n* instruction in sport and gymnastics as part of a school or college curriculum.

physical geography *n* the study of the earth's natural features, e.g. mountain ranges, ocean currents, etc.

physical jerks *n* (*pl*; *coll*) bodily exercises, esp. done regularly to keep fit.

physical science *n* any of the sciences dealing with non-living matter, e.g. astronomy, physics, chemistry and geology.

physician *n* a doctor who specialises in medical as distinct from surgical treatment of patients. [**physic**]

physics *n* (*sing*) the science that embraces the study of heat, light, sound, electricity, mechanics and magnetism; the science of the properties of matter and energy and their interactions; such properties and interactions. — *n* **physicist**. [Gr *ta physika*, natural things]

physio *n* ***-os*** (*coll*) a physiotherapist.

physio- or **physi-** *comb fm* physical or physiological. [Gr, from *physis*, nature, make-up]

physiognomy *n* ***-ies*** **1** the face or features, esp. as a key to personality. **2** the general appearance of something, e.g. the countryside. [Gr *physis*, nature, *gnomon*, interpreter]

physiology *n* the study of the processes by which animals and plants stay alive, e.g. respiration, blood circulation, nutrition, digestion and reproduction. — *adj* **physiological**. — *n* **physiologist**. [Gr *physis*, nature + **-logy**]

physiotherapy *n* the treatment of injury and disease by massage, physical exercise, etc. rather than medicines. — *n* **physiotherapist**.

physique *n* the structure of the body with regard to size, shape, proportions and muscular development. [Fr, orig. adj. physical, from Gr *physikos*, of nature]

phytomenadione *n* vitamin K. [From the names of related chemicals]

pi *n* **1** the 16th letter of the Greek alphabet (π, Π). **2** (*math*) this as a symbol representing the ratio of the circumference of a circle to its diameter, in numerical terms 3·14159.

pia mater *n* ***piae matres*** *n* (*anat*) the delicate innermost membrane enclosing the brain and spinal cord. [Lat, tender mother]

pianissimo *adj* & *adv* (*mus*) (played) very softly. [Ital, superlative of *piano*, quiet]

piano[1] *n* ***-os*** a large musical instrument with a keyboard, the keys being pressed down to operate a set of hammers that strike tautened wires to produce the sound. — *n* **pianist**. [**pianoforte**]

piano accordion *n* an accordion with a keyboard like a piano's.

piano[2] *adj & adv* (*mus*) (played) softly. [Ital]

pianoforte *n* the full formal term for a piano. [Ital *piano e forte*, soft and loud]

Pianola® *n* a mechanical piano operated by means of interchangeable paper rolls bearing coded music in the form of perforations.

piazza *n* a public square in an Italian town. [Ital, from Lat *platea* & Gr *plateia*, street]

pibroch *n* (a piece of) classical music for the Scottish bagpipes. [Gaelic *piobaireachd*]

pic *n* ***pics*** or ***pix*** (*coll*) a photograph or picture.

pica *n* (*printing*) an old type size, giving about six lines to the inch. [Lat *pica*, magpie]

picador *n* (*bullfighting*) a horseman who weakens the bull by wounding it with a lance. [Span, from *pica*, lance]

picaresque *adj* (of a novel, etc.) telling of the adventures of a usu. likeable rogue in separate, only loosely connected, episodes. [Span *picaro*, rogue]

piccalilli *n* a pickle consisting of mixed vegetables in a mustard sauce.

piccaninny or (esp. *US*) **pickaninny** *n* ***-ies*** (now *offensive*) a Negro or Aboriginal child. [Perhaps Port *pequenino*, dimin. of *pequeno*, little]

piccolo *n* ***-os*** a musical wind instrument similar to, but smaller and with a higher register than, the flute. [Ital, little]

pick[1] *v* **1** (*tr & intr*) to choose or select. **2** (*tr*) to detach and gather (flowers from a plant, fruit from a tree, etc.). **3** (*tr*; **up, off, out**, etc.) to lift, remove, detach or extract: *picked a crumb off the carpet*. **4** (*tr*) to open (a lock) with a device other than a key. **5** (*tr*) to get, take or extract whatever is of use or value from: *pick a bone* (*clean*); *pick someone's brains*. **6** (*tr*) to steal money or valuables from (someone's pocket). **7** (*tr*) to undo; to unpick: *pick a dress to pieces*. **8** (*tr*) to make (a hole) by unpicking. **9** (*tr*) to remove pieces of matter from (one's nose, teeth, a scab, etc.) with one's fingernails, etc. **10** (*tr*) to provoke (a fight, quarrel, etc.) with someone. — *n* **1** (*sing* or *pl*) the best of a group; *the pick of the bunch*. **2** one's own preferred selection: *have* or *take one's pick*. — *n* **picker**. — **pick and choose** to keep selecting and rejecting until one is satisfied. — *v* **pick at** (*tr*) **1** to eat only small quantities of (one's food). **2** to keep pulling at (a scab, etc.) with one's fingernails. — **pick holes in** to find fault with. — *v* **pick off** (*tr*) to shoot down one by one. — *v* **pick on** (*tr*) **1** to blame unfairly. **2** to bully. **3** to choose for an unpleasant job. **4** to choose; to light on. — *v* **pick out** (*tr*) **1** to select from a group. **2** to spot, recognise or distinguish amongst a group or crowd. **3** to play (a tune) uncertainly, esp. by ear. **4** to mark so as to distinguish from its surroundings: *beige walls with the picture rail picked out in brown*. — *v* **pick over** (*tr*) to examine one by one and reject whatever is unwanted. — **pick to pieces** to criticise severely. — *v* **pick up 1** (*tr*) to lift or raise. **2** (*tr*) to restore (oneself) to an upright position after a fall. **3** (*tr*) to learn or acquire (a habit, skill, language, etc.) over a time. **4** (*tr*) to notice or become aware of: *picked up a faint odour*. **5** (*tr*) to stop one's vehicle for, and give a lift to or take (someone or something) where required. **6** (*tr*) to obtain or acquire casually, by chance, etc.: *pick up a bargain, infection, ideas*, etc. **7** (*tr*) to go and fetch (someone or something waiting to be collected). **8** (*tr*; *radio, radar*, etc.) to receive (a signal, programme, etc.) on one's apparatus. **9** (*tr*) to arrest or seize: *picked up by the police*. **10** (*intr*) (of a person, or his or her health, etc.) to recover or improve. **11** (*tr & intr*) to increase; to improve: *pick up speed*; *Sales picked up*. **12** (*tr*; *coll*) to approach and make the acquaintance of, esp. with a view to sexual relations. **13** (*tr*) to refer back to (a point, etc.) in order to deal with it. **14** (*intr & tr*) to resume: *pick up where one left off*; *pick up the threads of a relationship*; *pick up the trail*. **15** (*tr*; *coll*) to agree to pay (a bill).— **pick up the pieces** to try to restore things to normality or make things better after some trouble or disaster. — **pick someone up on something** to point out someone's error to him or her. — **pick one's way** to go carefully so as to avoid hazards. [MidE *piken*]

pickings *n* (*pl*) (*coll*) profits made easily or casually from something.

pick-me-up *n* **1** a stimulating drink. **2** anything that revives and invigorates.

pick-up *n* **1** the stylus on a record-player. **2** a small lorry, truck or van. **3** (*coll*) an acquaintance made casually, esp. with a view to sexual relations; the making of such an acquaintance. **4** a halt to load goods or passengers; the goods or passengers so loaded.

pick[2] *n* **1** a tool with a long metal head pointed at one or both ends, for breaking ground, rock, ice, etc. **2** a poking or cleaning tool: *a toothpick*. **3** a plectrum. [MidE *pikke*]

pickaback. See **piggyback**.

pickaxe *n* a large pick, esp. with a point at one end of its head and a cutting edge at the other. [OFr *picois*]

picket *n* **1** (any one of) a group of strikers stationed outside their place of work to persuade other employees not to go in. **2** a body of soldiers on patrol or sentry duty. **3** a stake fixed in the ground, e.g. as part of a fence. — *v* ***-t-*** (*tr*) **1** to station pickets, or act as a picket, at (a factory, etc.). **2** to protect, guard or patrol with, or as, a military picket. [Fr *piquet*, dimin. of *pic*, pick]

picket line *n* a line of people acting as pickets in an industrial dispute.

pickle *n* **1** a preserve of vegetables, e.g. onions, cucumber or cauliflower, in vinegar, salt water or a tart sauce. **2** a vegetable so preserved. **3** the liquid used for this preserve. **4** (*coll*) a mess; a quandary: *get oneself in a pickle*. — *v* (*tr*) to preserve in vinegar, salt water, etc. [OGer *pekel*]

pickled *adj* **1** preserved in pickle. **2** (*coll*) drunk.

pickpocket *n* a thief who steals from people's pockets. [**pick**[1]]

picky *adj* **-ier**, **-iest** (*coll*) choosy; difficult to please. [**pick**[1]]

picnic *n* **1** an outing on which one takes food for eating in the open; the food so taken or eaten. **2** (*coll*; esp. with *neg*) an agreeable job or situation: *Indexing books is no picnic*. — *v* **-ck-** (*intr*) to have a picnic. — *n* **picnicker**. [Fr *pique-nique*]

pico- *comb fm* a millionth of a millionth part, or 10^{-12}. [Span *pico*, a small quantity]

Pict *n* a member of an ancient race inhabiting Britain, esp. NE Scotland. — *adj* **Pictish**. [Lat *picti*, painted men]

pictograph or **pictogram** *n* **1** a picture or symbol representing a word, as in Chinese writing. **2** a pictorial or diagrammatic representation of values, statistics, etc. [Lat *pictus*, painted + **-graph**, **-gram**]

pictorial *adj* relating to, or consisting of, pictures. — *n* a periodical with a high proportion of pictures. — *adv* **pictorially**. [Lat *pictor*, painter]

picture *n* **1** a representation of someone or something on a flat surface; a drawing, painting or photograph. **2** someone's portrait. **3** a view; a mental image: *a clear picture of the battle*. **4** a situation or outlook: *a gloomy financial picture*. **5** a person or thing strikingly like another: *She is the picture of her mother*. **6** a visible embodiment: *was the picture of happiness*. **7** an image of beauty: *looks a picture*. **8** the image received on a television screen. **9** a film; a motion picture. **10** (*coll;* in *pl* with **the**) the cinema. — *v* (*tr*) **1** to imagine or visualise. **2** to describe vividly; to depict. **3** to represent or show in a picture or photograph. — **in the picture** equipped with all the relevant facts. [Lat *pictura*]

picture postcard *n* a postcard with a picture on the front.

picture rail *n* a narrow moulding running round the walls of a room just below the ceiling, from which to hang pictures.

picture window *n* a large window with a plate-glass pane, framing a beautiful view.

picturesque *adj* **1** (of places or buildings) charming to look at, esp. if rather quaint. **2** (of language) colourful, expressive, graphic, vivid or (*facet*) strong to the point of offensiveness. — *adv* **picturesquely**. [Fr *pittoresque*, influenced by **picture**]

piddle *v* (*intr*; *coll*) **1** to urinate. **2** (**about**, **around**) to mess about or waste time. — *n* urine or the act of urinating.

piddling *adj* trivial; trifling.

pidgin *n* **1** (also **pidgin language**) any of the simplified languages used esp. for trading purposes between speakers of different languages, consisting of a combination and often simplification of the vocabulary, grammar and pronunciation systems of both (or many, or all) of the languages concerned. ◇ See also **creole**. **2** (*coll;* often **pigeon**) one's own affair, business or concern. [Said to be a Chinese pronunciation of *business*]

pidgin English *n* a pidgin in which one element is English, esp. that formerly spoken between the Chinese and Europeans.

pie *n* a savoury or sweet dish, usu. cooked in a container, consisting of a quantity of food with a covering and/or base of pastry. — **easy as pie** very easy. — **pie in the sky** some hoped-for but unguaranteed future prospect.

pie chart *n* a diagram in which proportional quantities are represented as sectors of a circle.

pie-eyed *adj* (*coll*) drunk.

piebald *adj* having contrasting patches of colour, esp. black and white. — *n* a piebald horse. [*pie*, magpie + **bald**]

piece *n* **1** a portion of some material; a bit. **2** any of the sections into which something (e.g. a cake) is divided; a portion taken from a whole. **3** a component part: *a jigsaw piece*. **4** an item in a set: *an 18-piece teaset*. **5** an individual member of a class of things represented by a collective noun: *a piece of fruit*, *furniture*, *clothing*, etc. **6** a specimen: *a fine piece of Chippendale*. **7** an instance: *a piece of nonsense*. **8** a musical, artistic, literary or dramatic work. **9** an article in a newspaper, etc. **10** a coin: *a 50-penny piece*. **11** (*chess*, etc.) one of the tokens or men used in a board game. **12** a cannon or firearm. **13** (*offensive coll*) a woman. — *v* (*tr*) **1** (with **together**) to join together to form a whole. **2** (with **up**) to patch or insert pieces into (a garment). — **all of a piece** forming an indivisible whole. — **go to pieces** (*coll*) to lose one's ability to cope. — **(all) in one piece** undamaged, unhurt or intact. — **in pieces 1** separated into a number of component parts. **2** broken; shattered. — **of a piece with** consistent or uniform with. — **say one's piece** to make one's contribution to a discussion. — **to pieces 1** into its component parts: *take to pieces*. **2** into fragments, shreds, tatters, etc. [OFr]

piecemeal *adv* a bit at a time.

piece of eight *n* ***pieces of eight*** an old Spanish gold coin worth eight reals.

piece rate *n* a fixed rate of pay for a particular amount of work done.

piecework *n* work paid for according to the amount done, not the time taken to do it.

pièce de résistance *n* ***pièces*** the best or most impressive item. [Fr]

pied *adj* (of birds) having variegated plumage, esp. of black and white. [*pie*, magpie]

pied-à-terre *n* ***pieds-*** a house or apartment, e.g. in a city, that one keeps as a lodging for one's occasional visits there. [Fr, literally 'foot on the ground']

pier *n* **1** a structure built of stone, wood or iron, projecting into water for use as a landing-stage or breakwater. **2** a pillar supporting a bridge or arch. **3** the masonry between two openings in the wall of a building. [MidE *per*, from Lat *pera*]

pierce *v* (*tr* or *intr*; **through, into**) **1** (of a sharp object, or a person using one) to make a hole in or through; to puncture; to make (a hole) with something sharp. **2** to penetrate or force a way through or into: *The wind pierced through her thin clothing*. **3** (of light or sound) to burst through (darkness or silence). **4** to affect or touch (someone's heart, soul, etc.) keenly or painfully. — *adj* **piercing**. [OFr *percer*]

Pierrot *n* a traditional male character from French pantomime, with a whitened face, white frilled outfit and pointed hat. [Fr name, dimin. of *Pierre*, Peter]

pietà *n* a painting or sculpture of the Virgin Mary holding the dead Christ on her lap. [Ital, piety]

piety *n* the quality of being pious, dutiful or religiously devout. [Lat *pietas*]

pietism *n* pious feeling, or an exaggerated show of piety. — *n* **pietist**. — *adj* **pietistic**.

piezoelectricity *n* **1** electricity produced through the application of mechanical stress to quartz and other crystalline materials. **2** stress or deformation in crystals produced by an electric current. — *adj* **piezoelectric**. [Gr *piezein*, to press]

piffle *n* nonsense; rubbish.

piffling *adj* trivial, trifling or petty.

pig *n* **1** a plump short-legged farm animal with a long head, mobile snout and pink or black skin sparsely covered with coarse hair. **2** an abusive term for a person, esp. someone greedy, dirty, selfish, or brutal. **3** (*slang*) a nasty job or situation. **4** (*offensive slang*) a policeman. **5** a quantity of metal cast into an oblong mass. — *v* ***-gg-*** (*tr*) to stuff (oneself) greedily. — **make a pig of oneself** (*coll*) to eat greedily. — **make a pig's ear of** (*coll*) to make a mess of; to botch. — **a pig in a poke** (*coll*) a purchase made without preliminary investigation as to suitability. — **pig it** (*coll*) **1** to eat greedily. **2** to live squalidly. — **pigs might fly** (*coll*) (as an expression of scepticism) that is highly unlikely. [MidE *pigge*]

piggery *n* ***-ies*** **1** a place where pigs are bred. **2** (*coll*) greediness or otherwise disgusting behaviour.

piggish *adj* (*derog*) greedy, dirty, selfish, mean or ill-mannered. — *n* **piggishness**.

piggy *n* ***-ies*** a child's diminutive for a pig; a little pig. — *adj* ***-ier***, ***-iest*** **1** pig-like. **2** (*derog*) (of eyes) small and mean-looking.

piggyback see separate entry.

piggy bank *n* a child's pig-shaped china container for saving cash in.

pigheaded *adj* stupidly obstinate. — *adv* **pigheadedly**. — *n* **pigheadedness**.

pig-in-the-middle *n* **1** a game in which one person stands between two others and tries to intercept the ball they are throwing to each other. **2** any person helplessly caught between two contending parties.

pig iron *n* iron from the blast furnace, poured, still in a crude state, into moulds.

piglet *n* a baby pig.

pigskin *n* **1** leather made from the skin of a pig. **2** (*NAm coll*) a football.

pigsty *n* ***-ies*** **1** a pen on a farm, etc. for pigs; a sty. **2** a place of filth and disorder.

pigswill *n* kitchen or brewery waste fed to pigs.

pigtail *n* a plaited length of hair, esp. one of a pair, worn hanging at the sides or back of the head.

pigeon[1] *n* **1** a plump-bodied bird of the dove family. **2** (*slang*) a dupe or simpleton. [OFr *pijon*, from Lat *pipio*, from *pipare*, to cheep]

pigeonhole *n* **1** any of a set of compartments, e.g. in a desk, for filing letters or papers. **2** a compartment of the mind or memory. — *v* (*tr*) **1** to put into a pigeonhole. **2** to put mentally into a category, esp. too readily. **3** to set aside for future consideration.

pigeon-toed *adj* (of a person) standing and walking with the toes turned in.

pigeon[2]. Another spelling of **pidgin** (sense 2).

piggyback or **pickaback** *n* or *adj* (of) a ride on someone's back, with the legs supported by the bearer's arms.

pigment *n* **1** any colouring matter used as dye, in paint, etc. **2** a substance in the tissues of plants and animals that produces their natural colouring. — *v* (*tr*) to colour with pigment; to dye or stain. [Lat *pigmentum*]

pigmentation *n* coloration or discoloration caused by pigments in the tissues.

pigmy. Another spelling of **pygmy**.

pike[1] *n* ***pike*** or ***pikes*** a fierce freshwater fish with a long pointed snout. [OE *pic*, point, pick]

pike[2] *n* (*hist*) a weapon like a spear, consisting of a metal point mounted on a long shaft. [OE *pic*, point]

pikestaff *n* the shaft of a pike. — **plain as a pikestaff** all too obvious.

pilaff, **pilaf** or **pilau** *n* an oriental dish of spiced rice with chicken, fish, etc. [Turk *pilaw*]

pilaster *n* a rectangular column standing out in relief from the façade of a building, as a decorative feature. [Fr *pilastre*, from Lat *pila*, pillar]

pilau. See **pilaff**.

pilchard *n* an edible sea fish of the herring family, but smaller, thicker and rounder.

pile[1] *n* **1** a number of things lying on top of each other; a quantity of something in a heap or mound. **2** (*coll*; often in *pl*) a large quantity. **3** a fortune: *made a* or *her pile on the horses*. **4** a massive or imposing building. **5** (also **funeral pile**) a pyre. **6** (also **atomic pile**) a nuclear reactor. **7** (*electr*) a vertical series of plates of two different metals arranged alternately to produce an electric current. — *v* **1** (*tr* & *intr*; **up**) to accumulate into a pile. **2** (*intr* with **in**, **into**, **off**, **out**, etc.) to move in a crowd or confused bunch. — **pile it on** (*coll*) to exaggerate. [Lat *pila*, stone pier]

pile-up *n* a multi-vehicle collision.

pile[2] *n* the raised cropped threads that give a soft thick surface to carpeting, velvet, etc.; a nap. [Lat *pilus*, hair]

pile[3] *n* a heavy wooden shaft, stone or concrete pillar, etc. driven into the ground as a support for a building, bridge, etc. [Lat *pilum*, javelin]

pile-driver *n* a machine for driving piles into the ground.

pile[4] *n* (usu. in *pl*) a haemorrhoid. [Lat *pila*, ball]

pilfer *v* **-r-** (*tr* & *intr*) to steal in small quantities. — *n* **pilferer**. [OFr *pelfre*, booty]

pilgrim *n* **1** a person who makes a journey to a holy place as an act of reverence and religious faith. **2** a traveller. [Lat *peregrinus*, foreigner, stranger]

pilgrimage *n* a journey to a shrine or other holy place, or to a place celebrated or made special by its associations.

Pilgrim Fathers *n* (*pl*) the English Puritans who sailed to America and founded Plymouth, Massachusetts in 1620.

pill *n* **1** a small ball or tablet of medicine, for swallowing. **2** something unpleasant that one must accept. **3** (with **the**) any of various oral contraceptives. — **sugar** or **sweeten the pill** to make something unpleasant easier to accept or cope with. [Lat *pila*, ball]

pillbox *n* **1** a small round container for pills. **2** (*mil*) a small usu. circular concrete shelter for use as a lookout post and gun emplacement. **3** (also **pillbox hat**) a small round flat-topped hat.

pillage *v* (*tr* & *intr*) to plunder or loot. — *n* **1** the act of pillaging. **2** loot, plunder or booty. — *n* **pillager**. [OFr *piller*, to pillage]

pillar *n* **1** a vertical post of wood, stone, metal or concrete serving as a support; a column. **2** any slender vertical mass, e.g. of smoke, rock, etc. **3** a strong and reliable supporter (of an organisation). — **from pillar to post** from one place to another, esp. in desperation, frustration, etc. [OFr *piler*, from Lat *pila*, pillar]

pillar box *n* a free-standing cylindrical public letter box.

pillion *n* a seat for a passenger on a motorcycle or horse, behind the rider. — *adv* on a pillion. [Gaelic *pillinn* or Irish *pillin*, dimin. of *peall*, skin or blanket]

pillory *n* **-ies** (*hist*) a wooden frame with holes for the hands and head into which wrongdoers were locked as a punishment, and publicly ridiculed. — *v* **-ies**, **-ied** (*tr*) **1** to hold up to public ridicule. **2** to put in a pillory. [OFr *pilori*]

pillow *n* a cushion for the head, esp. a large rectangular one on a bed. — *v* (*tr*) **1** to rest (one's head) as though on a pillow: *pillowed her head on her arms*. **2** to serve as pillow for. [OE *pylwe*, from Lat *pulvinus*, cushion]

pillowcase *n* (also **pillowslip**) a washable cover for a pillow.

pillow lace *n* lace worked over a cushion-like support, using bobbins.

pilot *n* **1** a person who flies an aircraft. **2** a person employed to conduct or steer ships into and out of harbour. **3** a guide. **4** (*machinery*) a device that guides a tool or machine part. — *adj* (of a scheme) serving as a preliminary test; experimental. — *v* **-t-** (*tr*) **1** to act as pilot to. **2** to direct, guide or steer (a project, etc.). [OFr *pillote*, from OItal *pilota*, earlier *pedota*, from Gr *pedon*, oar]

pilot light *n* **1** a small permanent gas flame, e.g. on a gas cooker, that ignites the main burners when they are turned on. **2** an indicator light on an electrical apparatus, showing when it is switched on.

pilot officer *n* the lowest-ranking officer in the Royal Air Force.

pimento *n* **-os** **1** the dried unripe fruit of a West Indian tree of the myrtle family; allspice. **2** the pimiento. [Altered from Span *pimiento*; see ety. for **pimiento**]

pimiento *n* **-os** **1** the red mild-tasting fruit of the sweet pepper, used as a relish, a stuffing for olives, etc. **2** the pimento or allspice. [Span, from Lat *pigmenta*, spiced drink, spice, pepper]

pimp *n* a man who finds customers for a prostitute or a brothel, and lives off the earnings. — *v* (*intr*) to act as a pimp.

pimpernel *n* a sprawling plant with small five-petalled flowers on long slender stems. [OFr *pimprenelle*]

pimple *n* a small raised pus-containing swelling on the skin; a spot. — *adj* **pimply**, **-ier**, **-iest**. [OE *pyplian*, to break out in pimples]

PIN *abbrev* personal identification number (also **PIN number**), a multi-digit number used to authorise cash withdrawal from a cash dispenser at a bank, etc.

pin *n* **1** a short slender usu. stainless steel implement with a sharp point and small round head, for fastening, attaching, etc., used esp. in dressmaking. **2** (usu. *in cmpds*) any of several fastening devices consisting of or incorporating a slender metal or wire shaft: *a hatpin, safety pin, drawing-pin*, etc. **3** a narrow brooch. **4** (usu. *in cmpds*) any of several cylindrical wooden or metal objects with various functions: *a rolling-pin*. **5** a peg of any of various kinds. **6** any or either of the cylindrical or square-sectioned legs on an electric plug. **7** (*skittles, ninepins*, etc.) a club-shaped object set upright for toppling with a ball. **8** the clip on a grenade, removed before throwing. **9** (*golf*) the metal shaft of the flag marking a hole. **10** (in *pl*; *coll*) one's legs. **11** (*old*) the least bit: *doesn't care a pin*. — *v* ***-nn-*** (*tr*) **1** (**together**, **back**, **up**, etc.) to secure with a pin. **2** (**down**, etc.) to hold fast or trap: *pinned to the ground by a fallen tree*. **3** (with **on**; *coll*) to put the blame for (a crime or offence) on someone. **4** (with **on**) to fix (one's hopes or faith) on (someone or something). — **for two pins** (*coll*) with minimum persuasion. — *v* **pin down** (*tr*) **1** to identify or define precisely. **2** to force a commitment or definite expression of opinion from.

pinball *n* a game played on a slot machine in which a small metal ball is propelled round a course, the score depending on what hazards it avoids and targets it hits; a form of bagatelle.

pincushion *n* a pad into which to stick dressmaking pins for convenient storage.

pinhead *n* the little rounded or flattened head of a pin, proverbial for smallness.

pin money *n* extra cash earned for spending on oneself, on luxury items, etc.

pinpoint *v* (*tr*) to place, define or identify precisely.

pinprick *n* **1** a tiny hole made by, or as if by, a pin. **2** a slight irritation or annoyance.

pins and needles *n* (*pl*) a prickling sensation in a limb, etc., felt as the flow of blood returns to it after being temporarily obstructed.

pinstripe *n* a narrow stripe in cloth.

pin tuck *n* a narrow decorative tuck in a garment.

pin-up *n* **1** a picture of a glamorous or otherwise admirable person that one pins on one's wall. **2** the person in such a picture.

pinwheel *n* **1** a whirling firework; Catherine wheel. **2** (*US*) a toy windmill.

pinafore *n* **1** an apron, esp. one with a bib. **2** (also **pinafore dress**) a sleeveless dress for wearing over a blouse, sweater, etc. [**pin** *v* + **afore**]

pince-nez *n* (*pl*) spectacles that are held in position by gripping the nose instead of being supported over the ears. [Fr, pinch-nose]

pincers *n* (*pl*) **1** a hinged tool with claw-like jaws for gripping things. **2** the hinged end of a crab's or lobster's claw, adapted for gripping. [OFr *pincer*, to pinch]

pincer movement *n* (*mil*) an advance that closes in on a target from both sides simultaneously.

pinch *v* **1** (*tr*) to squeeze or nip the flesh of, between thumb and finger. **2** (*tr*) to compress or squeeze painfully. **3** (*tr* & *intr*) (of tight shoes) to hurt or chafe. **4** (*tr* & *intr*; *coll*) to steal. **5** (*intr*) (of controls, restrictions, shortages, etc.) to cause hardship. **6** (*tr*; **off**, **out**, **back**) to prune (a plant) by removing the tips of shoots. **7** (*intr*) to economise: *pinch and scrape*. **8** (*tr*; *coll*) to arrest. — *n* **1** an act of pinching; a nip or squeeze. **2** a quantity of e.g. salt that can be held between thumb and finger; a small amount. — **at a pinch** if absolutely necessary. [OFr *pincier*, to pinch]

pinchbeck *n* a copper alloy with the appearance of gold, used in cheap jewellery. — *adj* cheap, artificial, sham, counterfeit or imitation.

pinched *adj* **1** (of someone's appearance) pale and haggard from tiredness, cold or other discomfort. [**pinch**]

pine[1] *n* **1** a cone-bearing evergreen tree with dark green needle-like leaves. **2** its pale wood, used for furniture. [Lat *pinus*]

pine cone *n* the fruit of the pine.

pine marten *n* an animal of esp. coniferous forests, related to the weasel and having dark brown fur with yellowish underparts.

pine[2] *v* (*intr*) **1** (**for**) to long or yearn. **2** (**away**) to waste away from grief or longing. [OE *pinian*, to torment]

pineal gland *n* (also **pineal body**) a small gland in the base of the brain that produces the hormone melatonin and in animals plays a part in seasonal breeding patterns. [Lat *pinea*, pine cone, from its shape]

pineapple *n* a large tropical fruit with juicy yellow flesh, not unlike a large pine cone in its shape and segmented skin pattern. [MidE *pinappel*, pine cone, the name passing in the 17th cent. to the tropical fruit]

ping *n* a sharp ringing sound like that made by plucking a taut wire, lightly striking glass or metal, etc. — *v* (*intr* & *tr*) to (cause to) make this sound. [Imit.]

ping-pong *n* **1** (also *caps*; ®) table tennis. [Imit. of the sound of the ball]

pinion[1] *v* ***-n-*** (*tr*) **1** to immobilise by holding or binding the arms of; to hold or bind (someone's arms). **2** to hold fast or bind: *pinioned against a wall*. — *n* the outer extremity of a bird's wing, including its flight feathers. [OFr *pignon*, wing]

pinion[2] *n* a small cogwheel that engages with a larger wheel or rack. [OFr *pignon*, cogwheel]

pink[1] *n* **1** a colour between red and white. **2** a genus of plants with fragrant red, pink or variegated flowers, including the carnation and sweet william. **3** a scarlet hunting-coat or its colour. **4** the highest point; the acme: *in the pink of condition*. **5** (also *coll derog* **pinko**, ***-os*** or ***-oes***) someone of mildly left-wing or communist views. — *adj* **1** of the colour pink. **2** slightly left-wing or communist. — *adj* **pinkish**. — *adj*

pinky, **-*ier***, **-*iest***. — **in the pink** (*coll*) in the best of health.

pink eye *n* an inflamed condition of the membrane covering the eye; conjunctivitis.

pink gin *n* gin flavoured with and stained pink by angostura bitters.

pink[2] *v* (*tr*) to cut (cloth) with a notched or serrated edge that frays less readily than a straight edge. [OE *pyngan*, to prick]

pinking shears *n* (*pl*) scissors for cutting such an edge.

pink[3] *v* (*intr*) (of a vehicle engine) to make a metallic knocking noise due to faulty combustion timing. [Imit.]

pinkie or **pinky** *n* **-*ies*** (*Scot* & *US*) the little finger. [Dut *pinkje*]

pinko. See **pink**[1].

pinnace *n* a small boat carried on a larger ship; a ship's boat. [OFr *pinace*, from OSpan *pinaza*, something of pine]

pinnacle *n* **1** a slender spire crowning a buttress, gable, roof or tower. **2** a rocky peak. **3** a high point of achievement. [Lat *pinnaculum*, dimin. of *pinna*, feather]

pinnate *adj* (*bot*) (of a leaf) made up of pairs of leaflets growing opposite to each other up a central stem. [Lat *pinnatus*, feathered]

pinny *n* **-*ies*** (*coll*) a pinafore.

pint *n* **1** a unit of liquid measure, $\frac{1}{8}$ of a gallon. **2** (*coll*) a drink of beer of this quantity. [OFr *pinte*]

pint-size or **pint-sized** *adj* (*humorous*) (of a person) small.

pinta *n* (*coll*) a pint of milk. [Contraction of *pint of*]

Pinyin *n* a system for writing Chinese with letters of the Roman alphabet. [Chin, phonetic spelling]

pioneer *n* **1** an explorer of, or settler in, hitherto unknown or wild country. **2** someone who breaks new ground in anything; an innovator or initiator. — *v* **1** (*intr*) to be a pioneer; to be innovative. **2** (*tr*) to explore and open up (a route, etc.). **3** (*tr*) to try out, originate or develop (a new technique, etc.). [OFr *peonier*, from Lat *pedo*, foot soldier]

pious *adj* **1** religiously devout. **2** dutiful. **3** (*derog*) ostentatiously virtuous; sanctimonious. — *adv* **piously**. — *n* **piousness**. [Lat *pius*, dutiful]

pip[1] *n* the small seed of a fruit such as an apple, pear, orange or grape. [**pippin**]

pip[2] *n* (usu. in *pl*) one of a series of short high-pitched signals on the radio, telephone, etc. [Imit.]

pip[3] *v* **-*pp-*** (*tr*) to defeat narrowly. — **pipped at the post** (*coll*) overtaken narrowly in the closing stages of a contest, etc.

pip[4] *n* **1** one of the emblems or spots on playing-cards, dice or dominoes. **2** (*mil*) in the British army, a star on a uniform indicating rank.

pip[5] *n* a disease of poultry and other fowl. — **give (someone) the pip** (*coll*) to irritate someone. [MidE *pippe*]

pipe *n* **1** a tubular conveyance for water, gas, oil, etc. **2** a little bowl with a hollow stem for smoking tobacco, etc.; a quantity of tobacco so smoked. **3** a wind instrument consisting of a simple wooden or metal tube. **4** (in *pl*) the bagpipes. **5** any of the vertical metal tubes through which sound is produced on an organ. **6** (esp. *old*; esp. *in cmpds*) any of the air passages in an animal body: *the windpipe*. — *v* **1** (*tr*) to convey (gas, water, oil, etc.) through pipes. **2** (*tr* & *intr*) to play on a pipe or the pipes. **3** (*tr*) to welcome or convoy with music from the bagpipes. **4** (*intr* & *tr*) (of a child) to speak or say in a small shrill voice. **5** (*tr*) using a bag with a nozzle, to force (icing or cream) into long strings for decorating a cake or dessert; to make (designs, etc.) on a cake, etc. by this means. — *v* **pipe down** (*intr*; *coll*) to stop talking; to be quiet. — *v* **pipe up** (*intr*) to speak unexpectedly, breaking a silence, etc. — **put that in one's pipe and smoke it** (*coll offensive*) to accept something whether one likes it or not. [OE, from Lat *pipare*, to chirp or play a pipe]

pipeclay *n* fine white clay for making tobacco pipes and delicate crockery.

pipe-cleaner *n* a piece of wire with a woolly tufted covering, for cleaning a tobacco pipe.

piped music *n* (*derog*) the non-stop medley of recorded music played through loudspeakers in restaurants, etc.

pipe dream *n* a delightful fantasy of the kind indulged in while smoking a pipe, orig. one filled with opium.

pipeline *n* a series of connected pipes laid underground to convey gas, water, oil, etc. — **in the pipeline** (*coll*) under consideration, in preparation or shortly forthcoming.

pipe of peace see **peace pipe**.

piper *n* a player of a pipe or the bagpipes.

piping *n* **1** the art of playing a pipe or the bagpipes. **2** a length of pipe, or system or series of pipes conveying water, oil, etc. **3** covered cord forming a decorative edging on upholstery or clothing. **4** strings and knots of icing or cream decorating a cake or dessert. — *adj* (of a voice) small and shrill. — **piping hot** (of food) very, or satisfyingly, hot.

pipette *n* a narrow glass tube into which liquid can be sucked for transferring or measuring. [Fr, dimin. of *pipe*, pipe]

pipistrelle *n* a reddish-brown bat, the smallest in Britain. [Fr, from Ital *pipistrello*, from Lat *vespertilio*, bat, from *vesper*, evening]

pipit *n* any of several lark-like songbirds related to the wagtail. [Imit. of its call]

pippin *n* any of several sweet apples, usu. rosy-skinned. [OFr *pepin*]

pipsqueak *n* (*coll derog*) someone or something insignificant or contemptible. [Perhaps **peep**[2], to cheep]

piquant *adj* **1** having a pleasantly spicy taste or tang. **2** amusing, intriguing, provocative or stimulating. — *n* **piquancy**. [Fr *piquer*, to prick]

pique *n* resentment; hurt pride. — *v* (*tr*) **1** to hurt the pride of; to offend or nettle. **2** to arouse (curiosity or interest). **3** to pride (oneself) on: *piqued himself on his good taste*. [Fr *piquer*, to prick]

piqué *n* stiff corded esp. cotton fabric. [Fr *piquer*, to prick]

piquet *n* (*cards*) a game for two, played with 32 cards. [Fr, from *pic*, the score of 30 points in this game, literally 'prick']

piracy. See **pirate**.

piranha *n* a small fierce carnivorous S American freshwater fish. [Port, from Tupí (S American Indian language) *piranya*]

pirate *n* **1** someone who attacks and robs ships at sea. **2** the ship used by pirates. **3** someone who publishes material without permission from the copyright-holder, or otherwise uses someone else's work illegally. **4** someone who runs a radio station without a licence. — *v* (*tr*) to publish, reproduce or use (someone else's literary or artistic work, or ideas) without legal permission. — *n* **piracy**. — *adj* **piratical**. [Gr *peirates*, from *peiraein*, to try one's fortune]

pirouette *n* a spin or twirl executed on tiptoe in dancing. — *v* (*intr*) to execute a pirouette or a series of them. [Fr, orig. a spinning top]

piscatorial *adj* (*formal* or *humorous*) relating to fish, fishing or fishermen. [Lat *piscatorius*, fisherman]

Pisces *n* **-es** a constellation and the twelfth sign of the zodiac, the Fishes. **2** a person born between 20 February and 20 March, under this sign. — *n* & *adj* **Piscean**. [Lat, fishes]

pisciculture *n* the rearing of fish by artificial methods or under controlled conditions. [Lat *piscis*, fish + **culture**]

piscina *n* a basin with a drain, found in older churches, in which to empty water used for rinsing the sacred vessels. [Lat, basin, orig. fish pond]

piss (*coll vulg*) *v* **1** (*intr*) to urinate. **2** (*tr*) to discharge (e.g. blood) in the urine. **3** (*tr*) to wet with one's urine: *piss the bed*. **4** (*intr*; **down**) to rain hard. — *n* **1** urine. **2** an act of urinating. — *v* **piss about** or **around** (*intr*) to mess about; to waste time. — *v* **piss off 1** (*intr*) to go away. **2** (*tr*) to irritate, annoy or bore. — **take the piss out of** to ridicule. [Fr *pisser*, from a colloquial Latin word; imit.]

pissed *adj* (*coll vulg*) drunk.

pistachio *n* **-os** the edible nut of a Eurasian tree, of the cashew family, with a green kernel. [Ital *pistacchio*]

piste *n* a ski slope or track of smooth compacted snow. [Fr, race track]

pistil *n* the female, seed-producing part of a flower, comprising the ovary, style and stigma. [Lat *pistillum*, pestle]

pistol *n* a small gun held in one hand when fired. [OFr *pistole*, from OCzech]

piston *n* **1** in steam engines, internal combustion engines or pumps, a disc or solid metal cylinder that slides up and down or to and fro within a hollow cylinder. **2** a sliding valve on a brass wind instrument. [Fr, from Ital *pistone*, from *pestare*, to pound]

piston ring *n* a split metal ring fitting into a groove round a piston and forming an airtight seal between it and its containing cylinder.

piston rod *n* in a vehicle engine, a rod attached to the piston, that transfers its motion by means of a crankshaft to the wheels.

pit[1] *n* **1** a big deep hole in the ground. **2** a coalmine. **3** a cavity sunk into the ground from which to inspect vehicle engines, etc. **4** (*car-racing*) any of a set of compartments beside a racetrack, where vehicles can refuel, etc. **5** an enclosure in which fighting animals or birds are put. **6** the floor of the auditorium in a theatre, or the people sitting there. **7** (also **orchestra pit**) the sunken area just in front of a stage, for the accommodation of an orchestra. **8** (*anat*, etc.) a hollow, indentation or depression: *the pit of the stomach* (i.e. the small hollow below the breastbone). **9** a scar left by a smallpox or acne pustule. **10** (*old*; with **the**) hell. **11** (in *pl*; with **the**; *slang*) the absolute depths of awfulness. — *v* **-tt-** (*tr*) **1** (**against**) to set or match in competition or opposition. **2** (**with**) marked by scars and holes: *pitted with craters*. **3** to put in a pit. [OE *pytt*, from Lat *puteus*, well]

pit bull terrier *n* a large breed of bull terrier orig. developed for dogfighting.

pithead *n* the entrance to a mineshaft and the machinery round it.

pitstop *n* a pause made at a refuelling pit by a racing driver.

pit[2] *n* (esp. *US*) the stone in a peach, apricot, plum, etc. — *v* **-tt-** to remove the stone from. [Dut, kernel]

pit-a-pat *n* a noise of pattering. — *adv* with this noise. [Imit.]

pitch[1] *v* **1** (*tr*) to set up (a tent or camp). **2** (*tr*) to throw or fling. **3** (*tr* & *intr*) to (cause to) fall heavily forward. **4** (*intr*) (of a ship) to plunge and lift alternately at bow and stern. **5** (*tr* & *intr*) (of a roof) to slope: *pitched at a steep angle*. **6** (*tr*) to give a particular musical pitch to (a note) in singing or playing, or to set (a song, etc.) at a higher or lower level within a possible range: *pitched too high for me*. **7** to choose a level, e.g. of difficulty, sophistication, etc. at which to present (a talk, etc.). **8** (*tr*) (*cricket*) to bowl (the ball) so that it lands where the batsman can hit it, or (*golf*) to hit (the ball) high and gently, so that it stays where it is on landing, or (*baseball*;

also *intr*) as pitcher, to throw to the batter overarm or underarm. — *n* **1** the field or area of play in any of several sports. **2** an act or style of pitching or throwing. **3** a degree of intensity; a level: *reached such a pitch*. **4** the angle of steepness of a slope. **5** (*mus*) the degree of highness or lowness of a note that results from the frequency of the vibrations producing it. **6** a street trader's station. **7** a line in sales talk, esp. one often made use of. **8** the distance between points on a saw, or between threads on a screw. **9** the plunging and rising motion of a ship. — *v* **pitch in** (*intr*; *coll*) **1** to set to enthusiastically. **2** to join in; to make a contribution. — *v* **pitch into** (*tr*; *coll*) to attack or blame bitterly. [MidE *picchen*, throw, put up]

perfect pitch or **absolute pitch** *n* the ability to recognise a note from its pitch, or spontaneously sing any note with correct pitch.

pitched battle *n* **1** a battle between armies that are prepared and drawn up in readiness. **2** a fierce dispute.

pitched roof *n* a sloping roof as distinct from a flat one.

pitcher *n* (*baseball*) the player who throws the ball to the batter to hit.

pitchfork *n* a long-handled fork with two or three sharp prongs, for tossing hay.

pitch[2] *n* **1** a thick black sticky substance obtained from tar, used for filling ships' seams, etc. **2** any of various bituminous or resinous substances. **3** resin from certain pine trees. — *v* (*tr*) to coat or treat with pitch. [OE *pic*]

pitch-black or **pitch-dark** *adj* utterly, intensely or unrelievedly black or dark.

pitchblende *n* a soft black mineral, the source of uranium and radium. [Ger *Pechblende*]

pitcher[1] *n* a large, esp. earthenware jug with one or two handles. [OFr *pichier*, from Lat *bicarium*, beaker]

pitcher plant *n* a plant with pitcher-shaped leaves that trap insects.

pitcher[2], **pitchfork**. See **pitch**[1].

piteous *adj* rousing one's pity; moving, poignant, heart-rending or pathetic. [**pity**]

pitfall *n* a hidden danger, unsuspected hazard or unforeseen difficulty. [**pit**[1]]

pith *n* **1** the soft white substance lining the rind of an orange or other citrus fruit. **2** the soft spongy substance at the centre of a plant stem. **3** the most important part of an argument, etc. **4** substance, forcefulness or vigour as a quality in writing, etc. [OE *pitha*]

pith helmet *n* a large light rigid hat made from the pith of the sola plant, worn esp. formerly in the tropics to protect the head from the sun.

pithy *adj* **-ier, -iest** (of a saying, comment, etc.) brief, forceful and to the point.

pitiable *adj* **1** arousing pity. **2** miserably inadequate; contemptible. [**pity**]

pitiful *adj* **1** arousing pity; wretched or pathetic. **2** sadly inadequate or ineffective. — *adv* **pitifully**. [**pity**]

pitiless *adj* showing no pity; merciless, cruel or relentless. [**pity**]

piton *n* (*mountaineering*) a metal peg or spike with an eye for passing a rope through, hammered into a rockface as an aid to climbers. [Fr, ringbolt]

pitta *n* (also **pitta bread**) a Middle-Eastern slightly leavened bread, usu. baked in hollow ovals that can be filled with other foods; one such oval. [Modern Gr, cake, pie]

pittance *n* a meagre allowance or wage. [OFr *pietance*, ration]

pitter-patter *n* the sound of pattering. — *adv* with this sound. [Imit.]

pituitary *n* **-ies** (also **pituitary gland**) a gland at the base of the brain that controls the body's growth and development. — *adj* of or relating to this gland. [Lat *pituita*, phlegm, rheum]

pity *n* **1** a feeling of sorrow for the troubles and sufferings of others; compassion. **2** a cause of sorrow or regret. — *v* **-ies, -ied** (*tr*) to feel or show pity for. — *adj* **pitying**. — *adv* **pityingly**. — **for pity's sake** an expression of earnest entreaty or of exasperation. — **have** or **take pity on** to feel or show pity for, esp. in some practical way. — **more's the pity** (*coll*) unfortunately; I'm sorry to say. [OFr *pite*, from Lat *pietas*, piety, dutifulness]

pivot *n* **1** a central pin, spindle or shaft round which something turns, swivels or revolves. **2** someone or something crucial, on which everyone or everything else depends. — *v* **-t-** (*intr*; **on**) **1** to turn, swivel or revolve; *pivot on one's heel*. **2** to depend. — *adj* **pivotal**. [Fr]

pix. See **pic**.

pixel *n* (*comput*, *TV*, etc.) the smallest element that goes to compose the picture on a television screen, etc. [**pix** + **element**]

pixie or **pixy** *n* **-ies** a kind of fairy, traditionally with mischievous tendencies. [Orig. dialect]

pizza *n* a circle of dough spread with cheese, tomatoes, etc. and baked, made orig. in Italy. [Ital]

pizzazz, **pizazz** or **pzazz** *n* (*coll*) a quality that is a combination of boldness, vigour, dash and flamboyance. [Coined by Diana Vreeland, U.S. fashion editor (*c*. 1903–89)]

pizzeria *n* a restaurant specialising in pizzas. [Ital, from **pizza**]

pizzicato *adj* & *adv* (of music for stringed instruments) (played) using the fingers to pluck the strings. [Ital, twitched]

Pk *abbrev* (in street names) Park.

Pl *abbrev* (in street names) Place.

pl *abbrev* plural.

placard *n* a board or stiff card bearing a notice, advertisement, slogan, message of protest, etc., carried or displayed in public. — *v* (*tr*) **1** to put placards on (a wall, etc.). **2** to announce (a forthcoming event, etc.) by placard. [OFr]

placate *v* (*tr*) to soothe, pacify or appease (an angry person, etc.). — *n* **placation**. — *adj* **placatory**. [Lat *placere*, to appease]

place *n* **1** an area, region, district, locality, etc.; a country, city, town, village, building, room, etc. **2** (*coll*) one's home or lodging. **3** (often *in cmpds*) somewhere with a certain association or function: *one's birthplace*; *a hiding-place*. **4** a seat or space, e.g. at table: *lay three places*. **5** an area on the surface of something, e.g. the body: *point to the sore place*. **6** something or someone's customary position: *put it back in its place*. **7** a point reached, e.g. in a conversation, narrative, series of developments, etc.: *a good place to stop*. **8** a point in a book, etc., esp. where one stopped reading: *made me lose my place*. **9** a position within an order e.g. of competitors in a contest, a set of priorities, etc.: *finished in third place*; *lost his place in the queue*; *lets her family take second place*. **10** social or political rank: *know* or *keep one's place*; *corruption in high places*. **11** a vacancy at an institution, on a committee, in a firm, etc.: *gain a university place*. **12** one's role, function, duty, etc.: *not my place to tell him*. **13** a useful role: *There's a place for judicious lying*. **14** (often in street names) an open square, or row of houses: *the market place*. **15** (*math*) the position of a number in a series, esp. of decimals after the point. — *v* (*tr*) **1** to put. **2** to submit: *place an order*, *advertisement*, etc. **3** to find a place, home, job, publisher, etc. for. **4** to assign final positions to (contestants, etc.): *was placed fourth*. **5** to identify or categorise: *a familiar voice that I couldn't quite place*. — **all over the place** in disorder or confusion. — **be placed 1** (*racing*, *athletics*) to finish as one of the first three. **2** to be in a position to do something: *was well placed to influence the decision*. — **fall into place** to become clear; to make sense. — **give place to** to make way for or yield to. — **go places** (*coll*) **1** to travel. **2** to be successful. — **in the first place** anyway: *never loved her in the first place*. — **in the first**, **second**, etc. **place** used to introduce successive points. — **in place** in the correct position. — **in place of** instead of. — **in places** here and there. — **in your**, etc. **place** if I were you, etc. — **out of place 1** not in the correct position. **2** inappropriate. — **put someone in his** or **her place** to humble someone as he or she deserves. — **take place** to happen, occur, be held, etc. — **take the place of** to replace or supersede. [OE *plæce* and OFr *place*, open place or street]

place card *n* a small card at someone's place at table, bearing his or name.

place kick *n* (*Rugby*) a kick made with the ball placed ready on the ground.

place mat *n* a table mat for use in a place setting.

placement *n* **1** the act or process of placing or positioning. **2** the finding of a job or home for someone. **3** a temporary job providing work experience, esp. for someone on a training course.

place name *n* the name of a town, village, hill, lake, etc.

place setting see **setting**.

placebo *n* **-os 1** a substance administered as a drug but having no medicinal content, given to a patient for its reassuring effect. **2** in a controlled trial of a drug, an inactive substance given without their knowledge to certain participants, so as to provide untreated subjects for comparison with those treated by the drug. [Lat, I shall please]

placenta *n* **-*tae*** or **-*tas*** an organ that develops in the womb of a pregnant mammal, from which the foetus receives its nutrition. [Lat, flat cake]

placid *adj* calm; tranquil. — *n* **placidity**. — *adv* **placidly**. [Lat *placidus*, from *placere*, to please]

plagiarise or **-ize** *v* (*tr* & *intr*; **from**) to steal (ideas, passages of text, etc.) from someone else's work, and use them as if they were one's own. — *n* **plagiarism**. — *n* **plagiarist**. [Lat *plagiarius*, kidnapper]

plague *n* **1** any of several highly infectious and frequently fatal diseases of which outbreaks tend to occur on an epidemic scale, esp. bubonic plague. **2** an overwhelming invasion by something unwelcome: *a plague of tourists*. **3** (*coll*) a nuisance. — *v* (*tr*) **1** to afflict: *plagued by headaches*. **2** (**with**) to pester; to annoy continually. [MidE *plage*, from Lat *plaga*, blow, disaster, pestilence]

plaice *n* ***plaice*** an edible brown flatfish with orange spots. [OFr *plais*, from Lat *platessa*, flatfish]

plaid *n* **1** tartan cloth. **2** (esp. *hist*) a long piece of this worn over the shoulder with a kilt. [Gaelic *plaide*, blanket]

plain *adj* **1** all of one colour; unpatterned; undecorated. **2** simple; unsophisticated; without improvement: *plain food*; *not Dr or Professor – just plain Mr*. **3** obvious; clear. **4** straightforward; direct: *plain language*, *dealing*, etc. **5** (**with**) frank; open. **6** (of a person) lacking beauty. **7** sheer: *plain selfishness*. — *n* **1** a large level expanse of land. **2** (*knitting*) the simpler of two basic stitches, with the wool passed round the front of the needle. ◇ See also **purl**. — *adv* utterly; quite: *plain ridiculous*. — *adv* **plainly**. — *n* **plainness**. [OFr, from Lat *planus*, level]

plain chocolate *n* dark chocolate made without milk.

plain clothes *n* (*pl*) ordinary clothes worn by police detectives on duty, as distinct from a uniform. — *adj* **plain-clothes**.

plain flour *n* flour containing no raising agent.

plain sailing 1 easy, unimpeded progress. **2** (*naut*) sailing in unobstructed waters.

plainsong *n* (also **plainchant**) in the mediaeval church, music for unaccompanied voices, sung in unison.

plain-spoken *adj* frank to the point of bluntness.

plaint *n* **1** (*poet*) an expression of woe; a lamentation. **2** (*legal*) a written statement of grievance against someone, submitted to a court of law. [OFr, from Lat *planctus*, a blow]

plaintiff *n* a person who brings a case against someone else in a court of law. ◇ See also **defendant**. [OFr *plaintif*, complaining]

plaintive *adj* mournful-sounding; sad; wistful. — *adv* **plaintively**. [OFr *plaintif*]

plait *v* (*tr*) to arrange (esp. hair) by interweaving three or more lengths. — *n* a length of hair or other material so interwoven. [OFr *pleit*, from Lat *plicare*, to fold]

plan *n* **1** a thought-out arrangement or method for doing something. **2** (usu. in *pl*) intentions. **3** a sketch, outline, scheme or set of guidelines. **4** a drawing or diagram of a floor of a house, the streets of a town, etc. done as though from above. — *v* ***-nn-*** **1** (*tr*) to devise a scheme for. **2** (*intr*) to prepare; to make plans: *plan ahead.* **3** (*tr* or *intr*; **for**) to make preparations or arrangements for. **4** (*tr* or *intr*; **on**) to intend. **5** (*intr* with **on** or **for**; usu. in *negative*) to allow for: *hadn't planned on triplets.* **6** (*tr*) to draw up plans for; to design. [Fr, ground plan, from Lat *planus*, flat]

planner *n* **1** someone who draws up plans or designs: *a town planner*. **2** a wall calendar showing the whole year, on which holidays, etc. can be marked.

planning *n* control exercised by a local authority over the erection and alteration of buildings and use of land.

plane[1] *n* an aeroplane. [**plane**[2]]

plane[2] *n* **1** (*math*, etc.) a surface such that a line joining any two points on it lies on it completely. **2** a level surface. **3** a level or standard: *on a higher intellectual plane*. — *adj* **1** flat; level. **2** (*math*) lying in one plane: *a plane figure*; *plane geometry*. — *v* (*intr*) **1** (of a boat) to skim over the surface of the water. **2** (of a bird) to wheel or soar with wings motionless. [Lat *planum*, level surface]

plane[3] *n* a carpenter's tool for smoothing wood by shaving away unevennesses. — *v* (*tr*) **1** (**down**) to smooth (wood) with a plane. **2** (with **off**, **away**) to remove with a plane. [Fr, from Lat *planare*, to smooth]

plane[4] *n* (also **plane tree**) **1** a tree with large, lobed leaves and flaking bark. **2** (*Scot*) the sycamore tree. [Fr *plane*, from Gr *platanos*]

planet *n* **1** any of the nine heavenly bodies – Mercury, Venus, Mars, Earth, Jupiter, Saturn, Uranus, Neptune and Pluto – that revolve round the sun. **2** any similar body revolving round any star. — *adj* **planetary**. [Fr *planète*, from Gr *planetes*, wanderer]

planetarium *n* ***-ria*** or ***-riums*** (a building housing) an apparatus that shows the motion of the planets by means of images projected on to a domed ceiling. [Lat *planetarius*, planetary]

plangent *adj* (of a sound) deep, ringing and mournful. — *n* **plangency**. — *adv* **plangently**. [Lat *plangere*, to beat]

plank *n* **1** a long flat piece of timber. **2** any of the policies forming the platform or programme of a political party. — *v* (*tr*) **1** to fit or cover with planks. **2** (**down**; *coll*) to put down roughly or noisily. — **walk the plank** to be made to walk blindfold along a plank projecting over a ship's side until one falls into the sea and drowns. [Lat *planca*, board]

planking *n* planks, or a surface, etc. constructed of them.

plankton *n* tiny plants and animals that drift about near the water surface, in seas or lakes. [Gr *planktos*, wandering]

plant *n* **1** any member of the vegetable kingdom, i.e. any living thing that gets its nourishment from inorganic substances and has no power of voluntary movement, typically growing from the ground, having a stem, root and leaves; one of the smaller members of this class, as distinct from a tree or shrub. **2** a factory, its buildings and equipment. **3** machinery, esp. mobile mechanical equipment used in building and road construction. **4** (*coll*) something deliberately placed for others to find and be misled by. — *v* (*tr*) **1** (**out**) to put (seeds or plants) into the ground to grow. **2** (**out**, **with**) to put plants or seeds into (ground, a garden, bed, etc.). **3** to introduce (an idea, doubt, etc.) into someone's mind. **4** to place firmly. **5** (**on**) to administer (a kiss or blow). **6** to post (someone) as a spy, in an office, factory, etc. **7** (*coll*) to place (something) deliberately so as to mislead the finder, e.g. as a means of incriminating an innocent person. **8** to establish (a colony, etc.). [Lat *planta*, shoot, sprig]

planter *n* **1** the owner or manager of a plantation. **2** a device for planting bulbs, etc. **3** a container for house plants.

plant pot *n* a pot for growing a plant in.

plantain[1] *n* a tropical green-skinned fruit like a large banana. [Span *plátano*]

plantain[2] *n* a plant that presses its leaves close to the ground, having a flower on a tall slender stem. [Lat *plantago*, from *planta*, sole of the foot]

plantation *n* **1** an estate growing crops such as tea, coffee, rubber and cotton on a large scale. **2** a stretch of land planted with a certain kind of tree. **3** (*hist*) a colony. [Lat *plantatio*, a planting]

plantigrade *adj* (*zool*) walking fully on the soles of the feet, as humans do. [Lat *planta*, sole + *gradi*, to walk]

plaque *n* **1** a commemorative inscribed tablet fixed to or set into a wall. **2** a wall ornament made of pottery, etc. **3** a substance composed of saliva and bacteria, that forms on the teeth. [Fr]

plasma *n* **1** the liquid content of blood, in which the blood cells are suspended. **2** the liquid content of milk and of lymph. **3** protoplasm. **4** (*physics*) a hot ionised gas, having a roughly equal content of positive ions and electrons. [Gr *plasma*, something moulded]

plaster *n* **1** a material consisting of lime, sand and water, that is applied to walls when soft and dries to form a hard smooth surface. **2** plaster of Paris. **3** (also **sticking-plaster**) a piece of sticky tape, usu. with a dressing attached, for protecting a wound. — *v* **-r-** (*tr*) **1** to apply plaster to (walls). **2** (*coll*; **down, on, with**) to coat or spread thickly: *plaster gel on one's hair*; *plaster one's hair with gel*. **3** (**down, to**) to fix with some wet or sticky substance: *hair plastered to his skull*. **4** (**with**) to cover liberally: *walls plastered with photos*. [Lat *plastrum*, from Gr *emplastron*, salve]

plasterboard *n* board consisting of a layer of plaster between two layers of fibreboard, used for making partitions, ceilings, etc.

plastered *adj* (*coll*) drunk.

plasterer *n* a person who applies plaster to walls, ceilings, etc.

plaster of Paris *n* powdered gypsum, mixed with water to make a material that dries hard, used for sculpting and for making casts for broken limbs.

plastic *n* **1** any of many durable synthetic materials mouldable to any shape when soft. **2** (*coll*) credit cards. — *adj* **1** made of plastic. **2** easily moulded or shaped; pliant. **3** easily influenced. **4** (*facet derog*) artificial; lacking genuine substance. **5** (of money) in the form of credit cards. **6** relating to sculpture and modelling. — *n* **plasticity**.

plastic arts *n* (*pl*) the sculptural arts.

plastic bomb *n* a bomb made with plastic explosive.

plastic bullet *n* a small solid plastic cylinder fired by the police to disperse riots.

plastic explosive *n* a mouldable explosive substance of jelly-like consistency.

plastic surgery *n* surgery to repair or replace damaged flesh, or to improve the appearance, esp. of the face. — *n* **plastic surgeon**.

Plasticine® *n* a non-hardening modelling material, used esp. by children.

plate *n* **1** a shallow dish, esp. of earthenware or porcelain, for serving food on. **2** the amount held by this; a plateful. **3** a shallow vessel in which to take the collection in church. **4** a sheet of metal, glass or other rigid material. **5** a flat piece of metal, plastic, etc. inscribed with a name, etc. **6** gold and silver vessels or cutlery; a gold or silver cup as the prize in a horse race, etc. **7** (also **plating**) a thin coating of gold, silver or tin applied to a base metal. **8** an illustration on glossy paper in a book. **9** (*photography*) a sheet of glass prepared with a light-sensitive coating for receiving an image. **10** a sheet of metal with an image engraved on it, or a print taken from it. **11** any of various surfaces set up with type ready for printing. **12** a moulded plastic fitting for the mouth with false teeth attached; a denture. **13** any of the rigid sections that make up the earth's crust. **14** (*anat*) a thin flat piece of bone or horn. — *v* (*tr*) **1** to coat (a base metal) with a thin layer of a precious one. **2** to cover with metal plates. — **on a plate** (*coll*) (presented to one) without one's having to make the least effort. — **on one's plate** (*coll*) for dealing with or attending to. [OFr, something flat]

plateful *n* **-fuls** **1** the amount that a plate will hold. **2** (usu. in *pl*; *coll*) a lot.

plate glass *n* glass made in stout sheets for shop windows, mirrors, etc.

platelayer *n* a person who lays and repairs railway lines.

plate tectonics *n* (*pl*) the interrelating movements of the rigid sections that make up the earth's crust, riding on the semi-molten rock of the interior.

plateau *n* **-teaux** or **-teaus** **1** an area of high land, more or less uniformly level. **2** a stable, unvarying condition of prices, etc. after a rise. [Fr, from OFr *platel*, something flat]

platelet *n* any of the plate-shaped cells in the blood that promote clotting when bleeding occurs. [Dimin. of **plate**]

platen *n* **1** a plate in some printing-presses that pushes the paper against the type. **2** the roller of a typewriter. [OFr *platine*]

platform *n* **1** a raised floor for speakers, performers, etc. **2** the raised walkway alongside the track at a railway station, giving access to trains. **3** a floating installation moored to the sea bed, for oil-drilling, marine research, etc. **4** an open step at the back of some, esp. older, buses, for passengers getting on or off. **5** a thick rigid sole for a shoe. **6** the publicly declared principles and intentions of a political party, forming the basis of its policies. **7** any situation giving one access to an audience, that one can exploit to promote one's views. [OFr *platte forme*, flat figure]

platinum *n* an element (symbol **Pt**), a heavy silvery-white precious metal, widely used for industrial purposes and in jewellery.

platinum-blond *adj* (of hair) of a silvery fairness. — *n* **platinum blonde** a woman with hair of this colour.

platitude *n* an empty, unoriginal or redundant comment, esp. made as though it were important. — *adj* **platitudinous**. [Fr, flatness]

Platonic *adj* **1** of or relating to *Plato*, the Greek philosopher (c. 400 BC). **2** (usu. without *cap*) (of love or a relationship) not involving sexual relations. **3** restricted to theorising; not involving action. — *adv* **platonically**.

platoon *n* **1** (*mil*) a subdivision of a company. **2** a squad of people acting in co-operation. [Fr *peloton*, dimin. of *pelote*, ball]

platter *n* **1** a large flat dish. **2** (*NAm coll*) a gramophone record. [OFr *plater*, from *plat*, plate]

platypus *n* **-*puses*** (also **duck-billed platypus**) a furry Australian egg-laying water mammal, with a ducklike beak and webbed feet. [Gr *platys*, wide + *pous*, foot]

plaudit *n* (esp. in *pl*) a commendation; an expression of praise. [Lat *plaudite*, imperative of *plaudere*, to praise]

plausible *adj* **1** (of an explanation, etc.) credible, reasonable or likely. **2** (of a person) having a pleasant and persuasive manner; smooth-tongued or glib. — *n* **plausibility**. — *adv* **plausibly**. [Lat *plausibilis*, deserving applause]

play *v* **1** (*intr*) (esp. of children) to spend time in recreation. **2** (*intr*; **about**, **around**, **with**) to fiddle or meddle with; to behave irresponsibly towards (someone, someone's affections, etc.). **3** (*tr* & *intr*; **at**) to take part in (a recreative pursuit, game, sport, match, round, etc.). **4** (*tr* or *intr*; **against**) to compete against in a game or sport. **5** (*intr*; *coll*) to co-operate: *refuse to play*. **6** (*tr*) to include as a team member: *playing McGuire in goal*. **7** (*tr*) to hit or kick (the ball), deliver (a shot), etc. in a sport. **8** (*tr*; *cards*) to use (a card) in the course of a game. **9** (*tr*) to speculate or gamble on (the Stock Exchange, etc.). **10** (*tr*; **on**) to perpetrate (a trick or joke) against someone. **11** (*intr* with **on**) to make a pun on. **12** (*tr* & *intr*) to act or behave: *play it cool*; *not playing fair*. **13** (*tr*) to act (a role) in a play, etc. **14** (*tr* & *intr*; **in**) to perform in (a play). **15** (*tr* & *intr*) to perform in (a place). **16** (*tr*) (of a film, play, etc.) to be presented: *playing all next week*. **17** (*tr* & *intr*) to pretend to be: *play the dumb blonde*. **18** (*tr*) to act as: *play host to the delegates*. **19** (*tr* & *intr*) to perform (music) on an instrument; to perform on (an instrument). **20** (*tr*) to turn on (a radio, tape-recording, etc.). **21** (*intr*) (of recorded music, etc.) to issue from a radio, etc; (of a radio, etc.) to produce sound. **22** (*intr* with **over**, **across**, etc.) (of e.g. light, a facial expression, etc.) to flicker over, across, etc. **23** (*intr*) (of a fountain) to be in operation. **24** (*tr*; **on**) to direct (a hose, etc.). **25** (*tr*) to allow (a fish) to tire itself by its struggles to get away. — *n* **1** recreation; playing games: *children at play*. **2** the playing of a game, performance in a sport, etc.: *Rain stopped play*. **3** (*coll*) behaviour; conduct: *fair* or *foul play*. **4** a dramatic piece for the stage, or a performance of it. **5** fun; jest: *said in play*. **6** range; scope: *give full play to the imagination*. **7** freedom of movement; looseness: *too much play in the brake*. **8** action or interaction: *play of sunlight on water*; *play of emotions*. **9** use: *bring all one's cunning into play*. — **in** (or **out of**) **play** (of the ball) in (or not in) a position where it may be played. — **make great play of** to emphasise or stress. — **make a play for** to try to get (e.g. someone's attention). — **make play with** to make effective or over-obvious use of. — *v* **play about** or **around** (*intr*; **with**) to behave ineffectively or irresponsibly. — *v* **play along** (*intr*; **with**) to co-operate for the time being; to humour (someone). — *v* **play at** (*tr*) **1** to make a pretence of, esp. in play: *play at being cowboys*, *a great financier*, etc. **2** to indulge in without seriousness: *play at politics*. **3** (*ironic*) to try to achieve: *What are they playing at?* — *v* **play back** (*tr*) to play (a film or sound recording) through immediately after making it (*n* **playback**). — *v* **play down** (*tr*) to represent as unimportant; to minimise, make light of or discount. — *v* **play off 1** (*intr*) to replay a match, etc. after a draw (*n* **play-off**). **2** (*tr* with **against**) to set (one person) off against (another), for one's own advantage. — *v* **play on** (*tr*) **1** to exploit (someone's fears, feelings, sympathies, etc.) for one's own benefit. **2** to make a pun on; *play on two senses of 'draw'*. — *v* **play out** (*tr*) **1** to act out in real life (a part, scene, etc. so predictable that it could have come from a play). **2** (usu. in *passive*; *coll*) to exhaust or overuse (*adj* **played-out**). — *v* **play up 1** (*intr*; *coll*) to behave unco-operatively. **2** (*intr*; *coll*) to cause one pain or discomfort. **3** (*intr*; *coll*) to function faultily. **4** (*intr* with **to**) to flatter; to ingratiate oneself with. **5** (*tr*) to highlight or give prominence to. **6** (*intr*) to try one's hardest in a game, match, etc. — *v* **play with** (*tr*) to contemplate: *played with the idea of becoming a writer*. [OE *plegan*]

playable *adj* **1** (of a pitch, ground, etc.) fit to be played on. **2** (of a ball) lying where it can be played.

play-act *v* (*intr*) to behave in an insincere fashion, disguising one's true feelings or intentions (*n* **play-acting**).

playbill *n* a poster advertising a play or show.

playboy *n* a man of wealth, leisure and frivolous lifestyle.

player *n* **1** a participant in a game or sport. **2** a performer on a musical instrument. **3** (*old*) an actor.

player piano *n* a Pianola®.

playfellow *n* a playmate.

playful *adj* **1** full of fun; frisky. **2** (of a remark, etc.) humorous. — *adv* **playfully**. — *n* **playfulness**.

playground *n* **1** an area for children's recreation, esp. as part of a school's grounds. **2** a resort for people who take frivolous recreation seriously.

playgroup *n* a number of children organised into a group for regular supervised play together.

playhouse *n* (*old* or in titles) a theatre.

playing-card *n* one of a pack of usu. 52 cards used in card games.

playing-field *n* a grassy expanse prepared and marked out for playing games.

playmate *n* one's companion in play.

play on words *n* a pun; punning.

playpen *n* a collapsible frame that when erected forms an enclosure inside which a baby may safely play.

playschool *n* a playgroup, or a school for children between two and five.

plaything *n* a toy.

playtime *n* a period for recreation, esp. as part of a school timetable.

playwright *n* an author of plays.

plaza *n* **1** a large public square or market place esp. in a Spanish town. **2** (esp. *NAm*) a shopping centre or complex. [Span, a square or market place]

plc or **PLC** *abbrev* public limited company.

plea *n* **1** an earnest appeal. **2** a statement made in a court of law by or on behalf of the defendant. **3** an excuse: *refused the invitation on the plea of a headache*. [OFr *plaid*]

plead *v* ***pleaded*** or (*Scot* or *US*) ***pled*** **1** (*intr*; **for, with**) to appeal earnestly. **2** (*intr*) (of an accused person) to state in a court of law that one is (guilty or not guilty). **3** (*tr* & *intr*; **for**) to argue in defence of: *plead someone's case*. **4** (*tr*) to give as an excuse: *plead ignorance*. — *adj* **pleading**. — *adv* **pleadingly**. [OFr *plaidier*]

pleadings *n* (*pl*) the formal statements submitted by defendant and plaintiff in a lawsuit.

pleasant *adj* **1** giving pleasure; enjoyable; agreeable. **2** (of a person) friendly; affable. — *adv* **pleasantly**. — *n* **pleasantness**. [OFr *plaisant*, from *plaisir*, to please]

pleasantry *n* ***-ies*** **1** (usu. in *pl*) a remark made for the sake of politeness or friendliness. **2** humour; teasing.

please *v* **1** (*tr* & *intr*) to give satisfaction, pleasure or enjoyment; to be agreeable to. **2** (*tr*) (with **it** as subject) to be the inclination of: *if it should please you to join us*. **3** (*tr* & *intr*) to choose; to like: *do what* or *as you please*. — *adv* used politely to accompany a request, order, acceptance of an offer, protest, a call for attention, etc. — *adj* **pleasing**. — *adv* **pleasingly**. — **if you please 1** (*old*) please. **2** (*ironic*) of all things: *is engaged to a baronet, if you please*. — **please oneself** to do as one likes. [OFr *plaisir*]

pleased *adj* **1** (**about, with**) happy; satisfied. **2** glad; delighted. — **pleased with oneself** (*derog*) self-satisfied; conceited.

pleasure *n* **1** a feeling of enjoyment or satisfaction: *take pleasure in one's surroundings*. **2** a source of such a feeling: *have the pleasure of your company*. **3** one's will, desire, wish, preference or inclination. **4** recreation: *combine business with pleasure*. **5** gratification of a sensual kind: *pleasure and pain*. — *v* (*tr*; *old*) to give (esp. sexual) pleasure to. — *adj* used for or done for pleasure: *a pleasure boat*; *a pleasure trip*. — **a** or **my pleasure** you're welcome; not at all; it's no trouble. — **at pleasure** when or as one likes. — **with pleasure** gladly; willingly; of course. [OFr *plaisir*, orig. infinitive]

pleasurable *adj* enjoyable; pleasant. — *adv* **pleasurably**.

pleat *n* a fold sewn or pressed into cloth, etc. — *v* (*tr*) to make pleats in. — *adj* **pleated**. [Variant of **plait**]

pleb *n* (*derog*) a person of coarse or vulgar tastes, manners or habits. [**plebeian**]

plebeian *n* **1** a member of the common people, esp. of ancient Rome. **2** (*derog*) a person lacking refinement or culture. — *adj* **1** of or belonging to the common people. **2** (*derog*) coarse; vulgar; unrefined. [Lat *plebeius*, from *plebs*, the people]

plebiscite *n* a vote of all the electors, taken to decide a matter of public importance; a referendum. [Lat *plebiscitum*, decree of the plebs]

plectrum *n* a small flat implement of metal, plastic, horn, etc., used for plucking the strings of a guitar. [Lat, from Gr *plectron*, from *plessein*, to strike]

pled. See **plead**.

pledge *n* **1** a solemn promise. **2** something left as security with someone to whom one owes money, etc. **3** something put into pawn. **4** a token or symbol: *a ring as a pledge of love*. **5** (**to**) a toast drunk as proof of friendship, etc. — *v* (*tr*) **1** to promise (money, loyalty, etc.) to someone. **2** to bind or commit (oneself, etc.). **3** to offer or give as a pledge or guarantee. **4** (*old*) to drink the health of. — **take** or **sign the pledge** (*old facet*) to promise to abstain forever from alcohol. [OFr *plege*]

Pleiocene. Another spelling of **Pliocene**.

Pleistocene *adj* & *n* (denoting) a period in the earth's history lasting from about two million to ten thousand years ago, during which ice advanced over the northern hemisphere, man evolved, small mammals abounded, and the mammoth became extinct. [Gr *pleisto-*, most + *kainos*, recent]

plenary *adj* **1** full; complete: *plenary powers*. **2** (of a meeting of a body) attended by all members. [Lat *plenarius*, from *plenus*, full]

plenipotentiary *adj* entrusted with, or conveying, full authority to act on behalf of one's government or other organisation. — *n* ***-ies*** someone, e.g. an ambassador, invested with such authority. [Lat *plenus*, full + *potentia*, power]

plenitude *n* **1** abundance; profusion. **2** completeness; fullness. [Lat *plenitudo*, from *plenus*, full]

plenteous *adj* plentiful; abundant. — *adv* **plenteously**. — *n* **plenteousness**. [MidE *plentivous*, from OFr *plentif*, from *plente*, plenty]

plentiful *adj* in good supply; abundant. — *adv* **plentifully**. [**plenty**]

plenty *pron* **1** enough, or more than enough. **2** a lot: *Plenty of folk would agree.* — *n* wealth or sufficiency: *in times of plenty.* — *adv* (*coll*) fully: *plenty wide enough.* — **in plenty** in abundant quantities. [OFr *plente*, from Lat *plenitas*, abundance]

pleonasm *n* **1** the use of more words than are needed to express something. **2** a superfluous word or words. — *adj* **pleonastic**. — *adv* **pleonastically**. [Gr *pleonasmos*, superfluity]

plethora *n* a large or excessive amount. [Gr, fullness]

pleura *n* (*anat*) the delicate membrane that covers the lungs and lines the chest cavity. [Gr, side, rib]

pleurisy *n* inflammation of the pleura. [OFr *pleurisie*]

plexus *n* (*anat*) a network of nerves, such as the *solar plexus* behind the stomach. [Lat, a weaving]

pliable *adj* **1** easily bent; flexible. **2** adaptable or alterable. **3** easily persuaded or influenced. — *n* **pliability**. — *adv* **pliably**. [Fr *plier*, to fold]

pliant *adj* **1** bending easily; pliable, flexible or supple. **2** easily influenced. — *n* **pliancy**. [OFr, from *plier*, to fold]

pliers *n* (*pl*) a hinged tool with jaws for gripping, bending or cutting wire, etc. [*ply*, to bend or fold]

plight[1] *n* a danger, difficulty or situation of hardship that one finds oneself in; a predicament. [MidE *plit*, fold, condition, influenced by the spelling of **plight**[2]]

plight[2] *v* (*tr*) to promise solemnly; to pledge. — **plight one's troth** to pledge oneself in marriage. [OE *pliht*, peril, risk]

plimsoll *n* (*old*) a light rubber-soled canvas shoe worn for gymnastics, etc.; a gymshoe. [From the resemblance of the line of the sole to the Plimsoll line]

Plimsoll line *n* a line painted round a ship's hull showing how far down into the water it may safely sit when loaded. [Suggested by Samuel *Plimsoll* (1824–98)]

plinth *n* **1** (*archit*) a square block serving as the base of a column, pillar, etc. **2** a base or pedestal for a statue or other sculpture, or a vase. [Gr *plinthos*, brick, stone block]

Pliocene *adj* & *n* (denoting) a period in the earth's history lasting from about five million to two million years ago, during which continents and oceans assumed their present shape, ice caps developed, and apes and monkeys flourished. [Gr *pleion*, more + *kainos*, recent]

PLO *abbrev* Palestine Liberation Organisation.

plod *v* **-*dd*-** (*intr*) **1** to walk slowly with a heavy tread. **2** to work slowly, methodically and thoroughly, if without inspiration. — *n* **plodder**. [Imit.]

plonk[1] (*coll*) *n* the resounding thud made by a heavy object falling. — *v* **1** (*tr*) to put or place with a thud or with finality: *plonked himself in the best chair.* **2** (*intr*) to place oneself, fall, etc. with a plonk. — *adv* with a thud: *landed plonk beside her.* [Imit.]

plonk[2] *n* (*coll*) cheap, undistinguished wine. [Said to be from Fr *vin blanc*, white wine]

plop *n* the sound of a small object dropping into water. — *v* **-*pp*-** (*intr* & *tr*) to fall or drop with this sound. — *adv* with a plop. [Imit.]

plosive *n* & *adj* (a consonant or consonantal sound) made by the sudden release of breath after stoppage. [Short for **explosive**]

plot[1] *n* **1** a secret plan, esp. laid jointly with others, for contriving something illegal or evil; a conspiracy. **2** the story of a play, film, novel, etc. — *v* **-*tt*-** **1** (*tr* & *intr*) to plan (something, esp. illegal or evil), usu. with others. **2** (*tr*) to make a plan or graph of; to mark the course or progress of. — *n* **plotter**. [**plot**[2], but influenced by Fr *complot*, conspiracy]

plot[2] *n* a piece of ground for any of various uses. [OE]

plough *n* **1** a bladed farm implement of any of various designs for turning up the soil in ridges and furrows. **2** any similar implement, esp. one for shovelling snow off roads. **3** (*cap*; also **Great Bear**) a constellation of seven stars whose configuration roughly suggests a plough. — *v* **1** (*tr*; **up**) to till or turn over (soil, land, etc.) with a plough. **2** (*tr*) to make (a furrow) with, or as if with, a plough. **3** (*intr*; **through**) to move with a ploughing action. **4** (*intr*; **through**, **on**; *coll*) to make laborious progress. **5** (*intr* with **into**; *coll*) (of a vehicle) to crash into. **6** (*tr*; *old coll*) to fail (a candidate in an exam); (of a candidate) to fail (an exam). — *v* **plough back** (*tr*) to re-invest (profits) in a business. — *v* **plough in** (*tr*) to dig into the soil (the remains of a crop after harvesting) with a plough. [OE *plog*, *ploh*]

ploughman *n* a person who steers the plough.

ploughshare *n* a blade of a plough.

plover *n* any of various, esp. seashore, birds, most with long wings and a short straight beak. [OFr *plovier*, rain bird]

plow *n* the US spelling of **plough**.

ploy *n* a stratagem, dodge or manoeuvre to gain an advantage. [Poss. from Lat *plicare*, to bend]

pluck *v* **1** (*tr*) to pull the feathers off (a bird) before cooking. **2** (*tr*) to pick (flowers or fruit) from a plant or tree. **3** (*tr*; **out**) to remove by pulling: *plucked out her grey hairs.* **4** (*tr*) to shape by removing hairs from (eyebrows). **5** (*tr* or *intr*; **at**) to pull or tug. **6** (*tr*) to sound (the strings of a violin, etc.) using the fingers or a plectrum. **7** (*tr*) to grab or save at the last minute: *plucked from the jaws of death.* **8** (*tr* with **up**) to summon up (courage). — *n* **1**

courage; guts. **2** a little tug. **3** the heart, liver and lungs of an animal. [OE *pluccian*, to pluck or tear]

plucky *adj* **-ier, -iest** (*coll*) courageous; spirited. — *adv* **pluckily**. — *n* **pluckiness**.

plug *n* **1** a piece of rubber, plastic, etc. shaped to fit a hole as a stopper, e.g. in a bath or sink. **2** (often *in cmpds*) any device or piece of material for a similar purpose: *earplugs*. **3** the plastic or rubber device with metal pins, fitted to the end of the flex of an electrical apparatus, that is pushed into a socket to connect with the power supply; also (*coll*) the socket. **4** (*coll*) a piece of favourable publicity given to a product, programme, etc., e.g. on television. **5** a spark plug. **6** a lump of tobacco for chewing. — *v* **-gg- 1** (*tr*; **up**) to stop or block up (a hole, etc.) with something. **2** (*tr*; *coll*) to give favourable publicity to (a product, programme, etc.), esp. repeatedly. **3** (*tr*; *slang*) to shoot with a gun. **4** (*intr* with **away, along**; *coll*) to work or progress steadily. — *v* **plug in** (*tr*) to connect (an electrical appliance) to the power supply by means of an electrical plug. [Dut, bung, peg]

plughole *n* the hole in a bath or sink through which water flows into the waste-pipe.

plum *n* **1** an oval red, purple, green or yellow fruit with soft, juicy flesh and a stone; the small tree bearing it. **2** a raisin used in cakes, etc.: *plum pudding*. **3** (*coll*) something of special desirability or superiority. — *adj* (*coll*) (of e.g. a job) desirable; choice. [OE *plume*, from Gr *proumnon*]

plummy *adj* **-ier, -iest 1** (*coll*) (of a job, etc.) desirable; worth having; choice. **2** (*derog*) (of a voice) rich, deep and usu. upper-class.

plumage *n* a bird's feathers, esp. with regard to colour. [OFr, from *plume*, feather]

plumb[1] *n* a lead weight hanging on the end of a line, used for measuring water depth or for testing a wall, etc. for perpendicularity. — *adj & adv* straight, vertical or perpendicular. — *adv* **1** (*coll*) exactly: *plumb in the middle*. **2** (esp. *US*; *coll*) utterly: *plumb crazy*. — *v* (*tr*) **1** to measure the depth of (water), test (a structure) for verticality, or adjust to the vertical, using a plumb. **2** to penetrate, probe or understand (a mystery, etc.). — **out of plumb** not vertical. — **plumb the depths of** to reach the worst extreme of. [Lat *plumbum*, lead]

plumb bob *n* a plumb.

plumbline *n* a line with a plumb on it for measuring depth or testing for verticality.

plumb[2] *v* (*tr*; **in**) to connect (a water-using appliance) to the water supply or waste pipe. [Lat *plumbum*, lead, used for making pipes]

plumber *n* a person who fits and repairs water pipes, and water- or gas-using appliances.

plumbing *n* **1** the system of water and gas pipes in a building, etc. **2** the work of a plumber. **3** (*facet*) the lavatory.

plume *n* **1** an imposing feather. **2** such a feather, or a tuft or bunch of feathers, worn as an ornament or crest, represented in a coat of arms, etc. **3** a curling column (of smoke etc.) — *v* (*tr*) **1** (of a bird) to clean or preen (itself or its feathers). **2** to decorate with plumes. **3** (**on**) to pride or congratulate (oneself) on something. — *adj* **plumy, -ier, -iest**. [OFr, from Lat *pluma*, soft feather]

plummet *v* **-t-** (*intr*) to fall or drop rapidly; to plunge or hurtle downwards. — *n* the weight on a plumbline or fishing-line. [OFr *plommet*, dimin. of *plomb*, lead]

plummy. See **plum**.

plump[1] *adj* full, rounded, fleshy, chubby, or not unattractively fat. — *v* (*tr*; **up**) to shake (cushions or pillows) to give them their full soft bulk. — *adv* **plumply**. — *n* **plumpness**. [ODut *plomp*, blunt]

plump[2] *v* (*tr & intr*; **down**) to put down, drop, fall or sit heavily. — *n* a sudden heavy fall, or the sound of it. — *adv* with a plump. — *v* **plump for** (*tr*) to decide on, opt for, or choose. [Imit.]

plunder *v* **-r-** (*tr & intr*; **of**) to steal (valuable goods), or loot (a place), esp. with open force during a war; to rob or ransack. — *n* the goods plundered; loot; booty. — *n* **plunderer**. [Dut *plunderen*]

plunge *v* **1** (*intr*; **in, in to**) to dive, throw oneself, fall or rush headlong. **2** (*intr*; **in, into**) to involve oneself rapidly and enthusiastically. **3** (*tr*) to thrust or push. **4** (*tr*) to put into a particular state or condition. **5** (*tr*) to dip briefly into water or other liquid. **6** (*intr*) to dip steeply: *plunging necklines*; *The ship plunged and rose*. — *n* **1** an act of plunging; a dive. **2** (*coll*) a dip or swim. — **take the plunge** (*coll*) to commit oneself finally after hesitation; to take an irreversible decision. [OFr *plungier*, from Lat *plumbum*, lead]

plunger *n* **1** a rubber cup at the end of a long handle, used with thrusting action to clear blocked drains, etc. **2** a part of a mechanism that moves up and down like a piston.

pluperfect (*gram*) *adj* denoting a tense, formed in English by *had* and a past participle, referring to action already accomplished at the time of the past action being related, as in *She had often been before, but it was different this time*. — *n* (a verb in) the pluperfect tense. [Lat *plus quam perfectum* (*tempus*), more than perfect (time)]

plural *n* (*gram*) the form of a noun, pronoun, adjective or verb used for two or more people, things, etc. ◇ See also **singular**. — *adj* **1** (*gram*) denoting or in the plural. **2** consisting of more than one, or of different kinds. [Lat *plus*, more]

pluralism *n* **1** the existence within a society of a variety of ethnic, cultural and religious groups. **2** the holding of more than one post, esp. in the Church. — *n* **pluralist**. — *adj* **pluralistic**.

plurality *n* **-ies 1** the fact of being plural or more than one. **2** a large number or variety. **3** a majority that is not absolute, i.e. a winning number of votes that represents less than half of the votes cast; any majority.

plus *prep* **1** (*math*) with the addition of: *2 plus 5*. **2** in combination with; with the added factor of: *bad luck, plus his own obstinacy*. **3** (used after a noun, with an unstated object) with something more besides: *earns £20 000 plus*; *has personality plus*. — *adj* **1** denoting the symbol '+': *the plus sign*. **2** mathematically positive; above zero: *plus 3°*. **3** advantageous: *a plus factor*. **4** (in schoolwork grades) denoting a slightly higher mark: *B plus*. **5** (*physics*, *electr*, etc.) electrically positive. — *n* ***pluses* 1** (also **plus sign**) the symbol (+) denoting addition or positive value. **2** (*coll*) something positive or good; a bonus, advantage, surplus or extra. — *conj* (*coll*) in addition to the fact that. [Lat, more]

plus fours *n* (*pl*) loose breeches gathered below the knee, once popular as golfing wear. [*plus 4* inches of fabric extending below the knee]

plush *n* cotton, silk, etc. fabric with a long velvety pile. — *adj* **1** made of plush. **2** (*coll*) plushy. [Fr *pluche*, earlier *peluche*, from Lat *pilus*, hair]

plushy *adj* **-ier**, **-iest** (*coll*) luxurious, opulent, stylish, or costly.

plutocracy *n* **-ies 1** government or domination by the wealthy. **2** a state governed by the wealthy. **3** an influential group whose power is backed by their wealth. [Gr *ploutos*, wealth + **-cracy**]

plutocrat *n* **1** a member of a plutocracy. **2** (*coll*) a wealthy person. — *adj* **plutocratic**.

plutonium *n* a radioactive metallic element (symbol **Pu**). [After the planet *Pluto*]

ply[1] *n* ***plies* 1** thickness of yarn, rope, or wood, measured by the number of strands or layers that compose it: *3-ply wool*. **2** a strand or layer. [OFr *pli*, fold]

plywood *n* wood made up of thin layers glued together.

ply[2] *v* ***plies***, ***plied* 1** (*tr*; **with**) to keep supplying or importuning (someone): *plied them with drinks* or *questions*. **2** (*tr & intr*; **between**) to travel (a route) regularly; to go regularly to and fro between destinations. **3** (*tr*; *old*) to work at (a trade). **4** (*tr*; *old*) to use (a tool, etc.): *ply one's needle*. [**apply**]

PM *abbrev* **1** Prime Minister. **2** Paymaster. **3** Postmaster. **4** post mortem.

Pm *symbol* (*chem*) promethium.

p.m. *abbrev* for *post meridiem* (Lat), after midday; in the afternoon. ◇ See also **a.m.**

PMS *abbrev* premenstrual syndrome.

PMT *abbrev* premenstrual tension.

pneumatic *adj* **1** of or relating to air or gases. **2** containing or inflated with air: *pneumatic tyres*. **3** worked or driven by compressed air: *pneumatic drills*. — *adv* **pneumatically**. [Gr *pneuma*, wind, breath]

pneumonia *n* inflammation of one or both lungs. [Gr *pneumon*, lung]

PO *abbrev* **1** Post Office. **2** Petty Officer. **3** Pilot Officer.

PO box *n* a numbered box, pigeonhole, etc. at a post office, to which mail may be sent for collection by a recipient without a permanent address.

Po *symbol* (*chem*) polonium.

po[1] *n* ***pos*** (*coll*) a chamberpot.

po[2] *abbrev* postal order.

poach[1] *v* (*tr*) **1** to cook (an egg without its shell) in or over boiling water. **2** to simmer (fish) in milk or other liquid. [OFr *pocher*, to pocket (the egg yolk inside the white), from *poche*, pocket]

poach[2] *v* **1** (*tr & intr*) to catch (game or fish) illegally on someone else's property. **2** (*intr* with **on**) to intrude on (another's territory or area of responsibility). **3** (*tr*) to steal (ideas, etc.). **4** (*tr*) to lure away (personnel at a rival establishment) to work for one's own. — *n* **poacher**. — *n* **poaching**. [OFr *pocher*, to gouge]

pock *n* **1** a small inflamed area on the skin, containing pus, esp. one caused by smallpox. **2** a pockmark. [OE *poc*]

pockmark *n* (also **pock**) a small pit or hollow in the skin left by a pock (sense **1**), esp. a smallpox one. — *adj* **pockmarked**.

pocket *n* **1** an extra piece sewn into or on to a garment to form an enclosed section for carrying things in. **2** any container similarly fitted or attached. **3** one's financial resources: *well beyond my pocket*. **4** a rock cavity filled with ore. **5** in conditions of air turbulence, a place in the atmosphere where the air pressure drops or rises abruptly. **6** an isolated patch or area of something: *pockets of unemployment*. **7** (*billiards*, etc.) any of the nets or pouches hanging from the side of the table, into which balls are played. — *adj* designed, or small enough, to be carried in a pocket; smaller than standard. — *v* **-t-** (*tr*) **1** to put in one's pocket. **2** (*coll*) to take dishonestly; to steal. **3** (*billiards*) to drive (a ball) into a pocket. **4** to swallow or suppress (one's pride), e.g. to make a humble request. — **in one another's pocket** in close intimacy with, or dependence on, one another. — **in one's pocket** in one's power. — **in** (or **out of**) **pocket** having gained (or lost) money on a transaction (**out-of-pocket expenses** those one has incurred on behalf of one's employer). — **line one's pocket** to make money, esp. dishonestly or immorally, from something. — **put one's hand in one's pocket** to be willing to contribute money. [OFr *poquet*, dimin. of *poque*, from ODut *poke*, pocket]

pocketbook *n* **1** (*US*) a wallet for money and papers. **2** (*US*) a woman's strapless handbag or purse. **3** a notebook.

pocket borough *n* (*hist*) in the UK before the 1832 Reform Act, an electoral constituency under the control of one person or family.

pocketful *n* **-*fuls*** as much as will fit into a pocket.

pocket knife *n* a knife with folding blades; a penknife.

pod *n* **1** the long seedcase of a pea, bean, etc. **2** a container, e.g. for fuel, fitted under the wings or fuselage of an aircraft. — *v* **-*dd*-** **1** (*tr*) to extract (peas, beans, etc.) from their pods. **2** (*intr*) (of a plant) to produce pods.

podgy *adj* **-*ier***, **-*iest*** (*derog*) plump or chubby; short and squat. [*podge*, a short fat person]

podiatry *n* (*NAm*) chiropody. — *n* **podiatrist**. [Gr *pod-* foot + *iatros*, doctor]

podium *n* **-*dia*** or **-*diums*** **1** a small platform for a public speaker, orchestra conductor, etc. **2** (*archit*) a projecting base for a colonnade, wall, etc. [Lat, platform, from Gr *pous*, foot]

poem *n* **1** a composition in verse, often of elevated and imaginatively expressed content. **2** an object, scene or creation of inspiring beauty. [Gr *poiema*, creation, poem, from *poieein*, to make]

poesy *n* (*old*) poetry. [Gr *poiesis*, from *poieein*, to make]

poet *n* a writer of poems. [Gr *poietes*, from *poieein*, to make]

poetess *n* a female poet.

poetic *adj* **1** of, relating or suitable to, poets or poetry. **2** having grace, beauty or inspiration suggestive of poetry. — *adv* **poetically**.

poetical *adj* **1** poetic. **2** written in verse: *the complete poetical works*. — *adv* **poetically**.

poetic justice *n* a situation in which evil is punished or good rewarded in a strikingly fitting way.

poetic licence *n* a poet's or writer's departure from strict fact or correct grammar, for the sake of effect.

poet laureate *n* ***poets laureate*** (*formal*) or ***poet laureates*** (in Britain) an officially appointed court poet, commissioned to produce poems for state occasions.

poetry *n* the art of composing poems. **2** poems collectively. **3** poetic quality, feeling, beauty or grace. [Lat *poetria*, from *poeta*, poet]

po-faced *adj* (*coll derog*) wearing a disapproving expression.

pogo stick *n* a spring-mounted pole with a handlebar and foot rests, on which to bounce, or progress by bounces.

pogrom *n* an organised massacre, orig. of Jews in 19th-cent. Russia. [Russ, destruction]

poignant *adj* **1** painful to the feelings: *a poignant reminder*. **2** deeply moving; full of pathos. — *n* **poignancy**. — *adv* **poignantly**. [OFr, present participle of *poindre*, to sting]

poinsettia *n* a Central American shrub, popular because of its scarlet leaves. [J R *Poinsett* (1779–1851), American Minister to Mexico]

point *n* **1** a sharp or tapering end or tip. **2** a dot, e.g. that inserted before a decimal fraction, as in *2.1* or *2·1* (*two point one*). **3** a punctuation mark, esp. a full stop. **4** (*geom*) a position found by means of coordinates. **5** a position, place or location: *a look-out point*. **6** a moment: *lost his temper at that point*. **7** a stage in a process, etc. **8** a stage, temperature, etc.: *boiling-point*. **9** the right moment for doing something: *lost courage when it came to the point*. **10** a feature or characteristic: *her good points*. **11** a detail or particular. **12** aim or intention: *the point of this procedure*. **13** use or value: *no point in trying*. **14** the significance (of a remark, story, joke, etc.). **15** a unit or mark in scoring. **16** any of the 32 directions marked on, or indicated by, a compass. **17** (usu. in *pl*) an adjustable tapering rail by means of which a train changes lines. **18** (*electr*) a socket or power point. **19** (usu. in *pl*) in an internal combustion engine, either of the two electrical contacts completing the circuit in the distributor. **20** (*printing*) a unit of type measurement, equal to $\frac{1}{12}$ of a pica. **21** (*cricket*) an off-side fielding position at right angles to the batsman. **22** (*ballet*; usu. in *pl*) the tip of the toe, or a block inserted into the toe of a ballet shoe. **23** a headland or promontory. **24** (usu. in *pl*) any of an animal's extremities, e.g. ears, tail and feet. **25** the tip of a deer's horn or antler. — *v* **1** (*tr*; **at**) to aim: *pointed a gun at her*. **2** (*tr* or *intr*; **to, towards, at**) to extend (one's finger or a pointed object) towards someone or something, so as to direct attention there; (of a sign, etc.) to indicate a certain direction. **3** (*intr*) to extend or face in a certain direction: *lay with toes pointing upward*. **4** (*intr*) (of a gun dog) to stand with the nose turned to where the dead game lies. **5** (*tr*; sometimes *facet*) to direct (someone): *Point me towards a pub*. **6** (*intr* with **to**) to indicate or suggest: *points to one solution*. **7** (*tr*) to extend (the toes) to form a point, as in dancing. **8** (*tr*) to fill gaps or cracks in (stonework or brickwork) with cement or mortar. — **beside the point** irrelevant. — **carry** or **gain one's point** to persuade others of the validity of one's opinion. — **come** or **get to the point** to cut out the irrelevancies and say what one wants to say. — **in point of fact** actually; in truth. — **make a point of** or **make it a point to** to be sure of (doing something) or take care to (do something). — **make one's point** to state one's opinion forcefully. — **on the point of** (doing) about to (do something). — *v* **point out** (*tr*) to indicate or draw attention to. — *v* **point up** (*tr*) to highlight or emphasise. — **score points off** to argue cleverly and successfully against (someone), often with regard to only minor details of his or her arguments. — **to the point** relevant. — **to the point of** to a degree that could be fairly described as: *brave to the point of recklessness*. — **up to a point** to a limited degree. [OFr, from Lat *pungere*, to pierce]

point-blank *adj* **1** (of a shot) fired at very close range. **2** (of a question, refusal, etc.) bluntly worded and direct. — *adv* **1** at close range. **2** in a blunt, direct manner. [**point**, *v* + *blank*, the white centre of a target, from Fr *blanc*, white]

point duty *n* the task or station of a policeman who is directing traffic.

pointed *adj* **1** having, or ending in, a point. **2** (of a remark, etc.) intended for, though not directly addressed to, a particular person; intended to convey a particular meaning or message although not directly expressing it. — *adv* **pointedly**. — *n* **pointedness**.

pointer *n* **1** a rod used by a speaker for indicating positions on a wall map, chart, etc. **2** the indicating finger or needle on a measuring instrument. **3** (*coll*) a suggestion or hint. **4** a breed of gun dog trained to point its muzzle in the direction where the dead game lies.

pointing *n* the cement or mortar filling the gaps between the bricks or stones of a wall.

pointless *adj* lacking purpose or meaning. — *adv* **pointlessly**.

point of no return *n* a stage reached in a process, etc. after which there is no possibility of stopping or going back.

point of order *n* ***points of order*** a question raised in an assembly as to whether the business is being done according to the rules.

point of sale *n* ***points of sale*** the place in a shop, etc. where goods are paid for; a till, pay desk or checkout. — *adj* **point-of-sale**.

point of view *n* ***points of view*** one's own way of seeing something, influenced by personal considerations and experience; one's standpoint or viewpoint.

point-to-point *n* ***point-to-points*** *n* a horse race across open country, from landmark to landmark.

pointillism *n* a method, used by some Impressionist painters, of suggesting shapes and colour tones by means of small dabs of unmixed colour painted side by side. — *n* **pointillist**. [Fr *pointiller*, to dot]

poise *n* **1** self-confidence, calm or composure. **2** grace of posture or carriage. **3** a state of equilibrium, balance or stability e.g. between extremes. — *v* **1** (*tr*, often in *passive*, or *intr*) to balance; to hold or be suspended or in a state of readiness. [OFr *pois*, weight]

poised *adj* (of behaviour, etc.) calm and dignified.

poison *n* **1** a substance that causes illness or death when swallowed or absorbed into the tissues. **2** any destructive or corrupting influence: *a poison spreading through society*. — *v* **-n-** (*tr*) **1** to harm or kill with poison. **2** to put poison into (food, etc.). **3** to contaminate or pollute: *rivers poisoned by effluents*. **4** to corrupt or pervert (someone's mind). **5** (**against**) to influence (someone's mind) against someone else. **6** to spoil in a nasty way: *poison a relationship*. **7** (usu. in *passive*; *coll*) to infect: *a poisoned toe*. — *n* **poisoner**. [OFr *puisun*, from Lat *potio*, drink, potion]

poison gas *n* any of several gases used in chemical warfare, that cause injury or death through contact or inhalation.

poison ivy *n* an American climbing plant whose leaves produce a juice that causes intense skin irritation.

poisonous *adj* **1** liable to cause injury or death if swallowed or absorbed. **2** producing, or able to inject, a poison: *poisonous snakes*. **3** (*coll*) (of a person, remark, etc.) malicious. — *adv* **poisonously**.

poison-pen letter *n* a malicious anonymous letter.

poke[1] *v* **1** (*tr*; **into, through**, etc.) to thrust (something pointed): *poke one's finger, a stick*, etc. *into a hole*, etc. **2** (*tr*) to prod or jab: *poke the fire*; *poked her in the ribs with his elbow*. **3** (*tr*) to make (a hole) by prodding. **4** (*tr & intr*; **out, through**) to (cause to) project: *poked his head out of the door*; *Her big toe poked through a hole in her sock*. **5** (*intr*; **about, around**) to search; to pry or snoop. **6** (*tr*) to make (a fire) burn more brightly by stirring it with a poker. — **poke one's nose into** (*coll*) to pry into or interfere in. [MidE, from a Germanic source]

poker *n* a metal rod for stirring a fire to make it burn better.

poke[2] *n* (esp. *Scot*) a paper bag. [MidE, from ODut]

poker[1]. See **poke**[1].

poker[2] *n* a card game in which players bet on the hands they hold, relying on bluff to outwit their opponents.

poker face *n* the expressionless countenance of an experienced poker-player, or of anyone who gives nothing away. — *adj* **poker-faced**.

poky *adj* **-ier, -iest** (*coll*) (of a room, house, etc.) small, confined or cramped. — *n* **pokiness**. [**poke**[1]]

polar *adj* **1** relating to the earth's North or South Pole or the regions round them. **2** relating to, or having, electric or magnetic poles. **3** as different as possible: *polar opposites*. [Lat *polaris*, from *polus*, from Gr *polos*, pivot, axis, pole]

polar bear *n* a large white bear found in the Arctic.

polarise or **-ize** *v* **1** (*tr*) to give magnetic or electric polarity to. **2** (*tr*) to restrict the vibrations of (light waves) to one plane. **3** (*tr & intr*) (of people or opinions) to split into two opposing camps. — *n* **polarisation** or **-z-**.

polarity *n* **-ies** **1** the state of having two opposite poles: *magnetic polarity*. **2** the status, i.e. whether positive or negative, of an electrode, etc.: *negative polarity*. **3** the tendency to develop, or be drawn, in opposite directions; oppositeness or an opposite: *the political polarities of left and right*.

Polaroid® *n* a plastic material able to polarise light, used in sunglasses, etc. to reduce glare.

Polaroid camera *n* a camera that, by means of an internal developing and printing process, produces a print within seconds of exposure.

polder *n* an area of land lying below sea level, from which the sea has been drained; a piece of reclaimed land. [ODut *polre*]

pole[1] *n* **1** either end of the earth's axis or the axis of any rotating sphere: *the North Pole*. **2** in the apparent sphere of the heavens, the points directly opposite to the North and South Pole, round which the stars appear to turn. **3** either extremity of a magnet, the one having a repelling, the other an attracting, force. **4** either of the two terminals, negative or positive, of an electric cell or battery. **5** either of two opposite positions in argument, opinion, etc. — **poles apart** (*coll*) as different or as far apart as possible. [Lat *polus*, from Gr *polos*, axis, pivot]

Pole Star *n* a star at the North Pole of the heavens, directly above the earth's North Pole.

pole[2] *n* **1** a rod, esp. cylindrical in section and fixed in the ground as a support. **2** an old measure of length equal to 5½ yards; a perch or rod. — **up the pole** (*coll*) mad; crazy. [OE *pal*, from Lat *palus*, stake]

pole position *n* the position at the inside of the front row of cars at the start of a race; an advantageous position at the start of any contest.

pole vault *n* an athletic event consisting of a jump over a high horizontal bar with the help of a long flexible pole to haul one's body into the air. — *n* **pole-vaulter**.

poleaxe *n* **1** a short-handled axe with a spike or hammer opposite the blade, used, esp. formerly, for slaughtering cattle. **2** (*hist*) a long-handled battleaxe. — *v* (*tr*) to strike, fell or floor (as if) with a poleaxe. [MidE *pollax*, head axe, from **poll**, head]

polecat *n* **1** a dark-brown animal of the weasel family, that emits a foul smell. **2** (*US*) a skunk. [MidE *polcat*]

polemic *n* a piece of writing or a speech fiercely attacking or defending an idea, opinion, etc.; writing or oratory of this sort. — *adj* (also **polemical**) relating to or involving polemic or polemics. — *adv* **polemically**. — *n* **polemicist**. [Gr *polemikos*, from *polemos*, war]

polemics *n* (*sing* or *pl*) the art of verbal wrangling; the cut and thrust of fierce disputation.

police *n* (*pl*) **1** the body of men and women employed by the government of a country to keep order, enforce the law, prevent crime, etc. **2** members of this body: *Over 200 police were on duty*. — *v* (*tr*) **1** to keep law and order in (an area) using the police, army, etc. **2** to supervise (an operation, etc.) to ensure that it is fairly or properly run. [Fr, from Gr *politeia*, political constitution]

police constable *n* a police officer of the lowest rank.

police dog *n* a dog trained to work with policemen.

policeman or **policewoman** *n* a police officer.

police officer *n* a member of a police force.

police state *n* a state with a repressive government that operates through secret police to eliminate opposition to it.

police station *n* the office of a local police force.

policy[1] *n* **-ies** **1** a plan of action, usu. based on certain principles, decided on by a body or individual. **2** a principle or set of principles on which to base decisions: *It's not our policy to imprison children*. **3** a course of conduct for following: *Your best policy is to keep quiet*. [OFr *policie*, from Gr *politeia*, political constitution]

policy[2] *n* **-ies** (also **insurance policy**) (a document confirming) an insurance agreement. — *n* **policy-holder**. [OFr *police*, from Lat *apodixis*, receipt, from Gr *apodeixis*, proof]

polio *n* (*coll*) poliomyelitis.

poliomyelitis *n* a viral disease of the brain and spinal cord, in some cases resulting in permanent paralysis. [Gr *polios*, grey + *myelos*, marrow + **-itis**]

Polish *adj* of or relating to Poland, its language, culture or people. — *n* the language of Poland.

polish *v* **1** (*tr & intr*; **up**) to make or become smooth and glossy by rubbing. **2** (*tr*; **up**) to improve or perfect. **3** (*tr*) to make cultivated, refined or elegant: *polished manners*. — *n* **1** a substance used for polishing surfaces. **2** a smooth shiny finish; a gloss. **3** an act of polishing. **4** refinement or elegance. — *n* **polisher**. — *v* **polish off** (*tr*; *coll*) to complete (work, etc.) or consume (food) at speed. — *v* **polish up** (*tr*) to improve (a skill, etc.) by working at it. [OFr *polir*, from Lat *polire*]

politburo *n* **-os** (sometimes *cap*) the policy-forming committee of a Communist party. [Russ]

polite *adj* **1** well-mannered; considerate towards others; courteous. **2** well-bred, cultivated or refined: *polite society*. — *adv*

politely. — *n* **politeness**. [Lat *politus*, from *polire*, to polish]

politic *adj* **1** (of a move) prudent; wise; shrewd. **2** (of a person) cunning; crafty. **3** (*old*) political: *the body politic* (= the people of a state considered as a political group). — *v* **-ck-** (*intr*; *derog*) to indulge in politics. [OFr *politique*, from Gr *politikos*, civic]

political *adj* **1** of or relating to government or public affairs. **2** relating to politics. **3** interested or involved in politics. **4** (of a move, etc.) made in the interests of gaining or keeping power. — *adv* **politically**.

political asylum *n* protection given by a government to a foreigner who has fled his or her own country for political reasons.

political prisoner *n* a person imprisoned for dissenting from the government.

political science *n* the study of politics and government.

politician *n* **1** someone engaged in politics, esp. as a member of parliament. **2** (*derog*) someone who goes in for power-seeking manoeuvres. [Fr *politicien*, from Gr *politikos*, civic]

politicise or **-ize** *v* **1** (*intr*) to go in for political activities or discussion. **2** (*tr*) to give a political nature to: *the politicising of sport*. **3** (*tr*) to make (someone) aware of or informed about politics. — *n* **politicisation** or **-z-**.

politics *n* **1** (*sing*) the science or business of government. **2** (*sing*) political science. **3** (*sing*) a political life as a career. **4** (*sing* & *pl*) political activities, wrangling, etc. **5** (*pl*) moves and manoeuvres concerned with the acquisition of power or getting one's way, e.g. in business. **6** (*pl*) one's political sympathies or principles: *What are your politics?*

politico *n* **-os** or **-oes** (*derog*) a politician or someone keen on politics. [Ital or Span]

politico- *comb fm* politics or political: *politico-philosophical writings*.

polity *n* **-ies 1** a politically organised body such as a state, church or association. **2** any form of political institution or government. [Gr *politeia*, political constitution]

polka *n* (a piece of music for) a lively dance performed usu. with a partner, with a pattern of three steps followed by a hop. — *v* **-kaing**, **-kaed** (*intr*) to dance a polka. [Czech *pulka*, half-step, or *Polka*, polish woman]

polka dot *n* any of numerous regularly spaced dots forming a pattern on fabric, etc.

poll *n* **1** (in *pl*) a political election: *victory at the polls*. **2** the voting, or votes cast, at an election: *a heavy poll*. **3** (also **opinion poll**) a survey of public opinion carried out by directly questioning a representative sample of the populace. **4** (esp. *old*) the head; this as a unit in numbering. — *v* **1** (*tr*) to win (a number of votes) in an election. **2** (*tr*) to register the votes of (a population). **3** (*tr* & *intr*) to cast (one's vote). **4** (*tr*) to conduct an opinion poll among. **5** (*tr*) to cut off the horns of (cattle). **6** (*tr*) to cut the top off (a tree); to make a pollard of. [MidE *polle*, (the hair of) the head]

polling-booth *n* an enclosed compartment at a polling-station in which to mark one's ballot paper in private.

polling-station *n* the centre one attends to cast one's vote.

pollster *n* a person who organises opinion polls.

poll tax *n* **1** a fixed tax levied on each member of a population. **2** a name (orig. *derog*) given to the community charge.

pollack *n* **-ack** or **-acks** an edible fish of northern waters, related to the cod.

pollard *n* **1** a tree whose branches have been lopped off so that it produces a bushy growth at the top of the trunk. **2** an animal whose horns, etc. have been shed naturally or deliberately removed. — *v* (*tr*) to make a pollard of (a tree or animal). [**poll** + sfx. *-ard* denoting a person, animal, etc. of a certain type]

pollen *n* the fertilising powder produced by the anthers of flowers. [Lat, flour]

pollen count *n* a measure of the amount of pollen in the air at any particular time, published for the benefit of those who have a pollen allergy.

pollinate *v* (*tr*) (of e.g. an insect) to carry pollen to the stigma of (a flower). — *n* **pollination**. [Lat *pollen*, flour]

pollster. See **poll**.

pollute *v* (*tr*) **1** to contaminate with harmful substances; to make impure. **2** to corrupt (someone's mind, etc.). — *n* & *adj* **pollutant**. — *n* **pollution**. [Lat *polluere*, to soil, defile]

polo *n* a ball game played on horseback using long-handled hammers to propel the ball along the ground. [Tibetan dialect, ball]

polo neck *n* **1** a high, close-fitting neck band on a sweater or shirt, worn folded over. **2** a sweater or shirt with such a neck. — *adj* **polo-neck**.

polonaise *n* (a piece of music for) a stately Polish promenading dance. [Fr, feminine of *polonais*, Polish]

polonium *n* a radioactive element (symbol **Po**), discovered in uranium ore by Marie Curie. [Lat *Polonia*, Poland, Mme Curie's native country]

polony *n* **-ies** a dry sausage made of partly cooked meat. [Probably *Bologna*, Italy]

poltergeist *n* a type of household ghost responsible for otherwise unaccountable noises, given also to shifting objects about. [Ger *poltern*, to make a racket + *Geist*, spirit, ghost]

poltroon *n* a despicable coward. [Ital *poltrone*, lazybones]

poly *n* ***polys*** (*coll*) a polytechnic.

poly- *comb fm* **1** many or much. **2** (*chem*) polymerised. [Gr, many, much]

polyandrous *adj* **1** having more than one husband at the same time. **2** (*bot*) having many stamens. — *n* **polyandry**. ◇ See also **monandrous**. [**poly-** (sense **1**) + Gr *aner*, man, husband]

polyanthus *n* ***-uses*** a cultivated hybrid plant related to the primrose, with several brightly coloured flowers to each stem. [**poly-** (sense **1**) + Gr *anthos*, flower]

polychromatic *adj* **1** multicoloured. **2** (of radiation) having more than one wavelength. [**poly-** (sense **1**) + Gr *chroma*, colour]

polyester *n* a synthetic polymer from which a fibre used in cloth manufacture is produced. [**poly-** (sense **2**) + **ester**]

polyethylene *n* polythene. [**poly-** (sense **2**) + **ethylene**]

polygamy *n* the custom or practice of having more than one wife or husband at the same time. ◇ See also **monogamy**. — *n* **polygamist**. — *adj* **polygamous**. — *adv* **polygamously**. [Gr *poly-*, many + *gamos*, marriage]

polyglot *adj* speaking, using, or written in, many languages. — *n* a person who speaks many languages. [Gr *poly-*, many + *glotta*, tongue, language]

polygon *n* (*geom*) a two-dimensional figure with many, esp. more than five, sides. — *adj* **polygonal**. [Gr *poly-*, many + *gonia*, angle]

polygraph *n* a machine that registers physiological data, e.g. pulse rate, used e.g. as a lie-detector. [Gr *poly-*, much + *graphein*, to write]

polygyny *n* the condition or custom of having more than one wife at the same time. [**poly-** (sense **1**) + Gr *gyne*, woman, wife]

polyhedron *n* ***-drons*** or ***-dra*** (*geom*) a solid with many, esp. more than seven, faces. — *adj* **polyhedral**. [Gr *poly-*, many + *hedra*, seat, base, face]

polymath *n* a person who is learned in a large variety of subjects. [Gr *poly-*, much + *manthanein*, to learn]

polymer *n* a chemical substance composed of molecules simply constructed from recurring units. — *adj* **polymeric**. [Gr *poly-*, many + *meros*, part]

polymerise or **-ize** *v* (*tr* & *intr*) to form into a polymer. — *n* **polymerisation** or **-z-**.

polymorphous or **polymorphic** *adj* existing in, or passing through, a variety of forms. [**poly-** (sense **1**) + Gr *morphe*, shape]

polyp *n* **1** (*zool*) a tiny tube-shaped sea creature with a ring of tentacles round its mouth. **2** (*pathol*) a small growth with a stalk-like base, projecting from the mucous membrane, e.g. inside the nose. — *adj* **polypous**. [Gr *polypous*, many-footed, from *poly-*, many + *pous*, foot]

polyphony *n* a type of music, typically for voices, in which each part has its independent melody; contrapuntal music. — *adj* **polyphonic**. [Gr *poly-*, many + *phone*, voice, sound]

polypropylene *n* a tough plastic, a polymer of propylene, with properties similar to those of polythene. [**poly-** (sense **2**)]

polystyrene *n* a light plastic used esp. in cellular form as a packing and insulating material. [**poly-** (sense **2**) + *styrene*, a hydrocarbon]

polysyllable *n* a word of three or more syllables. — *adj* **polysyllabic**. [**poly-** (sense **1**)]

polytechnic *n* a college of higher education in which courses in a large range of subjects, esp. of a technical or vocational kind, are available. — *adj* relating to technical training. [**poly-** (sense **1**) + Gr *techne*, art]

polytheism *n* belief in, or worship of, more than one god. — *n* **polytheist**. — *adj* **polytheistic**. [**poly-** (sense **1**) + Gr *theos*, god]

polythene *n* a light tough thermoplastic, a polymer of ethylene, used for making plastic bags, kitchenware, etc. [**poly-** **ethylene**]

polyunsaturated *adj* **1** (*chem*) containing more than one carbon–carbon double bond in the molecule. **2** (of esp. fish or vegetable oils and fats) free of cholesterol, therefore not liable to cause fatty deposits in the blood vessels. [**poly-** (sense **1**) + **unsaturated**]

polyurethane *n* any of various polymers used to make plastic foam, waterproof paints, etc., fillings, coatings, etc. [**poly-** (sense **2**) + *urethane*, an ester]

polyvinyl chloride *n* a plastic used for coating electric wires and as a clothing material; PVC. [**poly-** (sense **2**)]

pom *n* (*coll*; *Austr* & *NZ*) a pommy.

pomace *n* **1** crushed apples for cider-making; the residue of these or of any similar fruit after pressing. **2** anything crushed or ground to a pulp. [Lat *pomum*, fruit, apple]

pomade *n* (*hist*) a perfumed ointment for the hair and scalp. [Fr, from Ital *pomata*, from Lat *pomum*, apple, a one-time ingredient]

pomander *n* a perfumed ball composed of various substances, used to scent wardrobes, orig. carried to ward off infection; a perforated container for this or, now more commonly, a mixture of scented flower-petals, etc. [OFr *pomme d'ambre*, apple of amber]

pomegranate *n* a round seedy fruit with red juicy flesh and a tough reddish skin; the tree on which it grows. [Lat *pomum granatum*, seedy apple]

pomelo *n* ***-os*** a yellow citrus fruit similar to a grapefruit, native to SE Asia. [Dut *pompelmoes*, shaddock, grapefruit]

Pomeranian *n* a small breed of dog with a sharp-pointed face and thick long silky coat. [*Pomerania*, Baltic coastal region of central Europe]

pomfret *n* (also **pomfret cake**) a disc-shaped liquorice sweet traditionally made in *Pontefract*, Yorkshire. [OFr *Pontfret*, Pontefract, from Lat *pons*, bridge + *fractus*, broken]
pommel *n* **1** the raised forepart of a saddle. **2** a rounded knob forming the end of a sword hilt. — *v* **-ll-** (*tr*) to pummel. [OFr *pomel*, knob]
pommy *n* **-ies** (*Austr & NZ coll derog*) a British, or esp. English, person.
pomp *n* **1** ceremonial grandeur. **2** vain ostentation. [Lat *pompa*, procession]
pompom or **pompon** *n* a ball of cut wool or other yarn, used as a trimming on clothes or upholstery. [Fr *pompon*]
pom-pom *n* an automatic quick-firing gun; a machine gun; a multi-barrelled anti-aircraft gun. [Imit.]
pompous *adj* **1** solemnly self-important. **2** (of language) inappropriately grand and flowery; pretentious. — *n* **pomposity**.— *adv* **pompously**. [Lat *pomposus*, from *pompa*, procession]
ponce *n* (*offensive slang*) **1** an effeminate man. **2** a pimp. — *v* (*intr* with **about, around**) **1** to mince about in an effeminate manner. **2** to mess around.
poncho *n* **-os** an orig. S American outer garment made of, or like, a blanket with a hole for the head to go through. [Span]
pond *n* a small body of water, whether natural or artificial. [MidE *ponde*, enclosure]
ponder *v* (*tr & intr*; **on**) **-r-** to consider or contemplate. [Lat *ponderare*, to weigh]
ponderous *adj* **1** (of someone's speaking or writing style, humour, etc.) heavy-handed, laborious, over-solemn or pompous. **2** heavy or cumbersome; lumbering in movement. **3** weighty; important. — *adv* **ponderously**. — *n* **ponderousness**. [Lat *ponderosus*, from *ponderare*, to weigh]
pong (*coll*) *n* a stink; a bad smell. — *v* (*intr*; **of**) to smell badly. — *adj* **pongy, -ier, -iest**.
poniard *n* a slim-bladed dagger. [Fr *poignard*, from *poing*, fist]
pontiff *n* a title for the Pope, formerly applied to any Roman Catholic bishop. [Lat *pontifex*, high priest]
pontifical *adj* **1** belonging, or relating, to a pontiff. **2** (*derog*) pompously opinionated; dogmatic. — *adv* **pontifically**. [Lat *pontificalis*, from *pontifex*, high priest]
pontificals *n* (*pl*) the ceremonial dress of a bishop or pope.
pontificate *v* (*intr*; **on, about**) to pronounce one's opinion with pompous solemnity, as if it were the only correct one. — *n* the (period of) office of a pope. [Lat *pontificatus*, high-priesthood, from *pontifex*, priest]
pontoon[1] *n* any of a number of flat-bottomed craft, punts, barges, etc., anchored side by side across a river, to support a temporary bridge. [Fr *ponton*, from Lat *ponto*, punt]
pontoon bridge *n* a bridge supported on pontoons.
pontoon[2] *n* (*cards*) a game in which the object is to collect sets of cards that add up to 21 and no more. [Alteration of Fr *vingt-et-un*, twenty-one]
pony *n* **-ies** a horse of any of several small breeds, usu. under 14·2 hands (1·44 m) in height. [Scot *powney*, from Fr *poulenet*, dimin. of *poulain*, colt]
ponytail *n* (a hairstyle with the hair drawn back into) a bunch high up on the back of the head.
pony-trekking *n* the recreational activity of cross-country pony-riding in groups.
poodle *n* a breed of dog whose curly coat is traditionally clipped in an elaborate style. [Ger *Pudel(hund)*, from *pudeln*, to splash]
poof *n* (*offensive slang*) a male homosexual. [Fr *pouffe*, puff]
pooh *interj* (*coll*) an exclamation of scorn or of disgust, e.g. at a smell. [Imit.]
pooh-pooh *v* (*tr*; *coll*) to express scorn for (a suggestion, etc.).
pool[1] *n* **1** a small area of still water: *a rock pool*. **2** a puddle; a patch of spilt liquid: *pools of blood*. **3** a swimming-pool. **4** a deep part of a stream or river. [OE *pol*]
pool[2] *n* **1** a reserve of money, personnel, vehicles, etc. used as a communal resource: *a typing pool*. **2** the combined stakes of those betting on something; a jackpot. **3** (*commerce*) a group of businesses with a common arrangement to maintain high prices, so eliminating competition and preserving profits. **4** a game like billiards played with a white cue ball and usu. 15 numbered coloured balls, the aim being to shoot specified balls into specified pockets using the cue ball. **5** (in *pl*) football pools, i.e. betting by post on the results of a number of football games. — *v* (*tr*) to put (money or other resources) into a common supply for general use. [Fr *poule*, hen, stakes]
poop[1] *n* the raised, enclosed part at the stern of old sailing ships. [Lat *puppis*]
poop deck *n* the deck surmounting the poop.
poop[2] (*coll*) *v* **1** (*tr*, usu. in *passive*) to exhaust. **2** (*intr*) to become exhausted. — *v* **poop out** (*intr*) to give up from exhaustion.
poor *adj* **1** not having sufficient money or means to live comfortably. **2** (with **in**) not well supplied with: *a country poor in minerals*. **3** not good; weak; unsatisfactory. **4** unsatisfactorily small or sparse: *a poor attendance*. **5** used in expressing pity or sympathy: *Poor fellow!* — *n* **poorness**. — **poor man's** (often *derog*) denoting what is considered, often scornfully, to be a cheap or common substitute for (something expensive, rare or of a higher quality or value): *a flower called poor man's orchid*. [OFr *povre*, from Lat *pauper*, poor]

poorhouse *n* (*hist*) an institution maintained at public expense, for sheltering the poor; a workhouse.

poor law *n* (*hist*) a law or (usu. with *caps*) the set of laws concerned with the public support of the poor.

poorly *adv* not well; badly. — *adj* (*old coll* or *dialect*) ill.

poor white *n* (*derog*) a member of an impoverished and deprived class of white people living amongst blacks in the southern US or S Africa.

pop[1] *n* **1** a sharp, explosive noise, like that of a cork coming out of a bottle. **2** (*coll*) sweet non-alcoholic fizzy drinks. — *v* **-pp-** **1** (*tr* & *intr*) to (cause to) make a pop. **2** (*tr* & *intr*) to burst with a pop. **3** (*intr*; **out**) to spring out; to protrude; *popping eyes*. **4** (*intr*; *coll*; **in**, **out**, etc.) to go quickly: *pop next door*. **5** (*tr*; *coll*; **in**, etc.) to put quickly. — *adv* with a pop. — *v* **pop off** (*intr*; *coll*) to die.— **pop the question** (*coll facet*) to propose marriage. — *v* **pop up** (*intr*) to appear or occur, esp. unexpectedly. [Imit.]

popcorn *n* maize grains heated till they puff up and burst open.

pop-eyed *adj* (*coll*) with eyes protruding, esp. in amazement.

popgun *n* a toy gun that fires a cork or pellet with a pop.

popper *n* a press stud.

popping-crease *n* (*cricket*) the line behind which the batsman must stand, parallel to, and four feet in front of, the wicket.

pop-up *adj* (of a picture book) having cut-out parts designed to stand upright as the page is opened.

pop[2] *n* (also **pop music**) modern music popular esp. among young people, usu. with a strong beat, often played with electronic equipment (guitars, keyboards, etc.). — *adj* **1** performing or featuring pop music. **2** popular: *pop culture*. [**popular**]

pop art *n* a kind of art fashionable in the 1960s, using garish colours and drawing its images from advertising and comic strips.

pop[3] *n* (esp. *NAm coll*) (a form of address for) one's father or an elderly man. [**papa**]

pop. *abbrev* population.

pope *n* **1** (often with *cap*) the bishop of Rome, the head of the Roman Catholic church. **2** a priest in the Eastern Orthodox Church. [Gr *pappas*, papa, in the early church used respectfully to bishops]

popery *n* (*offensive*) Roman Catholicism.

popinjay *n* (*old derog*) someone vain or conceited; a dandy or fop. [OFr *papegai*, parrot]

popish *adj* (*offensive*) Roman Catholic; of Roman Catholicism. [**pope**]

poplar *n* a tall, slender tree of the willow family. [Lat *populus*]

poplin *n* a strong cotton cloth with a finely ribbed finish. [Fr *popeline*, from Ital *papalina*, papal (cloth), because made in the *papal* city of Avignon]

poppadum or **poppadom** *n* a paper-thin pancake grilled till crisp for serving with Indian dishes. [Tamil]

poppet *n* **1** a term of endearment for someone lovable. **2** in vehicle engines, a valve that rises and falls in its housing. [Earlier form of **puppet**]

poppy *n* **-ies** **1** a cornfield plant with large scarlet flowers and a hairy, wiry stem; any of several related plants, e.g. one from which opium is obtained. **2** an artificial red poppy, worn for Poppy Day, symbolising the poppies that grew on the battlefields of Flanders after World War I. [OE *popig*]

Poppy Day *n* (also **Remembrance Sunday**) the Sunday closest to 11 November, the date of the World War I armistice in 1918, when the dead of both world wars are remembered.

poppycock *n* (*coll*) nonsense. [Dut dialect *pappekak*, soft dung]

popsy *n* **-ies** (*old coll derog*) a girlfriend.

populace *n* the body of ordinary citizens; the common people. [Fr, from Ital *popolaccio*, from Lat *populus*, people]

popular *adj* **1** (**with**, **among**) liked or enjoyed by most people: *a pastime still popular with the young*. **2** (of beliefs, etc.) accepted by many people. **3** catering for the tastes and abilities of ordinary people as distinct from specialists, etc.: *a popular history of science*. **4** (of a person; **with**) generally liked and admired. **5** involving the will or preferences of the public in general: *by popular demand*. — *n* **popularity**. — *adv* **popularly**. [Lat *popularis*, from *populus*, people]

popular front *n* a left-wing group or faction, e.g. any of those set up from the 1930s onwards to oppose fascism.

popularise or **-ize** *v* (*tr*) **1** to make popular: *popularise a fashion*. **2** to present in a simple, easily understood way, so as to have general appeal. — *n* **popularisation** or **-z-**.

populate *v* (*tr*) **1** (usu. in *passive*) (of people or animals) to inhabit or live in: *areas populated by Chinese immigrants*. **2** to supply (uninhabited places) with inhabitants. [Lat *populare*, from *populus*, people]

population *n* **1** all the people living in a particular country, area, etc. **2** the number of people living in a particular area, etc.: *a population of 2 million*. **3** people, animals, etc. of a specified class in an area: *the elephant population of Malawi*. **4** the process of populating an area.

populism *n* political activity or notions that (are claimed to) reflect the opinions and interests of ordinary people. — *n* **populist**. [Lat *populus*, people]

populous *adj* thickly populated. [Lat *populosus*, from *populus*, people]

porcelain *n* **1** a fine white translucent earthenware, orig. made in China. **2** objects made of this. [OFr *porcelaine*, from Ital *porcellana*, cowrie shell]

porch *n* **1** a structure forming a covered entrance to the doorway of a building. **2** (*NAm*) a verandah. [OFr *porche*]

porcine *adj* of or like a pig. [Lat *porcus*, pig]

porcupine *n* an animal of the rodent type, covered with long spines interspersed with coarse hair. [OFr *porc d'espine*, literally 'spiny pig']

pore[1] *n* **1** a tiny opening in skin or in a plant surface, through which fluids can pass. **2** any tiny cavity, gap, etc. e.g. in soil or rock. [Lat *porus*, from Gr *poros*, passage, duct]

pore[2] *v* (*intr* with **over**) to study (books, etc.) with intense concentration. [MidE *pouren*]

pork *n* the flesh of a pig used as food. [OFr *porc*, from Lat *porcus*, pig]

porker *n* **1** a young pig. **2** a pig fattened for slaughter.

porky *adj* **-ier**, **-iest** **1** of or like pork. **2** (*coll*) plump.

porn *n* (*coll*) pornography.

porno (*coll*) *n* pornography. — *adj* pornographic.

pornography *n* books, pictures, films, etc. designed to be sexually arousing, often offensive owing to their explicit nature. — *n* **pornographer**. — *adj* **pornographic**. — *adv* **pornographically**. [Gr *pornographos*, writing about prostitutes, from *porne*, prostitute + *graphein*, to write]

porous *adj* **1** having pores or cavities. **2** that liquids can pass through. — *n* **porosity**. [Lat *porosus*, from *porus*, pore]

porphyry *n* **1** a hard purplish-red rock containing small feldspar crystals. **2** any fine-grained igneous rock containing large crystals. — *adj* **porphyritic**. [Gr *porphyrites*, purplish]

porpoise *n* a sea mammal of the whale family, similar to the dolphin, but with a blunt snout. [Lat *porcus*, pig + *piscis*, fish]

porridge *n* **1** a dish of oatmeal boiled in water, or of some other cereal boiled in water or milk. **2** (*slang*) time served by a criminal in prison. [Variation of **pottage**]

porringer *n* a bowl for soup or porridge, with a handle. [MidE *potinger*, variation of *potager*, soup bowl]

port[1] *n* **1** harbour. **2** a town with a harbour. [Lat *portus*]

port of call *n* ***ports of call*** a place called at during a journey.

port[2] *n* the left side of a ship or aircraft.

port[3] *n* **1** an opening in a ship's side for loading, etc. **2** a porthole. **3** (*comput*) a socket on a computer through which electronic information can pass to and from peripheral units. **4** (*old Scot*) a town gate. [Lat *porta*, gate]

port[4] *n* a dark-red or tawny fortified wine of Portugal. [*Oporto*, orig. the place from which it was exported]

port[5] *v* (*tr*; *mil*) to hold (a rifle, etc.) across the body with both hands, the barrel close to the left shoulder. [Fr *porter*, to carry]

portable *adj* **1** (designed to be) easily carried or moved. **2** (*comput*) (of a program) adaptable for use in a variety of systems. — *n* a portable radio, television, typewriter, etc. — *n* **portability**. [**port**[5]]

portage *n* **1** the carrying of ships, equipment, etc. overland from one waterway to another. **2** the route used for this. — *v* (*tr*) to transport (ships, etc.) overland. [Fr, from *porter*, to carry]

portal *n* an entrance, gateway or doorway, esp. an imposing or awesome one. [OFr, from Lat *portale*, from *porta*, gate]

portcullis *n* (*hist*) a vertical iron or wooden grating fitted into a town gateway or castle entrance, lowered to bar intruders. [OFr *porte coleïce*, sliding gate]

portend *v* (*tr*) to warn of; to signify or foreshadow; to be an omen of. [Lat *portendere*]

portent *n* **1** a prophetic sign; an omen. **2** fateful significance: *an event of grim portent*. **3** a marvel or prodigy. [Lat *portentum*]

portentous *adj* **1** ominous or fateful; of or relating to portents. **2** weighty, solemn or pompous.

porter[1] *n* a doorman, caretaker or janitor at college, office or factory. [Lat *portarius*, gatekeeper]

porter[2] *n* **1** a person employed to carry luggage or parcels, e.g. at a railway station. **2** a heavy, dark-brown beer formerly reputed popular with porters. **3** (*NAm*) a sleeping-car attendant. [OFr *porteour*, from Lat *portator*, from *portare*, to carry]

porterhouse *n* (also **porterhouse steak**) a choice cut of beefsteak from the back of the sirloin. [Orig. a public house or chophouse]

portfolio *n* ***-os*** **1** a case for carrying papers, drawings, photographs, etc.; the contents of such a case. **2** the post of a government minister with responsibility for a specific department (*n* **minister without portfolio** a government minister without such responsibility). **3** a list of one's investments. [Ital *portafoglio*, from *portare*, to carry + *foglio*, leaf]

porthole *n* a usu. round opening in a ship's side to admit light and air. [**port**[3] + **hole**]

portico *n* ***-os*** or ***-oes*** (*archit*) a colonnade forming a porch or covered way alongside a building. [Ital, from Lat *porticus*, porch]

portion *n* **1** a piece or part of a whole: *divide into 12 equal portions*. **2** a share; a part allotted to one. **3** an individual helping of food. **4** one's destiny or fate. **5** (*legal*) a woman's dowry. — *v* ***-n-*** (*tr*; **out**) to distribute portion by portion. [Lat *portio*]

portly *adj* ***-ier***, ***-iest*** (esp. of a man) somewhat stout. [Old word *port*, deportment]

portmanteau *n* ***-teaus*** or ***-teaux*** a leather travelling-bag that opens flat in two halves. [Fr *portemanteau*, from *porter*, to carry + *manteau*, coat, cloak]

portmanteau word *n* an invented word composed of parts of two words and conveying the sense of both, e.g. *brunch* (*br*eakfast + l*unch*), *chortle* (*ch*uckle + sn*ort*), or *galumph* (*gal*lop + tri*umph*).

portrait *n* **1** a drawing, painting or photograph of a person, esp. of the face only. **2** a written description, film depiction, etc. of someone or something: *a portrait of country life*. [OFr, past participle of *portraire*, to portray]

portraiture *n* the art of making portraits, or of depiction in writing, film, etc.

portray *v* **1** to make a portrait of. **2** to describe or depict. **3** to act the part of (a character) in a play, film, etc. — *n* **portrayal**. [OFr *portraire*, to portray]

Portuguese *adj* **1** of, or belonging to, Portugal or its inhabitants. **2** of, or belonging to, the Portuguese language. — *n* **1** a native or citizen of Portugal. **2** (*pl*; with **the**) the people of Portugal. **3** the language of Portugal, also spoken in Brazil, Angola and Mozambique.

Portuguese man-of-war *n* a jellyfish with an inflated sail-like crest, whose sting is highly poisonous.

pose *n* **1** a position or attitude of the body: *adopt a relaxed pose*. **2** an artificial way of behaving, adopted for effect: *His punk style is just a pose*. — *v* **1** (*intr* & *tr*) to take up a position oneself, or position (someone else), for a photograph, portrait, etc. **2** (*intr*; *derog*) to behave in an exaggerated or artificial way so as to draw attention to oneself. **3** (*intr* with **as**) to pretend to be. **4** (*tr*) to ask or put forward (a question). **5** (*tr*) to cause (a problem, etc.) or present (a threat, etc.). — **strike a pose** to adopt a position or attitude, esp. a commanding or impressive one. [OFr *poser*, to place, from Lat *pausare*, to cease, pause, but influenced by Lat *ponere*, to place]

poser *n* **1** (*derog*) someone who tries to impress others by putting on an act; a poseur. **2** (*coll*) a difficult problem; a puzzle.

poseur *n* (*derog*) a poser (sense **1**). [Fr]

posh (*coll*) *adj* **1** high-quality, expensive, smart or stylish. **2** upper-class. — *adv* in a posh manner: *talk posh*. — *v* (*tr* with **up**) to smarten. [Perhaps related to *posh*, a dandy]

posit *v* **-*t*-** (*tr*) to lay down, or assume, as a basis for discussion; to postulate. [Lat *ponere*, to place]

position *n* **1** a place where something or someone is: *a fine position overlooking the bay*. **2** the right or proper place: *in* or *out of position*. **3** the relationship of things to one another in space; arrangement. **4** a way of sitting, standing, lying, facing, being held or placed, etc.: *an upright position*. **5** (*mil*) a place occupied for strategic purposes. **6** one's opinion or viewpoint. **7** a job or post: *a senior position at the bank*. **8** rank; status; importance in society: *wealth and position*. **9** the place of a competitor in the finishing order, or at an earlier stage in a contest: *lying in fourth position*. **10** (*games*) one's allotted place on the pitch, as a team member: *the centre-forward position*. **11** the set of circumstances in which one is placed: *not in a position to help*. — *v* **-*n*-** (*tr*) to place; to put in position. — *adj* **positional**. — **be in no position to** (*ironic*) to have no right to (complain, criticise, etc.). [Lat *positio*, from *ponere*, to place]

positive *adj* **1** sure; certain; convinced. **2** definite; allowing no doubt: *positive proof of her guilt*. **3** expressing agreement or approval: *a positive response*. **4** optimistic: *feeling more positive*. **5** forceful or determined; not tentative. **6** constructive; contributing to progress or improvement; helpful. **7** clear and explicit: *positive directions*. **8** (*coll*) downright: *a positive scandal*. **9** (of a chemical test result) confirming the existence of the suspected condition, etc. **10** (*math*) (of quantities) greater than zero. **11** (*physics*, *electr*) charged with electricity because of an absence of electrons; (of one of two terminals) having the higher electrical potential. **12** (*photography*) having light and shade, or colours, as in the actual image, not reversed, etc. **13** (*gram*) expressing quality in the simple form, as distinct from the comparative or superlative forms. — *n* **1** (*photography*) a print in which light, shade and colour correspond to those of the actual image. **2** (*gram*) a positive adjective or adverb; the positive form or degree in comparison. **3** something positive, e.g. (*math*) a quantity, or (*electr*) a terminal. — *adv* **positively**. — *n* **positiveness**. [Lat *positivus*, from *ponere*, to place]

positive discrimination *n* the creation of special employment opportunities, etc. for those previously disadvantaged or discriminated against.

positive vetting *n* investigation of the connections and sympathies of a person being considered for a position of trust, e.g. in the senior civil service.

positivism *n* a school of philosophy maintaining that knowledge can come only from observable phenomena and positive facts; (also **logical positivism**) a 20th-cent. development of this, concerned with the meaningfulness and verifiability of statements. — *n* & *adj* **positivist**.

positron *n* (*physics*) a particle that has the same mass as an electron, and an equal, but opposite, charge. [**positive electron**]

poss *adj* (*coll*) possible. — *abbrev* (usu. **poss.**) **1** possible or possibly. **2** (*gram*) possessive.

posse *n* (*US hist*) a mounted troop of men at the service of a local sheriff. [Lat *posse*, to be able]

possess *v* (*tr*) **1** to own. **2** to have as a feature or quality: *possesses a quick mind*. **3** (of an emotion, evil spirit, etc.) to take hold of (someone): *What possessed you to* *behave like that?* — *n* **possessor**. [OFr *possesser*, from Lat *possessio*, possession]

possessed *adj* **1** (*formal*; with **of**) owning; having: *possessed of great wealth*. **2** controlled or driven by demons, etc.

possession *n* **1** the condition of possessing something; ownership: *take possession of*; *come into one's possession*. **2** the crime of possessing something illegally: *charged with possession of firearms*. **3** occupancy of property: *take possession of the house*. **4** (*football*) control of the ball by one or other team in a match. **5** something owned. **6** (in *pl*) one's property or belongings. **7** (in *pl*) a country's dominions abroad: *foreign possessions*. — **be in possession of** to hold or possess.

possessive *adj* **1** relating to possession. **2** (**about**) unwilling to share, or allow others use of, things one owns: *possessive about my car*. **3** inclined to dominate, monopolise, and allow no independence to, e.g. one's wife, husband, child, etc.: *a possessive husband*. **4** (*gram*) denoting the form of a noun, pronoun or adjective that shows possession, e.g. *Jack's*, *its* or *her*. — *n* (*gram*) **1** the possessive form of a word. **2** a word in the possessive. — *adv* **possessively**. — *n* **possessiveness**.

possible *adj* **1** achievable; able to be done. **2** that may happen: *the possible outcome*. **3** imaginable; conceivable: *a possible explanation*; *It's possible that he's dead*. — *n* a person or thing potentially selectable; a possibility. [Lat *possibilis*, from *posse*, to be able]

possibility *n* **-ies 1** something that is possible. **2** the state of being possible. **3** a candidate for selection, etc. **4** (in *pl*) promise or potential: *an idea with possibilities*.

possibly *adv* **1** perhaps; maybe. **2** within the limits of possibility: *doing all we possibly can*. **3** used for emphasis: *How could you possibly think that?*

possum *n* (*coll*) an opossum. — **play possum** to pretend to be unconscious, dead or unaware of what is happening.

post[1] *n* **1** a shaft or rod fixed upright in the ground, as a support, marker, etc.; (often *in cmpds*) a vertical timber supporting a horizontal one: *a doorpost*. **2** an upright pole marking the beginning or end of a race track. — *v* (*tr*) **1** (**up**) to stick up (a notice, etc.) for public viewing. **2** to announce the name of (someone) among others in a published list: *posted missing*. [Lat *postis*]

post[2] *n* **1** a job: *a teaching post*. **2** a position to which one is assigned for military duty: *never left his post*. **3** a settlement or establishment, esp. in a remote area: *a trading-post*, *military post*, etc. **4** (*mil*) a bugle call (**first** or **last post**) summoning soldiers to their quarters at night, or (**last post**) blown at funerals. — *v* (*tr*) to station (someone) somewhere on duty; to transfer (personnel) to a new location: *posted abroad*. [Ital *posto*, from Lat *positum*, from *ponere*, to place]

post[3] *n* **1** the official system for the delivery of mail. **2** letters and parcels delivered by this system; mail. **3** a collection of mail, e.g. from a postbox: *catch the next post*. **4** a delivery of mail: *came by the second post*. **5** a place for mail collection; a postbox or post office: *took it to the post*. **6** used as a newspaper title: *the Washington Post*. — *v* (*tr*) **1** to put (mail) into a postbox; to send by post. **2** (*book-keeping*) to enter in a ledger, or (with **up**) update (a ledger). **3** to supply with the latest news: *Keep us posted*. [Ital *posta*, from Lat *posita*, from *ponere*, to place]

postage *n* the charge for sending a letter, etc. through the post.

postage stamp *n* (also **stamp**) a small printed label stuck on a letter, etc. showing that the appropriate postage has been paid.

postal *adj* **1** of or relating to the post office or delivery of mail. **2** sent by post: *a postal vote*.

postal order *n* a money order available from, and payable by, a post office.

postbag *n* **1** a mailbag. **2** the letters received by e.g. a radio or television programme, magazine, or celebrated person.

postbox *n* a public box in which to post letters; a letter box.

postcard *n* a card for writing messages on, often with a picture on one side, designed for sending through the post without an envelope.

postcode or **postal code** *n* a code, often a combination of letters and numbers, specific to a particular section of housing, added to addresses to ease the task of sorting mail for delivery. ◇ See also **zip code**.

post-free *adj* **1** with postage prepaid. **2** without charge for postage.

postman or **postwoman** *n* a man or woman whose job is to deliver mail.

postmark *n* a mark stamped on mail by the post office, cancelling the stamp and showing the date and place of posting.

postmaster or **postmistress** *n* a man or woman in charge of a local post office.

Postmaster General *n* ***-masters General*** a Government minister in charge of the country's postal services.

post office *n* **1** a local office handling postal business, issuing various types of licence, etc. **2** (*caps*) the government department in charge of postal services.

post-paid *adj* with postage prepaid.

post- *comb fm* after: *postwar*. [Lat *post*, after, behind]

post chaise *n* (*hist*) a fast usu. four-wheeled coach carrying up to four passengers, and mail, drawn by posthorses. [**post**[3]]

postdate *v* (*tr*) **1** to put a future date on (a cheque, etc.). **2** to assign a later date than that previously accepted to (an event, etc.). **3** to occur at a later date than. [**post-**]

poster *n* **1** a large notice or advertisement for public display. **2** a large printed picture. [**post**[1]]
poster paint or **colour** *n* a water-based paint in a bright, opaque colour.
poste restante *n, adv* (a department of a post office, care of which mail may be) sent to an addressee temporarily without a permanent address, and kept till collected. [Fr, post remaining]
posterior *n* (*facet*) one's buttocks. — *adj* (esp. *anat* or *archit*) placed behind or after. [Lat, comparative of *posterus*, coming after]
posterity *n* **1** future generations. **2** one's descendants. [Lat *posteritas*, from *posterus*, coming after]
postern *n* (*hist*) a back door, back gate, or private entrance. [OFr *posterne*]
postgraduate *n* a person studying for an advanced degree or qualification after obtaining a first degree. — *adj* of or pertaining to such a person or degree. [**post-**]
posthaste *adv* with all speed. [*post*, a courier + **haste**]
posthouse *n* (*hist*) an inn where **post-horses** were kept for conveying the mail and for the use of travellers wishing to change horses, etc. [**post**[3]]
posthumous *adj* **1** published after the death of the author, composer, etc. **2** (of a child) born after its father's death. **3** awarded or coming after death: *posthumous decoration* or *acclaim*. — *adv* **posthumously**. [Lat *postumus*, superlative of *posterus*, coming after; *h* inserted by mistaken association with *humus*, earth, i.e. burial]
postilion or **postillion** *n* (*hist*) a rider on the nearside horse of one of the pairs of posthorses drawing a carriage, who, in the absence of a coachman, guides the team. [Ital *postiglione*, from *posta*, post, i.e. **post**[3]]
post-Impressionism *n* a loosely applied term embracing the work of late 19th-cent. French painters such as Cézanne, Gauguin, Matisse and Van Gogh.
post meridiem after noon. — *adj* **post-meridian**. [Lat]
post-mortem *n* **1** a medical examination of a dead person to establish the cause of death. **2** (*facet*) an after-the-event discussion. [Lat, after death]
post-natal *adj* belonging to, or occurring in, the period immediately after birth, or after giving birth: *post-natal depression*. [**post-**]
post-operative *adj* belonging to, or occurring in, the period immediately following a surgical operation: *post-operative discomfort*. [**post-**]
postpone *v* (*tr*) to defer or put off till later. — *n* **postponement**. [Lat *postponere*, to place after]
postprandial *adj* (esp. *facet*) following a meal: *a postprandial doze*. [**post-** + Lat *prandium*, breakfast, lunch]
postscript *n* **1** a message added to a letter as an afterthought, after one's signature. **2** anything serving as an addition or follow-up to something. [Lat *postscribere*, to write after]
postulant *n* a candidate for holy orders or for admission to a religious community. — *n* **postulancy**. [Lat *postulare*, to ask]
postulate *v* (*tr*) to assume or suggest as the basis for discussion; to take for granted. — *n* something postulated. — *n* **postulation**. [Lat *postulare*, to demand]
posture *n* **1** the way one holds one's body in standing, sitting or walking. **2** a particular position or attitude of the body. **3** an attitude adopted towards a particular issue, etc. **4** a pose adopted for effect. — *v* (*intr*; *derog*) to pose, strike attitudes, etc. so as to draw attention to oneself. — *adj* **postural**. — *n* **posturer**. [Lat *positura*, from *ponere*, to place]
postviral syndrome *n* a condition following viral infection, characterised by fatigue, poor concentration, depression and dizziness. [**post-**]
postwar *adj* of, or belonging to, the period following a war. [**post-**]
posy *n* **-ies** a small bunch of flowers. [A variant of *poesy*]
pot[1] *n* **1** any of various usu. deep and round domestic containers used as cooking or serving utensils or for storage. **2** the amount held by such a container: *a pot of tea*. **3** (*pottery*) any handmade vessel. **4** the pool of accumulated bets in any gambling game. **5** (*billiards*, etc.) a shot that pockets a ball. **6** a casual shot: *take a pot at something*. **7** a chamberpot. **8** a flowerpot or plant pot. **9** (in *pl*; *coll*) lots (of money). **10** (*coll*) a trophy, esp. a cup. **11** a pot-belly. — *v* **-tt-** **1** (*tr*) to plant in a plant pot. **2** (*tr*) to preserve (a type of food) in a pot. **3** (*tr*) to summarise, esp. in a popular style: *a potted history*. **4** (*tr*; *billiards*) to shoot (a ball) into a pocket. **5** (*tr*; *coll*) to shoot or (*intr* with **at**) shoot at (animals, etc.). — **go to pot** (*coll*) to degenerate badly. — **keep the pot boiling** (*coll*) to sustain public interest in something. [OE *pott*]
pot-belly *n* **-ies** (*coll derog*) a large overhanging belly. — *adj* **pot-bellied**.
potboiler *n* (*derog*) an inferior work of literature or art produced by a writer or artist capable of better work, simply to make money and stay in the public view.
potbound *adj* (of a plant) with its roots cramped by too small a pot.
potherb *n* a plant whose leaves or stems are used in cooking to season or garnish food.
pothole see separate entry.
pothook *n* **1** a hook on which to hang a pot over a fire. **2** a hooked stroke in handwriting.
pot luck *n* whatever is available.
pot roast *n* a cut of meat braised with a little water in a covered pot.
potsherd *n* a fragment of pottery.

pot-shot *n* **1** an easy shot at close range. **2** a shot made without taking careful aim.
potter *n* a person who makes pottery.
potter's wheel *n* an apparatus with a heavy rotating stone platter, on which clay pots can be shaped by hand before firing.
pottery *n* **1** vessels or other objects of baked clay. **2** the art of making such objects. **3** a factory where such objects are produced commercially.
potting-shed *n* a shed in which to keep garden tools, put plants into pots, etc.

pot[2] *n* (*coll*) marijuana. [Mexican Span *potiguaya*]

potable *adj* fit for drinking; drinkable. [Lat *potabilis*]

potash *n* any of various compounds of potassium, esp. the fertiliser potassium carbonate or (also **caustic potash**) potassium hydroxide. [**pot**[1] + **ash**]

potassium *n* an element (symbol **K**), a soft silvery-white alkali metal. [**potash**]

potation *n* (usu. *facet*) **1** the act of drinking. **2** an esp. alcoholic drink. [Lat *potatio*]

potato *n* **-oes** a starchy tuber widely used as a vegetable; the plant it belongs to, of the nightshade family. [Span *batata*, from a S American language]
potato crisp *n* a crisp.

poteen *n* (*Irish*) illicitly distilled Irish whiskey. [Irish *poitin*]

potent *adj* **1** strong; effective; powerful. **2** (of an argument, etc.) persuasive; convincing. **3** (of a drug or poison) powerful and swift in effect. **4** (of a male) capable of sexual intercourse. — *n* **potency, -ies**. [Lat *potens*, present participle of *posse*, to be able]

potentate *n* (*literary*) a powerful ruler; a monarch. [Lat *potentatus*, from *potens*, powerful]

potential *adj* possible or likely, though as yet not tested or actual. — *n* **1** the range of capabilities that a person or thing has; powers or resources not yet developed or made use of: *fulfil one's potential*. **2** (*physics*) (of a point in a field of force) the energy required to bring a unit of mass, electricity, etc. from infinity to that point. — *adv* **potentially**. [Lat *potentialis*, from *potentia*, power]
potential difference *n* a difference in the electrical states existing at two points, which causes a current to tend to flow between them.

pothole *n* **1** a rounded hole worn in the rock bed of a fast-flowing stream by swirling pebbles, etc. **2** a cave or deep hole eroded in limestone. **3** a hole worn in a road surface. [**pot**[1]]
potholing *n* the sport of exploring potholes (sense **2**). — *n* **potholer**.

potion *n* a draught of medicine, poison or some magic elixir. [Lat *potio*, from *potare*, to drink]

potpourri *n* **1** a fragrant mixture of dried flowers, leaves, etc. placed in containers and used to scent rooms. **2** a medley or mixture: *a potpourri of old tunes*. [Fr, literally 'rotten pot']

potter[1]. See **pot**[1].

potter[2] *v* **-r-** (*intr*) **1** (**about**) to busy oneself in a mild way with trifling tasks. **2** (**along, about**) to progress in an unhurried manner; to dawdle. [OE *potian*, to thrust]

potty[1] *adj* **-ier, -iest** (*coll*) **1** mad; crazy. **2** (with **about**) madly keen on (someone or something). — *n* **pottiness**.

potty[2] *n* **-ies** (*coll* or *childish*) a child's (usu. plastic) chamberpot. [Dimin. of **pot**[1]]

pouch *n* **1** (esp. *old*) a purse or small bag. **2** in marsupials such as thc kangaroo, a pocket of skin on the belly, in which the young are carried till weaned. **3** a fleshy fold in the cheek of hamsters and other rodents, for storing undigested food. **4** a puffy bulge under the eyes. [OFr *poche*, pocket]

pouffe *n* a firmly stuffed drum-shaped or cube-shaped cushion for use as a low seat. [Fr]

poulterer *n* a dealer in poultry and game. [*poult*, a chicken]

poultice *n* a hot, semi-liquid mixture spread on a bandage and applied to the skin to reduce inflammation, formerly used as a treatment for boils. [Lat *pultes*, plural of *puls*, porridge]

poultry *n* **1** farmyard fowl such as hens, ducks or geese. **2** the meat of such fowl. [*poult*, chicken, from OFr *poulet*, chicken]

pounce *v* **1** (*intr*; **on**) to leap (on one's victim or prey). **2** (*intr* with **on**) to seize upon; to grab eagerly. — *n* an act of pouncing.

pound[1] *n* **1** (also **pound sterling**; *symbol* **£**) the currency unit of the United Kingdom, divided into 100 pence. **2** the standard unit of currency in several other countries, e.g. Malta, Cyprus, Egypt and Ireland. **3** (*abbrev* **lb**) a measure of weight equal to 16 ounces (453 grams) avoirdupois, or 12 ounces (373 grams) troy. [OE *pund*]
poundage *n* a fee or commission charged per pound in weight or money.
-pounder *in cmpds* **1** something weighing a certain number of pounds: *The trout was a three-pounder*. **2** a field gun designed to fire shot weighing a certain number of pounds: *a twenty-four-pounder*.
pound of flesh *n* the strict exacting of one's due in the fulfilment of a bargain, to the extent of causing unreasonable suffering to the other party.

pound[2] *n* an enclosure where stray animals or illegally parked cars that have been taken into police charge are kept for collection. [OE *pund-*, enclosure]

pound[3] *v* **1** (*tr* & *intr*; **at, on**) to beat or bang vigorously. **2** (*tr* with **out**) to produce by pounding: *pounding out articles on her typewriter*. **3** (*intr*) to walk or run with heavy thudding steps. **4** (*tr*) to crush or grind to a powder. [OE *punian*]

pour *v* **1** (*tr* & *intr*) to (cause to) flow in a downward stream. **2** (*intr* & *tr*) (of a jug, etc.) to discharge (liquid) in a certain way: *doesn't pour very well.* **3** (*intr* & *tr*; **out**) to serve (wine, etc.) by pouring. **4** (*intr*) to rain heavily. **5** (*intr*; **in**, **out**, etc.) to come or go in large numbers: *people pouring out of the cinema.* **6** (*intr*; **in**, **out**, etc.) to flow or issue plentifully: *Donations poured in. Words poured from her pen.* **7** (*tr* with **out**) to reveal uninhibitedly: *pour out one's feelings.* **8** (*tr* with **into**) to invest (money, energy, etc.) liberally in something. **9** (*tr* with **on**) to heap (scorn or contempt) on something. — *n* **pourer**.

pouring *adv* (of rain) heavily, *pouring wet.*

pourboire *n* a tip or gratuity. [Fr]

pout *v* (*intr* & *tr*) to stick out (the lower lip or both lips) as an indication of sulkiness or seductiveness; (of the lips) to stick out in this way. — *n* an act of pouting or a pouting expression.

pouter *n* a variety of pigeon that can puff out its crop.

poverty *n* **1** the condition of being poor; want. **2** poor quality: *poverty of the soil.* **3** inadequacy; deficiency: *poverty of imagination.* [OFr *poverte*]

poverty line *n* the minimum income needed to purchase the basic needs of life.

poverty-stricken *adj* suffering from poverty.

poverty trap *n* the inescapable poverty of someone who, in achieving an improvement in income, has his or her state benefits cut.

POW *abbrev* prisoner of war.

powder *n* **1** any substance in the form of fine dust-like particles. **2** (also **face powder**) a cosmetic patted on to the skin to give it a soft, smooth appearance. **3** gunpowder. **4** a dose of medicine in powder form. — *v* **-r-** (*tr*) **1** to apply powder to; to sprinkle or cover with powder. **2** to reduce to a powder by crushing; to pulverise. — *adj* **powdery**. [OFr *poudre*]

powder puff *n* a pad of velvety or fluffy material for patting powder on to the skin.

powder room *n* a women's toilet in a restaurant, hotel, etc.

power *n* **1** control and influence exercised over others. **2** strength, vigour, force or effectiveness. **3** military strength: *sea power.* **4** the physical ability, skill, opportunity, or authority, to do something: *if it is within my power.* **5** an individual faculty or skill: *the power of speech; at the height of one's powers* (= at the time of one's life or career when one's skill is greatest). **6** a right, privilege, prerogative or responsibility: *the power of arrest; power of attorney.* **7** political control: *be in, come into,* or *take, power.* **8** a state that has an influential role in international affairs. **9** a person or group exercising control or influence: *the real power behind the prime minister.* **10** (*coll*) a great deal: *did her a power of good.* **11** any of the forms of energy; any of these as the driving force of a machine, etc.: *nuclear power; turn off the power.* **12** (*electr*) the rate, measured in watts, at which a system absorbs energy from, or passes energy into, another system. **13** (*math*) the value of a quantity when multiplied by itself a specified number of times: *12^4, or 12 to the power of 4 = $12 \times 12 \times 12 \times 12$.* **14** (*physics, mechanics*) the rate of doing mechanical work measured as a unit of work done per unit of time. **15** mechanical or electrical energy, as distinct from manual effort: *power-assisted steering.* **16** (*optics*) the magnifying strength of a lens. — *adj* using mechanical or electrical power; motor-driven: *power tools.* — *v* **-r-** (*tr*) to supply with power: *nuclear-powered warships.* [OFr *poer*, orig. an infinitive, related to Lat *posse*, to be able]

power cut *n* a break in the electricity supply.

powerful *adj* having great power, strength, vigour, authority, influence, force or effectiveness. — *adv* **powerfully**. — *n* **powerfulness**.

powerhouse *n* **1** a power station. **2** (*coll*) a forceful or vigorous person.

powerless *adj* deprived of power or authority. — *n* **powerlessness**.

power pack *n* a device for adjusting an electric current to the voltages required by a piece of electronic equipment.

power plant *n* **1** a power station. **2** the engine and parts making up the unit that supplies the propelling power in a vehicle.

power point *n* a socket for connecting an electrical device to the mains.

power station *n* an electricity generating station.

the powers that be *n* (*pl; facet*) the people in authority.

powwow *n* **1** (*coll*) a meeting for discussion. **2** (*hist*) a meeting of N American Indians. — *v* (*intr*) to hold a powwow. [Narragansett (N American Indian language) *powwaw*, priest]

pox *n* **1** (esp. *in cmpds*) a virus disease characterised by pocks or pustules: *smallpox; chickenpox.* **2** (*old coll*) syphilis. [Variant of **pocks**]

pp *abbrev* **1** *per procurationem* (Lat), by the agency of. **2** pages. **3** (*mus*) pianissimo.

ppm *abbrev* parts per million.

PPS *abbrev* **1** Parliamentary Private Secretary. **2** *post postscriptum* (Lat), after the postscript, i.e. an additional postscript.

PR *abbrev* **1** public relations. **2** proportional representation.

Pr *symbol* (*chem*) praseodymium.

practicable *adj* **1** capable of being done, used or successfully carried out; feasible. **2** (of e.g. a road) usable. — *n* **practicability**. — *adv* **practicably**. [Lat *practicare*, to practise; see ety. for **practise**]

practical *adj* **1** concerned with action with some purpose or result in contrast to theory: *put one's knowledge to practical use.*

2 (capable of being) effective in actual use: *practical ideas*; *a practical knowledge of German*. **3** (of e.g. clothes) designed for tough or everyday use; sensibly plain. **4** (of a person) sensible and efficient in deciding and acting; good at doing manual jobs. **5** in effect; virtual: *a practical walkover*. — *n* a practical lesson or examination, e.g. in a scientific subject. — *n* **practicality, -*ies***. [Old word *practic*, practical, from Gr *praktikos*]

practical joke *n* a trick played on someone, as distinct from a joke told.

practically *adv* **1** almost. **2** in a practical manner.

practice *n* **1** the process of carrying something out: *easier in theory than in practice*; *put one's ideas into practice*. **2** a habit, activity, procedure or custom: *Don't make a practice of it*. **3** repeated exercise to improve one's technique in an art, sport, etc. **4** a doctor's or lawyer's business or clientele. — **be in** (or **out of**) **practice** to have maintained (or failed to maintain) one's skill in an art, sport, etc. [**practise**]

practise *v* **1** (*tr* & *intr*) to do exercises repeatedly in (an art, sport, etc.) so as to improve one's performance. **2** (*tr*) to make a habit of: *practise self-control*. **3** (*tr*) to go in for as a custom: *tribes that practise bigamy*. **4** (*tr*) to work at, or follow (an art or profession, esp. medicine or law). **5** (*tr*; **on**) to execute (a wrongful act) against someone: *had practised a cruel deception on them*. [Lat *practicare*, from Gr *praktikos*, practical]

practised *adj* skilled; experienced; expert.

practitioner *n* someone practising an art or profession, esp. medicine. [Altered from earlier *practician*]

pragmatic *adj* concerned with what is practicable, expedient and convenient, rather than with theories and ideals; matter-of-fact; realistic. [Gr *pragma*, deed]

pragmatism *n* **1** a practical, matter-of-fact approach to dealing with problems, etc. **2** (*philos*) a school of thought that assesses concepts' truth in terms of their practical implications. — *n* **pragmatist**.

prairie *n* in N America, a treeless, grass-covered plain. [Fr, meadow]

prairie dog *n* a N American rodent similar to a marmot, that lives in labyrinthine burrows and barks like a dog.

praise *v* (*tr*) **1** to express admiration or approval of. **2** to worship or glorify (God) with hymns, thanksgiving, etc. — *n* **1** the expression of admiration or approval; commendation. **2** worship of God. — **sing the praises of** to commend enthusiastically. [OFr *preisier*, from Lat *pretiare*, to value]

praiseworthy *adj* deserving praise; commendable. — *adv* **praiseworthily**. — *n* **praiseworthiness**.

praline *n* a sweet consisting of nuts in caramelised sugar. [Marshal du Plessis *Praslin* (1598–1675), French soldier whose cook invented it]

pram *n* a wheeled carriage for a baby, pushed by someone on foot. [Shortened from **perambulator**]

prance *v* (*intr*) **1** (esp. of a horse) to walk with lively springing steps. **2** to frisk or skip about. **3** to parade about in a swaggering manner. [MidE *praunce*]

prang (*coll*) *v* (*tr*) to crash (a vehicle). — *n* a vehicle crash. [Imit.]

prank *n* a trick; a practical joke. — *n* **prankster**.

praseodymium *n* (*chem*) a metallic element (symbol **Pr**) that has green salts. [Gr *prasios*, leek-green]

prat (*slang*) **1** (*offensive*) someone stupid. **2** the buttocks.

prate *v* (*intr* & *tr*) to talk or utter foolishly. [ODut *praeten*]

prattle *v* (*intr* & *tr*) to chatter or utter childishly or foolishly. — *n* childish or foolish chatter. — *n* **prattler**. [OGer *pratelen*, to chatter]

prawn *n* an edible shellfish like a large shrimp. [MidE *prane*]

pray *v* **1** (*intr*) to address one's god, making earnest requests or giving thanks. **2** (*tr*; esp. *old*) to entreat or implore. **3** (*tr*) to hope desperately. — *interj* meaning 'please', or 'may I ask', uttered with quaint politeness or cold irony: *Pray come in. Who asked you, pray?* [OFr *preier*, from Lat *precari*, to pray]

prayer *n* **1** an address to one's god, making a request or giving thanks: *say one's prayers*. **2** the activity of praying. **3** an earnest hope, desire or entreaty.

prayer book *n* a book of set prayers appropriate for various occasions and types of church service.

prayer rug or **mat** *n* a small carpet on which a Muslim kneels when praying.

prayer wheel *n* (*Buddhism*) a drum that turns on a spindle, inscribed with prayers that are regarded as uttered as the drum is rotated.

praying mantis *n* a mantis.

pre- *pfx* before in **1** time (e.g. *pre-war*), **2** position (e.g. *premolar*) or **3** importance (e.g. *pre-eminent*). [Lat *prae-*]

preach *v* **1** (*intr* & *tr*) to deliver (a sermon) as part of a religious service. **2** (*intr*; **at**) to give advice in a tedious or obtrusive manner. **3** (*tr*) to advise; to advocate: *preach caution*. [Lat *praedicare*, to give advice, command]

preamble *n* an introduction or preface, e.g. to a speech or document; an opening statement. [Lat *praeambulare*, to walk before]

prearrange *v* (*tr*) to arrange in advance: *a prearranged signal*. — *n* **prearrangement**. [**pre-** (sense **1**)]

prebend *n* an allowance paid out of the revenues of a cathedral or collegiate church to its canons or chapter members. — *adj* **prebendal**. [Lat *praebenda*, allowance]

prebendary *n* **-*ies*** a clergyman in receipt of a prebend.

Precambrian *adj & n* (denoting) the earliest geological era, lasting from 4600 million to 590 million years ago, during which the earth's crust and oceans formed, and early forms of marine life appeared. [**pre-** (sense **1**)]

precancerous *adj* denoting a condition that could become cancerous if untreated. [**pre-** (sense **1**)]

precarious *adj* **1** unsafe; insecure; dangerous. **2** uncertain; chancy. — *adv* **precariously**. — *n* **precariousness**. [Lat *precarius*, obtained by prayer, uncertain, from *prex*, prayer]

precast *adj* (of concrete, etc.) made into blocks, etc. ready for use in building. [**pre-** (sense **1**)]

precaution *n* a measure taken to ensure a satisfactory outcome, or to avoid a risk or danger. — *adj* **precautionary**. [Lat *praecautio*]

precede *v* (*tr & intr*) **1** to go or be before, in time, order, position, rank or importance. **2** (*tr* with **with**) to preface or introduce: *preceded her lecture with a word of explanation*. [Lat *praecedere*, to go before]

precedence *n* **1** priority: *Safety takes precedence over all else*. **2** the fact of preceding, in order, rank, importance, etc.; the right to precede others: *were introduced in order of precedence*.

precedent *n* a previous incident, legal case, etc. that is parallel to one under consideration; the measures taken or judgement given in that case, serving as a basis for a decision in the present one.

precentor *n* a person who leads the singing of a church congregation, or leads the prayers in a synagogue. [Lat *praecentor*, from *prae-*, before + *canere*, to sing]

precept *n* a rule or principle, esp. of a moral kind, that guides one's behaviour. [Lat *praeceptum*]

precession *n* **1** (*astronomy*) (also **precession of the equinoxes**) the progressively earlier occurrence of the equinoxes, resulting from the slight daily change in the earth's angle of spin, comparable to the cone-shaped wobble of a spinning top. **2** the act of preceding. — *adj* **precessional**. [Lat *praecessio*, from *praecedere*, to precede]

precinct *n* **1** (also in *pl*) the enclosed grounds of a large building, etc.: *the cathedral precinct*; *within the university precincts*. **2** (in *pl*) the neighbourhood or environs of a place. **3** a traffic-free zone in a town, etc.: *a pedestrian precinct*. **4** (*US*) any of the districts into which a city is divided for administrative or policing purposes. [Lat *praecinctum*, from *praecingere*, to surround]

preciosity *n* affectedness or exaggerated refinement in speech or manner. [Lat *pretiositas*, from *pretiosus*, valuable]

precious *adj* **1** valuable. **2** (**to**) dear; beloved; treasured: *memories still precious to her*. **3** (*derog*) (of speech or manner) affected or over-precise. **4** (*ironic*) confounded: *Him and his precious brats!* — *adv* **preciously**. — *n* **preciousness**. — **precious few** or **little** almost none. [Lat *pretiosus*, valuable]

precious metal *n* gold, silver or platinum.

precious stone *n* a mineral valued for its beauty and rarity; a gem.

precipice *n* a sheer cliff. [Lat *praecipitium*, from *praecipitare*, to fall headlong]

precipitate *v* (*tr*) **1** to cause, or hasten the advent of: *precipitate a war*. **2** to throw or plunge: *precipitated himself into the controversy*. — *adj* (of actions or decisions) recklessly hasty or ill-considered. — *n* **1** (*chem*) a substance that separates from a solution or suspension, usu. sinking to the bottom. **2** moisture deposited as rain, snow, etc. — *adv* **precipitately**. [Lat *praecipitare*, to fall or throw headlong]

precipitation *n* **1** rash haste. **2** moisture deposited on the earth's surface as rain, snow, etc.; the amount of this. **3** the act of precipitating or process of being precipitated. **4** (*chem*) the formation of a precipitate.

precipitous *adj* **1** dangerously steep. **2** (of actions or decisions) precipitate. [Fr *précipiteux*]

précis *n* **-*cis*** a summary of a piece of writing. — *v* **-*cising***, **-*cised*** (*tr*) to make a précis of. [Fr, cut short]

precise *adj* **1** exact; very: *at this precise moment*. **2** clear; detailed: *precise instructions*. **3** accurate: *precise timing*. **4** (of a person) careful over details. — *n* **preciseness**. [Lat *praecisus*, shortened]

precisely *adv* **1** exactly. **2** in a precise manner. **3** (as a rejoinder) you're quite right.

precision *n* accuracy. — *adj* (of tools, etc.) designed to operate with minute accuracy.

preclude *v* (*tr*) **1** to rule out, eliminate or make impossible. **2** (**from**) to prevent: *precluded from attending the meeting*. — *n* **preclusion**. [Lat *praecludere*, to impede]

precocious *adj* **1** (of e.g. a child) unusually advanced in mental development, speech, behaviour, etc. **2** (of behaviour, achievements, etc.) indicating such advanced development. — *adv* **precociously**. — *n* **precocity**. [Lat *praecox*, ripening early, precocious]

precognition *n* the supposed ability to foresee events; foreknowledge. — *adj* **precognitive**. [Lat *praecognitio*]

preconceive *v* (*tr*; usu. in *past participle*) to form (an idea) of something before actually experiencing it. [**pre-** (sense **1**)]

preconception *n* an assumption about something not yet experienced; a preconceived idea. [**pre-** (sense **1**)]

precondition *n* a condition to be satisfied in advance. [**pre-** (sense **1**)]

precursor *n* something that precedes, and is a sign of, an approaching event. [Lat *praecursor*, forerunner, advance guard]

predacious *adj* predatory. [Altered from **predatory**]

pre-date *v* (*tr*) **1** to write a bygone date on (a document, etc.). **2** to occur at an earlier date than. [**pre-** (sense **1**)]

predator *n* **1** a bird or animal that kills and feeds on others. **2** (*derog*) a predatory person. [Lat *praedator*, plunderer, hunter]

predatory *adj* **1** (of creatures) killing and feeding on others. **2** (*derog*) (of people) cruelly exploiting the weakness or good will of others for personal gain. — *n* **predatoriness**.

predecease *v* (*tr*) to die before (someone). [**pre-** (sense **1**)]

predecessor *n* **1** the person who preceded one in one's job or position. **2** the previous version, model, etc. of a particular thing or product. **3** an ancestor. [Lat *praedecessor*, from *prae-*, before + *decedere*, to withdraw, give place]

predestine *v* (*tr*; usu. in *passive*) to destine or doom: *predestined to meet*. **2** to ordain or decree by fate: *happened as if predestined*. [Lat *praedestinare*, to determine in advance]

predestination *n* **1** the act of predestining or fact of being predestined. **2** (*relig*) the doctrine that whatever is to happen has been unalterably fixed by God from the beginning of time, esp. with regard to which souls are to be saved and which damned.

predetermine *v* (*tr*) **1** to decide, settle or fix in advance. **2** to influence, shape or cause to tend a certain way. — *n* **predetermination**. [**pre-** (sense **1**)]

predicament *n* a difficulty that one finds oneself in; a plight or dilemma. [Lat *praedicamentum*, something asserted]

predicate *n* **1** (*gram*) the word or words in a sentence or clause that say something about, but are not part of, its subject, as *knew what to do* in *The men knew what to do*. **2** (*logic*) what is stated as a property of the subject of a proposition. — *v* (*tr*) **1** to assert. **2** to imply; to entail the existence of. **3** (*logic*) to state as a property of the subject of a proposition. **4** (usu. in *passive*; **on**) to make the viability of (an idea, etc.) depend on something else being true. — *n* **predication**. [Lat *praedicare*, to assert]

predicative *adj* **1** (*gram*) (of an adjective) forming, esp. regularly, part of a predicate, as *asleep* in *She's asleep*. ◇ See also **attributive**. **2** relating to predicates. — *adv* **predicatively**.

predict *v* (*tr*) to prophesy, foretell or forecast. [Lat *praedicare*, to foretell]

predictable *adj* **1** able to be predicted; easily foreseen. **2** (*derog*) boringly consistent in one's behaviour or reactions, etc.; unoriginal. — *n* **predictability**. — *adv* **predictably**.

prediction *n* **1** the act or art of predicting. **2** something foretold.

predilection *n* (often *facet*; **for**) a special liking or preference (for something). [Lat *praediligere*, to prefer]

predispose *v* (*tr*) **1** to incline (someone) to react in a particular way: *Clear handwriting will predispose the examiners in your favour*. **2** to make susceptible to (esp. illness). — *n* **predisposition**. [**pre-** (sense **1**)]

predominate *v* (*intr*; **over**) **1** to be more numerous: *Girls predominate over boys in this class*. **2** to be more noticeable or prominent. **3** to have more influence: *The 'green' lobby is beginning to predominate*. [Lat *prae-*, above others + *dominari*, to have mastery]

predominant *adj* more numerous, prominent or powerful. — *n* **predominance**. — *adv* **predominantly**.

pre-eminent *adj* outstanding; excelling all others. — *n* **pre-eminence**. — *adv* **pre-eminently**. [Lat *praeeminere*, to be prominent]

pre-emption. *n* **1** the buying of, or right to buy, property, before others get the chance. **2** the act of pre-empting. [Lat *praeemere*, to buy before]

pre-empt *v* (*tr*) **1** to forestall and so make pointless (an action planned by someone else). **2** to obtain in advance for oneself.

pre-emptive *adj* **1** having the effect of pre-empting. **2** (*mil*) (of an attack or strike) effectively destroying the enemy's weapons before they can be used.

preen *v* **1** (*tr* & *intr*) (of a bird) to clean and smooth (its feathers) with its beak. **2** (*tr*) to groom (oneself), esp. in a vain manner. **3** (*tr* with **on**) to pride or congratulate (oneself) on. [MidE *prene*]

prefab *n* a prefabricated building, esp. a dwelling.

prefabricate *v* (*tr*) to manufacture standard sections of (a building) for later quick assembly. — *n* **prefabrication**. [**pre-** (sense **1**)]

preface *n* (**to**) **1** an explanatory statement at the beginning of a book. **2** anything of an introductory or preliminary character. — *v* (*tr*; **with**) **1** to provide (a book, etc.) with a preface. **2** to introduce or precede with some preliminary matter: *prefaced her speech by welcoming the guests*. — *adj* **prefatory**. [Lat *praefatio*, from *praefari*, to say beforehand]

prefect *n* **1** a senior pupil with minor disciplinary powers in a school. **2** in some countries, the senior official of an administrative district. [Lat *praefectus*, an official in charge, overseer, director, etc.]

prefecture *n* the (period of) office of, or the district presided over by, a prefect.

prefer *v* *-rr-* (*tr*) **1** (**to**) to like better: *prefer tea to coffee*. **2** (*legal*) to submit (a charge, accusation, etc.) to a court of law for consideration. **3** to promote (a person) over his or her colleagues. [Lat *praeferre*, to place before, esp. in esteem]

preferable *adj* more desirable, suitable or advisable; better. — *adv* **preferably**. [Fr *préférable*]

preference *n* **1** the preferring of one thing, etc. to another: *chose pink in preference to purple*. **2** (**for**) one's choice of, or liking for, someone or something particular: *have no special preferences*. **3** favourable consideration: *give preference to experienced applicants*.

preference shares *n* (*pl*) shares on which the dividend must be paid before that on ordinary shares.

preferential *adj* bestowing special favours or advantages: *preferential treatment*.

preferment *n* promotion to a more responsible position.

prefigure *v* (*tr*) to be an advance sign or representation of something that is to come; to foreshadow. — *n* **prefiguration**. [Lat *praefigurare*]

prefix *n* **1** (*gram*) an element such as *un-*, *re-*, *non-*, *de-* added to the beginning of a word to create a new word. **2** a title such as *Mr*, *Dr*, *Ms*, used before a person's name. — *v* (*tr*) **1** (**to**) to add at the beginning. **2** (**to**) to attach as a prefix. **3** (**with**, **by**) to add a prefix to.

pregnant *adj* **1** carrying an unborn child or young in the womb. **2** (of a remark, pause, silence, etc.) loaded with a significance only too obvious to those present. — *n* **pregnancy**, **-*ies***. [Lat *praegnans*]

prehensile *adj* (of e.g. a tail) capable of grasping. [Lat *prehendere*, to grasp]

prehistoric *adj* belonging or relating to the time before there were written historical records. — *adv* **prehistorically**. — *n* **prehistory**. [**pre-** (sense **1**)]

prejudge *v* (*tr*) **1** to form an opinion on (an issue, etc.) without having all the relevant facts. **2** to condemn (someone) unheard. — *n* **prejudgement**. [**pre-** (sense **1**)]

prejudice *n* **1** a biased opinion, based on insufficient knowledge. **2** (**against**) unthinking hostility, e.g. towards a particular racial or religious group. **3** (*legal*, etc.; **to**) harm; detriment: *without prejudice to your parental rights*. — *v* (*tr*) **1** (esp. in *passive*) to cause (someone) to feel prejudice; to bias: *prejudiced against*, or *in favour of, something*. **2** to harm or endanger: *Bad handwriting prejudices your chances of passing*. [Lat *praejudicium*, harm]

prejudicial *adj* **1** (**to**) harmful. **2** causing prejudice.

prelate *n* a bishop, abbot or other high-ranking ecclesiastic. [Lat *praelatus*, from *praeferre*, to prefer]

prelacy *n* **-*ies*** **1** the office of a prelate. **2** the entire body of prelates. **3** administration of the church by prelates.

preliminary *adj* occurring at the beginning; introductory or preparatory. — *n* **-*ies*** (esp. in *pl*) **1** something done or said by way of introduction or preparation. **2** a preliminary round in a competition. [Lat *prae-*, before + *limen*, threshold]

prelims *n* (*pl*; *coll*) **1** a set of preliminary examinations; the first public examinations in certain universities. **2** (*printing*) the title page, contents page and other matter preceding the main text of a book.

prelude *n* **1** (*mus*) an introductory passage or first movement, e.g. of a fugue or suite. **2** a name sometimes given to a short musical piece, a poetical composition, etc. **3** (**to**) some event that precedes, and prepares the ground for, one of greater significance: *talks that are being seen as a prelude to peace*. [Lat *praeludium*, from *prae-*, before + *ludere*, to play]

premarital *adj* belonging to, or occurring in, the period before marriage. [**pre-** (sense **1**)]

premature *adj* **1** (of a baby) born between three and twelve weeks before the expected date: *was a month premature*. **2** occurring before the usual or expected time: *premature senility*. **3** (of a decision, etc.) overhasty. — *adv* **prematurely**. [Lat *praematurus*]

premed *n* (*coll*) premedication.

premedication *n* the drugs given to a surgical patient in preparation for a general anaesthetic. [**pre-** (sense **1**)]

premeditate *v* (*tr*) to plan; to think out beforehand: *premeditated murder*. [Lat *praemeditari*]

premenstrual *adj* belonging to the time just before a menstrual period. [**pre-** (sense **1**)]

premenstrual tension or **syndrome** *n* a group of symptoms including depression and breast pain, associated with the hormonal changes preceding a menstrual period.

premier *adj* first in rank; most important; leading. — *n* a prime minister. — *n* **premiership**. [OFr, first, of first rank]

première *n* the first public performance of a play or showing of a film. — *v* **-*èring***, **-*èred*** (*tr*) to present a première of. [Fr, feminine of *premier*, first]

premise *n* **1** (also **premiss**) something assumed to be true as a basis for stating something further, esp. (*logic*) either of the propositions introducing a syllogism. **2** (in *pl*; *legal*) the preliminary matter in a document, etc; matters explained, or property referred to, earlier in the document. **3** (in *pl*) a building and its grounds. [Lat *praemissa*, things preceding, premise]

premium *n* **1** an amount paid usu. annually on an insurance agreement. **2** an extra sum added to wages or to interest. — **be at a premium** to be scarce and greatly in demand. — **put a premium on** to attach special importance to: *put a premium on punctuality*. [Lat *praemium*, prize]

Premium (Savings) Bond *n* a government bond yielding no interest, but carrying the chance of a cash prize.

premolar *n* any of the four teeth between the canines and first molars. [**pre-** (sense **2**)]

premonition *n* (**of, about**) an uncanny feeling that something is about to happen, before it actually does; an intuition or presentiment. [Lat *praemonitio*, forewarning]

prenatal *adj* belonging to the period before childbirth. [**pre-** (sense **1**)]

preoccupy *v* **-ies, -ied** (*tr*) to occupy the attention of wholly; to engross or obsess. — *n* **preoccupation**. — *adj* **preoccupied** (**by, with**). [Lat *praeoccupare*, to occupy beforehand]

preordain *v* (*tr*) to decree or determine in advance. [Lat *praeordinare*, to ordain in advance]

prep *n* (*coll*) preparation (sense **3**).

prep school *n* (*coll*) a preparatory school.

prep. *abbrev* (*gram*) preposition.

prepare *v* **1** (*tr* & *intr*; **for**) to make or get ready. **2** (*tr*) to make (a meal). **3** (*tr*) to clean or chop (vegetables or fruit). **4** (*tr*; **for**) to get (someone or oneself) into a fit state to receive a shock, etc. **5** (*intr*) to brace oneself (to do something): *prepare to jump*. [Lat *praeparare*, to prepare]

preparation *n* **1** the process of preparing or being prepared. **2** (esp. in *pl*) something done by way of preparing or getting ready. **3** follow-up, or preparatory, work done by students; homework. **4** a medicine, cosmetic, or other such prepared substance.

preparatory *adj* serving to prepare for something; introductory; preliminary. — **preparatory to** before; in preparation for: *checked the windows preparatory to leaving*.

preparatory school *n* **1** in Britain, a private school for children aged between seven and thirteen, usu. preparing them for public school. **2** in the US, a private secondary school, preparing pupils for college.

prepared *adj* willing: *not prepared to lend any more*.

prepay *v* **-paid** (*tr*) **1** to pay for in advance. **2** to pay the postage on in advance. — *n* **prepayment**. [**pre-** (sense **1**)]

preponderance *n* **1** the circumstance of being more numerous. **2** a superior number; a majority. — *adj* **preponderant**. [Lat *praeponderare*, to outweigh]

preponderate *v* (*intr*) to be more numerous; to predominate.

preposition *n* (*gram*) a word such as *to, from, into, against*, that deals with the position, movement, etc. of things or people in relation to one another, and is followed by an object. — *adj* **prepositional**. [Lat *praepositio*, from *praeponere*, to put before]

prepossess *v* (*tr*; esp. in *passive*) **1** to charm: *I was not prepossessed by his manners*. **2** to win over; to incline or bias: *was prepossessed in her favour*. [**pre-** (sense **1**)]

prepossessing *adj* attractive; winning.

preposterous *adj* ridiculous, absurd or outrageous. — *adv* **preposterously**. [Lat *praeposterus*, literally 'back to front']

Pre-Raphaelite *adj* denoting a mid-19th-cent. school of English painters who claimed to revive the simplicity, naturalism and realistic colour-use of painters before Raphael. — *n* a member of this school. [**pre-** (sense **1**)]

prerecord *v* (*tr*) to record (a programme for radio or television) in advance of its scheduled broadcasting time. [**pre-** (sense **1**)]

prerequisite *n* a preliminary requirement that must be satisfied. — *adj* (**to**) (of a condition, etc.) that must be satisfied beforehand. [**pre-** (sense **1**)]

prerogative *n* an exclusive right or privilege arising from one's rank or position. [Lat *praerogativa*, privilege]

Pres. *abbrev* President.

presage *v* (*tr*) to be a warning sign of; to foreshadow, forebode or portend. — *n* a portent, warning or omen. [Lat *praesagire*, to forebode]

presbyopia *n* difficulty in focusing the eye, a defect common in old age. [Gr *presbys*, old + *-opia*, condition of the eyes]

presbyter *n* **1** in the early church, an administrative official with some teaching and priestly duties. **2** in episcopal churches, another word for a priest. **3** in presbyterian churches, an elder. [Gr *presbyteros*, elder]

presbyterian *adj* **1** denoting church administration by presbyters or elders. **2** (*cap*) designating a church governed by elders. — *n* (*cap*) a member of a Presbyterian church. — *n* **Presbyterianism**.

presbytery *n* **-ies** **1** in a presbyterian church, an area of local administration. **2** a body of elders or presbyters, esp. one sitting as a local church court. **3** the eastern section of a church, beyond the choir. **4** the residence of a Roman Catholic priest.

pre-school *adj* (of, or catering for, children) not yet old enough to attend school. [**pre-** (sense **1**)]

prescient *adj* having or showing an understanding of what the future will bring. — *n* **prescience**. [Lat *praescientia*, from *praescire*, to know beforehand]

prescribe *v* (*tr*) **1** (esp. of a doctor) to advise as a remedy. **2** to recommend officially (e.g. a text for academic study). **3** to lay down or establish officially (a duty, penalty, etc.). [Lat *praescribere*, to write down beforehand]

prescript *n* a law, rule, principle, etc. that has been laid down. [Lat *praescriptum*, from *praescribere*, to write down beforehand]

prescription *n* **1** a set of instructions from a doctor for preparing and taking a medicine, etc. **2** the medicine, etc. so prescribed by a doctor. **3** the act of prescribing. — **on prescription** (of drugs) (available) only on the presentation to the pharmacist of a prescription from a doctor. [Lat *praescriptio*, order]

prescriptive *adj* **1** having an authoritative role or purpose; laying down rules: *Dictionaries should be descriptive of word use, not prescriptive*. **2** (of a right, etc.) established by custom. [Lat *praescribere*, to write down beforehand]

presence *n* **1** the state, or circumstance, of being present. **2** one's attendance at an event, etc.: *Your presence is requested.* **3** someone's company or nearness: *said so in my presence*. **4** one's physical bearing, esp. if commanding or authoritative: *people with presence*. **5** a being felt to be present, esp. in a supernatural way. **6** (activities demonstrating) one's influence or power in a place: *maintain a military presence in the area*. [Lat *praesentia*, from *praesens*, present]

presence of mind *n* calmness and the ability to act sensibly, esp. in an emergency.

present *adj* **1** (**at**) being here; being at the place or occasion in question. **2** (**in**) existing, detectable or able to be found: *gases present in the atmosphere*. **3** existing now: *the present situation, prime minister*, etc. **4** now being considered: *the present subject*. **5** (*gram*) (of the tense of a verb) denoting action now, or action that is continuing or habitual. — *n* **1** the present time. **2** (*gram*) (a verb in) the present tense. **3** (in *pl*; *old* or *legal*; with **these**) the present document; this statement, these words, etc. — **at present** now. — **for the present** for the time being. [Lat *praesens*]

present-day *adj* modern; of nowadays.

presently *adv* **1** soon; shortly. **2** (esp. *US*) at the present time; now.

present[1]. See **presence**.

present[2] *v* **1** (*tr*; **with**) to give, esp. formally or ceremonially: *presented her with, was presented with, a medal*. **2** (*tr*; **to**) to introduce (a person), esp. to someone distinguished. **3** (*tr*) to introduce or compère (a television or radio show). **4** (*tr*) to stage (a play), show (a film), etc. **5** (*tr*) to offer for consideration: *presented proposals*. **6** (*tr*; **with**) to pose; to set: *shouldn't present any problem*; *presented us with a few problems*. **7** (*tr*) (of an idea) to suggest (itself). **8** (*tr*) to hand over (a cheque) for acceptance or (a bill) for payment. **9** (*tr*) to set out: *presents her work neatly*. **10** (*tr*) to depict; to represent: *Her biographer presents her in an over-sympathetic light*. **11** (*tr*) to put on (e.g. a cheerful face) in public. **12** (*tr*) to offer (one's compliments) formally. **13** (*tr*) to hold (a weapon) in aiming position. **14** (*intr* with **with**; *med*) to report to a doctor with (certain symptoms or signs). **15** (*intr*; *med*) (of a baby's head or buttocks in childbirth) to be in a position to emerge first. — **present arms** to hold a rifle or other weapon vertically in front of one as a salute. — **present oneself** to appear in person. [Lat *praesentare*, to present]

presentable *adj* **1** fit to be seen, appear in company, etc. **2** passable; satisfactory. — *n* **presentability**. — *adv* **presentably**.

presentation *n* **1** the act of presenting. **2** the manner in which something is presented, laid out, explained or advertised. **3** something performed for an audience; a play, show or other entertainment. **4** (*med*) the position of a baby in the womb just before birth, i.e. whether head or buttocks downward.

presenter *n* (*radio & TV*) a person who introduces a show and gives a linking commentary between items.

present[3] *n* something given; a gift. [**present**[1]]

presentiment *n* a feeling that something, esp. bad, is about to happen, just before it does. [Fr, earlier spelling of *pressentiment*, foreboding]

preserve *v* (*tr*) **1** to save from loss, damage, decay or deterioration. **2** to treat (food), e.g. by freezing, smoking, drying, pickling or boiling in sugar, so that it will last. **3** to maintain (e.g. peace, the status quo, standards, etc.). **4** to keep safe from danger or death. — *n* **1** an area of work or activity restricted to certain people: *Politics was once a male preserve*. **2** an area of land or water where creatures are protected for private hunting, shooting or fishing: *a game preserve*. **3** a jam, pickle or other form in which fruit or vegetables are preserved by cooking in sugar, salt, vinegar, etc. — *n* **preservation**. — *n* **preserver**. [Lat *praeservare*, to guard]

preservative *adj* having the effect of preserving. — *n* a substance used to treat food or a perishable material, to prevent it decaying.

preset *v* **-*tt*-**, **-*set*** (*tr*) to adjust (a piece of electronic equipment, etc.) so that it will operate at the required time. [**pre-** (sense **1**)]

preside *v* (*intr*) **1** (**at, over**) to take the lead at an event, the chair at a meeting, etc.; to be in charge: *preside at the gathering*. **2** (with **over**) to dominate; to be a dominating presence in: *His statue presided over the park*. [Lat *praesidere*, to command, preside]

president *n* **1** (often *cap*) the elected head of state in a republic. **2** the chief office-bearer in a society or club. **3** the head of a business organisation. **4** the head of a college or other higher-education institution. — *adj* **presidential**. [Lat *praesidens*, present participle of *praesidere*, to preside]

presidency *n* **-*ies*** the rank or (period of) office of a president.

presidium *n* **-*iums*** or **-*ia*** a standing executive committee in a Communist state. [Lat, guard, garrison]

press[1] *v* **1** (*tr*) to push steadily, esp. with the finger: *press the bell*. **2** (*tr*; **against, to,**

etc.) to hold firmly against something; to flatten: *press one's nose against the glass.* **3** (*intr*; **against**, **down**, **on**, etc.) to push; to apply pressure: *press down on the accelerator.* **4** (*tr*) to compress or squash. **5** (*tr*) to squeeze (e.g. someone's hand) affectionately. **6** (*tr*) to preserve (plants) by flattening and drying, e.g. between the pages of a book. **7** (*tr*) to squeeze (fruit) to extract juice; to extract (juice) from fruit by squeezing. **8** (*tr*) to iron (clothes, etc.). **9** (*tr*; **for**) to urge or compel; to ask insistently. **10** (*tr*) to insist on; to urge recognition or discussion of: *press one's claim; press the point.* **11** (*intr* with **for**) to demand: *press for a pay rise.* **12** (*tr*; **on**) to insist on giving: *press gifts on someone.* **13** (*tr*; *legal*) to bring (charges) officially against someone. **14** (*intr*; **round**, **through**, etc.) to crowd. **15** (*intr*; **on**, **ahead**, **forward**) to hurry. **16** (*tr*) to produce (e.g. a gramophone record) from a mould by a compressing process. — *n* **1** an act of pressing. **2** any apparatus for pressing, flattening, squeezing, etc. **3** a printing-press. **4** the process or art of printing. **5** a printing-house. **6** newspapers or journalists in general. **7** newspaper publicity or reviews received by a show, book, etc.: *got a poor press.* **8** a crowd: *the press of onlookers.* **9** (*old* or *Scot*) a cupboard. — **go to press** to be sent for printing. [OFr *presser*]

press agent *n* a person who arranges newspaper advertising or publicity for a performer or other celebrity, etc.

press conference *n* an interview granted to reporters by a politician or other person in the news, for the purpose of announcing something, answering questions, etc.

press cutting *n* a paragraph or article cut from a newspaper, etc.

pressed *adj* under pressure; in a hurry. — **be hard pressed** to be in difficulties: *will be hard pressed to find a replacement.* — **be pressed for** (*coll*) to be short of (time or money).

press gallery *n* in Britain, the gallery reserved for journalists in parliament or the law courts.

pressing *adj* urgent: *pressing engagements.* — *n* a number of gramophone records produced from a single mould.

pressman or **presswoman** *n* a journalist or reporter.

press officer *n* a person employed by an organisation to give information about it to journalists.

press release *n* an official statement given to the press by an organisation, etc.

press stud *n* a type of button-like fastener, one part of which is pressed into the other.

press-up *n* an exercise performed face down, raising and lowering the body on the arms while keeping the trunk and legs rigid.

press[2] *v* (*tr*) **1** to force (men) into the army or navy. **2** to put to esp. emergency use: *press something or someone into service.* [From older *prest*, to recruit, orig. 'enlistment money']

pressgang *n* a gang employed to seize men and force them into the army or navy. — *v* (*tr*) **1** to force into the army or navy. **2** (*facet*) to force into service: *pressganged into helping with the party.*

pressure *n* **1** the act of pressing or process of being pressed. **2** the force produced by pressing. **3** the force exerted on a surface by gas or liquid, measured as so much weight on a unit of area: *blood pressure.* **4** force or coercion; forceful persuasion: *put pressure*, or *bring pressure to bear, on her to resign; under pressure to sell.* **5** the need to perform a great deal at speed: *work under pressure.* **6** tension, strain or stress: *the pressures of family life.* — *v* (*tr*) to try to persuade; to coerce, force or pressurise. [Lat *pressura*]

pressure cooker *n* a thick-walled pan with an airtight lid, in which food is cooked at speed by steam under high pressure.

pressure group *n* a number of people who join together to influence public opinion and government policy on some issue.

pressurise or **-ize** *v* (*tr*) **1** to adjust the pressure within (an enclosed compartment such as an aircraft cabin) so that nearly normal atmospheric pressure is constantly maintained. **2** (**into**) to put pressure on; to force or coerce: *pressurised into resigning.*

prestidigitator *n* someone expert at sleight of hand; a conjurer. — *n* **prestidigitation**. [Fr *prestidigitateur*, conjurer, 19th-cent. coinage from *preste*, adroit + Lat *digitus*, finger]

prestige *n* **1** fame, distinction or reputation due to rank or success. **2** standing and influence: *a job with prestige.* — *adj* (of a job, etc.) considered to give prestige. — *adj* **prestigious**. [Lat *praestigiae*, sleight of hand, magic]

presto *n* (**-*os***), *adj* & *adv* (*mus*) (a passage to be played) very fast. [Ital]

pre-stressed *adj* (of concrete) strengthened internally by stretched wires, as distinct from the steel bars in reinforced concrete. [**pre-** (sense **1**)]

presume *v* **1** (*tr*) to suppose (something to be the case) though one has no proof; to take for granted: *presumed he was dead.* **2** (*tr*) to be so bold as (to do something) without the proper right or knowledge; to venture: *wouldn't presume to advise the experts.* **3** (*intr* with **on**, **upon**) to count on (e.g. someone's goodwill), esp. without justification; to take unfair advantage of (someone's good nature, etc.). [Lat *praesumere*, to take in advance, suppose]

presumably *adv* I suppose.

presumption *n* **1** the act of presuming. **2** something presumed: *remarried on the presumption that her first husband was dead.* **3** grounds or justification for presuming something. **4** (*derog*) unsuitable boldness in one's behaviour towards others; insolence or arrogance. [Lat *praesumptio*]

presumptive *adj* presumed rather than absolutely certain. ◇ See also under **heir**.

presumptuous *adj* (*derog*) over-bold in one's behaviour towards others; insolent or arrogant. — *adv* **presumptuously**. [Lat *praesumptuosus*]

presuppose *v* (*tr*) **1** to take for granted; to assume as true. **2** to require as a necessary condition; to imply the existence of: *Forgiveness presupposes offence.* — *n* **presupposition**. [**pre-** (sense **1**)]

pretence *n* **1** the act of pretending. **2** make-believe. **3** an act one puts on deliberately to mislead: *His anger was mere pretence.* **4** a claim, esp. an unjustified one: *make no pretence to expert knowledge.* **5** show, affectation or ostentation; pretentiousness. **6** (esp. in *pl*) a misleading declaration of intention: *won their support under false pretences.* **7** show or semblance: *abandoned all pretence of fair play.* [OFr *pretensse*, from Lat *praetendere*, to pretend]

pretend *v* **1** (*tr* & *intr*) to make believe; to act as if, or give the impression that, something is the case when it is not: *pretend it's winter; pretend to be asleep.* **2** (*tr* & *intr*) to imply or claim falsely: *pretended not to know.* **3** (*intr* with **to**) to claim to have (a skill, etc.), esp. falsely; to lay esp. doubtful claim to (e.g. the throne). **4** (*tr*) to claim to feel; to profess falsely: *pretend friendship towards someone.* — *adj* (*coll*, esp. used by or to children) imaginary: *a pretend cave.* [Lat *praetendere*, to give as an excuse, pretend]

pretender *n* someone who lays esp. dubious claim to something, esp. the throne.

pretension *n* **1** foolish vanity, self-importance or affectation; pretentiousness. **2** a claim or aspiration: *a house with no pretensions to elegance.* [Lat *praetensio*]

pretentious *adj* **1** pompous, self-important or foolishly grandiose. **2** phoney or affected. **3** showy; ostentatious. — *adv* **pretentiously**. — *n* **pretentiousness**. [Formerly *pretensious*, from Lat *praetensio*, pretension]

preterite *n* (*gram*) **1** a verb tense that expresses past action, e.g. *ran, hit, moved.* **2** a verb in this tense. — *adj* denoting this tense. [Lat *praeteritum* (*tempus*), past (time)]

preternatural *adj* **1** exceeding the normal; uncanny; extraordinary. **2** supernatural. — *adv* **preternaturally**. [Lat *praeternaturalis*, from *praeter naturam*, beyond nature]

pretext *n* a false reason given for doing something, to disguise the real one; an excuse. [Lat *praetextum*, from *praetexere*, to fringe, adorn, give as an excuse]

prettify *v* **-ies**, **-ied** (*tr*) to attempt to make prettier by superficial ornamentation. — *n* **prettification**. [**pretty**]

pretty *adj* **-ier**, **-iest** **1** (usu. of women or girls) facially attractive, esp. in a feminine way. **2** charming to look at; decorative. **3** (of music, sound, etc.) delicately melodious. **4** neat, elegant or skilful: *a pretty solution.* **5** (*ironic*) grand; fine: *a pretty mess.* — *adv* fairly; satisfactorily; rather; decidedly. — *adv* **prettily**. — *n* **prettiness**. — **pretty much** (*coll*) more or less. — **pretty nearly** almost. — **pretty well** (*coll*) almost; more or less. — **sitting pretty** (*coll*) happily unaffected by problems besetting others; in an advantageous position. [OE *prættig*, astute]

a pretty pass (*coll*) a deplorable state of affairs.

pretty-pretty *adj* (*coll derog*) pretty in an over-sweet way.

pretzel *n* a salted and glazed biscuit in the shape of a knot. [Ger]

prevail *v* (*intr*) **1** (**over**, **against**) to be victorious; to win through. **2** to be common, usual or generally accepted: *the prevailing opinion, custom,* etc. **3** to be predominant: *the prevailing mood.* **4** (with **on**, **upon**) to persuade: *prevail on you to stay.* [Lat *praevalere*, to prove superior]

prevailing wind *n* the wind most commonly blowing in a region: *the prevailing south-west wind.*

prevalent *adj* (**among**) common; widespread. — *n* **prevalence**. — *adv* **prevalently**. [Lat *praevalere*, to prevail]

prevaricate *v* (*intr*) to avoid stating the truth or coming directly to the point; to behave or speak evasively. — *n* **prevarication**. — *n* **prevaricator**. [Lat *praevaricari*, to walk with splayed legs, behave dishonestly]

prevent *v* (*tr*) **1** (**from**) to stop (someone from doing something, or something from happening); to hinder. **2** to stop the occurrence of; to make impossible; to avert: *prevent war, disease,* etc. — *adj* **preventable** or **preventible**. — *n* **prevention**. [Lat *praevenire*, to anticipate, prevent]

preventive or **preventative** *adj* tending, or intended, to prevent something, e.g. illness: *preventive medicine, treatment, dentistry; preventive measures.* — *n* **1** a preventive drug. **2** a precautionary measure taken against something.

preventive detention *n* a term of imprisonment for a habitual or dangerous criminal.

preview *n* an advance showing of a film, play, exhibition, etc., before presentation to the general public. — *v* (*tr*) to show or view in advance to a select audience. [**pre-** (sense **1**)]

previous *adj* **1** earlier: *a previous occasion.* **2** former: *the previous chairman.* **3** prior: *a previous engagement.* **4** (*facet*) premature; over-prompt or over-hasty. — *adv* **previously**. — **previous to** before. [Lat *praevius*, leading the way]

pre-war *adj* belonging to the period before a war, esp. World War II. [**pre-** (sense **1**)]
prey *n* **1** a creature, or the creatures, that a predatory beast hunts and kills as food: *in search of prey*. **2** a victim or victims: *easy prey for muggers*. **3** (with **to**) a sufferer from (depression, anxiety, fears, etc.). — *v* (*intr* with **on, upon**) **1** to attack as prey. **2** to bully, exploit or terrorise as victims. **3** to afflict: *preyed on by anxieties*. [OFr *preie*, from Lat *praeda*, booty]
price *n* **1** the amount, usu. in money, for which a thing is sold or offered. **2** what one must give up or suffer in gaining something: *Loss of freedom is the price of celebrity*. **3** the sum by which one may be bribed. **4** (*gambling*) odds. — *v* (*tr*) **1** to fix a price for, or mark a price on. **2** to find out the price of. — **a price on someone's head** a reward offered for capturing or killing someone. — **at a price** at great expense. — **beyond** or **without price** priceless; invaluable. [OFr *pris*, from Lat *pretium*]
price control *n* a maximum or, rarely, minimum limit set on prices by the government.
price-fixing *n* the fixing of a price by agreement between suppliers.
priceless *adj* **1** too valuable to have a price; inestimably precious. **2** (*coll*) hilariously funny.
price tag *n* **1** a label showing a price. **2** the cost of something, e.g. a proposed building, etc.
pricey or **pricy** *adj* ***-ier, -iest*** (*coll*) expensive.
prick *v* **1** (*tr*) to pierce slightly with a fine point. **2** (*tr*) to make (a hole) by this means. **3** (*tr* & *intr*) to hurt by this means. **4** (*intr* & *tr*) to (cause to) smart: *feel one's eyes pricking*. **5** (*tr* & *intr* with **up**) (of a dog) to stick (its ears) upright, or (of its ears) to stand erect, in response to sound. **6** (*tr*) to mark out (a pattern) in punctured holes. — *n* **1** an act of pricking or feeling of being pricked; the pain of this. **2** a puncture made by pricking. **3** (*vulg*) a penis. **4** (*vulg offensive*) an abusive term for a man, esp. a self-important fool. — **kick against the pricks** to react against discipline or authority. — **prick up one's ears** (*coll*) to start listening attentively. [OE *prica*, point]
prickle *n* **1** a sharp point or thorn-like growth on a plant or creature, e.g. a hedgehog. **2** a pricking sensation: *a prickle of fear*. — *v* (*intr* & *tr*) to cause, affect with, or be affected with, a pricking sensation. [OE *pricel*]
prickly *adj* ***-ier, -iest*** **1** having prickles. **2** causing prickling. **3** (*coll*) (of a person) irritable; over-sensitive. **4** (of a topic) liable to cause controversy. — *n* **prickliness**.
prickly heat *n* an itchy skin condition, with inflammation around the sweat glands, occurring in intensely hot weather.
prickly pear *n* a prickly reddish pear-shaped fruit; the cactus on which it grows.
pride *n* **1** a feeling of pleasure and satisfaction at one's own or another's accomplishments, one's possessions, etc. **2** whatever inspires this feeling: *It's my pride and joy*. **3** self-respect; personal dignity. **4** an unjustified assumption of superiority; arrogance. **5** (*poetic*) the finest state; prime or bloom. **6** the finest item: *the pride of the collection*. **7** a number of lions keeping together as a group. — *v* (*tr* with **on**) to congratulate (oneself) on: *prided himself on his youthful figure*. — **swallow one's pride** to be forced to humble oneself. — **take (a) pride in 1** to be proud of. **2** to be conscientious about maintaining high standards in (one's work, etc.). [OE *pryde*]
pride of place *n* special prominence; the position of chief importance.
priest *n* **1** in the Roman Catholic and Orthodox churches, an ordained minister; in the Anglican church a minister ranking between deacon and bishop. **2** in non-Christian religions, an official who performs sacrifices and other religious rites. — *adj* **priestly**. [OE *preost*, from Lat *presbyter*, elder]
priestess *n* in non-Christian religions, a female priest.
priesthood *n* **1** the (period of) office of a priest. **2** the role or character of a priest. **3** priests collectively: *members of the priesthood*.
prig *n* a person who is too sure of his or her own moral blamelessness, and too critical of others' moral failings; a self-righteous person. — *adj* **priggish**. — *adv* **priggishly**. — *n* **priggishness**. [Orig. a coxcomb]
prim *adj* **1** stiffly formal, over-modest or over-proper. **2** prudishly disapproving. — *adv* **primly**. — *n* **primness**. [17th-cent. slang]
prima ballerina *n* the leading female dancer in a ballet company. [Ital, first ballerina]
primacy *n* ***-ies*** **1** the condition of being first in rank, importance or order. **2** the rank, (period of) office, or area of jurisdiction of a primate of the Church. [Lat *primatia*, from *primus*, first]
prima donna *n* **1** a leading female opera singer. **2** someone difficult to please, esp. if given to melodramatic tantrums when displeased. [Ital, first lady]
primaeval or **primeval** *adj* **1** belonging to earth's beginnings. **2** primitive. **3** instinctive. [Lat *primaevus*, young, from *primus*, first + *aevum*, age]
prima facie *adv* at first sight; on the evidence available; on the face of it. — *adj* apparent; based on first impressions: *prima facie evidence*. [Lat]
primal *adj* **1** relating to the beginnings of life; original: *man's primal innocence*. **2** basic; fundamental. [**prime**]
primary *adj* **1** first or most important; principal: *our primary concern*. **2** earliest in order or development: *the primary stage*. **3**

(*cap*; *geol*) Palaeozoic. **4** basic; fundamental: *primary causes*. **5** of the elementary stage or level. **6** (of education) for children aged between 5 and 11: *primary schools*. ◇ See also **secondary** and **tertiary**. **7** (of a bird's wing feather) outermost and longest. **8** firsthand; direct: *primary sources of information*. **9** (of products) being, or (of industries) concerned with, produce in its raw, natural state. **10** (*electr*) (of a battery or cell) producing electricity by an irreversible chemical reaction; (of a circuit or current) inducing a current in a neighbouring circuit. — *n* **-ies 1** something that is first in order, importance, etc. **2** a primary school. **3** (also **primary election**) in the US, a preliminary election at state level in which voters choose candidates for political office. **4** a bird's primary feather. [Lat *primarius*, principal]

primarily *adv* **1** chiefly; mainly. **2** in the first place; initially.

primary colour *n* one of a small number from which all others can be produced by mixing, those of light being red, green and blue, those of pigment (i.e. paint, etc.) being red, yellow and blue. ◇ See also **secondary colour**.

primary stress (*linguistics*) the main stress on a word; heaviest. ◇ See also **secondary stress**.

primate *n* **1** an archbishop. **2** a member of the highest order of mammals, including monkeys, lemurs, apes and humans. [Lat *primas*, from *primus*, first]

prime *adj* **1** chief; fundamental. **2** of best quality: *prime beef*. **3** excellent: *in prime condition*. **4** supremely typical: *a prime example*. **5** having the greatest potential for attracting interest or custom: *prime viewing time*; *prime sites on the high street*. — *n* the best, most productive or active stage in the life of a person or thing: *vehicles past their prime*; *cut off in her prime* or *in the prime of life*. — *v* (*tr*) **1** to prepare (something), e.g. (wood for painting) by applying a sealing coat of size, etc., (a gun or explosive device for firing or detonating) by inserting the igniting material, or (a pump for use) by filling it with water, etc. **2** to supply (someone) with the necessary facts in advance; to brief. **3** (*facet*) to supply (someone) with drink or food by way of relaxing, emboldening, or bribing him or her. [Lat *primus*, first]

prime lending rate *n* the lowest rate of interest charged by a bank at any time to creditworthy customers.

prime meridian *n* the 0° line of longitude, passing through Greenwich.

prime minister *n* the chief minister of a government.

prime mover *n* the force that is most effective in setting something in motion.

prime number *n* a number that is exactly divisible only by itself and 1, e.g. 3, 5, 7, 31.

primer *n* **1** a substance for sealing wood with, before painting. **2** an igniting or detonating device for firing the main charge in a gun or mine.

primer[1] *n* a first, or introductory, book of instruction. [Lat *primarium*, from *primarius*, primary]

primer[2]. See **prime**.

primeval. See **primaeval**.

primitive *adj* **1** belonging to earliest times, or the earliest stages of development: *primitive stone tools*. **2** simple, rough, crude or rudimentary: *living in primitive conditions*. **3** (*art*) simple, naïve or unsophisticated in style. — *n* (a work by) an artist in naïve style. — *adv* **primitively**. — *n* **primitiveness**. [Lat *primitivus*]

primogeniture *n* the circumstance of being the first-born child. **2** the right, or the principle, of succession or inheritance of an eldest son. [Lat *primogenitura*, first birth]

primordial *adj* existing from the beginning, esp. of the world; formed earliest: *primordial matter*. — *adv* **primordially**. [Lat *primordialis*, from *primus*, first + *ordiri*, to begin]

primp *v* (*tr* & *intr*) to groom, preen or titivate (oneself). [Perhaps related to **prim**]

primrose *n* **1** a small, low-growing wild plant with pale yellow flowers that appear in spring. **2** the pale yellow colour of these flowers. [Lat *prima rosa*, first rose]

primrose path *n* an untroubled, pleasure-seeking way of life.

primula *n* **-lae** or **-las** any of a genus of plants that includes the primrose and cowslip, esp. a low-growing cultivated variety with white, pink or purple five-petalled flowers. [Lat *primula* (*veris*), first little one of the spring]

Primus® *n* **-uses** (also **Primus stove**) a portable camping stove fuelled by vapourised oil.

prince *n* **1** the son of a sovereign. **2** a non-reigning male member of a royal or imperial family. **3** a sovereign of a small territory. **4** a ruler or sovereign generally. **5** a nobleman in certain countries. **6** someone or something celebrated or outstanding within a type or class: *the prince of highwaymen*. — *n* **princedom**. ◇ See also **principality**. [Lat *princeps*, leader, ruler]

Prince Charming *n* the prince in the tale of Cinderella, symbolising, for the romantic woman, the ideal handsome husband.

prince consort *n* the title given to a reigning queen's husband, who is himself a prince.

princely *adj* **1** of, or suitable to, a prince. **2** (often *ironic*) lavish; generous.

Prince of Wales *n* the title given to the eldest son of the British sovereign.

prince regent *n* a prince ruling on behalf of a sovereign who is too ill, young, etc. to rule.

princess *n* **1** the wife or daughter of a prince. **2** the daughter of a sovereign, or a non-reigning female member of a royal or imperial family.
Princess Royal *n* a title that may be conferred on the British sovereign's eldest daughter.
principal *adj* first in rank or importance. **2** chief; main. — *n* **1** the head of an educational institution. **2** a leading actor, singer or dancer in a theatrical production. **3** (*legal*) the person on behalf of whom an agent is acting. **4** (*legal*) a person ultimately responsible for fulfilling an obligation. **5** a person who commits or participates in a crime. **6** (*finance*) the sum of money on which interest is paid. — *adv* **principally**. [Lat *principalis*, chief, principal]
principal boy *n* the part of the young male hero in a pantomime, usu. played by a woman.
principal clause *n* a main clause.
principal parts *n* (*pl*; *gram*) the main forms of a verb from which all other forms can be deduced, e.g. in English the infinitive, the past tense and the past participle.
principality *n* **-ies 1** a territory ruled by a prince, or one that he derives his title from. **2** (*cap* with **the**) Wales. [Lat *principalitas*]
principle *n* **1** a general truth or assumption from which to argue. **2** a scientific law, esp. as explaining a natural phenomenon or the way a machine works. **3** a general rule of morality that guides one's conduct; the having of or holding to such rules: *a woman of principle*. **4** a norm of procedure: *the principle of primogeniture*. **5** a fundamental element or source: *the vital principle*. **6** (*chem*) a constituent of a substance that gives it its distinctive characteristics. — **in principle** in general, as opposed to in detail; broadly or basically. — **on principle** on the grounds of a particular principle of morality or wisdom. [Lat *principium*, beginning, source]
principled *adj* having, or proceeding from, esp. high moral principles.
prink *v* (*tr* & *intr*) to dress (oneself) up; to smarten (oneself) up. [Perhaps related to older *prank*, to dress up]
print *v* **1** (*tr*) to reproduce (text or pictures) on paper with ink, using a printing-press or other mechanical means. **2** (*tr*) to publish (a book, article, etc.). **3** (*tr* & *intr*) to write in separate, as opposed to joined-up, letters, in the style of mechanically printed text. **4** (*tr*) to make (a positive photograph) from a negative. **5** (*tr*) to mark designs on (fabric). **6** (*tr*) to fix (a scene) indelibly (on the memory, etc.). — *n* **1** (often *in cmpds*) a mark made on a surface by the pressure of something in contact with it: *footprints*; *fingerprints*. **2** a fingerprint. **3** hand-done lettering with each letter written separately. **4** mechanically printed text, esp. produced on a printing-press: *small print*. **5** a printed publication. **6** a design printed from an engraved wood block or metal plate. **7** a positive photograph made from a negative. **8** a fabric with a printed or stamped design. — **be in** (or **out of**) **print** (of books) to be currently available (or no longer available) from a publisher. — *v* **print out** (*tr* & *intr*; *comput*) to produce a print-out of (data). [MidE *prenten*, from OFr *priente*, a print]
printable *adj* **1** capable of being printed. **2** fit to be published.
printed circuit *n* a wiring circuit free of loose wiring, formed by printing the wiring design on copper foil bonded to a flat base and etching away the unprinted foil.
printer *n* **1** a person or business engaged in printing books, newspapers, etc. **2** a machine that prints, e.g. photographs. **3** (*comput*) a device that produces print-outs of data.
printing *n* **1** the art or business of producing books, etc. in print. **2** the run of books, etc. printed all at one time; an impression. **3** the form of handwriting in which the letters are separately written.
printing-press *n* a machine for printing books, newspapers, etc., operating in any of various ways.
print-out *n* (*comput*) (a piece of) printed output.
print run *n* the number of copies of a book, newspaper, etc. printed at a time.
prior[1] *adj* **1** (of an engagement) already arranged for the time in question; previous. **2** more urgent or pressing: *a prior claim*. — **prior to** before: *prior to departure*. [Lat, previous]
prior[2] *n* **1** the head of a community of certain orders of monks and friars. **2** in an abbey, the deputy of the abbot. [Lat, head]
prioress *n* a female prior.
priory *n* **-ies** a religious house under the supervision of a prior or prioress.
priority *n* **-ies 1** the circumstance of being earlier. **2** the right to be or go first; precedence or preference. **3** something that must be attended to before anything else. — **get one's priorities right** to give appropriate attention to things in the appropriate order. [Lat *prioritas*, from *prior*, previous]
prioritise or **-ize** *v* (*tr*) to schedule for immediate, or earliest, attention.
priory. See **prior**[1].
prise *v* (*tr*) to lever (something) open, off, out, etc.: *prised open the lid*; *prised the shell off the rock*. [OFr, something captured]
prism *n* **1** (*geom*) a solid figure whose two ends are matching parallel polygons and whose sides are parallelograms. **2** a transparent solid of this shape, esp. one with triangular ends, that separates a beam of white light into the colours of the spectrum. [Gr *prisma*, something sawn]
prismatic *adj* **1** of, like or using a prism: *a prismatic compass*. **2** (of colours or light) produced or separated (as though) by means of a prism; bright and clear.

prison *n* **1** a public building for the confinement of convicted criminals and accused persons waiting to be tried. **2** any place of confinement or situation of intolerable restriction. **3** custody; imprisonment: *no alternative to prison.* [OFr *prisun*, from Lat *prehensio*, right of arrest]

prison camp *n* an enclosed guarded camp where prisoners of war or political prisoners are kept.

prisoner *n* **1** a person who is under arrest or confined in prison. **2** a captive, esp. in war. — **take prisoner** to capture and hold as a prisoner.

prisoner of war *n* **-ers of war** someone taken prisoner during a war, esp. a member of the armed forces.

prissy *adj* **-ier**, **-iest** insipidly prim and prudish. — *adv* **prissily**. — *n* **prissiness**. [Prob. **prim** + **sissy**]

pristine *adj* **1** former: *restore to its pristine glory*. **2** original; unchanged or unspoilt: *still in its pristine state*. **3** fresh, clean, unused or untouched. [Lat *pristinus*, former, early]

privacy *n* **1** (one's right to) freedom from intrusion by the public: *respect her privacy*. **2** seclusion: *in the privacy of one's own home*. [**private**]

private *adj* **1** not open to, or available for the use of, the general public: *a private bathroom*. **2** not holding public office: *private individuals*. **3** kept secret from others; confidential: *private discussions*. **4** relating to one's personal, as distinct from one's professional, life: *a private engagement*. **5** (of thoughts or opinions) personal and usu. kept to oneself. **6** quiet and reserved by nature. **7** (of a place) secluded. **8** not coming under the state system of education, health care, social welfare, etc.; paid for, or paying, individually by fee, etc.: *private nursing-homes, pupils*, etc. **9** (of industries, etc.) owned and run by private individuals, not by the state. **10** (of a soldier) not an officer or NCO. **11** (of a member of parliament) not holding government office. — *n* **1** a private soldier. **2** (*coll*; in *pl*) private parts. — *adv* **privately**. — **in private** not in public; in secret; confidentially. [Lat *privare*, to withdraw or separate from public life]

private detective or **investigator** *n* someone who is not a member of the police force, engaged by a private individual to do detective work.

private enterprise *n* the management and financing of industry, etc. by private individuals or companies, not the state.

private means *n* (*pl*) or **income** *n* income from investments, etc., not from one's employment.

private parts *n* (*pl*; *euph*) the external genitals and excretory organs.

private sector *n* that part of a country's economy consisting of privately owned and operated businesses, etc.

privatise or **-ize** *v* (*tr*) to transfer a nationally owned business to private ownership. — *n* **privatisation** or **-z-**.

privateer *n* (*hist*) **1** a privately owned ship engaged by a government to seize and plunder an enemy's ships in wartime. **2** the commander, or a crew member, of such a ship. [**private**]

privation *n* the condition of not having, or being deprived of, life's comforts or necessities; a lack of something particular. [Lat *privatio*, deprivation]

privet *n* a type of bush of which hedges are commonly composed.

privilege *n* **1** a right granted to an individual or a select few, bestowing an advantage not enjoyed by others. **2** advantages and power enjoyed by people of wealth and high social class. **3** an opportunity to do something that brings one delight; a pleasure or honour: *have the privilege of meeting you*. [Lat *privilegium*, prerogative]

privileged *adj* **1** enjoying the advantages of wealth and class. **2** favoured with the opportunity (to do something).

privy *adj* **1** (with **to**) allowed to share in (secret discussions, etc.) or be in the know about (secret plans, happenings, etc.). **2** (*old*) secret; hidden. — *n* **-ies** (*old*) a lavatory. — *adv* **privily**. [OFr *privé*, private, a private place or close friend]

Privy Council *n* a private advisory council appointed by the sovereign, consisting chiefly of current and former members of the Cabinet, whose functions are mainly formal. — *n* **Privy Councillor**.

Privy Purse *n* an allowance granted to the sovereign by Parliament, for his or her private expenses.

prize[1] *n* **1** something won in a competition, lottery, etc. **2** a reward given in recognition of excellence. **3** something striven for, or worth striving for. **4** something captured or taken by force, esp. a ship in war; a trophy. — *adj* **1** deserving, or having won, a prize. **2** valued highly by a person: *her prize possession*. **3** (*ironic*) perfect; great: *a prize fool*. — *v* (*tr*) to value highly.

prize fight *n* a boxing-match fought for a money prize. — *n* **prize-fighter**. — *n* **prize-fighting**. [Partly OFr *pris*, price, partly OFr *prise*, something captured]

prize[2]. Another spelling of **prise**.

PRO *abbrev* Public Relations Officer.

pro[1] *adv* in favour. — *prep* in favour of. — *n* **pros** a reason, argument or choice in favour of something. [Lat, in favour of].

pros and cons *n* (*pl*) advantages and disadvantages. [**con** from Lat *contra*, against]

pro[2] *n* **pros** (*coll*) **1** a professional. **2** a prostitute.

pro-am *n* & *adj* (*golf*) (a competition) involving both professionals and amateurs.

pro- *pfx* **1** in favour of; admiring or supporting: *pro-French*. **2** serving in place of; acting for: *procathedral*; *proconsul*. [Lat]

probable *adj* **1** likely to happen: *the probable outcome.* **2** likely to be the case; likely to have happened: *probable that she's left.* **3** (of an explanation, etc.) likely to be correct. — *n* a person or thing likely to be selected. [Lat *probabilis*, from *probare*, to prove]

probability *n* **-ies 1** the state of being probable; likelihood. **2** something that is probable. **3** (*statistics*) a measure of the likelihood of something occurring, expressed as a ratio of positive cases to total potential cases: *a probability of one in four.* — **in all probability** most probably.

probably *adv* almost certainly; in all likelihood.

probate *n* **1** (*legal*) the process of establishing that a will is valid. **2** an official copy of a will, with the document certifying its validity. [Lat *probare*, to prove]

probation *n* **1** the system whereby (esp. young or first) offenders are allowed their freedom under supervision, on condition of good behaviour: *was put on probation for six months.* **2** in certain types of employment, a period during which a new employee is observed on the job, to confirm whether or not he or she can do it satisfactorily. — *adj* **probationary**. [Lat *probatio*, trial, test]

probationer *n* a person on probation.

probation officer *n* a person with responsibility as supervisor for an offender on probation.

probe *n* **1** a long slender usu. metal instrument used by doctors to examine a wound, locate a bullet, etc. **2** an investigation: *a police probe into drug-dealing.* **3** (also **space probe**) an unmanned spacecraft that records and transmits back to earth data about the environment it is passing through. **4** an act of probing; a poke or prod. — *v* (*tr* & *intr*; **into**) **1** to examine with a probe. **2** to poke or prod. **3** to investigate closely. [Lat *probare*, to test, prove]

probity *n* integrity; honesty. [Lat *probitas*]

problem *n* **1** a situation or matter that is difficult to understand or deal with. **2** a person or thing that is difficult to deal with. **3** a puzzle or mathematical question set for solving. — *adj* **1** (of a child, etc.) difficult to deal with, esp. in being disruptive or anti-social. **2** (of a play, etc.) dealing with a moral or social problem. — **no problem** (*coll*) **1** (in response to a request, or thanks) it's a pleasure, no trouble, etc. **2** easily: *found our way, no problem.* [Gr *problema*, question for solving]

problematic or **problematical** *adj* **1** causing problems. **2** uncertain. — *adv* **problematically**.

proboscis *n* **1** a flexible, elongated nose or snout, e.g. the trunk of an elephant. **2** the elongated mouth part of certain insects. **3** (*facet*) the human nose. [Gr *proboskis*, from *pro*, in front + *boskein*, to nourish]

procedure *n* **1** the method and order followed in doing something. **2** an established routine for conducting business at a meeting or in a law case. **3** a course of action; a step or measure taken. — *adj* **procedural**. — *adv* **procedurally**. [Fr *procédure*, from Lat *procedere*, to advance, proceed]

proceed *v* (*intr*) **1** to make one's way: *proceeding along the road.* **2** (**with**) to go on; to continue after stopping: *proceed with one's work*; *Please proceed.* **3** to set about a task, etc.: *instructions on how to proceed.* **4** (*coll*) to begin: *proceeded to question her.* **5** (with **from**) to arise from: *Fear proceeds from ignorance.* **6** (*legal*; with **against**) to take legal action against. [Lat *procedere*, to advance, proceed]

proceeding *n* **1** an action; a piece of behaviour. **2** (in *pl*) (a published record of) things said and done at a meeting of a society, etc. **3** (in *pl*) legal action: *begin divorce proceedings.*

proceeds *n* (*pl*) money made by an event, sale, etc.

process *n* **1** a series of operations performed on something during manufacture, etc. **2** a series of stages passed through, resulting in development or transformation. **3** an operation or procedure: *a slow process.* **4** (*anat*) a projection or prominence, e.g. on a bone: *the mastoid process.* — *v* (*tr*) **1** to put through the required process; to deal with appropriately: *process a film*; *process an application.* **2** to prepare (agricultural produce) for marketing, e.g. by canning, bottling or treating chemically. **3** to analyse (data) by computer. — **in the process of** in the course of. [Lat *processus*, progression]

processor *n* **1** a machine or person that processes something: *a word processor.* **2** (*comput*) a central processing unit.

procession *n* **1** a file of people or vehicles proceeding ceremonially in orderly formation. **2** this kind of succession or sequence: *moving in procession.* [Lat *processio*, an advance]

proclaim *v* (*tr*) **1** to announce publicly. **2** to declare (someone) to be (something): *proclaimed a traitor.* **3** to attest or prove all too clearly: *Cigarette smoke proclaimed his presence.* [Lat *proclamare*, to cry out]

proclamation *n* **1** an official public announcement of something nationally important. **2** the act of proclaiming. [Lat *proclamatio*]

proclivity *n* **-ies** (**for**) a tendency towards certain behaviour, esp. of an unsuitable kind: *a proclivity for chasing women.* [Lat *proclivitas*, from *proclivis*, sloping]

procrastinate *v* (*intr*) to keep putting off doing something that should be done straight away. — *n* **procrastination**. — *n* **procrastinator**. [Lat *procrastinare*, to delay or defer, from *cras*, tomorrow]

procreate *v* (*tr* & *intr*) to produce (offspring); to reproduce. — *n* **procreation**. [Lat *procreare*, to beget]

proctor *n* an official in some English universities whose functions include enforcement of discipline. [Contraction of **procurator**]

procurator *n* **1** in the Roman empire, a financial agent or administrator in a province. **2** an agent with power of attorney in a law court. — *n* **procuratorship** or **procuracy**, **-*ies***. [Lat, agent, manager]

procurator fiscal *n* in Scotland, a district official who combines the roles of coroner and public prosecutor.

procure *v* **1** (*tr*) to manage to obtain or bring about. **2** (*tr* & *intr*) to provide (prostitutes) for clients. — *n* **procurement**. [Lat *procurare*, from *pro*, on behalf of + *curare*, to attend to]

procurer or **procuress** *n* a man or woman who provides prostitutes for clients.

prod *v* **-*dd*- 1** (*tr* or *intr*; **at**) to poke or jab. **2** (*tr*) to nudge, prompt or spur into action. — *n* **1** a poke, jab or nudge. **2** a reminder. **3** a goad or similar pointed instrument.

prodigal *adj* **1** heedlessly extravagant or wasteful. **2** (**of**) lavish; generous: *be prodigal of praise*. — *n* **1** a squanderer, wastrel or spendthrift. **2** (also **prodigal son**) a repentant ne'er-do-well or a returned wanderer. — *n* **prodigality**. — *adv* **prodigally**. [Lat *prodigus*, wasteful]

prodigious *adj* **1** extraordinary or marvellous. **2** enormous; vast: *prodigious wealth*. — *adv* **prodigiously**. [Lat *prodigiosus*, from *prodigium*, wonder]

prodigy *n* **-*ies* 1** something that causes astonishment; a wonder; an extraordinary phenomenon. **2** a person, esp. a child, of extraordinary brilliance or talent. [Lat *prodigium*, portent, wonder]

produce *v* (*tr*) **1** to bring out or present to view. **2** to bear (children, young, leaves, etc.). **3** to yield (crops, fruit, etc.). **4** to secrete (a substance), give off (a smell), etc. **5** to make or manufacture. **6** to give rise to or prompt (a reaction) from people: *produced a subdued response*. **7** to direct (a play), arrange (a radio or television programme) for presentation, or finance and schedule the making of (a film). **8** (*geom*) to extend (a line). — *n* what is produced, esp. from land or livestock: *farm produce*. — *n* **producer**. — *adj* **producible**. [Lat *producere*, to bring forth]

product *n* **1** something produced, e.g. through manufacture or agriculture. **2** a result: *the product of hours of thought*. **3** (*math*) the quantity got by multiplying: *The product of 2 and 4 is 8*. [Lat *producere*, to produce]

production *n* **1** the act of producing; the process of producing or being produced: *goes into production next year*. **2** the quantity produced or rate of producing it. **3** something created; a literary or artistic work. **4** a particular presentation of a play, opera, ballet, etc. [Lat *productio*, from *producere*, to produce]

productive *adj* **1** yielding a lot; fertile; fruitful. **2** useful; profitable: *a productive meeting*. **3** (**of**) giving rise to; resulting in: *productive of ideas*. — *adv* **productively**.

productivity *n* rate and efficiency of work in industrial production, etc.

proem *n* an introduction, prelude or preface. [Gr *prooimion*, from *pro*, before + *oime*, song]

prof *n* (*coll*) a professor.

profane *adj* **1** showing disrespect for sacred things; irreverent. **2** not sacred or spiritual; temporal or worldly. — *v* (*tr*) **1** to treat (something sacred) irreverently. **2** to violate or defile (what should be respected). — *n* **profanation**. — *adv* **profanely**. [Lat *profanus*, not holy]

profanity *n* **-*ies* 1** lack of respect for sacred things. **2** blasphemous language; a blasphemy, swear word, oath, etc.

profess *v* (*tr*) **1** to make an open declaration of (beliefs, etc.). **2** to declare one's adherence to: *profess Christianity*. **3** to claim or pretend: *profess ignorance*; *profess to be an expert*. [Lat *profiteri*, to declare]

professed *adj* **1** self-acknowledged; self-confessed: *a professed agnostic*. **2** claimed by oneself; pretended: *a professed indifference to money*. — *adv* **professedly**.

profession *n* **1** an occupation, esp. one that requires specialist academic and practical training, e.g. medicine, law, teaching, engineering. **2** the body of people engaged in a particular one of these: *the medical profession*. **3** an act of professing; a declaration: *a profession of loyalty*.

professional *adj* **1** earning one's living in the performance, practice or teaching of something that is a pastime for others. **2** belonging to a trained profession: *professional skills*. **3** having the competence, expertise or conscientiousness of someone with professional training: *a professional performance*, *attitude*, etc. — *n* someone who is professional. — *adv* **professionally**.

professor *n* **1** a teacher of the highest rank in a university; the head of a university department. **2** (*US*) a university teacher. — *adj* **professorial**. — *n* **professorship**. [Lat, public teacher]

proffer *v* **-*r*-** (*tr*) to offer. [OFr *proffrir*]

proficient *adj* fully trained and competent; expert. — *n* **proficiency**. — *adv* **proficiently**. [Lat *proficere*, to make progress]

profile *n* **1** a side view of something, esp. a face or head; a side face. **2** a brief outline, sketch or assessment, esp. of a person. **3** the extent to which one advertises one's presence or involvement: *keep a low*, or *maintain a high*, *profile*. [Ital *profilo*, from *profilare*, to outline]

profit 1 *n* money gained from selling something for more than one paid for it. **2** an excess of income over expenses. **3** advantage or benefit. — *v* **-t-** (*intr*; **from, by**) to benefit.

profitable *adj* **1** (of a business, etc.) making a profit. **2** useful; fruitful. — *n* **profitability**. — *adv* **profitably**.

profiteer *n* a person who takes advantage of a shortage or other emergency to make exorbitant profits. — *v* (*intr*) to make excessive profits in such a way.

profit margin *n* the difference between the buying or production price and the selling price.

profit-sharing *n* an agreement whereby employees receive a proportion, fixed in advance, of a company's profits.

profiterole *n* a small sweet or savoury confection of choux pastry. [Fr, said to be a diminutive from *profiter*, to profit]

profligate *adj* **1** immoral and irresponsible; licentious or dissolute. **2** scandalously extravagant. — *n* a profligate person. — *n* **profligacy**. — *adv* **profligately**. [Lat *profligare*, to strike down]

pro forma *n* (also **pro-forma invoice**) an invoice sent in advance of the goods ordered. [Lat, for the sake of form]

profound *adj* **1** (of sleep) deep; sound. **2** (of a feeling) deeply felt or rooted. **3** (of comments, etc.) showing understanding or penetration. **4** intense; impenetrable: *profound deafness, silence*, etc. **5** radical, extensive or far-reaching: *profound changes*. — *adv* **profoundly**. — *n* **profundity**, ***-ies***. [Lat *profundus*, deep, profound]

profuse *adj* **1** overflowing; exaggerated; excessive: *offered profuse apologies*. **2** copious: *profuse bleeding*. — *adv* **profusely**. — *n* **profusion**. [Lat *profusus*, lavish]

progenitor *n* **1** an ancestor, forebear or forefather. **2** the begetter or originator of a movement, etc. [Lat, from *progignere*, to beget]

progeny *n* (*pl*) **1** children; offspring; descendants. **2** what results from or is generated by something; derivatives and offshoots. [Lat *progenies*, offspring]

progesterone *n* a female sex hormone produced by the ovaries, that prepares the womb for, and maintains, pregnancy. [Gr *pro-*, before + **gestation** + **sterol**]

prognosis *n* ***-oses*** **1** an informed forecast of developments in any situation. **2** a doctor's prediction on the course of a patient's illness and his or her chances of recovery. [Gr, knowing before]

prognosticate *v* (*tr*) to foretell. **2** to indicate in advance; to be a sign of. — *n* **prognostication**. — *n* **prognosticator**. [Lat *prognosticare*, to foretell, from Gr *prognostikon*, sign of the future]

programme or (*US* & *comput*) **program** *n* **1** (a leaflet showing) the schedule of proceedings for, and list of participants in, a theatre performance, entertainment, ceremony, etc. **2** an agenda, plan or schedule: *What's the programme for this morning?* **3** a series of planned projects to be undertaken: *the building programme for 1993*. **4** a scheduled radio or television presentation. **5** (**program**) (a set of coded instructions to a computer for the performance of) a series of operations. — *v* **-mm-** (*tr*) **1** to include in a programme; to schedule. **2** to draw up a programme for. **3** to set (a computer) by program to perform a set of tasks. **4** to set so as to operate at the required time: *heating programmed to come on at 7.00 pm*. — *n* **programmer**. [Gr *programma*, the order of the day, schedule]

programmable *adj* capable of being programmed to perform a task automatically.

progress *n* **1** movement while travelling in any direction. **2** course: *watched her erratic progress, followed the progress of the trial*, etc. **3** movement towards a destination, goal or state of completion: *make slow progress*. **4** advances or development: *make progress in the treatment of cancer*. **5** (*old*) a journey made in state by a sovereign, etc. — *v* **1** (*intr*) to move forwards or onwards; to proceed towards a goal. **2** (*intr*) to advance or develop. **3** (*intr*) to improve. **4** (*tr*) to put (something planned) into operation; to expedite. — **in progress** taking place. [Lat *progressus*, from *progredi*, to move forward]

progression *n* **1** the process of moving forwards or advancing in stages. **2** (*mus*) a succession of chords, or (*math*) a series of terms, the advance from one to the next being determined on a fixed pattern.

progressive *adj* **1** advanced in outlook; using, or favouring, new methods. **2** moving forward or advancing continuously or by stages: *progressive loss of memory*. **3** (of a disease) continuously increasing in severity or complication. **4** (of a dance or game) involving changes of partner at intervals. **5** (of taxation) increasing as the sum taxed increases. **6** (*gram*) denoting the forms of a verb that express continuing action, in English formed with the present participle, e.g. *I am sitting* or *she was going*. — *n* **1** a person with progressive ideas. **2** (*gram*) a verb in a progressive form. — *adv* **progressively**.

prohibit *v* **-t-** (*tr*) **1** to forbid, esp. by law; to ban. **2** to prevent or hinder. [Lat *prohibere*, to hinder, forbid]

prohibition *n* **1** the act of prohibiting or state of being prohibited. **2** a law or decree prohibiting something. **3** a ban by law on the manufacture and sale of alcoholic drinks, esp. (*cap*) that in force in the US from 1920 to 1933. — *n* **prohibitionist**.

prohibitive *adj* **1** banning; prohibiting. **2** tending to prevent or discourage. **3** (of prices, etc.) unaffordably high.

prohibitory *adj* prohibiting; restraining.

project *n* **1** a plan, scheme or proposal. **2** a research or study assignment. — *v* **1** (*intr*) to jut out; to protrude. **2** (*tr*) to throw forwards; to propel. **3** (*tr*) to throw (a shadow or image) on to a surface. **4** (*tr*) to propose or plan. **5** (*tr*) to forecast from present trends and other known data; to extrapolate. **6** (*tr*) to imagine (oneself) in another situation, esp. a future one. **7** (*tr*; **on to**) to ascribe (feelings of one's own) to other people. **8** (*tr*) to cause (one's voice) to be heard clearly at some distance. **9** (*intr*; *coll*) to make good contact with an audience through the strength of one's personality. [Lat *projicere*, to throw forward]

projection *n* **1** the act of projecting or process of being projected. **2** something that protrudes from a surface. **3** the showing of a film or transparencies on a screen. **4** a forecast based on present trends and other known data. **5** (*math*, *maps*) the representation of a solid object, esp. part of the earth's sphere, on a flat surface. **6** (*psychol*) a mental process by which a subjective mental image is perceived as belonging to the external world.

projectionist *n* a person who operates a projector, esp. in a cinema.

projector *n* a machine for projecting films or transparencies on to a screen.

projectile *n* an object designed to be propelled with force, esp. a missile such as a bullet or rocket. — *adj* hurling, or (designed to be) hurled, forwards. [Modern Lat *projectilis*, from Lat *projicere*, to throw forward]

prole *n* & *adj* (*coll derog*) proletarian.

proletarian *n* & *adj* (a member) of the proletariat. [Lat *proletarius*, a citizen who has nothing to offer society but his offspring, from *proles*, offspring]

proletariat *n* the working class, esp. unskilled labourers and industrial workers.

proliferate *v* **1** (*intr*) (of a plant or animal species) to reproduce rapidly. **2** (*intr*) to increase in numbers; to multiply. **3** (*tr*) to reproduce (cells, etc. rapidly). — *n* **proliferation**. [Lat *prolifer*, bearing offspring]

prolific *adj* **1** abundant in growth; producing plentiful fruit or offspring. **2** (of a writer, artist, etc.) constantly productive of new work. **3** (with **of**, **in**) productive of; abounding in. — *adv* **prolifically**. [Lat *prolificus*, fertile]

prolix *adj* (of speech or writing) tediously long-winded; wordy; verbose. — *n* **prolixity**, **-*ies***. [Lat *prolixus*, stretched out]

prologue *n* **1** a speech addressed to the audience at the beginning of a play; the actor delivering it. **2** a preface to a literary work. **3** (**to**) an event serving as an introduction or prelude. [Gr *prologos*, from *pro-*, before + *logos*, discourse]

prolong *v* (*tr*) to make longer; to extend or protract. — *n* **prolongation**. [Lat *prolongare*]

prom *n* (*coll*) **1** a promenade (sense **1**). **2** a promenade concert.

promenade *n* **1** a broad paved walk, esp. along a sea front. **2** (*facet*) a stately stroll. — *v* (now usu. *facet*) **1** (*intr*) to stroll in a stately fashion. **2** (*tr*) to walk (the streets, etc.). **3** (*tr*) to take for an airing; to parade: *promenaded her children through the park*. [Fr, from *promener*, to lead about]

promenade concert *n* a concert at which part of the audience is accommodated in a standing area and can move about.

promenade deck *n* an upper deck on board a ship, along which passengers can promenade.

promenader *n* an esp. regular attender at promenade concerts.

prominent *adj* **1** jutting out; projecting; protruding; bulging: *a prominent chin*; *prominent eyes*. **2** noticeable; conspicuous: *a prominent landmark*. **3** leading; notable: *a prominent politician*, *role*, etc. — *n* **prominence**. — *adv* **prominently**. [Lat *prominere*, to jut out]

promiscuous *adj* **1** (*derog*) indulging in casual or indiscriminate sexual relations. **2** haphazardly mixed. — *n* **promiscuity**. — *adv* **promiscuously**. [Lat *promiscuus*, mixed up]

promise *v* (*tr*) **1** to give an undertaking (to do or not do something). **2** to undertake to give (someone something). **3** to show signs of bringing: *clouds that promise rain*. **4** to look likely (to do something): *promises to have a great future*. **5** to assure or warn: *will be heavy going, I promise you*. — *n* **1** an undertaking to give, do or not do, something. **2** a sign: *a promise of spring in the air*. **3** signs of future excellence: *shows promise*. — **promise well** (or **badly**) to give grounds for hope (or despondency). [Lat *promissum*, from *promittere*, to send forth, promise]

promised land *n* **1** (*Bible*) the fertile land promised by God to the Israelites. **2** any longed-for place of contentment and prosperity.

promising *adj* **1** showing promise; talented; apt. **2** seeming to bode well for the future. — *adv* **promisingly**.

promissory *adj* expressing a promise, esp. in **promissory note**, a signed promise to pay a stated sum of money. [Lat *promissorius*, from *promissum*, promise]

promontory *n* **-*ies*** a usu. hilly part of a coastline that projects into the sea; a headland. [Lat *promontorium*, mountain ridge, promontory]

promote *v* (*tr*) **1** (**to**) to raise to a more senior position: *promoted to lieutenant*. **2** to contribute to: *Exercise promotes health*. **3** to work for the cause of: *promote peace*. **4** to publicise; to try to boost the sales of (a product) by advertising. **5** to be the organiser or financer of (an undertaking). — *n* **promotion**. — *adj* **promotional**. [Lat *promovere*, to cause to advance]

promoter *n* the organiser or financer of a sporting event or other undertaking.

prompt *adj* **1** immediate; quick; punctual. **2 (with)** instantly willing; ready; unhesitating; *prompt to offer help, with offers of help*. — *adv* punctually: *at 2.15 prompt*. — *n* **1** something serving as a reminder. **2** words supplied by a prompter to an actor. **3** a prompter. — *v* **1** (*tr*) to cause, lead or remind (someone to do something). **2** (*tr*) to produce or elicit (a reaction or response): *What prompted that remark?* **3** (*tr* & *intr*) to help (an actor) to remember his or her next words by supplying the first few. — *n* **promptitude**. — *adv* **promptly**. — *n* **promptness**. [Lat *promptus*, ready, quick, and *promptare*, to incite]

prompter *n* a person positioned offstage to prompt actors when they forget their lines.

promulgate *v* (*tr*) **1** to make (a decree, etc.) effective by means of an official public announcment. **2** to publicise or promote (an idea, theory, etc.) widely. — *n* **promulgation**. — *n* **promulgator**. [Lat *promulgare*, to make known]

pron. *abbrev* pronoun.

prone *adj* **1** lying flat, esp. face downwards. **2 (to)** predisposed to, or liable to suffer from: *prone to bronchitis*; *accident-prone*. **3** inclined or liable (to do something): *prone to make mistakes*. — *n* **proneness**. [Lat *pronus*, bent forwards]

prong *n* a point or spike, esp. one of those making up the head of a fork. [MidE *pronge*, pang]

pronged *adj* having (a certain number of) prongs: *a three-pronged attack* (i.e. one made by forces attacking from three directions).

pronominal *adj* of, or being, a pronoun; relating to pronouns. — *adv* **pronominally**. [Lat *pronominalis*, from *pronomen*, pronoun]

pronoun *n* a word such as *she*, *him*, *they*, *it* used in place of, and to refer to, a noun or noun phrase. ◇ See also **pronominal**. [Lat *pronomen*, from *pro-*, on behalf of + *nomen*, noun]

pronounce *v* **1** (*tr*) to say or utter (words, sounds, letters, etc.); to articulate or enunciate. **2** (*tr*) to declare officially, formally or authoritatively: *pronounced her innocent*. **3** (*tr*) to pass or deliver (judgement). **4** (*intr*; **on**) to give one's opinion or verdict on. — *adj* **pronounceable**. ◇ See also **pronunciation**. [Lat *pronuntiare*, to declaim, pronounce]

pronounced *adj* noticeable; distinct: *a pronounced limp*. — *adv* **pronouncedly**.

pronouncement *n* **1** a formal announcement. **2** a declaration of opinion; a verdict.

pronto *adv* (*coll*) immediately. [Span, quick]

pronunciation *n* the act, or a manner, or the usual way, of pronouncing words, sounds, letters, etc. [Lat *pronuntiatio*, expression, delivery]

proof *n* **1** evidence, esp. conclusive, that something is true or a fact. **2** (*legal*) the accumulated evidence on which a verdict is based. **3** (the activity or process of) testing or proving: *capable of proof*. **4** a test, trial or demonstration: *as a proof of her love*. **5** (*math*) a step-by-step verification of a proposition. **6** (*printing*) a trial copy of a sheet of printed text for examination or correction. **7** a trial print from a photographic negative. **8** a trial impression from an engraved plate. **9** the alcoholic content of distilled liquors, expressed as a percentage of that of proof spirit. — *adj* (with **against**, or *in cmpds*) able, or designed, to withstand, resist, deter or be free from: *proof against storms*; *leakproof*. — *v* (*tr*) **1** (sometimes *in cmpds*) to make resistant to, or proof against, something; to waterproof: *fully (water) proofed*; *soundproofing*. **2** to take a proof of (printed material). [Fr *preuve*, from Lat *proba*, test, proof]

proof-read *v* (*tr* & *intr*) to read and mark for correction the proofs of (a text, etc.). — *n* **proof-reader**.

proof spirit *n* a mixture of alcohol and water in which the alcohol content is 49·28% of the weight or 57·1% of the volume.

prop[1] *n* a rigid, esp. vertical, support of any of various kinds: *a clothes prop* (= for holding up a rope of washing to dry). **2** a person or thing that one depends on for help or emotional support. **3** (*Rugby*; also **prop forward**) a forward at either end of the front row of the scrum. — *v* ***-pp-*** (*tr*) **1 (up)** to support or hold upright with, or as if with, a prop. **2 (against)** to lean: *propped her bike against the wall*. **3** to serve as a prop to. [MidE *proppe*]

prop[2] *n* (*coll*) **1** a propeller. **2** (*theatre*; esp. in *pl*) a stage property. ◇ See also **props**.

propaganda *n* (the organised circulation by a political group, etc. of) information, misinformation, rumour or opinion, presented so as to influence public feeling. [From the Roman Catholic *Congregatio de propaganda fide* 'congregation for propagating the faith', responsible for foreign missions and training missionaries]

propagandise or **-ize** *v* (*tr*) to subject to propaganda. **2** (*intr*) to circulate propaganda.

propagandist *n* a person who prepares or circulates propaganda.

propagate *v* **1** (*intr* & *tr*) (of a plant or animal) to reproduce (itself); to grow or multiply. **2** (*tr*) to grow (plants) from seed, or by grafting, taking cuttings, etc. **3** (*tr*) to spread or popularise (ideas, etc.). **4** (*physics*) to transmit (sound, electromagnetism, etc.) in wave form. — *n* **propagation**. — *n* **propagator**. [Lat *propagare*, to grow plants by grafting, etc.]

propane *n* a gas got from petroleum and used for heating, lighting and cooking. [*propionic acid*, a fatty acid]

propel *v* **-ll-** (*tr*) **1** to drive or push forward. **2** to steer or send in a certain direction. [Lat *propellere*, to drive forward]

propellant *n* **1** something that propels. **2** the gas in an aerosol can that expels the contents. **3** the fuel in a jet engine. **4** an explosive for propelling a projectile, e.g. a rocket.

propeller *n* a device consisting of a shaft with radiating blades that rotate to propel a ship or an aircraft.

propelling-pencil *n* a type of pencil in which the lead is held in a casing and can be propelled forward as it is worn down.

propensity *n* **-ies** (**for, to, towards**) a tendency or inclination. [Lat *propendere*, to be inclined]

proper *adj* **1** real; genuine; that can rightly be described as: *have a proper holiday*. **2** right; correct: *learn the proper grip*. **3** appropriate: *at the proper time*. **4** own particular; correct: *everything in its proper place*. **5** socially accepted; respectable: *the proper way to behave*. **6** (*derog*) morally strict; prim: *is a bit proper*. **7** (with **to**) belonging to; suitable to: *the form of address proper to her rank*. **8** (used after a noun) strictly so called; itself: *now entering the city proper*. **9** (*coll*) utter: *felt a proper fool*. [OFr *propre*, own]

proper fraction *n* (*math*) a fraction such as $\frac{1}{2}$ and $\frac{3}{7}$ in which the number above the line is smaller than the one below. ◇ See also **improper fraction**.

properly *adv* **1** suitably; appropriately; correctly. **2** with strict accuracy: *Spiders can't properly be called insects*. **3** fully; thoroughly; completely. **4** (*coll*) utterly.

proper noun or **name** *n* (*gram*) the name of a particular person, place or thing. ◇ See also **common noun**.

property *n* **-ies** **1** something one owns: *That book is my property*. **2** one's possessions collectively. **3** the concept of ownership. **4** (a piece of) land or real estate. **5** a quality or attribute: *the properties of copper sulphate*. **6** (*theatre*) an object or piece of furniture used on stage during a performance. [MidE *proprete*, from Lat *proprietas*, attribute, ownership]

propertied *adj* owning property, esp. land.

property man or **mistress** *n* (*theatre*) a person in charge of stage properties.

prophecy *n* **-ies** **1** the interpretation of divine will or the foretelling of the future; a gift or aptitude for this. **2** a prophetic utterance; something foretold; a prediction. [OFr *prophecie*, from Gr *propheteia*]

prophesy *v* **-ies, -ied** **1** (*tr* & *intr*) to foretell (future happenings); to predict. **2** (*intr*) to utter prophecies; to interpret divine will. [Variant of **prophecy**]

prophet *n* **1** a person inspired to express the divine will or reveal the future. **2** (*Bible*; usu. *cap*) any of the writers of prophecy in the Old Testament, or the books attributed to them. **3** (*cap* with **the**) Mohammed. **4** someone (claiming to be) able to tell what will happen in the future: *prophets of mass destruction*. **5** a leading advocate of, or spokesperson for, a movement or cause: *a prophet of the green revolution*. [Gr *prophetes*, an expounder of divine will]

prophetess *n* a female prophet.

prophetic *adj* **1** foretelling the future: *prophetic remarks*. **2** of or relating to prophets or prophecy. — *adv* **prophetically**.

prophylactic *adj* guarding against, or preventing, disease or other mishap. — *n* a prophylactic drug or device; a precautionary measure. [Gr *prophylassein*, to take precautions against]

prophylaxis *n* action or treatment to prevent something unwanted; precautionary measures.

propinquity *n* **1** nearness in place or time; proximity. **2** closeness of kinship. [Lat *propinquitas*, from *propinquus*, near]

propitiate *v* to appease or placate (an angry person or god). — *adj* **propitiable**. — *n* **propitiation**. — *n* **propitiator**. — *adj* **propitiatory**. [Lat *propitiare*, to appease]

propitious *adj* **1** favourable; auspicious; advantageous: *a propitious moment to sell*. **2** (with **for, to**) likely to favour or encourage: *circumstances propitious to development*. — *adv* **propitiously**. [Lat *propitius*, favourable]

proponent *n* a supporter or advocate: *a proponent of recycling*. [Lat *proponere*, to propose]

proportion *n* **1** a part of a total: *a large proportion of the population*. **2** the size of one element or group in relation to the whole or total: *Only a small proportion of lawyers are women*. **3** the size of one group or component in relation to another: *mixed in a proportion of two parts to one*. **4** the correct balance between parts or elements: *The hands are out of proportion with the head*; *get things into proportion*; *anger out of all proportion to the offence*; *a sense of proportion*. **5** (in *pl*) size; dimensions: *a building, task*, etc. *of huge proportions*. **6** (*math*) correspondence between the ratios of two pairs of quantities, as expressed in *2 is to 8 as 3 is to 12*. — *v* **-n-** (*tr*) **1** to adjust the proportions, or balance the parts, of: *a well-proportioned room, body*, etc. **2** (with **to**) to adjust the proportion of (one thing to another). — **in proportion to** **1** in relation to; in comparison with. **2** in parallel with; in correspondence with; at the same rate as. [Lat *proportio*, proportion, symmetry]

proportional *adj* (**to**) **1** corresponding or matching in size, rate, etc. **2** in correct proportion; proportionate. — *adv* **proportionally**.

proportional representation *n* an electoral system in which each political party is represented in parliament in proportion to the votes it receives.

proportionate *adj* (**to**) being in correct proportion: *wages proportionate to the work done.* — *adv* **proportionately**.

propose *v* **1** (*tr*) to offer (a plan, etc.) for consideration; to suggest. **2** (*tr*) to suggest or nominate (someone for a position, task, etc.). **3** (*tr* & *intr*) to be the proposer of (the motion in a debate). **4** (*tr*) to intend: *don't propose to sell.* **5** (*tr*) to announce the drinking of (a toast) or of (someone's health). **6** (*intr*; **to**) to make an offer of marriage. [Lat *proponere*, to propose]

proposal *n* **1** the act of proposing something. **2** something proposed or suggested; a plan. **3** an offer of marriage.

proposer *n* **1** someone who proposes or advocates something. **2** the leading speaker in favour of the motion in a debate.

proposition *n* **1** a proposal or suggestion. **2** something to be dealt with or undertaken: *an awkward proposition.* **3** (*coll euph*) an invitation to have sexual intercourse. **4** (*logic*) a form of statement affirming or denying something, that can be true or false; a premise. **5** (*math*) a statement of a problem or theorem, esp. incorporating its solution or proof. — *v* **-n-** (*tr*; *coll euph*) to propose sexual intercourse to. [Lat *propositio*, a setting forth, premise, proposition]

propound *v* (*tr*) to put forward (an idea, theory, etc.) for consideration or discussion. [Lat *proponere*, to propose]

proprietary *adj* **1** (of e.g. rights) belonging to an owner or proprietor. **2** suggestive or indicative of ownership: *had a proprietary attitude towards his wife.* **3** (of medicines, etc.) marketed under a tradename. **4** privately owned and managed. [Lat *proprietarius*, from *proprietas*, ownership]

proprietary name *n* a tradename.

proprietor *n* an owner, esp. of a shop, hotel, business, etc. — *adj* **proprietorial**. [Lat *proprietarius*, from *proprietas*, ownership]

proprietress *n* a female proprietor.

propriety *n* **-ies** **1** socially acceptable behaviour, esp. between the sexes; modesty or decorum. **2** rightness; moral acceptability: *the dubious propriety of getting children to report on their teachers.* **3** (in *pl*) the details of correct behaviour; accepted standards of conduct: *observe the proprieties.* [MidE *propriete*, one's own nature, from OFr, from Lat *proprietas*, ownership]

props *n* (*theatre*) a property man or property mistress. ◇ See also **prop**.

propulsion *n* the process of driving, or of being driven, forward; a force that propels: *jet propulsion.* — *adj* **propulsive**. [Lat *propulsio*]

pro rata *adv* in proportion; in accordance with a certain rate. [Lat]

prorogue *v* **1** (*tr*) to discontinue the meetings of (a legislative assembly) for a time, without dissolving it. **2** (*intr*) (of a legislative assembly) to suspend a session. — *n* **prorogation**. [Lat *prorogare*, to propose, continue, defer]

prosaic *adj* **1** unpoetic; unimaginative. **2** dull, ordinary and uninteresting. — *adv* **prosaically**. [Lat *prosaicus*, from *prosa*, prose]

proscenium *n* **-iums** or **-ia** (*theatre*) **1** the part of a stage in front of the curtain. **2** (also **proscenium arch**) the arch framing the stage and separating it from the auditorium. [Gr *proskenion*, from *pro-*, in front + *skene*, stage]

proscribe *v* (*tr*) **1** to prohibit or condemn (something, e.g. a practice). **2** (*hist*) to outlaw or exile (someone). — *n* **proscription**. — *adj* **proscriptive**. [Lat *proscribere*, to outlaw]

prose *n* **1** ordinary written or spoken language as distinct from verse or poetry. **2** a passage of prose set for translation into a foreign language. [Lat *prosa oratio*, straightforward speech]

prosy *adj* **-ier**, **-iest** (of speech or writing) tediously long-winded.

prosecute *v* **1** (*tr* & *intr*) to bring a criminal action against (someone). **2** (*tr*; *formal*) to carry on or carry out: *prosecuting her enquiries.* [Lat *prosequi*, to pursue]

prosecution *n* **1** the act of prosecuting or process of being prosecuted. **2** the bringing of a criminal action against someone. **3** (*sing* or *pl*) (the lawyers acting for) the prosecuting party in a criminal case. **4** (*formal*) the process of carrying something out: *in the prosecution of my duties.*

prosecutor *n* a person who brings or conducts a criminal action against someone.

proselyte *n* a convert, esp. to Judaism. [Gr *proselytos*, new arrival, convert to Judaism]

proselytism *n* **1** the process of becoming a convert; conversion. **2** the practice of making converts.

proselytise or **-ize** *v* (*tr* & *intr*) to try to convert; to make converts.

prosody *n* **1** the study of verse-composition, esp. poetic metre. **2** (also **prosodics** *n sing*) the study of rhythm, stress and intonation in speech. — *adj* **prosodic**. — *n* **prosodist**. [Gr *prosoidia*, from *pros*, to + *oide*, song]

prospect *n* **1** a visualisation of something due, or likely, to happen: *the prospect of losing her job.* **2** an outlook for the future. **3** (in *pl*) chances of success, improvement, recovery, etc. **4** (in *pl*) opportunities for advancement: *a job with prospects.* **5** a potentially selectable candidate, team member, etc.: *is a doubtful prospect for Saturday's match.* **6** a potential client or customer. **7** a broad view: *a prospect of the bay.* **8** (*gold-mining*) (an area with potential as) a mine. — *v* (*intr*; **for**) **1** to search for (gold, etc.). **2** to hunt for or look out for (e.g. a job). — **in prospect** expected soon. [Lat *prospectus*, view]

prospective *adj* likely or expected; future: *a prospective buyer.*

prospector *n* a person prospecting for oil, gold, etc.

prospectus *n* **-*uses*** **1** a booklet giving information about a school or other institution; a brochure. **2** a document outlining a proposal for something, e.g. a literary work, or an issue of shares. [Lat, prospect]

prosper *v* **-*r*-** (*intr*) to do well, esp. financially; to thrive or flourish. [Lat *prosperari*, to prosper]

prosperity *n* the state of being prosperous; success; wealth.

prosperous *adj* wealthy and successful. — *adv* **prosperously**.

prostate *n* (also **prostate gland**) a gland at the neck of the bladder in male mammals. [Gr *prostates*, literally 'one that stands in front']

prosthesis *n* **-*eses*** (the fitting of) an artificial substitute for a part of the body removed by surgery, etc., e.g. an eye, limb, tooth or breast. [Gr, from *pros*, to + *tithenai*, to put]

prostitute *n* a person, esp. a woman or homosexual man, who accepts money in return for sexual intercourse or sexual acts. — *v* (*tr*) **1** to put (e.g. one's talents) to an unworthy use. **2** to offer (oneself or someone else) as a prostitute. — *n* **prostitution**. [Lat *prostituere*, to offer for sale]

prostrate *adj* **1** lying face downwards in an attitude of abject submission, humility or adoration. **2** lying flat. **3** exhausted by illness, grief, etc. — *v* (*tr*) **1** to throw (oneself) face down in submission or adoration. **2** to exhaust physically or emotionally. — *n* **prostration**. [Lat *prosternere*, to throw forwards]

prosy. See **prose**.

prot-. See **proto-**.

protactinium *n* an element (symbol **Pa**), a poisonous radioactive metal. [**prot-** + **actinium**]

protagonist *n* **1** the main character in a play or story. **2** the person, or any of the people, at the centre of a story or event. **3** a leader or champion of a movement, cause, etc. [Gr *protagonistes*, from *protos*, first + *agonistes*, combatant]

protean *adj* **1** readily able to change shape or appearance; variable; changeable. **2** versatile; diverse. [*Proteus*, a Greek sea god able to assume different shapes]

protect *v* (*tr*) **1 (from, against) 1** to shield from danger; to guard against injury, destruction, etc.; to keep safe. **2** to cover against loss, etc. by insurance. **3** to shield (home industries) from foreign competition by taxing imports. [Lat *protegere*, to cover in front, protect]

protection *n* **1 (from, against)** the action of protecting or condition of being protected; shelter, refuge, cover, safety or care. **2 (from, against)** something that protects: *grow a hedge as a protection against the wind.* **3** the system of protecting home industries against foreign competition by taxing imports. **4** the criminal practice of extorting money from shop-owners, etc. in return for leaving their premises unharmed; (also **protection money**) the money so extorted. **5** insurance cover.

protectionism *n* the policy of protecting home industry from foreign competition. — *n* **protectionist**.

protective *adj* **1** giving, or designed to give, protection. **2 (towards)** inclined or tending to protect: *feel protective towards one's children.* — *adv* **protectively**. — *n* **protectiveness**.

protective custody *n* the detention of someone in prison, officially for his or her own safety.

protector *n* **1** a person or thing that protects. **2** a patron or benefactor. **3** a person ruling a country during the childhood of the sovereign, or in the absence of a sovereign; a regent.

protectorate *n* **1** the office, or period of rule, of a protector. **2** protectorship of a weak or backward country assumed by a more powerful one; the status of a territory that is so protected without actual annexation.

protectress *n* a female protector.

protégé or **protégée** *n* a man or woman under the guidance, protection and patronage of a more important or wiser person. [Fr *protéger*, to protect]

protein *n* any of a group of organic compounds essential to the make-up of all living cells, consisting of amino acids in various combinations. [Gr *proteios*, primary]

pro tem (*coll*) short for **pro tempore** (Lat), for the time being.

protest *v* **1** (*intr*; **against, at, about**) to express an objection, disapproval, opposition or disagreement. **2** (*tr*; *US*) to challenge or object to (e.g. a decision or measure). **3** (*tr*) to declare solemnly, e.g. in response to an accusation: *protest one's innocence*. **4** (*tr*; *legal*) to obtain or write a protest with reference to (a bill). — *n* **1** a declaration of disapproval or dissent; an objection. **2** an organised public demonstration of disapproval. **3** (*legal*) a written statement that a bill has been presented and payment refused. — *n* **protester** or **protestor**. — **under protest** unwillingly. — [Lat *protestari*, to declare, testify]

Protestant *n* a member of any of the Christian churches that in the 16th century embraced the principles of the Reformation and, rejecting the authority of the pope, separated from the Roman Catholic church; a member of any body descended from these. — *adj* of, belonging to, or relating to, Protestants. — *n* **Protestantism**. [Orig. applied to those princes and others who in 1529 protested against an edict denouncing the Reformation]

protestation *n* **1** a protest or objection. **2** a solemn declaration or avowal.

proto- or **prot-** *comb fm* first or earliest: *prototype*. [Gr *protos*, first]
protocol *n* **1** correct formal or diplomatic etiquette or procedure. **2** a first draft of a diplomatic document, e.g. setting out the terms of a treaty. **3** (*US*) a plan of a scientific experiment or other procedure. [Gr *protokollon*, a note of the contents of a document, glued to the front sheet, from *protos*, first + *kolla*, glue]
proton *n* a particle with a positive electrical charge forming part (and in hydrogen the whole) of the atomic nucleus. [Gr *protos*, first]
protoplasm *n* (also **plasma**) the translucent, colourless, semi-liquid substance of which living cells are chiefly composed. [**proto-** + *plasma*, form]
prototype *n* **1** an original model from which later forms are copied, developed or derived. **2** a first working version, e.g. of a vehicle, aircraft, etc. **3** a person or thing that exemplifies a type. **4** a primitive or ancestral form of something. [Gr *prototypos*, primitive, original]
protozoon *n* **-zoa** a microscopic single-celled creature such as the amoeba, representing the lowest and simplest form of animal. — *n & adj* **protozoan**. [**proto-** + Gr *zoion*, animal]
protract *v* (*tr*) to prolong; to cause to last a long time. [Lat *protrahere*, to drag forth, prolong]
protracted *adj* lasting longer than usual or longer than expected.
protractor *n* (*geom*) an instrument, usu. a transparent plastic semicircle marked in degrees, for drawing and measuring angles. [Lat, from *protrahere*, to draw forth]
protrude *v* **1** (*intr*) to project; to stick out. **2** (*tr*) to push out or forward. — *n* **protrusion**. — *adj* **protrusive**. [Lat *protrudere*, to thrust forward]
protuberant *n* projecting; bulging; swelling out. — *n* **protuberance**. [Lat *protuberare*, to swell out]
proud *adj* **1** (**of**) feeling pride at one's own or another's accomplishments, one's possessions, etc. **2** being a cause or occasion for pride: *a proud day*; *her proudest possession*. **3** arrogant; conceited: *too proud to talk to us*. **4** concerned for one's dignity and self-respect: *too proud to accept help*. **5** honoured; gratified; delighted: *proud to be invited*. **6** splendid; imposing: *a proud sight*. **7** (*poetic*) lofty; high: *trees waving their proud tops*. **8** (**of**) projecting slightly from the surrounding surface. **9** (of flesh) forming a protuberant mass round a healing wound. — *adv* **proudly**. — **do (someone) proud** to entertain (someone) grandly. — **do oneself proud** to succeed gloriously. [OE *prud*]
prove *v* ***proved***, ***proved*** or (esp. *US* & *Scot*) ***proven*** **1** (*tr*) to show to be true, correct or a fact. **2** (*tr*) to show to be: *was proved innocent*; *drugs of proven effectiveness*. **3** (*intr*) to be found to be, when tried; to turn out to be: *Her advice proved sound*. **4** (*tr*) to show (oneself) to be: *has proved himself reliable*. **5** (*tr*) to show (oneself) capable or daring. **6** (*tr*; *legal*) to establish the validity of (a will). **7** (*tr*) (of dough) to (cause to) rise. — *adj* **provable** or **proveable**. — **not proven** (*legal*; *Scot*) the form of verdict resorted to where there is insufficient evidence to prove guilt. [Lat *probare*, to test, prove]
proving-ground *n* a place used for scientific testing; a place where something is tried out for the first time.
provenance *n* the place of origin, or source, of e.g. a work of art, archaeological find, etc. [Fr, from Lat *provenire*, to come forth]
Provençal *adj* of or relating to Provence in the south of France, its inhabitants, culture or language. — *n* **1** a language spoken in Provence, related to French and Spanish. **2** a native of Provence.
provender *n* **1** fodder for horses or cattle. **2** (*facet*) food. [OFr *provendre*, from Lat *praebenda*, payment]
proverb *n* any of a body of well-known, neatly expressed sayings that give advice or express a supposed truth. [Lat *proverbium*]
proverbial *adj* **1** of, like or being a proverb. **2** referred to in a proverb; traditionally quoted; well known: *a cat's proverbial nine lives*. — *adv* **proverbially**.
provide *v* **1** (*tr*; **with**) to supply. **2** (*tr*) (of e.g. a circumstance, situation, etc.) to offer: *provide enjoyment*, *an opportunity*, etc. **3** (*intr* with **for, against**) to prepare for (an emergency, etc.). **4** (*intr* with **for**) to support or keep (a family, etc.). **5** (*tr*; esp. *legal*) to stipulate or require (that something should be done, etc.). **6** (*intr* with **for**; esp. *legal*) to specify (something) as a requirement, or enable (something to be done). — *n* **provider**. [Lat *providere*, to see ahead, provide for]
provided or **providing (that)** *conj* **1** on the condition or understanding that. **2** if and only if.
providence *n* **1** a mysterious power or force that operates to keep one from harm, etc.; the benevolent foresight of God. **2** (*cap*) God as an all-seeing protector of His creatures. **3** the quality of being provident; prudent foresight or thrifty planning. [Lat *providentia*, foresight]
provident *adj* careful and thrifty in planning ahead. — *adv* **providently**.
providential *adj* due to providence; fortunate; lucky; opportune. — *adv* **providentially**.
province *n* **1** an administrative division of a country. **2** (*Roman hist*) a territory outside Italy, governed by Rome as part of its empire. **3** one's allotted range of duties, or one's field of knowledge or experience: *a task outside my province*. **4** (in *pl* with **the**) the parts of a country away from the capital, typically thought of as

culturally backward. [Lat *provincia*, official charge, province]

provincial *adj* **1** of, belonging to, or relating to a province. **2** relating to the parts of a country away from the capital: *a provincial accent*. **3** supposedly typical of provinces in being culturally backward, unsophisticated, or narrow in outlook. — *n* **provincialism**. — *adv* **provincially**. [Lat *provincialis*, from *provincia*, province]

provision *n* **1** the act of providing. **2** (**for**) something provided or made available; facilities: *provision for disabled pupils*. **3** (**for**) preparations; measures taken in advance: *make provision for the future*. **4** (in *pl*) food and other necessaries. **5** (esp. *legal*) a condition or requirement; a clause stipulating or enabling something. — *v* **-n-** (*tr*) to supply with food. [Lat *provisio*, forethought, precaution]

provisional *adj* temporary; conditional; for the time being, or immediate purposes, only; liable to be altered. — *adv* **provisionally**.

proviso *n* **-os 1** a condition: *agreed, with one proviso*. **2** (esp. *legal*) a clause stating a condition. — *adj* **provisory**. [Lat *proviso quod*, it being provided that]

provocateur. See **agent provocateur**.

provocation *n* **1** the act of provoking or state of being provoked; incitement. **2** a cause of anger, irritation or indignation. [Lat *provocatio*, calling forth, challenge]

provocative *adj* **1** tending, or intended, to cause anger; deliberately infuriating. **2** (designed to be) sexually arousing or stimulating: *provocative clothes, behaviour*, etc. — *adv* **provocatively**.

provoke *v* (*tr*) **1** to annoy or infuriate, esp. deliberately. **2** (**into**) to incite or goad. **3** to rouse (someone's anger, etc.). **4** to cause, stir up or bring about: *provoked a storm of protest*. [Lat *provocare*, to call forth, challenge, stimulate]

provoking *adj* annoying.

provost *n* **1** the head of some university colleges. **2** in Scotland, the chief magistrate of a burgh. [OFr, from Lat *propositus*, placed at the head]

provost marshal *n* an officer in charge of military police.

prow *n* the projecting front part of a ship; the bow. [Fr *proue*]

prowess *n* **1** skill; ability; expertise. **2** valour; dauntlessness. [OFr *proesse*]

prowl *v* (*intr*) **1** to go about stealthily, e.g. in search of prey. **2** to pace restlessly. — *n* an act of prowling. — *n* **prowler**. — **on the prowl** prowling about on the look-out for something. [MidE *prollen*]

proximate *adj* nearest; immmediately before or after in time, place, or order of occurrence. [Lat *proximare*, to approach]

proximity *n* (**to**) nearness; closeness in space or time: *lives in close proximity to the station*. [Lat *proximitas*, from *proximus*, next]

proxy *n* **-ies 1** a person authorised to act or vote on another's behalf; the agency of such a person. **2** (a document giving) the authority to act or vote for someone else. [Contraction of **procuracy**]

prude *n* a person who is or affects to be shocked by improper behaviour, mention of sexual matters, etc.; a prim or priggish person. — *n* **prudery**. — *adj* **prudish**. — *adv* **prudishly**. — *n* **prudishness**. [Fr *prude femme*, respectable woman]

prudent *adj* **1** wise or careful in conduct. **2** shrewd or thrifty in planning ahead. **3** wary; discreet: *a prudent withdrawal*. — *n* **prudence**. — *adv* **prudently**. [Lat *prudens*, contracted from *providens*, from *providere*, to see ahead]

prudential *adj* (*old*) characterised by, or exercising, careful forethought. [Lat *prudentialis*, from *prudentia*, prudence]

prune[1] *v* **1** to cut off (unneeded branches, etc.) from (a tree or shrub) to improve its growth. **2** to cut out (superfluous matter) from (a piece of writing, etc.); to trim or edit. — *n* an act of pruning. [OFr *proognier*, to prune (vines)]

pruning-hook *n* a garden tool with a curved blade, for pruning.

prune[2] *n* a dried plum. [Lat *prunum*, plum]

prurient *adj* **1** unhealthily or excessively interested in sexual matters. **2** tending to arouse such unhealthy interest. — *n* **prurience**. — *adv* **pruriently**. [Lat *prurire*, to itch, lust after]

Prussian *adj* (*hist*) of or relating to Prussia, a former north-central European state, part of the German empire. — *n* a native or inhabitant of Prussia.

Prussian blue *n* a deep blue pigment first made in Berlin; its colour.

prussic acid *n* a deadly poison first obtained from Prussian blue; a solution of hydrogen cyanide in water.

pry[1] *v* ***pries, pried*** (*intr*) **1** (**into**) to investigate matters that do not concern one, esp. the personal affairs of others; to nose or snoop. **2** to peer or peep inquisitively. [MidE *prien*]

pry[2] *v* ***pries, pried*** (*tr; US*) to prise. [**prise**]

PS *abbrev* postscript.

psalm *n* a sacred song, esp. one from the Book of Psalms in the Old Testament, traditionally attributed to King David. [Gr *psalmos*, song sung to a harp]

psalmist *n* a composer of psalms.

psalmody *n* **1** the art of singing psalms. **2** a collected body of psalms. [Gr *oide*, song]

psalter *n* **1** (*cap*) the Book of Psalms. **2** a book containing the Biblical psalms. [Gr *psalterion*, stringed instrument]

psaltery *n* **-ies** (*hist*) a zither-like stringed instrument played by plucking. [Gr *psalterion*, stringed instrument, harp]

PSBR *abbrev* public-sector borrowing requirement, the money needed by the public sector to finance services, etc. not covered by revenue.

psephology *n* the study of elections and voting patterns. — *adj* **psephological**. — *n* **psephologist**. [Gr *psephos*, pebble, vote + **-logy**]

pseud (*coll*) *n* a pretentious person; a bogus intellectual; a phoney. — *adj* bogus, sham or phoney. [**pseudo-**]

pseudo *adj* (*coll*) false; sham; phoney. [**pseudo-**]

pseudo- or **pseud-** *comb fm* **1** false. **2** pretending to be: *pseudo-intellectuals*. **3** deceptively resembling: *pseudo-scientific jargon*. [Gr *pseudes*, false]

pseudonym *n* a false name used by an author; a pen name or nom de plume. — *adj* **pseudonymous**. [Gr *pseudes*, false + *onyma*, name]

psi *abbrev* pounds per square inch, a unit of pressure measurement.

psittacosis *n* a disease of parrots that can be transmitted to human beings. [Gr *psittakos*, parrot + **-osis**]

psoriasis *n* a skin disease characterised by red scaly patches. [Gr, from *psora*, itch]

PSV *abbrev* public service vehicle.

psych *v* (*tr*; *coll*) **1** (**up**) to prepare, steel or brace (oneself) for a challenge, etc. **2** (**out**) to undermine the confidence of (one's opponent, etc.); to intimidate mentally. **3** to psychoanalyse. [**psych-**]

psych-. See **psycho-**.

psyche *n* one's mind, esp. with regard to the deep feelings and attitudes that account for one's opinions and behaviour. [Gr]

psychedelic *adj* **1** denoting a state of mind with heightened perceptions and increased mental powers. **2** (of drugs) inducing such a state. **3** (of perceived phenomena, e.g. colours) startlingly clear and vivid. [**psyche** + Gr *delos*, clear]

psychiatry *n* (the study of) the diagnosis and treatment of mental illness. — *adj* **psychiatric**. — *n* **psychiatrist**. [**psych-** + Gr *iatros*, doctor]

psychic *adj* **1** (also **psychical**) relating to mental processes or experiences that are not scientifically explainable, e.g. telepathy. **2** (of a person) sensitive to influences producing such experiences; having mental powers that are not scientifically explainable. [Gr *psychikos*, relating to the psyche]

psycho *n* **-os** (*coll*) a psychopath. — *adj* psychopathic.

psycho- or **psych-** *comb fm* the mind and its workings.

psychoanalyse or **-yze** *v* (*tr*) to examine or treat by psychoanalysis. — *n* **psychoanalyst**. — *adj* **psychoanalytic** or **psychoanalytical**. [**psycho-** + **analyse**]

psychoanalysis *n* the investigation and treatment of mental illness through discussions with the patient about his or her feelings, early life and past experiences, so that the cause, usu. hidden in the unconscious, can be identified and dealt with.

psychology *n* **1** the study of the human mind and the reasons for human behaviour. **2** the mental attitudes and associated behaviour characteristic of a certain individual or group: *mob psychology*. **3** the ability to understand how people's minds work, useful when trying to influence them: *good* or *bad psychology*. — *n* **psychologist**. [**psycho-** + **-logy**]

psychological *adj* relating to the mind or to psychology. — *adv* **psychologically**.

psychological moment *n* the moment at which one is most likely to succeed in influencing someone to react as one wants.

psychological warfare *n* propaganda and other methods used in wartime to influence enemy opinion and sap enemy morale.

psychopath *n* **1** (*tech*) a person with a personality disorder characterised by extreme callousness, who is liable to behave antisocially or violently in getting his or her own way. **2** (*coll*) a person who is dangerously unstable mentally or emotionally. — *adj* **psychopathic**. — *adv* **psychopathically**. [**psycho-** + **-path**]

psychopathy *n* **1** the condition of a psychopath. **2** mental illness generally.

psychosis *n* **-oses** a mental disorder causing the sufferer to lose hold on reality. — *adj* & *n* **psychotic**. — *adv* **psychotically**. [Gr, animation; in modern use, condition of the psyche]

psychosomatic *adj* (of bodily disorders) having a mental or emotional cause such as stress. — *adv* **psychosomatically**. [**psycho-** + Gr *soma*, body]

psychosurgery *n* the treatment of mental illness by brain surgery.

psychotherapy *n* the treatment of mental or nervous illness by psychological means, rather than by surgery or drugs. — *n* **psychotherapist**.

PT *abbrev* physical training.

Pt[1] *abbrev* Port.

Pt[2] *symbol* (*chem*) platinum.

pt *abbrev* **1** part. **2** pint. **3** point.

PTA *abbrev* Parent-Teacher Association.

ptarmigan *n* a mountain-dwelling grouse with white winter plumage. [Gaelic *tàrmachan*; the *p* wrongly added under the influence of Greek words beginning with *pt-*]

Pte *abbrev* (*mil*) Private, the title for an ordinary soldier.

pterodactyl *n* a extinct flying reptile with a bird-like skull and leathery wings. [Gr *pteron*, wing + *daktylos*, finger]

PTO *abbrev* please turn over.

ptomaine *n* any of several organic substances, some poisonous, that form in decaying animal tissues. [Ital *ptomaina*, from Gr *ptoma*, corpse]

pty *abbrev* proprietary.

Pu *symbol* (*chem*) plutonium.

pub *n* a public house, a place where alcoholic drinks may be bought for consumption on the premises.

puberty *n* the stage in life during which the reproductive organs develop, bringing about sexual maturity. [Lat *pubertas*]

pubes *n* **-bes** **1** the lower part of the abdomen; the groin. **2** the hair that grows on this part at puberty. [Lat]

pubescence *adj* **1** the onset of puberty. **2** a soft downy covering on plants. — *adj* **pubescent**. [Lat *pubescere*, to reach puberty, become downy]

pubic *adj* relating to the pubis or pubes. **[pubes]**

pubis *n* **-bes** (*anat*) the name of two bones at either side of the lower forepart of the pelvis. [Lat *os pubis*, bone of the pubes]

public *adj* **1** of, or concerning, all the people of a country or community: *public health*, *opinion*, etc. **2** relating to the organisation and administration of a community: *the public prosecutor*. **3** provided for the use of the community: *public parks*. **4** well known through exposure in the media: *public figures*. **5** made, done, held, etc. openly, for all to see, hear or participate in: *a public announcement*, *enquiry*, *meeting*, etc. **6** known to all: *when the facts became public*; *is public knowledge*; *make one's views public*. **7** watched or attended by an audience, spectators, etc.: *her last public appearance*. **8** open to view; not private or secluded: *It's too public here*. — *n* (*sing* or *pl*) **1** the people or community. **2** a particular class of people: *the concert-going public*. **3** an author's, performer's, etc. audience or group of devotees: *mustn't disappoint my public*. — **go public** to become a public company. — **in public** in the presence of other people. — **in the public eye** (of a person, etc.) well known through media exposure. [Lat *publicus*, from *populus*, people]

public-address system *n* the system of microphones, amplifiers and loudspeakers by means of which public announcements, etc. can be communicated to everyone within a large building, etc.

publication *n* **1** the act of publishing a printed work; the process of publishing or of being published. **2** a book, magazine, newspaper or other printed and published work. **3** the act of making something known to the public.

public bar *n* a bar less well furnished and serving drinks more cheaply than a lounge bar.

public company *n* a company whose shares are available for purchase by the public.

public convenience *n* a public toilet.

public enemy *n* someone whose behaviour makes him or her a menace to the community.

public holiday *n* a day kept as an official holiday, on which businesses, etc. are closed.

public house *n* an establishment where alcoholic drinks are sold for consumption on the premises; a pub.

publicise or **-ize** *v* (*tr*) **1** to make generally or widely known. **2** to advertise.

publicity *n* **1** advertising or other activity designed to rouse public interest in something. **2** public interest so attracted. **3** the condition of being the object of public attention.

public lending right *n* the right of authors to a fee whenever their books are borrowed from a public library.

public nuisance *n* an illegal act causing trouble or danger to the general public.

public prosecutor *n* a public official whose function is to prosecute those charged with criminal offences.

public relations *n* **1** (*pl* or *sing*) the relationship of an organisation, etc. with the public, esp. with regard to its reputation and its communication of information about itself. **2** (*sing*) the department of an organisation responsible for this.

public school *n* **1** in Britain, a secondary school run independently of the state, financed by endowments and by pupils' fees. **2** in the US, a school run by a public authority.

public sector *n* that part of a country's economy consisting of nationalised industries and of institutions and services run by the state or local authorities.

public servant *n* an elected or appointed holder of public office; a government employee.

public-spirited *adj* acting from, or showing, concern for the general good of all.

public transport *n* the buses, trains, etc. provided for public use by the state or by local authorities.

public utility *n* a supply e.g. of gas, water or electricity, or other service, provided for a community.

public works *n* (*pl*) buildings, roads, etc. built by the state for public use.

publican *n* **1** (*Bible*) a tax-collector. **2** (orig. *facet*) the keeper of a public house. [Lat *publicanus*, tax-farmer]

publish *v* (*tr* & *intr*) **1** to prepare, produce and distribute (printed material, computer software, etc.) for sale to the public. **2** (*intr* & *tr*) (of an author) to have (one's work) published. **3** (*tr*) to publish the work of (an author). **4** (*tr*) to announce publicly: *published their engagement*. **5** (*tr*; *legal*) to circulate (a libel). [OFr *publier*, from Lat *publicare*, to make public]

publisher *n* **1** a person or company engaged in the business of publishing books, newspapers, music, software, etc. **2** (*NAm*) a newspaper proprietor.

puce *n* a colour anywhere in the range between deep purplish pink and purplish brown. [Fr *couleur de puce*, flea colour]

puck *n* a thick disc of hard rubber used in ice-hockey in place of a ball. [Perhaps connected with **poke**[1]]

pucker *v* **-r-** (*tr* & *intr*) to gather into creases, folds or wrinkles; to wrinkle. — *n* a wrinkle, fold or crease. [Possibly connected with **poke**[2]]

puckish *adj* mischievous; impish. [Old word *puck*, sprite, devil]

pudding *n* **1** any of several sweet or savoury foods usu. made with flour and eggs and cooked by steaming, boiling or baking. **2** any sweet food served as dessert; the dessert course. **3** a type of sausage made with minced meat, spices, blood, oatmeal, etc.: *black pudding*. [MidE *poding*]

puddle *n* **1** a small pool, esp. of rainwater on the road. **2** a non-porous material composed of wet clay and sand kneaded together. — *v* (*tr*) **1** to knead (clay and sand) to form puddle. **2** to stir and expel carbon from (molten pig-iron) so as to produce wrought iron. [Prob. dimin. of OE *pudd*, ditch]

pudendum *n* **-*da*** (often in *pl*) the external sexual organs, esp. of a woman. [Lat, something to be ashamed of]

pudgy *adj* **-*ier*, -*iest***. Another form of **podgy**.

puerile *adj* childish; silly; immature. — *n* **puerility**. [Lat *puerilis*, from *puer*, boy]

puerperal *adj* connected with childbirth. [Lat *puerpera*, woman in labour]

puerperal fever *n* (fever accompanying) blood-poisoning caused by infection of the uterus or birth canal during childbirth.

puff *n* **1** a small rush, gust or blast of air, wind, etc.; the sound made by it. **2** a small cloud of smoke, dust or steam emitted from something. **3** (*coll*) breath: *quite out of puff*. **4** an act of inhaling and exhaling smoke from a pipe or cigarette; a drag or draw. **5** a light pastry: *jam puffs*. **6** a powder puff. **7** a bit of publicity intended, or serving, as an advertisement. — *v* (*tr* & *intr*) **1** to blow or breathe in small blasts. **2** (*intr*) (of smoke, steam, etc.) to emerge in small gusts or blasts. **3** (*intr* or *tr*; **at**) to inhale and exhale smoke from, or draw at (a cigarette, etc.). **4** (*intr*; **along**, etc.) (of a train, boat, etc.) to go along emitting puffs of steam. **5** (*intr*) to pant, or go along panting: *puffing up the hill*. **6** (*tr*; usu. in *passive*; **out**) to make breathless: *I'm puffed (out)*. **7** (*tr* & *intr*; **up**, **out**) to (cause to) swell: *puffed out its feathers*; *a puffed-up eye*. **8** (*tr* with **up**; usu. in *passive*) to fill with self-importance. **9** (*tr*) to praise extravagantly by way of advertisement. [OE *pyffan*; imit.]

puff adder *n* a large African viper that inflates the upper part of its body when startled.

puff ball *n* a ball-shaped edible fungus containing a powdery mass of spores.

puffer *n* (*Scot*; *hist*) a small steam-boat used to carry cargo around the west coast and western isles of Scotland.

puff pastry *n* light flaky pastry made with a high proportion of fat.

puffy *adj* **-*ier*, -*iest*** swollen as a result of injury or ill health. — *n* **puffiness**.

puffin *n* a black and white sea bird of northern regions, with a large brightly coloured beak.

pug *n* a small dog with a flattened snout and curly tail.

pug nose *n* a short upturned nose. — *adj* **pug-nosed**.

pugilism *n* (*old*) the sport of boxing or prize-fighting. — *n* **pugilist**. [Lat *pugil*, boxer]

pugnacious *adj* given to fighting; quarrelsome, belligerent or combative. — *adv* **pugnaciously**. — *n* **pugnacity**. [Lat *pugnax*, from *pugnare*, to fight]

puissance *n* (*showjumping*) a competition testing the horse's ability to jump high fences. [OFr, power]

puissant *adj* (*old* or *poetic*) strong, mighty or powerful. [OFr, from Lat *potens*, present participle of *posse*, to be able]

puke (*coll*) *v* (*tr* & *intr*) to vomit. — *n* **1** vomit. **2** an act of vomiting. [Possibly imit.]

pukka *adj* (*coll*) **1** superior; high-quality. **2** upper-class; well-bred. **3** genuine. [Hindi *pakka*, cooked, firm, ripe]

pulchritude *n* (*literary*) beauty of face and form. [Lat *pulchritudo*, beauty]

pull *v* **1** (*tr* & *intr*; **at**) to grip strongly and draw or force towards oneself; to tug or drag. **2** (*tr*) to remove or extract (a cork, tooth, weeds, etc.) with this action. **3** (*tr*) to operate (a trigger, lever or switch) with this action. **4** (*tr*; **on**) to put on (clothes) hastily. **5** (*tr*) to draw (a trailer, etc.). **6** (*tr*) to open or close (curtains or a blind). **7** (*tr*) to tear or take apart with a tugging action: *pulled it to pieces*. **8** (*tr* with **on**) to produce (a weapon) as a threat to: *pulled a gun on us*. **9** (*tr* & *intr*; **away**) to row (a boat). **10** (*intr*; **at**) to execute strokes with (an oar). **11** (*tr*) to pour (a pint of beer, etc.) by operating a lever. **12** (*intr*) (of a driver or vehicle) to steer or move in a particular direction: *pulled right*. **13** (*tr*) to hit (a ball) so that it veers off its intended course, e.g. (in *golf*) to the left and (in *cricket*) to the leg side. **14** (*intr*) (of an engine or vehicle) to produce the required propelling power: *isn't pulling well*. **15** (*intr* with **at**) to inhale and exhale smoke from (a cigarette, etc.); to draw or suck at. **16** (*tr*) to attract (a crowd, votes, etc.). **17** (*tr*) to strain (a muscle or tendon). **18** (*tr*) to practise or execute (esp. a trick) successfully: *pull a fast one*. **19** (*tr*; *printing*) to print (a proof). — *n* **1** an act of pulling. **2** attraction; attracting force: *magnetic pull*; *the pull of one's homeland*. **3** useful influence: *has some pull with the education department*. **4** a drag at a pipe; a swallow of liquor, etc. **5** a tab, etc. for pulling. **6** a stroke made with an oar. **7** (*printing*) a proof. — **pull ahead (of)** or **away (from)** to get in front; to gain a lead. — **pull apart 1** to tear; to reduce to pieces. **2** to criticise severely. — *v* **pull back** (*tr* & *intr*) to (cause to) withdraw or retreat. — *v* **pull down** (*tr*) to demolish (a building, etc.). — *v* **pull in 1** (*intr*) (of a train) to halt at a station. **2** (*intr*; also **pull over**) (of a vehicle) to move off, or to the side of, the road. **3** (*tr*; *slang*) to make (money, esp. a lot). **4** (*tr*; *coll*) to arrest. — *v* **pull off** (*tr*; *coll*) to arrange or accomplish sucessfully: *pull off a deal*. — *v* **pull out 1** (*tr*) to extract. ◇ See also **pull-out** below. **2** (*intr* & *tr*) to withdraw from combat, from a competition, project, etc. ◇ See also **pull-out** below. **3** (*intr*) (of a driver or vehicle) to move away from the kerb, or into the centre of the road to overtake. — **pull over** see **pull in** above. — **pull round** see **pull through** below. — *v* **pull together** (*intr*) to work together towards a common aim; to co-operate. — **pull oneself together** to reassert control over (oneself). — *v* **pull through** (*intr* & *tr*) (also **pull round**) to (help to) survive an illness. — *v* **pull up 1** (*intr*) (of a driver or vehicle) to stop. **2** (*tr*) to reprimand: *was pulled up for being late*. **3** (*tr*) to uproot (plants). **4** (*intr* with **on, with**) to catch up with. — **pull up short 1** to check (oneself). **2** to take aback. [OE *pullian*, to pluck, draw, pull]

pull-out *n* **1** a self-contained detachable section of a magazine designed to be kept for reference. **2** a withdrawal (from combat, etc.).

pullet *n* a young hen that has begun to lay but has not yet moulted. [OFr *poulet*, chicken]

pulley *n* **-eys 1** a device for lifting and lowering weights, consisting of a wheel with a grooved rim over which a rope or belt runs. **2** a clothes-drying frame suspended by ropes from the ceiling, lowered and raised by means of such a device. [OFr *polie*]

pullover *n* a knitted garment pulled on over one's head; a sweater or jumper.

pullulate *v* (*intr*) **1** to sprout or breed. **2** (**with**) to teem or abound. [Lat *pullulare*, from *pullulus*, chick]

pulmonary *adj* **1** of, relating to, or affecting the lungs. **2** having the function of a lung. [Lat *pulmonarius*, from *pulmo*, lung]

pulp *n* **1** the flesh of a fruit or vegetable. **2** a soft wet mass of mashed food or other material: *wood pulp*. **3** (*derog*) worthless literature, novels, magazines, etc., printed on poor paper. — *v* (*tr* & *intr*) to reduce, or be reduced, to a pulp. — *adj* **pulpy**, **-ier**, **-iest**. [Lat *pulpa*, flesh, pulp]

pulpit *n* **1** a small enclosed platform in a church, from which the preacher delivers the sermon. **2** church preachers in general: *the message from the pulpit*. [Lat *pulpitum*, platform]

pulsar *n* any of several star-like entities in the heavens, emitting regular pulses of radiation. [*puls*ating st*ar*]

pulsate *v* (*intr*) **1** to beat or throb. **2** to contract and expand rhythmically. **3** to vibrate. **4** (*physics*) to vary in force or intensity in a regularly recurring pattern. — *n* **pulsation**. [Lat *pulsare*, to beat]

pulse[1] *n* **1** the regular contraction and expansion of the arteries, detectable as a rhythmical beat where an artery nears the skin surface, e.g. at the wrist. **2** the rate of this beat, e.g. as an indicator of health: *feel* or *take someone's pulse*. **3** a regular throbbing beat in music. **4** (*physics, astronomy*, etc.) a regularly recurring vibration or brief signal. **5** the hum or bustle of a busy place. **6** a thrill of excitement, etc. **7** the attitude or feelings of a group or community at any one time: *check the pulse of the electorate*. — *v* (*intr*) to throb or pulsate. [Lat *pulsus*, a beating]

pulse[2] *n* the edible seeds of leguminous plants such as beans, peas and lentils, or of any particular one of these. [Lat *puls*, meal porridge or bean pottage]

pulverise or **-ize** *v* **1** (*tr* & *intr*) to crush or crumble to dust or powder. **2** (*tr*; *facet*) to defeat utterly; to annihilate. — *n* **pulverisation** or **-z-**. [Lat *pulverizare*, from *pulvis*, dust]

puma *n* one of the big cats of America, with a plain red-brown coat; the mountain lion or cougar. [Span, from Quechua (a S American Indian language)]

pumice *n* (also **pumice stone**) light porous volcanic lava, used as an abrasive and, in powdered form, for polishing. [Lat *pumex*]

pummel *v* **-ll-** (*tr*) to beat repeatedly with the fists. [**pommel**]

pump[1] *n* **1** any of various piston-operated or other devices for forcing or driving liquids or gases into or out of something, etc. **2** a standing device with a handle that is worked up and down for raising water from beneath the ground, esp. one serving as the water supply to a community. **3** a device for forcing air into a tyre. **4** (also **petrol pump**) a device for raising petrol from an underground storage tank to fill a vehicle's petrol tank. — *v* **1** (*tr* & *intr*) to raise, force or drive (liquids or gases) out of or into something with a pump. **2** (*tr*; **up**) to inflate (a tyre, etc.) with a pump. **3** (*tr*) to force in large gushes or flowing amounts: *pumping waste into the sea*. **4** (*tr*; **into**) to pour (money or other resources) into a project, etc. **5** (*tr*) to force out the contents of (someone's stomach) to rid it of a poison, etc. **6** (*tr*) to try to extract information from (someone) by persistent questioning. **7** (*tr*) to work (something) vigorously up and down, as though operating a pump handle: *pumped my hand in greeting*. **8** (*tr*; **into**) to fire (bullets); to fire bullets into: *pumped bullets into her*; *pumped her full of bullets*. — **pump iron** (*coll*) to exercise with weights; to go in for weight-training. [ODut *pumpe*, pipe]

pump[2] *n* **1** a rubber-soled canvas sports shoe; a gymshoe or plimsoll. **2** a light dancing shoe for men. **3** (esp. *US*) a plain, low-cut shoe for women; a court shoe.

pumpernickel *n* a dark heavy coarse rye bread, eaten esp. in Germany. [Ger, lout, perhaps literally 'stink-devil' or 'fart-devil']

pumpkin *n* a large round thick-skinned yellow fruit with edible flesh, used as a vegetable. [OFr *pompon*, from Gr *pepon*, melon]

pun *n* a form of joke consisting of a play on words, esp. one where an association is created between words of similar sound but different meaning, e.g. *A pun is a punishable offence*. — *v* **-nn-** (*intr*) to make a pun.

punster *n* a person who goes in for making puns.

Punch *n* a humpbacked, wife-beating puppet character in the traditional children's **Punch and Judy show**. — **pleased as Punch** highly gratified. [Ital *Pulcinella*, a commedia dell'arte character]

punch[1] *v* (*tr* & *intr*) to hit with one's fist. — *n* **1** a blow with the fist. **2** vigour and effectiveness in speech or writing: *lacks punch*. — **pack a punch** (*coll*) to be capable of delivering a powerful blow; to be forceful or effective. — **pull one's punches** to be deliberately less hard-hitting than one might be. [MidE *punchen*, variant of **pounce**]

punch-bag *n* a heavy stuffed leather bag hanging from the ceiling on a rope, used for boxing practice.

punch-ball *n* a leather ball mounted on a flexible stand, used for boxing practice.

punch-drunk *adj* **1** (of a boxer) brain-damaged from repeated blows to the head, with resultant unsteadiness and confusion. **2** dazed from over-intensive work or other shattering experience.

punchline *n* the words that conclude a funny story and contain its point.

punch-up *n* (*coll*) a fight.

punchy *adj* **-ier**, **-iest** (of speech or writing) vigorous and effective; forcefully expressed. — *n* **punchiness**.

punch[2] *n* **1** a tool for cutting holes or notches, or stamping designs, in leather, paper, metal, etc. **2** a tool for driving nail heads well down into a surface. — *v* (*tr*) **1** to pierce, notch or stamp with a punch: *punched our tickets*; *punch a hole*. **2** (*comput*) to use a key punch to record (data) on (a card or tape). — *v* **punch in** (or **out**) (*intr*; *US*) to clock in (or out). [MidE *puncheon*, piercing tool]

punched card or **punch card** *n* (*comput*) a card bearing coded data or instructions in the form of punched holes.

punch[3] *n* a drink made orig. from five ingredients — spirits, water, lemon juice, sugar and spice — but now also from a variety of others. [Said to be from Hindi *panch*, five]

punch bowl *n* **1** a large bowl for mixing and serving punch in. **2** a bowl-shaped hollow in the mountains.

punctilio *n* **-os 1** strictness in observing the finer details of etiquette, ceremony, or correct formal behaviour. **2** a fine detail of this kind. [Ital *puntiglio*, from Span dimin. of *punto*, point]

punctilious *adj* carefully attentive to details of correct, polite or considerate behaviour; making a point of observing a rule or custom: *always punctilious about remembering birthdays*. — *adv* **punctiliously**.

punctual *adj* **1** arriving or happening at the arranged time; not late. **2** (of a person) making a habit of not being late. — *n* **punctuality**. — *adv* **punctually**. [Lat *punctualis*, from *punctus*, point]

punctuate *v* **1** (*tr* & *intr*) to put punctuation marks into (a piece of writing). **2** (*tr*) to interrupt repeatedly: *a speech punctuated by bursts of applause*. **3** (*tr*) to give emphasis to: *punctuating her comments with taps on the desk*. [Lat *punctuare*, to prick, point, from *punctus*, point]

punctuation *n* **1** the system of marks used in a text to clarify its meaning for the reader. **2** the use of such marks, or the process of inserting them.

punctuation mark *n* any of the set of marks such as the full stop, comma, question mark, colon, etc. that in written matter indicate the pauses and intonations that would be used in speech, and make the meaning clear to the reader.

puncture *n* **1** a small hole pierced in something with a sharp point. **2** a perforation in an inflated object, esp. a pneumatic tyre; the resulting flat tyre. — *v* **1** (*tr* & *intr*) to make a puncture in, or be punctured. **2** (*tr*) to deflate (someone's pride, self-importance, etc.). [Lat *punctura*, pricking]

pundit *n* **1** a (would-be) authority on a particular subject who is consulted, or pronounces, on matters connected with it. **2** a Hindu learned in Hindu culture, philosophy and law. [Hindi *pandit*]

pungent *adj* **1** (of a taste or smell) sharp and strong. **2** (of remarks, wit, etc.) cleverly caustic or biting. — *n* **pungency**. — *adv* **pungently**. [Lat *pungere*, to prick]

punish *v* (*tr*) **1** to cause (an offender) to suffer for an offence. **2** to impose a penalty for (an offence). **3** (*coll*) to treat roughly: *really punishes that car of hers*. **4** to beat or defeat (an opponent, etc.) soundly. [Fr *punir*]

punishable *adj* (of offences) liable to be punished, esp. by law.

punishing *adj* harsh; severe: *punishing conditions*.

punishment *n* **1** the act of punishing or process of being punished. **2** any method of punishing; a type of penalty. **3** (*coll*) rough treatment, suffering or hardship.

punitive *adj* **1** relating to, inflicting, or intended to inflict, punishment: *punitive measures*. **2** severe; inflicting hardship: *punitive taxation*. — *adv* **punitively**. [Lat *punitivus*, from *punire*, to punish]

punk *n* **1** an anti-Establishment movement among the youth of the 1970s and 1980s, manifesting itself in aggressive weirdness of dress and hairstyle, and the wearing of cheap utility articles, e.g. safety pins, as ornament. **2** a follower of punk styles or punk rock. **3** punk rock. **4** (esp. *NAm*) a worthless or stupid person. — *adj* **1** relating to, or characteristic of, punk as a movement. **2** (esp. *NAm*) worthless; inferior. [Perhaps a combination of older *punk*, prostitute + *punk*, fire-lighting tinder]

punk rock *n* loud aggressive rock music popular in the 1970s and 1980s, with violent, sometimes obscene, lyrics, expressing disgust at the ugliness of life.

punnet *n* a small basket or container, usu. of cardboard or plastic, for soft fruit.

punster. See **pun**.

punt[1] *n* a long flat-bottomed open boat with square ends, propelled by a pole pushed against the bed of the river, etc. — *v* **1** (*intr*) to travel by, or operate, a punt. **2** (*tr*) to propel (a punt, etc.) with a pole. **3** (*tr*) to convey (passengers) in a punt. — *n* **punter**. [Lat *ponto*, punt, pontoon]

punt[2] *n* (*Rugby*, etc.) a kick given with the toe of the boot to a ball dropped directly from the hands. — *v* (*tr & intr*) to kick in this way.

punt[3] *v* (*intr*) **1** (*coll*) to bet on horses. **2** (*cards*) to bet against the bank. [Fr *ponter*, to bet]

punter *n* (*coll*) **1** someone who bets on horses; a gambler. **2** the average consumer, customer, or member of the public.

punt[4] *n* the pound (money) of the Republic of Ireland. [Irish Gaelic, pound]

puny *adj* ***-ier***, ***-iest*** **1** small, weak, or undersized. **2** feeble or ineffective. — *adv* **punily**. [OFr *puisne*, born later]

pup *n* **1** a young dog. **2** the young of other animals, e.g. the seal, wolf and rat. — *v* ***-pp-*** (*intr*) to give birth to pups. — **be sold a pup** (*coll*) to be swindled. — **in pup** (of a bitch) pregnant. [Shortened from **puppy**]

pupa *n* ***-pae*** or ***-pas*** the tightly compressed form an insect takes during its immobile stage when it is changing from larva to adult. — *adj* **pupal**. [Lat, doll]

pupil[1] *n* **1** someone who is being taught; a schoolchild or student. **2** someone studying under a particular master, etc.: *a pupil of Beethoven's*. **3** (*legal*) a ward. [OFr *pupille*, from Lat *pupillus*, *pupilla*, dimins. of *pupus*, boy, *pupa*, girl]

pupil[2] *n* the contracting and expanding circular opening in the middle of the eye through which the light passes to the retina. [Lat *pupilla*, dimin. of *pupa*, girl, doll]

puppet *n* **1** a doll that can be made to move in a lifelike way, of any of several types, e.g. operated by strings or sticks attached to its limbs, or designed to fit over the hand and operated by the fingers and thumb. **2** a person who is being controlled or manipulated by someone else. [Variant of **poppet**, from Lat *pupa*, doll]

puppeteer *n* a person skilled in manipulating puppets and giving puppet shows.

puppetry *n* the art of making and manipulating puppets.

puppet show *n* an entertainment with puppets as performers.

puppet state *n* an apparently independent country actually under the control of another.

puppy *n* ***-ies*** **1** a young dog. **2** a conceited young man. [Related to Fr *poupée*, doll]

puppy fat *n* a temporary plumpness in children, usu. at the pre-adolescent stage.

puppy love *n* the romantic love of an adolescent for an older person of the opposite sex; calf love.

purblind *adj* **1** nearly blind; dim-sighted. **2** dull-witted; obtuse. [Orig. completely blind, from **pure** + **blind**]

purchase *v* (*tr*) **1** to obtain in return for payment; to buy. **2** to get or achieve through labour, effort, sacrifice or risk. — *n* **1** something that has been bought. **2** the act of buying. **3** firmness in holding or gripping; a sure grasp or foothold. **4** (*mechanics*) the advantage given by a device such as a pulley or lever. — *n* **purchaser**. [OFr *pourchacier*, to seek to obtain]

purchase tax *n* a tax included in the price of goods considered non-essential.

purdah *n* the seclusion or veiling of women from public view in some Muslim and Hindu societies. [Hindi & Urdu *pardah*, curtain]

pure *adj* **1** consisting of itself only; unmixed with anything else: *pure gold*; *pure white*. **2** unpolluted; uncontaminated; wholesome: *pure water*, *air*, etc. **3** virtuous; chaste; free from sin or guilt: *pure thoughts*. **4** utter; nothing but: *pure lunacy; pure coincidence*. **5** (of mathematics or science) dealing with theory and abstractions rather than practical applications. **6** of unmixed blood or descent: *of pure Manx stock*. **7** (of sound, e.g. a sung note) clear, unwavering and exactly in tune. **8** absolutely true to type or style: *pure Art Deco*. **9** (of speech or language) free of imported, intrusive or debased elements. **10** (of a vowel) simple in sound quality, like the *o* in *box*, as distinct from a diphthong like the *oy* in *boy*. — *n* **pureness**. — **pure and simple** and nothing else: *It's jealousy pure and simple*. ◇ See also **purify**, **purist**, **purity**. [Lat *purus*]

pure-bred *adj* (of animals) of unmixed breed.

purely *adv* **1** in a pure way. **2** wholly; entirely: *won purely on her merits*. **3** merely: *purely a formality*.

purée *n* a quantity of fruit or vegetables reduced to a pulp by liquidising or rubbing through a sieve. — *v* ***-rées***, ***-réed*** (*tr*) to reduce to a purée. [Fr *purer*, to strain]

purgative *n* a medicine that causes the bowels to empty. — *adj* (of a medicine, etc.) having this effect. [Lat *purgativus*, from *purgare*, to clean out]

purgatory *n* **1** (*cap*; esp. *RC*) a place or state into which the soul passes after death to be cleansed of pardonable sins before going to heaven. **2** (esp. *coll facet*) any state of discomfort or suffering; an excruciating experience. [Lat *purgatorium*, from *purgare*, to cleanse]

purge *v* **1** (*tr*) to rid (e.g. the soul or body) of unwholesome thoughts or substances; to get rid of (impure elements) from (anything). **2** (*tr*) to rid (a political party, community, etc.) of (undesirable members). **3** (*tr & intr*; *old*) to take or give a purgative to empty (the bowels), or the bowels of (a person). **4** (*tr*; *legal*) to rid (oneself) of guilt by atoning for one's offence. **5** (*tr*; *legal*) to clear (oneself or someone else) of an accusation. — *n* **1** an act of purging. **2** the process of purging a party or community of undesirable members. **3** the process of purging the bowels. **4** a medicine to empty the bowels. [Lat *purgare*, to cleanse, purify]

puri *n* a small cake of unleavened Indian bread, deep-fried and served hot. [Hindi]

purify *v* **-ies**, **-ied** (*tr*) **1** to make pure. **2** to cleanse of contaminating or harmful substances. **3** to rid of intrusive elements. **4** (*relig*) to free from sin or guilt. — *n* **purification**. — *n* **purifier**. [Lat *purus*, pure + *facere*, to make]

purist *n* a person who insists on correctness of word usage, grammar, etc. or authenticity of detail in design, etc. — *n* **purism**. **[pure]**

puritan *n* **1** (*cap*; *hist*) a supporter of the 16th- to 17th-cent. Protestant movement in England and America that sought to rid church worship of ritual. **2** a person of strict, esp. over-strict, moral principles; someone who disapproves generally of luxuries and amusements. — *adj* **puritanical**. [Lat *puritas*, purity]

purity *n* **1** the state of being pure or unmixed. **2** freedom from contamination, pollution or unwholesome or intrusive elements. **3** chasteness or innocence. [Lat *puritas*, from *purus*, pure]

purl[1] *n* **1** (*knitting instructions*) the more complex of two basic stitches, with the wool passed behind the needle. ◇ See also **plain**. **2** cord made from gold or silver wire. **3** a decorative looped edging on lace, braid, etc. — *v* (*tr*) to knit in purl. [MidE *pirl*, to twist, *purl*, to embroider]

purl[2] *v* (*intr*) **1** to flow with a murmuring sound. **2** to eddy or swirl. [Related to Norw *purla*, to babble]

purlieus *n* (*pl*) the surroundings, or immediate neighbourhood, of a place. [OFr *puralé*, a going through]

purlin *n* (*building*) a beam lying lengthways inside a roof, parallel to its ridge or sides, supporting the rafters forming its slopes.

purloin *v* (*tr*) to steal, filch or pilfer. [OFr *purloigner*, to remove to a distance]

purple *n* **1** a colour that is a mixture of blue and red. **2** (*hist*) a crimson dye got from various shellfish. **3** crimson cloth, or a robe made from it worn by e.g. emperors and cardinals, symbolic of their authority. — *adj* **1** of either of these colours. **2** (of prose) self-consciously fine in style; over-elaborate; flowery. — **born in the purple** born into a ruling, royal or noble family. [Gr *porphyra*, dye-yielding shellfish]

purple heart *n* **1** (*coll*) a heart-shaped violet pill containing a stimulant drug. **2** (*caps*) a US military medal.

purple patch *n* a passage of purple prose.

purport *n* meaning, significance, point or gist. — *v* (*intr*) to (be presented so as to) seem: *a work purporting to have been written by Charles I.* [OFr *purporter*, to convey]

purpose *n* **1** one's object or aim in doing something. **2** the function for which something is intended: *a multi-purpose gadget.* **3** one's intentions, aspirations, aim or goal: *one's purpose in life*; *a sense of purpose.* **4** determination; resolve: *a woman of purpose.* — *v* (*tr*) to intend (to do something). — *adj* **purposeless**. — **on purpose** intentionally; deliberately. — **to little** (or **no**) **purpose** with few (or no) useful results. — **to the purpose** relevant; to the point. [OFr *pourpos*, from Lat *proponere*, to intend]

purpose-built *adj* designed to meet specific requirements: *a purpose-built medical centre.*

purposeful *adj* determined; intent; resolute; showing a sense of purpose. — *adv* **purposefully**.

purposely *adv* intentionally; on purpose.

purposive *adj* **1** having a clear purpose. **2** purposeful.

purr *v* **1** (*intr*) (of a cat) to make a soft, low, vibrating sound when happy. **2** (*intr*) (of a vehicle, engine or other machinery) to make a sound similar to this. **3** (*intr & tr*) to express pleasure, or say, in a tone vibrating with satisfaction. — *n* a purring sound. [Imit.]

purse *n* **1** a small container carried in the pocket or handbag, for keeping one's cash, etc. in. **2** (*NAm*) a woman's handbag. **3** the funds available to one for spending: *beyond my purse.* — *v* (*tr*) to draw (the lips) together in disapproval or deep thought. — **hold the purse strings** to be the person in control of spending, e.g. in a family or organisation. [OE *purs*]

purser *n* the ship's officer responsible for keeping the accounts and, on a passenger ship, seeing to the welfare of passengers.

pursue 1 (*tr & intr*) to follow in order to overtake, capture, attack, etc.; to chase. **2** (*tr*) to proceed along (a course or route). **3** (*tr*) to put one's efforts into achieving (a goal or aim). **4** (*tr*) to occupy oneself with (one's career, etc.). **5** (*tr*) to continue with, or follow up (investigations, enquiries, etc.). [OFr *pursuer*]

pursuance *n* the process of pursuing: *in pursuance of his duties*.

pursuer *n* **1** someone pursuing one: *escaped their pursuers*. **2** (*Scot legal*) a plaintiff or prosecutor.

pursuit *n* **1** the act of pursuing or chasing: *the pursuit of happiness*; *followed in hot pursuit*. **2** an occupation or hobby. [OFr *purseute*]

pursuivant *n* (*heraldry*) an officer of the College of Arms ranking below a herald. [Fr *poursuivre*, to follow]

purulent *adj* full of, or discharging, pus. — *n* **purulence**. [Lat *purulentus*, from *pus*, pus]

purvey *v* **-eys**, **-eyed** (*tr* & *intr*) (of a trader) to supply (food, provisions, etc.). — *n* **purveyance**. — *n* **purveyor**. [OFr *purveier*, from Lat *providere*, to provide for]

purview *n* **1** scope of responsibility or concern, e.g. of a court of law. **2** the range of one's knowledge, experience or activities. [OFr *purveu*, provided]

pus *n* the thick, yellowish liquid that forms in abscesses or infected wounds, composed of dead white blood cells, serum, bacteria and tissue debris. [Lat]

push *v* **1** (*tr* & *intr*; **against**, **at**, **on**) to (try to) force away from one using pressure; to press, thrust or shove. **2** (*tr*) to touch or grasp and move forward in front of one: *push a pram*. **3** (*intr* & *tr*; **through**, **past**, **in**, etc.) to force (one's way), thrusting aside people or obstacles. **4** (*intr*) to progress esp. laboriously: *pushing forward through the unknown*. **5** (*tr*; **down**, **up**) to force: *push up prices*. **6** (*tr*; **into**) to coax, urge, persuade or goad: *pushed her into applying*. **7** (*tr*) to pressurise into working harder, achieving more, etc.: *pushes himself too hard*. **8** (*intr* with **for**) to recommend strongly; to campaign or press for. **9** (*tr*) to promote (products) or urge acceptance of (ideas). **10** (*tr*) to sell (drugs) illegally. — *n* **1** an act of pushing; a thrust or shove. **2** a burst of effort towards achieving something. **3** determination, aggression or drive. — **at a push** if forced; at a pinch. — **be pushed for** (*coll*) to be short of (e.g. time or cash). — **be pushing (50, 60, etc.)** (*coll*) to be nearly (the specified age). — **give** (or **get**) **the push** (*coll*) to dismiss (or be dismissed) from a job, etc.; to reject (or be rejected by) someone. — *v* **push along** (*intr*; *coll*) to make one's departure. — *v* **push around** or **about** (*tr*; *coll*) **1** to bully; to treat roughly. **2** to dictate to; to order about. — *v* **push off** (*intr; coll*) to make one's departure; to go away. — *v* **push on** (*intr*) to continue on one's way, etc. — *v* **push over** (*tr*) to knock down. ◇ See also **pushover** below. — *v* **push through** (*tr*) to force acceptance of (a proposal, bill, etc.) by a legislative body, etc. [OFr *pousser*]

pushbike *n* (*coll*) a bicycle propelled by pedals alone.

push button *n* a button pressed to operate a machine, etc. — *adj* **push-button** operated by pressing a button.

push-chair *n* a small folding perambulator for a toddler.

pusher *n* (*coll*) a person who sells illegal drugs.

pushover *n* (*coll*) **1** someone easily got the better of. **2** a task easily accomplished.

pushy *adj* **-ier**, **-iest** aggressively self-assertive or ambitious.

pusillanimous *adj* timid, cowardly, weak-spirited or faint-hearted. — *n* **pusillanimity**. — *adv* **pusillanimously**. [Lat *pusillus*, diffident + *animus*, spirit]

puss *n* **1** (*coll*) a cat. **2** (*slang*) a girl. [Related to Dut *poes*]

pussy *n* **-ies 1** (*coll*) a cat. **2** (*vulg slang*) the female genitals; the vulva. **[puss]**

pussyfoot *v* (*intr*) **1** to behave indecisively; to avoid committing oneself. **2** to pad about stealthily.

pussy willow *n* a willow tree with silky grey catkins.

pustule *n* a small inflammation on the skin, containing pus; a pimple. — *adj* **pustular**. [Lat *pustula*]

put *v* **-tt-**, ***put*** **1** (*tr*) to place in, or convey to, a position or situation. **2** (*tr*) to fit: *put a new lock on the door*. **3** (*tr*) to cause to be: *put someone in a good mood*. **4** (*tr*) to apply: *put pressure on them*; *put paint on the brush*. **5** (*tr*) to set or impose: *put a tax on luxuries*; *put an end to free lunches*. **6** (*tr*) to lay (blame, reliance, emphasis, etc.) on something. **7** (*tr*) to set (someone) to work, etc. or apply (something) to a good purpose, etc. **8** (*tr*) to translate: *put this into French*. **9** (*tr*) to invest or pour (energy, money or other resources) into something. **10** (*tr*) to classify, categorise or put in order: *wouldn't put Verdi in the first rank*; *would put accuracy before speed*. **11** (*tr*; **at**) to estimate: *put the costs at £10 000*. **12** (*tr*) to submit (questions for answering, ideas for considering) to someone; to suggest: *put it to her that she was lying*. **13** (*tr*) to express: *don't know how to put it*; *a disaster, to put it mildly*. **14** (*tr*) to write: *don't know what to put*. **15** (*intr*; *naut*) to sail in a certain direction: *put out to sea*, *back to port*, etc. **16** (*tr*; *athletics*) to throw (the shot). — *v* **put about** (*tr*) to spread (reports or rumours); to rumour. **2** (*intr*; *naut*) to turn round; to change course. — *v* **put across** (*tr*) to communicate (ideas, etc.) to others. — *v* **put aside** (*tr*) **1** to save (e.g. money), esp. regularly, for future use. **2** to discount or deliberately disregard (problems, differences of opinion, etc.) for the sake of convenience, peace, etc. — *v* **put away** (*tr*) **1** to replace tidily. **2** to save for future use. **3** (*coll*) to consume (food or drink), esp. in quantity. **4** (*euph*) to imprison, or confine in a mental institution. **5** (*old*) to reject, discard or renounce. — *v* **put back** (*tr*) **1** to replace. **2** to postpone: *put the meeting back a month*, or *to next month*. **3** to adjust (a clock, etc.) to an earlier time. — *v* **put by** (*tr*) to save for the future. — *v* **put down** **1** (*tr*) to crush (a revolt, etc.). **2** (*tr*) to humiliate or snub (*n* **put-down**). **3** (*tr*) to kill (an animal, esp. one near death) painlessly. **4** (*tr*) to write down: *put down suggestions*. **5** (*intr*) (of an aircraft) to land. **6** (*tr*) to hand over (money) as a deposit on an intended purchase. **7** (*tr* with **for**) to sum up or dismiss as: *had put him down for a playboy*. **8** (*tr*; **for**) to include in a list of participants, subscribers, etc.: *put me down for the trip*. **9** (*tr* with **to**) to attribute: *errors put down to inexperience*. — *v* **put forward** (*tr*) **1** to offer (a proposal or suggestion). **2** to propose (someone's name) for a post, etc.; to nominate. **3** to advance the time or date of: *put the wedding forward a month*. **4** to adjust (a clock, etc.) to a later time. — *v* **put in** **1** (*tr*) to fit or install. **2** (*tr*) to spend (time) working at something: *puts in four hours' violin practice daily*. **3** (*intr* with **for**) to apply for. **4** (*tr*) to submit (a claim, etc.). **5** (*intr*; *naut*; **to**, **at**) to enter a port or harbour. **6** (*tr*) to interpose (a comment, etc.). — *v* **put off** (*tr*) **1** to switch off. **2** to postpone. **3** to cancel one's engagement with (someone): *have to put the Smiths off*. **4** to cause to lose concentration; to distract. **5** to cause to lose enthusiasm, or feel disgust, for (something): *Her accident put me off climbing. He was put off the cheese by its smell*. — *v* **put on** (*tr*) **1** to switch on (an electrical device, etc.). **2** to dress oneself in. **3** to gain (weight or speed). **4** to present (a play, show, etc.). **5** to provide (e.g. transport). **6** to adopt (e.g. an accent, manner, etc.) for effect or to deceive (*adj* **put-on**). **7** to bet (money) on (a horse, etc.). **8** (with **to**) to recommend to try: *A friend put me on to these biscuits*. **9** (with **to**) to lead in the directon of: *What put the police on to her?* — **put one over on** (*coll*) to trick or take in. — *v* **put out** (*tr*) **1** to extinguish (a light or fire). **2** to inconvenience. **3** to offend or annoy. **4** to issue (e.g. a distress call). **5** to publish (e.g. a leaflet). **6** to strain or dislocate (a part of the body). **7** (*cricket*) to dismiss (a player or team) from the batting. — *v* **put over** (*tr*) to communicate (ideas, etc.); to put across. — **put right** to mend or make better. — *v* **put through** (*tr*) **1** to arrange (a deal, agreement, etc.). **2** to make (a telephone call). **3** to connect by telephone: *was put through to the manager*. — **put together** to join up the parts of. — *v* **put up** **1** (*tr*) to build; to erect. **2** (*tr*) to raise (prices). **3** (*tr* & *intr*) to accommodate, or be accommodated, overnight: *put up at the inn*. **4** (*tr*) to present (a plan, etc.). **5** (*tr*) to offer (one's house, etc.) for sale. **6** (*tr*) to provide (funds) for a project, etc. **7** (*tr*) to show (resistance); to offer (a fight). **8** (*tr* & *intr*; **for**, **as**) to nominate, or offer oneself, as candidate: *putting you up for chairman*. **9** (*tr* with **to**) to manoeuvre (someone) into (doing something, esp. unwise or dishonest). **10** (*intr* with **with**) to bear or tolerate. — *v* **put upon** (*tr*; usu. in *passive*) to presume on the good will of; to take unfair advantage of (*adj* **put-upon**). [OE *putian*]

put-up job *n* something dishonestly prearranged to give a false impression.

putative *adj* supposed; assumed: *the putative father of the child*. [Lat *putativus*, from *putare*, to think]

putrefy *v* **-ies**, **-ied** (*intr*) to go bad, rot or decay, esp. with a foul smell. — n **putrefaction**. [Lat *putrefacere*, to rot]

putrescent *adj* decaying; rotting; putrefying. [Lat *putrescere*, to rot]

putrid *adj* **1** decayed; rotten. **2** stinking; foul; disgusting. **3** (*coll*) repellent; worthless. [Lat *putridus*, rotten]

putsch *n* a secretly planned, sudden attempt to remove a government from power. [Swiss Ger]

putt *v* (*tr* & *intr*; *golf*, *putting*) to send (the ball) gently forward along the ground towards the hole. — *n* a putting stroke. [Scot form of **put**]

putter *n* **1** a golf club used for putting. **2** a person who putts.

putting *n* **1** the act of putting a ball towards a hole. **2** a game somewhat similar to golf, played on a putting-green (sense **2**) using only putting strokes.

putting-green *n* **1** (also **green**) on a golf course, a smoothly mown patch of grass surrounding a hole. **2** an area of mown turf laid out like a tiny golf course, on which to play putting.

putty *n* **-ies** a paste of ground chalk and linseed oil, used for fixing glass in window frames, filling holes in wood, etc. [Fr *potée*, potful]

puzzle *v* **1** (*tr*) to perplex, mystify, bewilder or baffle. **2** (*intr*; **over**, **about**) to brood, ponder, wonder or worry. **3** (*tr* with **out**) to solve after prolonged thought. — *n* **1** a baffling problem. **2** a game or toy taking the form of something for solving, designed to test one's knowledge, memory, powers of reasoning or observation, manipulative skill, etc. — *n* **puzzlement**. — *adj* **puzzling**. — **puzzle one's brains**, **head**, etc. to think hard (about a problem).

puzzler *n* **1** a challenging problem or question; a poser. **2** a person who enjoys solving puzzles.

PVC *abbrev* polyvinyl chloride.

PW *abbrev* policewoman.

pyaemia or **pyemia** *n* blood poisoning in which abscesses form at a number of different sites in the body. [Gr *pyon*, pus + *haima*, blood]

pye-dog or **pie-dog** *n* a stray mongrel in Oriental regions; a pariah dog. [Hindi *pahi*, outsider]

pygmy or **pigmy** *n* **-ies 1** (*cap*) a member of one of the unusually short peoples of equatorial Africa. **2** an undersized person; a dwarf. **3** (*derog*) someone of no significance: *an intellectual pygmy*. — *adj* of a small-sized breed: *pygmy hippopotamuses*. [Gr *pygmaios*, literally 'measuring a *pygme* (= the distance from knuckle to elbow)']

pyjamas or (*US*) **pajamas** *n* (*pl*) a sleeping-suit consisting of a loose jacket or top, and trousers. [Persian and Hindi *payjamah*, leg-clothing]

pylon *n* **1** a tall steel structure for supporting electric power cables. **2** a post or tower to guide a pilot at an airfield. **3** an external structure on an aircraft for supporting an engine, etc. **4** (*Egyptian archaeol*) a gate tower or ornamental gateway. [Gr *pylon*, from *pyle*, gate]

pyorrhoea or **pyorrhea** *n* a discharge of pus, esp. from the gums or tooth sockets. [Gr *pyon*, pus + *rheein*, to flow]

pyramid *n* **1** any of the huge ancient Egyptian royal tombs built on a square base, with four sloping triangular sides meeting in a common apex. **2** (*geom*) a solid of this shape, with a square or triangular base. **3** any structure, pile, etc. of similar shape. — *adj* **pyramidal**. [Gr *pyramis*]

pyramid selling *n* the sale of goods in bulk to a distributor who divides them and sells them to sub-distributors at a profit, and so on.

pyre *n* a pile of wood on which a dead body is ceremonially cremated. [Gr *pyra*, from *pyr*, fire]

pyrethrum *n* **1** a flower of the chrysanthemum family. **2** an insecticide prepared from its flower-heads. [Gr *pyrethron*, a plant of the nettle family]

pyretic *adj* (*med*) relating to, or accompanied by, fever. [Gr *pyretos*, fever]

Pyrex® *n* a type of heat-resistant glass used esp. for ovenware.

pyridoxine *n* vitimin B_6. [The chemical *pyridine* + **oxygen**]

pyro- *comb fm* fire: *pyromania*; *pyrotechnics*. [Gr, from *pyr*, fire]

pyromania *n* (*psychol*) an obsessive urge to set fire to things. [**pyro-** + **-mania**]

pyrotechnics *n* **1** (*sing*) the art of making fireworks. **2** (*pl*) a fireworks display. **3** (*pl*) a display of fiery brilliance in speech, music, etc. [**pyro-**]

Pyrrhic victory *n* a victory won at so great a cost in lives, etc. that it can hardly be regarded as a triumph at all. [*Pyrrhus*, king of Epirus in Greece, who won such victories against the Romans in the 3rd cent. BC]

Pythagoras's theorem *n* the theorem that in a right-angled triangle the square on the hypotenuse is equal to the sum of the squares on the other two sides. [*Pythagoras* of Samos, Gr philosopher of 6th cent. BC]

python *n* any of several large non-poisonous snakes, including the boa constrictor, that kill their prey by crushing. [*Python*, a dragon killed by the Gr god Apollo]

pyx *n* **1** (*Christianity*) a container in which the consecrated Communion bread is kept. **2** a box at the Royal Mint in which sample coins for testing are kept. [Gr *pyxis*, a box of boxwood]

pzazz. See **pizzazz**.

Q

Q[1] or **q** *n* ***Qs*** or ***Q's***, ***q's*** the 17th letter of the English alphabet.
Q[2] *abbrev* **1** Queen or Queen's. **2** (*chess*) queen. **3** question.
QC *abbrev* Queen's Counsel.
QED *abbrev* for *quod erat demonstrandum* (Lat), which was what had to be proved.
QM *abbrev* quartermaster.
qq.v. or **qqv** *abbrev* for *quae vide* (Lat), which see, see these words (the form of **q.v.** used when referring to more than one item).
qr *abbrev* quarter.
qt *abbrev* quart.
q.t.: on the q.t. (*coll*) on the quiet; secretly.
qua *prep* considered as; as being: *the cartoonist's art, qua art*. [Lat, feminine ablative singular of *qui*, who]
quack[1] *n* the cry of a duck. — *v* (*intr*) **1** (of a duck) to make this cry. **2** to talk in a loud silly voice. [Imit.]
quack[2] *n* **1** a medically unqualified person who claims a doctor's knowledge and skill. **2** (*coll*, often *derog*) a doctor. — *n* **quackery**. [ODut *quacksalver*]
quad[1] *n* (*coll*) a quadruplet.
quad[2] *n* (*coll*) a quadrangle.
quad[3] (*coll*) *adj* quadraphonic. — *n* quadraphonics.
quadr- or **quadri-** *comb fm* four. [Lat, from *quattuor*, four]
Quadragesima *n* in the Christian calendar, the first Sunday in Lent. [Lat *quadragesima* (*dies*), fortieth (day)]
quadrangle *n* **1** (*geom*) a square, rectangle or other four-sided two-dimensional figure. **2** an open rectangular court within the buildings of a college, school, etc. [Lat *quadrangulum*, from *quadr-*, four + *angulus*, angle]
quadrant *n* **1** (*geom*) a quarter of the circumference of a circle. **2** (*geom*) a quarter of a circle, i.e. an area bounded by two radii meeting at right angles. **3** (*geom*) a quarter of a sphere, i.e. a section cut by two planes intersecting at right angles at the centre. **4** any device or mechanical part in the shape of a 90° arc. **5** (*naut* & *astron*) an instrument incorporating a graduated 90° arc, used for measuring altitude, e.g. of the stars.
quadraphonic *adj* (of sound reproduction) using four loudspeakers fed by four separate channels. — *n* **quadraphonics** (*sing*). — *n* **quadraphony**. [**quadr-** + **stereophonic**]
quadrate *n* a square, rectangle or cube; an object or instrument of any of these shapes. — *adj* square, rectangular or cube-shaped. [Lat *quadrare*, to make square]
quadratic (*math*) *adj* involving the square, but no higher power, of an unknown quantity or variable: *$x^2 + x - 4 = 8$ is a quadratic equation*. — *n* a quadratic equation.
quadrennial *adj* **1** lasting four years. **2** occurring every four years. — *adv* **quadrennially**. [Lat *quadriennium*, four-year period, from *quadri-*, four + *annus*, year]
quadrilateral *n* (*geom*) a four-sided two-dimensional figure. — *adj* four-sided. [Lat *quadrilaterus*, from *quadri-*, four + *latus*, side]
quadrille[1] *n* a square dance for four couples, in five or six movements; music for this. [Span *cuadrilla*, troop]
quadrille[2] *n* (*cards*) a game for four players using 40 cards. [Span *cuartillo*]
quadriplegia *n* paralysis affecting the arms and legs. — *adv* **quadriplegic**. [**quadri-** + Gr *plege*, blow, stroke]
quadruped *n* a four-footed animal, esp. a mammal. [Lat *quadrupes*, from *quadru-*, four + *pes*, foot]
quadruple *v* (*tr* & *intr*) to multiply by four or increase fourfold. — *adj* **1** four times as many or much. **2** composed of four parts. **3** (*mus*) (of time) having four beats to the bar. — *n* a quadruple number or amount. — *adv* **quadruply**. [Lat *quadruplus*, fourfold]
quadruplet *n* one of four children born to a mother at one birth.
quadruplicate *v* (*tr*) to make quadruple or fourfold. — *adj* fourfold; copied four times. — **in quadruplicate** copied four times. [Lat *quadruplicare*, to multiply by four]
quaff *v* (*tr* & *intr*; *literary* or *facet*) to drink eagerly or deeply.
quagga *n* an extinct S African wild ass, related to the zebra but striped on head and shoulders only. [Hottentot]
quagmire *n* an area of soft marshy ground; a bog. [*quag*, bog + **mire**]
quaich *n* (*Scot*) a two-handled drinking-cup usu. of silver or pewter. [Gaelic *cuach*, cup]
quail[1] *v* (*intr*; **at**) to lose courage or feel fear; to flinch.
quail[2] *n* a small bird of the partridge family. [Fr *quaille*]
quaint *adj* charmingly or pleasingly odd or old-fashioned. [OFr *cointe*, from Lat *cognitus*, known]
quake[1] *v* (*intr*) **1** (of people) to shake or tremble with fear, etc. **2** (of a building, etc.) to rock or shudder. — *n* a shudder or tremor, of fear, etc. [OE *cwacian*]
quake[2] *n* (*coll*) an earthquake.
Quaker *n* a member of a Christian sect, the Religious Society of Friends, founded by

George Fox in the 17th cent. [From their *quaking* at the name of the Lord]

qualify *v* **-ies**, **-ied** **1** (*intr*; **as**) to complete a training, pass an examination, etc., that gives one professional status. **2** (*tr*) to make suitable for a task, job, etc.: *is hardly qualified to judge*. **3** (*intr* with **for**) to fulfil requirements that give one a right to: *doesn't qualify for a grant*. **4** (*intr* with **as**) to be seen as having the right characteristics to be: *what qualifies as news these days*. **5** (*tr*) to add something to (a statement, etc.) that restricts or limits it. **6** (*tr*) to modify, tone down or restrict: *qualified approval*. **7** (*tr*; *gram*) (of an adjective) to define or describe (a noun). **8** (*intr*; *sport*) to reach a standard in a preliminary round that entitles one to participate in subsequent ones. — *n* **qualifier**. [Lat *qualis*, of what kind + *facere*, to make]

qualification *n* **1** an official record that one has completed a training, performed satisfactorily in an examination, etc. **2** a skill or ability that fits one for some job, etc. **3** the act, process or fact of qualifying. **4** an addition to a statement, etc. that narrows or restricts it; a condition, limitation or modification.

quality *n* **-ies** **1** standard of goodness. **2** excellence; high standard: *novels of quality*. **3** a characteristic or attribute: *has a silky quality*. **4** the character given to a voice or other sound by attributes other than pitch or loudness. **5** (*old*; often with **the**) (such people as have) high social status. **6** a quality newspaper. — *adj* of high quality or standard: *quality newspapers*. [Lat *qualitas*, from *qualis*, of what kind]

qualitative *adj* relating to, investigating or affecting the qualities or standard of something.

qualm *n* **1** a sudden feeling of nervousness or apprehension. **2** a feeling of uneasiness about whether what one is doing is right; a scruple, misgiving or pang of conscience. **3** a feeling of faintness or nausea. [OE *cwealm*, death, murder, slaughter, plague]

quandary *n* **-ies** a situation in which one is at a loss what to do; a dilemma or predicament.

quango *n* **-os** a government-funded body responsible for some area of public concern, its senior appointments being made by the government. [*qu*asi-*a*utonomous *n*on-*g*overnmental *o*rganisation]

quantify *v* **-ies**, **-ied** (*tr*) to find out the quantity of; to express as a quantity. [Lat *quantus*, how much + *facere*, to make]

quantity *n* **-ies** **1** the property things have that makes them measurable or countable; size or amount. **2** an amount that can be counted or measured; a specified amount: *a tiny quantity*. **3** largeness of amount; bulk: *buy in quantity*; *Quality, not quantity, is what counts*. **4** (in *pl*) a large amount: *quantities of food*. **5** (*math*) a value that may be expressed as a number, or the symbol or figure representing it. **6** (esp. *prosody*) the length or duration of a vowel sound or syllable. — **an unknown quantity** a person or thing whose importance or influence cannot be foreseen. [Lat *quantitas*, from *quantus*, how much]

quantitative *adj* **1** relating to quantity. **2** estimated, or measurable, in terms of quantity.

quantity surveyor *n* a person who estimates the quantities of materials needed to build something, and their probable cost.

quantum *n* **-ta** **1** an amount or quantity. **2** (*physics*) an indivisible unit of any form of physical energy. [Lat *quantus*, how much]

quantum leap or **jump** *n* a sudden transition; a spectacular advance.

quantum theory *n* the theory that energy exists in indivisible units or quanta.

quarantine *n* the isolation of people or animals to prevent the spread of any infectious disease that they could be developing; the duration of such isolation. — *v* (*tr*) to impose such isolation on; to put into quarantine. [Ital *quarantina*, period of 40 days]

quark *n* (*physics*) the name given to a particle believed to be the basic component of baryons and mesons, so far existing only in theory. [Coined by the Irish novelist James Joyce (1882–1941) in *Finnegans Wake*; adopted for scientific use by the American physicist Murray Gell-Mann (1929–)]

quarrel *n* **1** (**about**, **over**) an angry disagreement or argument. **2** (**with**) a cause of such disagreement; a complaint: *I've no quarrel with the management*. **3** a break in a friendship; a breach or rupture. — *v* **-ll-** (*intr*; **with**) **1** to argue or dispute angrily. **2** to disagree and fall out. **3** to find fault: *can't quarrel with her reasoning*. [Lat *querela*, complaint]

quarrelsome *adj* inclined to quarrel or dispute.

quarry[1] *n* **-ies** **1** an open excavation for the purpose of extracting stone or slate for building. **2** any source from which a supply of information or other material is obtained. — *v* **-ies**, **-ied** (*tr*) **1** to extract (stone, etc.) from a quarry. **2** to excavate a quarry in (land). **3** to get a supply of (material or information) from a source. [Lat *quadrare*, to square]

quarry tile *n* an unglazed floor tile.

quarry[2] *n* **-ies** **1** a hunted animal or bird; a prey. **2** someone or something that is the object of pursuit. [OFr *cuiree*, from *cuir*, hide]

quart *n* a liquid measure equivalent to quarter of a gallon or two pints (1·136 litres). [Lat *quartus*, fourth]

quarter *n* **1** one of four equal parts into which an object or quantity may be divided; the fraction $\frac{1}{4}$, one divided by four. **2** any of the three-month divisions of the year, esp. beginning or ending on a quarter day. **3** a unit of weight equal to a quarter of a hundredweight or 28 lbs. **4** (*coll*) 4 ozs, or a quarter of a pound. **5** a unit of measure for grain, equal to eight bushels. **6** (*NAm*) (a coin worth) 25 cents. **7** a period of 15 minutes; a point of time 15 minutes after or before any hour. **8** a fourth part of the moon's cycle; either of the visible shapes (phases) of the moon when half its surface is lit, at the point between the first and second, and the third and fourth, quarters of its cycle. **9** any of the four compass directions; any direction. **10** a district of a city, etc., e.g. identified by the predominant nationality of its population: *living in the Spanish quarter*. **11** (often in *pl*) a section of the public; certain people or a certain person: *disapproval in certain quarters; no sympathy from that quarter*. **12** (in *pl*) lodgings or accommodation, e.g. for soldiers and their families: *married quarters*. **13** (*old*) mercy shown to someone in one's power, e.g. a defeated enemy: *give no quarter*. **14** (*heraldry*) any of the four parts into which a shield is divided by intersecting horizontal and vertical lines. **15** any limb of a four-limbed animal: *hindquarters*. **16** (*sport*) any of four equal parts into which a match in some sports is divided. — *v* ***-r-*** (*tr*) **1** to divide into quarters. **2** to accommodate or billet in lodgings. **3** (*hist*) to divide (the body of a hanged traitor, etc.) into four parts. **4** (*heraldry*) to fill each quarter of (a shield) with bearings. **5** (of hounds) to cross and recross (an area) searching for game. — *adj* being one of four equal parts: *a quarter hour*. [OFr *quartier*, from Lat *quartarius*, fourth part]

quarterback *n* (*American football*) a player between the forwards and halfbacks, who directs his team's attacking play.

quarter day *n* (esp. *hist*) any of the four days beginning or ending one of the year's quarters, on which rent or interest are paid.

quarterdeck *n* the stern part of a ship's upper deck, usu. reserved for officers.

quarter final *n* (often in *pl*) the round before the semi-final of a competition. — *n* **quarter-finalist**.

quartering *n* (*heraldry*; usu. in *pl*) the coats of arms displayed on a shield to indicate family alliances.

quarterlight *n* a small window in either front door of a car, that pivots open for ventilation.

quarterly *adj* done, occurring, or published once every quarter of a year. — *adv* once every quarter. — *n* ***-ies*** a quarterly publication.

quartermaster *n* **1** an army officer responsible for soldiers' accommodation, food and clothing. **2** (*naut*) a petty officer responsible for navigation and signals.

quarter note *n* (*NAm*) a crotchet.

quarter sessions *n* (*pl*; *hist*) a local court of law presided over by a justice of the peace, formerly held quarterly.

quarterstaff *n* (*hist*) a six-foot pole used as a weapon.

quartet or **quartette** *n* **1** an ensemble of four singers or instrumental players. **2** a piece of music for four such performers. **3** any group or set of four. [Ital *quartetto*, from Lat *quartus*, fourth]

quarto *n* ***-os*** & *adj* (*printing*) (a book) of a size produced by folding a sheet of paper into four leaves or eight pages. [Lat *in quarto*, in one-fourth]

quartz *n* a common rock-forming mineral, silicon dioxide, occurring as hexagonal crystals or in a microscopically crystalline structure. [Ger *Quarz*]

quartz clock or **watch** *n* one operated by the vibrations of a quartz crystal.

quartz crystal *n* a disc or rod cut from a piece of piezoelectric quartz and ground so that it vibrates naturally at a particular frequency.

quasar *n* a distant, highly luminous star-like source of radio waves, outside our galaxy. [*qua*si-stell*ar* object]

quash *v* (*tr*) **1** to reject (a verdict, etc.) as invalid. **2** to annul (a law, etc.). **3** to subdue, crush or suppress (a rebellion, etc.). [Lat *quassare*, to shake]

quasi- *pfx* **1** to some extent; virtually: *a quasi-official role*. **2** in many respects similar to; virtual: *a quasi-deity*. **3** seeming(ly) but not actual(ly): *quasi-technical jargon; quasi-experts*. [Lat, as if]

quassia *n* **1** a S American tree whose bitter wood and bark are used as a tonic. **2** a W Indian tree of the same family. [Graman *Quassi*, 18th-cent. Negro slave in Surinam who discovered its medicinal properties]

quaternary *adj* **1** having four parts. **2** (*cap*) denoting the most recent period of geological history, beginning about two million years ago, following the Tertiary period in the Cenozoic era. — *n* (*cap*) the Quaternary period. [Lat *quaterni*, four each]

quatrain *n* (*poetry*) a verse or poem of four lines, usu. rhyming alternately. [Fr, from *quatre*, four]

quatrefoil *n* **1** a leaf composed of four lobes or leaflets. **2** (*archit*, etc.) a four-lobed design used esp. in open stonework. [OFr *quatic*, four + *foil*, leaf]

quattrocento *n* the 15th century, usu. with reference to Italian Renaissance art. [Ital, four (for fourteen) hundred]

quaver *v* ***-r-*** **1** (*intr*) (of someone's voice) to be unsteady; to shake or tremble. **2** (*tr*) to say or sing in a trembling voice. — *n* **1** (*mus*) a note that lasts half as long as a crotchet. **2** a tremble in the voice. — *adj* **quavery**. [Perhaps imit.]

quay *n* a wharf for the loading and unloading of ships. [OFr *kay*]

queasy *adj* ***-ier***, ***-iest*** **1** feeling slightly sick. **2** (of the stomach or digestion) easily upset. **3** (of food) causing feelings of nausea. **4** (of the conscience) readily made uneasy. — *adv* **queasily**. — *n* **queasiness**.

Quechua *n* a S American Indian language, one of the official languages of Peru.

queen *n* **1** a woman who rules a country, having inherited her position by birth. **2** the wife of a king. **3** a woman supreme in her field; a place or thing considered supreme in some way. **4** a large female ant, bee or wasp that lays eggs. **5** the most powerful chess piece, able to move forwards, backwards, sideways or diagonally. **6** a playing-card bearing the picture of a queen. **7** (*offensive slang*) an effeminate male homosexual. — *v* (*tr* & *intr*; *chess*) to make (a pawn) into a queen; (of a pawn) to be converted into a queen. — *adj* **queenly**. — **queen it** (*coll*) (of a woman) to behave overbearingly.

Queen Anne *n* an early 18th-cent. simple classical style of furniture and architecture.

queen consort *n* the wife of a reigning king.

queen mother *n* the widow of a king who is the mother of a reigning king or queen.

queen post *n* (*building*) one of two upright posts in a trussed roof, supporting the principal rafter.

Queen's (or **King's**) **Bench** *n* a division of the High Court of Justice.

Queen's (or **King's**) **Counsel** *n* in Britain, an honorary rank awarded to a barrister or advocate.

Queen's (or **King's**) **English** *n* correct standard English speech.

Queen's (or **King's**) **evidence** *n* evidence given by a criminal against his or her accomplices. — **turn Queen's** or **King's evidence** (of a criminal) to give such evidence.

Queen's Guide *n* the rank awarded to a Guide who has reached the highest level of proficiency.

Queen's (or **King's**) **highway** *n* any public road.

Queen's (or **King's**) **Scout** *n* a Scout who has reached the highest level of proficiency.

Queensberry Rules *n* (*pl*) the code of rules used in boxing, drawn up in 1867 for the Marquess of *Queensberry*.

queer *adj* **1** odd, strange or unusual. **2** (*coll*) slightly mad. **3** faint or ill: *feeling queer*. **4** (*coll*) suspicious; shady: *queer doings*. **5** (*offensive slang*) (of a man) homosexual. — *adv* **queerly**. — *n* **queerness**. — **in queer street** (*coll*) in debt or financial difficulties. — **queer someone's pitch** (*coll*) to spoil someone's plans; to thwart someone.

quell *v* (*tr*) **1** to crush or subdue (riots, disturbances, opposition, etc.). **2** to suppress or overcome (unwanted feelings, etc.). [OE *cwellan*, to kill]

quench *v* (*tr*) **1** to get rid of (one's thirst) by drinking. **2** to extinguish (a fire). **3** to damp or crush (ardour, enthusiasm, desire, etc.). **4** to plunge (hot metal) into water or oil to cool it. [OE *acwencan*]

quenelle *n* a dumpling of fish, chicken, veal, etc. [Fr]

quern *n* (*hist* or *archaeol*) a stone implement of any of several kinds for grinding grain by hand. [OE *cweorn*]

querulous *adj* **1** inclined to complain. **2** (of a voice, tone, etc.) complaining, grumbling or whining. [Lat *querulus*, from *queri*, to complain]

query *n* **-ies 1** a question, esp. one that raises a doubt. **2** a request for information; an inquiry. **3** a question mark. — *v* **-ies, -ied** (*tr*) **1** to raise a doubt about: *query a bill*. **2** to ask: *'How much?' she queried*. [Lat *quaere*, imperative of *quaerere*, to ask]

quest *n* **1** a search or hunt. **2** the object of one's search; one's goal. — *v* (*intr*; **about, for**) **1** to search about; to roam around in search of something. **2** (of a dog) to search for game. — **in quest of** looking for. [Lat *quaerere*, to seek]

question *n* **1** an utterance which requests information or other answer; the interrogative sentence or other form of words in which this is expressed. **2** a doubt or query: *raises questions about their loyalty*. **3** an uncertainty: *no question about the cause*. **4** a problem or difficulty: *the Northern Ireland question*. **5** a problem set for discussion or solution in an examination paper, etc. **6** an investigation or search for information: *still pursuing the question*. **7** a matter or issue: *when it's a question of safety*. **8** an issue on which something is dependent: *a question of time rather than money*. — *v* **-n-** (*tr*) **1** to ask (someone) questions; to interrogate. **2** to raise doubts about; to query: *would question her motives*; *question whether it's possible*. — *n* **questioner**. — **beyond question** not in doubt; beyond doubt. — **bring into question** to focus attention on. — **call in** or **into question** to suggest reasons for doubting. — **in question 1** presently under discussion or being referred to: *has an alibi for the time in question*. **2** in doubt: *Her ability is not in question*. — **no question of** no possibility or intention of. — **out of the question** impossible and so not worth considering. — **without question** unhesitatingly. [Lat *quaestio*, from *quaerere*, to ask]

questionable *adj* **1** doubtful; dubious; suspect: *questionable motives*. **2** of dubious value or benefit: *questionable schemes*.

question mark *n* **1** the punctuation mark (?) placed after a question. **2** a doubt: *still a question mark over funds*.

question master *n* the person who asks the questions in a quiz, etc.

question time *n* in parliament, a daily period set aside for members' questions to government ministers.

questionnaire *n* a set of questions, usu. in the form of a printed leaflet, for distribution to a number of people, as a means of collecting information, surveying opinions, etc. [Fr]

queue *n* a line or file of people or vehicles waiting for something. — *v* (*intr*; **up**, **for**) to form, or wait in, a queue. [Fr, tail]

quibble *v* (*intr*) to argue over trifles; to make petty objections. — *n* **1** a trifling objection. **2** (*old*) a pun.

quiche *n* a tart with a savoury filling usu. made with eggs. [Fr, from Ger *Küchen*, cake]

quick *adj* **1** taking little time; speedy. **2** lasting briefly: *a quick glance*. **3** not delayed; immediate: *a quick response*. **4** intelligent; alert; sharp: *quick-witted*. **5** (of the temper) easily roused: *quick tempered*. **6** nimble, deft or brisk. **7** not reluctant or slow (to do something); apt or ready: *quick to take offence*. — *adv* rapidly: *came as quick as we could*; *a quick-acting drug*. — *n* **1** an area of sensitive flesh, esp. at the base of the finger- or toenail. **2** (*old*; *pl*) those who are alive: *the quick and the dead*. — *adv* **quickly**. — *n* **quickness**. [OE *cwic*, living]

quicken *v* **-n- 1** (*intr* & *tr*) to make or become quicker. **2** (*tr*) to stimulate or stir (someone's interest, imagination, etc.). **3** (*intr*) (of a baby in the womb) to begin to move perceptibly, or (of a pregnant woman) to begin to feel her baby's movements.

quick-freeze *v* **-*froze*, -*frozen*** (*tr*) to freeze (food) rapidly so as to preserve all its natural qualities.

quickie *n* (*coll*) something quickly dealt with or done, e.g. an easy question.

quicklime *n* calcium oxide, a white crystalline solid, used in the manufacture of glass and steel.

quick one *n* (*coll*) a quickly consumed alcoholic drink.

quicksand *n* loose, wet sand that sucks down people or heavy objects standing on it.

quickset *adj* (of cuttings, etc.) planted so as to grow into a hedge. — *n* a hedge so formed.

quicksilver *n* (*old*) mercury.

quickstep *n* a ballroom dance with fast steps; a piece of music for this.

quid[1] ***quid*** (*slang*) a pound (£1). — **quids in** (*slang*) in a profitable or advantageous position.

quid[2] *n* a bit of tobacco for chewing. [Dialect, cud]

quiddity *n* **-*ies* 1** the essence of anything. **2** a quibble; a trifling detail or point. [Lat *quidditas*, essence]

quid pro quo *n* ***quid pro quos*** something given or taken in recompense or retaliation for something. [Lat, something for something]

quiescent *adj* quiet; silent; at rest; in an inactive state, esp. one unlikely to last. — *n* **quiescence**. [Lat *quiescere*, to rest]

quiet *adj* **1** making little or no noise; soft. **2** (of a place, etc.) peaceful; tranquil; without noise or bustle. **3** silent; saying nothing: *kept quiet about it*. **4** (of a person) reserved; unassertive. **5** (of weather) calm. **6** not disturbed by trouble or excitement: *a quiet life*. **7** without fuss or publicity: *a quiet wedding*. **8** (of business or trade) poor; not flourishing. **9** secret; private: *had a quiet word with her*. **10** undeclared: *quiet satisfaction*. **11** (of humour) subtle; not overdone. **12** enjoyed in peace: *a quiet read*. **13** (of the mind or conscience) untroubled by anxiety, guilt, etc. — *n* absence of, or freedom from, noise, commotion, etc.; calm, tranquillity or repose: *longing for peace and quiet*. — *v* **-t-** (*tr* & *intr*) to make or become quiet or calm. — *adv* **quietly**. — *n* **quietness**. — **on the quiet** secretly. [Lat *quietus*, quiet]

quieten *v* **-n- 1** (*tr* & *intr*) to make or become quiet. **2** to calm (doubts, fears, etc.)

quietism *n* calm, passive acceptance of events. — *n* **quietist**.

quietude *n* quietness; tranquillity.

quietus *n* **1** release from life; death. **2** release or discharge from debts or duties. [Lat *quietus est*, he is at peace]

quiff *n* a lock of hair brushed up into a point over the forehead.

quill *n* **1** a large stiff feather from a bird's wing or tail; the hollow base part of this. **2** a pen made from a bird's feather. **3** one of the long spines on a porcupine. [Related to Ger dialect *quiele*]

quilt *n* **1** a bedcover containing padding or a filling of feathers, etc., kept in place by intersecting seams. **2** a duvet; a continental quilt. — *v* (*tr* & *intr*) to sew (material, garments, etc.) in two layers with a filling, esp. with decorative seaming. — *adj* **quilted**. [OFr *cuilte*, from Lat *culcita*, mattress, cushion]

quin *n* (*coll*) a quintuplet.

quince *n* the round or pear-shaped acid fruit of an Asian tree, used to make jams, jellies, etc. [Orig. pl. of MidE *quyne*, quince, from Gr *melon Kydonion*, apple of Cydonia, in Crete]

quincentenary *n* **-*ies*** a 500th anniversary. [Lat *quinque*, five + **centenary**]

quincunx *n* **1** an arrangement of five things at the corners and centre of a square. **2** a repeating pattern based on this arrangement, e.g. in tree-planting. [Lat, five-twelfths]

quinine *n* a bitter-tasting drug obtained from cinchona bark, used to reduce pain and fever, e.g. in malaria. [Span *quina*, cinchona bark]

Quinquagesima *n* in the Christian calendar, the Sunday before Lent. [Lat, fiftieth (day before Easter Day)]

quinquennial *adj* **1** lasting five years. **2** occurring every five years. — *adv* **quinquennially**. [Lat *quinque*, five + *annus*, year]

quinquereme *n* (*coll*) a galley of the ancient world with five oarsmen to each oar, or five banks of oars. [Lat *quinque*, five + *remus*, oar]

quinsy *n* inflammation of the throat with an abscess on the tonsils. [Lat *quinancia*, from Gr *kynanche*, 'throttle-dog', from *kyon*, dog + *anchein*, to strangle]

quintal *n* **1** a metric unit of weight equal to 100 kg. **2** (*formerly*) a hundredweight, 112 lbs. [Arabic *qintar*, from Lat *centum*, 100]

quintessence *n* **1** the central, essential nature of something. **2** a perfect example or embodiment of something. **3** (*old*) the purest, most concentrated extract of a substance. — *adj* **quintessential**. — *adv* **quintessentially**. [Lat *quinta essentia*, fifth essence]

quintet or **quintette** *n* **1** an ensemble of five singers or instrumental players. **2** a piece of music for five such performers. **3** any group or set of five. [Ital *quintetto*, from Lat *quintus*, five]

quintuple *v* (*tr* & *intr*) to multiply by five or increase fivefold. — *adj* **1** five times as many or much. **2** composed of five parts. — *n* a quintuple number or amount. [Lat *quintuplus*, fivefold]

quintuplet *n* one of five children born to a mother at one birth.

quip *n* a witty remark. — *v* **-pp-** **1** (*intr*) to make a quip or quips. **2** (*tr*) to say in jest. [Perhaps Lat *quippe*, to be sure]

quire *n* **1** a paper measure, 25 (formerly 24) sheets. **2** (*old*) a set of folded sheets fitting inside one another for binding into book form. [OFr *quaier*, from Lat *quattuor*, four]

quirk *n* **1** an odd habit, mannerism or aspect of personality that someone has. **2** an odd twist in affairs or turn of events; a strange coincidence: *quirks of fate*. — *adj* **quirky**, **-ier**, **-iest**.

quisling *n* a traitor who co-operates with an enemy force occupying his or her own country; a collaborator. [Vidkun *Quisling* (1887–1945), who did this in Norway]

quit *v* **-tt-**, ***quitted*** or ***quit*** **1** (*tr*) to leave (a place, etc.). **2** (*tr* & *intr*) to leave, give up or resign (a job). **3** (*tr*; *coll*; esp. *US*) to cease (something, or doing something): *quit that racket*. **4** (*tr* & *intr*) (of a tenant) to move out of (rented premises). — *adj* (with **of**) free of; rid of. [OFr *quiter*, from Lat *quietare*, to pay]

quits *adj* (*coll*) even with one another; on an equal footing. — **call it quits** to acknowledge the one is even with one's opponent, etc. and agree to stop fighting, arguing, etc.

quittance *n* (a document acknowledging) a person's release from debt or other obligation.

quitter *n* (*coll*) **1** someone who gives up too easily. **2** a shirker.

quitch *n* couch grass. [OE *cwice*]

quite *adv* **1** completely; entirely: *don't quite understand*; *not quite clear*. **2** to a high degree: *quite exceptional*. **3** rather; fairly; to some, or a limited, degree: *quite promising*; *quite a nice day*; *quite enjoyed it*. **4** (used in reply) I agree, see your point, etc. — **quite a** or **some** a striking, impressive, daunting, challenging: *That's quite a* or *some task you have there*. — **quite so** I agree; you're right. — **quite something** something impressive. [Variant of **quit**]

quiver[1] *v* **-r-** (*intr*) to shake or tremble slightly; to shiver. — *n* a tremble or shiver. [Perhaps from older meaning, nimble]

quiver[2] *n* a long narrow case for carrying arrows in. [OFr *cuivre*]

quixotic *adj* **1** absurdly generous or chivalrous. **2** unrealistically romantic or idealistic. [Don *Quixote*, hero of a romance by the Spanish writer Cervantes (1547–1616)]

quiz *n* **-zzes** **1** an entertainment, e.g. on radio or television, in which the knowledge of a panel of contestants is tested. **2** any series of questions as a test of general or specialised knowledge. **3** an interrogation. — *v* **-zz-** (*tr*) to question; to interrogate.

quiz-master *n* the question-master in a television quiz, etc.

quizzical *adj* (of a look, expression, etc.) mocking; questioning; amused. — *adv* **quizzically**. [**quiz**]

quod *n* (*slang*) jail; prison.

quoin *n* **1** the angle of a building. **2** a cornerstone. **3** a wedge, e.g. (*printing*) for locking type into a frame. [Variant of *coin*]

quoit *n* **1** a ring of metal, rubber or rope used in the game of quoits. **2** (in *pl* with *sing* verb) a game in which such rings are thrown at pegs, with the aim of encircling them.

quondam *adj* former: *his quondam secretary*. [Lat, formerly]

quorum *n* the minimum number of members who must be present at a meeting for any business to be carried out. [Lat, of whom]

quorate (of a meeting, etc.) attended by enough people to amount to a quorum.

quota *n* **1** a total number or quantity that is permitted or required. **2** someone's allocated share, e.g. of work. [Lat *quotus*, of what number]

quote *v* **1** (*tr* & *intr*) to repeat the exact words of: *quote Milton, a poem, from a speech*, etc. **2** (*tr*) to refer to (a law, etc.) as authority or support. **3** (*tr* & *intr*; **for**) (of a contractor) to submit (a price) for a particular job. — *n* **1** a quotation. **2** a price quoted. **3** (in *pl*) quotation marks. — *interj* (*coll*) used in speech to indicate that one is quoting: *her quote 'reluctance' unquote*. [Lat *quotare*, to mark passages with numbers]

quotable *adj* worth quoting.

quotation *n* **1** something quoted. **2** the act of quoting. **3** an estimated price for a job submitted by a contractor to a client.

quotation marks *n* (*pl*) the punctuation marks (" " or ' ') used to show the beginning and end of a quotation, or on either side of a word or phrase on which attention is focused for some reason.

quoth (*old*) said: *quoth she, he* or *I.* [OE *cwæth*]
quotidian *adj* everyday; commonplace. **2** daily. **3** (of a fever) recurring daily. [Lat *quotidianus*, daily]
quotient *n* the number of times one number is contained in another, found by dividing the latter by the former. [Lat *quotiens*, how often?]
Qur'an or **Quran** *n.* Same as **Koran**.
q.v. or **qv** *abbrev* for *quod vide* (Lat), which see, see this word (used to refer a reader from a word used in a dictionary or encyclopaedia text, etc. to the entry dealing with it).
qwerty *n* the standard arrangement of keys on a typewriter or keyboard designed for English-language users, with the letters *q, w, e, r, t, y*, in that order, at the top left of the letters section of the keyboard.

R

R[1] or **r** *n* ***R's*** or ***Rs***, ***r's*** the eighteenth letter of the English alphabet.

the three R's *n* (*pl*) reading, writing and arithmetic.

R[2] *abbrev* **1** *Regina* (Lat), Queen. **2** *Rex* (Lat), King. **3** River. **4** (*chess*) rook.

® *symbol* registered trademark.

r *abbrev* **1** right. **2** recto. **3** radius.

RA *abbrev* **1** (*Br*) Royal Academy or Academician. **2** Rear Admiral.

Ra *symbol* (*chem*) radium.

rabbet *n* a groove cut along the edge of a piece of wood, etc., usu. to join with a tongue or projection in a matching piece. — *v* **-t-** (*tr*) **1** to cut a rabbet in. **2** to join by a rabbet. [OFr *rabattre*, to beat down]

rabbi *n* **1** a Jewish religious leader. **2** a Jewish scholar or teacher of the law. — *adj* **rabbinical**. [Hebr, my master]

rabbit *n* **1** a small, long-eared, burrowing animal with a fluffy white tail. **2** (*Br coll*) a poor performer in any sport or game. — *v* **-t-** (*intr*) **1** to hunt rabbits. **2** (**on, away**) to talk at great length; to chatter. [MidE *rabet*]

rabbit punch *n* a sharp blow on the back of the neck.

rabbit warren *n* a system of burrows in which wild rabbits live.

rabble *n* **1** a noisy, disorderly crowd. **2** (with **the**) the lowest class of people. [MidE]

rabble-rouser *n* a person who makes speeches, esp. calling for social or political change, which are meant to arouse feelings of anger and violence in those listening. — *adj* & *n* **rabble-rousing**.

Rabelaisian *adj* of or like the works of the 16th-century French writer François *Rabelais*, esp. in being satirical and coarsely humorous.

rabid *adj* **1** (of dogs, etc.) suffering from rabies. **2** fanatical; unreasoning. — *n* **rabidity**. — *adv* **rabidly**. — *n* **rabidness**. [Lat *rabidus*]

rabies *n* a disease of the nervous system that causes madness and usu. death, and which is transmitted by the bite of an infected animal. [Lat, from *rabere*, to rave]

RAC *abbrev* (*Br*) Royal Automobile Club, a British organisation which helps drivers with breakdowns or technical problems, gives travel information, etc. ◇ See also **AA**.

raccoon or **racoon** *n* a small, furry, N American animal, with a black striped tail and face. [A native American Indian name]

race[1] *n* **1** a contest of speed between runners, horses, cars, etc. **2** (in *pl*) a series of such contests over a fixed course, esp. for horses or dogs. **3** any contest or rivalry, esp. to be the first to do or get something. **4** a strong or rapid current of water in the sea or a river. **5** a channel conveying water to and from a mill wheel. **6** a groove in which something, e.g. ball-bearings, moves or slides. — *v* **1** (*intr*) to take part in a race. **2** (*tr*) to have a race with (someone). **3** (*tr*) to enter (a horse, car, etc.) in a race. **4** (*intr*; **about, along, around**, etc.) to run or move quickly. **5** (*tr* & *intr*) to (cause to) move more quickly than usual. **6** (*intr*) to own racehorses, or watch horse racing as a hobby. — *n* **racing**. [Norse *ras*]

racecard *n* a list of all the competitors and races at a race meeting.

racecourse or **racetrack** *n* a course or track used for racing horses, cars, bicycles, runners, etc.

racehorse *n* a horse bred and used for racing.

race meeting *n* a series of horse races taking place over the same course and on the same day.

racer *n* (*coll*) a bicycle or horse used for racing.

race[2] *n* **1** a major division of mankind having a particular set of physical characteristics, such as size, hair type or skin colour. **2** a tribe, nation or other group of people thought of as distinct from others. **3** human beings as a group: *the human race*. **4** a group of animals or plants within a species, which have characteristics which make them distinct from other members of that species. ◇ See also **racial**. [Ital *razza*]

race relations *n* (*pl*) social relations between people of different races in the same community or country.

race riot *n* a riot caused by bad feeling between people of different races or discrimination against people of a particular race.

raceme *n* a cluster of flowers formed by individual flowers attached to a long stalk by short stalks of equal length, as in the bluebell. [Lat *racemus*, bunch of grapes]

racial *adj* **1** of or relating to a particular race. **2** based on race. — *adv* **racially**. [**race**[2]]

racialism or **racism** *n* **1** a belief that a particular race is inherently superior to others. **2** abusive, oppressive behaviour, discrimination and prejudice caused by such a belief. — *n* & *adj* **racialist** or **racist**.

rack[1] *n* **1** a framework with rails, shelves, hooks, etc. for holding or storing things. **2** a framework for holding hay, etc. from which livestock can feed. **3** a bar with teeth which connect with teeth on a cogwheel to change the position of something, or to convert linear motion into rotary motion or vice versa. ◇ See also **pinion**[2]. **4** (*hist*) an instrument for torturing people by stretching their bodies. — *v* (*tr*) **1** to cause pain or suffering to: *be racked with guilt*. **2** to put in a rack. **3** (*hist*) to torture on a rack. — **rack one's brains** to think as hard as one can. [MidE *rakke*]

rack railway *n* a mountain railway with a rack (sense **3**) which engages with the cogged wheels of the locomotive.

rack rent *n* an excessive or unreasonably high rent.

rack[2]: **go to rack and ruin** to get into a state of neglect and decay. [OE *wræc*, misery]

rack[3] *v* (*tr*) to draw off (wine or beer) from its sediment. [Provençal *raca*, dregs]

rack[4] *n* a joint of meat, esp. of lamb, including the neck and front ribs.

racket[1] or **racquet** *n* a wooden or metal oval frame with catgut or nylon strings stretched across it, used for playing tennis, badminton, squash, etc. [Fr *raquette*]

rackets *n* (*sing*) a game for two or four players played with rackets in a court with four walls.

racket[2] *n* **1** a loud, confused noise or disturbance; din. **2** a fraudulent, illegal means of making money. **3** (*slang*) job; occupation.

racketeer *n* a person who makes money in some illegal way, often by threats of violence. — *v* (*intr*) to make money as a racketeer. — *n* **racketeering**.

raconteur *n* a person who tells anecdotes in an amusing or entertaining way. [Fr]

racoon. See **raccoon**.

racquet. See **racket**[1].

racy *adj* **-ier**, **-iest 1** lively or spirited. **2** slightly indecent; risqué. — *adv* **racily**. — *n* **raciness**. [**race**[2]]

RADA *abbrev* Royal Academy of Dramatic Art.

radar *n* **1** a method of detecting the direction, speed and distance away of an aircraft, ship, etc. by bouncing radio waves off it. **2** the equipment for sending out and receiving such radio waves. [*ra*dio *d*etection *a*nd *r*anging]

radar trap *n* a device using radar which allows the police to detect vehicles travelling faster than the speed limit.

raddled *adj* worn out and haggard-looking through debauchery. [*raddle*, red ochre]

radial *adj* **1** (of lines) spreading out from the centre of a circle, like rays. **2** of or relating to rays, a radius or radii. **3** along or in the direction of a radius or radii. **4** (*anat*) of the radius. — *n* **1** (in full **radial-ply tyre**) a tyre which has fabric cords laid at a right angle to the centre of the tread, allowing the walls to be flexible. ◇ See also **cross-ply**. **2** (*anat*) a radial artery or nerve. — *adv* **radially**. [Lat *radius*, spoke, ray]

radian *n* the angle, nearly 57·3°, formed at the centre of a circle by two radii which are as long as the arc they cut on the circle's circumference. [Lat *radius*, spoke, ray]

radiant *adj* **1** sending out rays of light; glowing or shining. **2** (**with**) beaming with great joy, love, hope and health. **3** transmitted by or as radiation. — *n* **1** a point or object which sends out light, heat or radiation. **2** (*astron*) the centre from which showers of meteors seem to come. — *n* **radiance**. — *adv* **radiantly**. [Lat *radiare*, to radiate]

radiant energy *n* energy given out as electromagnetic radiation.

radiant heat *n* heat transmitted by electromagnetic radiation.

radiate *v* **1** (*tr* & *intr*) to send out rays of (light, heat, electromagnetic radiation, etc.). **2** (*intr*) (of light, heat, electromagnetic radiation, etc.) to be emitted in rays. **3** (*tr*) to show a lot of (happiness, good health, etc.) clearly: *radiate vitality*. **4** (*tr* & *intr*) to (cause to) spread out from a central point as radii. — *adj* having rays, radii or a radial structure. [Lat *radiare*, to shine]

radiation *n* **1** the sending out of energy in the form of electromagnetic waves or particles, such as X-rays. **2** the energy sent out in this way. **3** the act of radiating or state of being radiated.

radiation sickness *n* an illness caused by absorbing too much radiation from radioactive material, X-rays, etc.

radiator *n* **1** an apparatus for heating, consisting of a series of pipes through which hot water (or hot oil) is circulated. **2** an apparatus for heating in which wires are made hot by electricity. **3** an apparatus for cooling an internal combustion engine, e.g. in a car, consisting of a series of tubes which water passes through, and a fan. [**radiate**]

radical *adj* **1** of or relating to the basic nature of something; fundamental. **2** far-reaching; thoroughgoing: *radical changes*. **3** in favour of or tending to produce thoroughgoing or extreme political and social reforms. **4** of a political group or party in favour of extreme reforms. **5** (*bot*) from or growing near the roots of a plant. **6** (*math*) of or relating to the roots of numbers. **7** (*linguistics*) of or relating to the roots of words. — *n* **1** a person who is a member of a radical political group, or who holds radical political views. **2** (*chem*) a group of atoms which behaves like a single atom. **3** (*math*) the root of a number. **4** (*linguistics*) the root of a word. — *n* **radicalism**. — *adv* **radically**. — *n* **radicalness**. [Lat *radix*, root]

radical sign *n* the sign $\sqrt{}$, showing a square root.

radicle *n* **1** the part of a seed which develops into the root. **2** a very small rootlike part, e.g. of a vein or nerve. [Lat *radicula*, small root]

radii. See **radius**.

radio *n* **-os 1** the sending and receiving of messages, etc. without connecting wires, using electromagnetic waves. **2** an electrical apparatus which receives, transmits or broadcasts signals using electromagnetic waves. **3** sound transmission or broadcasting by radio in general. **4** a company or organisation which broadcasts programmes on the radio: *Radio Forth.* — *adj* **1** of, for, transmitting or transmitted by radio. **2** controlled by radio. — *v* **-os, -oed 1** (*tr*) to send (a message) to (someone) by radio. **2** (*intr*) to broadcast or communicate by radio. [Lat *radius*, spoke, ray]

radio astronomy *n* astronomy based on detecting and interpreting radio waves generated by stars, planets, quasars, etc. in space.

radio frequency *n* a frequency of electromagnetic waves used for radio and television broadcasting.

radio-pager *n* a very small radio receiver which emits a bleeping sound in response to a signal, used for paging people. — *n* **radio-paging**.

radiotelephone *n* a telephone which works by radio waves, used esp. in cars and other vehicles.

radio telescope *n* a telescope which can pick up radio waves generated by stars, planets, etc. in space, used in radio astronomy.

radio- *comb fm* **1** radio or broadcasting. **2** radioactivity. **3** rays or radiation. [Lat *radius*, spoke, ray]

radioactivity *n* the spontaneous disintegration of the atomic nuclei of some elements, e.g. uranium, resulting in the giving off of radiation. — *adj* **radioactive**.

radiocarbon *n* a radioactive isotope of carbon, esp. carbon-14.

radiocarbon dating same as **carbon dating**.

radiochemistry *n* the chemistry of radioactive elements and compounds.

radiogram[1] *n* (*old*) an apparatus consisting of a radio and record-player. [**radio-** + **gramophone**]

radiogram[2] *n* a radiograph [**radio-** + **-gram**]

radiograph *n* a photograph taken using a form of radiation other than light, such as X-rays or gamma rays, esp. of the inside of the body. [**radio-** + **-graph**]

radiography *n* the production of radiographs for use in medicine. — *n* **radiographer**.

radioisotope *n* a radioactive isotope.

radiology *n* the scientific study of X-rays and other types of radiation, and its use in treating diseases. — *adj* **radiological**. — *n* **radiologist**. [**radio-** + **-logy**]

radiophonic *adj* of or relating to sound produced electronically. [**radio-** + Gr *phone*, sound]

radioscopy *n* the examination of the inside of the body, or of opaque objects, using X-rays. — *adj* **radioscopic**. [**radio-** + **-scopy**]

radiotherapy *n* the treatment of disease, esp. cancer, by X-rays and other forms of radiation.

radish *n* a plant of the mustard family, with pungent-tasting, red-skinned white roots, which are eaten raw in salads. [OE *rædic*, from Lat *radix*, root]

radium *n* a radioactive metallic element (symbol **Ra**), found in pitchblende and other minerals. [Lat *radius*, ray]

radius *n* **-ii** or **-ses 1** a straight line running from the centre of a circle to a point on its circumference. **2** the length of such a line. **3** a usu. specified distance from a central point, thought of as limiting an area: *all the houses within a radius of four miles.* **4** (*anat*) the shorter of the two bones in the human forearm, on the thumb side. **5** anything placed like a radius, such as a spoke in a wheel. [Lat, spoke, ray]

radon *n* an element (symbol **Rn**), a radioactive gas formed from the disintegration of radium. [**radium**]

RAF *abbrev* Royal Air Force.

raffia *n* ribbon-like fibre obtained from the leaves of certain palm trees, used for weaving mats, baskets, etc. [A native word from Madagascar]

raffish *adj* slightly shady or disreputable; rakish. — *adv* **raffishly**. — *n* **raffishness**. [**riff-raff**]

raffle *n* a lottery, often to raise money for charity, in which certain numbered tickets win prizes. — *v* (*tr*) to offer as a prize in a raffle. [MidE *rafle*, dice game]

raft *n* **1** a flat structure of logs, timber, etc. fastened together so as to float on water, used for transport or as a platform. **2** a flat, floating mass of ice, vegetation, etc. — *v* **1** (*tr*) to transport by raft. **2** (*intr*) to travel by raft. [Norse *raptr*, rafter]

rafter *n* any of several sloping beams supporting a roof. [OE *ræfter*]

rag[1] *n* **1** a scrap of cloth, esp. a piece which has been worn or torn off old clothes. **2** (usu. in *pl*) a piece of clothing, esp. when old and tattered. **3** (*coll derog*) a newspaper. — **lose one's rag** (*slang*) to lose one's temper. [OE *raggig*, shaggy]

rag-and-bone man *n* a person who collects and deals in old clothes and furniture, etc.

rag-bag *n* **1** (*coll*) a scruffy, untidy person. **2** a bag for storing rags and scraps of material.

ragged *adj* **1** (of clothes) old, worn and tattered. **2** dressed in old, worn, tattered clothing. **3** with a rough and irregular edge; jagged. **4** untidy; straggly. — *adv* **raggedly**. — *n* **raggedness**.

ragged Robin *n* a wild flower with pink, ragged-edged petals.

rag trade *n* the business of designing, making and selling clothes.

ragwort *n* a common plant with yellow flowers with ragged petals.

rag[2] *v* **-gg- 1** (*tr* & *intr*; esp. *Br*) to tease; to play rough tricks on (someone). **2** (*tr*) to scold. — *n* (*Br*) a series of noisy stunts and events put on by university or college students to raise money for charity: *rag week*.

rag[3] *n* a piece of ragtime music. [**ragtime**]

raga *n* **1** a traditional pattern of notes in Hindu classical music, around which melodies can be improvised. **2** a piece of music composed around such a pattern. [Sanskrit, colour, musical tone]

ragamuffin *n* a ragged, disreputable child. [MidE *Rugamoffyn*, the name of a demon in the poem *Piers Plowman*, by William Langland (*c*. 1332–*c*. 1400)]

rage *n* **1** (a fit of) violent anger. **2** violent, stormy action, e.g. of the wind, sea or a battle. **3** an intense desire or passion (for something). **4** a widespread, usu. temporary fashion or craze. — *v* (*intr*) **1** to be violently angry. **2** to speak wildly with anger or passion; to rave. **3** (of the wind, sea, a battle, etc.) to be stormy and unchecked. — *adj* **raging**. — **all the rage** (*coll*) very much in fashion. [Lat *rabies*, madness]

raglan *adj* **1** (of a sleeve) attached to a garment by two seams running diagonally from the neck to the armpit. **2** (of a garment) with such sleeves. [Lord *Raglan* (1788–1855), British commander in the Crimea]

ragout *n* a highly seasoned stew of meat and vegetables. [Fr *ragoût*]

ragtime *n* a type of jazz piano music with a highly syncopated rhythm, originated by Black American musicians in the 1890s. [*ragged* + *time*]

raid *n* **1** a sudden unexpected attack. **2** a sudden unexpected visit by the police searching for suspected criminals or illicit goods. **3** the selling of shares by a group of speculators in an attempt to lower share prices. — *v* **1** (*tr*) to make a raid on. **2** (*intr*) to go on a raid. — *n* **raider**. [OE *rad*, road]

rail[1] *n* **1** a usu. horizontal bar supported by vertical posts, forming a fence or barrier. **2** a horizontal bar used to hang things on. **3** either of a pair of lengths of steel forming a track for the wheels of a train. **4** the railway. — *v* (*tr*; **off**) to enclose (a space) within a rail or rails. — **off the rails** not functioning or behaving normally or properly. [OFr *reille*]

railcard *n* a special card, e.g. for students, the elderly, etc., giving the holder the right to reduced train fares.

railhead *n* **1** a railway terminal. **2** the furthest point reached by a railway under construction.

railing *n* **1** (usu. in *pl*) a fence or barrier. **2** material for building fences.

railroad *n* (*US*) a railway. — *v* (*tr*; *coll*; **into**) to rush (someone) unfairly (into doing something).

railway *n* **1** a track or set of tracks formed by two parallel steel rails fixed to sleepers, for trains to run on. **2** a system of such tracks, plus all the trains, buildings and people required for it to function. **3** a company responsible for operating such a system. **4** a similar set of tracks for a different type of vehicle: *funicular railway*.

rail[2] *v* (*intr*; **at, against**) to complain or criticise abusively or bitterly. [OFr *railler*, to deride]

rail[3] *n* any of various species of birds, usu. living near water, with a short neck and wings and long legs, such as the corncrake and coot. [OFr *rasle*]

raillery *n* (an instance of) good-humoured teasing. [**rail**[2]]

raiment *n* (*old* or *poetic*) clothing. [OFr *areer*, to array]

rain *n* **1** water falling from the clouds in drops. **2** (in *pl*) the season of heavy rainfall in tropical countries. **3** a heavy fall of something. — *v* **1** (*intr*) (of rain) to fall. **2** (*intr* & *tr*) to (cause to) fall like rain: *bullets raining down on them*; *rain down compliments on her head*. — **come rain or shine** whatever the weather or circumstances. — **rain cats and dogs** (*coll*) to rain very hard. — **right as rain** (*coll*) perfectly all right or in order. — *v* **rain off** (*tr*; *Br*) to cause (esp. a sporting event) to be cancelled because of rain. [OE *regn*]

rainbow *n* **1** a coloured arch, conventionally red, orange, yellow, green, blue, indigo and violet, sometimes seen in the sky, caused by light from the sun's rays being reflected and refracted through rain. **2** a collection or array of bright colours.

rainbow trout *n* a freshwater N American and European trout.

raincoat *n* a light waterproof coat worn to keep out the rain.

rainfall *n* **1** the amount of rain, hail and snow that falls in a certain place over a certain period. **2** a shower of rain.

rainforest *n* a dense tropical forest, with broad-leaved, evergreen trees and very heavy rainfall.

rainy *adj* **-ier, -iest 1** (of weather, etc.) having a lot of heavy showers of rain. **2** (of clouds, etc.) threatening rain.

a rainy day *n* a possible time of particular need in the future.

raise *v* (*tr*) **1** to move or lift to a high position or level. **2** to put in an upright or standing position. **3** to build. **4** to increase the value, amount or strength of: *raise prices*; *raise one's voice*. **5** to put forward for consideration or discussion: *raise an objection*. **6** to collect, levy or gather together. **7** to stir up or incite: *raise a protest*. **8** to bring into being; to provoke: *raise a laugh*; *raise the alarm*. **9** to promote to a higher rank. **10** to awaken or arouse from sleep or death. **11** to grow (vegetables, a crop, etc.). **12** to bring up or rear: *raise a family*. **13** to bring to an end or remove: *raise the siege*. **14** to cause (bread or dough) to rise with yeast. **15** to establish radio contact with. **16** (*math*) to increase (a quantity) to a given power: *3 raised to the power of 4 is 81*. **17** (*cards*) to bet more than (another player). **18** (*naut*) to cause (land) to come into sight by approaching. **19** to produce a nap on (cloth) by brushing. **20** to cause (a lump, blister, etc.) to form or swell. — *n* **1** an act of raising or lifting. **2** (*coll*, esp. *NAm*) an increase in salary. — *adj* **raised**. — *n* **raising**. — **raise hell** or **the devil** (*coll*) to make a lot of trouble. — **raise a person's hopes** to make a person more hopeful than he or she was or should be. — **raise someone's spirits** to make (a person) more cheerful or hopeful. [Norse *reisa*]

raisin *n* a dried grape. [OFr, grape]

raison d'être *n* ***raisons*** a purpose or reason that justifies a thing's or person's existence. [Fr, reason for being]

Raj *n* (*hist*) the British rule in India, 1858–1947. [Sanskrit *rajan*, king]

rajah or **raja** *n* (esp. *hist*) an Indian king or prince.

rake[1] *n* **1** a long-handled tool with a comb-like part at one end, used for smoothing or breaking up earth, gathering leaves together, etc. **2** any tool with a similar shape or use, e.g. a croupier's tool for gathering money together. — *v* **1** (*tr*; **up, together**) to collect, gather or remove with, or as if with, a rake. **2** (*tr*; **over**) to make smooth with a rake. **3** (*intr*) to work with a rake. **4** (*tr & intr*; **through, among**) to search carefully. **5** (*tr*) to sweep gradually along the length of, esp. with gunfire or (*fig*) one's eyes. **6** (*tr*) to scratch or scrape. — *v* **rake in** (*tr*; *coll*) to earn large amounts of (money) quickly. — *v* **rake up** (*tr*; *coll*) **1** to revive or uncover (something forgotten or lost): *rake up old memories*. **2** to find, esp. with difficulty: *rake up just enough people for the team*. [OE *raca*]

rake-off *n* (*slang*) a share of the profits, esp. when dishonest or illegal.

rake[2] *n* (*old*) a fashionable man who lives a dissolute and immoral life. — *adj* **rakish**. — *adv* **rakishly**. — *n* **rakishness**. [Abbrev. of obsolete *rakehell*]

rake[3] *n* **1** a sloping position, esp. of a ship's funnel or mast backwards towards the stern, of a ship's bow or stern in relation to the keel, or a theatre stage. **2** the amount by which something slopes. — *v* **1** (*tr & intr*) to set or be set at a sloping angle. **2** (*intr*) (of a ship's mast or funnel) to slope backwards towards the stern. **3** (*intr*) (of a ship's bow or stern) to project out beyond the keel.

rakish *adj* **1** (of a ship) looking as if it is built for speed. **2** confident, adventurous and jaunty.

rallentando *adj & adv* (*mus*) becoming gradually slower. — *n* ***-dos*** or ***-di*** a passage to be played in this way. [Ital]

rally *v* ***-ies, -ied*** **1** (*tr & intr*) to come or bring together again after being dispersed. **2** (*tr & intr*) to come or bring together for some common cause or action. **3** (*tr*) to revive (one's spirits, strength, abilities, etc.) by making an effort. **4** (*intr*) to recover one's lost health, fitness, strength, etc., esp. after an illness. **5** (*intr*) (of share prices) to increase again after a fall. — *n* ***-ies*** **1** a reassembling of forces to make a new effort. **2** a mass meeting of people with a common cause or interest. **3** a recovering of lost health, fitness, strength, esp. after an illness. **4** (*tennis*, etc.) a usu. long series of strokes between players before one of them finally wins the point. **5** a competition to test skill in driving, usu. held on public roads. — *v* **rally round** (*tr & intr*) to come together for a joint effort, esp. to help or support (someone). [OFr *rallier*, to re-join]

rallycross *n* motor racing over a course made up of both proper roads and rough ground.

RAM *abbrev* **1** (*comput*) random access memory, a temporary memory available to the user which allows programs to be loaded and run, and data to be changed. **2** Royal Academy of Music.

ram *n* **1** an uncastrated male sheep. **2** (*cap* with **the**) the constellation and sign of the zodiac Aries. **3** a battering-ram. **4** a pointed device on a warship's prow, for making holes in enemy ships. **5** the falling weight of a pile-driver. **6** a piston or plunger operated by hydraulic or other power. — *v* ***-mm-*** **1** (*tr*) to force down or into position by pushing hard. **2** (*tr & intr*) to strike or crash against violently: *ram the car into the wall*. — **ram something down someone's throat** (*coll*) to force someone to believe, accept or listen to (a statement, idea, etc.) by talking about it or repeating it constantly. — **ram (something) home** to emphasise (something) forcefully. [OE *ramm*]

ram-raid *n* a robbery, esp. from a shop, in which the thieves break into the premises by crashing a stolen vehicle through the window or door.

ramrod *n* **1** a rod for ramming charge down into, or for cleaning, the barrel of a gun. **2** a person who is strict, stern and inflexible, both physically and morally.

Ramadan or **Ramadhan** *n* **1** the ninth month of the Muslim year, during which Muslims fast between sunrise and sunset. **2** the fast itself. [Arabic]

ramble *v* (*intr*) **1** to go for a long walk or walks, esp. in the countryside, for pleasure. **2** (**on, on about**) to speak or write in an aimless or confused way. **3** to grow or extend in a straggling, trailing way. — *n* a walk, esp. in the countryside, for pleasure. — *n & adj* **rambling**. — *adv* **ramblingly**.

rambler *n* **1** a climbing plant, esp. a rose. **2** a person who goes walking in the country for pleasure.

RAMC *abbrev* (*Br*) Royal Army Medical Corps.

ramekin *n* **1** a small baking dish for a single serving of food. **2** an individual serving of food, esp. of a savoury dish containing cheese and eggs, served in a ramekin. [Fr *ramequin*]

ramification *n* **1** an arrangement of branches; a branched structure. **2** a single part or section of a complex subject, plot, etc. **3** a consequence, esp. a serious or complicated one. [Lat *ramus*, branch]

ramify *v* **-ies, -ied** (*tr* & *intr*) to separate or cause to separate into branches or sections.

ramp *n* **1** a sloping surface between two different levels, esp. one which can be used instead of steps. **2** a set of movable stairs for entering and leaving an aircraft. **3** (*Br*) a low hump lying across a road, designed to slow traffic down. **4** (*Br*) a place where the level of the road surface changes or is uneven due to roadworks. — *v* **1** (*tr*) to provide with a ramp. **2** (*intr*) to slope from one level to another. **3** (*intr*) to dash about in a wild, violent and threatening way. [OFr *ramper*, to creep]

rampage *v* (*intr*; **about, through,** etc.) to rush about wildly, angrily, violently or excitedly. — **on the rampage** rampaging, often destructively. [**ramp**]

rampant *adj* **1** uncontrolled; unrestrained: *rampant violence*. **2** (*heraldry*) in profile and standing erect on the left hind leg with the other legs raised. — *adv* **rampantly**. [**ramp**]

rampart *n* a broad mound or wall for defence, usu. with a wall or parapet on top. [OFr *remparer*, to defend]

ramrod. See **ram**.

ramshackle *adj* (esp. of buildings) badly made and likely to fall down; rickety. [Old word *ranshackle*, to ransack]

ran. See **run**.

ranch *n* **1** a large farm, esp. one in N America, for rearing cattle or horses. **2** (esp. *US*) a farm or area of land devoted to producing a particular crop or animal. — *v* (*intr*) to own, manage or work on a ranch. — *n* **rancher**. [Span *rancho*, mess-room]

rancid *adj* (of butter, oil, etc.) tasting or smelling sour. — *n* **rancidity** or **rancidness**. [Lat *rancidus*, stinking]

rancour *n* a long-lasting feeling of bitterness, dislike or hatred. — *adj* **rancorous**. — *adv* **rancorously**. [Lat *rancor*, from *rancere*, to be rancid]

rand *n* ***rand*** or ***rands*** the standard monetary unit used in S Africa and some neighbouring countries. [Witwaters*rand*, a large gold mining area near Johannesburg]

R & B *abbrev* rhythm and blues.

R & D *abbrev* research and development.

random *adj* lacking a definite plan, system or order; irregular; haphazard. — *adv* **randomly**. — *n* **randomness**. — **at random** without any particular plan, system or purpose. [OFr *randon*, gallop]

random access *n* access to a computer file which allows data in it to be read out of sequence.

random access memory see **RAM**.

randy *adj* **-ier, -iest** (*coll*) sexually excited; lustful. — *adv* **randily**. — *n* **randiness**. [A form of **rant**]

ranee. See **rani**.

rang. See **ring**[2].

range *n* **1** an area between limits within which things may move, function, etc.; the limits forming this area. **2** a number of items, products, etc. forming a distinct series. **3** the distance between the lowest and highest notes which may be produced by a musical instrument or a singing voice. **4** the distance to which a gun may be fired or an object thrown. **5** the distance between a weapon and its target. **6** the distance that can be covered by a vehicle without it needing to refuel. **7** an area where shooting may be practised and rockets tested. **8** a group of mountains forming a distinct series or row. **9** (esp. *NAm*) a large area of open land for grazing livestock. **10** the region over which a plant or animal is distributed. **11** (*math*) the set of values that a function or dependent variable may take. **12** an enclosed kitchen fireplace fitted with a large cooking stove with one or more ovens and a flat top surface for heating pans. — *v* **1** (*tr*) to put in a row or rows. **2** (*tr*) to put (someone, oneself, etc.) into a specified category or group: *He ranged himself among her enemies*. **3** (*intr*) to vary or change between specified limits. **4** (*tr* & *intr*; **over**) to roam freely (over). **5** (*intr*) to stretch or extend in a specified direction or over a specified area. [OFr, row, rank]

rangefinder *n* an instrument which can estimate how far away an object, esp. a target to be shot or photographed, is.

ranger *n* **1** a person who looks after a royal or national forest or park. **2** (*US*) a soldier who has been specially trained for raiding and combat; a commando. **3** (*US*) a member of a group of armed men who patrol and police a region. **4** (*cap*; also **Ranger Guide**; *Br*) a member of the senior branch of the Girl Guide Organisation.

rangy *adj* **-ier, -iest** (of a person) having long, thin limbs and a long, thin body.

rani or **ranee** *n* (esp. *hist*) the wife or widow of a rajah. [Sanskrit *rajni*, queen]

rank[1] *n* **1** a line or row of people or things. **2** a line of soldiers standing side by side. **3** a position of seniority within an organisation, society, the armed forces, etc. **4** a distinct class or group, e.g. according to ability. **5** high social position or status. **6** (in *pl*) ordinary soldiers (e.g. privates and corporals) as opposed to officers. **7** (*Br*) a place where taxis wait for passengers. **8** a row of squares along the player's side of a chessboard. — *v* **1** (*tr*) to arrange (people or things) in a row or line. **2** (*tr* & *intr*) to give or have a particular grade, position or status in relation to others. **3** (*tr*) to have a higher position, status, etc. than (someone); to outrank (someone). — **close ranks** (of a group of people) to keep their solidarity. — **pull rank** to use one's higher rank, status or position to get what one wants. — **the rank and file 1** the ordinary members of an organisation or society as opposed to the leaders or principal members. **2** the ordinary soldiers as opposed to the officers. [OFr *renc*]

ranker *n* a soldier who serves or has served in the ranks, esp. an officer who has been promoted up through the ranks.

rank[2] *adj* **1** coarsely overgrown and untidy. **2** offensively strong in smell or taste. **3** bold, open and shocking: *rank disobedience*. **4** complete: *a rank beginner*. — *adv* **rankly**. — *n* **rankness**. [OE *ranc*, proud, overbearing]

rankle *v* (*intr*) to continue to cause feelings of annoyance or bitterness: *His refusal still rankles.* [OFr *draoncle*, festering sore]

ransack *v* (*tr*) **1** to search thoroughly and often roughly. **2** to rob or plunder. [Norse *rannsaka*, from *rann*, house + *sækja*, to seek]

ransom *n* **1** money paid in return for the release of a kidnapped person. **2** the releasing of a kidnapped person in return for this. — *v* ***-m-*** (*tr*) **1** to pay a ransom for (someone's) release. **2** to demand a ransom before releasing (someone). — *n* **ransomer**. — **hold to ransom 1** to keep as a prisoner until a ransom is paid. **2** to blackmail into agreeing to one's demands. — **a king's ransom** a vast amount of money. [Lat *redemptio*, redemption]

rant *v* **1** (*intr*) to talk in a loud, angry, pompous way. **2** (*tr*) to declaim in a loud, pompous, self-important way. — *n* loud, pompous, empty speech. — *n* **ranter**. — *n* & *adj* **ranting**. [Dut *ranten*, to rave]

RAOC *abbrev* (*Br*) Royal Army Ordnance Corps.

rap[1] *n* **1** (the sound made by) a quick, sharp tap or blow. **2** (*slang*) blame or punishment: *take the rap*. **3** a fast, rhythmic monologue recited over a musical backing with a pronounced beat. **4** (in full **rap music**) a style of rock music based on such monologues. **5** (*coll*) a conversation. — *v* ***-pp-*** **1** (*tr*) to strike sharply. **2** (*intr*) to make a sharp tapping sound. **3** (*tr*; **out**) to utter (e.g. a command) sharply and quickly. **4** (*tr*) to criticise sharply. **5** (*tr*) to communicate (a message) by raps or knocks. **6** (*intr*; *coll*) to talk or have a discussion. **7** (*intr*; *coll*) to perform a fast, rhythmic monologue to music with a pronounced beat. — *n* **rapper**. — *n* **rapping**. — **beat the rap** (*US slang*) to escape punishment for a crime (whether guilty or not). [MidE *rappen*]

rap[2] *n* the least bit: *not care a rap.* [A former Irish counterfeit halfpenny]

rapacious *adj* **1** greedy and grasping, esp. for money. **2** (of an animal or bird) living by catching prey. — *adv* **rapaciously**. — *n* **rapaciousness** or **rapacity**. [Lat *rapere*, to seize and carry off]

rape[1] *n* **1** the crime of forcing a woman to have sex against her will. **2** the crime of sodomising a person against his or her will. **3** violation, despoiling or abuse. — *v* (*tr*) to commit rape on. — *n* **rapist**. [Lat *rapere*, to seize and carry off]

rape[2] *n* a plant related to the turnip, with brilliant yellow flowers, grown as food for sheep and for its seeds, from which **rapeseed oil** is made. [Lat *rapum*, turnip]

rapid *adj* moving, acting or happening quickly; fast. — *n* (in *pl*) a part of a river where the water flows quickly, usu. over dangerous, sharply descending rocks. — *n* **rapidity** or **rapidness**. — *adv* **rapidly**. [Lat *rapidus*]

rapid eye movement *n* a jerky movement of the closed eyes which can be observed in someone who is asleep and dreaming.

rapier *n* a long, thin, two-edged sword for thrusting. [Fr *rapière*]

rapine *n* plundering; robbery. [Lat *rapere*, to seize and carry off]

rapport *n* a feeling of sympathy and understanding; a close emotional bond. [Fr]

rapprochement *n* the establishment or renewal of a close, friendly relationship, esp. between states. [Fr]

rapscallion *n* (*old*) a rascal or scamp. [**rascal**]

rapt *adj* **1** enraptured; enchanted. **2** completely absorbed. [Lat *rapere*, to seize and carry off]

raptor *n* any bird of prey, e.g. an owl or falcon. — *adj* **raptorial**. [Lat, plunderer]

rapture *n* **1** great delight; ecstasy. **2** (in *pl*) great enthusiasm for or pleasure in (something): *go into raptures over her new car*. — *adj* **rapturous**. [**rapt**]

rare[1] *adj* **1** not done, found or occurring very often. **2** (of the atmosphere at high altitudes) thin; rarefied. **3** excellent; unusually good: *rare abilities*. **4** (*coll*) extreme; severe: *a rare old fright*. [Lat *rarus*, sparse]

rare earth *n* (*chem*) an oxide of a **rare earth element**, an element of the lanthanide series.

rarely *adv* **1** not often. **2** extremely well.

rare[2] *adj* (of meat) cooked on the outside but still raw on the inside. [OE *hrere*, lightly boiled]

rarebit. Same as **Welsh rarebit**.

rarefy *v* ***-ies***, ***-ied*** **1** (*tr* & *intr*) to make or become less dense or solid. **2** (*tr*) to refine or purify. [Lat *rarus*, rare + *facere*, to make]

rarefied *adj* **1** (of air, the atmosphere, etc.) thin; with a very low oxygen content. **2** select; exclusive: *move in rarefied circles*. **3** esoteric, mysterious, spiritual.

raring *adj* very keen and enthusiastic; *raring to go*. [**rear**[2]]

rarity *n* ***-ies*** **1** the state of being rare. **2** something valued because it is rare. [**rare**]

rascal *n* **1** a dishonest person; a rogue.

2 (*humorously*) a cheeky or mischievous child. — *adj* **rascally**. [OFr *rascaille*, rabble]

rase. Same as **raze**.

rash[1] *adj* acting, or done, with little caution or thought; hasty. — *adv* **rashly**. — *n* **rashness**. [MidE]

rash[2] *n* **1** a redness or outbreak of red spots on the skin. **2** a large number of instances of a thing happening at the same time: *a rash of burglaries*. [Lat *radere*, to scratch]

rasher *n* a thin slice of bacon or ham.

rasp *n* **1** a coarse, rough file. **2** a harsh, rough, grating sound. — *v* **1** (*tr*) to scrape roughly, esp. with a rasp. **2** (*tr*) to grate upon or irritate (e.g. someone's nerves). **3** (*tr*) to utter in a harsh, grating voice. **4** (*intr*) to speak in a harsh, grating voice. — *n* **rasper**. — *adj* **rasping**. — *adv* **raspingly**. — *adj* **raspy**, **-*ier***, **-*iest***. [OFr *raspe*]

raspberry *n* **-*ies*** **1** an edible red berry produced by a common European shrub. **2** (*slang*) a sound made by sticking the tongue out and blowing through the lips, usu. to express disapproval. [Earlier *raspis*]

Rasta *n* & *adj* (*coll*) Rastafarian. [Abbrev.]

Rastafarian *n* a follower of an orig. W Indian sect, which regards Blacks as the chosen people and reveres Haile Selassie, the former Emperor of Ethiopia, as God. — *adj* of Rastafarians. [*Ras Tafari*, the name and title of Haile Selassie (1891–1975)]

rat *n* **1** a rodent like a large long-tailed mouse. **2** (*coll*) a person who is disloyal towards his or her friends, party, etc. **3** (*coll*) a strike-breaker; a blackleg. — *v* **-*tt-*** (*intr*) **1** to hunt rats. **2** (**on**) to betray or desert one's friends or change sides. **3** to work as a blackleg. — **smell a rat** (*coll*) to sense that something is not as it should be. [OE *ræt*]

ratbag *n* (*slang*) a mean, despicable person.

rat race *n* (*coll*) the fierce, unending competition for success, wealth, etc. in business, society, etc.

ratter *n* a dog or other animal that catches and kills rats.

ratty *adj* **-*ier***, **-*iest*** **1** of or like a rat. **2** (*coll*) irritable.

ratable. Same as **rateable**.

ratan. Same as **rattan**.

rat-a-tat-tat *n* a sound of knocking on a door. [Imit.]

ratatouille *n* a southern French stew made with tomatoes, peppers, courgettes, aubergines, onions and garlic. [Fr]

ratchet *n* **1** a bar which fits into the notches of a toothed wheel so as to cause the wheel to turn in one direction only. **2** (also **rachet-wheel**) a wheel with a toothed rim. **3** the mechanism including the bar and toothed wheel together. [Fr *rochet*]

rate[1] *n* **1** the number of times something happens, etc. within a given period of time; the amount of something considered in relation to, or measured according to, another amount: *a high yearly suicide rate*; *at the rate of 20 miles an hour*. **2** a price or charge, often measured per unit: *the rate of pay for the job*. **3** a price or charge fixed according to a standard scale: *rate of exchange*. **4** class or rank: *second-rate*. **5** the speed of movement or change: *rate of progress*. **6** (in *pl*) (in the UK until 1990) a tax collected by a local authority, the amount of each person's contribution being based on the value of his or her property, used to pay for public services, such as libraries, rubbish collection, etc. ◇ See also **community charge**. — *v* **1** (*tr*) to give a value to: *be rated an excellent teacher*; *rate him number two in the world*. **2** (*tr*) to be worthy of; to deserve: *an answer not rating full marks*. **3** (*intr*; **as**) to be placed in a certain class or rank: *rates as the best book on the subject for years*. **4** (*tr*) (in the UK until 1990) to determine the value of (property) for the purposes of assessing the rates payable on it. — **at any rate** in any case; anyway. — **at this** or **that rate** if this or that is or continues to be the case. [Lat *rata*, from *reri*, to reckon]

rateable *adj* **1** able to have its value estimated for the purposes of rates. **2** (in the UK until 1990) having to pay rates.

rateable value *n* (in the UK until 1990) the fixed value of a piece of property used to calculate the rates to be paid on it.

rate-cap *v* **-*pp-*** (*tr*) (in the UK until 1990; of the government) to set an upper limit on the rate that can be levied by (a local authority). — *n* **rate-capping**.

ratepayer *n* (in the UK until 1990) a person who owns property on which rates must be paid.

rating *n* **1** a classification according to order, rank or value. **2** (esp. *Br*) an ordinary seaman. **3** an estimated value of a person's position, esp. as regards credit. **4** the proportion of viewers or listeners forming the estimated audience of a television or radio programme, used as a measure of that programme's popularity.

rate[2] *v* (*tr*) to scold severely. [MidE *raten*]

rather *adv* **1** more readily; from preference. **2** more truly or properly: *my parents, or rather my mother and stepfather*. **3** to a certain extent; somewhat. **4** on the contrary: *She said she'd help me; rather, she just sat around watching*. — *interj* yes indeed; very much. [OE *hrathor*]

ratify *v* **-*ies***, **-*ied*** (*tr*) to give formal consent to (e.g. a treaty, agreement, etc.), esp. by signature. — *n* **ratification**. [Lat *ratificare*]

ratio *n* **-*os*** **1** the number or degree of one class of things in relation to another, or between one thing and another, expressed as a proportion: *the ratio of dogs to cats is 5 to 3*. **2** the number of times one mathematical quantity can be divided by another. [Lat, reckoning]

ration *n* **1** a fixed allowance of food, clothing, petrol, etc. during a time of shortage. **2** (in *pl*) one's daily allowance of food, esp. in the army. — *v* **-n-** (*tr*) **1** (**out**) to distribute or share out (esp. something which is in short supply), usu. in fixed quantities. **2** to restrict the supply of (provisions) to (someone). — *n* **rationing**. [Lat *ratio*, reckoning]

ration book or **card** *n* a book or card containing coupons which can be exchanged for rationed goods.

rational *adj* **1** of or based on reason or logic. **2** able to think, form opinions, make judgements, etc. **3** sensible; reasonable. **4** sane. — *adv* **rationally**. — *n* **rationality**. [Lat *rationalis*]

rational number *n* (*math*) a number which can be expressed in the form of a fraction, e.g. $\frac{a}{b}$, where *a* and *b* are whole numbers, and *b* is not zero, e.g. $\frac{4}{5}$.

rationale *n* the underlying principles or reasons on which a decision, belief, action, etc. is based. [Lat *rationalis*]

rationalise or **-ize** *v* **1** (*tr*) to attribute (one's behaviour or attitude) to sensible, well-thought-out reasons or motives, esp. after the event. **2** (*intr*) to explain one's behaviour, etc. in this way. **3** (*tr*) to make logical or rational. **4** (*tr*) to make (an industry or organisation) more efficient and profitable by reorganising it to get rid of unnecessary costs and labour. — *n* **rationalisation** or **-z-**. **[rational]**

rationalism *n* the theory that one's actions and beliefs should be based on reason rather than on intuition or other people's teachings. — *n* **rationalist**. — *adj* **rationalistic**. **[rational]**

rattan *n* a climbing palm with very long, thin, tough stems which are used to make walking sticks and wickerwork. [Malay *rotan*]

rattle *v* **1** (*intr*) to make a series of short, sharp, hard sounds in quick succession. **2** (*tr*) to cause (e.g. crockery) to make such a noise. **3** (*intr*) to move along rapidly, often with a rattling noise. **4** (*intr*; **on**; **on about**) to chatter thoughtlessly or idly. **5** (*tr*; **off**, **out**, **through**) to say or recite rapidly, fluently or glibly. **6** (*tr*; *coll*) to make anxious, nervous and fidgety. — *n* **1** a series of short, sharp, hard sounds in quick succession. **2** a baby's toy consisting of a container filled with small pellets which rattle when the container is shaken. **3** a device for making a whirring sound, used esp. at football matches. **4** the loose rings on the tail of a rattlesnake which produce a rattling sound. **5** noisy, lively, empty chatter. **6** the rough, harsh breathing sound caused by air passing through mucus in the back of the throat, heard esp. on the approach of death. [MidE *ratelen*]

rattler *n* (*coll*) a rattlesnake.

rattlesnake *n* a poisonous American snake with loose rings on the tail which rattle.

rattletrap *n* (*coll*) a broken-down, rickety old vehicle, esp. a car.

rattling *adj* & *adv* (*old*) smart(ly); brisk(ly); very (good).

rattly *adj* **-ier**, **-iest** making a rattling noise; often rattling.

raucous *adj* hoarse, harsh. — *adv* **raucously**. — *n* **raucousness**. [Lat *raucus*]

raunchy *adj* **-ier**, **-iest** (*slang*) coarsely or openly sexual. — *adv* **raunchily**.

ravage *v* (*tr* & *intr*) to cause extensive damage (to); to destroy. — *n* (usu. in *pl*) damage or destruction: *the ravages of time*. [OFr *ravir*, to ravish]

rave *v* **1** (*intr*) to talk wildly as if mad or delirious. **2** (*intr*; **about**, **over**) to talk enthusiastically or passionately (about). — *n* (*coll*) **1** extravagant praise. **2** a rave-up. — *adj* (*coll*) extremely enthusiastic: *rave reviews*. [MidE *raven*]

raver *n* (*coll*) a person who leads a full, lively, uninhibited social life.

rave-up *n* (*coll*) a lively party or celebration.

raving *adj* & *adv* **1** frenzied; delirious. **2** (*coll*) great; extreme: *a raving beauty*. — *n* (usu. in *pl*) wild, frenzied or delirious talk.

ravel *v* **-ll-** **1** (*tr* & *intr*) to tangle or become tangled up. **2** (*tr*; **out**) to untangle, unravel or untwist. **3** (*intr*) to fray. — *n* **1** a tangle or knot. **2** a complication. **3** a loose or broken thread. [Dut *rafelen*]

raven *n* a large blue-black bird of the crow family. — *adj* glossy blue-black in colour: *raven-haired*. [OE *hræfn*]

ravening *adj* (esp. of meat-eating animals) hungrily seeking food. [*raven*, to devour, hunt for food]

ravenous *adj* **1** extremely hungry or greedy (for). **2** (of hunger, a desire, etc.) strong. **3** (of an animal, etc.) living on prey; predatory. — *adv* **ravenously**. — *n* **ravenousness**.

ravine *n* a deep, narrow, steep-sided gorge. [OFr, violent rushing]

ravioli *n* (*sing* or *pl*) small, square pasta cases with a savoury filling of meat, cheese, etc. [Ital]

ravish *v* (*tr*) **1** to cause to be overcome with joy, delight, etc.; to enrapture. **2** to rape. [Lat *rapere*, to seize and carry off]

ravishing *adj* delightful; lovely. — *adv* **ravishingly**.

raw *adj* **1** not cooked. **2** not processed, purified or refined. **3** (of alcoholic spirit) undiluted. **4** (of statistics, data, etc.) not analysed. **5** (of a person) not trained or experienced. **6** (of a wound, etc.) with a sore, inflamed surface. **7** (of the weather) cold and damp. — *n* a sore, inflamed or sensitive place. — *n* **rawness**. — **in the raw** **1** in a natural or crude state. **2** naked. [OE *hreaw*]

rawboned *adj* lean and gaunt.

raw deal *n* (*coll*) harsh, unfair treatment.

rawhide *n* **1** untanned leather. **2** a whip made from this.

raw material *n* any material, usu. in its natural state, out of which something is made or developed.

ray[1] *n* **1** a narrow beam of light or radioactive particles. **2** any of a set of lines fanning out from a central point. **3** a small amount of or the beginnings of (esp. hope or understanding). **4** any of the set of spines which support a fish's fin. [Lat *radius*, rod]

ray[2] *n* a fish with a broad, flat body, eyes on the top of its head, and a long narrow tail. [Lat *raia*]

ray[3]. Same as **re**[1].

rayon *n* an artificial silk fabric made from cellulose. [Prob. **ray**[1]]

raze *v* (*tr*) to destroy or demolish (buildings, a town, etc.) completely. [Lat *radere*, to scrape]

razor *n* a sharp-edged instrument used for shaving. [OFr *rasour*]

razorbill *n* a type of seabird with a sharp-edged bill.

razor edge *n* **1** a very fine, sharp edge. **2** a critical, delicately balanced situation.

razzle *n* (*slang*) a lively spree, outing or party, esp. involving a lot of drinking: *on the razzle*. [**dazzle**]

razzle-dazzle *n* (*slang*) **1** excitement, confusion, dazzling show, etc. **2** a lively spree.

razzmatazz *n* **1** razzle-dazzle. **2** humbug.

Rb *symbol* (*chem*) rubidium.

RC *abbrev* **1** Roman Catholic. **2** Red Cross.

Rd *abbrev* road.

Re *symbol* (*chem*) rhenium.

re[1] *n* (*mus*) the second note in the sol-fa scale. [From the first syllable of the word *resonare* in a mediaeval Latin hymn, certain syllables of which were used to name the notes]

re[2] *prep* with regard to; concerning. [Lat *res*, thing]

re- *pfx* **1** again: *reread*. **2** again and in a different or improved way: *rewrite*. **3** back or into a previous state: *replace*. [Lat]

reach *v* **1** (*tr*) to arrive at; to get as far as. **2** (*tr* & *intr*) to be able to touch or get hold of. **3** (*tr* & *intr*) to project or extend (to). **4** (*intr*; **across, after, for, out, up**) to stretch out (one's hand, etc.) to try to touch or get hold of. **5** (*tr*; *coll*) to hand or pass. **6** (*tr*) to make contact or communicate with, esp. by telephone. — *n* **1** the distance one can stretch one's arm, hand, etc.: *out of reach*; *within reach*. **2** the distance that can be travelled easily: *within reach of London*. **3** an act of reaching out. **4** range of influence, power, understanding or abilities. **5** (usu. in *pl*) a section within clear limits, e.g. part of a river or canal between two bends or locks. **6** (usu. in *pl*) a level: *the upper reaches of government*. — *adj* **reachable**. [OE *ræcan*]

reach-me-down *n* & *adj* (an item of clothing which is) second-hand or ready-made.

react *v* **1** (*intr*; **to**) to respond to something which has been done, said, has happened, etc. **2** (*intr*; **against**) to respond to something in a way which shows dislike or disapproval. **3** (*intr* & *tr*) to (cause to) undergo a chemical reaction. [Lat *reagere*]

reaction *n* (**to**) **1** a reacting or response to something. **2** opposition to change, esp. political change, and a desire to return to a former system. **3** a complete change of opinions, feelings, etc. to the opposite of what they were: *The idea was popular at first but then a reaction set in*. **4** a bodily response (to e.g. a drug). **5** (*chem*) a process of change which occurs in the atoms and molecules of substances when different substances are put together, usu. resulting in the creation of new substances. **6** (*physics*) the force which acts on a body whenever it exerts an equal force on another body.

reactionary *adj* (of a person or policies) opposed to change or progress and in favour of a return to a former system. — *n* **-ies** a reactionary person.

reactive *adj* showing a reaction; liable to react; sensitive to stimuli. — *n* **reactiveness**.

reactor same as **nuclear reactor**.

reactivate *v* (*tr*) to make active again. — *n* **reactivation**.

read *v* ***read*** **1** (*tr* & *intr*) to look at and understand (printed or written words). **2** (*tr* & *intr*; **out, aloud**) to speak (words which are printed or written). **3** (*tr* & *intr*) to learn or gain knowledge of by reading: *read the election results in the newspaper*. **4** (*tr* & *intr*) to pass one's leisure time reading (books): *I don't have much time for reading since having the baby*. **5** (*tr*) to look at or be able to see (something) and get information from it: *can't read the clock without my glasses*. **6** (*tr*) to interpret or understand the meaning of: *read a map*. **7** (*tr*) to interpret or understand (signs, marks, etc.) without using one's eyes: *read Braille*. **8** (*tr*) to know (a language) well enough to be able to understand something written in it: *speaks Chinese but can't read it*. **9** (*intr*) to have a certain wording: *The letter reads as follows*. **10** (*tr* & *intr*) to think that (a statement, etc.) has a particular meaning: *read it as criticism*. **11** (*intr*) (of writing) to be, or not be, coherent, fluent and logical: *an essay which reads well*, or *reads badly*. **12** (*tr*) (of dials, instruments, etc.) to show a particular measurement: *The barometer reads 'fair'*. **13** (*tr*) to put (a word, phrase, etc.) in place of another: *For 'three' read 'four'*. **14** (*tr*) to put into a specified condition by reading: *read the child to sleep*. **15** (*tr*) to study (a subject) at university. **16** (*tr*) to hear and understand, esp. when using two-way radio. **17** (*tr*; **in, out**; *comput*) to put (data) into or remove (data) from a storage device such as magnetic tape. ◇ See also **read-out**. — *n* **1** a period or act of reading. **2** a book, etc. thought of as being interesting, etc.: *This book is a good read*. — *adj* educated through reading: *well read.* — **read between the lines** to understand a meaning which is implied but not stated. — *v* **read into** (*tr*) to find (in a person's writing, words, etc.) a meaning which is not stated clearly and which may not have been intended. — *v* **read out** (*tr*) to read aloud. — *v* **read up** (*tr* & *intr*; **on**) to learn about (a subject) by reading lots of books on it. — **take as read** to accept or assume. [OE *rædan*]

readable *adj* **1** legible; able to be read. **2** pleasant or quite interesting to read. — *n* **readability** or **readableness**.

reader *n* **1** a person who reads. **2** (*Br*) a university lecturer ranking between professor and senior lecturer. **3** a person who reads prayers in a church. **4** a book containing usu. short texts, esp. one used for learning a foreign language. **5** a person who reads and reports on manuscripts for a publisher. **6** a person who reads and corrects proofs. **7** a machine which produces a magnified image from a microfilm so that it can be read.

readership *n* **1** the total number of people who read a newspaper, the novels of a particular author, etc. **2** (*Br*) the post of reader in a university.

reading *n* **1** the action of a person who reads. **2** the ability to read: *his reading is poor.* **3** books, material, etc. for reading. **4** an event at which a play, poetry, etc. is read to an audience. **5** any one of three stages in the passage of a bill through parliament. **6** the actual word or words that can be read in a text, esp. where more than one version is possible: *one of many disputed readings in the Bible.* **7** information, figures, etc. shown by an instrument or meter. **8** an understanding or interpretation: *one's reading of the situation.* — *adj* of, for or fond of reading.

read-only memory see **ROM**.

read-out *n* **1** information received from a computer, either on e.g. paper or displayed on a screen. **2** (a device used for) the act of getting information from a computer.

read-write head *n* (*comput*) a head in a disc drive which allows data to be written on to, or retrieved from, the disc.

read-write memory *n* a computer memory which allows data to be both read and changed.

ready *adj* **-ier**, **-iest** **1** prepared and available for action or use. **2** willing: *always ready to help.* **3** prompt; quick: *be too ready to find fault.* **4** likely or about to do: *a plant just ready to flower.* — *n* **-ies** (in *pl*; *coll*; also **ready money**) cash, esp. bank notes, for immediate use. — *adv* prepared or made beforehand: *ready cooked meals.* — *v* (*tr*) to make ready. — *adv* **readily**. — *n* **readiness**. — **at the ready 1** (of a gun) aimed and ready to be fired. **2** ready for immediate action. [OE *ræde*]

ready-made *adj* **1** (esp. of clothes) made to be worn by anyone, not made-to-measure. **2** convenient; useful: *a ready-made excuse.*

ready money *n* (*coll*) money available for immediate use.

ready reckoner *n* a book listing standard or useful calculations.

ready-to-wear *adj* (of clothes) made according to a standard size and not made-to-measure.

reafforest *v* (*tr*) to replant (former forest land) with trees. — *n* **reafforestation**.

reagent *n* a substance which behaves in a characteristic way in chemical reactions, used to detect the presence of other substances. [Lat *reagere*, to react]

real[1] *adj* **1** which actually exists; not imaginary. **2** not imitation; genuine. **3** actual; true: *the real reason.* **4** great, important or serious: *a real problem.* **5** (*law*) consisting of or relating to property which cannot be moved, such as land and houses. **6** (of an income, etc.) measured in terms of what it will buy rather than its nominal value. **7** (*math*) involving or containing real numbers. — *adv* (*NAm* & *Scot*) really. — **for real** (*slang*) in reality; seriously. [Lat *realis*, from *res*, thing]

real estate *n* (*NAm*) property in the form of houses or land.

realism *n* **1** in art and literature, a style that presents things as they really are. **2** (*philos*) the theory that physical objects exist even when they are not perceived by the mind. ◇ See also **idealism**. **3** an acceptance of or willingness to deal with things as they really are. — *n* **realist**. — *adj* **realistic**. — *adv* **realistically**.

reality *n* **-ies 1** the state or fact of being real. **2** the real nature (of something); the truth. **3** that which is real and not imaginary. — **in reality** in fact.

really *adv* **1** actually; in fact. **2** very; genuinely: *a really lovely day.* — *interj* an expression of surprise, doubt or mild protest.

real number *n* (*math*) any rational or irrational number.

real property *n* (*Br legal*) land or buildings. ◇ See also **personal property**, **real estate**.

real tennis *n* an early form of tennis played on a walled, indoor court. ◇ See also **lawn tennis**.

real-time *adj* (*comput*) of or relating to a system in which data is processed as it is generated.

realtor *n* (*NAm*; also *cap*) an estate agent, esp. one who is a member of the National Association of Realtors.

realty same as **real estate**.

real[2] *n* (*hist*) a small silver Spanish or Spanish-American coin. [Span, from Lat *regalis*, royal]

realign *v* (*tr*) **1** to group in a new or different way. **2** to bring back into line or alignment. — *n* **realignment**.

realise or **-ize** *v* **1** (*tr* & *intr*) to (come to) know or understand. **2** (*tr*) to make real; to make come true. **3** (*tr*) to cause to seem real; to act out: *realise the story on film*. **4** (*tr*) to convert (property or goods) into actual money: *realise one's assets*. **5** (*tr*) to gain (money): *realised £45 000 on the sale of the house*. — *adj* **realisable** or **-z-**. — *n* **realisation** or **-z-**. [OFr *realiser*]

realm *n* **1** a kingdom. **2** a field of interest, study or activity. [OFr *realme*]

realpolitik *n* politics based on the practical needs of life rather than on moral or ethical ideas. [Ger]

realtor. See **real**.

ream *n* **1** a number of sheets of paper equivalent to 20 quires, formerly 480, now usu. 500 or 516. **2** (in *pl*; *coll*) a large amount. [OFr *reame*, from Arabic *rizmah*, bale]

reap *v* (*tr* & *intr*) **1** to cut or gather (grain, etc.). **2** to clear (a field) by cutting a crop. **3** to receive as a consequence of one's actions. [OE *ripan*]

reaper *n* **1** a person or machine that reaps. **2** (with **the**; also **grim reaper**) death.

rear[1] *n* **1** the back part; the area at the back. **2** that part of an army which is farthest away from the enemy. **3** (*coll euph*) the buttocks. — *adj* at the back: *rear window*.

rear admiral *n* (a naval officer with) the rank below vice-admiral.

rearguard *n* a group of soldiers who protect the rear of an army, esp. in retreats.

rearguard action *n* **1** military action undertaken by the rearguard. **2** an effort to prevent or delay defeat, e.g. in an argument.

rearmost *adj* last of all.

rear-view mirror *n* a mirror fixed to a car's windscreen, or attached to a motorbicycle's handles, which allows the driver to see vehicles, etc. behind.

rearward *adj* at or to the rear. — *adv* (also **rearwards**) towards the rear.

rear[2] **1** (*tr*) to feed, care for and educate: *rear three children*. **2** (*tr*) to breed (animals) or grow (crops). **3** (*intr*; **up**) (esp. of a horse) to rise up on the hind legs. **4** (*tr*) to raise (the head, etc.) upright. **5** (*intr*) to tower (over the surroundings, etc.) [OE *rǣran*]

rearm *v* (*tr* & *intr*) to arm or become armed again with new or improved weapons. — *n* **rearmament**.

reason *n* **1** a justification or motive for an action, belief, etc. **2** an underlying explanation or cause. **3** the power of the mind to think, form opinions and judgements, reach conclusions, etc. **4** sanity. — *v* **-n-** **1** (*intr*) to use one's mind and reason to form opinions and judgements, reach conclusions, etc. **2** (*intr*; **with**) to try to persuade using careful argument. **3** (*tr*; **into, out of**, etc.) to persuade or influence using careful argument. **4** (*tr*; **out**) to think or set out logically. — **by reason of** because of; as a consequence of. — **it stands to reason** it is obvious or logical. — **within reason** within the bounds of what is sensible or possible. [OFr *reison*]

reasonable *adj* **1** sensible; showing reason or good judgement. **2** willing to listen to reason or argument. **3** in accordance with reason; fair; not extreme or excessive. **4** satisfactory or equal to what one might expect. — *n* **reasonableness**. — *adv* **reasonably**.

reasoning *n* **1** the forming of judgements or opinions using reason or careful argument. **2** the opinions or judgements formed in this way.

reassure *v* (*tr*) to relieve (someone) of anxiety and so give confidence to. — *n* **reassurance**. — *adj* **reassuring**. — *adv* **reassuringly**.

rebate *n* **1** a return of part of a sum of money paid. **2** a discount. [OFr *rabattre*, to beat back]

rebel *n* **1** a person who opposes or fights against people in authority or oppressive conditions. **2** a person who does not accept the rules of normal behaviour, dress, etc. — *adj* rebelling. — *v* **-ll-** (*intr*; **against**) **1** to resist authority or oppressive conditions openly and with force. **2** to reject the accepted rules of behaviour, dress, etc. **3** to feel aversion or dislike. [Lat *rebellis*, from *bellum*, war]

rebellion *n* an act of rebelling; a revolt.

rebellious *adj* rebelling or likely to rebel. — *adv* **rebelliously**. — *n* **rebelliousness**.

rebirth *n* a revival, renaissance or renewal, often a spiritual one.

rebound *v* (*intr*) **1** to bounce or spring back. **2** (**on, upon**) (of an action) to have a bad effect on the person performing the action. — **on the rebound 1** while still recovering from an emotional shock, esp. the end of a love affair. **2** while bouncing. [OFr *rebonder*]

rebuff *n* an unkind or unfriendly refusal to help someone or a rejection of help, advice, etc. from someone. — *v* (*tr*) to reject or refuse (an offer of or plea for help, a request, etc.) unkindly. [OFr *rebuffe*]

rebuke *v* (*tr*) to speak severely to (someone) because he or she has done wrong. — *n* the act of speaking severely to someone, or being spoken severely to. [OFr *rebuker*]

rebus *n* **-buses** a puzzle in which pictures and symbols are used to represent words and parts of words to form a message or phrase. [Lat, by things]

rebut *v* **-tt-** (*tr*) **1** to disprove (a charge or claim) esp. by offering opposing evidence. **2** to force to turn back. — *n* **rebuttal**. [OFr *rebouter*]

recalcitrant *adj* not willing to accept authority or discipline. — *n* **recalcitrance**. [Lat *recalcitare*, to kick back]

recall *v* (*tr*) **1** to order to return. **2** to remember. **3** to cancel or revoke. — *n* **1** an act of recalling. **2** the ability to remember accurately and in detail: *total recall*. —

beyond recall unable to be stopped or cancelled.

recant *v* **1** (*intr*) to reject one's (usu. religious or political) beliefs, esp. publicly. **2** (*tr & intr*) to withdraw (a statement). — *n* **recantation**. [Lat *recantare*, to revoke]

recap (*coll*) *v* ***-pp-*** (*tr & intr*) to recapitulate. — *n* recapitulation. [Abbrev.]

recapitulate *v* (*tr & intr*) to go over the chief points of (an argument, statement, etc.) again. [Lat *recapitulare*]

recapitulation *n* **1** an act or instance of recapitulating or summing up. **2** (*mus*) the final repetition of themes, after development, in a movement written in sonata form.

recapture *v* (*tr*) **1** to capture again. **2** to convey, produce or experience (images or feelings from the past): *recapture the atmosphere of Victorian London*. — *n* the act of recapturing or being recaptured.

recce (*coll*) *n* a reconnaissance. — *v* ***-ceing***, ***-ced*** or ***-ceed*** (*tr & intr*) to reconnoitre. [Abbrev.]

recede *v* (*intr*) **1** to go or move back or backwards. **2** to become more distant. **3** to grow less. **4** to bend or slope backwards. — *adj* **receding**. [Lat *recedere*]

receipt *n* **1** a written note saying that money or goods have been received. **2** the act of receiving or being received: *acknowledge receipt of the money*. **3** (usu. in *pl*) money received during a given period of time, esp. by a shop or business. [Lat *recipere*, to receive]

receive *v* **1** (*tr*) to get, be given or accept. **2** (*tr*) to experience or suffer: *receive injuries*. **3** (*tr*) to give attention to or consider: *receive a petition*. **4** (*tr*) to react in a specified way in response to: *receive the news well*. **5** (*tr*) to be awarded (an honour). **6** (*tr & intr*) to welcome or greet (guests), esp. formally. **7** (*tr*) to permit to become part of: *be received into the priesthood*. **8** (*tr & intr*; *tennis*, etc.) to be the player who returns (the opposing player's service). **9** (*tr & intr*; *Br*) to accept and often sell (goods one knows are stolen). **10** (*tr & intr*) to change (radio or television signals) into sounds or pictures. ◇ See also **reception**. [Lat *recipere*]

received *adj* generally accepted.

Received Pronunciation *n* the particular pronunciation of British English which is regarded by many as being least regionally limited, most socially acceptable, and most 'standard'.

receiver *n* **1** a person or thing that receives. **2** (also **official receiver**) a person who is appointed by a court to take control of the business of someone who has gone bankrupt or who is insane. **3** the part of a telephone which is held to one's ear. **4** the equipment in a telephone, radio or television that changes signals into sounds or pictures. **5** a person who receives stolen goods.

receivership *n* the state of being under the control of a receiver (sense **2**). **2** the post of a receiver (sense **2**).

recent *adj* happening, done, having appeared, etc. not long ago. — *adv* **recently**. [Lat *recens*, fresh]

receptacle *n* **1** a container. **2** (*bot*) the end of a stalk which bears a flower. **3** (*bot*) the part of a leaf which bears the reproductive organs in flowerless plants. [Lat *receptaculum*, reservoir]

reception *n* **1** the act of receiving or being received. **2** a response, reaction or welcome: *a hostile reception*. **3** a formal party or social gathering to welcome guests, esp. after a wedding. **4** the quality of radio or television signals received: *poor reception because of the weather*. **5** an office or desk where visitors or clients are welcomed on arrival, e.g. in a hotel or factory. [Lat *receptio*]

receptionist *n* a person who is employed e.g. in a hotel or factory to welcome visitors and guests and answer the telephone, etc.

receptive *adj* able, willing and quick to understand and accept new ideas. — *adv* **receptively**. — *n* **receptiveness** or **receptivity**.

recess *n* **1** an open space or alcove set in a wall. **2** (often in *pl*) a hidden, inner or secret place: *the dark recesses of her mind*. **3** a temporary break from work, esp. of a lawcourt, or of Parliament during a vacation. **4** (*NAm*) a short break between school classes. — *v* **1** (*tr*) to put in a recess. **2** (*tr*) to make a recess in. **3** (*intr*) to take a break or adjourn. [Lat *recessus*, retreat]

recession *n* **1** a temporary decline in economic activity, trade and prosperity. **2** the act of receding or state of being set back.

recessional *n* a hymn sung during the departure of the clergy and choir after a service.

recessive *adj* **1** tending to recede. **2** (*biol*) of or being a gene which carries a characteristic which will only be manifest if not overridden by another gene. ◇ See also **dominant**.

recherché *adj* **1** rare, exotic or particularly choice. **2** obscure and affected. [Fr]

recidivism *n* the habit of relapsing into crime. — *n & adj* **recidivist**. [Lat *recidivus*, falling back]

recipe *n* **1** a list of ingredients for and set of instructions on how to prepare and cook a particular kind of meal, cake, etc. **2** (**for**) a way of achieving (something desired): *a recipe for success*. [Lat *recipere*, to take]

recipient *n* a person or thing that receives. [Lat *recipere*, to receive]

reciprocal *adj* **1** given to and received from in return; mutual. **2** (of pronouns) expressing a relationship between two people or things, or mutual action, e.g. *one another* in *John and Mary love one another*. — *n* (*math*) either of a pair of numbers which produce 1 when multiplied together, e.g. $\frac{1}{4}$ and 4. — *adv* **reciprocally**.

reciprocate *v* **1** (*tr*) to return (affection, love, etc.). **2** (*intr*; **with**) to give in return: *reciprocate with an offer of money*. **3** (*intr*) (of part of a machine) to move backwards and forwards. — *n* **reciprocation**. [Lat *reciprocus*]

reciprocity *n* **1** reciprocal action. **2** a mutual exchange of privileges or advantages between countries, trade organisations, businesses, etc.

recite *v* (*tr* & *intr*) to repeat aloud from memory. **2** (*tr*) to make a detailed statement about or list: *recite one's grievances*. [Lat *recitare*]

recital *n* **1** a public performance (of music or songs) usu. by one person or a small number of people. **2** a detailed statement about or list of: *a recital of his grievances*. **3** an act of reciting. — *n* **recitalist**.

recitation *n* **1** something which is recited from memory. **2** an act of reciting.

recitative *n* a passage of speech in an opera or oratorio sung in a loud, passionate style.

reckless *adj* very careless; acting or done without any thought of the consequences. — *adv* **recklessly**. — *n* **recklessness**. [OE *receleas*]

reckon *v* **-n-** **1** (*tr*) to calculate, compute or estimate. **2** (*tr*) to think of as part of or belonging to: *reckon him among my friends*. **3** (*tr*; usu. in *passive*) to consider or think of in a specified way: *be reckoned a world authority*. **4** (*intr*; *coll*) to think or suppose. **5** (*intr*; **on, upon**) to rely on or expect: *reckon on his support*. **6** (*tr*; *slang*) to esteem or admire highly. — *v* **reckon up** (*tr*) to count or calculate: *reckon up the cost*. — *v* **reckon with** or **without** (*tr*) to expect, or not expect, trouble, difficulties or problems. — **to be reckoned with** not to be ignored. [OE *recenian*, to explain]

reckoning *n* **1** calculation; counting: *By my reckoning, we must be about eight miles from the town*. **2** a settling of accounts, debts, grievances, etc. — **day of reckoning** the time when one has to pay for, or be punished for, one's mistakes; a time of judgement.

reclaim *v* (*tr*) **1** to seek to regain possession of; to claim back. **2** to make (waste land) fit for use, esp. by draining. **3** to recover from a waste product. **4** (*old*) to reform (someone). — *adj* **reclaimable**. — *n* **reclamation**. [Lat *reclamare*, to cry out against]

recline *v* **1** (*intr*) to lean or lie on one's back or side. **2** (*tr*) to lean or lay (e.g. one's head) in a resting position. [Lat *reclinare*]

recliner *n* someone or something that reclines, esp. a comfortable chair with a back which can slope at different angles.

recluse *n* a person who lives alone and in seclusion; a hermit. [Lat *reclusus*, from *claudere*, to shut]

recognise or **-ize** *v* (*tr*) **1** to identify (a person or thing known or experienced before). **2** to admit or be aware of: *recognise one's mistakes*. **3** to show approval of and gratitude for: *recognise her courage by giving her a medal*. **4** to acknowledge the status or legality of (esp. a government or state). **5** to accept as valid: *recognise the authority of the court*. — *adj* **recognisable** or **-z-**. — *adv* **recognisably** or **-z-**. [Lat *recognoscere*]

recognisance or **-z-** *n* **1** a legally binding promise made to a magistrate or court to do or not do something specified. **2** money pledged as a guarantee of such a promise being kept.

recognition *n* the act or state of recognising or being recognised.

recoil *v* (*intr*) **1** (**at, from**) to move or jump back or away quickly or suddenly, usu. in horror or fear. **2** to spring back or rebound. **3** (of guns) to move backwards under the force of being fired. — *n* the act of recoiling, esp. the backwards movement of a gun when fired. [OFr *reculer*]

recollect *v* (*tr*) to remember, esp. with an effort. — *n* **recollection**. [Lat *recolligere*, to gather up]

recommend *v* (*tr*) **1** to advise. **2** to suggest as being suitable to be accepted, chosen, etc.; to commend. **3** to make acceptable, desirable or pleasing: *an applicant with very little to recommend him*. — *adj* **recommendable**. — *n* **recommendation**. [Lat *commendare*, to commend]

recompense *v* (*tr*; **for**) to pay or give (someone) compensation for injury or hardship suffered or reward for services, work done, etc. — *n* money, etc. given in compensation for injury or hardship suffered or as a reward for work done, etc. [Lat *compensare*]

reconcile *v* (*tr*) **1** (**with**) to make friendly again, e.g. after a quarrel. **2** (**with**) to bring (two or more different aims, points of view, etc.) into agreement; to harmonise. **3** (**to**) to make (oneself or someone else) accept (a situation, fact, etc.) patiently. — *n* **reconciliation**. — *adj* **reconciliatory**. [Lat *reconciliare*]

recondite *adj* **1** (of a subject or knowledge) little known. **2** dealing with profound, abstruse or obscure knowledge. [Lat *reconditus*, hidden]

recondition *v* **-n-** (*tr*) to repair or restore to original or good working condition, e.g. by cleaning or replacing broken parts. — *adj* **reconditioned**.

reconnaissance *n* **1** a survey of land, enemy troops, etc. to obtain information about the enemy. **2** a preliminary survey. [Fr]

reconnoitre *v* (*tr* & *intr*) to make a reconnaissance of (land, enemy troops, etc.). [OFr *reconnoître*, to examine, recognise]

reconsider *v* **-r-** (*tr* & *intr*) to consider (something) again and possibly change one's opinion or decision. — *n* **reconsideration**.

reconstitute *v* (*tr*) **1** to put or change back to the original form, e.g. by adding water. **2** to form or make up in a different way. — *n* **reconstitution**.

reconstruct *v* (*tr*) **1** to create a description or idea (of e.g. a crime) from the evidence available. **2** to rebuild. — *n* **reconstruction**.

record *n* **1** a usu. formal written report of facts, events or information. **2** (often in *pl*) information, facts, etc. collected over a usu. long period of time. **3** the state or fact of being recorded. **4** a round flat piece of usu. black plastic on which sound is recorded. **5** (in races, games, or almost any activity) a performance which has never yet been beaten. **6** a description of a person's, institution's, company's, etc. history and achievements. **7** a list of the crimes a person has been found guilty of. **8** (*comput*) a collection of related items of data which are handled as a single unit. **9** anything that recalls or commemorates past events. — *v* **1** (*tr*) to set down in writing or some other permanent form, esp. for use in the future. **2** (*tr* & *intr*) to register (sound, music, speech, etc.) on a record or tape so that it can be listened to in the future. **3** (*tr*) (of a dial, instrument, person's face, etc.) to show (a figure, feeling, etc.). — **go on record** to make a public statement. — **off the record** (of information, statements, etc.) not intended to be repeated or made public. — **on record** officially recorded; publicly known. — **set the record straight** to correct a mistake or false impression. [Lat *recordari*, to remember]

recorded delivery *n* a Post Office service in which the sending and receiving of a letter or parcel are recorded.

recorder *n* **1** a wooden or plastic wind instrument with a tapering mouthpiece and holes which are covered by the player's fingers. **2** a solicitor or barrister who sits as a part-time judge in a court. **3** a person who records something. **4** a tape-recorder.

recording *n* **1** the process of registering sounds or images on a record, tape, etc. **2** sound or images which have been recorded.

record-player *n* an apparatus which reproduces the sounds recorded on records.

recount *v* (*tr*) to tell (a story, etc.) in detail. [OFr *reconter*, from *conter*, to tell]

re-count *v* (*tr*) to count again. — *n* a re-counting, esp. of votes in an election.

recoup *v* (*tr*) **1** to recover or get back (something lost, e.g. money). **2** to compensate (e.g. for something lost). — *n* **recoupment**. [Fr *recouper*, to cut back]

recourse *n* **1** a source of help or protection. **2** the right to demand payment. — **have recourse to** to turn to for help, esp. in an emergency or in a case of extreme need. [Lat *recursus*, return]

recover *v* **-r- 1** (*tr*) to get or find again. **2** (*intr*; **from**) to regain one's good health, spirits or composure. **3** (*intr*) to regain a former and usu. better condition. **4** (*tr*) to regain control of (one's emotions, actions, etc.): *recover one's senses*. **5** (*tr*) to gain (compensation or damages) by legal action. **6** (*tr*) to get money to make up for (expenses, loss, etc.). **7** (*tr*) to obtain (a valuable or usable substance) from a waste product or by-product. — *n* **recoverability**. — *adj* **recoverable**. [Lat *recuperare*]

recovery *n* **-ies** an act, instance or process of recovering, or state of having recovered.

recreant *n* a cowardly or disloyal person. — *adj* cowardly or disloyal. [MidE]

recreate *v* (*tr*) to create again; to reproduce. — *n* **recreation**.

recreation *n* a pleasant, enjoyable and often refreshing activity done in one's spare time. — *adj* **recreational**.

recreation ground *n* an area of land for playing sports, games, etc. on.

recrimination *n* an accusation made by an accused person against his or her accuser. — *adj* **recriminatory**. [Lat *criminari*, to accuse]

recrudesce *v* (*intr*) (esp. of a disease) to appear or become active again. — *n* **recrudescence**. — *adj* **recrudescent**. [Lat *recrudescere*]

recruit *n* **1** a newly enlisted member of the army, air force, navy, etc. **2** a new member of a society, group, organisation, etc. — *v* (*tr* & *intr*) to enlist (people) as recruits. — *n* **recruitment**. [Fr *recrue*, new growth]

recta. See **rectum**.

rectal *adj* of the rectum. — *adv* **rectally**. [**rectum**]

rectangle *n* a four-sided figure with opposite sides which are equal and four right angles. [Lat *rectus*, straight + *angulus*, angle]

rectangular *adj* **1** of or like a rectangle. **2** placed at right angles.

rectify *v* **-ies**, **-ied** (*tr*) **1** to put right or correct (a mistake, etc.). **2** to purify (e.g. alcohol) by repeated distillation. **3** to change (an alternating current) into a direct current. **4** to determine the length of (a curve). — *adj* **rectifiable**. — *n* **rectification**. — *n* **rectifier**. [Lat *rectus*, straight + *facere*, to make]

rectilinear *adj* **1** in or forming a straight line. **2** bounded by straight lines. [Lat *rectus*, straight + *linea*, line]

rectitude *n* honesty; correctness of behaviour or judgement; moral integrity. [Lat *rectus*, straight]

recto *n* **-os** the right-hand page of an open book. ◇ See also **verso**. [Lat, on the right]

rector *n* **1** in the Church of England, a clergyman in charge of a parish where the tithes would formerly all have gone to him. **2** in the Roman Catholic Church, a priest in charge of a congregation or a religious house, esp. a Jesuit seminary. **3** the headmaster of some schools and colleges, esp.

in Scotland. **4** (*Scot*) a senior university official elected by and representing the students; occasionally in other countries, the head of a university or college. — *adj* **rectorial**. — *n* **rectorship**. [Lat, from *regere*, to rule]

rectory *n* **-ies** the house of a rector.

rectum *n* **-ta** or **-tums** the lower part of the alimentary canal, ending with the anus. [Lat *rectus*, straight]

recumbent *adj* lying down; reclining. [Lat *recumbere*, to recline]

recuperate *v* **1** (*intr*) to recover, esp. from illness. **2** (*tr*) to recover (something lost, one's health, etc.). — *adj* **recuperable**. — *n* **recuperation**. — *adj* **recuperative**. [Lat *recuperare*]

recur *v* **-rr-** (*intr*) **1** to happen or come round again or at intervals. **2** (of a thought, etc.) to come back into one's mind. — *n* **recurrence**. [Lat *recurrere*, to run back]

recurrent *adj* **1** happening often or regularly. **2** (of a nerve, vein, etc.) turning back to run in the opposite direction. — *adv* **recurrently**.

recurring decimal *n* a decimal fraction in which one figure or a group of figures is repeated to infinity: *One divided by three gives the recurring decimal 0·3333...*

recusant *n* **1** (*hist*) a person (esp. a Roman Catholic) who refused to attend Church of England services when these were compulsory (between c.1570 and c.1790). **2** a person who refuses to submit to authority. — *adj* of or like recusants. — *n* **recusancy**. [Lat *recusare*, to object]

recycle *v* (*tr*) to pass through a series of changes so as to return to a former state, esp. to process waste so that it can be used again. — *adj* **recyclable**.

red *adj* **-dd-** **1** of the colour of blood. **2** (of hair or fur) of a colour which varies between a golden brown and a deep reddish-brown. **3** (of eyes) bloodshot or with red rims. **4** having a red or flushed face, esp. from shame or anger. **5** (of wine) made with black grapes whose skins colour the wine. **6** (*coll derog*) communist. **7** (*cap*) of the former USSR; Soviet: *the Red Army*. — *n* **1** the colour of blood, or a similar shade. **2** red dye or paint. **3** red material or clothes. **4** the red traffic light, a sign that cars should stop. **5** anything that is red. **6** the debit side of an account; the state of being in debt e.g. to a bank. **7** (*coll derog*; often *cap*) a communist or socialist. — *adj* **reddish**. — *n* **redness**. — **paint the town red** (*coll*) to go out to enjoy oneself in a lively, noisy, and often drunken way. — **see red** (*coll*) to become angry. [OE *read*]

red admiral *n* a common N American and European butterfly which has broad red bands on its wings.

red blood cell or **red corpuscle** *n* a blood cell containing haemoglobin which carries oxygen to the tissues and which gives blood its red colour.

red-blooded *adj* active; manly; virile. — *n* **red-bloodedness**.

redbreast *n* a robin.

redbrick *adj* (of a British university) founded in the late nineteenth or early twentieth century.

red card *n* (*football*) a piece of red card or plastic shown by the referee to a player who is being sent off. ◇ See also **yellow card**.

red carpet *n* a strip of carpet put out for an important person to walk on; special treatment given to an important person or guest.

redcoat *n* **1** (*hist*) a British soldier. **2** an attendant at a Butlin's holiday camp.

red corpuscle see **red blood cell**.

Red Crescent *n* an organisation equivalent to the Red Cross in Muslim countries.

Red Cross *n* an international organisation which brings esp. medical relief to the victims of wars and natural disasters.

redcurrant *n* a small edible red berry which grows on a widely cultivated European shrub.

red deer *n* a large deer with a rich red-brown coat in the summer, found in Europe and Asia.

redden *v* **-n-** **1** (*tr* & *intr*) to make or become red or redder. **2** (*intr*) to blush.

red dwarf *n* a faint reddish star with a diameter which is about half that of the sun and a low surface temperature.

Red Ensign see **ensign**.

red flag *n* **1** a red banner used as a symbol of socialism or of revolution. **2** a flag used to warn of danger.

red giant *n* a star that has a large diameter relative to the sun and a low surface temperature.

red-handed *adj* in the act of committing a crime or immediately after having committed it: *caught red-handed.*

red hat *n* a cardinal's hat; a symbol of a cardinal's office.

redhead *n* a person, esp. a woman, with red (sense **2**) hair. — *adj* **redheaded**.

red herring *n* **1** a herring which has been cured and smoked to a dark reddish colour. **2** a subject, idea, clue, etc. introduced into a discussion, investigation, etc. to divert attention from the real issue or to mislead someone (from the fact that a red herring drawn across a track can put a dog off the scent).

red-hot *adj* **1** (of metal, etc.) heated until it glows red. **2** feeling or showing passionate or intense emotion or excitement: *red-hot anger*. **3** (*coll*) feeling or showing great enthusiasm: *a red-hot favourite*. **4** (of news, information, etc.) completely new and up to date.

red-hot poker *n* a garden plant with long spikes of usu. red or orange flowers.

Red Indian (often considered *offensive*) *n* a N American Indian. — *adj* of a N American Indian or Indians.

red lead *n* a bright red poisonous oxide of lead, used in making paints.

red-letter day *n* a day which will always be remembered because something particularly pleasant or important happened on it (from the custom of marking saints' days in red on ecclesiastical calendars).

red light *n* a red warning light, esp. one which warns vehicles to stop.

red-light district *n* (*coll*) a district where prostitutes work.

red pepper *n* **1** cayenne pepper. **2** a red capsicum or sweet pepper, eaten as a vegetable. ◇ See also **green pepper**.

red rag *n* anything which is likely to provoke someone or make him or her very angry.

red shift *n* a shift of lines in the spectrum towards the red end, usu. considered to occur because the source of light is moving away.

redskin *n* (*coll derog*) a N American Indian.

red squirrel *n* a native British squirrel with reddish-brown fur.

red tape *n* (*derog*) unnecessary rules and regulations which result in delay.

redwood *n* an extremely large Californian conifer with reddish wood.

redeem *v* (*tr*) **1** to buy back. **2** to recover (e.g. something that has been pawned or mortgaged) by payment or service. **3** to fulfil (a promise). **4** to set (a person) free or save (a person's life) by paying a ransom. **5** to free (someone, oneself) from blame or debt. **7** (of Christ) to free (humanity) from sin by his death on the cross. **8** to make up or compensate for (something bad or wrong). **9** to exchange (tokens, vouchers, etc.) for goods. **10** to exchange (bonds, shares, etc.) for cash. — *adj* **redeemable**. — *adj* **redeeming**. [Lat *redimere*, to buy back]

the Redeemer *n* Jesus Christ.

redemption *n* **1** the act of redeeming or state of being redeemed, esp. the freeing of humanity from sin by Christ. **2** anything which redeems. — *adj* **redemptive**. — **beyond** or **past redemption** too bad to be redeemed, improved or saved. [Lat *redemptio*, buying back]

redeploy *v* (*tr* & *intr*) to move (soldiers, workers, etc.) to another place or job. — *n* **redeployment**.

redevelop *v* **-p-** (*tr*) to build new buildings, etc. (in a run-down urban area). — *n* **redeveloper**. — *n* **redevelopment**.

redo *v* ***redoes***, ***redid***, ***redone*** (*tr*) **1** to do again. **2** to redecorate.

redolent *adj* **(of, with) 1** smelling strongly of. **2** suggesting strongly: *a street redolent of Victorian England*. — *n* **redolence**. — *adv* **redolently**. [Lat *redolere*, to give off a smell]

redouble *v* (*tr* & *intr*) **1** to make or become greater or more intense. **2** (*bridge*) to double (a bid that an opponent has already doubled).

redoubt *n* **1** a fortification, esp. a temporary one defending a pass or hilltop. **2** a stronghold. [Lat *reductus*, refuge]

redoubtable *adj* **1** causing fear or respect. **2** brave; valiant. — *adv* **redoubtably**. [OFr *redouter*, to fear greatly]

redound *v* (*intr*) **1** to have a direct, either advantageous or disadvantageous, effect (on). **2** to come back (to) as a consequence. [Lat *redundare*, to surge]

redress *v* (*tr*) **1** to set right or compensate for (something wrong). **2** to make even or equal again: *redress the balance*. — *n* **1** the act of redressing or being redressed. **2** money, etc. paid as compensation for loss or wrong done. [OFr *redrecier*, to straighten]

reduce *v* **1** (*tr* & *intr*) to make or become less, smaller, etc. **2** (*tr*; **to**) to change into a usu. worse or undesirable state or form: *reduced her to tears*. **3** (*tr*) to lower the rank, status or grade of. **4** (*tr*) to bring into a state of obedience; to subdue. **5** (*tr*) to make weaker or poorer: *reduced circumstances*. **6** (*tr*) to lower the price of. **7** (*intr*) to lose weight by dieting. **8** (*tr*) to convert (a substance) into a simpler form: *reduce chalk to a powder*. **9** (*tr*) to simplify or make more easily understood by considering only the essential elements: *reduce the plan to four main points*. **10** (*tr*) to thicken (a sauce) by boiling off excess liquid. **11** (*tr*; *math*) to simplify (a fraction, equation, etc.) by changing it to a form which cannot be further divided without a remainder. **12** (*tr* & *intr*; *chem*) to combine or cause to be combined with hydrogen. **13** (*tr* & *intr*; *chem*) to lose oxygen or remove oxygen from. **14** (*tr*) to convert (e.g. ore) into metal. — *n* **reducer**. — *n* **reducibility**. — *adj* **reducible**. ◇ See also **reduction**. [Lat *reducere*, to lead back]

reductio ad absurdum *n* **1** a way of proving that a premise is wrong by showing that its logical consequence is absurd. **2** the applying of a principle or rule so strictly that it is carried to absurd lengths. [Lat, reduction to the absurd]

reduction *n* **1** an act or instance of reducing; the state of being reduced. **2** the amount by which something is reduced. **3** a reduced copy of a picture, document, etc. [Lat *reductio*]

redundant *adj* **1** (of workers) no longer needed and therefore dismissed. **2** not needed; superfluous. **3** (of a word or phrase) expressing an idea which is already conveyed by another word or phrase, e.g. '*little*' in '*a little midget*' is redundant because '*midget*' already conveys the idea of smallness. — *n* **redundancy**, ***-ies***. [Lat *redundare*, to overflow]

reduplicate *v* (*tr*) **1** to repeat, copy or double. **2** (*gram*) to repeat (a word or syllable), often with some minor change, to form a new word, as in *hubble-bubble* or *riff-raff*. — *n* **reduplication**. [Lat *reduplicare*]

reed *n* **1** a tall, stiff grass growing on wet or marshy ground or in shallow water. **2** a mass of reeds used esp. for thatching. **3** a thin piece of cane or metal in certain musical instruments which vibrates and makes a sound when air passes over it. **4** (esp. in *pl*) a wind instrument or organ pipe with reeds. **5** a comb-like device on a loom for spacing the threads of the warp evenly and putting the weft into position. [OE *hreod*]

broken reed *n* a weak person that cannot be relied on.

reedy *adj* **-ier**, **-iest** **1** full of reeds. **2** having a tone like a reed instrument, esp. in being thin and piping. **3** thin and weak. — *adv* **reedily**. — *n* **reediness**.

reef[1] *n* **1** a ridge of rocks, sand, etc. just above or below the surface of the sea. **2** a vein containing ore, esp. gold. [Dut *rif*]

reef[2] *n* a part of a sail which may be folded in (in windy weather) or let out (in calm weather) to alter the area exposed to the wind. — *v* (*tr*) to reduce the area of (a sail) exposed to the wind. [MidE *refe*]

reefer *n* **1** (also **reefer-jacket** and **reefing-jacket**) a short, thick, woollen, double-breasted jacket. **2** (*slang*) a cigarette containing marijuana.

reef knot *n* a knot made by passing one end of the rope over and under the other end, and then back over and under it again.

reek *n* **1** a strong, unpleasant and often offensive smell. **2** (*Scot* & *dialect*) smoke. — *v* (*intr*) **1** to give off a strong, usu. unpleasant smell. **2** (**of**) to suggest or hint at something unpleasant: *This scheme reeks of racism.* **3** (*Scot* & *dialect*) to give off smoke. [OE *reocan*]

reel *n* **1** a round wheel-shaped or cylindrical object of plastic, metal, etc. on which thread, film, fishing-lines, etc. can be wound. **2** the quantity of film, thread, etc. wound on one of these. **3** a device for winding and unwinding a fishing-line. **4** (the music for) a lively Scottish, Irish or American dance. — *v* **1** (*tr*) to wind on a reel. **2** (*tr*; **in**, **up**) to pull in or up using a reel: *reel in a fish.* **3** (*intr*) to stagger or sway; to move unsteadily. **4** (*intr*) to whirl or appear to move: *The room began to reel and then she fainted.* **5** (*intr*; **back**) to be shaken physically or mentally: *reel back in horror*. **6** (*intr*) to dance a reel. — *v* **reel off** (*tr*) to say, repeat or write quickly and fluently. [OE *hreol*]

re-entry *n* **-ies** an act of entering again, esp. of a spacecraft entering the earth's atmosphere after flight in space.

reeve[1] *n* (*hist*) **1** the chief magistrate of a town or district. **2** an official who supervises a lord's manor or estate. [OE *refa*]

reeve[2] *v* ***rove*** or ***reeved*** (*tr*; **through**) to pass (a rope, etc.) through a hole, opening or ring. [Dut *reven*, to reef]

reeve[3] *n* a female ruff. ◇ See **ruff**[3].

ref *n* (*coll*) a referee (sense **1**).

refectory *n* **-ies** a dining-hall in a monastery or college. [Lat *reficere*, to refreshen]

refer *v* **-rr-** (**to**) **1** (*intr*) to talk or write (about); to mention: *refer to one's problems*. **2** (*intr*) to relate, concern, or apply to: *Does this refer to me?* **3** (*intr*) to look for information (in a place): *refer to one's notes*. **4** (*tr*) to direct (a person, etc.) to some authority for discussion, information, a decision, treatment, etc. **5** (*tr*) to explain (something) as being caused by. **6** (*tr*) to consider as belonging to a specified place, time or category. **7** (*tr*; *med*; usu. in *passive*) to feel (pain) in a different part of the body from its actual source. — *adj* **referable** or **referrable**. ◇ See also **referral**. [Lat *referre*, to carry back]

referee *n* **1** an umpire or judge, e.g. of a game or in a dispute. **2** a person who is willing to testify to a person's character, talents and abilities. — *v* (*tr* & *intr*) to act as a referee (for a game or in a dispute). [**refer**]

reference *n* **1** (**to**) a mention (of something); an allusion. **2** a direction in a book to another passage or book where information can be found. **3** a book or passage referred to. **4** the act of referring to a book or passage for information. **5** a written report on a person's character, talents and abilities, esp. of his or her aptitude for a particular job or position. **6** a person referred to for such a report. **7** the providing of facts and information: *a reference library*. **8** the directing of a person, question, etc. to some authority for information, a decision, etc. **9** a relation, correspondence or connection: *with reference to your last letter*. **10** a standard for measuring or judging: *a point of reference*. — *adj* **referential**. [**refer**]

terms of reference *n* (*pl*) a statement which describes the exact scope of the work to be carried out.

referendum *n* **-dums** or **-da** the act or principle of giving the people of a country the chance to state their opinion of some important matter by voting for or against it. [Lat *referre*, to carry back]

referral *n* the act of referring someone to an expert, esp. the sending of a patient by a GP to a specialist for treatment. [**refer**]

refill *n* (a container holding) the new filling for something which becomes empty through use. — *v* (*tr*) to fill again. — *adj* **refillable**.

refine *v* **1** (*tr*) to make pure by removing dirt, waste substances, etc. **2** (*tr* & *intr*) to make or become more elegant, polished or subtle.

refined *adj* **1** very polite; well-mannered; elegant. **2** having had all the dirt, waste substances, etc. removed. **3** improved; polished.

refinement *n* **1** the act or process of refining. **2** good manners or good taste;

polite speech; elegance. **3** an improvement or perfection. **4** a subtle distinction.

refinery *n* **-ies** a factory where raw materials such as sugar and oil are refined.

refit *v* **-tt- 1** (*tr*) to repair or fit new parts to (esp. a ship). **2** (*intr*) (of a ship) to be repaired or have new parts fitted. — *n* the act of refitting or of being refitted.

reflate *v* (*tr*) to cause reflation of (an economy). [**re-** + **inflation**]

reflation *n* an increase in the amount of money and credit available and in economic activity, designed to increase industrial production after a period of deflation. ◇ See also **deflation** and **inflation**. — *adj* **reflationary**.

reflect *v* **1** (*tr* & *intr*) (of a surface) to send back (light, heat, sound, etc.). **2** (*tr* & *intr*) (of a mirror, etc.) to give an image of. **3** (*intr*) (of a sound, image, etc.) to be reflected back from. **4** (*tr*) to have as a cause or be a consequence of: *Price increases reflect greater demand for the goods.* **5** (*tr*) to show or give an idea of: *a poem which reflects one's mood.* **6** (*tr* & *intr*; **on, upon**) (of an action, etc.) to bring praise, or blame, to: *Her behaviour reflects on* (= reflects badly on) *her mother. Your behaviour reflects well on you.* **7** (*intr*; **on, upon**) to consider carefully. [Lat *reflectere*, to bend back]

reflecting telescope *n* a large telescope which has a concave mirror for focusing light rays.

reflection *n* (also **reflexion**) **1** the act of reflecting. **2** the sound, heat, light, etc. reflected. **3** a reflected image. **4** careful and thoughtful consideration; contemplation. **5** blame, discredit or censure.

reflective *adj* **1** thoughtful; meditative. **2** (of a surface) able to reflect images, light, sound, etc. **3** reflected: *reflective glare of the sun on the water.* — *adv* **reflectively**.

reflector *n* **1** a polished surface which reflects light, heat, etc., esp. a piece of red plastic or glass on the back of a bicycle which glows when light shines on it. **2** a reflecting telescope.

reflex *n* **1** an immediate automatic response provoked by a given stimulus of which one is not conscious. **2** the ability to react with proper speed: *You need good reflexes to drive a car.* **3** reflected light, sound, heat, etc. or a reflected image. **4** a sign or expression (of something). **5** a word formed or element of speech which has developed from a corresponding earlier form. — *adj* **1** occurring as an automatic response without being thought about. **2** bent or turned backwards. **3** directed back on the source; reflected. **4** (of a thought) introspective. **5** (*math*) (of an angle) greater than 180° but less than 360°. [Lat *reflexus*, bent back]

reflex camera *n* a camera in which the image coming in through the lens is directed by a mirror to the viewfinder for focusing.

reflexion. See **reflection**.

reflexive *adj* (*gram*) **1** (of a pronoun) showing that the object of a verb is the same as the subject, e.g. in '*He cut himself*', '*himself*' is a reflexive pronoun. **2** (of a verb) used with a reflexive pronoun as object. — *adv* **reflexively**. [**reflex**]

reflexology *n* therapy for particular health problems and illnesses in which the soles of the feet are massaged, based on the belief that different parts of the soles relate to different parts of the body and different organs. — *n* **reflexologist**. [**reflex** + **-logy**]

reform *v* **1** (*tr*) to improve or remove faults from (a person, behaviour, etc.). **2** (*intr*) to give up bad habits, improve one's behaviour, etc. **3** (*tr*) to stop or abolish (misconduct, an abuse, etc.). — *n* **1** a correction or improvement, esp. in some social or political system. **2** improvement in one's behaviour or morals. — *adj* **reformable**. — *n* **reformer**. [Lat *reformare*]

reformation *n* **1** the act of reforming or state of being reformed; improvement. **2** (*cap*; *hist*) the 16th-century religious movement which began by trying to reform abuses in the Roman Catholic Church and which led to the development of the various Protestant churches in Europe.

reformative *adj* reforming.

reformatory *n* **-ies** (*old*; esp. *US*) a school for reforming the behaviour of young people who break the law.

Reformed Church *n* the Protestant Church, esp. the Calvinist church as distinct from the Lutheran.

Reform Judaism *n* a form of Judaism in which the Jewish Law is adapted so as to be relevant to contemporary life.

refract *v* (*tr*) (of water, glass, air, etc.) to deflect (a ray of light, sound, etc.) at a different angle when that ray enters it from another medium. — *n* **refraction**. — *adj* **refractive**. ◇ See also **refrangible**. [Lat *refringere*, to break up]

refracting telescope or **refractor** *n* a telescope which uses a series of lenses to focus light rays.

refractory *adj* **1** difficult to control; stubborn; unmanageable. **2** (of a disease, etc.) not responding to treatment. **3** (of metals, etc.) not melting under high temperatures. — *n* **refractoriness**. [Lat *refractarius*, stubborn]

refrain[1] *n* a phrase or group of lines, or the music for them, repeated at the end of each stanza or verse in a poem or song. [OFr *refrain*, from Lat *frangere*, to break]

refrain[2] *v* (*intr*; **from**) to keep oneself from acting in some way; to avoid. [Lat *refrenare*, from *frenum*, bridle]

refrangible *adj* able to be refracted. — *n* **refrangibility**. [Lat *refringere*, from *frangere*, to break]

refresh *v* (*tr*) **1** (of food, rest, etc.) to give renewed strength, energy and enthusiasm to. **2** to revive (someone, oneself, etc.) with food, rest, etc. **3** to provide a new supply of; to replenish. **4** to make cool. **5** to make (one's memory) clearer and stronger by reading or listening to the source of information again. [OFr *refreschir*]

refresher *n* **1** anything, e.g. a cold drink, that refreshes. **2** (*legal*) an extra fee paid to counsel during a long case or an adjournment.

refresher course *n* a course of study or training intended to increase or update a person's previous knowledge or skill.

refreshing *adj* **1** giving new strength, energy and enthusiasm; cooling. **2** particularly pleasing because different, unexpected or new. — *adv* **refreshingly**.

refreshment *n* **1** the act of refreshing or state of being refreshed. **2** anything which refreshes. **3** (in *pl*) food and drink.

refrigerant *n* a liquid used in the cooling mechanism of a refrigerator. — *adj* cooling. [**refrigerate**]

refrigerate *v* (*tr*) to make or keep (food) cold or frozen to prevent it from going bad. — *n* **refrigeration**. [Lat *refrigerare*, from *frigus*, cold]

refrigerator *n* a machine which keeps food cold and so prevents it from going bad.

refuel *v* **-ll- 1** (*tr*) to supply (an aircraft, etc.) with more fuel. **2** (*intr*) (of an aircraft, etc.) to take on more fuel.

refuge *n* **1** shelter or protection from danger or trouble. **2** any place, person or thing offering such shelter. [Lat *refugium*]

refugee *n* a person who seeks shelter, esp. from religious or political persecution, in another country.

refulgent *adj* (*literary*) shining brightly; radiant; beaming. — *n* **refulgence**. [Lat *refulgere*, to shine brightly]

refund *v* (*tr*) to pay (money, etc.) back to (someone). — *n* **1** the paying back of money, etc. **2** the money, etc. paid back. — *adj* **refundable**. [Lat *refundere*, to pour back]

refurbish *v* (*tr*) to renovate and redecorate. — *n* **refurbishment**.

refuse[1] *v* **1** (*tr* & *intr*) to declare oneself unwilling to do what one has been asked or told to do, etc.; to say 'no'. **2** (*tr*) not to accept (something): *refuse the offer of help*. **3** (*tr*) not to allow (access, etc.) or give (permission). **4** (*tr* & *intr*) to show or express unwillingness: *The car refused to start*. **5** (*tr* & *intr*) (of a horse) to decide not to jump over (a fence). [OFr *refuser*, to pour back]

refusal *n* an act of refusing. — **first refusal** the opportunity to buy, accept or refuse something before it is offered, given, sold, etc. to anyone else.

refusenik *n* a person, esp. a Jew, living in the countries of the former Soviet Union who was refused permission to emigrate (usu. to Israel).

refuse[2] *n* rubbish; anything thrown away; waste. [OFr *refus*, rejection]

refute *v* (*tr*) **1** to prove that (a person, statement, theory, etc.) is wrong. **2** (*coll*) to deny. — *adj* **refutable**. — *adv* **refutably**. — *n* **refutation**. [Lat *refutare*, to drive back]

regain *v* (*tr*) **1** to get back again or recover. **2** to get back to (a place).

regal *adj* of, like, or suitable for a king or queen. — *n* **regality**. — *adv* **regally**. [Lat *regalis*, royal]

regale *v* (*tr*) **1** (**with**) to entertain or amuse by telling stories, with clever conversation, etc. **2** (**with, on**) to entertain with food, drink and feasting. [Fr *régaler*]

regalia *n* (*pl*) **1** objects such as the crown and sceptre which are a sign of royalty, used at coronations, etc. **2** any ornaments, ceremonial clothes, etc. worn as a sign of a person's importance or authority, e.g. by a mayor. [Lat, things worthy of a king]

regard *v* (*tr*) **1** (**as**) to consider (someone or something) in a specified way. **2** to pay attention to; to take notice of. **3** to look at attentively or steadily. **4** to have a connection with or relate to. — *n* **1** thought or attention. **2** care or consideration; sympathy. **3** respect and affection: *be held in high regard*. **4** a gaze or look. **5** (in *pl*) greetings; good wishes. — **as regards** concerning; about; as far as (something) is concerned. — **with regard to** about; concerning. [MidE]

regardful *adj* (**of**) paying attention (to); taking notice (of).

regarding *prep* about; concerning,

regardless *adv* not thinking or caring about costs, problems, dangers, etc.; in spite of everything: *carry on regardless*. — *adj* (**of**) taking no notice (of): *regardless of the consequences*. — *adv* **regardlessly**.

regatta *n* a meeting for yacht or (small) boat races. [Ital]

regency *n* **-ies 1** the position of a regent. **2** (the period of) government by a regent. **3** (*cap*; *hist*) the period in Britain when the Prince of Wales ruled as regent, 1811–20. **4** (*cap*; *hist*) the period in France when Philip of Orleans ruled as regent, 1715–23. — *adj* (*cap*) (of architecture, furniture, dress, etc.) of or in the style of the Regency period in Britain or France. [Lat *regens*, from *regere*, to rule]

regent *n* a person who governs a country during a monarch's childhood or illness. — *adj* acting as regent; ruling.

regenerate *v* **1** (*tr* & *intr*) to (cause to) become morally or spiritually better. **2** (*tr* & *intr*) to develop or give new life or energy; to be brought back or bring back to life or original strength again. **3** (*tr*) to grow new tissue to replace (a damaged part of the body). **4** (*intr*) (of a damaged part of the body) to be replaced by new tissue. — *adj* having been regenerated, esp. in having improved morally, spiritually or physically. — *n* **regeneration**. — *adj*

regenerative. — *n* **regenerator**. [Lat *regenerare*, to bring forth again]

reggae *n* popular West Indian music which has a strong syncopated beat. [Jamaican English]

regicide *n* **1** the killing of a king. **2** a person who kills a king. [Lat *rex*, king + **-cide**]

regime *n* (also **régime**) **1** a system of government or a particular government. **2** a regimen. [Fr *régime*]

regimen *n* a course of treatment, esp. of diet and exercise, which is necessary for one's good health. [Lat, from *regere*, to rule]

regiment *n* **1** a permanent army unit consisting of several companies, etc. and commanded by a colonel. **2** a large number. — *v* (*tr*) **1** to organise or control strictly, usu. too strictly. **2** to form into a regiment or regiments. — *n* **regimentation**. — *adj* **regimented**. [Lat *regimentum*, from *regere*, to rule]

regimental *adj* of a regiment. — *n* (in *pl*) a military uniform, esp. of a particular regiment.

Regina *n* the reigning queen, now used mainly on coins and in official documents. [Lat, queen]

region *n* **1** an area of the world or a country with particular geographical, social, etc. characteristics. **2** an administrative area, esp. in Scotland. **3** an area of the body round or near a specific part, organ, etc.: *the abdominal region*. **4** any of the different layers which the atmosphere and sea are divided into according to height or depth. **5** an area of activity or interest. — **in the region of** approximately, nearly. [Lat *regio*, from *regere*, to rule]

regional *adj* **1** of a region. **2** (of a pain) affecting a particular area of the body. — *adv* **regionally**.

register *n* **1** (a book containing) a written list or record of names, events, etc. **2** a machine or device which records and lists information, esp. one in a shop (**cash register**) which lists sales and in which money is kept. **3** the range of tones produced by the human voice or a musical instrument. **4** the set of pipes controlled by an organ stop. **5** a style of speech or language suitable for and used in a particular situation. — *v* **-r- 1** (*tr*) to enter (an event, name, etc.) in an official register. **2** (*intr*) to enter one's name and address in a hotel register on arrival. **3** (*tr* & *intr*; **for**, etc.) to enrol formally. **4** (*tr*) to insure (a letter or parcel) against getting lost in the post. **5** (*tr*) (of a device) to record and usu. show (speed, information, etc.) automatically. **6** (*tr*) (of a person's face, etc.) to show (a particular feeling). **7** (*intr*) to make an impression on someone, e.g. being understood, remembered, etc.: *Her name didn't register*. **8** (*tr*) to obtain, achieve or win: *register one's first success*. — *adj* **registered**. — *n* **registration**. [Lat *regesta*, things recorded]

Registered General Nurse *n* a nurse who has passed the examination of the General Nursing Council for Scotland. ◇ See also **State Registered Nurse**.

register office *n* (*Br*) an office where records of births, deaths and marriages are kept and where marriages may be performed.

registration number *n* the sequence of letters and numbers by which a vehicle is registered, displayed on its number plate.

registrar *n* **1** a person who keeps an official register, esp. of births, deaths and marriages. **2** a senior administrator in a university responsible for student records, enrolment, etc. **3** (*Br*) a middle-ranking hospital doctor who is training to become a specialist, and who works under a consultant. [**register**]

registry *n* **-ies 1** an office or place where registers are kept. **2** registration.

registry office *n* same as **register office**.

Regius professor *n* (*Br*) a professor holding a chair which was founded by a king or queen. [Lat *regius*, royal]

regress *v* (*intr*) to return to a former less perfect, less desirable, less advanced, etc. state or condition. — *n* a return to a former less perfect, less advanced, etc. state or condition. — *adj* **regressive**. — *adv* **regressively**. [Lat *regressus*, return]

regression *n* **1** an act of regressing. **2** a return to an earlier stage of development, e.g. a return to childish behaviour by an adult.

regret *v* **-tt-** (*tr*) to feel sorry, repentant, distressed, disappointed, etc. about. — *n* **1** a feeling of sorrow, repentance, distress, disappointment, etc. **2** (in *pl*) a polite expression of disappointment, etc. used esp. when turning down an invitation. [OFr *regreter*]

regretful *adj* feeling or showing regret. — *adv* **regretfully**.

regrettable *adj* that should be regretted; unwelcome; unfortunate. — *adv* **regrettably**.

regt *abbrev* regiment.

regular *adj* **1** usual; normal; customary. **2** arranged, occurring, acting, etc. in a fixed pattern of predictable or equal intervals of space or time: *visit one's parents at regular intervals*. **3** agreeing with some rule, custom or normal practice, etc. and accepted as correct. **4** symmetrical or even; having all the faces, sides or angles, etc. the same. **5** having bowel movements or menstrual periods with normal frequency. **6** of ordinary size: *a regular portion of chips*. **7** (*coll*) complete; absolute: *That child is a regular little monster*. **8** (*gram*) (of a noun, verb, etc.) following one of the usual patterns of formation. **9** (of troops, the army, etc.) of or forming a permanent professional body. **10** officially qualified or recognised; professional. **11** belonging to a religious order and subject to the rule of that order. **12** (*NAm coll*) behaving in an acceptable, likable way: *a regular guy.* — *n* **1** a soldier in a professional, regular army. **2** (*coll*) a frequent customer. **3** a member of a religious order. — *n* **regularisation** or **-z-**. — *v* (*tr*) **regularise** or **-ize**.— *n* **regularity**. — *adv* **regularly**. [Lat *regula*, rule]

regulate *v* (*tr*) **1** to control or adjust (a piece of machinery, the heat or sound available, etc.) as required. **2** to control or direct (a person, thing, etc.) according to rules. [Lat *regula*, rule]

regulation *n* **1** a rule or instruction. **2** the act of regulating or state of being regulated. — *adj* conforming to or governed by rules or by stated standards.

regulator *n* a thing that regulates e.g. a piece of machinery.

regulo *n* each of several numbers in a series which indicate the temperature of a gas oven: *bake at regulo five.* [*Regulo*, orig. a trademark for a thermostatic control system for gas ovens]

regurgitate *v* **1** (*tr*) to bring back (food) into the mouth after it has been swallowed. **2** (*tr*; *derog*) to repeat exactly something already said). **3** (*intr*) to gush back up again. — *n* **regurgitation**. [Lat *regurgitare*]

rehabilitate *v* (*tr*) **1** to help (usu. a prisoner or someone who has been ill) re-adapt to normal life, esp. by providing vocational training. **2** to restore to a former state, rank, rights or privileges. — *n* **rehabilitation**. [Lat *rehabilitare*]

rehash (*coll*) *v* (*tr*) to use or present (subject matter which has been used before) in a slightly different form but with no improvements. — *n* a speech, book, etc. which uses subject matter which has been used before with little change and no improvements.

rehearse *v* **1** (*tr* & *intr*) to practise (a play, piece of music, etc.) before performing it in front of an audience. **2** (*tr*) to train (a person) for performing in front of an audience. **3** (*tr*) to give a list of or describe: *rehearse one's grievances.* **4** (*tr*) to repeat or say over again. [OFr *rehercier*, to harrow again]

rehearsal *n* **1** the act of rehearsing. **2** a performance of a play, etc. for practice.

rehouse *v* (*tr*) to provide with new and usu. better quality accommodation.

Reich *n* the German state until 1945, esp. the **Third Reich** (1933–45) under Nazi control. [Ger, kingdom]

reign *n* **1** the time during which a king or queen rules. **2** the time during which something rules or is in control: *reign of terror.*— *v* (*intr*) **1** to be a monarch. **2** to be present, exist or dominate: *Silence reigns.* [Lat *regnum*]

reigning *adj* (of a winner, champion, etc.) holding the title (of champion, etc.)

reimburse *v* (*tr*) to pay (a person) money to cover (expenses, losses, etc.). — *n* **reimbursement**. [**re-** + Lat *imbursare*, from *bursa*, purse]

rein *n* **1** (usu. in *pl*) one of two straps attached to a bridle for guiding a horse. **2** (in *pl*) a set of similar straps for guiding a young child. **3** a means of control or government: *take the reins.* — *v* (*tr*; **in**) to stop or restrain with or as if with reins. — **give a free rein to** to allow total freedom to act, operate, think, etc. — **keep a tight rein on** to keep strict control of. [OFr *resne*]

reincarnate *v* (*tr*) to cause (a person or soul) to be born again after death in a different body. — *adj* reborn. [Lat *incarnare*, to make flesh]

reincarnation *n* **1** (the belief in) the rebirth of the soul in another body after death. **2** a person who has been reincarnated. **3** an idea or principle presented in a different form.

reindeer *n* **-deer** or **-deers** a large deer found in northern Europe, Asia and America, both sexes of which have antlers, and which are often kept for pulling sledges and as a source of milk and meat. [Norse *hreindyri*]

reinforce *v* (*tr*) **1** to make stronger or give additional support to. **2** to make (an army, force, etc.) stronger by providing more soldiers and weapons, etc. [From earlier *renforce*]

reinforced concrete *n* concrete with steel bars or wire embedded in it to make it stronger.

reinforcement *n* **1** the act of reinforcing. **2** anything which reinforces. **3** (in *pl*) soldiers, etc. added to an army, force, etc. to make it stronger.

reinstate *v* (*tr*) to restore to a former, more powerful, position, status or rank. — *n* **reinstatement**. [**re-** + *instate*, to install]

reiterate *v* (*tr*) to repeat, esp. several times. — *n* **reiteration**. [Lat *reiterare*]

reject *v* (*tr*) **1** to refuse to accept, agree to, admit, believe, etc. **2** to throw away or discard. **3** (of the body) to fail to accept (new tissue or an organ from another body). — *n* a person or thing which is rejected. — *n* **rejection**. [Lat *rejicere*, from *jacere*, to throw]

rejig *v* **-gg-** (*tr*) **1** to re-equip. **2** to rearrange, often in a way which is considered dishonest or unethical.

rejoice *v* **1** (*intr*) to feel or show great happiness. **2** (*tr*) to give joy to; to make glad. — *n* **rejoicer**. — *n* & *adj* **rejoicing**. — *adv* **rejoicingly**. [OFr *rejouir*]

rejoin[1] *v* **1** (*tr*) to say in reply, esp. abruptly or wittily. **2** (*intr*; *legal*) to reply to a charge or pleading. [OFr *rejoindre*]

rejoinder *n* **1** an answer or remark, esp. one made abruptly or wittily in reply. **2** (*legal*) a defendant's answer to a plaintiff.

rejoin[2] *v* (*intr* & *tr*) to join again.

rejuvenate *v* (*tr*) to make (a person) feel, look, etc. young again. — *n* **rejuvenation**. [Lat *juvenis*, young]

relapse *v* (*intr*) to return to a former bad or undesirable state or condition such as ill health or bad habits. — *n* the act or process of relapsing, esp. a return to ill health after a partial recovery. [Lat *relabi*, from *labi*, to slide]

relate *v* **1** (*tr*) to tell or narrate (a story). **2** (*tr*; **to, with**) to show or form a connection or relationship between (facts, events, etc.): *relate his unhappiness to the fact that he never married.* **3** (*intr*; **to, with**) to have or form a connection or relationship: *Crime relates to poverty*. **4** (*intr*; **to**) to be about or concerned with: *information relating to the crime*. **5** (*intr*; *coll*; **to**) to get on well with; to react favourably to: *be unable to relate to modern music.* [Lat *relatus*, brought back]

related *adj* **1** belonging to the same family. **2** connected.

relation *n* **1** a connection or relationship between one person or thing and another. **2** a person who belongs to the same family through birth or marriage; a relative. **3** kinship. **4** reference; respect: *in relation to*. **5** a telling or narrating. **6** (in *pl*) the social, political or personal contact between people, countries, etc. **7** (in *pl*; *euph*) sexual intercourse.

relationship *n* **1** the state of being related. **2** the state of being related by birth or marriage. **3** the friendship, contact, communications, etc. which exist between people, countries, etc. **4** an emotional or sexual affair.

relative *n* a person who is related to someone else by birth or marriage. — *adj* **1** compared with something else; comparative: *the relative speeds of a car and train*. **2** existing only in relation to something else: *'Hot' and 'cold' are relative terms*. **3** (**to**) in proportion to: *salary relative to experience*. **4** which relates to; relevant: *information relative to the problem*. **5** (*gram*) (of a pronoun) referring to something real or implied which has already been stated and attaching a subordinate clause to it, as '*who*' in '*the children who are leaving*'. ◇ See also **antecedent**. **6** (*gram*) (of a clause) attached to a preceding word, phrase, etc. by a relative word such as *which* or *who*. ◇ See also **absolute**. **7** (*mus*) (of major and minor keys) having the same key signature. — *adv* **relatively**. [Lat *relativus*]

relative atomic mass *n* same as **atomic weight**.

relativity *n* **1** the state of being relative. **2** (also **special theory of relativity**) Einstein's theory that the mass of a body varies with its speed, based on the fundamental premises that all motion is relative and that the speed of light relative to an observer is constant. **3** (also **general theory of relativity**) this same theory extended to include gravitation and accelerated motion.

relax *v* **1** (*tr* & *intr*) to make or become less tense, nervous or worried. **2** (*tr* & *intr*) to give or take rest completely from work or effort. **3** (*tr* & *intr*) to make or become less strict or severe: *relax the rules*. **4** (*tr*) to lessen the force, strength or intensity of: *relax one's vigilance*. **5** (*intr*) to become weak or loose. — *adj* **relaxed**. — *adj* **relaxing**. [Lat *relaxare*]

relaxant *n* (*med*) a drug that can make a person feel less tense and help him or her relax.

relaxation *n* **1** the act of relaxing or state of being relaxed. **2** rest after work or effort. **3** a relaxing activity: *Golf is a popular relaxation.*

relay *n* **1** a set of people, supply of materials, etc. that replace others doing or being used for some task, etc. **2** (*old*) a supply of horses which relieve others on a journey. **3** a relay race. **4** an electrically operated device used to effect changes in an independent circuit, e.g. one in which a small change in current controls the switching on or off of an independent circuit. **5** a device which receives radio and television signals and then passes them further on. **6** something, esp. a signal or broadcast, which is relayed. — *v* ***-layed*** (*tr*) **1** to receive and pass on (news, a message, a television programme, etc.). **2** to pass along, supply or provide by relay. [OFr *relaier*, to leave behind]

relay race *n* a race between teams of runners, swimmers, etc. in which each member of the team runs, swims, etc. part of the total distance to be covered.

release *v* (*tr*) **1** (**from**) to free (a prisoner, etc.) from captivity. **2** (**from**) to relieve (someone) suffering from something unpleasant, a duty, burden, etc. **3** to loosen one's grip and stop holding. **4** to make (news, information, etc.) known publicly. **5** to offer (a film, record, book, etc.) for sale, performance, etc. **6** to move (a catch, brake, etc.) so that it no longer prevents something from moving, operating, etc. **7** to give off or emit (heat, gas, etc.). — *n* **1** the act of releasing or state of being released, from captivity, duty, oppression, etc. **2** the act of making available for sale, performance, publication, etc. **3** something made available for sale, performance, etc., esp. a new record or film. **4** (a document containing) an item of news which is made public. **5** an order or document allowing a prisoner, etc. to be released. **6** a handle or catch which holds and releases part of a mechanism. [OFr *relaissier*]

relegate *v* (*tr*) **1** to move (someone, a sports team, etc.) down to a lower grade, position, status, division, etc. **2** to refer (a decision, etc.) to (someone or something) for action to be taken. — *n* **relegation**. [Lat *relegare*, to send away]

relent *v* (*intr*) **1** to become less severe or unkind. **2** to give way and agree to something one initially would not accept. [Lat *re-*, back + *lentus*, flexible]

relentless *adj* **1** without pity; harsh. **2** never stopping; unrelenting: *a relentless fight against crime*. — *adv* **relentlessly**. — *n* **relentlessness**.

relevant *adj* directly connected with the matter in hand, being discussed, etc. — *n* **relevance** or **relevancy**. [Lat *relevare*, to raise up, relieve]

reliable *adj* able to be trusted or depended upon. — *n* **reliability**. — *adv* **reliably**. [**rely**]

reliance *n* (**on, upon**) the act or state of relying or depending upon, or trusting in, a person or thing. — *adj* **reliant**. [**rely**]

relic *n* **1** (often in *pl*) a part or fragment of an object left after the rest has decayed. **2** any object valued as being a memorial or souvenir of the past. **3** something left from a past time, esp. a custom, belief or practice, etc. **4** part of the body of a saint or martyr or of some object connected with him or her, preserved as holy. **5** (in *pl*) the remains of a dead person; a corpse. [Lat *reliquiae*, remains]

relief *n* **1** the lessening or removal of pain, worry, oppression or distress. **2** the calmness, relaxation, happiness, etc. which follows the lessening or removal of pain, worry, etc. **3** anything which lessens pain, worry, boredom or monotony. **4** help, often in the form of money, food, clothing and medicine, given to people in need. **5** a person who takes over a job or task from another person, usu. after a given period of time. **6** a bus, train, etc. which supplements public transport at particularly busy times. **7** the freeing of a besieged or endangered town, fortress or military post. **8** a method of sculpture in which figures project from a flat surface. **9** a clear, sharp outline caused by contrast. **10** the variations in height above sea level of an area of land. [OFr *relief*, from Lat *relevare*, to reduce the load]

relief map *n* a map which shows the variations in the height of the land, either by shading, or by being a three-dimensional model.

relieve *v* (*tr*) **1** to lessen or stop (a person's pain, worry, boredom, etc.). **2** (**of**) to take a burden from: *relieve her of the heavy bag*. **3** to give help or assistance to (someone in need). **4** to make less monotonous or boring, esp. by providing a contrast. **5** to free or dismiss from a duty or restriction. **6** to take over a job or task from (someone). **7** (**of**; esp. *facet*) to take something from (someone): *The thief relieved him of his wallet*. **8** to come to the help of (a besieged town, fortress, military post, etc.). — *adj* **relieved**. — **relieve oneself** to urinate or defecate. [Lat *relevare*, to reduce the load]

religion *n* **1** a belief in, or the worship of, a god or gods. **2** a particular system of belief or worship, such as Christianity or Judaism. **3** anything to which one is totally devoted and which rules one's life: *Mountaineering is his religion*. **4** the monastic way of life. [Lat *religio*]

religious *adj* **1** of or relating to religion. **2** following the rules or forms of worship of a particular religion very closely; pious; devout. **3** taking great care to do something properly; conscientious. **4** of or relating to the monastic way of life. — *n* ***religious*** a person bound by monastic vows, e.g. a monk or nun. — *adv* **religiously**. — *n* **religiousness**.

religious order see **order**.

relinquish *v* (*tr*) **1** to give up or abandon. **2** to release one's hold of. **3** to renounce possession or control of (a claim, right, etc.). — *n* **relinquishment**. [Lat *relinquere*, to leave behind]

reliquary *n* ***-ies*** a container for holy relics. [Lat *reliquiae*, remains]

relish *v* (*tr*) **1** to enjoy greatly or with discrimination. **2** to look forward to with great pleasure. — *n* **1** pleasure; enjoyment. **2** a spicy, appetising flavour, or a sauce or pickle which adds this to food. **3** zest, charm, liveliness or gusto. [OFr *reles*, remainder]

relive *v* (*tr*) to experience again, esp. in the imagination.

relocate *v* (*tr & intr*) to move (a business, one's home, etc.) from one place, town, etc. to another. — *n* **relocation**.

reluctance *n* **1** unwillingness; lack of enthusiasm. **2** (*physics*) a measure of the opposition to magnetic flux in a closed magnetic circuit. [Lat *reluctari*, to resist]

reluctant *adj* unwilling; not wanting. — *adv* **reluctantly**.

rely *v* ***-ies, -ied*** (*tr*; **on, upon**) **1** to depend on or need. **2** to trust (someone) to do something; to be certain of (something happening). ◇ See also **reliable, reliance**. [OFr *relier*, to bind together]

REM *abbrev* rapid eye movement.

remain *v* (*intr*) **1** to be left when something else, another part, etc. has been lost, taken away, used up, etc. **2** to stay in the same place; to not leave. **3** to be still (the same); to continue to be. **4** to still need (to be done, shown, dealt with, etc.): *That remains to be decided*. [Lat *remanere*, to stay behind]

remainder *n* **1** the number or part that is left after the rest has gone, been taken away, used up, etc. **2** (*math*) the amount left over when one number cannot be divided exactly by another number: *Seven divided by two gives three* (*with a*) *remainder* (*of*) *one*. **3** (*math*) the amount left when one number is subtracted from another. **4** a copy of a book which is sold at a reduced price when demand for that book comes to an end. **5** (*legal*) an interest in an estate which comes into effect only if another interest established at the same time ends. — *v* **-r-** (*tr*) to sell (a book) at a reduced price because demand for it has come to an end.

remains *n* (*pl*) **1** what is left after part has been taken away, eaten, destroyed, etc. **2** a dead body.

remake *n* something which is made again, esp. a new version of a film. — *v* **-*made*** (*tr*) to make again, esp. in a new way.

remand *v* (*tr*) to send (a person accused of a crime) back to prison or detain (him or her) on bail until more evidence can be collected and the case can be tried. — *n* the act of remanding. — **on remand** having been remanded in prison or on bail. [Lat *remandare*, to send back word, to repeat a command]

remand home *n* (*Br old*) a place to which a judge may send a child or young person who has broken the law, either on remand or as punishment.

remark *v* **1** (*tr* & *intr*; **on**) to notice and comment on (something). **2** (*tr*) to make a comment. — *n* a comment; an observation. [OFr *remarque*]

remarkable *adj* worth mentioning or commenting on; unusual; extraordinary. — *adv* **remarkably**.

REME *abbrev* Royal Electrical and Mechanical Engineers.

remedial *adj* **1** able to or intended to correct or put right. **2** (of teaching) intended to help those pupils with learning difficulties. ◇ See also **learning support**. — *adv* **remedially**. **[remedy]**

remedy *n* **-*ies*** (**for**) **1** any drug or treatment which cures or controls a disease. **2** anything which solves a problem or gets rid of something undesirable: *a remedy for the country's economic problems*. — *v* **-*ies***, ***ied-*** (*tr*) to put right or correct; to be a remedy for. — *adj* **remediable**. [Lat *remedium*]

remember *v* **-r-** **1** (*tr* & *intr*) to bring to mind (something or someone) that had been forgotten. **2** (*tr*) to keep (a fact, idea, etc.) in one's mind. **3** (*tr*) to reward or make a present to, e.g. in one's will. **4** (*tr*) to pass (a person's) good wishes and greetings to: *Remember me to your parents*. **5** (*tr*) to commemorate. [Lat *rememorari*]

remembrance *n* **1** the act of remembering or being remembered. **2** something which reminds a person of something or someone; a souvenir. **3** a memory or recollection: *a dim remembrance of the night's events*.

Remembrance Day or **Remembrance Sunday** *n* (in the UK) the Sunday nearest to 11 November, on which services are held to commemorate servicemen and -women who died in war. ◇ See also **Armistice Day**.

remind *v* (*tr*; **of**) **1** to cause (someone) to remember something. **2** to make (someone) think about someone or something else, esp. because of a similarity: *She reminds me of her sister*.

reminder *n* something that makes a person remember something or someone.

reminisce *v* (*intr*; **about**) to think, talk or write about things remembered from the past. [Lat *reminisci*, to remember]

reminiscence *n* **1** the act of thinking, talking or writing about the past. **2** an experience remembered from the past.

reminiscent *adj* **1** (**of**) similar (to); reminding one (of a person, place, thing, etc.) because of some similarity: *a painting reminiscent of van Gogh*. **2** thinking about the past a lot; given to reminiscing.

remiss *adj* careless; failing to pay attention; negligent. — *adj* **remissly**. — *n* **remissness**. [Lat *remittere*, to loosen]

remission *n* **1** a lessening in force or effect, esp. in the symptoms of a disease. **2** a reduction of a prison sentence. **3** pardon; forgiveness from sin. **4** an act of remitting. [Lat *remissio*, from *remittere*, to loosen]

remit *v* **-*tt-*** **1** (*tr*) to cancel or refrain from demanding (a debt, punishment, etc.). **2** (*tr* & *intr*) to make or become loose, slack or relaxed. **3** (*tr*) to send (money) in payment. **4** (*tr*) to refer (a matter for decision, etc.) to some other authority. **5** (*tr*) to refer (a case) to a lower court. **6** (*intr*) (of a disease, pain, rain, etc.) to become less severe for a period of time. **7** (*tr*) to send or put back into a previous state. **8** (*tr*) (of God) to forgive (sins). [Lat *remittere*, to loosen]

remittance *n* **1** the sending of money in payment. **2** the money sent.

remittent *adj* (of a disease) becoming less severe at times.

remix *v* (*tr*) to mix again in a different way, esp. to mix (a record) again, changing the balance of the different parts, etc. — *n* a remixed recording.

remnant *n* **1** a small piece or amount of something larger, or a small number of a large quantity of things left unsold, esp. a piece of material from the end of a roll. **2** a surviving trace or vestige. [OFr *remenoir*, to remain]

remonstrance *n* **1** an act of remonstrating. **2** a strong, usu. formal, protest. [Lat *remonstrare*, to demonstrate]

remonstrate *v* (*tr* & *intr*; **with**, **about**) to protest (to) or argue (with). — *n* **remonstration**. [Lat *remonstrare*, to demonstrate]

remorse *n* a deep feeling of guilt, regret and bitterness for something wrong or bad which one has done. — *adj* **remorseful**. — *adv* **remorsefully**. [Lat *remorsus*]

remorseless *adj* cruel; without pity. — *adv* **remorselessly**. — *n* **remorselessness**.

remote *adj* **1** far away or distant in time or place. **2** out of the way; away from civilisation. **3** operated or controlled from a distance. **4** distantly related. **5** very small or slight: *a remote chance*. **6** (of a person's manner) not friendly or interested; aloof. — *adv* **remotely**. — *n* **remoteness**. [Lat *remotus*, removed]

remote control *n* the control of a switch, device, model, etc. from a distance, by means of radio or electrical signals. — *adj* **remote-controlled**.

remould *v* (*tr*) to bond new tread on to (an old or worn tyre). — *n* a worn tyre which has had new tread bonded on to it.

remount *v* (*tr* & *intr*) to mount again, often on a fresh horse. — *n* a fresh horse.

remove *v* **1** (*tr*) to move (a person, thing, etc.) to a different place. **2** (*tr*) to take off (a piece of clothing). **3** (*tr*) to get rid of. **4** (*tr*) to dismiss (from a job, position, etc.). **5** (*intr*) to change one's position, place, location, etc., esp. to move to a new house. — *n* **1** a removal. **2** the degree of difference separating two things: *a form of government which is (at) only one remove from tyranny*. **3** (*Br*) an intermediate form or class in some schools. — *adj* **removable**. [Lat *removere*]

removal *n* **1** the act of removing or state of being removed. **2** the moving of furniture, etc. to a new home.

removed *adj* **1** separated or distant. **2** (of cousins) separated by a usu. specified number of generations: *A person's first cousin once removed is either the child of his or her first cousin or the first cousin of one of his or her parents.*

remover *n* a person or thing that removes, esp. who moves furniture, etc. from one house to another.

remunerate *v* (*tr*) **1** to pay for services done. **2** to recompense. — *n* **remuneration**. [Lat *remunerari*, from *munus*, gift]

remunerative *adj* bringing a good profit or having a good salary.

renaissance *n* **1** a rebirth or revival, esp. of learning, culture and the arts. **2** (*cap*) the revival of arts, literature and classical scholarship, and the beginnings of modern science, in Europe in the 14th to 16th centuries. — *adj* (*cap*) of the Renaissance. [Lat *renasci*, to be born again]

renal *adj* of, relating to or in the area of the kidneys. [Lat *renes*, kidneys]

renascent *adj* becoming active or lively again. — *n* **renascence**. [Lat *renasci*, to be born again]

rend *v* ***rent*** (*old*) **1** (*tr*) to tear, esp. using force or violence. **2** (*intr*) to become torn, esp. violently. [OE *rendan*]

render *v* ***-r-*** (*tr*) **1** to cause to become. **2** to give or provide (help, a service, etc.). **3** to pay (money) or perform (a duty), esp. in return for something: *render thanks to God.* **4** (**up**) to give up, release or yield: *The grave will never render up its dead.* **5** to translate. **6** to perform (the role of a character in a play, a piece of music, etc.). **7** to portray or reproduce, esp. in painting or music. **8** to present or submit for payment, approval, consideration, etc. **9** to cover (brick or stone) with a coat of plaster. **10** (**down**) to melt down (fat); to remove (fat) by melting. [OFr *rendre*]

rendering *n* **1** a coat of plaster. **2** a performance.

rendezvous *n* ***rendezvous*** **1** an appointment to meet, or the meeting itself, at a specified time and in a specified place. **2** the place where such a meeting is to be; a place where people meet. — *v* ***rendezvous***, ***rendezvoused*** (*intr*) to meet at an appointed place. [Fr, present yourselves]

rendition *n* **1** a performance or interpretation (of a piece of music or a dramatic role, etc.). **2** an act of rendering, esp. of translating. [OFr]

renegade *n* a person who deserts the religious, political, etc. group to which he or she belongs to join an enemy or rival group. [Span *renegado*]

renege *v* **1** (*intr*; **on**) to go back on a promise, agreement, one's word, etc. **2** (*tr*) to renounce (a promise, etc.) or desert (a person, faith, etc.). **3** (*intr*; *cards*) to revoke. — *n* **reneger**. [Lat *renegare*, from *negare*, to deny]

renew *v* **1** (*tr*) to make fresh or like new again; to restore to the original condition. **2** (*tr*) to begin (to do) again; to repeat. **3** (*tr*) to begin (some activity) again after a break. **4** (*tr* & *intr*) to make (a licence, lease, loan, etc.) valid for a further period of time. **5** (*tr*) to replenish or replace: *renew the water in the vases*. **6** (*tr*) to recover (youth, strength, etc.). — *adj* **renewable**. — *n* **renewal**. — *adj* **renewed**. — *n* **renewer**.

renewable energy *n* an energy source which is constantly being created and is constantly available, such as the sun, wind and waves.

rennet *n* a substance prepared from the stomachs of calves and used for curdling milk when making cheese. [MidE]

renounce *v* **1** (*tr*) to give up (a claim, title, right, etc.), esp. formally and publicly. **2** (*tr*) to refuse to recognise or associate with. **3** (*tr*) to give up (a bad habit). **4** (*intr*; *cards*) to fail to follow suit. — *n* **renouncement**. — *n* **renouncer**. ◇ See also **renunciation**. [Lat *renuntiare*]

renovate *v* (*tr*) to restore (esp. a building) to a former and better condition. — *n* **renovation**. — *n* **renovator**. [Lat *renovare*, from *novus*, new]

renown *n* fame. [OFr *renom*]

renowned *adj* famous; celebrated.

rent[1] *n* money paid to the owner of a property by a tenant in return for the use or occupation of that property. — *v* **1** (*tr*) to pay rent for (a building, etc.). **2** (*tr*; **out**) to allow (someone) to use (one's property) in return for payment of rent. **3** (*intr*) to be hired out for rent. [OFr *rente*]

rental *n* **1** money paid as rent. **2** the act of renting.

rent boy *n* a young male homosexual prostitute.

rent[2] *n* (*old*) an opening or split made by tearing, often violently. — *v past tense* of **rend**. **[rend]**

renunciation *n* **1** an act of renouncing. **2** a formal declaration of renouncing something. **3** self-denial. [Lat *renuntiatio*]

reopen *v* **-n- 1** (*tr* & *intr*) to open again. **2** (*tr*) to begin to discuss (a subject which has already been discussed) again.

rep *n* **1** a representative. **2** a repertory company or theatre. [Abbrev.]

repair[1] *v* (*tr*) **1** to restore (something damaged or broken) to good, working condition. **2** to put right, heal or make up for (something wrong that has been done). — *n* **1** an act of repairing. **2** a condition or state: *in good repair*. **3** a part or place that has been mended or repaired. — *adj* **repairable**. [Lat *reparare*]

repair[2] *v* (*intr*; **to**; *old*) to go (to); to take oneself off (to). [Lat *repatriare*, to return to one's homeland]

reparable *adj* able to be put right. [Lat *reparabilis*, able to be repaired]

reparation *n* **1** the act of making up for (something wrong that has been done). **2** money paid or something done for this purpose. **3** (usu. in *pl*) compensation paid after a war by a defeated nation for the damage caused. [Lat *reparatio*]

repartee *n* (skill at making) quick, witty replies; conversation having many such replies. [Fr *repartie*]

repast *n* (*formal* or *old*) a meal. [OFr *repaistre*, to eat a meal]

repatriate *v* (*tr*) to send (someone) back to his or her own country. — *n* **repatriation**. [Lat *repatriare*]

repay *v* **-*paid*** (*tr*) **1** to pay back (money). **2** to do or give something to (someone) in return for (something done or given to oneself): *repay his kindness*. — *adj* **repayable**. — *n* **repayment**.

repeal *v* (*tr*) to make (a law, etc.) no longer valid. — *n* the act of repealing (a law, etc.). — *adj* **repealable**. [OFr *repeler*]

repeat *v* **1** (*tr*) to say, do, etc. again. **2** (*tr*) to tell (something one has heard) to someone else, esp. when one ought not to. **3** (*tr*) to say (something) from memory. **4** (*intr*) (of food) to be tasted again after being swallowed. **5** (*intr*) to occur again; to recur: *The last bars of the music repeat*. **6** (*intr*) (of a gun) to fire several times without being reloaded. **7** (*intr*) (of a clock or watch) to strike the last hour or quarter hour when a spring is pressed. — *n* **1** an act of repeating. **2** something which is repeated, esp. a television programme which has been broadcast before. **3** (*mus*) (a sign which marks) a musical passage which is to be repeated. — *adj* repeated: *a repeat showing*. — *adj* **repeated**. — *adv* **repeatedly**. — **repeat itself** to happen in exactly the same way more than once. — **repeat oneself** to say the same thing more than once. ◇ See also **repetition**. [Lat *repetere*, to attack again]

repeatable *adj* **1** fit to be told to others. **2** able to be repeated.

repeater *n* **1** a clock or watch which strikes the last hour or quarter hour if a spring is pressed. **2** a gun which can be fired several times without having to be reloaded. **3** (*math*) a figure or sequence of figures in a decimal fraction which would recur infinitely.

repel *v* **-*ll*- 1** (*tr*) to force or drive back or away. **2** (*tr*) to cause a feeling of disgust or loathing. **3** (*tr* & *intr*) to fail to mix with, absorb or be attracted by (something else): *Oil repels water*. **4** (*tr*) to reject: *repel his advances*. [Lat *repellere*, to drive back]

repellent *n* something that repels, esp. insects. — *adj* repelling, esp. causing a feeling of disgust or loathing. — *adv* **repellently**.

repent *v* **1** (*tr* & *intr*; **of**) to feel great sorrow or regret (for something one has done); to wish (an action, etc.) undone. **2** (*intr*) to be sorry for all the evil or bad things one has done and decide to live a better life. — *n* **repentance**. — *adj* **repentant**. [OFr *repentir*]

repercussion *n* **1** (often in *pl*) a usu. bad unforeseen or indirect result or consequence of some action or event. **2** an echo or reverberation. — *adj* **repercussive**. [Lat *repercussio*]

repertoire *n* **1** the list of songs, plays, operas, etc. that a performer, singer, group of actors, etc. is able or ready to perform. **2** a range or stock of skills, techniques, talents, etc. that someone or something has, e.g. the total list of commands and codes that a computer can execute. [Fr]

repertory *n* **-*ies* 1** the complete list of plays that a theatre company is able and prepared to perform. **2** (also **repertory company**) a group of actors who perform a series of plays from their repertoire in the course of a season at one theatre. **3** (also **repertory theatre**) a theatre where a repertory company performs its plays. **4** repertory theatres in general: *worked in repertory for a few years*. [Lat *repertorium*, inventory]

repetition *n* **1** the act of repeating or being repeated. **2** a thing that is repeated. **3** a copy or replica. **4** something, e.g. a piece of music, which is played or recited from memory. [Lat *repetere*, to attack again]

repetitious or **repetitive** *adj* having too much repetition. — *adv* **repetitiously** or **repetitively**. — *n* **repetitiousness** or **repetitiveness**.

repine *v* (*intr*) to fret or feel discontented. **[pine**[2]**]**

replace (*tr*) **1** to put (something) back in a previous or proper position. **2** to take the place of or be a substitute for. **3** (**by, with**) to use or substitute one person or thing in place of (another): *replace the broken lock with a new one*. — *adj* **replaceable**.

replacement *n* **1** the act of replacing something. **2** a person or thing that replaces another.

replay *n* **1** the playing of a tape or recording again. **2** the playing of a football, etc. match again, usu. because neither team won the previous match. — *v* (*tr*) to play (a tape, recording, football match, etc.) again.

replenish *v* (*tr*) to fill up again or stock, esp. a supply of something which has been used up. — *n* **replenishment**. [OFr *replenir*, from Lat *plenus*, full]

replete *adj* **1** (**with**) completely or well supplied (with). **2** (*formal*) having eaten enough or more than enough. — *n* **repleteness** or **repletion**. [Lat *replere*, to refill]

replica *n* **1** an exact copy, esp. of a work of art, sometimes by the original artist, and often on a smaller scale. **2** a facsimile. [Lat *replicare*, to repeat]

replicate *v* **1** (*tr*) to make a replica of. **2** (*tr*) to repeat (an experiment). **3** (*intr*) (of a molecule, virus, etc.) to make a replica of itself. — *adj* **replicable**. [Lat *replicare*, to fold back]

reply *v* **-ies**, **-ied** **1** (*intr*) to respond in words, writing or action. **2** (*tr*) to say or do (something) in response. **3** (*intr*) to make a speech of thanks in answer to a speech of welcome. **4** (*intr*; *legal*) to answer a defendant's plea. — *n* **-ies** something said, written or done in answer or response. [Lat *replicare*, to fold back]

report *n* **1** a detailed statement, description or account, esp. after investigation. **2** a detailed and usu. formal account of the discussions and decisions of a committee, inquiry or other group of people. **3** (*Br*) a statement of a pupil's work and behaviour at school given to the parents, usu. at the end of each school year or each term. **4** rumour; general talk. **5** character or reputation. **6** a loud, explosive noise, e.g. of a gun firing. — *v* **1** (*tr*) to bring back as an answer, news or account. **2** (*tr* & *intr*) to give a formal or official account or description of, esp. after an investigation. **3** (*tr*; **for**) to make a complaint about (someone), esp. to a person in authority. **4** (*tr*) to make (something) known to a person in authority. **5** (*intr*; **for**, **to**) to present oneself at an appointed place, at an appointed time, for a particular purpose: *report to reception on arrival*. **6** (*intr*; **to**) to be responsible to or under the authority of. **7** (*intr*) to account for oneself in a particular way: *report sick*. **8** (*intr*) to act as a news reporter. — *adv* **reportedly**. [Lat *reportare*, to carry back]

reported speech *n* (*gram*) indirect speech.

reporter *n* a person who writes articles and reports for a newspaper, or for broadcast on television or radio.

repose[1] *n* a state of rest, calm, or peacefulness. — *v* **1** (*intr*) to lie resting. **2** (*tr*) to lay (oneself, one's head, etc.) to rest. **3** (*intr*) to lie dead. [Lat *repausare*]

repose[2] *v* **1** (*tr*) to place (confidence, trust, etc.) in a person or thing. **2** (*intr*) to be placed (in a person or thing). [Lat *reponere*, to replace]

repository *n* **-ies** **1** a place or container where things may be stored, esp. a museum or warehouse. **2** a person or thing thought of as a store of information, knowledge, etc. **3** a trusted person to whom one can confide secrets. [Lat *reponere*, to replace]

repossess *v* (*tr*) to regain possession of or take back (esp. goods sold on hire purchase because the buyer has not made the required payments or of property for which mortgage or rent has not been paid). — *n* **repossession**.

reprehend *v* (*tr*) to find fault with; to blame or reprove. [Lat *reprehendere*, to seize, blame]

reprehensible *adj* deserving blame or criticism. — *adv* **reprehensibly**. [Lat *reprehensibilis*]

represent *v* (*tr*) **1** to serve as a symbol or sign for; to stand for or correspond to: *Letters represent sounds. A thesis represents years of hard work*. **2** to speak or act on behalf of. **3** to be a good example of; to typify: *What he said represents the feelings of many people*. **4** to present an image of or portray, esp. through painting or sculpture. **5** to bring clearly to mind: *a film representing all the horrors of war*. **6** (**as**) to describe (as); to attribute a specified character or quality to: *represent oneself as an expert on roses*. **7** to show, state or explain: *represent the difficulties forcibly to the committee*. **8** to be an elected member of Parliament for. **9** to act out or play the part of on stage. [Lat *repraesentare*]

representation *n* **1** the act of representing or state of being represented. **2** a person or thing (esp. a painting) which represents someone or something else. **3** a body of representatives. **4** (often in *pl*) a strong statement made to present facts, opinions, complaints, demands or a petition. — *adj* **representational**.

representative *adj* **1** representing. **2** being a good example (of something); typical. **3** standing or acting as a deputy for someone. **4** (of government) carried on by elected people. — *n* **1** a person who represents someone or something else, esp. a person who represents, or sells the goods of, a business or company, or a person who represents a constituency in Parliament. **2** a typical example. — *adv* **representatively**. — *n* **representativeness**.

the House of Representatives *n* the lower house of the US Congress.

repress *v* (*tr*) **1** to keep (an impulse, a desire to do something, etc.) under control. **2** to put down, esp. using force: *repress the insurrection*. **3** to exclude (an unpleasant thought) from one's conscious mind. — *n* **repression**. — *n* **repressor**. [Lat *reprimere*, to keep back]

repressive *adj* severe; harsh. — *n* **repressiveness**.

reprieve *v* (*tr*) **1** to delay or cancel the punishment of (a prisoner condemned to death). **2** to give temporary relief from trouble, difficulty, pain, etc. — *n* **1** the act of delaying or cancelling a death sentence. **2** temporary relief from trouble, difficulty, pain, etc. [OFr *repris*, taken back]

reprimand *v* (*tr*) to criticise or rebuke angrily or severely, esp. formally. — *n* angry or severe and usu. formal criticism or rebuke. [Lat *reprimere*, to keep back]

reprint *n* **1** a copy of a book made by reprinting the original without any changes. **2** an occasion of reprinting. **3** the number of copies of a book which is reprinted. — *v* **1** (*tr*) to print more copies of (a book). **2** (*intr*) (of a book) to have more copies printed.

reprisal *n* **1** an act of taking revenge or retaliating. **2** the usu. forcible taking of foreign land in retaliation. [OFr *reprisaille*]

reprise *n* a repeated passage or theme in music. — *v* (*tr*) to repeat (an earlier passage or theme) in music. [OFr, a taking back]

reproach *v* (*tr*) to express disapproval of or disappointment with (a person) for a fault or some wrong done. — *n* **1** an act of reproaching. **2** (often in *pl*) an expression used to reproach or express disappointment. **3** a cause of disgrace or shame. — *adj* **reproachful**. — *adv* **reproachfully**. — **above** or **beyond reproach** too good to be criticised; excellent; perfect. [OFr *reprochier*]

reprobate *n* a person of immoral habits with no principles. — *adj* immoral and unprincipled. [Lat *reprobatus*, disapproved of]

reproduce 1 (*tr*) to make or produce a copy or imitation of; to duplicate. **2** (*tr*) to make or produce again or anew. **3** (*intr*) to turn out (well, badly, etc.) when copied. **4** (*intr* & *tr*) to produce offspring of the same kind as (itself): *an organism which can reproduce itself*. — *adj* **reproducible**.

reproduction *n* **1** the act or process of reproducing offspring. **2** a copy or imitation, esp. of a work of art. — *adj* (of furniture, etc.) made in imitation of an earlier style.

reproductive *adj* of or for reproduction. — *adv* **reproductively**. — *n* **reproductiveness** or **reproductivity**.

reproof *n* (words expressing) blame, criticism or a rebuke. [**reprove**]

reprove *v* (*tr*) to criticise, blame or condemn (someone) for a fault or some wrong done. — *adj* **reproving**. — *adv* **reprovingly**. [OFr *reprover*, from Lat *reprobare*, to disapprove of]

reptile *n* **1** any of the group of cold-blooded vertebrates which have a body covered with scales or bony plates, e.g. snakes, lizards, crocodiles and dinosaurs. **2** a mean, despicable person. [Lat *reptilis*, creeping]

reptilian *adj* of or like reptiles.

republic *n* **1** a form of government in which there is no monarch, and in which supreme power is held by the people or their elected representatives, esp. one in which the head of state is an elected or nominated president. **2** a country, state or unit within a state (e.g. in the former Soviet Union) having such a form of government. [Lat *respublica*, from *res*, concern, affair + *publicus*, public]

republican *adj* **1** of or like a republic. **2** in favour of or supporting a republican system of government. **3** (*cap*) of the Republican Party in the US. — *n* **1** a person who favours a republican system of government. **2** (*cap*) a member or supporter of the **Republican Party**, one of the two major political parties in the US, members of which support limited central government, the rights of individual states and interventionist foreign policy. ◇ See also **democratic**. — *n* **republicanism**.

repudiate *v* (*tr*) **1** to deny or reject: *repudiate the suggestion*. **2** to refuse to recognise or have anything to do with; to disown. **3** to refuse to acknowledge or pay (a debt, obligation, etc.). — *n* **repudiation**. [Lat *repudiare*]

repugnant *adj* **1** (**to**) causing a feeling of disgust or loathing. **2** (**with**) inconsistent; incompatible. — *n* **repugnance**. — *adv* **repugnantly**. [Lat *repugnare*, to fight against]

repulse *v* (*tr*) **1** to drive or force back (an enemy). **2** to reject (a person's offer of help, kindness, etc.) with coldness and discourtesy. **3** to cause a feeling of disgust, horror or loathing in. — *n* **1** an act of repulsing or state of being repulsed. **2** a cold, discourteous rejection. [Lat *repulsus*, driven back]

repulsion *n* **1** a feeling of disgust, horror or loathing. **2** a forcing back or being forced back. **3** (*physics*) a force which separates two objects, such as that between two electric charges or two magnetic poles which are the same.

repulsive *adj* causing a feeling of disgust, horror or loathing. — *adv* **repulsively**. — *n* **repulsiveness**.

reputable *adj* respectable; well thought of; trustworthy. — *adv* **reputably**. [Lat *reputabilis*]

reputation *n* **1** (**for**) the generally held opinion about a person with regard to his or her abilities, moral character, etc. **2** a high opinion generally held about a person or thing; a good name. [Lat *reputatio*]

repute *v* (*tr*; usu. in *passive*) to believe to be: *She is reputed to be a brilliant statistician*. — *n* reputation. — *adv* **reputedly**. — **by repute** reputedly. — **of repute** well thought of and respected by many people. [Lat *reputare*, to reckon]

request *n* **1** the act of asking for something. **2** something asked for. **3** the state of being asked for or sought after: *be in request*. —

v (*tr*) to ask (someone) for (something), esp. politely or as a favour. — **on request** if or when requested. [Lat *requirere*, to seek for]

request stop *n* a bus stop that a bus will only stop at if signalled to do so.

requiem *n* **1** (also *cap*) (in the Roman Catholic Church) a mass for the souls of the dead. **2** a piece of music written to accompany this service. [Lat *requiem*, rest, the first word of the Latin version of this mass]

require *v* (*tr*) **1** to need; to wish to have. **2** to have as a necessary or essential condition for success, fulfilment, etc. **3** to demand, exact or command by authority. [Lat *requirere*, to search for]

requirement *n* something that is needed, asked for, essential, ordered, etc.

requisite *adj* required; necessary; indispensable. — *n* something which is required, necessary or indispensable for some purpose: *toilet requisites*. [Lat *requisitus*, sought for]

requisition *n* **1** a (usu. written) formal and authoritative demand or request, esp. for supplies or the use of something, and esp. by the army. **2** the act of formally demanding, requesting or taking something. — *v* **-n-** (*tr*) to demand, take or order (supplies, the use of something, etc.) by official requisition. [Lat *requisitio*, a searching for]

requite *v* (*tr*; *formal*) **1** (**for**) to make a suitable return to or repay (a person) for some act. **2** (**with**) to repay (good with good or evil with evil); to avenge. — *n* **requital**. ◇ See also **unrequited**. [MidE *quitten*, to pay]

reredos *n* a usu. ornamental stone or wooden screen or partition wall behind an altar. [OFr *areredos*, from *arere*, behind + *dos*, back]

rerun *v* **-nn-**, **-ran**, **-run** (*tr*) **1** to run (a race) again. **2** to broadcast (a series of television or radio programmes) again. — *n* **1** a race that is run again. **2** a series of television or radio programmes which are broadcast again.

rescind *v* (*tr*) to cancel, annul or revoke (an order, law, custom, etc.). — *n* **rescindment** or **rescission**. [Lat *rescindere*, to cut off]

rescue *v* (*tr*; **from**) to free (a person or thing) from danger, evil, trouble, captivity, etc. — *n* the act of rescuing or state of being rescued. — *n* **rescuer**. [OFr *rescourre*]

research *n* a detailed and careful investigation into some area of study to (try to) discover and apply (new) facts or information. — *v* (*tr* & *intr*; **into**) to carry out such an investigation. — *n* **researcher**. [OFr *recercher*, to seek]

resemble *v* (*tr*) to be or look like or similar to. — *n* **resemblance**. [OFr *resembler*]

resent *v* (*tr*) to feel anger, bitterness or ill-will towards. — *adj* **resentful**. — *adv* **resentfully**. — *n* **resentfulness** or **resentment**. [OFr *ressentir*]

reserve *v* (*tr*) **1** to obtain or order in advance. **2** to keep back or set aside for the use of a particular person or for a particular purpose. **3** to delay or postpone (a legal judgement, taking a decision, etc.). — *n* **1** something which is kept back or set aside for later use or possible need. **2** the state or condition of being reserved or an act of reserving. **3** an area of land set aside for a particular purpose, esp. for the protection of animals, for hunting or fishing, or (esp. in Australia) for the original native inhabitants. **4** shy, cool, cautious and distant manner. **5** (often in *pl*) one of those members of a nation's armed forces who are not part of the regular services, but who are called up when needed. **6** an extra player or participant who can take the place of another if needed. **7** (often in *pl*) a company's money or assets, or a country's gold and foreign currency, held at a bank to meet liabilities. [Lat *reservare*, to keep back]

reservation *n* **1** the act of reserving something for future use. **2** a booking; something (e.g. a hotel room, a table in a restaurant) which has been reserved. **3** (usu. in *pl*) a doubt or objection which prevents one being able to accept or approve something wholeheartedly. **4** a limiting condition or proviso. **5** an area of land set aside for a particular purpose, esp. (in the US and Canada) for the original native inhabitants. **5** (*Br*) a strip of land between the two carriageways of a dual carriageway or motorway. **6** in some Christian churches, the practice of keeping back part of the consecrated bread and wine for some particular purpose after the service, e.g. for taking to the sick. **7** the right of the Pope to nominate someone to a vacant benefice.

reserved *adj* **1** booked. **2** shy, cool, cautious and distant; not open and friendly.

reserve price *n* the lowest price that the owner of something which is being sold by auction is prepared to accept.

reservist *n* a member of a nation's reserve forces.

reservoir *n* **1** a place, usu. a man-made lake, where water is collected and stored for use by the community. **2** a part of a machine, etc. where liquid is stored. **3** a large store or supply of something. [Fr]

reshuffle *v* (*tr*) **1** to shuffle (cards) again. **2** to reorganise or redistribute (e.g. posts in the cabinet). — *n* an act of reshuffling.

reside *v* (*intr*; **in**) **1** to live or have one's home (in), esp. permanently. **2** (of power, authority, a quality, etc.) to be present or found (in). [Lat *residere*, to settle down]

residence *n* **1** a house or dwelling, esp. a large, impressive and imposing one. **2** the act of living in a place. **3** the period of time one lives in a place. — **in residence 1** living in a particular place, esp. officially. **2** (esp. of a creative artist) working in a particular place for a period of time: *The* *university has an artist in residence.* [Lat *residere*, to settle down]

residency *n* **-ies 1** a residence, esp. the official dwelling of a governor, etc. in a colony, etc. **2** a period of advanced, specialised medical training in hospitals for doctors.

resident *n* **1** a person who lives in a place. **2** a bird or animal that does not migrate. **3** a guest staying in a hotel. **4** a doctor undergoing advanced, specialised training in a hospital. — *adj* **1** living or dwelling (in). **2** living or required to live in the place where one works. **3** (of birds and animals) not migrating.

residential *adj* **1** containing houses rather than factories and businesses, etc. **2** requiring residence in the same place as one works or studies: *a residential course.* **3** used as a residence: *a residential home for the elderly.* **4** relating to or connected with residence or residences: *residential qualifications.* — *adv* **residentially**.

residue *n* **1** what remains or is left over when a part has been taken away. **2** (*legal*) what is left of a dead person's estate after all of the debts and legacies have been paid. **3** (*chem*) a substance which remains after evaporation, combustion or distillation. [Lat *residuus*, remaining]

residual *adj* remaining; left over. — *n* something which remains or is left over.

resign *v* **1** (*intr*; **from**) to give up one's job, etc. **2** (*tr*) to give up or relinquish (a right, claim, etc.). **3** (*tr*; **to**) to bring (oneself) to accept something with patience and without resistance. [Lat *resignare*, to unseal]

resignation *n* **1** the act of resigning. **2** a formal letter or notice of one's intention to resign. **3** the state or quality of having or showing patient and calm acceptance.

resigned *adj* having or showing patient and calm acceptance of something thought of as inevitable. — *adv* **resignedly**.

resilient *adj* **1** (of people) quickly recovering from bad luck, illness, etc. **2** (of an object) quickly returning to its original shape after being bent, twisted, stretched, etc. — *n* **resilience** or **resiliency**. [Lat *resilire*, to leap back]

resin *n* a sticky solid or semi-solid substance produced by certain trees (e.g. firs, pines) and some other plants, or synthetically, used in making plastics, etc. — *adj* **resinous**. [Lat *resina*]

resist *v* **1** (*tr* & *intr*) to fight against (someone or something); to refuse to give in (to) or comply (with). **2** (*tr*) to remain undamaged by or withstand: *a metal which resists corrosion.* **3** (*tr*) to be unaffected by in spite of temptation or attraction: *He just can't resist chocolate.* — *adj* **resistible**. [Lat *resistere*, to oppose, resist]

resistance *n* **1** the act of resisting. **2** the ability or power to be unaffected or undamaged by something, esp. disease. **3** the force that one object exerts on the movement of another, causing it to slow down or stop. **4** the opposition to the passage of heat, electricity, etc. through a substance. **5** a resistor. **6** (often *cap*) an underground organisation which fights for the freedom of a country which has been conquered by a foreign power.

resistant *adj* able to resist or remain unaffected or undamaged by something. — *n* a person or thing that resists.

resistor *n* a device which introduces a known value of resistance into a circuit, etc.

resoluble *adj* able to be resolved or analysed. [Lat *resolvere*, to loose]

resolute *adj* having a fixed purpose or belief, and determined and firm in pursuing it. — *adv* **resolutely**. — *n* **resoluteness**. [Lat *resolutus*]

resolution *n* **1** the act of making a firm decision. **2** a firm decision. **3** a formal expression of opinion, will, etc. by a group of people, e.g. at a public meeting. **4** determination or resoluteness. **5** the act of solving or finding the answer to (a problem, question, etc.). **6** the ability of a television screen, photographic film, etc. to reproduce an image in very fine detail. **7** (*mus*) the passing of a chord from discord to concord. **8** (also **resolving power**) the ability of a microscope, telescope, etc. to distinguish between objects which are very close together. **9** the act of separating something (e.g. a chemical compound) into its constituent parts. [Lat *resolutio*]

resolve *v* **1** (*intr*) to take a firm decision (to). **2** (*tr*) to pass (a resolution), esp. formally by vote. **3** (*tr*) to find an answer to (a problem, question, etc.). **4** (*tr*) to take away or bring an end to (a doubt, fear, etc.). **5** (*tr* & *intr*; **into**) to break up or cause to break up into separate or constituent parts. **6** (*tr*) (of a television screen, photographic film, etc.) to produce an image of in fine detail. **7** (*tr*; *mus*) to make (a chord) pass from discord into concord. **8** (*tr*) (of microscopes, telescopes, etc.) to distinguish clearly between (objects which are very close together). — *n* **1** determination or firm intention. **2** a firm decision; a resolution. [Lat *resolvere*, to loose]

resolved *adj* determined; fixed in purpose.

resolving power see **resolution** (sense **8**).

resonance *n* **1** the quality or state of being resonant. **2** the reinforced or prolonged vibration of sound caused by the reflection of that vibration or by two adjacent objects vibrating in sympathy together. **3** the ringing quality of the human voice when produced in such a way that the vibration of the vocal cords is accompanied by sympathetic vibration of air in areas in the head, chest and throat. [Lat *resonare*, to resound]

resonant *adj* **1** (of sounds) echoing; continuing to sound; resounding. **2** producing echoing sounds: *resonant walls*. **3** full of or made stronger by a ringing quality: *a resonant voice*. — *adv* **resonantly**.

resonate *v* (*tr* & *intr*) to (cause to) resound or echo. — *n* **resonator**.

resort *v* (*intr* with **to**) **1** to turn to as a way of solving a problem, etc. when other methods have failed. **2** to go to, esp. frequently or in great numbers. — *n* **1** a place visited by many people, esp. one providing accommodation and recreation for holidaymakers. **2** someone or something looked to for help. — **in the last resort** when all other methods, etc. have failed. [OFr *resortir*, to rebound]

resound *v* **1** (*intr*) (of sounds) to ring or echo. **2** (*intr*; **with, to**) to be filled with echoing or ringing sounds: *The hall resounded to their cheers*. **3** (*intr*) to be widely known: *Her fame resounded throughout the country*. **4** (*tr*) (of a place) to cause (a sound) to echo or ring. **5** (*tr*) to repeat or spread (the praises of a person or thing). [Lat *resonare*]

resounding *adj* **1** echoing and ringing; reverberating. **2** thorough, clear and decisive: *a resounding victory*. — *adv* **resoundingly**.

resource *n* **1** a person or thing which gives help, support, etc. when needed. **2** a means of solving difficulties, problems, etc. **3** skill at finding ways of solving difficulties, problems, etc. **4** a supply of something. **5** (usu. in *pl*) a means of support, e.g. money and property. **6** (usu. in *pl*) a country's or business's natural source of wealth or the income from it: *natural resources*. **7** a means of occupying one's spare time or amusing oneself. [Lat *resurgere*, to rise again]

resourceful *adj* good at finding ways of solving difficulties, problems, etc. — *adv* **resourcefully**. — *n* **resourcefulness**.

respect *n* **1** admiration; good opinion: *be held in great respect*. **2** the state of being admired or well thought of. **3** (**for**) consideration of or attention to: *show no respect for the law*. **4** (in *pl*) a greeting or expression of admiration, esteem and honour. **5** a particular detail, feature or characteristic. **6** reference or connection: *in respect of*; *with respect to*. — *v* (*tr*) **1** to show or feel admiration or high regard for. **2** to show consideration, attention or thoughtfulness to: *respect other people's feelings*. — **pay one's respects** (**to**) to visit as a sign of respect or out of politeness. [Lat *respicere*, to look back]

respectable *adj* **1** deserving respect. **2** having a good reputation or character, esp. as regards morals. **3** (of behaviour) correct, acceptable. **4** presentable, decent. **5** fairly or relatively good or large. — *n* **respectability**. — *adv* **respectably**.

respectful *adj* having or showing respect. — *adv* **respectfully**. — *n* **respectfulness**.

respecting *prep* about; concerning.

respective *adj* belonging to or relating to each person or thing mentioned; particular; separate: *our respective homes*.

respectively *adv* referring to each person or thing separately and in turn.

respire *v* **1** (*intr* & *tr*) to breathe (air, etc.) in and out. **2** (*intr*) to take breath. [Lat *respirare*]

respiration *n* **1** the process by which people, animals, living cells, etc. take in oxygen and send out carbon dioxide; breathing. **2** a single complete breath. **3** the process (in living organisms) by which energy and carbon dioxide are produced by the oxidation of complex organic substances.

respirator *n* **1** a mask worn over the mouth and nose to prevent poisonous gas, dust, etc. being breathed in. **2** apparatus used to help very ill or injured people breathe when they are unable to do so naturally.

respiratory *adj* related to, or of, breathing.

respite *n* **1** (a) pause; a period of rest or relief from, or a temporary stopping of, something unpleasant, difficult, etc. **2** a temporary delay; a reprieve. — *v* (*tr*) **1** to grant a respite to. **2** to delay (e.g. the execution of a sentence). [OFr *respit*]

resplendent *adj* brilliant or splendid in appearance. — *n* **resplendence**. — *adv* **resplendently**. [Lat *resplendere*, to shine brightly]

respond *v* **1** (*intr* & *tr*) to answer or reply; to say in reply. **2** (*intr*) to act or behave in reply or response: *I smiled at her, but she didn't respond*. **3** (*intr*; **to**) to react favourably or well: *respond to treatment*. [Lat *respondere*, to return like for like]

respondent *n* **1** a person who answers or makes replies. **2** (*legal*) a defendant, esp. in a divorce suit. — *adj* answering; making a reply or response.

response *n* **1** an act of responding, replying or reacting. **2** a reply or answer. **3** a reaction: *meet with little response*. **4** an answer or reply, esp. in the form of a short verse which is either sung or spoken, made by the congregation or the choir to something said by the priest or minister during a service. [OFr *respons*]

responsible *adj* **1** (**for**) having control over and being accountable for; having as a job: *responsible for ordering new books*. **2** (**to**) having to answer or account for something (to): *responsible to the headmistress*. **3** (of a job, position, etc.) having many important duties, esp. the taking of important decisions; involving a lot of responsibility: *a very responsible job*. **4** (**for**) being the cause. **5** (of a person) able to be trusted. **6** (of a person) able to answer for one's own conduct; capable of rational and morally acceptable behaviour. — *adv* **responsibly**. [Lat *respondere*, to respond]

responsibility *n* **-ies** **1** something or someone for which one is responsible. **2**

the state of being responsible or having important duties for which one is responsible.

responsive *adj* **1** (of a person) quick to react or respond. **2** (**to**) reacting well or favourably: *a disease responsive to drugs*. **3** made as or forming a response: *a responsive smile*. — *adv* **responsively**. — *n* **responsiveness**. [Lat *responsivus*]

rest[1] *n* **1** a (usu. short) period of relaxation or freedom from work, activity, worry, etc. **2** sleep; repose. **3** calm; tranquillity. **4** a state of not moving or working. **5** death thought of as repose: *lay someone to rest* (= to bury a corpse). **6** (often *in cmpds*) something which holds or supports (something): *a headrest on a car seat*. **7** a pause in reading, speaking, etc. **8** (a mark showing) an interval of silence in a piece of music. **9** a place for resting, esp. a lodging for sailors. — *v* **1** (*tr* & *intr*) to (cause to) stop working or moving. **2** (*intr*) to relax, esp. by sleeping. **3** (*tr* & *intr*) to set, place or lie on or against something for support. **4** (*intr*) to be calm and free from worry. **5** (*tr* & *intr*; **on**) to give or have as a basis or support. **6** (*tr* & *intr*) to (cause to) depend or be based on or in. **7** (*tr* & *intr*; **on**) to (cause to) remain looking at: *His eyes rested on the floor*. **8** (*intr*) to be left without further attention, discussion or action: *Let the matter rest there*. **9** (*intr*) to lie dead or buried. **10** (*intr*) (of farmland) to lie without a crop in order to regain its fertility. **11** (*tr* & *intr*; *legal*) to stop calling witnesses and conclude (one's case): *rest one's case*. — **at rest 1** not moving. **2** free from pain, worry, etc.: *set his mind at rest*. **3** dead. [OE]

restful *adj* **1** bringing rest or causing a person to feel calm, peaceful and rested. **2** relaxed; at rest. — *adv* **restfully**. — *n* **restfulness**.

restless *adj* **1** constantly moving or fidgeting; unable to stay still or quiet. **2** giving no rest: *a restless night*. **3** worried, nervous and uneasy. — *adv* **restlessly**. — *n* **restlessness**.

rest room *n* (*NAm*) a room with lavatories, wash basins, and sometimes a seating area, in a shop, theatre, factory, etc., for the use of the staff or public.

rest[2] : **the rest 1** what is left when part of something is taken away, finished, etc., the remainder. **2** the others. — *v* (*intr*) to continue to be: *rest assured*. [Lat *restare*, to remain]

restaurant *n* a place where meals may be bought and eaten. [Fr]

restaurant car *n* a carriage on a train in which meals are served to travellers.

restaurateur *n* the owner or manager of a restaurant. [Fr]

restitution *n* **1** the act of giving back to the rightful owner something lost or stolen. **2** the paying of compensation for loss or injury. [Lat *restituere*, to put up again]

restive *adj* **1** unwilling to accept control or authority. **2** restless; nervous. **3** (of a horse) unwilling to move forwards. — *adv* **restively**. — *n* **restiveness**. [OFr *restif*, inert]

restoration *n* **1** the act or process of restoring. **2** the act of giving back something lost or stolen. **3** something restored or given back. **4** a model or reconstruction (e.g. of a ruin, extinct animal, etc.). **5** the act of returning to a former and higher status, rank, etc. **6** (*cap*) the return of the monarchy to Britain with the accession of Charles II in 1660; the reign of Charles II (1660–85). — *adj* (*cap*) (of literature, etc.) from the period of the Restoration of the monarchy in 1660, or the reign of Charles II (1660–85). [Lat *restauratio*, from *restaurare*, to restore]

restorative *n* & *adj* (something, e.g. a food or medicine) tending or helping to improve health, strength, spirits, etc. [**restore**]

restore *v* (*tr*) **1** to return (a building, painting, etc.) to a former and usu. better, esp. original, condition by repairing, cleaning, etc. **2** to bring back, or bring back to, a normal, healthy or proper state: *be restored to health*; *restore discipline*. **3** to return (something) lost or stolen to the rightful owner. **4** to bring or put back to a former and higher status, rank, etc. **5** to reconstruct or make a model or representation of (a ruin, extinct animal, etc.). — *adj* **restorable**. — *n* **restorer**. [Lat *restaurare*]

restrain *v* (*tr*) **1** to prevent (someone, oneself, etc.) from doing something. **2** to keep (one's temper, ambition, etc.) under control. **3** to take away (a person's) freedom, esp. by arresting him or her. [Lat *restringere*, to draw back tightly]

restrained *adj* **1** controlling, or able to control, one's emotions. **2** showing restraint; without excess.

restraint *n* **1** the act of restraining or state of being restrained. **2** a limit or restriction. **3** the avoidance of exaggeration or excess; the ability to remain calm and reasonable.

restrict *v* (*tr*) **1** (**to**) to keep (someone or something) within certain limits. **2** to limit or regulate the use of, esp. to withhold from general use. [Lat *restrictus*, drawn back]

restricted *adj* **1** limited in space; narrow; confined. **2** not for general use, circulation, etc. **3** (of an area, place, etc.) which only certain people, esp. military personnel, may enter.

restricted area *n* an area in which a special speed limit is in force, or to which access is limited.

restriction *n* **1** an act or instance of restricting. **2** something which restricts. **3** a regulation or rule which restricts or limits.

restrictive *adj* restricting or intended to restrict, esp. excessively. — *adv* **restrictively**.

restrictive practice *n* (often in *pl*) **1** an agreement between manufacturers, companies, etc. to keep production of goods down or limit the supply of goods on the market to keep prices high. **2** a practice by a trade union which limits and restricts the activities of members of other trade unions.

result *n* **1** an outcome or consequence of something. **2** (often in *pl*) a positive or favourable outcome or consequence. **3** a number or quantity obtained by calculation, etc. **4** (in *pl*) a list of final scores (in a series of football matches, etc.). **5** (*coll*) (in games) a win. **6** (in *pl*) a list of marks a student has obtained in an examination or series of examinations. — *v* (*intr*) **1** (**from**) to be a consequence or outcome of (some action, event, etc.). **2** (**in**) to end in a specified way: *Carelessness results in mistakes.* [Lat *resultare*, to leap back]

resultant *adj* resulting. — *n* (*math* & *physics*) a single force which is the equivalent of two or more forces acting on an object.

resume *v* **1** (*tr* & *intr*) to return to or begin again after an interruption. **2** (*tr*) to take back or go to (a former position, etc.): *resume one's seat.* ◇ See also **resumption**. [Lat *resumere*]

résumé *n* **1** a summary. **2** (*NAm*) a curriculum vitae. [Fr]

resumption *n* the act of resuming. [Lat *resumptio*]

resurgence *n* the act of returning to life, to a state of activity, importance, influence, etc. after a period of decline. — *adj* **resurgent**. [Lat *resurgere*, to rise again]

resurrect *v* (*tr*) **1** to bring back to life from the dead. **2** to bring back into general use, view, activity, etc.

resurrection *n* **1** the act of resurrecting or bringing (something) back into use. **2** the act of coming back to life after death. **3** (*cap*) Christ's coming back to life three days after his death on the cross. **4** (*cap*) the coming back to life of all the dead at the Last Judgement. [Lat *resurgere*, to rise again]

resuscitate *v* (*tr* & *intr*) to bring or come back to consciousness; to revive. — *n* **resuscitation**. [Lat *resuscitare*, to raise again]

retail *n* the sale of goods either individually or in small quantities to customers who will not resell them. — *adj* of, relating to or concerned with such sale of goods. — *adv* by retail; at a retail price. — *v* **1** (*tr* & *intr*) to sell (goods) in small quantities to customers; (of goods) to be sold in this way. **2** (*tr*) to tell or recount (a story, gossip, etc.) in great detail. — *n* **retailer**. ◇ See also **wholesale**. [OFr *retailler*, to cut off]

retail price index *n* a monthly index of the retail prices of certain household goods, taken as indicative of the cost of living for that month, and as a way of monitoring changes in the cost of living over a period of time.

retain *v* (*tr*) **1** to continue to have, contain, hold, use, etc. **2** (of a person) to be able to remember. **3** to hold back or keep in place. **4** to secure the services of (a person, esp. a lawyer) by paying a preliminary fee, often before the actual work begins. ◇ See also **retention**. [Lat *retinere*, to hold back]

retainer *n* **1** a fee paid to secure a person's professional services, esp. those of a lawyer or barrister. **2** a domestic servant who has been with a family for a long time. **3** a reduced rent paid for property while it is not occupied.

retaining wall *n* a wall built to support and hold back a mass of earth, rock or water.

retake *v* **-took**, **-taken** (*tr*) **1** to capture again. **2** to take (e.g. an examination) again. **3** to photograph (e.g. a scene in a film) again. — *n* a second taking of a photograph, filming of a scene, or sitting of an exam.

retaliate *v* (*intr*) to repay an injury, wrong, etc. in kind; to get revenge. — *n* **retaliation**. — *adj* **retaliatory**. [Lat *retaliare*]

retard *v* (*tr*) **1** to make slow or delay. **2** to keep back the progress, development, etc. of (e.g. a person's mental abilities). — *n* **retardation**. [Lat *retardare*, from *tardus*, slow]

retardant *adj* making something slower or delayed.

retarded *adj* not having made the expected physical or esp. mental development.

retch *v* (*intr*) to strain to vomit or almost vomit, but not actually do so. — *n* an act of retching. [OE *hræcan*]

retention *n* **1** the act of retaining or state of being retained. **2** the ability to remember experiences and things learnt. **3** the failure to get rid of fluid from the body. [Lat *retentio*]

retentive *adj* able to retain or keep, esp. fluid, memories or information. — *adv* **retentively**. — *n* **retentiveness**.

retexture *v* (*tr*) to treat (a blanket, garment, etc.) with chemicals which restore the original texture of the material.

rethink *v* **-thought** (*tr*) to think about or consider (a plan, etc.) again, usu. with a view to changing one's mind. — *n* an act of rethinking.

reticent *adj* not saying very much; not willing to communicate; not communicating everything that one knows. — *n* **reticence**. [Lat *reticere*, to be silent]

reticulate *adj* like a net, esp. in having lines, veins, etc. crossing. — *v* (*tr* & *intr*) to form or be formed into a network; to mark or be marked with a network of lines, etc. [Lat *reticulatus*, like a net]

reticule *n* (*hist*) a woman's small, often netted or beaded, pouch-like bag which fastens with a drawstring. [Lat *reticulum*, little net]

retina *n* ***-nas*** or ***-nae*** the light-sensitive lining at the back of the eye which receives the image from the lens. — *adj* **retinal**. [Lat, from *rete*, net]

retinol *n* vitamin A. [Gr *rhetine*, resin]

retinue *n* the servants, officials, aides, etc. who travel with and attend to an important person. [OFr *retenue*]

retire *v* **1** (*tr* & *intr*) to stop or cause to stop working permanently, usu. on reaching an age at which a pension can be received. **2** (*intr*) to go away to rest, esp. to go to bed. **3** (*intr*) to go away from or to; to leave: *retire to the drawing room.* **4** (*tr* & *intr*) to withdraw or cause to withdraw from a sporting contest, esp. because of injury. **5** (*tr* & *intr*) (of soldiers, etc.) to move or be moved back away from a dangerous position. [Fr *retirer*]

retiral *n* an act of retiring (e.g. from work) or going away from (a place).

retired *adj* **1** having permanently stopped working because of age. **2** secluded.

retirement *n* **1** the act of retiring or state of being retired from work. **2** seclusion and privacy.

retirement pension *n* (*Br*) a weekly payment by the state to people who have retired from work.

retiring *adj* shy and reserved; not liking to be noticed. — *adv* **retiringly**.

retort *v* **1** (*intr*) to make a quick and clever or angry reply. **2** (*tr*) to turn (an argument, criticism, blame, etc.) back on the person who first used that argument, criticism, blame, etc. **3** (*tr*) to heat and purify (metal). — *n* **1** a quick and clever or angry reply. **2** an argument, criticism, blame, etc. which is turned back upon the originator. **3** a glass vessel with a long neck which curves downwards, used in distilling. **4** a vessel for heating metals such as iron and carbon to make steel, or for heating coal to produce gas. [Lat *retorquere*, to twist back]

retouch *v* (*tr*) to improve or repair (a photograph, negative, painting, etc.) by adding extra touches.

retrace *v* (*tr*) **1** to go back over (one's route, path, etc.). **2** to go over (recent events, etc.) again in one's memory. **3** to trace back: *retrace one's roots.*

retract *v* (*tr* & *intr*) **1** to withdraw (a statement, claim, charge, etc.) as wrong, offensive or unjustified. **2** to refuse to acknowledge (a promise, agreement, etc. that one has made). **3** to draw in or back or be drawn in or back. [Lat *retrahere*, to draw back]

retractable *adj* able to be drawn up, in or back.

retractile *adj* (*tech*) (of e.g. a cat's claws) able to be drawn up, in or back.

retraction *n* a retracting, esp. of something one has said, agreed or promised.

retread *v* ***-trod***, ***-trodden*** or ***-treaded*** (*tr*) to bond new tread on to (an old or worn tyre). — *n* an old or worn tyre which has had new tread bonded on to it.

retreat *v* **1** (*intr* & *tr*) (of soldiers, troops, etc.) to move back or away from, or be caused to move back or away from, a position or battle. **2** (*intr*) to slope backwards; to recede. — *n* **1** the act of retreating, esp. from battle, a military position, danger, etc. **2** a signal, esp. one given on a bugle, to retreat. **3** a place of privacy, safety and seclusion. **4** a period of retirement from the world, esp. for prayer, meditation and study. [Lat *retrahere*, to draw back]

retrench *v* (*tr* & *intr*) to reduce or cut down (expenses, money spent, etc.); to economise. — *n* **retrenchment**. [OFr *retrenchier*, to cut off or back]

retribution *n* deserved punishment, esp. for sin or wrongdoing. [Lat *retribuere*, to give back]

retributive *adj* being or forming a punishment which is deserved or suitable.

retrieve *v* **1** (*tr*) to get or bring back again; to recover. **2** (*tr*) to rescue or save: *retrieve the situation.* **3** (*tr*) to recover (information) from storage in a computer memory. **4** (*tr*) to remember or recall to mind. **5** (*tr* & *intr*) (of dogs) to search for and bring back (game which has been shot by a hunter, or a ball, stick, etc. which has been thrown). — *adj* **retrievable**. — *adv* **retrievably**. [OFr *retrouver*, to find again]

retrieval *n* the act or possibility of retrieving or getting back.

retriever *n* a breed of dog with a short golden or black water-resistant coat, trained to retrieve game.

retro- *pfx* **1** back or backwards in time or space. **2** behind. [Lat *retro*, backwards]

retroactive *adj* applying to or affecting things from a date in the past: *retroactive legislation.* — *adv* **retroactively**. — *n* **retroactivity**. [Lat *retroagere*, to drive back]

retrograde *adj* **1** being, tending towards or causing a worse, less advanced or less desirable state. **2** moving or bending backwards. **3** in a reversed or opposite order. **4** (*astron*) (of a planet, etc.) seeming to move in the opposite or contrary direction to other planets, etc. **5** (*astron*) (of a planet, etc.) seeming to move from east to west. — *v* (*intr*) **1** to move backwards. **2** to deteriorate or decline. **3** (*astron*) (of a planet) to show retrograde movement. [Lat *retrogradus*, going backwards]

retrogress *v* (*intr*) to go back to an earlier, worse or less advanced condition or state; to deteriorate. — *n* **retrogression**. — *adj* **retrogressive**. [Lat *retrogressus*, a movement backwards]

retro-rocket *n* a small secondary rocket on a spacecraft which produces thrust in the opposite direction to that in which the spacecraft is moving, used for slowing down.

retrospect: **in retrospect** when considering or looking back on what has happened in the past. [Lat *retrospicere*, to look back]

retrospection *n* **1** an act of looking back at the past. **2** a tendency to look back on one's past life.

retrospective *adj* **1** (of a law, etc.) applying to the past as well as to the present and to the future. **2** looking back on past events. — *n* an exhibition which shows how an artist's work has developed over the years. — *adv* **retrospectively**.

retrovirus *n* any of several viruses which carry their genetic information in RNA rather than DNA, including several cancer-causing viruses and the virus which causes AIDS. [*re*verse *tr*anscriptase (the active enzyme in these viruses) + **virus**]

retroussé *adj* (esp. of the nose) turned up at the end. [Fr, tucked up]

retsina *n* a Greek, white, resin-flavoured wine. [ModGr]

return *v* **1** (*intr*) to come or go back again to a former place, state or owner. **2** (*tr*) to give, send, put back, etc. in a former position. **3** (*intr*) to come back to in thought or speech: *return to the topic later*. **4** (*tr*) to repay with something of the same value: *return the compliment*. **5** (*tr* & *intr*) to answer or reply. **6** (*tr*) to report or state officially or formally. **7** (*tr*) to earn or produce (profit, interest, etc.). **8** (*tr*) to elect as a Member of Parliament. **9** (*tr*) (of a jury) to give (a verdict). **10** (*tr*) (*tennis*, *badminton*, etc.) to hit (a ball, etc.) served by one's opponent. — *n* **1** an act of coming back from a place, state, etc. **2** an act of returning something, esp. to a former place, state, ownership, etc. **3** something returned, esp. unsold newspapers and magazines returned to the publisher or a theatre ticket returned to the theatre for resale. **4** profit from work, a business or investment. **5** (often in *pl*) a statement of a person's income and allowances, used for calculating the tax which must be paid. **6** (usu. in *pl*) a statement of the votes polled in an election. **7** (*Br*) a return ticket. **8** an answer or reply. **9** a ball, etc. hit back after one's opponent's service in tennis, etc. — *adj* of, forming, causing or relating to a return. — *adj* **returnable**. — **by return (of post)** to be returned immediately or by the very next post. — **in return** in exchange; in reply; as compensation. — **many happy returns (of the day)** an expression of good wishes on a person's birthday. [OFr *retorner*]

returning officer *n* (*Br*) an official in charge of running an election in a constituency, counting the votes, and declaring the result.

return match *n* a second match played between the same (teams of) players, but at the other home pitch to that on which the first match was played.

return ticket *n* a ticket which allows a person to travel to a place and back again.

reunion *n* **1** a meeting of people (e.g. relatives or friends) who have not met for some time. **2** the act of reuniting or state of being reunited.

reunite *v* (*tr* & *intr*; **with**) to bring or come together after being separated.

Rev. *abbrev* (also **Revd**) Reverend.

rev (*coll*) *n* (usu. in *pl*) a revolution in an engine, esp. used as a way of measuring the speed an engine is running at: *2 000 revs per minute*. — *v* **-vv-** (*coll*) **1** (*tr*; **up**) to increase the speed of (a car engine, etc.). **2** (*intr*; **up**) (of a car engine, etc.) to run faster. [Abbrev.]

Revd. See **Rev.**

revamp *v* (*tr*) to revise, renovate, patch up, usu. with the aim of improving.

reveal *v* (*tr*) **1** to make known (a secret, etc.). **2** to show; to allow to be seen. **3** (esp. of God) to make known through divine inspiration or supernatural means. — *adj* **revealing**. ◇ See also **revelation**. [Lat *revelare*, to unveil]

reveille *n* a bugle or drum call at daybreak to waken soldiers, etc. [Fr *réveillez!*, wake up!]

revel *v* **-ll-** (*intr*) **1** (**in**) to take great delight (in). **2** to enjoy oneself in a noisy, lively way. — *n* (usu. in *pl*) noisy, lively enjoyment, festivities or merrymaking. — *n* **reveller**. [OFr *reveler*, to riot]

revelry *n* **-ies** (usu. in *pl*) noisy, lively enjoyment, festivities or merrymaking.

revelation *n* **1** the act of revealing (secrets, information, etc.). **2** that which is made known or seen. **3** something revealed to man by God through divine inspiration or supernatural means. **4** (also *coll* **Revelations**; in full **the Book of the Revelation of St John the Divine**) the last book of the New Testament, which contains prophecies of the end of the world. [Lat *revelatio*, from *revelare*, to unveil]

revelatory *adj* to revealing.

revelry. See **revel**.

revenge *n* **1** malicious injury, harm or wrong done in return for injury, harm or wrong received. **2** something done as a means of returning injury, harm, etc. for injury, harm, etc. received. **3** the desire to do such injury, harm, etc. — *v* (*tr*) **1** to do injury, harm, etc. in return for (injury, harm, etc.) received. **2** (**on**) to take revenge on someone on behalf of (oneself or someone else). — *adj* **revengeful**. [OFr *revenger*]

revenue *n* **1** money which comes to a person, etc. from any source (e.g. property, shares), esp. the money raised by the government from taxes, etc. **2** (often *cap.*) a government department responsible for collecting this money. [OFr, from *revenir*, to return]

reverberate *v* **1** (*intr*) (of a sound, light, heat, etc.) to be echoed, repeated or reflected repeatedly. **2** (*tr*) to echo, repeat or reflect (a sound, light, etc.) repeatedly. **3** (*intr*) (of a story, scandal, etc.) to be repeated continually. — *n* **reverberation**. [Lat *reverberare*, to beat back]

revere *v* (*tr*) to feel or show great affection and respect for. [Lat *revereri*, to stand in awe of]

reverence *n* **1** great respect, esp. that shown to something sacred or holy. **2** (*cap*; with **His**, **Your**, etc.; sometimes *facet*) a title used for some members of the clergy.

reverend *adj* worthy of being revered or respected. **2** (*cap*) used before proper names as a title for members of the clergy. — *n* (*coll*) a member of the clergy.

reverent *adj* showing or feeling great respect. — *adv* **reverently**.

reverential *adj* showing great respect or reverence. — *adv* **reverentially**.

reverie *n* **1** a state of pleasantly dreamy and absented-minded thought. **2** a daydream or absent-minded idea or thought. [OFr *reverie*, from *rever*, to speak wildly]

revers *n* ***revers*** (usu. in *pl*) any part of a garment that is turned back, esp. a lapel. [Fr, reverse]

reverse *v* **1** (*tr* & *intr*) to (cause to) move in an opposite or backwards direction. **2** (*tr*) to put into an opposite or contrary position, state, order, etc. **3** (*tr*) to change (a policy, decision, etc.) to the exact opposite or contrary. **4** (*tr*) to set aside or overthrow (a legal decision or judgement). — *n* **1** the opposite or contrary of something. **2** an act of changing to an opposite or contrary position, direction, state, etc. or of being changed in this way. **3** the back or rear side of something, esp. the back cover of a book. **4** the side of a coin, medal, note, etc. with a secondary design on. ◇ See also **obverse**. **5** a piece of bad luck; a defeat; a reversal. **6** a mechanism, e.g. a car gear, which makes a machine, vehicle, etc. move in a backwards direction. — *adj* opposite, contrary or turned round in order, position, direction, etc. — *adj* **reversed**. — **in reverse** in an opposite or backwards direction. — **reverse the charges** to make a telephone call (a **reverse-charge call**) which is paid for by the person who receives it instead of by the caller. [Lat *reversare*, to turn round]

reversal *n* **1** the act of reversing or state of being reversed. **2** a change in fortune, esp. for the worse.

reversible *adj* **1** able to be reversed. **2** (of clothes) able to be worn with either side out.

reversing light *n* a usu. white light on the rear of a vehicle which warns the drivers and pedestrians behind that the vehicle is going to move backwards.

reversion *n* **1** a return to an earlier state, belief, etc. **2** the legal right (e.g. of an original owner or his or her heirs) to possess a property once the present owner dies. **3** property to which a person has such a right. **4** insurance which is paid on a person's death. **5** (*biol*) a return to an earlier, ancestral, and usu. less advanced, type. [Lat *reversio*]

revert *v* **1** (*intr*) to return to a topic in thought or conversation. **2** (*intr*) to return to a former and usu. worse state, practice, etc. **3** (*intr*; *biol*) to return to an earlier, ancestral, and usu. simpler type. **4** (*intr*) (esp. of property) to return to an original owner or his or her heirs after belonging temporarily to someone else. **5** (*tr*) to turn (something) back. [Lat *revertere*, to turn back]

review *n* **1** an act of examining, reviewing or revising, or the state of being examined, reviewed or revised. **2** a general survey. **3** a survey of the past and past events: *the newspaper's annual review of the year*. **4** a critical report on a book, play, film, etc. **5** (a part of) a magazine or newspaper which contains mainly reviews of books, etc. and essays on related subjects. **6** a second or additional study or consideration of facts, events, etc. **7** a formal or official inspection of troops, ships, etc. **8** (*legal*) a re-examination of a case. — *v* **1** (*tr*) to examine or go over, esp. critically or formally. **2** (*tr*) to look back on and examine (events in the past). **3** (*tr*) to inspect (troops, ships, etc.), esp. formally or officially. **4** (*tr*) to write a critical report on (a book, play, film, etc.). **5** (*intr*) to write reviews. **6** (*tr*; *legal*) to re-examine (a case). [OFr *revue*, from *revoir*, to see again]

reviewer *n* a person who writes critical reviews of books, plays, etc.

revile *v* **1** (*tr*) to abuse or criticise (someone or something) bitterly or scornfully. **2** (*intr*) to speak scornfully or use abusive langauge. — *n* **revilement**. — *n* **reviler**. [OFr *reviler*, from Lat *vilis*, worthless]

revise *v* **1** (*tr*) to examine again in order to identify and correct faults, take new circumstances into account, or otherwise improve. **2** (*tr*) to correct faults in, make improvements in and bring up to date (a previously printed book) usu. to prepare a new edition. **3** (*tr* & *intr*) to study (a subject or one's notes on it) again, to prepare for an examination. **4** (*tr*) to change or amend (an opinion, etc.). — *n* **reviser**. [Lat *revisere*, to look back]

revision *n* **1** the act of revising or process of being revised. **2** a revised book, edition, article, etc.

revisionism *n* **1** a policy of revising a doctrine. **2** a form of Communism which favours evolution rather than revolution as a way of achieving socialism. — *n* & *adj* **revisionist**.

revitalise or **-ize** *v* (*tr*) to give new life and energy to.

revive *v* (*tr* & *intr*) **1** to come or bring back to consciousness, strength, health, vitality, etc. **2** to come or bring back to use, to an active state, to notice, etc.: *revive an old play*. [Lat *revivere*, to live again]

revival *n* **1** the act of reviving or state of being revived. **2** a renewed interest, esp. in old customs and fashions. **3** a new production or performance, e.g. of an old and almost forgotten play. **4** a period of renewed religious faith and spirituality. **5** a series of evangelistic and often emotional meetings to encourage renewed religious faith.

revivalism *n* the promotion of renewed religious faith and spirituality through evangelistic meetings. — *n* & *adj* **revivalist**.

revivify *v* **-ies**, **-ied** (*tr*) to put new life into. — *n* **revivification**.

revoke *v* **1** (*tr*) to cancel or make (a will, agreement, etc.) no longer valid. **2** (*intr*) to fail to follow suit in cards when able to do so. — *n* an act of revoking at cards. — *adj* **revocable**. — *n* **revocation**. [Lat *revocare*, to call back]

revolt *v* **1** (*intr*; **against**) to rebel (against a government, authority, etc.). **2** (*tr* & *intr*) to (cause to) feel disgust, loathing, horror or revulsion. — *n* an act of rebelling; a rebellion against authority. — *adj* **revolted**. ◇ See also **revulsion**. [Lat *revolvere*, to roll back]

revolting *adj* causing a feeling of disgust, loathing, etc.; nauseating. — *adv* **revoltingly**.

revolution *n* **1** the usu. violent overthrow of a government or political system by the governed. **2** in Marxism, the class struggle which will end in the working class becoming the ruling class and the establishment of Communism. **3** a complete, drastic and usu. far-reaching change in ideas, ways of doing things, etc.: *the Industrial Revolution*. **4** a complete circle or turn round an axis. **5** an act of turning or moving round an axis. **6** a planet's orbit, or the time taken to go round it once. **7** a cycle of events, or the time taken to go through all of them and return to the beginning. [Lat *revolutio*]

revolutionary *adj* **1** of or like a revolution. **2** in favour of and supporting revolution. **3** completely new or different; involving radical change. — *n* **-ies** a person who takes part in or is in favour of revolution in general or a particular revolution.

revolutionise or **-ize** *v* (*tr*) to cause great, radical or fundamental changes in.

revolve *v* **1** (*tr* & *intr*) to move or turn, or cause to move or turn in a circle around a central point; to rotate. **2** (*intr*; **around**, **about**) to have as a centre, focus or main point. **3** (*intr*) to occur in cycles or regularly. **4** (*tr* & *intr*) to consider or be considered in turn; to ponder: *revolve the ideas in her head*. — *adj* **revolvable**. — *n* & *adj* **revolving**. ◇ See also **revolution**. [Lat *revolvere*, to roll back]

revolver *n* a pistol with a revolving cylinder which holds several bullets, and which can be fired several times without needing to be reloaded.

revue *n* an amusing and varied show, with songs, sketches, etc. which are often satirical, and which usu. feature popular performers. [Fr, review]

revulsion *n* **1** a feeling of complete disgust, distaste or repugnance. **2** a sudden and often violent change of feeling, esp. from love to hate. [Lat *revulsio*]

reward *n* **1** something given or received in return for work done, a service rendered, good behaviour, etc. **2** something given or received in return for good or evil. **3** a sum of money offered usu. for finding or helping to find a criminal, stolen or lost property, etc. — *v* (*tr*) to give a reward of some form to (someone) for work done, services rendered, help, good behaviour, etc. [OFr *reguarder*]

rewarding *adj* giving personal pleasure or satisfaction.

rewind *v* (*tr*) to wind (tape, film, etc.) back to the beginning.

rewire *v* (*tr*) to fit (a house, etc.) with a new system of electrical wiring.

Rex *n* the reigning king, now used mainly on coins and in official documents. [Lat, king]

RFC *abbrev* **1** Rugby Football Club. **2** (*hist*) Royal Flying Corps.

RGN *abbrev* Registered General Nurse.

Rh *symbol* **1** rhesus. **2** (*chem*) rhodium.

rhapsody *n* **-ies** **1** an enthusiastic and highly emotional speech, piece of writing, etc. **2** an emotional piece of music usu. written to suggest a free form or improvisation. — *adj* **rhapsodic** or **rhapsodical**. — *adv* **rhapsodically**. [Gr *rhapsoidia*, an epic]

rhapsodise or **-ize** *v* (*tr* & *intr*) to speak or write with great enthusiasm or emotion.

rhea *n* a S American flightless bird resembling, but smaller than, the ostrich. [Gr *Rhea*, the mother of Zeus in Greek mythology]

rhenium *n* a rare metallic element, symbol **Re**, used in certain alloys, e.g. those which act as superconductors. [Lat *Rhenus*, the Rhine]

rheostat *n* a device which varies the flow of electric current through a circuit. — *adj* **rheostatic**. [Gr *rheos*, flow + *statos*, stationary]

rhesus *n* (also **rhesus monkey**) a small N Indian monkey. [Gr *Rhesos*, the king of Thrace in Greek mythology]

rhesus factor *n* an antigen usu. found in red blood cells in humans (but first identified in the blood of rhesus monkeys), **rhesus positive** blood having this factor, and **rhesus negative** blood lacking it.

rhetoric *n* **1** the art of speaking and writing well, elegantly and effectively, esp. when used to persuade or influence others. **2** language which is full of unnecessarily long, formal or literary words and phrases, and which is also often insincere or meaningless. — *adj* **rhetorical**. [Gr *rhetorike* (*techne*) rhetorical (art)]

rhetorical question *n* a question which is asked to produce an effect and not because the speaker wants an answer.

rheum *n* a watery discharge from the nose or eyes. [Gr *rheuma*, flow]

rheumatism *n* a disease marked by painful swelling of the joints (e.g. one's hips, knees, fingers, etc.) and which causes stiffness and pain when moving them. [Gr *rheumatismos*, from *rheuma*, flow]

rheumatic *n* **1** a person suffering from rheumatism. **2** (in *pl*; *coll*) (pain caused by) rheumatism. — *adj* of or caused by rheumatism.

rheumatic fever *n* a disease which causes fever, painful swelling of the joints and possible damage to the heart, found esp. in children.

rheumatoid *adj* of or like rheumatism or rheumatoid arthritis.

rheumatoid arthritis *n* a chronic disease which causes painful swelling in the joints and which gets progressively worse.

rhinestone *n* an imitation diamond usu. made from glass or plastic. [*Rhine*, a river in Germany + **stone**]

rhino *n* ***-os*** a rhinoceros.

rhinoceros *n* ***-ros*** or ***-roses*** a large thick-skinned plant-eating animal with one or two horns on its nose, found in Africa and Asia. [Gr *rhinokeros*, from *rhis*, nose + *keros*, horn]

rhizome *n* a thick, horizontal, underground stem which produces roots and leafy shoots. [Gr *rhiza*, root]

rhodium *n* a metallic element, symbol **Rh**, which belongs to the platinum group and is used for making alloys. [Gr *rhodon*, rose, from its rose-coloured salts]

rhododendron *n* a flowering shrub with thick evergreen leaves and large, showy, colourful flowers. [Gr *rhodon*, rose + *dendron*, tree]

rhomboid *n* a four-sided shape with opposite sides and angles equal, two angles being greater and two smaller than a right angle, and two sides being longer than the other two. — *adj* (also **rhomboidal**) shaped like a rhomboid or a rhombus. [Gr *rhomboeides*, from *rhombos*, rhombus]

rhombus *n* ***-uses*** or ***-bi*** a four-sided shape with all four sides equal, two opposite angles being greater than a right angle and two smaller; a diamond shape. [Gr *rhombos*, anything which may be spun round]

rhubarb *n* **1** a large-leaved garden plant with reddish, sour-tasting stalks which can be cooked, sweetened and eaten. **2** the roots of a type of rhubarb found in China and Tibet, dried and taken as a laxative. **3** (*coll*) the sound of continuous murmured background conversation made by a group of actors, esp. by repeating the word *rhubarb*. **4** (*coll*) nonsense; rubbish. [OFr *reubarbe*, from Gr *rheon barbaron*, foreign rhubarb]

rhyme *n* **1** a pattern of words which have the same final sounds at the ends of lines in a poem. **2** the use of such patterns in poetry, etc. **3** a word which has the same sound as another: *'Beef' is a rhyme for 'leaf'*. **4** a short poem, verse or jingle written in rhyme. — *v* **1** (*intr*) (of words) to have the same final sounds and so form rhymes. **2** (*tr*; **with**) to use (a word) as a rhyme for another. **3** (*intr*) to write using rhymes. **4** (*tr*) to put (a story, etc.) into rhyme. — **without rhyme or reason** without sense, reason or any discernible system. [Gr *rhythmos*, rhythm]

rhyming slang *n* slang in which the word meant is replaced by a phrase in which the last word rhymes with the word meant, the phrase then often being shortened to the first word, e.g. '*butcher's hook*' is rhyming slang for '*look*', normally shortened to '*butcher's*', as in '*have a butcher's*'.

rhythm *n* **1** a regular, repeated pattern, movement, beat or sequence of events. **2** the regular arrangement of stress, notes of different lengths and pauses in a piece of music. **3** a particular pattern of stress, notes, etc. in music: *tango rhythm*. **4** a regular arrangement of sounds and stressed and unstressed syllables in poetry or other writing, suggesting movement; metre. **5** an ability to sing, speak, move, etc. rhythmically. **6** (in full **rhythm section**) the group of instruments (e.g. drums, guitar and bass) in a dance or jazz band which supply the rhythm for the music. **7** (in painting, sculpture, architecture, etc.) a regular and harmonious pattern of shapes, colours, areas of shade and light, empty spaces, etc. [Gr *rhythmos*, from *rheein*, to flow]

rhythmic or **rhythmical** *adj* of or with rhythm. — *adv* **rhythmically**.

RI *abbrev* **1** religious instruction. **2** (or **R.I.**) Rhode Island.

rib[1] *n* **1** any one of the slightly flexible bones which curve round and forward from the spine, forming the chest wall and protecting the heart and lungs. **2** a cut of meat including one or more ribs. **3** a rod-like bar which supports and strengthens a layer of fabric, membrane, etc., e.g. in an umbrella, insect's wing or aircraft wing. **4** one of the pieces of wood which curve round and upward from a ship's keel to form the framework of the hull. **5** a raised ridge in knitted or woven material. — *v* ***-bb-*** (*tr*) **1** to provide or enclose with ribs. **2** to knit ribs in by alternating plain and purl stitches. — *adj* **ribbed**. [OE *ribbe*]

ribbing *n* a pattern or arrangement of ribs, esp. in knitting.

rib cage *n* the chest wall formed by the ribs which protects the heart and lungs.

rib[2] *v* ***-bb-*** (*tr*; *coll*) to tease. — *n* **ribbing**. [Perhaps from the phrase *rib tickle*, to make someone laugh]

ribald *adj* (of language, a speaker, humour, etc.) humorous in a rude, vulgar, indecent and disrespectful way. [OFr *ribauld*]
ribaldry *n* ribald talk or behaviour.

riband or **ribband** *n* a ribbon, esp. one awarded as a prize. [OFr *reubon*]

ribbon *n* **1** a long narrow strip of usu. coloured material used for decorating clothes, tying hair and parcels, etc. **2** any ribbon-like strip. **3** a small piece of coloured cloth worn to show membership of a team, or as a sign of having won an award. **4** a narrow strip of inked cloth used to produce print in a typewriter. **5** (in *pl*) a torn strip, tatter or shred: *hanging in ribbons*. [OFr *reubon*]
ribbon development *n* an (often haphazard) building of houses, etc. along the side of a main road leading out of a town.

riboflavin *n* a yellow-coloured vitamin of the B complex found in green vegetables, milk, fish, egg yolk and liver; also called vitamin $\mathbf{B}_2$. [*ribose* (a sugar) + Lat *flavus*, yellow]

ribonucleic acid *n* an acid found in all living cells, which plays an important part in the development of proteins and which can also hold genetic information. [*ribose* (a sugar) + **nucleic acid**]

rice *n* **1** a grass which grows in wet, marshy ground in warm climates. **2** its seed, highly valued as food. [Gr *oryza*]
rice paper *n* very thin paper made from the bark of an oriental tree, used in cookery and for painting on.

rich *adj* **1** having a lot of money, property or possessions. **2** costly and elaborate: *rich clothes*. **3** high in value or quality: *a rich harvest*. **4** (**in**) well supplied (with); having in great abundance. **5** (of a soil, a region, etc.) productive, fertile. **6** (of colours) vivid and deep. **7** (of esp. an alcoholic drink) with a full, mellow, well-matured flavour. **8** (of food) with a lot of seasoning, fat, oil, sugar or fruit. **9** (of odours) pungent, spicy and penetrating. **10** (of a voice) full, mellow and deep. **11** (of a suggestion) unacceptable; outrageous; ridiculous: *That's a bit rich!* **12** (of the mixture of fuel and air in an internal combustion engine) having a (too) high proportion of fuel. — *n* **richness**. [OE *rice*, strong, powerful]
riches *n* (*pl*) wealth. [OFr *richesse*]
richly *adv* **1** in a rich or elaborate way. **2** fully and suitably: *richly deserved*.

Richter scale *n* a scale used for measuring the strength of an earthquake, ranging from 0 to 10, 8 being a major quake. [Charles F *Richter* (1900–85), the American seismologist who invented it]

rick[1] *n* a stack or heap, esp. of hay or corn and usu. thatched. [OE *hreac*]

rick[2] *v* (*tr*) to sprain or wrench (one's neck, ankle, etc.). — *n* a sprain or wrench. [A form of **wrick**]

rickets *n* (*sing* or *pl*) a disease in children caused by a lack of vitamin D, causing the bones to become soft and bend, one result of which is bow legs.

rickety *adj* **1** having or affected by rickets. **2** unsteady and likely to collapse. [**rickets**]

rick-rack *n* a zigzag braid for decorating or trimming clothes, soft furnishings, etc. [**rack**[1]]

rickshaw or **ricksha** *n* a small, two-wheeled, hooded carriage drawn either by a person on foot, or attached to a bicycle or motorcycle. [Jap *jinrikisha*, from *jin*, man + *riki*, power + *sha*, carriage]

ricochet *n* (the sound of) an act of hitting a surface and then bouncing off at an angle, as of a stone hitting and then bouncing off water. — *v* **-t-** or **-tt-** (*intr*) to hit a flat surface and bounce off again at an angle. [Fr]

rid *v* **-dd-** (*tr*; **of**) to free or clear (oneself) from something undesirable or unwanted. — **get rid of** to free or relieve oneself of (something unwanted). [Norse *rythja*, to clear]
riddance *n* the act of freeing oneself from something undesirable or unwanted. — **good riddance** a welcome relief from an undesirable or unwanted person or thing.

ridden. See **ride**.

riddle[1] *n* **1** a short usu. humorous puzzle, often in the form of a question, which describes an object, person, etc. in a mysterious or misleading way, and which can only be solved using ingenuity. **2** a person, thing or fact which is puzzling or difficult to understand. — *v* **1** (*intr*) to speak in riddles. **2** (*tr*) to solve (a riddle). [OE *rædels*]

riddle[2] *n* a large coarse sieve used e.g. for sifting gravel or grain. — *v* (*tr*) **1** to pass (gravel, grain, etc.) through a riddle. **2** (**with**) to fill with holes, esp. with gunshot: *riddled with bullets*. **3** (**with**) to spread through; to fill: *a government department riddled with corruption*. [OE *hriddel*]

ride *v* ***rode***, ***ridden*** **1** (*tr*) to sit on and control (a bicycle, horse, etc.). **2** (*intr*; **in**, **on**) to travel or be carried in a car, train, etc. or on a bicycle, horse, etc. **3** (*tr*; esp. *NAm*) to travel on (a vehicle). **4** (*intr*) to go out on horseback, esp. regularly. **5** (*tr*) to ride a horse in (a race). **6** (*tr*) to move or float on: *a ship riding the waves*. **7** (*intr*) (of a ship) to float at anchor. **8** (*intr*) (esp. of the moon) to appear to float. **9** (*tr*) to travel over or across by car, horse, etc. **10** (*intr*; **in**, **on**) to rest on or be supported by while moving: *a kite riding on the wind*. **11** (*tr*; usu. in *passive*) to dominate or oppress: *ridden with guilt*. **12** (*intr*) to remain undisturbed or unchanged: *let matters ride*. **13** (*intr*; **on**) to depend. **14** (*tr*) to bend before (a blow, punch, etc.) to reduce its impact. **15** (*tr*; *vulg*) to have sexual intercourse with. — *n* **1** a journey on horseback or by vehicle. **2** a lift: *gave him a ride to the shop*. **3** the type of movement felt in a vehicle: *a smooth ride*. **4** a path, esp. one through a wood, for horseback riding. **5** a fairground entertainment, such as a roller-coaster or big wheel. — *v* **ride out** (*tr*) to survive or get through safely: *ride out the storm.* — *v* **ride up** (*intr*) (of an item of clothing) to move gradually up the body out of position. — **riding high** very successful, confident and excited. — **take for a ride** (*coll*) to trick, cheat or deceive. [OE *ridan*]

rider *n* **1** a person who rides, esp. a horse. **2** an addition to what has already been said or written, esp. an extra clause added to a document; a qualification or amendment.

riding *n* the art and practice of riding horses.

ridge *n* **1** a strip of ground raised either side of a ploughed furrow. **2** any long, narrow raised area on an otherwise flat surface. **3** the top edge of something where two upward sloping surfaces meet, e.g. on a roof. **4** a long narrow range of hills or hilltop. **5** (*meteorol*) a long narrow area of high pressure. — *v* (*tr* & *intr*) to form or make into ridges. — *adj* **ridged** and **ridgy**, **-ier**, **-iest**. [OE *hrycg*]

ridgepole *n* **1** (also **ridgepiece**) the beam along the ridge of a roof to which the upper ends of the rafters are attached. **2** the horizontal pole at the top of a tent.

ridicule *n* language, laughter, behaviour, etc. which makes someone or something appear foolish or humiliated; derision; mockery: *held him up to ridicule.* — *v* (*tr*) to laugh at, make fun of or mock. [Lat *ridere*, to laugh]

ridiculous *adj* very silly or absurd; deserving to be laughed at. — *adv* **ridiculously**. — *n* **ridiculousness**.

riding *n* (usu. *cap*) any of the three former administrative divisions of Yorkshire, the **East Riding**, the **West Riding** and the **North Riding**. [Norse *thridjungr*, third part]

Riesling *n* a dry white wine produced in Germany and Austria from a grape of the same name. [Ger]

rife *adj* **1** (esp. of bad or unpleasant things) very common. **2** (**with**) having a large amount or number of (something bad or undesirable). [OE *ryfe*]

riff *n* (*jazz*, *rock*, etc.) a short passage of music played repeatedly. [Perhaps from **refrain**[1]]

riffle *v* **1** (*tr* & *intr*; **through**) to flick or leaf through (the pages of a book, a pile of papers, etc.) rapidly, esp. in a casual search for something. **2** (*tr*) to shuffle (playing cards) by dividing the pack into two equal piles, bending the cards back slightly, and controlling the fall of the corners of the cards with the thumbs, so that cards from each pile fall alternately. — *n* **1** (the sound caused by) the action of riffling (e.g. cards). **2** (*NAm*) a section of a stream or river where shallow water flows swiftly over a rough, rocky surface. **3** (*NAm*) a ripple or patch of ripples on the surface of water. [A combination of **ripple** and **ruffle**]

riff-raff *n* worthless, disreputable or undesirable people. [OFr *rif et raf*]

rifle[1] *n* **1** a large gun fired from the shoulder, with a long barrel with a spiral groove on the inside which gives the gun greater accuracy over a long distance. **2** (usu. in *pl*) a body of soldiers armed with rifles. — *v* (*tr*) to cut spiral grooves in (a gun or its barrel). [OGer *rifeln*, to groove]

rifle[2] *v* **1** (*tr* & *intr*) to search through (a house, safe, etc.) thoroughly in order to steal something from it. **2** (*tr*) to steal (something). [OFr *rifler*, to plunder]

rift *n* **1** a split or crack, esp. one in the ground. **2** a breaking of friendly relations between previously friendly people. — *v* (*tr*) to tear apart or split. [Norse *ript*, breaking of an agreement]

rift valley *n* a long narrow valley formed by subsidence of a portion of the earth's crust between two faults.

rig *v* **-gg-** (*tr*) **1** to fit (a ship) with ropes, sails and rigging. **2** to control or manipulate for dishonest purposes, for personal profit or advantage. — *n* **1** the arrangement of sails, ropes and masts on a ship. **2** an oil-rig. **3** gear or equipment, esp. that used for a specific task. **4** clothing or a uniform worn for a particular occasion or task. — *v* **rig out** (*tr*) **1** (**in**) to dress (oneself, someone), esp. in clothes of a stated or special kind. ◇ See also **rig-out** below. **2** (**with**) to equip with esp. special gear. — *v* **rig up** (*tr*) to build or prepare, esp. quickly and with whatever material is available. [Prob. Scandinavian]

rigging *n* **1** the system of ropes, wires, etc. which support and control a ship's masts and sails. **2** the ropes and wires, etc. which support the structure of an airship or the wings of a biplane.

rig-out *n* (*coll*) a person's full set of clothes.

right *adj* **1** of or on the side of someone or something which is towards the east when the front is facing north. **2** on or close to a spectator's right side: *stage right.* **3** (of a river bank) on the right hand of a person going downstream. **4** correct; true. **5** morally or legally correct or good. **6** (**for**) suitable; appropriate. **7** in a correct, proper, satisfactory or healthy condition: *not in one's right mind; put things right.* **8** of or on the side of fabric, a garment, etc. which is intended to be seen: *turn the right side of the dress out.* **9** with an axis perpendicular to the base: *a right angle.* **10** (also *cap*) politically conservative. **11** socially acceptable: *know all the right people.* **12** (esp. *Br coll*) complete; utter; real: *a right mess.* — *adv* **1** exactly or precisely. **2** immediately; without delay: *He'll be right over.* **3** completely; all the way: *right round the field.* **4** straight; directly: *right to the top.* **5** to or on the right side. **6** correctly; properly; satisfactorily. **7** (*old* or *dialect*) very; to the full: *be right glad to see her.* — *n* **1** (often in *pl*) a power, privilege, etc. that a person may claim legally or morally. **2** (often in *pl*) a just or legal claim to something: *mineral rights*. **3** that which is correct, good or just: *the rights and wrongs of the case*. **4** fairness, truth and justice. **5** the right side, part or direction. **6** (*cap*) the political party, group of people within a party, etc. which has the most conservative views (from European parliaments in which members holding the most conservative views sit on the president's right). **7** (*boxing*) (a punch with) the right hand. **8** (in *pl*; *finance*) the privilege given to a company's existing shareholders to buy new shares, usu. for less than the market value. **9** (in *pl*) the legal permission to print, publish, film, etc. a book, usu. sold to a company by the author or by another company. — *v* **1** (*tr* & *intr*) to put or come back to the correct, esp. upright, position. **2** (*tr*) to avenge or compensate for (something wrong done). **3** (*tr*) to correct; to put in order. — *interj* an expression of agreement, assent or readiness. — **by right(s)** rightfully. — **in one's own right** because of one's own qualifications, abilities, work, possessions, etc. — **in the right** right; with justice on one's side. — **keep on the right side of (someone)** to maintain (someone's) goodwill towards oneself. — **put** or **set to rights** to put in a proper order, place or state. — **right away** or **right now** immediately; at once. — **serve (someone) right** to be what (someone) deserves, esp. when that person has done something he or she was advised not to do. [OE *riht*]

right angle *n* an angle of 90°, formed by two lines which are perpendicular to each other. — *adj* **right-angled**. — **at right angles** perpendicular.

rightful *adj* **1** having a legally just claim. **2** (of property, a privilege, etc.) held by just right. **3** fair; just; equitable. — *adv* **rightfully**. — *n* **rightfulness**.

right-hand *adj* **1** at, on or towards the right. **2** done with the right hand.

right-handed *adj* **1** using the right hand more easily than the left. **2** (of a tool, etc.) designed to be used by the right hand. **3** (of a blow, etc.) done with the right hand. **4** (of a screw) needing to be turned clockwise to be screwed in. — *n* **right-handedness**.

right-hander *n* **1** a right-handed person. **2** a blow with the right hand.

right-hand man or **woman** *n* a valuable, indispensable and trusted assistant.

Right Honourable *n* a title given to British peers below the rank of marquis, privy councillors, present and past cabinet ministers, and to some Lord Mayors and Lord Provosts.

rightism *n* (support for and promotion of) the political opinions of conservatives or the right. — *n* & *adj* **rightist**.

rightly *adv* **1** correctly. **2** justly. **3** fairly; properly. **4** with good reason; justifiably. **5** with certainty.

right-minded *adj* thinking, judging and acting according to principles which are just, honest and sensible.

right of way *n* ***rights of way*** **1** the right of the public to use a path that crosses private property. **2** a path used by this right. **3** the right of one vehicle to proceed before other vehicles coming from different directions at junctions, roundabouts, etc.

Right Reverend *n* a title of a bishop.

rightward *adj* or (also **rightwards**) *adv* on or towards the right.

right wing *n* **1** the more conservative members of a political party. **2** (a player playing on) the right-hand side of a football pitch, etc.

right-wing *adj* politically conservative. — *n* **right-winger**.

righteous *adj* **1** (of a person) virtuous, free from sin or guilt. **2** (of an action) morally good. **3** caused by justifiable anger: *righteous indignation*. — *adv* **righteously**. — *n* **righteousness**. [OE *rihtwis*, from *riht*, right + *wise*, manner]

rigid *adj* **1** completely stiff and inflexible. **2** not able to be moved. **3** (of a person) strictly and inflexibly adhering to one's ideas, opinions and rules. **4** (of rules, etc.) maintained very strictly and never relaxed. — *n* **rigidity** or **rigidness**. — *adv* **rigidly**. [Lat *rigidus*]

rigmarole *n* **1** an unnecessarily or absurdly long, complicated series of actions, instructions or procedures. **2** a long rambling or confused statement or speech. [From *ragman rolls*, a series of documents in which the Scottish nobles promised allegiance to Edward I of England in 1291–2 and 1296]

rigor mortis *n* the temporary stiffening of the body after death. [Lat, stiffness of death]

rigour *n* **1** stiffness; hardness. **2** strictness or severity of temper, behaviour or judgement. **3** strict enforcement of rules or the law. **4** (usu. in *pl*) a harsh or severe condition, esp. of weather or climate. **5** harshness or severity of life; austerity. **6** strict precision or exactitude, e.g. of thought. [Lat *rigor*, stiffness]

rigorous *adj* **1** showing or having rigour; strict; harsh; severe. **2** (of the weather or climate) cold, harsh, and extremely unpleasant. **3** strictly accurate. — *adv* **rigorously**. — *n* **rigorousness**.

rile *v* (*tr*) to anger or annoy. [Variant of *roil*, to make (water) muddy or turbid]

rill *n* a small stream or brook. [Ger *Rille*, channel]

rille *n* (also **rill**) a long narrow valley or furrow on the moon or on Mars. [Ger *Rille*, channel]

rim *n* **1** a raised and often curved edge or border. **2** the outer circular edge of a wheel to which the tyre is attached. — *v* ***-mm-***

(*tr*) to form or provide an edge or rim to. — *adj* **rimless**. — *adj* **rimmed**. [OE *rima*]

rime[1] *n* thick white frost formed esp. from frozen water droplets from cloud or fog. — *v* (*tr*) to cover with rime. — *adj* **rimy**, **-*ier***, **-*iest***. [OE *hrim*]

rime[2]. Same as **rhyme**.

rind *n* **1** a thick, hard outer layer or covering as on cheese or bacon, or the peel of fruit. **2** the bark of a tree or plant. — *v* (*tr*) to strip bark from. [OE]

ring[1] *n* **1** a small circle of gold, silver or some other metal or material, worn on the finger. **2** a circle of metal, wood, plastic, etc. for holding, keeping in place, connecting, hanging, etc. **3** any object, mark or figure which is circular in shape. **4** a circular course. **5** a group of people or things arranged in a circle. **6** an enclosed and usu. circular area for competitions or exhibitions, esp. at a circus. **7** a square area marked off by ropes on a platform, where boxers or wrestlers fight. **8** (with **the**) boxing as a profession. **9** a group of people who act together to control an antiques or drugs market, betting, etc. for their own profit. **10** a circular electric element or gas burner on top of a cooker. **11** (*chem*) a closed chain of atoms in a molecule. **12** a thin band of particles orbiting some planets, such as Saturn and Uranus. — *v* (*tr*) **1** to make, form, draw, etc. a ring round. **2** to put a ring on the leg of (a bird) as a means of identifying it. **3** to fit a ring in the nose of (a bull) to make it easy to lead. — *adj* **ringed**. — **run rings round** (*coll*) to beat or be much better than. — **throw one's hat into the ring** (*coll*) to offer oneself as a candidate or contestant. [OE *hring*]

ring binder *n* a loose-leaf binder with metal rings which can be opened to add more pages or take them out.

ringbolt *n* a bolt with a ring attached.

ring dove *n* a wood pigeon.

ring finger *n* the third finger, esp. on the left hand, on which a wedding ring is worn.

ringleader *n* the leader of a group of people who are doing something wrong or making trouble.

ringlet *n* a long spiral curl of hair.

ring main *n* a domestic electrical supply system in which power points are connected to the mains in a closed circuit.

ringmaster *n* a person who is in charge of performances in a circus ring.

ring ouzel see **ouzel**.

ring road *n* (*Br*) a road that goes round a town or through its suburbs to keep its centre relatively free of traffic.

ringside *n* **1** the seating area immediately by a boxing, circus, etc. ring. **2** any place that gives a good clear view.

ringworm *n* a fungal infection in which inflamed and itchy red circular patches form on the skin.

ring[2] *v* ***rang***, ***rung*** **1** (*tr* & *intr*) to (cause to) make a sound, esp. a ringing, bell-like sound. **2** (*tr* & *intr*; **up**; *Br*) to telephone (someone). **3** (*intr*; **for**) to ring a bell as a summons. **4** (*intr*; **to, with**) (of a place or building) to be filled with sound: *The office rang with the news*. **5** (*intr*) to sound repeatedly; to resound: *Criticisms rang in his ears*. **6** (*intr*) (of the ears) to be filled with a buzzing, humming or ringing sensation or sound. **7** (*intr*) (of words, etc.) to give a stated impression: *His promises ring false*. — *n* **1** the act or sound of ringing. **2** the act of ringing a bell. **3** the clear, resonant sound of a bell, or a similarly resonant sound. **4** (*Br*) a telephone call. **5** a suggestion or impression of a particular feeling or quality: *a story with a ring of truth about it*. **6** a set of bells, esp. in a church. — *adj* **ringing**. — *adv* **ringingly**. — *v* **ring back** (*intr* & *tr*) **1** to telephone (someone) again. **2** to telephone (someone who telephoned earlier). — **ring the changes 1** to vary the way something is done, used, said, etc. **2** to go through all the various orders possible when ringing a peel of church bells. — **ring down**, or **up, the curtain 1** to give the signal for lowering, or raising, the curtain in a theatre. **2** (**on**) to put an end to, or begin, (a project, etc.). — *v* **ring in** and **out** (*tr*) to announce the arrival or departure of with, or as if with, bell-ringing: *ring out the old year*. — *v* **ring off** (*intr*) to end a telephone call. — *v* **ring out** (*intr*) to make a sudden clear, loud sound: *Shots rang out*. — *v* **ring up 1** (*tr* & *intr*) to telephone. **2** (*tr*) to record (the price of an item sold) on a cash register. [OE *hringan*]

ringer *n* **1** a person or thing that rings. **2** (also **dead ringer**; *coll*) a person or thing that is almost identical to some other person or thing. **3** (esp. *US*) a horse or athlete entered into a race or competition under a false name or other false pretences. **4** (esp. *US*) an impostor or fake.

rink *n* **1** (a building containing) an area of ice prepared for skating, curling or ice-hockey. **2** (a building containing) an area of smooth floor for roller skating. **3** a strip of grass or ice allotted to a team or set of players in bowling and curling. [OFr *renc*, rank, row]

rinse *v* (*tr*) **1** (**out**) to wash (soap, detergent, etc.) out of (clothes, hair, dishes, etc.) with clean water. **2** to remove traces of dirt by washing lightly in clean water, usu. without soap. **3** (**out**) to clean (a cup, one's mouth, etc.) by filling it with water, swirling the water round and throwing or spitting it out. **4** (**away**) to remove (soap, detergent, dirt, etc.) from a place with clean water. — *n* **1** an act of rinsing. **2** liquid used for rinsing. **3** a solution used in hairdressing to give a temporary tint to the hair. — *n* **rinser**. [OFr *recincier*]

riot *n* **1** a noisy public disturbance or disorder by a usu. large group of people, or (*legal*) by three or more people. **2** uncontrolled or wild revelry and feasting. **3** a striking display (esp. of colour). **4** a very amusing person or thing. — *v* **-t-** (*intr*) to take part in a riot. — *n* **rioter**. — **read the riot act** to give an angry warning that bad behaviour must stop. — **run riot** to act, speak, grow, etc. in a wild and uncontrolled way. [OFr *riote*, debate, quarrel]

riotous *adj* **1** participating in, likely to start, or like, a riot. **2** very active, noisy, cheerful and wild. **3** filled with wild revelry, parties, etc.: *riotous living*. — *adv* **riotously**. — *n* **riotousness**.

RIP *abbrev* for *requiescat in pace* (Lat), may he or she rest in peace.

rip *v* **-pp-** **1** (*tr* & *intr*) to tear or come apart violently or roughly. **2** (*tr*; **off**, **out**) to remove quickly and violently. **3** (*intr*; *coll*) to rush along or move quickly without restraint. **4** (*tr*) to saw (wood or timber) along the grain. — *n* **1** a violent or rough tear or split. **2** an act of ripping. — *n* **ripper**. — *v* **rip off** (*tr*; *coll*) to cheat or steal from; to defraud.

ripcord *n* a cord which releases a parachute from its pack when pulled.

rip-off *n* (*coll*) **1** an act or instance of stealing from, cheating or defrauding someone. **2** an item which is outrageously overpriced.

rip-roaring *adj* wild, noisy and exciting.

ripsaw *n* a saw for cutting along the grain of timber.

riparian *adj* (*formal*) of, occurring on or living on a riverbank. [Lat *ripa*, riverbank]

ripe *adj* **1** (of fruit, grain, etc.) fully matured and ready to be picked and eaten. **2** (of cheese) having been allowed to age to develop its full flavour. **3** resembling ripe fruit, esp. in being plump and pink. **4** mature in mind and body; fully developed. **5** (**for**) suitable or appropriate. **6** (**for**) eager or ready. **7** (of language, etc.) slightly indecent; smutty. — *n* **ripeness**. — **ripe (old) age** a very old age. [OE]

ripen *v* **-n-** (*tr* & *intr*) to make or become ripe or riper.

riposte *n* **1** a quick, sharp reply; a retort. **2** a fencer's quick return thrust. — *v* (*intr*) to answer with a riposte. [Fr, from Ital *risposta*, reply]

ripple *n* **1** a slight wave or series of slight waves on the surface of water. **2** a sound that rises and falls quickly and gently like that of rippling water, esp. of laughter or applause. **3** a wavy appearance, e.g. of material. — *v* **1** (*intr* & *tr*) to (cause to) form or flow with ripples or a rippling motion. **2** (*intr*) to make a rippling sound. — *adj* **rippling** and **ripply**, **-ier**, **-iest**.

rise *v* ***rose***, ***risen*** (*intr*) **1** to get or stand up, esp. from a sitting, kneeling or lying position. **2** to get up from bed, esp. after a night's sleep. **3** to move upwards; to ascend. **4** to increase in size, amount, volume, strength, degree, intensity, etc. **5** (of the sun, moon, planets, etc.) to appear above the horizon. **6** to stretch or slope upwards: *ground which rises gently*. **7** (**up**, **against**) to rebel. **8** to move from a lower position, rank, level, etc. to a higher one. **9** to begin or originate: *a river that rises in the mountains*. **10** (esp. of a person's spirits) to become more cheerful. **11** (esp. of an animal's fur, a person's hair, etc.) to become straight and stiff, e.g. because of fear or anger. **12** (of a committee, court, Parliament, etc.) to finish a session; to adjourn. **13** to come back to life. **14** to come to the surface of water: *wait for the fish to rise*. **15** (of dough) to swell up. **16** to be built: *new office blocks rising all over town*. **17** (**to**) to respond (e.g. to teasing, provocation or criticism). — *n* **1** an act of rising. **2** an increase in size, amount, volume, strength, status, rank, etc. **3** (*Br*) an increase in salary. **4** a piece of rising ground; a slope or hill. **5** a beginning or origin. **6** the vertical height of a step or flight of stairs. — **get** or **take a rise out of** (*coll*) to make (someone) angry, upset, etc., esp. through teasing or provocation. — **give rise to** to cause. — *v* **rise above** (*intr*) to remain unaffected by (teasing, provocation, criticism, etc.). — **rise to the bait** to do what someone else suggests by means of suggestions, hints, etc. that one should do. [OE *risan*]

riser *n* **1** a person who gets out of bed: *an early riser*. **2** any of the vertical parts between the horizontal steps of a set of stairs.

rising *n* **1** the act of rising. **2** a rebellion. — *adj* **1** moving or sloping upwards; getting higher. **2** approaching greater age, maturity, status, reputation or importance. **3** approaching a stated age: *the rising sevens*.

rising damp see **damp**.

risible *adj* **1** causing laughter; ludicrous; ridiculous. **2** inclined to laughter. — *n* **risibility**. [Lat *risibilis*]

risk *n* **1** the chance or possibility of suffering loss, injury, damage or failure. **2** a person or thing likely to cause loss, injury, damage, etc. **3** a person or thing thought of as likely (a **bad risk**) or unlikely (a **good risk**) to suffer loss, injury, damage, etc. — *v* (*tr*) **1** to expose to danger or risk. **2** to take the chance of (risk, danger, etc. occurring): *not risk being late*. — *adv* **riskily**. — *adj* **risky**, **-ier**, **-iest**. — **at one's own risk** accepting personal responsibility for any loss, injury, etc. which might occur. — **at risk** in danger; in a position which might lead to loss, injury, etc. — **at the risk of** with the possibility of (loss, injury or some other unfortunate consequence). — **run the risk of** to risk: *run the risk of being late*. — **run** or **take a risk** to act without worrying about the danger or risk involved. [Fr *risque*]

risotto *n* **-os** an Italian dish of rice cooked in a meat or seafood stock with onions, tomatoes, cheese, etc. [Ital *riso*, rice]

risqué *adj* (of a story, joke, etc.) bordering on the rude or indecent. [Fr, risked]

rissole *n* a small fried cake or ball of chopped meat coated in breadcrumbs. [OFr *roissole*]

ritardando *adj*, *adv* & *n* (**-dos** or **-di**; *mus*). Same as **rallentando**. [Ital]

rite *n* **1** a religious ceremony or observance. **2** the required words or actions for such a ceremony. **3** a body of such acts or ceremonies which are characteristic of a particular church: *the Latin rite of the Roman Catholic church.* [Lat *ritus*]

ritual *n* **1** the set order or words used in a religious ceremony. **2** a body of such rituals, esp. of a particular church. **3** the use of rituals in a religious ceremony. **4** an often repeated series of actions or procedure. — *adj* relating to or like rites or ritual. — *adv* **ritually**. [Lat *ritualis*]

ritualism *n* excessive belief in the importance of, or excessive practice of, ritual. — *n* **ritualist**. — *adj* **ritualistic**. — *adv* **ritualistically**.

ritzy *adj* **-ier**, **-iest** (*coll*) very smart and elegant. [*Ritz*, a name often used for luxury hotels]

rival *n* **1** a person or group of people that tries to compete with another for the same goal or in the same field. **2** a person or thing which equals another in quality, ability, etc.: *be without equal.* — *adj* being a rival; in competition for the same goal or in the same field. — *v* **-ll-** (*tr*) **1** to try to gain the same goal as (someone else); to be in competition with. **2** to try to equal or be better than. **3** to be able to be compared with as being equal or nearly so. [Lat *rivalis*, one who uses the same stream as another]

rivalry *n* **-ies** **1** the state of being a rival or rivals. **2** an act of rivalling.

riven *adj* having been violently torn or split apart. [Norse *rifa*]

river *n* **1** a large natural stream that usu. flows along a definite course. **2** an abundant or plentiful stream or flow. [OFr *riviere*, from Lat *ripa*, riverbank]

riverine *adj* of, on or near a river.

rivet *n* a metal bolt for fastening plates of metal together, with a headless end which can be beaten to form a second head to hold the bolt securely in place. — *v* **-t-** (*tr*) **1** to fasten with rivets. **2** to flatten or beat down (the head of a nail, etc.). **3** to fix securely. **4** to attract and hold firmly, to engross (e.g. a person's attention). **5** to cause (a person) to be fixed, esp. with horror or fear: *be riveted to the spot.* — *n* **riveter**. [OFr *river*, to attach]

riveting *adj* fascinating; enthralling.

riviera *n* a coastal area with a warm climate, esp. the SE coast of France and NW coast of Italy. [Ital, coast]

rivulet *n* a small stream or river. [Lat *rivulus*]

RM *abbrev* **1** Royal Mail. **2** Royal Marines. **3** Resident Magistrate.

rm *abbrev* room.

RN *abbrev* Royal Navy.

Rn *symbol* (*chem*) radon.

RNA *abbrev* ribonucleic acid.

RNLI *abbrev* Royal National Lifeboat Institution.

roach[1] *n* a silvery freshwater fish of the carp family. [OFr *roche*]

roach[2] *n* (esp. *NAm*) **1** a cockroach. **2** (*slang*) the butt of a marijuana cigarette. [Abbrev. of **cockroach**]

road *n* **1** an open, usu. specially surfaced or paved way, for people, vehicles or animals to travel on from one place to another. **2** (**to**, **for**) a route or way: *the road to ruin.* **3** (usu. in *pl*) a relatively sheltered area of water near the shore where ships may be anchored. — **get out of (someone's) road** (*coll*, esp. *Scot*) to get out of (someone's) way. — **one for the road** a final, usu. alcoholic, drink before leaving. — **on the road** travelling from place to place, esp. as a commercial traveller or tramp. [OE *rad*]

roadbed *n* **1** the foundation of a railway track on which the sleepers are laid. **2** the material laid down to form a road, and which forms a foundation for the road surface.

roadblock *n* a barrier put across a road (e.g. by the police or army) to stop and check vehicles and drivers.

road-hog *n* (*coll*) an aggressive and selfish driver, esp. one who tries to intimidate other drivers.

roadholding *n* the extent to which a vehicle remains stable when turning corners at high speed, in wet conditions, etc.

roadhouse *n* a public house or inn on the side of a major road.

roadie *n* (*coll*) a person who helps move the instruments and equipment which belong to esp. a rock or pop group.

road metal *n* broken stone or rock used for building or mending roads.

roadside *n* a strip of ground or land beside or along a road.

roadstead same as **road** (sense **3**).

roadster *n* **1** an open sports car for two people. **2** a strong bicycle. **3** a horse for riding or pulling carriages on roads.

roadway *n* the part of a road or street used by cars.

roadwork *n* **1** (in *pl*) the building or repairing of a road. **2** training, e.g. for marathons, boxing matches, etc. in the form of long runs on roads.

roadworthy *adj* in a suitable condition and safe to be used on the road. — *n* **roadworthiness**.

roam *v* (*tr* & *intr*; **about**, **over**) to ramble or wander about (over). — *n* the act of roaming; a ramble. — *n* **roamer**. [MidE *romen*]

roan *adj* (usu. of horses or cattle) having a reddish-brown or bay coat thickly flecked with grey or white hairs. — *n* an animal, esp. a horse, with a coat of this type. [OSpan *roano*]

roar *v* **1** (*intr*) to give a loud growling cry. **2** (*intr*) to laugh loudly, deeply and wildly. **3** (*intr*) to make a deep, loud, reverberating sound, as of cannons, busy traffic, wind and waves in a storm, or a fiercely burning fire. **4** (*tr*) to say (something) with a deep, loud cry, esp. as in anger. **5** (*intr*; **about**, **away**, **past**, etc.) to travel on or in a vehicle at high speed and with a roaring engine. **6** (*tr* with **on**) to shout encouragement to. **7** (*intr*) (of a horse) to breathe with a loud noise as a sign of disease. — *n* **1** a loud, deep, prolonged cry, as of lions, a cheering crowd, a person in pain or anger, etc. **2** a loud, deep, prolonged sound, as of cannons, busy traffic, an engine made to roar, the wind or waves in a storm, or a fiercely burning fire. — *adj* **roaring**. — *adv* **roaringly**. — **do a roaring trade** to do very brisk and profitable business. [OE *rarian*]

roaring drunk (*coll*) very drunk.

roaring forties see **forty**.

roast *v* **1** (*tr* & *intr*) to cook (meat or other food) by exposure to dry heat, esp. in an oven. **2** (*tr*) to dry and make brown (coffee beans, nuts, etc.) by exposure to dry heat. **3** (*intr*) (of meat, coffee beans, nuts, etc.) to be cooked or dried and made brown by being exposed to dry heat. **4** (*tr* & *intr*; *coll*) to (cause to) be or become extremely or excessively hot. **5** (*tr*; *coll*) to criticise severely. — *n* **1** a piece of meat which has been roasted or is suitable for roasting. **2** (*NAm*) a party in the open air at which food is roasted and eaten. — *adj* roasted: *roast potatoes*. [OFr *rostir*]

roaster *n* **1** an oven or dish for roasting food in. **2** a vegetable, fowl, etc. suitable for roasting.

roasting (coll) *adj* very hot. — *n* a dose of severe criticism.

rob *v* **-*bb*-** **(of)** **1** (*tr*) to steal something from (a person or place), esp. by force or threats. **2** (*tr*) to deprive (someone) of something expected as a right or due. **3** (*intr*) to commit robbery. — *n* **robber**. [OFr *robber*]

robbery *n* **-*ies*** the act of robbing, esp. theft with threats, force or violence.

robe *n* **1** (often in *pl*) a long, loose, flowing garment, esp. one worn for special cermonies by peers, judges, mayors, academics, etc. **2** (esp. *NAm*) a dressing-gown or bathrobe. — *v* (*tr* & *intr*) to clothe (oneself or someone) in a robe or robes. [OFr, booty]

robin *n* **1** (also **robin redbreast**) a small brown European thrush with a red breast. **2** a N American thrush with an orange-red breast, larger than the European robin. [A diminutive of *Robert*]

robot *n* **1** (esp. in science fiction stories, etc.) a machine which looks and functions like a human. **2** an automatic machine that can be programmed to perform specific tasks. **3** a person who works efficiently but who lacks human warmth or sensitivity. — *adj* **robotic**. [Czech *robota*, work]

robotics *n* (*sing*) **1** the science dealing with the design, construction and use of robots. **2** a form of dancing in which dancers imitate the stiff, jerky and sharp movements of robots.

robust *adj* **1** strong and healthy; with a strong constitution. **2** strongly built or constructed. **3** (of exercise, etc.) requiring strength and energy. **4** rough, earthy and slightly rude. **5** (of wine) with a full, rich quality. — *adv* **robustly**. — *n* **robustness**. [Lat *robustus*, from *robur*, oak, strength]

roc *n* an enormous bird in Arabian legends, strong enough to carry off an elephant. [Persian *rukh*]

rock[1] *n* **1** the hard mineral matter which forms part of the earth's crust. **2** a mass of this mineral matter forming a cliff, peak, reef, etc. **3** a large stone or boulder. **4** (*NAm*) a stone of any size. **5** someone or something which provides a firm foundation or support and can be depended upon. **6** (usu. in *pl*) a cause or source of difficulty, danger or disaster. **7** (*Br*) a hard sweet usu. made in the form of long, cylindrical sticks, which is brightly coloured and flavoured with peppermint, etc. **8** (*slang*) a precious stone, esp. a diamond. — **on the rocks** (*coll*) **1** (of a marriage) in a state where the husband and wife wish to separate or be divorced. **2** (of an alcoholic drink) served with ice cubes. **3** (of a business firm) in a state of great financial difficulty. [OFr *rocque*]

rock bottom *n* the lowest level possible. — *adj* **rock-bottom** (of prices, etc.) having reached the lowest they will ever be.

rock cake *n* a small round cake with a rough surface, made with fruit and spices.

rock crystal *n* a transparent colourless quartz.

rockery *n* **-*ies*** a garden made with both rocks and earth, and where rock plants are grown.

rock garden *n* a rockery, or a garden containing rockeries.

rock plant *n* any small alpine plant which grows among rocks and needs very little soil.

rock salmon *n* the dogfish or other fish, esp. when sold as food.

rock salt *n* common salt occurring as a mass of solid mineral.

rocky *adj* **-*ier***, **-*iest*** **1** full of rocks; made of or like rock. **2** full of problems and obstacles. — *n* **rockiness**.

rock[2] *v* **1** (*tr* & *intr*) to (cause to) sway gently backwards and forwards or from side to side: *rock the baby to sleep*. **2** (*tr* & *intr*) to (cause to) move or shake violently. **3** (*tr*) to disturb, upset or shock. **4** (*intr*) to dance to or play rock music. — *n* **1** a rocking movement. **2** (also **rock music**) a form of popular music with a very strong beat, usu. played on electronic instruments and derived from rock and roll. **3** rock and roll. — *adj* of rock music. [OE *roccian*]

rockabilly *n* a style of music which combines elements from both rock and roll and hillbilly.

rock and roll or **rock 'n' roll** *n* a form of popular music with a lively jive beat and simple melodies. — *v* (*intr*) to dance to or play rock and roll music.

rocker *n* **1** one of usu. two curved supports on which a chair, cradle, etc. rocks. **2** something that rocks on such supports, esp. a rocking chair. **3** a person or thing that rocks. **4** a device which is operated with a movement from side to side, backwards and forwards or up and down, esp. a switch between the 'on' and 'off' positions. **5** (*Br*; *cap*) (in the 1960s) a member of a sometimes violent teenage gang, typically wearing leather jackets and riding motorcycles. ◇ See also **mod**. **6** an object with a part which is curved like a rocker, esp. a skate with a curved blade. — **off one's rocker** (*coll*) mad; crazy.

rocking chair *n* a chair which rocks backwards and forwards on two curved supports.

rocking horse *n* a toy horse mounted on two curved supports on which a child can sit and rock backwards and forwards.

rocky *adj* **-ier**, **-iest** shaky; unsteady. — *adv* **rockily**. — *n* **rockiness**.

rocket *n* **1** a self-propelling, cylindrical projectile which is driven forwards and upwards by the gas it expels from burning fuel, e.g. one forming the basis of a jet engine. **2** such a device used as a firework or distress signal. **3** anything which is propelled by such a device, e.g. a bomb, missile or spacecraft. **4** (esp. *Br*; *coll*) a severe reprimand. — *v* **-t- 1** (*intr*) to move (esp. upwards) extremely quickly, as if with the speed of a rocket. **2** (*tr*) to attack with rockets. [Ital *rochetta*]

rococo *n* **1** an 18th-century style of architecture, decoration and furniture-making, characterised by elaborate ornamental details and asymmetrical patterns. **2** the corresponding style of music, characterised by a decline in the use of counterpoint and an extreme use of ornamentation. — *adj* **1** of or in this style. **2** unnecessarily florid and elaborate. [Fr]

rod *n* **1** a long slender stick or bar of wood, metal, etc. **2** a stick or bundle of twigs used to beat people as a punishment. **3** a stick, wand or sceptre carried as a symbol of office or authority. **4** a fishing-rod. **5** a unit of length equivalent to 5½ yards (*c.* 5 m). **6** a rod-shaped light-sensitive receptor in the retina in the eye. **7** (*vulg slang*) a penis. **8** (*US slang*) a pistol. [OE *rodd*]

rode. See **ride**.

rodent *n* any of the group of relatively small mammals with strong incisors for gnawing, including mice, rats, squirrels and beavers. [Lat *rodere*, to gnaw]

rodeo *n* **-os** a show or contest of cowboy skills, including riding, lassoing and animal-handling. [Span, from *rodear*, to go round]

rodomontade *n* **1** boastful or bragging words or behaviour. **2** a boastful or bragging speech. — *v* (*intr*) to talk boastfully; to brag. [Ital *Rodomonte*, the boastful king of Algiers in Ariosto's *Orlando Furioso* (1516)]

roe[1] *n* **1** (also **hard roe**) an ovary of a female fish and the eggs contained in it. **2** (also **soft roe**) the testis of a male fish and the mature sperm contained in it. [MidE *rowe*]

roe[2] *n* (also **roe deer**) a small deer found in Europe and Asia. [OE *ra*]

roentgen. Same as **röntgen**.

Rogation Day *n* any of the three days before Ascension Day. [Lat *rogatio*, from *rogare*, to ask]

roger *interj* (in radio communications and signalling) message received and understood. — *v* **-r-** (*tr*; *vulg slang*) (of a man) to have sexual intercourse with. [The name *Roger*]

rogue *n* **1** a dishonest person. **2** a person, esp. a child, who is playfully mischievous. **3** someone or something, esp. a plant, which is not true to its type and is inferior. **4** a vicious wild animal which lives apart from or has been driven from its herd. — *adj* of or like a rogue. — *adj* **roguish**. — *adv* **roguishly**. — *n* **roguishness**. [A cant word]

roguery *n* **-ies** the behaviour or an action which is typical of a rogue.

rogues gallery *n* a police collection of photographs of known criminals, used to identify suspects.

roister *v* **-r-** (*intr*) to enjoy oneself noisily. — *n* **roisterer**. [OFr *rustre*, ruffian]

role or **rôle** *n* **1** an actor's part in a play, film, etc. **2** a part played in life, business, etc.; a person's function. [Fr]

role model *n* a person whose life and behaviour is taken as an example to follow by someone else.

roll *n* **1** anything flat (such as paper, fabric, etc.) which is rolled up to form a cylinder or tube. **2** a small portion of bread for one person, often with a specified filling. **3** a folded piece of pastry or cake with a specified filling: *a sausage roll*. **4** a rolled mass of something: *rolls of fat*. **5** an official list of names, e.g. of school pupils, members of a club or people eligible to vote. **6** an act of rolling. **7** a swaying or rolling movement, e.g. in walking or dancing, or of a ship. **8** a long, low, prolonged sound. **9** a series of quick beats on a drum. **10** a complete rotation around its longitudinal axis by an aircraft. **11** a roller or cylinder used to press, shape or apply something. — *v* **1** (*tr* & *intr*; **back**, **down**, etc.) to (cause to) move by turning over and over, as if on an axis, and often in a specified direction. **2**

(*tr & intr*) to (cause to) move on wheels, rollers, etc., or in a vehicle with wheels. **3** (*tr & intr*; **over**) (of a person or animal, etc. lying down) to turn with a rolling movement to face in another direction. **4** (*tr & intr*) to (cause to) move or flow gently and steadily. **5** (*intr*; **down**) to seem to move like or in waves: *a garden rolling down to the river*. **6** (*intr*; **by, on**) to follow steadily one after the other: *The weeks rolled by*. **7** (*intr*) (e.g. of a ship) to sway or rock gently from side to side. **8** (*intr*) to walk with a swaying movement. **9** (*intr & tr*) to begin to operate or work: *The cameras rolled.* **10** (*tr & intr*) to move or cause (one's eyes) to move in a circle, esp. in disbelief, despair or amazement. **11** (*tr & intr*) to form or cause to form a tube or cylinder by winding or being wound round and round. **12** (*tr & intr*; **up**) to wrap or be wrapped by rolling. **13** (*tr*; **out**) to spread out or make flat or flatter, esp. by pressing and smoothing with something heavy. **14** (*intr*) to make a series of long, low, rumbling sounds. **15** (*tr*) to pronounce (esp. an 'r' sound) with a trill. **16** (*intr*; **with**) to move in the same direction as something so as to reduce its strength or impact: *roll with the punches*. — **be rolling in** (*coll*) to have large amounts of (e.g. money). — *v* **roll in** (*intr*) to come or arrive in large quantities. — **roll on** *interj* may (a particular or specified time) come soon. — *v* **roll up 1** (*tr & intr*) to (cause to) form into a roll. **2** (*intr*; *coll*) to arrive. **3** (*intr*; usu. as an *imperative*) to come in large numbers. [OFr *rolle*]

roll-call *n* the calling out of names from a list at an assembly, meeting, etc. to check who is present.

rolled gold *n* metal covered with a thin coating of gold.

roller *n* **1** any of a number of cylindrical objects or machines used for flattening, crushing, spreading, printing, applying paint, etc. **2** a rod for rolling cloth, etc. round. **3** a small cylinder on which hair is rolled for curling. **4** a solid wheel or cylinder attached to heavy machinery, etc. which make it easier to move. **5** a long heavy sea wave.

rollercoaster *n* a raised railway with sharp curves and steep inclines, ridden on for pleasure and excitement, and usu. found at funfairs.

roller skate *n* a series of wheels attached to a framework which can be fitted over one's shoe, or a shoe with wheels attached to the sole. — *v* **roller-skate** (*intr*) to move, dance, etc. on roller skates. — *n* **roller-skater**. — *n* **roller-skating**.

roller towel *n* a usu. long towel with the ends sewn together, hung on a roller.

rolling *adj* **1** (of land, countryside, etc.) with low, gentle hills and valleys, and without steep slopes and crags. **2** (of a contract) subject to review at regular intervals.

rolling mill *n* a factory or machine for rolling metal ingots into sheets, bars, etc. between rollers.

rolling-pin *n* a wooden, pottery, etc. cylinder for flattening out pastry.

rolling stock *n* the engines, wagons, coaches, etc. used on a railway.

rolling stone *n* a person who leads a restless or unsettled life.

rollneck *adj* (of a garment) having a high neck which is turned down over itself.

roll-on *n* **1** a woman's light elastic corset. **2** a liquid deodorant or antiperspirant in a small container with a rotating ball at the top.

roll-on-roll-off *adj* (of a passenger ferry, etc.) with entrances at both the front and back of the ship, so that cars, etc. may be driven on through one entrance and off through the other.

roll-top desk *n* a desk with a flexible cover of slats that may be rolled down when the desk is not being used.

roll-up *n* (*Br coll*) a cigarette which one makes oneself by rolling paper round loose tobacco.

rollicking *adj* boisterous, noisy and carefree. [Perhaps **romp** + **frolic**]

rollmop *n* a fillet of herring rolled up usu. round a slice of onion, and pickled in spiced vinegar. [Ger *Rollmops*, from *rollen*, to roll + *Mops*, pug-dog]

roly-poly *adj* round and podgy. — *n* **-*polies*** a strip of suet pastry filled with jam and rolled up, then baked or steamed. [Prob. **roll**]

ROM *abbrev* (*comput*) read-only memory, a memory which holds data permanently and allows it to be read and used but not changed.

Roman *adj* **1** of or related to modern or ancient Rome and the Roman Empire, its history, culture or inhabitants. **2** of the Roman Catholic Church. **3** (no *cap*) (of printing type) written in ordinary upright letters (as opposed to italics). — *n* **1** an inhabitant of modern or ancient Rome. **2** a Roman Catholic. **3** (no *cap*) roman letters or type. [Lat *Romanus*, from *Roma*, Rome]

Roman alphabet *n* the alphabet developed by the ancient Romans for writing Latin, and now used for most writing in Western European languages including English.

Roman Catholic *adj* of the Christian church which recognises the Pope as its head. — *n* a member of this church. — *n* **Roman Catholicism**.

Roman law *n* the system of laws developed by the ancient Romans, which forms the basis for the laws used in many modern countries.

Roman nose *n* a nose with a high bridge.

Roman numeral *n* any of the figures used to represent numbers in the system developed by the ancient Romans, e.g. *I* (= 1), *V* (= 5), *X* (= 10), etc. ◇ See also **Arabic numerals**.

romance n **1** a love affair. **2** sentimentalised or idealised love, valued esp. for its beauty, purity and the mutual devotion of the lovers. **3** an atmosphere, the feelings or behaviour associated with romantic love. **4** a sentimental account, esp. in writing or on film, of a love affair. **5** such writing, films, etc. as a group or genre. **6** a fictitious story which deals with imaginary, adventurous and mysterious events, characters, places, etc. **7** a mediaeval verse narrative dealing with chivalry, highly idealised love and fantastic adventures. **8** an exaggeration or absurd account or lie. **9** (*cap*) the group of languages, including French, Spanish and Italian, which have developed from Latin. **10** a short, informal, ballad-like piece of music. — *adj* (*cap*) of or relating to the languages which have developed from Latin, such as French, Spanish and Italian. — *v* **1** (*tr*) to try to win the love of. **2** (*intr*) to talk or write extravagantly, romantically or fantastically. **3** (*intr*) to lie. [OFr *romanz*]

Romanesque *adj* & *n* (of or in) the style of architecture found in W and S Europe from the 9th to the 12th centuries, characterised by round arches and vaults. [Fr]

Romanian *n* **1** the official language of Romania. **2** an inhabitant of or person from Romania. — *adj* of or relating to the Romanian people, their country, language, history or culture.

romantic *adj* **1** of, like, inclined towards or feeling sentimental and idealised love. **2** dealing with or suggesting adventure, mystery and sentimentalised love: *romantic fiction*. **3** highly impractical or imaginative, and often also foolish. **4** (often *cap*) (of literature, art, music, etc.) of, relating to or in the style of romanticism. — *n* **1** a person with a romantic, idealised and sentimental idea of love. **2** a person who writes, paints, etc. in the style of romanticism. — *adv* **romantically**. [OFr *romanz*, romance]

romanticise or **-ize** *v* **1** (*tr*) to make seem romantic. **2** (*tr* & *intr*) to describe or think of in a romantic, idealised, unrealistic and sometimes misleading way. **3** (*intr*) to hold romantic ideas or act in a romantic way.

romanticism *n* (often *cap*) the late 18th- and early 19th-century movement in art, literature and music, characterised by an emphasis on feelings and emotions, often using imagery taken from nature, and creating forms which are relatively free from rules and set orders. — *n* **romanticist**.

Romany *n* **-ies** **1** a gipsy. **2** the language spoken by gipsies, belonging to the Indic branch of Indo-European. — *adj* of the Romanies, their language and culture. [Romany *rom*, man]

Romeo *n* **-os** an ardent young male lover. [After the hero of Shakespeare's play *Romeo and Juliet*]

Romish *adj* (*derog*) Roman Catholic. [Rome]

romp *v* (*intr*) to play in a lively, boisterous way. **2** (**in, through**, etc.) to succeed (in a race, competition, task, etc.) quickly and easily. — *n* **1** an act of romping; boisterous play. **2** a swift pace. **3** a young person, esp. a girl, who romps. [Perhaps a variant of **ramp**]

rompers *n* (*pl*) (also **romper suit**) a suit for a baby, with short-legged trousers and either a short-sleeved top or a bib top.

rondeau *n* **-eaux** a poem of ten or thirteen lines with only two rhymes, and with the first line used as a refrain after the eighth and thirteenth lines. [OFr *rondel*, from *rond*, round]

rondo *n* **-os** a piece of music, esp. one forming the last movement of a sonata or a concerto, with a principal theme which recurs or is repeated as a refrain. [Ital]

röntgen *n* a unit used for measuring the dose of X-rays. [Wilhelm Conrad *Röntgen* (1845–1923), the German physicist who discovered X-rays]

rood *n* **1** a cross or crucifix, esp. a large one at the entrance to a church. **2** (*literary*) the cross on which Christ was crucified. [OE *rod*]

rood screen *n* an ornamental wooden or stone screen separating the choir from the nave.

roof *n* **roofs** **1** the top, usu. rigid, covering of a building or vehicle. **2** the top inner surface of an oven, refrigerator, the mouth, etc. **3** a dwelling or home: *two families sharing a single roof*. **4** a high, or the highest, level: *the roof of the world*. — *v* (*tr*) to cover with a roof. **2** to serve as a roof or shelter for. — **go through** or **hit the roof** (*coll*) to become very angry. — **raise the roof** (*coll*) to be very noisy. [OE *hrof*]

roof garden *n* a garden on a building's flat roof.

roofing *n* materials for building a roof.

roof rack *n* a frame for attaching to the roof of a car to carry luggage.

rook[1] *n* a large, crow-like bird which nests in colonies in the tops of trees, found in Europe and Asia. — *v* (*tr*; *coll*) to cheat or defraud, esp. at cards. [OE *hroc*]

rookery *n* **-ies** **1** a colony of rooks. **2** a colony of penguins, other sea birds, or seals.

rook[2] (*chess*). See **castle**. [Persian *rukh*]

rookie *n* (*coll*) a new or raw recruit. [A corruption of **recruit**]

room *n* **1** a part of a building which is separated from the rest of the building by having a ceiling, floor and walls. **2** a space or area which is occupied by or is available to someone or something. **3** all of the people present in a room: *the room suddenly became silent*. **4** (**for**) opportunity, scope or possibility: *room for improvement*. **5** (in *pl*) rented lodgings. — *v* (*intr*; esp. *US*) to lodge or share a room with. — *n* **roomful**, **-fuls**. [OE *rum*]

roommate *n* a person who shares a room with another person, esp. in a students' hostel.

room service *n* the serving of food, drinks, etc. to a hotel guest in his or her bedroom or suite.

roomy *adj* **-ier**, **-iest** having plenty of room; spacious. — *n* **roominess**.

roost *n* **1** a branch, perch, etc. on which birds, esp. domestic fowl, rest at night. **2** a group of birds, esp. domestic fowl, resting together on the same branch or perch. **3** a place offering temporary sleeping accommodation. — *v* (*intr*) (esp. of birds) to settle on a roost, esp. for sleep. — **come home to roost** (of a scheme, etc.) to have unpleasant consequences for or a bad effect on the originator. — **rule the roost** to be dominant. [OE *hrost*]

rooster *n* (esp. *NAm*) a farmyard cock.

root[1] *n* **1** the usu. underground part of a plant that secures it in the ground and which absorbs water and nourishment from the soil. **2** any underground and edible part of a plant, such as a bulb or tuber. **3** the part by which anything is attached to or embedded in something larger. **4** the part of a tooth, hair, nail, etc. which attaches it to the body. **5** the basic cause, source or origin of something. **6** (in *pl*) one's ancestry or family origins. **7** (in *pl*) one's feeling of belonging to a community or in a place. **8** the basic element in a word which remains after all the affixes have been removed, and which may form the basis of a number of related words: *'Love' is the root of 'lovable', 'loveliness' and 'lover'.* ◇ See also **stem**. **9** (*math*) a factor of a quantity that when taken a given number of times produces that quantity: *2 is the cube root of 8* (i.e. $2 \times 2 \times 2 = 8$). **10** (*math*) the value of an unknown quantity for which an equation is true. **11** (*mus*) the fundamental note on which a chord is built. — *v* **1** (*intr*) to grow roots; to become firmly established. **2** (*tr*; **up**) to dig up by the roots. **3** (*tr*) to fix with or as if with roots. **4** (*tr*) to provide with roots. — *adj* **rootless**. — *v* **root out** (*tr*) to remove or destroy completely. — **take root 1** to grow roots. **2** to become firmly established. [OE *rot*]

root beer *n* (*US*) a fizzy drink made from the roots of certain plants, e.g. dandelions, and flavoured with herbs.

root crop *n* a crop grown for its edible roots, e.g. carrots and turnips.

rooted *adj* fixed by or as if by roots; firmly established.

roots music *n* popular music of a style showing the influence of folk music and having a certain ethnic identity.

rootstock *n* a rhizome.

root[2] *v* **1** (*intr*) (esp. of pigs) to dig up the ground with the snout in search of food. **2** (*intr*; **around**, **about**) to poke about in looking for something; to rummage. **3** (*tr*; **up**, **out**) to find, fetch, move, etc. usu. by poking about, rummaging, etc.: *root him out of bed.* [OE *wrotan*, from *wrot*, snout]

root[3] *v* (*intr*; **for**; esp. *NAm coll*) to shout loud support or encouragement to or for.

rope *n* **1** (a length of) strong thick cord made by twisting fibres together. **2** a number of objects, esp. pearls or onions, strung together. **3** a hangman's noose. **4** a long, thin, sticky strand. — *v* **1** (*tr*) to tie, fasten or bind with a rope. **2** (*tr*; **off**) to enclose, separate or divide with a rope. **3** (*tr* & *intr*; **up**) to attach (climbers) or be attached to a rope for safety. **4** (*tr*; esp. *NAm*) to catch with a rope; to lasso. — **know the ropes** to have a thorough knowledge and experience of what needs to be done in a particular circumstance or for a particular job. — *v* **rope in** (*tr*) to persuade (someone) to take part. [OE *rap*]

rope walk *n* a long narrow shed or covered alley where ropes are made.

ropy or **ropey** *adj* **-ier**, **-iest 1** (*coll*) poor in quality. **2** forming sticky strands.

Roquefort *n* a strong, soft, blue-veined cheese made from ewes' milk. [The village in S France where it was orig. made]

ro-ro *adj* (of a passenger ferry, etc.) roll-on-roll-off. [Abbrev.]

Rorschach test *n* (*psychol*) a test designed to show intelligence, type of personality, mental state, etc. in which the subject is asked to describe the pictures formed by a number of inkblots. [Hermann *Rorschach* (1884–1922), Swiss psychiatrist]

rosaceous *adj* (*bot*) of or belonging to the plant family which includes the rose, apple, strawberry, cherry and almond. [Lat *rosa*, rose]

rosary *n* **-ies** (esp. *RC*) **1** a string of beads used to count prayers as they are recited. **2** a series of prayers with a set form and order counted on a string of beads. [Lat *rosarium*, rose garden]

rose[1] *n* **1** any of a family of shrubs with prickly stems and often sweet-smelling flowers. **2** the ornamental, often sweet-smelling, flower from any such shrub. **3** this flower as the national emblem of England. **4** any similar flowering plant, such as the Christmas rose. **5** a darkish pink colour. **6** (in *pl*) a light pink, glowing complexion: *put the roses back in one's cheeks*. **7** a nozzle with holes, usu. attached to the end of a hose, watering can, shower, etc. to make the water come out in a spray. **8** a circular fitting in a ceiling through which an electric light flex hangs. **9** a rose-like design, e.g. round the sound hole of a guitar or lute, or on a compass card. **10** a cut diamond with a flat base and many small triangular facets forming a rounded shape which rises to a point. **11** a rose window. **12** a rosette. — *adj* of or like roses, esp. in colour or scent. [OE, from Lat *rosa*]

roseate *adj* **1** like a rose, esp. in colour. **2** unrealistically hopeful or cheerful.

rosebay willowherb *n* a common wild plant that has spikes of dark pink flowers and produces many fluffy seeds.

rose-coloured *adj* pink. — **look at** or **see (something) through rose-coloured glasses** to have an unrealistically hopeful or cheerful view of (something).

rosehip *n* the red, berry-like fruit of the rose.

rose water *n* water distilled from rose petals.

rose window *n* a circular window with ornamental tracery coming out in a symmetrical pattern from the centre.

rosewood *n* a valuable dark red or purplish wood used in making furniture of the highest quality.

rosy *adj* **-ier**, **-iest** **1** rose-coloured; pink. **2** hopeful; optimistic; cheerful. — *adv* **rosily**. — *n* **rosiness**.

rose[2]. See **rise**.

rosé *n* a light pink wine made by removing the skins of red grapes after fermentation has begun. [Fr, pink]

rosemary *n* an evergreen fragrant shrub with stiff needle-like leaves used in cookery and perfumery. [Lat *rosmarinus*, from *ros*, dew + *marinus*, sea]

rosette *n* a badge or decoration made in coloured ribbon to resemble the shape and form of a rose, often awarded as a prize or worn as a sign of affiliation. [Fr, little rose]

Rosh Hashanah *n* the Jewish festival of New Year. [Hebr, head of the year]

rosin *n* a clear hard resin produced by distilling turpentine prepared from dead pine wood, rubbed on the bows of stringed musical instruments. — *v* **-n-** (*tr*) to rub rosin on (a violin bow, etc.) [A variant of **resin**]

roster *n* a list of people showing the order in which they are to do various duties, go on leave, etc. — *v* **-r-** (*tr*) to put (a name) on a roster. [Dut *rooster*, list]

rostrum *n* **-rums** or **-ra** **1** a platform on which a public speaker stands. **2** a raised platform, e.g. that on which a conductor stands before the orchestra, or for carrying a camera. **3** (*bot*) a hard beak-like part on an insect. — *adj* **rostral**. [Lat, beak]

rosy. See **rose**[1].

rot *v* **-tt-** **1** (*tr* & *intr*; **down**) to (cause to) decay. **2** (*intr*) to become corrupt. **3** (*intr*) to become physically weak. — *n* **1** decay; something which has rotted or decomposed. **2** (*coll*) nonsense; rubbish. **3** (usu. *in cmpds*) any of several plant or animal diseases which cause tissue to decay, such as *foot-rot* in sheep. ◇ See also **rotten**. [OE *rotian*]

rotgut *n* (*slang*) cheap, poor-quality alcoholic drink, esp. spirits.

rotter *n* (*old slang*) a worthless, despicable or depraved person.

rota *n* (esp. *Br*) a list of duties that are to be done and the names and order of the people who are to take turns in doing them. [Lat, wheel]

rotary *adj* turning on an axis like a wheel. — *n* **-ies** **1** a rotary machine. **2** (*NAm*) a traffic roundabout. [Lat *rota*, wheel]

Rotary Club *n* a local branch of **Rotary International**, an international charitable organisation whose members are mostly businessmen.

Rotarian *n* a member of this organisation.

rotate *v* **1** (*tr* & *intr*) to (cause to) turn on an axis like a wheel. **2** (*tr*) to arrange in an ordered sequence. **3** (*intr*) to take turns according to an ordered sequence. [Lat *rota*, wheel]

rotation *n* **1** an act of rotating or state of being rotated. **2** one complete turn around an axis. **3** a regular and recurring sequence. **4** (also **crop rotation**) the growing of different crops on a field, usu. in an ordered sequence, to help keep the land fertile.

rote *n* the mechanical use of the memory without necessarily understanding what is memorised. — **by rote** by memory; by heart. [MidE]

rotisserie *n* **1** a cooking apparatus with a spit on which meat, poultry, etc. may be cooked by direct heat. **2** a shop or restaurant which sells or serves meat cooked in this way. [Fr *rôtisserie*, from *rôtir*, to roast]

rotor *n* **1** a rotating part of a machine, esp. in an internal combustion engine. **2** a system of blades projecting from a cylinder which rotate at high speed to provide the force to lift and propel a helicopter.

Rotovator® or **Rotavator**® *n* a machine with a rotating blade for breaking up the soil. [**rotary cultivator**]

rotten *adj* **1** having gone bad, decayed, rotted or fallen to pieces. **2** morally corrupt. **3** (*coll*) miserably unwell. **4** (*coll*) unsatisfactory: *a rotten plan*. **5** (*coll*) unpleasant; disagreeable: *rotten weather*. — *n* **rottenness**. [Norse *rotinn*]

rotten borough *n* (*hist*) (before 1832) a borough that could elect an MP even though it had few or no inhabitants.

rotter. See **rot**.

Rottweiler *n* a large powerfully built black and tan dog, orig. from Germany. [*Rottweil* in SW Germany]

rotund *adj* **1** round. **2** plump. **3** impressive or grandiloquent. — *n* **rotundity** or **rotundness**. — *adv* **rotundly**. [Lat *rotundus*, from *rota*, wheel]

rotunda *n* a round, usu. domed, building or hall. [Ital *rotonda* (*camera*), round (room)]

rouble or **ruble** *n* the standard unit of currency in the countries of the former Soviet Union, equal to 100 kopecks. [Russ *rubl*]

roué *n* (*old*) a disreputable man; a rake. [Fr, a man deserving to be broken on a wheel (= a former method of torture or capital punishment in which a person was stretched out on a wheel and then his or her arms and legs were broken with an iron bar)]

rouge *n* a pink or red powder or cream used to colour the cheeks. — *v* **1** (*intr*) to use rouge. **2** (*tr*) to apply rouge to. [Fr, red]

rough *adj* **1** (of a surface) not smooth, even or regular. **2** (of ground) covered with stones, tall grass, bushes and/or scrub. **3** covered with shaggy or coarse hair. **4** harsh or grating: *a rough voice.* **5** (of a person's character, behaviour, etc.) noisy, coarse or violent. **6** stormy. **7** requiring hard work or considerable physical effort, or involving great difficulty, tension, etc.: *a rough day at work.* **8** (**on**) unpleasant and hard to bear: *a decision which is rough on the employees.* **9** (of a guess, calculation, etc.) approximate. **10** not polished or refined: *a rough draft.* **11** (*coll*) slightly unwell and tired, esp. because of heavy drinking or lack of sleep. — *n* **1** rough ground, esp. the uncut grass at the side of a golf fairway. **2** the unpleasant or disagreeable side of something: *take the rough with the smooth.* **3** a rough or crude state. **4** a crude preliminary sketch. **5** a hooligan, thug or bully. — *adv* **roughly.** — *n* **roughness.** — **rough it** (*coll*) to live primitively, without the usual comforts of life. — *v* **rough out** (*tr*) to do a preliminary sketch of or give a preliminary explanation of. — *v* **rough up** (*tr*; *coll*) to beat up. — **sleep rough** to sleep out-of-doors without proper shelter. [OE *ruh*]

roughage *n* coarse, bulky material, e.g. fibre, in food, which helps digestion.

rough-and-ready *adj* **1** quickly prepared and not polished or perfect but good enough. **2** (of people) friendly and pleasant but not polite or refined.

rough-and-tumble *n* (an instance of) disorderly but usu. friendly fighting or scuffling.

roughcast *n* a mixture of plaster and small stones used to cover outside walls. — *v* ***roughcast*** (*tr*) to cover with roughcast.

rough diamond *n* **1** an uncut and unpolished diamond. **2** a good-natured person with rough, unrefined manners.

roughen *v* **-n-** (*tr* & *intr*) to make or become rough.

rough-hew *v* (*tr*) to shape crudely and without refining, polishing or perfecting in any way.

rough-hewn *adj* crude, unpolished, unrefined.

roughhouse *n* (*coll*) a disturbance or brawl.

roughneck *n* **1** a worker on an oil rig. **2** a rough and rowdy person.

roughshod *adj* (of a horse) having horseshoes with projecting nails which prevent the horse from slipping in wet weather. — **ride roughshod over** to treat (someone) arrogantly and without regard for his or her feelings.

roulette *n* **1** a gambling game in which a ball is dropped into a spinning wheel divided up into many small, numbered compartments coloured black and red alternately, with the players betting on which compartment the ball will come to rest in. **2** a small tool with a toothed wheel, used for making a line of dots and perforating paper. [Fr]

round *adj* **1** shaped like, or approximately, a circle or a ball. **2** not angular; curved and plump. **3** moving in or forming a circle. **4** (of numbers) complete and exact: *a round dozen.* **5** (of a number) without a fraction. **6** (of a number) approximate, without taking minor amounts into account. **7** (of a sum of money) considerable; substantial. **8** plain-spoken; candid. — *adv* **1** in or to the opposite direction, position or opinion: *win someone round.* **2** in a circular direction or with a circular or revolving movement. **3** in, by or along a circuitous or indirect route. **4** on all sides so as to surround: *gather round.* **5** from one person to another: *pass it round.* **6** in rotation, so as to return to the starting point: *wait until spring comes round.* **7** from place to place: *drive round for a while.* **8** in circumference: *measures six feet round.* **9** to a particular place, esp. a person's home: *come round for supper.* — *prep* **1** on all sides of so as to surround or enclose. **2** so as to move or revolve around a centre or axis and return to the starting point: *run round the field.* **3** (*coll*) having as a central point or basis: *a film based round her experiences.* **4** from place to place in. **5** in all or various directions from; close to (a place). **6** so as to pass, or having passed, in a curved course: *drive round the corner.* — *n* **1** something round (and often flat) in shape. **2** a complete revolution round a circuit or path. **3** a single complete slice of bread. **4** a sandwich, or set of sandwiches, made from two complete slices of bread. **5** the playing of all 18 holes on a golf course in a single session. **6** one of a recurring series of events, actions, etc.: *a round of talks.* **7** a series of regular activities: *one's daily round.* **8** a regular route followed, esp. for the delivery of something: *a milk round.* **9** (usu. in *pl*) a doctor's visits to his patients, either in hospital or (of a general practitioner) in their own homes. **10** a stage in a competition. **11** a single period of play, competition, etc. in a group of several, e.g. in boxing. **12** a burst of applause or cheering. **13** a single bullet or charge of ammunition. **14** a set of drinks bought at the same time for all the members of a group. **15** an unaccompanied song in which different people all sing the same part continuously but start (and therefore end) at different times. — *v* **1** (*tr* & *intr*) to make or become round. **2** (*tr*) to go round: *The car rounded the corner.* — *n* **roundness.** — **go the rounds** (of news, information, etc.) to be passed round from person to person. — **in the round 1** with all details shown or considered. **2** (*theatre*) with the audience seated on at least three, and often four, sides of the stage. — **round about 1** on all sides; in a ring surrounding. **2** approximately. — **round the clock** (lasting) all day and all night; for twenty-four hours (*adj* **round-the-clock**). — *v* **round down** (*tr*) to lower (a number) so that it can be expressed as a round number: *round 15·47 down to 15*. — *v* **round off** (*tr*) **1** to make (corners, angles, etc.) smooth. **2** to complete successfully and pleasantly: *round off the meal with a glass of old brandy*. — *v* **round on** (*tr*) to turn on in anger and attack, usu. in speech. — *v* **round up** (*tr*) **1** to raise (a number) so that it can be expressed as a round number: *round 15·89 up to 16*. **2** to collect (people, or things such as livestock or facts) together (*n* **round-up**). [Lat *rotundus*]

roundabout *n* **1** (*Br*) a revolving platform, usu. with seats, on which one can ride for pleasure; a merry-go-round. **2** (*Br*) a circular road junction, usu. with an island in the middle, where several roads meet, and round which traffic must travel in the same direction. — *adj* not direct; circuitous.

rounded *adj* curved.

rounders *n* a team game similar to baseball, in which each team sends players in to bat in turn while the other team bowls and fields, with the batter scoring a run if he or she successfully runs round a square course in one go.

Roundhead *n* (*hist*) a supporter of the parliamentary party against Charles I in the English Civil War (1642–9).

roundly *adv* plainly and often rudely; bluntly; thoroughly.

round robin *n* **1** a petition or protest, esp. one in which the names are written in a circle to conceal the ringleader. **2** a tournament in which each competitor plays each of the others in turn.

round-shouldered *adj* with stooping shoulders and a back which bends forward slightly at the top.

round table *n* **1** (*cap*) the table at which King Arthur and his knights sat, round in shape so that no individual knight should have precedence. **2** a meeting or conference at which the participants meet on equal terms.

round trip *n* a trip to a place and back again, usu. by a different route.

round-up see **round up** (sense **2**) above.

roundel *n* **1** a small circular window or design. **2** a coloured round identification disc on the wing of a military aircraft. [OFr *rondel*, little circle]

roundelay *n* a simple song with a refrain. [OFr *rondelet*, from *rondel*, little circle]

rouse *v* (*tr* & *intr*) **1** to arouse (someone or oneself) or become aroused from sleep, listlessness or lethargy. **2** to excite or provoke, or be excited or provoked.

rousing *adj* stirring; exciting.

roustabout *n* an unskilled labourer, e.g. on an oil-rig or a farm.

rout[1] *v* (*tr*) to defeat completely and cause to flee in confusion. — *n* **1** a complete and overwhelming defeat. **2** a confused and disorderly retreat. **3** (*legal*) a group of three or more people gathered together to commit a crime or some unlawful act. **4** a disorderly and noisy group of people. [OFr *route*, from Lat *rumpere*, to break]

rout[2] *v* **1** (*tr* & *intr*) to dig up, esp. with the snout. **2** (*tr*; **out**, **up**) to find, fetch, etc. by searching, poking about, etc. [A variant of **root**[2]]

route *n* **1** the way travelled on a regular journey. **2** a particular group of roads followed to get to a place. — *v* (*tr*) to arrange a route for; to send by a selected route. [Lat *rupta* (*via*) broken (road)]

route march *n* a long and tiring march, esp. one for soldiers in training.

routine *n* **1** a regular or fixed way of doing things. **2** a set series of movements in a dance, performance, etc. **3** a part of a computer program which performs a specific function. — *adj* unvarying; regular; ordinary; done as part of a routine. — *adv* **routinely**. **[route]**

roux *n* ***roux*** a cooked mixture of flour and fat, used to thicken sauces. [Fr (*beurre*) *roux*, brown (butter)]

rove *v* **1** (*tr* & *intr*) to wander or roam over aimlessly. **2** (*intr*) (of the eyes) to keep looking in different directions.

rover *n* a wanderer, esp. a wandering pirate or robber.

roving *adj* wandering; likely to ramble or stray. — **have a roving eye** to be very interested sexually or romantically in many successive members of the opposite sex.

row[1] *n* **1** a number of people or things, such as theatre seats, numbers, vegetables, etc. arranged in a line. **2** a street with a line of houses on one or both sides. — **a hard row to hoe** a difficult job or destiny. — **in a row** in an unbroken sequence; in succession. [OE *raw*]

row[2] *v* **1** (*tr* & *intr*) to move (a boat) through the water using oars. **2** (*tr*) to carry (people, goods, etc.) in a rowing boat. **3** (*intr*) to race in rowing boats for sport. **4** (*tr*) to compete in (a race) in a rowing boat. — *n* **1** an act of rowing a boat. **2** a trip in a rowing boat. — *n* **rower**. [OE *rowan*]

rowboat *n* (*NAm*) a rowing boat.

rowing boat *n* (*Br*) a small boat which is moved by oars.

row[3] *n* **1** a noisy quarrel. **2** a loud unpleasant noise or disturbance. **3** a severe reprimand. — *v* (*intr*; **with**) to quarrel noisily.

rowan *n* **1** (also **rowan tree** or **mountain ash**) a European tree with clusters of white flowers and bright red berries. **2** (also **rowan berry**) a small red berry from this tree. [Scandinavian]

rowdy *adj* **-ier**, **-iest** noisy and rough. — *n* (*coll*) a noisy, rough person. — *adv*

rowdily. — *n* **rowdiness**. [Perhaps from **row**[3]]
rowdyism *n* rowdy behaviour.
rowel *n* a small spiked wheel on a spur. [OFr *roel*, small wheel]
rowlock *n* a device for holding an oar in place and serving as a pivot for it to turn on. [A variant of *oarlock*, from OE *arloc*]
royal *adj* **1** of or suitable for a king or queen. **2** under the patronage or in the service of the king or queen: *Royal Geographical Society*. **3** belonging to the king or queen. **4** being a member of the king's or queen's family. **5** regal; magnificent. **6** larger and more splendid than usual. — *n* **1** (*coll*) a member of the royal family. **2** a sail immediately above the topgallant sail. **3** a stag with antlers of twelve or more points. **4** a size of paper, either 19 by 24 inches (of writing paper) or 20 by 25 inches (of printing paper). — *adv* **royally**. [OFr *roial*, from Lat *regalis*]
Royal Air Force *n* the British air force.
royal blue *n* a rich, bright, deep-coloured blue.
royal commission *n* in the UK, a group of people appointed by the Crown at the request of the Government to inquire into and report on some matter.
royalist *n* **1** a supporter of the monarchy. **2** (*hist*; *cap*) a supporter of Charles I during the English Civil war (1642–9). — *adj* of royalists. — *n* **royalism**.
royal jelly *n* a substance secreted by worker bees which is fed to all larvae when young, and to larvae destined to become queens throughout their lives.
Royal Marines *n* (*pl*; *Br*) a corps of soldiers who have received special training, esp. in amphibious techniques which may be used in war.
Royal Navy *n* the British navy.
royal prerogative *n* the rights of the monarch, in theory not restricted in any way, but in practice laid down by custom.
royalty *n* **-ies 1** the character, state, office or power of a king or queen. **2** members of the royal family, either individually or collectively. **3** a percentage of the profits from each copy of a book, piece of music, invention, etc. sold, performed or used, which is paid to the author, composer, inventor, etc. **4** a payment made by companies who mine minerals, oil or gas to the person who owns the land or owns the mineral rights to the land that the company is mining. **5** a right (esp. to minerals) granted by a king or queen to an individual or company.
royal warrant *n* an official authorisation to a tradesman to supply goods to a royal household.
rozzer *n* (*old Br slang*) a policeman.
RP *abbrev* Received Pronunciation.
RPI *abbrev* (*Br*) retail price index, a list of the prices of selected consumer goods which is compiled regularly to show how prices are changing and how the cost of living is rising.
rpm *abbrev* revolutions per minute.
RR *abbrev* Right Reverend.
RSA *abbrev* **1** (*Br*) Royal Scottish Academy, or Academician. **2** (*Br*) Royal Society of Arts. **3** Republic of South Africa.
RSC *abbrev* Royal Shakespeare Company.
RSM *abbrev* regimental sergeant-major.
RSPB *abbrev* Royal Society for the Protection of Birds.
RSPCA *abbrev* Royal Society for the Prevention of Cruelty to Animals.
RSVP *abbrev* for *répondez s'il vous plaît* (Fr), please reply.
Rt Hon *abbrev* Right Honourable.
Rt Rev *abbrev* Right Reverend.
Ru *symbol* (*chem*) ruthenium.
rub *v* **-bb- 1** (*tr*) to move one's hand, an object, etc. back and forwards over the surface of (something) with pressure and friction. **2** (*tr*; **along, against, on**) to move (one's hand, an object, etc.) backwards and forwards over a surface with pressure and friction. **3** (*intr*; **against, on**) to move backwards and forwards over a surface with pressure and friction. **4** (*tr*; **in, on**) to apply (ointment, lotion, polish, etc.). **5** (*tr*) to clean, polish, dry, smooth, etc. **6** (*tr* & *intr*; **away, off, out**) to remove or be removed by pressure and friction. **7** (*tr* & *intr*) to make (something) sore by pressure and friction. **8** (*tr* & *intr*) to fray by pressure and friction. — *n* **1** an act of rubbing. **2** an obstacle or difficulty. — *v* **rub along** (*intr*; *coll*) **1** to manage to get along, make progress, etc. without any particular difficulties. **2** (**with**) to be on more or less friendly terms. — *v* **rub down** (*tr*) **1** to rub (one's body, a horse, etc.) briskly from head to foot, e.g. to dry it. **2** to prepare (a surface) to receive new paint or varnish by rubbing the old paint or varnish off (*n* **rub-down**). — *v* **rub in** (*tr*) **1** to apply (ointment, etc.) by rubbing. **2** (*coll*) to insist on talking about or emphasising (something that the person one is talking to finds unpleasant or embarrassing, esp. a mistake). — *v* **rub off on** (*intr*) to have an effect on or be passed to someone else by close association: *Some of his bad habits have rubbed off on you*. — *v* **rub out** (*tr*) **1** to remove by rubbing, esp. with a rubber. **2** (esp. *US slang*) to murder. — *v* **rub up** (*tr*) **1** to polish. **2** to refresh one's memory or knowledge of. — **rub (up) the wrong way** to annoy or irritate (someone). [MidE *rubben*]
rubbing *n* an impression or copy made by placing paper over a raised surface and rubbing the paper with crayon, wax, chalk, etc.
rubber[1] *n* **1** a strong elastic substance obtained from the latex of various trees or plants or produced synthetically. **2** (esp. *Br*) a small piece of rubber or plastic used for rubbing out pencil or ink marks on

paper; an eraser. **3** (esp. *NAm slang*) a condom. **4** (usu. in *pl*; *NAm*) waterproof rubber overshoes; galoshes. **5** any person, device or machine part that rubs. — *adj* of or producing rubber. — *adj* **rubbery**. [**rub**]

rubber band see **elastic band**.

rubberise or **-ize** *v* (*tr*) to treat or coat with rubber.

rubberneck *n* (*NAm slang*) a person who stares or gapes inquisitively or stupidly, esp. a tourist on a guided tour. — *v* (*intr*) to behave in this way.

rubber plant *n* **1** a house plant with large, shiny, dark green leaves. **2** (also **rubber tree**) any of several tropical trees grown for their latex, a valuable source of rubber.

rubber stamp *n* **1** an instrument made of rubber with figures, letters, names, etc. on it, used to stamp a name, date, etc. on books or papers. **2** an automatic, unthinking or routine agreement or authorisation. **3** a person or group of people required to approve or authorise another person's or group's decisions and actions without having the power, courage, etc. to withhold this approval or authorisation.

rubber-stamp *v* (*tr*) to give automatic, unthinking or routine approval of or authorisation for.

rubber tree see **rubber plant**.

rubber[2] *n* (esp. in bridge or whist) a match, consisting of either three or five games.

rubbish *n* **1** waste material; things that have been or are to be thrown away. **2** worthless or useless material or objects. **3** nonsense. — *adj* **rubbishy**. [MidE *rubbes*]

rubble *n* **1** broken stones, bricks, plaster, etc. from ruined or demolished buildings, **2** small, rough stones used in building, esp. as a filling between walls. [MidE *rubel*]

rubella *n* German measles. [Lat *rubeus*, red]

Rubicon *n* a boundary which, once crossed, commits the person crossing it to an irrevocable course of action. — **cross the Rubicon** to take an irrevocable decision. [Lat *Rubico*, a stream in N Italy separating Italy and the province of Cisalpine Gaul where Caesar was serving; Caesar's crossing of the stream with his army in 49 BC was tantamount to a declaration of war on the Roman republic, and began a civil war]

rubicund *adj* (esp. of the face or complexion) red or rosy; ruddy. [Lat *rubicundus*]

rubidium *n* (*chem*) a naturally occurring soft, radioactive, silvery-white metallic element (symbol **Rb**), used in photoelectric cells. [Lat *rubidus*, red, so called because of the two red lines in its spectrum]

ruble. See **rouble**.

rubric *n* **1** a heading in a book or manuscript, esp. one written or underlined in red. **2** an authoritative rule, esp. one for the conduct of divine service added in red to the liturgy. [Lat *rubrica*, red ochre]

ruby *n* **-ies** **1** a corundum varying in colour from deep red to pink, prized as a gemstone and also used in lasers and watchmaking. **2** the rich, deep red colour characteristic of this stone. — *adj* of this colour. [Lat *rubinus* (*lapis*), red (stone)]

ruby wedding *n* a fortieth wedding anniversary.

RUC *abbrev* Royal Ulster Constabulary.

ruche *n* a pleated or gathered frill of lace, ribbon, etc. used as a trimming. — *adj* **ruched**. [Fr, beehive]

ruck[1] *n* **1** a heap or mass of indistinguishable people or things. **2** (*Rugby*) a loose scrum that forms around a ball on the ground. [MidE *ruke*]

ruck[2] *n* a wrinkle or crease. — *v* (*tr & intr*; **up**) to wrinkle or crease. [Norse *hrukka*]

rucksack *n* a bag carried on the back by means of straps over the shoulders, used esp. by climbers and walkers. [Ger, back bag]

ruction *n* **1** a noisy disturbance; uproar. **2** (in *pl*) a noisy and usu. unpleasant or violent argument.

rudder *n* **1** a flat piece of wood, metal, etc. fixed vertically to a ship's stern for steering. **2** a movable aerofoil attached to the fin of an aircraft which helps control its movement along a horizontal plane. — *adj* **rudderless**. [OE *rothor*]

ruddy *adj* **-ier**, **-iest** **1** (of the face, complexion, etc.) having a healthy, glowing, rosy or pink colour. **2** red; reddish. [OE *rudig*]

rude *adj* **1** impolite; showing bad manners; discourteous. **2** roughly made; lacking refinement or polish: *build a rude shelter*. **3** ignorant, uneducated or primitive: *rude chaos*. **4** sudden and unpleasant: *a rude awakening*. **5** vigorous; robust: *rude health*. **6** vulgar; indecent. — *adv* **rudely**. — *n* **rudeness**. [Lat *rudis*, unwrought, rough]

rudiment *n* **1** (usu. in *pl*) a first or fundamental fact, rule or skill: *the rudiments of cooking*. **2** (usu. in *pl*) anything in an early and incomplete stage of development. **3** (*biol*) an organ or part which does not develop fully, usu. because it no longer has a function, such as the breast in male mammals. [Lat *rudimentum*]

rudimentary *adj* **1** basic; fundamental. **2** primitive or undeveloped; only partially developed because now useless.

rue[1] *v* ***ruing*** or ***rueing*** (*tr*) to regret; to wish that (something) had not happened. [OE *hreowan*]

rueful *adj* regretful or sorrowful, either genuinely so or not. — *adv* **ruefully**. — *n* **ruefulness**.

rue[2] *n* a strongly scented evergreen plant with bitter leaves which were formerly used in medicine, taken (punningly, because of **rue**[1]) as a symbol of repentance. [Gr *rhyte*]

ruff[1] *n* **1** a circular pleated or frilled linen collar worn round the neck in the late 16th and early 17th centuries, or in modern times by some choirs. **2** a fringe or frill of feathers or hair growing on a bird's or animal's neck. [Perhaps from **ruffle**]

ruff[2] *v* (*tr* & *intr*) to trump at cards. — *n* an act of trumping at cards. [Orig. the name of a card game, Fr *rouffle*]

ruff[3] *n* **1** a bird of the sandpiper family, the male of which grows a large ruff of feathers during the breeding season. **2** the male of this species (the female is called a **reeve**). [Perhaps **ruff**[1]]

ruffian *n* a violent, brutal and lawless person. — *adj* **ruffianly**. [OFr]

ruffle *v* **1** (*tr*) to make wrinkled or uneven; to spoil the smoothness of. **2** (*tr* & *intr*) to make or become irritated, annoyed or discomposed. **3** (*tr*; **up**) (of a bird) to erect (its feathers), usu. in anger or display. **4** (*tr*) to gather lace, linen, etc. into a ruff or ruffle. — *n* **1** a frill of lace, linen, etc. worn either round one's neck or round one's wrists. **2** any ruffling or disturbance of the evenness and smoothness of a surface or of the peace, a person's temper, etc. **3** the feathers round a bird's neck which are ruffled in anger or display. [MidE *ruffelen*]

rufous *adj* (esp. of a bird or animal) reddish or brownish-red in colour. [Lat *rufus*, red, reddish]

rug *n* **1** a thick, heavy mat or small carpet for covering (part of) the floor. **2** a thick blanket or wrap, esp. used when travelling or for horses. **3** (esp. *US slang*) a toupee or hairpiece. — **pull the rug (out) from under (someone)** to leave (a person) without defence, support, etc., esp. by some sudden discovery, action or argument. [Norse *rogg*, wool]

Rugby *n* (also **Rugby football**; also without *cap*) a form of football played with an oval ball which players may pick up and run with and may pass from hand to hand. [*Rugby*, the public school in Warwickshire where the game was first played]

Rugby League *n* (also without *caps*) the partly professional form of the game, played with teams of thirteen.

Rugby Union *n* (also without *caps*) the amateur form of the game, played with teams of fifteen.

rugged *adj* **1** (of hills, ground, etc.) having a rough, uneven surface; steep and rocky. **2** (of the face) having features that are strongly marked, irregular and furrowed and which suggest physical strength. **3** (esp. of a person's character) stern, austere and unbending. **4** involving physical hardships: *a rugged life*. **5** (of equipment, a machine, etc.) strongly or sturdily built to withstand vigorous use. — *adv* **ruggedly**. — *n* **ruggedness**. [MidE]

rugger *n* (*Br coll*) Rugby (Union).

ruin *n* **1** a broken, destroyed, decayed or collapsed state. **2** something which has been broken, destroyed or caused to decay or collapse, esp. (in *pl*) a building. **3** a complete loss of wealth, social position, power, etc. **4** a person, company, etc. that has lost all of his, her or its wealth, social position, power, etc. **5** a cause of a complete loss of wealth, social position, etc., or of physical destruction, decay, etc. — *v* **-n-** (*tr*) **1** to cause ruin to; to destroy. **2** to spoil (e.g. a child by treating him or her too indulgently). — *adj* **ruined**. — **in ruins** in a ruined state; completely wrecked or destroyed. [Lat *ruina*, from *ruere*, to tumble down]

ruination *n* the act of ruining or state of being ruined.

ruinous *adj* **1** likely to cause ruin: *ruinous prices*. **2** ruined; decayed; destroyed. — *adv* **ruinously**.

rule *n* **1** a principle, regulation, order or direction which governs or controls some action, function, form, use, etc. **2** government or control, or the period during which government or control is exercised. **3** a general principle, standard, guideline or custom: *make it a rule always to be punctual*. **4** the laws and customs which form the basis of a monastic or religious order and are followed by all members of that order: *the Benedictine rule*. **5** a strip of wood, metal or plastic with a straight edge marked off in units, used for measuring. **6** (*printing*) a thin straight line or dash. **7** an order made by a court and judge which applies to a particular case only. — *v* **1** (*tr* & *intr*) to govern; to exercise authority (over). **2** (*tr*) to keep control of or restrain. **3** (*tr*) to make an authoritative and usu. official or judicial decision. **4** (*intr*) to be common or prevalent: *Anarchy ruled after the war*. **5** (*tr*) to draw (a straight line). **6** (*tr*) to draw a straight line or a series of parallel lines on (e.g. paper). — **as a rule** usually. — *v* **rule off** (*tr*) to draw a line in order to separate. — **rule of thumb** a method of doing something, based on experience rather than theory or careful calculation. — *v* **rule out** (*tr*) **1** to leave out or not consider. **2** to make no longer possible; to preclude. [Lat *regula*, straight stick]

ruler *n* **1** a person, e.g. a sovereign, who rules or governs. **2** a strip of wood, metal or plastic with straight edges which is marked off in units (usu. inches or centimetres), and is used for drawing straight lines and measuring.

ruling *n* an official or authoritative decision. — *adj* **1** governing; controlling. **2** most important or strongest; predominant.

rum[1] *n* a spirit distilled from sugar cane.

rum baba see **baba**.

rum[2] *adj* **-mm-** (*Br coll*) strange; odd; queer; bizarre.

Rumanian. Same as **Romanian**.

rumba *n* **1** an orig. Cuban dance, popular as a ballroom dance, with pronounced hip movements produced by transferring the weight from one foot to the other. **2** music for the dance, with a stressed second beat. [American Span]

rumble *v* **1** (*intr*) to make a deep, low, grumbling sound. **2** (*intr*; **along, by, past**) to move making such a noise. **3** (*tr*) to say or utter with a rumbling voice or sound. **4** (*tr*; *Br slang*) to find out about (someone or something). — *n* **1** a deep, low grumbling sound. **2** (esp. *NAm slang*) a street fight, esp. one between gangs. — *adj* **rumbling**. [MidE *romblen*]

rumbustious *adj* (esp. *Br coll*) noisy and cheerful; boisterous. [Prob. **robust**]

ruminant *n* any mammal which chews the cud and has a stomach with three or four compartments, such as cattle, sheep, goats, antelope and giraffe. — *adj* **1** of or belonging to this group of mammals. **2** meditating or contemplating. [Lat *ruminari*, to chew the cud]

ruminate *v* (*intr*) **1** (of ruminants) to chew the cud. **2** (**on**, **upon**, **over**) to think deeply (about). — *n* **rumination**. — *adj* **ruminative**. [Lat *ruminari*, to chew the cud]

rummage *v* **1** (*intr*; **in**, **through**) to search for something by turning things out or over untidily. **2** (*tr*) to search thoroughly or turn things over untidily in: *rummage one's drawers*. — *n* **1** a thorough search. **2** things found by rummaging, esp. (*US*) jumble. [OFr *arrumage*, stowing of cargo on a ship]

rummy *n* a card game in which each player tries to collect sets or sequences of three or more cards.

rumour *n* **1** an item of news or information which is passed from person to person and which may or may not be true. **2** general talk or gossip; hearsay. — *v* (*tr*; in *passive*) to report or spread by rumour: *It is rumoured that she is going to have a baby*. [Lat *rumor*, noise]

rump *n* **1** the rear part of an animal's or bird's body; a person's buttocks. **2** (also **rump steak**) a cut of beef from the rump. **3** (usu. *contemptuous*) a small or inferior remnant. [MidE *rumpe*]

rumple *v* (*tr* & *intr*) to make or become untidy, creased or wrinkled. — *n* a wrinkle or crease. — *adj* **rumpled**. [Dut *rompel*, wrinkle]

rumpus *n* a noisy disturbance, brawl or uproar.

run *v* ***-nn-***, ***ran***, ***run*** **1** (*intr*) (of a person or animal) to move on foot so quickly that both or all feet are off the ground together for an instant during each step. **2** (*tr*) to cover or perform by, or as if by, running: *run a mile*; *run errands*. **3** (*intr*) to move quickly and easily on, or as if on, wheels. **4** (*intr*) to flee. **5** (*tr* & *intr*) to (cause to) move in a specified way or direction or with a specified result: *run the car up the ramp*; *let the dog run free*; *run him out of town*. **6** (*intr*) (of water, etc.) to flow: *rivers running to the sea*. **7** (*tr*) to cause or allow (liquid) to flow: *run cold water into the bath*. **8** (*tr* & *intr*) to cause (a container, tap, etc.) to give out liquid; (of a container, tap, etc.) to give out liquid: *run the tap*; *leave the tap running*. **9** (*tr*) to fill (a bath) with water: *run a hot bath*. **10** (*intr*) to come into a specified condition by, or as if by, flowing or running: *run dry*; *run short of time*; *Her blood ran cold*. **11** (*tr*) to be full of or flow with. **12** (*tr* & *intr*) to operate or work. **13** (*tr*) to organise or manage. **14** (*intr*; **over**, **round**, **up**) to make a short, brief, casual visit: *run up to town for the afternoon*. **15** (*intr* & *tr*) to (cause to) travel on a regular route: *a train running between Glasgow and Edinburgh*; *run an extra train*. **16** (*intr* & *tr*) to (cause to) continue or extend in a specified direction, for a specified time or distance, or over a specified range: *a road running south*; *colours running from pink to deep red*; *The play ran for ten years*. **17** (*intr*) to continue to have legal force: *a lease with a year still to run*. **18** (*tr*) to drive (someone) in a vehicle, usu. to a specified place. **19** (*tr* & *intr*; **along**, **over**, **through**, etc.) to (cause to) move or pass quickly, lightly or freely: *run one's eyes over the report*; *Excitement ran through the audience*. **20** (*intr*) to race or finish a race in a specified position. **21** (*intr*; **for**; esp. *NAm*) to stand as a candidate. **22** (*tr*) to enter (a contestant) in a race or as a candidate for office. **23** (*intr*) to spread, dissolve or circulate quickly: *the colour in his shirt ran*; *The rumour ran through the office*. **24** (*intr*) to be worded: *The report runs as follows*. **25** (*tr*) to be affected by or subjected to, or likely to be affected by: *run a high temperature*; *run risks*. **26** (*intr*) to develop relatively quickly in a specified direction; to tend (towards): *run to fat*. **27** (*intr*) to have as or be an inherent or recurring part of: *Blue eyes run in the family*. **28** (*tr*) to own, drive and maintain (a car). **29** (*tr*) to publish: *run the story in the magazine*. **30** (*tr* & *intr*) to accumulate or allow to accumulate: *run up debts at the bank*. **31** (*intr*) (of stitches) to become undone or (of a garment, e.g. hosiery) to have stitches come undone and form a ladder. **32** (*tr*) to graze (cattle): *run cattle in the valley*. **33** (*tr*) to hunt or track down. **34** (*tr*) to get past or through: *run a blockade*. **35** (*tr*) to smuggle: *run guns*. **36** (*intr*) (of fish) to migrate upstream, esp. to spawn. **37** (*tr*) to score (a run) by, or as if by, running. — *n* **1** an act of running. **2** the distance covered or time taken up by an act of running. **3** a rapid running movement: *break into a run*. **4** a trip in a vehicle, esp. one taken for pleasure. **5** a continuous and unbroken period or series of something: *a run of bad luck*; *The play had a run of six weeks*. **6** freedom to move about or come and go as one pleases: *have the run of the house*. **7** a high or urgent demand (for a currency, money, etc.). **8** a route which is regularly travelled: *a coach on the London to Glasgow run*. **9** a row of unravelled stitches, esp. in hosiery; a ladder. **10** the average type, class or kind: *the usual run of new students*. **11** (in *pl* with **the**; *coll*) diarrhoea. **12** a number produced in a single period of production: *a print run*. **13** three or more playing cards for a series or sequence. **14** an inclined course, esp. one covered with snow used for skiing. **15** a point scored in cricket either by a batter running from one wicket to the other or in any of certain other ways. **16** a unit of scoring in baseball made by the batter successfully completing a circuit of four bases. **17** (often *in cmpds*) an enclosure or pen for domestic fowls or animals: *a chicken-run*. **18** a shoal of migrating fish. **19** a track used regularly by wild animals. — **on the run** fleeing, esp. from the police. — *v* **run across** (*tr*) to meet unexpectedly. — *v* **run after** (*tr*) to chase. — *v* **run along** (*intr*; *coll*; usu. as *interj*) to go away. — *v* **run away** (*intr*) **1** to escape or flee. **2** (**with**) to elope. **3** (**with**) (of a horse) to gallop off uncontrollably (with someone on its back). **4** (with **with**) to steal. **5** (with **with**) to be over-enthusiastic about or carried away by (an idea, etc.). **6** (with **with**) to win an easy victory in: *run away with the competition*. **7** (with **with**) to use up. — *v* **run down 1** (*intr*) (of a clock, battery, etc.) to cease to work because of a gradual loss of power. **2** (*tr*) (of a vehicle or its driver) to knock to the ground. **3** (*tr*) to allow to be gradually reduced or closed: *run down the company's operations overseas*. **4** (*tr*) to speak badly of, usu. without good reason. **5** (*tr*) to chase or search for until the person or thing being sought is exhausted, found or captured. **6** (*tr*; usu. in *passive*) to cause (a person) to become weak and exhausted, usu. through overwork or a lack of proper food. — **run for it** (*coll*) to try to escape. — **run high** (of feelings) to be very strong. — *v* **run in 1** (*tr* & *intr*) to run (a new car or a car with a new engine) gently to prevent damage to the engine. **2** (*tr*; *coll*) to arrest. — *v* **run into 1** (*tr*; *coll*) to meet unexpectedly. **2** (*tr* & *intr*) to (cause to) crash into or collide with. **3** (*intr*) to suffer from or be beset by: *plans which ran into difficulties*. **4** (*intr*) to reach as far as; to extend into: *His debts run into hundreds*. — *v* **run off 1** (*tr*) to produce, esp. to print or duplicate, quickly. **2** (*intr*) to leave quickly; to run away. **3** (*tr*) to drain (liquid). **4** (*intr*) (of liquid) to be drained. **5** (*intr*; **with**) to steal. **6** (*intr*; **with**) to elope (with). **7** (*tr*) to decide (a race) by making the competitors, esp. people who have tied, run again. — *v* **run on 1** (*intr*) to talk without stopping or at length. **2** (*tr* & *intr*; *printing*) to continue or be continued in the same line without starting a new paragraph. — *v* **run out 1** (*intr*) (of a supply) to come to an end; to be used up. **2** (*intr*; **of**) to use up (a supply of): *run out of money*. **3** (*tr* & *intr*) to (allow to) leak out. **4** (*tr*; *cricket*) to put out (a batter running towards a wicket) by breaking that wicket with the ball. **5** (*intr*; **on**; *coll*) to abandon or desert. **6** (*tr*; esp. *NAm coll*) to force to leave: *run them out of town*. — *v* **run over 1** (*tr*) (of a vehicle or driver) to knock down and drive over, and injure or kill. **2** (*intr*) to overflow; to go beyond a limit. **3** (*tr*) to repeat or glance over quickly, esp. for practice. **4** (*intr*; **to**) to make a quick brief visit. — *v* **run through** (*tr*) **1** to look at, read, perform, etc. quickly, esp. for practice or as a rehearsal (*n* **run-through**). **2** to pierce with a sword or similar weapon. **3** to use up (money, resources, etc.) quickly and carelessly. — *v* **run to** (*intr*) **1** to have enough money for: *We can't run to a holiday this year*. **2** (of money, resources, etc.) to be sufficient for. — *v* **run up** (*tr*) **1** to make (esp. a garment) quickly. **2** to amass or accumulate (bills, debts, etc.). **3** to hoist (a flag). — *v* **run up against** (*tr*) to meet or be faced with (a difficulty). [OE *rinnan*]

runabout *n* a small light car, boat or aircraft.

runaway *n* a person or animal that has run away or fled. — *adj* **1** that is running away or out of control. **2** (of a race, victory, etc.) easily and convincingly won. **3** done or managed as a result of running away.

run-down *adj* **1** (of a person) tired or exhausted; in weakened health. **2** (of a building) shabby; dilapidated. — *n* **1** a gradual reduction in numbers, size, etc. **2** a brief statement of the main points or items; a summary.

run-in *n* (*coll*) a quarrel or argument.

runner *n* **1** a person or thing that runs. **2** a messenger. **3** a groove or strip along which a drawer, sliding door, etc. slides. **4** either of the strips of metal or wood running the length of a sledge, on which it moves. **5** a blade on an ice skate. **6** a long stem that grows along the surface of the ground and puts down new shoots, e.g. on the strawberry. **7** a long narrow strip of cloth or carpet used to decorate or cover a table, dresser, floor, etc. **8** a runner bean. **9** a smuggler. — **do a runner** (*slang*) to leave a place quickly, esp. a shop or restaurant without paying, or where one has done some damage.

runner bean *n* a climbing plant which produces bright red flowers and long, green, edible beans.

runner-up *n* ***runners-up*** a competitor who finishes in second place.

running *n* **1** the act of moving quickly. **2** the act of managing, organising or operating. — *adj* **1** of or for running. **2** done or performed while running, working, etc.: *running repairs*; *a running jump*. **3** continuous. **4** consecutive: *two days running*. **5** flowing. **6** giving out pus. — **in** or **out of the running** having, or not having, a chance of success.

running-board *n* a footboard along the side of a vehicle.

running head *n* a title occurring at the top of every page in a book.

running knot *n* a knot that changes the size of a noose as it is pulled.

running mate *n* (esp. *NAm*) a candidate standing for election to a post of secondary importance when considered as the partner of the candidate for a more important post; esp. the candidate for the post of vice-president of the USA.

runny *adj* **-ier, -iest 1** tending to run or flow, esp. (of the nose) with mucus. **2** liquid; watery.

run-off *n* an extra race, contest, etc. between two people or teams who have tied, to decide the winner.

run-of-the-mill *adj* ordinary; not special.

run time *n* the time needed to run a computer program completely.

run-up *n* an approach or period of preparation (e.g. for some event).

runway *n* a wide, hard surface from which aircraft take off and on which they land.

rune *n* **1** any of the letters of an early alphabet used by the Germanic peoples between about 200–600 AD, used esp. in carvings. **2** a mystical symbol or inscription. — *adj* **runic**. [Norse *run*, secret]

rung[1] *n* **1** a step on a ladder. **2** a crosspiece on a chair. [OE *hrung*]

rung[2]. See **ring**[2].

runnel *n* a small stream [OE *rynel*]

runt *n* **1** the smallest animal in a litter. **2** an undersized and weak person.

rupee *n* the standard unit of currency in India, Pakistan, Bhutan, Nepal, Sri Lanka, Mauritius and the Seychelles. [Sanskrit *rupya*, wrought silver]

rupture *n* **1** the act of breaking or bursting or state of being broken or burst. **2** a breach of harmony or friendly relations. **3** a hernia. — *v* (*tr* & *intr*) **1** to break, tear or burst. **2** to (cause to) suffer a breach of harmony or friendly relations. **3** to cause (someone or oneself) to suffer, or to be affected by, a hernia. [Lat *rumpere*, to break]

rural *adj* of the countryside; pastoral or agricultural. [Lat *ruralis*, from *rus*, country]

rural dean see **dean**.

ruse *n* a clever trick or plan intended to deceive or trick. [OFr *ruser*, to retreat]

rush[1] **1** (*tr* & *intr*) to (cause to) hurry or go quickly. **2** (*tr*) to perform or deal with too quickly or hurriedly. **3** (*tr*) to attack suddenly. **4** (*intr*; **at**) to approach or carry out hastily and impetuously: *rush at one's work*. **5** (*tr*) to force (someone) to act more quickly than he or she wants to. — *n* **1** a sudden quick movement, esp. forwards. **2** a sudden general movement, usu. towards a single goal: *a gold rush*. **3** haste; hurry: *be in a dreadful rush*. **4** a period of great activity. **5** a sudden demand (for something). **6** (*slang*) a feeling of euphoria after taking a drug. — *adj* done, or needing to be done, quickly. — **rush one's fences** to act too hastily. [OFr *ruser*, from Lat *recusare*, to push back]

rush hour *n* a period at the beginning or end of the day when traffic is at its busiest because people are travelling to or from work.

rush[2] *n* any of several tall grass-like plants which grow in or near water and which have slender cylindrical leaves used for making chair seats and plaited into mats. — *adj* **rushy**. [OE *risc*]

rush candle or **light** *n* a candle or night-light with a wick of rush.

rusk *n* a slice of bread which has been rebaked, or a hard dry biscuit resembling this, given as a food to babies. [Span or Port *rosca*, twist of bread]

russet *n* **1** a reddish-brown colour. **2** a variety of apple with a reddish-brown skin. — *adj* reddish-brown in colour. [Lat *russus*, red]

Russian *n* **1** a person born in or living in Russia or (*loosely*) the other former Soviet republics. **2** the Slavonic language spoken in Russia and the main official language of the former Soviet Union. — *adj* of Russia or (*loosely*) the former Soviet republics, their people, culture or language.

Russian roulette *n* an act of daring, esp. that in which one spins the cylinder of a revolver which is loaded with one bullet only, points the revolver at one's own head, and pulls the trigger.

Russian tea *n* tea served with lemon instead of milk.

Russo- *comb fm* of Russia or (*loosely*) the former Soviet republics: *a Russo-American treaty*.

rust *n* **1** a reddish-brown brittle coating which forms on iron and steel, caused by the action of oxygen and moisture. **2** a similar coating which forms on other metals. **3** the colour of rust, usu. a reddish-brown. **4** (a fungus causing) a plant disease in which leaves take on a rusty appearance. **5** a weakening or injurious influence or consequence, esp. mental or physical laziness or inactivity. — *v* **1** (*tr* & *intr*) to (cause to) become coated with rust. **2** (*intr*) to become weaker and inefficient, usu. through lack of use. **3** (*intr*) (of a plant) to be affected by rust. **4** (*intr*) (e.g. of bracken) to become reddish-brown in colour. [OE]

rustproof *adj* that will not rust or will prevent rust from forming.

rusty *adj* **-ier, -iest 1** covered with or affected by rust. **2** (of a skill, knowledge of a subject, etc.) not as good as it used to be through lack of practice. **3** rust-coloured. **4** (esp. of black clothes) discoloured, often with a brownish sheen, through age. — *adv* **rustily**. — *n* **rustiness**.

rustic *adj* **1** of or living in the country. **2** having the characteristics of country life or country people, esp. in being simple and unsophisticated, or awkward and uncouth. **3** made of rough, untrimmed branches: *rustic furniture*. — *n* a person from or living in the country, esp. one who is thought of as being simple and unsophisticated. — *adv* **rustically**. — *n* **rusticity**. [Lat *rusticus*, from *rus*, country]

rusticate *v* **1** (*tr* & *intr*) to live, go to live or send to live in the country. **2** (*tr*) to suspend (a student) from college or university temporarily because of some wrongdoing. **3** (*tr*) to make rustic or rural. [Lat *rusticari*, to live in the country]

rustle *v* **1** (*tr* & *intr*) to (cause to) make a soft whispering sound as of dry leaves. **2** (*intr*) to move with such a sound. **3** (*tr* & *intr*; esp. *NAm*) to steal (cattle or horses). — *n* a quick succession of soft, dry, crisp, whisper-like sounds. — *v* **rustle up** (*tr*) to arrange, gather together or prepare quickly. [MidE *rustlen*]

rustler *n* (esp. *NAm*) a person who steals cattle or horses.

rut[1] *n* **1** a deep track or furrow in soft ground made by wheels. **2** an established and usu. boring or dreary routine. — *adj* **rutted**.

rut[2] *n* **1** a period of sexual excitement in male deer and some other ruminants. **2** (also **rutting season**) the time of the year when this occurs. — *v* **-tt-** (*intr*) (of male animals) to be in a period of sexual excitement. [OFr *rut*, roar]

ruthenium *n* a hard white metallic element (symbol **Ru**) of the platinum group, used in certain alloys. [Lat *Ruthenia*, Russia, so called because it was discovered in ore from the Urals]

ruthless *adj* without pity. — *adv* **ruthlessly**. — *n* **ruthlessness**. [MidE *ruthe*, pity + **-less**]

rye *n* **1** a grass-like cereal which produces a grain used for making bread and whiskey, and as food for animals. **2** (also **rye whiskey**) whiskey distilled from fermented rye. [OE *ryge*]

S

S[1] or **s** *n* ***S's*** or ***Ss***, ***s's*** **1** the nineteenth letter in the English alphabet. **2** a thing shaped like this letter.
S[2] *abbrev* **1** Society. **2** South. **3** soprano.
S[3] *symbol* (*chem*) sulphur.
s *abbrev* **1** second(s) (of time). **2** (*formerly* in the UK) shilling(s) [Lat *solidus*]. ◇ See also **d**[1].
-s[1] or **-es** *sfx* used to form plurals of nouns, as in *cats, dogs, churches*.
-s[2] or **-es** *sfx* used to form the third person singular of the present tense of verbs, as in *walks, runs, reaches*.
's[1] *sfx* **1** used to form the possessive, as in *John's, the children's*. **2** used to form the plural of numbers and symbols, as in *3's, X's*.
's[2] **1** the shortened form of **is**, as in *he's not here*. **2** the shortened form of **has**, as in *she's taken it*. **3** the shortened form of **us**, as in *let's go*.
SA *abbrev* **1** Salvation Army. **2** South Africa. **3** South America. **4** South Australia.
Sabbath *n* (usu. with **the**) a day of the week set aside for religious worship and rest, Saturday among the Jews and Sunday among most Christians. [Hebr *shabbath*, rest]
sabbatical *adj* **1** of or being a period of leave given esp. to teachers in higher education, esp. for study. **2** relating to or typical of the Sabbath. — *n* a period of sabbatical leave. [Ety. as for **Sabbath**]
sable[1] *n* **1** a small flesh-eating mammal of northern Europe and Asia, related to the marten. **2** its shiny dark-brown fur. **3** an artist's paintbrush made of this. [OFr]
sable[2] *adj* **1** (*poetic*) dark. **2** (*heraldry*) black.
sable antelope *n* a large S African antelope, the male of which is mostly black.
sabot *n* a wooden clog, or a shoe with a wooden sole. [Fr]
sabotage *n* **1** deliberate damage or destruction, esp. carried out for military or political reasons. **2** action designed to disrupt any plan or scheme. — *v* (*tr*) to destroy, damage or disrupt deliberately. [Fr *saboter*, to ruin through carelessness]
saboteur *n* a person carrying out sabotage.
sabre *n* **1** a curved single-edged cavalry sword. **2** a lightweight fencing sword with a tapering blade. [Fr]
sabre-rattling *n* aggressive talk or action, esp. from politicians or military leaders, intended as a show of power.
sac *n* (*biol*) any (esp. fluid-filled) bag-like part in a plant or animal. [Lat *saccus*, bag]
saccharin or **saccharine** *n* a non-fattening artificial sweetener used instead of sugar. — *adj* over-sentimental or over-sweet; cloying. [Gr *sakcharon*, sugar]
sacerdotal *adj* **1** of or relating to priests. **2** resembling a priest; priestly. [Lat *sacerdos*, priest]
sachet *n* **1** a small sealed packet containing a liquid or powder. **2** a small bag containing a scented substance, used to perfume wardrobes, drawers, etc. [Fr, dimin. of *sac*, bag]
sack[1] *n* **1** a large bag, esp. of coarse cloth or paper. **2** (also **sackful**, ***-fuls***) the amount contained in such a bag. **3** (*coll*; with **the**) dismissal from employment: *give (someone)*, or *get, the sack*. **4** (*slang*) bed. — *v* (*tr*) **1** (*coll*) to dismiss from employment. **2** to put into a sack or sacks. — **hit the sack** (*slang*) to go to bed. [Lat *saccus*, bag]
sackcloth *n* **1** sacking (sense **1**). **2** a garment made from this, formerly worn in mourning or as a self-punishment for sin. — **sackcloth and ashes** a display of sorrow or remorse.
sacking *n* **1** coarse cloth used to make sacks. **2** (*coll*) dismissal from, or the act of dismissing from, employment.
sack[2] *v* (*tr*) to plunder and destroy (a town). — *n* the act of sacking a town. [Fr *mettre à sac*, to put (plunder) into a bag]
sack[3] *n* (*hist*) a dry white wine from Spain, Portugal and the Canary Islands. [Fr *sec*, dry]
sackbut *n* an early trombone-like wind instrument. [Fr *saquebute*]
sacra. See **sacrum**.
sacral[1] *adj* relating to sacred rites.
sacral[2] *adj* of or relating to the sacrum.
sacrament *n* **1** (*Christianity*) any of various symbolic ceremonies, e.g. marriage or baptism. **2** (*Christianity*; *cap*) the service of the Eucharist or Holy Communion; the consecrated bread and wine consumed. **3** a sign, token or pledge. — *adj* **sacramental**. [Lat *sacrare*, to consecrate]
sacred *adj* **1** devoted to God or a god and therefore regarded with deep and solemn respect. **2** connected with religion or worship: *sacred music*. **3** traditional and greatly respected; (of rules, etc.) not to be challenged or broken. — **sacred to** dedicated to. [Lat *sacer*, holy]
sacred cow *n* a thing, esp. a custom or institution, regarded as above criticism.
sacrifice *n* **1** the slaughter of a person or animal as an offering to God or a god; the person or animal slaughtered. **2** any offering made to God or a god. **3** any (esp. valuable) thing given up or given away for the sake of another thing or person. — *v* (*tr*) **1** to offer as a sacrifice to God or a god. **2** to give up or give away for the sake of some other person or thing. — *adj*

sacrificial. [Lat *sacer*, sacred + *facere*, to make]

sacrilege *n* wilful damage to or disrespect for something holy or something regarded with great respect by others. — *adj* **sacrilegious**. [Lat *sacrilegus*, stealer of sacred things]

sacristan or **sacrist** *n* **1** a person responsible for the safety of the contents of a church. **2** a person who looks after the church buildings and churchyard; a sexton. [Lat *sacer*, holy]

sacristy *n* **-ies** a room in a church where sacred utensils and garments are kept. [Lat *sacristia*, vestry]

sacrosanct *adj* supremely holy or sacred; not to be violated. — *n* **sacrosanctity**. [Lat *sacer*, holy + *sanctus*, hallowed]

sacrum *n* **-ra** a large triangular bone in the lower back, forming part of the pelvis. [Lat (*os*) *sacrum*, holy (bone), from its use in sacrifices]

sad *adj* **-dd- 1** feeling unhappy. **2** causing unhappiness: *sad news*. **3** expressing or suggesting unhappiness: *sad music*. **4** very bad; deplorable: *a sad state*. — *adv* **sadly**. — *n* **sadness**. [OE *sæd*, weary]

sadden *v* **-n-** (*tr* & *intr*) to make or become sad.

saddle *n* **1** a horse-rider's (usu. leather) seat, fitting on the horse's back and tying under its belly. **2** a fixed seat on a bicycle or motorcycle. **3** a cut of meat consisting of the two loins with a section of the backbone. **4** a mountain ridge connecting two peaks. — *v* (*tr*) **1** (**up**) to put a saddle on (a horse). **2** (**with**) to burden. — **in the saddle 1** on horseback. **2** in a position of power or control. [OE *sadol*]

saddleback *n* **1** an animal or bird with a saddle-shaped marking on its back. **2** a roof or mountain peak that dips in the middle. — *adj* **saddlebacked**.

saddler *n* a maker of saddles and harnesses for horses. — *n* **saddlery**, **-ies**.

saddle soap *n* soft soap for cleaning and preserving leather.

Sadducee *n* a member of an ancient Jewish sect influential around the time of Jesus Christ, opposing the progressive Pharisees, emphasising traditional written law, and rejecting the notion of life after death. [Hebr *Tsaduqim*]

sadhu *n* a wandering Hindu holy man, living on charity. [Sanskrit, pious]

sadism *n* **1** the practice of gaining sexual pleasure from inflicting pain on others. **2** (*loosely*) the inflicting of suffering on others for one's own satisfaction. — *n* **sadist**. — *adj* **sadistic**. [Comte (called Marquis) de *Sade* (1740–1814), Fr novelist]

sado-masochism *n* the practice of obtaining sexual pleasure from inflicting pain on oneself and others. — *n* **sado-masochist**. — *adj* **sado-masochistic**. [**sadism** + **masochism**]

SAE or **sae** *abbrev* stamped addressed envelope.

safari *n* an expedition or tour to hunt or observe wild animals, esp. in Africa: *on safari*. [Swahili, journey]

safari jacket *n* a long, square-cut jacket with four pleated pockets.

safari park *n* a large enclosed area in which (esp. non-native) wild animals roam freely and can be observed from a vehicle.

safe *adj* **1** free from danger. **2** unharmed. **3** giving protection from harm; secure: *a safe place*. **4** not dangerous: *It's safe to go out*. **5** involving no risk of loss; assured: *a safe bet*. **6** cautious: *better safe than sorry*. — *n* a sturdily constructed metal cabinet in which valuables can be locked away. — *adv* **safely**. — **be** or **err on the safe side** to be doubly cautious; to choose the safer alternative. [Lat *salvus*]

safe-conduct *n* (a document stating) official permission to pass or travel without arrest or interference, esp. in wartime.

safe-deposit or **safety-deposit** *n* a vault, e.g. in a bank, in which valuables can be locked away.

safeguard *n* a device or arrangement giving protection against danger or harm. — *v (tr)* protect; to ensure the safety of.

safekeeping *n* care and protection.

safe sex *n* sexual activity in which the transmission of disease, esp. Aids, is guarded against, e.g. by the use of a condom or the avoidance of penetration.

safety *n* the quality or condition of being safe.

safety belt *n* any strap for securing a person and preventing accidents, esp. a seat belt in a vehicle.

safety curtain *n* a fireproof curtain above a theatre stage, lowered to control the spread of fire.

safety-deposit see **safe-deposit**.

safety-lamp *n* a miner's oil lamp designed not to ignite any flammable gases encountered in the mine.

safety match *n* a match that ignites only when struck on a specially prepared surface.

safety net *n* **1** a large net positioned to catch a trapeze artist accidentally falling. **2** any measure protecting against loss or failure.

safety pin *n* a U-shaped pin with an attached guard fitting over the point.

safety razor *n* a shaving razor with a guard over the blade to prevent deep cuts.

safety valve *n* **1** a valve designed to open when a pressure level becomes dangerously high. **2** a way of harmlessly releasing emotion, e.g. anger or frustration.

safflower *n* a Eurasian plant with large orange-yellow flowers, yielding a dye and an oil used in cooking. [OFr *saffleur*]

saffron *n* **1** a species of crocus with purple or white flowers whose pollen-receiving parts, or stigmas, are bright orange. **2** the dried powdered stigmas, used to colour and flavour food. **3** a bright orange-yellow colour. [Arabic *zafaran*]

sag *v* **-gg-** (*intr*) **1** to sink or bend, esp. in the middle, under or as if under weight. **2** to hang loosely or bulge downwards through lack of firmness. — *n* a sagging state or position. — *adj* **saggy, -ier, -iest**. [Norse]

saga *n* **1** a mediaeval Scandinavian tale of legendary heroes and events. **2** any long and detailed artistic work, esp. a piece of modern fiction, often serialised, depicting successive generations of the same family. **3** (*coll*) a long series of events. [Norse]

sagacious *adj* (*formal*) having or showing intelligence and good judgement; wise. — *n* **sagacity**. [Lat *sagax*]

sage[1] *n* a Mediterranean plant with aromatic grey-green leaves; the leaves used as a flavouring in cooking. [Lat *salvia*, healing plant]

sagebrush *n* a white-flowered aromatic shrub growing in clumps in the deserts of the US.

sage[2] *n* a (usu. old) man of great wisdom, esp. an ancient philosopher. — *adj* wise; prudent. [Lat *sapere*, to be wise]

saggar or **sagger** *n* a large clay box in which pottery is packed for firing in a kiln.

Sagittarius *n* **1** a constellation and the ninth sign of the zodiac, the Archer. **2** a person born under the sign, between 22 November and 20 December. — *n & adj* **Sagittarian**. [Lat, from *sagitta*, arrow]

sago *n* a starchy grain or powder prepared from the pith of certain tropical palms, used in puddings and as a thickener. [Malay *sagu*]

sahib *n* a term equivalent to Mr or sir, used after a man's surname, or (esp. formerly) on its own to address or refer to a European man. ◇ See also **memsahib**. [Arabic, lord or friend]

said past tense and past participle of **say**. — *adj* (with **the**) previously mentioned or named.

sail *n* **1** a sheet of canvas spread to catch the wind as a means of propelling a ship. **2** a trip in a boat or ship (with or without sails); the distance travelled by boat or ship. **3** (*naut*; *pl* usu. ***sail***, esp. after a number) a ship with sails. **4** any of a windmill's revolving arms. — *v* **1** (*tr & intr*) to travel by boat or ship (across): *sail the Pacific*. **2** (*tr*) to control (a boat or ship). **3** (*intr*) to depart by boat or ship: *We sail at noon*. **4** (*intr*; **along, past**, etc.) to move smoothly and swiftly. **5** (*intr* with **through**) to get through effortlessly: *sailed through the interview*. — **sail close to the wind 1** to arrange a ship's sails to catch as much wind as is safely possible. **2** to come dangerously close to overstepping a limit, e.g. of good taste or decency. — **set sail** to begin a journey by boat or ship. [OE *segel*]

sailboard *n* a windsurfing board, like a surfboard with a sail attached. — *n* **sailboarding**.

sailcloth *n* **1** strong cloth, e.g. canvas, used to make sails. **2** heavy cotton cloth used for garments.

sailor *n* **1** any member of a ship's crew, esp. one who is not an officer. **2** a person considered in terms of ability to travel on water without becoming seasick: *a good sailor*.

sainfoin *n* a flowering Eurasian plant of the pea family, grown as animal fodder. [Fr, healthy hay]

saint *n* **1** a person whose profound holiness is formally recognised after death by a Christian church, and who is declared worthy of everlasting praise. **2** (*coll*) a very good and kind person. — *n* **sainthood**. [Lat *sanctus*, holy]

Saint Bernard *n* a very large dog with a thick brown and white coat, orig. kept by monks to rescue snowbound travellers in the St Bernard Pass in the Alps.

sainted *adj* **1** formally declared a saint. **2** greatly respected; hallowed.

saintly *adj* **1** of or relating to a saint. **2** very good or holy. — *n* **saintliness**.

saint's day *n* a date in the church calendar on which a particular saint is honoured.

Saint Vitus's dance *n* chorea.

saith (*old*) says.

sake[1] *n* benefit; behalf; account: *for my sake*. — **for God's, heaven's**, etc. **sake** expressions used in annoyance or when begging, e.g. for forgiveness. — **for the sake of** for the purpose of; in order to. [OE *sacu*, lawsuit]

sake[2] or **saki** *n* a Japanese alcoholic drink made from rice. [Jap]

salaam *n* **1** a word used as a greeting in Eastern countries, esp. by Muslims. **2** a low bow with the palm of the right hand on the forehead, a Muslim greeting or show of respect. **3** (in *pl*) greetings; compliments. — *v* (*tr & intr*) to perform a salaam (to). [Arabic *salam*, peace]

salable. See **saleable** under **sale**.

salacious *adj* **1** seeking to arouse sexual desire, esp. crudely or obscenely. **2** unnaturally preoccupied with sex; lecherous. — *n* **salaciousness**. [Lat *salax*, fond of leaping]

salad *n* a cold dish of usu. raw vegetables, usu. served with a dressing, often accompanying other foods.

fruit salad *n* a dish of mixed chopped fruits, usu. eaten as a dessert.

salad days *n* (*pl*; *literary*) years of youthful inexperience and carefree innocence.

salad dressing *n* any sauce served with a salad, e.g. mayonnaise or a mixture of oil and vinegar.

salamander *n* **1** a lizard-like amphibious creature of central and S Europe, formerly believed poisonous. **2** a mythical reptile or spirit living in fire. [Gr *salamandra*]

salami *n* **-is** a highly seasoned type of sausage, usu. served sliced. [Ital]

salary *n* **-ies** a fixed regular payment for (esp. non-manual) work, usu. made monthly. — *adj* **salaried**. ◇ See also **wage**. [Lat *salarium*, soldier's allowance to buy salt]

sale *n* **1** the act or practice of selling. **2** the selling of an item. **3** an item sold. **4** (usu. in *pl*) the value of the items sold. **5** a period during which goods are offered at reduced prices. **6** any event at which goods can be bought: *a book sale*. **7** (in *pl*) the operations associated with, or the staff responsible for, selling. — *adj* intended for selling, esp. at reduced prices or by auction. — **for** or **on sale** available for buying. [OE *sala*]

saleable or **salable** *adj* **1** fit to be sold. **2** for which there is a demand.

sale of work *n* a sale of items made in the community, to raise money for a charity or other organisation.

saleroom *n* a room in which public auctions are held, or goods to be auctioned displayed.

salesman, saleswoman and **salesperson** *n* a person who sells goods to customers, esp. in a shop.

salesmanship *n* the techniques involved in persuading people to buy things.

sales talk *n* persuasive talk used by salespeople.

salicylic acid *n* an acid in the form of white crystals, used in the manufacture of aspirin, fungicide and perfumes. [Lat *salyx*, willow, from whose bark it was orig. prepared]

salient *adj* **1** striking; outstanding. **2** (*archit*) jutting out or up. — *n* a projecting part or section, e.g. of a fortification or a defensive line of troops. [Lat *salire*, to leap]

saline *adj* of the nature of, or containing, salt: *saline solution*. — *n* **1** a solution of salt and water. 2 a lake, marsh, etc. of salt water. — *n* **salinity**. [Lat *sal*, salt]

saliva *n* the watery liquid produced by glands in the mouth to aid digestion. — *adj* **salivary**. [Lat]

salivate *v* (*intr*) **1** to have (esp. excessive amounts of) saliva in the mouth, as at the thought or sight of food. **2** (**over**) to drool. — *n* **salivation**.

sallow *adj* (of a person's complexion) yellowish-brown, often through poor health. — *v* (*tr* & *intr*) to make or become sallow. [OE *salo* or *salu*]

sally *n* **-ies** **1** a sudden attack by troops rushing forward. **2** an excursion. — *v* **-ies, -ied** (*intr*) **1** (of troops) to carry out a sally. **2** (*old* or *humorous*; **forth**) to rush out or surge forward; to set off. [Lat *salire*, to leap]

salmon *n* **-mon** or **-mons** **1** a large silvery marine fish that lays its eggs in fresh water. **2** its edible orange-pink flesh, highly prized. **3** any of various related fishes, and others unrelated but similar in appearance. **4** (also **salmon pink**) an orange-pink colour. [Lat *salmo*, from *salire*, to leap]

salmon ladder *n* a series of steps built in a river to help salmon swim upstream to lay eggs.

salmonella *n* **-ae** **1** any of various types of bacteria that contaminate food. **2** food poisoning caused by the presence of such bacteria. [Daniel E *Salmon* (1850–1914), US veterinary surgeon]

salon *n* **1** a shop or other establishment where clients are beautified in some way: a *hairdressing salon*. **2** a drawing-room, esp. in a large continental house. **3** a gathering of arts celebrities in a fashionable (esp. 17th- or 18th-century Parisian) household. **4** an art exhibition. [Fr]

saloon *n* **1** a large public room, e.g. for functions or some other specified purpose: *a billiard saloon*. **2** a large public room on a passenger ship. **3** (*old*) a lounge bar. **4** (*US*) any bar where alcohol is sold. **5** (*coll*; also **saloon car**) any motor car not an estate, coupé, convertible or sports model. [**salon**]

Salop *n* a form used as an abbreviation of Shropshire. [OFr *Salopescira*, Shropshire]

salopettes *n* (*pl*) quilted skiing trousers reaching to the chest, held up by shoulder-straps. [Fr]

salsa *n* **1** rhythmic dance music of S American origin, mixing jazz with rock. **2** a dance performed to such music. [Span, sauce]

salsify *n* **-ies** a purple-flowered Mediterranean plant with a long cylindrical edible root; the root. [Ital *sassefrica*]

SALT *abbrev* Strategic Arms Limitation Talks or Treaty.

salt *n* **1** (also **common salt**) sodium chloride, a white crystalline substance occurring as a mineral (**rock-salt**) or in solution in sea water (**sea-salt**), used to season and preserve food. **2** a chemical compound in which one or more hydrogen atoms have been replaced by a metal atom or atoms. **3** (in *pl*) any substance resembling salt in appearance or taste, esp. a medicine: *Epsom salts*. **4** liveliness; interest; wit. **5** (usu. **old salt**) an experienced sailor. — *v* (*tr*) **1** to season or preserve (food) with salt. **2** to cover (an icy road) with a scattering of salt to melt the ice. — *adj* **1** preserved with salt: *salt pork*. **2** containing salt: *salt water*. **3** tasting of salt; not bitter, sweet or sour. — *adj* **salted**. — **rub salt in someone's wounds** to add to someone's discomfort. — *v* **salt away** (*tr*) to store up for future use; to hoard. — **the salt of the earth** (among) the most worthy of all people. — **take (something) with a pinch of salt** to treat (usu. someone's words) sceptically or with suspicion. — **worth one's salt** competent; worthy of respect. [OE]

salt cellar *n* a container holding salt for use at the dinner table.

salty *adj* **-ier, -iest** **1** containing salt. **2** tasting (too strongly) of salt. **3** (of humour) sharp. — *n* **saltiness**.

saltpetre *n* potassium nitrate. [Lat *salpetra*, salt of rock]

salubrious *adj* **1** (*formal*) health-giving; promoting well-being: *a salubrious climate*. **2** respectable; pleasant: *not a very salubrious neighbourhood*. [Lat *salus*, health]

saluki *n* **-is** a tall slender silky-haired dog of Arabian origin, with a tufty tail and ears. [Arabic *seluqi*]

salutary *adj* **1** (intended to be) beneficial: *salutary warning*. **2** healthy; wholesome. — *adv* **salutarily**. [Lat *salus*, health]

salute *v* **1** (*tr* & *intr*; *mil*) to pay formal respect to (someone) with a set gesture, esp. with the right arm or a weapon. **2** (*tr*) to pay tribute to: *We salute your bravery*. **3** (*tr*) to greet with a show of friendship or respect. — *n* **1** a military gesture of respect. **2** a greeting. [Lat *salutare*, to greet]

salutation *n* an act, gesture or phrase of greeting. — *adj* **salutatory**.

salvage *v* (*tr*) **1** to rescue (e.g. property or a vessel) from potential damage or loss, e.g. in a fire or shipwreck, or from disposal as waste. **2** to recover (a sunken ship). **3** to manage to retain (e.g. one's pride) in adverse circumstances. — *n* **1** the act of salvaging property, a vessel, etc. **2** property salvaged. **3** payment made as a reward for saving a ship from destruction or loss. — *adj* **salvageable**. [Lat *salvare*, to save]

salvation *n* **1** the act of saving a person or thing from harm. **2** a person or thing that saves another from harm. **3** (*relig*) liberation from the influence of sin, or its consequences for the human soul. [Lat *salvare*, to save]

Salvation Army *n* a Christian organisation, with a semi-military structure of ranks, aiming to help the poor and spread Christianity.

salve *n* **1** ointment to heal or soothe. **2** anything that comforts or consoles. — *v* (*tr*) to ease or comfort: *salve one's conscience*. [OE *sealf*]

salver *n* a small ornamented (esp. silver) tray. [Fr *salve*, tray for presenting the king's food for tasting]

salvo *n* **-os** or **-oes** **1** a burst of gunfire from several guns firing at the same time. **2** a sudden round of applause. **3** a ferocious outburst of criticism or insults. [Ital *salva*, salute]

sal volatile *n* ammonium carbonate, esp. in solution in alcohol for use as smelling salts. [Lat, volatile salt]

Samaritan *n* **1** (also **good Samaritan**) a kind or helpful person. **2** a worker with the **Samaritans**, a voluntary organisation giving help and advice to people in distress. [Lat *Samaritanus*; from the story of the good Samaritan told by Jesus (Luke 10.30–37)]

samarium *n* an element (symbol **Sm**), a silvery metal used in the nuclear industry and in lasers. [Colonel *Samarski*, 19th-century Russian mines inspector]

samba *n* **1** a lively Brazilian dance, or a short-stepping ballroom dance developed from it. **2** a piece of music for either. [Port]

same *adj* **1** exactly alike or very similar. **2** not different. **3** unchanged or unchanging. **4** previously mentioned; the actual one in question: *this same man*. — *pron* (with **the**) the same person or thing, or the one previously mentioned: *She drank whisky, and I drank the same*. — *adv* (with **the**) **1** similarly; likewise: *I feel the same*. **2** (*coll*) equally: *We love each of you the same*. — *n* **sameness**. — **all** or **just the same** nevertheless. — **at the same time** however; on the other hand. — **be all the same to** to make no difference to. — **same here!** (*coll*) me too!; I agree! [Norse *samr*]

samey *adj* (*coll*) boringly similar or unchanging.

samizdat *n* formerly in the former Soviet Union, the secret printing and distribution of writings banned by the government; the writings themselves. [Russ, self-published]

samosa *n* a small deep-fried triangular spicy meat or vegetable pasty of Indian origin. [Hindi]

samovar *n* a Russian urn boiling water for tea, often elaborately decorated, traditionally heated by a central charcoal-filled pipe. [Russ]

Samoyed *n* **1** a member of a people of northern Siberia. **2** their language, distantly related to Finnish and Hungarian. **3** a sturdy dog of Siberian origin, with a thick cream or white coat and an upward-curling tail. [Russ *Samoed*]

sampan *n* any small flat-bottomed oriental boat propelled by oars rather than sails. [Chin *san*, three + *pan*, plank]

samphire *n* a flowering cliff plant whose fleshy leaves are used in pickles. [Fr (*herbe de*) *Saint Pierre*, (herb of) St Peter]

sample *n* a unit or part taken, displayed or considered as representative of others or of a whole. — *v* (*tr*) **1** to take or try as a sample. **2** to get experience of: *sampled life abroad*. [OFr *essample*, from Lat *exemplum*, example]

sampler *n* a piece of embroidery produced as a show or test of skill.

Samson *n* an exceptionally strong man. [Biblical character of this name]

samurai *n* **-ai** **1** (a member of) an aristocratic class of Japanese warriors between the 11th and 19th centuries. **2** (*loosely*) a samurai's sword, a two-handed sword with a curved blade. [Jap]

sanatorium *n* **-iums** or **-ia** **1** a hospital for the chronically ill, or for patients recovering from illnesses treated elsewhere. **2** a sickroom in a school, etc. [Lat, from *sanare*, to heal]

sanctify *v* **-ies**, **-ied** (*tr*) **1** to make sacred. **2** to free from sin. **3** to declare legitimate or binding in the eyes of the Church: *sanctify a marriage*. — *n* **sanctification**. [Lat *sanctus*, holy + *facere*, to make]

sanctimonious *adj* displaying exaggerated holiness or virtuousness, esp. hypocritically. — *n* **sanctimoniousness**. [Lat *sanctimonia*, sanctity]

sanction *n* **1** official permission or authority. **2** an economic or military measure taken by one nation to persuade another to adopt a particular policy. **3** a means of encouraging adherence to a social custom, e.g. a penalty or reward. **4** any penalty attached to an offence. — *v* **-n-** (*tr*) **1** to authorise or confirm formally. **2** to allow or agree to. **3** to encourage. [Lat *sancire*, to decree]

sanctity *n* **1** the quality of being holy or sacred. **2** the quality of deserving to be respected, and not violated or flouted. [Lat *sanctitas*]

sanctuary *n* **-ies 1** a holy or sacred place, e.g. a church or temple. **2** the most sacred area within such a place, e.g. around an altar. **3** a place, historically a church, giving immunity from arrest or other interference. **4** freedom from disturbance: *the sanctuary of the garden*. **5** a nature reserve in which the animals or plants are protected by law. [Lat *sanctuarium*, from *sanctus*, holy]

sanctum *n* **-tums** or **-ta 1** a sacred place. **2** a place providing total privacy. [Lat, holy]

sand *n* **1** a grainy substance forming beaches and deserts, consisting of rock and other minerals powdered by the action of the sea. **2** (in *pl*) an area covered with this substance, esp. a seashore or desert. — *v* (*tr*) to smooth or polish with sandpaper or a sander. [OE]

sandbag *n* a sand-filled sack used with others to form a barrier against gunfire or flood, or as ballast. — *v* (*tr*) to barricade or weigh down with sandbags.

sandbank *n* a bank of sand in a river or sea, formed by currents, often exposed at low tides.

sandblast *n* a jet of sand forced from a tube by air or steam pressure. — *v* (*tr*) to clean (e.g. stonework) with a sandblast.

sandboy: **as happy as a sandboy** extremely happy.

sandcastle *n* a pile of sand moulded for fun into a (perhaps only approximate) castle shape.

sander *n* a power-driven tool to which sandpaper or an abrasive disc can be fitted for speedy sanding of wood.

the sandman *n* a man in folklore who supposedly sprinkles sand on children's eyes to make them sleepy.

sandpaper *n* abrasive paper with a coating orig. of sand, now usu. of crushed glass, for smoothing and polishing wood. — *v* (*tr*) to smooth or polish with sandpaper.

sandpiper *n* any of various wading birds of northern shores, with a high-pitched piping call.

sandpit *n* a shallow pit filled with sand for children to play in.

sandstone *n* a type of soft rock formed from compressed sand, widely used in building.

sandstorm *n* a strong wind sweeping along clouds of sand.

sandy *adj* **-ier**, **-iest 1** containing sand. **2** of the colour of sand, a pale yellowish-brown or (of hair) reddish-brown.

sandal *n* a light shoe with little or no upper and straps attached for holding it on the foot. [Gr *sandalon*]

sandalwood *n* **1** a light-coloured fragrant wood from the heart of a SE Asian tree, used for carving, and yielding an oil used in perfumes. **2** the tree. [Sanskrit *candana*]

sandwich *n* a snack consisting of two slices of bread or a roll with a filling of cheese, meat, etc. — *v* (*tr*) to place, esp. with little or no gaps, between two other things. [4th Earl of *Sandwich*, who ate such snacks rather than leave the gambling table for meals]

sandwich board *n* either of two boards carried against a person's chest and back by means of shoulder straps, for the purpose of displaying advertisements.

sandwich course *n* an education course involving alternate periods of study and work experience.

sane *adj* **1** sound in mind; not mad. **2** sensible. — *adv* **sanely**. ◇ See also **sanity**. [Lat *sanus*, healthy]

sang. See **sing**.

sangfroid *n* cool-headedness; calmness; composure. [Fr, cold blood]

sangria *n* a Spanish drink of red wine, fruit juice and sugar. [Span *sangria*, bleeding]

sanguinary *adj* **1** bloody; involving much bloodshed. **2** bloodthirsty. [Ety. as for **sanguine**]

sanguine *adj* **1** cheerful and full of hope. **2** (of a complexion) ruddy. [Lat *sanguis*, blood]

sanitary *adj* **1** promoting good health and the prevention of disease; hygienic. **2** relating to health, esp. waste and sewage disposal. [Lat *sanitas*, health]

sanitary towel *n* an absorbent pad worn next to the vagina to catch menstrual fluids.

sanitation *n* **1** standards of public hygiene. **2** measures taken to preserve public health, esp. waste and sewage disposal. [Ety. as for **sanitary**]

sanitise or **-ize** *v* (*tr*) **1** to make hygienic. **2** to make less controversial by removing potentially offensive elements. — *n* **sanitisation** or **-z-**. [**sanitary**]

sanity *n* **1** soundness of mind. **2** good sense. [Lat *sanitas*, health]

sank. See **sink**.

sanserif *n* (also **sans serif**) a style of printing in which the letters have no serifs. [Old *sans*, without (from Fr) + **serif**]

Sanskrit *n* a language of ancient India, the religious language of Hinduism since ancient times. — *adj* relating to or expressed in this language. [Sanskrit *samskrta*, perfected]

Santa Claus *n* Father Christmas, a jolly old man dressed in red who, in folklore, brings children presents on Christmas Eve or St Nicholas' Day. [Dut dialect *Sante Klaas*, St Nicholas]

sap[1] *n* **1** a thin liquid circulating in plants, carrying food and water. **2** vitality. **3** (*slang*) a weak or easily fooled person. — *v* **-pp-** (*tr*) **1** to drain sap from (esp. a tree). **2** to weaken or exhaust; to drain (e.g. a person's energy). [OE *sæp*]

sapling *n* a young tree.

sappy *adj* **-ier**, **-iest 1** (of plants) full of sap. **2** full of energy. — *n* **sappiness**.

sap[2] *n* a hidden trench by means of which an attack is made on an enemy position. — *v* **-pp-** (*tr*) **1** to attack by means of a sap. **2** to undermine or weaken. [Ital *zappa*, spadework]

sapper *n* (*Br*) a soldier, esp. a private, in the Royal Engineers.

sapient *adj* (*formal*; often *ironic*) having or showing good judgement; wise. — *n* **sapience**. [Lat *sapere*, to be wise]

sapphic *adj* **1** (*literary*) lesbian. **2** (*poetry*) written in verses of four lines, with a short fourth line. [*Sappho*, poetess of ancient Greece, and reputed lesbian]

sapphire *n* **1** a precious stone of a transparent dark blue colour. **2** this colour. [Gr *sappheiros*]

saprophyte *n* (*bot*) any plant that lives on decaying organic matter, e.g. a fungus. [Gr *sapros*, rotten + *phyton*, plant]

saraband *n* **1** a slow formal dance of 17th-century Spain. **2** a piece of music for, or in the rhythm of, this dance. [Span *zarabanda*]

Saracen *n* **1** a member of a wandering Syrian people of Roman times. **2** a Muslim defending the Holy Land from mediaeval Christian crusaders. [Gr *Sarakenos*]

sarcasm *n* **1** bitter, usu. ironical remarks expressing scorn or contempt. **2** the use of such remarks. **3** their bitter, contemptuous quality. [Gr *sarkazein*, to tear the flesh]

sarcastic *adj* **1** containing sarcasm. **2** tending to use sarcasm. — *adv* **sarcastically**.

sarcoma *n* **-mas** or **-mata** (*med*) a cancerous tumour developing in connective tissue. [Gr *sarkoma*, fleshy growth]

sarcophagus *n* **-gi** or **-guses** a stone coffin or tomb, esp. one decorated with carvings. [Gr *sarkophagos*, flesh-eating, a supposed quality of the limestone often used]

sardine *n* a young pilchard or other similar fish, commonly packed tightly into small tins. — **like sardines** crowded closely together. [Gr *sardinos*]

sardonic *adj* mocking or scornful. [Gr *sardonion*, bitter-tasting Mediterranean plant]

sardonyx *n* a type of onyx with alternating bands of white and orange-red. [Gr]

sargasso *n* **-os** or **-oes** a brown ribbon-like seaweed that floats in huge masses. [Port *sargaço*]

sarge *n* (*coll*) sergeant.

sari *n* **-is** (also **saree**) a traditional garment of Hindu women, a single long piece of fabric wound round the body and draped over one shoulder, and sometimes the head. [Hindi]

sarky *adj* **-ier**, **-iest** (*coll*) sarcastic.

sarnie *n* (*slang*) a sandwich.

sarong *n* a Malaysian garment worn by both sexes, a single piece of fabric wrapped around the body to cover it from the waist or chest down. [Malay *sarung*]

sarsaparilla *n* **1** a tropical American climbing plant with heart-shaped leaves. **2** its dried root, used medicinally. **3** a soft drink flavoured with the root. **4** a liquid medicine prepared from the root. [Span *zarzaparilla*]

sartorial *adj* relating to tailoring, or to clothes in general: *sartorial elegance*. [Lat *sartor*, patcher]

SAS *abbrev* Special Air Service, a British Army unit of highly trained troops specialising in secret operations.

sash[1] *n* a broad band of cloth worn round the waist or over one shoulder, as part of a uniform. [Arabic *shash*]

sash[2] *n* either of two glazed frames forming a sash window. [Fr *châssis*, frame]

sash cord *n* a cord connecting the system of weights and pulleys by which a sash window is opened and held open.

sash window *n* a window consisting of two sashes, one or either of which can slide vertically past the other.

sassafras *n* **1** a N American deciduous tree of the laurel family. **2** its aromatic bark, used as a flavouring and in perfumes and medicine. [Span *sasafrás*]

Sassenach *n* (*Scot*; usu. *derog*) an English person. — *adj* English. [Gaelic *Sassunach*, from Lat *Saxones*, Saxons]

Sat. *abbrev* Saturday.

sat. See **sit**.

Satan *n* the Devil, the primary evil spirit and the enemy of God. [Hebr, enemy]

satanic *adj* **1** of or relating to Satan. **2** evil; abominable.

Satanism *n* the worship of Satan. — *n* **Satanist**.

satchel *n* a small briefcase-like bag for schoolbooks, usu. with a shoulder strap. [OFr *sachel*, little bag]

sate *v* (*tr*) to satisfy (a desire or appetite) to the full or to excess. [OE *sadian*]

satellite *n* **1** a heavenly body that orbits a larger planet or star, as the Earth does the Sun. **2** a man-made device set in orbit round the Earth, e.g. as an aid to communication or global television transmission. **3** a nation or state dependent, esp. economically or politically, on a larger neighbour. **4** a follower or hanger-on. [Lat *satelles*, attendant]

satellite dish *n* a dish-shaped aerial for receiving television programmes broadcast via satellite.

satellite town *n* a small town near a larger city, esp. one orig. developed to prevent the city becoming undesirably large.

satiate *v* (*tr*) to satisfy fully or to excess. — *n* **satiability**. — *adj* **satiable**. — *n* **satiation**. [Lat *satiare*, from *satis*, enough]

satiety *n* the state of being satiated.

satin *n* silk or rayon closely woven to produce a shiny finish. — *adj* **satiny**. [*Zaitun*, Arabic form of the Chinese name of the town where it was orig. produced]

satinwood *n* **1** a shiny light-coloured hardwood used for fine furniture. **2** the E Indian tree that produces it.

satire *n* **1** a variety of humour aiming at mockery or ridicule, often using sarcasm and irony. **2** any work, e.g. a play or film, using this kind of humour. — *adj* **satirical**. [Lat *satira*, mixture]

satirise or **-ize** *v* (*tr*) to mock or ridicule using satire. — *n* **satirisation** or **-z-**.

satirist *n* **1** a writer or performer of satires. **2** a person who frequently uses satire.

satisfy *v* **-ies**, **-ied 1** (*tr*) to fulfil the needs, desires or expectations of; to fulfil (e.g. a desire). **2** (*tr*) to meet the requirements of; to meet (a requirement). **3** (*tr*) to remove the doubts of; to convince. **4** (*intr*) to please; to remove all desire for others: *the taste that satisfies*. **5** (*tr*) to compensate for; to give compensation to. — *adj* **satisfied**. — *adj* **satisfying**. [Lat *satis*, enough + *facere*, to make]

satisfaction *n* **1** the act of satisfying, or the state or feeling of being satisfied. **2** compensation for mistreatment.

satisfactory *adj* giving satisfaction; adequate; acceptable. — *adv* **satisfactorily**.

satsuma *n* a thin-skinned seedless type of mandarin orange. [*Satsuma*, former Japanese province]

saturate *v* (*tr*) **1** to make soaking wet. **2** (**with**) to fill or cover with a large amount of (something). **3** to cause (a chemical compound) to combine fully and exclusively with another, allowing no further combinations. — *adj* **saturated**. — *n* **saturation**. [Lat *satur*, full]

saturation point *n* a limit beyond which no more can be added or accepted.

Saturday *n* the seventh day of the week. [OE *Sæterndæg*, Saturn's day]

saturnalia *n* **1** (*cap*) the ancient Roman festival of the god Saturn in mid-December, a time of merry-making and gift-giving. **2** (*literary*) a scene of rowdy celebration; a wild party.

saturnine *n* (*literary*) **1** grim-faced; unsmiling. **2** melancholy in character. [From the supposed gloomy influence of the planet in astrology]

satyr *n* **1** a mythological woodland god, part man, part goat, noted for lechery. **2** a lustful man. [Gr *satyros*]

sauce *n* **1** any seasoned liquid that food is cooked or served in or flavoured with after serving. **2** added interest or excitement. **3** (*coll*) impertinence; cheek. — *v* (*tr*; *coll*) to be cheeky to. [Lat *salsa*, from *sal*, salt]

sauce boat *n* a long shallow jug for serving sauce in.

saucepan *n* a deep (usu. lidded) cooking pot with a long handle.

saucy *adj* **-ier**, **-iest** (*coll*) **1** impertinent or cheeky; attractively bold or forward. **2** dealing with sex, esp. in an amusing way: *saucy postcards*. **3** (of clothes) smart. — *n* **sauciness**.

saucer *n* **1** a small shallow round dish for placing under a tea or coffee cup. **2** something shaped like this. [OFr *saussiere*]

sauerkraut *n* shredded cabbage pickled in salt water, a popular German dish. [Ger, sour cabbage]

sauna *n* **1** a Finnish-style steam bath, the steam created by pouring water on hot coals. **2** a building or room equipped for this. [Finn]

saunter *v* **-r-** (*intr*; **along**, **past**, etc.) to walk at a leisurely pace, often aimlessly; to stroll. — *n* **1** a lazy walking pace. **2** a leisurely walk; an amble.

saurian (*biol*) *adj* of or relating to lizards; lizard-like. — *n* a lizard. [Gr *sauros*, lizard]

sausage *n* **1** a mass of minced and seasoned meat enclosed in a thin tube-shaped casing, usu. served hot and whole when small, and cold and in slices when large. **2** any vaguely cylindrical object, esp. with rounded ends. — **not a sausage** (*coll*) nothing at all. [OFr *saussiche*]

sausage meat *n* minced meat of the kind used for making sausages.

sausage roll *n* a small pastry case filled with sausage meat and baked.

sauté *v* **-és**, **-éing** or **-éeing**, **-éd** or **-éed** (*tr*) to fry lightly for a short time. — *adj* fried in this way: *sauté potatoes*. [Fr, tossed]

savage *adj* **1** untamed; uncivilised. **2** ferocious: *savage temper*. **3** cruel; barbaric. **4** uncultivated; rugged. — *n* **1** (now *offensive*) a member of a primitive people. **2** an uncultured, brutish or cruel person. — *v* (*tr*) to attack with ferocity, causing severe injury. — *adv* **savagely**. — *n* **savageness**. [OFr *sauvage*, wild, from Lat *silvaticus*, of the woods]

savagery *n* **-ies 1** (an act of) cruelty or barbarousness. **2** the state of being wild or uncivilised.

savanna or **savannah** *n* a grassy plain of tropical or subtropical areas, with little or no other vegetation. [Span *zavana*]

savant *n* a male learned person. [Fr, from *savoir*, to know]

savante *n* a female learned person.

save *v* **1** (*tr*) to rescue from danger, harm, loss or failure. **2** (*tr*; **up**) to set aside for future use. **3** (*intr*; **up**, **for**) to set money aside for future use. **4** (*tr*) to use economically so as to avoid waste. **5** (*tr*) to cause or allow to escape potential unpleasantness or inconvenience; to spare: *That will save you the trouble of making the trip*. **6** (*tr*; *sport*) to prevent (a ball or shot) from reaching the goal; to prevent (a goal) from being scored. **7** (*tr*; *relig*) to free from the influence or consequences of sin. **8** (*tr* & *intr*; *comput*, **to**) to transfer (data) to storage on hard disk or tape, or to print-out on paper. — *n* **1** an act of saving a ball or shot, or preventing a goal. **2** an instruction for a computer to store data on a disk or tape. — *prep* (**for**) except: *burned all the books save (for) one*. — *conj* (*old* with **that**) were it not (that): *I would have gone with her, save that she had already left*. [Lat *salvare*]

saving *n* **1** a thing saved, esp. an economy made. **2** (in *pl*) money saved up. — *prep* (*formal*) except; save.

saving grace *n* a desirable feature that compensates for undesirable ones.

saveloy *n* a spicy smoked pork sausage. [Fr *cervelat*]

saviour *n* **1** a person who saves someone or something from danger or destruction. **2** a person who frees others from sin or evil. **3** (*Christianity*; *cap*) Christ. [MidE *sauveur*]

savoir-faire *n* **1** expertise. **2** tact. [Fr]

savory *n* ***-ies*** any of various aromatic plants of the mint family whose leaves are widely used as a flavouring in cooking. [Lat *satureia*]

savour *v* **1** (*tr*) to taste or smell with relish. **2** (*tr*) to take pleasure in. **3** (*tr*) to flavour or season (food). **4** (*intr* with **of**) to show signs of; to smack of. — *n* **1** taste or smell as possessed by something. **2** a faint but unmistakable quality. **3** a hint or trace. [Lat *sapere*, to taste]

savoury *adj* **1** having a salty or sharp taste or smell; not sweet. **2** pleasant, esp. morally pleasing or acceptable: *not a very savoury character*. **3** appetising. — *n* ***-ies*** a savoury food, esp. served as an hors d'oeuvre. — *n* **savouriness**.

savoy *n* a winter variety of cabbage with wrinkled leaves. [*Savoie*, region of France where it was orig. grown]

savvy (*slang*) *v* ***-ies***, ***-ied*** (*tr* & *intr*) to know or understand. — *n* **1** common sense; shrewdness. **2** know-how. [Span *saber*, to know]

saw[1]. See **see**[1].

saw[2] *n* any of various tools with a toothed metal blade for cutting, hand-operated or power-driven. — *v* ***sawed***, ***sawn*** **1** (*tr*) to cut (as if) with a saw. **2** (*intr*) to move to and fro, like a hand-operated saw. [OE *sagu*]

sawdust *n* dust in the form of tiny fragments of wood, made by sawing.

sawfish *n* a large ray that has a long snout edged with tooth-like spikes.

sawmill *n* a factory in which timber is cut.

sawn-off shotgun *n* a shotgun with the end of the barrel cut off, making it easier to carry concealed.

sawyer *n* a person who saws timber in a sawmill.

sax *n* (*coll*) a saxophone.

saxifrage *n* any of a family of rock plants with tufted or mossy leaves and small white, yellow or red flowers. [Lat *saxifraga*, rock-breaker]

Saxon *n* **1** a member of a Germanic people that conquered much of Britain in the 5th and 6th centuries. **2** any of various Germanic dialects spoken by them. **3** a native or inhabitant of the region of Saxony in modern Germany. — *adj* of or relating to the (esp. ancient) Saxons. [Lat *Saxones*, Saxons]

saxophone *n* a wind instrument with a long metal body, vaguely S-shaped, and finger-keys along its length. — *n* **saxophonist**. [Adolphe *Sax* (1814–94), Belgian instrument-maker]

say *v* ***said*** **1** (*tr*) to utter or pronounce. **2** (*tr*) to express in words: *say what you mean*. **3** (*tr*) to state as an opinion: *I say we should refuse*. **4** (*tr*) to suppose: *Say he doesn't come, what do we do then?* **5** (*tr*) to recite or repeat: *say a blessing*. **6** (*tr*) to judge or decide: *difficult to say which is best*. **7** (*tr*; **for**, **against**) to argue in favour of or against: *a lot to be said for it*. **8** (*tr*) to communicate: *She talked for ages but didn't actually say much. What is the poem trying to say?* **9** (*tr*) to indicate: *clock says ten o'clock*. **10** (*tr*) to report or claim: *said to be still alive*. **11** (*intr* & *tr*) to make a statement (about); to tell: *I'd rather not say*. — *n* **1** a chance to express an opinion: *You've had your say*. **2** the right to an opinion; the power to influence a decision: *have no say in the matter*. — *interj* (esp. *US*) an expression of surprise, protest or sudden joy. — **go without saying** to be obvious. — **not to say** indeed; even: *expensive, not to say extortionate*. — **that is to say** in other words. — **there's no saying** it is impossible to guess or judge. [OE *secgan*]

saying *n* **1** a proverb or maxim. **2** an expression.

say-so *n* **1** the right to make the final decision. **2** an unsupported claim or assertion.

Sb *symbol* (*chem*) antimony. [Lat *stibium*]

SC or **S.C.** *abbrev* South Carolina.

Sc *symbol* (*chem*) scandium.

scab *n* **1** a crust of dried blood formed over a healing wound. **2** a contagious skin disease of sheep. **3** a plant disease caused by a fungus, producing crusty spots. **4** (*slang derog*) a worker who defies a union's instruction to strike. — *v* ***-bb-*** (*intr*) **1** (**over**) to become covered by a scab. **2** (*slang*) to work as a scab. [OE *sceabb*]

scabby *adj* **-ier**, **-iest 1** covered with scabs. **2** (*coll derog*) contemptible; worthless. — *n* **scabbiness**.

scabbard *n* a sheath for a sword or dagger. [MidE *scauberc*]

scabies *n* a contagious skin disease causing severe itching. [Lat, from *scabere*, to scratch]

scabious *n* any of a family of Mediterranean flowering plants with long stalks and dome-shaped flower heads. [Lat *scabiosa herba*, scabies plant, from its use in curing scabies]

scabrous *adj* **1** (of skin, etc.) rough and flaky or scaly. **2** bawdy; smutty. [Lat *scaber*, rough]

scaffold *n* **1** a framework of metal poles and planks used as a temporary platform from which building repair or construction is carried out. **2** a makeshift platform from which a person is hanged. **3** any temporary platform. [OFr *escadafault*]

scaffolding *n* **1** a scaffold (sense **1**) or arrangement of scaffolds. **2** materials used for building scaffolds.

scalar (*tech*) *adj* having magnitude only, with no direction. — *n* a scalar quantity, e.g. temperature. [Lat *scala*, ladder]

scalawag. Same as **scallywag**.

scald *v* (*tr*) **1** to injure with hot liquid or steam. **2** to treat with hot water so as to sterilise. **3** to heat to just short of boiling point. — *n* an injury caused by scalding. [Lat *excaldare*, to bathe in warm water]

scale[1] *n* **1** a series of markings or divisions at regular known intervals, for use in measuring; a system of such markings or divisions. **2** a measuring instrument with such markings. **3** the relationship between actual size and size as represented on a model or drawing. **4** a complete sequence of notes in music, esp. of those between two octaves. **5** any graded system, e.g. of employees' salaries. **6** extent or level relative to others: *on a grand scale*. — *v* (*tr*) **1** to climb. **2** to change the size of (something), making it larger (**scale up**) or smaller (**scale down**) while keeping to the same proportions. — **to scale** with all sizes and distances in correct proportion to the real thing. [Lat *scala*, ladder]

scale[2] *n* **1** any of the small thin plates that cover the skin of fish and reptiles. **2** a flaky piece of anything, esp. skin. **3** tartar on the teeth. **4** a crusty white deposit formed when hard water is heated, e.g. in kettles. — *v* **1** (*tr*) to remove the scales from (e.g. a fish), or scale from (e.g. a kettle). **2** (*tr*) to remove in thin layers. **3** (*intr*) to come off in thin layers or flakes. — *adj* **scaly**, **-ier**, **-iest**. [OFr *escale*, husk]

scale[3] *n* **1** (in *pl*) an instrument for weighing. **2** either of the pans of a balance. **3** (in *pl*; *cap* with **the**) the constellation and sign of the zodiac Libra. — **tip** or **turn the scales 1** to prompt a firm decision; to be the decisive factor. **2** (**at**) to have one's weight measured (at): *tip the scales at 250 pounds*. [Norse *skal*, pan of a balance]

scalene *adj* (of a triangle) having each side a different length. [Gr *skalenos*, uneven]

scallion *n* any vegetable of the onion family that has a small bulb and long edible leaves, e.g. the leek and the spring onion. [OFr *escalogne*]

scallop *n* **1** an edible shellfish that has a pair of hinged, fan-shaped shells. **2** one of these shells, esp. when served filled with food. **3** any of a series of curves that together form a wavy edge, e.g. on fabric. — *v* **-p-** (*tr*) **1** to shape (an edge) in scallops. **2** to bake in a scallop shell or small shallow dish. [OFr *escalope*]

scallywag *n* (*coll*) a naughty child; a rascal.

scalp *n* **1** the part of the head covered, or usu. covered, by hair; the skin at this part. **2** a piece of this skin with its hair, formerly taken from slain enemies as a trophy, esp. by some tribes of N American Indians. — *v* (*tr*) **1** to remove the scalp of. **2** (*coll*) to buy up (e.g. theatre tickets) for resale at inflated prices. [MidE]

scalpel *n* a small surgical knife with a thin blade. [Lat *scalpellum*, small knife]

scamp *n* a mischievous person, esp. a child. [OFr *escamper*, to decamp]

scamper *v* **-r-** (*intr*) to run quickly taking short steps, esp. in play. — *n* **1** an act of scampering. **2** a scampering movement or pace. [Ety. as for **scamp**]

scampi *n* **1** (*pl*) large prawns. **2** a dish of these, usu. deep-fried in breadcrumbs. [Plural of Ital *scampo*, shrimp]

scan *v* **-nn- 1** (*tr*) to read through or examine carefully. **2** (*tr*) to look over quickly. **3** (*tr*; *med*) to produce an image of (an internal part of the body) using any of various electronic devices. **4** (*tr*) to search (an area) using radar, or by sending out a beam of light. **5** (*tr*) to examine the rhythm of (a piece of poetry). **6** (*intr*) (of a poem) to conform to a pattern of rhythm. ◇ See also **scansion**. — *n* **1** an act of scanning. **2** (*med*) an image produced by scanning. — *n* **scanner**. [Lat *scandere*, to climb]

scandal *n* **1** widespread public outrage and loss of reputation; an event or fact causing this. **2** any extremely objectionable fact or situation. **3** malicious gossip. [Gr *skandalon*, stumbling-block]

scandalise or **-ize** *v* (*tr*) to shock or outrage.

scandalmonger *n* a person who spreads malicious gossip.

scandalous *adj* disgraceful; outrageous. — *adv* **scandalously**.

Scandinavian *adj* of or relating to Scandinavia, the countries of Sweden, Norway and Denmark collectively, sometimes also including Finland and Iceland. — *n* **1** a native or inhabitant of Scandinavia. **2** the group of northern Germanic languages spoken in Scandinavia. [Lat *Scandinavia*]

scandium *n* an element (*symbol* **Sc**), a rare silvery-white metal found in various minerals. [*Scandinavia*, where it was discovered]

scansion *n* **1** the act or practice of scanning poetry. **2** a poem's particular pattern of rhythm. [Lat *scansio*]

scant *adj* **1** in short supply. **2** meagre; inadequate. [Norse *skamt*]

scanty *adj* **-ier**, **-iest** (too) small in size or amount; hardly enough: *scanty clothing*; *a scanty meal*. — *adv* **scantily**. — *n* **scantiness**.

scapegoat *n* a person made to take the blame or punishment for the mistakes of others. [**escape** + **goat**, from the biblical Jewish practice of symbolically loading the sins of the people on to a goat which was then released into the wilderness]

scapula *n* **-lae** or **-las** (*med*) the shoulder-blade. [Lat]

scapular *adj* (*med*) of the scapula. — *n* a monk's garment consisting of a broad cloth strip with a hole for the head, hanging loosely over a habit in front and behind.

scar[1] *n* **1** a mark left on the skin after a wound has healed. **2** a permanent damaging emotional effect. **3** a blemish. **4** a mark on a plant where a leaf was formerly attached. — *v* **-rr-** (*tr & intr*) to mark or become marked with a scar. [Gr *eschara*]

scar[2] *n* a steep rocky outcrop on the side of a hill or mountain. [Norse *sker*, low reef]

scarab *n* **1** any of various dung-beetles, esp. the black dung-beetle, regarded as sacred by the ancient Egyptians. **2** an image or carving of the sacred beetle, or a gemstone carved in its shape. [Lat *scarabaeus*]

scarce *adj* **1** not often found; rare. **2** in short supply. — *adv* scarcely: *could scarce see it through the mist*. — *n* **scarcity**, **-ies**. — **make oneself scarce** (*coll*) to leave or stay away. [OFr *eschars*]

scarcely *adv* **1** only just. **2** hardly ever. **3** not really; not at all: *scarcely a reason to hit him*.

scare *v* **1** (*tr & intr*) to make or become afraid. **2** (*tr*) to startle. **3** (*tr* with **away**, **off**) to drive away by frightening. — *n* **1** a fright. **2** a sudden and widespread (often unwarranted) feeling of alarm provoked by foreboding news: *a bomb scare*. [Norse *skirra*, to avoid]

scarecrow *n* **1** a rough model of a human figure set up in a field, etc. to scare birds off crops. **2** (*coll*) a raggedly dressed person. **3** (*coll*) a very thin person.

scaremonger *n* a person who causes alarm by spreading rumours of (esp. imminent) disaster. — *n* **scaremongering**.

scary *adv* **-ier**, **-iest** (*coll*) causing fear or alarm.

scarf[1] *n* **-fs** or **-ves** a strip or square of fabric worn around the neck, shoulders or head for warmth or decoration. [Perhaps OFr *escarpe*, sash or sling]

scarf[2] *n* a glued or bolted joint made between two ends, esp. of timber, cut so as to overlap and produce a continuous flush surface. — *v* (*tr*) to join by means of such a joint.

scarify *v* **-ies**, **-ied** (*tr*) **1** to make scratches or shallow cuts on the surface of. **2** to loosen and break up the surface of (e.g. soil). **3** to hurt with severe criticism. — *n* **scarification**. [Gr *skariphos*, etching tool]

scarlatina *n* (*med*) scarlet fever. [Ital *scarlattina*]

scarlet *n* a bright red colour. [Persian *saqalat*, scarlet cloth]

scarlet fever *n* an infectious disease causing fever, inflammation of the nose, throat and mouth, and a rash on the body.

scarlet woman *n* (*old* or *humorous*) a sexually promiscuous woman, esp. a prostitute.

scarp *n* **1** an escarpment. **2** the inner side of a defensive ditch, nearest to or flush with the wall of a castle, etc. [Ital *scarpa*]

scarper *v* **-r-** (*intr*; *coll*) to run away; to leave quickly and unnoticed. [Ital *scappare*, to escape]

scarves. See **scarf**[1].

scary. See **scare**.

scat[1] *v* **-tt-** (*intr*; *coll*; esp. in the *imperative*) to go away; to run off. [Perhaps from **scatter**]

scat[2] *n* jazz singing consisting of improvised sounds, not words. — *v* **-tt-** (*intr*) to sing jazz in this way. [Perhaps imit.]

scathing *adj* scornfully critical. — *adv* **scathingly**. [Norse *skathe*, injury]

scatology *n* **1** preoccupation with the obscene, esp. with excrement and related bodily functions. **2** (*med*) the study of excrement for the purpose of diagnosis. — *adj* **scatological**. [Gr *skor*, dung + **-logy**]

scatter *v* **-r-** **1** (*tr*) to lay or throw haphazardly. **2** (*tr & intr*) to (cause to) rush off in different directions. — *n* **1** an act of scattering. **2** a quantity of scattered things. — *n* **scattering**. [MidE]

scatterbrain *n* (*coll*) a person incapable of organised thought. — *adj* **scatterbrained**.

scatty *adj* **-ier**, **-iest** (*coll*) **1** mentally disorganised. **2** crazy; daft. [From **scatterbrained**]

scavenge *v* **1** (*intr*) to search among waste for usable things. **2** (*tr*; *chem*) to remove impurities from. [OFr *scawage*, inspection]

scavenger *n* **1** an animal that feeds on refuse or decaying flesh. **2** a person who searches among rubbish for usable things.

ScD *abbrev* for *Scientiae Doctor* (Lat), Doctor of Science.

scenario *n* **-os** **1** a rough written outline of a dramatic work, e.g. a film; a synopsis. **2** a detailed script. **3** a hypothetical situation or sequence of events. [Ital]

scene *n* **1** the setting in which a real or imaginary event takes place. **2** a unit of action in a play or film. ◇ See also **act. 3** (any of the pieces making up) a stage or film set. **4** a landscape, situation, etc. as seen by someone: *a delightful scene met their eyes*. **5** an embarrassing display of emotion in public: *make a scene*. **6** (*coll*) a state of affairs with regard to a particular activity: *the current music scene*. **7** (*coll*) a liked or preferred area of interest or activity: *not my scene*. — **behind the scenes 1** out of sight of the audience. **2** unknown to, or out of sight of, the public. — **come on the scene** to arrive; to become part of the current situation. — **set the scene** to describe the situation in which an event takes place. [Gr *skene*, tent, stage]

scenery *n* **1** landscape, esp. when attractively rural. **2** the items making up a stage or film set.

scenic *adj* **1** of, being or including attractive natural landscapes: *a scenic trip*. **2** of or relating to scenery on stage or in film.

scent *n* **1** the distinctive smell of a person, animal or plant. **2** a trail of this left behind: *dogs on the scent*. **3** a series of findings leading to a major discovery: *police on the scent of the drug baron*. **4** perfume. — *v* (*tr*) **1** to smell; to discover by the sense of smell. **2** to sense; to be aware of by instinct or intuition. **3** to give a smell, esp. a pleasant one, to. [Lat *sentire*, to perceive]

sceptic *n* **1** a person who believes that nothing can be known with absolute certainty. **2** a person who questions widely accepted (esp. religious) beliefs. — *adj* **sceptical**. — *n* **scepticism**. [Gr *skeptikos*, thoughtful]

sceptre *n* a ceremonial rod carried by a monarch as a symbol of sovereignty. [Gr *skeptron*, staff]

Sch *abbrev* schilling.

schedule *n* **1** a list of activities or events planned to take place at specific times. **2** the state of happening on time according to plan: *behind schedule*. **3** any list or inventory. **4** a timetable. **5** a supplement to a document. — *v* (*tr*) **1** to plan (something) to happen at a specific time. **2** to put on a schedule. [Lat *schedula*, from *scheda*, strip of papyrus]

schema *n* **-*mata*** **1** a diagram or plan. **2** an outline or synopsis. [Gr, form]

schematic *adj* **1** following a particular plan or arrangement. **2** in the form of a diagram or plan.

schematise or **-ize** *v* (*tr*) to represent by means of a diagram or plan. — *n* **schematisation** or **-z-**.

scheme *n* **1** a plan of action. **2** a system or programme: *a pension scheme*. **3** a careful arrangement of different parts: *a colour scheme*. **4** a secret plan to cause harm or damage. **5** a diagram or table. — *v* (*intr*; **for**) to plan or act secretly and usu. maliciously. — *n* **schemer**. [**schema**]

scherzo *n* **-*zos*** or **-*zi*** a lively piece of music, esp. a vigorous or light-hearted movement in a symphony or sonata. [Ital, joke]

schilling *n* the standard unit of currency in Austria, divided into 100 groschen. [Ger]

schism *n* **1** (esp. *relig*) separation from the main group, or into opposing groups. **2** the act of encouraging such separation. **3** a breakaway group formed. — *adj* **schismatic**. [Gr *schisma*, split]

schist *n* any metamorphic rock that can be split into roughly parallel layers. [Gr *schistos*, split]

schizo *n* **-*os*** & *adj* (*coll*) (a person who is) schizophrenic.

schizoid *adj* showing some of the qualities of schizophrenia, e.g. extreme shyness and indulgence in fantasy, but without definite mental disorder. — *n* a schizoid person. [Gr *schizein*, to split + **-oid**]

schizophrenia *n* a severe mental disorder marked by feelings of extreme insecurity, a withdrawal into one's own mind, and an inability to distinguish between reality and fantasy. [Gr *schizein*, to split + *phren*, mind]

schizophrenic *n* & *adj* (a person) suffering from schizophrenia.

schmaltz *n* (*coll*) excessive sentimentality, esp. in music or other art. — *adj* **schmaltzy**, **-*ier***, **-*iest***. [Yiddish, from Ger *Schmalz*, cooking fat]

schnapps *n* (in N Europe) any strong dry alcoholic spirit, esp. Dutch gin distilled from potatoes. [Ger *Schnapps*, dram of liquor]

schnitzel *n* a veal cutlet. [Ger]

scholar *n* **1** a learned person, esp. an academic. **2** a person who studies; a pupil or student. **3** a person receiving a scholarship. [Lat *scholaris*; see ety. at **school**]

scholarly *adj* **1** showing evidence of extensive study. **2** typical of work produced by scholars: *a book too scholarly to be popular*.

scholarship *n* **1** a sum of money awarded for the purposes of further study, usu. to an outstanding student. **2** the achievements or methods of a scholar.

scholastic *adj* **1** of or relating to learning; academic; educational. **2** of or relating to scholasticism. [Gr *scholastikos*; see ety. at **school**]

scholasticism *n* **1** the system of (esp. religious and moral) teaching, based on the writings of the Greek philosopher Aristotle, that dominated W Europe in the Middle Ages. **2** stubborn adherence to traditional teaching methods and values.

school[1] *n* **1** a place where a formal general education is received esp. as a child or teenager. **2** a place offering formal instruction in a particular subject, often part of a university: *art school*. **3** the body of students and teachers that occupy any such place. **4** the period of the day or year during which such a place is open to students: *stay behind after school*. **5** a group of painters, writers or other artists sharing the same style or master. **6** any activity or set of surroundings as a provider of experience: *Factories are the schools of life*. **7** (*coll*) a group of people meeting regularly for some purpose, e.g. gambling: *a card school*. — *v* (*tr*) **1** to educate in a school. **2** (**in**) to give training (of a particular kind) to. **3** to discipline. [Gr *schole*, leisure, lecture-place]

schoolchild *n* a child who attends a school.

schoolhouse *n* **1** a building used as a school, esp. in a rural area. **2** a house for a teacher within the grounds of a school.

schooling *n* education or instruction, esp. received at school.

school-leaver *n* a young person recently completing a course of education and no longer attending a school.

schoolmarm *n* (*coll*) **1** (esp. *US*) a schoolmistress. **2** a woman with old-fashioned manners or attitudes, esp. regarding sex. — *adj* **schoolmarmish**.

schoolmaster *n* a male schoolteacher or head of a school.

schoolmistress *n* a female schoolteacher or head of a school.

schoolteacher *n* a person who teaches in a school.

school[2] *n* a group of fish, whales or other marine animals swimming together. — *v* (*intr*) to form, or move about in, a school. [Dut]

schooner *n* **1** a fast sailing-ship with two or more masts. **2** a large sherry glass. **3** (*US*) a large beer glass. [In 18th-century English *skooner* or *scooner*, poss. from dialect *scoon*, to skim]

schottische *n* **1** a folk dance, orig. from Germany, with short steps and hops, like a slow polka. **2** a piece of music for such a dance. [Ger *der schottische Tanz*, the Scottish dance]

schwa *n* **1** the English vowel sound that occurs in unstressed syllables, e.g. in tog*e*th*er*. **2** the phonetic symbol ə used to represent this sound. [Heb *schewa*]

sciatic *adj* **1** of (the region around) the hip. **2** affected by sciatica. [Lat *sciaticus*, from Gr *ischion*, hip-joint]

sciatica *n* intense and intermittent pain in the lower back, buttocks, and backs of the thighs caused by pressure on the sciatic nerve that runs from the pelvis to the thigh.

science *n* **1** the formal study of (a particular aspect of) the natural world, through observation and experiment. **2** the knowledge gained by such study. **3** any area of knowledge obtained using, or arranged according to, formal principles: *political science*. **4** acquired skill or technique, as opposed to natural ability. [Lat *scientia*, knowledge]

science fiction *n* fiction presenting a view of life in the future, esp. incorporating space travel and other technological developments the writer imagines will be current at the future time portrayed.

science park *n* a group of establishments combining scientific research with commerce, often attached to a university.

scientific *adj* **1** of, relating to or used in science. **2** displaying the kind of principled approach characteristic of science: *not very scientific but it works*. — *adv* **scientifically**.

scientist *n* a student of or expert in science.

sci-fi *n* (*coll*) science fiction.

scilicet *adv* (*formal*; usu. in writing) namely; that is to say. [Lat *scire licet*, it is permitted to know]

scimitar *n* a Middle-Eastern sword with a curved single-edged blade, usu. broadening towards the tip. [Perhaps Persian *shimshir*]

scintilla *n* (*literary*) a hint or trace; an iota. [Lat, spark]

scintillate *v* (*intr*) **1** to sparkle or send out sparks. **2** to capture attention with one's vitality or wit. — *adj* **scintillating**. — *n* **scintillation**. [Lat *scintilla*, spark]

scion *n* **1** a plant cutting used for propagation, esp. by grafting. **2** a descendant or offspring. [OFr *cion*]

scissors *n* (*pl*) a one-handed cutting tool with two long blades joined in the middle so as to pivot with cutting edges coming together. [Lat *cisorium*, cutting tool]

sclera *n* the membrane forming the outer covering of the eyeball. [Gr *skleros*, hard]

sclerosis *n* abnormal hardening or thickening of body tissue, organs, or blood vessels. — *adj* **sclerotic**. [Gr *skleros*, hard]

scoff[1] *v* (*intr*; **at**) to express scorn or contempt; to jeer. — *n* an expression of scorn; a jeer. — *adj* **scoffing**.

scoff[2] *v* (*tr* & *intr*; *coll*) to eat (food) rapidly and greedily. — *n* (*slang*) food. [Scots *scaff*, food]

scold *v* (*tr*) to reprimand angrily. — *n* (*old*) a nagging or quarrelsome person, esp. a woman. — *n* **scolding**. [Norse *skald*]

scollop. Same as **scallop**.

sconce *n* a candlestick with a handle, or one fixed by bracket to a wall. [Lat *absconsa*, dark lantern]

scone *n* a small round flattish plain cake, usu. halved and spread with butter and jam. [Scot]

scoop *v* (*tr*) **1** (**up**) to lift or dig with a sweeping circular movement. **2** (**out**) to empty or hollow with such movements. **3** to defeat (rival newspapers) in being the first to publish a particular story. — *n* **1** any of various spoon-like implements for handling or serving food. **2** a hollow shovel-like part of a mechanical digger. **3** a scooping movement. **4** a quantity scooped. **5** a news story printed by one newspaper in advance of all others. [ODut *schoppe*, shovel]

scoot *v* (*intr*; *coll*) to go away quickly.

scooter *n* **1** a child's toy vehicle consisting of a board on a two-wheeled frame with tall handlebars, propelled by pushing against the ground with one foot while standing on the board with the other. **2** (also **motor-scooter**) a small-engined motorcycle with a protective front shield curving back at the bottom to form a supporting board for the feet which joins the casing containing the engine at the back of the vehicle.

scope *n* **1** the size (of a subject or topic). **2** the range of topics dealt with. **3** the limits within which there is the freedom or opportunity to act. **4** range of understanding: *beyond his scope.* [Gr *skopos*, point watched]

-scope *comb fm* an instrument for viewing, examining or detecting: *telescope*. [Gr *skopein*, to view]

-scopic *comb fm* **1** relating to (features of) instruments ending in **-scope**: *telescopic.* **2** relating to observation or observed size: *microscopic.*

-scopy *n* observation or examination, usu. with the use of instruments ending in **-scope**: *microscopy.*

scorbutic *adj* (*med*) relating to or suffering from scurvy. [Lat *scorbuticus*]

scorch *v* **1** (*tr* & *intr*) to burn or be burned slightly on the surface. **2** (*tr*) to dry up or wither. **3** (*tr*) to injure with severe criticism or scorn. — *n* **1** a scorched area. **2** a mark made by scorching. — *adj* **scorching.** [MidE *skorken*]

scorcher *n* (*coll*) an extremely hot day.

score *v* **1** (*tr* & *intr*) to achieve (a point, etc.) in games. **2** (*tr* & *intr*) to keep a record of points gained during (a game). **3** (*tr*) to make cuts or scratches in the surface of; to mark (e.g. a line) by a shallow cut. **4** (*tr* with **out**) to cancel with a line drawn through. **5** (*tr*) to be equivalent to (a number of points): *black king scores three.* **6** (*tr*) to break down (music) into parts for individual instruments or voices; to adapt (music) for instruments or voices other than those orig. intended. **7** (*tr*) to compose music for (a film or play). **8** (*intr*) to achieve a rating; to be judged or regarded: *always score low in written tests*; *This film scores high for entertainment value.* **9** (*intr*; *slang*) to obtain drugs for illegal use. **10** (*intr*; *slang*; **with**) to succeed in having sex. — *n* **1** a number of points, etc. scored. **2** an act of scoring a point, etc. **3** a scratch or shallow cut, esp. made as a mark. **4** a set of twenty: *three score.* **5** (in *pl*) lots: *scores of letters to write.* **6** (*coll*; with **the**) the current situation; the essential facts: *What's the score?* **7** a written copy of music scored. **8** the music from a film or play. **9** (with **the**) a reason; grounds: *accepted on the score of suitability.* **10** matter; concern; aspect: *no worries on that score.* **11** a grievance or grudge: *settle old scores.* **12** a record of amounts owed. **13** (*slang*) a successful attempt to obtain drugs for illegal use. **14** (*slang*) a successful attempt to have sex. — **over the score** (*coll*) beyond reasonable limits; unfair. — *v* **score off** (*tr*) to humiliate (someone) in order to gain the admiration of others. [OE *scoru*]

scoreboard *n* a board on which the score in a game is displayed, altered as the score changes.

scorer *n* **1** a person who scores a point, etc. **2** a person who keeps a written record of the score during a game.

scorn *n* mocking contempt. — *v* (*tr*) **1** to treat with scorn. **2** to reject with scorn. — *adj* **scornful.** — *adv* **scornfully.** [OFr *escarn*, mockery]

Scorpio *n* **-os** **1** a constellation and the eighth sign of the zodiac, the Scorpion. **2** a person born under the sign, between 23 October and 21 November.

scorpion *n* **1** a desert creature with an insect-like body, four pairs of legs, pincers, and an upward-curling tail delivering a poisonous sting. **2** (*cap* with **the**) the constellation and sign of the zodiac Scorpio. [Gr *skorpios*]

Scot *n* a native of Scotland. [Lat *Scottus*]

Scot. *abbrev* **1** Scotland. **2** Scottish.

Scotch *adj* (of things, esp. products; not now used of people) Scottish. — *n* Scotch whisky. [From **Scottish**]

Scotch broth *n* a thick soup made with barley and chopped vegetables.

Scotch egg *n* a hard-boiled egg in a sausage-meat case, fried in breadcrumbs.

Scotch mist *n* very fine rain, common in the Scottish Highlands.

Scotch terrier *n* a short-legged terrier with a thick wiry (usu. black) coat.

Scotch whisky *n* whisky distilled in Scotland from barley or other grain.

scotch *v* (*tr*) **1** to ruin or hinder (e.g. plans). **2** to reveal (esp. rumours) to be untrue. — *n* any of the lines marked on the ground for hopscotch.

scot-free *adj* unpunished or unharmed. [Obsolete *scot*, payment, tax]

Scots *adj* (esp. of law and language) Scottish. — *n* any of the dialects related to English used in (esp. Lowland) Scotland. [Scots *Scottis*, Scottish]

Scotsman and **Scotswoman** *n* a native of Scotland.

Scots pine *n* a coniferous tree of Europe and Asia, the only native British pine.

Scottie *n* a Scotch terrier.

Scottish *adj* of Scotland or its people. [OE *Scottisc*]

scoundrel *n* a person without principles or morals; a rogue or villain.

scour[1] *v* (*tr*) **1** to clean by hard rubbing. **2** to flush clean with a jet or current of water. — *n* **1** an act of scouring. **2** diarrhoea or dysentery in cattle. — *n* **scourer.** [Lat *excurare*, to cleanse]

scour[2] *v* (*tr*) to make an exhaustive search of (e.g. an area). [Norse *skur*, storm, shower]

scourge *n* **1** a cause of great suffering to many people: *Cancer is the scourge of Western society*. **2** a whip used for punishing. — *v* (*tr*) **1** to cause suffering to; to afflict. **2** to whip. [Lat *excoriare*, to flay]

Scouse (*coll*) *n* **1** the dialect of English spoken in Liverpool. **2** a Scouser. — *adj* of Liverpool, its people or their dialect. [Short form of *lobscouse*, a sailor's stew]

Scouser *n* (*coll*) a native of Liverpool.

scout *n* **1** (*mil*) a person or group sent out to observe the enemy and bring back information. **2** (also **talent scout**) a person whose job is to discover and recruit talented people, esp. in the fields of sport and entertainment. **3** (often *cap*; *formerly* **Boy Scout**) a member of the Scout Association, a worldwide youth organisation promoting outdoor skills and community spirit. **4** (*coll*) a search: *have a scout around for it in my bag*. — *v* (*intr*) **1** to act as a scout. **2** (*coll*; **about, around**) to make a search: *scouting about for new premises*. [OFr *escouter*]

Scouter *n* an adult leader in the Scout Association.

scow *n* a large flat-bottomed barge for freight. [Dut *schouw*]

scowl *v* (*intr*) **1** to wrinkle the brow in displeasure or anger. **2** (**at**) to look disapprovingly, angrily or threateningly. — *n* a scowling expression. [MidE]

Scrabble® *n* a board game in which lettered tiles are used to form words in crossword fashion, points being scored according to the tiles used and their position on the board.

scrabble *v* (*intr*; **at, for**) to scratch, grope or struggle frantically. — *n* an act of scrabbling. [Dut *schrabben*, to scratch]

scrag *n* **1** (also **scrag-end**) the thin part of a neck of mutton or veal, providing poor-quality meat. **2** an unhealthily thin person or animal. — *v* **-gg-** (*tr*; *coll*) **1** to wring the neck of; to throttle. **2** to attack angrily; to beat up. [Perhaps from **crag**]

scraggy *adj* **-ier, -iest** unhealthily thin; scrawny. — *n* **scragginess.**

scram *v* **-mm-** (*intr*; *coll*; often in the *imperative*) to go away at once. [Perhaps from **scramble**]

scramble *v* **1** (*tr*) to crawl or climb using hands and feet, esp. frantically. **2** (*intr*) to struggle violently against others: *starving people scrambling to grab food*. **3** (*tr*) to cook (eggs) whisked up with milk. **4** (*tr*) to throw together haphazardly; to jumble. **5** (*tr*) to rewrite (a message) in code form, for secret transmission; to transmit (a message) in a distorted form via an electronic scrambler. **6** (*intr*) (of aircraft or air crew) to take off immediately in response to an emergency. — *n* **1** an act of scrambling. **2** a violent struggle to beat others in getting something. **3** a walk or half-climb over rough ground. **4** an immediate take-off in an emergency. **5** a cross-country motorcycle race. [Perhaps from **scrabble**]

scrambler *n* an electronic device that alters the frequency of messages transmitted by telephone or radio, making them unintelligible to third parties.

scrap[1] *n* **1** a small piece; a fragment. **2** the smallest piece or amount: *not a scrap of advice*. **3** waste material; waste metal for recycling or re-using. **4** (in *pl*) leftover pieces of food. — *v* **-pp-** (*tr*) to discard as useless or abandon as unworkable. [Norse *skrap*]

scrapbook *n* a book with blank pages on which newspaper cuttings, etc. can be mounted.

scrap heap *n* **1** a place where unwanted objects, e.g. old furniture, are collected. **2** the state of being discarded or abandoned: *consign the idea to the scrap heap*.

scrappy *adj* **-ier, -iest** not uniform, continuous, or flowing; disjointed; fragmented; bitty. — *adv* **scrappily**. — *n* **scrappiness.**

scrap[2] (*coll*) *n* a fight or quarrel. — *v* **-pp-** (*intr*) to fight or quarrel.

scrape *v* **1** (*tr*) to push or drag (something, esp. a sharp object) along (a hard or rough surface). **2** (*intr*) to move along a surface with a grazing action. **3** (*tr*; **off**) to remove (something) from a surface with such an action. **4** (*tr*) to damage by such contact: *scraped his elbow*. **5** (*intr*) to make savings through hardship: *scrimp and scrape*. **6** (*intr*) to slide the foot backwards when bowing: *bow and scrape*. — *n* **1** an instance, or the action, of dragging or grazing. **2** a part damaged or cleaned by scraping. **3** (*coll*) a difficult or embarrassing situation; a predicament. **4** (*coll*) a fight or quarrel. — *n* **scraper**. — *v* **scrape through** or **by** (*tr* & *intr*) to manage or succeed (in doing something) narrowly or with difficulty: *just scraped through* (*the interview*). — *v* **scrape together** or **up** (*tr*) to collect little by little, through enormous effort. [OE *scrapian*]

scratch *v* **1** (*tr*) to rub or drag (a sharp or pointed object) across (a surface), causing damage or making marks. **2** (*tr*) to make (e.g. a mark) by such action. **3** (*tr* & *intr*) to rub (the skin) lightly with the fingernails, e.g. to relieve itching. **4** (*tr* with **out, off**) to cross out or cancel. **5** (*intr*) to make a grating noise. **6** (*intr*) to withdraw from a contest. — *n* **1** a mark made by scratching. **2** an act of scratching. **3** a superficial wound or minor injury. — *adj* **1** hastily got together; improvised: *a scratch meal*. **2** (of a competitor) not given a handicap. — **from scratch** from the beginning; without the benefit of preparation or previous experience. — **scratch the surface** to deal only superficially with an issue or problem. — **up to scratch** (*coll*) meeting the required or expected standard. [MidE]

scratchy *adj* **-ier, -iest 1** making the marks or noises of scratching. **2** causing or likely to cause itching. — *adv* **scratchily**. — *n* **scratchiness**.

scrawl *v* (*tr* & *intr*) to write or draw untidily or hurriedly. — *n* untidy or illegible handwriting. — *adj* **scrawly**, ***-ier***, ***-iest***.

scrawny *adj* ***-ier***, ***-iest*** very thin and bony. — *n* **scrawniness**.

scream *v* **1** (*tr* & *intr*; **at, to, with**) to utter or cry out in a loud high-pitched voice, e.g. in fear, pain or anger. **2** (*intr*) to laugh uproariously. **3** (*intr*; **past, through**, etc.) to speed, esp. making a shrill noise: *The train screamed through the tunnel.* **4** (*intr* with **at**) to be patently (often unpleasantly) obvious: *His incompetence screamed at him.* **5** (*intr* with **at**) to be intensely (esp. unpleasantly) bright in colour: *The curtains scream at you.* — *n* **1** a loud piercing cry or other sound. **2** (*coll*) an extremely amusing person, thing or event. [OE *scræmen*]

scree *n* loose stones covering a hill or mountain slope; a slope covered with loose stones. [Norse *skritha*, landslip]

screech *n* a harsh shrill cry, voice or noise. — *v* **1** (*tr* & *intr*) to utter a screech or as a screech. **2** (*intr*) to make a screech: *screeching brakes.* — *adj* **screechy**, ***-ier***, ***-iest***. [MidE *scrichen*]

screech owl *n* the barn owl, whose call is more of a screech than a hoot.

screed *n* a long, often tedious, speech or piece of writing. [OE *screade*, shred]

screen *n* **1** a movable set of hinged panels, used to partition part of a room off for privacy. **2** a single panel used for protection against strong heat or light. **3** the part of a television set on which the images are formed. **4** a white (usu. cloth) surface on to which films or slides are projected. **5** (with **the**) the medium of films or television: *a star of stage and screen.* **6** (*cricket*) a sight-screen. **7** a windscreen. — *v* (*tr*) **1** (**off**) to separate or partition with a screen. **2** to show at the cinema or on television. **3** to subject to an examination, e.g. to test trustworthiness or check for the presence of disease. [OFr *escran*]

screenplay *n* the text of a film, comprising dialogue, stage directions, and details for sets, etc.

screen printing *n* (also **screen process**) a printing technique in which ink is forced through a fine silk or nylon mesh, with areas to be left blank blocked chemically.

screen test *n* a filmed audition to test an actor's suitability for a film role.

screw *n* **1** a type of nail with a spiral ridge down its shaft and a slot in its head, driven firmly into place using a twisting action with a special tool. **2** any object similar in shape or function. **3** (*snooker*, *billiards*) a shot in which sidespin or backspin is put on the ball. **4** (*slang*) a prison officer. **5** (*vulg slang*) an act of sexual intercourse. **6** (*vulg slang*) a person judged by sexual prowess or suitability as a sexual partner. **7** (*slang*) wages. — *v* **1** (*tr*) to twist (a screw) into place. **2** (*intr* & *tr*; **up, together**, etc.) to attach or assemble, or become attached or assembled, by means of screws. **3** (*tr*) to push or pull with a twisting action. **4** (*tr*; *coll*; **from, out of**) to obtain by persuasion or threat: *screw more money out of him.* **5** (*tr*; *coll*) to swindle. **6** (*snooker*, *billiards*) to put sidespin or backspin on (the cue ball). **7** (*tr* & *intr*; *vulg slang*) to have sex with (someone). — **have one's head screwed on (the right way)** (*coll*) to be a sensible person. — **have a screw loose** (*coll*) to be slightly mad or crazy. — **put the screws on** (*coll*) to use pressure on, esp. in the form of threats of violence. — **screw up 1** (*tr*) to press or squash together or into a ball. **2** (*tr*) to summon up: *screwed up all her courage.* **3** (*tr* & *intr*; *coll*) to ruin or bungle (something). **4** (*tr*; *coll*; esp. *US*) to cause to become extremely anxious, nervous or psychologically disturbed (*adj* **screwed-up**). [OFr *escroue*]

screwball *n* (*slang*; esp. *US*) a crazy person; an eccentric.

screwdriver *n* a hand-held tool with a metal shaft whose shaped end fits into the slot on a screw's head, turned repeatedly to twist a screw into position.

screw top *n* **1** a round lid that is screwed off and on to open and re-seal a bottle or other container. **2** a container with such a top. — *adj* **screw-top**.

screwy *adj* ***-ier***, ***-iest*** (*coll*) crazy; eccentric.

scribble *v* **1** (*tr* & *intr*) to write quickly or untidily. **2** (*intr*) to draw meaningless lines or shapes absent-mindedly. — *n* **1** untidy or illegible handwriting. **2** meaningless written lines or shapes. — *adj* **scribbly**, ***-ier***, ***-iest***. [Lat *scribere*, to write]

scribbler *n* (*derog*) a worthless writer.

scribe *n* **1** a person employed to make handwritten copies of documents before printing was invented. **2** a Jewish lawyer or teacher of law in biblical times. **3** a tool with a pointed blade for scoring lines on wood or metal. [Lat *scriba*, from *scribere*, to write]

scrim *n* heavy cotton fabric used as lining in upholstery, and in bookbinding.

scrimmage *n* a fist-fight or brawl. — *v* (*intr*) to take part in a scrimmage. [Variant of **skirmish**]

scrimp *v* (*intr*) to live economically; to be frugal or sparing: *scrimp and save.* — *adj* **scrimpy**, ***-ier***, ***-iest***. [Scot]

scrimshank *v* (*intr*; *coll*) to evade work or duties. — *n* **scrimshanker**.

scrip *n* **1** a scrap of writing paper. **2** (*coll*) a doctor's prescription. **3** (*finance*) a provisional certificate issued before a formal share certificate is drawn up. [Shortened form of **prescription** and **subscription**]

script *n* **1** the printed text, or the spoken dialogue, of a play, film or broadcast. **2** a system of characters used for writing; an alphabet: *Chinese script.* **3** handwriting. **4** an examination candidate's answer paper. — *v* (*tr*) to write the script of (a play, film or broadcast). — *n* **scriptwriter**. [Lat *scriptum*, from *scribere*, to write]

scripture *n* **1** the sacred writings of a religion. **2** (*cap*; in *pl*) the Christian Bible. — *adj* **scriptural**. [Lat *scriptura*, from *scribere*, to write]

scrivener *n* (*hist*) a person who drafts, or makes handwritten copies of, (esp. legal) documents. [Ety. as for **scribe**]

scrofula *n* (*old*) tuberculosis, esp. of the lymphatic glands. — *adj* **scrofulous**. [Lat *scrofulae*, from *scrofa*, a sow, apparently prone to it]

scroll *n* **1** a roll of paper or parchment written on, now only a ceremonial format, e.g. for academic degrees. **2** an ancient text in this format: *the Dead Sea scrolls*. **3** a decorative spiral shape, e.g. in stonework or handwriting. — *v* (*tr* & *intr*; **up, down**) to move (the displayed text on a computer screen) up or down to bring into view data that cannot all be seen at the same time. [MidE *scrowle*]

Scrooge *n* a miserly person. [A miserly character in Dickens's story *A Christmas Carol*]

scrotum *n* **-ta** or **-tums** the bag of skin enclosing the testicles in mammals. — *adj* **scrotal**. [Lat]

scrounge *v* (*tr* & *intr*; *coll*; **off**) to get (something) by shamelessly asking or begging; to cadge or sponge. — *n* **scrounger**. [Dialect *scrunge*, to steal]

scrub[1] *v* **-bb-** **1** (*tr* & *intr*) to rub hard, esp. with a brush, to remove dirt. **2** (*tr*) to clean by hard rubbing. **3** (*intr* with **up**) to wash the hands and arms thoroughly before taking part in a surgical operation. **4** (*tr*; *coll*) to cancel or abandon (e.g. plans). — *n* an act of scrubbing. [OGer *schrubben*]

scrubber *n* (*offensive slang*) **1** an unattractive woman. **2** a woman who regularly indulges in casual sex.

scrub[2] *n* **1** (land covered with) low-growing bushes and shrubs. **2** a small animal, or one of inferior breed. **3** a small or insignificant person. — *adj* **scrubby, -ier, -iest**. — *n* **scrubland**. [Variant of **shrub**]

scruff[1] *n* the back (of the neck); the nape.

scruff[2] *n* (*coll*) a scruffy person.

scruffy *adj* **-ier, -iest** shabbily dressed and untidy-looking. — *adv* **scruffily**. — *n* **scruffiness**.

scrum *n* **1** (*Rugby*) a formation of players from both teams, hunched and with arms and heads tightly interlocked; a re-starting of play in which the ball is thrown into such a formation and struggled for with the feet. **2** (*coll*) a riotous struggle. — *v* **-mm-** (*intr*; **down**) to form a scrum. [Short form of **scrummage**]

scrum half *n* (*Rugby*) the player from each side who puts the ball into scrums.

scrummage *n* & *v* (*intr*) (to form) a scrum. [Variant of **scrimmage**]

scrummy *adj* **-ier, -iest** (*coll*) scrumptious.

scrumptious *adj* (*coll*) **1** delicious. **2** delightful.

scrumpy *n* **-ies** strong dry cider with a harsh taste, esp. as brewed in SW England. [Dialect *scrump*, withered apples]

scrunch *v* **1** (*tr* & *intr*; **up**) to crunch or crumple, or become crunched or crumpled. **2** (*intr*) to make a crunching sound. — *n* an act, or the sound, of scrunching.

scrunch-dry *v* (*tr*) to squeeze (hair) into bunches during blow-drying to give it more body.

scruple *n* **1** (usu. in *pl*; **about, over**) a sense of moral responsibility that makes one reluctant or unwilling to do wrong: *has no scruples*. **2** a unit of weight equal to 20 grains. — *v* (*intr*) to be hesitant or unwilling because of scruples: *wouldn't scruple to steal if we were starving*. [Lat *scrupulus*, pebble, anxiety]

scrupulous *adj* **1** taking great care to do nothing morally wrong. **2** paying careful attention to even the smallest details. — *adv* **scrupulously**.

scrutiny *n* **-ies** **1** a close and thorough examination or inspection. **2** a penetrating or critical look. [Lat *scrutari*, to search]

scrutineer *n* a person who scrutinises something, esp. the collecting and counting of votes.

scrutinise or **-ize** *v* (*tr*) to subject to scrutiny; to look at carefully.

scuba *n* a breathing device for underwater divers, consisting of cylinders of compressed air connected to a mouthpiece. [*s*elf-*c*ontained *u*nderwater *b*reathing *a*pparatus]

scud *v* **-dd-** (*intr*) **1** (esp. of clouds) to sweep quickly across the sky. **2** (*naut*) to sail swiftly under the force of a strong wind. — *n* cloud, rain or spray driven by the wind.

scuff *v* (*tr* & *intr*) **1** to graze or scrape, or become grazed or scraped, through wear. **2** to drag (the feet) when walking. — *n* an area worn away by scuffing. [Imit.]

scuffle *n* & *v* (*intr*) (to take part in) a confused fight or struggle.

scull *n* **1** either of a pair of short light oars used by a lone rower. **2** a racing boat propelled by a solitary rower using a pair of such oars. **3** a large single oar at the stern, moved from side to side to propel a boat. — *v* (*tr*) to propel with a scull or sculls. — *n* **sculler**.

scullery *n* **-ies** a room, attached to the kitchen in a large house, where basic kitchen work, e.g. washing up and chopping vegetables, is done. [OFr *escuelerie*]

sculpt *v* **1** (*tr* & *intr*) to carve or model (clay, etc.). **2** (*tr*) to create (a solid model of something) in clay, etc. **3** (*tr*) to create a solid model of (someone or something) in clay, etc. [Lat *sculpere*, to carve]

sculptor *n* a person who practises sculpture.

sculpture *n* **1** the art of carving or modelling with clay, wood, stone, plaster, etc. **2** a work or works of art produced in this way. — *v* (*tr* & *intr*) to sculpt. — *adj* **sculptural**.

sculptured *adj* (of physical features) fine and regular, like those of figures in classical sculpture.

scum *n* **1** dirt or waste matter floating on the surface of a liquid. **2** (*coll derog*) a contemptible person or people. — *v* ***-mm-*** (*tr*) to remove the scum from (a liquid). [ODut *schum*, foam]

scumbag *n* (*derog vulg slang*) a contemptible person.

scummy *adj* ***-ier***, ***-iest*** **1** covered with a layer of scum. **2** (*slang*) contemptible; despicable.

scupper[1] *v* ***-r-*** (*tr*) **1** (*coll*) to ruin or put an end to (e.g. plans). **2** to deliberately sink (a ship).

scupper[2] *n* (*naut*) a hole or pipe in a ship's side through which water is drained off the deck.

scurf *n* **1** dandruff. **2** any flaking or peeling substance. — *adj* **scurfy**, ***-ier***, ***-iest***. [OE]

scurrilous *adj* insulting or abusive, and unjustly damaging to the reputation: *scurrilous remarks*. — *n* **scurrility**. [Lat *scurrilis*, from *scurra*, buffoon]

scurry *v* ***-ies***, ***-ied*** (*intr*; **along**, **away**, etc.) to move hurriedly, esp. with short quick steps. — *n* ***-ies*** **1** an act, or the sound, of scurrying. **2** a sudden brief gust or fall, e.g. of wind or snow; a flurry. [From **hurry-scurry**, reduplication of **hurry**]

scurvy *n* a disease marked by bleeding under the skin and sponginess of the gums, caused by lack of vitamin C. — *adj* ***-ier***, ***-iest*** vile; contemptible. — *n* **scurviness**. [OE *scurf*]

scut *n* a short tail, esp. of a rabbit, hare or deer. [MidE]

scuttle[1] *n* (also **coal scuttle**) a container for a small amount of coal, usu. kept near a fire. [OE *scutel*]

scuttle[2] *v* (*intr*) to move quickly with short steps; to scurry. — *n* a scuttling pace or movement. [Related to **scud**]

scuttle[3] *v* (*tr*) **1** to deliberately sink (a ship) by making holes in it. **2** to ruin (e.g. plans). — *n* a lidded opening in a ship's side or deck. [OFr *escoutille*, hatchway]

Scylla and Charybdis *n* (*pl*; *Gr mythol*) a sea monster and a whirlpool (or in some accounts two monsters) in the strait between Italy and Sicily, so situated that the avoidance of one would force a ship closer to the other. — **between Scylla and Charybdis** faced with danger on both sides, so that to avoid one means to be more exposed to the other.

scythe *n* a tool with a handle and a long curved blade, for cutting tall crops or grass by hand with a sweeping action. — *v* (*tr*) to cut with a scythe. [OE *sithe*]

SD *abbrev* (also **S. Dak.**) South Dakota.

SE *abbrev* south-east or south-eastern.

Se *symbol* (*chem*) selenium.

sea *n* **1** (usu. with **the**) the great mass of salt water that covers most of the Earth's surface and surrounds its land masses. **2** any named part of this, usu. smaller than an ocean. **3** an area of this with reference to its calmness or turbulence: *choppy seas*. **4** a large inland saltwater lake: *the Dead Sea*. **5** a vast expanse or crowd: *a sea of worshippers*. — **all at sea** completely disorganised or at a loss. — **at sea** in a ship on the sea. — **go to sea** to become a sailor. — **put**, or **put out**, **to sea** to start a journey by sea. [OE *sæ*]

sea anchor *n* a device, esp. a canvas funnel, dragged by a moving ship to slow it or prevent it drifting off course.

sea anemone *n* a sea creature whose round body and petal-like tentacles give it the appearance of a flower.

the sea bed *n* the bottom or floor of the sea.

seaboard *n* a coast.

sea breeze *n* a breeze blowing inland from the sea.

sea change *n* a complete change or transformation.

sea cow *n* a dugong or manatee.

sea dog *n* an old or experienced sailor.

seafaring *adj* travelling by or working at sea. — *n* **seafarer**.

seafood *n* shellfish and other edible marine fish.

seagoing *adj* (of a ship) designed for sea travel.

seagull. Same as **gull**[1].

sea horse *n* any of various small fish with a curling tail, a horse-like head, and an upright swimming position.

sea kale *n* a plant of European coastal waters, with edible spiky green leaves.

sea legs *n* (*pl*) ability to resist seasickness and walk steadily on the deck of a rolling ship.

sea level *n* the average level of the sea's surface between high and low tides, the point from which land height is measured.

sea-lion *n* any of various Pacific seals with large ears.

seaman *n* a sailor below the rank of officer.

seamanship *n* sailing skills, including navigation.

sea pink *n* same as **thrift** (sense **2**).

seaplane *n* an aeroplane designed to take off from and land on water.

seaport *n* (a town with) a port on the coast.

seascape *n* a picture of a scene at sea.

Sea Scout *n* a member of a division of the Scout Association that provides training in seamanship.

seashell *n* the empty shell of an oyster, mussel or other mollusc.

seashore *n* land next to the sea.

seasick *adj* suffering from nausea brought on by the rolling or dipping motion of a ship. — *n* **seasickness**.

the seaside *n* any coastal area, esp. a holiday resort.

sea urchin *n* a sea creature with a small rounded body protected by a hard spiky shell.

seaward *adj* facing or moving toward the sea. — *adv* (also **seawards**) towards the sea.

seaweed *n* **1** any plant growing in the sea or among rocks on the seashore. **2** such plants collectively.

seaworthy *adj* (of a ship) fit to be sailed at sea. — *n* **seaworthiness**.

seal[1] *n* **1** a device, e.g. a strip of plastic or metal, serving to keep something closed, damage to which is proof of interference. **2** a piece of rubber or other material serving to keep a joint airtight or watertight. **3** a piece of wax or other material attached to a document and stamped with an official mark to show authenticity. **4** such a mark: *the royal seal.* **5** an engraved metal stamp or ring for making such a mark. **6** an object given, or a gesture made, as a pledge or guarantee. **7** a decorative adhesive label or stamp. — *v* (*tr*) **1** (**up**) to make securely closed, airtight or watertight with a seal. **2** to fix a seal to, or stamp with a seal. **3** to decide or settle: *seal someone's fate*; *seal a business agreement*. **4** to paint (e.g. wood) with a substance that protects against damage, e.g. by weather. — *v* **seal off** (*tr*) to isolate (an area), preventing entry by unauthorised persons. — **set one's seal on** or **to** to authorise, approve or formally endorse. [Lat *sigillum*, from *signum*, mark]

sealant *n* any material used for sealing, esp. one painted on to protect against weathering or wear.

sealing-wax *n* a waxy mixture of shellac and turpentine used for seals on documents.

seal of approval *n* (often *facet*) official approval.

seal[2] *n* **1** any of several types of smallish fish-eating sea mammal, smooth-skinned or furry, with four flippers and webbed feet, breeding on land. **2** sealskin. — *v* (*intr*) to hunt seals. [OE *seolh*]

sealskin *n* **1** the skin of a furry seal, or an imitation of it. **2** a garment made from this.

seam *n* **1** a join between edges, esp. one sewn or welded. **2** a layer of coal or ore in the earth. **3** a wrinkle or scar. — *v* (*tr*) **1** to join edge to edge. **2** to scar or wrinkle. [OE]

seamless *adj* **1** having no seams; made from a single piece. **2** seeming to be a unified whole; showing no signs of having been pieced together.

seamstress *n* a woman who sews, esp. professionally.

seamy *adj* **-ier**, **-iest** sordid; disreputable. — *n* **seaminess**. **[seam]**

séance or **seance** *n* a meeting at which a person attempts to contact the spirits of dead people on behalf of other people present. [Fr, sitting]

sear *v* (*tr*) **1** to scorch. **2** to wither. — *n* a mark made by scorching. [OE *searian*, to dry up]

searing *adj* burning; intense.

search *v* **1** (*tr* & *intr*; **for**, **through**) to carry out a thorough exploration (of) to try to find something. **2** (*tr*) to check the clothing or body of for concealed objects. **3** (*tr*) to examine closely: *search one's conscience*. **4** (*tr* with **out**) to uncover after a thorough check or exploration. — *n* an act of searching. — **in search of** searching for. — **search me** (*coll*) I don't know; I have no idea. [OFr *cerchier*, from Lat *circare*, to go around]

searching *adj* that seeks to discover the truth by intensive examination or observation: *a searching inquiry*.

searchlight *n* **1** a pivoting exterior light with a powerful beam, used to monitor an area in darkness. **2** its beam.

search party *n* a group of people taking part in an organised search for a missing person or thing.

search warrant *n* a document, issued by a justice of the peace, giving a police officer the legal right to search premises.

season *n* **1** any of the four major periods — spring, summer, autumn and winter — into which the year is divided according to differences in weather patterns and other natural phenomena. **2** a period of the year during which a particular sport is played or some other activity carried out: *fishing season*; *holiday season*. **3** any period having particular characteristics: *rainy season*; *our busy season*. **4** a period during which a particular fruit or vegetable is in plentiful supply. — *v* **-n-** (*tr*) **1** to flavour (food) by adding salt, pepper or other herbs and spices. **2** to prepare (e.g. timber) for use. **3** to make mature or experienced: *seasoned travellers*. **4** to tone down or temper. **5** to add interest or liveliness to. — *adj* **seasoned**. — **in season 1** (of food) available, as determined by its growing season. **2** (of game animals) for which the legal right to hunt exists, according to the time of year. **3** (of a female animal) ready to mate; on heat. — **out of season 1** (of food) not yet available. **2** (of game animals) not yet to be hunted. [OFr *seson*]

seasonable *adj* **1** (of weather) appropriate to the season. **2** coming at the right time; opportune.

seasonal *adj* available, happening or taking place only at certain times of the year.

seasoning *n* any substance used to season food.

season ticket *n* a ticket giving the right to a specified or unlimited number of visits or journeys during a fixed period.

seat *n* **1** a thing designed for sitting on, e.g. a chair or bench. **2** the part of it on which one sits. **3** a place for sitting, e.g. in a cinema or theatre, often reserved; a reservation for such a place. **4** the buttocks.

5 the part of a garment covering the buttocks. **6** the base of an object, or any part on which it rests or fits. **7** a position in Parliament or local government; a position on a committee or other administrative body. **8** an established centre: *seats of learning*. **9** a large country house. — *v* (*tr*) **1** to assign a seat to, e.g. at a dinner table. **2** to provide seats for: *The car seats five*. **3** to place in any situation or location. **4** to fit firmly and accurately. — **be seated** to sit down. — **take a** or **one's seat** to sit down. [Norse *sæti*]

seat belt *n* a safety belt that prevents a passenger in a vehicle from being thrown violently forward in the event of a crash.

-seater *in cmpds* having seats for (a certain number of people): *a three-seater sofa*.

seating *n* the number or arrangement of seats, e.g. in a dining-room.

sebaceous *adj* of, like or secreting sebum. [Lat *sebaceous*]

sebum *n* an oily substance secreted by the body to lubricate the hair and skin. [Lat]

Sec. *abbrev* Secretary.

sec[1] *n* (*coll*) a second: *wait a sec*.

sec[2] *adj* **1** (of wine) dry. **2** (of champagne) medium sweet. [Fr, dry]

sec[3] *abbrev* secant.

sec. *abbrev* second.

secant *n* (*math*) **1** a straight line that cuts a curve in two or more places. **2** in a right-angled triangle, the ratio of the length of the hypotenuse to that of the side adjacent to the angle under consideration. ◇ See also **cosecant**, **cosine**, **cotangent**. [Lat *secans*, from *secare*, to cut]

secateurs *n* (*pl*) small sharp shears for pruning bushes. [Fr]

secede *v* (*intr*; **from**) to withdraw formally, e.g. from a political or religious body or alliance. — *n* **secession**. [Lat *secedere*, to go apart]

seclude *v* (*tr*) **1** to keep away from others; to isolate. **2** to keep out of view. [Lat *secludere*]

secluded *adj* **1** away from people and noise; private and quiet. **2** hidden from view.

seclusion *n* the state of being secluded; peacefulness and privacy.

second[1] *adj* **1** next after the first, in order of sequence or importance. **2** alternate: *every second week*. **3** additional; supplementary: *have a second go*. **4** subordinate; inferior: *second to none*. **5** so similarly talented as to be worthy of the same name: *a writer described as a second Shakespeare*. **6** (*mus*) indicating an instrument or voice with a subordinate role to, or a slightly lower pitch than, another: *second soprano*. — *n* **1** a person or thing next in sequence after the first. **2** the second gear in an engine. **3** a second-class honours degree. **4** an assistant to a boxer or duellist. **5** (in *pl*) flawed goods sold at reduced prices. **6** (in *pl*; *coll*) a second helping of food. **7** (in *pl*; *coll*) the second course of a meal. **8** the Cub Scout or Brownie Guide next in rank to a sixer. — *v* (*tr*) **1** to declare formal support for (a proposal, or the person making it). **2** to give support or encouragement of any kind to. **3** to act as second to (a boxer or duellist). — *adv* in second place: *came second in the race*. [Lat *secundus*]

second best *n* the next after the best. — *adj* **second-best**. — **come off second best** (*coll*) to lose.

second childhood *n* senility; dotage.

second class *n* the class or category below the first in quality or value. — *adj* (**second-class**) **1** of or relating to the class below the first. **2** of a poor standard; inferior. **3** not having as many privileges as others: *a second-class citizen*. — *adv* (**second-class**) in carriages, etc. of a standard below that of the top class: *travel second-class*.

second cousin *n* the child of a parent's cousin.

seconder *n* a person who seconds a proposal or seconds the person making it.

second-hand *adj* **1** previously owned or used by someone else. **2** not directly received or obtained, but coming via an intermediary: *second-hand information*. — *adv* **1** in a second-hand state: *buy furniture second-hand*. **2** not directly, but from someone else: *heard it second-hand*.

second lieutenant *n* an army or navy officer of the lowest commissioned rank, the rank below lieutenant.

secondly *adv* in the second place; as a second consideration.

second nature *n* a habit so firmly fixed as to seem an innate part of a person's nature.

second person see **person**.

second-rate *adj* inferior; substandard.

second sight *n* the supposed power to see into the future or to see things happening elsewhere.

second thoughts *n* (*pl*) **1** doubts: *having second thoughts*. **2** a process of reconsidering and reaching a different decision: *on second thoughts*.

second wind *n* **1** the recovery of normal breathing after exertion. **2** a burst of renewed energy or enthusiasm.

second[2] *n* **1** a sixtieth part of a minute of time. **2** a sixtieth part of a minute of an angle, $\frac{1}{360}$ of a degree. **3** a moment: *wait a second*. [Lat *secunda* (*minuta*), secondary (minute)]

second hand *n* the pointer on a watch or clock that measures the time in seconds.

second[3] *v* (*tr*) to transfer temporarily to a different post, place or duty. — *n* **secondment**. [Fr *en second*, in the second rank]

secondary *adj* **1** of lesser importance than the principal or primary concern; subordinate. **2** developed from something earlier or original: *a secondary infection*. **3** (of education) between primary and higher or further; for pupils between ages 11 and 18. ◇ See also **primary**, **tertiary**. [Lat *secundarius*]

secondary colour *n* a colour obtained by mixing two primary colours.

secondary picketing *n* picketing of firms that have business connections with the employer against whom action is being taken.

secondary stress *n* (*linguistics*) the second-strongest stress in a word, etc. ◇ See also **primary stress.**

secrecy *n* **1** the state or fact of being secret. **2** the ability or tendency to keep information secret. [MidE *secretie*, from *secre*, secret]

secret *adj* **1** hidden from or undisclosed to others, or to all but a few. **2** whose activities are unknown to or unobserved by others: *a secret army*. **3** tending to conceal things from others; secretive. — *n* **1** a piece of information not revealed, or not to be revealed, to others. **2** an unknown or unrevealed method of achievement: *the secret of eternal youth*. **3** a fact or purpose that remains unexplained; a mystery. — *adv* **secretly**. — **in secret** secretly; unknown to others. ◇ See also **secrecy**. [Lat *secretus*, set apart]

secret agent *n* a member of the secret service; a spy.

secretive *adj* inclined not to reveal things to others; fond of secrecy. — *n* **secretiveness**.

secret police *n* a police force operating in secret to stamp out opposition to the government.

secret service *n* a government department responsible for espionage and matters of national security.

secretaire *n*. Same as **escritoire**. [Fr, secretary]

secretariat *n* **1** the administrative department of any large organisation, esp. a legislative body. **2** its staff or premises. [Fr *secrétariat*]

secretary *n* **-*ies*** **1** a person employed to perform administrative or clerical tasks. **2** the member of a club or society responsible for its correspondence and business records. **3** a senior civil servant assisting a government minister or ambassador. — *adj* **secretarial**. [Lat *secretarius*, person spoken to in confidence]

secretary-bird *n* a long-legged, long-tailed, snake-eating African bird of prey.

secretary-general *n* the principal administrative official in a large (esp. political) organisation.

Secretary of State *n* **1** in the UK, a minister at the head of a major government department. **2** in the US, the head of the department dealing with foreign affairs.

secrete[1] *v* (*tr*) (of a gland or similar organ) to form and release (a substance) for use in the body, or as an excretion. — *adj* **secretory**. [Ety. as for **secret**]

secretion *n* **1** a substance secreted. **2** the process of secreting.

secrete[2] *v* (*tr*) to hide away or conceal. [Ety. as for **secret**]

sect *n* a small (esp. religious) group whose views and practices are regarded as extreme, usu. part of, or separated from, some larger body. [Lat *secta*, a following]

sectarian *adj* **1** of, relating to or belonging to a sect. **2** having, showing or caused by hostility towards those outside one's own group or belonging to a particular group: *sectarian violence*. — *n* a member of a sect, esp. a bigoted person. — *n* **sectarianism**.

section *n* **1** any of the parts into which a thing is or can be divided, or from which it is constructed. **2** a subdivision of an army platoon. **3** the surface formed by cutting through a solid geometric figure. **4** the act of cutting through a solid figure. **5** a plan or diagram showing a view of an object as if it had been cut through. [Lat *secare*, to cut]

sectional *adj* **1** made in sections. **2** relating, or restricted, to a particular group or area.

sector *n* **1** a part of an area divided up for military purposes. **2** a separate part into which any sphere of activity, e.g. a nation's economy, can be divided: *the public and private sectors*. **3** a portion of a circle formed by two radii and the part of the circumference lying between them. [Lat, cutter]

secular *adj* **1** not religious or ecclesiastical; civil or lay. **2** relating to this world; not heavenly or spiritual. **3** (of members of the clergy) not bound by vows to a particular religious order. **4** occurring only once in a lifetime, century or age. [Lat *saecularis*, from *saeculum*, generation, century]

secularism *n* the view that society's values and standards should not be influenced or controlled by religion or the Church. — *v* (*tr*) **secularise** or **-ize**. — *n* **secularist**.

secure *adj* **1** free from danger; providing freedom from danger. **2** free from trouble or worry. **3** firmly fixed or attached. **4** not likely to be lost or taken away; assured: *a secure job*. — *v* (*tr*) **1** to fasten or attach firmly. **2** to get or get possession of. **3** to make free from danger or risk. **4** to guarantee. — *adv* **securely**. [Lat *securus*, from *se-*, without + *cura*, care]

security *n* **-*ies*** **1** the state of being secure. **2** freedom from the possibility of future financial difficulty. **3** protection from physical harm, esp. assassination. **4** freedom from vulnerability to political or military takeover: *national security*. **5** something given as a guarantee, e.g. of repayment of a loan. **6** (usu. in *pl*) a certificate stating ownership of stocks or shares; the monetary value represented by such certificates.

security blanket *n* **1** a blanket or other familiar piece of cloth carried around by a toddler for comfort. **2** any familiar object whose presence provides a sense of security or comfort.

security risk *n* a person or activity considered to be a threat to a nation's security, e.g. because of a likelihood of giving away military secrets.

sedan *n* **1** (*hist*; also **sedan chair**) a large enclosed chair which can be lifted and carried on horizontal poles. **2** (*US*) a saloon car.

sedate[1] *adj* **1** calm and dignified in manner. **2** slow and unexciting. — *adv* **sedately**. [Lat *sedare*, to still]

sedate[2] *v* (*tr*) to make calm by means of a sedative. — *n* **sedation**. [Lat *sedare*, to still]

sedative *n* & *adj* (a drug) having a soothing or calming effect.

sedentary *adj* **1** (of work) involving much sitting down. **2** (of a person) spending a lot of time sitting down; taking little exercise. [Lat *sedere*, to sit]

sedge *n* any of various grass-like plants of marshy areas, with triangular stems and clusters of tiny flowers. [OE *secg*]

sediment *n* **1** solid matter that settles at the bottom of a liquid. **2** material deposited by water, wind or ice and formed into rock. — *adj* **sedimentary**. [Lat *sedimentum*, from *sedere*, to sit]

sedition *n* speech, writing or action encouraging public disorder, esp. rebellion against the government. — *adj* **seditious**. [Lat *seditio*, a going apart]

seduce *v* (*tr*) **1** to charm into having sex. **2** to tempt, esp. into wrongdoing. — *n* **seduction**. [Lat *seducere*, to lead aside]

seductive *adj* **1** sexually very attractive and charming. **2** creating, or designed to create, the mood for sex: *seductive lighting*. **3** tempting; enticing. — *adv* **seductively**. — *n* **seductiveness**.

sedulous *adj* (*formal*) **1** steadily hard-working and conscientious; diligent. **2** painstakingly carried out. — *n* **sedulity**. [Lat *sedulus*]

sedum *n* any of a family of rock plants with fleshy leaves and white, yellow or pink flowers. [Lat]

see[1] *v* ***saw***, ***seen*** **1** (*tr*) to perceive with the eyes. **2** (*intr*) to have the power of vision. **3** (*tr*) to watch: *see a play*. **4** (*tr* & *intr*) to understand: *I don't see* (*what you mean*). **5** (*tr*) to be aware of or know, esp. by looking: *I see* (*from your letter*) *that you're married*. **6** (*tr* & *intr*) to find out: *wait and see*. **7** (*tr*) to meet up with; to be in the company of: *not seen her for ages*. **8** (*tr*) to spend time with, esp. romantically: *seeing a married woman*. **9** (*tr*) to speak to or consult: *asking to see the manager*. **10** (*tr*) to receive as a visitor: *The manager refused to see me*. **11** (*tr* & *intr*; **to**) to make sure (of): *See that you lock the door. I've seen to it*. **12** (*tr*) to imagine, esp. to regard as likely; to picture in the mind: *can't see him agreeing*; *can still see her as a little girl*. **13** (*tr*) to consider: *see her more as a writer than a politician*. **14** (*intr* with **in**) to find attractive: *don't know what he sees in her*. **15** (*tr*) to be witness to as a sight or event: *don't want to see her hurt*; *now seeing huge increases in unemployment*. **16** (*tr*) to escort: *see you home*. **17** (*tr*) to refer to for information: *see page 5*. **18** (*tr*; *cards*) to match the bet of by staking the same sum: *see you and raise you five*. — *v* **see about** (*tr*) to attend to the matter of. — **see fit to** to think it appropriate or proper to (do something). — *v* **see into** (*tr*) to investigate; to look into. — **see the light 1** to discover religious feelings within oneself. **2** to recognise the merits of, and adopt, some widely held point of view. — *v* **see off** (*tr*) **1** to accompany to a place of departure. **2** (*coll*) to get rid of by force. — *v* **see out** (*tr*) **1** to escort out. **2** to stay until the end of. **3** to outlive. — *v* **see over** (*tr*) to inspect; to look over. — **see things** to have hallucinations. — *v* **see through** (*tr*) **1** to be able to see what is behind or under (something). ◇ See also **see-through** below. **2** to recognise an essential truth underlying (a lie, trick, etc.). **3** to participate in to the end. — **see you (later)** (*coll*) goodbye for now.

seeing *n* the ability to see; the power of vision. — *conj* (**that**) given (that); since: *Seeing you're opposed to my plan, I won't pursue it*.

see-through *adj* (esp. of a garment) through which what is inside, underneath or beyond can be seen. ◇ See also **see through** above.

see[2] *n* **1** the post of bishop. **2** the area under the religious authority of a bishop or archbishop. [Lat *sedes*, seat]

seed *n* ***seeds*** or ***seed*** **1** (the part of) the fruit of a plant from which a new plant grows. **2** source or origin: *the seeds of the idea*. **3** (*literary*) offspring; descendants. **4** (*literary*) semen. **5** (*sport*) a seeded player. — *v* **1** (*intr*) (of a plant) to produce seeds. **2** (*tr*) to plant (seeds). **3** (*tr*) to remove seeds from (e.g. a fruit). **4** (*tr*; *sport*) to rank (a player in a tournament) according to his or her likelihood of winning; to arrange (a tournament) so that high-ranking players only meet each other in the latter stages of the contest. — *adj* **seeded**. — *adj* **seedless**. — **go to seed 1** (also **run to seed**) (of a plant) to grow rapidly and untidily prior to producing seed. **2** (*coll*) to allow oneself to become unkempt or unhealthy through lack of care. [OE *sæd*]

seedbed *n* **1** a piece of ground prepared for the planting of seeds. **2** an environment in which something (esp. undesirable) develops.

seedhead *n* a compact mass or cluster of seeds on a plant.

seedling *n* a young plant grown from seed.

seed-pearl *n* a tiny pearl.

seed-potato *n* a potato kept for planting, from which a new potato plant grows.

seedy *adj* ***-ier***, ***-iest*** **1** (of a fruit, etc.) full of seeds. **2** (of a plant) at the stage of producing seeds. **3** (*coll*) mildly ill. **4** (*coll*) shabby; run-down, dirty or disreputable: *seedy areas of town.*

seek *v* ***sought*** (*tr*) **1** to look for. **2** to try to get or achieve. **3** to try or endeavour: *seeking to please.* **4** to take oneself off to; to go to get: *seek shelter in a cave.* **5** to ask for: *sought his advice.* — *v* **seek out** (*tr*) to search intensively for and find. [OE *secan*]

seem *v* (*intr*) **1** to appear to the eye; to give the impression of (being). **2** to be apparent; to appear to the mind: *There seems* (*to be*) *no good reason for refusing.* **3** to think or believe oneself (to be, do, etc.): *I seem to know you from somewhere.* [Norse *soemr*, fitting]

seeming *adj* apparent. — *adv* **seemingly**.

seemly *adj* ***-ier***, ***-iest*** (*old*) fitting; suitable.

seen. See **see**[1].

seep *v* (*intr*) (of a liquid) to escape slowly, through or as if through a narrow opening. — *n* **seepage**. [Perhaps OE *sipian*, to soak]

seer *n* **1** a person who predicts future events; a clairvoyant. **2** a person of great wisdom and insight; a prophet. [**see**]

seersucker *n* lightweight cotton or linen cloth with a crinkly appearance. [Persian *shir o shakkar*, milk and sugar]

seesaw *n* **1** a plaything consisting of a plank balanced in the middle, allowing people, esp. children, seated on its ends to propel each other up and down by pushing off the ground with the feet. **2** an alternate up-and-down or back-and-forth movement. — *v* ***-sawed*** (*intr*) to move alternately up-and-down or back-and-forth. [Reduplication of **saw**[2], from a sawing action]

seethe *v* (*intr*) **1** (of a liquid) to churn and foam because or as if boiling. **2** to be extremely agitated, esp. with anger. — *adj* **seething**. [OE *seothan*]

segment *n* **1** a part, section or portion. **2** a part of a circle or sphere separated off by an intersecting line or plane. — *v* (*tr*) to divide into segments. — *n* **segmentation**. [Lat *segmentum*, from *secare*, to cut]

segregate *v* (*tr*) to separate (a group or groups) from others or from each other. — *adj* **segregated**. [Lat *se-*, apart + *grex*, flock]

segregation *n* **1** enforced separation into groups. **2** systematic isolation of one group, esp. a racial or ethnic minority, from the rest of society. — *adj* **segregational**.

seigneur *n* a feudal lord, esp. in France. [Fr]

seine *n* a large fishing net kept hanging vertically underwater by means of floats and weights. — *v* (*tr* & *intr*) to catch (fish) with a seine. [OE *segne*]

seismic *adj* **1** of or relating to earthquakes. **2** (*coll*) gigantic: *an increase of seismic proportions.* [Gr *seismos*, a shaking]

seismograph *n* an instrument that measures and records the force of earthquakes. — *n* **seismography**. [Gr *seismos*, a shaking + **-graph**]

seismology *n* the scientific study of earthquakes. — *adj* **seismological**. — *n* **seismologist**. [Gr *seismos*, a shaking + **-logy**]

seize *v* **1** (*tr*) to take or grab suddenly. **2** (*tr*) to affect suddenly and deeply; to overcome: *seized by panic.* **3** (*tr*) to take by force; to capture. **4** (*tr*) to take legal possession of. **5** (*tr* & *intr*; **on, upon**) to take (up) eagerly: *She seized the chance to point out my failings.* — *v* **seize up** (*intr*) to become stiff or jammed, e.g. through overuse or lack of lubrication. [OFr *saisir*]

seizure *n* **1** the act of seizing. **2** a sudden attack of an illness, esp. producing spasms or loss of movement.

seldom *adv* rarely. [OE *seldum*]

select *v* (*tr*) to choose from among several. — *adj* **1** picked out in preference to others. **2** to which entrance or membership is restricted; exclusive. — *n* **selectness**. — *n* **selector**. [Lat *seligere*]

select committee *n* a committee of Members of Parliament set up temporarily to look into a specific subject, e.g. education or defence.

selection *n* **1** the act or process of selecting or being selected. **2** a thing or set of things selected. **3** a range from which to choose. **4** the (naturally occurring or artificially stimulated) process by which certain animals or plants survive while others do not, leading, according to evolutionary theory, to the development of certain physical characteristics.

selective *adj* **1** exercising the right to reject some in favour of others. **2** able or tending to select; discriminating. **3** involving only certain people or things; exclusive. — *n* **selectivity**.

selenium *n* an element, symbol **Se**, a non-metallic, light-sensitive solid used e.g. in solar batteries. [Gr *selene*, moon]

self *n* ***selves*** **1** personality, or a particular aspect of it. **2** a person as a whole, a combination of characteristics of appearance and behaviour: *his usual happy self.* **3** personal interest or advantage. — *pron* (*coll*) myself, yourself, himself or herself. [OE *seolf*]

selfish *adj* **1** tending to be concerned only with personal welfare, not the welfare of others. **2** (of an act) revealing such a tendency. — *n* **selfishness**.

selfless *adj* **1** tending to consider the welfare of others before one's own. **2** (of an act) revealing such a tendency. — *n* **selflessness**.

self- *in cmpds* **1** of, by, for, in, to, or in relation to oneself: *self-doubt*; *self-inflicted.* **2** acting automatically: *self-closing.*

self-abuse *n* masturbation.

self-addressed *adj* addressed by the sender for return to him- or herself.

self-appointed *adj* acting on one's own authority, without being asked or chosen by others.

self-assertive *adj* always ready to make others aware of one's presence or opinions, esp. arrogantly or aggressively. — *n* **self-assertion**.

self-assurance *n* self-confidence. — *adj* **self-assured**.

self-catering *adj* (with accommodation) in which the guest or resident is responsible for providing and preparing his or her own meals.

self-centred *adj* interested only in oneself and one's own affairs.

self-coloured *adj* **1** of the same colour all over. **2** in its natural colour; undyed.

self-confessed *adj* as openly admitted by oneself: *a self-confessed cheat*.

self-confidence *n* total absence of shyness; confidence in one's own abilities. — *adj* **self-confident**.

self-conscious *adj* (tending to be) ill at ease in company as a result of feeling oneself to be observed by others. — *n* **self-consciousness**.

self-contained *adj* **1** (of accommodation) of which no part is shared with others. **2** content to be on one's own; independent. **3** needing nothing added; complete.

self-control *n* the ability to control one's emotions and impulses. — *adj* **self-controlled**.

self-defence *n* **1** the act or techniques of defending oneself from physical attack. **2** the act of defending one's own rights or principles.

self-denial *n* the act or practice of denying one's own needs or wishes.

self-determination *n* **1** the freedom to make one's own decisions without interference from others. **2** a nation's freedom to govern itself, without outside control.

self-drive *adj* (of a hired vehicle) to be driven by the hirer.

self-effacing *adj* tending to avoid making others aware of one's presence or one's achievements, because of shyness or modesty. — *n* **self-effacement**.

self-employed *adj* working on one's own behalf and under one's own control, rather than as an employee.

self-esteem *n* one's opinion, esp. good opinion, of oneself; self-respect.

self-evident *adj* clear enough to need no explanation or proof.

self-explanatory *adj* easily understood; needing no further explanation.

self-fulfilling *adj* (of a forecast, etc.) which, simply by being made, has the effect of bringing about the results it predicts: *a self-fulfilling prophecy*.

self-governing *adj* controlling itself, not controlled from outside by others. — *n* **self-government**.

self-help *n* the practice of solving one's own problems using abilities developed in oneself, rather than relying on assistance from others.

self-important *adj* having an exaggerated sense of one's own importance; arrogant; pompous. — *n* **self-importance**.

self-imposed *adj* forced on oneself by oneself, not imposed by others.

self-indulgent *adj* giving in, or tending to give in, to one's own wishes or whims. — *n* **self-indulgence**.

self-inflicted *adj* inflicted by oneself on oneself.

self-interest *n* (a desire to preserve or improve) one's own personal welfare or advantage. — *adj* **self-interested**.

self-made *adj* having acquired wealth or achieved success through one's own efforts, rather than through advantages given by birth.

self-opinionated *adj* tending to insist that one's own opinions, forcefully stated, are superior to all others.

self-pity *n* excessive grumbling or moaning about one's own misfortunes.

self-possessed *adj* calm and controlled, esp. in an emergency. — *n* **self-possession**.

self-preservation *n* (care or action taken for) the protection of one's own life; the instinct underlying this.

self-raising *adj* (of flour) containing an ingredient to make dough or pastry rise.

self-reliant *adj* never needing or seeking help from others; independent. — *n* **self-reliance**.

self-respect *n* respect for oneself and concern for one's dignity and reputation. — *adj* **self-respecting**.

self-restraint *n* the act of controlling, or the capacity to control, one's own desires or feelings.

self-righteous *adj* having too high an opinion of one's own goodness, and intolerant of other people's faults. — *n* **self-righteousness**.

self-sacrifice *n* the sacrifice of one's own wishes or interests for the sake of other people's. — *adj* **self-sacrificing**.

selfsame *adj* very same; identical.

self-satisfied *adj* feeling or showing complacent or arrogant satisfaction with oneself or one's achievements; smug. — *n* **self-satisfaction**.

self-sealing *adj* **1** (of an envelope) whose flap is coated with an adhesive which sticks without being moistened. **2** (e.g. of a tyre) capable of automatically sealing small punctures.

self-seeking *n* & *adj* (behaviour that shows one to be) preoccupied with one's own interests and the possibility of personal advantage. — *n* **self-seeker**.

self-service *n* a system, e.g. in a restaurant, in which customers themselves gather together what is to be bought or consumed. — *adj* (of a restaurant, etc.) operating such a system.

self-serving *adj* benefiting or seeking to benefit oneself, often to the disadvantage of others.

self-starter *n* **1** an electric starting device in a vehicle's engine. **2** (*coll*) a person who requires little supervision in a job, being able to motivate himself or herself and use his or her own initiative.

self-styled *adj* called or considered so only by oneself: *a self-styled superstar*.

self-sufficient *adj* (of a person or thing) able to provide oneself or itself with everything needed to live on or survive. — *n* **self-sufficiency**.

self-supporting *adj* **1** earning enough money to meet all one's own expenses. **2** self-sufficient. **3** needing no additional supports or attachments to stay firmly fixed or upright.

self-willed *adj* strongly or stubbornly determined to do or have what one wants.

sell *v* ***sold*** **1** (*tr*; **for**, **to**) to give (to someone) in exchange for money. **2** (*tr*) to have available for buying. **3** (*intr* with **at**, **for**) to be available for buying at (a given price). **4** (*intr*) to be bought by customers; to be in demand. **5** (*tr*) to cause to be bought; to promote the sale of: *The author's name sells the book*. **6** (*tr*; **on**) to cause to be accepted; to persuade to accept: *sell the scheme*; *sell him on the idea*. ◇ See also **sold on**. **7** (*tr*; **for**) to lose or betray (e.g. one's principles) in the process of getting something (esp. dishonourable). — *n* **1** the style of persuasion used in selling: *the hard sell*. **2** (*coll*) a trick or deception. — *n* **seller**. — **sell down the river** (*coll*) to betray. — *v* **sell off** (*tr*) to sell (remaining goods) quickly and cheaply. — *v* **sell out** **1** (*tr* & *intr*; **of**) to sell one's entire stock (of). **2** (*intr*; *coll*; **to**) to betray one's principles or associates: *He sold out to the opposition*. ◇ See also **sell-out** below. — **sell short** (*coll*) to understate the good qualities of, unfairly or with modesty. — *v* **sell up** (*intr*) to sell one's house or business. [OE *sellan*, to hand over]

sell-out *n* an event for which all the tickets have been sold. ◇ See also **sell out** above.

Sellotape® *n* a type of transparent adhesive tape, esp. for use on paper. — *v* (*tr*) to stick with Sellotape.

selvage or **selvedge** *n* an edge of a length of fabric woven so as to prevent fraying. [**self** + **edge**]

selves. See **self**.

semantic *adj* of or relating to meaning. — *adv* **semantically**. [Gr *semantikos*, significant]

semantics *n* (*sing*) the branch of linguistics that deals with meaning.

semaphore *n* **1** a system of signalling in which flags, or simply the arms, are held in positions that represent individual letters and numbers. **2** a signalling device, esp. a pole with arms that can be set in different positions. — *v* (*tr* & *intr*) to signal using semaphore or a semaphore. [Gr *sema*, sign + *-phoros*, bearer]

semblance *n* **1** appearance, esp. superficial or deceiving. **2** a hint or trace. [OFr *sembler*, to seem]

semen *n* a thick whitish liquid containing sperm, ejaculated by the penis. ◇ See also **seminal**. [Lat, seed]

semester *n* an academic term lasting half an academic year. [Lat *semestris*, six-monthly]

semi *n* ***-is*** (*coll*) a semi-detached house.

semi- *pfx* **1** half: *semiquaver*. **2** partly: *semiconscious*. **3** occurring twice in the stated period: *semiannual*. [Lat, half]

semiautomatic *adj* **1** partially automatic. **2** (of a firearm) continuously reloading bullets, but only firing one at a time.

semibreve *n* the longest musical note in common use, equal to half a breve, two minims, or four crotchets.

semicircle *n* (an arrangement in the shape of) one half of a circle. — *adj* **semicircular**.

semicolon *n* a punctuation mark (;) indicating a pause stronger than that marked by a comma and weaker than a full stop, used between items in lists and between related clauses.

semiconductor *n* a substance, such as silicon, that conducts electricity only when heated.

semi-detached *n* & *adj* (a house) with another house attached on one side.

semi-final *n* in competitions, either of two matches the winners of which play each other in the final. — *n* **semi-finalist**.

seminal *adj* **1** highly original and at the root of a trend or movement: *seminal writings*. **2** of or relating to seed, semen or reproduction in general. — *adv* **seminally**. [Lat *semen*, seed]

seminar *n* **1** a small class for the discussion of a particular topic between students and a tutor. **2** any meeting set up for the purpose of discussion. [Lat *seminarium*, seed-plot]

seminary *n* ***-ies*** **1** a college for the training of members of the clergy. **2** (*old*) a school, esp. for girls. — *n* **seminarian**. [Ety. as for **seminar**]

semiotics *n* (*sing*; also **semiology**) the study of human communication, esp. the relationship between words and the objects or concepts they refer to. — *adj* **semiotic**. [Gr *semeiotikos*, of signs; *semeion*, sign + **-logy**]

semi-permeable *adj* (of a plant or animal membrane) allowing small molecules to pass through but not large ones.

semi-precious *adj* (of a gem) considered less valuable than a precious stone.

semi-professional *adj* **1** engaging only part-time in a professional activity. **2** (of an activity) engaged in only as a part-time profession. — *n* a semi-professional person.

semiquaver *n* a musical note equal to half a quaver or one-sixteenth of a semibreve.

semi-skilled *adj* having or requiring a degree of training less advanced than that needed for specialised work.

Semite *n* a member of any of the Afro-Asian peoples said to be descended from the biblical character Shem, including Jews and Arabs. [Gr *Sem*, Shem (a son of Noah)]

Semitic *n* any of a group of Afro-Asiatic languages that includes Hebrew, Arabic and Aramaic. — *adj* **1** of, relating to or speaking any such language. **2** of or relating to Semites. **3** of or relating to the Jews; Jewish.

semitone *n* half a tone in the musical scale, the interval between adjacent notes on a keyboard instrument.

semi-tropical *adj* subtropical.

semivowel *n* **1** a speech sound having the qualities of both a vowel and a consonant, such as the sounds represented by the letters *y* and *w*. **2** a letter representing such a sound.

semolina *n* hard particles of wheat not ground into flour during milling, used to thicken soups and make puddings. [Ital *semolino*, dimin. of *semola*, bran]

SEN *abbrev* State Enrolled Nurse.

Sen. *abbrev* **1** senate. **2** senator. **3** senior.

senate *n* (often *cap*) **1** a law-making body, esp. the upper chamber of the national assembly in the US, Australia and some other countries. **2** the governing council in some British universities. **3** the chief legislative and administrative body in ancient Rome. [Lat *senatus*, from *senex*, old man]

senator *n* (often *cap*) a member of a senate. — *adj* **senatorial**.

send *v* ***sent*** (*tr*) **1** (**away**, **back**, **to**, etc.) to cause or order to go or be conveyed or transmitted. **2** to force or propel: *sent me flying*. **3** (**to**, **into**) to cause to become or pass into a state of: *sent him into fits of laughter*; *sent me mad*. **4** to bring about: *a plague sent by God*. **5** (*old slang*) to put into a state of ecstasy; to thrill. — *n* **sender**. — *v* **send away for** (*tr*) to order (goods) by post. — *v* **send down** (*tr*) **1** (*coll*) to send to prison. **2** to expel from university. — *v* **send for** (*tr*) **1** to ask or order to come; to summon. **2** to order to be brought or delivered. — *v* **send in** (*tr*) to offer or submit by post. — *v* **send off** (*tr*) **1** to dispatch, esp. by post. **2** to dismiss, esp. from the field of play in sport. **3** (**for**) to send away (for). ◇ See also **send-off** below. — *v* **send on** (*tr*) **1** to re-address and re-post (e.g. a letter); to forward. **2** to post, or cause to depart, so as to arrive in advance of oneself. — *v* **send out 1** (*tr*) to distribute by post. **2** (*tr*) to dispatch. **3** (*intr* & *tr*; **for**) to send (someone) to fetch. — *v* **send up** (*tr*; *coll*) to ridicule through exaggerated imitation (*n* **send-up**). [OE *sendan*]

send-off *n* a (lively) display of good wishes from an assembled crowd to a departing person or group.

send-up see **send up** above.

senescent *adj* (*formal*) growing old; ageing. — *n* **senescence**. [Lat *senescere*, to grow old]

seneschal *n* a steward in charge of the household or estate of a mediaeval lord or prince. [OFr, old servant]

senile *adj* **1** displaying the feebleness of mind or body brought on by old age. **2** of or caused by old age. — *n* **senility**. [Lat *senilis*, from *senex*, old]

senile dementia *n* mental decay brought on by old age.

senior *adj* **1** (**to**) older (than). **2** (**to**) higher in rank or authority (than). **3** of or for schoolchildren over the age of 11. **4** (*US*) of final-year college or university students. **5** older than a person of the same name, esp. distinguishing parent from child: *Jim Smith, Senior*. — *n* **1** a person who is older or of a higher rank. **2** a pupil in (the upper classes of) a senior school. **3** (*US*) a final-year student. [Lat, older]

senior citizen *n* an elderly person, esp. one retired.

seniority *n* **1** the state of being senior. **2** a privileged position earned through long service in a profession or with a company.

the senior service *n* the Royal Navy.

senna *n* **1** any of a family of tropical trees and shrubs that produce long seed pods. **2** a laxative prepared from the dried pods. [Arabic *sana*]

sensation *n* **1** awareness, or the ability to be aware, by means of the nervous system, of the physical existence or characteristics of things or of their contact with other things. **2** a physical feeling: *a burning sensation in my mouth*. **3** an emotion or general feeling. **4** (the cause of) a sudden widespread feeling of excitement, lively interest or shock. [Lat *sensatio*, from *sentire*, to feel]

sensational *adj* **1** causing, or intended to cause, widespread excitement, intense interest or shock. **2** (*coll*) excellent; marvellous. **3** of the senses. — *adv* **sensationally**.

sensationalism *n* the practice of, or methods used in, deliberately setting out to cause widespread excitement, intense interest or shock. — *n* **sensationalist**.

sense *n* **1** any of the five powers — hearing, taste, sight, smell and touch — used to perceive the physical world or the condition of the body. **2** an awareness or appreciation of, or an ability to make judgements regarding, some specified thing: *sense of direction*; *bad business sense*. **3** (often in *pl*) soundness of mind; reasonableness: *lost his senses*. **4** wisdom; practical worth: *no sense in doing it now*. **5** a general feeling, not perceived using any of the five natural powers: *a sense of guilt*. **6** overall meaning: *understood the sense of* *the passage, if not all the words.* **7** specific meaning. **8** general opinion; consensus: *the sense of the meeting.* — *v* (*tr*) **1** to perceive using any of the five senses. **2** to be aware of by means other than the five senses: *sensed that someone was following me.* **3** to realise or comprehend. — **come to one's senses 1** to begin acting wisely after a period of foolishness. **2** to regain consciousness. — **in a sense** in one respect; in a way. — **make sense 1** to be able to be understood. **2** to be wise or reasonable. [Lat *sensus*, from *sentire*, to feel]

senseless *adj* **1** unconscious. **2** unwise; foolish. — *adv* **senselessly**. — *n* **senselessness**.

sense organ *n* a bodily organ whose special function is to receive information about the physical world.

sensibility *n* **-ies 1** the ability to feel or have sensations. **2 (to)** the capacity to be affected emotionally; sensitivity: *sensibility to his grief.* **3** (in *pl*) feelings, when easily offended or hurt. **[sensible]**

sensible *adj* **1** wise; having or showing reasonableness or good judgement. **2** perceptible by the senses. **3 (to)** able to feel; sensitive: *sensible to pain.* — *adv* **sensibly**. [Lat *sensibilis*]

sensitise or **-ize** *v* (*tr*; **to**) to make sensitive. — *n* **sensitisation** or **-z-**.

sensitive *adj* **1 (to)** responding readily, strongly or painfully (to). **2 (to)** able to feel or respond (to). **3** easily upset or offended. **4** about which there is much strong feeling or difference of opinion: *sensitive issues.* **5** (of documents, etc.) not for public discussion or scrutiny, e.g. because involving matters of national security or embarrassing to the government. **6** (of scientific instruments) reacting to or recording very small changes. **7** (*photography*) responding to the action of light. **8** (*physics*, etc.) responding to the action of some force or stimulus: *pressure-sensitive.* — *adv* **sensitively**. — *n* **sensitivity**. [Lat *sensitivus*, from *sentire*, to feel]

sensor *n* a device that detects a physical quantity, e.g. light, either recording it or being activated by it to operate a switch. **[sense + -or]**

sensory *adj* of the senses or sensation. [Lat *sensorium*, brain, seat of the senses]

sensual *adj* **1** of the senses and the body rather than the mind or the spirit. **2** suggesting, enjoying or providing physical (esp. sexual) pleasure. **3** pursuing physical pleasures, esp. those derived from sex or food and drink. [Lat *sensus*, sense]

sensuality *n* **1** the quality of being sensual. **2** indulgence in physical pleasures.

sensuous *adj* **1** appealing to or designed to stimulate the senses, with no suggestion of sexual pleasure. **2** pleasing to the senses. **3** very aware of what is perceived by the senses. — *adv* **sensuously**. — *n* **sensuousness**. [Lat **sensus**, sense + **-ous**]

sent. See **send**.

sentence *n* **1** a sequence of words forming a complete and meaningful grammatical structure, beginning with a capital letter in writing (in the Roman and other European alphabets) and ending with a full stop or its equivalent. **2** a punishment determined by a court or judge; its announcement in court. — *v* (*tr*) **1** to announce the punishment to be given to. **2 (to)** to condemn (to), as punishment: *sentenced him to five years' imprisonment.* — **pass sentence (on)** to announce the punishment to be given (to). [Lat *sententia*, opinion]

sententious *adj* **1** tending to lecture others on morals. **2** full of, or fond of using, sayings or proverbs. — *n* **sententiousness**. [Lat *sententiosus*, full of meaning]

sentient *adj* able to feel; capable of sensation: *sentient beings.* — *n* **sentience**. [Lat *sentire*, to feel]

sentiment *n* **1** an emotion, esp. when expressed. **2** emotion or emotional behaviour in general, esp. when considered excessive, self-indulgent or insincere. **3** (often in *pl*) an opinion or view. [Lat *sentimentum*, from *sentire*, to feel]

sentimental *adj* **1** easily feeling and expressing tender emotions, esp. love, friendship and pity. **2** provoking or designed to provoke such emotions, esp. in large measure and without subtlety. **3** closely associated with, or moved (to tears) by, fond memories of the past: *objects of sentimental value.* — *n* **sentimentalism**. — *n* **sentimentalist**. — *n* **sentimentality**. — *adv* **sentimentally**.

sentimentalise or **-ize** *v* **1** (*intr*) to behave sentimentally. **2** (*tr*) to react to emotionally, rather than taking a frank and practical approach.

sentinel *n* a sentry. [Fr *sentinelle*]

sentry *n* **-ies** a soldier or other person on guard to control entry or passage.

sentry-box *n* a small open-fronted shelter for a sentry.

sepal *n* any of a group of leaf-like parts protecting an unopened flower bud, lying under the petals of the opened flower. [Fr *sépale*]

separable *adj* able to be separated. — *n* **separability**. [Lat *separabilis*]

separate *v* **1** (*tr*; **from, off, out**) to set, take, keep or force apart (from others or each other). **2** (*intr*) to move apart; to become detached; to cease to be or live together. **3** (*tr & intr*; **up**) to divide or become divided into parts. — *adj* **1** distinctly different or individual; unrelated: *a separate issue.* **2** physically unattached; isolated. — *n* (usu. in *pl*) a garment intended for wear with a variety of others, not forming part of a suit. — *n* **separateness**. — *n* **separator**. [Lat *separare*]

separation *n* **1** the act of separating or the state or process of being separated. **2** a place or line where there is a division. **3** a gap or interval that separates. **4** an arrangement, approved mutually or by a court, under which a husband and wife live apart while remaining married, usu. prior to divorce.

separatist *n* a person who encourages, or takes action to achieve, independence from a country or an established institution, e.g. a church. — *n* **separatism**.

sepia *n* **1** a yellowish-brown tint used in photography. **2** a dark reddish-brown colour. **3** a pigment of this colour, obtained from a fluid secreted by the cuttlefish. [Gr, cuttlefish]

sepoy *n* (*hist*) an Indian soldier in service with a European (esp. British) army. [Urdu and Persian *sipahi*, horseman]

sepsis *n* ***sepses*** (poisoning caused by) the spread of harmful bacteria from a point of infection. [Gr, putrefaction]

Sept. *abbrev* **1** September. **2** Septuagint.

sept *n* a clan, esp. in Ireland. [Alteration of **sect**]

septa. See **septum**.

September *n* the ninth month of the year. [Lat, seventh (month in the original Roman calendar)]

septennial *adj* **1** occurring once every seven years. **2** lasting seven years. [Lat *septem*, seven + *annus*, year]

septet *n* **1** a group of seven musicians. **2** a piece of music for seven performers. **3** any group or set of seven. [Lat *septem*, seven]

septic *adj* caused or affected by harmful bacteria. [Gr *septikos*; see ety. at **sepsis**]

septic tank *n* a tank, usu. underground, in which (esp. household) sewage is broken down by the action of bacteria.

septicaemia *n* blood-poisoning. [Gr *septikos*, putrefied + *haima*, blood]

septuagenarian *adj* between 70 and 79 years old. — *n* a septuagenarian person. [Lat *septuaginta*, seventy]

Septuagint *n* the ancient Greek version of the Old Testament, including the Apocrypha, traditionally thought to have been made by seventy-two scholars. [Lat *septuaginta*, seventy]

septum *n* ***-ta*** (*anat* & *biol*) any partition between cavities, e.g. nostrils, or areas of soft tissue. [Lat *saeptum*, fence]

septuple *adj* being seven times as much or as many; sevenfold. — *v* (*tr* & *intr*) to multiply or increase sevenfold. [Lat *septuplus*]

septuplet *n* any of seven children born at the same time to the same mother.

sepulchre *n* a grave or burial vault. — *v* (*tr*) to bury in a sepulchre; to entomb. [Lat *sepulcrum*]

sepulchral *adj* **1** of a tomb; of burial. **2** suggestive of death or burial; gloomy; funereal.

sequel *n* **1** (**to**) a book, film or play that continues an earlier story. **2** a result or consequence. [Lat *sequi*, to follow]

sequence *n* **1** a series of things following each other in a particular order; the order they follow. **2** a succession of short pieces of action making up a scene in a film. **3** (*math*) a set of values in which each is a fixed amount greater or smaller than its predecessor, as determined by a given rule. [Lat *sequi*, to follow]

sequential *adj* **1** following a particular order. **2** consequent; of which each element is a direct consequence of its predecessor.

sequester *v* ***-r-*** (*tr*) **1** to set apart or isolate. **2** to seclude: *a sequestered garden*. **3** (*legal*) to sequestrate. [Lat, depository]

sequestrate *v* (*tr*; *legal*) to remove from someone's possession until a dispute or debt has been settled. — *n* **sequestration**. — *n* **sequestrator**. [Lat *sequestrare*, from *sequester*, depository]

sequin *n* a tiny round shiny disc of foil or plastic, sewn on a garment for decoration. — *adj* **sequined**. [Ital *zecchino*]

sequoia *n* either of two types of giant Californian coniferous tree, the big tree or the redwood. [After the Cherokee Indian scholar *Sequoiah*]

seraglio *n* ***-os*** **1** a harem. **2** (*hist*) a Turkish palace, esp. that of the sultans at Constantinople. [Ital *serraglio*, from Persian *saray*, palace]

seraph *n* ***-aphs*** or ***-aphim*** an angel of the highest of the nine celestial orders. — *adj* **seraphic**. [Hebr]

Serbo-Croat *n* the main language of Croatia and Yugoslavia.

serenade *n* **1** a song or tune performed at night under a woman's window by her suitor. **2** any musical piece with a gentle tempo suggestive of romance. **3** a piece of classical music of symphony length but lighter in tone and for a smaller orchestra. — *v* (*tr*) to entertain (a person) with a serenade. [Lat *serenus*, bright clear sky]

serendipity *n* the state of frequently making lucky finds. — *adj* **serendipitous**. [From the folk tale 'The Three Princes of *Serendip*' (= Sri Lanka)]

serene *adj* **1** (of a person) calm; at peace. **2** (of a sky) cloudless. **3** (*cap*) a word incorporated in the titles of members of some European royal families: *Her Serene Highness*. — *adv* **serenely**. — *n* **serenity**. [Lat *serenus*, clear]

serf *n* in mediaeval Europe, a worker of near-slave status, bought and sold with the land on which he or she worked. — *n* **serfdom**. [Lat *servus*, slave]

serge *n* hard-wearing twilled (esp. woollen) fabric. [OFr]

sergeant *n* **1** a non-commissioned officer of the rank next above corporal in the armed forces. **2** a police officer of the rank between constable and inspector. [OFr *sergent*, from Lat *serviens*, servant]

sergeant-at-arms *n* (also **serjeant-**) an officer of a court or parliament, responsible for keeping order.

sergeant-major *n* a non-commissioned officer of the highest rank in the armed forces.

serial *n* **1** a story published or broadcast in regular instalments. **2** a periodical. — *adj* **1** appearing in instalments. **2** forming (part of) a series. [Ety. as for **series**]

serialise or **-ize** *v* (*tr*) to present in regular instalments. — *n* **serialisation** or **-z-**.

serial killer *n* a person committing a succession of murders.

serial number *n* any of a set of consecutive numbers printed on identical products to identify them as a batch.

series *n* ***series*** **1** a number of similar, related or identical things arranged or produced one after the other. **2** a television or radio programme in which the same characters appear, or a similar subject is addressed, in regularly broadcast shows. **3** (*math*) a sum of numbers or values in a sequence. **4** a set of electrical devices arranged so that a current passes undiminished through each in turn. **5** a set of layers of rock all formed during the same geological epoch. [Lat, chain, row]

serif *n* a short decorative line or stroke on the end of a printed letter, as in E as opposed to the sanserif (= without serifs) **E**.

seriocomic *adj* having both serious and comic elements or qualities.

serious *adj* **1** solemn; not light-hearted or flippant. **2** dealing with important issues: *a serious newspaper*. **3** severe: *a serious accident*. **4** important; significant: *serious differences of opinion*. **5** (**about**) earnest; sincere; not joking: *I'm serious about doing it*. — *adv* **seriously**. — *n* **seriousness**. [Lat *serius*]

serjeant. See **sergeant**.

sermon *n* **1** a public speech about morals, religious duties or some aspect of religious doctrine, esp. one forming part of a church service. **2** a lengthy (often pompous) speech telling others how to behave. [Lat *sermo*, discourse]

sermonise or **-ize** *v* (*intr*) to moralise.

seropositive *adj* (of a person) whose blood, after testing, has been shown to be infected by the specific disease tested for, usu. Aids.

serous. See **serum**.

serpent *n* **1** a snake. **2** a sneaky or malicious person. [Lat *serpens*, creeping thing]

serpentine *adj* **1** snake-like. **2** winding; full of twists and bends. — *n* a soft dark-green mineral, often mottled like a snake's skin.

serrated *adj* having notches or teeth like the blade of a saw. — *n* **serration**. [Lat *serra*, saw]

serried *adj* closely packed or grouped together: *soldiers in serried ranks*. [Fr *serrer*, to put close together]

serum *n* **1** (also **blood serum**) the yellowish watery part of blood, the liquid in which the corpuscles are carried, separated out when the blood clots. **2** this liquid containing antibodies to a specific disease, used in immunisation. **3** any watery liquid in animals' bodies or plants. [Lat, whey]

serous *adj* **1** of or relating to serum. **2** (of a liquid) resembling serum; watery.

servant *n* **1** a person employed by another to do household work. **2** a person who acts for the good of others in any capacity: *public servant*.

serve *v* **1** (*tr*) to work for the benefit of: *served the community well*. **2** (*intr*; **on**) to carry out duties as a member (of some body): *serve on a committee*. **3** (*intr*; **in**) to act as a member of the armed forces: *served in the marines*; *served in France*. **4** (*tr* & *intr*) to give assistance to (customers); to provide to customers. **5** (*tr* & *intr*) to respond to the needs or demands of (someone): *shoes have served me well*; *if my memory serves* (or *serves me*). **6** (*tr* & *intr*; **up, out**) to bring, distribute or present (food or drink) to (someone). **7** (*tr*) to provide specified facilities to: *trams serving the entire city*. **8** (*intr* & *tr*; **as**) to be of use; to fulfil (a need); to suffice: *There's no chair, but this box will serve. It will serve our purpose*. **9** (*intr* with **to**) to have the effect or result (of): *His long speech served to delay proceedings*. **10** (*tr*) to undergo as a requirement: *serve an apprenticeship*. **11** (*tr* & *intr*) to put (the ball) into play in racket sports. **12** (*tr*) to work for as a domestic servant. **13** (*tr*; **on, with**) to deliver or present (a legal document) to (someone): *served him with a writ*; *served a summons on her*. — *n* (*sport*) an act of serving. — *n* **server**. — **serve someone right** (*coll*) to be the misfortune or punishment that someone deserves. [Lat *servire*, to serve]

serving *n* a portion of food served at one time; a helping.

service *n* **1** (often in *pl*) work performed for or on behalf of others; use or usefulness; a favour, or any act with beneficial results: *do someone a service*; *Your services are no longer required. The car has given me good service. Can I be of service?* **2** employment or engagement as a member of an organisation working to serve or benefit others in some way; such an organisation: *a public service*; *the civil service*. **3** assistance given to customers. **4** a facility provided: *The bus company runs a great service*. **5** an occasion of worship or other religious ceremony; the words, etc. used on such an occasion: *the marriage service*. **6** a complete set of crockery: *a dinner service*. **7** a periodic check of the workings of a vehicle or other machine. **8** an act of putting the ball into play in racket sports; the game in which it is a particular player's turn to do so; the stroke used: *lose one's service*; *sliced service*. **9** a service charge: *service not included*. **10** (often in *pl*) any of the armed forces. **11** employment as a domestic servant. — *v* (*tr*) **1** to subject to a periodic (esp. mechanical) check. **2** (of a male animal) to mate with (a female). — *adj* **1** for use by domestic servants: *service entrance*. **2** of the army, navy or air force. — **at someone's service** ready to serve or give assistance to someone. — **be of service (to)** to help; to be useful (to). — **in service 1** in use; operating. **2** working as a domestic servant. [Lat *servitium*, from *servire*, to serve]

serviceable *adj* **1** capable of being used. **2** giving long-term use; durable. — *n* **serviceability**.

service area *n* a group of establishments near a motorway or major road, providing refuelling, restaurant and toilet facilities.

service charge *n* a percentage of a restaurant or hotel bill added on to cover (at least nominally) the cost of service.

service flat *n* a rented flat with the cost of certain services, e.g. domestic cleaning, included in the rent.

service industry *n* an industry whose business is providing services, e.g. dry-cleaning, rather than manufacturing goods.

serviceman and **servicewoman** *n* a member of any of the armed forces.

service station *n* a petrol station providing additional facilities for motorists, e.g. car-washing.

serviette *n* a table napkin. [OFr]

servile *adj* **1** slavishly respectful, obedient or attentive; fawning. **2** of, relating to or suitable for slaves: *servile tasks*. — *n* **servility**. [Lat *servilis*]

servitude *n* **1** slavery. **2 (to)** dependency (on): *servitude to drugs*. [Lat *servitudo*, from *servus*, slave]

servo *n* (*-os*; also **servo-mechanism**) a device able to perform very powerful mechanical tasks with a relatively small amount of energy: *servo-assisted brakes*. [Lat *servus*, servant]

sesame *n* a SE Asian plant cultivated for its edible seeds, used in cooking and cooking-oil production. [Gr *sesamon*]

sessile *adj* **1** (of a flower or leaf) attached directly to the plant, rather than by a short stalk. **2** (of a part of the body) attached directly to the body. **3** (of an animal) stationary; immobile. [Lat *sessilis*, low, squat]

session *n* **1** a meeting of a court, council or parliament; a period during which such meetings are regularly held. **2** a period of time spent engaged in one particular activity. **3** an academic term or year. — *adj* **sessional**. — **in session** conducting or engaged in a meeting. [Lat *sessio*, a sitting]

sestet *n* **1** a poem or verse of six lines. **2** the last six lines of a sonnet. **3** a group of six people or things; a sextet. [Ital *sestetto*, from Lat *sextus*, sixth]

set[1] *v* ***setting, set* 1** (*tr*) to put into a certain position or condition: *set high up*; *set free*; *set fire to*. **2** (*tr & intr*) to (cause to) become solid, rigid, firm or motionless: *cement hasn't set*; *set her jaw*. **3** (*tr*) to fix, establish or settle: *set a date*. **4** (*tr*) to put into a state of readiness: *set the table*. **5** (*tr*) to adjust (an instrument) to the correct reading: *set a clock*. **6** (*tr*) to adjust (a device) so that its controls are activated at a fixed time. **7** (*tr*) to fix (a broken bone) in its normal position, for healing. **8** (*tr*) to impose or assign as an exercise or duty: *set a test*. **9** (*tr*) to present or fix as a lead to be followed: *set an example*; *set the tone*. **10** (*tr*) to place on or against a background, or in surroundings: *diamonds set in a gold bracelet*; *poem set to music*; *story set in France*. **11** (*tr*) to stir, provoke or force into activity: *set me thinking*; *set her to work*. **12** (*tr*) to treat (hair) so as to stay firm in the required style. **13** (*tr*) to place as a value or consideration of worth: *set a high price on honesty*; *set great store by*. **14** (*intr*) (of the sun or moon) to disappear below the horizon. **15** (*tr*) to arrange (type) for printing. **16** (*tr*) (of a plant) to produce (seed). **17** (*tr*; **with**) to decorate: *a bracelet set with diamonds*. — *n* **1** form; shape: *the set of his jaw*. **2** posture or bearing. **3** the area within which filmed action takes place; the scenery and props used to create a particular location in filming. **4** the process of setting hair; a hairstyle produced by setting: *a shampoo and set*. — *adj* **1** fixed; allowing no alterations or variations: *a set menu*. **2** never changing: *set in his ways*. **3** predetermined or conventional: *set phrases*. **4 (to)** ready: *all set*. **5 (for)** about to receive or experience; due: *set for a pay rise*. **6 (on, upon)** determined: *dead set on resigning*. **7** assigned; prescribed: *set texts for study*. — *v* **set about** (*tr*) **1** to start or begin: *set about digging the garden*. **2** to attack. — *v* **set against** (*tr*) **1** to compare. **2** to make hostile towards: *set him against his own family*. **3** to deduct from: *set this against your tax bill for 1992*. — *v* **set apart** (*tr*) to reveal to be different, usu. better. — *v* **set aside** (*tr*) **1** to disregard or reject. **2** to put away for later use. — *v* **set back** (*tr*) **1** to delay or hinder the progress of (*n* **setback**). **2** to cause to return to an earlier and less advanced stage: *changes that will set the health service back decades*. **3** (*slang*) to cost: *set me back a fiver*. — *v* **set down** (*tr*) **1** to record in writing. **2** to allow (passengers) to get off or out. **3** to judge or view: *set the scheme down as a failure*. — *v* **set forth** (*old* or *formal*) **1** (*intr*; **on**) to begin a journey. **2** (*tr*) to put forward or explain: *set forth her views*. — *v* **set in** (*intr*) to become firmly established: *Winter has set in*. — *v* **set off 1** (*intr*; **on**) to start out (on a journey). **2** (*tr*) to provoke into action or behaviour of a particular kind; to start or cause: *set her off crying*; *set off a terrible argument*. **3** (*tr*) to detonate. **4** (*tr*) to show off to good advantage; to enhance the appearance of. **5** (*tr*) to deduct from another source; to offset. — *v* **set on** (*tr*) **1** to order to attack: *set the dogs on* *him*. **2** to attack. — *v* **set out 1** (*tr*) to present, explain or outline: *set out her proposals*. **2** (*tr*) to lay out for display. **3** (*intr*; **on**) to begin a journey. **4** (*tr*) to intend from the start (to): *set out to make me look foolish*. — *v* **set to** (*intr*) **1** to begin working; to apply oneself to a task. **2** to start fighting or arguing (*n* **set-to**). — *v* **set up** (*tr*) **1** to bring into being or operation; to establish. **2** to arrange (e.g. a meeting). **3** to erect: *set the tents up over here*. **4** to put into a position of guaranteed security: *His new job has set him up for life*. **5** to improve or restore the health of; to perk up. **6** (*slang*) to trick into becoming a target for blame or accusations. ◇ See also **set-up** below. [OE *settan*]

setback see **set back** above.

set piece *n* **1** a carefully prepared performance or sequence of movements. **2** an arrangement of fireworks on a scaffold, etc.

set square *n* a triangular (usu. plastic) plate used as an aid to drawing lines and angles.

setter *n* any of various breeds of dog orig. trained to stand rigid to signal that a hunted animal has been scented.

setting *n* **1** a position in which an instrument's controls are set. **2** a situation or background within or against which action takes place; the scenery and props used in filming a scene. **3** (also **place setting**) a set of cutlery, crockery and glassware laid out for use by one diner. **4** the mounting for a jewel.

set-to see **set to** above.

set-up *n* **1** (*coll*) an arrangement or set of arrangements. **2** (*slang*) a trick to get a person unjustly blamed or accused.

set[2] *n* **1** a group of related or similar things regarded as a complete unit. **2** a complete collection of pieces needed for a particular activity: *a chess set*; *a train set*. **3** one of the major divisions of a match in some sports, e.g. tennis, subdivided into games. **4** a group of people with common characteristics or interests. **5** an instrument for receiving television or radio broadcasts. **6** the songs or tunes performed at a concert. [OFr *sette*]

set[3] or **sett** *n* **1** a badger's burrow. **2** a block of stone or wood used in paving. [**set**[1]]

settee *n* a sofa. [From **settle**[2]]

settle[1] *v* **1** (*tr & intr*; **in**) to make or become firmly, comfortably or satisfactorily positioned or established. **2** (*tr & intr*; **on**) to come to an agreement (about): *settle* (*on*) *a date*; *settle an argument*. **3** (*intr*; **on**) to come lightly to rest. **4** (*tr & intr*; **down**) to (cause to) become calm, stable or disciplined after a period of noisy excitement or upheaval. **5** (*tr & intr*) to establish a permanent home or colony (in). **6** (*tr & intr*; **up, with**) to pay off or clear (a debt): *settle a bill*; *settle up with her*. **7** (*intr*) to sink to the bottom of something; to sink lower. **8** (*tr* with **on**) to transfer ownership of legally: *settled her estate on her son*. — *v* **settle for** (*tr*) to accept as a compromise or less-than-ideal option. [OE *setlan*, to place]

settlement *n* **1** the act of settling or the state of being settled. **2** a community or colony of recently settled people. **3** an agreement, esp. ending an official dispute. **4** subsidence. **5** an act of legally transferring ownership of property; a document enforcing this.

settler *n* a person who settles in a country that is being newly populated.

settle[2] *n* a wooden bench with arms and a solid high back, often with a storage chest fitted below the seat. [OE *setl*]

seven *n* **1** the number or figure 7; any symbol for this number. **2** the age of 7. **3** something, e.g. a garment or a person, whose size is denoted by the number 7. **4** a playing-card with 7 pips. **5** a set of 7 people or things. **6** 7 o'clock. **7** a score of 7 points. — *adj* **1** 7 in number. **2** aged 7. — *n, adj & adv* **seventh**. — *adv* **seventhly**. [OE *seofon*]

sevenfold *adj* **1** equal to seven times as much or as many. **2** divided into, or consisting of, seven parts. — *adv* by seven times as much.

the seven seas *n* (*pl*) all the oceans of the world.

seventh heaven *n* a state of intense happiness or joy.

seventeen *n* **1** the number or figure 17; any symbol for this number. **2** the age of 17. **3** something, e.g. a garment or a person, whose size is denoted by the number 17. **4** a set of 17 people or things. — *adj* **1** 17 in number. **2** aged 17. — *n, adj & adv* **seventeenth**. [OE *seofon*, seven + *tien*, ten]

seventy *n* **-ies 1** the number or figure 70; any symbol for this number. **2** the age of 70. **3** a set of 70 people or things. — *adj* **1** 70 in number. **2** aged 70. — *n, adj & adv* **seventieth**. [OE *seofontig*]

seventies *n* (*pl*) **1** the period of time between one's seventieth and eightieth birthdays. **2** the range of temperatures between seventy and eighty degrees. **3** the period of time between the seventieth and eightieth years of a century.

sever *v* **-r-** (*tr*) **1** to cut off physically: *severed limbs*. **2** to break off or end: *severed relations with them*. — *n* **severance**. [Lat *separare*, to separate]

severance pay *n* compensation paid by an employer to an employee dismissed through no fault of his or her own.

several *adj* **1** more than a few, but not a great number. **2** different and distinct; respective: *went their several ways*. — *pron* quite a few people or things. [OFr, separate]

severally *adj* (*formal*) separately or singly: *travelling severally*.

severe *adj* **1** extreme and difficult to endure; marked by extreme conditions. **2**

(**with**) very strict towards others. **3** suggesting seriousness and a lack of informality; austere. **4** having serious consequences; grave. **5** rigorous; demanding. — *adv* **severely**. — *n* **severity**. [Lat *severus*]

sew *v* ***sewn*** or ***sewed*** **1** (*tr*; **on**, **up**) to stitch, attach or repair (esp. fabric) with thread, by hand with a needle or by machine. **2** (*tr*) to make (garments) by stitching pieces of fabric together. **3** (*intr*) (to have the necessary skill) to perform such tasks: *Can he sew?* — *n* **sewing**. — *v* **sew up** (*tr*; *slang*) to arrange or complete successfully. [OE *siwian*]

sewing-machine *n* a machine for sewing, esp. an electric machine for sewing clothes, etc.

sewage *n* waste matter, esp. excrement, carried away in drains. [Back-formation from **sewer**]

sewage farm *n* a place where sewage is treated so as to be usable as manure.

sewer *n* a large underground pipe or channel for carrying away sewage from drains and water from road surfaces; a main drain. [OFr *essever*, to drain off]

sewerage *n* **1** a network of sewers. **2** drainage of sewage and surface water using sewers.

sex *n* **1** either of the two classes — male and female — into which animals and plants (or certain parts of plants) are divided according to their role in reproduction. **2** (the qualities that determine) membership of one of these classes. **3** sexual intercourse, often including other love-making activities. — *adj* **1** of or relating to sexual matters in general: *sex education*. **2** of or based on the fact of being male or female: *sex discrimination*. — *v* (*tr*) to identify the sex of (an animal). [Lat *sexus*]

sex appeal *n* sexual attractiveness.

sexed *adj* having a (great or small) desire to engage in sexual activity: *highly sexed*.

sexism *n* contempt shown for a particular sex, usu. by men of women, based on prejudice or stereotype. — *n* & *adj* **sexist**.

sexless *adj* **1** neither male nor female. **2** having no desire to engage in sexual activity. **3** (usu. *derog*) sexually unattractive.

sexology *n* the study of (human) sexual behaviour. — *n* **sexologist**.

sexual *adj* **1** concerned with or suggestive of sex or love-making. **2** of or relating to reproduction. **3** of, relating to, or according to membership of, the male or female sex. — *n* **sexuality**.

sexual harassment *n* harassment in the form of unwelcome, often offensive, sexual advances or remarks, usu. made by men towards women, esp. in the workplace.

sexual intercourse *n* the insertion of a man's penis into a woman's vagina, usu. with the release of semen into the vagina.

sexy *adj* ***-ier***, ***-iest*** (*coll*) **1** sexually attractive; arousing sexual desire. **2** currently popular or interesting: *sexy products*. — *adv* **sexily**. — *n* **sexiness**.

sexagenerian *n* & *adj* (a person) aged between sixty and sixty-nine. [Lat *sexaginta*, sixty]

sext *n* the fourth of the canonical hours. ◇ See also **compline, lauds, matins, none**[2], **terce**, **vespers**. [Lat *sexta (hora)*, the sixth (hour)]

sextant *n* an instrument like a small telescope mounted on a graded metal arc, used in navigation and surveying for measuring distance by means of angles. [Lat *sextans*, sixth, the arc being one-sixth of a full circle]

sextet *n* **1** (a piece of music for) a group of six singers or musicians. **2** any set of six. [Variant of **sestet**]

sexton *n* a person who looks after church property, often also having bell-ringing, grave-digging and other duties. [From **sacristan**]

sextuple *n* a value or quantity six times as much. — *adj* **1** sixfold. **2** made up of six parts. — *v* (*tr* & *intr*) to multiply or increase sixfold. [Lat *sextuplus*]

sextuplet *n* any of six children born at the same time to the same mother.

SF *abbrev* (also **sf**) science fiction.

sf or **sfz** *abbrev* sforzando.

sforzando *adv* & *adj* (*mus*) to be played with sudden emphasis. [Ital]

Sgt *abbrev* Sergeant.

sh *interj* hush; be quiet. [Imit.]

shabby *adj* ***-ier***, ***-iest*** **1** (esp. of clothes or furnishings) old and worn; threadbare; dingy. **2** (of a person) wearing such clothes. **3** nasty; mean: *shabby conduct*. — *adv* **shabbily**. — *n* **shabbiness**. [OE *sceabb*]

Shabuoth *n* the Jewish 'Feast of Weeks', celebrated 7 weeks after the first day of Passover to commemorate the giving of the Law to Moses. [Hebr]

shack *n* a roughly built hut. — *v* **shack up** (*intr*; *slang*; **with**, **together**) to live (together or with), without being married.

shackle *n* **1** either of a pair of metal bands, joined by a chain, locked round a prisoner's wrists or ankles to limit movement. **2** anything that restricts freedom. **3** a U-shaped metal loop closed over by a bolt, used for fastening ropes or chains together. — *v* (*tr*) to restrain with, or as if with, shackles. [OE *sceacul*]

shad *n* ***shad*** or ***shads*** any of a family of edible herring-like fish. [OE *sceadd*]

shade *n* **1** (dimness or coolness caused by) the (partial) blocking out of sunlight. **2** an area from which sunlight has been (partially) blocked. **3** such an area represented in a drawing or painting. **4** the state of appearing comparatively unimpressive: *lived in the shade of his brother's achievements*; *His painting puts mine in the shade*. **5** any device used as a shield from direct light; a lampshade. **6** a colour, esp. one similar to but slightly different from a principal colour. **7** a small amount; a touch. — *v* **1** (*tr*) to (partially) block out sunlight from. **2** (*tr*) to draw or paint so as to give the impression of shade. **3** (*intr*; **off**, **away**) to change gradually or unnoticeably. [OE *sceadu*]

shades *n* (*pl*) **1** (*slang*) sunglasses. **2** (**of**) qualities reminiscent (of).

shading *n* the representation of areas of shade, e.g. by close parallel lines in a drawing.

shady *adj* **-*ier***, **-*iest*** **1** sheltered, or giving shelter, from sunlight. **2** (*coll*) disreputable; probably dishonest or illegal. — *n* **shadiness.**

shadow *n* **1** a dark shape on a surface, produced when an object stands between the surface and a source of light. **2** an area darkened by the blocking out of light. **3** a slight amount; a hint or trace. **4** a sense of gloom or foreboding: *cast a shadow over the proceedings*. **5** a greatly weakened or otherwise reduced version: *a shadow of her former self*. **6** a constant companion. **7** a person following another closely and secretively. — *v* (*tr*) **1** to follow closely and secretively. **2** to put into darkness by blocking out light. — *adj* denoting a spokesperson or persons with the main opposition political party, who would become minister if the party were elected to power: *shadow Foreign Secretary*. [OE *sceadwe*, accusative case of *sceadu* (see **shade**)]

shadow-boxing *n* boxing against an imaginary opponent as training. — *v* (*intr*) **shadow-box.**

shadowy *adj* **1** dark and not clearly visible. **2** darkened by shadows. — *n* **shadowiness.**

shaft *n* **1** the long straight handle of a tool or weapon. **2** any long straight part, e.g. a revolving rod that transmits motion in vehicle engines. **3** a vertical passageway, esp. one through which a lift moves. **4** either of the projecting parts of a cart, etc. to which a horse or other animal is fastened. **5** a thing moving or aimed with the directness or violent force of an arrow or missile: *shaft of light*; *shafts of sarcasm*. **6** (*archit*) the long middle part of a column, between the base and the capital. [OE *sceaft*]

shag[1] *n* **1** a ragged mass of hair. **2** a long coarse pile or nap on fabric. **3** tobacco coarsely cut into shreds. [OE *sceacga*]

shaggy *adj* **-*ier***, **-*iest*** (covered with hair or fur that is) rough and untidy in appearance. — *n* **shagginess.**

shaggy dog story *n* a rambling story or joke amusing only because of its ridiculous length and pointlessness.

shag[2] *n* a species of cormorant which has a shaggy tuft on its head. [**shag**[1]]

shag[3] (*vulg slang*) *v* **-*gg-*** (*tr*) **1** to have sexual intercourse with. **2** (**out**) to tire (out). — *n* an act of sexual intercourse.

shagreen *n* **1** coarse grainy leather, esp. made from the skin of a horse or donkey. **2** the rough skin of a shark or ray, used as an abrasive. [Turk *sagri*, horse's rump]

shah *n* a ruler in various Middle Eastern countries, esp. (formerly) Iran. [Persian]

shake *v* ***shook***, ***shaken*** **1** (*tr*) to move with quick, often violent to-and-fro or up-and-down movements. **2** (*tr*; **up**) to mix in this way. ◇ See also **shake up** below. **3** (*tr*) to wave violently and threateningly. **4** (*tr & intr*) to (cause to) tremble, totter or shiver. **5** (*tr*) to cause intense shock or agitation within: *revelations that shook the nation*. **6** (*tr*; **up**) to greatly disturb or upset. ◇ See also **shake up** below. **7** (*tr*) to cause to waver; to weaken: *shook my confidence*. **8** (*intr*) to shake hands. — *n* **1** an act or the action of shaking. **2** (*coll*) a very short while; a moment. **3** (in *pl*; *coll*; with **the**) a fit of uncontrollable trembling. **4** a milk shake. — **no great shakes** (*coll*; **at**) of no great importance, ability or worth. — **shake a leg** (*coll*) to hurry up or get moving. — *v* **shake down** (*slang*) **1** (*tr*) to search thoroughly. **2** (*tr*) to extort money from. **3** (*intr*) to go to bed, esp. in a makeshift bed (*n* **shakedown**). — **shake hands** (**with**) to greet (each other or someone else) by clasping (usu. right) hands. — **shake one's head** to move one's head from side to side as a sign of rejection or disagreement. — *v* **shake off** (*tr*) **1** to get rid of; to free oneself from. **2** to escape from. — *v* **shake up** (*tr*; *coll*) **1** to reorganise thoroughly (*n* **shake-up**). **2** to stimulate into action, from a state of lethargy or apathy. [OE *sceacan*]

shakedown see **shake down** above.

shaker *n* a container from which something, e.g. salt, is dispensed by shaking, or in which something, e.g. a cocktail, is mixed by shaking.

shake-up see **shake up** above.

shaky *adj* **-*ier***, **-*iest*** **1** trembling, as with weakness or illness. **2** (*coll*) not solid, sound or secure. — *adv* **shakily.** — *n* **shakiness.**

Shakespearean or **Shakespearian** *adj* of, relating to or resembling the literary works or style of the English writer William *Shakespeare* (1564–1616).

shako *n* **-*os*** or **-*oes*** a tall nearly cylindrical military cap with a plume. [Hung *csákó*]

shale *n* soft rock formed from compressed clay, splitting easily into layers. — *adj* **shaly.** [OE *scealu*]

shall *v* (*aux*) expressing **1** the future tense of other verbs, esp. when the subject is *I* or *we*. **2** determination, intention, certainty and obligation, esp. when the subject is *you, he, she, it* or *they*: *They shall succeed*; *You shall have what you want*; *He shall become king*; *You shall not kill*. **3** a question implying future action, often with the sense of an offer or suggestion, esp. when the subject is *I* or *we*: *What shall we do? Shall I give you a hand?* ◇ See also **should**, **will**, **would**. [OE *sceal*]

shallot *n* a plant of the onion family, with a smallish oval bulb growing in clusters. [OFr *eschalote*]

shallow *adj* **1** having little depth. **2** not profound or sincere; superficial. — *n* (often in *pl*) a shallow place or part, esp. in water. [MidE *schalowe*]

shalom *n* & *interj* (an expression used as) a Jewish greeting or farewell. [Hebr, peace (be with you)]

shalt the form of the verb **shall** used after *thou*.

sham *adj* false; pretended; insincere. — *v* **-mm-** (*tr* & *intr*) to pretend or fake. — *n* **1** anything not genuine. **2** a person who shams, esp. an impostor.

shaman *n* **-mans** a priest who uses magic, esp. his ability to make his spirit leave his body, to cure illness, commune with gods and spirits, prophesy, influence the weather and food supply, etc. [Russ]

shamanism *n* a religion, esp. of N Asia, dominated by shamans and belief in their powers. — *adj* **shamanistic**.

shamble *v* (*intr*; **along**, **past**, etc.) to walk with slow, awkward, tottering steps. — *n* such a walk or pace. — *n* & *adj* **shambling**. [From **shambles**, suggesting trestle-like legs]

shambles *n* (*sing*) **1** (*coll*) a confused mess; (something in) a state of total disorder. **2** a meat market. **3** a slaughterhouse. **4** a scene of slaughter or carnage. [OE *scamel*, stool]

shambolic *adj* (*coll*) totally disorganised; chaotic.

shame *n* **1** an embarrassing or degrading sense of guilt, foolishness or failure as a result of one's own actions or those of another person associated with one. **2** the capacity to feel this. **3** disgrace or loss of reputation; a person or thing bringing this. **4** a regrettable or disappointing event or situation. — *v* (*tr*) **1** to cause to feel shame. **2 (into)** to provoke (into taking action) by inspiring feelings of shame: *shamed him into telling the truth*. **3** to bring disgrace on. — **put to shame** to cause to seem embarrassingly inadequate by comparison. [OE *sceamu*]

shamefaced *adj* **1** showing shame or embarrassment. **2** modest or bashful. — *adv* **shamefacedly**. [Orig. *shamefast*, held by shame]

shameful *adj* bringing or deserving shame; disgraceful. — *adv* **shamefully**.

shameless *adj* **1** showing no shame; not capable of feeling shame. **2** done entirely without shame; blatant. — *adv* **shamelessly**. — *n* **shamelessness**.

shammy *n* **-ies** (*coll*; also **shammy leather**) a chamois (sense **3**).

shampoo *n* **-oos** **1** a soapy liquid for washing the hair and scalp. **2** a similar liquid for cleaning carpets or upholstery. **3** a treatment with either liquid. — *v* **-oos**, **-ooed** (*tr*) to wash or clean with shampoo. [Hindi *cha(m)po*, squeeze]

shamrock *n* any of various plants whose green leaves have three rounded leaflets, e.g. clover, used as the national emblem of Ireland. [Irish Gaelic *seamrog*]

shandy *n* **-ies** a mixture of beer and lemonade or ginger beer.

shanghai *v* **-haiing**, **-hais**, **-haied** (*tr*; *coll*) **1** to kidnap and send to sea as a sailor. **2** to trick into any unpleasant situation. [*Shanghai*, city in China, from the former use of this method in recruiting sailors for trips to the East]

shank *n* **1** the part of the leg between the knee and the ankle; the corresponding part in an animal. **2** a cut of meat from the (esp. upper) leg of an animal. **3** a shaft, stem or other long straight part. [OE *sceanca*, leg]

shanks's pony *n* (*coll*) one's own legs as a means of travelling.

shan't shall not.

shantung *n* plain (usu. undyed) silk fabric with a rugged, slightly coarse finish. [*Shantung*, province in China where it was orig. made]

shanty[1] *n* **-ies** a roughly built hut; a shack. [Canadian Fr *chantier*, woodcutter's cabin]

shanty town *n* an area in which poor people live in makeshift or ramshackle housing.

shanty[2] *n* **-ies** a rythmical song of a kind formerly sung by sailors working in unison. [Fr *chanter*, to sing]

shape *n* **1** the outline or form of anything. **2** a person's body or figure. **3** form, person, etc.: *an assistant in the shape of my brother*. **4** a desired form or (esp. physical) condition: *get the contract into shape*; *keep in shape*. **5** condition generally: *in bad shape*. **6** an unidentifiable figure: *shapes lurking in the dark*. **7** a mould or pattern. **8** a figure, esp. geometric. — *v* (*tr*) **1** to give a particular form to; to fashion. **2** to influence to an important extent: *shaped history*. **3** to devise or develop to suit a particular purpose. — *v* **shape up** (*intr*; *coll*) **1** to appear to be developing (in a particular way). **2** to be promising; to progress or develop well. — **take shape** **1** to take on a definite form. **2** to become recognisable as the desired result of plans or theories. [OE *scieppan*]

shapeless *adj* **1** not having a regular describable shape. **2** unattractively shaped. — *n* **shapelessness**.

shapely *adj* (esp. of a person's body, or part of it) attractively shaped. — *n* **shapeliness**.

shard or **sherd** *n* a fragment of something brittle, usu. pottery, esp. when found on an archaeological site. [OE *sceard*]

share[1] *n* **1** a portion given to or contributed by each of several people or groups. **2** any of the units into which the total wealth of a business company is divided, ownership of which gives the right to a portion of the company's profits. — *v* **1** (*tr* & *intr*; **in**) to have joint use of or responsibility for, with another or others. **2** (*tr*; **out**) to divide into portions, distributed to each of several people or groups (*n* **share-out**). [OE *scearu*]

shareholder *n* a person who owns shares in a company.

share[2] *n* a ploughshare. [OE *scear*]

shark *n* **1** any of various kinds of large, usu. fierce, flesh-eating fish. **2** (*coll*) a ruthless or dishonest person, esp. one who swindles or exploits. [Perhaps Ger *Schurke*, scoundrel]

sharkskin *n* **1** (leather made from) a shark's skin. **2** smooth rayon fabric with a dull sheen.

sharp *adj* **1** having a thin edge that can cut or a point that can pierce. **2** having a bitter pungent taste. **3** severely felt: *sharp pain.* **4** (sudden and) acute: *sharp increases*; *a sharp bend.* **5** quick to perceive, act or react; keenly intelligent: *sharp-witted.* **6** (**with**) abrupt or harsh in speech (towards). **7** easily perceived; clear-cut: *in sharp contrast.* **8** sarcastic: *sharp-tongued.* **9** (*coll*) stylish. **10** (*mus*) higher in pitch by a semitone: *C sharp.* **11** (*mus*) out of tune by being slightly too high in pitch. — *n* **1** (*mus*) a sharp note. **2** (*coll*) a practised cheat: *a card sharp.* — *adv* **1** punctually; on the dot. **2** suddenly: *pulled up sharp.* **3** (*mus*) untunefully high in pitch. — *adv* **sharply**. — *n* **sharpness**. — **look sharp** (*coll*) to hurry up. [OE *scearp*]

sharpen *v* **-n-** (*tr* & *intr*) to make or grow sharp. — *n* **sharpener**.

sharper *n* (*coll*) a practised cheat; a sharp.

sharp practice *n* dishonesty; cheating.

sharpshooter *n* a good marksman. — *n* & *adj* **sharpshooting**.

shatter *v* **-r-** **1** (*tr* & *intr*) to break into tiny pieces, usu. suddenly or forcefully. **2** (*tr*) to destroy completely, or cause to break down: *shattered hopes*, *nerves.* **3** (*tr*) to upset greatly. **4** (*tr*; *coll*) to tire out; to exhaust. — *adj* **shattered**. — *adj* **shattering**.

shave *v* **1** (*tr*) to cut off (hair) from (the face or other part of the body) with a razor or shaver. **2** (*intr*) to remove one's growth of beard in this way. **3** (*tr*) to remove thin slivers from the surface of (esp. wood) with a bladed tool. **4** (*tr*) to graze the surface of, or narrowly miss, in passing. — *n* **1** an act or the process of shaving one's growth of beard. **2** a narrow miss or escape: a *close shave.* **3** a tool for shaving wood. — *n* **shaving**. [OE *sceafan*]

shaven *adj* shaved.

shaver *n* **1** an electrical device with a moving blade or set of blades for shaving hair. **2** (*old coll*) a young boy.

shavings *n* (*pl*) thin slivers, esp. of wood, removed from a surface.

shawl *n* a large single piece of fabric used as a loose covering for the head or shoulders, or for wrapping a baby in. [Persian *shal*]

she *pron* the female person or animal, or thing thought of as female (e.g. a ship), named before or understood from the context. — *n* **shes** a female person or animal: *a she-wolf.* [OE *seo*]

sheaf *n* **sheaves** a bundle, esp. of reaped corn, tied together. — *v* (*tr*; also **sheave**) to tie up in a bundle. [OE *sceaf*]

shear *v* **sheared**, **shorn** (*tr*) **1** to clip or cut off with a large pair of clippers. **2** to cut the fleece off (a sheep). **3** (**of**) to strip or deprive (of): *shorn of all authority.* **4** (*tr* & *intr*; **off**) (of metal) to twist or break under strain. — *n* **1** (in *pl*) a two-bladed cutting-tool like a large pair of scissors; clippers. **2** a twisting or breaking of metal under strain. — *n* **shearer**. [OE *sceran*]

sheath *n* **1** a covering for the blade of a sword or knife. **2** (anything forming) a long close-fitting covering. **3** (*old*) a condom. **4** a straight tight-fitting dress. [OE *sceath*]

sheathe *v* (*tr*) to put into, or protect or cover with, a sheath.

sheave and **sheaves**. See **sheaf**.

shebang *n* (*slang*) affair; matter: *the whole shebang.*

shed[1] *n* a wooden or metal outbuilding of any size, for working in or for storage or shelter. [From **shade**]

shed[2] *v* **-dd-**, **shed** (*tr*) **1** to release or cause to flow: *shed tears.* **2** to cast off or get rid of: *shed a skin*; *shed jobs.* **3** to cast: *shed light on.* **4** to allow to flow off: *This fabric sheds water.* [OE *sceadan*]

she'd **1** she had. **2** she would.

sheen *n* shine; glossiness; lustre. [OE *scene*]

sheep *n* **sheep** **1** an animal of the goat family, widely farmed for its edible flesh and its fleece from which wool is obtained. **2** a meek person, esp. one who follows or obeys unquestioningly. **3** a member of a congregation (thought of as being looked after by the pastor). [OE *sceap*]

sheep-dip *n* **1** a liquid disinfectant and insecticide used for washing sheep. **2** a trough full of this through which sheep are driven.

sheepdog *n* **1** a dog trained to herd sheep. **2** any of various breeds of dog orig. trained to herd sheep.

sheepish *adj* embarrassed because of having done something wrong or foolish. — *adv* **sheepishly**. — *n* **sheepishness**.

sheepshank *n* a knot used for shortening a rope.

sheepskin *n* **1** (a garment or rug made from) sheep's skin with the wool left on it. **2** leather made from sheep's skin.

sheer[1] *adj* **1** complete; absolute; nothing but: *sheer madness.* **2** (of a cliff, etc.) (nearly) vertical. **3** so fine as to be almost transparent. — *adv* **1** completely. **2** (almost) vertically: *rock face rising sheer.* [MidE *schere*]

sheer[2] *v* (*intr*; **off, away from**) **1** to change course suddenly; to swerve. **2** to move (away), esp. from a person or thing disliked or feared.

sheet[1] *n* **1** a large broad piece of fabric, esp. for covering the mattress of a bed. **2**

any large broad piece or expanse. **3** a piece (of paper), esp. of a size for writing on. **4** a pamphlet or newspaper. — *v* **1** (*tr*) to provide or cover with sheets. **2** (*intr*) (of rain, ice, etc.) to form, or fall in, a sheet-like mass. [OE *scete*]

sheeting *n* fabric used for making sheets.

sheet music *n* music printed on loose sheets of paper.

sheet[2] *n* (*naut*) a controlling rope attached to the lower corner of a sail. [OE *sceata*, corner]

sheet-anchor *n* **1** an extra anchor for use in an emergency. **2** a person or thing relied on for support, esp. in a crisis; a last hope. [Orig. *shoot-anchor*]

sheikh or **sheik** *n* **1** the head of an Arab tribe, village or family. **2** a Muslim leader. — *n* **sheikhdom** or **sheikdom**. [Arabic *shaikh*, old man]

sheila *n* (*coll*; *Austr* & *NZ*) a woman or girl. [From the name]

shekel *n* **1** the standard unit of currency in Israel, divided into 100 agorot. **2** an ancient Jewish coin and weight. **3** (in *pl*; *slang*) money. [Hebr *sheqel*]

shelduck *n* a large brightly coloured duck of Europe, Africa and Asia. [Dialect *sheld*, pied + **duck**]

sheldrake *n* a male shelduck.

shelf *n* ***shelves*** **1** a (usu. narrow) horizontal board for laying things on, fixed to a wall or as part of a cupboard, etc. **2** a sandbank or rocky ledge, esp. partially submerged. — **on the shelf 1** no longer used, employed or active. **2** no longer likely to have the opportunity to marry, esp. because of being too old. [OE *scylf*]

shelf-life *n* the length of time that a stored product remains usable.

shell *n* **1** the hard protective outer covering of numerous organisms, e.g. an egg, a nut, or a mollusc. **2** the empty covering of a mollusc, found on the seashore. **3** any hard outer case. **4** a round of ammunition for a large-bore gun, e.g. a mortar; a shotgun cartridge. **5** an empty framework or outer case, the early stage of construction or the undestroyed remains of something, e.g. a building. **6** a person very much weaker than before in body or personality. **7** a narrow light rowing-boat for racing. — *v* (*tr*) **1** to remove the shell from. **2** to bombard with (e.g. mortar) shells. — *n* **shelling**. — **out of one's shell** from a state of shyness and reserve to one of openness and sociableness. — *v* **shell out** (*tr*; *coll*) to pay out or spend. [OE *scell*]

shellfish *n* any of numerous (esp. edible) sea creatures with an outer shell, e.g. prawns and mussels.

shell-shock *n* nervous breakdown caused by prolonged exposure to combat conditions. — *adj* **shell-shocked**.

shell suit *n* a tracksuit of very lightweight multi-coloured fabric, commonly used as everyday casual wear.

she'll she will; she shall.

shellac *n* **1** a yellow or orange resin produced by the lac insect and others. **2** a solution of this in alcohol, used as a varnish. — *v* ***-ck-*** (*tr*) to coat with shellac. [**shell** + **lac**]

shelter *n* **1** protection against weather or danger. **2** a place or structure giving this. — *v* ***-r-*** **1** (*tr*) to protect from danger or the effects of weather. **2** (*intr*) to take cover.

sheltered *adj* **1** protected from the effects of weather. **2** kept ignorant of the world's unpleasantnesses: *a sheltered upbringing*.

sheltered housing *n* flats or bungalows specially designed for the elderly or disabled, esp. in a safe enclosed complex, with a resident attendant.

shelve *v* **1** (*tr*) to store on a shelf. **2** (*tr*) to fit with shelves. **3** (*tr*) to postpone the use or implementation of; to abandon. **4** (*tr*) to remove from active service. **5** (*intr*) (of ground) to slope gently.

shelves see **shelf**.

shelving *n* **1** material for use as shelves. **2** shelves collectively.

shenanigans *n* (*pl*; *coll*) **1** boisterous misbehaviour. **2** foolish behaviour; nonsense. **3** underhand dealings; trickery.

shepherd *n* **1** a person who looks after sheep. **2** (*literary*) a religious minister. — *v* (*tr*) to guide or herd (a group or crowd). [OE *sceaphirde*, sheep herd]

shepherdess *n* (*old*) a female shepherd.

shepherd's pie *n* a baked dish of minced meat with mashed potatoes on the top.

sherbet *n* **1** a fruit-flavoured powder, or a fizzy drink made from it. **2** a drink of sweetened fruit juices in Middle Eastern countries. [Turk and Persian *serbet*]

sherd. See **shard**.

sheriff *n* **1** the chief police officer in a US county. **2** the chief judge of a sheriff court. **3** the chief representative of the monarch in an English county, whose duties are now mainly ceremonial. [OE *scir*, shire + *gerefa*, reeve]

sheriff court *n* a court in a Scottish town or region dealing with civil actions and trying all but the most serious crimes.

Sherpa *n* a member of an Eastern Tibetan people living high on the south side of the Himalayas. [Tibetan *shar*, east + *pa*, inhabitant]

sherry *n* ***-ies*** a fortified wine ranging in colour from pale gold to dark brown, strictly speaking one produced in or near the S Spanish town of *Jerez*.

she's 1 she is. **2** she has.

Shetland pony *n* ***-ies*** a breed of small sturdy pony with a long thick coat, orig. bred in the Shetland Isles to the north of Scotland.

Shia or **Shiah** *n* one of the two main branches of Islam, the branch which regards Mohammed's son-in-law, Ali, as his true successor as leader of Islam. — *n* & *adj* **Shiite**. ◇ See also **Sunni**. [Arabic *shia*, sect]

shibboleth *n* **1** a common saying. **2** a slogan, custom or belief, esp. if considered outdated. **3** a use of a word, phrase or pronunciation that characterises members of a particular group. [In the Biblical story (Judges 12), the word used by Gileadites to identify Ephraimites, who pronounced *s* for *sh*]

shield *n* **1** a piece of armour carried to block an attack with a weapon. **2** a representation of this, usu. a vertical rectangle with a rounded bottom, used as an emblem. **3** a medal or trophy shaped (perhaps only vaguely) like this. **4** a protective plate or screen. **5** a person or thing that protects from danger or harm. — *v* (*tr*) to protect from harm or danger. [OE *sceld*]

shift *v* **1** (*tr* & *intr*) to change the position or direction of; to change position or direction. **2** (*tr*) to transfer, switch or re-direct: *shift the blame on to someone else*. **3** (*tr*) to change (gear in a vehicle). **4** (*tr*) to remove or dislodge. **5** (*intr*; *coll*) to move quickly. — *n* **1** a change, or change of position. **2** one of a set of consecutive periods into which a 24-hour working day is divided. ◇ See also **back shift**, **day shift**, **night shift**. **3** the group of workers on duty during any one of these periods. **4** a handy method of proceeding or dealing with something; an expedient. **5** a trick or other underhand scheme. — **shift one's ground** to adopt a new opinion, position in an argument, etc. [OE *sciftan*, to divide]

shiftless *adj* **1** having no motivation or initiative. **2** inefficient.

shifty *adj* **-ier**, **-iest** (suggesting a person to be) sly, untrustworthy or dishonest. — *adv* **shiftily**. — *n* **shiftiness**.

Shiite. See **Shia**.

shilling *n* **1** (*formerly*, before the introduction of decimal currency) (a British coin worth) one-twentieth of £1 or twelve old pence (12d). **2** the standard unit of currency in several E African countries. [OE *scilling*]

shilly-shally *v* **-ies**, **-ied** (*intr*) to be slow to make up one's mind; to be indecisive. [Reduplication of *shall I?*]

shim *n* a thin washer, or a metal or plastic strip, used to fill a gap between machine parts, esp. gears. — *v* **-mm-** (*tr*) to fill or adjust with a shim.

shimmer *v* **-r-** (*intr*) to shine quiveringly with reflected light. — *n* a quivering gleam of reflected light. — *adj* **shimmery**. [OE *scimerian*]

shin *n* **1** the bony front part of the leg below the knee. **2** the lower part of a leg of beef. — *v* **-nn-** (*tr* & *intr*; **up**) to climb by gripping with the hands and legs. — *n* **shinbone**. [OE *scinu*]

shindig *n* (*coll*) **1** a lively party or celebration. **2** a noisy disturbance; a commotion. [Perhaps from **shinty**]

shine *v* **shone** or (sense **3**) **shined 1** (*intr*) to give out or reflect light. **2** (*tr*) to direct the light from: *shone the torch in my face*. **3** (*tr*) to make bright and gleaming by polishing. **4** (*intr*; **at**) to command attention or be outstandingly impressive: *She shines at maths*. — *n* **1** shining quality; brightness; lustre. **2** sunny weather: *rain or shine*. — **take a shine to** (*coll*) to quickly or immediately come to like. [OE *scinan*]

shiner *n* (*coll*) a black eye.

shiny *adj* **-ier**, **-iest 1** reflecting light; polished to brightness. **2** (of part of a garment) at which the fabric has been badly worn, leaving a glossy surface.

shingle[1] *n* small pebbles on a seashore or river bank. — *adj* **shingly**.

shingle[2] *n* **1** a thin rectangular (esp. wooden) roof-tile. **2** a woman's short hairstyle, cropped at the back. — *v* (*tr*) **1** to tile with shingles. **2** to cut in a shingle. [Lat *scindula*, wooden tile]

shingles *n* (*sing*) an infectious disease of the nerve-cells, producing a rash of painful blisters on the body, esp. round the waist. [Lat *cingulum*, belt]

Shinto *n* the principal religion of Japan, involving the worship of many gods associated with aspects of nature. — *n* **Shintoism**. — *n* & *adj* **Shintoist**. [Jap, from Chin *shen*, god + *tao*, way]

shinty *n* **-ies 1** a hockey-like game of Scottish origin, played by two teams of twelve. **2** the stick or ball used for this game.

ship *n* **1** any large boat intended for sea travel. **2** (*coll*) a spaceship or airship. — *v* **-pp-** (*tr*) **1** to send or transport by ship, or any other means. **2** (*coll*; **off**) to send away: *shipped the children off to their grandparents'*. **3** (*naut*) (of a boat) to have (water, e.g. waves) coming on board over the side. **4** (*naut*) to bring on board a boat or ship: *ship oars*. — **when one's ship comes in** or **home** when one becomes rich. [OE *scip*]

shipboard *adj* taking place, or situated, on board a ship.

shipmate *n* a fellow sailor.

shipment *n* **1** a cargo or consignment (not necessarily one sent by ship). **2** the act or practice of shipping cargo.

shipping *n* **1** ships as traffic. **2** the commercial transporting of freight, esp. by ship.

shipshape *adj* in good order; neat and tidy.

shipwreck *n* **1** the accidental sinking or destruction of a ship. **2** the remains of a sunken or destroyed ship. **3** ruin; disaster. — *v* **1** (*tr* & *intr*) to (cause to) be the victim of accidental sinking or destruction. **2** (*tr*) to ruin (e.g. plans).

shipwright *n* a person who builds or repairs (esp. wooden) ships.

shipyard *n* a place where ships are built and repaired.

-ship *sfx* **1** rank, position or status: *lordship*. **2** a period of office or rule: *during his chairmanship*. **3** a state or condition: *friendship*. **4** a type of skill: *craftsmanship*.

5 a group of individuals: *membership*. [OE *-scipe*]

shire *n* a county. [OE *scir*, authority]

shire horse *n* a large strong horse bred for pulling carts, etc., orig. in the Midlands.

the Shires *n* (*pl*) the rural areas of England as opposed to the towns, specifically the Midland counties or the fox-hunting counties of Leicestershire and Northamptonshire.

shirk *v* (*tr* & *intr*) to avoid doing (work) or carrying out (a duty). — *n* **shirker**. [Perhaps Ger *Schurke*, scoundrel]

shirt *n* any of various styles of (long- or short-sleeved) garment for the upper body, usu. with a collar, esp. worn by men. — **in one's shirtsleeves** not wearing a jacket or coat. — **keep one's shirt on** (*slang*) to control one's temper. — **put one's shirt on** (*slang*) to bet all one has on. [OE *scyrte*]

shirt dress *n* (also **shirtwaister**) a woman's dress with a shirt-like bodice.

shirt-tail *n* the flap hanging down at the back of a shirt.

shirty *adj* **-ier**, **-iest** (*coll*) bad-tempered; annoyed.

shish kebab. See **kebab**.

shit or **shite** (*vulg*) *n* **1** faeces. **2** an act of defecating. **3** (*derog*) rubbish; nonsense. **4** (*derog*) a despicable person. — *v* ***shitting*** or ***shiting***; ***shit***, ***shitted*** or ***shat*** (*intr*) to defecate. — *interj* an expression of annoyance or disappointment. [OE *scitan*, to defecate]

shitty *adj* **-ier**, **-iest** (*vulg*) **1** filthy; soiled with, or as if with, shit. **2** (*derog*) mean; despicable.

shiver[1] *v* **-r-** (*intr*) to quiver or tremble (e.g. with cold or fear). — *n* an act of shivering; a shivering sensation. — *adj* **shivery**. — **the shivers** (*coll*) a fit of shivering. [MidE *chivere*]

shiver[2] *n* a splinter or other small fragment. — *v* **-r-** (*tr* & *intr*) to shatter. [MidE *scifre*]

shoal[1] *n* **1** a large number of fish swimming together. **2** a huge crowd; a multitude or swarm. — *v* (*intr*) to gather or move in a shoal. [OE *scolu*, a troop]

shoal[2] *n* **1** an area of shallow water. **2** an underwater sandbank or rocky ledge, esp. one exposed at low tide. — *v* (*tr* & *intr*) to make or become shallow. [OE *sceald*, shallow]

shock[1] *n* **1** (something that causes) a strong emotional disturbance, esp. a feeling of extreme surprise, outrage or disgust. **2** a convulsion caused by the passage of electricity through the body. **3** a heavy jarring blow or impact. **4** a temporary breakdown of all physical functions, e.g. as a result of extreme pain or sudden extreme emotional disturbance: *suffering from shock*. — *v* **1** (*tr* & *intr*) to (cause to) feel extreme surprise, outrage or disgust. **2** (*tr*) to shake or jar suddenly and forcefully. [Fr *choc*]

shock absorber *n* a device that absorbs impact, esp. fitted in vehicles to deaden the effects of travelling on bumpy roads.

shocking *adj* **1** extremely surprising, outrageous or disgusting. **2** (*coll*) very bad.

shock tactics *n* (*pl*) any course of action that seeks to achieve its object by means of suddenness and force.

shock therapy or **treatment** *n* the treatment of certain mental disorders using shocks induced by electric current or drugs.

shock[2] *n* a bushy mass (of hair).

shock[3] *n* a number of sheaves of corn propped up against each other to dry. — *v* (*tr*) to set up to dry in this way. [MidE *schokke*]

shod. See **shoe**.

shoddy *adj* **-ier**, **-iest 1** of poor quality; carelessly done or made. **2** of the nature of a cheap imitation. — *adv* **shoddily**. — *n* **shoddiness**.

shoe *n* **1** either of a pair of shaped outer coverings for the feet, esp. made of leather or other stiff material, usu. finishing below the ankle. **2** anything like this in shape or function. **3** a horseshoe. — *v* ***shoeing***, ***shod*** (*tr*) to fit (usu. a horse) with shoes. — **in someone's shoes** in the same situation as someone; in someone's place. [OE *scoh*]

shoehorn *n* a curved shaped piece of metal, plastic or (orig.) horn, used for gently levering a foot into a shoe.

shoelace *n* a string or cord for fastening a shoe.

shoestring *n* (esp. *US*) a shoelace. — **on a shoestring** (*coll*) with or using a very small amount of money.

shoe tree *n* a support put inside a shoe to preserve its shape when not being worn.

shogun *n* (*hist*) any of a dynasty of Japanese military rulers between the 12th and 19th centuries, who reduced the Emperor to a mere figurehead. [Jap, army leader]

shone. See **shine**.

shoo *interj* an expression used to chase away a person or animal. — *v* ***shooed*** (*tr*; **off**) to chase away by, or as if by, shouting 'Shoo!'. [Imit.]

shook. See **shake**.

shoot *v* ***shot*** **1** (*tr* & *intr*; **at**) to fire (a gun or other weapon, or bullets, arrows or other missiles). **2** (*tr*) to hit, wound or kill with a weapon or missile. **3** (*tr*) to direct forcefully and rapidly: *shot questions at them*. **4** (*tr* & *intr*) to (cause to) move or progress extremely fast: *That last victory shot them to the top of the table*. **5** (*intr*; **up**) to grow or increase extremely quickly. **6** (*tr* & *intr*; *sport*) to strike (the ball, etc.) at goal. **7** (*tr* & *intr*) to film, or take photographs (of). **8** (*intr*) (of pain) to dart with a stabbing sensation. **9** (*intr*) (of a plant) to produce new growth; (esp. of a vegetable) to produce unwanted flowers and seeds. **10** (*tr*; *coll*) to pass through (a set of traffic lights at red) without stopping. **11**

(*tr*; *coll*) to pass quickly through: *shoot rapids*. **12** (*tr*; *slang*) to play a game of (e.g. pool or golf); to have as a score at golf. **13** (*tr*; *slang*) to inject (esp. oneself) with (drugs) illegally. — *n* **1** an act of shooting. **2** a new or young plant growth. **3** an outing to hunt animals with firearms; an area of land within which animals are hunted in this way. — *n* **shooter**. — *v* **shoot down** (*tr*) **1** to cause (an aircraft) to crash with gunfire. **2** to kill with gunfire. **3** to mercilessly dismiss with criticism or ridicule. — **shoot one's mouth off** (*slang*) to speak indiscreetly or boastfully. [OE *sceotan*]

shooting brake *n* (*old*) an estate car.

shooting star *n* a meteor.

shooting-stick *n* a sturdy pointed walking-stick whose two-part handle folds out to form a small seat.

shop *n* **1** a place where goods (or services) are sold. **2** a place in which (esp. manual) work of a particular kind is carried out: *machine shop*. — *v* **-pp-** **1** (*intr*) (to visit a shop or shops in order) to buy goods. **2** (*tr*; *slang*) to inform on (someone), e.g. to the police. — *n* **shopper**. — **all over the shop** (*coll*) (scattered) everywhere; in numerous places. — *v* **shop around** (*intr*) **1** to compare the price and quality of goods in various shops before deciding to buy. **2** (*coll*) to explore the full range of options available before committing oneself to any. — **shut up shop** (*coll*) to stop trading, whether at the end of the working day or permanently. — **talk shop** (*coll*) to talk about one's work. [OE *sceoppa*, treasury]

shop assistant *n* a person serving customers in a shop.

shop floor *n* **1** the part of a factory where the manual work is carried out. **2** the workers in a factory, as opposed to the management.

shopkeeper *n* a person who owns and manages a shop.

shoplifting *n* stealing goods from shops. — *n* **shoplifter**.

shopping *n* **1** the activity of visiting shops (and buying things). **2** goods bought in shops.

shopping centre *n* **1** an area containing a large number of shops of different kinds. **2** a collection of different shops under one roof, often providing other facilities, e.g. restaurants and toilets.

shop-soiled *adj* slightly dirty or spoiled from being used as a display in a shop.

shop steward *n* a worker elected by others to be an official trade union representative in negotiations with the management.

shopwalker *n* a person who supervises shop assistants in a large department store.

shore[1] *n* **1** land bordering on the sea or any area of water. **2** (in *pl*; *literary*) lands; countries: *foreign shores*. [MidE *schore*]

shoreline *n* the line formed where land meets water.

shore[2] *n* a prop. — *v* (*tr*; **up**) **1** to support with props. **2** to give support to; to sustain or strengthen. [ODut *schore*]

shorn. See **shear**.

short *adj* **1** of little physical length; not long. **2** of little height. **3** brief; concise. **4** (of a temper) easily lost. **5** (**with**) rudely or angrily abrupt; curt. **6** (**of, on**) lacking (in); not having enough (of); deficient. **7** (of a memory) tending not to retain things for long. **8** (of pastry) crisp and crumbling easily. **9** (of betting odds) providing the winner with only a small profit; near even. **10** (of a vowel sound) being the briefer of two possible lengths of vowel. ◇ See also **long**[1]. **11** (of fielding positions in cricket) relatively near the batsman. — *adv* **1** abruptly: *stopped short*. **2** (with **of**) without going as far as; except: *tried every kind of persuasion short of threats*. — *n* **1** a drink of an alcoholic spirit. **2** a short cinema film shown before the main feature. **3** a short circuit. — *v* (*tr* & *intr*) to short-circuit. — *n* **shortness**. — **be caught** or **taken short** (*coll euph*) to have an urgent need to go to the toilet. — **fall short** to be less than a required, expected or stated amount. — **for short** as an abbreviated form. — **go** or **run short (of)** not to have enough (of). — **in short** concisely stated. — **short and sweet** (*coll*) agreeably brief. — **short for** an abbreviated form of. [OE *sceort*]

shortage *n* a lack or deficiency.

shortbread *n* a rich sweet crumbly biscuit made with flour, butter and sugar.

shortcake *n* **1** shortbread. **2** a dessert cake consisting of a biscuit base topped with fruit, served with cream.

short-change *v* (*tr*) **1** to give (a customer) less than the correct amount of change, whether by accident or intentionally. **2** (*coll*) to treat dishonestly; to cheat.

short circuit *n* a (usu. accidental) connection between two incompatible points in an electrical circuit, causing the current to be deflected from its normal path and resulting in the breakdown of the circuit. — *v* (**short-circuit**) **1** (*tr* & *intr*) to (cause to) break down through the formation of a short circuit.

shortcoming *n* a fault or defect.

short cut *n* **1** a quicker route between two places. **2** a method that saves time or effort.

shorten *v* **-n-** (*tr* & *intr*) to make or become shorter.

shortening *n* butter, lard or other fat used for making pastry more crumbly.

shortfall *n* **1** a failure to reach a desired or expected level. **2** (**of**) the amount or margin failed by.

shorthand *n* **1** any of various systems of strokes and dots representing speech sounds and groups of sounds, used as a fast way of recording speech in writing. **2** any method of abbreviated writing. — *adv* using any such system.

short-handed *adj* understaffed.

shorthorn *n* a breed of cattle with short horns.

shortie same as **shorty**.

shortlist *n* a selection of the best candidates from the total number submitted or nominated, from which the successful candidate will be chosen. — *v* (*tr*) to place on a shortlist.

short-lived *adj* lasting only for a short time.

shortly *adv* **1** soon. **2** in a curt or abrupt manner.

shorts *n* (*pl*) trousers extending from the waist to anywhere between the upper thigh and the knee.

short shrift *n* discourteously brief or disdainful consideration: *His suggestions were given short shrift*.

short-sighted *adj* **1** seeing clearly only things that are near. **2** lacking foresight; showing a lack of foresight. — *n* **short-sightedness**.

short-tempered *adj* easily made angry.

short-term *adj* **1** concerned only with the near future. **2** lasting only a short time.

short wave *n* a radio wave with a wavelength of between 10 and 100 metres.

short-winded *adj* easily running out of breath.

shorty *n* **-ies** (*coll*) a shorter-than-average person or thing.

shot[1] *n* **1** an act of firing a gun; the sound of a gun being fired. **2** small metal pellets fired in clusters from a shotgun. **3** a person considered in terms of ability to fire a gun accurately: *a good shot*. **4** (*sport*) an act of shooting or playing a stroke. **5** a photograph. **6** a single piece of filmed action recorded without a break by one camera. **7** a heavy metal ball thrown as a field event in athletics; this event. ◇ See also **shot put** below. **8** (*coll*) an attempt: *have a shot at*. **9** (*coll*) a turn or go: *It's my shot now*. **10** (*coll*) an injection. **11** (*coll*; esp. *US*) a drink of alcoholic spirit. **12** (*old*) the launch of a spacecraft, esp. a rocket: *moon shot*. — **call the shots** (*coll*) to give the orders; to be in charge. — **like a shot** extremely quickly; without hesitating. — **a shot in the arm** an uplifting or reviving influence; a boost. — **a shot in the dark** a wild guess. [OE *sceot*]

shotgun *n* a gun with a long wide smooth barrel for firing clusters of pellets.

shotgun wedding or **marriage** *n* a marriage into which the couple has been forced, esp. because of the woman's pregnancy.

shot put *n* an athletics event in which a heavy metal ball is thrown from the shoulder as far as possible. — *n* **shot-putter**.

shot[2] past tense and past participle of **shoot**. — *adj* **1** (of fabric) woven with different-coloured threads and in such a way that movement produces the effect of changing colours. **2** streaked (with a different colour). — **shot of** (*coll*) rid of.

should *v* (*aux*) expressing **1** obligation, duty or recommendation; ought to: *You should brush your teeth regularly*. **2** likelihood or probability: *He should have left by now*. **3** condition: *if I should die before you*. **4** (with *1st person pronouns*) a past tense of *shall* in reported speech: *I told them I should be back soon*. **5** statements in clauses with *that*, following expressions of feeling or mood: *It seems odd that we should both have had the same idea*. **6** (with *1st person pronouns*) doubt or polite indirectness in statements: *I should imagine he's left*; *I should think I'll get the job*. **7** (*literary*) purpose: *in order that we should not have to leave*. ◇ See also **shall**, **will**, **would**. [OE *sceolde*]

shoulder *n* **1** the part of the body between the neck and upper arm. **2** the part of a garment covering this. **3** the part of an animal's or bird's body where the foreleg or wing joins the trunk. **4** a cut of meat consisting of the animal's upper foreleg. **5** (in *pl*) the person as a bearer of burdens; capacity to bear burdens: *a lot of responsibility on his shoulders*; *have broad shoulders*. **6** any object or part resembling a human shoulder. **7** either edge of a road. — *v* **-r-** (*tr*) **1** to bear (e.g. a responsibility). **2** to carry on one's shoulders. **3** to thrust with the shoulder. — **(straight) from the shoulder** (*coll*) frankly and forcefully. — **put one's shoulder to the wheel** to get down to some hard work; to begin making a great effort. — **rub shoulders with** (*coll*) to meet or associate with. — **shoulder arms** to bring one's rifle to a vertical position tight in to the right side with the barrel against the shoulder. — **a shoulder to cry on** a person to tell one's troubles to. — **shoulder to shoulder** together in friendship or agreement; side by side. [OE *sculdor*]

shoulder blade *n* the broad flat triangular bone behind either shoulder; the scapula.

shoulder strap *n* a strap worn over the shoulder to support a garment or bag.

shouldn't should not.

shout *n* **1** a loud cry or call. **2** (*coll*) a turn to buy a round of drinks. — *v* (*tr & intr*; **out**) to utter (with) a loud cry or call. — *v* **shout down** (*tr*) to force to give up speaking, or make impossible to hear, with persistent shouting.

shove *v* **1** (*tr & intr*) to push or thrust with force. **2** (*tr*; *coll*) to place or put, esp. roughly: *Shove it in the bag*. — *n* a forceful push. — *v* **shove off** (*intr*) **1** to start one's boat moving by pushing against the shore or jetty. **2** (*coll*) to go away. [OE *scufan*]

shovel *n* **1** a tool with a deep-sided spade-like blade and a (long or short) handle, for lifting and carrying loose material. **2** (a part of) a machine with a scooping action. — *v* **-ll-** (*tr*) **1** to lift or carry with, or as if with, a shovel. **2** to take crudely, rapidly and in huge quantities: *shovelling* *food into her mouth.* [OE *scofl*, from *scufan*, to shove]

show *v* ***showed***; ***shown*** or ***showed*** **1** (*tr & intr*) to (cause to) be or become visible or noticeable. **2** (*tr*) to present or give to be viewed. **3** (*tr*) to display or exhibit. **4** (*tr*) to prove, indicate or reveal. **5** (*tr*) to teach by demonstrating: *showed me how to draw.* **6** (*tr*) to lead, guide or escort: *show you to your room.* **7** (*tr*) to give: *show him some respect.* **8** (*tr*) to represent or manifest: *exam results show a marked improvement.* **9** (*intr*) (of a cinema film) to be part of a current programme: *now showing in cinema 3.* **10** (*intr*; *slang*) to appear or arrive: *What time did he show?* — *n* **1** an entertainment or spectacle of any kind. **2** an exhibition. **3** a pretence: *a show of friendship between sworn enemies.* **4** a display of true feeling: *no show of emotion.* **5** (the sake of) grand appearance: *all done for show.* **6** (*coll*) proceedings; affair: *Who's running the show?* **7** (*old coll*) effort; attempt: *jolly good show.* — **on show** on display; available to be seen. — *v* **show off 1** (*tr*) to display proudly, inviting admiration. **2** (*intr*) to display oneself or one's talents openly, inviting attention or admiration. ◇ See also **show-off** below. **3** (*tr*) to display to good effect: *The cream rug shows off the red carpet nicely.* — *v* **show up 1** (*tr & intr*) to (cause to) be clearly visible. **2** (*tr*) to embarrass or humiliate in public. **3** (*tr*) to cause to seem inadequate or inferior by comparison. **4** (*intr*; *coll*) to arrive; to turn up. — **to show for** as reward for or a useful result of (e.g. one's efforts). [OE *sceawian*, to look]

showbiz *n* & *adj* (*coll*) (of or in) show business.

show business *n* the entertainment industry.

showcase *n* **1** a glass case for displaying objects, e.g. in a museum or shop. **2** any setting in which a person or thing is displayed to good advantage.

showdown *n* (*coll*) a fight or other contest settling a long-term dispute.

showing *n* **1** an act of exhibiting or displaying. **2** a screening of a cinema film. **3** a performance. **4** a display of behaviour as evidence of a fact: *On this showing, he certainly won't get the job.*

showjumping *n* a competitive sport in which riders on horseback take turns to jump a variety of obstacles, often against time. — *n* **showjumper**.

showman *n* **1** a person who owns or manages a circus, (a stall at) a fairground, or other entertainment. **2** a person skilled in displaying things, often his or her own abilities, so as to attract maximum attention. — *n* **showmanship**.

show-off *n* (*coll*) a person who behaves in such a way as to deliberately attract attention or admiration. ◇ See also **show off** above.

showpiece *n* **1** an item in an exhibition. **2** a thing presented as an excellent example of its type, to be copied or admired.

showroom *n* a room where (samples of) goods for sale are displayed.

showy *adj* ***-ier***, ***-iest*** **1** attractively and impressively bright. **2** stentatious; gaudy; flashy. — *n* **showiness**.

shower *n* **1** a sudden but brief fall of rain, snow or hail. **2** a device producing a stream of water for bathing under, usu. while standing. **3** (often in *pl*) a room or cubicle fitted with such a device or devices. **4** an act of bathing under such a device. **5** a sudden (esp. heavy) burst or fall: *a shower of abuse, of bullets; a meteor shower.* **6** (*coll*) a bunch of worthless people. — *v* ***-r-*** **1** (*tr & intr*) to cover, bestow, fall or come abundantly: *showered them with gifts; arrows showering (down) from the battlements.* **2** (*intr*) to bathe under a shower. **3** (*intr*) to rain in showers. [OE *scur*]

showery *adj* ***-ier***, ***-iest*** raining in showers.

shown. See **show**.

shrank. See **shrink**.

shrapnel *n* **1** flying fragments of the casing of any exploding shell. **2** an explosive shell, filled with pellets or metal fragments, detonated shortly before impact. [H *Shrapnel* (1761–1842), British inventor of the pellet-filled shell]

shred *n* **1** a thin strip cut or ripped off. **2** the smallest piece or amount: *not a shred of evidence.* — *v* ***shredding***; ***shredded*** or ***shred*** (*tr*) to reduce to shreds by cutting or ripping. — *n* **shredder**. [OE *screade*]

shrew *n* **1** a small mouse-like animal with a long pointed snout. **2** a quarrelsome or scolding woman. — *adj* **shrewish**. [OE *screawa*]

shrewd *adj* having or showing good judgement gained from practical experience. — *adv* **shrewdly**. — *n* **shrewdness**.

shriek *v* (*tr & intr*) to utter (with) a piercing scream. — *n* such a scream.

shrift. See **short shrift** under **short**.

shrike *n* any of various hook-billed songbirds that feed on insects or small birds and animals, some species being noted for impaling their prey on thorns, etc. [OE *scric*]

shrill *adj* (of a sound, voice, etc.) high-pitched and piercing. — *v* (*tr*) to utter in such a voice. — *n* **shrillness**.

shrimp *n* **1** a small edible long-tailed shellfish, smaller than a prawn. **2** (*coll*) a very small slight person. — *v* (*intr*) to fish for shrimps.

shrine *n* **1** a sacred place of worship. **2** the tomb of a saint or other holy person, or a monument erected near it. **3** any place or thing greatly respected because of its associations. [OE *scrin*]

shrink *v* ***shrank***, ***shrunk*** or (esp. as *adj*) ***shrunken*** **1** (*tr & intr*) to make or become smaller, esp. through exposure to heat, cold or moisture. **2** (*intr*; **from**) to move away in horror or disgust. **3** (*intr*; **from**) to be reluctant (to do or carry out). — *n* (*slang*) a psychiatrist. [OE *scrincan*]

shrinkage *n* the act or amount of shrinking.

shrink-wrap *v* (*tr*) to wrap in clear plastic film that is then shrunk, e.g. by heating, so as to fit tightly.

shrivel *v* **-*ll*-** (*tr* & *intr*; **up**) to (cause to) become shrunken and wrinkled, esp. through drying out.

shroud *n* **1** a cloth in which a dead body is wrapped. **2** anything that obscures, masks or hides: *shrouds of fog*. — *v* (*tr*) **1** to wrap in a shroud. **2** to obscure, mask or hide: *proceedings shrouded in secrecy*. [OE *scrud*, garment]

Shrove Tuesday *n* the day in the Christian calendar before Ash Wednesday, on which it was customary to confess one's sins; Pancake Day. [OE *scrifan*, to confess sins]

shrub *n* a bushy plant with a woody stem or stems. — *adj* **shrubby**, **-*ier***, **-*iest***. [OE *scrybb*, scrub]

shrubbery *n* **-*ies*** a place, esp. a part of a garden, where shrubs are grown.

shrug *v* **-*gg*-** (*tr* & *intr*) to raise (the shoulders) briefly as an indication of doubt or indifference. — *n* an act of shrugging. — *v* **shrug off** (*tr*) **1** to get rid of with ease. **2** to dismiss (e.g. criticism) with calm confidence.

shrunk, **shrunken**. See **shrink**.

shudder *v* **-*r*-** (*intr*) to tremble, esp. with fear or disgust. — *n* **1** such a trembling movement or feeling. **2** a heavy vibration or shaking. — **shudder to think** to be greatly embarrassed, alarmed or disgusted when imagining (e.g. what might happen).

shuffle *v* **1** (*tr* & *intr*) to move (one's feet) with short quick sliding movements; to walk in this way. **2** (*tr*) to rearrange or mix up roughly or carelessly. **3** (*tr*) to jumble up (playing cards) into a random order. — *n* **1** an act or sound of shuffling. **2** a short quick sliding of the feet in dancing.

shufti *n* (*coll*) a look or glance: *have a shufti at*. [Arabic, literally 'have you seen?']

shun *v* **-*nn*-** (*tr*) to avoid or keep away from. [OE *scunian*]

shunt *v* (*tr*) **1** to move (a train or carriage) from one track to another. **2** to move around; to change the place or places of. **3** to transfer (e.g. a task) on to someone else, as an evasion. — *n* **1** an act of shunting or being shunted. **2** a conductor diverting part of an electric current. **3** a railway siding. **4** (*coll*) a minor collision between vehicles.

shush *interj* be quiet! — *v* (*tr*) to command to be quiet by, or as if by, saying 'Shush!' [Imit.]

shut *v* **-*tt*-**, ***shut*** (*tr* & *intr*) **1** to place or move so as to close an opening: *shut a door*; *The door shut*. **2** to (cause to) close over, denying open access to the contents: *shut the cupboard*; *The book shut*. **3** not to allow access (to): *shut the shop*; *The office shuts at weekends*. — *adj* not open; closed. — *v* **shut down** (*tr*) to (cause to) stop working or operating, for a time or permanently (*n* **shutdown**). — *v* **shut in** (*tr*) to enclose or confine. — *v* **shut off** (*tr*) to switch off; to stop the flow of. — *v* **shut out** (*tr*) **1** to prevent entry by. **2** to exclude. **3** to block out (e.g. light). — *v* **shut up 1** (*tr* & *intr*; *coll*) to (cause to) stop speaking. **2** (*tr*) to close, for a time or permanently: *shut up shop*. **3** (*tr*) to confine. [OE *scyttan*, to bar]

shutdown see **shut down** above.

shuteye *n* (*slang*) sleep.

shutter *n* **1** a movable exterior cover for a window, esp. either of a pair of hinged wooden panels. **2** a device in a camera that opens and closes at a variable speed, exposing the film to light. — *v* **-*r*-** (*tr*) to fit or cover (a window) with a shutter or shutters. — **put up the shutters** (*coll*) to stop trading, for the day or permanently.

shuttle *n* **1** in weaving, the device carrying the horizontal thread (the **weft**) backwards and forwards between the vertical threads (the **warp**). **2** the device carrying the lower thread through the loop formed by the upper in a sewing-machine. **3** an aircraft, train or bus running a frequent service between two places (relatively) near to each other. — *v* (*tr* & *intr*) to (cause to) move or travel back and forth. [OE *scytel*, dart]

shuttlecock *n* a cone of feathers (or a plastic imitation) with a rounded cork fixed on its narrow end, hit back and forth in badminton.

shy[1] *adj* ***shyer*** or ***shier***, ***shyest*** or ***shiest*** **1** (showing oneself to be) embarrassed or unnerved by the company or attention of others. **2** easily scared; timid. **3** (**of**) wary or distrustful (of), or reluctant (towards): *workshy*. **4** (*coll*) short in payment: *You're 10p shy*. — *v* **-*ies***, **-*ied*** (*intr*) **1** to jump suddenly aside or back, startled. **2** (**away**) to move away mentally, showing reluctance: *shied away from taking the job*. — *n* **-*ies*** an act of shying. — *adv* **shyly**. — *n* **shyness**. [OE *sceoh*, timid]

shy[2] *v* **-*ies***, **-*ied*** (*tr*) to throw (e.g. a stone). — *n* **-*ies*** **1** a throw. **2** a fairground stall where balls are thrown to knock over objects, esp. coconuts.

shyster *n* (*slang*; esp. *US*) an unscrupulous or disreputable person, esp. in business. [Probably *Scheuster*, a disreputable 19th-century US lawyer]

SI *abbrev* the international system of units of measurement, whose standard units include the metre, kilogram and second, used for most scientific and technical purposes. [Fr *S*ystème *I*nternational (d'Unités)]

Si *symbol* (*chem*) silicon.

si. Same as **ti**.

Siamese *adj* of *Siam* (now Thailand), its people or their language; Thai. — *n* **1** a native of Siam; a Thai. **2** the language of Siam; Thai. **3** a Siamese cat.

Siamese cat *n* a fawn-coloured smooth-haired domestic cat with blue eyes and a small head.

Siamese twins *n* **1** twins born with a piece of flesh joining one to the other. **2** any two people always together.

sibilant *adj* of, like or pronounced with a hissing sound. — *n* a consonant with such a sound, e.g. *s* and *z*. — *n* **sibilance** or **sibilancy**. [Lat *sibilare*, to hiss]

sibling *n* a brother or sister. [OE *sibb*, relationship + **-ling**]

sic *adv* a term used in brackets after a word or phrase in a quotation that appears to be a mistake, to indicate that it is in fact quoted accurately. [Lat, thus, so]

sick *adj* **1** vomiting; feeling the desire to vomit. **2** ill; unwell. **3** relating to ill health: *sick pay*. **4** extremely annoyed; disgusted. **5** mentally deranged. **6** (also **sick and tired**; **of**) thoroughly weary or fed up. **7** (of humour) exploiting subjects like death and disease in an unpleasant way. **8** (*coll*) very inadequate in comparison: *makes my effort look a bit sick*. — *n* (*coll*) vomit. — *v* (*tr* & *intr*; **up**) to vomit. [OE *seoc*]

sick-bay *n* a room where ill or injured people are treated, e.g. in a place of work.

sicken *v* **-n- 1** (*tr*) to cause to feel like vomiting. **2** (*tr*) to annoy greatly or disgust. **3** (*intr* with **for**) to show symptoms (of): *sickening for the flu*. — *adj* **sickening**. — *adv* **sickeningly**.

sick-leave *n* time taken off because of sickness.

sickly *adj* **-ier**, **-iest 1** susceptible to illness; often ill. **2** of or suggesting illness. **3** inducing the desire to vomit: *a sickly smell*. **4** unhealthy-looking: *a sickly plant*. **5** weakly and contemptibly sentimental. — *adv* to an extent that suggests illness: *sickly pale*.

sickness *n* **1** an illness; ill-health. **2** vomiting. **3** nausea.

sickle *n* a tool with a short handle and a curved blade for cutting grain crops with a sweeping action. [OE *sicol*]

side *n* **1** any of the usu. flat or flattish surfaces that form the shape of something; any of these surfaces other than the top and bottom; any of these surfaces other than the front, back, top or bottom: *A cube has six sides. A barn has four sides. no windows in the sides of the house, just at the front and back*. **2** (the area forming) an edge or border: *at the side of the road*. **3** either of the parts or areas produced when the whole is divided up the middle: *the right side of your body*. **4** either of the broad surfaces of a flat or flattish object: *two sides of a coin*. **5** any of the lines forming a geometric figure. **6** any of the groups or teams, or opposing positions, in a conflict or competition. **7** (**to**) an aspect: *a different side to him*. **8** the slope of a hill. **9** the part of the body between armpit and hip. **10** a part of an area of land; district: *the north side of the town*. **11** father's or mother's family or ancestors: *related to him on her mother's side*. **12** (*coll*) television channel: *on the other side*. **13** (*slang*) a pretentious or superior air: *to put on side*. — *adj* **1** located at the side: *side entrance*. **2** subsidiary or subordinate: *side road*. — *v* (*intr* with **with**) to adopt the position (of), or join forces (with). — **let the side down** to disappoint one's own group, or frustrate its efforts, by falling below the standards set by its other members. — **on** or **to one side** in or to a position removed from the main concern; aside. — **on the side** as a secondary job or source of income, often dishonestly or illegally. — **on the ... side** (*coll*) rather ...; of a ... nature: *found his comments a bit on the offensive side*. — **side by side 1** close together. **2** with sides touching. — **take sides** to support one particular side in a conflict or argument. [OE]

sideboard *n* **1** a large piece of furniture consisting of shelves or cabinets mounted above drawers or cupboards. **2** a sideburn.

sideburn *n* the line of short hair growing down in front of each of a man's ears.

sidecar *n* a small carriage for one or two passengers, fixed to the side of a motorcycle.

side effect *n* an additional unexpected (usu. undesirable) effect, esp. of a drug.

sidekick *n* (*coll*) a close friend, partner or deputy.

sidelight *n* **1** a small light fitted on each outside edge of the front and rear of a motor vehicle, used in fading daylight. **2** a light on each side of a moving boat or ship, one red, one green. **3** light coming from the side.

sideline *n* **1** a line marking either side boundary of a sports pitch. **2** (in *pl*) the areas just outside these boundaries; the area to which non-participants in any activity are confined. **3** a business, etc. carried on in addition to regular work.

sidelong *adj* & *adv* from or to one side; not direct or directly: *a sidelong glance*.

side-saddle *n* a horse's saddle enabling a woman in a skirt to sit with both legs on the same side. — *adv* sitting in this way.

sideshow *n* a stall with some form of amusement or game at a fair, beside a circus, etc.

sidespin *n* a spinning motion imparted to a struck ball that causes it to rotate about its vertical axis while going forward. ◇ See also **backspin**, **topspin**.

side-splitting *adj* provoking uproarious laughter.

side-step *v* to avoid by, or as if by, stepping aside. — *n* a step taken to one side.

sideswipe *n* **1** a blow coming from the side, not head-on. **2** a criticism or rebuke made in passing, incidentally to the main discussion.

sidetrack *v* (*tr*) to divert the attention of away from the matter in hand.

sidewalk *n* (*US*) a pavement.

sideways *adv* & *adj* **1** from, to or towards one side. **2** with one side foremost: *slid sideways into the wall.*

side whiskers *n* (*pl*) sideburns.

sidereal *adj* (*formal*) of, relating to, or determined by the stars: *sidereal year.* [Lat *sidus*, star]

siding *n* a short dead-end railway line on to which wagons, etc. can be moved temporarily from the main line.

sidle *v* (*intr*) to go or move slowly and cautiously or secretively, avoiding notice. [Back-formation from obsolete *sideling*, sideways]

SIDS *abbrev* sudden infant death syndrome, also known as **cot death**.

siege *n* **1** an attempt to capture a fort or town by surrounding it with troops and forcing surrender. **2** a police operation using similar tactics, e.g. to force a criminal out of a building. — **lay siege to** to subject to a siege. [OFr *sege*, seat]

siemens *n* the standard unit of electrical conductance. [E W von *Siemens* (1816–92), German engineer]

sienna *n* **1** a pigment obtained from a type of earth with a high clay and iron content. **2** its colour, browny-yellow in its original state (**raw sienna**), reddish-brown when roasted (**burnt sienna**). [*Siena*, Italian city]

sierra *n* a mountain range in Spanish-speaking countries and the US, esp. when jagged. [Span, a saw]

siesta *n* a sleep or rest after the midday meal in hot countries. [Span]

sieve *n* a utensil with a meshed or perforated bottom, used to separate solids from liquids or large particles from smaller ones. — *v* (*tr*) to strain or separate with a sieve. — **have a head** or **memory like a sieve** to be very forgetful. [OE *sife*]

sift *v* (*tr*) **1** to pass through a sieve in order to separate out lumps or larger particles. **2** to separate out by, or as if by, passing through a sieve. **3** to examine closely and discriminatingly. [OE *siftan*, from *sife*, sieve]

sigh *v* **1** (*intr*) to release a long deep breath, esp. indicating sadness, longing, or relief. **2** (*intr*) to make a similar sound, esp. suggesting breakdown or failure: *heard the engine sigh.* **3** (*tr*) to express with such a sound. — *n* an act or the sound of sighing. — *v* **sigh for** (*tr*; *literary*) to regret, grieve over, or yearn for. [OE *sican*]

sight *n* **1** the power of seeing; vision. **2** a thing seen. **3** (**of**) (the opportunity to see something because it is within) one's field of vision: *catch sight of*; *within*, or *out of*, *sight.* **4** (usu. in *pl*) a thing that is particularly interesting to see: *seeing the sights of the town.* **5** a device on a firearm through or along which one looks to take aim. **6** opinion or judgement: *just a failure in his sight.* **7** (*coll*) a person or thing unpleasant to look at: *looked a sight without his teeth in.* — *v* (*tr*) **1** to get a look at or glimpse of. **2** to adjust the sight of (a firearm). **3** to aim (a firearm) using the sight. — **at** or **on sight 1** as soon as seen. **2** without previous view or study. — **lose sight of 1** to no longer be able to see. **2** to fail to keep in mind; to no longer be familiar with. — **a sight** (*coll*) a great deal or great many: *a sight more people than expected.* — **a sight for sore eyes** a very welcome sight. — **set one's sights on** to decide on as an ambition or aim. — **sight unseen** without seeing or having seen the thing in question beforehand: *buy a house sight unseen.* [OE *sihth*]

sighted *adj* having the power of sight; not blind.

sightless *adj* blind.

sight-reading *n* playing or singing from printed music that one has not seen before. — *v* (*tr* & *intr*) **sight-read**.

sight-screen *n* any of a set of large white movable screens at either end of a cricket ground, providing a background against which the batsman can see the ball clearly.

sightseeing *n* visiting places of interest. — *v* (*intr*) **sightsee**. — *n* **sightseer**.

sign *n* **1** a printed mark with a meaning; a symbol: *a multiplication sign.* **2** an indication: *signs of improvement.* **3** a board or panel displaying information for public view. **4** a signal: *gave me the sign to enter by waving his hat.* **5** a sign of the zodiac. — *v* **1** (*tr*) to write a signature on; to confirm one's assent to with a signature. **2** (*tr*) to write (one's name) as a signature. **3** (*tr* & *intr*; **for**) to employ or become employed with the signing of a contract: *They've signed a new player. She's signed for another team.* **4** (*tr* & *intr*) to give a signal (to) or indication (of). **5** (*tr* & *intr*) to communicate using sign language. — *v* **sign away** (*tr*) to give away or transfer by signing a legally binding document. — *v* **sign in 1** (*intr*) to record one's arrival, e.g. at work, by writing one's name. **2** (*tr*) to give (e.g. a non-member) official permission to enter a club, etc. by signing one's name. — *v* **sign off 1** (*intr*) to bring a broadcast to an end. **2** (*tr*) to dismiss from employment. **3** (*intr*) to remove oneself from the register of unemployed people. — *v* **sign on 1** (*tr* & *intr*) to engage, e.g. for work; to engage oneself. **2** (*intr*; *coll*) to register oneself as unemployed; to sign one's name as a formal declaration that one is (still) unemployed, as part of a regular report to an unemployment office. — *v* **sign up 1** (*intr*) to engage oneself, e.g. with an organisation (esp. the army) or for a task, by writing one's name. **2** (*tr*) to engage (someone) for work by signing a contract. [Lat *signum*]

sign language *n* any form of communication using bodily gestures to represent words and ideas, esp. a formal system of hand gestures used by deaf people.

sign of the zodiac see **zodiac**.

signpost *n* a post carrying a sign giving information to motorists or pedestrians. — *v* (*tr*) to mark (a route) with signposts.

signal *n* **1** a message in the form of a gesture, light, sound, etc., conveying information or indicating the time for action. **2** (often in *pl*) the apparatus used to send such a message, e.g. coloured lights or movable arms on metal poles on a railway network. **3** (**for**) an event (seen as) marking the moment for action to be taken: *Her resignation was the signal for me to resign also.* **4** any set of transmitted electrical impulses received as a sound or image, e.g. in television, or the message conveyed by them. — *v* **-ll- 1** (*tr* & *intr*) to transmit (a message) using signals. **2** (*tr*) to indicate: *A fall in interest rates signalled increased trading in sterling.* — *adj* notable: *a signal triumph.* [Lat *signum*]

signal-box *n* the building from which signals on a railway line are controlled.

signalise or **-ize** *v* (*tr*) to distinguish; to make notable.

signally *adv* notably.

signalman *n* a controller of railway signals.

signatory *n* **-ies** & *adj* (a person, organisation or state) signing a contract, treaty or other document: *signatory nations.* [Ety. as for **signature**]

signature *n* **1** one's name written by oneself as a formal mark of authorisation, acceptance, etc. **2** an indication of key (**key signature**) or time (**time signature**) at the beginning of a line of music. **3** a large sheet of paper with a number of printed pages on it, folded to form a section of a book; a letter or number at the foot of such a sheet, indicating the sequence in which such sheets are to be put together. [Lat *signare*, to sign]

signature tune *n* a tune used to identify or introduce a particular radio or television programme or performer.

signet *n* a small seal used for stamping documents, etc. [Lat *signum*, sign]

signet-ring *n* a finger ring carrying a signet.

significance *n* meaning or importance. [Ety. as for **signify**]

significant *adj* **1** important; worth noting. **2** having some meaning; indicating or implying something. — *adv* **significantly**.

signify *v* **-ies**, **-ied 1** (*tr*) to be a sign of; to suggest or mean. **2** (*tr*) to denote; to be a symbol of. **3** (*intr*) to be important or significant. [Lat *signum*, sign + *facere*, to make]

Sikh *n* a follower of a religion founded by Nának in 16th-century India, worshipping one God. — *adj* of the Sikhs, their beliefs or their customs. — *n* **Sikhism**. [Hindi, disciple]

silage *n* animal fodder preserved in a fresh green state in a silo. [**silo**]

silence *n* **1** (a period of) absence of sound or speech. **2** failure or unwillingness to disclose information or give away secrets. — *v* (*tr*) to cause to stop speaking, stop making a noise, or stop giving away information. — *interj* be quiet. — **in silence** without speaking. [Lat *silere*, to be quiet]

silencer *n* a device fitted to a gun barrel or engine exhaust to muffle noise.

silent *adj* **1** free from noise. **2** not speaking; not mentioning or divulging something. **3** unspoken but expressed: *silent joy*. **4** not pronounced: *the silent p in pneumonia.* **5** (of a film) that has no soundtrack. — *n* a silent film. — *adv* **silently**.

silent partner see **sleeping partner** under **sleep**.

silhouette *n* **1** a dark shape seen against a light background. **2** an outline drawing of a person, esp. a portrait in profile, usu. filled in with black. — *v* (*tr*) to represent, or cause to appear, as a silhouette. [E de *Silhouette* (1709–67), Fr finance minister]

silicon *n* an element (symbol **Si**), a non-metallic component of silica much used in electronics. [Lat *silex*, flint]

silica *n* a hard mineral occurring naturally as quartz and opal, used in the manufacture of glass.

silicate *n* any of various (usu. insoluble) compounds of silicon, oxygen and a metal.

silicon chip *n* a minute piece of silicon on which electronic microcircuits can be, or are, formed.

silicone *n* any of various compounds of silicon used in lubricants, paints and rubbers for their resistance to heat, water and electricity.

silicosis *n* a lung disease caused by prolonged inhaling of dust containing silica. [**silica** + **-osis**]

silk *n* **1** a fine soft fibre produced by the silkworm. **2** thread or fabric made from such fibres. **3** (esp. in *pl*) a garment made from such fabric. **4** the silk gown worn by a Queen's or King's Counsel; the rank of QC or KC. — **take silk** to become a QC or KC. [OE *seolc*, from Lat *sericum*]

silken *adj* (*literary*) **1** made of silk. **2** as soft or smooth as silk.

silk screen printing same as **screen printing**.

silkworm *n* **1** the larva of a Chinese moth, that spins silk to form its cocoon. **2** the moth.

silky *adj* **-ier**, **-iest 1** soft and shiny like silk. **2** (of a person's manner or voice) suave. — *n* **silkiness**.

sill *n* (a ledge of wood, stone or metal forming) the bottom part of a framework around an opening such as a window or door. [OE *syll*]

sillabub. See **syllabub**.

silly *adj* **-ier**, **-iest 1** not sensible; foolish; frivolous. **2** dazed; senseless. **3** (*cricket*) in a position very near the batsman: *silly mid-on.* **4** senseless: *knocked him silly.* — *n* **-ies**

(*coll*) a foolish person. — *adv* **sillily**. — *n* **silliness**. [OE *sælig*, happy]

silo *n* **-*os*** **1** an airtight pit or tall round tower for storing grain or silage. **2** an underground chamber housing a missile ready for firing. [Span, from Gr *siros*, pit]

silt *n* fine sand and mud deposited by flowing water. — *v* (*tr* & *intr*; **up**) to (cause to) become blocked by silt. [MidE *sylt*]

Silurian *adj* of, relating to or formed in the geological period that ended about 390 million years ago, the third period of the Paleozoic era. — *n* (with **the**) this period. [Lat *Silures*, an ancient people of Wales]

silvan. Same as **sylvan**.

silver *n* **1** an element (symbol **Ag**), a precious shiny grey metal widely used in making jewellery and coins. **2** coins made of this metal. **3** articles made of (or coated with) this metal, esp. cutlery and other tableware. **4** a silver medal. — *adj* **1** of a whitish-grey colour: *silver-haired*. **2** (of a wedding or other anniversary) 25th. — *v* **-*r*-** (*tr*) **1** to apply a thin coating of silver to. **2** to give a whitish metallic sheen to. [OE *seolfor*]

silver birch *n* a species of birch tree with silvery-white peeling bark.

silverfish *n* a small wingless silver-coloured insect common in houses.

silver lining *n* a positive aspect of an otherwise unpleasant or unfortunate situation.

silver medal *n* a medal of silver awarded esp. in sporting competitions, usu. to the person in second place.

silver plate *n* **1** a thin coating of silver on metal objects, e.g. cutlery. **2** such objects coated with silver. — *adj* **silver-plated**.

the silver screen *n* (*coll*) the film industry or films in general.

silverside *n* a fine cut of beef from just below the rump.

silversmith *n* a person who makes or repairs articles made of silver.

silvery *adj* **1** having the colour or shiny quality of silver. **2** having a pleasantly light ringing sound: *silvery bells*.

silviculture *n* (*tech*) the cultivation of forest trees. [Lat *silva*, wood + **culture**]

simian *n* & *adj* (of or resembling) a monkey or ape. [Lat *simia*, ape]

similar *adj* (**to**) alike; having a resemblance (to); of the same kind, but not identical. — *n* **similarity**, **-*ies***. — *adv* **similarly**. [Lat *similis*, like]

simile *n* any phrase in which a thing is described by being likened to something, usu. using 'as' or 'like', as in 'eyes sparkling like diamonds'. [Ety. as for **similar**]

similitude *n* (*formal*) similarity; resemblance. [Ety. as for **similar**]

simmer *v* **-*r*-** **1** (*tr* & *intr*) to (cause to) cook gently at just below boiling point. **2** (*intr*) to be near to an outburst of emotion, usu. anger. — *n* a simmering state. — *v* **simmer down** (*intr*) to calm down after a commotion, esp. an angry outburst. [MidE *simperen*]

simnel *n* a sweet marzipan-covered fruit cake, traditionally baked at Easter or Mid-Lent. [Lat *simila*, fine flour]

simony *n* the practice of buying or selling a religious post or other privilege. [*Simon* Magus, biblical sorcerer who offered money for the power to convey the gift of the Holy Spirit]

simper *v* **-*r*-** **1** (*intr*) to smile in a foolishly weak manner. **2** (*tr*) to express by or while smiling in this way. — *n* a simpering smile.

simple *adj* **1** easy; not difficult. **2** straightforward; not complex or complicated. **3** plain or basic; not elaborate or luxurious. **4** down-to-earth; unpretentious. **5** (often *ironic*) foolish; gullible; lacking intelligence. **6** plain; mere; not altered or adulterated: *The simple fact is, you're wrong*. **7** (*gram*) (of a sentence) consisting of only one clause. ◇ See also **compound** and **complex**. — *n* **simplicity**. [Lat *simplus*, *simplex*]

simple fracture *n* a fracture of the bone only, with no breaking of the skin.

simple interest *n* interest paid only on the basic sum initially borrowed, rather than on an ever-increasing amount which is this basic sum with interest progressively added. ◇ See also **compound interest**.

simple-minded *adj* **1** lacking intelligence; foolish. **2** over-simple; unsophisticated. — *n* **simple-mindedness**.

simpleton *n* a foolish or unintelligent person.

simply *adv* **1** in a straightforward, uncomplicated way. **2** just: *simply not true*. **3** absolutely: *simply marvellous*. **4** merely: *simply wanted to help*.

simplify *v* **-*ies***, **-*ied*** (*tr*) to make less complicated or easier to understand. — *n* **simplification**. [Lat *simplus*, *simplex*, simple + *facere*, to make]

simplistic *adj* unrealistically straightforward or uncomplicated. — *adv* **simplistically**. **[simple]**

simulate *v* (*tr*) **1** to produce a convincing re-creation of (a real-life event or set of conditions). **2** to pretend to have, do or feel. — *n* **simulation**. [Lat *simulare*]

simulated *adj* imitation: *simulated leather*.

simulator *n* a device that simulates required conditions, e.g. for training purposes: *flight simulator*.

simulcast *n* **1** a programme broadcast simultaneously on radio and television. **2** the transmission of a programme in this way. [*simul*taneous + broad*cast*]

simultaneous *adj* happening, or done, at exactly the same time. — *adv* **simultaneously**. — *n* **simultaneousness** or **simultaneity**. [Lat *simul*, at the same time]

simultaneous equations *n* (*pl*; *math*) two or more equations whose variables have the same values in both or all the equations.

sin[1] *n* **1** an act that breaks religious law or teaching. **2** the condition of being not fully at one with God through having broken religious law or (**original sin**) being born with an inherited sinful nature. **3** an act that offends common standards of morality or decency; an outrage. **4** (*coll*) a great shame. — *v* **-nn-** (*intr*) to commit a sin. — *adj* **sinful**. — *n* **sinner**. — **live in sin** (*old coll*) to live together as husband and wife without being married. [OE *synn*]

sin[2] *abbrev* sine.

since *conj* **1** during or throughout the period between now and some earlier stated time. **2** as; because. — *prep* during or throughout the period between now and some earlier stated time. — *adv* **1** from that time onwards. **2** ago: *five years since*. [MidE *sithens*]

sincere *adj* genuine; not pretended or affected. — *adv* **sincerely**. — *n* **sincerity**. [Lat *sincerus*, clean]

sine *n* (*math*) in a right-angled triangle, the ratio of the length of the side opposite the angle under consideration to the length of the hypotenuse. ◇ See also **cosine**, **tangent**, **cosecant**. [Lat *sinus*, curve, bay]

sinecure *n* a paid job involving little or no work. [Lat *sine*, without + *cura*, care]

sine die *adv* indefinitely; with no future time fixed. [Lat, without a day]

sine qua non *n* an essential condition or requirement. [Lat, without which not]

sinew *n* **1** a strong piece of fibrous tissue joining a muscle to a bone; a tendon. **2** (in *pl*) physical strength; muscle. **3** (often in *pl*) (a source of) strength or power of any kind. [OE *sinu*]

sinewy *adj* **1** (lean and) muscular. **2** strong; tough; vigorous.

sing *v* ***sang***, ***sung*** **1** (*tr* & *intr*; **about**, **of**) to speak (words) in a musical, rhythmic fashion, esp. to the accompaniment of music. **2** (*tr*; **to**) to cause to pass into a particular state with such sound: *sang him to sleep*. **3** (*intr*) to make a sound like a musical voice; to hum, ring or whistle: *the kettle singing on the stove*; *bullets singing past his ears*. **4** (*intr*) to suffer a ringing sound: *My ears were singing*. **5** (*intr*; *slang*) to inform or confess. — *n* **singer**. — *n* **singing**. — *v* **sing out** (*intr*) to shout or call out. — **sing someone's praises** to praise someone enthusiastically. [OE *singan*]

singsong *n* an informal bout of singing for pleasure. — *adj* (of a speaking voice, etc.) musical; up-and-down in tone or pitch.

sing. *abbrev* singular.

singe *v* ***singeing*** (*tr* & *intr*) to burn lightly on the surface; to scorch or become scorched. — *n* a light surface burn. [OE *sengan*]

single *adj* **1** of which there is only one; solitary. **2** unmarried, esp. never having been married. **3** for use by one person only: *a single room*. **4** valid for an outward journey only; not return. **5** (used for emphasis with **a** or **one**) even one: *not a single person*. **6** (of a flower) having only one set of petals. — *n* **1** a single room. **2** a ticket for an outward journey only. **3** a record with only one track on each side. **4** a pound coin or note. **5** (*cricket*) one run. — *v* (*tr* with **out**) to pick from among others. [Lat *singuli*, one by one]

single-breasted *adj* (of a coat or jacket) having only one row of buttons and a slight overlap at the front.

single combat *n* fighting between two individuals.

single figures *n* (*pl*) the numbers between 1 and 9 inclusive. — *adj* **single-figure**.

single file *n* a line of people standing or moving one behind the other.

single-handed *adj* & *adv* (done, etc.) by oneself, without help from others. — *adv* **single-handedly**.

single-minded *adj* determinedly pursuing a single aim or object. — *adv* **single-mindedly**. — *n* **single-mindedness**.

single parent *n* a mother or father bringing up a child alone.

singles *n* a sports match with one player on each side.

singles bar *n* a bar intended as a meeting place for unmarried or unattached people.

singly *adv* one at a time; individually.

singlet *n* a man's vest or other vest-like garment. [**single**]

singleton *n* a solitary person or thing, esp. the only playing-card of a particular suit in a hand.

singular *adj* **1** single; unique. **2** extraordinary; exceptional. **3** strange; odd. **4** (*gram*) denoting or referring to one person, thing, etc. as opposed to two or more than two. ◇ See also **plural**. — *n* (*gram*) a word or form of a word expressing the idea of one person, thing, etc. as opposed to two or more than two. — *n* **singularity**. [Lat *singularis*]

singularly *adv* **1** extraordinarily. **2** strangely. **3** singly. **4** very.

Sinhalese *n* **1** (*sing* & *pl*) (a member of) a people living in Sri Lanka. **2** the Indo-European language spoken by this people, derived from Sanskrit. — *adj* of this people or their language. [Sanskrit *Simhala*, Sri Lanka]

sinister *adj* **1** suggesting or threatening evil or danger. **2** (*heraldry*) on the left side of the shield, from the bearer's point of view, not the observer's. ◇ See also **dexter**. [Lat, left, thought by the Romans to be the unlucky side]

sink *v* ***sank***, ***sunk*** or (esp. as *adj*) ***sunken*** **1** (*tr* & *intr*) to (cause to) fall (and perhaps remain) below the surface of water. **2** (*intr*) to collapse downwardly or inwardly; to fall because of a collapsing base or foundation. **3** (*intr*) to produce the sensation of a downward collapse within the body: *My heart sank at the news*. **4** (*tr*) to embed: *sank the* *pole into the ground*. **5** (*intr*; **into**) to pass steadily (and often dangerously) into a worse state. **6** (*intr*; **in**) to penetrate or be absorbed. ◇ See also **sink in** below. **7** (*tr*) to invest (money) heavily. **8** (*tr*; *coll*) to ruin the plans of; to ruin (plans): *We're sunk*. **9** (*intr*) (of the sun) to disappear slowly below the horizon. **10** (*tr*; *coll*) to get (a ball) into the hole in snooker, billiards, etc. and golf. — *n* a wall-mounted basin with built-in water supply and drainage. — *v* **sink in** (*intr*; *coll*) to be fully understood or realised. [OE *sincan*]

sinker *n* a weight used to make something, e.g. a fishing-line, sink.

sink unit *n* a piece of kitchen furniture consisting of a sink and draining-board with cupboards underneath.

Sino- *comb fm* Chinese: *Sino-Soviet*. [Gr *Sinai*, Chinese]

Sinology *n* the study of China in all its aspects, e.g. cultural and political. — *n* **Sinologist**. **[Sino- + -logy]**

sinuous *adj* **1** having many curves or bends; meandering. **2** having a twisting and turning motion. — *n* **sinuosity** or **sinuousness**. [Ety. as for **sinus]**

sinus *n* any of several air-filled hollows in the bones of the skull, connected with the nose. [Lat, curve]

sinusitis *n* inflammation of the lining of the sinuses.

sip *v* **-*pp*-** (*tr* & *intr*) to drink in very small mouthfuls. — *n* **1** an act of sipping. **2** an amount sipped at one time. [Perhaps a variation of **sup]**

siphon or **syphon** *n* **1** a bent pipe or tube through which, by atmospheric pressure, a liquid is drawn from one container into a second container placed at a lower level. **2** a bottle from which a liquid, esp. soda water, is forced by pressure of gas. — *v* **-*n*-** (*tr* with **off**) **1** to draw off (a liquid) using a siphon. **2** to take slowly and continuously from a store or fund. [Gr]

sir *n* **1** (*cap*) a title used before the Christian name of a knight or baronet. **2** a term of politeness or respect used in addressing a man. **[sire]**

sire *n* **1** the father of a horse or other animal. **2** (*old*) a term of respect used in addressing a king. — *v* (*tr*) (of animals) to father. [OFr, from Lat *senior*, elder]

siren *n* **1** a device that gives out a loud wailing noise, usu. as a warning signal. **2** (*Gr mythol*) any of various sea-nymphs, part woman, part bird, whose songs lured sailors to their death on the rocks. **3** an irresistible woman thought capable of ruining men's lives. [Gr *Seiren*]

sirloin *n* a fine cut of beef from the upper side of the part of the back just in front of the rump. [Fr *surlonge*, from *sur*, above + *longe*, loin]

sirocco *n* **-*os*** a dry hot dust-carrying wind blowing into S Europe from N Africa. [Ital, from Arabic *sharq*, east wind]

sis *n* (*coll*) (a name for) a sister.

sisal *n* a strong fibre from the leaves of the agave plant of central America, used to make rope. [*Sisal*, Mexican port from where it was first exported]

siskin *n* a yellowish-green Eurasian songbird of the finch family. [ODut *siseken*]

sissy or **cissy** *n* **-*ies*** (*derog*) a weak, cowardly person. **[sister]**

sister *n* **1** a female child of the same parents as another. **2** a nun. **3** a senior female nurse, esp. one in charge of a ward. **4** a close female associate; a fellow female member of a profession, class or racial group. — *adj* of the same origin or design: *a sister ship*. [OE *sweostor* or Norse *systir*]

sisterhood *n* **1** the state of being a sister or sisters. **2** a religious community of women; a body of nuns. **3** a group of women with common interests or beliefs.

sister-in-law *n* ***sisters-*** **1** the sister of one's husband or wife. **2** the wife of one's brother.

sisterly *adj* (of a woman or her behaviour) like a sister, esp. in being kind and affectionate. — *n* **sisterliness**.

sit *v* **-*tt*-, *sat*** **1** (*intr*) to rest the body on the buttocks or hindquarters; (of a bird) to perch or lie. **2** (*intr*) to lie, rest or hang: *a cup sitting on the shelf*; *The dress sits nicely around her waist*. **3** (*intr*) to lie unused: *tools sitting in the shed*. **4** (*intr*) to hold a meeting or other session: *court sits tomorrow*. **5** (*intr*; **on**) to be a member, taking regular part in meetings: *sit on a committee*. ◇ See also **sit on** below. **6** (*tr*) to take (an examination); to be a candidate for (a degree or other award). **7** (*tr*) to conduct to a seat; to assign a seat to: *sat me next to him*. **8** (*intr*; **with**) to be or exist in comparison or relation: *His smoking sits awkwardly with his being a doctor*. **9** (*intr*) to serve as an artist's or photographer's model. — **be sitting pretty** (*coll*) to be in a very advantageous position. — *v* **sit back** (*intr*) **1** to sit comfortably, esp. with the back rested. **2** to merely observe, taking no action, esp. when action is needed. — *v* **sit down 1** (*tr* & *intr*) to (cause to) adopt a sitting position. **2** (*intr*; **under**) to give in or submit meekly. ◇ See also **sit-down** below. — *v* **sit in** (*intr*) **1** (**on**) to be present (at), esp. without taking part. **2** (**for**) to act as a substitute or deputy (for). ◇ See also **sit-in** below. — *v* **sit on** (*tr*; *coll*) **1** to delay taking action about (a matter in one's care). **2** to keep secret; to suppress. **3** to force into saying or doing nothing. — *v* **sit out** (*tr*) **1** to stay until the end of. **2** to take no part in (a dance or game). — **sit tight 1** to maintain one's position determinedly. **2** to wait patiently. — *v* **sit up** (*intr*) **1** to bring oneself from a slouching or lying position into an upright sitting position. **2** to remain out of bed longer than usual. **3** to take notice suddenly or show a sudden interest. ◇ See also **sit-up** below. [OE *sittan*]

sit-down *n* (*coll*) a short rest in a seated position. — *adj* **1** (of a meal) for which the diners are seated. **2** (of a strike) in which the workers occupy the workplace until an agreement is reached. ◇ See also **sit down** above.

sit-in *n* an occupation of a building, etc. as a protest. ◇ See also **sit in** above.

sitter *n* **1** a person who poses for an artist or photographer. **2** a baby-sitter.

sitting *n* **1** a period of continuous action: *wrote it at one sitting.* **2** a turn to eat for any of two or more groups too numerous to eat at the same time in the same place. **3** a period of posing for an artist or photographer. **4** a session or meeting of an official body.

sitting duck or **target** *n* a person or thing in a defenceless position, easily attacked, criticised, etc.

sitting-room *n* a room, esp. in a private house, for relaxing in; a living-room.

sitting tenant *n* a tenant presently occupying a property.

sit-up *n* a physical exercise in which, from a lying position, the torso is raised up and over the thighs, often with the hands behind the head.

sitar *n* a guitar-like instrument of Indian origin, with a long neck, rounded body and two sets of strings. [Hindi]

sitcom *n* (*coll*) a situation comedy.

site *n* **1** the place where something was, is, or is to be situated. **2** an area set aside for a specific activity: *camping site.* [Lat *situs*, position]

situate *v* (*tr*) to put in a certain position or set of circumstances. [Lat *situare*, to position]

situation *n* **1** a set of circumstances; a state of affairs. **2** a position or location. **3** a job: *situations vacant.*

situation comedy *n* a comedy in series form in which the same characters are featured in a more or less fixed set of surroundings.

six *n* **1** the number or figure 6; any symbol for this number. **2** the age of 6. **3** something, e.g. a garment or a person, whose size is denoted by the number 6. **4** a group of 6 people or things. **5** a playing-card with 6 pips. **6** 6 o'clock. **7** a score of 6 points. **8** (*cricket*) a hit scoring 6 runs. **7** a team of (more or less) 6 Cub Scouts or Brownie Guides. — *adj* **1** 6 in number. **2** aged 6. — *adj, n & adv* **sixth.** — *adv* **sixthly.** — **at sixes and sevens** in a state of total disorder or confusion. — **knock for six** (*coll*) **1** to defeat or ruin completely. **2** to shock or surprise greatly. — **six (of one) and half a dozen (of the other)** equal; equally acceptable or unacceptable; the same on both sides. [OE *siex*]

sixer *n* the Cub Scout or Brownie Guide leader of a six.

sixfold *adj* **1** equal to six times as much or as many. **2** divided into, or consisting of, six parts. — *adv* by six times as much.

six-pack *n* a pack containing six items sold as one unit, esp. a pack of six cans of beer.

sixpence *n* a former small British silver coin worth six old pennies (6d), equivalent in value to 2½p.

sixpenny *adj* worth or costing six old pennies.

sixth form *n* (the pupils belonging to) classes in which school subjects are taught to a level that prepares for higher education, in the sixth, or sixth and seventh, years of secondary education. — *n* **sixth-former.**

sixth sense *n* an unexplained power of intuition by which one is aware of things not seen, heard, touched, smelled or tasted.

sixteen *n* **1** the number or figure 16; any symbol for this number. **2** the age of 16. **3** something, e.g. a garment or a person, whose size is denoted by the number 16. **4** a set of 16 people or things. — *adj* **1** 16 in number. **2** aged 16. — *adj, n & adv* **sixteenth.** [OE *siextene*]

sixty *n* **-ies 1** the number or figure 60; any symbol for this number. **2** the age of 60. **3** a set of 60 people or things. — *adj* **1** 60 in number. **2** aged 60. — *adj, n & adv* **sixtieth.** [OE *siextig*]

sixties *n* (*pl*) **1** the period of time between one's sixtieth and seventieth birthdays. **2** the range of temperatures between sixty and seventy degrees. **3** the period of time between the sixtieth and seventieth years of a century.

size[1] *n* **1** length, breadth, height or volume, or a combination of all or any of these. **2** largeness: *astonished by its size.* **3** any of a range of graded measurements, e.g. of garments. — *v* (*tr*) **1** to measure in order to determine size. **2** to sort or arrange according to size. **3** (**up**) to judge the nature, quality or worth of. [OFr *sise*]

sizeable or **sizable** *adj* fairly large.

size[2] *n* a weak kind of glue used to stiffen paper and fabric, and to prepare walls for plastering and wallpapering. — *v* (*tr*) to treat with size.

sizzle *v* (*intr*) **1** to make a hissing sound when, or as if when, frying in hot fat. **2** (*coll*) to be in a state of intense emotion, esp. anger or excitement. — *n* a sizzling sound. [Imit.]

skate[1] *n* **1** a boot with a device fitted to the sole for gliding smoothly over surfaces, either a steel blade for use on ice (**ice-skate**) or a set of small wheels for use on wooden and other surfaces (**roller-skate**). **2** the blade of an ice-skate. — *v* (*intr*) to move around on skates. — *n* **skater.** — *n* **skating.** — **get one's skates on** (*coll*) to hurry up. — **skate on thin ice** to risk danger or harm, esp. through lack of care or good judgement. — *v* **skate over** or **round** (*tr*) to avoid dealing with or considering (a difficulty). [OF *eschasse*, stilt]

skateboard *n* a narrow shaped board mounted on sets of small wheels, for riding on in a standing or crouching position.

skate[2] *n* ***skate*** or ***skates*** a large flat edible fish of the ray family. [Norse *skata*]

skedaddle *v* (*intr*; *coll*) to run away quickly.

skein *n* a loose coil of wool or thread. [OFr *escaigne*]

skeleton *n* **1** the framework of bones supporting a human or animal body. **2** an initial basic structure or idea upon or around which anything is built. **3** (*coll*) an unhealthily thin person. — *adj* **skeletal**. [Gr *skeleton* (*soma*), dried (body)]

skeleton in the cupboard or **closet** *n* a shameful fact concerning oneself or one's family that one tries to keep secret.

skeleton key *n* a key filed in such a way that it can open many different locks.

skeleton staff *n* a set of staff reduced to a bare minimum.

sketch *n* **1** a rough drawing quickly done. **2** a rough plan or outline. **3** any of several short pieces of comedy presented as a programme. — *v* **1** (*tr* & *intr*) to do a rough drawing or drawings (of). **2** (*tr*) to give a rough outline of. [Gr *schedios*, offhand]

sketchy *adj* ***-ier***, ***-iest*** lacking detail; not complete or substantial. — *adv* **sketchily**. — *n* **sketchiness**.

skew *adj* slanted; oblique; askew. — *v* **1** (*tr* & *intr*) to (cause to) slant. **2** (*tr*) to distort. — *n* a slanting position: *on the skew*. [OFr *eschuer*]

skew-whiff *adj* & *adv* (*coll*) (lying) in a slanted position; awry.

skewbald *adj* (of an animal, esp. a horse) with patches of white and another colour (other than black). — *n* a skewbald horse.

skewer *n* a long wooden or metal pin pushed through chunks of meat, etc. which are to be roasted. — *v* ***-r-*** (*tr*) to fasten or pierce with, or as if with, a skewer. [Dialect *skiver*]

ski *n* ***skis*** **1** a long narrow strip of wood, metal or plastic, upturned at the front, for gliding over snow, attached to each of a pair of boots or to a vehicle. **2** (also **water-ski**) a similar object worn on each foot for gliding over water. — *v* ***skis***, ***skiing***, ***skied*** or ***ski'd*** (*intr*) to move on skis, esp. as a sport or leisure activity. — *n* **skier**. — *n* **skiing**. [Norse *skith*, piece of split wood]

ski lift *n* a device for carrying skiers to the top of a slope so that they can ski down.

skid *v* ***-dd-*** (*intr*) **1** (of a wheel, etc.) to slide along without revolving. **2** (of a vehicle) to slide at an angle, esp. out of control. — *n* an instance of skidding. — **put the skids under** (*coll*) **1** to cause to hurry. **2** to speed up the downfall of.

skid pan *n* a special slippery track on which drivers learn to control skidding vehicles.

skid row *n* the poorest or most squalid part of a town.

skiff *n* a small light boat. [Fr *esquif*]

skill *n* **1** expertness; dexterity. **2** a talent or accomplishment, naturally acquired or developed through training. — *adj* **skilled**. [Norse *skil*, distinction]

skilful *adj* having or showing skill. — *adv* **skilfully**.

skillet *n* a small long-handled frying-pan or saucepan. [Perhaps Norse *skjola*, bucket]

skim *v* ***-mm-*** **1** (*tr*) to remove (floating matter) from the surface of (a liquid). **2** (*tr* & *intr*) to (cause to) brush against or glide lightly over (a surface): *skimming stones on the sea*; *bird's wings skimming* (*over*) *the water*. **3** (*tr* & *intr*; **through**) to read superficially. [OFr *escume*, scum]

skimmed milk or **skim milk** *n* milk from which the cream has been removed.

skimp *v* (*intr*; **on**) to spend, use or give too little or only just enough. [Perhaps **scant** + **scrimp**]

skimpy *adj* ***-ier***, ***-iest*** **1** inadequate; barely enough. **2** (of clothes) leaving much of the body uncovered. — *adv* **skimpily**. — *n* **skimpiness**.

skin *n* **1** the tissue forming the outer covering on the bodies of humans and animals. **2** the outer covering of some fruits and vegetables. **3** complexion: *greasy skin*. **4** an animal hide, with or without fur or hair attached. **5** a semi-solid coating on the surface of a liquid. **6** a container for liquids made from an animal hide. — *v* ***-nn-*** (*tr*) **1** to strip the skin from. **2** to injure by scraping the skin from. **3** (*slang*) to cheat or swindle. — **by the skin of one's teeth** very narrowly; only just. — **get under someone's skin** (*coll*) **1** to greatly annoy and upset someone. **2** to become a consuming passion with someone. — **no skin off one's nose** (*coll*) not a cause of even slight concern or nuisance to one. — **save someone's skin** to save someone from death or other harm. [Norse *skinn*]

skin-deep *adj* superficial.

skin-diving *n* underwater swimming with no wet suit and only simple breathing and other equipment. — *n* **skin-diver**.

skin flick *n* (*slang*) a pornographic film.

skinflint *n* (*coll*) a very ungenerous person.

skinful *n* ***-fuls*** (*slang*;) a large amount of alcohol, enough to make one thoroughly drunk.

skinhead *n* a person with closely cropped hair, esp. a white youth with tight jeans, heavy boots and anti-establishment attitudes.

skinny *adj* ***-ier***, ***-iest*** (of a person) very thin.

skinny-dipping *n* (*coll*) naked swimming. — *v* (*intr*) **skinny-dip**.

skin-tight *adj* (of a garment) very tight-fitting.

skint *adj* (*slang*) without money; hard up. [**skinned**]

skip[1] *v* ***-pp-*** **1** (*intr*) to go along with light springing or hopping steps on alternate feet. **2** (*intr*) to make jumps over a skipping-rope. **3** (*tr*) to omit, leave out or pass over. **4** (*tr*; *coll*) not to attend (e.g. a class in school). — *n* a skipping movement. — **skip it!** (*coll*) forget it; ignore it; it is not important. [MidE *skippen*]

skipping-rope *n* a rope swung backwards and forwards or twirled in a circular motion by the person skipping or by two other people each holding an end, for jumping over as exercise or as a children's game.

skip[2] *n* **1** a large metal container for rubbish from e.g. building work. **2** a large (esp. wicker) chest, e.g. for storing theatrical costumes. **3** a lift in a coal mine. [Variant of *skep*, beehive]

skipper *n* the captain of a ship, aeroplane or team. — *v* **-r-** (*tr*) to act as skipper of. [ODut *schipper*, shipper]

skirl *v* (*intr*) & *n* (to make) the high-pitched screaming sound of the bagpipes.

skirmish *n* **1** a brief battle during a war, esp. away from the main fighting. **2** any minor fight or dispute. — *v* (*intr*) to engage in a skirmish. [OFr *escarmouche*]

skirt *n* **1** a woman's garment that hangs from the waist. **2** the part of a woman's dress from the waist down. **3** any part or attachment resembling a skirt, e.g. the flap around the base of a hovercraft. **4** a cut of beef from the rear part of the belly; the flank. **5** (*offensive slang*; also **bit of skirt**) a woman regarded as an object of sexual desire. — *v* (*tr*) **1** to border. **2** to pass along or around the edge of. **3** to avoid confronting (e.g. a problem). [Norse *skyrta*, shirt]

skit *n* a short satirical piece of writing or drama.

skittish *adj* **1** lively and playful. **2** frequently changing mood or opinion; capricious. **3** (of a horse) easily frightened.

skittle *n* any of several free-standing bottle-shaped (esp. wooden) targets at which a ball is aimed in the game of **skittles**.

skive *v* (*intr*; *coll*; **off**) to evade work or a duty, esp. through laziness. — *n* **skiver**.

skivvy (*coll*) *n* (*derog*) **-ies** a servant, esp. a woman, who does unpleasant household jobs. — *v* **-ies**, **-ied** (*intr*) to work as, or as if, a skivvy.

skua *n* any of various large predatory gull-like birds. [Norse *skufr*]

skulduggery *n* unscrupulous or dishonest behaviour; trickery. [Scots *sculduddery*, unchastity]

skulk *v* (*intr*) **1** to sneak (off). **2** to hide or lurk, planning mischief. [Norse]

skull *n* **1** the head's framework of bone. **2** (*coll*) the head or brain. [Norse]

skull and crossbones *n* a representation of a human skull with two bones arranged in an X underneath, used formerly as a pirate's symbol, now as a symbol of death or danger.

skullcap *n* a small brimless cap fitting closely on the head.

skunk *n* **1** a N American mammal like a large squirrel with a black-and-white coat, which defends itself by squirting out an unpleasant-smelling liquid. **2** (*derog*) a despised person. [From an Algonquian (N American Indian) language *segonku*]

sky *n* **-ies** (often in *pl*) **1** the vast area of space visible above the earth, in which the sun, moon and stars can be seen; the heavens. **2** the appearance of this area as a reflection of weather: *dismal skies*. — *v* **-ies**, **-ied** (*tr*) to mishit (a ball) high into the air. — **the sky's the limit** there is no upper limit, e.g. to the amount of money that may be spent. — **to the skies** in a lavish or extremely enthusiastic manner: *praise him to the skies*. [Norse, cloud]

sky-blue *n* bright light blue, the colour of a cloudless sky.

sky-diving *n* free-falling from an aircraft, often involving performing manoeuvres in mid-air, with a long delay before the parachute is opened. — *n* **sky-diver**.

sky-high *adv* & *adj* very high. ◇ See also **blow sky-high** at **blow**[1].

skyjack *v* (*tr*; *slang*) to hijack (an aircraft).

skylark *n* the common lark, which sings when flying vertically and hovering. — *v* (*intr*; *old*) to lark about.

skylight *n* a (usu. small) window in a roof or ceiling.

skyline *n* the outline of buildings, hills and trees seen against the sky.

skyscraper *n* an extremely tall building.

skyward *adj* towards the sky. — *adv* (also **skywards**) towards the sky.

Skye terrier *n* a small long-haired terrier orig. bred on the Scottish island of *Skye*.

slab *n* a thick flat rectangular piece, slice or object. — *v* **-bb-** (*tr*) to pave with concrete slabs.

slack[1] *adj* **1** loose; not pulled or stretched tight. **2** not careful or diligent; remiss. **3** not busy. **4** (of the tide, etc.) still; neither ebbing nor flowing. — *n* **1** a loosely hanging part. **2** a period of little trade or other activity. — *v* (also **slacken**, **-n-**) **1** (*intr*; **off**, **up**) to become slower; to slow one's working pace through tiredness or laziness. **2** (*tr* & *intr*; **off**) to make or become looser. **3** (*intr*; **off**) to become less busy. **4** (*tr* & *intr*; **off**) to make or become less rigid and more easy or relaxed. [OE *slæc*]

slacker *n* a person who does not work hard enough; a shirker.

slacks *n* (*pl*; *old*) a type of loose casual trousers.

slack[2] *n* coal dust or tiny fragments of coal. [OGer *slecke*]

slag[1] *n* **1** waste material formed on the surface of molten metal ore. **2** waste left over from coal mining. — *v* **-gg-** (*intr*) (of molten metal ore) to throw up a surface layer of slag. [OGer *slagge*]

slag[2] *v* **-gg-** (*tr*; *slang*; **off**) to criticise harshly or speak disparagingly about.

slag[3] *n* (*derog slang*) a person, esp. a woman, who regularly has casual sex with different people.

slain. See **slay**.
slake *v* (*tr*) **1** (*literary*) to satisfy or quench (thirst, desire or anger). **2** to cause (lime) to crumble by adding water. [OE *slacian*]
slalom *n* a race, on skis or in canoes, in and out of obstacles on a winding course. [Norw]
slam[1] *v* **-mm- 1** (*tr* & *intr*) to shut loudly and with violence. **2** (*tr* & *intr*; *coll*; **into**, **against**, etc.) to (cause to) make loud heavy contact. **3** (*tr*; *slang*) to criticise severely. — *n* the act or sound of slamming.
the slammer *n* (*slang*) prison.
slam[2]. See **grand slam** and **little slam**.
slander *n* (the making of) a false spoken (not written) statement about a person, intended to damage his or her reputation. — *v* **-r-** (*tr*) to speak about in such a way. — *adj* **slanderous**. ◇ See also **libel**. [OFr *esclandre*, from Gr *skandalon*, snare, scandal]
slang *n* words and phrases used only very informally, not usu. in writing or polite speech, and often only by members of a particular social group or profession. — *v* (*tr*) to speak abusively to using coarse language. — *adj* **slangy**, **-ier**, **-iest**.
slanging match *n* (*coll*) an angry exchange of abuse.
slant *v* **1** (*intr*) to be at an angle, not horizontal or vertical; to slope. **2** (*tr*; **towards**) to present in a biased way. **3** (*tr*; **towards**) to present so as to invite an audience or readership of a particular kind. — *n* a sloping position, surface or line. — *adj* sloping; lying at an angle. — *adj* **slanting**. [MidE *slent*]
slap *n* **1** a blow with the palm of the hand or anything flat. **2** the sound made by such a blow, or by the impact of one flat surface with another. — *v* **-pp-** (*tr*) **1** to strike with the open hand or anything flat. **2** to bring or send with a slapping sound: *slapped the newspaper down on the table*. **3** (*coll*; **on**) to apply thickly and carelessly: *slapped make-up on her face*. — *adv* (*coll*) **1** exactly or precisely: *slap in the middle*. **2** heavily; with a slap: *fell slap on his face*. — *v* **slap down** (*tr*; *coll*) to abruptly dismiss the suggestions or interference of. — **a slap in the face** (*coll*) an insult or rebuff. — **a slap on the back** (*coll*) congratulations. — **a slap on the wrist** (*coll*; often *facet*) a mild reprimand. [Ger dialect *slapp*; orig. imit.]
slap and tickle *n* (*coll humorous*) kissing and cuddling; sexual activity of any kind.
slap-bang *adv* (*coll*) **1** exactly or precisely: *slap-bang in the middle*. **2** directly and with force: *drove slap-bang into the wall*.
slapdash *adj* careless and hurried.
slap-happy *adj* (*coll*) **1** cheerfully carefree or careless. **2** punch-drunk.
slapstick *n* comedy in which the humour is derived from boisterous antics of all kinds.
slap-up *adj* (*coll*) (of a meal) lavish; extravagant.
slash[1] *v* **1** (*tr* & *intr*; **at**) to make sweeping cuts or cutting strokes (in or at), esp. repeatedly. **2** (*tr*; *coll*) to reduce suddenly and drastically. — *n* **1** a long (esp. deep) cut. **2** a sweeping cutting stroke. **3** (also **slash mark**) an oblique line in writing or printing; a solidus.
slash[2] (*vulg slang*) *v* (*intr*) to urinate. — *n* an act of urinating. [Perhaps Scot dialect, large splash]
slat *n* a thin strip, esp. of wood or metal. — *adj* **slatted**. [OFr *esclat*]
slate[1] *n* **1** (a piece of) a fine-grained, usu. dull grey rock splitting easily into thin layers, used e.g. to make roofing tiles. **2** a roofing tile made of this. **3** (esp. *formerly*) a piece of this for writing on. **4** a record of credit given to a customer: *put it on my slate*. **5** a dull grey colour. — *v* (*tr*) to cover (a roof) with slates. [OFr *esclate*]
a clean slate *n* a fresh start, with all previous grievances or faults forgotten or ignored, no debts owing, etc.
slate[2] *v* (*tr*; *coll*) to criticise extremely harshly. — *adj* **slating**. [Norse]
slattern *n* (*old*) a woman of dirty or untidy appearance or habits. — *n* **slatternliness**. — *adj* **slatternly**. [Dialect *slatter*, to slop]
slaughter *n* **1** the killing of animals for food. **2** cruel and violent murder. **3** the large-scale indiscriminate killing of people or animals. — *v* **-r-** (*tr*) **1** to subject to slaughter. **2** (*coll*) to defeat resoundingly; to trounce. [Norse *slatr*, butchers' meat]
slaughterhouse *n* a place where animals are killed to be sold for food; an abattoir.
Slav *n* a member of any of various Central and Eastern European peoples speaking Slavonic languages such as Russian, Bulgarian and Polish. — *adj* **Slavic**. [Lat *Sclavus*]
slave *n* **1** (*hist*) a person owned by and acting as servant to another, with no personal freedom. **2** a person who works extremely hard for another; a drudge. **3** a person submissively devoted to another. **4** (**to**) a person whose life is dominated by some activity or thing: *a slave to her work*. — *v* (*intr*; **away**, **at**) to work hard and ceaselessly. [OFr *esclave*, orig. 'Slav', the Slavs being much-conquered peoples in the Middle Ages]
slave-driver *n* **1** (*hist*) a person employed to ensure that slaves work hard. **2** (*coll*) a person who demands very hard work from others.
slaver *n* (*hist*) **1** a person engaging in the buying and selling of slaves. **2** a ship for transporting slaves.
slavery *n* **1** the state of being a slave. **2** the practice of owning slaves. **3** extremely hard work; toil.
slavish *adj* **1** rigid or unwavering in following rules or instructions. **2** very closely copied or imitated; unoriginal. **3** of or like a slave. — *adv* **slavishly**.

slaver[1] *n* spittle running from the mouth. — *v* **-r-** (*intr*) **1** to let spittle run from the mouth; to dribble. **2** (*coll*) to talk nonsense.

slaver[2], **slavish**. See **slave**.

Slavonic *n* a group of Central and Eastern European languages that includes Russian, Polish, Czech, Slovak, Serb and Slovenian. — *adj* of these languages, the peoples speaking them, or their cultures. [Ety. as for **Slav**]

slay *v* ***slew***, ***slain*** (*tr*; *archaic* or *literary*) to kill. — *n* **slayer**. [OE *slean*]

sleazy *adj* ***-ier***, ***-iest*** (*coll*) **1** dirty and neglected-looking. **2** cheaply suggestive of sex or crime; disreputable. — *n* **sleaziness** or **sleaze**.

sled *n* a sledge. — *v* ***-dd-*** (*intr*) to sledge. [OGer *sledde*]

sledge *n* **1** a vehicle with ski-like runners for travelling over snow, drawn by horses or dogs. **2** a child's toy vehicle of similar design, propelled by the hands or feet; a toboggan. — *v* (*intr*) **1** to travel by sledge. **2** to play on a sledge. [ODut *sleedse*]

sledgehammer *n* a large heavy hammer swung with both arms. [OE *slecg*, from *slean*, to strike]

sleek *adj* **1** (of hair, fur, etc.) smooth, soft and glossy. **2** having a well-fed and prosperous appearance. **3** insincerely polite or flattering. — *v* (*tr*; **down, back**) to smooth (esp. hair). [Form of **slick**]

sleep *n* **1** rest in a state of (near) unconsciousness, with the eyes closed. **2** a period of such rest. **3** (*coll*) mucus that collects in the corners of the eyes during such rest. **4** (*poetic*) death. — *v* ***slept*** **1** (*intr*) to rest in a state of sleep. **2** (*intr*) to be motionless, inactive or dormant. **3** (*tr*) to provide or contain sleeping accommodation for: *The caravan sleeps four*. **4** (*intr*; *coll*) to be in a dreamy state, not paying attention. **5** (*intr*; *poetic*) to be dead. — **go to sleep 1** to pass into a state of sleep. **2** (*coll*) (of a limb) to be temporarily numb through lack of circulation of blood. — **lose sleep over** (*coll*) to worry about. — **put to sleep 1** to anaesthetise. **2** (*euph*) to kill (an animal) painlessly with an injected drug. — *v* **sleep around** (*intr*) to engage in casual sex frequently and with different people. — *v* **sleep in** (*intr*) **1** to fail to wake up on time; to oversleep. **2** to sleep at one's place of work; to live in. — *v* **sleep off** (*tr*) to recover from by sleeping. — *v* **sleep on** (*tr*) to delay taking a decision about until the following morning. — *v* **sleep out** (*intr*) **1** to sleep out of doors. **2** to sleep away from one's place of work; to live out. — *v* **sleep with** (*tr*; *euph*) to have, or to be in the habit of having, sexual relations with. [OE *slæp*]

sleeper *n* **1** a person who sleeps: *a light sleeper*. **2** any of the horizontal wooden or concrete beams supporting the rails on a railway track. **3** a railway carriage providing sleeping accommodation for passengers; a train with such carriages.

sleeping-bag *n* a large quilted sack for sleeping in when camping, etc.

sleeping partner *n* (also **silent partner**) a partner who invests money in a business without taking part in its running.

sleeping-pill *n* a pill that induces sleep.

sleeping sickness *n* a disease, often fatal, causing violent fever and extreme drowsiness, transmitted by the tsetse fly of Africa.

sleepless *adj* **1** during which one did not sleep. **2** unable to sleep.

sleepwalk *v* (*intr*) to walk about while asleep. — *n* **sleepwalker**. — *n* **sleepwalking**.

sleepy *adj* ***-ier***, ***-iest*** **1** feeling the desire to sleep; drowsy. **2** suggesting sleep or drowsiness: *sleepy music*. **3** characterised by quietness and a lack of activity: *a sleepy village*. — *adv* **sleepily**. — *n* **sleepiness**.

sleepyhead *n* (*coll*) **1** a person who often feels sleepy, or who needs a lot of sleep. **2** a person who tends to daydream a lot.

sleet *n* rain mixed with snow or hail. — *v* (*intr*) to rain simultaneously with snow or hail. — *adj* **sleety, *-ier*, *-iest***.

sleeve *n* **1** the part of a garment that covers the arm. **2** any tube-like cover. **3** the cardboard or paper envelope in which a record is stored. — *adj* **sleeveless**. — **up one's sleeve** held secretly in reserve, for possible later use. [OE *slefe*]

sleigh *n* a large horse-drawn sledge. — *v* (*intr*) to travel by sleigh. [Dut *slee*]

sleight of hand *n* skill in moving the hands quickly and deceptively, in the performing of magic tricks. [Norse *slægth*, cunning]

slender *adj* **1** attractively slim. **2** narrow; slight: *by a slender margin*. **3** meagre: *slender means*.

slept. See **sleep**.

sleuth (*humorous*) *n* & *v* (*intr*) (to do the work of) a detective. [Norse *sloth*, trail]

slew[1]. See **slay**.

slew[2] *v* (*tr* & *intr*) to (cause to) twist or swing round, esp. suddenly and uncontrollably. — *n* an instance of slewing.

slewed *adj* (*slang*) extremely drunk.

slice *n* **1** a thin broad piece, or a wedge, cut off. **2** (*coll*) a share or portion: *a slice of the business*. **3** a kitchen tool with a broad flat blade for sliding under and lifting solid food. **4** (*sport*) a stroke causing a ball to spin sideways and curve away in a particular direction; the spin imparted. — *v* **1** (*tr*) to cut up into slices. **2** (*tr*; **off**) to cut as, or as if as, a slice: *sliced a piece off his finger*. **3** (*intr*; **through, into**) to cut deeply and easily; to move easily and forcefully, as if cutting with a knife: *a boat slicing through the water*. **4** (*tr*) to strike (a ball) with a slice. — *n* **slicer**. [OGer *slizan*, to split]

slick *adj* **1** dishonestly or slyly clever. **2** impressively (but often only superficially) smart or efficient: *slick organisation*. **3** smooth and glossy; sleek. — *v* (*tr*; **down**, **back**) to smooth (esp. hair). — *n* (also **oil slick**) a wide layer of spilled oil floating on the surface of water. [OE *slician*, to smooth]

slicker *n* **1** a sophisticated city-dweller. **2** a shifty or swindling person.

slide *v* ***slid*** **1** (*tr* & *intr*) to (cause to) move or run smoothly along a surface. **2** (*tr* & *intr*) to move or place softly and unobtrusively: *slid the letter into his pocket*. **3** (*intr*) to lose one's footing; to slip. **4** (*intr*) to pass gradually, esp. through neglect or laziness: *slid back into his old habits*. — *n* **1** an act or instance of sliding. **2** any part that glides smoothly, e.g. the moving part of a trombone. **3** an apparatus for children to play on, usu. with a ladder to climb up and a narrow sloping part to slide down. **4** a small glass plate on which specimens are placed to be viewed through a microscope. **5** a small transparent photograph viewed in magnified size by means of a projector. **6** a large decorative hair-clip. — **let (something) slide** to allow (something) to get worse. [OE *slidan*]

slide-rule *n* a ruler-like instrument with a sliding central section and different sets of markings, used for numerous types of mathematical calculation.

sliding scale *n* a scale, e.g. of fees charged, that varies according to changes in conditions, e.g. unforeseen difficulties in performing the service requested.

slight *adj* **1** small in extent, significance or seriousness. **2** slender. **3** lacking solidity; flimsy. **4** lacking substance or value: *slight works of literature*. — *v* (*tr*) to insult by ignoring or dismissing abruptly; to snub. — *adv* **slightly**. — **not in the slightest** not at all; not even to the smallest degree. [From the root seen in OE *eorthslihtes*, close to the ground]

slily. See **sly**.

slim *adj* ***-mm-*** **1** attractively thin; slender. **2** of little thickness or width. **3** not great; slight: *a slim chance*. — *v* ***-mm-*** (*intr*) to make oneself slim, esp. by diet and exercise. — *n* **slimmer**. — *n* & *adj* **slimming**. [Dut, crafty]

slime *n* **1** any thin unpleasantly slippery or gluey mud-like substance. **2** any mucus-like substance secreted, e.g. by snails. [OE *slim*]

slimy *adj* ***-ier***, ***-iest*** **1** like, covered with or consisting of slime. **2** (*coll*) exaggeratedly and unpleasantly obedient or attentive; obsequious. — *adv* **slimily**. — *n* **sliminess**.

sling[1] *n* **1** a cloth hoop supporting an injured arm, one end hanging round the neck and the arm passed through the other end. **2** a primitive weapon for launching stones, consisting of a strap or pouch in which the stone is placed and swung round fast. **3** a strap or loop for hoisting, lowering or carrying a weight. — *v* ***slung*** (*tr*) **1** (*coll*) to throw, esp. with force; to fling. **2** to hang loosely: *jacket slung over his shoulder*. **3** to launch from a sling. — **sling one's hook** (*slang*) to go away.

slingback *n* a shoe with no cover for the heel, just a strap passing round it to hold the shoe on.

slingshot *n* (esp. *US*) a catapult.

sling[2] *n* a drink of alcoholic spirit (esp. gin) and water, sweetened and flavoured.

slink *v* ***slunk*** (*intr*) to go or move sneakingly or ashamedly. [OE *slincan*]

slinky *adj* ***-ier***, ***-iest*** (*coll*) **1** (of a garment) clinging attractively to the body. **2** slender. **3** walking with slow rolling movements that emphasise the body's curves. — *adv* **slinkily**. — *n* **slinkiness**.

slip[1] *v* ***-pp-*** **1** (*intr*) to lose one's footing and slide accidentally. **2** (*intr*) to slide, move or drop accidentally. **3** (*tr*) to place smoothly, quietly or secretively: *slipped the envelope into her pocket*. **4** (*intr*; **in**, **out**, etc.) to move quietly and unnoticed. **5** (*tr* & *intr*) to (cause to) move smoothly with a sliding motion. **6** (*tr*) to pull free from smoothly and swiftly; to suddenly escape from: *The dog slipped its lead. The name has slipped my mind*. **7** (*intr*; **up**) to make a slight mistake inadvertently. **8** (*tr*; *coll*) to give or pass secretly: *slipped him a fiver*. **9** (*intr*; *coll*) to lose one's former skill or expertise, or control of a situation. **10** (*tr*) to dislocate (esp. a spinal disc). — *n* **1** an instance of losing one's footing and sliding accidentally. **2** (also **slip-up**) a slight and inadvertent mistake: *a slip of the tongue* or *pen*. **3** a woman's loose undergarment worn under a dress or skirt. **4** a loose covering for a pillow. **5** a slipway. **6** (*cricket*) a fielder standing near to and (roughly) in line with the wicketkeeper on the on side; (often in *pl*) this fielding position. — **give (someone) the slip** (*coll*) to escape from (someone) with cunning. — **let slip 1** to reveal in speech accidentally. **2** to fail to take advantage of (e.g. an opportunity). [OGer dialect *slippen*]

slip-knot *n* **1** a knot undone simply by pulling one end of the cord. **2** a knot finishing off a noose, and slipping along the cord to adjust the noose's size.

slip-on *n* & *adj* (a garment, esp. a shoe) that is easily put on, without laces, buttons or other fastenings.

slipped disc *n* a dislocation of the layer of cartilage between any of the vertebrae, causing painful pressure on a spinal nerve.

slipper *n* a soft loose laceless indoor shoe. — *adj* **slippered**.

slippery *adj* **1** (also **slippy**, ***-ier***, ***-iest***) so smooth as to cause slipping. **2** (also **slippy**) difficult to catch or keep hold of. **3** unpredictable or untrustworthy. — *n* **slipperiness**.

slip road *n* a road for joining or leaving a motorway.

slipshod *adj* untidy and careless or carelessly done.

slipstream *n* **1** an area of decreased wind resistance immediately behind a moving vehicle or other object. **2** a stream of air driven back by a moving vehicle, esp. an aircraft.

slip-up see **slip** (*n* sense **2**) above.

slipway *n* a ramp that slopes into water, for launching boats.

slip[2] *n* **1** a small strip or piece (of paper). **2** a small pre-printed form. **3** a mere youngster; an exceptionally slender person: *just a slip of a girl.* [MidE *slippe*]

slip[3] *n* a creamy mixture of clay and water used for decorating and casting pottery. [OE *slipa*, paste]

slit *n* a long narrow cut or opening. — *v* **-tt-** (*tr*) **1** to cut a slit in. **2** to cut into strips. [MidE *slitten*]

slither *v* **-r-** (*intr*) **1** to slide or slip unsteadily while walking, e.g. on ice. **2** to move slidingly, like a snake. — *n* a slithering movement. — *adj* **slithery**. [OE *slidrian*]

sliver *n* a long thin piece cut or broken off. — *v* **-r-** (*intr*) to become broken or cut into slivers. [OE *slifan*, to cleave]

slivovitz *n* a dry colourless plum brandy from E Europe. [Serbo-Croat *šljivovica*, from *šljiva*, plum]

slob (*coll*) *n* a lazy, untidy or coarse person. — *v* **-bb-** (*intr*; **about**, **around**) to move or behave in a lazy, untidy or slovenly way. — *adj* **slobbish** or **slobby**, **-ier**, **-iest**. [Irish Gaelic *slab*, mud]

slobber *v* **-r-** (*intr*) **1** to let saliva run from the mouth; to dribble or slaver. **2** (*coll*; **over**) to express extreme (esp. unreasoning) enthusiasm or admiration (for). — *n* dribbled saliva. — *adj* **slobbery**. [MidE]

sloe *n* the blackthorn fruit or bush. [OE *sla*]

sloe gin *n* gin flavoured by having sloes soaked in it.

slog (*coll*) *v* **-gg-** **1** (*tr*) to hit hard and wildly. **2** to labour or toil. — *n* **1** a hard wild blow or stroke. **2** extremely tiring work.

slogan *n* a phrase used to identify a group or organisation, or to advertise a product. [Gaelic *sluagh*, army + *gairm*, cry]

sloop *n* a single-masted sailing boat with fore-and-aft sails. [Dut *sloep*]

slop *v* **-pp-** (**about**, **around**) **1** (*tr* & *intr*) to (cause to) splash or spill violently. **2** (*intr*; *coll*) to move or behave in an untidy or slovenly way. — *n* **1** spilled liquid. **2** (often in *pl*) unappetising watery food. **3** (in *pl*) waste food. **4** (in *pl*) liquid food fed to pigs. **5** (in *pl*) bedpan waste. **6** gushy sentiment. — *adj* **sloppy**, **-ier**, **-iest**. — *adv* **sloppily**. — *n* **sloppiness**. — *v* **slop out** (*intr*) (of prisoners) to empty bedpans. [OE (*cu-*)*sloppe*, (cow) droppings]

slope *n* **1** a position or direction that is neither level nor upright; an upward or downward slant. **2** a slanting surface; an incline; the side of a hill or mountain. **3** a specially prepared track for skiing, on the side of a snow-covered hill or mountain. — *v* (*intr*) **1** to rise or fall at an angle. **2** to be slanted or inclined. — *v* **slope off** (*intr*; *coll*) to leave, esp. furtively. [OE *aslupan*, to slip away]

slosh *v* **1** (*tr* & *intr*; **about**, **around**) to (cause to) splash or spill noisily. **2** (*tr*; *slang*) to strike with a heavy blow. — *n* **1** the sound of splashing or spilling. **2** slush; a watery mess. **3** (*slang*) a heavy blow. [A form of **slush**]

sloshed *adj* (*coll*) drunk.

slot *n* **1** a small narrow rectangular opening into which something is fitted or inserted. **2** a time, place or position within a schedule, e.g. of broadcasts or airport take-offs and landings. — *v* **-tt-** (*tr*) **1** (**in**) to fit, insert or place in a slot. **2** to make a slot in. [OFr *esclot*]

slot machine *n* a machine operated by inserting a coin in a slot, e.g. a vending machine or fruit machine.

sloth *n* **1** a long-haired slow-moving tree-dwelling mammal of S America. **2** the desire to avoid all activity or exertion; laziness; indolence. — *adj* **slothful**. [OE *slæwth*, from *slaw*, slow]

slouch *v* (*intr*) to sit, stand or walk with a tired or lazy drooping posture. — *n* **1** such a posture. **2** (*coll*; **at**; usu. with a *negative*) an incompetent person: *She's no slouch at snooker*.

slough[1] *n* **1** a mud-filled hollow. **2** an area of boggy land; a mire. **3** (*literary*; **of**) a state of deep and gloomy emotion: *in a slough of depression*. [OE *sloh*]

slough[2] *n* any part of an animal cast off or moulted, esp. a snake's dead skin. — *v* (*tr*; **off**) **1** to shed (e.g. a dead skin). **2** to cast off or dismiss (e.g. worries). [MidE *sloh*]

sloven *n* a slovenly person.

slovenly *adj* careless, untidy or dirty in appearance, habits or methods of working. — *adv* in a slovenly manner. — *n* **slovenliness**.

slow *adj* **1** having little speed or pace; not moving fast or quickly. **2** taking a long time, or longer than usual or expected. **3** (of a watch or clock) showing a time earlier than the correct time. **4** not quickly or easily learning, understanding or appreciating. **5** progressing at a boringly gentle pace: *a slow film*. **6** not allowing fast progress or movement: *traffic was slow*; *a golf course with slow greens*. **7** needing much provocation (in order to): *slow to get angry*. **8** (of business) slack. **9** (of photographic film) needing a relatively long exposure time. — *adv* in a slow manner. — *v* (*tr* & *intr*; **down**, **up**) to (cause to) reduce speed, pace, or rate of progress. — *adv* **slowly**. — *n* **slowness**. [OE *slaw*]

slowcoach *n* (*coll*) a person who moves or works at a slow pace.

slow motion *n* **1** a speed of movement in film or television that is much slower than real-life movement, created by increasing the speed at which the camera records the action. **2** an imitation of this in real-life movement. — *adj* **slow-motion**.

slow-worm *n* a small legless Eurasian lizard with a snake-like body. [OE *slawyrm*; the first part not related to *slow* but assimilated to it]

sludge *n* **1** soft slimy mud. **2** muddy sediment. **3** sewage. **4** half-melted snow; slush. — *adj* **sludgy**, **-*ier***, **-*iest***. [Probably from **slush**]

slug[1] *n* a land mollusc like a snail but with no shell.

sluggard *n* (*old*) a lazy, inactive person.

sluggish *adj* **1** unenergetic; lazy; inactive. **2** less lively, active or responsive than usual: *The engine is a bit sluggish.*

slug[2] *n* **1** (*coll*) a bullet. **2** (*printing*) a solid line or section of metal type produced by a composing machine.

slug[3] (*coll*) *n* & *v* **-*gg*-** (*tr*) (to strike with) a heavy blow.

slug[4] *n* (*coll*) a large gulped mouthful of liquid, esp. alcohol spirit.

sluice *n* **1** a channel or drain for water. **2** (also **sluice-gate**) a valve or sliding gate for controlling the flow of water in such a channel. **3** a trough for washing gold or other minerals out of sand, etc. **4** an act of washing down or rinsing. — *v* (*tr*) **1** to drain by means of a sluice. **2** to wash down or rinse by throwing water on. [OFr *escluse*, from Lat *excludere*, to shut out]

slum *n* **1** a run-down, dirty, usu. overcrowded house. **2** (often in *pl*) an area of such housing. — *v* **-*mm*-** (*intr*) **1** to visit a socially deprived area, esp. out of curiosity or for amusement. **2** to adopt the tastes or behaviour of members of a lower social class, out of pretentiousness. — **slum it** (*coll*; often *facet*) to experience circumstances less sophisticated or more squalid than one is used to.

slummy *adj* **-*ier***, **-*iest*** (*coll*) like a slum; run-down or squalid.

slumber (*poetic*) *n* & *v* **-*r*-** (*intr*) (to) sleep. — *adj* **slumbering**. — *adj* **slumberous**. [MidE *slumeren*]

slump *v* (*intr*) **1** to drop or sink suddenly and heavily, e.g. with tiredness: *slumped into an armchair*. **2** (of trade, etc.) to decline suddenly and sharply. — *n* a serious (esp. long-term) decline, e.g. in a nation's economy.

slung. See **sling**.

slunk. See **slink**.

slur *v* **-*rr*-** **1** (*tr* & *intr*) to pronounce (words) unclearly, e.g. through drunkenness. **2** (*tr*) to speak or write about very disparagingly. **3** (*tr*; **over**) to mention only briefly or deal with only superficially. **4** (*tr*; *mus*) to sing or play as a flowing sequence without pauses. — *n* **1** a disparaging remark intended to damage a reputation. **2** a slurred word or slurring way of speaking. **3** (*mus*) a flowing pauseless style of singing or playing.

slurp *v* (*tr*) to eat or drink noisily with a sucking action. — *n* a slurping sound. [Dut *slurpen*, to sip audibly]

slurry *n* **-*ies*** **1** a runny mixture of solid particles and water, esp. watery concrete. **2** liquid manure used in farming.

slush *n* **1** half-melted snow. **2** any watery half-liquid substance. **3** sickly sentimentality. — *adj* **slushy**, **-*ier***, **-*iest***.

slush fund *n* a fund of money used for dishonest purposes, e.g. bribery, esp. by a political party.

slut *n* (*derog*) **1** a woman who regularly engages in casual sex. **2** a prostitute. **3** an untidy or dirty woman. — *adj* **sluttish**.

sly *adj* ***slyer*** or ***slier***, ***slyest*** or ***sliest*** **1** clever; cunning. **2** secretive; secretively deceitful or dishonest. **3** playfully mischievous: *a sly smile*. — *adv* **slyly** or **slily**. — **on the sly** (*coll*) secretly or furtively. [Norse *slægr*]

Sm *symbol* (*chem*) samarium.

smack[1] *v* **1** (*tr*) to slap, esp. with the hand. **2** (*tr* & *intr*; *coll*) to hit loudly and heavily: *Her head smacked against the wall.* **3** (*tr*) to part (the lips) loudly, with relish or in pleasant anticipation. — *n* **1** an act, or the sound, of smacking. **2** a loud enthusiastic kiss. — *adv* (*coll*) **1** directly and with force: *drove smack into the tree*. **2** precisely: *smack in the middle*. [ODut *smacken*]

smacker *n* **1** (*coll*) a loud enthusiastic kiss. **2** (*slang*) a pound sterling or a dollar.

smack[2] *v* (*intr* with **of**) **1** to have the flavour of. **2** to have a suggestion or trace of. — *n* **1** taste; distinctive flavour. **2** a hint or trace. [OE *smæc*]

smack[3] *n* a small single-masted fishing boat. [Dut *smak*]

smack[4] *n* (*slang*) heroin.

small *adj* **1** little in size or quantity. **2** little in extent, importance or worth; not great. **3** humble: *small beginnings*. **4** petty: *small-minded*. **5** young: *a small child*. **6** (of a letter) lower-case; not capital. **7** humiliated: *feel small*. — *n* **1** the narrow part, esp. of the back. **2** (in *pl*; *coll*) underclothes. — *adv* **1** on a small scale. **2** into small pieces. — *n* **smallness**. [OE *smæl*]

small ads *n* (*pl*; *coll*) short advertisements in a newspaper, advertising items for sale, etc.

small arms *n* (*pl*) hand-held firearms.

small change *n* coins of little value.

small fry *n* (*coll*) **1** (*sing* or *pl*) a person or thing, or people or things, of little importance or influence. **2** (*pl*) young children.

smallholding *n* a piece of cultivated land smaller than a farm, usu. under fifty acres. — *n* **smallholder**.

the small hours *n* (*pl*) the hours immediately after midnight.

small-minded *adj* narrow-minded; petty-minded.

smallpox *n* a highly contagious disease characterised by fever and a severe rash of large blisters that usu. leave permanent scars.

small print *n* the details of a contract or other undertaking, often printed very small, esp. when considered likely to contain unattractive conditions that the writer of the contract does not want to be noticed.

the small screen *n* television, as opposed to cinema.

small talk *n* polite conversation about trivial matters.

small-time *adj* operating on a small scale.

smarm *v* **1** (*tr*; **down**) to smooth or flatten (the hair) with an oily substance. **2** (*intr*; *coll*) to be exaggeratedly and insincerely flattering or respectful. — *n* (*coll*) exaggerated or insincere flattery.

smarmy *adj* **-ier**, **-iest** (*coll*) **1** ingratiatingly flattering or respectful. **2** self-consciously suave or charming. — *adv* **smarmily**. — *n* **smarminess**.

smart *adj* **1** neat and well-dressed. **2** clever; astute; shrewd. **3** expensive and sophisticated: *a smart hotel*. **4** (of pain, etc.) sharp and stinging. **5** brisk: *at a smart pace*. **6** computer-guided or electronically controlled: *a smart bomb*. **7** (*coll*) impressive; excellent. — *v* (*intr*) **1** to feel or be the cause of a sharp stinging pain. **2** to feel or be the cause of acute irritation or distress. **3** (*intr*; **for**) to suffer the harsh consequences (of) or punishment (for). — *n* a sharp stinging pain. — *adv* in a smart manner. — *adv* **smartly**. — *n* **smartness**. — **look smart** to hurry up. [OE *smeortan*]

smart alec or **aleck** *n* (*coll*) a person who thinks himself or herself cleverer than others; a know-all. — *adj* **smart-alecky**.

smarten *v* **-n-** (*tr* & *intr*; **up**) to make or become smarter; to brighten (up).

smash *v* **1** (*tr* & *intr*; **up**) to break violently into pieces; to destroy or be destroyed in this way. ◇ See also **smash-up** below. **2** (*tr* & *intr*) to strike with violence, often causing damage; to burst with great force: *smashed his fist down on the table*; *smashed through the door*. **3** (*tr*; *coll*) to break up or ruin completely: *smash an international drugs ring*. **4** (*tr*) to hit (a ball) with a smash. — *n* **1** an act, or the sound, of smashing. **2** a powerful overhead stroke in racket sports. **3** (*coll*) a road traffic accident. **4** (*coll*) a smash hit. — *adv* with a smashing sound. [Imit.]

smash-and-grab (*coll*) *n* & *adj* (a robbery) carried out by smashing a shop window and snatching the items on display.

smashed *adj* (*coll*) extremely drunk.

smasher *n* (*coll*) a person or thing very much liked or admired.

smashing *adj* (*coll*) excellent; splendid.

smash hit *n* (*coll*) (a song, play, film, etc. that is) an overwhelming success.

smash-up *n* (*coll*) a violent road traffic accident.

smattering *n* **1** a few scraps of knowledge. **2** a small amount scattered around. [MidE *smateren*, to rattle]

smear *v* **1** (*tr*) to spread (something sticky or oily) thickly over (a surface). **2** (*tr* & *intr*) to make or become blurred; to smudge. **3** (*tr*) to say or write abusively damaging things about (someone). — *n* **1** a greasy mark or patch. **2** a damaging criticism or accusation; a slur. **3** an amount of a substance, esp. of cervical tissue, placed on a slide for examination under a microscope. **4** (*coll*) a smear test. — *adj* **smeary**. [OE *smeru*, fat, grease]

smear test *n* an examination, under a microscope, of a small amount of tissue from a woman's cervix, to test for the presence of cervical cancer.

smell *n* **1** the sense by which one becomes aware of the odour of things, located in the nose. **2** the quality perceived by this sense; (an) odour or scent. **3** an unpleasant odour. **4** an act of using this sense: *have a smell of this*. — *v* ***smelled*** or ***smelt*** **1** (*tr*) to be aware of, or take in, the odour of. **2** (*intr*; **of**) to give off an odour (of). **3** (*intr*) to give off an unpleasant odour. **4** (*tr*) to be aware of by intuition; to recognise signs or traces of: *I smell a government cover-up*. **5** (*intr* with **of**) to show signs or traces (of): *an organisation smelling of corruption*. — *v* **smell out** (*tr*) to find, track down or uncover by, or as if by, smell. [MidE *smel*]

smelling-salts *n* (*pl*) crystals of ammonium carbonate, whose strong sharp odour stimulates consciousness after fainting.

smelly *adj* **-ier**, **-iest** (*coll*) unpleasant-smelling. — *n* **smelliness**.

smelt[1] *v* (*tr*) to melt (ore) in order to separate out (the metal it contains). — *n* **smelter**. [OGer *smelten*]

smelt[2]. See **smell**.

smelt[3] *n* ***-elts*** or ***-elt*** any of various small silvery edible fish of the salmon family. [OE *smylt*]

smile *v* **1** (*intr*) to turn up the corners of the mouth, often showing the teeth, usu. as an expression of pleasure, favour or amusement. **2** (*intr* with **at**) to react (to) with such an expression. **3** (*tr*) to show with such an expression: *smiled his agreement*. **4** (*intr* with **on**) to show favour towards. — *n* an act or way of smiling. — *adj* **smiling**. [MidE *smilen*]

smirch *v* (*tr*) **1** to make dirty; to soil or stain. **2** to damage or sully (a reputation, etc.); to besmirch. — *n* **1** a stain. **2** a smear on a reputation. [OFr *esmorcher*, to hurt]

smirk *v* (*intr*) to smile in a self-satisfied or foolish manner. — *n* such a smile. [OE *smercian*]

smite *v* ***smote***, ***smitten*** (*old* or *literary*) **1** (*tr*) to strike or beat with a heavy blow or blows. **2** (*tr*) to kill. **3** (*tr*; **with**) to afflict. **4** (*tr*) to cause to fall immediately and overpoweringly in love: *not fail to be smitten by such beauty*. **5** (*intr* with **on**, **upon**) to come suddenly and forcefully: *The king's authority smote down on him*. [OE *smitan*, to smear]

smith *n* (esp. *in cmpds*) **1** a person who makes articles in (a particular) metal: *silversmith*. **2** a blacksmith. **3** a person who makes skilful use of something: *wordsmith*. [OE]

smithy *n* **-ies** a blacksmith's workshop.

smithereens *n* (*pl*; *coll*) tiny fragments: *smashed it to smithereens*. [Irish Gaelic *smidirin*, dimin. of *smiodar*, fragment]

smitten *past participle* of **smite**. — *adj* in love (with); obsessed (by).

smock *n* **1** any loose shirt-like garment worn, e.g. by artists, over other clothes for protection, esp. one slipped over the head. **2** a woman's long loose-fitting blouse. **3** (*hist*) a loose-fitting overall of coarse linen worn by farm-workers. [OE *smoc*]

smocking *n* decorative stitching used on gathered or tucked material.

smog *n* fog mixed with smoke and fumes. — *adj* **smoggy**, **-ier**, **-iest**. [**smoke** + **fog**]

smoke *n* **1** the gases and fine particles given off by something burning. **2** visible fumes or vapours. **3** (*coll*) the act of or time spent smoking tobacco. **4** (*coll*) a cigarette or cigar. — *v* **1** (*intr*) to give off smoke or visible fumes or vapours. **2** (*tr* & *intr*) to inhale the smoke from the burning tobacco in (a cigarette, cigar or pipe); to do this as a habit. **3** (*tr*) to preserve or flavour (food) by the action of smoke. — *adj* **smoked**. — **go up in smoke 1** to be completely destroyed by fire. **2** (of plans, etc.) to be ruined completely; to come to nothing. — **the (Big) Smoke** (*coll*) the nearby big city; a country's capital city. — *v* **smoke out** (*tr*) **1** to drive (an animal) into the open by filling its burrow with smoke. **2** to uncover by persistent searching or investigation. [OE *smoca*]

smokeless *adj* **1** (of fuel) producing little or no smoke. **2** (of an area) in which the use of smoke-producing fuel is not allowed; in which tobacco-smoking is not allowed.

smoker *n* **1** a person who smokes tobacco products. **2** a railway carriage in which tobacco-smoking is permitted.

smokescreen *n* **1** a cloud of smoke used to conceal the movements of troops, etc. **2** anything said or done to hide or deceive.

smokestack *n* **1** a tall industrial chimney. **2** a funnel on a ship or steam train.

smoking *n* tobacco-smoking. — *adj* in which tobacco-smoking is allowed.

smoky *adj* **-ier**, **-iest 1** giving out (too much) smoke. **2** filled with (esp. tobacco) smoke. **3** having a smoked flavour. **4** hazy, esp. in colour: *smoky blue*. **5** made dirty by smoke. — *n* **smokiness**.

smolt *n* a young salmon migrating from fresh water to the sea. [Scot]

smooch (*coll*) *v* (*intr*) **1** to kiss and cuddle (with or together). **2** to dance slowly in an embrace (with or together). — *n* a period of smooching. — *adj* **smoochy**, **-ier**, **-iest**.

smooth *adj* **1** having an even regular surface; not rough, coarse, bumpy or wavy. **2** having few or no lumps; of even texture. **3** free from problems or difficulties: *a smooth journey*. **4** characterised by steady movement and a lack of jolts: *a smooth ferry crossing*. **5** not sharp or bitter: *a smooth sherry*. **6** very elegant or charming, esp. self-consciously or insincerely so. — *v* (*tr*) **1** (**out**, **down**) to make smooth. **2** (**out**, **over**) to cause (problems, etc.) to seem less serious or important. **3** to make easier: *smooth the way to promotion*. — *adv* smoothly: *a smooth-running system*. — *n* the easy, pleasurable or trouble-free part or aspect: *take the rough with the smooth*. — *adv* **smoothly**. — *n* **smoothness**. [OE *smoth*]

smoothie or **smoothy** *n* **-ies** (*coll*) a very elegant or charming person, esp. one self-consciously or insincerely so.

smooth-talking or **smooth-tongued** *adj* **1** exaggeratedly and insincerely flattering. **2** (seeking to be) charmingly persuasive.

smorgasbord *n* an assortment of hot and cold savoury dishes served as a buffet. [Swed, from *smörgås*, open sandwich + *bord*, table]

smote. See **smite**.

smother *v* **-r- 1** (*tr* & *intr*) to kill with or die from lack of air, esp. with an obstruction over the mouth and nose; to suffocate. **2** (*tr*) to extinguish (a fire) by cutting off the air supply, e.g. by throwing a blanket over it. **3** (*tr*; **with**) to cover with a thick layer: *bread smothered with jam*. **4** (*tr*; **with**) to give an oppressive or stifling amount to: *smothered the children with love*. **5** (*tr*) to suppress or contain (e.g. laughter). [MidE *smorther*, from OE *smorian*]

smoulder *v* **-r-** (*intr*) **1** to burn slowly or without flame. **2** to linger on in a suppressed state: *smouldering anger*. — *n* a smouldering fire or emotion. [MidE *smolder*]

smudge *n* **1** a mark or blot spread by rubbing. **2** a faint or blurred shape, e.g. an object seen from afar. — *v* **1** (*tr*) to make a smudge on or of. **2** (*intr*) to become a smudge. — *adj* **smudgy**, **-ier**, **-iest**.

smug *adj* **-gg-** (showing oneself to be) arrogantly pleased with oneself; self-satisfied. — *adv* **smugly**. — *n* **smugness**. [Ger dialect *smuck*, neat]

smuggle *v* (*tr*; **into**, **out of**) **1** to take (goods) into or out of a country secretly and illegally, e.g. to avoid paying duty. **2** to bring or take secretly, usu. breaking a rule or restriction. — *n* **smuggler**. — *n* **smuggling**. [Ger dialect *smuggeln*]

smut *n* **1** soot. **2** a speck of dirt or soot. **3** mildly obscene language, pictures or images. **4** a fungal disease of plants, esp. cereal crops. — *v* **-tt-** (*tr*) to dirty or affect with smut. [MidE *smotten*, to stain]

smutty *adj* **-ier**, **-iest 1** dirtied by smut. **2** mildly obscene. — *n* **smuttiness**.

Sn *symbol* (*chem*) tin. [Lat *stannum*]

snack *n* a light meal quickly taken, or a bite to eat between meals. [Perhaps ODut *snacken*, to snap]

snack bar *n* a café, kiosk or counter serving snacks.

snaffle *n* a simple bridle-bit for a horse. — *v* (*tr*) **1** to fit (a horse) with a snaffle. **2** (*coll*) to take sneakily or without permission.

snag *n* **1** a problem or drawback. **2** a sharp or jagged edge on which clothes, etc. could get caught. **3** a hole or tear in clothes, etc. caused by such catching. **4** a part of a tree submerged in water, hazardous to navigation. — *v* ***-gg-*** (*tr*) to catch or tear on a snag. [Perhaps Norse *snagi*, peg]

snail *n* any of various small slow-crawling soft-bodied legless creatures with a spiral shell into which the whole body can be coiled. — **at a snail's pace** extremely slowly. [OE *snæl*]

snake *n* **1** any of numerous species of legless crawling reptiles with long narrow bodies, many of which have a poisonous bite. **2** any long and flexible or winding thing or shape. **3** (*coll*; also **snake in the grass**) a treacherous person; a supposed friend revealed to be an enemy. — *v* (*intr*) to move windingly or follow a winding course. [OE *snaca*]

snakebite *n* **1** the wound or poisoned condition caused by the bite of a venomous snake. **2** (*coll*) a drink of cider and beer or lager in equal measures.

snake-charmer *n* a street entertainer who (seemingly) induces snakes to perform rhythmical movements, esp. by playing music.

snakes and ladders *n* (*sing*) a game played with counters and dice on a board marked with an ascending path on which ladders allow short cuts to the goal and snakes force one to go back towards the beginning.

snaky *adj* ***-ier***, ***-iest*** **1** like a snake, esp. long, thin and flexible or winding. **2** treacherous or cruelly deceitful. — *adv* **snakily**.

snap *v* ***-pp-*** **1** (*tr & intr*) to break suddenly and cleanly with a sharp cracking noise: *snapped the stick over his knee*. **2** (*tr & intr*) to move quickly and forcefully with a sharp sound: *The lid snapped shut*. **3** (*intr*; **at**) to make a biting or grasping movement. **4** (*tr & intr*; **at**) to speak or express abruptly with anger or impatience. **5** (*tr*; *coll*) to take a photograph of, esp. spontaneously and with simple equipment. **6** (*intr*; *coll*) to lose one's senses or self-control suddenly and with disturbing results. — *n* **1** the act or sound of snapping. **2** (*coll*) a photograph, esp. taken spontaneously and with simple equipment. **3** a catch or other fastening that closes with a snapping sound. **4** a crisp biscuit or savoury. **5** (also **cold snap**) a sudden brief period of cold weather. **6** a card game in which all the cards played are collected by the first player to shout 'snap' whenever matching cards are laid down by consecutive players. — *interj* **1** the word shouted in the card game. **2** the word used to highlight any matching pair. — *adj* taken or made spontaneously, without long consideration: *a snap decision*. — *adv* with a snapping sound. — **snap one's fingers 1** to make a short loud snapping sound by flicking one's fingers sharply, usu. to attract attention. **2** (**at**) to show contempt (for) or defiance (at). — **snap out of it** (*coll*) to immediately bring oneself out of a state or condition, e.g. of sulking or depression. — *v* **snap up** (*tr*) to seize eagerly: *snapped up the opportunity*. [Prob. Dut *snappen*]

snapdragon *n* an antirrhinum, a garden plant whose flower, when pinched, opens and closes like a mouth.

snappy *adj* ***-ier***, ***-iest*** **1** irritable; inclined to snap. **2** smart and fashionable: *a snappy dresser*. **3** lively: *at a snappy tempo*. — *adv* **snappily**. — *n* **snappiness**. — **make it snappy!** (*coll*) hurry up!; be quick about it!

snapshot *n* a photograph, esp. taken spontaneously and with simple equipment.

snare *n* **1** an animal trap, esp. one with a string or wire noose to catch the animal's foot. **2** anything that traps or entangles. **3** the set of wires fitted to a snare drum. — *v* (*tr*) to trap or entangle in, or as if in, a snare. [OE *sneare*]

snare drum *n* a medium-sized drum sitting horizontally, with a set of wires fitted to its underside that rattle sharply when the drum is struck.

snarl[1] *v* **1** (*intr*) (of an animal) to growl angrily, showing the teeth. **2** (*tr & intr*) to speak or say aggressively in anger or irritation. — *n* **1** an act of snarling. **2** a snarling sound or facial expression.

snarl[2] *n* **1** a knotted or tangled mass. **2** a confused or congested situation or state. — *v* (*tr & intr*; **up**) to make or become knotted, tangled, confused or congested. [Ety. as for **snare**]

snarl-up *n* (*coll*) any muddled or congested situation, esp. a traffic jam.

snatch *v* **1** (*tr*) to seize or grab suddenly. **2** (*intr* with **at**) to make a sudden grabbing movement. **3** (*tr*) to pull suddenly and forcefully: *snatched her hand away*. **4** (*tr*; *coll*) to take or have as soon as the opportunity arises: *snatch a bite to eat*. — *n* **1** an act of snatching. **2** a fragment overheard or remembered: *a few snatches of the old song*. **3** a brief period: *snatches of rest between long shifts*. **4** (*coll*) a robbery. [MidE *snacchen*]

snazzy *adj* ***-ier***, ***-iest*** (*coll*) fashionably smart or elegant. — *adv* **snazzily**.

sneak *v* **1** (*intr*) to move or go quietly and avoiding notice. **2** (*tr*; **in**, **out**, etc.) to bring or take secretly, esp. breaking a rule or prohibition: *sneaked a girl into his room*; *sneak a look at the letter*. **3** (*intr*; *coll*; **on**) to tell tales: *sneak on a schoolmate*. — *n* (*coll*) a person who sneaks; a tell-tale. [Perhaps OE *snican*, to creep]

sneakers *n* (*pl*; esp. *US*) sports shoes; training shoes.

sneaking *adj* (of a feeling, etc.) slight but not easy to suppress.
sneak thief *n* a thief who gets in through unlocked doors or windows, without breaking in.
sneaky *adj* **-ier**, **-iest** done or operating with secretive unfairness or dishonesty; underhand. — *adv* **sneakily**.

sneer *v* **1** (*intr*; **at**) to show scorn or contempt (for), esp. by drawing the top lip up at one side. **2** (*tr*) to say scornfully or contemptuously. — *n* an expression of scorn or contempt made with a raised lip, or otherwise. — *adj* **sneering**.

sneeze *v* (*intr*) to blow air out through the nose suddenly, violently and involuntarily, esp. because of irritation in the nostrils. — *n* an act or the sound of sneezing. — **sneeze at** (*coll*) to regard or dismiss as being of little value: *an opportunity not to be sneezed at.* [OE *fnesan*]

snick *n* **1** a small cut; a nick. **2** (*cricket*) a glancing contact with the edge of the bat. — *v* (*tr*) **1** to make a small cut in. **2** (*cricket*) to hit with a snick.

snicker. Same as **snigger**.

snide *adj* expressing criticism or disapproval in an indirect way intended to offend.

sniff *v* **1** (*intr*) to draw in air through the nose in short sharp bursts, e.g. when crying. **2** (*tr* & *intr*; **at**) to smell (at) in this way. **3** (*tr*) to inhale the fumes from (a dangerous or addictive substance): *sniffing glue.* — *n* an act or the sound of sniffing. — *v* **sniff at** (*tr*; *coll*) to regard or dismiss as being of little value: *an offer not to be sniffed at.* — *v* **sniff out** (*tr*) to discover or detect by, or as if by, the sense of smell. [Imit.]
sniffle *v* (*intr*) to sniff repeatedly, e.g. because of having a cold. — *n* **1** an act or the sound of sniffling. **2** (in *pl*; *coll*; with **the**) a slight cold.
sniffy *adj* **-ier**, **-iest** (*coll*) **1** (habitually) contemptuous or disdainful. **2** sniffing repeatedly, or feeling that one wants to, because of having a cold. — *adv* **sniffily**.

snifter *n* (*slang*) a drink of alcohol, esp. alcoholic spirit; a tipple or dram. [Dialect *snift*, to sniff]

snigger *v* **-r-** (*intr*) to laugh quietly in a foolish or mocking way. — *n* such a laugh. [Imit.]

snip *v* **-pp-** (*tr*) to cut, esp. with a single quick action or actions with scissors. — *n* **1** an act or the action of snipping. **2** a small piece snipped off. **3** a small cut or notch. **4** (*coll*) a bargain. **5** (*coll*) a certainty; a thing easily done. [Dut *snippen*]

snipe *n* **1** a marshland wading-bird with a long straight bill. **2** a quick verbal attack or criticism. — *v* (*intr*; **at**) **1** to shoot from a hidden position, targeting individuals. **2** to launch a quick verbal attack or criticism. — *n* **sniper**. [MidE]

snippet *n* a scrap, e.g. of information. [**snip**]

snitch (*slang*) *n* **1** the nose. **2** an informer. — *v* **1** (*intr*) to betray others; to inform. **2** (*tr*) to steal; to pilfer. — *n* **snitcher**.

snivel *v* **-ll-** (*intr*) **1** to whine or complain tearfully. **2** to have a runny nose. — *n* an act of snivelling. — *adj* **snivelling**. [OE *snofl*, mucus]

snob *n* **1** a person who places too high a value on social status, admiring those higher up the social ladder and despising those lower down. **2** a person who judges a thing solely according to the values of those people regarded as socially or intellectually superior: *a wine snob.* — *n* **snobbery**. — *adj* **snobbish**. — *n* **snobbishness**. — *adj* **snobby**, **-ier**, **-iest**.

snog (*slang*) *v* **-gg-** (*intr*) to kiss and cuddle. — *n* a kiss and cuddle.

snood *n* a pouch of netting or fabric worn by women on the back of the head, to keep hair in a bundle. [OE *snod*]

snook: **cock a snook at** (*coll*) **1** to put the thumb to the nose and wave the fingers at, as a gesture of contempt or defiance. **2** to express open contempt for.

snooker *n* **1** a game in which long leather-tipped sticks are used to force a white ball to knock coloured balls into holes on the corners and sides of a large cloth-covered table. **2** in this game, a position in which the path between the white ball and the target ball is obstructed by another ball. — *v* **-r-** (*tr*) **1** in snooker, to force (an opponent) to attempt to hit an obstructed target ball. **2** (*coll*) to thwart (a person or plan).

snoop *v* (*intr*) to go about inquisitively; to pry. — *n* **1** an act of snooping. **2** a person who snoops. — *n* **snooper**. [Dut *snoepen*, to eat or steal]

snooty *adj* **-ier**, **-iest** (*coll*) haughty; snobbish. — *adv* **snootily**. — *n* **snootiness**.

snooze *v* (*intr*) to sleep lightly; to doze. — *n* a period of light sleeping, esp. when brief; a nap.

snore *v* (*intr*) to breathe heavily and with a snorting sound while sleeping. — *n* an act or the sound of snoring. [Imit.]

snorkel *n* **1** a rigid tube through which air from above the surface of water can be drawn into the mouth while one is swimming just below the surface. **2** a set of tubes on a submarine extended above the surface of the sea to take in air and release exhaust gases. — *v* **-ll-** (*intr*) to swim with a snorkel. [Ger *Schnorchel*]

snort *v* **1** (*intr*) (esp. of animals) to force air violently and noisily out through the nostrils; to make a similar noise while taking air in. **2** (*tr* & *intr*) to speak or say in this way, esp. expressing contempt or anger. **3** (*tr*; *slang*) to inhale (a powdered drug, esp. cocaine) through the nose. — *n* **1** an act or the sound of snorting. **2** (*coll*) a small drink of alcoholic spirit. **3** (*slang*) an amount of a powdered drug inhaled in one breath. [MidE *snorten*]

snot *n* (*coll*) **1** (*vulg*) mucus of the nose. **2** (*derog*) a contemptible person. [OE *gesnot*]
snotty *adj* **-ier**, **-iest** (*coll*) **1** (*vulg*) covered or dripping with nasal mucus: *snotty-nosed kids.* **2** haughty; having or showing contempt. **3** (*derog*) contemptible; worthless: *I don't want your snotty advice.* — *adv* **snottily**. — *n* **snottiness**.

snout *n* **1** the projecting nose and mouth parts of certain animals, e.g. the pig. **2** (*coll*) the human nose. **3** any projecting part. [OGer *snut*]

snow *n* **1** frozen water vapour falling to the ground in soft white flakes, or lying on the ground as a soft white mass. **2** a fall of this: *heavy snows.* **3** (*coll*) flickering white speckles on a television screen caused by interference or a poor signal. **4** (*slang*) cocaine. — *v* **1** (*intr*) (of snow) to fall. **2** (*tr*; **in, up**) to bury or block with snow. — *adj* **snowy**, **-ier**, **-iest**. — **snowed under** (**with**) overwhelmed (by): *snowed under with work.* [OE *snaw*]
snowball *n* a small mass of snow pressed hard together, used by children as a missile. — *v* **1** (*tr* & *intr*) to throw snowballs (at). **2** (*intr*) to develop or increase rapidly and uncontrollably.
snow blindness *n* severely (but temporarily) impaired eyesight cause by prolonged exposure of the eyes to bright sunlight reflected by snow. — *adj* **snow-blind**.
snowboard *n* a type of wide ski on which one stands with both feet. — *n* **snowboarding**.
snowbound *adj* shut in or prevented from travelling because of heavy falls of snow.
snow-capped *adj* (esp. of mountains) with a covering of snow on the top.
snowdrift *n* a bank of snow blown together by the wind.
snowdrop *n* a European plant of the daffodil family producing small white drooping flowers in early spring.
snowfall *n* **1** a fall of snow. **2** an amount of fallen snow.
snowflake *n* any of the single small feathery clumps of crystals of frozen water vapour that snow is made up of.
snow leopard *n* same as **ounce**[2].
snowline *n* the level or height on a mountain above which there is a permanent layer of snow.
snowman *n* a crude human figure made of packed snow.
snowmobile *n* a motorised vehicle, on skis or tracks, for travelling on snow.
snowplough *n* (a vehicle or train fitted with) a large shovel-like device for clearing snow from roads or tracks.
snowshoe *n* either of a pair of racket-like frameworks strapped to the feet for walking over deep snow.

SNP *abbrev* Scottish National Party.

Snr or **snr** *abbrev* senior.

snub *v* **-bb-** (*tr*) to insult by openly ignoring, rejecting or otherwise showing contempt. — *n* an act of snubbing. — *adj* (of a nose) short and flat. [Norse *snubba*, to scold]

snuff[1] *n* powdered tobacco for inhaling through the nose. — *v* (*intr*) to take snuff. [ODut *snuffen*, to snuffle]
snuffbox *n* a small lidded (esp. metal) container for snuff.

snuff[2] *v* (*tr*) **1** (**out**) to extinguish (a candle). **2** to snip off the burnt part of the wick of (a candle or lamp). **3** (**out**) to put an end to: *snuff out all opposition.* — *n* the burnt part of the wick of a lamp or candle. — **snuff it** (*slang*) to die. [MidE *snoffe*]
snuff movie or **film** *n* (*slang*) a pornographic film in which the climax is the real-life murder of one of the participants.

snuffle *v* **1** (*intr*) to breathe, esp. breathe in, through a partially blocked nose. **2** (*tr* & *intr*) to say or speak in a nasal tone. **3** (*intr*) to snivel. — *n* **1** the sound of breathing through a partially blocked nose. **2** (in *pl*; *coll*; with **the**) a slight cold. [**snuff**[1]]

snug *adj* **-gg-** **1** enjoying or providing warmth, comfort and shelter; cosy. **2** comfortably close-fitting. — *n* (also **snuggery**, **-ies**) a small comfortable room or compartment in a pub. — *adv* **snugly**.
snuggle *v* (*intr*; **down, in**, etc.) to settle oneself into a position of warmth and comfort.

so[1] *adv* **1** to such an extent: *so expensive that nobody buys it.* **2** to this, that, or the same extent; as: *This one is lovely, but that one is not so nice.* **3** extremely: *She is so talented!* **4** in that state or condition: *promised to be faithful, and has remained so.* **5** also; likewise: *She's my friend and so are you.* **6** used to avoid repeating a previous statement: *You've to take your medicine because I said so.* — *conj* **1** therefore; thereafter: *He insulted me, so I hit him.* **2** (often **so that**) in order (that): *Lend me the book, so (that) I can read it.* — *adj* true: *You think I'm mad, but it's not so.* — *interj* used to express discovery: *So, that's what you've been doing!* — **and so on** or **forth** (also **and so on and so forth**) and more of the same; continuing in the same way. — **just so** neatly, precisely or perfectly: *with her hair arranged just so.* — **or so** approximately: *five or so days ago.* — **so as to** in order to; in such a way as to. — **so be it** used to express acceptance or defiant resignation. — **so much** or **many** **1** such a lot: *just so much work to do!* **2** just; mere: *politicians squabbling like so many children.* — **so much for** nothing has come of; that has disposed of or ruined: *So much for all our plans!* — **so to speak** or **say** if one can use, or if you will forgive the use of, such an expression. — **so what?** (*coll*) that is of no importance or consequence at all. [OE *swa*]
so-and-so *n* (*coll*) **1** a person whose name one does not know or cannot remember. **2**

used in place of a vulgar word: *You crafty little so-and-so!*

so-called *adj* known or presented as such (with the implication that the term is wrongly or inappropriately used): *a panel of so-called experts.*

so-so *adj* & *adv* (*coll*) (in a way that is) neither very good nor very bad; passable; middling.

so[2]. Same as **soh**.

soak *v* **1** (*tr* & *intr*) to (leave to) stand in a liquid for some time. **2** (*tr*) to make thoroughly wet; to drench. **3** (*intr*; **in, through**) to penetrate or pass (through). **4** (*tr* with **up**) to absorb. — *n* **1** an act of soaking. **2** (*coll*) a long period of lying in a bath. **3** (*coll*) a person who habitually drinks a lot of alcohol. — *adj* **soaked**. — *n* & *adj* **soaking**. [OE *socian*]

soap *n* **1** a mixture of oils or fats, in the form of a liquid, powder or solid block, used with water to remove dirt. **2** a block of such a substance. **3** (*coll*) a soap opera. — *v* (*tr*) **1** to apply soap to. **2** (*coll*; **up**) to charm or persuade with flattery. — *adj* **soapy**, **-*ier***, **-*iest***. [OE *sape*]

soapbox *n* an improvised platform for public speech-making, orig. an upturned crate for carrying soap.

soap opera *n* a radio or television series dealing with the daily life and troubles of a regular group of characters, orig. applied to those sponsored in the US by soap manufacturing companies.

soapstone *n* a soft (usu. grey or brown) variety of the talc mineral, widely used for ornamental carvings.

soar *v* (*intr*) **1** to fly high into the air. **2** to glide through the air at a high altitude. **3** to rise sharply to a great height or level: *temperatures soaring.* [OFr *essorer*, to expose to air by raising up]

sob *v* **-*bb*- 1** (*intr*) to cry uncontrollably with intermittent gulps for breath. **2** (*tr*) to say while crying in this way. — *n* a gulp for breath between bouts of crying. [Imit.]

sob-story *n* (*coll*) a story of personal misfortune told in order to gain sympathy.

sober *adj* **1** not at all drunk. **2** serious or solemn; not frivolous. **3** suggesting sedateness or seriousness rather than exuberance or frivolity: *sober clothes.* **4** plain; unembellished: *the sober truth.* — *v* **-*r*-** (*tr* & *intr* with **up**) to make or become free from the effects of alcohol. [Lat *sobrius*, from *se-*, not + *ebrius*, drunk]

sobering *adj* provoking serious reflection: *a sobering thought.*

sobriety *n* the state of being sober, esp. not drunk. [Lat *sobrietas*]

sobriquet or **soubriquet** *n* (*literary*) a nickname. [Fr]

Soc. *abbrev* **1** Socialist. **2** Society.

soccer *n* a form of football played between teams of eleven players with a round ball, in which the players attempt to kick or head the ball into the opposing team's goal. [Association football]

sociable *adj* **1** fond of the company of others; friendly. **2** characterised by friendliness: *a sociable meeting.* — *n* **sociability** or **sociableness**. — *adv* **sociably**. [Lat *sociabilis*; see **social**]

social *adj* **1** of or for (the welfare of) people or society as a whole: *social policies.* **2** relating to the organisation and behaviour of people in societies or communities: *social studies.* **3** tending or needing to live with others; not solitary: *social creatures.* **4** intended for or promoting friendly gatherings of people: *a social club.* — *n* **1** a social gathering, esp. one organised by a club or other group. **2** (*coll*; with **the**) social security. — *adv* **socially**. [Lat *socius*, companion]

social climber *n* (often *derog*) a person who seeks to gain higher social status, often by despicable methods.

social contract *n* a (supposed) agreement between individuals within a society to work together for the benefit of all, often involving the sacrifice of some personal freedoms.

social democracy *n* support for political policies that promote a gradual and voluntary change from a capitalist to a socialist society. — *n* **social democrat**.

Social Democratic Party *n* in the UK, a political party founded by former members of the Labour Party in 1981, reduced in influence when the majority of its members amalgamated with the Liberal Party in 1988, and formally wound up in 1990.

socialise or **-ize** *v* **1** (*intr*) to meet with people on an informal, friendly basis. **2** (*intr*) to circulate among guests at a party; to mingle. **3** (*tr*) to organise into societies or communities. — *n* **socialisation** or **-z-**.

socialism *n* the theory or system according to which a nation's wealth, e.g. its land, industries and transport systems, belongs to the people as a whole rather than being owned by private individuals. — *n* & *adj* **socialist**.

socialite *n* a person who mixes with people of high social status.

social sciences *n* those subjects that deal with the organisation and behaviour of people in societies and communities, including sociology, anthropology, economics and history. — *n* **social scientist**.

social security *n* **1** a system by which members of a society pay money into a common fund, from which payments are made to individuals in times of unemployment, illness and old age. **2** a payment or scheme of payments from such a fund.

social services *n* services provided by local or national government for the general welfare of people in society, e.g. housing, education and health.

social work *n* work in any of the services provided by local government for the care of underprivileged people. — *n* **social worker**.

society *n* **-*ies*- 1** mankind as a whole, or a part of it such as one nation, considered as a single community. **2** a division of mankind with common characteristics, e.g. of nationality, race or religion. **3** an organised group or association. **4** the rich, fashionable section of the upper class: *a society wedding*. **5** (*formal*) company: *prefers the society of women*. [Lat *societas*]

socio- *comb fm* social; of society or sociology: *socioeconomic*.

sociology *n* the scientific study of the nature, structure and workings of human society. — *adj* **sociological**. — *n* **sociologist**. [Lat *socius*, companion + **-logy**]

sock[1] *n* a fabric covering for the foot and ankle, sometimes reaching to the knee, worn inside a shoe or boot. — **pull one's socks up** (*coll*) to make an effort to do better. — **put a sock in it** (*slang*) to become silent; to be quiet [OE *socc*, light shoe]

sock[2] (*slang*) *n* & *v* (*tr*) (to hit with) a powerful blow. — **sock it to** (*slang*) to make a powerful impression on.

socket *n* **1** a specially-shaped hole or set of holes into which something is fitted: *an electrical socket*. **2** a hollow structure in the body into which another part fits: *a ball-and-socket joint*. [OFr *soket*]

Socratic *adj* of or relating to the Greek philosopher *Socrates* (died 399 BC), his philosophy, or his method of teaching or inquiry by a series of questions and answers.

sod[1] *n* **1** a slab of earth with grass growing on it; a turf. **2** (*poetic*) the ground. [OGer *sode*]

sod[2] (*vulg slang*) *n* **1** an unpleasant, badly behaved or despicable person. **2** a person: *lucky sod*. — **sod all** (*vulg slang*) nothing at all. — **sod it, them**, etc. (*vulg slang*) an expression of annoyance. — *v* **sod off**, **-*dd*-** (*intr*; *vulg slang*) to go away. [**sodomite**]

sodding *adj* (*vulg slang*) a general term of disparagement.

Sod's law *n* (*slang*) the facetious saying stating that if something can go wrong, it will go wrong, or that the most inconvenient thing that could happen is what is most likely to happen.

soda *n* **1** a common name given to any of various compounds of sodium in everyday use, e.g. sodium carbonate (**washing soda**) or sodium bicarbonate (**baking soda**). **2** soda water. **3** (*US*) a fizzy soft drink of any kind. [Lat]

soda bread *n* bread in which the raising ingredient is baking soda, not yeast.

soda fountain *n* (*US*) a counter in a shop from which fizzy drinks, ice-cream and snacks are served.

soda water *n* water made fizzy by the addition of carbon dioxide, widely used as a mixer with alcoholic spirits.

sodden *adj* **1** heavy with moisture; thoroughly soaked. **2** made lifeless or sluggish, esp. through excessive consumption of alcohol: *drink-sodden brain*.

sodium *n* an element (symbol **Na**), a bluish-white metal of which many compounds exist as everyday substances, including common salt (**sodium chloride**). [**soda**]

sodomy *n* **1** a form of intercourse in which the penis is inserted into the anus of a man or woman; buggery. **2** sexual intercourse between a man and an animal. [*Sodom*, biblical city renowned for vice]

sodomise or **-ize** *v* (*tr*) to practise sodomy on.

sodomite *n* a person who engages in sodomy.

sofa *n* an upholstered seat with a back and arms, for two or more people. [Arabic *suffah*]

soft *adj* **1** easily yielding or changing shape when pressed; pliable. **2** (of fabric, etc.) having a smooth surface producing little or no friction. **3** quiet: *a soft voice*. **4** of little brightness: *soft colours*. **5** kind or sympathetic, esp. excessively so. **6** not able to endure rough treatment or hardship. **7** lacking strength of character; easily influenced. **8** weak in the mind; simple: *soft in the head*. **9** weakly sentimental. **10** (of water) low in or free from mineral salts and so lathering easily. **11** tender; loving: *soft words*. **12** (*coll*) requiring little effort; easy: *a soft job*. **13** (of drugs) not (severely) addictive. **14** with moderate rather than hardline or extreme policies: *the soft left*. **15** (of the consonants *c* and *g*) pronounced as in *dance* and *age* respectively. — *adv* softly: *speaks soft*. — **soft on** (*coll*) **1** lenient towards. **2** infatuated with. [OE *softe*]

softball *n* a game similar to baseball, played with a larger, softer ball.

soft-boiled *adj* (of eggs) boiled for a short while only, leaving the yolk soft.

soft drink *n* a non-alcoholic drink.

soften *v* **-*n*-** (*tr* & *intr*; **up**) to make or become soft or softer. — *n* **softener**.

soft furnishings *n* (*pl*) curtains, rugs and other articles made of fabric.

soft-hearted *adj* kind-hearted and generous; compassionate.

soft option *n* the easier or easiest course of action or job.

soft pedal *n* a pedal on a piano pressed to make the sound from the strings less lingering or ringing

soft-pedal *v* **-*ll*-** (*tr*; *coll*) to tone down, or avoid emphasising or mentioning: *The government were soft-pedalling the scheme's disadvantages*.

soft porn *n* (*coll*) pornography in which sexual acts are not shown or described explicitly.

soft sell *n* the use of gentle persuasion as a selling technique, rather than heavy-handed pressure.

soft-soap *v* (*tr*; *coll*) to speak flatteringly to, esp. in order to persuade or deceive.

soft-spoken *adj* having a soft voice (and usu. mild manner).

soft spot *n* a fondness: *have a soft spot for*.

soft touch *n* (*slang*) a person easily taken advantage of, esp. one giving money willingly.

software *n* computer programs, and the floppy disks, tapes, etc. on which information is recorded, as opposed to the machines themselves. ◇ See also **hardware**.

softwood *n* wood from conifers, e.g. the pine, easily sawn.

softy or **softie** *n* ***-ies*** (*coll*) **1** a person easily upset. **2** a weakly sentimental person. **3** a person not able to endure rough treatment or hardship.

soggy *adj* ***-ier***, ***-iest*** **1** thoroughly wet; saturated. **2** (of ground) waterlogged; boggy. — *adv* **soggily**. — *n* **sogginess**. [Dialect *sog*, bog]

soh *n* (*mus*) in tonic sol-fa, the fifth note of the major scale. [From the first syllable of the word *solve* in a mediaeval Latin hymn, certain syllables of which were used to name the notes of the scale]

soil[1] *n* **1** the upper layer of the earth's land surface, in which plants grow. **2** (*literary*) country; land: *on foreign soil*. [Lat *solum*, ground]

soil[2] *v* (*tr*) **1** to dirty or stain. **2** to bring discredit on; to sully: *soiled reputation*. — *n* **1** a stain. **2** dirt. **3** dung; sewage. [OFr *souil*, wallowing-place]

soirée or **soiree** *n* **1** a formal party held in the evening. **2** (often *facet*) an evening of entertainment of any kind. [Fr *soirée*, evening]

sojourn (*formal*) *n* a short stay. — *v* (*intr*) to stay for a short while. [OFr *sojorner*]

sol[1]. Same as **soh**.

sol[2] *n* (*chem*) a liquid with extremely small particles of a solid suspended in it.

sola *n* an Indian plant, the pith of which was used to make pith helmets. [Hindi]

solace *n* (a source of) comfort in time of disappointment or sorrow. — *v* (*tr*) **1** to provide with such comfort. **2** to bring relief from. — *n* **solacement**. [Lat *solari*, to comfort in distress]

solar *adj* **1** of or relating to the sun. **2** of, by or using energy from the sun's rays: *solar-powered*. [Lat *sol*, sun]

solar battery or **solar panel** *n* a device for converting the sun's light into electrical power, comprising a number of **solar cells**.

solarium *n* ***-riums*** or ***-ria*** **1** a room or establishment equipped with sun-beds. **2** a conservatory or other room designed to allow exposure to sunlight.

solar plexus *n* an area in the abdomen in which there is a concentration of nerves radiating from a central point.

solar system *n* the system of planets, asteroids and comets that radiate around our sun.

sold *past tense* and *past participle* of **sell**. — **sold on** (*coll*) extremely enthusiastic or convinced about.

solder *n* an alloy melted over the join between two metals, hardening quickly to form a seal. — *v* ***-r-*** (*tr*) to join with solder. [Lat *solidare*, to strengthen]

soldering-iron *n* a tool with a probe-like part, usu. electrically heated, used to melt and apply solder.

soldier *n* **1** a member of a fighting force, esp. a national army. **2** a member of an army below officer rank. — *v* ***-r-*** (*intr*) to serve as a soldier. — *v* **soldier on** (*intr*) to continue determinedly in spite of difficulties. — *adj* **soldierly**. [OFr *soudier*, from *soude*, pay]

soldier of fortune *n* a person willing to serve in any army that pays him or her.

sole[1] *n* **1** the underside of the foot. **2** the underside of a shoe or boot, esp. the part not including the heel. **3** the flattish underside of anything. — *v* (*tr*) to fit (a shoe or boot) with a sole. [Lat *solum*, bottom]

sole[2] *n* ***sole*** or ***soles*** a small edible flat-bodied fish of warm waters. [Lat *solea*]

sole[3] *adj* **1** only. **2** exclusive: *has sole rights to the story*. [Lat *solus*, alone]

solely *adv* **1** alone; without others: *solely to blame*. **2** only; excluding all else: *done solely for profit*.

solecism *n* **1** a mistake in the use of language. **2** an instance of bad or incorrect behaviour. — *adj* **solecistic**. [Gr *soloikismos*]

solemn *adj* **1** done, made, etc. in earnest: *a solemn vow*. **2** of a very serious and formal nature; suggesting seriousness: *a solemn occasion*; *solemn music*. **3** (looking) glum or sombre. — *n* **solemnity**. — *adv* **solemnly**. [Lat *sollemnis*, annual, customary, appointed]

solemnise or **-ize** *v* (*tr*) **1** to perform (esp. a marriage) with a formal or religious ceremony. **2** to make solemn. — *n* **solemnisation** or **-z-**.

solenoid *n* a coil of wire made magnetic by passing an electric current through it. [Gr *solen*, tube]

sol-fa *n* a system of musical notation in which the notes of a scale are represented by syllables, esp. *doh*, *ray*, *me*, *fa*, *soh*, *lah* and *ti*, written down or sung. [**sol** (a form of **soh**) + **fa**]

solicit *v* ***-t-*** **1** (*tr*; *formal*) to ask for, or for something from: *solicit aid from other countries*; *solicited me for advice*. **2** (*intr*) (of a prostitute) to approach people with open offers of sex for money. **3** (*tr*; *formal*) to require or call for. — *n* **solicitation**. [Lat *solicitare*]

solicitor *n* a lawyer who prepares legal documents, gives legal advice, and (in the lower courts only) speaks on behalf of clients.

Solicitor General *n* **-*tors*** the government law officer next in rank below the Attorney General or Lord Advocate.

solicitous *adj* **1 (about, for)** very anxious or concerned (about or for). **2 (to)** very willing or eager (to). — *adv* **solicitously**.

solicitude *n* **1** anxiety or uneasiness of mind. **2** the state of being solicitous.

solid *adj* **1** in a form other than a liquid or a gas, and resisting changes in shape. **2** of the same nature or material throughout; pure: *a solid oak table*. **3** firmly constructed or attached; not easily breaking or loosening. **4** difficult to undermine or destroy; sound: *solid support for the scheme*. **5** not hollow. **6** without breaks; continuous: *waited for four solid hours*. **7** competent, rather than outstanding: *a solid piece of work*. — *n* **1** a substance that is neither liquid nor gas. **2** a three-dimensional geometric figure. **3** (in *pl*) non-liquid food. **4** (in *pl*) particles of solid matter in a liquid. — *n* **solidity**. — *adv* **solidly**. [Lat *solidus*]

solidarity *n* mutual support and unity of interests and actions among members of a group.

solidify *v* **-*ies*, -*ied*** (*tr* & *intr*) to make or become solid. — *n* **solidification**.

solid-state *adj* (of an electronic device) in which the current flows through solid materials, e.g. transistors or silicon chips, rather than through a vacuum, as it does in electron valves.

solidus *n* a printed line sloping from right to left, e.g. separating alternatives, as in *and/or*; a stroke or slash mark. [Lat]

soliloquy *n* **-*ies*** **1** an act of talking to oneself, esp. a speech in a play, etc. in which a character reveals thoughts or intentions to the audience by talking aloud to him- or herself. **2** the use of such speeches as a device in drama. [Lat *solus*, alone + *loqui*, to speak]

soliloquise or **-ize** *v* (*intr*) to speak a soliloquy.

solipsism *n* (*philos*) the theory that one's own self is the only thing whose existence one can be sure of. — *n* **solipsist**. [Lat *solus*, alone + *ipse*, self]

solitaire *n* **1** any of several games for one player only, esp. one whose object is to eliminate pegs or marbles from a board and leave only one. **2** a single gem in a setting on its own. **3** (esp. *US*) the card game patience. [Fr; see ety. for **solitary**]

solitary *adj* **1** single; lone. **2** preferring to be alone; not social. **3** without companions; lonely. **4** remote; secluded. — *n* **1** a person who lives alone, esp. a hermit. **2** (*coll*) solitary confinement. — *n* **solitariness**. [Lat *solitarius*, from *solus*, alone]

solitary confinement *n* imprisonment in a cell by oneself.

solitude *n* the state of being (esp. pleasantly) alone or secluded. [Lat *solitudo*, from *solus*, alone]

solo *n* **-*os*** a piece of music, or a passage within it, for a single voice or instrument, with or without accompaniment. — *adj* performed alone, without assistance or accompaniment. — *adv* alone: *fly solo*. — *n* **soloist**. [Ital, from Lat *solus*, alone]

solstice *n* either of the times when the sun is furthest from the equator, the longest day (**summer solstice**, around June 21 in the northern hemisphere) and the shortest day (**winter solstice**, around December 21 in the northern hemisphere). [Lat *solstitium*, the standing still of the sun]

soluble *adj* **1** capable of being dissolved. **2** capable of being solved or resolved. — *n* **solubility**. [Lat *solubilis*]

solute *n* a dissolved substance. [Lat *solutus*, from *solvere*, to loosen]

solution *n* **1** (the act of finding) an answer to a problem or puzzle. **2** a liquid which has a solid or gas dissolved in it. **3** the act of dissolving or the state of being dissolved: *the solution of*; *in solution*. [Lat *solutio*]

solve *v* (*tr*) to discover the answer to (a puzzle) or a way out of (a problem). — *adj* **solvable**. [Lat *solvere*, to loosen]

solvent *adj* **1** able to pay all one's debts. **2** able to dissolve one or more substances. — *n* a solvent substance. — *n* **solvency**.

solvent abuse *n* the inhaling of the fumes from certain solvents, e.g. glues, for their intoxicating effects.

Som. *abbrev* Somerset.

somatic *adj* (*med*, *biol*, etc.) **1** of the body, rather than the mind. **2** of the body, as opposed to reproduction: *somatic cells*. [Gr *soma*, body]

sombre *adj* **1** sad and serious; grave. **2** dark and gloomy. **3** suggesting seriousness, rather than light-heartedness. — *adv* **sombrely**. [Fr, perhaps from Lat *sub*, under + *umbra*, shade]

sombrero *n* **-*os*** a man's straw or felt hat with a very wide brim, popular in Mexico. [Span, from *sombra*, shade]

some *adj* **1** denoting an unknown or unspecified amount or number of. **2** of unknown or unspecified nature or identity: *some problem with the engine*. **3** quite a lot of: *been waiting for some time*. **4** at least a little: *Try to feel some excitement*. **5** a poor example of: *Some friend you are!* **6** (*coll*) an excellent or impressive example of: *That was some shot!* — *pron* **1** certain unspecified things or people: *Some say he should resign*. **2** an unspecified amount or number: *Give him some, too*. — *adv* **1** to an unspecified extent: *play some more*. **2** approximately: *some twenty feet deep*. [OE *sum*]

somebody *pron* **1** an unknown or unspecified person; someone. **2** a person of importance: *tried to be somebody*.

someday *adv* at an unknown or unspecified time in the future.

somehow *adv* **1** in some way not yet known. **2** for a reason not easy to explain.

someone *pron* somebody.

something *pron* **1** a thing not known or not stated: *Take something to eat*. **2** an amount or number not known or not stated: *something short of a thousand people*; *aged about forty something*. **3** a person or thing of importance: *make something of oneself*; *make something out of a casual remark*. **4** a certain truth or value: *There is something in what you say*. **5** (*coll*) an impressive person or thing: *That meal was really something!* — *adv* to some degree; rather: *The garden looks something like a scrapyard.* — **something of** to some extent: *She's something of a local celebrity*.

sometime *adv* at an unknown or unspecified time in the future or the past.

sometimes *adv* occasionally.

somewhat *adv* rather; a little. — **somewhat of** to some extent.

somewhere *adv* in or to some place or degree, or at some point, not known or not specified.

-some *sfx* **1** causing or producing: *troublesome*. **2** inviting: *cuddlesome*. **3** tending to: *quarrelsome*. **4** a group of the specified number of people or things: *a foursome*. [OE *-sum]*

somersault *n* a leap or roll in which the whole body turns a complete circle forwards or backwards, leading with the head. — *v* (*intr*) to perform such a leap or roll. [Lat *supra*, over + *saltus*, leap]

somnambulism *n* (*formal*) sleepwalking. — *n* **somnambulist**. [Lat *somnus*, sleep + *ambulare*, to walk]

somnolent *adj* (*formal*) sleepy or drowsy; causing sleepiness or drowsiness. — *n* **somnolence**. [Lat *somnus*, sleep]

son *n* **1** a male child. **2** a male person closely associated with, or seen as developing from, a particular activity or set of circumstances: *a son of the Russian revolution*. **3** a familiar (often patronising) term of address used to a boy or man. **4** (*relig*; *cap* with **the**) Jesus Christ considered as the second person in the Holy Trinity. [OE *sunu*]

son-in-law *n* ***sons-*** the husband of one's daughter.

sonar *n* **1** (the equipment used in) a system of underwater navigation and missile targeting in which the echoes from projected sound waves indicate the presence of objects. **2** an echo-sounding navigation technique used by bats and some marine animals. [*so*und *na*vigation *a*nd *r*anging]

sonata *n* a piece of classical music, in three or more movements, for a solo instrument, esp. the piano. [Ital, from *sonare*, to sound]

son et lumière *n* a dramatic night-time outdoor spectacle with lights, music and narration on a particular theme, often staged at and presenting the history of a famous building. [Fr, sound and light]

song *n* **1** a set of words to be sung, usu. with accompanying music. **2** the musical call of certain birds. **3** singing: *poetry and song*. **4** a bargain price: *going for a song*. — **make a song and dance about** (*coll*) to make an unnecessary fuss about. [OE *sang*]

songbird *n* any of various kinds of bird with a musical call.

songster *n* (*old*) a talented (esp. male) singer.

songstress *n* (*old*) a talented female singer.

song thrush *n* a common European thrush, well known for its tuneful call.

sonic *adj* **1** relating to or using sound or sound waves. **2** travelling at (approximately) the speed of sound. [Lat *sonus*]

sonic boom *n* a loud explosive noise heard when the shock wave produced by an aircraft travelling faster than the speed of sound reaches the ground.

sonnet *n* a poem with fourteen lines of ten or eleven syllables each and a regular rhyming pattern. [Ital *sonetto*]

sonny *n* a familiar (often condescending) term of address used to a boy or man. [**son**]

sonorous *adj* **1** sounding impressively loud and deep. **2** giving out a deep clear sound when struck: *a sonorous bell*. **3** (of language) impressively eloquent. — *n* **sonority** or **sonorousness**. [Lat *sonare*, to sound]

soon *adv* **1** in a short time from now or from a stated time. **2** quickly; with little delay. **3** willingly: *would sooner pay the fine than go to prison*. — **as soon as** at or not before the moment when: *will pay you as soon as I receive the goods*. — **as soon ... as** used to state that the first alternative is slightly preferable to the second: *would just as soon die as marry him*. — **no sooner ... than** immediately after: *No sooner had I mentioned his name than he appeared*. — **no sooner said than done** (of a request, promise, etc.) immediately fulfilled. — **sooner or later** eventually. [OE *sona*]

soot *n* a black powdery substance produced when coal or wood is burned; smut. — *adj* **sooty, *-ier*, *-iest***. [OE *sot*]

soothe *v* (*tr*) **1** to bring relief from (a pain, etc.). **2** to comfort or calm (someone). — *adj* **soothing**. [OE *gesothian*, to confirm as true]

soothsayer *n* a person who predicts the future; a seer. — *v* (*intr*) **soothsay**. [Archaic *sooth*, truth + **say**]

sop *n* **1** (often in *pl*) a piece of food, esp. bread, dipped in a liquid, e.g. soup. **2** something given or done as a bribe or in order to pacify someone. — *v* ***-pp-*** (*tr*; **up**) to mop or soak (up). [OE *sopp*]

sophism *n* a convincing but false argument or explanation, esp. one intended to deceive. — *n* **sophist**. — *n* **sophistry, *-ies***. [Gr *sophisma*, clever device, from *sophia*, wisdom]

sophisticate *v* (*tr*) to make sophisticated. — *n* a sophisticated person. — *n* **sophistication**. [Lat *sophisticare*, to adulterate]

sophisticated *adj* **1** having or displaying a broad knowledge and experience of the world, esp. of artistic and intellectual things; appealing to or frequented by people with such knowledge and experience. **2** complex and subtle: *sophisticated weaponry*; *sophisticated arguments*.

sophomore *n* (esp. *US*) a second-year student at a school or university. [Gr *sophos*, wise + *moros*, foolish]

soporific *adj* **1** causing sleep. **2** extremely slow and boring: *a soporific speech*. — *n* a sleep-inducing drug. [Lat *sopor*, deep sleep + *facere*, to make]

sopping *adj* & *adv* thoroughly (wet); soaking. [**sop**]

soppy *adj* **-ier**, **-iest** (*coll*) weakly sentimental. — *adv* **soppily**. — *n* **soppiness**. [**sop**]

soprano *n* **-os** **1** (a person with) a singing voice of the highest pitch for a woman or a boy. **2** a musical part for such a voice. **3** a musical instrument high or highest in pitch in relation to others in its family. [Ital, from Lat *supra*, above]

sorbet *n* a dish of sweetened fruit juice, frozen and served as a kind of ice-cream; a water ice. [Fr, from Arabic *sharbah*, drink]

sorcery *n* the performing of magic using the power of supernatural forces, esp. of black magic using the power of evil spirits. — *n* **sorcerer**. — *n* **sorceress**. [OFr *sorcerie*]

sordid *adj* **1** repulsively filthy; squalid. **2** morally revolting; ignoble. [Lat *sordidus*, dirty]

sore *adj* **1** painful when touched; tender. **2** (esp. *US*) angry or resentful. — *n* a diseased spot or area, esp. an ulcer or boil. — **stick out like a sore thumb** (*coll*) to be embarrassingly obvious or noticeable; to be awkwardly different or out of place. [OE *sar*]

sorely *adv* acutely; very much.

sore point *n* a subject causing much anger or resentment when raised.

sorghum *n* a thick-stemmed Eastern tropical grass whose grain is used as a cereal and to make syrup. [Ital *sorgo*]

sorority *n* **-ies** a women's club or society, esp. any of several such societies in a US university. [Lat *soror*, sister]

sorrel[1] *n* any of various sour-tasting herbs of the dock family, used medicinally and in salads. [OFr *sorele*, from *sur*, sour]

sorrel[2] *adj* of a reddish-brown or light chestnut colour. — *n* a horse of this colour. [OFr *sorel*]

sorrow *n* **1** (**for**) grief or deep sadness because of one's own or another's loss or disappointment. **2** (**to**) a cause of this. — *v* (*intr*) to have or express such feelings. — *adj* **sorrowful**. — *adv* **sorrowfully**. [OE *sorg*]

sorry *adj* **-ier**, **-iest** **1** (**for**) feeling regret or shame. **2** (**for**) feeling pity or sympathy, often implying contempt. **3** pitifully bad: *in a sorry state*. **4** contemptibly bad; extremely poor: *a sorry excuse*. — *interj* **1** used as an apology. **2** (as a question) used to ask for what was just said to be repeated. [OE *sarig*, wounded, influenced in meaning by **sorrow**]

sort *n* **1** a kind, type or class. **2** (*coll*) a person: *not a bad sort*. — *v* (*tr*) **1** to arrange into different groups according to type or kind. **2** (*coll*) to put right. **3** (*coll*) to deal with, esp. to punish. — **a sort of** something like a: *a sort of bottle with a tube attached*. — **of a sort** or **of sorts** of an inferior or not-altogether-typical kind: *an author of a sort*; *a container of sorts*. — **out of sorts** (*coll*) **1** slightly unwell. **2** in a bad mood. — **sort of** (*coll*) rather; in a way; to a certain extent: *feeling sort of embarrassed*. — *v* **sort out** (*tr*) **1** to separate out from a mixed collection into a group or groups according to kind. **2** to put into order; to arrange. **3** to resolve the difficulties relating to; to put right. **4** (*coll*) to deal with, usu. by punishing. [Lat *sortis*, a lot, from *sortiri*, to draw lots]

sortie *n* **1** a sudden attack by besieged troops. **2** an operational flight by a single military aircraft. **3** (*coll*) a short trip to an unpleasant or unfamiliar place. — *v* **-ieing** (*intr*) to make a sortie. [Fr, from *sortir*, to go out]

SOS *n* **1** a ship's or aircraft's call for help, consisting of these letters repeated in Morse code. **2** (*coll*) any call for help. [Letters chosen for ease of transmission and recognition in Morse code]

sostenuto *adv* & *adj* (*mus*) in a steady flowing way, without cutting short any notes. [Ital, sustained]

sot *n* (*old*) a person who is continually drunk. — *adj* **sottish**. [OFr]

sotto voce *adv* **1** in a quiet voice, so as not to be overheard. **2** (*mus*) very softly. [Ital, below the voice]

sou *n* **1** a former French coin of low value. **2** (*coll*) the smallest amount of money: *haven't a sou*. [Fr]

sou' *in cmpds* (esp. *naut*) south: *a sou'wester*.

soubrette *n* a minor female part in a play, esp. that of an impudent, flirtatious or intriguing maid. [Fr, from Provençal *soubreto*, coy]

soubriquet. See **sobriquet**.

soufflé *n* a light sweet or savoury baked dish, a frothy mass of whipped egg-whites with other ingredients mixed in. [Fr, from *souffler*, to puff up]

sough *n* & *v* (*intr*) (to make) the sighing sound of wind blowing through trees. [OE *swogan*, to rustle]

sought *past tense* and *past participle* of **seek**.

sought-after *adj* desired; in demand.

souk *n* a market-place in Muslim countries. [Arabic *suq*]

soul *n* **1** the non-physical part of a person, with personality, emotions and intellect, widely believed to survive in some form after the death of the body. **2** emotional sensitivity; ordinary human feelings of sympathy: *a singer with no soul*; *cruelty* *committed by brutes with no soul.* **3** essential nature: *recognise the soul of the political movement.* **4** motivating force; leader: *the soul of the revolution.* **5** **(of)** a perfect example; a personification: *She's the soul of discretion.* **6** (*coll*) a person: *a kind old soul.* **7** soul music. — *adj* of or relating to Black American culture: *soul food.* [OE *sawol]*

soul-destroying *adj* **1** extremely dull, boring or repetitive. **2** extremely difficult to tolerate or accept emotionally.

soulful *adj* having or expressing deep feelings, esp. of sadness. — *adv* **soulfully**.

soulless *adj* **1** having no emotional sensitivity or ordinary human sympathy. **2** (of a task, etc.) for which no human qualities are required; extremely monotonous or mechanical. **3** (of a place) bleak; lifeless.

soul mate *n* a person with whom one shares the same feelings, thoughts and ideas.

soul music *n* a jazzier, more mainstream type of blues music, typically earthy and emotional in tone, usu. dealing with love.

soul-searching *n* critical examination of one's own conscience, motives, actions, etc.

sound[1] *n* **1** disturbances in the air caused by vibrations, information on which is transmitted to the brain by the sense of hearing. **2** a thing heard; a noise. **3** audible quality: *The guitar has a nice sound.* **4** the mental impression created by something heard: *don't like the sound of that.* **5** aural material, e.g. spoken commentary and music, accompanying a film or broadcast: *sound editor.* **6** (*coll*) volume or volume control, esp. on a television set. **7** (often in *pl*; *slang*) music, esp. pop: *sounds of the 60s.* — *v* **1** (*tr* & *intr*) to (cause to) produce a sound. **2** (*intr*) to create an impression in the mind when heard: *sounds like fun.* **3** (*tr*) to pronounce: *doesn't sound his h's.* **4** (*tr*) to announce or signal with a sound: *sound the alarm.* **5** (*tr*; *med*) to examine by tapping or listening. ◇ See also **sound**[3] (sense **2**). — *v* **sound off** (*intr*; *coll*) to state one's opinions forcefully, esp. one's complaints angrily. [Lat *sonus*]

sound barrier *n* increased air resistance met by an aircraft at around the speed of sound, requiring a huge increase in power for a small increase in speed.

soundbite *n* a brief segment on television news in which a reporter, or a political figure, etc., delivers a short succinct report or statement.

sound-box *n* the hollow body of a violin, guitar, etc.

sound effects *n* (*pl*) artificially produced sounds matching actions in film, broadcasting or theatre.

sounding-board *n* **1** a board over a stage or pulpit directing the speaker's voice towards the audience. **2** a means of testing the acceptability or popularity of ideas or opinions.

soundtrack *n* **1** a band of magnetic tape along the edge of a cinematographic film, on which the sound is recorded. **2** a recording of the music from a film or broadcast.

sound[2] *adj* **1** not damaged or injured; in good condition; healthy. **2** sensible; well-founded; reliable: *sound advice.* **3** acceptable or approved of. **4** thorough: *a sound beating.* **5** (of sleep) deep and undisturbed. — *adv* deeply: *sound asleep.* — *adv* **soundly**. [OE *gesund*]

sound[3] *v* (*tr*) **1** to measure the depth of (esp. the sea). **2** (*med*) to examine (a hollow organ, etc.) with a probe. ◇ See also **sound**[1] (sense **5**). — *n* a probe for examining hollow organs. — *v* **sound out** (*tr*) to try to discover the thoughts or intentions of. [OFr *sonder*]

sounding *n* **1** the act of measuring depth, esp. of the sea. **2** a depth measured. **3** (often in *pl*) a sampling of opinions or (e.g. voting) intentions.

sound[4] *n* a narrow passage of water connecting two seas or separating an island and the mainland; a strait. [OE *sund*]

soup *n* a liquid food made by stewing meat, vegetables or grains. — *adj* **soupy**, ***-ier***, ***-iest***. — **in the soup** (*slang*) in trouble or difficulty. — *v* **soup up** (*tr*; *coll*) to make changes to (a vehicle or its engine) to bring increases in speed or power. [OFr *soupe*]

soup kitchen *n* a place where volunteer workers supply free food to people in need.

soupçon *n* (*literary* or *facet*) the slightest amount; a hint or dash. [Fr, suspicion]

sour *adj* **1** having an acid taste or smell, similar to that of lemon juice or vinegar. **2** rancid or stale because of fermentation: *sour milk.* **3** sullen; miserable: *sour-faced old man.* **4** bad, unsuccessful or inharmonious: *The marriage turned sour.* — *v* (*tr* & *intr*) to make or become sour, esp. bad, unsuccessful or inharmonious. — *adv* **sourly**. [OE *sur*]

sour cream *n* cream deliberately made sour by the action of bacteria, for use in savoury dishes.

sour grapes *n* (*sing*) envy and resentment in the form of pretended dislike or disapproval of the thing or person envied.

sourpuss *n* (*coll*) a habitually sullen or miserable person.

source *n* **1** the place, thing, person or circumstance from which anything begins or develops; origin. **2** the point where a river or stream begins. **3** a person, or a book or other document, providing information or evidence. [Lat *surgere*, to rise]

souse *v* (*tr*) **1** to soak or cook in liquid. **2** to pickle. **3** to plunge in a liquid. **4** to make thoroughly wet; to drench. — *n* **1** an act of sousing. **2** the liquid in which food is soused. **3** (esp. *US*) pickle; any pickled food. [OGer *sulza*]

soused *adj* (*slang*) drunk.

soutane *n* the robe or cassock worn by a Roman Catholic priest. [Fr, from Lat *subtus*, beneath]

south *n* (often with **the**; sometimes *cap*) the direction to the right of a person facing the rising sun in the northern hemisphere, directly opposite north, or any part of the earth, a country, a town, etc. lying in this direction. — *adv* towards the south. — *adj* **1** of, facing or lying in the south; on the side or in the part nearest the south. **2** (of wind) blowing from the south. [OE *suth*]

southbound *adj* travelling south; of or for traffic travelling south: *southbound carriageway*.

south-east and **south-west** *n* **1** the direction midway between south and east or south and west. **2** (with **the**; often *cap*) an area lying in this direction. — *adv* in this direction. — *adj* of, facing or lying in the south-east or south-west. — *adj* **south-eastern** and **south-western**.

south-easterly and **south-westerly** *adj* & *adv* **1** south-east or south-west. **2** (blowing) from the south-east or south-west. — *n* **-ies** a wind blowing from the south-east or south-west.

southerly *adj* & *adv* south. — *n* **-ies** a south wind.

southern *adj* south; of, facing or lying in the south. — *adj* **southernmost**.

southerner *n* a native or inhabitant of a southern region or country.

the southern lights *n* (*pl*) the aurora australis.

southpaw (*coll*) *n* a left-handed person, esp. a left-handed boxer (i.e. one who leads with the right hand). — *adj* left-handed.

the South Pole *n* the southernmost point of the earth's axis of rotation, in Antarctica.

the South Sea *n* the southern part of the Pacific Ocean.

southward *adj* travelling towards the south. — *adv* (also **southwards**) towards the south.

south-west, **south-westerly** and **south-western** see **south-east**, **south-easterly**.

souvenir *n* a thing bought, kept or given as a reminder of a place, person or occasion; a memento. [Fr]

sou'wester *n* a seaman's waterproof hat with a large flap-like brim at the back. [Contraction of **south-wester**]

sovereign *n* **1** a supreme ruler or head, esp. a monarch. **2** a former British gold coin worth £1. — *adj* **1** having supreme power or authority: *a sovereign ruler*. **2** politically independent: *a sovereign state*. **3** outstanding; unrivalled; utmost: *sovereign intelligence*. [OFr *sovrain*]

sovereignty *n* **-ies** **1** supreme and independent political power or authority. **2** a politically independent state.

soviet *n* **1** any of the councils that made up the local and national governments in the former Soviet Union. **2** (usu. *cap*) a native or inhabitant of the former Soviet Union. — *adj* (*cap*) of the former Soviet Union. [Russ *sovet*, council]

sow[1] *v* ***sowed***, ***sown*** or ***sowed*** (*tr*) **1** to plant (seed); to plant (land) with (crops of a particular kind). **2** to introduce or arouse: *sowed (the seeds of) doubt in his mind*. [OE *sawan*]

sow[2] *n* an adult female pig. [OE *sugu*]

soya bean *n* an Asian bean eaten as a vegetable and as a meat substitute when processed, and used as a source of oil and flour. [Jap *sho-yu*]

soy sauce *n* a salty brown sauce made from soya beans, widely used in Eastern (esp. Chinese) cooking. [Chin *shi-yu*, salt bean oil]

sozzled *adj* (*coll*) drunk.

spa *n* **1** a mineral water spring. **2** a town where such a spring is (or was once) located. [*Spa*, Belgian town]

space *n* **1** the three-dimensional medium in which all physical things exist. **2** a portion of this; room: *enough space in the garden for a pool*. **3** an interval of distance; a gap. **4** an empty place: *a space at our table*. **5** a period of time: *within the space of ten minutes*. **6** (also **outer space**) the region beyond the earth, in which other planets and stars are located; the universe. — *in cmpds* of, or for use or travel in, the region beyond the earth: *spacesuit*; *spaceship*. — *v* (*tr*; **out**) to arrange with intervals, or greater intervals, of distance or time between each. — **spaced out** (*slang*) in a dazed or stupefied state because of, or as if through, taking drugs. ◇ See also **spatial**. [Lat *spatium*]

the space age *n* the present period in history, in which travel in space has become possible. — *adj* (**space-age**) **1** technologically very advanced. **2** having a futuristic appearance.

Space Invaders® *n* any of various video games in which players use buttons or levers to fire at invading creatures descending the screen.

spaceman and **spacewoman** *n* a male or female traveller in space.

space platform or **station** *n* a large structure built in space, for use as a stopping-off point in space travel or as a base for observation and research.

space shuttle *n* an aircraft-like space vehicle designed to make repeated journeys into space.

space-time continuum *n* reality regarded as having four dimensions — length, breadth, height and time.

spacious *adj* having ample room or space; extending over a large area. — *n* **spaciousness**.

spade[1] *n* **1** a long-handled digging tool with a broad metal blade which is pushed into the ground with the foot. **2** a child's toy version of this, usu. of plastic: *bucket and spade*. — **call a spade a spade** to speak plainly, without politely softening the impact of one's words. [OE *spadu*]

spadework *n* hard or boring preparatory work.

spade[2] *n* **1** any of the suit of playing-cards that carries an emblem like a black inverted heart. **2** (in *pl*) this suit. **3** (*offensive slang*) a Black person. [Gr *spathe*, broad blade]

spaghetti *n* pasta in the form of long thin string-like strands. [Ital, from *spago*, cord]

spaghetti western *n* a western film shot in Europe with an international cast, typically by an Italian director, typically violent and melodramatic.

spake (*old*) *past tense* of **speak**.

Spam® *n* tinned processed meat made mainly from pork. [*sp*iced h*am*]

span *n* **1** the length between the supports of a bridge or arch. **2** a measure of length equal to the distance between the tips of thumb and little finger on an extended hand, conventionally taken as nine inches. **3** (often *in cmpds*) length from end to end in distance or time: *the wingspan of an aircraft*; *the timespan of the war*. — *v* **-nn-** (*tr*) to extend across or over. [OE *spann*]

spangle *n* a small piece of glittering material, esp. a sequin. — *v* **1** (*tr*) to decorate (e.g. a garment) with spangles. **2** (*intr*) to glitter. [OE *spang*, clasp]

Spaniard *n* a native or citizen of Spain. ◇ See also **Spanish**. [OFr *Espaignart*]

spaniel *n* any of several breeds of dog with long drooping ears and a silky coat. — *adj* expressing unwavering devotion or subservience: *his spaniel eyes*. [OFr *espaigneul*, Spanish dog]

Spanish *n* **1** (*pl*) the people of Spain. **2** their language, also spoken in the southern US and Central and S America. — *adj* of the people or their language. [*Spain* + **-ish**]

Spanish guitar *n* the type of guitar usu. used for playing classical and folk music.

the Spanish Main *n* (*formerly*) (the coast of) the Caribbean Sea.

spank *v* (*tr*) to strike or slap with the flat of the hand, esp. on the buttocks, usu. as a punishment. — *n* such a slap. [Imit.]

spanking *n* a series of spanks. — *adv* (*coll*) absolutely; strikingly: *a spanking new watch*. — *adj* (*coll*) **1** brisk: *a spanking pace*. **2** impressively fine; striking.

spanner *n* a tool for turning a nut or bolt, a lever with a shaped end. — **throw a spanner in the works** to frustrate or upset a plan or system. [Ger, from *spannen*, to stretch]

spar[1] *n* a strong thick pole of wood or metal, esp. one used as a mast or beam on a ship. [Norse *sperra*]

spar[2] *v* **-rr-** (*intr*; **with**) **1** to engage in boxing practice (with a partner); to box against an imaginary opponent, for practice. **2** to engage in lively (esp. friendly) argument. [Perhaps OFr *esparer*, to kick out]

sparring partner *n* **1** a person with whom a boxer practises. **2** a person with whom one enjoys a lively argument.

spar[3] *n* (usu. *in cmpds*) any of various translucent non-metallic minerals splitting easily into layers: *feldspar*; *fluorspar*. [OGer]

spare *adj* **1** held in reserve as a replacement. **2** available for use; unoccupied: *a spare seat next to me*. **3** lean; thin. **4** frugal; scanty. — *v* (*tr*) **1** to afford to give or give away. **2** to refrain from harming, punishing, killing or destroying: *spare his life*, *his feelings*. **3** to avoid causing or bringing on: *will spare your blushes*. **4** to avoid incurring: *no expense spared*. — *n* a duplicate kept in reserve for use as a replacement. — **go spare** (*slang*) to become mad with anger. — **to spare** left over; surplus to what is required. [OE *sparian*]

spare part *n* a part, for a machine, etc., held in reserve to replace an existing identical part that becomes faulty.

spare ribs *n* (*pl*) ribs of pork with only a small amount of meat on them.

spare tyre *n* **1** an extra tyre carried to replace a punctured tyre. **2** (*coll*) a band of fat just above a person's waist.

sparing *adj* economical or frugal, often to the point of inadequacy or meanness. — *adv* **sparingly**.

spark *n* **1** a tiny red-hot glowing particle thrown off by burning material, or by the friction between two hard (esp. metal or stone) surfaces. **2** an electrical charge flashing across a gap between two conductors. **3** a trace, hint or glimmer: *not a spark of intelligence*. **4** a lively, witty or intelligent person: *a bright spark*. — *v* (*intr*) to throw off sparks. — *v* **spark off** (*tr*) to cause to begin; to stimulate or provoke. [OE *spærca*]

spark plug or **sparking plug** *n* an electrical device in a vehicle engine that produces a spark to ignite the air and petrol mixture.

sparkle *v* (*intr*) **1** to give off sparks. **2** to shine with tiny points of bright light. **3** (of wine, etc.) to give off bubbles of carbon dioxide; to effervesce. **4** to be impressively lively or witty. — *n* **1** an act of sparkling; sparkling appearance. **2** liveliness; vivacity; wit. — *adj* **sparkling**. [Dimin. of **spark**]

sparkler *n* **1** a hand-held firework that gives off sparks. **2** (*coll*) a diamond or other impressive jewel.

sparrow *n* **1** any of a family of small brown or grey birds similar to finches. **2** (*in cmpds*) applied to some similar small birds: *hedge sparrow*. [OE *spearwa*]

sparrow-hawk *n* a short-winged bird of prey of the falcon family.

sparse *adj* thinly scattered or dotted about; scanty. — *adv* **sparsely**. — *n* **sparseness** or **sparsity**. [Lat *spargere*, to scatter]

spartan *adj* **1** (e.g. of living conditions) austere; frugal; harshly basic. **2** militaristic. — *n* a spartan person. [*Sparta*, ancient Greek city]

spasm *n* **1** a sudden uncontrollable jerk caused by a contraction of the muscles. **2** a short period of activity; a spell. **3** a sudden burst of emotion: *spasm of anger*. [Gr *spasma*, contraction]

spasmodic *adj* occurring in or consisting of short periods; not constant or regular; intermittent. — *adv* **spasmodically**.

spastic *n* **1** a person suffering from spastic paralysis. **2** (*derog slang*) a clumsy or useless person. — *adj* affected with spastic paralysis. [Gr *spastikos*; see ety. for **spasm**]

spastic paralysis *n* permanent uncontrollable jerky muscle movement caused by injury to the muscle-controlling part of the brain.

spat[1]. See **spit**[1].

spat[2] (*coll*) *n* & *v* **-tt-** (*intr*) (to engage in) a minor fight or quarrel. [Probably imit.]

spat[3] *n* either of a pair of cloth coverings fitting round the ankles and over the tops of the shoes. [Abbrev. of obsolete *spatterdash*, long gaiter protecting trousers from mud splashes]

spate *n* a sudden rush or increased quantity; a burst. — **in spate** (of a river) fast-flowing due to flooding.

spatial *adj* of or relating to space. [Lat *spatium*, space]

spatter *v* **-r-** (*tr* & *intr*) to splash in scattered drops or patches. — *n* **1** a quantity spattered. **2** the act of spattering.

spatula *n* a mixing or spreading tool with a broad blunt (often flexible) blade. [Lat *spatula*, broad blade]

spawn *n* the eggs of frogs, fish and molluscs, laid in water in a soft transparent jelly-like mass. — *v* **1** (*intr*) (of frogs, fish, etc.) to lay eggs. **2** (*tr*) to give rise to; to lead to: *The film's success spawned several sequels*. [OFr *espandre*, to shed]

spay *v* (*tr*) to remove the ovaries from (a female animal). [OFr *espeier*, to cut with a sword]

speak *v* ***spoke*, *spoken*** **1** (*tr* & *intr*; **to, with**) to utter (words); to talk. **2** (*intr*; **to**) to (be willing to) talk to (someone, each other): *They haven't spoken for years*. **3** (*intr*) to make a speech. **4** (*tr*) to (be able to) communicate in (a particular language): *speaks French*. **5** (*intr* with **of**) to make mention (of); to refer (to): *folk songs speaking of ancient customs*. **6** (*intr*) to convey meaning: *Actions speak louder than words*. — **be on speaking terms** to be sufficiently friendly or familiar to hold a conversation. — *v* **speak for** (*tr*) to speak (esp. to give an opinion) on behalf of: *I like it, but I can't speak for them*. — **speak for itself** to have an obvious meaning; to need no further explanation or comment. — **speak one's mind** to say boldly what one thinks. — *v* **speak out** (*intr*) **1** to speak openly; to state one's views forcefully. **2** to speak up. — *v* **speak up** (*intr*) to speak more loudly. — **to speak of** worth mentioning: *received no education to speak of*. [OE *specan*]

speakeasy *n* ***-ies*** (*slang*) a bar or other place selling alcohol illicitly during Prohibition.

speaker *n* **1** a person who speaks, esp. one making a formal speech. **2** a loudspeaker. **3** (*cap*) the person presiding over debate in a law-making assembly, e.g. the House of Commons.

spear *n* **1** a weapon consisting of a long pole with a sharp (esp. metal) point, for throwing from the shoulder. **2** a spiky plant shoot, e.g. a blade of grass. — *v* (*tr*) to pierce with, or as if with, a spear. [OE *spere*]

spearhead *n* the leading part of an attacking force. — *v* (*tr*) to lead (a movement, campaign or attack).

spearmint *n* **1** a common variety of mint plant, from which a flavouring is made for use in sweets, toothpaste, etc. **2** the flavouring.

spec[1]: **on spec** (*coll*) as a gamble, in the hope of success: *wrote to them on spec, asking for a job*. **[speculation]**

spec[2] *n* (*coll*) specification.

special *adj* **1** distinct from, esp. better than, others of the same kind; exceptional. **2** designed for a particular purpose. **3** not ordinary or common: *special circumstances*. **4** particular; great: *make a special effort*. — *n* a special thing or person, e.g. an extra edition of a newspaper or a train running a particular service. — *adv* **specially**. [Lat *specialis*]

Special Branch *n* a British police department dealing with matters of political security.

special constable *n* a member of a reserve police force, called upon e.g. in times of national emergency.

special delivery *n* a delivery of post outside normal delivery times.

special education the education of children with special needs, esp. those physically or mentally handicapped.

specialise or **-ize** *v* **1** (*intr*; **in**) to devote all one's efforts to, or reserve one's best efforts for, one particular activity, field of study, etc. **2** (*tr*) to adapt to be used for a specific purpose. — *n* **specialisation** or **-z-**. — *adj* **specialised** or **-z-**. — *n* **specialist**.

specialism *n* **1** a subject of study one specialises in. **2** the act of specialising in some subject.

speciality *n* ***-ies*** (also, esp. *NAm*, **specialty**) **1** a thing specialised in: *Seafood is the restaurant's speciality*. **2** a special feature, service or product.

special licence *n* a licence allowing a marriage to take place at short notice, without the usual legal formalities.

special school *n* a school designed for the teaching of children with particular needs, esp. arising from physical or mental handicaps.

specie *n* (*tech*) money in coin form, as distinct from notes. [Lat *in specie*, in kind]

species *n* **-ies 1** a group of closely related organisms able to breed together; a subdivision of a genus. **2** a kind or type. [Lat, kind, appearance]

specific *adj* **1** of a particular nature; precisely identified. **2** precise in meaning; not vague. — *n* **1** (usu. in *pl*) a specific detail, e.g. of a plan or scheme. **2** a drug used to treat a specific disease. — *adv* **specifically**. [Lat *species*, kind + *facere*, to make]

specification *n* **1** (often in *pl*) a detailed description of a thing built or constructed. **2** the nature and quality of the parts that it is made up of: *a car with a hi-tech specification.* **3** the act of specifying.

specific gravity *n* a measure of the density of a liquid, e.g. beer, consisting of the ratio of the weight of a fixed volume of the liquid to the weight of the same volume of water.

specify *v* **-ies**, **-ied** (*tr*) **1** to refer to or identify precisely. **2** to state as a condition or requirement. [Ety. as for **specific**]

specimen *n* **1** a sample or example of something, esp. an object studied or put in a collection. **2** a sample of blood, urine or tissue on which medical tests are carried out. **3** (*coll*) a person of a particular kind: *an ugly specimen.* [Lat, from *specere*, to see]

specious *adj* seeming to be good, sound or just, but really false or flawed: *specious arguments.* — *n* **speciousness** or **speciosity**. [Lat *species*, appearance]

speck *n* a small spot, stain or particle. [OE *specca*]

speckle *n* a little spot, esp. one of several on a different-coloured background. — *v* (*tr*) to mark with speckles. — *adj* **speckled**. [Dimin. of **speck**]

specs *n* (*pl*; *coll*) spectacles.

spectacle *n* **1** a thing seen; a sight, esp. impressive, wonderful or ridiculous. **2** a public display or exhibition. **3** (in *pl*) a pair of lenses held in a frame over the eyes, used to correct faulty eyesight. — **make a spectacle of oneself** to behave in a way that attracts public ridicule or scorn. [Lat *spectaculum*, from *specere*, to look at]

spectacular *adj* **1** impressively striking to see or watch. **2** remarkable; dramatic. — *n* a spectacular show or display. — *adv* **spectacularly**. [Ety. as for **spectacle**]

spectator *n* a person who watches an event or incident. [Lat, from *spectare*, to look]

spectate *v* (*intr*) to be a spectator; to look on.

spectre *n* **1** a visible ghost; an apparition. **2** a haunting fear; the threat of something unpleasant. — *adj* **spectral**. [Fr, from Lat *specere*, to look at]

spectrometer *n* an instrument for measuring spectra in terms of wavelength and energy. [**spectrum** + **-meter**]

spectroscope *n* an instrument for producing and observing spectra. [**spectrum** + **-meter**]

spectrum *n* ***spectra*** or **-*rums* 1** the range of colours — red, orange, yellow, green, blue, indigo and violet — that make up white light, separately visible when the light is passed through a prism. **2** any full range: *the whole spectrum of human emotions.* [Lat, appearance]

speculate *v* (*intr*) **1** (**on**, **about**) to make guesses; to consider possibilities. **2** to make (risky) purchases, e.g. of property or stocks and shares, in the hope of quickly making profitable sales. — *n* **speculation**. — *adj* **speculative**. — *n* **speculator**. [Lat *speculari*, to look out]

sped. See **speed**.

speech *n* **1** the ability to speak. **2** a way of speaking: *slurred speech.* **3** that which is spoken; spoken language. **4** a talk addressed to other people. [OE *spec*]

speechify *v* **-ies**, **-ied** (*intr*; *coll*) to make (esp. long and boring) speeches.

speechless *adj* temporarily unable to speak, because of surprise, shock, emotion, etc.

speech therapy *n* the treatment of speech and language disorders. — *n* **speech therapist**.

speed *n* **1** rate of movement or action. **2** quickness; rapidity: *with speed.* **3** a gear setting on a vehicle: *five-speed gearbox.* **4** a photographic film's sensitivity to light. **5** (*slang*) amphetamines. — *v* ***sped*** (*intr*) **1** to move quickly. **2** to drive at a speed higher than the legal limit. — **at speed** quickly. — *v* **speed up** (*tr* & *intr*) to (cause to) increase in speed. [OE *sped*]

speedboat *n* a motor boat capable of high speeds.

speed bump *n* a low hump across a road intended to slow down traffic.

speed limit *n* the maximum speed a vehicle may legally travel at on a given (stretch of) road.

speedometer *n* an instrument in a vehicle that shows the speed the vehicle is travelling at.

speed trap *n* a stretch of road over which the police (often secretly) monitor vehicles' speeds in order to catch drivers exceeding the limit.

speedway *n* **1** racing on lightweight motorcycles round a cinder track. **2** the track used.

speedy *adj* **-ier**, **-iest** fast; prompt; without delay. — *adv* **speedily**.

speedo *n* **-os** (*coll*) a speedometer.

speedwell *n* a plant of the foxglove family, with small blue or pink flowers.

spelaeology or **speleology** *n* **1** the scientific study of caves. **2** cave-exploring. [Gr *spelaion*, cave + **-logy**]

spell[1] *v* ***spelt*** or ***spelled*** **1** (*tr* & *intr*) to write or name the letters making up (a word or words) in their correct order. **2** (*tr*) to form (a word) when written in sequence: *B, A, D spells 'bad'*. **3** (*tr*) to indicate: *His angry expression spelt trouble*. — *v* **spell out** (*tr*) **1** to explain clearly and in detail. **2** to read, write or speak the letters of (a word) one by one. [OFr *espeller*]

spelling *n* **1** ability to spell. **2** a way a word is spelt.

spell[2] *n* **1** a set of words which, esp. when spoken, is believed to have magical power. **2** the influence of such power: *cast a spell on someone*. **3** a strong attracting influence; a fascination. [OE, narrative, from *spellian*, to speak or announce]

spellbinding *adj* causing one to be spellbound.

spellbound *adj* completely charmed or fascinated, as if held by magical power.

spell[3] *n* a period, e.g. of illness, work, or weather of a particular kind. [OE *spelian*, to act for another]

spelt. See **spell**[1].

spend *v* ***spent*** **1** (*tr* & *intr*) to use up or pay out (money). **2** (*tr*; **on**) to use or devote (e.g. time or energy). **3** (*tr*) to use up completely; to exhaust: *Her passion was spent*. — **spend a penny** (*coll euph*) to urinate. [Lat *expendere*]

spendthrift *n* a person who spends money freely and carelessly.

spent *past tense* and *past participle* of **spend**. — *adj* used up; exhausted.

sperm *n* **1** any of the millions of fertilising cells contained in semen. **2** semen. [Gr *sperma*, seed]

spermaceti *n* a waxy substance obtained from the head of the sperm whale, used in cosmetics.

spermatozoon *n* ***-zoa*** (*biol*) a sperm (sense **1**).

spermicide *n* a substance that kills sperm, used in conjunction with various methods of contraception, e.g. the condom and the diaphragm.

sperm whale *n* a large whale with a bulbous head that contains the spermaceti for which it is hunted, along with the ambergris in its intestines.

spew *v* (*tr* & *intr*) **1** to vomit. **2** to (cause to) pour or stream out. — *n* vomit. [OE *spiowan*, to spit]

sphagnum *n* ***-na*** a moss growing in boggy areas. [Gr *sphagnos*]

sphere *n* **1** a round solid figure with a surface on which all points are an equal distance from the centre; a globe or ball. **2** a field of activity. **3** range or extent: *extend one's sphere of influence*. **4** a class or circle within society: *moves in a different sphere*. [Gr *sphaira*]

spherical *adj* sphere-shaped.

spheroid *n* a solid figure that is nearly spherical, but not quite.

sphincter *n* a ring of muscle that expands and contracts to open and close the entrance to a cavity in the body: *anal sphincter*. [Gr *sphingein*, to bind tight]

sphinx *n* **1** (*cap*; *Gr mythol*) a monster with the head of a woman and the body of a lioness, that killed travellers who could not solve the riddles it set. **2** a stone carving or other representation of such a monster, esp. (*cap*) the huge monument near the Egyptian pyramids. **3** a mysterious or enigmatic person.

spice *n* **1** any of numerous strong-smelling vegetable substances used to flavour food, e.g. pepper, ginger and nutmeg. **2** such substances collectively. **3** something that adds interest or enjoyment: *Variety is the spice of life*. — *v* (*tr*) **1** to flavour with spice. **2** (**up**) to add interest or enjoyment to. [OFr *espice*]

spicy *adj* ***-ier***, ***-iest*** **1** tasting or smelling of spices; pungent; piquant. **2** (*coll*) dealing with (esp. sexual) scandal.

spick and span *adj* neat, clean and tidy. [From obsolete *spick and span new*, extension of MidE *span new*, brand new]

spider *n* **1** any of numerous varieties of small eight-legged creature, many of which spin silky webs to catch insects for food. **2** a thing resembling this creature, e.g. a multi-pointed rest used in snooker. — *adj* **spidery**. [OE *spithra*, from *spinnan*, to spin]

spider monkey *n* an American tree-dwelling monkey with long thin limbs and a long tail.

spiel *n* (*coll*) **1** a long rambling story, esp. given as an excuse: *gave me this whole spiel about missing the train*. **2** plausible talk, esp. sales patter. [Ger, play]

spiffing *adj* (*old coll*) excellent; splendid.

spigot *n* **1** a plug used to stop up the vent hole in a cask. **2** a tap fitted to a cask. [Provençal *espigot*]

spike[1] *n* **1** a thin sharp point. **2** a pointed piece of metal, e.g. one of several on railings or the soles of running-shoes. **3** (in *pl*) running-shoes with such soles. **4** a large metal nail. — *v* (*tr*) **1** to strike, pierce or impale with a pointed object. **2** (*coll*) to make (a drink) stronger by adding (extra) alcohol. — **spike someone's guns** (*coll*) to spoil someone's plans. [OE *spicing*]

spiky *adj* ***-ier***, ***-iest*** **1** having spikes or pointed ends. **2** (*coll*) bad-tempered. — *adv* **spikily**. — *n* **spikiness**.

spike[2] *n* **1** a long thin flower-head with several small stemless flowers along its length. **2** an ear of corn. [Lat *spica*, ear of corn]

spikenard *n* **1** a sweet-smelling Indian plant with purple flowers. **2** an oil or ointment made from it. [Lat *spica nardi*]

spill[1] *v* ***spilt*** or ***spilled*** **1** (*tr* & *intr*) to (cause to) run or flow out from a container, esp. accidentally. **2** (*intr*) to come or go in large crowds, esp. quickly: *spectators spilling out of the stadium*. **3** (*tr*) to shed (blood, esp. of other people). **4** (*tr*; *coll*) to throw from a vehicle or saddle. — *n* **1** an act of spilling. **2** (*coll*) a fall, esp. from a vehicle or horse. — **spill the beans** (*coll*) to give away information, esp. a secret, usu. inadvertently. [OE *spillan*]

spillage *n* **1** the act of spilling. **2** an amount spilt.

spill[2] *n* a thin strip of wood or twisted paper for lighting a fire, candle, etc.

spilt. See **spill**[1].

spin *v* **-nn-**; ***spun*** **1** (*tr* & *intr*) to (cause to) rotate repeatedly, esp. quickly. **2** (*tr*) to draw out and twist (fibres, etc.) into thread. **3** (*tr*) to construct from thread: *spiders spinning webs*. **4** (*tr*) to throw or strike (a ball) so that it rotates while moving forward, causing deviation through the air or on impact with the ground or a second ball. **5** (*intr*) to have a revolving sensation that disorientates: *My head was spinning*. **6** (*tr*) to dry in a spin-drier. — *n* **1** an act of spinning or a spinning motion. **2** rotation in a ball thrown or struck. **3** a nose-first spiral descent in an aircraft, esp. uncontrolled. **4** (*coll*) a short trip in a vehicle, for pleasure. — *v* **spin out** (*tr*) **1** to prolong. **2** to cause to last longer by economical use. — **spin a yarn** to tell a story, esp. a long improbable one. [OE *spinnan*]

spin bowler *n* (*cricket*) a slow bowler who spins the ball sharply with his fingers as he releases it.

spin-drier or **-dryer** *n* a machine that forces the water out of wet laundry by spinning it at high speed in a revolving drum. — *v* (*tr*) **spin-dry**.

spinner *n* **1** a spin-drier. **2** an angler's lure shaped so as to spin in the water when the line is pulled. **3** (*cricket*) (a ball bowled by) a spin bowler.

spinning-jenny *n* an early type of spinning machine, with several spindles.

spinning-wheel *n* a machine for spinning thread, consisting of a spindle driven by a hand- or foot-operated wheel.

spin-off *n* **1** a side-effect or by-product, esp. valuable. **2** a thing developed from an earlier product or idea, e.g. a television series derived from a successful film.

spina bifida *n* protrusion of the spinal cord through the backbone, a condition existing from birth and often causing permanent paralysis. [Lat, split spine]

spinach *n* **1** a plant of the beet family. **2** its dark green succulent leaves eaten as a vegetable. [OFr *espinache*, from Arabic *isfanakh*]

spinal. See **spine**.

spindle *n* **1** a rod with a notched or tapered end, for twisting the thread in spinning. **2** a pin or axis on which anything turns. [OE *spinel*, from *spinnan*, to spin]

spindly *adj* **-ier**, **-iest** (*coll*) long, thin and frail-looking.

spindrift *n* spray blown from the crests of waves. [Scot variation of obsolete *spoondrift*, from *spoon*, to be blown by the wind + **drift**]

spine *n* **1** the series of small interlinking bones forming a flexible column along the backs of many animals. **2** the narrow middle section of a book's cover, covering the part where the pages are fastened in. **3** a projecting thorn-like growth on a plant or animal. **4** (*coll*) courage; strength of character: *He's got no spine*. [Lat *spina*, thorn]

spinal *adj* of or relating to the spine.

spinal column *n* the spine.

spinal cord *n* a cord-like mass of nerve tissue running along the spine and connecting the brain to nerves in all other parts of the body.

spine-chilling *adj* (*coll*) frightening; scary. — *n* **spine-chiller**.

spineless *adj* **1** having no spine; invertebrate. **2** (*coll*) lacking courage or strength of character.

spiny *adj* **-ier**, **-iest** **1** (of plants or animals) covered with spines. **2** troublesome; difficult to deal with: *a spiny problem*.

spinet *n* a musical instrument like a small harpsichord. [Ital *spinetta*]

spinnaker *n* a large triangular sail set at the front of a yacht.

spinney *n* **-eys** a small wood. [Lat *spinetum*, thorn-hedge]

spinster *n* a woman who has never been married, esp. when elderly. — *n* **spinsterhood**. [MidE *spinnestere*, woman who spins thread]

spiny. See **spine**.

spiral *n* **1** the pattern made by a line winding outwards from a central point in near-circles of ever-increasing size. **2** the pattern made by a line winding downwards from a point in near-circles of the same or ever-increasing size, as if round a cylinder or cone. **3** a curve or course following such a pattern. **4** a gradual but continuous rise or fall, e.g. of prices. — *adj* of the shape or nature of a spiral. — *v* **-ll-** (*intr*) to follow a spiral course or pattern. — *adv* **spirally**. [Gr *speira*, coil]

spire *n* a tall thin structure tapering upwards to a point, esp. a tower on a church roof. [OE *spir*, shoot, sprout]

spirit *n* **1** the force within a person that is or provides the will to live: *sad news broke his spirit*. **2** this force as an independent part of a person, widely believed to survive the body after death, and sometimes visible as a ghost. **3** a supernatural being without a body: *evil spirits*. **4** one's thoughts, concerns, etc. (as opposed to one's actual presence): *be with you in spirit, though not in person*. **5** (usu. in *pl*) emotional state; mood: *in high spirits*. **6** overall atmosphere or feeling generated by several people together: *enter into the spirit of the party*; *team spirit*. **7** courage; liveliness or vivacity. **8** the underlying essential meaning or intention as distinct from literal interpretation: *in accordance with the spirit, not the letter, of the law*. **9** a distilled alcoholic liquid for drinking, e.g. whisky, brandy or gin. **10** (*chem*) a volatile liquid obtained by distillation. — *v* **-t-** (*tr*; **away, off**) to carry or convey mysteriously or magically. [Lat *spiritus*, breath]

spirited *adj* **1** full of courage or liveliness. **2** (*in cmpds*) showing a particular kind of spirit, mood or attitude: *high-spirited*; *public-spirited.*

spirit-lamp *n* a lamp fuelled by methylated or other spirit as opposed to oil.

spirit level *n* a flat-edged bar with a short liquid-filled glass tube set inside it, showing the perfect levelness of a surface on which it is placed when a large bubble in the liquid lies between two markings on the tube.

spiritual *adj* **1** of or relating to the spirit or soul, rather than to the body or to physical things. **2** religious: *a spiritual leader*. — *n* (also **Negro spiritual**) a religious song (of a kind) developed from the communal singing traditions of Black people in the southern US. — *n* **spirituality**. — *adv* **spiritually**. [Lat *spiritualis*; see **spirit**]

spiritualism *n* belief in, or the practice of, communication with the spirits of dead people through a medium, a specially sensitive person. — *n* **spiritualist**.

spirituous *adj* containing alcohol obtained by distillation. **[spirit]**

spit[1] *v* **-tt-**, ***spat*** **1** (*intr*) to throw out saliva from the mouth, often as a gesture of contempt. **2** (*tr*; **out**) to force (e.g. food) out of the mouth. **3** (*tr*) to emit in a short explosive burst: *The frying pan spat hot oil on me*. **4** (*tr*) to speak or utter with hate or violence. **5** (*intr*) (of rain) to fall in light intermittent drops. — *n* **1** saliva spat from the mouth; spittle. **2** (*coll*) spitting image: *He's his father's spit*. — **spit it out** (*coll*) to say what one is thinking, or is hesitating to say. [OE *spittan*]

spit and polish *n* (*coll*) rigorous attention to cleanliness and tidiness, esp. in the armed forces.

spit-and-sawdust *adj* lacking luxury or refinement, like the sawdust-covered floors of many pubs in former times.

spitfire *n* a hot-tempered person, esp. a woman or girl.

spitting image *n* (*coll*) an exact likeness; a double.

spit[2] *n* **1** a long thin metal rod on which meat is skewered and held over a fire for roasting. **2** a long narrow strip of land jutting out into the sea. [OE *spitu*]

spite *n* the desire to hurt or offend; ill-will. — *v* (*tr*) to annoy or offend intentionally. — *adj* **spiteful**. — *adv* **spitefully**. — *n* **spitefulness**. — **in spite of** in opposition to the efforts of; regardless of. **[despite]**

spittle *n* saliva, esp. when spat from the mouth; spit. [OE *spætl*]

spittoon *n* a container for spitting into, esp. a bucket on the floor of a pub in former times.

spiv *n* (*coll*) a man, typically flashily dressed, engaging in small-time trade in illicit or stolen goods. — *adj* **spivvy**, ***-ier***, ***-iest***.

splash *v* **1** (*tr* & *intr*) to cause large drops of (a liquid or semi-liquid substance) to be thrown about. **2** (*intr*) (of such a substance) to fly around or land in large drops. **3** (*tr*) to make wet or dirty with such drops. **4** (*tr*) to print or display boldly: *photograph splashed across the front page*. — *n* **1** a sound of splashing. **2** an amount splashed. **3** a stain made by splashing. **4** an irregular spot or patch: *splashes of colour*. **5** (*coll*) a small amount of liquid; a dash. — **make a splash** to attract much attention, esp. deliberately. — *v* **splash out** (*intr*; *coll*; **on**) to spend a lot of money (on). [Orig. *plash*, probably imit.]

splashdown *n* a landing at sea of the crew capsule of a space rocket. — *v* **splash down** (*intr*).

splat *n* the sound made by a soft wet object striking a surface. — *adv* with this sound: *fell splat on the floor*. [Imit.]

splatter *v* **-r-** (*tr* & *intr*) to splash with or in small scattered drops. — *n* a splashing sound, esp. when repeated or continuous.

splay *v* (*tr*) to spread (e.g. fingers). **[display]**

spleen *n* **1** a small soft organ near the stomach, responsible for purifying the blood. **2** bad temper; spitefulness. [Gr *splen*]

splendid *adj* **1** magnificent; impressively grand or sumptuous. **2** very good; excellent. — *adv* **splendidly**. [Lat *splendidus*, shining, brilliant]

splendiferous *adj* (*coll*) splendid. **[splendour** + *-ferous* from other words with this ending (from Lat *ferre*, to carry)]

splendour *n* the state or quality of being splendid. [Lat *splendor*]

splenetic *adj* **1** (also **splenic**) of or relating to the spleen. **2** bad-tempered; spiteful; full of spleen. **[spleen]**

splice *v* (*tr*) **1** to join (two pieces of rope) by weaving the strands of one into the other. **2** to join (two pieces of film, magnetic tape, etc.) end to end with an adhesive. — *n* a join made in either of these ways. — **get spliced** (*coll*) to get married. [Dut *splissen*]

splint *n* a piece of wood strapped to a broken limb to fix it in position while the bone heals. [ODut *splinte*]

splinter *n* a small thin sharp piece broken off a hard substance, e.g. wood or glass. — *v* **-r-** (*tr* & *intr*) to break into splinters. [Ety. as for **splint**]

splinter group *n* a small (esp. political) group formed by individuals breaking away from a larger one.

split *v* **-tt-**, ***split*** **1** (*tr* & *intr*) to (cause to) break apart or into pieces, esp. lengthways. **2** (*tr* & *intr*; **up**) to divide up or make into separate smaller amounts or groups. **3** (*tr* & *intr*; **up**) to (cause to) break away from each other or from a group through disagreement. **4** (*intr*; *slang*) to go away or leave. **5** (*intr*; **on**; *slang*) to tell tales or inform. — *n* **1** a lengthways break or crack. **2** a separation or division through disagreement. **3** a dessert of fruit, esp. a banana, sliced open and topped with cream or ice-cream. **4** (in *pl* with **the**) an acrobatic leap or drop to the floor with legs splayed in a straight line, each leg at right angles to the torso. — **split the difference 1** to compromise by each making an equal concession. **2** to divide a remaining amount equally. — **split hairs** to make, or argue about, extremely fine and trivial distinctions. — **split one's sides** (*coll*) to laugh uncontrollably. [Dut *splitten*]

split infinitive *n* an infinitive with an adverb between 'to' and the verb, as in *to boldly go*, considered grammatically incorrect by some people.

split-level *adj* consisting of, or existing on, more than one level.

split pea *n* a dried pea split in half, used in soups and stews.

split personality *n* the displaying of two (or more) distinct types of behaviour by a single person, a feature of various mental disorders, esp. schizophrenia.

split second *n* & *adj* (made or occurring in) a fraction of a second: *a split-second decision*.

splitting *adj* (of a headache) very severe.

splodge *n* a large splash, stain or patch. — *v* (*tr*) to mark with splodges.

splurge *n* a spending spree or other extravagance. — *v* (*intr*; **on**) to spend money extravagantly.

splutter *v* **-r- 1** (*intr*) to make spitting sounds and throw out drops of liquid, sparks, etc. **2** (*tr* & *intr*) to speak or say haltingly or incoherently, e.g. through embarrassment. — *n* the act or noise of spluttering. [Orig. **sputter**]

spoil *v* ***spoilt*** or ***spoiled*** **1** (*tr*) to impair, ruin or make useless or valueless. **2** (*tr*) to make selfish and unable to accept hardship or disappointment by consistently indulging all demands or wishes: *a spoilt child*. **3** (*intr*) (of food) to become unfit to eat. — *n* (in *pl*) **1** possessions taken by force; plunder: *the spoils of war*. **2** any benefits or rewards. — **be spoiling for** to seek out (esp. a fight) eagerly. [Lat *spolium*, plunder]

spoiler *n* **1** a flap on an aircraft wing that reduces lift and so assists descent. **2** a fixed horizontal fin on a car that increases its roadholding at high speeds.

spoilsport *n* (*coll*) a person who spoils, or refuses to join in, the fun of others.

spoke[1]. See **speak**.

spoke[2] *n* any of the radiating rods or bars attaching the rim of a wheel to its centre. — **put a spoke in someone's wheel** to upset someone's plans. [OE *spaca*]

spoken *past participle* of **speak**. — *adj* **1** uttered or expressed in speech. **2** (*in cmpds*) speaking in a particular way: *soft-spoken*. — **spoken for 1** reserved; taken. **2** married, engaged, or in a steady relationship.

spokesman (**-men**), **spokeswoman** (**-men**) and **spokesperson** *n* a person chosen to speak on behalf of others. [**speak**]

spoliation *n* robbing; plundering. [Lat *spoliare*]

spondee *n* a foot (= unit of poetical rhythm) consisting of two long syllables. — *adj* **spondaic**. [Gr *spondeios*]

sponge *n* **1** any of various simple sea creatures with porous bodies that attach themselves permanently to rock. **2** the springy fibrous skeleton of any such creature, able to absorb water. **3** a piece of this, or a man-made substitute, used in washing and cleaning. **4** a sponge cake or pudding. **5** an act of cleaning with a sponge. **6** (*coll*) a person who is regularly drunk. — *v* **1** (*tr*) to wash or clean with a sponge and water. **2** (*intr*; **off**, **on**) to live by taking advantage of the generosity of others. **3** (*tr*; **off**) to get by taking such advantage. [Gr *spongia*]

sponge bag *n* a small waterproof bag for carrying toiletries in when travelling.

sponge cake and **sponge pudding** *n* a very light cake or steamed cake-like pudding.

sponger *n* (*coll*) a person who sponges off others.

spongy *adj* **-ier**, **-iest** soft and springy, and perhaps absorbent, like a sponge.

sponsor *n* **1** a person or organisation that finances an event or broadcast in return for advertising. **2** a person who promises a sum of money to a participant in a forthcoming fund-raising event. **3** a person who offers to be responsible for another, esp. a godparent. **4** a person who submits a proposal, e.g. for new legislation. — *v* **-r-** (*tr*) to act as a sponsor for. — *adj* **sponsored**. — *n* **sponsorship**. [Lat *spondere*, to promise]

spontaneous *adj* **1** unplanned and voluntary or instinctive, not provoked or invited by others. **2** occurring naturally or by itself, not caused or influenced from outside. **3** (of a manner or style) natural; not affected or studied. — *n* **spontaneity**. [Lat *sponte*, of one's own accord]

spontaneous combustion *n* the catching fire of a substance as a result of heat generated within it, not applied from outside.

spoof (*coll*) *n* **1** a satirical imitation; a parody. **2** a light-hearted hoax or trick. — *v* (*tr*) to subject to a spoof. [Orig. the name of a hoaxing game]

spook (*coll*) *n* a ghost. — *v* (*tr*) to frighten or startle. [OGer *spok*]

spooky *adj* **-ier**, **-iest** (*coll*) suggestive of ghosts or the supernatural; eerie.

spool *n* a small cylinder on which thread, photographic film, tape, etc. is wound; a reel. [OGer *spole*]

spoon *n* **1** a kitchen utensil with a handle and a round or oval shallow bowl-like part, for eating, serving or stirring food. **2** (also **spoonful**, ***-fuls***) the amount held by a spoon. — *v* **1** (*tr*) to lift (food) with a spoon. **2** (*intr*; *old*) to kiss and cuddle. [OE *spon*]

spoon-feed *v* (*tr*) **1** to feed (e.g. a baby) with a spoon. **2** to supply (someone) with everything needed or required, making any personal effort unnecessary.

spoonerism *n* an accidental, and often comic, slip in speech which reverses the positions of the first sounds of a pair of words, as in *shoving leopard* for *loving shepherd*. [Rev. W A *Spooner* (1844–1930)]

spoor *n* the track or scent left by an animal. [Dut, track]

sporadic *adj* occurring from time to time, at irregular intervals; intermittent. — *adv* **sporadically**. [Gr *sporados*, scattered]

spore *n* a reproductive cell produced by many plants and some micro-organisms, e.g. bacteria, growing into a new individual alone or by fusing with another. [Gr *spora*, seed]

sporran *n* a leather pouch worn hanging in front of the kilt in Scottish Highland dress. [Gaelic *sporan*]

sport *n* **1** any activity or competition designed to test physical skills. **2** such activities collectively. **3** the pleasure or amusement gained from such an activity: *hunting for sport*. **4** good-humoured fun: *did it in sport*. **5** (*coll*) a person who cheerfully accepts defeat, inconvenience or being the butt of jokes: *a good sport*. **6** (*literary*) a person or thing manipulated or controlled by outside influences; a plaything. **7** (*biol*) an animal or plant that varies from the normal type. — *v* (*tr*) to wear or display, esp. proudly. — **make sport of** (*old*) to make fun of. [Shortened from **disport**]

sporting *adj* **1** of or relating to sport: *sporting achievements*. **2** having or displaying fairness or generosity of character. — *adv* **sportingly**. — **a sporting chance** an even chance of success or failure.

sportive *adj* playful.

sports car *n* a small fast car, esp. a two-seater, whose body sits close to the ground.

sports jacket *n* a man's jacket for casual wear.

sportsman or **sportswoman** *n* **1** a person who takes part in sport. **2** a person who plays fair and accepts defeat cheerfully. — *adj* **sportsmanlike**. — *n* **sportsmanship**.

sporty *adj* ***-ier***, ***-iest*** **1** fond of, and often taking part in, sport. **2** (of a car) that looks like or handles like a sports car.

spot *n* **1** a small mark or stain. **2** a drop of liquid. **3** a small amount (esp. of liquid). **4** an eruption on the skin; a pimple. **5** a place. **6** (*coll*) a small amount (of work): *did a spot of ironing*. **7** a place or period within a schedule or programme: *a five-minute comedy spot*. **8** (*coll*) a spotlight. — *v* ***-tt-*** **1** (*tr*) to mark with spots. **2** (*tr*) to see; to catch sight of. **3** (*tr*) to watch for and record the sighting of (e.g. trains). **4** (*tr*) to search for (new talent). **5** (*intr*) (of rain) to fall lightly. — *adj* **spotted**. — *n* **spotter** (esp. *in cmpds*) a person who spots (e.g. trains). — *n* **spotting** (esp. *in cmpds*). — **in a (tight) spot** (*coll*) in trouble or difficulty. — **knock spots off** (*coll*) to be overwhelmingly better than. — **on the spot 1** immediately, and often without warning. **2** at the scene (of some event). **3** in an awkward situation, esp. one requiring immediate action or response: *put someone on the spot*. [Norse *spotti*, small bit]

spot check *n* an inspection made at random and without warning.

spotless *adj* absolutely clean; unblemished. — *adv* **spotlessly**. — *n* **spotlessness**.

spotlight *n* **1** (a lamp casting) a concentrated circle of light on a small area, esp. of a theatre stage. **2** (with **the**) the attention or gaze of others: *put him in the spotlight*. — *v* ***-lit*** or ***-lighted*** (*tr*) **1** to illuminate with a spotlight. **2** to direct attention to; to highlight.

spot-on *adj* (*coll*) **1** exactly right; perfectly accurate. **2** precisely what was required; excellent.

spotted dick *n* suet pudding containing dried fruit.

spotty *adj* ***-ier***, ***-iest*** **1** marked with a pattern of spots. **2** whose skin, esp. of the face, has many spots on it. — *n* **spottiness**.

spouse *n* a husband or wife. [Lat *sponsus*, from *spondere*, to promise]

spout *n* **1** a projecting tube or lip through which liquid flows or is poured. **2** a jet or stream of liquid, e.g. from a fountain or the blowhole of a whale. — *v* **1** (*tr*) to (cause to) flow out in a jet or stream. **2** (*tr & intr*; **on**) to speak or say, esp. at length and boringly. — **up the spout** (*slang*) **1** ruined or damaged beyond repair. **2** (*vulg*) pregnant. [MidE *spouten*]

sprain *v* (*tr*) to injure the muscles of by a sudden twisting or wrenching. — *n* such an injury, causing swelling.

sprang. See **spring**.

sprat *n* a small edible fish of the herring family. [OE *sprot*]

sprawl *v* (*intr*) **1** to sit, lie or fall lazily with the arms and legs spread out wide. **2** to spread or extend in an irregular, straggling, untidy way: *sprawling towns*. — *n* a sprawling position. [OE *spreawlian*, to move convulsively]

spray[1] *n* **1** a fine mist of small flying drops of liquid. **2** a liquid designed to be applied as a mist: *hairspray*. **3** a device for dispensing a liquid as a mist; an atomiser or aerosol. — *v* (*tr*) **1** to apply or dispense (a liquid) in spray form. **2** to apply a spray to. **3** (**with**) to subject to a heavy and widespread stream (of): *sprayed the car with bullets*. [ODut *sprayen*]

spray-gun *n* a container with a trigger-operated aerosol attached, for dispensing liquid, e.g. paint, in spray form.

spray[2] *n* a small branch of a tree or plant with leaves and flowers attached, used for decoration. [Perhaps OE *spræc*, twig]

spread *v* ***spread*** **1** (*tr* & *intr*) to apply, or be capable of being applied, in a smooth coating over a surface. **2** (*tr* & *intr*; **out**) to (cause to) extend or scatter, often more widely or more thinly. **3** (*tr*; **out**) to open (out) or unfold. **4** (*tr* & *intr*) to (cause to) be transmitted or distributed: *spread disease* or *rumours*. — *n* **1** the act or extent of spreading. **2** a food in paste form, for spreading on bread, etc. **3** a pair of facing pages in a newspaper or magazine. **4** (*coll*) a lavish meal. **5** (*coll*) increased fatness around the waist and hips: *middle-aged spread*. [OE *sprædan*]

spread-eagled *adj* with arms and legs stretched wide.

spreadsheet *n* a computer program displaying different batches of figures simultaneously.

spree *n* a period of extravagance or excess, esp. in spending money or drinking alcohol. [Perhaps Scots *spreath*, cattle raid]

sprig *n* a small shoot or twig: *sprig of heather*.

sprightly *adj* **1** lively and quick-moving. **2** performed at a brisk pace. — *n* **sprightliness**. [**sprite**]

spring *v* ***sprang***, ***sprung*** **1** (*intr*) to leap with a sudden quick launching action. **2** (*intr*) to move suddenly and swiftly by elastic force. **3** (*intr*; **up**) to appear or come into being suddenly. **4** (*intr*; **from**) to develop or originate. **5** (*tr*; **on**) to present or reveal suddenly and unexpectedly: *spring a surprise on someone*. **6** (*tr*) to fit (e.g. a mattress) with springs. **7** (*tr*; *slang*) to secure the escape of (a prisoner) from jail. — *n* **1** a metal coil that expands and contracts freely, returning to its original shape when released. **2** a natural outflow of water from the ground. **3** the season between winter and summer, when most plants begin to grow. **4** a sudden vigorous leap. **5** capacity to return to an original shape after pressure is released: *The mattress has lost its spring*. **6** a lively bouncing or jaunty quality: *a spring in his step*. [OE *springan*]

spring balance *n* a device that measures weight by the downward pull on a large spring to which the weighed object is attached.

springboard *n* **1** a board that springs up after being jumped on, used by divers and gymnasts as a launching device. **2** anything that serves to get things moving.

springbok *n* a South African antelope renowned for its high springing leap when running.

spring chicken *n* **1** a very young chicken valued for its tender edible flesh. **2** (*coll*) a young person.

spring cleaning *n* a thorough cleaning of a house, traditionally carried out in spring. — *v* (*tr* & *intr*) **spring-clean**.

springer *n* a large spaniel with a domed head.

spring onion *n* an onion picked when young, while just a tiny white bulb with long thin shoots, usu. eaten raw in salads.

spring tide *n* a tide at which there is the greatest difference between the high and low points, coming after a new and a full moon.

springtime *n* the season of spring.

springy *adj* **-ier**, **-iest** readily springing back into its original shape when released; elastic; resilient. — *n* **springiness**.

sprinkle *v* (*tr*) **1** to scatter in, or cover with a scattering of, tiny drops or particles. **2** to arrange or distribute in a thin scattering: *houses sprinkled around the valley*. [OE *springan*, to spring]

sprinkler *n* a device that sprinkles, esp. one sprinkling water over plants or on a fire to extinguish it.

sprinkling *n* a small amount thinly scattered.

sprint *n* **1** a race at high speed over a short distance. **2** a burst of speed e.g. at the end of a long race. — *v* (*tr* & *intr*) to run at full speed. — *n* **sprinter**. [Norse *sprinta*]

sprit *n* a small diagonal spar used to spread a sail. [OE *spreot*, pole]

spritsail *n* a sail spread wide by a sprit.

sprite *n* a playful fairy; an elf or imp. [OFr *esprit*, spirit]

spritzer *n* a drink of white wine and soda water. [Ger *spritzen*, to spray]

sprocket *n* **1** any of a set of teeth on the rim of a driving wheel, e.g. fitting into the links of a chain or the holes on a strip of film. **2** a wheel with sprockets.

sprout *v* **1** (*tr* & *intr*) to develop (a new growth, e.g. of leaves or hair). **2** (*intr*; **up**) to grow or develop; to spring (up). — *n* **1** a new growth; a shoot or bud. **2** a Brussels sprout. [OE *sprutan*]

spruce[1] *n* **1** an evergreen cone-bearing tree with a thick pyramid-shaped growth of needle-like leaves. **2** the wood of this tree. [Obsolete *Pruce*, Prussia]

spruce[2] *adj* neat and smart, esp. in appearance and dress. — *v* **spruce up** (*tr* & *intr*) to make or become spruce. [From smart 16th-century clothing made of *spruce leather* from *Pruce*, Prussia]

sprung. See **spring**.

spry *adj* **-yer**, **-yest** **1** lively; active. **2** light on one's feet; nimble. — *adv* **spryly**. — *n* **spryness**.

spud *n* (*coll*) a potato. [MidE *spudde*, short knife]

spume *n* & *v* (*intr*) (to make) foam or froth. — *adj* **spumy**, **-ier**, **-iest**. [Lat *spuma*, from *spuere*, to spew]

spun. See **spin**.

spunk *n* **1** (*coll*) courage; mettle. **2** (*vulg slang*) semen. [Irish Gaelic *sponc*, tinder]
spunky *adj* **-ier**, **-iest** (*coll*) courageous; spirited.

spur *n* **1** a device with a spiky metal wheel, fitted to the heel of a horse-rider's boot, dug into the horse's side to make it go faster. **2** anything that urges or encourages greater effort or progress. **3** a spike or pointed part, e.g. on a cock's leg. **4** a ridge sticking out from a range of hills or mountains. — *v* **-rr-** (*tr* with **on**) to urge on. — **on the spur of the moment** suddenly; on an impulse. [OE *spura*]

spurge *n* any of various plants producing a bitter, often poisonous, milky juice formerly used as a laxative. [OFr *espurge*, from Lat *expurgare*, to purge]

spurious *adj* **1** not what it seems or claims to be; false. **2** based on false or mistaken reasoning. [Lat *spurius*, false]

spurn *v* (*tr*) to reject (e.g. a person's love) scornfully. [OE *spurnan*]

spurt *v* (*tr* & *intr*) to (cause to) flow out in a sudden sharp jet. — *n* **1** a jet of liquid suddenly flowing out. **2** a short spell of intensified activity or increased speed.

sputnik *n* a Soviet satellite orbiting the earth. [Name of the first Soviet satellite, literally 'travelling companion']

sputter. Same as **splutter**. [Imit.]

sputum *n* **-ta** saliva, esp. mingled with mucus. [Lat, from *spuere*, to spit]

spy *n* **-ies 1** a person employed by a government or organisation to secretly gather information about political enemies or competitors. **2** a person observing others in secret. — *v* **-ies**, **-ied 1** (*intr*; **on**) to work as a spy. **2** (*intr*; **on**) to watch from a position of hiding. **3** (*tr*) to catch sight of; to spot. — *v* **spy out** (*tr*) to discover or uncover by spying. [OFr *espier*]
spyglass *n* a small telescope.
spyhole *n* a peephole.

sq. *abbrev* square.

squab *n* **1** a young unfledged bird, esp. a pigeon. **2** a short fat person.
squabby *adj* **-ier**, **-iest** short and fat; stumpy.

squabble *v* (*intr*) to quarrel noisily, esp. about something trivial. — *n* a noisy (esp. petty) quarrel.

squad *n* **1** a small group of soldiers, often twelve, drilling or working together. **2** any group of people working together. **3** a set of players from which a sporting team is selected. [Ital *squadra*, square]
squaddy or **squaddie** *n* **-ies** (*slang*) an ordinary soldier; a private.

squadron *n* **1** a group of between 10 and 18 military aircraft, the principal unit of an air force. **2** a group of warships sent on a particular mission. **3** a division of an armoured regiment of soldiers. [Ital *squadrone*; see ety. for **squad**]
squadron leader *n* an air force officer of the rank below wing commander, in charge of a squadron.

squalid *adj* **1** disgustingly filthy and neglected. **2** morally repulsive; sordid. ◇ See also **squalor**. [Lat *squalidus*, dirty]

squall *n* **1** a sudden and short-lived violent wind or storm. **2** a loud cry; a yell. — *v* **1** (*tr* & *intr*) to yell. **2** (of wind) to blow in a squall. — *adj* **squally**.

squalor *n* the state of being squalid. [Lat, roughness]

squander *v* **-r-** (*tr*) to use up wastefully.

square *n* **1** a two-dimensional figure with four sides of equal length and four right angles. **2** anything shaped like this. **3** an open space in a town, shaped (perhaps only vaguely) like this, often including the surrounding buildings. **4** an L- or T-shaped instrument with which angles can be measured or straight lines drawn. **5** the figure produced when a number is multiplied by itself. **6** (*coll*) a person with traditional or old-fashioned values or tastes. — *adj* **1** square-shaped. **2** measured in length and breadth; of an area equal to a square whose sides are the stated length: *an area of three square metres*; *One room is three metres square*. **3** less rounded than normal: *a square jaw*. **4** measuring almost the same in breadth as in length or height: *a squat, square-framed man*. **5** fair; honest: *a square deal*. **6** (also **all square**) equal; with each side owing nothing. **7** complete; outright: *a square denial*. **8** (*coll*) having traditional or old-fashioned values or tastes. — *v* **1** (*tr*) to make square in shape, esp. to make right-angled. **2** (*tr*) to multiply (a number) by itself. **3** (*tr* & *intr*; **up**) to pay off or settle (a debt). ◇ See also **square up to** below. **4** (*tr*) to make the scores in (a match) level. **5** (*tr*; **with**) to get approval or permission for. **6** (*intr*; **with**) to agree or correspond. **7** (*tr*) to mark with a pattern of squares. — *adv* **1** solidly and directly: *hit me square on the jaw*. **2** fairly; honestly. — *adv* **squarely**. — **back to square one** (*coll*) back to the beginning, with no progress made. — **square the circle** to do the impossible. — *v* **square up to** (*tr*) to face up to and prepare to tackle. ◇ See also **square** (*v* sense **3**). [OFr *esquarre*, from Lat *quadra*]
square-bashing *n* (*slang*) military drill on a barracks square.
square bracket *n* either of a pair of printed brackets of the kind used to enclose the etymologies in this dictionary.
square dance *n* a folk dance performed by couples in a square formation.
square leg *n* (*cricket*) (a fielder at) a fielding position level with the batsman, at some distance from him, and facing his back.
square meal *n* a good nourishing meal.
square root *n* the number which, when multiplied by itself, gives the number in question.

squash[1] *v* **1** (*tr*) to crush or flatten by pressing or squeezing. **2** (*intr*; **into**) to force one's body (into a confined space). **3** (*tr*) to suppress or put down (e.g. a rebellion). **4** (*tr*) to force into silence with a cutting reply. — *n* **1** (a drink made by diluting) a concentrated fruit syrup. **2** a crushed or crowded state. **3** (also **squash rackets**) a game for two players on a walled indoor court, played with small-headed long-handled rackets and a small rubber ball. [OFr *esquacer*, to crush]

squashy *adj* **-ier**, **-iest** (*coll*) soft and easily squashed.

squash[2] *n* (esp. *US*) **1** any marrow-like vegetable of the cucumber family. **2** any of the plants bearing them. [Narragansett (N American Indian language) *askutasquash*]

squat *v* **-tt-** (*intr*) **1** to take up, or be sitting in, a low position with the knees fully bent and the weight on the soles of the feet. **2** to occupy an empty building without legal right. — *n* **1** a squatting position. **2** an empty building unlawfully occupied. **3** (*coll*) a squat thrust. — *adj* short and broad or fat. [OFr *esquatir*, to crush]

squatter *n* a person unlawfully occupying an empty building.

squat thrust *n* a fitness exercise in which, from an all-fours position, the feet are jumped forwards so the knees touch the elbows, then back again.

squaw *n* a N American Indian woman or wife. [Massachusett (N American Indian language) *squa*]

squawk *n* & *v* (*intr*) **1** (to utter) a loud croaky cry, like that of a parrot. **2** (to make) a loud protest or complaint. — *adj* **squawky**, **-ier**, **-iest**. [Imit.]

squeak *n* **1** a short high-pitched cry or sound, like that of a mouse or a rusty gate. **2** (also **narrow squeak**) a narrow escape; a victory or success achieved by the slimmest of margins. — *v* (*tr* & *intr*) to utter a squeak or with a squeak. — *n* **squeakiness**. — *adj* **squeaky**, **-ier**, **-iest**. — *v* **squeak through** (*intr*) to succeed or win by the slimmest of margins. [Imit.]

squeal *n* a long high-pitched cry or yelp, like that of a pig or a child in pain. — *v* **1** (*tr* & *intr*) to utter a squeal or with a squeal. **2** (*intr*; *coll*) to inform or tell tales. **3** (*intr*) to complain or protest loudly. — *n* **squealer**. [Imit.]

squeamish *adj* **1** slightly nauseous. **2** easily made nauseous. [OFr *escoymous*]

squeegee *n* a device with a rubber blade for scraping water off a surface, e.g. a window. [**squeeze**]

squeeze *v* **1** (*tr*) to grasp or embrace tightly. **2** (*tr*) to press forcefully, esp. from at least two sides. **3** (*tr*) to press or crush so as to extract (e.g. juice); to extract (e.g. toothpaste) by pressing or crushing. **4** (*intr*; **into**, **through**) to force one's body (into or through a confined space). **5** (*tr*; **out of**) to obtain (something) from (someone) by extortion or persuasion. — *n* **1** an act of squeezing. **2** a crowded or crushed state: *a bit of a squeeze with four on the sofa.* **3** an amount (of fruit juice, etc.) got by squeezing. **4** a restriction, esp. on spending or borrowing money. — *n* **squeezer**. — **put the squeeze on** (*coll*) to pressurise (someone) into giving something. [OE *cwysan*, to press]

squeeze-box *n* (*coll*) an accordion or concertina.

squelch *n* a loud gurgling or sucking sound made by contact with a thick sticky substance, e.g. wet mud. — *v* (*intr*) to make this sound. — *adj* **squelchy**, **-ier**, **-iest**. [Imit.]

squib *n* **1** a small firework that jumps around on the ground before exploding. **2** a satirical criticism or attack; a lampoon. — **a damp squib** a thing that fails to produce the impressive effect expected. [Perhaps imit.]

squid *n* **-id** or **-ids** a sea creature with a long rounded body and ten trailing tentacles.

squiffy *adj* **-ier**, **-iest** (*coll*) slightly drunk; tipsy.

squiggle *n* a wavy scribbled line. — *adj* **squiggly**, **-ier**, **-iest**. [Perhaps **squirm** and **wriggle**]

squint *n* **1** the condition of having one or both eyes set slightly off-centre, preventing parallel vision. **2** (*coll*; **at**) a quick look; a peep. — *v* (*intr*) **1** to be affected by a squint. **2** to look with eyes half-closed; to peer. — *adj* **1** squinting. **2** (*coll*) not properly straight or centred. [Perhaps Dut *schuinte*, slant]

squire *n* **1** an owner of a large area of rural land, esp. the chief landowner in a district. **2** (*coll*) a term of address used between men. [**esquire**]

squirm *v* (*intr*) **1** to wriggle. **2** to feel or show embarrassment, shame or nervousness, often with slight wriggling movements of the body. — *n* a squirming movement. [Perhaps connected with **worm**]

squirrel *n* a tree-dwelling rodent with a large bushy tail and grey or reddish-brown fur. [Gr *skiouros*, from *skia*, shade + *oura*, tail]

squirt *v* (*tr* & *intr*) to (make a liquid) shoot out in a narrow jet. — *n* **1** an act of squirting or an amount of liquid squirted. **2** (*coll*) a small or insignificant person, esp. when arrogant. [Imit.]

squish *n* & *v* (*intr*) (to make, or move with) a gentle splashing or squelching sound. [Imit.]

Sr *abbrev* Senior (after a name).

Sr *symbol* (*chem*) strontium.

SRN *abbrev* State Registered Nurse.

SS *abbrev* **1** *Schutzstaffel* (Ger), a paramilitary police force in Nazi Germany. **2** steamship. **3** Saints.

St *abbrev* **1** Saint. **2** Street.

st. *abbrev* stone (the unit of weight).

stab *v* **-bb-** **1** (*tr*) to wound or pierce with a pointed instrument or weapon. **2** (*intr*; **at**) to make a quick thrusting movement with something sharp. **3** (*intr*) to produce a sharp piercing sensation: *stabbing pain.* — *n* **1** an act of stabbing. **2** a stabbing sensation. **3** (*coll*) a try: *have a stab at.* — **stab in the back** to make a treacherous attack on. [MidE]

stabilise or **-ize** *v* (*tr* & *intr*) to make or become (more) stable. — *n* **stabilisation** or **-z-**.

stabiliser or **-izer** *n* **1** a device that steadies a ship or aircraft. **2** (in *pl*) two small wheels fitted to the back wheel of a child's bicycle to give it added stability. **3** a chemical substance added to food to preserve its shape and texture.

stability *n* the state or quality of being stable. [Lat *stabilitas*]

stable[1] *adj* **1** firmly balanced or fixed; not likely to wobble or fall. **2** firmly established; not likely to be abolished, overthrown or destroyed: *a stable government.* **3** regular or constant; not erratic or changing: *The patient's condition is stable.* [Lat *stabilis*]

stable[2] *n* **1** a building in which horses are kept. **2** a place where horses are bred and trained. **3** (*coll*) a number of people or things with a common background or origin, e.g. a number of athletes trained by the same coach. [Lat *stabulum*]

staccato *adj* & *adv* **1** (*mus*) with notes played as a series of short, abrupt, audibly separate units rather than as a flowing sequence. **2** with, or consisting of, a series of short distinct sounds. [Ital, from *distaccare*, to separate]

stack *n* **1** a large neat pile of hay or straw. **2** any large neat pile. **3** (*coll*; often in *pl*) a large amount. **4** a large industrial chimney: *smokestack.* — *v* (*tr*) **1** to arrange in a stack or stacks. **2** to pre-arrange (playing-cards) in a pack so as to allow cheating. **3** to arrange (circumstances, etc.) to favour or disadvantage a particular person. **4** to arrange (aircraft waiting to land) into a queue in which each circles the airport at a different altitude. [Norse *stakkr*, haystack]

stadium *n* **-iums** or **-ia** a large sports arena with spectators' seats on different tiers. [Gr *stadion*]

staff *n* **1** the total number of employees working in an establishment or organisation. **2** the employees working for or assisting a manager. **3** (*mil*) the officers assisting a senior commander. **4** (***staffs*** or ***staves***) any stick or rod carried in the hand. **5** (also **stave**, ***staves***) the set of lines and spaces on which music is written. — *v* (*tr*) to provide (an establishment) with staff.

staff nurse *n* a qualified nurse next below a sister in rank.

staff sergeant *n* the senior sergeant in an army company.

Staffs. *abbrev* Staffordshire.

stag *n* **1** an adult male deer, esp. a red deer. **2** (*slang*) a person who buys shares in the hope of selling them immediately for a profit. — *adj* male; of or for men only. [OE *stagga*]

stag beetle *n* a beetle with large antler-like jaw parts.

stag party or **night** *n* a party for men only, esp. in honour of a man about to be married.

stage *n* **1** a platform on which a performance takes place. **2** any of several distinct and successive periods. **3** a part of a journey or route. **4** (**the**) the theatre as a profession or art form. **5** (*coll*) a stagecoach. — *v* (*tr*) **1** to present as a performance; to present a performance of (a play). **2** to pre-arrange to happen in a particular way. **3** to organise or hold as an event. [OFr *estage*, storey, tier]

stagecoach *n* a large horse-drawn coach formerly carrying passengers and mail on a regular fixed route.

stage directions *n* (*pl*) instructions relating to actors' movements, and often sound and lighting effects, written as part of the script of a play.

stage fright *n* nervousness felt by an actor (or any other person) about to appear in front of an audience, esp. for the first time.

stagehand *n* a person responsible for moving scenery and props in a theatre.

stage-manage *v* (*tr*) **1** to be the stage manager of (a play). **2** to pre-arrange to happen in a certain way, in order to create a particular effect.

stage manager *n* a person supervising the arrangement of scenery and props for a play.

stage-struck *adj* having an overwhelming desire to be an actor.

stage whisper *n* **1** an actor's loud whisper intended to be heard by the audience. **2** any loud whisper (intended to be) heard by people other than the person addressed.

staging *n* **1** scaffolding, or the planks used for walking on; any temporary platform. **2** the putting on of a play or other spectacle.

stagy *adj* ***-ier***, ***-iest*** theatrical; artificial or affected. — *n* **staginess**.

stagflation *n* inflation in an economy without the expected growth in employment or demand for goods. [**stagnation** + **inflation**]

stagger *v* **-r-** **1** (*intr*) to walk or move unsteadily. **2** (*tr*) to cause extreme shock or surprise to. **3** (*tr*) to arrange so as to take place or begin at different times: *a staggered start to a rally.* — *n* **1** an act of staggering. **2** (in *pl*) a disease of the brain in horses and cattle, causing staggering. **3** (in *pl* with **the**) giddiness. — *adj* **staggering**. [Norse *staka*, to push]

stagnant *adj* **1** (of water) not flowing; dirty and foul-smelling because of not flowing. **2** not moving or developing; dull and inactive. [Lat *stagnum*, pond]

stagnate *v* (*intr*) to be or become stagnant. — *n* **stagnation**.

stagy. See **stage**.

staid *adj* serious or sober in character or manner, esp. to the point of being dull. [Obsolete past participle of **stay**]

stain *v* **1** (*tr* & *intr*) to make or become marked or discoloured, often permanently. **2** (*tr*) to change the colour of (e.g. wood) by applying a liquid chemical. — *n* **1** a mark or discoloration. **2** a liquid chemical applied (e.g. to wood) to bring about a change of colour. **3** (**on**) a cause of shame or dishonour: *a stain on his reputation.* [MidE *steynen*, to paint]

stained glass *n* decorative glass coloured by a chemical process, esp. used in church windows.

stainless steel *n* an alloy of steel and chromium, very resistant to rust.

stair *n* **1** any of a set of indoor steps connecting the floors of a building. **2** (in *pl*) a set of these. [OE *stæger*]

staircase or **stairway** *n* a set of stairs, often including the stairwell.

stairwell *n* the vertical shaft containing a staircase.

stake[1] *n* **1** a stick or post, usu. with one end pointed, knocked into the ground as a support, e.g. for a young tree or a fence. **2** (with **the**; *formerly*) a post to which a person is tied to be burned alive as a punishment; the punishment. — *v* (*tr*) to support or fasten to the ground with a stake. — **stake a claim** to assert or establish a right or ownership. — *v* **stake out** (*tr*) **1** to mark the boundary of (a piece of land) with stakes. **2** (*coll*) to place (a person or a building) under surveillance (*n* **stake-out**). [OE *staca*]

stake[2] *n* **1** a sum of money risked in betting. **2** (**in**) an interest, esp. financial: *have a stake in the project's success.* **3** (in *pl*) a prize, esp. in horse-racing. — *v* (*tr*) **1** to risk as a bet. **2** to give (esp. financial) support to. — **at stake 1** to be won or lost; wagered. **2** at risk; in danger. [Perhaps ODut *staken*, to place]

stalactite *n* an icicle-like mass of limestone attached to the roof of a cave, etc., formed by the dripping of water containing limestone. [Gr *stalaktos*, a dripping]

stalagmite *n* a spiky mass of limestone sticking up from the floor of a cave, etc., formed by the dripping of water from a stalactite. [Gr *stalagma*, a drop]

stale *adj* **1** (of food) not fresh, and therefore dry and tasteless. **2** (of air) not fresh; musty. **3** overused and no longer interesting or original. **4** out of condition because of over-training or overstudy. — *n* **staleness**. [OFr *estaler*, to halt]

stalemate *n* **1** (*chess*) a position from which a player cannot move without leaving his or her king in check, resulting in a draw. **2** a position, in any contest or dispute, from which no progress can be made nor winner emerge; a deadlock. [MidE *stale*, stalemate + **mate**[2]]

stalk[1] *n* **1** the principal stem of a plant, or the stem by which a leaf, flower or fruit attaches itself to the plant. **2** any slender connecting part. [OE *stalu*]

stalk[2] *v* **1** (*tr*) to hunt, follow or approach stealthily. **2** (*intr*) to walk or stride stiffly or proudly. — *n* **stalker**. [OE *stealcian*]

stalking-horse *n* **1** a horse behind which a hunter hides while approaching the hunted animal. **2** a person or thing used to conceal real plans or intentions, esp. a planned attack.

stall[1] *n* **1** a compartment for housing a single animal in a cowshed, stable, etc. **2** a platform or stand on which goods or services for sale are displayed or advertised. **3** a church seat with arms, esp. one in the choir or chancel. **4** (in *pl*) the seats on the ground floor of a theatre or cinema. **5** an act of stalling a vehicle or its engine. — *v* **1** (*tr* & *intr*) to (cause a motor vehicle or its engine to) cut out through jerky use of the clutch. **2** (*tr*) to put (an animal) into a stall. [OE]

stall[2] *v* **1** (*tr*) to delay. **2** (*intr*) to do something in order to delay something else; to be evasive. — *n* an act of stalling; a delaying tactic. [Obsolete *stale*, decoy]

stallion *n* an uncastrated adult male horse, esp. one kept for breeding. [OFr *estalon*]

stalwart *adj* **1** strong and sturdy. **2** unwavering in commitment and support; reliable. — *n* a stalwart supporter. [OE *stælwierthe*, serviceable]

stamen *n* any of the small stalk-like pollen-bearing parts on the inside of a flower. [Lat, warp thread]

stamina *n* energy needed to withstand prolonged physical (or mental) exertion. [Old plural of **stamen**]

stammer *n* an inability to utter, without hesitation, certain speech sounds at the beginning of words, resulting in a repetition of the sound; the resulting repetition. — *v* **-r-** (*tr* & *intr*) to speak or say with a stammer. [OE *stamerian*]

stamp *v* **1** (*tr* & *intr*; **on**) to bring (the foot) down with force (on). **2** (*intr*) to walk with a heavy tread. **3** (*tr*) to imprint or impress (a mark or design); to imprint or impress (something) with a mark or design. **4** (*tr*) to fix or mark deeply: *The number was stamped on his memory*. **5** (*tr*) to prove to be; to characterise: *His lies stamp him as untrustworthy*. **6** (*tr*) to stick a postage or other stamp on. — *n* **1** (also **postage stamp**) a small piece of gummed paper bearing the official mark of a nation's postal system, stuck to mail to show that postage has been paid. **2** any similar adhesive device. **3** an instrument for stamping a mark or design; the mark or design stamped. **4** a characteristic mark or sign: *The crime bears the stamp of a professional*. **5** an act of stamping the foot. — *v* **stamp out** (*tr*) **1** to put out (a fire) by stamping on it. **2** to put an end to or destroy (e.g. an uprising). [OE *stampian*]

stamp duty *n* a tax on the drawing up of certain legal documents, e.g. those transferring ownership of property.

stamping-ground *n* a place where a certain person or (orig.) wild animal can usu. be found.

stampede *n* a sudden wild rush of frightened animals (or of a frightened or excited crowd of people). — *v* (*intr*) to rush in a herd or crowd. [Span *estampar*, to stamp]

stance *n* **1** position or manner of standing, e.g. when preparing to play a stroke in sport. **2** point of view. [Lat *stare*, to stand]

stanch. Same as **staunch**[2].

stanchion *n* an upright beam or pole serving as a support. [OFr *estançon*]

stand *v* ***stood*** **1** (*intr*; **up**) to be in, or move into, an upright position supported by the legs or a base. **2** (*tr* & *intr*) to place or situate, or be placed or situated. **3** (*intr*) to be a particular height: *The tower stands 300 feet tall.* **4** (*tr*) to tolerate or put up with: *can't stand him.* ◇ See also **stand for** below. **5** (*intr*) to be in a particular state or condition: *I stand corrected. The score stands at 3–1.* **6** (*intr* with **to**) to be in a position (to): *stand to make a lot of money.* **7** (*intr*) to continue to apply or be valid: *The decision stands.* **8** (*intr* with **for**) to be a symbol or representation of. **9** (*intr*; **for**) to be a candidate. **10** (*tr*) to withstand or survive: *stood the test.* **11** (*tr*; *coll*) to buy (something) for (someone): *stood me lunch.* — *n* **1** a base on which something is supported: *a cake-stand.* **2** a stall displaying or advertising goods or services for sale. **3** a structure with sitting or standing accommodation for spectators. **4** a rack or other device on which coats, hats, umbrellas, etc. may be hung. **5** (**against**, **on**) (action indicating) an attitude or opinion resolutely adopted: *take a stand against further building.* **6** an act of resisting attack: *make a stand.* **7** (*cricket*) a partnership between batsmen, expressed in terms of the time it lasts or the runs scored. — *v* **stand by 1** (*intr*; **to**) to be in a state of readiness to act (*n* **standby**). **2** (*tr*) to give support to, or continue to be faithful to, in time of difficulty. **3** (*intr*) to look on without taking the required or expected action: *stood by and watched her drown.* — *v* **stand down** (*intr*) to resign. — *v* **stand for** (*tr*) to tolerate or allow. — *v* **stand in** (*intr*; **for**) to act as a substitute (*n* **stand-in**). — *v* **stand off** (*intr*) to stay some distance away. — **stand one's ground** to maintain one's position resolutely; to refuse to give in. — *v* **stand out** (*intr*) **1** to be noticeable or prominent. **2** (**for**, **against**) to continue to be resolutely in favour of or opposed to. **3** (*intr* with **for**) to refuse to agree or give in, in the expectation of further concessions; to hold out. — *v* **stand up 1** (*intr*) to assume a standing position; to stand. **2** (*intr*) to prove to be valid on examination: *an argument that will stand up in court.* **3** (*tr*; *coll*) to fail to keep an appointment with (esp. a romantic partner). **4** (*intr* with **for**) to be outspoken in one's support for or defence of. **5** (*intr* with **to**) to face or resist (e.g. an opponent) courageously; to withstand (e.g. hard wear or criticism). [OE *standan*]

stand-by, stand-in see **stand by, stand in** above.

standing *n* **1** position, status or reputation. **2** duration. — *adj* **1** done, taken, etc. in or from a standing position: *a standing ovation.* **2** permanent; regularly used: *a standing joke.*

standing order *n* **1** an instruction from an account-holder to a bank to make fixed payments from the account to a third party at regular intervals. **2** an order placed with a shopkeeper for a regular supply of something.

stand-off or **stand-off half** *n* (*Rugby*) a half-back who stands away from the scrum and acts as a link between the scrum-half and the three-quarters.

stand-offish *adj* unfriendly or aloof.

standpipe *n* a vertical pipe leading from a water supply, esp. one providing an emergency supply in the street when household water is cut off.

standpoint *n* a point of view.

standstill *n* a complete stop, with no progress being made at all.

standard *n* **1** an established or accepted model; a thing with which others are compared so as to be measured or judged. **2** a level of excellence, value or quality. **3** (often in *pl*) a principle of behaviour or morality adhered to. **4** a flag or other emblem, esp. one carried on a pole. **5** an upright pole or support. **6** something, esp. a song, that has remained popular over the years. — *adj* **1** of the normal or accepted kind, without variations or additions. **2** typical; average; unexceptional. **3** accepted as supremely authoritative: *the standard text on the subject.* **4** (of language) accepted as correct by educated native speakers. [OFr *estandart*]

standard-bearer *n* **1** a person carrying a flag. **2** the leader of a movement or cause.

Standard Grade *n* in Scotland, (a pass in) an examination replacing the former O grade, usu. taken by pupils after four years of secondary education.

standardise or **-ize** *v* (*tr*) to make (all examples of something) uniform in kind, size, shape, etc. — *n* **standardisation** or **-z-**.

standard lamp *n* a lamp on a pole with a base that sits on the floor.

stank. See **stink**.

stanza *n* a verse in poetry. [Ital]

staple[1] *n* **1** a U-shaped wire fastener for paper, forced through the paper from a special instrument into which it is loaded. **2** a U-shaped metal nail. — *v* (*tr*) to fasten or attach with a staple or staples. [OE *stapol*, post, support]

stapler *n* an instrument for driving staples through paper.

staple[2] *adj* **1** principal; main: *staple foods.* **2** of principal importance as a traded article. — *n* a staple product or ingredient. [ODut *stapel*, shop, warehouse]

star *n* **1** any of the innumerable bodies visible in the night sky as points of light, technically excluding, but loosely taken as including, the planets, comets and meteors. **2** a representation of such a body in the form of a figure with five or more radiating points, often used as a symbol of rank or excellence. **3** (in *pl*) the planets regarded as an influence on people's fortunes. **4** (in *pl*) a horoscope. **5** a celebrity, esp. from the entertainment world. **6** a principal performer. **7** an asterisk. — *v* **-rr- 1** (*tr* & *intr*) to feature or appear as a principal performer. **2** (*tr*) to decorate with stars. **3** (*tr*) to asterisk. — **see stars** to see spots of light before one's eyes, e.g. as a result of a heavy blow to the head. [OE *steorra*]

star-crossed *adj* (*literary*) ill-fated; doomed.

stardom *n* the state of being a celebrity.

stardust *n* an imaginary dust that blinds the eyes to reality and fills them with romantic illusions.

starfish *n* a sea creature with a flat body and usu. five radiating arms.

star fruit *n* the smooth-skinned yellow fruit of a SE Asian tree, the carambola, star-shaped in cross-section.

stargazer *n* (*coll*) **1** (*facet*) an astronomer or astrologer. **2** a daydreamer. — *n* **stargazing.**

starlet *n* a young (esp. film) actress regarded as a star of the future.

starlight *n* the light from the stars. — *adj* **starlit.**

Star of David *n* the symbol of Judaism, a six-pointed star formed by overlapping two equilateral triangles.

starry *adj* **-ier, -iest 1** filled or decorated with stars. **2** shining brightly.

starry-eyed *adj* **1** naïvely idealistic or optimistic. **2** radiantly happy or affectionate.

the Stars and Stripes *n* the national flag of the US.

star-studded *adj* (*coll*) (of the cast of a film, etc.) featuring many well-known performers.

star turn *n* the main item or principal performer in a show.

starboard *n* the right side of a ship or aircraft, as viewed when facing forwards. — *adj* & *adv* of, on or towards the right side. [OE *steorbord*, steering board]

starch *n* **1** a carbohydrate stored in plants in the form of tiny white granules, used in solution with water as a fabric stiffener. **2** food containing this carbohydrate in large quantities, e.g. potatoes and rice. **3** stiffness of manner; over-formality. — *v* (*tr*) to stiffen with starch. [OE *stercan*, to stiffen]

starchy *adj* **-ier, -iest 1** like or containing starch. **2** stiff in manner; over-formal. — *adv* **starchily.** — *n* **starchiness.**

stare *v* (*intr*) to look with a fixed gaze. — *n* **1** an act of staring. **2** a fixed gaze. — **be staring (someone) in the face 1** to be very easy for (someone) to see or realise, if only he or she were to look or think straight. **2** to be unpleasantly imminent. — *v* **stare out** or **down** (*tr*) to cause (a staring person or animal) to look away by staring more steadily and determinedly. [OE *starian*]

stark *adj* **1** severely bare, harsh or simple. **2** plain; unembellished: *the stark truth.* **3** utter; downright. — *adv* utterly; completely. [OE *stearc*, hard, strong]

starkers *adj* (*coll*) stark-naked.

stark-naked *adj* completely naked. [MidE *stert-naked*, from OE *steort*, tail + *nacod*, naked]

starling *n* a small common songbird with dark glossy speckled feathers and a short tail. [OE *stærling*]

start *v* **1** (*tr* & *intr*) to begin; to bring or come into being. **2** (*tr* & *intr*; **up**) to set or be set in motion, or put or be put into a working state. **3** (*intr*; **as, off as, out as**) to be at first. **4** (*intr*; **on, off on, out on**) to begin, e.g. on a journey or in a career. **5** (*tr*; **up**) to establish or set up. **6** (*tr*; **off**) to initiate or get going; to cause or set off. **7** (*intr*; **for, from**) to begin a journey. **8** (*intr*) to flinch or shrink back suddenly and sharply, e.g. in fear or surprise. **9** (*intr*; *coll*; **on, with**) to pick a quarrel. ◇ See also **start on** below. **10** (*tr*) to drive (an animal) from a lair or hiding-place. — *n* **1** the first or early part. **2** a beginning, origin or cause. **3** the time or place at which something starts. **4** an advantage given or held at the beginning of a race or other contest. **5** a help in or opportunity of beginning, e.g. in a career. **6** a sudden flinching or shrinking back. — **for a start** as an initial consideration; in the first place. — *v* **start on** (*tr*) to suddenly become violently hostile towards; to turn on. ◇ See also **start** (*v* sense **9**) above. — **to start with 1** in the beginning. **2** in the first place. [MidE *sterten*]

starter *n* **1** a person who gives the signal for a race to begin. **2** any of the competitors, horses, greyhounds, etc. assembled for the start of a race. **3** a device that puts a machine or engine into motion. **4** (*coll*; often in *pl*) the first course of a meal. — **for starters** (*coll*) in the first place; for a start.

startle *v* (*tr*) **1** to give a sudden fright to. **2** to surprise. — *adj* **startling.** [OE *steartlian*, to stumble or struggle]

starve *v* **1** (*tr* & *intr*) to (cause to) suffer extreme ill-health, or die, through lack of food. **2** (*intr*; *coll*) to be very hungry. **3** (*tr*; **of**) to cause to suffer a severe lack: *starved the project of funds.* **4** (*tr*; **into**) to force (into behaviour of a particular kind) by withholding or preventing access to food. — *n* **starvation**. [OE *steorfan*, to die]

stash (*slang*) *v* (*tr*) to put into a hiding-place. — *n* a hidden supply or store, or its hiding-place.

state *n* **1** the condition, e.g. of health, appearance or emotions, in which a person or thing exists at a particular time. **2** a territory governed by a single political body; a nation. **3** any of a number of locally governed areas making up a nation or federation under the ultimate control of a central government, as in the US. **4** (usu. *cap*; with **the**) the government and all its apparatus, e.g. the civil service and the armed forces. **5** (*coll*) an emotionally agitated condition. **6** (*coll*) a confused or untidy condition. — *adj* **1** of, relating to, or controlled or financed by the State, or a federal state. **2** ceremonial: *a state visit by the Queen*. — *v* (*tr*) **1** to express clearly; to affirm or assert. **2** to specify. — **lie in state** (of a corpse) to be ceremonially displayed to the public before burial. — **the States** the United States of America. [Lat *status*, from *stare*, to stand]

State Enrolled Nurse *n* a nurse qualified to perform many nursing tasks. ◇ See also **State Registered Nurse** below.

stateless *adj* having no nationality or citizenship.

stately *adj* **-ier**, **-iest** noble, dignified and impressive in appearance or manner. — *n* **stateliness**.

stately home *n* a large grand old private house, usu. one open to the public.

statement *n* **1** a thing stated, esp. a formal written or spoken declaration. **2** a record of finances, esp. one sent by a bank to an account-holder detailing the holder's transactions within a particular period. **3** the act of stating.

state of affairs *n* a situation or set of circumstances.

state of play *n* the situation at present.

state of the art *n* the current level of advancement achieved by the most modern, up-to-date technology or thinking in a particular field. — *adj* **state-of-the-art**.

State Registered Nurse *n* (in England and Wales) a nurse with advanced training, qualified to perform all nursing tasks. ◇ See also **State Enrolled Nurse** above and **Registered General Nurse** under **register**.

stateroom *n* **1** a large room in a palace, etc. used for ceremonial occasions. **2** a large private cabin on a ship.

statesman and **stateswoman** *n* an experienced and well-respected (male or female) politician. — *adj* **statesmanlike** and **stateswomanlike**. — *n* **statesmanship** and **stateswomanship**.

static *adj* **1** not moving; stationary. **2** fixed; not portable. **3** tending not to move around or change. **4** relating to statics. — *n* **1** (also **static electricity**) electricity not flowing but lying on a surface, e.g. hair or nylon fabric, produced as a result of friction. **2** atmospheric disturbance in television and radio reception. [Gr *statikos*, bringing to a standstill]

statics *n* (*sing*) the branch of physics dealing with stationary bodies and forces in equilibrium.

station *n* **1** a stopping-place for passenger trains or buses, with facilities for refuelling, ticket-purchasing, etc. **2** a local headquarters or depot, e.g. of a police force. **3** a building equipped for some particular purpose, e.g. electricity generation. **4** a radio or television channel, or the buildings from which it is broadcast. **5** a position within a class structure. **6** a post or place of duty. — *v* **-n-** (*tr*) to appoint to a post or place of duty. [Lat *statio*, from *stare*, to stand]

stationmaster *n* the official in charge of a railway station.

the stations of the Cross *n* (*pl*; *RC Church*) **1** a series of (usu. fourteen) pictures or carvings representing the stages of Christ's journey to Calvary, usu. situated around the inside of a church. **2** a series of prayers made at these.

station wagon *n* (*US*) an estate car.

stationary *adj* **1** not moving; still. **2** not changing. [Ety. as for **station**]

stationer *n* a person or shop selling stationery. [Lat *statio*, shop]

stationery *n* paper, envelopes, pens and other writing materials.

statistics *n* **1** (*sing*) the science dealing with the classification, presentation and interpretation of numerical information. **2** (usu. in *pl*) an item of numerical information collected and presented in an ordered way. — *adj* **statistical**. — *adv* **statistically**. — *n* **statistician**. [Ger *Statistik*, study of political facts and figures, from Lat *status*, state]

statue *n* a sculpted, moulded or cast figure, esp. of a person or animal, usu. life-size or larger, often erected in a public place. [Lat *statua*]

statuesque *adj* like a statue, esp. (of a woman) tall and well-proportioned in figure or dignified and imposing in appearance.

statuette *n* a small statue.

stature *n* **1** height of body. **2** greatness; eminence. [Lat *statura*, from *stare*, to stand]

status *n* **1** rank or position in relation to others, within society, an organisation, etc. **2** legal state, e.g. with regard to adulthood, marriage or citizenship. **3** importance. [Lat]

the status quo *n* the situation as it now is, unchanged. [Lat, the state in which]

status symbol *n* a possession or privilege regarded as an indication of a person's high (esp. social) status.

statute *n* **1** a law made by the legislative assembly of a country and recorded in a formal document. **2** a permanent rule drawn up by the leader or leaders of an organisation. [Lat *statutum*, that which is set up]

the statute book *n* the formal written record of all the laws passed by a parliament, etc.

statutory *adj* **1** required or prescribed by law or a rule. **2** usual or regular, as if prescribed by law. — *adv* **statutorily**.

staunch[1] *adj* loyal; trusty; steadfast. [OFr *estanche*, watertight]

staunch[2] *v* (*tr*) to stop the flow of (esp. blood from a wound). [OFr *estanchier*]

stave *n* **1** any of the vertical wooden strips joined to form a barrel or tub. **2** any (esp. wooden) bar, rod or shaft, e.g. a rung on a ladder. **3** (*mus*) a staff. **4** a verse of a poem or song. — *v* (*tr*) **1** (***staved*** or ***stove***; with **in**) to smash a hole in. **2** (***staved***; with **off**) to delay the onset of; to ward (off). [Back-formation from **staves**, plural of **staff**]

staves. *Pl* of **staff** and **stave**.

stay[1] *v* ***stayed*** **1** (*intr*) to remain in the same place or condition, without moving or changing. **2** (*intr*) to reside temporarily, e.g. as a guest. **3** (*intr*; **to**, **for**) to linger in order to share or join in something: *stay for dinner*. **4** (*tr*) to suspend or postpone (e.g. legal proceedings). **5** (*tr*) to control or restrain (e.g. anger). **6** (*intr*; *Scot*) to reside permanently; to live. — *n* **1** a period of temporary residence; a visit. **2** a suspension of legal proceedings, or a postponement of a legally enforceable punishment: *grant a stay of execution*. — *v* **stay in** (*intr*) to remain indoors, esp. not to go out socially. — **stay put** (*coll*) to remain where one or it is. — *v* **stay up** (*intr*) to remain out of bed beyond one's usual bedtime. [Lat *stare*, to stand]

stay-at-home (*coll*) *adj* tending to prefer the peaceful routine of domestic life to a busy and varied social life. — *n* a stay-at-home person.

stayer *n* (*coll*) a person or animal with great powers of endurance.

staying power *n* stamina; endurance.

stay[2] *n* **1** a prop or support. **2** any of a number of strips of bone or metal sewn into a corset to stiffen it. **3** (in *pl*) a corset stiffened in this way. [OFr *estaye*]

stay[3] *n* a rope or cable with which a pole, etc. is anchored to the ground to keep it upright. [OE *stæg*]

STD *abbrev* **1** subscriber trunk dialling. **2** sexually transmitted disease.

STD code *n* a telephone code for a town or other area, used before a subscriber's individual number when telephoning from outside the area.

stead: **in (someone's) stead** in place of (someone). — **stand (someone) in good stead** to prove useful to (someone). [OE *stede*, place]

steadfast *adj* firm; resolute; determinedly unwavering. — *adv* **steadfastly**. — *n* **steadfastness**. [OE *stede*, place + *fæst*, fixed]

steady *adj* ***-ier***, ***-iest*** **1** firmly fixed or balanced; not tottering or wobbling. **2** regular; constant; unvarying. **3** stable; not easily disrupted or undermined. **4** having a serious or sober character. — *v* ***-ies***, ***-ied*** (*tr* & *intr*) to make or become steady or steadier. — *adv* in a steady manner. — *interj* (also **steady on!**) be careful!; keep calm!; don't be foolish or hasty. — *adv* **steadily**. — *n* **steadiness**. — **go steady** (*coll*; **with**) to have a steady romantic relationship. [Ety. as for **stead**]

steak *n* **1** (a thick slice of) fine quality beef for frying or grilling. **2** beef for stewing or braising in chunks. **3** a thick slice of any meat or fish. [Norse *steik*, roast]

steakhouse *n* a restaurant specialising in beef steaks.

steal *v* ***stole***, ***stolen*** **1** (*tr* & *intr*) to take away (another person's property) without permission or legal right, esp. secretly. **2** (*tr*) to obtain by cleverness or trickery: *steal a kiss*. **3** (*tr*) to fraudulently present (another person's work, ideas, etc.) as one's own. **4** (*intr*) to go stealthily. — *n* (*coll*) **1** a bargain; a thing easily obtained. **2** (esp. *US*) an act of stealing. [OE *stelan*]

stealth *n* **1** softness and quietness of movement, avoiding notice. **2** secretive or deceitful behaviour. — *adv* **stealthily**. — *adj* **stealthy**, ***-ier***, ***-iest***. [Ety. as for **steal** + **-th**]

steam *n* **1** the gas into which water is converted by boiling, invisible but generally becoming visible as a white mist of fine water vapour; the water vapour itself. **2** this gas as a source of mechanical power: *steam-driven*. **3** (*coll*) power, energy or speed: *run out of steam*. — *v* **1** (*intr*) to give off steam. **2** (*tr*) to cook or otherwise treat by exposure to steam. **3** (*intr*) to move under the power of steam. **4** (*intr*; *coll*) to go at speed. — *adj* powered by steam. — **let off steam** to release anger or energy built up inside one. — *v* **steam up** (*tr* & *intr*) (of a transparent or reflective surface) to make or become clouded by tiny droplets of condensed steam. — **steamed up** (*coll*) very angry or excited. — **under one's own steam** by one's own efforts alone. [OE]

steam-boat see **steamship** below.

steamer *n* **1** a ship whose engines are powered by steam. **2** a two-tier pot in which food in the upper tier is cooked by the action of steam from water heated in the lower tier.

steam iron *n* an electric iron in which steam from a built-in water tank is released on to the laundry through holes in the iron's base, to help smooth out creases.

steamroller *n* a large vehicle, orig. and still often steam-driven, with wheels consisting of huge solid metal cylinders, driven over newly made roads to flatten the surface. — *v* (*tr*; *coll*) **1** to use overpowering force or persuasion to secure the speedy movement or progress of. **2** to crush (opposition, etc.).

steamship or **steam-boat** *n* a boat powered by steam.

steamy *adj* **-ier**, **-iest** **1** full of, or made cloudy by, steam. **2** (*coll*) involving or featuring sexual passion; erotic.

steed *n* (*literary*) a horse thought of as something to ride on. [OE *steda*, stallion]

steel *n* **1** a tough yet malleable metal alloy of iron and carbon, with numerous industrial uses. **2** a rough-surfaced rod made of this alloy, on which knives are sharpened by hand. **3** hardness or strength, esp. of a person's character. — *v* (*tr*) to develop, or call upon, qualities of strength and resilience in (esp. oneself). [OE *style*]

steel band *n* a band, of a kind originating in the W Indies, with percussion instruments made from steel petrol drums.

steel blue *n* a deep greyish-blue colour.

steel wool *n* thin strands of steel in a woolly mass, used for polishing and scouring.

steelworks *n* (*sing* or *pl*) a factory where steel is manufactured.

steely *adj* **-ier**, **-iest** **1** hard and unyielding: *a steely gaze*. **2** steel-blue.

steep[1] *adj* **1** rising or sloping sharply. **2** (*coll*) (of a price, rate, etc.) unreasonably high. — *adv* **steeply**. — *n* **steepness**. [OE *steap*]

steepen *v* **-n-** (*tr* & *intr*) to make or become steep or steeper.

steep[2] *v* (*tr* & *intr*) to soak thoroughly in liquid. — **steeped in** deeply and palpably associated with or influenced by. [MidE *stepen*]

steeple *n* **1** a tower forming part of a church or temple, esp. one with a spire. **2** the spire itself. [OE *stepel*]

steeplechase *n* **1** a horse race round a course with hurdles, usu. in the form of man-made hedges. **2** a track race for humans, with very high hurdles and a water jump. — *v* (*intr*) to take part in a steeplechase. — *n* **steeplechaser**.

steeplejack *n* a person who repairs steeples and tall chimneys.

steer[1] *v* **1** (*tr* & *intr*) to guide or control the direction of (a vehicle or vessel). **2** (*tr*) to guide the course or movements of, e.g. with tuition, persuasion or force. **3** (*tr*) to follow (a particular course). — **steer clear of** to avoid. [OE *styran*]

steerage *n* **1** (*old*) the cheapest accommodation on board a passenger ship, traditionally near the rudder. **2** the act or practice of steering.

steering committee *n* **1** a committee deciding on the nature and order of topics to be discussed by a parliament, etc. **2** a committee in charge of the overall direction pursued by a business or other organisation.

steering-wheel *n* a wheel turned by hand to control the wheels of a vehicle or the rudder of a vessel.

steer[2] *n* a young bull or male ox, esp. one castrated and reared for beef. [OE *steor*]

stegosaurus *n* a four-legged plant-eating dinosaur with two rows of diamond-shaped plates sticking up along its back. [Gr *stegos*, roof + *saurus*, lizard]

stein *n* a large metal or earthenware beer mug, often with a hinged lid. [Ger]

stele or **stela** *n* **-lae** an ancient stone pillar or upright slab, usu. carved or engraved. [Gr *stele*]

stellar *adj* of, like, or relating to a star or stars. [Lat *stella*, star]

stem[1] *n* **1** the central part of a plant, growing upward from the root, or the part by which a leaf, flower or fruit is attached to a branch. **2** the long thin supporting part of a wine glass. **3** any long slender part. **4** (*linguistics*) the usu. unchanging base of a word, to which inflectional affixes are added. ◇ See also **root**. — *v* **-mm-** (*intr* with **from**) to originate or spring (from). [OE *stemn*]

stem[2] *v* **-mm-** (*tr*) to stop (the flow of something). [Norse *stemma*]

stench *n* a strong and extremely unpleasant smell. [OE *stenc*, smell]

stencil *n* **1** a drawing or printing plate with parts cut out to form lettering or a design that is copied on to a surface by laying the plate on the surface and inking or painting over the cut out parts. **2** the lettering or design produced in this way. — *v* **-ll-** (*tr*) to print or produce by means of a stencil. [OFr *estinceller*, to sparkle]

sten gun *n* a lightweight portable machine-gun. [*S*hepherd and *T*urpin, designers, and *En*field as in **Bren gun**]

stenography *n* the skill or practice of writing in shorthand. — *adj* **stenographic**. [Gr *stenos*, narrow + *graphein*, to write]

stenographer *n* (*US*) a shorthand typist.

stentorian *adj* (*literary*) (of a voice) very loud, deep and carrying. [*Stentor*, a herald in Greek mythology]

step *n* **1** a single complete action of lifting then placing down the foot in walking or running. **2** the distance covered in the course of such an action. **3** a movement of the foot (usu. one of a pattern of movements) in dancing. **4** (often in *pl*) a single (often outdoor) stair, or any stair-like support used to climb up or down. **5** the sound of a foot being laid on the ground in walking. **6** a single action or measure taken in proceeding towards an end or goal. **7** a degree or stage in a scale or series. **8** a way of walking; gait. **9** (in *pl*) a step-ladder. — *v* **-pp-** (*intr*) **1** to move by taking a step or steps, esp. slowly, quietly or carefully. **2** (**on**) to lay one's foot, often heavily. **3** (**into**) to enter (into) or become involved (in), esp. easily, casually or carelessly. **4** to go or come: *step this way*. — **in step (with)**

1 walking or marching in unison, with corresponding feet hitting the ground at the same time. **2** in harmony or unison. — **out of step (with)** not in step. — **step by step** gradually. — *v* **step down 1** (*intr*) to resign from a position of authority. **2** (*tr*) to reduce the rate, intensity, etc. of. — *v* **step in** (*intr*) **1** to take up a position or role as a substitute or replacement. **2** to intervene in an argument. — *v* **step on** (*tr*; *coll*) to treat harshly or with contempt. — **step on it** (*coll*) to hurry up. — *v* **step out** (*intr*) **1** to walk quickly and confidently with long strides. **2** (*coll*) to go out socially. — *v* **step up** (*tr*) to increase the rate, intensity, etc. of. — **watch one's step 1** to walk with careful steps, avoiding danger. **2** to proceed with caution, taking care not to anger or offend others. [OE *steppe*]

stepladder *n* a short ladder with flat steps, not rungs, made free-standing by means of a supporting frame attached by a hinge at the ladder's top.

stepping-stone *n* **1** a large stone in a stream, etc., with a surface above the water level, stepped on to cross the stream. **2** a means of gradual progress.

step- *pfx* indicating a relationship not by blood but through a second or later marriage or partnership. [OE *steop*, orig. orphan]

stepbrother and **stepsister** *n* the son or daughter of a stepfather or stepmother.

stepchild *n* a stepson or stepdaughter.

stepfather and **stepmother** *n* the second or later husband of a mother or wife of a father.

step-parent *n* a stepfather or stepmother.

stepson and **stepdaughter** *n* the son or daughter of a second or later husband or wife, from an earlier marriage or partnership.

steppe *n* a vast dry grassy (usu. treeless) plain, esp. in SE Europe and Asia. [Russ *step*]

-ster *sfx* denoting a person with regard to some characteristic, activity, membership of a group, etc.: *youngster*; *trickster*; *gangster*.

stereo *n* **1** stereophonic reproduction of sound: *broadcast in stereo*. **2** ***-os*** a hi-fi system giving a stereophonic reproduction of sound. — *adj* stereophonic.

stereo- *comb fm* solid; three-dimensional. [Gr *stereos*, solid]

stereophonic *adj* (of sound) recorded so as to be reproduced with different elements fed through two (or more) loudspeakers, creating the effect of live sound. — *adv* **stereophonically**.

stereoscopic *adj* of, relating to or being the perception of objects as having depth and solidity, owing to a slight difference in point of view between two viewing agents, e.g. the eyes. — *adv* **stereoscopically**.

stereotype *n* **1** an over-generalised idea, impression or point of view allowing for no individuality or variation. **2** a person or thing conforming to such an idea, etc. **3** a solid metal printing plate cast from a mould taken from a plate on which the text consists of individual letters pieced together. — *v* (*tr*) to think of or characterise in an over-generalised way. — *adj* **stereotyped**.

sterile *adj* **1** biologically incapable of producing offspring, fruit or seeds. **2** made free of germs. **3** producing no results; having no new ideas. — *n* **sterility**. [Lat *sterilis*, barren]

sterilise or **-ize** *v* (*tr*) to make sterile. — *n* **sterilisation** or **-z-**.

sterling *n* British money. — *adj* **1** of British money. **2** good quality; worthy; reliable. **3** authentic; genuine. **4** (of silver) of at least 92·5 per cent purity. [OE *steorra*, star, from the markings on early Norman pennies]

stern[1] *adj* **1** extremely strict; authoritarian. **2** harsh, severe or rigorous. **3** unpleasantly serious or unfriendly in appearance or nature. — *adv* **sternly**. — *n* **sternness**. [OE *styrne*]

stern[2] *n* the rear of a ship or boat. [Norse *stjorn*, steering]

sternum *n* ***-nums*** or ***-na*** the breastbone, the broad vertical bone in the chest to which the ribs and collarbone are attached. — *adj* **sternal**. [Gr *sternon*, chest]

steroid *n* **1** any of numerous natural compounds containing carbon, including some vitamins and hormones, many of which control the workings of the body. **2** a drug containing such a compound, esp. one promoting muscle growth, used in medicine and sometimes taken (usu. illegally) by athletes. [**sterol** and **-oid**]

sterol *n* any of various solid naturally occurring insoluble alcohol substances, e.g. cholesterol. [Shortened from **cholesterol** and others]

stertorous *adj* (*formal*) (of breathing) noisy; with a snoring sound. [Lat *stertere*, to snore]

stet *v* ***-tt-*** (*tr*) (used esp. as an instruction in proof-reading) to ignore an earlier instruction to amend or delete (a word, letter, etc.). [Lat, let it stand]

stethoscope *n* an instrument for listening to sounds made inside the body, e.g. the heartbeat, consisting of a small concave disc, placed on the body, with attached tubes carrying the sound to earpieces. [Gr *stethos*, chest + *skopeein*, to look at]

stetson *n* a man's broad-brimmed felt hat with a high crown, concave at the top, worn esp. by cowboys. [John *Stetson* (1830–1903), American hat-maker]

stevedore *n* a person employed to load and unload ships; a docker. [Span *estibador*, packer]

stew *v* **1** (*tr*) to cook (esp. meat) by long simmering. **2** (*tr*) to cause (tea) to become bitter and over-strong by letting it brew for too long. **3** (*intr*; *coll*) to be in a state of worry or agitation. — *n* **1** a dish of food, esp. meat, cooked by stewing. **2** (*coll*) a state of worry or agitation. — **stew in one's own juice** (*coll*) to suffer the consequences of one's own (foolish) actions. [OFr *estuve*, stove]

stewed *adj* (*coll*) drunk.

steward *n* **1** an attendant on a passenger ship or aircraft. **2** a person supervising crowd movements during a sporting event or public march. **3** a person overseeing catering and associated arrangements in a hotel or club. **4** a person employed to manage another person's property and affairs, e.g. on a country estate. **5** a senior official monitoring the conduct of jockeys during a horse race. — *v* (*tr*) to serve as a steward of. [OE *stigweard*, hall-keeper]

stewardess *n* a female attendant on a passenger ship or aircraft.

stick[1] *n* **1** a twig or thin branch taken from or which has fallen from a tree. **2** any long thin piece of wood shaped for a particular purpose, e.g. striking the ball in hockey, or playing a percussion instrument. **3** a long thin piece of anything, e.g. celery. **4** (usu. in *pl*) a piece of furniture, esp. one of few. **5** (*coll*) verbal abuse, criticism or mockery. **6** (in *pl*; *coll*; with **the**) a rural area when considered remote or unsophisticated. **7** (*old coll*) a person. — **get (hold of) the wrong end of the stick** to misunderstand a situation, a statement, etc. [OE *sticca*]

stick insect *n* a tropical insect with a long twig-like body and legs.

stick[2] *v* ***stuck***, ***stuck*** **1** (*tr*; **through, into**, etc.) to push or thrust (esp. something pointed). **2** (*tr*; **on, up**, etc.) to fasten by piercing with a pin or other sharp object: *stick it up with drawing-pins.* **3** (*tr* & *intr*; **on, up**, etc.) to fix, or be or stay fixed, with an adhesive. **4** (*intr*) to remain: *an episode that sticks in my mind.* **5** (*tr* & *intr*) to make or be unable to move; to jam or lock. **6** (*tr*) to confine. **7** (*intr* with **to**) to remain faithful to (e.g. a promise); not to stray from (e.g. the matter under discussion). **8** (*intr*) (of criticism, etc.) to continue to be considered valid. **9** (*tr*; *coll*) to place or put. **10** (*tr*; *coll*) to bear or tolerate. — *v* **stick around** (*intr*; *coll*) to remain or linger. — *v* **stick at** (*tr*) **1** to continue doggedly with. **2** to hesitate or refuse to do for reasons of principle: *will stick at nothing in order to succeed.* — *v* **stick by** (*tr*) to remain loyal to. — **stick in one's throat** (*coll*) to be extremely difficult to say or accept, usu. for reasons of principle. — *v* **stick out 1** (*tr* & *intr*) to (cause to) project or protrude. **2** (*intr*) to be obvious or noticeable; to stand out. **3** (*tr*; *coll*) to endure. **4** (*intr* with **for**) to continue to insist (on), refusing to yield. — *v* **stick together** (*intr*) to remain loyal to and supportive towards each other. — *v* **stick up** (*intr*) **1** (*coll*) to project upwards; to stand up. **2 (for)** to speak or act in defence (of). [OE *stician*]

sticker *n* an adhesive label, esp. one displaying a message or advertisement in the window of a shop, a car, etc.

sticking-plaster *n* adhesive plaster used to dress wounds.

stick-in-the-mud *n* (*coll*) a person boringly opposed to anything new or adventurous.

sticky *adj* ***-ier***, ***-iest*** **1** able or likely to stick to other surfaces. **2** (of weather) warm and humid; muggy. **3** (*coll*) (of a situation, etc.) difficult; awkward; unpleasant. — *n* **stickiness**.

a sticky end *n* (*coll*) an unpleasant end or death.

sticky-fingered *adj* (*coll*) prone to pilfering.

sticky tape *n* a strong tape for binding, fastening or joining, with an adhesive substance on one side.

a sticky wicket *n* (*coll*) a difficult situation to cope with.

stickleback *n* a small spiny-backed fish of northern rivers. [OE *sticel*, prick + **back**]

stickler *n* (**for**) a person who always insists (on). [OE *stihtan*, to set in order]

stiff *adj* **1** not easily bent or folded; rigid. **2** (of limbs, joints, etc.) lacking suppleness; not moving or bending easily. **3** (of punishment, etc.) harsh; severe. **4** (of a task, etc.) difficult; arduous. **5** (of wind) blowing strongly. **6** (of a manner) not natural and relaxed; over-formal. **7** thick in consistency; viscous. **8** (*coll*) (of an alcoholic drink) strong. — *adv* (*coll*) to an extreme degree: *bored me stiff.* — *n* (*slang*) a corpse. — *adv* **stiffly**. — *n* **stiffness**. — **have** or **keep a stiff upper lip** to show or maintain self-control and resignation in the face of disappointment or unpleasantness. [OE *stif*]

stiffen *v* ***-n-*** (*tr* & *intr*) to make or become stiff or stiffer.

stiff-necked *adj* arrogantly obstinate.

stifle *v* **1** (*intr*) to experience difficulty in breathing, esp. because of heat and lack of air. **2** (*tr*) to kill by stopping the breathing; to smother. **3** (*tr*) to suppress (e.g. anger or opposition). [Perhaps OFr *estouffer*, to smother]

stifling *adj* unpleasantly hot or airless.

stigma *n* ***-mas*** or (sense **4**) ***-mata*** **1** shame or social disgrace. **2** a blemish or scar on the skin. **3** (*bot*) the part of a flower that receives pollen, on the end of the style. **4** (in *pl*) marks resembling Christ's crucifixion wounds, said to have appeared on the bodies of certain holy people. [Gr, tattoo-mark, brand]

stigmatise or **-ize** *v* (*tr*) to describe or regard as shameful. — *n* **stigmatisation** or **-z-**.

stile *n* a step, or set of steps, built into a fence or wall. [OE *stigel*]

stiletto *n* ***-os*** **1** (also **stiletto heel**) a high thin heel on a woman's shoe. **2** (*coll*) a shoe with such a heel. **3** a dagger with a narrow tapering blade. [Ital, dimin. of *stilo*, dagger]

still[1] *adj* **1** motionless; inactive. **2** quiet and calm; tranquil. **3** (of a drink) not fizzy. — *adv* **1** continuing as before, now or at some future time. **2** up to the present time, or the time in question; yet. **3** even then; nevertheless. **4** quietly and without movement: *sit still.* **5** (with comparatives) to a greater degree; even: *older still.* — *v* **1** (*tr* & *intr*) to make or become still. **2** (*tr*) to calm, appease or put an end to. — *n* **1** stillness; tranquillity. **2** a photograph, esp. of an actor in or a scene from a cinema film, used for publicity purposes. — *n* **stillness.** [OE *stille*]

stillborn *adj* **1** dead when born. **2** (of a project, etc.) doomed from the start.

still life *n* ***lifes*** **1** a painting, drawing or photograph of an object or objects, e.g. a bowl of fruit, rather than of a living thing. **2** this kind of art or photography.

still[2] *n* an apparatus in which an alcoholic spirit is distilled. **[distil]**

still room *n* **1** a room in which distilling is carried out. **2** a housekeeper's pantry in a large house.

stilt *n* **1** either of a pair of long poles with supports for the feet part way up, on which a person can walk around supported high above the ground. **2** any of a set of props on which a building, jetty, etc. is supported above ground or water level. [MidE *stilte*]

stilted *adj* (of language) unnatural-sounding, esp. over-formal. [Ety. as for **stilt**]

Stilton *n* a strong white English cheese, often with blue veins. [*Stilton*, Cambridgeshire]

stimulate *v* (*tr*) **1** to cause (increased) physical activity in (e.g. an organ of the body). **2** to initiate or get going. **3** to excite or arouse the senses of; to animate or invigorate. **4** to create interest and enthusiasm in (someone). — *adj* **stimulating.** — *n* **stimulation.** [Lat *stimulare*]

stimulant *n* & *adj* (a drug, alcoholic drink or other substance or thing) that has a stimulating effect on the body or mind.

stimulus *n* ***-li*** a thing that stimulates. [Lat, goad]

sting *n* **1** a plant or animal part that can pierce skin and inject poison. **2** the act of injecting poison in this way. **3** the poison injected or wound inflicted. **4** any sharp tingling pain. **5** any sharply wounding quality or effect, e.g. that of a vicious insult. **6** (*slang*) a trick, swindle or robbery. — *v* ***stung*** **1** (*tr*) to pierce, poison or wound with a sting. **2** (*intr*) to produce a sharp tingling pain. **3** (*tr* with **into**) to goad or incite (into action of a particular kind). **4** (*tr*; *slang*) to cheat, swindle or rob; to cheat by overcharging. — *adj* **stinging.** [OE *stingan*, to pierce]

stinging nettle same as **nettle.**

stingray *n* a ray with a long whip-like tail tipped with spikes capable of inflicting severe wounds.

stingy *adj* ***-ier***, ***-iest*** ungenerous; mean; miserly. — *adv* **stingily.** — *n* **stinginess.** [From *stinge*, a dialect form of **sting**]

stink *n* **1** a strong and very unpleasant smell. **2** (*coll*) an angry complaint or outraged reaction; a fuss: *kick up a stink.* — *v* ***stank*** or ***stunk***, ***stunk*** **1** (*intr*) to give off a stink. **2** (*tr*; **out**) to fill (a place) with a stink. **3** (*intr*; *coll*) to be contemptibly bad or unpleasant. **4** (*intr*; *coll*) to be morally disgusting. [OE *stincan*, to smell]

stink bomb *n* a small bomb-like container releasing a foul-smelling gas when broken as a practical joke.

stinker *n* (*coll*) **1** a very difficult task, question, etc. **2** a dishonest, cheating or otherwise unpleasant person.

stinking *adj* **1** that stinks. **2** (*coll*) very unpleasant. — *adv* (*coll*) extremely; disgustingly: *stinking rich.*

stint *v* (*tr* & *intr*; **on**) to be mean or grudging in the giving or supplying (of). — *n* an allotted amount of work. — **without stint** liberally; unreservedly. [OE *styntan*, to dull]

stipend *n* a salary or allowance, esp. one paid to a member of the clergy. [Lat *stipendium*, tax]

stipendiary *n* ***-ies*** & *adj* (a person) receiving a stipend.

stipple *v* (*tr*) **1** to paint or draw in dots or dabs, rather than lines or masses of colour. **2** to give a finish of tiny raised bumps to (wet cement, plaster, etc.), creating a grainy effect. — *n* a pattern produced by stippling. [Dut *stippelen*, dimin. of *stippen*, to dot]

stipulate *v* (*tr*) to state as a necessary condition. — *n* **stipulation.** [Lat *stipulari*]

stir[1] *v* ***-rr-*** **1** (*tr*) to mix or agitate (a liquid or semi-liquid substance) by repeated circular strokes with a spoon or other utensil. **2** (*tr*) to arouse the emotions of; to move. **3** (*intr*) to make a (slight or single) movement. **4** (*tr* with **up**) to cause or provoke (e.g. trouble). **5** (*intr*) to get up after sleeping; to become active after resting. **6** (*intr*; *coll*; also **stir it**) to make trouble. — *n* **1** an act of stirring (a liquid, etc.). **2** an excited reaction; a commotion: *cause a stir.* [OE *styrian*]

stir-fry *v* (*tr*) to cook lightly by brisk frying on a high heat with little oil. — *n* a dish of stir-fried food.

stirrer *n* (*coll*) a person who enjoys stirring up trouble.

stirring *adj* arousing strong emotions.

stir[2] *n* (*slang*) prison.

stir-crazy *n* (*slang*, esp. *US*) emotionally disturbed as a result of being confined, esp. in prison.

stirrup *n* **1** either of a pair of metal loops hanging on straps from a horse's saddle, serving as the rider's footrests. **2** any strap or loop supporting or passing under a foot. [OE *stigrap*, from *stigan*, to mount + *rap*, rope]

stirrup cup *n* an alcoholic drink given to a person, orig. a rider, about to leave.

stirrup pump *n* a portable hand-operated pump that draws water from a bucket, etc., used in fighting small fires.

stitch *n* **1** a single interlinking loop of thread or yarn in sewing or knitting. **2** a complete movement of the needle or needles creating such a loop. **3** any of various ways in which such loops are interlinked. **4** a single interlinking loop of surgical suture. **5** a sharp ache in the side resulting from physical exertion. **6** (*coll*) the least scrap of clothing: *without a stitch on*. — *v* (*tr*; **up**) to join, close (up), or decorate with stitches. — **in stitches** (*coll*) helpless with laughter. — *v* **stitch up** (*tr*; *slang*) to trick, esp. to betray or double-cross. [OE *stice*, prick]

stoat *n* a small brown flesh-eating mammal of the weasel family, called an ermine in its white winter fur. [MidE *stote*]

stock *n* **1** (often in *pl*; **of**) the total amount of goods (of a particular kind) stored in a shop, warehouse, etc. **2** a supply kept in reserve. **3** equipment or raw material in use: *rolling stock*. **4** liquid in which meat or vegetables have been cooked, used as a base for a soup, sauce, etc. **5** the shaped wooden or plastic part of a rifle or similar gun, held against the firer's shoulder. **6** farm animals; livestock. **7** the money raised by a company through the selling of shares. **8** the total shares issued by a particular company or held by an individual shareholder. **9** a group of shares bought or sold as a unit. **10** ancestry; descent: *of peasant stock*. **11** any of various Mediterranean plants of the wallflower family, cultivated for their bright flowers. **12** (in *pl*) a wooden device into which an offender was formerly fastened to be displayed for public ridicule, held by the head and wrists, or wrists and ankles. **13** reputation; standing. — *adj* **1** of a standard type, size, etc., constantly in demand and always kept in stock. **2** (of a phrase, etc.) much used, esp. so over-used as to be meaningless. — *v* **1** (*tr*) to keep a stock of for sale. **2** (*intr* with **up, up on**) to acquire or build up a stock (of). **3** (*tr*) to provide with a supply: *well-stocked drinks cabinet*. — **in stock** currently held for sale on the premises. — **out of stock** not in stock. — **take stock 1** to make an inventory of all stock held on the premises at a particular time. **2** (**of**) to make an overall assessment (e.g. of the present situation). [OE *stocc*, stick]

stockbroker *n* a person who buys and sells stocks and shares for customers in return for a fee. — *n* **stockbroking**.

stock car *n* a car modified for a kind of track racing in which deliberate colliding is allowed. — *n* **stock car racing**.

stock cube *n* a small cube of compressed meat or vegetable extract, added to water to make stock.

stock exchange *n* (the building housing) a market for the trading of stocks and shares by professional dealers on behalf of customers.

stock-in-trade *n* the basic equipment, techniques, personal qualities, etc. needed for a particular trade or activity.

stockist *n* a person or shop that stocks a particular item.

stockjobber *n* (*stock exchange*) until 1986, a middleman buying and selling stocks and shares for stockbrokers.

stock market *n* a stock exchange, or the trading carried on there.

stockpile *n* an accumulated reserve supply. — *v* (*tr*) to accumulate a (usu. large) reserve supply of.

stockroom *n* a storeroom, esp. in a shop.

stock-still *adj* & *adv* motionless.

stocktaking *n* **1** the process of making a detailed inventory of all stock held on the premises of a shop, factory, etc. at a particular time. **2** the process of making an overall assessment (e.g. of the present situation).

stockyard *n* a large yard or enclosure in which cattle are kept temporarily, e.g. to be sorted for market.

stockade *n* a fence or enclosure made from tall heavy posts, built for defence. — *v* (*tr*) to protect or defend with a stockade. [Span *estacada*]

stockinet or **stockinette** *n* a stretchy knitted fabric used esp. for undergarments. [Perhaps from **stocking-net**]

stocking *n* **1** either of a pair of close-fitting coverings for women's legs, made of fine semi-transparent nylon or silk. **2** a sock. [Ety. as for **stock**]

stockinged *adj* (of feet) with only socks, stockings or tights on, not shoes.

stocky *adj* **-ier**, **-iest** (of a person or animal) broad and strong-looking, esp. when not tall. — *adv* **stockily**. — *n* **stockiness**. [**stock**]

stodge *n* food that is heavy, filling and usu. fairly tasteless. — *v* (*tr*) to stuff with food.

stodgy *adj* **-ier**, **-iest 1** of the nature of stodge. **2** boringly conventional or serious. — *n* **stodginess**.

stoic *n* **1** a stoical person. **2** (*cap*) a disciple of the ancient Greek philosopher Zeno, who taught that true happiness is only achieved by accepting what is decided by fate or natural law. — *n* **stoicism** and **Stoicism**. [Gr *Stoa Poikile*, Painted Porch, where Zeno taught]

stoical *adj* **1** accepting suffering or misfortune uncomplainingly. **2** indifferent to both pain and pleasure. — *adv* **stoically**.

stoke *v* (**up**) **1** (*tr*) to put coal or other fuel in (e.g. the furnace of a boiler). **2** (*tr*) to arouse or intensify (e.g. passion or enthusiasm). **3** (*intr*; *coll*) to fill oneself with food. [Dut *stoken*]

stokehold *n* the boiler room on a steamship.

stoker *n* a person who stokes a furnace, esp. on a steamship or steam train.

stole[1]. See **steal**.

stole[2] *n* **1** a woman's scarf-like garment, often of fur, worn round the shoulders. **2** a scarf-like garment worn ceremonially by members of the clergy, with ends hanging down in front. [Gr]

stolen. See **steal**.

stolid *adj* showing little or no interest or emotion; impassive. — *n* **stolidity** or **stolidness**. — *adv* **stolidly**. [Lat *stolidus*, dull]

stoma *n* **-mata** **1** any of countless pores in plant leaves that control the passage of gases in and out. **2** (*tech*) a mouth or mouth-like opening in animals. [Gr, mouth]

stomach *n* **1** the bag-like organ of the body into which food passes when swallowed, and where initial digestion takes place. **2** (*loosely*) the area around the abdomen; the belly. **3** (*coll*; **for**) courage: *hasn't got the stomach for the fight*. **4** (*coll*; **for**) desire or inclination: *has no stomach for exercise*. — *v* (*tr*) **1** (*coll*) to bear or put up with: *can't stomach his arrogance*. **2** to digest easily, or eat without getting ill. [Gr *stomachos*, from *stoma*, mouth]

stomach-ache *n* a pain in the abdominal area, esp. from indigestion.

stomach pump *n* a device for drawing out stomach contents, usu. a syringe with an attached tube passed down the throat.

stomata. See **stoma**.

stomp *v* (*intr*) to stamp or tread heavily. — *n* a kind of lively jazz dancing with stamping movements. [**stamp**]

stone *n* **1** the hard solid mineral substance of which rocks are made. **2** a piece of this, esp. fairly small. **3** any piece of this shaped and used for a particular purpose, e.g. milling corn. **4** (also **gemstone**) a shaped and polished piece of a precious or semi-precious mineral. **5** the hard seed forming the central mass of any of various fruits, e.g. the peach. **6** any small hard (esp. rounded) mass, e.g. of hail, or of minerals and salts in a diseased organ, e.g. the kidneys. **7** ***stone*** a standard unit of weight equal to 14 pounds or 6·35 kilograms. **8** a dull light grey colour. — *v* (*tr*) **1** to pelt with stones. **2** to remove the stone from (fruit). — *adv* completely: *stone-deaf*; *stone-cold*. — **leave no stone unturned** to try all possibilities or make every possible effort. — **a stone's throw** (*coll*) a short distance. [OE *stan*]

the Stone Age *n* the earliest period in human history, during which primitive tools and weapons were made of stone.

stonechat *n* a small brownish European bird whose song is like two stones knocking together.

stoned *adj* (*slang*) **1** under the influence of drugs. **2** very drunk.

stonemason *n* a person skilled in shaping stone for building work.

stonewall *v* (*intr*) to hold up progress intentionally, e.g. by obstructing discussion or by batting extremely defensively in cricket.

stoneware *n* hard coarse pottery made of clay with a high silica content or of clay with flint mixed in.

stonewashed *adj* (of fabric) given an old faded appearance through the abrasive action of small pieces of pumice stone.

stony *adj* ***-ier***, ***-iest*** **1** covered with stones. **2** having a hard unfriendly or unfeeling appearance or quality: *stony-hearted*. **3** (*coll*) stony-broke. — *adv* **stonily**.

stony-broke *adj* (*coll*) having absolutely no money; penniless.

stood. See **stand**.

stooge *n* **1** a performer serving to provide a comedian with opportunities for making jokes, often also the butt of the jokes. **2** an assistant, esp. one given unpleasant tasks or otherwise exploited.

stool *n* **1** a seat without a back. **2** a footstool. **3** a single piece of faeces. — **fall between two stools** to lose two opportunities by hesitating between them or trying for both. [OE *stol*]

stool-pigeon *n* **1** a (real or dummy) pigeon used by a hunter to lure others. **2** a police informer.

stoop[1] *v* (*intr*) **1** to bend the upper body forward and down. **2** to walk with head and shoulders bent forward. **3** (**to**) to lower oneself; to deign or condescend (to do). — *n* a stooped posture. [OE *stupian*]

stoop[2] *n* (*US*) an open porch; a veranda. [Dut *stoep*]

stoop[3]. See **stoup**.

stop *v* ***-pp-*** **1** (*tr* & *intr*) to bring or come to rest, a standstill or an end; to (cause to) cease moving, operating or progressing. **2** (*tr*) to prevent. **3** (*tr*) to withhold or keep back. **4** (*tr*; **up**) to block, plug or close. **5** (*tr*) to deduct (money) from wages. **6** (*tr*) to instruct a bank not to honour (a cheque). **7** (*tr*; *coll*) to stay or reside temporarily. **8** (*tr*; *mus*) to adjust the vibrating length of (a string) by pressing down with a finger. **9** (*tr*; *slang*) to receive (a blow). — *n* **1** an act of stopping. **2** a place stopped at, e.g. on a bus route. **3** the state of being stopped; a standstill. **4** a device that prevents (further) movement. **5** a full stop. **6** a set of organ pipes of uniform tone; a keyboard knob that brings them all into use at once. **7** (also **f-stop**) any of a graded series of sizes that a camera's aperture can be adjusted to. **8** a speech sound made by suddenly releasing a build-up of air behind the lips, teeth, tongue, etc. — **pull out all the stops** to make one's best effort. — **put a stop to** to prevent (something) from continuing to happen. — **stop at nothing** to be prepared to do anything, no matter how unscrupulous (to achieve one's aim). — *v* **stop down** (*intr*) to reduce the size of the aperture in a camera. — *v* **stop off** or **over**

(*intr*) to break one's journey (*n* **stop-off** and **stop-over**). [OE *stoppian*]

stopcock *n* (the lever, etc. operating) a valve controlling the flow of liquid in a pipe.

stopgap *n* a temporary substitute.

stop-off and **stop-over** see **stop off** above.

stoppage *n* **1** an act of stopping or the state of being stopped. **2** an amount deducted from wages. **3** a stopping of work, as in a strike.

stopper *n* a cork, plug or bung.

stop press *n* **1** late news inserted into a newspaper after printing has begun, in a specially reserved space. **2** the space itself.

stopwatch *n* a watch fitted with a device that can instantly stop the hands, used for timing races, etc.

store *n* **1** a supply kept in reserve. **2** a shop, esp. when large and one of a chain. **3** (often in *pl*) a place where stocks or supplies are kept, e.g. a warehouse. **4** a computer's memory. — *v* (*tr*) **1** to put aside for future use. **2** (**up**) to build up a reserve supply of. **3** to put (e.g. furniture) into a warehouse for temporary safekeeping. **4** to put into a computer's memory. — **in store 1** kept in reserve; ready to be supplied. **2** (**for**) destined to happen (to); imminent. — **set** or **lay store by** to value highly. [Lat *instaurare*, to provide or restore]

storage *n* **1** the act of storing or the state of being stored. **2** space used for storing things. **3** the process of storing information in a computer's memory.

storage heater *n* a domestic heater that stores up heat generated by cheap electricity overnight, releasing it when required.

storehouse *n* a place where things are stored.

storey *n* **-eys** a level, floor or tier of a building. [Lat *historia*, picture, story, from the pictures with which mediaeval windows were decorated]

stork *n* **1** a large, predominantly white wading bird of warm countries, with a long reddish beak and legs. **2** (with **the**) this bird as the supposed bringer of babies. [OE *storc*]

storm *n* **1** an outbreak of violent weather, with severe winds and heavy falls of rain, hail or snow, often with thunder and lightning. **2** a violent reaction, outburst or show of feeling. **3** a furious burst, e.g. of gunfire or applause. — *v* **1** (*intr*) to go or come loudly and angrily. **2** (*tr*) to say or shout angrily. **3** (*tr*; *mil*) to make a sudden violent attack on. — **a storm in a teacup** (*coll*) a lot of fuss about something unimportant. — **take by storm 1** to enthral or captivate totally and instantly. **2** (*mil*) to capture by storming. — *adj* **stormy**, **-ier**, **-iest**. [OE]

storm centre *n* **1** the centre of a storm, where air pressure is lowest. **2** any focus of trouble or controversy.

storm door *n* a second outer door, giving extra protection from bad weather.

stormtrooper *n* **1** a soldier trained in methods of sudden violent attack. **2** (*hist*) a member of a branch of the Nazi army with a terrorist function.

story *n* **-ies 1** a written or spoken description of an event or series of events, real or imaginary. **2** (also **short story**) a piece of fiction much shorter than a novel, usu. published as one of a collection. **3** (also **storyline**) the plot of a novel, play or film. **4** a news article. **5** (*coll*) a lie. — **the story goes (that)** it is widely said or believed (that). [Lat *historia*]

stoup or **stoop** *n* a basin for holy water. [Norse *staup*]

stout *adj* **1** rather fat. **2** hard-wearing; robust. **3** (also **stout-hearted**) courageous; steadfastly reliable. — *n* dark beer with a strong malt flavour. — *adv* **stoutly**. — *n* **stoutness**. [Dut]

stove[1] *n* **1** a domestic cooker. **2** any cooking or heating apparatus, e.g. an industrial kiln. [OE *stofa*]

stove[2]. See **stave**.

stow *v* **1** (*tr*; **away**) to pack or store, esp. out of sight. **2** (*intr* with **away**) to hide on a ship, aircraft or vehicle in the hope of travelling free. [OE, place]

stowage *n* **1** a place for stowing things. **2** a charge made for stowing goods.

stowaway *n* a person who stows away on a ship, etc. — *adj* **1** travelling as a stowaway. **2** able to be folded up and carried or stored easily.

strabismus *n* (*med*) a squint. [Gr *strabismos*]

straddle *v* (*tr*) **1** to stand or sit with one leg or part on either side of. **2** to part (the legs) widely. **3** (*coll*) to adopt a neutral or non-committal attitude towards. [Related to **stride**]

strafe *v* (*tr*) to attack with heavy machine-gun fire from a low-flying aircraft. [Ger *strafen*, to punish]

straggle *v* (*intr*) **1** to grow or spread untidily. **2** to lag behind or stray from the main group or course. — *n* **straggler**. — *adj* **straggly**, **-ier**, **-iest**.

straight *adj* **1** not curved, bent, curly or wavy. **2** without deviations or detours; direct. **3** level; not sloping, leaning or twisted. **4** frank; open; direct. **5** respectable; not dishonest, disreputable or criminal. **6** neat; tidy; in good order. **7** successive; in a row. **8** (of a drink, esp. alcoholic) undiluted; neat. **9** with all debts and favours paid back. **10** not comic; serious. **11** (*coll*) conventional in tastes and opinions. **12** (*slang*) heterosexual. — *adv* **1** in or into a straight line, position or posture. **2** following an undeviating course; directly. **3** immediately. **4** honestly; frankly. — *n* **1** a straight line or part, e.g. of a race track. **2** (*slang*) a heterosexual person. **3** (*poker*) a running sequence of five cards, irrespective of suit. — **go straight**

(*coll*) to renounce criminal activities and live an honest life. — **the straight and narrow** an honest, respectable, sober way of life. — **straight away** immediately. — **straight up** (*coll*) honestly; really. [OE *streht*, from *streccan*, to stretch]

straighten *v* **-*n*-** **1** (*tr* & *intr*; **out**, **up**) to make or become straight. **2** (*tr* with **out**) to resolve, disentangle or put into order.

a straight face *n* an unsmiling face hiding a desire to laugh.

straight fight *n* a contest in which there are only two candidates or sides.

straightforward *adj* **1** without difficulties or complications; simple. **2** honest and frank.

straight man *n* a comedian's stooge.

strain[1] *v* **1** (*tr*) to injure or weaken (oneself or a part of one's body) through over-exertion. **2** (*intr*) to make violent efforts. **3** (*tr*) to make extreme use of or demands on. **4** (*tr*) to pass through or pour into a sieve or colander. **5** (*tr* with **off**) to remove by the use of a sieve or colander. **6** (*tr*) to stretch or draw tight. **7** (*intr* with **at**) to tug violently. **8** (*intr* with **at**) to feel or show reluctance or disgust; to balk. — *n* **1** an injury caused by over-exertion, esp. a wrenching of the muscles. **2** an extreme or excessive effort made by, or demand made on, the mind or (a part of) the body. **3** the tiredness resulting from such an effort. **4** an absence of friendliness and openness; tension. **5** tautness; the force that produces it. **6** (often in *pl*) (a fragment of) a melody or tune. **7** one's tone in speech or writing. [OFr *estraindre*, from Lat *stringere*, to stretch tight]

strained *adj* **1** (of an action, a person's manner, etc.) not natural or easy; forced. **2** (of an atmosphere) not friendly or relaxed; tense.

strainer *n* a sieve or colander.

strain[2] *n* **1** a breed or race of animals or plants. **2** a variety (of bacterium or other micro-organism). **3** an (esp. inherited) element of a person's character. [OE *streon*, a begetting]

strait *n* **1** (often in *pl*) a narrow strip of sea between two land masses. **2** (in *pl*) difficulty; hardship: *dire straits*. — *adj* (*old*) narrow; strict. [OFr *estreit*, from Lat *stringere*, to draw tight]

straitened: **in straitened circumstances** having very little money.

straitjacket *n* **1** a jacket used to restrain the arms of a person with violent tendencies, with long sleeves crossed at the chest and tied behind. **2** a thing that prevents freedom of development or expression.

strait-laced *adj* strictly correct in moral behaviour and attitudes; prudish or puritanical.

strand[1] *v* (*tr*) **1** to run (a ship) aground. **2** to leave in a helpless position, e.g. without transport. — *n* (*literary*) a shore or beach. [OE, seashore]

strand[2] *n* **1** a single thread, fibre, length of hair, etc., whether alone or twisted or plaited with others to form a rope, cord or braid. **2** a single element or component part.

strange *adj* **1** not known or experienced before; unfamiliar or alien. **2** not usual, ordinary or predictable; difficult to explain or understand; odd. **3** vaguely ill or ill at ease. — *adv* **strangely**. — *n* **strangeness**. [Lat *extraneus*, foreign]

stranger *n* **1** a person whom one does not know. **2** a person from a different place, home town, family, etc. **3** (with **to**) a person unfamiliar with or inexperienced in.

strangle *v* (*tr*) **1** to (attempt to) kill by squeezing the throat with the hands, a cord, etc. **2** to (partly) hold back or suppress (e.g. a scream or laughter). **3** to hinder or stop the development or expression of. — *n* **strangler**. [Lat *strangulare*]

stranglehold *n* **1** a choking hold in wrestling. **2** (**on**) a position of total control; a severely repressive influence.

strangulate *v* (*tr*) **1** (*med*) to press or squeeze so as to stop the flow of blood or air. **2** to strangle. — *n* **strangulation**. [Ety. as for **strangle**]

strap *n* **1** a narrow strip of leather or fabric by which a thing is hung, carried or fastened. **2** (also **shoulder strap**) either of a pair of strips of fabric by which a garment hangs from the shoulders. **3** a leather belt used to give a beating as punishment; (with **the**) such a beating. **4** a hanging loop providing a hand-hold for a standing passenger on a bus or train. — *v* **-*pp*-** (*tr*) **1** (**in**, **up**) to fasten or bind with a strap or straps. **2** to beat with a strap. [Dialect form of **strop**]

strapped *adj* (**for**) (*coll*) short (of).

strapping *adj* tall and strong-looking.

strata. See **stratum**.

stratagem *n* a trick or plan, esp. one for deceiving an enemy or gaining an advantage. [Gr *strategema*, act of generalship]

strategy *n* **-*ies*** **1** the process of, or skill in, planning and conducting a military campaign. **2** a long-term plan for future success or development. — *n* **strategist**. [Gr *strategia*, from *stratos*, army + *agein*, to lead]

strategic *adj* **1** of or relating to (a) strategy. **2** (of weapons) designed for a direct long-range attack on an enemy's homeland, rather than for close-range battlefield use. — *adv* **strategically**.

strath *n* (in Scotland) a broad flat valley. [Gaelic *srath*]

strathspey *n* **-*eys*** (a piece of music for) a Scottish folk dance similar to but slower than the reel. [*Strathspey* (the valley of the river Spey) in Scotland]

stratify *v* **-*ies***, **-*ied*** (*tr*) **1** (*geol*) to deposit (rock) in layers or strata. **2** to classify or arrange into different grades, levels or social classes. — *n* **stratification**. [Lat *stratum* (see ety. for **stratum**) + *facere*, to make]

stratosphere *n* the layer of the earth's atmosphere between about 5½ and 31 miles up (9 to 50 km), within which temperature increases with altitude. — *adj* **stratospheric**. [**stratum** + *-sphere* as in **atmosphere**]

stratum *n* **-ta** **1** a layer of sedimentary rock. **2** a layer of cells in living tissue. **3** a layer of the atmosphere or the ocean. **4** a level, grade or social class. [Lat, something spread]

stratus *n* **-ti** a wide sheet of low grey cloud. [**stratum**]

straw *n* **1** the dried cut stalks of corn and similar crops, used as bedding and fodder for cattle, and woven into hats, baskets, etc. **2** a single stalk. **3** a thin hollow tube for sucking up a drink. **4** a pale yellow colour. — **clutch at straws** to resort, in desperation, to an alternative that is unlikely to succeed. — **the last straw** the last in a whole series of disagreeable incidents, breaking one's tolerance or resistance. — **the short straw** the worst of all possible outcomes or options. [OE *streaw*]

straw poll or **vote** *n* an unofficial vote, esp. taken on the spot, to get some idea of general opinion.

strawberry *n* **-ies** **1** a small juicy pinkish-red fruit whose surface is dotted with brownish-yellow seeds. **2** the low-growing plant that bears it. **3** the flavour or colour of the fruit. [OE *streawberige*, perhaps from the straw-like appearance of the plant stem]

strawberry blonde *n* & *adj* (a woman with hair that is) reddish-blonde.

strawberry mark *n* a reddish birthmark.

stray *v* (*intr*) **1** to wander away (from the right path or place). **2** to move away (e.g. from the main issue) in thought, speech or writing, esp. carelessly. **3** to depart from an accepted or required pattern of (esp. moral) behaviour. — *n* a lost or homeless pet or child. — *adj* not the result of a regular or intended process; random; casual. [OFr *estraier*, to wander]

streak *n* **1** a long irregular stripe or band. **2** (of lightning) a flash. **3** an element or characteristic: *a cowardly streak*. **4** a short period; a spell: *a lucky streak*. **5** (*coll*) a naked or near-naked dash through a public place. — *v* **1** (*tr*) to mark with a streak or streaks. **2** (*intr*) to move at great speed; to dash. **3** (*intr*; *coll*) to run naked or nearly naked through a public place. — *adj* **streaked**. [OE *strica*, stroke]

streaker *n* (*coll*) a person who streaks (sense **3**).

streaky *adj* **-ier**, **-iest** **1** marked with streaks. **2** (of bacon) with alternate layers of fat and meat. — *n* **streakiness**.

stream *n* **1** a very narrow river; a brook or rivulet. **2** any constant flow of water or other liquid. **3** a continuously moving line or mass, e.g. of vehicles. **4** an uninterrupted burst or succession, e.g. of insults. **5** general direction, trend or tendency. **6** any of several groups into which school pupils are broadly divided according to ability, subdivided into classes. — *v* **1** (*intr*) to flow or move continuously and in large quantities or numbers. **2** (*intr*) to float or trail in the wind. **3** (*tr*) to divide (pupils) into streams. [OE]

streamer *n* **1** a long paper ribbon used to decorate a room. **2** a roll of coloured paper that uncoils when thrown. **3** a long thin flag.

streamline *v* (*tr*) to make streamlined.

streamlined *adj* **1** (of a vehicle, aircraft or vessel) shaped so as to move smoothly and efficiently with minimum resistance to air or water. **2** (of an organisation, process, etc.) extremely efficient, with little or no waste of resources, excess staff, unnecessary steps, etc.

street *n* **1** a public road, esp. one in a town with pavements and buildings at the side or sides. **2** the road and the buildings together. **3** the people in the buildings or on the pavements: *tell the whole street*. — **on the street** or **streets** (*coll*) **1** homeless. **2** practising prostitution, esp. soliciting. — **streets ahead of** (*coll*) very much more advanced than or superior to. — **up someone's street** (*coll*) suited to someone's tastes or abilities. — **walk the streets** **1** to walk from street to street. **2** to solicit as a prostitute on the street. [OE *stræt*]

streetcar *n* (*US*) a tram.

street credibility *n* (also *coll* **street cred**) popularity with, or acceptability in the eyes of, the fashionable or politically liberal youth of today. — *adj* **street-credible** (also, *coll*, **street-cred**).

streetwalker *n* (*coll*) a prostitute who solicits.

streetwise *adj* (*coll*) experienced in, and able to survive, the ruthlessness of urban life.

strength *n* **1** the quality or degree of being physically or mentally strong. **2** the ability to withstand pressure or force. **3** degree or intensity, e.g. of emotion or light. **4** potency, e.g. of a drug or alcoholic drink. **5** (of an argument) forcefulness. **6** a highly valued quality or asset. **7** the number of people, etc. needed or normally expected in a group, esp. in comparison to those actually present or available: *with the workforce only at half strength*. — **go from strength to strength** to improve through a series of successes each surpassing the previous one. — **on the strength of** on the basis of; judging by. [OE *strengthu*]

strengthen *v* **-n-** (*tr* & *intr*) to make or become stronger.

strenuous *adj* requiring, or performed with, great effort or energy. — *n* **strenuosity** or **strenuousness**. — *adv* **strenuously**. [Lat *strenuus*]

streptococcus *n* **-ci** any of various species of bacterium that cause serious illness. [Gr *streptos*, twisted + *kokkos*, berry]

streptomycin *n* an antibiotic used to treat various bacterial infections. [Gr *streptos*, twisted + *mykes*, fungus]

stress *n* **1** mental or emotional pressure; acute anxiety. **2** physical pressure or tension. **3** importance, emphasis or weight laid on or attached to something. **4** emphasis on a particular syllable or word. — *v* (*tr*) **1** to emphasise or attach importance to. **2** to pronounce with emphasis. **3** to subject to mental or physical stress. — *adj* **stressful**. [Shortened from **distress**]

stress-mark *n* a mark used to indicate stress.

stretch *v* **1** (*tr* & *intr*) to make or become (temporarily or permanently) longer or wider by pulling or drawing out. **2** (*intr*; **for, over**) to extend in space or time. **3** (*tr* & *intr*; **out**) to straighten and extend fully (a part of) one's body, e.g. when waking or reaching. **4** (*tr* & *intr*) to make or become tight or taut. **5** (*tr*; **out**) to lay (out) at full length. **6** (*intr*) to be extendable without breaking. **7** (*tr* & *intr*) to (cause to) last longer through economical use. **8** (*tr*; **out**) to prolong. **9** (*tr*) to make extreme demands on or severely test (e.g. resources or physical abilities). **10** (*tr*) to exaggerate (the truth). — *n* **1** an act of stretching, esp. (a part of) the body. **2** a period of time; a spell. **3** an expanse, e.g. of land or water. **4** capacity to extend or expand. **5** a straight part on a race-track or course. **6** (*coll*) a difficult task or test: *will be a bit of a stretch*. **7** (*slang*) a term of imprisonment. — **at a stretch 1** continuously; without interruption. **2** with difficulty. — **stretch a point** to agree to something not strictly in keeping with the rules; to bend the rules. — **stretch one's legs** to take a (usu. short) walk to invigorate oneself after inactivity. [OE *streccan*]

stretcher *n* a length of canvas or other sheeting with poles attached, for carrying a sick or wounded person in a lying position. — *n* **stretcher-bearer**.

stretchy *adj* **-ier, -iest** (of materials) able or tending to stretch. — *n* **stretchiness**.

strew *v* ***strewed, strewed*** or ***strewn*** (*tr*) **1** to scatter untidily. **2** (**with**) to cover with an untidy scattering (of). [OE *streowian*]

strewth *interj* (*coll*) an expression of surprise or annoyance. [*God's truth*]

stria *n* **-ae** (*geol* or *biol*) any of a series of parallel grooves in rock, or furrows or streaks of colour in plants and animals. — *adj* **striated**. — *n* **striation**. [Lat, furrow]

stricken *adj* deeply affected, overwhelmed or afflicted, e.g. by grief or disease. [Archaic past participle of **strike**]

strict *adj* **1** demanding obedience or close observance of rules; severe. **2** (of instructions, etc.) that must be obeyed. **3** observing rules or practices very closely: *strict Catholics*. **4** exact; precise: *the strict sense of the word*. **5** complete: *in the strictest confidence*. — *adv* **strictly**. — *n* **strictness**. [Lat *stringere*, to tighten]

stricture *n* **1** a severe criticism. **2** (*med*) abnormal narrowing of a passage. [Ety. as for **strict**]

stride *n* **1** a single long step in walking. **2** the length of such a step. **3** a way of walking in long steps. **4** (usu. in *pl*) a measure of progress or development: *make great strides*. **5** a rhythm, e.g. in working, aimed for or settled into: *put me off my stride*. **6** (in *pl*; *slang*) trousers. — *v* ***strode, stridden*** **1** (*intr*) to walk with long steps. **2** (*intr*) to take a long step. **3** (*tr*) to step or extend over. — **take (something) in one's stride** to carry out or cope with (something) effortlessly, as if part of a regular routine. [OE *stridan*]

strident *adj* **1** (of a sound, esp. a voice) loud and harsh. **2** forcefully assertive; compelling. — *n* **stridency**. — *adv* **stridently**. [Lat *stridere*, to creak]

strife *n* **1** bitter conflict or fighting. **2** (*coll*) trouble of any sort; hassle. [OFr *estrif*]

strike *v* ***struck*** **1** (*tr*) to hit; to give a blow to; to come or bring into heavy contact with. **2** (*tr*; **as**) to make a particular impression on. **3** (*tr*) to come into the mind of; to occur to. **4** (*tr*) to cause (a match) to ignite through friction. **5** (*intr* with **at, out**) to attempt to hit. **6** (*tr* & *intr*) (of a clock) to announce (the time) with a chime. **7** (*intr*) to happen suddenly: *Disaster struck*. **8** (*intr*) to make a sudden attack. **9** (*tr*) to afflict suddenly; to cause to become by affliction: *struck dumb*. **10** (*tr*; **into**) to introduce or inject suddenly: *struck terror into them*. **11** (*tr*) to arrive at or settle (e.g. a bargain or a balance). **12** (*tr*) to find a source of (e.g. oil). **13** (*intr* with **on**) to come upon or arrive at by chance: *struck on an idea*. **14** (*intr*) to (continue to) stop working as part of a collective protest against an employer. **15** (*tr*) to dismantle (a camp). **16** (*tr*) to make (a coin) by stamping metal. **17** (*tr*) to adopt (a posture or attitude). **18** (*tr*) to lower (a flag). **19** (*tr* & *intr*) to draw (a line) in order to cross something out. — *n* **1** an act of hitting or dealing a blow. **2** a usu. collective on-going refusal to work, as a protest against an employer. **3** an on-going refusal to engage in a regular or expected activity, e.g. eating, as a protest. **4** a military attack, esp. by aircraft. **5** a discovery of a mineral source, e.g. gold. **6** the knocking down of all pins with a single ball in tenpin bowling. **7** (*cricket*) the position of being the batsman bowled at: *take strike*. **8** (*baseball*) a ball swung at but missed by the batter. — **on strike** taking part in an industrial or other strike. — **strike it lucky** or **rich** to enjoy luck or become rich suddenly and unexpectedly. — *v* **strike off** (*tr*) to officially remove the name of from a professional register, e.g. of doctors, because of misconduct. — *v* **strike out 1** (*tr*) to cross out or efface. **2** (*intr*) to set out determinedly on a journey or effort (towards). **3** (*tr* & *intr*; *baseball*) to dismiss or be dismissed by means of three strikes (*n* **strike-out**). **4** (*intr*; *slang*) to fail completely (*n* **strike-out**). — *v* **strike up 1** (*intr*) (of musicians) to begin to play. **2** (*tr*) to start (e.g. a conversation). [OE *strican*]

strike-breaker *n* a person who continues to work while others strike, or who is brought in to do the job of a striking worker.

strike pay *n* an allowance paid by a trade union to a member on strike.

striker *n* **1** a worker taking part in a strike. **2** (*football*) a player with an attacking role.

striking *adj* **1** impressive or arresting. **2** noticeable; marked. **3** on strike.

string *n* **1** (a piece of) thin cord. **2** any of a set of pieces of stretched wire, catgut or other material vibrated to produce sound in various musical instruments. **3** (in *pl* with **the**) (the musicians playing) the orchestral instruments in which sound is produced in this way, usu. the violins, violas, cellos and double basses collectively. **4** a set (of things, e.g. pearls) threaded together. **5** a series or succession. **6** (in *pl*) undesirable conditions or limitations: *no strings attached.* **7** any cord-like thing, e.g. a nerve or tendon. — *v* ***strung*** **1** (*tr*) to fit or provide with a string or strings. **2** (*tr*; **up**) to hang, stretch or tie with, or as if with, string. ◇ See also **string up** below. **3** (*tr*) to thread (e.g. beads) on a string. **4** (*intr*; **out**) to extend or stretch in a long line. — **pull strings** (*coll*) to use one's influence, or relationships with influential people, to get something done. — **pull the strings** (*coll*) to be the ultimate, although not usu. apparent, controller of a situation or person. — *v* **string along 1** (*intr*; **with**) to go along for company. **2** (*tr*) to keep in a state of deception or false hope. — *v* **string up** (*tr*; *coll*) to kill by hanging. [OE *streng*]

stringer *n* **1** a horizontal beam in a framework. **2** a journalist employed part-time to cover a particular town or area.

stringy *adj* ***-ier***, ***-iest*** **1** like string, esp. thin and thread-like. **2** (of meat or other food) full of chewy fibres. — *n* **stringiness**.

stringent *adj* **1** (of rules, etc.) severe; rigorous; strictly enforced. **2** marked by a lack of money. — *n* **stringency**. — *adv* **stringently**. [Lat *stringere*, to draw together]

strip *n* **1** a long narrow piece. **2** a lightweight uniform worn by members of a sports team. **3** a striptease performance. — *v* ***-pp-*** **1** (*tr*; **off**) to remove by peeling or pulling off; to remove the surface or contents of in this way. **2** (*tr*; **of**) to divest or dispossess (of e.g. property or dignity). **3** (*tr*) to remove the clothes of. **4** (*intr*; **off**) to take one's clothes off. **5** (*tr*; **down**) to take to pieces; to dismantle. [OE *strypan*]

strip cartoon *n* a sequence of drawings, e.g. in a newspaper, telling a comic or adventure story.

strip club *n* a club in which striptease artistes perform.

strip lighting *n* lighting by tube-shaped fluorescent lamps, not bulbs.

stripper *n* **1** a striptease artiste. **2** a substance or appliance for removing paint, varnish, etc.

strip search *n* a thorough search of the body of a person who has been made to take off his or her clothes, to check for concealed drugs or smuggled items. — *v* (*tr*) **strip-search**.

striptease *n* an entertainment in which a person undresses to music in a slow and sexually exciting way.

stripe *n* **1** a band of colour. **2** a chevron or coloured band on a uniform, indicating rank. — *v* (*tr*) to mark with stripes. — *adj* **striped**. [ODut]

stripy *adj* ***-ier***, ***-iest*** marked with stripes; striped.

stripling *n* (*literary*) a boy or youth. [Dimin. of **strip**]

strive *v* ***strove***, ***striven*** (*intr*) **1** (**for**) to try extremely hard; to struggle. **2** (**with**, **against**) to contend; to be in conflict. [OFr *estriver*]

strobe *n* **1** strobe lighting. **2** a stroboscope. [Gr *strobos*, whirling]

strobe lighting *n* (the equipment producing) a powerful rapidly flashing light which, directed on a moving body, creates an effect of jerky movement, widely used in discotheques, etc.

stroboscope *n* an instrument that makes a repetitively moving (esp. revolving) thing seem stationary by flashing a light on it at the precise rate of movement, allowing it to be examined, photographed, etc. [Gr *strobos*, whirling + **-scope**]

strode. See **stride**.

stroke *n* **1** an act of striking; the way a thing is struck, esp. the technique used in striking a ball in sport. **2** a single movement with a pen, paintbrush, etc., or the line or daub produced. **3** a single complete movement in a repeated series, as in swimming, rowing or the action of pistons in an engine. **4** a particular named style of swimming. **5** the striking of a clock, or its sound. **6** a gentle caress or other touching movement. **7** (with **of**) an act or occurrence that reveals the presence of something, e.g. genius or luck. **8** a sloping line used to separate alternatives in writing or print; a solidus. **9** a sudden loss of consciousness caused by the bursting or blocking of a blood vessel in the brain, often resulting in permanent paralysis in part of the body. **10** (*coll*) the least amount of work: *not done a stroke all day.* — *v* (*tr*) **1** to caress in kindness or affection, often repeatedly. **2** to strike (a ball) smoothly and with seeming effortlessness. — **at a stroke** with a single action. — **on the stroke of** precisely at (a particular time). [OE *strac*]

stroll *v* (*intr*) to walk in a slow leisurely way. — *n* a leisurely walk. [Perhaps Ger *strolchen*, from *Strolch*, tramp]

strong *adj* **1** (capable of) exerting great force or power. **2** able to withstand rough treatment; robust. **3** (of views, etc.) firmly held or boldly expressed. **4** (of taste, light, etc.) sharply felt or experienced; intense; powerful. **5** (of coffee, alcoholic drink, etc.) relatively undiluted with water or other liquid; concentrated. **6** (of an argument) convincing. **7** (**on**) excelling (in); well-skilled or versed (in). **8** (of language) bold or straightforward; rude or offensive. **9** (of prices, values, etc.) steady or rising. **10** (of a syllable) stressed. **11** (of a group, etc.) numbering so many: *a gang fifty strong*. — *adv* **strongly**. — **come on strong** (*coll*) to be strongly, often disconcertingly, persuasive or assertive. — **going strong** (*coll*) flourishing; thriving. [OE *strang*]

strongarm *adj* (*coll*) **1** aggressively forceful. **2** making use of (threats of) physical violence. — *v* (*tr*) to compel with aggressive forcefulness or (threats of) physical violence.

strongbox *n* a safe, or other sturdy lockable box for storing money or valuables.

stronghold *n* **1** a fortified place of defence, e.g. a castle. **2** a place where there is strong support (e.g. for a political party).

strong point *n* a thing in which a person excels.

strongroom *n* a room in which valuables or prisoners are held for safekeeping, designed to be difficult to penetrate.

strong verb *n* in English, German, etc., an irregular verb with different vowels in different tenses, as *sing*, *sang*, *sung* and *write*, *wrote*, *written*. ◇ See also **weak verb**.

strontium *n* an element (symbol **Sr**), a soft malleable yellowish metal whose radioactive isotope **strontium-90** is used in nuclear power sources. [*Strontian* in Scotland, where it was discovered]

strop *n* a strip of coarse leather or other abrasive material on which razors are sharpened. — *v* ***-pp-*** (*tr*) to sharpen (a razor) on a strop. [Lat *struppus*, thong]

stroppy *adj* ***-ier***, ***-iest*** (*coll*) quarrelsome, bad-tempered and awkward to deal with. [Probably from **obstreperous**]

strove. See **strive**.

struck *past tense* and *past participle* of **strike**. — **struck on** (*coll*) infatuated with; enthusiastic about.

structure *n* **1** the way in which the parts of a thing are arranged or organised. **2** a thing built or constructed from many smaller parts. — *v* (*tr*) to put into an organised form or arrangement. [Lat *structura*, from *struere*, to build]

structural *adj* of or relating to structure, or a basic structure or framework. — *adv* **structurally**.

structuralism *n* an approach to various areas of study, e.g. literary criticism and linguistics, which seeks to identify underlying patterns or structures, esp. as they might reflect patterns of behaviour or thought in society as a whole. — *n* & *adj* **structuralist**.

strudel *n* a baked roll of thin pastry with a filling of fruit, esp. apple. [Ger, whirlpool, from the rolling]

struggle *v* (*intr*) **1** to move the body around violently in an attempt to get free. **2** to strive vigorously or make a strenuous effort under difficult conditions. **3** (**along**, **through**, etc.) to make one's way with great difficulty. **4** (**with**) to fight or contend. — *n* **1** an act of struggling. **2** a task requiring strenuous effort. **3** a fight or contest. [MidE *strogelen*]

strum *v* ***-mm-*** (*tr* & *intr*) to play (a stringed musical instrument, or a tune on it) with sweeps of the fingers or thumb rather than with precise plucking. — *n* an act or bout of strumming.

strumpet *n* (*old*) a prostitute, or a woman who engages in casual sex.

strung. See **string**.

strut[1] *v* ***-tt-*** (*intr*) to walk in a proud or self-important way. — *n* a strutting way of walking. — **strut one's stuff** (*slang*) **1** to dance. **2** to show off one's talent; to show off in general. [OE *strutian*]

strut[2] *n* a bar or rod used to support weight or take pressure; a prop.

strychnine *n* a deadly poison obtained from the seeds of a tropical Indian tree, used medicinally in small quantities as a nerve stimulant. [Gr *strychnos*, nightshade]

stub *n* **1** a short piece, e.g. of a cigarette or a pencil, left after the rest has been used up. **2** the part of a cheque or ticket kept by the issuer as a record. — *v* ***-bb-*** (*tr*) **1** to accidentally bump the end of (one's toe) against a hard surface. **2** (**out**) to put out (a cigarette or cigar) by pressing the end against a surface. [OE *stubb*]

stubby *adj* ***-ier***, ***-iest*** short and broad or thick-set. — *n* **stubbiness**.

stubble *n* **1** the mass of short stalks left in the ground after a crop has been harvested. **2** a short early growth of beard. — *adj* **stubbly**. [OFr *estuble*]

stubborn *adj* **1** (unreasonably) unwilling to change plans or opinions; obstinate. **2** determined; unyielding. **3** very difficult to treat, remove or deal with: *stubborn stains*. — *adv* **stubbornly**. — *n* **stubbornness**.

stucco *n* ***-os*** or ***-oes*** any kind of plaster or cement used for coating, or moulding decorative shapes on to, outside walls. — *v* ***-os*** or ***-oes***, ***-oed*** or ***-o'd*** (*tr*) to coat with or mould out of stucco. [Ital, from OGer *stucchi*, coating]

stuck *past tense* and *past participle* of **stick**[2]. — **be stuck** (*coll*) **1** (**for**) to be bewildered, helpless or at a loss. **2** (**with**) to be unable to escape (from a person or thing considered unpleasant). — **get stuck in** (*slang*) to set about an activity with energy or aggression. — **stuck on** (*coll*) fond of or infatuated with.

stuck-up *adj* (*coll*) snobbish; conceited.

stud[1] *n* **1** a rivet-like metal knob fitted on to a surface, e.g. of a garment, for decoration. **2** any of several knob-like projections on the sole of a sports boot, giving added grip. **3** a fastener, e.g. fixing a collar to a shirt, consisting of two small discs on either end of a short bar or shank. **4** a press stud. — *v* **-dd- 1** (*tr*) to fasten or decorate with a stud or studs. **2** (with **with**) to cover with a dense scattering of. [OE *studu*, post]

stud[2] *n* **1** a male animal, esp. a horse, kept for breeding. **2** (also **stud farm**) a place where animals, esp. horses, are bred. **3** a collection of animals kept for breeding. **4** (*coll*) stud poker. **5** (*slang*) a man who has (or thinks he has) great sexual energy and prowess. — **at stud** or **out to stud** kept for breeding purposes. [OE *stod*]

stud poker *n* a form of the game of poker in which bets are placed on hands in which some of the cards are laid face up.

student *n* **1** a person following a formal course of study, esp. at a college, polytechnic or university. **2** (**of**) a person with an informed interest (in). [Lat *studere*, to be zealous]

studio *n* **-os 1** the workroom of an artist or photographer. **2** a room in which music recordings, cinema films, or television or radio programmes are made. **3** (in *pl*) the premises of a company making any of these. [Ital; see **study**]

studio couch *n* a couch, often backless, that converts into a bed.

studio flat *n* a small flat with one main room acting as living, eating, sleeping and often cooking area.

studious *adj* **1** having a serious, hard-working approach to study. **2** painstaking or painstakingly carried out. — *adv* **studiously**. — *n* **studiousness**. [**study**]

study *v* **-ies, -ied 1** (*tr & intr*) to give time and attention to the gaining of knowledge (of); to take an educational course (in). **2** (*tr*) to look at or examine closely, or think about carefully. — *n* **-ies 1** the act or process of studying. **2** (in *pl*) work done in the process of acquiring knowledge. **3** (**of**) a careful and detailed examination or consideration. **4** a work of art produced for the sake of practice, or in preparation for a more complex or detailed work. **5** a piece of music intended to exercise and develop the player's technique. **6** a private room where quiet work or study is carried out. [Lat *studere*, to be zealous, from *studium*, zeal]

studied *adj* (of an attitude, expression, etc.) carefully practised and adopted or produced for effect; unspontaneous and affected.

stuff *n* **1** any material, substance or equipment. **2** luggage; belongings. **3** (*literary*) matter; essence: *the very stuff of life*. **4** (*old*) cloth, esp. woollen. — *v* (*tr*) **1** to fill the hollow or hollowed-out part of (e.g. a chicken or pepper) with a seasoned mixture of other foods. **2** to fill to capacity or over. **3** to cram or thrust (in). **4** to fill out the disembodied skin of (an animal) to recreate its living shape. **5** to feed (oneself) gluttonously. **6** (**up**) to block (e.g. a hole, or a nose with mucus). **7** (*slang*) to defeat overwhelmingly. **8** (*slang*) to dispose of (something angrily rejected) however one wishes: *Stuff your job!* **9** (*old vulg slang*) to have sexual intercourse with (a woman). — **do one's stuff** (*coll*) **1** to display one's talent or skill. **2** to perform the task required of one. — **get stuffed!** (*vulg slang*) an expression of anger or contemptuous dismissal. — **know one's stuff** (*coll*) to have a thorough knowledge of the subject with which one is concerned. [OFr *estoffe*]

stuffed shirt *n* (*coll*) a pompous person.

stuffing *n* **1** padding used to stuff children's toys, cushions, animal skins, etc. **2** a seasoned mixture of foods with which another item of food is stuffed. — **knock the stuffing out of** to deprive of strength or force (of any kind), esp. with a single swift action.

stuffy *adj* **-ier, -iest 1** lacking fresh, cool air; badly ventilated. **2** (*coll*) pompous. **3** (*coll*) boringly formal, conventional or unadventurous; staid. — *adv* **stuffily**. — *n* **stuffiness**.

stultify *v* **-ies, -ied** (*tr*) **1** to make (e.g. efforts) appear useless or foolish. **2** to dull the mind of, e.g. with boring tasks. — *adj* **stultifying**. [Lat *stultus*, foolish + *facere*, to make]

stumble *v* (*intr*) **1** to lose one's balance and pitch forwards after accidentally catching or misplacing one's foot. **2** to walk unsteadily. **3** to speak with frequent hesitations and mistakes. **4** to make a mistake in speech or action. **5** (**across, on**) to come by chance. — *n* an act of stumbling. [MidE *stomble*]

stumbling-block *n* **1** an obstacle or difficulty. **2** a cause of failure or faltering.

stump *n* **1** the part of a felled or fallen tree left in the ground. **2** the short part of anything, e.g. a limb, left after the larger part has been removed. **3** (*cricket*) any of the three thin vertical wooden posts forming the wicket; (in *pl*) the whole wicket, bails included. — *v* **1** (*tr*) to baffle or perplex. **2** (*intr*) to walk stiffly and unsteadily, or heavily and noisily. **3** (*tr; cricket*) to dismiss (a batsman stepping wholly beyond the crease) by disturbing the wicket with the ball. — *v* **stump up** (*tr & intr; coll*) to pay up. [MidE *stumpe*]

stumpy *adj* **-*ier***, **-*iest*** short and thick. — *n* **stumpiness**.

stun *v* **-*nn*-** (*tr*) **1** to make unconscious, e.g. by a blow to the head. **2** to make unable to speak or think clearly, e.g. through shock. **3** (*coll*) to impress greatly; to astound. [OFr *estoner*, to astonish]

stunner *n* (*coll*) a person or thing of overwhelming beauty or attractiveness.

stunning *adj* (*coll*) **1** outstandingly beautiful. **2** extremely impressive. — *adv* **stunningly**.

stung. See **sting**.

stunk. See **stink**.

stunt[1] *v* (*tr*) to prevent (growth or development) to the full, or prevent the full growth or development of. — *adj* **stunted**. [OE, dull, stupid]

stunt[2] *n* **1** a daring act or spectacular event intended to show off talent or attract publicity. **2** a dangerous or acrobatic feat performed as part of the action of a film or television programme.

stuntman or **stuntwoman** *n* a person hired to take the place of an actor when stunts are being filmed.

stupefy *v* **-*ies***, **-*ied*** (*tr*) **1** to make senseless, e.g. with drugs or alcohol. **2** to amaze or astound. **3** to confuse or bewilder. — *n* **stupefaction**. — *adj* **stupefying**. [Lat *stupere*, to be struck senseless + *facere*, to make]

stupendous *adj* **1** astounding. **2** (*coll*) astoundingly huge or excellent. — *adv* **stupendously**. [Lat *stupere*, to be stunned]

stupid *adj* **1** having or showing a lack of common sense, or a slowness to understand. **2** made senseless or stupefied, e.g. with drugs. **3** (*coll*) trivial; unimportant. — *n* **stupidity**. — *adv* **stupidly**. [Lat *stupidus*, senseless]

stupor *n* a half-conscious, dazed or lethargic condition, e.g. from taking drugs or alcohol. [Lat, insensibility]

sturdy *adj* **-*ier***, **-*iest*** **1** (of limbs, etc.) thick and strong-looking. **2** strongly built; robust. **3** healthy; vigorous; hardy. — *adv* **sturdily**. — *n* **sturdiness**. [OFr *estourdi*, stunned]

sturgeon *n* a large long-snouted fish of northern seas, from which caviar is obtained. [OFr]

stutter *n* **1** an inability to utter, without hesitation, certain speech sounds esp. at the beginnings of words, resulting in repetition of the sounds; a stammer. **2** the resulting repetition. — *v* **-*r*-** (*tr* & *intr*) to speak or say with a stutter. [Obsolete *stut*]

STV *abbrev* **1** single transferable vote (= a method of voting for proportional representation). **2** Scottish Television.

sty[1] *n* **-*ies*** a pen in which pigs are kept. [OE *stig*, pen, hall]

sty[2] or **stye** *n* **-*ies*** or **-*yes*** a tiny swelling on the eyelid, at the base of the lash. [OE *stigan*, to rise]

style *n* **1** a manner or way of doing something, e.g. writing, speaking, painting or designing buildings. **2** a distinctive manner that characterises a particular author, painter, film-maker, etc. **3** kind; type; make. **4** a striking quality, often elegance or lavishness, considered desirable or admirable: *She dresses with style*. **5** the state of being fashionable: *gone out of style*. **6** a pointed tool used for engraving. **7** a small stalk-like part on the inside of a flower, bearing the stigma. — *v* (*tr*) **1** to design, shape or groom in a particular way. **2** to name, designate or label: *a self-styled expert*. [Lat *stilus*, writing tool, literary style]

stylise or **-ize** *v* (*tr*) to give a distinctive or elaborate style to, esp. creating an impression of unnaturalness. — *adj* **stylised** or **-z-**.

stylish *adj* elegant; fashionable. — *adv* **stylishly**.

stylist *n* **1** a trained hairdresser. **2** a writer, artist, etc. who pays a lot of attention to style.

stylistic *adj* of or relating to (esp. artistic or literary) style. — *adv* **stylistically**.

stylus *n* **-*ses*** or **-*li*** **1** the needle-like part on the end of the arm of a record-player, that picks up the sound from the record's grooves. **2** the cutting tool used to produce the grooves in a record. [Ety. as for **style**]

stymie *v* **-*ies***, **-*mieing*** or **-*mying***, **-*ied*** (*tr*) to prevent, thwart or frustrate. — *n* **-*ies*** **1** (*golf*) a situation in which an opponent's ball blocks the path between one's own ball and the hole, possible before the introduction of markers. **2** any tricky situation.

styptic *adj* drawing skin tissue together, reducing or stopping bleeding; astringent. — *n* a styptic substance. [Gr *styptikos*, contracting]

suave *adj* **1** polite and charming, esp. insincerely so. **2** (*loosely*) smart and fashionable. — *adv* **suavely**. — *n* **suavity**. [Lat *suavis*, sweet]

sub (*coll*) *n* **1** a submarine. **2** a substitute player. **3** (also **subs**) a subscription fee. **4** a small loan or an advance payment of wages, to help one subsist. **5** a subeditor. — *v* **-*bb*-** **1** (*intr*) to act as a substitute. **2** (*tr* & *intr*) to subedit or work as a subeditor.

sub- *pfx* **1** under or below: *submarine*. **2** secondary; lower in rank or importance: *sublieutenant*. **3** imperfectly; less than: *subhuman*. **4** a part or division of: *subcommittee*. [Lat *sub*, under, near]

subaltern *n* any army officer below the rank of captain. [Lat *subalternus*, from *sub*, under + *alter*, another]

subaqua *adj* of, for, or for use in underwater activities. [**sub-** (sense **1**) + Lat *aqua*, water]

subatomic *adj* **1** smaller than an atom. **2** existing or occurring within an atom. [**sub-** (sense **4**)]

subconscious *n* & *adj* (existing or occurring in) the area of the mind that the individual is only dimly, or not at all, aware of, nevertheless capable of influencing behaviour. — *adv* **subconsciously**. [**sub-** (sense **3**)]

subcontinent *n* a large part of a continent that is distinctive in some way, e.g. by its shape or culture. [**sub-** (sense **4**)]

subcontract *n* a secondary contract, by which the hired person or company hires another to carry out the work. — *v* (*tr*) to employ (a worker), or pass on (work), under the terms of a subcontract. [**sub-** (sense **2**)]

subcontractor *n* a person or company employed under the terms of a subcontract.

subculture *n* the customs, tastes or activities of a particular group within society. [**sub-** (sense **4**)]

subcutaneous *adj* (*med*) under the skin. [Lat *sub*, under + *cutis*, skin]

subdivide *v* (*tr*) to divide (a part) into even smaller parts. — *n* **subdivision**. [**sub-** (sense **4**)]

subdue *v* (*tr*) to overpower and bring under control; to suppress or conquer (feelings or an enemy). [Lat *subducere*, to remove]

subdued *adj* **1** (of lighting, etc.) soft, or made softer; toned down. **2** (of a person) uncharacteristically quiet or in low spirits.

subedit *v* **-t-** (*tr* & *intr*) to act as a subeditor (of). [**sub-** (sense **2**)]

subeditor *n* **1** a person who selects and prepares material to be printed, e.g. in a newspaper or magazine, for the ultimate approval of an editor. **2** a person who assists with various editing tasks.

subject *n* **1** a matter or topic under discussion or consideration. **2** an area of learning that forms a course of study. **3** a person or thing represented by an artist or writer. **4** a person on whom an experiment or operation is performed. **5** a person under the ultimate rule of a monarch or government; a citizen. **6** (*gram*) a word or phrase referring to the person or thing that performs the action of an active verb or receives the action of a passive verb, as in '*He* dropped it' and '*It* was dropped by him'. ◇ See also **object**. — *adj* **1** (**to**) showing a tendency; prone. **2** (**to**) exposed; open. **3** (**to**) governed; dependent. **4** ruled by a monarch or government. — *adv* (with **to**) conditionally upon; on condition that one has. — *v* (*tr* with **to**) **1** to cause to undergo or experience (usu. something unpleasant). **2** to make subordinate (to) or bring under the control (of). — *n* **subjection**. [Lat *subjectus*, thrown under]

subjective *adj* **1** based on personal thoughts and feelings; not impartial or objective. ◇ See also **objective**. **2** (*gram*) indicating or referring to the subject of a verb; nominative. — *adv* **subjectively**.

sub judice *adj* under consideration by a court, and therefore not to be publicly discussed or remarked on. [Lat]

subjugate *v* (*tr*) to bring under one's control; to make obedient or submissive. — *n* **subjugation**. [Lat *sub*, under + *jugum*, yoke]

subjunctive (*gram*) *n* **1** a set of verb forms, or mood, used to express condition, wish or uncertainty, e.g. 'If I *were* you' and 'I suggest he *leave* now'. **2** a verb form of this kind. — *adj* in or of the subjunctive. [Lat *subjungere*, to join to]

sublet *v* **-tt-**, **-let** (*tr*) to rent out to another person (property one is renting from someone else). [**sub-** (sense **2**)]

sublimate *v* (*tr*) to transform (esp. a primitive or base emotion) into something considered nobler or of higher quality; to refine. — *n* **sublimation**. [Lat *sublimare*, to elevate or exalt]

sublime *adj* **1** of the highest or noblest nature, usu. morally or spiritually. **2** overwhelmingly great; supreme. — *v* (*tr* & *intr*; *chem*) to change from a solid to a vapour without passing through the liquid state. — **from the sublime to the ridiculous** (passing, e.g. in a comparison) from something of a very serious, intellectual or beautiful nature to something silly or trivial. — *adv* **sublimely**. — *n* **sublimity** . [Lat *sublimis*, in a high position]

subliminal *adj* existing or occurring below the threshold of ordinary awareness. — *adv* **subliminally**. [Lat *sub*, under + *limen*, threshold]

subliminal advertising *n* advertising in the form of pictures shown during a film or television programme for a split second only, so that the viewer's subconscious mind registers them without the viewer knowing.

submachine-gun *n* a lightweight portable machine-gun fired from the shoulder or hip. [**sub-** (sense **3**)]

submarine *n* a vessel, esp. military, able to travel beneath the surface of the sea. — *adj* under the surface of the sea. — *n* **submariner**. [**sub-** (sense **1**)]

submerge *v* **1** (*tr* & *intr*) to plunge or sink under the surface of water or other liquid. **2** (*tr*) to overwhelm or inundate, e.g. with work. — *n* **submersion**. [Lat *sub*, under + *mergere*, to plunge]

submersible *n* & *adj* (a vessel) able to operate under water.

submit *v* **-tt- 1** (*intr*; **to**) to give in, esp. to the wishes or control of another person; to stop resisting. **2** (*tr* & *intr*) to offer (oneself) as a subject of experiment or other treatment. **3** (*tr*) to offer or present (e.g. a proposal) for formal consideration by others. [Lat *sub*, beneath + *mittere*, to send]

submission *n* **1** an act of submitting. **2** a thing submitted, e.g. for consideration or approval. **3** submissiveness.

submissive *adj* willing or tending to submit; meek; obedient. — *adv* **submissively**. — *n* **submissiveness**.

subnormal *adj* less than normal, esp. with regard to intelligence. [**sub-** (sense **1**)]

subordinate *adj* (**to**) lower in rank or importance (than); secondary. — *n* a subordinate person or thing. — *v* (*tr*; **to**) to regard or treat as subordinate (to). — *n* **subordination**. [Lat *sub*, below + *ordo*, rank]

subordinate clause *n* (*gram*) a clause that acts like a noun, adjective or adverb and is not able to function as an independent sentence, as in 'The book *that you gave me for Christmas* was fascinating'. ◇ See also **main clause**.

suborn *v* (*tr*) to persuade (someone) to commit a crime or other wrong, e.g. with a bribe. [Lat *sub*, secretly + *ornare*, to equip]

subpoena *n* a written order legally obliging a person to appear in a court of law at a specified time; a summons. — *v* ***-naed*** or ***-na'd*** (*tr*) to serve with a subpoena. [Lat, under penalty]

subscribe *v* (*intr*) **1** (**to**) to (sign a contract binding oneself to) pay money, e.g. a membership fee or the cost of receiving regular issues of a magazine. **2** (with **to**) to agree with or believe in. — *n* **subscriber**. [Lat *sub*, at the bottom + *scribere*, to write]

subscriber trunk dialling *n* a telephone system in which customers make long-distance calls direct, without the help of an operator.

subscript *n* & *adj* (a printed character) set below the level of the line, as the number 2 in H_2O. ◇ See also **superscript**. [Ety. as for **subscribe**]

subscription *n* **1** a payment made in subscribing. **2** an advance order, esp. of a book before its official publication. **3** the act of subscribing. [Ety. as for **subscribe**]

subsequent *adj* & *adv* (**to**) happening after or following. — *adv* **subsequently**. [Lat *sub*, after + *sequi*, to follow]

subservient *adj* **1** (too) ready or eager to submit to the wishes of others. **2** (**to**) subordinate. — *n* **subservience**. [Lat *sub*, under + *servire*, to serve]

subside *v* (*intr*) **1** (of land, buildings, etc.) to sink to a lower level; to settle. **2** (of noise, feelings, etc.) to become less loud or intense; to die down. — *n* **subsidence**. [Lat *sub*, down + *sidere*, to settle]

subsidiary *adj* **1** (**to**) of secondary importance; subordinate. **2** serving as an addition or supplement; auxiliary. — *n* ***-ies*** **1** a subsidiary person or thing. **2** a company at least half-owned by another (usu. larger) organisation. [Ety. as for **subside**]

subsidise or **-ize** *v* (*tr*) **1** to provide or support with a subsidy. **2** to pay a proportion of the cost of (a thing supplied) in order to reduce the price paid by the customer. **3** (*loosely*) to pay the expenses of. [Ety. as for **subside**]

subsidy *n* ***-ies*** **1** a sum of money given, e.g. by a government to an industry, to help with running costs or to keep product prices low. **2** financial aid of this kind. [Ety. as for **subside**]

subsist *v* (*intr*) **1** (**on**) to live or (barely) manage to stay alive (by means of). **2** (*formal*; with **in**) to lie or be found in; to consist of: *The team's success subsists in their fitness*. [Lat *subsistere*, to stand still or firm]

subsistence *n* the means of existence; livelihood. — *adj* (of wages, etc.) just enough to provide basic necessities.

subsistence farming *n* farming in which most of the produce is consumed by the farmer's family.

subsoil *n* the layer of soil just beneath the surface soil. [**sub-** (sense **1**)]

subsonic *adj* relating to, being, or travelling at speeds below the speed of sound. [**sub-** (sense **3**)]

substance *n* **1** the matter or material that a thing is made of. **2** a particular kind of matter with a definable quality: *a sticky substance*. **3** the essence or basic meaning of something spoken or written. **4** touchable reality; tangibility: *Ghosts have no substance*. **5** solid quality or worth: *food with no substance*. **6** foundation; truth: *no substance in the rumours*. **7** wealth and influence: *woman of substance*. [Lat *substantia*]

substandard *adj* inferior; not up to the required or expected standard.

substantial *adj* **1** considerable in amount, extent or importance. **2** of real value or worth; (of food) nourishing. **3** solidly built. **4** existing as a touchable thing; material; corporeal. **5** relating to a thing's basic nature or essence; essential. **6** wealthy and influential; well-to-do. — *adv* **substantially**. [Ety. as for **substance**]

substantiate *v* (*tr*) to prove or support; to confirm the truth or validity of. — *n* **substantiation**. [Ety. as for **substance**]

substantive *adj* **1** of significant importance or value. **2** relating to the essential nature of something. — *n* (*gram*) a noun. — *adv* **substantively**. [Lat *substantivus*]

substitute *n* a person or thing that takes the place of, or is used instead of, another. — *v* (*tr*; **for**) to use or bring into use as a substitute. — *adj* acting as a substitute. — *n* **substitution**. [Lat *sub*, under + *statuere*, to set]

substratum *n* ***-ta*** (*tech*) **1** an underlying layer. **2** a foundation or foundation material. [**sub-** (sense **1**)]

subsume *v* (*tr*) **1** to take into, or regard as part of, a larger, more general group or category. **2** (*loosely*) to take over. — *n* **subsumption**. [Lat *sub*, under + *sumere*, to take]

subtend *v* (*tr*) (of a line or a side of a geometric figure) to be opposite to (an arc or an angle). [Lat *sub*, under + *tendere*, to stretch]

subterfuge *n* (the use of) a trick or deception that evades, conceals or obscures. [Lat *subter-*, secretly + *fugere*, to flee]

subterranean *adj* existing or operating underground, or in secret. [Lat *sub*, under + *terra*, earth]

subtitle *n* **1** (in *pl*) a printed translation of the dialogue of a foreign film, appearing bit by bit at the bottom of the screen. **2** a second title, usu. expanding on or explaining the main title. [**sub-** (sense **1**)]

subtle *adj* **1** not straightforwardly or obviously stated or displayed. **2** (of distinctions, etc.) difficult to appreciate or perceive. **3** (of flavours, etc.) extremely faint or delicate. **4** carefully or craftily discreet or indirect. — *n* **subtlety** , **-*ies***. — *adv* **subtly**. [Lat *sub*, under + *tela*, web]

subtract *v* (*tr*; **from**) to take (one number or quantity) from another; to deduct. — *n* **subtraction**. [Lat *sub*, away + *trahere*, to draw]

subtropical *adj* (belonging to or typical of those areas) bordering on the tropical regions of the world. [**sub-** (sense **3**)]

suburb *n* (often in *pl*) a district, esp. residential, on the edge of a town or city. [Lat *sub*, near + *urbs*, city]

suburban *adj* **1** of or in a suburb. **2** narrow in outlook; narrowly genteel or middle-class.

suburbia *n* (the people who live in) suburbs collectively.

subvention *n* a grant or subsidy. [Lat *subvenire*, to come to help]

subvert *v* (*tr*) **1** to overthrow (a government or other legally established body). **2** to corrupt (a person); to undermine (a principle, etc.). [Lat *subvertere*, to overturn]

subversion *n* the act or practice of subverting (usu. a government).

subversive *n* & *adj* (a person) likely, tending, or intending to subvert (usu. a government).

subway *n* **1** a passage under a road or railway, esp. for pedestrians, also for pipes, etc. **2** (*US*) an underground railway. [**sub-** (sense **1**)]

succeed *v* **1** (*intr*) to achieve an aim or purpose. **2** (*intr*) to develop or turn out as planned. **3** (*intr*) to do well in a particular area or field. **4** (*tr*) to come next after; to follow. **5** (*intr* with **to**) to take up (a position, etc.), following on from someone else. [Lat *succedere*, to go next after]

success *n* **1** the quality of succeeding or the state of having succeeded; a favourable development or outcome. **2** the attainment of fame, power or wealth. **3** a person who has attained any such quality, or who is judged favourably by others. **4** a thing that turns out as planned, or that is judged favourably by others. — *adj* **successful**. — *adv* **successfully**. [Ety. as for **succeed**]

succession *n* **1** a series of people or things coming one after the other. **2** the right or order by which one person or thing succeeds another. — **in succession** one after the other.

successive *adj* immediately following another or each other. — *adv* **successively**.

successor *n* a person who follows another, esp. who takes over the job or position of another.

succinct *adj* (of something written or said) brief and precise; concise. — *adv* **succinctly**. — *n* **succinctness**. [Lat *succinctus*]

Succoth. Same as **Sukkoth**.

succour (*formal*) *n* help or relief in time of distress or need. — *v* (*tr*) to give succour to. [Lat *succurrere*, to run to help]

succubus *n* **-*bi*** a female evil spirit which is supposed to have sexual intercourse with sleeping men. ◇ See also **incubus**. [Lat *succuba*, prostitute]

succulent *adj* **1** (of food) deliciously juicy. **2** (of a plant) with thick fleshy leaves or stems in which water can be stored for long periods. — *n* a succulent plant. — *n* **succulence**. [Lat *sucus*, juice]

succumb *v* (*intr*; **to**) **1** to give in (to pressure, temptation or desire). **2** to die (of). [Lat *sub*, under + *cumbere*, to lie down]

such *adj* **1** of that kind, or the same or a similar kind: *You can't reason with such a person.* **2** so great: *not such a fool as to believe that.* — *adv* extremely: *such a lovely present.* — *pron* a person or thing, or people or things, like that or those just mentioned: *chimps, gorillas and such.* — **as such 1** in or by itself alone. **2** as it is described. — **such as** for example. [OE *swilc*]

such-and-such *adj* & *pron* (a person or thing) of a particular but unspecified kind.

suchlike *adj* & *pron* (things) of the same kind.

suck *v* **1** (*tr* & *intr*; **in, up**) to draw (liquid) into the mouth. **2** (*tr*) to draw liquid from (e.g. a juicy fruit) with the mouth. **3** (*tr*; **in, up**) to draw in by suction. **4** (*tr*) to take (e.g. a thumb or a pencil) partly into the mouth and subject it to action similar to that for sucking in liquids. **5** (*tr*) to draw the flavour from (e.g. a sweet) with squeezing and rolling movements inside the mouth. **6** (*tr*) to draw milk from (a breast or udder) with the mouth. **7** (*intr*; *slang*; esp. *US*) to be contemptible or contemptibly bad. — *n* an act or bout of sucking. — *v* **suck up to** (*tr*; *coll*) to flatter or be obsequious to, in order to gain favour. [OE *sucan*]

sucker *n* **1** a cup-shaped organ in plants and animals that attaches itself to surfaces by suction. **2** a similar man-made device. **3** a shoot rising from underground and developing into a new plant. **4** (*coll*) a person easily deceived or taken advantage of. **5** (*coll*; with **for**) a person irresistibly attracted to.

suckle *v* **1** (*tr*) to feed (a baby) with milk from one's breast or udder. **2** (*tr* & *intr*) to

suck milk from (a breast or udder). [Ety. as for **suck**]
suckling *n* a young baby or animal still suckling its mother's breast.

sucrose *n* (*chem*) sugar of the kind generally used by people for sweetening food and drinks. [Fr *sucre*, sugar]

suction *n* **1** the act or power of sucking. **2** a drawing or adhering force created by a difference or reduction in air pressure. [Lat *sugere*, to suck]

sudden *adj* happening quickly or unexpectedly. — *adv* **suddenly**. — *n* **suddenness**. — **all of a sudden** suddenly. [OFr *soudain*]
sudden death *n* a method of deciding a tied contest by declaring the winner to be the player or team that scores first in an extra period.

sudorific *n* & *adj* (*med*) (a drug) causing sweating. [Lat *sudor*, sweat + *facere*, to make]

suds *n* (*pl*) a mass of bubbles produced on water when soap or other detergent is dissolved. [Perhaps ODut *sudse*, marsh]

sue *v* (*tr* & *intr*) to take legal proceedings against (a person or company). [OFr *suir*, from Lat *sequi*, to follow]

suede *n* soft leather given a velvet-like finish. [Fr (*gants de*) *Suède*, (gloves from) Sweden]

suet *n* hard fat from around the kidneys of sheep or cattle, used to make pastry and puddings. [Lat *sebum*, fat]

Suff. *abbrev* Suffolk.

suffer *v* **-r-** **1** (*tr* & *intr*) to undergo or endure (physical or mental pain or other unpleasantness). **2** (*intr* with **from**) to be afflicted (with an illness). **3** (*intr*) to deteriorate (as a result of something). **4** (*tr*) to tolerate: *not suffer fools gladly*. **5** (*tr*; *old*; **to**) to allow: *Suffer little children to come unto me*. — *n* **sufferer**. — *n* **suffering**. [Lat *sub*, under + *ferre*, to bear]
sufferance: **on sufferance** tolerated, but not welcomed or encouraged.

suffice *v* **1** (*intr*; **for**) to be enough, or be good enough (for a particular purpose). **2** (*tr*) to satisfy (a person). — **suffice it to say** I need only say. [Lat *sufficere*]

sufficient *adj* enough; adequate. — *adv* **sufficiently**. [Lat *sufficere*, to suffice]
sufficiency *n* **-ies** a sufficient amount.

suffix *n* a word element added to the end of a word or word stem to mark a grammatical inflection or form a derivative, e.g. the *-s* in *monkeys* and the *-tude* in *certitude*. — *v* (*tr*) to add as a suffix. [Lat *suffixus*, fixed underneath]

suffocate *v* **1** (*tr* & *intr*) to kill with or die from lack of air, e.g. with an obstruction over the mouth and nose. **2** (*intr*) to experience difficulty in breathing because of heat and lack of air; to stifle. **3** (*tr*; **with**) to subject to an oppressive amount (of). — *adj* **suffocating**. — *n* **suffocation**. [Lat *suffocare*, from *sub*, under + *fauces*, throat]

suffragan *n* **1** a bishop appointed as assistant to another bishop. **2** any bishop considered as an archbishop's subordinate. [Lat *suffraganeus*, assistant]

suffrage *n* the right to vote in political elections. [Lat *suffragium*, a vote]
suffragette *n* any of a group of women who campaigned strenuously for women's suffrage in Britain in the early 20th century.

suffuse *v* (*tr*) (of colour, light, etc.) to cover or spread throughout. — *n* **suffusion**. [Lat *suffundere*, to pour beneath]

sugar *n* **1** a sweet-tasting carbohydrate substance found in sugar-cane and other plants, refined into white or brown crystals, used to sweeten food and drinks. **2** any carbohydrate of the same family, e.g. glucose. **3** (*coll*) a term of endearment. — *v* **-r-** (*tr*) **1** to sweeten with sugar. **2** to sprinkle or coat with sugar. — **sugar the pill** to make something unpleasant easier to deal with or accept. — *adj* **sugared**. [Arabic *sukkar*]
sugar-beet *n* a variety of beet cultivated for its white roots which yield sugar.
sugar-cane *n* a tall tropical grass with thick woody stems from which sugar is obtained.
sugar daddy *n* (*coll*) an elderly man with a young girlfriend on whom he lavishes money and gifts.
sugar-maple *n* a N American maple tree from whose sap sugar is obtained.
sugar soap *n* a substance for cleaning or stripping paint.
sugary *adj* **1** like sugar in taste or appearance. **2** containing (too much) sugar. **3** (*coll*) exaggeratedly or insincerely pleasant or affectionate; cloying. — *n* **sugariness**.

suggest *v* (*tr*) **1** to put forward as a possibility or recommendation. **2** to make one think of; to create an impression of. **3** to cause one to think or conclude. [Lat *suggerere*, to put under]
suggestible *adj* easily influenced by suggestions made by others.
suggestion *n* **1** a thing suggested; a proposal or recommendation. **2** a hint or trace. **3** the creation of a belief or impulse in the mind of a hypnotised person. **4** the act of suggesting.
suggestive *adj* **1** (with **of**) causing one to think of; creating an impression of. **2** provoking thoughts or feelings of a sexual nature. — *adv* **suggestively**.

suicide *n* **1** the act, or an instance, of killing oneself deliberately. **2** a person who deliberately kills himself or herself. **3** the bringing about of one's own downfall, often unintentionally: *The minister's speech was political suicide*. — *adj* **suicidal**. [Lat *sui*, of oneself + *caedere*, to kill]

suit *n* **1** a set of clothes, usu. a jacket with trousers or a skirt, made from the same material and designed to be worn together. **2** an outfit worn on specific occasions or for a specific activity. **3** any of the four groups into which a pack of playing-cards is divided. **4** a legal action taken against someone; a lawsuit. — *v* **1** (*tr* & *intr*) to be acceptable to or what is required by. **2** (*tr*) to be appropriate to, in harmony with or attractive to. — **follow suit 1** to play a card of the same suit as the card first played. **2** to do the same as someone else has done. — **suit oneself** to do what one wants to do, esp. without considering others. [OFr *sieute*, from *sivre*, to follow]

suitable *adj* that suits; appropriate or agreeable. — *n* **suitability**. — *adv* **suitably**.

suitcase *n* a portable travelling case for clothes, with flat stiffened sides and a handle.

suite *n* **1** a set of rooms forming a self-contained unit within a larger building. **2** a matching set of furniture. **3** (*mus*) a set of instrumental movements in related keys. **4** a group of followers or attendants. [Fr]

suitor *n* **1** (*old*) a man courting a woman for love or marriage. **2** a person who sues; a plaintiff. [Ety. as for **suit**]

Sukkoth *n* (also **Feast of Tabernacles**) a Jewish harvest festival commemorating the period when the Israelites lived in tents in the desert during the Exodus from Egypt. [Hebr, huts]

sulk *v* (*intr*) to be silent or unsociable out of petty resentment or bad temper. — *n* (often in *pl* with **the**) a bout of sulking. — *adv* **sulkily**. — *n* **sulkiness**. — *adj* **sulky**, **-ier**, **-iest**. [Perhaps OE *aseolcan*, to slack or be slow]

sullen *adj* **1** silently and stubbornly angry or unsociable. **2** (of skies, etc.) dismal. — *adv* **sullenly**. — *n* **sullenness**. [Lat *solus*, alone]

sully *v* **-ies**, **-ied** (*tr*) **1** to tarnish or mar (a reputation, etc.). **2** (*literary*) to make dirty. [OE *sylian*, to defile]

sulphate *n* a salt of sulphuric acid. [**sulphur** + **-ate**]

sulphide *n* a compound containing sulphur and another element. [**sulphur** + **-ide**]

sulphur *n* an element (symbol **S**), a yellow brittle non-metallic mineral that burns with a blue flame and a choking smell. [Lat *sulfur*]

sulphuric acid *n* a very corrosive acid (H_2SO_4) widely used in industry.

sulphurous *adj* of, like, or containing sulphur.

sultan *n* the ruler of any of various Muslim countries, esp. the former ruler of the Ottoman empire. [Arabic]

sultana *n* **1** the wife or concubine of a sultan. **2** the mother, sister or daughter of a sultan. **3** a pale seedless raisin.

sultry *adj* **-ier**, **-iest 1** (whose appearance is) suggestive of sexual passion; sensual. **2** (of weather) hot and humid; close. — *adv* **sultrily**. — *n* **sultriness**. [Obsolete *sulter*, to swelter]

sum *n* **1** the amount produced when numbers or quantities are added together. **2** an amount of money. **3** an (esp. simple) arithmetical calculation. — *v* **-mm-** (**up**) **1** (*tr*) to summarise. **2** (*tr*) to express or embody the complete character or nature of. **3** (*tr*) to make a quick assessment of. **4** (*intr*) (of a court judge) to restate the main points of a case before the jury retires (*n* **summing-up**). — **in sum** briefly; to sum up. [Lat *summa*, top]

sum total *n* the complete or final total.

summary *n* **-ies** a short account outlining the main points. — *adj* done or performed quickly, without hesitation or (often proper) attention to details or formalities. — *adv* **summarily**. [Lat *summarium*]

summarise or **-ize** *v* (*tr*) to make or present a summary of.

summation *n* **1** the process of finding the sum; addition. **2** a summary or summing-up. [Lat *summare*, to sum up]

summer *n* **1** the warmest season of the year, between spring and autumn, extending from about May to September in the northern hemisphere. **2** (*literary*) a time of greatest energy, happiness, etc.; a heyday. — *adj* of, occurring in, or for use in the summer. — *adj* **summery**. [OE *sumer*]

summerhouse *n* any small building or shelter designed to provide shade in a park or garden.

summer school *n* a course of study held during the summer, e.g. at a university.

summertime *n* the season of summer.

summer time *n* time one hour ahead of Greenwich Mean Time, adopted in Britain during the summer months for daylight-saving purposes.

summit *n* **1** the highest point of a mountain or hill. **2** the highest (possible) level of achievement or development, e.g. in a career. **3** (also **summit meeting** or **summit conference**) a conference between heads of government or other senior officials. [Lat *summum*, highest]

summon *v* **-n-** (*tr*) **1** to order (a person) to come or appear, e.g. in a court of law. **2** to order or call upon (to do something). **3** (**up**) to gather or muster (e.g. one's strength or energy). [Lat *summonere*, to warn secretly]

summons *n* **-ses 1** a written order legally obliging a person to attend a court of law at a specified time. **2** any authoritative order to come or to do something. — *v* (*tr*) to serve with a summons.

sumo *n* traditional Japanese wrestling between contestants of great bulk, won by forcing the opponent to the ground or out of the circular unroped ring. [Jap]

sump *n* **1** a small tank inside a vehicle engine from which oil is carried around the moving parts. **2** any pit into which liquid drains or is poured. [Dut *somp*]

sumptuary *adj* **1** relating to or regulating expense. **2** controlling extravagance. [Lat *sumptuarius*, from *sumptus*, cost]

sumptuous *adj* superbly rich and luxurious. [Lat *sumptuosus*, from *sumptus*, cost]

sun *n* **1** (usu. *cap* with **the**) the star that is the source of light, heat and gravitational pull for all the planets in the earth's planetary system. **2** the heat or light from this star. **3** any star with a system of planets revolving around it. — *v* ***-nn-*** (*tr*) to expose (oneself) to the sun's rays. — **under the sun** anywhere; on earth. [OE *sunne*]

sunbathe *v* (*intr*) to expose one's body to the sun, in order to get a suntan. — *n* **sunbathing**.

sunbeam *n* a ray of sunlight.

sunbed *n* a bed-like device with sun-lamps fitted above (and often beneath a transparent screen one lies on), for artificially tanning the whole body.

sunburn *n* soreness and reddening of the skin caused by over-exposure to the sun.

sundial *n* an instrument that uses sunlight to tell the time, by the changing position of the shadow that a vertical arm casts on a horizontal plate with graded markings.

sundown *n* sunset.

sunfish *n* a large ocean fish with a flat body that is almost circular seen side on.

sunflower *n* an orig. N American plant that has large tall-stemmed flowers with yellow radiating petals and edible seeds yielding a cooking oil.

sunglasses *n* (*pl*) glasses with tinted lenses, worn to protect the eyes from sunlight, not to correct eyesight.

sun-lamp *n* a lamp emitting light similar in nature to sunlight, used therapeutically and for artificially tanning the skin.

sunlight *n* light from the sun. — *adj* **sunlit**.

sun lounge *n* a room with large windows for letting in maximum sunlight.

sunny *adj* ***-ier***, ***-iest*** **1** filled with sunshine or sunlight. **2** cheerful; good-humoured.

sunrise *n* (the time of) the sun's appearance above the horizon in the morning.

sunroof *n* a transparent panel in a car roof, for letting in sunlight, often opening for ventilation.

sunset *n* (the time of) the sun's disappearance below the horizon in the evening.

sunshade *n* **1** a sort of umbrella for protecting one from the sun. **2** an awning.

sunshine *n* **1** fair weather, with the sun shining brightly. **2** the light or heat of the sun. **3** a place where one can be in the light or heat of the sun. **4** an informal term of address, often used in a condescending or scolding tone.

sunspot *n* **1** an area of temporary coolness on the sun's surface, visible as a dark patch. **2** (*coll*) a holiday resort renowned for sunny weather.

sunstroke *n* a severe condition of collapse and fever brought on by over-exposure to the sun.

suntan *n* a browning of the skin through exposure to the sun or a sun-lamp. — *adj* **sun-tanned**.

sun-trap *n* an area, in a garden, etc., that receives a lot of sunlight and is sheltered from the wind.

sun-up *n* sunrise.

Sun. *abbrev* Sunday.

sundae *n* a portion of ice-cream topped with fruit, nuts, syrup, etc.

Sunday *n* **1** the first day of the week and for most Christians the day of worship and rest. **2** (*coll*) a newspaper appearing on this day. — **a month of Sundays** a very long time. [OE *sunnan dæg*, day of the sun]

Sunday best *n* one's best clothes, (esp. formerly) considered the most suitable for wearing to church.

Sunday school *n* a class for the religious instruction of children, held on Sundays, usu. in church buildings.

sundry *adj* various; assorted; miscellaneous. — *n* ***-ies*** (in *pl*) various small unspecified items; oddments. — **all and sundry** everybody. [OE *syndrig*]

sung. See **sing**.

sunk. See **sink**.

sunken former *past participle* of **sink**. — *adj* **1** situated or fitted at a lower level than the surrounding area. **2** (of cheeks, etc.) made hollow through ill health.

Sunni *n* one of the two main branches of the Islamic religion (the other being **Shia**), that regards the teachings of Mohammed himself as supremely authoritative. — *n & adj* **Sunnite**. [Arabic *sunnah*, rule]

sup *v* ***-pp-*** (*tr*) **1** to drink in small mouthfuls. **2** (*coll*) to drink (alcohol). — *n* a small mouthful; a sip. [OE *supan*]

super[1] *adj & interj (coll)* extremely good; excellent. — *n* something of superior quality or grade, e.g. petrol. [Lat, above]

super[2] *n* (*coll*) **1** a superintendent. **2** a supernumerary, esp. a supernumerary actor.

super- *pfx* **1** great or extreme in size or degree: *supertanker*. **2** above or beyond: *supernatural*. **3** outstanding: *superhero*. [Lat *super*, above]

superannuated *adj* **1** made to retire and given a pension; pensioned off. **2** old and no longer fit for use. [Lat *super*, above + *annus*, year]

superannuation *n* **1** an amount regularly deducted from wages as a contribution to a company pension. **2** the pension received. **3** retirement.

superb *adj* **1** (*coll*) outstandingly excellent. **2** magnificent; majestic. — *adv* **superbly**. [Lat *superbus*, proud]

supercharge *v* (*tr*) **1** to increase the power and performance of (a vehicle engine). **2** (**with**) to charge or fill (e.g. an atmosphere) with an intense amount of an emotion, etc. [**super-** (sense **1**)]

supercharger *n* a device that increases the pressure under which air is forced into a vehicle engine, increasing the engine's power and performance.

supercilious *adj* **1** self-important. **2** arrogantly disdainful. — *adv* **superciliously**. — *n* **superciliousness**. [Lat *super*, above + *cilium*, eyelid]

superconductivity *n* (*physics*) the complete absence of electrical resistance in some metals and ceramics at certain temperatures. [**super-** (sense **1**)] **superconductor** *n* (*physics*) a material which exhibits superconductivity.

supererogation *n* the doing of more than is required. — *adj* **supererogatory**. [Lat *super*, above + *erogare*, to pay out]

superficial *adj* **1** of, on or near the surface. **2** not thorough or in-depth; cursory. **3** only apparent; not real or genuine. **4** lacking the capacity for sincere emotion or serious thought; shallow. — *n* **superficiality**. — *adv* **superficially**. [Lat *super*, above + *facies*, face]

superfluous *adj* more than is needed or wanted; surplus. — *n* **superfluity**, ***-ies***. [Lat *superfluus*, overflowing]

supergrass *n* (*slang*) a police informer whose information has led to large numbers of arrests. [**super-** (sense **3**) + **grass** (sense **5**]

superhuman *adj* beyond ordinary human ability or knowledge. [**super-** (sense **2**)]

superimpose *v* (*tr*) to lay or set (one thing) on top of another. — *n* **superimposition**. [**super-** (sense **1**)]

superintend *v* (*tr*) to supervise. — *n* **superintendence**. [Lat *superintendere*] **superintendent** *n* **1** a police officer above the rank of chief inspector. **2** a person who superintends.

superior *adj* **1** (**to**) higher in rank or position. **2** (**to**) better in a particular way. **3** of high quality. **4** arrogant; self-important. **5** (of a printed character) set above the level of the line. — *n* **1** a person of higher rank or position. **2** the head of a religious community. — *n* **superiority**. [Lat *superus*, set above]

superlative *adj* **1** superior to all others; supreme. **2** (*gram*) (of an adjective or adverb) expressing the highest degree of a particular quality, e.g. *nicest* and *most beautiful*. — *n* (*gram*) (an adjective or adverb in) the superlative form. [Lat *superlativus*]

superman *n* ***-men*** **1** a man with extraordinary strength or ability. **2** a fictional man with superhuman powers. [**super-** (sense **3**)]

supermarket *n* a large self-service store selling food and other goods. [**super-** (sense **1**)]

supernatural *adj* of, relating to, or being phenomena that cannot be explained by the laws of nature or physics. — *n* (with **the**) supernatural phenomena. [**super-** (sense **2**)]

supernova *n* ***-vae*** or ***-vas*** a star that, on exploding, briefly becomes up to several hundred million times brighter than the sun. [**super-** (sense **1**) + **nova**]

supernumerary *adj* additional to the normal or required number; extra. — *n* ***-ies*** **1** a supernumerary person or thing. **2** an actor without a speaking part. [Lat *super*, above + *numerus*, number]

superpower *n* a nation with outstanding political, economic or military influence, esp. the United States or the former Soviet Union. [**super-** (sense **1**)]

superscript *n* & *adj* (a printed character) set above the level of the line, as the number 2 in πr^2. ◇ See also **subscript**. [Lat *super*, above + *scribere*, to write]

supersede *v* (*tr*) **1** to take the place of (often something outdated or no longer valid). **2** to set aside in favour of another. — *n* **supersession**. [Lat *supersedere*, to sit above]

supersonic *adj* (capable of travelling at speeds) faster than the speed of sound. — *adv* **supersonically**. [Lat *super*, above + *sonus*, sound]

superstar *n* an internationally famous celebrity, esp. from the world of film, popular music or sport. [**super-** (sense **3**)]

superstition *n* **1** belief in a mysterious influence that certain (esp. commonplace) objects, actions or occurrences have on events, people's lives, etc. **2** a particular opinion or practice based on such belief. **3** any widely held but unfounded belief. — *adj* **superstitious**. [Lat *superstitio*, fear of the supernatural]

superstructure *n* any part built above another (esp. main) part, e.g. those parts of a ship above the main deck. [**super-** (sense **1**)]

supertax *n* (*coll*) a surtax. [**super-** (sense **2**)]

supervene *v* (*intr*) to occur as an (esp. unexpected) interruption to some process. — *n* **supervention**. [Lat *supervenire*, to come upon]

supervise *v* (*tr*) to be in overall charge of; to oversee. — *n* **supervision**. — *n* **supervisor**. — *adj* **supervisory**. [Lat *supervidere*, to see over]

supine *adj* **1** lying on one's back. **2** passive or lazy. [Lat *supinus*]

supper *n* **1** a light evening meal. **2** a late-night snack taken in addition to and later than the main evening meal. [OFr *soper*]

supplant *v* (*tr*) to take the place of, often by force or unfair means. [Lat *supplantare*, to trip up]

supple *adj* **1** (of joints, etc.) bending easily; flexible. **2** (of a person) having flexible joints. — *adv* **supplely** or **supply**. — *n* **suppleness**. [Lat *supplex*, bending the knees]

supplement *n* **1** a thing added to make something complete or to make up a deficiency. **2** an extra section added to a book to give additional information or to correct previous errors. **3** a separate part added to a newspaper or magazine on certain occasions, e.g. on Sundays. — *v* (*tr*) to add to, or make up a lack of. — *adj*

supplementary. — *n* **supplementation**. [Lat *supplementum*, a filling up]

supplementary benefit *n* a former name for **income support**.

supplicate *v* (*tr* & *intr*; **to**, **for**) to make a humble and earnest request or entreaty to (someone); to beg. — *n* **supplication**. [Lat *supplicare*, to beg on one's knees]

supplicant *n* & *adj* (a person) who supplicates.

supply *v* **-ies**, **-ied** (*tr*) **1** (**to**, **with**) to provide or furnish. **2** to satisfy (e.g. a need); to make up (a deficiency). — *n* **-ies 1** an amount supplied, esp. regularly. **2** an amount that can be drawn from and used; a stock. **3** (in *pl*) necessary food or equipment gathered or taken on a journey, etc. **4** a source of some public utility, e.g. water or gas. **5** (*econ*) the total amount of a commodity being produced for sale. **6** degree of availability: *in short supply*. **7** a person, esp. a teacher, acting as a temporary substitute. **8** the act of supplying. — *n* **supplier**. [Lat *supplere*, to fill up]

support *v* (*tr*) **1** to keep upright or in place; to keep from falling; to bear the weight of. **2** to give active approval and encouragement to. **3** to provide with the means necessary for living or existing. **4** to maintain a loyal interest in the fortunes of (a sporting team), esp. by regular attendance at matches. **5** to reinforce the disputed accuracy or validity of (e.g. a theory or claim). **6** to speak in favour of (a proposal, etc.). **7** to play a part subordinate to (a leading actor). **8** to perform as an introduction to (the main item in a musical concert, etc.). **9** to bear or tolerate. — *n* **1** the act of supporting or the state of being supported. **2** a person, group or thing that supports; a supporting act in a concert, etc. — *adj* **supporting**. [Lat *supportare*, to hold up]

supporter *n* a person who supports (esp. a sporting team, a political party, a cause or a proposal).

supportive *adj* providing support, esp. active approval and encouragement.

suppose *v* (*tr*) **1** to consider likely or probable; to regard as a (near) certainty. **2** to treat (a possibility) as a fact for the purposes of forming an argument or plan: *Let us suppose he doesn't come*. **3** (of a theory) to require (something) to be true or be the case in order to be valid. [Lat *supponere*, to substitute]

supposed *adj* generally believed to be so or such (but considered doubtful by the speaker). — **supposed to 1** expected or required to. **2** reputed to (have or be). — *adv* **supposedly**.

supposition *n* **1** the act of supposing. **2** that which is supposed; a mere possibility or assumption, not a fact. — *adj* **suppositional**.

suppositious *adj* based on supposition; hypothetical.

suppository *n* **-ies** a small cylindrical tablet containing a medicinal substance, inserted into the anus or vagina and left to melt. [Lat *suppositorium*, from *supponere*, to place underneath]

suppress *v* (*tr*) **1** to hold in or restrain (feelings, etc.). **2** to put a stop to or crush (e.g. a rebellion). **3** to prevent from broadcasting or circulating; to prevent from being broadcast, circulated, or otherwise made known. **4** to moderate or eliminate (interference) in an electrical device. — *n* **suppression**. — *n* **suppressor**. [Lat *supprimere*, to press down]

suppurate *v* (*intr*) (of a wound, etc.) to gather or esp. release pus. — *n* **suppuration**. [Lat *suppurare*]

supra *adv* above; further up the page or earlier in the book. [Lat]

supra- *pfx* above. [Lat *supra*, above]

supreme *adj* **1** of highest rank, power or importance; greatest. **2** most excellent; best. **3** greatest in degree; utmost. — *adv* **supremely**. [Lat *supremus*, highest]

supremacy *n* **1** supreme power or authority. **2** the state of being supreme.

supremo *n* **-os** (*coll*) **1** a supreme head or leader. **2** a boss. [Span; see ety. for **supreme**]

sur-[1] *pfx* over, above or beyond; super-. [Fr]

sur-[2] *pfx* the form of **sub-** used before some word roots beginning with the letter *r*, as in **surrogate**.

sura or **surah** *n* a chapter of the Koran. [Arabic, step]

surcharge *n* **1** an extra charge. **2** an alteration printed on or over something, esp. a new valuation on a stamp. **3** an amount over a permitted load. — *v* (*tr*) **1** to impose a surcharge on. **2** to print a surcharge on or over. **3** to overload. [**sur-**[1]]

sure *adj* **1** (**of**, **about**) confident beyond doubt in one's belief or knowledge; convinced. **2** guaranteed or certain (to happen, etc.). **3** (**of**) unquestionably destined (for); assured (of). **4** undoubtedly true or accurate: *a sure sign*. **5** reliably stable or secure. — *adv* (*coll*) certainly; of course. — *n* **sureness**. — **be sure to** not to fail to (do something). — **for sure** definitely; undoubtedly. — **make sure** to take the necessary action to remove all doubt or risk; to be certain. — **sure enough** (*coll*) in fact; as was expected. — **to be sure** certainly; admittedly. [OFr *sur*, from Lat *securus*, with care]

sure-fire *adj* (*coll*) sure to succeed; infallible.

sure-footed *adj* **1** not stumbling or likely to stumble. **2** not making, or not likely to make, mistakes.

surely *adv* **1** without doubt; certainly. **2** (in questions and exclamations) it must be that; it is hoped or expected that: *Surely you're not leaving already!*

surety *n* **-ies 1** (a thing given as) security against loss or damage, or a guarantee that a promise will be fulfilled. **2** a person who agrees to become legally responsible for another person's behaviour. [Ety. as for **sure**]

surf *n* the foam produced by breaking waves. — *v* (*intr*) to go surfing. — *n* **surfer**.

surfboard *n* a long narrow shaped fibre-glass board that a surfer stands or lies on.

surfing *n* the sport of riding a surfboard along on the crests of large breaking waves.

surface *n* **1** the upper or outer side of anything, often with regard to texture or appearance. **2** the upper level of a body or container of liquid. **3** external appearance, rather than underlying reality. **4** a geometric figure that is flat or two-dimensional, not solid. — *adj* **1** at, on or relating to a surface. **2** superficial. — *v* **1** (*tr*) to give the desired finish or texture to the surface of. **2** (*intr*) to rise to the surface of a liquid. **3** (*intr*) to become apparent; to come to light. **4** (*intr*; *coll*) to get out of bed. [Fr]

surface tension *n* the combination of molecular forces within a liquid that causes its surface to behave like a thin elastic membrane, clinging to the sides of a container or other object.

surfeit *n* **1** an excess. **2** the stuffed or sickened feeling resulting from any excess, esp. over-eating or over-drinking. — *v* (*tr*) to feed or otherwise indulge until stuffed or disgusted. [OFr *surfait*, excess]

surge *n* **1** a violent rush (of emotion). **2** a sudden powerful mass movement, esp. forwards. **3** a sudden sharp increase. **4** a rising and falling of a large area of sea, without individual waves; a swell. — *v* (*intr*) to well up, move, increase or swell suddenly and with force. [Lat *surgere*, to rise]

surgeon *n* **1** a doctor specialising in surgery. **2** a military doctor. [OFr *surgien*, from Gr *kheirurgia*; see ety. for **surgery**]

surgery *n* **-ies** **1** the treatment of disease or injury by cutting into the patient's body to operate directly on, or remove, the affected part. **2** the place where, or period of the day during which, a community doctor or dentist carries out treatment. **3** a set period during which a local MP or councillor is available to be consulted by the public. [Gr *kheirurgia*, from *kheir*, hand + *ergon*, work]

surgical *adj* of, for use in, or by means of surgery. — *adv* **surgically**. [Ety. as for **surgeon**]

surgical spirit *n* methylated spirit, with small amounts of castor oil, oil of wintergreen and other substances, used for cleaning wounds and sterilising medical equipment.

surly *adj* **-ier**, **-iest** abrupt and impolite in manner or speech. — *n* **surliness**. [Obsolete *sirly*, haughty]

surmise *v* (*tr*) to conclude from the (incomplete or unverified) information available; to infer. — *n* **1** a conclusion drawn from such information. **2** the act of drawing such a conclusion; conjecture. [OFr *surmettre*, to accuse]

surmount *v* (*tr*) **1** to overcome (problems, obstacles, etc.). **2** to be set on top of; to crown. — *adj* **surmountable**. [OFr *surmunter*]

surname *n* a family name or last name, as opposed to a forename or Christian name. [Fr *surnom*]

surpass *v* (*tr*) **1** to go or be beyond in degree or extent; to exceed. **2** to be better than. — *adj* **surpassed**. [Fr *surpasser*]

surplice *n* a loose wide-sleeved white linen garment worn ceremonially over the robe of members of the clergy and choir singers. [Lat *superpellicium*, overgarment]

surplus *n* **1** an amount exceeding the amount required or used. **2** (*accounting*) the amount by which income is greater than expenditure. — *adj* left over after needs have been met; extra. [Fr]

surprise *n* **1** (the momentary feeling of mental disorientation caused by) an encounter with something sudden or unexpected. **2** the act of catching someone unawares; the state of being caught unawares. — *v* (*tr*) **1** to cause to experience surprise by presenting with or subjecting to something unexpected. **2** to come upon unexpectedly or catch unawares. **3** to capture or attack with a sudden unexpected manoeuvre. — **take (someone) by surprise** to surprise (someone); to catch (someone) unawares. — *adj* **surprised**. — *adj* **surprising**. [OFr *surprendre*, to take over]

surrealism *n* an early-20th-century movement in art, literature and cinema moving away from realistic representations of life, esp. by attempting to express thoughts or dreams. — *adj* **surreal**. — *n* & *adj* **surrealist**. — *adj* **surrealistic**. [Fr *sur*, above + *réalisme*, realism]

surrender *v* **-r-** **1** (*intr*) to admit defeat by giving oneself up to an enemy; to yield. **2** (*intr*; **to**) to allow oneself to be influenced or overcome (by a desire or emotion); to give in. **3** (*tr*) to give or hand over, voluntarily or under duress. — *n* the act of surrendering. [OFr *surrendre*]

surreptitious *adj* done secretly or sneakily. — *adv* **surreptitiously**. — *n* **surreptitiousness**. [Lat *sub*, secretly + *rapere*, to snatch]

surrogate *n* & *adj* (a person or thing) standing in for another. [Lat *sub*, in the place of + *rogare*, to ask]

surrogacy *n* **-ies** **1** the state of being (a) surrogate. **2** the use of a surrogate, esp. a surrogate mother.

surrogate mother *n* a woman who carries and gives birth to a baby on behalf of another couple, esp. through artificial insemination with the man's sperm.

surround *v* (*tr*) **1** to extend all around; to encircle. **2** to exist as a background situation to; to make up the particular context or environment of. **3** (**with**) to maintain around (oneself) a large following (of people) or collection (of things). — *n* (an ornamental structure fitted around) a border or edge. — *adj* **surrounding**. [OFr *suronder*]

surroundings *n* (*pl*) environment; the places and things round about.

surtax *n* an additional tax, esp. on incomes above a certain high level. [**sur-**[1]]

surveillance *n* the act of keeping a close watch over a person, e.g. a suspected criminal. [Fr; see ety. for **survey**]

survey *v* **-eys**, **-eyed** (*tr*) **1** to look at or examine at length or in detail, in order to get a general view. **2** to examine (a building) in order to assess its condition or value. **3** to measure land heights and distances in (an area) for the purposes of drawing a detailed map. — *n* **-eys 1** a detailed examination or investigation, e.g. to find out public opinion or customer preference. **2** an inspection of a building to assess condition or value. **3** a collecting of land measurements for map-making purposes. — *n* **surveyor**. [OFr *surveoir*, from Lat *super*, over + *videre*, to see]

survive *v* **1** (*tr* & *intr*) to remain alive or (relatively) undamaged in spite of (a dangerous experience); to come through. **2** (*tr*) to live on after the death of. **3** (*intr*) to remain alive or in existence. — *n* **survival**. — *adj* **surviving**. — *n* **survivor**. [Lat *super*, beyond + *vivere*, to live]

sus (*slang*) *n* **1** a suspect. **2** suspicion, or suspicious behaviour. — *v* **-ss-** (*tr*) same as **suss**. [**suspect** or **suspicion**]

susceptible *adj* **1** (**to**) suffering readily (from); prone (to). **2** in whom strong feelings, esp. of love, are easily aroused. **3** (**to**) capable of being influenced (e.g. by persuasion). **4** (with **of**) open (to); admitting (of): *a ruling susceptible of several interpretations*. [Lat *suscipere*, to take up]

susceptibility *n* **-ies 1** the state or degree of being susceptible. **2** (in *pl*) feelings; sensibilities.

sushi *n* a Japanese dish of small cakes of cold rice topped with raw fish or vegetables. [Jap]

suspect *v* (*tr*) **1** to consider likely. **2** to think (a person) possibly or probably guilty of a crime or other wrongdoing. **3** to doubt the truth or genuineness of. — *n* a person suspected of committing a crime, etc. — *adj* thought to be possibly false, untrue or dangerous; dubious. ◇ See also **suspicion**. [Lat *suspicere*]

suspend *v* (*tr*) **1** to hang or hang up. **2** to bring a halt to, esp. temporarily. **3** to delay or postpone. **4** to remove from a job, a team, etc. temporarily, as punishment or during an investigation of a possible misdemeanour. **5** to keep particles of (a solid) floating within the body of a liquid or gas by viscosity or molecular force. [Lat *suspendere*]

suspended animation *n* a state in which a body's main functions are temporarily slowed down to an absolute minimum, e.g. in hibernation.

suspended sentence *n* a sentence of imprisonment not actually served unless the offender commits another crime within a specified period.

suspenders *n* (*pl*) **1** elastic straps for holding up women's stockings. **2** elastic straps for holding up men's socks. **3** (*NAm*) braces for trousers.

suspender-belt *n* a woman's belt-like undergarment with attached suspenders.

suspense *n* a state of nervous or excited uncertainty. — *adj* **suspenseful**. [Ety. as for **suspend**]

suspension *n* **1** the act of suspending or the state of being suspended. **2** a system of springs and shock absorbers that supports a vehicle's body on its axles. **3** a mixture of solid particles suspended in a liquid or gas.

suspension bridge *n* a bridge in which the road or rail surface hangs on vertical cables themselves attached to thicker cables stretched between towers.

suspicion *n* **1** the feeling of suspecting. **2** an act of suspecting; a belief or opinion based on intuition or slender evidence. **3** a slight quantity; a trace. — **above suspicion** too highly respected to be suspected of a crime or wrongdoing. — **under suspicion** suspected of a crime or wrongdoing. [Ety. as for **suspect**]

suspicious *adj* **1** (**of**, **about**) suspecting or tending to suspect guilt, wrongdoing or danger. **2** arousing suspicion; dubious. — *adv* **suspiciously**.

suss *v* (*tr*; *slang*) **1** (**out**) to discover, or discover the character of, esp. by intuition. **2** (with **out**) to assess or establish by taking a look. [**suspect** or **suspicion**]

sustain *v* (*tr*) **1** to maintain the energy or spirits of; to keep going. **2** to suffer or undergo (e.g. an injury). **3** to judge (esp. a barrister's objection to an opposing barrister's question or comment in court) to be valid. **4** to bear the weight of; to support. **5** to keep in existence, esp. over a long period; to maintain. — *adj* **sustained**. [Lat *sustinere*]

sustenance *n* that which keeps up energy or spirits, esp. food and drink. [Ety. as for **sustain**]

suttee *n* **1** a former Hindu custom in which a widow sacrifices herself by being burned alive on her dead husband's funeral fire. **2** a Hindu woman who sacrifices herself in this way. [Sanskrit *sati*, true wife]

suture *n* **1** the thread used in sewing up wounds. **2** a stitch or seam made with such thread. — *v* (*tr*) to sew up (a wound). [Lat *sutura*, seam]

suzerain *n* **1** a nation or state that has control over another. **2** a feudal lord. — *n* **suzerainty**. [Fr]

svelte *adj* of attractively slim build. [Fr]

SW *abbrev* **1** short wave. **2** south-west or south-western.

swab *n* **1** a piece of cotton wool or gauze used to clean wounds, apply antiseptics, etc. **2** a sample of some bodily fluid taken for examination. **3** a mop used for cleaning floors, ships' decks, etc. **4** (*slang*) a worthless person. — *v* ***-bb-*** (*tr*) to clean or clean out (as if) with a swab. [ODut *swabbe*]

swaddle *v* (*tr*) **1** to bandage. **2** to wrap (a baby) in swaddling-clothes. [OE *swæthel*, bandage]

swaddling-clothes *n* (*pl*) strips of cloth formerly wrapped round a newborn baby to restrict movement.

swag *n* **1** (*slang*) stolen goods. **2** (*Austr*) a traveller's pack or rolled bundle of possessions. **3** a garland hung between two points, or a carved representation of one. — *v* ***-gg-*** (*intr*) to sway or sag. [Norse *sveggja*, to cause to sway]

swagman *n* (*Austr*) a traveller on foot, esp. an itinerant workman, who carries a swag.

swagger *v* ***-r-*** (*intr*) **1** to walk with an air of self-importance. **2** to behave arrogantly. — *n* **1** a swaggering way of walking or behaving. **2** (*coll*) the quality of being showily fashionable or smart. — *adj* (*coll*) showily fashionable or smart. [**swag**]

swagger-stick *n* a short cane carried by a military officer.

swain *n* (*old & poetic*) **1** a country youth. **2** a young male lover or suitor. [OE *swan*]

swallow[1] *v* **1** (*tr*) to allow (e.g. food) to pass down the throat to the stomach. **2** (*intr*) to move the muscles of the throat as if allowing such movement; to gulp. **3** (*tr*; **up**) to make an indistinguishable and inseparable part of a larger mass; to engulf or absorb. **4** (*tr*) to stifle or repress (one's pride, tears, etc.). **5** (*tr*) to accept (an insult, etc.) meekly and without retaliation. **6** (*tr*; *coll*) to believe unquestioningly. — *n* **1** an act of swallowing. **2** an amount swallowed at one time. [OE *swelgan*]

swallow[2] *n* a small fast-flying insect-eating bird with long pointed wings and a long forked tail. [OE *swalwe*]

swallow dive *n* a dive during which the arms are held out at chest level until just before the entry into water.

swam. See **swim**.

swami *n* a Hindu religious teacher. [Hindi *svami*, lord, master]

swamp *n* (an area of) permanently wet, spongy ground, esp. overgrown or forested. — *v* (*tr*) **1** (**with**) to overwhelm or inundate. **2** to cause (a boat) to fill with water. **3** to flood. — *adj* **swampy**, ***-ier***, ***-iest***. [ODut *somp*]

swan *n* a large, usu. white water-bird with a long flexible neck and shortish legs. — *v* ***-nn-*** (*intr*; *coll* with **off**, **around**, etc.) to go or wander irresponsibly or idly. [OE]

swan song *n* the last performance or piece of work by a musician, artist, etc. before death or retirement.

swank (*coll*) *v* (*intr*) to boast or show off. — *n* boastfulness.

swanky *adj* ***-ier***, ***-iest*** (*coll*) **1** boastful. **2** showily smart or fashionable.

swap or **swop** *v* ***-pp-*** (*tr* & *intr*; **for, with**) to exchange (one thing for another). — *n* **1** an exchange. **2** a thing exchanged or offered in exchange. [MidE *swappen*]

swarm[1] *n* **1** a large group of bees flying off in search of a new home. **2** any large group of insects or other small creatures on the move. **3** a crowd of people on the move. — *v* (*intr*) **1** (**round**) to gather, move or go in a swarm. **2** (**with**) to be crowded or overrun. [OE *swearm*]

swarm[2] *v* (*tr* & *intr*; **up**) to climb (esp. a rope or tree) by clasping with the hands and knees or feet.

swarthy *adj* ***-ier***, ***-iest*** of dark complexion. — *n* **swarthiness**. [OE *sweart*]

swashbuckling *adj* (of a film, tale, etc.) full of adventure and excitement. [Obsolete *swash*, to make noisy violent movements + **buckler**]

swastika *n* a plain cross with the ends bent at right angles, usu. clockwise, an ancient religious symbol and the adopted badge of the Nazi party. [Sanskrit *svastika*, from *svasti*, wellbeing]

swat *v* ***-tt-*** (*tr*) to crush (esp. a fly) with a heavy slapping blow. — *n* such a blow. [OFr *esquatir*, to crush]

swatch *n* **1** a sample, esp. of fabric. **2** a collection of fabric samples.

swath or **swathe** *n* **1** (the width of) a strip of grass or corn, etc. cut by a scythe, mower or harvester. **2** a broad strip, esp. of land. [OE *swæth*, track]

swathe[1] *v* (*tr*) to wrap or bind in fabric, e.g. clothes or bandages. — *n* a bandage; a wrapping, esp. of cloth. [OE *swathian*]

swathe[2]. See **swath**.

sway *v* **1** (*tr* & *intr*) to (cause to) swing from side to side, esp. slowly and smoothly. **2** (*intr*) to waver between two opinions or decisions. **3** (*tr*) to persuade to take a particular view or decision. — *n* **1** a swaying motion. **2** control or influence. — **hold sway** to have authority or influence. [Perhaps Norse *sveigja*, to bend]

swear *v* ***swore***, ***sworn*** **1** (*intr*) to use obscene or blasphemous language. **2** (*tr*) to promise or assert solemnly or earnestly, as if by taking an oath. **3** (*tr* with **to**) to solemnly state to be unquestionably true. **4** (*tr* with **to**) to make (someone) give a solemn promise: *I swore him to secrecy*. — *v* **swear by** (*tr*) **1** to appeal to (e.g. God) as a witness of one's solemn promise or statement. **2** (*coll*) to put complete trust in (e.g. a certain product or remedy). — *v* **swear in** (*tr*) to formally introduce into a post, or into the witness box, by requesting to take an oath. — *v* **swear off** (*tr*; *coll*) to promise to give up (e.g. cigarettes). [OE *swerian*]

swear-word *n* a word regarded as obscene or blasphemous.

sweat *n* **1** the salty moisture that the body gives off through the skin's pores during physical exertion, exposure to heat, nervousness or fear. **2** the state, or a fit, of giving off such moisture. **3** (*coll*) any activity that causes the body to give off such moisture. — *v* ***sweated*** or ***sweat*** **1** (*intr*) to give off sweat through one's pores. **2** (*intr*) to release a sweat-like moisture, as cheese does when warm. **3** (*intr*; *coll*) to be nervous, anxious or afraid. **4** (*tr*) to exercise (e.g. a racehorse) strenuously, to the point of producing sweat. **5** (*tr*) to cook (e.g. onions) slowly so as to release and retain the juices. — *adj* **sweaty**, ***-ier***, ***-iest***. — **in a sweat** (*coll*) in a worried or anxious state. — **no sweat!** (*slang*) **1** that presents no problems. **2** okay! — **sweat blood** (*coll*) **1** to work extremely hard. **2** to be in a state of extreme anxiety. — **sweat it out** (*coll*) to endure a difficult or unpleasant situation to the end, esp. to wait at length in nervous anticipation. [OE *swætan*]

sweatband *n* a strip of (often elasticated) fabric worn around the wrist or head to absorb sweat when playing sports.

sweated labour *n* (people carrying out) hard work for long hours with poor pay and conditions.

sweater *n* any (esp. heavy) knitted jersey or pullover.

sweatshirt *n* a long-sleeved jersey of a thick soft cotton fabric with a fleecy lining, orig. worn for sports.

sweatshop *n* a workshop or factory in which sweated labour is demanded.

sweatsuit *n* a loose-fitting suit of sweatshirt and trousers, usu. tight-fitting at the wrists and ankles, worn esp. by athletes.

Swede *n* a native or citizen of Sweden.

Swedish *n* **1** the language of Sweden. **2** (*pl*) Swedes. — *adj* of or relating to Sweden, its people or their language.

swede *n* a large turnip with yellow flesh, orig. introduced from Sweden. [**Swede**]

sweep *v* ***swept*** **1** (*tr* & *intr*; **up**) to clean (a room, a floor, etc.), or remove (dirt, dust, etc.), with a brush or broom. **2** (*tr*) to take, carry or push suddenly and with irresistible force. **3** (*tr*) to force or inspire into taking an unwanted or unintended direction or course of action. **4** (*tr*) to lift, gather or clear with a forceful scooping or brushing movement. **5** (*intr*) to move, pass or spread smoothly and swiftly, or uncontrollably. **6** (*intr*) to walk (esp. with garments flowing) impressively, arrogantly or indignantly. **7** (*tr*) to pass quickly over, making light contact. **8** (*intr*) to extend curvingly and impressively into the distance. **9** (*tr*) (of emotions, etc.) to affect suddenly and overpoweringly. **10** (*tr*) to cast or direct (e.g. one's gaze) with a scanning movement. — *n* **1** an act of sweeping. **2** a sweeping movement. **3** a sweeping line, e.g. of a road or landscape. **4** (*coll*) a sweepstake. **5** (*coll*) a chimney-sweep. — **sweep (something) under the carpet** to hide or ignore (unpleasant facts, problems, etc.). [OE *swapan*, to sweep]

sweeper *n* **1** a person who sweeps. **2** a device or machine used for sweeping. **3** (*sport*) a player covering the whole area behind a line of defenders.

sweeping *adj* **1** (of a search, a change, etc.) wide-ranging and thorough. **2** (of a statement) too generalised; indiscriminate. **3** (of a victory, etc.) impressive; decisive. — *n* (usu. in *pl*) a thing swept up. — *adv* **sweepingly**.

sweepstake *n* **1** a system of gambling in which the prize money is the sum of the stakes of all those betting. **2** a horse race in which the winning owner receives sums of money put up by all the other owners.

sweet *adj* **1** tasting like sugar; not sour, salty or bitter. **2** pleasing to any of the senses, esp. smell and hearing. **3** (of air or water) fresh and untainted. **4** (of wine) with a (perhaps only vague) taste of sugar or fruit; not dry. **5** likeable; charming. **6** (*coll* with **on**) fond (of); infatuated (with). — *n* **1** any small sugar-based confection for sucking or chewing. **2** a dessert. **3** a person one loves. — *adv* **sweetly**. — *n* **sweetness**. [OE *swete*]

sweet-and-sour *adj* cooked in a sauce that combines sugar with vinegar or fruit juice. — *n* a sweet-and-sour dish.

sweetbread *n* the pancreas of a young animal, esp. a calf, used as food.

sweetcorn *n* kernels of a variety of maize, eaten young while still sweet.

sweeten *v* ***-n-*** (*tr*) **1** to make (food) sweet or sweeter. **2** (*coll*; **up**) to make (a person) more agreeable or amenable, e.g. by flattery. **3** (*coll*) to make (e.g. an offer) more acceptable or inviting, by making changes or additions.

sweetener *n* **1** a non-fattening sweetening agent for food and drink. **2** (*coll*) a sweetening change or addition to an offer, etc., esp. a bribe.

sweetheart *n* **1** a term of endearment. **2** (*old*) a lover.

sweetie *n* (*coll*) **1** a sweet confection for sucking or chewing. **2** a term of endearment. **3** a lovable person.

sweetmeat *n* any small sugar-based confection or cake.

sweet nothings *n* (*pl*) the endearments that lovers say to each other.

sweet pea *n* a European climbing plant with delicate fragrant brightly-coloured flowers.

sweet pepper *n* **1** a fruit consisting of a hollow pod, usu. red, green or yellow in colour. **2** the plant which produces such fruit.

sweet potato *n* the potato-like root of a tropical American climbing plant, with pinkish skin and yellow, slightly sweet flesh.

sweet talk *n* (*coll*) flattery intended to persuade.
sweet-talk *v* (*tr*; *coll*) to persuade with flattery.
sweet tooth *n* a fondness for sweet foods. — *adj* **sweet-toothed**.

swell *v* ***swelled***, ***swollen*** or ***swelled*** **1** (*tr* & *intr*; **up, out**) to make or become bigger or fatter through injury, infection or filling with liquid or air. **2** (*tr* & *intr*) to (cause to) increase in number, size or intensity. **3** (*intr*) to become (visibly) filled with emotion, esp. pride. **4** (*intr*) (of the sea) to rise and fall in smooth masses, without forming individual waves. **5** (*intr*) (of a sound) to become louder, then die away. — *n* **1** a heaving of the sea without waves. **2** an increase in number, size or intensity. **3** an increase in volume of sound or music, followed by a dying away. **4** (*old coll*) a person who dresses smartly and fashionably. **5** (*old coll*) a prominent member of society. — *adj* & *interj* (*coll*; esp. *US*) excellent. [OE *swellan*]
swelling *n* an area on the body swollen through injury or infection.

swelter *v* ***-r-*** (*intr*) to sweat heavily or feel oppressively hot. — *n* a sweltering feeling or state. [OE *sweltan*, to die]
sweltering *adj* (of weather) oppressively hot.

swept. See **sweep**.

swerve *v* (*intr*) **1** to turn or move aside suddenly and sharply, e.g. to avoid a collision. **2** to deviate from a course of action. — *n* an act of swerving; a swerving movement. [MidE]

swift *adj* **1** fast-moving; able to move fast. **2** done, given, etc. quickly or promptly. — *n* a small fast-flying insect-eating bird similar to the swallow but with longer wings and a shorter tail. — *adv* **swiftly**. — *n* **swiftness**. [OE]

swig (*coll*) *v* ***-gg-*** (*tr* & *intr*) to drink in gulps, esp. from a bottle. — *n* a large draught, or gulp.

swill *v* (*tr*) **1** to rinse by splashing water round or over. **2** (*coll*) to drink (esp. alcohol) greedily. — *n* **1** any mushy mixture of scraps fed to pigs. **2** disgusting food or drink. **3** (*coll*) a gulp of beer or other alcohol. [OE *swilian*, to wash]

swim *v* ***-mm-***, ***swam***, ***swum*** **1** (*intr*) to propel oneself through water by moving the arms and legs or (in animals) other parts of the body. **2** (*tr*) to cover (a distance) or cross (a stretch of water) in this way. **3** (*intr*; **in, with**) to be flooded or awash (with). **4** (*intr*) to float. **5** (*intr*) to be affected by dizziness. **6** (*intr*) to (seem to) move about in waves or whirls. — *n* **1** a spell of swimming. **2** the general flow of events. — *n* **swimmer**. — **in the swim** (*old coll*) up to date with, and often involved in, what is going on around one. [OE *swimman*]
swimming-bath *n* (also in *pl*) a (usu. indoor) swimming-pool.
swimming-costume *n* a swimsuit.
swimmingly *adj* (*coll*) smoothly and successfully.
swimming-pool *n* an artificial pool for swimming in.
swimsuit *n* a garment worn for swimming.

swindle *v* (*tr*) to cheat or trick; to obtain by cheating or trickery. — *n* **1** an act of swindling. **2** anything that is not what it is presented as being. — *n* **swindler**. [Ger *schwindeln*, to be giddy]

swine *n* ***swine*** (sense **1**), ***swine*** or ***swines*** (sense **2**) **1** a pig. **2** a despicable person. — *adj* **swinish**. — *adv* **swinishly**. [OE *swin*, pig]

swing *v* ***swung*** **1** (*tr* & *intr*) to (cause to) open, close, or move to and fro in a curving motion, pivoting from a fixed point. **2** (*tr* & *intr*) to (cause to) move or turn with a sweeping or swaying movement or movements. **3** (*intr*) to undergo a sudden sharp change or changes, e.g. of opinion, mood or direction. **4** (*tr*; *coll*) to arrange or fix; to achieve the successful outcome of. **5** (*tr*; *coll*) to determine or settle the outcome of (e.g. an election in which voters were initially undecided). **6** (*intr*; *coll*; **for, at**) to throw a punch (at). **7** (*intr*; *slang*) (of a party, etc.) to be lively and exciting. **8** (*intr*; *old slang*) to enjoy oneself with vigour and enthusiasm. **9** (*intr*; *old slang*) to be promiscuous. **10** (*intr*; *slang*) to be hanged. **11** (*tr*; *mus*) to perform as swing. — *n* **1** an act, manner or spell of swinging. **2** a swinging movement. **3** a seat suspended from a frame or branch, for a child to swing on. **4** a sudden sharp change, e.g. in mood or pattern of voting. **5** a swinging stroke with a golf club, cricket bat, etc.; the technique of a golfer. **6** (*mus*) jazz or jazzy dance music with a simple regular rhythm, popularised by bands in the 1930s. **7** usual routine or pace: *get back into the swing of things*. — **in full swing** at the height of liveliness. — **swing the lead** (*slang*) to make up excuses to avoid work. — **swings and roundabouts** (*coll*) a situation in which advantages and disadvantages are equal. [OE *swingan*]
swingboat *n* a fairground ride in the form of a boat-shaped swinging carriage.
swing bridge *n* a bridge that swings open to let boats through.
swing door *n* a door hinged so as to open in both directions.
swinger *n* (*old slang*) **1** a person who has a very active social life, esp. with much dancing and drinking. **2** a promiscuous person.
swinging *adj* **1** moving or turning with a swing. **2** (*coll*) lively and exciting.

swingeing *adj* hard to bear; severe. [OE *swengan*, to shake]

swinish. See **swine**.

swipe *v* (*tr*) **1** to hit with a heavy sweeping blow. **2** (*coll*) to steal. — *n* a heavy sweeping blow. — *v* **swipe at** (*tr*) to try to hit. [OE *swipian*, to beat]

swirl *v* (*tr* & *intr*) to (cause to) flow or move with a whirling or circling motion. — *n* such a motion.

swish[1] *v* (*tr* & *intr*) to (cause to) move with a brushing or rustling sound. — *n* a brushing or rustling sound or movement. [Imit.]

swish[2] *adj* (*coll*) smart and stylish.

Swiss *adj* of or relating to Switzerland, its people, or the dialects of German and French spoken by them. — *n* ***Swiss*** **1** a native or citizen of Switzerland. **2** either of the dialects of German and French spoken in Switzerland.

Swiss roll *n* a cylindrical cake made by rolling up a thin slab of sponge spread with jam or cream.

switch *n* **1** (a button, knob or small lever that operates) a device that makes or breaks an electrical circuit, turning an appliance on or off. **2** a change; an exchange or change-over. **3** a long flexible twig or cane. **4** (*US*) a set of railway points. — *v* **1** (*tr* & *intr*; **on, off**) to turn (an appliance) on or off by means of a switch. **2** (*tr* & *intr*) to exchange (one thing or person for another), esp. quickly and without notice. **3** (*tr* & *intr*; **to, over to**) to transfer or change over (e.g. to a different system). **4** (*intr* with **off**; *coll*) to stop paying attention. **5** (*tr* with **on**; *coll*) to bring on (e.g. charm or tears) at will, to create the required effect. **6** (*tr* & *intr*; *slang*; **to**) to make or become aware (of) or sympathetic (to) (*adj* **switched-on**). **7** (*tr*) to whip with a switch.

switchback *n* **1** a road with many twists and turns and upward and downward slopes. **2** a roller-coaster.

switchboard *n* **1** a board on which incoming telephone calls are connected manually or electronically. **2** a board from which various pieces of electrical equipment are controlled.

swivel *n* a joint between two parts enabling one part to turn or pivot independently of the other. — *v* ***-ll-*** (*tr* & *intr*) to (cause to) turn or pivot (as if) on a swivel. [OE *swifan*, to turn round]

swivel chair *n* a chair in which the seat pivots on the base, and can be spun right round.

swizz *n* (*coll*) a thing that, in reality, is disappointingly inferior to what was cheatingly promised.

swizzle *n* **1** a frothy cocktail with a rum or gin base. **2** (*coll*) a swizz. — *v* (*tr*; *coll*) to cheat with a swizz.

swizzle-stick *n* a thin (usu. plastic) stick used to stir cocktails and other drinks.

swollen. See **swell**.

swoon *v* (*intr*) **1** to faint. **2** (**over**) to go into raptures or fits of adoration. — *n* an act of swooning. [MidE *iswowen*]

swoop *v* (*intr*) **1** to fly down with a fast sweeping movement. **2** (**on**) to make a sudden forceful attack; to descend or pounce. — *n* **1** an act of swooping. **2** a swooping movement. [OE *swapan*, to sweep]

swop. See **swap**.

sword *n* **1** a weapon like a large heavy knife, with a long blade sharpened on one or both edges. **2** (with **the**) violence, esp. military force. **3** (with **the**) destruction or death by war or violence. — **cross swords (with)** to fight or quarrel. [OE *sweord*]

sword dance *n* **1** in Scotland, a dance, often by a solo dancer, with steps over an arrangement of swords laid on the ground. **2** in northern England, a dance for a group of dancers carrying long flexible swords with which they perform a number of movements and create various patterns.

swordfish *n* a large sea-fish with a very long and pointed upper jaw used as a weapon.

sword of Damocles *n* (*literary*) any imminent danger or disaster.

swordplay *n* **1** the activity or art of fencing. **2** lively argument.

swordsman *n* a man skilled in fighting with a sword. — *n* **swordsmanship**.

swordstick *n* a hollow walking-stick containing a short sword or dagger.

swore. See **swear**.

sworn *past participle* of **swear**. — *adj* bound or confirmed by, or as if by, having taken an oath: *sworn enemies*.

swot (*coll*) *v* ***-tt-*** (*tr* & *intr*) **1** to study hard and seriously. **2** (**up**) to study intensively, esp. at the last minute. — *n* a person who studies hard, esp. single-mindedly or in order to impress a teacher. [Variant of **sweat**]

swum. See **swim**.

swung. See **swing**.

sybarite *n* a person devoted to a life of luxury and pleasure. — *adj* **sybaritic**. [Inhabitant of *Sybaris*, ancient Greek colony in S Italy, noted for luxury]

sycamore *n* **1** a deciduous tree of Europe and Asia, with large five-pointed leaves and seed-cases that spin when they fall. **2** (*NAm*) any American plane tree. **3** the wood of any of these trees. [Gr *sykomoros*, from *sykon*, fig]

sycophant *n* a person who flatters in a servile way; a crawler. — *n* **sycophancy**. — *adj* **sycophantic**. [Gr *sykophantes*, informer, swindler]

syllabi. See **syllabus**.

syllabic *adj* of or relating to syllables, or the division of words into syllables. [Ety. as for **syllable**]

syllabify *v* ***-ies, -ied*** (*tr*) to divide (a word) into syllables. — *n* **syllabification**.

syllable *n* **1** any of the parts, consisting of one or more sounds and usu. including a vowel, that a spoken word can be divided into: *The word 'telephone' has three syllables, 'te', 'le', and 'phone', and 'tiger' has two, 'ti' and 'ger'*. **2** a single word: *never uttered a syllable the whole evening*. — **in**

words of one syllable plainly; frankly. [Gr *syllabe*]

syllabub or **sillabub** *n* a frothy dessert made by whipping a sweetened mixture of cream or milk and wine.

syllabus *n* ***-buses*** or ***-bi*** (a sheet of paper or a booklet detailing) a series of topics covered in a course of study. [From a misreading of Lat *sittybas*, from Gr *sittyba*, book-label]

syllogism *n* an argument in which a conclusion, valid or invalid, is drawn from two independent statements using logic, as in *All dogs are animals, foxhounds are dogs, therefore foxhounds are animals*. — *adj* **syllogistic**. [Gr *syllogismos*, a reasoning together]

sylph *n* **1** in folklore, a spirit of the air. **2** a slender, graceful woman or girl. — *adj* **sylph-like**. [Word created by Paracelsus, a mediaeval alchemist]

sylvan *adj* (*literary*) of woods or woodland; wooded. [Lat *silva*, a wood]

symbiosis *n* ***-ses*** **1** an arrangement by which two animals or plants of different species live closely together, esp. one that benefits both of them. **2** any mutually beneficial relationship. — *adj* **symbiotic**. [Gr *syn*, together + *bios*, livelihood]

symbol *n* **1** a thing that represents or stands for another, usu. something concrete or material representing an idea or emotion, e.g. the colour red representing danger. **2** a letter or sign used to represent a quantity, idea, object, operation, etc., such as the × used in mathematics to represent the multiplication process or £ used for pound sterling. [Gr *symbolon*, token]

symbolic *adj* **1** (**of**) being a symbol; standing (for). **2** relating to symbols or their use. — *adv* **symbolically**.

symbolise or **-ize** *v* (*tr*) to be a symbol of; to stand for. — *n* **symbolisation** or **-z-**.

symbolism *n* **1** the use of symbols, esp. to express ideas or emotions in literature, cinema, etc. **2** (often *cap*) a 19th-century movement in art and literature making heavy use of symbols. — *n* **symbolist**.

symmetry *n* ***-ies*** **1** exact similarity between two parts or halves, as if one were a mirror image of the other. **2** (beauty resulting from) the arrangement of parts in pleasing proportion to each other. — *adj* **symmetrical**. — *adv* **symmetrically**. [Gr *syn*, together + *metron*, measure]

sympathetic *adj* **1** (**to**) feeling or expressing sympathy. **2** amiable, esp. because of being kind-hearted. **3** acting or done out of sympathy. **4** in keeping with one's mood or feelings; agreeable. — *adv* **sympathetically**. [**sympathy**]

sympathy *n* ***-ies*** **1** a deep and genuine understanding of the sadness or suffering of others, often shown in expressions of sorrow or pity. **2** (often in *pl*; **for, with**) loyal or approving support (for) or agreement (with): *on strike in sympathy with the nurses*. **3** affection between people resulting from their understanding of each other's personalities. ◇ See also **empathy**. [Gr *syn*, with + *pathos*, suffering]

sympathise or **-ize** *v* (*intr*; **with**) to feel or express sympathy. — *n* **sympathiser** or **-z-**.

symphony *n* ***-ies*** **1** a long musical work in several parts, or movements, played by a full orchestra. **2** an instrumental passage in a musical work which consists mostly of singing. **3** (*literary*) (anything consisting of, covered in or making up) a pleasing combination of parts, e.g. shapes or colours. — *adj* **symphonic**. [Gr *syn*, together + *phone*, sound]

symphony orchestra *n* a large orchestra capable of playing symphonies.

symposium *n* ***-ia*** **1** a conference held to discuss a particular (esp. academic) subject. **2** a collection of essays by different writers on a single topic. [Gr *symposion*, drinking-party with intellectual discussion]

symptom *n* **1** an indication of the presence of illness, technically something felt by the sufferer and not outwardly visible. **2** an indication of the existence of a (usu. unpleasant) state or condition: *falling church attendance as a symptom of society's moral decline*. [Gr *symptoma*, happening, attribute]

symptomatic *adj* serving as a symptom.

synagogue *n* **1** a Jewish place of worship and religious instruction. **2** a Jewish religious assembly or congregation. [Gr *synagoge*, assembly]

synch or **sync** (*coll*) *n* synchronisation, esp. of sound and picture in film and television. — *v* (*tr*) to synchronise.

synchromesh *n* a gear system which matches the speeds of the gear wheels before they are engaged, avoiding shock and noise in gear-changing. [*synchro*nised *mesh*]

synchronise or **-ize** *v* **1** (*tr* & *intr*; **with**) to (cause to) happen, move or operate in exact time with (something else or each other). **2** (*tr*) to project (a film) or broadcast (a television programme) so that the action, actors' lip movements, etc. precisely match the sounds or words heard. — *n* **synchronisation** or **-z-**. [Gr *syn*, together + *chronos*, time]

synchronous *adj* (**with**) in time (with); synchronised.

syncopate *v* (*tr*) to alter (the rhythm of music) by putting the stress on beats not usually stressed. — *n* **syncopation**. [Ety. as for **syncope**]

syncope *n* **1** (*med*) a fit of fainting. **2** the dropping of a letter or syllable in the middle of a word, e.g. in *o'er*, the poetic version of *over*. [Gr *synkope*, a cutting short]

syndic *n* the person representing a university or other body or company in business or legal matters. [Gr *syndikos*, advocate, representative]

syndicalism *n* a form of trade-unionism favouring the transfer of the ownership of factories, etc. to the workers themselves. — *n* & *adj* **syndicalist**. [Fr *syndicalisme*, from Gr *syndikos*, representative]

syndicate *n* **1** any association of people or groups working together on a single project. **2** a group of business organisations jointly managing or financing a single venture. **3** an association of criminals organising widespread illegal activities. **4** an association of journalists selling material to a variety of newspapers. — *v* (*tr*) **1** to form into a syndicate. **2** to organise or sell by means of a syndicate. — *n* **syndication**. [OFr *syndicat*, from Gr *syndikos*, representative]

syndrome *n* **1** a set of symptoms that represent a specific (physical or mental) illness. **2** a pattern or series of events, observed qualities, etc. characteristic of a particular problem or condition. [Gr, a running together]

synecdoche *n* a figure of speech in which a part of something is used to refer to or denote the whole thing, or the whole to refer to or denote a part, as *wiser heads* meaning *wiser people*. [Gr *synekdoche*, a receiving together]

synod *n* (a meeting of) a local or national council of members of the clergy. [Gr *synodos*, meeting]

synonym *n* a word having the same, or very nearly the same, meaning as another. [Gr *syn*, with + *onoma*, name]

synonymous *adj* (**with**) **1** having the same meaning. **2** very closely associated in the mind: *English football is no longer synonymous with hooliganism*.

synopsis *n* ***-opses*** *n* a brief outline, e.g. of the plot of a book; a summary. [Gr *syn*, together + *opsis*, view]

synoptic *adj* of the nature of a synopsis; giving or taking an overall view.

the Synoptic Gospels *n* (*pl*) the Gospels of Matthew, Mark and Luke, very alike in viewpoint and in their presentation of the account of Jesus's life.

synovia *n* an oily liquid produced by the body to lubricate the joints. — *adj* **synovial**. [Term invented by Paracelsus, a mediaeval physician and alchemist]

syntax *n* (the grammatical rules governing) the positioning of words in a sentence and their relationship to each other. — *adj* **syntactic** or **syntactical**. [Gr *syn*, together + *tassein*, to put in order]

synthesis *n* ***-eses*** **1** the process of putting together separate parts to form a complex whole. **2** the result of such a process. **3** the process of combining simple chemical substances to create a more complex one, esp. one resembling a naturally-occurring substance. [Gr *syn*, together + *thesis*, a placing]

synthesise or **-ize** *v* (*tr*) **1** to combine (simple parts) to form (a complex whole). **2** to create by chemical synthesis.

synthesiser or **-z-** *n* a musical instrument, esp. a keyboard, that produces sound electronically, esp. one also reproducing the sounds of other instruments.

synthetic *adj* **1** created artificially by combining chemical substances; not natural; man-made. **2** not sincere; sham. — *adv* **synthetically**. [Gr *synthetikos*, skilled at putting together]

syphilis *n* a sexually transmitted disease in which sores are produced on the sex organs, eventually spreading throughout the body. — *adj* **syphilitic**. [*Syphilus*, infected hero of a 16th-century Latin poem]

syphon. See **siphon**.

syringa *n* **1** the mock orange shrub. **2** the lilac shrub. [Ety. as for **syringe**]

syringe *n* a medical instrument for injecting or drawing off liquid, consisting of a hollow cylinder with a plunger inside and a thin hollow needle attached. — *v* (*tr*) to clean, spray or inject using a syringe. [Gr *syrinx*, tube]

syrup *n* **1** the thick sweet sticky concentrated juice of various plants, e.g. the sugar-cane and the maple, with various cooking and table uses. **2** a solution of water and sugar in which fruit is stored in tins. **3** any sugar-flavoured liquid medicine. **4** (*coll*) exaggerated sentimentality or pleasantness of manner. — *adj* **syrupy**. [Arabic *sharab*]

system *n* **1** a set of interconnected or interrelated parts forming a complex whole: *the transport system*; *the human digestive system*. **2** an arrangement of mechanical, electrical or electronic parts functioning as a unit. **3** a way of working; a method. **4** efficiency of organisation; methodicalness. **5** one's mind or body regarded as a set of interconnected parts: *get the illness out of your system*. **6** (with **the**) society, or the network of institutions that control it, regarded as repressing the power and freedom of the individual. [Gr *systema*]

systematic *adj* **1** making use of, or carried out according to, a clearly worked-out plan or method. **2** methodical. — *adv* **systematically**.

systematise or **-ize** *v* (*tr*) to organise or arrange in a methodical way. — *n* **systematisation** or **-z-**.

systemic *adj* (*med* or *biol*) relating to or affecting the whole body or the whole plant. — *adv* **systemically**.

systems analysis *n* the study of a particular (e.g. industrial) process and the designing of a computer program or programs to control it more efficiently. — *n* **systems analyst**.

systole *n* (*med*) a single contraction of the heart which, together with a **diastole**, forms a single beat. — *adj* **systolic**. [Gr]

T

T[1] or **t** *n* ***Ts*** or ***T's***, ***t's*** **1** the twentieth letter of the English alphabet. **2** something shaped like a T, e.g. a pipe which is used to join three separate pipes together. — **to a T** exactly; perfectly well.

T-junction *n* a junction at which one road meets another at a right angle but does not cross it.

T-shirt *n* (also **tee shirt**) a light, casual shirt, often made of stretchy material, with no collar and usu. short sleeves.

T-square *n* a T-shaped ruler for drawing right angles.

T[2] *abbrev* (*mus*) tenor.

T[3] *symbol* (*chem*) tritium.

t or **t.** *abbrev* **1** ton. **2** tonne. **3** troy (weight).

TA *abbrev* Territorial Army.

Ta *symbol* (*chem*) tantalum.

ta *interj* (*Br coll*) thank you. [Imit. of young child's pronunciation]

tab[1] *n* **1** a small flap, tag, strip of material, etc. attached to an article, for hanging it up, opening it, holding it, etc. for identification. **2** a small strip of material attached to a garment for hanging it up. **3** (*NAm*) a bill, e.g. in a restaurant. — *v* ***-bb-*** (*tr*) to fix a tab to. — **keep tabs on** (*coll*) to keep a close watch or check on. — **pick up the tab** (*NAm*) to pay the bill.

tab[2] *n* a key on a typewriter or word processor which sets and then automatically finds the position of the margins and columns needed to arrange information in a table. [Abbrev. of **tabulator**]

tabard *n* a short, loose, sleeveless jacket or tunic, worn esp. by a knight over his armour, or, with the arms of the king or queen on the front, by a herald. [OFr *tabart*]

Tabasco® *n* a hot sauce made from a pungent type of red pepper. [*Tabasco* in Mexico]

tabbouleh *n* a Mediterranean salad made with cracked wheat which has been soaked esp. in lemon juice and mixed with chopped vegetables, esp. tomatoes, cucumber and garlic. [Arabic *tabbula*]

tabby *n* ***-ies*** **1** (also **tabby cat**) a usu. grey or brown cat with darker stripes. **2** (also **tabby cat**) any female domestic cat. **3** a kind of silk with irregular wavy, shiny markings. — *adj* having darker stripes or wavy markings. [*Al-Attabiyah* in Baghdad where the silk was first made]

tabernacle *n* **1** (also *cap*; *hist*) the tent carried by the Israelites across the desert during the Exodus, used as a sanctuary for the Ark of the Covenant. **2** (esp. RC) a receptacle in which the consecrated bread and wine are kept. **3** a place of worship of certain nonconformist Christian denominations. — **Feast of Tabernacles** see **Sukkoth**. [Lat *tabernaculum*, tent]

tabla *n* a pair of small drums played with the hands in Indian music. [Hindi, from Arabic, drum]

table *n* **1** a piece of furniture consisting of a flat horizontal surface supported by a leg or legs. **2** the people sitting at a table. **3** the food served at a particular table or in a particular house: *keeps a good table.* **4** a group of words, figures, etc. arranged systematically in columns and rows. **5** a multiplication table. **6** any flat, level surface. **7** (*hist*) a slab of stone or wood inscribed with laws. **8** a tableland. **9** a broad flat surface cut on a gem. — *v* (*tr*) **1** (*Br*) to put forward for discussion. **2** (*NAm*) to postpone discussion (e.g. of a bill) indefinitely. **3** to make or enter into a table; to tabulate. — **at table** at a meal. — **on the table** under discussion. — **turn the tables on someone** to reverse a situation completely and put (someone) in a totally different, and usu. disadvantageous, position. [Lat *tabula*, board, tablet]

tablecloth *n* an often decorative cloth for covering a table, esp. during meals.

tableland *n* a broad high area of flat or gently undulating ground; a plateau.

table licence *n* a licence to sell and serve alcohol only with meals.

table linen *n* tablecloths and napkins.

table mat *n* a mat for protecting the top of a table from the heat of dishes from the oven and warmed plates.

tablespoon *n* **1** a spoon which is larger than a dessertspoon and is used for serving food. **2** (also **tablespoonful**, ***-fuls***) the amount a tablespoon will hold.

table tennis *n* a game based on tennis which is played indoors on a table with small bats and a light hollow ball.

tableware *n* dishes, plates, cutlery, etc. for use at table.

tableau *n* ***tableaux*** **1** a picture or pictorial representation of a group or scene. **2** (also **tableau vivant**, ***tableaux vivants***) a group of people on stage forming a silent, motionless scene from history, literature, etc. [Fr]

table d'hôte *n* ***tables d'hôte*** a meal with a set number of choices and a set number of courses offered for a fixed price, esp. to residents in a hotel. [Fr, host's table]

tablet *n* **1** a small, solid, measured amount of a medicine or drug; a pill. **2** a solid flat piece of something, e.g. soap. **3** a slab of stone or wood on which inscriptions may be carved. [OFr *tablete*, from Lat *tabula*, board]

tabloid *n* a newspaper with relatively small pages (approximately 12 × 16 in., 30 × 40 cm), esp. one written in an informal and often sensationalist style and with many photographs. ◇ See also **broadsheet**. [**tablet**]

taboo or **tabu** *n* **1** anything which is forbidden for religious reasons or by social custom. **2** any system which forbids certain actions as being unclean or holy. — *adj* forbidden or prohibited as being a taboo. — *v* (*tr*) to forbid (a custom, the use of a word, etc.) as a taboo. [Tongan (the language of Tonga) *tabu*, unclean, holy]

tabor *n* a small, single-headed drum played with one hand while the same player plays a pipe or fife with the other. [OFr *tabour*]

tabular *adj* arranged in systematic columns; in the form of or according to a table. [Lat *tabularis*, from *tabula*, board]

tabulate *v* (*tr*) to arrange (information) in tabular form. — *n* **tabulation**. [Lat *tabulare*, from *tabula*, board]

tabulator *n* **1** see **tab**². **2** a machine which reads data from a computer storage device, esp. punched cards, and prints it out on continuous sheets of paper.

tachograph *n* a device which records the speed a vehicle travels at and the distance travelled in a particular period of time, used esp. in lorries and coaches. [Gr *tachos*, speed + **-graph**]

tachometer *n* a device which measures the speed of a machine or vehicle. [Gr *tachos*, speed + **-meter**]

tacit *adj* understood but not actually stated; implied; inferred. — *adv* **tacitly**. — *n* **tacitness**. [Lat *tacitus*, silent]

taciturn *adj* saying little; quiet and uncommunicative. — *n* **taciturnity**. — *adv* **taciturnly**. [Lat *taciturnus*, from *tacere*, to be silent]

tack *n* **1** a short nail with a sharp point and a broad flat head. **2** a long loose temporary stitch used esp. to hold material together while it is being sewn properly. **3** the direction of a sailing ship which is sailing into the wind at an angle, stated in terms of the side of the sail that the wind is blowing against: *on the starboard tack*. **4** a sailing ship's zigzag course formed by sailing with first one side of the sail to the wind and then the other. **5** a direction, course of action or policy. **6** riding harness, saddle and bridle, etc. for a horse. **7** stickiness. — *v* **1** (*tr*; **down, on**) to fasten or attach with tacks. **2** (*tr*; **on, up**) to sew with long loose temporary stitches. **3** (*tr*; **on**) to attach or add as a supplement. **4** (*intr*) (of a sailing ship, or a person in control of such a ship) to sail into the wind at an angle with first one side of the sail to the wind and then the other so as to sail in a zigzag course and be able to progress forwards. **5** (*tr*) to change the tack of (a ship) to the opposite one. **6** (*intr*) to change one's direction, course of action or policy abruptly. [MidE *tak*]

tacky *adj* **-ier**, **-iest** sticky. — *n* **tackiness**.

tackle *n* **1** (*sport*) an act of trying to get the ball away from a player on the opposing team. **2** the equipment needed for a particular sport or occupation. **3** a system of ropes and pulleys for lifting heavy objects. **4** the ropes and rigging on a ship. — *v* **1** (*tr*) to grasp or seize and struggle with, esp. to try and restrain. **2** (*tr*) to try to deal with or solve (a problem). **3** (*tr* & *intr*; *sport*) to try to get the ball from (a player on the opposing team). [MidE *takel*, gear]

tacky¹. See **tack**.

tacky² *adj* **-ier**, **-iest** (*coll*) shabby; vulgar. — *adv* **tackily**. — *n* **tackiness**.

taco *n* **-os** in Mexican cooking, a thin, rolled pancake filled with meat and fried. [Mexican Span]

tact *n* **1** an awareness of the best or most considerate way to deal with others so as to avoid offence, upset, antagonism or resentment. **2** skill or judgement in handling difficult situations; diplomacy. — *adj* **tactful**. — *adv* **tactfully**. — *n* **tactfulness**. — *adj* **tactless**. — *adv* **tactlessly**. — *n* **tactlessness**. [Lat *tactus*, touch]

tactic *n* a tactical manoeuvre. [Gr *taktikos*, fit for arranging]

tactical *adj* **1** of, concerned with or forming tactics. **2** skilful; well executed and well planned. **3** (of bombs, missiles, etc.) used to support other military operations. — *adv* **tactically**.

tactical voting *n* the practice of voting for a candidate one does not support but who is the most likely to defeat another candidate that one supports even less.

tactician *n* a person who is good at tactics or successful planning.

tactics *n* **1** (*sing*) the art or science of employing and manoeuvring troops to win or gain an advantage over the enemy. **2** (*sing*) skill in or the art of using whatever means are available to achieve an end or aim. **3** (*pl*) the plans, procedure, means, etc. followed.

tactile *adj* **1** of or having a sense of touch. **2** perceptible to the sense of touch. [Lat *tactilis*, from *tangere*, to touch]

tadpole *n* the larva of the frog or toad, with a rounded body and long tail, which lives in water. [MidE *taddepol*, from *tadde*, toad + *pol*, head]

taffeta *n* & *adj* (made of) a stiff shiny cloth woven from silk or some silk-like material, e.g. rayon. [Persian *taftan*, to twist]

taffrail *n* a rail round a ship's stern. [Dut *tafereel*, panel]

Taffy *n* **-ies** (*slang*; usu. *derog*; often *offensive*) a Welshman. [Welsh *Dafydd*, David]

tag¹ *n* **1** a piece of material, paper, leather, etc. that carries information (e.g. washing instructions or the price) about the object to which it is attached. **2** an electronic device such as a bracelet or anklet which transmits radio signals and is used to supervise the movements of a prisoner or offender outside of prison. **3** a metal or plastic point on the end of a shoelace or cord. **4** a loose hanging flap or piece of loose hanging cloth. **5** a trite or common quotation used esp. for effect. **6** the final speech in a play, or refrain in a song, added to make the moral or point clear. — *v* **-gg- 1** (*tr*) to put a tag or tags on. **2** (*tr*; **on**) to attach or fasten (something). **3** (*intr*; **along, on**) to follow or accompany, esp. when uninvited. [MidE *tagge*]

tag[2] *n* a children's game in which one child chases the others and tries to catch or touch one of them, who then becomes the chaser. — *v* **-gg-** (*tr*) to catch or touch in or as if in the game of tag.

tagliatelle *n* pasta made in the form of long narrow ribbons. [Ital]

tahini *n* a thick paste made from ground sesame seeds. [Arabic *tahine*, from *tahan*, to grind]

t'ai chi or **t'ai chi ch'uan** *n* a Chinese system of exercise and self-defence in which good balance and co-ordination mean that minimum effort is used, developed esp. by doing extremely slow and controlled exercises. [Chin, great art of boxing]

taiga *n* the vast area of coniferous forests which stretches across much of those parts of N America, Europe and Asia which lie just south of the Arctic Circle. [Russ]

tail[1] *n* **1** the often quite long and relatively thin part of an animal's body that projects from the lower or rear end of the back; the feathers that project from the rear of a bird's body; the end part of a snake's body. **2** anything which has a similar form, function or position as a creature's tail: *the tail of a shirt* or *of a kite*. **3** a lower, last or rear part: *the tail of the storm*. **4** the rear part of an aircraft including the rudder and tailplane. **5** the trail of luminous particles following a comet. **6** (in *pl*) the reverse side of a coin, that side which does not bear a portrait or head. **7** (in *pl*) a tailcoat. **8** (in *pl*) evening dress for men, usu. including a tailcoat and white bow tie. **9** (*coll*) a person who follows and keeps a constant watch on someone else. **10** (*offensive slang*) women thought of as sexual objects. — *v* **1** (*tr*) to remove the stalks (from fruit or vegetables). **2** (*tr* & *intr*; **after**) to follow closely. — *adj* **tailed**. — *adj* **tailless**. — *v* **tail away** or **off** (*intr*) to become gradually less, smaller or weaker. — **turn tail** to turn round and run away. — **with one's tail between one's legs** completely defeated or humiliated. [OE *tægel*]

tailback *n* a long queue of traffic stretching back from an accident, roadworks, etc. blocking the road.

tailboard *n* a hinged or removable flap at the rear of a lorry, cart or wagon.

tailcoat *n* a man's formal black jacket which is cut away below the waist in the front and has a long divided, tapering tail which is slit to the waist.

tail end *n* the very end or last part.

tailgate *n* **1** the rear door which opens upwards on a hatchback vehicle. **2** the lower gate of a canal lock. **3** (esp. *NAm*) a tailboard.

tail-light *n* (esp. *NAm*) the usu. red light on the back of a car, train, bicycle, etc.

tailpiece *n* **1** a piece at the end or tail. **2** a design or engraving at the end of a chapter. **3** a strip of wood at the bottom of some stringed instruments (e.g. a violin) from which the strings are stretched across the bridge to the pegs.

tailplane *n* a small horizontal wing at the rear of an aircraft.

tailspin *n* an aircraft's spiral dive with the nose facing down.

tail wind *n* a wind blowing in the same direction as that in which a ship, aircraft, etc. is travelling.

tail[2] *n* (*legal*) a limiting of who may inherit property to one person and that person's heirs, or to some other particular class of heirs. [OFr *taillier*, to cut]

tailor *n* a person who makes suits, jackets, trousers, overcoats, etc. to measure, esp. for men. — *v* **-r- 1** (*tr* & *intr*) to make and style (garments) so that they fit well. **2** (*tr*) to make suitable for particular or special circumstances. [OFr *taillour*]

tailor-bird *n* a small Asian bird that sews leaves together to make a nest.

tailored *adj* **1** tailor-made. **2** (of a person) dressed in clothes which fit and hang impeccably.

tailoress *n* (*rare*) a female tailor.

tailor-made *adj* **1** (of clothes) made by a tailor to fit and hang impeccably. **2** very well suited or adapted for a particular purpose. — *n* a tailor-made garment.

taint *v* **1** (*tr* & *intr*) to affect or be affected by pollution, putrefaction or contamination. **2** (*tr*) to contaminate morally; to infect with evil. **3** (*tr*; **with**) to affect slightly with something bad. — *n* **1** a spot, mark or trace of decay, contamination, infection or something bad or evil. **2** a corrupt or decayed condition. — *adj* **tainted**. [MidE *taynt*, struck + OFr *teint*, from Lat *tingere*, to dye]

take *v* ***took***, ***taken*** **1** (*tr*; **down, out**, etc.) to (select and) reach out for and grasp, lift, pull, etc.; to (select and) grasp, enter, etc. for use: *Take the book down from the shelf. Take my car if you like.* **2** (*tr*; **away, in, off, out**, etc.) to carry, conduct or lead to another place: *take him some grapes*; *talents which will take her far*. **3** (*tr*) to do or perform: *take a walk*; *take one's revenge*. **4** (*tr*) to get, receive, occupy, obtain, rent or buy: *take a holiday*; *take two pounds of potatoes*. **5** (*tr*) to agree to have or accept: *take advice, responsibility*, etc.; *take office*; *won't take a cheque*. **6** (*tr*) to accept as true or valid: *take her word for it*. **7** (*tr*) to adopt or commit oneself to: *take a decision*; *take* *her side in the argument*. **8** (*tr*) to endure or put up with: *can't take his arrogance*. **9** (*tr*) to need or require: *take all day to finish*; *a verb which takes a direct object*. **10** (*tr*) to use as a means of transport: *take the bus*. **11** (*tr*) to make (a written note of): *take the minutes of the meeting*; *take notes*. ◇ See also **take down** below. **12** (*tr*) to make (a photographic record of): *take a photo*; *take that funny little man over there*. **13** (*tr*) to study or teach: *take French at night school*. **14** (*tr*) to remove, use or borrow without permission: *took her coat by mistake*. **15** (*tr*) to proceed to occupy: *take a seat*. **16** (*tr*) to come or derive from: *a quotation taken from Buchan*. **17** (*tr*) to have room or strength to support: *The shelf won't take any more books*. **18** (*tr*) to consider (as an example). **19** (*tr*; **for**) to consider or think of in a particular way; to mistakenly consider (someone) to be someone or something: *took her to be a teacher*; *Do you take him for a fool?* **20** (*tr*) to capture or win. **21** (*tr*, esp. in *passive*, & *intr* with **to**) to charm and delight or be charmed and delighted by: *be quite taken with him*; *He really took to his new family*. **22** (*tr*) to eat or drink: *take medicine*; *take sugar in coffee*. **23** (*tr*) to conduct or lead: *This road will take you the station*. **24** (*tr*) to be in charge or control of; to run: *take the meeting*. **25** (*tr*) to react to or receive in a specified way: *take the news well*. **26** (*tr*) to feel: *take pride in one's work*. **27** (*tr*) to turn to (someone or something) for (help, refuge, etc.). **28** (*tr*; **away**, **from**, **off**) to subtract. **29** (*tr*) to go down or into: *took the first road on the left*. **30** (*tr*) to deal with or consider: *take the first two questions together*. **31** (*intr*) to have or produce the expected or desired effect: *The vaccination didn't take*. **32** (*intr*) (of seeds, etc.) to begin to send out roots and grow. **33** (*tr*) to measure: *take a temperature*. **34** (*tr* in *passive* & *intr*) to become (ill), esp. suddenly. **35** (*tr*) to understand. **36** (*tr*) to have sexual intercourse with. — *n* **1** a scene filmed or piece of music recorded during an uninterrupted period of filming or recording. **2** the amount or number taken (e.g. of fish caught) at one time. **3** the amount of money taken in a shop, business, etc. over a particular period of time: *the day's take*. — *adj* **taken**. — *v* **take after** (*tr*) to be like (a parent or relation) in appearance or character. — *v* **take against** (*tr*) to take a dislike to. — *v* **take apart** (*tr*) **1** to separate into pieces or components. **2** to criticise or defeat severely. — *v* **take back** (*tr*) **1** to make (someone) remember the past. **2** to withdraw or retract (a statement or promise). **3** to gain possession of again. **4** to return (a person or object) to an original or former position. **5** to accept (a former lover, friend, etc.) as a lover, friend, etc. again. **6** to return (anything bought from a shop) to the shop for an exchange or refund. — **take a degree** to study for, be examined for and obtain a university or college degree. — *v* **take down** (*tr*) **1** to make a written note or record of. **2** to demolish, pull down or dismantle. **3** to lower. **4** to lead (someone) in to dinner. **5** to make less powerful or self-important; to humble: *take him down a peg or two*. — *v* **take in** (*tr*) **1** to include. **2** to give accommodation or shelter to. **3** to understand and remember. **4** to make (a garment) smaller. **5** to deceive or cheat. **6** to do (paid work) in one's home: *take in washing*. **7** (*coll*) to include a visit to: *take in a restaurant on the way home*. — **take it 1** to be able to bear (suffering, trouble, difficulty, etc.): *Tell me the worst, I can take it*. **2** to assume: *I take it that you'll be able to come*. — **take it from me** you can believe me. — **take it out of** (*coll*) to exhaust the strength or energy of. — **take it out on** (*coll*) to vent one's anger or frustration on (an innocent person or thing). — **take it upon oneself** to take responsibility (for). — *v* **take off 1** (*tr*) to remove. **2** (*tr*) to deduct. **3** (*intr*) (of an aircraft) to leave the ground. **4** (*intr*; *coll*) (of a scheme, product, etc.) to become popular and successful and expand quickly. **5** (*intr*; *coll*; **for**) to depart or set out. **6** (*tr*) to spend (a period of time) away from work on holiday, resting, etc. **7** (*tr*) to imitate or mimic. ◇ See also **take-off** below. — *v* **take on 1** (*tr*) to agree to do; to undertake. **2** (*tr*) to give employment to; to add to one's employees. **3** (*tr*; **at**) to challenge or compete against (esp. a stronger opponent). **4** (*tr*) to acquire (a new meaning, quality, appearance, etc.). **5** (*tr*) to receive (new passengers, fuel, cargo, etc.) on board. **6** (*intr*; *coll*) to be very upset or distraught. — *v* **take out** (*tr*) **1** to remove or extract. **2** to go out with or escort in public. **3** to obtain on application: *take out insurance*; *take out a warrant*. **4** (*slang*) to kill, defeat or destroy. — *v* **take over** (*tr* & *intr*; **from**) to assume control, management or ownership (of). ◇ See also **takeover** below. — *v* **take to** (*tr*) **1** to develop a liking for. **2** to begin to do regularly as a habit. **3** to turn to as a remedy or for refuge. — *v* **take up 1** (*tr*) to lift or raise. **2** (*tr*) to use or occupy (space or time). **3** (*tr*) to become interested in and begin to do: *take up the violin*. **4** (*tr*) to begin to be a patron of (someone). **5** (*tr*) to shorten (a garment). **6** (*tr* & *intr*) to continue (a story, account, etc.) from where one left off after a short break. **7** (*tr*) to begin to live in: *take up residence in July*. **8** (*tr*) to accept (an offer). **9** (*tr* with **on**) to accept the offer, proposal, challenge, etc. of. **10** (*tr* with **on**) to discuss something with: *take her up on a couple of points in her essay*. **11** (*tr*) to absorb. **12** (*tr*; **with**) to discuss (a matter): *take it up with one's MP*. ◇ See also **take-up** below. — *v* **take up with** (*tr*) to become friendly with; to begin to associate with. [OE *tacan*]

takeaway *n* **1** a cooked meal prepared and bought in a restaurant but taken away and eaten somewhere else, e.g. at home. **2** a restaurant which provides such meals. — *adj* **1** (of cooked meals) prepared and bought in a restaurant but eaten somewhere else. **2** (of a restaurant) providing such meals.

take-home pay *n* the salary that one actually receives after tax, national insurance and pension contributions have been deducted.

take-off *n* **1** an act of leaving the ground. **2** an act of imitating or mimicking. **3** a place from which one takes off, jumps, etc.; a starting-point. ◇ See also **take off** above.

takeover *n* the act of taking control of something, esp. a company by buying the majority of its shares. ◇ See also **take over** above.

taker *n* a person who takes or accepts something, esp. a bet.

take-up *n* the act of claiming or accepting something, e.g. state benefit. ◇ See also **take up** above.

take-up rate *n* the number of people who claim a benefit to which they are entitled or who accept an offer.

taking *adj* attractive; charming. — *n* (in *pl*) the amount of money taken at a concert, in a shop, etc.; receipts.

talc or **talcum** *n* **1** a soft, greasy grey or silver-white mineral used in talcum powder, making pottery, etc. **2** talcum powder. [Persian *talk*]

talcum powder *n* a fine, often perfumed, powder made from purified talc, used on the body.

tale *n* **1** a story or narrative. **2** a false or malicious story or piece of gossip; a lie. — **tell tales (about, on)** to give away secret or private information, esp. about another person's wrongdoing to someone in authority. [OE *talu*]

tale-bearer *n* a person who repeats malicious or false gossip.

talent *n* **1** a special or innate skill, aptitude or ability, esp. for art, music, etc. **2** high general or mental ability. **3** a person or people with such skill or ability. **4** (*coll*) attractive members of the opposite sex as a group. **5** (*hist*) a measure of weight and unit of currency used e.g. by the ancient Greeks and Romans. — *adj* **talented**. [OE *talente*, from Lat *talentum*]

talent scout or **spotter** *n* a person whose job is to find and recruit talented amateurs, esp. singers and dancers, for professional engagements.

talisman *n* **-mans** a small object such as a stone which is supposed to have magic powers to protect its owner from evil, bring good luck or work magic; a charm or amulet. — *adj* **talismanic**. [Gr *telesma*, rite, consecrated object]

talk *v* **1** (*intr*; **about, to, with**) to express one's ideas, feelings and thoughts (to someone) in words; to have a conversation or discussion (about something). **2** (*tr*) to discuss: *talk business*. **3** (*intr*) to use or be able to use speech: *Is the baby beginning to talk yet?* **4** (*tr*) to express in speech; to utter: *talk nonsense*. **5** (*intr*) to gossip. **6** (*intr*) to give away secret information. **7** (*tr*) to use or speak in (a language): *talk Dutch*. **8** (*tr*; **into, out of**) to bring into a specified state or position by talking: *talk oneself hoarse*; *talk him out of jumping*. **9** (*intr*) to have influence: *Money talks*. **10** (*intr*; **on**) to give a talk or lecture. — *n* **1** a conversation or discussion. **2** (often in *pl*) a formal discussion or series of negotiations. **3** an informal lecture. **4** (the subject of) gossip or rumour: *the talk of the town*. **5** boasting which will never be carried out; meaningless and useless discussion: *His ideas are all just talk*. **6** a particular way of speaking or communicating: *baby talk*. — *n* **talker**. — **now you're talking** (*coll*) now you are saying something that I want to hear. — *v* **talk back** (*intr*) to answer rudely, impudently or boldly. — **talk big** (*coll*) to talk boastfully. — *v* **talk down 1** (*intr* with **to**) to talk patronisingly or condescendingly to. **2** (*tr*) to silence by speaking more loudly or aggressively. **3** (*tr*) to help (a pilot or aircraft) to land by sending instructions over the radio. — *v* **talk out** (*tr*) **1** to resolve (a problem or difference of opinion) by discussion. **2** (*Br*) to defeat (a bill or motion in Parliament) by discussing it until it is too late to vote on it. — *v* **talk over** (*tr*) to discuss. — *v* **talk round** (*tr*) **1** to bring (someone) to one's own way of thinking by talking persuasively. **2** to discuss all aspects of (a subject, problem, etc.) but without reaching a decision or coming to a conclusion. — **you can't talk** (*coll*) you are in no position to criticise or disagree. [MidE *talken*]

talkative *adj* talking a lot.

talkie *n* (*coll*) a cinema film with sound, esp. one of the first such films.

talking-point *n* a subject for discussion.

talking-shop *n* a place for discussion and argument and not action.

talking-to *n* (*coll*) a ticking-off; a scolding or reproof.

tall *adj* **1** of above average height. **2** having a stated height: *six feet tall*. **3** difficult to believe; extravagant: *a tall story*. **4** difficult or demanding: *a tall order*. — *n* **tallness**. [MidE *tal*, from OE *getæl*, swift, ready]

tallboy *n* a tall high chest of drawers, sometimes with an upper and slightly smaller section standing on a larger lower one, or on short legs.

tallow *n* hard fat from sheep and cattle melted down and used to make candles, soap, etc. [MidE *talg*]

tally *n* **-ies 1** an account or reckoning, e.g. of work done, debts or the score in a game. **2** (*hist*) a stick which could have notches cut in it to show debts and accounts, and which could then be split in half lengthways so that each party had a record of the deal. **3** a distinguishing or identifying mark or label. **4** a counterpart; a corresponding part. — *v* ***-ies***, ***-ied*** **1** (*intr*; **with**) to agree, correspond or match. **2** (*tr*) to record or mark (a number, score, etc.) on, or as if on, a tally. [Lat *talea*, stick]

tally clerk *n* a person who checks a ship's cargo against an official list.

tallyman *n* **1** a person who keeps a tally. **2** a person who sells goods on credit, esp. from door to door.

tally-ho *interj* a cry to the hounds at a hunt when a fox has been sighted.

Talmud *n* the body of Jewish civil and canon law. — *adj* **Talmudic**. [Hebr, instruction]

Talmudist *n* a scholar of the Talmud.

talon *n* a hooked claw, esp. of a bird of prey. [Lat *talus*, heel]

tamarind *n* **1** a tropical evergreen tree which bears yellow flowers and brown seed pods. **2** the pod of this tree, filled with a reddish-black slightly acid pulp used as food and to make cooling drinks. [Arabic *tamr-hindi*, Indian date]

tamarisk *n* a tropical or Mediterranean shrub or tree with slender branches and small pink or white flowers, usu. found on seashores. [Lat *tamarix*]

tambour *n* **1** a drum. **2** a frame for embroidery consisting of two hoops which hold the fabric taut while stitches are sewn. **3** an embroidery done on such a frame. [OFr]

tambourine *n* a small round drum with skin stretched tight on one side only, with small discs of metal in the rim that jingle when the drum is struck with the hand. [ODut *tamborijn*, small drum]

tame *adj* **1** (of animals) used to living or working with people; not wild or dangerous. **2** (of land, etc.) changed by people from a natural wild state; cultivated. **3** docile, meek and submissive. **4** dull and unexciting; insipid: *a tame ending to an otherwise exciting story*. — *v* (*tr*) **1** to make (an animal) used to living or working with people. **2** to make meek and humble; to deprive the spirit of; to subdue. — *adj* **tamable** or **tameable**. — *adv* **tamely**. — *n* **tameness**. — *n* **tamer**. [OE *tam*]

Tamil *n* **1** a member of a people living in S India and Sri Lanka. **2** the language spoken by this people. — *adj* of or relating to this people or their language.

tam-o'-shanter *n* a Scottish flat round cloth or woollen cap which fits tightly round the brows and has a full crown, often with a bobble in the middle. [After the hero of Burns's poem *Tam o' Shanter*]

tamp *v* (*tr*) **1** to fill up (a hole containing explosive) with earth, cement, etc. before setting off the explosion. **2** to drive or force down (e.g. ballast on a railway) by repeated blows.

tamper *v* *-r-* (*intr*) **1** (**with**) to interfere or meddle with, esp. in such a way as to cause damage. **2** (with **with**) to (try to) corrupt or influence, esp. by bribery. [A form of **temper**]

tamper-evident *adj* (of packaging) designed in such a way that it is obvious when it has been tampered with.

tampon *n* a plug of cottonwool or other soft absorbent material inserted into a cavity or wound to absorb blood and other secretions, esp. one for use in the vagina during menstruation. — *v* ***-n-*** (*tr*) to insert a tampon in. [OFr, from *tape*, plug]

tan[1] *n* **1** the brown colour of the skin after exposure to the sun's ultraviolet rays. **2** a tawny brown colour. **3** oak bark or other material, used esp. for tanning hides. — *adj* tawny brown in colour. — *v* ***-nn-*** **1** (*tr* & *intr*) to (cause to) become brown in the sun. **2** (*tr*) to convert (hide) into leather by soaking it in a solution containing tannin, mineral salts or man-made chemicals. **3** (*tr*; *coll*) to beat. — *adj* **tanned**. — *n* **tanning**. [Lat *tannum*, oak bark]

tanner *n* a person whose job is to tan leather.

tannery *n* ***-ies*** a place where hides are tanned.

tannic acid or **tannin** *n* any of several substances obtained from certain tree barks and other plants, used in tanning leather, dyeing, ink-making and in medicine, also occurring in, and giving a distinctive flavour to, red wine and tea.

tan[2] *abbrev* tangent (sense **2**).

tandem *n* **1** a type of long three-wheeled bicycle for two people, with two seats and two sets of pedals placed one behind the other. **2** (a carriage drawn by) a team of two horses harnessed one behind the other. **3** any two people or things which follow one behind the other. — *adv* one behind the other, esp. on a bicycle, or with two horses harnessed one behind the other: *ride tandem*; *drive tandem*. — **in tandem 1** with one behind the other. **2** together or in partnership with. [A pun on Lat *tandem*, at length, at last]

tandoori *n* (food cooked by) an Indian method of cooking meat and vegetables on a spit over charcoal in a clay oven. [Hindi *tandoor*, clay oven]

tang *n* **1** a strong or sharp taste, flavour or smell. **2** a trace or hint. **3** the pointed end of a knife, sword, chisel, etc. that fits into and is held firmly by the handle. [Norse *tange*, point]

tangy *adj* ***-ier***, ***-iest*** having a fresh sharp smell or flavour.

tangent *n* **1** (*geom*) a straight line that touches a curve but does not cut through it. **2** (*math*) for either of the acute angles in a right-angled triangle, the ratio of the length of the side opposite the angle to the length of the side adjacent to it. ◇ See also **sine, cosine, cotangent**. — *adj* of, being or forming a tangent. — **at a tangent** in a completely different direction or course. [Lat *tangere*, to touch]

tangential *adj* **1** of or along a tangent. **2** not of central importance to; incidental; peripheral. — *adv* **tangentially**.

tangerine *n* **1** (a tree that produces) a variety of mandarin orange with a loose, reddish-orange skin and flesh. **2** the reddish-orange colour of this fruit. — *adj* reddish-orange. [*Tangier*, a port on the Moroccan coast]

tangible *adj* **1** able to be felt by touch. **2** real or definite; material: *tangible evidence*. — *n* **tangibility**. — *adv* **tangibly**. [Lat *tangibilis*]

tangle *n* **1** an untidy, confused or knotted state or mass, e.g. of hair or fibres. **2** a confused or complicated state or situation. — *v* **1** (*tr* & *intr*) (esp. of hair, fibres, etc.) to make or become untidy, knotted and confused. **2** (*intr*; **with**; *coll*) to become involved (with), esp. in conflict, a struggle or argument. **3** (*intr*; **with**; *coll*) to embrace. **4** (*tr*; *coll*) to trap or hamper the movement of. — *adj* **tangled**. [MidE *tangilen*]

tango *n* **-os** (a piece of music for) a dance of Argentinian origin with dramatic stylised body positions and long pauses. — *v* **-os**, **-oed** (*intr*) to perform this dance. [American Span]

tank *n* **1** a large container for holding, storing or transporting liquids or gas. **2** (also **tankful**, **-fuls**) the quantity contained in a tank. **3** a heavy steel-covered vehicle armed with guns and moving on caterpillar wheels. — *v* **1** (*tr*; **up**) to fill the tank of (a vehicle) with fuel. **2** (*tr* & *intr*; **up**; *slang*) to drink or cause to drink heavily and become very drunk. **3** (*tr*) to store in a tank. **4** (*intr*) to move like a tank, esp. quickly and heavily. [Gujurati (Indian language) *tankh*, reservoir & Port *tanque*, pond]

tanker *n* **1** a ship or large lorry which transports liquid in bulk. **2** an aircraft which transports fuel and is usu. able to refuel other aircraft in flight.

tankard *n* a large silver, pewter or pottery drinking-mug, often with a hinged lid, used esp. for drinking beer. [MidE]

tanker. See **tank**.

tanner[1] *n* (*Br old coll*) a sixpence.

tanner[2], **tannery**, **tannic acid** and **tannin**. See **tan**[1].

Tannoy® *n* a communication system with loudspeakers, used for making announcements in public buildings, e.g. railway stations.

tansy *n* **-ies** a wild plant with small heads of yellow flowers and pungent leaves used in cooking and formerly in medicine. [Gr *athanasia*, immortality]

tantalise or **-ize** *v* (*tr*) to tease or torment (someone) by keeping something wanted just out of reach. — *n* **tantalisation** or **-z-**. — *adj* **tantalising** or **-z-**. — *adv* **tantalisingly** or **-z-**. [*Tantalus*, in Greek mythology the king of Phrygia who was condemned to stand up to his chin in water which flowed away whenever he tried to drink and beneath hanging bunches of grapes that moved higher whenever he reached for them]

tantalum *n* (*chem*) a grey-white metallic element (symbol **Ta**), which is resistant to heat and acid and is used in electronic components and surgery. [Named after *Tantalus* (see etymology for **tantalise**), because of certain supposedly tantalising characteristics of its chemistry]

tantalus *n* a case in which decanters holding whisky, sherry, etc. are visible but locked up. [See etymology for **tantalise**]

tantamount *adj*: **tantamount to** having the same effect or result as; as good as; equivalent to. [OFr *tant amunter* or Ital *tanto montare*, to amount to as much]

tantrum *n* a fit of (esp. childish) bad temper.

Taoism *n* **1** a Chinese philosophical system based on the teachings of Lao-tzu (c. 6th cent. BC) and others, advocating a life of simplicity and non-interference with the natural course of events. **2** a religion supposedly based on this system of philosophy, but also including magic, superstition and the worship of many gods. — *n* & *adj* **Taoist**. [Chin *tao*, way]

tap[1] *n* **1** (the sound made by) a quick or light touch, knock or blow. **2** tap-dancing. **3** a piece of metal attached to the sole and heel of a shoe for tap-dancing. — *v* **-pp-** **1** (*tr*) to strike or knock lightly. **2** (*tr*) to strike or knock lightly with (something). **3** (*tr*; **out**) to produce by tapping: *tap out a message*. **4** (*intr*; **at**, **on**) to strike a light but audible blow.

tap-dance *n* a dance performed wearing shoes with metal on the soles and toes so that the dancer's rhythmical steps can be heard clearly. — *v* (*intr*) to perform a tap-dance. — *n* **tap-dancer**. — *n* **tap-dancing**. [MidE *tappen*]

tap[2] *n* **1** a device consisting of a valve, with a handle for opening and shutting it, attached to a pipe for controlling the flow of liquid or gas. **2** a peg or stopper, esp. in a barrel. **3** a receiver for listening to and recording private conversations, attached secretly to a telephone wire. **4** an act of attaching such a receiver to a telephone wire. **5** the withdrawal of fluid from a place, esp. (*med*) from a cavity in the body. **6** a screw for cutting an internal thread. — *v* **-pp-** (*tr*) **1** to get liquid from (a barrel, cavity in the body, etc.) by piercing it or opening it with, or as if with, a tap. **2** to let out (liquid) from a vessel by opening, or as if by opening, a tap. **3** to get sap from (a tree) by cutting into it. **4** to attach a receiver secretly to (a telephone wire) so as to be able to hear private conversations. **5** to start using (a source, supply, etc.). **6** (*coll*; **for**) to get money from (someone) as a loan or present. — **on tap 1** (of beer) stored in casks from which it is served. **2**

ready and available for immediate use. [OE *tæppa*]

taproom *n* a bar serving alcoholic drinks, esp. beer direct from casks.

taproot *n* a strong root of a plant that grows down vertically and sends out small roots horizontally.

tape *n* **1** a narrow strip of woven cloth used for tying, fastening, etc. **2** (often in *cmpds*; in full **magnetic tape**) a ribbon of thin plastic or metal used for recording sounds or images: *videotape*. **3** anything which has been recorded on magnetic tape; a tape- or video-recording. **4** (in full **adhesive tape**) a ribbon of thin paper or plastic with a sticky surface, used for fastening, sticking, etc. **5** a string or paper ribbon stretched above the finishing line on a race track. **6** a tape-measure. — *v* **1** (*tr*) to fasten, tie or seal with tape. **2** (*tr* & *intr*) to record (sounds or images) on magnetic tape. — **have** (**something** or **someone**) **taped** (*coll*) to understand (something or someone) perfectly. [OE *tæppe*]

tape deck *n* the part of a tape-recorder comprising the motor, the recording head, the support for the spools, etc.

tape-measure *n* a length of plastic, cloth or thin flexible metal tape, marked with inches, feet and yards or centimetres and metres, for measuring.

tape-record *v* (*tr*) to record (sounds) on magnetic tape. — *n* **tape-recording**.

tape-recorder *n* a machine which records sounds on magnetic tape and reproduces them when required.

tapeworm *n* a worm which lives as a parasite in the intestines.

taper *n* **1** a long thin candle. **2** a long waxed wick or spill for lighting candles or fires. **3** a gradual lessening of diameter or width towards one end. — *v* **-r-** (*tr* & *intr*; **off**) **1** to make or become gradually narrower towards one end. **2** to make or become gradually less. — *adj* **tapered** and **tapering**. [OE *tapor*]

tapestry *n* **-ies** **1** a thick woven textile with an ornamental design (often a picture) on it, used for curtains, wall-hangings, chair coverings, etc. **2** (a piece of) embroidery with usu. wool done on canvas which imitates designs and pictures found in and the heavy texture of tapestry. — *adj* **tapestried**. [OFr *tapisserie*, carpeting]

tapioca *n* hard white grains of starch from the cassava plant, often made into a pudding with sugar and milk. [Tupí (S American Indian language) *tipioca*, juice squeezed out]

tapir *n* ***tapir*** or ***tapirs*** a large hoofed mammal with a snout, found in S America and Malaysia. [Tupí (S American Indian language) *tapira*]

tappet *n* a lever or projection that transmits motion from one part of a machine to another, esp. in an internal-combustion engine from the camshaft to the valves. [**tap**[1]]

taps *n* (*pl*) **1** a bugle call for lights out, also used at military funerals. **2** (in the Guide movement) a song sung at the end of a meeting or round a campfire in the evening. [**tattoo**[2]]

tar[1] *n* **1** a thick dark sticky liquid obtained by distilling organic matter such as wood, peat or coal (in this case, also called **coal tar**), and used in making roads, preserving wood and as an antiseptic. **2** a similar substance, esp. the residue formed from smoke from burning tobacco. — *v* **-rr-** (*tr*) to cover with tar. — **tar and feather** to cover (a person) with tar and then feathers as a punishment. — **tarred with the same brush** having the same faults. [OE *teoru*]

tarry *adj* **-ier**, **-iest** of, like or covered with tar. — *n* **tarriness**.

tar[2] *n* (*old coll*) a sailor. [Perhaps abbrev. of **tarpaulin**]

taramasalata *n* a creamy pink pâté made from the smoked roe of fish, esp. cod, and olive oil and garlic. [Modern Gr]

tarantella *n* (a piece of music for) a lively country dance from S Italy. [*Taranto* in S Italy]

tarantula *n* **1** any of several large hairy tropical spiders, some of which are poisonous. **2** a large black spider found in S Europe. [Ital *tarantola*]

tarboosh *n* a hat like a fez, sometimes worn with a turban. [Arabic *tarbush*]

tardy *adj* **-ier**, **-iest** **1** slow to move, progress or grow; sluggish. **2** slower to arrive or happen than expected; late. — *adv* **tardily**. — *n* **tardiness**. [Lat *tardus*, slow]

tare[1] *n* **1** any of several vetches, esp. those grown for food or fodder. **2** (usu. in *pl*; *Bible*) a weed which grows in cornfields. [MidE]

tare[2] *n* and *adj* **1** (of) the weight of the wrapping paper or container in which goods are packed. **2** (of) an allowance made for this. **3** (of) the weight of a vehicle without its fuel, cargo or passengers. [Arabic *tarhah*, that which is thrown away]

target *n* **1** an object aimed at in shooting practice or competitions, esp. a flat round board marked with concentric circles and with a bull's-eye in the centre. **2** any object or area fired or aimed at. **3** a person or thing which is the focus of ridicule or criticism. **4** a result aimed at; a goal. **5** (*archaic*) a small buckler or round shield. — *v* **-t-** (*tr*) **1** to direct or aim (something). **2** to make (a person, place or thing) a target or the object of an attack. [OFr *targe*, shield]

tariff *n* **1** a list of prices or charges: *a hotel tariff*. **2** the tax or duty to be paid on a particular class of goods imported or exported. **3** a list of such taxes and duties. [Arabic *tarif*, explanation]

tarlatan *n* an open, transparent muslin, used for stiffening garments. [Fr *tarlatane*]

tarmac *n* **1** tarmacadam. **2** a surface covered with tarmac, esp. an airport runway. [**tar**[1] + **mac(adam)**]

tarmacadam *n* a mixture of small stones bound together with tar, used to make road surfaces, etc.

tarn *n* a small mountain lake. [Norse *tjörn*]

tarnish *v* **1** (*tr*) to make (metal) dull and discoloured, esp. through the action of air or dirt. **2** (*intr*) (of metal) to become dull and discoloured. **3** (*tr*) to spoil or damage (e.g. someone's reputation). — *n* **1** a loss of shine or lustre. **2** a discoloured or dull film on the surface of metal. — *adj* **tarnishable**. [OFr *ternir*, to make dull]

tarot *n* **1** a pack of 78 playing cards consisting of four suits of fourteen cards (the **minor arcana**) and a fifth suit of twenty-two trump cards (the **major arcana**), used for playing several different games or for fortune-telling. **2** any of the twenty-two trump cards in this pack, which are decorated with allegorical pictures. [Ital *tarocchi*]

tarpaulin *n* (a sheet of) heavy canvas which has been made waterproof, esp. with tar. [**tar**[1] + **pall**[1]]

tarragon *n* a European herb with narrow, pungent leaves used in cooking, e.g. for flavouring vinegar. [Gr *drakon*, dragon]

tarry[1]. See **tar**[1].

tarry[2] *v* ***-ies***, ***-ied*** (*intr*) **1** to linger or stay (in a place). **2** to be slow or late in coming, doing something, etc. [MidE *taryen*, to delay]

tarsus *n* **tarsi** **1** (*anat*) the bones forming the upper part of the foot and ankle. **2** (*biol*) (in insects) the final part of a limb, usu. a five-jointed foot. **3** (*anat*) a plate of dense connective tissue that supports and stiffens the eyelid. — *adj* **tarsal**. [Gr *tarsos*, the flat of the foot]

tart[1] *adj* **1** sharp or sour in taste. **2** (of a remark, etc.) brief and sarcastic; cutting. — *adv* **tartly**. — *n* **tartness**. [OE *teart*, rough]

tart[2] *n* **1** a pastry case, esp. one without a top, with a sweet filling such as fruit or jam. **2** (*derog slang*) a female prostitute or a promiscuous woman. — *v* **tart up** (*tr*; *slang*) to make superficially more attractive, esp. in a showy, vulgar or tasteless way. [OFr *tarte*]

tarty *adj* ***-ier***, ***-iest*** (*derog slang*) **1** (of a woman or women's clothing) blatantly sexual or promiscuous. **2** cheap, showy and vulgar.

tartan *n* **1** a distinctive checked pattern which can be produced with checks of different widths and different colours, esp. one of the very many designs each of which is associated with a different Scottish clan. **2** a woollen cloth or garment woven with such a design. [OFr *tiretaine*]

Tartar *n* **1** (also **Tatar**) a member of a group of peoples, including Mongols and Turks, which overran Asia and parts of Europe in the Middle Ages. **2** (usu. **Tatar**) a member of a people related to the Turks living esp. in central Asia. **3** (usu. **Tatar**) the language spoken by this people. **4** (no *cap*) a violent, fierce or irritable person. — *adj* of the Tartars or their language. [Lat *Tartarus*, from Persian *Tatar*, perhaps influenced by Gr *Tartaros*, hell]

tartar *n* **1** a hard deposit, consisting mostly of calcium salts, that forms on the teeth. **2** a deposit that forms a hard brownish-red crust on the insides of wine casks during fermentation. [Gr *tartaron*]

cream of tartar *n* a purified white powder obtained from tartar (sense **2**), used in baking.

tartaric acid *n* an acid which occurs naturally in fruits (e.g. unripe grapes) and some other plants, used in baking powders.

tartar sauce *n* (also **tartare sauce**) mayonnaise flavoured with chopped pickles, capers, olives and parsley, often served with fish. [Fr *sauce tartare*]

task *n* a piece of work to be done or required, esp. one which is unpleasant or difficult; a chore. — **take to task** to scold or criticise. [OFr *tasque*]

task-force *n* **1** (*mil*) a temporary grouping of different units, e.g. land, sea and air forces, under a single commander to undertake a specific mission. **2** any similar grouping of individuals for a specific purpose.

taskmaster or **taskmistress** *n* a man, or woman, who sets and supervises the work of others, esp. strictly or severely.

Tasmanian devil *n* a small, ferocious, bear-like marsupial now found only in Tasmania.

Tass *n* the official news agency of the former Soviet Union. [Acronym of Russ *Telegrafnoe Agentsvo Sovietskovo Soyuza*, Telegraph Agency of the Soviet Union]

tassel *n* **1** a decoration (e.g. on a curtain, cushion or lampshade) consisting of a hanging bunch of threads tied firmly at one end and loose at the other. **2** a tassel-like flower-head on some plants, esp. maize. — *v* ***-ll-*** **1** (*tr*) to adorn with tassels. **2** (*intr*) (of maize) to grow tassels. [OFr]

taste *v* **1** (*tr* & *intr*) to test or discover the flavour of (food or drink) by taking a small amount of it into one's mouth. **2** (*tr* & *intr*) to be aware of or recognise the flavour of: *I can taste nutmeg in this cake*. **3** (*intr* with **of**) to have a particular flavour. **4** (*tr*) to eat or drink, esp. in small quantities or with enjoyment: *hadn't tasted food for days*. **5** (*tr*) to experience: *taste defeat*. — *n* **1** the sense by which flavours are distinguished by the tongue and nose. **2** the flavour of anything that is known through this sense: *dislike the taste of onions*. **3** an act of tasting or a small quantity of food or drink tasted. **4** a first, usu. brief experience of something. **5** (**for**) a liking or preference: *a taste for exotic holidays*; *The film was not to her taste*. **6** the ability to judge, and appreciate, what is suitable as well as being fine, elegant or beautiful: *show good taste in clothes*; *a joke in poor taste*. — *adj*

tastable. — **to taste** as needed to give a pleasing flavour. [OFr *taster*]

taste bud *n* any of the cells on the surface of the tongue which are sensitive to flavour.

tasteful *adj* showing good judgement or taste. — *adv* **tastefully**. — *n* **tastefulness**.

tasteless *adj* **1** lacking flavour. **2** showing a lack of good taste or judgement. — *adv* **tastelessly**. — *n* **tastelessness**.

taster *n* a person whose job is to taste and judge the quality of food or drink.

tasting *n* an (often social) event at which a particular food or drink (esp. wine) is sampled.

tasty *adj* **-ier**, **-iest** **1** having a good, esp. savoury, flavour. **2** (*coll*) interesting or attractive. — *adv* **tastily**. — *n* **tastiness**.

tat[1] *n* (*Br coll*) rubbish or junk. [**tatty**]

tat[2] *v* **-tt-** (*tr* & *intr*) to make (lace for trimming) by hand with a small shuttle from sewing-thread.

tatting *n* **1** delicate knotted lace trimming made by hand with a small shuttle from sewing-thread. **2** the process of making such lace.

ta-ta *interj* (*Br coll*) (esp. used to or by young children) good-bye.

Tatar. See **Tartar**.

tatter *n* (usu. in *pl*) a torn, ragged shred of cloth, esp. of clothing. — **in tatters 1** (of clothes) in a torn and ragged condition. **2** (of an argument, discussion, etc.) in ruins; torn apart and useless. [MidE, from Norse *torturr*, rag]

tattered *adj* ragged or torn.

tattle *n* idle chatter or gossip. — *v* **1** (*intr*) to chat or gossip idly. **2** (*tr*) to give away (secrets) by chatting idly or gossiping. — *n* **tattler**. [ODut *tatelen*]

tattoo[1] *v* **-oos**, **-ooed** (*tr*) to mark (coloured designs or pictures) on (a person or part of the body) by pricking the skin and putting in indelible dyes. — *n* **-oos** a design tattooed on the skin. — *n* **tattooer** or **tattooist**. [Tahitian *tatau*]

tattoo[2] *n* **-oos** **1** a signal by drum or bugle calling soldiers to quarters, esp. in the evening. **2** an outdoor military entertainment with marching troops, military bands, etc., usu. given in the evening. **3** a rhythmic beating, tapping or drumming. [Earlier *taptoo*, from Dut *taptoe*, the tap of a barrel (is to be) shut]

tatty *adj* **-ier**, **-iest** (*coll*) shabby and untidy. — *adv* **tattily**. — *n* **tattiness**. [**tatter**]

taught. See **teach**.

taunt *v* (*tr*) to tease, say unpleasant things to or jeer at in a cruel and hurtful way. — *n* a cruel, unpleasant and often hurtful or provoking remark. — *n* & *adj* **taunting**. — *adv* **tauntingly**.

taupe *n* & *adj* (of) a brownish-grey colour. [Fr, mole]

Taurus *n* **1** a constellation and the second sign of the zodiac, the Bull. **2** a person born between 21 April and 20 May, under this sign. — *n* & *adj* **Taurean**. [Lat, bull]

taut *adj* **1** pulled or stretched tight. **2** showing nervous strain or anxiety. **3** (of a ship) in good condition. [MidE *toht*, tight]

tauten *v* **-n-** (*tr* & *intr*) to make or become taut.

tautology *n* **-ies** **1** (an example of) the use of words which merely repeat the meaning found in other words already used, as in *All of a sudden she suddenly remembered.* **2** (*logic*) a statement which is necessarily always true. — *adj* **tautological** or **tautologous**. [Gr *tautologos*, from *tauto*, same + *legein*, to say]

tavern *n* an inn or public house. [Lat *taberna*, shed]

tawdry *adj* **-ier**, **-iest** cheap and showy and of poor quality. — *adv* **tawdrily**. — *n* **tawdriness**. [From *St Audrey lace*, lace sold at fairs held on the feast day of St Audrey, 17 October]

tawny *n* & *adj* **-ier**, **-iest** (of) a yellowish-brown colour. [OFr *taune*]

tawny owl *n* a tawny-coloured European owl.

taws or **tawse** *n* (esp. *Scot*) a leather strap divided into strips at one end, formerly used for corporal punishment in schools. [Plural of obsolete *taw*, whip]

tax *n* (**on**) **1** a contribution towards a country's expenses raised by the government from people's salaries, property, and from the sale of goods and services. **2** a strain, burden or heavy demand. — *v* (*tr*) **1** to impose a tax on (a person, goods, etc.) or take tax from (a salary). **2** to put a strain on or make a heavy demand on. **3** (**with**) to accuse (of) or charge (with). **4** (*legal*) to assess (costs). — *adj* **taxable**. [Lat *taxare*, to appraise]

taxation *n* the act or system of taxing or the state of being taxed.

tax-deductible *adj* (of expenses, etc.) able to be deducted from one's income before it is assessed for tax.

tax-free *adj* & *adv* without payment of tax.

tax haven *n* a country or state with a low rate of taxation compared to one's own.

taxing *adj* requiring a lot of mental or physical effort; demanding.

taxpayer *n* a person who pays or is liable for tax or taxes.

taxi *n* **-is** (also **taxicab**) a car which may be hired together with its driver to carry passengers on usu. short journeys, and which is usu. fitted with a taximeter for calculating the fare. — *v* **-ies**, **-iing** or **-ying**, **-ied** **1** (*intr*) (of a pilot or aircraft) to move along the ground slowly before or after take-off or landing under its own power. **2** (*tr*) to cause (an aircraft) to move in this way. **3** (*intr* & *tr*) to travel or cause to be conveyed in a taxi. [Short for *taximeter cab*]

taxi rank *n* a place where taxis stand until hired.

taxidermy *n* the art of preparing, stuffing and mounting animal skins and birds so that they present a lifelike appearance. — *n* **taxidermist**. [Gr *taxis*, arrangement + *derma*, skin]

taximeter *n* a meter fitted to a taxi which calculates the distance travelled and the fare due. [Fr *taximètre*, from *taxe*, tax + *mètre*, meter]

taxonomy *n* the practice or science of classifying plants and animals into groups according to their differences and similarities. — *adj* **taxonomic**. — *n* **taxonomist**. [Gr *taxis*, arrangement + *nomia*, law]

TB *abbrev* tuberculosis.

Tb *symbol* (*chem*) terbium.

tbsp *abbrev* tablespoon or tablespoonful.

Tc *symbol* (*chem*) technetium.

TCP® *abbrev* trichlorophenylmethyliodasalicyl, an antiseptic and disinfectant.

Te *symbol* (*chem*) tellurium.

te. See **ti**.

tea *n* **1** an evergreen shrub or tree grown in Asia, esp. India, Ceylon and China. **2** the dried leaves of this plant prepared for sale. **3** a drink made by infusing these leaves in boiling water and served either hot or iced. **4** a similar drink made from the leaves or flowers of other plants or some totally different ingredient: *peppermint tea*; *beef tea*. **5** a light afternoon meal at which tea, sandwiches and cakes are served. **6** (*Br*) a light cooked meal, usu. less substantial than the midday meal, served early in the evening. [Southern Chin *te*]

tea bag *n* a small bag or sachet of thin paper containing tea, infused in boiling water in a pot or cup.

tea break *n* a pause for a cup of tea or other refreshment during working hours.

tea caddy *n* a small container for tea leaves.

teacake *n* a glazed currant bun, usu. eaten toasted.

tea chest *n* a tall light wooden box in which tea is packed for export, or for storing things in.

tea cloth *n* **1** a small cloth for decorating and protecting the surface of a table or trolley. **2** a tea towel.

tea-cosy *n* a cover to keep a teapot warm.

teacup *n* **1** a medium-sized cup used esp. for drinking tea. **2** (also **teacupful**, ***-fuls***) the amount that a teacup holds.

teahouse *n* a restaurant in China or Japan where tea and light refreshments are served.

tea leaf *n* **1** a leaf of the tea plant, or a part of the leaf. **2** (in *pl*) the leaves remaining in the pot or cup after the tea made from them has been drunk. **3** (*slang*) a thief.

teapot *n* a pot with a spout and handle used for making and pouring tea.

tearoom *n* a restaurant where tea, coffee, cakes, etc. are served.

tea rose *n* a hybrid rose which is supposed to smell of tea.

teaspoon *n* **1** a small spoon for use with a teacup. **2** (also **teaspoonful**, ***-fuls***) the amount that a teaspoon will hold.

tea towel *n* a cloth for drying dishes after they have been washed.

tea tray *n* a tray on which tea, usu. with sandwiches and cakes, is served.

tea trolley *n* a small trolley from which tea, sandwiches and cakes are served.

teach *v* ***taught*** **1** (*tr*) to give knowledge to; to instruct in a skill or help to learn. **2** (*tr*) to give lessons in (a subject). **3** (*intr*) to give lessons in a subject, esp. professionally. **4** (*tr*) to cause to learn or understand, esp. by example, experience or punishment: *Experience had taught her never to expect the train to be on time*. **5** (*tr*) to force (someone) to realise that particular behaviour is either required or not required at all: *That'll teach you to be so rude* or *to be a bit more polite*. — **teach school** (*NAm*) to be a teacher in a school. [OE *tæcan*]

teachable *adj* **1** able, willing or quick to learn. **2** capable of being taught.

teacher *n* a person who teaches, esp. professionally in a school.

teach-in *n* an informal lecture, demonstration and discussion, or a series of these given one after the other and usu. on the same day, by experts in a particular subject.

teaching *n* **1** the work or profession of a teacher. **2** (often in *pl*) that which is taught, esp. guidance or doctrine.

teaching hospital *n* a large hospital where medical students are taught.

teak *n* **1** a large tree which grows in India, Malaysia, etc. **2** its hard yellowish-brown wood used for making furniture. [Malayalam (S Indian language) *tekka*]

teal *n* any of several kinds of small freshwater duck of Europe and America. [MidE *tele*]

team *n* **1** a group of people forming one side in a game. **2** a group of people working together. **3** two or more animals working together, esp. in harness together. — *v* **1** (*intr* & *tr*; **up, up with**) to form or make into a team for some common action. **2** (*tr*) to harness (horses, oxen, etc.) together. **3** (*tr*; **with**) to match (clothes). [OE, child-bearing, offspring]

team spirit *n* willingness to work together as part of a team and suppress individual needs and desires.

teamster *n* **1** a driver of a team of animals. **2** (*US*) a lorry-driver.

team-work *n* cooperation between those who are working together on a task.

tear[1] *n* **1** a drop of clear salty liquid that moistens and washes the eye and eyelid and is often shed as a result of emotion, esp. grief. **2** any pear- or tear-shaped drop or blob. — *adj* **tearless**. — **in tears** crying; weeping. [OE]

teardrop *n* a single tear.

tear duct *n* a short tube opening in the inner corner of the eye, for carrying tears to the eye or draining them into the nose.

tearful *adj* **1** inclined to cry or weep. **2** with much crying or weeping; covered with tears. **3** causing tears to be shed; sad. — *adv* **tearfully**. — *n* **tearfulness**.

tear gas *n* a gas which causes stinging, blinding tears and temporary loss of sight, used e.g. to control riots.

tear-jerker *n* (*coll*) a sentimental play, film, book, etc. intended to make people feel sad and cry. — *adj* **tear-jerking**.

tear-stained *adj* (of the face or cheeks) marked with the traces of tears.

tear[2] *v* ***tore***, ***torn*** **1** (*tr*) to pull or rip apart by force. **2** (*tr*) to make (a hole, etc.) by, or as if by, tearing or ripping. **3** (*intr*) to come apart; to be (able to be) pulled or ripped apart: *material that tears easily*. **4** (*tr*; **away, from**) to remove or take by force; to force or persuade to leave. **5** (*intr*; **along, away, off**) to rush; to move with speed or violence. — *n* **1** a hole or other damage caused by tearing. **2** an act of tearing. **3** damage: *wear and tear*. — **be torn between** to be unable to decide between. — **tear a strip off** (*coll*) to rebuke or reprimand severely. — *v* **tear at** (*tr*) **1** to pull violently or attack with tearing movements. **2** (also **tear apart**) to cause severe suffering or distress to. — *v* **tear down** (*tr*) to pull down or demolish using force. — **tear one's hair (out)** to be in despair with impatience and frustration. — *v* **tear into** (*tr*) to attack, either physically or with criticism. — *v* **tear up** (*tr*) **1** to remove from a fixed position by violence: *The wind tore up several trees*. **2** to tear into pieces. [OE *teran*]

tearaway *n* (*Br coll*) an undisciplined and reckless young person.

tearing *adj* furious; overwhelming: *a tearing hurry*.

tease *v* **1** (*tr & intr*) to annoy or irritate on purpose or unkindly. **2** (*tr & intr*) to laugh at or make fun of playfully or annoyingly. **3** (*tr*) to persuade (someone) to agree to (something), esp. by continual coaxing. **4** (*tr & intr*) to arouse (someone) sexually without satisfying that desire. **5** (*tr*; **out**) to comb (wool, flax, hair, etc.) to remove tangles and open out the fibres. **6** (*tr*) to raise a nap on (cloth) by scratching or brushing, esp. with teasels. **7** (*tr*) to back-comb (the hair). — *n* **1** a person or thing that teases. **2** an act of teasing. [OE *tæsan*, to card]

teaser *n* **1** a puzzle or tricky problem. **2** a person who enjoys teasing others. — *n & adj* **teasing**. — *adv* **teasingly**.

teasel, **teazel** or **teazle** *n* **1** a plant whose prickly flower heads were formerly used to raise a nap on woollen or woven cloth. **2** an artificial substitute for the teasel. [OE *tæsel*]

teat *n* **1** the nipple of a breast or udder. **2** a piece of shaped rubber attached to a bottle through which a baby can suck milk. [OFr *tete*]

teazel, **teazle**. See **teasel**.

tec *n* (*coll*) a detective. [Abbrev.]

tech *n* (*coll*) a technical college.

tech. *abbrev* **1** technical. **2** technology.

technetium *n* (*chem*) an artificially produced radioactive metallic element (symbol **Tc**). [Gr *technetos*, artificial]

technical *adj* **1** having knowledge of, specialising in or relating to a practical skill or applied science, esp. those sciences which are useful to industry. **2** (esp. of language) relating to a particular subject or requiring knowledge of a particular subject to be understood. **3** according to a strict interpretation of the law or rules. **4** of or showing a quality of technique: *playing of technical brilliance*. — *adv* **technically**. [Gr *technikos*, from *techne*, art]

technical college *n* a college of further education that teaches practical skills and applied sciences necessary to industry and business.

technical drawing *n* **1** the drawing of plans, machinery, electrical circuits, etc. with compasses, rulers, etc. for business and industry. **2** a drawing done for business or industry.

technical hitch *n* a mechanical fault.

technicality *n* ***-ies*** **1** a technical detail or term. **2** a usu. trivial or petty detail caused by a strict interpretation of the law or rules. **3** the state of being technical.

technical knockout *n* a decision by a referee that a boxer has been defeated even though he or she has not been knocked out.

technician *n* **1** a person specialised or skilled in a practical art or science: *a dental technician*. **2** a person employed to do practical work in a laboratory. [Gr *techne*, art]

Technicolor® *n* a process of producing colour cine film by placing several copies of a scene, each one produced using different colour filters, on top of each other.

technique *n* **1** proficiency or skill in the practical or formal aspects of an art, esp. painting, music, sport, etc.: *a singer with a beautiful voice but poor technique*. **2** mechanical or practical skill or method: *study the techniques of film-making*. **3** a way of achieving one's purpose skilfully; a knack. [Fr, from Gr *technikos*, from *techne*, art]

technocracy *n* ***-ies*** the government of a country or management of an industry by technical experts. — *n* **technocrat**. — *adj* **technocratic**. [Gr *techne*, art + **-cracy**]

technology *n* ***-ies*** **1** (the study or use of) science which has a practical value, esp. in industry. **2** practical sciences as a group. **3** the technical skills and achievements of a particular time in history, civilisation or group of people. — *adj* **technological**. — *n* **technologist**. [Gr *technologia*, systematic treatment]

tectonics *n* (*sing*) **1** (*geol*) the study of structures which form the earth's crust and the forces which change it. ◇ See also **plate tectonics**. **2** the art or science of building and construction. [Gr *tekton*, builder]

Ted *n* (*Br coll*) a Teddy boy. [Abbrev.]

teddy[1] *n* **-*ies*** (also **teddy bear**) a child's stuffed toy bear. [*Teddy*, the pet-name of the American president Theodore Roosevelt (1858–1919), well known as a bear hunter]

teddy[2] *n* **-*ies*** a woman's one-piece undergarment consisting of a chemise and panties.

Teddy boy *n* (*Br coll*) an unruly or rowdy adolescent, esp. one in the 1950s who dressed in Edwardian-style clothes. [*Teddy*, a familiar form of *Edward*]

Te Deum *n* ***Deums*** (the music for) a Latin hymn of praise and thanksgiving. [From its first words *Te Deum laudamus*, You, God, we praise]

tedious *adj* boring because long-winded or dull; monotonous. — *adv* **tediously**. — *n* **tediousness**. [Lat *taedere*, to weary]

tedium *n* tediousness; boredom. [Lat *taedere*, to weary]

tee[1] *n* a phonetic spelling for the letter T. ◇ See also **T**[1].
tee shirt see **T-shirt** at **T**[1].

tee[2] *n* **1** a small peg with a concave top, or a small pile of sand, used to support a golf ball when the first shot is taken at the beginning of a hole. **2** the small area of level ground where the first shot is taken at the beginning of a hole. **3** a mark aimed at in quoits or curling. — *v* **tee off** (*intr*) to play one's first ball at the beginning of a golf hole. — *v* **tee up** (*tr & intr*) to place (a golf ball) on a tee.

teem[1] *v* (*intr*) **1** (**with**) to be full (of) or abound (with). **2** to be present in large numbers; to be plentiful. [OE *teman*, to give birth]

teem[2] *v* (*intr*; **down**) (of water, esp. rain) to pour in torrents. [Norse *toema*, to empty]

teen *n* **1** (in *pl*) the years of a person's life between the ages of thirteen and nineteen. **2** (in *pl*) the numbers from thirteen to nineteen. **3** (*coll*; usu. in *pl*) a teenager. [OE *tien*, ten]
teenage *adj* (also **teenaged**) **1** in one's teens. **2** of or suitable for people in their teens.
teenager *n* a person aged between thirteen and nineteen.
teenybopper *n* (*coll*) a young teenager, usu. a girl, who enthusiastically follows the latest trends in clothes and pop music.

teeny *adj* **-*ier***, **-*iest*** (*coll*; also **teensy -*ier***, **-*iest***) tiny. [**tiny** + **wee**]
teeny-weeny *adj* (*coll*; also **teensy-weensy**) very tiny.

teenybopper. See **teen**.

teepee. See **tepee**.

teeter *v* **-r-** (*intr*) **1** (**about**, **along**, etc.) to stand or move unsteadily; to wobble. **2** to hesitate or waver. [MidE *titeren*]

teeth. See **tooth**.

teethe *v* (*intr*) (of a baby) to grow one's first teeth. — *n* **teething**. [MidE *tethen*]
teething ring *n* a small hard ring for a baby to chew while teething.
teething troubles *n* (*pl*) problems or difficulties at the beginning of a project, or with a new piece of machinery, etc.

teetotal *adj* never taking alcoholic drink. — *n* **teetotaller**. [Presumably connected with '*total* abstinence (from alcohol)'; used by a campaigner for total abstinence in a speech in 1833]

TEFL *abbrev* teaching English as a foreign language.

tel. *abbrev* telephone.

tele- *comb fm* **1** at, over or to a distance: *telegram*. **2** television: *teletext*. **3** telephone: *telesales*. [Gr *tele*, far]

tele-ad *n* an advertisement placed in a newspaper by telephone.

telecast *v* **-*cast*** or **-*casted*** (*tr*) to broadcast by television. — *n* a television broadcast. — *n* **telecaster**. [**tele-** + **broadcast**]

telecommunication *n* communication of information or messages in written, verbal or pictorial form over a distance by telephone, television cable, etc. [**tele-** + **communication**]
telecommunications *n* (*sing*) the science or technology of such communication.

telegram *n* a message sent by telegraph and delivered in printed form, now used (in the UK) only for messages sent abroad and replaced by **Telemessage**® for inland messages. [**tele-** + **-gram**]

telegraph *n* a system of or instrument for sending messages or information to a distance, esp. by sending electrical impulses along a wire. — *v* **1** (*tr & intr*) to send (a message) to (someone) by telegraph. **2** (*tr*) to give a warning of (something which is to happen) without being aware of doing so. **3** (*intr*) to signal. — *n* **telegrapher** and **telegraphist**. [Fr *télégraphe*]
telegraphese *n* the jargon or abbreviated language used for telegrams.
telegraphic *adj* **1** of or by telegraph or telegram. **2** concisely worded. — *adv* **telegraphically**.
telegraphy *n* the science or practice of sending messages by telegraph.

telekinesis *n* the moving of objects at a distance without using physical force, e.g. by willpower. — *adj* **telekinetic**. [**tele** + Gr *kinesis*, movement]

Telemessage® *n* a message sent by telex or telephone and delivered in printed form, replacing the **telegram** within the UK.

telemeter *n* an apparatus which measures temperature, an electrical quantity, or other such information and transmits the measurement to a distant point. — *adj* **telemetric**. — *n* **telemetry**. [**tele-** + **-meter**]

teleology *n* the doctrine that the universe, all phenomena and natural processes are directed towards a goal or are designed according to some purpose. — *adj* **teleological**. — *n* **teleologist**. [Gr *telos*, end + **-logy**]

telepathy *n* the communication of thoughts directly from one person's mind to another's without using any of the five known senses. — *adj* **telepathic**. — *adv* **telepathically**. [**tele-** + Gr *pathos*, feeling]

telepathist *n* a person who studies or practises telepathy.

telephone *n* **1** an instrument, usu. consisting of a microphone and receiver mounted in a handset, which allows a person to speak to someone at a distance by transmitting sound in the form of electrical signals. **2** the system of communication which uses these instruments. — *v* **1** (*tr*) to (try to) contact and speak to (someone) by telephone. **2** (*tr*) to send (a message, etc.) by telephone. **3** (*intr*) to make a telephone call. — *adj* **telephonic**. — **on the telephone 1** connected to the telephone system. **2** talking to someone by means of the telephone. [**tele-** + **-phone** (sense **1**)]

telephone box or **booth** or **kiosk** *n* a small enclosed or partly-enclosed compartment containing a telephone for public use.

telephone directory or **book** *n* a book containing a list of the names, addresses and telephone numbers of all or most of the telephone-owners in a particular area.

telephone exchange see **exchange**.

telephonist *n* a telephone switchboard operator.

telephony *n* the use or system of communication by means of the telephone.

telephoto *adj* of telephotography. [Abbrev.]

telephoto lens *n* a camera lens which produces large images of distant or small objects.

telephotography *n* the photographing of distant objects with lenses which produce large images. — *adj* **telephotographic**.

teleprinter *n* an apparatus with a keyboard which types messages as they are received by telegraph and transmits them as they are typed.

Teleprompter® *n* a device next to a camera and out of sight of the audience which allows a television speaker to read the text as he or she is filmed.

telesales *n* (*pl*) (also **teleselling**) the selling of goods or services by telephone.

telescope *n* **1** an optical instrument usu. in the form of a tube with a combination of lenses and mirrors inside, which makes distant objects seem closer and larger. **2** a radio telescope. — *v* **1** (*intr*) to be in the form of several cylinders which slide into each other for opening and closing, like the sections of a folding telescope. **2** (*tr*) to slide or push one part (of something) into another. **3** (*tr* & *intr*) to crush or compress, or become crushed or compressed, under impact. [**tele-** + Gr *skopeein*, to see]

telescopic *adj* **1** of, like or performed with a telescope. **2** able to be seen only through a telescope. **3** (of a lens) able to discern and magnify distant objects. **4** made in sections which slide into each other. — *adv* **telescopically**.

telescopic sight *n* a small telescope used as a sight on a rifle.

teleselling. See **telesales**.

teletext *n* a news and information service which is produced and regularly updated by a television company and is transmitted to and viewable on televisions fitted with the necessary receiver and decoder. [**tele-** + **text**]

telethon *n* a usu. day-long television programme broadcast to raise money for charity. [**television** + **marathon**]

Teletype® *n* a type of teleprinter.

televangelist *n* (esp. *US*) an evangelical preacher who preaches and conducts religious services regularly on television. [**television** + **evangelist**]

televise *v* (*tr*) to broadcast by television. [**television**]

television *n* **1** the sending of images, usu. accompanied by sound, in the form of radio waves from a distance to be reproduced on a screen in a person's home, etc. **2** (also **television set**) an apparatus with a screen and speakers which is able to receive and decode radio waves and reproduce them in the form of images and sounds. **3** television broadcasting in general. [**tele-** + **vision**]

televisual *adj* of or suitable for being broadcast by television. — *adv* **televisually**. [**tele-** + **visual**]

telex (also *cap*) *n* **1** an international service whereby customers hire teleprinters which allow them to send messages to other customers. **2** a teleprinter which is used in this service. **3** a message received or sent by this service. — *v* (*tr* & *intr*) to send (a message) to (someone) in this way. [**teleprinter** + **exchange**]

tell *v* ***told*** **1** (*tr*; **about**, **to**) to inform or give information to (someone) in speech or writing. **2** (*tr* & *intr*; **of**) to relate or give an account of. **3** (*tr*) to order, command or instruct. **4** (*tr*) to express in words: *tell lies*. **5** (*tr*; **by**, **from**) to discover or distinguish: *tell Brie from Camembert*. **6** (*intr*; **on**) to give away secrets (about someone). **7** (*tr*) to make known or give away. **8** (*intr*; **on**) to have a noticeable effect (on). **9** (*intr* & *tr*) to know (something) definitely: *can never tell when he's lying*. **10** (*tr*) to assure. **11** (*intr*; **against**) to be evidence: *behaviour which will tell against him*. **12** (*tr*) to count: *an audience of nine all told*. — **take a telling** to do as one is told without having to be asked again. — *v* **tell apart** (*tr*) to distinguish between. — *v* **tell off** (*tr*) **1** to scold or reprimand (*n* **telling-off**). **2** to count off and detach on some special duty. — **you're telling me!** (*coll*) I know that only too well. [OE *tellan*]

teller *n* **1** a person who tells esp. stories. **2** a bank employee who receives money from and pays it out to members of the public. **3** a person who counts votes.

telling *adj* having a great or marked effect. — *adv* **tellingly**.

telltale *n* **1** a person who spreads gossip and rumours, esp. about another person's private affairs or misdeeds. **2** any of various devices for recording or monitoring a process, machine, etc. — *adj* revealing or indicating something secret or hidden.

tellurian *adj* of or living on the earth. — *n* (esp. in science fiction) an inhabitant of the earth. [Lat *tellus*, earth]

tellurium *n* (*chem*) a rare, silvery, non-metallic element (symbol **Te**), used for semiconductors and alloys. [Lat *tellus*, earth]

telly *n* **-ies** (*coll*) (a) television. [Abbrev.]

temerity *n* rashness or boldness; an unreasonable lack of fear. [Lat *temeritas*]

temp *n* an employee, esp. a secretary, typist or other office worker, employed on a temporary basis. — *v* (*intr*) to work as a temp. [Abbrev.]

temp. *abbrev* **1** temperature. **2** temporary.

temper *n* **1** a characteristic state of mind; mood or humour: *have an even temper*. **2** a state of calm; composure; self-control: *lose one's temper*. **3** a state of uncontrolled anger: *in a temper*. **4** a tendency to have fits of uncontrolled anger. **5** the degree of hardness and elasticity of metal and glass. — *v* **-r-** (*tr*) **1** (**with**) to soften or make less severe. **2** to harden (metal or glass) by heating and quenching it. **3** to bring (clay) to the proper consistency by adding water and kneading. **4** to tune (the notes on a keyboard instrument) so that the intervals between them are correct. — **out of temper** irritable; peevish; fractious. [Lat *temperare*, to mix in due proportion]

tempera *n* **1** a method of painting in which powdered pigment is mixed with an emulsion made usu. of egg yolks and water. **2** an emulsion, esp. one made with egg yolks and water, into which powdered pigments are mixed to produce paint. **3** a painting produced using tempera. [Ital *temperare*, to mix in due proportion]

temperament *n* **1** a person's natural character or disposition which governs the way he or she behaves and thinks. **2** a sensitive, creative and excitable or emotional personality. **3** an adjustment made to the intervals between notes on an instrument's keyboard to allow the instrument to play in any key. [Lat *temperamentum*, a mixing in due proportion, in this case of the four humours believed in the Middle Ages to govern one's physical and mental characteristics]

temperamental *adj* **1** given to extreme changes of mood; quick to show emotion, anger, irritability, etc. **2** (of a machine, etc.) not working reliably or consistently. **3** of or caused by temperament. — *adv* **temperamentally**.

temperance *n* **1** moderation, self-restraint, esp. in controlling one's appetite or desires. **2** moderation or complete abstinence from alcoholic drink. [Lat *temperantia*, moderation, sobriety]

temperate *adj* **1** moderate and self-restrained, esp. in appetite, consumption of alcoholic drink and behaviour. **2** not excessive; moderate. **3** (of a climate or region) having temperatures which are mild, and neither tropical nor polar. — *adv* **temperately**. — *n* **temperateness**. [Lat *temperatus*]

temperate zones *n* (*pl*) those parts of the earth having moderate temperatures, lying between the tropic of Cancer and the Arctic Circle, and the tropic of Capricorn and the Antarctic Circle.

temperature *n* **1** the degree of hotness, e.g. of air, water, etc., as measured e.g. by a thermometer. **2** one's level of body heat: *take his temperature*. **3** a level of body heat which is higher than normal: *have a temperature*. [Lat *temperatura*, proportion]

tempest *n* **1** a violent storm with very strong winds. **2** a violent uproar. [Lat *tempestas*, season, storm]

tempestuous *adj* **1** of or like a tempest; very stormy. **2** (of a person, behaviour, etc.) violently emotional; passionate. — *adv* **tempestuously**. — *n* **tempestuousness**.

tempi. See **tempo**.

template *n* (also **templet**) **1** a piece of metal, plastic or wood cut in a particular shape used as a pattern when cutting out material, drawing, etc. **2** a small wooden beam or block placed in a wall to help spread and support the weight or load. **3** the coded instructions carried by a molecule for the formation of a new molecule of the same type. [Lat *templum*, small piece of timber]

temple[1] *n* **1** a building in which people worship, esp. in ancient and non-Christian religions, and in particular Christian sects such as the Mormons. **2** (*hist*) either of the two successive religious buildings built by the Jews in Jerusalem, one before and one after their exile in Babylon. **3** a place devoted to a particular purpose: *a temple to literature*. **4** (with *cap*) either of the two inns of court in London on a site once occupied by the Knights Templars and their church. **5** (*US*) a synagogue, esp. in Reform or Conservative Judaism. [Lat *templum*]

temple[2] *n* either of the flat parts of the head at the side of the forehead in front of the ear. [Lat *tempus*]

temple[3] *n* a device in a loom which keeps the cloth stretched. [Lat *templum*, small piece of timber]

templet. See **template**.

tempo *n* ***-pos*** or ***-pi*** **1** the speed at which a piece of music should be or is played. **2** rate or speed. [Ital]

temporal[1] *adj* **1** of or relating to time, often in being relatively short. **2** of worldly or secular life as opposed to religious or spiritual life. **3** (*gram*) relating to tense or the expression of time. — *adv* **temporally**. [Lat *temporalis*, from *tempus*, time]

temporal[2] *adj* of or close to the temples on either side of the head. [Lat *tempus*, temple]

temporary *adj* lasting, acting, used, etc. for a limited period of time only. — *n* ***-ies*** a worker employed temporarily; a temp. — *adv* **temporarily**. — *n* **temporariness**. [Lat *temporarius*, from *tempus*, time]

temporise or **-ize** *v* (*intr*) **1** to avoid taking a decision or committing oneself to some course of action, to gain time and perhaps win a compromise. **2** to adapt oneself to circumstances or what the occasion requires. — *n* **temporisation** or **-z-**. — *n* **temporiser** or **-z-**. [Lat *tempus*, time]

tempt *v* (*tr*) **1** to (try to) attract and persuade (someone) to do something, esp. something wrong, evil or foolish. **2** to attract or allure. **3** to be strongly inclined (to do something). **4** to risk provoking, esp. by doing something foolhardy: *tempt fate*. [Lat *temptare*, to probe, test]

temptation *n* **1** an act of tempting or the state of being tempted. **2** something that tempts.

tempter *n* **1** (also **temptress**) *n* a man (or woman) who tempts. **2** (*cap*) the Devil.

tempting *adj* attractive; inviting; enticing. — *adv* **temptingly**.

Ten. *abbrev* Tennessee.

ten *n* **1** the number or figure 10; any symbol for this number. **2** the age of 10. **3** something, esp. a garment or a person, whose size is denoted by 10. **4** a playing-card with 10 pips. **5** a set of 10 things, people, etc. **6** 10 o'clock. **7** a score of 10 points. — *adj* **1** 10 in number. **2** aged 10. — *pron* 10 things or people. [OE]

the Ten Commandments *n* (*pl*) the commandments given by God to Moses which instruct people how to behave towards God and each other.

tenfold *adj* **1** ten times as much or as many. **2** divided into, or consisting of, ten parts. — *adv* by ten times as much.

ten-gallon hat *n* (*US*) a hat worn by cowboys, with a broad brim and high crown.

tenner *n* (*coll*) a ten-pound or ten-dollar note.

tenpin bowling *n* a game in which ten skittles are set up at the end of an alley and a ball is rolled at them with the aim of knocking as many down as possible.

tenth *n* **1** one of ten equal parts. **2** the last of ten; the next after the ninth. **3** (*mus*) an interval of an octave plus a third. **4** (*mus*) a note which is an octave plus a third above or below another. — *adj* being the last of ten or in an equivalent position. — *adv* **1** in tenth position. **2** (also **tenthly**) as the tenth point, etc.

tenable *adj* **1** able to be believed, upheld or maintained. **2** (**by**, **for**) (of a job) able to be held or occupied (e.g. for a specified period of time only or by a specified person). — *n* **tenability** or **tenableness**. [Lat *tenere*, to hold]

tenacious *adj* **1** holding or sticking firmly. **2** determined; persistent; obstinate. **3** (of memory) retaining information extremely well; retentive. — *adv* **tenaciously**. — *n* **tenaciousness** or **tenacity**. [Lat *tenere*, to hold]

tenant *n* **1** a person who pays rent to another for the use of property or land. **2** an occupant. — *v* (*tr*) to occupy as a tenant. — *adj* **tenanted**. [Lat *tenere*, to hold]

tenancy *n* ***-ies*** **1** the temporary renting of property or land by a tenant. **2** the period during which property or land is so rented.

tenant farmer *n* a farmer who farms land rented from another person, esp. on an estate.

tenantry *n* all of the tenants, usu. of an estate or a landlord.

tench *n* ***tench*** a European freshwater fish with a dark green or brownish body, related to the carp. [OFr *tenche*]

tend[1] *v* **1** (*tr*) to take care of; to look after; to wait on. **2** (*intr*; **to**) to attend to: *tend to his needs*. **[attend]**

tender *n* **1** (also *in cmpds*) a person who looks after something or someone: *bartender*. **2** a small boat which carries stores or passengers to and from a larger boat. **3** a railway wagon attached to a steam-engine to carry fuel and water.

tend[2] *v* (*intr*) **1** (**to, towards**) to be likely or inclined to. **2** to move slightly, lean or slope in a specified direction. [Lat *tendere*, to stretch]

tendency *n* ***-ies*** **1** a likelihood of acting or thinking, or an inclination to act or think, in a particular way. **2** a general course, trend or drift. **3** a faction or group within a political party or movement.

tendentious *adj* having a particular bias, tendency or underlying purpose. — *adv* **tendentiously**. — *n* **tendentiousness**.

tender[1] *adj* **1** soft and delicate; fragile. **2** (of meat) easily chewed or cut. **3** easily damaged or grieved; sensitive: *a tender heart*. **4** easily hurt when touched, esp. because of having been hurt before: *Her arm is still bruised and tender*. **5** loving and gentle: *tender words*. **6** easily moved to love, pity, guilt, etc.: *a tender conscience*. **7** youthful and vulnerable: *of tender years*. **8** requiring gentle, sensitive or careful handling. — *adv* **tenderly**. — *n* **tenderness**. [OFr *tendre*, from Lat *tener*]

tenderfoot *n* ***-feet*** or ***-foots*** an inexperienced newcomer or beginner.

tender-hearted *adj* kind and sympathetic; easily made to feel love or pity. —

adv **tender-heartedly**. — *n* **tender-heartedness**.

tenderise or **-ize** *v* (*tr*) to make (meat) tender by pounding it or by adding an acidic substance. — *n* **tenderiser** or **-z-**.

tenderloin *n* a cut from the tenderest part of the loin of pork, beef, etc.

tender[2] *v* **-r-** **1** (*tr*) to offer or present (an apology, resignation, etc.). **2** (*intr*; **for**) to make a formal offer to do (work) or supply (goods) for a stated amount of money and within a stated period of time. — *n* a formal offer, usu. in writing, to do work or supply goods for a stated amount of money and within a stated period of time. — **put out to tender** to invite tenders for a particular job. [Lat *tendere*, to stretch]

tender[3]. See **tend**[1].

tendon *n* a cord of strong, fibrous tissue that joins a muscle to a bone or some other structure. [Lat *tendo*]

tendinitis or **tendonitis** *n* inflammation of a tendon.

tendril *n* a thin, curling shoot by which some climbing plants attach themselves to supports. — *adj* **tendrilled**. [OFr *tendron*, shoot]

tenement *n* (esp. in Scotland) **1** a large building divided into several individual, self-contained flats or apartments. **2** a self-contained flat or room within such a building. [Lat *tenementum*, from *tenere*, to hold]

tenet *n* a belief, opinion, or doctrine. [Lat, he, she or it holds]

Tenn. *abbrev* Tennessee.

tenner. See **ten**.

tennis *n* **1** (also **lawn tennis**) a game in which two players or two pairs of players use rackets to hit a light ball across a net on a grass-covered or hard rectangular court. **2** real tennis. [OFr *tenetz*, hold!, take!]

tennis elbow *n* painful inflammation of the elbow caused by over-exercise (typically by playing tennis) or over-work.

tenon *n* a projection at the end of a piece of wood, etc., formed to fit into a socket or mortise in another piece. — *v* **-n-** (*tr*) **1** to fix with a tenon. **2** to cut a tenon in. [Lat *tenere*, to hold]

tenor *n* **1** (a singer with) a singing voice of the highest normal range for an adult man. **2** an instrument, e.g. a viola, recorder or saxophone, with a similar range. **3** music written for a voice or instrument with such a range. **4** the general course or meaning of something written or spoken. **5** a settled or general course or direction, e.g. of a person's life. — *adj* (of a singing voice or musical instrument) with this range. — *adv* with a tenor voice: *sing tenor*. [Lat, from *tenere*, to hold]

tense[1] *n* (*gram*) a form of verb that shows the time of its action in relation to the time of speaking and whether that action is completed or not. [Lat *tempus*, time]

tense[2] *adj* **1** feeling, showing or marked by emotional, nervous or mental strain. **2** tightly stretched; taut. — *v* (*tr* & *intr*; **up**) to make or become tense. — *adv* **tensely**. — *n* **tenseness**. [Lat *tendere*, to stretch]

tensile *adj* **1** able to be stretched. **2** of or relating to stretching or tension. — *n* **tensility**. [Lat *tensilis*, from *tendere*, to stretch]

tensile strength *n* a measure of the amount of stretching a material can bear, expressed as the greatest stress it can resist before breaking.

tension *n* **1** an act of stretching, the state of being stretched or the degree to which something is stretched. **2** mental or emotional strain, excitement or anxiety, usu. accompanied by physical symptoms. **3** strained relations or underlying hostility between people, countries, etc. **4** (*physics*) a force which causes a body to be stretched or elongated. **5** electromotive force. **6** (*knitting*) the tightness or looseness of wool as one knits, measured as the number of stitches to the inch. — *v* **-n-** (*tr*) to give the required tightness or tension to. [Lat *tensio*, from *tendere*, to stretch]

tent *n* **1** a shelter made of canvas or other material supported by poles or a frame and fastened to the ground with ropes and pegs, that can be taken down and carried from place to place. **2** anything like a tent in form or function, esp. a clear plastic device placed over the head and shoulders to control the oxygen supply to a sick person. — *v* **1** (*intr*) to camp in a tent. **2** (*tr*) to cover or shelter with a tent. [OFr *tente*, from Lat *tendere*, to stretch]

tentacle *n* **1** a long, thin, flexible organ growing on an animal's head or near its mouth, used to feel, grasp and feed. **2** a sensitive hair for catching insects on some insect-eating plants. — *adj* **tentacled**. — *adj* **tentacular**. [Lat *tentare*, to feel]

tentative *adj* **1** not finalised or completed; provisional. **2** uncertain; hesitant; cautious. — *adv* **tentatively**. — *n* **tentativeness**. [Lat *tentare*, to try]

tenter *n* a frame on which cloth is stretched, esp. so that it dries without losing its shape.

tenterhook *n* a sharp hooked nail used for fastening cloth to a tenter. — **on tenterhooks** in a state of impatient suspense or anxiety.

tenuous *adj* **1** slight; with little strength or substance. **2** thin; slim. — *adv* **tenuously**. — *n* **tenuousness**. [Lat *tenuis*, thin]

tenure *n* **1** the holding of an office, position or property. **2** the length of time an office, position or property is held. **3** the holding of a position, esp. a university teaching job, for a guaranteed length of time or permanently. **4** the conditions by which an office, position or property is held. — *adj* **tenured**. [Lat *tenere*, to hold]

tepee or **teepee** *n* an American Indian tent formed of skins stretched over a conical frame of poles. [Dakota (American Indian language) *tipi*]

tepid *adj* **1** slightly or only just warm; lukewarm. **2** not enthusiastic. — *n* **tepidity** or **tepidness**. — *adv* **tepidly**. [Lat *tepidus*]

tequila *n* a Mexican spirit used as the basis for many alcoholic drinks. [*Tequila*, a district in Mexico]

ter- *pfx* three; threefold; thrice. [Lat *ter*, thrice]

terbium *n* (*chem*) a soft silvery metallic element (symbol **Tb**), of the rare earth series, used in lasers. [From *Ytterby* in Sweden, where it was discovered]

terce *n* the third of the canonical hours. ◇ See also **compline, lauds, matins, none**[2], **sext, vespers**.

tercel or **tiercel** *n* a male hawk. [OFr *tercel*]

tercentenary *n* **-ies** (also **tercentennial**) a three-hundredth anniversary. — *adj* (also **tercentennial**) of three hundred years. [Lat *ter*, thrice + **centenary**]

tercet *n* a set of three lines in a poem which rhyme or which are connected by rhyme to a preceding or following group of three lines. [Ital *terzetto*, from *terzo*, third]

teredo *n* **-os** any of several molluscs which bore into wooden ships. [Gr *teredon*, boring worm]

tergiversate *v* (*intr*) **1** to turn one's back. **2** to change sides. **3** to speak or act evasively. — *n* **tergiversation**. — *n* **tergiversator**. [Lat *tergum*, back + *versare*, to turn]

term *n* **1** a word or expression, esp. one used with a precise meaning in a specialised field: *a scientific term*. **2** (in *pl*) language used; a particular way of speaking: *criticise him in no uncertain terms*. **3** a limited or clearly defined period of time. **4** the end of a particular time, esp. the end of pregnancy when the baby is about to be born. **5** (in *pl*) a relationship between people or countries: *be on good terms*. **6** (in *pl*) the rules or conditions of an agreement: *terms of sale*. **7** (in *pl*) fixed charges for work or a service. **8** one of the usu. three divisions into which the academic and school year is divided. **9** the time during which a court is in session. **10** (*math*) a quantity which is joined to another by either addition or subtraction. **11** (*math*) one quantity in a series or sequence. **12** (*logic*) a word or expression which may be a subject or a predicate of a proposition. — *v* (*tr*) to name or call. — **come to terms 1** to give way or submit; to yield. **2** (**with**) to come to an agreement or understanding (with). **3** (**with**) to find a way of living with or tolerating (some personal trouble or difficulty). — **in terms of** in relation to; using the language and value of as a basis. [Lat *terminus*, boundary]

termagant *n* a scolding, brawling and overbearing woman. [OFr *Tervagan*, a mythical deity believed in the Middle Ages to be worshipped by Muslims and introduced into morality plays as a scolding, overbearing character]

terminable *adj* able to come or be brought to an end. — *n* **terminability** or **terminableness**. [Lat *terminus*, boundary]

terminal *adj* **1** (of an illness) causing death; fatal. **2** (of a patient) having an illness which will cause death. **3** (*coll*) extreme; acute: *terminal sulking*. **4** forming or occurring at an end, boundary or terminus. **5** of a term or occurring every term. — *n* **1** an arrival and departure building at an airport. **2** a large station at the end of a railway line or for long-distance buses and coaches. **3** a point in an electric circuit or electrical device at which the current leaves or enters it, or by which it may be connected to another device. **4** a device consisting usu. of a keyboard and visual display unit, which allows a user to communicate with and use a distant computer. **5** an installation at the end of a pipeline or at a port where oil is stored and from where it is distributed. — *adv* **terminally**. [Lat *terminalis*, from *terminus*, boundary]

terminal velocity *n* the maximum speed reached by an object falling or fired through a fluid or gas, e.g. the atmosphere.

terminate *v* **1** (*tr* & *intr*) to bring or come to an end. **2** (*intr*; **in, with, at**; *formal*) to end or conclude (in a specified way or at a specified time): *The match terminated in a draw*. **3** (*tr*) to end (a pregnancy) artificially before its term. **4** (*tr*) to form a boundary or limit (of). **5** (*intr*; *formal*) to stop; to go no further: *The train terminates at Dundee*. [Lat *terminare*, to set a limit to]

termination *n* **1** an act of ending or the state of being brought to an end. **2** an artificially induced miscarriage or abortion. **3** a final result.

terminology *n* **-ies** the words and phrases used in a particular subject or field. — *adj* **terminological**. — *adv* **terminologically**. — *n* **terminologist**. [Lat *terminus*, term]

terminus *n* **-ni** or **-nuses 1** the end of a railway line or bus route, usu. with a station. **2** an extreme or final point. **3** a stone marking a boundary. [Lat, boundary, limit]

termite *n* a pale-coloured ant-like insect which feeds on wood, found mainly in the tropics. [Lat *termes*, white ant]

tern *n* any of several sea-birds which are smaller than gulls and have long wings and a long forked tail. [Scandinavian]

ternary *adj* **1** having three parts. **2** (*math*) using three as a base. [Lat *ternarius*]

terpsichorean *adj* of or relating to dancing. [Gr *Terpsichore*, the muse of dancing and choral singing]

terrace *n* **1** each one of a series of raised level banks of earth, like large steps on the side of a hill, used for cultivation. **2** a row of identical and connected houses, properly one overlooking a slope, or the street on to which they face. **3** a raised, level, paved area by the side of a house. **4** (usu. in *pl*) the open areas rising in tiers round a sports ground, where spectators stand. — *v* (*tr*) to form into a terrace or terraces. [Lat *terracea*]

terrace or **terraced house** *n* (*Br*) a house which is part of a terrace.

terracotta *n* **1** an unglazed brownish-orange earthenware made from a mixture of sand and clay and used for pottery, statuettes and building. **2** its brownish-orange colour. — *adj* made of, or the colour of, terracotta. [Ital, baked earth]

terra firma *n* dry land as opposed to water or air; solid ground. [Lat, firm land]

terrain *n* a stretch of land, esp. with regard to its physical features or as a battle area. [Lat *terrenus*, from *terra*, earth]

terrapin *n* any of several N American freshwater turtles. [From an American Indian language]

terrarium *n* **-ia** or **-iums** **1** an enclosed area or container in which small land animals are kept. **2** a large globe-shaped sealed glass jar in which plants are grown. [Lat *terra*, earth]

terrestrial *adj* **1** of the planet earth. **2** (of animals and plants) living or growing on dry land as opposed to in the water, in the air, in trees, etc. **3** of this world; worldly; mundane. **4** (of television signals) sent by a land transmitter and not by satellite. — *n* an inhabitant of the earth. [Lat *terrestris*, from *terra*, earth]

terrible *adj* **1** (*coll*) very bad: *a terrible singer*. **2** (*coll*) very great; extreme: *a terrible gossip*. **3** causing great fear or terror. **4** causing suffering or hardship and requiring great strength or fortitude. [Lat *terribilis*, from *terrere*, to frighten]

terribly *adv* **1** (*coll*) very: *terribly happy*. **2** in a terrible way; to a great degree: *hurts terribly*.

terrier *n* any of several breeds of small dog bred orig. to hunt animals in burrows. [OFr (*chien*) *terrier*, (dog) of the earth]

terrific *adj* **1** (*coll*) marvellous; excellent. **2** (*coll*) very great or powerful: *a terrific storm*. **3** very frightening; terrifying. — *adv* **terrifically**. [Lat *terrificus*, frightful]

terrify *v* **-ies**, **-ied** (*tr*) to make very frightened; to fill with terror. — *adj* **terrified**. — *adj* **terrifying**. [Lat *terrificare*]

terrine *n* **1** an oval or round earthenware dish in which food may be cooked and served. **2** food cooked or served in such a dish, esp. pâté. [OFr *terrin*, earthen]

territory *n* **-ies** **1** a stretch of land; a region. **2** the land under the control of a ruler, government or state. **3** an area of knowledge, interest or activity. **4** an area or district for which a travelling salesman or distributor is responsible. **5** an area which a bird or animal treats as its own and defends against others of the same species. **6** (often *cap*) part of a country (usu. a federal state such as the US) with an organised government but without the full rights of a state. [Lat *territorium*, the land round a town]

territorial *adj* **1** of or relating to a territory. **2** limited or restricted to a particular area or district. **3** (esp. of birds and animals) likely to establish its own territory and defend it from others of the same species. — *n* (*cap*; *Br*) a member of the Territorial Army.

Territorial Army *n* (*Br*) a reserve army of volunteers organised on a regional basis.

territorial waters *n* (*pl*) the sea surrounding a state, considered to belong to it.

terror *n* **1** very great fear or dread. **2** something or someone which causes such fear. **3** (*coll*) a troublesome or mischievous person, esp. a child. **4** a time of, or government by, terror. [Lat]

terrorise or **-ize** *v* (*tr*) **1** to frighten greatly. **2** to control or coerce (someone) by threatening violence. — *n* **terrorisation** or **-z-**.

terrorism *n* the systematic and organised use of violence and intimidation to force a government, community, etc. to act in a certain way or accept certain demands. — *n* & *adj* **terrorist**.

terror-stricken *adj* feeling very great uncontrollable fear.

terry *n* **-ies** an absorbent fabric with uncut loops on one side used esp. for towels. — *adj* made of this fabric.

terse *adj* **1** (of language) brief and concise; succinct. **2** abrupt and rude; curt. — *adv* **tersely**. — *n* **terseness**. [Lat *tersus*, rubbed clean]

tertiary *adj* **1** third in order, degree, importance, etc. **2** (of education) coming after secondary, e.g. university or college. ◇ See also **primary** and **secondary**. **3** (*cap*) of the Tertiary. — *n* **-ies** **1** (*cap*) the geological period that extends from 65 million to 2 million years ago, when mammals developed, flowering plants became widespread and the seas receded. **2** a lay person who is affiliated to a monastic order and who follows a slightly modified form of that order's rule. [Lat *tertius*, third]

Terylene® *n* a synthetic fabric of polyester fibres which is light, strong and crease-resistant.

TESSA *abbrev* Tax Exempt Special Savings Account.

tessellate *v* (*tr*) to form into or mark like a mosaic, esp. with tesserae or checks. [Lat *tessella*, small square piece of stone]

tessellated *adj* chequered.

tessera *n* **-rae** a square piece of stone, glass, etc. used in mosaics. [Lat]

test[1] *n* **1** a critical examination or trial of a person's or thing's qualities, abilities, etc. **2** anything used as the basis of such an examination or trial, e.g. a set of questions or exercises: *Marathon-running is a test of endurance*. **3** a short, minor, usu. written examination: *a spelling test*. **4** a test match. **5** (*chem*) anything used to distinguish, detect or identify a substance; a reagent. — *v* **1** (*tr*) to examine (someone or something, abilities, qualities, etc.), esp. by trial. **2** (*tr* & *intr*; **for**) to examine (a substance) to discover whether another substance is present or not: *test the water for microbes*. **3** (*intr*) to achieve a stated result in a test: *test positive for the virus*. — *adj* **testable**. — *n* **tester**. [OFr, from Lat *testa* or *testum*, earthenware pot]

test case *n* (*law*) a case whose outcome will serve as a precedent for all similar cases in the future.

test drive *n* a trial drive in a car to test its performance by a prospective owner.

test-drive *v* (*tr*) to test (a car) by taking a trial drive.

test match *n* (in various sports, esp. cricket) a match forming one of a series played by the same two international teams.

test paper *n* **1** a list of questions forming a short, minor examination. **2** paper which has been soaked in some substance so that it changes colour when it comes into contact with certain chemicals.

test pilot *n* a pilot who tests new aircraft by flying them.

test tube *n* a thin glass tube closed at one end, used in chemical tests or experiments.

test-tube baby *n* a baby conceived outside the mother's womb in a laboratory and replanted in the mother's womb to grow.

test[2] *n* (*biol*) a hard outer covering or shell of certain invertebrates. [Lat *testa*, tile]

testa *n* **-*tae*** (*biol*) the hard outer covering of a seed.

testaceous *adj* (*biol*) having a hard outer shell.

testament *n* **1** a written statement of one's wishes, esp. of what one wants to be done with one's property after death; a will: *last will and testament*. **2** proof, evidence or tribute. **3** a covenant between God and Man. **4** (*cap*) either of the two main divisions of the Bible, the **Old Testament** or the **New Testament**. **5** (*cap*) a copy of the New Testament. — *adj* **testamentary**. [Lat *testamentum*, from *testis*, witness]

testate *adj* (*legal*) having made and left a valid will. [Lat *testari*, to make a will]

testator or **testatrix** *n* (*legal*) a man, or woman, who leaves a will at death.

testes. See **testis**.

testicle *n* either of the two glands in the male body which produce sperm, in mammals usu. enclosed in the scrotum below the penis. — *adj* **testicular**. [Lat *testis*, witness (of male virility)]

testify *v* **-*ies***, **-*ied*** **1** (*intr*; **against**, **on behalf of**) to give evidence in court. **2** (*tr* & *intr*; **to**) to serve as evidence or proof (of). **3** (*intr*) to make a solemn declaration (e.g. of one's faith). **4** (*tr*) to declare solemnly: *testify one's sorrow*. [Lat *testificari*, from *testis*, witness]

testimony *n* **-*ies*** **1** a statement made under oath, esp. in a law court. **2** evidence: *a testimony to her intelligence*. **3** a declaration of truth or fact. [Lat *testimonium*, from *testis*, witness]

testimonial *n* **1** a letter or certificate giving details of one's character, conduct and qualifications. **2** a gift presented (often in public) as a sign of respect or as a tribute to personal qualities or services.

testis *n* **-*tes*** a testicle. [Lat]

testosterone *n* the main male sex hormone, a steroid secreted by the testes. [Lat *testis*, testicle]

testy *adj* **-*ier***, **-*iest*** irritable; bad-tempered; touchy. — *adv* **testily**. — *n* **testiness**. [OFr *testif*, headstrong]

tetanus *n* **1** an infectious disease usu. caused by a bacterium introduced into the body through a wound, which causes a painful stiffening or spasm of some muscles, esp. those of the jaw. **2** the state of prolonged contraction of a muscle caused by quickly repeated stimuli. [Gr *tetanos*, from *teinein*, to stretch]

tetchy *adj* **-*ier***, **-*iest*** irritable; peevish. — *adv* **tetchily**. — *n* **tetchiness**.

tête-à-tête *n* **-*têtes*** a private conversation or meeting between two people. — *adj* & *adv* (in) private; intimate(ly). [Fr, head to head]

tether *n* a rope or chain for tying an animal to a post or confining it to a particular spot. — *v* **-*r-*** (*tr*) to tie or restrain with a tether. — **at the end of one's tether** having reached the limit of one's patience, strength, resources, etc. [Norse *tjothr*]

tetra- *comb fm* four. [Gr]

tetrad *n* a group of four. [Gr *tetras*]

tetragon *n* a plane figure with four angles and four sides. [Gr *tetragonon*]

Tetragrammaton *n* the Hebrew name of God written using four letters, in the English alphabet given as either YHWH (Yahweh) or JHVH (Jehovah). [Gr, from *tetra-*, four + *gramma*, letter]

tetrahedron *n* **-*drons*** or **-*dra*** a solid figure having four plane faces with three angles each; a three-sided pyramid. [Gr *tetraedron*]

tetrameter *n* a line of verse with four measures. [Gr *tetrametros*, from *tetra-*, four + *metron*, measure]

Teuton *n* **1** any speaker of a Germanic language. **2** (*hist*) a member of an ancient Germanic tribe from N Europe. [Lat *Teutoni* or *Teutones*, the Teutons]

Teutonic *adj* **1** of the Germanic languages or peoples speaking these languages. **2** German. — *n* Germanic.

Tex. *abbrev* Texas.

Tex-Mex *adj* (of food, music, etc.) typically Mexican but with elements either taken from, or adapted through contact with, American culture. [**Texan** + **Mexican**]

text *n* **1** the main body of printed words in a book as opposed to the notes, illustrations, etc. **2** the actual words of an author or piece of written work as opposed to commentary on them. **3** a short passage from the Bible taken as the starting-point for a sermon or quoted in authority. **4** a theme or subject. **5** (often in *pl*) a book, novel, play, etc. forming part of a course of study. **6** the words written or displayed on a visual display unit. [Lat *texere*, to weave]

textbook *n* a book containing the standard principles and information of a subject. — *adj* (of an example, operation, etc.) exactly as it should be, esp. in being perfect or typical.

textile *n* **1** any cloth or fabric made by weaving or knitting. **2** fibre, yarn, etc. suitable for weaving into cloth. — *adj* of, relating to, manufacturing, or suitable for being woven into, such cloth. [Lat *textilis*, from *texere*, to weave]

textual *adj* of, relating to, found in or based on a text or texts. — *adv* **textually**. **[text]**

texture *n* **1** the way the surface of a material or substance feels when touched. **2** the way that a piece of cloth looks or feels, caused by the way in which it is woven. **3** the structure of a substance as formed by the size and arrangement of the smaller particles which form it, esp. as seen, touched or tasted: *cheese with a crumbly texture*. **4** the structure of a piece of music, writing, work of art, etc. as formed by the individual parts which form it. — *v* (*tr*; also **texturise** or **-ize**) to give a particular texture to (e.g. food or fabric). — *adj* **textural**. — *adj* **textured**. [Lat *texere*, to weave]

TGWU *abbrev* Transport and General Workers' Union.

Th *symbol* (*chem*) thorium.

Th. *abbrev* Thursday.

-th[1] *sfx* (also **-eth**) forming ordinal numbers and fractions from cardinal numbers greater than, or ending in a number greater than, three. [OE *-tha*, *-the*]

-th[2] *sfx* forming nouns meaning action or process, or state or condition: *death*; *filth*; *width*. [OE *-thu*, *-tho*, *-th*]

thalidomide *n* a drug formerly used as a sedative but withdrawn in 1961 because it was found to cause malformation of the foetus if taken by the mother in early pregnancy.

thallium *n* (*chem*) a soft, highly toxic, lead-like metallic element (symbol **Tl**), used in alloys. [Gr *thallos*, a green shoot, so-called because of the bright green line in its spectrum]

than *conj* **1** used to introduce the second part of a comparison, or that part which is taken as the basis of a comparison: *She is older than he is*. **2** used to introduce the second, and usu. less desirable or rejected, option in a statement of alternatives: *would rather go swimming than play football*. **3** except; other than: *be left with no alternative than to resign*. — *prep* in comparison with: *someone older than him*. [OE *thonne*]

thane *n* (*hist*) **1** (in Anglo-Saxon England) a person holding land from the king or some other superior in exchange for military service. **2** a person holding land from a Scottish king (but not in return for military service); a Scottish feudal lord. [OE *thegn*]

thank *v* (*tr*; **for**) **1** to express gratitude to: *thanked him for his help*. **2** to hold responsible for: *have only yourself to thank for your failure*. — *n* (in *pl*; **for**) **1** gratitude or an expression of gratitude. **2** thank you: *thanks for the present*. — **no thanks to** in spite of; no gratitude is due to. — **thank God** or **goodness** or **heavens** an expression of relief. — **thanks to** as a result of. — **thank you** a polite expression acknowledging a gift, help or offer. [OE *thancian*]

thankful *adj* grateful; relieved and happy. — *adv* **thankfully**. — *n* **thankfulness**.

thankless *adj* bringing no thanks, pleasure or profit. — *adv* **thanklessly**. — *n* **thanklessness**.

thanksgiving *n* **1** a formal act of giving thanks, esp. to God. **2** (*cap*; also **Thanksgiving Day**) a public holiday for giving thanks to God, occurring on the fourth Thursday in November in the US and the second Monday in October in Canada.

that *adj* ***those*** **1** indicating the thing, person or idea (already) mentioned, specified or understood. **2** indicating someone or something that is farther away or is in contrast: *not this book, that one*. — *pron* ***those*** **1** the person, thing or idea just mentioned, already spoken of or understood. **2** a relatively distant or more distant person, thing or idea. — *relative pron* used instead of **which**, **who** or **whom** to introduce a relative clause which defines, distinguishes or restricts the person or thing mentioned in the preceding clause: *all the children that were late*. — *conj* used to introduce a noun clause, or a clause showing reason, purpose, consequence, a result, or expressing a wish or desire: *spoke so quickly that no one could understand*; *Oh, that the holiday would never end!* — *adv* **1** to the degree or extent shown or understood: *won't reach that far*. **2** (*coll* or *dialect*) to such a degree that; so: *She's that unhappy she cries all day long*. — **all that** (*coll*) very: *not all that good*. — **that's that** that is the end of the matter. [OE *thæt*]

thatch *n* **1** a roof covering of straw, reeds, etc. **2** anything resembling such a roof, esp. thick hair on the head. — *v* (*tr* & *intr*) to cover (a roof or building) with thatch. — *n* **thatcher**. [OE *theccan*]

thaw *v* **1** (*tr* & *intr*) (of snow or ice) to (cause to) melt. **2** (*tr* & *intr*; **out**) (of anything frozen, e.g. food) to (cause to) become unfrozen; to defrost. **3** (*intr*) to become warm enough to begin to melt snow and ice: *It's beginning to thaw.* **4** (*tr* & *intr*; **out**) to make or become less stiff and numb with cold. **5** (*tr* & *intr*; **out**) to make or become more friendly or relaxed. — *n* **1** an act or process of thawing. **2** a period of weather warm enough to begin to thaw ice and snow. [OE *thawian*]

the[1] *definite article* **1** used to refer to a particular person or thing, or group of people or things, already mentioned, implied or known. **2** used to refer to a unique person or thing: *the Pope.* **3** used before a singular noun to refer to all the members of that group or class: *a history of the novel.* **4** used before certain titles and proper names. **5** used before an adjective or noun describing an identified person: *William the Conqueror.* **6** used after a preposition to refer to a unit of quantity, time, etc.: *a car which does forty miles to the gallon; paid by the hour.* [OE *the*, who, which, that, replacing *se*, that]

the[2] *adv* **1** used before comparative adjectives or adverbs to indicate (by) so much or (by) how much: *the sooner the better.* **2** used before superlative adjectives and adverbs to indicate an amount beyond all others: *like this book the best.* [OE *thy*, by that, by that much]

theatre *n* **1** a building or area outside specially designed for the performance of plays, operas, etc. **2** a large room with seats rising in tiers, e.g. for lectures. **3** (also with **the**) the writing and production of plays in general. **4** (*Br*) a specially equipped room in a hospital where surgery is performed. **5** a scene of action or place where events take place: *theatre of war.* **6** (with **the**) the world and profession of actors and theatre companies. **7** (*NAm*) a cinema. [Gr *theatron*, from *theaesthai*, to see]

theatrical *adj* **1** of theatres or acting. **2** (of behaviour, a gesture, etc.) done only for effect; artificial and exaggerated. — *n* (in *pl*) dramatic performances. — *n* **theatricality** — *adv* **theatrically**.

thee *pron* (*archaic*, *dialect* or *relig*) the object form of the pronoun **thou**: *Let me give thee the book.* [OE *the*]

theft *n* **1** (an act of) stealing. **2** something stolen. [OE *thiefth*]

their *adj* **1** of or belonging to them. **2** (*coll*, and considered wrong by some speakers) his or her: *Has anyone not got their book with them?* [Norse *thierra*]

theirs *pron* a person or thing that belongs to them. — **of theirs** belonging to them.

theism *n* the belief in the existence of God or a god, esp. one revealed supernaturally to man. — *n* **theist**. — *adj* **theistic**. ◇ See also **deism**. [Gr *theos*, god + **-ism**]

them or *pron* **1** people or things already mentioned or spoken about, or understood or implied; the object form of **they**. **2** (*coll* or *dialect*) those. **3** (*old*) themselves. — *adj* (*coll* or *dialect*) those. [Norse *thiem*]

themselves *pron* **1** the reflexive form of **them** and **they**: *They helped themselves.* **2** used for emphasis: *They did it themselves.* **3** their normal selves: *They aren't feeling themselves today.* **4** (*coll*; also **themself**; considered incorrect by some speakers) himself or herself: *If anyone has to blame themselves, it's her.* **5** (also **by themselves**) alone; without help.

theme *n* **1** the subject of a discussion, speech or piece of writing. **2** (*mus*) a short melody which forms the basis of a piece of music and which is developed and repeated with variations. **3** a repeated or recurring image or idea in literature or art. **4** a brief essay or written exercise. [Gr *thema*]

theme park *n* a large amusement park in which all of the rides and attractions are based on a particular theme, such as outer space.

theme song or **tune** *n* a song or melody that is associated with, and usu. played at the beginning and end of, a film, television or radio programme, or which is associated with a particular character.

then *adv* **1** at that time. **2** soon or immediately after that: *looked at him, then turned away.* **3** in that case; that being so; as a necessary consequence: *What would we do then? If you're tired, then you should rest.* **4** also; in addition. **5** used to continue a narrative after a break or digression: *By the time she got to the top, then, it had started to snow.* **6** used esp. at the end of questions which ask for an explanation, opinion, etc., or which ask for or assume agreement: *Your mind is made up, then? That was a bit of a shock, then, wasn't it?* — *n* that time: *until then.* — *adj* being or acting at that time: *the then Prime Minister.* — **then and there** at that very time and on that very spot. [OE *thonne*]

thence *adv* (*old* or *formal*) **1** from that place or time. **2** from that cause; therefore. [MidE *thennes*]

thenceforth or **thenceforward** *adv* (*old* or *formal*) from that time or place forwards.

theo- *comb fm* of God or a god. [Gr *theos*, god]

theocracy *n* **-ies** (a country or state having) government by God or a god directly, or by priests representing that god. — *n* **theocrat**. — *adj* **theocratic**. — *adv* **theocratically**. [Gr *theos*, god + *kratos*, power]

theodolite *n* an instrument for measuring horizontal and vertical angles when surveying land. [Lat *theodolitus*]

theology *n* **-ies** **1** the study of God, religion, religious belief and revelation. **2** a particular system of religious belief: *Catholic theology.* — *adj* **theological**. — *adv* **theologically**. [Gr *theos*, god + *logos*, word, reason]

theologian *n* a person who studies, or is an expert in, theology.

theorem *n* (esp. *math* & *logic*) a statement or proposition which is not self-evident but which has been or can be proved to be true by applying other more basic but generally accepted propositions. [Gr *theorema*, subject for contemplation]

theory *n* **-ies 1** a series of ideas and general principles which (seek to) explain some aspect of the world: *theory of relativity*. **2** an idea or explanation which has not yet been proved; a conjecture. **3** the general and usu. abstract principles or ideas of a subject: *music theory*. **4** an ideal, hypothetical or abstract situation; ideal, hypothetical or abstract reasoning: *a good idea in theory but one which probably wouldn't work in practice*. [Gr *theoria*, from *theoreein*, to view]

theoretical *adj* (also **theoretic**) **1** concerned with or based on theory rather than practical knowledge or experience. **2** existing in theory only; hypothetical. **3** dealing with theory only; speculative. — *adv* **theoretically**.

theoretician *n* someone who specialises in or is concerned with the theoretical aspects of a subject rather than its practical use.

theorise or **-ize** *v* (*intr*; **about**) to think up theories; to speculate.

theorist *n* **1** a person who speculates or invents theories. **2** a theoretician.

theosophy *n* **-ies** a religious philosophy which is based on the belief that a knowledge of God can be achieved through intuition, mysticism and divine inspiration, esp. a modern movement which combines this with elements from Hinduism and Buddhism, such as a belief in reincarnation. — *adj* **theosophic** or **theosophical**. — *adv* **theosophically**. — *n* **theosophist**. [Gr *theos*, god + *sophia*, wisdom]

therapeutic *adj* **1** of, concerning or contributing to the healing and curing of disease. **2** bringing a feeling of general well-being. — *adv* **therapeutically**. [Gr *therapeuein*, to take care of, to heal]

therapeutics *n* (*sing*) the branch of medicine concerned with the treatment and cure of disease.

therapy *n* **-ies** the treatment of physical or mental diseases and disorders by means other than surgery. — *n* **therapist**. [Gr *therapeuein*, to take care of, to heal]

there *adv* **1** at, in or to a place or position. **2** at that point in speech, a piece of writing, performance, etc.: *Don't stop there*. **3** in that respect: *agree with him there*. **4** used to begin a sentence when the subject of the verb follows the verb instead of coming before it: *There are no mistakes in this*. **5** used at the beginning of a sentence to emphasise or call attention to that sentence: *There goes the last bus*. **6** used after a noun for emphasis: *That book there is the one you need*. **7** (*coll & dialect*) used between a noun and *that*, etc. for emphasis: *that there tractor*. — *n* that place or point. — *interj* used to express sympathy, satisfaction, approval, encouragement, etc. or to comfort. — **have been there before** (*slang*) to have been in the same, esp. unpleasant, situation before. — **there and then** at that very time and on that very spot. — **there you are 1** (used when giving something to someone) this is what you need or want. **2** (used to express satisfaction or triumph) I told you so. [OE *thær*]

thereabouts *adv* (also **thereabout**) near that place, number, amount, degree or time.

thereafter *adv* (*formal*) from that time on.

thereby *adv* (*formal*) **1** by that means. **2** in consequence.

therefore *adv* for that reason; as a consequence.

therein *adv* (*formal*) in or into that or it.

thereof *adv* (*formal*) of or from that or it.

thereon *adv* (*formal*) on or on to that or it.

thereto *adv* (*formal*) to that or it; in addition.

thereunder *adv* (*formal*) under that or it.

thereupon *adv* (*formal*) **1** on that matter or point. **2** immediately after it or that.

thermo- *comb fm* of heat. [Gr *therme*, heat]

therm *n* a unit of heat equal to 100 000 British thermal units, used to measure gas used or sold. [Gr *therme*, heat]

thermal *adj* **1** of, caused by or producing heat. **2** (of clothing) designed to prevent the loss of heat from the body. — *n* a rising current of warm air, used by birds, gliders and hang-gliders to move upwards. — *adv* **thermally**. [Gr *therme*, heat]

British thermal unit *n* the amount of heat needed to raise the temperature of one pound of water by one degree Fahrenheit, equal to 252 calories or 1055 joules.

thermion *n* an electrically charged particle emitted by an extremely hot or incandescent substance. — *adj* **thermionic**. [Gr *therme*, heat]

thermionic valve or (esp. *NAm*) **tube** *n* a valve containing a heated cathode which emits electrons and carefully controls their flow.

thermo- *comb fm* heat. [Gr *therme*, heat]

thermocouple *n* a pair of wires of different metals joined at both ends, used for generating a current which can be used to measure temperature. [**thermo-** + **couple**]

thermodynamics *n* (*sing*) the branch of science concerned with the relationship between heat and other (e.g. mechanical and electrical) forms of energy. — *adj* **thermodynamic**. — *adv* **thermodynamically**. [**thermo-** + **dynamics**]

thermoelectricity *n* electricity generated by the presence of different temperatures within a single circuit, esp. by a pair of different metals brought into contact. — *adj* **thermoelectric**. [**thermo-** + **electricity**]

thermometer *n* an instrument for measuring temperature, esp. a thin glass tube with degrees marked along the side, filled with mercury which expands and contracts in response to heat. [**thermo-** + **meter**]

thermonuclear *adj* **1** of, using or showing nuclear reactions which can only be produced at extremely high temperatures. **2** relating to or involving thermonuclear weapons. [**thermo-** + **nuclear**]

thermoplastic *adj* (of a substance) able to be heated to be made plastic and cooled to be made hard repeatedly and without any appreciable change in quality or properties. — *n* a thermoplastic substance, esp. a resin. [**thermo-** + **plastic**]

Thermos® *n* (also **Thermos® flask**) a vacuum flask which keeps the temperature of its contents constant. [Gr, hot]

thermosetting *adj* (of plastics) becoming permanently hard after a single melting and moulding. [**thermo-** + **set**]

thermostat *n* an apparatus which automatically controls temperature (e.g. of a room, water or an oven) by switching the heating system off or on when the temperature reaches or falls below the required level. — *adj* **thermostatic**. — *adv* **thermostatically**. [**thermo-** + Gr *-states*, causing to stand]

thesaurus *n* ***-ruses*** or ***-ri*** **1** a book which lists words and their synonyms according to sense. **2** any book, e.g. a dictionary or encyclopaedia, which gives information about a particular field, quotations, etc. [Gr *thesauros*, treasury]

these. See **this**.

thesis *n* ***theses*** **1** a long written essay or report, esp. one based on original research and presented for an advanced university degree such as the MSc, MLitt or PhD. **2** an idea or proposition to be supported or upheld in argument. **3** an unproved statement put forward as a basis for argument or discussion. [Gr, a setting down]

Thespian *adj* of or relating to tragedy, or to drama and the theatre in general. — *n* (usu. *facet*) an actor or actress. [Gr *Thespis* (lived c.534 BC), Greek poet and reputed founder of Greek tragedy]

they *pron* **1** the people (not including the speaker or a person spoken to), animals or things already spoken about or being indicated. **2** people in general. **3** people in authority. **4** (*coll*, and considered wrong by some speakers; used usu. when the sex of the person in question is unknown) he or she: *Anyone can help if they want*. [Norse *their*]

they'd 1 they had. **2** they would.

they'll 1 they will. **2** they shall.

they're they are.

they've they have.

thiamine or **thiamin** *n* a vitamin of the B complex (**B**$_1$), found in yeast and cereal germs, beans and liver, a deficiency of which causes nervous disorders and beriberi. [Gr *theion*, sulphur + **amine**]

thick *adj* **1** having a relatively large distance between opposite sides. **2** having a specified distance between opposite sides: *one inch thick*. **3** having a large diameter: *a thick rope*. **4** (of a line, handwriting, etc.) broad. **5** (of liquids) containing a lot of solid matter; viscous: *thick soup*. **6** having many single units placed very close together; dense: *thick hair*. **7** difficult to see through: *thick fog*. **8** (**with**) covered with or full of: *a room thick with smoke*. **9** great in number: *insults were flying thick and fast*. **10** (of speech) not clear. **11** (of an accent) marked; pronounced. **12** (*coll*) (of a person) stupid; dull. **13** (*coll*; **with**) friendly or intimate: *be very thick with the new manager*. **14** (*coll*) unfair: *That's a bit thick!* — *adv* thickly. — *n* (with **the**) **1** the busiest, most active or most intense part. **2** the thickest part of anything. — *adv* **thickly**. — **as thick as thieves** very friendly. — **through thick and thin** whatever happens; in spite of any difficulties. [OE *thicce*]

thicken *v* ***-n-*** **1** (*tr* & *intr*) to make or become thick or thicker. **2** (*intr*) to become more complicated: *The plot thickens*.

thickening *n* **1** something used to thicken liquid. **2** the process of making or becoming thicker. **3** a thickened part.

thickhead *n* (*coll*) a stupid person.

thick-headed *adj* (*coll*) **1** stupid. **2** unable to think clearly because of a cold, too much alcohol, etc.

thickness *n* **1** the state, quality or degree of being thick. **2** a layer. **3** the thick part of something.

thickset *adj* **1** heavily built; having a thick, short body. **2** growing or planted close together.

thick-skinned *adj* not easily hurt by criticism or insults; insensitive.

thicket *n* a dense mass of bushes and trees. [**thick**]

thief *n* ***thieves*** a person who steals, esp. secretly and often without violence. [OE *theof*]

thieve *v* (*tr* & *intr*) to steal. — *n* & *adj* **thieving**.

thievish *adj* given to stealing. — *adv* **thievishly**. — *n* **thievishness**.

thigh *n* the fleshy part of the leg between the knee and hip in man, or the corresponding part in animals. [OE *theoh*]

thigh bone *n* the bone of the leg between the hip-joint and the knee.

thimble *n* **1** a small metal, ceramic or plastic cap worn on the finger to protect it and push the needle when sewing. **2** a metal ring with a concave groove on the outside, fitted into a loop formed by splicing a rope in order to prevent chafing. [OE *thymel*]

thimbleful *n* ***-fuls*** the amount a thimble will hold, esp. used for a very small quantity of liquid.

thin *adj* ***-nn-*** **1** having a relatively short distance between opposite sides. **2** having a relatively small diameter: *thin string*. **3**

(of a line, handwriting, etc.) narrow or fine. **4** (of people or animals) not fat; lean (often too lean). **5** (of liquids) containing very little solid matter. **6** set far apart; not dense or crowded: *thin hair*. **7** rarefied: *thin air*. **8** few in number: *Good books are thin on the ground*. **9** weak; lacking in body: *thin blood*. **10** not convincing or believable: *a thin disguise*. **11** (*coll*) difficult; uncomfortable; unpleasant: *have a thin time of it*. — *adv* thinly. — *v* ***-nn-*** (*tr* & *intr*; **out**) to make or become thin, thinner, sparser or less dense. — *adv* **thinly**. — *n* **thinness**. [OE *thynne*]

thin air *n* nowhere: *disappear into thin air*.

thinner *n* a liquid such as turpentine that is added to paint or varnish to dilute it.

thin-skinned *adj* sensitive; easily hurt or upset.

thine (*archaic*, *dialect* or *relig*) *pron* something which belongs to thee. — *adj* (used before a vowel instead of **thy**) of or belonging to thee. — **of thine** of or belonging to thee [OE *thin*]

thing *n* **1** any object, esp. one that is inanimate. **2** any object that cannot, need not or should not be named. **3** any fact, quality, idea, etc. that can be thought about or referred to. **4** an event, affair or circumstance: *Things are getting out of hand*. **5** a quality: *Generosity is a great thing*. **6** (*coll*) a person or animal, esp. when thought of as an object of pity: *poor thing!* **7** a preoccupation, obsession or interest: *have a thing about horses*. **8** what is needed or required: *It's just the thing*. **9** an aim: *The thing is to do better next time*. **10** (in *pl*) personal belongings, esp. clothes. — **do one's own thing** (*coll*) to do what one likes doing best, or what it is natural for one to do. — **make a thing of** to make a fuss about or exaggerate the importance of. — **(just) one of those things** something that must be accepted or cannot be avoided. [OE, object, act, assembly]

thingummy or **thingamy** *n* ***-ies*** (*coll*; also **thingummyjig**, **thingummybob**) someone or something whose name is unknown, forgotten, deliberately not used, or unmentionable. **[thing]**

think *v* ***thought*** **1** (*intr*; **about**) to have or form ideas in the mind (about); to have as a thought in one's mind. **2** (*tr* & *intr*; **about**, **of**) to consider, judge or believe: *thought the world was flat*; *think of oneself as a great singer*. **3** (*tr* & *intr*; **about**, **of**) to intend or plan; to form an idea of: *think about going to London*; *couldn't think of being so unkind*; *think no harm*. **4** (*tr* & *intr*; **of**) to imagine, expect or suspect: *didn't think there would be any trouble*. **5** (*intr* with **of**) to keep in one's mind; to consider: *think of the children first*. **6** (*tr* & *intr*; **of**) to remember: *didn't think to tell her*; *couldn't think of his name*. **7** (*tr*; **of**) to form or have an idea (of): *think of a plan*. **8** (*tr*) to have one's mind full of. **9** (*tr*) to bring into a specified condition by thinking. — *n* (*coll*) an act of thinking. — **think better of 1** to change one's mind about (something) on thinking about it again or further. **2** to think that (someone) would not be so bad (as to do something wrong): *I thought better of him than that*. — **think highly, well, badly**, etc. **of** to have a high, good, bad, etc. opinion of. — **think little of** and **not think much of** to have a very low opinion of. — *v* **think out** (*tr*) **1** to consider carefully; to plan. **2** to solve (a problem) by thinking about all the aspects of it. — *v* **think over** (*tr*) to consider all the advantages and disadvantages (of an action, decision, etc.); to reflect on. — *v* **think through** (*tr*) to think carefully about all the possible consequences of (a plan, idea, etc.), esp. so as to reach a conclusion as to its wisdom or value. — **think twice (about)** to hesitate before doing (something); to decide not to do (something). — *v* **think up** (*tr*) to invent or devise. [OE *thencan*]

thinker *n* a person who thinks, esp. deeply and constructively or in a specified way: *an original*, *shallow*, etc. *thinker*.

thinking *n* **1** the act of using one's mind to produce thoughts. **2** opinion or judgement: *What's your thinking on this?* — *adj* (of people) using the mind intelligently and constructively. — **put on one's thinking-cap** (*coll*) to think carefully or reflect, esp. to try to solve a problem or come up with an idea.

think tank *n* (*coll*) a group of experts who research into an area to find solutions to problems and think up new ideas.

third *adj* **1** coming next after second in time, place, order or rank; last of three. **2** being one of three equal parts. **3** being the forward gear which is one faster than second in a gearbox, e.g. in a motor vehicle. — *n* **1** one of three equal parts. **2** (also **third gear**) the gear which is one faster than second in a gearbox, e.g. in a motor vehicle. **3** (the person or thing occupying) the third position in time, place, order or rank. **4** (*mus*) an interval of three notes (counting inclusively) along the diatonic scale. **5** (*mus*) a note which is separated by such an interval from another. **6** (*Br*; also **third class**) an honours degree of the third, and usu. lowest, class. — *adv* in the third position: *come third in the race*. [OE *thridda*]

third class *n* the class or rank next (esp. in quality) after second.

third-class *adj* & *adv* of or in the position, class or rank next after or below the second.

third degree *n* long and severe questioning, sometimes involving torture.

third-degree (*adj*) see **degree**.

third dimension *n* the depth or thickness of an object which distinguishes a solid object from a flat one.

thirdly *adv* in the third place; as the third reason, etc.

third party *n* a person who is indirectly involved, or involved by chance, in a legal action, contract, etc. between usu. two principals.
third-party *adj* (of insurance) covering damage done by or injury done to a person other than the insured.
third person see **person**.
third-rate *adj* of very bad or inferior quality.
the Third World *n* the developing or underdeveloped countries in Africa, Asia and Latin America.

thirst *n* **1** the need to drink, or the feeling of dryness in the mouth that this causes. **2** (**for**) a strong and eager desire or longing (for). — *v* (*intr*) **1** (**for**) to have a great desire or longing (for). **2** (*old*) to be thirsty. [OE *thyrstan*]
thirsty *adj* **-ier**, **-iest** **1** needing or wanting to drink. **2** (**for**) eager or longing (for). **3** causing thirst. — *adv* **thirstily**. — *n* **thirstiness**.

thirteen *n* **1** the number or figure 13; any symbol for this number. **2** the age of 13. **3** something, esp. a garment or a person, whose size is denoted by the number 13. **4** a set of 13 people or things. — *adj* **1** 13 in number. **2** aged 13. — *n, adj & adv* **thirteenth**. [OE *threotine*]

thirty *n* **-ies** **1** the number or figure 30; any symbol for this number. **2** the age of 30. **3** a set of 30 people or things. — *adj* **1** 30 in number. **2** aged 30. — *n, adj & adv* **thirtieth**. [OE *thritig*]
thirties *n* (*pl*) **1** the period of time between one's thirtieth and fortieth birthdays. **2** the range of temperatures between thirty and forty degrees. **3** the period of time between the thirtieth and fortieth years of a century.

this *pron* ***these*** **1** a person, animal, thing or idea already mentioned, about to be mentioned, indicated, or otherwise understood from the context. **2** a person, animal, thing or idea which is nearby, esp. which is closer to the speaker than something else. **3** the present time or place. **4** an action, event, circumstance: *What do you think of this?* — *adj* **1** being the person, animal, thing or idea which is nearby, esp. closer than something else: *this book or that one*. **2** being the person, animal, thing or idea just mentioned, about to be mentioned, indicated, or otherwise understood. **3** relating to today, or time in the recent past ending today: *this morning*; *have been working on it these last few days*. **4** (*coll*) (used instead of **a** or **the** for emphasis) being a person, animal, thing or idea not yet mentioned: *Then I had this brilliant idea*. — *adv* to this (extreme) degree or extent: *I didn't think it would be this easy*. — **this and that** (*coll*) various minor unspecified actions, objects, etc. [OE *thes*]

thistle *n* any of several plants with prickly purple flowers, the national emblem of Scotland. [OE *thistel*]
thistledown *n* the fluffy hairs attached to thistle seeds.

thither *adv* (*old*, *literary* or *formal*) to or towards that place. [OE *thider*]

tho' (esp. *poetic*). Same as **though**.

thole[1] or **tholepin** *n* either one of a pair of pins in the side of a boat to keep an oar in place. ◇ See also **rowlock**. [OE *thol*]

thole[2] *v* (*tr*; *Scot* or *old*) to endure or tolerate. [OE *tholian*, to suffer]

thong *n* a narrow strip of leather used e.g. to fasten something, or as the lash of a whip. [OE *thwang*]

thorax *n* ***-axes*** or ***-aces*** the part of the body between the head and abdomen, in man the chest, and in insects the middle section that bears the wings and legs. — *adj* **thoracic**. [Gr, breastplate]

thorium *n* (*chem*) a dark grey radioactive metallic element (symbol **Th**), which can be used as a nuclear fuel. [*Thor*, the Scandinavian god of thunder]

thorn *n* **1** a hard, sharp point sticking out from the stem or branch of certain plants. **2** a shrub bearing thorns, esp. a hawthorn. **3** a constant irritation or annoyance: *a thorn in one's side*. [OE]
thorny *adj* **-ier**, **-iest** **1** full of or covered with thorns. **2** difficult; causing trouble or problems.

thorough *adj* **1** (of a person) extremely careful and attending to every detail. **2** (of a task, etc.) carried out with great care and great attention to detail. **3** complete; absolute: *a thorough waste of time*. — *adv* **thoroughly**. — *n* **thoroughness**. [OE *thurh*]
thoroughbred *n* **1** an animal, esp. a horse, bred from the best specimens carefully developed by selective breeding over many years. **2** (*cap*) a breed of racehorse descended from English mares and Arab stallions of the early eighteenth century. **3** a racehorse belonging to this breed. — *adj* **1** (of an animal, esp. a horse) bred from the best specimens; pure-bred. **2** (*cap*) of or being a Thoroughbred.
thoroughfare *n* **1** a public road or street. **2** (the right of passage through) a road or path open at both ends.
thoroughgoing *adj* **1** extremely thorough. **2** utter; out-and-out: *a thoroughgoing villain*.

those. See **that**.

thou[1] *pron* (*old*, *dialect* or *relig*) you (singular). [OE *thu*]

thou[2] *n* ***thou*** or ***thous*** **1** (*coll*) a thousand. **2** a unit of length equal to one thousandth of an inch. [Abbrev.]

though *conj* **1** despite the fact that. **2** if or even if: *wouldn't marry him though he was the richest man in the world*. **3** and yet; but: *like the new car, though not as much as the old one*. — *adv* however; nevertheless. — **as though** as if. [Norse *tho*]

thought *past tense* and *past participle* of **think**. — *n* **1** an idea, concept or opinion. **2** the act of thinking. **3** serious and careful consideration: *give some thought to the problem.* **4** the faculty or power of reasoning. **5** the intellectual ideas which are typical of a particular place, time, group, etc.: *recent scientific thought.* **6** intention, expectation or hope. [OE *thoht*]

thoughtful *adj* **1** (given to or appearing to be) thinking deeply; reflective. **2** showing careful or serious thought: *a thoughtful review of the book.* **3** thinking of other people; considerate. — *adv* **thoughtfully**. — *n* **thoughtfulness**.

thoughtless *adj* **1** not thinking about other people; inconsiderate. **2** showing a lack of careful or serious thought; rash. — *adv* **thoughtlessly**. — *n* **thoughtlessness**.

thousand *n* ***thousands*** or (after another number) ***thousand*** **1** the number or figure 1000; any symbol for this number, e.g. M. **2** anything having 1000 parts, etc. **3** (usu. in *pl*; *coll*) a very large, unspecified number or amount. — *adj* numbering 1000. — *n* & *adj* **thousandth**. — **one in a thousand** an extremely rare or special person or thing. [OE *thusend*]

thrall *n* **1** a person who is in the power of another person or thing; a slave. **2** (also **thraldom**) the state of being in the power of another person or thing; slavery: *be held in thrall by her beauty.* [OE *thræl*]

thrash *v* **1** (*tr*) to beat soundly, esp. with blows or a whip. **2** (*tr*) to defeat thoroughly or decisively. **3** (*tr* & *intr*; **about, around**) to move around violently or wildly. **4** (*tr* & *intr*) to thresh (corn, etc.). — *n* **1** an act of thrashing. **2** (*coll*) a party. — *n* **thrashing**. — *v* **thrash out** (*tr*) to discuss (a problem, etc.) thoroughly to try to solve it; to produce (a solution to a problem, etc.) by thorough discussion. [OE *therscan*]

thread *n* **1** a very thin strand of glass, silk, cotton or wool, esp. when several such strands are twisted together for sewing. **2** any naturally formed very thin strand of fibre, such as that forming a spider's web. **3** anything like a thread in length and narrowness. **4** the projecting spiral ridge round a screw, bolt or in a nut. **5** a continuous connecting element or theme in a story, argument, etc.: *lost the thread of what he was saying.* **6** a thin seam or vein of ore or coal. — *v* **1** (*tr*) to pass a thread through (e.g. the eye of a needle). **2** (*tr*) to pass (tape, film, etc.) into or through something to put it into its correct position. **3** (*tr*) to string (beads) on a thread or length of string. **4** (*tr* & *intr*; **through**) to make (one's way) carefully (through e.g. narrow streets or crowded areas). **5** (*tr*) to streak (hair, the sky, etc.) with narrow patches of a different colour. **6** (*tr*) to provide (e.g. a bolt) with a screw thread. — **hang by a thread** to be in a very precarious or dangerous state or position. [OE *thræd*]

threadbare *adj* **1** (of material or clothes) worn thin; shabby. **2** (of a person) wearing such clothes. **3** (of a word, excuse, etc.) commonly used and meaningless; hackneyed; feeble.

threadworm *n* any of several thread-like worms which live as parasites, often in humans.

threat *n* **1** a warning that one is going to or might hurt or punish (someone). **2** a sign that something dangerous or unpleasant is or may be about to happen. **3** (**to**) a source of danger (for). [OE, affliction]

threaten *v* **-n-** **1** (*tr*) to make or be a threat to. **2** (*tr*) to give warning that (something unpleasant or dangerous is or may be about to happen). **3** (*intr*) (of something unpleasant or dangerous) to seem likely to happen: *A storm was threatening.* — *adj* **threatening**. — *adv* **threateningly**.

three *n* **1** the number or figure 3; any symbol for this number, e.g. III. **2** the age of 3. **3** something, esp. a garment or a person, whose size is denoted by the number 3. **4** a playing-card with 3 pips. **5** a set of 3 things or people. **6** 3 o'clock. **7** a score of 3. — *adj* **1** 3 in number. **2** aged 3. — *pron* 3 things or people. [OE *thrie*]

three-dimensional *adj* **1** having or appearing to have three dimensions, i.e. height, width and depth. **2** (esp. of characters in stories) developed or described in detail and therefore lifelike.

threefold *adj* **1** three times as much or as great. **2** divided into, or consisting of, three parts. — *adv* by three times as much.

three-legged race *n* a race run between pairs of runners who have their adjacent legs tied together.

three-line whip *n* a written notice to politicians belonging to a particular party that they must attend a vote in parliament and vote in the way in which they are instructed.

threepence *n* (*Br hist*) the sum of three pence (3d) (before decimal currency was introduced).

threepenny *adj* (*Br hist*) **1** worth or costing threepence. **2** of little worth or value.

threepenny bit or **piece** *n* (*Br hist*) a coin worth threepence.

three-ply *n* anything which has three layers or strands bound together, esp. wood or wool. — *adj* having three layers or strands.

three-point turn *n* a reversing of the direction of a motor vehicle by moving forward, then backward, then forward again while turning round.

three-quarter *adj* being three-quarters of the full amount or length. — *n* (*Rugby*) any of the four players positioned between the full back and the scrum half and stand-off half.

the three Rs *n* (*pl*) reading, writing and arithmetic, regarded as the three most important skills to be taught in primary school.

threesome *n* a group of three.

threnody *n* **-ies** a song or ode of lamentation, esp. for a person's death. — *adj* **threnodial** or **threnodic**. — *n* **threnodist**. [Gr *threnos*, lament + *oide*, song]

thresh *v* (*tr* & *intr*) **1** to beat (stalks of corn) in order to extract the grain. **2** to beat or strike. **3** (**about**, **around**) to move violently or wildly. [OE *therscan*]

thresher *n* **1** a machine or person that threshes corn, etc. **2** a large shark with a long whip-like tail.

threshold *n* **1** a piece of wood or stone forming the bottom of a doorway. **2** any doorway or entrance. **3** a starting-point: *the threshold of a new career*. **4** the point, level or limit at which a stimulus (such as pain) begins to cause a response (e.g. be felt as painful). [OE *therscold*]

threw. See **throw**.

thrice *adv* (*old* or *literary*) three times; three times as much. [OE *thriwa*]

thrift *n* **1** careful spending, use or management of resources, esp. money. **2** a wild plant with narrow bluish-green leaves and dense round heads of pink flowers, usu. found near the coast. — *adj* **thriftless**. [Norse, prosperity]

thrifty *adj* **-ier**, **-iest** showing thrift; economical; frugal. — *adv* **thriftily**. — *n* **thriftiness**.

thrill *v* **1** (*tr* & *intr*) to feel or cause to feel a sudden strong glowing, tingling or throbbing sensation, esp. of excitement, emotion or pleasure. **2** (*tr* & *intr*) to vibrate or quiver. **3** (*intr*; **along**, **through**, etc.) (of a feeling) to pass quickly with a glowing, tingling or throbbing sensation: *Excitement thrilled through her*. — *n* **1** a sudden tingling feeling of excitement, happiness or pleasure. **2** something, e.g. an event, which causes such a feeling. **3** a shivering or trembling feeling caused esp. by fear, terror or distress. — *adj* **thrilling**. — *adv* **thrillingly**. [OE *thyrlian*, to pierce]

thriller *n* an exciting novel, play or film, usu. involving crime, espionage or adventure.

thrips *n* ***thrips*** or ***thripses*** a minute, slender black insect which lives on flowers. [Gr, woodworm]

thrive *v* ***throve*** or ***thrived***, ***thriven*** or ***thrived*** (*intr*) **1** to grow strong and healthy. **2** to prosper or be successful, esp. financially. — *adj* **thriving**. [Norse *thrifa*, to grasp]

thro' or **thro**. Same as **through**.

throat *n* **1** the top part of the passage which leads from the mouth and nose to the stomach. **2** the front part of the neck. **3** something resembling a throat in form or function, esp. a narrow passageway or opening. — **cut one's own throat** to cause one's own ruin or downfall. — **cut someone's throat** to kill or injure someone by slitting open his or her throat. — **stick in one's throat** to be impossible to say, believe or accept. [OE *throte*]

throaty *adj* **-ier**, **-iest** (of a voice) deep and hoarse. — *adv* **throatily**. — *n* **throatiness**.

throb *v* ***-bb-*** (*intr*) **1** to beat, esp. with unusual force in response to excitement, emotion, exercise or pain. **2** to beat or vibrate with a strong, regular rhythm. — *n* a regular beat; pulse. [MidE *throbben*]

throe *n* (usu. in *pl*) a violent pang or spasm, esp. during childbirth or before death. — **in the throes of** (*formal* or *facet*) involved in a difficult or painful struggle with; suffering under: *in the throes of a severe storm*. [MidE *throwe*]

thrombosis *n* ***-oses*** the forming of a clot in a blood vessel. — *adj* **thrombotic**. [Gr, curdling]

throne *n* **1** the ceremonial chair of a monarch or bishop, used on official occasions. **2** the office or power of the sovereign: *come to the throne*. — *v* (*tr*) to place on a throne. [Gr *thronos*, seat]

throng *n* a crowd of people or things, esp. in a small space; a multitude. — **1** (*tr*) to crowd or fill: *people thronging the streets*. **2** (*intr*) to move in a crowd; to come together in great numbers: *an audience thronging into a theatre*. [OE *gethrang*]

throstle *n* (*old* or *poetic*) a song thrush. [OE]

throttle *n* **1** (a pedal or lever which controls) a valve which regulates the amount of fuel, steam, etc. supplied to an engine. **2** the throat or windpipe. — *v* (*tr*) to injure or kill by choking or strangling. **2** to prevent from being said, expressed, etc.; to suppress. **3** to control the flow of (fuel, steam, etc. to an engine) using a valve. **4** (**back**, **down**) to reduce the speed of (an engine) by closing the throttle to reduce the amount of fuel, steam, etc. supplied to it. [MidE *throtelen*, to strangle]

through *prep* **1** going from one side or end of to the other: *a road through the village*. **2** from place to place within; everywhere within: *searched through the house*. **3** from the beginning to the end of: *read through the magazine*. **4** (esp. *NAm*) up to and including: *Tuesday through Thursday*. **5** because of: *lost his job through stupidity*. **6** by way of, means of or agency of; by: *related through marriage*. — *adv* **1** into and out of; from one side or end to the other. **2** from the beginning to the end. **3** into a position of having completed, esp. successfully: *sat the exam again and got through*. **4** to the core; completely: *soaked through*. **5** (esp. *Br*) in or into communication by telephone: *put the caller through*. — *adj* **1** (of a journey, route, train, ticket, etc.) going all the way to one's destination without requiring a change of line, train, etc. or a new ticket. **2** (of traffic) passing straight through an area, town, etc. without stopping. **3** going from one surface, side or end to another: *a through road*. — **be through 1** (**with**) to have finished or completed. **2** (**with**) to have no more to do with; to have no further dealings with: *be through with men.* **3** to have no further chance of success (as); to be finished (as): *be through as a dancer.* — **through and through** completely. [OE *thurh*]

throughout *prep* **1** in all parts of. **2** during the whole of. — *adv* **1** in every part; everywhere: *a house with carpets throughout.* **2** during the whole time: *remain friends throughout.*

throughput *n* the amount of material put through a process, esp. a computer or manufacturing process.

throw *v* ***threw***, ***thrown*** **1** (*tr* & *intr*) to propel or hurl through the air with force, esp. with a rapid forward movement of the hand and arm. **2** (*tr*; **against**, **in**, **on**, **on to**, **out**, etc.) to move or hurl into a specified position, esp. suddenly or violently. **3** (*tr*) to put into a specified condition, esp. suddenly: *threw them into confusion.* **4** (*tr*; **off**, **on**) to put (clothes, etc.) off or on quickly and carelessly. **5** (*tr*) to direct, cast or emit: *a candle throwing shadows on the wall*; *throw a glance.* **6** (*tr*; *coll*) to puzzle or confuse. **7** (*tr*) (of a horse) to make (its rider) fall off. **8** (*tr*; *wrestling*, *judo*, etc.) to bring (one's opponent) to the ground. **9** (*tr*) to move (a switch or lever) so as to operate a mechanism. **10** (*tr*) to make (pottery) on a potter's wheel. **11** (*tr*; **together**) to construct, esp. hurriedly or temporarily. **12** (*tr*; *coll*) to lose (a contest) deliberately, esp. in return for a bribe. **13** (*tr* & *intr*) to roll (dice) on to a flat surface. **14** (*tr*) to obtain (a specified number) by throwing dice. **15** (*tr*) to have or suffer: *throw a tantrum.* **16** (*tr*) to give (a party). **17** (*tr*) to deliver (a punch). **18** (*tr*) to cause (one's voice) to appear to come from elsewhere. — *n* **1** an act of throwing or instance of being thrown. **2** the distance something is thrown. **3** (*coll*) an article, item, turn, etc.: *sell them at £2 a throw.* **4** (*geol*) the amount by which a fault in a stratum is displaced vertically. — *v* **throw about** or **around** (*tr*) **1** to throw in various directions; to scatter. — *v* **throw away** (*tr*) **1** to get rid of. **2** to fail to take advantage of; to waste or lose through lack of care. — *v* **throw back 1** (*tr*) to delay or hinder the progress of. **2** (*tr*; **on**, **upon**) to force (someone) to rely (on). **3** (*intr*; **to**) to revert to some earlier, ancestral character or type. — *v* **throw in** (*tr*) **1** to include or add as a gift or as part of a bargain at no extra cost. **2** to break in with or contribute (a remark) to a discussion. — **throw in one's hand** (*coll*) to give up or abandon what one is doing. — **throw in the towel** or **sponge** (*coll*) to give up or abandon a struggle. — **throw oneself into** to begin (doing something) with great energy or enthusiasm. — *v* **throw off** (*tr*) **1** to get rid of or discard: *throw off a cold.* **2** to write or say in an offhand, careless way. — **throw oneself on** to rely or depend on (someone's goodwill, sympathies, mercy, etc.). — *v* **throw open** (*tr*) **1** to open suddenly and widely. **2** to allow anyone to enter, take part in, etc. — *v* **throw out** (*tr*) **1** to get rid of; to reject or dismiss. **2** to say in a casual or offhand manner. **3** to confuse or disconcert. **4** to cause to extend, project or stick out, esp. from a main body: *throw out a new wing.* — *v* **throw over** (*tr*) to leave or abandon (a lover). — *v* **throw together** (*tr*) **1** to bring (people) into contact by chance. **2** to put together in a hurry. — *v* **throw up 1** (*intr* & *tr*; *coll*) to vomit. **2** (*tr*) to give up or abandon. **3** (*tr*) to raise (one's hands) in the air quickly, usu. as a sign of despair, horror, etc. **4** (*tr*) to build or erect hurriedly. [OE *thrawan*, to twist]

throwaway *adj* **1** meant to be thrown away after use. **2** said or done casually or carelessly.

throwback *n* (a person, animal or plant that is an example of) reversion to earlier or ancestral characteristics.

throw-in *n* (*football*, *basketball*, etc.) an act of throwing the ball back into play from a sideline.

thru (*US*). Same as **through**.

thrum[1] *v* ***-mm-*** **1** (*tr* & *intr*) to strum idly (on a stringed instrument). **2** (*intr*) to drum or tap with the fingers. **3** (*intr*) to hum monotonously. — *n* (the sound of) repetitive strumming. [Imit.]

thrum[2] *n* **1** an unwoven end of thread remaining on a loom when the woven fabric has been cut away, or a group of such threads. **2** any loose thread or fringe. [OE]

thrush[1] *n* any of several common small or medium-sized songbirds with brown feathers and a spotted chest. [OE *thrysce*]

thrush[2] *n* **1** a fungal infection, esp. of children, which causes white blisters in the mouth, throat and lips. **2** a similar infection in the vagina. **3** an inflammation affecting the sole of a horse's hoof.

thrust *v* ***thrust*** **1** (*tr*) to push suddenly and violently. **2** (*tr*; **on**, **upon**) to force (someone) to accept (something); to impose (something) on (someone). **3** (*tr* with **through**) to pierce or stab. **4** (*intr* with **at**) to make a lunge (at). **5** (*intr*; **into**, **past**, **through**, etc.) to force one's way. — *n* **1** a sudden or violent movement forward; a push or lunge. **2** a force producing motion, esp. that produced by a rocket or jet engine which propels an aircraft or spacecraft forwards and upwards. **3** an attack or lunge with a pointed weapon; a stab. **4** an attack, esp. by a military force on the enemy's territory, or a verbal attack on a person. **5** the strong continuous pressure that one part of an object exerts against another. **6** the main theme, message or gist, e.g. of an argument. **7** determination; drive. [Norse *thrysta*]

thud *n* a dull sound like that of something heavy falling to the ground. — *v* ***-dd-*** (*intr*) to move or fall with a thud. [OE *thyddan*, to strike]

thug *n* **1** a violent, brutal man or criminal. **2** (*cap*; *hist*) a member of a religious organisation of robbers and murderers in India. — *n* **thuggery**. — *adj* **thuggish**. [Hindi *thag*, thief, cheat]

thulium *n* (*chem*) a soft metallic element (symbol **Tm**), one of the rare-earth elements. [Lat *Thule*, believed by the ancients to be the most northerly part of Europe]

thumb *n* **1** the short thick finger of the hand, set lower than and at a different angle from the other four. **2** the part of a glove or mitten covering this finger. **3** a digit of other animals corresponding to the human thumb. — *v* **1** (*tr* & *intr*; **through**) to turn over (the pages of a book, magazine, etc.) to glance at the contents. **2** (*tr*) to smudge or wear with the thumb. **3** (*tr*) to ask for or obtain (a lift) in a motor vehicle by signalling to passing drivers with the thumb. **4** (*intr*) to travel by thumbing lifts; to hitchhike. — **all thumbs** awkward and clumsy. — **thumbs down** a sign indicating failure, rejection or disapproval. — **thumbs up** a sign indicating success, best wishes for success, satisfaction or approval. — **under someone's thumb** completely controlled or dominated by someone. [OE *thuma*]

thumb index *n* a series of notches, each with a letter or word in them, cut into the outer edges of pages of a book for quick reference.

thumb-nail *n* the nail on the thumb. — *adj* brief and concise.

thumbscrew *n* (*hist*) an instrument of torture which crushes the thumbs.

thumbtack *n* (*NAm*) a drawing-pin.

thump *n* (the dull sound of) a heavy blow. — *v* **1** (*tr*) to beat or strike with dull-sounding heavy blows. **2** (*intr*) to throb or beat violently. **3** (*tr*; **out**) to play (a tune), esp. on a piano, by pounding heavily on the keys. **4** (*intr*; **along**, **around**, etc.) to move with heavy, pounding steps. [Imit.]

thumping (*coll*) *adj* very big: *a thumping lie*. — *adv* very: *a pair of thumping great boots*.

thunder *n* **1** a deep rumbling or loud cracking sound heard after a flash of lightning, caused by the lightning causing gases in the atmosphere to expand suddenly. **2** a loud, deep, rumbling noise. — *v* **-r-** **1** (*intr*) (of thunder) to sound or rumble. **2** (*intr*) to make a noise like thunder while moving: *tanks thundering over a bridge*. **3** (*tr*) to say or utter in a loud, often aggressive, voice. [OE *thunor*]

thunderbolt *n* **1** a flash of lightning immediately followed by thunder. **2** a sudden and unexpected event. **3** the supposed destructive stone, missile, etc. falling to earth in a flash of lightning.

thunderclap *n* (something as loud, violent and sudden as) a crash of thunder.

thundercloud *n* a large cloud charged with electricity which produces thunder and lightning.

thundering (*coll*) *adj* very great: *a thundering idiot*. — *adv* very: *a thundering great error*.

thunderous *adj* like thunder, esp. in being very loud, threatening or violent. — *adv* **thunderously**.

thunderstorm *n* a storm with thunder and lightning and usu. heavy rain.

thunderstruck *adj* overcome by surprise; astonished.

thundery *adj* warning of, or likely to have or bring, thunder.

Thur. or **Thurs.** *abbrev* Thursday.

thurible *n* a censer. [Lat *thus*, incense]

Thursday *n* the fifth day of the week. [OE *thunresdæg*, the day of Thunor, the Anglo-Saxon god of thunder]

thus *adv* **1** in the way or manner shown or mentioned; in this manner. **2** to this degree, amount or distance: *thus far*. **3** therefore; accordingly. [OE]

thwack *n* (the noise made by) a blow with something flat, such as a bat. — *v* (*tr*) to strike (something) with such a noise. [Imit.]

thwart *v* (*tr*) to stop, prevent or hinder (someone, or his or her plans, etc.). — *n* a seat for a rower lying across a boat. [Norse *thvert*, across]

thy *adj* (*old*, *dialect* or *relig*) of or belonging to thee. [**thine**]

thyself *pron* (*old*, *dialect* or *relig*) **1** the reflexive form of **thou** and **thee**. **2** used for emphasis. **3** your normal self. **4** (also **by thyself**) alone; without help.

thyme *n* any of several herbs and shrubs, esp. those with sweet-smelling leaves which are used to season food. [Gr *thymon*]

thymus *n* ***thymi*** (in full **thymus gland**) a gland near the base of the neck which produces white blood cells for the immune system. [Gr *thymos*]

thyroid *n* (in full **thyroid gland**) a large gland in the neck which produces hormones which control the body's metabolism. — *adj* **1** of the thyroid gland or thyroid cartilage. **2** shield-shaped. [Gr *thyreoeides*, shield-shaped]

thyroid cartilage *n* the principal cartilage in the larynx which projects in men to form the Adam's apple.

Ti *symbol* (*chem*) titanium.

ti or **te** *n* (*mus*) in tonic sol-fa, the seventh note of the major scale. [Earlier *si*, from the initial sounds of *S*ancte *I*ohannes in a mediaeval Latin hymn, certain syllables and sounds of which were used in naming the notes of the scale]

tiara *n* **1** a women's jewelled ornament for the head, similar to a crown. **2** the pope's three-tiered crown. [Gr]

Tibetan *n* **1** a citizen or inhabitant of Tibet (the Tibet Autonomous Region of China). **2** the main language of Tibet. — *adj* of or relating to Tibet, its people, their language, etc.

tibia *n* **-ias** or **-iae** **1** the inner and usu. larger of the two bones between the knee and ankle in man, or the bone corresponding to this in other animals; the shinbone. **2** the fourth joint of an insect's leg. [Lat, shinbone]

tic *n* **1** a habitual nervous, involuntary movement or twitch of a muscle, esp. of the face. **2** an habitual and usu. involuntary response or behaviour. [Fr]

tick[1] *n* **1** a usu. soft regular tapping or clicking sound, such as that made by a watch or clock. **2** (*Br coll*) a moment. **3** a small mark, usu. a line with an acute angle at the bottom, used to show that something is correct, to mark off items on a list which have been dealt with, etc. — *v* **1** (*intr*) (of e.g. a clock) to make a sound like a tick. **2** (*intr*; **away**) (of time) to pass. **3** (*tr*) to mark with a written tick. **4** (*tr*; **off**) to count (e.g. an item on a list) by putting a written tick beside it. — *v* **tick off** (*tr*; *coll*) to scold (*n* **ticking-off**). — *v* **tick over** (*intr*) **1** to function or work quietly and smoothly at a relatively gentle or moderate rate. **2** (of an engine) to idle. — **what makes someone tick** (*coll*) the reason why someone behaves and thinks in the way that he or she does. [MidE *tek*, little touch]

ticker *n* **1** anything that ticks, e.g. a watch. **2** (*coll*) the heart.

ticker-tape *n* (*formerly*) continuous paper tape with messages, esp. up-to-date share prices, printed by a telegraph instrument.

tick-tack *n* a system of communication based on hand signals, used e.g. by bookmakers at a racecourse to exchange information about the odds they are offering.

tick[2] *n* **1** any of several bloodsucking, spider-like insects living on the skin of some animals, e.g. dogs and cattle. **2** any of several bloodsucking flies living on the skins of e.g. sheep and birds. [OE *ticia*]

tick[3] *n* **1** the strong cover of a mattress, pillow or bolster. **2** (also **ticking**) the strong, coarse, usu. striped cotton fabric from which such covers are made. [Gr *theke*, case]

tick[4] *n* (*Br coll*) credit: *buy it on tick*. [Abbrev. of **ticket**]

ticket *n* **1** a printed piece of paper or card which shows that the holder has paid a fare (e.g. for travel on a bus or train) or for admission (e.g. to a theatre or cinema), or has the right to use certain services (e.g. a library). **2** an official notice issued to someone who has committed a motor offence, such as speeding or parking illegally. **3** a tag or label, esp. one showing the price, size, etc. of the item to which it is attached. **4** (*NAm*) a list of candidates put up for election by a particular political party. **5** the principles of a particular political party. **6** (*slang*) a certificate discharging a soldier from the army. **7** (*slang*) a licence or permit, esp. one allowing the holder to work as a ship's master or pilot. **8** (*coll*) exactly what is required, proper or best: *just the ticket*. — *v* **-t-** (*tr*) to give or attach a ticket or label to. [OFr *estiquier*, to attach, stick]

tickle *v* **1** (*tr*) to touch (a person or part of the body) lightly and so as to provoke a tingling or light prickling sensation or laughter. **2** (*intr*) (of a part of the body) to feel a tingling or light prickling sensation. **3** (*tr*; *coll*) to amuse or entertain. **4** (*tr*) to catch (a fish, esp. a trout) by rubbing it gently underneath so that it moves backwards into one's hands allowing one to put one's fingers into its gills. — *n* **1** an act of tickling. **2** a tingling or light prickling sensation. — **tickled pink** or **to death** (*coll*) very pleased or amused. [MidE *tikelen*]

ticklish *adj* **1** sensitive to tickling. **2** (of a problem, etc.) difficult to manage or deal with; needing careful handling. — *n* **ticklishness.**

tick-tack. See **tick**[1].

tidal. See **tide**.

tidbit *n* (esp. *NAm*) a titbit.

tiddler *n* (*Br coll*) **1** a small fish, esp. a stickleback or a minnow. **2** a small person or thing.

tiddly[1] *adj* **-ier**, **-iest** (*Br coll*) slightly drunk.

tiddly[2] *adj* **-ier**, **-iest** (*Br coll*) little.

tiddlywinks *n* (*sing*) a game in which players try to flick small flat plastic discs into a cup using larger discs.

tide *n* **1** the regular rise and fall in the level of a body of water, esp. the sea, caused by the pull of the sun and moon. **2** the level of the water, esp. the sea, as affected by this: *high tide*. **3** a sudden or marked trend: *the tide of public opinion*. **4** (usu. *in cmpds*) a time or season, esp. of some festival: *Whitsuntide*. — *v* (*intr*) to drift with or be carried on the tide. — *v* **tide (someone) over** (*tr*; *coll*) to help (someone) deal with a problem, difficult situation, etc. for a time. [OE *tid*]

tidal *adj* of, depending on or affected by tides. — *adv* **tidally**.

tidal wave *n* **1** (*tech*) an enormous wave driven by the forces producing the tides. **2** (not *tech*; properly called a **tsunami**) an enormous wave caused by movement of the sea floor, travelling very quickly and causing great destruction if it touches land.

tidemark *n* **1** a mark showing the highest level that the tide has reached or usu. reaches. **2** (esp. *Br coll*) a mark left on a bath which shows how high it was filled. **3** (esp. *Br coll*) a dirty mark on the skin which shows the limit of washing.

tideway *n* a channel in which a tide runs, esp. that part of a river which has a tide.

tidings *n* (*pl*) news. [OE *tidung*]

tidy *adj* **-ier**, **-iest** **1** neat and in good order. **2** methodical. **3** (*coll*) large; considerable. — *v* (*tr* & *intr*; **away**, **up**) to make neat; to put (things) away or arrange (them) neatly. — *adv* **tidily**. — *n* **tidiness**. [MidE, seasonable]

tie *v* ***tying*** **1** (*tr*) to fasten with a string, ribbon, rope, etc. **2** (*tr*) to make (string, ribbon, etc.) into a bow or knot, or to make a bow or knot in. **3** (*intr*) to be fastened with a knot, string, ribbon, etc.: *a dress that ties at the back*. **4** (*intr*; **with**) to have the same score or final position as another competitor or entrant (in a game, contest, etc.). **5** (*tr*; **down**) to limit or restrict the way (someone) leads his or her life: *be tied down by family responsibilities*. **6** (*tr*; *mus*) to mark (notes of the same pitch) with a curved line showing that they are to be played as a continuous sound rather than individually. **7** (*tr*; *mus*) to play (notes of the same pitch) in this way. — *n* **1** a narrow strip of material worn, esp. by men, round the neck under a shirt collar and tied in a knot or bow at the front. **2** a strip of ribbon, rope, cord, chain, etc. for binding and fastening. **3** something that limits or restricts one's freedom. **4** a link or bond: *ties of friendship*. **5** (a match, competition, etc. in which the result is) an equal final score or position for each team or competitor. **6** (*Br*) a game or match to be played, esp. in a knockout competition. **7** a rod or beam holding parts of a structure together. **8** (*mus*) a curved line above two or more notes of the same pitch showing that they are to be played as a continuous sound rather than individually. **9** (*NAm*) a railway sleeper. — *v* **tie down** (*tr*) to bind (e.g. to a decision). — *v* **tie in** (*tr & intr*; **with**) to be in or be brought into connection; to correspond or be made to correspond. — *v* **tie up 1** (*tr*) to attach and fasten securely with string, esp. to make into a parcel with string. **2** (*tr & intr*; **with**) to be in or be brought into connection; to correspond or be made to correspond. **3** (*tr & intr*) to moor or dock. **4** (*tr*) to invest (money, funds, etc.) so that it cannot be used for other purposes. **5** (*tr*) to keep busy. **6** to block or restrict progress, movement or operation. [OE *tiegan*]

tie beam *n* a horizontal beam connecting the lower ends of rafters so that they do not move apart.

tie-break or **tie-breaker** *n* an extra game, series of games, or question that decides which of the competitors or teams is to win a match which has ended in a draw.

tied cottage *n* (*Br*) a cottage on an employer's land which is rented out to employees.

tied house *n* (*Br*) a public house which may only sell the beer of a particular brewery.

tie-dyeing *n* a way of dyeing fabrics to produce patterns, in which parts of the fabric are tied tightly to stop them absorbing the dye. — *adj* **tie-dyed**.

tie-in *n* **1** a connection or link. **2** something which is presented at the same time as something else, esp. a book which is published to coincide with a film or television programme.

tie-pin or **-clip** *n* an ornamental clasp fixed to a tie to hold it in place.

tier *n* any series of levels placed one above the other, e.g. of seats in a theatre. — *v* (*tr*) to place in tiers. [OFr *tire*, sequence]

tiercel. See **tercel**.

tiff *n* a slight, petty quarrel. — *v* (*intr*) to have a tiff; to squabble.

tiffin *n* (*old*) a light meal taken in the middle of the morning, esp. by members of the British Raj in India. [From obsolete *tiff*, to sip]

tig, ***-gg-***. Same as **tag**^{2}.

tiger *n* **1** a very large wild cat with a striped tawny coat, found in Asia. **2** the male of this species. **3** a fierce, cruel person. — *adj* **tigerish**. ◇ See also **tigress**. [Gr *tigris*]

tiger lily *n* a tall lily with black- or purple-spotted orange flowers.

tiger moth *n* any of several moths with long striped and spotted wings.

tight *adj* **1** fitting very or too closely. **2** stretched so as not to be loose; tense; taut. **3** fixed or held firmly in place: *a tight knot*. **4** (usu. *in cmpds*) made so as to not let air, water, etc. pass in or out: *watertight*. **5** difficult or posing problems: *in a tight spot*. **6** strictly and carefully controlled: *keep a tight rein on one's emotions*. **7** (of a contest or match) closely or evenly fought. **8** (of a schedule, timetable, etc.) not allowing much time. **9** (*coll*) mean; miserly. **10** (*coll*) drunk. **11** (of money or some commodity) in short supply; difficult to obtain. — *adv* tightly; soundly; completely. — *adv* **tightly**. — *n* **tightness**. [Norse *thettr*]

tighten *v* ***-n-*** (*tr & intr*) to make or become tight or tighter.

tight-fisted *adj* mean and ungenerous with money.

tight-knit *adj* closely organised or united.

tight-lipped *adj* with the lips firmly closed in determination to say or reveal nothing.

tightrope *n* **1** a tightly-stretched rope or wire on which acrobats balance. **2** a difficult situation which requires careful, fair handling if a potential disaster is to be avoided.

tights *n* (*pl*) a close-fitting usu. nylon or woollen garment covering the feet, legs and body to the waist, worn by women, dancers, acrobats, etc.

tigress *n* **1** a female tiger. **2** a fierce or passionate woman. **[tiger]**

tike. Same as **tyke**.

tikka *adj* (in Indian cookery, of meat) marinated in yogurt and spices and cooked in a clay oven. [Hindi]

tilde *n* a mark (˜) placed over *n* in Spanish to show that it is pronounced *ny* and over *a* and *o* in Portuguese to show they are nasalised. [Span]

tile *n* **1** a flat, thin slab of fired clay, or a similar one of cork or linoleum, used to cover roofs, floors, walls, etc. **2** a tube-shaped piece of clay used for building drains. **3** a small, flat, rectangular piece used in some games. — *v* (*tr*) to cover with tiles. — **on the tiles** having a wild time socially, usu. including a lot of drinking and dancing. — *n* **tiler**. [OE *tigele*, from Lat *tegula*]

tiling *n* **1** tiles as a group. **2** a tiled area. **3** the act of covering a surface with tiles.

till[1] *prep* up to the time of: *wait till tomorrow*. — *conj* up to the time when: *Go on till you reach the station*. ◇ See also **until**. [OE *til*]

till[2] *n* a container or drawer in which money taken from customers is put, now usu. part of a cash register. [MidE *tylle*, to draw]

till[3] *v* (*tr*) to prepare and cultivate (land) for growing of crops. — *adj* **tillable**. — *n* **tiller**. [OE *tilian*, to aim at]

tillage *n* **1** the preparing and cultivating of land for crops. **2** land which has been tilled.

tiller[1] *n* the lever used to turn the rudder of a boat. [OFr *telier*, weaver's beam]

tiller[2] *n* **1** a sapling. **2** a shoot growing from the bottom of the original stalk. **3** a sucker. [OE *telgor*, twig]

tilt *v* **1** (*tr* & *intr*) to (cause to) slope; to be or put in a slanting position. **2** (*intr* with **at**) to charge at or attack. **3** (*intr*; **with**) to fight on horseback with a lance; to joust. **4** (*tr*; **at**) to point (a lance) or attack with (a lance) as if in a joust. **5** (*tr*) to forge (steel, etc.) using a tilt-hammer. — *n* **1** a slant; a sloping position or angle. **2** an act of tilting. **3** a joust. **4** a thrust, charge or attack with a lance during a joust. **5** an attack, disagreement or contest. — **at full tilt** at full speed or with full force. [OE *tealt*, tottering]

tilt-hammer *n* a heavy pivoted hammer lifted by a cam, used in forging.

tilth *n* **1** the tilling and cultivating of land. **2** the condition of land that has been tilled and cultivated. [OE]

timber *n* **1** wood, esp. prepared for building or carpentry. **2** trees suitable for this; forest- or woodland. **3** a wooden beam in the framework of esp. a ship or house. — *interj* used to warn that a tree has been cut and is going to fall. — *v* **-r-** (*tr*) **1** to provide timber or beams for. **2** to cover in timber. [OE]

timbered *adj* **1** built completely or partly of wood. **2** (of land) covered with trees; wooded.

timber line *n* (on mountains) the line or level above which trees do not grow.

timbre *n* the distinctive quality of the tone produced by a musical instrument or voice, as opposed to pitch and loudness. [OFr, bell]

timbrel *n* a small tambourine. [OFr *timbre*, bell]

time *n* **1** the continuous passing and succession of minutes, days, years, etc. **2** a particular point in time expressed in hours and minutes, or days, months and years, and as can be read from a clock or watch or told by a calendar. **3** any system for reckoning or expressing time: *British Summer Time*. **4** (often in *pl*) a point or period which is marked by some event or some particular characteristic: *at the time of her marriage*; *Edwardian times*. **5** the period required or available for, suitable for or spent doing some particular activity. **6** an unspecified interval or period: *stayed there for a time*. **7** one of a number or series of occasions or repeated actions: *been to Spain three times*. **8** (in *pl*) expressing multiplication: *Three times two is six*. **9** a period or occasion, esp. a personal one, characterised by some quality or experience: *a good time*; *hard times*. **10** a particular period being considered, esp. the present. **11** (*coll*) a prison sentence: *do time*. **12** an apprenticeship. **13** the point at which something ends, e.g. a section of a game. **14** (*Br*) the time when a public house must close. **15** the moment at which childbirth or death is expected. **16** the hours and days that one spends at work. **17** a rate of pay for work: *double time*. **18** (*mus*) any of several different rhythms and speeds: *polka time*. **19** (*mus*) the speed at which a piece of music is to be played. — *adj* that can be set to function at a particular moment or during a particular period: *a time switch on a heating system*. — *v* **1** (*tr*) to measure the time taken by (an event, journey, etc.). **2** (*tr*) to arrange, set or choose the time for. **3** (*tr* & *intr*) to keep or beat, or cause to keep or beat, time (with). — **against time** with as much speed as possible because of the need or wish to finish by a certain time. — **ahead of time** earlier than expected or necessary. — **all in good time** in due course; soon enough. — **all the time** continually. — **at times** occasionally; sometimes. — **behind time** late. — **behind the times** out-of-date; old-fashioned. — **for the time being** meanwhile; for the moment. — **from time to time** occasionally; sometimes. — **have no time for** to have no interest in or patience with; to despise. — **have the time of one's life** to enjoy oneself very much. — **in good time** early. — **in no time** very quickly. — **in one's own time 1** in one's spare time when not at work. **2** at the speed one prefers. — **in time 1** early enough. **2** (**with**) at the same speed or rhythm (as). — **kill time** to pass time aimlessly while waiting for some future event. — **make good time** to travel as quickly as, or more quickly than, one had expected or hoped. — **no time (at all)** (*coll*) a very short time. — **on time** at the right time; not late. — **pass the time of day (with)** to exchange greetings and have a brief, casual conversation (with). — **take one's time** not to hurry; to work as slowly as one wishes. — **time and (time) again** again and again; repeatedly. — **time out**

of mind for longer than anyone can remember. [OE *tima*]
time-and-motion study *n* a study of the way work is done in a factory, company, etc., with a view to increasing efficiency.
time bomb *n* a bomb that has been set to explode at a particular time.
time capsule *n* a box containing objects chosen as typical of the current age, buried or otherwise preserved for discovery in the future.
time clock *n* an apparatus with a clock which stamps on cards the time of arrival and departure of e.g. factory workers.
time exposure *n* a photograph taken by exposing the film to the light for a relatively long period of time, usu. a few seconds.
time-honoured *adj* respected and upheld because of being a custom or tradition.
timekeeper *n* **1** a person who records the time, e.g. that worked by employees or taken by a competitor in a game. **2** a clock or watch, esp. thought of in terms of its accuracy: *a good timekeeper*. **3** an employee thought of in turns of punctuality. — *n* **timekeeping**.
time lag *n* the interval or delay between connected events or phenomena.
timeless *adj* **1** not belonging to or typical of any particular time or date. **2** unaffected by time; ageless; eternal. — *adv* **timelessly**. — *n* **timelessness**.
time limit *n* a fixed length of time during which something must be done and finished.
timely *adj* coming at the right or a suitable moment. — *n* **timeliness**.
time out *n* (esp. *NAm*) a brief pause or period of rest, esp. in a game. — **take time out (from)** to take a break from some activity, e.g. work.
timepiece *n* an instrument for keeping time, esp. one which is larger than a watch but which does not chime.
timer *n* **1** a device like a clock which switches an appliance on or off at preset times. **2** a person or instrument that records the time taken by someone or something.
time-served *adj* having completed an apprenticeship; fully trained.
timeserver *n* a person who changes his or her behaviour or opinions to fit those held by people in general or by someone in authority.
time-sharing *n* **1** a scheme whereby a person buys the right to use a holiday home for the same specified period within the year for an agreed number of years. **2** a system which allows many users with individual terminals to use a single computer at the same time.
time signal *n* a signal, esp. broadcast on the radio, which gives the exact time.
time signature *n* (*mus*) a sign consisting of two numbers one above the other (the lower one indicating the value of the note used as the basic beat and the upper one the number of these to the bar), placed after the key signature at the beginning of a piece of music to show the rhythm it is to be played in, or in the middle of a piece where the rhythm changes.
timetable *n* **1** a list of the departure and arrival times of trains, coaches, buses, etc. **2** a plan showing the order of events, esp. of classes in a school. — *v* (*tr*) to arrange or include in a timetable; to schedule or plan.
timeworn *adj* worn through long use; old.
time zone *n* one of 24 longitudinal bands dividing the earth, each of which has a common standard time.
timing *n* the regulating and co-ordinating of actions and events to achieve the best possible effect, esp. the regulating of the speed of dialogue, action, and interaction between characters in a play, film, etc.

timid *adj* easily frightened or alarmed; nervous; shy. — *n* **timidity** or **timidness**. — *adv* **timidly**. [Lat *timidus*]

timorous *adj* very timid; frightened. — *adv* **timorously**. — *n* **timorousness**. [Lat *timere*, to fear]

timpani or **tympani** *n* (*pl*) a set of two or three kettledrums. — *n* **timpanist** or **tympanist**. [Ital]

tin *n* **1** a soft, silvery-white metallic element (symbol **Sn**), which resists corrosion and is used in alloys and to form tin plate. **2** an airtight metal container, often made of tin plate, for storing food. **3** any of several containers of different shapes and sizes made usu. of tin or aluminium and in which food is cooked. **4** (also **tinful, *-fuls***) the amount a tin will hold. **5** a strip of tin along the bottom of the front wall of a squash court. **6** (*Br slang*) money. — *adj* made of tin. — *v* ***-nn-*** (*tr*) **1** to pack (food) in tins; to can. **2** to cover or coat with tin. — *adj* **tinned**. [OE]
tinfoil *n* tin, aluminium or other metal in the form of very thin, paper-like sheets, used esp. for wrapping food.
tin god *n* **1** a self-important, pompous person. **2** a person or thing held in excessively or unjustifiably high esteem.
tin hat *n* (*slang*) a military steel helmet.
tinny *adj* ***-ier, -iest*** **1** of or like tin, esp. in appearance or taste. **2** not solid and durable; flimsy; shoddy. **3** (of sound) thin and high-pitched. — *adv* **tinnily**. — *n* **tinniness**.
tin-opener *n* any of several tools for opening tins of food.
tin plate *n* thin sheet iron or steel coated with tin.
tinpot *adj* (*Br coll*) cheap; of poor quality.
tinsmith *n* a worker in tin and tin plate.

tincture *n* **1** a slight flavour, trace or addition. **2** a slight trace of colour; hue; tinge. **3** a solution of a drug in alcohol for medicinal use. — *v* (*tr*) to give a trace of a colour, flavour, etc. to. [Lat *tinctura*, dyeing]

tinder *n* dry material, esp. wood, which is easily set alight and can be used as kindling. [OE *tynder*]

tinder-box *n* **1** (*hist*) a box containing tinder, a flint and steel for striking a spark to light a fire. **2** a volatile and potentially dangerous situation.

tine *n* a slender prong or tooth, e.g. of a comb, fork or antler. [OE *tind*]

ting *n* a high, metallic tinkling sound such as that made by a small bell. [Imit.]

ting-a-ling *n* a ringing or tinkling.

tinge *n* **1** a trace or slight amount of colour. **2** a trace or hint of (e.g. a quality or feeling). — *v* (*tr*) **1** to give a slight colour to. **2** to give a trace or hint of a feeling, quality, etc. to. [Lat *tingere*]

tingle *v* (*tr* & *intr*) to (cause to) feel a prickling or slightly stinging sensation, as with cold or embarrassment. — *n* a prickling or slightly stinging sensation. — *adj* **tingling** or **tingly**, ***-ier***, ***-iest***. [MidE *tinglen*, a variant of *tinklen*, to tinkle]

tinker *n* **1** a travelling mender of pots, pans and other household utensils. **2** (esp. *Scot* & *Irish*) a gypsy. **3** (*coll*) a mischievous or impish person, esp. a child. — *v* ***-r-*** (*intr*) **1** (**at, about, with, around**) to work in an unskilled way, meddle or fiddle with machinery, etc., esp. to try to improve it. **2** to work as a tinker. [MidE *tinkere*, worker in tin]

tinkle *v* **1** (*tr* & *intr*) to (cause to) make a sound of or like the ringing or jingling of small bells. **2** (*intr*; *coll*) to urinate. — *n* **1** a ringing or jingling sound. **2** (*coll*) a telephone call. **3** (*coll*) an act of urinating. — *adj* **tinkly**. [MidE *tinken*, to click or tink]

tinny. See **tin**.

tinsel *n* **1** a long strip of glittering coloured metal or plastic threads used as a decoration esp. at Christmas. **2** anything which is cheap and showy. — *adj* of or like tinsel, esp. in being cheap and showy. — *adj* **tinselly**. [OFr *estincele*, spark]

tint *n* **1** a variety or (usu. slightly) different shade of a colour. **2** a variety of a colour, esp. one made softer by adding white. **3** a pale or faint colour used as a background for printing. **4** shading produced by engraving parallel lines close together. **5** a hair dye. — *v* (*tr*) to give a tint to; to colour slightly. [Lat *tingere*, to colour]

tintinnabulation *n* a ringing of bells. [Lat *tintinnabulum*, bell]

tiny *adj* ***-ier***, ***-iest*** very small. — *n* **tininess**. [MidE *tine*]

tip[1] *n* **1** the usu. small pointed end of something. **2** a small piece forming an end or point: *a rubber tip on a walking-stick*. **3** a tea leaf-bud. — *v* ***-pp-*** (*tr*) **1** to put or form a tip on. **2** (**in**) to attach (a loose sheet) into a book. **3** to remove a tip from. — *adj* **tipped**. — **on the tip of one's tongue** about to be or almost said, but not able to be because not quite remembered. [MidE]

tip[2] *v* ***-pp-*** **1** (*tr* & *intr*; **up**) to (cause to) lean or slant. **2** (*tr*; **out**) to remove or empty (something) from its container, surface, etc. by overturning or upsetting that container or causing that surface to slant. **3** (*tr*; *Br*) to dump (rubbish). — *n* **1** a place for tipping rubbish, coal, etc. **2** (*coll*) a very untidy place. — *v* **tip over** (*tr* & *intr*) to knock or fall over; to overturn. [MidE *typen*, to overturn]

tip[3] *n* **1** a gift of money given to a servant, waiter, taxi driver, etc. in return for service done well. **2** a piece of useful information; a helpful hint or warning. **3** a piece of inside information which may lead to financial gain, such as the name of a horse likely to win a race, or a company whose shares are likely to become more valuable. — *v* ***-pp-*** (*tr*) to give a tip to. — *v* **tip off** (*tr*) to give a piece of useful or secret information, hint or warning to (*n* **tip-off**). [Perhaps from **tip**[4]]

tipster *n* a person who gives tips, esp. as to which horses to bet on.

tip[4] *n* a light blow or tap. — *v* ***-pp-*** (*tr*) to hit or strike lightly. [MidE]

tippet *n* **1** a shoulder-cape of fur or cloth. **2** a long band of cloth or fur worn as part of some official costumes, e.g. by the clergy over the surplice during morning and evening prayers. [**tip**[1]]

tipple (*coll*) *v* (*tr* & *intr*) to drink alcohol (often) in relatively small amounts. — *n* a person's favourite alcoholic drink. — *n* **tippler**.

tipstaff *n* ***-staffs*** or ***-staves*** **1** a metal-tipped staff which is a symbol of office. **2** a sheriff's officer. [**tip**[1] **+ staff**]

tipster. See **tip**[3].

tipsy *adj* ***-ier***, ***-iest*** (*coll*) slightly drunk. — *adv* **tipsily**. — *n* **tipsiness**. [**tip**[2]]

tiptoe *v* (*intr*) to walk quietly or stealthily on the tips of the toes. — *n* the tips of the toes. — *adv* on the tips of the toes. [**tip**[1] **+ toe**]

tiptop (*coll*) *adj* & *adv* excellent; first-class. — *n* the very best; the height of excellence. [**tip**[1] **+ top**[1]]

TIR *abbrev* for *Transports Internationaux Routiers* (Fr), International Road Transport, a continental haulage organisation.

tirade *n* a long angry speech, harangue or denunciation. [Fr]

tire[1] *v* **1** (*tr* & *intr*; **out**) to make or become physically or mentally weary and in need of rest. **2** (*tr*; **of**) to lose patience (with); to have had enough (of); to become bored (with). — *adj* **tiring**. [OE *teorian*]

tired *adj* **1** wearied; exhausted. **2** (**of**) no longer interested in; bored with. **3** lacking freshness and showing the effects of time and wear, esp. in being limp and grubby or hackneyed. — *adv* **tiredly**. — *n* **tiredness**.

tireless *adj* never becoming weary or exhausted. — *adv* **tirelessly**. — *n* **tirelessness**.

tiresome *adj* troublesome and irritating; annoying; tedious. — *adv* **tiresomely**. — *n* **tiresomeness**.

tire[2] (esp. *NAm*). Same as **tyre**.

tiro or **tyro** *n* **-os** a beginner or novice. [Lat, recruit]

'tis (*archaic* or *poetic*) it is.

tissue *n* **1** a group of cells with a similar structure and particular function in an animal or plant: *muscle tissue*. **2** a piece of thin, soft, disposable paper used as a handkerchief or as toilet paper. **3** (in full **tissue paper**) fine, thin, soft paper, used e.g. for protecting fragile objects. **4** fine, thin, delicate woven fabric. **5** an interwoven mass or collection: *a tissue of lies*. [OFr *tissu*, woven cloth]

tit[1] *n* any of several small agile songbirds. [MidE *tite*]

tit[2]: **tit for tat** blow for blow; repayment of injury with injury.

tit[3] *n* **1** (*slang*) a teat. **2** (*vulg slang*) a woman's breast. [OE *titt*]

titan *n* a person or thing of very great strength, size, intellect or importance. [Gr *Titan*, in Greek mythology one of a family of gods descended from Uranus and Gaea]

titanic *adj* having great strength or size; colossal; gigantic.

titanium *n* a white metallic element (symbol **Ti**) used to make strong, light alloys which resist corrosion. [**titan**]

titbit *n* a choice or small tasty morsel. e.g. of food or gossip. [**tide** (sense **4**) + **bit**[1]]

titfer *n* (*slang*) a hat. [Shortened from rhyming slang *tit for tat* (see **tit**[2])]

tithe *n* **1** (often in *pl*; *hist*) a tenth part of a person's annual income or produce, paid as a tax to support the church or clergy in a parish. **2** a tenth part. — *v* **1** (*tr*) to demand a tithe or tithes from. **2** (*intr*) to pay a tithe or tithes. — *adj* **tithable**. [OE *teotha*, tithe, tenth]

Titian *n* & *adj* (of, having or being) a bright reddish-gold colour. [*Titian* (*Tiziano* Vecellio, c. 1490–1576), the Venetian painter who used this colour]

titillate *v* (*tr*) **1** to excite gently, esp. in a sexual way. **2** to tickle. — *adj* **titillating**. — *n* **titillation**. [Lat *titillare*]

titivate *v* (*tr* & *intr*; *coll*) to smarten up or put the finishing touches (to). — *n* **titivation**. [Earlier *tidivate*, from **tidy** + *-vate* from words such as *elevate* and *cultivate*]

title *n* **1** the distinguishing name of a book, play, work of art, piece of music, etc. **2** an often descriptive heading, e.g. of a chapter in a book or a legal document. **3** a word of address used before a person's name to show acquired or inherited rank, an honour, occupation or attainment. **4** a title page. **5** (often in *pl*) written material on film giving credits, dialogue, etc. **6** (*legal*) a right to the possession or ownership of property. **7** (*sport*) a championship. **8** a book or publication. **9** a book or publication as distinct from a copy and as listed in a catalogue. — *v* (*tr*) to give a title to. [Lat *titulus*]

titled *adj* having a title, esp. one that shows noble rank.

title deed *n* a document proving legal ownership.

title page *n* the page at the beginning of a book which gives the name and address of the publisher, the title, author, and cataloguing information, etc.

title role *n* the role of the character in a play or film from which that play or film takes its name, e.g. *King Lear*.

titmouse *n* **-mice**. Same as **tit**[1]. [MidE *titemose*]

titrate *v* (*tr*; *chem*) to measure (a constituent of a solution) by titration. [Fr *titre*, title, qualification]

titration *n* (*chem*) measurement of the amount of one constituent in a solution by finding how much of a second substance of known strength is required to complete a chemical reaction.

titter (*coll*) *v* **-r-** (*intr*) to giggle or snigger. — *n* a giggle or snigger.

tittle *n* **1** a small written or printed sign, mark or dot. **2** a very small particle. [Lat *titulus*, title]

tittle-tattle *n* idle or petty gossip or chatter. — *v* (*intr*) to gossip or chatter idly.

titty *n* **-ies** (a child's word for) **tit**[3].

titular *adj* **1** having the title of an office or position but none of the authority or duties. **2** of, being or having a title. — *adv* **titularly**. [Lat *titulus*, title]

tizzy *n* **-ies** (*coll*) a nervous, highly excited or confused state.

Tl *symbol* (*chem*) thallium.

Tm *symbol* (*chem*) thulium.

TN *abbrev* Tennessee.

TNT *abbrev* trinitrotoluene, a highly explosive substance.

to *prep* **1** towards; in the direction of; with the destination of. **2** used to express as a resulting condition, aim or purpose: *turn to stone*; *boil the fruit to a pulp*; *made to order*; *to my surprise*. **3** as far as; until: *a lie from beginning to end*; *five miles from the house to the station*; *bear the scars of the attack to this day*. **4** used to introduce the indirect object of a verb: *He sent it to us*. **5** used to express addition: *add one to ten*. **6** used to express attachment, connection, contact or possession: *put his ear to the door*; *the key to the lock*. **7** before the hour of: *ten minutes to three*. **8** used to express response or reaction to a situation, event, etc.: *rise to the occasion*; *dance to the music*. **9** used to express comparison or proportion: *win by two goals to one*; *second to none*. **10** used before an infinitive or instead of a complete infinitive: *He asked her to stay but she didn't want to*. — *adv* **1** in or into a nearly closed position: *pulled the window to*. **2** back into consciousness: *He came to a few minutes later*. **3** near at hand. **4** in the direction required. — **to and fro** backwards and forwards. —

toing and froing movement backwards and forwards in an agitated way. [OE]

toad *n* **1** a tailless leaping amphibian with a dry, warty skin, related to the frog but larger and living more on land. **2** an obnoxious, repellent person. [OE *tade*]

toadflax *n* a plant with flax-like leaves and yellow flowers.

toad-in-the-hole *n* (*Br*) sausages cooked in Yorkshire pudding batter.

toadstool *n* any of several kinds of fungi, often poisonous, with round, umbrella-like tops. ◇ See also **mushroom**.

toady *n* **-ies** a person who flatters someone else, does everything he or she wants and hangs on his or her every word; a sycophant. — *v* **-ies, -ied** (*tr & intr*; **to**) to flatter and behave with slavish obedience (to). — *adj* **toadyish**. — *n* **toadyism**.

toast *v* **1** (*tr*) to make (esp. bread) brown by exposing it to direct heat, e.g. under a grill. **2** (*intr*) (of esp. bread) to become brown in this way. **3** (*tr & intr*) to make or become warm by being exposed to heat, e.g. a fire. **4** (*tr*) to drink ceremonially in honour of or to the health or future success of. — *n* **1** bread which has been browned by being exposed to direct heat, e.g. under a grill. **2** (a call for) an act of drinking to a person's honour, health or future success. **3** a person whose honour, health or future success is drunk to. **4** a very admired person or thing: *Her singing is the toast of the festival.* **5** the wish conveyed when drinking to someone's honour, etc. — *adj* **toasted**. [Lat *tostus*, roasted; sense **4** of the verb and senses **2**, **3**, **4** and **5** of the noun reflect the idea that a woman's name (i.e. as the person whose health is being drunk to) would flavour the wine like spiced toast]

toaster *n* an electric machine for toasting bread.

toasting-fork *n* a fork with a long handle, used to toast bread in front of a fire.

toastmaster or **toastmistress** *n* a man or woman who announces the toasts to be drunk at a ceremonial dinner.

toast rack *n* a small rack in which slices of toast can be served.

tobacco *n* **-os** or **-oes 1** any of several American plants with large leaves. **2** the narcotic leaves which are dried and rubbed and can be smoked in a pipe, made into cigarettes, etc. for smoking, a hard block for chewing, or snuff. [Span *tabaco*]

tobacconist *n* a person or shop that sells tobacco, cigarettes, cigars, pipes, etc.

-to-be *in cmpds* future; soon to become: *mother-to-be*.

toboggan *n* a long, light sledge which curves up at the front, used for riding over snow and ice. — *v* (*intr*) to ride on a toboggan. — *n* **tobogganing**. — *n* **tobogganist** or **tobogganer**. [Micmac (N American Indian language) *topagan*]

toby jug *n* a small jug or mug for drinking beer from, in the form of a stout old man wearing a three-cornered hat and smoking a pipe. [From the name *Tobias*]

toccata *n* a piece of music for a keyboard instrument intended to show off the performer's skill and touch in a series of runs and chords before breaking into a fugue. [Ital, from *toccare*, to touch]

Toc H *n* a society formed after the First World War to promote Christian fellowship. [*Toc* (telegrapher's code for *T*) + *H*, from *T*albot *H*ouse in Belgium where it held its first meetings]

tocopherol *n* vitamin E. [Gr *tokos*, offspring + *pherein*, to bear, from its apparent necessity for reproduction]

tocsin *n* an alarm bell or warning signal. [Fr]

tod: **on one's tod** (*Br coll*) alone. [Rhyming slang *on one's Tod Sloan*, on one's own]

today *n* **1** this day. **2** the present time. — *adv* **1** on or during this day. **2** nowadays; at the present time. [OE *to dæg*]

toddle *v* (*intr*) **1** to walk with unsteady steps, as or like a young child. **2** (*coll*) to take a casual walk; to stroll or saunter. **3** (*coll*; **off**) to leave; to depart (for). — *n* **1** a toddling walk. **2** (*coll*) a casual walk or stroll. [**totter** + **waddle**]

toddler *n* a very young child who is just beginning or has just learnt to walk.

toddy *n* **-ies** a drink made of spirits, sugar, hot water, lemon juice and sometimes spices. [Hindi *tari*, from *tar*, palm]

to-do *n* ***to-dos*** (*coll*) a fuss, commotion or bustle.

toe *n* **1** any of the five finger-like parts at the end of the foot. **2** the front part of a shoe, sock, etc. covering the toes. **3** the corresponding part of an animal's foot. **4** the lower, often projecting end of e.g. a tool or area of land. — *v* (*tr*) **1** to kick, strike or touch with the toes. **2** to provide (e.g. a stocking, sock or shoe) with a toe. — **on one's toes** alert and ready for action. — **toe the line** (*coll*) to act according to the rules. — **tread on someone's toes** to offend or upset (someone). — **turn up one's toes** (*coll*) to die. [OE *ta*]

toe-cap *n* a piece of metal or leather covering the toe of a boot or shoe.

toe-hold *n* **1** a place to anchor one's toes, e.g. when climbing. **2** a small initial or beginning position.

toenail *n* a nail covering a toe.

toerag *n* (*slang*) a despicable or contemptible person.

toff *n* (*Br slang*) an upper-class and usu. smartly dressed person. [From *tuft*, a titled undergraduate]

toffee *n* a sticky sweet which is usu. either chewy or hard, made from boiling sugar and butter, and sometimes nuts, etc.

toffee-apple *n* an apple covered with a thin layer of toffee on a stick.

toffee-nosed *adj* (*Br coll*) conceited; stuck-up.

tofu *n* a curd made from soya beans, with a creamy colour and bland flavour, used esp. in Japanese cooking. [Jap, from Chin *tou fu*, rotten beans]

tog[1] *n* (in *pl*) clothes. — *v* **-gg-** (*tr & intr*; **up**) to dress (oneself), esp. in one's best or warmest clothes. [MidE, from Lat *toga*, toga]

tog[2] *n* a unit for measuring the warmth of fabrics and clothes. [Perhaps from **tog**[1]]

toga *n* (*hist*) a loose outer garment worn draped round the body by a citizen of ancient Rome. — *adj* **togaed**. [Lat]

together *adv* **1** with someone or something else; in company: *travel together*. **2** at the same time: *all arrived together*. **3** so as to be in contact, joined or united. **4** by action with one or more other people: *managed to persuade him together*. **5** in or into one place: *gather together*. **6** continuously: *chatting on the phone for hours together*. **7** (*coll*) into a proper or suitable order or state of being organised: *get things together*. — *adj* (*coll*) well organised; competent. — **together with** in company with; in addition to. [OE *to gæthere*]

togetherness *n* a feeling of closeness, mutual sympathy and understanding and of belonging together.

toggle *n* **1** a fastening, e.g. for garments, consisting of a small bar of wood, plastic, etc. which will pass one way only through a loop of material, rope, etc. **2** a pin, bar or crosspiece placed through a link in a chain, loop in a rope, etc. to prevent the chain, rope, etc. from slipping. **3** (*comput*) a keyboard command which turns a particular feature (e.g. bold type or read-only mode) on or off. — *v* **1** (*tr*) to provide or fasten with a toggle. **2** (*tr*; **on, off**; *comput*) to turn (a particular feature, e.g. bold type or read-only mode) on or off using a keyboard command. **3** (*intr*; **between**; *comput*) to move between (different features, modes, files, etc.) using a keyboard command.

toggle switch *n* an electric switch with a small projecting lever which can be put into either of two positions (usu. up or down) representing a positive and negative state, e.g. on and off, used in many electricity switches.

toil[1] *v* (*intr*) **1** (**at**) to work long and hard; to labour. **2** to make progress or move forwards with great difficulty or effort. — *n* long, hard work. [OFr *toiler*, to contend]

toilsome *adj* involving long, hard work.

toilworn *adj* wearied by hard work.

toil[2] *n* (usu. in *pl*) a trap or snare. [Fr *toile*, cloth, from Lat *tela*, web]

toilet *n* **1** a bowl-like receptacle for the body's waste matter, with a water supply for washing this into a drain. **2** a room containing such a receptacle. **3** (also **toilette**) the act of washing, dressing and arranging one's hair. [Fr *toilette*, cloth]

toilet paper or **tissue** *n* thin absorbent paper used for cleaning the body after urination and defecation.

toilet roll *n* a roll of toilet paper.

toiletry *n* **-ies** (usu. in *pl*) any article or cosmetic used when washing, arranging the hair, and making up.

toilet water *n* a light perfume containing a lot of alcohol.

Tokay *n* a sweet, heavy, aromatic wine made at *Tokay* in Hungary.

token *n* **1** a mark, sign or distinctive feature. **2** anything serving as a reminder or souvenir; a keepsake. **3** a voucher worth a stated amount of money which can be exchanged for goods of the same value. **4** a small coin-like piece of metal or plastic which is used instead of money, e.g. in slot machines. — *adj* done or given as a token and therefore of no real value. — **by the same token** also; in addition; for the same reason. [OE *tacen*]

tokenism *n* the principle or practice of doing very little of something in pretence that one is committed to it, e.g. of employing one black person in order to seem to be committed to equal opportunities for all races.

tolbooth. See **toll**[2].

told. See **tell**.

tolerate *v* (*tr*) **1** to bear or endure (pain or hardship); to put up with. **2** to be able to resist the effects of (a drug). **3** to treat fairly and accept (a person with different religious, political, etc. beliefs or opinions). **4** to allow to be done or exist. [Lat *tolerare*]

tolerable *adj* **1** able to be borne or endured. **2** fairly good. — *n* **tolerability** or **tolerableness**. — *adv* **tolerably**.

tolerance *n* **1** the ability to be fair towards and accepting of other people's religious, political, etc. beliefs or opinions. **2** the ability to resist or endure pain or hardship. **3** the ability to resist or adapt to the effects of a drug so that the drug loses its effectiveness. **4** the permitted range of variation in values when measuring. — *adj* **tolerant**. — *adv* **tolerantly**.

toleration *n* **1** the act of tolerating. **2** the practice of allowing people to practise religions which are different to the established religion of the country.

toll[1] *v* **1** (*tr & intr*) to ring (a bell) with slow, measured strokes. **2** (*tr*) (of a bell) to announce, signal or summon by ringing with slow, measured strokes. — *n* the act or sound of tolling. [MidE *tollen*, to entice, lure]

toll[2] *n* **1** a fee or tax paid for the use of some bridges and roads. **2** the cost in damage, injury or lives of some disaster. [OE]

tolbooth or **tollbooth** *n* **1** an office where tolls are or were collected. **2** (*old Scot*) a town hall. **3** (*Scot*) a prison.

tollgate *n* a gate or barrier across a road or bridge which is not lifted until travellers have paid the toll.

tom *n* a male of various animals, esp. (in full **tomcat**) a male cat. — **Tom, Dick and Harry** anybody at all; people in general. [Abbrev. of the name *Thomas*]

tomahawk *n* a small axe used as a weapon by N American Indians. [Algonquian (N American Indian language group) *tamahaac*]

tomato *n* **-oes 1** a round or oval fleshy, juicy fruit, usu. red or yellow in colour, eaten as a vegetable e.g. in salads. **2** the plant bearing this fruit. [Aztec *tomatl*]

tomb *n* **1** a chamber or vault for a dead body, either below or above ground, and often serving as a monument; a grave. **2** a hole cut in the earth or rock for a dead body. **3** (*poetic*; with **the**) death. [Gr *tymbos*]

tombstone *n* an ornamental stone placed over a grave, on which the dead person's name, etc. is engraved.

tombola *n* a lottery in which winning tickets are drawn from a revolving drum. [Ital *tombolare*, to tumble]

tomboy *n* a girl who likes rough and adventurous games and activities. [**tom** + **boy**]

tomcat. See **tom**.

tome *n* a large, heavy and usu. learned book. [Gr *tomos*, slice]

tomfool *n* an absolute fool. — *adj* absolutely foolish. [MidE *Thome fole*, Tom the fool]

tomfoolery *n* **-ies** (a piece of) stupid or foolish behaviour; nonsense.

Tommy *n* **-ies** (*coll*) a private in the British army. [*Tommy* Atkins, the name used on specimens of official forms]

tommygun *n* a type of submachine gun. [J T *Thompson* (1860–1940), its American inventor]

tommy-rot *n* (*coll*) absolute nonsense.

tomorrow *n* **1** the day after today. **2** the future. — *adv* **1** on the day after today. **2** in the future. [OE *to morgen*]

tomtit *n* a tit, esp. a bluetit. [**tom** + **tit**[1]]

tom-tom *n* a usu. small-headed drum beaten with the hands. [Hindi *tam-tam*, imit.]

ton *n* **1** (*Br*; in full **long ton**) a unit of weight equal to 2240 lb (approximately 1016·05 kg). **2** (*NAm*; in full **short ton**) a unit of weight equal to 2000 lb (approximately 907·2 kg). **3** (in full **metric ton**; also **tonne**) a unit of weight equal to 1000 kg (approximately 2204·6 lb). **4** (in full **displacement ton**) a unit used to measure the amount of water a ship displaces, equal to 2240 lb or 35 cubic feet of seawater. **5** (in full **register ton**) a unit (orig. a *tun* of wine) used to measure a ship's internal capacity, equal to 100 cubic feet. **6** (in full **freight ton**) a unit for measuring the space taken up by cargo, equal to 40 cubic feet. **7** (usu. in *pl*; *coll*) a lot. **8** (*coll*) a speed, score, sum, etc. of one hundred. ◇ See also **tonnage**. [A variant of **tun**]

tonner *n* (*in cmpds* with a numeral) a ship, lorry, etc. that can carry the specified number of tons.

ton-up *adj* (*old slang*) (esp. of a motorcyclist) travelling or having travelled at more than 100 mph, esp. often and recklessly.

tone *n* **1** a musical or vocal sound with reference to its quality and pitch. **2** (*mus*) a sound having a definite pitch. **3** a quality or character of the voice expressing a particular feeling, mood, etc. **4** the general character or style of spoken or written expression. **5** (*mus*) the interval between, or equivalent to that between, the first two notes of the major scale. **6** high quality, style or character: *His coarse jokes lowered the tone of the meeting*. **7** the quality, tint or shade of a colour. **8** the harmony or general effect of colours. **9** firmness of the body, a bodily organ or muscle. — *v* **1** (*intr*; **in, with**) to fit in well or harmonise (with). **2** (*tr*) to give tone or the correct tone to. **3** (*intr*) to take on a tone or quality. — *v* **tone down** (*tr* & *intr*) to make or become softer or less harsh in tone, colour, force, etc. — *v* **tone up** (*tr* & *intr*) to make or become stronger, healthier, more forceful, etc. [Gr *tonos*, tension]

tonal *adj* of or relating to tone or tonality.

tonality *n* **-ies 1** (*mus*) the organisation of all of the notes and chords of a piece of music in relation to a single tonic. **2** the colour scheme and tones used in a painting.

tone-deaf *adj* unable to distinguish accurately between notes of different pitch. — *n* **tone-deafness**.

toneless *adj* without variation in sound, pitch, expression, etc. — *adv* **tonelessly**.

tone poem *n* a piece of music not divided into movements and based on a story or literary or descriptive theme.

tong *n* (also *cap*) a Chinese guild or secret society, esp. one responsible for organised crime and gang warfare. [S Chin dialect *tong*, meeting hall]

tongs *n* (*pl*) a tool consisting of two arms joined by a hinge or pivot, for holding and lifting objects. [OE *tang*]

tongue *n* **1** the fleshy, muscular organ attached to the floor of the mouth, used for eating, licking, tasting and (in people) speaking. **2** the tongue of some animals, e.g. the ox and sheep, used as food. **3** the ability to speak. **4** a particular language. **5** a particular manner of speaking: *a sharp tongue*. **6** (usu. in *pl*) speaking in wholly or partly unknown languages, esp. in Christian worship as a gift of the Holy Spirit: *speak in tongues*. **7** anything like a tongue in shape. **8** a narrow strip of land that reaches out into water. **9** the clapper in a bell. **10** a flap in the opening of a shoe or boot. **11** a projecting strip along the side of a board that fits into a groove in another. — *v* **1** (*tr*) to touch or lick with the tongue. **2** (*intr*; *mus*) to play a wind instrument by tonguing. **3** (*tr*; *mus*) to produce (notes) by means of tonguing. — **find one's tongue** to be able to speak again after a shock which has left one speechless. — **hold one's tongue** to say nothing; to keep quiet. — **lose one's tongue** to be left speechless with shock, horror, etc. — **(with one's) tongue in (one's) cheek** with ironic, insincere or humorous intention. [OE *tunge*]

tongue-tie *n* a speech impediment which is caused by an abnormally small fold of skin under the tongue not allowing full movement of the tongue.

tongue-tied *adj* **1** speechless, esp. because of shyness or embarrassment. **2** suffering from tongue-tie.

tongue-twister *n* a phrase or sentence that is difficult to say quickly, usu. because it contains a series of similar consonant sounds, e.g. *She sells sea shells on the sea shore.*

tonguing *n* (*mus*) a way of playing a wind instrument which allows individual notes to be articulated separately by the tongue opening and blocking the passage of air.

tonic *n* **1** a medicine that increases strength, energy and the general wellbeing of the body. **2** anything that is refreshing or invigorating. **3** (in full **tonic water**) a fizzy soft drink flavoured with quinine. **4** (*mus*) the first note of a scale, the note on which a key is based. — *adj* **1** increasing strength, energy and wellbeing. **2** invigorating. **3** (*mus*) of or being the tonic. **4** producing (esp. muscular) tension. [Gr *tonikos*]

tonic sol-fa *n* a way of teaching music which represents notes by syllables, with *doh* as the keynote for major keys and *lah* that for minor keys.

tonight *n* the night of this present day. — *adv* on or during the night of the present day. [OE *to niht*]

tonnage *n* **1** the space available in a ship for carrying cargo, measured in tons. **2** the total carrying capacity of a country's merchant shipping, measured in tons. **3** a duty or tax on ships based on their cargo-carrying capacity. **4** a duty on cargo by the ton. [Orig. a tax or duty levied on each *tun* of wine carried by a ship. ◇ See also **ton**]

tonne *n* (also **metric ton**) a unit of weight equal to 1000 kg (approximately 2204·6 lb). [Fr]

tonsil *n* either of two oval lumps of tissue on either side of the tongue at the back of the throat. [Lat *tonsillae* (*pl*)]

tonsillectomy *n* **-ies** a surgical operation to remove the tonsils. [**tonsil** + Gr *ektome*, a cutting out]

tonsillitis *n* inflammation of the tonsils. [**tonsil** + **-itis**]

tonsorial *adj* (often *humorous*) of a barber, barbering or hairdressing. [Lat *tondere*, to clip or shave]

tonsure *n* **1** a shaved patch on the crown of a monk's or priest's head. **2** the act of shaving the crown of a monk's or priest's head as part of the rite of entering a monastic order or the priesthood. — *v* (*tr*) to shave the head of, esp. as a tonsure. — *adj* **tonsured**. [Lat *tonsura*, from *tondere*, to clip or shave]

tontine *n* an annuity scheme in which several subscribers share a common fund, with their individual benefits increasing as members die until only one member is left alive and receives everything or until a specified date at which the proceeds will be shared amongst the survivors. [Lorenzo *Tonti* (c. 1653), the Italian-born Parisian banker who invented it]

too *adv* **1** to a greater extent or more than is required, desirable or suitable: *too many things to do*. **2** in addition; as well; also: *enjoy swimming and like cycling too*. **3** what is more; indeed: *She wants a new car, and her husband is buying her one, too!* [Stressed form of **to**]

took. See **take**.

tool *n* **1** an implement, esp. one used by hand, for cutting, digging, etc., such as a spade, hammer, etc. **2** the cutting part of a machine tool. **3** a thing used in or necessary to a particular trade or profession: *Books are the tools of a librarian's job*. **4** a person who is used or manipulated by another, esp. for selfish or dishonest reasons. **5** (*vulg slang*) a penis. — *v* **1** (*tr*) to work or engrave (e.g. stone or leather) with tools. **2** (*tr & intr*; **up**) to equip (e.g. a factory) or become equipped with the tools needed for production. **3** (*intr*; **along**, **around**, etc.; *coll*) to drive or ride, usu. casually. [OE *tol*]

toolmaker *n* a person who makes or repairs machine tools. — *n* **toolmaking**.

toot *n* a quick, sharp blast of a trumpet, whistle, horn, etc. — *v* (*tr & intr*) to sound or cause (a trumpet, horn, etc.) to sound with a quick, sharp blast. [Imit.]

tooth *n* ***teeth*** **1** any of the hard, bone-like, enamel-coated objects set in the jaws of most vertebrates and used for biting and chewing. **2** anything like a tooth in shape, arrangement or function, such as one of series of cogs on a wheel or points on a comb. **3** an appetite or liking, esp. for sweet foods: *a sweet tooth*. **4** (in *pl*) enough power or force to be effective. — *v* **1** (*tr*) to provide with teeth. **2** (*intr*) (of cogwheels) to interlock. — *adj* **toothless**. — **in the teeth of** against; in opposition to. — **long in the tooth** (*coll*) old — **set one's teeth on edge** to cause a sharp, stabbing pain in the teeth such as that caused by eating something very cold; to cause to wince; to irritate severely. — **take the teeth out of** to make harmless. — **tooth and nail** fiercely and with all one's strength. [OE *toth*]

toothache *n* a pain in or near a tooth.

toothbrush *n* a brush for cleaning the teeth.

toothpaste *n* a paste used to clean the teeth.

toothpick *n* a small sharp piece of wood, plastic, etc. for picking out food from between the teeth.

toothpowder *n* a powder used to clean the teeth.

toothsome *adj* appetising; delicious; attractive.

toothy *adj* **-ier**, **-iest** showing or having a lot of esp. large, prominent teeth. — *adv* **toothily**.

tootle *v* (*intr*) **1** to toot gently or continuously. **2** (**round**; *coll*) to go casually, esp. by car. — *n* **1** a tootling sound. **2** (*coll*) a trip or drive. [**toot**]

tootsie or **tootsy** *n* **-ies** (*coll*) **1** a foot. **2** a toe.

top[1] *n* **1** the highest part, point or level of anything. **2** (the person or thing having) the highest or most important rank or position: *top of the class.* **3** the upper edge or surface of something: *the table-top.* **4** a lid or piece for covering the top of something. **5** a garment for covering the upper half of esp. a woman's body. **6** the highest or loudest degree or pitch: *the top of one's voice.* **7** (in *pl* with **the**; *coll*) the very best person or thing. **8** (esp. in *pl*) the part of a root vegetable that is above the ground. **9** (*Br*) top gear. — *adj* of, at or being the highest or most important. — *v* **-pp-** (*tr*) **1** to cover or form the top of, esp. as a finishing or decorative touch: *top a cake with cream.* **2** to remove the top of. **3** to rise above or be better than; to surpass. **4** to reach the top of. **5** (*slang*) to kill. **6** (*golf*) to hit the upper half of (the ball). — **from top to toe** completely; from head to foot. — **on top of 1** in control of. **2** in addition to. **3** very close to. — **on top of the world** in the very best of spirits. — *v* **top off** (*tr*) to put a finishing or decorative touch to. — *v* **top out** (*tr*) to put the highest stone on (a building). — *v* **top up** (*tr*; **with**) **1** to refill (a glass, container, etc.) that has been partly emptied. **2** to refill the partly emptied glass, container, etc. of (someone): *Let me top you up with coffee.* **3** to provide money to bring (a grant, wage, money supply, etc.) to the required or desirable total. [OE]

top boot *n* a high boot with a band of different coloured leather round the top.

top brass *n* (*coll*) the highest-ranking (esp. military) officers or personnel.

topcoat *n* an overcoat.

top coat *n* a final coat of paint.

top dog *n* (*coll*) the most important or powerful person in a group.

top drawer *n* the highest level, esp. of society.

top-dressing *n* **1** manure or fertiliser spread over the surface of soil. **2** the spreading of manure or fertiliser on the surface of soil. — *v* **top-dress** (*tr*).

top-flight *adj* of the best or highest quality.

topgallant *n* & *adj* (the mast or sail) above the topmast and topsail.

top gear *n* (*Br*) the combination of gearwheels which allows a vehicle to travel at its fastest speeds.

top hat *n* a man's tall, cylindrical hat, often made of silk, worn as part of formal dress.

top-heavy *adj* **1** having the upper part too heavy for, or disproportionately large in comparison with, the lower. **2** (of a company, administration, etc.) having too many senior staff in proportion to junior staff.

top-knot *n* a knot of hair worn on top of the head.

topless *adj* **1** having no top. **2** (of a woman's garment) leaving the breasts exposed. **3** (of a woman) with her breasts exposed. **4** (of a place) where women go topless.

topmast *n* the second mast, usu. directly above the lower mast.

topmost *adj* being the very highest of all.

top-notch *adj* (*coll*) of the very best quality; superb.

topper *n* (*coll*) a top hat.

topping *n* something that forms a covering or garnish for food. — *adj* (*Br old coll*) excellent.

topsail *n* a square sail set across the topmast.

top-secret *adj* very secret, esp. officially classified so.

topside *n* **1** a lean cut of beef from the rump. **2** the side of a ship above the waterline. — *adj* & *adv* on deck.

topsoil *n* the upper layer of soil, turned over when ploughed.

topspin *n* a spin given to a ball by hitting it sharply on the upper half with a forward and upward stroke to make it travel higher, further or more quickly. ◇ See also **backspin, sidespin**.

top[2] *n* a wooden or metal toy which spins on a pointed base. — **sleep like a top** to sleep very soundly. [OE]

topaz *n* a hard, glassy, semi-precious stone, often yellow in colour. [Gr *topazos*]

tope[1] *v* (*intr*) to drink alcohol to excess. — *n* **toper**. [A variant of obsolete *top*, to drink]

tope[2] *n* a small shark found in European waters. [Norfolk dialect]

topi or **topee** *n* a helmet-like lightweight hat worn in hot countries as protection against the sun. [Hindi, hat]

topiary *n* **-ies 1** the art of cutting trees, bushes and hedges into ornamental shapes. **2** an example of this. — *adj* of or relating to topiary work. [Lat *topia*, landscape gardening]

topic *n* a subject or theme. [Gr *topos*, place]

topical *adj* **1** relating to matters of interest at the present time; dealing with current affairs. **2** relating to a particular place; local. **3** of a topic or topics. — *n* **topicality**. — *adv* **topically**.

topography *n* **-ies 1** (a description or map of) the natural and man-made features on the surface of land, such as rivers, mountains, valleys, bridges and railway lines. **2** the describing or mapping of such features. **3** the mapping or describing of the surface of any object or body. — *adj* **topographical**. — *adv* **topographically**. [Gr *topos*, place + *graphein*, to describe]

topology *n* the branch of geometry which studies those properties of a figure which do not change even when that figure is bent, stretched, etc. — *adj* **topological**. — *adv* **topologically**. [Gr *topos*, place + **-logy** (sense **1**)]

topple *v* (*tr* & *intr*) **1** (**over**) to cause to fall, fall, or make as if to fall as if top-heavy. **2** to overthrow or be overthrown. [**top**[1]]

topsy-turvy *adj* & *adv* **1** upside down. **2** in confusion. — *adv* **topsy-turvily**. — *n* **topsy-turviness**. [**top**[1] + obsolete *terve*, to turn over]

toque *n* a woman's small, close-fitting, brimless or nearly brimless hat. [Fr]

tor *n* a bare rocky hill. [OE *torr*]

Torah *n* (*Judaism*) **1** the Pentateuch. **2** the scroll on which this is written, used in a synagogue. **3** the whole body of Jewish literature and law, both written and oral, and including the Old Testament and Talmud. [Hebrew, instruction]

torc. See **torque**.

torch *n* **1** (*Br*) a small portable light powered by electric batteries. **2** a piece of wood or bundle of cloth, etc. used to give light. **3** any source of heat, light, illumination, enlightenment, etc. — **carry a torch for** to feel (esp. unrequited) love for. [OFr *torche*, from Lat *torquere*, to twist]

torchlight *n* the light of a torch or torches.

tore. See **tear**[2].

toreador *n* a bullfighter, esp. one on horseback. [Span]

torero *n* **-*os*** a bullfighter on foot. [Span]

torment *n* **1** very great pain, suffering or anxiety. **2** something that causes this. — *v* (*tr*) **1** to cause great pain, suffering or anxiety to. **2** to pester or harass (e.g. a child or animal). — *n* **tormentor**. [Lat *tormentum*]

torn. See **tear**[2].

tornado *n* **-*oes*** a violent destructive storm accompanied by whirlwinds. [Span *tronada*, thunderstorm]

torpedo *n* **-*os*** or **-*oes*** **1** a long, self-propelling, underwater missile which explodes on impact with its target (usu. a ship) and can be fired from submarines, ships and aircraft. **2** any of several rays found in warm seas with organs on the head which can give an electric shock. **3** (esp. *NAm*) a small container holding an explosive charge, used in warfare as e.g. a firework or fog-signal. — *v* **-*oes***, **-*oed*** (*tr*) **1** to attack with torpedos. **2** to wreck or destroy (e.g. a plan). [Lat, numbness, electric ray]

torpedo boat *n* a small, fast warship armed with torpedos.

torpid *adj* **1** sluggish and dull; lacking in energy. **2** unable to move or feel; numb. **3** (of a hibernating animal) dormant. — *n* **torpidity**. — *adv* **torpidly**. [Lat *torpidus*, from *torpere*, to be numb]

torpor *n* **1** drowsiness, sluggishness or apathy. **2** numbness. [Lat, from *torpere*, to be numb]

torque *n* **1** (also **torc**; *hist*) a necklace made of metal twisted into a band, worn by the ancient Britons and Gauls. **2** a force or series of forces causing or tending to cause rotation. **3** a measure of the turning effect of such a force or forces. [Lat *torquere*, to twist]

torr *n* a unit for measuring very low pressure, equal to 133·3 pascals. [E *Torricelli* (1608–47), the Italian mathematician who discovered the principle of the barometer]

torrent *n* **1** a great rushing stream or downpour of water, lava, etc. **2** a violent or strong flow, e.g. of questions, abuse, etc. — *adj* **torrential**. [Lat *torrens*, boiling]

torrid *adj* **1** (e.g. of the weather) so hot and dry as to scorch the land. **2** (of land) scorched and parched by extremely hot, dry weather. **3** passionate; intensely emotional. [Lat *torridus*, from *torrere*, to parch]

torsion *n* **1** the act or process of twisting something by applying force to one end while the other is held firm or twisted in the opposite direction. **2** the state of being twisted in this way. — *adj* **torsional**. [Lat *torsio*, from *torquere*, to twist]

torso *n* **-*os*** **1** the main part of the human body, without the limbs and head. **2** a nude statue of this. [Ital, from Lat *thyrsos*, stalk]

tort *n* (*legal*) any wrongful act other than breach of contract for which an action for damages or compensation may be brought. [Lat *tortum*, wrong]

tortilla *n* a Mexican thin round maize cake cooked on a griddle and usu. eaten hot with a filling or topping of meat or cheese. [Span *torta*, cake]

tortoise *n* a slow-moving reptile with a hard, bony or leathery shell covering the trunk and into which the head and legs may be drawn, living in fresh water and esp. on land. [Lat *tortuca*]

tortoiseshell *n* **1** the brown and yellow mottled shell of a sea turtle, used in making combs, jewellery and decorative inlay in furniture. **2** a butterfly with mottled orange or red and brown or black wings. **3** a domestic cat with a mottled orange and brown coat. — *adj* made of or mottled like tortoiseshell.

tortuous *adj* **1** full of twists and turns. **2** not straightforward, esp. in being devious or involved. — *adv* **tortuously**. — *n* **tortuousness**. [Lat *tortuosus*, from *torquere*, to twist]

torture *n* **1** the infliction of severe pain or mental suffering, esp. as a punishment or as a means of persuading someone to give information. **2** (something causing) great physical or mental suffering. — *v* (*tr*) **1** to subject to torture. **2** to cause to experience great physical or mental suffering. **3** to force out of a natural state or position; to distort. — *adj* **torturous**. — *adv* **torturously**. [Lat *tortura*, torment]

Tory *n* **-*ies*** **1** a member or supporter of the British Conservative Party. **2** (*hist*) a member or supporter of a major English political party from the 17th to mid-19th century which favoured royal authority over that of Parliament, supported the established Church and was against political and social reform, superseded by the Conservative Party. ◇ See also **Whig**. **3** (*US hist*) a supporter of the British Crown during the American Revolution. — *adj* **1** of, being or supporting the Tories. **2** Conservative. — *n* **Toryism**. [Irish Gaelic *tórai*, bandit, outlaw]

toss *v* **1** (*tr*) to throw up into the air. **2** (*tr*; **away**, **aside**, **out**, etc.) to throw lightly and carelessly. **3** (*intr*; **about**, **around**) to move restlessly or from side to side repeatedly: *toss sleeplessly all night*. **4** (*tr & intr*; **about**) to throw or be thrown from side to side repeatedly and violently: *a ship tossed by the storm*. **5** (*tr*) to jerk (the head), esp. as a sign of impatience or anger. **6** (*tr & intr*) to throw (a spinning coin) into the air and guess which side will land facing up, as a way of making a decision or settling a dispute. **7** (*tr*) to settle a dispute with (someone) by tossing a coin: *toss him for the last cake*. **8** (*tr*) to coat (food, esp. salad) by gently mixing it in a dressing. **9** (*tr*) (of a horse, etc.) to throw (its rider). **10** (*tr*) (of an animal) to throw (a person) into the air with its horns. **11** (*tr*) to discuss or consider in, or as if in, light-hearted or casual debate: *toss the different ideas back and forth in one's head*. — *n* **1** an act or an instance of tossing. **2** a fall from a horse. **3** (*vulg slang*) the slightest amount: *not give a toss*. — **argue the toss** to dispute a decision. — *v* **toss off 1** (*tr*) to drink quickly, esp. in a single swallow. **2** (*tr*) to produce quickly and easily. **3** (*intr & tr*; *Br vulg slang*) to masturbate. — *v* **toss up** (*intr*) to throw a spinning coin into the air and guess which side will land facing upwards, as a way of making a decision or settling a dispute.

toss-up *n* **1** (*coll*) an even chance or risk. **2** an acting of tossing a coin.

tot[1] **1** a small child; a toddler. **2** a small amount of spirits: *a tot of whisky*.

tot[2] *v* **-*tt*-** **1** (*tr*; **up**) to add together. **2** (*intr*; **up**) (of money, etc.) to increase. — *n* **totting-up**. [Abbrev. of **total**]

total *adj* whole; complete. — *n* the whole or complete amount, e.g. of various things added together. — *v* **-*ll*-** **1** (*tr & intr*; **up to**) to amount to. **2** (*tr*; **up**) to add up. **3** (*tr*; *US slang*) to wreck or destroy completely. — *adv* **totally**. [Lat *totalis*, from *totus*, all]

totalitarian *adj* of or relating to a system of government by a single party which allows no opposition and which demands complete obedience to the State. — *n* a person in favour of such a system. — *n* **totalitarianism**.

totalisator or **-z-** *n* (also **totaliser** or **-z-**) a machine which registers bets and calculates winnings in proportion to the amount of money staked.

totality *n* **1** completeness. **2** a complete number or amount.

tote[1] *n* a totalisator. [Abbrev.]

tote[2] *v* (*tr*; **about**, **around**; *coll*) to carry, drag or wear.

tote bag *n* a large bag for carrying shopping.

totem *n* **1** a natural object, esp. an animal, used as the badge or sign of a tribe or an individual person among North American Indians. **2** an image or representation of this. — *adj* **totemic**. [Ojibwa (N American Indian language) *nintotem*, my totem, from *ote-*, to live in a village]

totem pole *n* **1** a large wooden pole on which totems are carved and painted. **2** an order of rank; a hierarchy.

totter *v* **-*r*-** (*intr*) **1** to move unsteadily or weakly. **2** to sway or tremble as if about to fall. **3** (of a system of government, etc.) to be on the verge of collapse. — *n* a weak and unsteady movement or gait. — *adj* **tottery**, **-*ier***, **-*iest***. [MidE *toteron*]

toucan *n* a tropical American fruit-eating bird with a huge beak and brightly coloured feathers. [Tupí (S American Indian language) *tucana*, imit. of its cry]

touch *v* **1** (*tr*) to bring something (e.g. one's hand) into contact, esp. lightly, with (something), esp. so as to feel: *He touched her cheek gently*. **2** (*tr*) (of something) to come into contact with (something else): *The branch touched the window*. **3** (*intr*) to feel, push or strike something lightly, esp. with the hand or foot. **4** (*intr*) to be in contact with something else without overlapping. **5** (*tr*) to make (someone) feel pity, sympathy, quiet pleasure, etc.: *was touched by his sad story*. **6** (*tr*) to have an effect on. **7** (*tr*) to be of concern to: *a matter which doesn't touch you*. **8** (*tr*) to have dealings with: *wouldn't touch a job like that*. **9** (*tr*) to use, esp. to eat or drink: *I never touch chocolate*. **10** (*tr*) to reach: *The temperature touched 100°*. **11** (*tr*) to be as good as; to equal or rival: *No one can touch her at chess*. **12** (*tr*) to mark slightly or delicately; to make a usu. slight, sometimes harmful, impression on: *a sky touched with pink*. **13** (*tr*) to draw or paint with light strokes. **14** (*tr & intr*; **on**, **upon**) to speak of or discuss briefly or in passing. **15** (*tr*) to disturb by handling, meddling, etc.: *Someone's touched my papers*. **16** (*tr*; **for**; *slang*) to ask for and receive money as a loan or gift from: *touch him for £50*. — *n* **1** an act of touching or the sensation of being touched. **2** the sense by which the existence, nature, texture and quality of objects can be perceived through physical contact with the hands, feet, skin, lips, etc. **3** the particular texture and qualities of an object as perceived through contact with the hands, etc.: *the silky touch of the fabric against her skin.* **4** a small amount or quantity; a trace or hint. **5** a slight attack (e.g. of an illness). **6** a slight stroke or mark. **7** a detail which adds to or complements the general pleasing effect or appearance: *put the finishing touches to the portrait*; *A few vases of flowers are an elegant touch.* **8** a distinctive or characteristic style or manner: *a woman's touch.* **9** a musician's individual manner or technique of touching or striking the keys of a keyboard instrument or strings of a string instrument to produce a good tone. **10** an artist's or writer's individual style or manner of working. **11** the ability to respond or behave with sensitivity and sympathy: *have a wonderful touch with animals.* **12** contact; communication: *out of touch with recent developments*; *in touch with old school friends.* **13** (with **a**; *coll*) a bit: *a touch too much make-up.* **14** (*football*, etc.) the ground outside the touchlines. **15** (*slang*) an act of asking for and receiving money from someone as a gift or loan. **16** (*slang*) a person who can be persuaded to give or lend money: *a soft touch.* **17** a test with, or as if with, a touchstone. — **touch and go** of a very uncertain outcome. — *v* **touch down 1** (*intr*) (of aircraft or spacecraft) to land (*n* **touchdown**). **2** (*tr*; *Rugby*) to put (the ball) on the ground behind the goal-line, either behind one's own as a defensive move or behind the opponent's when scoring a try (*n* **touchdown**). — *v* **touch off** (*tr*) **1** to cause to explode, e.g. by touching with a flame. **2** to cause to begin; to trigger. — *v* **touch up** (*tr*) **1** to improve by adding small details to or correcting or hiding the minor faults of. **2** (*slang*) to touch so as to excite sexually; to molest sexually. [OFr *tuchier*]

touchdown see **touch down** above.

touched *adj* **1** feeling pity, sympathy, quiet pleasure, etc. **2** (*coll*) slightly mad.

touching *adj* causing one to feel pity or sympathy; moving. — *prep* concerning. — *adv* **touchingly**.

touch judge *n* (*Rugby*) a linesman.

touchline *n* (*football*, *Rugby*, etc.) either of the two lines marking the side boundaries of the pitch.

touchpaper *n* paper steeped in saltpetre for firing gunpowder.

touchstone *n* **1** a test or standard of judging the quality of something. **2** a hard, black, flint-like stone used for testing the purity and quality of gold and silver alloys which, when rubbed on this stone, leave a coloured mark which indicates the amount of alloy.

touch-type *v* (*intr*) to type without looking at the typewriter keyboard. — *n* **touch-typing**. — *n* **touch-typist**.

touchwood *n* wood which can be used as tinder, esp. because it is dry or decayed.

touchy *adj* **-ier**, **-iest** (*coll*) **1** easily annoyed or offended. **2** needing to be handled or dealt with with care and tact. — *adv* **touchily**. — *n* **touchiness**.

touché *interj* an expression used to acknowledge **1** a hit in fencing or **2** a point scored in an argument or made in retaliation. [Fr, touched]

tough *adj* **1** strong and durable; not easily cut, broken, torn or worn out. **2** (of food) difficult to chew. **3** (of people and animals) strong and fit and able to endure hardship. **4** difficult to deal with or overcome; testing. **5** severe and determined; unyielding; resolute. **6** rough and violent; criminal. **7** (*coll*) unlucky; unjust; unpleasant: *tough luck.* — *n* a rough, violent person, esp. a bully or criminal. — *adv* **toughly**. — *n* **toughness**. — **get tough with** (*coll*) to begin to deal more forcefully, strictly or severely with. [OE *toh*]

toughen *v* **-n-** (*tr* & *intr*; **up**) to make or become tough or tougher.

toupee *n* a small wig or hair-piece worn usu. by men to cover a bald patch. [Fr *toupet*, tuft of hair]

tour *n* **1** an extended journey round a place stopping at various places along the route and usu. returning to one's starting-point at the end: *a coach tour of Italy.* **2** a visit round a particular place: *a tour of the cathedral.* **3** a journey round a place with frequent stops for business or professional engagements along the route, e.g. by a theatre company or a sports team visiting from abroad. **4** an official period of duty or military service, esp. abroad. — *v* **1** (*tr* & *intr*) to make a tour of (a place). **2** (*tr*) (of a theatre company) to travel from place to place giving performances of (a play). [OFr, from Gr *tornos*, tool for making circles]

tourism *n* **1** the practice of travelling to and visiting places for pleasure and relaxation. **2** the industry providing services, e.g. accommodation and catering, for tourists.

tourist *n* **1** a person who travels for pleasure and relaxation. **2** a member of a sports team visiting from abroad. — *adj* of or suitable for tourists, often in being cheap or reasonably priced.

tourist class *n* the cheapest class of passenger accommodation on a ship or in an aircraft.

touristy *adj* (*derog*) designed for or full of tourists.

tour de force *n* ***tours de force*** a feat of strength or skill; an outstanding performance or effort. [Fr]

tourmaline *n* a mineral containing sodium, calcium, iron, magnesium and other metals, colourless, black or transparent blue or pink, sometimes used as a gemstone. [Sinhalese *tormalliya*, cornelian]

tournament *n* **1** a competition, e.g. in tennis or chess, between many players for a championship, usu. played in heats. **2** (*hist*) in the Middle Ages, a competition in which knights on horseback fought with usu. blunted lances and swords. [OFr *torneiement*]

tournedos *n* **-os** a small, round, thick fillet of beef. [Fr]

tourney *n* **-eys** a medieval tournament. — *v* **-eys**, **-eyed** (*intr*) to take part in a medieval tournament. [OFr *torneie*]

tourniquet *n* a bandage or other device for tying very tightly round an arm or leg to stop the flow of blood through an artery. [Fr, from *tourner*, to turn]

tousle *v* (*tr*) to make (esp. hair) untidy; to tangle or dishevel. — *n* a tousled mass. [MidE *touselen*]

tout *v* **1** (*intr*; **for**) to try persistently to persuade people to buy something, give support, etc.: *tout for trade*. **2** (*tr*) to try persistently to persuade (someone) to buy (something). **3** (*tr*) to advertise or praise strongly or aggressively. **4** (*intr*) to spy on racehorses in training to gain information about their condition and likely future performance. — *n* **1** a person who buys up large numbers of tickets for a popular sporting event, concert, etc. and sells them at vastly inflated prices to members of the public. **2** a person who spies on racehorses in training and passes information about their condition, etc. to people wishing to bet on them. **3** a person who touts for trade, esp. persistently or aggressively. [MidE *tuten*, to peep out]

tow[1] *v* (*tr*) **1** to pull (a ship, barge, car, trailer, etc.) by rope, chain or cable behind the vehicle one is driving. **2** (of a vehicle) to pull (a ship, barge, car, etc.) along by rope, chain or cable. — **1** an act of towing or the state of being towed. **2** something towed, e.g. a car. — **in tow 1** (also **on tow**, **under tow**) (of vehicles) being towed. **2** as a companion or escort: *She arrived late with several men in tow*. **3** under one's protection, guidance or control: *be taken in tow by a more experienced employee*. [OE *togian*]

towbar *n* a short rigid bar at the back of a car for towing a caravan or trailer.

towline or **towrope** *n* a rope, chain or cable used for towing.

towpath *n* a path beside a canal or river formerly used by horses towing barges.

tow[2] *n* the coarse, short or broken fibres of flax or hemp prepared for spinning into rope. [OE]

tow-coloured *adj* (of hair) very fair.

tow-head *n* a person with very fair or tousled hair. — *adj* **tow-headed**.

towards or **toward** *prep* **1** in the direction of: *travel towards Glasgow*; *turn towards him*. **2** in relation or regard to: *a strange attitude towards the new manager*. **3** as a contribution to: *donate £1000 towards the cost of a new hospital*. **4** near; just before: *towards midnight*. [OE *toweard*, future]

towel *n* **1** a piece of absorbent cloth or paper for drying oneself, washed dishes, etc. **2** a sanitary towel. — *v* **-ll-** (*tr*) **1** to rub, wipe or dry with a towel. **2** (*slang*) to thrash. [OFr *toaille*]

towelling *n* **1** an absorbent cotton cloth for making towels. **2** (*slang*) a thrashing.

tower *n* **1** a tall, narrow, usu. circular or square structure forming part of a larger, lower building such as a church or castle or standing alone, built for defence, as a lookout, for machinery, etc. **2** a fortress, esp. one with one or more towers: *the Tower of London*. — *v* **-r-** (*intr*; **above**) to reach a great height or rise high (above). — **a tower of strength** someone who is a great help, support or encouragement. — *v* **tower over** (*intr*) to be considerably taller than or superior to. [OE *torr*]

tower block *n* a very tall residential or office building.

towering *adj* **1** reaching a great height; very tall or elevated. **2** (of rage, fury, etc.) intense; violent.

town *n* **1** an urban area with relatively defined boundaries and a name, smaller than a city but larger than a village. **2** the central shopping or business area in a neighbourhood. **3** the principal town in an area, esp. (in SE England) London. **4** the people living in a town. **5** city or urban life in general as opposed to the countryside and rural life. **6** the permanent residents of a town as opposed to *gown*, the members of its university. — **go out on the town** (*coll*) to enjoy the entertainments offered by a town, esp. its restaurants and bars. — **go to town** (*coll*) to do something very thoroughly or with great enthusiasm or expense. [OE *tun*, enclosure, manor]

town clerk *n* (*Br hist*, until 1974) a secretary and legal advisor to a town council.

town council *n* an elected governing body of a town. — *n* **town councillor**.

town crier *n* (*hist*) a person whose job is to make public announcements in the streets of a town.

townee or **townie** *n* (*coll*, often *derog*) a person living in a town, esp. as opposed to a person living in the countryside or a member of a town's university.

town hall *n* the building where the official business of a town is carried out.

town house *n* **1** a terraced house, esp. a fashionable one, and often with the living room on an upper floor. **2** a person's house in town as opposed to his or her house in the country.

town planning *n* the planning and designing of the future development of a town.

townscape *n* the general appearance of or visual impression created by a town.

townsfolk *n* (*pl*) same as **townspeople**.

township *n* **1** (*SAfr*) an urban area where black and coloured citizens live. **2** (*Br hist*) a division of a large parish. **3** (*NAm*) a subdivision of a county with some degree of local government. **4** (*NAm*) an area of land or district thirty-six miles square. **5** (*Austr*) a small town or settlement.

townsman and **townswoman** *n* a man or woman living in a town or city.

townspeople *n* (*pl*) the people living in a town or city.

toxaemia *n* **1** blood-poisoning. **2** a serious condition occurring in late pregnancy characterised by a sudden rise in blood pressure. — *adj* **toxaemic**. [Gr *toxikon*, poison for the tips of arrows + *haima*, blood]

toxic *adj* **1** poisonous. **2** of or caused by a poison or toxin. [Gr *toxikon*, poison for the tips of arrows]

toxicity *n* **-*ies*** **1** the degree to which a substance is poisonous. **2** the state of being poisonous.

toxicology *n* the scientific study of poisons. — *n* **toxicologist**.

toxic shock syndrome *n* a potentially fatal condition in women, marked by flu-like symptoms and a drop in blood pressure, caused by blood-poisoning which is itself caused by a toxin developing in a high-absorbency tampon kept in the body during menstruation.

toxin *n* any poison produced naturally by plants, animals, bacteria, etc., esp. in a body. [**toxic**]

toxocara *n* a parasitic worm living in the intestines of dogs and cats and known when passed to humans to cause a disease (**toxocariasis**) often leading to eye damage. [Gr *toxikon*, poison for the tips of arrows + *kara*, head]

toy *n* **1** an object made, esp. for a child, to play with. **2** (often *derog*) anything, esp. a gadget, intended to be or thought of as being for amusement or pleasure rather than practical use. **3** something which is very small, esp. a dwarf breed of dog. — *adj* **1** made to be played with, esp. in imitation of something real: *a toy oven*. **2** being (a member of) a dwarf breed. — *v* (*intr*; **with**) **1** to play with in an idle way and without really being interested: *toy with one's food*. **2** to flirt or amuse oneself amorously (with). [MidE *toye*, dalliance]

toy boy *n* (*coll*) a usu. young man who is the lover of a woman much older than himself.

trace[1] *n* **1** a mark or sign that some person, animal or thing has been in that place. **2** a track or footprint. **3** a very small amount that can only just be detected. **4** a tracing. **5** a line marked by the moving pen of a recording instrument. **6** a visible line on a cathode ray tube showing the path of a moving spot. **7** a supposed physical change in the brain or cells of the nervous system caused by learning. — *v* **1** (*tr*) to track and discover by or as if by following clues, a trail, etc. **2** (*tr*) to follow step by step: *trace the development of medicine*. **3** (*tr*) to make a copy of (a drawing, design, etc.) by covering it with a sheet of semi-transparent paper and drawing over the visible lines. **4** (*tr*) to outline or sketch (an idea, plan, etc.). **5** (*tr & intr*; **back**) to date or be dated back: *can trace the name back to the 16th century*. [OFr, from Lat *trahere*, to draw]

trace element *n* a substance, esp. a metal such as copper, zinc or iron, which is needed in very small quantities by a body or plant.

tracer *n* **1** a person or device that traces. **2** a bullet, etc. which leaves a smoke-trail behind it by which its flight path can be seen. **3** a substance, esp. a radioactive element, whose course through the body, or effect on it, can be observed.

tracery *n* **-*ies*** **1** ornamental open stonework used to form a decorative pattern, esp. in the top part of a Gothic window. **2** a finely patterned decoration or design.

tracing *n* **1** a copy of a drawing made on semi-transparent paper. **2** an act of tracing.

tracing-paper *n* thin, semi-transparent paper used for tracing drawings.

trace[2] *n* either of two ropes, chains or straps attached to an animal's collar, etc. for pulling a carriage, cart, etc. — **kick over the traces** to become independent or rebellious. [OFr *trais*, from Lat *trahere*, to pull]

trachea *n* **-*eae*** the passage which carries air into and out of the lungs from the larynx; the windpipe. [Gr *tracheia* (*arteria*) rough (artery)]

tracheotomy *n* **-*ies*** a cut made in the trachea to help breathing. [**trachea** + Gr *tome*, a cutting]

trachoma *n* a contagious eye disease in which the inner eyelids become rough and inflamed. [Gr, roughness]

track *n* **1** a mark or trail left by the passing of a person, animal or thing, esp. a footprint. **2** a rough path, esp. one beaten by feet. **3** a specially prepared course, esp. for racing. **4** a railway line, i.e. the parallel rails, the space in between, and the sleepers and stones below. **5** a length of railing along which something, e.g. a curtain, moves. **6** any of several separate sections on a gramophone record containing a separate song, movement, etc. **7** the song, piece of music, etc. recorded on such a section. **8** one of a series of parallel paths on magnetic recording tape containing a single sequence of signals. **9** the line or course of travel or movement. **10** the line or course of thought, reasoning, etc. **11** the continuous band of metal plates used instead of wheels on heavy vehicles designed to travel over rough surfaces, e.g. a tank. **12** the distance between a pair of wheels as measured between those parts of the wheels which actually touch the ground. — *v* **1** (*tr*) to follow the marks, footprints, etc. left by (a person or animal).

2 (*tr*) to follow and usu. plot the course of (a spacecraft, satellite, etc.) by radar. **3** (*intr*) to move a television or film camera in towards, parallel to or away from the object being filmed. **4** (*intr*) (of a gramophone needle) to follow the grooves of a record. **5** (*intr*) (of a vehicle's rear wheels) to run exactly in the course of the front wheels. — **across the tracks** or **the wrong side of the tracks** (*coll*) a socially disadvantaged area of town. — **in one's tracks** exactly where one is standing. — **keep** (or **lose**) **track of** to keep (or not keep) oneself informed about the progress or whereabouts of. — **make tracks** (*coll*) **1** to leave. **2** (with **for**) to go towards. — **on the track of** following, pursuing, or looking for. — *v* **track down** (*tr*) to search for and find after a thorough search or by following a track. [OFr *trac*]

tracker dog *n* a dog specially trained to search for people, esp. criminals.

track event *n* (*athletics*) a race. ◇ See also **field event**.

tracking *n* **1** the balance of the arm on a gramophone so that the needle remains correctly positioned in the groove. **2** (*electr engin*) a leakage of current between two insulated points caused by moisture, dirt, etc.

tracking station *n* a station equipped with radar to follow and plot the courses of spacecraft, satellites, etc.

track record *n* a record of past performance.

track shoe *n* a shoe with a spiked sole worn by a runner.

tracksuit *n* a warm suit worn by athletes, etc. when exercising, or to keep the body warm before and after performing.

tract *n* **1** an area of land, usu. of indefinite extent. **2** a system in the body with a particular function formed by a series of connected organs and glands: *the digestive tract*. **3** a short essay or book, esp. on a religious subject. [Lat *trahere*, to draw]

tractable *adj* easily managed, controlled or used; pliant; docile. — *n* **tractability** or **tractableness**. — *adv* **tractably**. [Lat *tractabilis*]

traction *n* **1** the action of pulling, state of being pulled or the force used in pulling. **2** (*med*) a steady pulling on a muscle or limb using a series of pulleys and weights, to correct some condition or problem. **3** the grip of a wheel, tyre, etc. on the surface on which it moves. — *adj* **tractional** or **tractive**. [Lat *tractio*, from *trahere*, to pull]

traction engine *n* a steam- or diesel-powered engine or locomotive used, esp. formerly, for pulling heavy loads over rough ground.

tractor *n* **1** a slow-moving motor vehicle with two large rear wheels for pulling esp. farm machinery, heavy loads, etc. **2** a traction engine. [Lat, from *trahere*, to pull]

trad *n* (*Br coll*) traditional jazz, the style of jazz music first played in the 1920s and 1930s and which originated in New Orleans. — *adj* traditional. [Abbrev.]

trade *n* **1** the buying and selling of goods or services. **2** (people involved in and earning a living from) business and commerce, esp. as opposed to a profession or landed property. **3** a personal occupation or job, esp. one requiring skill; a craft: *a carpenter by trade*. **4** the people and companies engaged in a particular business or occupation: *the building trade*. **5** customers: *the lunch-time trade*. **6** business at a particular time or for a particular market: *the tourist trade*; *a seasonal trade in woolly hats*. **7** (in *pl*) the trade winds. — *v* **1** (*intr*; **in**) to buy and sell (a particular type of goods). **2** (*intr*; **with**) to engage in trade (with a person or country). **3** (*tr*) to exchange (one commodity) for another. — *v* **trade in** (*tr*; **for**) to give (something) as part payment (for) (*n* **trade-in**). — *v* **trade off** (*tr*) to give (something) in exchange for something else, usu. as a compromise (*n* **trade-off**). — *v* **trade on** (*tr*) to take usu. unfair advantage of (a person's generosity, kindness, etc.). [MidE, course, path]

trade gap *n* the amount by which a country's imports are greater than its exports.

trade-in see **trade in** above.

trademark *n* **1** a name, word or symbol, esp. one (**Registered Trademark**) that is officially registered and protected by law, used to represent a company or individual and shown on all of the goods made or sold by that company or individual. **2** a distinguishing characteristic or feature.

tradename *n* **1** a name given to an article or product, or group of these, by the trade which produces them. **2** a name under which a company or individual does business. **3** a name serving as a trademark.

trade-off see **trade off** above.

trader *n* **1** a person who trades, often one who owns or runs a shop, or who trades in a particular group of goods. **2** a ship used for trade.

tradesman or **tradeswoman** *n* **1** a shopkeeper, esp. one who will deliver to private houses. **2** a skilled worker.

tradespeople *n* (*pl*) people engaged in trade.

Trades Union Congress *n* a national organisation formed from representatives of trade unions, which meets annually to discuss working conditions and the economy in the country at large.

trade, or **trades, union** *n* an organisation of workers or employees formed to protect the workers' or employees' interests and generally try to improve working conditions and pay. — *n* **trade unionism**. — *n* **trade unionist**.

trade wind *n* a wind that blows continually towards the equator and is deflected westward by the eastward rotation of the earth.

trading estate *n* (esp. *Br*) an area in a town which is developed for industry and business.
trading post *n* a store in a remote or sparsely populated region.
trading stamp *n* a stamp given to a customer in return for a certain amount of money spent on goods in a store, and which may be collected and exchanged for an item supplied by the company issuing the trading stamp.

tradescantia *n* any of several widely cultivated plants with attractive, often variegated, leaves. [John *Tradescant* (c. 1567–1637), English gardener, naturalist and traveller]

tradition *n* **1** the handing down of doctrines, beliefs, customs, etc. from generation to generation. **2** a doctrine, belief, custom, story, etc. that is passed on. **3** a particular body of doctrines, beliefs, customs, etc. belonging to a particular group of people, religion, country, family, etc. **4** the continuous development of a body of artistic, literary or musical principles or conventions. — *adj* **traditional**. — *adv* **traditionally**. [Lat *traditio*, from *tradere*, to give up]
traditionalism *n* belief in the importance of, respect for and often excessive following of tradition. — *n* & *adj* **traditionalist**.
traditional jazz see **trad**.

traduce *v* (*tr*) to say or write unpleasant things about; to malign. — *n* **traducement**. — *n* **traducer**. [Lat *traducere*, to lead across]

traffic *n* **1** the vehicles, ships, aircraft, etc. moving along a route. **2** the movement of vehicles along a route. **3** illegal or dishonest trade. **4** trade; commerce. **5** the transporting of goods or people on a railway, air or sea route, etc. **6** the goods or people transported along a route. **7** dealings or communication between groups or individuals. — *v* ***-ficking, -ficked*** **1** (*intr*; **in**) to deal or trade in, esp. illegally or dishonestly. **2** (*tr*) to deal in (a particular type of goods). — *n* **trafficker**. [OFr *traffique*]
traffic island see **island**.
traffic lights *n* (*pl*) a system of red, amber and green lights which controls traffic at road junctions, pedestrian crossings, etc.
traffic warden *n* (*Br*) a person whose job is to control the parking of vehicles in towns and report parking offences.

tragedy *n* ***-ies*** **1** a serious drama, film, opera, etc. in which the main character or characters are eventually destroyed through a combination of events, circumstances and personality problems. **2** such plays as a group or genre. **3** any sad play, film, book, etc., esp. one ending with an unnecessary or untimely death. **4** a serious disaster. **5** any sad event. [Gr *tragoidia*, from *tragos*, goat + *oide*, song]
tragedian *n* **1** an actor who specialises in tragic roles. **2** a person who writes tragedies.
tragedienne *n* an actress who specialises in tragic roles.

tragic *adj* **1** sad; very distressing. **2** of, involving or in the style of tragedy. — *adv* **tragically**. [Gr *tragikos*]

tragicomedy *n* ***-ies*** a play or event which includes a mixture of both tragedy and comedy. — *adj* **tragicomic**. — *adv* **tragicomically**. [Lat *tragicomoedia*]

trail *v* **1** (*tr* & *intr*) to drag or be dragged loosely along the ground or other surface, esp. behind one. **2** (*intr*; **along, behind**) to walk or move along slowly and wearily. **3** (*tr*) to drag (a limb, etc.) esp. slowly and wearily: *a bird trailing a broken wing*. **4** (*tr* & *intr*) to fall or lag behind (e.g. a competitor) in e.g. a race or contest, often by a stated number of points. **5** (*tr*) to follow the track or footsteps of. **6** (*tr* & *intr*) to grow or encourage (a plant) to grow so long that it droops over or along a surface towards the ground. — *n* **1** a track, series of marks, footprints, etc. left by a passing person, animal or thing, esp. one followed in hunting. **2** a rough path or track through a wild or mountainous area. **3** anything which drags or is drawn behind. **4** the part of a gun carriage that rests on the ground when the limber is detached. — *v* **trail away** or **off** (*intr*) (esp. of a sound) to become fainter. [MidE *trailen*]
trailblazer *n* a person who is the first to do or discover something, or the first to go somewhere; a pioneer. — *n* & *adj* **trailblazing**. ◇ See also **blaze a trail** at **blaze**[2].
trailer *n* **1** a usu. two-wheeled cart for towing behind a car, used e.g. for transporting small boats. **2** the rear section of an articulated lorry, as opposed to the cab. **3** (*NAm*) a caravan. **4** a series of brief extracts from a film or programme prepared as an advertisement for it.

train *n* **1** a string of railway carriages or wagons with a locomotive; (*loosely*) a locomotive. **2** a back part of a long dress or robe that trails behind the wearer. **3** the attendants following or accompanying an important person. **4** a connected series of events, actions, ideas or thoughts. **5** a number of things in a string or connected line, e.g. a line of animals or vehicles carrying baggage. **6** a line of gunpowder, etc. laid to fire a charge. **7** a set of connected wheels which act on each other to transmit motion. — *v* **1** (*tr*) to teach (a person or animal) to do something or prepare (him, her or it) for something through instruction, practice or exercises. **2** (*intr*; **as**) to be taught, or prepare oneself to be, through instruction, practice or exercises. **3** (*tr* & *intr*; **for**) to prepare for performance (e.g. in a sport) by instruction, practice, exercise, diet, etc.: *train for the marathon*. **4** (*tr*; **on**) to point or aim (e.g. a gun) at or focus (e.g. a telescope) on a particular object or in a particular direction. **5** (*tr*) to make (a plant, tree, etc.) grow in a particular direction: *train the ivy along the wall.* **6** (*intr*) to travel by train. — *adj* **trained**. [OFr *trahiner*, to drag]

train-bearer *n* a person who carries the train of a person's dress or robe.

trainee *n* a person who is being trained for a job.

trainer *n* **1** a person who trains racehorses, athletes, sportsmen and -women, etc. **2** (*Br*) a soft running shoe with a thick sole. **3** a machine or device used in training, e.g. an aircraft with two sets of controls for training pilots.

training *n* **1** the act or process of being prepared for something, of being taught or learning a particular skill and practising it until the required standard is reached: *go into training for the marathon.* **2** the state of being physically fit: *out of training*.

train-spotter *n* a person who, for a hobby, notes the numbers of locomotives or carriages he or she sees. — *n* **train-spotting**.

traipse or **trapes** *v* (*intr*) to walk or trudge along idly or wearily. — *n* a long, tiring walk.

trait *n* a distinguishing feature or quality, esp. of a person's character. [Fr, from Lat *trahere*, to draw]

traitor *n* (**to**) **1** a person who commits treason and betrays his or her country to the enemy. **2** a person who betrays a friend's trust. — *adj* **traitorous**. — *adv* **traitorously**. [Lat *tradere*, to give up]

traitress *n* (*old*) a female traitor.

trajectory *n* **-ies** the path through which an object moves, esp. the curve of a projectile travelling through the air. [Lat *trajectorius*, casting over]

tram *n* **1** (also **tramcar**) an electrically-powered passenger vehicle which runs on rails laid in the streets. **2** a truck or wagon running on rails in a mine.

tramline *n* **1** (often in *pl*) either of a pair of rails forming the track on which trams run. **2** (in *pl*) the lines marking the sides of a tennis or badminton court and the lines parallel to them inside the court.

tramway *n* **1** a system of tracks for trams. **2** a tram system.

trammel *n* **1** a dragnet for fishing in which a fine inner mesh is carried by fish through the coarse outer mesh, thus trapping the fish in a pocket. **2** (usu. in *pl*) anything which hinders or prevents free action or movement. — *v* **-ll-** (*tr*) **1** to catch or entangle, esp. in a trammel. **2** to hinder or prevent the free movement of. [OFr *tramail*, net]

tramp *v* **1** (*intr*; **about**, **up**, etc.) to walk with firm, heavy footsteps. **2** (*intr*) to make a journey on foot, esp. heavily or wearily: *tramp over the hills.* **3** (*tr*) to walk heavily and wearily on or through: *tramp the streets.* **4** (*tr*) to walk (a specified distance) heavily and wearily: *tramp six miles across the open moor.* **5** (*intr*) to live as a tramp. **6** (*tr*) to tread or trample. — *n* **1** a person with no fixed home or job, who travels from place to place on foot and who lives by begging and doing odd jobs. **2** a long and often tiring walk esp. in the country. **3** the sound of heavy, rhythmic footsteps. **4** (also **tramp steamer**) a cargo boat with no fixed, regular route. **5** (*slang*) a promiscuous or immoral woman. **6** an iron plate on the sole of a shoe to protect it, e.g. when digging. [MidE *trampen*]

trample *v* (*tr* & *intr*; **on**, **upon**, **over**) **1** to tread heavily or roughly; to press or be pressed down by treading or being trodden on: *cigarette ash trampled into the carpet.* **2** to treat roughly or with contempt so as to bruise or injure: *trample all over her feelings.* — *n* an act of or the sound made by trampling. [MidE *tramplen*, to stamp]

trampoline *n* a piece of tough canvas attached to a framework by cords or rope and stretched tight, for acrobats, gymnasts, children, etc. to jump on. — *v* (*intr*) to jump, turn somersaults, etc. on a trampoline. [Ital *trampolino*, springboard]

trance *n* **1** a sleep-like or half-conscious state in which one loses the ability to react to stimuli such as pain. **2** a dazed or absorbed state. **3** a usu. self-induced state in which one may experience religious or mystical ecstasy. [Lat *transire*, to go across]

trannie or **tranny** *n* **-ies** (esp. *Br coll*) a transistor radio. [Abbrev.]

tranquil *adj* quiet; peaceful; undisturbed. — *n* **tranquillity**. — *adv* **tranquilly**. [Lat *tranquillus*]

tranquillise or -ize *v* (*tr* & *intr*) to make or become calm, peaceful or less tense or restore or be restored to such a state, esp. through drugs.

tranquilliser or **-z-** *n* a drug which calms the nerves, reduces anxiety, etc.

trans *abbrev* **1** transitive. **2** translation; translated.

trans- *pfx* **1** across; beyond; on the other side of: *transatlantic.* **2** through. **3** into another state or place: *transform.* [Lat *trans*, across]

transact *v* (*tr*) to conduct or carry out (business). — *n* **transactor** (*formal*). [Lat *transigere*, to force through]

transaction *n* **1** something transacted, esp. a business deal. **2** (in *pl*) the published reports of papers read, discussions, decisions taken, etc. at a meeting of a learned society. **3** an act of transacting.

transalpine *adj* situated or happening beyond the Alps (orig. as viewed from Rome). [Lat *transalpinus*]

transatlantic *adj* **1** crossing the Atlantic. **2** situated on the other side of the Atlantic. **3** of, belonging to or from the other side of the Atlantic. [**trans-** + **Atlantic**]

transceiver *n* a piece of radio equipment which both receives and transmits signals. [**transmitter** + **receiver**]

transcend *v* (*tr*) **1** to be beyond the limits or range of: *transcend the bounds of human experience*. **2** to be better or greater than; to surpass or excel. **3** to overcome or surmount: *transcend all difficulties*. [Lat *transcendere*, to climb over]

transcendent *adj* **1** going beyond in excellence; surpassing or excelling. **2** beyond usual human knowledge or experience. **3** (esp. of God) existing outside the material or created world and independent of it. — *n* **transcendence** or **transcendency**.

transcendental *adj* **1** going beyond usual human knowledge or experience. **2** going beyond in excellence; surpassing or excelling. **3** supernatural or mystical. **4** vague, abstract or abstruse. — *adv* **transcendentally**.

transcendentalism *n* any philosophical system concerned with what is constant, innate and a priori, independent of and a necessary prerequisite to experience.

transcendental meditation *n* a system of meditation for relieving anxiety, promoting spiritual wellbeing and achieving physical and mental relaxation through the (usu. silent) repetition of a mantra.

transcontinental *adj* (e.g. of a railway) crossing a continent. — *n* something that crosses a continent, e.g. a railway.

transcribe *v* (*tr*) **1** to write out (a text) in full, e.g. from notes: *take shorthand notes to be transcribed later*. **2** to copy (a text) from one place to another: *transcribed the poem into her album*. **3** to write out (a spoken text). **4** (*mus*) to arrange (a piece of music) for an instrument or voice that it was not originally composed for. **5** to record (a programme) for future broadcasting. **6** (*comput*) to transfer (information) from one storage device to another. [Lat *transcribere*]

transcript *n* a written or printed copy, esp. a legal or official copy of court proceedings. [Lat *transcriptum*]

transcription *n* **1** the act of transcribing. **2** something transcribed; a transcript. [Lat *transcriptio*]

transducer *n* a device that converts a physical quantity into an electrical signal, e.g. a microphone, which converts sound into an electrical signal. [Lat *transducere*, to lead across]

transept *n* (either of the two arms forming) that part of a cross-shaped church that is at right angles to the nave. [Lat *transeptum*, from *trans*, across + *saeptum*, enclosure]

transfer *v* *-rr-* **1** (*tr* & *intr*) to move from one place, person or group to another. **2** (*intr*) to change from one vehicle, line or passenger system to another. **3** (*tr*; *legal*) to give the right to or ownership of (property) to someone. **4** (*tr*) to move (a design) from one surface to another. — *n* **1** an act of transferring or the state of being transferred. **2** a design or picture that can be transferred from one surface to another. **3** any person or thing that is transferred. **4** (*legal*) the changing of the right to property from one person to another; conveyance. **5** (*legal*) any document which records such a change in the right to property. **6** (*NAm*) a ticket allowing a passenger to continue a journey on another route. — *adj* **transferable** or **transferrable**. [Lat *transferre*, to carry across]

transference *n* **1** the act of transferring from one person, place or group to another. **2** (*psychol*) an unconscious transferring of one's emotions, fears, anxieties, etc. to another person or thing, esp to a psychoanalyst during therapy.

transfigure *v* (*tr*) to change the appearance of, esp. so as to make more beautiful, glorious or exalted. [Lat *transfigurare*]

transfiguration *n* **1** a change in appearance, esp. becoming more beautiful, glorious or exalted. **2** (*cap*) the change in Christ's appearance, notably his becoming more radiant, on the mountain. **3** (*cap*) a Church festival held on 6 August to commemorate this.

transfix *v* (*tr*) **1** to cause (someone) to be unable to move through surprise, fear, horror, etc. **2** to pierce through with, or as if with, a pointed weapon. — *n* **transfixion**. [Lat *transfigere*, to pierce through]

transform *v* **1** (*tr*) to change the appearance, nature or function of completely and often dramatically. **2** (*intr*; **into, to**) to undergo a complete and often dramatic change of appearance, function or nature. **3** (*tr*; *math*) to change the form but not the value of (an equation or algebraic expression). **4** (*tr*) to change the voltage or type of (a current), e.g. from alternating to direct. — *n* **transformation**. [Lat *transformare*]

transformer *n* an apparatus which transfers an alternating current from one part or device to another, usu. with a change of voltage.

transfuse *v* (*tr*) **1** to transfer (blood or plasma from one person) into the blood vessels of another. **2** to cause to pass, enter or diffuse through. **3** to cause (fluid) to pass from one vessel to another. [Lat *transfundere*, to pour out]

transfusion *n* an act of transfusing, esp. of giving a person blood or plasma from someone else.

transgenic *adj* (*bot* & *zool*) containing genetic material introduced, usu. in the form of DNA, from another species. [**trans-** + **gene**]

transgress *v* **1** (*tr* & *intr*) to go beyond the limits set by, break or violate (divine law, a rule, etc.). **2** (*tr*) to overstep (a limit or boundary). — *n* **transgressor**. [Lat *transgredi*, to step across]

transgression *n* **1** the act of breaking rules, divine law, etc. **2** a fault, crime or sin.

tranship. Same as **transship**.

transient *adj* lasting, staying or visiting for a short time only; passing quickly. — *n* **1**

a temporary resident or worker. **2** a short, sudden surge of voltage or current. — *n* **transience** or **transiency**. — *adv* **transiently**. [Lat *transire*, to cross over]

transistor *n* **1** (*electronics*) a semiconductor device with three electrodes able to perform several functions including amplification and rectification. **2** (in full **transistor radio**) a small portable radio using several such devices. [**transfer resistor**]

transistorise or **-ize** *v* (*tr*) to fit with a transistor or transistors. — *adj* **transistorised** or **-z-**. — *n* **transistorisation** or **-z-**.

transit *n* **1** the carrying or movement of goods or passengers from place to place or across or through a place. **2** a route or passage: *transit by sea.* **3** (esp. *US*) the transport of passengers or goods on public, usu. local, routes. **4** the passage of a heavenly body across a meridian. — *v* **-t-** (*tr*) to pass across or through. — **in transit** (of goods or passengers) in the process of being taken from or travelling from one place to another. [Lat *transitus*, from *transire*, to cross over]

transit camp *n* a camp for the temporary accommodation of soldiers, refugees, etc. on the way to their permanent destination.

transit lounge *n* an airport lounge for passengers waiting for a connecting flight.

transit visa *n* a visa which allows a person to pass through a country but not to stop in it.

transition *n* **1** a change or passage from one place, state, subject, etc. to another. **2** (*mus*) a change from one key to another. **3** (*archit*) the gradual change from one style to another, esp. from Norman to Early English. — *adj* **transitional** or **transitionary**. — *adv* **transitionally**. [Lat *transitio*, from *transire*, to cross over]

transitive *adj* (*gram*) (of a verb) having a direct object, such as the verb *hit* in the phrase *hit the ball.* — *adv* **transitively**. ◇ See also **intransitive**. [Lat *transitivus*]

transitory *adj* lasting only for a short time; transient. — *adv* **transitorily**. — *n* **transitoriness**. [Lat. *transitorius*, from *transire*, to cross over]

translate *v* **1** (*tr*) to put (a word, speech, written text, etc.) into another language. **2** (*intr*) to do this, esp. as a profession. **3** (*intr*) (of a written text, etc.) to be able to be put into another language: *Poetry doesn't always translate well.* **4** (*tr*) to put or express (e.g. an idea) in plainer or simpler terms. **5** (*tr*) to interpret the significance or meaning of (an action, behaviour, etc.). **6** (*tr* & *intr*; **into**) to change or be changed into or show or be shown as: *translate her ideas into reality.* **7** (*tr*) to change or move from one state, condition, person, place, etc. to another. **8** (*tr*) to move (a bishop) from one see to another. **9** (*tr*) to move (the relics of a saint) from one place to another. **10** (*tr*) to remove to heaven, esp. without death. — *n* **translator**. [Lat *translatum*, from *transferre*, to carry across]

translation *n* **1** a word, speech, written text, etc. that has been put into one language from another. **2** the act of translating. **3** (*math*) change of place, such that each point moves in the same direction at the same speed. — *adj* **translational**.

transliterate *v* (*tr*) to write (a word, name, text, etc.) in the letters of another alphabet. — *n* **transliteration**. — *n* **transliterator**. [**trans-** + Lat *litera*, letter]

translucent *adj* **1** allowing light to pass and be diffused through; semi-transparent. **2** clear. — *n* **translucence** or **translucency**. — *adv* **translucently**. [Lat *translucere*, to shine through]

transmigrate *v* (*intr*) **1** (of a soul) to pass into another body at death. **2** to move from one home or abode to another; to migrate. — *n* **transmigration**. [Lat *transmigrare*]

transmission *n* **1** an act of transmitting or the state of being transmitted. **2** something transmitted, esp. a radio or television broadcast. **3** the system of parts in a motor vehicle which transfers power from the engine to the wheels. [Lat *transmissio*]

transmit *v* **-tt-** **1** (*tr*) to pass or hand on (esp. a message or infection). **2** (*tr* & *intr*) to send out (signals) by radio waves. **3** (*tr* & *intr*) to broadcast (a radio or television programme). **4** (*tr*) to allow the passage of (e.g. light or sound); to act as a medium for. — *adj* **transmissible**. [Lat *transmittere*]

transmitter *n* a person or thing that transmits, esp. an apparatus for transmitting radio signals.

transmogrify *v* **-ies**, **-ied** (*tr*; *facet* or *jocular*) to transform, esp. in shape or appearance and often in a surprising or bizarre way. — *n* **transmogrification**.

transmute *v* (*tr*) **1** to change the form, substance or nature of. **2** to change (one chemical element) into another. **3** (*alchemy*) to change (base metal) into gold or silver. — *adj* **transmutable**. — *n* **transmutation**. [Lat *transmutare*]

transom *n* **1** a horizontal bar of wood or stone dividing a window, or placed across the top of a door separating it from a window or fanlight above. **2** a lintel. **3** (in full **transom window**) a small window over the lintel of a door or larger window. **4** any of several crossbeams in the stern of a boat. [OFr *traversin*]

transparent *adj* **1** able to be seen through; clear. **2** easily seen through, understood or recognised; obvious; evident. **3** frank and open; candid. — *adv* **transparently**. [Lat *transparere*, to shine through]

transparency *n* **-ies** **1** the state of being transparent. **2** a small photograph on glass or rigid plastic mounted in a frame and viewed by being placed in a projector or other device which shines light behind it.

transpire *v* **1** (*intr*) (esp. of something secret) to become known; to come to light: *It later transpired that he had been in Paris.* **2** (*intr*; *loosely*) to happen. **3** (*tr* & *intr*) (of plants) to give off (water vapour) through leaves or (of some animals) to give off (waste material) through a skin or membrane. **4** (*tr*) to give off in the form of vapour. — *n* **transpiration**. [Lat *transpirare*, to breathe through]

transplant *v* (*tr*) **1** to transfer (an organ, skin, etc.) from one person or part of the body to another. **2** to move (esp. a growing plant) from one place to another. — *n* **1** an operation in which an organ, skin, etc. is transferred from one person or part of the body to another. **2** anything which has been transplanted, esp. an organ, skin or plant. — *n* **transplantation**. [Lat *transplantare*]

transport *v* (*tr*) **1** to carry (goods, passengers, etc.) from one place to another. **2** (*hist*) to send to a penal colony overseas. **3** (**with**) to affect with strong feelings: *transported with grief.* — *n* **1** (a system or business for) the transporting of people, goods, etc. from place to place. **2** a means of getting or being transported from place to place: *My car has broken down so I've got no transport at the moment.* **3** (often in *pl*) strong emotion, esp. of pleasure or delight; ecstasy. **4** a ship, aircraft, lorry, etc. used to carry soldiers or military equipment and stores. **5** (*hist*) a criminal or convict who has been sentenced to transportation. — *adj* **transportable**. [Lat *transportare*]

transportation *n* **1** the act or transporting or process of being transported. **2** a means of being transported; transport. **3** (*hist*) the punishment of prisoners by sending them to a penal colony overseas.

transport café *n* (*Br*) an inexpensive restaurant on or near a main road, used esp. by lorry drivers.

transporter *n* someone or something that transports, esp. a heavy vehicle for carrying large goods.

transpose *v* (*tr*) **1** to cause (two or more things, letters, words, etc.) to change places. **2** to change the position of (a thing) in a sequence or series. **3** (*mus*) to perform or rewrite in a different key. **4** (*math*) to move (a term) to the other side of an equation and reverse the sign accompanying it. — *adj* **transposable**. — *n* **transposition**. [MidE *transposen*, to transmute]

transship *v* **-pp-** (*tr* & *intr*) to transfer from one ship or form of transport to another. — *n* **transshipment**. [**trans-** + **ship**]

transubstantiate *v* (*tr*) to change into another substance. [Lat *transubstantiare*]

transubstantiation *n* the doctrine, esp. in the Roman Catholic and Eastern Orthodox churches, that the bread and wine become the actual body and blood of Christ when consecrated during the eucharist, but with their appearance remaining unchanged.

transuranic *adj* (*chem*) having an atomic number greater than that of uranium. [**trans-** + **uranium**]

transverse *adj* placed, lying, built, etc. crosswise or at right angles. — *adv* **transversely**. [Lat *transvertere*, to turn across]

transvestite *n* a person, esp. a man, who seeks (often sexual) pleasure by dressing up as a member of the opposite sex. — *n* **transvestism**. [Lat *trans*, across + *vestire*, to dress]

trap *n* **1** a device or hole, usu. with bait attached, for catching animals. **2** a plan or trick for surprising a person into speech or action, or catching someone unawares: *a speed trap.* **3** a trapdoor. **4** a bend in a pipe, esp. a drainpipe, which fills with liquid to stop foul gases passing up the pipe. **5** a light, two-wheeled carriage pulled by a single horse. **6** a device for throwing a ball or clay pigeon into the air. **7** a box-like compartment from which a greyhound is released at the beginning of a race. **8** a bunker or other hazard on a golf course. **9** (*slang*) the mouth. **10** (in *pl*; *jazz*) drums or other percussion instruments. ◇ See also **traps**. — *v* **-pp-** **1** (*tr*) to catch (an animal) in a trap. **2** (*tr*) to catch (a person) out or unawares, esp. with a trick. **3** (*tr*) to set traps in (a place). **4** (*tr*) to stop and hold in or as if in a trap. **5** (*intr*) to act as a trapper. [OE *treppe*]

trapdoor *n* a small door or opening in a floor or ceiling.

trapper *n* a person who traps animals and sells their fur.

trapes. See **traipse**.

trapeze *n* a swing-like apparatus consisting of a short horizontal bar hung on two ropes, on which gymnasts or acrobats perform tricks. [Fr *trapèze*, trapezium]

trapezium *n* **-ziums** or **-zia** **1** (*Br*) a quadrilateral with one pair of opposite sides parallel. **2** (*US*) a trapezoid (sense **1**). **3** any quadrilateral that is not a parallelogram. [Gr *trapezion*, from *trapeza*, table]

trapezoid *n* **1** (*Br*) a quadrilateral with no sides parallel. **2** (*US*) a trapezium (sense **1**). [Gr *trapeza*, table]

trappings *n* (*pl*) clothes or ornaments suitable for a particular occasion, ceremony, office or person. [OFr *drap*, cloth]

Trappist *n* a member of a branch of the Cistercian order of monks with a severe rule which includes a vow of silence. — *adj* of or relating to Trappists or their order. [*La Trappe*, in France, where the order was founded]

traps *n* (*pl*) personal luggage. [OFr *drap*, cloth]

trash *n* **1** (esp. *US*) rubbish; waste material or objects. **2** nonsense. **3** a worthless person or worthless people. **4** a worthless object or worthless objects. [MidE *trasches*]

trashcan *n* (*US*) a dustbin.

trashy *adj* **-ier**, **-iest** worthless. — *adv* **trashily**. — *n* **trashiness**.

trattoria *n* **-ias** or **-ie** an Italian restaurant. [Ital]

trauma *n* **-mas** or **-mata** **1** a physical injury or wound. **2** a state of shock caused by a physical wound or injury. **3** an emotional shock which may have long-term effects on behaviour or character. [Gr, wound]

traumatic *adj* **1** relating to, causing, or for physical wounds. **2** of or causing an emotional shock with long-term effects. **3** (*coll*) distressing; frightening; unpleasant. — *adv* **traumatically**.

traumatise or **-ize** *v* (*tr*) to cause physical or emotional trauma to.

travail *n* **1** painful or extremely hard work or labour. **2** the pain of childbirth; labour. — *v* (*intr*) to work hard or with pain, esp. in childbirth. [OFr]

travel *v* **-ll-** **1** (*intr*) to go from place to place; to journey, esp. abroad or far from home. **2** (*tr*) to journey through, across or over (a region, country, etc.). **3** (*tr*) to journey across (a stated distance). **4** (*intr*) to be capable of withstanding a usu. long journey: *Her children don't travel well.* **5** (*intr*) to journey from place to place as a sales representative. **6** (*intr*) to move: *Light travels in a straight line.* **7** (*intr*) to move or pass deliberately and steadily from one point to another: *Her eyes travelled over the horizon.* **8** (*intr*) (esp. of machinery) to move along a fixed course. **9** (*intr*; *coll*) to move quickly. — *n* **1** an act of travelling. **2** (usu. in *pl*) a journey or tour, esp. abroad: *get back from one's travels.* **3** the distance or speed travelled by machinery. [MidE]

travel agency *n* an office where one can arrange airline, coach, ship and train tickets, hotel accommodation, etc. for journeys and holidays. — *n* **travel agent**.

travelled *adj* (esp. *in cmpds*) **1** having travelled esp. abroad a lot. **2** travelled along; frequented: *a well-travelled road.*

traveller *n* **1** a person who travels. **2** (*old*) a travelling sales representative. **3** (*Br coll*) a gypsy.

traveller's cheque *n* a cheque issued by a bank, which can be exchanged for the currency of another country when in that country.

travelogue *n* a film, article, talk, etc. about travel, esp. an individual's trip to a particular place or region.

traverse *v* **1** (*tr*) to go across or through. **2** (*tr*) to lie or reach across: *a bridge traversing a deep gorge.* **3** (*tr* & *intr*) to climb, walk or ski at an angle across (a slope) rather than straight up or down. **4** (*intr*) to move sideways or to one side. **5** (*tr*) to examine or consider (a subject, problem, etc.) carefully and thoroughly. **6** (*tr*) to move (esp. the barrel of a large gun) to one side while keeping it horizontal. **7** (*tr*) to oppose or thwart. **8** (*tr*) to survey by traverse. — *n* **1** an act of crossing or traversing. **2** a path or passage across e.g. a rock face or slope. **3** something that lies across. **4** a sideways movement. **5** the movement of the barrel of a large gun to one side while being kept horizontal. **6** a survey by measuring straight lines from point to point and the angles between. **7** an obstruction. — *adj* being or lying across; oblique. — *adj* **traversal**. [Lat *traversare*]

travesty *n* **-ies** a ridiculous, crude, inadequate or distorted imitation: *a travesty of justice.* — *v* **-ies**, **-ied** (*tr*) to make a travesty of. [Fr *travestir*, to disguise]

trawl *n* **1** (in full **trawl-net**) a large, wide-mouthed, bag-shaped net used to catch fish in the sea. **2** a wide-ranging or extensive search. — *v* (*tr* & *intr*) **1** to search (the sea, an area of sea, etc.) for (fish) with a trawl. **2** to search through (a large number of things, people, etc.) thoroughly, esp. before finding the one required: *trawl through hundreds of applications before compiling a short-list.* [ODut *tragel*]

trawler *n* **1** a fishing-boat used in trawling. **2** a person who trawls.

tray *n* **1** a flat piece of wood, metal, plastic, etc. usu. with a low edge, for carrying dishes, crockery, etc. **2** a very shallow lidless box forming a drawer in e.g. a wardrobe or trunk, or used for displaying articles in a cabinet. [OE *trig*]

treacherous *adj* **1** not able to be trusted; ready or likely to betray. **2** having hidden hazards and dangers. — *adv* **treacherously**. — *n* **treacherousness**. [OFr *trechier*, to cheat]

treachery *n* **-ies** (an act of) betraying someone or their trust; disloyalty.

treacle *n* **1** a thick, dark, sticky liquid produced when refining sugar. **2** molasses. [Gr *theriake*, an antidote to the bites of wild beasts, with the word gradually coming to be applied to the sugary substance in which the antidote was taken rather than to the antidote itself]

tread *v* ***trod***, ***trodden*** or ***trod*** **1** (*intr*; **on**) to put a foot or feet (on); to walk or step (on). **2** (*tr*) to step or walk on, over or along. **3** (*tr*; **down**, **in**, **into**) to crush or press (e.g. into the ground) with a foot or feet; to trample: *tread grapes*; *tread the ash into the carpet.* **4** (*tr*) to wear or form (a path, hole, etc.) by walking. **5** (*tr*) to perform by walking. **6** (*intr*; **on**) to suppress. **7** (*tr*) (of a male bird) to copulate with (a female bird). — *n* **1** a manner, style or sound of walking: *a heavy tread.* **2** an act of treading. **3** a mark made by treading; a footprint or track. **4** the thick, grooved and patterned surface of a tyre that grips the road. **5** that part of a wheel that touches the rail. **6** that part of a rail that the wheels touch. **7** that part of the sole of a shoe that touches the ground. **8** the horizontal part of a step or stair on which the foot is placed. — **tread water** to keep oneself afloat and upright in water by making a treading movement with the legs as if walking and a circular movement with the hands and arms. [OE *tredan*]

treadmill *n* **1** an apparatus for producing motion consisting of a large wheel turned by people (esp. formerly prisoners) or animals treading on steps inside or around it. **2** a monotonous and dreary routine. **3** an exercise machine consisting of a continuous moving belt whose speed can be regulated to make the user walk, jog or run.

treadle *n* a pedal for one or both feet that drives a machine, e.g. a sewing-machine or loom. — *v* (*intr*) to work a treadle. [OE *tredel*, step]

treason *n* **1** (also **high treason**) disloyalty to or betrayal of one's country, sovereign or government. **2** any betrayal of trust or act of disloyalty. [OFr *traison*]

treasonable *adj* of, being or involving treason. — *adv* **treasonably**.

treasure *n* **1** wealth and riches, esp. in the form of gold, silver, precious stones and jewels, etc. which have been accumulated over a period of time and which can be hoarded. **2** any thing of great value. **3** (*coll*) a much loved and valued helper, friend, etc. — *v* (*tr*) **1** to value greatly or think of as very precious. **2** (**up**) to hoard up or collect (something) for future use or because it is considered valuable: *treasure up all the photographs of the children*. [OFr *tresor*]

treasure hunt *n* **1** a hunt for treasure. **2** a game in which players try to be the first to find a hidden prize by solving a series of clues whose answers lead to its location.

treasurer *n* **1** the person in a club, society, etc. who is in charge of the money and accounts. **2** an official responsible for public money, e.g. in a local council.

treasure-trove *n* (*legal*) treasure or money that is found hidden usu. in the earth and whose owner is unknown, deemed to be the property of the Crown. [OFr *trover*, to find]

treasury *n* **-ies 1** a place where treasure is stored. **2** (*cap*) (the building which houses) the government department in charge of a country's finances, esp. the collection and distribution of income from tax, etc. **3** the income or funds of a state, government, organisation or society. **4** a store of valued items, e.g. a book containing popular poems, stories or quotations.

Treasury bench *n* the front bench in the House of Commons where the Prime Minister, Chancellor of the Exchequer and other senior members of the Government sit.

treat *v* **1** (*tr*) to deal with or behave towards (a person or thing) in a certain manner: *treated him badly*; *treat it as a joke*. **2** (*tr*) to care for or deal with (a person, illness, injury, etc.) medically. **3** (*tr*; **with**) to put through a process or apply something to: *treat the wood with creosote*. **4** (*tr*; **to**) to provide (someone) with food, drink, entertainment or a present at one's own expense: *She treated herself to a new dress*. **5** (*tr*) to speak or write about; to discuss. **6** (*intr*; **of**) to deal with or discuss a subject, esp. in writing. **7** (*intr*; **with**) to negotiate (with another nation, person, etc.) to settle a dispute, end a war, etc. — *n* **1** an outing, meal, present, etc. given as a gift by one person to another. **2** any source of pleasure or enjoyment, esp. when unexpected. — **a treat** (*coll*) very good or well: *She looked a treat*. [OFr *traitier*]

treatment *n* **1** the medical or surgical care given to a patient, or to cure an illness. **2** an act or the manner of dealing with someone or something, often in a literary, musical or artistic treatment: *rough treatment*; *Monet's characteristic treatment of light and shadow*. — **the full treatment** (*coll*) the appropriate or usual treatment, complete in every detail.

treatise *n* a formal piece of writing which deals with a subject in depth. [OFr *tretis*, from *traitier*, to treat]

treaty *n* **-ies 1** a formal agreement between states or governments. **2** an agreement between two parties or individuals, esp. for the purchase of property. [OFr *trete*]

treble *n* **1** anything which is three times as much or as many. **2** (*mus*) soprano; a person, esp. a boy, having a soprano singing voice; a part written for this voice. **3** (*mus*) an instrument with a similar range, esp. in a family of instruments, the member with the highest range. **4** a high-pitched voice or sound. **5** the higher part of the audio frequency range of a radio, record, etc. **6** a bet on three races in which the original money bet and won on the first race is bet on the second, then the total bet on the third, so that the better either wins a lot of money or loses it all. **7** (a hit on) the narrow inner ring of a dartboard which scores three times the stated score. — *adj* **1** three times as much or as many; threefold; triple. **2** of, for, being or having a treble voice. **3** (of a voice) high-pitched. — *adv* with a treble voice: *sing treble*. — *v* (*tr* & *intr*) to make or become three times as much. — *adv* **trebly**. ◇ See also **triple**. [Lat *triplus*, triple]

treble chance *n* a way of betting with football pools in which the chance of winning depends on the number of draws and home and away wins forecast by the competitor.

treble clef *n* a sign at the beginning of a piece of written music which places on the second line of the staff the note G a fifth above middle C .

trecento *n* the 14th century, usu. with reference to Italian art. [Ital, three hundred (shortened from *mille trecento*, thirteen hundred)]

treddle. Same as **treadle**.

tree *n* **1** a tall, woody, perennial plant with a firm trunk which has branches usu. only on its upper part. **2** a similar plant or shrub with a single stem, such as a palm or rose tree. **3** anything like a tree, esp. in having branches leading from a main trunk, e.g. a diagram with a branched structure: *a family tree*. **4** (also *in cmpds*) a wooden frame or support, such as one for footwear (**shoe tree**) or mugs (**mug tree**). **5** (*old*) a cross for crucifixion. **6** (*old*) a gallows or gibbet. — *v* (*tr*) to drive or chase up a tree. — *adj* **treeless**. — **at the top of the tree** at the top of one's profession. — **up a tree** (esp. *NAm coll*) in difficulties. [OE *treow*]

tree creeper *n* a little bird that runs up tree trunks in search of insects on which to feed.

tree fern *n* a large fern with a tall, woody trunk.

tree line *n* same as **timber line**.

tree surgery *n* the art or practice of treating diseased or damaged trees to preserve them, e.g. by filling holes, cutting off dead branches and providing supports. — *n* **tree surgeon**.

trefoil *n* **1** a leaf which is divided into three sections. **2** any plant having such leaves, e.g. clover. **3** anything with three lobes or sections. **4** a carved ornament or decoration with three lobes or sections. [Lat *trifolium*, from *tres*, three + *folium*, leaf]

trek *v* **-kk-** (*intr*) **1** to make a long, hard journey. **2** (*SAfr*) to make a journey by ox-wagon. — *n* **1** a long, hard journey. **2** (*SAfr*) a journey by ox-wagon. [Dut, to draw (a vehicle or load)]

trellis *n* a frame or network of narrow wooden strips used to support climbing plants. — *v* **-s-** (*tr*) to provide or support with a trellis. — *adj* **trellised**. [OFr *trelis*]

tremble *v* (*intr*) **1** to shake, e.g. with cold, fear, weakness, etc. **2** to quiver or vibrate. **3** (**for**) to feel fear or anxiety (for). — *n* **1** a trembling movement; a shudder or tremor. **2** (in *pl*) a disease of livestock, esp. cattle, causing muscular weakness, shaking and constipation. — *adj* **trembling**. — *adv* **tremblingly**. — *adj* **trembly**, **-ier**, **-iest**. — **go in fear and trembling (of)** (often *facet*) to be very afraid (of). [Lat *tremere*, to shake]

trembling poplar *n* the aspen.

tremendous *adj* **1** enormous; huge. **2** (*coll*) very good or remarkable. — *adv* **tremendously**. [Lat *tremendus*, to be trembled at]

tremolo *n* **-os** (*mus*) **1** a trembling effect produced by rapidly repeating a note or notes, produced esp. by a stringed or keyboard instrument. **2** a similar effect produced in singing by fluctuating the pitch of the note sung. **3** a device in an organ for producing a trembling effect. [Ital]

tremor *n* **1** a shaking or quivering. **2** a slight vibration or trembling movement, esp. a slight earthquake. **3** a thrill. [Lat]

tremulous *adj* **1** trembling, esp. with fear, worry, nervousness or excitement. **2** (of a line drawn, words written, etc.) written by a shaky, hesitant hand and so weak and wavering. — *adv* **tremulously**. — *n* **tremulousness**. [Lat *tremulus*, from *tremere*, to shake]

trench *n* **1** a long narrow ditch dug in the ground, esp. one used to protect soliders from enemy gunfire. **2** a long, narrow and deep natural depression in the sea bed. — *v* (*tr*) **1** to dig a trench or trenches (in). **2** to provide (a place) with a trench as fortification. [OFr *trenche*, cut]

trench coat *n* a waterproof coat with a belt and epaulettes, based on the style of a military raincoat.

trench warfare *n* warfare in which each side uses trenches from which to attack the enemy.

trenchant *adj* **1** cutting; keen. **2** incisive; penetrating. **3** forthright; vigorous. — *n* **trenchancy**. — *adv* **trenchantly**. [OFr, cutting]

trencher *n* **1** (*hist*) a wooden plate or board for serving food on. **2** (in full **trencher-cap**) a square, flat hat worn by academics; a mortarboard. [OFr *trenchour*, from *trenchier*, to cut]

trencherman *n* a person who eats well or heartily.

trend *n* **1** a general direction or tendency. **2** the current general movement in fashion, style or taste. — *v* (*intr*; **towards**) to turn or have a tendency to turn in a usu. specified direction: *trend north*; *trend towards socialism*. [OE *trendan*]

trendsetter *n* a person who sets a fashion. — *n* **trendsetting**.

trendy *adj* **-ier**, **-iest** (esp. *Br coll*) following the latest fashions, often without thinking or using one's own discrimination or taste. — *n* **-ies** a trendy person. — *adv* **trendily**.

trepan *n* a small cylindrical saw formerly used for removing part of a bone, esp. the skull, during surgery. — *v* **-nn-** (*tr*) to remove (a piece of bone) with a trepan. ◇ See also **trephine**. [Gr *trypaein*, to bore]

trephine *n* a surgical instrument used for removing circular sections of bone, esp. from the skull, during surgery, now used instead of the trepan. — *v* (*tr*) to remove (a piece of bone) with a trephine. [Lat *tres fines*, three ends]

trepidation *n* fear or nervousness. [Lat *trepidare*, to hurry with alarm]

trespass *v* (*intr*; **on**) **1** to enter (someone else's property) without the right or permission to do so. **2** (*intr*; **on**, **upon**) to intrude into (a person's time, privacy, rights, etc.). **3** (*old*) to sin. — *n* **1** the act of entering someone else's property with the right or permission to do so. **2** an intrusion into someone's time, privacy, etc. **3** (*old*) a sin. — *n* **trespasser**. [Lat *transpassare*, to step across]

tress *n* **1** a long lock or plait of hair. **2** (in *pl*) a woman's or girl's long hair. [OFr *tresse*]

trestle *n* a support, e.g. for a table, consisting of a horizontal beam resting at each end on a pair of legs sloping outwards. [OFr *trestel*, from Lat *transtrum*, transom]

trestle table *n* a table consisting of a board or boards supported by trestles.

trews *n* (*pl*) trousers, esp. of tartan cloth. [Irish & Scottish Gaelic *triubhas*]

tri- *comb fm* three, three times or threefold. [Lat *tres* & Gr *treis*, three]

triad *n* **1** any group of three people or things. **2** a chord consisting of three notes, usu. a base note and those notes a third and a fifth above it. **3** (often *cap*) any of several Chinese secret societies, esp. one involved in organised crime or drug trafficking. **4** in Welsh literature, a group of three sayings, stories, etc. about related subjects. — *adj* **triadic**. [Gr *treis*, three]

trial *n* **1** a legal process by which a person accused of a crime or misdemeanour is judged in a court of law. **2** an act of trying or testing; a test. **3** (any person or thing causing) trouble, worry or vexation: *Her son is a great trial to her*. **4** (*sport*) a preliminary test of a player's or athlete's skill and fitness, esp. before choosing which players or athletes to include in a team. **5** a test of a vehicle's performance held esp. over rough ground or a demanding course. **6** a competition, usu. held over rough ground, to test car- or motorcycle-handling skills. **7** any competition testing the skills of animals: *sheepdog trials*. **8** an attempt. — **on trial 1** the subject of a legal action in court. **2** undergoing tests or examination before being permanently accepted or approved. — **trial and error** the trying of various methods, alternatives, etc. until the correct or suitable one is found. [OFr, from *trier*, to try]

trial run *n* a test of a vehicle, piece of machinery, etc. or rehearsal of a play, to assess effectiveness.

triangle *n* **1** a two-dimensional figure with three sides and three angles. **2** anything with a similar shape. **3** a musical percussion instrument consisting of a metal bar shaped into a triangle with one corner left open that is struck with a small hammer. **4** an emotional relationship or love affair involving three people. [Lat *triangulum*]

triangular *adj* **1** in the shape of a triangle. **2** involving three people or parties. — *n* **triangularity**. — *adv* **triangularly**.

triangulate *v* (*tr*) to survey (an area) by dividing it up into a series of triangles, e.g. when map-making. — *n* **triangulation**.

Triassic *n* the geological period that extends from approximately 250 to 215 million years ago, when the first dinosaurs and small mammals appeared. — *adj* of this geological period. [Lat *trias*, triad]

triathlon *n* an athletic contest consisting of three events, usu. swimming, running and cycling. — *n* **triathlete**. [**tri-** + **decathlon**]

tribe *n* **1** a group of families, clans or communities who are linked by social, economic and political ties, who often have a common ancestor and usu. have a common culture, dialect and leader. **2** a group of people with a common interest, profession, etc. **3** (*hist*) any of the three divisions of the ancient Romans, the Latins, Etruscans and Sabines. **4** (*hist*) any of the twelve divisions of the Israelites, each of which was believed to be descended from one of the twelve patriarchs. **5** (*biol*) in plant and animal classification, a group of related genera within a family. [Lat *tribus*, one of the divisions of the ancient Roman people]

tribal *adj* of a tribe or tribes. — *adv* **tribally**.

tribalism *n* **1** the system of tribes as a way of organising society. **2** the feeling of belonging to a tribe.

tribesman or **tribeswoman** *n* a man, or woman, who belongs to a tribe.

tribulation *n* (a cause of) great sorrow or trouble. [Lat *tribulatio*, from *tribulare*, to afflict]

tribunal *n* **1** a court of justice. **2** a group of people appointed to inquire into some matter or dispute and to adjudicate or give judgement. **3** a seat or bench in a court for a judge or judges. [Lat]

tribune[1] *n* **1** (*hist*) a high official elected by the ordinary people of ancient Rome to defend their rights and interests. **2** a champion or defender of the rights of the common people. [Lat *tribunus*]

tribune[2] *n* **1** a raised area, dais or stand. **2** a bishop's throne. [Lat *tribuna*]

tributary *n* **-ies 1** a stream or river flowing into a larger river or lake. **2** a person or nation paying tribute to another. — *adj* **1** (of a stream or river) being a tributary. **2** paid or owed as tribute. **3** paying tribute. [Lat *tributarius*]

tribute *n* **1** something given or said as an expression of praise, thanks, admiration or affection. **2** (**to**) a sign or evidence of (something valuable, effective, worthy of praise, etc.): *Her success was a tribute to all her hard work*. **3** (esp. *hist*) (a sum of) money paid regularly by one nation or ruler to another in return for protection or as an acknowledgement of submission: *pay tribute*. [Lat *tributum*]

trice: **in a trice** in a very short time; almost immediately. [MidE, to pull or haul]

triceps *n* any muscle attached to a bone or bones in three places, esp. the large muscle at the back of the arm which straightens the elbow. [Lat, three-headed]

triceratops *n* a large, heavily-built, four-legged plant-eating dinosaur, which had a bony frill round its neck, one horn over each eye and one on its nose. [Gr *trikeratos*, three-horned + *ops*, face]

trichology *n* the scientific study of the hair and its diseases. [Gr *trix*, hair + **-logy** (sense **1**)]

trick *n* **1** something which is done or said to cheat, deceive, fool or humiliate someone. **2** a deceptive appearance, esp. one caused by the light; an illusion. **3** a mischievous act or plan; a prank or joke. **4** a clever or skilful act or feat which astonishes, puzzles or amuses. **5** a habit or mannerism: *He has a trick of scratching his nose when he's angry*. **6** a special technique or knack: *a trick of the trade*. **7** a feat of skill which can be learned. **8** the cards played in one round of a card game and which are won by one of the players. **9** (*slang*) a prostitute's client. **10** (*naut*) a period of duty at the helm. — *adj* **1** intended to deceive or give a certain illusion: *trick photography*. **2** able to or designed for the performing of tricks. — *v* (*tr*) **1** to cheat, deceive or defraud. **2** (**into**, **out of**) to make (someone) do what one wants him or her to do, or gain something from (someone) by cheating or deception: *trick him out of his money*. **3** (**out**, **up**) to dress or decorate fancily. — **do the trick** (*coll*) to do or be what is necessary to achieve something. — **trick or treat** (esp. *NAm*) the children's practice of dressing up on Hallowe'en to call at people's houses to threaten to play a trick unless they are given some treat (e.g. sweets) by the householder. — **up to one's tricks** (*coll*) behaving in one's usual, esp. deceitful or amusing, way. [OFr *trique*]

trickery *n* **-ies** an act or the practice of deceiving or cheating.

trickster *n* a person who deceives or cheats, or plays tricks.

tricky *adj* **-ier**, **-iest** **1** difficult to handle or do; needing skill and care. **2** inclined to trickery; sly; deceitful. **3** clever in tricks; resourceful; adroit. — *adv* **trickily**. — *n* **trickiness**.

trickle *v* **1** (*tr* & *intr*) to (cause to) flow in a thin slow stream or drops. **2** (*intr*) to move, come or go slowly and gradually. — *n* a thin slow stream, flow or movement. [MidE *triklen*]

tricolour *n* a three-coloured flag, esp. one with three equal stripes of different colours, such as the French and Irish flags. — *adj* **tricoloured**. [Lat *tricolor*]

tricot *n* **1** a hand-knitted woollen fabric. **2** a soft, slightly ribbed cloth for women's garments. [Fr, knitting]

tricycle *n* **1** a vehicle with three wheels, two at the back and one at the front, driven by pedals. **2** a light, three-wheeled car for the use of a disabled person. — *v* (*intr*) to ride a tricycle. — *n* **tricyclist**. [**tri-** + **cycle**]

trident *n* **1** (*hist*) a spear with three prongs, esp. as carried by a sea-god, such as Neptune or Britannia, or a Roman gladiator. **2** (*cap*) a ballistic missile with several warheads which can each be programmed to attack a different target, fired from a submarine. [Lat *tridens*, having three teeth]

Tridentine *adj* of or relating to the Council of Trent (1545–63) or the traditional Catholic beliefs and doctrines reaffirmed there as a reaction to Protestantism and the Reformation. — *n* a member of the Roman Catholic Chruch who follows the traditional doctrine affirmed at the Council of Trent. [Lat *Tridentum*, Trent]

triennial *adj* **1** happening once every three years. **2** lasting three years. — *adv* **triennially**. [Lat *triennis*]

trifle *n* **1** anything of very little value. **2** a very small amount. **3** a dessert made typically of sponge-cake soaked in sherry and spread with jam or jelly and fruit and topped with custard and whipped cream. — *v* **1** (*intr*; **with**) to treat (e.g. a person or his or her feelings) without respect and as if worthless. **2** (*intr*) to act, behave or talk idly. **3** (*tr*; **away**) to spend or pass (e.g. time) idly. [OFr *trufe*, mockery, deceit]

trifling *adj* **1** unimportant; trivial. **2** frivolous.

trig *n* (*coll*) trigonometry. [Abbrev.]

trig point *n* (*coll*) same as **trigonometrical point**.

trigger *n* **1** a small lever which releases a catch or spring to set a mechanism going, esp. one which is squeezed to fire a gun. **2** anything which starts a train of actions or reactions. — *v* **-r-** (*tr*; **off**) to start (a train of actions, reactions, events, etc.). [Dut *trekken*, to pull]

trigger-happy *adj* (*coll*) likely to shoot or react violently without thinking or with very little provocation.

trigonometry *n* the branch of mathematics which studies the relationship between the sides and angles of triangles and the different functions (sines, tangents, etc.) of the angles, used e.g. in surveying. — *adj* **trigonometrical**. [Gr *trigonon*, triangle + *metron*, measure]

trigonometrical point *n* a fixed point, often a point on a hilltop, whose position as the vertex of a triangle is calculated astronomically and which is used as an aid to map-making.

trike *n* (*coll*) a tricycle. [Abbrev.]

trilateral *adj* having three sides. — *adv* **trilaterally**. [Lat *tri-*, three + *latus*, side]

trilby *n* **-ies** (esp. *Br*) a soft felt hat with an indented crown and narrow brim. [*Trilby*, the heroine of the novel of the same name by George du Maurier (1834–96), in the stage version of which such a hat was worn]

trilingual *adj* **1** able to speak three languages fluently, as or like a native speaker. **2** written or spoken in three languages. [**tri-** + Lat *lingua*, tongue]

trill *n* **1** (*mus*) a sound produced by playing or singing a note and a note higher than it repeatedly and in rapid succession. **2** a shrill warbling sound made by a songbird. **3** a consonant sound, esp. an 'r' sound, produced by rapidly vibrating the tongue. — *v* (*tr* & *intr*) to play, sing or pronounce (something) with a trill. [Ital *trillo*]

trillion *n* **1** in Britain and Europe, a million million millions (10^{18}). **2** in the US and Canada, a million millions (10^{12}). **3** (esp. in pl; *coll*) an enormous number or amount. — *n* & *adj* **trillionth**. **[tri- + million]**

trilobite *n* any of various extinct marine arthropods with a body divided into three lobes, now found as fossils. [Gr *trilobos*, three-lobed]

trilogy *n* ***-ies*** a group of three plays, novels, poems, operas, etc. which are related, often by theme. [Gr *trilogia*]

trim *v* ***-mm-*** **1** (*tr*) to make neat and tidy, esp. by clipping. **2** (*tr*; **away, off**) to remove by, or as if by, cutting: *trim hundreds of pounds off the cost*. **3** (*tr*) to make less by, or as if by, cutting: *trim costs*. **4** (*tr*) to decorate with ribbons, lace, ornaments, etc. **5** (*tr*) to adjust the balance of (a ship, submarine or aircraft) by moving its cargo, ballast, etc. **6** (*tr*) to arrange (a ship's sails) to suit the weather conditions. **7** (*intr*) to hold a neutral or middle course between two opposing individuals or groups. **8** (*intr*) to adjust one's behaviour to suit current trends or opinions, esp. for self-advancement. — *n* **1** a haircut which neatens but does not change a person's hairstyle. **2** proper order or condition: *in good trim*. **3** material, ornaments, etc. used as decoration. **4** the decorative additions to a car, including the upholstery, internal and external colour scheme and chrome and leather accessories. **5** the set or balance of a ship on the water. **6** (of a ship) the state of being ready, esp. with the sails in proper order, for sailing. **7** the inclination of an aircraft in flight, esp. with reference to the horizon. **8** parts removed by trimming. — *adj* ***-mm-*** **1** in good order; neat and tidy. **2** clean-cut; slim. — *adv* **trimly**. — *n* **trimness**. [OE *trymian*, to strengthen]

trimmer *n* **1** a person or thing that trims. **2** a person who adjusts his or her behaviour to suit current trends and opinions, esp. for self-advancement. **3** a short horizontal beam on a floor into which the ends of joists are fitted.

trimming *n* **1** ribbon, lace or some other decoration added e.g. to a garment. **2** (in *pl*) the traditional or usual sauce, garnish, accompanying vegetables, etc. served with a particular dish. **3** (in *pl*) parts cut or trimmed off.

trimaran *n* a boat with three hulls placed side by side. **[tri- + catamaran]**

trimester *n* a period of three months, esp. in the US one forming an academic term. [Lat *trimestris*, of three months]

Trinitarian *n* a person who believes in the doctrine of the Trinity. — *adj* of or believing in the doctrine of the Trinity. — *n* **Trinitarianism**. ◇ See also **Unitarian**. **[trinity]**

trinitrotoluene. See **TNT**. **[tri- + nitro- +** *toluene*, a liquid organic chemical]

trinity *n* ***-ies*** **1** the state of being or a group of three. **2** (*cap*; *Christian theol*) the unity of three persons, the Father, Son and Holy Spirit, in a single Godhead. **3** (*cap*; in full **Trinity Sunday**) the Sunday after Whit Sunday, kept as a festival in honour of the Trinity. **4** (*cap*; in full **Trinity Term**) the university or law term beginning after Easter. [Lat *trinitas*]

trinket *n* a small, worthless article, esp. a cheap ornament or piece of jewellery.

trinketry *n* a collection of such articles.

trio *n* ***-os*** **1** a group of three. **2** (*mus*) (a piece of music composed for) a group of three instruments, players or singers. **3** (*mus*) a division of a minuet, scherzo or march. [Ital]

trip *v* ***-pp-*** **1** (*tr* & *intr*; **on, over, up**) to (cause to) stumble. **2** (*tr* & *intr*; **up**) to (cause to) make a mistake or mistakes. **3** (*tr*) to catch (someone) in a fault or mistake. **4** (*intr*; **along**) to walk, skip or dance with short, light steps. **5** (*intr*) to move or flow smoothly and easily: *words tripping off the tongue*. **6** (*intr*) to take a trip or excursion. **7** (*intr*; *slang*) to experience the hallucinatory effects of a drug, esp. LSD. **8** (*tr* & *intr*) to activate or cause (a device or mechanism) to be activated, esp. suddenly. **9** (*tr*) to perform (a dance) with quick, light, agile steps. — *n* **1** a short journey or excursion, usu. to a place and back again. **2** a catching of the foot; a stumble. **3** a short, light step or skip. **4** a striking part or catch which activates a mechanism. **5** an error or blunder. **6** (*slang*) a hallucinatory experience caused by taking a drug, esp. LSD. **7** (*slang*) an intensely emotional experience. [OFr *triper*]

tripper *n* **1** (esp. *Br*; often *derog*) a person who goes on a journey for pleasure; a tourist. **2** (*slang*) a person who takes a drug, esp. LSD, and experiences its hallucinatory effects.

trip-wire *n* a hidden wire which sets off a mechanism of some kind, such as an alarm or bomb, when someone trips over it.

tripartite *adj* **1** divided into three parts. **2** involving or concerning three parts, groups, people, etc. [Lat *tripartitus*]

tripe *n* **1** parts of the stomach of a cow or sheep, used as food. **2** (*coll*) nonsense; rubbish. [OFr]

triple *adj* **1** three times as great, as much or as many. **2** made up of three parts or things. **3** (*mus*) having three beats to the bar. — *v* (*tr* & *intr*) to make or become three times as great, much or many. — *n* **1** three times the (usual) amount. **2** a group or series of three. — *adv* **triply**. ◇ See also **treble**. [Lat *triplus*]

triple jump *n* an athletic event in which competitors try to cover the greatest distance with a type of jump consisting of a hop, skip and a jump.

triple point *n* the temperature and pressure at which the solid, liquid and gaseous forms of a substance can co-exist.

triplet *n* **1** one of three children or animals born to the same mother at the same time. **2** a group or set of three. **3** (*mus*) a group of three notes played in the time usu. given to two. **4** a group of three rhyming verses in a poem. [**triple**]

triplicate *adj* **1** having three parts which are exactly alike. **2** being one of three identical copies. **3** tripled. — *n* any of three identical copies or three parts which are exactly alike. — *v* (*tr*) to make three copies of. — *n* **triplication**. — **in triplicate** three times; on three separate copies (of the same form). [Lat *triplicatus*]

tripod *n* **1** a stand with three legs for supporting a camera. **2** a stool or table with three legs or feet. [Lat *tripus*]

tripos *n* an honours examination for the BA degree at Cambridge University. [Lat *tripus*, tripod]

triptych *n* a picture or carving on three panels which are joined together by hinges to form a single work of art, often used as an altarpiece. ◇ See also **diptych**. [Gr *triptychos*, threefold]

trireme *n* an ancient Greek warship with three banks of rowers on each side. [Lat *triremis*]

trisect *v* (*tr*) to divide into three, usu. equal, parts. — *n* **trisection**. [**tri-** + Lat *secare*, to cut]

trite *adj* (of a remark, phrase, etc.) having no meaning or effectiveness because repeated or used so often; hackneyed. — *adv* **tritely**. — *n* **triteness**. [Lat *tritus*, rubbed]

tritium *n* (*chem*) a radioactive isotope of hydrogen (symbol **T**), with three times the mass of ordinary hydrogen. [Gr *tritos*, third]

triumph *n* **1** a great or notable victory, success or achievement. **2** the great joy or feeling of elation felt on winning a great victory, etc. **3** (*hist*) the procession accompanying the entry into ancient Rome of a general who had won a great victory over a foreign enemy. — *v* (*intr*) **1** (**over**) to win a victory or be successful. **2** to celebrate a victory or success. **3** (**over**) to enjoy a feeling of triumph (over someone). [Lat *triumphus*]

triumphal *adj* of or celebrating a triumph.

triumphant *adj* **1** having won a victory or achieved success. **2** feeling or showing great joy or elation at, or celebrating, a victory or success. — *adv* **triumphantly**.

triumvir *n* **-viri** or **-virs** any one of a group of three people sharing office or supreme power. — *adj* **triumviral**. [Lat, from *trium virorum*, of three men]

triumvirate *n* a group of three people sharing office or supreme power.

trivalent *adj* (*chem*) having a valency of three. — *n* **trivalence** or **trivalency**. [**tri-** + Lat *valere*, to be strong]

trivet *n* **1** a three-legged stand or bracket which hooks on to a grate for holding cooking vessels over a fire. **2** a stand for a hot dish, pot, teapot, etc. at table. [OE *trefet*]

trivia *n* (*pl*) unimportant or petty matters or details. [Lat *trivium*, place where three ways meet]

trivial *adj* **1** of very little importance. **2** (of a person) only interested in unimportant things; frivolous. **3** commonplace; ordinary. — *n* **triviality**, **-ies**. — *adv* **trivially**.

trivialise or **-ize** *v* (*tr*) to make or treat as if trivial or unimportant. — *n* **trivialisation** or **-z-**.

trochee *n* (*prosody*) a foot consisting of one long syllable followed by one short one. [Gr *trochaios* (*pous*), running (foot)]

trod, trodden. See **tread**.

troglodyte *n* a person who lives in a cave. [Gr *troglodytes*, one who creeps into holes]

troika *n* **1** a Russian vehicle drawn by three horses abreast. **2** a team of three horses harnessed abreast. **3** any group of three people working as a team, esp. sharing power. [Russ]

Trojan *n* **1** (*hist*) a citizen or inhabitant of ancient Troy in Asia Minor. **2** a person who works, fights, etc. extremely hard or courageously. — *adj* of ancient Troy, its inhabitants or citizens. [Lat *Trojanus*, from *Troja*, Troy]

troll[1] *n* (*Scandinavian mythol*) an imaginary, ugly, evil-tempered, human-like creature, usu. a dwarf or a giant. [Norse]

troll[2] *v* **1** (*tr* & *intr*) to fish (for or in) by trailing bait on a line through water. **2** (*intr*; *old* or *facet*) to stroll or saunter. — *n* (a line holding) the bait used in trolling. [MidE *trollen*, to roll or stroll]

trolley *n* **-eys** **1** (esp. *Br*) a small cart or basket on wheels used for conveying luggage, shopping, etc. **2** (esp. *Br*) a small table, usu. with a shelf underneath, mounted on castors or wheels, used for conveying food, crockery, etc. in the home or a restaurant. **3** a bed on wheels for transporting patients in hospital. **4** (esp. *Br*) a small wagon or truck running on rails. **5** a trolley wheel. **6** (*Br*) a trolley bus. **7** (*NAm*) a trolley car. — **off one's trolley** (*coll*) daft; crazy. [Prob. from **troll**[2]]

trolley bus *n* a vehicle providing public transport which receives power from a trolley wheel and overhead electric wires.

trolley car *n* (*NAm*) a vehicle providing public transport which runs on rails like a tram and receives power from a trolley wheel and overhead electric wires.

trolley wheel *n* a small grooved wheel which collects current from an overhead electric wire and transmits it down a pole to power the vehicle underneath.

trollop *n* a shameless, promiscuous, disreputable or untidy woman. [Perhaps from **troll**[2]]

trombone *n* a brass musical wind instrument, on which the pitch of notes is altered by sliding a tube in and out. — *n* **trombonist**. [Ital, from *tromba*, trumpet]

trompe l'oeil *n* ***trompe l'oeils*** a painting or decoration which gives a convincing illusion of reality. [Fr, deceives the eye]

troop *n* **1** (in *pl*) the armed forces; soldiers. **2** a group or collection, esp. of people or animals. **3** a division of a cavalry or armoured squadron. **4** a large group of Scouts, divided into patrols. — *v* (*intr*; **along, into, off, over**, etc.) to move as a group. — **troop the colour** to parade the regiment's flag ceremonially. [OFr *trope*]

trooper *n* **1** a private soldier, esp. one in a cavalry or armoured unit. **2** a cavalry soldier's horse. **3** (*US*) a policeman mounted on a horse or motorcycle. **4** (*Br*) a troop-ship.

troop-ship *n* a ship for transporting soldiers.

trope *n* a word or expression used figuratively. [Gr *tropos*, turn]

trophy *n* ***-ies*** **1** a cup, medal, plate, etc. awarded as a prize for victory or success in some contest, esp. in sport. **2** something which is kept in memory of a victory or success, e.g. in hunting. **3** a memorial of victory, esp. in ancient Greece or Rome, orig. captured weapons, armour and other spoils, set up on or near the field of victory. **4** a representation of such a memorial, e.g. on a medal or monument. [Gr *tropaion*]

tropic *n* **1** either of two imaginary circles running round the earth at 23° 27′ north (the **Tropic of Cancer**) or 23° 27′ south (the **Tropic of Capricorn**) of the equator. **2** (in *pl*) the part of the earth lying between these two circles, noted for its hot, dry weather. [Gr *tropikos*]

tropical *adj* (also **tropic**) **1** of, relating to, found in or from the tropics. **2** very hot; passionate. **3** luxuriant. — *adv* **tropically**.

tropism *n* (*biol*) the turning or curving of an animal or plant in response to an external stimulus, such as a plant turning towards the sun. [Gr *tropos*, turning]

troposphere *n* the lowest layer of the atmosphere extending from the earth's surface to a height of between nine kilometres (at the Poles) and seventeen kilometres (at the equator), in which the temperature decreases with height. [Gr *tropos*, turn + **sphere**]

Trot *n* (*coll derog*) **1** a Trotskyist. **2** any supporter of the extreme left. [Abbrev.]

trot *v* ***-tt-*** **1** (*intr*) (of a horse) to move at a steady, fairly fast pace, moving each diagonal pair of legs together to give a bouncy gait. **2** (*tr*) to cause (a horse) to move in this way. **3** (*intr*) to move or proceed at a steady, fairly brisk pace. — *n* **1** the pace at which a horse, rider, etc. moves when trotting. **2** an act of trotting. **3** (in *pl*; *slang*) diarrhoea. — **on the trot** (*coll*) **1** one after the other. **2** continually moving about; busy. — *v* **trot out** (*tr*; *coll*) to bring out, produce or present for approval, esp. repeatedly: *He trots out the same excuses every time he's late.* [OFr *troter*]

trotter *n* **1** a horse trained to trot in harness. **2** (usu. in *pl*) a pig's foot, used as food.

troth *n* (*old*) faith or fidelity. — **plight one's troth** to promise to be faithful and true in marriage. [OE *treowth*, truth]

Trotskyism *n* the political, social and economic theories of L *Trotsky* (1879–1940), including a belief in the need for a worldwide socialist revolution. — *n* & *adj* **Trotskyist** or **Trotskyite**.

troubadour *n* (*hist*) any of a number of lyric poets in southern France and northern Italy in the 11th to 13th centuries who wrote, usu. in Provençal, about a highly idealised form of love. [Provençal *trobar*, to find]

trouble *n* **1** (something which causes) distress, worry, concern or annoyance. **2** (something which causes) bother, effort or work: *go to a lot of trouble*; *The dog was no trouble*. **3** a problem or difficulty: *Your trouble is that you're too generous*. **4** (often in *pl*) public disturbances and unrest. **5** illness or weakness: *heart trouble*. **6** malfunction; failure: *engine trouble*. **7** the state of expecting a child when not married: *get into trouble*. — *v* **1** (*tr* & *intr*) to feel or cause to feel distress, worry, concern, anger or sadness to. **2** (*tr*) to cause physical distress or discomfort to. **3** (*tr*) (used when making polite, formal requests) to put to inconvenience: *Might I trouble you to open the window a little?* **4** (*intr*) to make any effort or take pains: *He didn't even trouble to tell me what had happened.* **5** (*tr*) to disturb or agitate (e.g. the surface of water). — *adj* **troubled**. — **be asking for trouble** (*coll*) to behave in a way likely to bring problems or difficulties on oneself. — **in trouble** in difficulties, esp. because of doing something wrong or illegal. — **take trouble** (**over, with**) to take a lot of care (over). [OFr *trubler*, from Lat *turbare*, to disturb]

troublemaker *n* a person who continually and usu. deliberately causes trouble, worry, problems, etc. to others.

troubleshooter *n* **1** a person who is employed to find and solve problems, e.g. with machinery or in a company. **2** a person employed to mediate in disputes. — *n* **troubleshooting**.

troublesome *adj* causing worry or difficulty. — *adv* **troublesomely**. — *n* **troublesomeness**.

troublous *adj* (*old* or *literary*) full of troubles; disturbed.

trough *n* **1** a long, low, narrow open container, esp. one for holding water or feed for animals. **2** a channel, drain or gutter. **3** a long, narrow hollow between two waves. **4** a long, narrow area of low atmospheric pressure. **5** a low point. [OE *trog*]

trounce *v* (*tr*) to beat or defeat completely. — *n* **trouncing**.

troupe *n* a group or company of performers. [Fr, from Lat *troppus*, troop]

trouper *n* **1** a member of such a group or company. **2** an experienced, hard-working and loyal colleague.

trousers *n* (*pl*) an outer garment for the lower part of the body, reaching from the waist and covering each leg separately down to the ankle. [Irish and Scottish Gaelic *triubhas*, trews]

trouser *in cmpds* of trousers: *trouser-buttons*.

trousseau *n* ***-eaux*** or ***-eaus*** a bride's set of new clothes (and sometimes household linen), traditionally bought for her wedding, honeymoon, and married life. [Fr, from *trousse*, bundle]

trout *n* ***trout*** or ***trouts*** **1** any of several usu. freshwater fish of the salmon family. **2** (*slang derog*) an unpleasant, interfering old person, usu. a woman. [OE *truht*]

trove. See **treasure-trove**.

trowel *n* **1** a small, hand-held tool with a flat blade, used for applying and spreading mortar, plaster, etc. **2** a similar tool with a slightly curved blade, used for potting plants, etc. [Lat *trulla*, scoop]

troy *n* (in full **troy weight**) a system of weights used for precious metals and gemstones, with twelve ounces or 5760 grains to the pound. [*Troyes*, in France]

truant *n* someone who stays away from school or work without good reason or without permission. — *v* (*intr*) to be a truant. — *n* **truancy**. — **play truant** to stay away from school without good reason and without permission. [OFr]

truce *n* **1** an agreement to stop fighting, usu. temporarily. **2** a temporary break in fighting, hostilities, feuding, etc. [MidE *trewes*, from OE *treow*, true]

truck[1] *n* **1** (*Br*) an open railway wagon for carrying goods. **2** (esp. *NAm*) a heavy motor vehicle for transporting goods; a lorry. **3** a frame with four or more wheels supporting a railway carriage. **4** any wheeled vehicle, trolley or cart for moving heavy goods. — *v* **1** (*tr*) to put on or transport by truck. **2** (*intr*; esp. *NAm*) to work as a truck driver. — *n* **trucking**.

trucker *n* (esp. *NAm*) a person who drives a lorry, esp. over long distances.

truck[2] *n* **1** exchange of goods; commercial dealings. **2** payment of wages in goods rather than money. **3** (*coll*) small goods or wares. **4** (*coll*) odds and ends; rubbish. **5** (*US*) market-garden produce, such as vegetables and fruit. — *v* (*tr* & *intr*) to give (goods) in exchange; to barter. — **have no truck with** to have no part in or dealings with. [OFr *troquer*, to exchange]

truckle *n* (in full **truckle-bed**) a low bed that may be wheeled under a larger bed for storage. — *v* (*intr*; **to**) to submit or give in passively or weakly. [Lat *trochlea*, pulley]

truculent *adj* aggressively defiant, quarrelsome or discourteous. — *n* **truculence** or **truculency**. — *adv* **truculently**. [Lat *trux*, wild, fierce]

trudge *v* **1** (*intr*; **along, over, up**, etc.) to walk with slow, heavy, weary steps. **2** (*tr*) to cover (a stated distance, ground, etc.) with slow, heavy, weary steps. — *n* a long, weary or tiring walk.

true *adj* **1** agreeing with fact or reality; not false or wrong: *a true story*. **2** real; genuine; properly so called: *The spider is not a true insect*. **3** accurate or exact: *A photograph doesn't give a true idea of the size of the building*. **4** faithful; loyal: *be true to one's word*. **5** conforming to a standard, pattern, type or expectation: *behave true to form*. **6** in the correct position; well-fitting; accurately adjusted. **7** (of a compass bearing) measured according to the earth's axis and not magnetic north. **8** honest; sincere: *twelve good men and true*. — *adv* **1** certainly: *True, she isn't very happy here*. **2** truthfully. **3** faithfully. **4** honestly. **5** accurately or precisely. **6** accurately in tune: *sing true*. **7** conforming to ancestral type: *breed true*. — *v* (*tr*) to bring or restore (e.g. machinery) into an accurate or required position. — *n* **trueness**. — **come true** (of a dream, hope, etc.) to actually happen. — **out of true** not in the correct position; not straight or properly balanced. ◇ See also **truth**. [OE *treow*]

true-blue *adj* **1** extremely loyal. **2** (*Br*) being an extremely orthodox supporter of the Conservative party. — *n* a true-blue person.

true-love *n* a beloved person; a sweetheart.

true north *n* the direction of the North Pole (rather than the direction of magnetic north).

truism *n* a statement which is obviously true; a commonplace.

truly *adv* **1** really: *truly believe it to be for the best*. **2** genuinely; honestly. **3** faithfully. **4** accurately; exactly. **5** properly; rightly.

truffle *n* **1** any of several dark round fungi which grow underground and are considered a delicacy. **2** a usu. round sweet made typically with cream, butter, chocolate and rum, and coated in cocoa. [Lat *tuber*, lump, swelling]

trug *n* (*Br*) a shallow rectangular basket used for carrying garden tools, plants, etc. [Perhaps a variant of **trough**]

truism, truly. See **true**.

trump[1] *n* **1** (in *pl*) the suit of cards which has been declared to have a higher value than any other suit. **2** (also **trump card**) a card belonging to this suit, which beats any card belonging to one of the other three suits. **3** (also **trump card**) a secret advantage. **4** (*coll*) a helpful, reliable or fine person. — *v* **1** (*tr* & *intr*) to defeat (an ordinary card or a trick with no trumps) by playing a trump. **2** (*tr*) to win a surprising victory or advantage over (a person, plan, idea, etc.). — **come** or **turn up trumps** to behave in an unexpectedly useful or helpful way when things are particularly difficult. — *v* **trump up** (*tr*) to invent or make up (false evidence, accusations, etc.) (*adj* **trumped up**). [A variant of **triumph**]

trump[2] *n* (*old* or *poetic*) a trumpet. — **the last trump** the trumpet call to wake the dead on the Day of Judgement. [OFr *trompe*]

trumpery *n* **-ies 1** showy but worthless articles. **2** rubbish. — *adj* showy but worthless. [OFr *tromper*, to deceive]

trumpet *n* **1** a brass musical instrument with a narrow tube and flared bell and a powerful, high, clear tone. **2** anything like this in shape, such as the corona of a daffodil or a horn, or sound. **3** the loud cry of an elephant. — *v* **-t- 1** (*intr*) (of an elephant) to make a loud cry. **2** (*intr*) to blow a trumpet. **3** (*tr*) to make known or proclaim loudly. — *n* **trumpeter**. [OFr *trompette*]

truncate *v* (*tr*) to cut so as to shorten. — *adj* (*bot* & *biol*) (e.g. of a leaf) with the base or tip cut square. — *adj* **truncated**. — *n* **truncation**. [Lat *truncare*]

truncheon *n* **1** a short, thick heavy stick, carried by police officers. ◇ See also **baton**. **2** a staff of authority or office. [OFr *tronchon*, stump]

trundle *v* (*tr* & *intr*; **along, through**, etc.) to move or roll heavily, clumsily and noisily on, or as if on, wheels. [OE *trendel*]

trunk *n* **1** the main stem of a tree without the branches and roots. **2** a person's or animal's body without the head and limbs. **3** the main part of anything. **4** a large rigid box or chest for storing or transporting clothes and personal items. **5** (*NAm*) the boot of a car. **6** the long, muscular nose of an elephant. **7** (in *pl*) men's close-fitting shorts or pants worn esp. for swimming. [Lat *truncus*]

trunk call *n* (esp. *Br*) a long-distance telephone call.

trunk line *n* **1** a main telephone line between large towns or cities. **2** a main railway line.

trunk road *n* a main road between large towns.

truss *n* **1** a framework, e.g. of wooden or metal beams, supporting a roof, bridge, etc. **2** a belt, bandage or other device worn to support a hernia. **3** a bundle of hay or straw. **4** a cluster of flowers or fruit at the top of a main stalk or stem. **5** (*archit*) a corbel. — *v* (*tr*) **1** (**up**) to tie up or bind (someone) tightly. **2** to tie up the wings and legs of (a fowl) before cooking. **3** to support (a roof, bridge, etc.) with a truss. [OFr *trousse*]

trust *n* **1** (**in**) belief or confidence in, or reliance on, the truth, goodness, character, power, ability, etc. of someone or something. **2** charge or care: *The child was placed in my trust.* **3** the state of being responsible for the conscientious performance of some task: *be in a position of trust.* **4** a task made the responsibility of someone in the belief that he or she will perform it well and conscientiously. **5** credit: *put it on trust.* **6** an arrangement by which money or property is managed by one person for the benefit of someone else. **7** an amount of money or property managed by one person for the benefit of another. **8** a group of business firms working together to control the market in a particular commodity, beat down competition and maximise profits. — *adj* held in trust. — *v* **1** (*tr* & *intr*; **in**) to have confidence or faith (in); to depend or rely (on): *trust her to be able to cope.* **2** (*tr*) to allow (someone) to use or do something in the belief that (he or she) will behave responsibly, honestly, etc.: *wouldn't trust him with your new car.* **3** (*tr*; **to**) to give to the care of: *trust the child to him.* **4** (*tr* & *intr*) to be confident, hope or suppose: *I trust you had a good journey.* **5** (*tr*) to give credit to. — **take (something or someone) on trust** to accept or believe (someone or something) without checking. [Norse *traust*]

trustee *n* **1** a person who manages money or property for someone else. **2** a member of a group of people managing the affairs and business of a company or institution. — *n* **trusteeship**.

trustful or **trusting** *adj* willing to have confidence or trust in others; confiding. — *adv* **trustfully** or **trustingly**. — *n* **trustfulness**.

trust fund *n* money or property held in trust, e.g. until the owner comes of age.

trustworthy *adj* able to be trusted or depended on. — *adv* **trustworthily**. — *n* **trustworthiness**.

trusty *adj* **-ier, -iest** able to be trusted or depended on. — *n* **-ies** a trusted person, esp. a convict given special privileges for good behaviour. — *adv* **trustily**. — *n* **trustiness**.

truth *n* ***truths*** **1** the state of being true, genuine or factual. **2** the state of being truthful; sincerity; honesty. **3** that which is true. **4** that which is established or generally accepted as true: *scientific truths.* **5** strict adherence to an original or standard. — **to tell the truth** or **truth to tell** really; actually. [OE *treowth*]

truthful *adj* **1** (of a person) telling the truth. **2** true; realistic. — *adv* **truthfully**. — *n* **truthfulness**.

try *v* ***tries, tried*** **1** (*tr* & *intr*) to attempt or make an effort (at); to seek to attain or achieve. **2** (*tr*; **out**) to test or experiment (with) in order to assess its usefulness, value, quality, etc. or whether one likes it or not. **3** (*tr*) to judge or conduct the trial of (someone). **4** (*tr*) to examine all the evidence (in a case) in a law court. **5** (*tr*) to put strain or stress (on): *try the limits of his patience*. — *n* ***-ies*** **1** an attempt or effort. **2** (*Rugby*) the score of three points (in Rugby League) or four points (in Rugby Union) gained by a player who succeeds in placing the ball over the opponent's goal line with his or her hand. — *n* **trier**. — **try one's hand at** to see if one can do (something), esp. at a first attempt. — **try it on** (*Br coll*) to indulge in bad or risky behaviour, or attempt to deceive or fool someone, to test that person's patience and see how far one can go without being hurt, told off, etc. (*n* **try-on**). — *v* **try on** (*tr*) to put (clothes, shoes, etc.) on to check the fit and appearance (*n* **try-on**). — *v* **try out** (*tr*) to test the qualities, value or abilities (of something or someone) by making (it, him or her) perform (*n* **try-out**). [OFr *trier*, to sift]

tried *adj* **1** tested and proved to be good, efficient, etc. **2** (in *phrases & cmpds*) having had one's patience put to strain: *sorely tried*.

trying *adj* causing strain or anxiety; stretching one's patience to the limit.

try-on see **try it on** and **try on** above.

try-out see **try out** above.

trysail *n* a small strong fore-and-aft sail used in a storm.

tryst (esp. *old Scot* or *literary*) *n* **1** an arrangement to meet someone, esp. a lover. **2** the meeting itself. **3** (also **trysting-place**) the place where such a meeting takes place. — *v* (*intr*; **with**) to arrange a tryst (with). [OFr *triste*, a hunter's station]

tsar or **czar** *n* (also **tzar**) **1** the title given to the emperor of Russia. **2** a despot or tyrant. [Lat *Caesar*, family name of the earliest Roman emperors]

tsarevitch or **czarevitch** *n* (also **tzarevitch**) the title given to the eldest son of a tsar or tsarina.

tsarina or **czarina** *n* (also **tzarina**) **1** the title given to a woman who rules Russia as empress. **2** the title given to the wife or widow of a tsar.

TSB *abbrev* Trustee Savings Bank.

tsetse *n* (in full **tsetse-fly**) an African fly which feeds on human and animal blood and transmits several dangerous diseases including sleeping sickness. [Name in Tswana (S African language)]

T-shirt, T-square. See **T**[1].

tsunami *n* ***-is*** an enormous wave caused by movements, e.g. earthquakes, of the sea floor, which travels very quickly and may cause great destruction if it touches land. [Jap *tsu*, harbour + *nami*, wave]

tub *n* **1** any of various large, low, round wooden, metal or plastic containers, usu. for holding water. **2** a small, round plastic or cardboard container for holding cream, ice-cream, yoghurt, etc. **3** a bath. **4** (also **tubful**, ***-fuls***) the amount a tub will hold. **5** (*coll*) a slow, often clumsy boat. [MidE *tubbe*]

tub-thumper *n* a passionate or ranting public speaker or preacher. — *n* **tub-thumping**.

tuba *n* a large brass musical instrument with a low-pitched tone. [Lat & Ital]

tubby *adj* ***-ier***, ***-iest*** (*coll*) plump; podgy. — *n* **tubbiness**. [**tub**]

tube *n* **1** a long hollow cylinder used for conveying liquids or as a container. **2** a similar long hollow structure in an animal or plant body: *bronchial tubes*. **3** a cylindrical container made from soft metal or plastic with a cap at one end, used for holding paste which is got out by squeezing. **4** (*Br*) (a train running on) an underground railway, esp. in London. **5** a cathode ray tube. **6** (esp. *NAm*) a thermionic valve. **7** (*slang*) a television set. — **go down the tubes** (*slang*) to fail dismally; to be ruined. [Lat *tubus*, pipe]

tubeless *adj* (of a tyre) having no inner tube.

tubing *n* (material for) a length of tube or system of tubes.

tuber *n* **1** a short, fleshy stem, often covered in bud-like growths and usu. found underground, such as the potato. **2** (*anat*) a rounded swelling or lump. — *adj* **tuberous**. [Lat, swelling]

tubercle *n* **1** a small round swelling or lump, e.g. on a bone. **2** a small round swelling in an organ, esp. one caused by a bacillus and characteristic of tuberculosis. [Lat *tuberculum*, small swelling]

tubercular *adj* (also **tuberculous**) **1** of, affected by or suffering from tuberculosis. **2** of or having tubercles. [Lat *tuberculum*, small swelling]

tuberculin *n* a preparation in the form of a sterile liquid prepared from a culture of the bacillus which causes tuberculosis, used to test for and treat the disease. [Lat *tuberculum*, small swelling]

tuberculin-tested *adj* (of milk) from cows that have been tested for and certified free from tuberculosis.

tuberculosis *n* an infectious disease caused by a bacillus and characterised by the formation of tubercles, esp. in the lungs. [Lat, from *tuberculum*, small swelling]

tuberculous. See **tubercular**.

tubular *adj* **1** made or consisting of tubes or tube-shaped pieces. **2** shaped like a tube. [**tube**]

tubule *n* a small tube in an animal or plant body. [**tube**]

TUC *abbrev* Trades Union Congress.

tuck *v* **1** (*tr*; **in, into, up**) to push, thrust or fold the outer edges of (something) together or into something, to make firm, secure or tidy: *tuck your shirt in*. **2** (*tr*; **up**) to draw or put into a folded position: *tucked her legs up*. **3** (*tr*; **in, up**) to fold the edges of the bedclothes tightly round (someone): *tuck the child in*. **4** (*tr*) to put in a confined, hidden and sometimes isolated place: *tuck it away out of sight*. **5** (*tr*) to make a tuck or tucks in (a garment, etc.). — *n* **1** a flat pleat or fold sewn in a garment or piece of material. **2** (*Br coll*) food, esp. sweets, cakes and pastries eaten by school children. — *v* **tuck away** (*tr*; *coll*) to eat esp. large quantities of (food) heartily. — *v* **tuck in** or **into** (*intr*; *coll*) to eat heartily or greedily: *tuck into supper*. [OE *tucian*, to disturb]

tuck shop *n* (*Br*) a small shop selling sweets, cakes, pastries, etc. in or near a school.

tucker *n* (*hist*) a piece of material, lace, etc. drawn over the bodice of a low-cut dress. — **best bib and tucker** (*coll*) best clothes. [**tuck**]

Tudor *adj* **1** of the royal family which ruled England from 1485 to 1603 or this period in English history. **2** in or of the style of architecture characteristic of this period, which involved using a lot of wood both internally and externally. — *n* a member of the Tudor royal family. [Owen *Tudor* (c. 1400–61), grandfather of the first Tudor monarch Henry VII]

Tues. *abbrev* Tuesday.

Tuesday *n* the third day of the week. [OE *Tiwesdaeg*, Tiw's day (Tiw being the Anglo-Saxon god of war)]

tufa *n* a porous rock formed from calcium carbonate deposited by springs rich in this mineral. — *adj* **tufaceous**. [Ital, from Lat *tofus*, soft stone]

tuff *n* a rock composed of fine volcanic fragments and dust. — *adj* **tuffaceous**. [Fr *tuf*, from Lat *tofus*, soft stone]

tuffet *n* **1** a low seat. **2** a small mound. [Variant of **tuft**]

tuft *n* a small bunch or clump of grass, hair, feathers, wool, etc. attached or growing together at the base. — *adj* **tufted**. — *adj* **tufty**, ***-ier***, ***-iest***. [MidE]

tug *v* ***-gg-*** (*tr* & *intr*) **1** **(at)** to pull sharply and strongly. **2** to tow (a ship) with a tugboat. — *n* **1** a strong, sharp pull. **2** a hard struggle. **3** (in full **tugboat**) a small boat with a very powerful engine, for towing larger ships and barges. [MidE *toggen*, from OE *teon*]

tug-of-love *n* a dispute over the guardianship of a child, e.g. between divorced parents.

tug-of-war *n* **1** a contest in which two people or teams pull at opposite ends of a rope, trying to pull their opponents over a centre line. **2** any hard struggle between two opposing sides.

tuition *n* **1** teaching or instruction, esp. when paid for, or in a college or university. **2** the fee paid for teaching or instruction. [Lat *tuitio*, protection]

tulip *n* **1** a plant of the lily family grown from a bulb. **2** one of the brightly-coloured cup-shaped flowers produced by this plant. [Turk *tulbend*, turban]

tulip tree *n* a tall N American tree of the magnolia family, with tulip-like flowers.

tulle *n* a delicate thin netted cloth made of silk or rayon. [*Tulle* in France, where it was first made]

tum *n* (a child's word for) a stomach. [Abbrev. of **tummy**]

tumble *v* **1** (*tr* & *intr*; **down**, **over**, etc.) to (cause to) fall, esp. suddenly, helplessly or clumsily, headlong, or as if turning end over end. **2** (*intr*) to fall or collapse suddenly, esp. in value or amount. **3** (*intr*; **about**, **around**) to roll over and over or toss around helplessly. **4** (*intr*) to perform as an acrobat, esp. turning somersaults. **5** (*intr*; **in**, **into**, **out**, **out of**) to move or rush in a confused, hasty way: *tumble out of the car*. **6** (*tr*) to rumple or disorder: *tumble the bedclothes*. **7** (*intr*; **to**; *coll*) to understand, realise or become aware of suddenly: *tumble to her intentions*. **8** (*tr*) to dry (wet clothes or washing) in a tumble-drier. — *n* **1** an act of tumbling. **2** a fall. **3** a somersault. **4** a confused or untidy state or heap. [OE *tumbian*]

tumbledown *adj* (of a building) falling to pieces; ramshackle.

tumble-drier or **-dryer** *n* a machine for drying wet clothes, washing, etc. with a drum which tosses the clothes, etc. around while blowing hot air into them. — *v* **tumble-dry** (*tr* & *intr*).

tumbler *n* **1** a large drinking glass without a stem or handle. **2** (also **tumblerful**, ***-fuls***) the amount such a glass holds. **3** an acrobat, esp. one who performs somersaults. **4** a tumble-drier. **5** the part of a lock which holds the bolt in place until it is moved by a key. **6** the part of a firearm which is released by the trigger and forces the hammer forward. **7** (also **tumbling-barrel** or **-box**) a machine with a revolving drum in which gemstones are polished.

tumbleweed *n* a plant that snaps off above the root, curls into a ball and rolls around in the wind.

tumbrel or **tumbril** *n* **1** a two-wheeled cart which tips over backwards to empty its load, used e.g. on farms. **2** (*hist*) a similar cart used to take those sentenced to death to the guillotine during the French Revolution. [OFr *tomberel*, from *tomber*, to fall]

tumescent *adj* swollen or becoming swollen, esp. with blood as a response to sexual stimulation. — *n* **tumescence**. [Lat *tumescere*, to swell up]

tumid *adj* **1** swollen or enlarged. **2** (of writing, speech, etc.) bombastic; inflated. — *n* **tumidity**. — *adv* **tumidly**. [Lat *tumidus*, from *tumere*, to swell]

tummy *n* ***-ies*** (a child's word for) a stomach. [Nursery pronunciation of **stomach**]

tummy-button *n* (a child's word for) a navel.

tumour *n* **1** an abnormal and usu. dangerous mass of tissue in the body formed by a new growth of cells. **2** a swelling, esp. one caused by such a growth. — *adj* **tumorous**. [Lat, from *tumere*, to swell]

tumular, tumuli. See **tumulus**.

tumult *n* **1** a great or confused noise, esp. made by a crowd; an uproar. **2** a violent or angry commotion or disturbance. **3** the state of feeling confused and usu. violent emotions: *a mind in tumult*. [Lat *tumultus*, from *tumere*, to swell]

tumultuous *adj* **1** with great noise or confusion: *a tumultuous welcome*. **2** disorderly; unruly. **3** agitated. — *adv* **tumultuously**.

tumulus *n* **-li** (*archaeol*) an ancient burial mound or barrow. [Lat, from *tumere*, to swell]

tun *n* **1** a large cask, esp. for ale or wine. **2** (*hist*) the amount such a cask holds, being 252 gallons of wine or 216 gallons of ale, used as a unit of measure for liquids. [MidE *tunne*]

tuna *n* **-na** or **-nas** **1** a large sea-fish of the mackerel family. **2** (also **tuna-fish**) its flesh used as food. [Gr *thynnos*]

tundra *n* a vast flat Arctic plain with permanently frozen subsoil, and sparse vegetation consisting mainly of lichens and mosses. [Lappish]

tune *n* **1** a pleasing succession of musical notes; a melody. **2** (the state of being set to) the correct, or a standard, musical pitch: *The guitar's out of tune*. **3** harmony; agreement: *in tune with current fashions*. — *v* **1** (*tr* & *intr*; **up**) to adjust (a musical instrument or instruments, their keys or strings, etc.) to the correct or a standard pitch. **2** (*tr* & *intr*; **in, to**) to adjust (a radio receiver) to pick up signals from a required frequency or station, or for a particular programme: *tune in to the Archers*. **3** (*tr*; **up**) to adjust (an engine, machine, etc.) so that it runs properly and efficiently. — **call the tune** (*coll*) to be in charge. — **change one's tune** to change one's attitude, opinions, approach or way of talking. — **in tune 1** (of a musical instrument or voice) having or producing the correct or a required pitch: *sing in tune*. **2** (**with**) having the same pitch (as other instruments or voices): *The two guitars aren't in tune*. — **out of tune** not in tune. — **to the tune of** (*coll*) amounting to the sum or total of. — *adj* **tunable** or **tuneable**. [MidE variant of **tone**]

tuneful *adj* **1** having a good, clear, pleasant, etc. tune; melodious. **2** full of music. — *adv* **tunefully**. — *n* **tunefulness**.

tuneless *adj* without a good, pleasant, etc. tune; not melodious. — *adv* **tunelessly**. — *n* **tunelessness**.

tuner *n* **1** a person whose profession is tuning instruments, esp. pianos. **2** a dial or knob on a radio used to tune in to different frequencies and stations. **3** a radio which is part of a stereo system.

tuning-fork *n* a piece of metal with two prongs, which gives out a pure note of a specified pitch when struck, used when tuning pianos, guitars, etc.

tungsten *n* (*chem*; also **wolfram**) a rare hard grey metallic element (symbol **W**), which is resistant to corrosion and has a very high melting point, used for making lamp filaments and for alloying steel. [Swed, heavy stone]

tunic *n* **1** a loose, sleeveless garment reaching usu. to the hip or knee and usu. with a belted or gathered waist, as worn in ancient Greece and Rome, or as a type of simple modern dress. **2** a close-fitting usu. belted jacket with a high collar worn as part of a soldier's or policeman's uniform. **3** (*biol*) a covering membrane or layer. [Lat *tunica*]

tunnel *n* **1** a man-made underground passage for pedestrians, vehicles, trains, etc. through or under some obstruction such as a hill or river. **2** an underground passage dug by an animal such as a mole. **3** a period of difficulty, problems, stress or exceptionally hard work: *light at the end of the tunnel*. — *v* **-ll-** **1** (*intr*; **through, under**, etc.) to make a tunnel through, under, etc. **2** (*intr*) to pass through, or as if through, a tunnel. **3** (*tr*) to make (one's way) by digging a tunnel. [OFr *tonel*, cask]

tunnel vision *n* **1** a medical condition in which one is unable to see objects other than those straight ahead. **2** the inability or unwillingness to consider other viewpoints on or the wider implications of a situation.

tunny *n* **-ies** (also **tunny-fish**) tuna. [Gr *thynnos*]

tup (esp. *Br*) *n* a ram. — *v* **-pp-** (*tr*) (of a ram) to copulate with (a ewe). [MidE *tupe*]

tuppence, tuppenny. See **twopence, twopenny**.

turban *n* **1** a man's headdress consisting of a long cloth sash wound round the head or a cap, worn esp. by Muslims and Sikhs. **2** a woman's headdress or hat similar to this. — *adj* **turbaned**. [Persian *dulband*]

turbid *adj* **1** (of liquid, etc.) cloudy; not clear. **2** thick or dense. **3** confused; disordered. — *n* **turbidity** or **turbidness**. — *adv* **turbidly**. [Lat *turbidus*, from *turba*, disturbance]

turbine *n* a rotary motor in which a wheel or drum with blades is driven by a flow water, steam, gas, etc. to produce power, esp. electricity. [Lat *turbo*, whirlwind]

turbo- *comb fm* having or driven by a turbine. [Lat *turbo*, whirlwind]

turbocharger *n* a supercharger operated by the exhaust gases of an engine, thereby boosting its power.

turbofan *n* a jet engine driven by a gas turbine in which part of the power developed is used to drive a fan which blows air out of the exhaust and so increases thrust.

turbojet *n* (an aircraft powered by) a jet engine consisting of a compressor and a turbine in which the gas energy produced is directed through a nozzle to produce thrust.

turboprop *n* (an aircraft powered by) a jet engine in which the turbine is attached to a propeller.

turbot *n* **-bot** or **-bots** (the flesh of) a large flatfish highly valued as food. [OFr]

turbulence *n* **1** a disturbed, wild or unruly state. **2** (*meteorol*) the irregular movement of large volumes of air, causing stormy conditions. **3** the irregular movement of particles in a liquid or gas. [Lat *turbulentia*, from *turba*, turmoil]

turbulent *adj* **1** violently disturbed; wild; unruly. **2** (*meteorol*) in a state of turbulence; stormy. **3** causing disturbance or unrest. — *adv* **turbulently**.

turd *n* **1** (*vulg slang*) a lump of excrement. **2** (*taboo*) a worthless or despicable person. [OE *tord*]

tureen *n* a large deep dish with a cover from which food, esp. soup, is served at table. [OFr *terrin*, earthen]

turf *n* ***turfs*** or ***turves*** **1** the surface of the soil consisting of grass and matted roots. **2** a square piece cut from this. **3** a slab of peat. **4** (with **the**) horse-racing, the racecourse or the racing world. **5** (*slang*) area of operation or influence; territory. — *v* (*tr*) **1** to cover with turf. **2** (esp. *Br coll*; **over**, **out**) to throw: *turfed him out of the house*; *Turf the book over here*. — *adj* **turfy**, ***-ier***, ***-iest***. [OE]

turf accountant *n* (*Br*) a bookmaker.

turgescent *adj* swelling; growing big. — *n* **turgescence**. [Lat *turgere*, to swell]

turgid *adj* **1** swollen; inflated or distended. **2** (of language) sounding important but meaning very little; pompous. — *n* **turgidity** or **turgidness**. — *adv* **turgidly**. [Lat *turgere*, to swell]

Turk *n* **1** a person from the modern state of Turkey or the former Ottoman Empire. **2** any speaker of a Turkic language. **3** (*derog*) a wild or unmanageable person. — *adj* Turkish. [Persian and Arabic]

Turkic *n* the family of Asian languages to which Turkish, Tartar, Uzbek, etc. belong. — *adj* of this family of languages or the people who speak them.

Turkish *adj* of Turkey, its people, language, etc. — *n* the official language of Turkey.

Turkish bath *n* a bath in which the bather first sweats in a hot room filled with steam, is then washed and massaged, and finally takes a cold shower.

Turkish coffee *n* strong, usu. very sweet, black coffee.

Turkish delight *n* a sticky, jelly-like sweet usu. flavoured with rose water or lemon and dusted with icing sugar.

turkey *n* **-eys** **1** (the flesh of) a large farmyard bird of the pheasant family, valued for its flesh as food, orig. from America. **2** (esp. *US slang*) a slow, stupid or inept person. **3** (*US slang*) a play, film, etc. that is a complete failure. — **talk turkey** (*US slang*) to talk bluntly or frankly; to talk business. [Orig. used of a guinea fowl imported from *Turkey*, and later wrongly applied to the American bird]

turmeric *n* **1** an E Indian plant of the ginger family. **2** the dried, powdered underground stem of this plant, used as a spice (e.g. in curry powder) and as a yellow dye. [Lat *terra merita*, merited earth]

turmoil *n* wild confusion, agitation or disorder; upheaval: *a mind in turmoil*.

turn *v* **1** (*tr* & *intr*) to move or go round in a circle or with a circular movement. **2** (*tr* & *intr*) to (cause to) change position so that a different side or part comes to the top or front: *turn the pages slowly*; *turn to face the sun*; *turn it inside out*. **3** (*intr*) to change direction or take a new direction: *turn left at the corner*. **4** (*tr* & *intr*) to direct, aim or point or be directed, aimed or pointed: *turn one's thoughts to supper*. **5** (*tr*) to go round: *turn the corner*. **6** (*tr* & *intr*; **into**, **to**) to (cause to) become or change to: *turn the book into a film*; *love which turned to hate*; *turn nasty*. **7** (*tr* & *intr*; **to**) to (cause to) change colour: *The shock turned his hair white*. *The leaves begin to turn in September*. **8** (*tr* & *intr*) (of milk) to make or become sour. **9** (*tr*) to make into a circular or rounded shape, esp. on a lathe or potter's wheel. **10** (*tr*) to perform with a rotating movement: *turn somersaults*. **11** (*intr*; **on**) to move or swing around a point or pivot: *a gate turning on its hinge*; *turn on one's heels*. **12** (*intr*; **on**) to depend (on): *The whole argument turns on a single point*. **13** (*tr*) to pass the age or time of: *turn forty*. **14** (*intr*; **to**) to appeal to for help or support; to have recourse to: *turn to drink*. **15** (*intr*; **to**) to come to consider or pay attention to: *turn to the washing-up*; *The conversation turned to discussing holiday plans*. **16** (*tr*; **out**, **into**, **on to**) to put (something) into by, or as if by, inverting; to tip out: *turn the dough out on to the table*. **17** (*tr* & *intr*) (of the stomach) to (cause to) feel nausea or queasiness. **18** (*tr* & *intr*) (of the head) to (cause to) become giddy. **19** (*tr*) to translate. **20** (*tr* & *intr*; **against**) to make or become unfriendly, dissatisfied (with) or hostile (to). **21** (*intr*; **on**, **upon**) to attack, esp. suddenly or violently. **22** (*tr*) to remake (part of a garment, sheet, etc.) by putting the worn outer part on the inside: *turn a collar*. **23** (*tr*) to give an elegant form to. **24** (*intr*) (of the tide) to begin to flow in the opposite direction. **25** (*tr*) to make (a profit, etc.). — *n* **1** an act of turning; a complete or partial rotation: *a turn of the wheel*. **2** a change of direction, course or position: *a turn to the right*. **3** a point or place where a change of direction occurs. **4** a direction, tendency or trend: *the twists and turns of the saga*. **5** a change in nature, character, condition, course, etc.: *a turn for the worse*; *an unfortunate turn of events*. **6** an opportunity or duty that comes to each of several people in rotation or succession: *her turn to bat*. **7** inclination or tendency: *be of a pessimistic* *turn of mind.* **8** a distinctive style or manner: *a blunt turn of phrase.* **9** an act of a stated kind, usu. good or malicious. **10** (*coll*) a sudden feeling of illness, nervousness, shock, faintness, etc.: *gave her quite a turn.* **11** a short walk or ride. **12** (a person performing) one of a series of short acts or performances, e.g. in a circus or variety theatre. **13** a single coil or twist of e.g. rope or wire. **14** (*mus*) an ornament in which the principal note is preceded by that next above it and followed by that next below it. — **at every turn** everywhere, at every stage; continually. — **by turns** or **in turn** one after another in order; in succession. — **on the turn 1** (of the tide) in the process of beginning to go in the opposite direction. **2** (of milk) on the point of going sour. — **out of turn 1** out of the correct order. **2** at a time when to speak or act is rude or impertinent: *apologise for speaking out of turn.* — **serve a turn** to be enough or adequate for present purposes or needs. — **take turns** or **take it in turn** (of two or more people) to share a task by acting or working one after the other in rotation. — **to a turn** (esp. cooked) to exactly the right degree. — **turn (and turn) about** one after the other; each taking a turn. — *v* **turn aside** (*tr* & *intr*) to turn (one's eyes, gaze, face, concentration, etc.) to look, face or be focused in another direction. — *v* **turn away 1** (*intr*) to move or turn to face the opposite direction. **2** (*tr*) to send away or reject; to refuse admittance to. — *v* **turn back** (*tr* & *intr*) to (cause to) return in the opposite direction. — **turn one's back on** to leave for ever; to have no more to do with. — *v* **turn down** (*tr*) **1** to refuse or reject. **2** to reduce (the level of light, noise, etc.) produced by (something) by or as if by turning a control. — **turn one's hand to** to (have the ability to) do (a job, etc.). — *v* **turn in 1** (*intr*; *coll*) to go to bed. **2** (*tr*) to hand over (a person or thing) to someone in authority. **3** (*tr*) to give, achieve or register (a good performance, score, etc.). **4** (*intr*) to bend inwards. — **turn loose** to set free. — *v* **turn off 1** (*tr*) to cause (water, electricity, etc. or a machine) to stop flowing or operating by, or as if by, turning a knob or pushing a button or switch. **2** (*tr*) to operate (a knob, button, tap, switch, etc.) so that something stops. **3** (*intr*) to leave a straight course or a main road: *followed the car until it turned off down a side street.* **4** (*intr*) (of a road) to lead from a main road. **5** (*tr*; *coll*) to cause (someone) to feel dislike, disgust or to lose (esp. sexual) interest. — **the turn of the month, year, century**, etc. the end of one month, year or century, etc. and the beginning of the next. — *v* **turn on 1** (*tr*) to cause (water, electricity, etc. or a machine) to flow or operate by or as if by turning a knob. **2** (*tr*) to operate (a knob, button, tap, switch, etc.) so that something begins to work. **3** (*intr*) to depend on. **4** (*tr*; *coll*) to cause (someone) to feel excitement, pleasure or (esp. sexual) interest. **5** (*tr* & *intr*; *coll*) to (cause to) feel a heightened sense of awareness, esp. with hallucinogenic drugs. **6** (*tr*) to attack physically or verbally. — *v* **turn out 1** (*tr*) to send away; to make leave; to expel. **2** (*tr*) to put (esp. a light) out or off by or as if by turning a knob. **3** (*tr*) to make or produce. **4** (*tr*) to empty or clear, esp. for cleaning or to check the contents. **5** (*intr*) to happen or prove to be: *She turned out to be right.* **6** (*intr*) to leave home for a public meeting or event: *Hundreds of people turned out to vote.* **7** (*tr*) to dress, equip or groom: *well turned out.* **8** (*intr*; *coll*) to get out of bed. **9** (*intr*) to bend outwards. **10** (*tr*) to call (soldiers, a guard, etc.) for duty. — *v* **turn over 1** (*tr* & *intr*) to turn so that the hidden or reverse side becomes visible or faces upwards: *turn over the page.* **2** (*tr* & *intr*) to roll from side to side. **3** (*tr*) to think about carefully. **4** (*tr*; **to**) to give up or surrender to. **5** (*tr* & *intr*) (of an engine) to start or be caused to start and run at low speed. **6** (*tr*) to handle or do business to the amount of. **7** (*tr*; *slang*) to rob. — *v* **turn round 1** (*intr*) to turn to face in the opposite direction. **2** (*tr*) to receive and deal with (a matter, the arrival of loaded vehicles, etc.) in the appropriate manner: *turn an order round in a couple of hours.* **3** (*intr*) (of a loaded vehicle) to arrive, be unloaded and depart again. — *v* **turn to** (*intr*) to get down to esp. hard work. — *v* **turn up 1** (*intr*) to appear or arrive. **2** (*intr*) to be found, esp. by accident or unexpectedly. **3** (*tr*) to increase the flow, intensity or strength of (sound, light, etc.) produced by (a machine) by, or as if by, turning a knob. **4** (*tr*) to discover (facts, evidence, etc.). **5** (*tr*) to shorten (a garment or the hem of a garment) by folding part up and stitching it in place. **6** (*tr*) to turn so as to make the hidden or reverse side visible. [OE *turnain* & OFr *torner*]

turnabout or **turnaround** *n* **1** an act of turning to face the opposite way. **2** a complete change or reversal of direction or opinion.

turncoat *n* a person who turns against or leaves his or her party, principles, etc. and joins the opposing side.

turner *n* a person or thing that turns, esp. a person who works with a lathe.

turning *n* **1** a place where one road branches off from another. **2** a road which branches off from another. **3** the art of using a lathe to form curves in wood, metal, etc. **4** (in *pl*) the shavings from an object turned on a lathe.

turning-circle *n* the smallest possible circle in which a vehicle can turn round.

turning-point *n* a time or place at which a turn or significant change is made.

turnkey *n* **-eys** (*hist*) a person who keeps the keys in a prison; a gaoler.

turnoff *n* **1** a road which branches off from a main road. **2** (*coll*) a person or thing that causes dislike or disgust.

turn-on *n* (*slang*) a person or thing that causes esp. sexual excitement.

turn-out *n* **1** the number of people attending a meeting, celebration, event, etc. **2** an outfit or set of clothes or equipment. **3** the quantity of goods produced or on display.

turnover *n* **1** the total value of sales in a business during a certain time. **2** the rate at which stock is sold and replenished. **3** the rate at which money or workers pass through a business. **4** a small pastry with a fruit or jam filling.

turnpike *n* **1** (*hist*) a gate or barrier across a road or bridge which is not lifted until travellers have paid the toll. **2** (esp. *US*) a motorway on which a toll is paid.

turnstile *n* a revolving gate with metal arms which allows only one person to pass through at a time, usu. after payment of a fee.

turntable *n* **1** the revolving platform on which a record turns on a record-player. **2** a revolving platform for turning railway engines and other vehicles.

turn-up *n* **1** (esp. *Br*) a piece of material folded up at the bottom of a trouser-leg. **2** (also **turn-up for the book**) an unexpected and usu. pleasant surprise; a surprising piece of good luck.

turnip *n* **1** a plant of the cabbage family with a large round white or yellowish root. **2** the root of this vegetable used as food or animal fodder. [From **turn**, with reference to its rounded shape + Lat *napus*, turnip]

turpentine *n* **1** a thick, oily resin obtained from certain trees, e.g. pines. **2** (also **oil of turpentine**) a clear essential oil distilled from this resin used in many commercial products, esp. solvent and paint thinners. [Gr *terebinthos*, a tree yielding turpentine]

turpitude *n* baseness; vileness; depravity. [Lat *turpitudo*]

turquoise *n* **1** a light greenish-blue gemstone. **2** its colour. [OFr *turkeis*, Turkish, as first brought from Persia through Turkey or Turkestan]

turret *n* **1** a small tower on a castle or other building. **2** (in full **gun-turret**) a small, revolving tower-like structure on warships, tanks, etc. on which guns are mounted. **3** that part of a lathe which holds the cutting tool. — *adj* **turreted**. [Lat *turris*, tower]

turtle *n* any of several marine or freshwater tortoise-like reptiles, with a hard shell and flippers for swimming. — **turn turtle** (of a boat, etc.) to turn upside down; to capsize. [Lat *tortuca*]

turtle-neck *n* (a garment, esp. a sweater, with) a high, round, close-fitting neck.

turtle soup *n* soup made from the flesh and fat of a female turtle.

turtledove *n* any of several wild doves noted for their soft cooing and apparent affection for mates and young. [Lat *turtur*]

turves. See **turf**.

tusk *n* one of a pair of long, curved, pointed teeth which project from the mouth of certain animals including the elephant, walrus and wild boar. — *adj* **tusked**. [OE *tusc*]

tusker *n* an elephant, walrus, wild boar, etc. with well-developed tusks.

tussle *n* a sharp or vigorous struggle or fight. — *v* (*intr*; **with**) to struggle or fight vigorously. [MidE *tusen*]

tussock *n* a clump of grass or other vegetation. — *adj* **tussocky**.

tut or **tut-tut** *interj* an expression of mild disapproval, annoyance or rebuke. — *v* **-*tt*-** (*intr*) to express mild disapproval, annoyance or rebuke by saying 'tut' or 'tut-tut'. — *n* an act of saying 'tut' or 'tut-tut'. [Orig. a conventional spelling representation of the sound, also represented by *tch* or *tsk*, made with the tongue against the inner gums to express mild disapproval, etc.]

tutelage *n* **1** the state or office of being a guardian. **2** the state of being under the care of a guardian. **3** tuition or instruction. [Lat *tutela*, guard]

tutelary *adj* **1** having the power or role of a guardian over someone. **2** of a guardian. **3** giving protection. [Lat *tutelaris*, from *tutela*, guardian]

tutor *n* **1** a university or college teacher who teaches students individually or in small groups, or who is responsible for the general welfare and progress of a certain number of students. **2** a private teacher. **3** (*Br*) an instruction book. — *v* **-*r*-** (*tr* & *intr*; **in**) to act as a tutor (to). — *n* **tutorship**. [Lat, guardian]

tutorial *n* a lesson given by a university or college tutor to an individual student or small group of students. — *adj* of a tutor or tuition by a tutor. — *adv* **tutorially**.

tutti (*mus*) *adv* with all the instruments and singers together. — *n* a piece of music to be played or sung by all the instruments and singers together. [Ital]

tutti-frutti *n* an ice cream or other sweet containing or flavoured with mixed fruits. [Ital, all fruits]

tut-tut. See **tut**.

tutu *n* a female ballet dancer's very short, stiff, spreading skirt. [Fr]

tu-whit tu-whoo *n* a conventional spelling representation of an owl's hoot.

tux *n* (esp. *NAm coll*) a tuxedo. [Abbrev.]

tuxedo *n* **-*os*** a dinner-jacket, or an evening suit which includes such a jacket. [From a fashionable club at *Tuxedo* Park, New York]

TV *abbrev* television.

TVEI *abbrev* Technical and Vocational Education Initiative, a scheme intended to give school students more job-oriented and technological courses.

TVP *abbrev* textured vegetable protein, a form of protein from vegetable sources which has a meat-like texture, used in food as a substitute for meat.

twaddle *n* (*coll*) nonsense; senseless or silly writing or talk. — *v* (*intr*) to speak or write nonsense.

twain *n* (*old*) two: *in twain.* [OE *twegen*]

twang *n* **1** a sharp ringing sound like that produced by plucking a tightly-stretched string. **2** a nasal quality or tone of voice. **3** (*coll*) a local or regional intonation. — *v* (*tr* & *intr*) to make or cause to make a twang. — *adj* **twangy**, **-ier**, **-iest**. [Imit.]

twat *n* (*vulg slang*) **1** a worthless, unpleasant or despicable person. **2** the female genitals.

tweak *v* (*tr*) to pull or twist with a sudden jerk. — *n* a sudden sharp pull or twist. [Related to **twitch**]

twee *adj* **tweer**, **tweest** (esp. *Br coll*) too pretty, sweet, quaint or sentimental. — *adv* **tweely**. — *n* **tweeness**. [From *tweet*, a childish pronunciation of **sweet**]

tweed *n* **1** a thick, rough woollen cloth usu. with coloured flecks in it, made orig. in Scotland and used for suits, jackets, etc. **2** (in *pl*) clothes, esp. a suit, made of this material. [Scots *tweedling*, twilling or *tweeled*, twilled]

tweedy *adj* **-ier**, **-iest** **1** of or like tweed. **2** typical of people who enjoy a hearty, outdoors life and pastimes such as fishing and shooting, for which it is traditional to wear tweed clothing.

'tween *prep* & *adv* (*old*) between.

tweet *n* a melodious chirping sound made by a small bird. — *v* (*intr*) to chirp melodiously. [Imit.]

tweeter *n* a loudspeaker used to reproduce high-frequency sounds. ◇ See also **woofer**.

tweezers *n* (*pl*) a small pair of pincers for pulling out individual hairs, holding small objects, etc. [Obsolete *tweeze*, a surgeon's case of instruments]

twelfth *n* **1** one of twelve equal parts. **2** the last of twelve; the next after the eleventh. — *adj* coming after the eleventh. — *adv* **1** in twelfth position. **2** (also **twelfthly**) as the twelfth point, etc. [OE *twelfta*]

the glorious twelfth *n* 12 August, the opening day of the grouse-shooting season.

Twelfth Day *n* the twelfth day after Christmas, 6 January.

twelfth man *n* (*cricket*) a reserve member of a team.

Twelfth Night *n* the evening before the twelfth day after Christmas (5 January) or the evening of the day itself (6 January).

twelve *n* **1** the number or figure 12; any symbol for this number. **2** the age of 12 years. **3** something, esp. a garment or a person, whose size is denoted by 12. **4** a set of 12 things, people, etc. **5** a score of 12 points. **6** 12 o'clock. **7** (a film with) a certificate from the censors stating that the film is suitable only for people of twelve years and over. — *adj* **1** 12 in number. **2** aged 12. — *pron* 12 people or things. ◇ See also **twelfth**. [OE *twelf*]

twelvefold *adj* **1** twelve times as much or as many. **2** divided into or consisting of twelve parts. — *adv* by twelve times as much.

twelvemonth *n* (*archaic*) a year.

twelve-tone *adj* (*mus*) of or relating to music based on a pattern formed from the twelve notes of the chromatic scale.

twenty *n* **-ies** **1** the number or figure 20; any symbol for this number. **2** the age of 20. **3** a set of 20 people, things, etc. **4** a bank note worth 20 pounds. **5** a score of 20 points. — *adj* **1** 20 in number. **2** aged 20. — *pron* 20 people or things. — *n*, *adj* & *adv* **twentieth**. [OE *twentig*]

twenties *n* (*pl*) **1** the period of time between one's 20th and 30th birthdays. **2** the range of temperatures between twenty and thirty degrees. **3** the period of time between the 20th and 30th years of a century.

twerp *n* (also **twirp**; *coll*) a silly or contemptible person.

twice *adv* **1** two times; on two occasions. **2** double in amount: *twice as much.* [MidE *twiges*, from OE *twige*]

twiddle *v* **1** (*tr*) to twist (something) round and round: *twiddle the knob on the radio.* **2** (*intr*; **with**) to play (with) or twist round and round idly. — *n* **1** an act of twiddling. **2** a curly mark or ornament. — **twiddle one's thumbs** **1** to move one's thumbs in a circular movement round and round each other, usu. as a sign of boredom. **2** to have nothing to do. — *n* **twiddler**. — *adj* **twiddly**, **-ier**, **-iest**. [Perhaps from **twirl**, **twist**, **twitch** + **fiddle**]

twig[1] *n* a small shoot branch of a tree, bush, etc. — *adj* **twiggy**. [OE]

twig[2] *v* **-gg-** (*tr* & *intr*; *coll*) to understand (a joke, situation, etc.) esp. suddenly. [Irish Gaelic *tuigim*, I understand]

twilight *n* **1** the faint light in the sky when the sun is just below the horizon immediately before sunrise or esp. immediately after sunset. **2** the time of day when this occurs. **3** dim light or partial darkness. **4** a period of decline in strength, health or importance, esp. after a period of vigorous activity: *the twilight of his life.* — *adj* of or at to twilight; shadowy; dim. — *adj* **twilit**. [OE *twi*, two + **light**]

twilight zone *n* **1** a decaying area of a city or town situated typically between the main business and commercial area and the suburbs. **2** any indefinite or intermediate state or position.

twill *n* a strong woven cloth worked to give an appearance of parallel diagonal lines. — *v* (*tr*) to weave (fabric) with a twill. — *adj* **twilled**. — *n* **twilling**. [OE *twilic*, woven of double thread]

twin *n* **1** either of two people or animals born of the same mother at the same time. **2** either or two people or things that are very like or closely associated with each other. **3** (in *pl*; *cap* with **the**) Gemini. **4** (also **twin crystal**) a compound crystal consisting of two crystals or parts of crystals which have grown together so that each one or part is a mirror image of the other. — *adj* **1** being one of or consisting of a pair born of the same mother at the same time. **2** being one of or consisting of very similar or closely connected parts. — *v* **-*nn*- 1** (*tr* & *intr*) to bring or come together closely or intimately. **2** (*tr*; **with**) to link (a town) with a counterpart in another country to encourage cultural, social and economic exchanges and co-operation. **3** (*intr*) to give birth to twins. **4** (*tr* & *intr*) to form into or grow as a twin crystal. [OE *twinn*]

twin bed *n* a single bed which is one of a matching pair.

twin-engined *adj* having a pair of engines.

twinset *n* (*Br*) a matching sweater and cardigan.

twin town *n* a town which has been linked to a town abroad to encourage cultural, social and economic exchanges and co-operation.

twine *n* **1** strong string or cord made of twisting two or more threads of cotton, hemp, etc. together. **2** a coil or twist. **3** an act of twisting or clasping. — *v* **1** (*tr*) to twist together; to interweave. **2** (*tr*) to form by twisting or interweaving. **3** (*tr* & *intr*; **round**) to twist or coil (round), e.g. for support: *ivy twining round the old tree trunk*. [OE *twin*, double or twisted thread]

twinge *n* **1** a sudden sharp stabbing or shooting pain. **2** a sudden sharp pang (of emotional pain, bad conscience, etc.). — *v* (*tr* & *intr*) to feel or cause to feel a sharp pain or pang. [OE *twengan*, to pinch]

twinkle *v* **1** (*intr*) (of a star, etc.) to shine with a bright, flickering light. **2** (*intr*) (of the eyes) to shine or sparkle with amusement or mischief. **3** (*tr*) to give off (light) with a flicker. — *n* **1** a gleam or sparkle in the eyes. **2** a flicker or glimmer of light. **3** an act of twinkling. — *adj* & *n* **twinkling**. — *adj* **twinkly**. — **in a twinkle, in a twinkling** or **in the twinkling of an eye** in a moment or very short time. [OE *twinclian*]

twirl *v* (*tr* & *intr*; **round**) to turn, spin or twist (round). — *n* **1** an act of twirling. **2** a curly mark or ornament, esp. one made with a pen. — *adj* **twirly**. [**twist** + **whirl**]

twirp. See **twerp**.

twist *v* **1** (*tr* & *intr*) to wind or turn round, esp. by moving only a single part, or different parts in opposite directions: *twist the knob*; *He twisted round in his seat*. **2** (*intr*) to follow a winding course: *a road twisting through the mountains*. **3** (*tr* & *intr*) to wind around or together: *twist the pieces of string together*; *A piece of wire was twisted round his leg*. **4** (*tr*) to force or wrench out of the correct shape or position with a sharp turning movement: *twist an ankle*. **5** (*tr*) to distort the form, meaning, implication or balance of: *twisted his face into an ugly sneer*; *twist her words*; *a twisted mind*. **6** (*tr*) to remove or break off with a sharp turning movement: *twist the button off*. **7** (*tr*) to form by winding or weaving. **8** (*intr*) to dance the twist. **9** (*tr* & *intr*) to take or give a spiral or coiled form (to). — *n* **1** the act of twisting. **2** something formed by twisting or being twisted. **3** a turn or coil; a bend. **4** a sharp turning movement which pulls something out of shape; a wrench. **5** an unexpected event, development or change, e.g. of direction. **6** a distortion of form, nature or meaning. **7** an eccentricity or perversion. **8** a length of thread, cord, silk, etc. formed by twisting two or more strands together. **9** a twisted roll of bread or tobacco. **10** a curl of citrus peel used to flavour a drink. **11** a screw of paper, esp. one containing a collection of small items such as sweets. **12** (usu. with **the**) a dance, popular in the 1960s, in which the dancer constantly twists the body. — *adj* **twisted**. — *adj* **twisty**, **-*ier***, **-*iest***. — **round the twist** (*coll*) mad; crazy. — **twist someone's arm** (*coll*) to apply esp. moral pressure to someone to make him or her act in the way one wants. [MidE *twisten*, to divide]

twister *n* **1** (*Br coll*) a dishonest or deceiving person; a swindler. **2** (*NAm*) a tornado.

twit[1] *n* (*coll*) a fool or idiot. [Perhaps from **twit**[2]]

twit[2] *v* **-*tt*-** (*tr*) to tease or criticise, usu. pleasantly or affectionately. [OE *ætwitan*, to reproach]

twitch *v* **1** (*intr*) to move jerkily. **2** (*tr* & *intr*; **at**) to pull or pluck sharply or jerkily. — *n* **1** a sudden sharp pull or jerking movement. **2** a sudden spasm of a muscle, esp. one caused by nervousness; a tic. [Related to OE *twiccian*, to pluck]

twitcher *n* **1** a person or thing that twitches. **2** (*coll*) a bird-watcher whose main interest is to spot as many rare birds as possible.

twitchy *adj* **-*ier***, **-*iest*** (*coll*) nervous. — *adv* **twitchily**.

twitter *n* **1** a light, repeated chirping sound made by esp. small birds. **2** (*coll*) a nervous or excited state: *be all of a twitter*. — *v* **-*r*- 1** (*intr*) (esp. of birds) to make a light, repeated chirping sound or similar high-pitched trembling sounds. **2** (*tr*) to say or utter with such a chirping sound. **3** (*intr*) to make small nervous or excited movements. — *adj* **twittery**. [Imit.]

two *n* **1** the number or figure 2; any symbol for this number. **2** the age of 2. **3** something, esp. a garment or a person, whose size is denoted by the number 2. **4** something with 2 parts or members. **5** a playing-card with 2 pips. ◇ See also **deuce**[1]. **6** 2 o'clock. **7** a score of 2. — *adj* **1** 2 in number. **2** aged 2. — *pron* two people or things. — **in two** in or into two pieces. — **put two and two together** to come to a usu. obvious conclusion from the available evidence. — **that makes two of us** (*coll*) the same is true of me too. [OE *twa*]

two-bit *adj* (*US coll*) cheap; petty; small-time.

two-edged *adj* double-edged.

two-faced *adj* deceitful; hypocritical; insincere.

twofold *adj* **1** twice as much or as many. **2** divided into or consisting of two parts. — *adv* by twice as much.

two-handed *adj* **1** having, needing or for two hands or people. **2** able to use both hands equally well.

twopence or **tuppence** *n* (*Br*) **1** the sum of two pence, esp. before the introduction of decimal coinage. **2** a coin of the value of two pence in decimal coinage. — **not care twopence** or **tuppence** (*coll*) to not care at all.

twopenny or **tuppenny** *adj* (*Br*) **1** worth or costing twopence. **2** (*coll*) cheap; worthless.

two-piece *n* & *adj* (a garment) having two matching or complementary pieces or parts: *a man's two-piece suit*.

two-ply *adj* having two strands or layers. — *n* **-ies** knitting wool or yarn made of two strands of wool twisted together.

two-seater *n* a vehicle, aircraft or seat for two people.

two-sided *adj* **1** having two sides which are different. **2** having two aspects; controversial.

twosome *n* (a game, dance, etc. for) two people or a couple.

two-step *n* (a tune for) a ballroom dance in duple time.

two-stroke *adj* (of an internal combustion engine) having a cycle consisting of one up and one down stroke of a piston.

two-time *v* (*tr* & *intr*; *coll*) to deceive (a husband, wife, lover, etc.) by having a relationship with someone else at the same time. — *n* **two-timer**. — *adj* **two-timing**.

two-tone *adj* having or made up of two colours or two shades of the same colour, or two sounds.

two-way *adj* **1** able to move, moving or allowing movement in two opposite directions: *a two-way street*. **2** (of a radio, telephone, etc.) able to both send and receive messages. **3** (of communication between two people or groups) in which both participate equally and responsibility and gains are shared. **4** able to be used in two ways.

TX *abbrev* Texas.

tycoon *n* a rich and powerful businessman or businesswoman. [Jap *taikun*, great prince]

tying. See **tie**.

tyke *n* **1** a dog, esp. a mongrel. **2** (*Br*; esp. *dialect*) a rough, rude, coarse man. **3** (*coll*) a small, often cheeky child. [Norse *tik*, bitch]

tympani, **tympanist**. See **timpani**.

tympanum *n* **-na** or **-nums** **1** the middle ear. **2** (also **tympanic membrane**) the eardrum. **3** a membrane covering the hearing organ of an insect. **4** (*archit*) the recessed usu. triangular face of a pediment. **5** (*archit*) a space between a lintel and an arch over it. **6** a drum or drumhead. — *adj* **tympanic**. [Gr *tympanon*, kettledrum]

Tynwald *n* the parliament of the Isle of Man. [Norse *thing*, assembly + *völlr*, field]

type *n* **1** a class or group of people, animals or things which share similar characteristics; a kind or variety: *Trains, cars and aircraft are all types of vehicle*. **2** the general character, nature or form of a particular class or group. **3** (*coll*) a person, esp. of a specified kind: *a quiet type of person*. **4** a person, animal or thing that is a characteristic example of its group or class. **5** a small metal block with a raised letter or character on one surface, used for printing. **6** a set of such blocks. **7** a set of such blocks of a particular kind: *italic type*. **8** printed letters, characters, words, etc. **9** (*biol*) the actual specimen on which the description of a new species or genus is based. — *v* **1** (*tr* & *intr*) to write (words, text, etc.) using a typewriter or word processor. **2** (*tr*) to be a characteristic example or type of; to typify. **3** (*tr*; *med* & *biol*) to decide the type of (e.g. a blood sample); to classify. — *n* **typing**. [Gr *typos*, blow, mark]

typecast *v* ***typecast*** to cast (an actor or actress) continually in the same kind of part. — *adj* **typecast**.

typeface *n* a set of letters, characters, etc. of a particular design or style.

typescript *n* any typewritten document, manuscript or copy.

typeset *v* **-tt-**, ***typeset*** (*tr*; *printing*) to arrange (type) or set (a page, etc.) in type ready for printing.

typesetter *n* a person or machine that sets type ready for printing.

typewrite *v* ***-wrote***, ***-written*** (*tr* & *intr*) to write with a typewriter. — *n* **typewriting**.

typewriter *n* a machine with a keyboard for writing in characters resembling print.

typist *n* a person who types, esp. as a job.

typhoid *n* (in full **typhoid fever**) a dangerous infectious disease characterised by fever, a red rash and severe intestinal problems including diarrhoea, caused by a bacterium in food or drinking water. — *adj* of or like typhus. [Gr *typhos*, fever + *eidos*, likeness]

typhoon *n* a violent storm occurring in the China Sea and W Pacific area. [Chin *ta feng*, great wind + Gr *typhon*, whirlwind]

typhus *n* a dangerous infectious disease characterised by a red rash, headaches and fever, spread by lice. [Gr *typhos*, fever]

typical *adj* (**of**) **1** having or showing the usual characteristics; being a characteristic or representative example. **2** showing the usual, expected, undesirable characteristics of behaviour, attitude, etc.: *A hostile reaction is typical of him.* **3** of, relating to or being a representative or characteristic specimen or type. **4** foreshadowing; symbolic. — *adv* **typically**. [Lat *typicalis*, from Gr *typos*, blow, mark]

typify *v* **-ies**, **-ied** (*tr*) **1** to be an excellent or characteristic example of. **2** to represent by a type or symbol; to symbolise. [Gr *typos*, blow, mark + Lat *facere*, to make]

typist. See **type**.

typo *n* **-os** an error made in the typesetting of a text, such as the use of one letter in mistake for another. [Abbrev. of *typographical error*]

typography *n* **1** the art or occupation of composing type and arranging texts for printing. **2** the style and general appearance of printed matter which has been typeset. — *adj* **typographic** or **typographical**. — *adv* **typographically**. [Lat *typographia*]

typographer *n* a person skilled in typography.

tyranny *n* **-ies 1** cruel, unjust and oppressive use of authority or power. **2** absolute, cruel and oppressive government by a single tyrant or group of tyrannical people. **3** a state under such government. **4** a cruel, unjust or oppressive act. [Lat *tyrannia*, from Gr *tyrannos*, tyrant]

tyrannical or **tyrannous** *adj* of or like a tyrant; oppressive; despotic. — *adv* **tyrannically** or **tyrannously**.

tyrannise or **-ize** *v* (*tr* & *intr*) to rule or treat (a person or people) in a cruel, unjust and oppressive way.

tyrannosaur or **tyrannosaurus** *n* a large flesh-eating dinosaur with two large hind legs for walking on and much smaller forelegs. [Gr *tyrannos*, tyrant + **dinosaur**]

tyrant *n* **1** a cruel, unjust and oppressive ruler with absolute power. **2** a person who uses authority or power cruelly and unjustly. [Gr *tyrannos*]

tyre *n* a thick, rubber, usu. air-filled or hollow ring placed over a wheel. [Variant of *tire*, headdress]

tyro. See **tiro**.

tzar, **tzarevitch**, **tzarina**. See **tsar**.

tzatziki *n* a Greek dish made of yoghurt with finely chopped cucumber and flavoured with mint and garlic, eaten as a dip. [Mod Gr]

tzigane *n* a Hungarian gypsy. [Hung *cigány*, gypsy]

U

U[1] or **u** *n* ***U's*** or ***Us***, ***u's*** **1** the twenty-first letter of the English alphabet. **2** anything shaped like the letter.

U-boat *n* a German submarine (esp. of World Wars I and II). [Ger *Unterseeboot*, undersea-boat]

U-turn *n* **1** a manoeuvre in which a vehicle is turned to face the other way in a single continuous movement. **2** a complete reversal of direction, e.g. of government policy.

U[2] *adj* (*coll*) typical of, suitable for, or used by people of the *u*pper class. ◇ See also **non-U**.

U[3] *abbrev* **1** unionist. **2** united. **3** universal, (a certificate designating) a film suitable for viewing by people of all ages.

U[4] *symbol* (*chem*) uranium.

UB40 *n* in the UK, a registration card issued by the Department of Employment to an unemployed person.

ubiquitous *adj* (seeming to be) found everywhere; ever-present. — *n* **ubiquity**. [Lat *ubique*, everywhere]

U-boat. See **U**[1].

UCCA *abbrev* Universities Central Council on Admissions.

udder *n* the bag-like milk-producing organ of a cow, sheep or goat, with several teats. [OE *uder*]

UDI *abbrev* Unilateral Declaration of Independence.

UEFA *abbrev* Union of European Football Associations.

UFO *n* ***-O's*** or ***-Os*** (*coll*) an *u*nidentified *f*lying *o*bject (i.e. something thought to be a spaceship from another world).

ugh *interj* an exclamation of dislike or disgust, also used to represent a cough or grunt.

ugli *n* ***-is*** or ***-ies*** a fruit that is a cross between a grapefruit, a tangerine and a seville orange, with wrinkly green and yellow skin. [**ugly**, from its appearance]

ugly *adj* ***-ier***, ***-iest*** **1** unpleasant to look at. **2** morally repulsive or offensive. **3** threatening or involving danger or violence. **4** bad-tempered.

ugly duckling *n* a person or thing initially thought ugly or worthless but growing to be outstandingly beautiful or highly valued.

UHF *abbrev* ultra-high frequency.

UHT *abbrev* ultra-heat-treated.

UK *abbrev* United Kingdom.

ukase *n* a command issued by a supreme ruler, esp. the Tsar in Imperial Russia. [Russ *ukaz*]

ukulele or **ukelele** *n* a small (usu. four-stringed) guitar. [Hawaiian, jumping flea]

ulcer *n* **1** a slow-healing internal or external wound. **2** a continuing source of harm or evil. — *adj* **ulcerous**. [Lat *ulceris*]

ulcerate *v* (*tr* & *intr*) to form an ulcer (on or in). — *n* **ulceration**.

ulna *n* ***-ae*** or ***-as*** (*med*) the inner and larger of the two bones of the human forearm, or the corresponding bone in an animal's forelimb or bird's wing. — *adj* **ulnar**. [Lat, elbow, arm]

ulster *n* a man's loose heavy double-breasted overcoat. [*Ulster*, i.e. Northern Ireland, where first made]

ult. *abbrev* **1** ultimate or ultimately. **2** ultimo.

ulterior *adj* (of motives, etc.) other than what is apparent or admitted. [Lat, from *uls*, beyond]

ultimate *adj* **1** last or final. **2** most important; greatest possible. **3** fundamental; basic. **4** (*coll*) best; most advanced. — *pron* (*coll*; with **the**) the best or most advanced one of its kind. [Lat *ultimus*, last]

ultimately *adv* in the end; finally.

ultimatum *n* ***-tums*** or ***-ta*** a final statement declaring an intention to take hostile action unless a specified condition is fulfilled. [Ety. as for **ultimate**]

ultimo *adj* (in business letters) of last month: *your letter of the 10th ultimo.* [Lat *ultimus*, last]

ultra- *pfx* **1** beyond in place, range or limit: *ultra-microscopic*. **2** extreme or extremely: *ultra-Conservative*. [Lat *ultra*, beyond]

ultra-heat-treated *adj* (of milk, etc.) sterilised by heating to a very high temperature, so increasing shelf-life. [**ultra-** (sense **2**)]

ultra-high frequency *n* a radio frequency between 300 and 3000 megahertz.

ultramarine *n* a deep blue pigment used in paints, orig. made by grinding lapis lazuli, a beautiful blue stone from Asia. [Lat *ultra marinus*, overseas, from where the stone was imported]

ultramontane *n* & *adj* **1** (a person living) beyond the mountains, esp. the Alps. **2** (a member) of a faction within the Roman Catholic Church strongly in favour of supreme rule by the Pope, rather than regional independence. [Lat *ultra*, beyond + *mons*, mountain]

ultrasonic *adj* relating to or producing ultrasound. — *adv* **ultrasonically**. [**ultra-** (sense **1**) + **sonic**]

ultrasonics *n* (*sing*) the study of ultrasound, a branch of physics.

ultrasound *n* sound waves with frequencies beyond the range of human hearing. [**ultra-** (sense **1**)]

ultrasound scan *n* a medical examination of an internal part, esp. a foetus, by directing ultrasound waves through it to produce an image on a screen.

ultraviolet *adj* relating to, consisting of, or emitting the kind of light that tans the skin, invisible because of its very short wavelength. [**ultra-** (sense **1**) + **violet** (because beyond the violet end of the visible spectrum]

ululate *v* (*intr*) to howl, wail or screech. — *n* **ululation**. [Lat *ululare*]

umbel *n* (*bot*) a flat- or round-topped cluster of flowers with stalks of equal length growing from the same point on the plant's main stem. — *adj* **umbellate**. [Lat *umbella*, sunshade]

umbelliferous *adj* (*bot*) with flowers growing in umbels.

umber *n* a dark yellowish-brown mineral in soil, used as a pigment in paints. [Ital (*terra di*) *umbra*, shadow (earth) or Umbrian (earth)]

burnt umber *n* umber heated to a dark reddish-brown colour.

raw umber *n* untreated umber.

umbilicus *n* (*med*) the navel. — *adj* **umbilical**. [Lat]

umbilical cord *n* a long flexible tube-like organ by which a foetus is attached to the placenta, and through which it receives nourishment.

umbra *n* **-rae** or **-ras 1** the darkest part of a shadow, at the centre. **2** any shadow, esp. that cast by the moon on the earth during an eclipse of the sun. [Lat, shade, shadow]

umbrage *n* offence, esp. in the phrases *give umbrage* and *take umbrage*. [OFr *ombrage*, from Lat *umbra*, shadow]

umbrella *n* **1** a device carried to give shelter against rain, etc., consisting of a rounded fabric canopy on a lightweight folding framework fitted around a central handle. **2** a thing, e.g. an organisation, providing protection or overall cover for a number of others. [Ital *ombrella*, from *ombra*, shade]

umlaut *n* (in Germanic languages) **1** a change in the pronunciation of a vowel under the influence of a front vowel in a following syllable (esp. in a suffix). **2** the two dots placed above a vowel that undergoes or has undergone this change. [Ger *um*, around + *Laut*, sound]

umpire *n* a person supervising play in various sports, e.g. cricket and tennis, enforcing the rules and deciding disputes. — *v* (*tr* & *intr*) to act as umpire (in). [OFr *nomper*, not a peer or equal]

umpteen *adj* (*coll*) very many; innumerable. — *adj* & *pron* **umpteenth**. [Obsolete *umpty*, a great deal + *-teen*, from *thirteen*, etc.]

UN *abbrev* United Nations.

'un *pron* (*coll*) one: *That's a nice 'un.*

un- *pfx* **1** not, or the opposite of: *unacceptable*; *unattractive*. **2** the reversal of a process: *unplug*; *unhook*. **3** a release from, or depriving of: *uncage*; *unthrone*. [OE]

unable *adj* not having sufficient strength, skill or authority; not able (to do).

unaccountable *adj* **1** impossible to explain. **2** (**to**) not answerable or accountable (to). — *adv* **unaccountably**.

unaccustomed *adj* **1** (**to**) not used (to) or accustomed (to). **2** not usual or customary.

unadopted *adj* (of a road) for which the local authority has no responsibility regarding maintenance, etc.

unadulterated *adj* **1** pure or neat; not mixed with anything else. **2** sheer; absolute.

unadvised *adj* **1** not advised; without advice. **2** unwise; ill-advised. — *adv* **unadvisedly**.

unaffected *adj* **1** sincere or genuine, not pretended or affected; free from pretentiousness. **2** (**by**) not affected.

unalienable. Same as **inalienable**.

unalloyed *adj* (of joy, pleasure, etc.) pure; sheer; not mixed with feelings of sadness or anxiety.

unanimous *adj* **1** all in complete agreement. **2** (of an opinion, decision, etc.) shared or arrived at by all, with none disagreeing. — *n* **unanimity**. [Lat *unus*, one + *animus*, mind]

unanswerable *adj* that can not be denied or disproved.

unapproachable *adj* whose manner discourages informality; unfriendly; standoffish.

unarmed *adj* without weapons.

unasked *adj* **1** not asked. **2** not asked for; uninvited.

unassailable *adj* not able to be challenged or destroyed.

unassuming *adj* modest or unpretentious.

unattached *adj* **1** not in a steady romantic or sexual relationship with another person. **2** not attached, associated or connected.

unattended *adj* **1** not accompanied or watched over. **2** not listened to or paid attention.

unavailing *adj* (of efforts, etc.) futile; of no avail.

unaware *adj* (**of, that**) having no knowledge; not aware (of or that).

unawares *adv* **1** unexpectedly; by surprise. **2** without knowing or realising.

unbalanced *adj* **1** not in a state of physical balance. **2** lacking mental balance; deranged. **3** lacking impartiality; biased.

unbearable *adj* too unpleasant to bear; intolerable. — *adv* **unbearably**.

unbecoming *adj* **1** not suited to the wearer. **2** not proper or fitting.

unbeknown *adv* (also **unbeknownst**; *coll*; **to**) unknown (to); without the knowledge of (a person).

unbelief *n* lack of (esp. religious) belief. — *n* **unbeliever**. — *adj* **unbelieving**.

unbelievable *adj* **1** too unusual or unexpected to be believed. **2** (*coll*) remarkable; astonishing. — *adv* **unbelievably**.

unbend *v* **-bent 1** (*intr*) to become less formal in manner or behaviour. **2** (*tr*) to straighten or release from a bent position.

unbending *adj* strict or severe; inflexible.

unbidden *adj* & *adv* (*literary*) not requested, solicited or summoned up; spontaneous or spontaneously.
unblushing *adj* shameless; brazen.
unborn *adj* **1** (of a baby) not yet born. **2** of or in the future.
unbosom *v* **-m-** (*tr*) to speak openly about (what is on one's mind); to free (oneself) from worries or troubles by talking about them.
unbounded *adj* limitless; infinite.
unbowed *adj* **1** not bowed or bent. **2** not conquered or forced to yield.
unbridled *adj* fully and freely felt or expressed; unrestrained.
unburden *v* **-n-** (*tr*) **1** to remove a load or burden from. **2** to relieve (oneself or one's mind) of troubles or worries by confessing them to another person.
uncalled-for *adj* (of a remark, etc.) not warranted or deserved, esp. unjustifiably rude or aggressive.
uncanny *adj* **1** strange or mysterious. **2** beyond ordinary human ability. — *adv* **uncannily**. — *n* **uncanniness**.
uncared-for *adj* not well looked-after; neglected.
unceremonious *adj* **1** without ceremony; informal. **2** with no regard for politeness or dignity; direct and abrupt. — *adv* **unceremoniously**.
uncertain *adj* **1** **(of, about)** not sure, certain or confident. **2** not definitely known or decided. **3** not to be depended upon. **4** likely to change. **5** lacking confidence; hesitant. — *n* **uncertainty, *-ies***.
uncharted *adj* **1** (of territory, etc.) which has never been fully explored or mapped in detail. **2** not yet examined or investigated.
unchristian *adj* against the principles or spirit of Christianity; uncharitable.
uncial *adj* (of a form of writing) in large rounded letters with flowing strokes, of a kind used in ancient manuscripts. — *n* **1** an uncial letter or form of writing. **2** a manuscript written in uncials. [Lat *uncia*, inch]
uncircumcised *adj* **1** not circumcised. **2** not Jewish; gentile.
uncivil *adj* lacking courtesy; rude. — *adv* **uncivilly**.
unclasp *v* **1** (*tr*) to unfasten the clasp on. **2** (*tr*) to relax one's clasp on. **3** (*tr* & *intr*) to (cause one's hand to) relax and open up.
uncle *n* **1** the brother or brother-in-law of a father or mother; the husband of an aunt. **2** (*coll*) a form of address used by a child to a male friend of his or her parents. **3** (*slang*) a pawnbroker. [Lat *avunculus*]
Uncle Sam *n* the United States or its government.
Uncle Tom *n* (*offensive derog*) a black person who behaves subserviently to whites.
unclean *adj* **1** morally or spiritually impure. **2** (of an animal) regarded for religious reasons as unfit to be used as food.
unclothe *v* (*tr*) **1** to take the clothes off. **2** to uncover or reveal.
uncomfortable *adj* **1** not comfortable. **2** feeling, involving or causing discomfort or unease. — *adv* **uncomfortably**.
uncommon *adj* **1** rare or unusual. **2** remarkably great; extreme. — *adv* **uncommonly**.
uncompromising *adj* **1** refusing to compromise or submit. **2** sheer; out-and-out. — *adv* **uncompromisingly**.
unconcern *n* lack of interest or concern; indifference. — *adj* **unconcerned**. — *adv* **unconcernedly**.
unconditional *adj* straightforward, with no conditions imposed; absolute. — *adv* **unconditionally**.
unconscionable *adj* **1** without conscience or scruples. **2** outrageous; unthinkable; unreasonable; excessive.
unconscious *adj* **1** without consciousness; senseless. **2** **(of)** not aware. **3** done, produced, etc. unintentionally and without the doer being aware of it: *He has unconscious charm.* — *n* (with **the**) the deepest part of the mind, containing thoughts and impulses one is not aware of. — *adv* **unconsciously**.
unconstitutional *adj* not allowed by or consistent with a nation's constitution. — *adv* **unconstitutionally**.
uncork *v* (*tr*) **1** to remove the cork from (a bottle). **2** (*coll*) to release (e.g. emotion) from a pent-up state.
uncouple *v* (*tr*) to undo the coupling of or between; to disconnect.
uncouth *adj* coarse in behaviour, manners or language. [OE *uncuth*, unfamiliar (i.e. with social graces)]
uncover *v* **-r-** **1** (*tr*) to remove the cover from. **2** (*tr*) to reveal or expose. **3** (*intr*) to take off one's hat as a mark of respect.
uncrowned *adj* (of a monarch) not yet crowned.
uncrowned king or **queen** *n* **(of)** a person widely and popularly (if not formally) acknowledged to be the most successful or influential (in a particular sphere).
unction *n* **1** (*RC*, *Orthodox & other eastern churches*) the act of ceremonially anointing a person with oil. **2** the oil used. **3** ointment of any kind. **4** soothing words or thoughts. **5** the kind of sincerity in language or tone of voice that provokes, or is the result of, deep emotion. **6** affected charm, sincerity, or religious feeling. [Lat *ungere*, to anoint]
extreme unction *n* (*RC*) the act of anointing a dying person with consecrated oil.
unctuous *adj* **1** insincerely and excessively charming. **2** oily; greasy. [Lat *unctuosus*]
uncut *adj* **1** not cut. **2** (of a book) whose pages have not been cut open. **3** (of a book, film, etc.) with no parts cut out. **4** (of a gemstone) not cut into a regular shape.
undeceive *v* (*tr*) to free from a mistaken belief; to reveal the truth to.

undecided *adj* **1** not having decided; not able to decide. **2** about which no decision has been made.

undeniable *adj* **1** not able to be denied; obviously true. **2** clearly and indisputably excellent. — *adv* **undeniably**.

under *prep* **1** below or beneath; on the downward-facing surface of. **2** at the foot of. **3** less than; short of. **4** lower in rank than. **5** during the reign or administration of. **6** subjected to, receiving or sustaining: *under consideration*; *under pressure*. **7** in the category or classification of. **8** according to: *under the terms of the agreement*. **9** in view of; because of: *under the circumstances*. **10** propelled by: *under sail*. **11** (of a field) planted with (a particular crop). — *adv* **1** in or to a lower place, position or rank. **2** into a state of unconsciousness. — *adj* **1** lower. **2** subordinate. — **under way** in motion; in progress. [OE]

under-age *adj* (carried on by people who are) below an age required by law.

underwater *adj* & *adv* (existing, carried out, etc.) below the surface of water.

under- *comb fm* **1** beneath or below: *underfoot*. **2** too little in quantity or degree; insufficient or insufficiently: *underexpose*; *underpay*. **3** lower in rank or importance: *under-secretary*. **4** less than: *underbid*. **5** less or lower than expectations or potential: *underdeveloped*.

underachieve *v* (*intr*) to be less successful than expected, esp. academically; to fail to fulfil one's potential. — *n* **underachiever**.

underarm *adj* & *adv* (of a style of throwing, bowling, etc. in sports) with the arm kept below the level of the shoulder.

underbelly *n* **-*ies*** **1** the part of an animal's belly facing the ground. **2** any underside that resembles a belly. **3** (also **soft underbelly**) any unprotected part vulnerable to attack.

undercarriage *n* **1** the landing-gear of an aircraft, including wheels, shock absorbers, etc. **2** the chassis of a road vehicle.

undercharge *v* (*tr*) **1** to charge (a person) too little money. **2** to put an insufficient charge in (e.g. an electrical circuit or explosive device).

underclothes *n* (*pl*) or **underclothing** *n* underwear.

undercoat *n* **1** a layer of paint applied as preparation for the top or finishing coat. **2** the kind of paint used. **3** a layer of fur or hair beneath the top layer. — *v* (*tr*) to apply an undercoat to.

undercover *adj* working, or carried out, in secret.

undercurrent *n* **1** an unseen current under the (often still) surface of a body of water. **2** an underlying trend or body of opinion, esp. different from the one perceived.

undercut *v* **-*tt*-**, **-*cut*** (*tr*) **1** to offer goods or services at a lower price than (a competitor). **2** to cut away the underside of. **3** to apply backspin to (a ball). — *n* the underside of a sirloin, i.e. the fillet.

underdog *n* **1** the less highly regarded competitor, not expected to win. **2** the losing competitor. **3** a person dominated by another.

underdone *adj* not cooked to the proper or required degree.

underemployed *adj* **1** given less work than could realistically be done. **2** given work that fails to make good use of the skills possessed. — *n* **underemployment**.

underestimate *v* (*tr*) to make too low an estimate of the value, capacity or extent of. — *n* too low an estimate.

underfelt *n* an old type of underlay, made of felt.

underfoot *adv* under the feet of a walking or running person or people.

undergarment *n* an item of underwear.

undergo *v* **-*goes***, **-*went***, **-*gone*** (*tr*) to endure, experience or be subjected to. [OE *undergan*]

undergraduate *n* a person studying for a first degree in a higher education establishment.

underground *n* (usu. with **the**) **1** a place or area below ground level. **2** a system of electric trains running in tunnels below ground. **3** a secret paramilitary organisation fighting a government or occupying force. **4** any artistic movement seeking to challenge or overturn established (usu. social as well as artistic) views and practices. — *adj* **1** existing or operating below the surface of the ground. **2** of or belonging to any political or artistic underground. — *adv* **1** to a position below ground level. **2** into hiding.

undergrowth *n* a thick growth of shrubs and bushes among trees.

underhand or **underhanded** *adj* **1** secretively deceitful or dishonest; sly. **2** underarm. — *adv* in an underhand way.

underlay *v* **-*laid*** (*tr*) to lay underneath, or support or provide with something laid underneath. — *n* a thing laid underneath another, esp. felt or rubber matting laid under a carpet for protection.

underlie *v* **-*lying***, **-*lay***, **-*lain*** (*tr*) **1** to lie underneath. **2** to be the hidden cause or meaning of (an attitude, event, etc.), beneath what is apparent, visible or superficial. — *adj* **underlying**.

underline *v* (*tr*) **1** to draw a line under (e.g. a word or piece of text). **2** to emphasise.

underling *n* (*derog*) a subordinate. [**-ling**]

undermentioned *adj* mentioned or named below or later in the text.

undermine *v* (*tr*) **1** to dig or wear away the base or foundation of. **2** to weaken or destroy, esp. gradually and imperceptibly.

underneath *prep* & *adv* beneath or below; under. — *n* a lower or downward-facing part or surface. [OE *underneothan*]

underpants *n* (*pl*) a man's undergarment covering the body from the waist or hips to (esp. the tops of) the thighs.

underpass *n* **1** a tunnel for pedestrians under a road or railway; a subway. **2** a road or railway passing under another.
underpin *v* **-nn-** (*tr*) **1** to support from beneath, usu. temporarily, with brickwork or a prop. **2** (*fig*) to give strength or support to.
underplay *v* (*tr*) to understate or reduce the emphasis on.
underprivileged *adj* deprived of the basic living standards and rights enjoyed by most people in society.
underproduce *v* (*tr* & *intr*) to produce less than the required or potential amount (of). — *n* **underproduction**.
underrate *v* (*tr*) to underestimate. — *adj* **underrated**.
underseal *n* an anti-rusting substance painted on to the underside of a motor vehicle. — *v* (*tr*) to apply such a substance to.
under-secretary *n* **-ies** a subordinate to a secretary (of state), esp. a junior minister or senior civil servant.
undersell *v* **-sold** (*tr*) to sell goods or services at a lower price than (a competitor).
undersexed *adj* experiencing sexual desire less frequently or less intensely than the average person.
undershoot *v* **-shot** (*tr*) **1** (of an aircraft) to land short of (a runway). **2** to fall short of (a target, etc.).
underside *n* the downward-facing side or surface.
undersigned *adj* & *n* (those) whose names are signed below.
undersized *adj* of less than the usual size.
underskirt *n* a thin skirt-like undergarment worn under a dress or skirt.
understaffed *adj* having insufficient staff.
understand *v* **-stood** **1** (*tr*) to grasp with the mind the meaning, nature, explanation or implication of. **2** (*tr*) to know, believe or infer, from information received. **3** (*tr*) to have a sympathetic awareness of the character or nature of. **4** (*intr*) to grasp what is said. **5** (*intr*) to be sympathetic. — *adj* **understandable**. — *adv* **understandably**. [OE *understandan*]
understanding *n* **1** the act of understanding, or the ability to understand. **2** a person's perception or interpretation of information received. **3** an informal agreement. **4** a sympathetic harmony of viewpoints. **5** a condition agreed upon: *on the understanding that you stay for six months.* — *adj* sympathetic to, or keenly aware of, the feelings and opinions of others.
understate *v* (*tr*) to describe as being less or more moderate than is really the case, or to express in very restrained or moderate terms, often for ironic or dramatic effect. — *n* **understatement**.
understood *past tense* and *past participle* of **understand**. — *adj* **1** implied but not expressed or stated. **2** realised without being, or needing to be, openly stated.
understudy *v* **-ies**, **-ied** (*tr* & *intr*) to study (a role), or study the role of (an actor), so as to be able to take over if the need arises. — *n* **-ies** a person who understudies.
undertake *v* **-took**, **-taken** (*tr*) **1** to accept (a duty, responsibility or task). **2** to promise or agree. [MidE *undertaken*, to entrap]
undertaker *n* a person whose job is organising funerals and preparing dead bodies for burial or cremation.
undertaking *n* **1** a duty, responsibility or task undertaken. **2** a promise or guarantee. **3** the work of an undertaker.
undertone *n* **1** a quiet tone of voice. **2** an underlying quality, emotion or atmosphere. **3** a subdued sound or shade of a colour.
undertook. See **undertake**.
undertow *n* **1** the strong outward-flowing current underneath a breaking wave. **2** an undercurrent flowing in the opposite direction to the surface current.
undervalue *v* (*tr*) to place too low a value on.
underwater. See **under**.
underwear *n* clothes worn under shirts, trousers, dresses and skirts.
underwent. See **undergo**.
underworld *n* **1** the world of organised crime. **2** (*mythol*) a world beneath the earth's surface, the home of the souls of the dead.
underwrite *v* **-wrote**, **-written** (*tr*) **1** to agree to finance (a commercial venture), and accept the loss in the event of failure. **2** to agree to buy, or find a buyer for, leftover shares from (a sale of shares to the public). **3** to issue (an insurance policy), accepting the risk involved. — *n* **underwriter**.
undesirable *n* & *adj* (a person or thing considered) unpleasant or objectionable in some way. — *adv* **undesirably**.
undid. See **undo**.
undies *n* (*pl*; *coll*) items of (esp. women's) underwear.
undo *v* **-does**, **-did**, **-done** **1** (*tr* & *intr*) to open, unfasten or untie. **2** (*tr*) to cancel or reverse the effect or result of. **3** (*tr*; *facet* or *literary*) to bring about the downfall of: *I am undone!*
undoing *n* (the cause of) downfall or ruin.
undone *adj* **1** unfinished. **2** unfastened. **3** ruined.
undoubted *adj* beyond doubt or question; clear; evident. — *adv* **undoubtedly**.
undreamed-of or **undreamt-of** *adj* not imagined, esp. thought never to be likely or possible.
undress *v* **1** (*tr*) to take the clothes off. **2** (*intr*) to take one's clothes off. — *n* **1** nakedness, or near-nakedness. **2** casual or informal dress. **3** ordinary uniform as opposed to full military dress.

undue *adj* inappropriately or unjustifiably great; excessive. — *adv* **unduly**.
undue influence *n* (*legal*) a strong influence over another person, considered to have prevented that person from exercising free will.

undulate *v* (*intr*) **1** to move in or like waves. **2** to be wavy. — *n* **undulation**. [Lat *unda*, wave]

unduly. See **undue**.

undying *adj* everlasting; eternal.

unearned *adj* **1** (of income) gained through investments, interest on savings, etc., rather than as wages or fees. **2** not deserved.

unearth *v* (*tr*) **1** to dig up out of the ground. **2** to discover by searching or rummaging.

unearthly *adj* **1** weird; ghostly. **2** (*coll*) outrageous, esp. outrageously early: *at this unearthly hour*. **3** not of this earth; heavenly or hellish. — *n* **unearthliness**.

uneasy *adj* **-ier**, **-iest** **1** nervous, anxious or unsettled; ill at ease. **2** unlikely to prove lasting; unstable. **3** causing anxiety; unsettling. — *n* **unease** or **uneasiness**. — *adv* **uneasily**.

uneconomic *adj* not conforming to the principles of sound economics, esp. unprofitable.

uneconomical *adj* not economical; wasteful.

unemployed *adj* **1** not having a paid job. **2** not in use. — *n* (with **the**) unemployed people.
unemployment *n* **1** the state of being unemployed. **2** the number of unemployed people.
unemployment benefit *n* a regular payment made to an unemployed worker through the national insurance scheme.

unequal *adj* **1** not equal in quantity, value or rank. **2** not evenly matched or balanced. **3** (with **to**) unable to carry out, deal with, etc. **4** not uniform; varying.
unequalled *adj* not matched by any other; without equal; supreme.

unequivocal *adj* clearly stated or expressed; unambiguous. — *adv* **unequivocally**.

unerring *adj* consistently true or accurate; never making an error or missing the mark.

UNESCO *abbrev* United Nations Educational, Scientific and Cultural Organisation.

uneven *adj* **1** not smooth or flat; bumpy. **2** (of a contest) with sides poorly matched; unequal. **3** not uniform or consistent; varying.

uneventful *adj* during which nothing interesting or out of the ordinary happens; (boringly) routine. — *adv* **uneventfully**.

unexampled *adj* **1** unprecedented. **2** unequalled.

unexceptionable *adj* so inoffensive, excellent or suitable as to make criticism or objection impossible.

unexceptional *adj* ordinary; run-of-the-mill.

unfailing *adj* remaining constant; never weakening or failing. — *adv* **unfailingly**.

unfair *adj* **1** not fair or just. **2** involving deceit or dishonesty. — *adv* **unfairly**. — *n* **unfairness**.

unfaithful *adj* **1** breaking faith with a sexual partner by having a sexual relationship with someone else. **2** not loyal. **3** not true to a promise. **4** not accurate as a copy or reproduction.

unfathomable *adj* **1** that cannot be understood or fathomed. **2** too deep to measure or fathom.

unfavourable *adj* **1** not encouraging or helping; adverse. **2** not liking, agreeing or approving. — *adv* **unfavourably**.

unfeeling *adj* unsympathetic; hard-hearted.

unfettered *adj* not controlled or restrained.

unfit *adj* **1** (**to**, **for**) not meeting required standards; not good enough. **2** not fit, esp. physically.

unfitted *adj* **1** not provided with fittings. **2** not adapted or suited.

unflappable *adj* (*coll*) never becoming agitated or alarmed; always remaining calm. — *n* **unflappability**. — *adv* **unflappably**.

unfledged *adj* **1** (of a bird) not yet having developed adult flight feathers. **2** (young and) inexperienced.

unflinching *adj* showing a fearless determination in the face of danger or difficulty.

unfold *v* **1** (*tr*) to open out the folds of; to spread out. **2** (*intr*) to be opened out or spread out. **3** (*intr*) to develop, or be revealed, gradually.

unfortunate *adj* **1** having bad luck. **2** resulting from or constituting bad luck: *an unfortunate injury*. **3** regrettable. — *n* an unfortunate person. — *adv* **unfortunately**.

unfounded *adj* not based on fact; without foundation; groundless.

unfreeze *v* **-froze**, **-frozen** **1** (*tr* & *intr*) to (cause to) thaw. **2** (*tr*) to free (e.g. prices or funds) from a restriction or control imposed, e.g. by a government.

unfrock. Same as **defrock**.

unfurl *v* (*tr* & *intr*) to open out from a rolled-up or tied-up state.

ungainly *adj* **-ier**, **-iest** awkward and ungraceful in movement. — *n* **ungainliness**. [Obsolete *gainly*, graceful]

ungodly *adj* **1** wicked or sinful. **2** (*coll*) outrageous, esp. outrageously early. — *n* **ungodliness**.

ungovernable *adj* (of a temper, etc.) uncontrollable.

unguarded *adj* **1** without guard; unprotected. **2** showing a lack of caution or alertness. — *adv* **unguardedly**.

unguent *n* ointment. [Lat *unguere*, to anoint]

ungulate (*biol*) *adj* hoofed. — *n* a hoofed mammal. [Lat *ungula*, hoof, claw]

unhand *v* (*tr*; *old* or *literary*) to let go of; to take one's hands off.

unhappy *adj* **-ier**, **-iest** **1** sad; in low spirits. **2** being the result of, or bringing, misfortune; unfortunate. — *adv* **unhappily**. — *n* **unhappiness**.

unhealthy *adj* **-ier**, **-iest** **1** suffering from, or showing evidence of, ill health. **2** damaging to health. **3** causing or likely to cause anxiety or worry; psychologically damaging. **4** flouting or corrupting moral standards. — *adv* **unhealthily**. — *n* **unhealthiness**.

unheard *adj* **1** not heard. **2** not heeded; ignored.

unheard-of *adj* **1** not known to have ever happened or been done before; unprecedented. **2** not at all famous; unknown.

unhinge *v* (*tr*) to cause (a person, or a person's mind) to become unbalanced. — *adj* **unhinged**.

unholy *adj* **-ier**, **-iest** **1** wicked; sinful; irreligious. **2** (*coll*) outrageous; frightful.

unholy alliance *n* an alliance that seems unnatural, esp. because it is between adversaries, often formed for malicious purposes against a third party.

unhorse *v* (*tr*) to throw or force (a rider) off a horse.

uni *n* (*coll*) a university.

uni- *pfx* one; a single: *unidirectional*. [Lat *unus*, one]

unicameral *adj* having only one lawmaking body or chamber.

UNICEF *abbrev* United Nations Children's Fund.

unicellular *adj* (of an organism) consisting of a single cell.

unicorn *n* a mythical animal in the form of a (usu. white) horse with a long straight horn on its forehead. [Lat *cornu*, horn]

unicycle *n* an acrobat's cycle consisting of a single wheel with a seat and pedals attached. — *n* **unicyclist**.

unidentified *adj* **1** not identified. **2** too strange to identify.

unidentified flying object *n* any unrecognisable flying vehicle presumed to be from another planet or outer space.

unification *n* the act of unifying, or the state of being unified. [Lat *unus*, one + *facere*, to make]

uniform *n* a distinctive set of clothing worn by members of a particular organisation or profession. — *adj* not changing or varying in form or nature. — *adj* **uniformed**. — *n* **uniformity**. — *adv* **uniformly**. [Lat *unus*, one + *forma*, form]

unify *v* **-ies**, **-ied** (*tr*) to bring together to form a single unit or whole. [Lat *unus*, one + *facere*, to make]

unilateral *adj* affecting, involving, or done by only one person or group among several. — *adv* **unilaterally**. [**uni-** + Lat *latus*, side]

unilateralism *n* (support for) unilateral action, esp. unilateral nuclear disarmament. — *n* & *adj* **unilateralist**.

unimpeachable *adj* indisputably reliable or honest.

uninspired *adj* (of a performance, etc.) lacking feeling or imagination; dull.

uninspiring *adj* that fails to inspire interest, enthusiasm or emotion.

uninterested *adj* not taking an interest; not interested. ◇ See also **disinterested**.

union *n* **1** the act of uniting or the state of being united. **2** an association of people or groups united in a common (esp. political) purpose. **3** a trade union. **4** (a building housing) an organisation concerned with the welfare of the students in a college, university, etc., often also the site of canteen and recreational facilities. **5** agreement or harmony. **6** (*formal*) marriage; wedlock. **7** (*math*) a set comprising the members of two smaller sets. **8** (*formal*) sexual intercourse. [Lat *unio*, from *unus*, one]

union flag *n* the Union Jack.

unionise or **-ize** *v* (*tr*) **1** to recruit into a trade union. **2** to organise (a workforce), or the workforce of (a company), into a trade union. — *n* **unionisation** or **-z-**.

unionist *n* **1** a person supporting or believing in trade unions. **2** a person in favour of creating or maintaining a political union between states or countries, esp. (*cap*) between Northern Ireland and Britain. — *n* **unionism**.

Union Jack *n* the national flag of the United Kingdom, combining the crosses of St George, St Andrew and St Patrick.

unique *adj* **1** being the only one of its kind; having no equal. **2** (**to**) found solely (in), or belonging solely (to). **3** (*coll*) extremely unusual or excellent. — *adv* **uniquely**. — *n* **uniqueness**. [Lat *unicus*, from *unus*, one]

unisex *adj* suited to, for use by, or wearable by, both men and women. [**uni-**]

unisexual *adj* (of an organism) possessing either male or female sex organs, but not both. ◇ See also **bisexual**. [**uni-**]

unison *n* **1** (*mus*) sameness of pitch in voices or instruments; the state of singing or playing all in the same pitch. **2** the state of acting all in the same way at the same time. **3** complete agreement. [Lat *unus*, one + *sonus*, sound]

unit *n* **1** a single item or element regarded as the smallest subdivision of a whole; a single person or thing. **2** a set of mechanical or electrical parts, or a group of workers, performing a specific function within a larger construction or organisation. **3** a standard measure in which a particular quantity, e.g. time or distance, is expressed. **4** an item of furniture combining with others to form a set; a set of such items. **5** any whole number less than 10. **6** any subdivision of a military force. [**unity**]

unit price *n* the price per item of goods supplied.

unit trust *n* (a financial organisation operating) an investment scheme in which clients' money is invested in various companies, with the combined shares purchased divided into units which are allocated in multiples to each client according to the individual amount invested.

Unitarian *n* & *adj* (a member) of a religious group orig. comprising Christians who believed God to be a single entity rather than a Trinity of Father, Son and Holy Spirit, now including members holding a very broad spectrum of beliefs. — *n* **Unitarianism**. [**unity**]

unitary *adj* **1** of a unit or units. **2** characterised by unity or uniformity. [**unit**]

unite *v* **1** (*tr* & *intr*) to make or become a single unit or whole. **2** (*tr* & *intr*; **in**) to bring or come together in a common purpose or belief. **3** (*tr*) to have (e.g. features or characteristics) in combination. — *adj* **united**. [Lat *unire*]

United Kingdom (of Great Britain and Northern Ireland) *n* the official name, since 1922, of the kingdom consisting of England, Scotland, Wales and Northern Ireland.

United Nations *n* (*pl* or *sing*) an organisation made up of representatives from most countries of the world, promoting international peace and co-operation.

United States (of America) *n* (*pl* or *sing*) a republic in N America consisting of a federation of 50 states and one district.

unity *n* **-ies 1** the state of being a single unified whole; oneness. **2** a single unified whole. **3** agreement or harmony between different members or elements. **4** (*math*) the number 1. [Lat *unitas*, from *unus*, one]

Univ. *abbrev* University.

univalent *adj* monovalent. — *n* **univalency**. [**uni-**]

universe *n* **1** everything that exists everywhere, on earth and in space; the (limitless) space in which all things exist. **2** the world; all people. [Lat *universus*, whole]

universal *adj* **1** of the universe. **2** of, relating to, or affecting the whole world or all people. **3** of, relating to, or affecting all the people or things in a particular group. **4** (*coll*) widespread; general; all-round. — *n* **universality**. — *adv* **universally**.

universal joint or **coupling** *n* a joint allowing movement in all directions.

university *n* **-ies 1** a higher education institution with the authority to award degrees, traditionally in non-vocational subjects. **2** its buildings, staff or students. [Lat *universitas*, group of scholars]

unkempt *adj* (of hair) uncombed. **2** (of general appearance) untidy; scruffy. [OE *uncembed*, uncombed]

unkind *adj* unsympathetic, cruel or harsh.

unknown *adj* **1** not known; unfamiliar. **2** not at all famous. — *adv* (with **to**) without the knowledge of. — *n* an unknown person or thing.

unknown quantity *n* a person or thing whose precise identity, nature or influence is not known or cannot be predicted.

unladen *adj* not carrying a load.

unleaded *adj* (of petrol) with a very low lead content, designed to reduce environmental pollution from exhaust fumes.

unlearn *v* **-learnt** or **-learned** (*tr*) **1** to try actively to forget; to rid one's memory of. **2** to free oneself from (e.g. an acquired habit).

unlearned[1] *adj* having no learning; uneducated.

unlearned[2] or **unlearnt** *adj* **1** (of a lesson, etc.) not learnt. **2** (of a skill, etc.) not acquired by learning; instinctive; innate.

unleash *v* (*tr*) **1** to release (e.g. a dog) from a leash. **2** to release or give free expression to (e.g. anger).

unleavened *adj* (of bread) made without yeast, and therefore rather flat and hard.

unless *conj* if not; except if. [MidE *unlesse*]

unlettered *adj* **1** uneducated. **2** illiterate.

unlike *prep* **1** different from. **2** not typical or characteristic of. — *adj* different; dissimilar.

unlikely *adj* **1** probably untrue. **2** not expected or likely (to). **3** not obviously suitable; improbable. — *n* **unlikelihood** or **unlikeliness**.

unlimited *adj* **1** not limited or restricted. **2** (*loosely*) very great or numerous.

unlisted *adj* not entered on a list, esp. on a list of telephone numbers or companies quoted on the Stock Exchange.

unload *v* **1** (*tr* & *intr*) to remove (cargo) from (a vehicle). **2** (*tr* & *intr*) to remove the ammunition from (a gun). **3** (*tr*) to dispose of. **4** (*tr*) to relieve (oneself or one's mind) of troubles or anxieties by telling them to another; to get rid of (troubles) in this way.

unlock *v* (*tr*) **1** to undo the lock of. **2** to free from being locked up. **3** to release or let loose.

unlooked-for *adj* **1** unexpected. **2** not deliberately encouraged or invited.

unloose *v* (*tr*; also **unloosen**, **-n-**) **1** to make less tight; to loosen. **2** to set free.

unlucky *adj* **-ier**, **-iest 1** bringing, resulting from, or constituting bad luck. **2** having, or tending to have, bad luck.

unluckily *adv* **1** in an unlucky way; as a result of bad luck. **2** I am sorry to say; unfortunately.

unmade *adj* **1** not yet made. **2** (of a bed) with bedclothes not re-arranged neatly after being slept in. **3** (of a road) with no proper surface (e.g. of tarmac).

unmake *v* (*tr*) to cancel or destroy the (esp. beneficial) effect of.

unman *v* **-nn-** (*tr*; *old* or *literary*) to cause to lose self-control, esp. to overcome with emotion.

unmanned *adj* **1** not manned, esp. (of a spacecraft, etc.) controlled remotely or automatically. **2** (*old* or *literary*) deprived of self-control.

unmannerly *adj* bad-mannered; impolite. — *n* **unmannerliness**.

unmarried *adj* not married, usu. when never having been married.

unmask *v* (*tr*) **1** to remove a mask or disguise from. **2** to reveal the true identity or nature of.
unmentionable *adj* not fit to be mentioned or talked about, esp. because considered indecent. — *n* (in *pl*; *humorous*) underwear.
unmerciful *adj* **1** merciless. **2** unpleasantly great or extreme.
unmistakable or **unmistakeable** *adj* too easily recognisable to be mistaken for anything or anyone else. — *adv* **unmistakably** or **unmistakeably**.
unmitigated *adj* **1** not lessened or made less severe. **2** unqualified; absolute; out-and-out: *an unmitigated rogue*.
unmoved *adj* **1** still in the same place. **2** not persuaded. **3** not affected by emotion.
unnatural *adj* **1** contrary to the way things usually happen in nature. **2** contrary to ordinary human nature, esp. intensely evil, cruel or disgusting. **3** insincere; affected. — *adv* **unnaturally**.
unnerve *v* (*tr*) **1** to weaken the courage or confidence of. **2** to cause to feel ill at ease. — *adj* **unnerving**.
unnumbered *adj* **1** not given a number. **2** too numerous to be counted; innumerable.
UNO *abbrev* United Nations Organisation.
unobtrusive *adj* not noticeable or prominent. — *adv* **unobtrusively**.
unpack *v* (*tr*) **1** to take out of a packed state. **2** to empty (e.g. a suitcase) of packed contents.
unparalleled *adj* so remarkable as to have no equal or parallel.
unparliamentary *adj* contrary to the established procedures by which, or to the spirit in which, a parliament is conducted.
unperson *n* a person whose existence is officially denied or ignored, often by removing his or her name from official records.
unpick *v* (*tr*) to undo (stitches); to take (a sewn article) to pieces by undoing the stitching.
unpleasant *adj* not pleasant; disagreeable. — *adv* **unpleasantly**.
unpleasantness *n* **1** the quality of being unpleasant. **2** (*euph*) an unpleasant incident, esp. a disagreement involving open hostility.
unpopular *adj* generally disliked. — *n* **unpopularity**.
unpractical *adj* having no practical skills; not good at practical tasks. ◇ See also **impractical**.
unpractised *adj* **1** having had little or no practice or experience. **2** not (yet) put into practice.
unprecedented *adj* not known to have ever happened before; without precedent.
unprepossessing *adj* **1** unappealing; unattractive. **2** not creating or likely to create a good impression.
unprincipled *adj* having or showing a lack of moral principles.
unprintable *adj* not fit to be printed, esp. because of being obscene or libellous.
unprofessional *adj* violating the rules governing, or the standards of conduct expected of, members of a particular profession.
unputdownable *adj* (*coll*) (of a book) so absorbing as to compel one to read to the end without a break.
unqualified *adj* **1** not having any formal qualifications; lacking the formal qualifications required for a particular job, etc. **2** not limited or moderated in any way. **3** absolute; out-and-out: *an unqualified success*. **4** not competent.
unquestionable *adj* beyond doubt or question. — *adv* **unquestionably**.
unquestioning *adj* not arguing or protesting; done, etc. without argument or protest. — *adv* **unquestioningly**.
unquiet (*literary*) *adj* anxious; ill at ease; restless. — *n* disquiet.
unquote *interj* used in speech to indicate the end of a quotation. ◇ See also **quote**.
unravel *v* **-ll-** (*tr* & *intr*) **1** to take or come out of a knitted or woven state back into a strand or strands. **2** to take or come out of a tangled state. **3** to make or become clear after being confusing or obscure.
unread *adj* **1** (of a book, etc.) that has not been read. **2** (of a person) having read few books.
unreadable *adj* **1** illegible. **2** too difficult to read. **3** not worth reading.
unready *adj* **1** not ready. **2** not acting quickly; hesitant.
unreal *adj* **1** not real; illusory or imaginary. **2** (*coll*) exceptionally strange, ridiculous or excellent. — *n* **unreality**.
unrelenting *adj* **1** refusing to change viewpoint or chosen course of action. **2** not softened by feelings of mercy or pity. **3** constant; relentless; never stopping.
unremitting *adj* not easing off or abating; constant; never stopping.
unrequited *adj* (of love) not felt in return by the loved person.
unreserved *adj* **1** not booked or reserved. **2** open and sociable in manner; showing no shyness or reserve. **3** not moderated or limited; unqualified. — *adv* **unreservedly**.
unrest *n* **1** a state of (esp. public) discontent bordering on riotousness. **2** anxiety; unease.
unrivalled *adj* far better than any other; unequalled.
unruffled *adj* **1** (of a surface) smooth. **2** (of a person) not agitated or flustered.
unruly *adj* **-ier**, **-iest** (tending to become) noisily disobedient or disorderly. — *n* **unruliness**.
unsaddle *v* (*tr*) **1** to take the saddle off (a horse). **2** to throw (a rider) from a horse; to unhorse.
unsaid *adj* not said, esp. when it might have been or should have been said. ◇ See also **unsay**.

unsaturated *adj* (of fats) containing carbon compounds able to undergo further chemical reactions, and thought less likely to cause heart disease than saturated fats.
unsavoury *adj* unpleasant or distasteful.
unsay *v* **-said** (*tr*) to take back or withdraw (something said). ◇ See also **unsaid**.
unscathed *adj* not harmed or injured.
unscramble *v* (*tr*) **1** to interpret (a coded or scrambled message). **2** to take out of a jumbled state and put in order.
unscrew *v* (*tr*) **1** to remove or loosen by taking out screws, or with a twisting or screwing action. **2** to loosen (a screw).
unscrupulous *adj* without scruples or moral principles.
unseasonable *adj* **1** not appropriate to the time of year. **2** coming at a bad time; inopportune.
unseat *v* (*tr*) **1** to remove from an official post or position, esp. a parliamentary seat. **2** to throw or knock off a seat, or off a horse.
unseemly *adj* not fitting, esp. because of being indecent. — *n* **unseemliness**.
unseen *adj* **1** not seen or noticed. **2** (of an examination text) not seen in advance by the examinee.
unselfish *adj* having or showing concern for others; generous-spirited. — *adv* **unselfishly**. — *n* **unselfishness**.
unsettle *v* (*tr*) **1** to disturb from a fixed or stable position or state. **2** to cause to become ill at ease.
unsettled *adj* **1** lacking stability; changing or likely to change. **2** not relaxed or at ease. **3** (of debts) unpaid.
unshakable or **unshakeable** *adj* (of beliefs, or the person holding them) firm; steadfast.
unsightly *adj* **-ier**, **-iest** not pleasant to look at; ugly. — *n* **unsightliness**.
unskilled *adj* not having or requiring any special skill or training.
unsociable *adj* disliking or avoiding the company of other people.
unsocial *adj* **1** annoying, or likely to annoy, other people; antisocial. **2** (of hours of work) falling outside the normal working day.
unsophisticated *adj* **1** not sophisticated. **2** free from insincerity or artificiality.
unsound *adj* **1** not reliable; not based on sound reasoning. **2** not firm or solid. — **of unsound mind** (*legal*) mentally ill; insane.
unsparing *adj* **1** giving generously or liberally. **2** showing no mercy.
unspeakable *adj* **1** not able to be expressed in words. **2** too bad, wicked or obscene to be spoken about. — *adv* **unspeakably**.
unstinting *adj* giving (e.g. praise) generously or liberally.
unstoppable *adj* (*coll*) whose progress can not be stopped.
unstrung *adj* **1** with strings removed. **2** unnerved.
unstuck *adj* loosened or released from a stuck state. — **come unstuck** (of a plan, etc.) to go wrong.
unstudied *adj* not affected; natural and spontaneous.
unsung *adj* (of people or their achievements) not praised or recognised.
unswerving *adj* not deviating from a belief or aim; steadfast.
untangle *v* (*tr*) to disentangle.
unthinkable *adj* **1** too unusual to be likely; inconceivable. **2** too unpleasant to think about.
unthinking *adj* **1** inconsiderate. **2** careless.
unthrone *v* (*tr*) to dethrone.
untie *v* (*tr*) **1** to undo from a tied state. **2** to remove the constraints on; to set free.
until *prep* **1** up to the time of. **2** up to the time of reaching (a place); as far as: *slept until Edinburgh*. **3** (with a *negative*) before. — *conj* **1** up to the time that. **2** (with a *negative*) before. **[till[1]]**
untimely *adj* **1** happening before the proper or expected time. **2** coming at an inappropriate or inconvenient time. — *n* **untimeliness**.
unto *prep* (*old*) to.
untold *adj* **1** not told. **2** too severe to be described. **3** too many to be counted.
untouchable *adj* **1** not to be touched or handled. **2** (having an aloofness) discouraging physical contact. **3** above the law. — *n* **1** an untouchable person or thing. **2** (*formerly*, in India) a member of the lowest social class, or caste, whose touch was regarded by members of higher castes as a contamination.
untoward *adj* **1** inconvenient; unfortunate. **2** adverse; unfavourable.
untrue *adj* **1** not true. **2** not accurate. **3** unfaithful.
untruth *n* **1** the fact of being untrue. **2** a lie. — *adj* **untruthful**.
unused *adj* **1** brand new; never used. **2** **(to)** not used (to) or accustomed (to).
unusual *adj* not usual; uncommon; rare. — *adv* **unusually**.
unutterable *adj* so extreme or intense as to be impossible to express in words.
unvarnished *adj* (of an account or report) not exaggerated or embellished.
unveil *v* **1** (*tr*) to remove a veil from (a person's face). **2** (*intr*) to remove one's veil. **3** (*tr*) to remove the (esp. cloth) covering from as part of a formal opening ceremony. **4** (*tr*) to reveal or make known for the first time. — *n* **unveiling**.
unvoiced *adj* **1** unspoken. **2** (*phon*) pronounced without vibrating the vocal cords; voiceless.
unwaged *adj* not in paid employment.
unwell *adj* ill.
unwieldy *adj* large and awkward to carry or manage; cumbersome. — *n* **unwieldiness**. **[wield]**
unwilling *adj* having or showing a lack of willingness; reluctant. — *adv* **unwillingly**. — *n* **unwillingness**.

unwind *v* **-*wound*** **1** (*tr* & *intr*) to take or come out of a coiled or wound position. **2** (*intr*; *coll*) to relax.

unwise *adj* not prudent; ill-advised; foolish. — *adv* **unwisely**.

unwitting *adj* **1** not realising or being aware. **2** done without being realised or intended. — *adv* **unwittingly**. **[wit]**

unwonted *adj* not usual or habitual. **[wont]**

unwound. See **unwind**.

unwritten *adj* **1** not recorded in writing or print. **2** (of a rule or law) not formally enforceable, but traditionally accepted and followed.

unzip *v* **-*pp*-** (*tr*) to unfasten or open by undoing a zip.

up *prep* at or to a higher position on, or a position further along: *climbed up the stairs*; *walking up the road*. — *adv* **1** at or to a higher position or level: *lift it up*; *turn up the volume*; *prices went up*. **2** at or to a place higher up, or a more northerly place. **3** in or to a more erect position: *stood up*. **4** fully or completely: *use up*; *eat up*. **5** into the state of being gathered together: *saved up for it*; *parcel up the presents*. **6** in or to a place of storage or lodging: *put them up for the night*. **7** out of bed: *got up*. **8** to or towards: *went up (to) the town*; *travelling up to London*; *walked up to him*. — *adj* **1** placed in, or moving or directed to, a higher position. **2** out of bed: *He's not up yet*. **3** having an advantage; ahead: *two goals up*; *£5 up after the first bet*. **4** (of a road) under repair. **5** appearing in court: *up before the judge*. **6** (of the sun) above the horizon. **7** relating to or providing (esp. rail) transport to, rather than away from, a major place: *the up train*. — *v* **-*pp*-** **1** (*tr*) to raise or increase. **2** (*intr*; *coll*) to proceed boldly or unexpectedly to act or speak; to get up (and do something): *He upped and left her*. — *n* **1** a success or advantage. **2** a spell of good luck or prosperity. — **be (well) up on** or **in** to have a (thorough) knowledge of. — **it's all up with** (*coll*) there is no hope for. — **on the up-and-up** (*coll*) **1** steadily becoming more successful. **2** honest; on the level. — **something is up** something is wrong or amiss. — **up against 1** situated or pressed close against. **2** faced with (difficulties, etc.). — **up and about** or **up and doing** out of bed and active. — **up for 1** presented or offered for (e.g. discussion or sale). **2** under consideration for (a job or post). — **up front** (*coll*) **1** openly or candidly. **2** (of money paid) in advance. ◇ See also **up-front** below. — **up to 1** immersed or embedded as far as. **2** dependent on: *It's up to you*. **3** capable of (doing); equal to (a task, etc.). **4** thinking about doing or engaged in doing: *be up to no good*. **5** as good as: *not up to his standard*. — **up to date 1** containing all the latest facts or statistics. **2** knowing or reflecting the latest trends (*adj* **up-to-date**). — **up to the minute** completely up to date (*adj* **up-to-the-minute**). — **up to much** (*coll*) good at all; any good. — **up with 1** abreast of. **2** even with. **3** an expression of enthusiastic approval (of) or support (for). — **up yours!** (*vulg slang*) an expression of vehement refusal or defiance, or aggressive contempt. — **what's up?** what's the matter? what's wrong? [OE *up* or *upp*]

up-and-coming *adj* beginning to become successful or well known.

upbeat *adj* (*coll*) cheerful; optimistic. — *n* (*mus*) the unstressed beat, at which a conductor raises the baton.

upbraid see separate entry.

upbringing *n* the all-round instruction and education of a child, intended to form his or her character and values.

up-country *adj* & *adv* to or in the regions away from the coast; inland. — *n* the inland regions.

update *v* (*tr*) to make or bring up to date. — *n* an act of updating.

up-end *v* (*tr*) **1** to turn upside down. **2** to put into disorder or disarray.

up-front *adj* (also **upfront**; *coll*) **1** candid; open. **2** (of money) paid in advance.

upgrade *v* (*tr*) **1** to promote (a person). **2** to increase the grade or status of (a job or post). **3** to improve the quality of.

upheaval *n* a change or disturbance that greatly disrupts.

upheld see **uphold**.

uphill *adj* **1** sloping upwards; ascending. **2** (of a task, etc.) requiring great effort; arduous. — *adv* up a slope.

uphold *v* **-*held*** (*tr*) **1** to support (an action), defend (a right) or maintain (the law). **2** to declare (e.g. a court judgement) to be correct or just; to confirm.

upholster see separate entry.

upkeep *n* (the cost of) the task of keeping something in good order or condition.

upland *n* (often in *pl*) a high or hilly region.

uplift *v* (*tr*) **1** to fill with an invigorating happiness, optimism, or awareness of the spiritual nature of things. **2** (*formal*) to lift up; to collect. — *n* an uplifting influence or effect. — *adj* **uplifting**.

up-market *adj* high in price, quality or prestige.

upmost *adj* & *adv* uppermost.

upright *adj* **1** standing straight up; erect or vertical. **2** having integrity or moral correctness. — *adv* into an upright position. — *n* **1** a vertical (usu. supporting) post or pole. **2** an upright piano.

upright piano *n* a piano with strings arranged vertically in a case above the keyboard.

uprising *n* a rebellion or revolt.

uproar see separate entry.

uproot *v* (*tr*) **1** to pull (a plant) out of the ground completely, with the root attached. **2** to take completely away from surroundings settled into.

ups and downs *n* (*pl*) spells of success and failure; changes of fortune.

upset see separate entry.
upshot *n* (with **the**) the final outcome or ultimate effect.
upside *n* **1** the upper part or side of anything. **2** (*coll*) a positive or favourable aspect.
upside-down or **upside down** *adj & adv* **1** with the top part at the bottom; (so as to be) upturned or inverted. **2** in or into complete confusion or disorder.
upsides (with) *adj* (*coll*) even (with), esp. through revenge or retaliation.
upstage *adj* & *adv* **1** at or towards the back of a theatre stage. **2** (*slang*) arrogant or arrogantly. — *v* (*tr*) **1** to move upstage and force (an actor) to turn his or her back to the audience when speaking to one. **2** to direct attention away from (a person) on to oneself.
upstairs *adj* & *adv* **1** on or to an upper floor. **2** (*coll*) in or to a (more) senior position. — *n* an upper floor, esp. the part of a house above the ground floor.
upstanding *adj* **1** honest; respectable; trustworthy. **2** having a healthily erect posture. — **be upstanding** (*formal*) to stand up.
upstart *n* (*derog*) a person, esp. young, with rapidly acquired power or wealth and an arrogant manner (as a result).
upstream *adv* towards the source of a river or stream and against the current.
upsurge *n* a sudden sharp rise or increase; a surging up.
uptake: **quick** or **slow on the uptake** (*coll*) quick or slow to understand or realise.
uptight *adj* (*coll*) **1** nervous; anxious; tense. **2** angry; irritated. **3** (esp. *US*) strait-laced; conventional.
up-to-date, **up-to-the-minute** see under **up** above.
upturn *n* an increase in (esp. economic) activity; an upward trend. — *v* (*tr*) to turn over, up or upside-down.
upward *adv* (also **upwards**) **1** to or towards a higher place, a more important or senior position, or an earlier era. — *adj* moving or directed upwards. — *adv* **upwardly**. — **upwardly mobile** (*coll*) moving, or in a position to move, into a higher social class or income bracket. — **upwards of** more than.
upwind *adv* **1** against the direction of the wind; into the wind. **2** **(of)** in front (of) in terms of wind direction; with the wind carrying one's scent to (e.g. an animal). — *adj* going against or exposed to the wind.

upbraid *v* (*tr*) to scold or reproach. [OE *upbregdan*]

upholster *v* *-r-* (*tr*) to fit with upholstery. — *adj* **upholstered**. — *n* **upholsterer**. [**uphold**, obsolete meaning 'to keep in good condition']
upholstery *n* **1** the springs, stuffing and covers of a chair or sofa. **2** the work of an upholsterer.

upon *prep* on or on to. — **upon my word!** (*old*) an exclamation of surprise. [**up** + **on**]

upper *adj* **1** higher; situated above. **2** high or higher in rank or status. — *n* **1** the part of a shoe above the sole. **2** (*slang*) (a pill containing) a drug that induces euphoria. — **on one's uppers** (*coll*) extremely short of money; destitute.
upper-case *adj* (of a printed letter) capital.
the upper class *n* (the people of) the highest social class; the aristocracy (*adj* **upper-class**).
the upper crust *n* (*coll*) the upper class (*adj* **upper-crust**).
uppercut *n* a forceful upward blow with the fist, usu. under the chin.
the upper hand *n* a position of advantage or dominance.
upper house *n* (often *cap*) a second (usu. smaller) law-making assembly in a country's administrative system, e.g. the House of Lords in the British parliament.
uppermost *adj* & *adv* at, in or into the highest or most prominent position.

uppish or **uppity** *adj* (*coll*) arrogant or snobbish. [**up**]

uproar *n* (an outbreak of) noisy and boisterous behaviour, esp. angry protest. [Dut *oproer*, from *oproeren*, to stir up]
uproarious *adj* **1** (of laughter) very loud and unrestrained. **2** provoking such laughter. — *adv* **uproariously**.

ups-a-daisy or **upsy-daisy** *interj* an expression of encouragement to a child one is lifting up, or helping up from a fall.

upset *v* *-tt-*, *-set* (*tr*) **1** to cause to be emotionally distressed. **2** to ruin or spoil (e.g. plans). **3** to disturb the proper balance or function of (a person's stomach). **4** to knock over. — *n* **1** a disturbance, e.g. of plans or digestion. **2** an unexpected result or outcome. — *adj* **upset**. — *adj* **upsetting**.
upset price *n* the lowest price a seller will accept, and the price at which bidding starts at an auction.

upsy-daisy. See **ups-a-daisy**.

uranium *n* an element (symbol **U**), a heavy silvery-white radioactive metal whose isotope **uranium-235** is used as a nuclear fuel. [After the planet *Uranus*, discovered shortly before the metal]

urban *adj* of, relating to, or situated in a town or city; not rural. [Lat *urbs*, city]
urban guerrilla *n* a person carrying out terrorist activities in urban areas.
urbanise or **-ize** *v* (*tr*) to make (a district) less rural and more town-like. — *n* **urbanisation** or **-z-**.

urbane *adj* **1** having refined manners; courteous. **2** sophisticated; civilised; elegant. — *n* **urbanity**. [Lat *urbanus*, of the town]

urchin *n* **1** a mischievous child. **2** a dirty, raggedly dressed child. **3** a sea-urchin. [OFr *heriçon*, from Lat *ericus*, hedgehog]

Urdu *adj* & *n* (of or relating to) the official literary language of Pakistan, related to Hindi but with many words from Arabic and Persian.

urea *n* a white salty soluble form of waste protein contained in urine, synthetically produced for use as a fertiliser and animal feed. [Gr *ouron*, urine]

ureter *n* the tube through which urine passes from the kidneys to the bladder. [Gr *oureter*, from *ouron*, urine]

urethra *n* **-*ras*** or **-*rae*** the tube through which urine passes from the bladder out of the body. [Gr *ourethra*, from *ouron*, urine]

urethritis *n* inflammation of the urethra.

urge *v* (*tr*) **1** to persuade forcefully or incite. **2** to beg or entreat. **3** to advise or recommend earnestly. **4** (**on**) to drive (e.g. horses) onwards. — *n* a strong impulse, desire or motivation. [Lat *urgere*]

urgent *adj* **1** needing immediate attention or action. **2** (of a request, etc.) forcefully and earnestly made. — *n* **urgency**. — *adv* **urgently**. [Lat *urgere*, to urge]

uric *adj* of, obtained from, or present in urine. [Fr *urique*; see ety. for **urine**]

urinal *n* **1** any receptacle designed for men to urinate into. **2** a room containing such receptacles. [OFr, from Lat *urinalis*, of urine]

urine *n* the pale yellowish liquid mixture of waste protein and salts produced by the kidneys and discharged from the body via the bladder. [Lat *urina*, from Gr *ouron*]

urinary *adj* of or relating to (the passing of) urine.

urinate *v* (*intr*) to discharge urine. — *n* **urination**.

urn *n* **1** a vase with a rounded body, a small narrow neck and a (usu. square) base. **2** such a vase used to contain a dead person's ashes. **3** a large metal cylinder with a tap and an internal element for heating water or making large quantities of tea or coffee. [Lat *urna*]

urology *n* the branch of medicine dealing with urinary diseases and abnormalities. [Gr *ouron*, urine + **-logy**]

ursine *adj* **1** of or relating to bears. **2** bear-like. [Lat *ursus*, bear]

US *abbrev* United States (of America).

us *pron* **1** the speaker or writer together with another person or other people; the object form of **we**. **2** all or any people; one. **3** (*coll*) me: *give us a hand*. — **be us** (*coll*) to be suited to us. [OE]

USA *abbrev* United States of America.

usage *n* **1** the act or way of using. **2** custom or practice. **3** the way language is used in practice; a word or expression commonly used. [OFr]

use[1] *v* (*tr*) **1** (**as, for**) to put to a particular purpose. **2** to consume; to take as a fuel. **3** to treat (a person) as a means to benefit oneself; to exploit. **4** (*slang*) to take (esp. drugs or alcohol) habitually. **5** (*old*) to behave (well or badly) towards. — *adj* **usable**. — *n* **user**. — **used to** accustomed to: *She's not used to exercising*. — *v* (*aux*) was or were formerly: *They used to be friends. She didn't used to be/never used to be/used not to be so grumpy*. — *v* **use up** (*tr*) **1** to exhaust (e.g. supplies). **2** to finish off (an amount left over). **3** (*slang*) to tire out (*adj* **used-up**). [Lat *uti*, to use]

used *adj* **1** not new; second-hand.

user-friendly *adj* designed to be easy or pleasant to use, or easy to follow or understand.

use[2] *n* **1** the act of using. **2** the state of being (able to be) used: *go out of use; not in use*. **3** (**for**) a practical purpose a thing can be put to. **4** the quality of serving a practical purpose: *It's no use complaining. Is this spanner any use?* **5** the ability or power to use (e.g. a limb). **6** the length of time for which a thing is, will be, or has remained serviceable: *should give you plenty of use*. **7** the habit of using; custom. — **have no use for 1** to have no need of. **2** (*coll*) to dislike or despise. — **make use of 1** to put to a practical purpose. **2** to exploit (a person). [Lat *usus*, from *uti*, to use]

useful *adj* **1** serving a helpful purpose, or various purposes. **2** (*coll*; **at**) rather good. — *adv* **usefully**. — *n* **usefulness**. — **come in useful** to prove to be useful.

useless *adj* **1** serving no practical purpose. **2** (*coll*; **at**) very poor. — *adv* **uselessly**. — *n* **uselessness**.

usher *n* **1** a person who shows people to their seats, e.g. in a church or theatre. **2** a court official who guards the door and maintains order. **3** an official who escorts, or introduces people to, dignitaries on ceremonial occasions. — *v* (*tr*) **1** (**in, out**) to conduct or escort (a person). **2** (*literary*; **in**) to be a sign of the imminent arrival of; to herald. [OFr *ussier*, from Lat *ostiarius*, doorkeeper]

usherette *n* a woman who shows people to their seats in a theatre or cinema.

USSR *abbrev* Union of Soviet Socialist Republics. ◇ See also **CIS**.

usual *adj* done, happening, etc. most often; customary. — *n* (*coll*; with **the**) the thing regularly requested, done, etc. — *adv* **usually**. — **as usual** as regularly happens. [Lat *usualis*]

usurp *v* (*tr*) to take (e.g. power) or assume (e.g. authority) by force, without right, or unjustly. — *n* **usurpation**. — *n* **usurper**. [Lat *usurpare*, to take possession of by use]

usury *n* **1** the practice of lending money at an unfairly or illegally high rate of interest. **2** such a rate of interest. — *n* **usurer**. — *adj* **usurious**. [Lat *usura*, from *uti*, to use]

UT or **Ut.** *abbrev* Utah.

utensil *n* an implement or container, esp. for everyday use. [Lat *utensilis*, fit for use]

uterus *n* **-*ri*** (*med*) the womb. — *adj* **uterine**. [Lat]

utilitarian *adj* **1** intended to be useful rather than beautiful. **2** caring (too much) about usefulness and not (enough) about beauty. **3** of or relating to utilitarianism. — *n* a supporter of utilitarianism. [**utility**]

utilitarianism *n* a set of values based on the belief that an action is morally right if it benefits the majority of people.

utilise or **-ize** *v* (*tr*) to make practical use of; to use. — *n* **utilisation** or **-z-**. [**utility**]

utility *n* **-*ies*** **1** usefulness. **2** a useful thing. ◇ See also **public utility** under **public**. — *adj* designed for usefulness, rather than beauty. [Lat *utilis*, useful, from *uti*, to use]

utmost *adj* **1** greatest possible. **2** furthest; outermost. — *n* the greatest possible degree or extent: *tried his utmost to win.* [OE *utemest*]

utopia *n* (often *cap*) any imaginary place or situation of ideal perfection. — *adj* **utopian**. [Sir Thomas More's book *Utopia* (1516), and its imaginary paradise of that name]

utricle *n* **1** (*med*) the larger of the cavities of the inner ear. **2** (*biol*) any pouch-like part in plants and animals. [Lat *utriculus*, small bag]

utter[1] *v* **-*r*-** (*tr*) **1** to express or give out as speech or a sound; to speak. **2** (*legal*) to put (counterfeit money) into circulation. [MidE *uttren*, from OE *ut*, out]

utterance *n* **1** the act of uttering; the ability to utter. **2** a thing uttered.

utter[2] *adj* complete; total; absolute. — *adv* **utterly**. [OE *utor*, outer]

uttermost *adj* utmost.

U-turn. See under **U**[1]

UV or **uv** *abbrev* ultraviolet.

uvula *n* **-*las*** or **-*lae*** the fleshy part of the soft palate that hangs over the back of the tongue at the entrance to the throat. — *adj* **uvular**. [Lat, small grape]

uxorious *adj* greatly or submissively fond of one's wife. [Lat *uxor*, wife]

V

V[1] or **v** *n* ***V's*** or ***Vs, v's*** **1** the twenty-second letter of the English alphabet. **2** a thing shaped like the letter.

V-neck *n* **1** the open neck of a garment cut or formed to a point at the front. **2** a garment, esp. a sweater, with such a neck. — *adj* **V-necked**.

V-sign *n* a sign made by raising the first two fingers, an expression of victory with the palm turned outwards or an offensive gesture of contempt with the palm inwards.

V[2] *abbrev* volt.

V[3] *symbol* **1** (*chem*) vanadium. **2** the Roman numeral for 5.

v *abbrev* **1** verb. **2** versus. **3** very. **4** *vide* (Lat), see, refer to.

VA or **Va.** *abbrev* Virginia.

vac *n* (*coll*) a vacation, esp. between terms at university or college.

vacant *adj* **1** empty or unoccupied. **2** having, showing or suggesting an absence of thought, concentration or intelligence. — *adv* **vacantly**. [Lat *vacare*, to be empty]

vacancy *n* ***-ies*** **1** the state of being vacant. **2** an unoccupied job or post. **3** an unoccupied room in a hotel, etc.

vacate *v* (*tr*) to leave or cease to occupy (e.g. a house or a job). [Lat *vacare*, to be empty]

vacation *n* **1** (esp. *US*) a holiday. **2** a holiday between terms at a university, college, or court of law. — *v* (*intr*; *US*) to take a holiday. [Lat *vacatio*, freedom, exemption]

vaccine *n* **1** a substance containing (usu. dead or impotent) bacteria or viruses, injected into the blood to stimulate the production of antibodies and give immunity to a specific disease. **2** a substance containing the cowpox virus, administered to humans to give immunity to smallpox. [Lat *vaccinus*, from *vacca*, cow]

vaccinate *v* (*tr*) to administer a vaccine to, giving immunity from a disease. — *n* **vaccination**.

vacillate *v* (*intr*) to change opinions or decisions frequently; to waver. — *n* **vaccillation**. [Lat *vacillare*]

vacuous *adj* **1** unintelligent; stupid; inane. **2** (of a gaze, etc.) blank; expressionless. **3** empty. **4** having no meaning or purpose. — *adv* **vacuously**. [Lat *vacuus*, empty]

vacuity *n* ***-ies*** **1** the state or quality of being vacuous. **2** a vacuous thing, e.g. a foolish idea. **3** (*formal*) an empty space.

vacuum *n* ***-uums*** or (except sense **5**) ***-ua*** **1** a space from which all matter has been removed. **2** a space from which (almost) all air or other gas has been removed. **3** (a feeling of) emptiness. **4** a condition of isolation from outside influences. **5** (*coll*) a vacuum cleaner. — *v* ***-m-*** (*tr & intr*; *coll*) to clean with a vacuum cleaner. [Lat, from *vacuus*, empty]

vacuum cleaner *n* an electrically powered cleaning device that lifts dust and dirt by suction.

vacuum flask *n* a container for keeping drinks hot or cold, consisting of a double-skinned glass bottle with a vacuum sealed in between the skins fitted inside a protective metal or plastic container.

vacuum-packed *adj* sealed in a container from which most of the air has been removed.

vacuum tube *n* a tube in which a near-vacuum has been created, esp. for the free passage of electricity.

vade-mecum *n* a useful handbook carried with one for frequent reference. [Lat, literally 'go with me']

vagabond *n* a person who lives a wandering life, settling nowhere, esp. one regarded as lazy or worthless. — *adj* wandering; roving. [Lat *vagari*, to wander]

vagary *n* ***-ies*** an unpredictable and erratic act or turn of events. [Lat *vagari*, to wander]

vagina *n* the passage connecting the external female sex organs to the womb. — *adj* **vaginal**. [Lat, sheath]

vagrant *n* a person who has no permanent home or place of work. — *adj* **1** wandering; roving. **2** uncertain; unsettled. — *n* **vagrancy**. [OFr *wakerant*, roaming]

vague *adj* **1** of an indistinct or imprecise nature. **2** thinking, expressing or remembering without clarity or precision. — *adv* **vaguely**. — *n* **vagueness**. [Lat *vagus*, wandering]

vain *adj* **1** having too much pride in one's appearance, achievements, or possessions; conceited. **2** having no useful effect or result; futile. — *adv* **vainly**. — **in vain** with no success; fruitlessly. — **take someone's name in vain** to speak the name of someone, esp. God, in a disrespectful way, usu. in an exclamation of anger or surprise. [Lat *vanus*, empty]

vainglory *n* extreme boastfulness; excessive pride in oneself. — *adj* **vainglorious**. [OFr *vaine gloire*]

valance *n* a decorative strip of fabric hung over a curtain rail or round the frame of a bed. [Perhaps OFr *valer*, to descend]

vale *n* (*old* or *literary*) a valley. [Lat *vallis*]

valediction *n* a farewell. — *adj* **valedictory**. [Lat *vale*, farewell + *dicere*, to say]

valency *n* ***-ies*** the power of an atom to combine with others, expressed as the number of atoms of hydrogen it can combine with. — *adj* (*in cmpds*) **-valent**. [Lat *valentia*, strength, capacity]

valentine *n* **1** a message of love sent (usu. anonymously) on 14 February, St *Valentine*'s Day. **2** the person it is sent to.

valerian *n* **1** any of a family of small flowering plants of Europe and Asia whose roots have many medicinal uses. **2** a sedative drug prepared from the root of one of these.

valet *n* a man's personal servant. — *v* **-t-** **1** (*intr*) to work as a valet. **2** (*tr*) to clean or clean out (esp. another person's car). [Fr]

valeta. See **veleta**.

valetudinarian *adj* **1** relating to or suffering from a long-term or chronic illness. **2** needlessly worried about one's own health; hypochondriac. — *n* a valetudinarian person. [Lat *valetudo*, state of health]

Valhalla *n* (*Scandinavian mythol*) the place where the souls of slain heroes live in eternal bliss. [Norse *Valhöll*, from *valr*, the slain + *höll*, hall]

valiant *adj* brave; courageous; heroic. — *adv* **valiantly**. [Lat *valere*, to be strong]

valid *adj* **1** based on truth or sound reasoning. **2** (of a ticket, passport, etc.) legally acceptable for use. **3** (of a contract, etc.) drawn up according to proper legal procedure. — *n* **validity**. [Lat *validus*, strong]

validate *v* (*tr*) to show to be valid; to confirm the validity of. — *n* **validation**.

valise *n* (esp. *US*) a small overnight case or bag. [Fr, suitcase]

Valium® *n* a type of tranquillising drug.

Valkyrie *n* (*Scandinavian mythol*) any of the beautiful goddesses who carry the souls of slain heroes to Valhalla. [Norse *Valkyrja*, from *valr*, the slain + *kjosa*, to choose]

valley *n* **-eys** **1** an area of low flat land between hills or mountains, often with a river running through. **2** any trough or hollow between ridges, e.g. on an M-shaped roof. [Lat *vallis*]

valour *n* courage or bravery, esp. in battle. — *adj* **valorous**. [Lat *valere*, to be strong]

valuable *adj* of considerable value or usefulness. — *n* (usu. in *pl*) an expensive item of personal property. — *adv* **valuably**. [**value**]

value *n* **1** worth in monetary terms. **2** the quality of being useful or desirable; the degree of usefulness or desirability. **3** the quality of being a fair exchange: *value for money*. **4** (in *pl*) moral principles or standards. **5** (*math*) a quantity represented by a symbol or set of symbols. **6** (*mus*) the duration of a note or rest. — *v* (*tr*) **1** to consider to be of (high or low) value; to esteem. **2** to consider to be of high value; to prize. **3** to assess the value of. — *adj* **valueless**. — *n* **valuer**. [Lat *valere*]

valuation *n* **1** an (esp. professional) assessment of the monetary value of something. **2** the value arrived at.

value-added tax *n* a tax on goods and services sold, charged on an amount that is the difference between the cost of raw materials and production, and the market value of the final product.

valued *adj* considered valuable or precious.

value judgement *n* an assessment of worth or merit based on personal opinion rather than objective fact.

valve *n* **1** a device that regulates the one-way flow of a liquid or gas in a pipe by opening and closing an aperture. **2** a structure in the body controlling the one-way flow of liquid or gas through an organ. **3** a vacuum tube containing a cathode which, when heated, releases a one-way flow of electric current. **4** any of a set of finger-operated devices that control the flow of air through some brass musical instruments, producing different notes. **5** a single piece forming a half or whole of the shell of a mollusc. ◇ See also **bivalve**. — *adj* **valvular**. [Lat *valva*, folding door]

vamoose *v* (*intr*; *slang*; esp. *US*) to depart hurriedly; to clear off. [Span *vamos*, let us go]

vamp[1] (*coll*) *n* a woman who flaunts her sexual charm, esp. in order to exploit men. — *v* **1** (*intr*) to behave like a vamp. **2** (*tr*) to seduce (a man) with intent to exploit. — *adj* **vampish**. [**vampire**]

vamp[2] *n* the part of a shoe or boot that covers the toes. — *v* (*tr*) **1** (**up**) to refurbish; to do up; to prepare (e.g. an old speech) for re-use by making alterations. **2** (**up**) to make (up) from bits and pieces. **3** to improvise (a simple musical accompaniment). [OFr *avanpié*, forefoot]

vampire *n* **1** orig. in E European folklore, a dead person who rises from the grave at night to suck the blood of the living. **2** a person who ruthlessly exploits others. [Ger *Vampir*]

vampire bat *n* a bat of Central and S America that pierces the skin of animals and humans and sucks their blood.

van[1] *n* **1** a road vehicle for transporting goods, smaller than a lorry or truck. **2** a railway carriage in which luggage and parcels are carried, often also where the guard travels. [Shortened from **caravan**]

van[2] *n* (*coll*) a vanguard.

vanadium *n* an element (symbol **V**), a silvery metal added to alloys to enhance their strength. [*Vanadis*, a name of the Norse goddess Freyja]

Van Allen belt *n* either of two zones of very high radiation partially encircling the earth at a height of about 1200 miles. [J A *Van Allen* (born 1914), US physicist]

vandal *n* a person who purposely and pointlessly damages or destroys things, esp. public property. — *n* **vandalism**. [Name of the war-like Germanic tribe who overran W Europe in the 4th and 5th centuries]

vandalise or **-ize** *v* (*tr*) to inflict wilful and senseless damage on (property).

vane *n* **1** a weathervane. **2** any of the blades of a windmill, propeller or revolving fan. [Obsolete *fane*, flag, weathercock]

vanguard *n* **1** the part of a military force that advances first. **2** (the person or group in) the position of leading the way, or of setting standards for others to follow. [Fr *avant-garde*, advance guard]

vanilla *n* **1** (the pod of) a Mexican climbing orchid. **2** a flavouring substance obtained from the pod, used in ice-cream, chocolate, and other foods. [Span *vainilla*, small pod]

vanish *v* (*intr*) **1** to disappear. **2** to cease to exist; to die out. [Lat *evanescere*, from *vanus*, empty]

vanishing cream *n* moisturising cream that leaves no trace on the skin.

vanishing point *n* the point at which parallel lines extending into the distance appear to meet.

vanity *n* **-ies 1** the quality of being vain or conceited. **2** a thing one is conceited about. **3** futility or worthlessness. [Lat *vanitas*]

vanity bag or **case** *n* a woman's handbag-style container for cosmetics, etc.

vanity unit *n* a piece of furniture combining a dressing-table and washbasin.

vanquish *v* (*tr*; *literary*) to defeat, conquer or overcome. [Lat *vincere*]

vantage *n* an advantage, esp. in tennis. [OFr]

vantage point *n* a position from which one has a clear overall view of a landscape or situation.

vapid *adj* **1** dull; uninteresting. **2** having little taste, colour or smell. — *n* **vapidity**. [Lat *vapidus*, flat-tasting]

vapour *n* **1** a mass of tiny droplets of moisture rising as a cloud or mist from a liquid or solid. **2** the gas produced by heating a substance that is normally a liquid or solid. **3** (*pl*; *old*; **the**) a feeling of depression, or of faintness, formerly thought to be caused by gases in the stomach. [Lat *vapor*]

vaporise or **-ize** *v* **1** (*tr*) to convert into vapour. **2** (*intr*) to become vapour; to evaporate. **3** (*tr*) to destroy by reducing to vapour. — *n* **vaporisation** or **-z-**.

vapour trail *n* a white trail of condensed water vapour from the engine exhausts of a high-flying aircraft.

variable *adj* **1** varying or tending to vary; not steady or regular; changeable. **2** that can be varied or altered. — *n* **1** a thing that can vary unpredictably in nature or degree. **2** (*math*) a symbol that can represent any of a range of quantities or values. — *n* **variability**. — *adv* **variably**.

variant *n* **1** a different form of the same thing, e.g. one of several possible spellings of a word. **2** an example that differs from a standard. — *adj* **1** different. **2** differing from a standard. **[vary]**

variance *n* (**between**, **with**) **1** (the state of being) a discrepancy: *sets of results at variance with each other*; *a variance between them*. **2** a state of disagreement; opposition; conflict: *two factions at variance* (*with each other*).

variation *n* **1** the act or process of varying or changing. **2** a thing that varies from a standard. **3** the extent to which a thing varies from a standard. **4** a passage of music in which the main melody is repeated with some (slight) changes. **[vary]**

varicoloured *adj* having parts in different colours. [Lat *varius*, various + **colour**]

varicose *adj* **1** (of a vein, esp. of the leg) permanently twisted and enlarged through poor blood circulation, often causing pain. **2** (of an ulcer) resulting from the development of such a vein. [Lat *varix*, varicose vein]

variegated *adj* with patches of different colours or shades of colour. — *n* **variegation**. [Lat *variegatus*, from *varius*, changing]

variety *n* **-ies 1** any of various types of the same thing; a kind or sort. **2** the quality of departing from a fixed pattern or routine; diversity. **3** a plant or animal differing from another in certain characteristics, but not enough to be classed as a separate species; a race, breed or strain. **4** a form of theatrical entertainment consisting of a succession of acts of different kinds; music hall. [Lat *varietas*]

various *adj* **1** several different: *worked for various companies*. **2** different; disparate; diverse: *Her interests are many and various*. [Lat *varius*, changing]

variously *adv* in different ways or at different times.

varlet *n* (*old*) **1** a menial servant. **2** a rascal or rogue. [OFr *vaslet*]

varmint *n* (*slang*; esp. *US*) a troublesome animal or person. [Variant of **vermin**]

varnish *n* **1** an oil-based liquid containing resin, painted on to a surface, esp. wood, to give a hard transparent (usu. glossy) finish. **2** any liquid providing a similar finish, e.g. on fingernails. **3** a superficial attractiveness or impressiveness, esp. masking underlying shoddiness or inadequacy; a gloss. — *v* (*tr*) **1** to apply varnish to. **2** to make superficially appealing or impressive. [Fr *vernis*]

varsity (*coll*) *n* **-ies** & *adj* (of) a university.

vary *v* **-ies**, **-ied 1** (*intr*) to change, or be of different kinds, esp. according to different circumstances. **2** (*tr* & *intr*) to make or become less regular or uniform and more diverse. — *adj* **varied**. — *adj* **varying**. ◇ See also **variable** and **variation**. [Lat *variare*, from *varius*, various]

vas *n* **vasa** (*med*) a vessel, tube or duct carrying liquid. [Lat, vessel]

vas deferens *n* **vasa deferentia** (*med*) the duct from each testicle that carries sperm to the penis. [Lat *deferre*, to carry away]

vascular *adj* (*biol*) of, relating to, or composed of vessels or tubes carrying liquids, e.g. blood or sap. [Lat *vasculum*, from *vas*, vessel]

vase *n* a (usu. rounded) ornamental glass or pottery container, esp. one for holding cut flowers. [Lat *vas*, vessel]

vasectomy *n* **-ies** a surgical operation to remove all or part of the vas deferens, esp. so as to sterilise a man. [Lat *vas*, vessel + **-ectomy**]

Vaseline® *n* a soothing and lubricating ointment consisting mainly of petroleum jelly.

vassal *n* **1** (*hist*) a person acting as a servant to, and fighting on behalf of, a mediaeval lord in return for land or protection. **2** a person or nation dependent on or subservient to another. — *n* **vassalage**. [Lat *vassus*, servant]

vast *adj* extremely great in size, extent or amount. — *adv* **vastly**. — *n* **vastness**. [Lat *vastus*, desolate, huge]

VAT *abbrev* value-added tax.

vat *n* a large barrel or tank for storing or holding liquids, esp. alcoholic drinks. [OE *fæt*]

Vatican *n* (with **the**) **1** the Pope's palace, on Vatican Hill in Rome. **2** the authority of the Pope. [Lat *Mons Vaticanus*, Vatican Hill]

vaudeville *n* (esp. *US*) variety entertainment; music hall. [Fr]

vault[1] *n* **1** an arched roof or ceiling, e.g. in a church. **2** an underground chamber used for storage, or as a burial tomb. **3** a wine cellar. **4** a fortified room for storing valuables, e.g. in a bank. **5** (*poetic*) the sky or heaven. — *v* (*tr*) **1** to build in the shape of an arch. **2** to provide with an arched roof or ceiling. [OFr *voute*, from Lat *volvere*, to roll]

vault[2] *v* (*tr & intr*) to spring or leap (over), esp. assisted by the hands or a pole. — *n* an act of vaulting. [Lat *volvere*, to roll]

vaulting *adj* (of ambition, pride, etc.) excessive; immoderate.

vaulting-horse *n* a padded wooden block on legs, vaulted over by gymnasts.

vaunt *v* (*tr & intr*) to boast or behave boastfully (about). — *n* a boast. — *adv* **vauntingly**. [Lat *vanitare*, from *vanus*, vain]

VC *abbrev* **1** Vice Chancellor. **2** Victoria Cross.

VCR *abbrev* video cassette recorder.

VD *abbrev* venereal disease.

VDU *abbrev* visual display unit.

've short for **have**.

veal *n* the flesh of a calf, used as food. [OFr *veel*, from Lat *vitulus*, calf]

vector *n* **1** (*physics*) a quantity that has direction as well as magnitude, e.g. velocity as opposed to temperature. **2** the course of an aircraft or missile. **3** (*med*) a carrier of a disease or infection, esp. an insect. [Lat, carrier]

Veda *n* any or all of the ancient scriptures of the Hindu religion. — *adj* **Vedic**. [Sanskrit *veda*, knowledge]

veer *v* (*intr*) **1** to move, esp. suddenly, in a (sharply) different direction. **2** (of wind) to change direction clockwise. — *n* a change of direction. [Fr *virer*]

veg *n* (*coll*) a vegetable or vegetables.

vegan *n* a person who does not eat meat, dairy products or any foods containing animal fats or extracts, often also avoiding wool, leather and other animal-based substances. — *adj* **1** of or for vegans. **2** (of a meal or diet) excluding such foods. — *n* **veganism**. [Contraction of **vegetarian**]

vegetable *n* **1** any part of a plant used for food, e.g. the tuber, root, leaves or fruit of any of numerous plants, used e.g. in salads or to accompany meat (and so distinguished from **fruit** (sense **1**) which are relatively sweet and used esp. as a dessert); any such plant. **2** (*coll offensive*) a person almost totally incapable of any physical or mental activity because of severe brain damage. [Lat *vegetabilis*, from *vegetus*, lively]

vegetable marrow *n* a marrow.

vegetable oil *n* any of various oils obtained from plants, esp. used in cooking and cosmetics.

vegetal *adj* of or relating to vegetables or to plant life in general. [Lat *vegetalis*]

vegetarian *n* a person who does not eat meat or fish. — *adj* **1** of or for vegetarians. **2** (of food or a diet) containing no meat or fish. — *n* **vegetarianism**. [**vegetable** + sfx. *-arian*]

vegetate *v* (*intr*) **1** to live a dull inactive life. **2** to live or grow as a vegetable. [Lat *vegetare*, to animate]

vegetation *n* **1** plants collectively. **2** plants growing in a mass.

vegetative *adj* **1** of plants or vegetation. **2** (*biol*) relating to an organism's growth, rather than its reproduction.

vehement *adj* expressed with strong feeling or firm conviction; forceful; emphatic. — *n* **vehemence**. — *adv* **vehemently**. [Lat *vehemens*, eager]

vehicle *n* **1** any (esp. self-propelling) contrivance for transporting people or things. **2** a person or thing used as a means or medium of expressing or communicating ideas or opinions: *newspapers as vehicles for political propaganda*. **3** a neutral substance in which a drug is mixed in order to be administered, e.g. a syrup. **4** a substance in which a pigment is transferred to a surface as paint, e.g. oil or water. — *adj* **vehicular**. [Lat *vehere*, to carry]

veil *n* **1** a fabric covering for a woman's head or face, forming part of traditional dress in some religions. **2** a covering of fine netting for a woman's head, attached to a hat or headdress, worn for decoration or ceremonially, e.g. by a bride. **3** the hood-like part of a nun's habit. **4** (with **the**; *literary*) the vocation of a nun. **5** anything that covers or obscures: *a veil of secrecy*. — *v* (*tr*) **1** to cover, or cover the face of, with a veil. **2** to (partly) conceal, disguise or obscure: *veiled threats*. — **draw a veil**

over to conceal discreetly; to avoid mentioning. — **take the veil** to become a nun. [Lat *velum*, curtain]

vein *n* **1** any of the vessels or tubes that carry blood back to the heart. **2** (*loosely*) any blood vessel. **3** a seam of a different mineral running through rock. **4** a streak of different colour, e.g. in cheese. **5** any of the fine tubes forming the framework of a leaf or an insect's wing. **6** a mood or tone: *written in a sarcastic vein.* **7** a distinct characteristic present throughout; a streak. — *adj* **veined**. — *adj* **veiny**, ***-ier***, ***-iest***. [Lat *vena*]

Velcro® *n* a fastening material consisting of two nylon surfaces, one of tiny hooks, the other of thin fibres, which bond tightly when pressed together but are easily pulled apart.

veld or **veldt** *n* a wide grassy plane with few or no trees, esp. in southern Africa. [Dut *veld*, field]

veleta or **valeta** *n* a ballroom dance or dance tune with a fast waltz-like rhythm. [Span, weathercock]

vellum *n* **1** a fine kind of parchment, orig. made from calfskin. **2** a manuscript written on such parchment. **3** thick cream-coloured writing-paper. [OFr *velin*, from *veel*, calf]

velocity *n* ***-ies*** **1** (*tech*) rate of motion in a particular direction. **2** (*loosely*) speed. [Lat *velox*, swift]

velour or **velours** *n* any fabric with a velvet-like pile, used esp. for upholstery. [Fr *velours*; see ety. at **velvet**]

velvet *n* **1** a fabric, usu. nylon or silk, with a very short soft closely woven pile on one side. **2** a covering of furry skin on a growing antler. — *adj* **1** made of velvet. **2** soft or smooth like velvet. — *adj* **velvety**. — **on velvet** (*coll*) in a comfortable position of safety or wealth. [Lat *velvettum*, from *villus*, tuft]

velvet glove *n* apparent gentleness or lenience concealing strength or strictness, esp. in the phrase *an iron hand in a velvet glove.*

velveteen *n* cotton fabric with a velvet-like pile.

Ven. *abbrev* Venerable.

venal *adj* **1** willing to be persuaded by corrupt means, esp. bribery. **2** (of behaviour) dishonest; corrupt. — *n* **venality**. — *adv* **venally**. [Lat *venum*, goods for sale]

vend *v* (*tr*) to sell or offer for sale. [Lat *vendere*, to sell]

vendee *n* (*legal*) a buyer, esp. of property.

vender *n* a seller, e.g. at a market.

vending machine *n* a coin-operated machine dispensing sweets, drinks, cigarettes, etc.

vendor *n* (*legal*) a seller, esp. of property.

vendetta *n* **1** a bitter feud in which the family of a murdered person takes revenge by killing the murderer or a relative. **2** any long-standing bitter feud or quarrel. [Ital, from Lat *vindicta*, revenge]

veneer *n* **1** a thin layer of a fine material fixed to the surface of an inferior material to give an attractive finish, esp. fine wood on cheaper wood. **2** (**of**) a false external appearance, e.g. of good quality or respectability. — *v* (*tr*) to put a veneer on. [OFr *fornir*, to furnish]

venerable *adj* **1** deserving to be greatly respected or revered, esp. on account of age or religious association. **2** (*cap*; *C of E*) a title given to an archdeacon. **3** (*cap*; *RC*) a title given to a person due to be declared a saint. [**venerate**]

venerate *v* (*tr*) to regard with deep respect or awe; to revere. — *n* **veneration**. [Lat *venerari*]

venereal *adj* **1** (of a disease or infection) transmitted by sexual intercourse. **2** relating to, resulting from, or for the treatment of such diseases. [Lat *venereus*, from *Venus*, Roman goddess of love]

venereal disease *n* any of several diseases transmitted by sexual intercourse, e.g. syphilis.

Venetian *adj* of or relating to Venice, a city in NE Italy. — *n* a native or citizen of Venice. [Lat *Venetia*, Venice]

Venetian blind *n* a window blind consisting of horizontal slats strung together, one beneath the other, and tilted to let in or shut out light.

vengeance *n* punishment inflicted as a revenge; retribution. — **with a vengeance 1** forcefully or violently. **2** to a great degree: *foolishness with a vengeance.* [OFr, from Lat *vindicare*, to avenge]

vengeful *adj* **1** eager for revenge. **2** carried out in revenge. [Old word *venge*, to avenge + **-ful**]

venial *adj* forgivable; excusable. — *n* **veniality**. [Lat *venia*, pardon]

venial sin *n* (esp. *RC*) a minor sin, which does not separate one from God's grace. ◇ See also **mortal sin**.

venison *n* the flesh of a deer, used as food. [OFr, from Lat *venari*, to hunt]

Venn diagram *n* (*math*) a diagram in which mathematical sets and their relationships are represented by overlapping circles. [John *Venn* (1834–1923), English mathematician]

venom *n* **1** a poisonous liquid that some creatures, e.g. scorpions and certain snakes, inject in a bite or sting. **2** spitefulness, esp. in language or tone of voice. — *adj* **venomous**. [Lat *venenum*, poison]

venous *adj* of, relating to, or contained in veins. [Lat *vena*, vein]

vent[1] *n* a slit in a garment, esp. upwards from the hem at the back of a jacket or coat, for style or ease of movement. [Fr *fente*, slit]

vent[2] *n* **1** an opening allowing air, gas or liquid into or out of a confined space. **2** the passage inside a volcano, through which lava and gases escape. **3** (*biol*) the anus of a bird or other small animal. — *v* (*tr*) **1** to make a vent in. **2** to let in or out through a vent. **3** to release (esp. emotion) freely. — **give vent to** to release (esp. emotion) in a violent outburst. [Fr *éventer*, to expose to air]

ventilate *v* (*tr*) **1** to allow fresh air to circulate throughout. **2** to cause (blood) to take up oxygen. **3** to supply air to (the lungs). **4** to expose to public examination or discussion. — *n* **ventilation**. [Lat *ventilare*, from *ventus*, wind]

ventilator *n* **1** a device that circulates or draws in fresh air. **2** a machine that ventilates the lungs of a person whose respiratory system is damaged.

ventral *adj* of, relating to, or situated on the abdomen or belly. — *adv* **ventrally**. [Lat *venter*, abdomen]

ventricle *n* **1** either of the muscular chambers in the heart that pump blood in or out. **2** any of the four main cavities of the brain. — *adj* **ventricular**. [Lat *ventriculus*]

ventriloquism *n* the art of speaking in a way that makes the sound appear to come from elsewhere, e.g. a dummy's mouth; throwing the voice. — *v* (*intr*) **ventriloquise** or **-ize**. — *n* **ventriloquist**. [Lat *venter*, belly + *loqui*, to speak]

venture *n* **1** an exercise or operation involving danger or uncertainty. **2** a business project, esp. one involving risk or speculation. **3** a thing attempted. — *v* **1** (*tr* & *intr*) to dare, or dare to go: *ventured to criticise the chairman*; *venture out in bad weather*. **2** (*tr*) to put forward or present in the face of possible opposition: *ventured a different opinion*. **3** (*tr*) to expose to danger or chance; to risk. — *n* **venturer**. — *v* **venture on** (*tr*) to attempt (something dangerous). [Shortened from **adventure**]

Venture Scout *n* a member of the senior branch of the Scout movement.

venturesome *adj* **1** prepared to take risks. **2** involving danger; risky.

venue *n* **1** the chosen location for a sports event, concert, etc. **2** (*legal*) the place where a court case is to be tried, or the district from which the jurors are chosen. **3** a meeting-place. [Lat *venire*, to come]

Venus fly trap *n* a plant that consumes insects which become trapped by its fleshy hinged leaves that snap shut when touched.

veracious *adj* (*formal*) truthful. [Lat *verus*, true]

veracity *n* (*formal*) truthfulness.

veranda or **verandah** *n* a sheltered terrace attached to a house or other building. [Port *varanda*, balcony]

verb *n* any of a grammatical class of words that represent an action, experience, occurrence or state, e.g. *do*, *feel*, *happen* and *remain*. [Lat *verbum*, word]

verbal *adj* **1** of, relating to or consisting of words: *verbal abuse*. **2** spoken, not written: *verbal communication*. **3** (*gram*) of or relating to verbs. — *adv* **verbally**.

verbalise or **-ize** *v* **1** (*tr*) to express in words. **2** (*intr*) to use too many words; to be verbose.

verbalism *n* great or excessive attention paid to words used, rather than to ideas expressed, e.g. by a critic dealing with a literary work.

verbal noun *n* a form of a verb used in a sentence as a noun, e.g. '*To err* is human' and '*Swimming* keeps you fit'.

verbatim *adj* & *adv* using exactly the same words; word-for-word. [Lat]

verbena *n* any of a group of plants of mild and tropical climates, with clusters of fragrant flowers, used in herbal medicine and cosmetics. [Lat, sacred bough]

verbiage *n* (the use of) language that is wordy or needlessly complicated, and often meaningless. [OFr *verbeier*, to chatter]

verbose *adj* using or containing too many words; boringly or irritatingly long-winded. — *n* **verbosity** . [Lat *verbosus*]

verdant *adj* **1** covered with lush green grass or vegetation. **2** of a rich green colour. **3** naïve or unsophisticated; green. — *n* **verdancy**. [OFr]

verdict *n* **1** the decision arrived at by the jury in a court of law. **2** any decision, opinion or judgement. [Lat *veredictum*, truly said]

verdigris *n* a green rust that forms on copper, brass or bronze. [OFr *verd de Grèce*, green of Greece]

verdure *n* (*literary*) (the rich colour of) lush green vegetation. [OFr]

verge[1] *n* **1** a limit, boundary or border. **2** a strip of grass bordering a road. **3** a point or stage immediately beyond or after which something lies or occurs: *on the verge of striking him*. — *v* **1** (*tr*) to serve as the border or boundary of. **2** (*intr* with **on**) to be very close (to being or becoming): *enthusiasm verging on obsession*. [Lat *virga*, rod]

verge[2] *v* (*intr*) **1** to slope or incline. **2** (**to**, **towards**) to move or tend (to or towards). [Lat *vergere*, to bend]

verger *n* **1** a church official who assists the minister and acts as caretaker. **2** an official who carries the ceremonial staff of a bishop or other dignitary. [Lat *virga*, rod]

verify *v* **-*ies***, **-*ied*** (*tr*) to check, or confirm, the truth or accuracy of. — *adj* **verifiable**. — *n* **verification**. [Lat *verus*, true + *facere*, to make]

verily *adv* (*old*) truly; really. [**very**]

verisimilitude *n* **1** the quality of appearing to be real or true. **2** a statement, etc. that merely sounds true. [Lat *verus*, true + *similis*, like]

veritable *adj* accurately described as such; real: *a veritable genius!* — *adv* **veritably**. [Lat *verus*, true]

verity *n* **-*ies*** **1** a true statement, esp. one of fundamental wisdom or importance; a maxim. **2** truthfulness. [Lat *verus*, true]

vermicelli *n* **1** pasta in very thin strands, thinner than spaghetti. **2** tiny splinters of chocolate used for cake decoration, etc. [Ital, little worms]

vermiform *adj* like a worm; worm-shaped. [Lat *vermis*, worm]

vermiform appendix *n* (*med*) the appendix.

vermilion *n* **1** a bright scarlet colour. **2** a pigment of this colour, consisting of sulphide of mercury. [Lat *vermiculus*]

vermin *n* **1** a collective name for wild animals that spread disease or generally cause a nuisance, esp. rats and other rodents. **2** detestable people. — *adj* **verminous**. [Lat *vermis*, worm]

vermouth *n* an alcoholic drink consisting of (esp. white) wine flavoured with aromatic herbs, orig. wormwood. [Ger *Wermut*, wormwood]

vernacular *n* (usu. with **the**) **1** the native language of a country or people, as opposed to a foreign language imposed from outside. **2** the form of a language as commonly spoken, as opposed to the formal or literary language. **3** the language or jargon of a particular group. **4** (*humorous*) slangy or obscene language. — *adj* **1** of or in the vernacular. **2** local; native. [Lat *vernaculus*, native]

vernal *adj* of, happening in, or appropriate to spring. — *adv* **vernally**. [Lat *ver*, spring]

vernier *n* a small sliding device on some measuring instruments, e.g. barometers and theodolites, used to measure fractions of units. [P *Vernier* (1580–1637), French mathematician]

veronica *n* a plant of the foxglove family, of mild and cold climates, with small blue, pink or white flowers. [After St *Veronica*]

verruca *n* **-cas** or **-cae** (*med*) a wart, esp. an in-growing one on the sole of the foot. [Lat, wart]

versatile *adj* **1** adapting easily to different tasks. **2** having numerous uses or abilities. — *n* **versatility**. [Lat *versatilis*, from *vertere*, to turn]

verse *n* **1** a division of a poem; a stanza. **2** poetry, as opposed to prose. **3** a poem. **4** a division of a song. **5** any of the numbered subdivisions of the chapters of the Bible. [Lat *versus*, line, row]

versed *adj* (**in**) familiar (with) or skilled (in).

versify *v* **-ies**, **-ied** **1** (*intr*) to write poetry. **2** (*tr*) to express as, or turn into, a poem. — *n* **versification**. — *n* **versifier**. [Lat *versificare*, to put into verse]

version *n* any of several types or forms in which a thing exists or is available, e.g. a particular edition or translation of a book, or one person's account of an incident. [Lat *versio*, from *vertere*, to turn]

verso *n* **-os** **1** the back of a loose sheet of printed paper. **2** the left-hand page of two open pages. ◇ See also **recto**. [Lat *verso* (*folio*), turned (leaf)]

versus *prep* **1** (in a contest or lawsuit) against. **2** (*coll*) in comparison to. [Lat]

vertebra *n* **-rae** any of the segments of bone that form the spine. — *adj* **vertebral**. [Lat]

vertebrate *adj* having a spine. — *n* any creature that has a spine, e.g. fishes, birds and mammals.

vertex *n* **-texes** or **-tices** **1** the highest point; the peak or summit. **2** (*math*) the point opposite the base of a geometric figure. **3** (*math*) the point at which any two sides of a geometric figure meet. [Lat, summit, whirlpool]

vertical *adj* **1** perpendicular to the horizon; upright. **2** running from top to bottom, not side to side. **3** of or at a vertex. **4** relating to, involving, or running through all levels within a hierarchy, all stages of a process, etc., rather than just one. — *n* a vertical line or direction. — *adv* **vertically**. [**vertex**]

vertical take-off *n* an aircraft's take-off direct from a stationary position, rather than from a run.

vertiginous *adj* **1** so high or whirling as to bring on vertigo; dizzying. **2** relating to vertigo.

vertigo *n* a whirling sensation felt when the sense of balance is disturbed; dizziness; giddiness. [Lat, from *vertere*, to turn]

vervain *n* a wild verbena. [OFr *vervaine*]

verve *n* great liveliness or enthusiasm. [Fr]

very *adv* **1** to a high degree or great extent: *very kind*. **2** (used with *own* and *same*, and with superlative adjectives) absolutely; truly: *the very same day*; *my very best effort*. — *adj* **1** absolute: *the very top*. **2** precise; actual: *this very minute*. **3** mere: *shocked by the very thought*. — **not very** not at all; the opposite of. — **very good** or **very well** expressions of consent and approval. [OFr *verai*, from Lat *verus*, true]

very high frequency *n* a band of radio frequencies between 30 and 300 megahertz.

Very light *n* a coloured flare fired from a pistol (**Very pistol**). [Invented by E W *Very* (1852–1910), US naval ordnance officer]

vesicle *n* **1** (*biol*) any cavity or pouch-like part, esp. one filled with liquid. **2** (*med*) a blister. [Lat *vesica*, bladder]

vespers *n* (*sing*) an evening service in some Christian churches; evensong. [Lat *vesper*, evening]. ◇ See also **compline**, **lauds**, **matins**, **none**[2], **sext**, **terce**.

vessel *n* **1** a container, esp. for liquid. **2** a ship or large boat. **3** a tube or duct carrying liquid, e.g. blood or sap, in animals and plants. [Lat *vasis*]

vest *n* **1** an undergarment for the top half of the body. **2** (esp. *US*) a waistcoat. — *v* **1** (*tr*; **in**, **with**) to give or bestow legally or officially: *by the power vested in me*; *The chairman is vested with absolute authority*. **2** (*intr*) to put on ecclesiastical robes. [Lat *vestis*, clothing]

vested interest *n* **1** a personal interest in the fortunes of a particular system, institution, company, etc., because one is directly affected or closely associated. **2** a person or company with such an interest.

vestal *adj* virginal; chaste. — *n* **1** a chaste woman, esp. a nun. **2** a vestal virgin. [Lat *vestalis*, of *Vesta*, the Roman goddess of the hearth and home]

vestal virgin *n* in ancient Rome, a young woman sworn to chastity and dedicated to tending the fire and other duties in the Temple of Vesta.

vestibule *n* an (esp. small) entrance hall. [Lat *vestibulum*]

vestige *n* **1** a slight amount; a hint or shred. **2** a surviving trace of what has almost disappeared. **3** (*biol*) a small, fairly functionless part in an animal or plant, once a fully developed organ in ancestors. — *adj* **vestigial**. [Lat *vestigium*, footprint]

vestment *n* **1** any of various garments worn ceremonially by members of the clergy and church choir. **2** any ceremonial robe. [Lat *vestis*, clothing]

vestry *n* **-*ies*** a room in a church where the vestments are kept, often also used for meetings, Sunday school classes, etc. [Lat *vestis*, clothing]

vet[1] *n* a veterinary surgeon. — *v* **-*tt*-** (*tr*) to examine or investigate (e.g. a candidate) thoroughly, esp. to check for suitability.

vet[2] *n* (*coll*; *US*) a veteran.

vetch *n* any of various climbing plants of the pea family with blue or purple flowers, and pods used as fodder. [Lat *vicia*]

veteran *n* **1** a person with many years of experience in a particular activity. **2** an old and experienced member of the armed forces. **3** (*US*) an ex-serviceman or -woman. [Lat *veteranus*, old]

veteran car *n* a very old motor car, specifically one made before 1905.

veterinary *adj* concerned with diseases of animals. — *n* **-*ies*** (*coll*) a veterinary surgeon. [Lat *veterinae*, cattle]

veterinary surgeon or **veterinarian** *n* a person qualified to treat diseases of animals.

veto *n* **-*oes*** **1** the right to formally reject a proposal or forbid an action, e.g. in a law-making assembly; the act of using such a right. **2** (*coll*) any prohibition or refusal of permission: *put a veto on smoking in the kitchen.* — *v* **-*oes***, **-*oed*** (*tr*) **1** to formally and authoritatively reject or forbid. **2** (*loosely*) to forbid. [Lat, I forbid]

vex *v* (*tr*) **1** to annoy or irritate. **2** to worry. — *adj* **vexing**. [Lat *vexare*, to shake, to annoy]

vexation *n* **1** the state or feeling of being vexed. **2** a thing that vexes.

vexatious *adj* vexing.

vexed *adj* (of an issue, etc.) much discussed or debated.

VHF *abbrev* very high frequency.

via *prep* by way of or by means of; through. [Lat, way]

viable *adj* **1** (of a plan, etc.) having a chance of success; feasible; practicable. **2** (of a plant, etc.) able to exist or grow in particular conditions. **3** (of a foetus or baby) able to survive independently, outside the womb. — *n* **viability**. — *adv* **viably**. [Fr, from Lat *vita*, life]

viaduct *n* a bridge-like structure of stone arches supporting a road or railway across a valley, etc. [Lat *via*, way + *ducere*, to lead]

vial. Same as **phial**.

viand *n* (usu. in *pl*; *formal*) an item of food. [OFr *viande*, food, from Lat *vivenda*]

viaticum *n* **-*cums*** or **-*ca*** **1** the Eucharist given to a dying person. **2** (*formal*) provisions for a journey. [Lat, from *via*, way]

vibes *n* (*pl*; *coll*) feelings, sensations, or an atmosphere experienced or communicated. [Shortened from **vibrations**]

vibrant *adj* **1** (**with**) extremely lively or exciting; made strikingly animated or energetic. **2** (of colour) very bright. **3** vibrating. — *n* **vibrancy**. — *adv* **vibrantly**. [**vibrate**]

vibraphone *n* a musical instrument in which horizontal metal bars of different lengths are made to resound electrically when struck with hammers. — *n* **vibraphonist**. [**vibrate + -phone**]

vibrate *v* **1** (*tr & intr*) to (cause to) move a short distance back and forth very rapidly. **2** (*intr*) to ring or resound when struck. **3** (*intr*) to shake or tremble. **4** (*intr*) to swing back and forth; to oscillate. — *adj* **vibratory**. [Lat *vibrare*, to tremble]

vibration *n* **1** a vibrating motion. **2** a single movement back and forth in vibrating. **3** (in *pl*; *coll*) feelings, sensations, or an atmosphere experienced or communicated.

vibrator *n* **1** any device that produces a vibrating motion, e.g. for massage. **2** a battery-powered vibrating dildo.

vibrato *n* **-*os*** a faint trembling effect in singing or the playing of string and wind instruments, achieved by vibrating the throat muscles or the fingers. [Ital]

vicar *n* **1** (*C of E*) the minister of a parish. **2** (*RC*) a bishop's deputy. — *adj* **vicarial**. [Lat *vicarius*, deputy, substitute]

vicarage *n* a vicar's residence or benefice.

vicar-apostolic *n* (*RC*) a member of the clergy appointed, with the rank of bishop, to a country with no established church structure.

vicar-general *n* (*RC*) an official assisting a bishop in administrative matters.

Vicar of Christ *n* the Pope, as representative of Christ on earth.

vicarious *adj* **1** experienced not directly but through witnessing the experience of another person: *vicarious excitement from watching his child learn.* **2** undergone on behalf of someone else. **3** standing in for another. **4** (of authority, etc.) delegated to someone else. [Lat *vicarius*, substituted]

vice[1] *n* a tool with heavy movable metal jaws, usu. fixed to a bench, for gripping an object being worked on. [Fr *vis*, screw]

vice[2] *n* **1** a habit or activity considered immoral, evil or depraved, e.g. prostitution or child-molesting. **2** such activities collectively. **3** (*humorous*) a bad habit; a fault in one's character. [Lat *vitium*, blemish]

vice squad *n* a branch of the police force investigating crimes relating to vice, e.g. illegal gambling and prostitution.

vice[3] *prep* **1** in place of. **2** following on from or succeeding. — **vice versa** with elements (of a situation, etc.) reversed; the other way round. [Lat, turn, alteration]

vice- *pfx* next in rank to, and acting as deputy for: *vice-admiral*; *vice-president*. [Ety. as for **vice**[3]]

vice-chancellor *n* the administrative head in certain universities, the chancellor being a figurehead only.

vice-regal see **viceroy**.

vicegerent *n* & *adj* (a person) appointed to act in place of a superior. — *n* **vicegerency**. [**vice**[3] + Lat *gerere*, to manage]

viceroy *n* a governor of a province or colony ruling in the name of, and with the authority of, a monarch or national government. — *adj* **viceregal**. — *n* **viceroyalty** or **viceroyship**. [Fr]

vice versa. See **vice**[3].

vicinity *n* **-ies** **1** a neighbourhood. **2** the area immediately surrounding. **3** the condition of being close; nearness. [Lat *vicinus*, neighbour]

vicious *adj* **1** violent or ferocious. **2** spiteful or malicious. **3** extremely severe or harsh. **4** (of reasoning, etc.) incorrect or faulty; unsound. — *adv* **viciously**. — *n* **viciousness**. [Lat *vitiosus*, faulty]

vicious circle *n* **1** a situation in which any attempt to resolve a problem creates others which in turn recreate the first one. **2** an incorrect form of reasoning in which one thing is supposedly proved on the basis of something else which itself depends for its proof on the truth of the first thing.

vicissitude *n* an unpredictable change of fortune or circumstance. [Lat *visis*, change]

victim *n* **1** a person or animal subjected to death, suffering, ill-treatment or trickery. **2** a person or animal killed as a (religious) sacrifice. [Lat *victima*, beast for sacrifice]

victimise or **-ize** *v* (*tr*) **1** to single out for bad or unfair treatment. **2** to cause to be a victim. — *n* **victimisation** or **-z-**.

victor *n* the winner or winning side in a war or contest. [Lat, from *vincere*, to conquer]

victoria *n* a large red sweet variety of plum, named after Queen *Victoria*.

Victoria Cross *n* the highest award for bravery in battle awarded to members of the British armed forces, founded by Queen *Victoria*.

Victorian *adj* **1** of, relating to, or characteristic of Queen *Victoria* or the period of her reign (1837–1901). **2** (of attitudes or values) typical of the strictness or conventionality of this period. — *n* a person who lived during this period.

Victoriana *n* (*pl*) objects from, or of a style typical of, the Victorian period.

victory *n* **-ies** (a) success against an opponent in a war or contest. [Ety. as for **victor**]

victorious *adj* **1** winning a war or contest. **2** marking or representing a victory.

victual *n* (usu. in *pl*) food; provisions. — *v* **-ll-** **1** (*tr*) to supply with victuals. **2** (*intr*) to obtain supplies. [Lat *victualis*, relating to living]

victualler *n* (*formal*) a shopkeeper selling food and drink.

(**licensed victualler** *n* a person authorised to sell food and alcoholic drink, e.g. in a pub, for consumption on the premises).

vicuña *n* **1** a S American mammal related to the llama. **2** a cloth or yarn made from its wool. [Span]

vide (as an instruction in a text) refer to; see. [Lat]

videlicet *adv* (*formal*; esp. in writing) namely; that is. [Lat]

video *adj* of or relating to the recording, reproducing or broadcasting of visual (esp. televised) images on magnetic tape. — *n* **-os** **1** the recording, reproducing or broadcasting of visual (esp. televised) images on magnetic tape. **2** a videocassette or videocassette recorder. **3** a film or programme pre-recorded on videocassette. — *v* **-os**, **-oed** (*tr*) to make a videocassette recording of. [Lat *videre*, to see]

video camera *n* a camera recording moving images and sound on to videotape.

videocassette *n* a cassette containing videotape.

videocassette recorder *n* a machine by means of which visual images, and sound, can be recorded on a videocassette, linked to a television set or video camera.

video game *n* an electronically-operated game involving the manipulation of images on a visual display unit.

video nasty *n* an explicitly horrific or pornographic film released, often exclusively, on videocassette.

video recorder *n* a videocassette recorder.

videotape *n* magnetic tape on which visual images and sound can be recorded.

videotext *n* any system in which computerised information is displayed on a television screen, e.g. teletext.

vie *v* **vying** (*intr*; **with**, **for**) to compete or struggle. [OFr *envier*, to challenge or invite]

view *n* **1** (**of**) an act or opportunity of seeing without obstruction: *a good view of the stage*. **2** something, esp. a landscape, seen from a particular point: *a magnificent view from the summit*. **3** range or field of vision: *out of view*. **4** a scene recorded in photograph or picture form. **5** (**of**) a description or impression: *The book gives* *a view of mediaeval life*. **6 (of, on)** an opinion; a point of view. **7 (of)** a way of considering or understanding something: *a short-term view of the situation*. **8 (to)** an intention or purpose: *bought the house with a view to moving in after retirement*. — *v* **1** (*tr*) to see or look at. **2** (*tr*) to inspect or examine. **3** (*tr*) to consider or regard. **4** (*tr* & *intr*) to watch (a programme) on television; to watch television. — **have in view** to have as a plan or aim. — **in view of** taking account of; because of. — **on view** displayed for all to see or inspect. [Fr *vue*]

viewdata *n* a system in which computerised information can be called up on to a television screen by telephone.

viewer *n* **1** any device used for viewing something, e.g. a photographic slide. **2** a person watching television.

viewfinder *n* a device on a camera through which one can see the field of vision covered by the lens.

viewing *n* an act or opportunity of seeing or inspecting something.

viewpoint *n* an interpretation of facts received; an opinion or point of view.

vigil *n* **1** a period of staying awake, usu. to guard or watch over a person or thing. **2** the day before a major religious festival, traditionally spent in prayer. **3** a night-time religious service or session of prayer. [Lat, awake, watchful]

vigilant *adj* ready for possible trouble or danger; alert; watchful. — *n* **vigilance**. [Lat *vigilare*, to keep awake]

vigilante *n* a self-appointed enforcer of law and order who feels that existing policing is inadequate. **[vigil]**

vignette *n* **1** a decorative design on a book's title page, traditionally of vine leaves. **2** a photographic portrait with the background deliberately faded. **3** a short literary essay, esp. describing a person's character. [Fr, little vine]

vigour *n* **1** great strength and energy of body or mind. **2** liveliness or forcefulness of action. **3** healthy growth (in plants, etc.). — *adj* **vigorous**. — *adv* **vigorously**. [Lat *vigor*]

viking *n* (often *cap*) any of the Danes, Norwegians and Swedes who raided by sea, and settled in, much of NW Europe between the 8th and 11th centuries. [Perhaps from OE *wicing*, pirate]

vile *adj* **1** evil or wicked. **2** physically repulsive; disgusting. **3** (*coll*) extremely bad or unpleasant. [Lat *vilis*, worthless, base]

vilify *v* **-ies**, **-ied** (*tr*) to say insulting or abusive things about; to malign or defame. — *n* **vilification**. [Lat *vilificare*, to make worthless or base]

villa *n* **1** a large country house or mansion. **2** a good-sized (esp. detached) suburban house. **3** a seaside house rented to holiday-makers. [Lat, country house]

village *n* **1** a cluster of houses and shops smaller than a town and larger than a hamlet, esp. in or near the countryside. **2** the people living in it. **3** a residential complex for participants in a (usu. international) sporting event. — *n* **villager**. [OFr, from Lat *villaticus*]

villain *n* **1** the principal wicked character in a story. **2** any violent, wicked or unscrupulous person. **3** (*slang*) a criminal. [OFr *vilein*, serf, from Lat *villanus*, worker on a country estate]

villain of the piece *n* **1** the villain in a story. **2** the person responsible for the trouble in question.

villainous *adj* **1** of, like, or worthy of a villain. **2** (*coll*) extremely bad.

villainy *n* **-ies** (an act of) wickedness or violence.

villein *n* (*hist*) a peasant worker of near-slave status, tied directly to a mediaeval lord, not to the lord's property. — *n* **villeinage**. [Ety. as for **villain**]

vim *n* (*coll*) energy; liveliness. [Lat, from *vis*, force]

vinaigrette *n* a salad dressing made by mixing oil, vinegar and seasonings, esp. mustard. [Fr, from *vinaigre*, vinegar]

vindicate *v* (*tr*) **1** to prove to be blameless or beyond criticism. **2** to show to have been worthwhile or justified: *The kidnapper's surrender vindicates the police tactic of negotiation*. — *n* **vindication**. — *adj* **vindicatory**. [Lat *vindicare*, to lay claim to, to avenge]

vindictive *adj* **1** feeling or showing spite or hatred. **2** seeking revenge. **3** serving as revenge or retribution. — *adv* **vindictively**. — *n* **vindictiveness**. [Ety. as for **vindicate**]

vine *n* **1** any of various climbing plants that produce grapes. **2** any climbing or trailing plant, e.g. ivy. [Lat *vinum*, wine]

vinegar *n* **1** a sour liquid made by fermenting diluted beer, wine or cider, used as a condiment and for pickling. **2** the quality of being bad-tempered or peevish. — *adj* **vinegary**. [Fr *vinaigre*, from *vin*, wine + *aigre*, sour]

vineyard *n* a plantation of grape-bearing vines, esp. for wine-making.

vingt-et-un *n* the card game pontoon. [Fr, twenty-one]

viniculture *n* the process or art of growing grapes (and making wine). — *n* **viniculturist**. [Lat *vinum*, wine + **culture**]

vino *n* **-os** (*slang*) wine. [Span and Ital]

vinous *adj* **1** of or like wine. **2** resulting from (esp. drinking too much) wine: *a vinous complexion*. [Lat *vinum*, wine]

vintage *n* **1** the grape-harvest of a certain year. **2** the wine produced from that harvest. **3** the time of year when grapes are harvested. **4** a particular period: *poetry of Elizabethan vintage*. — *adj* **1** (of wine) of good quality and from a specified year. **2** typical (of the best work or most characteristic behaviour of): *The remark was vintage Churchill*. [OFr, from Lat *vinum*, wine]

vintage car *n* an old motor car, specifically one built between 1919 and 1930.
vintner *n* (*formal*) a wine-merchant. [OFr *vinetier*]
vinyl *n* **1** any of a group of tough plastics manufactured in various forms, e.g. paint additives and carpet fibres. **2** (*coll*) the large thin (usu. black) plastic disc as one format in which recorded music is available, as distinct from cassette, compact disc, etc.
viol *n* any of a family of early musical instruments from which the violin family is descended. — *n* **violist**. [OProvençal *viola*]
viola[1] *n* a musical instrument very similar to, but slightly larger than, the violin. — *n* **violist**. [Ital]
viola[2] *n* any of a group of flowering plants of which the violet and pansy are members. [Lat]
violate *v* (*tr*) **1** to disregard or break (e.g. a law, a treaty or a promise). **2** to treat (something sacred or private) with disrespect; to profane. **3** to disturb or disrupt (e.g. a person's peace or privacy). **4** to rape or sexually abuse. — *n* **violation**. — *n* **violator**. [Lat *violare*, to treat violently]
violent *adj* **1** marked by or using great physical force. **2** using, or involving the use of, such force to cause physical harm. **3** impulsively aggressive and unrestrained in nature or behaviour. **4** intense, extreme or vehement: *violent dislike*. — *adv* **violently**. [Lat *violentus*, from *vis*, force]
violence *n* **1** the state or quality of being violent. **2** violent behaviour. — **do violence to 1** to harm physically. **2** to spoil or ruin. **3** to distort the meaning of.
violet *n* **1** any of a group of flowering plants of mild climates with large purple or blue petals; any of various similar but unrelated plants, e.g. the African violet. **2** a bluish-purple colour. [Lat *viola*]
shrinking violet *n* (*coll*) a shy, hesitant person.
violin *n* **1** a smallish musical instrument with a shaped body and a neck along which four strings are stretched, held with one end under the chin and played with a bow. **2** any of the violinists in an orchestra: *the second violins*. [Ital *violino*, little viola]
violinist *n* a violin player.
violoncello *n* **-os** (*formal*) a cello. — *n* **violoncellist**. [Ital]
VIP *abbrev* very important person.
viper *n* **1** any of a family of poisonous snakes, including the common viper or adder, Britain's only poisonous snake. **2** a treacherous or spiteful person. [Lat *vipera*]
virago *n* **-oes** or **-os** (*literary*) a loudly fierce or overbearing woman. [Lat, manlike woman]
viral. See **virus**.
virgin *n* **1** a person, esp. a woman, who has never had sexual intercourse. **2** a member of a religious order of women sworn to chastity. **3** (*cap*; with **the**) Mary, mother of Jesus Christ. **4** (*cap*) a portrait or statue of Mary. **5** (*cap*; with **the**) the sign or constellation Virgo. — *adj* **1** never having had sexual intercourse; chaste. **2** in its original state, e.g. never having been touched, cultivated, written on or walked on. [Lat *virgo*]
virginal *adj* **1** of or appropriate to a virgin. **2** in the state of virginity.
Virgin Birth *n* the birth of Christ, regarded by Christians as an act of God, since Christ's mother, Mary, was a virgin.
virginity *n* the state of being a virgin.
virginal[1]. See **virgin**.
virginal[2] *n* an early keyboard instrument like a small harpsichord. [Perhaps because mostly played by young women]
Virgo *n* **-os 1** a constellation and the sixth sign of the zodiac, the Virgin. **2** a person born under the sign, between 23 August and 22 September. [Lat, virgin]
virile *adj* **1** (of a man) having a high level of sexual desire. **2** displaying or requiring qualities regarded as typically masculine, esp. physical strength. **3** (of a man) able to produce children. **4** of, relating to, or possessing the features of, a mature adult male. — *n* **virility**. [Lat *virilis*, manly]
virology *n* the branch of medicine dealing with the study of viruses. — *adj* **virological**. [**virus** + **-logy**]
virtual *adj* **1** in effect or in practice, but not in name: *a virtual state of war*. **2** near: *the virtual collapse of the industry*. [Ety. as for **virtue**]
virtually *adv* **1** more or less, though not strictly speaking. **2** almost; nearly.
virtual reality *n* an illusory three-dimensional world created by computer, that one can have the impression of moving around in by wearing a computerised headset.
virtue *n* **1** a quality regarded as morally good. **2** moral goodness; righteousness. **3** an admirable quality or desirable feature. **4** virginity, esp. in women. — *adj* **virtuous**. — *adv* **virtuously**. — **by** or **in virtue of** because of; on account of. [Lat *virtus*, moral excellence, bravery]
virtuoso *n* **-os** a person with remarkable artistic skill, esp. a brilliant musical performer. — *n* **virtuosity**. [Ital, learned, skilful]
virtuous. See **virtue**.
virulent *adj* **1** (of a disease) having a very harmful effect very quickly. **2** (of a disease or the organism causing it) extremely infectious. **3** (of a substance) highly poisonous. **4** bitterly hostile; acrimonious. — *n* **virulence**. [Lat *virulentus*, venomous]
virus *n* **1** any of numerous types of micro-organism, smaller than bacteria, that grow on living cells and often cause disease. **2** the organism that causes and transmits an infectious disease. **3** a disease caused by such an organism. **4** anything that damages or corrupts. **5** (also **computer virus**) a piece of computer information inserted into a program to destroy or disrupt data,

passed on to all linked computers. [Lat, venom]

viral *n* **1** of or relating to viruses. **2** caused by a virus.

visa *n* a permit stamped into a passport to allow the holder to enter or leave the country issuing it. [Lat, from *videre*, to see]

visage *n* (*literary*) **1** the face. **2** the face's usual expression; a countenance. [Fr, face]

vis-à-vis *prep* in relation to; with regard to. — *adv* face-to-face. — *n* ***vis-à-vis*** a counterpart or opposite number. [Fr, face-to-face]

viscera *n* (*pl*; *med*) the body's large internal organs. [**viscus**]

visceral *adj* **1** of or relating to the viscera. **2** of the feelings, esp. the basic human instincts rather than the intellect.

viscid *adj* viscous. [Lat *viscum*, bird-lime]

viscose *n* **1** cellulose in a viscous state, able to be made into thread. **2** rayon, a fabric made from such thread. [Ety. as for **viscous**]

viscosity. See **viscous**.

viscount *n* a British nobleman below an earl and above a baron in rank. — *n* **viscountcy, *-ies*** or **viscountship**. [OFr *visconte*]

viscountess *n* **1** the wife or widow of a viscount. **2** a woman of the rank of viscount in her own right.

viscous *adj* **1** of a thick semi-liquid consistency, not flowing easily. **2** (of liquid) sticky. — *n* **viscosity**. [Lat *viscosus*, sticky, from *viscum*, bird-lime]

viscus *n* (*med*) any of the body's large internal organs. ◇ See also **viscera**. [Lat]

visible *adj* **1** able to be seen. **2** able to be realised or perceived; apparent. — *adv* **visibly**. [Lat *visibilis*, from *videre*, to see]

visibility *n* **1** the state or fact of being visible. **2** the extent to which one can see clearly in current weather conditions: *poor visibility*; *visibility down to 50 yards*.

vision *n* **1** the ability to see; the faculty of sight. **2** an image conjured up vividly in the imagination. **3** the ability to perceive what is likely, and plan wisely for it; foresight. **4** an image communicated supernaturally, esp. by God. **5** the (quality of) picture on a television screen. **6** a person or thing of overwhelming beauty. [Lat *visio*, sight]

visionary *adj* **1** showing or marked by great foresight or imagination. **2** possible only in the imagination; impracticable; fanciful. **3** capable of seeing supernatural images; seeing such images often. — *n* ***-ies*** **1** a person of great foresight. **2** a person to whom images are communicated supernaturally. **3** a person who dreams up fanciful schemes.

visit *v* ***-t-*** **1** (*tr* & *intr*) to go or come to see (a person or place) socially or professionally. **2** (*tr* & *intr*) to go or come to stay (with) temporarily. **3** (*tr* with **on**) to inflict (e.g. harm or a punishment). **4** (*tr*) to enter the mind of temporarily. **5** (*tr*; *old*; **with**) to afflict or trouble (with). — *n* **1** an act of visiting; a social or professional call. **2** a temporary stay. **3** a sightseeing excursion. — *n* **visitor**. [Lat *visitare*, from *visere*, to go to see]

visitant *n* **1** a person appearing in a supernatural vision; an apparition. **2** a migratory bird, staying temporarily.

visiting-card *n* a calling-card.

visitation *n* **1** an official visit or inspection. **2** an event regarded as a punishment or reward from God. **3** an instance of seeing a supernatural vision. **4** (*cap* with **the**) the visit made by the Virgin Mary to her cousin Elizabeth; the Christian festival commemorating this, held on 2 July.

visor *n* **1** the movable part of a helmet, covering the face. **2** (also **sun visor**) a device like a peaked cap with no head covering, often made of plastic, worn to shade the eyes. **3** a small movable panel above the windscreen on the inside of a motor vehicle, folded down to shade the eyes from sunlight. [OFr *viser*, from *vis*, face]

vista *n* **1** a view into the distance, esp. bounded narrowly on both sides, e.g. by rows of trees. **2** a mental vision extending far into the future or past. [Ital, view]

visual *adj* **1** of, relating to, or received through sight or vision: *a visual image*. **2** creating vivid mental images: *visual poetry*. **3** creating a strong impression through what is seen, rather than what is said or heard: *a very visual play*. — *adv* **visually**. [Lat *visus*, sight]

visual aid *n* a picture, diagram, film, etc. used as an aid to teaching or presenting information.

the visual arts *n* (*pl*) painting, sculpture, films, etc., as opposed to literature, music, etc.

visual display unit *n* a screen on which information from a computer is displayed.

visualise or **-ize** *v* (*tr*) to form a clear mental image of. — *n* **visualisation** or **-z-**.

vital *adj* **1** of, relating to, or essential for life: *the vital organs*. **2** determining life or death, or success or failure: *a vital error*. **3** essential; of the greatest importance. **4** full of life; energetic. — *n* (*pl*) the vital organs, e.g. the brain, the heart and the lungs. — *adv* **vitally**. [Lat *vita*, life]

vitalise or **-ize** *v* (*tr*) to fill with life or energy. — *n* **vitalisation** or **-z-**.

vitality *n* **1** liveliness and energy. **2** the state of being alive; the ability to stay alive.

vital statistics *n* (*pl*) **1** statistics concerning births, marriages, deaths and other matters relating to population. **2** (*coll*) a woman's bust, waist and hip measurements.

vitamin *n* any of a group of substances essential for healthy life, present in small quantities in various natural foods, and commonly referred to by the letters A, B, C, D, E, etc. [Lat *vita*, life + **amine**]

vitamin A *n* (also **retinol**) a vitamin found in dairy products, etc. and required for the correct functioning of the eyes.

vitamin B *n* any of the vitamins of the vitamin B complex: **vitamin B_1** (also **thiamine**) a vitamin found in seeds and grains, and a lack of which causes beri-beri; **vitamin B_2** (also **riboflavin**) found in milk, cheese, liver, etc.; **vitamin B_6** (also **pyridoxine**) found in cereals, meat, fruit, etc., and a lack of which causes skin diseases; **vitamin B_{12}** (also **cyanocobalamin**) found in meat and milk, and a lack of which causes anaemia; **niacin** or **nicotinic acid** found in meat, fish and cereals, and a lack of which causes pellagra; **folic acid** found in liver and green vegetables, and a lack of which causes anaemia; **pantothenic acid**, occurring widely in animal and vegetable sources, and **biotin**, found in liver and kidney, etc., a lack of which causes skin disease.

vitamin C *n* (also **ascorbic acid**) found in citrus fruits, green vegetables, etc., a lack of which causes scurvy.

vitamin D *n* either of the vitamins **D_2** (or **calciferol**) and **D_3** (or **cholecalciferol**) occurring in fish and essential to the prevention of rickets.

vitamin E *n* (also **tocopherol**) any of a group of substances obtained from various plant and animal sources, with various functions.

vitamin K *n* any of a group of vitamins, esp. **K_1** (also **phytomenadione**) found in green vegetables, etc. and necessary for blood-clotting.

vitamin P *n* (also **citrin** or **bioflavonoid**) any of a group of substances found e.g. in citrus fruit, required for the correct functioning of blood capillaries.

vitiate *v* (*tr*) **1** to impair the quality or effectiveness of (e.g. an argument); to make faulty or defective. **2** to make (e.g. a legal contract) ineffectual or invalid. — *n* **vitiation**. [Lat *vitiare*, from *vitium*, blemish]

viticulture *n* viniculture. [Lat *vitis*, vine + **culture**]

vitreous *adj* **1** of, relating to, or consisting of glass. **2** like glass in hardness, shine or transparency: *vitreous china.* [Lat *vitrum*, glass]

vitreous humour *n* a jelly-like substance inside the eye, between the lens and the retina.

vitrify *v* **-ies**, **-ied** (*tr* & *intr*) to (cause to) become glass or glass-like, esp. by heat. — *n* **vitrification**. — *adj* **vitrified**. [Lat *vitrum*, glass + *facere*, to make]

vitriol *n* **1** concentrated sulphuric acid. **2** a sulphate of a metal, orig. one of a glassy appearance. **3** extremely bitter or hateful speech or criticism. [Lat *vitreus*, of glass]

vitriolic *adj* extremely bitter or hateful.

vituperate *v* **1** (*tr*) to attack with abusive criticism or disapproval. **2** (*intr*) to use abusive language. — *n* **vituperation**. — *adj* **vituperative**. [Lat *vituperare*, to blame]

viva[1] *interj* long live —; — forever. [Span and Ital]

viva[2] *n* (also **viva voce**) an examination in which questions and answers are spoken, not written; an oral examination. — *v* **-vaed** (*tr*) to examine orally. [Lat *viva voce*, by the living voice]

viva voce *adv* in speech; orally.

vivacious *adj* having an attractively lively personality. — *n* **vivacity**. [Lat *vivax*, lively]

vivarium *n* **-iums** or **-ia** any place or enclosure in which live animals are kept, esp. in conditions resembling their natural habitat. [Lat, from *vivere*, to live]

vivid *adj* **1** (of colour) very bright. **2** creating, forming or retaining a clear mental picture: *a vivid account of the match*; *a vivid imagination.* **3** full of life; vivacious. — *adv* **vividly**. — *n* **vividness**. [Lat *vividus*, lively]

viviparous *adj* (of animals) giving birth to a fully alive, developed offspring, rather than an egg. — *n* **viviparity**. — *adv* **viviparously**. ◇ See also **oviparous**. [Lat *vivus*, alive + *parere*, to produce]

vivisection *n* **1** the practice of cutting open live animals for the purposes of experimentation. **2** an experiment of this kind. — *v* (*tr*) **vivisect**. [Lat *vivus*, living + *secare*, to cut]

vivisectionist *n* a person who practises, or defends the practice of, vivisection.

vixen *n* **1** a female fox. **2** a fierce or spiteful woman. [OE *fyxen*]

viz *adv* namely; that is. [Abbrev. of **videlicet**]

vizier *n* a high-ranking government official in certain Muslim countries. [Arabic *wazir*, porter, bearer of a burden]

voc. *abbrev* vocative.

vocab *n* (*coll*) vocabulary.

vocable *n* (*linguistics*) **1** a spoken word or single sound in a word. **2** a (spoken or written) word regarded as a series of sounds or letters, rather than as a unit of meaning. [Ety. as for **vocabulary**]

vocabulary *n* **-ies** **1** (the sum of) the words of a particular language. **2** the range of words known to or used by a particular person. **3** the words used by a particular group or in a particular sphere. **4** a list of words with translations alongside. **5** a range of (esp. artistic) forms and techniques. [Lat *vocabulum*, from *vox*, voice]

vocal *adj* **1** of, relating to, or produced by the voice. **2** expressing opinions, criticism, etc. freely and forcefully. — *n* (*pl*) the parts of a song, etc. that are sung, not played by instruments; words, rather than music. — *adv* **vocally**. [Lat *vocalis*, from *vox*, voice]

vocal cords *n* (*pl*) folds in the membrane lining the larynx, vibrated by the breath to produce sound.

vocalise or **-ize** *v* (*tr*) **1** to utter or produce with the voice. **2** to express in words; to articulate. — *n* **vocalisation** or **-z-**.

vocalist *n* a singer, esp. in a pop group.

vocation *n* **1** a particular occupation or profession. **2** a feeling of being destined to do, or especially suited for, a particular type of work. **3** a feeling of being called by God to adopt a religious life or perform good works. [Lat *vocare*, to call]

vocational *adj* concerned with, or in preparation for, a particular trade or profession.

vocative (*gram*) *n* **1** in some languages, the particular form of a word used when a person or thing is addressed directly. **2** a word in this form. — *adj* in the vocative. [Lat *vocare*, to call]

vociferate *v* (*tr* & *intr*) **1** to exclaim loudly and forcefully. **2** to shout or cry in a loud voice; to bawl. [Lat *vox*, voice + *ferre*, to carry]

vociferous *adj* loud and forceful in stating opinions, etc.; (of opinions, etc.) expressed loudly and forcefully. — *adv* **vociferously**. — *n* **vociferousness**. [Ety. as for **vociferate**]

vodka *n* a clear alcoholic spirit of Russian origin, traditionally made from rye, sometimes from potatoes. [Russ, from *voda*, water]

vogue *n* **1** the current fashion or trend in any sphere: *in vogue*. **2** a period of being fashionable or popular: *enjoyed a long vogue*. — *adj* currently popular or fashionable. [Fr]

voice *n* **1** the ability to speak; the power of speech: *lost his voice*. **2** a way of speaking or singing peculiar to each individual, and by which he or she can be identified. **3** a tone of speech reflecting a particular emotion: *in a nervous voice*. **4** the sound of a person speaking: *heard a voice*. **5** the ability to sing, esp. well. **6** expression in the form of spoken words: *gave voice to his feelings*. **7** a means of expression or communication: *Parliament's role as the voice of the people*. **8** (*gram*) the state of a verb's being either active or passive. — *v* (*tr*) **1** to express in speech. **2** (*phon*) to pronounce with a vibration of the vocal cords. — **in good voice** singing well. — **with one voice** unanimously. [Lat *vox*]

voice-box *n* (*coll*) the larynx.

voiced *adj* **1** expressed in speech. **2** (*phon*) pronounced with a vibration of the vocal cords, as is the sound *z*, but not the sound *s*.

voiceless *adj* (*phon*) not voiced.

voice-over *n* the voice of an unseen narrator in a film or television advertisement or programme.

void *adj* **1** not valid or legally binding: *declared the contract null and void*. **2** containing nothing; empty or unoccupied. **3** (**of**) lacking (in); free (from); devoid (of). — *n* **1** an empty space. **2** a space left blank or unfilled. **3** a feeling of absence or emptiness strongly felt. — *v* (*tr*) **1** to make empty or clear. **2** to invalidate or nullify. **3** to empty (the bladder or bowels). [OFr *voide*, empty]

voile *n* any very thin semi-transparent fabric. [Fr, veil]

vol. *abbrev* volume.

volatile *adj* **1** changing quickly from a solid or liquid into a vapour. **2** explosive. **3** easily becoming angry or violent. **4** (of a situation, etc.) liable to change quickly, esp. verging on violence. — *n* **volatility**. [Lat *volare*, to fly]

volatilise or **-ize** *v* (*tr* & *intr*) to (cause to) change from a solid or liquid into a vapour. — *n* **volatilisation** or **-z-**.

vol-au-vent *n* a small round puff-pastry case with a savoury filling. [Fr, literally 'flight in the wind']

volcano *n* **-oes** **1** an opening in the earth's crust, typically a cone-shaped mountain with a central crater, through which molten rock, ash and gases erupt or have erupted periodically. **2** a situation, or a person, likely to erupt into anger or violence. [Lat *Vulcanus*, Roman god of fire]

volcanic *adj* **1** of, relating to, or produced by a volcano or volcanoes. **2** easily erupting into anger or violence: *a volcanic temper*.

vole *n* any of various small, blunt-nosed, short-eared, mouse-like rodents. [Orig. *vole-mouse*, from Norw *voll*, field + *mus*, mouse]

volition *n* the act of willing or choosing; the exercising of one's will: *did it of her own volition*. — *adj* **volitional**. [Lat *velle*, to will]

volley *n* **-eys** **1** a firing of several guns or other weapons simultaneously. **2** an outburst of several things, e.g. insults, launched at once or in rapid succession. **3** (*sport*) a striking of the ball before it bounces. — *v* (*tr*) **1** to fire (weapons) in a volley. **2** (*sport*) to strike (a ball) before it bounces. [Fr *volée*, flight]

volleyball *n* a game, for two teams of six players each, in which a large ball is volleyed over a high net with the hands.

volt *n* the standard unit of potential difference, the force that carries an electric current of one ampere between two points in a circuit against a resistance of one ohm. [Alessandro *Volta* (1745–1827), Italian scientist]

voltage *n* potential difference expressed as a number of volts.

voltmeter *n* an instrument that measures voltage.

volte-face *n* a sudden and complete reversal, esp. of opinion. [Fr]

voluble *adj* **1** speaking or spoken insistently, uninterruptedly, or with ease. **2** tending to talk a lot; very talkative. — *n* **volubility**. — *adv* **volubly**. [Lat *volubilis*, from *volvere*, to roll]

volume *n* **1** the amount of three-dimensional space occupied by an object, gas or liquid. **2** loudness of sound; the control that adjusts it on a radio, hi-fi system, etc. **3** a book, whether complete in itself or one of several forming a larger work. **4** an (esp. large) amount, quantity or mass: *the volume of traffic*. — **speak volumes** to be very significant; to say a lot: *Her refusal to answer spoke volumes*. [Lat *volumen*, roll, scroll]

voluminous *adj* **1** (of garments) flowing or billowing out; ample. **2** producing great quantities of writing; (of writing) enough to fill many volumes. [**volume**]

voluntary *adj* **1** done, given, taken, etc. by choice, not by accident or compulsion. **2** working with no expectation of being paid or otherwise rewarded; (of work) unpaid. **3** (of an organisation) staffed by unpaid workers; supported by donations of money freely given. **4** (of a movement, muscle or limb) produced or controlled by the will. — *n* ***-ies*** a piece of (esp. organ) music played before, during or after a church service. — *adv* **voluntarily**. [Lat *voluntarius*, from *velle*, to will]

volunteer *v* **1** (*tr* & *intr*; **for**) to offer (one's help or services) willingly, without being persuaded or forced. **2** (*intr*) to go into military service by choice, without being conscripted. **3** (*tr*) to give (information, etc.) unasked. **4** (*tr*; *facet*; **for**) to order (someone) to perform a task or give help. — *n* **1** a person who volunteers. **2** a person carrying out voluntary work. **3** a member of a non-professional army of voluntary soldiers set up during wartime. [**voluntary**]

voluptuary *n* ***-ies*** a person addicted to luxury and sensual pleasures. — *adj* promoting or characterised by luxury and sensual pleasures. [Lat *voluptas*, pleasure]

voluptuous *adj* **1** of, consisting of, or suggestive of sensual pleasure. **2** (of a woman) sexually very attractive, esp. having a very shapely figure. — *n* **voluptuousness**. [Lat *voluptas*, pleasure]

volute *n* **1** a spiral. **2** a scroll carved in stone, esp. at the top of a column. **3** one single twist in a spiral shell. [Lat *volvere*, to roll]

vomit *v* ***-t-*** **1** (*tr* & *intr*) to throw out (the contents of the stomach) through the mouth; to be sick. **2** (*tr*) to emit or throw out with force or violence. — *n* matter vomited from the stomach. [Lat *vomere*]

voodoo *n* **1** witchcraft of a type orig. practised by the Black peoples of the West Indies and southern US. **2** the beliefs and practices of the religious cult that developed it, including serpent-worship and human sacrifice. — *v* (*tr*) to bewitch using, or as if using, voodoo methods. [(in various W African languages) *vodu*, spirit, demon]

voracious *adj* **1** eating or craving food in large quantities. **2** extremely eager in some respect: *a voracious reader*. — *adv* **voraciously**. — *n* **voracity**. [Lat *vorare*, to devour]

vortex *n* ***-texes*** or ***-tices*** **1** a whirlpool or whirlwind; any whirling mass or motion. **2** a situation into which all surrounding people or things are helplessly and dangerously drawn. — *adj* **vortical**. [Lat, from *vortere*, to turn]

votary *n* ***-ies*** **1** a person bound by solemn vows to a religious life. **2** a person dedicated to a particular cause or activity. [Lat *vovere*, to vow]

vote *n* **1** a formal indication of choice or opinion, e.g. in an election or debate. **2** the right to express a choice or opinion, esp. in a national election. **3** a (collective) choice or opinion expressed in this way: *a vote in favour of the motion*. **4** the support given by a certain sector of the population, or to a particular candidate or group, in this way: *attract the middle-class vote*; *an increase in the Liberal vote*. — *v* **1** (*intr*) to cast a vote (for or against). **2** (*tr*) to decide, state, grant or bring about by casting votes. **3** (*tr*) to declare support for by casting a vote. **4** (*tr*; *coll*) to declare or pronounce by general consent: *The show was voted a success*. **5** (*tr*; *coll*) to propose or suggest. — *n* **voter**. — *v* **vote down** (*tr*) to reject or defeat by voting. — *v* **vote in** (*tr*) to appoint by voting; to elect. [Lat *votum*, wish]

votive *adj* done or given in thanks to God, or to fulfil a vow or promise. [Lat *vovere*, to vow]

vouch *v* (*intr* with **for**) to give a firm assurance or authoritative guarantee of the truth, authenticity, trustworthiness, etc. (of someone or something). [OFr *voucher*, to call upon to defend]

voucher *n* **1** any ticket or paper serving as proof, e.g. of the purchase or receipt of goods. **2** a ticket exchangeable for goods or services of a specified value; a token: *a gift voucher*. [Ety. as for **vouch**]

vouchsafe *v* (*tr* & *intr; old* or *literary*) to agree or condescend (to do, give, grant or allow): *vouchsafed me no reply*; *did not vouchsafe to reply*. [**vouch** + **safe**]

vow *n* a solemn and binding promise, esp. one made to or in the name of God. — *v* (*tr*) to promise or declare solemnly, or threaten emphatically; to swear. [Lat *vovere*]

vowel *n* **1** any speech-sound made with an open mouth and no contact between mouth, lips, teeth or tongue. **2** a letter, used alone or in combination, representing such a sound —in English the letters *a*, *e*, *i*, *o*, *u* and in some words *y*. [Lat *vocalis*, from *vox*, voice]

vox populi *n* (also **vox pop**) the voice of the people, i.e. public opinion. [Lat]

voyage *n* a long journey to a distant place, esp. by sea or in space. — *v* (*intr*) to go on a voyage; to travel. — *n* **voyager**. [Fr, from Lat *viaticum*]

voyeur *n* **1** a person who gets sexual pleasure from watching (esp. secretly) others undressing or having sex. **2** a person who observes, esp. with fascination or intrusively, the distress, misery, pain, etc. of others. — *n* **voyeurism**. — *adj* **voyeuristic**. [Fr, one who sees]

vs *abbrev* versus.

VSO *abbrev* Voluntary Service Overseas.

VSOP *abbrev* very special old pale, a port, sherry or brandy between 20 and 25 years old.

VT or **Vt.** *abbrev* Vermont.

VTOL *abbrev* vertical take-off and landing.

vulcanise or **-ize** *v* (*tr*) to treat (rubber) with sulphur at high temperature or pressure, to enhance strength or elasticity. — *n* **vulcanisation** or **-z-**. [Ety. as for **volcano**]

vulcanite *n* hard black vulcanised rubber.

vulg. *abbrev* vulgar.

vulgar *adj* **1** marked by a lack of politeness or social or cultural refinement; coarse. **2** of or relating to the form of a language commonly spoken, rather than to formal or literary language; vernacular. — *adv* **vulgarly**.

vulgar fraction *n* a fraction expressed as one number above another, rather than in decimal form.

vulgarise or **-ize** *v* (*tr*) **1** to make vulgar. **2** to make, or spoil by making, common or popular. — *n* **vulgarisation** or **-z-**.

vulgarism *n* **1** a vulgar expression in speech. **2** an example of vulgar behaviour.

vulgarity *n* **-ies** (an example of) coarseness in speech or behaviour.

Vulgate *n* (with **the**) a Latin version of the Bible written in the 4th century. [Lat *vulgata* (*editio*), popular (edition)]

vulnerable *adj* **1** easily hurt physically or emotionally. **2** easily tempted or persuaded. **3** (**to**) unprotected against attack, e.g. with weapons or criticism. — *n* **vulnerability**. [Lat *vulnerare*, to wound]

vulpine *adj* **1** of, relating to, or resembling a fox or foxes. **2** cunning, like a fox. [Lat *vulpes*, fox]

vulture *n* **1** a very large bird of prey of hot regions, feeding chiefly on dead animals. **2** a person who exploits, or prepares to exploit, the downfall or death of another. [Lat *vultur*]

vulva *n* (*med*) the parts surrounding the opening to the vagina; the female genitals. [Lat, wrapping, womb]

vv *abbrev* **1** versus. **2** vice versa.

vying *present participle* of **vie**.

W

W[1] or **w** *n* ***Ws*** or ***W's***, ***w's*** the 23rd letter of the English alphabet.

W[2] *symbol* (*chem*) tungsten. [Ger *Wolfram*]

W[3] *abbrev* **1** watt. **2** West. **3** (*physics*) work.

w *abbrev* **1** (*cricket*) wicket. **2** wide. **3** wife. **4** with.

WA *abbrev* Washington.

wacky *adj* ***-ier***, ***-iest*** (*coll*, orig. *US*) eccentric; crazy. [Perhaps from **whack**]

wad *n* **1** a compressed mass of soft material used for packing, padding, stuffing, etc. **2** a thick sheaf or bundle of banknotes, etc. [Lat *wadda*, from Arabic]

wadding *n* material used as padding or stuffing.

waddle *v* (*intr*) (of a duck, or *derog* of a person, esp. if short and plump) to sway from side to side in walking. [**wade**]

wade *v* **1** (*tr* & *intr*) **1** to walk through deep water; to cross (a river, etc.) by wading. **2** (*intr* with **through**) to make one's way laboriously through: *wading through legal documents*. **3** (*intr* with **into**) to attack or criticise fiercely. — *v* **wade in** (*intr*) to involve oneself unhesitatingly and enthusiastically in a task, etc. [OE *wadan*, to go]

wader *n* **1** any long-legged bird that wades in shallow waters in search of food. **2** (usu. in *pl*) a thigh-high waterproof boot used by anglers, etc.

wadi *n* a rocky river bed in N Africa and Arabia, dry except during the rains. [Arabic]

wafer *n* **1** a thin, light, finely layered kind of biscuit, served e.g. with ice cream. **2** a thin disc of unleavened bread or rice paper served to communicants at Holy Communion. **3** (*hist*) a thin disc of sticky paste or other adhesive material for sealing letters. **4** (*hist*) a small flat edible capsule of medicine. [MidE *wafre*, from ODut *wafer*, variant of *wafel*, waffle]

waffle[1] *n* a light-textured cake made of batter, with a distinctive grid-like surface pattern. [ODut *wafel*]

waffle iron *n* a flat double-sided hinged mould for cooking waffles in.

waffle[2] *v* (*intr*) to talk or write at length but to little purpose. — *n* talk or writing of this kind. — *n* **waffler**.

waft *v* (*tr* & *intr*) to (cause to) float or drift gently, esp. through the air. — *n* a whiff, e.g. of perfume. [MidE *waughter or wafter*, escort vessel]

wag *v* ***-gg-*** **1** (*tr* & *intr*) to wave to and fro vigorously; (of a dog) to wave (its tail), or (of its tail) to wave, as a sign of pleasure. **2** (*tr*) to shake (one's finger) up and down at someone, while giving advice, a warning or rebuke. **3** (*intr*) (of tongues, chins or beards) to move busily in chatter. — *n* **1** a wagging movement. **2** a habitual joker; someone with a roguish sense of humour; a wit. — *adj* **waggish**. [OE *wagian*]

wage *v* (*tr*; **against**) to fight (a war or battle). — *n* **1** (in *sing* or *pl*) a regular, esp. daily or weekly rather than monthly, payment from an employer to an esp. unskilled or semi-skilled employee. ◇ See also **salary**. **2** (in *pl* with *sing* verb; *old literary*) reward, recompense or repayment. [OFr *wagier*, to pledge]

wager (*old*) *n* a bet on the outcome or result of something. — *v* ***-r-*** (*tr*) to bet; to stake in a bet. [OFr *wagier*, to pledge]

waggle *v* (*tr* & *intr*) to (cause to) move to and fro. [**wag**]

wagon or **waggon** *n* **1** a four-wheeled vehicle for carrying loads, esp. horse-drawn; a cart. **2** an open truck or closed van for carrying railway freight. **3** a tea trolley. — **on** (or **off**) **the wagon** (*coll*) temporarily abstaining (or no longer abstaining) from alcohol. [Dut *wagen*]

wagoner or **waggoner** *n* the driver of a wagon.

waif *n* **1** an orphaned, abandoned or homeless child. **2** any pathetically undernourished-looking child. **3** something unclaimed and apparently ownerless. — *adj* **waif-like**. [OFr *waif*, *guaif*, stray beast]

waifs and strays *n* (*pl*) **1** homeless people, esp. children. **2** unclaimed articles; odds and ends.

wail *n* a long-drawn-out mournful or complaining cry. — *v* (*intr* & *tr*) to make, or utter with, such a cry. **2** (of e.g. a siren) to make a similar noise. [Perhaps related to Norse *wæla*, to wail]

wainscot *n* (esp. *hist*) wooden panelling or boarding covering the lower part of the walls of a room. [Perhaps Dut *wagenschot*, wagon partition]

wainscoting or **wainscotting** *n* (material for constructing) a wainscot.

waist *n* **1** the narrow part of the human body between the ribs and hips. **2** the part of a garment covering this. **3** a narrow middle part of something such as a violin or wasp. **4** the middle part of a ship. [OE *wæstm*, form, figure]

waistband *n* the reinforced strip of cloth on a skirt, trousers, etc., that goes round the waist.

waistcoat *n* a close-fitting, sleeveless waist-length garment worn esp. by men under a jacket.

wait *v* **1** (*intr*; **for**) to delay action, or remain in a certain place, in expectation of, or readiness for, something: *wait for the bus*; *Wait till you're older*. **2** (*intr*) (of a task, etc.) to remain temporarily undealt with: *That can wait*. **3** (*tr*) to postpone action for (a period of time). **4** (*tr*) to await (one's turn, etc.). **5** (*tr*; *coll*) to delay eating (a meal) till someone arrives: *won't wait dinner*. **6** (*intr*) to park one's vehicle briefly at the kerb, etc.: *No waiting*. **7** (*intr*) to serve people with food at a restaurant, etc.; to act as a waiter or waitress. — *v* **wait on** (*tr*) **1** to serve food to (esp. restaurant guests); to act as a waiter or waitress to. **2** to act as a servant or attendant to. **3** (*dialect*) to wait for. **4** (*old*) to pay a respectful visit to. — *v* **wait up** (*intr*; **for**) to stay out of bed at night waiting for someone's arrival or return, or some other event. — **you wait!** an expression used to warn or threaten. [OFr *waitier*, *guaitier*, from OGer *wahten*, to watch]

waiter or **waitress** *n* a man, or woman, who serves people with food at a restaurant, etc.

waiting-list *n* a list of people waiting for something currently unavailable.

waiting-room *n* a room for people to wait in, e.g. at a railway station, doctor's surgery, etc.

waive *v* (*tr*) **1** to refrain from insisting upon; to give up (a claim, right, etc.). **2** to refrain from enforcing (a rule, penalty, etc.). [OFr *weyver*, *guaiver*, to abandon]

waiver *n* (a written statement confirming) the relinquishment of one's right, etc.

wake[1] *v* ***woke***, ***woken*** **1** (*tr* & *intr*; **up**) to rouse or be roused from sleep. **2** (*tr* & *intr*; **up**) to stir or be stirred out of a state of inactivity, lethargy, etc. **3** (*intr* & *tr* with **up to**) to become or make aware of (a fact, circumstance, situation, etc.). — *n* **1** a watch or vigil kept beside a corpse. **2** (*dialect*) an annual holiday. [MidE *waken*, from OE *wacan*, to become awake, & *wacian*, to stay awake]

wakeful *adj* **1** not asleep; unable to sleep. **2** (of a night) sleepless. **3** vigilant; alert; watchful. — *adv* **wakefully**.

waking hours *n* (*pl*) the part of the day that one spends awake.

wake[2] *n* a trail of disturbed water left by a ship, or of disturbed air left by an aircraft. — **in one's wake** wherever one has been. — **in the wake of** coming after; resulting from. [Norse *vök*, hole or channel in the ice]

waken *v* **-n- 1** (*tr* & *intr*; **up**) to rouse or be roused from sleep, or from inactivity or lethargy. **2** (*intr* with **to**) to become aware of (a fact, situation, etc.). [OE *wæcnan*]

wale *n* **1** a raised mark on the skin; a weal. **2** a ridge on cloth, e.g. the rib on corduroy. **3** (*naut*) a course of planking running along the top edge of a ship's side. [OE *walu*, ridge]

walk *v* **1** (*intr*) to go in some direction on foot, moving one's feet alternately and always having one or other foot on the ground. **2** (*intr*; **in, out**, etc.) to go or travel on foot; to do this for exercise. **3** (*tr*) to travel (a distance) thus. **4** (*tr*) to go about (the streets, countryside, etc.) on foot. **5** (*tr*) to accompany, support, or propel (someone who is on foot). **6** (*tr*) to take (a dog) out for exercise. **7** (*intr*; *old*) to live one's life or behave in a certain manner: *walk in fear*; *walk tall*. **8** (*intr*; *facet*) to disappear; to be stolen: *My pen has walked*. — *n* **1** the motion, or pace, of walking: *She slowed to a walk*. **2** an outing or journey on foot, esp. for exercise. **3** a distance walked or for walking: *a three-minute walk*. **4** one's distinctive manner of walking: *recognised his walk*. **5** a path, esp. a broad formal one. **6** a route for walking: *some nice walks in these parts*. — **walk all over** (*coll*) to treat inconsiderately or arrogantly. — *v* **walk away** (*intr*) **1** (with **from**; *coll*) to outdistance. **2** (with **from**) to ignore or abandon: *walk away from one's responsibilities*. **3** (with **from**) to escape unhurt from (an accident, etc.). **4** (with **with**) to win (prizes) effortlessly. — *v* **walk into** (*tr*) to involve oneself in (trouble, etc.) through one's own unwariness. — *v* **walk off** (*intr*) **1** to depart. **2** (with **with**) to win (prizes) effortlessly. **3** (with **with**; *coll*) to steal. — *v* **walk out** (*intr*) **1** (of factory workers, etc.) to leave the workplace in a body, in declaration of a strike (*n* **walk-out**). **2** to depart abruptly from a meeting, etc. in protest. **3** (with **on**) to abandon or desert. **4** (**with**; *old*) to pay court to (someone of the opposite sex). [OE *wealcan*]

walkabout *n* **1** a casual stroll through a crowd of ordinary people by a celebrity, esp. a member of the royal family. **2** (*Austr*; usu. in **go walkabout**) a walk alone in the bush by an Australian Aboriginal.

walker *n* a person who walks, esp. for pleasure.

walking *adj* **1** in human form: *a walking encyclopaedia*. **2** for the use of walkers: *walking shoes*.

walking-stick *n* a stick used for support or balance in walking.

walk of life *n* one's occupation or profession.

walk-on *adj* (of a part in a play, opera, etc.) not involving any speaking or singing.

walkover *n* (*coll*) an easy victory.

walkway *n* a paved path or passage for pedestrians.

walkie-talkie *n* (*coll*) a portable two-way radio carried by police, etc.

wall *n* **1** a solid vertical brick or stone construction of narrow width, substantial length, and variable height, serving e.g. as a barrier, territorial division or protection. **2** the side of a building or room. **3** anything in some way suggestive of a wall: *a wall of fire*, *secrecy*, etc. **4** (*biol*, etc.) an outer covering, e.g. of a cell; the side of a hollow organ or cavity. **5** a sheer rock face. — *v* (*tr*) **1** to surround with a wall: *a walled garden*. **2** (**off**, **in**) to separate or enclose with a wall. **3** (**up**) to block (an opening) with, or seal (something) behind, brick-work, etc.; to shut in (a person) in this way. — **go to the wall** (of a business) to fail. — **have one's back to the wall** to be making one's last desperate stand. — **up the wall** (*coll*) crazy. — **walls have ears** we might be overheard. [OE *weall*, from Lat *vallum*, rampart]

wallbars *n* (*pl*) a series of horizontal wooden bars supported by uprights lining the walls of a gymnasium, for climbing, hanging from, etc.

wallflower *n* **1** a sweet-smelling plant with yellow, orange or red flowers. **2** (*coll*) a person who sits all evening at the edge of the dance floor, waiting in vain to be asked to dance.

wallpaper *n* paper used to decorate the interior walls and ceilings of houses, etc. — *v* (*tr*) to cover (walls) or the walls of (a room) with wallpaper.

wall-to-wall *adj* **1** (of carpeting) covering the entire floor of a room. **2** (*facet*) ever-present; inescapable: *wall-to-wall Muzak*.

wallaby *n* **-ies** a plant-eating Australian marsupial similar to, but smaller than, the kangaroo. [Dharuk (an Aboriginal language) *walaba*]

wallah *n* (*Anglo-Indian*; *in cmpds*) a person performing a specified task: *the tea wallah*. [Hindi *-wala*]

wallet *n* **1** a flat folding case made e.g. of leather, for holding banknotes, etc., carried in the pocket or handbag. **2** any of various kinds of esp. plastic folders or envelopes for holding papers, etc. [MidE]

walleye *n* **1** an eye in which the iris has a chalky appearance. **2** an eye that squints away from the nose, so that an abnormal amount of the white shows. — *adj* **walleyed**. [Norse *wagleygr*]

Walloon *n* **1** a member of the French-speaking population of southern Belgium. **2** their language, a dialect of French. — *adj* relating to, or belonging to, the Walloons. [Fr *Wallon*, from Germanic; literally 'foreigner']

wallop (*coll*) *v* **-p-** (*tr*) to hit or spank vigorously. — *n* a hit or a thrashing. [OFr *waloper*, *galoper*, to gallop]

walloping *n* a thrashing. — *adj* great; whopping: *a walloping (great) hole*.

wallow *v* (*intr*) **1** to lie or roll about (in water, mud, etc.) **2** (with **in**) to revel or luxuriate (in admiration, etc.). **3** (with **in**) to indulge excessively (in self-pity, etc.). **4** (of a ship) to roll from side to side making poor headway. **5** to get bogged down and fail to progress with speed and economy. [OE *wealwian*]

wally *n* **-ies** (*coll*) an ineffectual or foolish person. [From the name *Walter*]

walnut *n* **1** an edible nut formed in two corresponding hemispherical sections, with a hard, wrinkled shell. **2** the tree bearing it, whose wood is used for furniture-making. [OE *wealhhnutu*, foreign nut]

walrus *n* **-ruses** or **-rus** a large sea mammal with a whiskery muzzle and large downward-pointing tusks, related to the seal. [Dut, literally 'whale-horse']

walrus moustache *n* a thick drooping moustache.

waltz *n* **1** a slow or fast ballroom dance in triple time. **2** a piece of music for this dance. — *v* (*intr*) **1** to dance a waltz. **2** (*coll*) to go or move with easy confidence. [Ger *Walzer*, from *walzen*, to roll, dance]

wampum *n* (*hist*) shells strung together for use as money among the American Indians. [Algonquian (N American Indian language group) *wampumpeag*, white string of beads]

wan *adj* **-nn-** pale and pinched-looking from illness, exhaustion or grief. — *adv* **wanly**. — *n* **wanness**. [OE *wann*, dusky, lurid]

wand *n* **1** a slender rod used e.g. by magicians or fairies for performing magic. **2** a conductor's baton. **3** a rod carried as a symbol of authority. **4** a slender young shoot; a flexible cane or switch. [Norse *vöndr*, shoot]

wander *v* **-r-** (*tr*) **1** to walk or travel about, heading for no particular destination; to ramble. **2** (of a stream, etc.) to follow a meandering course. **3** (**from**) to stray, e.g. from the right path, or from the point of an argument, etc. **4** (of people, their wits, etc.) to become confused, incoherent or irrational, e.g. in delirium or advanced age. **5** (of one's thoughts, etc.) to flit randomly. — *n* a ramble or stroll. — *n* **wanderer**. [OE *wandrian*]

wanderlust *n* an urge to rove; a liking for keeping on the move. [Ger, from *wandern*, to travel + *Lust*, desire]

wane *v* (*intr*) **1** (of the moon) to grow narrower as the sun illuminates less of its surface. **2** to decline in glory or influence. — *n* the process of waning or declining. — **on the wane** decreasing or declining. [OE *wanian*, to lessen]

wangle *v* (*tr*) to contrive or obtain by persuasiveness or subtle manipulation. — *n* an act of wangling.

wank *v* (*intr*; *vulg slang*) to masturbate. — *n* **wanker** (used also as a general term of abuse).

want *v* **1** (*tr*) to feel a desire for. **2** (*tr*) to wish (to do something, someone to do something, etc.): *wants to go*; *doesn't want you to leave*. **3** (*intr*; *coll*) to desire to get (in, on, off, out, etc.). **4** (*tr*; *coll*) ought; need: *You want to take more care. We want to turn left at the school.* **5** (*tr*; *coll*) to need (a certain treatment, etc.): *He wants his head examined.* **6** (*tr*, or (*old*) *intr* with **for**) to feel the lack of: *want for nothing*. **7** (*tr*) to require the presence of: *You're wanted next door.* **8** (*tr*) to desire (someone) sexually. **9** (*tr*; *old*) to fall short by (a certain amount): *It wants two minutes to*, or *of*, *midnight*. — *n* **1** a need or requirement. **2** (*old*) lack: *a want of discretion*. **3** a state of need; destitution: *those in want*. — **for want of** in the absence of: *for want of a* *better word*. — **in want of** needing. [Norse *vanta*, to be lacking]

wanted *adj* being sought by the police on suspicion of having committed a crime, etc.

wanting *adj* **1** missing; lacking. **2** (**in**) not having enough of: *wanting in tact*. **3** not up to requirements: *has been found wanting*.

wanton *adj* **1** motivelessly cruel. **2** motiveless: *wanton destruction*. **3** (*old*) (of a woman) sexually immoral. **4** (*old*) playfully fanciful; whimsical. — *n* (*old*) a wanton woman. — *v* **-n-** (*intr*; *old*) to play about, flirt, or trifle wantonly. — *adv* **wantonly**. — *n* **wantonness**. [MidE *wantowen*, from OE *wan-*, not + *togen*, disciplined]

wapiti *n* a large deer of N America. [Algonquian (N American Indian language group)]

war *n* **1** an openly acknowledged state of armed conflict, esp. between nations: *declared war on the French*. **2** a particular armed struggle: *the Iran–Iraq war*. **3** fighting as a science: *the arts of war*. **4** open hostility between people. **5** any long-continued struggle or campaign: *the war against drug-dealing*. **6** fierce rivalry or competition in business: *a trade war*. — *v* **-rr-** (*intr*; **with**) **1** to fight wars. **2** to conflict one with another: *warring emotions*. — **go to war** to begin an armed conflict. — **have been in the wars** (*coll*) to have, or show signs of having, sustained injuries. [OFr *werre*]

war crime *n* a crime, e.g. ill-treatment of prisoners, massacre of civilians or racial minorities, etc., committed during, and in connection with, a war. — *n* **war criminal**.

war cry *n* **1** a cry used to rally or hearten troops, or as a signal for charging. **2** a slogan or watchword.

war dance *n* a dance performed by primitive tribes before going into battle, or after victory.

warfare *n* **1** the activity of waging war. **2** violent conflict.

war game *n* **1** a mock battle or military exercise providing training in tactics, etc. **2** an elaborate game in which players use model soldiers, knights, etc. to enact imaginary battles, etc.

warhead *n* the front part of a missile, etc. containing the explosives.

warhorse *n* **1** (*hist*) a powerful horse on which a knight rode into battle. **2** an old soldier or politician still full of fight. **3** a standard, reliable, frequently used, overfamiliar musical composition, etc.

warlike *adj* **1** fond of fighting; aggressive; belligerent. **2** relating to war; military.

warlord *n* a powerful military leader.

war memorial *n* a monument commemorating members of the armed forces who died in war.

warmonger *n* a person who tries to precipitate war, or whips up enthusiasm for it.

warpaint *n* paint put on the face by primitive peoples when going to war.

warpath *n* the march to war, esp. (*hist*) among American Indians. — **on the warpath 1** setting off to fight. **2** (*coll*) in a fighting mood; in angry pursuit.

warship *n* a ship equipped with guns, etc. for naval battles.

wartime *n* a period during which a war is going on.

warble[1] *v* (*intr* & *tr*) **1** (of a bird) to sing melodiously. **2** (of a person) to sing in a high, tremulous voice; to trill. [OFr *werbler*]

warbler *n* any of several small songbirds.

warble[2] *n* a swelling under the hide of horses or cattle, esp. one containing a maggot.

-ward. See **-wards**.

ward *n* **1** any of the rooms in a hospital with beds for patients. **2** any of the areas into which a town, etc. is divided for administration or elections. **3** (*legal*) a person, esp. a minor, under the protection of a guardian or court. **4** a projection inside a lock that fits into a notch in its key, ensuring that the lock cannot be turned by the wrong key. **5** (*old*) a watch or guard kept over something. — *v* (*tr* with **off**) **1** to fend off, turn aside, or parry (a blow). **2** to keep (trouble, hunger, disease, etc.) away. [OE *weard*, protector]

warden *n* **1** a person in charge of a hostel, student residence, old people's home, etc. **2** (*in cmpds*) a public official responsible in any of various ways for maintaining order: *a traffic warden*, *game warden*, etc. **3** (esp. *NAm*) the officer in charge of a prison. [OFr *wardein*]

warder or **wardress** *n* a male, or female, prison officer. [MidE *wardere*, from OFr *warder*, *garder*, to guard]

wardrobe *n* **1** a cupboard in which to hang clothes. **2** one's personal stock of garments. **3** the stock of costumes belonging to a theatrical company. [OFr *garderobe*]

wardrobe mistress or **master** *n* the woman or man in charge of a theatrical company's costumes.

wardroom *n* the officers' quarters on board a warship. [**ward**]

-wards *sfx* (also **-ward**) in the direction of; towards: *westwards*; *backwards*. [OE *-weardes*, genitive of *-weard*, towards]

-ward *sfx* going towards: *an eastward direction*.

ware *n* **1** (*in cmpds*) manufactured goods of a specified material (*glassware*, *silverware*), range of use (*kitchenware*), etc. **2** (often *in cmpds*) a particular type of pottery: *Delft ware*, *Samian ware*, etc. **3** (in *pl*) goods that one has for sale. [OE *waru*]

warehouse *n* **1** a building in which goods are stored. **2** a large, esp. wholesale, shop.

warlock *n* a wizard, male magician or sorcerer. [OE *warloga*]

warm *adj* **1** moderately, comfortably or pleasantly hot. **2** (of clothes) providing and preserving heat. **3** (of work) making one hot. **4** kind-hearted and affectionate. **5** (of an environment, etc.) welcoming and congenial. **6** enthusiastic; whole-hearted: *warm support*. **7** (esp. *old*) vehement; indignant: *was warm in her denial of the charge*. **8** (of colours) suggestive of comfortable heat — typically deep and containing red or yellow. **9** (of a trail or scent) still fresh enough to follow. **10** (in a children's game, etc.) close to guessing correctly or finding the thing sought. **11** (esp. *old*) (of one's situation) awkward or dangerous. — *v* **1** (*tr* & *intr*) to make or become warm or warmer. **2** (*intr* with **to**) to gain in enthusiasm for (a task) as one performs it. **3** (*intr* with **to**) to gain in affection or approval for (a person). — *adv* **warmly**. — *v* **warm up 1** (*tr* & *intr*) to make or become warm or warmer. **2** (*tr*) to re-heat (food). **3** (*intr* & *tr*) (of a party, etc.) to make or get livelier. **4** (*intr* & *tr*) (of an engine) to reach, or bring up to, an efficient working temperature. **5** (*intr*) to exercise the body gently in preparation for a strenuous workout, race, athletic contest, etc. (*n* **warm-up**). [OE *wearm*]

warm-blooded *adj* **1** (of animals, etc.) having a blood temperature that is higher than that of the surrounding atmosphere and remains constant. **2** (of a person) passionate, impulsive or ardent.

warm front *n* (*meteorol*) the edge of a mass of warm air pushing against a mass of cold air.

warm-hearted *adj* kind, affectionate and generous.

warming-pan *n* (*hist*) a long-handled copper or brass lidded container for hot coals, slid into a bed to warm it up.

warmth *n* **1** the condition of being warm; moderate, pleasant or comfortable heat. **2** affection or kind-heartedness. **3** passion; vehemence: *the warmth of her denial*. **4** strength or intensity: *the warmth of her love for him*.

warn *v* (*tr*) **1** (**of, about**) to make aware of possible or approaching danger or difficulty. **2** to advise strongly: *warned them to book early*. **3** to rebuke or admonish, with the threat of punishment for a repetition of the offence; to caution. **4** to inform in advance: *warned him she might be late*. **5** (**off**) to order to go away. [OE *wearnian*]

warning *n* something that happens, or is said or done, that serves to warn. — *adj* intended, or serving, to warn. — *adv* **warningly**.

warp (*tr* & *intr*) **1** (of e.g. wood) to (cause to) become twisted out of shape through the shrinking and expanding effects of damp and heat. **2** to (cause to) become distorted, corrupted or perverted. **3** (*naut*) to move (a vessel) by hauling on a rope fixed e.g. to a post on a wharf; (of a vessel) to be manoeuvred by this method. — *n* **1** an unevenness or twist in wood, etc. **2** a distortion or abnormal twist in personality, etc. **3** a shift or displacement in a continuous dimension, esp. time: *caught in a time warp*. **4** (*naut*) a rope used for warping a vessel. **5** (*weaving*) the set of threads stretched lengthways in a loom, under and over which the widthways set of threads (the **weft** or **woof**) are passed. [OE *weorpan*, to throw]

warrant *n* **1** a written legal authorisation for doing something, e.g. arresting someone, or searching property. **2** a certificate such as a licence, voucher or receipt, that authorises, guarantees or confirms something. **3** a justification: *has no warrant for making such an accusation*. **4** a certificate appointing a warrant officer in the armed services. — *v* (*tr*) **1** to justify: *The circumstances are suspicious enough to warrant a full investigation*. **2** (*old*) to assert with confidence; to be willing to bet: *I'll warrant he knows nothing of this*. **3** to guarantee (goods, etc.) as being of the specified quality or quantity; to confirm as genuine, worthy, etc. — *adj* **warrantable**. [OFr *warant*, *guarant*]

warrant officer *n* in the armed services, an officer intermediate between a commissioned and non-commissioned officer.

warrantor *n* a person who gives a warrant or warranty.

warranty *n* **-ies 1** an assurance of the quality of goods being sold, usu. with an acceptance of responsibility for repairs during an initial period of use; a guarantee. **2** an undertaking or assurance expressed or implied in certain contracts.

warren *n* **1** an underground labyrinth of interconnecting tunnels linking numerous rabbit burrows. **2** an overcrowded dwelling or district. **3** any maze of passages. [OFr *warenne*]

warrior *n* **1** a skilled fighting man, esp. of earlier times. **2** any distinguished soldier. **3** a person notable for stoutness of spirit or indomitability. [OFr *werreieor*]

wart *n* **1** a small hard roundish growth of horny skin, e.g. on the hands or face, caused by a virus. **2** a similar projection on the surface of a plant or the skin of an animal. — **warts and all** with all blemishes or defects frankly displayed. [OE *wearte*]

warthog *n* a hairy wild pig of Africa with wart-like lumps on its face, and two tusks.

Warwicks. *abbrev* Warwickshire.

wary *adj* **-ier**, **-iest 1** alert; vigilant; cautious; on one's guard. **2** distrustful or apprehensive. **3** (with **of**) suspicious: *should be wary of such invitations*. — *adv* **warily**. — *n* **wariness**. [OE *wær*, to beware]

was. See **be**.

Wash. *abbrev* Washington.

wash 1 (*tr*) to cleanse with water and usu. soap or detergent. **2** (*intr*) to cleanse oneself, or one's hands and face, with water, etc. **3** (*intr*) (of a fabric) to withstand washing without damage, or (of a dye) to be unaffected by washing in water. **4** (*tr & intr*; **out**, **away**, **off**) to get rid of (a stain, dirt, etc.), or (of a stain, dirt, etc.) to disappear, through washing. **5** (*intr & tr*) (of an animal) to lick (itself, its young, etc.) clean. **6** (*tr*) to moisten or flush (e.g. an injured part) with liquid. **7** (*tr* or *intr*; **against**, **over**, etc.) (of a river, the sea, waves, etc.) to flow against, over, etc.: *Hamelin, with its walls washed by the Weser*. **8** (*tr & intr*; **down**, **away**, etc.) (of flowing water) to sweep (objects) along with it, or (of substances, etc.) to be swept along by water. **9** (*tr*) (of flowing water) to gouge out (a channel, etc.) in the landscape. **10** (*tr*) to apply watercolour thinly to (a surface, e.g. a wall). **11** (*intr*; *coll*) to stand the test; to bear investigation: *That excuse won't wash*. **12** (*tr*; *mining*) to separate (ore) from earth with a flow of water. **13** (*tr*; *literary*) to spread over: *washed with the pale light of morning*. — *n* **1** the process of washing or being washed. **2** this process undertaken by a laundry. **3** a quantity of clothes, etc. for washing, or just washed. **4** the breaking of waves against something; the sound of this. **5** the rough water or disturbed air left by a ship or aircraft. **6** a lotion or other preparation for cleansing or washing. **7** kitchen slops or brewery waste, etc. for giving to pigs; pigswill. **8** a thin application of water colour. — **come out in the wash** to turn out satisfactorily in the end. — *v* **wash down** (*tr*) **1** (**with**) to ease (a pill) down one's throat, or accompany (food), with a drink. **2** to wash (walls, etc.) from top to bottom. — **washed out 1** (of a person) worn out and faded-looking (*adj* **washed-out**). **2** (of fabric) faded through washing (*adj* **washed-out**). — **washed up** (*coll*) **1** (of a person) finished; incapable of further productivity (*adj* **washed-up**). **2** (of plans, etc.) having come to nothing. — **wash one's hands of** to abandon responsibility for. — *v* **wash out** (*tr*) (of rain) to cause the cancellation of (a match, etc.). ◇ See also **washout** below. — *v* **wash up** (*tr & intr*) to wash (dishes) (*n* **washing-up**). [OE *wæscan*]

washable *adj* able to be washed without damage.

washbasin or **washhand basin** *n* a shallow sink in which to wash one's face and hands.

washcloth *n* (*NAm*) a facecloth or flannel.

washer *n* **1** (esp. *in cmpds*) a machine for washing: *a dishwasher*. **2** a flat ring of rubber or metal for keeping a joint tight, or one of linen for reinforcing the punched holes in ring-binder paper.

washerwoman *n* (esp. *hist*) a woman paid to wash clothes.

washhouse *n* (esp. *hist*) **1** an outhouse or basement room for washing clothes. **2** a public building for washing clothes in.

washing *n* clothes to be, or which have just been washed.

washing-machine *n* a machine for washing clothes.

washing-powder *n* powdered detergent for washing clothes.

washing soda *n* sodium carbonate crystals, used for washing and cleaning.

wash leather *n* a chamois leather.

washout *n* **1** (*coll*) a failure or flop. **2** a rained-off event, e.g. a match.

washroom *n* (*NAm*) a lavatory.

washstand *n* (*hist*) a small table in a bedroom for holding a jug and basin for washing oneself.

washy *adj* **-ier**, **-iest** (*coll*) **1** (of a drink) watery; weak. **2** feeble; lacking liveliness or vigour. **3** (of colours) faded-looking or pallid.

wasn't was not.

wasp *n* a stinging insect with a thin waist and in many species a black-and-yellow-striped abdomen. [OE *wæsp*]

waspish *adj* sharp-tongued; caustic.

wasp waist *n* a tiny waist, esp. in a curvaceous human female body. — *adj* **wasp-waisted**.

WASP *abbrev* (*NAm*; often *derog*) White Anglo-Saxon Protestant.

wassail *n* (*old*) **1** a festive bout of drinking. **2** a toast made at such an occasion. [Norse *ves heill*, be in good health]

wast a form of the past tense of the verb *be* used with the pronoun *thou*.

waste *v* **1** (*tr*; **on**) to use or spend purposelessly, extravagantly, or to too little useful effect; to squander. **2** (*tr*) to fail to use or make the best of (an opportunity, etc.). **3** (*tr*) to throw away unused. **4** (*tr*; **on**) to offer (advice, sympathy, etc.) where it is unheeded or unappreciated. **5** (*tr & intr*; esp. with **away**) to (cause to) lose flesh or strength. **6** (*tr*; *old*) to devastate (territory); to lay waste. — *adj* **1** rejected as useless or excess to requirements. **2** (of ground) lying unused, uninhabited or uncultivated. **3** (*physiol*) excreted from the body in the urine or faeces. — *n* **1** the act, or an instance, of wasting; the condition of being wasted. **2** failure to take advantage of something: *a waste of talent*, *opportunity*, etc. **3** materials and substances discarded during a manufacturing process. **4** refuse; rubbish. **5** (*physiol*) matter excreted from the body. **6** a devastated or barren region: *reduced to a muddy waste*. **7** (esp. in *pl*) a vast tract of uncultivated land, expanse of ocean, etc.: *the Arctic wastes*. — **go** or **run to waste** to be wasted. [OFr *wast*, *guast*]

wastage *n* **1** the process of wasting; loss through wasting. **2** the amount so lost. **3** loss or reduction through use, natural decay, etc. **4** (also **natural wastage**) reduction of staff through retirement or resignation, as distinct from dismissal or redundancy.

wasteful *adj* causing waste; extravagant.

wasteland *n* a desolate and barren region.

waste paper *n* paper discarded as rubbish.

wastepaper basket or **bin** *n* a basket or other container for waste paper and other office or household waste.

waste pipe *n* a pipe carrying waste material or waste water from a sink, etc.

waste product *n* **1** a useless by-product of a manufacturing process, etc. **2** a substance excreted from the body during the metabolic and physiological processes.

waster *n* an idler, good-for-nothing or wastrel.

wastrel *n* an idle spendthrift; a good-for-nothing. **[waste]**

watch *v* **1** (*tr* & *intr*) to look at or focus one's attention on (someone or something moving, doing something, etc.). **2** (*tr* & *intr*) to pass time looking at (television, a programme, entertainment, sports event, etc.). **3** (*tr*) to guard, look after or keep an eye on. **4** (*tr*) to keep track of, follow or monitor: *watch developments in the Middle East*. **5** (*tr*) to keep (e.g. a building or person) under observation or surveillance. **6** (*tr* & *intr*; **for**) to await (one's chance, opportunity, etc.). **7** (*tr*) to keep checking on, in case controlling measures or adjustments are necessary. **8** (*tr*; *coll*) to take (oneself) in hand. **9** (*tr*) to pay proper attention to: *Watch where you're going!* **10** (*tr*) to take care: *Watch you don't slip*. — *n* **1** a small instrument for telling the time, usu. worn strapped to the wrist or in the waistcoat pocket. **2** the activity or duty of watching or guarding: *Keep watch*; *stayed on watch*. **3** (*naut*) any of the four-hour shifts during which particular crew members are on duty; those on duty in any shift. **4** (*old*) a body of sentries on look-out duty; a watchman or body of watchmen. — **keep a watch on** to keep under observation. — **on the watch for** seeking or looking out for. — **watch it!** be careful! — *v* **watch out** (*intr*) **1** to be careful. **2** (with **for**) to be on one's guard against; to look out for. — *v* **watch over** (*tr*) to guard, look after or tend to. [OE *wæccan* or *wacian*, to watch]

watchdog *n* **1** a dog kept to guard premises, etc. **2** a person or group of people guarding against unacceptable standards, behaviour, etc.

watchful *adj* alert, vigilant and wary. — *adv* **watchfully**. — *n* **watchfulness**.

watching brief *n* an instruction to a barrister to follow a case on behalf of a client not directly involved.

watchmaker *n* a person who makes and repairs watches and clocks.

watchman *n* a man employed to guard premises at night.

watchnight service *n* a church service lasting through midnight on Christmas Eve or New Year's Eve.

watchtower *n* a tower from which a sentry keeps watch.

watchword *n* **1** a catchphrase encapsulating the principles, or used to inspire the members, of a party, group, profession, etc. **2** (*old*) a password.

water *n* **1** a colourless, transparent, tasteless and odourless liquid that is a compound of hydrogen and oxygen, falls as rain, and forms seas, lakes and rivers. **2** (sometimes in *pl*) an expanse of this; a sea, lake, river, etc. **3** (in *pl*) the sea round a country's coasts, considered part of its territory. **4** the level or state of the tide: *at high* or *low water*. **5** a solution of something in water: *rose water*, *ammonia water*, etc. **6** (in *pl*) water at a spa, etc., containing minerals and formerly considered good for one's health. **7** (*physiol*) any of several fluids secreted by the body, esp. urine. **8** (in *pl*) the liquid surrounding the foetus in the womb; amniotic fluid: *Her waters broke at 5.05 a.m.* **9** (*gems*) the degree of brilliance and transparency of a diamond. — *v* **1** (*tr*) to wet, soak or sprinkle with water. **2** (*tr*) to irrigate (land). **3** (*tr*) to dilute (wine, etc.). **4** (*intr*) (of the mouth) to produce saliva in response to a stimulus activated by the expectation of food. **5** (*intr*) (of the eyes) to fill with tears when irritated. **6** (*tr* & *intr*) to let (animals) drink, or (of animals) to drink: *fed and watered*. **7** (*tr*) to give a wavy appearance to the surface of, by wetting and pressing: *watered silk*. — **by water** by ship. — **hold water** to prove sound; to be valid. — **in** (or **into**) **deep water** in (or into) trouble, danger or difficulty; out of one's depth. — **like water** (*coll*) in large quantities; freely; lavishly: *spending money like water*. — **make one's mouth water** to make one's saliva flow; to stimulate one's appetite for something. — **of the first water** (sometimes *ironic*) of the highest class; first-class; prize: *an idiot of the first water*. — **pass water** (*euph*) to urinate. — **test the water** or **waters** to see what the response might be to what one intends to do, before doing it. — **throw cold water on** (*coll*) to be discouraging or unenthusiastic about. — **tread water** to keep oneself afloat and upright in deep water, gently moving one's legs and arms to maintain the position. — **under water** under the surface of the water. — *v* **water down** (*tr*) **1** to dilute or thin with water. **2** to reduce the impact of; to tone down; to make less controversial or offensive. — **water under the bridge** experiences that are past and done with. [OE *wæter*]

water bed *n* (a bed having) a waterproof mattress filled with water.

water biscuit *n* a plain crisp biscuit made from water and flour, eaten with cheese, etc.

waterborne *adj* carried by water.
water buffalo *n* the common domestic buffalo of India and S Asia, with backward-curving horns.
water bus *n* a passenger boat sailing regularly across a lake, along a river, etc.
water cannon *n* a device that sends out a powerful jet of water, used for dispersing crowds.
Water-carrier (with **the**) the constellation and sign of the zodiac Aquarius.
water chestnut *n* the edible tuber of a Chinese plant of the sedge family.
water closet *n* (*formal* or *tech*) a lavatory whose pan is mechanically flushed with water.
watercolour *n* **1** a paint thinned with water, not oil. **2** a painting done in such paint. — *n* **water-colourist**.
water-cooled *adj* (of an engine, etc.) cooled by circulating water.
watercourse *n* the bed or channel of a stream, river or canal.
watercress *n* a cress that grows in water, whose sharp-tasting leaves are used in salads, etc.
water-diviner *n* a person who detects underground sources of water, usu. with a divining-rod; a dowser.
waterfall *n* a place in a river or stream where the water drops a considerable height down steep rocks, over a precipice, etc.; a cascade.
waterfowl *n* **1** a bird living on or near water, esp. a swimming bird such as a duck. **2** (*pl*) swimming game birds in general.
waterfront *n* the buildings or part of a town along the edge of a river, lake, or the sea.
waterglass *n* a solution of potassium or sodium silicate in water, used as protective coating, an adhesive and, esp. formerly, for preserving eggs.
waterhole *n* a pond, pool or spring in a desert area, where animals can drink.
water ice *n* sweetened fruit purée frozen and served as a dessert; a sorbet.
watering-can *n* a water-container with a handle and spout, for watering plants.
watering-hole *n* **1** a waterhole. **2** (*facet*) a public house.
watering-place *n* (esp. *hist*) a spa or other place where people go to drink mineral water or bathe.
water jump *n* in a steeplechase, etc., a jump over a water-filled ditch.
water level *n* **1** the height reached by the surface of a body of water. **2** the level below which the ground is waterlogged; a water table. **3** a waterline.
water lily *n* a floating plant with large flat circular leaves and cup-shaped flowers.
waterline *n* the level reached by the water on the hull of a floating vessel.
waterlogged *adj* **1** saturated with water. **2** (of a boat) so filled or saturated with water as to be unmanageable.
water main *n* a large underground pipe carrying a public water supply.
watermark *n* **1** the limit reached by the sea at high or low tide. **2** a manufacturer's distinctive mark in paper, visible when the paper is held up to the light. — *v* (*tr*) to impress (paper) with a watermark.
water meadow *n* a meadow kept fertile by periodic flooding from a stream.
water melon *n* a melon native to Africa, with dark green coarse skin and red flesh.
watermill *n* a mill whose machinery is driven by a water wheel.
water pistol *n* a toy pistol that fires squirts of water.
water polo *n* a seven-a-side ball game for swimmers; a similar game for canoeists.
water power *n* the power of water that is falling or moving, usable as a mechanical force for driving machinery, etc.
waterproof *adj* impenetrable by water; treated or coated so as to resist water. — *v* (*tr*) to treat so as to make waterproof. — *n* a raincoat.
water rat *n* (also **water vole**) a swimming rodent inhabiting stream banks.
water rate *n* a charge made for the use of the public water supply.
watershed *n* **1** the high land separating two river basins. **2** a crucial point after which events take a different turn.
waterside *n* the edge of a river, lake or sea.
water ski *n* a ski on which to glide over water, towed by a powered boat. — *v* (**water-ski**) ***-skis***, ***-skied*** or ***-ski'd*** (*intr*) to travel on water skis. — *n* **water-skiing**.
water-softener *n* a substance or device used in water to remove minerals, esp. calcium, that cause hardness and prevent lathering.
waterspout *n* a small tornado over water, taking the form of a revolving column of mist and spray.
water table *n* (*geol*) the level below which fissures and pores in the ground are filled with water.
watertight *adj* **1** so well sealed as to be impenetrable by water. **2** (of an argument, etc.) without flaw, weakness or opening for misinterpretation; completely sound.
water tower *n* a tower supporting an elevated water tank, from which water can be distributed at uniform pressure.
water vapour *n* water in the form of droplets suspended in the atmosphere, esp. where evaporation has occurred at a temperature below boiling point.
water vole see **water rat**.
waterway *n* a channel, e.g. a canal or river, used by ships or smaller boats.
waterwheel *n* a wheel driven by water to work machinery, etc.
water wings *n* (*pl*) an inflatable device that supports the chest and terminates in wing-like projections, used by children learning to swim.

waterworks *n* **1** (*sing* or *pl*) an installation where water is purified and stored for distribution to an area. **2** (*pl*; *euph*) one's bladder and urinary system. **3** (*pl*; *facet*) tears; weeping.

watery *adj* **1** of, or consisting of, water: *the watery depths*. **2** containing too much water; over-diluted; weak or thin: *watery tea*. **3** (of the sun or sunlight) weak and pale, as when alternating with showers. **4** (of eyes) inclined to water. **5** (of a smile, etc.) half-hearted; feeble.

Waterloo *n* the challenge that finally defeats one: *meet one's Waterloo*. [The battle of *Waterloo*, 1815, Napoleon's final defeat]

watt *n* a unit of power, equal to one joule per second. [J *Watt*, engineer, 1736–1819]

wattage *n* electrical power expressed in watts.

watt hour *n* a unit of electrical energy, the amount of work done by one watt in one hour.

wattle *n* **1** rods, branches, etc. forming a framework for a wall, esp. when interwoven. **2** a loose fold of skin hanging from the throat of certain birds, fish and lizards. **3** any of various Australian acacia trees.

wattle and daub *n* wattle plastered with mud, as a building material.

wave *v* **1** (*intr* & *tr*) to move (one's hand) to and fro in greeting, farewell, or as a signal; to hold up and move (some other object) in this way for this purpose: *waved (her hand) to her father*; *waved their handkerchiefs*. **2** (*tr*) to say (esp. goodbye) thus: *waved them farewell*. **3** (*tr* with **off**) to see off on a journey thus: *waved him off*. **4** (*tr* & *intr*) to (cause to) move or sway to and fro. **5** (*tr*) to direct with a gesture of the hand: *waved the waiter away*. **6** (*tr*) to put a gentle curl into (hair) by artificial means. — *n* **1** any of a series of ridges moving across the sea or other expanse of water; such a ridge as it arches and breaks on the shore, etc. **2** (*physics*) any of the series of similar surges of disturbance that pass through the particles of other fluid media such as air, generating energy sufficient for the transmission of heat, light, sound, etc. **3** any of the circles of disturbance moving outwards from the site of a shock such as an earthquake. **4** a loose soft curl, or series of such curls, in the hair. **5** a surge or sudden feeling: *a wave of nausea*. **6** a sudden increase in something: *a wave of car thefts*; *a heat wave*. **7** an advancing body of people: *waves of invaders*. **8** any of a series of curves in an upward-and-downward-curving line or outline. **9** an act of waving the hand, etc. — *v* **wave aside** (*tr*) to dismiss (an objection, etc.) as unimportant. [OE *wafian*, to wave]

waveband *n* a range of wavelengths occupied by radio transmission of a particular type.

wavelength *n* (*physics*, *radio*) **1** the distance from a point on one wave to the corresponding point on the next. **2** the length of the radio wave used by a particular broadcasting station. — **on the same wavelength** (of two or more people) having views that harmonise rather than conflict.

wavy *adj* **-ier**, **-iest** **1** (of hair) falling in waves. **2** (of a line or outline) curving alternately upward and downward.

waver *v* **-r-** (*intr*) **1** to falter, lessen, weaken, etc. **2** to hesitate through indecision. **3** (of the voice) to become unsteady through emotion, etc. **4** to shimmer or flicker. **5** to vary or fluctuate between extremes: *wavering between elation and despair*. [Norse *vafra*, to flicker]

wavy. See **wave**.

wax[1] *n* **1** any of various fatty substances of plant, animal or mineral origin, typically shiny, easily moulded, insoluble in water, and softening when heated, used e.g. to make candles and polishes. **2** beeswax. **3** sealing-wax. **4** the sticky, yellowish matter that forms in the ears. [OE *weax*]

waxen *adj* made of, or similar to, wax.

waxwork *n* **1** a lifelike model, esp. of someone celebrated, made of wax. **2** (in *pl*) an exhibition of these.

waxy *adj* **-ier**, **-iest** like wax in appearance or feel.

wax[2] *v* (*intr*) **1** (of the moon) to appear larger as more of its surface is illuminated by the sun. **2** to increase in size, strength or power. **3** (*facet*) to become (e.g. eloquent, lyrical) in one's description of something. [OE *weaxan*, to grow]

way[1] *n* **1** (a route, entrance, exit, etc. providing) passage or access somewhere: *the way in*. **2** the route, road or direction taken for a particular journey: *on the way to school*; *Going my way?* **3** (often *in cmpds*) a track or road: *a motorway*; *Watling Way*. **4** a direction: *a one-way street*; *a two-way radio*. **5** position: *the wrong way up*. **6** a distance in space or time: *a little way ahead*; *Christmas is a long way off*. **7** one's district: *if you're round our way*. **8** the route or path ahead; room to move or progress: *block*, or *get in*, *someone's way*; *moved out of her way*; *clear the way for reform*. **9** a means. **10** a distinctive manner or style: *a funny way of walking*. **11** a method: *an easy way to cook fish*; *do it your own way*. **12** (in *pl*) customs: *Their ways are not ours*. **13** a characteristic piece of behaviour: *can't stand the way he ignores women*. **14** a habit or routine: *get into the way of taking regular exercise*. **15** a typical pattern or course: *It's always the way*. **16** what one wants oneself, as opposed to what others want: *always wanting*, *getting*, or *having*, *his own way*. **17** a mental approach: *different ways of looking at it*. **18** a respect: *correct in some ways*. **19** an alternative course, possibility, choice, etc.: *can't have it both ways*; *That way we'll save money*. **20** a state or condition: *is in a bad way*. **21** scale: *is in business in a big way*. **22** used with **the** to mean 'how' or 'as', and with **this** or **that** to mean 'thus': *if that's the way you feel*; *didn't know you felt that way*. **23** used with many verbs to indicate progress: *ate their way through the food*. **24** (*naut*) headway: *made little way that day*. **24** used in indicating the number of portions something is divided into: *divided it three ways*. — **be** or **get on one's way** to make a start on a journey. — **by the way** incidentally; let me mention while I remember. — **by way of 1** by the route that passes through; via. **2** as a form or means of: *He grinned by way of apology*. — **come one's way** (of an opportunity, etc.) to become available to one. — **give way 1** to collapse or subside. **2** to fail or break down under pressure, etc. **3** to yield to persuasion or pressure. — **go out of one's way** to make special efforts. — **have something one's own way** to get what one wants with something. — **have a way with** to be good at handling: *has a way with customers*. — **have a way with one** (*coll*) to have an attractive manner. — **have one's way with** (*old euph*) to have sexual intercourse with. — **in its**, etc. **way** as far as it, etc. goes; within limits: *OK in its way*. — **in no way** not at all. — **in the way of** in the nature of: *haven't got much in the way of cash*. — **lead** or **show the way** to act as a guide or inspiration to others. — **learn one's way around** to accustom oneself to one's new environment, duties, etc. — **look the other way** to pretend not to notice something. — **lose one's way** to leave one's intended route by mistake. — **make one's way 1** to go. **2** to progress or prosper: *making her way in life*. — **make way for 1** to stand aside, or make room, for. **2** to be replaced by. — **no two ways about it** that's certain; no doubt about it. — **no way** (*slang*) absolutely no possibility. — **on the way out** becoming unfashionable. — **on the way to** progressing towards: *well on the way to becoming a millionaire*. — **pay one's way** to pay one's own debts and living expenses. — **put out of the way** (*coll euph*) to kill. — **see one's way clear to** to be agreeable to (e.g. lending money). — **That's the way!** (used to applaud a response) Good! — **under way** in motion; progressing. [OE *weg*]

way of life *n* a style of living; the living of one's life according to certain principles.

ways and means *n* (*pl*) methods, esp. of obtaining funds; resources.

wayside *n* (the land at) the edge of a road. — *adj* growing or lying near the edge of roads. — **fall by the wayside** to fail or give up in one's attempt to do something; to drop out.

way² *adv* (*coll*) far; a long way: *way back in the 60s*. — **way out** (*old slang*) excitingly unusual, exotic or new (*adj* **way-out**). [**away**]

waybill *n* a list giving details of goods or passengers being carried. [**way**¹]

wayfarer *n* (*old*) a traveller, esp. on foot. — *n* & *adj* **wayfaring**. [**way**¹ + **fare**]

waylay *v* **-laid** (*tr*) **1** to lie in wait for and ambush. **2** to wait for and delay with conversation. [**way**¹ + **lay**²]

wayleave *n* permission given to pass over another's ground, usu. on payment of a fee. [**way**¹ + **leave**²]

-ways *comb fm* direction or manner: *lengthways*, *edgeways*, etc. [**way**¹]

wayward *adj* undisciplined, self-willed, headstrong, wilful or rebellious. [**away** + **-ward**]

WC *abbrev* ***WCs*** or ***WC's*** water closet.

W/Cdr *abbrev* Wing Commander.

we *pron* used **1** to refer to oneself in company with another or others. **2** to refer to people in general: *the times we live in*. **3** (by newspaper editors and esp. formerly by monarchs) to refer to themselves. **4** (*patronisingly* or *affably*) to mean 'you': *How are we today, Mr Brown?* [OE]

WEA *abbrev* Workers' Educational Association.

weak *adj* **1** lacking physical strength. **2** not functioning effectively: *a weak heart*. **3** liable to give way: *a weak link*. **4** lacking power: *militarily weak*. **5** (*finance*) dropping in value: *a weak dollar*. **6** too easily influenced by others. **7** yielding too easily to temptation. **8** lacking full flavour: *weak tea*. **9** (of an argument) unsound or unconvincing. **10** faint: *a weak signal*. **11** half-hearted: *a weak smile*. **12** (**on, in**) defective in some respect; having insufficient of something. [Norse *veikr*]

weaken *v* **-n- 1** (*tr* & *intr*) to (cause to) become weaker. **2** (*intr*) to yield to pressure or persuasion.

weak-kneed *adj* cowardly; feeble.

weakling *n* **1** a physically weak person or animal. **2** someone weak in a certain respect: *a moral weakling*.

weak-minded *adj* **1** of feeble intelligence. **2** lacking will or determination.

weak moment *n* a lapse of self-discipline.

weakness *n* **1** the condition of being weak. **2** a fault or failing. **3** (**for**) a liking.

weak verb *n* (*gram*) a verb inflected by the addition of a regular suffix, e.g. *walk* (*walked*), rather than by change of the main vowel, as with *sing* (*sang*, *sung*). ◇ See also **strong verb**.

weal¹ *n* a long, raised, reddened mark on the skin caused e.g. by a slash with a whip or sword. [Variant of **wale**, ridge]

weal² *n* (*old*) welfare: *the common weal*. [OE *wela*]

wealth *n* **1** (the possession of) riches and property. **2** abundance of resources: *the country's mineral wealth*. **3** a large quantity: *a wealth of examples*. [MidE *welthe*, from OE *wela*, weal²]

wealthy *adj* **-ier, -iest 1** possessing riches and property; rich. **2** (with **in**) well supplied with; rich in: *wealthy in timber*.

wean[1] *v* **1** to accustom (a baby) to taking food other than its mother's milk: *weaned on to solid foods*. **2** (**from**) to break (someone) gradually of a bad habit, etc.: *how to wean him from drugs*. [OE *wenian*, to accustom]

wean[2] *n* (*Scot*) a child. [**wee** + *ane*, one]

weapon *n* **1** an instrument or device used to kill or injure people in a war or fight. **2** something one can use to get the better of others: *Patience is our best weapon*. — *n* **weaponry**. [OE *wæpen*]

wear *v* ***wore, worn* 1** (*tr*) to be dressed in, or have on one's body. **2** (*tr*) to have (one's hair, beard, etc.) cut a certain length or in a certain style. **3** (*tr*) to have (a certain expression). **4** (*intr*) (of a carpet or garment) to become thin or threadbare through use. **5** (*tr*) to make (a hole, bare patch, etc.) in something through heavy use. **6** (*intr*) to bear intensive use; to last in use: *doesn't wear well*. **7** (*tr*; *coll*) to accept (an excuse, story, etc.) or tolerate (a situation, etc.). **8** (*tr*) to tire: *worn to a frazzle*. **9** (*intr*; **on**) to irritate. — *n* **1** (often *in cmpds*) clothes suitable for a certain purpose, person, occasion, etc.: *menswear*. **2** the amount or type of use that e.g. clothing, carpeting, etc. gets: *subjected to heavy wear*. **3** damage caused through use: *machinery showing signs of wear*. — *adj* **wearable**. — *n* **wearer**. — *v* **wear away** (*tr* & *intr*) to become thin or disappear completely through rubbing, weathering, etc. — *v* **wear down 1** (*tr* & *intr*) to make or become shallower or shorter through rubbing, friction, etc. — **wearing thin** (of an excuse, etc.) becoming unconvincing or ineffective through over-use. — *v* **wear off** (*intr*) (of a feeling, pain, etc.) to become less intense; to disappear gradually. — *v* **wear on** (*intr*) (of time) to pass: *as the year wore on*. — *v* **wear out 1** (*tr* & *intr*) to make or become unusable through use (*adj* **worn-out**). **2** (*tr*) to tire utterly; to exhaust (*adj* **worn-out**). — *v* **wear through** (*intr*) to develop a hole through heavy wear. [OE *werian*]

wearing *adj* exhausting.

wear and tear *n* damage sustained in the course of continual or normal use.

wearisome *adj* tiring, tedious, boring or frustrating. [**weary**]

weary *adj* **-ier, -iest 1** tired out; exhausted. **2** (**of**) tired; fed up. **3** tiring, dreary or irksome. — *v* **1** (*tr* & *intr*) to make or become weary. **2** (*intr* with **of**) to get tired of. — *adv* **wearily**. — *n* **weariness**. [OE *werig*]

weasel *n* a small slender short-legged reddish-brown animal that feeds on frogs, mice, etc. [OE *wesle*]

weather *n* the atmospheric conditions in any area at any time, with regard to sun, cloud, temperature, wind, rain, etc. — *adj* (*naut*) on the side exposed to the wind. — *v* **-r- 1** (*tr* & *intr*) to expose or be exposed to the effects of wind, sun, rain, etc.; to alter or be altered in colour, texture, shape, etc. through such exposure. **2** (*tr*) to come safely through (a storm or stormy situation). **3** (*tr*; *naut*) to get to the windward side of (a headland, etc.). — **keep a weather eye open** to keep alert for developments. — **make heavy weather of** to make unnecessarily slow and difficult progress with. — **under the weather** (*coll*) not in good health. [OE *weder*]

weatherbeaten *adj* **1** (of the skin or face) tanned by exposure to sun and wind. **2** worn or damaged by exposure to the weather.

weatherboard *n* **1** a sloping board fitted to the bottom of a door, to exclude rain. **2** any of a series of overlapping horizontal boards covering an exterior wall.

weathercock *n* **1** a weathervane in the form of a farmyard cock. **2** (*derog*) a fickle, unreliable person who frequently changes loyalties.

weatherman *n* (*coll*) a person who presents the weather forecast on radio or television.

weatherproof *adj* designed or treated so as to keep out wind and rain.

weathervane *n* a revolving arrow that turns to point in the direction of the wind, having a fixed base with arms for each of the four compass points, mounted e.g. on a church spire.

weave[1] *v* ***wove, woven* 1** (*tr* & *intr*) to make (cloth or tapestry) in a loom, passing threads under and over the threads of a fixed warp; to interlace (threads) thus. **2** (*tr*) to construct anything (e.g. a basket, fence, etc.) by passing flexible strips in and out between fixed canes, etc.; to make by interlacing or intertwining. **3** to devise (a story, plot, etc.); to work (details, facts, etc.) into a story, etc. — *n* the pattern or compactness of the weaving in a fabric: *an open weave*.

weaver *n* a person who weaves. [OE *wefian*]

weave[2] *v* ***weaved*** (*intr*) to move to and fro or wind in and out. — **get weaving** (*coll*) to get busy; to hurry. [MidE *weve*]

web *n* **1** a network of slender threads constructed by a spider to trap insects. **2** (*old*) a piece of weaving or tapestry on a loom. **3** a membrane connecting the toes of a swimming bird or animal. **4** (*printing*) a continuous roll of paper fed through rollers in an offset lithographic printing process. **5** any intricate network: *a web of lies, intrigue*, etc. — *adj* **webbed**. [OE *webb*]

webbing *n* strong jute or nylon fabric woven into strips for use as belts, straps and supporting bands in upholstery.

web-footed or **-toed** *adj* having webbed feet.

wed *v* **-dd-**; ***wedded*** or ***wed*** **1** (*tr* or *intr*; *old*) to marry. **2** (*tr*; *old*) to join in marriage. **3** (*tr*; **to, with**) to unite or combine: *wed firmness with compassion*. [OE *weddian*, to promise, marry]

wedded *adj* **1** (with **to**) devoted to (one's job, work, etc.). **2** (with **to**) firmly committed to (an idea, belief, etc.). **3** married; in marriage: *wedded bliss*.

Wed. *abbrev* Wednesday.

we'd we would or we should.

wedding *n* **1** a marriage ceremony. **2** any of the notable anniversaries of this, i.e. the **silver** (25 years), **ruby** (40 years), **golden** (50 years), or **diamond** (60 years) **wedding**. **[wed]**

wedding breakfast *n* the celebratory meal served after a wedding ceremony.

wedding cake *n* a rich iced fruit cake usu. in several tiers, served to wedding guests.

wedding ring *n* a ring, esp. in the form of a plain gold band, given by a bridegroom to his bride, or by a bride and bridegroom to each other, for wearing as an indication of married status.

wedge *n* **1** a piece of solid wood, metal or other material, tapering to a thin edge, driven into e.g. wood to split it, or pushed into a narrow gap between moving parts to immobilise them. **2** a wedge-shaped section usu. cut from something circular. **3** a shoe heel in the form of a wedge, tapering towards the sole. **4** (*golf*) a club with a steeply angled wedge-shaped head for lofting. — *v* (*tr*) **1** to fix or immobilise in position with, or as if with, a wedge. **2** (**in, into**, etc.) to thrust or insert: *wedged herself into the corner*. — **drive a wedge between** to cause ill-feeling or division between (people formerly friendly or united). — **the thin end of the wedge** something that looks like the small beginning of a significant, usu. unwanted, development. [OE *wecg*]

Wedgwood® *n* a type of pottery decorated with white classical figures applied over a distinctive blue background. [Josiah *Wedgwood*, English potter (1730–95)]

wedlock *n* (esp. *old*) the condition of being married. — **born out of wedlock** born to parents not married to each other; illegitimate. [OE *wedlac*]

Wednesday *n* the fourth day of the week. [OE *Wodnes dæg*, the day of Woden (the chief god of the Germanic peoples)]

wee[1] *adj* ***weer***, ***weest*** (*coll*, esp. *Scot*) small; tiny. [MidE *we*, bit, from OE *wæg*, weight]

wee[2] (*coll*, esp. *childish*) *v* ***wees***, ***weed*** (*intr*) to urinate. — *n* (also **wee-wee**) **1** an act of urinating. **2** urine.

weed *n* **1** a wild plant growing among cultivated plants or elsewhere where unwanted. **2** (*coll*) marijuana. **3** (with **the**; *old* or *facet*) tobacco. **4** (*derog*) an unmanly man, esp. of gangling build. — *v* **1** (*tr* & *intr*) to uproot weeds from (a garden, flowerbed, etc.). **2** (with **out**) to identify and eliminate (e.g. those who are unwanted or incompetent) from an organisation or other group. [OE *weod*]

weedkiller *n* a substance used to kill (plant) weeds.

weedy *adj* ***-ier***, ***-iest*** **1** overrun with weeds. **2** (of a plant) straggly in growth. **3** (*derog*) (of a man) of gangling or otherwise unmanly build. **4** feeble; ineffectual.

weeds n (*pl*) the black mourning clothes worn by a widow. [OE *wæd*, garment]

week *n* **1** a sequence of seven consecutive days, usu. beginning on Sunday. **2** any period of seven consecutive days. **3** the working days of the week, as distinct from the weekend. **4** the period worked per week: *works a 45-hour week*. — *adv* seven days after a specified day: *She's arriving Tuesday week*. — **a week last Friday, Tuesday**, etc. the Friday, Tuesday, etc. before the last one. — **a week on** or **next Friday, Tuesday**, etc. the Friday, Tuesday, etc. after the next one. — **week in, week out** endlessly. [OE *wice*]

Feast of Weeks *n* Shabuoth.

weekly *adj* **1** occurring, produced, or issued every week, or once a week. — *adv* every week, or once a week. — *n* ***-ies*** a magazine or newspaper published once a week.

weekday *n* any day except Sunday, or except Saturday and Sunday.

weekend *n* the non-working period from Friday evening to Sunday night.

weeny *adj* ***-ier***, ***-iest*** (*coll*) tiny. **[wee + tiny** or **teeny]**

weep *v* ***wept*** **1** (*intr*) to shed tears as an expression of grief or other emotion. **2** (*intr* with **for**, or (*poetic*) *tr*) to lament or bewail: *wept for her lost youth*; *No poet wept his passing*. **3** (*intr* & *tr*) (of a wound, seal, etc.) to exude (matter); to ooze. — *n* a bout of weeping. [OE *wepan*]

weeping *adj* (of a tree variety) having low-drooping branches.

weepy *adj* ***-ier***, ***-iest*** **1** tearful. **2** (of a story, etc.) making one weep; poignant; sentimental. — *n* ***-ies*** (*coll*) a film, novel, etc. of this kind.

weevil *n* any of several beetles with an elongated proboscis, that as both adults and larvae can damage fruit, grain, nuts and trees; any insect that damages stored grain. [OE *wifel*]

wee-wee. See **wee**[2].

weft *n* (*weaving*) the threads that are passed over and under the fixed threads of the warp in a loom. [OE]

weigh *v* **1** (*tr*) to measure the weight of. **2** (*tr* & *intr*) to have (a certain weight): *weighs 8 kilos*; *Books weigh heavy*. **3** (*tr* with **out**) to measure out a specific weight of: *weighed out a pound of flour*. **4** (*tr*; **up**) to consider or assess (facts, possibilities, etc.). **5** (*tr*) to balance (something) in one's hand so as to feel its weight. **6** (*intr* with **on, upon**) to oppress: *Her worries weighed (heavily) on* *her*. **7** (*intr* with **with**) to impress favourably: *Your previous experience should weigh with the appointments board.* **8** (*tr*) to raise (the anchor) of a ship before sailing: *weighed anchor at dawn.* — *v* **weigh down** (*tr*) to burden, overload, or oppress. — *v* **weigh in** (*intr*) **1** (of a wrestler or boxer before a fight, or of a jockey after a race) to be weighed officially (*n* **weigh-in**). **2** (with **with**; *coll*) to contribute (a comment, etc.) to a discussion. [OE *wegan*]

weighbridge *n* an apparatus for weighing vehicles with their loads, consisting of a metal plate set into a road surface and connected to a weighing device.

weight *n* **1** the heaviness of something; the amount anything weighs. **2** the property a body has that causes it to fall to earth. **3** any system of units for measuring and expressing weight: *imperial weight*; *troy weight*. **4** a piece of metal of a standard weight, against which to measure the weight of other objects. **5** (often *in cmpds*) a heavy object used to compress, hold down or counterbalance: *a paperweight*, *counterweight*, etc. **6** a heavy load. **7** (*athletics*) a heavy object for lifting, throwing or tossing. **8** a mental burden: *took a weight off my mind.* **9** strength or significance in terms of amount: *the weight of evidence*, *support*, etc. **10** the main thrust or force: *the weight of the argument.* **11** influence, authority or credibility: *opinions that carry little weight.* **12** (*statistics*) a number denoting the frequency of some element within a frequency distribution. — *v* (*tr*) **1** (**down**) to add weight to, e.g. to restrict movement: *weighted the tent down with stones.* **2** (**down**) to burden or oppress: *weighted down by care.* **3** to arrange so as to have an unevenness or bias: *a tax system weighted in favour of the better-off.* — **pull one's weight** to do one's full share of work, etc. — **throw one's weight about** (*coll*) to behave domineeringly. — **throw one's weight behind** to give one's full support to. — **worth one's weight in gold** exceptionally useful or helpful. [OE *wiht*]

weighting *n* a supplement to a salary, usu. to compensate for high living costs: *London weighting.*

weightless *adj* **1** weighing nothing or almost nothing. **2** (of astronauts in space) not subject to earth's gravity, so able to float free. — *n* **weightlessness.**

weightlifting *n* the sport or exercise of lifting barbells. — *n* **weightlifter.**

weight-training *n* muscle-strengthening exercises performed with the aid of weights and pulleys.

weighty, **-ier**, **-iest** *adj* **1** heavy. **2** important, significant or grave.

weir *n* **1** a shallow dam constructed across a river to control its flow. **2** a fish-trap built across a river in the form of a fence. [OE *wer*, enclosure]

weird *adj* **1** eerie; uncanny; supernatural. **2** queer; strange; bizarre. — *adv* **weirdly.** — *n* **weirdness.** [OE *wyrd*, fate]

weirdo *n* **-os** (*coll*) someone who behaves or dresses bizarrely.

welch. Another spelling of **welsh**.

welcome *v* (*tr*) **1** to receive (a guest, visitor, etc.) with a warm greeting or kindly hospitality. **2** to encourage visits from: *The museum welcomes children.* **3** to invite (suggestions, contributions, etc.). **4** to approve of (an action, etc.): *welcomed her intervention.* **5** to respond with pleasure to: *welcomed the long summer evenings.* — *interj* an expression of pleasure on receiving someone: *Welcome home!* — *n* the act of welcoming; a reception. — *adj* **1** warmly received: *was made welcome.* **2** gladly permitted or encouraged (to do or keep something): *You're welcome to borrow it*; *She's welcome to my old bicycle.* **3** much appreciated: *a welcome cup of tea.* — **welcome with open arms** to receive warmly, gladly, gratefully or thankfully. — **you're welcome!** (used in response to thanks) not at all; it's a pleasure. [OE *wilcuma*, a welcome guest]

weld *v* (*tr*) **1** to join (pieces of metal or plastic) by pressure, first heating the edges to soften them. **2** to join (pieces of metal) by fusion, using an electric arc. **3** to unite or blend together: *welded them into a competent choir.* — *n* a joint made by welding. — *n* **welder.** [Past participle of older *well*, to melt, weld]

welfare *n* **1** the health, comfort, happiness and general wellbeing of a person, group, etc. **2** social work concerned with helping those in need. **3** financial support given to those in need. [**well**[1] + **fare**]

welfare state *n* a system in which the government uses tax revenue to look after citizens' welfare, with the provision of free health care, old-age pensions, and financial support for the disabled or unemployed.

well[1] ***better***, ***best*** *adv* **1** competently; skilfully. **2** satisfactorily: *All went well.* **3** kindly: *was well treated.* **4** thoroughly; properly; carefully; fully: *wash it well*; *wasn't attending very well.* **5** intimately: *don't know her well.* **6** successfully; prosperously: *do*, *live*, etc. *well.* **7** approvingly: *thinks well of you.* **8** by a long way: *well past midnight*; *well ahead.* **9** justifiably: *can't very well ignore him.* **10** conceivably; quite possibly: *may well be right.* **11** understandably: *if she objects, as well she may.* **12** very much: *well worth doing.* **13** used in combination with *quite*, *perfectly*, *damn*, for emphasis: *I'm damn well going to.* — *adj* **1** healthy. **2** in a satisfactory state. **3** sensible; advisable: *would be well to check.* — *interj* **1** used enquiringly in expectation of a response, explanation, etc. **2** used variously in conversation, e.g. to resume a narrative, preface a reply, express surprise, indignation, doubt, etc. — **all very well** (*ironic*) fine for some. — **as well**

1 too; in addition. **2** (also **just as well**) for all the difference it makes: *I may as well tell you.* **3** (also **just as well**) advisable; sensible: *would be as well to buy it now.* **4** (also **just as well**) a good thing; lucky: *It was just as well you came when you did.* — **as well as** in addition to. — **do well out of** to profit from (a situation, etc.). — **leave** or **let well alone** not to interfere where things will do as they are. — **mean well** to have helpful or kindly intentions. — **very well** (in complying with an order, accepting a point, etc.) yes, all right, agreed, in that case, etc. — **well and good** used to show acceptance of facts or a situation. — **well and truly** thoroughly; completely. — **well away 1** making rapid progress; having got into one's stride. **2** (*coll*) drunk, asleep, etc. — **well done!** used to congratulate someone on an achievement, etc. — **well enough** satisfactory within limits. — **well off 1** wealthy; financially comfortable (*adj* **well-off**). **2** in circumstances that should content one. — **well out of** lucky to be free of. — **well up in** having a thorough knowledge of. [OE *wel*]

well-advised *adj* sensible: *You'd be well-advised to comply.*

well-appointed *adj* (of a house, etc.) well furnished or equipped.

well-balanced *adj* **1** satisfactorily proportioned. **2** sane, sensible and stable.

well-behaved *adj* behaving with good manners or due propriety.

wellbeing *n* welfare.

well-born *adj* descended from an aristocratic family.

well-bred *adj* having good manners; showing good breeding.

well-built *adj* **1** strongly built. **2** of muscular or well-proportioned bodily build.

well-connected *adj* having influential or aristocratic friends and relations.

well-disposed *adj* (**towards**) inclined to be friendly.

well-earned *adj* thoroughly deserved.

well-founded *adj* (of suspicions, etc.) justified; based on good grounds.

well-groomed *adj* (of a person) of smart, neat appearance.

well-grounded *adj* **1** (of an argument, etc.) soundly based. **2** (**in**) having had a good basic training.

well-heeled *adj* (*coll*) wealthy.

well-informed *adj* **1** having sound, reliable information on something particular. **2** full of varied knowledge.

well-intentioned *adj* having good intentions, if an unfortunate effect.

well-judged *adj* neatly calculated; judicious.

well-knit *adj* **1** (of a person) sturdily and compactly built. **2** compactly or soundly constructed.

wellknown *adj* familiar or famous.

well-mannered *adj* polite.

well-meaning *adj* well-intentioned. — *adj* **well-meant**.

well-nigh *adv* almost; nearly.

well-oiled *adj* **1** (*coll*) drunk. **2** (*fig*) operating smoothly from thorough practice.

well-preserved *adj* **1** in good condition; not decayed. **2** youthful in appearance; showing few signs of age.

well-read *adj* having read and learnt much.

well-rounded *adj* **1** pleasantly plump. **2** having had a broadly based, balanced upbringing and education. **3** well constructed and complete.

well-spoken *adj* having a courteous, fluent and usu. refined way of speaking.

well-thought-of *adj* approved of; respected.

well-timed *adj* timely; opportune.

well-to-do *adj* wealthy; financially comfortable.

well-tried *adj* found reliable from frequent testing.

well-turned *adj* **1** (*old*) attractively formed: *a well-turned ankle.* **2** neatly expressed: *a well-turned phrase.*

well-versed *adj* (**in**) thoroughly trained.

well-wisher *n* someone concerned for one's welfare.

well-worn *adj* **1** much worn or used; showing signs of wear. **2** (of an expression, etc.) over-familiar from frequent use; trite.

well[2] *n* **1** a shaft or hole bored into the ground to give access to a supply of water, oil or gas. **2** (a pool fed by) a natural spring of water. **3** a shaft, or shaft-shaped cavity, e.g. that made through the floors of a building to take the staircase: *a stairwell.* **4** (*naut*) an enclosure in a ship's hold round the pumps. **5** (esp. *in cmpds*) a reservoir or receptacle: *an inkwell.* **6** (*legal*) the open space in the centre of a law court. **7** a plentiful source of something: *She's a well of information.* — *v* (*intr*; **up**) (of a liquid) to spring, flow or flood to the surface. [OE *wella*]

wellhead *n* **1** the source of a stream; a spring. **2** an origin or source. **3** the rim or structure round the top of a well.

wellspring *n* **1** a spring or fountain. **2** a rich or bountiful source.

we'll we will or we shall.

wellington *n* a waterproof rubber or plastic boot loosely covering the foot and calf. [After the first Duke of *Wellington* (1769–1852)]

welly *n* **-ies** (*coll*) a wellington.

Welsh *adj* **1** of or belonging to Wales. **2** of, or in, the language of Wales. — *n* **1** the Celtic language of Wales. **2** (*pl*; with **the**) the people of Wales. [OE *welisc*, from *wealh*, Briton, foreigner]

Welshman or **Welshwoman** *n* a person from Wales.

Welsh rabbit or **rarebit** *n* a dish of melted cheese served on toast.

welsh or **welch** *v* (*intr* with **on**) **1** to fail to pay (one's debts) or fulfil (one's obligations). **2** to fail to keep one's promise to (a person).

welt *n* **1** a reinforcing band or border, e.g. the ribbing at the waist of a knitted garment. **2** (*shoemaking*) a strip of leather fitted round the upper, as a means of attaching it to the sole. **3** a weal raised by a lash or blow. — *v* (*tr*) **1** to fit a welt. **2** to beat or thrash.

welter *n* a confused mass. — *v* **-r-** (*intr*; **in**) to lie, roll or wallow. [ODut *welteren*]

welterweight *n* **1** a class for boxers and wrestlers of not more than a specified weight (66·7 kg in professional boxing, similar but different weights in amateur boxing and wrestling). **2** a boxer or wrestler of this weight. — *adj* (for contestants) of the prescribed weight.

wen *n* a cyst on the skin, usu. of the scalp. [OE *wenn*]

wench *n* (*old coll*) **1** a girl; a woman. **2** a servant girl. **3** a prostitute. — *v* (*intr*) **1** to associate with prostitutes. **2** to go courting girls. [OE *wencel*, a child]

wend *v* to make (one's way). [OE *wendan*, to go]

Wendy house *n* a small playhouse for children constructed of wood or cloth. [*Wendy*, character in J M Barrie's *Peter Pan*, 1904]

went. See **go**.

wept. See **weep**.

were. See **be**.

we're we are.

weren't were not.

werewolf *n* **-wolves** (*folklore*) a person who changes periodically into a wolf. [OE *werwulf*, man-wolf]

wert (*old*) a form of the past tense of the verb *be* used with the pronoun *thou*.

Wesleyan *adj* relating to John *Wesley* (1703–91), or to Methodism, the Protestant movement founded by him. — *n* a follower of Wesley or Methodism.

west *n* (sometimes *cap*; often with **the**) the direction in which the sun sets, or any part of the earth, a country, town, etc. lying in that direction. ◇ See also **the West** below. — *adj* **1** in the west; on the side that is on or nearer the west. **2** (of a wind) blowing from the west. — *adv* toward the west. — **the West 1** the countries of Europe and N America, in contrast to those of Asia, esp., formerly, the non-communist bloc as distinct from the communist or former communist countries of the East. **2** (esp. *hist*) the part of the US to the west of the Mississippi.— **go west** (*coll*) to be lost or destroyed. [OE]

westbound *adj* heading west.

the West Country *n* the south-western counties of England — Somerset, Devon and Cornwall.

the West End *n* the fashionable shopping and theatre district in west central London.

westering *adj* moving, or (of the sun) sinking, towards the west.

westerly *adj* **1** (of a wind) coming from the west. **2** of, or in, the west. **3** looking, lying, etc. towards the west. — *n* **-ies** a westerly wind.

western *adj* of the west or the West. — *n* a film or story about 19th-cent. cowboys in the west of the US.

westerner *n* a person who lives in or comes from the west, esp. the western US.

westernmost *adj* situated furthest west.

westward *adv* (also **westwards**) & *adj* towards the west.

West Indian *n* & *adj* (a native or inhabitant) of the West Indies.

wet *adj* **-tt- 1** covered or soaked in water, rain, perspiration or other liquid. **2** (of weather) rainy. **3** (of paint, cement, etc.) not yet dried. **4** covered with tears: *wet cheeks*. **5** (of a baby) having a urine-soaked nappy. **6** (*coll derog*) (of a person) feeble; ineffectual. **7** (*US hist*) allowing the sale of alcoholic drink. **8** (*chem*) (of processes, etc.) using liquid. — *n* **1** moisture. **2** rainy weather; rain. **3** (*derog*) a feeble, ineffectual person. **4** (*coll*) a moderate Conservative. ◇ See also **dry**. — *v* **-tt-**, ***wet*** or ***wetted*** (sense **1**), ***wet*** (sense **2**) (*tr*) **1** to make wet; to splash or soak. **2** to urinate involuntarily on: *wet the bed*. — **wet behind the ears** (*coll*) immature, naive or inexperienced. — **wet through** soaked to the skin. [OE *wæt*]

wet blanket *n* a dreary, pessimistic person who dampens the enthusiasm and enjoyment of others; a killjoy.

wet dream *n* a dream involving an erotic experience, that causes actual ejaculation of semen.

wet nurse *n* (*hist*) a woman employed to breastfeed another's baby.

wet suit *n* a tight-fitting rubber suit permeable by water, but conserving body heat, worn by divers, canoeists, yachtsmen, etc.

wether *n* a castrated ram. [OE]

we've we have.

whack (*coll*) *v* (*tr*) to hit sharply and resoundingly. — *n* **1** (the sound of) a sharp, resounding blow. **2** one's share of the profits, work, etc. — **have a whack at** to try. [Imit.]

whacked *adj* exhausted.

whacking *adj* huge: *a whacking* (*great*) *salary*.

whale *n* any of several huge sea mammals shaped similarly to fish but with flippers and horizontal tail blades, breathing air through an opening on top of the head. — *v* (*intr*) to hunt whales. — *n* **whaling**. — **a whale of a** (*coll*) a hugely enjoyable (time, evening, etc.). [OE *hwæl*]

whalebone *n* the light flexible horny substance of which the plankton-filtering plates in the mouths of toothless whales are composed, used esp. formerly for stiffening corsets, etc.

whale oil *n* oil obtained from whale blubber.

whaler *n* a person or ship engaged in whaling.

wharf *n* **wharfs** or **wharves** a landing-stage built along a waterfront for loading and unloading vessels. [OE *hwearf*]

wharfage *n* **1** dues paid for the use of a wharf. **2** accommodation for vessels at a wharf.

wharfinger *n* the owner or supervisor of a wharf.

what **1** used in requesting identification, spccification or classification of a thing or person, as an *adj* (*What street are we in? Tell me what flowers these are*) or as a *pron* (*What's that bird?*). **2** used in exclamations, as an *adj* (*What lies she tells! What a fool!*), as an *adv* (*What awful clothes! What a silly suggestion! What does it matter?*) or as a *pron* (*What on earth will he say next? What she puts up with!*). **3** used relatively, meaning the, all or any (things or people) that, as a *pron* (*just what I wanted*; *What you need is a holiday*), as an *adj* (*invited what friends she could*) or as an *adv* (*What little money they have goes on drugs*). — **give someone what for** (*coll*) to scold or punish someone. — **so what?** (*coll*) what of it? — **what about ...? 1** do you fancy (something, or doing something)? **2** what is your opinion of ...? **3** aren't you forgetting ...? **4** (also **what of...?**) what plans, news or information have you about ...? — **what ... for?** why? — **what if ...?** what will happen if ...? — **what ... like?** used in requesting a description: *What's she like? What does it look like?* — **what of it?** (*coll*) does it really matter? — **what's more** and, more importantly. — **what's what** (*coll*) what really goes on, counts, etc.; the truth of the matter. — **what's with ...?** (*coll*; esp. *US*) what's the matter with ...? — **what the devil, hell, dickens**, etc. (*coll*) what ever, on earth, etc. — **what with** because of. [OE *hwæt*]

what-d'you-call-it *n* (*coll*) a thing whose name one can't remember.

whatever *relative pron & relative adj* any (things or quantity) that: *Take whatever you want, whatever money you need.* — *pron & adj* no matter what: *must finish, whatever difficulties crop up* or *whatever else I do.* — *adj* **1** whatsoever; at all: *has nothing whatever to do with you.* **2** (*coll*) some or other: *has disappeared, for whatever reason.*— *pron* **1** an emphatic form of **what**: *Whatever shall I do?* **2** used when one is not sure what something is: *a didgeridoo, whatever that is.* — **or whatever** (*coll*) or some such thing. — **whatever you say** as you wish.

what have you *n* other such things.

whatnot *n* **1** a stand with shelves for ornaments, etc. **2** (*coll*) a whatsit. **3** (*coll*) and other similar things: *grammar and whatnot.*

what's-his-(or **-her-**, **-its-**, etc.)**name** *n* (*coll*) a person or thing whose name one can't remember.

whatsit *n* (*coll*) some unspecified thing, or one whose name one can't remember. [*what is it?*]

whatsoever *pron & adj* **1** (*poetic*) whatever: *whatsoever things are lovely.* **2** (used after noun or pronoun in *neg* sentences) at all: *had no encouragement whatsoever*; *none whatsoever.*

wheat *n* any of a genus of grasses, or their grain, providing flour for bread, etc. [OE *hwæte*]

wheaten *adj* **1** made of wheat flour or grain. **2** wholemeal.

wheat germ *n* the vitamin-rich embryo of wheat, present in the grain.

wheatmeal *n* wheat flour with some of the bran and germ removed, intermediate between wholemeal flour and white flour.

wheatsheaf *n* a sheaf of wheat.

wheatear *n* a migratory songbird with a white belly and rump. [Probably changed from *white arse*]

wheedle *v* (*intr & tr*) to coax or cajole. — *n* **wheedler**.

wheel *n* **1** a circular object of varying design rotating on an axle, on which a vehicle moves along the ground. **2** such an object serving as part of a machine or mechanism. **3** a steering-wheel, spinning-wheel or water wheel. **4** (in *pl*; *coll*, esp. *US*) a motor vehicle for personal use. **5** (in *pl*) workings (of an organisation, etc.): *the wheels of justice.* **6** (*hist*) a circular instrument of torture on which the victim was stretched. **7** (*gambling*) a disc or drum on the results of whose random spin bets are made: *a roulette wheel.* **8** a circling or pivoting movement, e.g. of troops. **9** any progression that appears to go round in a circle: *the wheel of fortune, fashion,* etc. — *v* **1** (*tr*) to fit with wheels: *wheeled vehicles.* **2** (*tr*) to push (a wheeled vehicle or conveyance) or (someone or something) in or on it. **3** (*intr*) (of troops, birds, etc.) to sweep round in a curve. **4** (*intr*; **round**) to turn round suddenly; to pivot on one's heel. — **at** or **behind the wheel 1** in the driver's seat. **2** in charge. — **wheel and deal** to be a wheeler-dealer. — *v* **wheel out** (*tr*) to put forward for consideration (ideas, etc. too often suggested before). [OE *hweol*]

wheelbarrow *n* a hand-pushed cart with a wheel in front and two legs at the rear.

wheelbase *n* the distance between the front and rear axles of a vehicle.

wheelchair *n* a chair with wheels in which invalids can be conveyed or convey themselves.

wheel clamp *n* a locking device fitted by the police to one wheel of, and so immobilising, an illegally parked vehicle, removed only on payment of a fine.

wheeler-dealing or **wheeling and dealing** *n* tough dealing and bargaining in pursuit of one's political or business interests. — *n* **wheeler-dealer**.

wheelhouse *n* the shelter on a ship's bridge in which the steering-gear is housed.
wheelwright *n* a craftsman who makes and repairs wheels and wheeled carriages.
wheeze *v* (*intr*) to breathe in a laboured way with a gasping or rasping noise, when suffering from a lung infection, etc. — *n* **1** a wheezing breath or sound. **2** (*coll*) a bright idea; a clever scheme. — *adv* **wheezily**. — *adj* **wheezy, *-ier, -iest***. [Norse *hvæza*]
whelk *n* an edible shellfish with a thick spiral shell. [OE *weoloc*]
whelp *n* **1** the young of a dog or wolf; a puppy. **2** (*old*) an impudent boy or youth. — *v* (*intr*) to give birth to puppies or cubs. [OE *hwelp*]
when *adv* at what time?; during what period?; how soon?: *When does the plane arrive? I can't remember when ruffs were in fashion.* — *conj* **1** at the time, or during the period, that: *locks the door when she goes to bed*; *It happened when I was abroad.* **2** as soon as: *I'll come when I've finished.* **3** at any time that; whenever: *come when you can.* **4** but just then: *was about to leave when the telephone rang.* **5** at which time; for at that time: *Ring tomorrow, when I'll have more information.* **6** in spite of the fact that; considering that: *Why stand when you can sit?* — *pron* what time: *They stayed talking, until when I can't say.* — *relative pron* which time; at or during which: *since when she hasn't spoken to me*; *an era when life was harder.* [OE *hwænne*]
whenever *conj* **1** at any or every time that: *gets furious whenever he fails to get his way.* **2** if ever; no matter when: *I'll be here whenever you need me.* — *adv* **1** an emphatic form of **when**: *Whenever could I have said that?* **2** used to indicate that one does not know when: *at Pentecost, whenever that is.* — **or whenever** (*coll*) or some such time.
whensoever *adv* if ever; no matter when.
whence (also **from whence**) *adv* **1** from what place?: *enquired whence they had come.* **2** from what cause or circumstance?: *can't explain whence the mistake arose.* — *conj* **1** to the place from which; from where: *returned (to the village) whence they had come.* **2** from which cause or circumstance: *has red hair, whence his nickname 'Ginger'.* [MidE *hwannes*]
where *adv* **1** in, at or to which place?; in what direction?: *Where is she going? don't know where this road takes us.* **2** in what respect?: *showed me where I'd gone wrong.* — *pron* what place?: *Where have you come from?* — *conj* or *relative pron* **1** in, at or to the, or any, place that; in, at or to which: *went where he pleased*; *the village where I was born*, etc. **2** in any case in which: *keep families together where possible.* **3** the aspect or respect in which: *That's where you're wrong.* **4** and there: *stopped at Bradford, where we picked up Jane.* [OE *hwær*]
whereabouts *adv* roughly where? — *n* (*sing* or *pl*) the (rough) position of a person or thing.
whereas *conj* **1** when in fact: *She thought she'd failed, whereas she'd done well.* **2** but, by contrast: *I'm a pessimist, whereas my husband is an optimist.*
whereby *relative pron* by means of which.
wherefore *conj* & *adv* (esp. *old* or *legal*) for what reason? — *n* a reason, as in *the whys and wherefores.*
wherein (esp. *old* or *legal*) *adv* & *conj* in what place?; in what respect?: *Wherein is the justification?* — *relative pron* in which place or thing.
whereof *relative pron* (esp. *old*) of which: *the circumstances whereof I told you.*
whereon *relative pron* (esp. *old*) on which.
wheresoever *adv* (*old*) no matter where.
whereupon *conj* at which point.
wherever *relative pron* in, at or to any or every place that: *takes it wherever she goes.* — *conj* in, at or to whatever place: *They were welcomed wherever they went.* — *adv* **1** no matter where: *I won't lose touch, wherever I go.* **2** an emphatic form of **where**: *Wherever can they be?* **3** used to indicate that one does not know where: *St Adamnan's Church, wherever that is.* — **or wherever** (*coll*) or some such place.
wherewithal *relative pron* (*old*) with which. — *n* (with **the**) the means, resources, necessary equipment or cash.
wherry *n* ***-ies*** **1** a long light rowing-boat, esp. for transporting passengers. **2** a light barge.
whet *v* ***-tt-*** (*tr*) **1** to sharpen (a bladed tool) by rubbing it against stone, etc. **2** to intensify (someone's appetite or desire). [OE *hwettan*]
whetstone *n* a stone for sharpening bladed tools.
whether *conj* **1** used to introduce an indirect question: *asked whether it was raining.* **2** used to introduce an indirect question involving alternative possibilities: *was uncertain whether or not he liked her.* **3** used to state the certainty of something, whichever of two circumstances applies: *promised to marry her, whether or not his parents agreed*; *The rules, whether fair or unfair, are not our concern.* [OE *hwæther*]
whew *interj* (*coll*) an expression of relief or amazement.
whey *n* the watery content of milk, separated from the curd in making cheese, junket, etc. [OE *hwæg*]
which used in requesting identification or specification of a thing or person from a known set or group, as an *adj* (*Which twin did you mean? can't decide which map is better*), or as a *pron* (*Which did you choose?*). — *relative pron* **1** (replaceable by **that** when not following a preposition) used to introduce a defining clause: *animals which (or that) hibernate*; *the evidence on which she based it.* **2** used to add a commenting clause: *her car, which usually sat*

out in the street. — *relative adj & relative pron* any that; whichever: *Take which books you want. Take which you fancy.* — **can't tell, see**, etc. **which is which** can't distinguish one from the other. [OE *hwilc*]

whichever *relative pron & relative adj* **1** the one or ones that; any that: *Take whichever are suitable, whichever coat fits better*, etc. **2** according to which: *at 10.00 or 10.30, whichever is more convenient.* — *adj & pron* no matter which: *We'll be late, whichever way we go. I'll be satisfied, whichever you choose.*

whiff *n* **1** a slight smell. **2** a puff or slight rush: *a whiff of smoke.* **3** a hint: *at the first whiff of scandal.* [Imit.]

Whig (*Br hist*) *n* a member of a political party favouring constitutional government and popular reform, superseded in the 19th cent. by the Liberal party. ◇ See also **Tory**. — *adj* of or relating to the Whigs. — *n* **Whiggery**. — *adj* **Whiggish**. — *n* **Whiggism**. [Probably *whiggamore*, a 17th-cent. Scottish Presbyterian rebel]

while *conj* **1** at the same time as. **2** for as long as; for the whole time that: *guards us while we sleep.* **3** during the time that: *happened while we were abroad.* **4** whereas: *He likes camping, while she prefers sailing.* **5** although: *While I see your point, I still cannot agree.* — *adv* at or during which: *all the months while I was ill.* — *n* a space or lapse of time: *after a while.* — *v* (*tr* with **away**) to pass (time) without boredom. — **in between whiles** during the intervals. — **make it worth someone's while** (*coll*) to pay someone well for his or her trouble. — **worth one's while** worth one's time and trouble.

whilst *conj* while.

whim *n* a sudden fanciful idea; a caprice.

whimper *v* **-r- 1** (*intr*) to cry feebly or plaintively. **2** (*tr*) to say plaintively. — *n* a feebly plaintive cry. [Imit.]

whimsy *n* **-ies 1** quaint, fanciful humour. **2** a whim. [**whim**]

whimsical *adj* **1** delicately fanciful or playful. **2** odd, weird or fantastic. **3** given to having whims. — *n* **whimsicality**. — *adv* **whimsically**.

whin *n* gorse. [Prob. Norse]

whine *v* **1** (*intr*) to whimper. **2** (*intr*) to cry fretfully. **3** (*intr*) to complain peevishly. **4** (*intr*) to speak in a thin, ingratiating or servile voice. **5** (*tr*) to say peevishly. — *n* **1** a whimper. **2** a continuous high-pitched noise. **3** a thin, ingratiating nasal tone of voice. [OE *hwinan*]

whinge *v* (*intr*; *coll*) to complain irritably. — *n* a peevish complaint. [OE *hwinsian*, to whine]

whinny *v* **-ies**, **-ied** (*intr*) (of a horse) to neigh softly. — *n* **-ies** a gentle neigh. [Imit.]

whip *n* **1** a lash with a handle, for driving animals or thrashing people. **2** a member of a parliamentary party responsible for members' discipline, and for their attendance to vote on important issues. **3** a notice sent to members by a party whip requiring their attendance for a vote, urgency being indicated by the number of underlinings: *a three-line whip.* **4** a dessert of any of various flavours made with beaten egg-whites or cream. **5** a whipper-in. — *v* **-pp- 1** (*tr*) to strike or thrash with a whip. **2** (*tr*) to lash with the action or force of a whip: *A sharp wind whipped their faces.* **3** (*tr & intr*) to (cause to) move with a whip-like motion: *The branch whipped back.* **4** (*tr*; **out**, **off**, etc.) to take or snatch: *whipped out a revolver.* **5** (*intr & tr*) to move smartly: *whipped out of sight.* **6** (*tr*; **into**) to rouse, goad, drive or force into a certain state: *whipped the crowd into a fury.* **7** (*tr* with **up**) to arouse (support, enthusiasm or other feelings). **8** (*tr* with **up**) to prepare (a meal) hastily. **9** (*tr*; *coll*) to steal. **10** (*tr*) to beat (egg-whites, cream, etc.) till stiff. **11** (*tr*) to wind cord round (a rope, etc.) to prevent fraying. **12** (*tr*) to oversew. **13** (*tr*; *coll*) to outdo, outwit or defeat. — **have the whip hand over** (*coll*) to have an advantage over. [MidE *whippe*]

whipcord *n* **1** strong, fine, tightly twisted cord. **2** cotton or worsted cloth with a diagonal rib.

whiplash *n* **1** the lash of a whip, or the motion it represents. **2** (also **whiplash injury**) an injury to the neck caused by the sharp forwards-and-backwards wrenching it suffers in a vehicle collision.

whipper-in *n* an assistant to a huntsman, who controls the hounds.

whipping-boy *n* **1** (*hist*) a boy who is educated with a prince and given whatever beatings the prince has deserved. **2** anyone on whom the blame for others' faults falls.

whipping cream *n* cream that will thicken when whipped.

whipping-top *n* a top kept spinning by the lash of a whip.

whippy *adj* **-ier**, **-iest** (of a stick or cane) springy; flexible.

whip-round *n* a collection of money hastily made among a group of people.

whipstock *n* the handle of a whip.

whipper-snapper *n* (*old coll*) a cheeky young lad; any lowly person who behaves impudently.

whippet *n* a slender dog like a small greyhound, used for racing.

whippoorwill *n* a species of nightjar native to N America. [Imit. of call]

whirl *v* **1** (*intr*) to spin or revolve rapidly. **2** (*tr & intr*) to move with a rapid circling or spiralling motion. **3** (*intr*) (of one's head) to feel dizzy from excitement, etc. — *n* **1** a circling or spiralling movement or pattern: *whirls of smoke, colour*, etc. **2** a round of intense activity: *a whirl of parties.* **3** a dizzy state. [Norse *hvirfla*, to turn]

whirlpool *n* a fast-circling current that draws ships, etc. down into its centre.

whirlwind *n* a violently spiralling column of air. — *adj* rapid: *a whirlwind courtship.*

whirligig *n* **1** a spinning toy, esp. a top. **2** a merry-go-round. **3** a dizzying round of activity, progression of events, etc. [MidE *whirligigge*, spinning toy]

whirlybird *n* (*coll*) a helicopter.

whirr or **whir** *v* **-rr-** (*intr*) to turn or spin with a humming noise. — *n* a whirring sound. [Prob. Scandinavian]

whisk *v* (*tr*) **1** (**off**, **away**) to brush or sweep lightly: *whisked the crumbs off the table*. **2** to transport rapidly: *was whisked into hospital*. **3** to move with a brisk waving motion: *whisked its tail from side to side*. **4** to beat (egg-whites, cream, etc.) till stiff. — *n* **1** a whisking movement or action. **2** a hand-held implement for whisking egg-whites, etc. **3** (also **fly whisk**) a flexible implement for swatting flies. [Related to Norse *visk*, wisp]

whisker *n* **1** any of the long coarse hairs growing round the mouth of a cat, mouse, etc. **2** (in *pl*) a man's beard, esp. the parts growing on his cheeks. **3** the tiniest possible margin; a hair's breadth: *within a whisker of death*; *escaped by a whisker*. — *adj* **whiskery**. [Related to Norse *visk*, wisp]

whiskey *n* **-*eys*** (*Irish & US*) whisky.

whisky *n* **-*ies*** an alcoholic spirit distilled from a fermented mash of cereal grains, e.g. barley, wheat or rye. [Gaelic *uisge beatha*, literally 'water of life']

whisper *v* **-*r*-** **1** (*intr & tr*) to speak or say quietly, breathing rather than voicing the words. **2** (*intr & tr*) to speak or say in secrecy or confidence. **3** (*intr & tr*) to spread a rumour; to rumour: *It's whispered that she's leaving him*. **4** (*intr*) (of a breeze, etc.) to make a rustling sound in leaves, etc. — *n* **1** a whispered level of speech: *spoke in a whisper*. **2** (often in *pl*) a rumour or hint; whispered gossip: *have been whispers about their divorce*. **3** a soft rustling sound: *the whisper of the breeze*. [OE *hwisprian*]

whist *n* a card game for usu. two pairs of players, in which the object is to take a majority of 13 tricks, each trick over six scoring one point. [Orig. *whisk*]

whist drive *n* a gathering for whist-playing, with a change of partner after every four games.

whistle *n* **1** a shrill sound produced through pursed lips or through the teeth, used to signal, to express surprise, etc. **2** any of several similar sounds, e.g. the call of a bird, or the shrill sigh of the wind. **3** any of many devices producing a similar sound, etc., e.g. one operated by steam on a railway locomotive or kettle, or one blown by a referee to regulate play on the pitch. **4** a simple wind instrument consisting of a wooden or metal pipe with finger holes. — *v* **1** (*intr & tr*) to produce a whistle through pursed lips or teeth; to perform (a tune), signal, communicate or summon with this sound. **2** (*intr & tr*) to blow a whistle, or play on a whistle. **3** (*intr*) (of a kettle or locomotive) to emit a whistling sound. **4** (*intr*) (of the wind) to make a shrill sound. **5** (*intr & tr*) (of a bird) to sing. **6** (*intr*) (of a bullet, etc.) to whizz through the air. — **blow the whistle on** (*coll*) **1** to expose (illegal or dishonest practices) to the authorities. **2** to declare illegal. — **wet one's whistle** (*coll*) to have a drink; to quench one's thirst. — *v* **whistle for** (*tr*; *coll*) to expect in vain. [OE *hwistlian*, to whistle]

whistle-stop *adj* **1** (of a politician's tour) with a number of short stops, orig. at railway stations, for delivering electioneering addresses to local communities. **2** (of any tour) very rapid, with a number of brief stops.

whit *n* (with a *neg*) the least bit. [Variant of *wight*, creature]

Whit *n* Whitsuntide. — *adj* of or belonging to Whitsuntide.

white *adj* **1** of the colour of snow, the colour that reflects all light. **2** (often *cap*) (of people) belonging to one of the pale-skinned races; relating to such people. **3** abnormally pale, from shock or illness. **4** (of e.g. a rabbit or mouse) albino. **5** (of hair) lacking pigment, as in old age. **6** (of a variety of anything) pale-coloured, as distinct from darker types: *white grapes*. **7** (of wine) made from white grapes or from skinned black grapes. **8** (of flour) having had the bran and wheat germ removed; (of bread) made with white flour. **9** (of coffee or tea) with milk or cream added. **10** (*poetic*) (of the soul, etc.) pure; innocent. — *n* **1** white colour or colouring matter, e.g. paint; white clothes: *dressed all in white*. **2** (often *cap*) a White person. **3** (also **egg-white**) the clear fluid surrounding the yolk of an egg; albumen. **4** the white part of the eyeball, surrounding the iris. **5** (*games*, etc.) something white, e.g. a playing-piece in chess or draughts, a ball in snooker, or ring on an archery target; the player of the white pieces in a board game. **6** (in *pl*) household linen, or white clothes, worn e.g. for cricket or tennis. — *n* **whiteness**. — *adj* **whitish**. — **bleed white** to drain, or deprive gradually, of resources, wealth, etc. [OE *hwit*]

white ant *n* a termite.

whitebait *n* the young of various fish, e.g. herrings, fried and eaten whole.

white blood cell or **white corpuscle** *n* one of the colourless cells in blood and lymph, that protect the body against disease and infection; a leucocyte.

white-collar *adj* denoting non-manual workers, in clerical or other professions. ◇ See also **blue-collar**.

white dwarf *n* one of a number of dense, but faint, stars.

white elephant *n* a possession or piece of property that is useless or unwanted, esp. if inconvenient or expensive to keep.

White Ensign see **ensign**.

white feather *n* a symbol of cowardice. — **show the white feather** to behave in a cowardly fashion.

white fish *n* a general name for white-fleshed sea fish, including whiting, cod, sole, haddock and halibut.

white flag *n* the signal used for offering surrender or requesting a truce.

white gold *n* a pale lustrous alloy of gold, containing e.g. platinum or palladium.

white goods *n* (*pl*) large, traditionally white, kitchen appliances such as washing machines, dishwashers and cookers.

white-headed boy *n* (*ironic*) a favourite or protégé.

white heat *n* **1** a temperature of metals, etc. greater than red heat, at which white light is emitted. **2** (*coll*) the intensest possible keenness, activity or excitement: *the white heat of technology*. — *adj* **white-hot**.

white hope *n* someone of whom great achievements are expected.

white horse *n* a white wave crest on a choppy sea.

white lead *n* a mixture of lead carbonate and lead hydroxide in the form of a white powder, used as colouring matter, etc.

white lie *n* a forgivable lie, esp. one told to avoid hurting someone's feelings.

white light *n* light, such as that of the sun, containing all the wavelengths in the visible range of the spectrum.

white magic *n* magic used for beneficial purposes, e.g. to oppose evil, cure disease, etc.

white matter *n* pale fibrous nerve tissue in the brain and spinal cord.

white meat *n* pale-coloured meat, e.g. veal, chicken and turkey; (in a chicken, etc.) the paler meat of the breast as opposed to the darker meat of the leg, etc.

whiten *v* **-n-** (*tr* & *intr*) to make or become white or whiter; to bleach. — *n* **whitener**.

white noise *n* noise in which there are a large number of frequencies of roughly equal intensity.

white-out *n* **1** conditions of poor visibility in snowy weather, when the overcast sky blends imperceptibly with the white landscape. **2** a dense blizzard.

white paper *n* (also *caps*) a government policy statement printed on white paper, issued for the information of parliament. ◇ See also **green paper**.

white pepper *n* light-coloured pepper made from peppercorns from which the dark outer husk has been removed

white pudding *n* a spicy sausage made from minced pork, oatmeal and suet.

white sauce *n* thick sauce made from flour, fat and milk.

white slave *n* a girl or woman held against her will, and forced into prostitution.

white spirit *n* a colourless liquid distilled from petroleum, used as a substitute for turpentine, e.g. for thinning paint.

white sugar *n* refined sugar.

white tie *n* **1** a white bow tie, part of men's formal evening dress. **2** (as an instruction on an invitation) formal evening dress for men.

whitewash *n* **1** a mixture of lime and water, for giving a white coating to esp. outside walls. **2** measures taken to cover up e.g. a disreputable affair, clear a stained reputation, etc. — *v* (*tr*) to coat, clean up or conceal with whitewash.

white whale *n* a white toothed whale of arctic waters, related to the dolphin.

whitewood *n* **1** the light-coloured timber of any of various trees. **2** unstained wood; wood prepared for staining.

whither (esp. *old*) *adv* **1** to what place? *whither did they go?* **2** in what direction? towards what state?: *Whither education?* — *conj* or *relative pron* **1** to the, or any, place that; towards which: *went whither he was instructed*; *the mountain pass whither they were headed*. **2** towards which place: *Some miles away lay London, whither they turned their steps next day*. [OE *hwider*]

whiting[1] *n* a small edible fish related to the cod. [MidE *hwitling* or ODut *witinc*]

whiting[2] *n* ground and washed white chalk, used in putty, whitewash and silver-cleaner. [**white**]

whitlow *n* an inflammation of the finger or toe, esp. near the nail. [MidE *whitflawe*, white flaw]

Whitsun *n* Whitsuntide. — *adj* of or relating to Whitsuntide or Whit Sunday.

Whit Sunday or **Whitsunday** *n* in the Christian church, the seventh Sunday after Easter, commemorating the day of Pentecost, on which by tradition those newly baptised wore white robes. [OE *hwita sunnandæg*, white Sunday]

Whitsuntide *n* the week beginning with Whit Sunday.

whittle *v* (*tr*) **1** to cut, carve or pare (a stick, piece of wood, etc.). **2** to shape or fashion by this means. **3** (with **away**) to consume bit by bit, eat away at or erode. **4** (with **down**) to reduce, by cutting something out repeatedly: *whittled down the guest list*. [OE *thwitan*, to cut]

whizz or **whiz** (*coll*) *v* **-zz-** (*intr*) **1** to fly through the air, esp. with a whistling noise. **2** to move fast. — *n* (**at**) an expert.

whizz kid *n* (*coll*) someone who achieves success early, through ability, inventiveness, dynamism or ambition.

who *pron* what person or people?: *Who did you give it to? asked who else he had seen*. — *relative pron* **1** (used to introduce a defining clause; replaceable by **that**) **1** (the person or people) that: *anyone who* (or *that*) *thinks that*; *the lady who* (or *that*) *you were dancing with*. **2** used to add a commenting clause: *Bellini, who was born 190 years ago today*. **3** any (person or people) that; whoever: *Complain who dares!* ◇ See also **whom**. — **who's who** who or what everyone is, esp. everyone important. — *n* a book of brief biographies of famous people. [OE *hwa*]

whoever *relative pron* any person or people that; whomever: *Whoever is appointed* (or *whoever we appoint, whoever the job goes to*) *must face this challenge.* — *pron* **1** no matter who: *Whoever calls, I'm not available.* **2** an emphatic form of **who**: *Whoever told you that?* **3** used to indicate that one does not know who: *St Fiacre, whoever he was.* — **or whoever** (*coll*) or some other such person or people.
whosoever *pron* whoever.
WHO *abbrev* World Health Organisation.
whoa *interj* (used esp. to a horse) stop!
who'd 1 who would. **2** who had.
whodunit or **whodunnit** *n* (*coll*) a detective novel, play, etc.; a mystery. [*Who done it?*, facetiously illiterate for *who did it?*]
whoever. See **who**.
whole *n* **1** all of; not less than. **2** something complete in itself, esp. if consisting of integrated parts: *elements that together form a whole.* — *adj* **1** all of; no less than. **2** in one piece: *swallowed it whole.* **3** unbroken: *only two cups left whole.* **4** (of food) processed as little as possible. **5** (*old*) healthy; well: *the miracle that made him whole.* **6** (*coll*) huge; vast: *a whole pile of work to do.* — *adv* (*coll*) completely; altogether; wholly: *a whole new approach.* — *n* **wholeness**. — **a whole lot** (*coll*) a great deal. — **as a whole** in general; taken as a complete group, etc. rather than as individuals. — **on the whole** considering everything. [OE *hal*, healthy]
wholehearted *adj* sincere and enthusiastic. — *adv* **wholeheartedly**.
wholemeal *adj* **1** (of flour) made from the entire wheat grain. **2** (of bread) made from wholemeal flour.
wholesale *n* the sale of goods in large quantities to a retailer. — *adj* & *adv* **1** of, or by, this type of sale. **2** on a huge scale and without discrimination: *wholesale destruction.* — *n* **wholesaler**. ◇ See also **retail**.
wholesome *adj* **1** attractively healthy: *a wholesome appearance.* **2** promoting health. **3** (esp. *old*) morally beneficial. **4** sensible; prudent: *a wholesome respect for mountains.* — *adv* **wholesomely**. — *n* **wholesomeness**.
wholly *adv* completely; altogether.
whom (used as the object of a verb or preposition; now often replaced by **who**) *pron* what person or people?: *Whom do you want?*; *To whom are you referring?* — *relative pron* **1** (used to introduce a defining clause; replaceable by **that** when not following a preposition) (the person or people) that: *another person whom* (or *that*) *I must thank.* **2** used to add a commenting clause: *her sister, whom secretly she hated.* **3** any (person or people) that; whomever: *to whom it may concern.* [OE *hwam*]
whomever *relative pron* (*old* or *formal*) (used as the object of a verb or preposition) any (person or people) that: *Whomever he asked, agreed.* — *pron* no matter whom: *Whomever they appoint, I'm resigning.*
whomsoever *pron* whomever.
whoop *n* **1** a loud cry of delight, triumph, etc. **2** a noisy indrawn breath typical in whooping cough. — *v* (*intr* & *tr*) to utter, or say with, a whoop. — **whoop it up** (*coll*) to celebrate noisily.
whooping cough *n* an infectious disease, esp. of children, with bouts of violent coughing punctuated by noisy gasps as the breath is drawn in again.
whoopee *interj* expressing exuberant delight. — **make whoopee** to celebrate exuberantly. [**whoop**]
whoops *interj* an exclamation of surprise or concern made when one has a slight accident, makes an error, etc. or sees someone else do so.
whop *v* ***-pp-*** (*tr*; *coll*) **1** to hit; to thrash. **2** to defeat soundly.
whopper (*old coll*) *n* **1** anything very large: *a whopper of a fish.* **2** a lie.
whopping *adj* huge: *a whopping* (*great*) *bill.*
whore *n* (*old offensive*) **1** a prostitute. **2** a sexually immoral or promiscuous woman. — *v* (*intr*; *old vulg*) **1** (of a man) to have sexual relations with prostitutes. **2** (of a woman) to be a prostitute. [OE *hore*]
whorehouse *n* (*old coll*) a brothel.
who're who are.
whorl *n* **1** (*bot*) a ring of leaves round a stem. **2** one of the turns on a spiral shell. **3** (a fingerprint having) a ridge forming a complete circle. [OE *hwyrfel*]
who's 1 who is. **2** who has.
whose *pron* & *adj* belonging to which person or people: *Whose is this jacket? don't know whose these are.* — *relative pron* & *relative adj* **1** (used to introduce a defining clause) of whom or which (the): *children whose parents are divorced*; *buildings whose foundations are sinking.* **2** used to add a commenting clause: *my parents, without whose help I couldn't have succeeded.* **3** (the thing, etc.) of whoever or whichever: *Take whose advice you will.*
why *adv* for what reason: *Why do you ask? said why she was leaving.* — *relative pron* for, or because of, which: *no reason why I should get involved.* — *interj* **1** expressing surprise, indignation, impatience, recognition, etc.: *Why, you little monster!* **2** used to challenge an implied criticism: *Why, have you any objection?* — *n* a reason: *the whys and wherefores.* — **why not** used to make, or agree to, a suggestion: *Why don't you ask her? 'Like a drink?' 'Why not.'* [OE *hwi*]
WI *abbrev* **1** West Indies. **2** Wisconsin. **3** (in Britain) Women's Institute.
wick *n* the string running up through a candle and projecting at the top, that burns when lit and draws up the wax into the flame. — **get on someone's wick** (*slang*) to be a source of irritation to someone. [OE *weoce*]

wicked *adj* **1** evil; sinful; immoral. **2** mischievous; playful; roguish. **3** (*coll*) bad: *wicked weather*. — *adv* **wickedly**. — *n* **wickedness**. [OE *wicca*, wizard]

wicker *adj* (of a fence, basket, etc.) made of interwoven twigs, canes, rushes, etc. [From Scandinavian]

wickerwork *n* articles made of such material.

wicket *n* **1** (*cricket*) a row of three small wooden posts stuck upright in the ground behind either crease; the playing area between these; a batsman's stand at the wicket, or his or her dismissal by the bowler: *45 runs for two wickets*. **2** a small door or gate, esp. one that can open separately within a large door or gate. [OFr *wiket*]

wicket-keeper *n* (*cricket*) the fielder who stands immediately behind the wicket.

wide *adj* **1** large in extent from side to side. **2** measuring a certain amount from side to side. **3** (of eyes) open to the fullest extent. **4** (of a range, selection, etc.) covering a great variety. **5** extensive; widespread: *wide support*. **6** (of a gap) large: *a wide difference*. **7** general, as opposed to particular: *consider the wider implications*. **8** (**of**) off the mark: *His aim was wide* (*of the target*). — *adv* **1** over an extensive area: *travelling far and wide*. **2** to the fullest extent: *with legs wide apart*. **3** (**of**) off the mark: *shot wide* (*of the target*). — *n* (*cricket*) a ball bowled out of the batsman's reach. — *adv* **widely**. — *n* **wideness**. — **wide awake** fully awake or alert. — **wide open 1** open to the fullest extent. **2** (*coll*) vulnerable; exposed to attack. [OE *wid*]

-wide *in cmpds* throughout the extent of: *nationwide support*; *travelled worldwide*.

wide-angle lens *n* a camera lens with an extra-wide range of view.

wide boy *n* (*coll*) a shrewd but dishonest operator in business undertakings.

widen *v* **-n-** (*tr* & *intr*) to make, or become, wide or wider.

wide-ranging *adj* (of interests, discussions, etc.) covering a large variety of subjects or topics.

widespread *adj* **1** extending over a wide area. **2** affecting or involving large numbers of people: *widespread agreement*.

widgeon. See **wigeon**.

widow *n* **1** a woman whose husband is dead and who has not remarried. **2** (*coll*) a woman whose husband spends much time away from her on some esp. sporting pursuit: *golf widows*. — *v* (*tr*) to leave (someone) a widow or widower. [OE *widewe*]

widower *n* a man whose wife is dead, and who has not remarried.

width *n* **1** extent from side to side. **2** wideness. **3** the distance from side to side across a swimming-pool. [**wide**]

widthways *adv* & *adj*: across the width: *folded widthways*.

wield *v* (*tr*) **1** to (lift ready to) use (a tool, weapon, etc.). **2** to have or exert (power, authority, influence, etc.). [OE *wieldan*, to control]

wife *n* ***wives*** **1** the woman to whom a man is married; a married woman. **2** (*old, dialect* or *in cmpds*) a woman: *a housewife*, *fishwife*, etc. [OE *wif*]

wifely *adj* of, or considered suitable to, a wife.

wig *n* an artificial covering of hair for the head. — *adj* **wigged**. [**periwig**]

wigeon or **widgeon** *n* a wild duck of marshy regions.

wigging *n* (*coll*) a scolding. [**wig**[1]]

wiggle *v* (*tr* & *intr*; *coll*) to move, esp. jerkily, from side to side or up and down. — *adj* **wiggly**, ***-ier***, ***-iest***. [Related to OE *wegan*, to move & Dut *wiggelen*, to totter]

wight *n* (*old*) a human creature. [OE *wiht*]

wigwam *n* **1** a domed tent-like N American Indian dwelling made of arched poles covered with skins, bark or mats. **2** often applied to the cone-shaped dwelling more correctly known as a tepee. [Abenaki (N American Indian language) *wikewam*, house]

wild *adj* **1** (of animals) untamed; undomesticated; not dependent on man. **2** (of plants) growing in a natural, uncultivated state. **3** (of country) desolate, rugged, inhospitable or uninhabitable. **4** (of tribes, etc.) savage; uncivilised. **5** unrestrained; uncontrolled: *wild fury*. **6** frantically excited: *The spectators went wild*. **7** distraught: *wild with grief*. **8** dishevelled; disordered: *wild attire*. **9** (of eyes) staring; scared-looking. **10** (of weather) stormy: *a wild night*. **11** (of plans, hopes, schemes, etc.) crazy; impracticable; unrealistic: *succeeded beyond their wildest dreams*. **12** (of a guess) very approximate, or quite random. **13** (with **about**) intensely keen on. **14** (*coll*) furious. **15** (*slang*) enjoyable; terrific. — *n* **1** (with **the**) a wild animal's or plant's natural environment or life in it: *returned the cub to the wild*. **2** (often in *pl*; with **the**) lonely, sparsely inhabited regions away from the city. — *adv* **wildly**. — *n* **wildness**. — **run wild 1** (of a garden or plants) to revert to a wild, overgrown, uncultivated state. **2** (of e.g. children) to live a life of freedom, with little discipline or control. [OE *wilde*]

wild card *n* **1** a competitor lacking the usual or statutory qualifications. **2** (*comput*) a character substitutable for any other in a file.

wildcat *n* a fierce undomesticated variety of cat living in the wild. — *adj* **1** (of an industrial strike) not called or approved by trade union officials. **2** (of a business scheme) financially unsound or risky; speculative. **3** (of an oil well) exploratory; experimental.

wildfire *n* (*hist*) a highly flammable liquid used in warfare. — **spread like wildfire** (of e.g. news, plague, etc.) to spread fast.

wildfowl *n* (*sing* or *pl*) a game bird or game birds, esp. waterfowl. — *n* **wildfowler**. — *n* **wildfowling**.

wild-goose chase *n* a search that is doomed, esp. for reasons unknown to the searcher, to be unsuccessful.

wildlife *n* wild animals, birds and plants in general.

the Wild West *n* (*hist*) the part of the US west of the Mississippi, settled during the 19th cent. and legendary for the adventures of its cattlemen and the struggle to gain territory from the Indian population.

wildebeest *n* **-*beest*** or **-*beests*** a gnu. [Afrikaans, from Dut *wilde*, wild + *beest*, ox]

wilderness *n* **1** an uncultivated or uninhabited region. **2** a desolate, pathless area. **3** an overgrown tangle of weeds, etc. **4** (*hist*) a part of a garden or estate deliberately left wild for romantic effect. **5** any daunting maze. **6** (*politics*) the state of being without office or influence after playing a leading role. — **a voice crying in the wilderness** someone with an important message or warning who goes unheeded. [OE *wilddeor*, wild beast]

wile *n* **1** (in *pl*) charming personal ways. **2** a piece of cunning; a ruse, trick, manoeuvre or stratagem. — *v* (*tr*) **1** (*old*; **away**, etc.) to lure, beguile or entice. **2** (with **away**) to pass (time) pleasantly; to while away. [OE *wil*; related to **guile**]

wilful *adj* **1** deliberate; intentional. **2** headstrong, obstinate or self-willed. — *adv* **wilfully**. — *n* **wilfulness**. [**will**[2]]

will[1] *v* (*aux*) used **1** esp. in the second and third persons, to form a future tense. **2** in the first person, to express intention or determination: *We will not give in.* **3** to make requests: *Please will you shut the door?* **4** to express commands: *You will apologise to your mother immediately!* **5** to indicate ability: *The table will seat ten.* **6** to indicate readiness or willingness: *Any of our branches will exchange the goods. The car simply will not start.* **7** to make an invitation: *Will you have a coffee?* **8** to indicate what is bound to be the case: *Accidents will happen. The experienced teacher will know when a child is unhappy.* **9** to state what applies in certain circumstances: *An unemployed young person living at home will not receive housing benefit.* **10** to express an assumption or probability: *That will be Ted at the door.* **11** to suggest obstinate resistance to advice: *She will leave her clothes on the floor.* **12** to mean 'will be so good' or 'wish': *Consider, if you will...*; *Make what you will of that.* ◇ See also **shall, won't**. [OE *wyllan*]

will[2] *n* **1** the power of conscious decision and deliberate choice of action: *free will*; *exercise one's will.* **2** (one's determination in effecting) one's own preferences: *a clash of wills*; *I did it against my will.* **3** desire or determination: *the will to live.* **4** a wish or desire: *What is your will?* **5** (a document containing) one's instructions for the disposal of one's property, etc. after one's death. **6** one's feeling towards someone else: *felt no ill-will towards her.* — *v* (*tr*) **1** to try to compel by, or as if by, exerting one's will: *willed herself to keep going.* **2** (**formal**) to desire, request and expect (that something will be done, etc.): *Her Majesty wills it.* **3** to bequeath in one's will. — **at will** as and when one wishes. — **with a will** eagerly; enthusiastically. — **with the best will in the world** (with a *negative*) no matter how willing one is or how hard one tries. [OE *willa*]

willpower *n* the determination, persistence and self-discipline needed to accomplish something.

willies *n* (*pl*; *coll*; with **the**) a feeling of fear.

willing *adj* **1** ready, glad, or not disinclined (to do something). **2** eager and cooperative. **3** voluntarily given. — *adv* **willingly**. — *n* **willingness**. [**will**[2]]

will-o'-the-wisp *n* **1** a phosphorescence sometimes seen over marshes, caused by the combustion of marsh gas. **2** something elusive, such as an unattainable goal. [Literally 'Will of the torch']

willow *n* **1** a tree with slender pliant branches. **2** its wood, used e.g. to make cricket bats, basketwork, etc. [OE *welig*]

willow herb *n* a plant with willow-like leaves and purple flowers.

willow pattern *n* a design used on pottery, usu. in blue on a white background, showing a Chinese landscape with a willow tree, bridge, and figures.

willowy *adj* (of a person, esp. a woman) slender, lithe and graceful.

willy or **willie** *n* **-*ies*** (*coll*, esp. *childish*) a penis.

willy-nilly *adv* whether one wishes or not; regardless. [Orig. *will I, nill I* (or *will ye, he*, etc.), will I, will I not]

wilt *v* (*intr*) **1** (of flowers) to droop or wither, e.g. from heat or lack of water. **2** to droop from fatigue or heat. **3** to lose courage or confidence. — *n* a plant disease causing wilting. [Variant of *wilk*, to wither]

Wilts. *abbrev* Wiltshire.

wily *adj* **-*ier***, **-*iest*** cunning. — *n* **wiliness**. [**wile**]

win *v* **-*nn*-**, ***won*** **1** (*tr* & *intr*) to be victorious, come first, or beat one's opponent or rivals in (a contest, race, conflict, war, bet, election, etc.). **2** (*tr*) to compete or fight for, and obtain (a victory, prize, etc.). **3** (*tr*) to obtain by struggle or effort: *win someone's heart, a contract*, etc. **4** (*tr*) to earn and get: *win respect.* **5** (*tr*; *old*) to gain the hand of in marriage: *wooed and won her.* **6** (*tr*) to secure for: *Her dazzling smile won her the part.* **7** (*intr* with **through, out**) to be successful, or succeed in getting somewhere, after a struggle. — *n* a victory or success. — *n* **winner.** — **you can't win** there's no way to succeed, please someone, etc. — *v* **win over** or **round** (*tr*) to persuade over to one's side or one's opinion. [OE *winnan*]

winning *adj* **1** attractive or charming: *a winning smile.* **2** securing victory: *the winning shot.* — *n* (in *pl*) money won, esp. in gambling. — *adv* **winningly**.

winning-post *n* (esp. *horse-racing*) the post marking the point where a race finishes.

wince *v* (*intr*) to shrink back, start or grimace, e.g. in pain or anticipation of it; to flinch. — *n* a start or grimace in reaction to pain, etc. [OFr *wencier*, *guenchier*]

winceyette *n* a soft cotton cloth with a raised brushed surface on both sides. [Scot *wincey*, linen or cotton cloth with a mixture of wool]

winch *n* **1** a drum-shaped roller round which a rope or chain is wound for hoisting or hauling heavy loads; a windlass. **2** a crank or handle for setting a wheel, axle or machinery in motion. — *v* (*tr*; **up**, **in**) to hoist or haul with a winch. [OE *wince*]

wind[1] *n* **1** a current of air moving or blowing from any direction across the earth's surface. **2** a current of air produced artificially, by a fan, etc. **3** an influence that seems to pervade events: *a wind of change.* **4** one's breath or breath supply: *short of wind.* **5** (wind carrying) the scent of game, or, for animals, the scent of a hunter or predator. **6** a hint, suggestion, suspicion or intimation of something: *if the Press gets wind of this deal.* **7** gas built up in the intestines; flatulence. **8** empty, pompous or trivial talk. **9** the wind instruments of an orchestra; their players. — *v* (*tr*) to deprive of breath temporarily: *winded by her fall.* — **before the wind** (of a ship) (sailing) with the wind coming from behind it. — **break wind** to discharge intestinal gas through the anus. — **down wind from** receiving, or liable to receive, air laden with the smell, pollutants, etc., from. — **get** (or **put**) **the wind up** (*coll*) to become (or make) anxious or alarmed. — **get one's second wind** to recover breath after initial exertion sufficiently to carry on with ease. — **in the wind** about to happen. — **like the wind** swiftly. — **sail close to the wind** to be in danger of going beyond an approved limit. — **see which way the wind blows** to assess current opinions, likely developments, etc. — **take the wind out of someone's sails** to thwart someone's confident progress; to deflate or humble someone. [OE]

windbag *n* (*coll*) a person full of pompous, tedious or trivial talk.

wind band *n* a musical ensemble made up of wind instruments.

windbreak *n* a barrier, e.g. in the form of a fence or line of trees, giving protection from the wind.

windcheater *n* a windproof jacket usu. of close-woven fabric.

windchill *n* the extra chill given to air temperature by the wind.

wind cone *n* a windsock.

windfall *n* **1** a fruit, esp. an apple, blown down from its tree. **2** an unexpected financial gain, or other piece of good fortune.

wind farm *n* a place where electricity is generated by wind power.

wind instrument *n* a musical instrument such as a clarinet, flute or trumpet, played by blowing air through it.

windjammer *n* (*hist*) a large fast merchant sailing-ship.

windmill *n* **1** a mill for grinding grain, or a machine for pumping water or generating electricity, operated by wind-driven sails or vanes. **2** a toy with a set of plastic or paper sails mounted on a stick, that revolve in the wind. — **tilt at windmills** to attack imaginary foes.

windpipe *n* the passage running from the back of the throat to the lungs, through which air is drawn into, and expelled from, the body; the trachea.

wind power *n* wind used as a driving force or source of energy.

windscreen *n* the front window of a motor vehicle.

windshield *n* (esp. *NAm*) a windscreen.

windsock *n* an open-ended cone of fabric flying from a mast, e.g. at an airport, showing the direction and speed of the wind.

windsurfing *n* the sport of riding the waves on a sailboard; sailboarding.

windswept *adj* **1** exposed to strong winds. **2** dishevelled from, or otherwise showing the effects of, exposure to the wind.

wind tunnel *n* a tunnel-like chamber inside which models are exposed to a steady airstream, used for gauging the effects of wind pressure on aircraft, etc.

windward *n* & *adj* (the side of a boat, etc.) facing the wind.

windy *adj* ***-ier***, ***-iest*** **1** exposed to, or characterised by, strong wind: *a windy place*, *day*, etc. **2** (*coll*) (of speech or writing) long-winded or pompous. **3** (*coll*) nervous; uneasy.

wind[2] *v* ***wound*** **1** (*tr* & *intr*; **round**, **up**) to wrap or coil, or be wrapped or coiled. **2** (*intr* & *tr*) to progress on a path with many twists and turns: *winding lanes*; *The procession wound its way through the streets.* **3** (*tr*; **up**) to tighten the spring of (a clock, watch or other clockwork device) by turning a knob or key. — *n* **winder**. — *v* **wind down 1** (*tr*) to lower (e.g. a vehicle window) by turning a handle. **2** (*intr*) (of a clock or clockwork device) to slow down and stop working. **3** (*tr*) to reduce the activities and number of employees of (a business). **4** (*intr*) to get rid of built-up tension; to relax gradually; to unwind. — *v* **wind up 1** (*tr*) to tighten the spring of (a clock or clockwork device). **2** (*tr*) to raise (e.g. a vehicle window) by turning a handle. **3** (*tr*) to close down (a business). **4** (*tr*) to bring to a close or conclusion. **5** (*tr*) to make tense, nervous or excited: *all wound up*. **6** (*tr*; *coll*) to taunt or tease. **7** (*intr*; *coll*) to end up: *wind up in jail*. [OE *windan*]

winding-sheet *n* a sheet for wrapping a corpse in; a shroud.

windlass *n* a drum-shaped axle round which a rope or chain is wound for hauling or hoisting weights. [Norse *windass*, from *vinda*, to wind + *ass*, beam]

window *n* **1** a opening in a wall to look out through, or let in light and air; a wooden or metal frame fitted with panes of glass for placing in such an opening; a pane. **2** the area behind a shop's window, in which to display goods on sale: *the skirt in the window*. **3** a glass-covered opening e.g. at a railway, theatre, etc., at which to purchase one's ticket. **4** a gap in a schedule, etc. available for some purpose. [Norse *windauga*, literally 'wind eye']

window box *n* a box fitted along an exterior window ledge, for growing plants in.

window-dressing *n* **1** the art of arranging goods in a shop window. **2** the art or practice of giving something superficial appeal by skilful presentation.

window-shopping *n* the activity of eyeing goods in shop windows as the next-best thing to buying them.

windowsill or **window ledge** *n* the interior or exterior ledge running along the bottom of a window.

wine *n* **1** an alcoholic drink made from the fermented juice of grapes, or one made from other fruits, plants, etc. **2** the dark red colour of red wine. [OE *win*, from Lat *vinum*]

winebibber *n* (*old*) someone who drinks wine to excess.

wine cellar *n* **1** a cellar in which to store wines. **2** the stock of wine stored there.

wine glass *n* a drinking-glass typically consisting of a bowl on a stem, with a wide base flaring out from the stem.

wineskin (*hist*) the skin of a goat or sheep sewn up and used for holding wine.

winy *adj* **-ier**, **-iest** having a wine-like flavour.

wing *n* **1** one of the arm-like limbs of a bird or bat that are adapted for flying; an insect's similar flying-organ. **2** one of the similar structures projecting from either side of an aircraft body. **3** any of the corner sections of a vehicle body, forming covers for the wheels. **4** a part of a building projecting from the central or main section. **5** the left or right flank of an army or fleet in battle formation. **6** (*football*, etc.) either edge of the pitch, or the player at either extreme of the forward line. **7** (in *pl*) the area at each side of a stage, where performers wait to enter, out of sight of the audience. **8** a group with its own distinct views and character, within a political party or other body. **9** in the Royal Air Force, a unit consisting of several squadrons. **10** (in *pl*; *literary*) a miraculous surge of speed: *Fear lent him wings*. — *v* (*tr*) **1** to wound in the wing, arm or shoulder; to wound superficially. **2** (*tr*) to make (one's way) by flying. **3** (*tr*; esp. *poetic*) to fly over, or skim lightly. **4** (*tr*) to send (e.g. an arrow) swiftly on its way. — *adj* **wingless**. — **in the wings** waiting for one's turn to perform. — **on the wing** flying; in flight. — **spread one's wings 1** to use one's potential fully. **2** to escape from a confining environment in order to do this. — **take wing** to fly off. — **under someone's wing** under someone's protection or guidance. [Norse *vængre*]

wing chair *n* an armchair that has a high back with forward-projecting lugs.

wing commander *n* in the Royal Air Force, (an officer of) the rank below group captain.

winger *n* (esp. *football*) a player in wing position.

wing nut *n* a nut (sense **2**) with flattened projections for easy turning by finger and thumb.

wingspan *n* the distance from tip to tip of the wings of an aircraft, or a bird's wings when outstretched.

wink *v* (*intr* & *tr*; **at**) to shut (an eye) briefly as a form of informal communication with someone, esp. as a conspiratorial signal. **2** (*intr* with **at**) to ignore (e.g. an offence or improper procedure) deliberately; to pretend not to notice. **3** (of lights, stars, etc.) to flicker or twinkle. — *n* an act of winking. — **tip (someone) the wink** to give (someone) a useful hint, valuable information, etc., esp. discreetly. [OE *wincian*]

forty winks *n* (*pl*; *coll*) a short sleep.

winker *n* (*old coll*) a flashing direction-indicator on a motor vehicle.

winkle *n* a small edible snail-shaped shellfish; a periwinkle. — *v* (*tr* with **out**) to force or prise out. [**periwinkle**[2]]

winkle-picker *n* (*coll*) a shoe with a long narrow pointed toe.

winnow *v* (*tr*) **1** to separate chaff from (grain) by blowing a current of air through it or fanning it. **2** (with **out, from**, etc.) to blow (chaff) from grain; to identify and reject (what is unwanted) from a group or mass. **3** to sift (evidence, etc.). [OE *windwian*, from *wind*, wind]

wino *n* **-os** (*slang*) someone, esp. a down-and-out, addicted to cheap wine. [**wine**]

winsome *adj* (esp. *old*) charming; captivating. — *adv* **winsomely**. — *n* **winsomeness**. [OE *wynsum*, joyous]

winter *n* the coldest season of the year, coming between autumn and spring. — *adj* of or belonging to winter. — *v* **-r-** (*intr*; **at, in**) to spend winter somewhere, esp. somewhere warm. [OE]

wintergreen *n* **1** an evergreen plant from which an aromatic oil, used medicinally and as a flavouring, is obtained. **2** this oil.

winter sports *n* (*pl*) sports held on snow or ice, e.g. skiing and tobogganing.

wintertime *n* the season of winter.

wintry *adj* **-ier**, **-iest** **1** (of weather, etc.) of, like, or characteristic of, winter. **2** unfriendly, cold or hostile: *a wintry expression.* — *n* **wintriness**.

winy. See **wine**.

wipe *v* (*tr*) **1** to clean or dry with a cloth, on a mat, etc. **2** to dry (dishes). **3** (**off**, **away**) to remove by wiping. **4** (*comput*, *audio* or *video*) to erase (material) from a tape or disk; to erase material from (a tape or disk). **5** to remove or get rid of: *wiped the incident from his memory.* **6** to pass (a cloth, etc.) over, or rub (a liquid, etc.) on to, a surface. — *v* **wipe out** (*tr*) **1** to clean out the inside of. **2** to remove or get rid of: *wipe out the memory.* **3** to destroy or obliterate. [OE *wipian*]

wiper *n* (also **windscreen-wiper**) a mechanical arm that swings to and fro across a vehicle windscreen for clearing it.

wire *n* **1** metal drawn out into a narrow flexible strand. **2** a length of this, usu. wrapped in insulating material, used for carrying an electric current. **3** (sometimes in *pl*) the cable connecting point with point in a telecommunications system. **4** a telegram or telegraph. **5** a fence, barrier, etc. made of wire; wire netting. — *v* (*tr*) **1** to send a telegram to; to send (a message) by telegram. **2** (**up**) to fit up or connect up (an electrical apparatus, system, etc.) with wires. **3** (**up**) to fasten or secure with wire. — **get one's wires crossed** to get things confused. [OE *wir*]

wire-haired *adj* (of a dog breed) having a coarse, usu. wavy coat.

wireless *n* (*old*) **1** a radio. **2** wireless telegraphy. [**wire** + **-less**]

wireless telegraphy *n* the transmission of signals by means of electromagnetic waves.

wire netting *n* wires twisted into network for use as fencing, etc.

wiretap *v* **-pp-** (*tr*) to tap (a telephone) or the telephone of.

wire wool *n* a mass of fine wire used for scouring.

wireworm *n* the hard-bodied worm-like larva of certain beetles, destructive to plant roots.

wiring *n* the (arrangement of) electrical wires used in a circuit or system.

wiry *adj* **-ier**, **-iest** **1** of slight build, but strong and agile. **2** resembling wire; (of hair) coarse and wavy.

Wis. *abbrev* Wisconsin.

wisdom *n* **1** the ability to make sensible judgements and decisions, esp. on the basis of one's knowledge and experience; prudence and common sense. **2** learning; knowledge. **3** the weight of informed opinion: *the current wisdom on whether or not to smack children.* **4** (*old*) wise sayings. [OE]

wisdom tooth *n* any of the last four molar teeth to come through, at the back of each side of the upper and lower jaw.

wise[1] *adj* **1** having or showing wisdom; prudent; sensible. **2** learned. **3** astute; shrewd; sagacious. **4** (*in cmpds*) knowing the ways of: *streetwise*; *worldly-wise.* — *adv* **wisely**. ◇ See also **wisdom**. — **be** (or **get**, or **put**) **wise to** (*coll*) to be (or become, or make) aware of. — **none the wiser** knowing no more than before. — *v* **wise up** (*intr*) to find out the facts about something. [OE *wis*]

wisecrack *n* a smart, clever, knowing remark.

wise guy *n* (*coll*) someone full of smart comments; a know-all.

wise man *n* (*old*) **1** a wizard. **2** one of the Magi.

wise[2] *n* (*old*) way: *in no wise to blame.* [OE *wise*, manner]

-wise[1] *in cmpds* **1** denoting direction or manner: *lengthwise*; *clockwise*; *likewise*; *otherwise.* **2** as regards: *money-wise*; *business-wise.* [**wise**[2]]

-wise[2]. See **wise**[1] (sense **4**).

wiseacre *n* (*derog*) someone who assumes an air of superior wisdom. [ODut *wijsegghe*r, soothsayer]

wish *v* **1** (*tr*) to want; used esp. in expressing one's desire. **2** (*tr*) to desire, esp. vainly or helplessly (that something were the case): *I wish you'd sit still. I wish I'd known.* **3** (*intr* with **for**) to long, esp. vainly, for: *often wished for a quieter life.* **4** (*intr*; **for**) to make a wish (sense **4**): *wished for a new bicycle.* **5** (*tr*) to express a desire for (luck, success, happiness, etc.) to come to: *wish you all the best.* **6** (*tr*) to say (good afternoon, etc.) to: *wished them good day.* **7** (*tr* with **on**; with a *negative*) to desire (something) to be inflicted on: *wouldn't wish it on my worst enemy.* **8** (*tr*; *coll*) to impose or inflict: *expect she'll wish herself on us for Christmas.* — *n* **1** a desire. **2** (esp. in *pl*) what one wants to be done, etc. **3** (in *pl*) a hope expressed for someone's welfare: *best wishes to your parents.* **4** in fairy tales, traditional ritual, etc., the stating of a desire in expectation or hope of its being magically fulfilled: *make a wish.* — **wish someone joy of** (*ironic*) to hope someone has pleasure or satisfaction from (something one is glad one does not have). [OE *wyscan*]

wishbone *n* a V-shaped bone in the breast of poultry.

wishful thinking *n* an over-optimistic expectation that something will happen, arising from one's desire that it should.

wishy-washy *adj* **1** (of e.g. colours) insipidly pale. **2** characterless; insipid. **3** watery; weak. [**wash**]

wisp *n* **1** a strand; a thin fine tuft or shred. **2** something slight or insubstantial: *a wisp of a child.* — *adj* **wispy**, **-ier**, **-iest**.

wistful *adj* sadly or vainly yearning. — *adv* **wistfully**. — *n* **wistfulness**. [Old word *wist*, intent]

wit[1] *n* **1** humour; the ability to express oneself amusingly. **2** a person with this ability. **3** humorous speech or writing. **4** (in *sing* or *pl*) common sense; intelligence; resourcefulness. — **at one's wits' end** (*coll*) reduced to despair; utterly at a loss. — **have** or **keep one's wits about one** to be, or stay, alert. — **live by one's wits** to live by cunning. — **scared**, etc. **out of one's wits** frantic with terror. [OE, mind, thought]

wit[2]: **to wit** (*old* or *legal*) that is to say; namely. [OE *witan*, to know]

witch *n* **1** a person, esp. a woman, supposed to have magical powers used usually, but not always, malevolently. **2** a frighteningly ugly or wicked old woman. **3** a dangerously or irresistibly fascinating woman. [OE *wicca*]

witchcraft *n* magic or sorcery of the kind practised by witches.

witch doctor *n* a member of a tribal society who is believed to have magic powers, and to be able to cure or harm people by means of them.

witchery *n* **1** the activities of witches. **2** a bewitching or spellbinding influence; fascination.

witch hunt *n* the hunting down and persecution of an individual or number of individuals, for alleged political or other types of heresy, behaviour considered dangerous to society, etc.

witch hazel *n* **1** a N American shrub with narrow-petalled yellow flowers, from whose bark an astringent lotion is produced, used to treat bruises, etc. **2** another name for wych-elm. [OE *wice*]

with *prep* **1** in the company of: *went with her*. **2** used after verbs of partnering, co-operating, associating, etc.: *danced with him*, *plays with Arsenal*, etc. **3** used after verbs of mixing: *mingled with the crowd*. **4** by means of; using: *raised it with a crowbar*. **5** used after verbs of covering, filling, etc.: *plastered with mud*; *filled with rubbish*. **6** used after verbs of providing: *equipped with firearms*. **7** as a result of: *shaking with fear*. **8** bearing; announcing: *rang with bad news*. **9** in the same direction as: *drift with the current*. **10** at the same time or rate as: *Discretion comes with age*. **11** used after verbs of conflict: *quarrelled with her brother*; *clashes with the curtains*. **12** used after verbs of agreeing, disagreeing and comparing: *compared with last year*; *agrees* (or *disagrees*) *with the evidence*. **13** used in describing: *a man with a limp*. **14** used in stating manner: *won with ease*, *answered with a nod*, etc. **15** because of having: *With your talents, you'll surely get the job*. **16** in spite of having: *With all his money he's still unhappy*. **17** in (the specified circumstances): *I can't go abroad with my mother so ill*. **18** featuring; starring: *'Treasure Island' with Robert Newton*. **19** in the care of: *left it with the porter*. **20** used after verbs of parting: *parted with her sadly*, *dispensed with his crutches*, etc. **21** regarding: *What shall we do with this? can't do a thing with my hair*; *What's wrong with you?* **22** used after adverbs and adverbial phrases in exclamations expressing a wish or order: *Down with tyranny! Into bed with you!* **23** (*coll*) understanding: *Are you with me?* **24** loyal to; supporting: *We're with you all the way*. — **with it** (*old coll*) fashionable; trendy. — **with that** at that point; thereupon. [OE]

withal (*old*) *adv* **1** as well; into the bargain. **2** for all that; nevertheless. — *prep* with: *flesh to bait fish withal*. [**with** + **all**]

withdraw *v* ***-drew***, ***-drawn*** **1** (*intr*) to move somewhere else, esp. more secluded: *withdrew into her bedroom*. **2** (*tr* & *intr*) (of troops) to move back; to (order to) retreat. **3** (*tr*) to pull in or back: *withdrew his head into the carriage*; *withdrew her hand from his*. **4** (*tr*) to take (money) from a bank account for use. **5** (*intr* & *tr*) to back out or pull out of an activity: *withdrew from the contest*. **6** (*tr*) to take back, or say that one doesn't mean (what one has said): *I withdraw that remark*. **7** (*intr* with **from**) to stop oneself taking (a drug to which one is addicted). **8** (*intr*) to become uncommunicative or unresponsive. **9** (*tr*) to discontinue or cancel: *withdraw a service*, *offer*, etc. [**with** (= away from) + **draw**]

withdrawal *n* **1** the act or process of withdrawing. **2** a removal of money from a bank account. **3** the breaking of a drug addiction, with associated discomfort. **4** a retreat into silence and self-absorption.

withdrawn *adj* unresponsive, shy or reserved.

withhold, within, without, withstand see separate entries.

withe *n* a pliable branch or twig, esp. from the willow tree. [OE *withthe*]

wither *v* ***-r-*** (*intr* & *tr*) **1** (of plants) to (cause to) fade, dry up and die. **2** to (cause to) fade and disappear: *Love that never withers*. **3** to (cause to) shrivel and decay: *withered old bodies*. [Possibly variant of **weather**]

withered *adj* (of a limb) thin and stunted, from illness, etc.

withering *adj* (of a glance, remark, etc.) such as makes one shrivel up; bitterly contemptuous.

withers *n* (*pl*) the ridge between the shoulder blades of a horse. [Older *wither*, against]

withhold *v* ***-held*** (*tr*) to refuse to give or grant; to hold back: *withhold evidence*, *permission*, *payment*, etc. [**with** (=away from) + **hold**]

within *prep* **1** inside; enclosed by: *within these four walls*; *circles within circles*. **2** not outside the limits of; not beyond: *live within one's means*; *within sight*, *earshot*, *reach*. **3** in less than (a certain time or distance):

finished within a week; *within a hair's breadth of death*. — *adv* (esp. *old*) inside: *Apply within*; *a voice from within*. [OE *withinnan*]

without *prep* **1** not having the company of: *went home without him*. **2** deprived of: *can't live without her*. **3** not having: *a blue sky without a cloud*. **4** lacking: *books without covers*. **5** not (behaving as expected or in a particular way): *answered without smiling*; *did it without being told*. **6** not giving, showing, etc.: *complied without a murmur*. **7** not encountering (some expected circumstance): *managed without difficulty*, *without anyone getting hurt*, etc. **8** not having (something required); in neglect of (a usual procedure): *entered without permission*; *imprisoned without trial*. **9** not using; not having the help of: *opened it without a key*. **10** if it had not been for: *would have died without their help*. **11** (*old*) outside: *without the walls*. — *adv* (*old*) outside. [OE *withutan*]

withstand *v* (*tr*) to resist or brave: *withstand storms*, *insults*, etc. [OE *withstandan*]

withy *n* **-*ies*** a withe.

witless *adj* **1** stupid; brainless. **2** crazy. [**wit**[1]]

witness *n* **1** someone who sees, and can therefore give a direct account of, an event, occurrence, etc. **2** a person who gives evidence in a court of law. **3** a person who adds his or her own signature to confirm the genuineness of a signature just put on a document, etc. **4** (something that is) proof or evidence of anything. — *v* **1** (*tr*) to be present as an observer at (an event, etc.). **2** (*tr*) to add one's own signature to confirm the genuineness of (a signature on a document, etc.). **3** (*tr*) (of a period or place) to be the setting for, or (of a person) to live through (certain events): *a century that witnessed great medical advances*. **4** (*tr* & *intr*; **to**) to confirm: *will witness* (*to*) *his instability*. — *prep* as shown by: *Doctors can't cure everything, witness their helplessness over AIDS*. — **bear witness (to)** to be evidence; to give confirmation: *a chaotic mess that bore witness to the struggle*; *was at home all evening, as my husband will bear witness*. — **be witness to** to be in a position to observe: *have never before been witness to such cruelty*. [OE *witnes*, from *witan*, to know]

witness-box or **-stand** *n* the enclosed stand from which a witness gives evidence in a court of law.

witticism *n* a witty remark. [**witty**]

witty *adj* **-*ier***, **-*iest*** able to express oneself cleverly and amusingly. — *adv* **wittily**. — *n* **wittiness**. [**wit**[1]]

wittingly *adv* knowingly; consciously. [OE *witan*, to know]

wives . See **wife**.

wizard *n* **1** a man supposed to have magic powers; a magician or sorcerer. **2** (*coll*; **at**, **with**) a person extraordinarily skilled in some way. — *adj* (*old coll*) marvellous. [MidE *wisard*, from *wis*, wise]

wizened *adj* shrivelled or wrinkled, esp. with age. [OE *wisnian*, to dry up]

woad *n* **1** a plant from whose leaves a blue dye is obtained. **2** this dye used by ancient Britons to paint their bodies. [OE *wad*]

wobble *v* **1** (*intr* & *tr*) to (cause to) rock, sway or shake unsteadily. **2** (*intr*) (of the voice) to be unsteady. **3** (*intr*) to be undecided; to waver. — *n* a wobbling, rocking or swaying motion. [Ger *wabbeln*]

wobbly *adj* **-*ier***, **-*iest*** unsteady; shaky. — *n* **wobbliness**.

wodge *n* (*coll*) a lump, wad or chunk. [**wedge**]

woe *n* **1** grief; misery. **2** affliction; calamity. — *interj* (*old*) an exclamation of grief. — **woe betide** (*old* or *facet*) may evil befall, or evil will befall (whoever offends in some specified way). — **woe is me** (*old* or *facet*) alas! [OE *wa*]

woebegone *adj* dismally sorrowful. [*begone*, surrounded]

woeful *adj* **1** mournful; sorrowful. **2** causing woe. **3** disgraceful; pitiful. — *adv* **woefully**. — *n* **woefulness**.

wog *n* (*Br offensive slang*) any non-white person. [Perhaps **golliwog**]

wok *n* an almost hemispherical pan used in Chinese cookery. [Southern Chin]

woke, **woken**. See **wake**.

wold *n* a tract of open rolling upland. [OE *wald*, *weald*, forest]

wolf *n* ***wolves*** **1** a wild animal of the dog family, a predator that hunts in packs. **2** (*coll*) a man with an insatiable appetite for sexual conquests. — *v* (*tr*; **down**; *coll*) to gobble greedily. — *adj* **wolfish**. — *adv* **wolfishly**. — **cry wolf** to give a false alarm. — **keep the wolf from the door** to ward off hunger. — **wolf in sheep's clothing** someone who behind a bland exterior is dangerously unscrupulous. [OE]

wolfcub *n* **1** a young wolf. **2** (*cap*; *old*) a Cub Scout.

wolfsbane see separate entry.

wolf whistle *n* a whistle usu. directed at a woman by a man, as a coarse expression of admiration for her appearance.

wolfram *n* tungsten, or the ore containing it. [Ger]

wolfsbane *n* a poisonous yellow-flowered plant; the aconite.

wolverine *n* a large carnivorous animal of the weasel family, found in the forests of N America, Europe and Asia. [**wolf**]

woman *n* ***women*** **1** an adult human female. **2** women generally. **3** one's wife or girlfriend. **4** (*old* or *condescending*) a female servant or domestic daily help. **5** feminine instincts: *The woman in her longed for a child*. — *adj* female: *a woman doctor*. [OE *wifman*, from *wif*, wife + *man*, man, human]

-woman *in cmpds* **1** a woman performing a specified job: *a needlewoman*, *charwoman*, *chairwoman, policewoman*, etc. **2** a woman of a specified place or nationality: *a Frenchwoman.*

womanhood *n* **1** the state of being a woman; female adulthood. **2** womankind.

womanise or **-ize** *v* (*intr; coll derog*) (of a man) to frequent the company of, or have casual affairs with, women. — *n* **womaniser**.

womanish *adj* (*derog*) **1** associated with women. **2** (of a man, his behaviour or appearance) effeminate; unmanly.

womankind *n* women generally.

womanly *adj* **1** feminine. **2** considered natural or suitable to a woman. — *n* **womanliness**.

womenfolk *n* (*pl*) **1** women generally. **2** the female members of a family or society. **3** a man's female relations.

women's liberation *n* a movement, started by women, aimed at freeing them from the disadvantages they suffer in a male-dominated society.

womb *n* **1** the uterus, the organ in female mammals in which the young develop till birth. **2** a place of origin: *the womb of civilisation.* **3** (*literary*) a deep dark centre: *in the womb of the earth.* [OE *wamb*]

wombat *n* a burrowing Australian herbivorous marsupial. [Dharuk (Australian Aboriginal language) *wambat*]

women. See **woman**.

won. See **win**.

wonder *n* **1** the state of mind produced by something extraordinary, new or unexpected; amazement; awe. **2** something that is a cause of awe, amazement or bafflement; a marvel. — *adj* notable for accomplishing marvels: *a wonder drug.* — *v* **-r-** **1** (*tr & intr*) to be curious: *often wondered about her background.* **2** (*tr & intr*; **at**) to be surprised: *shouldn't wonder if she won; hardly to be wondered at.* **3** (*tr & intr*; **about**) to be uncertain or undecided: *wonder whether to go.* **4** (*tr*) used politely to introduce requests: *I wonder if you could help me?* — *n* **wonderment**. — **do** or **work wonders** to achieve marvellous results. — **no, little** or **small wonder** I'm not surprised. [OE *wundor*]

wonderful *adj* **1** arousing wonder; extraordinary. **2** excellent; splendid. — *adv* **wonderfully**.

wonderland *n* **1** an imaginary place full of marvels. **2** a scene of strange unearthly beauty.

wondrous *adj* wonderful, strange or awesome. — *adv* **wondrously**. [**wonder**]

wonky *adj* **-ier**, **-iest** (*coll*) unsound, unsteady, wobbly, crooked or ill-made.

wont (esp. *old*) *adj* habitually inclined, or accustomed. — *n* **1** a habit that one has: *It was her wont to rise early.* [OE *gewunod*, accustomed]

wonted *adj* customary: *with none of his wonted cheerfulness.*

won't will not.

woo *v* **woos**, **wooed** (*tr*) **1** (esp. *old*) (of a man) to try to win the love of (a woman) esp. in the hope of marrying her. **2** to try to win the support of: *woo the voters.* **3** to pursue or seek (fame, success, fortune, etc.). — *n* **wooer**. [OE *wogian*]

wood *n* **1** the material of which the trunk and branches of trees are composed; this used in building, for making furniture, etc., or as a fuel; timber; firewood. **2** (in *sing* or *pl*) an expanse of growing trees. **3** a golf club whose head is made of wood. **4** (*bowls*) a bowl. **5** casks or barrels made of wood, for wine or beer: *matured in wood.* — *adj* made of, or using, wood. — **not see the wood for the trees** to be so overwhelmed, or so over-concerned, with detail as to fail to see the obvious or general point. — **out of the woods** free at last of trouble or danger. — **touch wood** (usu. as *interj*) to touch something wooden as a superstitious guard against bad luck: *no problems so far, touch wood!* [OE *wudu*]

wood alcohol *n* methanol.

woodcock *n* a long-billed game bird related to the snipe, but with a bulkier body and shorter, stronger legs.

woodcut *n* a design cut into a wooden block, or a print taken from it.

woodcutter *n* a person who fells trees and chops wood.

wooded *adj* (of land) covered with trees.

wooden *adj* **1** made of wood. **2** (of an actor, performance, etc.) stiff, unnatural and inhibited; lacking expression and liveliness. — *adv* **woodenly**. — *n* **woodenness**.

wooden-headed *adj* dull-witted; unintelligent.

wooden spoon *n* a booby prize.

woodland *n* (often in *pl*) land largely covered with woods.

woodlouse *n* **-lice** an insect-like creature with a grey, oval, plated body, found in damp places, under stones, bark, etc.

woodpecker *n* a bird with a long, strong, sharp beak with which it bores into tree bark searching for insects to eat.

wood pigeon *n* a common pigeon of the woods, with a white marking round its neck; the ring dove.

wood pulp *n* crushed wood fibres used in paper-making.

woodwind *n* orchestral wind instruments made, or formerly made, of wood, including the flute, oboe, clarinet and bassoon; the section of the orchestra composed of these.

woodwork *n* **1** the art of making things out of wood; carpentry. **2** the wooden parts of any structure.

woodworm *n* **-worm** or **-worms** the larva of any of several beetles, that bores into wood.

woody *adj* **-ier**, **-iest** **1** (of countryside) wooded. **2** composed of wood: *plants with woody stems.*

woody nightshade *n* a purple-flowered climbing plant with poisonous red berries.
woodbine *n* honeysuckle. [OE *wudubinde*]
woodchuck *n* a N American marmot. [Cree (N American Indian language) *otchek*, marten]
woodruff *n* a white-flowered, sweet-smelling plant. [OE *wuduroffe*]
woof[1] *n* the sound of a dog's bark. — *v* (*intr*) to give a bark. [Imit.]
woofer *n* (*audio*) a large loudspeaker for reproducing low-frequency sounds. ◇ See also **tweeter**.
woof[2] *n* (*weaving*) the weft. [MidE *oof*, with *w* added by association with **weft** and **warp**]
wool *n* **1** the soft wavy hair of sheep and certain other animals. **2** this spun into yarn for knitting or weaving. **3** fluffy, curly or tangled material resembling this: *steel wool*. — *adj* made of, or relating to, wool. — **pull the wool over someone's eyes** (*coll*) to deceive someone. [OE *wull*]
wool-gathering *n* absent-mindedness; day-dreaming.
woollen *adj* **1** made of wool. **2** producing, or dealing in, goods made of wool: *woollen manufacturers, merchants*, etc. — *n* **1** (often in *pl*) a woollen, esp. knitted, garment. **2** a woollen fabric.
woolly *adj* **-ier, -iest** **1** made of wool, like wool, or covered with wool or wool-like fibres, etc.; fluffy and soft. **2** vague and muddled: *woolly thinking*; *woolly-minded*. — *n* (*coll*) a woollen, usu. knitted garment. — *n* **woolliness**.
woolsack *n* the seat of the Lord Chancellor in the House of Lords, a large square wool-stuffed sack.
woozy *adj* **-ier, -iest** (*coll*) feeling dazed, dizzy or confused, with senses blurred and hazy. — *adv* **woozily**. — **wooziness**.
wop *n* (*offensive slang*) a member of a Latin or Mediterranean race, e.g. an Italian, esp. as an immigrant or visitor. [Perhaps Ital dialect *guappo*, swaggerer]
Worcester sauce *n* a strong-tasting sauce used as a seasoning, made with soy sauce, vinegar and spices. [*Worcester*, in England, where orig. made]
word *n* **1** the smallest unit of spoken or written language that can be used independently, usu. separated off by spaces in writing and printing. **2** a brief conversation on a particular matter: *I'd like a word with you*. **3** any brief statement, message or communication: *a word of caution*; *a word to all pet-owners*. **4** news or notice: *any word of Kate? sent word she'd arrive tomorrow*. **5** a rumour: *The word is they're bankrupt*. **6** one's solemn promise: *give one's word*; *word of honour*. **7** an order: *expects her word to be obeyed*; *just say the word*. **8** a word given as a signal for action: *Wait till I give the word*. **9** what someone says: *remembered her mother's words*. **10** (in *pl*) language as a means of communication: *impossible to convey in words*. **11** (in *pl*) discussion in contrast to action. **12** (in *pl*) the lyrics of a song, etc.; the speeches an actor must learn for a particular part. **13** (*cap*; with **the**) (the teachings contained in) the Bible. **14** a watchword: *Mum's the word!* **15** (*comput*) a set of bits stored and used as a single unit of meaning. — *v* (*tr*) to express in carefully chosen words: *worded her refusal tactfully*. — **as good as one's word** careful to keep one's promise. — **have words** (*coll*; **with**) to quarrel. — **in a word** briefly. — **in other words** saying the same thing in a different way. — **in so many words** explicitly; bluntly. — **of many** (or **few**) **words** inclined to be talkative (or reserved). — **say the word** to give one's consent or approval for some action to proceed. — **take someone at his** (or **her**) **word** to take someone's offer, etc. literally. — **take someone's word for it** to accept what someone says as true, when one has no means of knowing personally. — **(upon) my word** (*old*) an exclamation of surprise. — **word for word** (repeated) in exactly the same words, or (translated) into exactly corresponding words. [OE]
word-blindness *n* dyslexia.
word game *n* any game or puzzle in which words are constructed, deciphered, etc.
wording *n* one's choice and arrangement of words in expressing something.
word of honour *n* one's solemn promise.
word of mouth *n* spoken, in contrast to written, communication.
word-perfect *adj* able to repeat something accurately from memory.
word processor *n* an electronic machine with screen, by means of which text entered by keyboard can be organised, stored, updated and printed out. — *n* **word-processing**.
wordy *adj* **-ier, -iest** using too many words to say something; long-winded, esp. pompously so. — *adv* **wordily**. — *n* **wordiness**.
wore. See **wear**.
work *n* **1** physical or mental effort made in order to achieve or make something; labour, study, research, etc. **2** employment: *out of work*. **3** one's place of employment: *leaves work at 4.30*. **4** tasks to be done: *often brings work home with her*; *housework*. **5** the product of mental or physical labour: *His work has improved*; *a splendid piece of work*. **6** a literary, artistic, musical or dramatic composition or creation: *the complete works of Milton*. **7** anything done, managed, made, achieved, etc.; activity for some purpose: *Good work! works of charity*. **8** (esp. *in cmpds*) things made in the material or with the tools specified; the production of such things: *basketwork*; *needlework*. **9** (esp. *in cmpds*) the parts of a building, etc. using a specified material: *stonework, paintwork*, etc. **10** (in *pl*) building or repair operations: *roadworks*; *the clerk of works*. **11** (often *in cmpds* in *pl*;

esp. *archaeol*) a rampart or defence: *earthworks*. **12** (in *pl*; *coll*) the operating parts of e.g. a watch or machine; the mechanism. **13** (in *pl* often *in cmpds*, usu. with *sing* verb) the place of manufacture of a specified product: *gasworks*. **14** (*coll*; with **the**) everything possible, available or going; the lot: *has a headache, fever, cold—the works!* **15** (*physics*) the transfer of energy that occurs when force is exerted on a body to move it. — *adj* relating to, suitable for, etc., work: *work clothes*. — *v* **1** (*intr*; **at, on, for, with**, etc.) to do work; to exert oneself mentally or physically; to toil, labour or study. **2** (*intr* & *tr*) to be employed; to have a job; to perform the tasks and duties involved in a job; to do this for (so many hours a day, etc.): *stop working at 65*; *works a nine-hour day*. **3** (*tr*) to impose tasks on; to cause to labour: *works her staff hard*. **4** (*tr* & *intr*) to operate, esp. satisfactorily: *learn to work a drill*; *Does this radio work?* **5** (*intr*) (of a plan, idea, etc.) to be successful or effective. **6** (*intr*) to function in a particular way: *Most relationships don't work like that*. **7** (*intr* with **in**) (of a craftsman) to specialise in the use of (a specified material): *works in brass*. **8** (*tr*) to shape or fashion (metals or other materials); to make by doing this: *earrings worked in silver*. **9** (*tr*) to cultivate (land). **10** (*tr*) to extract materials from (a mine). **11** (*tr*) to knead (e.g. dough). **12** (*tr*) to cover (an area) as a salesman, etc. **13** (*tr*; *old*) to sew, embroider, etc. (e.g. a handkerchief). **14** (*tr*) to achieve (miracles, wonders, etc.). **15** (*tr*; *coll*) to manipulate (a system, rules, etc.) to one's advantage. **16** (*tr*; **up**) to rouse or stir up: *work oneself into a rage*; *too worked-up to think*. **17** (*tr* & *intr*) to make (one's way), or (cause to) shift gradually: *work one's way forward*; *worked the nail out of his sole*. **18** (*intr*) (of e.g. a screw) to become gradually (loose, free, etc.). **19** (*intr*) (of someone's face or features) to move uncontrollably with emotion; to contort. **20** (*tr*) to exercise (a part of the body). **21** (*tr*) to earn (one's sea passage) by unpaid work on board. — **give someone the works** (*slang*) to use every measure available in dealing with someone, by way of e.g. punishment, coercion, ceremonious welcome, beauty treatment, etc. — **have one's work cut out** (*coll*) to be faced with a challenging task. — **make short work of** to accomplish, dispose of, or consume, speedily. — **a piece** or **bit of work** (*coll*, usu. *derog*) a person, esp. with regard to character or disposition: *a nasty bit of work*. — **place of work** the office, factory or other premises where one is employed. — *v* **work in 1** (*tr*) to add and mix (an ingredient) into a mixture. **2** (*tr*) to find a place for; to fit in: *work the idea in somewhere in your thesis*. **3** (*intr*) (of workers protesting against closure, redundancy, etc.) to occupy work premises and take over the running of the business (*n* **work-in**). — *v* **work off** (*tr*) to get rid of (energy) or the effects of (a heavy meal) by energetic activity. — *v* **work on** (*tr*) **1** to try to perfect or improve. **2** (*coll*) to use one's powers of persuasion on. **3** to use as a basis for one's decisions and actions: *working on that assumption*. — *v* **work out 1** (*tr*) to solve, sort out or reason out. **2** (*intr*) to go successfully: *if things work out*. **3** (*intr*) to perform a set of energetic physical exercises (*n* **work-out**). — *v* **work over** (*tr*; *slang*) to beat (someone) up. — **work to rule** to slow work down deliberately by keeping strictly to the rules laid down for its performance, as an alternative to going on strike (*n* **work-to-rule**). — *v* **work up 1** (*tr*) to excite or agitate. **2** (*tr*) to summon up (an appetite, enthusiasm, energy, etc.). **3** (*intr* with **to**) to approach (something hard) by easy steps. [OE *weorc*]

workable *adj* **1** (of a scheme, etc.) able to be carried out; practicable. **2** (of e.g. a material, mineral source, etc.) able to be worked. — *n* **workability**.

workaday *adj* **1** ordinary; commonplace. **2** suitable for a work day; practical or everyday; not fine.

workaholic *adj* & *n* (*coll*) (a person) addicted to work. [After *alcoholic*]

workbasket or **workbox** *n* a basket or box for holding sewing materials and implements.

workbench *n* a usu. purpose-built table for a mechanic or craftsman.

workday *n* (esp. *NAm*) a working day.

worker *n* **1** a person who works. **2** a person employed in manual work. **3** an employee as opposed to an employer. **4** amongst social insects such as bees or ants, one of a number of sterile females that do the work of the colony.

workforce *n* the number of workers engaged in a particular industry, factory, etc.; the total number of workers potentially available.

workhouse *n* (*hist*) an institution where the poor can be housed and given work to do.

working *n* **1** (sometimes in *pl*) the (mode of) operation of something. **2** the steps, usu. noted down, by which the answer to a mathematical problem is reached. **3** (in *pl*) excavations at a mine or quarry. — *adj* **1** (of a period of time) devoted to, or denoting that part that is devoted to, work. **2** adequate for one's purposes: *a working knowledge of French*. — **in working order** functioning properly.

working class *n* (*pl* or *sing*) the wage-earning section of the population, employed esp. in manual labour. — *adj* **working-class**.

working day *n* **1** a day on which people go to work as usual. **2** the part of the day during which work is done: *an eight-hour working day*.

working-party *n* a group of people appointed to investigate and report on something.

workload *n* the amount of work expected of a person or machine.

workman *n* **1** a man employed to do manual work. **2** anyone performing a craft.

workmanlike *adj* suitable to, or characteristic of, a good workman.

workmanship *n* the skill of a craftsman, esp. where evident in the appearance of a finished product.

workmate *n* (*coll*) someone who works alongside one in one's place of work; a fellow-worker or colleague.

work of art *n* **1** a painting or sculpture of high quality. **2** anything constructed or composed with obvious skill.

workpiece *n* an object that is being worked on with a machine or tool.

workshop *n* **1** a room or building where construction and repairs are carried out. **2** a course of study or work, esp. of an experimental kind, for a group of people on a particular project.

workshy *adj* (*coll*) lazy; inclined to avoid work.

work station *n* a person's seat at a computer terminal.

work study *n* an investigation of the most efficient way of doing a job, esp. with regard to time and effort.

work surface or **worktop** *n* a flat surface constructed along the top of kitchen installations such as fridge and cupboards, on which to prepare food, etc.

world *n* **1** the earth; the planet we inhabit. **2** any other planet or potentially habitable heavenly body. **3** the people inhabiting the earth; mankind: *tell the world.* **4** human affairs: *the present state of the world.* **5** (*cap*) a group of countries characterised in a certain way: *the Third World, New World,* etc. **6** (*cap*) the people of a particular period, and their culture: *the Ancient World.* **7** a state of existence: *in this world or the next.* **8** the busy, crowded, materialistic life of people in general, esp. from the point of view of someone who has not experienced it, or who rejects it: *go out into the world; escape from the world; the outside world.* **9** one's individual way of life or range of experience: *one's own narrow world.* **10** an atmosphere or environment: *enter a world of make-believe.* **11** a particular area of activity: *the world of politics.* **12** a class of living things: *the insect world.* **13** (*coll*) a great deal; a lot: *did her a world of good; are worlds apart.* — *adj* of, relating to, affecting, or important throughout, the whole world: *world championships; a world power.* — **be** or **mean all the world to** to be important or precious to. — **the best of both worlds** the benefits of both alternatives with the drawbacks of neither. — **bring into the world** to give birth to or deliver (a baby). — **come into the world** to be born. — **come** or **go up** (or **down**) **in the world** to rise (or fall) in social status. — **for all the world as if** exactly as if. — **in the world** used for emphasis: *how in the world ...? without a care in the world.* — **not for the world** not for anything: *wouldn't hurt her for the world.* — **on top of the world** (*coll*) supremely happy. — **out of this world** (*coll*) extraordinarily fine; marvellous. — **think the world of** to love or admire immensely. [OE *weorold*]

man or **woman of the world** *n* a socially experienced person; someone not easily shocked or surprised.

world-beater *n* a person, product, etc. that is supreme in its class.

world-class *adj* (esp. *sport*) of the highest standard in the world.

world-famous *adj* well known throughout the world.

worldly *adj* **-ier**, **-iest 1** relating to this world; material, not spiritual or eternal: *worldly possessions.* **2** over-concerned with possessions, money, luxuries, etc.; materialistic. **3** shrewd about the ways of the world; knowing and sophisticated in one's outlook. — *n* **worldliness.**

worldly-wise *adj* knowledgeable about life; not easily impressed.

world music *n* popular folk music originating in non-western, esp. African, cultures.

world-shaking *adj* (*coll*) important; significant; momentous.

world war *n* a war in which most of the major world powers take part, esp. the Great War (**World War I**) of 1914–18 or that of 1939–45 (**World War II**).

worldweary *adj* tired of the world; bored of life.

worldwide *adj* & *adv* (extending or known) throughout the world.

worm *n* **1** a small long slender cylindrical animal without backbone or limbs, found esp. in soil; an earthworm. **2** any superficially similar but unrelated animal, such as a flatworm or tapeworm. **3** the similar larva of any of various insects; a grub: *woodworm.* **4** a mean, contemptible, weak or worthless person. **5** (*mech*) the spiral thread of a screw. **6** (in *pl* with *sing* verb) a disease caused by parasitic worms in the intestines. — *v* (*tr*) **1** to wriggle (one's way): *wormed their way to the front.* **2** (**into**) to work (one's way) into (someone's favour, affections, etc.). **3** (**out**) to extract little by little: *wormed the secret out of him.* **4** (*tr*) to treat (an animal) for worms. — *adj* **wormy, -ier, -iest.** [OE *wyrm*]

wormcast *n* a coiled heap of sand or earth excreted by a burrowing worm.

worm-eaten *adj* (e.g. of furniture) riddled with wormholes.

worm gear *n* **1** a gear consisting of a shaft with a spiral thread that engages with and drives a toothed wheel. **2** (also **worm wheel**) the toothed wheel so driven.

wormhole *n* a hole left by a burrowing grub, in e.g. furniture, books or fruit.

wormwood *n* **1** a bitter-tasting herb from which the flavouring for absinthe is obtained. **2** (*old*) (a cause of) acute bitterness or chagrin. [OE *wermod*]

worn *past participle* of **wear**. — *adj* **1** haggard with weariness. **2** showing signs of deterioration through long use or wear. — **worn out 1** exhausted. **2** too badly worn to be any further use; threadbare.

worrisome *adj* (*old*) causing worry; perturbing; vexing. [**worry**]

worry *v* **-ies**, **-ied 1** (*intr*) to be anxious. **2** (*tr*) to cause anxiety to. **3** (*tr*) to bother or harass. **4** (*tr*) (of a dog) to tear and pull about with the teeth; to chase and bite (sheep, etc.). **5** (*intr* with **at**) to try to solve (a problem, etc.). — *n* **-ies 1** a state of anxiety. **2** a cause of anxiety. — *adj* **worried (about)**. — *n* **worrier**. — **not to worry** (*coll*) an expression of reassurance. [OE *wyrgan*, to strangle]

worry beads *n* a string of beads for fiddling with, to calm the nerves.

worse *adj* (*comparative* of **bad**) **1** more bad: *To be blind or deaf —which is worse?* **2** more ill. **3** more grave, serious or acute. **4** inferior in standard. — *n* something worse: *Worse was to follow.* — *adv* less well; more badly. — **go from bad to worse** to get worse; to deteriorate. — **might do worse than** should consider (doing something). — **none the worse for** unharmed by (an accident, bad experience, etc.). — **the worse for** showing the bad effects of. — **the worse for wear 1** worn or shabby from use. **2** in poor condition. — **worse off** in a worse situation, esp. financially. [OE *wyrsa*]

worsen *v* **-n-** (*intr* & *intr*) to (cause to) grow worse.

worship *v* **-pp- 1** (*tr* & *intr*) to honour (God or a god) with praise, prayer, hymns, etc. **2** (*tr*) to love or admire, esp. blindly; to idolise. **3** (*tr*) to glorify or exalt (material things, e.g. money). — *n* **1** the activity of worshipping. **2** (*cap* with **His**, **Your**, etc.; *Br*) the title by which to refer to or address a mayor or magistrate. — *n* **worshipper**. [OE *weorthscipe*, 'worthship']

worshipful *adj* **1** full of reverence or adoration. **2** (usu. *cap*) used as a term of respect in the titles of certain dignitaries. **3** worshipping; adoring.

worst *adj* **1** most bad, awful, unpleasant, etc. **2** most grave, severe, acute or dire. **3** most inferior; lowest in standard. — *n* the worst thing, part or possibility: *hope the worst is over.* — *adv* most severely; most badly: *the worst I've ever played.*— *v* (*tr*) to defeat; to get the better of. — **at its**, etc. **worst** in the worst state or severest degree. — **at (the) worst** taking the most unfavourable or pessimistic view. — **do your worst** do what you threaten — see if I care! — **get the worst of** to lose (a fight, argument, etc.). — **if the worst comes to the worst** supposing the worst happens. [OE *wyrst*]

worsted *n* **1** a fine strong woollen yarn. **2** fabric woven from this. [*Worstead*, in Norfolk]

wort *n* **1** (esp. *in cmpds*) a plant: *liverwort*. **2** (*brewing*) a dilute solution or infusion of malt, fermented to make beer and whisky. [OE *wyrt*, plant, root]

worth *n* **1** value; importance; usefulness. **2** financial value. **3** the quantity of anything that can be bought for a certain sum, accomplished in a certain time, etc.: *lost a thousand pounds' worth of equipment*; *three days' worth of work.* — *adj* **1** having a value of: *a stamp worth £15.* **2** (*coll*) having money and property to the value of: *She's worth two million.* **3** justifying, deserving, meriting, repaying or warranting: *worth consideration.* — **for all one is worth** with all one's might. — **for all it's**, etc. **worth** to the utmost. — **for what it's**, etc. **worth** worthless though it, etc. may be. — **worth it** worthwhile. [OE *weorth*]

worthless *adj* of no value or merit. — *adv* **worthlessly**. — *n* **worthlessness**.

worthwhile *adj* worth the time, money or energy expended; useful, beneficial or rewarding.

worthy *adj* **-ier**, **-iest 1** (often rather *condescending*) admirable; excellent; deserving: *support worthy causes.* **2 (of)** deserving (of something, or to be or do something). **3** (with **of**) suitable to. — *n* (often rather *condescending*) an esteemed person; a dignitary: *the village worthies.* — *adv* **worthily**. — *n* **worthiness**. [**worth**]

would *v* (*aux*) *past tense* of **will**, used **1** in reported speech: *said she would leave at 10.* **2** to indicate willingness, readiness or ability: *was asked to help, but would not. The radio simply would not work.* **3** in expressing probability: *They would surely have heard.* **4** in indicating habitual action: *would always telephone at six.* **5** in implying that some happening is predictable or unsurprising: *'She refused.' 'She would.'* **6** to suggest obstinate resistance to advice: *He would have his own way.* **7** in expressing frustration at some happening: *It would rain, just as we're setting out.* **8** in expressing condition: *In your place, I would have told her.* **9** in making polite invitations, offers or requests: *Would you like to go? Would you rather have a red one? Would you ring her back?* **10** in formulating a desire: *wish she would stop talking.* **11** in politely expressing and seeking opinions: *I would suggest, would you not agree*, etc. — **would (that)** (*old*) if only: *Would* (*that*) *I were twenty again.* [OE *wolde*, past tense of *wyllan*]

would-be *adj* trying, hoping, or merely pretending, to be.

wouldn't would not.

wound[1]. See **wind**[2].

wound[2] *n* **1** an injury to living animal or plant tissue, caused by a cut, blow, etc.; a surgeon's incision. **2 (to)** an injury caused to pride, feelings, reputation, etc. — *v* (*tr* & *intr*) **1** to inflict a wound on (a person, creature, limb, etc.). **2** to injure (feelings, etc.). [OE *wund*]

wove, woven. See **weave**.

wow[1] (*coll*) *interj* an exclamation of astonishment or admiration. — *n* a huge success. — *v* (*tr*) to impress hugely. [Perhaps orig. Scot]

wow[2] *n* (*audio*) a repeated waver in the pitch of reproduced sound, usu. caused by an irregularity in the operating speed of the recording or reproducing apparatus. [Imit.]

WPC *abbrev* woman police constable.

wpm *abbrev* words per minute.

WRAC *abbrev* Women's Royal Army Corps.

wrack *n* **1** seaweed, esp. one of the large brown varieties, floating, cast-up, or growing on the beach. **2** (variant of **rack**[2]) destruction. **3** a wreck or wreckage. [ODut or OGer *wrak*, related to OE *wræc*, misery, & *wrecan*, to wreak]

WRAF *abbrev* Women's Royal Air Force.

wraith *n* **1** a ghost; a spectre. **2** a person of spectral thinness and pallor. [Orig. Scot]

wrangle *v* (*intr*) to quarrel or argue noisily or bitterly. — *n* a bitter dispute. [Ger *wrangeln*, related to **wring**]

wrap *v* ***-pp-*** *v* (*tr*) **1 (round)** to fold or wind (something) round something. **2 (up)** to cover or enfold (something) in something. — *n* **1** a shawl or stole for the shoulders. **2** a protective covering. — **keep under wraps** (*coll*) to keep secret. — **take the wraps off** (*coll*) to reveal to the public for the first time. — **wrapped up in** absorbed in; engrossed by. — *v* **wrap round 1** (*intr* & *tr*) (of e.g. a garment) to pass right round with an overlap (*adj* **wrapround** or **wraparound**). **2** (*comput*) (of screen text) to start a new line as soon as the last character space on the previous line is filled (*adj* & *n* **wrapround** or **wraparound**). — *v* **wrap up 1** (*tr*; *coll*) to finish off or settle finally. **2** (*intr* & *tr*) to dress warmly. **3** (*intr*; *slang*) to be quiet.

wrapper *n* **1** a paper or cellophane cover round a packet, sweet, etc. **2** the dust jacket of a book.

wrapping *n* (esp. in *pl*) any of various types of cover, wrapper or packing material.

wrasse *n* a brightly coloured bony sea fish. [Cornish *wrach*]

wrath *n* anger; fury. — *adj* **wrathful**. — *adv* **wrathfully**. [OE *wræththo*]

wreak *v* (*tr*; esp. *old*) **1** to cause (havoc, damage, etc.) on a disastrous scale. **2 (on, upon)** to take (vengeance or revenge) ruthlessly on. **3** to give unrestrained expression to (one's anger or hatred). [OE *wrecan*]

wreath *n* **1** a ring-shaped garland of flowers and foliage placed on a grave as a tribute, or hung up as a decoration. **2** a victor's crown of esp. laurel leaves. **3** (usu. in *pl*) a ring, curl or spiral of smoke, mist, etc. [OE *writha*, something coiled, related to **writhe**]

wreathe *v* **1** (*tr*) to coil, twine or intertwine. **2** (*tr*) to hang or encircle with flowers, etc. **3** (*tr*) to cover or surround (in smoke, mist, etc.). **4** (*intr*) (of smoke, etc.) to curl, coil or spiral. — **wreathed in smiles** smiling broadly or joyously.

wreck *n* **1** the destruction, esp. accidental, of a ship at sea. **2** a hopelessly damaged sunken or grounded ship. **3** a crashed aircraft; a ruined vehicle. **4** (*coll*) someone in a pitiful state of fitness or mental health. **5** something in so advanced a state of deterioration that it cannot be salvaged. **6** (*coll*) a mess or shambles. **7** the remains of something destroyed: *a wreck of his former self*. — *v* (*tr*) **1** to break; to destroy. **2** to spoil (e.g. plans, hopes, a holiday, relationship, etc.). **3** to cause the wreck of (a ship, etc.). [MidE *wrec*, from ODan *wræce*]

wreckage *n* (the remains of) things that have been wrecked.

wrecker *n* **1** someone who criminally ruins anything; (*hist*) someone who deliberately causes a wreck in order to plunder the wreckage. **2** (*NAm*) a person whose job is to demolish buildings, vehicles, etc. **3** (*NAm*) a breakdown vehicle.

Wren *n* a member of the Women's Royal Naval Service. [From the initials **WRNS**]

wren *n* a very small songbird with short wings and an erect tail. [OE *wrenna*]

wrench *v* (*tr*) **1 (out, off)** to pull or twist violently. **2 (away)** to drag; to persuade forcibly to leave. **3** to sprain (an ankle, etc.). — *n* **1** a violent pull or twist. **2** a spanner-like tool for gripping and turning nuts and bolts, etc. **3** a painful parting or separation: *Leaving home was always a wrench*. [OE *wrencan*]

wrest *v* (*tr*; **from**) **1** to pull or wrench away, esp. from someone else's grasp or possession. **2** to extract with force or difficulty: *wrested an admission from her*. **3** to grab (victory) from the expected victor. **4** to distort or twist (words) from their true meaning. [OE *wræstan*]

wrestle *v* **1** (*tr* & *intr*) to fight by trying to grip, throw and pinion (one's opponent); to do this as a sport; to force to some position in this way: *wrestled him to the floor*. **2** (*intr*; **with**) to struggle. — *n* **1** a spell of wrestling. **2** a struggle. — *n* **wrestler**. — *n* **wrestling**. [OE *wrestlian*]

wretch *n* **1** a miserable, unfortunate, pitiful creature. **2** (esp. *humorous*) a shamelessly wicked person. [OE *wrecca*]

wretched *adj* **1** pitiable. **2** miserable; unhappy; distressed; distraught. **3** inferior; poor; lowly: *a wretched hovel*. **4** infuriating: *a wretched bore*. — *adv* **wretchedly**. — *n* **wretchedness**.

wrick . Another spelling of **rick**[2].

wriggle *v* **1** (*intr* & *tr*) to twist to and fro. **2** (*intr* & *tr*) to make (one's way) by this means. **3** (*intr* with **out of**) to manage cleverly to get out of (an awkward situation, disagreeable obligation, etc.). — *n* a wriggling action. — *adj* **wriggly**, ***-ier***, ***-iest***. [OGer *wriggeln*]

wright *n* (esp. *in cmpds*) a maker or repairer: *a playwright*, *shipwright*, *wheelwright*, etc. [OE *wryhta*]

wring *v* ***wrung*** (*tr*) **1** (**out**) to force (liquid) from (something) by twisting or squeezing. **2** (**from**, **out of**) to force (information, a consent, etc.) from someone. **3** to break (the neck) of a bird, etc. by twisting. **4** to keep clasping and twisting (one's hands) in distress. **5** to crush (someone's hand) in one's own, by way of greeting. **6** to tear at (the heart as the supposed seat of the emotions). — **wringing wet** soaking wet; saturated. [OE *wringan*]

wringer *n* (esp. *hist*) a machine with two rollers for squeezing water out of wet clothes.

wrinkle[1] *n* **1** a crease or line in the skin, esp. of the face, appearing with advancing age. **2** a slight crease or ridge in any surface. — *v* (*tr* & *intr*) to (cause to) develop wrinkles. — *adj* **wrinkly**, ***-ier***, ***-iest***. [OE *wrinclian*, to wind round]

wrinkle[2] *n* (*coll*) a useful tip; a handy hint. [Perhaps from OE *wrenc*, trick]

wrist *n* **1** the joint between wrist and forearm. **2** the part of a sleeve covering this. [OE]

wristlet *n* a decorative or supporting band for the wrist.

wristwatch *n* a watch worn strapped to the wrist.

writ *n* a legal document by which one is summoned, or required to do or refrain from doing something. [OE]

write *v* ***wrote***, ***written*** **1** (*tr* & *intr*) to produce (letters, symbols, numbers, words, sentences, etc.) on a surface, esp. paper, usu. using a pen or pencil. **2** (*tr*) to compose or create (a book, music, etc.) in manuscript, typescript, on computer, etc.; to be the author or composer of. **3** (*intr*) to compose novels, contribute articles to newspapers, etc., esp. as a living. **4** (*tr*) to put down; to inscribe. **5** (*tr*) to make or fill in (a document, form, etc.): *write a prescription*. **6** (*tr* & *intr*) to compose (a letter, etc.). **7** (*tr*) to say in a letter, article, book, etc. **8** (*tr*) to put up-to-date information in (one's diary, etc.). **9** (*tr*) to fill (pages, sheets, etc.) with writing. **10** (*tr*) to display all too clearly: *guilt written all over his face*. **11** (*tr*; *comput*) to transfer (data) to a memory or storage device. — *v* **write down 1** (*tr*) to put down or record in writing. **2** (*intr*; **to**) to write in a simplified style, as if for people less intelligent than oneself. 3 (*tr*) to reduce the accounting value of. — *v* **write in** (*intr*) to write a letter (to an organisation, television programme, etc.). — *v* **write into** (*tr*) to include (a condition, etc.) in a contract, etc. — *v* **write off 1** (*intr*; **for, to**) to write and send a letter of request. **2** (*tr*) to damage (a vehicle) beyond repair (*n* **write-off**). **3** (*tr*) to cancel (a long-unpaid debt). **4** (*tr*) to discontinue (a project, etc.) because likely to fail. **5** (*tr*) to dismiss as something of no importance. — *v* **write out** (*tr*) **1** to write in full; to copy or transcribe. **2** (*tr*) to remove (a character or scene) from a film, serial, etc. — *v* **write up** (*tr*) **1** to write or rewrite in orderly, easily readable form: *write up one's report*, *notes*, etc. **2** to bring (one's diary, accounts, etc.) up to date. **3** to write about or review, esp. approvingly (*n* **write-up**). [OE *writan*]

writer *n* **1** a person who writes, esp. as a living; an author. **2** someone who has written a particular thing.

writer's cramp *n* painful cramp of the hand brought on by intensive writing.

writing *n* **1** written or printed words. **2** handwriting. **3** (the art or activity of) literary composition. **4** (usu. in *pl*) a literary work: *Bacon's writings*. **5** a form of script: *Chinese writing*. — **in writing** (of a promise, etc.) in written form, esp. as being undeniable proof of intention, etc.

writing-paper *n* paper for writing letters on.

writhe *v* (*intr*) **1** to twist violently to and fro, esp. in pain or discomfort; to squirm. **2** (*coll*) to feel painfully embarrassed or humiliated. [OE *writhan*, to twist]

written *past participle* of **write**. — *adj* expressed in writing, and so undeniable: *a written undertaking*.

the written word *n* written, as distinct from spoken, language.

WRNS *abbrev* Women's Royal Naval Service.

wrong *adj* **1** not correct. **2** (**about**) mistaken: *quite wrong about her motives*. **3** not appropriate or suitable: *always saying the wrong thing*; *wrong way up*. **4** not good; not sensible; unjustifiable: *wrong to waste the good weather*. **5** morally bad: *wrong to tell lies*. **6** (**with**) defective or faulty: *something wrong with the radio*. **7** (**with**) amiss; causing trouble, pain, etc.: *wouldn't cry unless something was wrong with her*. **8** (of one side of a fabric, garment, etc.) intended as the inner, unseen, side. **9** not socially acceptable: *get in with the wrong class of people*. — *adv* **1** incorrectly: *spelt wrong*. **2** improperly; badly: *timed it wrong*. — *n* **1** whatever is not right or just: *know right from wrong*; *do wrong*. **2** any injury done to someone else: *did her wrong*. — *v* (*tr*) **1** to treat unjustly. **2** to judge unfairly. — *adv* **wrongly**. — **get on the wrong side of** (*coll*) to antagonise. — **get wrong 1** to give the incorrect answer to, or do incorrectly. **2** to misunderstand. — **go wrong 1** (of plans, etc.) to fail to go as intended. **2** to make an error. **3** to stray morally; to fall into bad ways. **4** (of a mechanical device) to stop functioning properly. — **in the wrong** guilty of an error or injustice. [OE *wrang*]

wrongdoer *n* a person guilty of an immoral or illegal act. — *n* **wrongdoing**.

wrongfoot *v* (*tr*) **1** (e.g. *tennis*) to catch (one's opponent) off balance by making an unpredictable shot, etc. to a point away from the direction in which he or she is moving or preparing to move. **2** to contrive to place (an opponent in a dispute, etc.) at a tactical or moral disadvantage; to disconcert.

wrongful *adj* unlawful; unjust. — *adv* **wrongfully**.

wrote. See **write**.

wroth *adj* (*old*) angry; full of wrath. [OE *wrath*]

wrought *adj* **1** (*old*) made, formed, shaped or fashioned. **2** (*old*) decorated or ornamented. **3** (of metal) beaten into shape as distinct from being cast. [Old past participle of **work**]

wrought iron *n* a pure form of iron suitable for beating and bending into shape. ◇ See also **cast iron**. — *adj* **wrought-iron**.

wrought-up *adj* over-excited; agitated.

wrung. See **wring**.

WRVS *abbrev* Women's Royal Voluntary Service.

wry *adj* **1** slightly mocking or bitter; ironic. **2** (of a facial expression) with the features twisted into a grimace, in reaction to a bitter taste, etc. **3** twisted to one side; awry. [OE *wrigian*, to turn, twist]

wryneck *n* a small bird related to the woodpecker, that twists its head to look backwards over its shoulder.

wt *abbrev* weight.

wuther *v* **-r-** (*intr*; *dialect*) (of the wind) to roar or bluster. [Related to Norse *hvitha*, squall]

WV or **W. Va.** *abbrev* West Virginia.

WWF *abbrev* World Wide Fund for Nature.

WY or **Wy.** *abbrev* Wyoming.

wych-elm *n* a tree of the elm family native to N Europe and Asia, with drooping branches and smooth bark. [OE *wice*]

wych hazel. Another spelling of **witch hazel**.

Wyo. *abbrev* Wyoming.

WYSIWYG *abbrev* (*comput*) what you see is what you get, i.e. the type and characters appearing on screen are as they will appear on the print-out. — *n* a word-processing facility giving text on screen that closely approximates to printed text, with italic and bold type, etc. as required.

X

X[1] or **x** *n* ***X's*** or ***Xs***, ***x's*** **1** the twenty-fourth letter of the English alphabet. **2** anything in the shape of an X. **3** an unknown or unnamed person.

X[2] *symbol* **1** (esp. *math*; also **x**) an unknown quantity. ◇ See also **Y** and **Z**. **2** the Roman numeral for 10. **3** (*US*, and formerly *Br*; *films*) a symbol used to indicate that people under the age of 17 (in the US) or 18 (in the UK) will not be admitted to a showing of the film (replaced in the UK by '18'). **4** a mark used to symbolise a kiss, to indicate an error, the signature of an illiterate person, etc.

X-chromosome *n* (*biol*) a chromosome involved in the determination of an animal's sex, two X-chromosomes usu. occurring in females, one X- and one Y-chromosome in males.

X-ray *n* **1** (usu. in *pl*) an electromagnetic ray which can pass through many substances that light cannot pass through, producing on photographic film an image of the object passed through. **2** a photograph taken using X-rays. **3** a medical examination using X-rays. — *v* (*tr*) to take a photograph of (something) using X-rays.

x (esp. *math*). See **X**[2].

X-chromosome. See **X**[2].

Xe *symbol* (*chem*) xenon.

xenon *n* an element (symbol **Xe**), a colourless, odourless gas occurring in very small quantities in the earth's atmosphere. [Gr *xenos*, stranger]

xenophobia *n* intense fear or dislike of foreigners or strangers. — *n* **xenophobe**. — *adj* **xenophobic**. [Gr *xenos*, stranger + **phobia**]

xerography *n* a photocopying process in which fine dry electrically charged coloured powder is dusted over, and adheres to, an electrically charged image of the matter to be copied, and is then fixed by heat. — *adj* **xerographic**. [Gr *xeros*, dry + **-graphy**]

xerophyte *n* (*bot*) a plant able to live where water is in scarce supply or difficult to absorb for chemical reasons. [Gr *xeros*, dry + *phyton*, plant]

Xerox® *n* **1** a type of photographic process used for copying documents. **2** a copying-machine using this process. **3** (also without *cap*) a photocopy made by such a process. — *v* (*tr*; also without *cap*) to photocopy (something) using this process. [**xerography**]

Xmas *n* (*coll*) short for **Christmas**. [*X*, an abbrev. for **Christ** + *-mas*]

X-ray. See **X**[2].

xylem *n* (*bot*) the woody tissue of trees and plants that conducts water from the roots. [Gr *xylon*, wood]

xylene or **xylol** *n* a hydrocarbon existing in three isomeric forms, a colourless liquid obtained from coal tar, etc. and used e.g. as a solvent and in the preparation of specimens for microscopy. [Gr *xylon*, wood]

xylophone *n* a musical instrument consisting of a series of wooden, or sometimes metal, bars of different lengths, played by being struck by wooden hammers. — *n* **xylophonist**. [Gr *xylon*, wood + *phone*, sound]

Y

Y[1] or **y** *n* ***Y's*** or ***Ys***, ***y's*** **1** the twenty-fifth letter of the English alphabet. **2** anything of the shape of this letter.

Y-fronts *n* (*pl*) men's or boys' underpants with a Y-shaped front seam.

Y[2] *abbrev* yen.

Y[3] *symbol* **1** (*chem*) yttrium. **2** (esp. *math*; also **y**) the second of two unknown quantities. ◇ See also **X** and **Z**.

Y-chromosome *n* (*biol*) a chromosome involved in the determination of an animal's sex, occurring only in males. ◇ See also **X-chromosome**.

y *symbol* (esp. *math*). See **Y**[3].

-y[1] *sfx* forming adjectives with the sense of 'full of', 'characterised by', 'having the quality of', 'keen on', etc.: *spotty*; *icy*; *shiny*; *horsey*. [OE **-ig**]

-y[2] *sfx* forming **1** diminutives or nouns used as terms of affection: *doggy*; *daddy*. **2** nouns denoting people or things with a particular characteristic: *fatty*. [Orig. Scots, used in names]

-y[3] *sfx* forming nouns denoting **1** a quality or state: *jealousy*; *modesty*. **2** an action: *entreaty*; *expiry*. [OFr **-*ie***]

yacht *n* a boat or small ship, usu. with sails, often with an engine, built and used for racing or cruising. — *n* **yachting**.

yachtsman and **yachtswoman** *n* a person who sails a yacht.

yacht club *n* a club for yacht-owners.

yack (*derog slang*) *v* (also **yak**, ***-kk-***; *intr*) to talk at length and often foolishly or annoyingly. — *n* persistent foolish or annoying chatter. [Imit.]

yah *interj* **1** an exclamation of scorn or contempt. **2** (*coll*) yes.

yahoo *n* a lout or ruffian. [From the manlike brutish creatures in Swift's *Gulliver's Travels*]

yak[1] *n* ***yaks*** or ***yak*** a type of long-haired ox found in Tibet. [Tibetan *gyag*]

yak[2]. See **yack**.

Yale lock® or **Yale**® *n* a type of lock operated by a flat key with a notched upper edge. [Linus *Yale* (1821–68), US locksmith]

yam *n* **1** a large edible potato-like root. **2** any of several kinds of tropical plant producing these roots. **3** (esp. *southern US*) a sweet potato. [Port *inhame*]

yammer *v* ***-r-*** **1** (*intr*) to complain whiningly; to grumble. **2** (*intr*) to talk loudly and at length. 3 (*tr*) to say, esp. to make (a complaint), loudly and longly. — *n* the act or sound of yammering. [OE *geomrian*]

yang. See **yin**.

Yank *n* (*coll*) a person from the United States. [**Yankee**]

yank (*coll*) *n* a sudden, sharp pull. — *v* (*tr* & *intr*; **on**, **at**, etc.) to pull suddenly and sharply.

Yankee *n* **1** (*Br coll*) a Yank. **2** (*US*) a person from New England or from any of the northern states of America. [Perhaps Dut *Jan Kees*, John Cheese, the nickname given by the New York Dutch to the British settlers in Connecticut]

yap *v* ***-pp-*** (*intr*) **1** (**at**) (of a puppy or small dog) to give a high-pitched bark. **2** (*coll derog*; **on**, **away**, etc.) (of a person) to talk continually in a shrill voice, often about trivial matters. — *n* a short, high-pitched bark. — *adj* **yappy**, ***-ier***, ***-iest***. [Imit.]

yard[1] *n* **1** a unit of length equal to 3 feet (0·9144 m). **2** (*naut*) a long beam hung on a mast, from which to hang a sail. [OE *gierd*, rod]

yardage *n* the length (or, rarely, the area or volume) of something, measured in yards.

yard-arm *n* (*naut*) either of the tapering end-sections of a yard.

yardstick *n* **1** a standard for comparison. **2** a stick exactly one yard long, used for measuring.

yard[2] *n* **1** (often *in cmpds*) an area of (enclosed) ground near a building. **2** (often *in cmpds*) an area of enclosed ground used for a special (business) purpose: *a shipyard*. **3** (*NAm*) a garden. [OE *geard*, fence, enclosure]

the Yard *n* (*coll*) New Scotland Yard, the headquarters of the London Metropolitan Police.

yarmulka or **yarmulke** *n* a skullcap worn by Jewish men. [Yiddish, from Pol, small cap]

yarn *n* **1** thread spun from wool, cotton, etc. **2** a story or tale, often lengthy and incredible. **3** (*coll*) a lie. — **spin a yarn** (*coll*) to tell a yarn (senses **2** and **3**).

yarrow *n* a strong-scented composite plant with heads of small white flowers. [OE *gearwe*]

yashmak *n* a veil worn by Muslim women, covering the face below the eyes. [Arabic *yashmaq*]

yaw *v* (*intr*) **1** (of a ship) to move temporarily from, or fail to keep to, the direct line of its course. **2** (of an aircraft) to deviate horizontally from the direct line of its course. **3** to move unsteadily; to zigzag. — *n* an act of yawing.

yawl *n* **1** a type of small fishing- or sailing-boat, esp. one with two masts. **2** a ship's small boat, usu. with four or six oars. [Dut *jol*]

yawn *v* (*intr*) **1** to open the mouth wide and take a deep, involuntary breath when tired or bored. **2** (of a hole, gap, etc.) to be or become wide open. — *n* **1** an act of yawning. **2** (*coll*) a boring event, person, etc. [OE *ganian*, to yawn, and *geonian*, to gape widely]

yawning *adj* (of a hole, etc.) wide; large.

yaws *n* (*sing*) an infectious skin disease of tropical countries, causing red swellings.

Yb *symbol* (*chem*) ytterbium.

Y-chromosome. See **Y**[3].

yd *abbrev* yard.

ye[1] *pron* (*old* or *dialect*) you (plural). [OE *ge*]

ye[2] *definite article* (*old*, or used to give an impression of an older form of English) the: *Ye Olde Englishe Tea Shoppe*. [From the use of *y* by mediaeval printers as a substitute for the old letter þ representing the *th*-sound]

yea *interj* (*old*) yes. [OE *gea*]

yeah *interj* (*coll*) yes.

year *n* **1** the period of time the earth takes to go once round the sun, about $365\frac{1}{4}$ days; the equivalent time for any other planet. **2** (also **calendar year**) the period from 1 January to 31 December, being 365 days, except in a leap year, when it is 366 days. **3** any period of twelve months. **4** a period of less than twelve months during which some activity is carried on: *At this college, the academic year runs from September to June*. **5** a period of study at school, college, etc. over an academic year: *She's in third year now*. **6** students at a particular stage in their studies, considered as a group: *had a meeting with the third year this morning*. ◇ See also **years** below. — **year in, year out** (happening, done, etc.) every year, with great, and often tedious, regularity. [OE *gear*]

year-book *n* a book of information updated and published every year, esp. one recording the events, etc. of the previous year.

yearling *n* an animal which is a year old. — *adj* (of an animal) one year old.

yearly *adj* **1** happening, etc. every year. **2** valid for one year. — *adv* every year.

years *n* (*pl*) **1** age: *He is wise for his years*. **2** (*coll*) a very long time. **3** some period of time in the past or future: *in years gone by*.

yearn *v* (*intr*) **1** (**for, after**) to feel a great desire; to long. **2** (**for, to**) to feel compassion. — *n* **yearning**. [OE *giernan*, to desire]

yeast *n* a substance consisting of minute fungi which cause fermentation, used in the production of alcoholic drinks and to make dough rise in bread-making, etc. [OE *gist*]

yeasty *adj* **-ier, -iest 1** (tasting or smelling) of yeast. **2** frothy. **3** trivial.

yell *n* a loud shout or cry. — *v* (*intr* & *tr*; **at, to**) to shout or cry out. [OE *gellan*]

yellow *adj* **1** of the colour of gold, butter, egg-yolk, a lemon, etc. **2** (*derog coll*) cowardly: *a yellow streak* (= a tendency to cowardice). **3** (often considered *offensive* when used as a term of racial description) having a yellow or yellowish skin. — **1** (any shade of) the colour of gold, butter, egg-yolk, etc. **2** something (e.g. material or paint) yellow in colour. — *v* (*tr* & *intr*) to make or become yellow. — *adj* **yellowish**. — *n* **yellowness**. [OE *geolu*]

yellow-bellied *adj* (*slang*) cowardly.

yellow card *n* (*football*) a yellow-coloured card shown by the referee as a warning to a player being cautioned for a serious violation of the rules. ◇ See also **red card**.

yellow fever *n* an acute viral disease of tropical America and West Africa transmitted by the bite of a mosquito, causing high fever, jaundice and haemorrhaging.

yellowhammer *n* a small brownish bunting, the male of which has a yellow head, neck and breast.

Yellow Pages® *n* (*pl*) a telephone directory, or a section of one, printed on yellow paper, in which entries are classified and arranged together according to the nature of the trade or profession of the individuals or companies listed and the services they offer.

yelp *v* (*intr*) & *n* (of a dog, etc.) (to give) a sharp, sudden cry. [OE *gielpan*, to boast]

yen[1] (*coll*; **for**) *n* a desire. — *v* **-nn-** to feel a longing. [S Chin dialect *yeen*]

yen[2] *n* ***yen*** the standard unit of Japanese currency. [Jap]

yeoman *n* ***yeomen*** **1** (*hist*) a farmer who owns and works his own land, often serving as a foot-soldier when required. **2** (*mil*) a member of the yeomanry (sense **2**). [MidE *yoman*; perhaps from earlier *yongman*, young man]

yeomanry *n* **-ies 1** (*hist*) the class of land-owning farmers. **2** a volunteer cavalry force formed in the 18th century, now mechanised and forming part of the Territorial Army.

Yeomen of the Guard *n* **1** the company of men who form the bodyguard of the British monarch on certain ceremonial occasions. **2** (more correctly **Yeomen Warders of the Tower of London**) the company of men who guard the Tower of London.

yep *interj* (*coll*) yes.

yes *interj* used to express agreement or consent. — *n* ***yesses*** an expression of agreement or consent.

yes-man *n* (*derog*) a person who always agrees with the opinions and follows the suggestions of a superior, employer, etc., esp. to curry favour with them.

yesterday *n* **1** the day before today. **2** the recent past. — *adv* **1** on the day before today. **2** in the recent past. [OE *giestran dæg*]

yesteryear *n* (esp. *literary*) **1** the past, esp. the recent past. **2** last year.

yet *adv* **1** (also **as yet**) up till now or then; by now or by that time: *He had not yet arrived*. **2** at this time; now: *You can't leave yet*. **3** at some time in the future; before the matter is finished; still: *She may yet make* *a success of it*. **4** (used for emphasis with **another**, **more** or a *comparative adj*) even; still: *yet greater progress*; *yet another mistake*. — *conj* but; however; nevertheless. — **nor yet** and not ... either. — **yet again** once more. [OE *giet*]

yeti *n* the abominable snowman, an ape-like creature supposed to live in the Himalayas. [Tibetan]

yew *n* **1** (also **yew tree**) a type of evergreen tree with dark needle-like leaves and red berries. **2** its wood. [OE *iw*]

Y-fronts. See **Y**.

YHA *abbrev* Youth Hostels Association.

Yid *n* (*offensive*) a Jew. [**Yiddish**]

Yiddish *n* & *adj* (of or in) a language spoken by many Jews, based on mediaeval German, with elements from Hebrew and several other, esp. Slavic, languages. [Ger *jüdisch*, Jewish]

yield *v* **1** (*tr*) to produce or supply as a crop or natural product: *Cows yield milk*. **2** (*tr*) to give or produce: *Shares yield dividends*. **3** (*tr* & *intr*; **to**) to give up or give in; to surrender. **4** (*intr*; **to**) to break or give way (under force or pressure). — *n* the amount produced. [OE *gieldan*, to pay]

yielding *adj* **1** submissive. **2** flexible. **3** able to or tending to give way.

yin *n* (*Chinese philos*) one of the two opposing and complementary principles of traditional Chinese philosophy, religion, medicine, etc., being the negative, feminine, dark, cold, passive element or force as opposed to the positive, masculine, light, warm, active **yang**. [Chin *yin*, dark, *yang*, bright]

yippee *interj* (*coll*) used to show excitement, delight, etc.

YMCA *abbrev* Young Men's Christian Association. ◇ See also **YWCA**.

yob *n* (*slang*; also **yobbo**, ***-os*** or ***-oes***) a bad-mannered, aggressive young person; a lout or hooligan. [A slang reversed form of *boy*]

yodel *v* ***-ll-*** (*tr* & *intr*) to sing (a melody, etc.), changing frequently from a normal to a falsetto voice and back again. — *n* an act of yodelling. — *n* **yodeller**. [Ger dialect *jodeln*]

yoga *n* **1** a system of Hindu philosophy showing how to free the soul from reincarnation and reunite it with God. **2** any of several systems of physical and mental discipline based on this, esp. (in western countries) a particular system of physical exercises. [Sanskrit, union]

yogi *n* a person who practises the yoga philosophy and the physical and mental disciplines associated with it.

yoghurt, **yogurt** or **yoghourt** *n* a type of semi-liquid food made from fermented milk, often flavoured with fruit. [Turk *yoghurt*]

yoke *n* **1** a wooden frame placed over the necks of oxen to hold them together when they are pulling a plough, cart, etc. **2** a frame placed across a person's shoulders, for carrying buckets. **3** something oppressive; a great burden: *the yoke of slavery*. **4** (*tech*) the part of a garment that fits over the shoulders and round the neck. — *v* (*tr*; **to, together**) **1** to join under or with a yoke (sense **1**). **2** to join or unite. [OE *geoc*]

yokel *n* (usu. *derog*) an unsophisticated (usu. male) person from the country.

yolk *n* the yellow part of a bird's or reptile's egg. [OE *geolca*, from *geolu*, yellow]

Yom Kippur *n* the Day of Atonement, an annual Jewish religious festival devoted to repentance for past sins and celebrated with fasting and prayer. [Hebr]

yon *adj* (*literary* or *dialect*) that or those. [OE *geon*]

yonder *adj* & *adv* (situated) in or at that place over there. [MidE]

yonks *n* (*coll*) a long time.

yoo-hoo *interj* (*coll*) used to attract someone's attention.

yore: **days of yore** (*literary*) times past or long ago. [OE *geara*, formerly]

yorker *n* (*cricket*) a ball pitched to a point directly under the bat. [Prob. *Yorkshire*]

Yorkist *n* & *adj* (*Br hist*) (a person) adhering to the House of York in the Wars of the Roses. ◇ See also **Lancastrian**.

Yorks. *abbrev* Yorkshire.

Yorkshire pudding *n* a baked cake-like pudding of unsweetened batter, served esp. with roast beef. [*Yorkshire* in England]

Yorkshire terrier *n* a small long-haired breed of dog.

you *pron* **1** the person or persons, etc. spoken or written to. **2** any or every person: *You don't often see that nowadays*. — **be you** (*coll*) to suit you: *That hat is just you*. [OE *eow*, orig. accusative and dative of *ge*, ye]

you'd **1** you would. **2** you had.

you'll **1** you will. **2** you shall.

young *adj* **1** in the first part of life, growth, development, etc.; not old. **2** in the early stages: *The evening is still young*. — *n* (*pl*) **1** young animals or birds: *Some birds feed their young on insects*. **2** (with **the**) young people in general. [OE *geong*]

youngster *n* (*coll*) a young person.

your *adj* belonging to you. [OE *eower*, genitive of *ge*, ye]

yours *pron* **1** something belonging to you. **2** (also **yours faithfully**, **sincerely** or **truly**) expressions written before one's signature at the end of a letter. ◇ See also **yours truly** below. — **of yours** of or belonging to you.

yourself *pron* ***-selves*** **1** the reflexive form of **you**. **2** used for emphasis. **3** your normal self: *don't seem yourself this morning*. **4** (also **by yourself**) alone; without help.

yours truly *n* (*coll*) I or me.

you're you are.

yourself. See **your**.

youth *n* **1** (the state of being in) the early part of life, between childhood and adulthood. **2** the enthusiasm, rashness, etc. associated with people in this period of life.

3 a boy or young man. **4** (*pl*) young people in general.

youth club *n* a place or organisation providing leisure activities for young people.

youth custody centre *n* a place where young offenders between the ages of 15 and 21 are detained and given education and training.

youthful *adj* **1** young, esp. in manner or appearance. **2** (of someone who is not young) young-looking, or having the energy, enthusiasm, etc. of a young person. **3** of or associated with youth: *youthful pleasures*. — *adv* **youthfully**. — *n* **youthfulness**.

youth hostel *n* a place for young people, esp. hikers, on holiday, where cheap and simple accommodation is provided. — *n* **youth hosteller**.

Youth Training Scheme see **YTS**.

you've you have.

yowl *v* (*intr*) & *n* (esp. of an animal) (to make) a sad cry or howl. [MidE *youlen*]

yo-yo *n* **-yos 1** a toy consisting of a pair of wooden, metal or plastic discs joined at their centre with a deep groove between them, and with a piece of string attached to and wound round the joining axis within the groove, the toy being repeatedly made to unwind from the string by the force of its weight and rewind by its momentum. **2** anything which resembles such an object in upward and downward movement or variation. — *v* **-yos** (*intr*) to rise and fall repeatedly; to fluctuate repeatedly in any way. [Orig. a trademark]

yr *abbrev* **1** year. **2** your.

YTS *abbrev* Youth Training Scheme, a British government-sponsored scheme to give training and work-experience to unemployed school-leavers.

ytterbium *n* (*chem*) a silvery-white metallic element, symbol **Yb**, one of the rare earth metals. [*Ytterby*, a quarry in Sweden]

yttrium *n* (*chem*) a silvery metallic element, symbol **Y**, used in alloys and in optical and electronic devices. [Same as for **Ytterbium**]

yucca *n* any of a number of household and garden plants, orig. from the southern US and central America, grown for their attractive sword-like leaves and clusters of white flowers.

yucky or **yukky** *adj* **-ier**, **-iest** (*coll*) disgusting; unpleasant; messy. [*Yuck* or *yuk*, an expression of disgust]

Yule *n* (*old*, *literary* or *dialect*) **1** Christmas. **2** (also **Yuletide**) the Christmas period. [OE *geol*]

yummy *adj* **-ier**, **-iest** (*coll*) delicious. [**yum-yum**]

yum-yum *interj* an expression of delight at or appreciative anticipation of something, esp. delicious food. [Imit.]

yuppie or **yuppy** *n* **-ies** (*coll*; usu. *derog*) an ambitious young professional person carving out a career for himself or herself in a city job. [*Y*oung *u*rban *p*rofessional, or *y*oung *u*pwardly-mobile *p*rofessional]

YWCA *abbrev* Young Women's Christian Association. ◇ See also **YMCA**.

Z

Z[1] or **z** *n* ***Z's*** or ***Zs, z's*** **1** the last letter of the English alphabet. **2** anything in the shape of this letter.

Z[2] *symbol* (esp. *math*; also **z**) a third unknown quantity. ◇ See also **X** and **Y**.

zabaglione *n* a dessert made from egg-yolks, sugar and wine whipped together. [Ital]

zany *adj* ***-ier***, ***-iest*** amusingly crazy. [*Zanni*, a N Ital dialect form of *Gianni* or *Giovanni*, John, name of a character in mediaeval comedies]

zap *v* ***-pp-*** (*coll*) **1** (*tr*) to hit, destroy, shoot, etc., esp. suddenly. **2** (*tr*; *comput*) to erase or correct (a fault). **3** (*intr*) to change television channels frequently using a remote-control device. **4** (*tr* & *intr*) to move quickly or suddenly. [Imit.]

zeal *n* (**for**) great, sometimes excessive, enthusiasm or keenness. [Gr *zelos*]

zealot *n* **1** (*cap*; *hist*) a member of a militant Jewish group opposed to the Roman occupation of Palestine. **2** (often *derog*) a single-minded, determined supporter of a political cause, religion, etc.

zealous *adj* enthusiastic; keen. — *adv* **zealously**.

zebra *n* ***-bras*** or ***-bra*** a black-and-white striped animal of the horse family, found wild in Africa. [From an African language]

zebra crossing *n* (*Br*) a pedestrian crossing marked by black and white stripes.

zebu *n* a domesticated ox found in parts of Africa and Asia. [Fr *zébu*]

zed (*Br*) *n* the name of the letter Z. [Fr *zède*, from Gr *zeta*]

zee (*US*) *n* the name of the letter Z.

Zen *n* (also **Zen Buddhism**) a school of Buddhism found esp. in Japan, teaching that the way to enlightenment is through meditation and an intuitive understanding of reality. [Jap]

Zend-Avesta *n* the Zoroastrian sacred writings, comprising the scriptures (the **Avesta**) and the commentary on them (the **Zend**). [OPersian *zand*, commentary, *avastak*, text]

zenith *n* **1** the point in the sky directly above one. **2** the highest point. [Arabic *samt-ar-ras*, direction of the head]

zephyr *n* (*literary*) a light, gentle breeze. [Gr *Zephyros*, the west wind]

zeppelin *n* (also *cap*; *hist*) a type of rigid cigar-shaped hydrogen-filled airship designed by Count Ferdinand von *Zeppelin* (1838–1917).

zero *n* ***-os*** **1** the number or figure 0. **2** the point on a scale (e.g. on a thermometer) which is taken as the base from which measurements may be made: *5 degrees below zero.* **3** zero hour. ◇ See also **absolute zero**. — *adj* **1** of no measurable size. **2** (*coll*) not any; no. — *v* ***-os*** (*tr*) to set to zero on a scale. — *v* **zero in on** (*tr*) **1** to aim for; to move towards. **2** to focus one's attention on. **3** to aim a weapon at. [Fr *zéro*, from Arabic *sifr*]

zero hour *n* **1** the exact time fixed for something to happen. **2** the time at which a military operation, etc. is fixed to begin.

zero-rated *adj* (of goods) on which the buyer pays no VAT, and on which the seller can claim back any VAT he or she has paid.

zest *n* **1** keen enjoyment; enthusiasm. **2** something that adds to one's enjoyment of something. **3** (*cooking*) the peel of an orange or lemon, used for flavouring.

zestful *adj* keen; full of enjoyment. — *adv* **zestfully**.

zeugma *n* a figure of speech in which an adjective or verb is applied to two nouns although strictly it is appropriate to only one of them. [Gr, yoking together]

ziggurat *n* a pyramid-like temple in ancient Mesopotamia. [Assyrian *ziqquratu*, mountain-top]

zigzag *n* **1** (usu. in *pl*) one of two or more sharp bends to right and left in a path, etc. **2** a path, road, etc. with a number of such bends. — *adj* (of a path, road, etc.) having sharp bends to right and left. — *v* ***-gg-*** (*tr*) to move in a zigzag path or manner. [Fr, from Ger *Zickzack*]

zilch *n* (*slang*) nothing.

zillion *n* (*coll*) a very large but unspecified number. [By analogy with *million*, *billion*, etc.]

Zimmer® *n* a three-sided tubular metal frame held in front of one, used as a support for walking by the disabled or infirm. [Name of the original manufacturer]

zinc *n* a bluish-white metallic element, symbol **Zn**, a constituent of brass and other alloys, and also used in galvanising, etc. [Ger *Zink*]

zinc ointment *n* a soothing antiseptic ointment containing zinc oxide.

zing *n* **1** a short, high-pitched humming sound, as made by a bullet or vibrating string. **2** (*coll*) zest or vitality. — *v* (*intr*) to move very quickly, esp. making a high-pitched hum. [Imit.]

zinnia *n* an orig. tropical American plant cultivated for its showy flowers. [J G *Zinn* (1727–59), Ger botanist]

Zion *n* **1** the hill on which part of Jerusalem stands, often taken as representing Jerusalem itself. **2** the Jewish people. **3** Palestine or Israel as the homeland of the Jewish people. **4** the Christian church. **5** heaven. [Hebr *tsiyon*]

Zionism *n* the movement which worked for the establishment of a national homeland in Palestine for Jews and now supports the state of Israel. — *n & adj* **Zionist**.

zip[1] *n* **1** (also **zip fastener** &, esp. *NAm*, **zipper**) a device for fastening clothes, bags, etc., in which two rows of metal or nylon teeth are made to fit into each other when a sliding tab is pulled along them. **2** a whizzing sound. **3** (*coll*) energy; vitality. — *v* ***-pp-*** **1** (*tr & intr*; **up**) to fasten, or be fastened, with a zip fastener. **2** (*intr*) to make, or move with, a whizzing sound. [Imit.]

zip fastener see **zip** (sense **1**).

zippy *adj* ***-ier***, ***-iest*** (*coll*) lively; quick.

zip code *n* in the US, a postal code, having the form of a five-figure number. [*z*one *i*mprovement *p*lan]

zipper, **zippy**. See **zip**[1].

zircon *n* a colourless, blue, green, grey or reddish-orange gemstone of zirconium silicate. [Ger *Zirkon*; orig. from Persian *zargun*, golden]

zirconium *n* a greyish metallic element, symbol **Zr**, highly resistant to corrosion. [**zircon**]

zither *n* a musical instrument consisting of a flat wooden sound-box, one section of which has frets on it, over which strings (usu. metal) are stretched, the instrument being played resting on a table or on the player's knees. [Ger *Zither*]

Zn *symbol* (*chem*) zinc.

zodiac *n* **1** (with **the**) an imaginary belt across the sky through which the sun, moon and planets appear to move, divided into twelve equal parts called the **signs of the zodiac**, each of which is named after a constellation which used to lie in it (although the signs and constellations now no longer match up) and corresponds in astrology to a different part of the year and to a particular human character-type. **2** (*astrol*) a usu. circular diagram representing this belt. [OFr *zodiaque*, from Gr *zoidiakos*, from *zoidion*, a figure of a small animal]

zombie or **zombi** *n* **1** a corpse brought to life again by magic. **2** (*coll derog*) a slow-moving, stupid, unresponsive or apathetic person. [Kongo (W African language) *zumbi*, fetish]

zone *n* **1** an area or region of a country, town, etc., esp. one marked out for a special purpose or by a particular feature. **2** any of the five horizontal bands into which the Earth's surface is divided by the Arctic Circle, the Tropic of Cancer, the Tropic of Capricorn and the Antarctic Circle. — *v* (*tr*) **1** (**off**) to divide into zones; to mark as a zone. **2** to assign to a particular zone. — *adj* **zonal**. [Lat *zona*, girdle]

time zone *n* any one of the 24 more or less parallel sections into which the world is divided longitudinally, all places within a given zone generally being at the same standard time.

zonked *adj* **1** (*coll*) exhausted. **2** (*slang*) under the influence of drugs or alcohol. [Imit.]

zoo *n* a place where wild animals are kept for the public to see, and for study, breeding, etc. [**zoological garden**]

zoology *n* the scientific study of animals. — *adj* **zoological**. — *adv* **zoologically**. — *n* **zoologist**. [Gr *zoion*, animal + **-logy**]

zoological garden *n* a zoo.

zoom *v* **1** (*intr & tr*; **past**, **over**, **up**, etc.) to (cause to) move very quickly, making a loud, low-pitched, buzzing noise. **2** (*intr*; **away**, **off**, etc.) to move very quickly. **3** (*intr*) to increase quickly: *Prices have zoomed in the past year*. — *n* the act or sound of zooming. — *v* **zoom in** (*intr*; **on**) to direct a camera towards (someone or something) using a zoom lens to make the person or thing appear to come closer. [Imit.]

zoom lens *n* a type of camera lens which can be used to make a distant object appear gradually closer or further away without the camera being moved and without loss of focus.

zoophyte *n* (*biol*) any of various invertebrate animals which resemble plants, such as sponges, corals and sea anemones. [Gr *zoion*, animal + *phyton*, plant]

Zoroastrianism *n* an ancient orig. Persian religion founded or reformed by *Zoroaster* (6th century BC), which teaches the existence of two continuously opposed divine beings, one good and one evil. — *n & adj* **Zoroastrian**. ◇ See also **Parsee**.

Zr *symbol* (*chem*) zirconium.

zucchini *n* (*NAm & Austr*) ***-ni*** or ***-nis*** a courgette. [Ital]

Zulu *n* **1** a member of a Bantu people of S Africa. **2** the language of this people. — *adj* of or pertaining to the Zulus, their language, etc.

zygote *n* (*biol*) the cell resulting from the union of two gametes, or the individual that develops from that cell. [Gr *zygon*, yoke]

zymase *n* any of the enzymes which cause fermentation of carbohydrates into alcohol. [Gr *zyme*, leaven]

zymotic *n* **1** relating to or causing fermentation. **2** relating to, causing or like an infectious disease. [Gr *zymosis*, fermentation]

Appendices

Symbols

In mathematics

$+$	plus; positive; underestimate
$-$	minus; negative; overestimate
$\pm$	plus or minus; positive or negative; degree of accuracy
$\mp$	minus or plus; negative or positive
$\times$	multiplies (coll. 'times') (6×4)
$\cdot$	multiplies (coll. 'times') $(6\cdot4)$
$\div$	divided by $(6\div4)$
$/$	divided by; ratio of (6/4)
$\frac{}{}$	divided by; ratio of $(\frac{6}{4})$
$=$	equals
$\neq$, $\ne$	not equal to
$\equiv$	identical with
$\not\equiv$, $\not\equiv$	not identical with
$:$	ratio of (6:4)
$::$	proportionately equals (1:2::2:4)
$\approx$	approximately equal to; equivalent to; similar to
$>$	greater than
$\gg$	much greater than
$\ngtr$	not greater than
$<$	less than
$\ll$	much less than
$\nless$	not less than
$\geqslant$, $\geqq$, $\eqslantgtr$	equal to or greater than
$\leqslant$, $\leqq$, $\eqslantless$	equal to or less than
$\propto$	directly proportional to
( )	parentheses
[ ]	brackets
{ }	braces
$\overline{}$	vinculum: division $(\overline{a-b})$; chord of circle or length of line $(\overline{AB})$; arithmetic mean $(\overline{X})$
∞	infinity
$\rightarrow$	approaches the limit
$\sqrt{}$	square root
$\sqrt[3]{}$, $\sqrt[4]{}$	cube root, fourth root, etc.
!	factorial $(4!=4\times3\times2\times1)$
%	percent
$'$	prime; minute(s) of arc; foot/feet
$''$	double prime; second(s) of arc; inch(es)
$\frown$	arc of circle
$^\circ$	degree of arc
$\angle$, $\angle$s	angle(s)
$\veebar$	equiangular
$\perp$	perpendicular
$\parallel$	parallel
$\bigcirc$, Ⓢ	circle(s)
$\triangle$, $\triangle$s	triangle(s)
$\square$	square
▭	rectangle
▱	parallelogram
$\cong$	congruent to
$\therefore$	therefore
$\because$	because
$\stackrel{m}{=}$	measured by
$\triangle$	increment
$\sum$	summation
$\int$	integral sign
$\bigcup$	union
$\bigcap$	interaction

In general use

&	ampersand (*and*)
&c.	et cetera
@	at; per (in costs)
×	by (measuring dimensions) (3×4)
©	copyright
®	registered as a trademark
¶	new paragraph
§	(new) section
″	ditto
†	died
☠	poison; danger
♂, □	male
♀, ○	female
✠	bishop's name follows
☏	telephone number follows
☛	this way
✂ ··· ✂ ···	cut here

In astronomy

●	new moon
☽	moon, first quarter
○	full moon
☾	moon, last quarter

In cards

♥	hearts
♦	diamonds
♠	spades
♣	clubs

Countries of the world

Country	Adjective and name of national

A

Afghanistan Afghan
Albania Albanian
Algeria Algerian
America *see* **United States of America**
Andorra Andorran
Angola Angolan
Antigua and Barbuda Antiguan, Barbudan
Argentina Argentine *or* Argentinian (*person* = an Argentinian)
Armenia Armenian
Aruba Aruban
Australia Australian
Austria Austrian
Azerbaijan Azerbaijani

B

Bahamas Bahamian
Bahrain Bahraini
Bangladesh Bangladeshi
Barbados Barbadian
Belgium Belgian
Belize Belizian
Benin Beninese
Bermuda Bermudan *or* Bermudian
Bhutan Bhutanese
Bolivia Bolivian
Botswana
Brazil Brazilian
Brunei Bruneian
Bulgaria Bulgarian
Burkina Faso Burkinese
Burma *see* Myanma
Burundi Burundian
Byelarus Byelarussian

C

Cambodia (Kampuchea) Cambodian
Cameroon Cameroonian
Canada Canadian
Cape Verde Cape Verdean
Cayman Islands (*person* = a Cayman Islander)
Central African Republic
Chad Chadian
Chile Chilean
China Chinese
Colombia Colombian
Comoros Comorian *or* Comoran (*person* = a Comoran)
Congo Congolese
Cook Islands (*person* = a Cook Islander)
Costa Rica Costa Rican
Côte d'Ivoire (Ivory Coast) Ivorian
Croatia Croat *or* Croatian
Cuba Cuban
Cyprus Cypriot
Czechoslovakia Czech *or* Czechoslovak

D

Denmark Danish (*person* = a Dane)
Djibouti Djiboutian
Dominica Dominican
Dominican Republic Dominican

E

Ecuador Ecuadorian
Egypt Egyptian
El Salvador Salvadorean
Equatorial Guinea (*person* = an Equatorial Guinean)
Estonia Estonian
Ethiopia Ethiopian

F

Faeroe Islands Faeroese
Falkland Islands (*person* = a Falkland Islander)
Fiji Fijian
Finland Finnish (*person* = a Finn)
France French (*person* = a Frenchman, *fem* Frenchwoman)
French Guyana French Guyanan
French Polynesia French Polynesian

Country	Adjective and name of national

G

Gabon Gabonese
The Gambia Gambian
Georgia Georgian
Germany German
Ghana Ghanaian
Great Britain *see* **United Kingdom**
Greece Greek
Greenland Greenlandic (*person* = a Greenlander)
Grenada Grenadian
Guatemala Guatemalan
Guinea Guinean
Guinea-Bissau
Guyana Guyanese

H

Haiti Haitian
Holland *see* **The Netherlands**
Honduras Honduran
Hong Kong
Hungary Hungarian

I

Iceland Icelandic (*person* = an Icelander)
India Indian
Indonesia Indonesian
Iran Iranian
Iraq Iraqi
Ireland, Republic of Irish (*person* = an Irishman, *fem* Irishwoman)
Israel Israeli
Italy Italian
Ivory Coast *see* **Côte d'Ivoire**

J

Jamaica Jamaican
Japan Japanese
Jordan Jordanian

K

Kampuchea *see* **Cambodia**
Kazakhstan Kazakh
Kenya Kenyan
Kirgizstan Kirgiz
Kiribati
Korea, North North Korean
Korea, South South Korean
Kuwait Kuwaiti

Country	Adjective and name of national

L

Laos Laotian
Latvia Latvian
Lebanon Lebanese
Lesotho (*person* = a Mosotho, *pl* Basotho)
Liberia Liberian
Libya Libyan
Liechtenstein (*person* = a Liechtensteiner)
Lithuania Lithuanian
Luxembourg Luxembourgian (*person* = a Luxembourger *or* Luxemburger)

M

Macau
Madagascar Malagasy *or* Madagascan
Malawi Malawian
Malaysia Malaysian
Maldives Maldivian
Mali Malian
Malta Maltese
Mauritania Mauritanian
Mauritius Mauritian
Mexico Mexican
Micronesia Micronesian
Moldova Moldovan
Monaco Monégasque *or* Monacan
Mongolia Mongolian
Morocco Moroccan
Mozambique Mozambican
Myanma (Burma) Myanman *or* Burmese

N

Namibia Namibian
Nauru Nauruan
Nepal Nepalese *or* Nepali
The Netherlands Dutch (*person* = a Dutchman, *fem* Dutchwoman, both a Netherlander)
New Zealand (*person* = a New Zealander)
Nicaragua Nicaraguan
Niger (*person* = a Nigerian)
Nigeria Nigerian
Norway Norwegian

Country	Adjective and name of national

O
Oman Omani

P
Pakistan Pakistani
Panama Panamanian
Papua New Guinea Papua New Guinean *or* Papuan
Paraguay Paraguayan
Peru Peruvian
Philippines Filipino *or* Philippine (*person* = a Filipino, *fem* Filipina)
Poland Polish (*person* = a Pole)
Portugal Portuguese
Puerto Rico Puerto Rican

Q
Qatar Qatari

R
Romania Romanian
Russia Russian
Rwanda Rwandan *or* Rwandese

S
St Helena and dependencies St Helenian
St Kitts and Nevis
St Lucia St Lucian
St Vincent and the Grenadines
San Marino San Marinese
São Tomé and Principe São Tomean
Saudi Arabia Saudi Arabian *or* Saudi
Senegal Senegalese
Seychelles Seychellois
Sierra Leone Sierra Leonian
Singapore Singaporean
Slovenia Slovene *or* Slovenian
Solomon Islands (*person* = a Solomon Islander)
Somalia Somali
South Africa South African
Spain Spanish (*person* = a Spaniard)
Sri Lanka Sri Lankan
Sudan Sudanese
Suriname Surinamese
Swaziland Swazi
Sweden Swedish (*person* = a Swede)
Switzerland Swiss
Syria Syrian

T
Tadzhikistan Tadzhik
Taiwan Taiwanese
Tanzania Tanzanian
Thailand Thai
Togo Togolese
Tonga Tongan
Trinidad and Tobago Trinidadian and Tobagan *or* Tobagonian
Tunisia Tunisian
Turkey Turkish (*person* = a Turk)
Turkmenistan Turkmen
Turks and Caicos Islands
Tuvalu Tuvaluan

U
Uganda Ugandan
Ukraine Ukrainian
United Arab Emirates
United Kingdom British (*person* = a Briton)
United States of America American
Uruguay Uruguayan
Uzbekistan Uzbek

V
Vanuatu Vanuatuan
Vatican Vatican
Venezuela Venezuelan
Vietnam Vietnamese

W
Western Samoa Western Samoan

Y
Yemen Yemeni *or* Yemenite
Yugoslavia Yugoslav

Z
Zaïre Zaïrean
Zimbabwe Zimbabwean

Punctuation rules

A **full stop (.)** is used at the end of a statement and often after a command; a **question mark (?)** comes after a question and an **exclamation mark (!)** after an exclamation or interjection, and sometimes after a command:

This is a useful report. Show it to the Chairman tomorrow.

Would you make a copy for me?

Cheerio! Don't forget what I said!

A **comma (,)** shows a slight break in a sentence. It is used:

1 between two clauses joined by *but* or *or* if the second one has a subject:
I'll come to see you tomorrow, but I don't know when I will arrive.

2 after a subordinate clause:
When he returned, I made a cup of tea.

3 around the kind of relative clause that gives *additional information*:
The salesman, who had driven from Southampton, was tired.
but *not* around the kind of relative clause that *identifies* a person or thing:
Those people who would like tickets should write to the secretary.

4 around a descriptive or explanatory phrase referring to a person or thing:
Mrs Cook, our local councillor, has joined the committee.

5 after introductory words, or around words which form a comment:
However, I wasn't late after all.
I must leave now, unfortunately.
Philip, I'm sorry to say, has left the company.

6 before *please*, after *yes* and *no*, and before or after the name of the person who is being spoken to:
May I see the file, please?
No, I'm sorry.
Hurry up, Christopher.

7 in a list of more than two things and often between adjectives preceding a noun, where there are two or more:
a pen, a pencil and a rubber
a busy, overcrowded room (but no commas in e.g. a *cheerful old man*, because *old man* is regarded as a single unit).

A **colon (:)** is used to introduce the answer that the first part of the sentence expects:
There's one thing I'd really like: a new car.
You'll need the following: passport, ticket, boarding pass.

A **semicolon (;)** separates parts of a sentence that are equally important and are not linked by *and*, *but*, *or*, etc. Sometimes a semicolon is used to separate items in a list:
One tray of sandwiches will be sufficient; to prepare more would be wasteful.
I have three ambitions: to set up my own business; to buy a boat and sail around the world; to live in Sydney.

Quotation marks (' ') or **(" ")** are used before and after direct speech; a **comma** is usually put before or after the direct speech:
Mary said, 'You're late'.
'You're late', said Mary.

Both single and double quotes are correct, but modern usage prefers single quotes. However, if there is a quotation or highlighted passage within another quotation, both single and double quotes must be used:
'Did she say "You're late"?', John asked.

An **apostrophe (')** is used:

1 to form possessive nouns; it is placed before the *s* with singular nouns and with plural nouns not ending in *–s*, and after the *s* with plural nouns ending in *–s*:
Anne's desk; the women's coats; the residents' car park.

2 in shortened forms, showing where part of a word has been left out:

I've only two appointments today.
Aren't you coming with us?

A **hyphen (-)** is used:

1 in many nouns (others are written as one word or as two words without a hyphen):

air-conditioning (but *aircraft* and *air force*).

2 in compound adjectives placed before the noun:

a six-page contract; a twenty-year-old building: a well-deserved award.

3 sometimes with a prefix:

The votes must be re-counted.

Spelling rules

To a large extent the ability to spell English words correctly depends on becoming familiar with the *look* of them when they are spelt in the accepted way.

There are, however, a few general rules, *though one must always be on the watch for exceptions.*

Derivatives of words ending in -*y*

1 The plural of a noun in **-y, -ey** (also **-ay, -oy, -uy**):

A noun in **-y** following a consonant has its plural in **-ies.**

baby babies country countries

Nouns in **-ey,** etc., have their plural in **-eys,** etc.

donkey donkeys valley valleys
day days Monday Mondays
alloy alloys guy guys

2 The parts of a verb when the verb ends in **-y, -ey** (etc.):

The formation is similar to that of noun plurals in (1) above.

cry cries cried
certify certifies certified

but

convey conveys conveyed
delay delays delayed
destroy destroys destroyed
buy buys

3 Comparison of adjectives, or the formation of nouns or adverbs from them:

A rule similar to the above holds for words in **-y,** and in some cases for those in **-ey** (etc.).

shady shadier shadiest
shadiness shadily
pretty prettier prettiest
prettiness prettily

but

grey greyer greyest
greyness greyly
coy coyer coyest
coyness coyly

There are, however, exceptions and irregularities (such as *wryly* and *gluier*) for which the dictionary should be consulted.

Derivatives of words ending in -*c*

When a suffix beginning with a vowel is added, and the consonant still has a hard *k* sound, **-c** becomes **-ck-**:

picnic picnicking
picnicked picnicker
mimic mimicking
mimicked mimicker

-k- is not added in words such as *musician*, *electricity*, etc., where the consonant has the soft sound of *sh* or *s*.

-ie- or -ei-?

i before *e*
except after *c*.

(This rule applies only to words in which the sound is long *ee*.)

e.g.
belief believe grief pier siege
ceiling conceit deceit deceive

Exceptions are *seize*, *weird* and personal names (e.g. *Neil*, *Sheila*) and certain surnames.

Derivatives of words with final -*e*

1 Before a vowel (including **y**), **-e** is usually dropped:

e.g.
come coming hate hating
fame famous pale palish
use usable ice icy
noise noisy

Some exceptions are intended to distinguish one word from another: e.g. *holey* (= full of holes), *holy*; *dyeing*, *dying*.

2 Before a consonant, **-e** is usually kept:

e.g.
hateful useless movement paleness

but see *true*, *whole*, *judge* for exceptions.

3 **-e-** is kept after soft **-c-** or **-g-** before **-a-**, **-o-**:

e.g.
noticeable traceable
manageable advantageous

The doubling of a final consonant before a following vowel

1 In a word of one syllable with a short vowel, the final consonant is doubled:

e.g.
man manning manned mannish
red redder reddest redden
sin sinning sinned sinner
stop stopping stopped stopper
drum drumming drummed drummer

2 In a word of more than one syllable with a short final vowel, the final consonant is doubled only if the accent is on the final syllable:

e.g.
entrap entrapping entrapped
regret regretting regretted
begin beginning beginner
occur occurring occurred occurrence

but
enter entering entered
profit profiting profited
gallop galloping galloped
hiccup hiccuping hiccuped

3 In British English (but not in American) **-l** is doubled no matter where the accent falls:

e.g.
compel compelling compelled

and also
travel travelling travelled traveller

4 Some derivatives of words ending in **-s** can be spelt in two ways, e.g. *bias*. Certain words ending in **-p** are not treated strictly in accordance with the rule stated in (2) above, e.g. *kidnap*, *handicap*.

Plural of words ending in *-f*

It is usual to add *s* to make the plural form, e.g. *roof*, *roofs*, but there are several exceptions, e.g. *calves*, *elves*, *knives*, *leaves*.

Some words have optional spellings:
e.g.
hoof (*hoofs*, or *hooves*), *scarf*, *wharf*, *handkerchief*.

Irregular plurals

Where a noun has an irregular plural form it is usually shown in its entry in the dictionary.